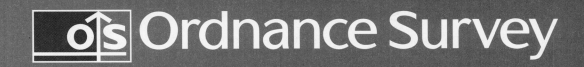

STREET ATLAS
West Yorkshire

Contents

II *Explanation of street index reference system*

II *Key to town, village and rural locality abbreviations in index*

III *Key to map symbols*

IV-V *Key to map pages*

VI *Administrative and post code boundaries*

1 *Street maps*

201 *Index of hospitals, railway stations, schools, shopping centres, street names and universities*

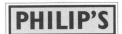

First edition published 1996 by

Ordnance Survey
Romsey Road
Maybush
Southampton SO16 4GU

and

George Philip Ltd.
an imprint of Reed Books
Michelin House, 81 Fulham Road, London SW3 6RB
and Auckland, Melbourne, Singapore and Toronto

ISBN 0-540-06329-0 (Philip's, hardback)
ISBN 0-540-06327-4 (Philip's, wire-o)

ISBN 0-319-00842-8 (Ordnance Survey, hardback)
ISBN 0-319-00843-6 (Ordnance Survey, wire-o)

Printed and bound in Spain by Cayfosa

EXPLANATION OF THE STREET INDEX REFERENCE SYSTEM

Street names are listed alphabetically and show the locality, the Post Office Postcode District, the page number and a reference to the square in which the name falls on the map page.

Example: Rutland St. Han ST4.....................57 D3 8

Rutland St   This is the full street name, which may have been abbreviated on the map.

Han   This is the abbreviation for the town, village or locality in which the street falls.

ST4   This is the Post Office Postcode District for the street name.

57   This is the page number of the map on which the street name appears.

D3   The letter and figure indicate the square on the map in which the centre of the street falls. The square can be found at the junction of the vertical column carrying the appropriate letter and the horizontal row carrying the appropriate figure.

8   In congested areas numbers may have been used to indicate the location of a street. In certain circumstances, the number used to represent a street will follow the reference in the gazetteer entry.

ABBREVIATIONS USED IN THE INDEX
Road Names

Approach	App	Corner	Cnr	Heights	Hts
Arcade	Arc	Cottages	Cotts	Industri al Estate	Ind Est
Avenue	Ave	Court	Ct	Interchange	Intc
Boulevard	Bvd	Courtyard	Ctyd	Junction	Junc
Buildings	Bldgs	Crescent	Cres	Lane	La
Business Park	Bsns Pk	Drive	Dr	North	N
Business Centre	Bsns Ctr	Drove	Dro	Orchard	Orch
Bungalows	Bglws	East	E	Parade	Par
Causeway	Cswy	Embankment	Emb	Park	Pk
Centre	Ctr	Esplanade	Espl	Passage	Pas
Circle	Circ	Estate	Est	Place	Pl
Circus	Cir	Gardens	Gdns	Precinct	Prec
Close	Cl	Green	Gn	Promenade	Prom
Common	Comm	Grove	Gr	Retail Park	Ret Pk

Road	Rd
Roundabout	Rdbt
South	S
Square	Sq
Stairs	Strs
Steps	Stps
Street,Saint	St
Terrace	Terr
Trading Estate	Trad Est
Walk	Wlk
West	W
Yard	Yd

Key to abbreviations of Town, Village and Rural locality names used in the index of street names.

Locality	Abbr	Pg	Ref	Locality	Abbr	Pg	Ref	Locality	Abbr	Pg	Ref
Aberford	Aber	64	E7	Cullingworth	Cull	52	C6	Huddersfield	Hud	154	C6	Royston	Roy	179	D3
Ackworth Moor Top	Ack M T	163	E6	Darrington	Dar	147	C5	Hunger Hill	H Hill	8	B8	Ryhill	Ryhill	162	B1
Addingham	Add	6	E8	Dearne	Dearne	194	D1	Ilkley	Ilkley	8	C4	Saxton	Saxton	65	E8
Adwick Le Street	Ad Le S	184	E2	Denby Dale	D Dale	192	B6	Ingbirchworth	Ing	191	E1	Scarcroft	Scar	45	D8
Arthington	Arth	25	D6	Denholme	Denh	52	D1	Keighley	Keigh	35	D6	Shafton	Shaf	180	B3
Askwith	Ask	9	F5	Denshaw	Densh	167	B3	Kexbrough	Kex	177	A1	Shelf	Shelf	93	D6
Bacup	Bacup	106	B4	Denton	Denton	9	A6	Kippax	Kippax	83	B2	Shepley	Shep	190	F8
Badsworth	Bad	164	E2	Dewsbury	Dew	139	C7	Kirk Deighton	K Deig	13	C8	Sherburn in Elmet	S in Elm	65	E1
Baildon	Bail	38	C3	Diggle	Diggle	185	B4	Kirk Smeaton	K Smea	166	D5	Shipley	Ship	55	B7
Bardsey	Bard	28	D4	Draughton	Draug	1	D5	Kirkburton	Kirkb	173	E6	Sicklinghall	Sickl	12	C5
Barnsley	Barn	178	F1	Dunford Bridge	Dun Br	199	D1	Kirkheaton	Kirkhe	137	C1	Silkstone	Silk	193	F1
Barwick in Elmet	B in Elm	63	E7	East Ardsley	E Ard	120	B7	Knottingley	Knot	127	B4	Silsden	Sil	5	E1
Batley	Batley	118	C4	East Carlton	E Carl	23	D3	Leathley	Leath	24	C8	Skelmanthorpe	Skel	175	B2
Beal	Beal	127	F6	East Keswick	E Kes	28	C6	Ledsham	Ledsh	104	D8	Skipton	Skip	1	A4
Beamsley	Beam	2	F5	Eccup	Eccup	25	F1	Ledston	Ledst	103	E6	Slaithwaite	Slai	152	A1
Bickerton	Bick	15	C7	Elland	Elland	134	E6	Leeds	Leeds	79	A7	South Elmsall	S Elm	183	A2
Bingley	Bing	37	C4	Embsay	Embsay	1	A8	Lepton	Lepton	155	E3	South Hiendley	S Hie	180	D6
Birkenshaw	Birk	96	B5	Emley	Emley	175	C7	Lindley	Lind	11	E7	South Kirkby	S Kirk	182	C1
Birkin	Birkin	127	D7	Fairburn	Fair	105	B4	Littleborough	Litt	129	B2	South Milford	S Mil	84	F3
Blackshaw Head	B Head	87	F4	Farnhill	Farnh	4	D1	Liversedge	Liver	117	A6	Sowerby Bridge	Sow Br	112	C3
Bolton Abbey	B Abby	2	E8	Farnley	Farnley	11	D4	Lofthouse Gate	Loft G	121	D6	Spofforth	Spof	12	C8
Boston Spa	B Spa	30	D7	Featherstone	Feath	145	C7	Low Bradley	L Brad	4	D5	Steeton	Stee	17	D5
Bradford	Brad	74	E8	Flockton	Floc	157	C2	Mapplewell	Mapp	178	C1	Stutton	Stut	48	C5
Bramham	Bramham	30	E3	Garforth	Gar	83	B5	Marsden	Mars	168	E3	Sutton-in-Craven	S-in-Cra	16	E5
Bramhope	Bramho	24	D3	Gildersome	Gild	97	D8	Meltham	Mel	170	E3	Swillington	Swil	82	B1
Brierley	Bri	181	A3	Glusburn	Glu	16	C6	Menston	Men	22	A4	Tadcaster	Tad	31	E3
Brighouse	Brig	115	B2	Great Houghton	G Hou	194	A3	Mickfield	M'field	84	A7	Thorner	Thorner	45	E5
Brodsworth	Brod	195	F2	Grimethorpe	Grim	181	B1	Mickletown	M'town	102	D3	Thornton	Thorn	72	E6
Brotherton	Broth	126	D8	Guiseley	Guise	39	C8	Middleton	Midd	99	D4	Thorp Arch	Th Arch	14	F1
Burghwallis	Burg	184	E4	Halifax	Hali	113	D6	Mirfield	Mir	138	A6	Thorpe Audlin	Th Aud	165	B4
Burley in Wharfdale	Bur in W	9	D1	Halton East	Hal E	1	E8	Monk Fryston	M Fry	105	E8	Tintwistle	Tint	197	A2
Burton Salmon	B Sal	105	E3	Hampole	Ham	184	B1	Morley	Morley	98	C3	Todmorden	Tod	108	C6
Byram	Byram	126	E7	Harden	Harden	36	B1	Nesfield	Nes	7	C8	Trawden	Traw	32	A2
Carlecotes	Carl	200	B3	Harewood	Hare	27	A7	Netherton	Neth	158	E6	Upton	Upton	183	A8
Castleford	Castle	124	F8	Haworth	Haw	51	B7	Normanton	Nor	123	B1	Wadsworth Moor	Wad M	68	E6
Castley	Cast	25	B8	Hazlewood	Hazl	3	B8	Northowram	Northo	93	B2	Wakefield	Wake	142	E5
Cawthorne	Caw	193	D4	Hebden Bridge	Heb Br	89	B3	Norton	Norton	166	F1	Walton	Walton	161	B6
Clayton	Clay	194	C4	Hemsworth	Hem	181	C8	Notton	Notton	178	F6	West Bretton	W Bret	176	E8
Clayton West	Clay W	175	E2	Heptonstall	Hep	67	C2	Ossett	Ossett	140	E6	West Hardwick	W Har	165	B1
Cleckheaton	Clec	116	C6	High Hoyland	H Hoy	176	C1	Otley	Otley	23	B8	Wetherby	Weth	13	C6
Clifton	Clift	10	E5	Hillam	Hillam	105	F7	Oxenhope	Oxen	51	D2	Whitley Common	Wh Com	200	E7
Collingham	Coll	29	B8	Holme	Holme	197	B6	Penistone	Pen	192	E1	Whitworth	Whit	106	E1
Cononley	Con	4	A3	Holme Chapel	H Chap	85	B6	Pontefract	Pont	146	B6	Wighill	Wig	15	F3
Cowling	Cowl	32	C7	Holmfirth	Holmfi	189	B5	Pool	Pool	24	D7	Wilsden	Wil	53	D5
Cridling Stubbs	C Stub	127	D1	Honley	Honley	171	E4	Pudsey	Pudsey	76	D7	Womersley	Wom	147	F3
Crigglestone	Crig	159	E5	Hooton Pagnell	H Pag	195	C5	Queensbury	Queen	72	F2	Woolley	Wool	177	F7
Crofton	Crof	143	F1	Horbury	Hor	141	B2	Ripponden	Rip	132	D4	Worsthorne	Worst	66	A4
Cudworth	Cud	180	B1	Horsforth	Hors	41	A2	Rothwell	Roth	100	E5	Yeadon	Yeadon	40	D5

Key to map symbols

Motorway	
Primary Routes (Dual carriageway and single)	
A Roads (Dual carriageway and single)	
B Roads (Dual carriageway and single)	
C Roads (Dual carriageway and single)	
Minor Roads	
Roads under construction	
County boundaries	
All Railways	
Track or private road	
Gate or obstruction to traffic (restrictions may not apply at all times or to all vehicles)	
All paths, bridleways, BOAT's, RUPP's, dismantled railways, etc.	

The representation in this atlas of a road, track or path is no evidence of the existence of a right of way

174 Adjoining page indicator

Abbr.	Full	Abbr.	Full
Acad	Academy	Mon	Monument
Cemy	Cemetery	Mus	Museum
C Ctr	Civic Centre	Obsy	Observatory
CH	Club House	Pal	Royal Palace
Coll	College	PH	Public House
Ex H	Exhibition Hall	Resr	Reservoir
Ind Est	Industrial Estate	Ret Pk	Retail Park
Inst	Institute	Sch	School
Ct	Law Court	Sh Ctr	Shopping Centre
L Ctr	Leisure Centre	Sta	Station
LC	Level Crossing	TH	Town Hall/House
Liby	Library	Trad Est	Trading Estate
Mkt	Market	Univ	University
Meml	Memorial	YH	Youth Hostel

British Rail station	
Private railway station	
Bus, coach station	
Ambulance station	
Coastguard station	
Fire station	
Police station	
Casualty entrance to hospital	
Churches, Place of worship	
H Hospital	
i Information Centre	
P Parking	
Post Office	
Public Convenience	
Important buildings, schools, colleges, universities and hospitals	
River Soar — Water Name	
Stream	
River or canal (minor and major)	
Water Fill	
Tidal Water	
Woods	
Houses	

0	¼	½	¾	1 mile
0	250 m 500 m 750 m		1 Kilometre	

The scale of the maps is 5.52 cm to 1 km (3½ inches to 1 mile)

The small numbers around the edges of the maps identify the 1 kilometre National Grid lines

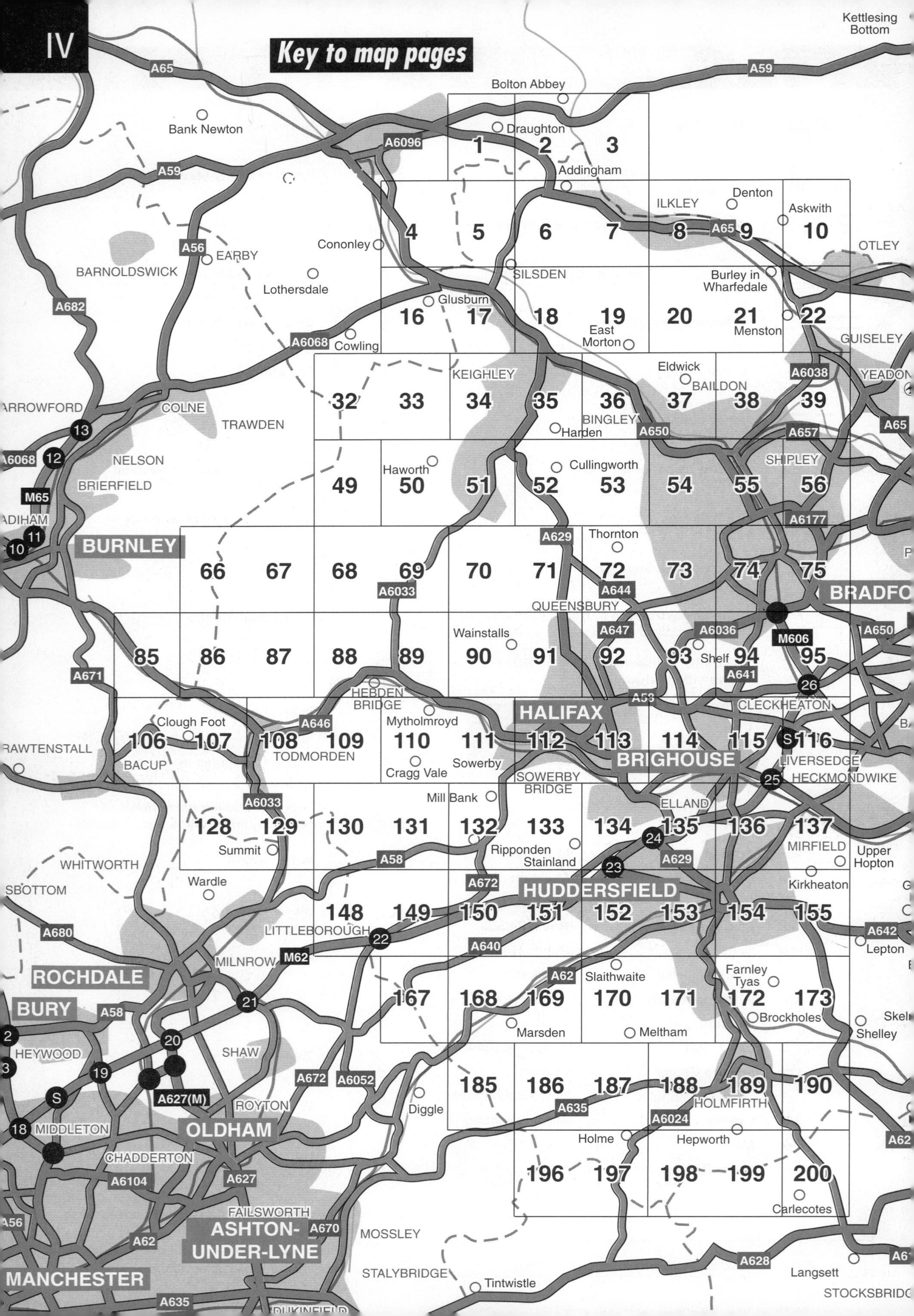
IV
Key to map pages
Kettlesing Bottom
A65
A59
Bolton Abbey
Bank Newton
Draughton
A6096
1
2
3
Addingham
A59
ILKLEY
Denton
Askwith
A56
EARBY
Cononley
4
5
6
7
8
A65
9
10
OTLEY
BARNOLDSWICK
Lothersdale
SILSDEN
Burley in Wharfedale
A682
Glusburn
16
17
18
19
East Morton
20
21
Menston
22
GUISELEY
A6068
Cowling
KEIGHLEY
Eldwick
BAILDON
A6038
YEADON
32
33
34
35
36
37
38
39
ARROWFORD
COLNE
TRAWDEN
BINGLEY
Harden
A650
A657
A65
13
A6068
12
NELSON
Cullingworth
SHIPLEY
Haworth
BRIERFIELD
49
50
51
52
53
54
55
56
M65
A6177
ADIHAM
11
10
BURNLEY
A629
Thornton
66
67
68
69
70
71
72
73
74
75
A6033
A644
BRADFO
QUEENSBURY
A647
A6036
M606
A650
Wainstalls
85
86
87
88
89
90
91
92
93
Shelf
94
95
A671
A641
26
HEBDEN BRIDGE
A58
CLECKHEATON
Clough Foot
A646
HALIFAX
Mythholmroyd
106
107
108
109
110
111
112
113
114
115
S
116
RAWTENSTALL
BACUP
TODMORDEN
Cragg Vale
Sowerby
BRIGHOUSE
LIVERSEDGE
SOWERBY BRIDGE
25
HECKMONDWIKE
A6033
Mill Bank
ELLAND
128
129
130
131
132
133
134
24
135
136
137
Summit
Ripponden
Stainland
MIRFIELD
Upper Hopton
WHITWORTH
A58
23
A629
Wardle
A672
Kirkheaton
SBOTTOM
HUDDERSFIELD
148
149
150
151
152
153
154
155
LITTLEBOROUGH
22
A642
A680
A640
Lepton
MILNROW
M62
A62
Slaithwaite
Farnley Tyas
ROCHDALE
167
168
169
170
171
172
173
21
BURY
A58
Brockholes
Marsden
Meltham
Shelley
20
HEYWOOD
SHAW
19
A672
A6052
185
186
187
188
189
190
S
A627(M)
ROYTON
Diggle
A635
HOLMFIRTH
18
MIDDLETON
OLDHAM
A6024
Holme
Hepworth
CHADDERTON
A62
A6104
A627
196
197
198
199
200
Carlecotes
FAILSWORTH
A56
ASHTON-UNDER-LYNE
A670
MOSSLEY
A62
A628
Langsett
STALYBRIDGE
MANCHESTER
Tintwistle
STOCKSBRID
A635
DUKINFIELD

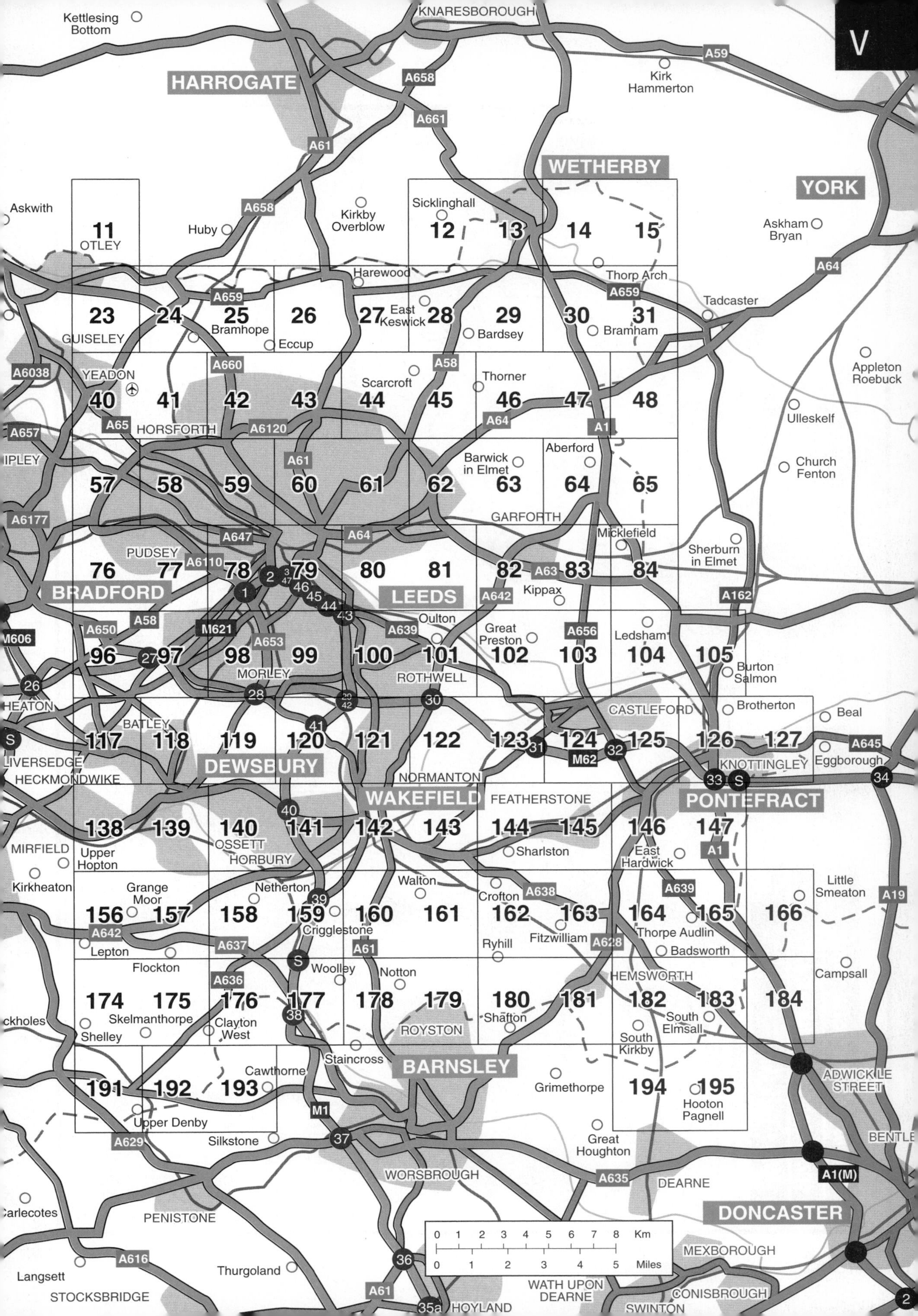
V
Kettlesing Bottom
KNARESBOROUGH
A59
HARROGATE
A658
Kirk Hammerton
A661
A61
WETHERBY
YORK
Askwith
A658
Huby
Kirkby Overblow
Sicklinghall
Askham Bryan
11
OTLEY
12
13
14
15
Harewood
Thorp Arch
A64
A659
A659
Tadcaster
23
24
25
26
27
East Keswick
28
29
30
31
GUISELEY
Bramhope
Eccup
Bardsey
Bramham
A6038
YEADON
A660
A58
Appleton Roebuck
Scarcroft
Thorner
40
41
42
43
44
45
46
47
48
A65
HORSFORTH
A6120
A64
A1
Ulleskelf
A657
IPLEY
A61
Barwick in Elmet
Aberford
Church Fenton
57
58
59
60
61
62
63
64
65
A6177
GARFORTH
A647
A64
Micklefield
Sherburn in Elmet
PUDSEY
A6110
76
77
78
79
80
81
82
A63
83
84
BRADFORD
LEEDS
A642
Kippax
A162
A650
A58
M621
A639
Oulton
Great Preston
A656
Ledsham
M606
A653
96
97
98
99
100
101
102
103
104
105
MORLEY
ROTHWELL
Burton Salmon
HEATON
CASTLEFORD
Brotherton
Beal
BATLEY
117
118
119
120
121
122
123
124
125
126
127
A645
LIVERSEDGE
DEWSBURY
M62
KNOTTINGLEY
Eggborough
HECKMONDWIKE
NORMANTON
WAKEFIELD
FEATHERSTONE
PONTEFRACT
138
139
140
141
142
143
144
145
146
147
MIRFIELD
Upper Hopton
OSSETT
HORBURY
Sharlston
East Hardwick
A1
Kirkheaton
Grange Moor
Netherton
Walton
Crofton
A638
A639
Little Smeaton
A19
156
157
158
159
160
161
162
163
164
165
166
A642
Crigglestone
A61
Ryhill
Fitzwilliam
A628
Thorpe Audlin
Lepton
A637
Badsworth
Flockton
Woolley
Notton
HEMSWORTH
Campsall
A636
174
175
176
177
178
179
180
181
182
183
184
Skelmanthorpe
Clayton West
Shafton
South Elmsall
ckholes
Shelley
ROYSTON
South Kirkby
Staincross
BARNSLEY
Cawthorne
ADWICK LE STREET
Grimethorpe
191
192
193
194
195
Hooton Pagnell
M1
Upper Denby
A629
Silkstone
Great Houghton
BENTLE
A1(M)
WORSBROUGH
A635
DEARNE
Carlecotes
DONCASTER
PENISTONE
0 1 2 3 4 5 6 7 8 Km
0 1 2 3 4 5 Miles
MEXBOROUGH
A616
Langsett
Thurgoland
WATH UPON DEARNE
CONISBROUGH
STOCKSBRIDGE
A61
HOYLAND
SWINTON

VI

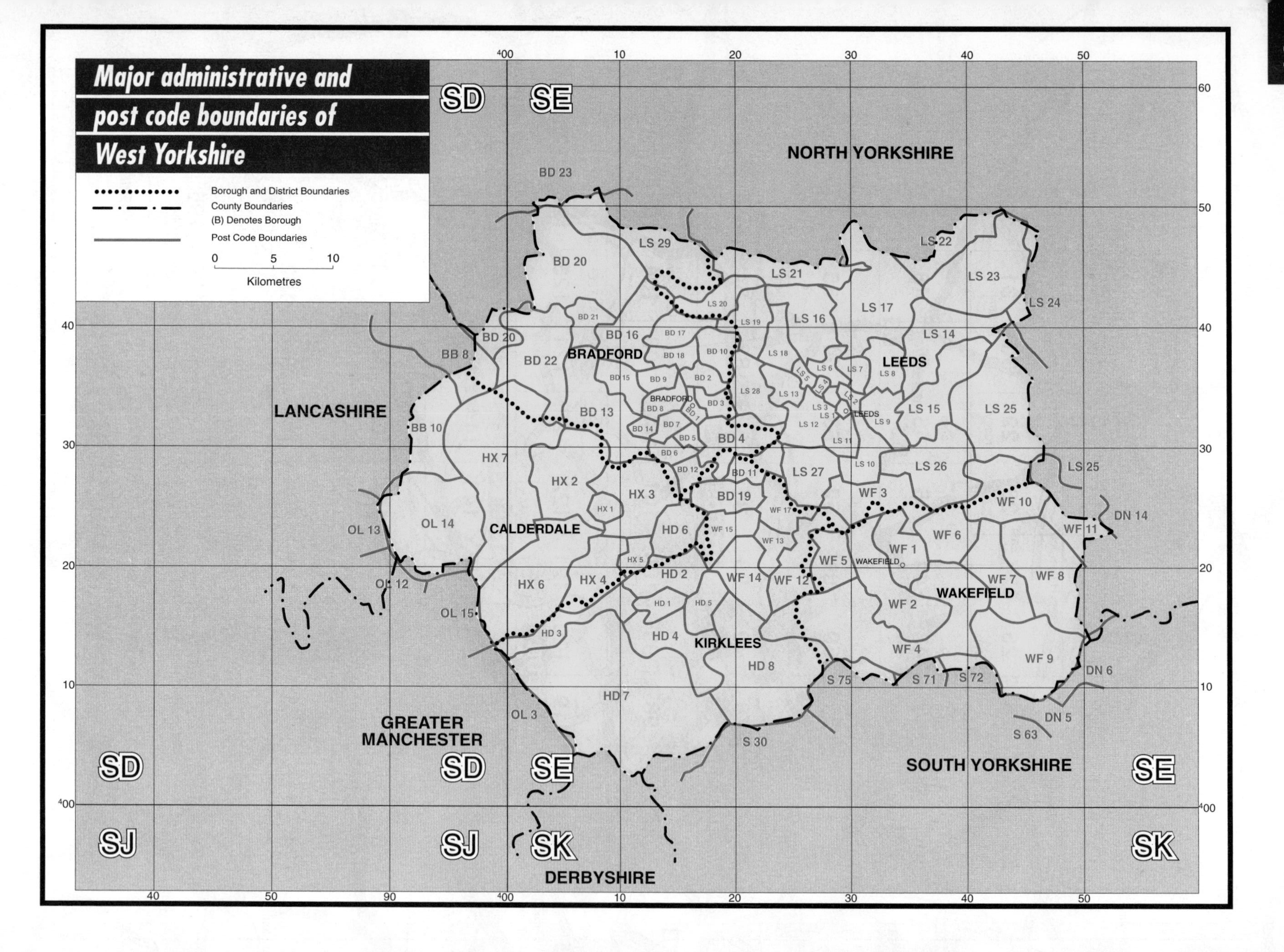

Major administrative and post code boundaries of West Yorkshire

Borough and District Boundaries

County Boundaries

(B) Denotes Borough

Post Code Boundaries

0   5   10

Kilometres

NORTH YORKSHIRE

SOUTH YORKSHIRE

LANCASHIRE

GREATER MANCHESTER

DERBYSHIRE

LEEDS

WAKEFIELD

BRADFORD

KIRKLEES

CALDERDALE

SD   SE   SK   SJ

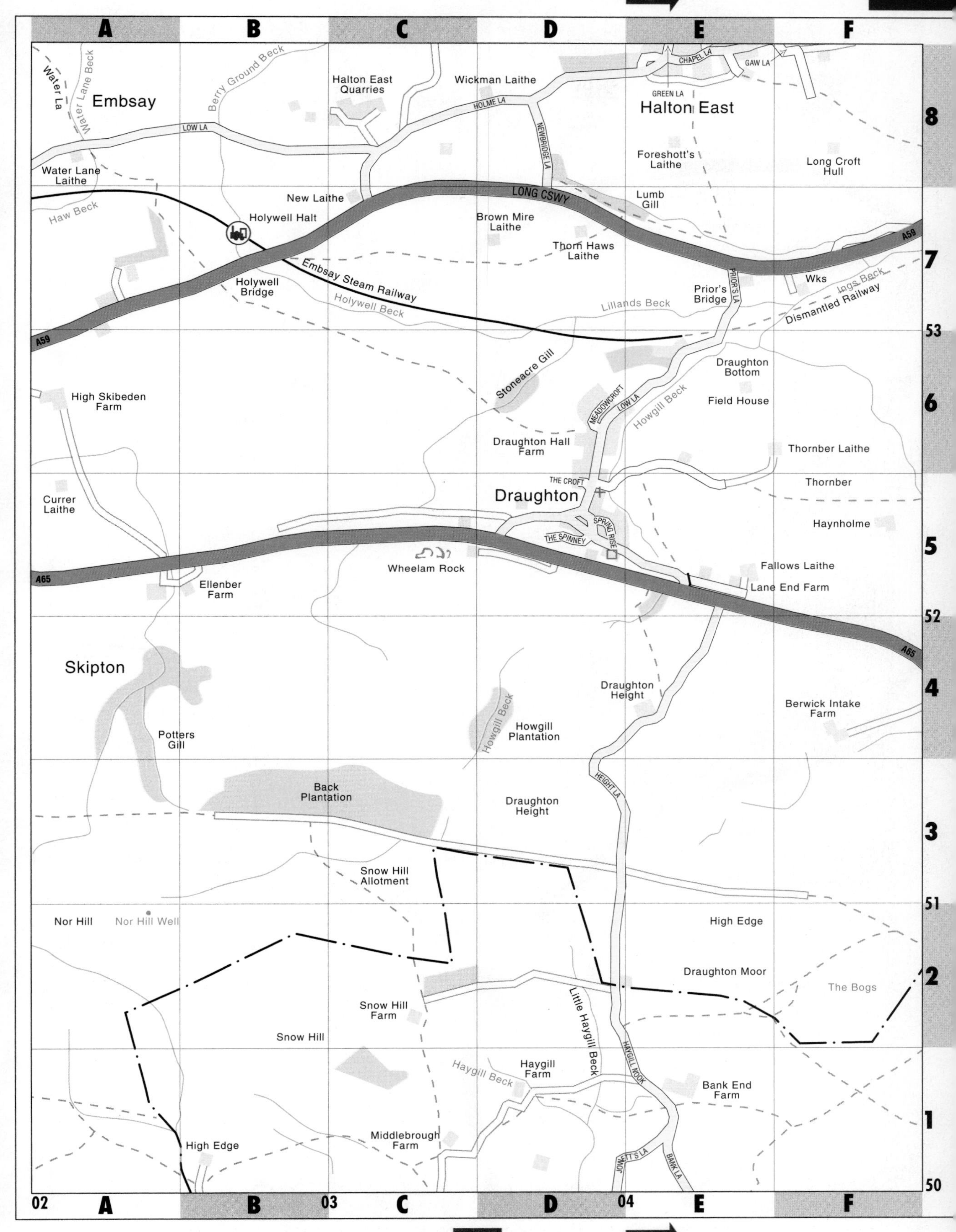
2
A
B
C
D
E
F
Water La
Water Lane Beck
Berry Ground Beck
Embsay
Halton East Quarries
Wickman Laithe
CHAPEL LA
GAW LA
GREEN LA
Halton East
HOLME LA
LOW LA
NEWBRIDGE LA
Water Lane Laithe
Foreshott's Laithe
Long Croft Hull
New Laithe
LONG CSWY
Lumb Gill
Haw Beck
Holywell Halt
Brown Mire Laithe
Thorn Haws Laithe
A59
Embsay Steam Railway
Holywell Bridge
Holywell Beck
Lillands Beck
Prior's Bridge
PRIOR'S LA
Wks
Ings Beck
Dismantled Railway
A59
Stoneacre Gill
Draughton Bottom
High Skibeden Farm
MEADOWCROFT
LOW LA
Howgill Beck
Field House
Draughton Hall Farm
Thornber Laithe
THE CROFT
Thornber
Currer Laithe
Draughton
SPRING RISE
THE SPINNEY
Haynholme
A65
Wheelam Rock
Fallows Laithe
Ellenber Farm
Lane End Farm
A65
Skipton
Draughton Height
Howgill Beck
Berwick Intake Farm
Howgill Plantation
Potters Gill
Back Plantation
HEIGHT LA
Draughton Height
Snow Hill Allotment
Nor Hill
Nor Hill Well
High Edge
Draughton Moor
The Bogs
Little Haygill Beck
Snow Hill Farm
Snow Hill
Haygill Beck
Haygill Farm
HAYGILL NOOK
Bank End Farm
High Edge
Middlebrough Farm
JOWETT'S LA
BANK LA
8
7
53
6
5
52
4
3
51
2
1
50
02
03
04
5
2

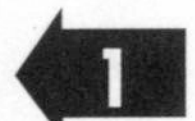

1

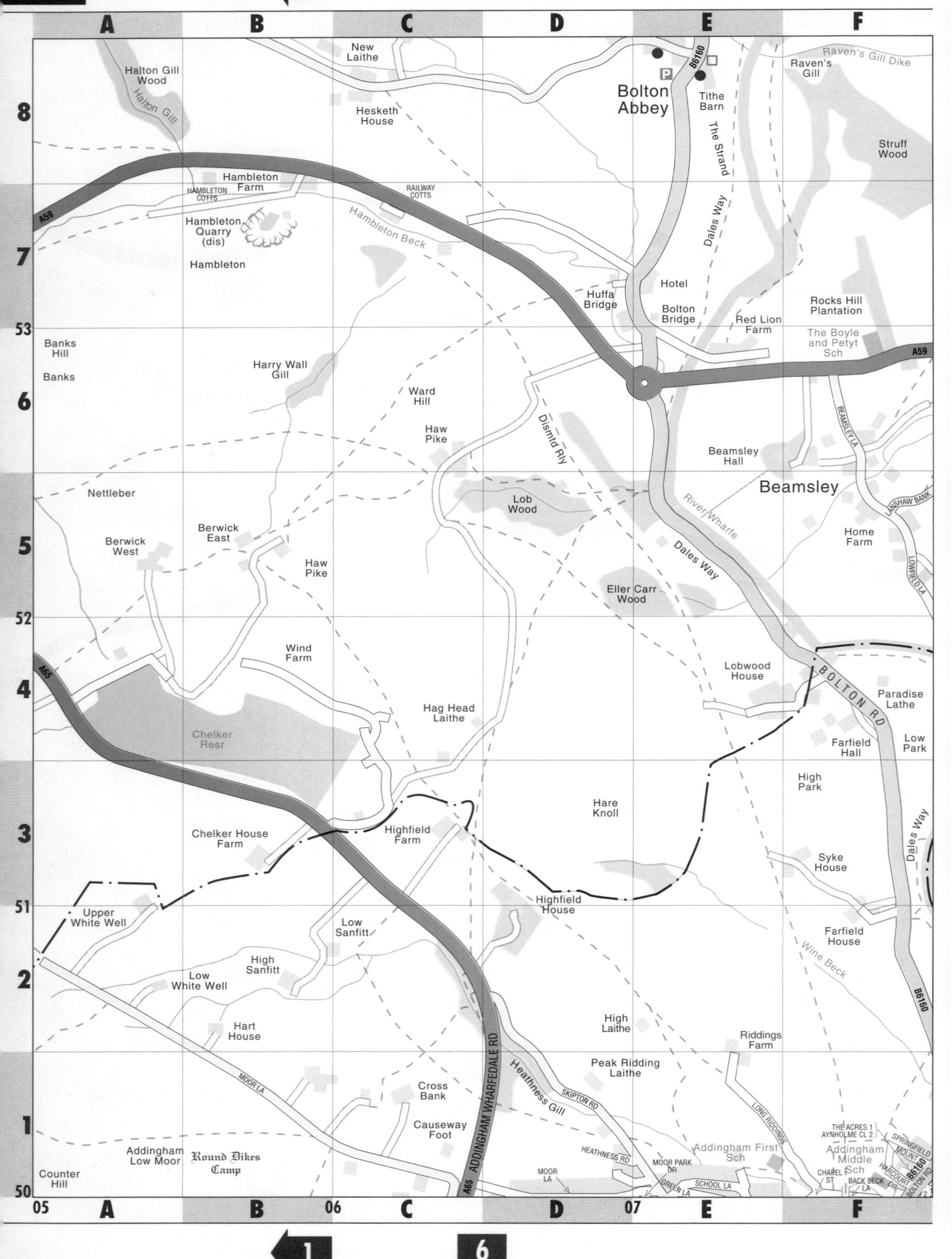

A
B
C
D
E
F
8
7
53
6
5
52
4
3
51
2
1
50
05
06
07
New Laithe
Halton Gill Wood
Halton Gill
Hesketh House
Bolton Abbey
B6160
Tithe Barn
Raven's Gill Dike
Raven's Gill
The Strand
Struff Wood
Hambleton Farm
HAMBLETON COTTS
RAILWAY COTTS
A59
Hambleton Quarry (dis)
Hambleton Beck
Hambleton
Dales Way
Hotel
Huffa Bridge
Bolton Bridge
Red Lion Farm
Rocks Hill Plantation
The Boyle and Petyt Sch
Banks Hill
Banks
Harry Wall Gill
Ward Hill
Haw Pike
Dismtd Rly
BEAMSLEY LA
Beamsley Hall
Beamsley
Nettleber
Lob Wood
River Wharfe
LANSHAW BANK
Berwick East
Berwick West
Haw Pike
Dales Way
Home Farm
Eller Carr Wood
LOWFIELD LA
Wind Farm
Lobwood House
BOLTON RD
Paradise Lathe
A65
Hag Head Laithe
Chelker Resr
Farfield Hall
Low Park
High Park
Hare Knoll
Highfield Farm
Chelker House Farm
Syke House
Dales Way
Highfield House
Upper White Well
Low Sanfitt
Farfield House
Wine Beck
High Sanfitt
Low White Well
B6160
High Laithe
Hart House
Riddings Farm
ADDINGHAM WHARFEDALE RD
Peak Ridding Laithe
Heathness Gill
SKIPTON RD
MOOR LA
Cross Bank
LONG RIDDINGS
Causeway Foot
THE ACRES 1
AYNHOLME CL 2
SPRINGFIELD MOUNT
Addingham Low Moor
Round Dikes Camp
HEATHNESS RD
Addingham First Sch
Addingham Middle Sch
HARCOURT DR
Counter Hill
MOOR LA
MOOR PARK DR
GREEN LA
SCHOOL LA
CHAPEL ST
BACK BECK LA
BOLTON RD

1
6

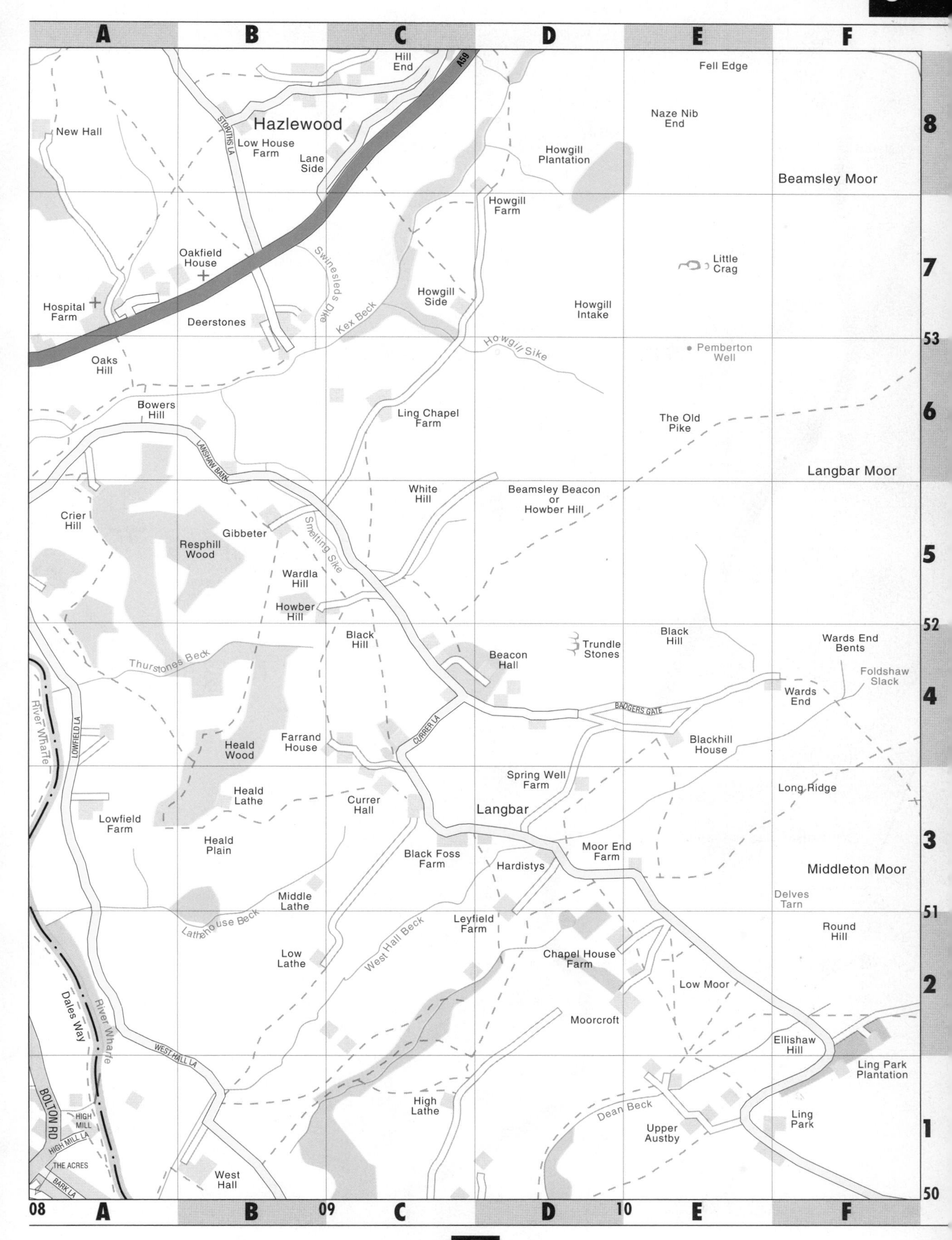

A   B   C   D   E   F

8

Fell Edge

Hazlewood

Hill
End

New Hall

Low House
Farm

Lane
Side

Howgill
Plantation

Naze Nib
End

Beamsley Moor

Oakfield
House

Swinesleds Dike

Kex Beck

Howgill
Farm

Howgill
Side

Little
Crag

7

Hospital
Farm

Deerstones

Howgill
Intake

Oaks
Hill

Howgill Sike

Pemberton
Well

53

Bowers
Hill

Ling Chapel
Farm

The Old
Pike

6

LANGSHAW BANK

White
Hill

Beamsley Beacon
or
Howber Hill

Langbar Moor

Crier
Hill

Gibbeter

Smelting Sike

Resphill
Wood

Wardla
Hill

5

Howber
Hill

52

Black
Hill

Black
Hill

Wards End
Bents

Thurstones Beck

Beacon
Hall

Trundle
Stones

Foldshaw
Slack

CURRER LA

BADGERS GATE

Wards
End

4

River Wharfe

LOWFIELD LA

Heald
Wood

Farrand
House

Blackhill
House

Heald
Lathe

Curren
Hall

Spring Well
Farm

Long Ridge

Lowfield
Farm

Langbar

Heald
Plain

Black Foss
Farm

Hardistys

Moor End
Farm

Middleton Moor

3

Middle
Lathe

Lathenouse Beck

West Hall Beck

Leyfield
Farm

Delves
Tarn

51

Low
Lathe

Chapel House
Farm

Round
Hill

Dales Way

River Wharfe

WEST HALL LA

Low Moor

2

Moorcroft

Ellishaw
Hill

BOLTON RD

HIGH
MILL

HIGH MILL LA

THE ACRES

PARK LA

High
Lathe

Dean Beck

Upper
Austby

Ling
Park

Ling Park
Plantation

1

West
Hall

50

08   A   B   09   C   D   10   E   F

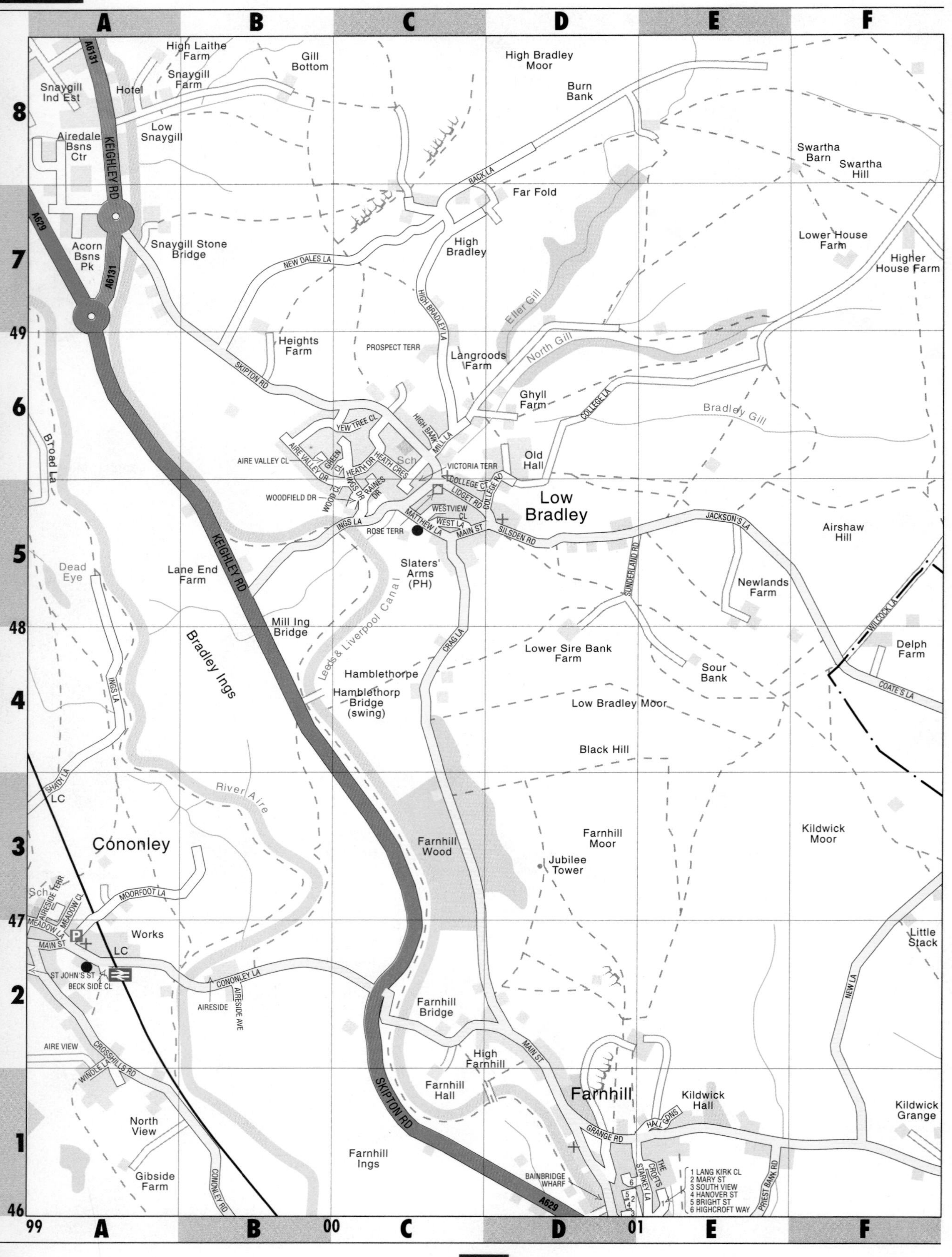

A6131

Snaygill Ind Est

High Laithe Farm

Gill Bottom

High Bradley Moor

Burn Bank

Hotel

Snaygill Farm

Airedale Bsns Ctr

Low Snaygill

Swartha Barn

Swartha Hill

KEIGHLEY RD

BACK LA

Far Fold

Acorn Bsns Pk

Snaygill Stone Bridge

A629

A6131

Lower House Farm

Higher House Farm

NEW DALES LA

High Bradley

HIGH BRADLEY LA

Eller Gill

49

Heights Farm

PROSPECT TERR

Langroods Farm

North Gill

SKIPTON RD

Bradley Gill

6

YEW TREE CL

Ghyll Farm

COLLEGE LA

BROAD LA

AIRE VALLEY CL

GREEN

HIGH PARK LA

MILL LA

Sch

AIRE VALLEY DR

HEATH DR HEATH CRES

Victoria Terr

Old Hall

WOOD DR

WEST LA

RAINES DR

COLLEGE RD

WOODFIELD DR

INGS LA

COLLEGE RD

LIDGET RD

Low Bradley

Airshaw Hill

MATTHEW LA

WESTVIEW CL

ROSE TERR

WEST LA

MAIN ST

SILSDEN RD

JACKSON'S LA

5

Dead Eye

Lane End Farm

Slaters' Arms (PH)

Newlands Farm

SUNDERLAND RD

WILCOCK LA

Mill Ing Bridge

Leeds & Liverpool Canal

CRAG LA

Lower Sire Bank Farm

Sour Bank

Delph Farm

48

Bradley Ings

Hamblethorpe

Low Bradley Moor

COATE'S LA

4

Hamblethorp Bridge (swing)

Black Hill

INGS LA

SHARP LA

LC

River Aire

Farnhill Wood

Farnhill Moor

Kildwick Moor

3

Cononley

Jubilee Tower

MOORFOOT LA

AIRESIDE TERR

MEADOW CL

Works

SKIPTON RD

Farnhill Bridge

MAIN ST

Little Stack

47

Sch

MEADOW CL

P

LC

CONONLEY LA

MAIN ST

AIRESIDE AVE

MAIN LA

ST JOHN'S ST

BECK SIDE CL

AIRESIDE

2

Aire View

Farnhill Hall

Farnhill

High Farnhill

Kildwick Hall

WINDLE ST

CROSSHILLS RD

Kildwick Grange

GRANGE RD

THE GREES

STARKEY LA

PRIEST BANK RD

North View

Farnhill Ings

HAY GARS

1 LANG KIRK CL
2 MARY ST
3 SOUTH VIEW
4 HANOVER ST
5 BRIGHT ST
6 HIGHCROFT WAY

1

Gibside Farm

CONONLEY RD

BAINBRIDGE WHARF

A629

46

1
6

A
B
C
D
E
F
8
7
49
6
5
48
4
3
47
2
1
46
02
03
04
Lower Edge Farm
Carr Bog Farm
Woofa Bank
Moorgate
Schoolmaster Place Farm
Cowburn Farm
JOWETT'S LA
Woofa Bank
Moorcock Hall
BANK LA
Crow Trees
Jenkin Cottage
RIDGE LA
Edge Beck
WALKER'S LA
Cowburn Beck
Walton Hole
Parson's La
CRINGLES LA
High Marchup Barn
Peel's Laithe
Silsden Moor
High Bracken Hill Farm
GREEN LA
Great Gill
Far Cringles Farm
Old Tower
Foster Cliffe Farm
Foster Cliff Beck
Cocklick Hill
Kiln Hill
KILN HILL LA
KIT LA
Lane House
A6034
Cringles
Cocklick Laithe
Horne House
LOW LA
Beck House Farm
Dales Bank Farm
Great Gill Beck
Smoulden Farm
Heights Farm
HEIGHTS LA
Dover Cottage
Lower Heights
HORN LA
FISHBECK LA
Far Stake Hill
Upper Hay Hills
Fishbeck
Hayhills Farm North
Hayhills Beck
Silsden Resr
COATE'S LA
HAYHILLS LA
Bloomer Hill Farm
DENNIS LA
HOLE LA
Hayhills Farm South
Bridge House
Hole Farm
Raikes Head
BOLTON RD
Hutter Hill
NEW LA
Low Bracken Hill
Raikes Hall
GHYLLBANK 8
BROWFIELD TERR 9
BRIDGE RD 10
BRIERDENE 11
NICOLSONS PL 12
BROWN BANK LA
Tar Topping
BRADLEY RD
Town Head
THROSTLE NEST RD 1
FARDENE ST 2
TILLOTSON ST 3
BARRETT ST 4
HAWTHORNE ST 5
STRAWBERRY ST 6
MILLFIELDS 7
High Crossmoor Farm
High Mark
SKIPTON RD
Liby
Silsden
KIRKGATE
Kildwick Grange
Grange House
Grange La
Lane House
Near Woodside Farm
Airedale House Farm
WESTERLEY
Leeds & Liverpool Canal
MILL BANKS
SYKES LA
KEIGHLEY RD
A6034
HAINSWORTH RD
CLOG BRIDGE
BRUNTHWAITE LA
HAWBER LA
Cemy

17
6

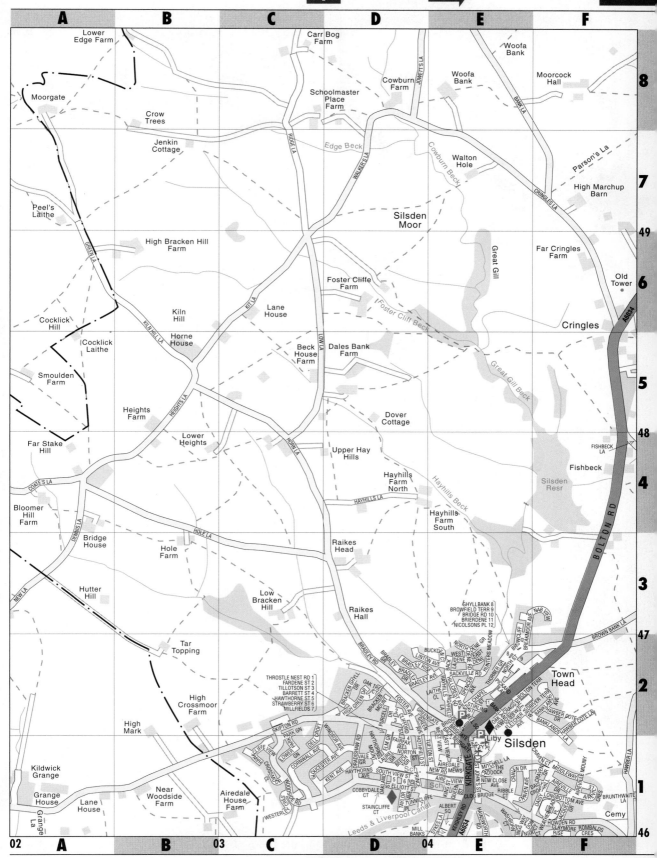

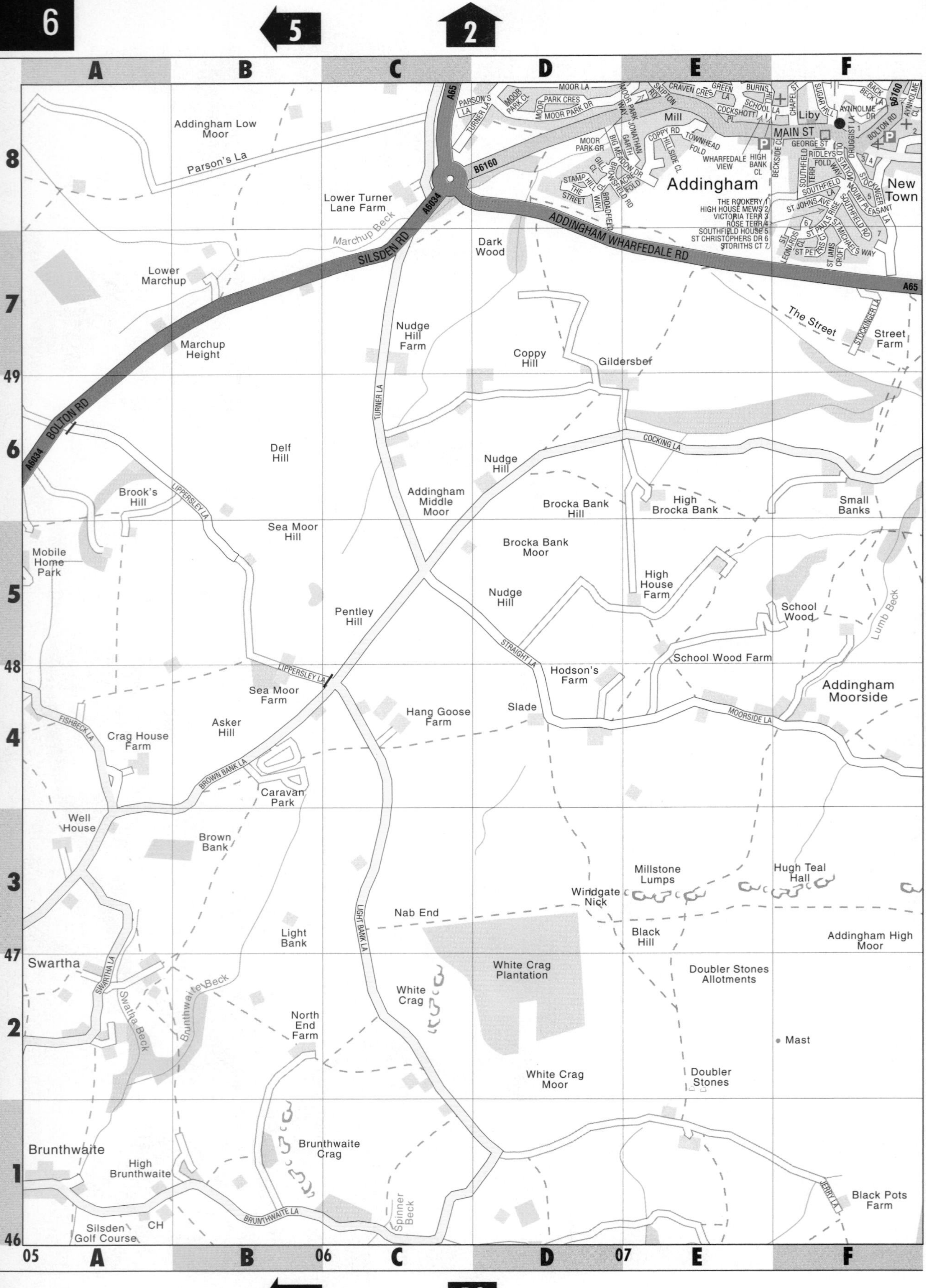

A   B   C   D   E   F

8

Addingham Low Moor

Parson's La

A65

PARSON'S LA

TURNER LA

MOOR PARK CL

MOOR PARK CRES

MOOR PARK DR

B6160

MOOR PARK GR

COPPY RD

TOWNHEAD FOLD

WHARFEDALE FOLD

HIGH BANK CL

STAMP HILL CL

THE STREET

SKIPTON RD

CRAVEN CRES

GREEN LA

BURNS LA

SCHOOL LA

COCKSHOTT LA

CHAPEL ST

SUGAR HILL CL

Liby

BACK BECK LA

AYNHOLME DR

BOLTON RD

B6160

AYNHOLME CL

Mill

MAIN ST

GEORGE ST

RIDLEYS CT

SOUTHFIELD TERR

DRUGGIST LA

STOCKINGER LA

New Town

Addingham

THE ROOKERY 1
HIGH HOUSE MEWS 2
VICTORIA TERR 3
ROSE TERR 4
SOUTHFIELD HOUSE 5
ST CHRISTOPHERS DR 6
STORITHS CT 7.

ST JOHNS AVE
ST PAULS RISE
ST PAULS CL
ST PETS
LEOPARDS
ST JOHNS CL
ST MICHEL'S RD
SOUTHFIELD
MOUNT PLEASANT
MICHEL'S WAY

Lower Turner Lane Farm

Marchup Beck

SILSDEN RD

Dark Wood

ADDINGHAM WHARFEDALE RD

A65

The Street

Street Farm

7

Lower Marchup

Marchup Height

Nudge Hill Farm

Coppy Hill

Gildersber

49

BOLTON RD

A6034

Brook's Hill

LIPPERSLEY LA

Delf Hill

TURNER LA

Nudge Hill

Addingham Middle Moor

Brocka Bank Hill

COCKING LA

High Brocka Bank

Small Banks

6

Mobile Home Park

Sea Moor Hill

Brocka Bank Moor

High House Farm

School Wood

Lumb Beck

5

Pentley Hill

LIPPERSLEY LA

Sea Moor Farm

Nudge Hill

STRAIGHT LA

School Wood Farm

Addingham Moorside

48

Crag House Farm

FISHBECK LA

Asker Hill

Hang Goose Farm

Hodson's Farm

Slade

MOORSIDE LA

4

Well House

BROWN BANK LA

Caravan Park

Brown Bank

Millstone Lumps

Hugh Teal Hall

3

Nab End

Windgate Nick

Black Hill

Addingham High Moor

47

Swartha

SWARTHA LA

Swartha Beck

Brunthwaite Beck

LIGHT BANK LA

Light Bank

White Crag

White Crag Plantation

Doubler Stones Allotments

2

North End Farm

• Mast

Brunthwaite

High Brunthwaite

Brunthwaite Crag

White Crag Moor

Doubler Stones

1

Spinner Beck

JERRY LA

Black Pots Farm

46

Silsden Golf Course

CH

BRUNTHWAITE LA

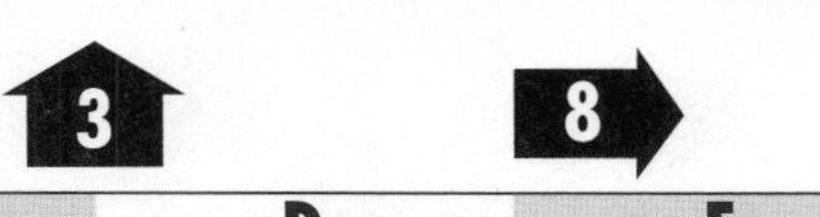

3
8

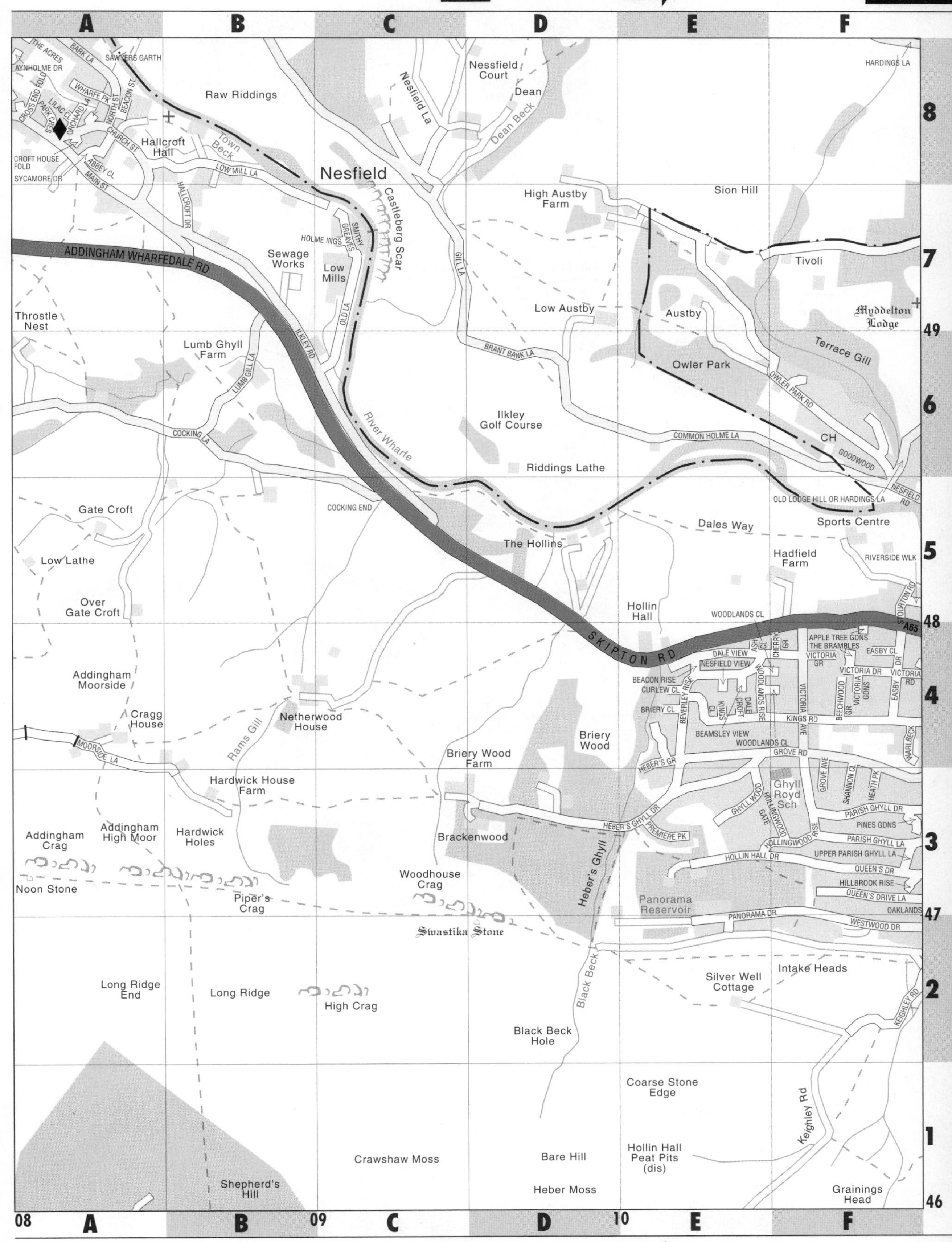

A
B
C
D
E
F
8
7
49
6
5
48
4
3
47
2
1
46
08
09
10
THE ACRES
BARK LA
SAWYERS GARTH
AYNHOLME DR
WHARFE PK
CROSS END FOLD
PARK CRES
LILAC CL
ORCHARD LA
NORTH ST
BEACON ST
CHURCH ST
CROFT HOUSE FOLD
ABBEY CL
SYCAMORE DR
MAIN ST
Raw Riddings
Hallcroft Hall
Town Beck
LOW MILL LA
HALLCROFT DR
Nesfield
Nessfield Court
Dean
Dean Beck
Nesfield La
Castleberg Scar
HOLME INGS
SMITHY GREAVES
Sewage Works
Low Mills
OLD LA
GILL LA
High Austby Farm
Sion Hill
Tivoli
HARDINGS LA
ADDINGHAM WHARFEDALE RD
Throstle Nest
Lumb Ghyll Farm
LUMB GILL LA
ILKLEY RD
Low Austby
Austby
Myddelton Lodge
BRANT BANK LA
Owler Park
Terrace Gill
OWLER PARK RD
Ilkley Golf Course
River Wharfe
COCKING LA
COMMON HOLME LA
CH
GOODWOOD
Riddings Lathe
NESFIELD RD
OLD LODGE HILL OR HARDINGS LA
COCKING END
Gate Croft
Dales Way
Sports Centre
The Hollins
Low Lathe
Hadfield Farm
RIVERSIDE WLK
Over Gate Croft
Hollin Hall
WOODLANDS CL
STOURTON RD
A65
SKIPTON RD
APPLE TREE GDNS
THE BRAMBLES
EASBY CL
DALE VIEW
NESFIELD VIEW
VICTORIA GR
VICTORIA DR
VICTORIA RD
Addingham Moorside
BEACON RISE
CURLEW CL
BRIERY CL
BEVERLEY RISE
KINGS CL
DALE CROFT
WOODLANDS RISE
ASH CL
CHERRY GR
VICTORIA AVE
BEECHWOOD DR
VICTORIA GDNS
EASBY DR
KINGS RD
Cragg House
Netherwood House
BEAMSLEY VIEW
WOODLANDS CL
Briery Wood
MARLBECK
MOORSIDE LA
Rams Gill
Briery Wood Farm
HEBER'S GR
GROVE RD
Hardwick House Farm
GROVE AVE
SHANNON CL
HEATH PK
Ghyll Royd Sch
GHYLL WOOD
HOLLINGWOOD GATE
HOLLINGWOOD RISE
PARISH GHYLL DR
PINES GDNS
Addingham Crag
Addingham High Moor
Hardwick Holes
Brackenwood
HEBER'S GHYLL DR
PREMIERE PK
PARISH GHYLL LA
HOLLINGWOOD RISE
UPPER PARISH GHYLL LA
HOLLIN HALL DR
QUEEN'S DR
HILLBROOK RISE
QUEEN'S DRIVE LA
Noon Stone
Piper's Crag
Woodhouse Crag
Heber's Ghyll
Panorama Reservoir
OAKLANDS
PANORAMA DR
WESTWOOD DR
Swastika Stone
Black Beck
Intake Heads
Long Ridge End
Long Ridge
High Crag
Silver Well Cottage
KEIGHLEY RD
Black Beck Hole
Coarse Stone Edge
Keighley Rd
Crawshaw Moss
Bare Hill
Hollin Hall Peat Pits (dis)
Shepherd's Hill
Heber Moss
Grainings Head

7

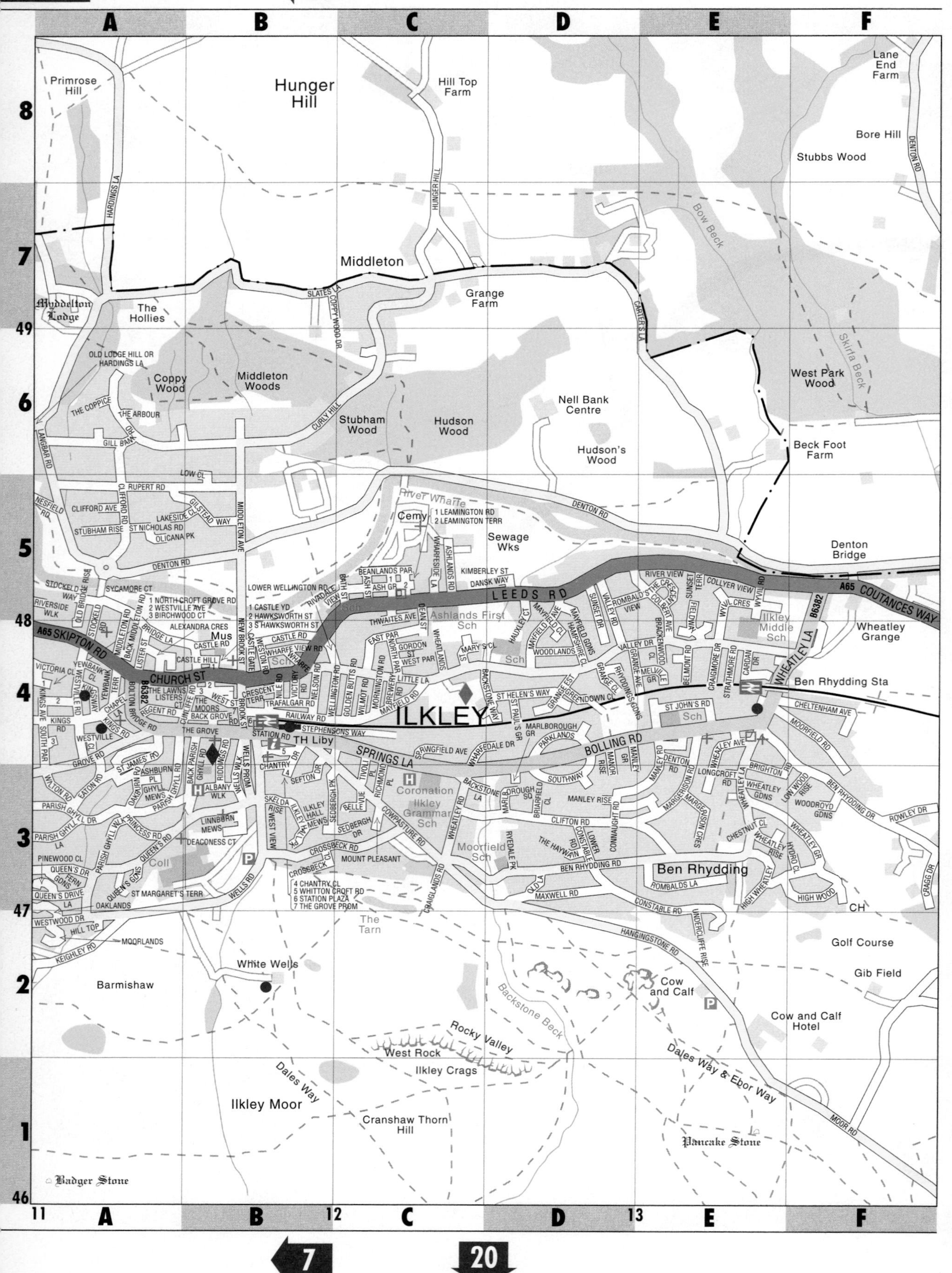

A
B
C
D
E
F
8
7
49
6
5
48
4
3
47
2
1
46
11
12
13
Primrose Hill
Hunger Hill
Hill Top Farm
Lane End Farm
Bore Hill
Stubbs Wood
DENTON RD
HUNGER HILL
HARDINGS LA
Bow Beck
Middleton
Myddelton Lodge
The Hollies
SLATES LA
COPPY WOOD DR
Grange Farm
CARTER'S LA
Skirfa Beck
OLD LODGE HILL OR HARDINGS LA
Coppy Wood
Middleton Woods
THE COPPICE
THE ARBOUR
CURLY HILL
Stubham Wood
Hudson Wood
Nell Bank Centre
West Park Wood
Hudson's Wood
Beck Foot Farm
GILL BANK
LANGBAR RD
LOW CL
RUPERT RD
CLIFFORD RD
NESFIELD RD
CLIFFORD AVE
LAKESIDE CL
GILSTEAD WAY
STUBHAM RISE
ST NICHOLAS RD
OLICANA PK
MIDDLETON AVE
River Wharfe
Cemy
1 LEAMINGTON RD
2 LEAMINGTON TERR
DENTON RD
Sewage Wks
Denton Bridge
DENTON RD
STOCKELD WAY
SYCAMORE CT
OLD BRIDGE RISE
RIVERSIDE WLK
1 NORTH CROFT GROVE RD
2 WESTVILLE AVE
3 BIRCHWOOD CT
LOWER WELLINGTON RD
1 CASTLE YD
2 HAWKSWORTH ST
3 S HAWKSWORTH ST
ALEXANDRA CRES
Mus
CASTLE RD
CASTLE HILL
WHARFE VIEW RD
BEANLANDS PAR
ASH GR
KIMBERLEY ST
DANSK WAY
WHARFESIDE LA
ASHLANDS RD
LEEDS RD
Sch
THWAITES AVE
Ashlands First Sch
RIVER VIEW
THE CRESCENT
SUNSET TERR
COLLYER VIEW
WYVIL RD
WYVIL CRES
A65
COUTANCES WAY
B6382
Ilkley Middle Sch
Wheatley Grange
A65 SKIPTON RD
STOCKELD RD
MIDDLETON RD
BACK MIDDLETON RD
BRIDGE LA
LISTER ST
EAST PAR
GORDON ST
WEST PAR
ST MARY'S CL
HAUXLEY CT
MAYFIELD AVE
MAYFIELD CL
HAMPSHIRE CL
MAYFIELD GDNS
SUNSET DR
VALLEY RD
ROMBALDS VIEW
COLBERT AVE
BRACKENWOOD CL
FIELDWAY
WOODLANDS
VALLEY DR
BELMONT RD
CRAIGMORE DR
STRATHMORE RD
CARDAN DR
WHEATLEY LA
VICTORIA CL
YEWBANK CL
YEWBANK TERR
CHURCH ST
NEW BROOK ST
CASTLE GATE
WESTON RD
WHARFE VIEW
NILE RD
VICTORIA RD
NELSON RD
WELLINGTON RD
GOLDEN BUTTS RD
WILMOT RD
MORNINGTON RD
NORTH PAR
BREWERY RD
LITTLE LA
MAYFIELD RD
BACKSTONE WAY
ST HELEN'S WAY
GRANGE EST
GRANGE CL
GRANGE AVE
RHYDDINGS GDNS
MELVILLE GR
GREENDOWN CL
Ben Rhydding Sta
KINGS AVE
WESTVILLE RD
KINGS GDNS
CHAPEL
BOLTON BRIDGE RD
B6382
THE LAWNS
LISTERS CT
REGENT RD
THE MOORS
WEST ST
BACK GROVE RD
BROOK ST
CRESCENT TERR
TRAFALGAR RD
RAILWAY RD
ILKLEY
ST PAUL'S GR
MARLBOROUGH GR
ST JOHN'S RD
Sch
CHELTENHAM AVE
MOORFIELD RD
KINGS RD
SOUTH PAR
WESTVILLE CL
THE GROVE
STATION RD
STEPHENSONS WAY
TH Liby
SPRINGS LA
SPRINGFIELD AVE
WHARFEDALE DR
PARKLANDS
BOLLING RD
WHEATLEY AVE
GROVE RD
ST JAMES' RD
BACK PARISH GHYLL RD
RIDDINGS RD
WELLS PROM
CHANTRY DR
SEFTON DR
TIVOLI PL
RICHMOND PL
Coronation
SOUTHWAY
MANOR RISE
MANLEY GR
MANLEY RD
DENTON RD
LONGCROFT RD
BRIGHTON RD
LOW WOOD RISE
BEN RHYDDING DR
ROWLEY DR
WILTON RD
EATON RD
ASHBURN PL
GHYLL MEWS
PARISH GHYLL RD
ALBANY WLK
SKELDA RISE
ILKLEY HALL MEWS
SEDBERGH PK
BELLE VUE
Ilkley Grammar Sch
BACKSTONE LA
MARLBOROUGH SQ
BRIARFIELD CL
MANLEY RISE
CONNAUGHT RD
MARGERISON RD
MARGERISON CRES
WHEATLEY GDNS
WOODROYD GDNS
PARISH GHYLL DR
PARISH GHYLL LA
LINNBURN MEWS
DEACONESS CT
WEST VIEW
SEDBERGH DR
COWPASTURE RD
WHEATLEY RD
CLIFTON RD
CHESTNUT CL
WHEATLEY RISE
HYDRO CL
WHEATLEY GR
CRAGG DR
PINEWOOD CL
Coll
P
CROSSBECK RD
CROSSBECK CL
MOUNT PLEASANT
Moorfield Sch
RYEDALE PK
THE HAYWAIN
LOWER CONSTABLE RD
BEN RHYDDING RD
Ben Rhydding
QUEEN'S DR
FERN GDNS
QUEEN'S GDNS
QUEEN'S RD
ST MARGARET'S TERR
WELLS RD
4 CHANTRY CL
5 WHITTON CROFT RD
6 STATION PLAZA
7 THE GROVE PROM
CRAIGLANDS RD
OLD LA
MAXWELL RD
ROMBALDS LA
HIGH WHEATLEY
HIGH WOOD
CH
QUEEN'S DRIVE LA
OAKLANDS
CONSTABLE RD
UNDERCLIFFE RISE
WESTWOOD DR
HILL TOP
MOORLANDS
The Tarn
HANGINGSTONE RD
Golf Course
KEIGHLEY RD
White Wells
Barmishaw
Cow and Calf
Gib Field
Backstone Beck
P
Cow and Calf Hotel
Rocky Valley
West Rock
Ilkley Crags
Dales Way
Dales Way & Ebor Way
Ilkley Moor
Cranshaw Thorn Hill
MOOR RD
Pancake Stone
Badger Stone
7
20

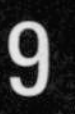

10

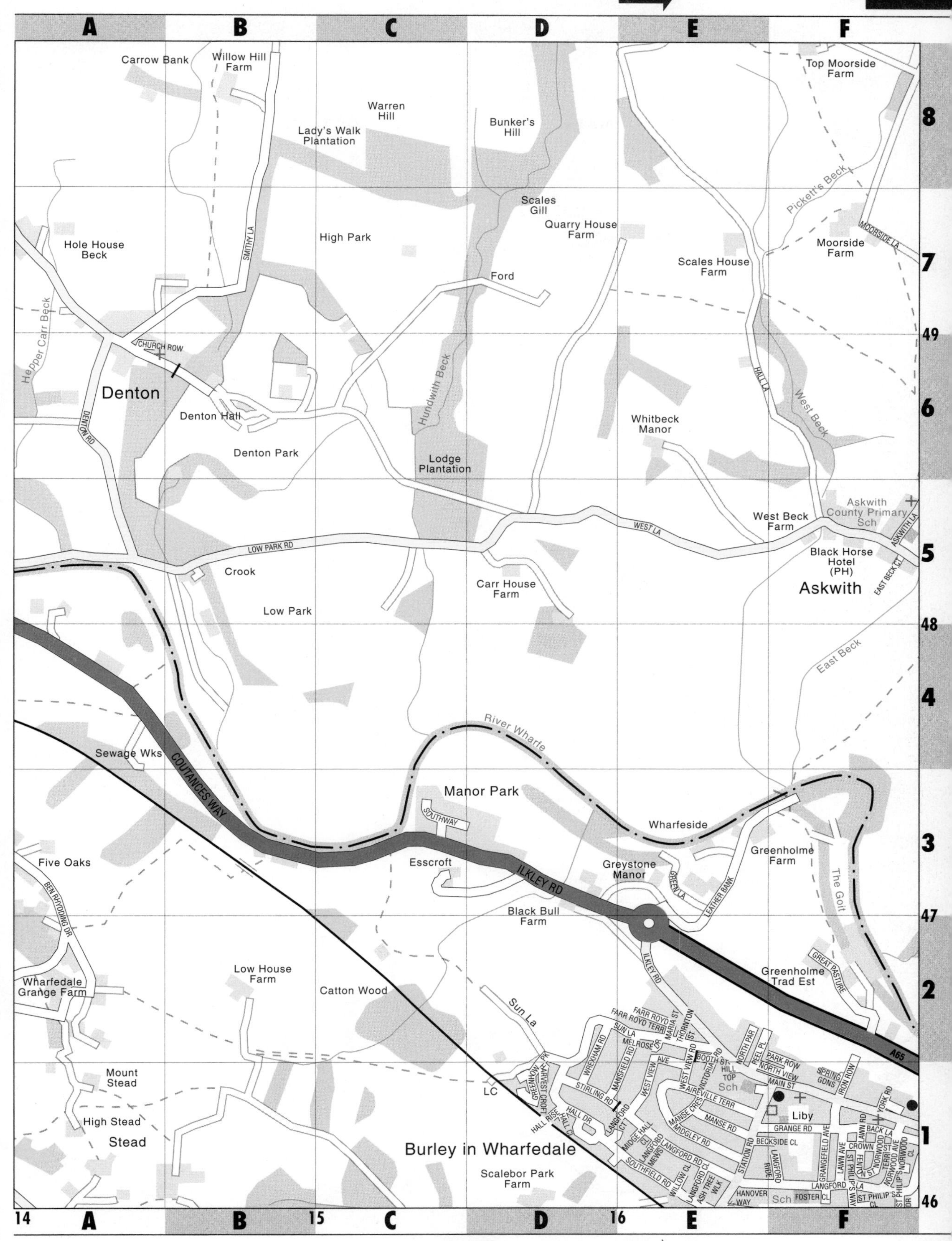

A
B
C
D
E
F
8
7
49
6
5
48
4
3
47
2
1
46
14
15
16
Carrow Bank
Willow Hill Farm
Warren Hill
Lady's Walk Plantation
Bunker's Hill
Top Moorside Farm
Pickett's Beck
Scales Gill
Quarry House Farm
Hole House Beck
SMITHY LA
High Park
Moorside Farm
MOORSIDE LA
Scales House Farm
Ford
Hepper Carr Beck
CHURCH ROW
Denton
Denton Hall
Hundwith Beck
HALL LA
West Beck
Whitbeck Manor
DENTON RD
Denton Park
Lodge Plantation
Askwith County Primary Sch
West Beck Farm
WEST LA
ASKWITH LA
LOW PARK RD
Black Horse Hotel (PH)
EAST BECK CT
Crook
Carr House Farm
Askwith
Low Park
East Beck
River Wharfe
Sewage Wks
COUTANCES WAY
Manor Park
SOUTHWAY
Wharfeside
Five Oaks
Esscroft
Greenholme Farm
Greystone Manor
ILKLEY RD
GREEN LA
LEATHER BANK
The Goit
BEN RHYDDING DR
Black Bull Farm
Low House Farm
GREAT PASTURE
Greenholme Trad Est
Wharfedale Grange Farm
Catton Wood
ILKLEY RD
Sun La
A65
Mount Stead
High Stead
Stead
LC
Burley in Wharfedale
Scalebor Park Farm
Sch
Liby
Sch
FARR ROYD
FARR ROYD TERR
SUN LA
MELROSE DR
WREXHAM RD
MANSFIELD RD
WEST VIEW AVE
WEST VIEW RD
VICTORIA RD
THORNTON ST
MARIA ST
BOOTH ST
HILL TOP
NORTH PAR
PEEL PL
PARK ROW
NORTH VIEW
MAIN ST
SPRING GDNS
IRON ROW
YORK RD
STIRLING RD
AIREVILLE TERR
MANSE CRES
MANSE RD
MIDGLEY RD
GRANGE RD
BACK LA
GREENHOW PK
HARVEST CROFT
HALL RISE
HALL CL
HALL DR
LANGFORD CT
MIDGE HALL CL
LANGFORD MEWS
LANGFORD RD
SOUTHFIELD RD
WILLOW CL
LANGFORD CL
ASH TREE WLK
STATION RD
LANGFORD RIDE
BECKSIDE CL
GRANGEFIELD AVE
LAWN AVE
LAWN RD
CROWN ST
FENTON ST
NORWOOD TERR
NORWOOD AVE
ST PHILIP'S WAY
LANGFORD LA
HANOVER WAY
FOSTER CL
ST PHILIP'S CL
ST PHILIP'S DR

21
10

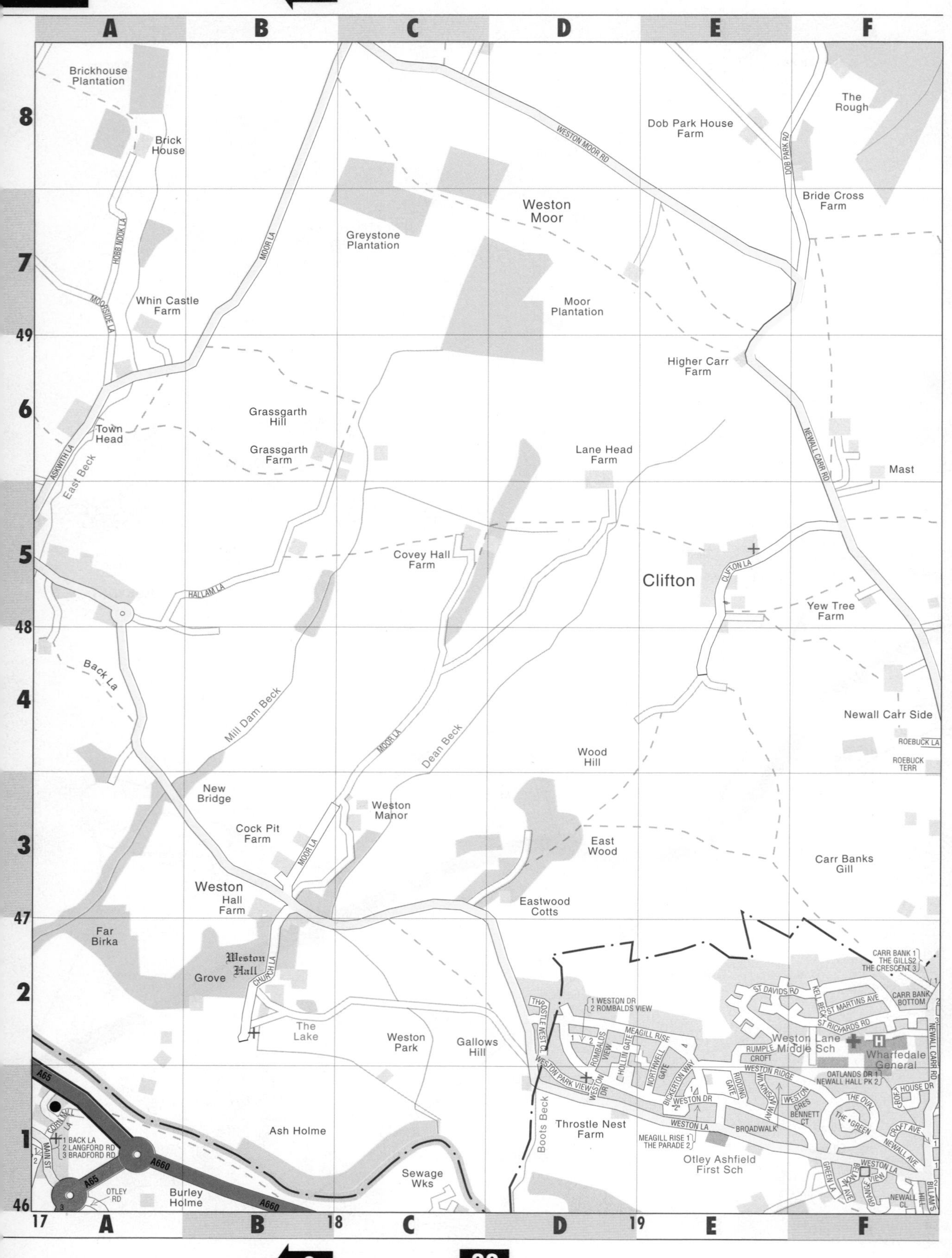

A B C D E F

8

Brickhouse
Plantation

Brick
House

The Rough

Weston Moor Rd

Dob Park House
Farm

Dob Park Rd

Bride Cross
Farm

Weston
Moor

Moor La

Greystone
Plantation

7

Hobb Wood La

Moorside La

Whin Castle
Farm

Moor
Plantation

49

Higher Carr
Farm

Newall Carr Rd

6

Town
Head

East Beck

Grassgarth
Hill

Grassgarth
Farm

Lane Head
Farm

Mast

Askwith La

5

Hallam La

Covey Hall
Farm

Clifton

Clifton La

Yew Tree
Farm

48

Back La

Newall Carr Side

Roebuck La

4

Mill Dam Beck

Moor La

Dean Beck

Wood
Hill

Roebuck
Terr

New
Bridge

Weston
Manor

East
Wood

Carr Banks
Gill

3

Cock Pit
Farm

Moor La

Weston
Hall Farm

Eastwood
Cotts

47

Far
Birka

Weston
Hall

Grove

Church La

CARR BANK 1
THE GILLS 2
THE CRESCENT 3

St Davids Rd

Kell Beck

St Martins Ave

CARR BANK
BOTTOM

2

The
Lake

Weston
Park

Gallows
Hill

1 WESTON DR
2 ROMBALDS VIEW

Meagill Rise

St Richards Rd

Weston Lane
Middle Sch

Wharfedale
General

Newall Carr Rd

Castle West

Weston Park View

Rombalds
View

Hollin Gate

Martinwell

Bickerton Way

Riding
Gate

Kinson Way

Rumple
Croft

Chris
Bennett
Ct

Oatlands Dr 1
Newall Hall Pk 2

The
Green

The Oval

House Dr

Croft Ave

A65

1

Ash Holme

Boots Beck

Throstle Nest
Farm

Weston Dr

Weston La

Broadwalk

MEAGILL RISE 1
THE PARADE 2

Otley Ashfield
First Sch

Green La

Newall Ave

Weston La

Skay Ave

Billams

1 BACK LA
2 LANGFORD RD
3 BRADFORD RD

Cornmill

Main St

A660

Otley
Rd

46

Burley
Holme

A65

A660

Sewage
Wks

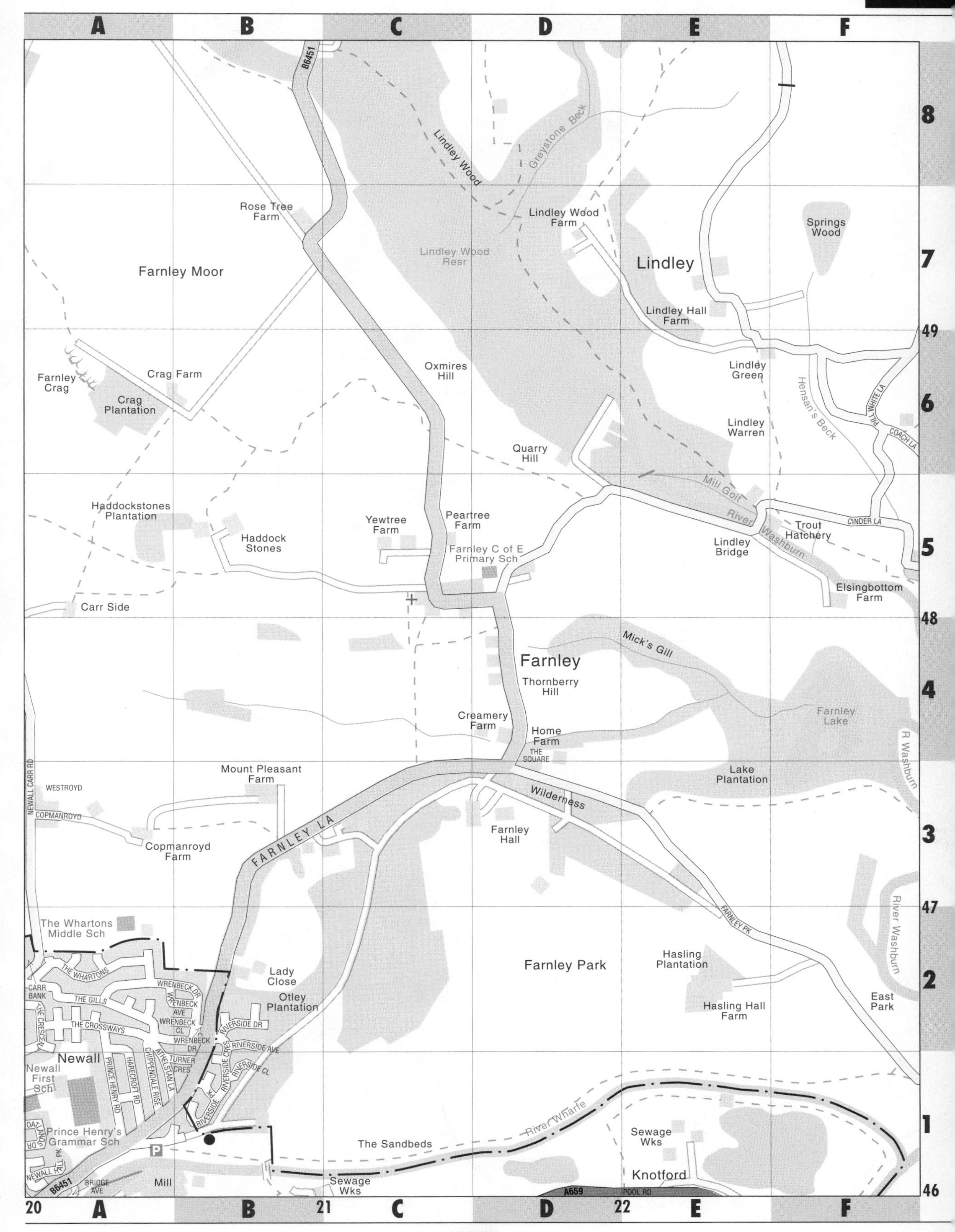
A
B
C
D
E
F
8
7
49
6
5
48
4
3
47
2
1
46
20
21
22
B6451
Lindley Wood
Greystone Beck
Rose Tree Farm
Lindley Wood Farm
Lindley Wood Resr
Springs Wood
Farnley Moor
Lindley
Lindley Hall Farm
Farnley Crag
Crag Farm
Crag Plantation
Oxmires Hill
Lindley Green
Hensan's Beck
PILL WHITE LA
COACH LA
Lindley Warren
Quarry Hill
Mill Goit
River Washburn
Haddockstones Plantation
Yewtree Farm
Peartree Farm
Haddock Stones
Farnley C of E Primary Sch
Trout Hatchery
CINDER LA
Lindley Bridge
Elsingbottom Farm
Carr Side
Mick's Gill
Farnley
Thornberry Hill
Farnley Lake
Creamery Farm
Home Farm
THE SQUARE
R Washburn
Mount Pleasant Farm
Lake Plantation
NEWALL CARR RD
WESTROYD
COPMANROYD
Wilderness
FARNLEY LA
Farnley Hall
Copmanroyd Farm
FARNLEY PK
River Washburn
The Whartons Middle Sch
Farnley Park
Hasling Plantation
THE WHARTONS
Lady Close
Otley Plantation
CARR BANK
WRENBECK DR
THE GILLS
WRENBECK AVE
Hasling Hall Farm
East Park
THE CROSSWAYS
WRENBECK CL
RIVERSIDE DR
WRENBECK DR
RIVERSIDE AVE
Newall
PRINCE HENRY RD
HARECROFT RD
CHIPPENDALE RISE
ATHELSTAN LA
TURNER CRES
RIVERSIDE CRES
RIVERSIDE CL
Newall First Sch
RIVERSIDE
River Wharfe
Sewage Wks
Prince Henry's Grammar Sch
P
The Sandbeds
NEWALL HALL PK
B6451
BRIDGE AVE
Mill
Sewage Wks
Knotford
A659
POOL RD

23

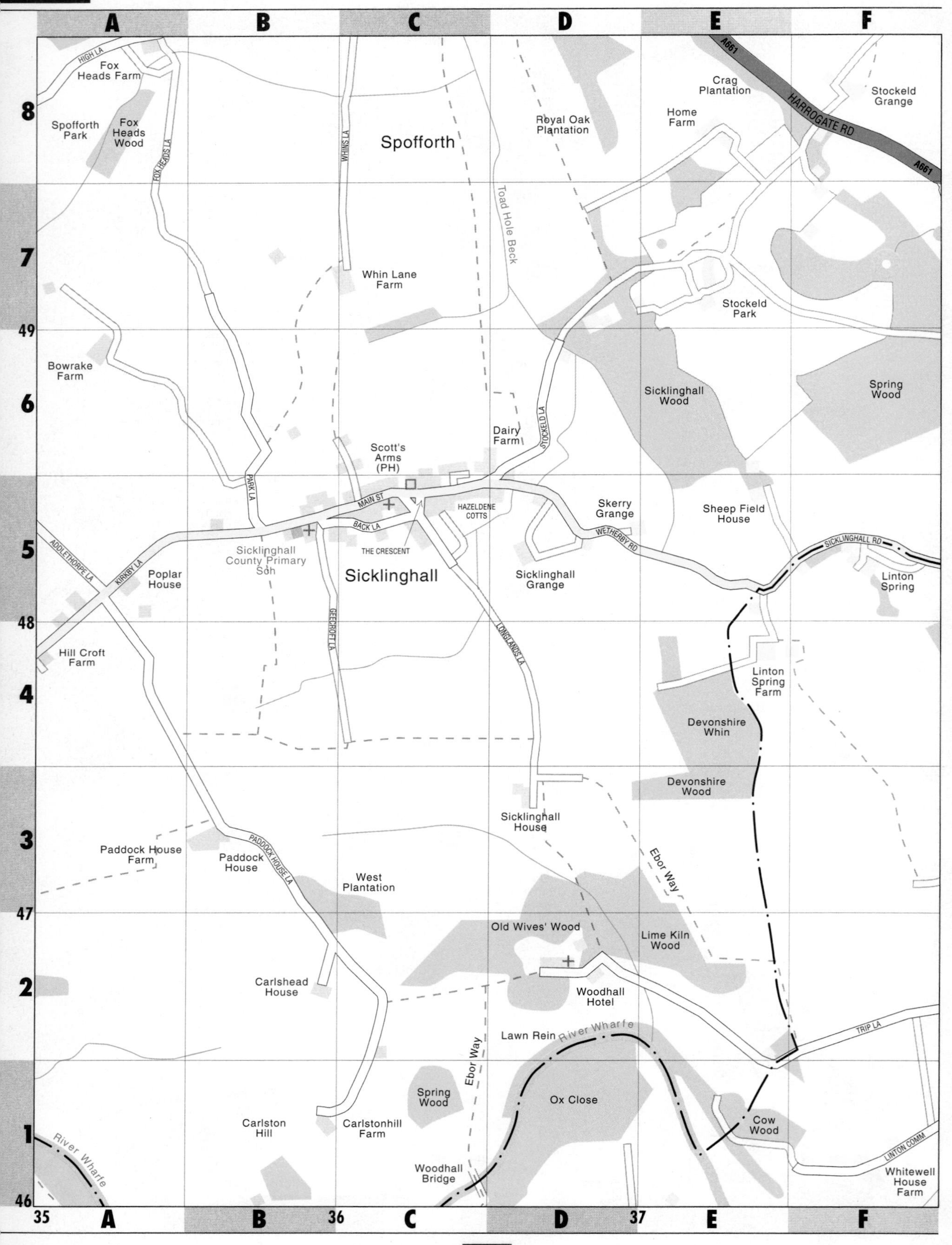
A
B
C
D
E
F
8
7
49
6
5
48
4
3
47
2
1
46
35
36
37
HIGH LA
Fox Heads Farm
Spofforth Park
Fox Heads Wood
FOX HEADS LA
WHINS LA
Spofforth
Royal Oak Plantation
Toad Hole Beck
Crag Plantation
Home Farm
A661
HARROGATE RD
Stockeld Grange
Whin Lane Farm
Stockeld Park
Bowrake Farm
Sicklinghall Wood
Spring Wood
Dairy Farm
STOCKELD LA
Scott's Arms (PH)
PARK LA
MAIN ST
BACK LA
HAZELDENE COTTS
THE CRESCENT
Skerry Grange
WETHERBY RD
Sheep Field House
SICKLINGHALL RD
ADDLETHORPE LA
KIRKBY LA
Poplar House
Sicklinghall County Primary Sch
Sicklinghall
Sicklinghall Grange
Linton Spring
Hill Croft Farm
GEECROFT LA
LONGLANDS LA
Linton Spring Farm
Devonshire Whin
Devonshire Wood
Sicklinghall House
Paddock House Farm
Paddock House
PADDOCK HOUSE LA
West Plantation
Ebor Way
Old Wives' Wood
Lime Kiln Wood
Carlshead House
Woodhall Hotel
Lawn Rein
River Wharfe
TRIP LA
Spring Wood
Ox Close
Cow Wood
Carlston Hill
Carlstonhill Farm
LINTON COMM
Woodhall Bridge
Whitewell House Farm

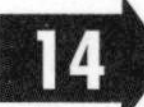

14

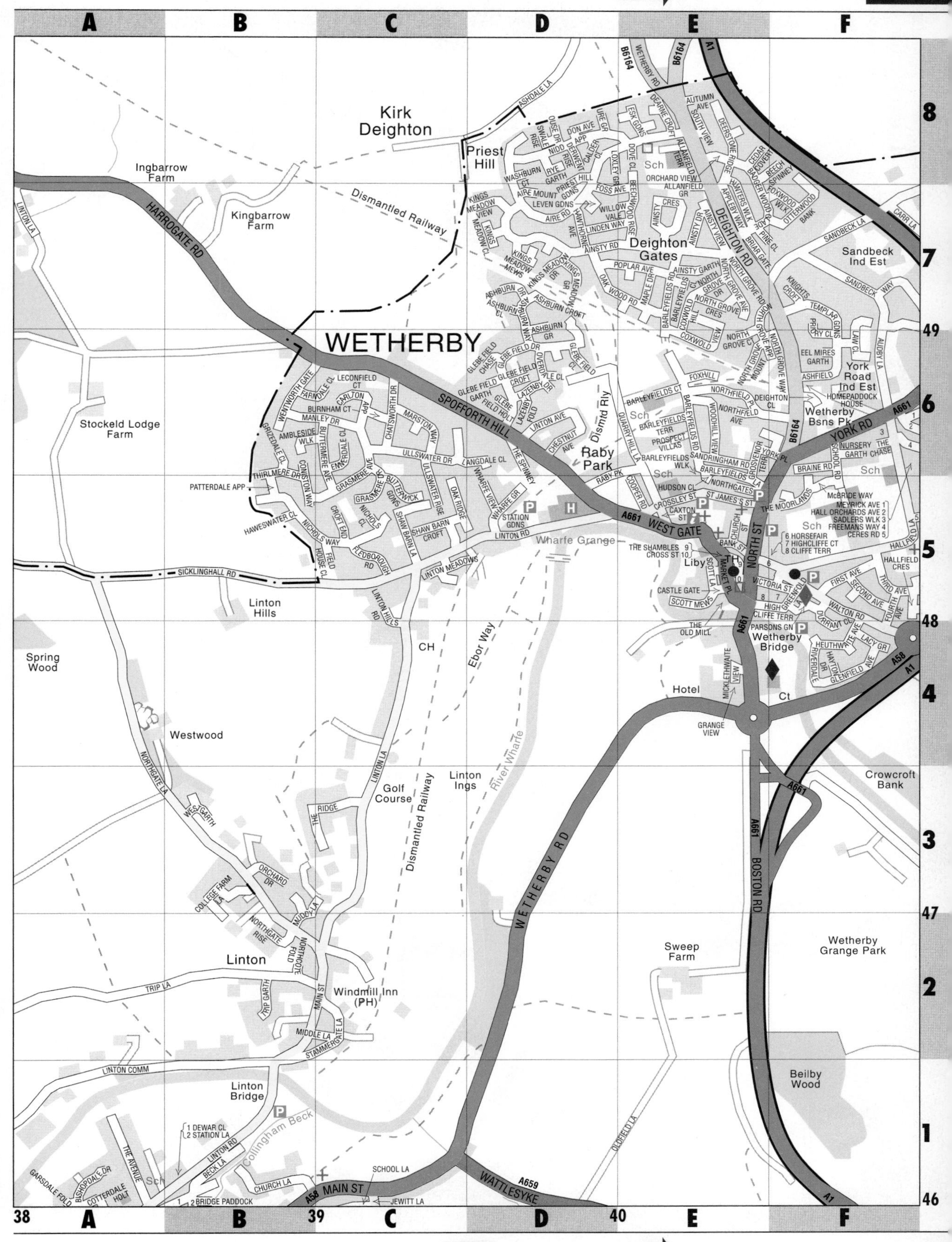

A
B
C
D
E
F
8
7
6
5
4
3
2
1
49
48
47
46
38
39
40
Kirk Deighton
Priest Hill
Ingbarrow Farm
Kingbarrow Farm
Dismantled Railway
HARROGATE RD
LINTON LA
WETHERBY
Deighton Gates
Sandbeck Ind Est
York Road Ind Est
Wetherby Bsns Pk
Stockeld Lodge Farm
SPOFFORTH HILL
Raby Park
Dismtd Rly
PATTERDALE APP
HAWESWATER CL
SICKLINGHALL RD
Linton Hills
A661 WEST GATE
Wharfe Grange
NORTH ST
DEIGHTON RD
YORK RD
A661
B6164
A1
Liby
TH
Wetherby Bridge
Hotel
GRANGE VIEW
Ct
CH
Ebor Way
Spring Wood
Westwood
NORTHGATE LA
Golf Course
Linton Ings
River Wharfe
WETHERBY RD
BOSTON RD
Crowcroft Bank
A58
Wetherby Grange Park
Sweep Farm
Linton
TRIP LA
Windmill Inn (PH)
MAIN ST
MIDDLE LA
STAMMERGATE LA
LINTON COMM
Linton Bridge
Collingham Beck
1 DEWAR CL
2 STATION LA
THE AVENUE
LINTON RD
BECK LA
CHURCH LA
SCHOOL LA
A58 MAIN ST
JEWITT LA
1 2 BRIDGE PADDOCK
GARSDALE FOLD
BISHOPDALE DR
COTTERDALE HOLT
WATTLESYKE
A659
OLDFIELD LA
Beilby Wood
Sch
6 HORSEFAIR
7 HIGHCLIFFE CT
8 CLIFFE TERR
McBRIDE WAY
MEYRICK AVE 1
HALL ORCHARDS AVE 2
SADLERS WLK 3
FREEMANS WAY 4
CERES RD 5
THE SHAMBLES 9
CROSS ST 10
CASTLE GATE
SCOTT MEWS
THE OLD MILL
PARSONS GN
MICKLETHWAITE VIEW

29
14

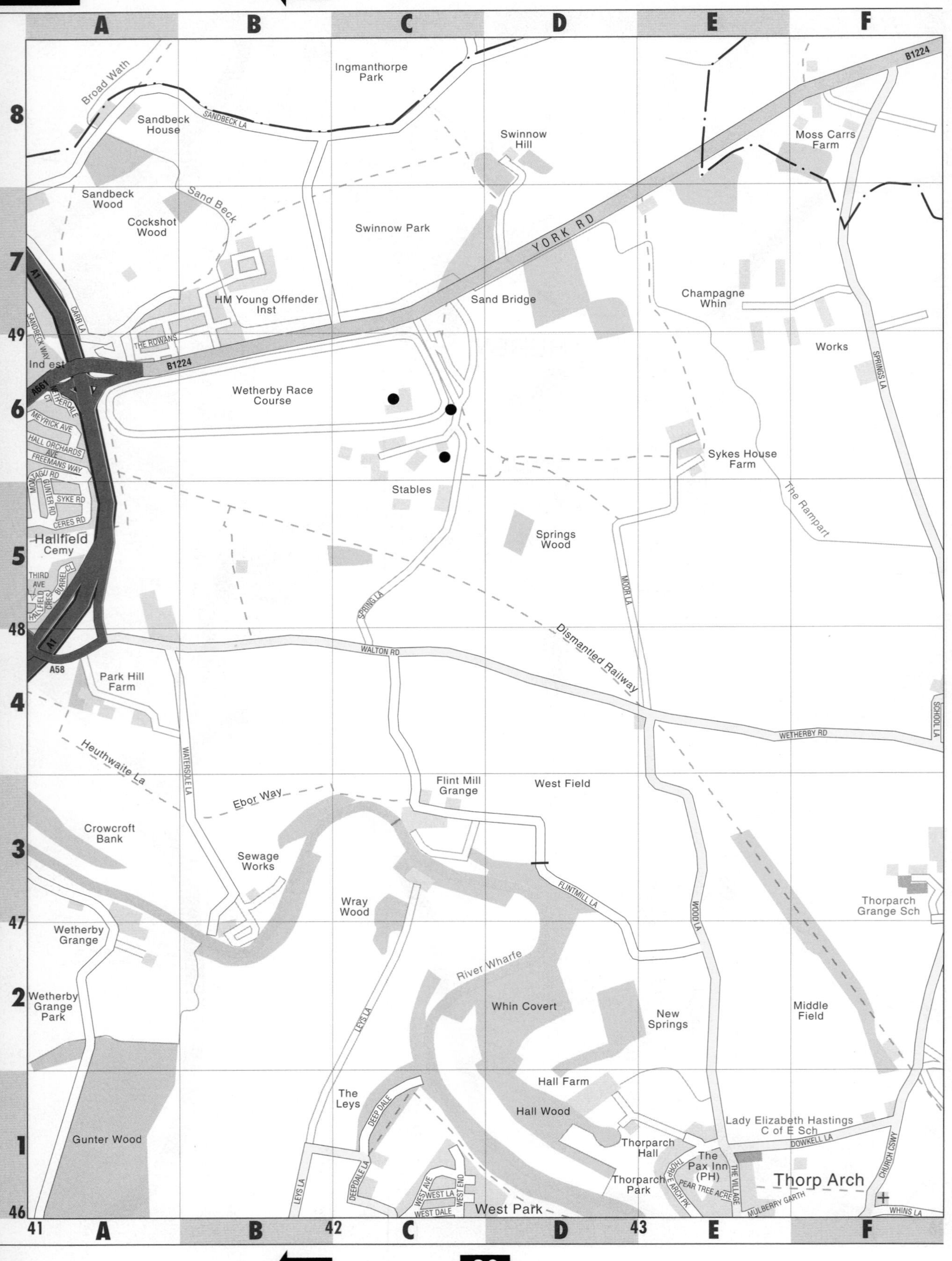

A B C D E F

8 Broad Wath

Ingmanthorpe Park

Moss Carrs Farm

B1224

Sandbeck House

SANDBECK LA

Swinnow Hill

Sandbeck Wood

Sand Beck

Cockshot Wood

Swinnow Park

YORK RD

7

A1

HM Young Offender Inst

Sand Bridge

Champagne Whin

49

THE ROWANS

SANDBECK WAY

CARR LA

B1224

Works

SPRINGS LA

Ind est

6 A661

MEYRICK AVE

HALL ORCHARDS AVE

FREEMANS WAY

Wetherby Race Course

Sykes House Farm

The Rampart

MONTAGU RD

GUNTER RD

SYKE RD

CERES RD

Stables

Springs Wood

MOOR LA

Hallfield Cemy

5

THIRD AVE

SPRING LA

48

A1

WALTON RD

Dismantled Railway

Park Hill Farm

A58

4

Heuthwaite La

WETHERBY RD

SCHOOL LA

WATERSIDE LA

Ebor Way

Flint Mill Grange

West Field

Crowcroft Bank

Sewage Works

FLINTMILL LA

WOOD LA

Thorparch Grange Sch

47

Wray Wood

Wetherby Grange

River Wharfe

2

LEYS LA

Whin Covert

New Springs

Middle Field

Wetherby Grange Park

Hall Farm

46 Gunter Wood

The Leys

DEEP DALE

Hall Wood

Thorparch Hall

Lady Elizabeth Hastings C of E Sch

DOWKELL LA

Thorparch Park

The Pax Inn (PH)

THE VILLAGE

PEAR TREE ACRE

CHURCH CSWY

Thorp Arch

ARCH PK

MULBERRY GARTH

WHINS LA

LEYS LA

DEEPDALE LA

WEST AVE

WEST END

WEST DALE

West Park

41 A B 42 C D 43 E F

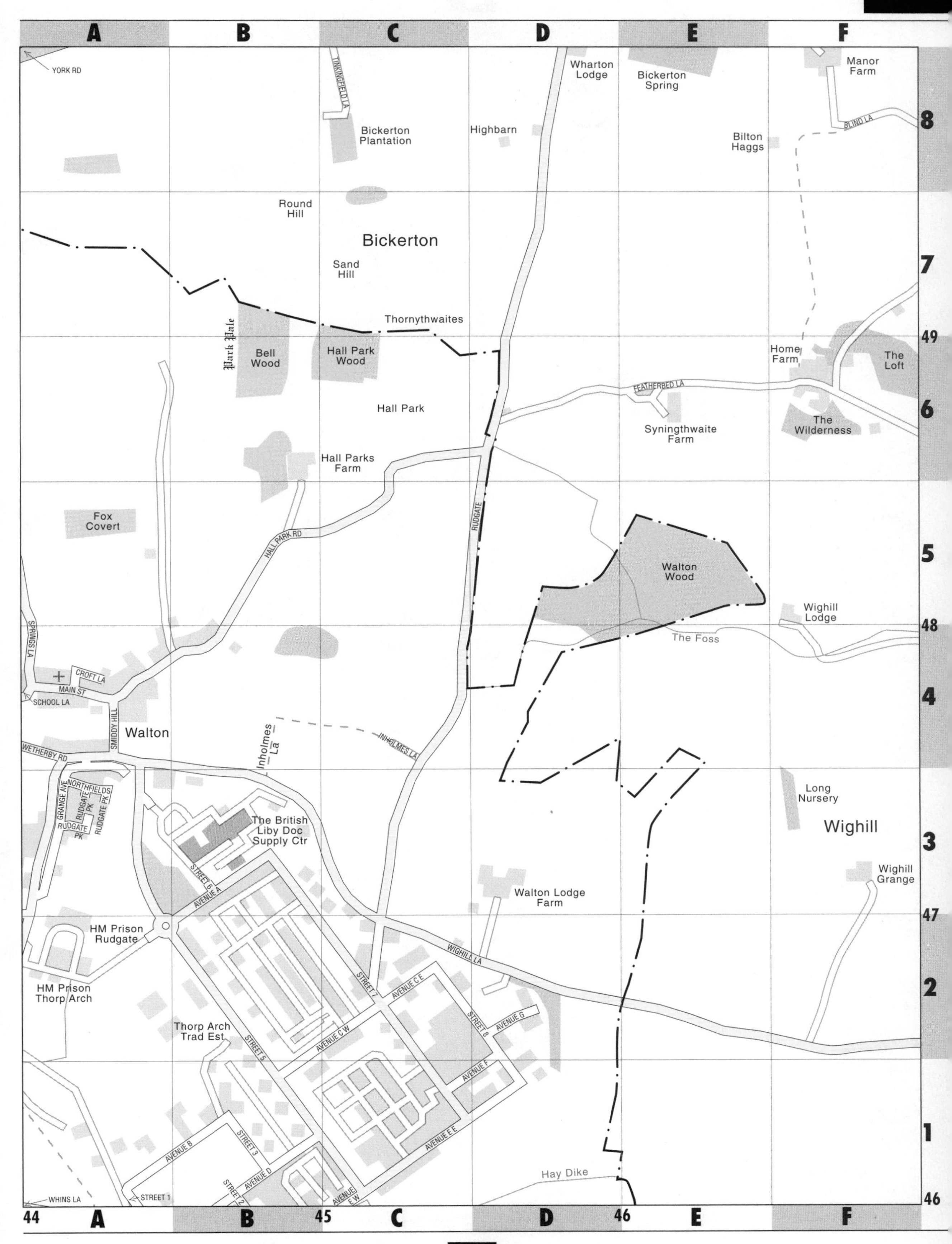

York Rd

Bickerton
Plantation

Tinkingfield La

Wharton
Lodge

Bickerton
Spring

Highbarn

Manor
Farm

Blind La

Bilton
Haggs

8

Round
Hill

Bickerton

Sand
Hill

7

Park Vale

Thornythwaites

49

Home
Farm

The
Loft

Bell
Wood

Hall Park
Wood

Featherbed La

6

Hall Park

Syningthwaite
Farm

The
Wilderness

Hall Parks
Farm

Fox
Covert

Hall Park Rd

Rudgate

Walton
Wood

5

Wighill
Lodge

48

The Foss

Croft La

Main St

School La

4

Springs La

Smiddy Hill

Walton

Inholmes La

Inholmes La

Wetherby Rd

Long
Nursery

Wighill

Grange Ave

Northfields

Rudgate Pk

Rudgate Pk

The British
Liby Doc
Supply Ctr

3

Wighill
Grange

Rudgate Pk

Street G A

Avenue A

47

HM Prison
Rudgate

Walton Lodge
Farm

2

HM Prison
Thorp Arch

Street S

Street Z

Avenue C E

Wighill La

Avenue C W

Street B

Avenue G

Thorp Arch
Trad Est

Avenue F

Avenue E E

Avenue B

Street 3

Avenue D

Avenue E W

1

Avenue E W

Whins La

Street 1

Street 2

Hay Dike

46

44   A   B   45   C   D   46   E   F

4

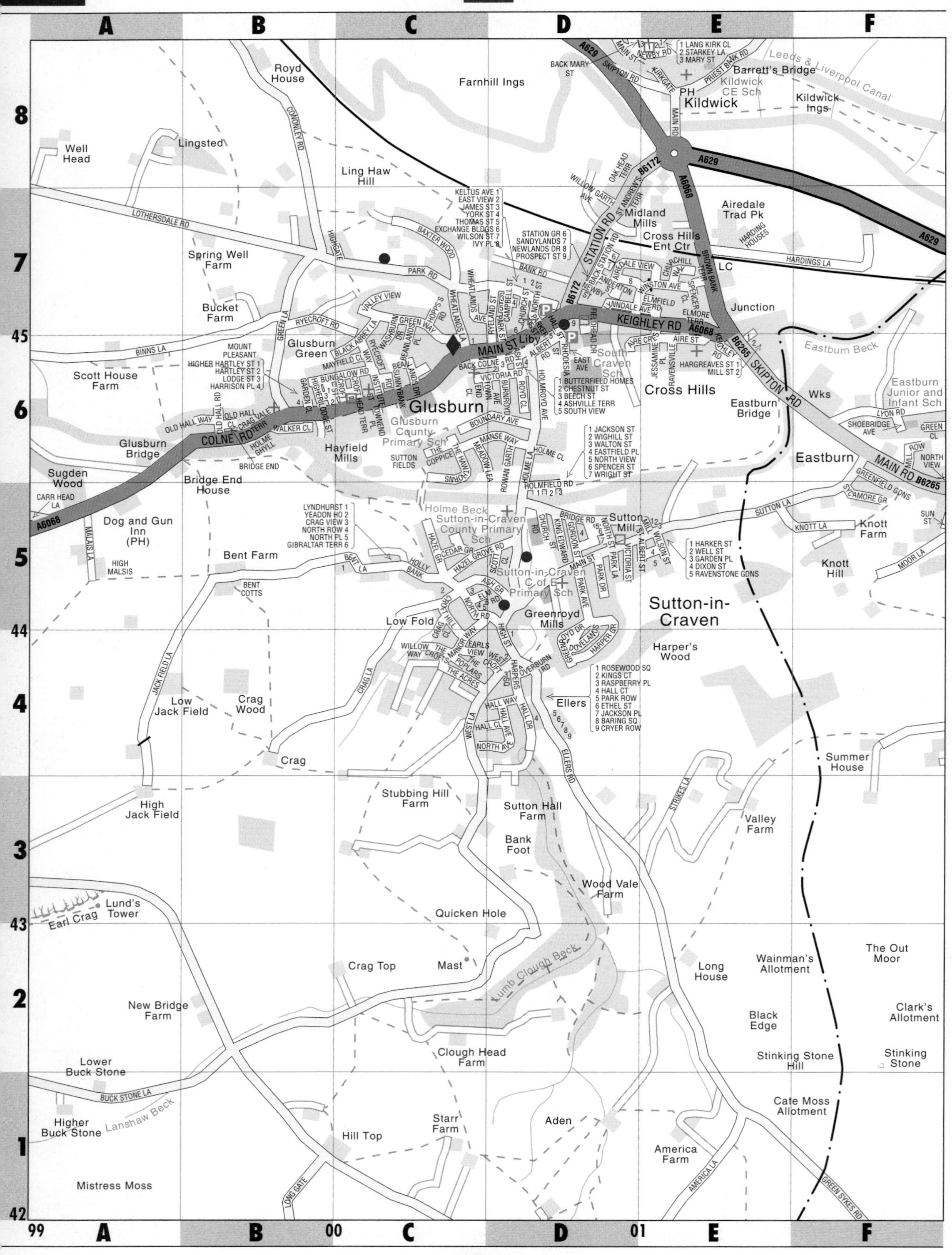
A
B
C
D
E
F
8
7
45
6
5
44
4
3
43
2
1
42
99
00
01
Royd House
Farnhill Ings
Kildwick
Kildwick CE Sch
Barrett's Bridge
Leeds & Liverpool Canal
Kildwick Ings
Well Head
Lingsted
Ling Haw Hill
Midland Mills
Airedale Trad Pk
Cross Hills Ent Ctr
Spring Well Farm
Bucket Farm
Junction
Glusburn Green
Scott House Farm
Glusburn
Glusburn County Primary Sch
South Craven Sch
Cross Hills
Eastburn Bridge
Eastburn Beck
Eastburn Junior and Infant Sch
Wks
Glusburn Bridge
Hayfield Mills
Eastburn
Sugden Wood
Bridge End House
Holme Beck
Sutton-in-Craven County Primary Sch
Dog and Gun Inn (PH)
Sutton Mill
Knott Farm
Bent Farm
High Malsis
Knott Hill
Sutton-in-Craven C of E Primary Sch
Sutton-in-Craven
Low Fold
Greenroyd Mills
Harper's Wood
Low Jack Field
Crag Wood
Ellers
Crag
Summer House
High Jack Field
Stubbing Hill Farm
Sutton Hall Farm
Valley Farm
Bank Foot
Wood Vale Farm
Lund's Tower
Earl Crag
Quicken Hole
Crag Top
Mast
Lumb Clough Beck
Long House
Wainman's Allotment
The Out Moor
New Bridge Farm
Black Edge
Clark's Allotment
Lower Buck Stone
Clough Head Farm
Stinking Stone Hill
Stinking Stone
Higher Buck Stone
Lanshaw Beck
Cate Moss Allotment
Hill Top
Starr Farm
Aden
America Farm
Mistress Moss
A629
A6068
B6172
B6265
A6068
KEIGHLEY RD
MAIN ST
COLNE RD
SKIPTON RD
MAIN RD
STATION RD
LOTHERSDALE RD
PARK RD
BINNS LA
RYECROFT RD
SUTTON LA
HARDINGS LA
BUCK STONE LA
ELLERS RD
JACK FIELD LA
CRAG LA
BENT LA
HOLLY BANK
LONG GATE
AMERICA LA
GREEN SYKES RD
1 LANG KIRK CL
2 STARKEY LA
3 MARY ST
KELTUS AVE 1
EAST VIEW 2
JAMES ST 3
YORK ST 4
THOMAS ST 5
EXCHANGE BLDGS 6
WILSON ST 7
IVY PL 8
STATION GR 6
SANDYLANDS 7
NEWLANDS DR 8
PROSPECT ST 9
MOUNT PLEASANT
HIGHER HARTLEY ST 1
HARTLEY ST 2
LODGE ST 3
HARRISON PL 4
1 BUTTERFIELD HOMES
2 CHESTNUT ST
3 BEECH ST
4 ASHVILLE TERR
5 SOUTH VIEW
1 JACKSON ST
2 WIGHILL ST
3 WALTON ST
4 EASTFIELD PL
5 NORTH VIEW
6 SPENCER ST
7 WRIGHT ST
HARGREAVES ST 1
MILL ST 2
LYNDHURST 1
YEADON HO 2
CRAG VIEW 3
NORTH ROW 4
NORTH PL 5
GIBRALTAR TERR 6
1 HARKER ST
2 WELL ST
3 GARDEN PL
4 DIXON ST
5 RAVENSTONE GDNS
1 ROSEWOOD SQ
2 KINGS CT
3 RASPBERRY PL
4 HALL CT
5 PARK ROW
6 ETHEL ST
7 JACKSON PL
8 BARING SQ
9 CRYER ROW

33

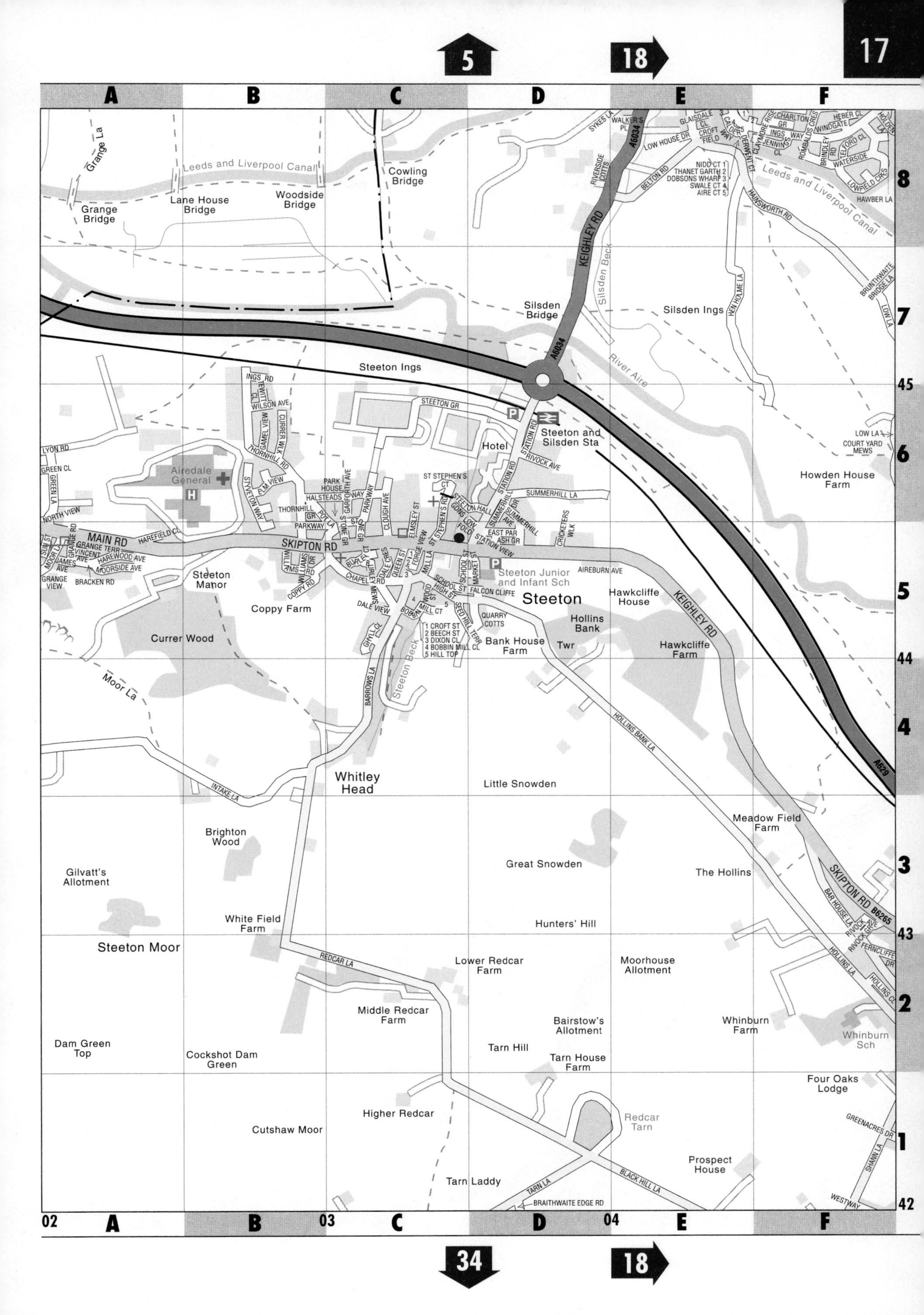
5
18
A
B
C
D
E
F
8
7
45
6
5
44
4
3
43
2
1
42
02
03
04
34
18
Grange La
Leeds and Liverpool Canal
Grange Bridge
Lane House Bridge
Woodside Bridge
Cowling Bridge
Silsden Bridge
Silsden Ings
Silsden Beck
KEIGHLEY RD
A6034
River Aire
Steeton Ings
Steeton and Silsden Sta
Hotel
Airedale General
Steeton Manor
Coppy Farm
Currer Wood
Moor La
Steeton Junior and Infant Sch
Steeton
Hawkcliffe House
Hollins Bank
Bank House Farm
Twr
Hawkcliffe Farm
Howden House Farm
SKIPTON RD
MAIN RD
KEIGHLEY RD
HOLLINS BANK LA
A629
Whitley Head
Little Snowden
INTAKE LA
Brighton Wood
Gilvatt's Allotment
Great Snowden
Meadow Field Farm
The Hollins
SKIPTON RD B6265
White Field Farm
Hunters' Hill
Steeton Moor
REDCAR LA
Lower Redcar Farm
Moorhouse Allotment
Middle Redcar Farm
Bairstow's Allotment
Whinburn Farm
Whinburn Sch
Dam Green Top
Cockshot Dam Green
Tarn Hill
Tarn House Farm
Four Oaks Lodge
Higher Redcar
Cutshaw Moor
Redcar Tarn
Prospect House
Tarn Laddy
TARN LA
BLACK HILL LA
BRAITHWAITE EDGE RD
GREENACRES DR
SHANN LA
WESTWAY
NIDD CT 1
THANET GARTH 2
DOBSONS WHARF 3
SWALE CT 4
AIRE CT 5
1 CROFT ST
2 BEECH ST
3 DIXON CL
4 BOBBIN MILL CL
5 HILL TOP
STEETON GR
STATION RD
RIVOCK AVE
SUMMERHILL LA
ST STEPHEN'S CT
HALSTEADS
PARK HOUSE
THORNHILL
PARKWAY
CLOUGH AVE
ELMSLEY ST
FORGE VIEW
MILL LA
SCHOOL ST
MARKET ST
HIGH ST
FALCON CLIFFE
QUARRY COTTS
SEED HILL TERR
CHAPEL RD
DALE VIEW
BARROWS LA
AIREBURN AVE
CRICKETERS WLK
EAST PAR
ASH GR
STATION VIEW
INGS RD
WILSON AVE
CURRER WLK
THORNHILL RD
STYVETON WAY
LYON RD
GREEN CL
NORTH VIEW
HAREFIELD CL
GRANGE TERR
HAREWOOD AVE
MOORSIDE AVE
BRACKEN RD
GRANGE VIEW
COPPY RD
LOW HOUSE DR
BELTON RD
HAINSWORTH RD
BRUNTHWAITE BRIDGE LA
LOW LA
COURT YARD MEWS
HAWBER LA
BAR HOUSE LA
HOLLINS LA
HOLLINS CL
FERNCLIFFE DR

17 6

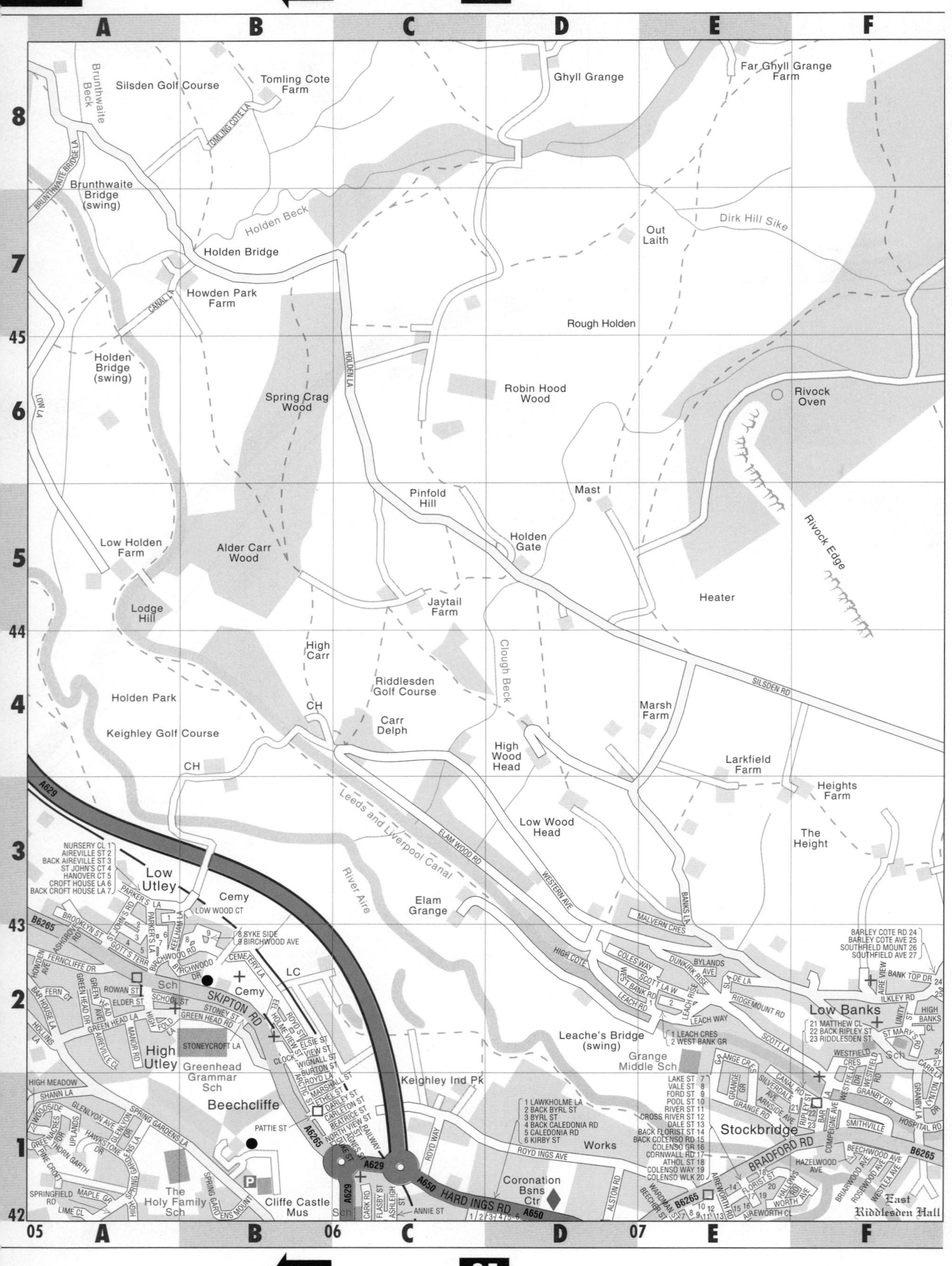

A B C D E F
8
7
45
6
5
44
4
3
43
2
1
42
05 06 07
Silsden Golf Course
Brunthwaite Beck
Tomling Cote Farm
TOMLING COTE LA
Ghyll Grange
Far Ghyll Grange Farm
BRUNTHWAITE BRIDGE LA
Brunthwaite Bridge (swing)
Holden Beck
Holden Bridge
Howden Park Farm
CANAL LA
Out Laith
Dirk Hill Sike
Rough Holden
Holden Bridge (swing)
LOW LA
HOLDEN LA
Spring Crag Wood
Robin Hood Wood
Rivock Oven
Pinfold Hill
Mast
Rivock Edge
Low Holden Farm
Alder Carr Wood
Holden Gate
Lodge Hill
Jaytail Farm
Heater
High Carr
Clough Beck
SILSDEN RD
Riddlesden Golf Course
Holden Park
CH
Carr Delph
Marsh Farm
Keighley Golf Course
High Wood Head
Larkfield Farm
CH
A629
Leeds and Liverpool Canal
Heights Farm
Low Wood Head
ELAM WOOD RD
The Height
NURSERY CL 1
AIREVILLE ST 2
BACK AIREVILLE ST 3
ST JOHN'S CT 4
HANOVER CT 5
CROFT HOUSE LA 6
BACK CROFT HOUSE LA 7
Low Utley
River Aire
WESTERN AVE
Cemy
LOW WOOD CT
Elam Grange
BANKS LA
B6265
8 SYKE SIDE
9 BIRCHWOOD AVE
MALVERN CRES
BARLEY COTE RD 24
BARLEY COTE AVE 25
SOUTHFIELD MOUNT 26
SOUTHFIELD AVE 27
HIGH COTE
COLES WAY
DUNKIRK RISE
BYLANDS AVE
LC
Sch
Cemy
SKIPTON RD
SCOTT LA W
RIDGEMOUNT RD
BANK TOP DR
ILKLEY RD
Low Banks
LEACH WAY
HIGH BANKS CL
21 MATTHEW CL
22 BACK RIPLEY ST
23 RIDDLESDEN ST
STONEYCROFT LA
Leache's Bridge (swing)
1 LEACH CRES
2 WEST BANK GR
ST MARY'S RD
High Utley
Greenhead Grammar Sch
Grange Middle Sch
SCOTT LA
WESTFIELD CRES
HIGH MEADOW
Keighley Ind Pk
LAKE ST 7
VALE ST 8
FORD ST 9
POOL ST 10
RIVER ST 11
CROSS RIVER ST 12
DALE ST 13
BACK FLORIST ST 14
BACK COLENSO RD 15
COLENSO GR 16
CORNWALL RD 17
ATHOL ST 18
COLENSO WAY 19
COLENSO WLK 20
Beechcliffe
1 LAWKHOLME LA
2 BACK BYRL ST
3 BYRL ST
4 BACK CALEDONIA RD
5 CALEDONIA RD
6 KIRBY ST
GRANBY DR
SMITHVILLE
HOSPITAL RD
Stockbridge
PATTIE ST
A6265
ROYD INGS AVE
Works
BRADFORD RD
B6265
BEECHWOOD AVE
HAZELWOOD AVE
ROSEWOOD AVE
WESTLEA AVE
A629
Coronation Bsns Ctr
A650 HARD INGS RD
A650
ANNIE ST
The Holy Family Sch
Cliffe Castle Mus
ALSTON RD
AIREWORTH RD
AIREWORTH CL
East Riddlesden Hall

17 35

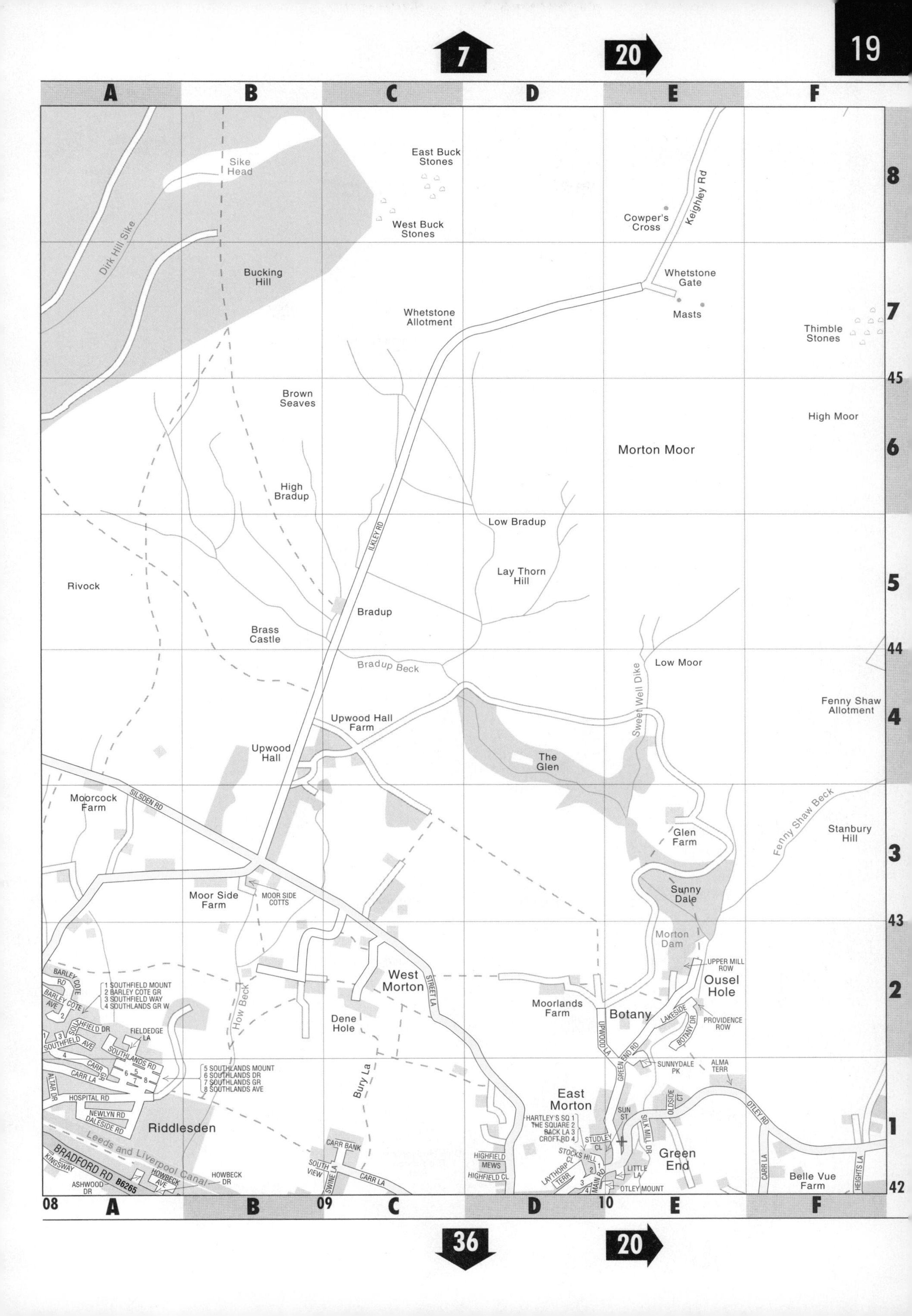
7
20
A B C D E F
East Buck Stones
Sike Head
West Buck Stones
Cowper's Cross
Keighley Rd
Dirk Hill Sike
Bucking Hill
Whetstone Gate
Masts
Whetstone Allotment
Thimble Stones
Brown Seaves
High Moor
Morton Moor
High Bradup
Low Bradup
ILKLEY RD
Rivock
Lay Thorn Hill
Bradup
Brass Castle
Bradup Beck
Low Moor
Sweet Well Dike
Fenny Shaw Allotment
Upwood Hall Farm
Upwood Hall
The Glen
Moorcock Farm
SILSDEN RD
Stanbury Hill
Fenny Shaw Beck
Glen Farm
Moor Side Farm
MOOR SIDE COTTS
Sunny Dale
Morton Dam
UPPER MILL ROW
Ousel Hole
West Morton
STREET LA
Moorlands Farm
Botany
LAKESIDE
BOTANY DR
PROVIDENCE ROW
Dene Hole
UPWOOD LA
GREEN END RD
SUNNYDALE PK
ALMA TERR
1 SOUTHFIELD MOUNT
2 BARLEY COTE GR
3 SOUTHFIELD WAY
4 SOUTHLANDS GR W
BARLEY COTE RD
BARLEY COTE AVE
SOUTHFIELD DR
SOUTHFIELD AVE
FIELDEDGE LA
SOUTHLANDS RD
CARR GR
CARR LA
How Beck
5 SOUTHLANDS MOUNT
6 SOUTHLANDS DR
7 SOUTHLANDS GR
8 SOUTHLANDS AVE
ALTAR DR
HOSPITAL RD
NEWLYN RD
DALESIDE RD
Riddlesden
Leeds and Liverpool Canal
Bury La
East Morton
HARTLEY'S SQ 1
THE SQUARE 2
BACK LA 3
CROFT RD 4
SUN ST
SILK MILL DR
OLDSIDE CT
OTLEY RD
STUDLEY CL
STOCKS HILL CL
LAYTHORP TERR
MAIN RD
LITTLE LA
OTLEY MOUNT
Green End
CARR LA
HEIGHTS LA
Belle Vue Farm
CARR BANK
SOUTH VIEW
SWINE LA
CARR LA
HIGHFIELD MEWS
HIGHFIELD CL
BRADFORD RD B6265
KINGSWAY
ASHWOOD DR
HOWBECK AVE
HOWBECK DR
8 7 45 6 5 44 4 3 43 2 1 42
08 09 10
36
20

19
8

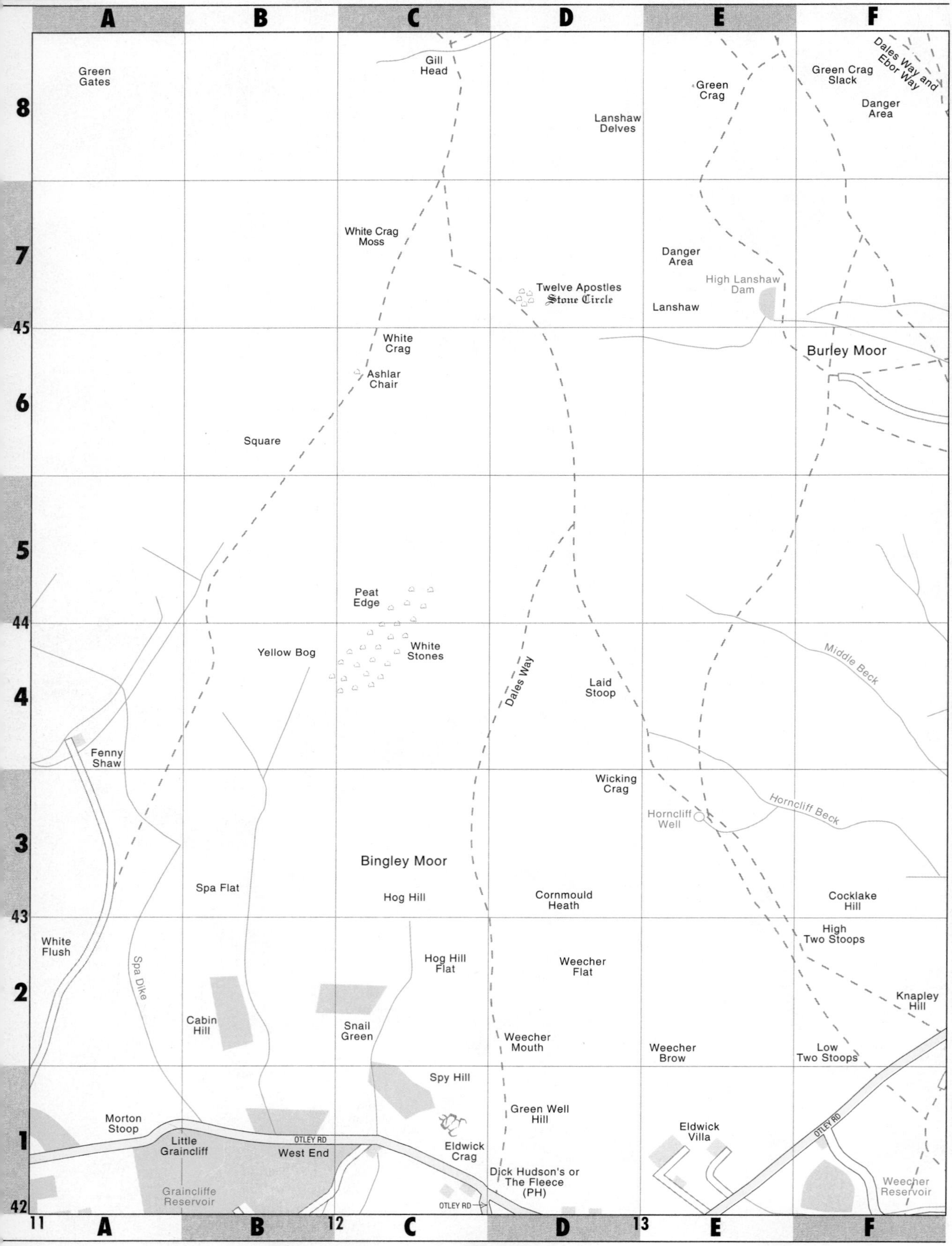

	A	B	C	D	E	F

8

Green Gates

Gill Head

Lanshaw Delves

Green Crag

Green Crag Slack

Dales Way and Ebor Way

Danger Area

7

White Crag Moss

Danger Area

High Lanshaw Dam

45

Twelve Apostles Stone Circle

Lanshaw

Burley Moor

White Crag

6

Ashlar Chair

Square

5

Peat Edge

44

Yellow Bog

White Stones

Middle Beck

4

Dales Way

Laid Stoop

Fenny Shaw

Wicking Crag

Horncliff Beck

3

Horncliff Well

Bingley Moor

Spa Flat

Hog Hill

Cornmould Heath

Cocklake Hill

43

White Flush

High Two Stoops

Hog Hill Flat

Weecher Flat

Knapley Hill

2

Spa Dike

Cabin Hill

Snail Green

Weecher Mouth

Weecher Brow

Low Two Stoops

Spy Hill

Green Well Hill

1

Morton Stoop

Little Graincliff

OTLEY RD

West End

Eldwick Crag

Eldwick Villa

OTLEY RD

Weecher Reservoir

Graincliffe Reservoir

Dick Hudson's or The Fleece (PH)

OTLEY RD

42

11	A		B	12	C		D	13	E		F

19
37

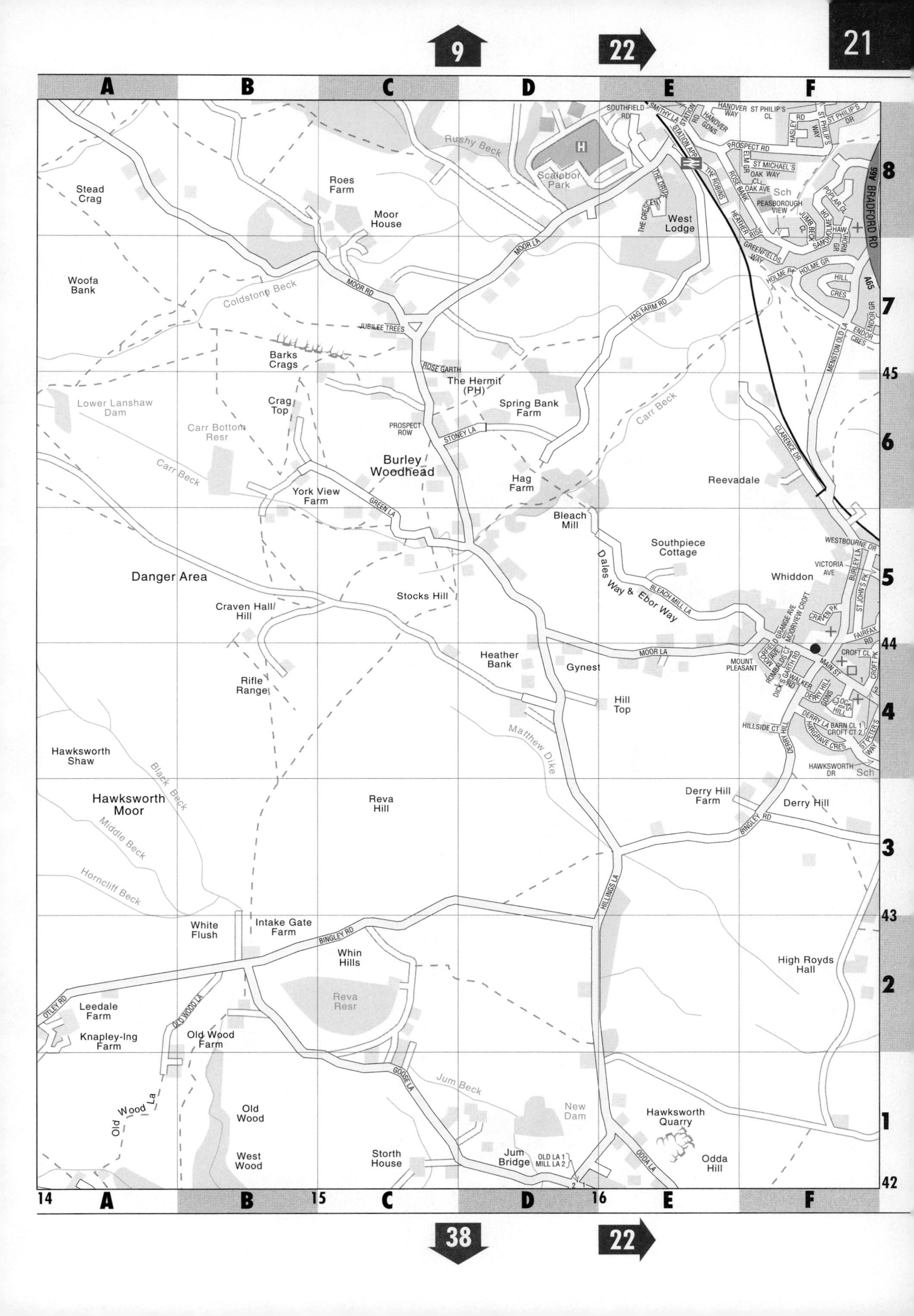
9
22
A
B
C
D
E
F
Stead Crag
Roes Farm
Moor House
Rushy Beck
Scalebor Park
West Lodge
Woofa Bank
Coldstone Beck
MOOR RD
MOOR LA
JUBILEE TREES
HAG FARM RD
Barks Crags
ROSE GARTH
The Hermit (PH)
Spring Bank Farm
Lower Lanshaw Dam
Crag Top
Carr Bottom Resr
PROSPECT ROW
STONEY LA
Carr Beck
Burley Woodhead
York View Farm
GREEN LA
Hag Farm
Reevadale
CLARENCE DR
Bleach Mill
Southpiece Cottage
Danger Area
Dales Way & Ebor Way
BLEACH MILL LA
Whiddon
Craven Hall Hill
Stocks Hill
Heather Bank
MOOR LA
Gynest
MOUNT PLEASANT
Rifle Range
Hill Top
Matthew Dike
Hawksworth Shaw
Black Beck
Hawksworth Moor
Middle Beck
Reva Hill
Derry Hill Farm
Derry Hill
BINGLEY RD
Horncliff Beck
HILLINGS LA
White Flush
Intake Gate Farm
BINGLEY RD
Whin Hills
High Royds Hall
Leedale Farm
OTLEY RD
OLD WOOD LA
Reva Resr
Knapley-Ing Farm
Old Wood Farm
GOOSE LA
Jum Beck
Old Wood La
Old Wood
New Dam
Hawksworth Quarry
West Wood
Storth House
Jum Bridge
OLD LA 1
MILL LA 2
ODDA LA
Odda Hill
SOUTHFIELD RD
SMITHY LA
STATION RD
STATION APP
HANOVER GDNS
HANOVER WAY
ST PHILIP'S CL
ST PHILIP'S DR
PROSPECT RD
ST MICHAEL'S CL
OAK WAY
OAK AVE
Sch
PEASBOROUGH VIEW
THE ROBINS
ROSE BANK
HEATHER RISE
GREENFIELDS WAY
HOLME RI
HOLME GR
HILL CRES
ENDOR GR
ENDOR CRES
MENSTON OLD LA
A65 BRADFORD RD
A65
THE DRIVE
THE CRESCENT
WESTBOURNE DR
VICTORIA AVE
BURLEY LA
ST JOHN'S PK
CRAVEN PK
FAIRFAX RD
CROFT CL
CROFT PK
MAIN ST
WALKER RD
DERRY HILL GDNS
STOCKS HILL
DERRY LA
BARN CL 1
CROFT CT 2
HARGRAVE CRES
ST PETER'S WAY
HILLSIDE CT
DERRY HILL
HAWKSWORTH DR
Sch
8
7
45
6
5
44
4
3
43
2
1
42
14
15
16
38
22

21
10

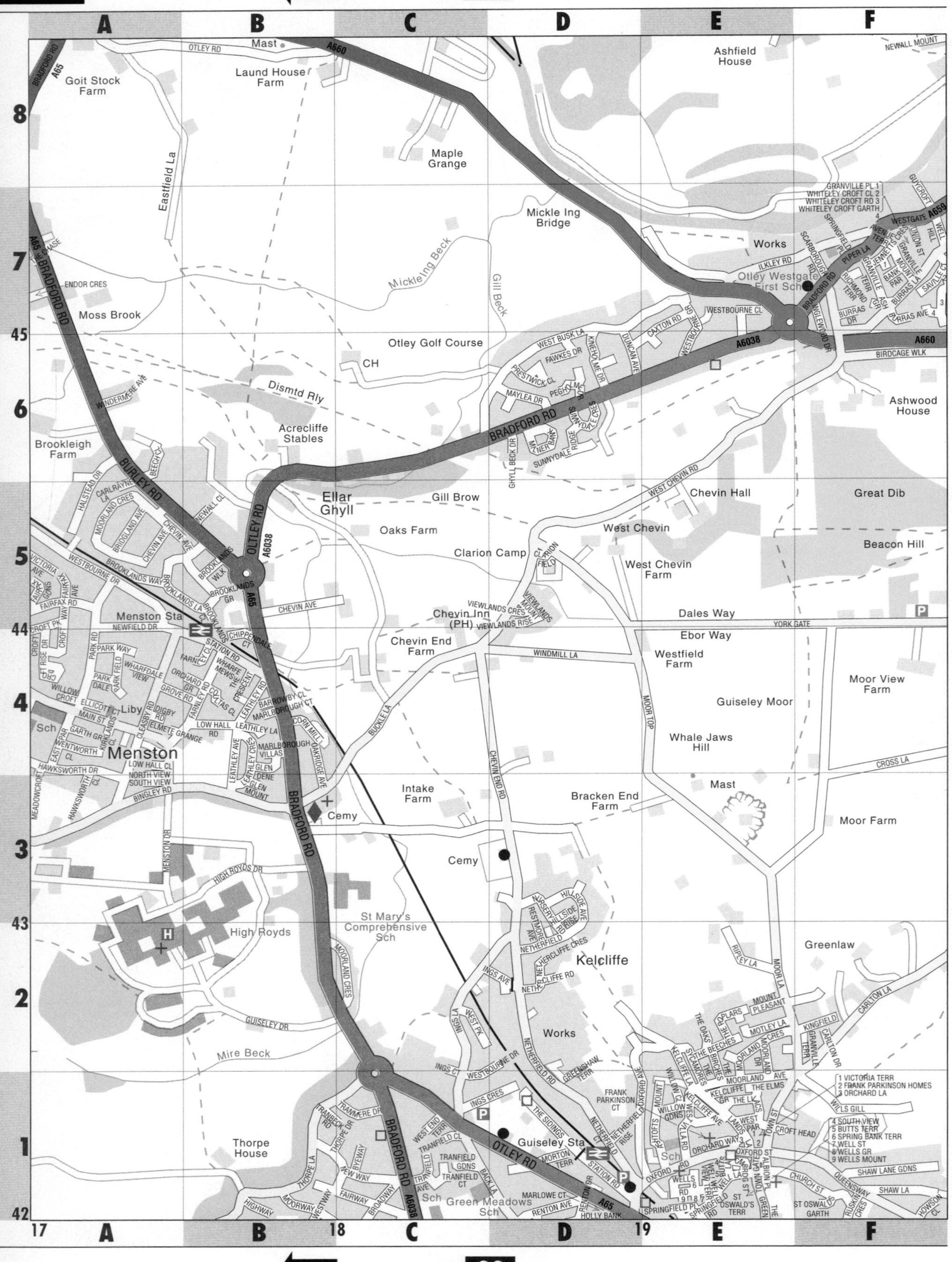
A
B
C
D
E
F
8
7
6
5
4
3
2
1
45
44
43
42
17
18
19
Goit Stock Farm
Laund House Farm
Mast
OTLEY RD
A660
BRADFORD RD
A65
Ashfield House
NEWALL MOUNT
Eastfield La
Maple Grange
Mickle Ing Bridge
Mickleing Beck
Gill Beck
Works
ILKLEY RD
Otley Westgate First Sch
WESTBOURNE CL
GRANVILLE PL 1
WHITELEY CROFT CL 2
WHITELEY CROFT RD 3
WHITELEY CROFT GARTH
WESTGATE
A659
PIPER LA
ENDOR CRES
Moss Brook
Otley Golf Course
CH
A6038
A660
BIRDCAGE WLK
WEST BUSK LA
FAWKES DR
CAXTON RD
DUNCAN AVE
WESTBOURNE GR
PRESTWICK CL
MAYLEA DR
Dismtd Rly
WINDERMERE AVE
Ashwood House
BRADFORD RD
Acrecliffe Stables
Brookleigh Farm
SUNNYDALE RIDGE
GHYLL BECK DR
WEST CHEVIN RD
Chevin Hall
Great Dib
Ellar Ghyll
Gill Brow
BURLEY RD
HALSTEAD DR
CARLRAYNE LA
MOORLAND CRES
BRIDGLAND AVE
CHEVIN AVE
NEWALL CL
OLTLEY RD
A6038
Oaks Farm
West Chevin
Beacon Hill
Clarion Camp
CLARION FIELD
West Chevin Farm
VICTORIA AVE
WESTBOURNE DR
BROOKLANDS WAY
BROOKLANDS LA
BROOKLANDS GR
CHEVIN AVE
VIEWLANDS CRES
VIEWLANDS MOUNT
VIEWLANDS RISE
Chevin Inn (PH)
Dales Way
YORK GATE
Ebor Way
FAIRFAX RD
Menston Sta
NEWFIELD DR
CHIPPENDALE CT
STATION RD
Chevin End Farm
WINDMILL LA
Westfield Farm
Moor View Farm
CROFT PK
PARK RD
PARK WAY
WHARFEDALE VIEW
ORCHARD GR
GROVE RD
BARROWBY CL
MARLBOROUGH CT
Guiseley Moor
WILLOW CROFT
ELLICOTT CT
MAIN ST
Liby
DIGBY RD
Sch
GARTH GR
WENTWORTH
ELMETE GRANGE
LOW HALL RD
LEATHLEY LA
CORN MILL
MARLBOROUGH VILLAS
BUCKLE LA
MOOR TOP
Whale Jaws Hill
Menston
HAWKSWORTH DR
LOW HALL CL
NORTH VIEW
SOUTH VIEW
BINGLEY RD
GLEN DENE
GLEN MOUNT
OAKRIDGE AVE
CHEVIN END RD
CROSS LA
Mast
Intake Farm
Bracken End Farm
Cemy
Moor Farm
MENSTON DR
HIGH ROYDS DR
Cemy
St Mary's Comprehensive Sch
High Royds
MOORLAND CRES
NETHERFIELD
NETHERCLIFFE CRES
Kelcliffe
Greenlaw
RIPLEY LA
MOOR LA
INGS AVE
NETHERCLIFFE RD
CARLTON LA
GUISELEY DR
Mire Beck
INGS LA
WEST PK
Works
MOUNT PLEASANT
MOTLEY LA
KINGFIELD
CARLTON DR
INGS CT
WESTBOURNE DR
NETHERFIELD RD
GREENSHAW TERR
FRANK PARKINSON CT
MOORLAND AVE
THE ELMS
1 VICTORIA TERR
2 FRANK PARKINSON HOMES
3 ORCHARD LA
WILLS GILL
INGS CRES
TRANMERE DR
THE SIDINGS
KELCLIFFE AVE
4 SOUTH VIEW
5 BUTTS TERR
6 SPRING BANK TERR
7 WELL ST
8 WELLS GR
9 WELLS MOUNT
WEST END TERR
TRANFIELD CL
Guiseley Sta
ORCHARD WAY
CROFT HEAD
Thorpe House
TRANFIELD GDNS
TRANFIELD CT
OTLEY RD
MORTON TERR
STATION RD
OXFORD ST
SHAW LANE GDNS
THORPE LA
BYEWAY
NEW WAY
FAIRWAY
BROADWAY
BACK LA
Sch
Green Meadows Sch
MARLOWE CT
RENTON AVE
HOLLY BANK
A65
OXFORD RD
WELLS RD
CHURCH ST
SHAW LA
HIGHWAY
MOORWAY
WESTWAY
BRADFORD RD
A6038
SPRINGFIELD PL
ST OSWALD'S TERR
ST OSWALDS GARTH
QUEENSWAY
RUSKIN CRES
HOWSON CL

21
39

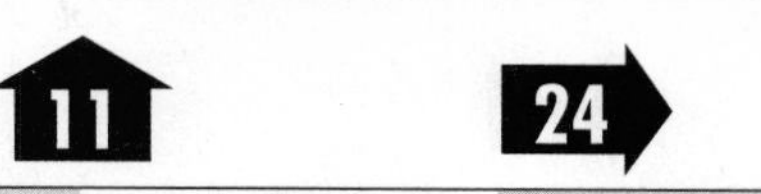

11
24

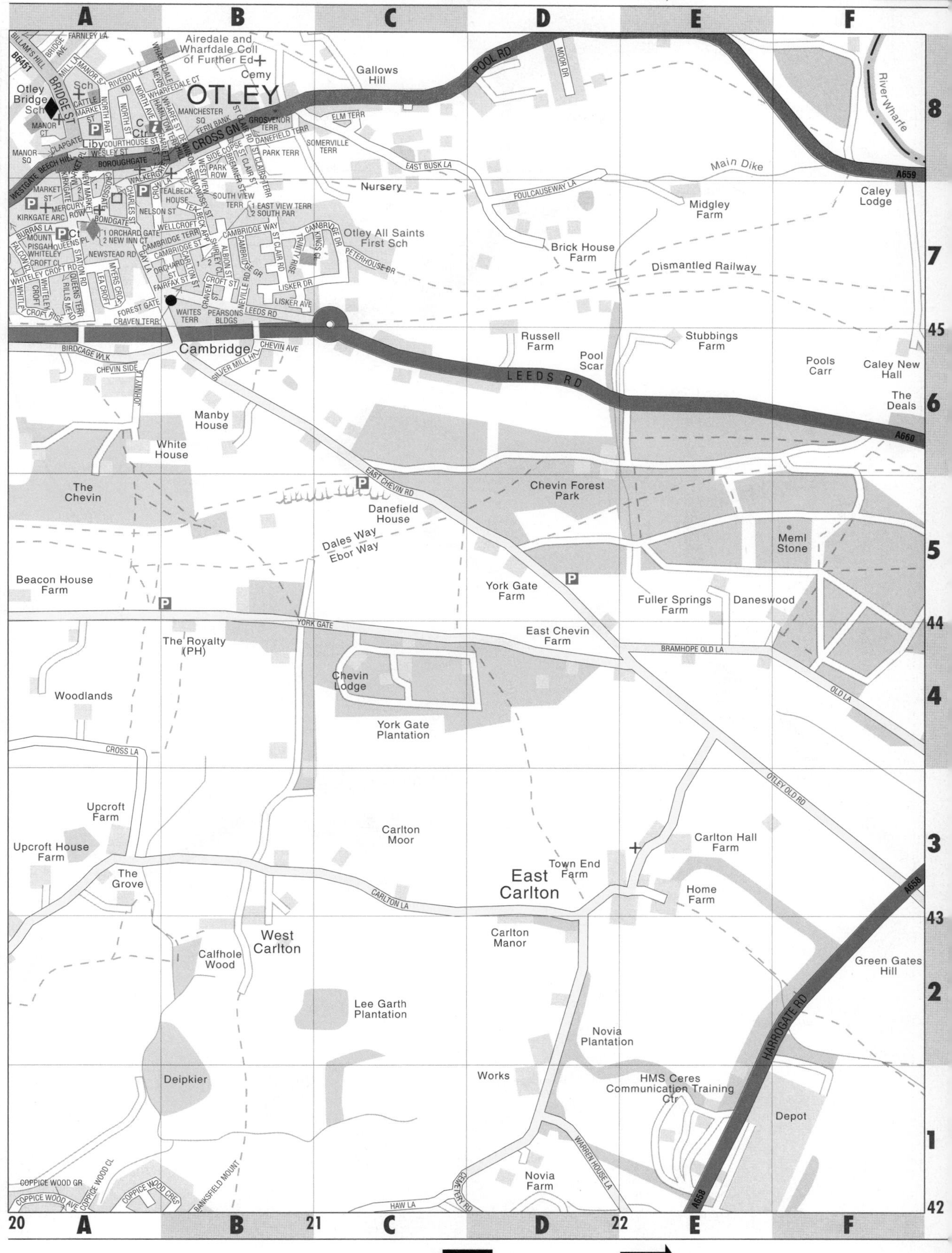

OTLEY
Airedale and Wharfdale Coll of Further Ed
Cemy
Gallows Hill
POOL RD
MOOR DR
River Wharfe
Otley Bridge Sch
BRIDGE ST
CROSS GN
BOROUGHGATE
WESTGATE
ELM TERR
SOMERVILLE TERR
PARK TERR
EAST BUSK LA
Main Dike
A659
Nursery
FOULCAUSEWAY LA
Midgley Farm
Caley Lodge
Otley All Saints First Sch
Brick House Farm
Dismantled Railway
PETERHOUSE DR
LEEDS RD
Russell Farm
Pool Scar
Stubbings Farm
Pools Carr
Caley New Hall
The Deals
Cambridge
CHEVIN AVE
BIRDCAGE WLK
CHEVIN SIDE
SILVER MILL HILL
Manby House
White House
A660
The Chevin
EAST CHEVIN RD
Danefield House
Chevin Forest Park
Dales Way
Ebor Way
Meml Stone
Beacon House Farm
York Gate Farm
Fuller Springs Farm
Daneswood
YORK GATE
The Royalty (PH)
East Chevin Farm
BRAMHOPE OLD LA
OLD LA
Woodlands
Chevin Lodge
York Gate Plantation
CROSS LA
OTLEY OLD RD
Upcroft Farm
Carlton Moor
Carlton Hall Farm
Upcroft House Farm
The Grove
Town End Farm
East Carlton
Home Farm
CARLTON LA
A658
West Carlton
Carlton Manor
Calfhole Wood
Green Gates Hill
Lee Garth Plantation
HARROGATE RD
Novia Plantation
Deipkier
Works
HMS Ceres Communication Training Ctr
Depot
WARREN HOUSE LA
Novia Farm
COPPICE WOOD GR
COPPICE WOOD AVE
COPPICE WOOD CL
COPPICE WOOD CRES
BANKSFIELD MOUNT
HAW LA
CEMETERY RD
A B C D E F
8 7 6 5 4 3 2 1
45 44 43 42
20 21 22
40
24

23

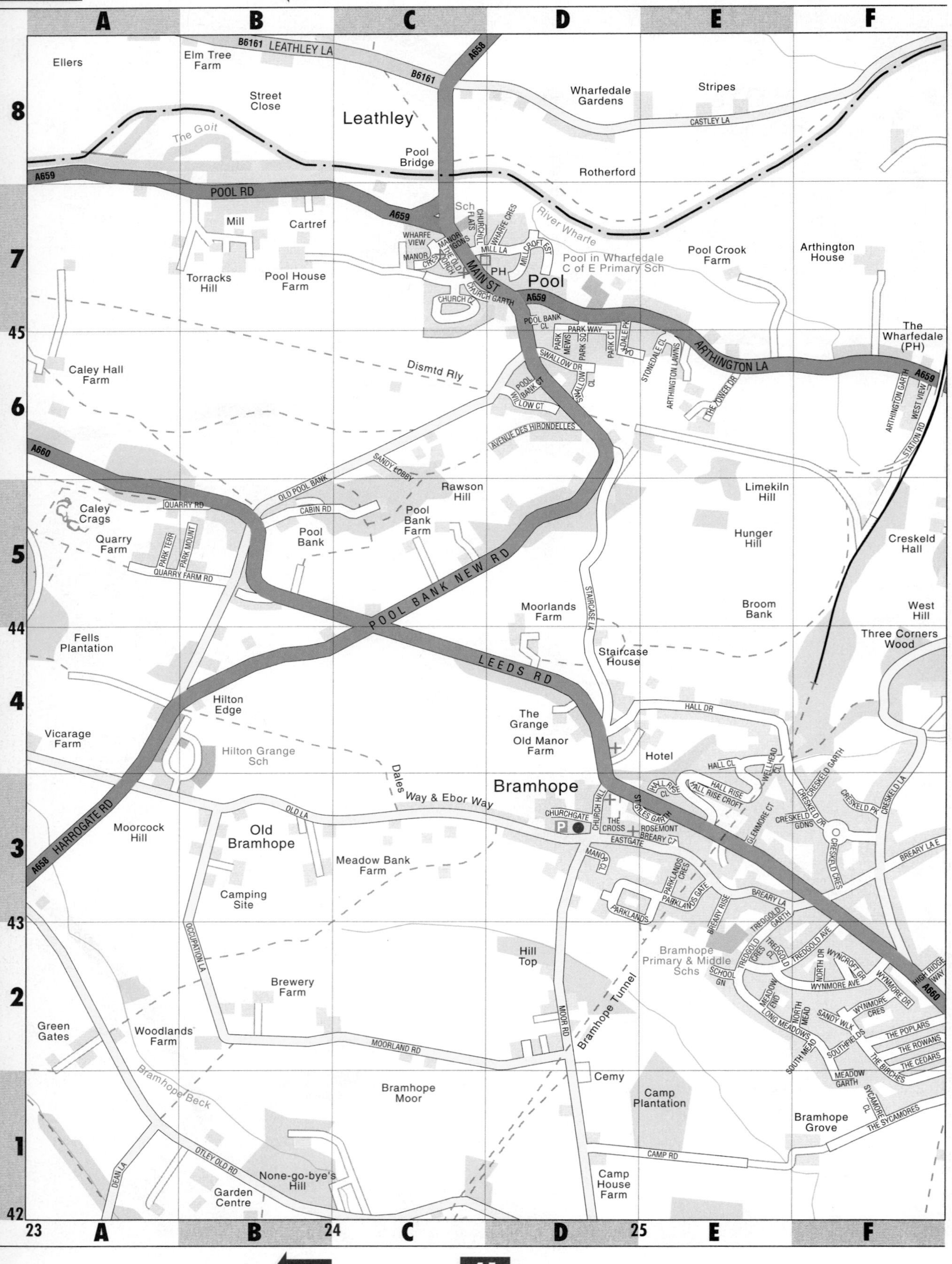
A
B
C
D
E
F
Ellers
Elm Tree Farm
Street Close
Leathley
B6161 LEATHLEY LA
A658
Wharfedale Gardens
Stripes
CASTLEY LA
The Goit
Pool Bridge
Rotherford
A659
POOL RD
Mill
Cartref
River Wharfe
Pool Crook Farm
Arthington House
Torracks Hill
Pool House Farm
Pool in Wharfedale C of E Primary Sch
Pool
MAIN ST
CHURCH CL
CHURCH GARTH
ARTHINGTON LA
The Wharfedale (PH)
Caley Hall Farm
Dismtd Rly
AVENUE DES HIRONDELLES
A660
Caley Crags
QUARRY RD
OLD POOL BANK
SANDY LOBBY
Rawson Hill
CABIN RD
Pool Bank Farm
Limekiln Hill
Quarry Farm
PARK TERR
PARK MOUNT
QUARRY FARM RD
Pool Bank
Hunger Hill
Creskeld Hall
POOL BANK NEW RD
STAIRCASE LA
Moorlands Farm
Broom Bank
West Hill
Fells Plantation
Three Corners Wood
LEEDS RD
Staircase House
Hilton Edge
The Grange
Vicarage Farm
HALL DR
Old Manor Farm
Hilton Grange Sch
Hotel
Dales Way & Ebor Way
Bramhope
OLD LA
Moorcock Hill
Old Bramhope
A658 HARROGATE RD
CHURCHGATE
EASTGATE
Meadow Bank Farm
Camping Site
PARKLANDS
BREARY LA
BREARY LA E
Hill Top
Bramhope Primary & Middle Schs
OCCUPATION LA
Brewery Farm
Bramhope Tunnel
MOOR RD
WYNMORE AVE
Green Gates
Woodlands Farm
MOORLAND RD
THE POPLARS
THE ROWANS
THE CEDARS
Bramhope Beck
Cemy
Bramhope Moor
Camp Plantation
Bramhope Grove
THE SYCAMORES
CAMP RD
OTLEY OLD RD
DEAN LA
None-go-bye's Hill
Garden Centre
Camp House Farm
8
7
45
6
5
44
4
3
43
2
1
42
23
24
25

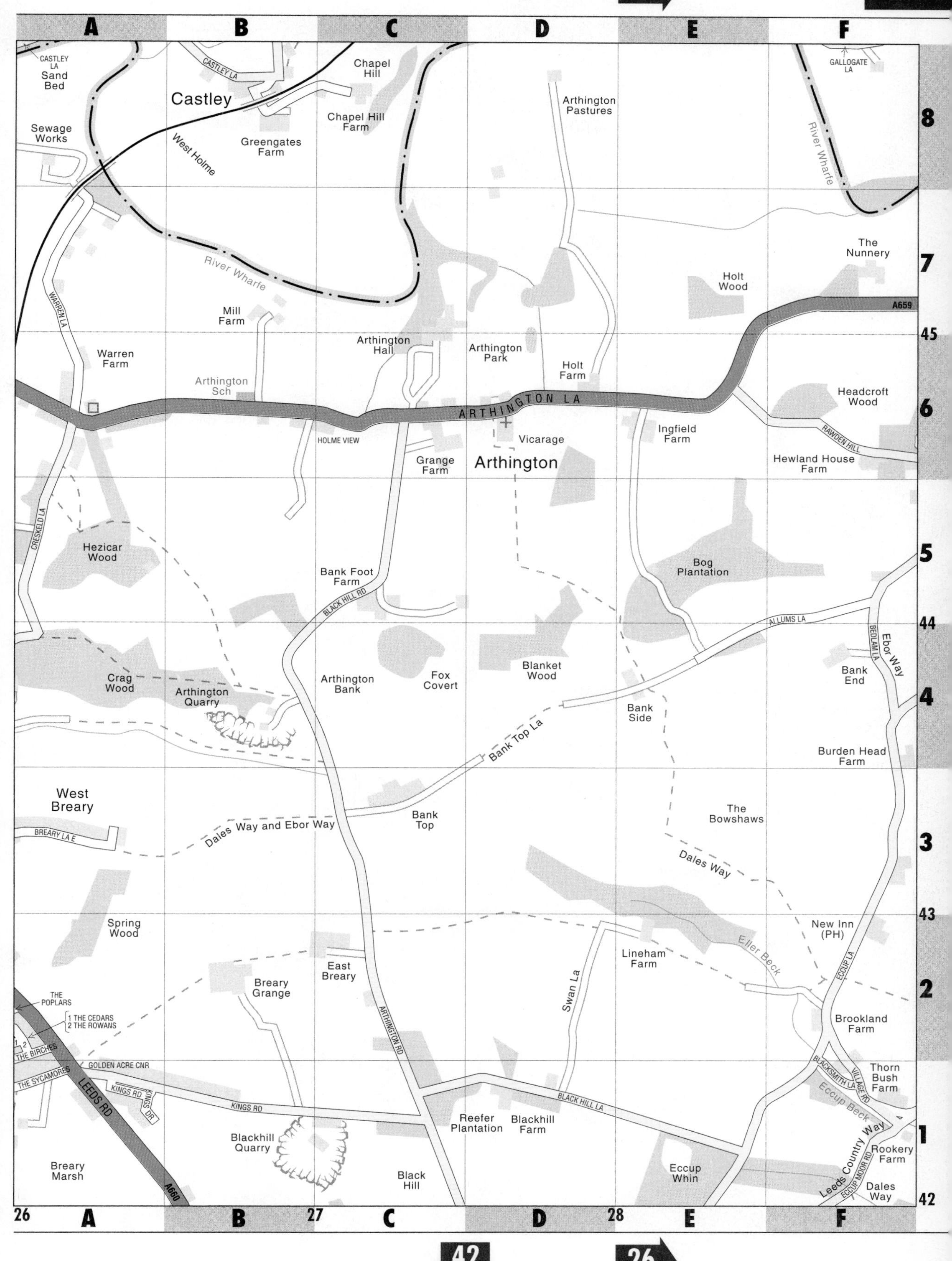

CASTLEY LA
Sand Bed
CASTLEY LA
Chapel Hill
Castley
Chapel Hill Farm
GALLOGATE LA
Sewage Works
Greengates Farm
West Holme
River Wharfe
Arthington Pastures
River Wharfe
The Nunnery
Mill Farm
Holt Wood
A659
Warren Farm
Arthington Hall
Arthington Sch
Arthington Park
Holt Farm
Headcroft Wood
WARREN LA
ARTHINGTON LA
HOLME VIEW
Vicarage
Ingfield Farm
RAWDEN HILL
Grange Farm
Arthington
Hewland House Farm
CRESKELD LA
Hezicar Wood
Bank Foot Farm
Bog Plantation
BLACK HILL RD
AL LUMS LA
Crag Wood
Arthington Bank
Fox Covert
Blanket Wood
Bank End
Ebor Way
BEDLAM LA
Arthington Quarry
Bank Side
Burden Head Farm
West Breary
Bank Top La
The Bowshaws
BREARY LA E
Dales Way and Ebor Way
Bank Top
Dales Way
Eller Beck
New Inn (PH)
ECCUP LA
Spring Wood
Lineham Farm
Breary Grange
East Breary
Swan La
Brookland Farm
THE POPLARS
1 THE CEDARS
2 THE ROWANS
ARTHINGTON RD
Thorn Bush Farm
THE BIRCHES
THE SYCAMORES
GOLDEN ACRE CNR
KINGS DR
KINGS RD
Black Hill La
BLACKSMITH LA
VILLAGE RD
Eccup Beck
Leeds Country Way
Rookery Farm
LEEDS RD
KINGS RD
Blackhill Quarry
Reefer Plantation
Blackhill Farm
ECCUP MOOR RD
Dales Way
Breary Marsh
A660
Black Hill
Eccup Whin

25

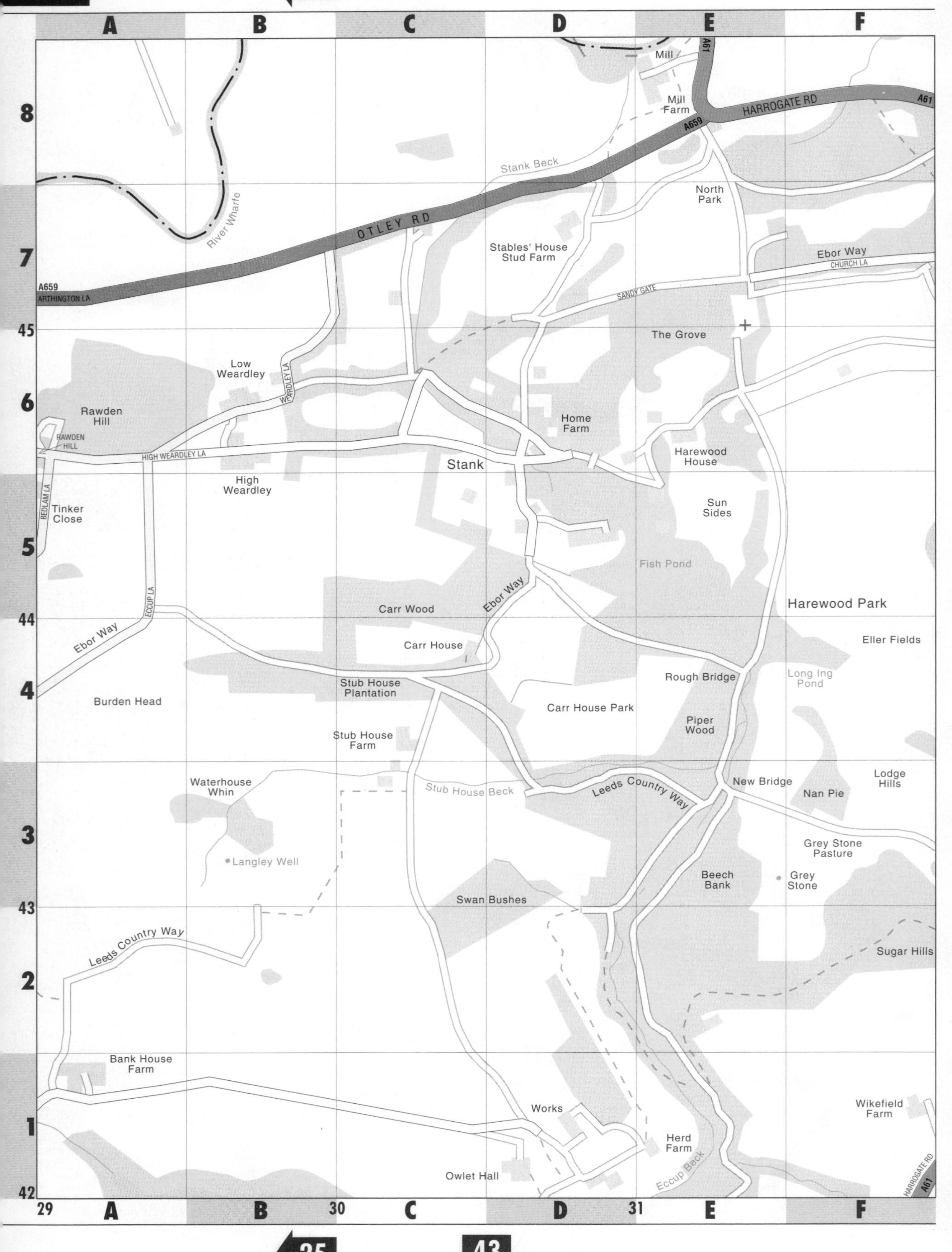
A
B
C
D
E
F
8
7
45
6
5
44
4
3
43
2
1
42
29
30
31
Mill
Mill Farm
A61
A659
HARROGATE RD
Stank Beck
River Wharfe
OTLEY RD
North Park
Stables' House Stud Farm
Ebor Way
CHURCH LA
SANDY GATE
A659
ARTHINGTON LA
The Grove
Low Weardley
WEARDLEY LA
Rawden Hill
RAWDEN HILL
Home Farm
Harewood House
HIGH WEARDLEY LA
Stank
High Weardley
BEDLAM LA
Tinker Close
Sun Sides
Fish Pond
ECCUP LA
Ebor Way
Carr Wood
Harewood Park
Ebor Way
Eller Fields
Carr House
Rough Bridge
Long Ing Pond
Stub House Plantation
Burden Head
Carr House Park
Piper Wood
Stub House Farm
Waterhouse Whin
Stub House Beck
Leeds Country Way
New Bridge
Lodge Hills
Nan Pie
Grey Stone Pasture
Langley Well
Beech Bank
Grey Stone
Swan Bushes
Leeds Country Way
Sugar Hills
Bank House Farm
Works
Wikefield Farm
Herd Farm
Eccup Beck
Owlet Hall
HARROGATE RD
A61

25
43

28

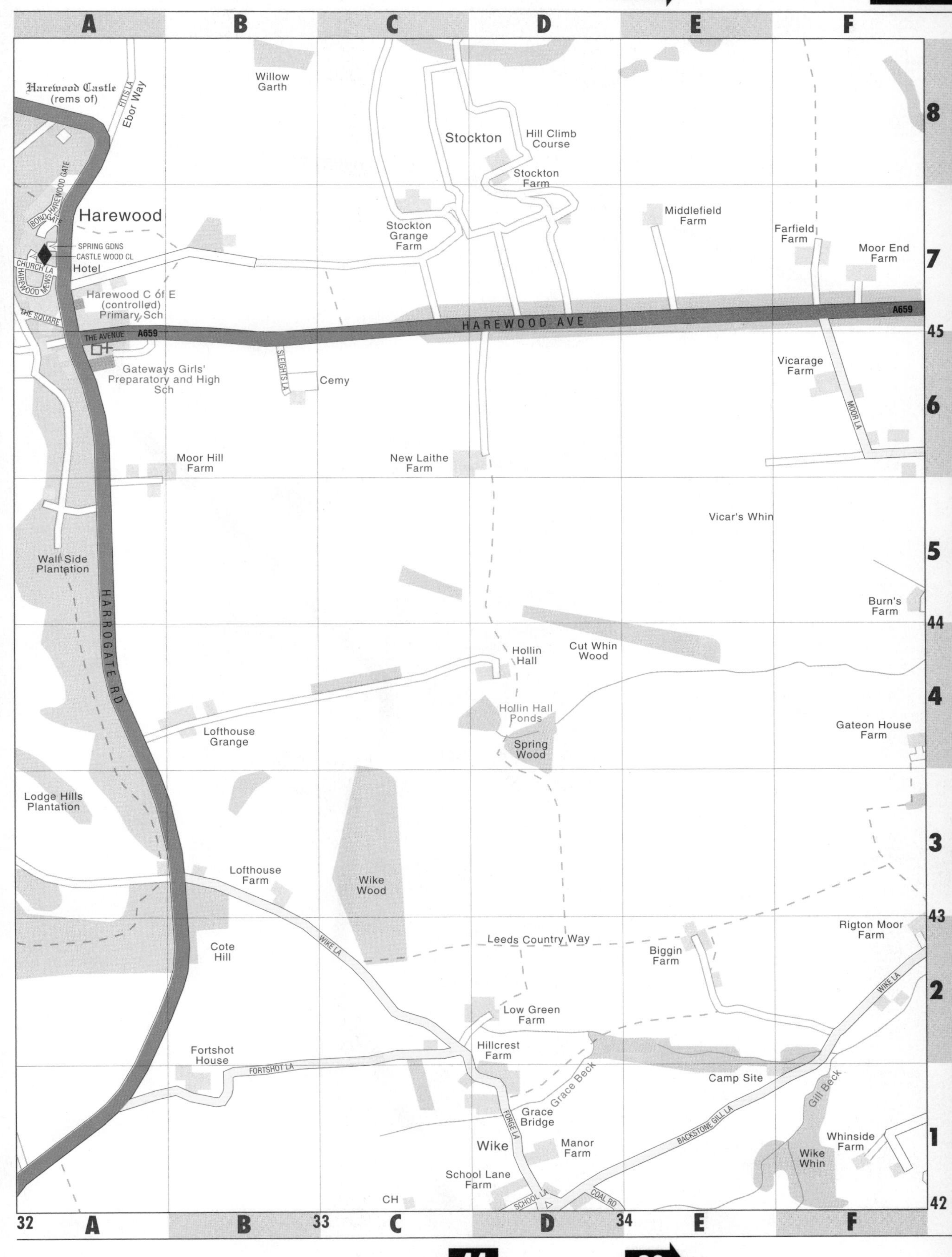

A
B
C
D
E
F
Harewood Castle (rems of)
Ebor Way
Willow Garth
Stockton
Hill Climb Course
Stockton Farm
Harewood
Stockton Grange Farm
Middlefield Farm
Farfield Farm
Moor End Farm
SPRING GDNS
CASTLE WOOD CL
Hotel
CHURCH LA
HAREWOOD MEWS
Harewood C of E (controlled) Primary Sch
THE SQUARE
THE AVENUE
A659
HAREWOOD AVE
Gateways Girls' Preparatory and High Sch
SLEIGHTS LA
Cemy
Vicarage Farm
MOOR LA
Moor Hill Farm
New Laithe Farm
Vicar's Whin
Wall Side Plantation
HARROGATE RD
Burn's Farm
Hollin Hall
Cut Whin Wood
Hollin Hall Ponds
Spring Wood
Lofthouse Grange
Gateon House Farm
Lodge Hills Plantation
Lofthouse Farm
Wike Wood
Cote Hill
WIKE LA
Leeds Country Way
Biggin Farm
Rigton Moor Farm
Low Green Farm
Fortshot House
FORTSHOT LA
Hillcrest Farm
Grace Beck
Camp Site
Gill Beck
FORGE LA
Grace Bridge
BACKSTONE GILL LA
Wike
Manor Farm
Whinside Farm
Wike Whin
School Lane Farm
CH
SCHOOL LA
COAL RD
8
7
45
6
5
44
4
3
43
2
1
42
32
33
34

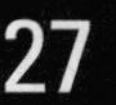

44

28

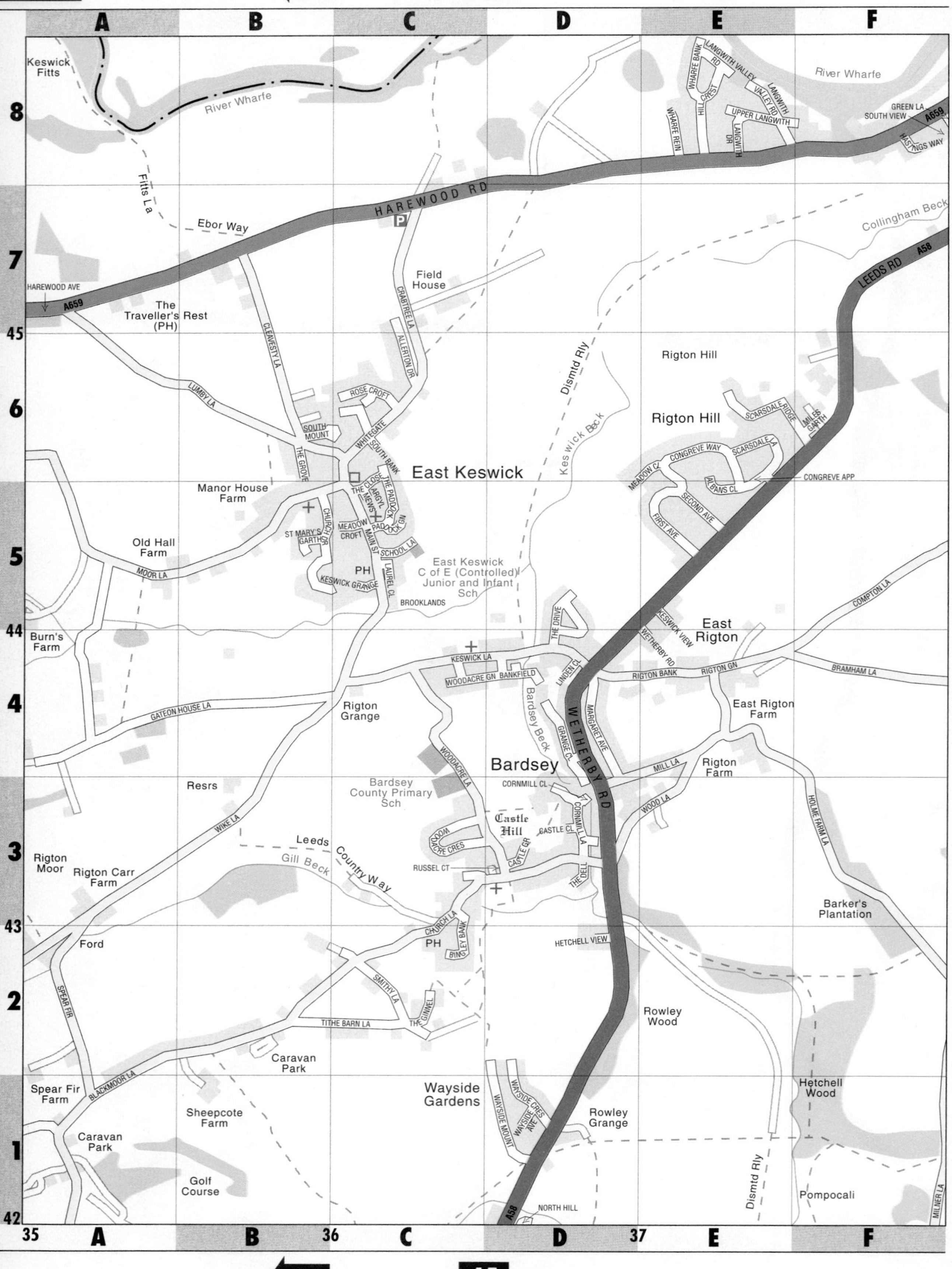

A **B** **C** **D** **E** **F**

Keswick Fitts

River Wharfe

River Wharfe

8

LANGWITH VALLEY
WHARFE BANK
LANGWITH RD
HILL CREST
VALLEY RD
WHARFE RHN
UPPER LANGWITH
LANGWITH DR
GREEN LA
SOUTH VIEW
A659
HASTINGS WAY

HAREWOOD RD

Fitts La

Ebor Way

P

Field House

Collingham Beck

LEEDS RD A58

7

HAREWOOD AVE

A659

The Traveller's Rest (PH)

CRABTREE LA

Dismtd Rly

Rigton Hill

45

LUMBY LA

ALLERTON DR

CLAREBESTY LA

THE GROVE

ROSE CROFT

WHITEGATE

SOUTH BANK

Keswick Beck

Rigton Hill

SCARSDALE RIDGE
SCARSDALE LA
LINDLES GARTH

6

SOUTH MOUNT

MEADOW CL
CONGREVE WAY
ALBANS CL
CONGREVE APP

East Keswick

THE CLOSE
ARGYL
PAD
NO 2
SECOND AVE

Manor House Farm

CHURCH ST
MEADOW CROFT
ST MARY'S GARTHS
MARY ST
SCHOOL LA
LAUREL CL
FIRST AVE

Old Hall Farm

5

MOOR LA

PH
KESWICK GRANGE

BROOKLANDS

East Keswick C of E (Controlled) Junior and Infant Sch

COMPTON LA

Burn's Farm

44

THE DRIVE

KESWICK LA

WOODACRE GN BANKFIELD

KESWICK VIEW

East Rigton

LINDEN CL

WETHERBY RD

RIGTON BANK

RIGTON GN

BRAMHAM LA

4

GATEON HOUSE LA

Rigton Grange

WOODACRE GN

Bardsey Beck

GRANGE CL

MARGARET AVE

WETHERBY RD

East Rigton Farm

Resrs

Bardsey County Primary Sch

Bardsey

CORNMILL CL

MILL LA

Rigton Farm

WIKE LA

WOODACRE CRES

CORNMILL LA

WOOD LA

HOLME FARM LA

3

Rigton Moor

Rigton Carr Farm

Leeds Country Way

Gill Beck

Castle Hill

CASTLE CL

CASTLE GR

HETCHELL VIEW

Barker's Plantation

RUSSEL CT

THE BELL

43

Ford

CHURCH LA

PH

BINGLEY BANK

Rowley Wood

2

SPEAR FIR

SMITHY LA

THE GUNNEL

TITHE BARN LA

Caravan Park

Sheepcote Farm

Wayside Gardens

WAYSIDE CRES

WAYSIDE MOUNT

WAYSIDE DRIVE

Rowley Grange

Hetchell Wood

Pompocali

1

Spear Fir Farm

BLACKMOOR LA

Caravan Park

Golf Course

Dismtd Rly

MILNER LA

42

NORTH HILL

A58

35 **A** **B** 36 **C** **D** 37 **E** **F**

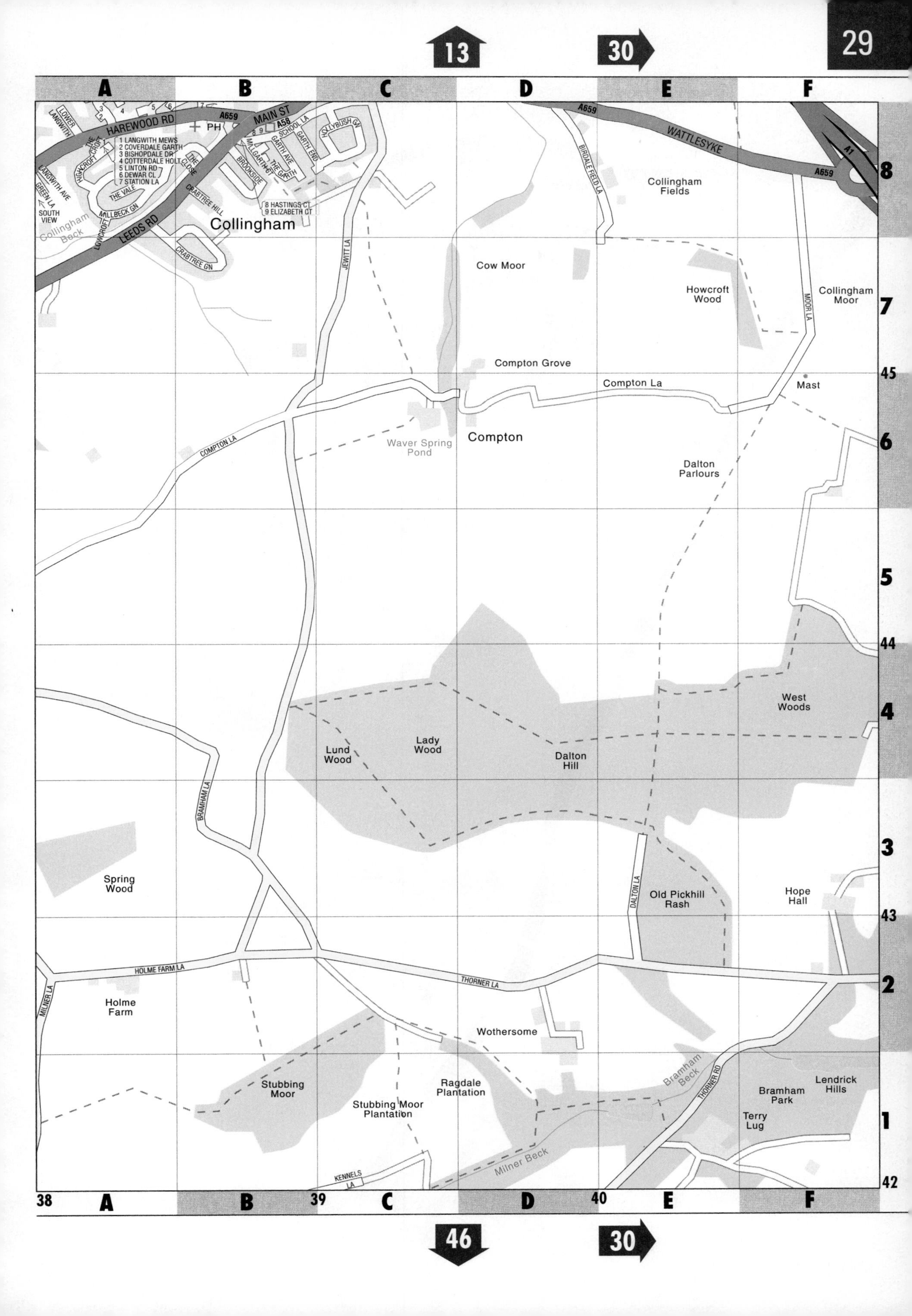

Collingham

1 LANGWITH MEWS
2 COVERDALE GARTH
3 BISHOPDALE DR
4 COTTERDALE HOLT
5 LINTON RD
6 DEWAR CL
7 STATION LA

8 HASTINGS CT
9 ELIZABETH CT

HAREWOOD RD
MAIN ST
A659
A58
LEEDS RD
A659
WATTLESYKE
A1
A659

Collingham Fields

Cow Moor

Howcroft Wood

Collingham Moor

Compton Grove

Compton La

Mast

Compton

Waver Spring Pond

Dalton Parlours

Lund Wood

Lady Wood

Dalton Hill

West Woods

Spring Wood

Old Pickhill Rash

Hope Hall

Holme Farm La

Thorner La

Holme Farm

Wothersome

Bramham Beck

Stubbing Moor

Ragdale Plantation

Bramham Park

Lendrick Hills

Stubbing Moor Plantation

Terry Lug

Milner Beck

KENNELS LA

29
14

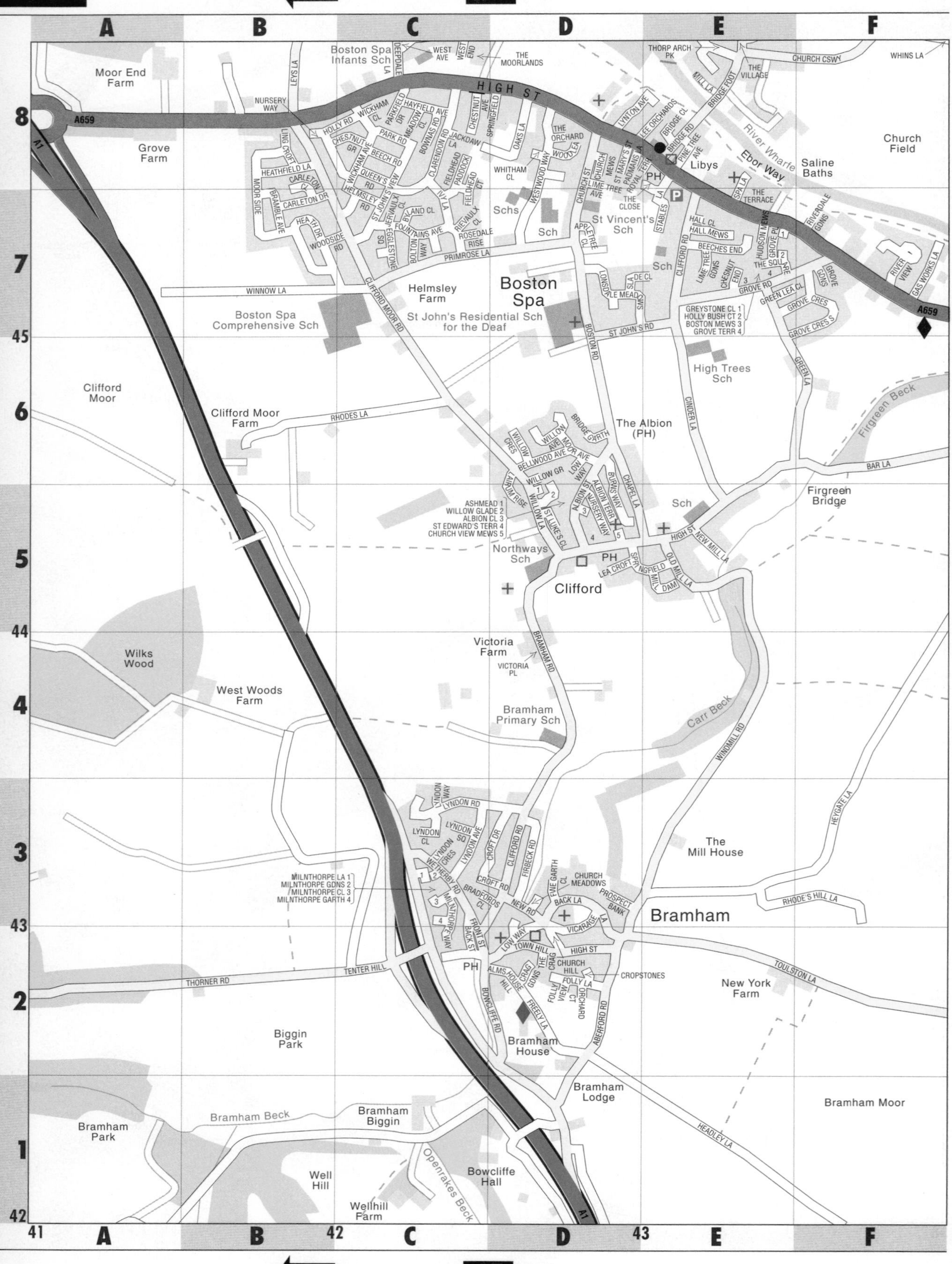
A
B
C
D
E
F
8
7
45
6
5
44
4
3
43
2
1
42
41
42
43
Moor End Farm
Grove Farm
A659
A1
HIGH ST
Boston Spa Infants Sch
WEST AVE
WEST END
THE MOORLANDS
DEEPDALE
LEYS LA
NURSERY WAY
HOLLY RD
WICKHAM CL
PARKFIELD DR
HAYFIELD AVE
MEADOW CL
CHESTNUT AVE
SPRINGFIELD
JACKDAW LA
BOWNAS RD
CLARENDON RD
OAKS LA
PARK RD
BEECH RD
HEATHFIELD LA
CARLETON CL
CARLETON DR
MOOR SIDE
BRAMBLE AVE
HEATH DR
WOODSIDE RD
QUEEN'S RD
HELMSLEY RD
WICKHAM AVE
ST JOHN'S VIEW
FIELDHEAD PADDOCK
FIELDHEAD CT
IVY LA
BYLAND CL
FOUNTAINS AVE
BOLTON WAY
EGGLESTONE SQ
RIEVAULX CL
ROSEDALE RISE
PRIMROSE LA
WHITHAM CL
WESTWOOD WAY
THE ORCHARD
WOOD LA
Schs
Sch
CHURCH ST
LIME TREE AVE
THE CLOSE
ST MARY'S ST
PADMANS LA
ROYAL TERR
LYNTON AVE
LEE ORCHARDS
BRIDGE CL
BRIDGE RD
PINE TREE AVE
St Vincent's Sch
APPLETREE CL
STABLES LA
PH
Libys
THORP ARCH PK
THE VILLAGE
MILL LA
BRIDGE FOOT
CHURCH CSWY
WHINS LA
River Wharfe
Ebor Way
Saline Baths
Church Field
SPA LA
THE TERRACE
HALL CL
HALL MEWS
BEECHES END
HUDSON MEWS
CLIFFORD RD
LIME TREE GDNS
CHESNUT END
THE SQUARE
GROVE PL
GROVE RD
GREEN LEA CL
GROVE GDNS
GROVE CRES
GROVE CRES S
RIVERDALE GDNS
RIVER VIEW
GAS WORKS LA
WINNOW LA
Helmsley Farm
Boston Spa
St John's Residential Sch for the Deaf
Boston Spa Comprehensive Sch
CLIFFORD MOOR RD
LONSDALE MEADOWS
DE CL
BOSTON RD
ST JOHN'S RD
GREYSTONE CL 1
HOLLY BUSH CT 2
BOSTON MEWS 3
GROVE TERR 4
High Trees Sch
GREEN LA
Clifford Moor
Clifford Moor Farm
RHODES LA
The Albion (PH)
CINDER LA
Firgreen Beck
BAR LA
BRIDGE GARTH
WILLOW AVE
WILLOW CRES
BELLWOOD AVE
MOOR AVE
LOW WAY
WILLOW GR
LARKIN RISE
WILLOW LA
ST LUKE'S CL
ALBION ST
ALBION TERR
NURSERY WAY
BURNS WAY
CHAPEL LA
ASHMEAD 1
WILLOW GLADE 2
ALBION CL 3
ST EDWARD'S TERR 4
CHURCH VIEW MEWS 5
Northways Sch
Clifford
LEA CROFT
SPRINGFIELD
MILL DAM
OLD MILL LA
HIGH ST
NEW MILL LA
Sch
Firgreen Bridge
Wilks Wood
Victoria Farm
VICTORIA PL
BRAMHAM RD
West Woods Farm
Bramham Primary Sch
Carr Beck
WINDMILL RD
HEYGATE LA
LYNDON WAY
LYNDON RD
LYNDON CL
LYNDON SQ
LYNDON CRES
LYNDON AVE
CROFT DR
CLIFFORD RD
FIRBECK RD
The Mill House
MILNTHORPE LA 1
MILNTHORPE GDNS 2
MILNTHORPE CL 3
MILNTHORPE GARTH 4
WETHERBY RD
MILNTHORPE WAY
CROFT RD
BRADFORDS CL
FIVE GARTH CL
CHURCH MEADOWS
PROSPECT BANK
BACK LA
NEW RD
VICARAGE LA
RHODE'S HILL LA
Bramham
FRONT ST
BACK ST
LOW WAY
TOWN HILL
HIGH ST
THE CRAG
CHURCH HILL
CROPSTONES
TENTER HILL
THORNER RD
ALMS HOUSE HILL
CRAG GDNS
FOLLY LA
FOLLY VIEW
ORCHARD CT
FREELY LA
TOULSTON LA
New York Farm
BOWCLIFFE RD
ABERFORD RD
Biggin Park
Bramham House
Bramham Lodge
HEADLEY LA
Bramham Moor
Bramham Park
Bramham Beck
Bramham Biggin
Openrakes Beck
Well Hill
Bowcliffe Hall
Wellhill Farm

29
47

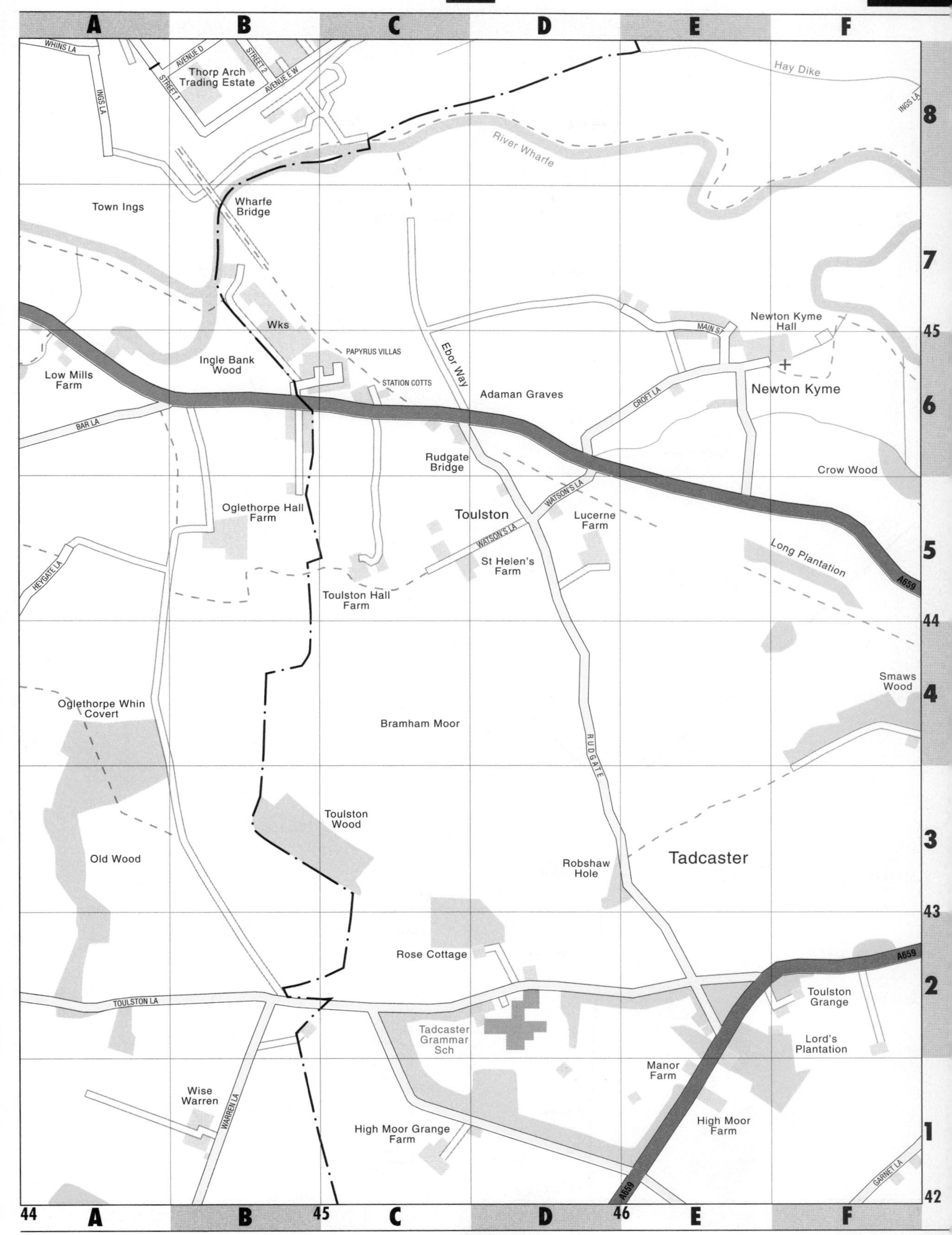

WHINS LA

INGS LA

AVENUE D

STREET 2

STREET 1

AVENUE E W

Thorp Arch
Trading Estate

Hay Dike

INGS LA

8

River Wharfe

Town Ings

Wharfe
Bridge

7

45

Wks

Newton Kyme
Hall

MAIN ST

Ingle Bank
Wood

PAPYRUS VILLAS

STATION COTTS

Ebor Way

Newton Kyme

Low Mills
Farm

Adaman Graves

CROFT LA

6

BAR LA

Rudgate
Bridge

Crow Wood

Oglethorpe Hall
Farm

Toulston

WATSON'S LA

Lucerne
Farm

Long Plantation

A659

5

HEYGATE LA

St Helen's
Farm

44

Toulston Hall
Farm

Smaws
Wood

Oglethorpe Whin
Covert

4

Bramham Moor

RUDGATE

Toulston
Wood

3

Old Wood

Robshaw
Hole

Tadcaster

43

A659

Rose Cottage

Toulston
Grange

TOULSTON LA

Lord's
Plantation

Tadcaster
Grammar
Sch

Manor
Farm

WARREN LA

Wise
Warren

High Moor
Farm

1

High Moor Grange
Farm

GARNET LA

A659

42

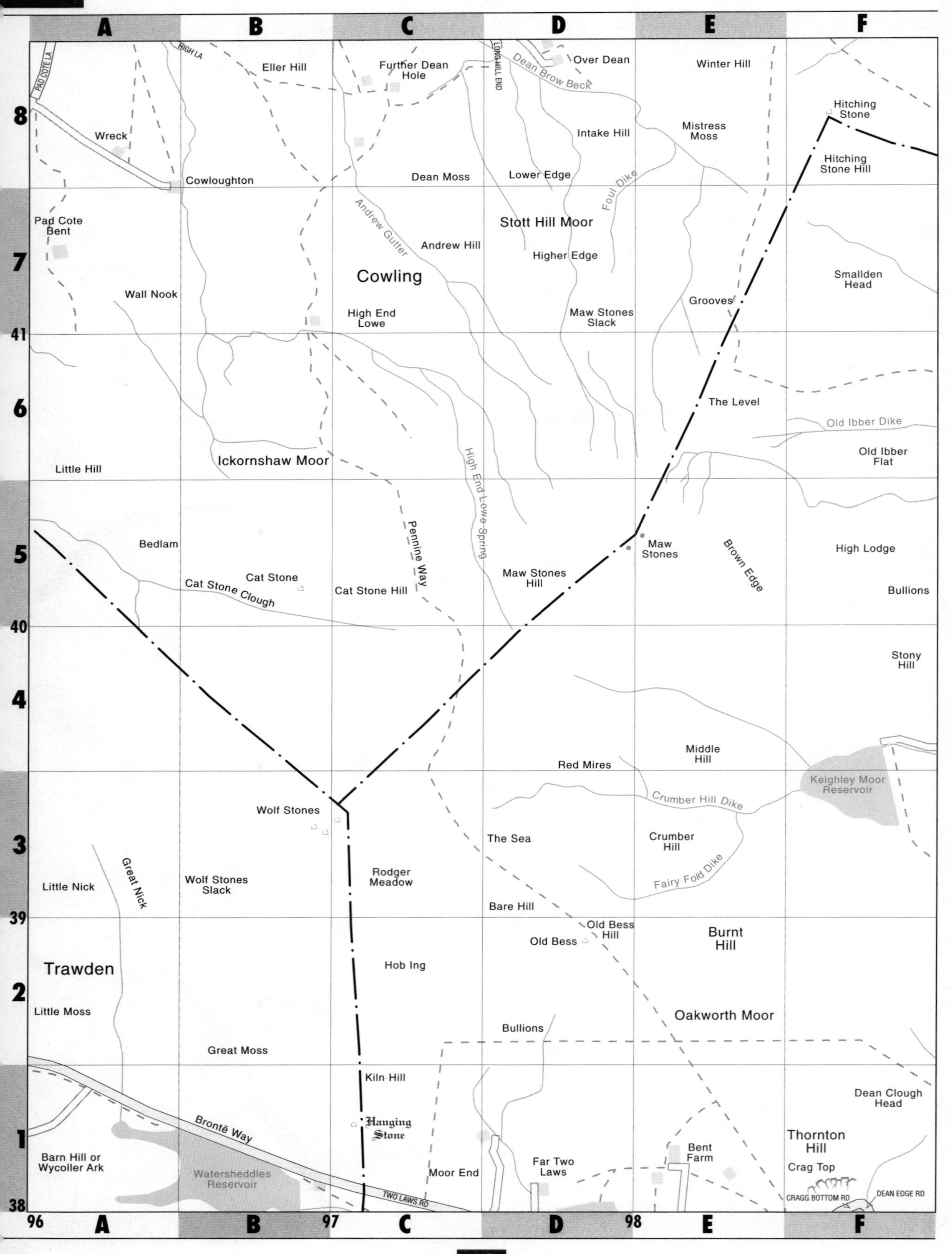

A
B
C
D
E
F
PAD COTE LA
HIGH LA
Eller Hill
Further Dean Hole
LONG HILL END
Dean Brow Beck
Over Dean
Winter Hill
Hitching Stone
Wreck
Cowloughton
Intake Hill
Mistress Moss
Hitching Stone Hill
Dean Moss
Lower Edge
Foul Dike
Pad Cote Bent
Andrew Gutter
Andrew Hill
Stott Hill Moor
Higher Edge
Cowling
Smallden Head
Wall Nook
High End Lowe
Maw Stones Slack
Grooves
The Level
Old Ibber Dike
Old Ibber Flat
Ickornshaw Moor
Little Hill
High End Lowe Spring
Pennine Way
Bedlam
Maw Stones
Brown Edge
High Lodge
Cat Stone
Cat Stone Clough
Cat Stone Hill
Maw Stones Hill
Bullions
Stony Hill
Middle Hill
Red Mires
Keighley Moor Reservoir
Crumber Hill Dike
Wolf Stones
The Sea
Crumber Hill
Great Nick
Little Nick
Wolf Stones Slack
Rodger Meadow
Fairy Fold Dike
Bare Hill
Old Bess Hill
Old Bess
Burnt Hill
Trawden
Hob Ing
Little Moss
Oakworth Moor
Bullions
Great Moss
Kiln Hill
Dean Clough Head
Brontë Way
Hanging Stone
Thornton Hill
Barn Hill or Wycoller Ark
Bent Farm
Far Two Laws
Crag Top
Watersheddles Reservoir
Moor End
TWO LAWS RD
CRAGG BOTTOM RD
DEAN EDGE RD
8
7
41
6
5
40
4
3
39
2
1
38
96
97
98

49

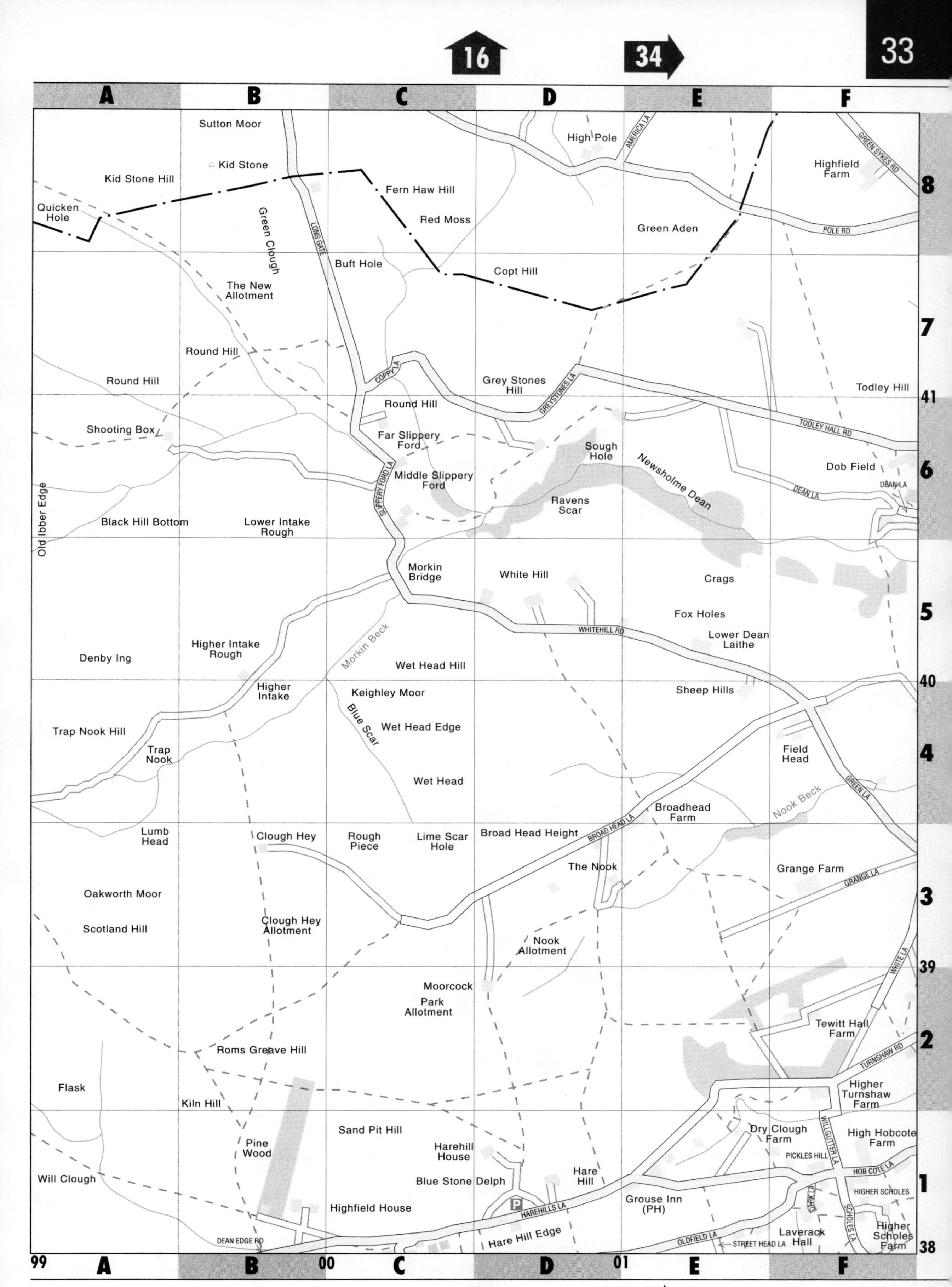
16
34
A
B
C
D
E
F
Sutton Moor
Kid Stone
Kid Stone Hill
Quicken Hole
Green Clough
LONG GATE
Fern Haw Hill
Red Moss
High Pole
AMERICA LA
GREEN SYKES RD
Highfield Farm
Green Aden
POLE RD
Buft Hole
Copt Hill
The New Allotment
Round Hill
Round Hill
COPPY LA
Grey Stones Hill
GREYSTONES LA
Todley Hill
Round Hill
TODLEY HALL RD
Shooting Box
Far Slippery Ford
Sough Hole
Newsholme Dean
Dob Field
Middle Slippery Ford
DEAN LA
DEAN LA
SLIPPERY FORD LA
Ravens Scar
Old Ibber Edge
Black Hill Bottom
Lower Intake Rough
Morkin Bridge
White Hill
Crags
Fox Holes
WHITEHILL RD
Lower Dean Laithe
Higher Intake Rough
Morkin Beck
Denby Ing
Wet Head Hill
Higher Intake
Keighley Moor
Sheep Hills
Blue Scar
Wet Head Edge
Trap Nook Hill
Trap Nook
Field Head
Wet Head
GREEN LA
Nook Beck
Broadhead Farm
BROAD HEAD LA
Lumb Head
Clough Hey
Rough Piece
Lime Scar Hole
Broad Head Height
The Nook
Grange Farm
GRANGE LA
Oakworth Moor
Scotland Hill
Clough Hey Allotment
Nook Allotment
WHITE LA
Moorcock
Park Allotment
Tewitt Hall Farm
TURNSHAW RD
Roms Greave Hill
Higher Turnshaw Farm
Flask
Kiln Hill
Sand Pit Hill
Dry Clough Farm
High Hobcote Farm
Pine Wood
Harehill House
PICKLES HILL
WILLGUTTER LA
HOB COTE LA
Hare Hill
Will Clough
Blue Stone Delph
HIGHER SCHOLES
Grouse Inn (PH)
Highfield House
HAREHILLS LA
DARK LA
SCHOLES LA
Higher Scholes Farm
Laverack Hall
DEAN EDGE RD
Hare Hill Edge
OLDFIELD LA
STREET HEAD LA
8
7
41
6
5
40
4
3
39
2
1
38
99
00
01

33
17

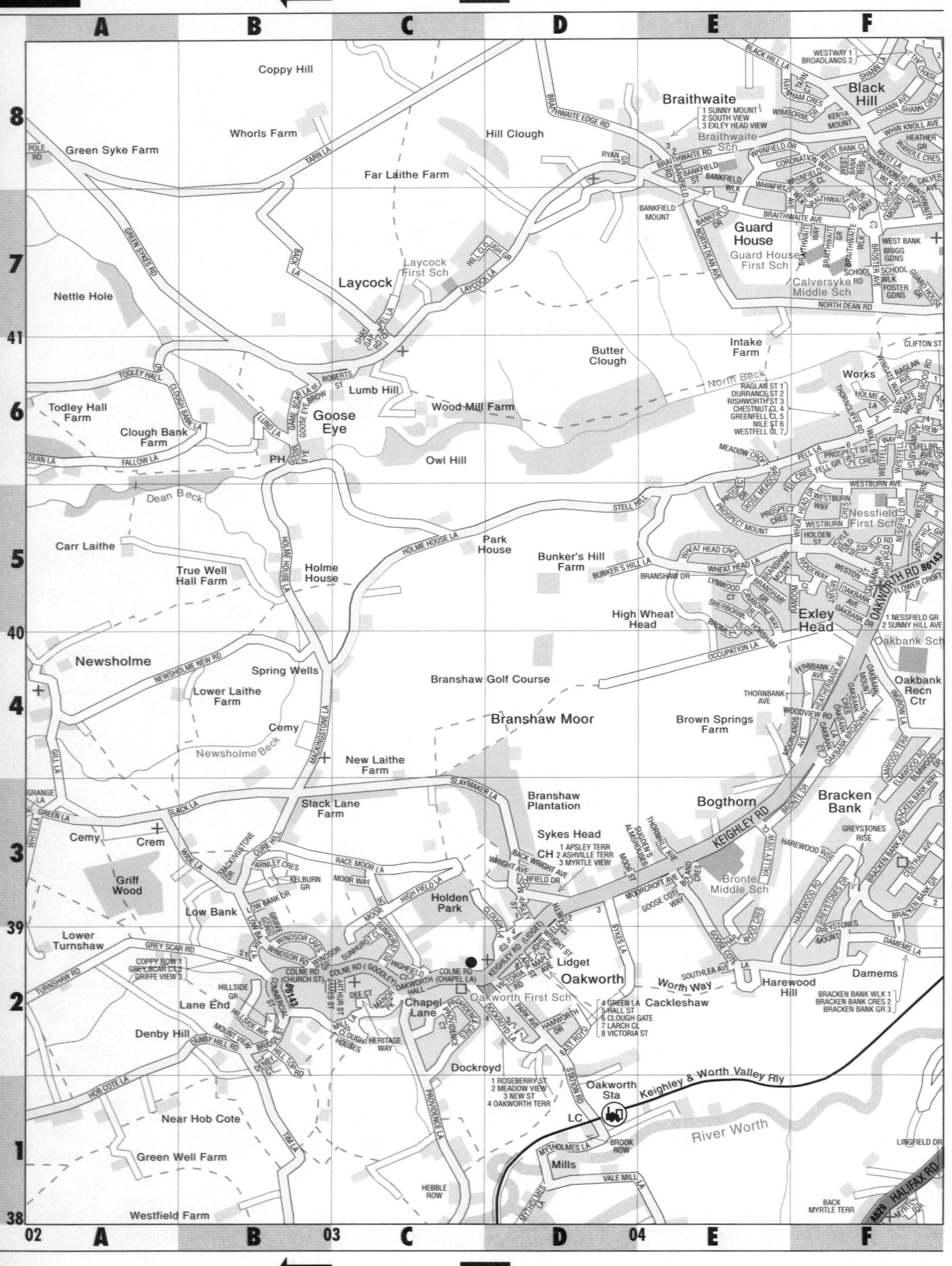
Coppy Hill
Whorls Farm
Green Syke Farm
Hill Clough
Far Laithe Farm
Braithwaite
Black Hill
Braithwaite Sch
Guard House
Guard House First Sch
Calversyke Middle Sch
Laycock
Laycock First Sch
Nettle Hole
Butter Clough
Intake Farm
Works
Todley Hall Farm
Clough Bank Farm
Lumb Hill
Goose Eye
Wood Mill Farm
Owl Hill
Dean Beck
North Beck
Carr Laithe
Park House
Bunker's Hill Farm
True Well Hall Farm
Holme House
Nessfield First Sch
High Wheat Head
Exley Head
Newsholme
Spring Wells
Lower Laithe Farm
Branshaw Golf Course
Oakbank Sch
Oakbank Recn Ctr
Branshaw Moor
Brown Springs Farm
Cemy
Newsholme Beck
New Laithe Farm
Branshaw Plantation
Slack Lane Farm
Bogthorn
Bracken Bank
Sykes Head
Cemy
Crem
Griff Wood
Holden Park
Bronte Middle Sch
Low Bank
Lower Turnshaw
Lidget
Oakworth
Damems
Harewood Hill
Worth Way
Lane End
Chapel Lane
Oakworth First Sch
Cackleshaw
Denby Hill
Dockroyd
Keighley & Worth Valley Rly
Oakworth Sta
Near Hob Cote
River Worth
Green Well Farm
Mills
Westfield Farm
KEIGHLEY RD
OAKWORTH RD B6143
HALIFAX RD A629
B6143
A B C D E F
8 7 6 5 4 3 2 1
41 40 39 38
02 03 04

33
51

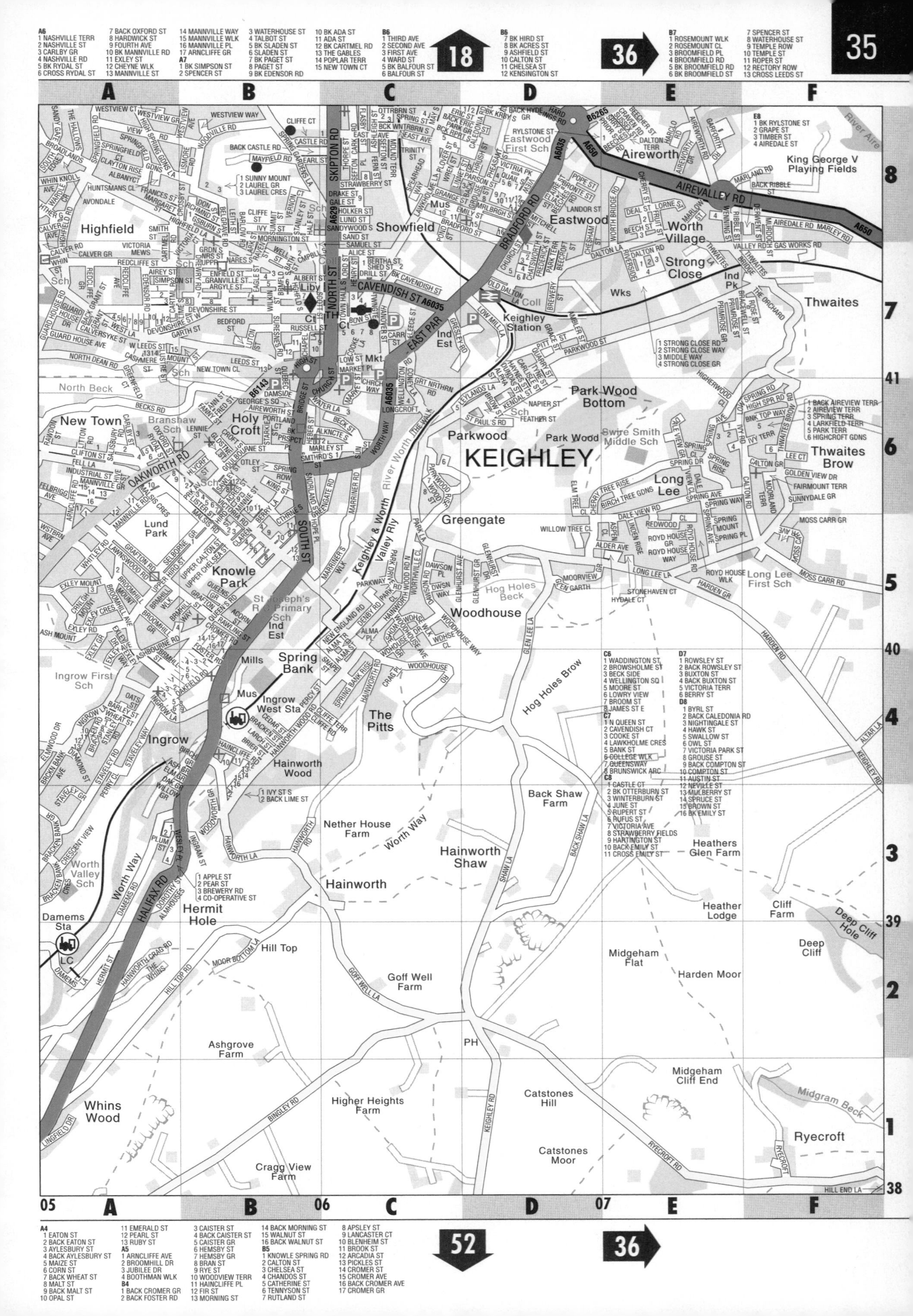

A6
1 NASHVILLE TERR
2 NASHVILLE ST
3 CARLBY GR
4 NASHVILLE RD
5 BK RYDAL ST
6 CROSS RYDAL ST
7 BACK OXFORD ST
8 HARDWICK ST
9 FOURTH AVE
10 BK MANNVILLE RD
11 EXLEY ST
12 CHEYNE WLK
13 MANNVILLE ST
14 MANNVILLE WAY
15 MANNVILLE WLK
16 MANNVILLE PL
17 ARNCLIFFE GR
A7
1 BK SIMPSON ST
2 SPENCER ST
3 WATERHOUSE ST
4 TALBOT ST
5 BK SLADEN ST
6 SLADEN ST
7 BK PAGET ST
8 PAGET ST
9 BK EDENSOR RD
10 BK ADA ST
11 ADA ST
12 BK CARTMEL RD
13 THE GABLES
14 POPLAR TERR
15 NEW TOWN CT
B6
1 THIRD AVE
2 SECOND AVE
3 FIRST AVE
4 WARD ST
5 BK BALFOUR ST
6 BALFOUR ST
18
B6
7 BK HIRD ST
8 BK ACRES ST
9 ASHFIELD ST
10 CALTON ST
11 CHELSEA ST
12 KENSINGTON ST
36
B7
1 ROSEMOUNT WLK
2 ROSEMOUNT CL
3 BROOMFIELD PL
4 BROOMFIELD RD
5 BK BROOMFIELD RD
6 BK BROOMFIELD ST
7 SPENCER ST
8 WATERHOUSE ST
9 TEMPLE ROW
10 TEMPLE ST
11 ROPER ST
12 RECTORY ROW
13 CROSS LEEDS ST
A B C D E F
E8
1 BK RYLSTONE ST
2 GRAPE ST
3 TIMBER ST
4 AIREDALE ST
KEIGHLEY
Highfield
Showfield
Eastwood
Aireworth
Worth Village
Strong Close
Thwaites
King George V Playing Fields
Keighley Station
New Town
Holy Croft
Park Wood Bottom
Parkwood
Thwaites Brow
Long Lee
Greengate
Lund Park
Knowle Park
Woodhouse
Spring Bank
Ingrow First Sch
Ingrow West Sta
The Pitts
Ingrow
Hainworth Wood
Nether House Farm
Back Shaw Farm
Hainworth Shaw
Heathers Glen Farm
Worth Valley Sch
Hainworth
Hermit Hole
Damems Sta
Hill Top
Goff Well Farm
Midgeham Flat
Harden Moor
Heather Lodge
Cliff Farm
Deep Cliff
Ashgrove Farm
Midgeham Cliff End
Catstones Hill
Whins Wood
Higher Heights Farm
Ryecroft
Catstones Moor
Cragg View Farm
C6
1 WADDINGTON ST
2 BROWSHOLME ST
3 BECK SIDE
4 WELLINGTON SQ
5 MOORE ST
6 LOWRY VIEW
7 BROOM ST
8 JAMES ST E
C7
1 N QUEEN ST
2 CAVENDISH CT
3 COOKE ST
4 LAWKHOLME CRES
5 BANK ST
6 COLLEGE WLK
7 QUEENSWAY
8 BRUNSWICK ARC
C8
1 CASTLE CT
2 BK OTTERBURN ST
3 WINTERBURN ST
4 JUNE ST
5 RUPERT ST
6 RUFUS ST
7 VICTORIA AVE
8 STRAWBERRY FIELDS
9 HARTINGTON ST
10 BACK EMILY ST
11 CROSS EMILY ST
D7
1 ROWSLEY ST
2 BACK ROWSLEY ST
3 BUXTON ST
4 BACK BUXTON ST
5 VICTORIA TERR
6 BERRY ST
D8
1 BYRL ST
2 BACK CALEDONIA RD
3 NIGHTINGALE ST
4 HAWK ST
5 SWALLOW ST
6 OWL ST
7 VICTORIA PARK ST
8 GROUSE ST
9 BACK COMPTON ST
10 COMPTON ST
11 AUSTIN ST
12 NEVILLE ST
13 MULBERRY ST
14 SPRUCE ST
15 BROWN ST
16 BK EMILY ST
05 A B 06 C D 07 E F
A4
1 EATON ST
2 BACK EATON ST
3 AYLESBURY ST
4 BACK AYLESBURY ST
5 MAIZE ST
6 CORN ST
7 BACK WHEAT ST
8 MALT ST
9 BACK MALT ST
10 OPAL ST
11 EMERALD ST
12 PEARL ST
13 RUBY ST
A5
1 ARNCLIFFE AVE
2 BROOMHILL DR
3 JUBILEE DR
4 BOOTHMAN WLK
B4
1 BACK CROMER GR
2 BACK FOSTER RD
3 CAISTER ST
4 BACK CAISTER ST
5 CAISTER GR
6 HEMSBY ST
7 HEMSBY GR
8 BRAN ST
9 RYE ST
10 WOODVIEW TERR
11 HAINCLIFFE PL
12 FIR ST
13 MORNING ST
14 BACK MORNING ST
15 WALNUT ST
16 BACK WALNUT ST
B5
1 KNOWLE SPRING RD
2 CALTON ST
3 CHELSEA ST
4 CHANDOS ST
5 CATHERINE ST
6 TENNYSON ST
7 RUTLAND ST
8 APSLEY ST
9 LANCASTER CT
10 BLENHEIM ST
11 BROOK ST
12 ARCADIA ST
13 PICKLES ST
14 CROMER ST
15 CROMER AVE
16 BACK CROMER AVE
17 CROMER GR
52
36

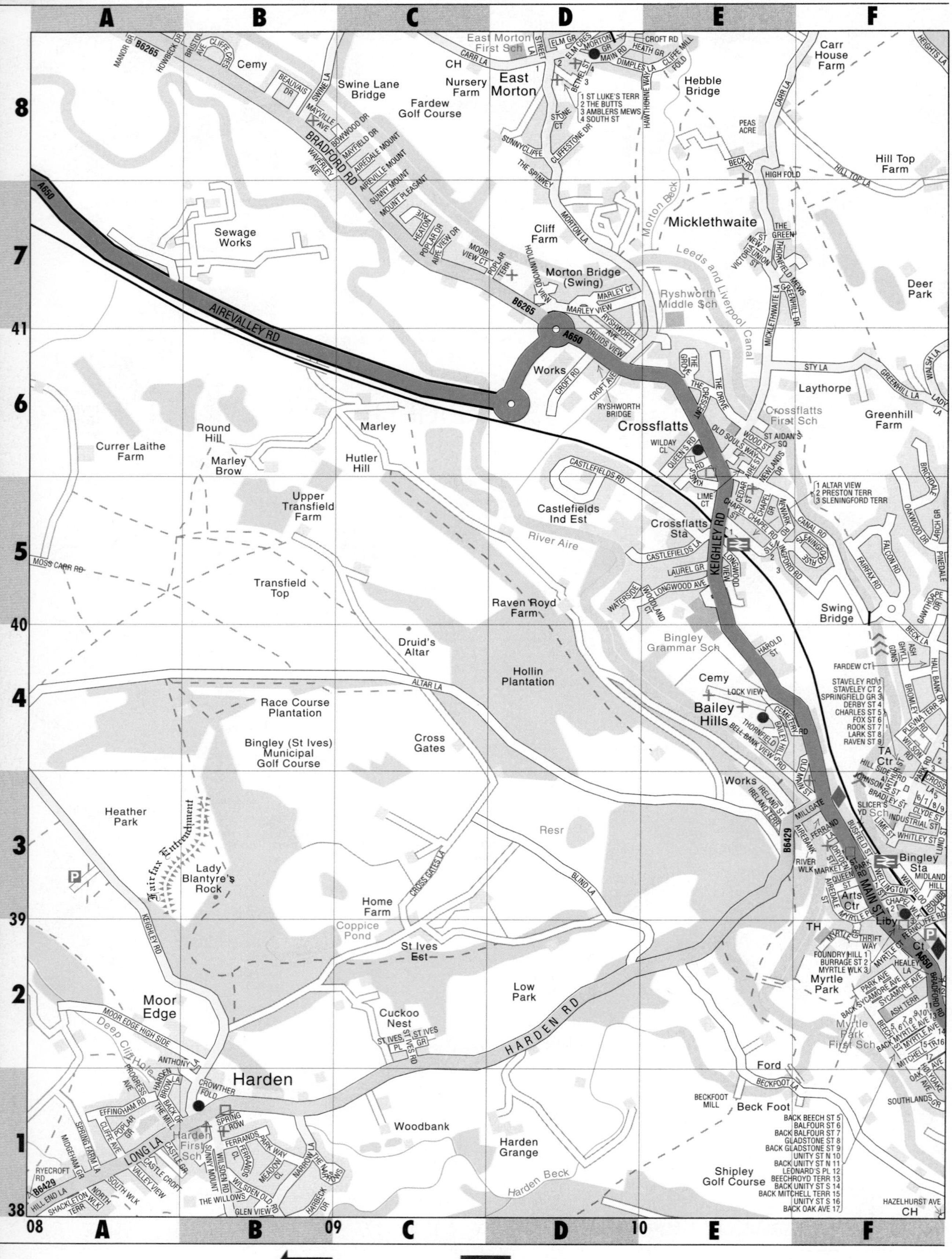
A
B
C
D
E
F
8
7
41
6
5
40
4
3
39
2
1
38
08
09
10
East Morton First Sch
CH
East Morton
Nursery Farm
Fardew Golf Course
Swine Lane Bridge
Cemy
Carr House Farm
Hebble Bridge
PEAS ACRE
HIGH FOLD
Hill Top Farm
HILL TOP LA
1 ST LUKE'S TERR
2 THE BUTTS
3 AMBLERS MEWS
4 SOUTH ST
MANOR GR
B6265
HOWBECK DR
BRISTOL AVE
CLIFFE CRES
BEAUVAIS DR
SWINE LA
MAYVILLE AVE
BOWWOOD DR
MAYFIELD DR
AIREDALE MOUNT
AIREVILLE MOUNT
SUNNY MOUNT
MOUNT PLEASANT
BRADFORD RD
WAVERLEY AVE
HEATON AVE
POPLAR DR
AIRE VIEW DR
MOOR VIEW CT
POPLAR TERR
ELM GR
CROFT RD
MAIN RD
HEATH GR
DIMPLES LA
CLIFFE MILL FOLD
HAWTHORNE WAY
CARR LA
BECK RD
STONE CT
CLIFFESTONE DR
SUNNYCLIFFE
THE SPINNEY
MORTON LA
HOLLINWOOD VIEW
Cliff Farm
Morton Bridge (Swing)
Sewage Works
A650
AIREVALLEY RD
Morton Beck
Micklethwaite
Leeds and Liverpool Canal
Ryshworth Middle Sch
MARLEY CT
MARLEY VIEW
RYSHWORTH AVE
DRUIDS VIEW
CROFT AVE
RYSHWORTH BRIDGE
Works
THE GREEN
VICTORIA ST
NEW ST
UNION ST
THORNFIELD MEWS
GREENHILL DR
MICKLETHWAITE LA
Deer Park
STY LA
Laythorpe
GREENHILL LA
WALSH LA
LADY LA
Greenhill Farm
Crossflatts First Sch
Crossflatts
THE GROVE
THE CRESCENT
THE DRIVE
OLD SOULS WAY
WOOD ST
ST AIDAN'S SQ
WILDAY CL
QUEEN'S RD
KING'S RD
AIRE ST
NEWLANDS DR
1 ALTAR VIEW
2 PRESTON TERR
3 SLENINGFORD TERR
Round Hill
Marley
Hutler Hill
Currer Laithe Farm
Marley Brow
Upper Transfield Farm
Castlefields Ind Est
CASTLEFIELDS RD
LIME CT
CEDAR ST
CHAPEL ST
CHAPEL GR
CHAPEL RD
NEWARK RD
Crossflatts Sta
KEIGHLEY RD
CANAL RD
SLENINGFORD RISE
SLENINGFORD RD
River Aire
CASTLEFIELDS LA
LAUREL GR
LONGWOOD VIEW
LONGWOOD AVE
WATERSIDE
WOODLAND CT
MOSS CARR RD
Transfield Top
Raven Royd Farm
FALCON RD
FAIRFAX RD
BIRCHDALE
OAKWOOD DR
LARCH GR
PINEDALE
Swing Bridge
GAWTHORPE DR
BECK LA
ASH GHYLL GDNS
HALL BANK DR
Bingley Grammar Sch
HAROLD ST
Druid's Altar
Hollin Plantation
Cemy
LOCK VIEW
Bailey Hills
CEMETERY RD
THORNFIELD
BAILEY HILL
BELL BANK VIEW
ALTAR LA
Race Course Plantation
Bingley (St Ives) Municipal Golf Course
Cross Gates
FARDEW CT
STAVELEY RD 1
STAVELEY CT 2
SPRINGFIELD GR 3
DERBY ST 4
CHARLES ST 5
FOX ST 6
ROOK ST 7
LARK ST 8
RAVEN ST 9
BROMLEY RD
PLEVNA TERR
WILSON RD
TA Ctr
HILL SIDE RD
JOHNSON ST
BRADLEY ST
SLICER'S YD
Sch
INDUSTRIAL ST
CLYDE ST
WHITLEY ST
LIME ST
PARK RD
CROSS
Works
OLD MAIN ST
IRELAND ST
IRELAND TERR
MILLGATE
B6429
AIREBANK
FERRAND LA
Heather Park
Fairfax Entrenchment
Lady Blantyre's Rock
Resr
RIVER WLK
MARKET ST
DRYDEN ST
QUEEN ST
PARK RD
Bingley Sta
MIDLAND HILL
MAIN ST
BUSFIELD ST
WELLINGTON ST
WATERLOO
CHAPEL LA
Arts Ctr
AIREDALE ST
MYRTLE PL
Liby
FERNCLIFFE RD
Ct
A650
BRADFORD RD
P
KEIGHLEY RD
Home Farm
CROSS GATES LA
BLIND LA
Coppice Pond
St Ives Est
TH
MYRTLE GR
THRIFT WAY
FOUNDRY HILL 1
BURRAGE ST 2
MYRTLE WLK 3
MYRTLE ST
HEALEY LA
Myrtle Park
Moor Edge
MOOR EDGE HIGH SIDE
Deep Cliff Hole
Low Park
Cuckoo Nest
ST IVES PL
ST IVES GR
ST IVES RD
HARDEN RD
PARK AVE
SYCAMORE AVE
ASH TERR
Myrtle Park First Sch
MYRTLE AVE
MITCHELL TERR
OAK AVE
ANTHONY LA
Harden
PROGRESS AVE
HARDEN BROW
BACK OF THE MILL
CROWTHER FOLD
Ford
BECKFOOT LA
BECKFOOT MILL
Beck Foot
SOUTHLANDS GR
EFFINGHAM RD
POPLAR GR
SPRING ROW
Harden First Sch
FERRANDS CL
FERRANDS PARK WAY
MEADOW CL
Woodbank
Harden Grange
SPRING FARM LA
MIDGEHAM GR
CLIFFE AVE
LONG LA
CASTLE CROFT
SUNNY MOUNT
WILSDEN RD
WILSDEN OLD RD
NARROW LA
THE NARROWS
RYECROFT RD
HILL END LA
SHACKLETON TERR
NORTH WLK
SOUTH WLK
VALLEY VIEW
THE WILLOWS
GLEN VIEW
HARBECK DR
Harden Beck
Shipley Golf Course
BACK BEECH ST 5
BALFOUR ST 6
BACK BALFOUR ST 7
GLADSTONE ST 8
BACK GLADSTONE ST 9
UNITY ST N 10
BACK UNITY ST N 11
LEONARD'S PL 12
BEECHROYD TERR 13
BACK UNITY ST S 14
BACK MITCHELL TERR 15
UNITY ST S 16
BACK OAK AVE 17
HAZELHURST AVE
CH

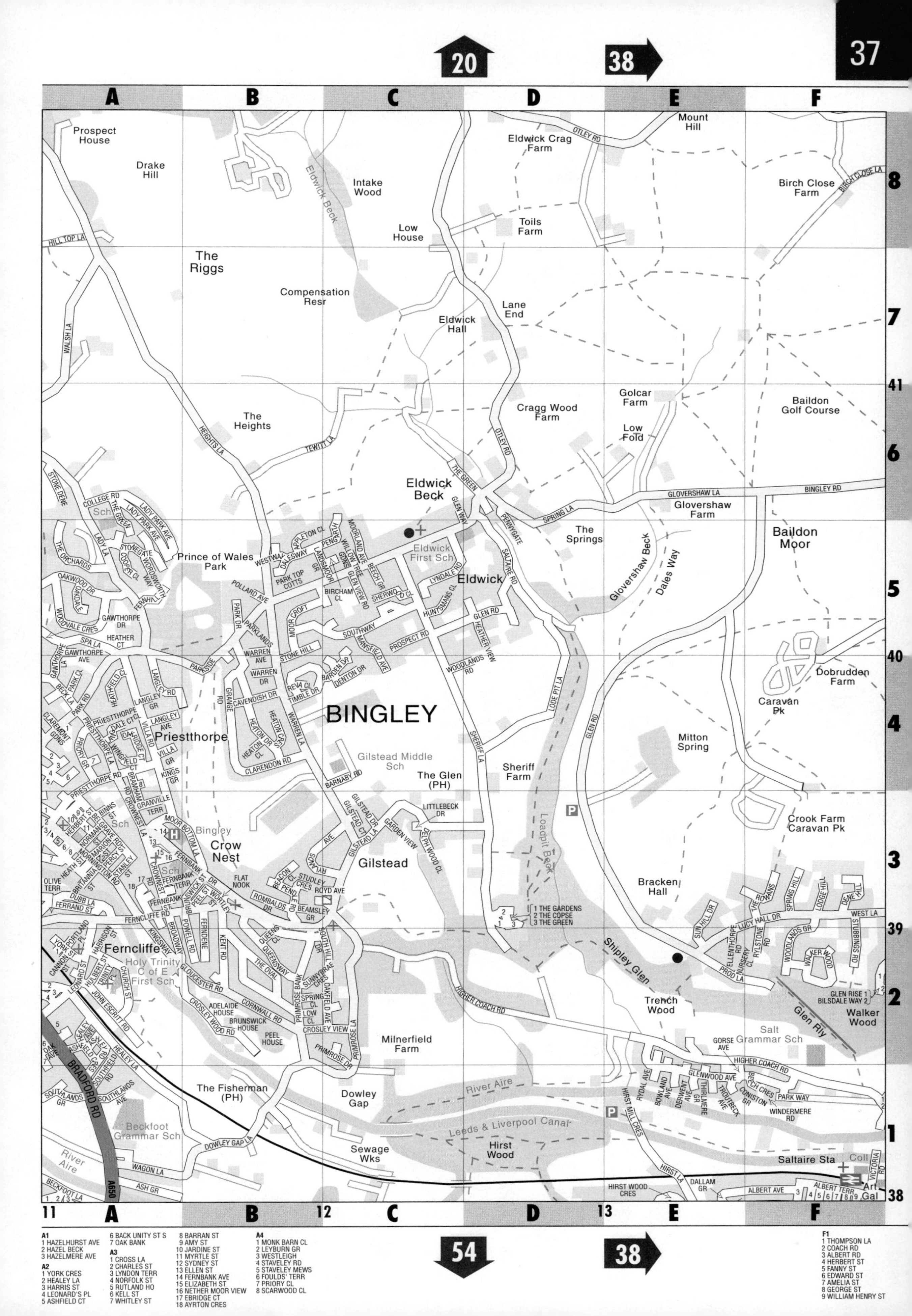

A B C D E F

11 A 12 B C 13 D E 38 F

Prospect House

Drake Hill

The Riggs

HILL TOP LA

WALSH LA

The Heights

HEIGHTS LA

TEWITT LA

COLLEGE RD

The Green

Sch

LADY PARK LA

THE ORCHARDS

LADY LA

OAKWOOD DR

GAWTHORPE DR

HEATHER CT

SPA LA

GAWTHORPE AVE

GANTHORPE AVE

BECK LA

PARK CRES

PRIESTTHORPE RD

CLAREMONT GDNS

Priestthorpe

PRIESTTHORPE RD

FIELD CL

DALE CTO

LANGLEY RD

LANGLEY AVE

LANGLEY GR

KINGS GR

GRANVILLE TERR

BARNABY RD

Sch

MOOR BOTTOM LA

HERBERT ST

Bingley
Sch

H

Crow Nest

Intake Wood

Low House

Compensation Resr

Eldwick Hall

Eldwick Beck

Prince of Wales Park

WESTNAL

PENS

APPLETON RD

GLESWAY

PARK TOP COTTS

PARK DR

PARKLANDS

WARREN AVE

WARREN DR

PARKSIDE

MOOR CROFT

STONE HILL

CAVENDISH DR

HEATON GR

HEATON CL

CLARENDON RD

BIRCHAM CL

SHERWOOD CL

MANSFIELD AVE

HUNTSMANS LA

LYNDALE RD

GLEN VIEW RD

WILSON RD

BEECH GR

MOORLAND AVE

LARKSMOOR

SOUTHWAY

BARDEN DR

DENTON DR

Eldwick First Sch

Eldwick

GLEN RD

HEATHER VIEW

PROSPECT RD

WOODLANDS RD

Gilstead Middle Sch

BINGLEY

GILSTEAD DR

GILSTEAD LA

GARDEN VIEW

The Glen (PH)

LITTLEBECK DR

Gilstead

BEECH WOOD CL

REVA CL

TIMBLE DR

BEECON

STUDLEY CRES

PENDLE

ROYD AVE

FLAT NOOK

ROMBALDS GR

BEAMSLEY GR

FERNCLIFFE

KENT RD

POWELL RD

BROADWAY

KINGSWAY

FERNCLIFFE RD

Ferncliffe

Holy Trinity C of E First Sch

CANNON

CROSS

HARRISON

HULBERT

ST

JOHN ESCRITT RD

CHURCH ST

BRADFORD RD

A650

HEALEY LA

SOUTHLANDS

SOUTHLANDS AVE

BECKFOOT LA

River Aire

Beckfoot Grammar Sch

WAGON LA

ASH GR

The Fisherman (PH)

DOWLEY GAP LA

Dowley Gap

PRIMROSE BANK

SUNNYDALE AVE

SUNNYDALE CRES

OAKFIELD AVE

LOW CL

SPRING CL

PRIMROSE DR

CROSLEY VIEW

ADELAIDE HOUSE

BRUNSWICK HOUSE

PEEL HOUSE

CROSLEY WOOD RD

CORNWALL RD

GLOUCESTER RD

QUEENS CL

QUEENSWAY

THE OVAL

SOUTH HILL

HIGHER COACH RD

Milnerfield Farm

Sewage Wks

River Aire

Leeds & Liverpool Canal

Hirst Wood

OTLEY RD

Eldwick Crag Farm

Toils Farm

Lane End

Cragg Wood Farm

Mount Hill

Birch Close Farm

BIRCH CLOSE LA

Golcar Farm

Low Fold

Baildon Golf Course

THE GREEN

GLEN WAY

PENIGATE

SALTAIRE RD

SHERIFF LA

LODE PIT LA

OTLEY RD

SPRING LA

GLOVERSHAW LA

BINGLEY RD

Gloveshaw Farm

The Springs

Gloveshaw Beck

Dales Way

Baildon Moor

Mitton Spring

Sheriff Farm

GLEN RD

P

Loadpit Beck

1 THE GARDENS
2 THE COPSE
3 THE GREEN

Bracken Hall

Crook Farm Caravan Pk

Caravan Pk

Dobrudden Farm

40

4

SUN HILL DR

ELLENTHORPE

LUCY HALL DR

NURSERY RD

PROD LA

THE ROYDS

SPRIG HILL

RYLSTONE

LODGE HILL

GENE KELL

WOODLANDS GR

STIBBINGS RD

WALKER WOOD

WEST LA

Shipley Glen

Glen Rly

Trench Wood

Salt Gorse Grammar Sch

GORSE AVE

HIGHER COACH RD

HIRST MILL CRES

P

RYDAL AVE

BOWLAND AVE

DERWENT AVE

THIRLMERE GR

GLENWOOD AVE

TROTBECK GR

CONISTON AVE

BRCH CRES

PARK WAY

WINDERMERE RD

HIRST LA

DALLAM GR

ALBERT AVE

Saltaire Sta

Coll

ALBERT TERR

Art Gal

HIRST WOOD CRES

GLEN RISE 1
BILSDALE WAY 2

Walker Wood

8

7

41

6

5

3

39

2

1

38

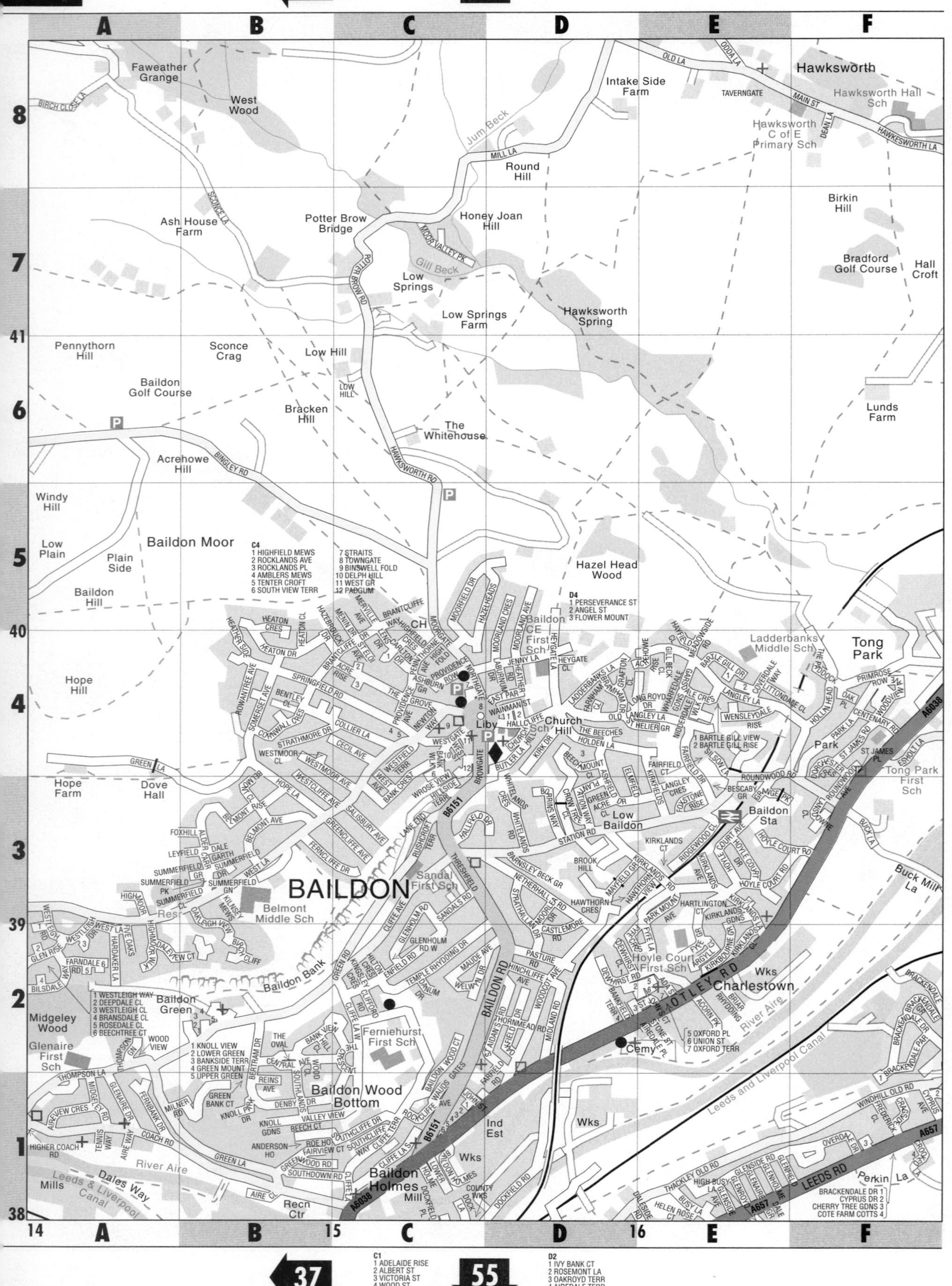

A B C D E F

8

Faweather Grange

West Wood

Intake Side Farm

OLD LA ODDA LA

TAVERNGATE

MAIN ST

Hawksworth

Hawksworth Hall Sch

DEAN LA

HAWKSWORTH LA

Hawksworth C of E Primary Sch

Jum Beck

MILL LA

Round Hill

7

Ash House Farm

SCONCE LA

POTTER BROW RD

Potter Brow Bridge

MOORS VALLEY PK

Gill Beck

Honey Joan Hill

Low Springs

Low Springs Farm

Hawksworth Spring

Birkin Hill

Bradford Golf Course

Hall Croft

41

Pennythorn Hill

Sconce Crag

Low Hill

LOW HILL

6

P

Baildon Golf Course

Bracken Hill

The Whitehouse

HAWKSWORTH RD

P

Acrehowe Hill

BINGLEY RD

Lunds Farm

5

Windy Hill

Low Plain

Plain Side

Baildon Moor

Baildon Hill

Hazel Head Wood

C4
1 HIGHFIELD MEWS
2 ROCKLANDS AVE
3 ROCKLANDS PL
4 AMBLERS MEWS
5 TENTER CROFT
6 SOUTH VIEW TERR

7 STRAITS
8 TOWNGATE
9 BINSWELL FOLD
10 DELPH HILL
11 WEST GR
12 PADGUM

D4
1 PERSEVERANCE ST
2 ANGEL ST
3 FLOWER MOUNT

Ladderbanks Middle Sch

Tong Park

40

Hope Hill

HEATON CRES

HEATON DR

BRANTCLIFFE

MOORFIELD DR

MOORLAND CRES

MOOR AVE

Baildon CE First Sch

HEYGATE CL

Tong Park First Sch

St James Pl

4

SPRINGFIELD RD

BENTLEY CL

COLLIER LA

Liby

CHURCH HILL

P

Church Hill

BARTLE GILL VIEW
BARTLE GILL RISE

Park

Tong Park First Sch

3

Hope Farm

Dove Hall

GREEN LA

WESTMOOR CL

CECIL AVE

WESTCLIFFE AVE

SALISBURY AVE

GREENCLIFFE AVE

FERNCLIFFE AVE

BROWGATE

B6151

BUTLER LA

Low Baildon

KIRKLANDS CT

Baildon Sta

Buck Mill La

BAILDON

FOXHILL

LEYFIELD

BELMONT AVE

Belmont Middle Sch

Sandal First Sch

Brook Hill

39

WESTFIELD RD

GLEN RISE

FIVE OAKS

FARNDALE

BILSDALE

Midgeley Wood

SUMMERFIELD

HIGHFIELD

OAKLEIGH RD

Baildon Bank

CLIFFE AVE

GREEN RD

SANDALS RD

Hawthorn Cres

CASTLEMORE AVE

Hoyle Court First Sch

OTLEY RD

Charlestown

5 OXFORD PL
6 UNION ST
7 OXFORD TERR

BRACKENDALE

2

1 WESTLEIGH WAY
2 DEEPDALE CL
3 WESTLEIGH CL
4 BRANSDALE CL
5 ROSEDALE CL
6 BEECHTREE CT

Baildon Green

WOOD VIEW

Ferniehurst First Sch

CLIFFE LA

BAILDON RD

MIDLAND RD

River Aire

Cemy

Leeds and Liverpool Canal

Wks

1

Glenaire First Sch

HIGHER COACH RD

COACH RD

GREEN LA

River Aire

1 KNOLL VIEW
2 LOWER GREEN
3 BANKSIDE TERR
4 GREEN MOUNT
5 UPPER GREEN

THE OVAL

Baildon Wood Bottom

SOUTHCLIFFE DR

B6157

Ind Est

Wks

WINDHILL OLD RD

A657

38

Dales Way

Leeds & Liverpool Canal

Mills

Baildon Holmes

DOCKFIELD RD

Recn Ctr

A6038

LEEDS RD

Perkin La

BRACKENDALE DR 1
CYPRUS DR 2
CHERRY TREE GDNS 3
COTE FARM COTTS 4

14 A 15 B C 16 D E F

C1
1 ADELAIDE RISE
2 ALBERT ST
3 VICTORIA ST
4 WOOD ST
5 QUEEN ST
6 GEORGE ST

D2
1 IVY BANK CT
2 ROSEMONT LA
3 OAKROYD TERR
4 AIREDALE TERR

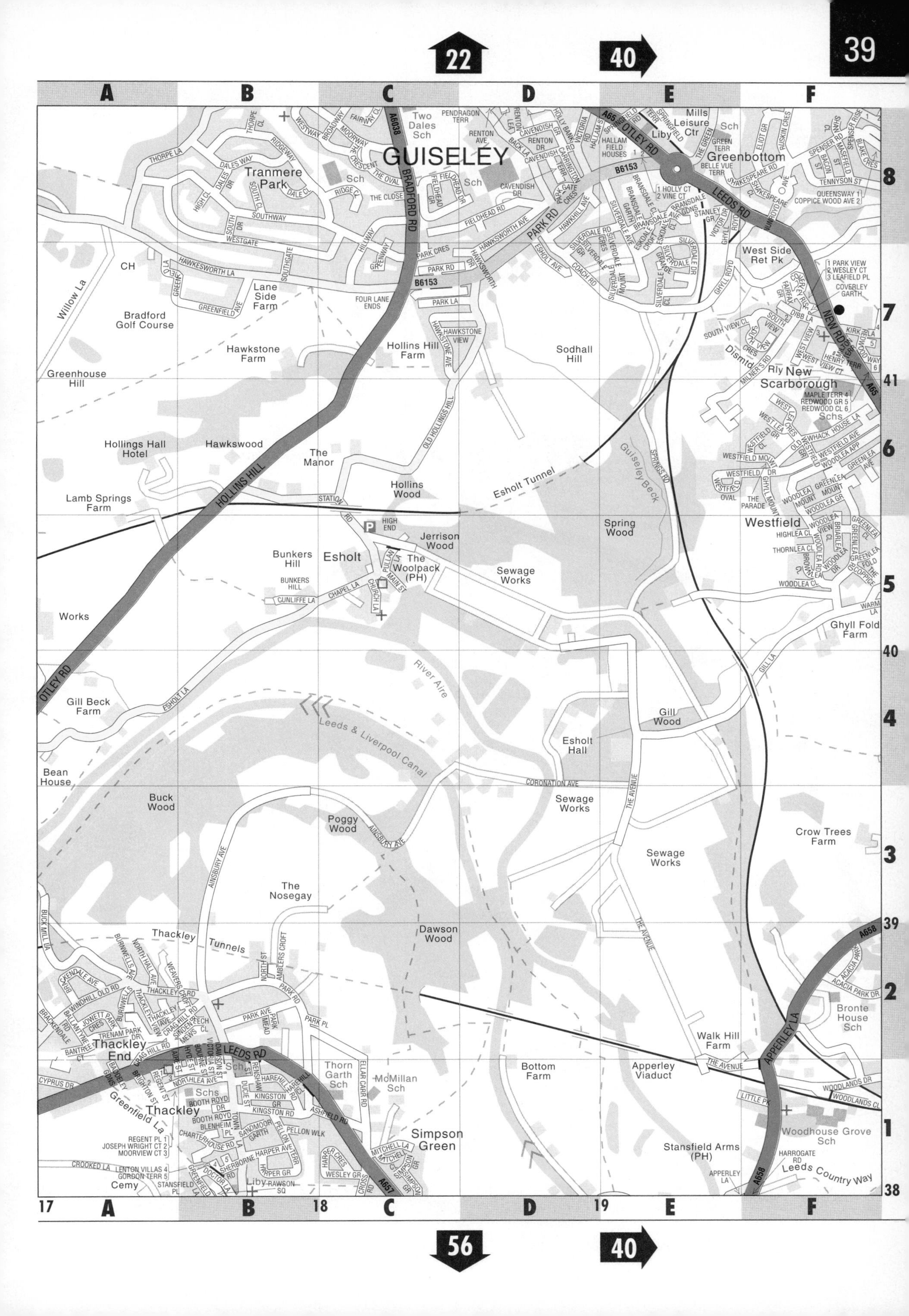
22
40
A
B
C
D
E
F
GUISELEY
Two Dales Sch
Mills Leisure Ctr
Liby
Sch
Greenbottom
Tranmere Park
Sch
Sch
OTLEY RD
BRADFORD RD
A6038
A65
B6153
LEEDS RD
PARK RD
HAWKSWORTH AVE
HAWKESWORTH LA
West Side Ret Pk
CH
Lane Side Farm
Bradford Golf Course
Willow La
FOUR LANE ENDS
Hawkstone Farm
Hollins Hill Farm
Sodhall Hill
Greenhouse Hill
Dismtd Rly
New Scarborough
Schs
Hollings Hall Hotel
Hawkswood
The Manor
Hollins Wood
Esholt Tunnel
Guiseley Beck
Lamb Springs Farm
HOLLINS HILL
Westfield
Spring Wood
Bunkers Hill
Esholt
The Woolpack (PH)
Jerrison Wood
Sewage Works
Works
Ghyll Fold Farm
River Aire
OTLEY RD
Gill Beck Farm
ESHOLT LA
Gill Wood
Leeds & Liverpool Canal
Esholt Hall
Bean House
Buck Wood
CORONATION AVE
Sewage Works
Poggy Wood
THE AVENUE
Crow Trees Farm
Sewage Works
The Nosegay
Dawson Wood
Thackley Tunnels
A658
APPERLEY LA
Bronte House Sch
Walk Hill Farm
Thackley End
LEEDS RD
Thorn Garth Sch
McMillan Sch
Bottom Farm
Apperley Viaduct
Schs
Thackley
Greenfield La
Woodhouse Grove Sch
Simpson Green
Stansfield Arms (PH)
Leeds Country Way
Cemy
A657
A658
8
7
41
6
5
40
4
3
39
2
1
38
17
18
19
A
B
C
D
E
F
56
40

39
23

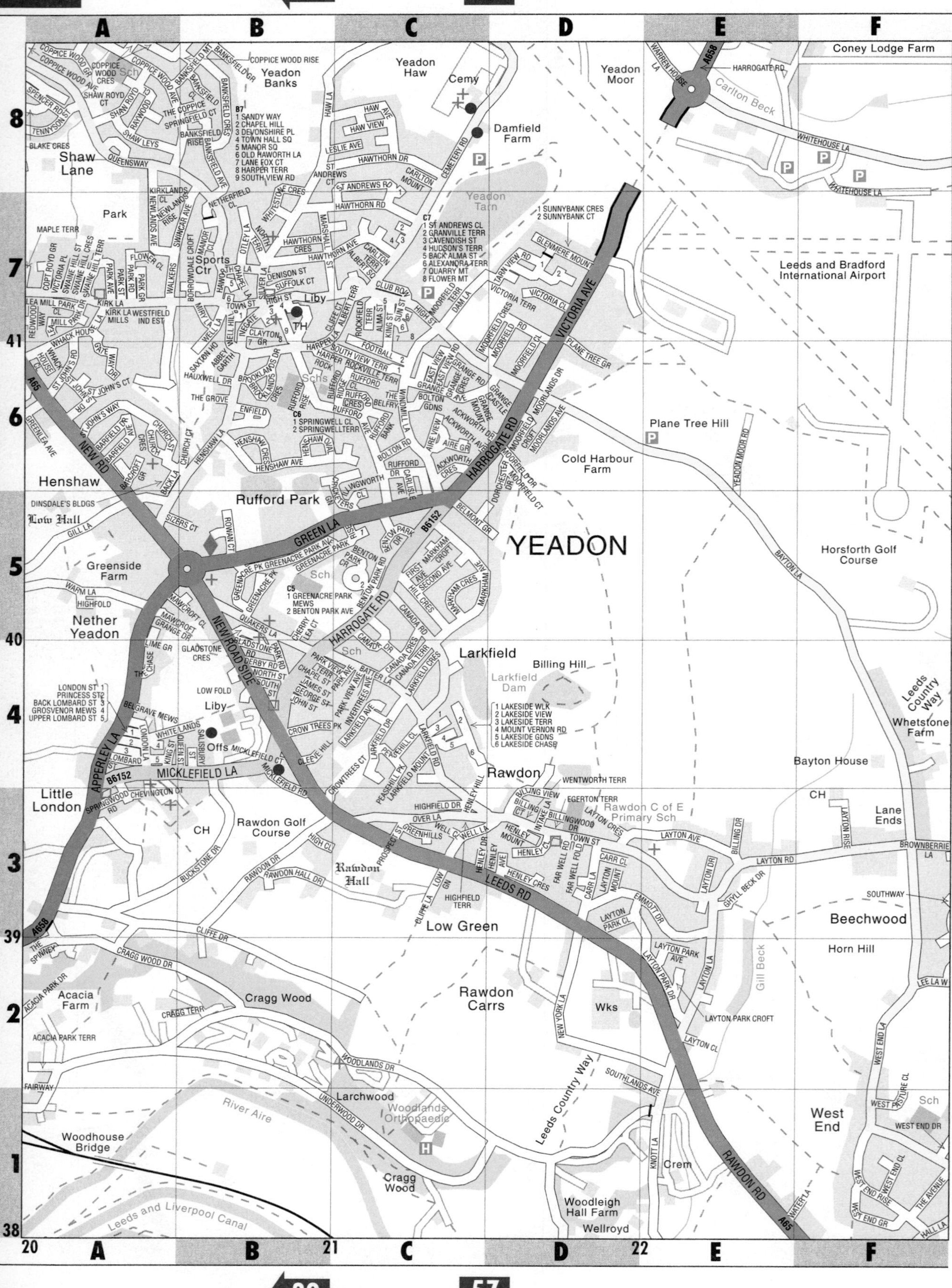
YEADON
Yeadon Banks
Yeadon Haw
Yeadon Moor
Shaw Lane
Damfield Farm
Yeadon Tarn
Leeds and Bradford International Airport
Coney Lodge Farm
Henshaw
Rufford Park
Low Hall
Greenside Farm
Nether Yeadon
Plane Tree Hill
Cold Harbour Farm
Horsforth Golf Course
Larkfield
Billing Hill
Larkfield Dam
Rawdon
Little London
Rawdon Golf Course
Rawdon Hall
Low Green
Beechwood
Horn Hill
Whetstone Farm
Bayton House
Lane Ends
Acacia Farm
Cragg Wood
Rawdon Carrs
Wks
Larchwood
Woodlands Orthopaedic
Woodhouse Bridge
Cragg Wood
River Aire
Leeds and Liverpool Canal
Leeds Country Way
Crem
Woodleigh Hall Farm
Wellroyd
West End
NEW RD
GREEN LA
HARROGATE RD
VICTORIA AVE
LEEDS RD
RAWDON RD
APPERLEY LA
MICKLEFIELD LA
NEW ROAD SIDE
BAYTON LA
LAYTON RD
CLIFFE DR
CRAGG WOOD DR
UNDERWOOD DR
WOODLANDS DR
A65
A658
B6152

39
57

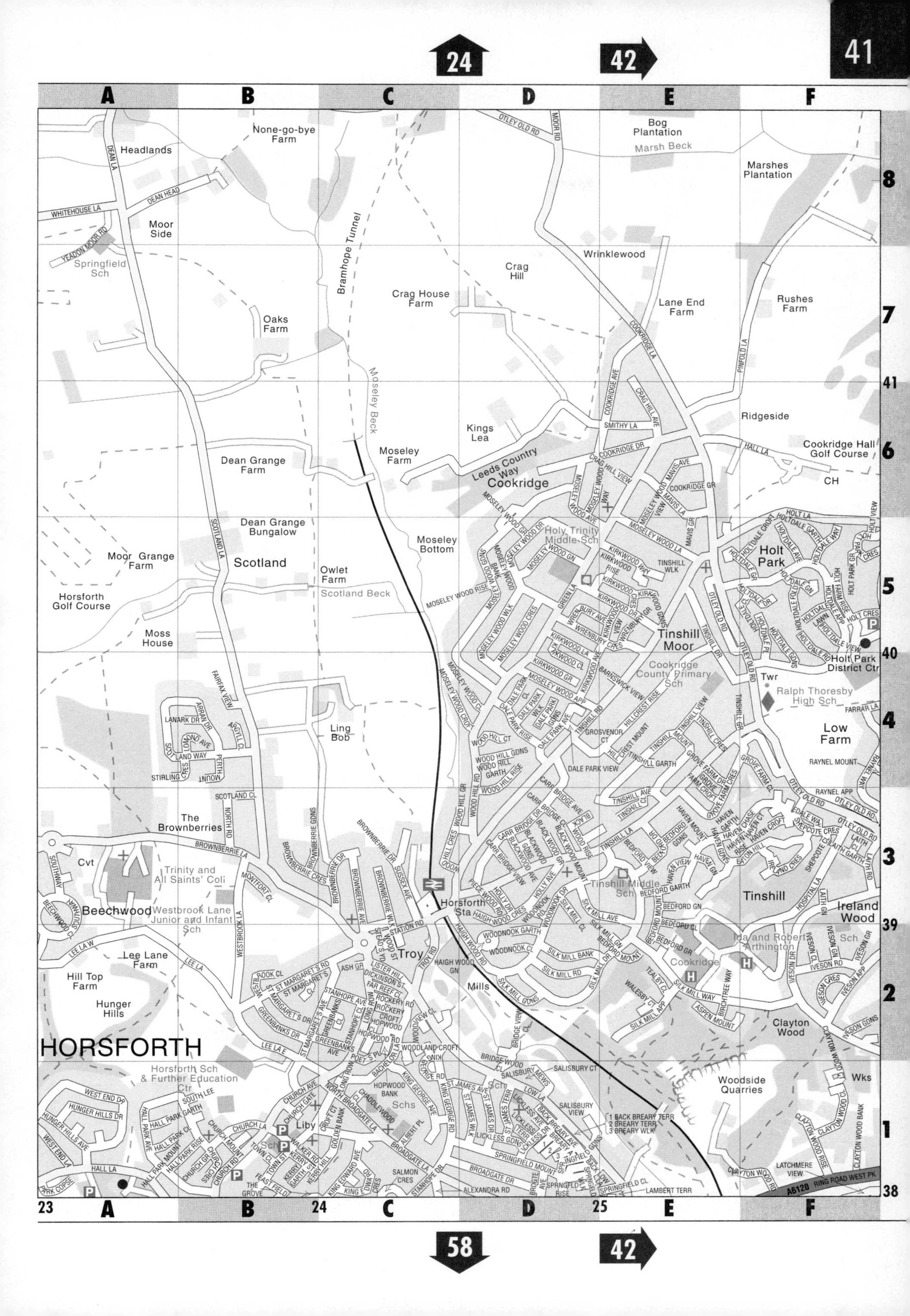

41
24
42
58
42
A
B
C
D
E
F
8
7
41
6
5
40
4
3
39
2
1
38
23
24
25
None-go-bye Farm
Headlands
Bog Plantation
Marsh Beck
Marshes Plantation
DEAN LA
DEAN HEAD
WHITEHOUSE LA
YEADON MOOR RD
Moor Side
Springfield Sch
OTLEY OLD RD
MOOR RD
Bramhope Tunnel
Wrinklewood
Crag Hill
Crag House Farm
Lane End Farm
Rushes Farm
Oaks Farm
COOKRIDGE LA
PINFOLD LA
Moseley Beck
COOKRIDGE AVE
CRAG HILL AVE
Ridgeside
Kings Lea
SMITHY LA
HALL LA
Cookridge Hall Golf Course
Dean Grange Farm
Moseley Farm
Leeds Country Way
Cookridge
COOKRIDGE DR
CRAG HILL VIEW
MAVIS AVE
COOKRIDGE GR
MAVIS LA
MAVIS GR
CH
Dean Grange Bungalow
Moseley Bottom
Holy Trinity Middle Sch
MOSELEY WOOD LA
TINSHILL WLK
HOLT LA
Holt Park
Moor Grange Farm
Scotland
SCOTLAND LA
Owlet Farm
Scotland Beck
Horsforth Golf Course
MOSELEY WOOD RISE
KIRKWOOD WAY
KIRKWOOD RISE
GREEN LA
WRENBURY AVE
WRENBURY CRES
Tinshill Moor
OTLEY OLD RD
TINSHILL DR
Moss House
KIRKWOOD LA
KIRKWOOD CL
KIRKWOOD GR
Holt Park District Ctr
Cookridge County Primary Sch
Twr
Ralph Thoresby High Sch
FARRAR LA
FAIRFAX VIEW
LANARK DR
ARRAN DR
ARGYLL CL
MOSELEY WOOD APP
BARNSWICK VIEW
HILLCREST RISE
Ling Bob
DALE PARK AVE
TINSHILL RD
GROSVENOR CT
HILLCREST MOUNT
TINSHILL GARTH
TINSHILL CRES
TINSHILL GR
Low Farm
STIRLING CRES
PERTH MOUNT
WOOD HILL CT
WOOD HILL GDNS
WOOD HILL GARTH
WOOD HILL RISE
DALE PARK VIEW
GROVE FARM DR
RAYNEL MOUNT
SCOTLAND CL
NORTH RD
CARR BRIDGE AVE
TINSHILL AVE
TINSHILL CL
RAYNEL APP
OTLEY OLD RD
BROWNBERRIE GDNS
The Brownberries
BROWNBERRIE LA
BROWNBERRIE DR
SUSSEX AVE
WOOD HILL GR
WOOD HILL RD
TINSHILL LA
BEDFORD VIEW
HAVEN MOUNT
HAVEN GARTH
HAVEN CHASE
HAVEN CT
HAVEN CROFT
SHEPCOTE CRES
SOUTHWAY
Cvt
Trinity and All Saints' Coll
MONTFORT CL
BROWNBERRIE CRES
BROWNBERRIE AVE
BROWNBERRIE WLK
Horsforth Sta
PIECE WOOD RD
HOLLY AVE
Tinshill Middle Sch
BEDFORD GARTH
Tinshill
HOSPITAL LA
LAITH RD
Ireland Wood
Beechwood
Westbrook Lane Junior and Infant Sch
WESTBROOK LA
STATION RD
HAIGH WOOD CRES
WOODNOOK DR
SILK MILL AVE
BEDFORD GN
LEE LA W
Lee Lane Farm
LEE LA
ASH GR
Troy
TROY RD
HAIGH WOOD RD
WOODNOOK GARTH
WOODNOOK CL
SILK MILL BANK
SILK MILL RD
BEDFORD MOUNT
BEDFORD GR
Cookridge
Ida and Robert Arthington
Sch
IVESON RD
Hill Top Farm
ST MARGARET'S RD
ST MARGARET'S CL
LISTER HILL
DICKINSON ST
FAR REEF CL
ROCKERY RD
HAIGH WOOD GN
Mills
SILK MILL GDNS
WALESBY CT
TEALBY CL
SILK MILL WAY
BIRCHTREE WAY
IVESON APP
Hunger Hills
GREENBANKS DR
STANHOPE AVE
HOPWOOD RD
SILK MILL APP
ASPEN MOUNT
Clayton Wood
HORSFORTH
LEE LA E
WOODLAND CROFT
BRIDGE WOOD CL
SALISBURY CT
SALISBURY MEWS
CLAYTON WOOD RD
Horsforth Sch & Further Education Ctr
Woodside Quarries
Wks
WEST END DR
SOUTH LEE
CHURCH AVE
CHURCH GATE
NORTH BROADGATE LA
HOPWOOD BANK
Schs
KING GEORGE RD
ST JAMES AVE
ST JAMES DR
LOW LA
SALISBURY VIEW
1 BACK BREARY TERR
2 BREARY TERR
3 BREARY WLK
HUNGER HILLS DR
HUNGER HILLS AVE
HALL PARK GARTH
CHURCH LA
Liby
GOLDEN BANK
ALBERT PL
ST JAMES WLK
LICKLESS GDNS
CLAYTON WOOD BANK
CLAYTON WOOD RISE
WEST END LA
HALL PARK AVE
HALL PARK RISE
CHURCH MOUNT
TOWN ST
BROADGATE LA
SPRINGFIELD MOUNT
HALL LA
PARK COPSE
KING EDWARD AVE
SALMON CRES
STANHOPE DR
BROADGATE DR
ALEXANDRA RD
SPRINGFIELD CL
LAMBERT TERR
CLAYTON WOOD RD
LATCHMERE VIEW
A6120 RING ROAD WEST PK

41
25

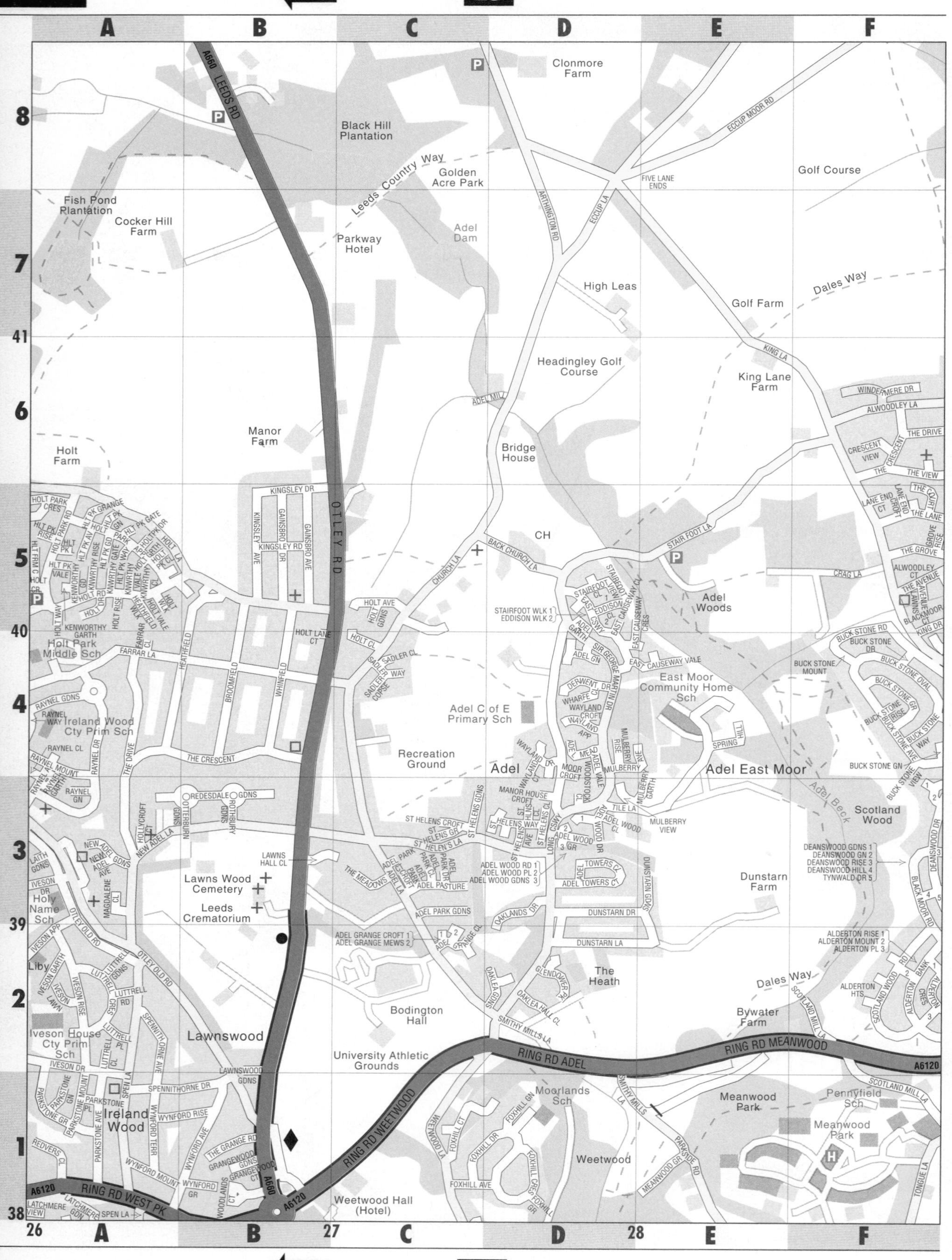
Clonmore Farm
Black Hill Plantation
Golden Acre Park
Leeds Country Way
Fish Pond Plantation
Cocker Hill Farm
Parkway Hotel
Adel Dam
FIVE LANE ENDS
Golf Course
High Leas
Golf Farm
Dales Way
Headingley Golf Course
King Lane Farm
Manor Farm
Holt Farm
Bridge House
CH
Adel Woods
Holt Park Middle Sch
East Moor Community Home Sch
Ireland Wood Cty Prim Sch
Adel C of E Primary Sch
Recreation Ground
Adel
Adel East Moor
Scotland Wood
Adel Beck
Lawns Wood Cemetery
Leeds Crematorium
Dunstarn Farm
Holy Name Sch
The Heath
Bodington Hall
Bywater Farm
Iveson House Cty Prim Sch
Lawnswood
University Athletic Grounds
RING RD ADEL
RING RD MEANWOOD
RING RD WEETWOOD
RING RD WEST PK
Moorlands Sch
Meanwood Park
Pennyfield Sch
Ireland Wood
Weetwood
Weetwood Hall (Hotel)
OTLEY RD
A660 LEEDS RD
A6120

41
59

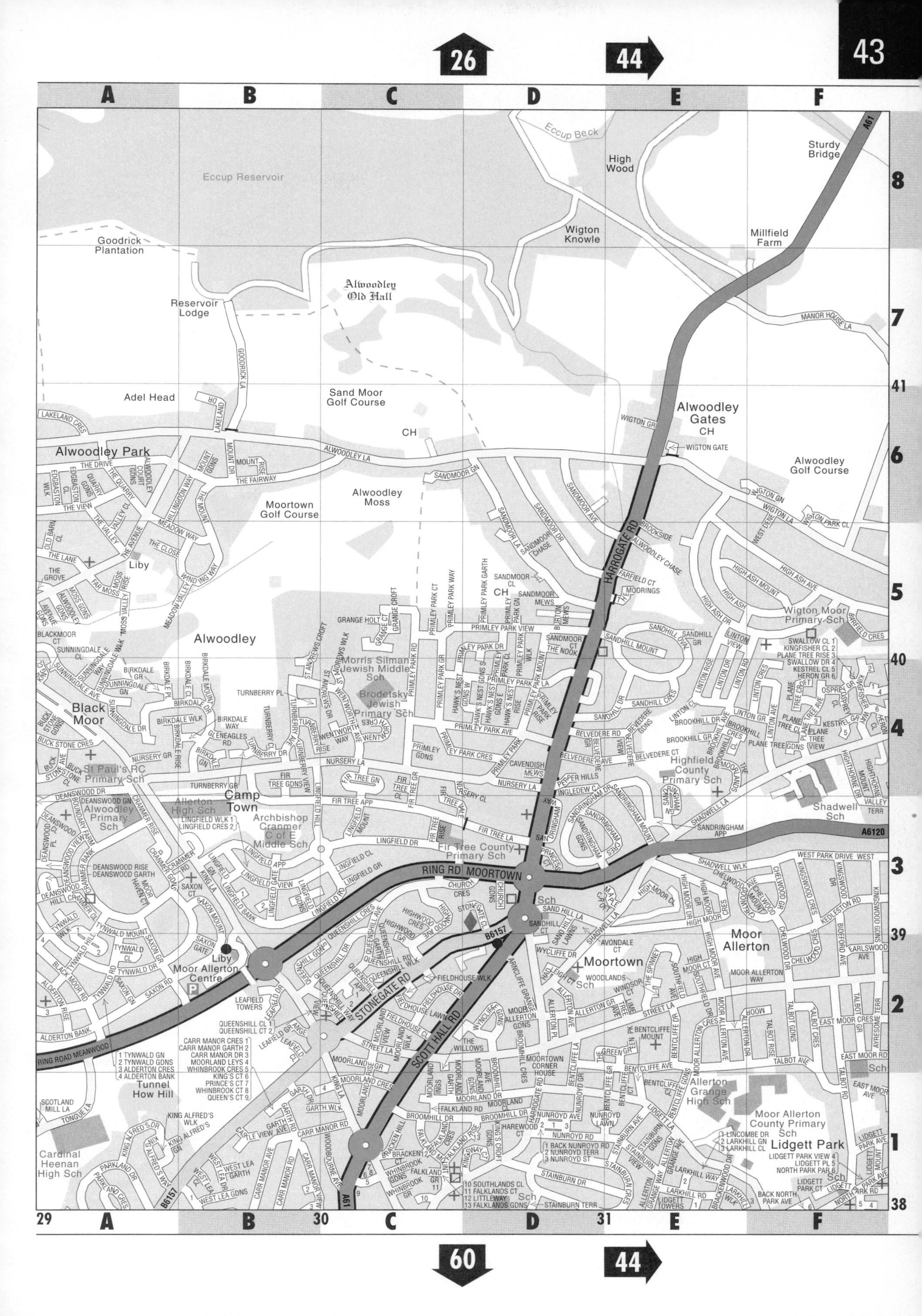

43
26
44
60
A
B
C
D
E
F
8
7
41
6
5
40
4
3
39
2
1
38
29
30
31
Eccup Reservoir
Eccup Beck
High Wood
Sturdy Bridge
A61
Goodrick Plantation
Wigton Knowle
Millfield Farm
Alwoodley Old Hall
Reservoir Lodge
GOODRICK LA
MANOR HOUSE LA
Adel Head
Sand Moor Golf Course
Alwoodley Gates
CH
WIGTON GATE
WIGTON GR
LAKELAND CRES
Alwoodley Park
ALWOODLEY LA
Alwoodley Golf Course
Alwoodley Moss
Moortown Golf Course
SANDMOOR GN
WIGTON GN
WIGTON LA
WIGTON PARK CL
HARROGATE RD
BROOKSIDE
ALWOODLEY CHASE
FARFIELD CT
MOORINGS
HIGH ASH AVE
HIGH ASH MOUNT
HIGH ASH DR
Liby
Alwoodley
Wigton Moor Primary Sch
Morris Silman Jewish Middle Sch
Brodetsky Jewish Primary Sch
PRIMLEY PARK VIEW
SANDHILL MOUNT
SANDHILL OVAL
SANDHILL CRES
Black Moor
PRIMLEY PARK AVE
BELVEDERE RD
Highfield County Primary Sch
St Paul's RC Primary Sch
NURSERY LA
Camp Town
Allerton High Sch
Alwoodley Primary Sch
Archbishop Cranmer C of E Middle Sch
Shadwell Sch
SHADWELL LA
A6120
Fir Tree County Primary Sch
FIR TREE LA
LINGFIELD DR
RING RD MOORTOWN
Sch
Moor Allerton
Moortown
Liby
Moor Allerton Centre
B6157
STONEGATE RD
SCOTT HALL RD
STREET LA
RING ROAD MEANWOOD
Tunnel How Hill
Allerton Grange High Sch
Moor Allerton County Primary Sch
Lidgett Park
Cardinal Heenan High Sch
SCOTLAND MILL LA
TONGUE LA
CARR MANOR RD
STAINBURN DR
STAINBURN TERR

43
27

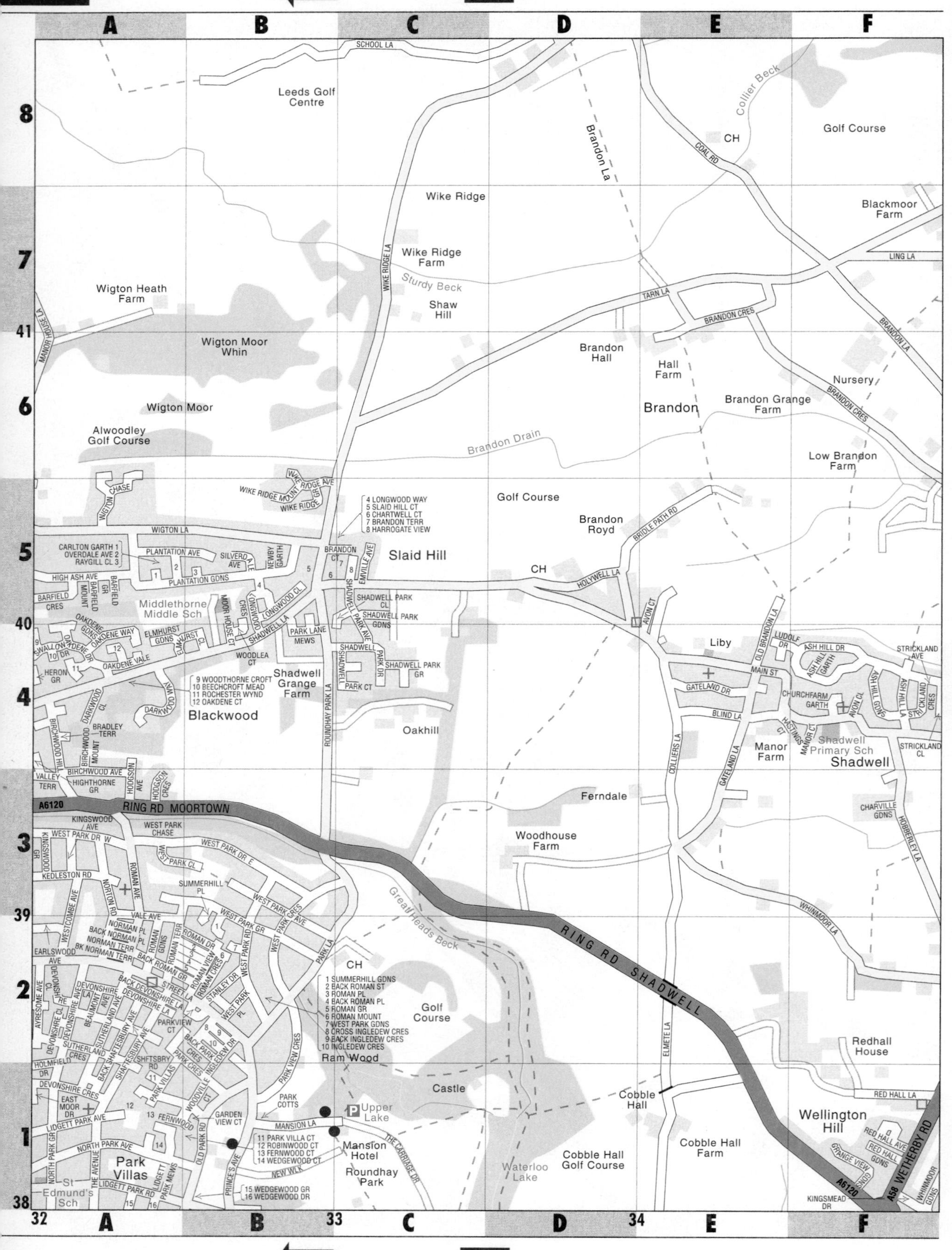
A
B
C
D
E
F
8
7
41
6
5
40
4
3
39
2
1
38
32
33
34
SCHOOL LA
Leeds Golf
Centre
Collier Beck
CH
Golf Course
Brandon La
COAL RD
Wike Ridge
Blackmoor
Farm
Wike Ridge
Farm
LING LA
WIKE RIDGE LA
Sturdy Beck
Wigton Heath
Farm
Shaw
Hill
TARN LA
BRANDON CRES
BRANDON LA
MANOR HOUSE LA
Wigton Moor
Whin
Brandon
Hall
Hall
Farm
Nursery
Wigton Moor
Brandon
Brandon Grange
Farm
Alwoodley
Golf Course
Brandon Drain
Low Brandon
Farm
WIGTON CHASE
WIKE RIDGE MOUNT
WIKE RIDGE AVE
WIKE RIDGE GR
4 LONGWOOD WAY
5 SLAID HILL CT
6 CHARTWELL CT
7 BRANDON TERR
8 HARROGATE VIEW
Golf Course
Brandon
Royd
BRIDLE PATH RD
WIGTON LA
CARLTON GARTH 1
OVERDALE AVE 2
RAYGILL CL 3
PLANTATION AVE
SILVERDALE AVE
NEWBY GARTH
BRANDON CT
EMVILLE AVE
Slaid Hill
CH
HOLYWELL LA
HIGH ASH AVE
PLANTATION GDNS
BARFIELD CRES
BARFIELD MOUNT
BARFIELD GR
Middlethorne
Middle Sch
MOOR HOUSE CT
LONGWOOD CL
SHADWELL PARK CL
SHADWELL PARK GDNS
SHADWELL PARK AVE
AVON CT
OAKDENE GDNS
OAKDENE WAY
ELMHURST GDNS
ELMHURST CL
SHADWELL LA
PARK LANE MEWS
Liby
OLD BRANDON LA
LUDOLF DR
ASH HILL DR
STRICKLAND AVE
SWALLOW DR
OAKDENE DR
OAKDENE VALE
WOODLEA CT
SHADWELL WALK
PARK DR
SHADWELL PARK GR
ASH HILL GARTH
HERON GR
9 WOODTHORNE CROFT
10 BEECHCROFT MEAD
11 ROCHESTER WYND
12 OAKDENE CT
Shadwell
Grange
Farm
PARK CT
MAIN ST
GATELAND DR
CHURCHFARM GARTH
ASH HILL GDNS
ASH HILL LA
STRICKLAND CRES
AVON CL
DARKWOOD WAY
DARKWOOD CL
Blackwood
ROUNDHAY PARK LA
BLIND LA
BIRCHWOOD HILL
BIRCHWOOD MOUNT
BRADLEY TERR
Oakhill
HASTINGS CT
MANOR CT
Manor
Farm
Shadwell
Primary Sch
Shadwell
STRICKLAND CL
COLLIERS LA
GATELAND LA
VALLEY TERR
BIRCHWOOD AVE
HIGHTHORNE GR
HODGSON AVE
HODGSON CRES
Ferndale
A6120
RING RD MOORTOWN
KINGSWOOD AVE
WEST PARK CHASE
CHARVILLE GDNS
WEST PARK DR W
KINGSWOOD GR
WEST PARK DR E
WEST PARK CL
Woodhouse
Farm
HOBBERLEY LA
KEDLESTON RD
NORTON RD
ROMAN AVE
SUMMERHILL PL
Great Heads Beck
WESTCOMBE AVE
VALE AVE
WEST PARK CRES
WEST PARK AVE
WEST PARK GR
NORMAN PL
BACK NORMAN PL
NORMAN TERR
BK NORMAN TERR
ROMAN GDNS
ROMAN TERR
ROMAN DR
BACK ROMAN GR
EARLSWOOD AVE
WEST PARK RD
PARK LA
RING RD SHADWELL
WHINMOOR LA
CH
DEVONSHIRE CL
DEVONSHIRE AVE
DEVONSHIRE LA
BACK DEVONSHIRE LA
ROMAN VIEW
ROMAN CRES
STANLEY DR
1 SUMMERHILL GDNS
2 BACK ROMAN ST
3 ROMAN PL
4 BACK ROMAN PL
5 ROMAN GR
6 ROMAN MOUNT
7 WEST PARK GDNS
8 CROSS INGLEDEW CRES
9 BACK INGLEDEW CRES
10 INGLEDEW CRES
AYRESOME AVE
BEAUMONT AVE
SUTHERLAND AVE
SHAFTESBURY AVE
PARKVIEW CT
WEST PARK PL
Golf
Course
ELMETE LA
SUTHERLAND CRES
BACK SHAFTESBURY AVE
SHFTSBRY RD
PARK CRES
BACK PARK CRES
INGLEDEW DR
PARK VIEW CRES
Ram Wood
Redhall
House
HOLMFIELD DR
DEVONSHIRE CRES
PARK VILLAS
WOODVILLE CT
Castle
Cobble
Hall
RED HALL LA
EAST MOOR DR
FERNWOOD
GARDEN VIEW CT
PARK COTTS
MANSION LA
Upper
Lake
Wellington
Hill
LIDGETT PARK AVE
OLD PARK RD
11 PARK VILLA CT
12 ROBINWOOD CT
13 FERNWOOD CT
14 WEDGEWOOD CT
Mansion
Hotel
THE CARRIAGE DR
RED HALL AVE
RED HALL GDNS
GRANGE VIEW
WETHERBY RD
NORTH PARK AVE
PRINCE'S AVE
NEW WLK
Cobble Hall
Golf Course
Cobble Hall
Farm
Park
Villas
THE AVENUE
LIDGETT PARK MEWS
Roundhay
Park
Waterloo
Lake
A6120
A58
WHINMOOR GDNS
NORTH PARK GR
St
Edmund's
Sch
LIDGETT PARK RD
15 WEDGEWOOD GR
16 WEDGEWOOD DR
KINGSMEAD DR

43
61

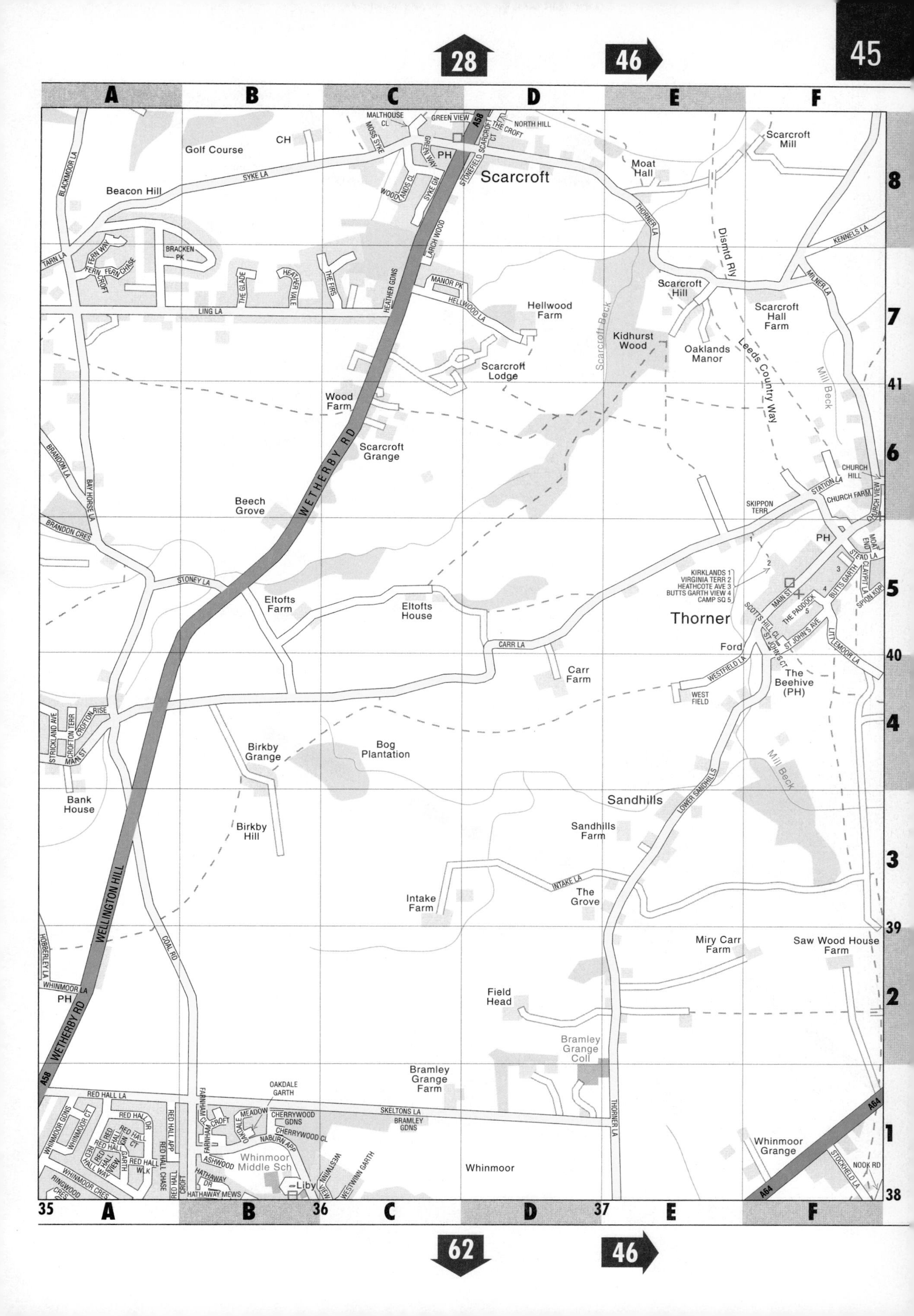
28
46
A
B
C
D
E
F
Golf Course
CH
MALTHOUSE CL
MOSS SYKE
GREEN VIEW
A58
THE CROFT
NORTH HILL
PH
Scarcroft
SYKE LA
Beacon Hill
Moat Hall
Scarcroft Mill
THORNER LA
Dismtd Rly
KENNELS LA
TARN LA
FERN WAY
FERN CROFT
FERN CHASE
BRACKEN PK
THE GLADE
HEATHER VALE
THE FIRS
HEATHER GDNS
LARCH WOOD
MANOR PK
HELLWOOD LA
LING LA
Hellwood Farm
Scarcroft Hill
Scarcroft Hall Farm
MILNER LA
Kidhurst Wood
Oaklands Manor
Leeds Country Way
Scarcroft Beck
Scarcroft Lodge
Mill Beck
Wood Farm
Scarcroft Grange
WETHERBY RD
BRANDON LA
BAY HORSE LA
Beech Grove
CHURCH HILL
STATION LA
CHURCH FARM
CHURCH VIEW
SKIPPON TERR
BRANDON CRES
PH
MOAT END
STEAD LA
CLAYPIT LA
BUTTS GARTH
SPION KOP
KIRKLANDS 1
VIRGINIA TERR 2
HEATHCOTE AVE 3
BUTTS GARTH VIEW 4
CAMP SQ 5
STONEY LA
Eltofts Farm
Eltofts House
MAIN ST
THE PADDOCK
SCOTTS HILL CL
ST JOHN'S AVE
Thorner
CARR LA
Ford
ST JOHN'S CT
LITTLEMOOR LA
Carr Farm
WESTFIELD LA
WEST FIELD
The Beehive (PH)
STRICKLAND AVE
CROFTON TERR
CROFTON RISE
MAIN ST
Birkby Grange
Bog Plantation
Mill Beck
Bank House
Sandhills
LOWER SANDHILLS
Birkby Hill
Sandhills Farm
INTAKE LA
Intake Farm
The Grove
WELLINGTON HILL
COAL RD
Miry Carr Farm
Saw Wood House Farm
HOBBERLEY LA
WHINMOOR LA
PH
Field Head
WETHERBY RD
A58
Bramley Grange Coll
Bramley Grange Farm
RED HALL LA
OAKDALE GARTH
SKELTONS LA
THORNER LA
A64
WHINMOOR GDNS
WHINMOOR CT
RED HALL DR
RED HALL APP
RED HALL CHASE
FARNHAM CL
FARNHAM CROFT
MEADOW
OAKDALE
CHERRYWOOD GDNS
BRAMLEY GDNS
CHERRYWOOD CL
NABURN APP
Whinmoor Grange
RED HALL WAY
RED HALL VIEW
RED HALL GARTH
RED HALL GN
RED HALL CT
RED HALL WLK
RED HALL CROFT
ASHWOOD
Whinmoor Middle Sch
WESTWINN VIEW
WESTWINN GARTH
Whinmoor
STOCKHELD LA
NOOK RD
WHINMOOR CRES
RINGWOOD CRES
HATHAWAY DR
HATHAWAY MEWS
Liby
A64
8
7
41
6
5
40
4
3
39
2
1
38
35
36
37
62
46

45
29

A B C D E F

8

The Shambles

Privet
Plantation

Bramham
Park

Milner
Wood

Norwood
Bottoms

The
Gardens

KENNELS LA

Milner Beck

Bramham
Park

Thorner Beck

7

Norwood House
Farm

BRAMHAM RD

41

Nova
Scotia

Bramham Moor

6

Whittle Car

KENSINGTON AVE

MANOR GDNS

Kellfield
Grange

KIRKFIELD CRES

CHURCH HILL

KIRKFIELD LA

KIRKFIELD AVE

ELLERKER RD

KIRKFIELD RD

YORKFIELD LA

ST PETER'S GARTH

THE CLOSE

KIRK HILLS

KIRKFIELD LA

MANGRILL LA

Jenny Sober
Plantation

STEAD LA

Thorner C of E
Junior and Infant Sch

Thorner Moor

5

ELLERKER LA

Leeds Country Way

Potterton Moor

40

Park House
Farm

A64

4

Kiddal Lane
End

The
Fox and Grapes
(PH)

Woodlands
Farm

Kiddal
Wood

Redhills
Plantation

Old
Plantation

3

Kiddal
Hall

KIDDAL LA

Potterton

Saw Wood

Kiddal
Bridge

Potterton
Hall

39

POTTERTON LA

Morgan
Cross

Potterton Park

Potterton Beck

Leeds Country Way

Flying Horse
Farm

2

MIRY LA

A64

1

Potterton
Bridge

Rake Beck

Whinmoor
Nook
Farm

Woodhouse
Farm

NOOK RD

Limekiln
Hill

38

Arthursdale

DARK LA

38 A B 39 C D 40 E F

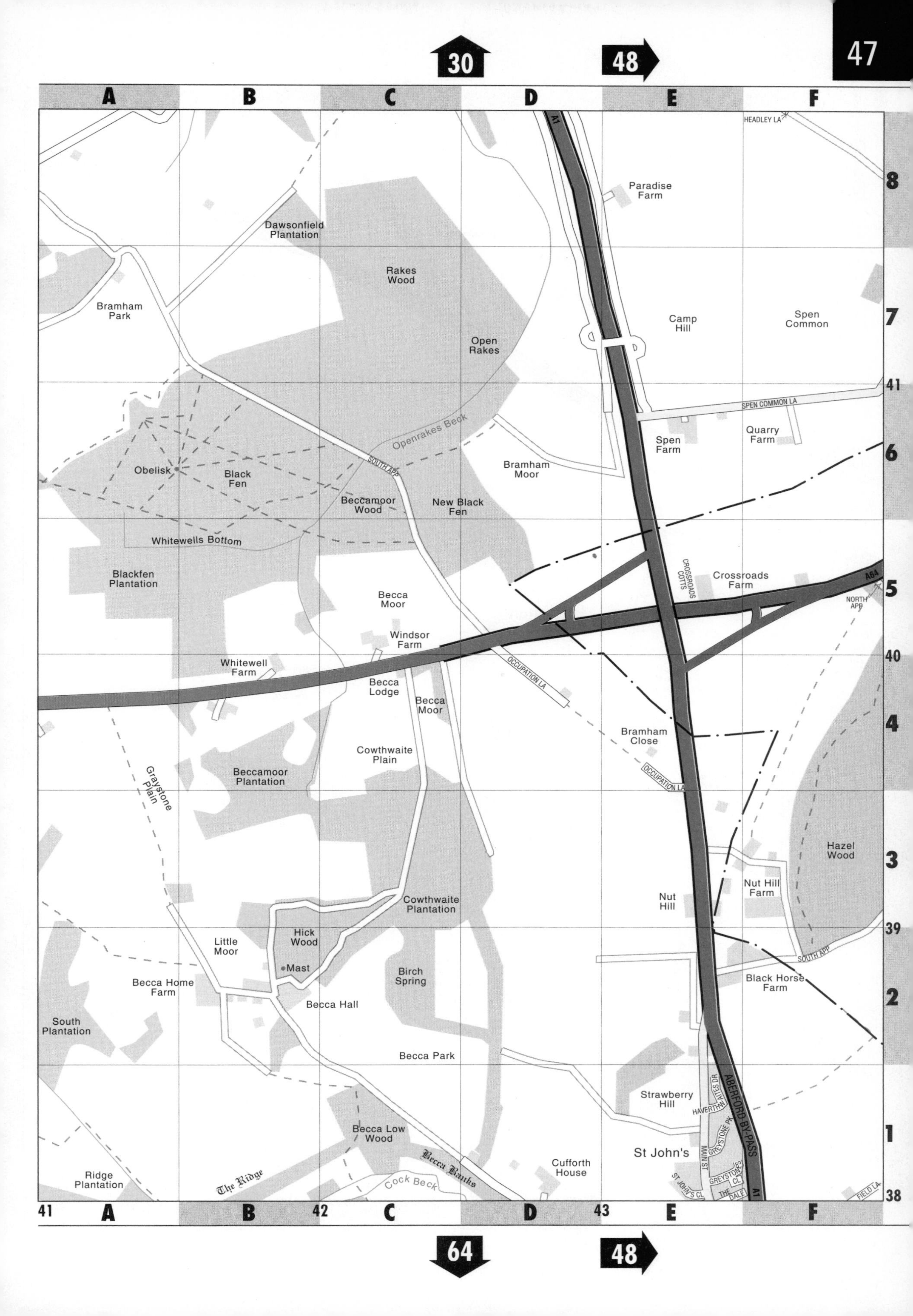
30
48
A
B
C
D
E
F
A1
HEADLEY LA
Paradise Farm
Dawsonfield Plantation
Rakes Wood
Bramham Park
Camp Hill
Spen Common
Open Rakes
SPEN COMMON LA
Openrakes Beck
Spen Farm
Quarry Farm
SOUTH APP
Obelisk
Black Fen
Bramham Moor
Beccamoor Wood
New Black Fen
Whitewells Bottom
CROSSROADS COTTS
Crossroads Farm
A64
Blackfen Plantation
Becca Moor
NORTH APP
Windsor Farm
Whitewell Farm
OCCUPATION LA
Becca Lodge
Becca Moor
Bramham Close
Cowthwaite Plain
Beccamoor Plantation
Graystone Plain
OCCUPATION LA
Hazel Wood
Nut Hill
Nut Hill Farm
Cowthwaite Plantation
Little Moor
Hick Wood
Mast
Birch Spring
SOUTH APP
Black Horse Farm
Becca Home Farm
Becca Hall
South Plantation
Becca Park
Strawberry Hill
WAITES DR
HAVERTHW
ABERFORD BY-PASS
GREYSTONE PK
Becca Low Wood
St John's
MAIN ST
Cufforth House
Becca Banks
Ridge Plantation
The Ridge
Cock Beck
ST JOHN'S CL
GREYSTONES CL
THE DALE
FIELD LA
8
7
41
6
5
40
4
3
39
2
1
38
41
42
43
64
48

47 31

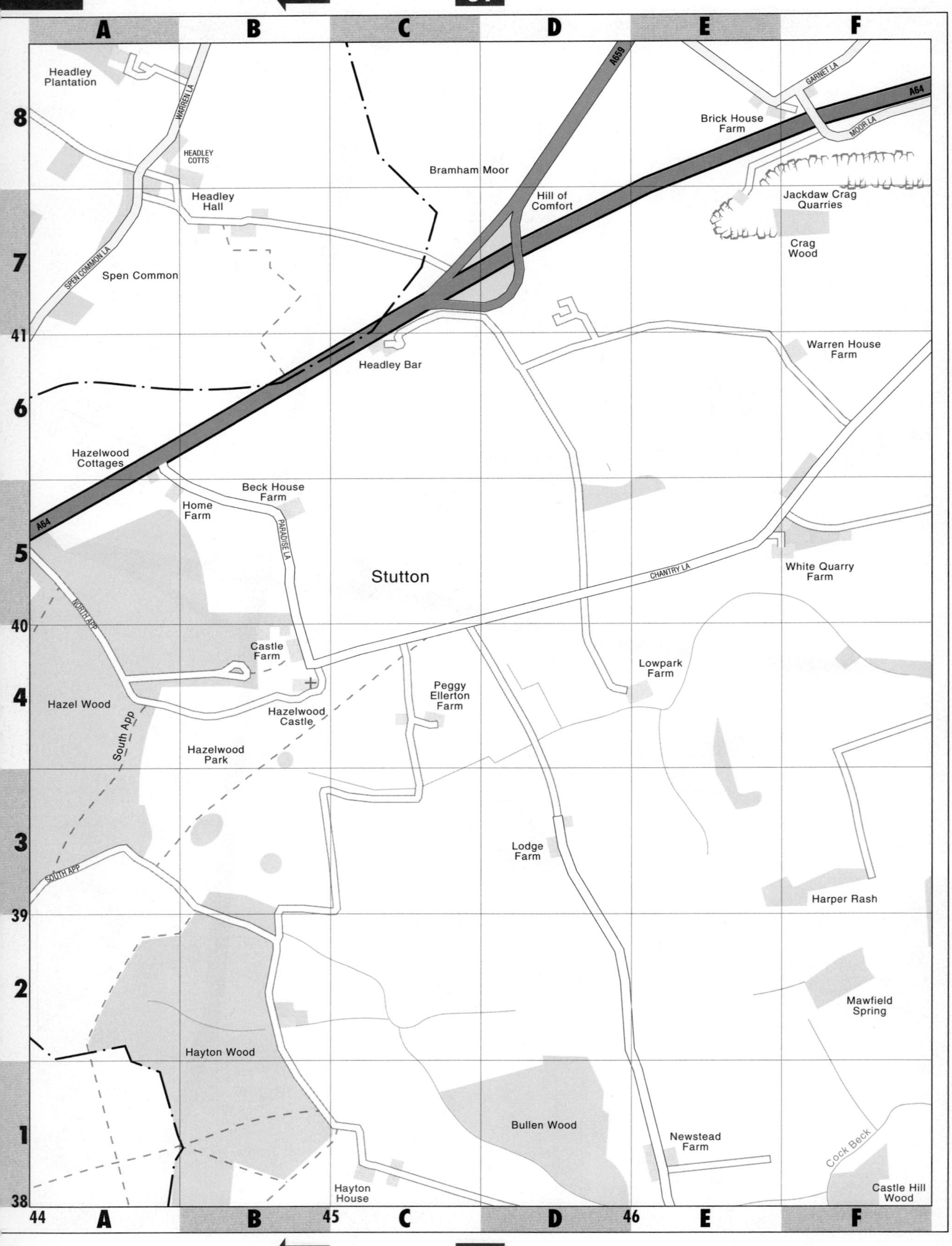
A
B
C
D
E
F
8
7
41
6
5
40
4
3
39
2
1
38
44
45
46
Headley Plantation
WARREN LA
HEADLEY COTTS
Headley Hall
Bramham Moor
A659
GARNET LA
A64
Brick House Farm
MOOR LA
Jackdaw Crag Quarries
Crag Wood
Hill of Comfort
SPEN COMMON LA
Spen Common
Headley Bar
Warren House Farm
Hazelwood Cottages
Beck House Farm
Home Farm
PARADISE LA
Stutton
CHANTRY LA
White Quarry Farm
NORTH APP
Castle Farm
Lowpark Farm
Peggy Ellerton Farm
Hazel Wood
Hazelwood Castle
South App
Hazelwood Park
Lodge Farm
SOUTH APP
Harper Rash
Mawfield Spring
Hayton Wood
Bullen Wood
Newstead Farm
Cock Beck
Castle Hill Wood
Hayton House

47 65

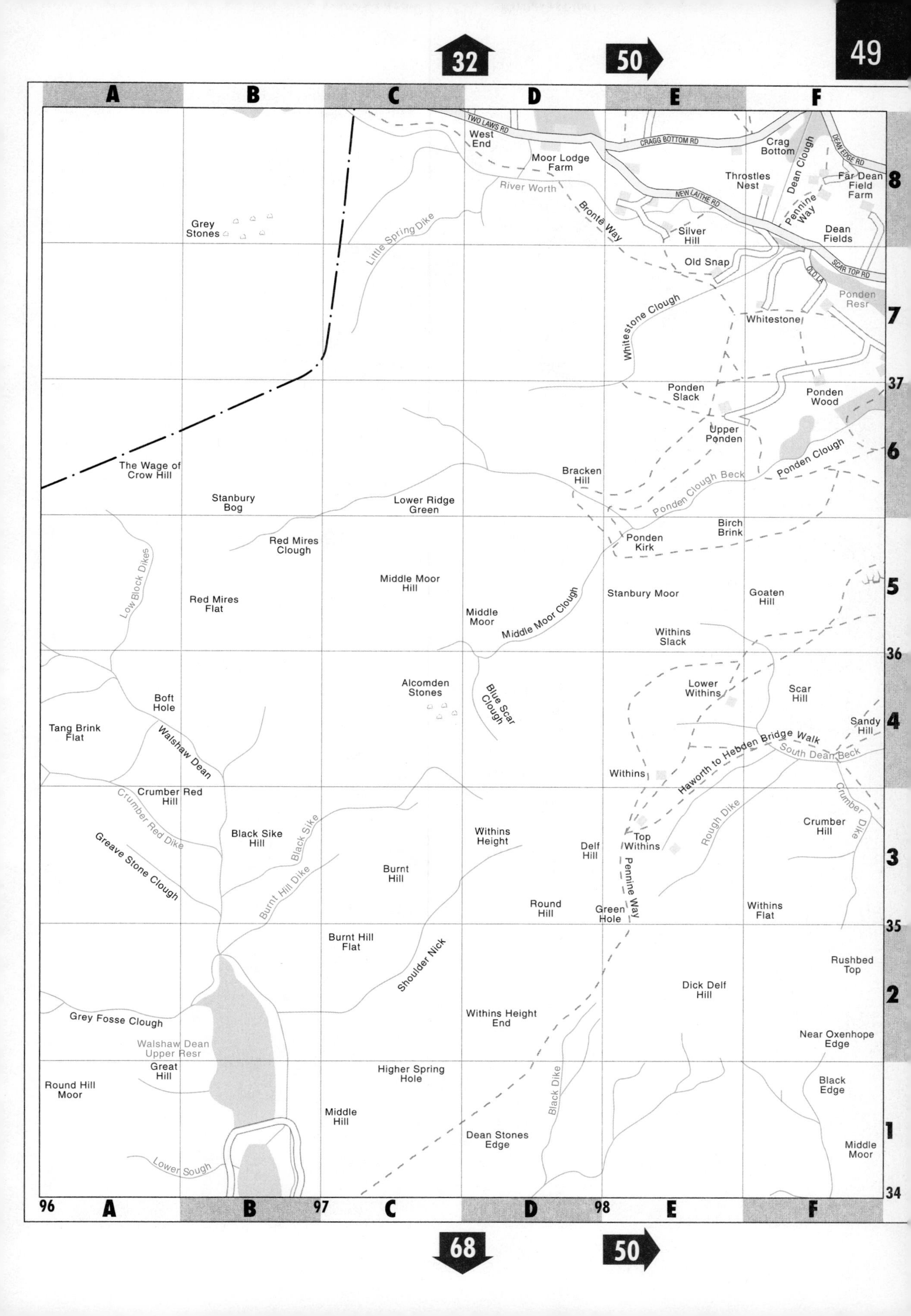
32
50
A
B
C
D
E
F
TWO LAWS RD
West End
CRAGG BOTTOM RD
Crag Bottom
Moor Lodge Farm
Throstles Nest
Dean Clough
DEAN EDGE RD
Far Dean Field Farm
River Worth
NEW LAITHE RD
Pennine Way
Bronte Way
Grey Stones
Little Spring Dike
Silver Hill
Dean Fields
Old Snap
SCAR TOP RD
OLD LA
Ponden Resr
Whitestone Clough
Whitestone
Ponden Slack
Ponden Wood
Upper Ponden
The Wage of Crow Hill
Bracken Hill
Ponden Clough Beck
Ponden Clough
Stanbury Bog
Lower Ridge Green
Birch Brink
Red Mires Clough
Ponden Kirk
Low Block Dikes
Middle Moor Hill
Red Mires Flat
Stanbury Moor
Goaten Hill
Middle Moor
Middle Moor Clough
Withins Slack
Alcomden Stones
Lower Withins
Scar Hill
Boft Hole
Blue Scar Clough
Tang Brink Flat
Walshaw Dean
Sandy Hill
Haworth to Hebden Bridge Walk
South Dean Beck
Withins
Crumber Red Hill
Crumber Red Dike
Crumber Dike
Crumber Hill
Black Sike Hill
Black Sike
Withins Height
Top Withins
Greave Stone Clough
Delf Hill
Rough Dike
Burnt Hill
Burnt Hill Dike
Pennine Way
Round Hill
Green Hole
Withins Flat
Burnt Hill Flat
Shoulder Nick
Rushbed Top
Dick Delf Hill
Grey Fosse Clough
Withins Height End
Near Oxenhope Edge
Walshaw Dean Upper Resr
Great Hill
Higher Spring Hole
Black Edge
Round Hill Moor
Black Dike
Middle Hill
Dean Stones Edge
Middle Moor
Lower Sough
8
7
37
6
5
36
4
3
35
2
1
34
96
97
98
68
50

49 33

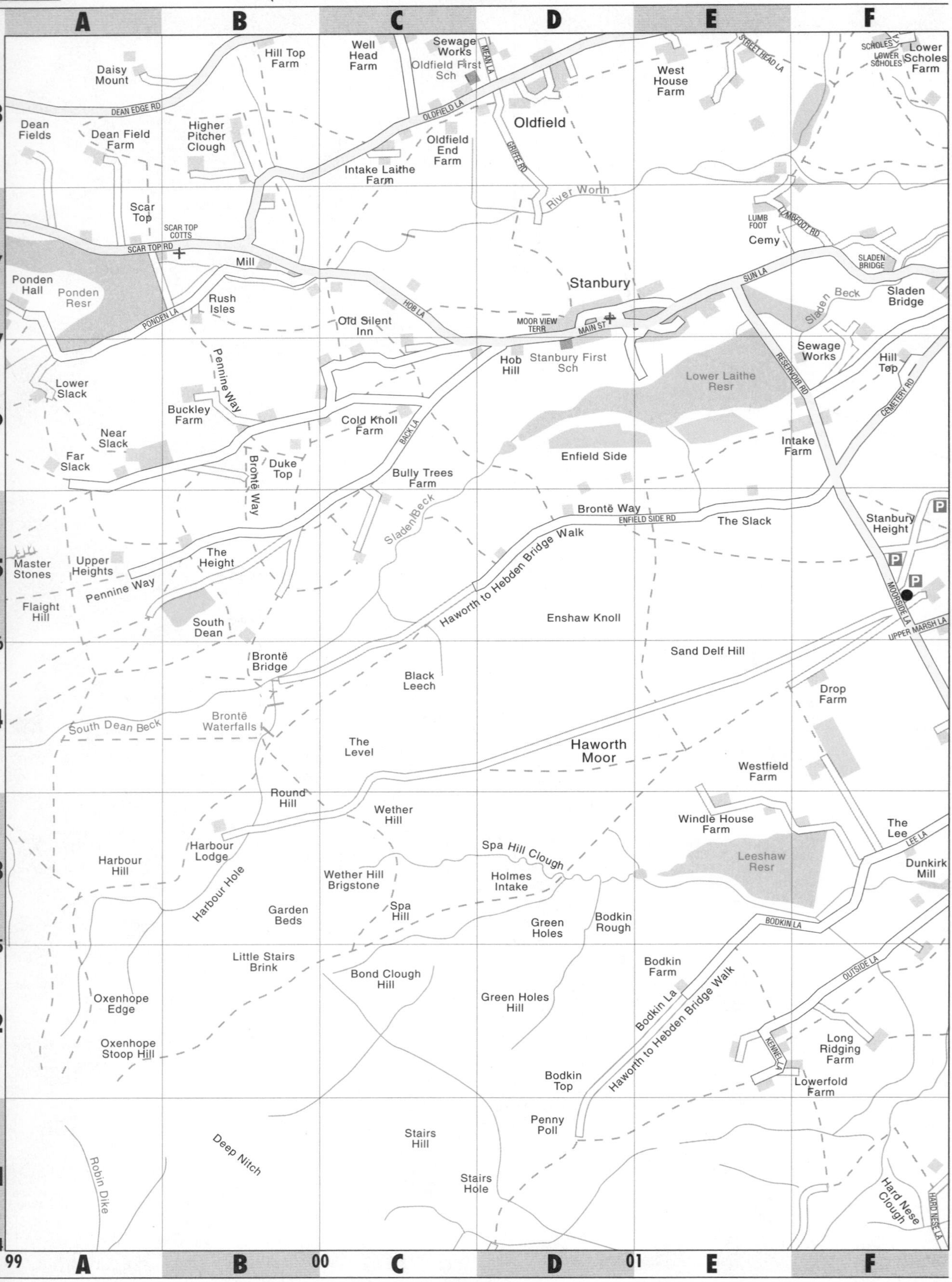

A B C D E F

8

Daisy Mount
Dean Fields
Dean Field Farm
Higher Pitcher Clough
Hill Top Farm
Well Head Farm
Sewage Works
Oldfield First Sch
MEAL LA
West House Farm
SCHOLES LA
LOWER SCHOLES
Lower Scholes Farm
DEAN EDGE RD
OLDFIELD LA
Oldfield
Oldfield End Farm
GRIFFE RD
STREET HEAD LA

Scar Top
SCAR TOP COTTS
Intake Laithe Farm
River Worth
LUMB FOOT
LUMBFOOT RD
Cemy

7

Ponden Hall
Ponden Resr
SCAR TOP RD
Mill
Rush Isles
Old Silent Inn
HOB LA
Stanbury
MOOR VIEW TERR
MAIN ST
SUN LA
Sladen Beck
SLADEN BRIDGE
Sladen Bridge

PONDEN LA

37

Lower Slack
Pennine Way
Buckley Farm
Hob Hill
Stanbury First Sch
Lower Laithe Resr
RESERVOIR RD
Sewage Works
Hill Top
CEMETERY RD

6

Near Slack
Far Slack
Cold Knoll Farm
BACK LA
Duke Top
Brontë Way
Bully Trees Farm
Enfield Side
Intake Farm

Sladen Beck

5

Master Stones
Upper Heights
The Height
Pennine Way
Brontë Way
Enfield Side Rd
The Slack
Haworth to Hebden Bridge Walk
Stanbury Height
P P P
MOORSIDE LA
UPPER MARSH LA

Flaight Hill
South Dean
Enshaw Knoll

36

Brontë Bridge
Black Leech
Sand Delf Hill
Drop Farm

4

South Dean Beck
Brontë Waterfalls
The Level
Haworth Moor
Westfield Farm
The Lee
LEE LA

Round Hill
Wether Hill
Windle House Farm
Leeshaw Resr
Dunkirk Mill

3

Harbour Hill
Harbour Lodge
Harbour Hole
Wether Hill Brigstone
Spa Hill Clough
Holmes Intake
Bodkin Rough
BODKIN LA

Garden Beds
Spa Hill
Green Holes

35

Little Stairs Brink
Bond Clough Hill
Bodkin Farm
OUTSIDE LA

Oxenhope Edge
Green Holes Hill
Bodkin La
Haworth to Hebden Bridge Walk
Long Ridging Farm
KENNEL LA

2

Oxenhope Stoop Hill
Lowerfold Farm

Robin Dike
Deep Nitch
Stairs Hill
Bodkin Top
Penny Poll
Stairs Hole
Hard Nese Clough
HARD NESE LA

1

34

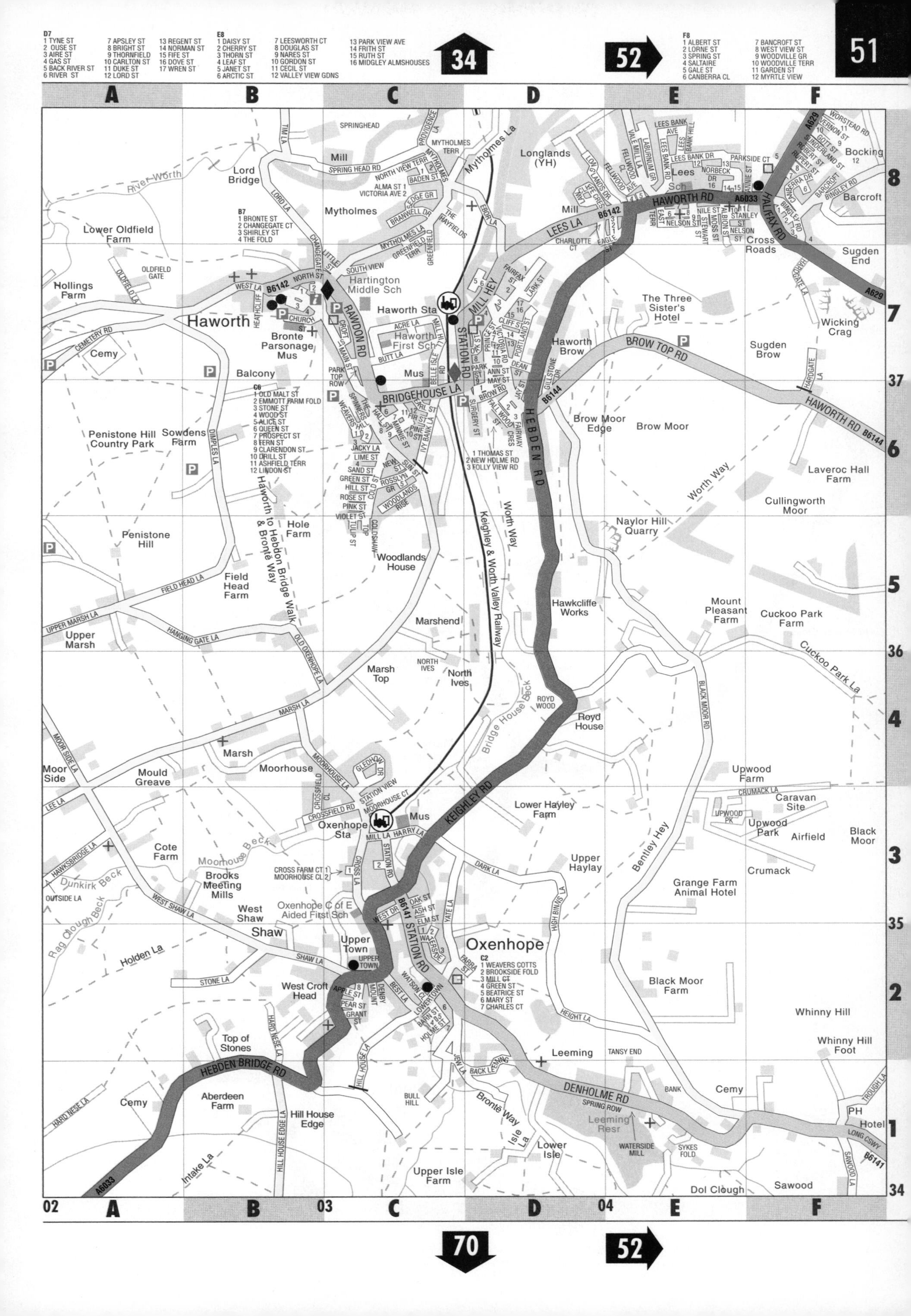

51
D7
1 TYNE ST
2 OUSE ST
3 AIRE ST
4 GAS ST
5 BACK RIVER ST
6 RIVER ST
7 APSLEY ST
8 BRIGHT ST
9 THORNFIELD
10 CARLTON ST
11 DUKE ST
12 LORD ST
13 REGENT ST
14 NORMAN ST
15 FIFE ST
16 DOVE ST
17 WREN ST
E8
1 DAISY ST
2 CHERRY ST
3 THORN ST
4 LEAF ST
5 JANET ST
6 ARCTIC ST
7 LEESWORTH CT
8 DOUGLAS ST
9 NARES ST
10 GORDON ST
11 CECIL ST
12 VALLEY VIEW GDNS
13 PARK VIEW AVE
14 FRITH ST
15 RUTH ST
16 MIDGLEY ALMSHOUSES
34
52
F8
1 ALBERT ST
2 LORNE ST
3 SPRING ST
4 SALTAIRE
5 GALE ST
6 CANBERRA CL
7 BANCROFT ST
8 WEST VIEW ST
9 WOODVILLE GR
10 WOODVILLE TERR
11 GARDEN ST
12 MYRTLE VIEW
A B C D E F
8 7 37 6 5 36 4 3 35 2 1 34
02 03 04
Springhead
Mill
Lord Bridge
River Worth
Mytholmes
Mytholmes La
Longlands (YH)
Lees
Mill
Haworth Rd
Lees La
B6142
A6033
Halifax Rd
A629
Bocking
Barcroft
Cross Roads
Sugden End
Lower Oldfield Farm
Hollings Farm
B7
1 BRONTE ST
2 CHANGEGATE CT
3 SHIRLEY ST
4 THE FOLD
Haworth
Hartington Middle Sch
Haworth Sta
Haworth First Sch
Bronte Parsonage Mus
Cemy
Balcony
Mus
Rawdon Rd
Station Rd
Mill Hey
Bridgehouse La
Cemetery Rd
The Three Sister's Hotel
Wicking Crag
Haworth Brow
Brow Top Rd
Sugden Brow
B6144
C6
1 OLD MALT ST
2 EMMOTT FARM FOLD
3 STONE ST
4 WOOD ST
5 ALICE ST
6 QUEEN ST
7 PROSPECT ST
8 FERN ST
9 CLARENDON ST
10 DRILL ST
11 ASHFIELD TERR
12 LINDON ST
1 THOMAS ST
2 NEW HOLME RD
3 FOLLY VIEW RD
Penistone Hill Country Park
Sowdens Farm
Brow Moor Edge
Brow Moor
Hebden Rd
Haworth Rd
Laveroc Hall Farm
Worth Way
Cullingworth Moor
Haworth to Hebden Bridge Walk & Brontë Way
Keighley & Worth Valley Railway
Hole Farm
Naylor Hill Quarry
Penistone Hill
Woodlands House
Field Head Farm
Field Head La
Upper Marsh La
Upper Marsh
Hanging Gate La
Marshend
Hawkcliffe Works
Mount Pleasant Farm
Cuckoo Park Farm
Cuckoo Park La
Marsh Top
North Ives
Royd Wood
Royd House
Bridge House Beck
Black Moor Rd
Marsh La
Marsh
Moorhouse
Moor Side
Mould Greave
Upwood Farm
Crumack La
Caravan Site
Keighley Rd
Lower Hayley Farm
Upwood Park
Airfield
Black Moor
Oxenhope Sta
Mus
Cote Farm
Moorhouse Beck
Dunkirk Beck
Brooks Meeting Mills
Upper Haylay
Bentley Hey
Crumack
Grange Farm Animal Hotel
West Shaw
Shaw
Oxenhope C of E Aided First Sch
Rag Clough Beck
Holden La
Upper Town
Oxenhope
C2
1 WEAVERS COTTS
2 BROOKSIDE FOLD
3 MILL CT
4 GREEN ST
5 BEATRICE ST
6 MARY ST
7 CHARLES CT
West Croft Head
Black Moor Farm
Whinny Hill
Top of Stones
Leeming
Tansy End
Whinny Hill Foot
Hebden Bridge Rd
Denholme Rd
Aberdeen Farm
Cemy
Hill House Edge
Bull Hill
Brontë Way
Leeming Resr
Waterside Mill
Sykes Fold
Bank
Cemy
PH
Hotel
Lower Isle
Upper Isle Farm
Intake La
A6033
Dol Clough
Sawood
B6141
70
52

51
35

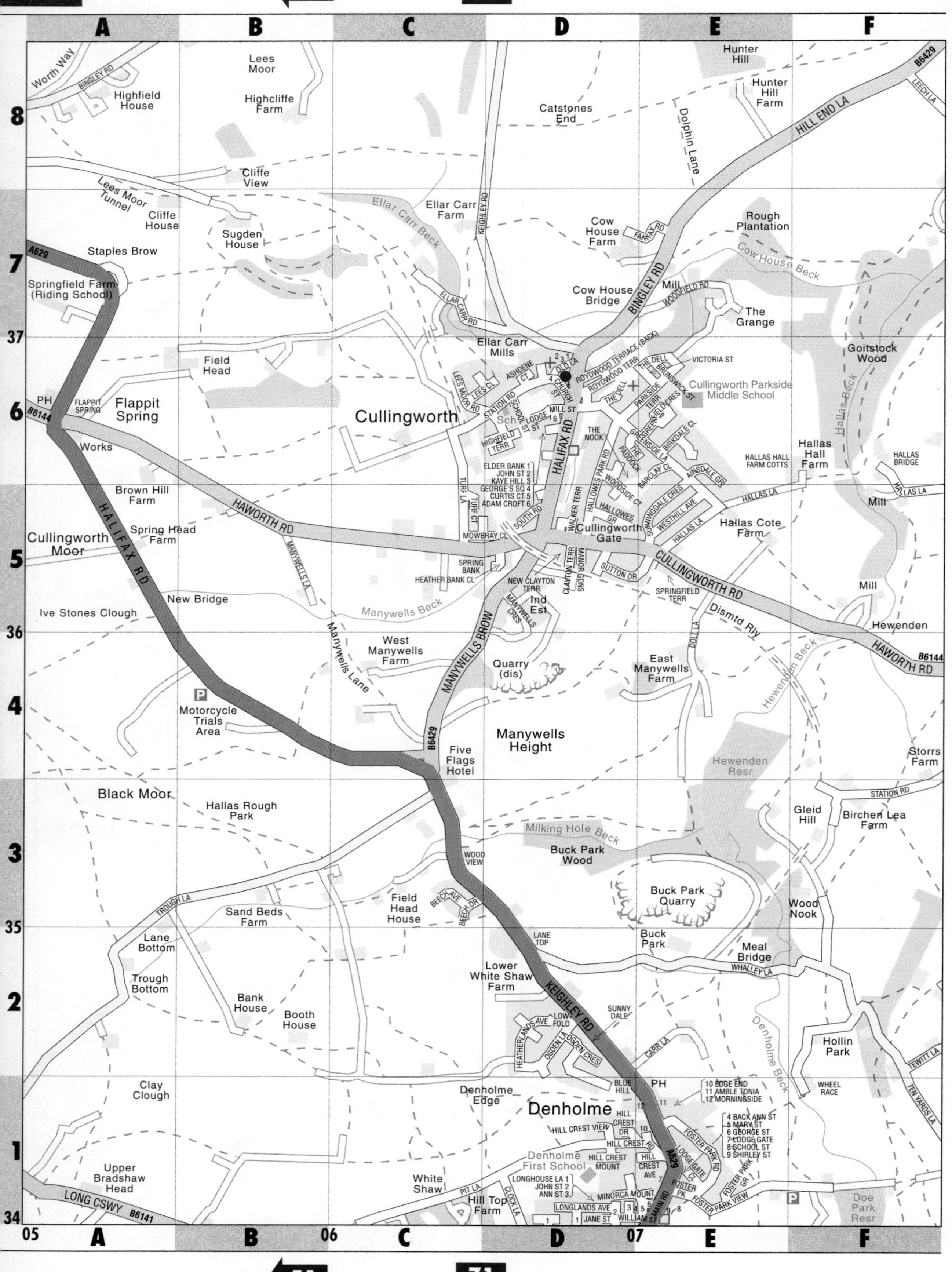
A
B
C
D
E
F
8
7
37
6
5
36
4
3
35
2
1
34
05
06
07
Worth Way
BINGLEY RD
Highfield House
Lees Moor
Highcliffe Farm
Catstones End
Dolphin Lane
Hunter Hill
Hunter Hill Farm
B6429
LEECH LA
HILL END LA
Cliffe View
Lees Moor Tunnel
Cliffe House
Sugden House
Ellar Carr Beck
Ellar Carr Farm
KEIGHLEY RD
Cow House Farm
FAIRFAX RD
Rough Plantation
Cow House Beck
A629
Staples Brow
Springfield Farm (Riding School)
ELLAR CARR RD
BINGLEY RD
Mill
WOODFIELD RD
Cow House Bridge
The Grange
Field Head
Ellar Carr Mills
ASHDENE CT
OLD LA
CHURCH ST
ROYDWOOD TERRACE (BACK)
ROYDWOOD TERR
THE DELL
BRUNSWICK ST
VICTORIA ST
Cullingworth Parkside Middle School
Goitstock Wood
PH
FLAPPIT SPRING
Flappit Spring
B6144
Cullingworth
LEES MOOR RD
LEES CL
STATION RD
SCHOOL ST
LODGE ST
MILL ST
PARKSIDE TERR
GREENFIELD CRES
BIRKDALE CL
Hallas Beck
Sch
HALIFAX RD
THE NOOK
THE PADDOCK
GREENSIDE LA
Works
HIGHFIELD TERR
ELDER BANK 1
JOHN ST 2
KAYE HILL 3
GEORGE'S SQ 4
CURTIS CT 5
ADAM CROFT 6
HALLOWES PARK RD
WOODSIDE CT
BARCLAY CL
AINSDALE GR
Hallas Hall Farm
HALLAS HALL FARM COTTS
HALLAS BRIDGE
Brown Hill Farm
HALIFAX RD
HAWORTH RD
TURF LA
TURF CT
SOUTH RD
WALKER TERR
HALLOWES GR
SUNNINGDALE CRES
WESTHILL AVE
HALLAS LA
Mill
Spring Head Farm
Cullingworth Moor
MANYWELLS LA
MOWBRAY CL
Cullingworth Gate
HALLAS LA
Hallas Cote Farm
SPRING BANK
HEATHER BANK CL
CLAYTON TERR
MANOR GDNS
SUTTON DR
CULLINGWORTH RD
New Bridge
NEW CLAYTON TERR
Ind Est
MANYWELLS CRES
SPRINGFIELD TERR
Mill
Ive Stones Clough
Manywells Beck
Dismtd Rly
Hewenden
Manywells Lane
West Manywells Farm
MANYWELLS BROW
DOLL LA
HAWORTH RD
B6144
Quarry (dis)
East Manywells Farm
Hewenden Beck
P
Motorcycle Trials Area
Manywells Height
Storrs Farm
B6429
Five Flags Hotel
Hewenden Resr
Black Moor
Hallas Rough Park
STATION RD
Gleid Hill
Birchen Lea Farm
Milking Hole Beck
WOOD VIEW
Buck Park Wood
Buck Park Quarry
TROUGH LA
Sand Beds Farm
Field Head House
BEECH AVE
BEECH DR
Wood Nook
Lane Bottom
LANE TOP
Buck Park
Meal Bridge
WHALLEY LA
Trough Bottom
Lower White Shaw Farm
KEIGHLEY RD
Bank House
Booth House
SUNNY DALE
HEATHERLANDS AVE
LOW FOLD
OGDEN LA
OGDEN CRES
CARR LA
Denholme Beck
Hollin Park
TEWITT LA
Clay Clough
BLUE HILL
PH
10 EDGE END
11 AMBLE TONIA
12 MORNINGSIDE
WHEEL RACE
TEN YARDS LA
Denholme Edge
Denholme
HILL CREST VIEW
HILL CREST DR
HILL CREST RD
FOSTER PARK RD
4 BACK ANN ST
5 MARY ST
6 GEORGE ST
7 LODGE GATE
8 SCHOOL ST
9 SHIRLEY ST
Denholme First School
HILL CREST MOUNT
HILL CREST AVE
LODGE GATE CL
FOSTER PARK GR
Upper Bradshaw Head
White Shaw
PIT LA
CLOCK LA
LONGHOUSE LA 1
JOHN ST 2
ANN ST 3
MINORCA MOUNT
FOSTER PK
FOSTER PARK VIEW
P
Doe Park Resr
LONG CSWY
B6141
Hill Top Farm
LONGLANDS AVE
JANE ST
WILLIAM ST
MAIN RD
A629

51
71

36
54

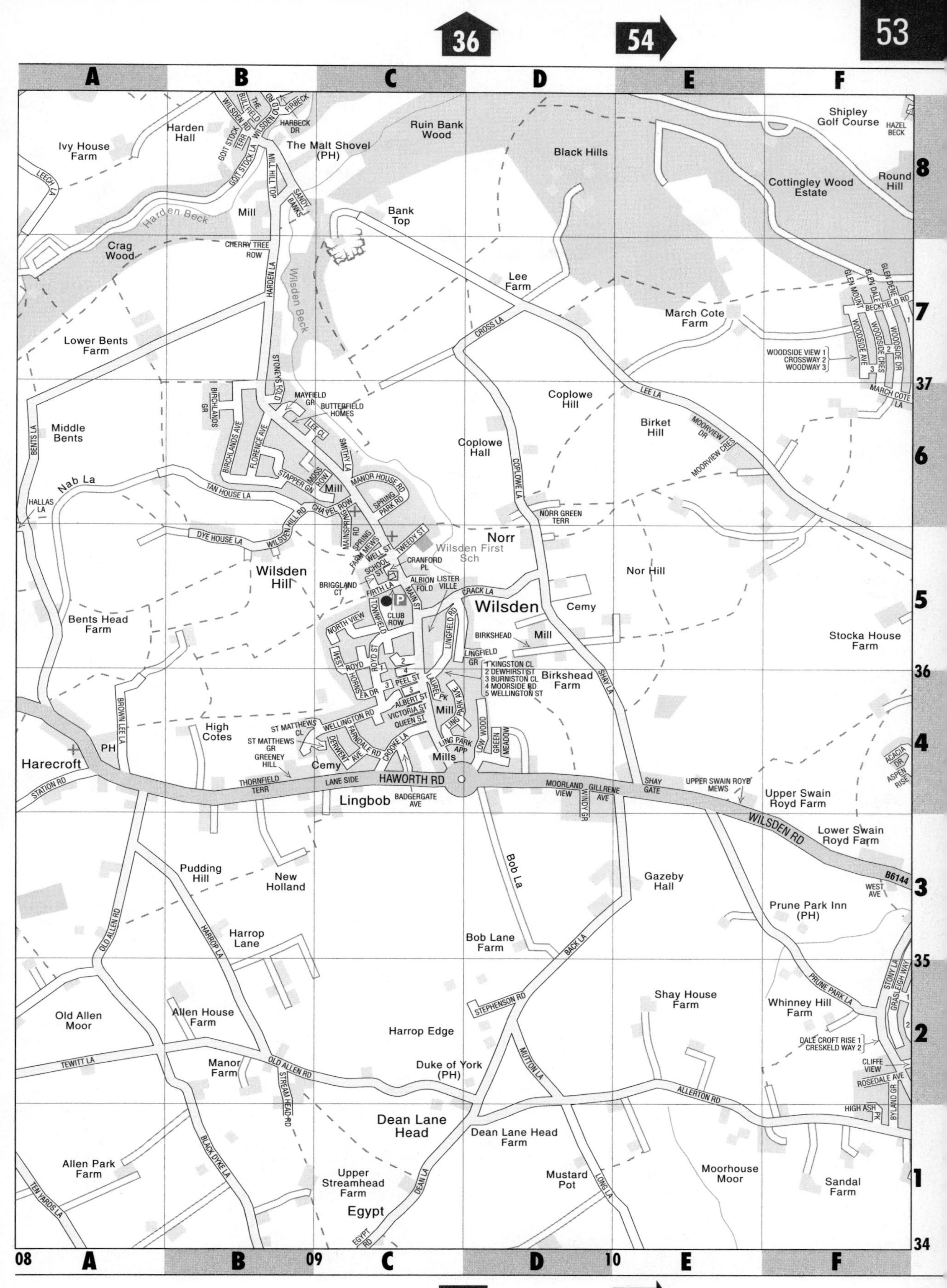
Harden Hall
Ivy House Farm
The Malt Shovel (PH)
Ruin Bank Wood
Black Hills
Shipley Golf Course
Cottingley Wood Estate
Round Hill
Mill
Crag Wood
Bank Top
Lee Farm
March Cote Farm
Lower Bents Farm
Middle Bents
Coplowe Hill
Coplowe Hall
Birket Hill
Nab La
Norr
Wilsden First Sch
Wilsden Hill
Nor Hill
Wilsden
Cemy
Bents Head Farm
Stocka House Farm
Birkshead Farm
High Cotes
Harecroft
Lingbob
HAWORTH RD
Upper Swain Royd Farm
Lower Swain Royd Farm
WILSDEN RD
Pudding Hill
New Holland
Bob La
Gazeby Hall
Prune Park Inn (PH)
Harrop Lane
Bob Lane Farm
Shay House Farm
Whinney Hill Farm
Old Allen Moor
Allen House Farm
Harrop Edge
Manor Farm
Duke of York (PH)
Dean Lane Head
Dean Lane Head Farm
Allen Park Farm
Upper Streamhead Farm
Egypt
Mustard Pot
Moorhouse Moor
Sandal Farm

72
54

53
37

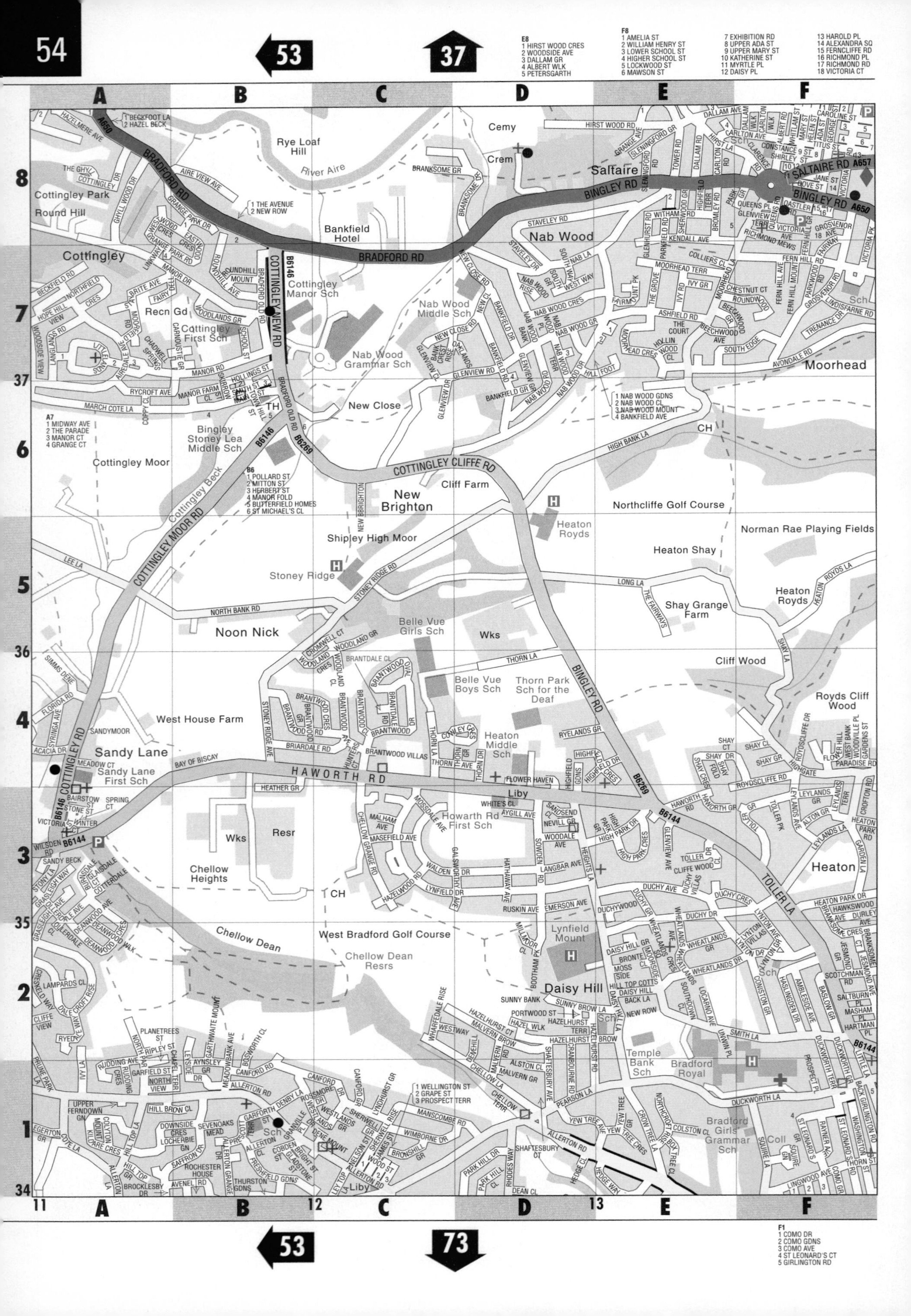
E8
1 HIRST WOOD CRES
2 WOODSIDE AVE
3 DALLAM GR
4 ALBERT WLK
5 PETERSGARTH
F8
1 AMELIA ST
2 WILLIAM HENRY ST
3 LOWER SCHOOL ST
4 HIGHER SCHOOL ST
5 LOCKWOOD ST
6 MAWSON ST
7 EXHIBITION RD
8 UPPER ADA ST
9 UPPER MARY ST
10 KATHERINE ST
11 MYRTLE PL
12 DAISY PL
13 HAROLD PL
14 ALEXANDRA SQ
15 FERNCLIFFE RD
16 RICHMOND PL
17 RICHMOND RD
18 VICTORIA CT
A7
1 MIDWAY AVE
2 THE PARADE
3 MANOR CT
4 GRANGE CT
B6
1 POLLARD ST
2 MITTON ST
3 HERBERT ST
4 MANOR FOLD
5 BUTTERFIELD HOMES
6 ST MICHAEL'S CL
1 NAB WOOD GDNS
2 NAB WOOD CL
3 NAB WOOD MOUNT
4 BANKFIELD AVE
1 THE AVENUE
2 NEW ROW
1 BECKFOOT LA
2 HAZEL BECK
1 WELLINGTON ST
2 GRAPE ST
3 PROSPECT TERR
F1
1 COMO DR
2 COMO GDNS
3 COMO AVE
4 ST LEONARD'S CT
5 GIRLINGTON RD
Rye Loaf Hill
Cemy
Crem
River Aire
Saltaire
Cottingley Park
Round Hill
Bankfield Hotel
Nab Wood
Cottingley
Cottingley Manor Sch
Nab Wood Middle Sch
Recn Gd
Cottingley First Sch
Nab Wood Grammar Sch
Moorhead
New Close
Bingley Stoney Lea Middle Sch
Cottingley Moor
New Brighton
Cliff Farm
Northcliffe Golf Course
Heaton Royds
Shipley High Moor
Norman Rae Playing Fields
Heaton Shay
Stoney Ridge
Shay Grange Farm
Noon Nick
Belle Vue Girls Sch
Wks
Cliff Wood
Belle Vue Boys Sch
Thorn Park Sch for the Deaf
Royds Cliff Wood
West House Farm
Heaton Middle Sch
Sandy Lane
Sandy Lane First Sch
Howarth Rd First Sch
Resr
Chellow Heights
Heaton
Chellow Dean
West Bradford Golf Course
Chellow Dean Resrs
Lynfield Mount
Daisy Hill
Temple Bank Sch
Bradford Royal
Bradford Girls' Grammar Sch
Coll
BRADFORD RD
BINGLEY RD
SALTAIRE RD
COTTINGLEY NEW RD
COTTINGLEY CLIFFE RD
COTTINGLEY MOOR RD
HAWORTH RD
TOLLER LA
HIGH BANK LA
LONG LA
NORTH BANK RD
LEE LA
A650
A657
B6146
B6269
B6144

53
73

38 56

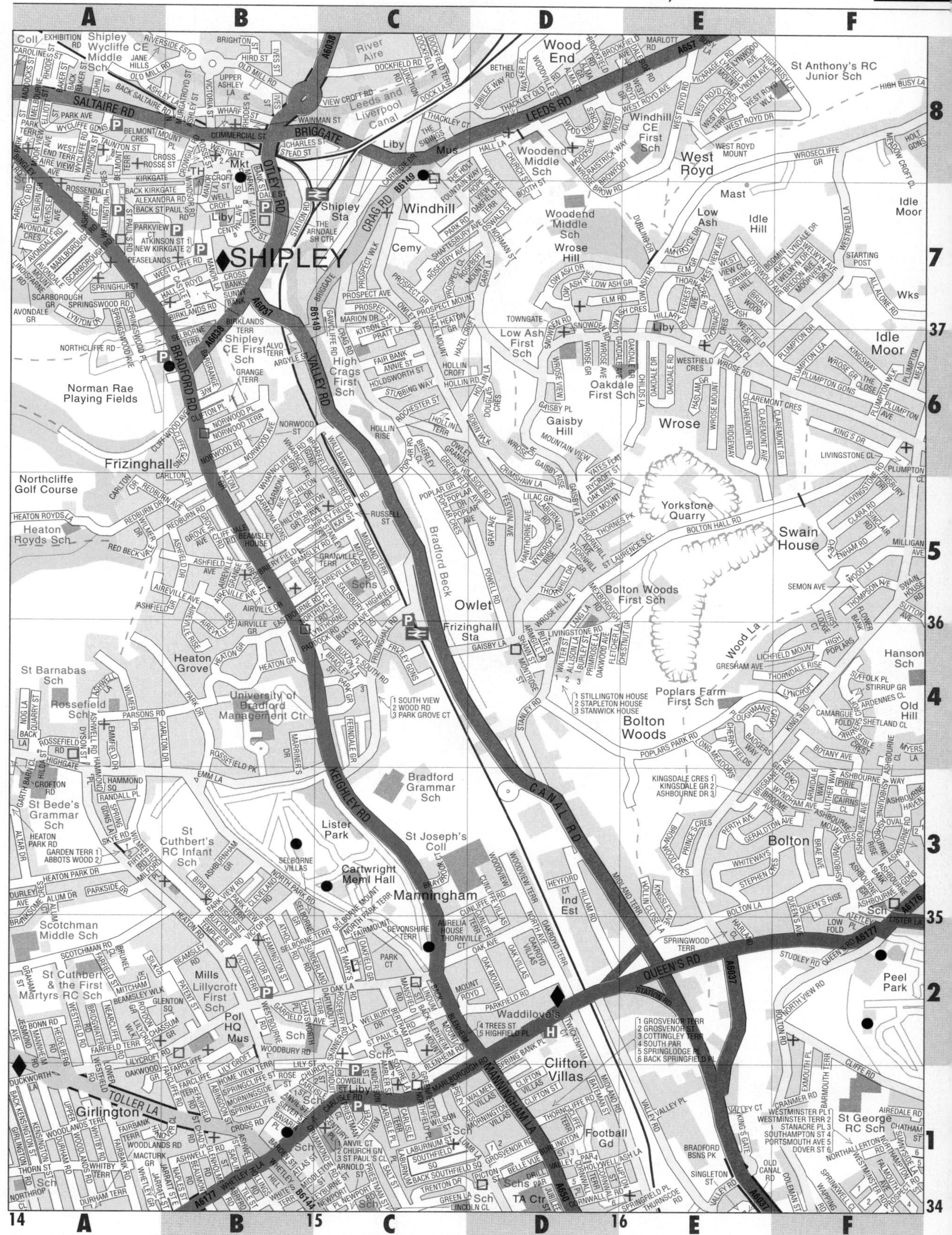
A
B
C
D
E
F
SHIPLEY
Shipley Wycliffe CE Middle Sch
River Aire
Leeds and Liverpool Canal
SALTAIRE RD
BRIGGATE
LEEDS RD
Wood End
St Anthony's RC Junior Sch
Windhill CE First Sch
Woodend Middle Sch
West Royd
Mkt
Liby
Mus
Shipley Sta
THE ARNDALE SH CTR
Windhill
Cemy
OTLEY RD
CRAG RD
Mast
Low Ash
Idle Hill
Idle Moor
Wrose Hill
Wks
Low Ash First Sch
Oakdale First Sch
Shipley CE First Sch
High Crags First Sch
Norman Rae Playing Fields
BRADFORD RD
VALLEY RD
Gaisby Hill
Wrose
Frizinghall
Northcliffe Golf Course
Heaton Royds Sch
Yorkstone Quarry
Swain House
Bradford Beck
Owlet
Bolton Woods First Sch
Frizinghall Sta
Heaton Grove
St Barnabas Sch
Rossefield Sch
University of Bradford Management Ctr
Hanson Sch
Poplars Farm First Sch
Old Hill
Bolton Woods
CANAL RD
KEIGHLEY RD
Bradford Grammar Sch
St Bede's Grammar Sch
Lister Park
St Cuthbert's RC Infant Sch
St Joseph's Coll
Cartwright Meml Hall
Bolton
Manningham
Scotchman Middle Sch
Ind Est
St Cuthbert & the First Martyrs RC Sch
Mills
Lillycroft First Sch
Pol HQ Mus
QUEEN'S RD
Peel Park
Waddilove's
Clifton Villas
TOLLER LA
Girlington
MANNINGHAM LA
Football Gd
St George RC Sch
TA Ctr
14
15
16
34
35
36
37
1
2
3
4
5
6
7
8

74 56

55
39

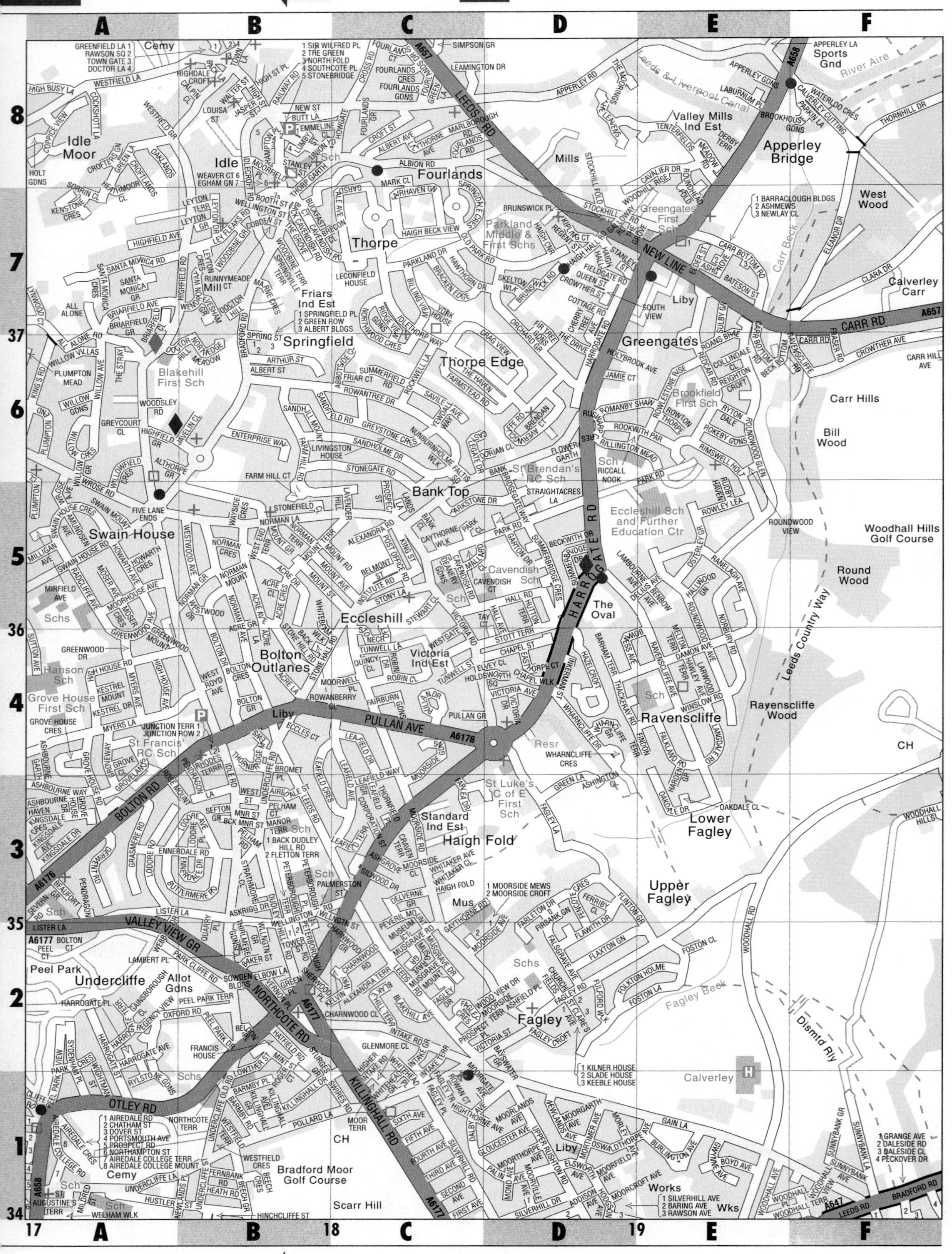
A
B
C
D
E
F
8
7
37
6
5
36
4
3
35
2
1
34
17
18
19
Idle Moor
Idle
Fourlands
Thorpe
Apperley Bridge
Valley Mills Ind Est
Mills
West Wood
Sports Gnd
River Aire
Leeds & Liverpool Canal
Parkland Middle & First Schs
Greengates First Sch
Friars Ind Est
Mill
Springfield
Thorpe Edge
Greengates
Liby
Calverley Carr
Blakehill First Sch
Brookfield First Sch
Carr Hills
Bill Wood
Bank Top
St Brendan's RC Sch
Eccleshill Sch and Further Education Ctr
Woodhall Hills Golf Course
Swain House
Cavendish Sch
The Oval
Round Wood
Eccleshill
Bolton Outlanes
Victoria Ind Est
Leeds Country Way
Hanson Sch
Grove House First Sch
Ravenscliffe
Ravenscliffe Wood
St Francis' RC Sch
Resr
St Luke's C of E First Sch
Standard Ind Est
Haigh Fold
Lower Fagley
Upper Fagley
Mus
Peel Park
Undercliffe
Allot Gdns
Schs
Fagley
Fagley Beck
Dismtd Rly
Calverley
Francis House
Bradford Moor Golf Course
Scarr Hill
Cemy
Works
Wks
LEEDS RD
NEW LINE
CARR RD
HARROGATE RD
PULLAN AVE
BOLTON RD
VALLEY VIEW GR
NORTHCOTE RD
KILLINGHALL RD
OTLEY RD
LISTER LA
A657
A658
A6176
A6177
A647

55
75

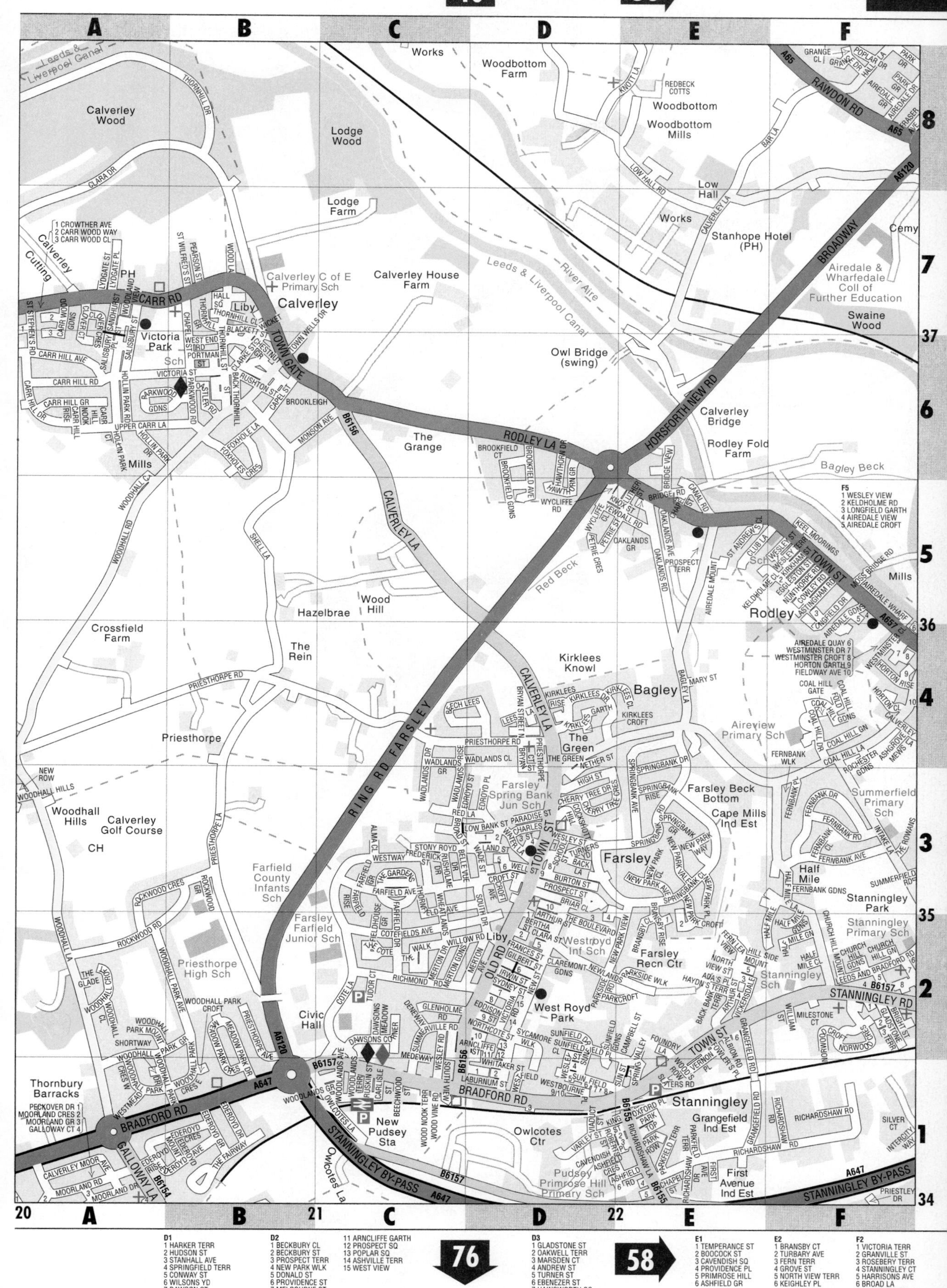

D1	D2		D3	E1	E2	F2
1 HARKER TERR	1 BECKBURY CL	11 ARNCLIFFE GARTH	1 GLADSTONE ST	1 TEMPERANCE ST	1 BRANSBY CT	1 VICTORIA TERR
2 HUDSON ST	2 BECKBURY ST	12 PROSPECT SQ	2 OAKWELL TERR	2 BOOCOCK ST	2 TURBARY AVE	2 GRANVILLE ST
3 STANHALL AVE	3 PROSPECT TERR	13 POPLAR SQ	3 MARSDEN CT	3 CAVENDISH SQ	3 FERN TERR	3 ROSEBERY TERR
4 SPRINGFIELD TERR	4 NEW PARK WLK	14 ASHVILLE TERR	4 ANDREW ST	4 PROVIDENCE PL	4 GROVE ST	4 STANNINGLEY CT
5 CONWAY ST	5 DONALD ST	15 WEST VIEW	5 TURNER ST	5 PRIMROSE HILL	5 NORTH VIEW TERR	5 HARRISONS AVE
6 WILSONS YD	6 PROVIDENCE ST		6 EBENEZER ST	6 ASHFIELD GR	6 KEIGHLEY PL	6 BROAD LA
7 DAWSON ST	7 MELBOURNE ST		7 HAINSWORTH SQ			7 BRITANNIA ST
8 WILLIAM ST	8 TENNYSON ST		8 GAMBLES HILL			8 BRITANNIA CL
9 WEST TERRACE ST	9 ARMSTRONG ST		9 OLD FOLD			
10 WEST GROVE ST	10 ANDREW ST		10 ST JOHN'S AVE			

B7
1 FEATHERBANK WLK
2 BACK FEATHERBANK TERR
3 FEATHERBANK TERR
4 SUNNYBANK AVE
5 BACK SUNNYBANK AVE
6 SUNNYBANK RD
7 BACK CLARENCE RD
8 WATERHOUSE CT
9 NEWLAY WOOD FOLD

C8
1 FEAST FIELD
2 STONEYTHORPE
3 STONEYCROFT
4 BROADWAY DR
5 FEATHERBANK GR
6 FEATHERBANK MOUNT

C7
1 WARWICK CT
2 NEWLAY BRIDGE PATH
3 NEWLAY WOOD GDNS
4 THROSTLE NEST VIEW
5 BACK OUTWOOD LA
6 BACK CRAGGWOOD RD
7 CRAGGWELL TERR
8 CRAGGWOOD TERR
9 WOODBINE TERR
10 REGENT CT

D8
1 WOODVILLE GR
2 WOODVILLE AVE
3 WOODVILLE TERR
4 WOODVILLE CRES

E8
1 BIRCH HILL RISE
2 TAN-HOUSE HILL
3 PARADISE PL
4 OAKFIELD TERR
5 WOODVILLE CT
6 WOODVILLE PL

F8
1 RING RD WEST PK
2 CLAYTON GRANGE
3 LATCHMERE CROSS
4 LATCHMERE CREST
5 LATCHMERE GN
6 OLD FARM WLK
7 LINTON CROFT
8 MOOR GRANGE CT

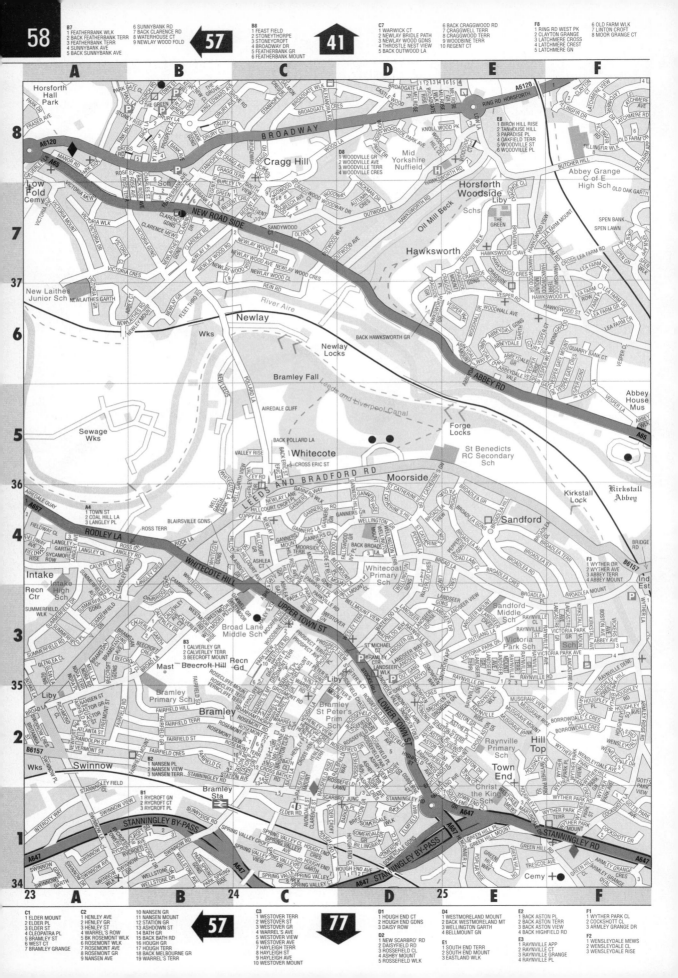

C1
1 ELDER MOUNT
2 ELDER PL
3 ELDER ST
4 CLEOPATRA PL
5 BRAMLEY ST
6 WEST CT
7 BRAMLEY GRANGE

C2
1 HENLEY AVE
2 HENLEY GR
3 HENLEY ST
4 WARREL'S ROW
5 BK ROSEMONT WLK
6 ROSEMONT WLK
7 ROSEMONT AVE
8 ROSEMONT GR
9 NANSEN AVE
10 NANSEN GR
11 NANSEN MOUNT
12 STATION GR
13 ASHDOWN ST
14 BATH GR
15 BACK BATH RD
16 HOUGH GR
17 HOUGH TERR
18 WARREL'S TERR

C3
1 WESTOVER TERR
2 WESTOVER ST
3 WESTOVER GR
4 WARREL'S AVE
5 WESTOVER VIEW
6 WESTOVER GDNS
7 HAYLEIGH TERR
8 HAYLEIGH ST
9 HAYLEIGH AVE
10 WESTOVER MOUNT

D1
1 HOUGH END CT
2 HOUGH END GDNS
3 DAISY ROW

D2
1 NEW SCARBRO' RD
2 DAISYFIELD RD
3 ROSSEFIELD CL
4 ASHBY MOUNT
5 ROSSEFIELD WLK

D4
1 WESTMORELAND MOUNT
2 BACK WESTMORELAND MT
3 WELLINGTON GARTH
4 BELLMOUNT GN

E1
1 SOUTH END TERR
2 SOUTH END MOUNT
3 EASTLAND WLK

E2
1 BACK ASTON PL
2 BACK ASTON TERR
3 BACK ASTON VIEW
4 BACK HIGHFIELD RD

E3
1 RAYNVILLE APP
2 RAYNVILLE CL
3 RAYNVILLE GRANGE
4 RAYNVILLE PL

F1
1 WYTHER PARK CL
2 COCKSHOTT CL
3 ARMLEY GRANGE DR

F2
1 WENSLEYDALE MEWS
2 WENSLEYDALE CL
3 WENSLEYDALE RISE

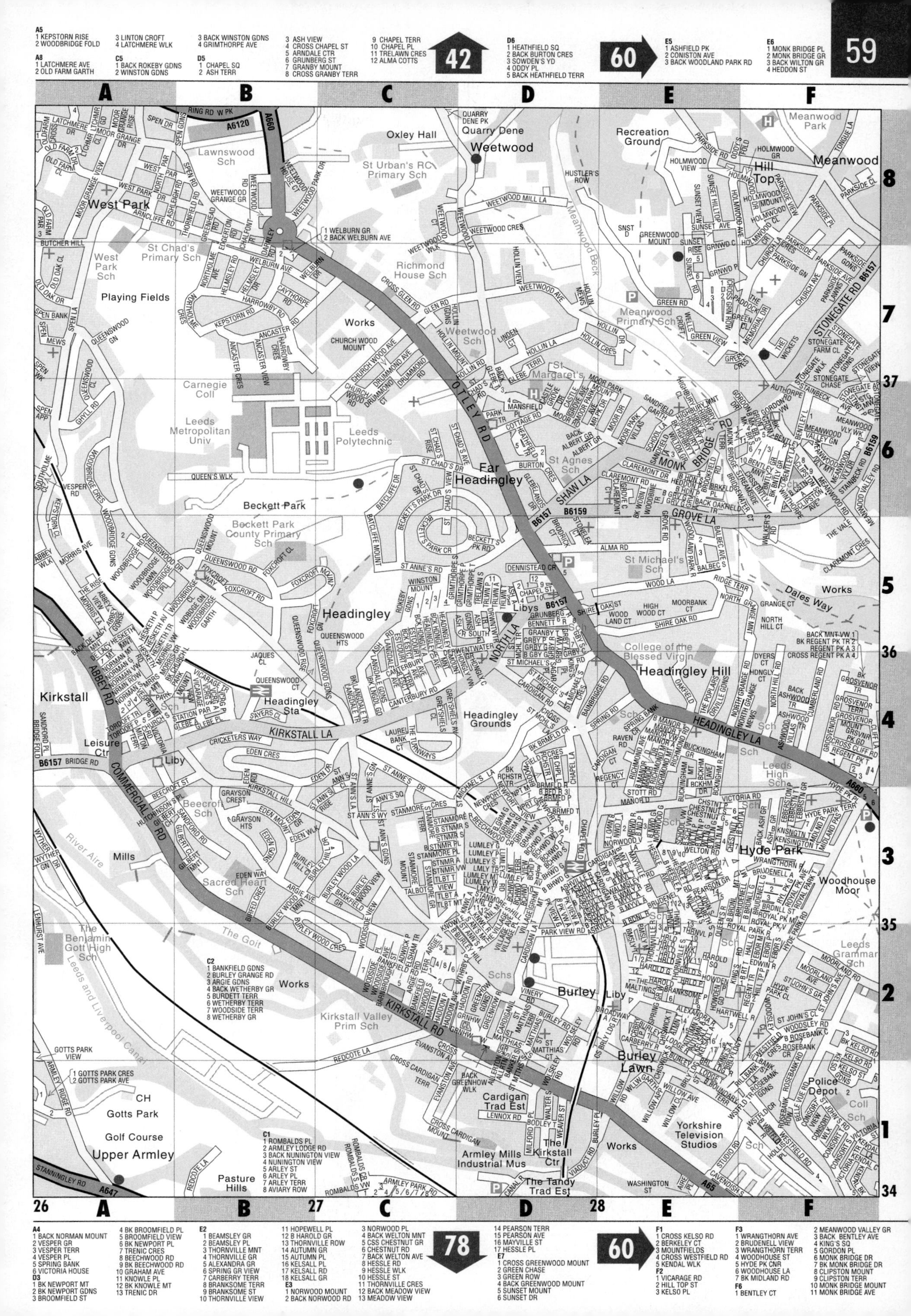

59
A5
1 KEPSTORN RISE
2 WOODBRIDGE FOLD
A8
1 LATCHMERE AVE
2 OLD FARM GARTH
3 LINTON CROFT
4 LATCHMERE WLK
C5
1 BACK ROKEBY GDNS
2 WINSTON GDNS
3 BACK WINSTON GDNS
4 GRIMTHORPE AVE
D5
1 CHAPEL SQ
2 ASH TERR
3 ASH VIEW
4 CROSS CHAPEL ST
5 ARNDALE CTR
6 GRUNBERG ST
7 GRANBY MOUNT
8 CROSS GRANBY TERR
9 CHAPEL TERR
10 CHAPEL PL
11 TRELAWN CRES
12 ALMA COTTS
42
D6
1 HEATHFIELD SQ
2 BACK BURTON CRES
3 SOWDEN'S YD
4 ODDY PL
5 BACK HEATHFIELD TERR
60
E5
1 ASHFIELD PK
2 CONISTON AVE
3 BACK WOODLAND PARK RD
E6
1 MONK BRIDGE PL
2 MONK BRIDGE GR
3 BACK WILTON GR
4 HEDDON ST
A B C D E F
West Park
Lawnswood Sch
Oxley Hall
Quarry Dene
Weetwood
St Urban's RC Primary Sch
Recreation Ground
Meanwood Park
Meanwood
Hill Top
St Chad's Primary Sch
West Park Sch
Playing Fields
Richmond House Sch
Meanwood Primary Sch
Works
Weetwood Sch
Carnegie Coll
Leeds Metropolitan Univ
Leeds Polytechnic
St Margaret's
St Agnes Sch
Far Headingley
Beckett Park
Beckett Park County Primary Sch
St Michael's Sch
Headingley
Libys
Dales Way
College of the Blessed Virgin
Headingley Hill
Kirkstall
Headingley Sta
Headingley Grounds
Leisure Ctr
Liby
Leeds High Sch
Beecroft Sch
Hyde Park
Woodhouse Moor
Mills
River Aire
Sacred Heart Sch
The Goit
The Benjamin Gott High Sch
Leeds Grammar Sch
Leeds and Liverpool Canal
Works
Kirkstall Valley Prim Sch
Burley
Schs
Burley Lawn
Police Depot
Coll Sch
Cardigan Trad Est
Yorkshire Television Studios
CH
Gotts Park
Golf Course
Upper Armley
Pasture Hills
Armley Mills Industrial Mus
The Kirkstall Ctr
The Tandy Trad Est
OTLEY RD
KIRKSTALL LA
KIRKSTALL RD
HEADINGLEY LA
ABBEY RD
COMMERCIAL RD
GROVE LA
SHAW LA
MONK BRIDGE RD
STONEGATE RD
A660
A65
A647
A6120
B6157
B6159
RING RD W PK
8 7 6 5 4 3 2 1
37 36 35 34
26 27 28
C2
1 BANKFIELD GDNS
2 BURLEY GRANGE RD
3 ARGIE GDNS
4 BACK WETHERBY GR
5 BURDETT TERR
6 WETHERBY TERR
7 WOODSIDE TERR
8 WETHERBY GR
C1
1 ROMBALDS PL
2 ARMLEY LODGE RD
3 BACK NUNINGTON VIEW
4 NUNINGTON VIEW
5 ARLEY ST
6 ARLEY PL
7 ARLEY TERR
8 AVIARY ROW
A4
1 BACK NORMAN MOUNT
2 VESPER GR
3 VESPER TERR
4 VESPER PL
5 SPRING BANK
6 VICTORIA HOUSE
D3
1 BK NEWPORT MT
2 BK NEWPORT GDNS
3 BROOMFIELD ST
4 BK BROOMFIELD PL
5 BROOMFIELD VIEW
6 BK NEWPORT PL
7 TRENIC CRES
8 BEECHWOOD RD
9 BK BEECHWOOD RD
10 GRAHAM AVE
11 KNOWLE PL
12 BK KNOWLE MT
13 TRENIC DR
E2
1 BEAMSLEY GR
2 BEAMSLEY PL
3 THORNVILLE MNT
4 THORNVILLE GR
5 ALEXANDRA GR
6 SPRING GR VIEW
7 CARBERRY TERR
8 BRANKSOME TERR
9 BRANKSOME ST
10 THORNVILLE VIEW
11 HOPEWELL PL
12 B HAROLD GR
13 THORNVILLE ROW
14 AUTUMN GR
15 AUTUMN PL
16 KELSALL PL
17 KELSALL RD
18 KELSALL GR
E3
1 NORWOOD MOUNT
2 BACK NORWOOD RD
3 NORWOOD PL
4 BACK WELTON MNT
5 CSS CHESTNUT GR
6 CHESTNUT RD
7 BACK WELTON AVE
8 HESSLE RD
9 HESSLE WLK
10 HESSLE ST
11 THORNVILLE CRES
12 BACK MEADOW VIEW
13 MEADOW VIEW
78
14 PEARSON TERR
15 PEARSON AVE
16 MAYVILLE ST
17 HESSLE PL
E7
1 CROSS GREENWOOD MOUNT
2 GREEN CHASE
3 GREEN ROW
4 BACK GREENWOOD MOUNT
5 SUNSET MOUNT
6 SUNSET DR
60
F1
1 CROSS KELSO RD
2 BERKELEY CT
3 MOUNTFIELDS
4 CROSS WESTFIELD RD
5 KENDAL WLK
F2
1 VICARAGE RD
2 HILL TOP ST
3 KELSO PL
F3
1 WRANGTHORN AVE
2 BRUDENELL VIEW
3 WRANGTHORN TERR
4 WOODHOUSE ST
5 HYDE PK CNR
6 WOODHOUSE LA
7 BK MIDLAND RD
F6
1 BENTLEY CT
2 MEANWOOD VALLEY GR
3 BACK BENTLEY AVE
4 KING'S SQ
5 GORDON PL
6 MONK BRIDGE DR
7 BK MONK BRIDGE DR
8 CLIPSTON MOUNT
9 CLIPSTON TERR
10 MONK BRIDGE MOUNT
11 MONK BRIDGE AVE

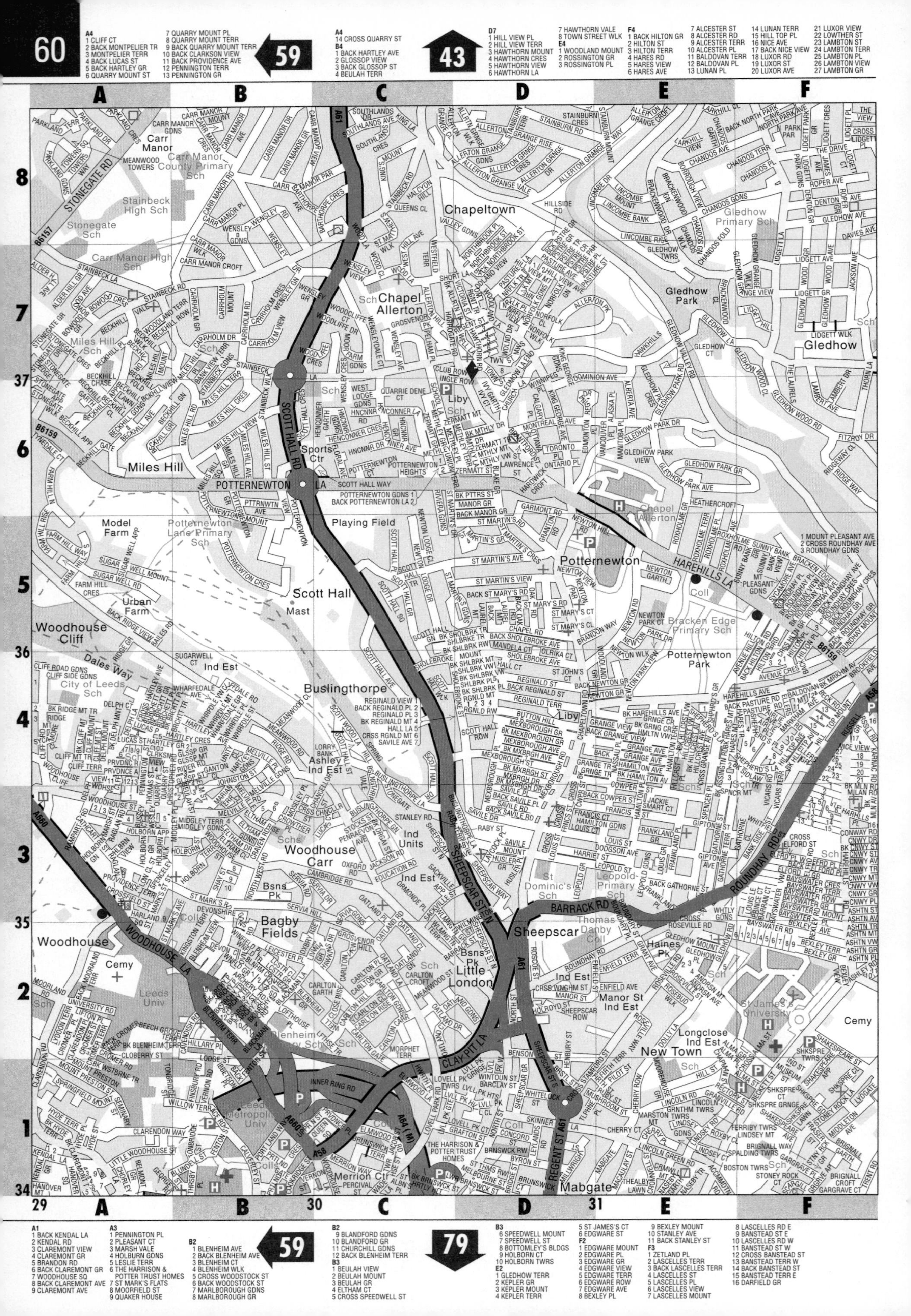
60
A4
1 CLIFF CT
2 BACK MONTPELIER TR
3 MONTPELIER TERR
4 BACK LUCAS ST
5 BACK HARTLEY GR
6 QUARRY MOUNT ST
7 QUARRY MOUNT PL
8 QUARRY MOUNT TERR
9 BACK QUARRY MOUNT TERR
10 BACK CLARKSON VIEW
11 BACK PROVIDENCE AVE
12 PENNINGTON TERR
13 PENNINGTON GR
59
A4
14 CROSS QUARRY ST
B4
1 BACK HARTLEY AVE
2 GLOSSOP VIEW
3 BACK GLOSSOP ST
4 BEULAH TERR
43
D7
1 HILL VIEW PL
2 HILL VIEW TERR
3 HAWTHORN MOUNT
4 HAWTHORN CRES
5 HAWTHORN VIEW
6 HAWTHORN LA
7 HAWTHORN VALE
8 TOWN STREET WLK
E4
1 WOODLAND MOUNT
2 ROSSINGTON GR
3 ROSSINGTON PL
F4
1 BACK HILTON GR
2 HILTON ST
3 HILTON TERR
4 HARES RD
5 HARES VIEW
6 HARES AVE
7 ALCESTER ST
8 ALCESTER RD
9 ALCESTER TERR
10 ALCESTER PL
11 BALDOVAN TERR
12 BALDOVAN PL
13 LUNAN PL
14 LUNAN TERR
15 HILL TOP PL
16 NICE AVE
17 BACK NICE VIEW
18 LUXOR RD
19 LUXOR ST
20 LUXOR AVE
21 LUXOR VIEW
22 LOWTHER ST
23 LAMBTON ST
24 LAMBTON TERR
25 LAMBTON PL
26 LAMBTON VIEW
27 LAMBTON GR
A B C D E F
8 7 37 6 5 36 4 3 35 2 1 34
Carr Manor
Chapeltown
Chapel Allerton
Gledhow Park
Gledhow
Miles Hill
Model Farm
Urban Farm
Woodhouse Cliff
Scott Hall
Potternewton
Potternewton Park
Buslingthorpe
Woodhouse Carr
Bagby Fields
Sheepscar
Little London
Woodhouse
Leeds Univ
Leeds Metropolitan Univ
New Town
Mabgate
Merrion Ctr
SCOTT HALL RD
POTTERNEWTON LA
HAREHILLS LA
SHEEPSCAR ST N
BARRACK RD
ROUNDHAY RD
WOODHOUSE LA
CLAY PIT LA
INNER RING RD
REGENT ST
STONEGATE RD
Dales Way
29 30 31
A1
1 BACK KENDAL LA
2 KENDAL RD
3 CLAREMONT VIEW
4 CLAREMONT GR
5 BRANDON RD
6 BACK CLAREMONT GR
7 WOODHOUSE SQ
8 BACK CLAREMONT AVE
9 CLAREMONT AVE
A3
1 PENNINGTON PL
2 PLEASANT CT
3 MARSH VALE
4 HOLBURN GDNS
5 LESLIE TERR
6 THE HARRISON & POTTER TRUST HOMES
7 ST MARK'S FLATS
8 MOORFIELD ST
9 QUAKER HOUSE
59
B2
1 BLENHEIM AVE
2 BACK BLENHEIM AVE
3 BLENHEIM CT
4 BLENHEIM WLK
5 CROSS WOODSTOCK ST
6 BACK WOODSTOCK ST
7 MARLBOROUGH GDNS
8 MARLBOROUGH GR
B2
9 BLANDFORD GDNS
10 BLANDFORD GR
11 CHURCHILL GDNS
12 BACK BLENHEIM TERR
B3
1 BEULAH VIEW
2 BEULAH MOUNT
3 BEULAH GR
4 ELTHAM CT
5 CROSS SPEEDWELL ST
79
B3
6 SPEEDWELL MOUNT
7 SPEEDWELL ST
8 BOTTOMLEY'S BLDGS
9 HOLBORN CT
10 HOLBORN TWRS
E2
1 GLEDHOW TERR
2 KEPLER GR
3 KEPLER MOUNT
4 KEPLER TERR
5 ST JAMES'S CT
6 EDGWARE ST
F2
1 EDGWARE MOUNT
2 EDGWARE PL
3 EDGWARE GR
4 EDGWARE VIEW
5 EDGWARE TERR
6 EDGWARE ROW
7 EDGWARE AVE
8 BEXLEY PL
9 BEXLEY MOUNT
10 STANLEY AVE
11 BACK STANLEY ST
F3
1 ZETLAND PL
2 LASCELLES TERR
3 BACK LASCELLES TERR
4 LASCELLES ST
5 LASCELLES PL
6 LASCELLES VIEW
7 LASCELLES MOUNT
8 LASCELLES RD E
9 BANSTEAD ST E
10 LASCELLES RD W
11 BANSTEAD ST W
12 CROSS BANSTEAD ST
13 BANSTEAD TERR W
14 BACK BANSTEAD ST
15 BANSTEAD TERR E
16 DARFIELD GR

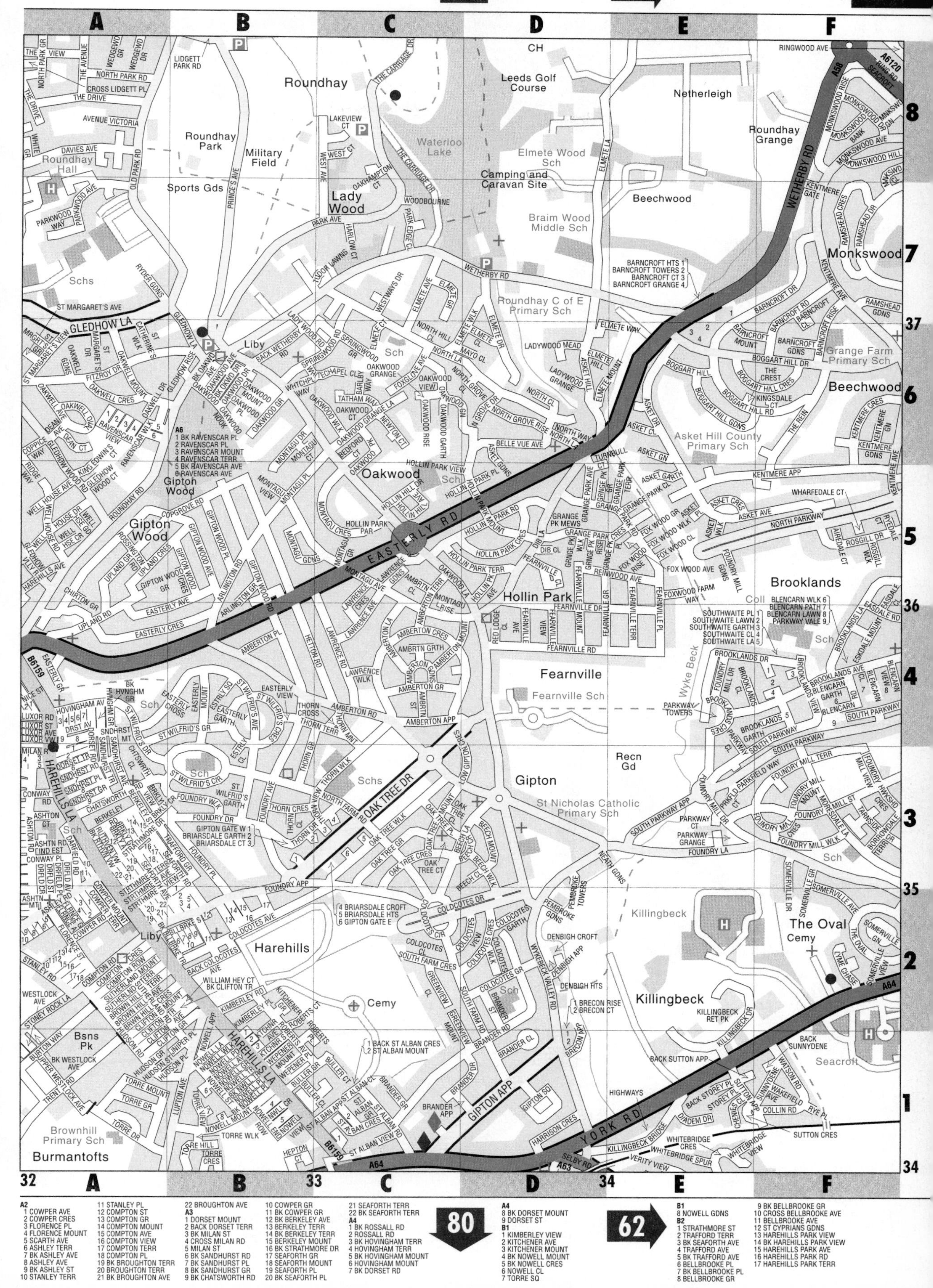

80   62 ►

A2
1 COWPER AVE
2 COWPER CRES
3 FLORENCE PL
4 FLORENCE MOUNT
5 SCARTH AVE
6 ASHLEY TERR
7 BK ASHLEY AVE
8 ASHLEY AVE
9 BK ASHLEY ST
10 STANLEY TERR
11 STANLEY PL
12 COMPTON ST
13 COMPTON GR
14 COMPTON MOUNT
15 COMPTON AVE
16 COMPTON VIEW
17 COMPTON TERR
18 COMPTON PL
19 BK BROUGHTON TERR
20 BROUGHTON TERR
21 BK BROUGHTON AVE

22 BROUGHTON AVE
A3
1 DORSET MOUNT
2 BACK DORSET TERR
3 BK MILAN ST
4 CROSS MILAN RD
5 MILAN ST
6 BK SANDHURST RD
7 BK SANDHURST PL
8 BK SANDHURST GR
9 BK CHATSWORTH RD

10 COWPER GR
11 BK COWPER GR
12 BK BERKELEY AVE
13 BERKELEY TERR
14 BK BERKELEY TERR
15 BERKELEY MOUNT
16 BK STRATHMORE DR
17 COMPTON TERR
18 SEAFORTH MOUNT
19 SEAFORTH PL
20 BK SEAFORTH PL

21 SEAFORTH TERR
22 BK SEAFORTH TERR
A4
1 BK ROSSALL RD
2 ROSSALL RD
3 BK HOVINGHAM TERR
4 HOVINGHAM TERR
5 BK HOVINGHAM MOUNT
6 HOVINGHAM MOUNT
7 BK DORSET RD

A4
8 BK DORSET MOUNT
9 DORSET ST
B1
1 KIMBERLEY VIEW
2 KITCHENER AVE
3 KITCHENER MOUNT
4 TRAFFORD AVE
5 BK NOWELL CRES
6 NOWELL CL
7 TORRE SQ

B1
8 NOWELL GDNS
B2
1 STRATHMORE ST
2 TRAFFORD TERR
3 BK SEAFORTH AVE
4 TRAFFORD AVE
5 BK TRAFFORD AVE
6 BELLBROOKE PL
7 BK BELLBROOKE PL
8 BELLBROOKE GR

9 BK BELLBROOKE GR
10 CROSS BELLBROOKE AVE
11 BELLBROOKE AVE
12 ST CYPRIANS GDNS
13 HAREHILLS PARK VIEW
14 BK HAREHILLS PARK VIEW
15 HAREHILLS PARK AVE
16 HAREHILLS PARK RD
17 HAREHILLS PARK TERR

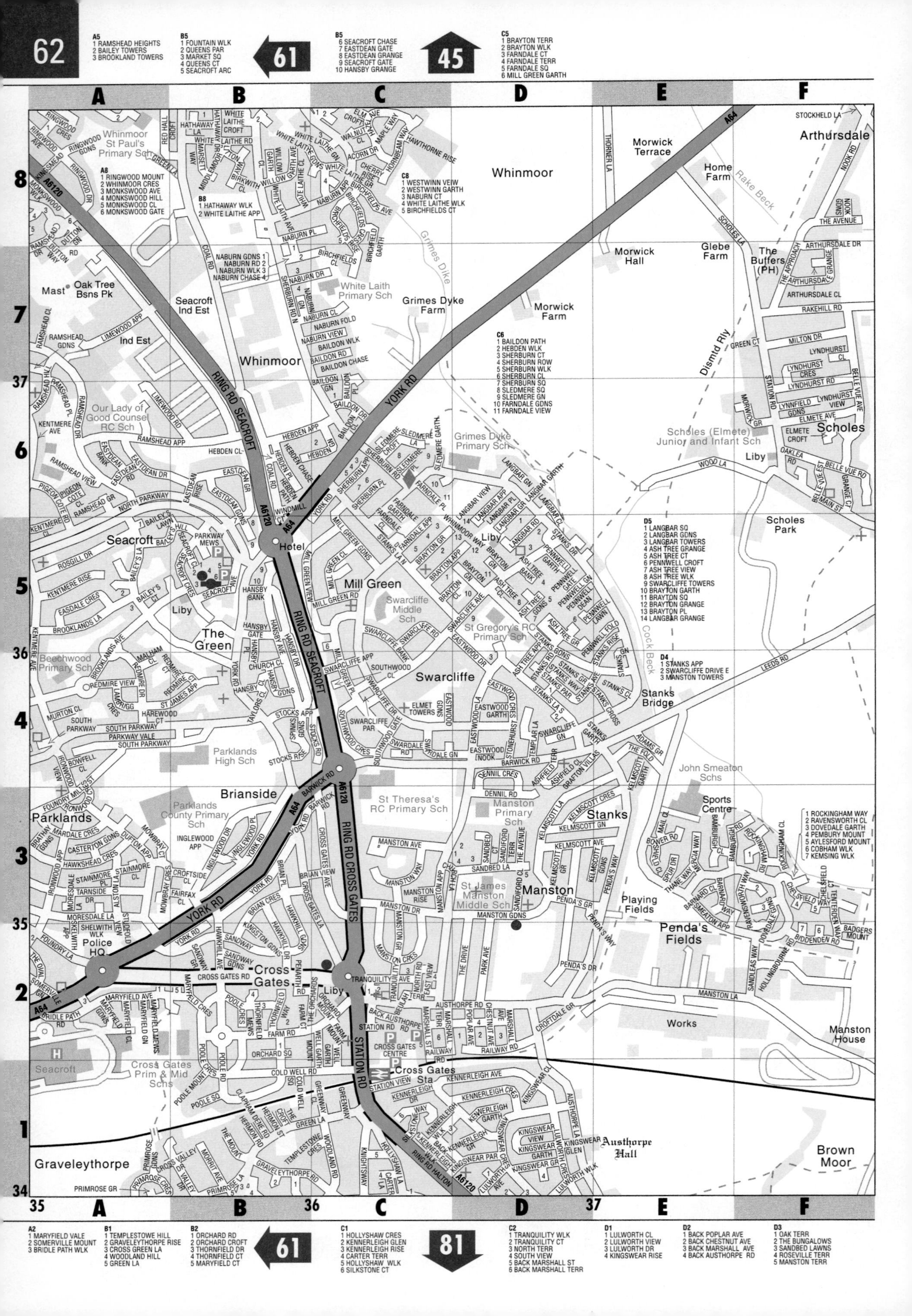
A5
1 RAMSHEAD HEIGHTS
2 BAILEY TOWERS
3 BROOKLAND TOWERS
B5
1 FOUNTAIN WLK
2 QUEENS PAR
3 MARKET SQ
4 QUEENS CT
5 SEACROFT ARC
61
B5
6 SEACROFT CHASE
7 EASTDEAN GATE
8 EASTDEAN GRANGE
9 SEACROFT GATE
10 HANSBY GRANGE
45
C5
1 BRAYTON TERR
2 BRAYTON WLK
3 FARNDALE CT
4 FARNDALE TERR
5 FARNDALE SQ
6 MILL GREEN GARTH
A
B
C
D
E
F
8
7
37
6
5
36
4
3
35
2
1
34
35
36
37
A8
1 RINGWOOD MOUNT
2 WHINMOOR CRES
3 MONKSWOOD AVE
4 MONKSWOOD HILL
5 MONKSWOOD CL
6 MONKSWOOD GATE
B8
1 HATHAWAY WLK
2 WHITE LAITHE APP
C8
1 WESTWINN VIEW
2 WESTWINN GARTH
3 NABURN CT
4 WHITE LAITHE WLK
5 BIRCHFIELDS CT
NABURN GDNS 1
NABURN RD 2
NABURN WLK 3
NABURN CHASE 4
C6
1 BAILDON PATH
2 HEBDEN WLK
3 SHERBURN CT
4 SHERBURN ROW
5 SHERBURN WLK
6 SHERBURN CL
7 SHERBURN SQ
8 SLEDMERE SQ
9 SLEDMERE GN
10 FARNDALE GDNS
11 FARNDALE VIEW
D5
1 LANGBAR SQ
2 LANGBAR GDNS
3 LANGBAR TOWERS
4 ASH TREE GRANGE
5 ASH TREE CT
6 PENNWELL CROFT
7 ASH TREE VIEW
8 ASH TREE WLK
9 SWARCLIFFE TOWERS
10 BRAYTON GARTH
11 BRAYTON SQ
12 BRAYTON GRANGE
13 BRAYTON PL
14 LANGBAR GRANGE
D4
1 STANKS APP
2 SWARCLIFFE DRIVE E
3 MANSTON TOWERS
1 ROCKINGHAM WAY
2 RAVENSWORTH CL
3 DOVEDALE GARTH
4 PEMBURY MOUNT
5 AYLESFORD MOUNT
6 COBHAM WLK
7 KEMSING WLK
Whinmoor
St Paul's
Primary Sch
Whinmoor
Morwick
Terrace
Arthursdale
Home
Farm
Rake Beck
Morwick
Hall
Glebe
Farm
The
Buffers
(PH)
Mast
Oak Tree
Bsns Pk
Seacroft
Ind Est
White Laith
Primary Sch
Grimes Dyke
Farm
Morwick
Farm
Grimes Dike
Ind Est
Whinmoor
Dismtd Rly
Our Lady of
Good Counsel
RC Sch
Grimes Dyke
Primary Sch
Scholes (Elmete)
Junior and Infant Sch
Scholes
Liby
Scholes
Park
Seacroft
Hotel
Liby
Mill Green
Swarcliffe
Middle
Sch
Liby
The
Green
St Gregory's RC
Primary Sch
Cock Beck
Beechwood
Primary Sch
Swarcliffe
Stanks
Bridge
Parklands
High Sch
John Smeaton
Schs
Brianside
St Theresa's
RC Primary Sch
Sports
Centre
Parklands
County Primary
Sch
Manston
Primary
Sch
Stanks
Parklands
St James
Manston
Middle Sch
Manston
Playing
Fields
Police
HQ
Penda's
Fields
Cross
Gates
Liby
Works
Manston
House
Seacroft
Cross Gates
Prim & Mid
Schs
Cross Gates
Sta
CROSS GATES
CENTRE
Austhorpe
Hall
Graveleythorpe
Brown
Moor
RING RD SEACROFT
RING RD CROSS GATES
YORK RD
STATION RD
RING RD HALTON
A6120
A64
LEEDS RD
STOCKHELD LA
THORNER LA
SCHOLES LA
WOOD LA
MANSTON LA
BARWICK RD
NORTH PARKWAY
SOUTH PARKWAY
CROSS GATES RD
A2
1 MARYFIELD VALE
2 SOMERVILLE MOUNT
3 BRIDLE PATH WLK
B1
1 TEMPLESTOWE HILL
2 GRAVELEYTHORPE RISE
3 CROSS GREEN LA
4 WOODLAND HILL
5 GREEN LA
B2
1 ORCHARD RD
2 ORCHARD CROFT
3 THORNFIELD DR
4 THORNFIELD CT
5 MARYFIELD CT
61
81
C1
1 HOLLYSHAW CRES
2 KENNERLEIGH GLEN
3 KENNERLEIGH RISE
4 CARTER TERR
5 HOLLYSHAW WLK
6 SILKSTONE CT
C2
1 TRANQUILITY WLK
2 TRANQUILITY CT
3 NORTH TERR
4 SOUTH VIEW
5 BACK MARSHALL ST
6 BACK MARSHALL TERR
D1
1 LULWORTH CL
2 LULWORTH VIEW
3 LULWORTH DR
4 KINGSWEAR RISE
D2
1 BACK POPLAR AVE
2 BACK CHESTNUT AVE
3 BACK MARSHALL AVE
4 BACK AUSTHORPE RD
D3
1 OAK TERR
2 THE BUNGALOWS
3 SANDBED LAWNS
4 ROSEVILLE TERR
5 MANSTON TERR

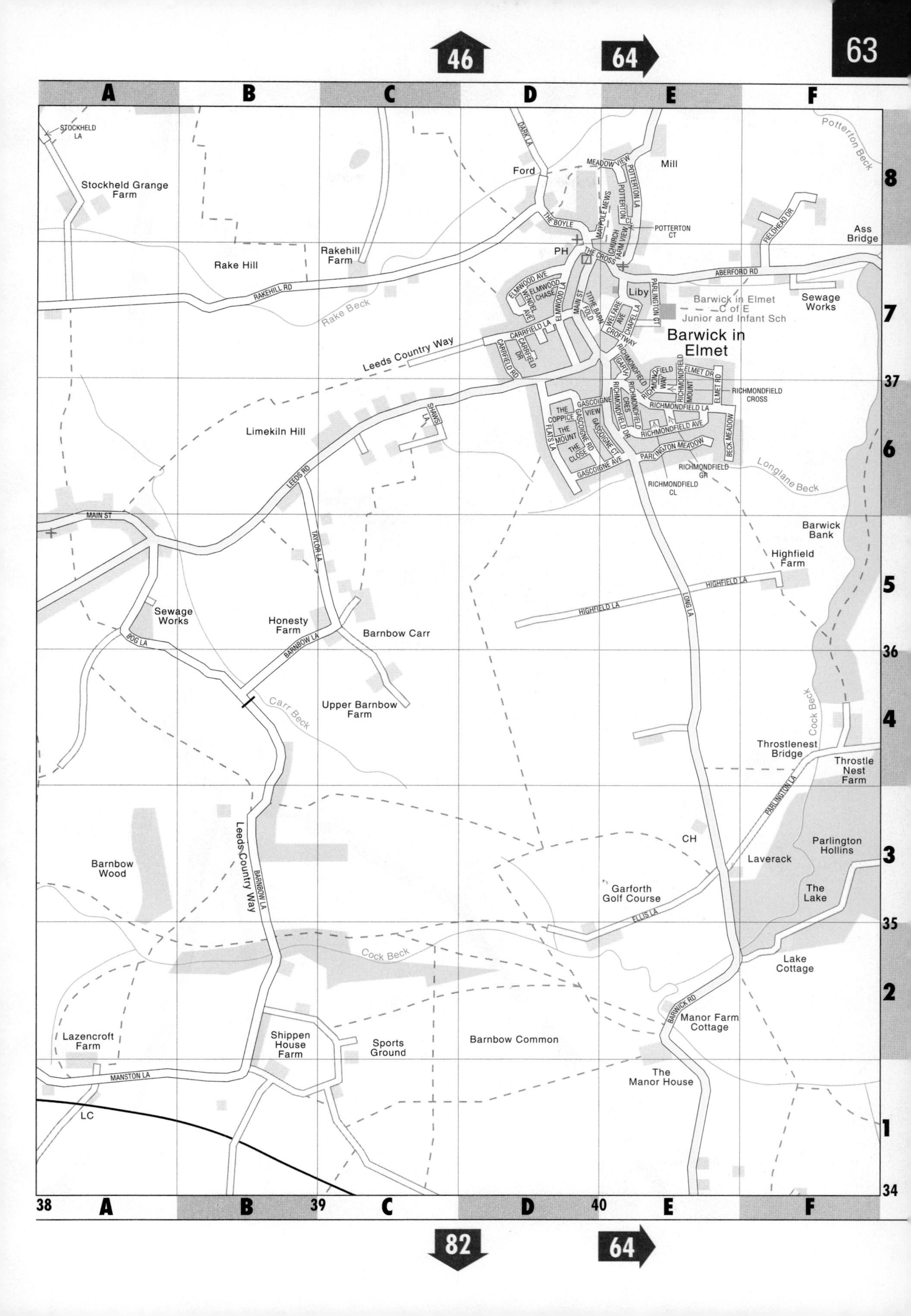

63
46
64
82
64
A
B
C
D
E
F
8
7
6
5
4
3
2
1
37
36
35
34
38
39
40
STOCKHELD LA
Stockheld Grange Farm
Rake Hill
Rakehill Farm
RAKEHILL RD
Rake Beck
Leeds Country Way
Ford
Mill
DARK LA
MEADOW VIEW
POTTERTON LA
MAYPOLE MEWS
POTTERTON CL
CHURCH FARM VIEW
POTTERTON CT
THE BOYLE
PH
THE CROSS
FIELDHEAD DR
Ass Bridge
Potterton Beck
ABERFORD RD
Sewage Works
ELMWOOD AVE
ELMWOOD CHASE
WENDEL AVE
ELMWOOD LA
MAIN ST
TITHE BARN FOLD
WELFARE AVE
CHAPEL LA
PARLINGTON CT
Liby
Barwick in Elmet C of E Junior and Infant Sch
Barwick in Elmet
CROFTWAY
CARRFIELD LA
CARRFIELD DR
CARRFIELD RD
RICHMONDFIELD GARTH
RICHMONDFIELD WAY
RICHMONDFIELD MOUNT
ELMET DR
ELMET RD
RICHMONDFIELD CROSS
RICHMONDFIELD LA
RICHMONDFIELD AVE
RICHMONDFIELD CRES
RICHMONDFIELD DR
GASCOIGNE VIEW
GASCOIGNE RD
GASCOIGNE CT
GASCOIGNE AVE
THE COPPICE
THE MOUNT
THE CLOSE
FLATS LA
PARLINGTON MEADOW
BECK MEADOW
RICHMONDFIELD GR
RICHMONDFIELD CL
Longlane Beck
Limekiln Hill
SHAWS LA
LEEDS RD
MAIN ST
TAYLOR LA
Barwick Bank
Highfield Farm
HIGHFIELD LA
LONG LA
Sewage Works
Honesty Farm
Barnbow Carr
BOG LA
BARNBOW LA
Carr Beck
Upper Barnbow Farm
Cock Beck
Throstlenest Bridge
Throstle Nest Farm
PARLINGTON LA
CH
Barnbow Wood
Leeds Country Way
Laverack
Parlington Hollins
Garforth Golf Course
The Lake
ELLIS LA
Cock Beck
Lake Cottage
BARWICK RD
Manor Farm Cottage
Lazencroft Farm
Shippen House Farm
Sports Ground
Barnbow Common
The Manor House
MANSTON LA
LC

63
47

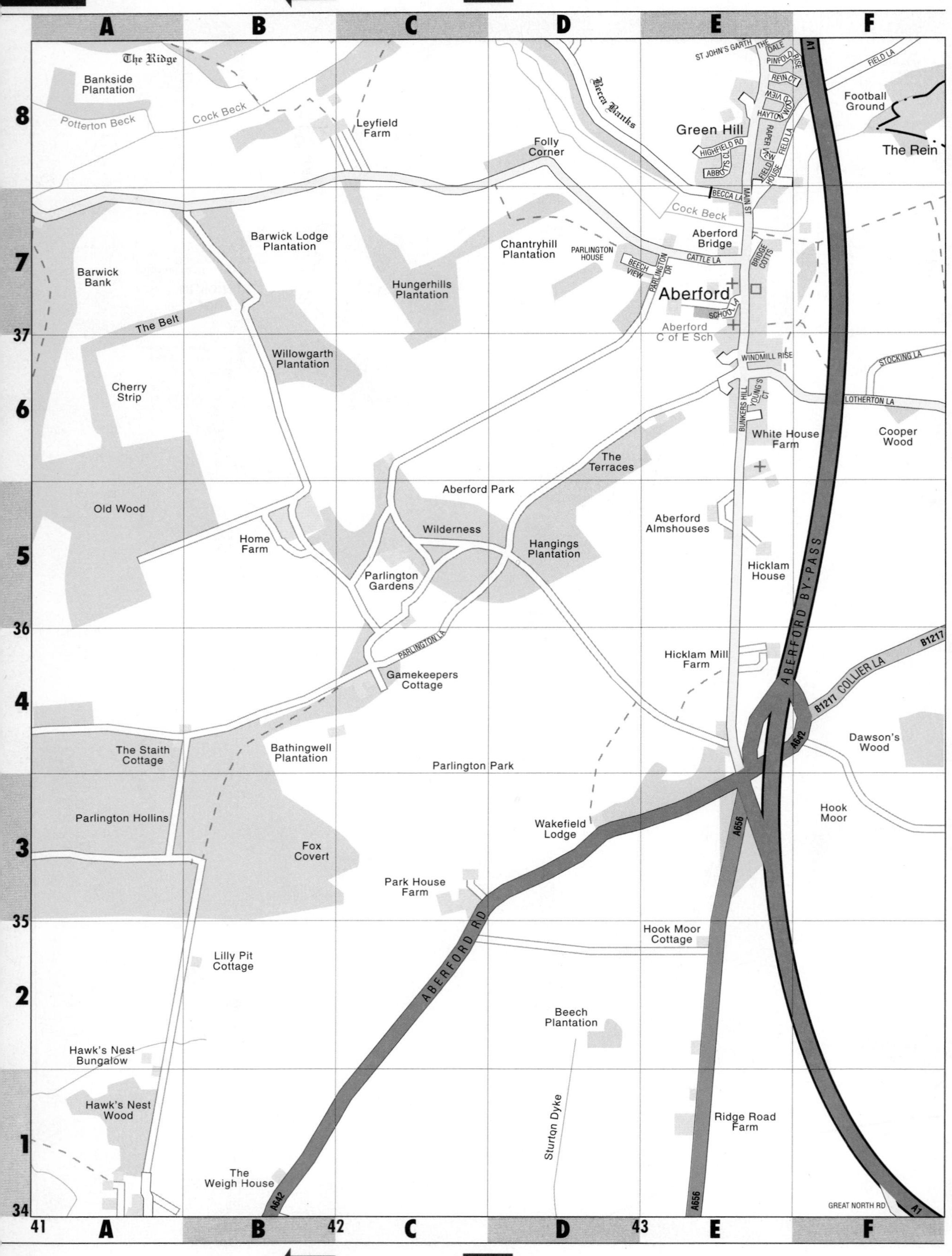
A
B
C
D
E
F
The Ridge
Bankside Plantation
Potterton Beck
Cock Beck
Leyfield Farm
Becca Banks
ST JOHN'S GARTH
THE DALE
PINFOLD RISE
REIN CT
FIELD LA
Green Hill
HAYTON WOOD VIEW
HIGHFIELD RD
ABBOTTS CL
RAPER VIEW
FIELD HOUSE
FIELD LA
Football Ground
The Rein
Folly Corner
BECCA LA
MAIN ST
Cock Beck
Aberford Bridge
BRIDGE COTTS
Barwick Lodge Plantation
Chantryhill Plantation
PARLINGTON HOUSE
BEECH VIEW
PARLINGTON DR
CATTLE LA
Barwick Bank
Hungerhills Plantation
Aberford
SCHOOL LA
The Belt
Aberford C of E Sch
Willowgarth Plantation
WINDMILL RISE
STOCKING LA
Cherry Strip
BUNKERS HILL
YOUNG'S CT
LOTHERTON LA
White House Farm
Cooper Wood
The Terraces
Aberford Park
Old Wood
Aberford Almshouses
Wilderness
Home Farm
Hangings Plantation
Parlington Gardens
Hicklam House
ABERFORD BY-PASS
PARLINGTON LA
Hicklam Mill Farm
B1217
B1211 COLLIER LA
Gamekeepers Cottage
A642
Dawson's Wood
The Staith Cottage
Bathingwell Plantation
Parlington Park
Hook Moor
Parlington Hollins
Wakefield Lodge
A656
Fox Covert
Park House Farm
ABERFORD RD
Hook Moor Cottage
Lilly Pit Cottage
Beech Plantation
Hawk's Nest Bungalow
Hawk's Nest Wood
Sturton Dyke
Ridge Road Farm
The Weigh House
A642
A656
GREAT NORTH RD
A1
8
7
37
6
5
36
4
3
35
2
1
34
41
42
43

63
83

48

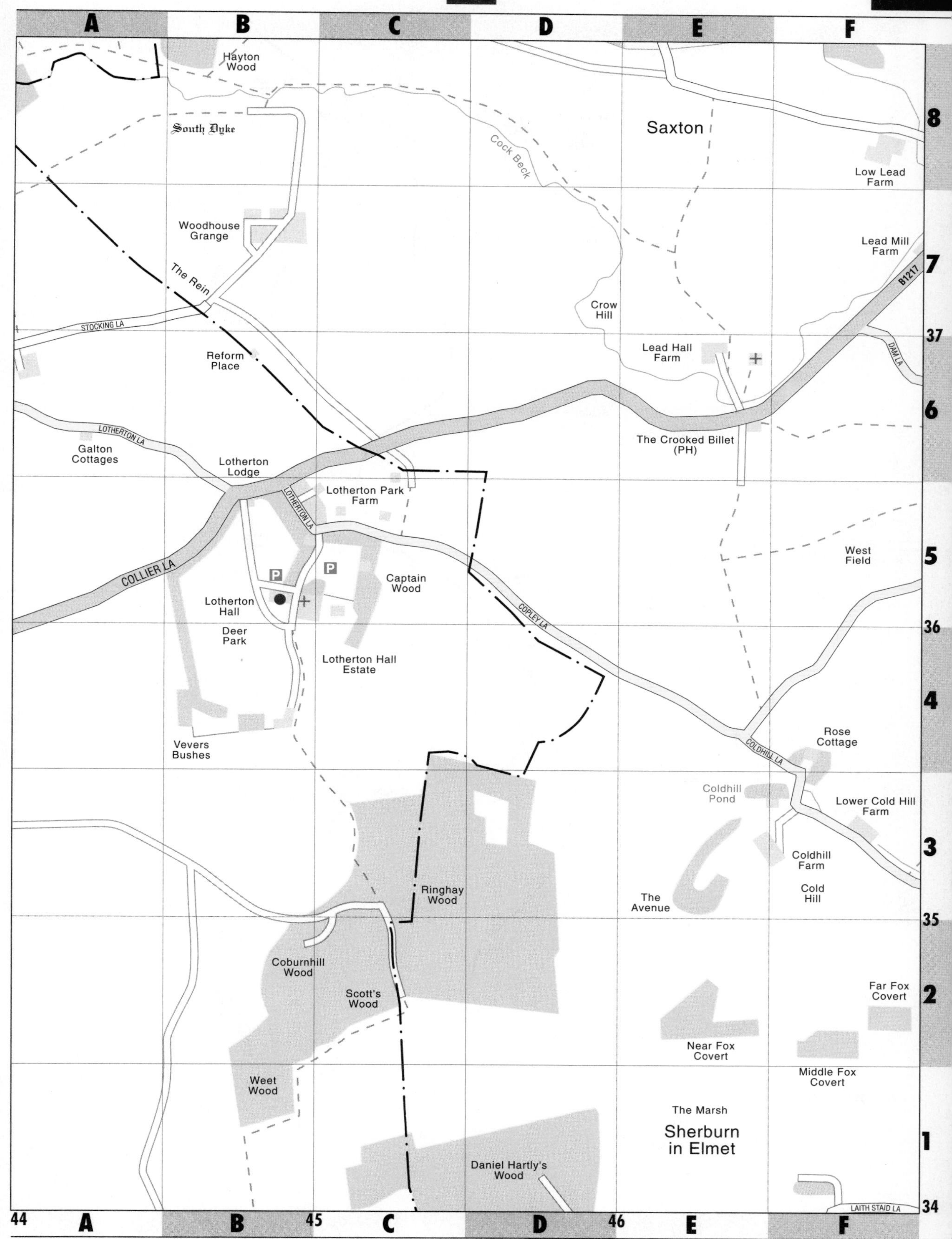

A
B
C
D
E
F
Hayton Wood
South Dyke
Saxton
Cock Beck
Low Lead Farm
Woodhouse Grange
Lead Mill Farm
The Rein
B1217
Crow Hill
STOCKING LA
Reform Place
Lead Hall Farm
DAM LA
LOTHERTON LA
Galton Cottages
Lotherton Lodge
The Crooked Billet (PH)
LOTHERTON LA
Lotherton Park Farm
COLLIER LA
West Field
P
P
Captain Wood
Lotherton Hall
COPLEY LA
Deer Park
Lotherton Hall Estate
Vevers Bushes
Rose Cottage
COLDHILL LA
Coldhill Pond
Lower Cold Hill Farm
Coldhill Farm
Ringhay Wood
The Avenue
Cold Hill
Coburnhill Wood
Scott's Wood
Far Fox Covert
Near Fox Covert
Middle Fox Covert
Weet Wood
The Marsh
Sherburn in Elmet
Daniel Hartly's Wood
LAITH STAID LA
8
7
37
6
5
36
4
3
35
2
1
34
44
45
46

84

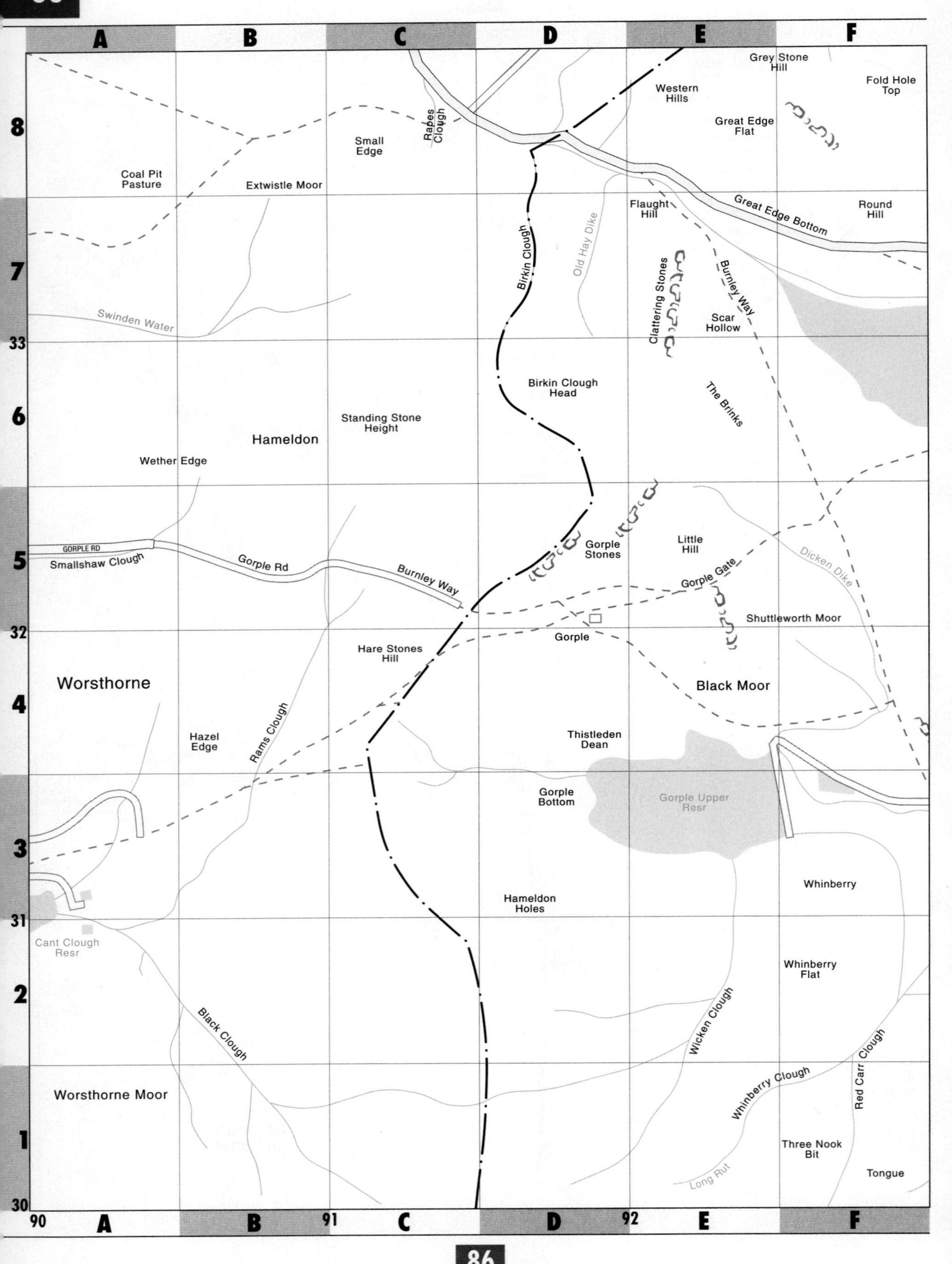

A B C D E F

Grey Stone Hill

Fold Hole Top

Western Hills

Great Edge Flat

Small Edge

Rapes Clough

Coal Pit Pasture

Extwistle Moor

Flaught Hill

Great Edge Bottom

Round Hill

Birkin Clough

Old Hay Dike

Clattering Stones

Burnley Way

Scar Hollow

Swinden Water

Birkin Clough Head

The Brinks

Standing Stone Height

Hameldon

Wether Edge

Gorple Stones

Little Hill

Dicken Dike

GORPLE RD

Gorple Rd

Burnley Way

Gorple Gate

Smallshaw Clough

Shuttleworth Moor

Hare Stones Hill

Gorple

Worsthorne

Black Moor

Hazel Edge

Rams Clough

Thistleden Dean

Gorple Bottom

Gorple Upper Resr

Whinberry

Cant Clough Resr

Hameldon Holes

Whinberry Flat

Black Clough

Wicken Clough

Red Carr Clough

Worsthorne Moor

Whinberry Clough

Three Nook Bit

Long Rut

Tongue

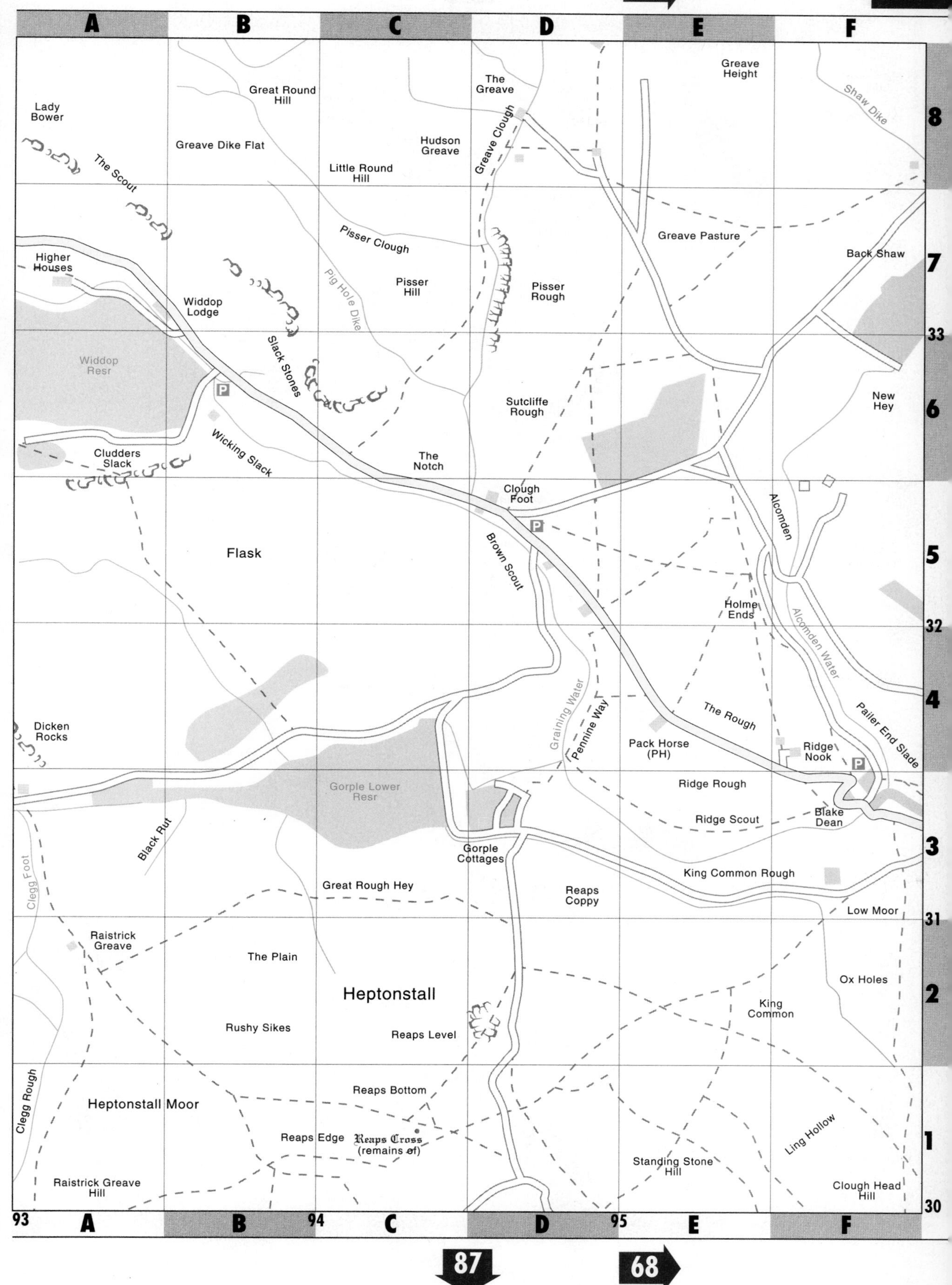

68
A
B
C
D
E
F
Greave Height
Shaw Dike
Great Round Hill
The Greave
Lady Bower
8
Greave Dike Flat
Hudson Greave
Greave Clough
The Scout
Little Round Hill
Greave Pasture
Pisser Clough
Back Shaw
Higher Houses
7
Pig Hole Dike
Pisser Hill
Pisser Rough
Widdop Lodge
33
Widdop Resr
Slack Stones
New Hey
Sutcliffe Rough
6
Wicking Slack
Cludders Slack
The Notch
Clough Foot
Alcomden
Brown Scout
Flask
5
Holme Ends
32
Alcomden Water
Graining Water
4
Pennine Way
The Rough
Pailer End Slade
Dicken Rocks
Pack Horse (PH)
Ridge Nook
Gorple Lower Resr
Ridge Rough
Black Rut
Ridge Scout
Blake Dean
3
Gorple Cottages
Clegg Foot
King Common Rough
Great Rough Hey
Reaps Coppy
Low Moor
31
Raistrick Greave
The Plain
Ox Holes
2
Heptonstall
King Common
Rushy Sikes
Reaps Level
Clegg Rough
Reaps Bottom
Heptonstall Moor
1
Ling Hollow
Reaps Edge
Reaps Cross
(remains of)
Standing Stone Hill
Raistrick Greave Hill
Clough Head Hill
30
93
94
95
87
68

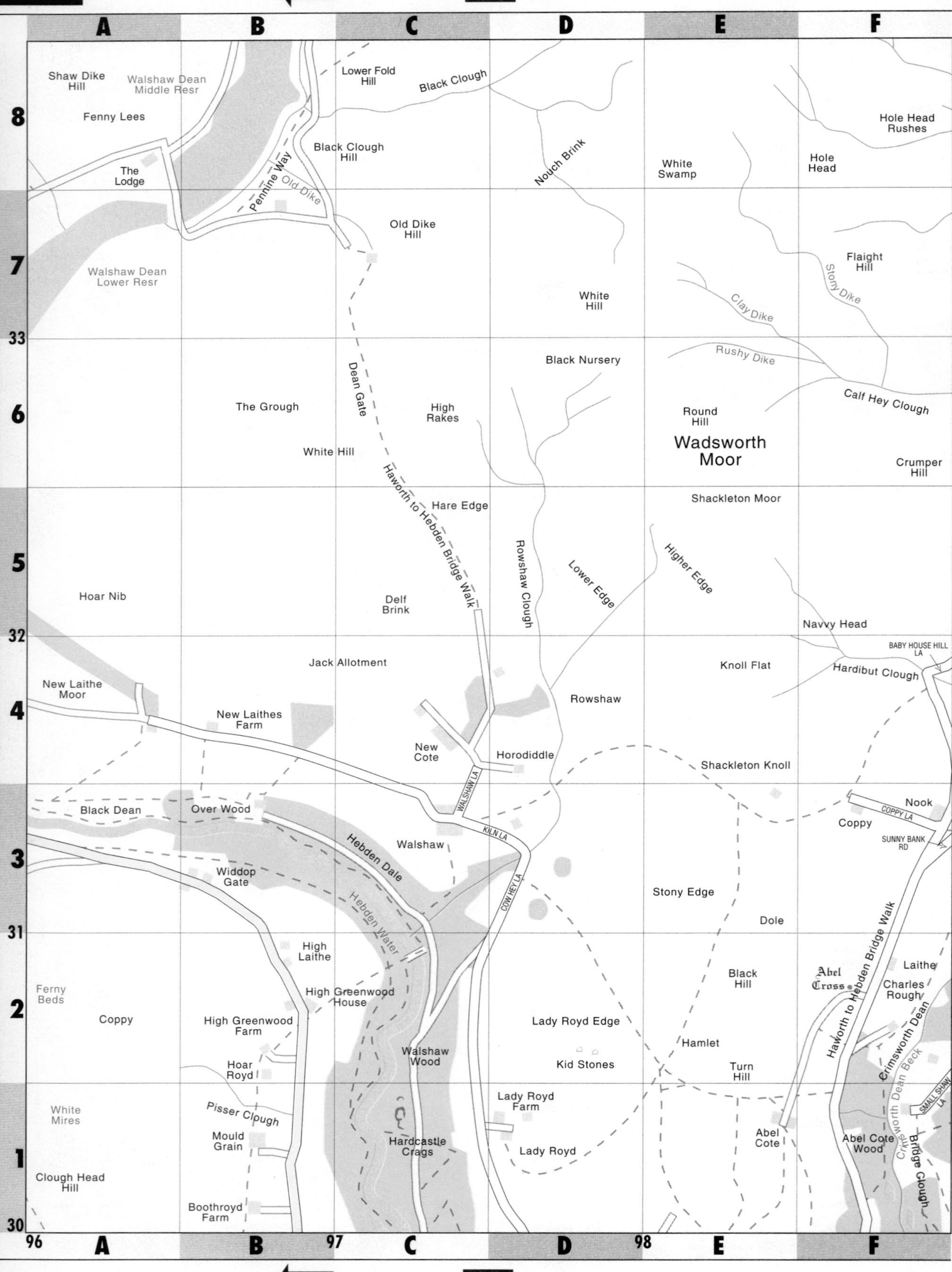

	A	B	C	D	E	F

8

Shaw Dike Hill

Walshaw Dean Middle Resr

Lower Fold Hill

Black Clough

Nouch Brink

White Swamp

Hole Head Rushes

Fenny Lees

Black Clough Hill

The Lodge

Pennine Way

Old Dike

Hole Head

7

Walshaw Dean Lower Resr

Old Dike Hill

White Hill

Flaight Hill

Stony Dike

Clay Dike

33

Black Nursery

Rushy Dike

Calf Hey Clough

6

The Grough

High Rakes

Round Hill

Wadsworth Moor

Crumper Hill

White Hill

Haworth to Hebden Bridge Walk

Dean Gate

Hare Edge

Shackleton Moor

5

Hoar Nib

Delf Brink

Rowshaw Clough

Lower Edge

Higher Edge

Navvy Head

32

Jack Allotment

Knoll Flat

BABY HOUSE HILL LA

Hardibut Clough

4

New Laithe Moor

New Laithes Farm

New Cote

Horodiddle

Rowshaw

Shackleton Knoll

3

Black Dean

Over Wood

Walshaw

WALSHAW LA

KILN LA

COW HEY LA

Stony Edge

Nook

COPPY LA

Coppy

SUNNY BANK RD

Hebden Dale

Dole

31

Widdop Gate

Hebden Water

High Laithe

Black Hill

Abel Cross

Laithe

Charles Rough

2

Ferny Beds

Coppy

High Greenwood Farm

High Greenwood House

Walshaw Wood

Lady Royd Edge

Kid Stones

Hamlet

Turn Hill

Haworth to Hebden Bridge Walk

Crimsworth Dean Beck

Crimsworth Dean

SMALL SHAW LA

Hoar Royd

1

White Mires

Pisser Clough

Mould Grain

Hardcastle Crags

Lady Royd Farm

Lady Royd

Abel Cote

Abel Cote Wood

Bridge Clough

Clough Head Hill

Boothroyd Farm

30

96	A	B	97	C	D	98	E	F

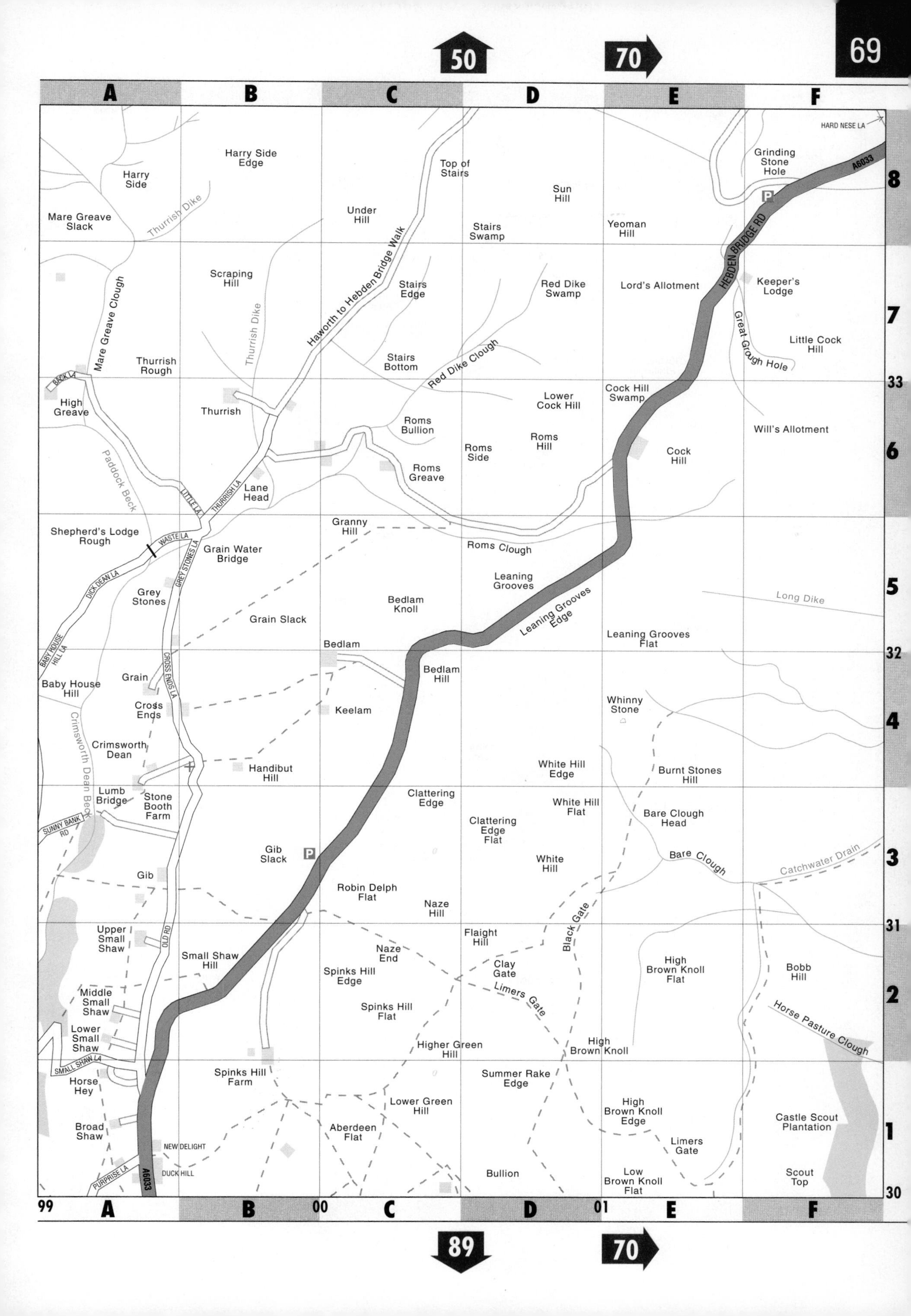
50
70
A B C D E F
8 7 33 6 5 32 4 3 31 2 1 30
99 00 01
HARD NESE LA
A6033
Grinding Stone Hole
Harry Side Edge
Harry Side
Top of Stairs
Sun Hill
Mare Greave Slack
Thurrish Dike
Under Hill
Stairs Swamp
Yeoman Hill
HEBDEN BRIDGE RD
Scraping Hill
Haworth to Hebden Bridge Walk
Stairs Edge
Red Dike Swamp
Lord's Allotment
Keeper's Lodge
Mare Greave Clough
Great Grough Hole
Little Cock Hill
Thurrish Rough
Stairs Bottom
Red Dike Clough
BACK LA
High Greave
Thurrish
Lower Cock Hill
Cock Hill Swamp
Roms Bullion
Will's Allotment
Roms Hill
Roms Side
Cock Hill
Paddock Beck
Roms Greave
Lane Head
LITTLE LA
THURRISH LA
Shepherd's Lodge Rough
Granny Hill
WASTE LA
Grain Water Bridge
Roms Clough
DICK DEAN LA
GREY STONES LA
Leaning Grooves
Grey Stones
Bedlam Knoll
Long Dike
Grain Slack
Leaning Grooves Edge
Leaning Grooves Flat
BABY HOUSE HILL LA
Bedlam
CROSS ENDS LA
Grain
Bedlam Hill
Baby House Hill
Whinny Stone
Cross Ends
Keelam
Crimsworth Dean Beck
Crimsworth Dean
White Hill Edge
Burnt Stones Hill
Handibut Hill
Lumb Bridge
Stone Booth Farm
Clattering Edge
White Hill Flat
Bare Clough Head
SUNNY BANK RD
Clattering Edge Flat
Gib Slack
White Hill
Bare Clough
Catchwater Drain
Gib
Robin Delph Flat
Naze Hill
Upper Small Shaw
OLD RD
Flaight Hill
Black Gate
Small Shaw Hill
Naze End
Clay Gate
High Brown Knoll Flat
Bobb Hill
Spinks Hill Edge
Limers Gate
Middle Small Shaw
Spinks Hill Flat
Horse Pasture Clough
Lower Small Shaw
Higher Green Hill
High Brown Knoll
SMALL SHAW LA
Horse Hey
Spinks Hill Farm
Summer Rake Edge
Lower Green Hill
High Brown Knoll Edge
Castle Scout Plantation
Broad Shaw
Aberdeen Flat
Limers Gate
NEW DELIGHT
PURPRISE LA
DUCK HILL
Bullion
Low Brown Knoll Flat
Scout Top
89
70

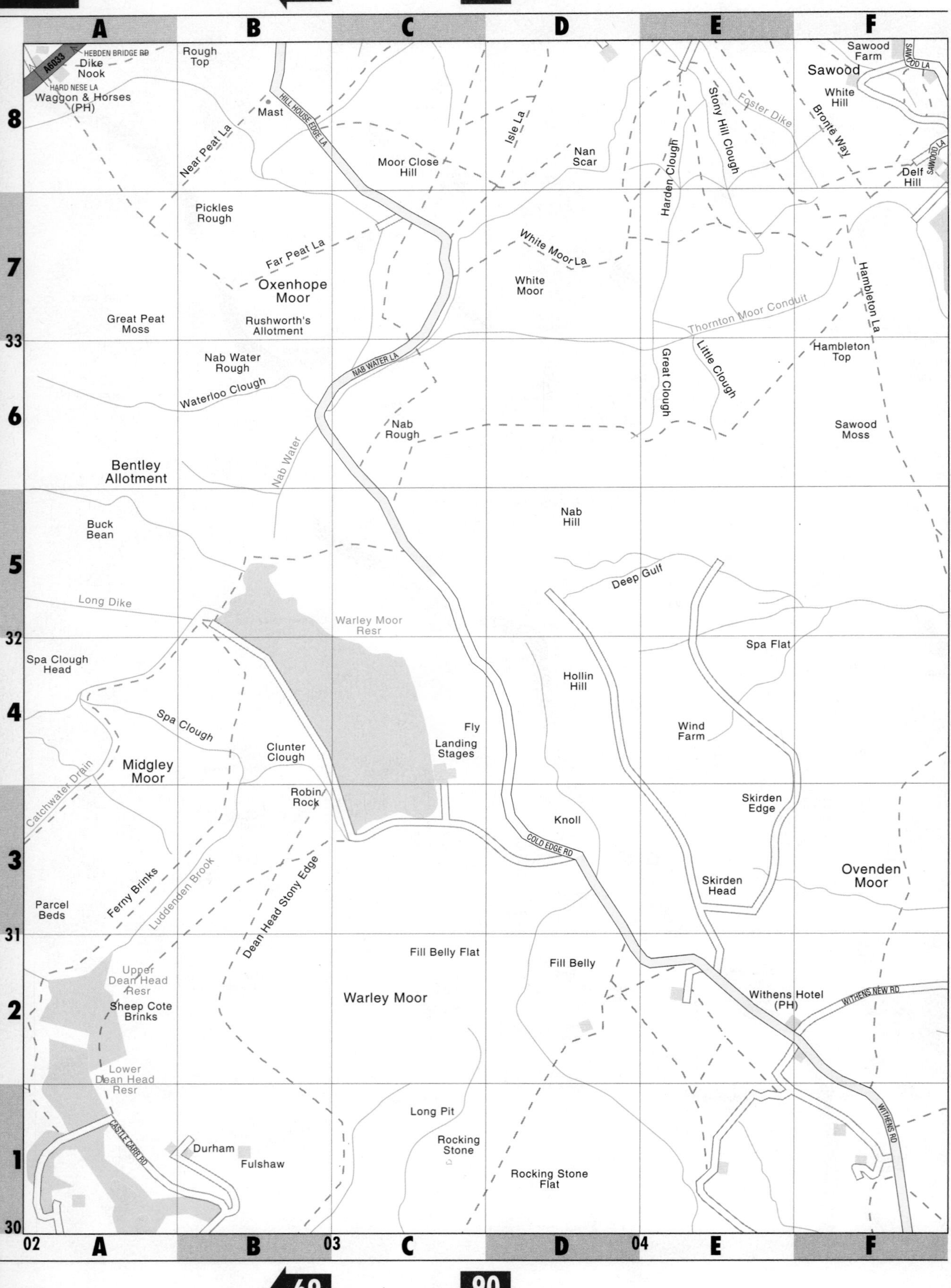

A6033

HEBDEN BRIDGE BB

Dike Nook

HARD NESE LA

Waggon & Horses (PH)

Rough Top

Near Peat La

Mast

HILL HOUSE EDGE LA

Sawood Farm

SAWOOD LA

Sawood

White Hill

Bronte Way

Stony Hill Clough

Foster Dike

SAWOOD LA

Delf Hill

Moor Close Hill

Isle La

Nan Scar

Harden Clough

Pickles Rough

Far Peat La

Oxenhope Moor

White Moor La

White Moor

Hambleton La

Great Peat Moss

Rushworth's Allotment

Thornton Moor Conduit

Hambleton Top

Nab Water Rough

NAB WATER LA

Little Clough

Hambleton Top

Waterloo Clough

Nab Rough

Great Clough

Sawood Moss

Nab Water

Bentley Allotment

Buck Bean

Nab Hill

Long Dike

Deep Gulf

Spa Flat

Warley Moor Resr

Spa Clough Head

Hollin Hill

Spa Clough

Fly Landing Stages

Wind Farm

Midgley Moor

Clunter Clough

Skirden Edge

Catchwater Drain

Robin Rock

Knoll

COLD EDGE RD

Skirden Head

Ovenden Moor

Parcel Beds

Ferny Brinks

Luddenden Brook

Dean Head Stony Edge

Fill Belly Flat

Fill Belly

Withens Hotel (PH)

WITHENS NEW RD

Upper Dean Head Resr

Warley Moor

Sheep Cote Brinks

Lower Dean Head Resr

CASTLE CARR RD

Durham

Fulshaw

Long Pit

Rocking Stone

Rocking Stone Flat

WITHENS RD

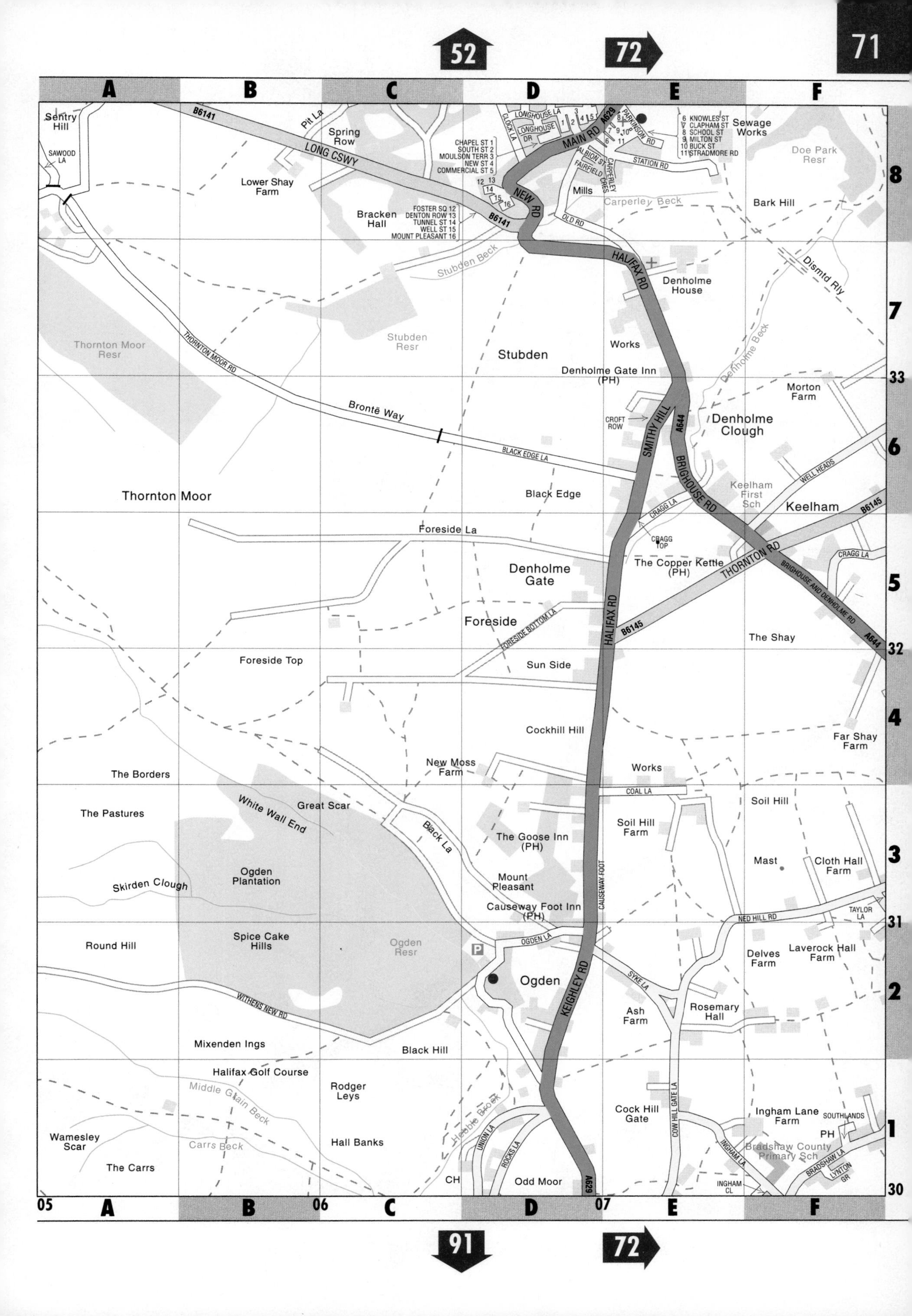
52
72
A
B
C
D
E
F
Sentry Hill
SAWOOD LA
Pit La
Spring Row
LONG CSWY
B6141
Lower Shay Farm
Bracken Hall
CHAPEL ST 1
SOUTH ST 2
MOULSON TERR 3
NEW ST 4
COMMERCIAL ST 5
FOSTER SQ 12
DENTON ROW 13
TUNNEL ST 14
WELL ST 15
MOUNT PLEASANT 16
LONGHOUSE LA
CLOCK LA
LONGHOUSE DR
MAIN RD
A629
PARKINSON RD
NEW RD
6 KNOWLES ST
7 CLAPHAM ST
8 SCHOOL ST
9 MILTON ST
10 BUCK ST
11 STRADMORE RD
Sewage Works
STATION RD
ALBION ST
FAIRFIELD CRES
CARPERLEY CRES
Mills
Carperley Beck
Doe Park Resr
Bark Hill
OLD RD
Stubden Beck
HALIFAX RD
Denholme House
Dismtd Rly
Thornton Moor Resr
THORNTON MOOR RD
Stubden Resr
Stubden
Works
Denholme Gate Inn (PH)
Denholme Beck
Morton Farm
Brontë Way
CROFT ROW
SMITHY HILL
A644
Denholme Clough
BLACK EDGE LA
BRIGHOUSE RD
WELL HEADS
Thornton Moor
Black Edge
Keelham First Sch
Keelham
B6145
CRAGG LA
Foreside La
CRAGG TOP
Denholme Gate
The Copper Kettle (PH)
THORNTON RD
BRIGHOUSE AND DENHOLME RD
Foreside
FORESIDE BOTTOM LA
B6145
The Shay
Foreside Top
Sun Side
Cockhill Hill
Far Shay Farm
New Moss Farm
Works
The Borders
COAL LA
Great Scar
White Wall End
Soil Hill
The Pastures
Black La
Soil Hill Farm
The Goose Inn (PH)
Mast
Cloth Hall Farm
Ogden Plantation
Skirden Clough
Mount Pleasant
CAUSEWAY FOOT
Causeway Foot Inn (PH)
TAYLOR LA
NED HILL RD
Round Hill
Spice Cake Hills
Ogden Resr
OGDEN LA
P
Delves Farm
Laverock Hall Farm
Ogden
SYKE LA
KEIGHLEY RD
WITHENS NEW RD
Ash Farm
Rosemary Hall
Mixenden Ings
Black Hill
Halifax Golf Course
Middle Grain Beck
Rodger Leys
Hebble Brook
Cock Hill Gate
COW HILL GATE LA
Ingham Lane Farm
SOUTHLANDS
PH
Wamesley Scar
Carrs Beck
Hall Banks
UNION LA
ROCKS LA
INGHAM LA
Bradshaw County Primary Sch
BRADSHAW LA
LYNTON GR
The Carrs
CH
Odd Moor
INGHAM CL
8
7
33
6
5
32
4
3
31
2
1
30
05
06
07
91
72

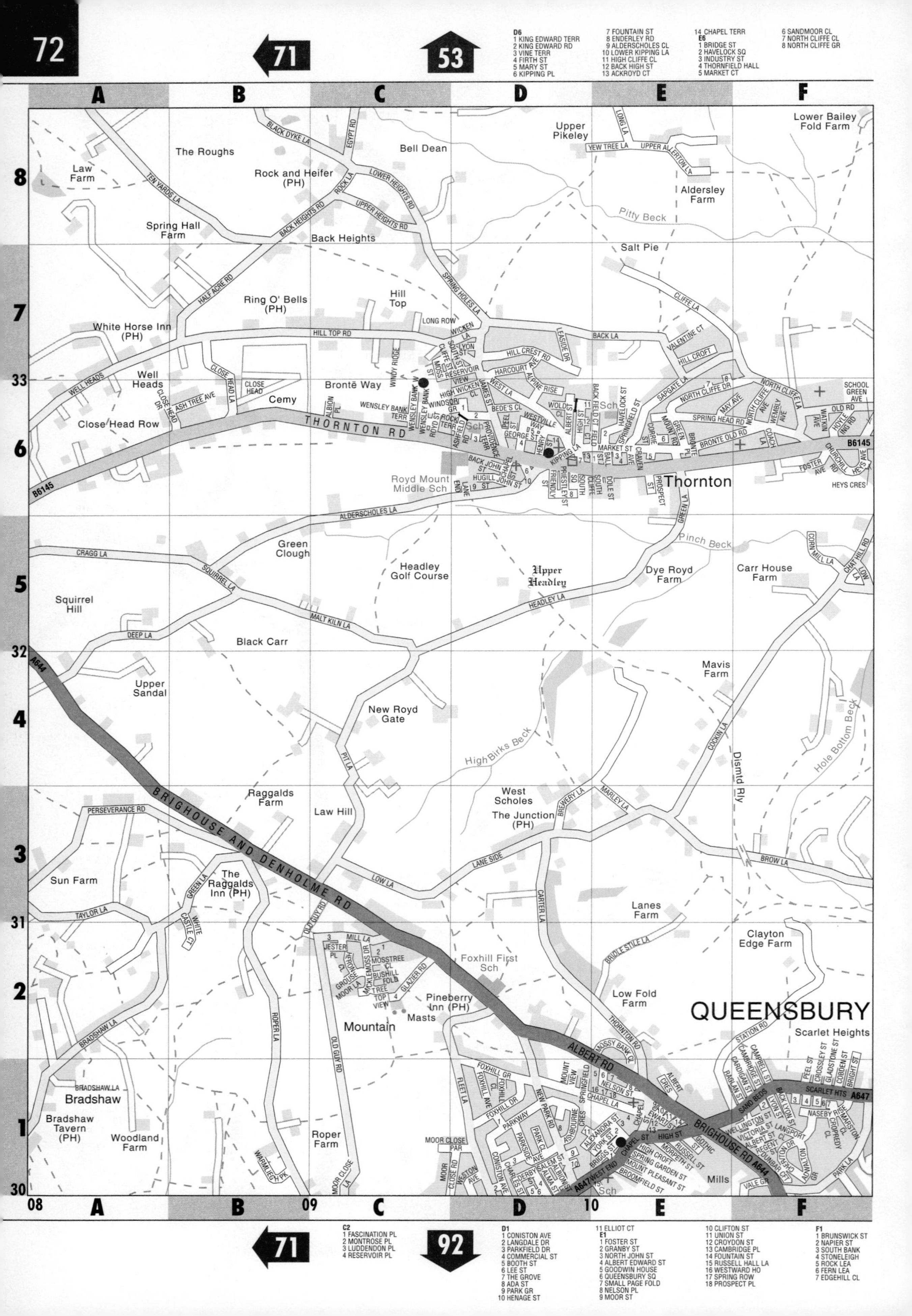

← 71

↑ 53

D6
1 KING EDWARD TERR
2 KING EDWARD RD
3 VINE TERR
4 FIRTH ST
5 MARY ST
6 KIPPING PL

7 FOUNTAIN ST
8 ENDERLEY RD
9 ALDERSCHOLES CL
10 LOWER KIPPING LA
11 HIGH CLIFFE CL
12 BACK HIGH ST
13 ACKROYD CT

14 CHAPEL TERR
E6
1 BRIDGE ST
2 HAVELOCK SQ
3 INDUSTRY ST
4 THORNFIELD HALL
5 MARKET CT

6 SANDMOOR CL
7 NORTH CLIFFE CL
8 NORTH CLIFFE GR

Law Farm

The Roughs

Bell Dean

Upper Pikeley

Lower Bailey Fold Farm

Rock and Heifer (PH)

Spring Hall Farm

Back Heights

Salt Pie

Aldersley Farm

Pitty Beck

White Horse Inn (PH)

Ring O' Bells (PH)

Hill Top

Close Head Row

Well Heads

Cemy

Brontë Way

THORNTON RD

Thornton

Royd Mount Middle Sch

Cragg La

Green Clough

Headley Golf Course

Upper Headley

Pinch Beck

Dye Royd Farm

Carr House Farm

Squirrel Hill

Black Carr

Upper Sandal

New Royd Gate

High Birks Beck

Mavis Farm

Hole Bottom Beck

Raggalds Farm

Law Hill

West Scholes

The Junction (PH)

Dismid Rly

Sun Farm

BRIGHOUSE AND DENHOLME RD

Lanes Farm

Clayton Edge Farm

The Raggalds Inn (PH)

Pineberry Inn (PH)

Mountain

Masts

Foxhill First Sch

Low Fold Farm

QUEENSBURY

Scarlet Heights

Bradshaw

Bradshaw Tavern (PH)

Woodland Farm

Roper Farm

ALBERT RD

Mills

BRIGHOUSE RD A644

SCARLET HTS A647

← 71

↓ 92

C2
1 FASCINATION PL
2 MONTROSE PL
3 LUDDENDON PL
4 RESERVOIR PL

D1
1 CONISTON AVE
2 LANGDALE DR
3 PARKFIELD DR
4 COMMERCIAL ST
5 BOOTH ST
6 LEE ST
7 THE GROVE
8 ADA ST
9 PARK GR
10 HENAGE ST

11 ELLIOT CT
E1
1 FOSTER ST
2 GRANBY ST
3 NORTH JOHN ST
4 ALBERT EDWARD ST
5 GOODWIN HOUSE
6 QUEENSBURY SQ
7 SMALL PAGE FOLD
8 NELSON PL
9 MOOR ST

10 CLIFTON ST
11 UNION ST
12 CROYDON ST
13 CAMBRIDGE PL
14 FOUNTAIN ST
15 RUSSELL HALL LA
16 WESTWARD HO
17 SPRING ROW
18 PROSPECT PL

F1
1 BRUNSWICK ST
2 NAPIER ST
3 SOUTH BANK
4 STONELEIGH
5 ROCK LEA
6 FERN LEA
7 EDGEHILL CL

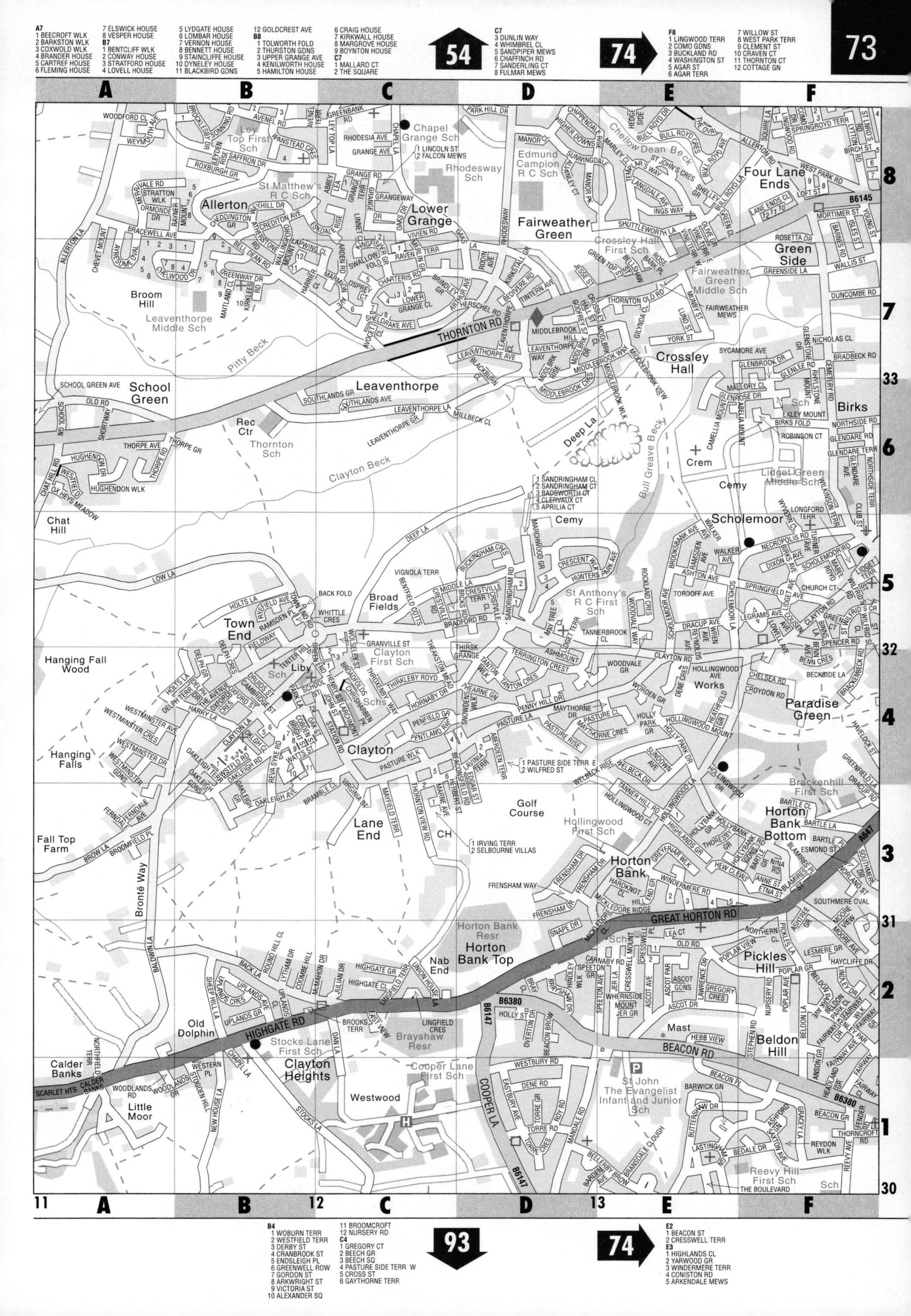

73
54
74
93
74
A7
1 BEECROFT WLK
2 BARKSTON WLK
3 COXWOLD WLK
4 BRANDER HOUSE
5 CARTREF HOUSE
6 FLEMING HOUSE
7 ELSWICK HOUSE
8 VESPER HOUSE
B7
1 BENTCLIFF WLK
2 CONWAY HOUSE
3 STRATFORD HOUSE
4 LOVELL HOUSE
5 LYDGATE HOUSE
6 LOMBAR HOUSE
7 VERNON HOUSE
8 BENNETT HOUSE
9 STAINCLIFFE HOUSE
10 DYNELEY HOUSE
11 BLACKBIRD GDNS
12 GOLDCREST AVE
B8
1 TOLWORTH FOLD
2 THURSTON GDNS
3 UPPER GRANGE AVE
4 KENILWORTH HOUSE
5 HAMILTON HOUSE
6 CRAIG HOUSE
7 KIRKWALL HOUSE
8 MARGROVE HOUSE
9 BOYNTON HOUSE
C7
1 MALLARD CT
2 THE SQUARE
C7
3 DUNLIN WAY
4 WHIMBREL CL
5 SANDPIPER MEWS
6 CHAFFINCH RD
7 SANDERLING CT
8 FULMAR MEWS
F8
1 LINGWOOD TERR
2 COMO GDNS
3 BUCKLAND RD
4 WASHINGTON ST
5 AGAR ST
6 AGAR TERR
7 WILLOW ST
8 WEST PARK TERR
9 CLEMENT ST
10 CRAVEN CT
11 THORNTON CT
12 COTTAGE GN
A B C D E F
8 7 33 6 5 32 4 3 31 2 1 30
11 12 13
Allerton
Ley Top First Sch
Chapel Grange Sch
St Matthew's R C Sch
Lower Grange
Edmund Campion R C Sch
Rhodesway Sch
Fairweather Green
Chellow Dean Beck
Four Lane Ends
Crossley Hall First Sch
Green Side
Fairweather Green Middle Sch
Broom Hill
Leaventhorpe Middle Sch
THORNTON RD
Pitty Beck
Crossley Hall
School Green
Leaventhorpe
Rec Ctr
Thornton Sch
Deep La
Clayton Beck
Bull Greave Beck
Crem
Birks
Lidget Green Middle Sch
Cemy
Chat Hill
Scholemoor
Broad Fields
St Anthony's R C First Sch
Town End
Hanging Fall Wood
Liby
Clayton First Sch
Works
Paradise Green
Hanging Falls
Clayton
Golf Course
Brackenhill First Sch
Horton Bank Bottom
Lane End
Hollingwood First Sch
Fall Top Farm
CH
Horton Bank
Brontë Way
GREAT HORTON RD
Horton Bank Resr
Horton Bank Top
Nab End
Pickles Hill
Old Dolphin
HIGHGATE RD
Brayshaw Resr
Mast
BEACON RD
Beldon Hill
Stocks Lane First Sch
Calder Banks
Clayton Heights
Cooper Lane First Sch
St John The Evangelist Infant and Junior Sch
Little Moor
Westwood
COOPER LA
Reevy Hill First Sch
B6145
A647
B6380
B6147
B4
1 WOBURN TERR
2 WESTFIELD TERR
3 DERBY ST
4 CRANBROOK ST
5 ENDSLEIGH PL
6 GREENWELL ROW
7 GORDON ST
8 ARKWRIGHT ST
9 VICTORIA ST
10 ALEXANDER SQ
11 BROOMCROFT
12 NURSERY RD
C4
1 GREGORY CT
2 BEECH GR
3 BEECH SQ
4 PASTURE SIDE TERR W
5 CROSS ST
6 GAYTHORNE TERR
E2
1 BEACON ST
2 CRESSWELL TERR
E3
1 HIGHLANDS CL
2 YARWOOD GR
3 WINDERMERE TERR
4 CONISTON RD
5 ARKENDALE MEWS

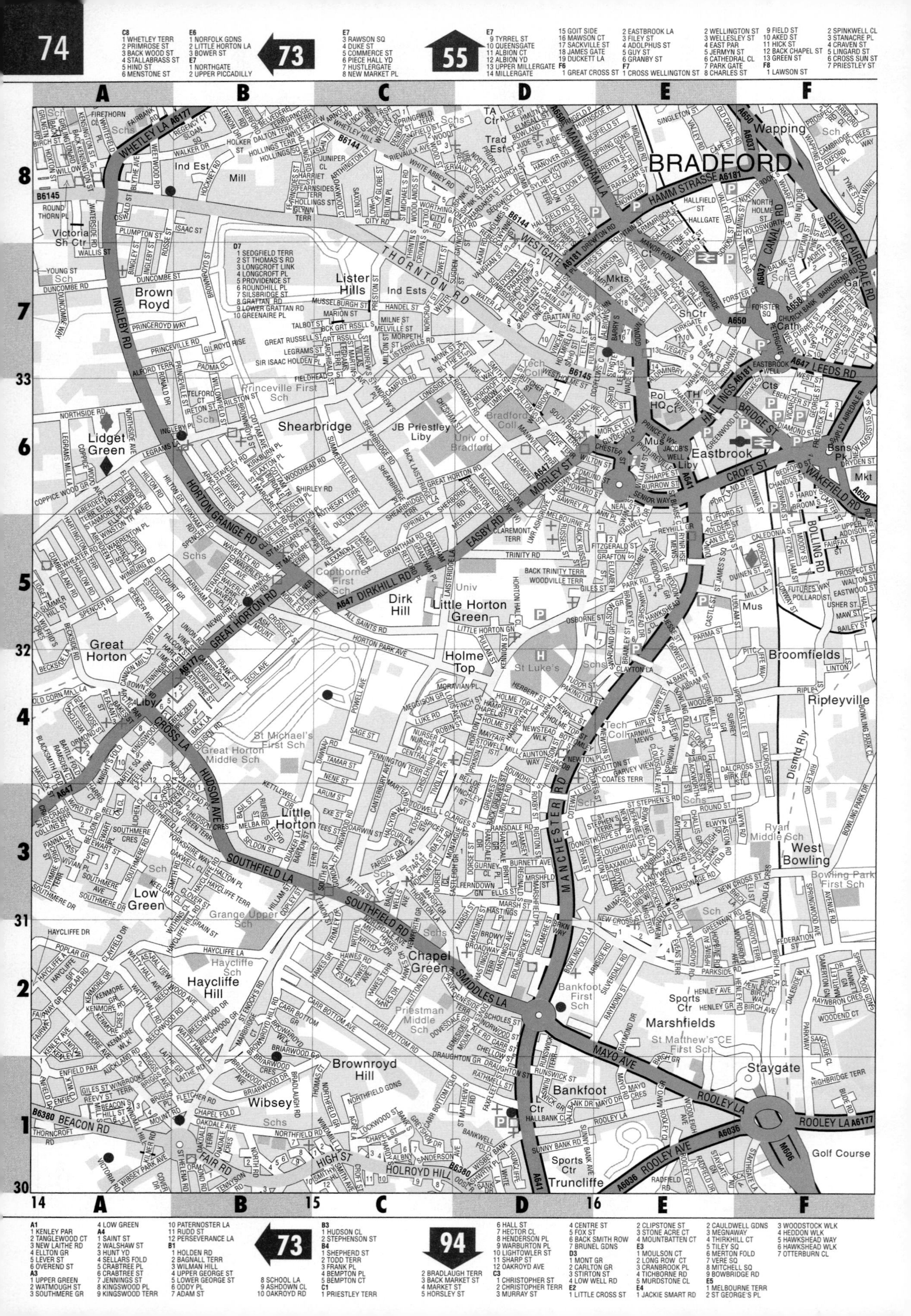
C8
1 WHETLEY TERR
2 PRIMROSE ST
3 BACK WOOD ST
4 STALLABRASS ST
5 HIND ST
6 MENSTONE ST
E6
1 NORFOLK GDNS
2 LITTLE HORTON LA
3 BOWER ST
E7
1 NORTHGATE
2 UPPER PICCADILLY
73
E7
3 RAWSON SQ
4 DUKE ST
5 COMMERCE ST
6 PIECE HALL YD
7 HUSTLERGATE
8 NEW MARKET PL
55
E7
9 TYRREL ST
10 QUEENSGATE
11 ALBION CT
12 ALBION YD
13 UPPER MILLERGATE
14 MILLERGATE
15 GOIT SIDE
16 MAWSON CT
17 SACKVILLE ST
18 JAMES GATE
19 DUCKETT LA
F6
1 GREAT CROSS ST
2 EASTBROOK LA
3 FILEY ST
4 ADOLPHUS ST
5 GUY ST
6 GRANBY ST
F7
1 CROSS WELLINGTON ST
2 WELLINGTON ST
3 WELLESLEY ST
4 EAST PAR
5 JERMYN ST
6 CATHEDRAL CL
7 PARK GATE
8 CHARLES ST
9 FIELD ST
10 AKED ST
11 HICK ST
12 BACK CHAPEL ST
13 GREEN ST
F8
1 LAWSON ST
2 SPINKWELL CL
3 STANACRE PL
4 CRAVEN ST
5 LINGARD ST
6 CROSS SUN ST
7 PRIESTLEY ST
A B C D E F
8 7 33 6 5 32 4 3 31 2 1 30
14 15 16
BRADFORD
Wapping
Ind Est
Mill
Victoria Sh Ctr
Brown Royd
Lister Hills
Ind Ests
THORNTON RD
D7
1 SEDGFIELD TERR
2 ST THOMAS'S RD
3 LONGCROFT LINK
4 LONGCROFT PL
5 PROVIDENCE ST
6 ROUNDHILL PL
7 SILSBRIDGE ST
8 GRATTAN RD
9 LOWER GRATTAN RD
10 GREENAIRE PL
Trad Est
TA Ctr
MANNINGHAM LA
HAMM STRASSE
WESTGATE
Mkts
ShCtr
Cath
LEEDS RD
Princeville First Sch
Shearbridge
JB Priestley Liby
Univ of Bradford
Bradford Coll
Tech Coll
Pol HQ
TH
Ct
Cts
Mus
Eastbrook
Bsns Pk
Mkt
Lidget Green
INGLEBY RD
HORTON GRANGE RD
GREAT HORTON RD
MORLEY ST
EASBY RD
DIRKHILL RD
Copthorne First Sch
Dirk Hill
Univ
Little Horton Green
Great Horton
Holme Top
St Luke's
Broomfields
Ripleyville
WAKEFIELD RD
BOLLING RD
St Michael's First Sch
Great Horton Middle Sch
Little Horton
HUDSON AVE
SOUTHFIELD LA
SOUTHFIELD RD
MANCHESTER RD
Low Green
Grange Upper Sch
Ryan Middle Sch
West Bowling
Bowling Park First Sch
Dismtd Rly
Haycliffe Sch
Haycliffe Hill
Chapel Green
SMIDDLES LA
Bankfoot First Sch
Sports Ctr
Marshfields
St Matthew's CE First Sch
Priestman Middle Sch
Brownroyd Hill
Wibsey
Staygate
MAYO AVE
ROOLEY LA
Bankfoot
BEACON RD
Schs
HIGH ST
HOLROYD HILL
Ctr
Truncliffe
ROOLEY AVE
Golf Course
14 A B 15 C D 16 E F
A1
1 KENLEY PAR
2 TANGLEWOOD CT
3 NEW LAITHE RD
4 ELLTON GR
5 LEVER ST
6 OVEREND ST
A3
1 UPPER GREEN
2 WATMOUGH ST
3 SOUTHMERE GR
4 LOW GREEN
A4
1 SAINT ST
2 WALSHAW ST
3 HUNT YD
4 SELLARS FOLD
5 CRABTREE PL
6 CRABTREE ST
7 JENNINGS ST
8 KINGSWOOD PL
9 KINGSWOOD TERR
10 PATERNOSTER LA
11 RUDD ST
12 PERSEVERANCE LA
B1
1 HOLDEN RD
2 BAGNALL TERR
3 WILMAN HILL
4 UPPER GEORGE ST
5 LOWER GEORGE ST
6 ODDY PL
7 ADAM ST
73
8 SCHOOL LA
9 ASHDOWN CL
10 OAKROYD RD
B3
1 HUDSON CL
2 STEPHENSON ST
B4
1 SHEPHERD ST
2 TODD TERR
3 FRANK PL
4 BEMPTON PL
5 BEMPTON CT
C1
1 PRIESTLEY TERR
94
2 BRADLAUGH TERR
3 BACK MARKET ST
4 MARKET ST
5 HORSLEY ST
6 HALL ST
7 HECTOR CL
8 HENDERSON PL
9 WARBURTON PL
10 LIGHTOWLER ST
11 SHARP ST
12 OAKROYD AVE
C3
1 CHRISTOPHER ST
2 CHRISTOPHER TERR
3 MURRAY ST
4 CENTRE ST
5 FOX ST
6 BACK SMITH ROW
7 BRUNEL GDNS
D3
1 MONT GR
2 CARLTON GR
3 STIRTON ST
4 LOW WELL RD
E2
1 LITTLE CROSS ST
2 CLIPSTONE ST
3 STONE ACRE CT
4 MOUNTBATTEN CT
E3
1 MOULSON CT
2 LONG ROW CT
3 CRANBROOK PL
4 TICHBORNE RD
5 MURDSTONE CL
E4
1 JACKIE SMART RD
2 CAULDWELL GDNS
3 MEGNAWAY
4 THIRKHILL CT
5 TILEY SQ
6 MERTON FOLD
7 VERE SQ
8 MITCHELL SQ
9 BOWBRIDGE RD
E5
1 MELBOURNE TERR
2 ST GEORGE'S PL
3 WOODSTOCK WLK
4 HEDDON WLK
5 HAWKSHEAD WAY
6 HAWKSHEAD WLK
7 OTTERBURN CL

56
76

A
B
C
D
E
F
8
7
6
5
4
3
2
1
33
32
31
30
17
18
19
Carlton-Bolling Sch
Bradford Moor Golf Course
Bradford Moor First Sch
Lapage Middle Sch
Windmill Hill
Works
Thornbury
Phoenix Park Sports Grounds
Leeds Country Way
Barkerend
Bradford Moor
Golf Course
Leeds Road
Laisterdyke
Mills
St James's Mkt
Essex Pk Ind Est
Gasholder Station
Birksland Ind Est
Bowling Court Ind Est
Swain Green
Tyersal First Sch
Pudsey Tyersal Primary Sch
Mast
Cityway Ind Est
Dismtd Rly
Tyersal
Tyersal Gate
Bowling
Cutler Heights
Holme Bank Farm
Holmefield First Sch
Lower Fields Middle Sch
Bolling Hall (Mus)
Fairfax Community Sch
Lindley House Sch
Bowling Park
Dudley Hill
Holme Wood
Holme
East Bowling
St Columba's RC First Sch
Goose Hill
Cemy
Tong Street
Bierley
St Blaise RC Secondary Sch
West Bowling Golf Course
Broomwood Middle Sch
West Yorkshire Ind Est
Works
LEEDS RD
LEEDS OLD RD
BARKEREND RD
NEW OTLEY RD
OTLEY RD
KILLINGHALL RD
LAISTERDYKE
STICKER LA
WAKEFIELD RD
TONG ST
ROOLEY LA
BOWLING BACK LA
GIPSY ST
DICK LA
A658
A650
A6177
A647
B6381

95
76

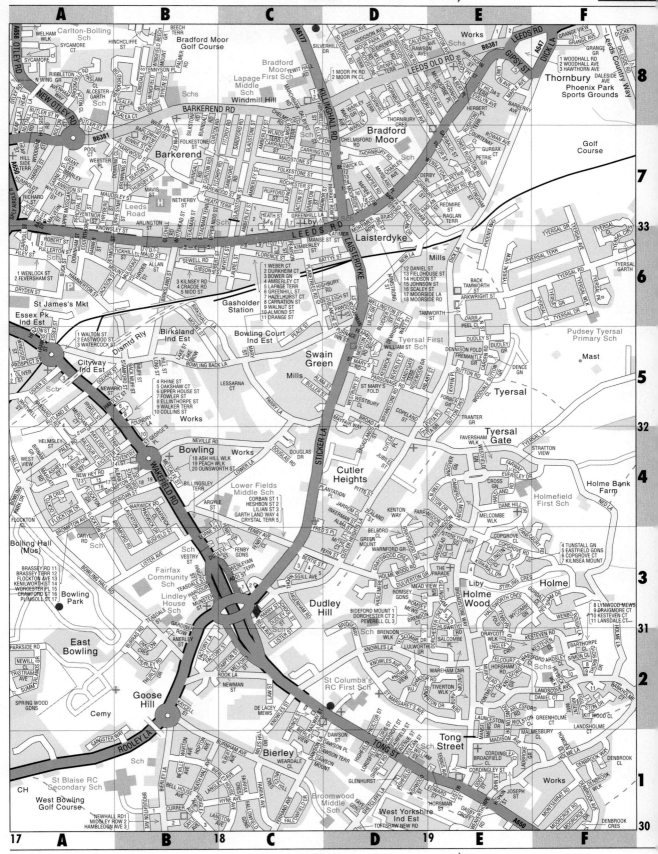

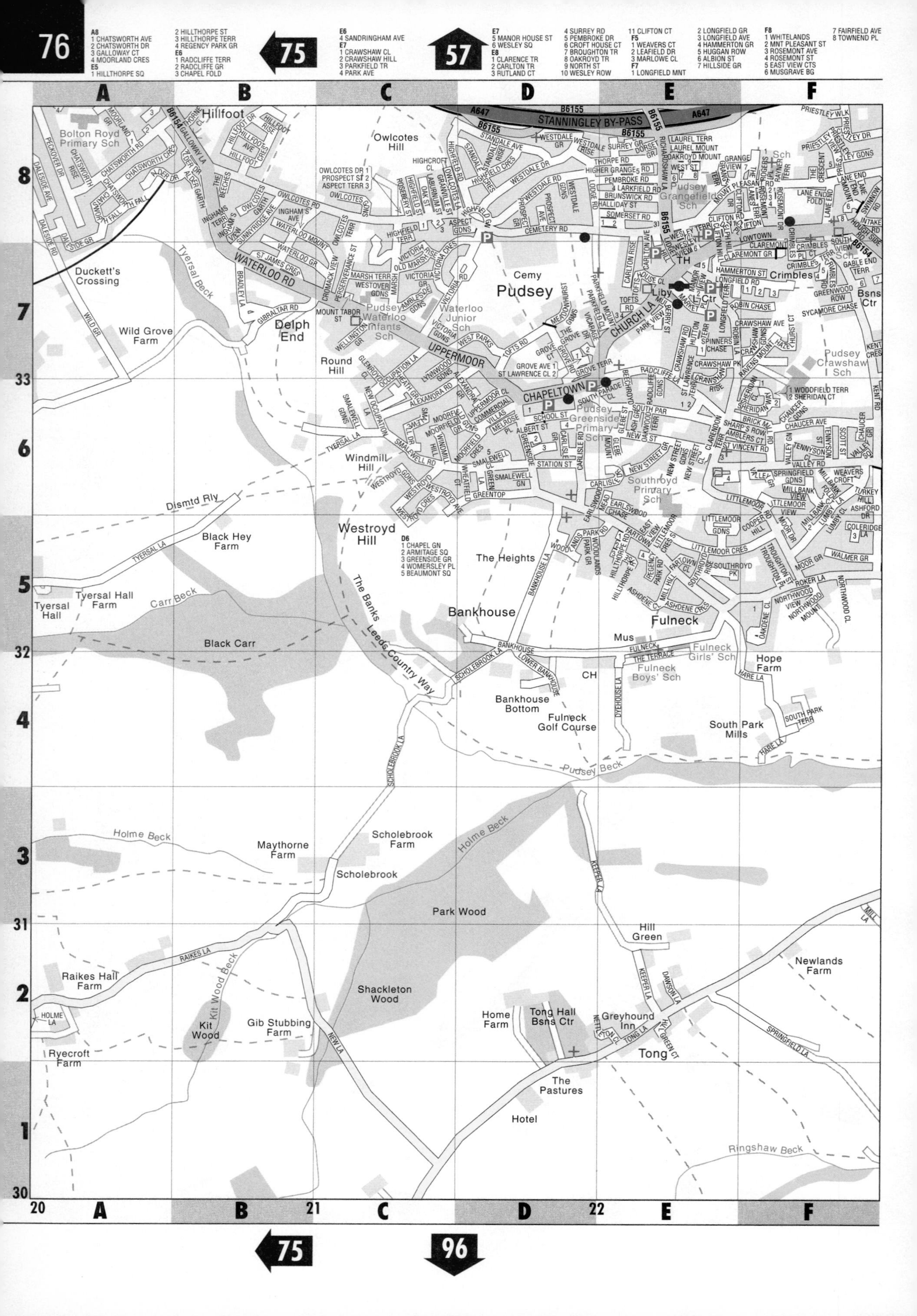
76
A8
1 CHATSWORTH AVE
2 CHATSWORTH DR
3 GALLOWAY CT
4 MOORLAND CRES
E5
1 HILLTHORPE SQ
2 HILLTHORPE ST
3 HILLTHORPE TERR
4 REGENCY PARK GR
E6
1 RADCLIFFE TERR
2 RADCLIFFE GR
3 CHAPEL FOLD
75
E6
4 SANDRINGHAM AVE
E7
1 CRAWSHAW CL
2 CRAWSHAW HILL
3 PARKFIELD TR
4 PARK AVE
57
E7
5 MANOR HOUSE ST
6 WESLEY SQ
E8
1 CLARENCE TR
2 CARLTON TR
3 RUTLAND CT
4 SURREY RD
5 PEMBROKE DR
6 CROFT HOUSE CT
7 BROUGHTON TR
8 OAKROYD TR
9 NORTH ST
10 WESLEY ROW
11 CLIFTON CT
F5
1 WEAVERS CT
2 LEAFIELD DR
3 MARLOWE CL
F7
1 LONGFIELD MNT
2 LONGFIELD GR
3 LONGFIELD AVE
4 HAMMERTON GR
5 HUGGAN ROW
6 ALBION ST
7 HILLSIDE GR
F8
1 WHITELANDS
2 MNT PLEASANT ST
3 ROSEMONT AVE
4 ROSEMONT ST
5 EAST VIEW CTS
6 MUSGRAVE BG
7 FAIRFIELD AVE
8 TOWNEND PL
A
B
C
D
E
F
8
7
33
6
5
32
4
3
31
2
1
30
20
21
22
Hillfoot
Bolton Royd Primary Sch
Owlcotes Hill
STANNINGLEY BY-PASS
A647
B6155
B6154
Duckett's Crossing
Tyersal Beck
WATERLOO RD
Wild Grove Farm
Delph End
Pudsey Waterloo Infants Sch
Waterloo Junior Sch
Cemy
Pudsey
UPPERMOOR
CHURCH LA
Round Hill
Pudsey Grangefield Sch
TH
Liby
L Ctr
Crimbles
Bsns Ctr
Pudsey Crawshaw Sch
CHAPELTOWN
Pudsey Greenside Primary Sch
Southroyd Primary Sch
Windmill Hill
Dismtd Rly
Westroyd Hill
D6
1 CHAPEL GN
2 ARMITAGE SQ
3 GREENSIDE GR
4 WOMERSLEY PL
5 BEAUMONT SQ
Black Hey Farm
The Heights
Tyersal Hall
Tyersal Hall Farm
Carr Beck
Black Carr
The Banks
Leeds Country Way
Bankhouse
Fulneck
Mus
Fulneck Girls' Sch
Fulneck Boys' Sch
Hope Farm
CH
Bankhouse Bottom
Fulneck Golf Course
South Park Mills
Pudsey Beck
Holme Beck
Maythorne Farm
Scholebrook Farm
Scholebrook
Park Wood
Hill Green
Raikes Hall Farm
RAIKES LA
Kit Wood Beck
Kit Wood
Shackleton Wood
Gib Stubbing Farm
Newlands Farm
Home Farm
Tong Hall Bsns Ctr
Greyhound Inn
Tong
Ryecroft Farm
The Pastures
Hotel
Ringshaw Beck
KEEPER LA
NEW LA
SPRINGFIELD LA
SCHOLEBROOK LA
TYERSAL LA
75
96

58
78

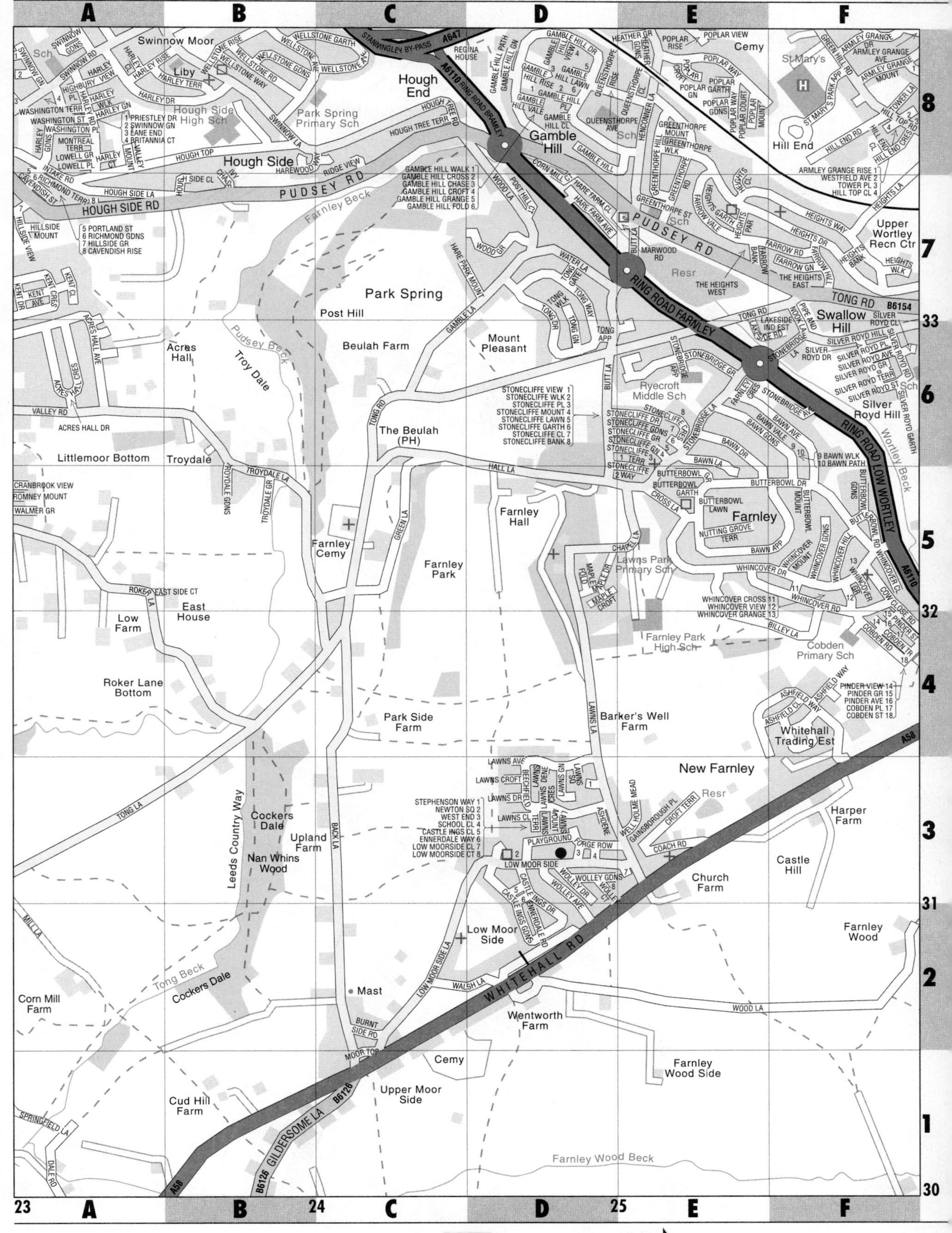
A
B
C
D
E
F
8
7
33
6
5
32
4
3
31
2
1
30
23
24
25
Swinnow Moor
Sch
SWINNOW GDNS
SWINNOW GN
SWINNOW RD
HIGHBURY VIEW
HARLEY PL
HARLEY RD
HARLEY WLK
HARLEY GN
WASHINGTON TERR
WASHINGTON ST
WASHINGTON PL
1 PRIESTLEY DR
2 SWINNOW GN
3 LANE END
4 BRITANNIA CT
MONTREAL TERR
LOWELL GR
LOWELL PL
HARLEY CT
VALLEY MOUNT
INTAKE RD
RICHMOND TERR
CAVENDISH ST
HOUGH SIDE RD
HILLSIDE VIEW
HILLSIDE MOUNT
5 PORTLAND ST
6 RICHMOND GDNS
7 HILLSIDE GR
8 CAVENDISH RISE
Liby
HARLEY CL
HARLEY RISE
HARLEY TERR
HARLEY DR
WELLSTONE RISE
WELLSTONE GARTH
WELLSTONE RD
WELLSTONE GDNS
WELLSTONE AVE
WELLSTONE WAY
Hough Side High Sch
Park Spring Primary Sch
SWINNOW LA
HOUGH TOP
Hough Side
HAREWOOD WAY
RIDGE VIEW
IVY CHASE
H SIDE CL
HOUGH SIDE LA
PUDSEY RD
Farnley Beck
STANNINGLEY BY-PASS
A647
A6110 RING ROAD BRAMLEY
REGINA HOUSE
Hough End
HOUGH TREE RD
HOUGH TREE TERR
GAMBLE HILL PATH
GAMBLE HILL GN
GAMBLE HILL DR
GAMBLE HILL VIEW
GAMBLE HILL RISE
GAMBLE HILL LAWN
GAMBLE HILL PL
GAMBLE HILL VALE
GAMBLE HILL CT
Gamble Hill
GAMBLE HILL
GAMBLE HILL WALK 1
GAMBLE HILL CROSS 2
GAMBLE HILL CHASE 3
GAMBLE HILL CROFT 4
GAMBLE HILL GRANGE 5
GAMBLE HILL FOLD 6
WOOD LA
POST HILL CT
CORN MILL
HARE FARM CL
HARE FARM AVE
WOOD GR
HARE PARK MOUNT
WATER LA
TONG GATE
TONG WAY
TONG WLK
TONG DR
TONG GN
TONG APP
Park Spring
Post Hill
GAMBLE LA
Mount Pleasant
Beulah Farm
Acres Hall
Pudsey Beck
Troy Dale
QUEENSTHORPE RISE
QUEENSTHORPE CL
QUEENSTHORPE AVE
HENCONNER LA
HEATHER GR
HEATHER GDNS
Sch
GREENTHORPE MOUNT
GREENTHORPE WLK
GREENTHORPE
GREENTHORPE HILL
GREENTHORPE RD
GREENTHORPE ST
Sch
BUTT LA
MARWOOD RD
PUDSEY RD
RING ROAD FARNLEY
Resr
THE HEIGHTS WEST
POPLAR VIEW
POPLAR RISE
Cemy
POPLAR CROFT
POPLAR WAY
POPLAR GN
POPLAR GDNS
POPLAR COURT
POPLAR MOUNT
HEIGHTS CL
HEIGHTS GARTH
FARROW VALE
HEIGHTS PAR
HEIGHTS BANK
FARROW BANK
FARROW RD
FARROW GN
FARROW HILL
HEIGHTS DR
HEIGHTS WAY
HEIGHTS LA
HEIGHTS WLK
THE HEIGHTS EAST
TONG RD
B6154
St Mary's
H
GREEN HILL RD
ARMLEY GRANGE DR
ARMLEY GRANGE AVE
ARMLEY GRANGE MOUNT
ST MARY'S PARK APP
TOWER LA
HILL TOP RD
HILL END RD
HILL END CL
HILL END CRES
Hill End
ARMLEY GRANGE RISE 1
WESTFIELD AVE 2
TOWER PL 3
HILL TOP CL 4
Upper Wortley Recn Ctr
Swallow Hill
LAKESIDE IND EST
PIPE AND NOOK LA
LAKESIDE RD
SILVER ROYD CL
SILVER ROYD HILL
SILVER ROYD DR
SILVER ROYD AVE
SILVER ROYD GR
SILVER ROYD TERR
SILVER ROYD ST
SILVER ROYD RD
SILVER ROYD GARTH
Sch
Silver Royd Hill
RING ROAD LOW WORTLEY
Wortley Beck
A6110
STONEBRIDGE APP
STONEBRIDGE GR
STONEBRIDGE LA
STONEBRIDGE AVE
Ryecroft Middle Sch
FARNLEY CRES
STONECLIFFE VIEW 1
STONECLIFFE WLK 2
STONECLIFFE PL 3
STONECLIFFE MOUNT 4
STONECLIFFE LAWN 5
STONECLIFFE GARTH 6
STONECLIFFE CL 7
STONECLIFFE BANK 8
STONECLIFFE DR
STONECLIFFE GDNS
STONECLIFFE CRES
STONECLIFFE GR
STONECLIFFE GN
STONECLIFFE TERR
STONECLIFFE WAY
BAWN AVE
BAWN VALE
BAWN GDNS
BAWN DR
BAWN LA
9 BAWN WLK
10 BAWN PATH
BUTTERBOWL GR
BUTTERBOWL GARTH
BUTTERBOWL LAWN
BUTTERBOWL DR
BUTTERBOWL MOUNT
BUTTERBOWL GDNS
BUTTERBOWL RD
CROSS LA
Farnley
NUTTING GROVE TERR
BAWN APP
VALLEY RD
ACRES HALL AVE
ACRES HALL CRES
ACRES HALL DR
KENT CRES
KENT CL
KENT AVE
KENT DR
Littlemoor Bottom
Troydale
TROYDALE GDNS
TROYDALE GR
TROYDALE LA
TONG RD
The Beulah (PH)
HALL LA
CRANBROOK VIEW
ROMNEY MOUNT
WALMER GR
Farnley Cemy
GREEN LA
Farnley Hall
Farnley Park
CHAPEL LA
Lawns Park Primary Sch
MAPLE FOLD
MAPLE DR
MAPLE CROFT
WHINCOVER DR
WHINCOVER MOUNT
WHINCOVER GDNS
WHINCOVER HILL
WHINCOVER GDNS
WHINCOVER CL
WHINCOVER RD
WHINCOVER CROSS 11
WHINCOVER VIEW 12
WHINCOVER GRANGE 13
BILLEY LA
COW CLOSE RD
COBDEN RD
COBDEN GR
COBDEN TERR
PINDER ST
Farnley Park High Sch
Cobden Primary Sch
ROKER LA
EAST SIDE CT
Low Farm
East House
Roker Lane Bottom
Park Side Farm
LAWNS LA
Barker's Well Farm
ASHFIELD WAY
ASHFIELD CL
PINDER VIEW 14
PINDER GR 15
PINDER AVE 16
COBDEN PL 17
COBDEN ST 18
Whitehall Trading Est
A58
New Farnley
Resr
TONG LA
Leeds Country Way
Cockers Dale
Nan Whins Wood
Upland Farm
BACK LA
LAWNS AVE
LAWNS CROFT
LAWNS DR
LAWNS CL
BEECHFIELD
LAWNS DENE
LAWNS GN
LAWNS SQ
LAWNS TERR
LAWNS MOUNT
STEPHENSON WAY 1
NEWTON SQ 2
WEST END 3
SCHOOL CL 4
CASTLE INGS CL 5
ENNERDALE WAY 6
LOW MOORSIDE CL 7
LOW MOORSIDE CT 8
PLAYGROUND
FORGE ROW
LOW MOOR SIDE
ASHDENE
WELL HOLME MEAD
GAINSBOROUGH PL
CROFT TERR
COACH RD
WOLLEY DR
WOLLEY AVE
WOLLEY GDNS
WOLLEY CT
CASTLE INGS DR
CASTLE INGS GDNS
ENNERDALE RD
Harper Farm
Castle Hill
Church Farm
Low Moor Side
LOW MOOR SIDE LA
WHITEHALL RD
WALSH LA
MILL LA
Farnley Wood
Tong Beck
Cockers Dale
Corn Mill Farm
Mast
BURNT SIDE RD
MOOR TOP
Wentworth Farm
WOOD LA
Cemy
Farnley Wood Side
Upper Moor Side
B6126
GILDERSOME LA
Cud Hill Farm
SPRINGFIELD LA
DALE RD
A58
Farnley Wood Beck

97
78

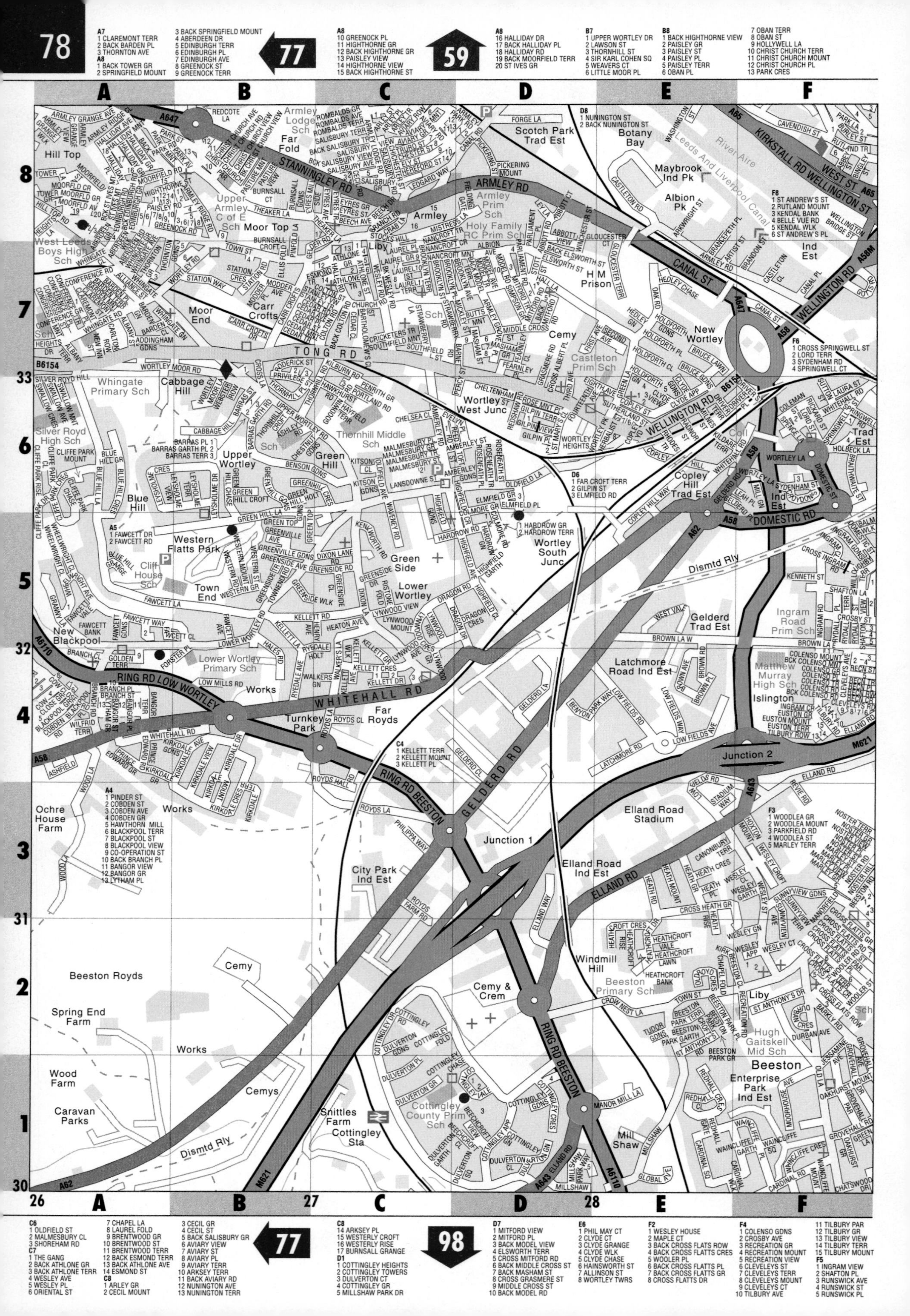
78
A7
1 CLAREMONT TERR
2 BACK BARDEN PL
3 THORNTON AVE
A8
1 BACK TOWER GR
2 SPRINGFIELD MOUNT
3 BACK SPRINGFIELD MOUNT
4 ABERDEEN DR
5 EDINBURGH TERR
6 EDINBURGH PL
7 EDINBURGH AVE
8 GREENOCK ST
9 GREENOCK TERR
77
A8
10 GREENOCK PL
11 HIGHTHORNE GR
12 BACK HIGHTHORNE GR
13 PAISLEY VIEW
14 HIGHTHORNE VIEW
15 BACK HIGHTHORNE ST
59
A8
16 HALLIDAY DR
17 BACK HALLIDAY PL
18 HALLIDAY RD
19 BACK MOORFIELD TERR
20 ST IVES GR
B7
1 UPPER WORTLEY DR
2 LAWSON ST
3 THORNHILL ST
4 SIR KARL COHEN SQ
5 WEAVERS CT
6 LITTLE MOOR PL
B8
1 BACK HIGHTHORNE VIEW
2 PAISLEY GR
3 PAISLEY ST
4 PAISLEY PL
5 PAISLEY TERR
6 OBAN PL
7 OBAN TERR
8 OBAN ST
9 HOLLYWELL LA
10 CHRIST CHURCH TERR
11 CHRIST CHURCH MOUNT
12 CHRIST CHURCH PL
13 PARK CRES
A B C D E F
8 7 33 6 5 32 4 3 31 2 1 30
Hill Top
West Leeds Boys High Sch
Armley Lodge Sch
Far Fold
Upper Armley C of E Sch
Moor Top
Armley
Armley Prim Sch
Holy Family RC Prim Sch
Scotch Park Trad Est
Botany Bay
Maybrook Ind Pk
Albion Pk
River Aire
Leeds And Liverpool Canal
Ind Est
H M Prison
New Wortley
Moor End
Carr Crofts
Cemy
Castleton Prim Sch
Whingate Primary Sch
Cabbage Hill
Silver Royd High Sch
Upper Wortley
Green Hill
Thornhill Middle Sch
Wortley West Junc
Copley Hill Trad Est
Trad Est
Blue Hill
Western Flatts Park
Cliff House Sch
Town End
Green Side
Lower Wortley
Wortley South Junc
Dismtd Rly
Ingram Road Prim Sch
New Blackpool
Lower Wortley Primary Sch
Gelderd Trad Est
Latchmore Road Ind Est
Matthew Murray High Sch
Islington
Works
Turnkey Park
Far Royds
Junction 2
Ochre House Farm
Elland Road Stadium
Junction 1
City Park Ind Est
Elland Road Ind Est
Beeston Royds
Cemy
Windmill Hill
Beeston Primary Sch
Cemy & Crem
Liby
Spring End Farm
Hugh Gaitskell Mid Sch
Beeston
Wood Farm
Enterprise Park Ind Est
Caravan Parks
Cemys
Snittles Farm
Cottingley Sta
Cottingley County Prim Sch
Mill Shaw
STANNINGLEY RD
ARMLEY RD
TONG RD
CANAL ST
KIRKSTALL RD
WELLINGTON RD
WELLINGTON ST
WEST ST
WHITEHALL RD
RING RD LOW WORTLEY
RING RD BEESTON
GELDERD RD
DOMESTIC RD
ELLAND RD
A647 A65 A58M A58 B6154 A6110 A62 A643 M621
D8
1 NUNINGTON ST
2 BACK NUNINGTON ST
F8
1 ST ANDREW'S ST
2 RUTLAND MOUNT
3 KENDAL BANK
4 BELLE VUE RD
5 KENDAL WLK
6 ST ANDREW'S PL
F6
1 CROSS SPRINGWELL ST
2 LORD TERR
3 SYDENHAM RD
4 SPRINGWELL CT
D6
1 FAR CROFT TERR
2 GILPIN ST
3 ELMFIELD RD
A5
1 FAWCETT DR
2 FAWCETT RD
C4
1 KELLETT TERR
2 KELLETT MOUNT
3 KELLETT PL
A4
1 PINDER ST
2 COBDEN ST
3 COBDEN AVE
4 COBDEN GR
5 HAWTHORN MILL
6 BLACKPOOL TERR
7 BLACKPOOL ST
8 BLACKPOOL VIEW
9 CO-OPERATION ST
10 BACK BRANCH PL
11 BANGOR VIEW
12 BANGOR GR
13 LYTHAM PL
F3
1 WOODLEA GR
2 WOODLEA MOUNT
3 PARKFIELD RD
4 WOODLEA ST
5 MARLEY TERR
26 A B 27 C D 28 E F
C6
1 OLDFIELD ST
2 MALMESBURY CL
3 SHOREHAM RD
C7
1 THE GANG
2 BACK ATHLONE GR
3 BACK ATHLONE TERR
4 WESLEY AVE
5 WESLEY PL
6 ORIENTAL ST
7 CHAPEL LA
8 LAUREL FOLD
9 BRENTWOOD GR
10 BRENTWOOD ST
11 BRENTWOOD TERR
12 BACK ESMOND TERR
13 BACK ATHLONE AVE
14 ESMOND ST
C8
1 ARLEY GR
2 CECIL MOUNT
3 CECIL GR
4 CECIL ST
5 BACK SALISBURY GR
6 AVIARY VIEW
7 AVIARY ST
8 AVIARY PL
9 AVIARY TERR
10 ARKSEY TERR
11 BACK AVIARY RD
12 NUNINGTON AVE
13 NUNINGTON TERR
77
C8
14 ARKSEY PL
15 WESTERLY CROFT
16 WESTERLY RISE
17 BURNSALL GRANGE
D1
1 COTTINGLEY HEIGHTS
2 COTTINGLEY TOWERS
3 DULVERTON CT
4 COTTINGLEY GR
5 MILLSHAW PARK DR
98
D7
1 MITFORD VIEW
2 MITFORD PL
3 BACK MODEL VIEW
4 ELSWORTH TERR
5 CROSS MITFORD RD
6 BACK MIDDLE CROSS ST
7 BACK MASHAM ST
8 CROSS GRASMERE ST
9 MIDDLE CROSS ST
10 BACK MODEL RD
E6
1 PHIL MAY CT
2 CLYDE CT
3 CLYDE GRANGE
4 CLYDE WLK
5 CLYDE CHASE
6 HAINSWORTH ST
7 ALLINSON ST
8 WORTLEY TWRS
F2
1 WESLEY HOUSE
2 MAPLE CT
3 BACK CROSS FLATS ROW
4 BACK CROSS FLATTS CRES
5 WOOLER PL
6 BACK CROSS FLATTS PL
7 BACK CROSS FLATTS GR
8 CROSS FLATTS DR
F4
1 COLENSO GDNS
2 CROSBY AVE
3 RECREATION GR
4 RECREATION MOUNT
5 RECREATION VIEW
6 CLEVELEYS ST
7 CLEVELEYS TERR
8 CLEVELEYS MOUNT
9 CLEVELEYS CT
10 TILBURY AVE
11 TILBURY PAR
12 TILBURY GR
13 TILBURY VIEW
14 TILBURY TERR
15 TILBURY MOUNT
F5
1 INGRAM VIEW
2 SHAFTON PL
3 RUNSWICK AVE
4 RUNSWICK ST
5 RUNSWICK PL

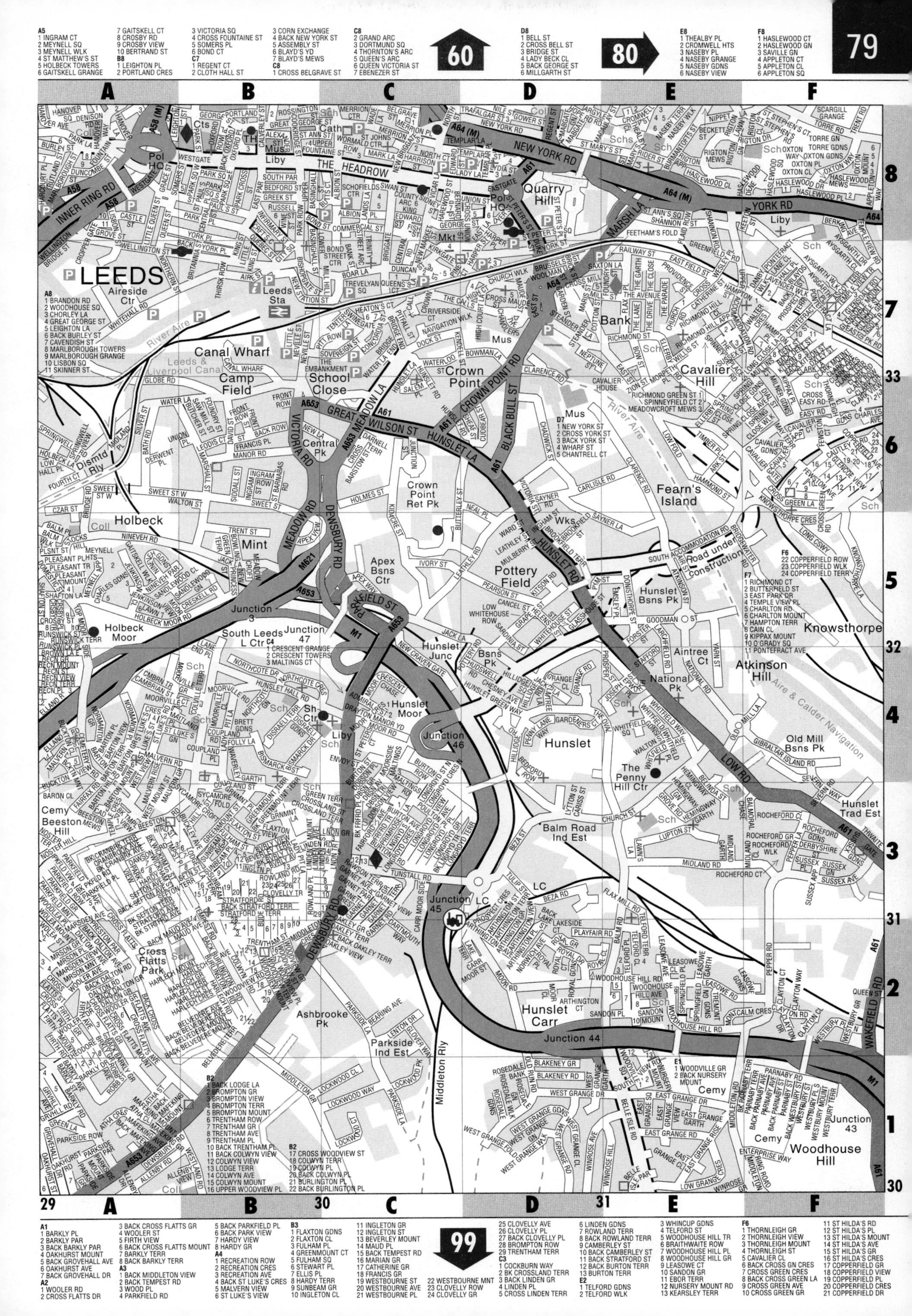
79
A5
1 INGRAM CT
2 MEYNELL SQ
3 MEYNELL WLK
4 ST MATTHEW'S ST
5 HOLBECK TOWERS
6 GAITSKELL GRANGE
7 GAITSKELL CT
8 CROSBY RD
9 CROSBY VIEW
10 BERTRAND ST
B8
1 LEIGHTON PL
2 PORTLAND CRES
3 VICTORIA SQ
4 CROSS FOUNTAINE ST
5 SOMERS PL
6 BOND CT
C7
1 REGENT CT
2 CLOTH HALL ST
3 CORN EXCHANGE
4 BACK NEW YORK ST
5 ASSEMBLY ST
6 BLAYD'S YD
7 BLAYD'S MEWS
C8
1 CROSS BELGRAVE ST
C8
2 GRAND ARC
3 DORTMUND SQ
4 THORNTON'S ARC
5 QUEEN'S ARC
6 QUEEN VICTORIA ST
7 EBENEZER ST
60
D8
1 BELL ST
2 CROSS BELL ST
3 BRIDGE ST
4 LADY BECK CL
5 BACK GEORGE ST
6 MILLGARTH ST
80
E8
1 THEALBY PL
2 CROMWELL HTS
3 NASEBY PL
4 NASEBY GRANGE
5 NASEBY GDNS
6 NASEBY VIEW
F8
1 HASLEWOOD CT
2 HASLEWOOD GN
3 SAVILLE GN
4 APPLETON CT
5 APPLETON CL
6 APPLETON SQ
A B C D E F
LEEDS
Leeds Sta
Aireside Ctr
River Aire
Canal Wharf
Leeds & Liverpool Canal
Camp Field
School Close
Crown Point
Quarry Hill
Bank
Cavalier Hill
Fearn's Island
Holbeck
Mint
Apex Bsns Ctr
Crown Point Ret Pk
Pottery Field
Hunslet Bsns Pk
Knowsthorpe
Atkinson Hill
Aintree Ct
National Pk
Holbeck Moor
South Leeds L Ctr
Junction 3
Junction 47
Hunslet Junc
Bsns Pk
Hunslet Moor
Junction 46
Hunslet
The Penny Hill Ctr
Old Mill Bsns Pk
Aire & Calder Navigation
Hunslet Trad Est
Cemy Beeston Hill
Balm Road Ind Est
Junction 45
Cross Flatts Park
Ashbrooke Pk
Parkside Ind Est
Hunslet Carr
Junction 44
Middleton Rly
Cemy
Junction 43
Woodhouse Hill
INNER RING RD
NEW YORK RD
THE HEADROW
YORK RD
GREAT WILSON ST
HUNSLET LA
HUNSLET RD
CROWN POINT RD
LOW RD
DEWSBURY RD
WAKEFIELD RD
A8
1 BRANDON RD
2 WOODHOUSE SQ
3 CHORLEY LA
4 GREAT GEORGE ST
5 LEIGHTON LA
6 BACK BURLEY ST
7 CAVENDISH ST
8 MARLBOROUGH TOWERS
9 MARLBOROUGH GRANGE
10 LISBON SQ
11 SKINNER ST
D7
1 NEW YORK ST
2 CROSS YORK ST
3 BACK YORK ST
4 WHARF ST
5 CHANTRELL CT
C4
1 CRESCENT GRANGE
2 CRESCENT TOWERS
3 MALTINGS CT
F6
22 COPPERFIELD ROW
23 COPPERFIELD WLK
24 COPPERFIELD TERR
F7
1 RICHMOND CT
2 BUTTERFIELD ST
3 EAST PARK DR
4 TEMPLE VIEW PL
5 CHARLTON RD
6 CHARLTON MOUNT
7 HAMPTON TERR
8 CAIN CL
9 KIPPAX MOUNT
10 O'GRADY SQ
11 PONTEFRACT AVE
B2
1 BACK LODGE LA
2 BROMPTON GR
3 BROMPTON VIEW
4 BROMPTON TERR
5 BROMPTON MOUNT
6 TRENTHAM ROW
7 TRENTHAM GR
8 TRENTHAM AVE
9 TRENTHAM PL
10 BACK TRENTHAM PL
11 BACK COLWYN VIEW
12 COLWYN VIEW
13 LODGE TERR
14 COLWYN AVE
15 COLWYN MOUNT
16 UPPER WOODVIEW PL
B2
17 CROSS WOODVIEW ST
18 COLWYN TERR
19 COLWYN PL
20 BACK COLWYN PL
21 BURLINGTON PL
22 BACK BURLINGTON PL
E1
1 WOODVILLE GR
2 BACK NURSERY MOUNT
8 7 6 5 4 3 2 1
33 32 31 30
29 30 31
99
A1
1 BARKLY PL
2 BARKLY PAR
3 BACK BARKLY PAR
4 OAKHURST MOUNT
5 BACK GROVEHALL AVE
6 OAKHURST AVE
7 BACK GROVEHALL DR
A2
1 WOOLER RD
2 CROSS FLATTS DR
3 BACK CROSS FLATTS GR
4 WOOLER ST
5 FIRTH VIEW
6 BACK CROSS FLATTS MOUNT
7 BARKLY TERR
8 BACK BARKLY TERR
A3
1 BACK MIDDLETON VIEW
2 BACK TEMPEST RD
3 WOOD PL
4 PARKFIELD RD
5 BACK PARKFIELD PL
6 BACK PARK VIEW
7 HARDY VIEW
8 HARDY GR
A4
1 RECREATION ROW
2 RECREATION CRES
3 RECREATION AVE
4 BACK ST LUKE'S CRES
5 MALVERN VIEW
6 ST LUKE'S VIEW
B3
1 FLAXTON GDNS
2 FLAXTON CL
3 FULHAM PL
4 GREENMOUNT CT
5 FULHAM SQ
6 STEWART PL
7 ELLIS PL
8 HARDY TERR
9 SUNBEAM GR
10 INGLETON CL
11 INGLETON GR
12 INGLETON ST
13 BEVERLEY MOUNT
14 MAUD PL
15 BACK TEMPEST RD
16 MARIAN GR
17 CATHERINE GR
18 FRANCIS GR
19 WESTBOURNE ST
20 WESTBOURNE AVE
21 WESTBOURNE PL
22 WESTBOURNE MNT
23 CLOVELLY ROW
24 CLOVELLY GR
25 CLOVELLY AVE
26 CLOVELLY PL
27 BACK CLOVELLY PL
28 BROMPTON ROW
29 TRENTHAM TERR
C3
1 COCKBURN WAY
2 BK CROSSLAND TERR
3 BACK LINDEN GR
4 LINDEN PL
5 CROSS LINDEN TERR
6 LINDEN GDNS
7 ROWLAND TERR
8 BACK ROWLAND TERR
9 CAMBERLEY ST
10 BACK CAMBERLEY ST
11 BACK STRATFORD ST
12 BACK BURTON TERR
13 BURTON TERR
E2
1 TELFORD GDNS
2 TELFORD WLK
3 WHINCUP GDNS
4 TELFORD ST
5 WOODHOUSE HILL TR
6 BRAITHWAITE ROW
7 WOODHOUSE HILL PL
8 WOODHOUSE HILL GR
9 LEASOWE CT
10 SANDON GR
11 EBOR TERR
12 NURSERY MOUNT RD
13 KEARSLEY TERR
F6
1 THORNLEIGH GR
2 THORNLEIGH VIEW
3 THORNLEIGH MOUNT
4 THORNLEIGH ST
5 CAVALIER CL
6 BACK CROSS GN CRES
7 CROSS GREEN CRES
8 BACK CROSS GREEN LA
9 CROSS GREEN AVE
10 CROSS GREEN GR
11 ST HILDA'S RD
12 ST HILDA'S PL
13 ST HILDA'S MOUNT
14 ST HILDA'S AVE
15 ST HILDA'S GR
16 ST HILDA'S CRES
17 COPPERFIELD GR
18 COPPERFIELD VIEW
19 COPPERFIELD PL
20 COPPERFIELD CRES
21 COPPERFIELD DR

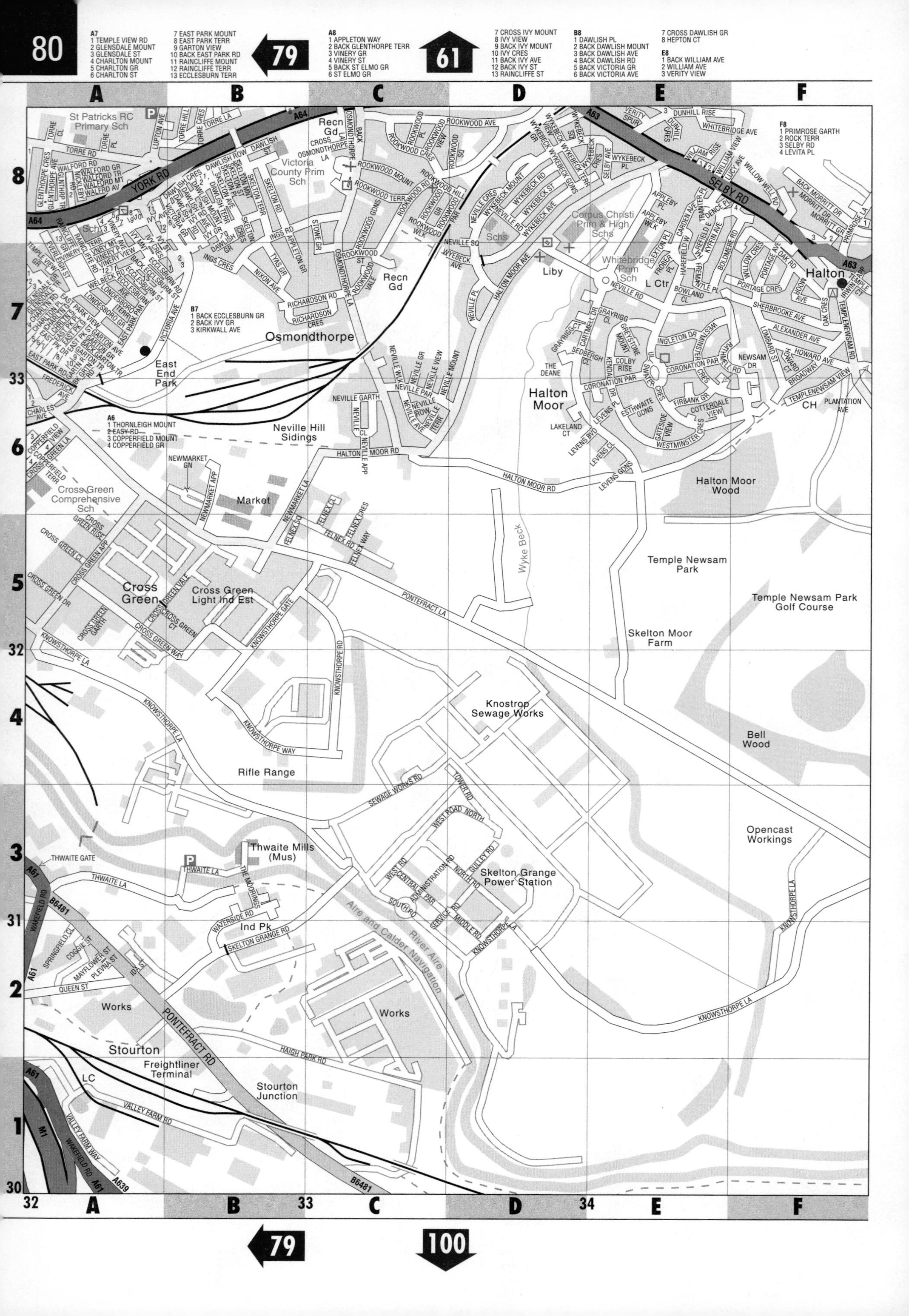
A7
1 TEMPLE VIEW RD
2 GLENSDALE MOUNT
3 GLENSDALE ST
4 CHARLTON MOUNT
5 CHARLTON GR
6 CHARLTON ST
7 EAST PARK MOUNT
8 EAST PARK TERR
9 GARTON VIEW
10 BACK EAST PARK RD
11 RAINCLIFFE MOUNT
12 RAINCLIFFE TERR
13 ECCLESBURN TERR
79
A8
1 APPLETON WAY
2 BACK GLENTHORPE TERR
3 VINERY GR
4 VINERY ST
5 BACK ST ELMO GR
6 ST ELMO GR
61
7 CROSS IVY MOUNT
8 IVY VIEW
9 BACK IVY MOUNT
10 IVY CRES
11 BACK IVY AVE
12 BACK IVY ST
13 RAINCLIFFE ST
B8
1 DAWLISH PL
2 BACK DAWLISH MOUNT
3 BACK DAWLISH AVE
4 BACK DAWLISH RD
5 BACK VICTORIA GR
6 BACK VICTORIA AVE
7 CROSS DAWLISH GR
8 HEPTON CT
E8
1 BACK WILLIAM AVE
2 WILLIAM AVE
3 VERITY VIEW
F8
1 PRIMROSE GARTH
2 ROCK TERR
3 SELBY RD
4 LEVITA PL
B7
1 BACK ECCLESBURN GR
2 BACK IVY GR
3 KIRKWALL AVE
A6
1 THORNLEIGH MOUNT
2 EASY RD
3 COPPERFIELD MOUNT
4 COPPERFIELD GR
A B C D E F
8 7 6 5 4 3 2 1
33 32 31 30 34
St Patricks RC Primary Sch
Victoria County Prim Sch
Recn Gd
Osmondthorpe
East End Park
Neville Hill Sidings
Cross Green Comprehensive Sch
Market
Cross Green
Cross Green Light Ind Est
Corpus Christi Prim & High Schs
Schs
Liby
Whitebridge Prim Sch
L Ctr
Halton
Halton Moor
CH
Halton Moor Wood
Temple Newsam Park
Temple Newsam Park Golf Course
Skelton Moor Farm
Wyke Beck
Knostrop Sewage Works
Bell Wood
Rifle Range
Opencast Workings
Thwaite Mills (Mus)
Skelton Grange Power Station
Ind Pk
Aire and Calder Navigation
River Aire
Works
Stourton
Freightliner Terminal
Stourton Junction
LC
YORK RD
SELBY RD
A64
A63
A61
A639
B6481
M1
PONTEFRACT LA
PONTEFRACT RD
HALTON MOOR RD
HALTON MOOR AVE
KNOWSTHORPE LA
KNOWSTHORPE RD
KNOWSTHORPE WAY
KNOWSTHORPE GATE
SEWAGE WORKS RD
TOWER RD
WEST ROAD NORTH
THWAITE LA
THWAITE GATE
WAKEFIELD RD
VALLEY FARM RD
VALLEY FARM WAY
HAIGH PARK RD
SKELTON GRANGE RD
WATERSIDE RD
QUEEN ST
TEMPLENEWSAM RD
TEMPLENEWSAM VIEW
NEVILLE RD
NEVILLE PL
ROOKWOOD AVE
OSMONDTHORPE LA
NEWMARKET LA
CROSS GREEN LA
CROSS GREEN WAY
100
79

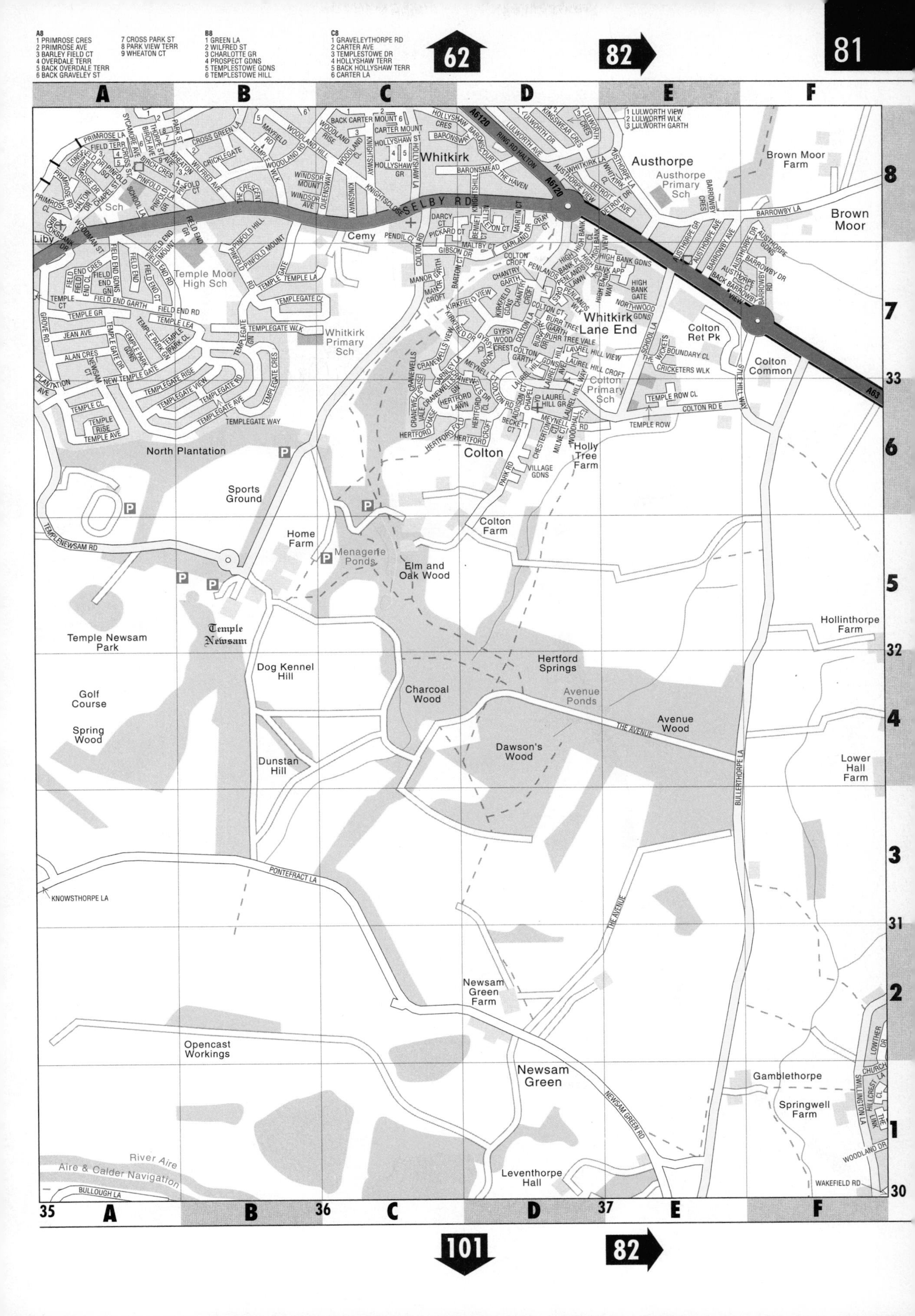

81
62
82
101
82
A8
1 PRIMROSE CRES
2 PRIMROSE AVE
3 BARLEY FIELD CT
4 OVERDALE TERR
5 BACK OVERDALE TERR
6 BACK GRAVELEY ST
7 CROSS PARK ST
8 PARK VIEW TERR
9 WHEATON CT
B8
1 GREEN LA
2 WILFRED ST
3 CHARLOTTE GR
4 PROSPECT GDNS
5 TEMPLESTOWE GDNS
6 TEMPLESTOWE HILL
C8
1 GRAVELEYTHORPE RD
2 CARTER AVE
3 TEMPLESTOWE DR
4 HOLLYSHAW TERR
5 BACK HOLLYSHAW TERR
6 CARTER LA
1 LULWORTH VIEW
2 LULWORTH WLK
3 LULWORTH GARTH
Whitkirk
Austhorpe
Austhorpe Primary Sch
Brown Moor Farm
Brown Moor
SELBY RD
A6120
RING RD HALTON
A63
BARROWBY LA
Cemy
Liby
Sch
Temple Moor High Sch
Whitkirk Primary Sch
Whitkirk Lane End
Colton Ret Pk
Colton Common
Colton Primary Sch
TEMPLE ROW
COLTON RD E
Holly Tree Farm
Colton
North Plantation
TEMPLEGATE WAY
Sports Ground
TEMPLENEWSAM RD
Home Farm
Menagerie Ponds
Elm and Oak Wood
Colton Farm
Temple Newsam
Temple Newsam Park
Hollinthorpe Farm
Dog Kennel Hill
Hertford Springs
Avenue Ponds
Charcoal Wood
Golf Course
Spring Wood
THE AVENUE
Avenue Wood
Dawson's Wood
Dunstan Hill
Lower Hall Farm
BULLERTHORPE LA
PONTEFRACT LA
KNOWSTHORPE LA
Newsam Green Farm
Opencast Workings
Newsam Green
NEWSAM GREEN RD
Gamblethorpe
Springwell Farm
SWILLINGTON LA
WOODLAND DR
WAKEFIELD RD
River Aire
Aire & Calder Navigation
BULLOUGH LA
Leventhorpe Hall
35
36
37
30
31
32
33

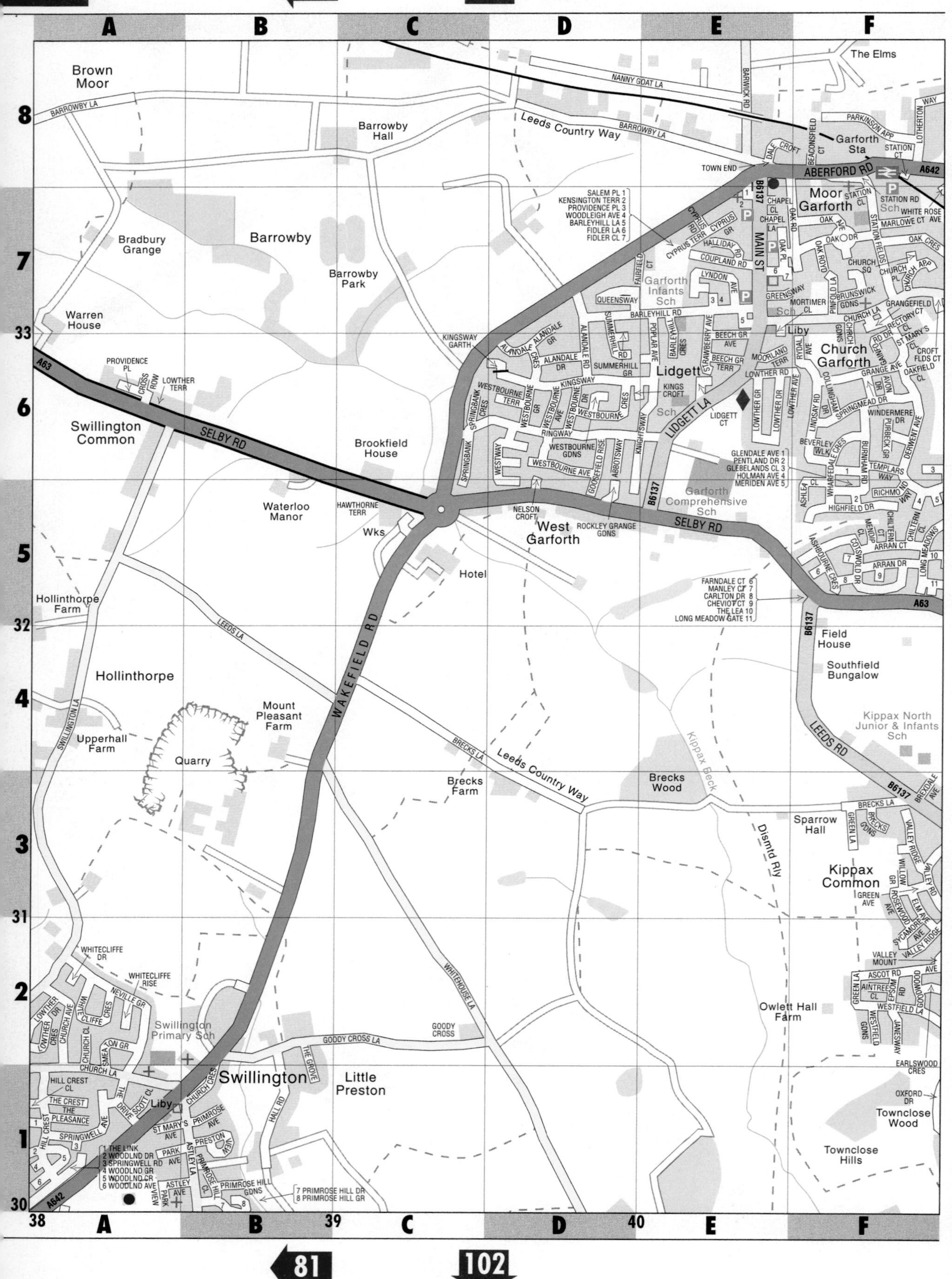

81
63

A   B   C   D   E   F

8

Brown
Moor

Barrowby
Hall

Leeds Country Way

The Elms

NANNY GOAT LA

BARWICK RD

PARKINSON APP

Garforth
Sta

STATION
CT

LOTHERTON WAY

BARROWBY LA

BARROWBY LA

7

Bradbury
Grange

Barrowby

Barrowby
Park

SALEM PL 1
KENSINGTON TERR 2
PROVIDENCE PL 3
WOODLEIGH AVE 4
BARLEYHILL LA 5
FIDLER LA 6
FIDLER CL 7

TOWN END

ABERFORD RD

A642

Moor
Garforth

STATION RD

STATION
CT

WHITE ROSE
AVE

MARLOWE CT

OAK
AVE

OAK CR

CHURCH
SQ

OAK CRES

33

Warren
House

Kingsway
Garth

CYPRUS TERR

CYPRUS

CHAPEL
CL

CHAPEL
LA

MAIN ST

HALLIDAY

COUPLAND RD

LYNDON

GREENSWAY

MORTIMER
CL

BRUNSWICK

GRANGEFIELD

CHURCH

CHURCH APP

St MARY's

RECTORY DR

CROFT
FLDS CT

OAKFIELD

Church
Garforth

6

Swillington
Common

SELBY RD

Providence
PL

CROSS
ROW

LOWTHER TERR

Brookfield
House

Garforth
Infants
Sch

QUEENSWAY

FAIRFIELD

BARLEYHILL RD

SUMMERHILL
GR

POPLAR AVE

STRAWBERRY AVE

BEECH GR
AVE

BARLEYHILL
CRES

Lidgett

KINGS
CROFT

Sch

LIDGETT LA

LIDGETT
CT

MOORLAND

LOWTHER RD

LOWTHER DR

RYDAL

AVON

COLLINGHAM

GRANGE DR

BEVERLEY
WLK

WHARFEDALE
CL

BURNHAM

PURBECK
GR

SPRINGMEAD DR

WINDERMERE
DR

DERWENT AVE

Liby

SPRINGBANK

WESTBOURNE
TERR

WESTBOURNE
GR

WESTBOURNE
AVE

WESTBOURN
CL

RINGWAY

ABBOTSWAY

KNIGHTSWAY

KINGSWAY

GLENDALE AVE 1
PENTLAND DR 2
GLEBELANDS CL 3
HOLMAN AVE 4
MERIDEN AVE 5

TEMPLARS
WAY

HIGHFIELD DR

RICHMO

CHILTERN

CHILTERN

LONG MEADOWS

ASHLEA

32

Hollinthorpe
Farm

LEEDS LA

WESTWAY

WESTBOURNE
GDNS

WESTBOURNE AVE

GODERILL RISE

SPRINGBANK

NELSON
CROFT

West
Garforth

ROCKLEY GRANGE
GDNS

SELBY RD

B6137

Garforth
Comprehensive
Sch

ASHBOURNE CRES

ARRAN CT

ARRAN DR

A63

Field
House

Southfield
Bungalow

5

Hotel

FARNDALE CT 6
MANLEY CT 7
CARLTON DR 8
CHEVIOT CT 9
THE LEA 10
LONG MEADOW GATE 11

B6137

Kippax Beck

Kippax North
Junior & Infants
Sch

4

Hollinthorpe

Upperhall
Farm

SWILLINGTON LA

Mount
Pleasant
Farm

WAKEFIELD RD

BRECKS LA

Leeds Country Way

Brecks
Wood

Dismtd Rly

LEEDS RD

B6137

BREXDALE CL

3

Quarry

Brecks
Farm

Sparrow
Hall

BRECKS LA

GREEN LA

VALLEY RIDGE

BRECKS
GDNS

WILLOW

VALLEY RIDGE

Kippax
Common

GREEN
AVE

ROSEWOOD

ELM LA

SYCAMORE

31

WHITECLIFFE
DR

WHITECLIFFE
RISE

WHITEHOUSE LA

VALLEY
MOUNT

ASCOT RD

GREEN LA

AINTREE

WESTFIELD
GDNS

JANEWAY

WESTFIELD

2

LOWTHER
CRES

NEVILLE GR

WHITE
CLIFFE
CRES

CHURCH CL

STATION GR

Swillington
Primary Sch

GODDY CROSS LA

THE GROVE

HALL RD

GOODY
CROSS

Owlett Hall
Farm

EARLSWOOD
CRES

OXFORD
DR

Townclose
Wood

1

HILL CREST
CL

THE CREST
THE
PLEASANCE

CHURCH LA

DRIVE SCOTT CL

Liby

St MARY's
AVE

SPRINGWELL
AVE

Swillington

PARK
AVE

PRIMROSE
AVE

ASTLEY LA

PRESTON

Little
Preston

Townclose
Hills

1 THE LINK
2 WOODLND DR
3 SPRINGWELL RD
4 WOODLND GR
5 WOODLND CR
6 WOODLND AVE

7 PRIMROSE HILL DR
8 PRIMROSE HILL GR

PRIMROSE HILL
GDNS

30

A642

38   A   B   39   C   D   40   E   F

81
102

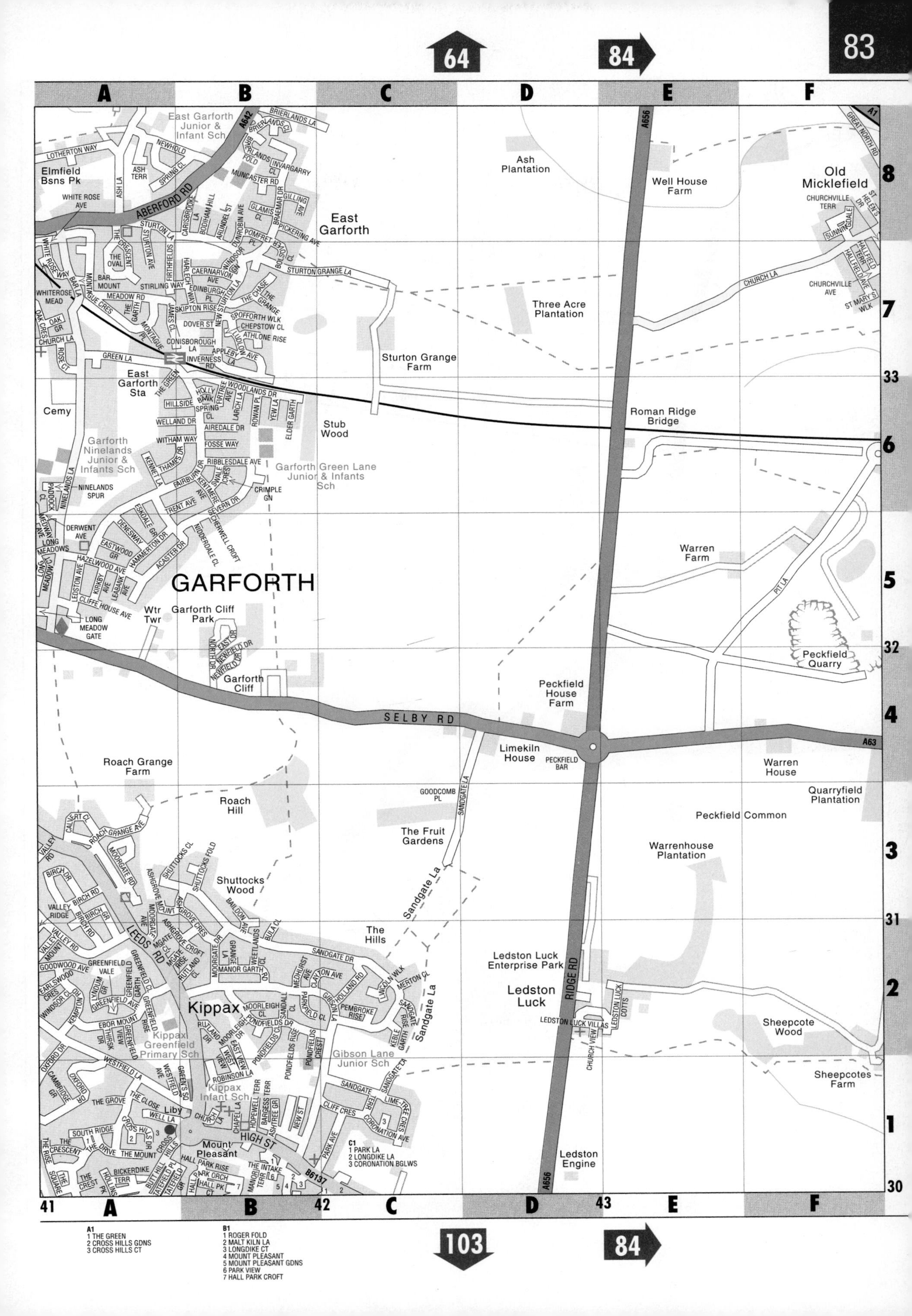
64
84
A
B
C
D
E
F
East Garforth Junior & Infant Sch
Elmfield Bsns Pk
Ash Plantation
Well House Farm
Old Micklefield
East Garforth
Three Acre Plantation
Sturton Grange Farm
East Garforth Sta
Cemy
Roman Ridge Bridge
Stub Wood
Garforth Ninelands Junior & Infants Sch
Garforth Green Lane Junior & Infants Sch
Warren Farm
GARFORTH
Wtr Twr
Garforth Cliff Park
Garforth Cliff
Peckfield Quarry
Peckfield House Farm
SELBY RD
Limekiln House
PECKFIELD BAR
Warren House
Roach Grange Farm
Roach Hill
Quarryfield Plantation
Peckfield Common
The Fruit Gardens
Warrenhouse Plantation
Shuttocks Wood
Sandgate La
The Hills
Ledston Luck Enterprise Park
Ledston Luck
RIDGE RD
Kippax
Kippax Greenfield Primary Sch
Sheepcote Wood
Gibson Lane Junior Sch
Sheepcotes Farm
Kippax Infant Sch
Liby
Mount Pleasant
HIGH ST
Ledston Engine
ABERFORD RD
LEEDS RD
CHURCH LA
GREEN LA
A642
A656
A63
A1
B6137
8
7
33
6
5
32
4
3
31
2
1
30
41
42
43
C1
1 PARK LA
2 LONGDIKE LA
3 CORONATION BGLWS
A1
1 THE GREEN
2 CROSS HILLS GDNS
3 CROSS HILLS CT
B1
1 ROGER FOLD
2 MALT KILN LA
3 LONGDIKE CT
4 MOUNT PLEASANT
5 MOUNT PLEASANT GDNS
6 PARK VIEW
7 HALL PARK CROFT
103
84

83
65

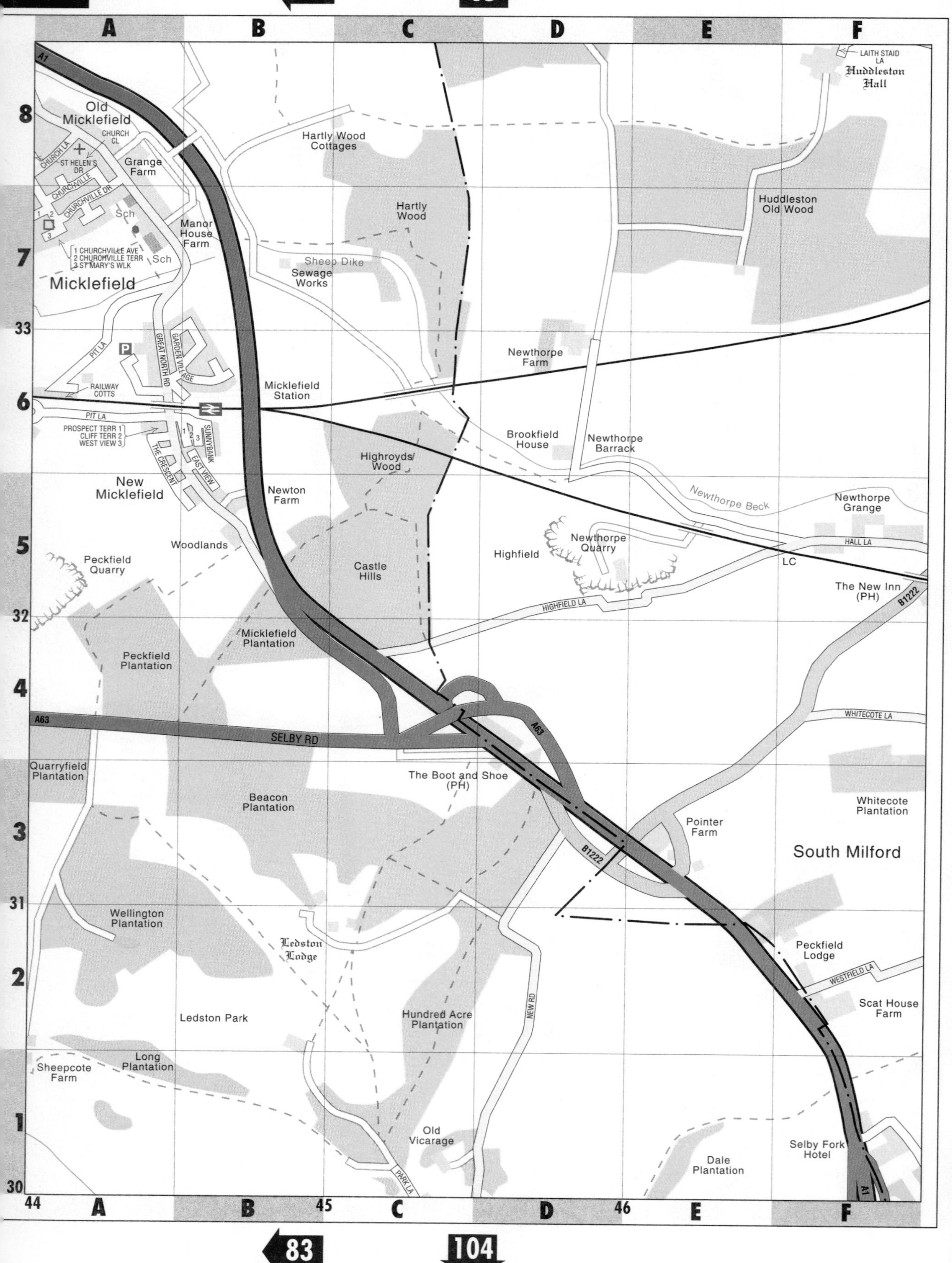
A
B
C
D
E
F
8
7
33
6
5
32
4
3
31
2
1
30
44
45
46
A1
Old Micklefield
CHURCH CL
CHURCH LA
ST HELEN'S DR
CHURCHVILLE
CHURCHVILLE DR
Grange Farm
Sch
Manor House Farm
1 CHURCHVILLE AVE
2 CHURCHVILLE TERR
3 ST MARY'S WLK
Sch
Micklefield
PIT LA
GREAT NORTH RD
GARDEN VILLAGE
RAILWAY COTTS
PIT LA
PROSPECT TERR 1
CLIFF TERR 2
WEST VIEW 3
SUNNYBANK
THE CRESCENT
EAST VIEW
New Micklefield
Woodlands
Peckfield Quarry
Hartly Wood Cottages
Hartly Wood
Sheep Dike
Sewage Works
Micklefield Station
Newton Farm
Highroyds Wood
Castle Hills
Micklefield Plantation
Peckfield Plantation
A63
SELBY RD
Quarryfield Plantation
Beacon Plantation
The Boot and Shoe (PH)
Wellington Plantation
Ledston Lodge
Ledston Park
Hundred Acre Plantation
NEW RD
Long Plantation
Sheepcote Farm
Old Vicarage
PARK LA
LAITH STAID LA
Huddleston Hall
Huddleston Old Wood
Newthorpe Farm
Brookfield House
Newthorpe Barrack
Newthorpe Beck
Newthorpe Grange
Newthorpe Quarry
Highfield
HALL LA
LC
The New Inn (PH)
B1222
HIGHFIELD LA
WHITECOTE LA
A63
Pointer Farm
Whitecote Plantation
South Milford
B1222
Peckfield Lodge
WESTFIELD LA
Scat House Farm
Selby Fork Hotel
Dale Plantation
A1

83
104

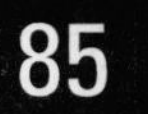

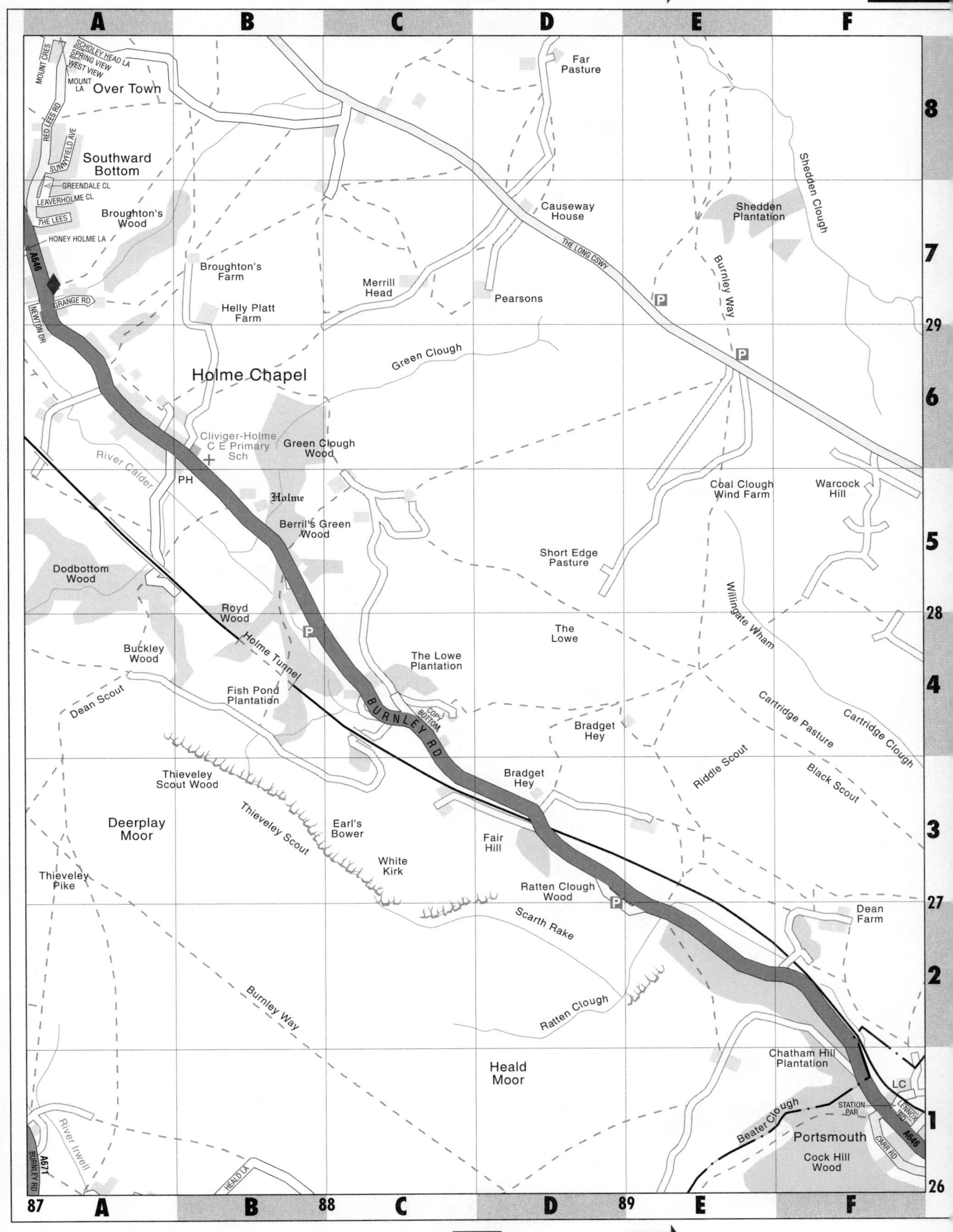

86
A
B
C
D
E
F
Over Town
Southward Bottom
Broughton's Wood
Broughton's Farm
Helly Platt Farm
Holme Chapel
Merrill Head
Far Pasture
Causeway House
Pearsons
Shedden Plantation
Shedden Clough
Burnley Way
THE LONG CSWY
Green Clough
Cliviger-Holme C E Primary Sch
Green Clough Wood
River Calder
PH
Holme
Berril's Green Wood
Coal Clough Wind Farm
Warcock Hill
Short Edge Pasture
Dodbottom Wood
Royd Wood
The Lowe
Willingate Wham
Buckley Wood
Holme Tunnel
The Lowe Plantation
Dean Scout
Fish Pond Plantation
BURNLEY RD
COPY BOTTOM
Bradget Hey
Cartridge Pasture
Cartridge Clough
Riddle Scout
Black Scout
Thieveley Scout Wood
Deerplay Moor
Thieveley Scout
Earl's Bower
Fair Hill
White Kirk
Thieveley Pike
Ratten Clough Wood
Scarth Rake
Dean Farm
Burnley Way
Ratten Clough
Heald Moor
Chatham Hill Plantation
Beater Clough
Portsmouth
Cock Hill Wood
River Irwell
A646
A671
BURNLEY RD
HEALD LA
STATION PAR
LENNOX RD
CARR RD
LC
SCHOLEY HEAD LA
SPRING VIEW
WEST VIEW
MOUNT CRES
MOUNT LA
RED LEES RD
SUNNYFIELD AVE
GREENDALE CL
LEAVERHOLME CL
THE LEES
HONEY HOLME LA
GRANGE RD
NEWTON DR
8
7
29
6
5
28
4
3
27
2
1
26
87
88
89
106
86

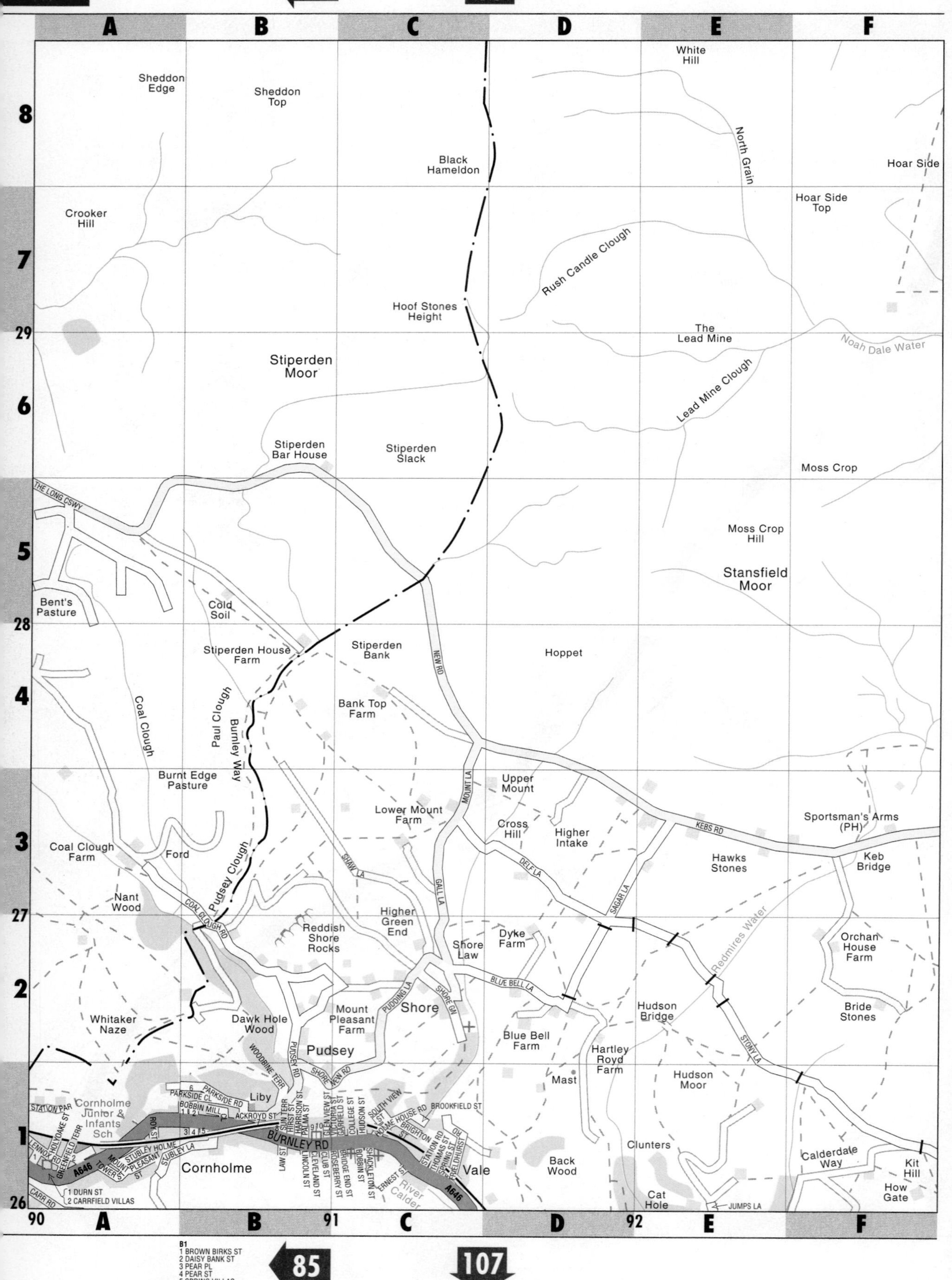

B1
1 BROWN BIRKS ST
2 DAISY BANK ST
3 PEAR PL
4 PEAR ST
5 SPRING VILLAS
6 STANSFIELD TERR
7 CORNHOLME TERR
8 OAKLEIGH TERR
9 SUNNY BANK TERR
10 GLADSTONE ST

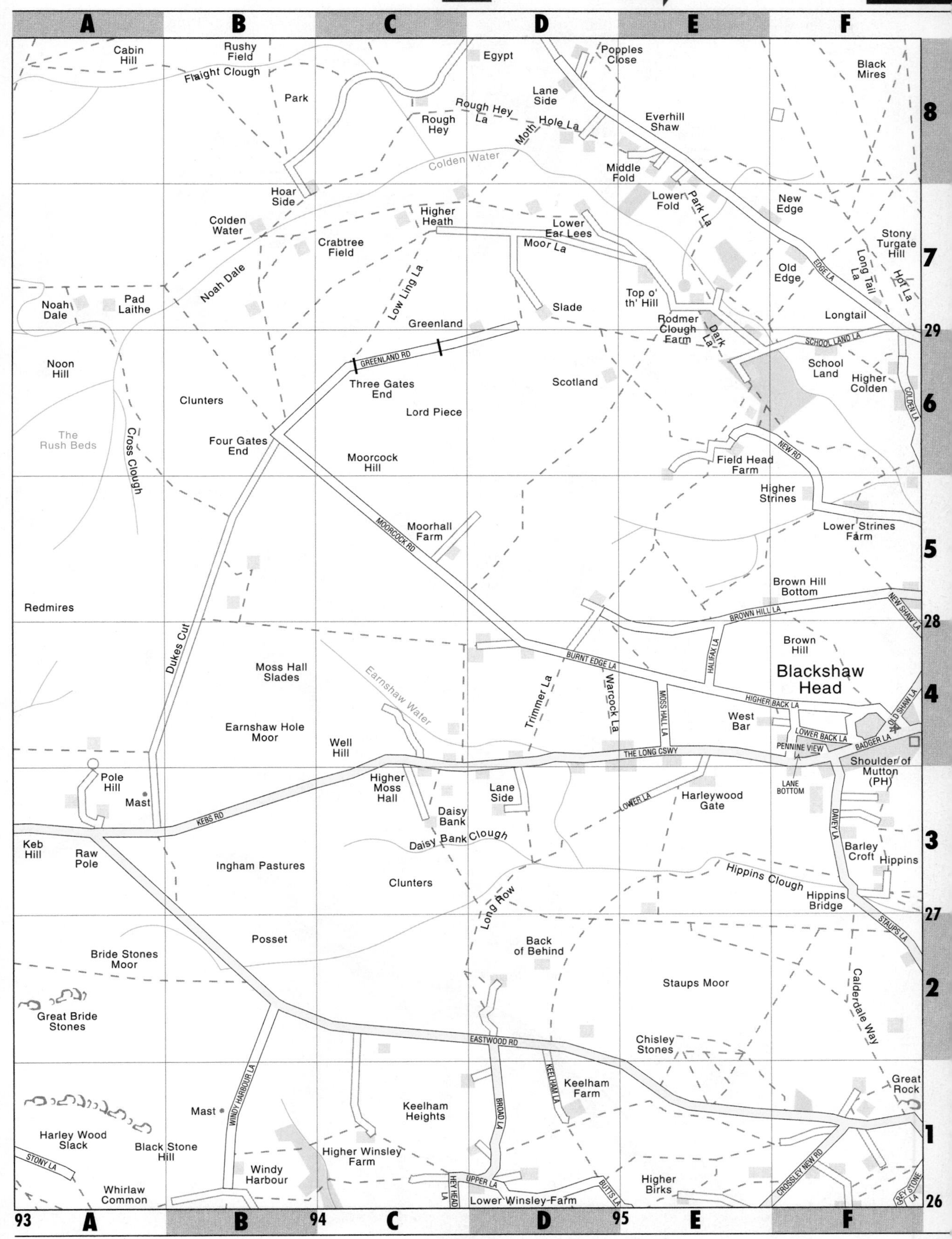

67
88
108
88

A   B   C   D   E   F

Cabin Hill
Rushy Field
Flaight Clough
Park
Egypt
Popples Close
Lane Side
Everhill Shaw
Rough Hey La
Hole La
Black Mires

8

Rough Hey
Colden Water
Middle Fold
Lower Fold
Park La
New Edge

Hoar Side
Higher Heath
Lower Ear Lees
Old Edge
Stony Turgate Hill
Long Tail La
Hot La

7

Colden Water
Crabtree Field
Moor La
Edge La

Noah Dale
Top o' th' Hill
Rodmer Clough Farm
Longtail

29

Noah Dale
Pad Laithe
Low Ling La
Slade
Dark La
School Land La

Noon Hill
Greenland
Scotland
School Land
Higher Colden
COLDEN LA

6

GREENLAND RD
Clunters
Three Gates End
Lord Piece

The Rush Beds
Cross Clough
Four Gates End
Moorcock Hill
Field Head Farm
NEW RD

Higher Strines

5

MOORCOCK RD
Moorhall Farm
Lower Strines Farm

Redmires
Dukes Cut
Brown Hill Bottom
BROWN HILL LA
NEW SHAW LA

28

Moss Hall Slades
Earnshaw Water
BURNT EDGE LA
Brown Hill

Earnshaw Hole Moor
Trimmer La
Warcock La
MOSS HALL LA
HALIFAX LA
Blackshaw Head
HIGHER BACK LA
OLD SHAW LA

4

Well Hill
West Bar
LOWER BACK LA
BADGER LA

Pole Hill
Mast
KEBS RD
Higher Moss Hall
Daisy Bank
Lane Side
Lower La
Harleywood Gate
PENNINE VIEW
LANE BOTTOM
Shoulder of Mutton (PH)

Keb Hill
Raw Pole
Clunters
Daisy Bank Clough
Hippins Clough
DAVEY LA
Barley Croft
Hippins

3

Ingham Pastures
Long Row
Hippins Bridge
STAUPS LA

27

Posset
Back of Behind
Staups Moor
Calderdale Way

2

Bride Stones Moor
EASTWOOD RD
Chisley Stones

Great Bride Stones
WINDY HARBOUR LA
Keelham Heights
BROAD LA
KEELHAM LA
Keelham Farm
Great Rock

1

Mast
Higher Winsley Farm
Higher Birks
CROSSLEY NEW RD
GREY STONE

Harley Wood Slack
Black Stone Hill
STONY LA
Windy Harbour
HEY HEAD LA
UPPER LA
Lower Winsley Farm
BUTTS LA

Whirlaw Common

26

93   A   B   94   C   D   95   E   F

87
68

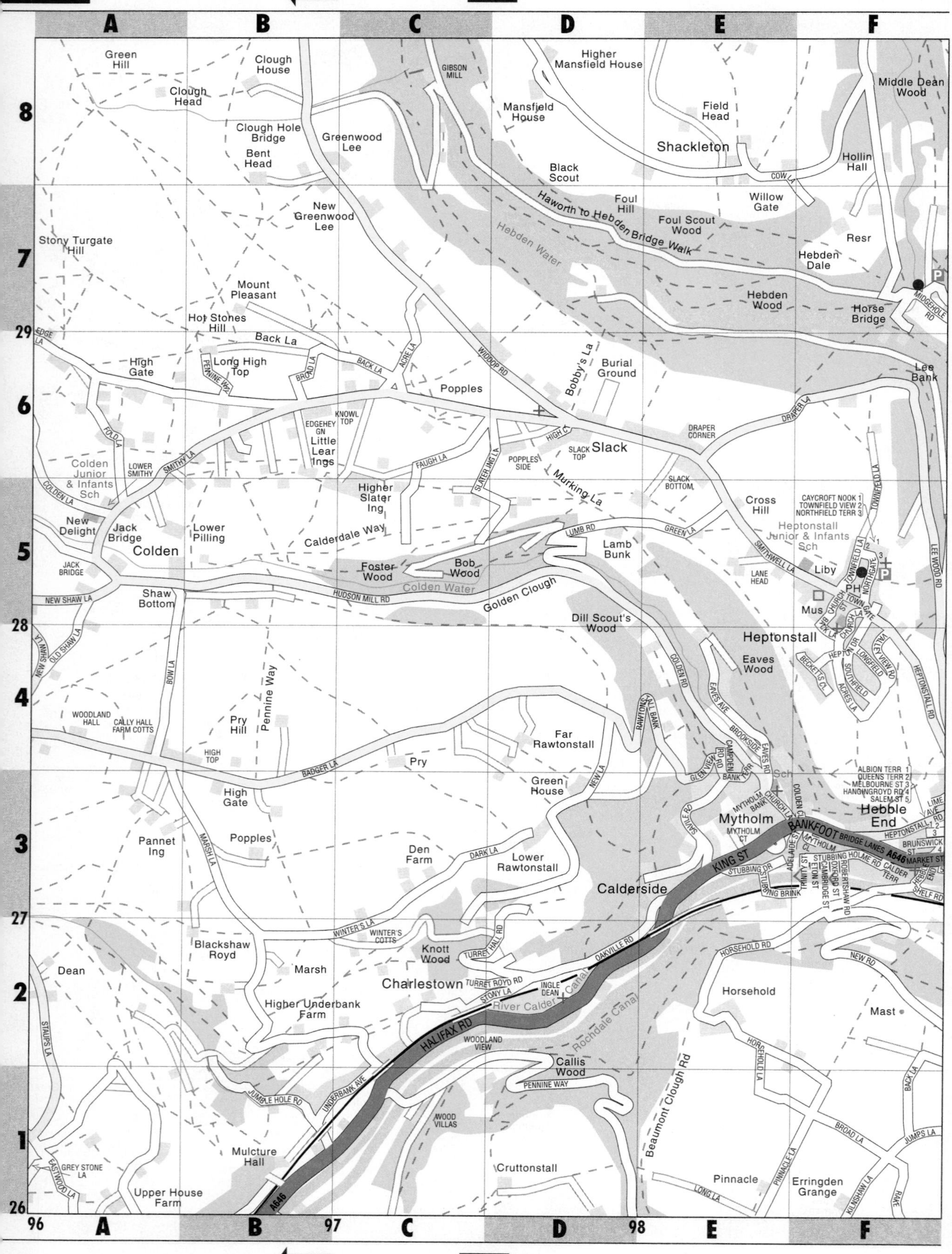
A
B
C
D
E
F
8
7
29
6
5
28
4
3
27
2
1
26
96
97
98
Green Hill
Clough House
Clough Head
Gibson Mill
Higher Mansfield House
Middle Dean Wood
Mansfield House
Field Head
Clough Hole Bridge
Greenwood Lee
Shackleton
Hollin Hall
Bent Head
Black Scout
Cow La
Foul Hill
Willow Gate
New Greenwood Lee
Haworth to Hebden Bridge Walk
Foul Scout Wood
Hebden Water
Resr
Stony Turgate Hill
Hebden Dale
Mount Pleasant
Hebden Wood
Horse Bridge
Midgehole Rd
Hot Stones Hill
Edge La
Back La
High Gate
Long High Top
Pennine Way
Broad La
Acre La
Widdop Rd
Bobby's La
Burial Ground
Lee Bank
Popples
Draper La
Knowl Top
Edgehey Gn
Little Lear Ings
High C
Draper Corner
Slack
Fold La
Colden Junior & Infants Sch
Lower Smithy
Smithy La
Faugh La
Slater Ing Rd
Popples Side
Slack Top
Slack Bottom
Higher Slater Ing
Murking La
Colden La
Cross Hill
Caycroft Nook 1
Townfield View 2
Northfield Terr 3
Townfield La
New Delight
Jack Bridge
Lower Pilling
Calderdale Way
Lumb Rd
Green La
Lamb Bunk
Heptonstall Junior & Infants Sch
Colden
Smithwell La
Foster Wood
Bob Wood
Liby
Lee Wood Rd
Jack Bridge
Lane Head
PH
Northgate
Colden Water
Golden Clough
Shaw Bottom
New Shaw La
Hudson Mill Rd
Mus
Church St
Town Gate
Dill Scout's Wood
Back La
Church La
Heptonstall
New Shaw La
Old Shaw La
Hepton Dr
Longfield
Valley View Rd
Eaves Wood
Becketts Cl
Southfield
Acres La
Colden Rd
Heptonstall Rd
Bow La
Pennine Way
Eaves Ave
Rawtonstall Bank
Woodland Hall
Cally Hall Farm Cotts
Pry Hill
Far Rawtonstall
Brookside
High Top
Camden Rd
Eaves Rd
Pry
Badger La
Glen View
Bank Terr
Sch
Green House
New La
Albion Terr 1
Queens Terr 2
Melbourne St 3
Hangingroyd Rd 4
Salem St 5
High Gate
Mytholm Bank
Church La
Colden Cl
Hebble End
Savile Rd
Mytholm
Lime Ave
Mytholm Ct
Bankfoot
Bridge Lanes
Heptonstall Rd
Pannet Ing
Popples
Marsh La
Brunswick St
Market St
Den Farm
Dark La
Mytholm Cl
A646
Lower Rawtonstall
King St
Adelaide St
Stubbing Holme Rd
Calder Terr
Hebble End
Stubbing Dr
Trinity St
Eton St
Cambridge St
Oxford St
Robertshaw Rd
Calderside
Stubbing Brink
Shelf Rd
Winter's La
Winter's Cotts
Turret Hall Rd
Blackshaw Royd
Knott Wood
Oakville Rd
Horsehold Rd
New Rd
Dean
Marsh
Charlestown
Turret Royd Rd
Ingle Dean
Horsehold
Canal
Stony La
River Calder
Rochdale Canal
Higher Underbank Farm
Mast
Staups La
Halifax Rd
Woodland View
Horsehold La
Callis Wood
Beaumont Clough Rd
Back La
Jumble Hole Rd
Underbank Ave
Pennine Way
Wood Villas
Broad La
Jumps La
Mulcture Hall
Grey Stone La
Eastwood La
Cruttonstall
Pinnacle
Pinnacle La
Erringden Grange
Kilnshaw La
Rake
Upper House Farm
Long La

87
109

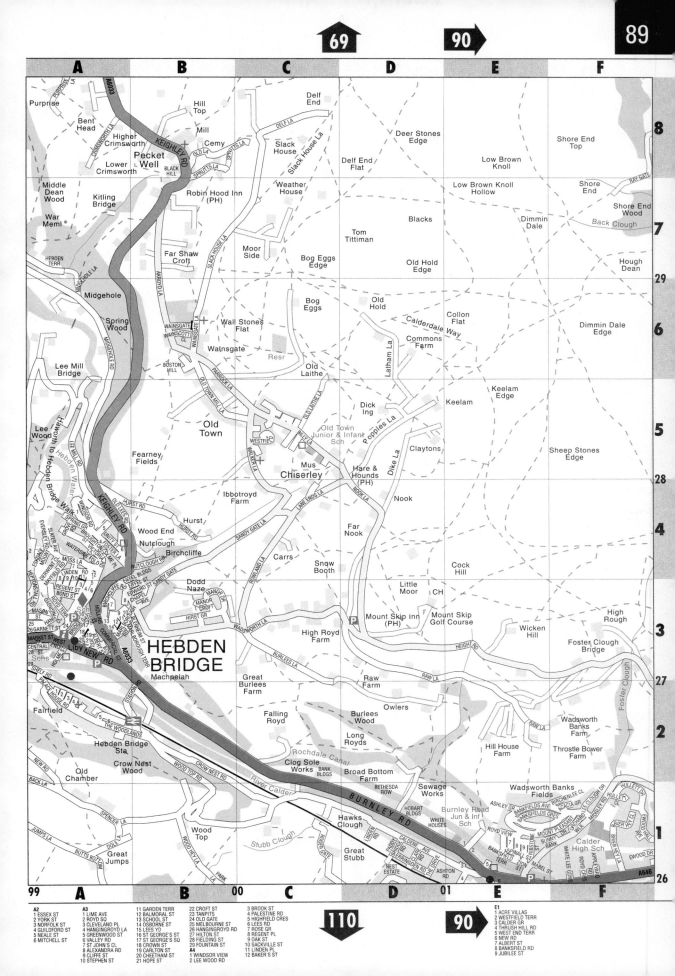

A B C D E F

8
7
29
6
5
28
4
3
27
2
1
26

Purprise
Bent Head
Higher Crimsworth
Pecket Well
Lower Crimsworth
Middle Dean Wood
Kitling Bridge
War Meml
HEBDEN TERR
Midgehole
Spring Wood
Lee Mill Bridge
Lee Wood
Haworth to Hebden Bridge Walk
KEIGHLEY RD
Fairfield
Hebden Bridge Sta
Crow Nest Wood
Old Chamber
NEW RD
BACK LA
JUMPS LA
BUTTS BOTTOM
DOLE
Great Jumps
SPENCER LA

Hill Top
Mill
Cemy
BLACK HILL
OLD LA
SPRUTTS LA
KEIGHLEY RD
AKROYD LA
Robin Hood Inn (PH)
Far Shaw Croft
WAINSGATE LA
WAINSCOTT CL
Boston Hill
OLD TOWN MILL LA
Old Town
Fearney Fields
Wood End
Nutlough
Birchcliffe
HURST RD
Hurst
EIFFEL BLDGS
EDWARD ST
CHAPEL AVE
MANOR CROFT
Dodd Naze
HIRST GR
BLACKCLIFFE LA
HEBDEN BRIDGE
Machpelah
COMMERCIAL ST
A6033
STATION RD
THE WOODLANDS
CROW NEST RD
WOOD TOP RD
Wood Top
WOOD HEY LA
PARK
ROBIN GATE

Delf End
DELF LA
Slack House
SLACK HOUSE LA
Weather House
Moor Side
Bog Eggs Edge
Bog Eggs
Wall Stones Flat
PABROCK LA
Wainsgate
Resr
Old Laithe
OLD LAITHE LA
WESTFIE
WALKER LA
Chiserley
Mus
BILLY LA
Ibbotroyd Farm
LANE ENDS LA
ROWLAND LA
SANDY GATE LA
Carrs
Snow Booth
SANDY GATE
Great Burlees Farm
BURLEES LA
WADSWORTH LA
Falling Royd
Long Royds
Rochdale Canal
Clog Sole Works
BANK BLDGS
River Calder
Stubb Clough
Great Stubb
NEST ESTATE
PADDY BRIDGE RD
GERRINGDEN RD

Delf End Flat
Deer Stones Edge
Low Brown Knoll
Low Brown Knoll Hollow
Blacks
Tom Tittiman
Old Hold Edge
Old Hold
Calderdale Way
Collon Flat
Commons Farm
Dick Ing
LATHAM LA
Keelam
POPPLES LA
Old Town Junior & Infant Sch
Hare & Hounds (PH)
DIKE LA
Claytons
Little Moor
Nook
NOOK LA
Far Nook
Cock Hill
CH
Mount Skip Inn (PH)
Mount Skip Golf Course
High Royd Farm
HEIGHT RD
Raw Farm
RAW LA
Owlers
Burlees Wood
Broad Bottom Farm
Sewage Works
BETHESDA ROW
BURNLEY RD
Hawks Clough
LINDEN RD
Broad Bottom Farm
HOBART BLDGS
WHITE HOUSES
Burnley Road Jun & Inf Sch
CALDENE AVE
ASHTON RD
CLARE RD
THE DRIVE

Shore End Top
RAY GATE
Shore End
Shore End Wood
Back Clough
Dimmin Dale
Hough Dean
Dimmin Dale Edge
Keelam Edge
Sheep Stones Edge
High Rough
Foster Clough Bridge
Foster Clough
Wicken Hill
Wadsworth Banks Farm
Throstle Bower Farm
Hill House Farm
Wadsworth Banks Fields
ASHLEY GR
BANKSFIELDS AVE
BIRCHENLEE CL
ACACIA GR
MOUNT PLEASANT
ROYD VIEW
SUNNY BANK
ASPINALL ST
ZION
MABEL ST
BANKSFIELD TERR
FIRSTONE
WHITE LEE GDNS
Calder High Sch
BIRCH HEY LA
ROYD CRES
APPLEYARD
EWOOD DR
A646

99 A 00 B C 01 D E F 26

A2
1 ESSEX ST
2 YORK ST
3 NORFOLK ST
4 GUILDFORD ST
5 NEALE ST
6 MITCHELL ST

A3
1 LIME AVE
2 ROYD SQ
3 CLEVELAND PL
4 HANGINGROYD LA
5 GREENWOOD ST
6 VALLEY RD
7 ST JOHN'S CL
8 ALEXANDRA RD
9 CLIFFE ST
10 STEPHEN ST

11 GARDEN TERR
12 BALMORAL ST
13 SCHOOL ST
14 OSBORNE ST
15 LEES YD
16 ST GEORGE'S SQ
17 ST GEORGE'S SQ
18 CROWN ST
19 CARLTON ST
20 CHEETHAM ST
21 HOPE ST

22 CROFT ST
23 TANPITS
24 OLD GATE
25 MELBOURNE ST
26 HANGINGROYD RD
27 HILTON ST
28 FIELDING ST
29 FOUNTAIN ST

A4
1 WINDSOR VIEW
2 LEE WOOD RD

3 BROOK ST
4 PALESTINE RD
5 HIGHFIELD CRES
6 LEES RD
7 ROSE GR
8 REGENT PL
9 OAK ST
10 SACKVILLE ST
11 LINDEN PL
12 BAKER'S ST

E1
1 ACRE VILLAS
2 WESTFIELD TERR
3 CALDER GR
4 THRUSH HILL RD
5 WEST END TERR
6 NEW RD
7 ALBERT ST
8 BANKSFIELD RD
9 JUBILEE ST

89
70

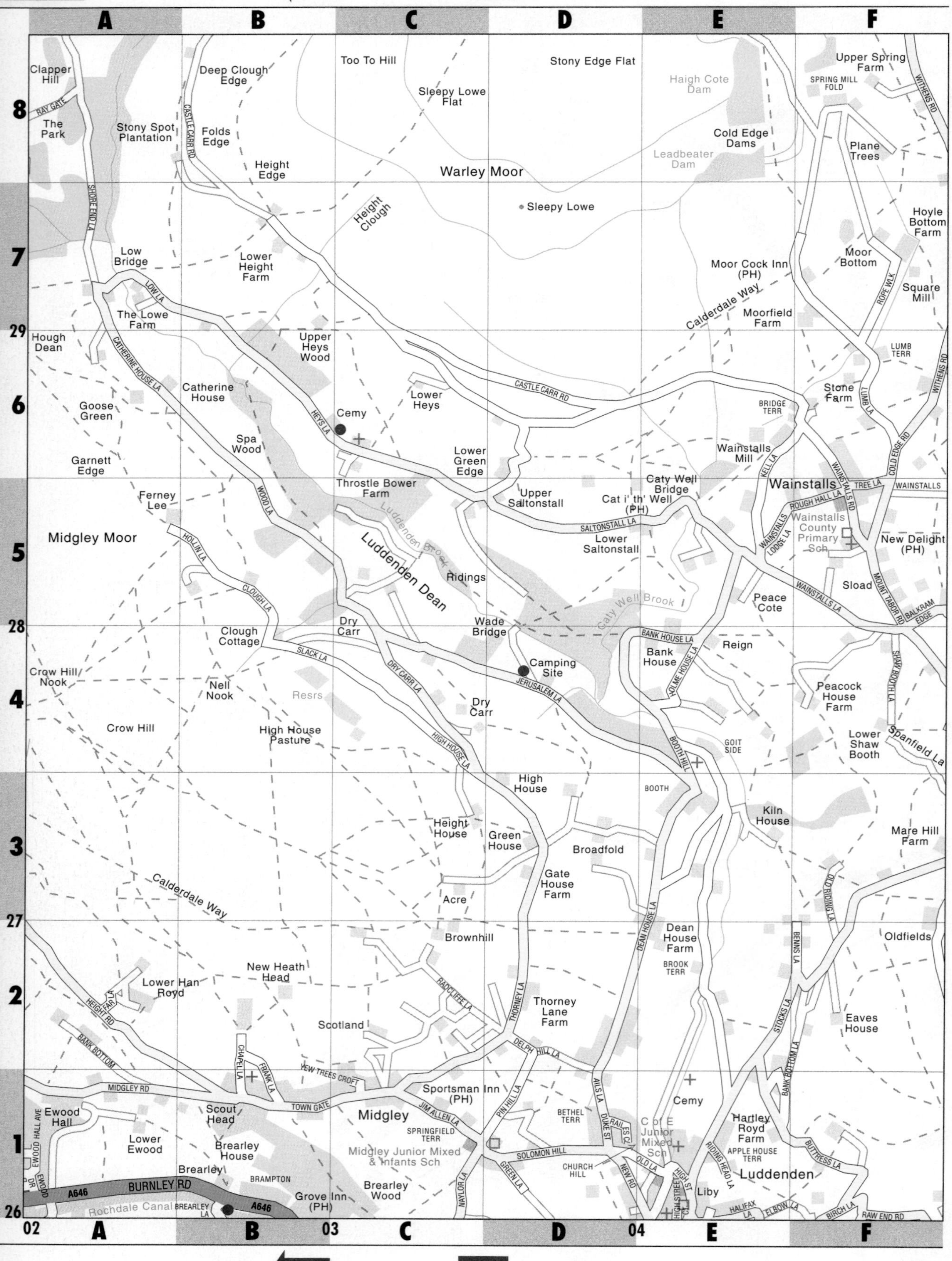
Clapper Hill
Deep Clough Edge
Too To Hill
Stony Edge Flat
Upper Spring Farm
Haigh Cote Dam
Spring Mill Fold
Sleepy Lowe Flat
The Park
Stony Spot Plantation
Folds Edge
Cold Edge Dams
Plane Trees
Leadbeater Dam
Height Edge
Warley Moor
Sleepy Lowe
Hoyle Bottom Farm
Height Clough
Low Bridge
Lower Height Farm
Moor Cock Inn (PH)
Moor Bottom
Square Mill
Calderdale Way
Moorfield Farm
The Lowe Farm
Hough Dean
Upper Heys Wood
Catherine House
Goose Green
Cemy
Lower Heys
Stone Farm
Spa Wood
Garnett Edge
Lower Green Edge
Wainstalls Mill
Caty Well Bridge
Wainstalls
Throstle Bower Farm
Ferney Lee
Upper Saltonstall
Cat i' th' Well (PH)
Wainstalls County Primary Sch
New Delight (PH)
Midgley Moor
Luddenden Dean
Luddenden Brook
Lower Saltonstall
Ridings
Sload
Peace Cote
Caty Well Brook
Wade Bridge
Dry Carr
Clough Cottage
Reign
Bank House
Camping Site
Crow Hill Nook
Nell Nook
Resrs
Peacock House Farm
Crow Hill
High House Pasture
Lower Shaw Booth
Spanfield La
Goit Side
High House
Booth
Kiln House
Height House
Green House
Broadfold
Mare Hill Farm
Gate House Farm
Acre
Calderdale Way
Brownhill
Dean House Farm
Oldfields
Brook Terr
New Heath Head
Lower Han Royd
Thorney Lane Farm
Scotland
Eaves House
Sportsman Inn (PH)
Cemy
Ewood Hall
Scout Head
Midgley
Bethel Terr
Springfield Terr
C of E Junior Mixed Sch
Hartley Royd Farm
Lower Ewood
Brearley House
Midgley Junior Mixed & Infants Sch
Church Hill
Apple House Terr
Brearley
Brampton
Luddenden
Burnley Rd
A646
Brearley Wood
Grove Inn (PH)
Liby
Rochdale Canal
Ray Gate
Castle Carr Rd
Shore End La
Withens Rd
Low La
Rope Wlk
Lumb Terr
Catherine House La
Castle Carr Rd
Bridge Terr
Lumb La
Heys La
Cold Edge Rd
Kell La
Wainstalls Rd
Tree La
Wainstalls
Rough Hall La
Wood La
Saltonstall La
Wainstalls Lodge La
Hollin La
Mount Tabor Rd
Clough La
Wainstalls La
Balkram Edge
Bank House La
Slack La
Holme House La
Dry Carr La
Jerusalem La
Shay Booth La
Booth Hill
High House La
Old Riding La
Dean House La
Benns La
Radcliffe La
Height Far
Thorney La
Stocks La
Bank Bottom
Chapel La
Delph Hill La
Bank Bottom La
Frank La
Yew Trees Croft
Midgley Rd
Town Gate
Ails La
Pin Hill La
Jim Allen La
Duke St
Rail Es Cl
Ewood Hall Ave
Solomon Hill
Riding Head La
Buttress La
Old La
Ewood Dr
Green La
Naylor La
New Rd
High St
Halifax La
Elbow La
Birch La
Raw End Rd
Brearley La
8
7
29
6
5
28
4
3
27
2
1
26
02
03
04
A
B
C
D
E
F

89
111

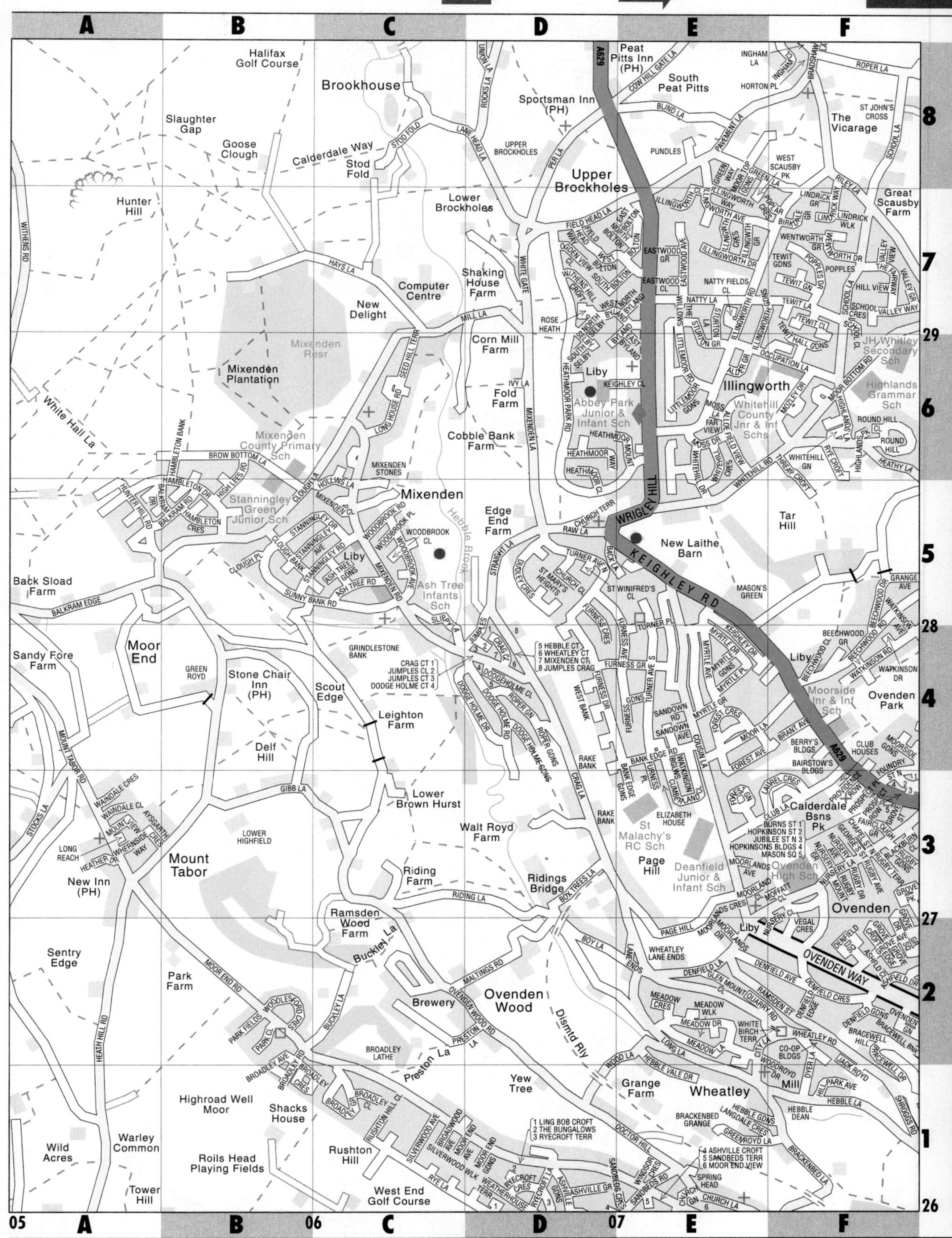
A
B
C
D
E
F
Halifax Golf Course
Brookhouse
Peat Pitts Inn (PH)
South Peat Pitts
Ingham La
Roper La
Horton Pl
Slaughter Gap
Goose Clough
Calderdale Way
Stod Fold
Sportsman Inn (PH)
Blind La
The Vicarage
St John's Cross
Upper Brockholes
Pundles
Pavement La
West Scausby Pk
Hunter Hill
Lower Brockholes
Great Scausby Farm
Withens Rd
Field Head La
Illingworth Cl
Illingworth Ave
Illingworth Dr
Eastwood Gr
Eastwood Cl
Eastwood Ave
Hays La
Computer Centre
Shaking House Farm
White Gate
Natty Fields Cl
Natty La
Tewit Gdns
Tewit Gn
Tewit La
Tewit Hall Gdns
Popples
Hill View
School La
School Cres
Valley Way
New Delight
Mill La
Rose Heath
Corn Mill Farm
Mixenden Resr
Mixenden Plantation
Occupation La
JH Whitley Secondary Sch
Liby
Ivy La
Fold Farm
Keighley Cl
Abbey Park Junior & Infant Sch
Illingworth
Whitehill County Jnr & Inf Schs
Highlands Grammar Sch
Moor Bottom Rd
Round Hill
White Hall La
Mixenden County Primary Sch
Cobble Bank Farm
Heathmoor Park Rd
Heathmoor Way
Heathmoor Cl
Whitehill Rd
Whitehill Gn
Threap Croft
Rye Croft
Heathy La
Hambleton Bank
Brow Bottom La
Mixenden Stones
Mixenden
Hambleton Dr
Balkram Rd
Hunter Hill Rd
Stanningley Green Junior Sch
Stanningley Dr
Woodbrook Rd
Woodbrook Cl
Edge End Farm
Church Terr
Wrigley Hill
Raw La
Tar Hill
New Laithe Barn
Clough Pl
Clough Bank
Sunny Bank Rd
Ash Tree Rd
Mixenden Rd
Hebble Brook
Ash Tree Infants Sch
Straight La
Turner Ave N
St Mary's Heights
St Winifred's Cl
Keighley Rd
Mason's Green
Grange Ave
Back Sload Farm
Balkram Edge
Slippy La
Turner Pl
Beechwood Dr
Watkinson Ave
Moor End
Sandy Fore Farm
Grindlestone Bank
5 Hebble Ct
6 Wheatley Ct
7 Mixenden Ct
8 Jumples Crag
Crag Ct 1
Jumples Cl 2
Jumples Ct 3
Dodge Holme Ct 4
Furness Gr
Beechwood Gr
Watkinson Rd
Watkinson Dr
Green Royd
Stone Chair Inn (PH)
Scout Edge
Leighton Farm
Dodge Holme Dr
Roper Gn
Furness Dr
Turner Ave S
Sandown Rd
Sandown Ave
Myrtle Gr
Forest Cres
Moor La
Brant Ave
Moorside Jnr & Inf Sch
Ovenden Park
Delf Hill
Roper Gdns
Crag La
West Bank
Rake Bank
Bank Edge Rd
Cousin La
Forest Ave
Berry's Bldgs
Bairstow's Bldgs
Club Houses
Moorside Gdns
Foundry
Mount Tabor Rd
Waindale Cres
Gibb La
Lower Brown Hurst
Laurel Cres
Club La
Calderdale Bsns Pk
Providence Row
Prospect Pl
Stocks La
Long Reach
Heather Dr
Whernside Way
Lower Highfield
Mount Tabor
Walt Royd Farm
Rake Bank
Elizabeth House
St Malachy's RC Sch
Burns St 1
Hopkinson St 2
Jubilee St N 3
Hopkinsons Bldgs 4
Mason Sq 5
New Inn (PH)
Riding Farm
Ridings Bridge
Page Hill
Deanfield Junior & Infant Sch
Moorlands Ave
Ovenden High Sch
Riding La
Box Trees La
Moorland Cres
Moffatt Cl
Ovenden
Sentry Edge
Ramsden Wood Farm
Buckley La
Page Hill
Wheatley Lane Ends
Nursery Cl
Vegal Cres
Ovenden Way
Boy La
Lane Ends
Denfield La
Denfield Ave
Glen Mount Cl
Ramsden St
Quarry Rd
Denfield Cres
Park Farm
Moor End Rd
Maltings Rd
Ovenden Wood
Brewery
Ovenden Wood Rd
Meadow Cres
Meadow Wlk
Meadow Dr
White Birch Terr
Co-op Bldgs
Wheatley Rd
Bracewell Hill
Heath Hill Rd
Park Fields
Woodlesford Cres
Dismtd Rly
Preston La
Broadley Lathe
Long La
City La
Dyer La
Jack Royd
Broadley Ave
Broadley Cres
Yew Tree
Wood La
Hebble Vale Dr
Grange Farm
Woodroyd Dr
Wheatley
Mill
Park Ave
Hebble La
Highroad Well Moor
Shacks House
Rushton Hill Cl
Silverwood Ave
Broadwood Ave
Moor End Gdns
1 Ling Bob Croft
2 The Bungalows
3 Ryecroft Terr
Doctor Hill
Brackenbed Grange
Langdale Cres
Greenroyd La
Hebble Dean
Shroggs Rd
Warley Common
Wild Acres
Rushton Hill
Roils Head Playing Fields
Silverwood Wlk
Ryecroft Cres
Ashville Gr
Sandbeds Cres
Sandbeds Rd
4 Ashville Croft
5 Sandbeds Terr
6 Moor End View
Spring Head
Brackenbed La
Tower Hill
West End Golf Course
Rye La
Weatherhouse Terr
Ryecroft La
Church Gn
Church La
A629
8
7
29
6
5
28
4
3
27
2
1
26
05
06
07

91
72

C8
1 OLD GUY RD
2 MOOR CLOSE FARM MEWS
3 CLARENDON PL
4 SUNNY VIEW TERR
5 MYRTLE GR
6 OXFORD RD

D8
1 CONISTON AVE
2 CONISTON CL
3 LEE ST
4 HAINSWORTH MOOR GARTH
5 HAINSWORTH MOOR CRES
6 HAINSWORTH MOOR DR

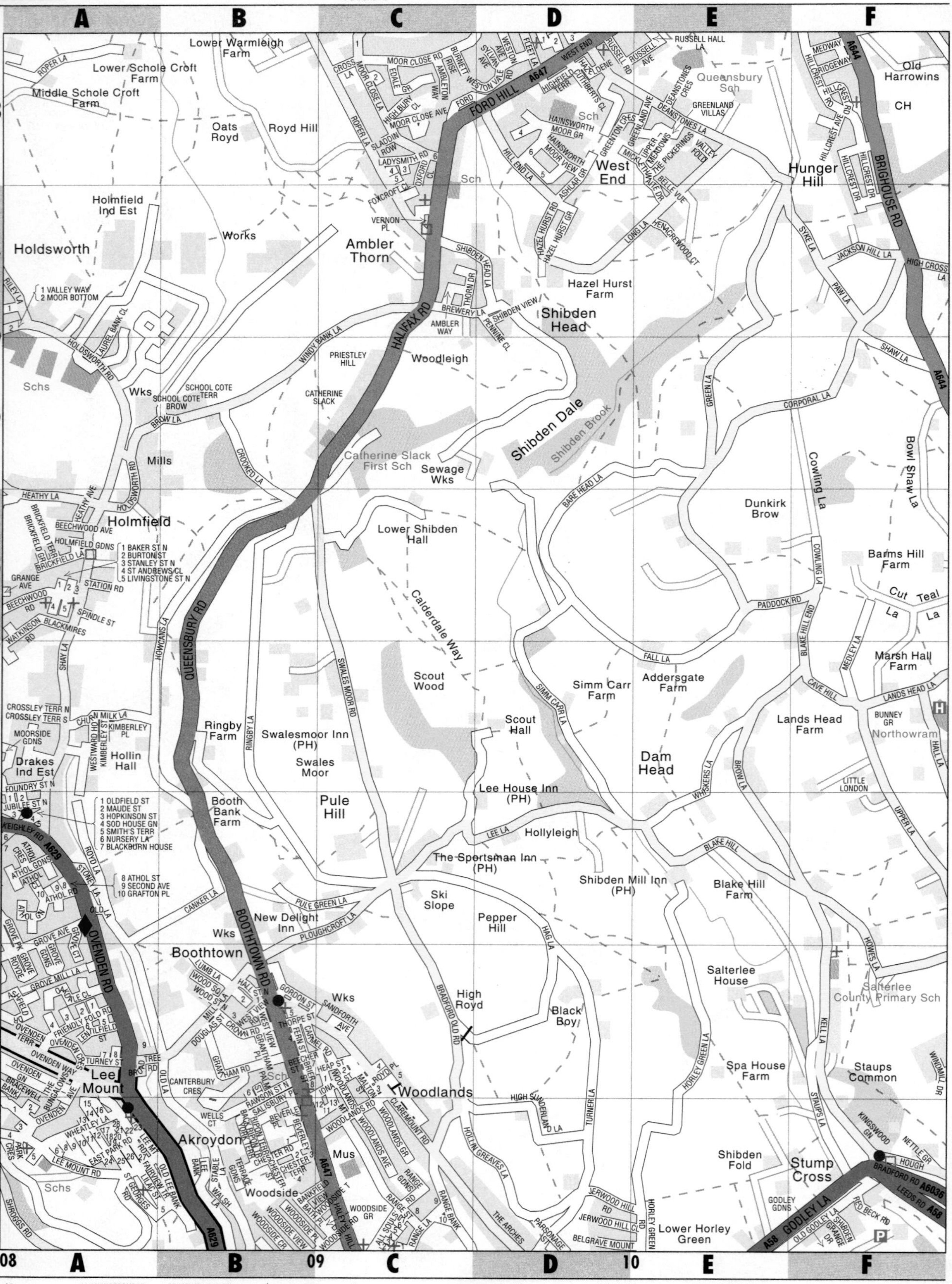
A
B
C
D
E
F
8
7
29
6
5
28
4
3
27
2
1
26
08
09
10
Lower Warmleigh Farm
Lower Schole Croft Farm
Middle Schole Croft Farm
Oats Royd
Royd Hill
Holmfield Ind Est
Holdsworth
Works
Ambler Thorn
Queensbury Sch
West End
Hunger Hill
Old Harrowins
CH
Hazel Hurst Farm
Shibden Head
Woodleigh
Priestley Hill
Catherine Slack
Catherine Slack First Sch
Sewage Wks
Shibden Dale
Shibden Brook
Schs
Wks
Mills
Holmfield
Lower Shibden Hall
Calderdale Way
Dunkirk Brow
Cowling La
Bowl Shaw La
Barms Hill Farm
Cut La
Teal La
Marsh Hall Farm
Scout Wood
Simm Carr Farm
Addersgate Farm
Lands Head Farm
Northowram
Ringby Farm
Swalesmoor Inn (PH)
Swales Moor
Scout Hall
Dam Head
Hollin Hall
Drakes Ind Est
Booth Bank Farm
Pule Hill
Lee House Inn (PH)
Hollyleigh
The Sportsman Inn (PH)
Shibden Mill Inn (PH)
Blake Hill Farm
Little London
New Delight Inn
Ski Slope
Pepper Hill
Boothtown
Salterlee House
Salterlee County Primary Sch
High Royd
Black Boy
Spa House Farm
Staups Common
Lee Mount
Woodlands
Akroydon
Mus
Woodside
Shibden Fold
Stump Cross
Lower Horley Green
Schs
QUEENSBURY RD
HALIFAX RD
BOOTHTOWN RD
OVENDEN RD
BRIGHOUSE RD
FORD HILL
GODLEY LA
A647
A644
A629
A6036
A58

A1
1 BRACEWELL DR
2 BRACEWELL GR
3 WHEATLEY CL
4 WHEATLEY RD
5 LEE MOUNT GDNS
6 PEABODY ST
7 ELLISON ST
8 BUXTON ST
9 MATLOCK ST
10 GRANGE ST
11 LIVINGSTONE ST
12 TENNYSON ST
13 CLIFTON ST
14 LAWRENCE ST
15 OVENDEN CL
16 RUSHWORTH ST
17 GARFIELD ST
18 COLUMBUS ST
19 ASHVILLE ST
20 WASHINGTON ST
21 BRIGHTON ST
22 MELBOURNE ST
23 INGHAMS CT
24 RUSKIN TERR
25 WOODVILLE ST
26 MELROSE ST
27 CONCRETE ST
28 BATLEY ST

A2
1 FRIENDLY ST
2 BETHEL ST
3 AMY ST
4 CLEVEDON PL
5 EARL TERR
6 LENTILFIELD TERR
7 EASTWOOD ST
8 ROBERT ST
9 OVENDEN ROAD TERR

B1
1 CHESTER CT
2 CHESTER GR
3 CHESTER CL
4 CHESTRE PL
5 GILMOUR ST

B2
1 TURNER'S CT
2 McBURNEY CL
3 BRUNEL CT
4 UTTLEY ST
5 SIMPSON ST
6 CATHCART ST
7 FERNFIELD TERR
8 IONA PL

C1
1 SUNNY SIDE ST
2 ALL SOULS' TERR
3 ALL SOULS' ST
4 SUNNY BANK TERR
5 LAURA ST
6 ADA ST
7 BACK LYTTON ST
8 WOODLANDS VIEW
9 LOWER RANGE
10 AMBLERS TERR
11 BROUGHAM RD
12 BROUGHAM ST
13 BROUGHAM TERR

C2
1 BREWERY ST
2 ROBERT ST N
3 CLAREMOUNT TERR
4 ROYD MOUNT
5 THORN VIEW

91
113

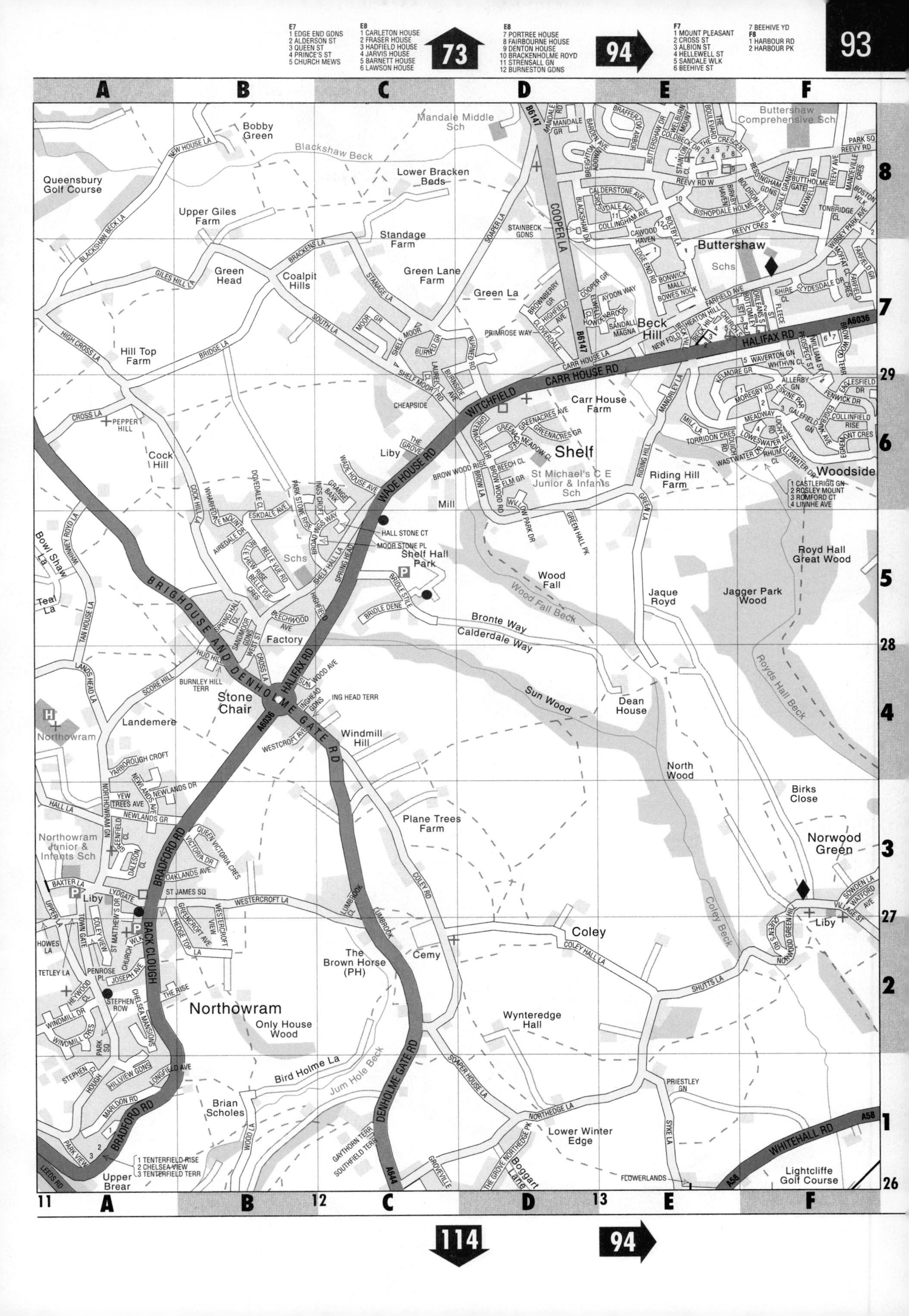

93
E7
1 EDGE END GDNS
2 ALDERSON ST
3 QUEEN ST
4 PRINCE'S ST
5 CHURCH MEWS
E8
1 CARLETON HOUSE
2 FRASER HOUSE
3 HADFIELD HOUSE
4 JARVIS HOUSE
5 BARNETT HOUSE
6 LAWSON HOUSE
73
E8
7 PORTREE HOUSE
8 FAIRBOURNE HOUSE
9 DENTON HOUSE
10 BRACKENHOLME ROYD
11 STRENSALL GN
12 BURNESTON GDNS
94
F7
1 MOUNT PLEASANT
2 CROSS ST
3 ALBION ST
4 HELLEWELL ST
5 SANDALE WLK
6 BEEHIVE ST
7 BEEHIVE YD
F8
1 HARBOUR RD
2 HARBOUR PK
A
B
C
D
E
F
Bobby Green
Mandale Middle Sch
Buttershaw Comprehensive Sch
Blackshaw Beck
Queensbury Golf Course
Lower Bracken Beds
Upper Giles Farm
Standage Farm
Buttershaw
Schs
Green Head
Coalpit Hills
Green Lane Farm
Green La
Beck Hill
Hill Top Farm
Carr House Farm
Liby
Shelf
St Michael's C E Junior & Infants Sch
Woodside
Riding Hill Farm
Cock Hill
Mill
1 CASTLERIGG GN
2 ROSLEY MOUNT
3 ROMFORD CT
4 LINNHE AVE
Shelf Hall Park
Royd Hall Great Wood
Wood Fall
Jaque Royd
Jagger Park Wood
Bowl Shaw La
Teal La
Factory
Bronte Way
Calderdale Way
Wood Fall Beck
Royds Hall Beck
Stone Chair
Sun Wood
Dean House
Landemere
Northowram
Windmill Hill
North Wood
Birks Close
Plane Trees Farm
Norwood Green
Northowram Junior & Infants Sch
Coley
Coley Beck
Cemy
The Brown Horse (PH)
Northowram
Only House Wood
Wynteredge Hall
Bird Holme La
Jum Hole Beck
Brian Scholes
Lower Winter Edge
Boggart Lane
Upper Brear
Lightcliffe Golf Course
1 TENTERFIELD RISE
2 CHELSEA VIEW
3 TENTERFIELD TERR
BRIGHOUSE AND DENHOLME GATE RD
HALIFAX RD
WADE HOUSE RD
WITCHFIELD
CARR HOUSE RD
COOPER LA
BRADFORD RD
BACK CLOUGH
DENHOLME GATE RD
WHITEHALL RD
A6036
A644
A58
B6147
8
7
29
6
5
28
4
3
27
2
1
26
11
12
13
114
94

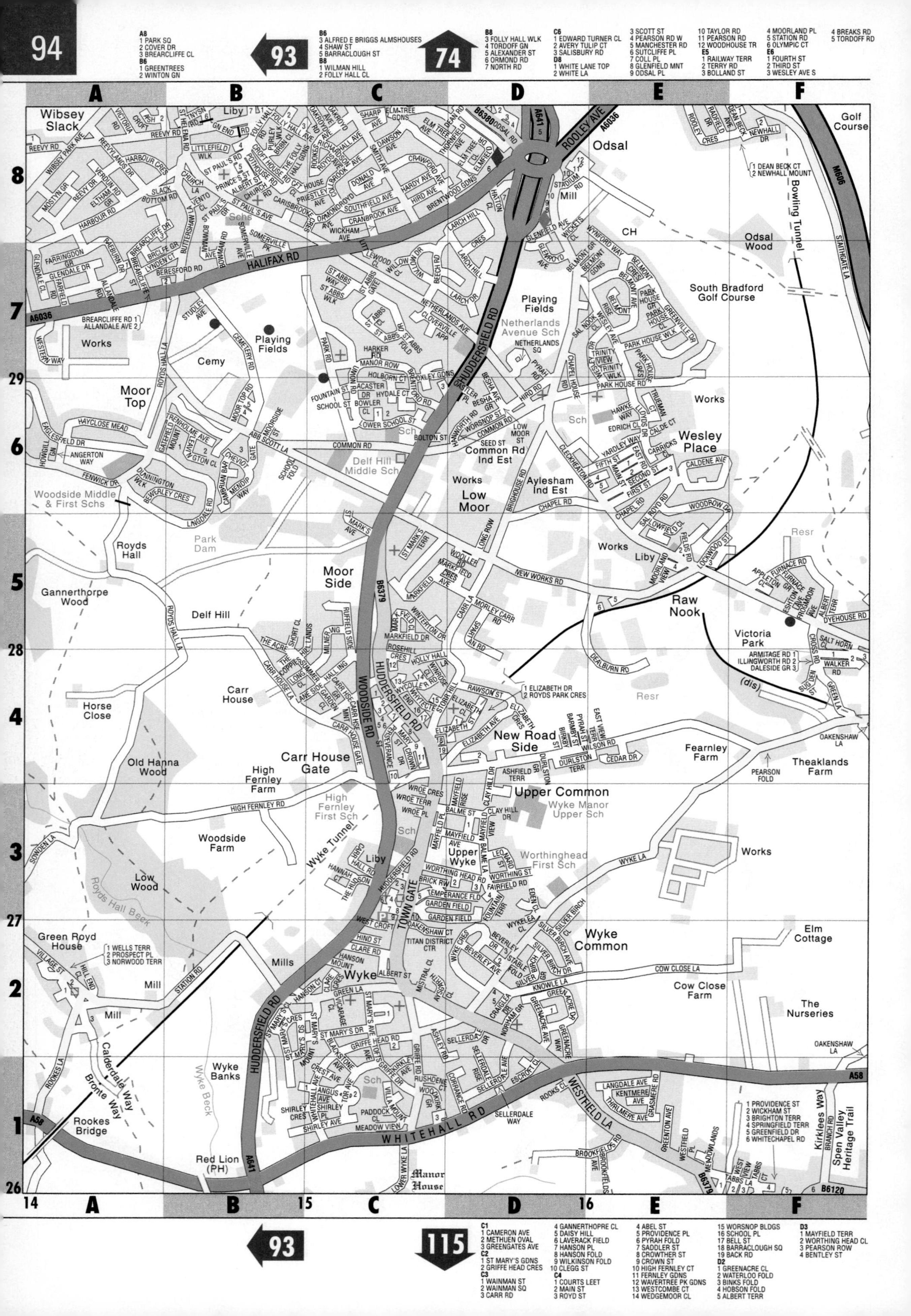
A8
1 PARK SQ
2 COVER DR
3 BREARCLIFFE CL
B6
1 GREENTREES
2 WINTON GN
93
B6
3 ALFRED E BRIGGS ALMSHOUSES
4 SHAW ST
5 BARRACLOUGH ST
B8
1 WILMAN HILL
2 FOLLY HALL CL
74
B8
3 FOLLY HALL WLK
4 TORDOFF GN
5 ALEXANDER ST
6 ORMOND RD
7 NORTH RD
C6
1 EDWARD TURNER CL
2 AVERY TULIP CT
3 SALISBURY RD
D8
1 WHITE LANE TOP
2 WHITE LA
3 SCOTT ST
4 PEARSON RD W
5 MANCHESTER RD
6 SUTCLIFFE PL
7 COLL PL
8 GLENFIELD MNT
9 ODSAL PL
10 TAYLOR RD
11 PEARSON RD
12 WOODHOUSE TR
E5
1 RAILWAY TERR
2 TERRY RD
3 BOLLAND ST
4 MOORLAND PL
5 STATION RD
6 OLYMPIC CT
E6
1 FOURTH ST
2 THIRD ST
3 WESLEY AVE S
4 BREAKS RD
5 TORDOFF RD
A B C D E F
Wibsey Slack
Odsal
Golf Course
Mill
CH
Odsal Wood
Bowling Tunnel
South Bradford Golf Course
Playing Fields
Netherlands Avenue Sch
Works
Cemy
Moor Top
Delf Hill Middle Sch
Common Rd Ind Est
Low Moor
Aylesham Ind Est
Wesley Place
Woodside Middle & First Schs
Royds Hall
Park Dam
Moor Side
Gannerthorpe Wood
Delf Hill
Raw Nook
Victoria Park
Resr
Horse Close
Carr House
New Road Side
Fearnley Farm
Theaklands Farm
Old Hanna Wood
High Fernley Farm
Carr House Gate
Upper Common
Wyke Manor Upper Sch
High Fernley First Sch
Woodside Farm
Upper Wyke
Worthinghead First Sch
Low Wood
Royds Hall Beck
Wyke Tunnel
Green Royd House
Wyke Common
Elm Cottage
Mills
Wyke
Cow Close Farm
The Nurseries
Calderdale Way
Bronte Way
Wyke Banks
Wyke Beck
Rookes Bridge
Red Lion (PH)
Manor House
Kirklees Way
Spen Valley Heritage Trail
HALIFAX RD
HUDDERSFIELD RD
WOODSIDE RD
WHITEHALL RD
WESTFIELD LA
A6036
A641
A58
B6379
B6380
B6120
M606
8 7 29 6 5 28 4 3 27 2 1 26
14 15 16
93
115
C1
1 CAMERON AVE
2 METHUEN OVAL
3 GREENGATES AVE
C2
1 ST MARY'S GDNS
2 GRIFFE HEAD CRES
C3
1 WAINMAN ST
2 WAINMAN SQ
3 CARR RD
4 GANNERTHOPRE CL
5 DAISY HILL
6 LAVERACK FIELD
7 HANSON PL
8 HANSON FOLD
9 WILKINSON FOLD
10 CLEGG ST
C4
1 COURTS LEET
2 MAIN ST
3 ROYD ST
4 ABEL ST
5 PROVIDENCE PL
6 PYRAH FOLD
7 SADDLER ST
8 CROWTHER ST
9 CROWN ST
10 HIGH FERNLEY CT
11 FERNLEY GDNS
12 WAVERTREE PK GDNS
13 WESTCOMBE CT
14 WEDGEMOOR CL
15 WORSNOP BLDGS
16 SCHOOL PL
17 BELL ST
18 BARRACLOUGH SQ
19 BACK RD
D2
1 GREENACRE CL
2 WATERLOO FOLD
3 BINKS FOLD
4 HOBSON FOLD
5 ALBERT TERR
D3
1 MAYFIELD TERR
2 WORTHING HEAD CL
3 PEARSON ROW
4 BENTLEY ST

75
96

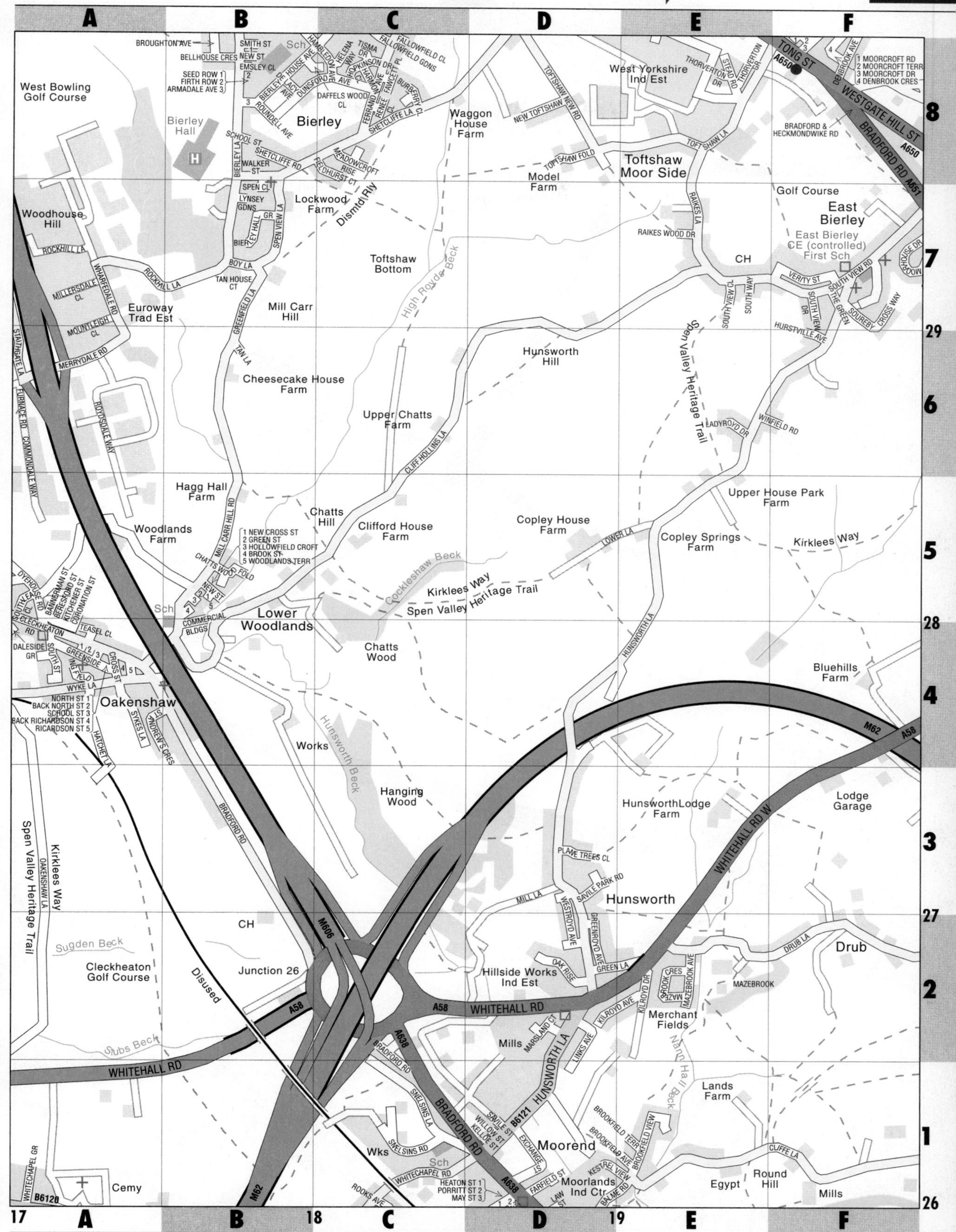

West Bowling Golf Course
Bierley Hall
Bierley
Woodhouse Hill
Euroway Trad Est
Lockwood Farm
Dismtd Rly
Waggon House Farm
West Yorkshire Ind Est
Toftshaw Moor Side
Model Farm
Toftshaw Bottom
Mill Carr Hill
Golf Course
East Bierley
East Bierley CE (controlled) First Sch
Cheesecake House Farm
Upper Chatts Farm
Hunsworth Hill
Spen Valley Heritage Trail
Hagg Hall Farm
Woodlands Farm
Chatts Hill
Clifford House Farm
Copley House Farm
Copley Springs Farm
Upper House Park Farm
Kirklees Way
Cockleshaw Beck
Lower Woodlands
Chatts Wood
Oakenshaw
Bluehills Farm
Works
Hunsworth Beck
Hanging Wood
HunsworthLodge Farm
Lodge Garage
Hunsworth
Drub
Cleckheaton Golf Course
Sugden Beck
Junction 26
Disused
Hillside Works Ind Est
Merchant Fields
Mills
Lands Farm
Moorend
Moorlands Ind Ctr
Egypt
Round Hill
Wks
Cemy
WHITEHALL RD
WHITEHALL RD W
BRADFORD RD
HUNSWORTH LA
M62
M606
A58
A638
A650
A651
B6120
B6121
TONG ST
WESTGATE HILL ST
BRADFORD & HECKMONDWIKE RD
1 MOORCROFT RD
2 MOORCROFT TERR
3 MOORCROFT DR
4 DENBROOK CRES
1 NEW CROSS ST
2 GREEN ST
3 HOLLOWFIELD CROFT
4 BROOK ST
5 WOODLANDS TERR
NORTH ST 1
BACK NORTH ST 2
SCHOOL ST 3
BACK RICHARDSON ST 4
RICARDSON ST 5
HEATON ST 1
PORRITT ST 2
MAY ST 3
A B C D E F
17 18 19
8 7 6 5 4 3 2 1
29 28 27 26

116
96

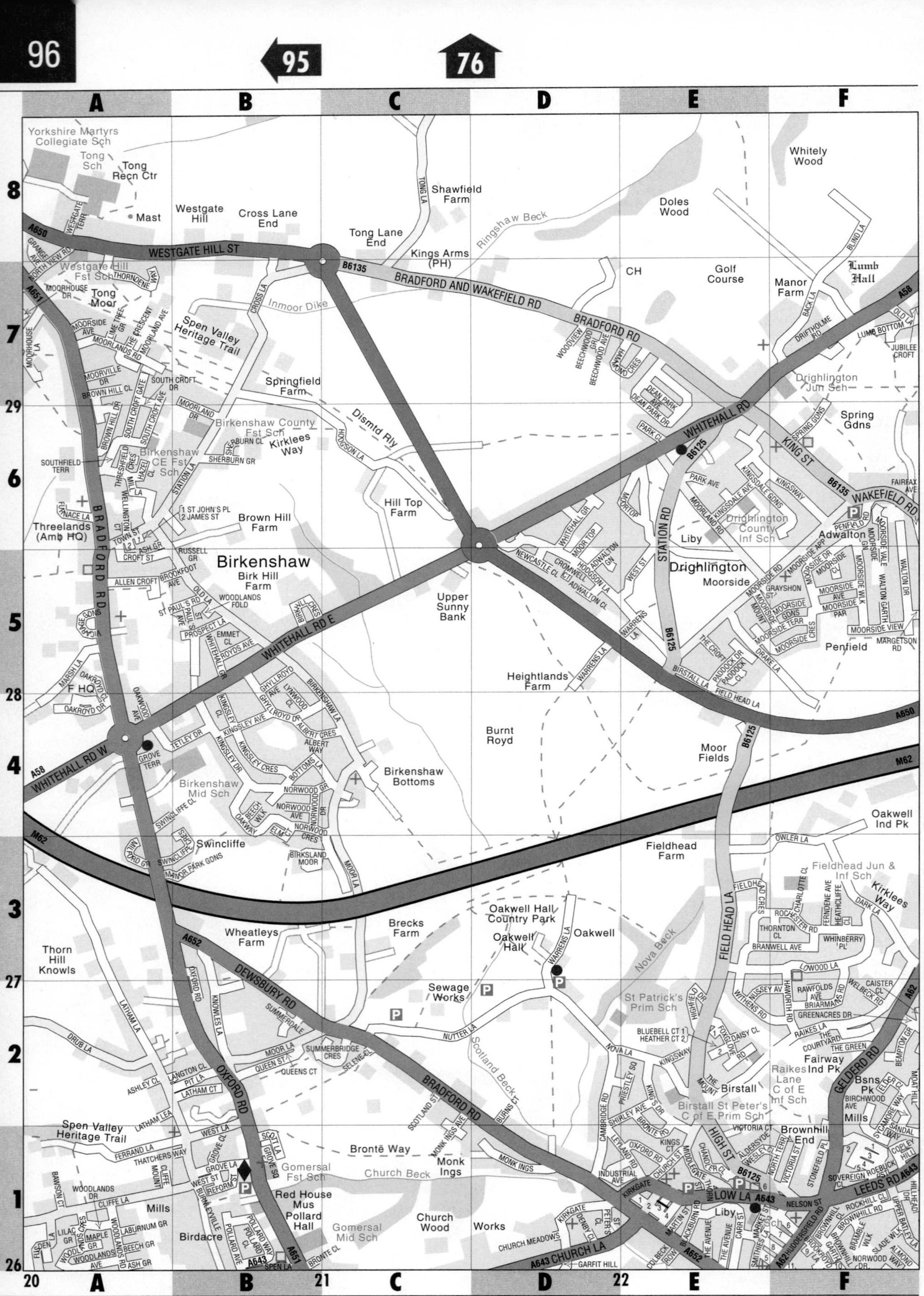

77

98

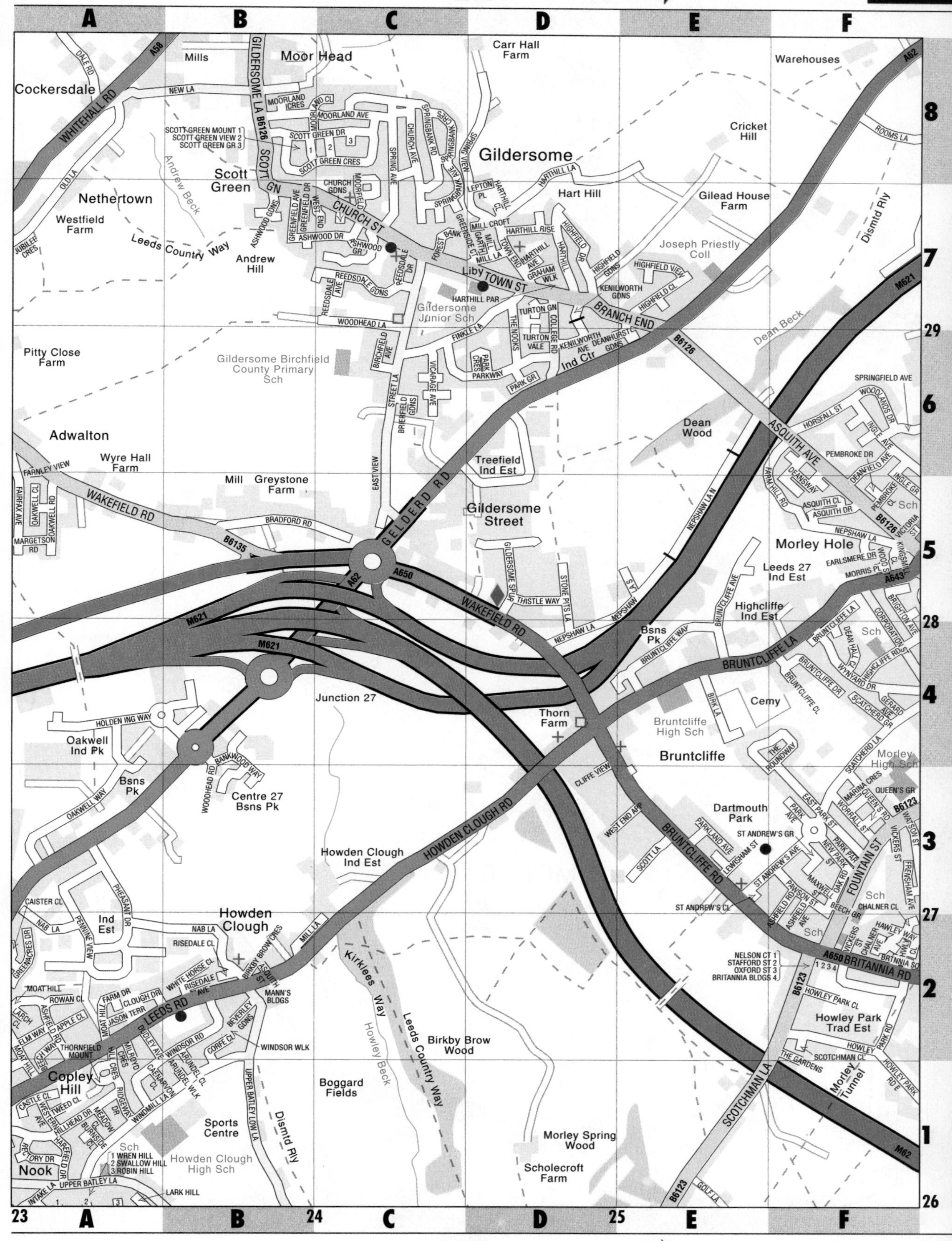

Cockersdale
Mills
Moor Head
Carr Hall Farm
Warehouses
Gildersome
Scott Green
Nethertown
Westfield Farm
Cricket Hill
Hart Hill
Gilead House Farm
Joseph Priestly Coll
Andrew Hill
Leeds Country Way
Andrew Beck
Gildersome Junior Sch
Gildersome Birchfield County Primary Sch
Pitty Close Farm
Adwalton
Wyre Hall Farm
Mill
Greystone Farm
Treefield Ind Est
Gildersome Street
Dean Wood
Dean Beck
Morley Hole
Leeds 27 Ind Est
Highcliffe Ind Est
Bsns Pk
Junction 27
Thorn Farm
Bruntcliffe High Sch
Cemy
Bruntcliffe
Oakwell Ind Pk
Bsns Pk
Centre 27 Bsns Pk
Dartmouth Park
Morley High Sch
Howden Clough Ind Est
Howden Clough
Ind Est
Kirklees Way
Leeds Country Way
Howley Beck
Birkby Brow Wood
Howley Park Trad Est
Morley Tunnel
Copley Hill
Boggard Fields
Sports Centre
Howden Clough High Sch
Morley Spring Wood
Scholecroft Farm
Nook
Dismtd Rly
M621
M62
A62
A650
A58
A643
B6126
B6135
B6123
GELDERD RD
WAKEFIELD RD
HOWDEN CLOUGH RD
BRUNTCLIFFE RD
BRUNTCLIFFE LA
ASQUITH AVE
BRITANNIA RD
SCOTCHMAN LA
LEEDS RD
WHITEHALL RD
CHURCH ST
TOWN ST
BRANCH END
FOUNTAIN ST
NEPSHAW LA
NEPSHAW LA N
OAKWELL WAY
HOLDEN ING WAY
UPPER BATLEY LOW LA
UPPER BATLEY LA
LARK HILL
INTAKE LA
SCOTT GREEN MOUNT 1
SCOTT GREEN VIEW 2
SCOTT GREEN GR 3
NELSON CT 1
STAFFORD ST 2
OXFORD ST 3
BRITANNIA BLDGS 4
1 WREN HILL
2 SWALLOW HILL
3 ROBIN HILL
A B C D E F
8 7 6 5 4 3 2 1
23 24 25 26 27 28 29

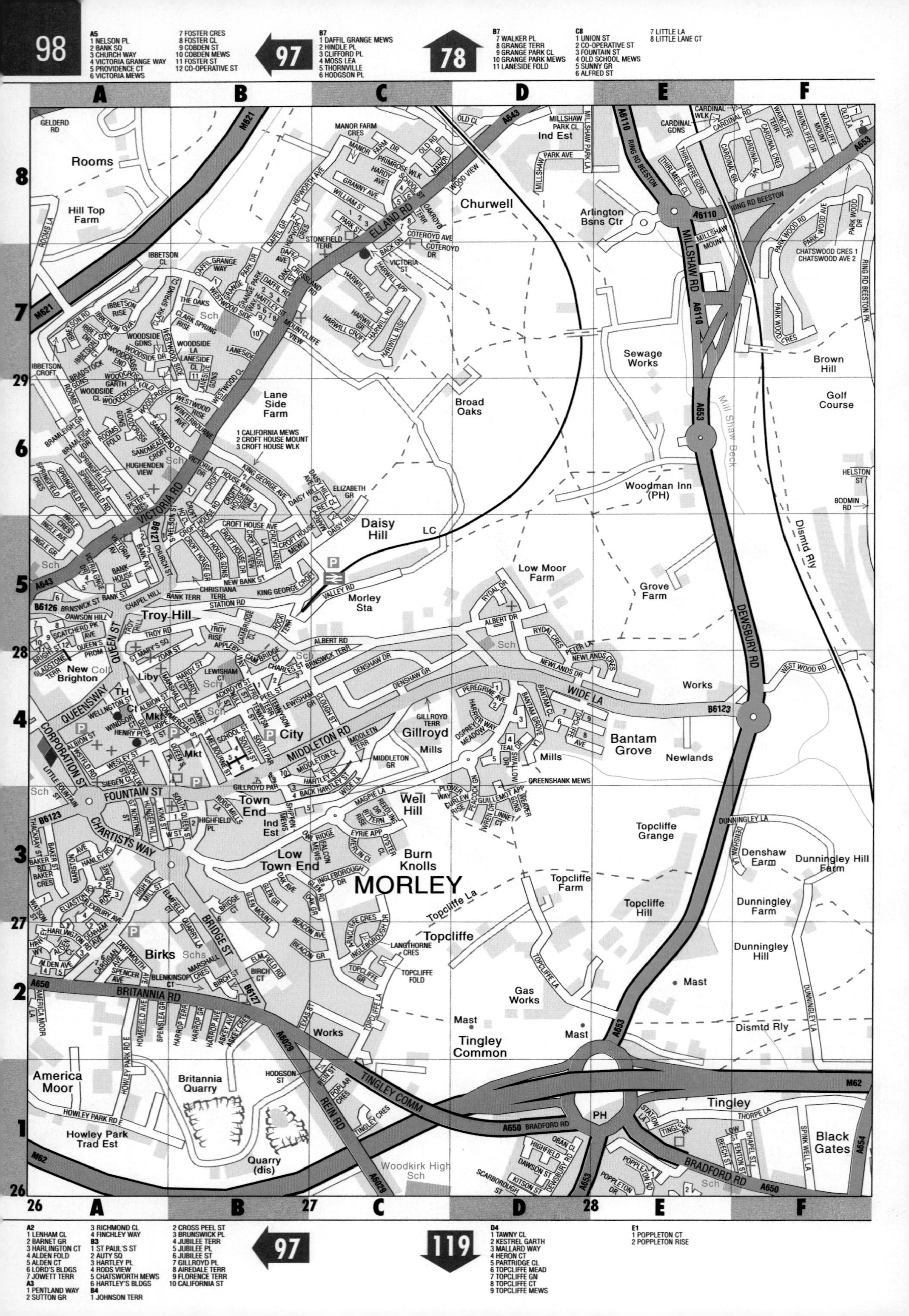

98

A5
1 NELSON PL
2 BANK SQ
3 CHURCH WAY
4 VICTORIA GRANGE WAY
5 PROVIDENCE CT
6 VICTORIA MEWS

7 FOSTER CRES
8 FOSTER ST
9 COBDEN ST
10 COBDEN MEWS
11 FOSTER ST
12 CO-OPERATIVE ST

B7
1 DAFFIL GRANGE MEWS
2 HINDLE PL
3 CLIFFORD PL
4 MOSS LEA
5 THORNVILLE
6 HODGSON PL

97

78

B7
7 WALKER PL
8 GRANGE TERR
9 GRANGE PARK CL
10 GRANGE PARK MEWS
11 LANESIDE FOLD

C8
1 UNION ST
2 CO-OPERATIVE ST
3 FOUNTAIN ST
4 OLD SCHOOL MEWS
5 SUNNY GR
6 ALFRED ST

7 LITTLE LA
8 LITTLE LANE CT

26 A 27 B C 27 D 28 E F

A2
1 LENHAM CL
2 BARNET GR
3 HARLINGTON CT
4 ALDEN FOLD
5 ALDEN CT
6 LORD'S BLDGS
7 JOWETT TERR
A3
1 PENTLAND WAY
2 SUTTON GR

3 RICHMOND CL
4 FINCHLEY WAY
B3
1 ST PAUL'S ST
2 AUTY SQ
3 HARTLEY PL
4 RODS VIEW
5 CHATSWORTH MEWS
6 HARTLEY'S BLDGS
B4
1 JOHNSON TERR

2 CROSS PEEL ST
3 BRUNSWICK PL
4 JUBILEE TERR
5 JUBILEE PL
6 JUBILEE ST
7 GILLROYD PL
8 AIREDALE TERR
9 FLORENCE TERR
10 CALIFORNIA ST

97

119

D4
1 TAWNY CL
2 KESTREL GARTH
3 MALLARD WAY
4 HERON CT
5 PARTRIDGE CL
6 TOPCLIFFE MEAD
7 TOPCLIFFE GN
8 TOPCLIFFE CT
9 TOPCLIFFE MEWS

E1
1 POPPLETON CT
2 POPPLETON RISE

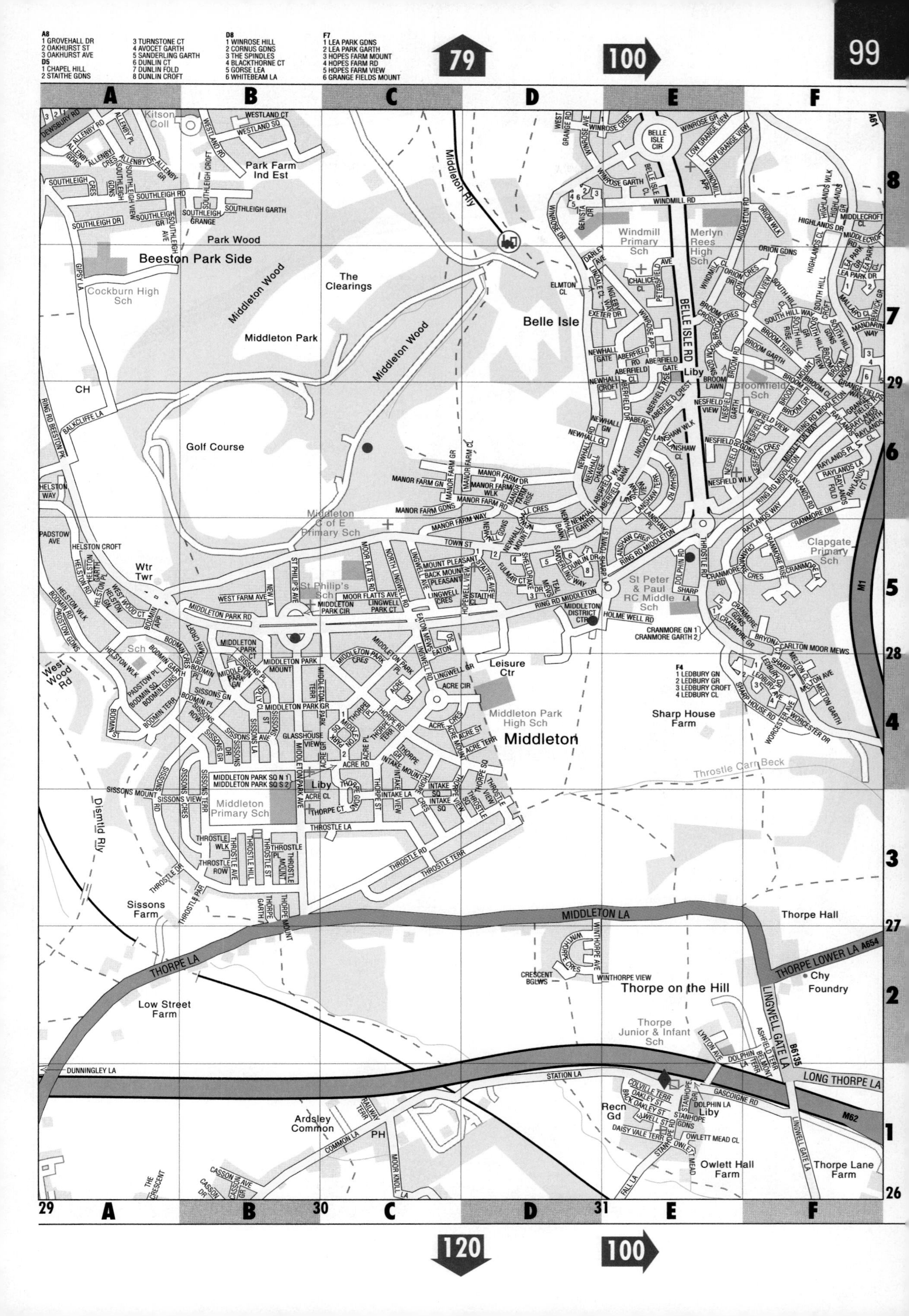
A8
1 GROVEHALL DR
2 OAKHURST ST
3 OAKHURST AVE
D5
1 CHAPEL HILL
2 STAITHE GDNS
3 TURNSTONE CT
4 AVOCET GARTH
5 SANDERLING GARTH
6 DUNLIN CT
7 DUNLIN FOLD
8 DUNLIN CROFT
D8
1 WINROSE HILL
2 CORNUS GDNS
3 THE SPINDLES
4 BLACKTHORNE CT
5 GORSE LEA
6 WHITEBEAM LA
F7
1 LEA PARK GDNS
2 LEA PARK GARTH
3 HOPES FARM MOUNT
4 HOPES FARM RD
5 HOPES FARM VIEW
6 GRANGE FIELDS MOUNT
79
100
A
B
C
D
E
F
Kitson Coll
Park Farm Ind Est
Park Wood
Beeston Park Side
Cockburn High Sch
Middleton Wood
The Clearings
Middleton Park
Middleton Rly
Belle Isle
Windmill Primary Sch
Merlyn Rees High Sch
BELLE ISLE RD
Liby
Broomfield Sch
CH
Golf Course
Middleton C of E Primary Sch
Wtr Twr
St Philip's Sch
St Peter & Paul RC Middle Sch
Clapgate Primary Sch
M1
Leisure Ctr
Middleton Park High Sch
Middleton
Sharp House Farm
F4
1 LEDBURY GN
2 LEDBURY GR
3 LEDBURY CROFT
4 LEDBURY CL
CRANMORE GN 1
CRANMORE GARTH 2
Throstle Carr Beck
Middleton Primary Sch
Dismtld Rly
Sch
West Wood Rd
Sissons Farm
MIDDLETON LA
Thorpe Hall
THORPE LA
THORPE LOWER LA A654
Chy Foundry
Low Street Farm
CRESCENT BGLWS
Thorpe on the Hill
LINGWELL GATE LA
Thorpe Junior & Infant Sch
B6135
DUNNINGLEY LA
STATION LA
LONG THORPE LA
M62
Recn Gd
Ardsley Common
PH
COMMON LA
Owlett Hall Farm
Thorpe Lane Farm
8
7
29
6
5
28
4
3
27
2
1
26
29
30
31
120
100

99
80

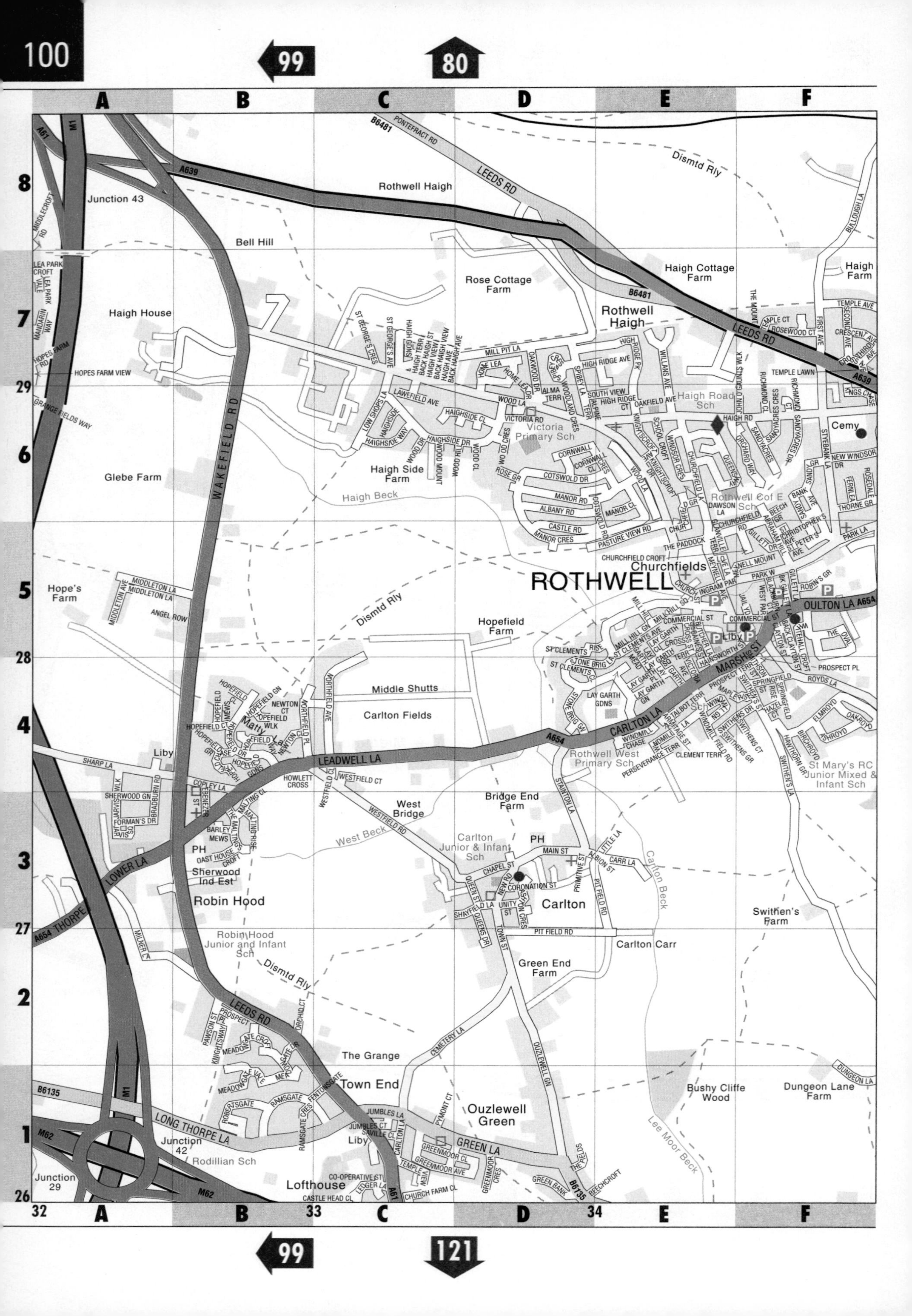
A
B
C
D
E
F
8
7
29
6
5
28
4
3
27
2
1
26
32
33
34
ROTHWELL
Rothwell Haigh
Junction 43
Bell Hill
Haigh House
Glebe Farm
Hope's Farm
Rose Cottage Farm
Haigh Cottage Farm
Haigh Farm
Haigh Side Farm
Haigh Beck
Victoria Primary Sch
Haigh Road Sch
Rothwell C of E Sch
Churchfields
Cemy
Dismtd Rly
Hopefield Farm
Middle Shutts
Carlton Fields
Matty La
Liby
West Bridge
West Beck
Bridge End Farm
Carlton Junior & Infant Sch
PH
Carlton
Carlton Carr
Carlton Beck
Rothwell West Primary Sch
St Mary's RC Junior Mixed & Infant Sch
Swithen's Farm
Sherwood Ind Est
Robin Hood
Robin Hood Junior and Infant Sch
Green End Farm
The Grange
Town End
Ouzlewell Green
Bushy Cliffe Wood
Dungeon Lane Farm
Lee Moor Beck
Junction 42
Junction 29
Rodillian Sch
Lofthouse
LEEDS RD
WAKEFIELD RD
LEADWELL LA
CARLTON LA
OULTON LA A654
MARSH ST
LOWER LA
A654 THORPE LA
LONG THORPE LA
GREEN LA
OUZLEWELL GN
CEMETERY LA
PIT FIELD RD
M1
M62
A61
A639
B6481
B6135
PONTEFRACT RD

99
121

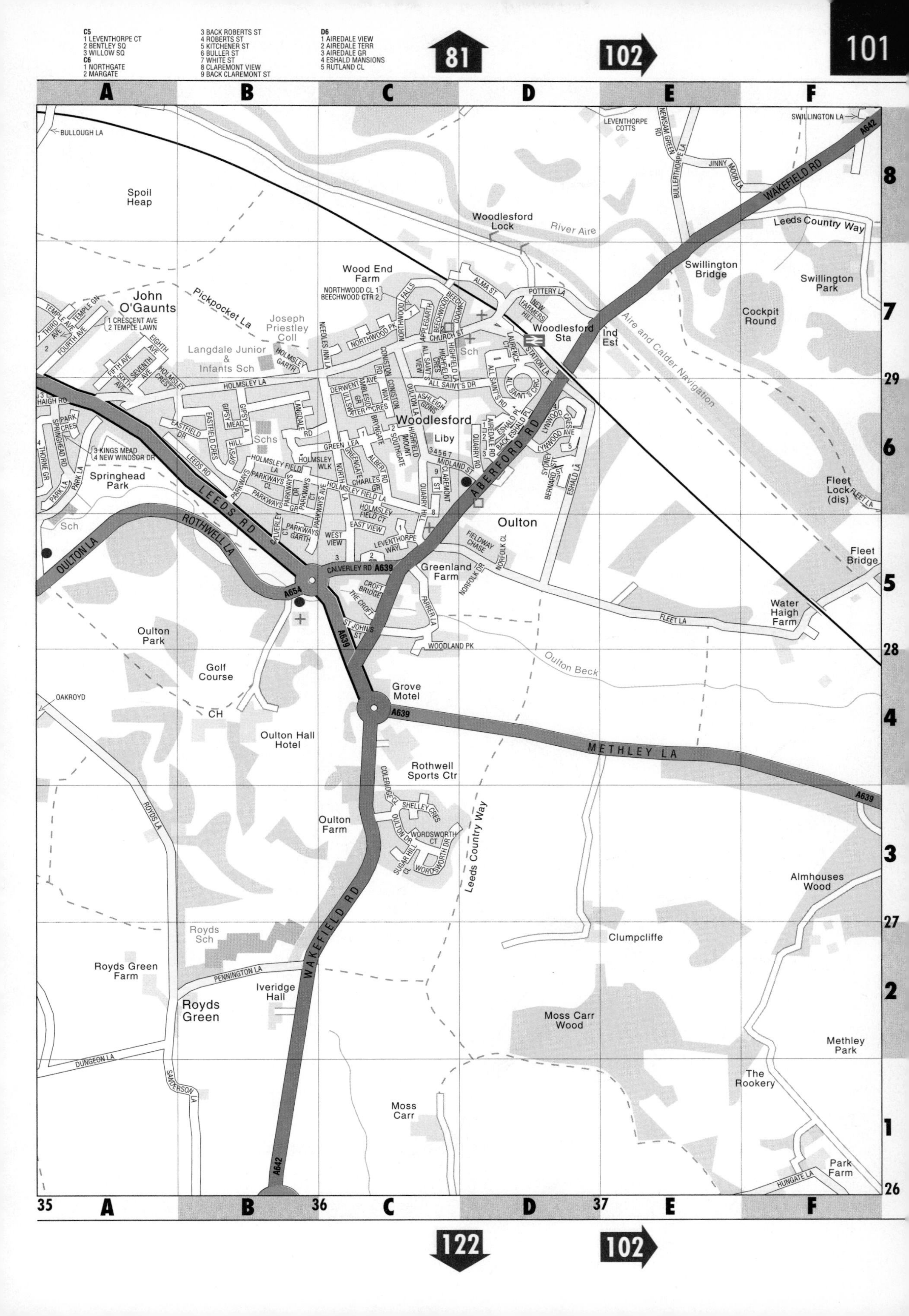

101
82

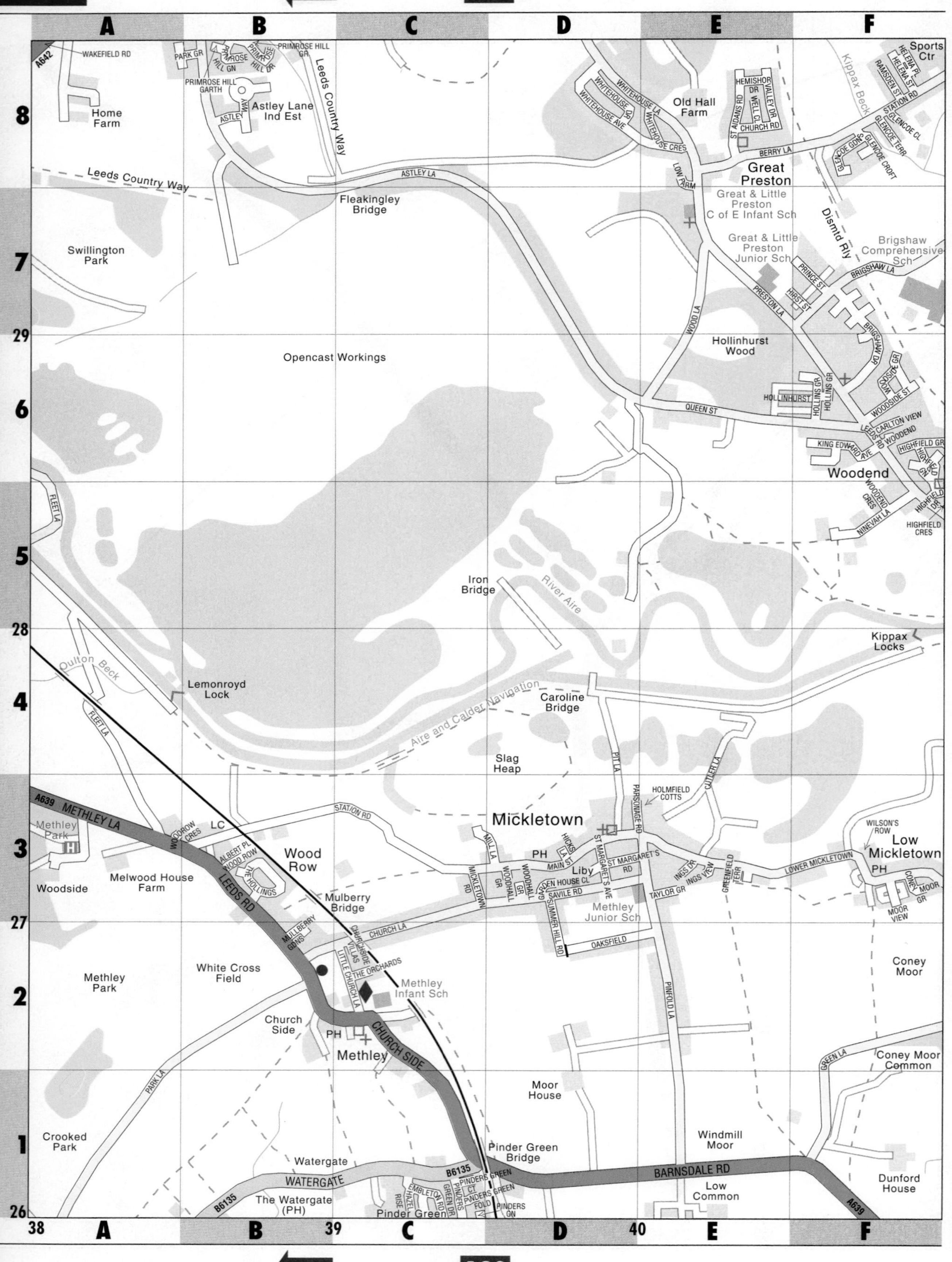
A
B
C
D
E
F
8
7
29
6
5
28
4
3
27
2
1
26
38
39
40
Home Farm
Astley Lane Ind Est
Leeds Country Way
Old Hall Farm
Great Preston
Great & Little Preston C of E Infant Sch
Great & Little Preston Junior Sch
Sports Ctr
Kippax Beck
Dismtd Rly
Brigshaw Comprehensive Sch
Swillington Park
Fleakingley Bridge
Opencast Workings
Hollinhurst Wood
Woodend
Iron Bridge
River Aire
Kippax Locks
Oulton Beck
Lemonroyd Lock
Caroline Bridge
Aire and Calder Navigation
Slag Heap
Mickletown
Low Mickletown
Methley Park
Woodside
Melwood House Farm
Wood Row
Mulberry Bridge
Liby
Methley Junior Sch
Coney Moor
White Cross Field
Methley Infant Sch
Church Side
Methley
Coney Moor Common
Moor House
Crooked Park
Windmill Moor
Pinder Green Bridge
Watergate
The Watergate (PH)
Pinder Green
Low Common
Dunford House
ASTLEY LA
QUEEN ST
BERRY LA
PRESTON LA
WOOD LA
STATION RD
METHLEY LA
LEEDS RD
CHURCH LA
CHURCH SIDE
MAIN ST
PINFOLD LA
BARNSDALE RD
WATERGATE
LOWER MICKLETOWN
A639
A642
B6135

101
123

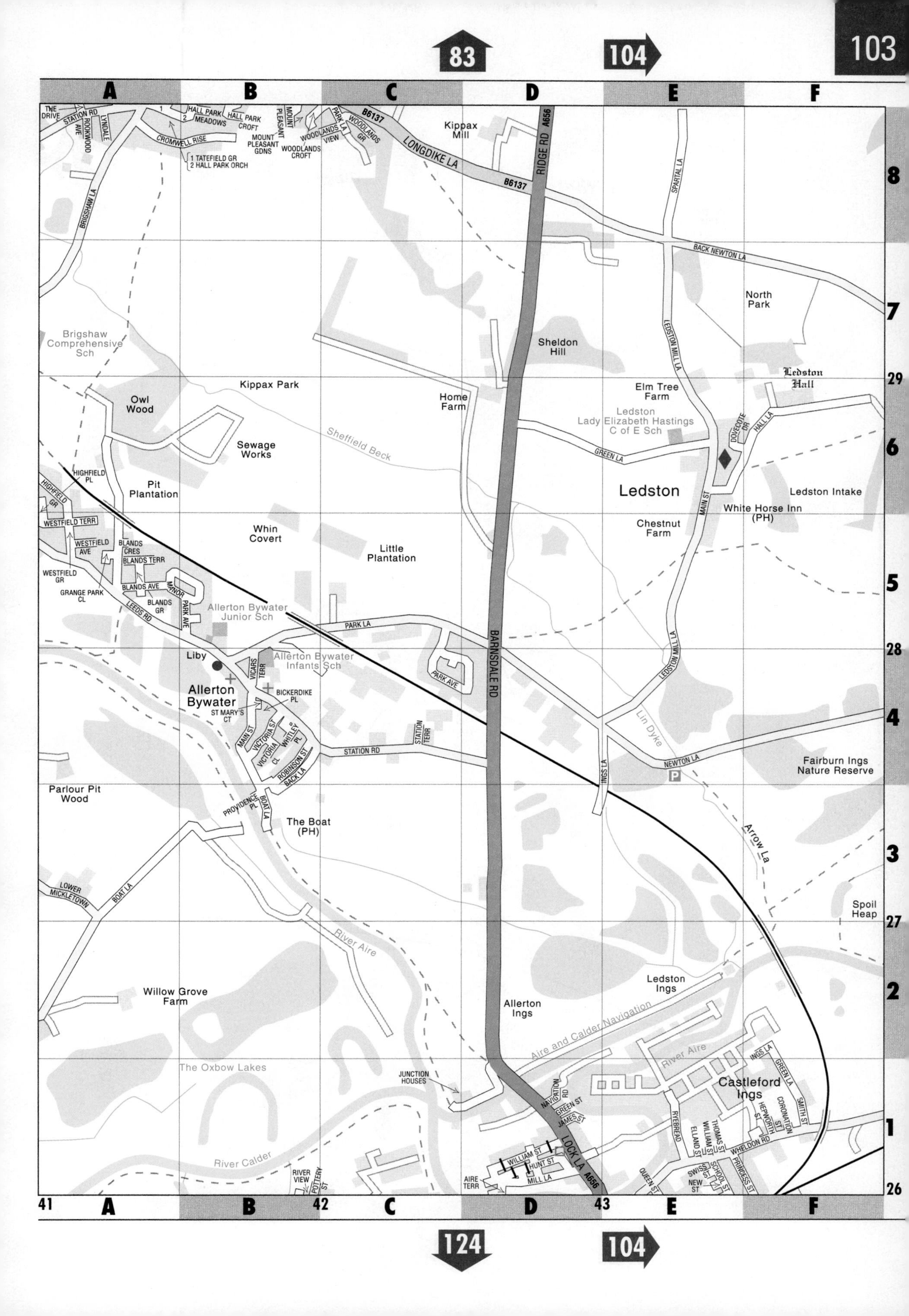
83
104
Kippax Mill
RIDGE RD A656
LONGDIKE LA
B6137
SPARTAL LA
BACK NEWTON LA
North Park
Sheldon Hill
LEDSTON MILL LA
Ledston Hall
Brigshaw Comprehensive Sch
Kippax Park
Owl Wood
Home Farm
Elm Tree Farm
Ledston Lady Elizabeth Hastings C of E Sch
Sewage Works
Sheffield Beck
GREEN LA
HALL LA
DOVECOTE DR
Ledston
Ledston Intake
White Horse Inn (PH)
Pit Plantation
Chestnut Farm
Whin Covert
Little Plantation
Allerton Bywater Junior Sch
PARK LA
BARNSDALE RD
Liby
Allerton Bywater Infants Sch
Allerton Bywater
PARK AVE
Lin Dyke
STATION RD
NEWTON LA
INGS LA
Fairburn Ings Nature Reserve
Parlour Pit Wood
The Boat (PH)
Arrow La
Spoil Heap
BOAT LA
LOWER MICKLETOWN
River Aire
Willow Grove Farm
Allerton Ings
Ledston Ings
Aire and Calder Navigation
The Oxbow Lakes
JUNCTION HOUSES
Castleford Ings
River Calder
LOCK LA A656
WHELDON RD
41
42
43
A B C D E F
1 2 3 4 5 6 7 8
26 27 28 29

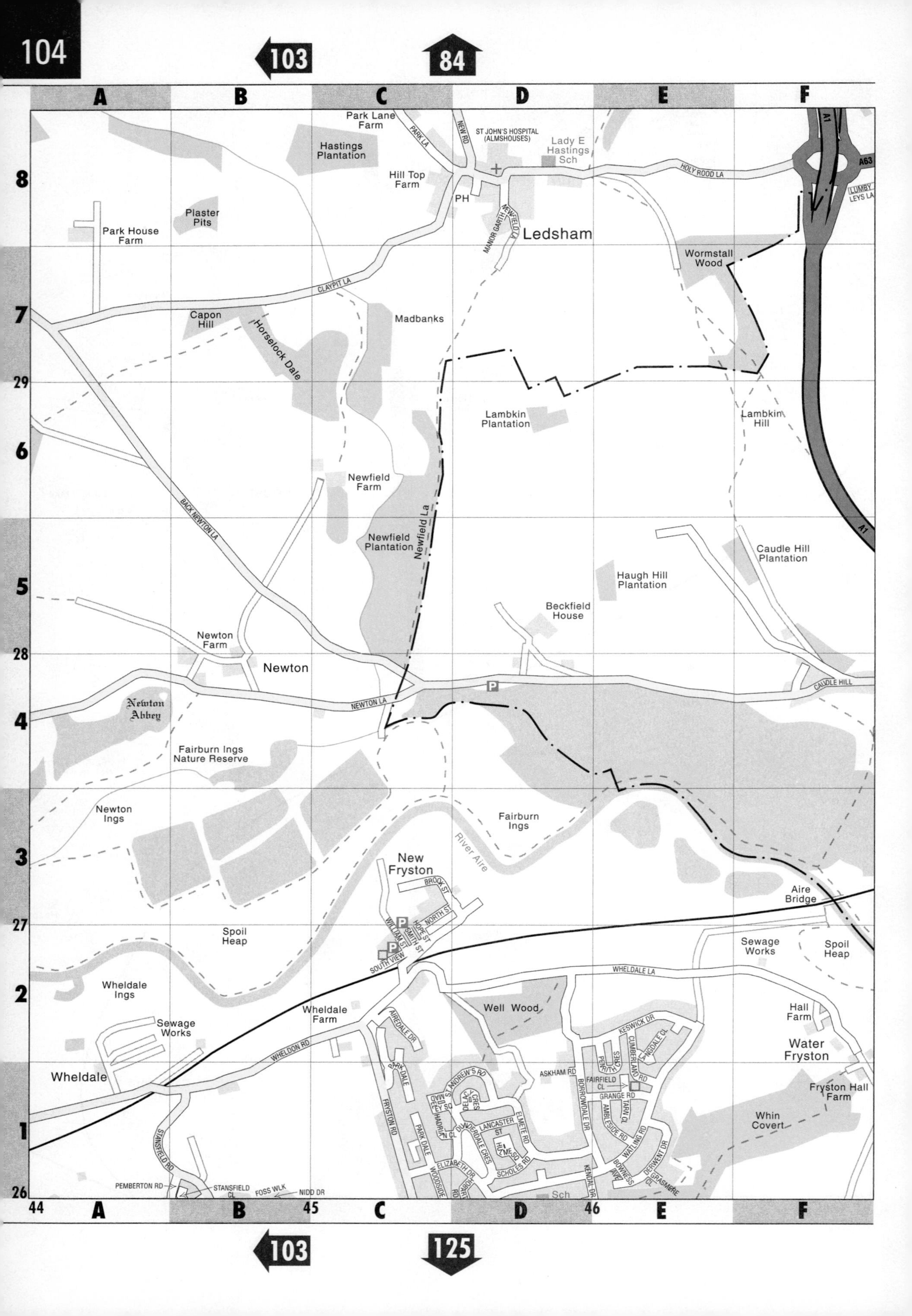
Park Lane Farm
Hastings Plantation
Hill Top Farm
ST JOHN'S HOSPITAL (ALMSHOUSES)
Lady E Hastings Sch
HOLY ROOD LA
A63
LUMBY LEYS LA
A1
PH
Plaster Pits
Park House Farm
Ledsham
Wormstall Wood
CLAYPIT LA
Capon Hill
Horselock Dale
Madbanks
Lambkin Plantation
Lambkin Hill
Newfield Farm
BACK NEWTON LA
Newfield Plantation
Newfield La
Caudle Hill Plantation
Haugh Hill Plantation
Beckfield House
Newton Farm
Newton
NEWTON LA
CAUDLE HILL
Newton Abbey
Fairburn Ings Nature Reserve
Newton Ings
Fairburn Ings
River Aire
New Fryston
Aire Bridge
Spoil Heap
Sewage Works
Spoil Heap
WHELDALE LA
Wheldale Ings
Wheldale Farm
Well Wood
Hall Farm
Water Fryston
Sewage Works
WHELDON RD
Wheldale
Fryston Hall Farm
Whin Covert
FRYSTON RD
PARK DALE
WOODSIDE
ELIZABETH DR
LANCASTER ST
SCHOLES RD
BORROWDALE DR
KENDAL DR
AMBLESIDE RD
WATLING RD
DERWENT DR
GRASMERE
BOWNESS AVE
GRANGE RD
FAIRFIELD CL
CUMBERLAND RD
KESWICK DR
ASKHAM RD
STANSFIELD RD
PEMBERTON RD
STANSFIELD CL
FOSS WLK
NIDD DR
Sch
A B C D E F
8 7 6 5 4 3 2 1
29 28 27 26
44 45 46

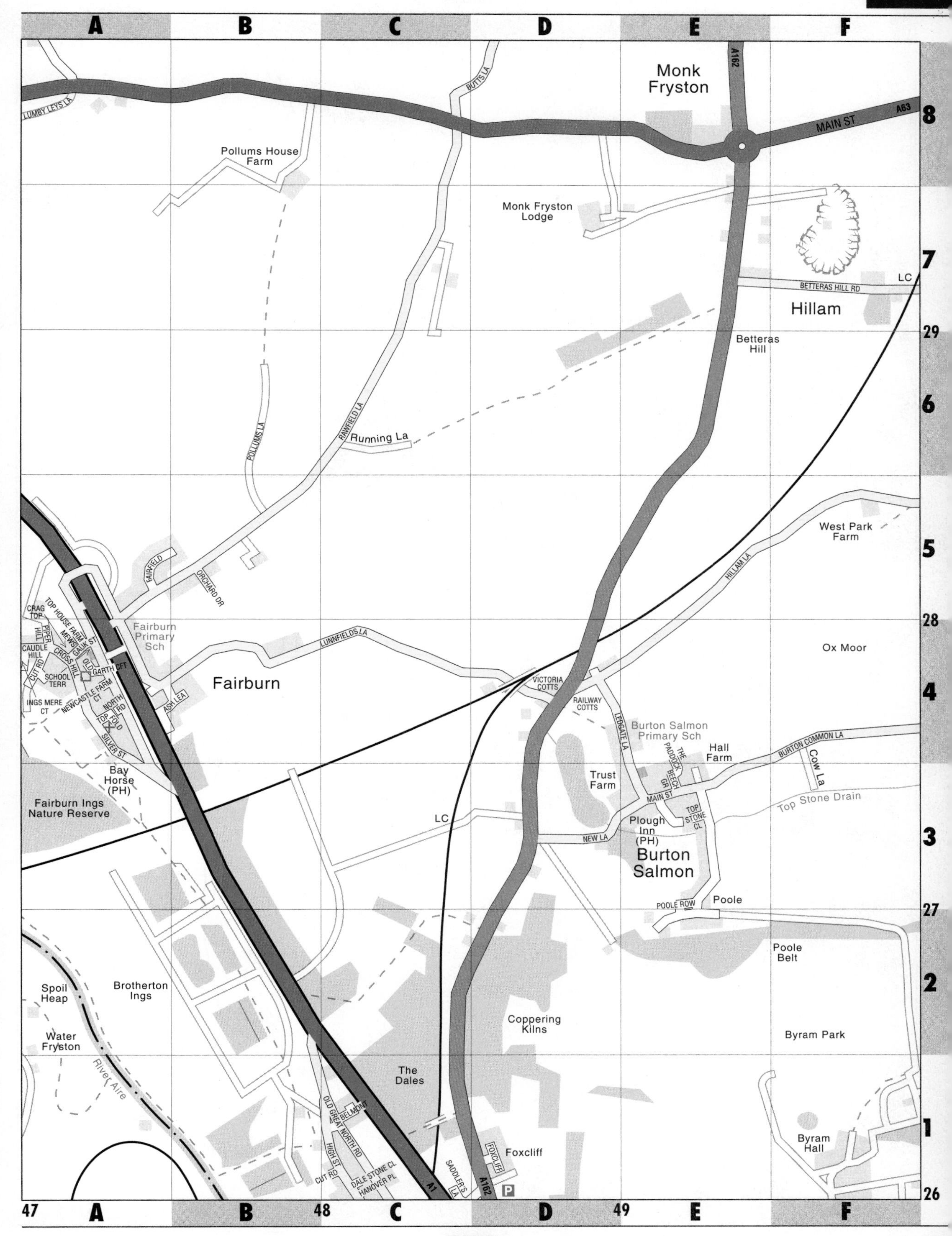

Monk Fryston

A162

A63

Main St

Lumby Leys La

Pollums House Farm

Butts La

Monk Fryston Lodge

Betteras Hill Rd

LC

Hillam

Betteras Hill

Pollums La

Rainfield La

Running La

West Park Farm

Hillam La

Ox Moor

Fairfield

Orchard Dr

Fairburn Primary Sch

Lunnfields La

Fairburn

Crag Tor

Top House Farm

Piper Hill

Main St

Chalk St

Old Garth

Cross Hill

Caudle Hill

School Terr

Newcastle Farm Ct

Garth Cft

Ash Lea

Ings Mere Ct

North

Top Rd

Silver St

Victoria Cotts

Railway Cotts

Burton Salmon Primary Sch

Hall Farm

Burton Common La

Cow La

Leggate La

The Paddock

Beech Gr

Top Stone Drain

Trust Farm

Bay Horse (PH)

Fairburn Ings Nature Reserve

LC

New La

Main St

Plough Inn (PH)

Top Stone Cl

Burton Salmon

Poole Row

Poole

Poole Belt

Spoil Heap

Brotherton Ings

Byram Park

Water Fryston

River Aire

The Dales

Coppering Kilns

Byram Hall

Old Great North Rd

Belmont

High St

Cut Rd

Dale Stone Cl

Hanover Pl

Saddlers La

A1

A162

P

Foxcliff

LC

47   48   49

26 27 28 29

85

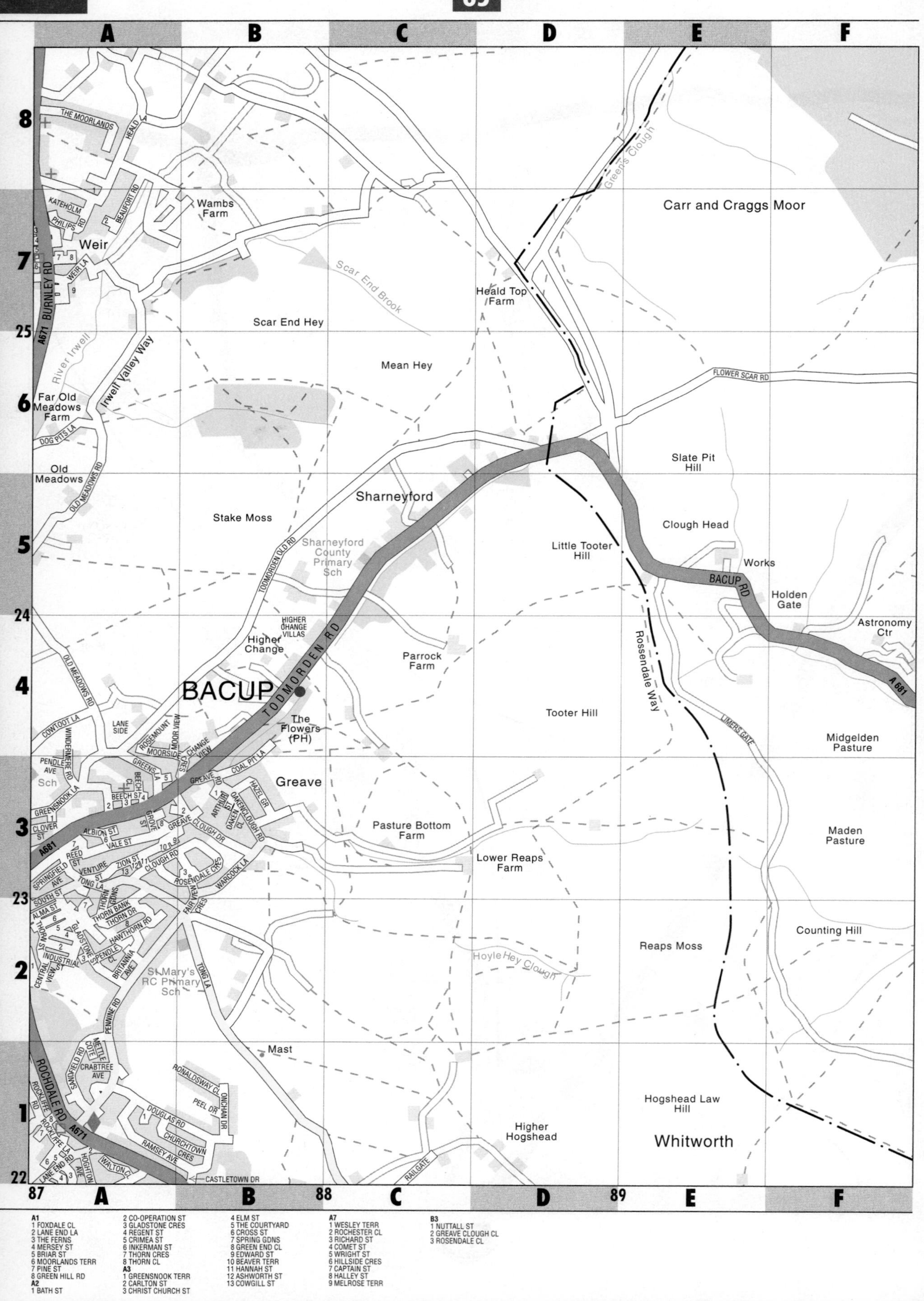

A1
1 FOXDALE CL
2 LANE END LA
3 THE FERNS
4 MERSEY ST
5 BRIAR ST
6 MOORLANDS TERR
7 PINE ST
8 GREEN HILL RD
A2
1 BATH ST

2 CO-OPERATION ST
3 GLADSTONE CRES
4 REGENT ST
5 CRIMEA ST
6 INKERMAN ST
7 THORN CRES
8 THORN CL
A3
1 GREENSNOOK TERR
2 CARLTON ST
3 CHRIST CHURCH ST

4 ELM ST
5 THE COURTYARD
6 CROSS ST
7 SPRING GDNS
8 GREEN END CL
9 EDWARD ST
10 BEAVER TERR
11 HANNAH ST
12 ASHWORTH ST
13 COWGILL ST

A7
1 WESLEY TERR
2 ROCHESTER CL
3 RICHARD ST
4 COMET ST
5 WRIGHT ST
6 HILLSIDE CRES
7 CAPTAIN ST
8 HALLEY ST
9 MELROSE TERR

B3
1 NUTTALL ST
2 GREAVE CLOUGH CL
3 ROSENDALE CL

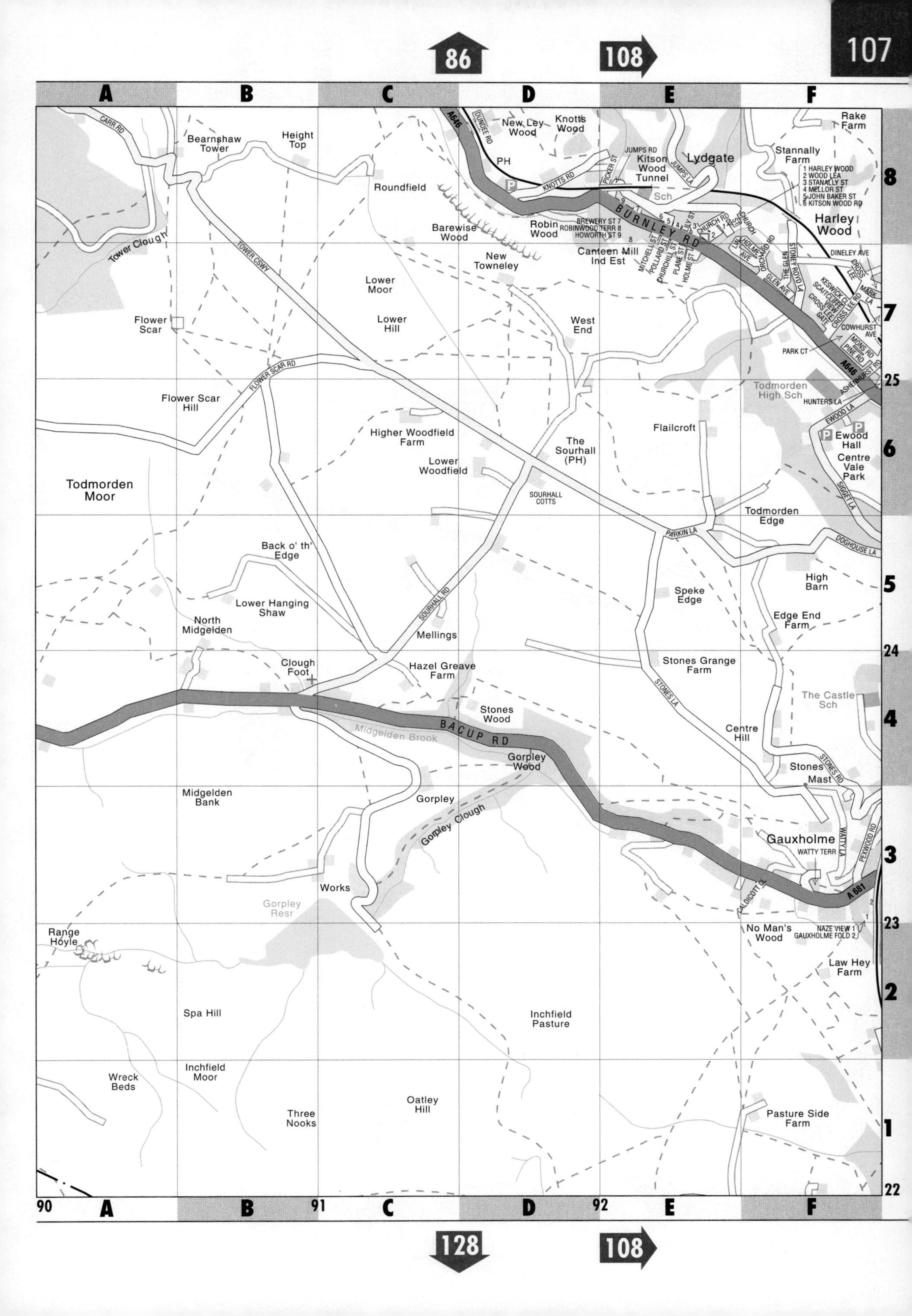

86
108
128
108

CARR RD

Bearnshaw
Tower

Height
Top

Roundfield

A646

DUMFIE RD

New Ley
Wood

Knotts
Wood

PICKER ST

KNOTTS RD

JUMPS RD

JUMPS LA

Kitson
Wood
Tunnel

Lydgate

Stannally
Farm

Rake
Farm

1 HARLEY WOOD
2 WOOD LEA
3 STANALLY ST
4 MELLOR ST
5 JOHN BAKER ST
6 KITSON WOOD RD

Tower Clough

TOWER CSWY

Barewise
Wood

Robin
Wood

PH

Sch

BREWERY ST 7
ROBINWOOD TERR 8
HOWORTH ST 9

BURNLEY RD

MITCHELL ST

POLLARD ST

CHURCHILL ST

PLANE ST

HOLME ST

CHURCH RD

LIV ST

CHURCH RD

ST CHOLM ROAD

GLEN AVE

THE GLEN

STONEY ROYD LA

DINELEY AVE

Harley
Wood

KESWICK CL
SCAR FOLD
CROSS LEE
CROSS LEE

MARK

DEE

8

New
Towneley

Canteen Mill
Ind Est

West
End

COWHURST
AVE

MDNS RD

PINE RD

ASHENHURST RD

A646

7

Flower
Scar

Lower
Moor

Lower
Hill

The
Sourhall
(PH)

Flailcroft

PARK CT

Todmorden
High Sch

HUNTERS LA

EWOOD LA

P

P

Ewood
Hall

25

Flower Scar
Hill

FLOWER SCAR RD

Higher Woodfield
Farm

Lower
Woodfield

SOURHALL
COTTS

Centre
Vale
Park

SIGGET LA

6

Todmorden
Moor

PARKIN LA

Todmorden
Edge

DOGHOUSE LA

Back o' th'
Edge

SOURHALL RD

Speke
Edge

High
Barn

5

Lower Hanging
Shaw

North
Midgelden

Mellings

Hazel Greave
Farm

Stones Grange
Farm

STONES LA

Edge End
Farm

24

Clough
Foot

Stones
Wood

The Castle
Sch

Midgelden Brook

BACUP RD

Gorpley
Wood

Centre
Hill

Stones
Mast

STONES RD

4

Midgelden
Bank

Gorpley

Gorpley Clough

Gauxholme

WATTY LA

WATTY TERR

PEXWOOD RD

3

Works

Gorpley
Resr

CALDICOTT CL

A 681

No Man's
Wood

NAZE VIEW 1
GAUXHOLME FOLD 2

2

1

23

Range
Hoyle

Spa Hill

Law Hey
Farm

2

Wreck
Beds

Inchfield
Moor

Three
Nooks

Oatley
Hill

Inchfield
Pasture

Pasture Side
Farm

1

90

A

B

91

C

D

92

E

F

22

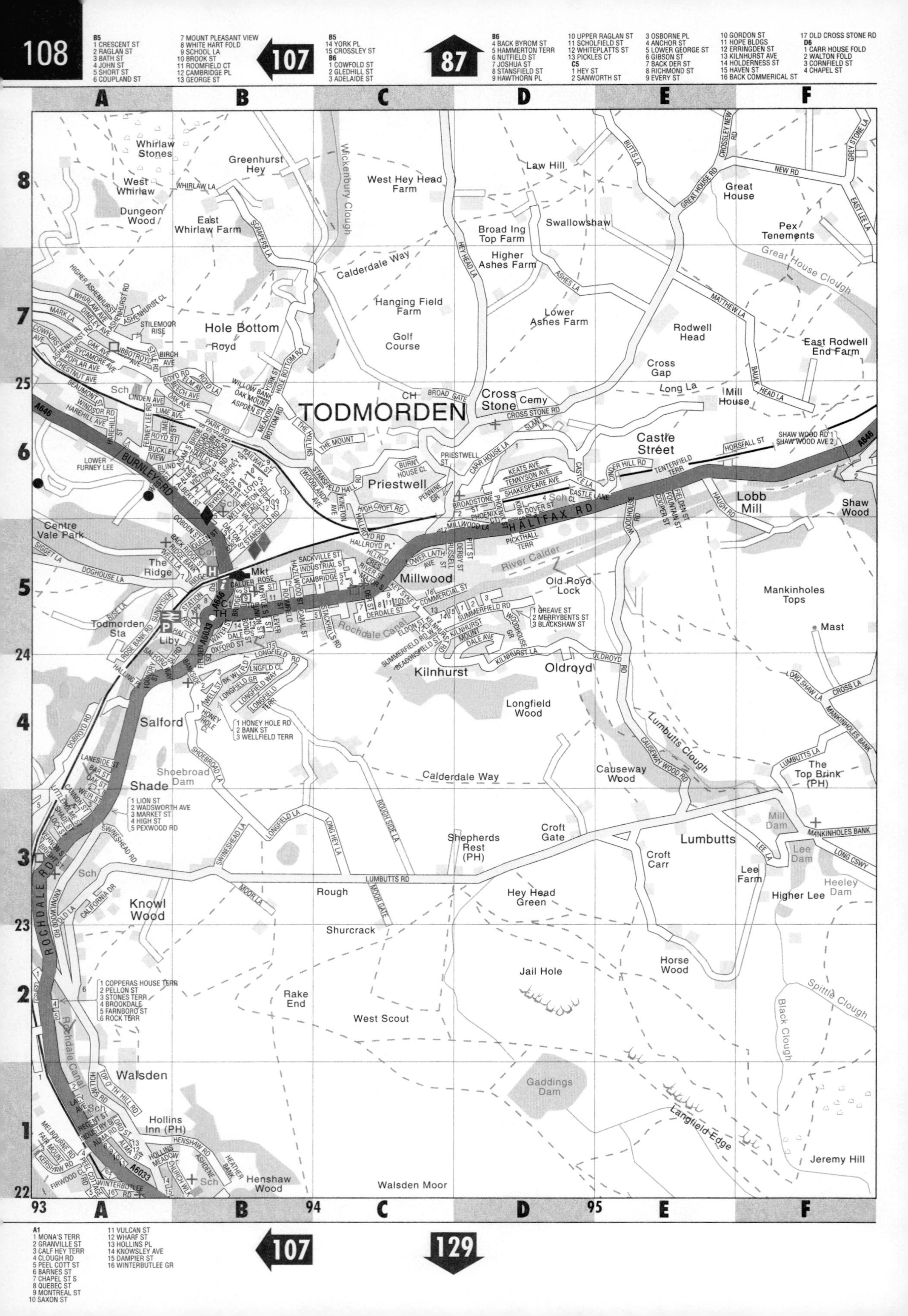
108
B5
1 CRESCENT ST
2 RAGLAN ST
3 BATH ST
4 JOHN ST
5 SHORT ST
6 COUPLAND ST
7 MOUNT PLEASANT VIEW
8 WHITE HART FOLD
9 SCHOOL LA
10 BROOK ST
11 ROOMFIELD CT
12 CAMBRIDGE PL
13 GEORGE ST
107
B5
14 YORK PL
15 CROSSLEY ST
B6
1 COWFOLD ST
2 GLEDHILL ST
3 ADELAIDE ST
87
B6
4 BACK BYROM ST
5 HAMMERTON TERR
6 NUTFIELD ST
7 JOSHUA ST
8 STANSFIELD ST
9 HAWTHORN PL
10 UPPER RAGLAN ST
11 SCHOLFIELD ST
12 WHITEPLATTS ST
13 PICKLES CT
C5
1 HEY ST
2 SANWORTH ST
3 OSBORNE PL
4 ANCHOR ST
5 LOWER GEORGE ST
6 GIBSON ST
7 BACK DER ST
8 RICHMOND ST
9 EVERY ST
10 GORDON ST
11 HOPE BLDGS
12 ERRINGDEN ST
13 KILNHURST AVE
14 HOLDERNESS ST
15 HAVEN ST
16 BACK COMMERICAL ST
17 OLD CROSS STONE RD
D6
1 CARR HOUSE FOLD
2 WALTON FOLD
3 CORNFIELD ST
4 CHAPEL ST
TODMORDEN
Whirlaw Stones
West Whirlaw
Dungeon Wood
Greenhurst Hey
East Whirlaw Farm
West Hey Head Farm
Wickenbury Clough
Law Hill
Broad Ing Top Farm
Higher Ashes Farm
Swallowshaw
Great House
Pex Tenements
Great House Clough
Calderdale Way
Hanging Field Farm
Golf Course
Lower Ashes Farm
Rodwell Head
East Rodwell End Farm
Cross Gap
Long La
Mill House
Hole Bottom
Royd
Cross Stone
Cemy
Castle Street
Priestwell
Lobb Mill
Shaw Wood
Centre Vale Park
The Ridge
Mkt
Millwood
River Calder
Old Royd Lock
Mankinholes Tops
Mast
Todmorden Sta
Liby
Rochdale Canal
Kilnhurst
Oldroyd
Longfield Wood
Salford
Shoebroad Dam
Shade
Lumbutts Clough
Causeway Wood
The Top Brink (PH)
Mill Dam
Croft Gate
Shepherds Rest (PH)
Lumbutts
Croft Carr
Lee Farm
Lee Dam
Heeley Dam
Higher Lee
Knowl Wood
Rough
Hey Head Green
Shurcrack
Rake End
West Scout
Jail Hole
Horse Wood
Spittle Clough
Black Clough
Walsden
Gaddings Dam
Langfield Edge
Hollins Inn (PH)
Henshaw Wood
Walsden Moor
Jeremy Hill
BURNLEY RD
HALIFAX RD
ROCHDALE RD
A646
A6033
LUMBUTTS RD
1 GREAVE ST
2 MERRYBENTS ST
3 BLACKSHAW ST
1 HONEY HOLE RD
2 BANK ST
3 WELLFIELD TERR
1 LION ST
2 WADSWORTH AVE
3 MARKET ST
4 HIGH ST
5 PEXWOOD RD
1 COPPERAS HOUSE TERR
2 PELLON ST
3 STONES TERR
4 BROOKDALE
5 FARNBORO ST
6 ROCK TERR
93 A B 94 C D 95 E F
A1
1 MONA'S TERR
2 GRANVILLE ST
3 CALF HEY TERR
4 CLOUGH RD
5 PEEL COTT ST
6 BARNES ST
7 CHAPEL ST S
8 QUEBEC ST
9 MONTREAL ST
10 SAXON ST
11 VULCAN ST
12 WHARF ST
13 HOLLINS PL
14 KNOWSLEY AVE
15 DAMPIER ST
16 WINTERBUTLEE GR
107
129

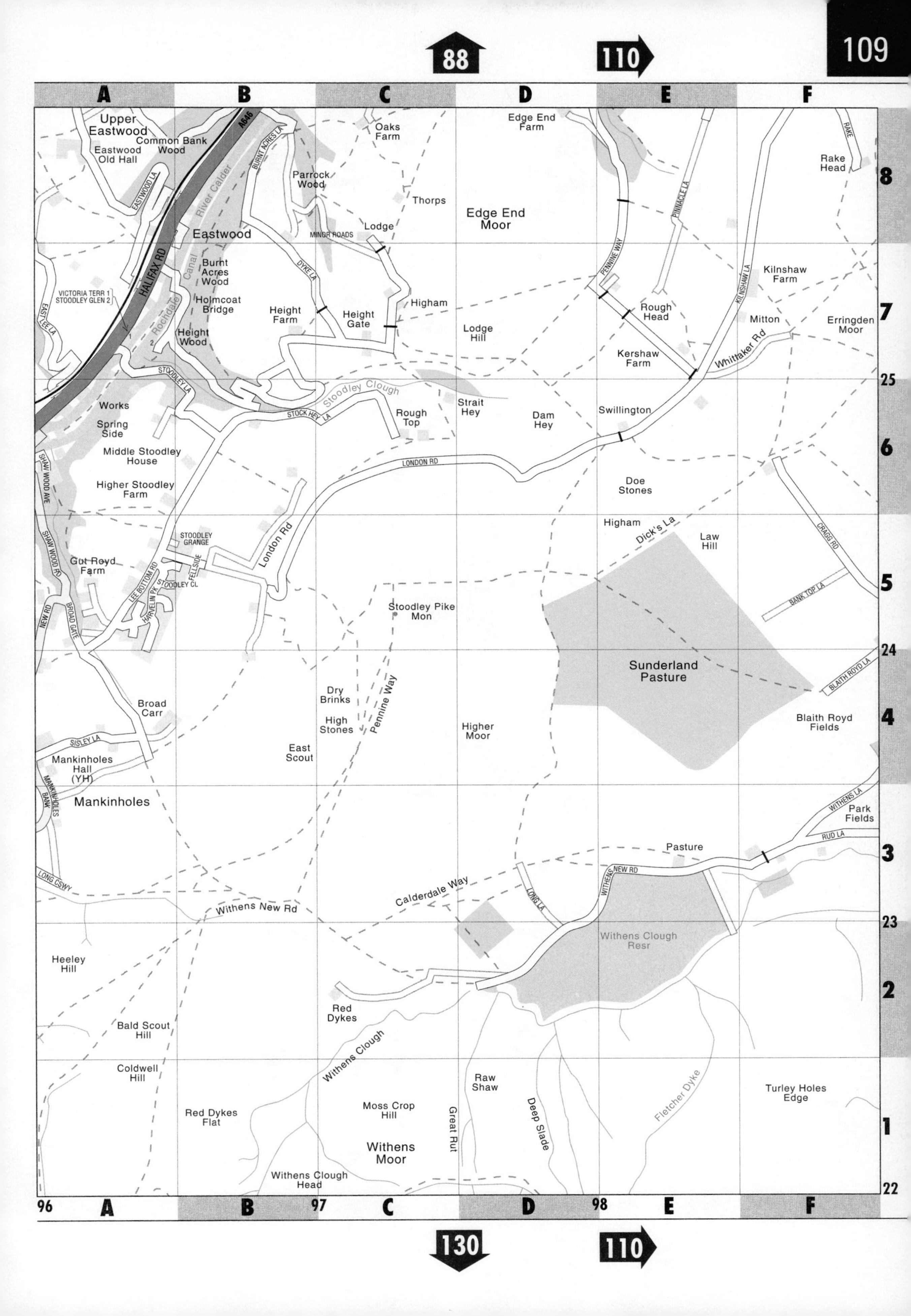
88
110
A
B
C
D
E
F
Upper Eastwood
Common Bank Wood
Eastwood Old Hall
EASTWOOD LA
A646
BURNT ACRES LA
River Calder
Oaks Farm
Parrock Wood
Edge End Farm
Thorps
Edge End Moor
RAKE
Rake Head
PINNACLE LA
Eastwood
MINOR ROADS
Lodge
HALIFAX RD
Canal
Burnt Acres Wood
DYKE LA
PENNINE WAY
Kilnshaw Farm
KILNSHAW LA
VICTORIA TERR 1
STOODLEY GLEN 2
EAST LEE LA
Rochdale
Holmcoat Bridge
Height Farm
Height Gate
Higham
Rough Head
Mitton
Erringden Moor
Height Wood
Lodge Hill
Kershaw Farm
Whitaker Rd
STOODLEY LA
Stoodley Clough
Works
STOCK HEY LA
Rough Top
Strait Hey
Dam Hey
Swillington
Spring Side
Middle Stoodley House
SHAW WOOD AVE
LONDON RD
Doe Stones
Higher Stoodley Farm
Higham
Dick's La
Law Hill
CRAGG RD
STOODLEY GRANGE
London Rd
Gut Royd Farm
LEE BOTTOM RD
FELLSIDE
STOODLEY CL
HARVELIN PK
BANK TOP LA
NEW RD
BROAD GATE
Stoodley Pike Mon
Sunderland Pasture
BLAITH ROYD LA
Dry Brinks
Pennine Way
Broad Carr
High Stones
Higher Moor
Blaith Royd Fields
SISLEY LA
East Scout
Mankinholes Hall (YH)
MANKINHOLES BANK
Mankinholes
WITHENS LA
Park Fields
RUD LA
Pasture
LONG CSWY
WITHENS NEW RD
Calderdale Way
LONG LA
Withens New Rd
Withens Clough Resr
Heeley Hill
Red Dykes
Bald Scout Hill
Withens Clough
Coldwell Hill
Raw Shaw
Fletcher Dyke
Turley Holes Edge
Red Dykes Flat
Moss Crop Hill
Great Rut
Deep Slade
Withens Moor
Withens Clough Head
8
7
25
6
5
24
4
3
23
2
1
22
96
97
98
130
110

109
89

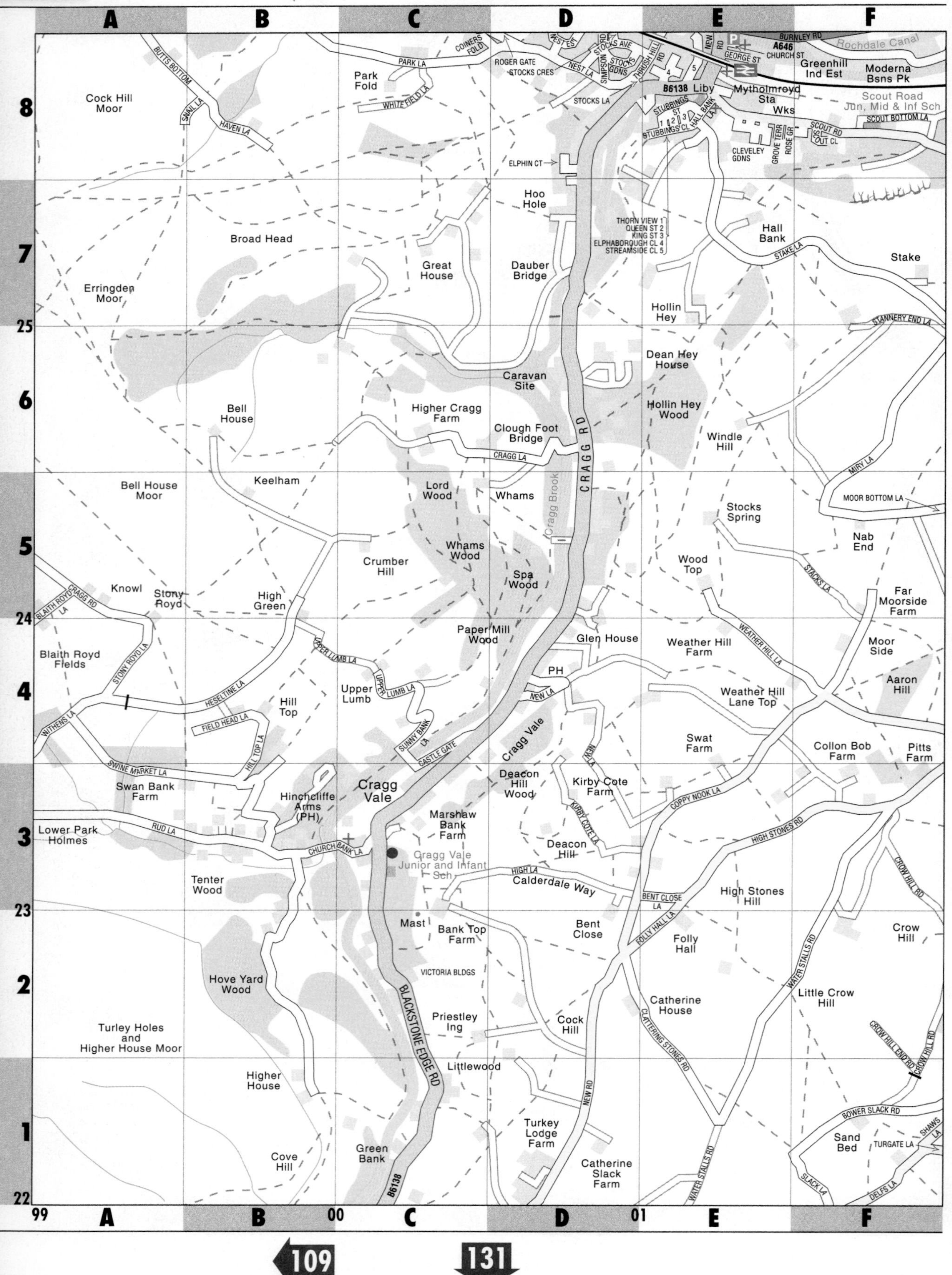
Cock Hill Moor
Park Fold
Broad Head
Erringden Moor
Great House
Hoo Hole
Dauber Bridge
Hollin Hey
Hall Bank
Stake
Mytholmroyd Sta
Greenhill Ind Est
Moderna Bsns Pk
Scout Road Jun, Mid & Inf Sch
Rochdale Canal
Dean Hey House
Hollin Hey Wood
Caravan Site
Bell House
Higher Cragg Farm
Clough Foot Bridge
Windle Hill
Bell House Moor
Keelham
Lord Wood
Whams
Stocks Spring
Nab End
Crumber Hill
Whams Wood
Spa Wood
Wood Top
Far Moorside Farm
Knowl
Stony Royd
High Green
Paper Mill Wood
Glen House
Weather Hill Farm
Moor Side
Blaith Royd Fields
Upper Lumb
Hill Top
Weather Hill Lane Top
Aaron Hill
Swat Farm
Collon Bob Farm
Pitts Farm
Swan Bank Farm
Cragg Vale
Hinchcliffe Arms (PH)
Deacon Hill Wood
Kirby Cote Farm
Lower Park Holmes
Marshaw Bank Farm
Deacon Hill
Cragg Vale Junior and Infant Sch
Tenter Wood
Calderdale Way
High Stones Hill
Mast
Bank Top Farm
Bent Close
Folly Hall
Crow Hill
Hove Yard Wood
Catherine House
Little Crow Hill
Turley Holes and Higher House Moor
Priestley Ing
Cock Hill
Littlewood
Higher House
Turkey Lodge Farm
Sand Bed
Cove Hill
Green Bank
Catherine Slack Farm
VICTORIA BLDGS
CRAGG RD
BLACKSTONE EDGE RD
B6138
A646
Cragg Brook
PH
BURNLEY RD
GEORGE ST
CHURCH ST
SCOUT RD
SCOUT CL
SCOUT BOTTOM LA
CLEVELEY GDNS
GROVE TERR
ROSE GR
STUBBINGS ST
STUBBINGS CL
HALL BANK LA
ELPHIN CT
THORN VIEW 1
QUEEN ST 2
KING ST 3
ELPHABOROUGH CL 4
STREAMSIDE CL 5
STAKE LA
STANNERY END LA
MIRY LA
MOOR BOTTOM LA
STACKS LA
WEATHER HILL LA
PARK LA
COINERS FOLD
ROGER GATE
STOCKS CRES
NEST EST
NEST LA
STOCKS AVE
STOCKS GDNS
SIMPSON RD
THRISH HILL RD
STOCKS LA
NEW RD
WHITE FIELD LA
BUTTS BOTTOM
SNAIL LA
HAVEN LA
CRAGG LA
CRAGG RD
BLAITH ROYD LA
STONY ROYD LA
HESELTINE LA
WITHENS LA
FIELD HEAD LA
HILL TOP LA
SWINE MARKET LA
RUD LA
CHURCH BANK LA
UPPER LUMB LA
SUNNY BANK LA
CASTLE GATE
NEW LA
KIRBY COTE LA
COPPY NOOK LA
HIGH STONES RD
HIGH LA
BENT CLOSE LA
FOLLY HALL LA
CROW HILL RD
WATER STALLS RD
CLATTERING STONES RD
CROW HILL END RD
BOWER SLACK RD
TURGATE LA
SHAWS LA
SLACK LA
DELFS LA
A B C D E F
8 7 6 5 4 3 2 1
25 24 23 22
99 00 01

109
131

90
112

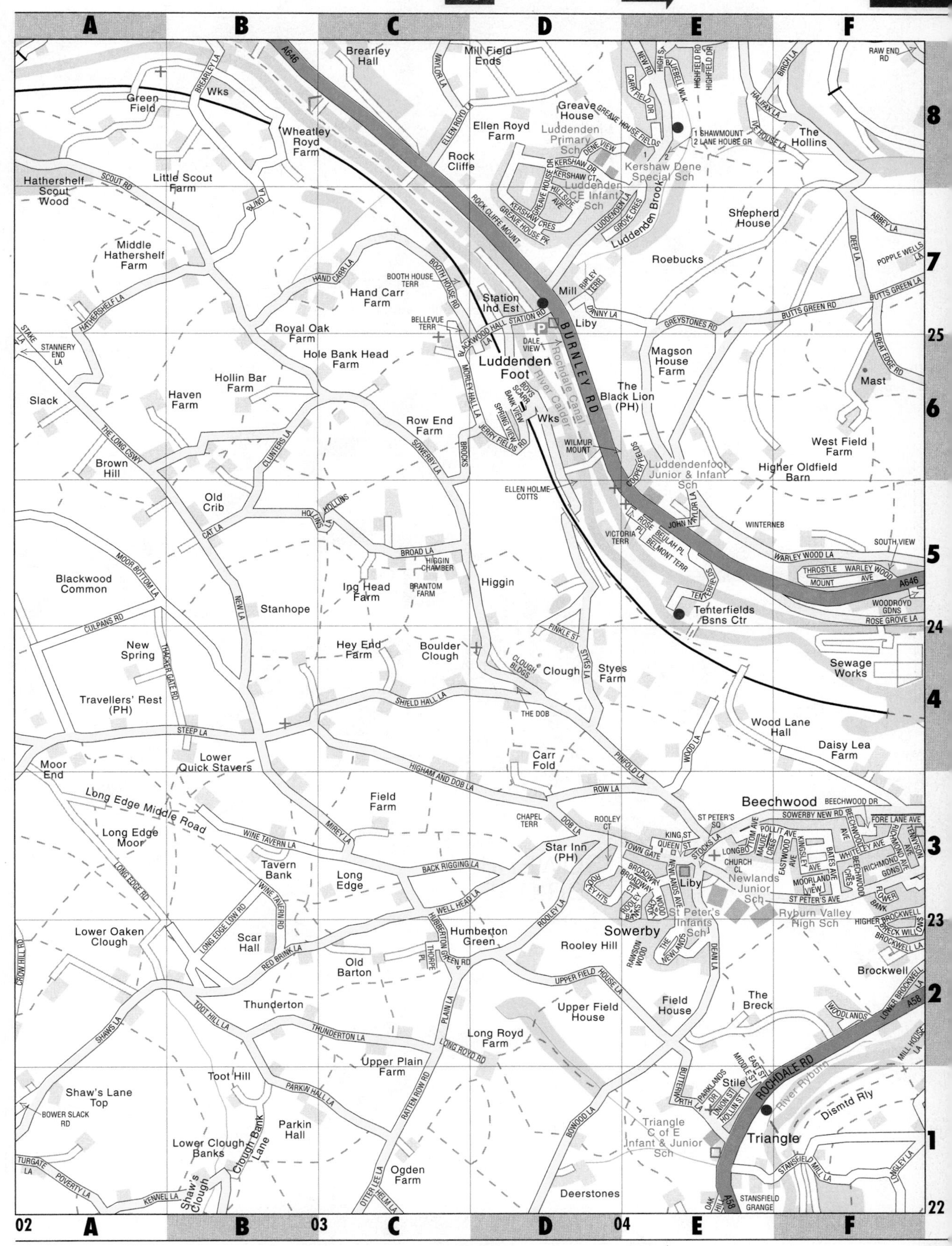
A
B
C
D
E
F
8
7
25
6
5
24
4
3
23
2
1
22
02
03
04
A646
A58
Brearley Hall
Mill Field Ends
Green Field
Wks
Wheatley Royd Farm
Ellen Royd Farm
Rock Cliffe
Greave House
Luddenden Primary Sch
Kershaw Dene Special Sch
Luddenden CE Infant Sch
Luddenden Brook
The Hollins
Hathershelf Scout Wood
Little Scout Farm
Middle Hathershelf Farm
Shepherd House
Roebucks
Hand Carr Farm
Station Ind Est
Mill
Liby
Royal Oak Farm
Hole Bank Head Farm
Luddenden Foot
Rochdale Canal
River Calder
BURNLEY RD
Magson House Farm
The Black Lion (PH)
Mast
Slack
Hollin Bar Farm
Haven Farm
Row End Farm
Wks
West Field Farm
Brown Hill
Luddendenfoot Junior & Infant Sch
Higher Oldfield Barn
Old Crib
WINTERNEB
Blackwood Common
Higgin
Ing Head Farm
Stanhope
Tenterfields Bsns Ctr
New Spring
Hey End Farm
Boulder Clough
Clough
Styes Farm
Sewage Works
Travellers' Rest (PH)
Wood Lane Hall
Daisy Lea Farm
Moor End
Lower Quick Stavers
Carr Fold
Long Edge Middle Road
Field Farm
Beechwood
Long Edge Moor
Star Inn (PH)
Tavern Bank
Long Edge
Liby
Newlands Junior Sch
Lower Oaken Clough
Scar Hall
Humberton Green
Sowerby
St Peter's Infants Sch
Ryburn Valley High Sch
Rooley Hill
Old Barton
Brockwell
Thunderton
Upper Field House
Field House
The Breck
Long Royd Farm
Upper Plain Farm
Toot Hill
Stile
Shaw's Lane Top
Dismtd Rly
River Ryburn
Parkin Hall
Triangle C of E Infant & Junior Sch
Triangle
Lower Clough Banks
Clough Bank Lane
Shaw's Clough
Ogden Farm
Deerstones
ROCHDALE RD
SCOUT RD
HATHERSHELF LA
STANNERY END LA
THE LONG CSWY
CAT LA
MOOR BOTTOM LA
CULPANS RD
NEW LA
STEEP LA
HIGHAM AND DOB LA
SHIELD HALL LA
SOWERBY LA
BROAD LA
WINE TAVERN LA
BACK RIGGING LA
WELL HEAD LA
RED BRINK LA
LONG EDGE RD
SHAWS LA
TOOT HILL LA
THUNDERTON LA
LONG ROYD RD
PARKIN HALL LA
RATTEN ROW RD
PLAIN LA
ROOLEY LA
UPPER FIELD HOUSE LA
DEAN LA
BOWOOD LA
WOOD LA
PINFOLD LA
ROW LA
BUTTS GREEN RD
GREYSTONES RD
WARLEY WOOD LA
ROSE GROVE LA
STANSFIELD MILL LA
LONGLEY LA
TURGATE LA
POVERTY LA
KENNEL LA
OTTER LEE LA
BOWER SLACK RD
CROW HILL RD

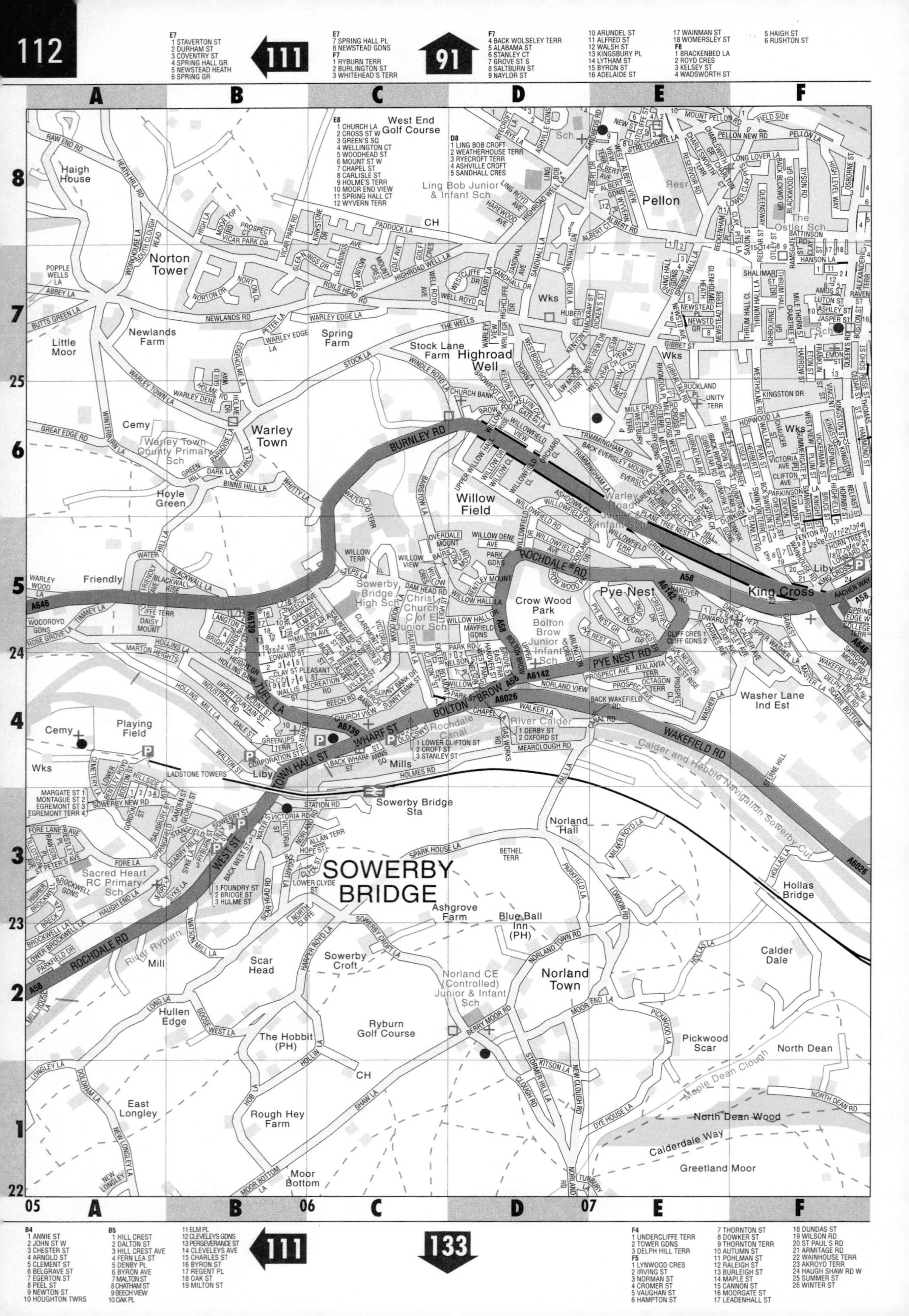
E7
1 STAVERTON ST
2 DURHAM ST
3 COVENTRY ST
4 SPRING HALL GR
5 NEWSTEAD HEATH
6 SPRING GR
111
E7
7 SPRING HALL PL
8 NEWSTEAD GDNS
F7
1 RYBURN TERR
2 BURLINGTON ST
3 WHITEHEAD'S TERR
91
F7
4 BACK WOLSELEY TERR
5 ALABAMA ST
6 STANLEY CT
7 GROVE ST S
8 SALTBURN ST
9 NAYLOR ST
10 ARUNDEL ST
11 ALFRED ST
12 WALSH ST
13 KINGSBURY PL
14 LYTHAM ST
15 BYRON ST
16 ADELAIDE ST
17 WAINMAN ST
18 WOMERSLEY ST
F8
1 BRACKENBED LA
2 ROYD CRES
3 KELSEY ST
4 WADSWORTH ST
5 HAIGH ST
6 RUSHTON ST
A
B
C
D
E
F
8
7
25
6
24
4
3
23
2
1
22
05
06
07
E8
1 CHURCH LA
2 CROSS ST W
3 GREEN'S SQ
4 WELLINGTON CT
5 WOODHEAD ST
6 MOUNT ST W
7 CHAPEL ST
8 CARLISLE ST
9 HOLME'S TERR
10 MOOR END VIEW
11 SPRING HALL CT
12 WYVERN TERR
D8
1 LING BOB CROFT
2 WEATHERHOUSE TERR
3 RYECROFT TERR
4 ASHVILLE CROFT
5 SANDHALL CRES
West End Golf Course
Ling Bob Junior & Infant Sch
Haigh House
Norton Tower
Popple Wells La
Newlands Farm
Little Moor
Spring Farm
Stock Lane Farm
Highroad Well
Pellon
Resr
The Ostler Sch
Wks
Sch
Cemy
Warley Town County Primary Sch
Warley Town
Hoyle Green
Willow Field
Warley Road Junior & Infant Sch
Friendly
Sowerby Bridge High Sch
Christ Church C of E Junior Sch
Crow Wood Park
Bolton Brow Junior & Infant Sch
Pye Nest
King Cross
Liby
Washer Lane Ind Est
Playing Field
Rochdale Canal
River Calder
Calder and Hebble Navigation Sowerby Cut
Mills
Sowerby Bridge Sta
Norland Hall
Sacred Heart RC Primary Sch
SOWERBY BRIDGE
Ashgrove Farm
Blue Ball Inn (PH)
Hollas Bridge
Scar Head
Sowerby Croft
River Ryburn
Mill
Calder Dale
Norland CE (Controlled) Junior & Infant Sch
Norland Town
Hullen Edge
The Hobbit (PH)
Ryburn Golf Course
Pickwood Scar
North Dean
CH
Maple Dean Clough
East Longley
Rough Hey Farm
North Dean Wood
Calderdale Way
Greetland Moor
Moor Bottom
A646
A58
A6139
A6142
A6026
BURNLEY RD
ROCHDALE RD
WAKEFIELD RD
PYE NEST RD
BOLTON BROW
TUEL LA
TOWN HALL ST
WHARF ST
WEST ST
NEWLANDS RD
HIGHROAD WELL LA
B4
1 ANNIE ST
2 JOHN ST W
3 CHESTER ST
4 ARNOLD ST
5 CLEMENT ST
6 BELGRAVE ST
7 EGERTON ST
8 PEEL ST
9 NEWTON ST
10 HOUGHTON TWRS
B5
1 HILL CREST
2 DALTON ST
3 HILL CREST AVE
4 FERN LEA ST
5 DENBY PL
6 BYRON AVE
7 MALTON ST
8 CHATHAM ST
9 BEECH VIEW
10 OAK PL
11 ELM PL
12 CLEVELEYS GDNS
13 PERSEVERANCE ST
14 CLEVELEYS AVE
15 CHARLES ST
16 BYRON ST
17 REGENT PL
18 OAK ST
19 MILTON ST
111
133
F4
1 UNDERCLIFFE TERR
2 TOWER GDNS
3 DELPH HILL TERR
F5
1 LYNWOOD CRES
2 IRVING ST
3 NORMAN ST
4 CROMER ST
5 VAUGHAN ST
6 HAMPTON ST
7 THORNTON ST
8 DOWKER ST
9 THORNTON TERR
10 AUTUMN ST
11 POHLMAN ST
12 RALEIGH ST
13 BURLEIGH ST
14 MAPLE ST
15 CANNON ST
16 MOORGATE ST
17 LEADENHALL ST
18 DUNDAS ST
19 WILSON RD
20 ST PAUL'S RD
21 ARMITAGE RD
22 WAINHOUSE TERR
23 AKROYD TERR
24 HAUGH SHAW RD W
25 SUMMER ST
26 WINTER ST

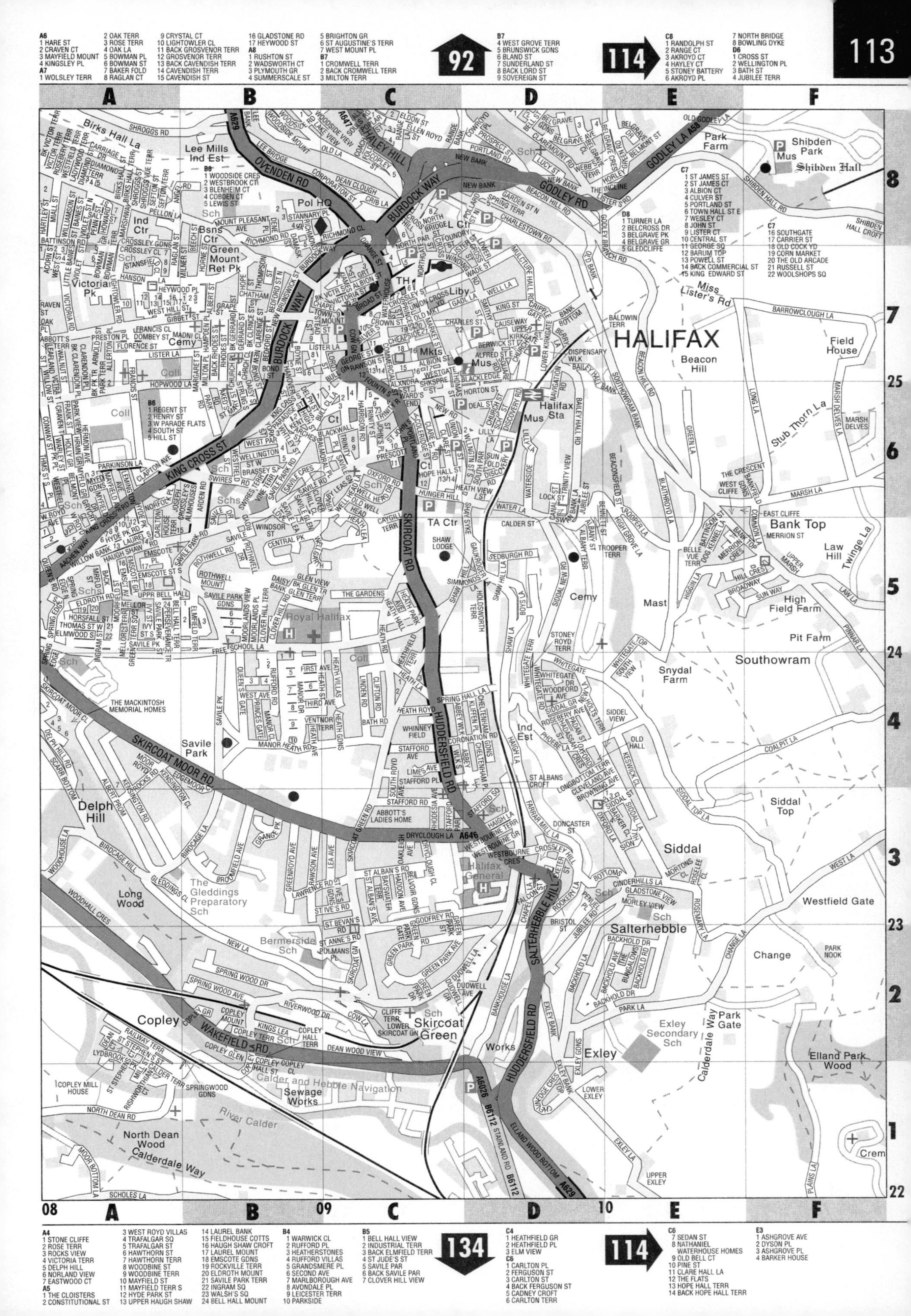

A6
1 HARE ST
2 CRAVEN CT
3 MAYFIELD MOUNT
4 KINGSLEY PL

A7
1 WOLSLEY TERR

2 OAK TERR
3 ROSE TERR
4 OAK LA
5 BOWMAN PL
6 BOWMAN ST
7 BAKER FOLD
8 RAGLAN CT

9 CRYSTAL CT
10 LIGHTOWLER CL
11 BACK GROSVENOR TERR
12 GROSVENOR TERR
13 BACK CAVENDISH TERR
14 CAVENDISH TERR
15 CAVENDISH ST

16 GLADSTONE RD
17 HEYWOOD ST

A8
1 RUSHTON ST
2 WADSWORTH CT
3 PLYMOUTH ST
4 SUMMERSCALE ST

5 BRIGHTON GR
6 ST AUGUSTINE'S TERR
7 WEST MOUNT PL

B7
1 CROMWELL TERR
2 BACK CROMWELL TERR
3 MILTON TERR

B7
4 WEST GROVE TERR
5 BRUNSWICK GDNS
6 BLAND ST
7 SUNDERLAND ST
8 BACK LORD ST
9 SOVEREIGN ST

C8
1 RANDOLPH ST
2 RANGE CT
3 AKROYD CT
4 HAYLEY CT
5 AKROYD PL

7 NORTH BRIDGE
8 BOWLING DYKE

D6
1 CROSS ST
2 WELLINGTON PL
3 BATH ST
4 JUBILEE TERR

92   114

C7
1 ST JAMES ST
2 ST JAMES CT
3 CULVER ST
4 CULVER ST
5 PORTLAND ST
6 TOWN HALL ST E
7 WESLEY CT
8 JOHN ST
9 LISTER CT
10 CENTRAL ST
11 GEORGE SQ
12 BARUM TOP
13 POWELL ST
14 BACK COMMERCIAL ST
15 KING EDWARD ST

D8
1 TURNER LA
2 BELCROSS DR
3 BELGRAVE PK
4 BELGRAVE GR
5 GLEDCLIFFE

C7
16 SOUTHGATE
17 CARRIER ST
18 OLD COCK YD
19 CORN MARKET
20 THE OLD ARCADE
21 RUSSELL ST
22 WOOLSHOPS SQ

HALIFAX

A4
1 STONE CLIFFE
2 ROSE TERR
3 ROCKS VIEW
4 VICTORIA TERR
5 DELPH HILL
6 NORLAND VIEW
7 EASTWOOD CT

A5
1 THE CLOISTERS
2 CONSTITUTIONAL

3 WEST ROYD VILLAS
4 TRAFALGAR SQ
5 TRAFALGAR ST
6 HAWTHORN ST
7 HAWTHORN TERR
8 WOODBINE ST
9 WOODBINE TERR
10 MAYFIELD ST
11 MAYFIELD TERR
12 HYDE PARK ST
13 UPPER HAUGH SHAW

14 LAUREL BANK
15 FIELDHOUSE COTTS
16 HAUGH SHAW CROFT
17 LAUREL MOUNT
18 EMSCOTE GDNS
19 ROCKVILLE TERR
20 ELDROTH MOUNT
21 SAVILE PARK TERR
22 INGRAM SQ
23 WALSH'S SQ

B4
1 WARWICK CL
2 RUFFORD PL
3 HEATHERSTONES
4 RUFFORD VILLAS
5 GRANDSMERE PL
6 SECOND AVE
7 MARLBOROUGH AVE
8 AVONDALE PL
9 LEICESTER TERR
10 PARKSIDE

B5
1 BELL HALL VIEW
2 INDUSTRIAL TERR
3 BACK ELMFIELD ST
4 ST JUDE'S ST
5 SAVILE PAR
6 BACK SAVILE PAR
7 CLOVER HILL VIEW

C4
1 HEATHFIELD GR
2 HEATHFIELD PL
3 ELM VIEW

C6
1 CARLTON PL
2 FERGUSON ST
3 CARLTON ST
4 BACK FERGUSON ST
5 CADNEY CROFT
6 CARLTON TERR

C6
7 SEDAN ST
8 NATHANIEL WATERHOUSE HOMES
9 OLD BELL CT
10 PINE ST
11 CLARE HALL LA
12 THE FLATS
13 HOPE HALL TERR
14 BACK HOPE HALL TERR

E3
1 ASHGROVE AVE
2 DYSON PL
3 ASHGROVE PL
4 BARKER HOUSE

134   114

113
93

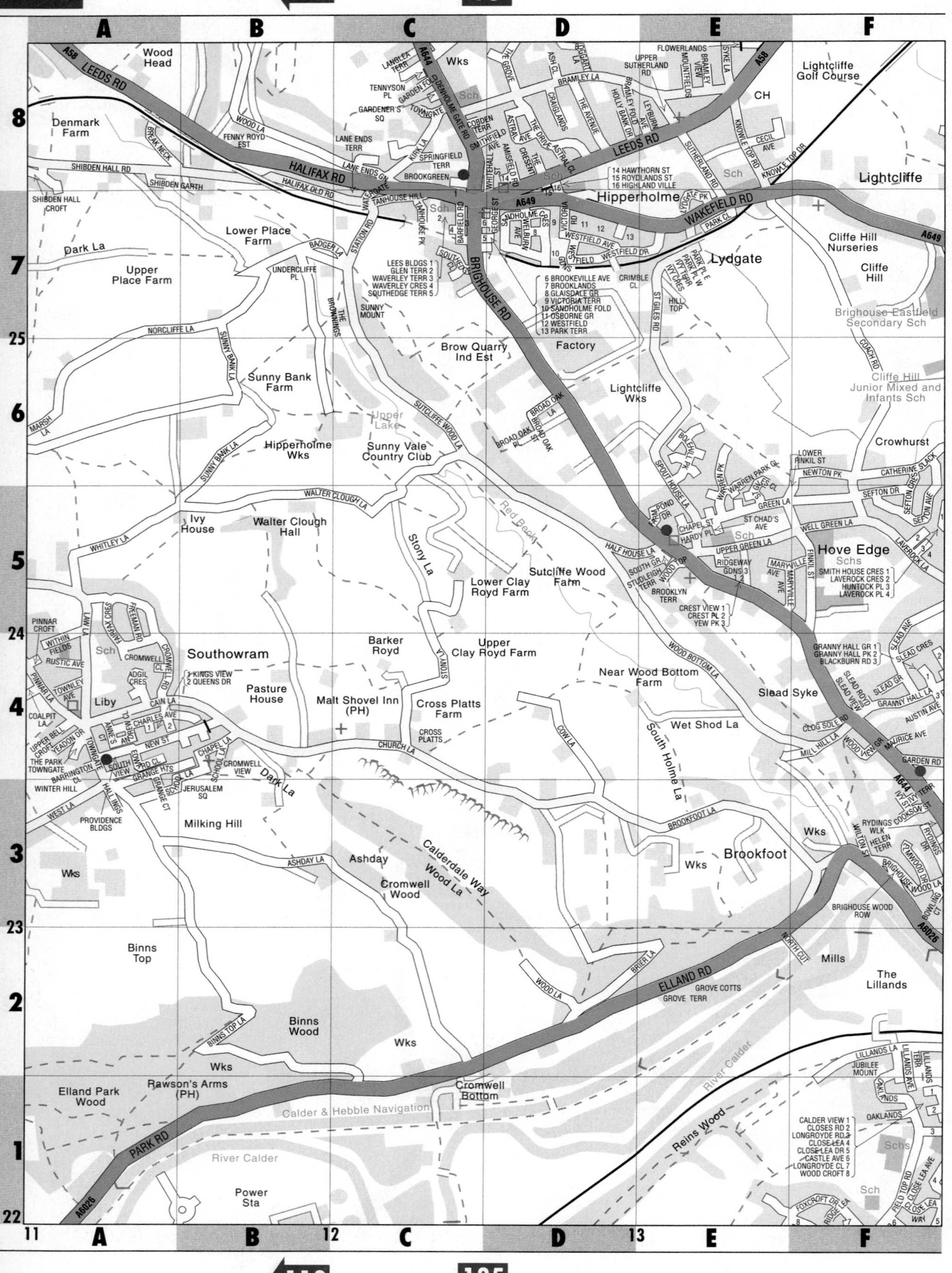
A
B
C
D
E
F
LEEDS RD
A58
Wood Head
Denmark Farm
WOOD LA
FENNY ROYD EST
BREAK NECK
SHIBDEN HALL RD
SHIBDEN GARTH
SHIBDEN HALL CROFT
HALIFAX RD
HALIFAX OLD RD
LANGLEA TERR
TENNYSON PL
GARDEN FOLD
GARDENER'S SQ
TOWNGATE
LANE ENDS TERR
KIRK LA
SPRINGFIELD TERR
LANE ENDS GN
BROOKGREEN
WATERGATE
TANHOUSE HILL
TANHOUSE PK
A644
Wks
DENHOLME GATE RD
Sch
COBDEN TERR
SMITHFIELD
WHITEHALL ST
AMISFIELD RD
ASTRAL AVE
THE CRESENT
THE DRIVE
ASTRAL CL
THE GROVE
ASH CL
CRAIGLANDS
BRAMLEY LA
THE AVENUE
HOLLY BANK DR
BRAMLEY FOLD
UPPER SUTHERLAND RD
FLOWERLANDS
MOUNTFIELDS
BRAMLEY VIEW
SYKE LA
LEYBURN AVE
LEEDS RD
SUTHERLAND RD
KNOWLE TOP RD
CECIL AVE
KNOWLE TOP DR
CH
Lightcliffe Golf Course
Lightcliffe
14 HAWTHORN ST
15 ROYDLANDS ST
16 HIGHLAND VILLE
Hipperholme
A649
WAKEFIELD RD
LYDGATE PK
PARK CL
A649
Lower Place Farm
Dark La
Upper Place Farm
BADGER LA
STATION RD
UNDERCLIFFE PL
BARFIELD RD
GEORGE ST
SANDHOLME CRES
WELBURN AVE
VICTORIA RD
WESTFIELD AVE
WESTFIELD DR
WEST GDNS
SOUTHEDGE CL
BRIGHOUSE RD
LEES BLDGS 1
GLEN TERR 2
WAVERLEY TERR 3
WAVERLEY CRES 4
SOUTHEDGE TERR 5
6 BROOKEVILLE AVE
7 BROOKLANDS
8 GLAISDALE GR
9 VICTORIA TERR
10 SANDHOLME FOLD
11 OSBORNE GR
12 WESTFIELD
13 PARK TERR
CRIMBLE CL
Lydgate
PARK PLE
PARK PL W
IVY TERR
IVY CRES
HILL TOP
ST GILES RD
Cliffe Hill Nurseries
Cliffe Hill
Brighouse Eastfield Secondary Sch
THE BROWNINGS
SUNNY MOUNT
NORCLIFFE LA
SUNNY BANK LA
Brow Quarry Ind Est
Factory
COACH RD
Cliffe Hill Junior Mixed and Infants Sch
Sunny Bank Farm
MARSH LA
Lightcliffe Wks
BROAD OAK LA
BROAD OAK ST
BROAD OAK PL
Upper Lake
SUTCLIFFE WOOD LA
Hipperholme Wks
Sunny Vale Country Club
SUNNY BANK LA
BOLEHILL PK
SPOUT HOUSE LA
WARREN PARK CL
ST GILES CL
LOWER RINKIL ST
NEWTON PK
CATHERINE SLACK
Crowhurst
SEFTON DR
SEFTON CRES
SEFTON AVE
WALTER CLOUGH LA
Ivy House
Walter Clough Hall
Red Beck
Stony La
POND DR
CHAPEL ST
HARDY PL
ST CHAD'S AVE
GREEN LA
WELL GREEN LA
Sch
Hove Edge
Schs
WHITLEY LA
HALF HOUSE LA
SOUTH GR
STUDLEIGH TERR
WOOD TOP
UPPER GREEN LA
RIDGEWAY GDNS
MARYVILLE AVE
FINKIL ST
LAVEROCK LA
SMITH HOUSE CRES 1
LAVEROCK CRES 2
HUNTOCK PL 3
LAVEROCK PL 4
Lower Clay Royd Farm
Sutcliffe Wood Farm
BROOKLYN TERR
CREST VIEW 1
CREST PL 2
YEW PK 3
PINNAR CROFT
WITHIN FIELDS
RUSTIC AVE
PINNAR LA
TOWNLEY AVE
LAW LA
FAIRFAX CRES
FREEMAN RD
Sch
CROMWELL CL
CROMWELL RD
ADGIL CRES
Southowram
1 KINGS VIEW
2 QUEENS DR
Barker Royd
Upper Clay Royd Farm
STONY LA
WOOD BOTTOM LA
Near Wood Bottom Farm
GRANNY HALL GR 1
GRANNY HALL PK 2
BLACKBURN RD 3
SLEAD AVE
SLEAD CRES
SLEAD GR
GRANNY HALL LA
SLEAD ROYD
SLEAD VIEW
Slead Syke
AUSTIN AVE
Liby
CAIN LA
CHARLES AVE
ANNE'S CT
Pasture House
Malt Shovel Inn (PH)
Cross Platts Farm
CROSS PLATTS
COW LA
South Holme La
Wet Shod La
CLOG SOLE RD
MILL HILL LA
WOOD VIEW GR
MAURICE AVE
GARDEN RD
COALPIT LA
UPPER BELL CROFT
YEADON DR
THE PARK
TOWNGATE
BARRINGTON CL
WINTER HILL
NEW ST
SOUTH VIEW
EDWARD CL
GRANGE HTS
CHAPEL LA
CROMWELL VIEW
SCHOOL LA
JERUSALEM SQ
GRANGE CT
HALL INGS
WEST LA
PROVIDENCE BLDGS
CHURCH LA
Dark La
Milking Hill
BROOKFOOT LA
Wks
A644
IVY ST
IVY TERR
COOKSON ST
RYDINGS WLK
HELEN TERR
WILTON ST
RYDINGS DR
FERNWOOD DR
BRIGHOUSE WOOD LA
BOWLING CT
Brookfoot
Wks
Wks
ASHDAY LA
Ashday
Calderdale Way
Wood La
Cromwell Wood
BRIGHOUSE WOOD ROW
A6026
NORTH CUT
Mills
The Lillands
Binns Top
BRIER LA
WOOD LA
ELLAND RD
GROVE COTTS
GROVE TERR
Binns Wood
BINNS TOP LA
Wks
Wks
LILLANDS LA
LILLANDS TERR
LILLANDS AVE
JUBILEE MOUNT
OAKLANDS
Elland Park Wood
Rawson's Arms (PH)
Cromwell Bottom
Calder & Hebble Navigation
River Calder
Reins Wood
CALDER VIEW 1
CLOSES RD 2
LONGROYDE RD 3
CLOSE LEA 4
CLOSE LEA DR 5
CASTLE AVE 6
LONGROYDE CL 7
WOOD CROFT 8
Schs
PARK RD
A6026
River Calder
Power Sta
FOXCROFT DR
RIDGE LEA
FIELD TOP RD
CLOSE LEA AVE
CLOSE LEA WAY
Sch
8
7
25
6
5
24
4
3
23
2
1
22
11
12
13

113
135

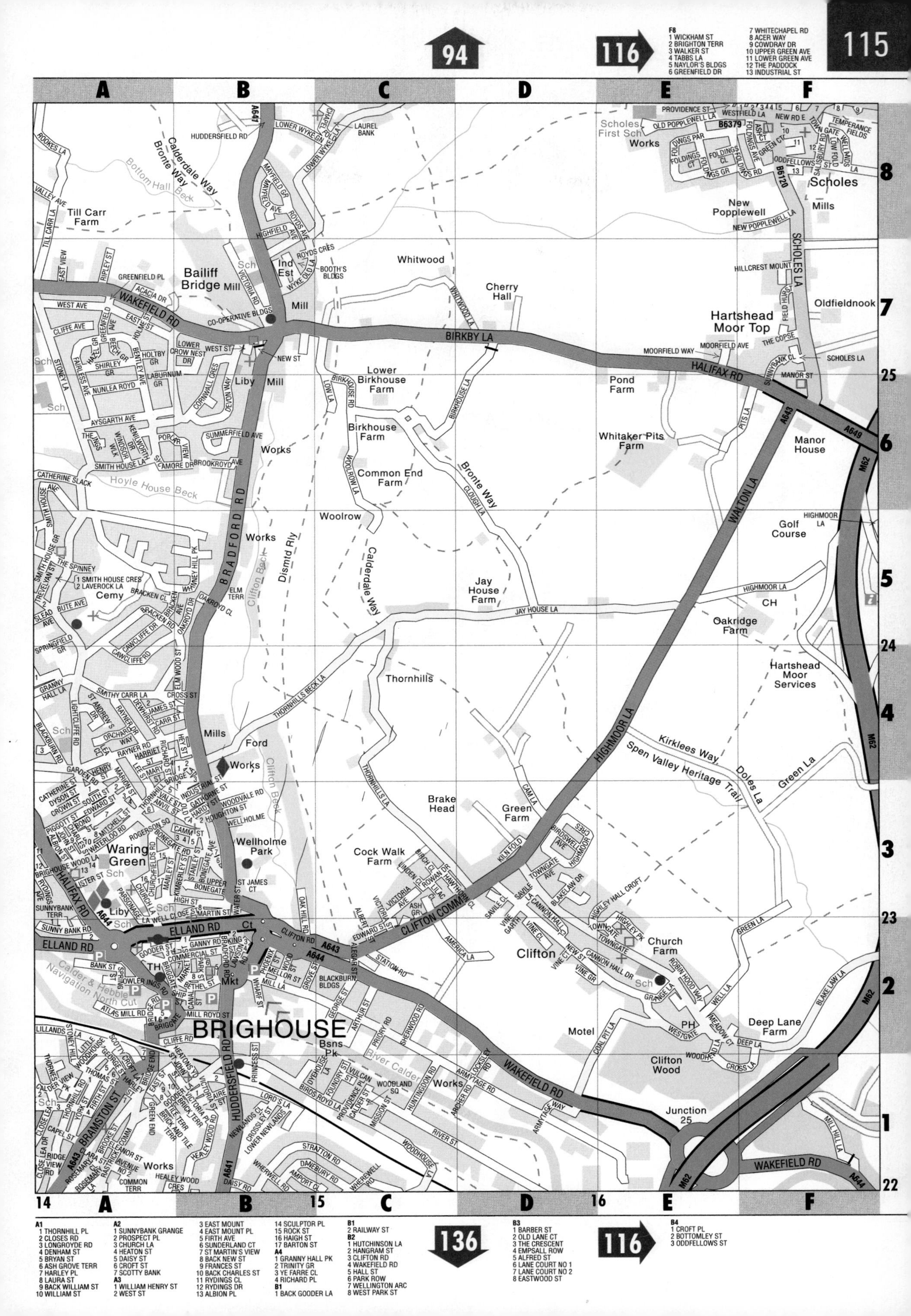
115
94
116
F8
1 WICKHAM ST
2 BRIGHTON TERR
3 WALKER ST
4 TABBS LA
5 NAYLOR'S BLDGS
6 GREENFIELD DR
7 WHITECHAPEL RD
8 ACER WAY
9 COWDRAY DR
10 UPPER GREEN AVE
11 LOWER GREEN AVE
12 THE PADDOCK
13 INDUSTRIAL ST
A
B
C
D
E
F
8
7
25
6
5
24
4
3
23
2
1
22
14
15
16
Scholes First Sch
Works
Scholes
Mills
New Popplewell
NEW POPPLEWELL LA
PROVIDENCE ST
WESTFIELD LA
OLD POPPLEWELL LA
B6379
NEW RD E
TEMPERANCE FIELDS
TOWN GATE
FOLDINGS PAR
FOLDINGS CT
FOLDINGS CL
FOLDINGS AVE
FOLDINGS GR
FOLDINGS RD
GREEN CT
ODDFELLOWS ST
SALISBURY RD
LOW FOLD
WELLANDS
B6120
SCHOLES LA
HILLCREST MOUNT
FIELD HURST
Oldfieldnook
Hartshead Moor Top
THE COPSE
MOORFIELD WAY
MOORFIELD AVE
SCHOLES LA
SUNNYBANK CL
MANOR ST
HALIFAX RD
Pond Farm
A643
A649
M62
Manor House
Whitaker Pits Farm
PITS LA
HIGHMOOR LA
Golf Course
HIGHMOOR LA
CH
Oakridge Farm
Hartshead Moor Services
Kirklees Way
Spen Valley Heritage Trail
Doles La
Green La
GREEN LA
BLAKE LAW LA
WELL LA
Deep Lane Farm
DEEP LA
CROSS LA
MEADOW CT
ROBIN HOOD WAY
Church Farm
Sch
PH
WESTGATE
Motel
COAL PIT LA
Clifton Wood
Junction 25
WAKEFIELD RD
MILL HILL LA
A644
ROOKES LA
HUDDERSFIELD RD
A641
Calderdale Way
Bronte Way
Bottom Hall Beck
VALLEY AVE
Till Carr Farm
TILL CARR LA
EAST VIEW
RIPLEY ST
GREENFIELD PL
Bailiff Bridge
Mill
Sch
VICTORIA RD
Ind Est
ROYDS CRES
BOOTH'S BLDGS
WYKE OLD LA
HIGHFIELD AVE
MAYFIELD GR
MAYFIELD AVE
ROYDS AVE
LOWER WYKE GN
LOWER WYKE LA
CHAPEL FOLD
LAUREL BANK
Whitwood
Cherry Hall
WHITWOOD LA
WEST AVE
WAKEFIELD RD
ACACIA DR
CO-OPERATIVE BLDGS
Mill
BIRKBY LA
CLIFFE AVE
EAST ST
HOLME ST
BENTLEY AVE
BEECH GR
HAZEL GR
GREENFIELD AVE
LOWER CROW NEST DR
WEST ST
NEW ST
HOLTBY GR
SHIRLEY GR
LABURNUM GR
CORNWALL CRES
DEVON WAY
Liby
Mill
FAIRLESS AVE
STONEY LA
NUNLEA ROYD
Sch
AYSGARTH AVE
KENILWORTH DR
WINDSOR WLK
THE INGS
POPLAR VIEW
SUMMERFIELD AVE
SMITH HOUSE LA
SYCAMORE DR
BROOKROYD AVE
Works
LOW LA
BIRKHOUSE RD
Lower Birkhouse Farm
Birkhouse Farm
BIRKHOUSE LA
WOOLROW LA
Common End Farm
Bronte Way
CLOUGH LA
CATHERINE SLACK
Hoyle House Beck
SMITH HOUSE AVE
SMITH HOUSE GR
BRADFORD RD
Woolrow
Works
Dismtd Rly
Calderdale Way
WALTON LA
THE SPINNEY
1 SMITH HOUSE CRES
2 LAVEROCK LA
TREVELYAN ST
BUTE AVE
Cemy
BRACKEN CL
BRACKEN RD
WHINNEY HILL PK
OAKROYD DR
OAKROYD CL
ELM TERR
Clifton Beck
Jay House Farm
JAY HOUSE LA
SLEAD AVE
SPRINGFIELD GR
CAWCLIFFE DR
CAWCLIFFE RD
ELM WOOD ST
CROSS ST
Thornhills
THORNHILLS BECK LA
GRANNY HALL LA
LIGHTCLIFFE RD
SMITHY CARR LA
ST ANDREW'S DR
RAYNER DR
JAMES ST
CARR ST
BLACKBURN RD
Sch
ORCHARD WAY
RAYNER RD
HARRIET ST
RICHARD ST
Mills
Ford
Works
HIGHMOOR LA
THORNHILLS LA
CAM LA
Brake Head
Green Farm
GARDEN RD
HENRY ST
MARION ST
CATHERINE ST
DYSON ST
CROWN ST
SOUTH ST
EDWARD ST
THORNHILL BRIDGE LA
INDUSTRIAL ST
GATHORNE ST
WOODVALE RD
HOUGHTON ST
WELLHOLME
ANVIL ST
PIGGOTT ST
BOND ST
ALBION ST
WATERLOO RD
MITCHELL ST
ROGERSON SQ
BONEGATE RD
BONEGATE AVE
CAMM ST
Wellholme Park
Waring Green
KILN FOLD
BIRDSWELL AVE
HIGHMOOR CRES
Cock Walk Farm
BIRCH CL
LINDEN CL
ROWAN DR
HAWTHORN CL
LILAC CL
VICTORIA AVE
ASH GR
BRIGHOUSE WOOD LA
HALIFAX RD
Sch
LISTER ST
KIMBERLEY ST
STANLEY ST
UPPER BONEGATE
ST JAMES CT
TOWNGATE AVE
BLAKELAW DR
HIGHLEY HALL CROFT
HIGHLEY PK
TOWNGATE
SUNNYBANK TERR
PARSONAGE LA
Liby
A644
Sch
HIGH ST
MARTIN ST
WATER ST
OAK HILL RD
CLIFTON COMM
SAVILE CL
SAVILE
VINE GARTH
VINE CL
CANNON HALL
NEW ST
VINE CT
Clifton
CANNON HALL DR
VINE GR
GRANGE LA
SUNNY BANK RD
ELLAND RD
Ct
CLIFTON RD
A643
EDWARD ST
VICTORIA ST
ALBERT ST
AMERICA LA
STATION RD
ELLAND RD
GOODER ST
GANNY RD
COMMERCIAL ST
BRADFORD RD
KING ST
BANK ST
SPRING ST
TH
PARK ST
BETHEL ST
PHOENIX ST
MELLOR ST
WOOD ST
ROCK ST
MILL LA
WHARF ST
GROVE ST
BLACKBURN BLDGS
ALEGAR ST
Calder & Hebble Navigation North Cut
BOWLER INGS RD
SHIP ST
CANAL ST
Mkt
GEORGE ST
ARTHUR ST
PRIORY RD
SHERWOOD RD
ATLAS MILL RD
BRIDGE RD
BRIGGATE
MILL ROYD ST
BRIGHOUSE
LILLANDS LA
STONEY HILL
LITTLE WOODHOUSE
SCOTTY CROFT LA
BRIDGE END
CLIFFE RD
HEATONS CT
JOHN ST
Bsns Pk
River Calder
LOCKSLEY RD
THORNES PK
CALDER VIEW
THOMAS ST
GEORGE ST
HARLEY ST
FIRTH ST
YORK ST
HUDDERSFIELD RD
PRINCESS ST
DYEHOUSE LA
FOUNDRY ST
VULCAN ST
WOODLAND SQ
Works
ARMYTAGE RD
HUNTINGDON RD
ARCHER RD
CLOSE LEA DR
CAPEL ST
BRAMSTON ST
A643
EAST ST
VICTORIA ST
BRICK TERR
GREEN END
BRICK AND TILE TERR
NEWLANDS CL
LORD'S LA
CROSSLEY ST
LOWER NEWLANDS
BIRDS ROYD LA
PROVIDENCE PL
CALDER ST
MISSION ST
RIVER ST
ARMYTAGE WAY
RIDGE VIEW RD
BROOKE ST
ELEANOR ST
AVENUE NO 2
ROSEMARY LA
RASTRICK COMM
COMMON TERR
Works
HEALEY WOOD RD
HEALEY WOOD CRES
DAISY RD
A641
WHERWELL RD
AMPORT CL
DANBURY RD
STRATTON RD
WHEREWELL RD
WOODHOUSE LA
M62
WAKEFIELD RD
A644
136
116
A1
1 THORNHILL PL
2 CLOSES RD
3 LONGROYDE RD
4 DENHAM ST
5 BRYAN ST
6 ASH GROVE TERR
7 HARLEY PL
8 LAURA ST
9 BACK WILLIAM ST
10 WILLIAM ST
A2
1 SUNNYBANK GRANGE
2 PROSPECT PL
3 CHURCH LA
4 HEATON ST
5 DAISY ST
6 CROFT ST
7 SCOTTY BANK
A3
1 WILLIAM HENRY ST
2 WEST ST
3 EAST MOUNT
4 EAST MOUNT PL
5 FIRTH AVE
6 SUNDERLAND CT
7 ST MARTIN'S VIEW
8 BACK NEW ST
9 FRANCES ST
10 BACK CHARLES ST
11 RYDINGS CL
12 RYDINGS DR
13 ALBION PL
14 SCULPTOR PL
15 ROCK ST
16 HAIGH ST
17 BARTON ST
A4
1 GRANNY HALL PK
2 TRINITY GR
3 YE FARRE CL
4 RICHARD PL
B1
1 BACK GOODER LA
B1
2 RAILWAY ST
B2
1 HUTCHINSON LA
2 HANGRAM ST
3 CLIFTON RD
4 WAKEFIELD RD
5 HALL ST
6 PARK ROW
7 WELLINGTON ARC
8 WEST PARK ST
B3
1 BARBER ST
2 OLD LANE CT
3 THE CRESCENT
4 EMPSALL ROW
5 ALFRED ST
6 LANE COURT NO 1
7 LANE COURT NO 2
8 EASTWOOD ST
B4
1 CROFT PL
2 BOTTOMLEY ST
3 ODDFELLOWS ST

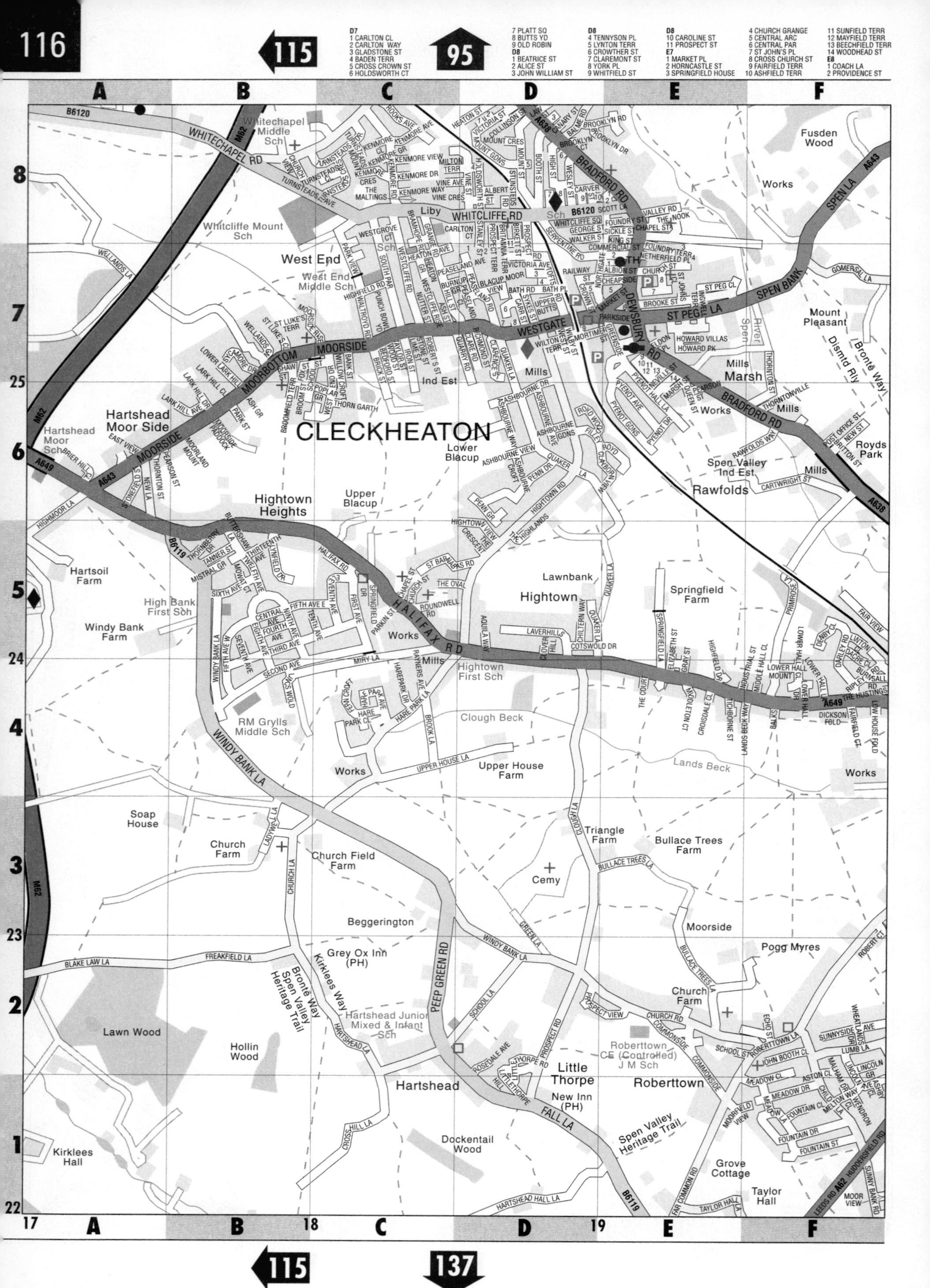
115
95
D7
1 CARLTON CL
2 CARLTON WAY
3 GLADSTONE ST
4 BADEN TERR
5 CROSS CROWN ST
6 HOLDSWORTH CT
7 PLATT SQ
8 BUTTS YD
9 OLD ROBIN
D8
1 BEATRICE ST
2 ALICE ST
3 JOHN WILLIAM ST
D8
4 TENNYSON PL
5 LYNTON TERR
6 CROWTHER ST
7 CLAREMONT ST
8 YORK PL
9 WHITFIELD ST
D8
10 CAROLINE ST
11 PROSPECT ST
E7
1 MARKET PL
2 HORNCASTLE ST
3 SPRINGFIELD HOUSE
4 CHURCH GRANGE
5 CENTRAL ARC
6 CENTRAL PAR
7 ST JOHN'S PL
8 CROSS CHURCH ST
9 FAIRFIELD TERR
10 ASHFIELD TERR
11 SUNFIELD TERR
12 MAYFIELD TERR
13 BEECHFIELD TERR
14 WOODHEAD ST
E8
1 COACH LA
2 PROVIDENCE ST
A
B
C
D
E
F
8
7
25
6
5
24
4
3
23
2
1
22
17
18
19
CLECKHEATON
WHITECHAPEL RD
Whitechapel Middle Sch
Whitcliffe Mount Sch
West End
West End Middle Sch
WHITCLIFFE RD
BRADFORD RD
DEWSBURY RD
WESTGATE
MOORSIDE
MOORBOTTOM
ST PEG LA
SPEN LA
SPEN BANK
Fusden Wood
Works
Mount Pleasant
Marsh
Mills
Ind Est
Hartshead Moor Side
Hartshead Moor Sch
Lower Blacup
Upper Blacup
Hightown Heights
Spen Valley Ind Est
Rawfolds
Royds Park
Hartsoil Farm
High Bank First Sch
Windy Bank Farm
Lawnbank
Hightown
Springfield Farm
HALIFAX RD
Hightown First Sch
RM Grylls Middle Sch
Clough Beck
Lands Beck
Upper House Farm
WINDY BANK LA
Soap House
Church Farm
Church Field Farm
Triangle Farm
Bullace Trees Farm
Cemy
Beggerington
Grey Ox Inn (PH)
Moorside
Pogg Myres
Church Farm
Lawn Wood
Hollin Wood
Brontë Way Spen Valley Heritage Trail
Kirklees Way
Hartshead Junior Mixed & Infant Sch
PEEP GREEN RD
Roberttown CE (Controlled) J M Sch
Little Thorpe
Roberttown
Hartshead
New Inn (PH)
Spen Valley Heritage Trail
FALL LA
Dockentail Wood
Kirklees Hall
Grove Cottage
Taylor Hall
115
137

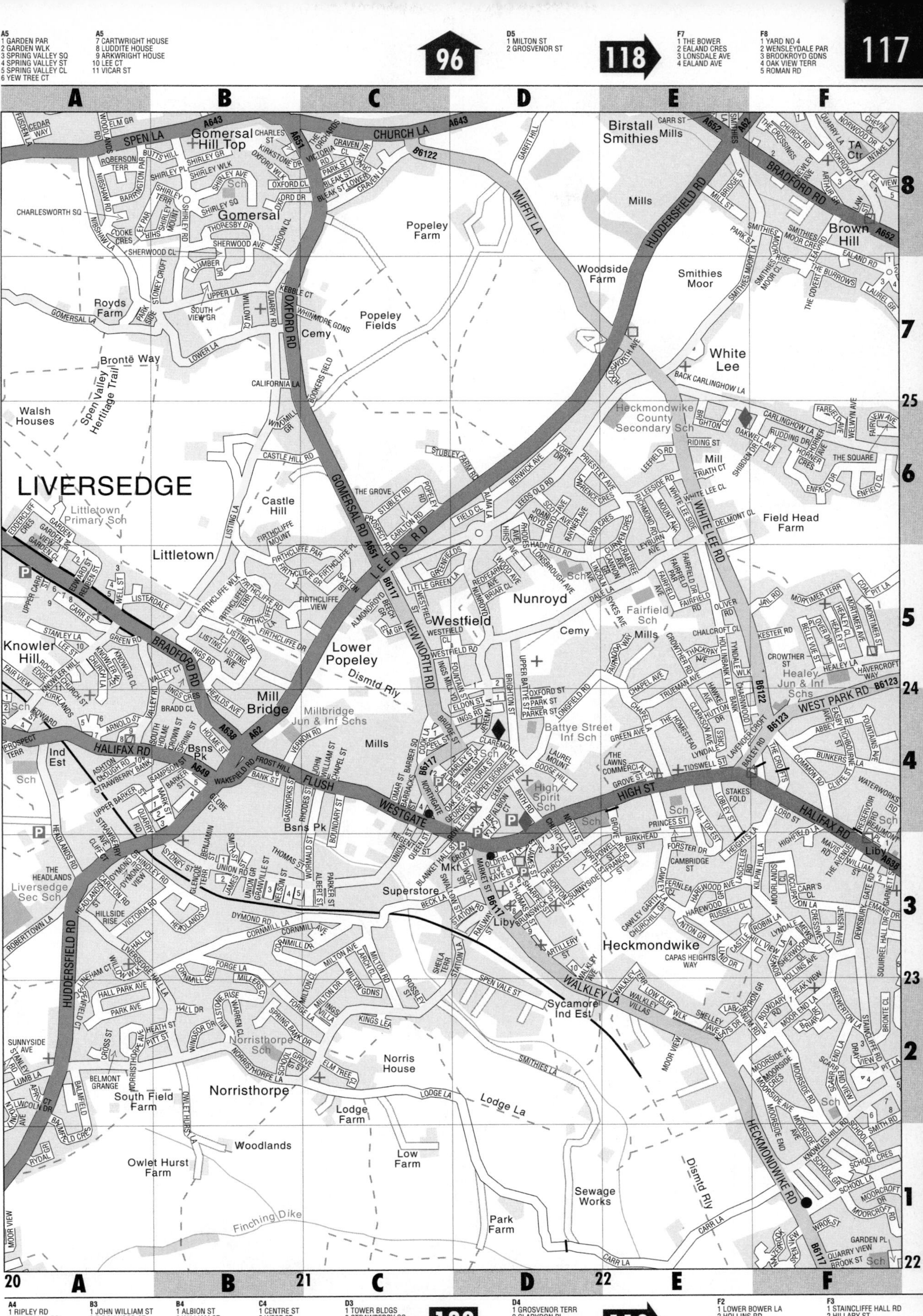

A
B
C
D
E
F
8
7
25
6
5
24
4
3
23
2
1
22
20
21
22
Gomersal Hill Top
Gomersal
Birstall Smithies
Mills
Popeley Farm
Royds Farm
Popeley Fields
Cemy
Woodside Farm
Smithies Moor
Brown Hill
White Lee
Bronte Way
Spen Valley Heritage Trail
Walsh Houses
Heckmondwike County Secondary Sch
LIVERSEDGE
Littletown Primary Sch
Castle Hill
Littletown
Field Head Farm
Nunroyd
Westfield
Fairfield Sch
Knowler Hill
Lower Popeley
Dismtd Rly
Mill Bridge
Millbridge Jun & Inf Schs
Healey Jun & Inf Schs
Battye Street Inf Sch
High Spirit Sch
Ind Est
Bsns Pk
Mkt
Superstore
Liby
THE HEADLANDS
Liversedge Sec Sch
Heckmondwike
Sycamore Ind Est
Norristhorpe Sch
Norris House
Norristhorpe
South Field Farm
Lodge Farm
Lodge La
Woodlands
Low Farm
Owlet Hurst Farm
Sewage Works
Park Farm
Finching Dike
SPEN LA
CHURCH LA
BRADFORD RD
HUDDERSFIELD RD
MUFFIT LA
OXFORD RD
GOMERSAL RD
LEEDS RD
NEW NORTH RD
WHITE LEE RD
HALIFAX RD
WESTGATE
HIGH ST
FLUSH
WALKLEY LA
HECKMONDWIKE RD
WEST PARK RD
A643
A651
A652
A62
A638
A649
B6122
B6117
B6123

C5
1 CHURCHFIELD ST
2 HENRIETTA ST
3 BK HENRIETTA ST
4 BK PROVIDENCE ST
5 MARKET SQ
6 BRUNSWICK ST
7 HUME CREST
8 COBDEN CL
9 BAYLDONS PL
10 WARDS HILL CT

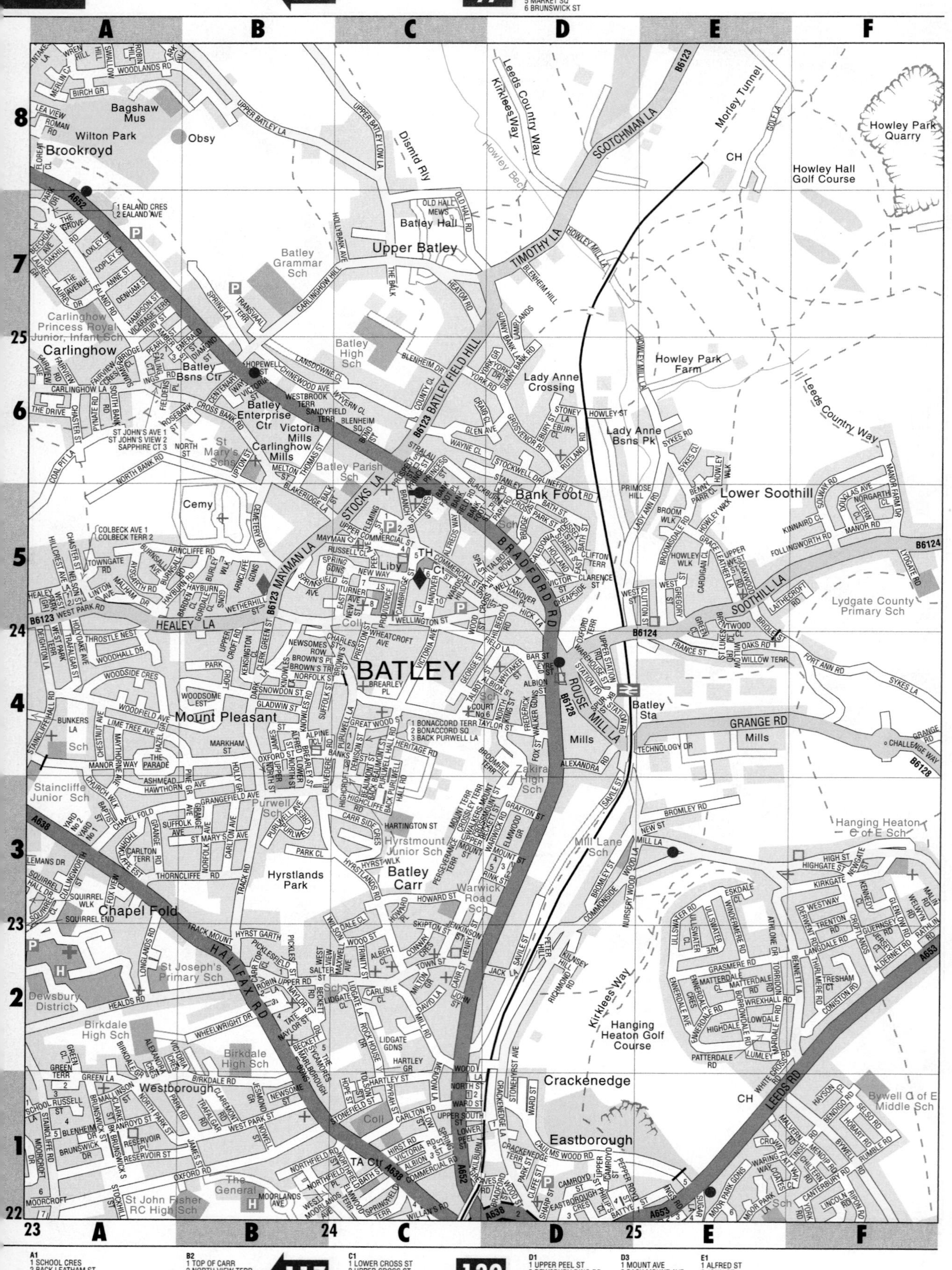

A1
1 SCHOOL CRES
2 BACK LEATHAM ST
3 GLADSTONE CT
4 HANOVER CT
5 FAIRFIELD CRES
6 FIR BANK
7 STAINCLIFFE CL

B2
1 TOP OF CARR
2 NORTH VIEW TERR
3 MITCHELL AVE
4 SOUTH VIEW TERR
5 MARLBRO' TERR

C1
1 LOWER CROSS ST
2 UPPER CROSS ST
3 BRIGHT ST
4 SPINKWELL RD

D1
1 UPPER PEEL ST
2 DEWSBURY RING RD
3 ERNEST ST
4 BACK MARRIOT ST

D3
1 MOUNT AVE
2 BACK MOUNT AVE
3 CROSS RINK ST
4 RINK TERR
5 RINK PAR

E1
1 ALFRED ST
2 JOHN ST
3 WELL ST
4 HOLLINROYD RD
5 VICTORIA BLDGS
6 MOOR PARK CT

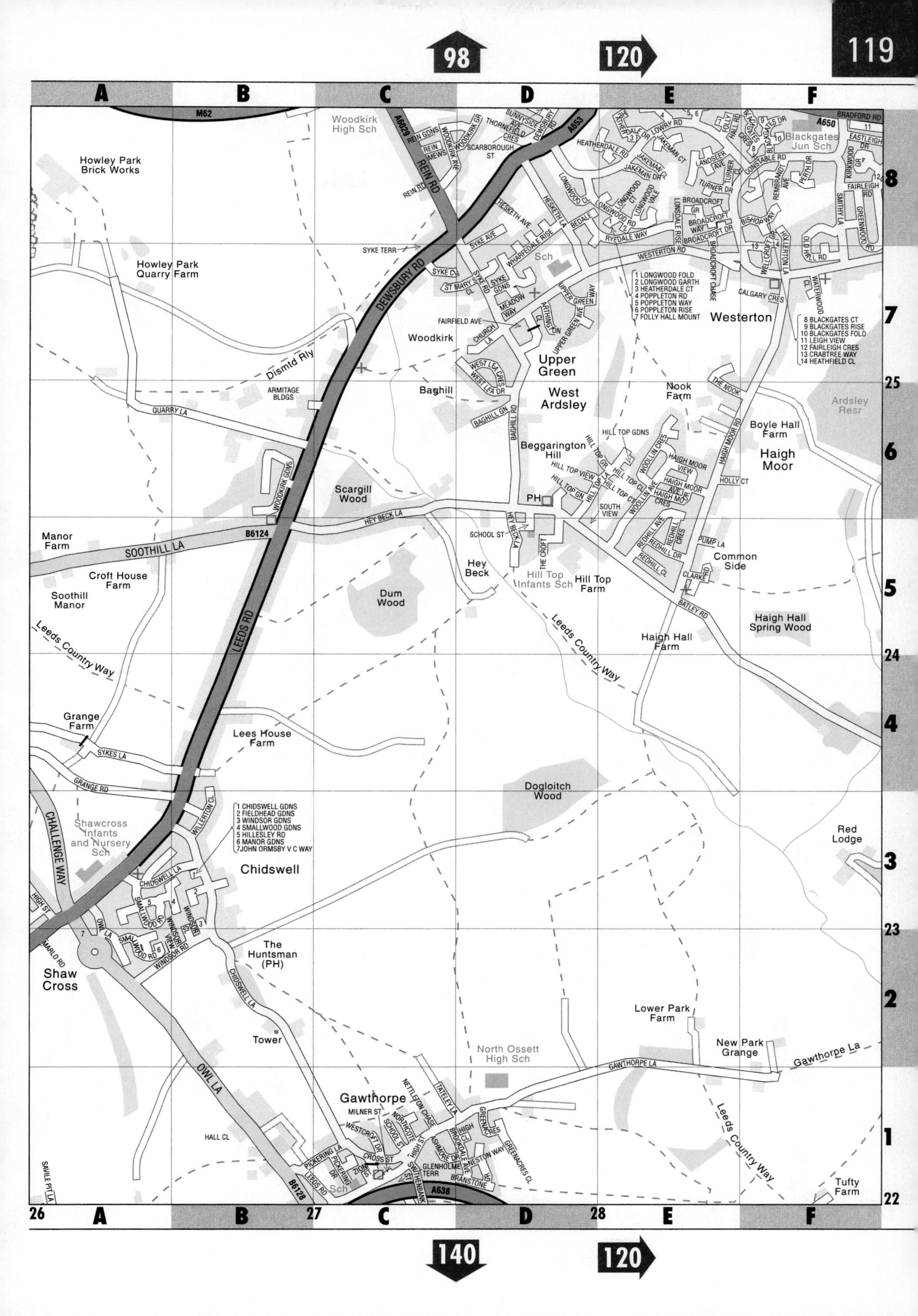
98
120
119
A B C D E F
M62
Woodkirk High Sch
A6029
REIN RD
REIN GDNS
REIN MEWS
WOODKIRK AVE
WOODKIRK GR
THORNEFIELD CRES
SUNNYSIDE AVE
DEWSBURY RD
SCARBOROUGH ST
A653
Howley Park Brick Works
Howley Park Quarry Farm
SYKE TERR
DEWSBURY RD
HESKETH AVE
HESKETH LA
BEDALE
SYKE AVE
WHARFEDALE RISE
SYKE CL
ST MARY'S CL
SYKE RD
SYKE GDNS
MEADOW WAY
Sch
UPPER GREEN WAY
UPPER GREEN AVE
ARTHINGTON CL
FAIRFIELD AVE
CHURCH LA
Woodkirk
Dismtd Rly
WEST LEA CRES
WEST LEA DR
Upper Green
Baghill
West Ardsley
ARMITAGE BLDGS
QUARRY LA
BAGHILL GN
BAGHILL RD
HEATHERDALE RD
LOWRY RD
JAKEMAN CT
JAKEMAN CL
JAKEMAN DR
LANDSEER AVE
TURNER AVE
TURNER DR
FOLLY HALL RD
BLACKGATES CRES
BLACKGATES DR
CONSTABLE RD
Blackgates Jun Sch
A650
BRADFORD RD
EASTLEIGH DR
KIRKWOOD GR
FAIRLEIGH RD
PERTH DR
REMBRANDT AVE
LONGWOOD CL
LONGWOOD CT
LONGWOOD VALE
LONGWOOD RD
RYEDALE WAY
LONSDALE RISE
BROADCROFT GR
BROADCROFT WAY
BROADCROFT DR
BROADCROFT CHASE
BISHOP WAY
WELLCROFT GR
HOLMESTON LA
SMITHY LA
GREENWOOD RD
OLD HALL RD
WESTERTON RD
1 LONGWOOD FOLD
2 LONGWOOD GARTH
3 HEATHERDALE CT
4 POPPLETON RD
5 POPPLETON WAY
6 POPPLETON RISE
7 FOLLY HALL MOUNT
CALGARY CRES
WATERWOOD CL
Westerton
8 BLACKGATES CT
9 BLACKGATES RISE
10 BLACKGATES FOLD
11 LEIGH VIEW
12 FAIRLEIGH CRES
13 CRABTREE WAY
14 HEATHFIELD CL
THE NOOK
Nook Farm
Ardsley Resr
Boyle Hall Farm
Haigh Moor
HAIGH MOOR RD
HOLLY CT
HILL TOP GDNS
HILL TOP GR
HILL TOP VIEW
HILL TOP CL
HILL TOP CT
HILL TOP GN
HILL TOP LA
WOOLLIN CRES
WOOLLIN AVE
HAIGH MOOR VIEW
HAIGH MOOR AVE
HAIGH MOOR CRES
SOUTH VIEW
Beggarington Hill
PH
WOODKIRK GDNS
Scargill Wood
HEY BECK LA
Manor Farm
B6124
SOOTHILL LA
SCHOOL ST
THE CROFT
REDHILL AVE
REDHILL CRES
REDHILL DR
REDHILL CL
PUMP LA
Common Side
CLARKE
Croft House Farm
Soothill Manor
Hey Beck
Dum Wood
Hill Top Infants Sch
Hill Top Farm
BATLEY RD
LEEDS RD
Leeds Country Way
Haigh Hall Farm
Haigh Hall Spring Wood
Grange Farm
SYKES LA
Lees House Farm
GRANGE RD
Dogloitch Wood
CHALLENGE WAY
Shawcross Infants and Nursery Sch
WILLERTON CL
1 CHIDSWELL GDNS
2 FIELDHEAD GDNS
3 WINDSOR GDNS
4 SMALLWOOD GDNS
5 HILLESLEY RD
6 MANOR GDNS
7 JOHN ORMSBY V C WAY
Chidswell
CHIDSWELL LA
Red Lodge
HIGH ST
OWL LA
SMALLWOOD RD
WINDSOR VIEW
WINDSOR CL
WINDSOR RD
MARLO RD
Shaw Cross
The Huntsman (PH)
Lower Park Farm
Tower
New Park Grange
Gawthorpe La
GAWTHORPE LA
North Ossett High Sch
Gawthorpe
MILNER ST
NETTLETON CHASE
TATEFIELD CL
WESTCROFT DR
SCHOOL ST
NORTHCOTE
HIGH ST
ASHMORE DR
BROOKDALE AVE
GREENACRES
GREENACRES CL
HIGH CL
NESTON WAY
HALL CL
PICKERING LA
PICKERING DR
CROSS ST
ZION ST
GLENHOLME TERR
BRANSTONE
SMITHIENBANK
A638
B6128
LEEDS RD
SAVILE PIT LA
Sch
Tufty Farm
8 7 6 5 4 3 2 1
25 24 23 22
26 27 28

119
99

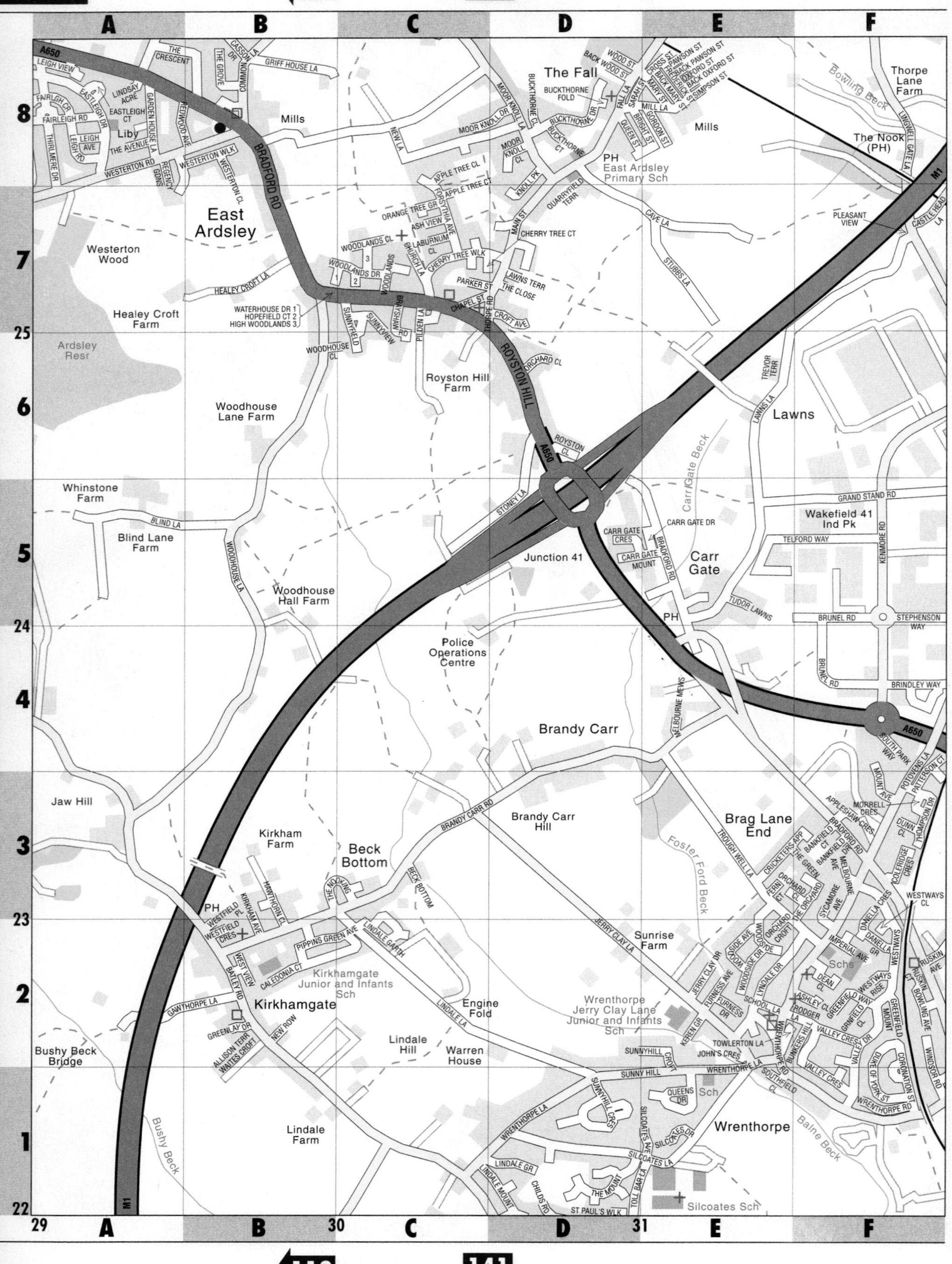
A
B
C
D
E
F
8
7
25
6
5
24
4
3
23
2
1
22
29
30
31
A650
M1
The Fall
Thorpe Lane Farm
Bowling Beck
Mills
Liby
The Nook (PH)
PH
East Ardsley Primary Sch
East Ardsley
Westerton Wood
Healey Croft Farm
Ardsley Resr
Woodhouse Lane Farm
Royston Hill Farm
Lawns
Whinstone Farm
Blind Lane Farm
Wakefield 41 Ind Pk
Carr Gate
Junction 41
Woodhouse Hall Farm
Police Operations Centre
Brandy Carr
Jaw Hill
Brag Lane End
Kirkham Farm
Beck Bottom
Brandy Carr Hill
Foster Ford Beck
Sunrise Farm
Kirkhamgate Junior and Infants Sch
Kirkhamgate
Engine Fold
Wrenthorpe Jerry Clay Lane Junior and Infants Sch
Bushy Beck Bridge
Lindale Hill
Warren House
Lindale Farm
Bushy Beck
Wrenthorpe
Balne Beck
Silcoates Sch
Sch
Schs
GRIFF HOUSE LA
BRADFORD RD
ROYSTON HILL
HEALEY CROFT LA
WOODHOUSE LA
BLIND LA
BRANDY CARR RD
JERRY CLAY LA
TROUGH WELL LA
LINDALE LA
WRENTHORPE LA
SUNNY HILL
WRENTHORPE RD
SILCOATES LA
GRAND STAND RD
TELFORD WAY
BRUNEL RD
STEPHENSON WAY
BRINDLEY WAY
KENMORE RD
CAVE LA
STUBBS LA
CARR GATE DR
TUDOR LAWNS
MELBOURNE MEWS
GAWTHORPE LA
STONEY LA
WATERHOUSE DR 1
HOPEFIELD CT 2
HIGH WOODLANDS 3

119
141

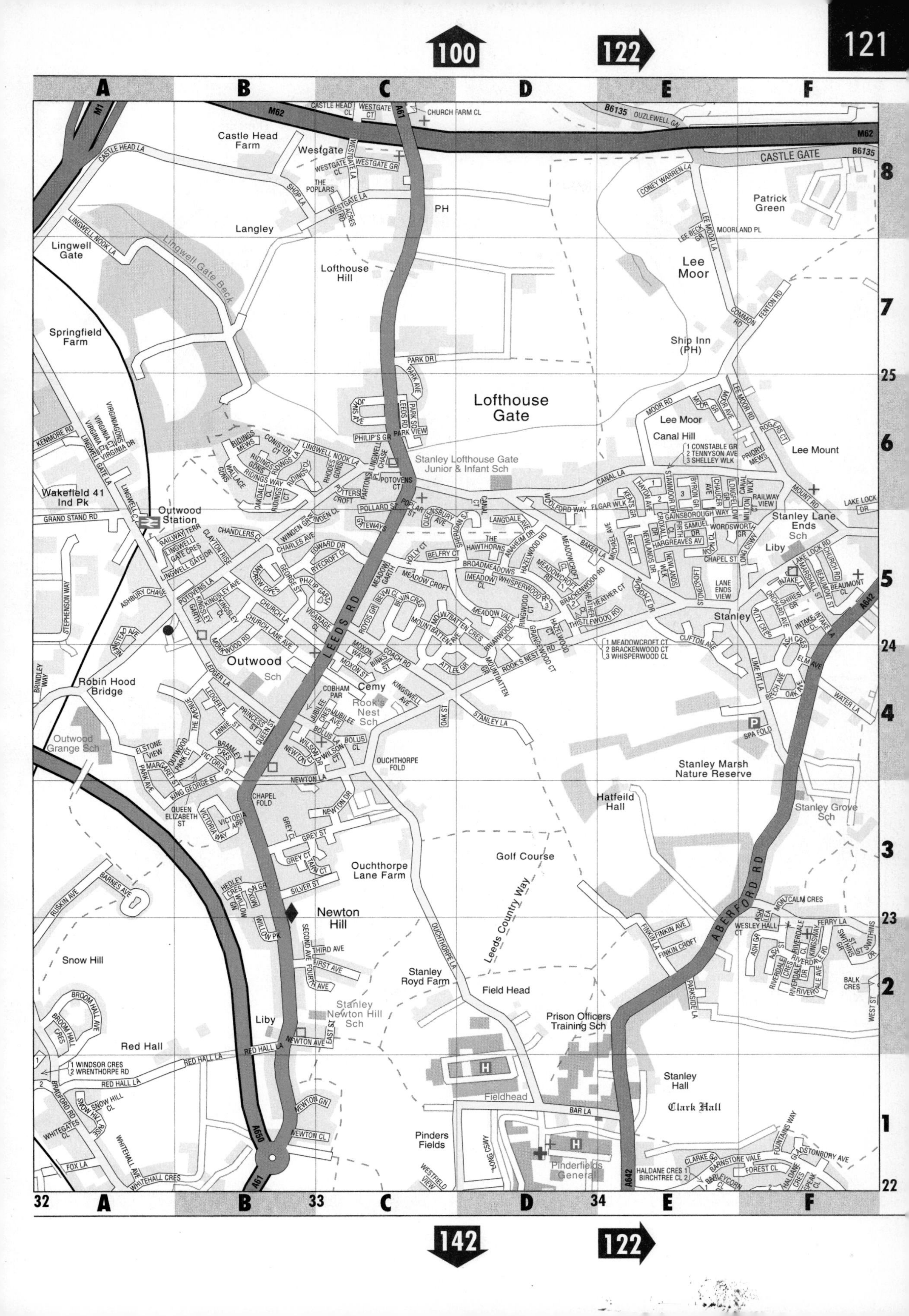
100
122
M62
A61
M1
B6135
Castle Head Farm
Westgate
Langley
Lingwell Gate
Lofthouse Hill
Springfield Farm
Lofthouse Gate
Stanley Lofthouse Gate Junior & Infant Sch
Patrick Green
Lee Moor
Ship Inn (PH)
Canal Hill
Lee Mount
Stanley Lane Ends
Wakefield 41 Ind Pk
Outwood Station
Outwood
Robin Hood Bridge
Outwood Grange Sch
Rook's Nest Sch
Cemy
Stanley
Stanley Marsh Nature Reserve
Hatfeild Hall
Stanley Grove Sch
Golf Course
Leeds Country Way
Ouchthorpe Lane Farm
Newton Hill
Snow Hill
Stanley Royd Farm
Field Head
Stanley Newton Hill Sch
Prison Officers Training Sch
Red Hall
Stanley Hall
Clark Hall
Fieldhead
Pinders Fields
Pinderfields General
LEEDS RD
ABERFORD RD
CASTLE GATE
A650
A642
32
33
34
22
23
24
25
142
122

121
101

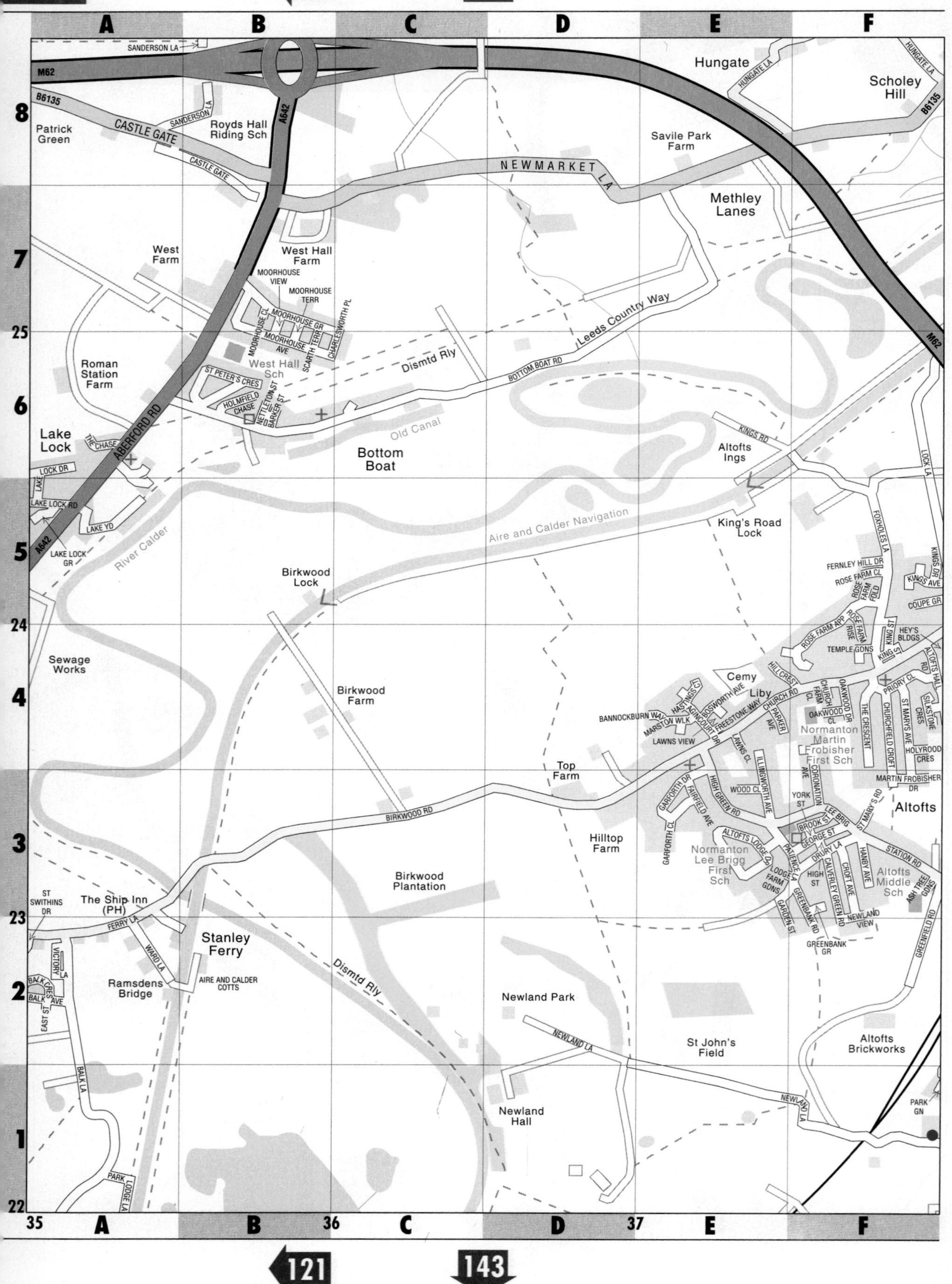
A
B
C
D
E
F
SANDERSON LA
M62
Hungate
HUNGATE LA
Scholey
Hill
B6135
8
Patrick
Green
CASTLE GATE
SANDERSON LA
Royds Hall
Riding Sch
A642
Savile Park
Farm
CASTLE GATE
NEWMARKET LA
Methley
Lanes
7
West
Farm
West Hall
Farm
MOORHOUSE
VIEW
MOORHOUSE
TERR
MOORHOUSE GR
MOORHOUSE CL
MOORHOUSE
AVE
SCARTH TERR
CHARLESWORTH PL
Leeds Country Way
25
Roman
Station
Farm
West Hall
Sch
ST PETER'S CRES
Dismtd Rly
BOTTOM BOAT RD
M62
6
HOLMFIELD
CHASE
NETTLETON ST
BARKER ST
Lake
Lock
THE CHASE
ABERFORD RD
Old Canal
Bottom
Boat
KINGS RD
Altofts
Ings
LOCK DR
LAKE
LAKE LOCK RD
LAKE YD
A642
Aire and Calder Navigation
King's Road
Lock
FOXHOLES LA
LOCK LA
5
LAKE LOCK
GR
River Calder
Birkwood
Lock
FERNLEY HILL DR
ROSE FARM CL
ROSE FARM FOLD
KINGS DR
KINGS AVE
COUPE GR
24
ROSE FARM APP
ROSE FARM RISE
KING ST
HEY'S
BLDGS
TEMPLE GDNS
KING S
ALTOFTS HALL RD
Sewage
Works
Cemy
HILL CREST
4
Birkwood
Farm
Liby
BOSWORTH AVE
HASTINGS CT
CHURCH RD
CHURCH FARM CL
OAKWOOD DR
PRIORY CL
BANNOCKBURN WAY
MARSTON WLK
AGINCOURT DR
TREESTONE WAY
PARKER AVE
OAKWOOD CL
THE CRESCENT
CHURCHFIELD CROFT
ST MARY'S AVE
SILKSTONE CRES
LAWNS VIEW
LAWNS CL
Normanton
Martin
Frobisher
First Sch
HOLYROOD CRES
Top
Farm
ILLINGWORTH AVE
MARTIN FROBISHER DR
GARFORTH DR
FAIRFIELD AVE
HIGH GREEN RD
WOOD CL
YORK ST
CORONATION AVE
ST MARY'S RD
Altofts
BIRKWOOD RD
LEE BRIG
BROOK ST
GARFORTH CL
Hilltop
Farm
ALTOFTS LODGE DR
GEORGE ST
3
Normanton
Lee Brigg
First
Sch
PATIENCE LA
DRURY LA
HANBY AVE
STATION RD
LODGE FARM GDNS
HIGH ST
CAVERLEY GREEN RD
CROFT AVE
Altofts
Middle
Sch
ASH TREE GDNS
ST
SWITHINS
DR
The Ship Inn
(PH)
Birkwood
Plantation
GARDEN ST
GREENBANK RD
NEWLAND VIEW
GREENFIELD RD
23
FERRY LA
GREENBANK
GR
Stanley
Ferry
VICTORY LA
WARD LA
Dismtd Rly
2
BALK CRES
BALK AVE
Ramsdens
Bridge
AIRE AND CALDER
COTTS
Newland Park
EAST ST
NEWLAND LA
St John's
Field
Altofts
Brickworks
BALK LA
NEWLAND LA
PARK
GN
Newland
Hall
1
PARK
LODGE LA
22
35
A
B
36
C
D
37
E
F

121
143

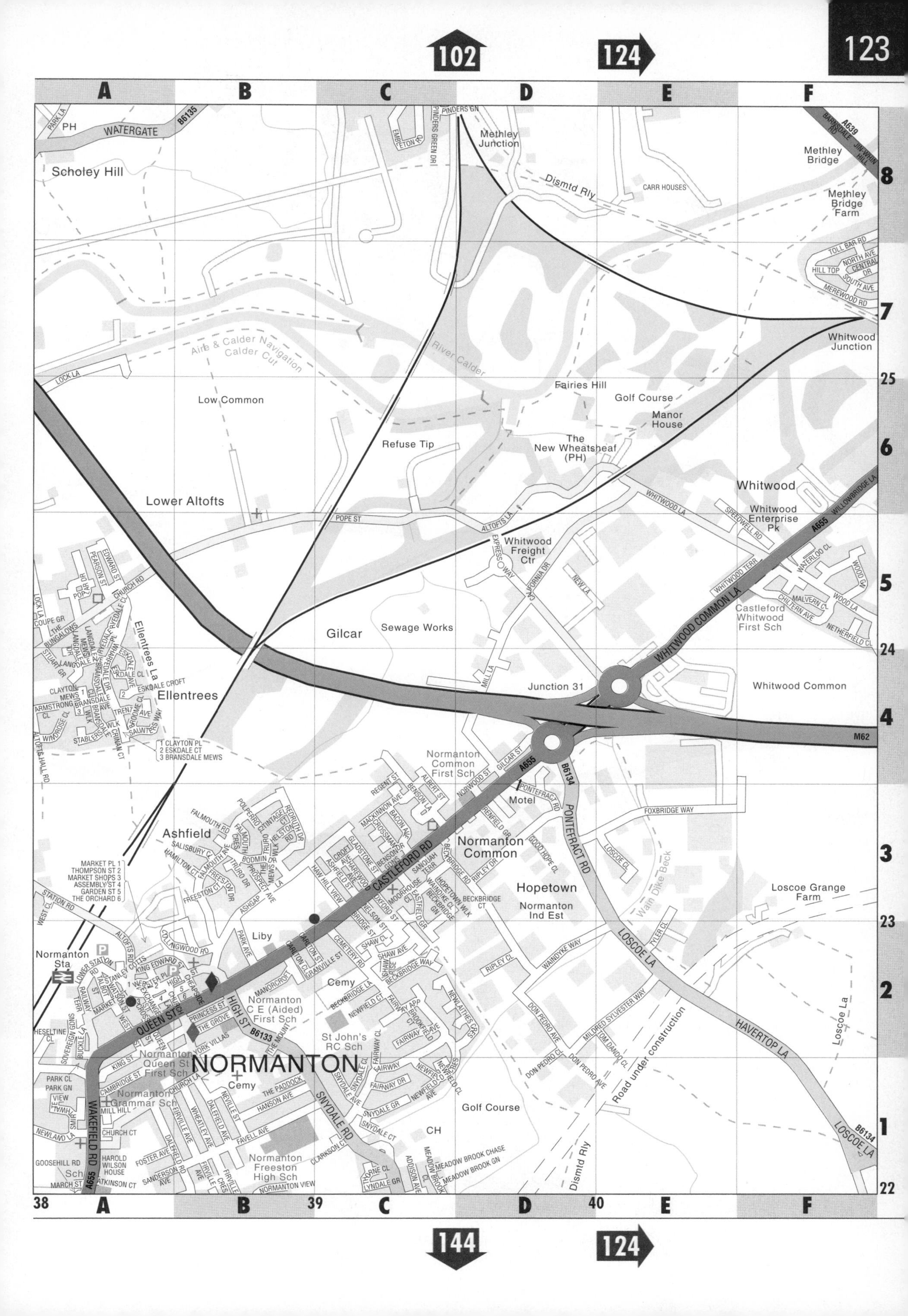

102
124
A
B
C
D
E
F
8
7
25
6
5
24
4
3
23
2
1
22
38
39
40
144
Scholey Hill
WATERGATE
B6135
PARK LA
PH
PINDERS GN
PINDERS GREEN DR
EMBLETON RD
Methley Junction
Dismtd Rly
CARR HOUSES
Methley Bridge
Methley Bridge Farm
A639
BARNSDALE RD
TOLL BAR RD
HILL TOP
NORTH AVE
CENTRAL DR
SOUTH AVE
MEREWOOD RD
Whitwood Junction
Aire & Calder Navigation
Calder Cut
River Calder
LOCK LA
Low Common
Fairies Hill
Golf Course
Manor House
The New Wheatsheaf (PH)
Refuse Tip
Lower Altofts
POPE ST
ALTOFTS LA
WHITWOOD LA
Whitwood
Whitwood Enterprise Pk
SPEEDWELL RD
A655
WILLOWBRIDGE LA
Whitwood Freight Ctr
EXPRESS WAY
CALIFORNIA DR
NEW LA
WHITWOOD TERR
WATERLOO CL
WOOD GR
WOOD LA
MALVERN CL
CHILTERN AVE
NETHERFIELD CL
WHITWOOD COMMON LA
Castleford Whitwood First Sch
EDWARD ST
PEARSON ST
CHURCH RD
POP
LOCK LA
COUPE GR
THE BUNGALOWS
Ellentrees La
Gilcar
Sewage Works
MILL LA
Junction 31
Whitwood Common
M62
ESKDALE CROFT
Ellentrees
CLAYTON MEWS
ARMSTRONG CL
STUART GR
WINDROSE CL
STABLERS WLK
SAUNTERS WAY
ALTOFTS HALL RD
1 CLAYTON PL
2 ESKDALE CT
3 BRANSDALE MEWS
Normanton Common First Sch
GILCAR ST
NORWOOD ST
ALBERT ST
BENSON LA
REGENT ST
B6134
PONTEFRACT RD
Motel
FOXBRIDGE WAY
Ashfield
FALMOUTH RD
POLPERRO CL
TINTAGEL CT
REDRUTH RD
SALISBURY CL
HAMILTON CT
FREESTON CT
Normanton Common
RENFIELD GR
GOOD HOPE CL
RIPLEY DR
LOSCOE CL
Wain Dike Beck
Hopetown
Normanton Ind Est
BECKBRIDGE CT
HOPETOWN WLK
CASTLEFORD RD
MARKET PL 1
THOMPSON ST 2
MARKET SHOPS 3
ASSEMBLY ST 4
GARDEN ST 5
THE ORCHARD 6
STATION RD
WEST CL
Loscoe Grange Farm
LOSCOE LA
TYLER CL
Normanton Sta
Liby
COLLINGWOOD RD
PARK AVE
CARLTON ST
GRANVILLE ST
CEMETERY RD
SHAW AVE
BECKBRIDGE WAY
RIPLEY CL
WAINDYKE WAY
Cemy
MANORCROFT
Normanton C E (Aided) First Sch
BECKBRIDGE LA
NEWFIELD CT
QUEEN ST
HIGH ST
B6133
PRINCESS ST
THE GROVE
YORK VILLAS
St John's RC Sch
NEWLAITHES GR
DON PEDRO AVE
MILDRED SYLVESTER WAY
TOM DANDO CL
Road under construction
HAVERTOP LA
Loscoe La
HESELTINE CL
SOVEREIGN GDNS
KING ST
Normanton Queen St First Sch
NORMANTON
Cemy
CAMBRIDGE ST
PARK CL
PARK GN
VIEW
MILL HILL
Normanton Grammar Sch
WAKEFIELD RD
NEWLAND LA
CHURCH CT
GOOSEHILL RD
HAROLD WILSON HOUSE
Sch
MARCH ST
ATKINSON CT
FOSTER AVE
SANDERSON AVE
FIRVILLE AVE
WHEATLEY AVE
DALEFIELD AVE
NEVILLE ST
HANSON AVE
THE PADDOCK
FAVELL AVE
Normanton Freeston High Sch
NORMANTON VIEW
SNYDALE RD
SNYDALE AVE
SNYDALE GR
SNYDALE CT
FAIRWAY
FAIRWAY DR
Golf Course
CH
CLARKSON CT
THORNE CL
LYNDALE GR
ADDISON AVE
MEADOW BROOK CHASE
MEADOW BROOK GN
Dismtd Rly
DON PEDRO CL
DON PEDRO AVE
LOSCOE LA
B6134

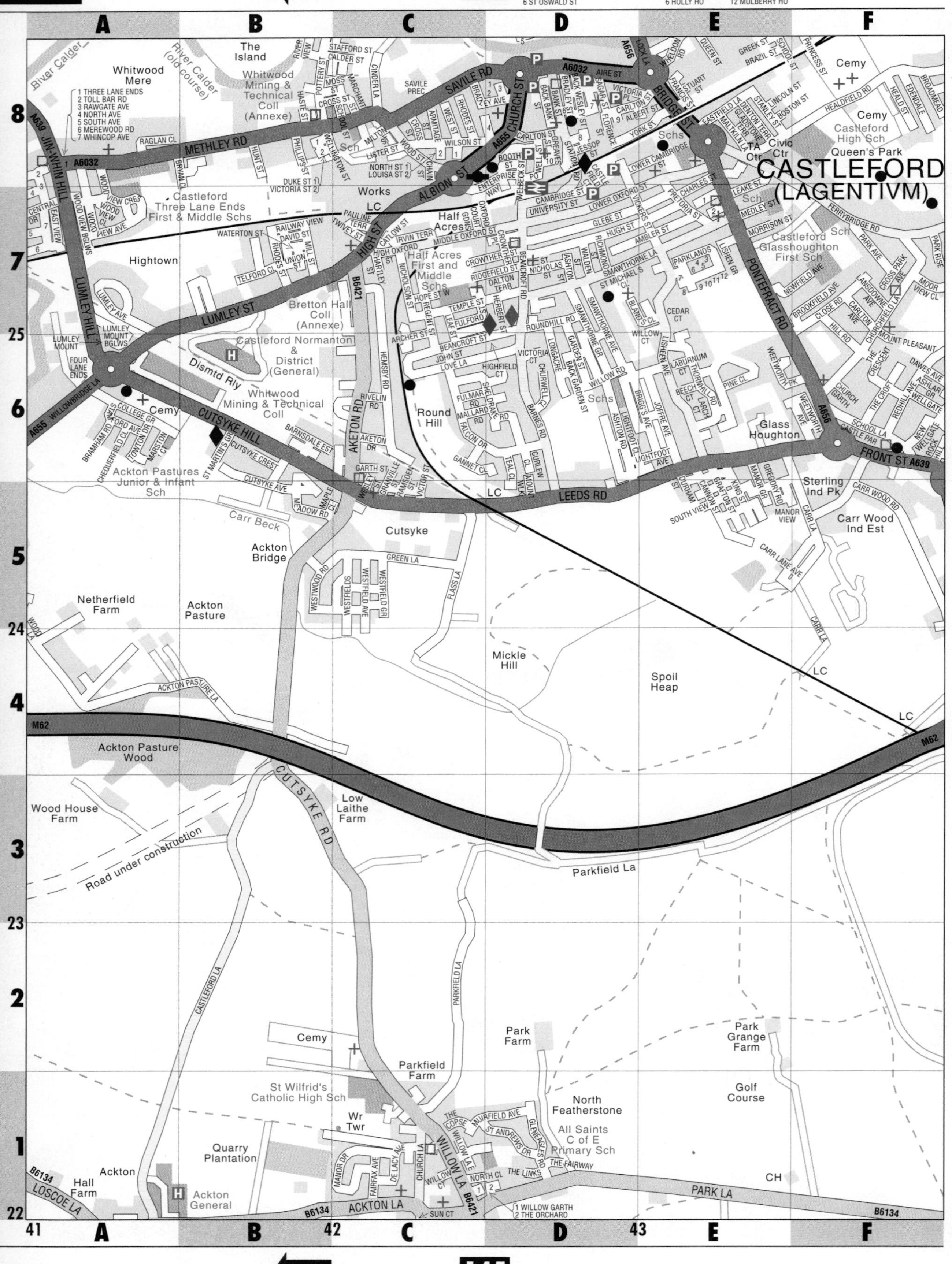

D8
1 ST MARY'S PL
2 RECTORY AVE
3 RECTORY ST
4 PERSEVERANCE ST
5 AIRE TERR
6 ST OSWALD ST

7 WESLEY ST
8 COMMERCIAL ST
9 SYKES ST
10 HOPE ST E

E7
1 ROBIN HOOD ST
2 ST HELENS PL
3 POPLAR HO
4 LAUREL HO
5 SYCAMORE HO
6 HOLLY HO

7 BIRCH HO
8 ACACIA HO
9 OAK HO
10 CYPRESS HO
11 MAGNOLIA HO
12 MULBERRY HO

CASTLEFORD
(LAGENTIVM)

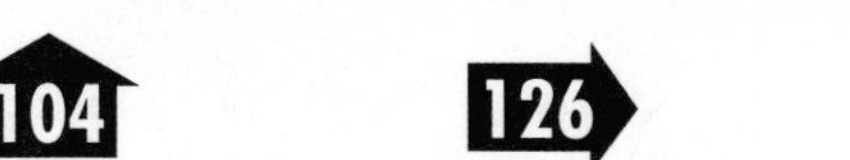

104
126

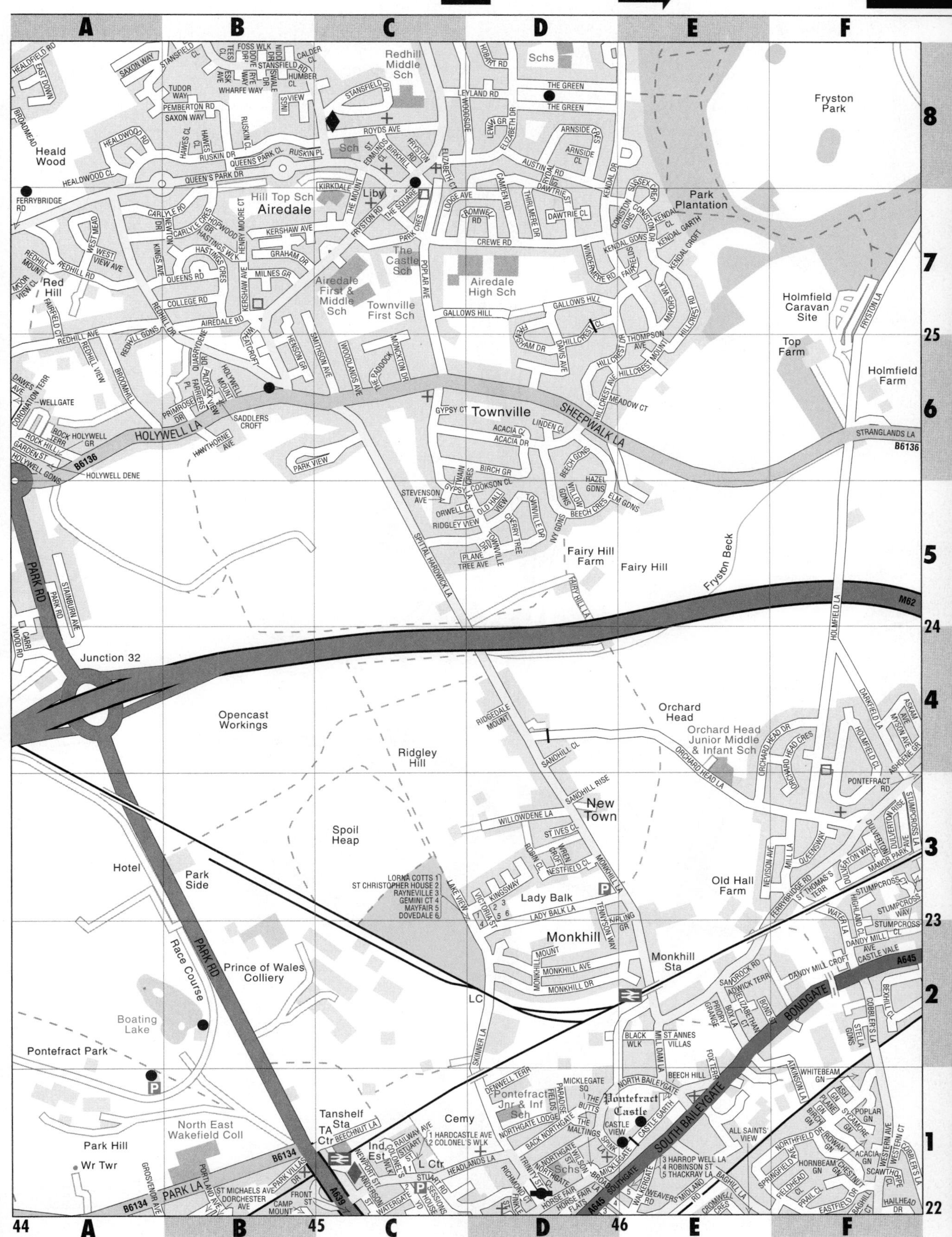

A
B
C
D
E
F
8
7
25
6
5
24
4
3
23
2
1
22
44
45
46
Redhill Middle Sch
Schs
THE GREEN
Fryston Park
Heald Wood
FERRYBRIDGE RD
HEALDWOOD CL
QUEEN'S PARK DR
QUEENS PARK CL
RUSKIN DR
RUSKIN PL
SAXON WAY
STANSFIELD CL
TUDOR WAY
PEMBERTON RD
WHARFE WAY
HUMBER CL
STANSFIELD DR
ROYDS AVE
LEYLAND RD
HOBART RD
WOODSIDE
LEWIN GR
ELIZABETH DR
ELIZABETH CT
ARNSIDE CRES
ARNSIDE CL
AUSTIN RD
DAWTRIE ST
DAWTRIE CL
KENDAL DR
Park Plantation
Hill Top Sch
Airedale
Liby
THE SQUARE
KIRKDALE
THE MOUNT
FRYSTON RD
PARK CRES
LODGE AVE
CAMDEN RD
CROMWELL RD
THIRLMERE DR
CREWE RD
WINDERMERE RD
CONISTON DR
KENDAL GDNS
KENDAL GARTH
KENDAL CROFT
Red Hill
REDHILL DR
REDHILL AVE
REDHILL VIEW
REDHILL GDNS
CARLYLE RD
CARLYLE CRES
HOPWOOD
HASTINGS WLK
HASTINGS CRES
HENRY MOORE CT
KERSHAW AVE
GRAHAM DR
MILNES GR
QUEENS RD
COLLEGE RD
AIREDALE RD
WEST MEAD
WEST VIEW AVE
FAIRFIELD CT
The Castle Sch
Airedale First & Middle Sch
Townville First Sch
Airedale High Sch
POPLAR AVE
GALLOWS HILL
HILLCREST CL
HILLCREST AVE
HILLCREST MOUNT
HILLCREST RD
THOMPSON AVE
MEADOW CT
DAVIS AVE
Holmfield Caravan Site
FRYSTON LA
Top Farm
Holmfield Farm
HENSON GR
SMITHSON AVE
WOODLANDS AVE
THE PADDOCK
MONCKTON DR
QUARRYDENE
PADDOCK VIEW
HOLYWELL MOUNT
PRIMROSE DR
FARRIERS
SADDLERS CROFT
HAWTHORNE AVE
HOLYWELL LA
B6136
WELLGATE
CORONATION TERR
DAWES AVE
ROCK HILL
GARDEN ST
HOLYWELL GDNS
HOLYWELL DENE
PARK VIEW
BROOMHILL
Townville
GYPSY CT
ACACIA CL
ACACIA DR
LINDEN CL
SHEEPWALK LA
STRANGLANDS LA
BIRCH GR
BEECH GDNS
HAZEL GDNS
ELM GDNS
BEECH CRES
WILLOW GDNS
COOKSON CL
STEVENSON AVE
ORWELL CL
OLD HALL VIEW
RIDGLEY VIEW
CHERRY TREE
TOWNVILLE DR
IVY GDNS
PLANE TREE AVE
SPITTAL HARDWICK LA
Fairy Hill Farm
Fairy Hill
FAIRY HILL LA
Fryston Beck
M62
PARK RD
STAINBURN AVE
CARR WOOD RD
Junction 32
Opencast Workings
Ridgley Hill
RIDGEDALE MOUNT
SANDHILL CL
SANDHILL RISE
Orchard Head
Orchard Head Junior Middle & Infant Sch
ORCHARD HEAD LA
ORCHARD HEAD DR
ORCHARD HEAD CRES
HOLMFIELD LA
DARKFIELD LA
HOLMFIELD CL
ASKAM AVE
PONTEFRACT RD
New Town
Spoil Heap
WILLOWDENE LA
ST IVES CL
NESTFIELD CL
MONKHILL LA
LORNA COTTS 1
ST CHRISTOPHER HOUSE 2
RAYNEVILLE 3
GEMINI CT 4
MAYFAIR 5
DOVEDALE 6
KINGSWAY
VICTORIA ST
LAKE VIEW
Lady Balk
LADY BALK LA
TENNYSON WAY
STIRLING GR
Monkhill
MONKHILL MOUNT
MONKHILL AVE
MONKHILL DR
Monkhill Sta
Old Hall Farm
NEVISON AVE
MILL LA
QUEENSWAY
FERRYBRIDGE RD
ST THOMAS'S TERR
DULVERTON WAY
MANOR PARK AVE
STUMPCROSS LA
STUMPCROSS WAY
STUMPCROSS CL
WATER LA
HIGHLAND CL
DANDY MILL AVE
CASTLE VALE
DANDY MILL CROFT
A645
Hotel
Park Side
Race Course
Prince of Wales Colliery
LC
Boating Lake
Pontefract Park
SKINNER LA
SANDROCK RD
ADWICK TERR
PRIORY GRANGE
BONDGATE
BEXHILL CL
COBBLER'S LA
STELLA GDNS
BLACK WLK
ST ANNES VILLAS
MILL DAM LA
BEECH HILL
NORTH BAILEYGATE
DENWELL TERR
MICKLEGATE SQ
Pontefract Jnr & Inf Sch
PARADISE FIELDS
THE BUTTS
Pontefract Castle
CASTLE GARTH
CASTLE VIEW
SOUTH BAILEYGATE
ATKINSON LA
WHITEBEAM GN
ALL SAINTS' VIEW
Tanshelf Sta
TA Ctr
BEECHNUT LA
Cemy
1 HARDCASTLE AVE
2 COLONEL'S WLK
NORTHGATE LODGE
BACK NORTHGATE
THE MALTINGS
Ind Est
L Ctr
HEADLANDS LA
NORTHGATE
Schs
3 HARROP WELL LA
4 ROBINSON ST
5 THACKRAY LA
BAGHILL LA
MIDLAND RD
WEAVERS
CROMWELL CRES
North East Wakefield Coll
Park Hill
Wr Twr
B6134
PARK LA
ST MICHAELS AVE
DORCHESTER AVE
GROSVENOR AVE
PORTLAND AVE
PARK VILLAS
CAMP MOUNT
FRONT ST
A639
NEWPORT ST
WATERGATE
SESSIONS HOUSE YD
RICHMOND CT
HORSE FAIR
HORSE FAIR FLATS
MICKLEGATE
SOUTHGATE
WALKERGATE
SPRINGFIELD AVE
NORTHFIELD DR
HORNBEAM GN
ROWAN GN
ACACIA GN
CHESTNUT GN
SCAWTHORPE CL
WESTERN AVE
COBBLER'S LA
EASTFIELD DR
HAILHEAD DR
FIELDHEAD CL
PLANE GN
SYCAMORE GN
POPLAR GN
ASH GN
BIRCH GN

125
105

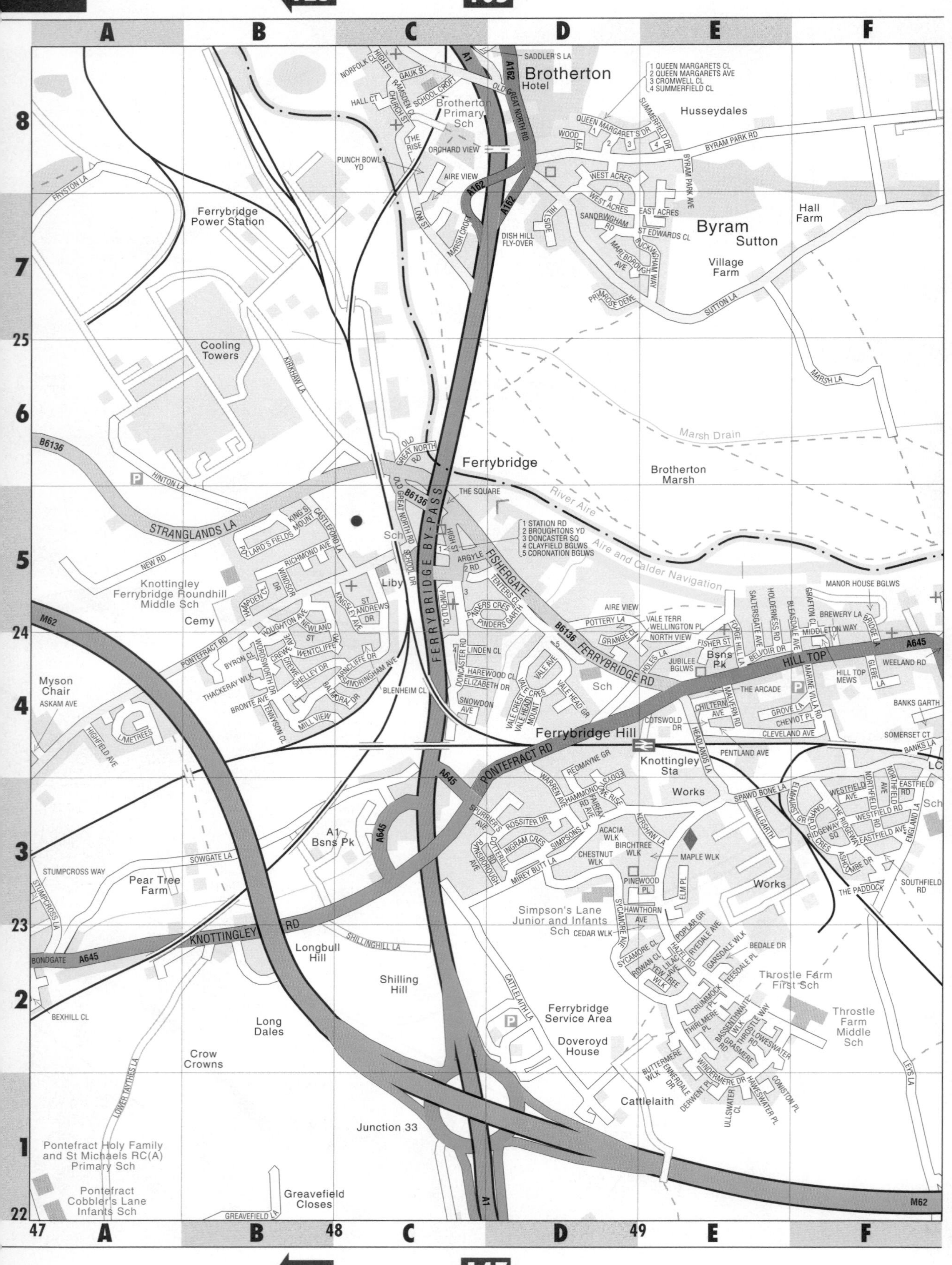
Brotherton
Hotel
Brotherton Primary Sch
Husseydales
1 QUEEN MARGARETS CL
2 QUEEN MARGARETS AVE
3 CROMWELL CL
4 SUMMERFIELD CL
BYRAM PARK RD
Byram
Sutton
Hall Farm
Village Farm
Ferrybridge Power Station
Cooling Towers
DISH HILL FLY-OVER
Marsh Drain
Ferrybridge
Brotherton Marsh
River Aire
Aire and Calder Navigation
1 STATION RD
2 BROUGHTONS YD
3 DONCASTER SQ
4 CLAYFIELD BGLWS
5 CORONATION BGLWS
STRANGLANDS LA
FERRYBRIDGE BY-PASS
FISHERGATE
FERRYBRIDGE RD
HILL TOP
Knottingley Ferrybridge Roundhill Middle Sch
Cemy
Myson Chair
Ferrybridge Hill
Knottingley Sta
Works
PONTEFRACT RD
A1 Bsns Pk
Pear Tree Farm
KNOTTINGLEY RD
Longbull Hill
Shilling Hill
Simpson's Lane Junior and Infants Sch
Ferrybridge Service Area
Doveroyd House
Throstle Farm First Sch
Throstle Farm Middle Sch
Long Dales
Crow Crowns
Cattlelaith
Junction 33
Pontefract Holy Family and St Michaels RC(A) Primary Sch
Pontefract Cobbler's Lane Infants Sch
Greavefield Closes
M62
A1
A645
B6136
A162

125
147

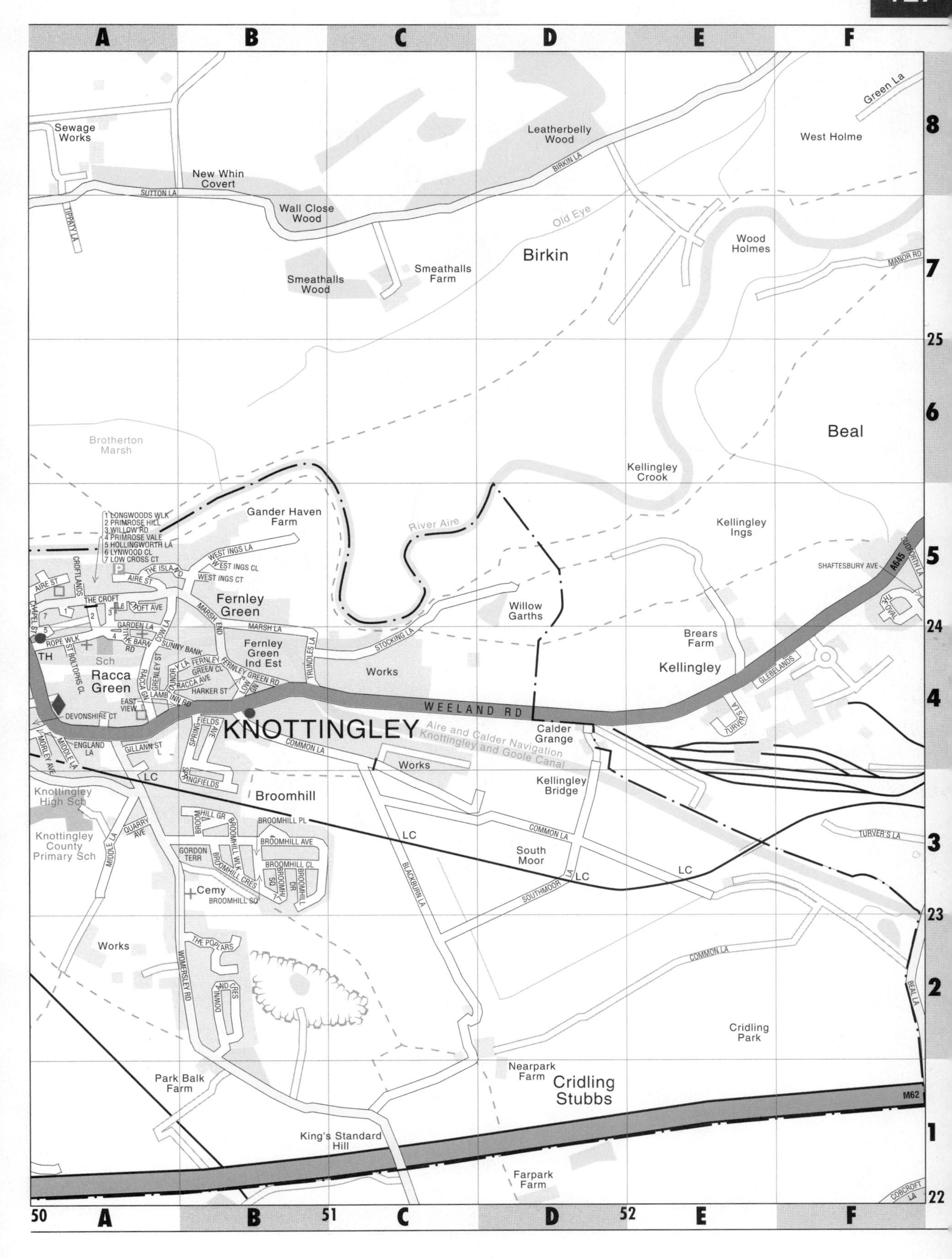

A **B** **C** **D** **E** **F**

8

Sewage
Works

Leatherbelly
Wood

West Holme

Green La

New Whin
Covert

BIRKIN LA

SUTTON LA

Wall Close
Wood

Old Eye

7

Birkin

Smeathalls
Wood

Smeathalls
Farm

Wood
Holmes

MANOR RD

25

Brotherton
Marsh

Beal

6

Kellingley
Crook

Gander Haven
Farm

River Aire

Kellingley
Ings

SHAFTESBURY AVE

A645

SUDFORTH LA

5

1 LONGWOODS WLK
2 PRIMROSE HILL
3 WILLOW RD
4 PRIMROSE VALE
5 HOLLINGWORTH LA
6 LYNWOOD CL
7 LOW CROSS CT

WEST INGS LA

WEST INGS CL

WEST INGS CT

Willow
Garths

AIRE ST

THE ISLA

CROFTLANDS

AIRE ST

THE CROFT

CROFT AVE

Fernley
Green

MARSH END

MARSH LA

Brears
Farm

24

GARDEN LA

SUNNY BANK

Fernley
Green Ind Est

FERNLEY GREEN RD

STOCKING LA

Works

Kellingley

GLEBELANDS

TURVERS LA

CHEVIN

Sch

ROPE WLK

ST BOLTOPHS CL

RACCA GN

FERNLEY GREEN AVE

HARKER ST

TRUNDLES LA

WEELAND RD

4

TH

Racca
Green

DEVONSHIRE CT

EAST
VIEW

LAMB INN RD

KNOTTINGLEY

Aire and Calder Navigation
Knottingley and Goole Canal

Calder
Grange

MORLEY LA

MIDDLE LA

ENGLAND
LA

GILLANN ST

SPRINGS

FIELDS

COMMON LA

Works

Kellingley
Bridge

LC

SPRINGFIELDS

Broomhill

South
Moor

COMMON LA

LC

TURVER'S LA

3

Knottingley
High Sch

Knottingley
County
Primary Sch

QUARRY AVE

BROOMHILL GR

BROOMHILL WLK

BROOMHILL PL

BROOMHILL AVE

BROOMHILL CRES

BROOMHILL CL

BROOMHILL DR

BLACKBURN LA

LC

SOUTHMOOR

LC

LC

GORDON
TERR

Cemy

BROOMHILL SQ

BEAL LA

23

Works

THE POPLARS

WOMERSLEY RD

MID CRES

LINWOOD

COMMON LA

Cridling
Park

2

Park Balk
Farm

Nearpark
Farm

Cridling
Stubbs

M62

1

King's Standard
Hill

Farpark
Farm

CORCROFT LA

22

50 **A** **B** 51 **C** **D** 52 **E** **F**

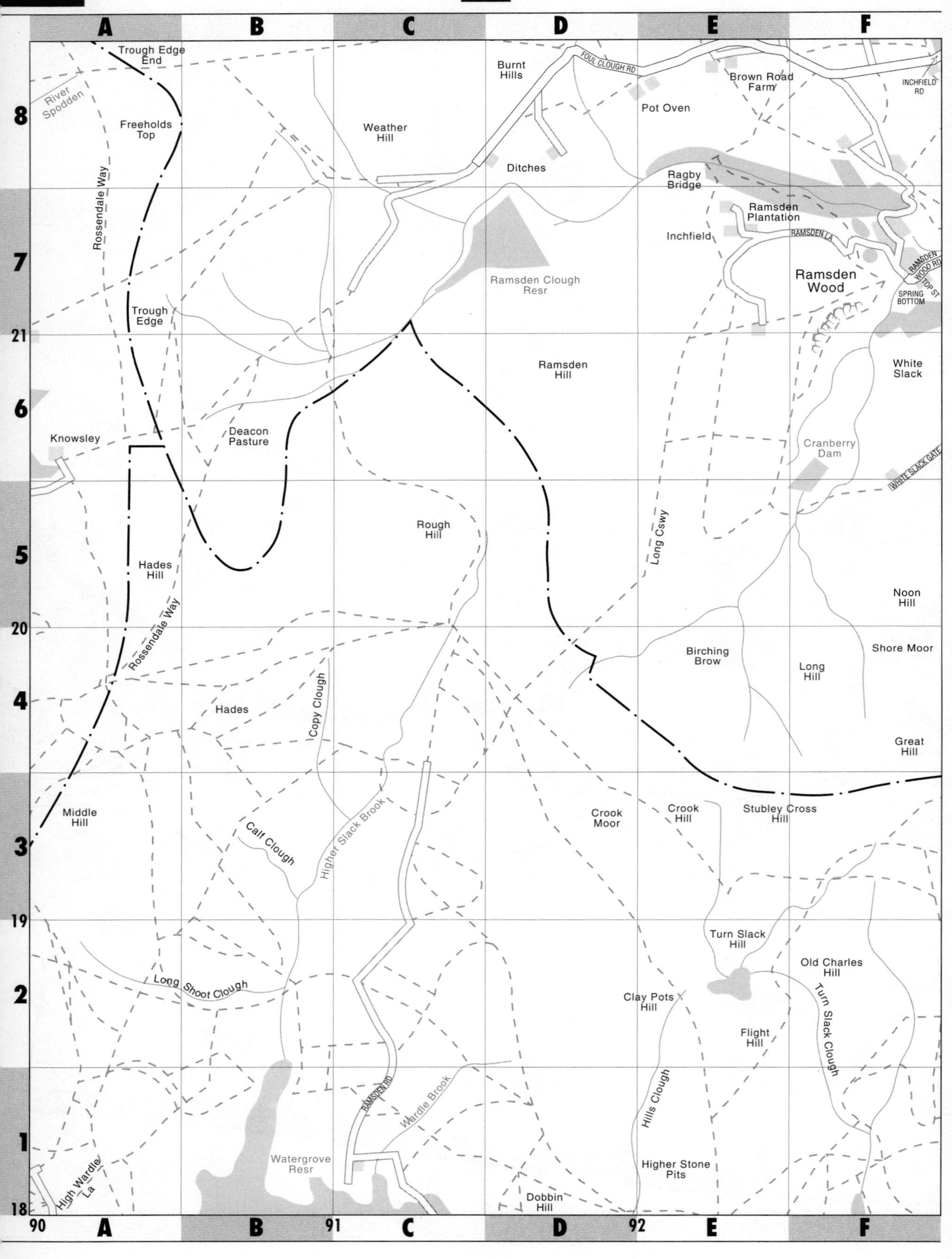

A B C D E F

8

River Spodden

Trough Edge End

Freeholds Top

Burnt Hills

FOUL CLOUGH RD

Brown Road Farm

Pot Oven

INCHFIELD RD

Weather Hill

Ditches

Ragby Bridge

Ramsden Plantation

7

Rossendale Way

Inchfield

RAMSDEN LA

Ramsden Wood

RAMSDEN WOOD RD

TOP ST

21

Trough Edge

Ramsden Clough Resr

SPRING BOTTOM

6

Ramsden Hill

White Slack

Knowsley

Deacon Pasture

Cranberry Dam

WHITE SLACK GATE

Rough Hill

Long Cswy

5

Hades Hill

Noon Hill

20

Rossendale Way

Birching Brow

Shore Moor

4

Hades

Copy Clough

Long Hill

Great Hill

Middle Hill

Calf Clough

Higher Slack Brook

Crook Moor

Crook Hill

Stubley Cross Hill

3

19

Turn Slack Hill

Old Charles Hill

2

Long Shoot Clough

Clay Pots Hill

Flight Hill

Turn Slack Clough

Hills Clough

RAMSDEN RD

Wardle Brook

1

High Wardle La

Watergrove Resr

Higher Stone Pits

18

Dobbin Hill

90 A B 91 C D 92 E F

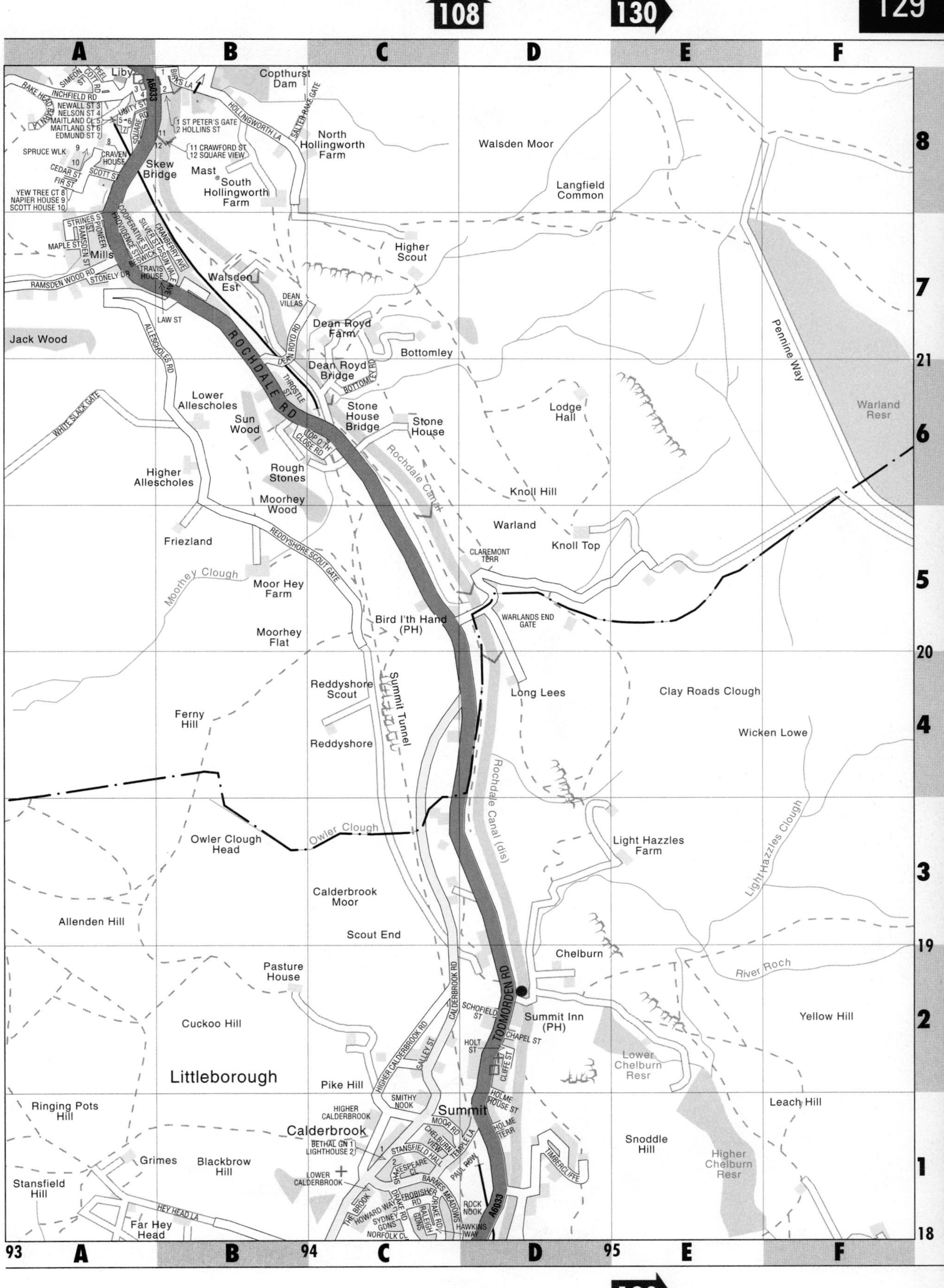
A B C D E F
8 7 21 6 5 20 4 3 19 2 1 18
93 94 95
Liby
Copthurst Dam
North Hollingworth Farm
Walsden Moor
Langfield Common
Skew Bridge
Mast
South Hollingworth Farm
Higher Scout
Mills
Walsden Est
Dean Villas
Dean Royd Farm
Bottomley
Jack Wood
Dean Royd Bridge
Pennine Way
Lower Allescholes
Sun Wood
Stone House Bridge
Stone House
Lodge Hall
Warland Resr
Higher Allescholes
Rough Stones
Moorhey Wood
Knoll Hill
Rochdale Canal
Friezland
Warland
Knoll Top
Claremont Terr
Moorhey Clough
Moor Hey Farm
Bird I'th Hand (PH)
Warlands End Gate
Moorhey Flat
Reddyshore Scout
Summit Tunnel
Long Lees
Clay Roads Clough
Ferny Hill
Reddyshore
Wicken Lowe
Owler Clough
Owler Clough Head
Rochdale Canal (dis)
Light Hazzles Farm
Light Hazzles Clough
Calderbrook Moor
Allenden Hill
Scout End
Chelburn
River Roch
Pasture House
Summit Inn (PH)
Yellow Hill
Cuckoo Hill
Lower Chelburn Resr
Littleborough
Pike Hill
Leach Hill
Ringing Pots Hill
Summit
Calderbrook
Snoddle Hill
Grimes
Blackbrow Hill
Higher Chelburn Resr
Stansfield Hill
Far Hey Head
Rock Nook
Rochdale Rd
Todmorden Rd
A6033
Calderbrook Rd
Higher Calderbrook Rd
Hey Head La
Timbercliffe
Allescholes Rd
Reddyshore Scout Gate
White Slack Gate
Hollingworth La
Salter Rake Gate
Inchfield Rd
Ramsden Wood Rd
Stonely Dr
Law St
Newall St 3
Nelson St 4
Maitland Cl 5
Maitland St 6
Edmund St 7
Spruce Wlk
Cedar St
Fir St
Scott St
Craven House
Yew Tree Ct 8
Napier House 9
Scott House 10
1 St Peter's Gate
2 Hollins St
11 Crawford St
12 Square View
Maple St
Strines St
Ramsden St
Pioneer St
Cooperative St
Providence St
Silver St
Cranberry Ave
Travis House
Dean Royd Rd
Throstle St
Bottomley Rd
Top o'th' Close Rd
Schofield St
Chapel St
Holt St
Cliffe St
Salley St
Holme House St
Holme Terr
Smithy Nook
Higher Calderbrook
Moor Rd
Chelburn View
Temple La
Bethal Gn 1
Lighthouse 2
Stansfield Hall
Lower Calderbrook
Paul Row
Barnes Meadows
Frobisher Rd
Drake Rd
Raleigh Gdns
Drake Ct
Howard Way
Sydney Gdns
Norfolk Cl
The Brook
Hawkins Way

129
109

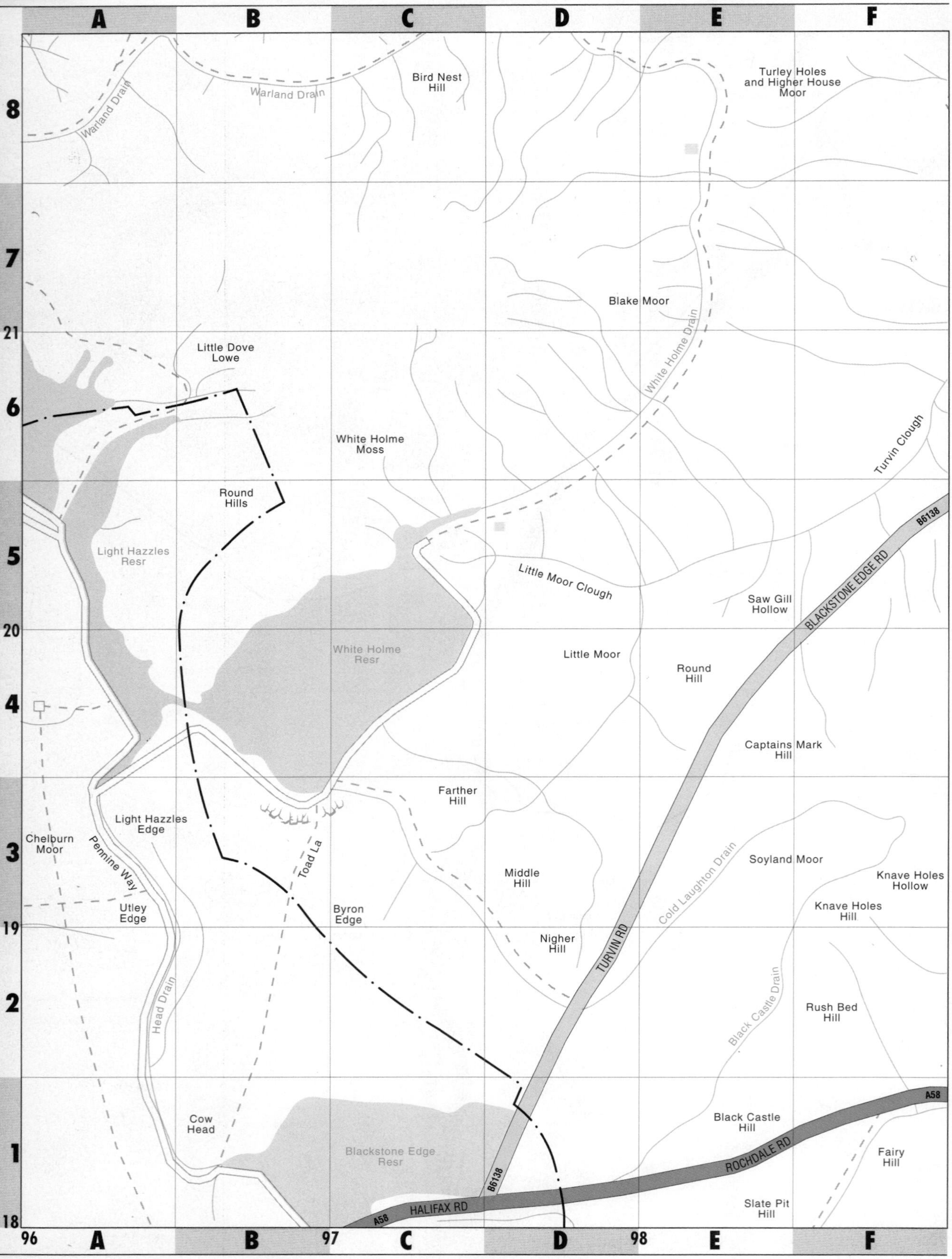

A B C D E F

8

Warland Drain
Warland Drain
Bird Nest Hill
Turley Holes and Higher House Moor

7

Blake Moor

21

6
Little Dove Lowe
Round Hills
White Holme Moss
White Holme Drain
Turvin Clough

Light Hazzles Resr

5
Little Moor Clough
Saw Gill Hollow
BLACKSTONE EDGE RD
B6138

20
White Holme Resr
Little Moor
Round Hill

4
Captains Mark Hill
Chelburn Moor
Pennine Way
Light Hazzles Edge
Farther Hill
Soyland Moor
Knave Holes Hollow

3
Toad La
Middle Hill
Knave Holes Hill
Utley Edge
Byron Edge
Cold Laughton Drain
TURVIN RD

19
Nigher Hill
Black Castle Drain

2
Head Drain
Rush Bed Hill

Cow Head
Black Castle Hill
A58

1
Blackstone Edge Resr
B6138
ROCHDALE RD
Fairy Hill

18
A58
HALIFAX RD
Slate Pit Hill

96 A B 97 C D 98 E F

110

132

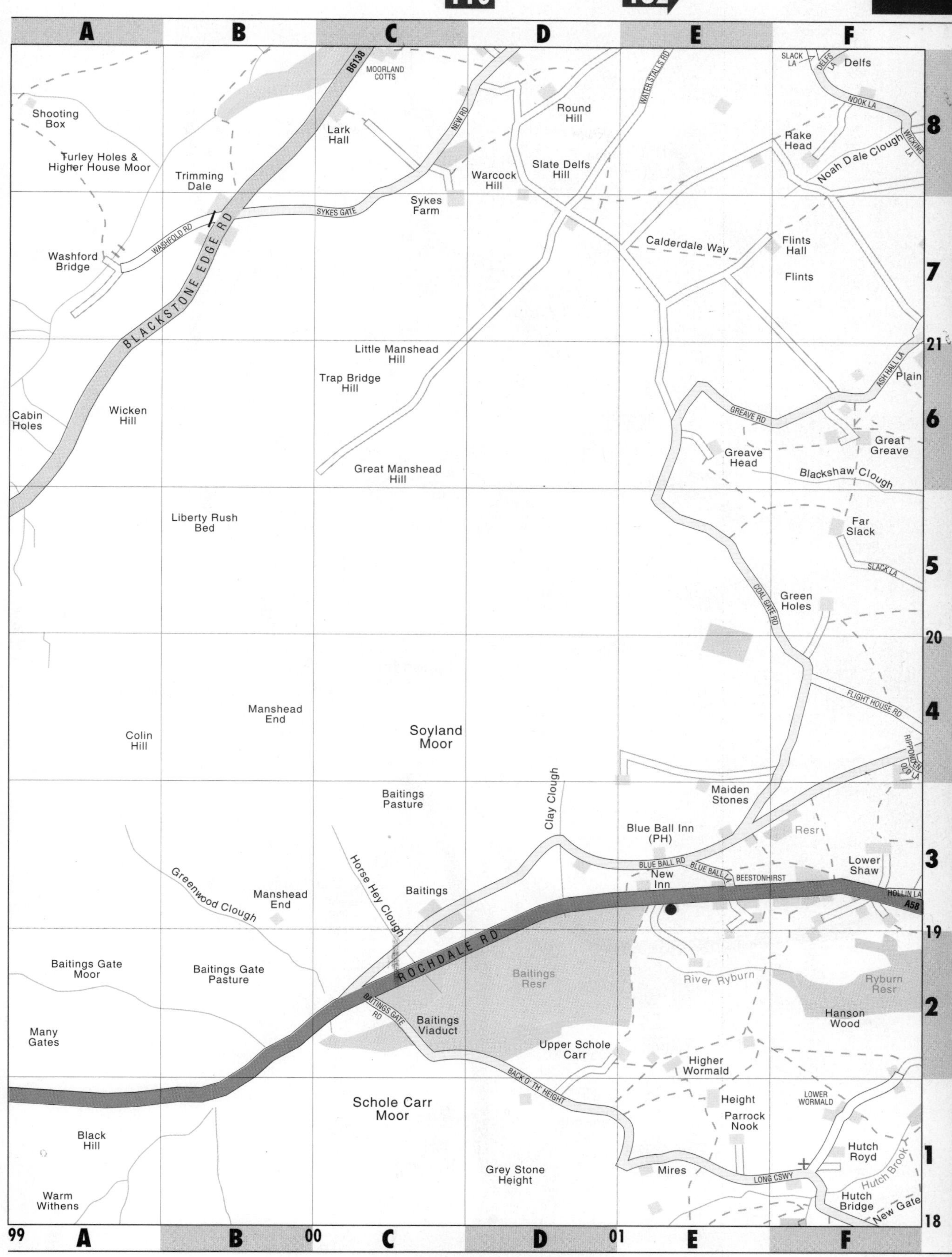

A
B
C
D
E
F
B6138
MOORLAND COTTS
SLACK LA
DELFS LA
Delfs
NOOK LA
Shooting Box
Round Hill
Lark Hall
NEW RD
WATER STALLS RD
Rake Head
Turley Holes & Higher House Moor
Trimming Dale
Warcock Hill
Slate Delfs Hill
Noah Dale Clough
WICKING LA
Sykes Farm
SYKES GATE
WASHFOLD RD
BLACKSTONE EDGE RD
Washford Bridge
Calderdale Way
Flints Hall
Flints
Little Manshead Hill
Trap Bridge Hill
ASH HALL LA
Plain
Cabin Holes
Wicken Hill
GREAVE RD
Great Greave
Greave Head
Blackshaw Clough
Great Manshead Hill
Liberty Rush Bed
Far Slack
SLACK LA
COAL GATE RD
Green Holes
FLIGHT HOUSE RD
Manshead End
Soyland Moor
Colin Hill
RIPPONDEN OLD LA
Baitings Pasture
Clay Clough
Maiden Stones
Blue Ball Inn (PH)
Resr
Horse Hey Clough
Greenwood Clough
Manshead End
Baitings
BLUE BALL RD
BLUE BALL LA
BEESTONHIRST
New Inn
Lower Shaw
HOLLIN LA
A58
ROCHDALE RD
Baitings Gate Moor
Baitings Gate Pasture
Baitings Resr
River Ryburn
Ryburn Resr
BAITINGS GATE RD
Baitings Viaduct
Hanson Wood
Many Gates
Upper Schole Carr
Higher Wormald
BACK O' TH' HEIGHT
Schole Carr Moor
Height
LOWER WORMALD
Parrock Nook
Black Hill
Hutch Royd
Grey Stone Height
Mires
LONG CSWY
Hutch Brook
Warm Withens
Hutch Bridge
New Gate
8
7
21
6
5
20
4
3
19
2
1
18
99
00
01

131

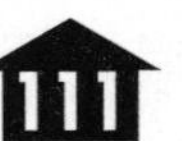

111

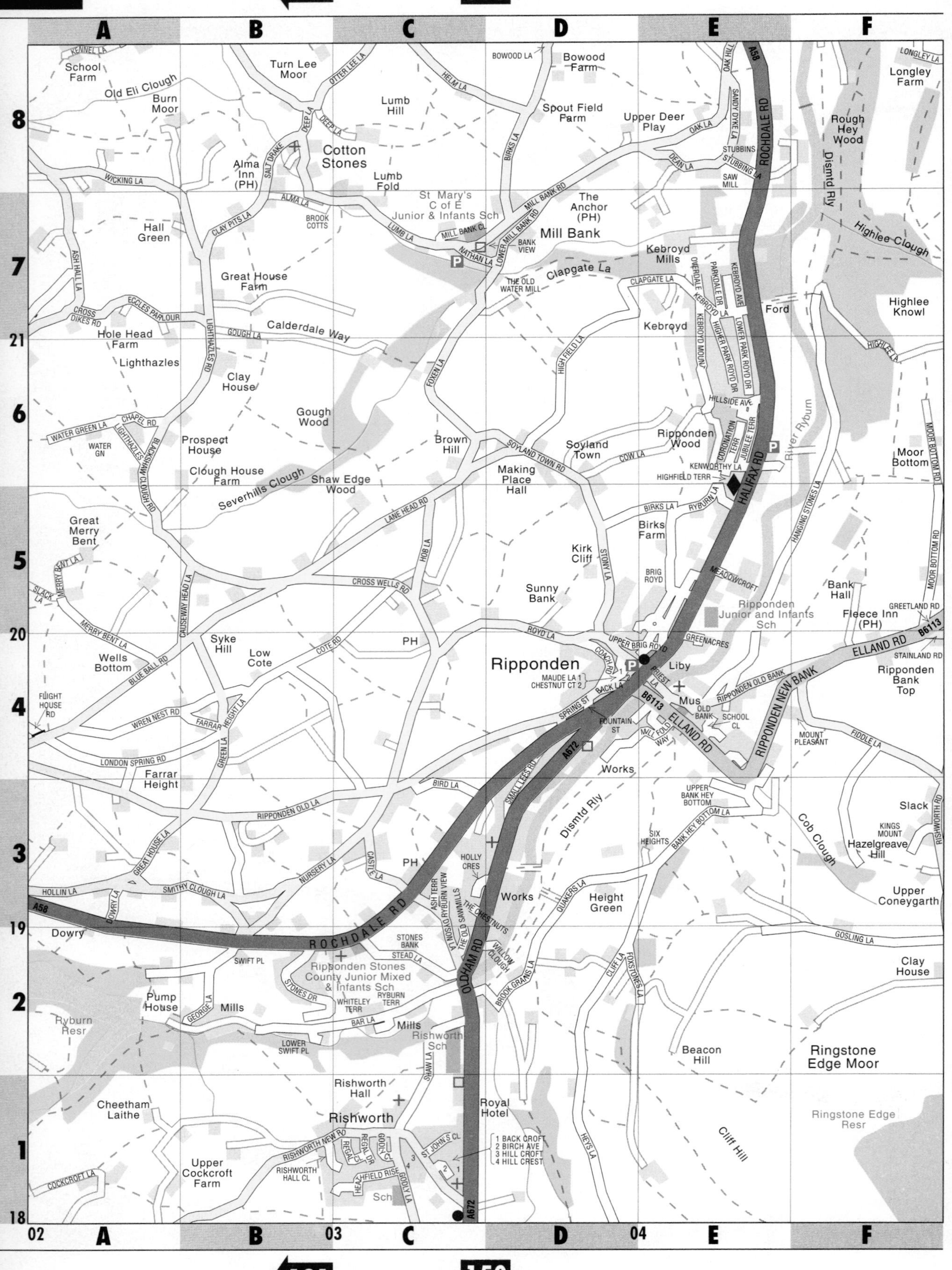

A
B
C
D
E
F
School Farm
Old Eli Clough
Burn Moor
Turn Lee Moor
Lumb Hill
Bowood Farm
Spout Field Farm
Upper Deer Play
Longley Farm
Rough Hey Wood
Cotton Stones
Alma Inn (PH)
Lumb Fold
St Mary's C of E Junior & Infants Sch
The Anchor (PH)
Mill Bank
Kebroyd Mills
Hall Green
Great House Farm
Clapgate La
Highlee Clough
Highlee Knowl
Ford
Kebroyd
Hole Head Farm
Calderdale Way
Lighthazles
Clay House
Gough Wood
Brown Hill
Soyland Town
Ripponden Wood
Prospect House
Clough House Farm
Severhills Clough
Shaw Edge Wood
Making Place Hall
Moor Bottom
Great Merry Bent
Birks Farm
Kirk Cliff
Sunny Bank
Bank Hall
Ripponden Junior and Infants Sch
Fleece Inn (PH)
Syke Hill
Low Cote
PH
Wells Bottom
Ripponden
Liby
Mus
Ripponden Bank Top
Works
Farrar Height
Slack
Cob Clough
Hazelgreave Hill
Dismtd Rly
Six Heights
PH
Holly Cres
Works
Height Green
Upper Coneygarth
Dowry
Rochdale Rd
Ripponden Stones County Junior Mixed & Infants Sch
Clay House
Pump House
Mills
Ryburn Resr
Mills
Rishworth Sch
Beacon Hill
Ringstone Edge Moor
Cheetham Laithe
Rishworth Hall
Royal Hotel
Rishworth
Ringstone Edge Resr
Cliff Hill
Upper Cockcroft Farm
Sch
1 Back Croft
2 Birch Ave
3 Hill Croft
4 Hill Crest
02
03
04
18
19
20
21

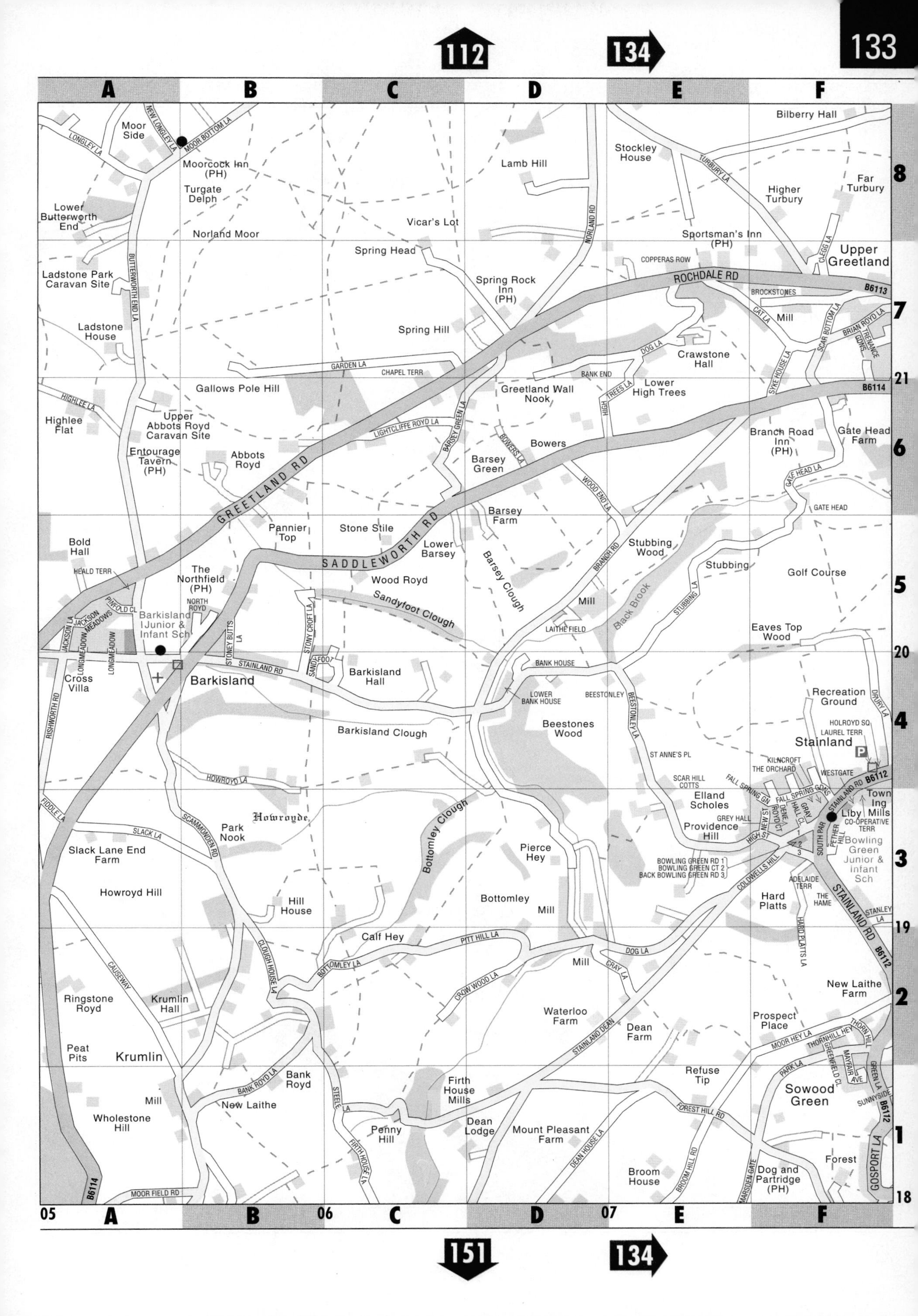
133
112
134
151
134
A
B
C
D
E
F
8
7
21
6
5
20
4
3
19
2
1
18
05
06
07
Moor Side
LONGLEY LA
NEW LONGLEY LA
MOOR BOTTOM LA
Moorcock Inn (PH)
Turgate Delph
Lower Butterworth End
Norland Moor
Ladstone Park Caravan Site
BUTTERWORTH END LA
Ladstone House
Gallows Pole Hill
HIGHLEE LA
Highlee Flat
Upper Abbots Royd Caravan Site
Entourage Tavern (PH)
Abbots Royd
GREETLAND RD
Pannier Top
Bold Hall
HEALD TERR
The Northfield (PH)
NORTH ROYD
PINFOLD CL
JACKSON MEADOWS
JACKSON LA
Barkisland Junior & Infant Sch
LONGMEADOW
STONEY BUTTS LA
STAINLAND RD
Cross Villa
Barkisland
RISHWORTH RD
FIDDLE LA
SLACK LA
Slack Lane End Farm
Howroyd Hill
SCAMMONDEN RD
Park Nook
Howroyde
HOWROYD LA
CAUSEWAY
Ringstone Royd
Krumlin Hall
Peat Pits
Krumlin
Mill
Wholestone Hill
B6114
MOOR FIELD RD
Lamb Hill
Vicar's Lot
Spring Head
Spring Rock Inn (PH)
Spring Hill
GARDEN LA
CHAPEL TERR
LIGHTCLIFFE ROYD LA
BARSEY GREEN LA
Stone Stile
SADDLEWORTH RD
Lower Barsey
Wood Royd
Sandyfoot Clough
STONY CROFT LA
SANDYFOOT
Barkisland Hall
Barkisland Clough
NORLAND RD
Greetland Wall Nook
BOWERS LA
Bowers
Barsey Green
Barsey Farm
Barsey Clough
Bottomley Clough
Hill House
Calf Hey
PITT HILL LA
BOTTOMLEY LA
CLOUGH HOUSE LA
CROW WOOD LA
Bank Royd
BANK ROYD LA
New Laithe
STEELE LA
Penny Hill
FIRTH HOUSE LA
Firth House Mills
Dean Lodge
Mount Pleasant Farm
DEAN HOUSE LA
Pierce Hey
Bottomley Mill
Waterloo Farm
STAINLAND DEAN
Dean Farm
DOG LA
CRAY LA
Stockley House
TURBURY LA
Sportsman's Inn (PH)
COPPERAS ROW
ROCHDALE RD
BANK END
HIGH TREES LA
Lower High Trees
Crawstone Hall
WOOD END LA
BRANCH RD
Stubbing Wood
Black Brook
LAITHE FIELD
BANK HOUSE
LOWER BANK HOUSE
BEESTONLEY
BEESTONLEY LA
Beestones Wood
ST ANNE'S PL
SCAR HILL COTTS
Elland Scholes
GREY HALL
Providence Hill
BOWLING GREEN RD 1
BOWLING GREEN CT 2
BACK BOWLING GREEN RD 3
COLDWELLS HILL
Refuse Tip
FOREST HILL RD
BROOM HILL RD
Broom House
MARSDEN GATE
Bilberry Hall
Far Turbury
Higher Turbury
CLEGG LA
Upper Greetland
B6113
BROCKSTONES
CAT LA
Mill
SCAR BOTTOM LA
BRIAN ROYD LA
TRENANCE GDNS
SYKE HOUSE LA
B6114
Branch Road Inn (PH)
Gate Head Farm
GATE HEAD LA
GATE HEAD
Stubbing
STUBBING LA
Golf Course
Eaves Top Wood
Recreation Ground
DRURY LA
HOLROYD SQ
LAUREL TERR
Stainland
KILNCROFT
THE ORCHARD
WESTGATE
B6112
FALL SPRING GN
FALL SPRING GDNS
DENE
ROYD CT
GRAY HALL CL
NEW ST
HIGH ST
Town Ing Mills
Liby
CO-OPERATIVE TERR
SOUTH PAR
PETHER HILL
Bowling Green Junior & Infant Sch
ADELAIDE TERR
Hard Platts
THE HAME
HARD PLATTS LA
STANLEY LA
New Laithe Farm
Prospect Place
MOOR HEY LA
THORNHILL HEY
THORN HILL
GREENFIELD CL
MAYFAIR AVE
PARK LA
GREEN LA
Sowood Green
SUNNYSIDE
GOSPORT LA
Forest
Dog and Partridge (PH)

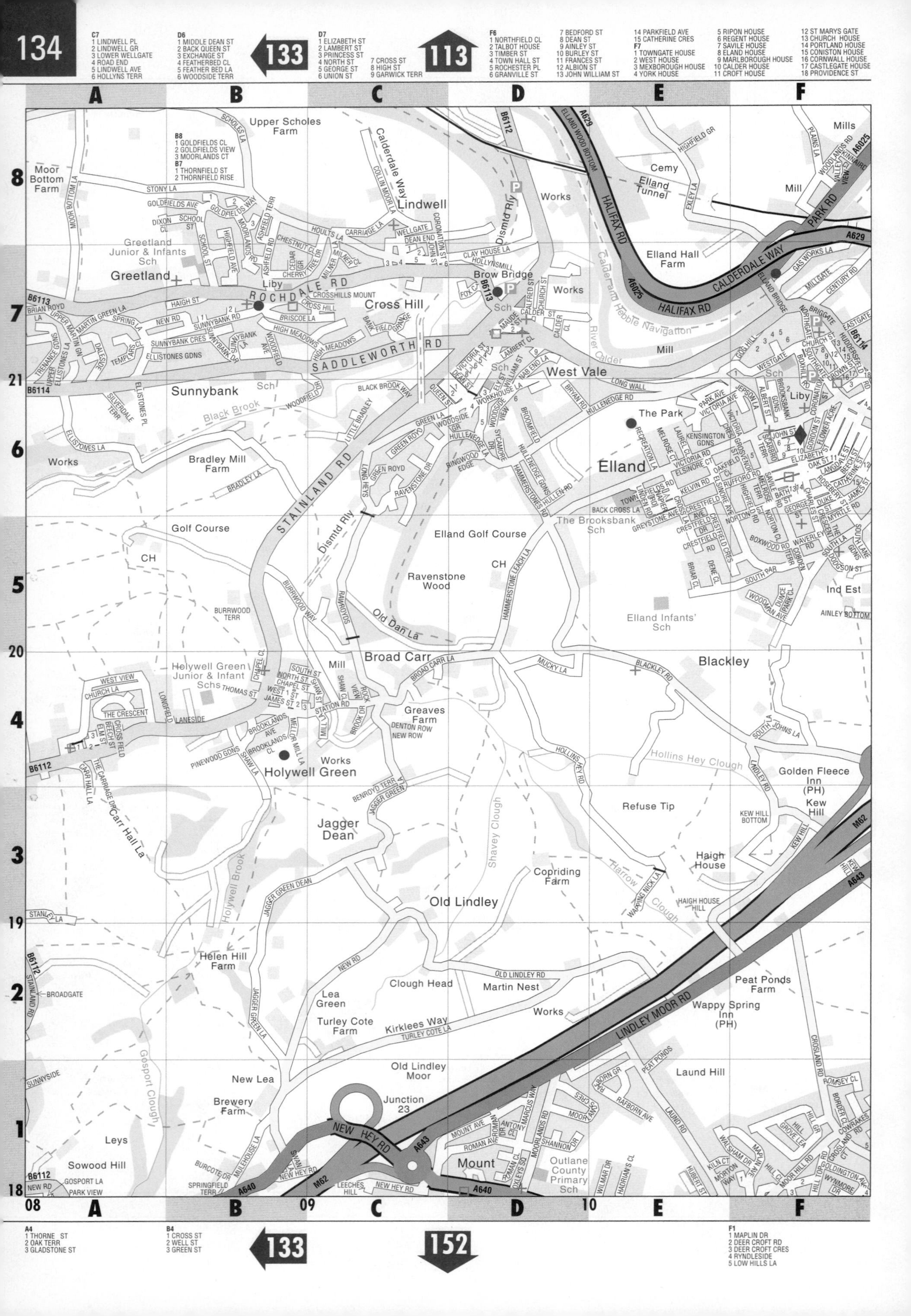
134
C7
1 LINDWELL PL
2 LINDWELL GR
3 LOWER WELLGATE
4 ROAD END
5 LINDWELL AVE
6 HOLLYNS TERR
D6
1 MIDDLE DEAN ST
2 BACK QUEEN ST
3 EXCHANGE ST
4 FEATHERBED CL
5 FEATHER BED LA
6 WOODSIDE TERR
133
D7
1 ELIZABETH ST
2 LAMBERT ST
3 PRINCESS ST
4 NORTH ST
5 GEORGE ST
6 UNION ST
7 CROSS ST
8 HIGH ST
9 GARWICK TERR
113
F6
1 NORTHFIELD CL
2 TALBOT HOUSE
3 TIMBER ST
4 TOWN HALL ST
5 ROCHESTER PL
6 GRANVILLE ST
7 BEDFORD ST
8 DEAN ST
9 AINLEY ST
10 BURLEY ST
11 FRANCES ST
12 ALBION ST
13 JOHN WILLIAM ST
14 PARKFIELD AVE
15 CATHERINE CRES
F7
1 TOWNGATE HOUSE
2 WEST HOUSE
3 MEXBOROUGH HOUSE
4 YORK HOUSE
5 RIPON HOUSE
6 REGENT HOUSE
7 SAVILE HOUSE
8 ELAND HOUSE
9 MARLBOROUGH HOUSE
10 CALDER HOUSE
11 CROFT HOUSE
12 ST MARYS GATE
13 CHURCH HOUSE
14 PORTLAND HOUSE
15 CONISTON HOUSE
16 CORNWALL HOUSE
17 CASTLEGATE HOUSE
18 PROVIDENCE ST
A B C D E F
8 7 21 6 5 20 4 3 19 2 1 18
Upper Scholes Farm
B8
1 GOLDFIELDS CL
2 GOLDFIELDS VIEW
3 MOORLANDS CT
B7
1 THORNFIELD ST
2 THORNFIELD RISE
Moor Bottom Farm
Calderdale Way
Lindwell
Works
Cemy
Elland Tunnel
Mill
Mills
Greetland Junior & Infants Sch
Greetland
Liby
ROCHDALE RD
Cross Hill
Brow Bridge
Sch
Works
Elland Hall Farm
HALIFAX RD
CALDERDALE WAY
Calder and Hebble Navigation
River Calder
Mill
SADDLEWORTH RD
West Vale
Sunnybank
Sch
Black Brook
The Park
Liby
Elland
Works
Bradley Mill Farm
STAINLAND RD
Dismtd Rly
Golf Course
CH
Elland Golf Course
The Brooksbank Sch
CH
Ravenstone Wood
Ind Est
Old Dan La
Elland Infants' Sch
Broad Carr
Mill
Blackley
Holywell Green Junior & Infant Schs
Greaves Farm
Hollins Hey Clough
Golden Fleece Inn (PH)
Kew Hill
Works
Holywell Green
Refuse Tip
Jagger Dean
Shavey Clough
Haigh House
Copriding Farm
Old Lindley
Harrow Clough
Holywell Brook
Helen Hill Farm
Peat Ponds Farm
LINDLEY MOOR RD
Clough Head
Martin Nest
Wappy Spring Inn (PH)
Lea Green
Works
Turley Cote Farm
Kirklees Way
Old Lindley Moor
Laund Hill
New Lea
Gosport Clough
Brewery Farm
Junction 23
Leys
NEW HEY RD
Sowood Hill
Mount
Outlane County Primary Sch
08 09 10
A4
1 THORNE ST
2 OAK TERR
3 GLADSTONE ST
B4
1 CROSS ST
2 WELL ST
3 GREEN ST
133
152
F1
1 MAPLIN DR
2 DEER CROFT RD
3 DEER CROFT CRES
4 RYNDLESIDE
5 LOW HILLS LA

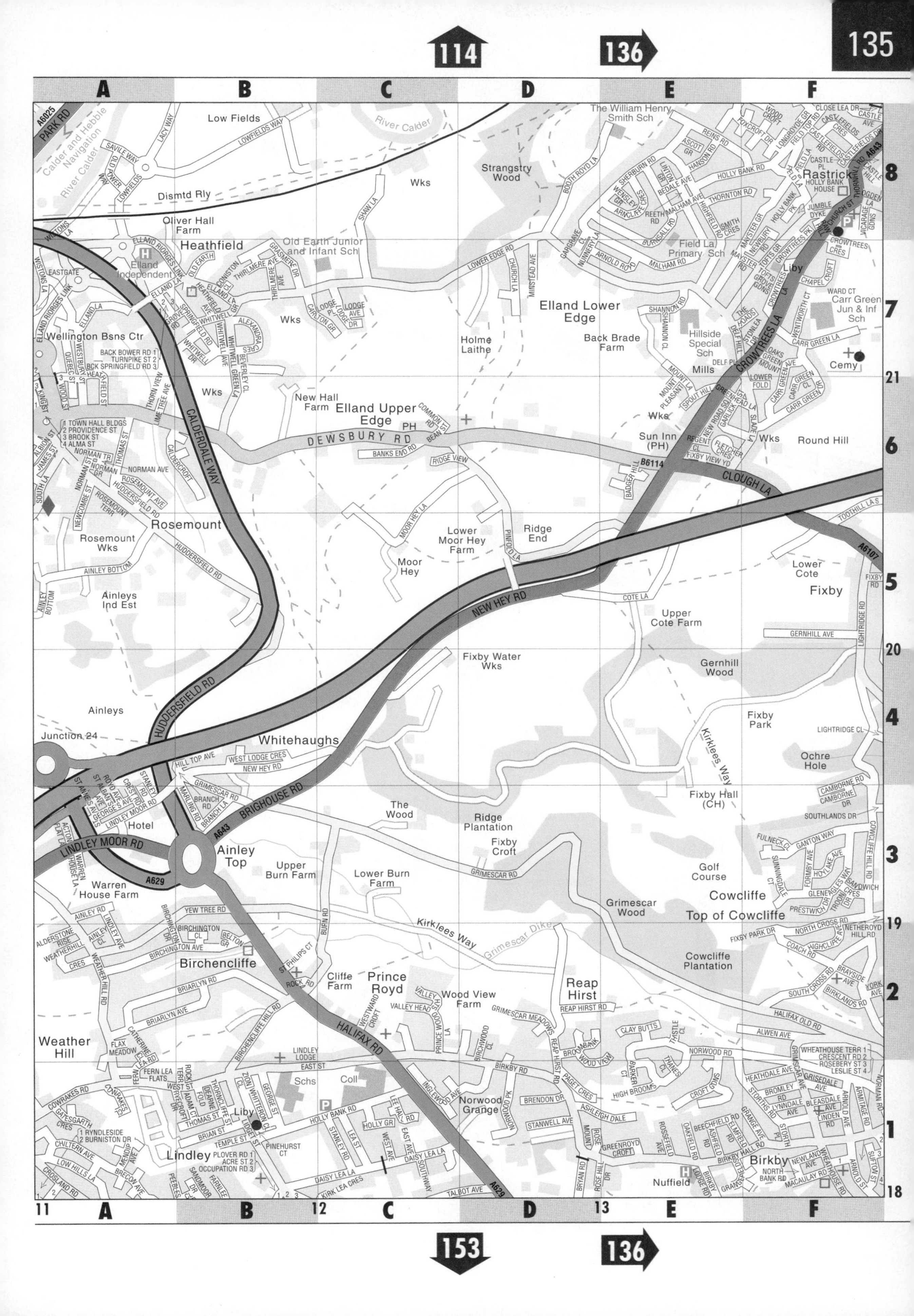
114
136
A
B
C
D
E
F
Low Fields
River Calder
The William Henry Smith Sch
Calder and Hebble Navigation
River Calder
Strangstry Wood
Wks
Dismtd Rly
Rastrick
Oliver Hall Farm
Heathfield
Old Earth Junior and Infant Sch
Elland Independent
Field La Primary Sch
Wellington Bsns Ctr
Wks
Elland Lower Edge
Holme Laithe
Back Brade Farm
Hillside Special Sch
Carr Green Jun & Inf Sch
Cemy
Mills
New Hall Farm
Elland Upper Edge
PH
DEWSBURY RD
Sun Inn (PH)
Wks
Round Hill
CALDERDALE WAY
CLOUGH LA
Rosemount
Rosemount Wks
Lower Moor Hey Farm
Ridge End
Moor Hey
Lower Cote
Fixby
Ainleys Ind Est
NEW HEY RD
Upper Cote Farm
Fixby Water Wks
Gernhill Wood
HUDDERSFIELD RD
Ainleys
Fixby Park
Junction 24
Whitehaughs
Kirklees Way
Ochre Hole
BRIGHOUSE RD
Fixby Hall (CH)
The Wood
Ridge Plantation
Hotel
LINDLEY MOOR RD
Ainley Top
Fixby Croft
Upper Burn Farm
Lower Burn Farm
Golf Course
Warren House Farm
Cowcliffe
Grimescar Wood
Top of Cowcliffe
Kirklees Way
Grimescar Dike
Birchencliffe
Cowcliffe Plantation
Cliffe Farm
Prince Royd
Reap Hirst
Wood View Farm
Weather Hill
HALIFAX RD
Schs
Coll
Norwood Grange
Liby
Lindley
Birkby
Nuffield
8
7
21
6
5
20
4
3
19
2
1
18
11
12
13
153
136

135
115

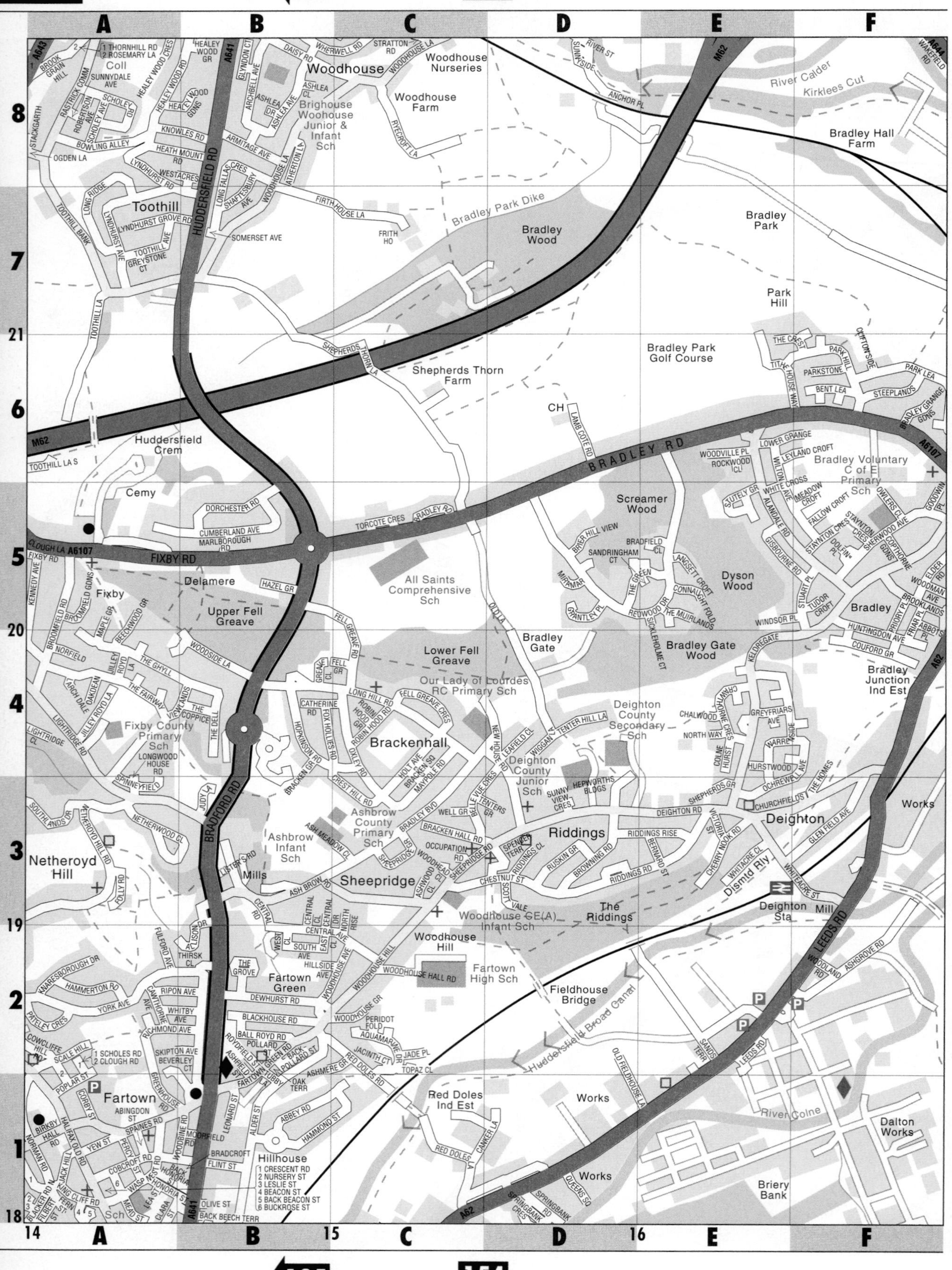
Woodhouse
Woodhouse Nurseries
Woodhouse Farm
Brighouse Woohouse Junior & Infant Sch
Toothill
Bradley Park Dike
Bradley Wood
Bradley Park
Bradley Hall Farm
River Calder
Kirklees Cut
Park Hill
Bradley Park Golf Course
Shepherds Thorn Farm
Huddersfield Crem
Cemy
HUDDERSFIELD RD
BRADLEY RD
FIXBY RD
Screamer Wood
Dyson Wood
Bradley Voluntary C of E Primary Sch
Bradley
All Saints Comprehensive Sch
Delamere
Fixby
Upper Fell Greave
Lower Fell Greave
Bradley Gate
Bradley Gate Wood
Bradley Junction Ind Est
Our Lady of Lourdes RC Primary Sch
Deighton County Secondary Sch
Brackenhall
Fixby County Primary Sch
Deighton County Junior Sch
Ashbrow County Primary Sch
Ashbrow Infant Sch
Riddings
Deighton
Netheroyd Hill
Mills
Sheepridge
Dismtd Rly
Deighton Sta
Mill
Woodhouse CE(A) Infant Sch
The Riddings
Woodhouse Hill
Fartown High Sch
Fartown Green
Fieldhouse Bridge
Huddersfield Broad Canal
BRADFORD RD
LEEDS RD
Red Doles Ind Est
Works
Fartown
River Colne
Dalton Works
Hillhouse
Briery Bank
Sch
1 CRESCENT RD
2 NURSERY ST
3 LESLIE ST
4 BEACON ST
5 BACK BEACON ST
6 BUCKROSE ST
1 THORNHILL RD
2 ROSEMARY LA
1 SCHOLES RD
2 CLOUGH RD
M62
A62
A641
A6107
A643
A644

135
154

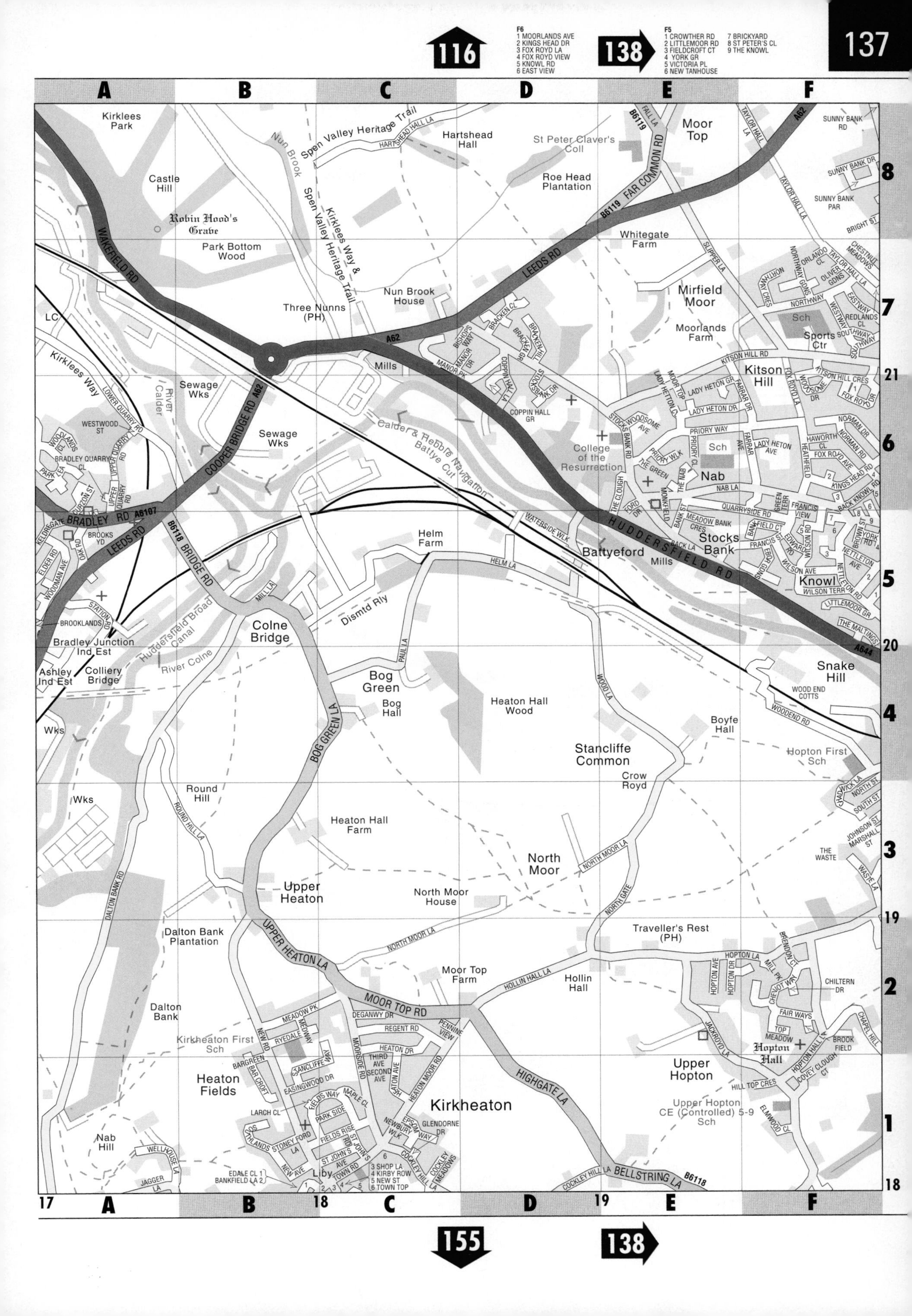
116
138
F6
1 MOORLANDS AVE
2 KINGS HEAD DR
3 FOX ROYD LA
4 FOX ROYD VIEW
5 KNOWL RD
6 EAST VIEW
F5
1 CROWTHER RD
2 LITTLEMOOR RD
3 FIELDCROFT CT
4 YORK GR
5 VICTORIA PL
6 NEW TANHOUSE
7 BRICKYARD
8 ST PETER'S CL
9 THE KNOWL
A
B
C
D
E
F
Kirklees Park
Castle Hill
Robin Hood's Grave
Park Bottom Wood
Spen Valley Heritage Trail
Nun Brook
Kirklees Way & Spen Valley Heritage Trail
Hartshead Hall
St Peter Claver's Coll
Roe Head Plantation
Moor Top
FAR COMMON RD
B6119
LEEDS RD
Whitegate Farm
Mirfield Moor
Moorlands Farm
Sch
Sports Ctr
Kitson Hill
Nun Brook House
Three Nunns (PH)
A62
Mills
WAKEFIELD RD
LC
Kirklees Way
Sewage Wks
River Calder
COOPER BRIDGE RD
Calder & Hebble Navigation
Battye Cut
College of the Resurrection
Nab
Stocks Bank
Knowl
Battyeford
Mills
HUDDERSFIELD RD
A644
BRADLEY RD
A6107
B6118
BRIDGE RD
Helm Farm
HELM LA
Dismtd Rly
Colne Bridge
Huddersfield Broad Canal
River Colne
Bradley Junction Ind Est
Ashley Ind Est
Colliery Bridge
Wks
Bog Green
Bog Hall
BOG GREEN LA
Heaton Hall Wood
WOOD LA
Boyfe Hall
Stancliffe Common
Crow Royd
Snake Hill
WOOD END COTTS
WOODEND RD
Hopton First Sch
Round Hill
ROUND HILL LA
Heaton Hall Farm
North Moor
NORTH MOOR LA
NORTH GATE
THE WASTE
Upper Heaton
North Moor House
DALTON BANK RD
Dalton Bank Plantation
UPPER HEATON LA
Traveller's Rest (PH)
Moor Top Farm
HOLLIN HALL LA
Hollin Hall
Dalton Bank
MOOR TOP RD
Kirkheaton First Sch
Heaton Fields
Kirkheaton
HIGHGATE LA
Upper Hopton
Hopton Hall
Upper Hopton CE (Controlled) 5-9 Sch
Nab Hill
Liby
BELLSTRING LA
COCKLEY HILL LA
EDALE CL 1
BANKFIELD LA 2
3 SHOP LA
4 KIRBY ROW
5 NEW ST
6 TOWN TOP
17
18
19
21
20
1
2
3
4
5
6
7
8
155
138

A B C D E F

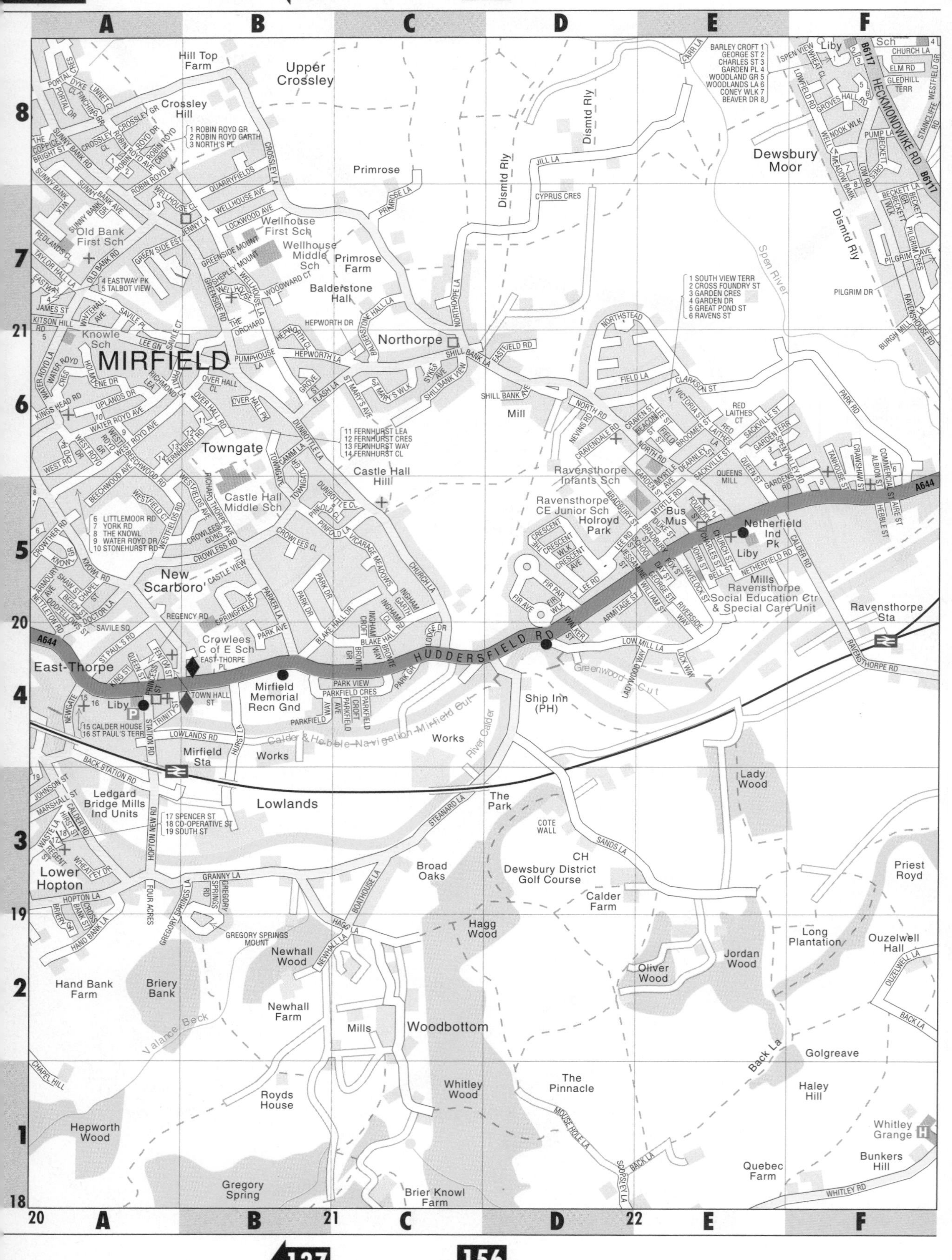
MIRFIELD
Hill Top Farm
Upper Crossley
Crossley Hill
Primrose
Wellhouse First Sch
Wellhouse Middle Sch
Old Bank First Sch
Primrose Farm
Balderstone Hall
Northorpe
Knowle Sch
Dewsbury Moor
Dismtd Rly
Spen River
Towngate
Castle Hall Hill
Castle Hall Middle Sch
Mill
Ravensthorpe Infants Sch
Ravensthorpe CE Junior Sch
Holroyd Park
Bus Mus
Netherfield Ind Pk
Liby
Mills
Ravensthorpe Social Education Ctr & Special Care Unit
Ravensthorpe Sta
New Scarboro'
Crowlees C of E Sch
East-Thorpe
Mirfield Memorial Recn Gnd
Ship Inn (PH)
HUDDERSFIELD RD
A644
B6117
HECKMONDWIKE RD
Greenwood Cut
Calder & Hebble Navigation Mirfield Cut
River Calder
Works
Mirfield Sta
Lowlands
Ledgard Bridge Mills Ind Units
The Park
Lady Wood
Lower Hopton
Broad Oaks
CH
Dewsbury District Golf Course
Calder Farm
Priest Royd
Hagg Wood
Long Plantation
Ouzelwell Hall
Newhall Wood
Oliver Wood
Jordan Wood
Hand Bank Farm
Briery Bank
Newhall Farm
Woodbottom
Golgreave
Valance Beck
Back La
Whitley Wood
The Pinnacle
Haley Hill
Royds House
Hepworth Wood
Whitley Grange
Bunkers Hill
Quebec Farm
Gregory Spring
Brier Knowl Farm
1 ROBIN ROYD GR
2 ROBIN ROYD GARTH
3 NORTH'S PL
BARLEY CROFT 1
GEORGE ST 2
CHARLES ST 3
GARDEN PL 4
WOODLAND GR 5
WOODLANDS LA 6
CONEY WLK 7
BEAVER DR 8
4 EASTWAY PK
5 TALBOT VIEW
1 SOUTH VIEW TERR
2 CROSS FOUNDRY ST
3 GREEN CRES
4 GARDEN DR
5 GREAT POND ST
6 RAVENS ST
11 FERNHURST LEA
12 FERNHURST CRES
13 FERNHURST WAY
14 FERNHURST CL
6 LITTLEMOOR RD
7 YORK RD
8 THE KNOWL
9 WATER ROYD DR
10 STONEHURST RD
15 CALDER HOUSE
16 ST PAUL'S TERR
17 SPENCER ST
18 CO-OPERATIVE ST
19 SOUTH ST
8 7 21 6 5 20 4 3 19 2 1 18
20 21 22

A B C D E F

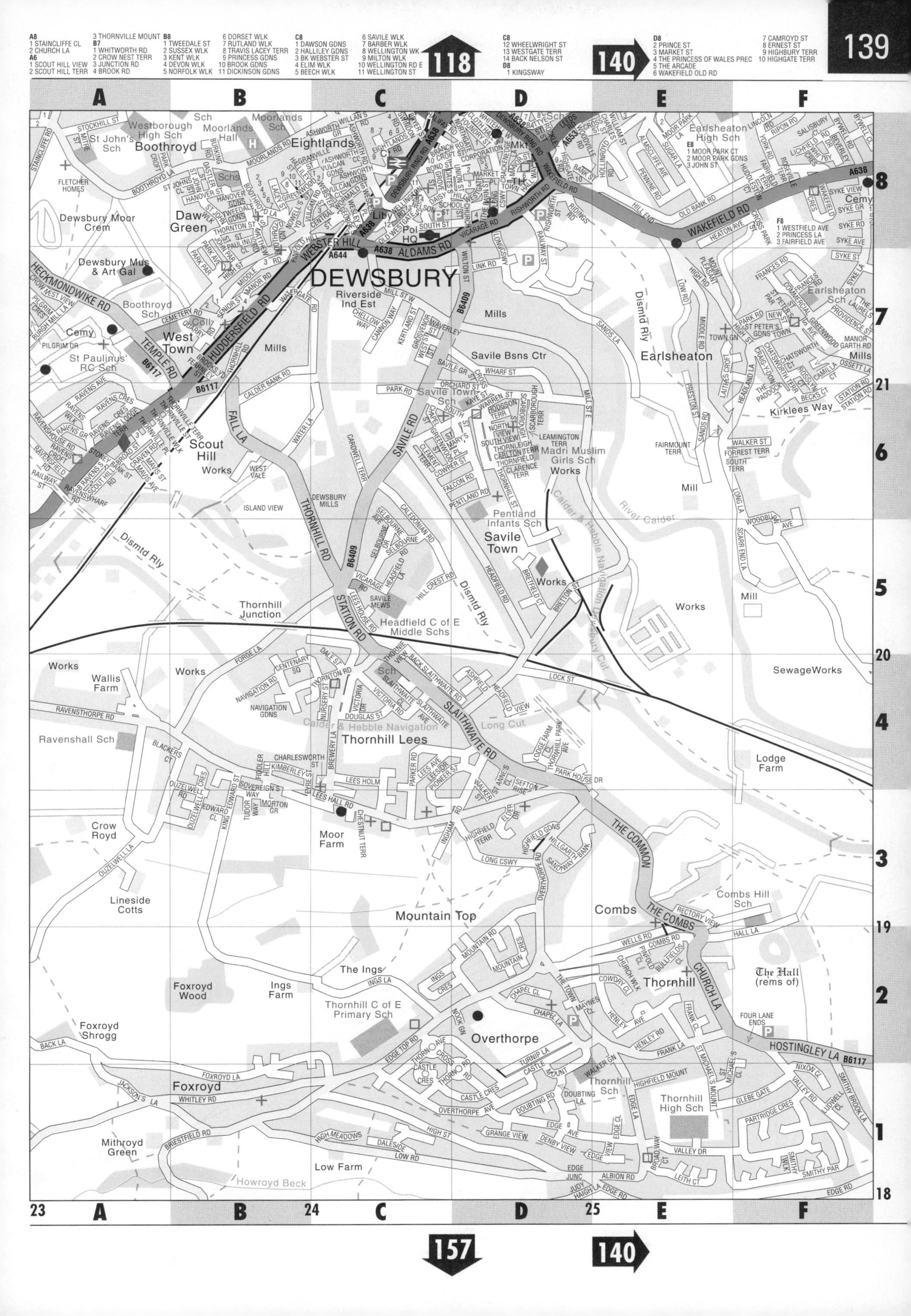
A8
1 STAINCLIFFE CL
2 CHURCH LA
A6
1 SCOUT HILL VIEW
2 SCOUT HILL TERR
3 THORNVILLE MOUNT
B7
1 WHITWORTH RD
2 CROW NEST TERR
3 JUNCTION RD
4 BROOK RD
B8
1 TWEEDALE ST
2 SUSSEX WLK
3 KENT WLK
4 DEVON WLK
5 NORFOLK WLK
6 DORSET WLK
7 RUTLAND WLK
8 TRAVIS LACEY TERR
9 PRINCESS GDNS
10 BROOK GDNS
11 DICKINSON GDNS
C8
1 DAWSON GDNS
2 HALLILEY GDNS
3 BK WEBSTER ST
4 ELIM WLK
5 BEECH WLK
6 SAVILE WLK
7 BARBER WLK
8 WELLINGTON WK
9 MILTON WLK
10 WELLINGTON RD E
11 WELLINGTON ST
118
C8
12 WHEELWRIGHT ST
13 WESTGATE TERR
14 BACK NELSON ST
D8
1 KINGSWAY
140
D8
2 PRINCE ST
3 MARKET ST
4 THE PRINCESS OF WALES PREC
5 THE ARCADE
6 WAKEFIELD OLD RD
7 CAMROYD ST
8 ERNEST ST
9 HIGHBURY TERR
10 HIGHGATE TERR
139
A
B
C
D
E
F
Westborough High Sch
St John's Sch
Boothroyd
Moorlands Hall
Moorlands Sch
Eightlands
Earlsheaton High Sch
E8
1 MOOR PARK CT
2 MOOR PARK GDNS
3 JOHN ST
FLETCHER HOMES
Dewsbury Moor Crem
Daw Green
Liby
Pol HQ
Mkt
TH
WAKEFIELD RD
Cemy
F8
1 WESTFIELD AVE
2 PRINCESS LA
3 FAIRFIELD AVE
8
WEBSTER HILL
ALDAMS RD
Dewsbury Mus & Art Gal
DEWSBURY
Riverside Ind Est
Dismtd Rly
Earlsheaton Sch
HECKMONDWIKE RD
Boothroyd Sch
Cemy
West Town
Mills
Mills
HUDDERSFIELD RD
St Paulinus' RC Sch
Savile Bsns Ctr
Earlsheaton
Mills
7
TEMPLE RD
21
Kirklees Way
Savile Town Sch
Scout Hill
Works
Madri Muslim Girls Sch
Works
6
SAVILE RD
THORNHILL RD
Mill
River Calder
Pentland Infants Sch
Savile Town
Dismtd Rly
Works
Calder & Hebble Navigation
5
Thornhill Junction
STATION RD
Headfield C of E Middle Schs
Mill
Works
Dewsbury Cut
Works
Wallis Farm
Works
20
SewageWorks
Calder & Hebble Navigation
Long Cut
Ravenshall Sch
Thornhill Lees
SLAITHWAITE RD
4
Lodge Farm
Crow Royd
Moor Farm
THE COMMON
3
Lineside Cotts
Mountain Top
Combs
Combs Hill Sch
19
THE COMBS
The Ings
Thornhill
The Hall (rems of)
Foxroyd Wood
Ings Farm
Thornhill C of E Primary Sch
CHURCH LA
2
Foxroyd Shrogg
Overthorpe
FOUR LANE ENDS
HOSTINGLEY LA
B6117
Foxroyd
Thornhill Sch
Thornhill High Sch
1
Mithroyd Green
Low Farm
Howroyd Beck
18
23
A
B
24
C
D
25
E
F
157
140

139
119

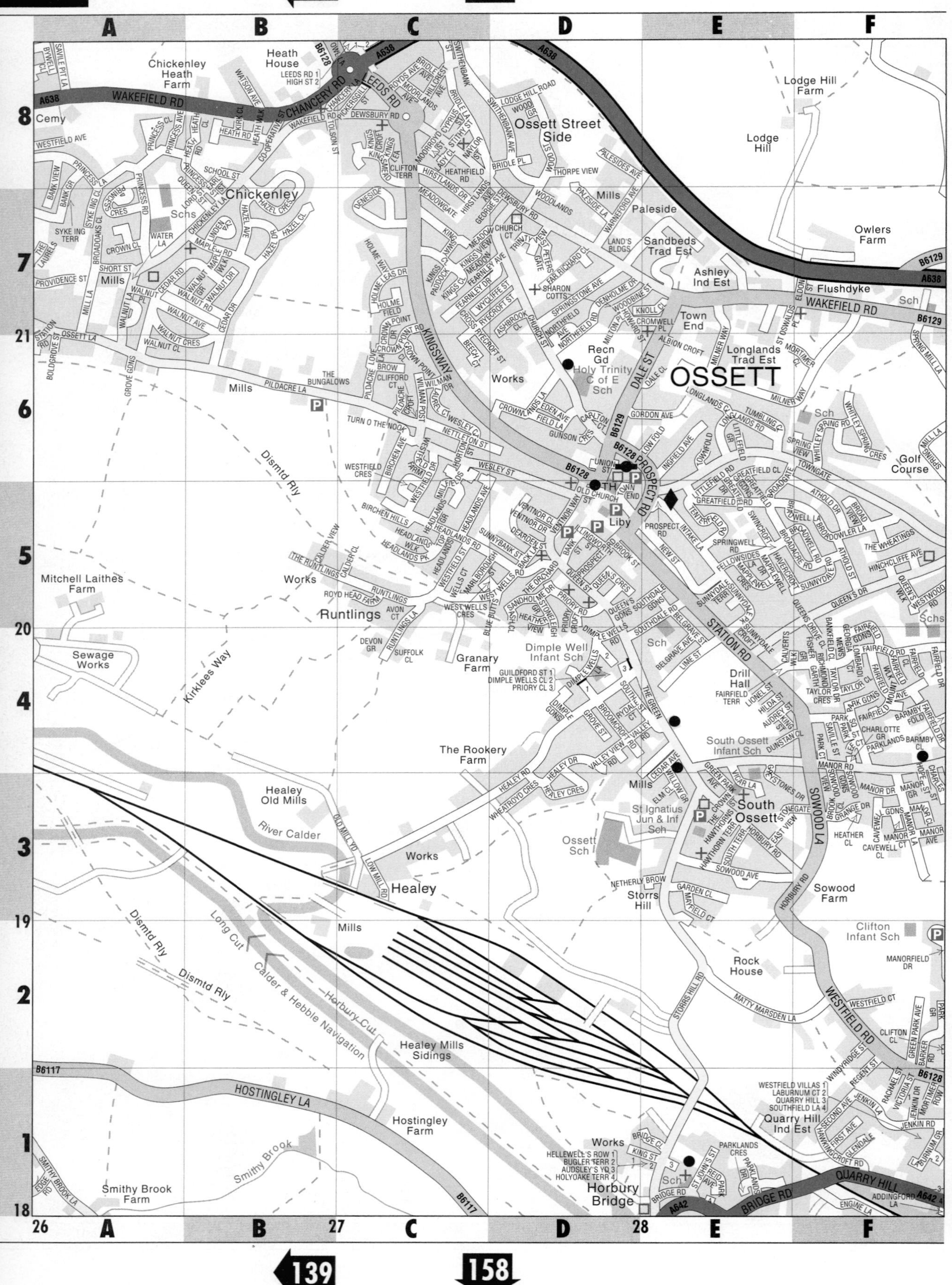
A
B
C
D
E
F
8
7
21
6
5
20
4
3
19
2
1
18
26
27
28
Chickenley Heath Farm
Heath House
A638
WAKEFIELD RD
CHANCERY RD
LEEDS RD
B6128
Cemy
WESTFIELD AVE
Chickenley
Schs
Mills
SHORT ST
PROVIDENCE ST
OSSETT LA
WALNUT RD
WALNUT AVE
WALNUT CRES
WALNUT CL
CEDAR DR
HAZEL AVE
HAZEL DR
SCHOOL ST
PILDACRE LA
THE BUNGALOWS
Dismtd Rly
Mitchell Laithes Farm
Sewage Works
Kirklees Way
Works
Runtlings
THE RUNTLINGS
ROYD HEAD FARM
KINGSWAY
Ossett Street Side
LODGE HILL ROAD
THORPE VIEW
Mills
Paleside
WOODLANDS
Sandbeds Trad Est
Ashley Ind Est
Lodge Hill Farm
Lodge Hill
Owlers Farm
B6129
Flushdyke
Sch
Town End
Recn Gd
Holy Trinity C of E Sch
Works
DALE ST
OSSETT
Longlands Trad Est
MILNER WAY
WAKEFIELD RD
SPRINGSTONE AVE
B6129
TOWNGATE
Golf Course
B6128
PROSPECT RD
WESLEY ST
Liby
UNION ST
TN END
STATION RD
THE WHEATINGS
QUEEN'S DR
Schs
Dimple Well Infant Sch
Granary Farm
Sch
Drill Hall
FAIRFIELD TERR
South Ossett Infant Sch
The Rookery Farm
HEALEY RD
HEALEY CRES
WHEATROYD CRES
Mills
St Ignatius Jun & Inf Sch
South Ossett
Ossett Sch
SOWOOD LA
SOWOOD AVE
HORBURY RD
Sowood Farm
Healey Old Mills
River Calder
Works
Healey
LOW MILL RD
OLD MILL YD
NETHERLY BROW
Storrs Hill
GARDEN CL
Mills
Clifton Infant Sch
MANORFIELD DR
Rock House
STORRS HILL RD
MATTY MARSDEN LA
WESTFIELD RD
WESTFIELD CT
CLIFTON CL
Long Cut
Dismtd Rly
Dismtd Rly
Calder & Hebble Navigation
Horbury Cut
Healey Mills Sidings
B6117
HOSTINGLEY LA
Hostingley Farm
Smithy Brook
Smithy Brook Farm
SMITHY BROOK LA
B6117
Works
HELLEWELL'S ROW 1
BUGLER TERR 2
AUDSLEY'S YD 3
HOLYOAKE TERR 4
KING ST
Horbury Bridge
BRIDGE RD
A642
Sch
PARKLANDS CRES
Quarry Hill Ind Est
WESTFIELD VILLAS 1
LABURNUM CT 2
QUARRY HILL 3
SOUTHFIELD LA 4
QUARRY HILL
BRIDGE RD
ENGINE LA
ADDINGFORD LA
JENKIN RD
B6128

139
158

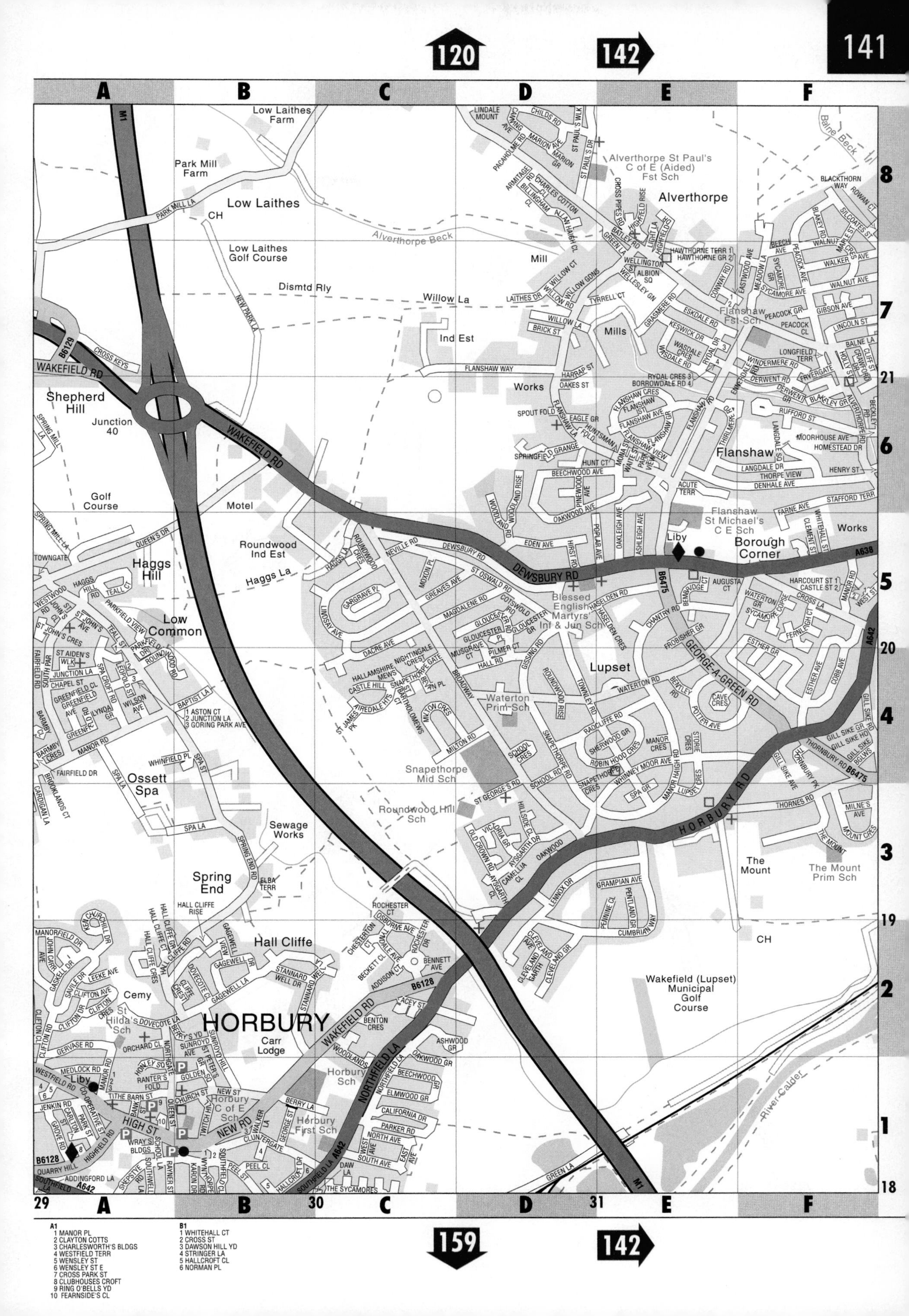

141
120
142
159
142
A
B
C
D
E
F
8
7
6
5
4
3
2
1
21
20
19
18
29
30
31
Low Laithes Farm
Park Mill Farm
Low Laithes
CH
Alverthorpe Beck
Low Laithes Golf Course
Dismtd Rly
Willow La
Ind Est
FLANSHAW WAY
WAKEFIELD RD
Shepherd Hill
Junction 40
Golf Course
Motel
Roundwood Ind Est
Haggs La
Haggs Hill
Low Common
Ossett Spa
Sewage Works
Spring End
Hall Cliffe
Cemy
HORBURY
Carr Lodge
Horbury Sch
Horbury C of E Sch
Horbury First Sch
St Hilda's Sch
Liby
HIGH ST
NEW RD
B6128
A642
NORTHFIELD LA
SOUTHFIELD LA
QUARRY HILL
Alverthorpe
Alverthorpe St Paul's C of E (Aided) Fst Sch
Mill
Mills
Works
Flanshaw Fst Sch
Flanshaw
Flanshaw St Michael's C E Sch
Borough Corner
DEWSBURY RD
A638
B6475
Blessed English Martyrs' Inf & Jun Sch
Lupset
GEORGE-A-GREEN RD
Waterton Prim Sch
Snapethorpe Mid Sch
Roundwood Hill Sch
HORBURY RD
The Mount
The Mount Prim Sch
CH
Wakefield (Lupset) Municipal Golf Course
River Calder
M1
A1
1 MANOR PL
2 CLAYTON COTTS
3 CHARLESWORTH'S BLDGS
4 WESTFIELD TERR
5 WENSLEY ST
6 WENSLEY ST E
7 CROSS PARK ST
8 CLUBHOUSES CROFT
9 RING O'BELLS YD
10 FEARNSIDE'S CL
B1
1 WHITEHALL CT
2 CROSS ST
3 DAWSON HILL YD
4 STRINGER LA
5 HALLCROFT CL
6 NORMAN PL

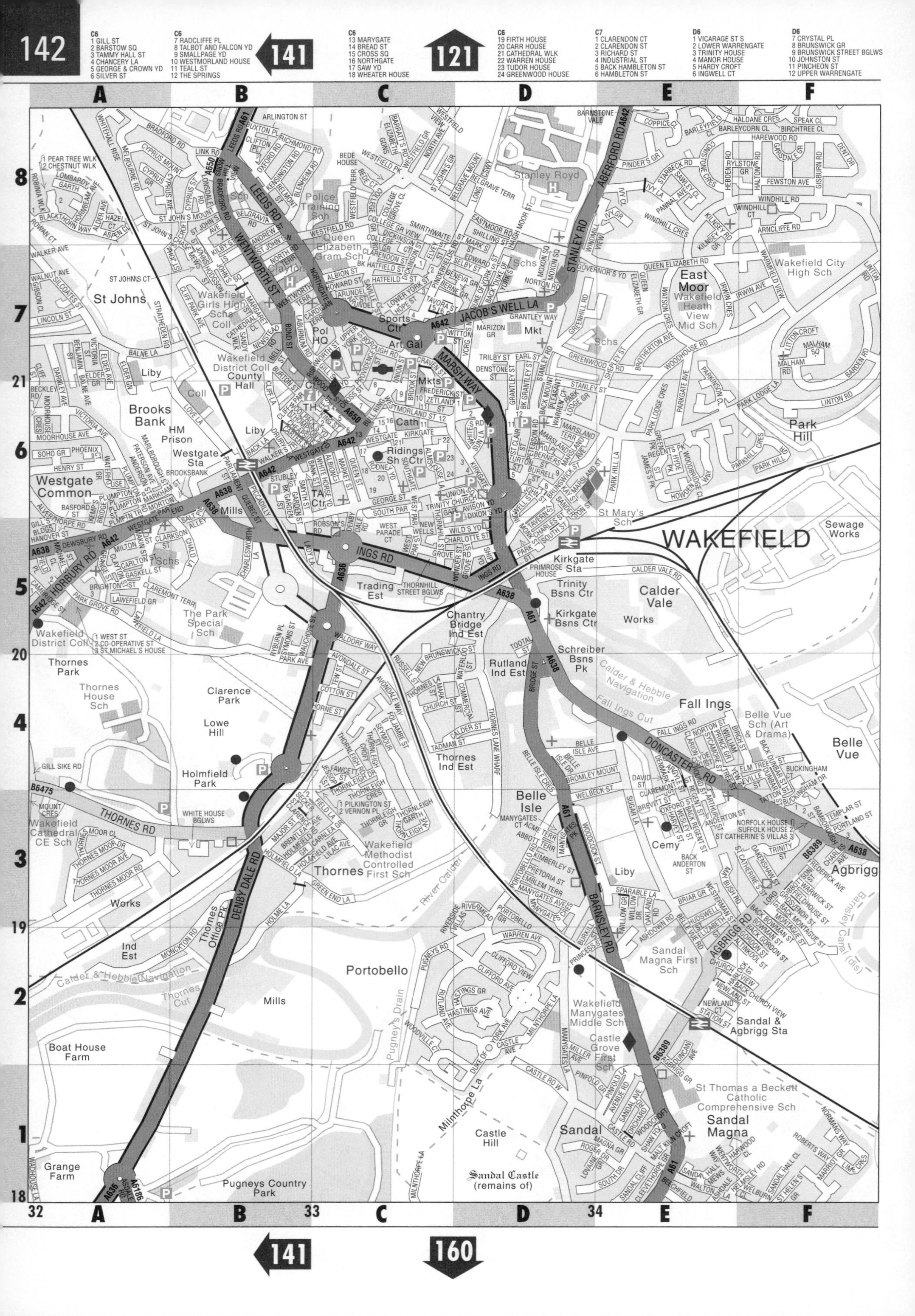

141
121
141
160

C6
1 GILL ST
2 BARSTOW SQ
3 TAMMY HALL ST
4 CHANCERY LA
5 GEORGE & CROWN YD
6 SILVER ST

C6
7 RADCLIFFE PL
8 TALBOT AND FALCON YD
9 SMALLPAGE YD
10 WESTMORLAND HOUSE
11 TEALL ST
12 THE SPRINGS

C6
13 MARYGATE
14 BREAD ST
15 CROSS SQ
16 NORTHGATE
17 SAW YD
18 WHEATER HOUSE

C6
19 FIRTH HOUSE
20 CARR HOUSE
21 CATHEDRAL WLK
22 WARREN HOUSE
23 TUDOR HOUSE
24 GREENWOOD HOUSE

C7
1 CLARENDON CT
2 CLARENDON ST
3 RICHARD ST
4 INDUSTRIAL ST
5 BACK HAMBLETON ST
6 HAMBLETON ST

D6
1 VICARAGE ST S
2 LOWER WARRENGATE
3 TRINITY HOUSE
4 MANOR HOUSE
5 HARDY CROFT
6 INGWELL CT

D6
7 CRYSTAL PL
8 BRUNSWICK GR
9 BRUNSWICK STREET BGLWS
10 JOHNSTON ST
11 PINCHEON ST
12 UPPER WARRENGATE

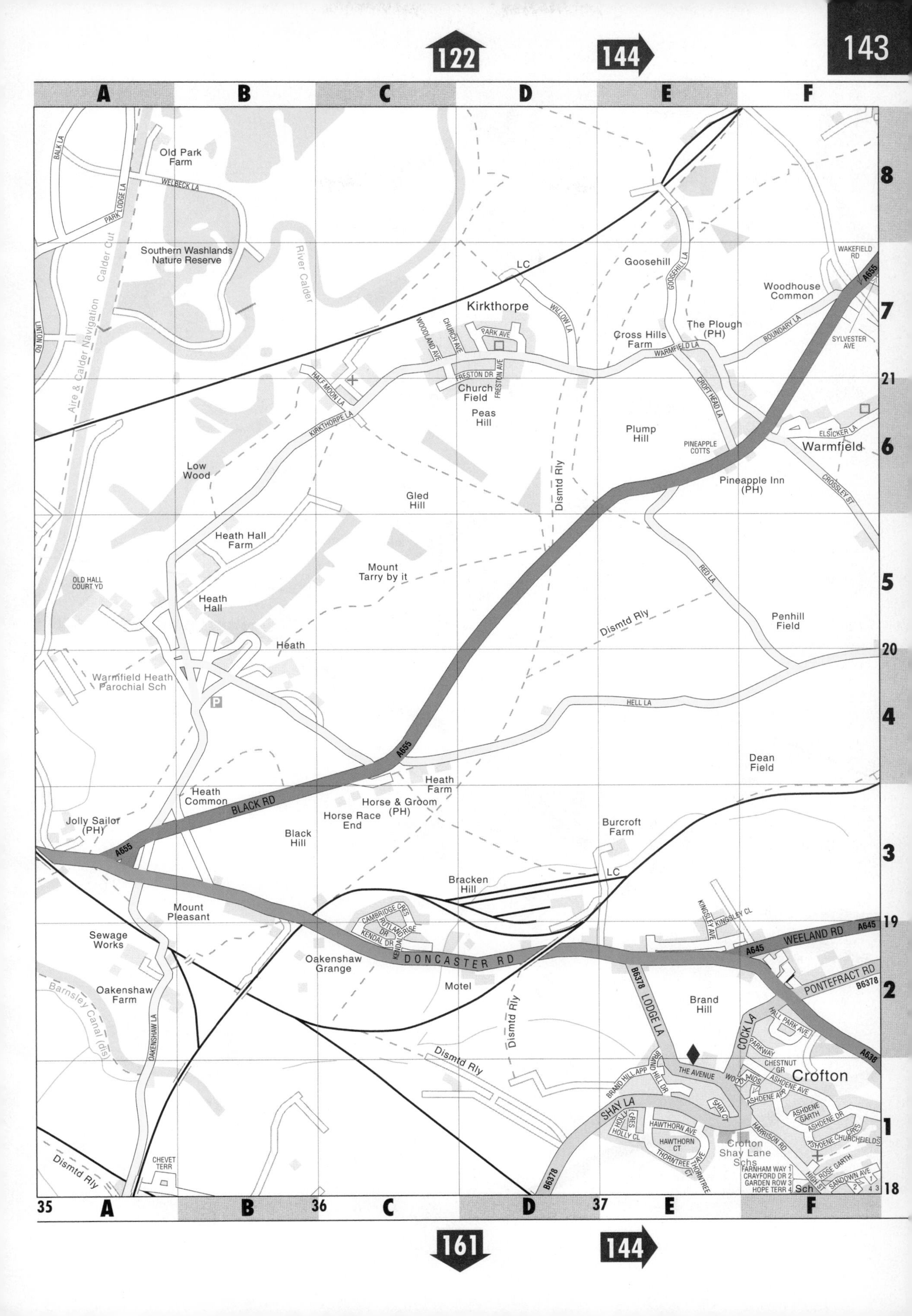
122
144
A
B
C
D
E
F
Old Park Farm
WELBECK LA
PARK LODGE LA
BALK LA
Southern Washlands Nature Reserve
Calder Cut
River Calder
Aire & Calder Navigation
LINTON RD
LC
Goosehill
GOOSEHILL LA
Kirkthorpe
WILLOW LA
WOODLAND AVE
CHURCH AVE
PARK AVE
FRESTON DR
FRESTON AVE
Church Field
HALF MOON LA
KIRKTHORPE LA
Cross Hills Farm
The Plough (PH)
WARMFIELD LA
CROFT HEAD LA
BOUNDARY LA
Woodhouse Common
WAKEFIELD RD
A655
SYLVESTER AVE
Peas Hill
Plump Hill
PINEAPPLE COTTS
ELSICKER LA
Warmfield
Pineapple Inn (PH)
CROSSLEY ST
Low Wood
Gled Hill
Dismtd Rly
Heath Hall Farm
OLD HALL COURT YD
Mount Tarry by it
RED LA
Heath Hall
Heath
Penhill Field
Warmfield Heath Parochial Sch
P
HELL LA
A655
Dean Field
Heath Farm
Heath Common
BLACK RD
Horse & Groom (PH)
Horse Race End
Jolly Sailor (PH)
Black Hill
Burcroft Farm
A655
LC
Bracken Hill
Mount Pleasant
CAMBRIDGE CRES
RUTLAND DR
KENDAL DR
KENDAL RISE
KINGSLEY AVE
KINGSLEY CL
WEELAND RD
A645
Sewage Works
Oakenshaw Grange
DONCASTER RD
B6378
LODGE LA
PONTEFRACT RD
B6378
Oakenshaw Farm
Barnsley Canal (dis)
Motel
Dismtd Rly
Brand Hill
COCK LA
HALL PARK AVE
PARKWAY
OAKENSHAW LA
A638
Dismtd Rly
BRAND HILL APP
BRAND HILL DR
THE AVENUE
WOOD
LANDS
CHESTNUT GR
ASHDENE AVE
ASHDENE APP
Crofton
SHAY LA
SHAY CT
ASHDENE GARTH
ASHDENE DR
HOLLY CRES
HOLLY CL
HAWTHORN AVE
HAWTHORN CT
HARRISON RD
ASHDENE
CHURCHFIELDS
CRES
Crofton Shay Lane Schs
THORNTREE CT
THORNTREE AVE
ROSE GARTH
Dismtd Rly
CHEVET TERR
B6378
FARNHAM WAY 1
CRAYFORD DR 2
GARDEN ROW 3
HOPE TERR 4
HIGH ST
SANDOWN AVE
Sch
8
7
21
6
5
20
4
3
19
2
1
18
35
36
37
161
144

143
123

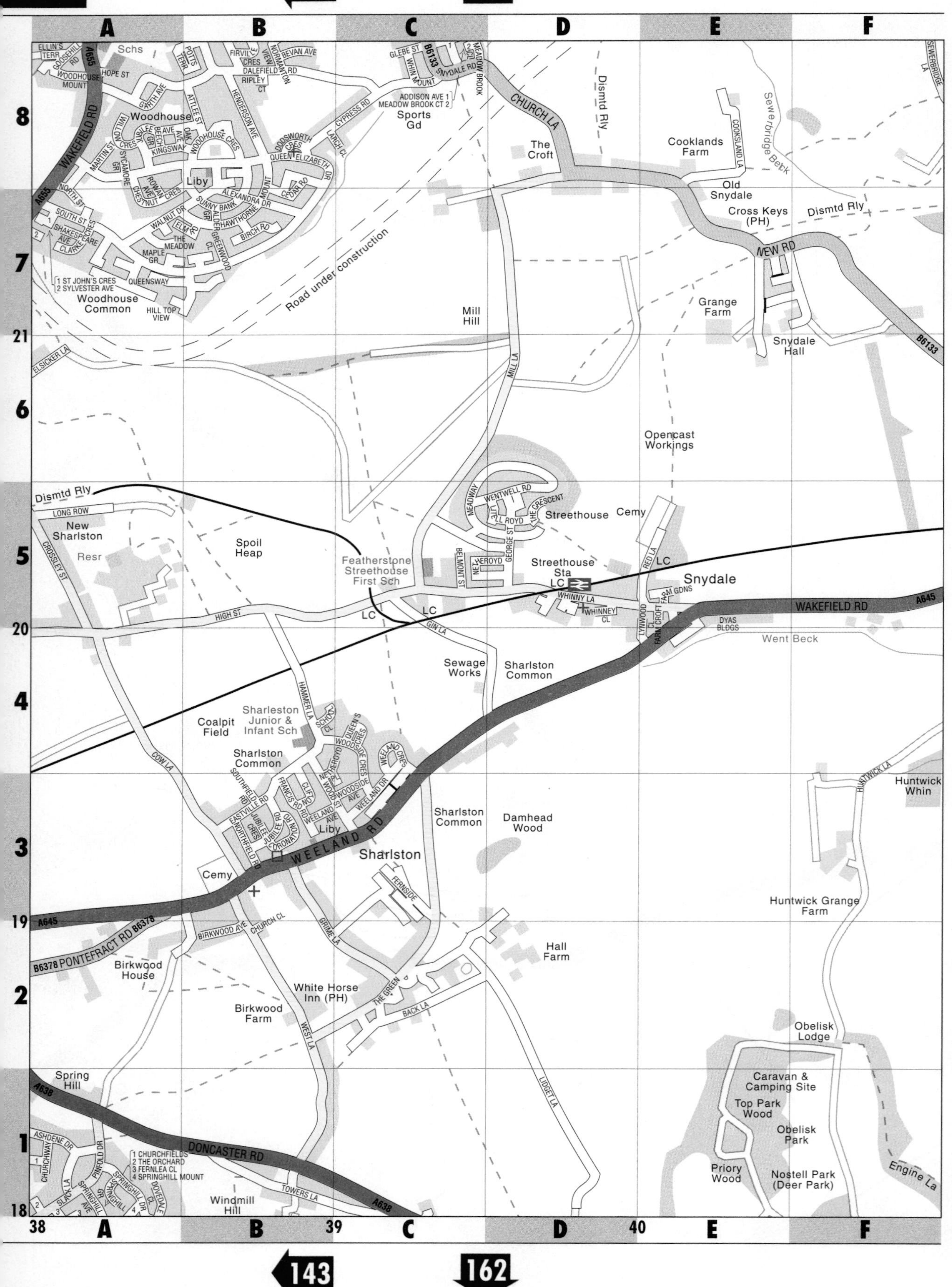
A
B
C
D
E
F
Woodhouse
Liby
Woodhouse Common
WAKEFIELD RD
A655
Schs
HOPE ST
GARTH AVE
POTTS TERR
ATTLEE ST
HENDERSON AVE
WOODHOUSE CRES
DALEFIELD RD
RIPLEY CT
NORMANTON VIEW
BEVAN AVE
FIRVILLE CRES
GLEBE ST
B6133
SNYDALE RD
WHIN MOUNT
MEADOW BROOK
ADDISON AVE
MEADOW BROOK CT
Sports Gd
CYPRESS RD
LARCH CL
QUEEN ELIZABETH DR
DODSWORTH CRES
CEDAR RD
ALEXANDRA DR
HAWTHORNE MOUNT
BIRCH RD
SUNNY BANK
WALNUT DR
MAPLE GR
QUEENSWAY
HILL TOP VIEW
1 ST JOHN'S CRES
2 SYLVESTER AVE
SOUTH ST
NORTH ST
MARTIN ST
SYCAMORE GR
KINGSWAY
ROWAN AVE
CHESTNUT CRES
Road under construction
CHURCH LA
The Croft
Dismtd Rly
Cooklands Farm
COOKSLAND LA
Sewerbridge Beck
SEWERBRIDGE LA
Old Snydale
Cross Keys (PH)
NEW RD
Grange Farm
Snydale Hall
B6133
Mill Hill
MILL LA
ELSICKER LA
Opencast Workings
Dismtd Rly
LONG ROW
New Sharlston
Resr
CROSSLEY ST
Spoil Heap
Featherstone Streethouse First Sch
MEADWAY
WENTWELL RD
THE CRESCENT
Streethouse
Cemy
BELMONT ST
GEORGE ST
Streethouse Sta
LC
WHINNY LA
WHINNEY CL
RED LA
Snydale
FARM GDNS
HIGH ST
GIN LA
WAKEFIELD RD
A645
DYAS BLDGS
Went Beck
LYNWOOD CL
FARM CROFT
Sewage Works
Sharlston Common
HAMMER LA
Coalpit Field
Sharleston Junior & Infant Sch
Sharlston Common
COW LA
SCHOOL CL
QUEEN'S CRES
WOODSIDE CRES
WEELAND CRES
WEELAND DR
WOODSIDE AVE
SOUTHFIELD RD
EASTVILLE RD
FRANCIS RD
CLIFF RD
WEELAND AVE
JUBILEE RD
CORONATION RD
NORTHFIELD RD
Liby
WEELAND RD
Sharlston
Sharlston Common
Damhead Wood
Cemy
FERNSIDE
A645
HUNTWICK LA
Huntwick Whin
Huntwick Grange Farm
B6378 PONTEFRACT RD
BIRKWOOD AVE
CHURCH CL
Birkwood House
GRIME LA
Hall Farm
White Horse Inn (PH)
THE GREEN
BACK LA
Birkwood Farm
WEST LA
Obelisk Lodge
Spring Hill
A638
LIDGET LA
Caravan & Camping Site
Top Park Wood
Obelisk Park
Priory Wood
Nostell Park (Deer Park)
Engine La
ASHDENE DR
CHURCHWAY
SLACK LA
PINFOLD DR
SPRINGHILL
1 CHURCHFIELDS
2 THE ORCHARD
3 FERNLEA CL
4 SPRINGHILL MOUNT
DOVEDALE CL
DONCASTER RD
TOWERS LA
Windmill Hill
A638
8
7
21
6
5
20
4
3
19
2
1
18
38
39
40

143
162

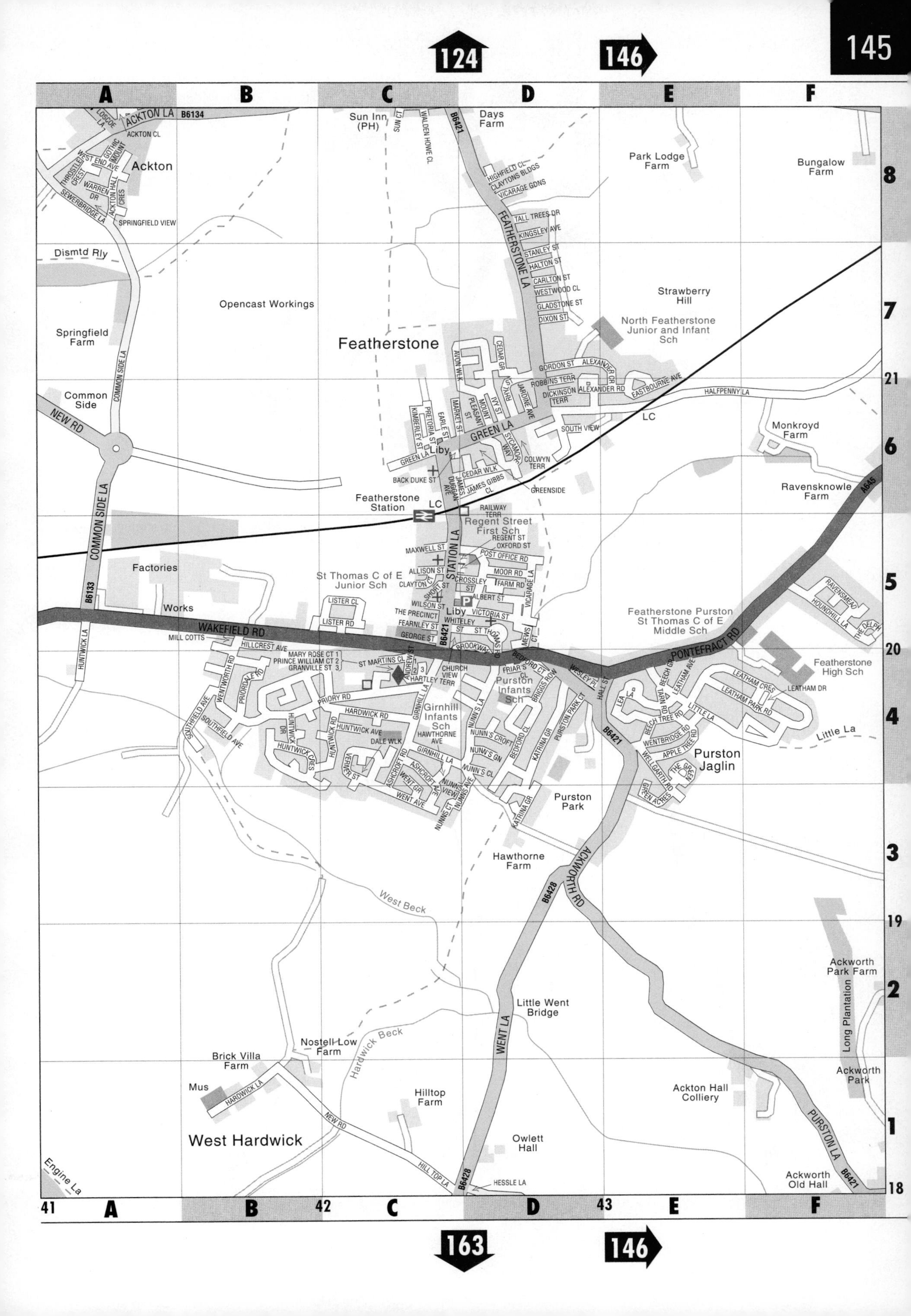
124
146
A
B
C
D
E
F
Ackton
Ackton La
B6134
Ackton Cl
Loscoe La
Throstle Crest
West End Ave
Gothic Mount
Warren Dr
Ackton Hall Cres
Sewerbridge La
Springfield View
Dismtd Rly
Opencast Workings
Springfield Farm
Common Side
Common Side La
New Rd
Sun Inn (PH)
Sun Ct
Walden Howe Cl
B6421
Days Farm
Highfield Cl
Claytons Bldgs
Vicarage Gdns
Featherstone La
Tall Trees Dr
Kingsley Ave
Stanley St
Halton St
Carlton St
Westwood Cl
Gladstone St
Dixon St
Park Lodge Farm
Bungalow Farm
Strawberry Hill
North Featherstone Junior and Infant Sch
Featherstone
Cedar Gr
Avon Wlk
Gordon St
Alexander Cr
Robbins Terr
Dickinson Terr
Alexander Rd
Eastbourne Ave
Halfpenny La
LC
Green La
Liby
Kimberley St
Pretoria St
Earle St
Market St
Pleasant St
Mount
Ivy St
Holly Ct
Jardine Ave
Sycamore Way
South View
Colwyn Terr
Cedar Wlk
Back Duke St
Duggan Ave
James St
James Gibbs Cl
Greenside
Monkroyd Farm
Ravensknowle Farm
A645
Featherstone Station
Railway Terr
Regent Street First Sch
Regent St
Oxford St
Station La
Maxwell St
Post Office Rd
Moor Rd
Farm Rd
Allison St
Clayton Ct
Short St
Crossley St
Vicarage La
Albert St
Wilson St
The Precinct
Victoria St
Whiteley St
St Thomas Rd
Fearnley St
George St
Mews Ct
Brookway
Factories
Works
St Thomas C of E Junior Sch
Lister Cl
Lister Rd
B6133
Common Side La
Huntwick La
Wakefield Rd
Mill Cotts
Hillcrest Ave
Mary Rose Ct 1
Prince William Ct 2
Granville St 3
St Martins Cl
Andrew St
Church View
Hartley Terr
Bedford Ct
Friar's Cl
Wesley Pl
Hall St
Pontefract Rd
Featherstone Purston St Thomas C of E Middle Sch
Featherstone High Sch
Ravensmead
Houndhill La
The Delph
Leatham Cres
Leatham Dr
Leatham Park Rd
Leatham Ave
Beech Gr
Tarn Rd
Lea La
Little La
Beech Tree Rd
Wentbridge Rd
Apple Tree Rd
Wellgarth Rd
The Gr
Green Acres
Purston Jaglin
Wentworth Rd
Priordale Rd
Southfield Ave
Priory Rd
Hardwick Rd
Huntwick Ave
Huntwick Dr
Huntwick Cres
Huntwick Rd
Dale Wlk
Verner St
Ashcroft Rd
Ashcroft Ave
Went Gr
Went Ave
Girnhill La
Girnhill Infants Sch
Hawthorne Ave
Nunn's La
Nunn's Croft
Nunn's Gn
Nunn's Cl
Nunns View
Nunns Ct
Nunns Ave
Purston Infants Sch
Briggs Row
Bedford Cl
Katrina Gr
Purston Park Ct
B6421
Purston Park
Hawthorne Farm
Ackworth Rd
B6428
West Beck
Little Went Bridge
Went La
Ackworth Park Farm
Long Plantation
Ackworth Park
Nostell Low Farm
Hardwick Beck
Brick Villa Farm
Mus
Hardwick La
New Rd
Hilltop Farm
West Hardwick
Hill Top La
Owlett Hall
Hessle La
Ackton Hall Colliery
Purston La
Ackworth Old Hall
Engine La
8
7
21
6
5
20
4
3
19
2
1
18
41
42
43
163
146

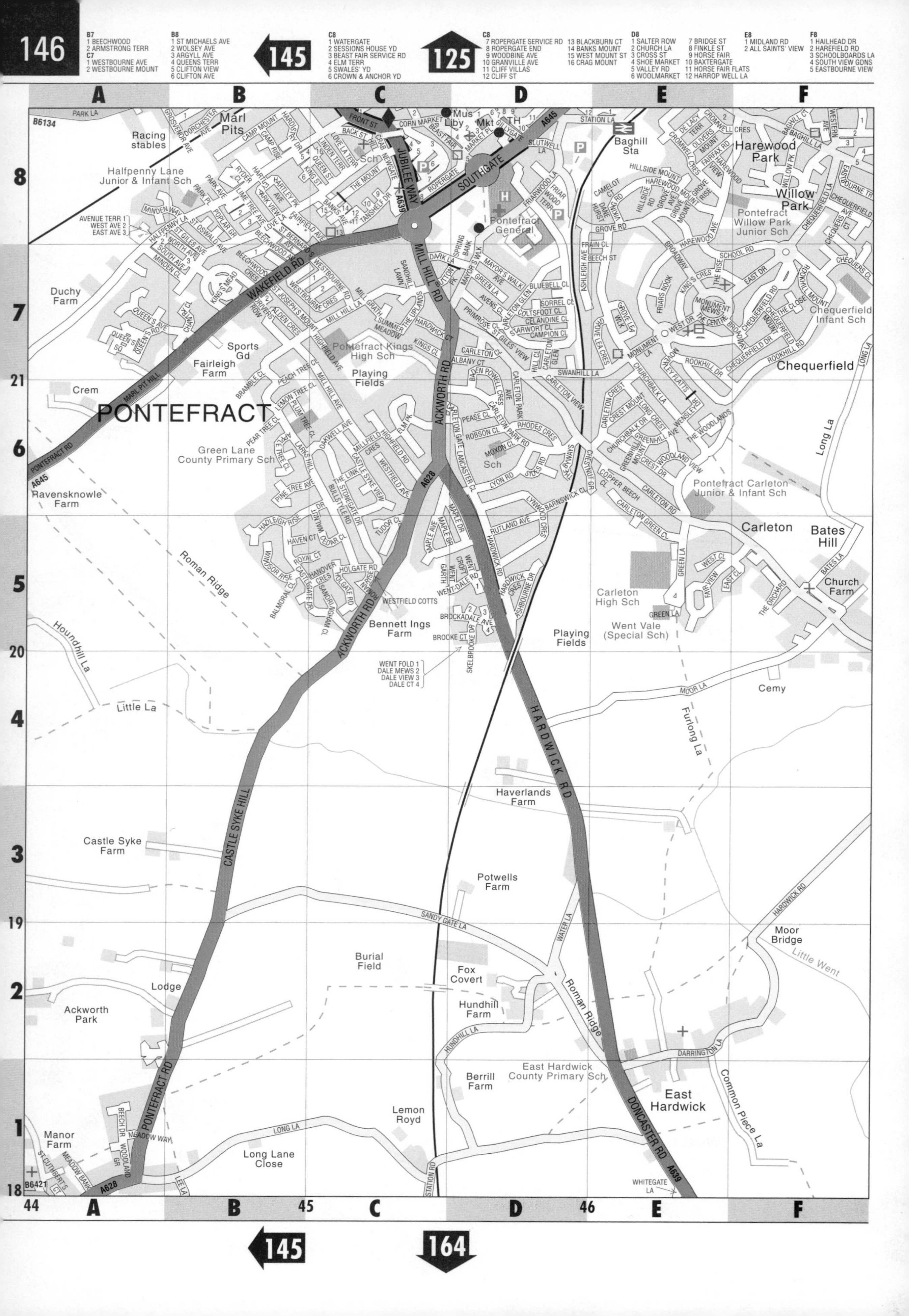

146
B7
1 BEECHWOOD
2 ARMSTRONG TERR
C7
1 WESTBOURNE AVE
2 WESTBOURNE MOUNT
B8
1 ST MICHAELS AVE
2 WOLSEY AVE
3 ARGYLL AVE
4 QUEENS TERR
5 CLIFTON VIEW
6 CLIFTON AVE
145
C8
1 WATERGATE
2 SESSIONS HOUSE YD
3 BEAST FAIR SERVICE RD
4 ELM TERR
5 SWALES' YD
6 CROWN & ANCHOR YD
125
C8
7 ROPERGATE SERVICE RD
8 ROPERGATE END
9 WOODBINE AVE
10 GRANVILLE AVE
11 CLIFF VILLAS
12 CLIFF ST
13 BLACKBURN CT
14 BANKS MOUNT
15 WEST MOUNT ST
16 CRAG MOUNT
D8
1 SALTER ROW
2 CHURCH LA
3 CROSS ST
4 SHOE MARKET
5 VALLEY RD
6 WOOLMARKET
7 BRIDGE ST
8 FINKLE ST
9 HORSE FAIR
10 BAXTERGATE
11 HORSE FAIR FLATS
12 HARROP WELL LA
E8
1 MIDLAND RD
2 ALL SAINTS' VIEW
F8
1 HAILHEAD DR
2 HAREFIELD RD
3 SCHOOLBOARDS LA
4 SOUTH VIEW GDNS
5 EASTBOURNE VIEW
A
B
C
D
E
F
8
7
21
6
5
20
4
3
19
2
1
18
44
45
46
Racing stables
Marl Pits
Halfpenny Lane Junior & Infant Sch
Mus
Liby
Mkt
TH
Sch
Baghill Sta
Harewood Park
Willow Park
Pontefract Willow Park Junior Sch
Pontefract General
Duchy Farm
Sports Gd
Fairleigh Farm
Pontefract Kings High Sch
Playing Fields
Chequerfield Infant Sch
Chequerfield
Crem
PONTEFRACT
Green Lane County Primary Sch
Ravensknowle Farm
Sch
Pontefract Carleton Junior & Infant Sch
Carleton
Bates Hill
Church Farm
Carleton High Sch
Went Vale (Special Sch)
Playing Fields
Bennett Ings Farm
Roman Ridge
Houndhill La
Little La
Cemy
Furlong La
Moor La
Long La
Haverlands Farm
Castle Syke Farm
Potwells Farm
Moor Bridge
Little Went
Burial Field
Fox Covert
Lodge
Ackworth Park
Hundhill Farm
Roman Ridge
Berrill Farm
East Hardwick County Primary Sch
East Hardwick
Common Piece La
Lemon Royd
Manor Farm
Long Lane Close
WAKEFIELD RD
MILL HILL RD
ACKWORTH RD
SOUTHGATE
JUBILEE WAY
CASTLE SYKE HILL
HARDWICK RD
DONCASTER RD
PONTEFRACT RD
SANDY GATE LA
DARRINGTON LA
WHITEGATE LA
WENT FOLD 1
DALE MEWS 2
DALE VIEW 3
DALE CT 4
AVENUE TERR 1
WEST AVE 2
EAST AVE 3
A645
A628
A639
B6134
B6421
145
164

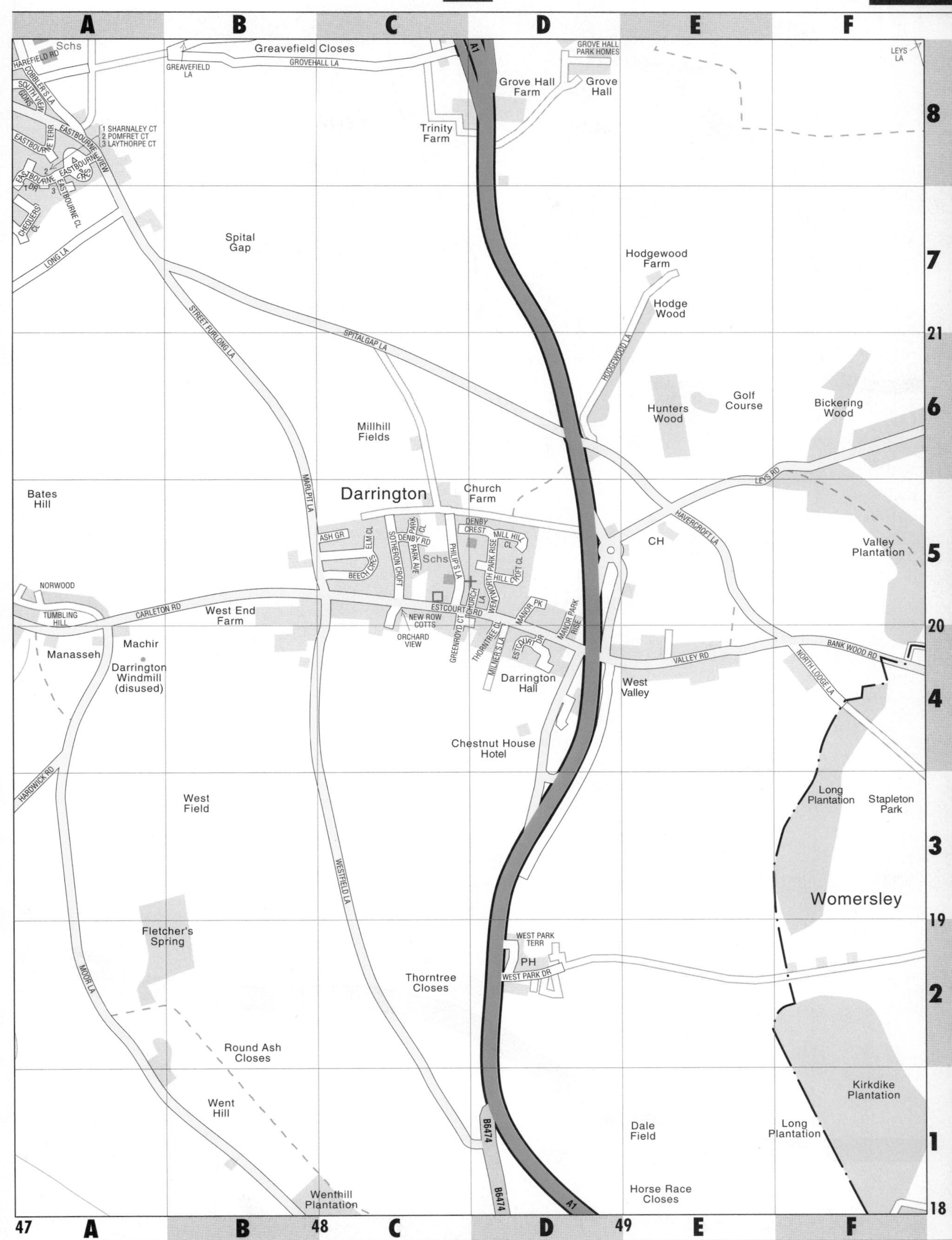

Schs
Greavefield Closes
GREAVEFIELD LA
GROVEHALL LA
GROVE HALL
PARK HOMES
LEYS LA

HAREFIELD RD
COBBLERS LA
SOUTHVIEW GDNS
EASTBOURNE TERR
EASTBOURNE VIEW
EASTBOURNE DR
EASTBOURNE CL
CHEQUERS CL
LONG LA

1 SHARNALEY CT
2 POMFRET CT
3 LAYTHORPE CT

Grove Hall
Farm
Grove
Hall

Trinity
Farm

Spital
Gap

Hodgewood
Farm

Hodge
Wood

SPITALGAP LA
STREET FURLONG LA

Millhill
Fields

Hunters
Wood

Golf
Course

Bickering
Wood

Bates
Hill

Darrington

Church
Farm

LEYS RD

Valley
Plantation

NORWOOD
TUMBLING
HILL

MARAPIT LA
ASH GR
ELM CL
BEECH CRS
SOTHERON CROFT
DENBY PK
DENBY RD
HIGH RD
DENBY CREST
MILL HILL CL
WENTWORTH PARK RISE
HILL CL
CROFT CL
PHILIP'S LA
Schs

HAVERCROFT LA
CH

CARLETON RD
West End
Farm

Machir
Manasseh
Darrington
Windmill
(disused)

GREENHOLD CL
THORNTREE CL
NEW ROW
COTTS
ORCHARD
VIEW
ESTCOURT RD
CHURCH RD
MILNERS LA
ESTCOURT DR

MANOR PK
MANOR PARK RISE

West
Valley

VALLEY RD
BANK WOOD RD
NORTH LODGE LA

HARDWICK RD

Darrington
Hall

Chestnut House
Hotel

Long
Plantation

Stapleton
Park

West
Field

WESTFIELD LA

Womersley

Fletcher's
Spring

MOOR LA

Thorntree
Closes

WEST PARK
TERR
PH
WEST PARK DR

Long
Plantation

Round Ash
Closes

Kirkdike
Plantation

Went
Hill

B6474

Dale
Field

Wenthill
Plantation

B6474
A1

Horse Race
Closes

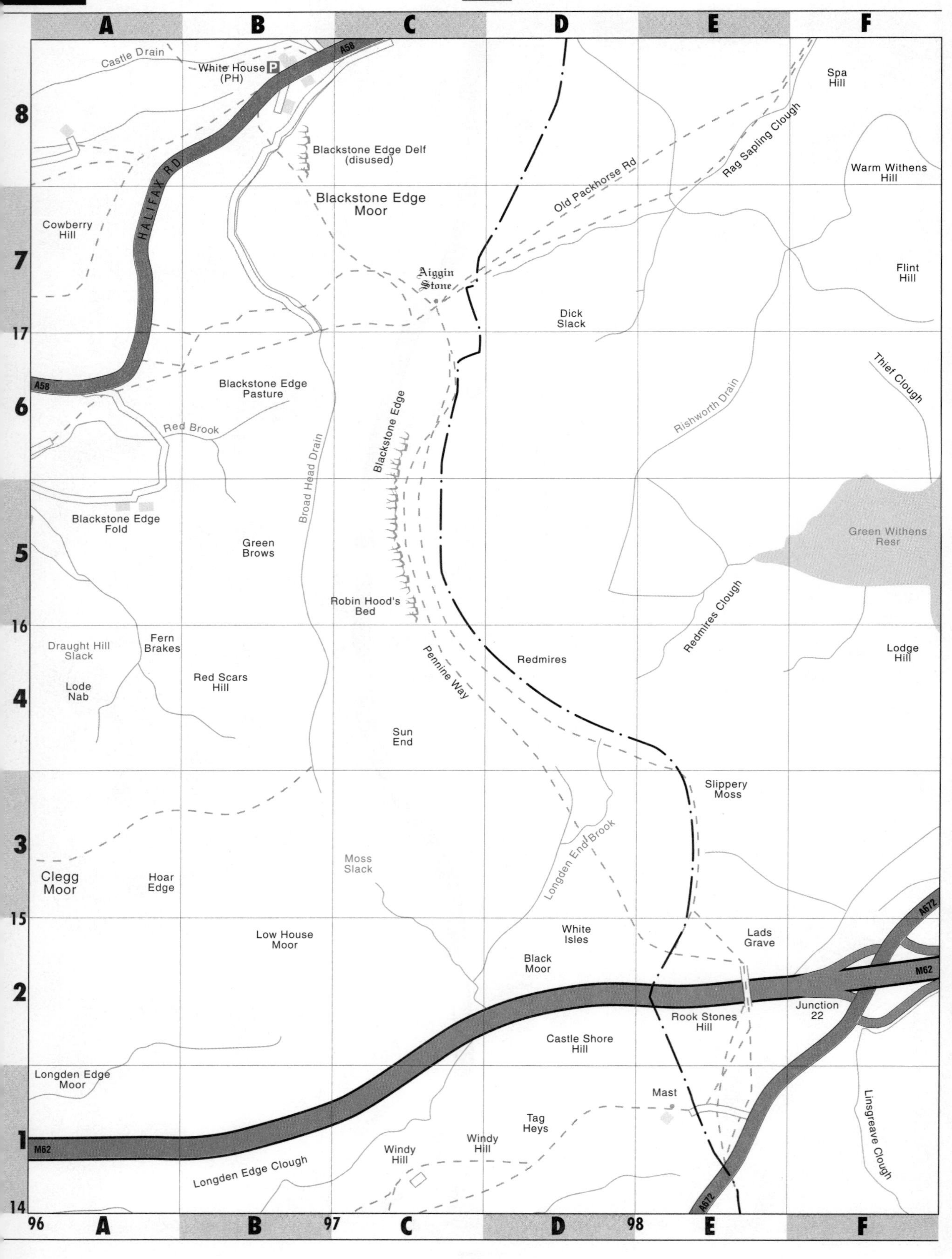

A   **B**   **C**   **D**   **E**   **F**

Castle Drain

White House (PH)

8

Blackstone Edge Delf (disused)

Blackstone Edge Moor

HALIFAX RD

Spa Hill

Warm Withens Hill

Cowberry Hill

7

Aiggin Stone

Flint Hill

Old Packhorse Rd

Rag Sapling Clough

17

Dick Slack

A58

Blackstone Edge Pasture

6

Red Brook

Blackstone Edge

Thief Clough

Broad Head Drain

Rishworth Drain

Blackstone Edge Fold

Green Brows

Green Withens Resr

5

Robin Hood's Bed

Redmires Clough

16

Draught Hill Slack

Fern Brakes

Lodge Hill

Lode Nab

Red Scars Hill

Pennine Way

Redmires

4

Sun End

Slippery Moss

Clegg Moor

Hoar Edge

3

Moss Slack

Longden End Brook

15

Low House Moor

White Isles

Lads Grave

A672

Longden Edge Moor

Black Moor

2

Rook Stones Hill

Junction 22

M62

Castle Shore Hill

Mast

M62

1

Tag Heys

Linsgreave Clough

Longden Edge Clough

Windy Hill

Windy Hill

A672

14

96   **A**   **B**   97   **C**   **D**   98   **E**   **F**

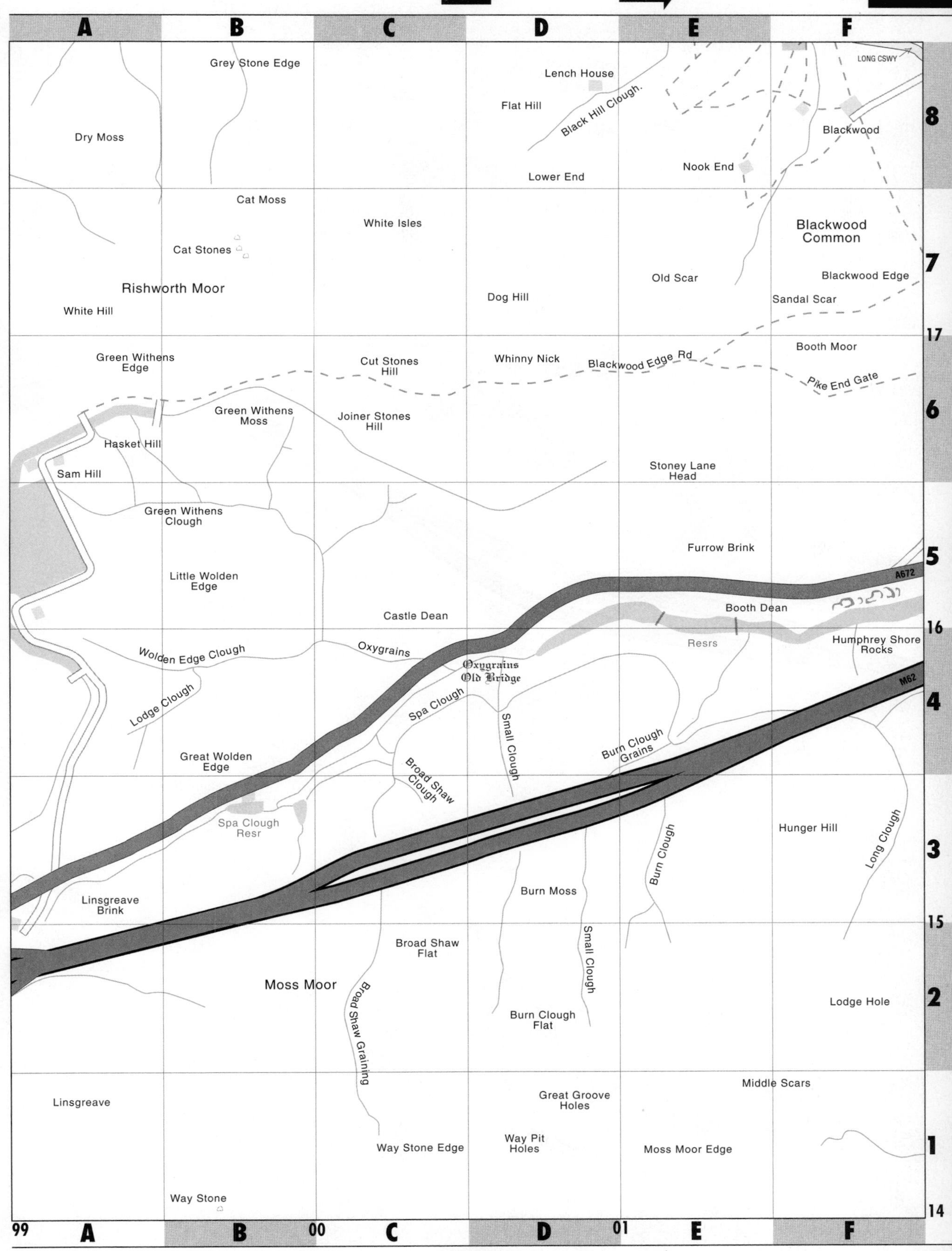

Grey Stone Edge

Lench House

Flat Hill

Black Hill Clough.

LONG CSWY

Blackwood

8

Dry Moss

Lower End

Nook End

Cat Moss

White Isles

Blackwood
Common

Cat Stones

Old Scar

Blackwood Edge

7

Rishworth Moor

Dog Hill

Sandal Scar

White Hill

17

Green Withens
Edge

Cut Stones
Hill

Whinny Nick

Blackwood Edge Rd

Booth Moor

Pike End Gate

Green Withens
Moss

Joiner Stones
Hill

6

Hasket Hill

Stoney Lane
Head

Sam Hill

Green Withens
Clough

Furrow Brink

5

Little Wolden
Edge

Booth Dean

A672

Castle Dean

Resrs

16

Wolden Edge Clough

Oxygrains

Oxygrains
Old Bridge

Humphrey Shore
Rocks

M62

Lodge Clough

Spa Clough

Small Clough

Burn Clough
Grains

4

Great Wolden
Edge

Broad Shaw
Clough

Burn Clough

Hunger Hill

Long Clough

3

Spa Clough
Resr

Burn Moss

Linsgreave
Brink

Small Clough

15

Broad Shaw
Flat

Moss Moor

Broad Shaw Graining

Burn Clough
Flat

Lodge Hole

2

Linsgreave

Great Groove
Holes

Middle Scars

Way Stone Edge

Way Pit
Holes

Moss Moor Edge

1

Way Stone

14

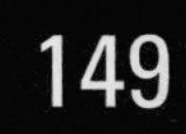

149
132

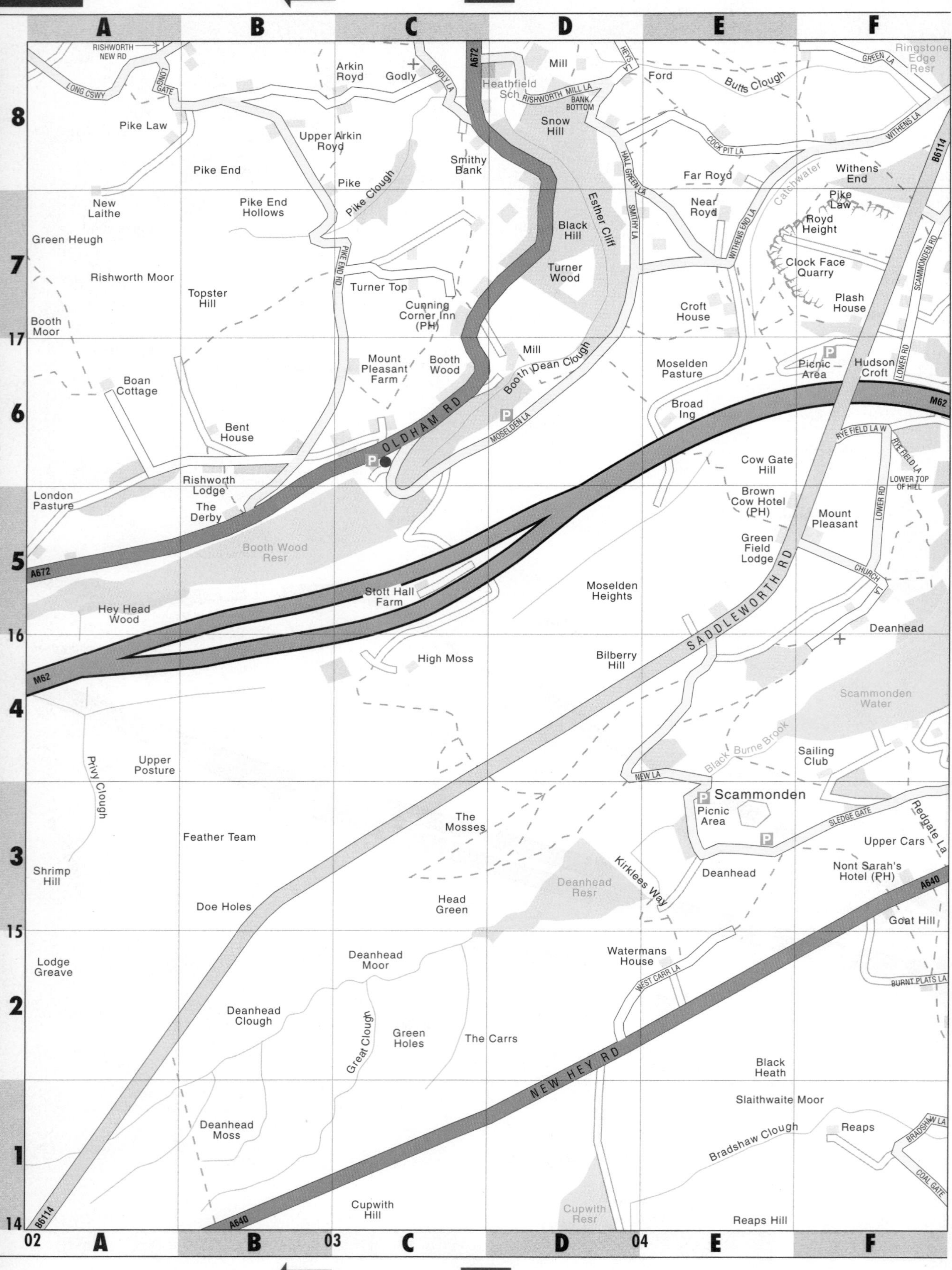
A
B
C
D
E
F
RISHWORTH NEW RD
LONG CSWY
GATE
Arkin Royd
Godly
GODLY LA
A672
Heathfield Sch
Mill
HEYS LA
Ford
Butts Clough
GREEN LA
Ringstone Edge Resr
RISHWORTH MILL LA
BANK BOTTOM
Snow Hill
Pike Law
Upper Arkin Royd
COCK PIT LA
WITHENS LA
B6114
Smithy Bank
Pike End
Pike
Pike Clough
HALL GREEN LA
Far Royd
Catchwater
Withens End
New Laithe
Pike End Hollows
Esther Cliff
SMITHY LA
Near Royd
WITHENS END LA
Pike Law
Royd Height
Green Heugh
Black Hill
Clock Face Quarry
PIKE END RD
Rishworth Moor
Turner Wood
SCAMMONDEN RD
Turner Top
Topster Hill
Cunning Corner Inn (PH)
Croft House
Plash House
Booth Moor
Mill
Booth Dean Clough
Moselden Pasture
Picnic Area
Hudson Croft
LOWER RD
Mount Pleasant Farm
Booth Wood
Boan Cottage
OLDHAM RD
Broad Ing
M62
MOSELDEN LA
Bent House
RYE FIELD LA W
RYE FIELD LA
Cow Gate Hill
LOWER TOP OF HILL
Rishworth Lodge
Brown Cow Hotel (PH)
London Pasture
The Derby
Mount Pleasant
LOWER RD
Green Field Lodge
Booth Wood Resr
A672
CHURCH LA
Moselden Heights
Stott Hall Farm
Hey Head Wood
SADDLEWORTH RD
Deanhead
Bilberry Hill
High Moss
M62
Scammonden Water
Black Burne Brook
Sailing Club
Upper Posture
Privy Clough
NEW LA
Scammonden
Picnic Area
Redgate La
SLEDGE GATE
The Mosses
Feather Team
Upper Cars
Shrimp Hill
Deanhead
Kirklees Way
Nont Sarah's Hotel (PH)
Deanhead Resr
A640
Head Green
Doe Holes
Goat Hill
Deanhead Moor
Watermans House
Lodge Greave
WEST CARR LA
BURNT PLATS LA
Deanhead Clough
Green Holes
Great Clough
The Carrs
NEW HEY RD
Black Heath
Slaithwaite Moor
Deanhead Moss
Reaps
BRADSHAW LA
Bradshaw Clough
COAL GATE
Cupwith Hill
Cupwith Resr
Reaps Hill
B6114
A640
8
7
17
6
5
16
4
3
15
2
1
14
02
03
04

149
168

133
152

A
B
C
D
E
F
8
7
17
6
5
16
4
3
15
2
1
14
05
06
07
SADDLEWORTH RD
B6114
WITHENS LA
MOOR FIELD RD
Banquet House
Springfield
FIRTH HOUSE LA
Wood Head
SCAMMONDEN RD
Upper Wood House
Upper Firth House Mills
DEAN HOUSE LA
New Manor House
New Peel Castle
BROOM HILL RD
Crow Edge
Prospect House
FOREST HILL RD
Wilderness Farm
PROSPECT PL
Stainland Moor
Lower Nook
Dean House
Vicars Lot
MARSDEN GATE
The Commercial (PH)
A640
WINTER HILL 1
HORSE POND LA 2
ROUND INGS RD 3
M62
ROUND INGS RD
Black Brook
Upper Hey House
Hey House Clough
Red Lane Dike
Hollin Hey
Hey Wood
Lower Moulson Place
Lower Hey House
Leyfield Farm
Outlane Moor
Hey Clough
Hey Croft Clough
Han Head
Heycroft Farm
HEY LA
Valve Tower
Owlet Edge
Round Hill
Low Platt
CHAPEL HILL LA
LOW PLATT LA
Wholestone Moor
Wholestone Hill
CROFT HOUSE RD
Scammonden Water
CAMP HILL
Lower Royal George (PH)
PINFOLD LA
GREEN SLACKS LA
Spring Royd
Croft House Moss
Quebec
Rocking Stone Hill
Delph Hill
Hardenby Farm
NEW HEY RD
WOODHOUSE COTTS
Rocking Stones
ROCHDALE RD
CAUSEWAY
O'COT LA
O'Cot
POLE GATE BRANCH
Pole Moor
WALLER CLOUGH RD
SLEDGE GATE
POLE GATE
MELLOR BRK
Pleasant Pasture
The Sun
Nab
WORTS HILL LA
WORTS HILL SIDE
Far Worts Hill
CRIMEA LA
New Hey Carrs
Carr House
Kirklees Way
Mast
HIGHFIELD RD
Moorside Edge
Worts Hill
GREAT BEN LA
BACK O' WALL
Poor House
Mast
Bunkers Hill
Heath
Onely House
Goat Hill Moor
West End
Laund
Stonyfield
ROCK LA
BURNT PLATS LA
Barrett
MOOR SIDE LA
Cartgate Foot
LAUND RD
TIDING FIELD LA
SURAT RD
INTAKE RD
Gosling Green
Wilberlee
CASTLE LA
MEAL HILL LA
MEAL HILL
Colne Valley Circular Walk
AINLEY PL
Goat Hill
Wilberlee County Primary School
Castle
PIGHILL TOP LA
PICKLE TOP
SANDWELL ST 1
WAVERLEY ST 2
HILL TOP FOLD 3
HILL TOP RD 4
CRIMBLE BANK 5
STATION RD 6
TYAS LA
Birks
HEYS LA
BRADSHAW LA
CLOUGH HOUSE
Heys
Hill Top
MEADOW LA
HAWTHORN RD
CLOUGH HOUSE LA
CASTLE LA
Bradshaw
Merry Dale
ING HEAD
LONGROYD CRES
LONGLANDS AVE
MONA ST
Merry Dale Clough
LONGLANDS RD
PRETORIA ST
LORD ST
OLNEY ST
Scout Wood
Clough House Bridge
ROYD ST
NETHEREND RD
GROVE ST
UNION ST
WOOD ST
SCOUT LA
NORTH LA
LEWISHAM RD 7
CARR LA 8
CHURCHWOOD CL 9
BANK GATE
NEW CL
FOLLINGWORTH LA
Slaithwaite Resr
TWO GATES
Mills
Slaithwaite Sta
COAL GATE
Upper House Farm
NEW CLOSE LA
Follingworth
Lower Holme
HOLME LA
BLAKEHOLME CL
NABBS LA
IVY MOUNT
Sch
Sch

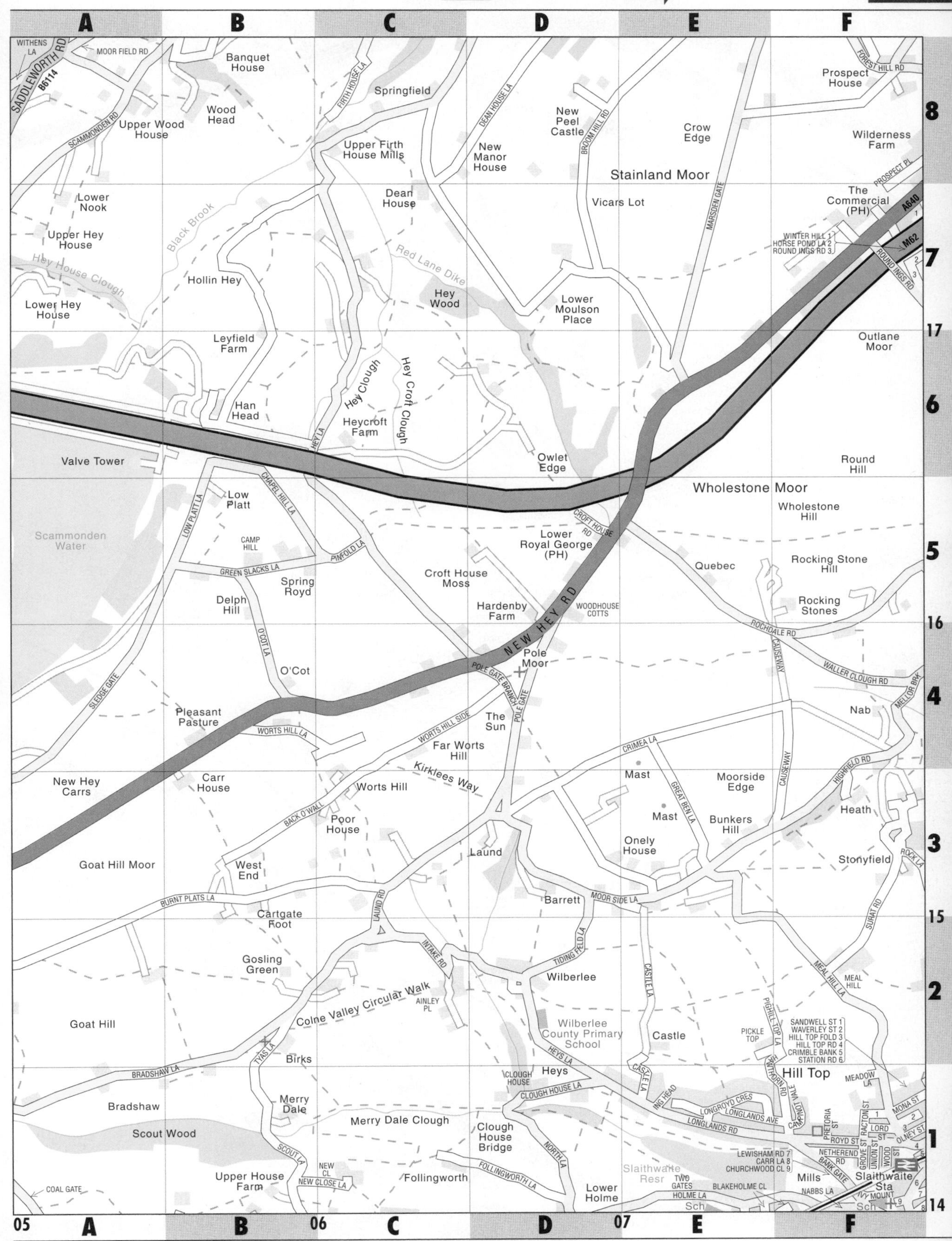

169
152

151
134

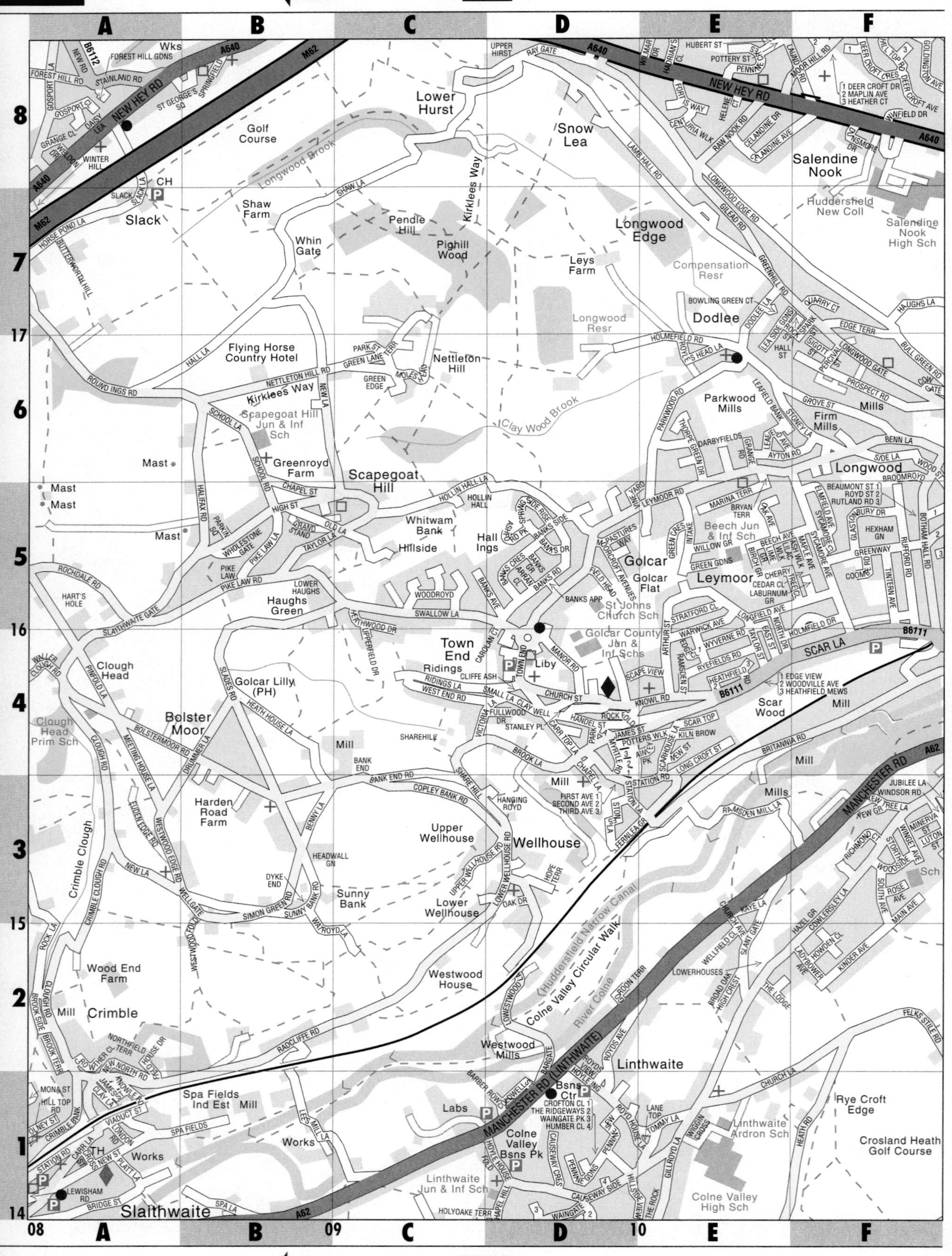
A
B
C
D
E
F
8
7
17
6
5
16
4
3
15
2
1
14
08
09
10
M62
A640
NEW HEY RD
B6112
FOREST HILL GDNS
FOREST HILL RD
STAINLAND RD
Wks
GOSPORT LA
ST GEORGE'S SQ
SPRINGFIELD
GRANGE CL
DAISY LEA
WINTER HILL
SLACK
CH
Slack
HORSE POND LA
BUTTERNORTH HILL
Golf Course
Longwood Brook
Shaw Farm
SHAW LA
Whin Gate
Lower Hurst
UPPER HIRST
RAY GATE
Pendle Hill
Pighill Wood
Kirklees Way
Snow Lea
LAMB HALL RD
Longwood Edge
Leys Farm
Compensation Resr
Longwood Resr
HUBERT ST
POTTERY ST
PENNINE CL
MOOR HILL RD
1 DEER CROFT DR
2 MAPLIN AVE
3 HEATHER CST
DEER CROFT CRES
DEER CROFT AVE
GOLDINGTON AVE
FORTIS WAY
HELENE CT
RAW NOOK RD
CELANDINE DR
CELANDINE AVE
Salendine Nook
Huddersfield New Coll
Salendine Nook High Sch
LONGWOOD EDGE RD
GILEAD RD
GREENHILL RD
BOWLING GREEN CT
Dodlee
DODLEE LA
QUARRY CT
HAUGHS LA
EDGE TERR
BULL GREEN RD
HOLMEFIELD RD
HALL ST
LONGWOOD GATE
PROSPECT RD
COW GATE
Mills
Flying Horse Country Hotel
HALL LA
ROUND INGS RD
NETTLETON HILL RD
GREEN LANE TERR
PARK CT
GREEN EDGE
MOLES HEAD
Nettleton Hill
Kirklees Way
NEW LA
SCHOOL LA
Scapegoat Hill Jun & Inf Sch
Clay Wood Brook
Parkwood Mills
PARKWOOD RD
THORPE GREEN DR
DARBYFIELDS
LEAFIELD BANK
STONEY LA
GROVE ST
Firm Mills
BENN LA
AYTON RD
SIDE LA
Longwood
WOOD ST
BROOMROYD
Mast
Greenroyd Farm
SCHOOL RD
CHAPEL ST
Scapegoat Hill
HOLLIN HALL LA
HOLLIN HALL
HALIFAX RD
HIGH ST
PARKIN SQ
WHOLESTONE GATE
GRAND STAND
OLD LA
TAYLOR LA
PIKE LAW LA
Whitwam Bank
Hillside
Hall Ings
SPRING SIDE RISE
BANKS SIDE
BANKS DR
BANKS CRES
BANKS GR
BANKS RD
BANKS AVE
LEYMOOR RD
MARINA TERR
BRYAN TERR
Beech Jun & Inf Sch
WILLOW GR
GREEN GDNS
Golcar
Golcar Flat
Leymoor
CHERRY TREE CL
CEDAR CL
LABURNUM GR
BEAUMONT ST 1
ROYD ST 2
RUTLAND RD 3
HEXHAM GN
GREENWAY
COOMBE RD
TINTERN AVE
RUFFORD RD
BOTHAM HALL RD
Mast
PIKE LAW
PIKE LAW RD
ROCHDALE RD
HART'S HOLE
LOWER HAUGHS
Haughs Green
WOODROYD
SWALLOW LA
BANKS APP
St Johns Church Sch
Golcar County Jun & Inf Schs
STRATFORD CL
WARWICK AVE
WYVERNE RD
RYEFIELDS RD
HEATHFIELD RD
HOLMFIELD DR
SCAR LA
B6111
1 EDGE VIEW
2 WOODVILLE AVE
3 HEATHFIELD MEWS
SLAITHWAITE GATE
HEATHWOOD DR
UPPERFIELD DR
Town End
Ridings
CLIFFE ASH
Liby
MANOR RD
CHURCH ST
SCAPE VIEW
KNOWL RD
Scar Wood
Mill
Clough Head
WALLER CLOUGH RD
PINFOLD LA
Golcar Lilly (PH)
SLADES RD
HEATH HOUSE LA
RIDINGS LA
WEST END RD
SMALL LA
CLAY WELL
FULLWOOD DR
STANLEY PL
VICTORIA LA
HANDEL ST
ROCK FOLD
JAMES ST
POTTERS WLK
KILN BROW
SCAR TOP
NEW ST
LONG CROFT ST
BRITANNIA RD
Clough Head Prim Sch
Bolster Moor
BOLSTERMOOR RD
DRUMMER LA
MEETING HOUSE LA
CLOUGH RD
Mill
SHAREHILL
BANK END
BANK END RD
COPLEY BANK RD
SHARE HILL
BROOK LA
CARR TOP LA
CHAPEL LA
STATION RD
Mill
FIRST AVE 1
SECOND AVE 2
THIRD AVE 3
STATION LA
A62
MANCHESTER RD
JUBILEE LA
WINDSOR RD
NEW GR
TREE LA
MINERVA ST
LUTON ST
Mill
Mills
RAMSDEN MILL LA
Harden Road Farm
EUDEN EDGE RD
WESTWOOD EDGE RD
BENNY LA
HANGING ROYD
Upper Wellhouse
Wellhouse
Crimble Clough
CRIMBLE CLOUGH RD
NEW LA
HEADWALL GN
DYKE END
Sunny Bank
UPPER WELLHOUSE RD
LOWER WELLHOUSE RD
HOPE TERR
Lower Wellhouse
OAK DR
RICHMOND CL
WINGET AVE
STORTHS RD
WOODSIDE RD
Sch
SOUTH AVE
ROSE AVE
MAIN AVE
WELLGATE
SIMON GREEN RD
SUNNY BANK RD
WAYROYD LA
WESTWOOD FOLD
ROCK LA
Huddersfield Narrow Canal
Colne Valley Circular Walk
CHURCH AVE
KAYE LA
SLANT GATE
HAZEL GR
COWLERSLEY LA
HOWDEN CL
LADYBOWER AVE
KINDER AVE
Wood End Farm
Westwood House
LOWERHOUSES
WELLFIELD CL
BROAD OAK
HIGH CREST
THE LODGE
Mill
Crimble
CLOUGH RD
BROOK SIDE
BROOK TERR
LOWESTWOOD LA
River Colne
GORDON TERR
FELKS STILE RD
NORTHFIELD TERR
CROWTHER CL
HOUSE DR
RADCLIFFE RD
Westwood Mills
BARGATE
ROYDS AVE
Linthwaite
MONA ST
HILL TOP RD
NORTH RD
JAMES ST
CLAY LA
Spa Fields Ind Est
Mill
BARBER ROW
CROWELL CL
Bsns Ctr
MANCHESTER RD (LINTHWAITE)
HOYLE ING
CROFTON CL 1
THE RIDGEWAYS 2
WAINGATE PK 3
HUMBER CL 4
LANE TOP
TOMMY LA
CHURCH LA
Rye Croft Edge
OLNEY ST
CRIMBLE BANK
VIADUCT ST
SPA FIELDS
LEE'S MILL LA
Labs
ROYD HOUSE LA
Linthwaite Ardron Sch
HEATH RD
STATION RD
CARR LA
TH
NEW ST
PLATT LA
Works
Works
Colne Valley Bsns Pk
HOYLE HOUSE FOLD
CAUSEWAY CRES
PENNINE GDNS
GILLROYD LA
WIGGIN CROSS
Crosland Heath Golf Course
LEWISHAM RD
BRIDGE ST
Slaithwaite
SPA LA
Linthwaite Jun & Inf Sch
CHAPEL HILL
HOLYOAKE TERR
WAINGATE
CAUSEWAY SIDE
HILLSIDE VIEW
THE ROCK
Colne Valley High Sch

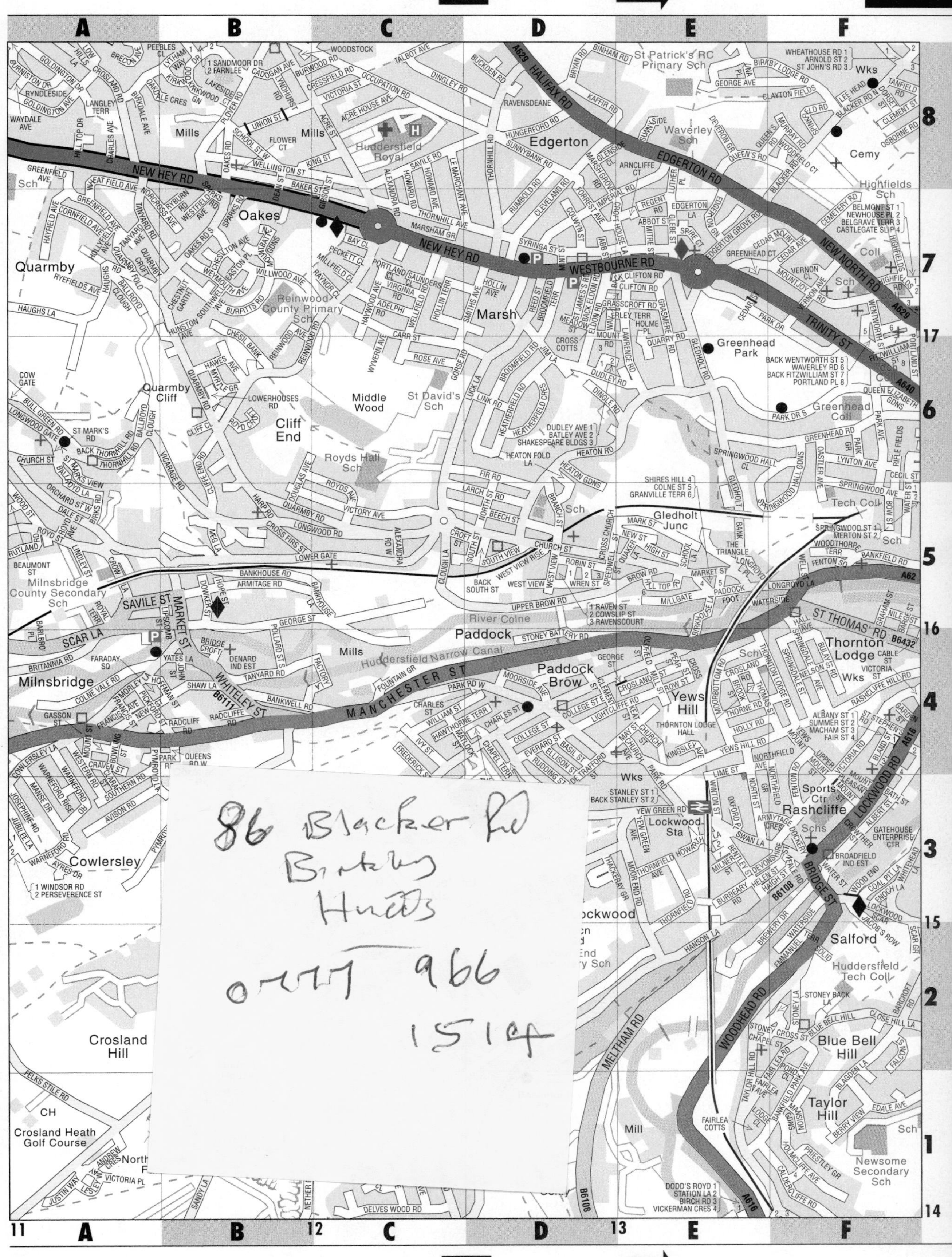

Handwritten note:
86 Blacker Rd
Birkby
Hudds

01777 966
1514

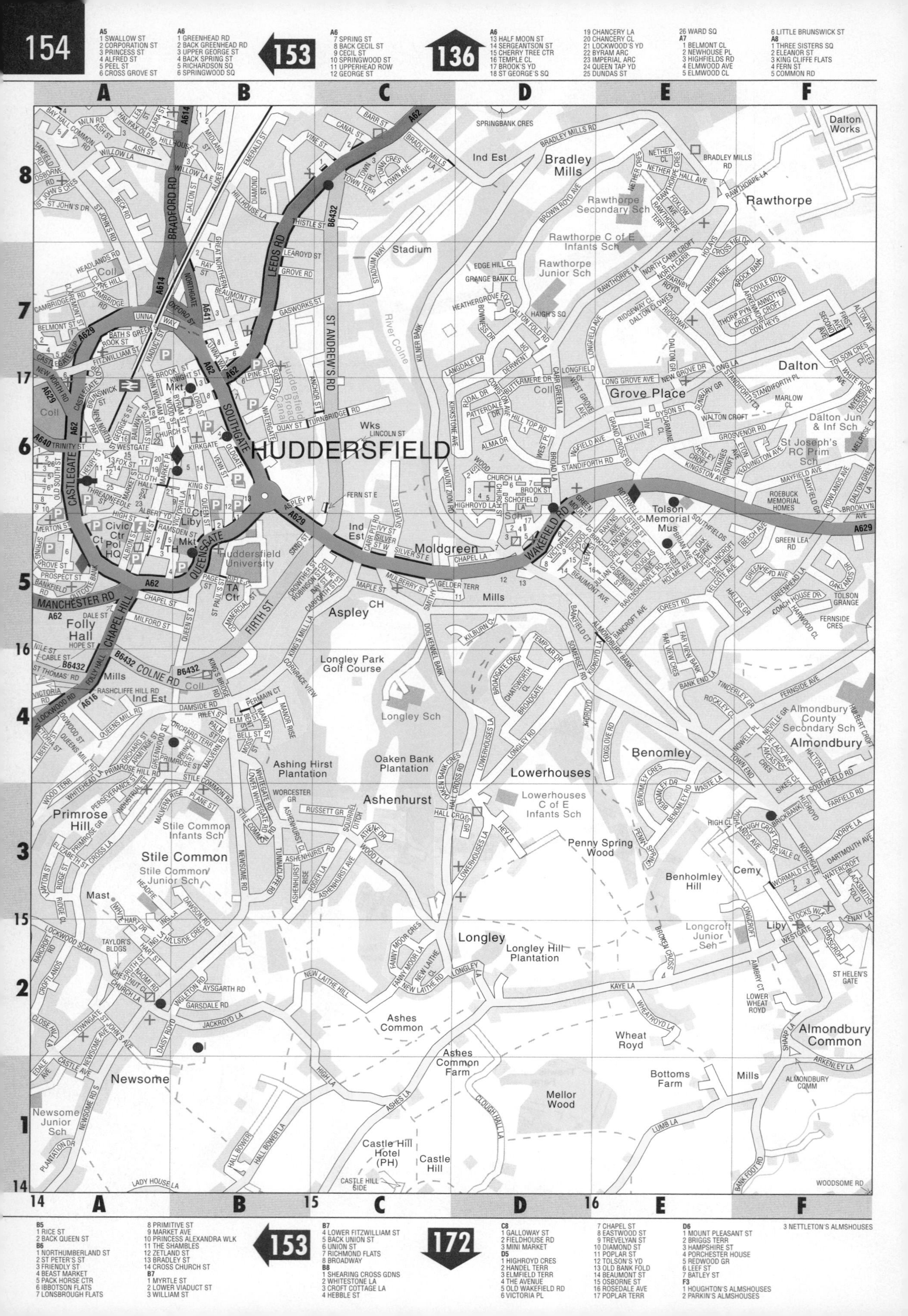
154
A5
1 SWALLOW ST
2 CORPORATION ST
3 PRINCESS ST
4 ALFRED ST
5 PEEL ST
6 CROSS GROVE ST
A6
1 GREENHEAD RD
2 BACK GREENHEAD RD
3 UPPER GEORGE ST
4 BACK SPRING ST
5 RICHARDSON SQ
6 SPRINGWOOD SQ
153
A6
7 SPRING ST
8 BACK CECIL ST
9 CECIL ST
10 SPRINGWOOD ST
11 UPPERHEAD ROW
12 GEORGE ST
136
A6
13 HALF MOON ST
14 SERGEANTSON ST
15 CHERRY TREE CTR
16 TEMPLE CL
17 BROOK'S YD
18 ST GEORGE'S SQ
19 CHANCERY LA
20 CHANCERY CL
21 LOCKWOOD'S YD
22 BYRAM ARC
23 IMPERIAL ARC
24 QUEEN TAP YD
25 DUNDAS ST
26 WARD SQ
A7
1 BELMONT CL
2 NEWHOUSE PL
3 HIGHFIELDS RD
4 ELMWOOD AVE
5 ELMWOOD CL
6 LITTLE BRUNSWICK ST
A8
1 THREE SISTERS SQ
2 ELEANOR ST
3 KING CLIFFE FLATS
4 FERN ST
5 COMMON RD
A
B
C
D
E
F
8
7
17
6
5
16
4
3
15
2
1
14
HUDDERSFIELD
Bradley Mills
Ind Est
Dalton Works
Rawthorpe
Rawthorpe Secondary Sch
Rawthorpe C of E Infants Sch
Rawthorpe Junior Sch
Stadium
River Colne
Huddersfield Broad Canal
Dalton
Grove Place
Coll
Dalton Jun & Inf Sch
St Joseph's RC Prim Sch
Roebuck Memorial Homes
Tolson Memorial Mus
Moldgreen
Mills
Aspley
Wks
Mkt
Civic Ctr
Pol HQ
Ct
Liby
TH
Huddersfield University
TA Ctr
Folly Hall
Longley Park Golf Course
Longley Sch
Oaken Bank Plantation
Ashing Hirst Plantation
Ashenhurst
Lowerhouses
Lowerhouses C of E Infants Sch
Benomley
Almondbury County Secondary Sch
Almondbury
Penny Spring Wood
Benholmley Hill
Cemy
Longcroft Junior Sch
Primrose Hill
Stile Common Infants Sch
Stile Common
Stile Common Junior Sch
Mast
Longley
Longley Hill Plantation
Ashes Common
Ashes Common Farm
Wheat Royd
Bottoms Farm
Almondbury Common
Newsome
Newsome Junior Sch
Mellor Wood
Castle Hill Hotel (PH)
Castle Hill
A62
A629
A614
A641
A640
A616
B6432
MANCHESTER RD
CASTLEGATE
CHAPEL HILL
BRADFORD RD
LEEDS RD
ST ANDREW'S RD
SOUTHGATE
QUEENSGATE
WAKEFIELD RD
FIRTH ST
COLNE RD
WESTGATE
KIRKGATE
NEW NORTH RD
TRINITY ST
LOCKWOOD RD
DOG KENNEL BANK
LOWERHOUSES LA
KAYE LA
LUMB LA
WOODSOME RD
LADY HOUSE LA
CASTLE HILL SIDE
14
15
16
B5
1 RICE ST
2 BACK QUEEN ST
B6
1 NORTHUMBERLAND ST
2 ST PETER'S ST
3 FRIENDLY ST
4 BEAST MARKET
5 PACK HORSE CTR
6 IBBOTSON FLATS
7 LONSBROUGH FLATS
8 PRIMITIVE ST
9 MARKET AVE
10 PRINCESS ALEXANDRA WLK
11 THE SHAMBLES
12 ZETLAND ST
13 BRADLEY ST
14 CROSS CHURCH ST
B7
1 MYRTLE ST
2 LOWER VIADUCT ST
3 WILLIAM ST
153
B7
4 LOWER FITZWILLIAM ST
5 BACK UNION ST
6 UNION ST
7 RICHMOND FLATS
8 BROADWAY
B8
1 SHEARING CROSS GDNS
2 WHITESTONE LA
3 CROFT COTTAGE LA
4 HEBBLE ST
172
C8
1 GALLOWAY ST
2 FIELDHOUSE RD
3 MINI MARKET
D5
1 HIGHROYD CRES
2 HANDEL TERR
3 ELMFIELD TERR
4 THE AVENUE
5 OLD WAKEFIELD RD
6 VICTORIA PL
7 CHAPEL ST
8 EASTWOOD ST
9 TREVELYAN ST
10 DIAMOND ST
11 POPLAR ST
12 TOLSON'S YD
13 OLD BANK FOLD
14 BEAUMONT ST
15 OSBORNE ST
16 ROSEDALE AVE
17 POPLAR TERR
D6
1 MOUNT PLEASANT ST
2 BRIGGS TERR
3 HAMPSHIRE ST
4 PORCHESTER HOUSE
5 REDWOOD GR
6 LEEF ST
7 BATLEY ST
F3
1 HOUGHTON'S ALMSHOUSES
2 PARKIN'S ALMSHOUSES
3 NETTLETON'S ALMSHOUSES

155

137

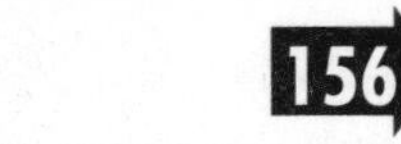

156

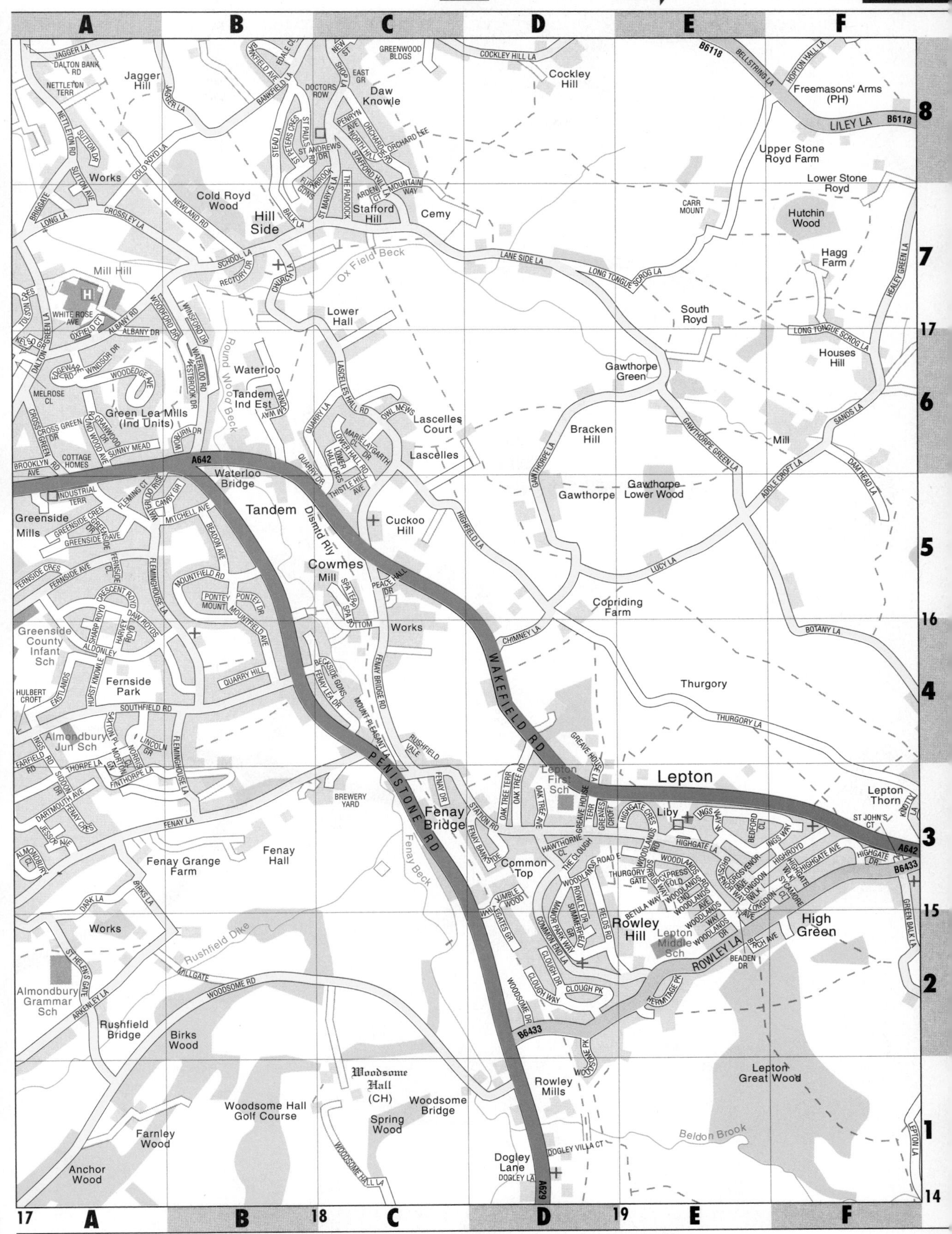

A
B
C
D
E
F
8
7
6
5
4
3
2
1
17
16
15
14
18
19
Jagger Hill
Daw Knowle
Cockley Hill
Freemasons' Arms (PH)
LILEY LA
B6118
Upper Stone Royd Farm
Lower Stone Royd
Works
Cold Royd Wood
Hill Side
Stafford Hill
Cemy
Carr Mount
Hutchin Wood
Hagg Farm
Mill Hill
Ox Field Beck
LANE SIDE LA
LONG TONGUE SCROG LA
Lower Hall
South Royd
Houses Hill
Waterloo
Tandem Ind Est
Gawthorpe Green
Green Lea Mills (Ind Units)
Lascelles Court
Lascelles
Bracken Hill
Mill
Round Wood Beck
A642
Waterloo Bridge
Tandem
Dismtd Rly
Gawthorpe
Gawthorpe Lower Wood
Greenside Mills
Cuckoo Hill
Cowmes Mill
LUCY LA
Copriding Farm
Works
Greenside County Infant Sch
Fernside Park
Thurgory
WAKEFIELD RD
PENISTONE RD
Almondbury Jun Sch
Lepton
Lepton First Sch
Lepton Thorn
Liby
Brewery Yard
Fenay Bridge
Fenay Hall
Fenay Grange Farm
Common Top
Fenay Beck
Rowley Hill
Lepton Middle Sch
High Green
ROWLEY LA
B6433
Works
Rushfield Dike
Almondbury Grammar Sch
Rushfield Bridge
Birks Wood
Rowley Mills
Lepton Great Wood
Woodsome Hall (CH)
Woodsome Hall Golf Course
Woodsome Bridge
Spring Wood
Farnley Wood
Beldon Brook
Anchor Wood
Dogley Lane
A629

155
138

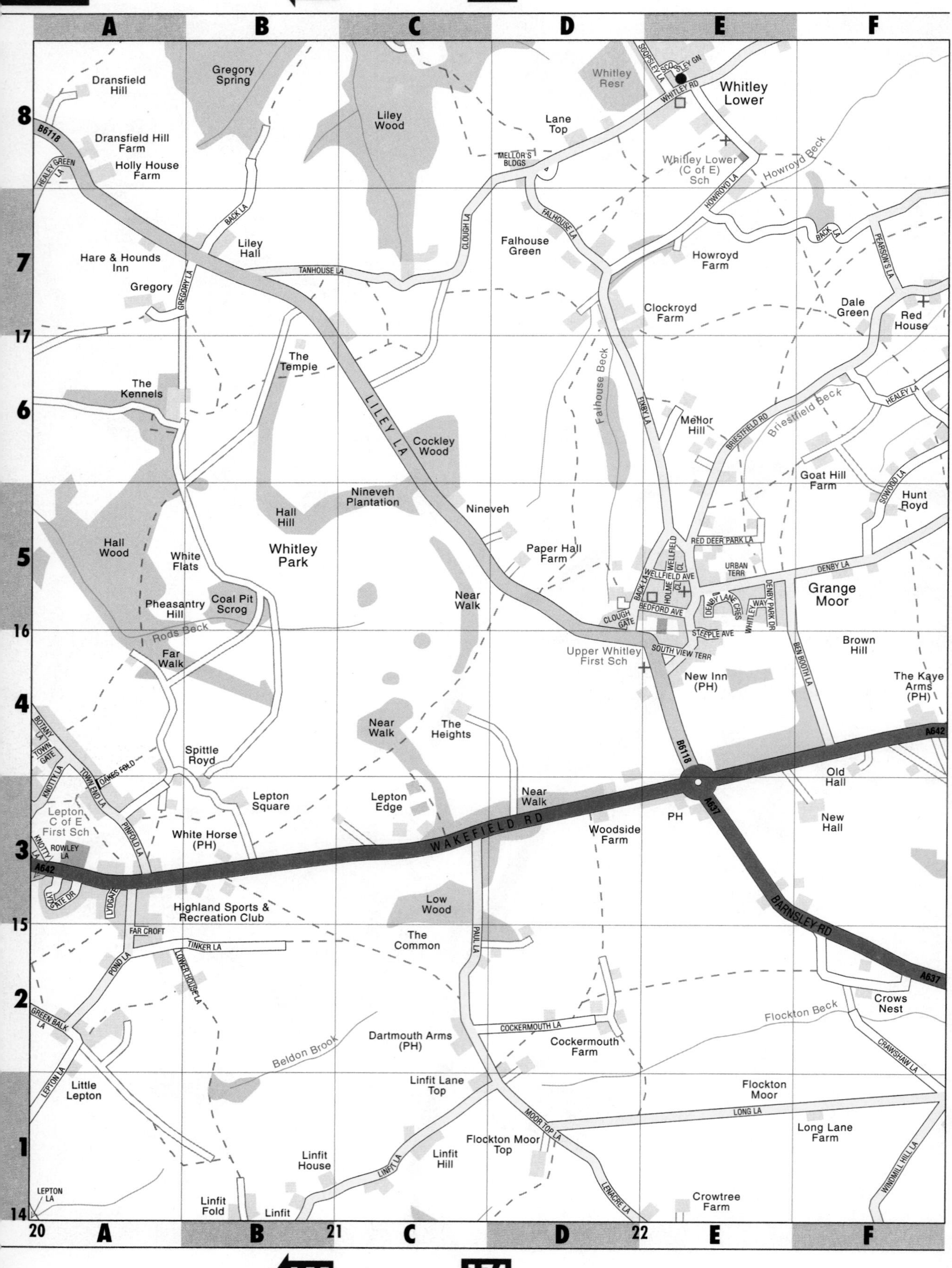
A
B
C
D
E
F
8
7
17
6
5
16
4
3
15
2
1
14
20
21
22
Dransfield Hill
Gregory Spring
Liley Wood
Whitley Resr
Whitley Lower
Lane Top
Dransfield Hill Farm
Holly House Farm
MELLOR'S BLDGS
Whitley Lower (C of E) Sch
Howroyd Beck
B6118
HEALEY GREEN LA
BACK LA
CLOUGH LA
FALHOUSE LA
HOWROYD LA
WHITLEY RD
SCOPSLEY LA
SCOPSLEY GN
Liley Hall
Hare & Hounds Inn
Gregory
GREGORY LA
TANHOUSE LA
Falhouse Green
Howroyd Farm
PEARSON'S LA
Clockroyd Farm
Dale Green
Red House
The Temple
The Kennels
Falhouse Beck
FINBY LA
LILEY LA
Cockley Wood
Mellor Hill
BRIESTFIELD RD
Briestfield Beck
HEALEY LA
Goat Hill Farm
SOWOOD LA
Hunt Royd
Nineveh Plantation
Nineveh
Hall Hill
Hall Wood
White Flats
Whitley Park
Paper Hall Farm
RED DEER PARK LA
WELLFIELD AVE
URBAN TERR
DENBY LA
Grange Moor
Near Walk
Pheasantry Hill
Coal Pit Scrog
Rods Beck
CLOUGH GATE
BEDFORD AVE
STEEPLE AVE
DENBY LANE CRES
DENBY PARK DR
WHITLEY WAY
SOUTH VIEW TERR
Upper Whitley First Sch
Brown Hill
Far Walk
New Inn (PH)
BEN BOOTH LA
The Kaye Arms (PH)
Near Walk
The Heights
A642
BOTANY LA
TOWN GATE
KNOTTY LA
DAMES FOLD
TOWN END LA
Spittle Royd
Old Hall
Lepton Square
Lepton Edge
Near Walk
Lepton C of E First Sch
PINFOLD LA
WAKEFIELD RD
PH
New Hall
A637
ROWLEY LA
White Horse (PH)
Woodside Farm
LYDGATE DR
LYDGATE
Highland Sports & Recreation Club
Low Wood
BARNSLEY RD
FAR CROFT
TINKER LA
The Common
PAUL LA
POND LA
LOWER HOUSE LA
GREEN BALK LA
Crows Nest
Flockton Beck
COCKERMOUTH LA
Dartmouth Arms (PH)
Beldon Brook
Cockermouth Farm
CRAWSHAW LA
LEPTON LA
Little Lepton
Linfit Lane Top
Flockton Moor
LONG LA
MOOR TOP LA
Long Lane Farm
Flockton Moor Top
Linfit House
Linfit Hill
LINFIT LA
WINDMILL HILL LA
LENACRE LA
LEPTON LA
Linfit Fold
Linfit
Crowtree Farm

155
174

139
158

A
B
C
D
E
F
8
7
6
5
4
3
2
1
17
16
15
14
23
24
25
Edge Rd
Poplar Farm
Smithy Brook
Briestfield Rd
Judy Haigh La
Mug Mill La
Carr La
Carr Farm
Ash-Lea
Blackerhill Farm
Shoulder of Mutton Inn (PH)
Back La
Briestfield
Mug Mill Farm
Haigh House
Bank House Farm
Lower Dimpledale
Upper Dimpledale
Briggs La
Healey Farm
Healey La
Wood La
Cemy
Hepper Wood
Timmins Shrogg
Lower Denby Farm
Sowood La
Denby La
Birk Wood
A642
Green La
Crossfield Ct
Overton
Wood Mount
Highfield Cres
Denby Wood
New Rd
Mus
Old Rd
Smithy La
Upper Denby
Woodlands Farm
The Reindeer (PH)
Kirklees Way
Grange Wood
Hayne La
Low Farm
Denby Grange La
Pit Hill Plantation
Grange La
New Hall Farm
Denby Grange
Grange Park
Fish Ponds Plantation
New Hall App
The Rookery
Wakefield Rd
The Rough
Hardcastle La
Dial Wood
HM Prison & Young Offender Inst
New Hall La
New Hall Way
Manor Dr
Lady Beatrice Plantation
Hawthorne Cl
Ash Brow
Rutland Rd
Park Side
Hill Top Rd
Hazel Gr
Chessington Dr
PH
Flockton Green
Barnsley Rd
Bar La
A637
Flockton (C of E) First Sch
Pinfold Cl
Doctor La
Mill La
Flockton
Flockton Mill Farm
Pinfold La
Mill Beck
Haigh La
Common End
Highfield House
Common La
Kirkby Wood
Mouse House Dike
Six Lanes End
Epley Wood
Furnace Grange
Crawshaw La
Clough Rd
Clough Dike
Bank Wood Beck
Kirkby La
Kirkby Grange Farm

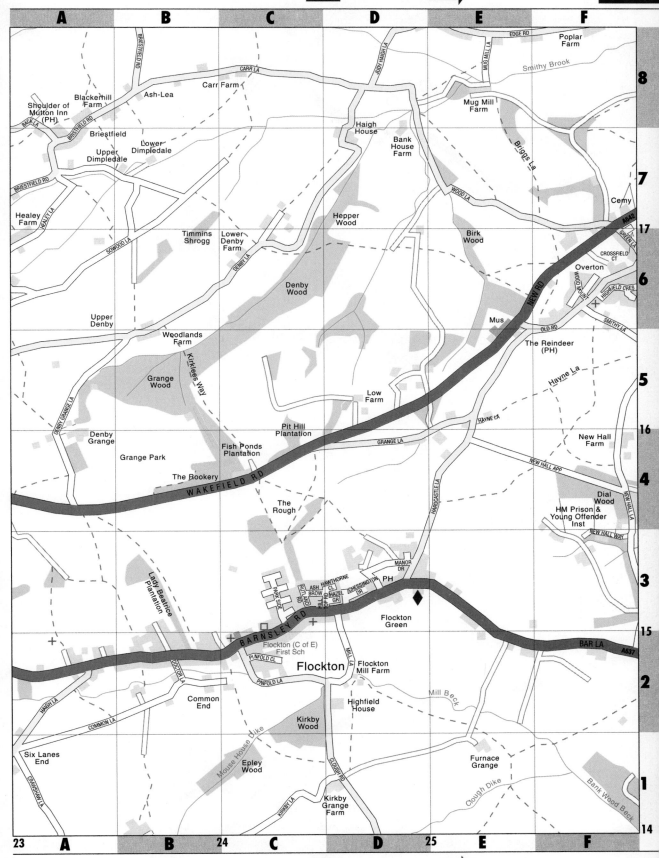

157
140

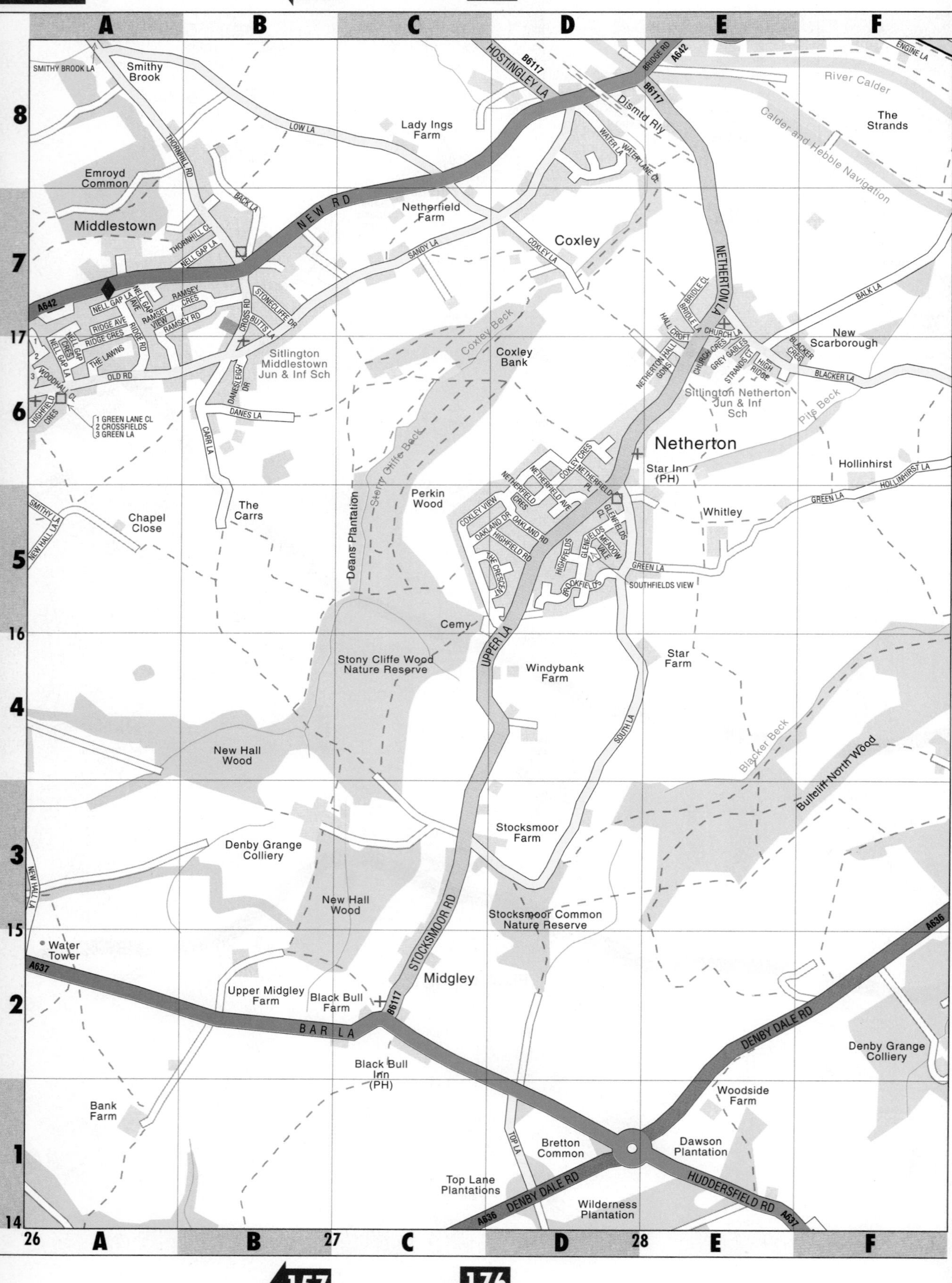
A
B
C
D
E
F
8
7
17
6
5
16
4
3
15
2
1
14
26
27
28
SMITHY BROOK LA
Smithy Brook
Emroyd Common
Middlestown
Lady Ings Farm
Netherfield Farm
Coxley
HOSTINGLEY LA
B6117
A642
BRIDGE RD
Dismtd Rly
River Calder
The Strands
Calder and Hebble Navigation
ENGINE LA
NEW RD
LOW LA
THORNHILL RD
BACK LA
THORNHILL CL
NELL GAP LA
SANDY LA
COXLEY LA
WATER LA
WATER LANE CL
NETHERTON LA
BRIDLE CL
BRIDLE LA
HALL CROFT
CHURCH LA
CHURCH CRES
GREY GABLES
STRANDS CT
HIGH RIDGE
BLACKER CRES
BLACKER LA
BALK LA
New Scarborough
NETHERTON HALL GDNS
Sitlington Netherton Jun & Inf Sch
Pits Beck
Netherton
Star Inn (PH)
Hollinhirst
HOLLINHIRST LA
GREEN LA
Whitley
Coxley Beck
Coxley Bank
Sitlington Middlestown Jun & Inf Sch
RAMSEY CRES
RAMSEY VIEW
RAMSEY RD
RIDGE AVE
RIDGE CRES
RIDGE RD
THE LAWNS
OLD RD
NELL GAP AVE
NELL GAP CRES
STONECLIFFE DR
CROSS RD
BUTTS LA
DANESLEIGH DR
DANES LA
CARR LA
WOODHALL CL
HIGHFIELD CRES
1 GREEN LANE CL
2 CROSSFIELDS
3 GREEN LA
Stony Cliffe Beck
Perkin Wood
Deans Plantation
The Carrs
Chapel Close
SMITHY LA
NEW HALL LA
COXLEY VIEW
NETHERFIELD CRES
NETHERFIELD AVE
NETHERFIELD PL
COXLEY CRES
OAKLAND DR
OAKLAND RD
HIGHFIELD RD
THE CRESCENT
HIGHFIELDS
GLENFIELDS
GLENFIELDS CL
MEADOW VALE
BROOKFIELDS
SOUTHFIELDS VIEW
Cemy
UPPER LA
Windybank Farm
Star Farm
Stony Cliffe Wood Nature Reserve
SOUTH LA
Blacker Beck
Bullcliff North Wood
New Hall Wood
Stocksmoor Farm
Denby Grange Colliery
New Hall Wood
STOCKSMOOR RD
Stocksmoor Common Nature Reserve
Water Tower
A637
A636
Midgley
Upper Midgley Farm
Black Bull Farm
BAR LA
Black Bull Inn (PH)
DENBY DALE RD
Denby Grange Colliery
Woodside Farm
Bank Farm
Bretton Common
Dawson Plantation
TOP LA
Top Lane Plantations
Wilderness Plantation
HUDDERSFIELD RD

157
176

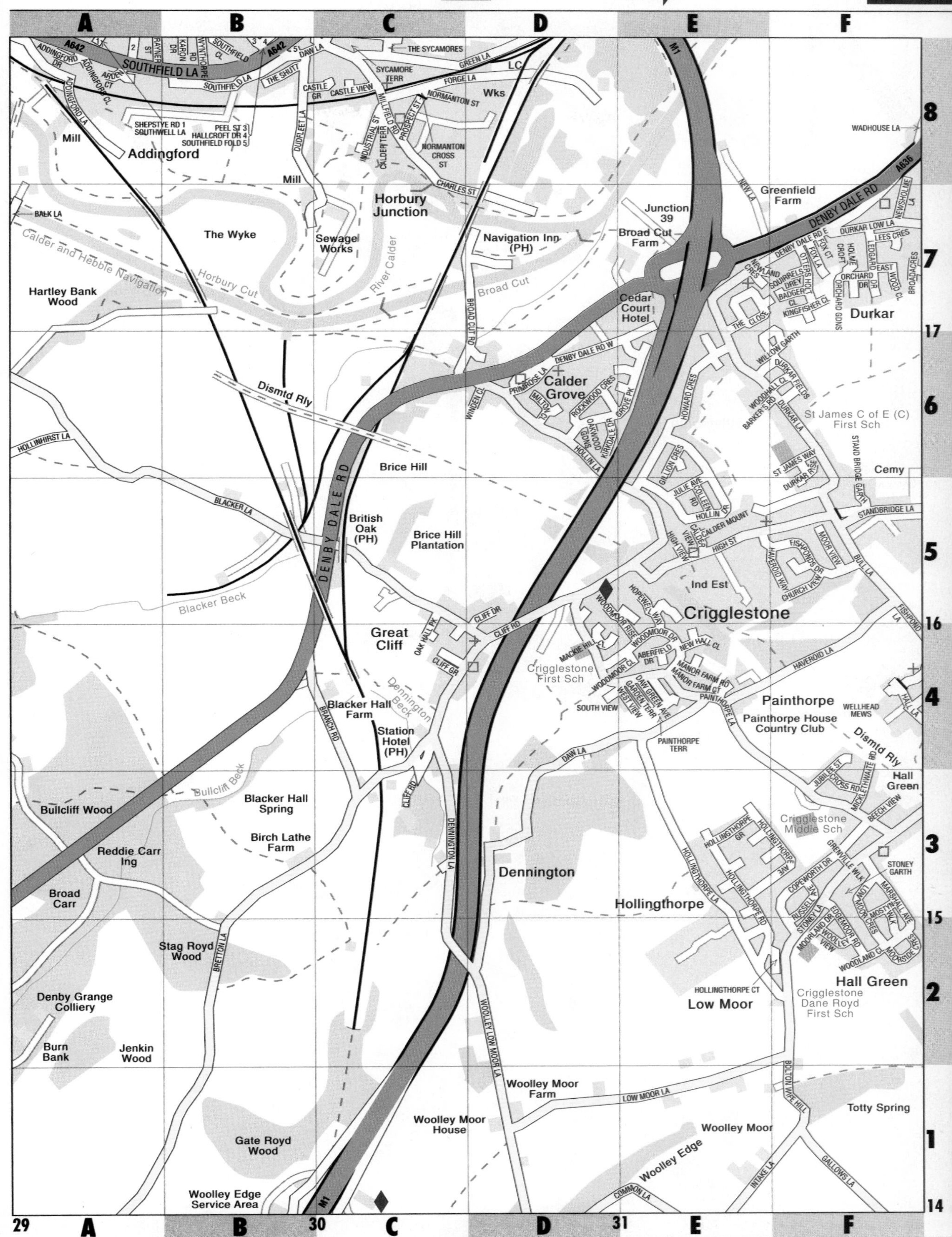
A B C D E F
8
7
17
6
5
16
4
3
15
2
1
14
29 30 31
Addingford
Mill
The Wyke
Sewage Works
Horbury Junction
Navigation Inn (PH)
Junction 39
Broad Cut Farm
Greenfield Farm
Cedar Court Hotel
Durkar
Calder Grove
Hartley Bank Wood
Calder and Hebble Navigation
Horbury Cut
River Calder
Broad Cut
Dismtd Rly
Brice Hill
British Oak (PH)
Brice Hill Plantation
St James C of E (C) First Sch
Cemy
Ind Est
Crigglestone
Great Cliff
Crigglestone First Sch
Blacker Beck
Blacker Hall Farm
Dennington Beck
Station Hotel (PH)
Painthorpe
Painthorpe House Country Club
Hall Green
Bullcliff Beck
Bullcliff Wood
Blacker Hall Spring
Birch Lathe Farm
Reddie Carr Ing
Broad Carr
Crigglestone Middle Sch
Dennington
Hollingthorpe
Stag Royd Wood
Denby Grange Colliery
Low Moor
Crigglestone Dane Royd First Sch
Burn Bank
Jenkin Wood
Woolley Moor Farm
Woolley Moor House
Woolley Moor
Totty Spring
Gate Royd Wood
Woolley Edge
Woolley Edge Service Area
Wks
LC
M1
A642
A636
SOUTHFIELD LA
DENBY DALE RD
THE SYCAMORES
SYCAMORE TERR
GREEN LA
FORGE LA
NORMANTON ST
NORMANTON CROSS ST
CHARLES ST
CASTLE GR
CASTLE VIEW
THE SHUTT
DAW LA
DUDFLEET LA
INDUSTRIAL ST
CALDER TERR
MILLFIELD RD
PROSPECT ST
SHEPSTYE RD 1
SOUTHWELL LA 2
PEEL ST 3
HALLCROFT DR 4
SOUTHFIELD FOLD 5
ADDINGFORD DR
ADDINGFORD CL
ADDINGFORD LA
ARDEN CT
BALK LA
HOLLINHIRST LA
BLACKER LA
BROAD CUT RD
WINDEN CL
PRIMROSE LA
MILTON
DENBY DALE RD W
ROCKWOOD CRES
OAKWOOD GDNS
HOLLIN LA
KIRKDALE DR
GROVE PK
HOWARD CRES
NEW LA
WADHOUSE LA
NEWSHOLME LA
DURKAR LOW LA
LEES CRES
DENBY DALE RD E
FOX LA
FOX CT
HOLME CROFT
LEDGARD DR
EAST WOOD CL
BROADACRES
NEWLAND CRES
OTTERS HOLT
SQUIRRELS DREY
BADGER CL
KINGFISHER CL
ORCHARD DR
ORCHARD GDNS
THE CLOSE
WILLOW GARTH
DURKAR FIELDS
WOODHALL CL
BARKER'S RD
DURKAR LA
STAND BRIDGE GARTH
STANDBRIDGE LA
ST JAMES WAY
DURKAR RISE
GILLION CRES
JULIE AVE
COLLEEN RD
HOLLIN DR
CALDER MOUNT
CALDER VIEW
HIGH VIEW
HIGH ST
HAVEROID WAY
FISHPONDS DR
MOOR VIEW
CHURCH VIEW
BULL LA
FISHPOND LA
HAVEROID LA
HOPEWELL WAY
WOODMOOR RISE
WOODMOOR DR
WOODMOOR CL
MACKIE HILL CL
ABERFIELD DR
NEW HALL CL
MANOR FARM RD
MANOR FARM CT
DAW GREEN AVE
GARDEN TERR
WEST VIEW
SOUTH VIEW
PAINTHORPE LA
PAINTHORPE TERR
CLIFF DR
CLIFF RD
CLIFF GR
OAK HALL PK
BRANCH RD
CLIFF RD
DENNINGTON LA
HALL LA
WELLHEAD MEWS
JUBILEE ST
CROSS RD
MICKLETHWAITE RD
BEECH VIEW
HOLLINGTHORPE GR
HOLLINGTHORPE AVE
HOLLINGTHORPE RD
HOLLINGTHORPE LA
HOLLINGTHORPE CT
GRENVILLE WLK
STONEY GARTH
COPEWORTH DR
RUSSELL AVE
STONEY LA
MARSHALL AVE
MOSTYN WLK
MOOR CRES
EDGEMOOR RD
MOORLAND DR
WOOLLEY VIEW
WOODLAND CL
MOORSIDE CL
WOOLLEY LOW MOOR LA
LOW MOOR LA
BOLTON WIFE HILL
BRETTON LA
INTAKE LA
GALLOWS LA
COMMON LA

159
142

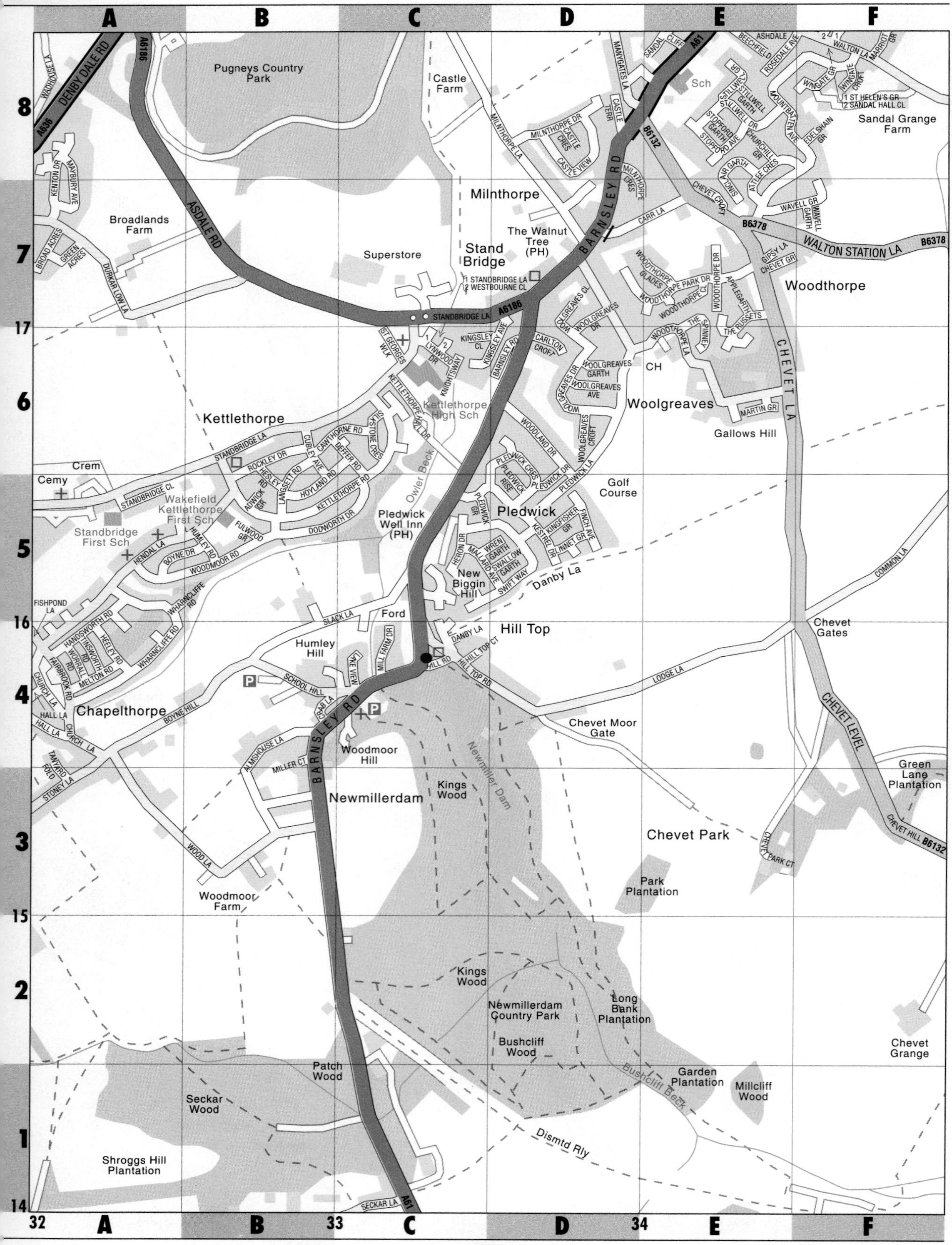

A   B   C   D   E   F

8

Pugneys Country Park

Castle Farm

Milnthorpe

WADDINGLEY LA
DENBYDALE RD
A636
A6186

Sandal Grange Farm

ASHDALE
BEECHFIELD
ROSEDALE AV
WALTON LA MARRIOT
WINGATE GR
WINGATE CROFT
1 ST HELEN'S GR
1 SANDAL HALL CL

Sch

BARNSLEY RD
A61
B6132

MILNTHORPE DR
CASTLE TERR
CASTLE CRES
CASTLE VIEW

7

Broadlands Farm

ASDALE RD

Superstore

Stand Bridge

The Walnut Tree (PH)

1 STANDBRIDGE LA
2 WESTBOURNE CL

CARR LA

CHEVET CROFT
B6378
WALTON STATION LA
B6378

Woodthorpe

MAYBURY AVE
KENTON DR
BROAD ACRES
GREEN ACRES
DURHAM LOW LA

17

STANDBRIDGE LA
A6186

WOODTHORPE GLADES
WOODTHORPE PARK DR
WOODTHORPE CL
WOODTHORPE LA

ST GEORGE'S WLK
LYNMOOR DR
KNIGHTSWAY
KINGSLEY AVE
KINGSLEY CL
BARNSLEY RD
CARLTON CROFT

CH

THE SPINNEY
THE RUSSETS

CHEVET LA

6

Kettlethorpe

STANDBRIDGE LA
ROCKLEY DR
RUDLEY
RAWICK
LANGSETT RD
CAWTHORNE RD
DEFER RD
HOYLAND RD

Kettlethorpe High Sch

WOODLAND DR
PLEDWICK CRES
PLEDWICK RISE
PLEDWICK GR

WOOLGREAVES DR
WOOLGREAVES GARTH
WOOLGREAVES AVE
WOOLGREAVES COM
WOOLGREAVES CROFT

Woolgreaves

Gallows Hill
MARTIN GR

Crem

Cemy

Wakefield Kettlethorpe First Sch

Standbridge First Sch

FULWOOD GR
DODWORTH DR
KETTLETHORPE RD

Owler Beck

PLEDWICK LA
ST PLEDWICK

Pledwick Well Inn (PH)

Golf Course

Pledwick

FINCH AVE
KESTREL GR
KINGFISHER GR
LINNET GR

5

FISHPOND LA
HANDSWORTH RD
NORRALL RD
HEELEY RD
FAIRBROOK RD
MELTON RD
WHARNCLIFFE RD
HUMLEY LA
BOYNE DR
WOODMOOR RD
HENDAL LA

New Biggin Hill

HERON DR
ALMAN GARTH
LARK DR
WREN GARTH
SWALLOW GARTH
SWIFT WAY

Danby La

16

SLACK LA

Ford

Humley Hill

Danby La

Hill Top

Chevet Gates

CHURCH LA
HALL LA

Chapelthorpe

BOYNE HILL
SCHOOL HILL
CARR LA
PIKE VIEW
MILL FARM DR
MILL RD
HILL TOP CT
HILL TOP RD

LODGE LA

CHEVET LEVEL

4

HALL LA
HAYFORD
STONEY LA

BARNSLEY RD

Woodmoor Hill

Chevet Moor Gate

Green Lane Plantation

3

ALMSHOUSE LA
MILLER CT
WOOD LA

Newmillerdam

Kings Wood

Newmiller Dam

Chevet Park

CHEVET PARK CT
CHEVET HILL B6132

15

Woodmoor Farm

Park Plantation

2

Kings Wood

Newmillerdam Country Park

Long Bank Plantation

Chevet Grange

Bushcliff Wood

Garden Plantation

Millcliff Wood

Bushcliff Beck

1

Patch Wood

Seckar Wood

Shroggs Hill Plantation

Dismtd Rly

14

32   A   B   33   C   D   34   E   F

SECKAR LA
A61

159
178

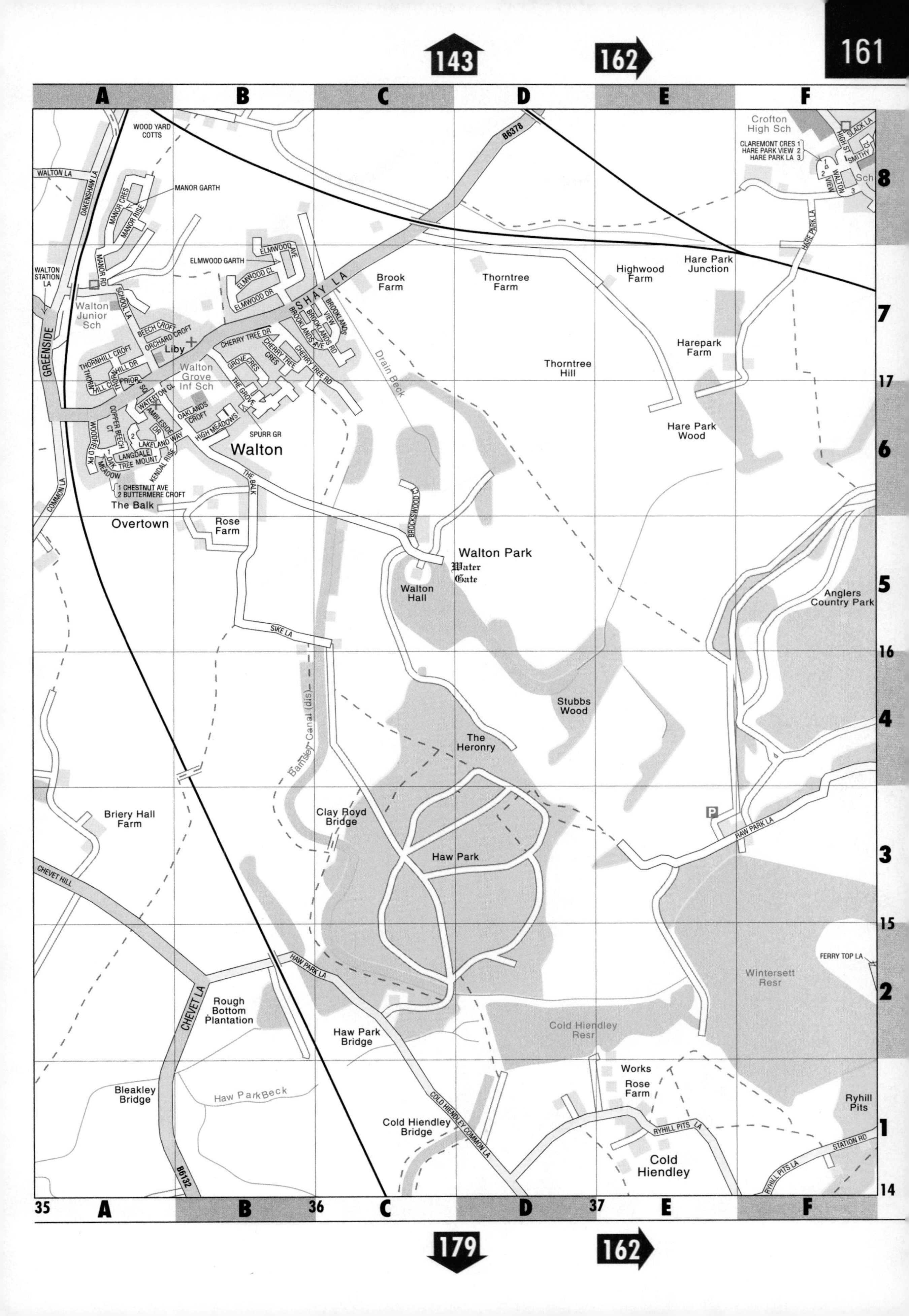

143
162
A B C D E F
8 7 17 6 5 16 4 3 15 2 1 14
35 36 37
179
162
WOOD YARD COTTS
WALTON LA
OAKENSHAW LA
MANOR GARTH
MANOR CRES
MANOR RISE
MANOR RD
WALTON STATION LA
SCHOOL LA
Walton Junior Sch
GREENSIDE
ELMWOOD GARTH
ELMWOOD AVE
ELMWOOD CL
ELMWOOD DR
SHAY LA
B6378
BROOKLANDS VIEW
BROOKLANDS RD
BROOKLANDS AVE
BEECH CROFT
ORCHARD CROFT
Liby
CHERRY TREE DR
CHERRY TREE CRES
CHERRY TREE RD
THORNHILL CROFT
THORNHILL DR
PRIORY SQ
Walton Grove Inf Sch
GROVE CRES
THE GROVE
WATERTON CL
OAKLANDS CROFT
HIGH MEADOWS
SPURR GR
AMBLESIDE DR
LAKELAND WAY
COPPER BEECH CT
WOODFIELD PK
LANGDALE
OAK TREE MOUNT
MEADOW
KENDAL RISE
Walton
1 CHESTNUT AVE
2 BUTTERMERE CROFT
The Balk
THE BALK
COMMON LA
Overtown
Rose Farm
Brook Farm
Thorntree Farm
Highwood Farm
Hare Park Junction
Crofton High Sch
CLAREMONT CRES 1
HARE PARK VIEW 2
HARE PARK LA 3
HIGH ST
SLACK LA
SMITHY
WALTON VIEW
Sch
HARE PARK LA
Harepark Farm
Thorntree Hill
Drain Beck
Hare Park Wood
BROCKSWOOD CT
Walton Park
Water Gate
Walton Hall
SIKE LA
Anglers Country Park
Stubbs Wood
Barnsley Canal (dis)
The Heronry
Briery Hall Farm
Clay Royd Bridge
Haw Park
HAW PARK LA
CHEVET HILL
CHEVET LA
Rough Bottom Plantation
Haw Park Bridge
Cold Hiendley Resr
Wintersett Resr
FERRY TOP LA
Works
Rose Farm
Bleakley Bridge
Haw Park Beck
COLD HIENDLEY COMMON LA
Cold Hiendley Bridge
RYHILL PITS LA
Ryhill Pits
STATION RD
Cold Hiendley
B6132

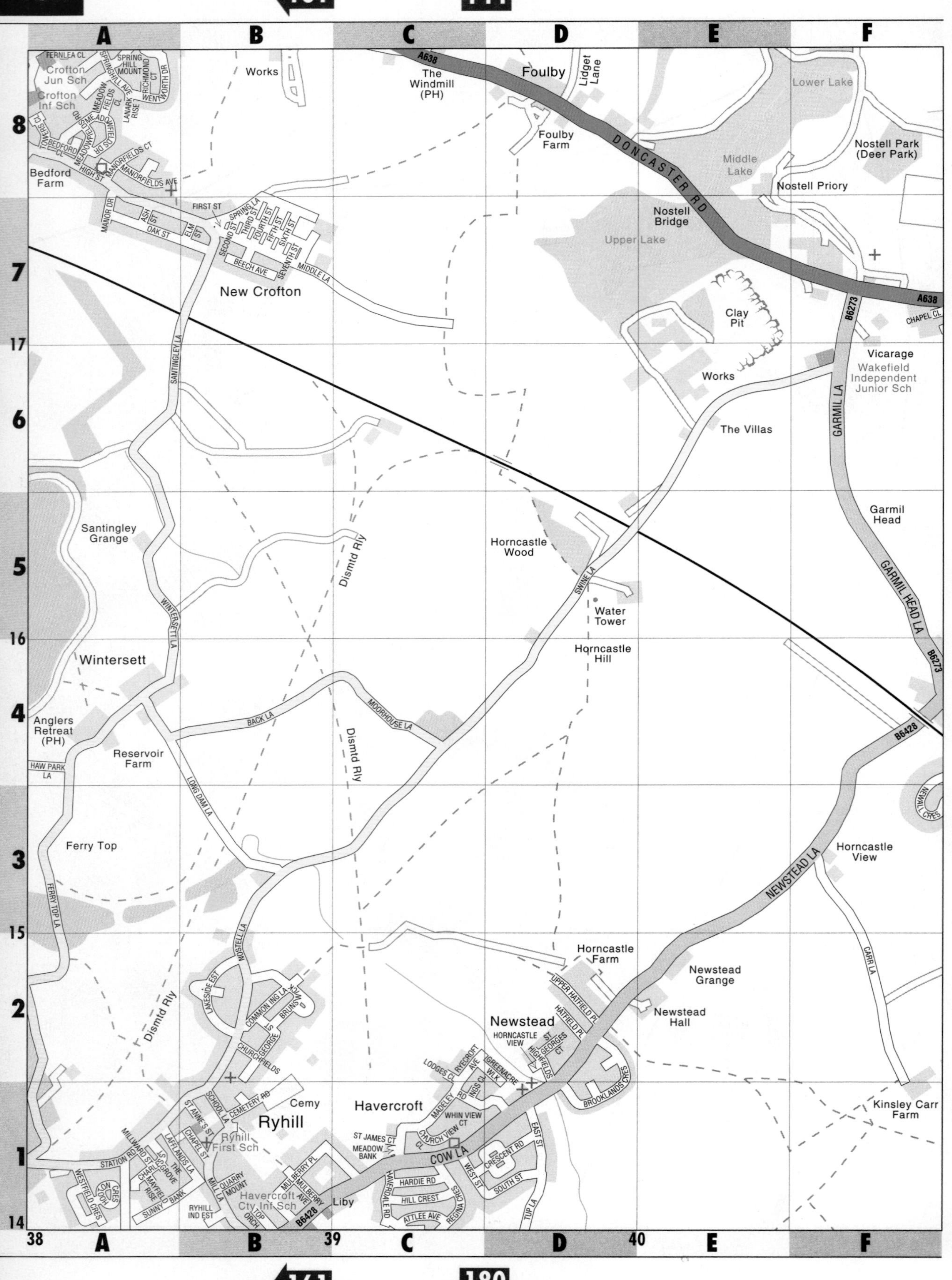

161
144

A B C D E F

8
7
17
6
5
16
4
3
15
2
1
14

FERNLEA CL
Crofton Jun Sch
Crofton Inf Sch
SPRING HILL MOUNT
RICHMOND WORTH DR
SPRINGHILL AVE
LANARK RISE
GREEN MEADOW
DISMEL ADFIELDS
BEDFORD CL
SHAPE
Bedford Farm
HIGH ST
MANOR DR
MANORFIELDS CT
MANORFIELDS AVE
FIRST ST
OAK ST
ASH ST
ELM ST
SECOND ST
SPRING LA
THIRD ST
FOURTH ST
FIFTH ST
SIXTH ST
SEVENTH ST
BEECH AVE
MIDDLE LA

Works

New Crofton

Santingley Grange

SANTINGLEY LA

WINTERSETT LA

Wintersett

Anglers Retreat (PH)

HAW PARK LA

Reservoir Farm

BACK LA

Ferry Top

FERRY TOP LA

LONG DAM LA

Dismtd Rly

Dismtd Rly

Dismtd Rly

MOORHOUSE LA

The Windmill (PH)

A638

Foulby

Lidget Lane

Foulby Farm

DONCASTER RD

Nostell Bridge

Upper Lake

Middle Lake

Lower Lake

Nostell Park (Deer Park)

Nostell Priory

B6273

A638

CHAPEL CL

Vicarage
Wakefield Independent Junior Sch

GARMIL LA

The Villas

Works

Clay Pit

Horncastle Wood

SWINE LA

Water Tower

Horncastle Hill

Garmil Head

GARMIL HEAD LA

B6273

B6428

Horncastle View

NEWSTEAD LA

CARR LA

Horncastle Farm

UPPER HATFIELD PL

Newstead

HORNCASTLE VIEW

HATFIELD PL

HIGH ST FLDS

ST GEORGES CT

BROOKLANDS CRES

Newstead Grange

Newstead Hall

Kinsley Carr Farm

Ryhill

WESTELLA

LAKESIDE EST

COMMON ING LA

BRUNSW

LS

CHURCHFIELDS

GEORGE

SCHOOL LA

CEMETERY RD

STANEY ST

CHAPEL LA

Cemy

Havercroft

LODGES CL
RYECROFT
AVE
GREENACRE
WLK
MAUDS LEY CL
WHIN VIEW CT
ST JAMES CT
MEADOW BANK
CHURCH VIEW CT
CL

COW LA

WEST ST

CRESCENT RD

EAST ST

SOUTH ST

TOLL LA

MILLWARD ST
STATION RD
LAFTLANDS LA
CHARLES
LATIMORE
THE
SUNNY
BANK
RYHILL IND EST
MULBERRY PL
QUARRY MOUNT
MILL LA
Havercroft Cty Inf Sch
Liby
HAVERDALE RD
HILL CREST
HARDIE RD
ATTLEE AVE
REGINA
WESTFIELD CRES
ON CRES
Ryhill First Sch
B6428

38 A B 39 C D 40 E F

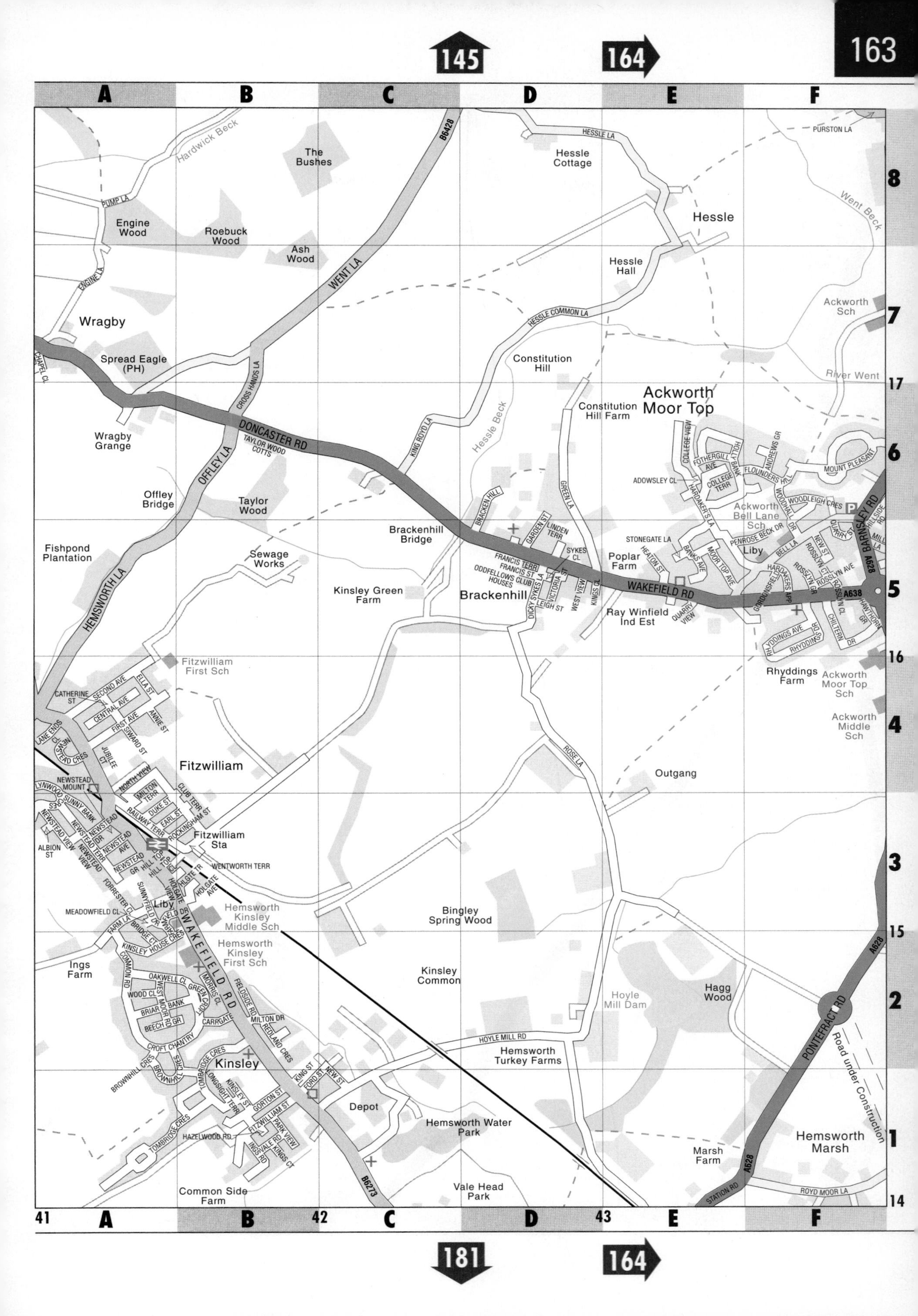
145
164
A
B
C
D
E
F
Wragby
Engine Wood
Roebuck Wood
Ash Wood
The Bushes
Hardwick Beck
Spread Eagle (PH)
Wragby Grange
Offley Bridge
Taylor Wood
Fishpond Plantation
Sewage Works
Brackenhill Bridge
Kinsley Green Farm
Brackenhill
Constitution Hill
Constitution Hill Farm
Hessle Cottage
Hessle
Hessle Hall
Ackworth Moor Top
Ackworth Sch
River Went
Went Beck
Poplar Farm
Liby
Ackworth Bell Lane Sch
Ray Winfield Ind Est
Rhyddings Farm
Ackworth Moor Top Sch
Ackworth Middle Sch
Outgang
Fitzwilliam
Fitzwilliam First Sch
Fitzwilliam Sta
Hemsworth Kinsley Middle Sch
Hemsworth Kinsley First Sch
Ings Farm
Kinsley
Bingley Spring Wood
Kinsley Common
Hoyle Mill Dam
Hagg Wood
Hemsworth Turkey Farms
Depot
Hemsworth Water Park
Vale Head Park
Common Side Farm
Marsh Farm
Hemsworth Marsh
Road under Construction
DONCASTER RD
WAKEFIELD RD
HEMSWORTH LA
OFFLEY LA
WENT LA
B6428
CROSS HANDS LA
KING ROYD LA
HESSLE COMMON LA
HESSLE LA
PUMP LA
ENGINE LA
CHAPEL CL
PURSTON LA
BARNSLEY RD
A628
A638
B6273
PONTEFRACT RD
HOYLE MILL RD
ROSE LA
GREEN LA
STATION RD
ROYD MOOR LA
TAYLOR WOOD COTTS
8
7
6
5
4
3
2
1
17
16
15
14
41
42
43
181
164

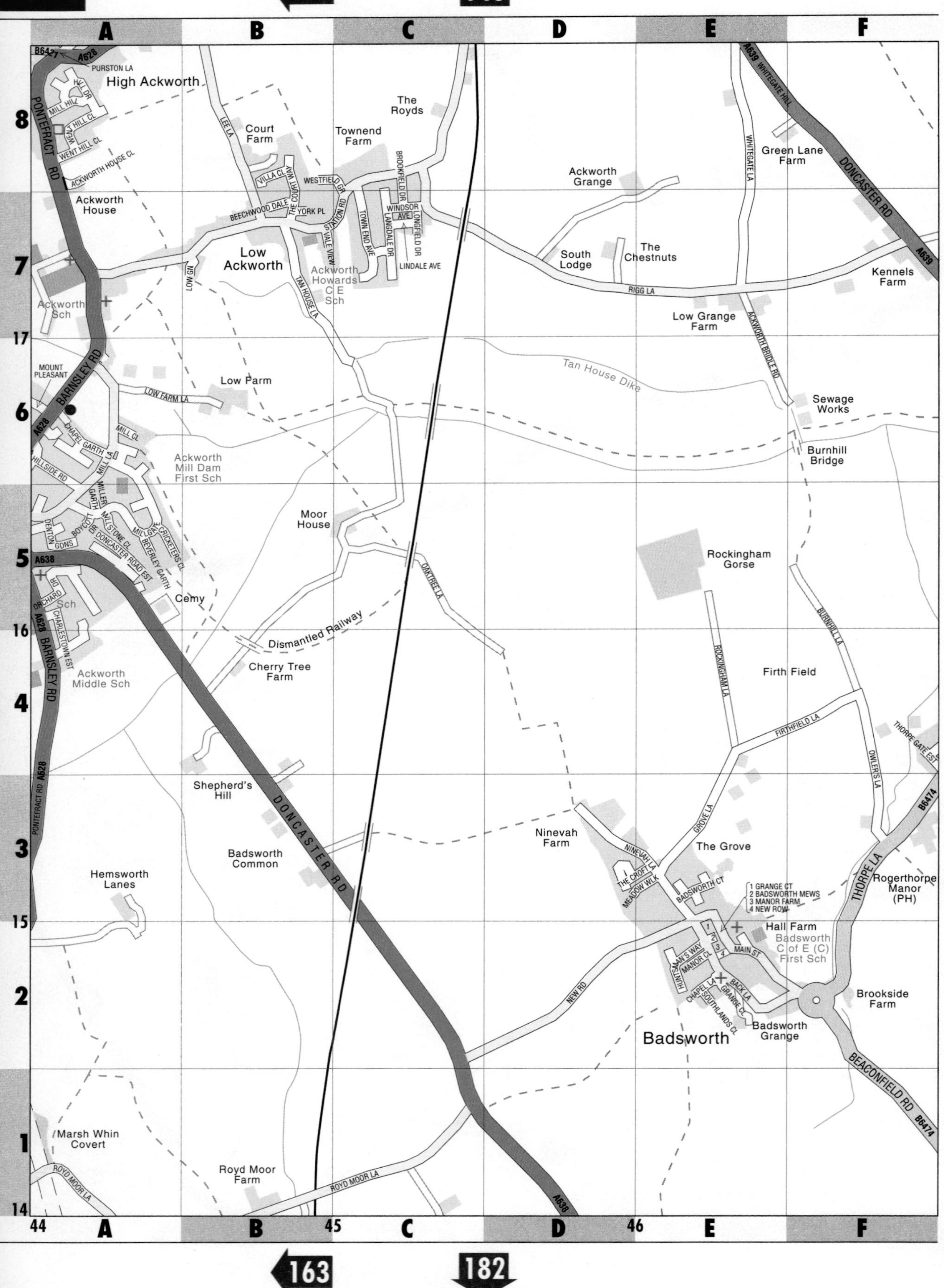
High Ackworth
PURSTON LA
PONTEFRACT RD
MILL HILL
WENT HILL CL
ACKWORTH HOUSE CL
Ackworth House
Court Farm
LEE LA
Townend Farm
The Royds
VILLA CL
THE COURT WAY
WESTFIELD GR
BROOKFIELD DR
WINDSOR AVE
LONGFIELD DR
LANGDALE DR
TOWN END AVE
STATION RD
YORK PL
BEECHWOOD DALE
VIALE VIEW
LINDALE AVE
Low Ackworth
LOW GN
TAN HOUSE LA
Ackworth Howards C E Sch
Ackworth Sch
Ackworth Grange
South Lodge
The Chestnuts
RIGG LA
WHITEGATE LA
WHITEGATE HILL
Green Lane Farm
DONCASTER RD
Kennels Farm
Low Grange Farm
ACKWORTH BRIDLE RD
MOUNT PLEASANT
BARNSLEY RD
Low Farm
LOW FARM LA
Tan House Dike
Sewage Works
Burnhill Bridge
MILL CL
CHAPEL GARTH
HILLSIDE RD
MILLER GARTH
Ackworth Mill Dam First Sch
Moor House
MILLSTONE CL
MILLGATE
BEVERLEY GARTH
CRICKETERS CL
DENTON GDNS
BOYCOTT DR
DONCASTER ROAD EST
Rockingham Gorse
OAKTREE LA
Cemy
ORCHARD DR
CHARLESTOWN EST
Sch
Dismantled Railway
Cherry Tree Farm
Ackworth Middle Sch
ROCKINGHAM LA
BURNHILL LA
Firth Field
FIRTHFIELD LA
THORPE GATE EST
OWLERS LA
Shepherd's Hill
DONCASTER RD
Ninevah Farm
GROVE LA
The Grove
NINEVAH LA
THE CROFT
MEADOW WLK
BADSWORTH CT
1 GRANGE CT
2 BADSWORTH MEWS
3 MANOR FARM
4 NEW ROW
Hall Farm
Badsworth C of E (C) First Sch
MAIN ST
THORPE LA
Rogerthorpe Manor (PH)
Badsworth Common
Hemsworth Lanes
HUNTSMAN'S WAY
MANOR CL
CHAPEL LA
SOUTHLANDS CL
GRANGE CL
BACK LA
NEW RD
Brookside Farm
Badsworth
Badsworth Grange
BEACONFIELD RD
Marsh Whin Covert
ROYD MOOR LA
Royd Moor Farm
A628
A638
A639
B6421
B6474

147

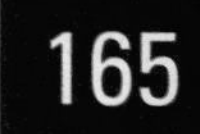

166

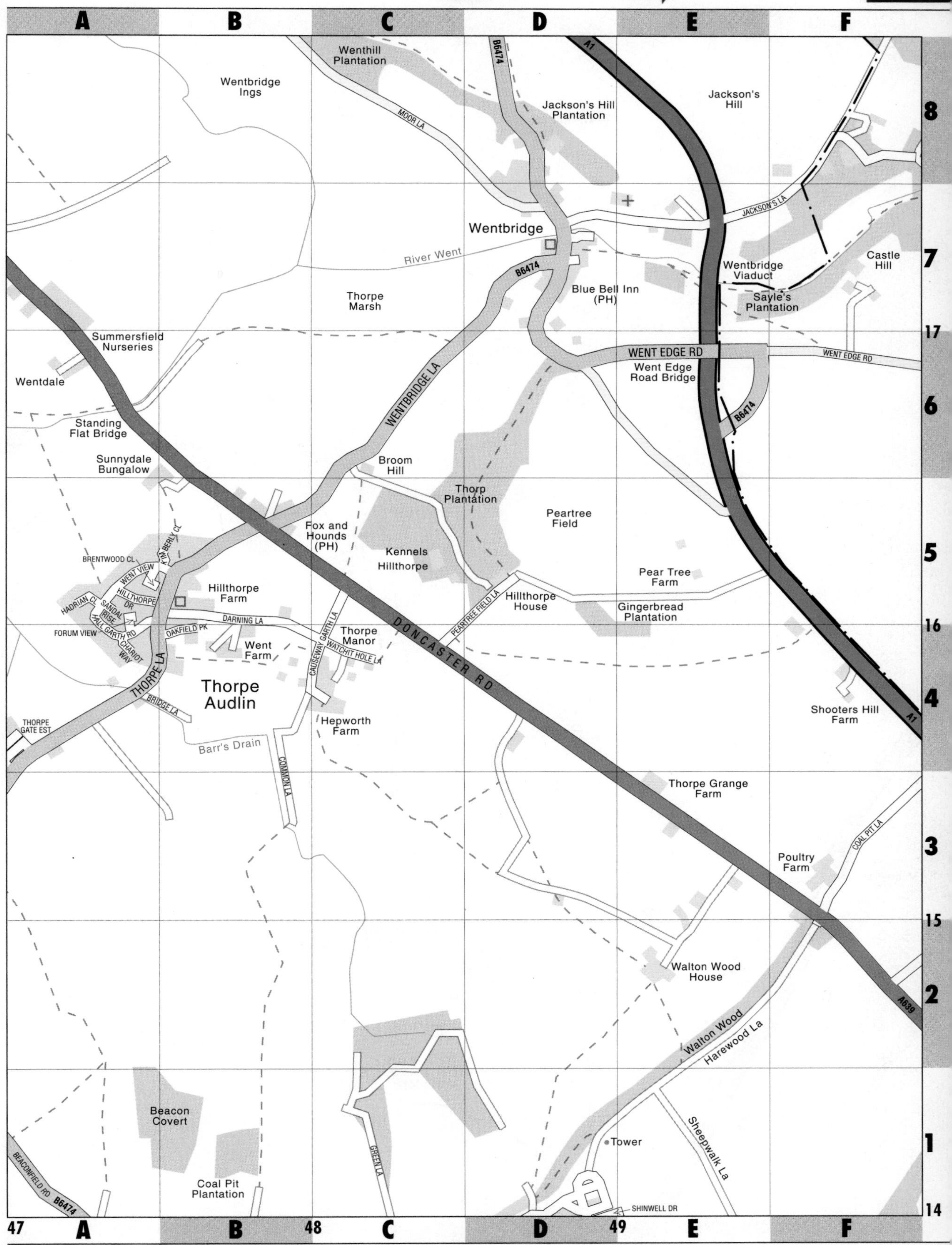

A
B
C
D
E
F
Wenthill Plantation
Wentbridge Ings
Jackson's Hill Plantation
Jackson's Hill
MOOR LA
B6474
A1
Wentbridge
River Went
JACKSON'S LA
Wentbridge Viaduct
Castle Hill
Thorpe Marsh
Blue Bell Inn (PH)
Sayle's Plantation
Summersfield Nurseries
WENT EDGE RD
Went Edge Road Bridge
Wentdale
Standing Flat Bridge
WENTBRIDGE LA
Sunnydale Bungalow
Broom Hill
Thorp Plantation
Peartree Field
Fox and Hounds (PH)
Kennels
Hillthorpe
BRENTWOOD CL
KIMBERLY CL
WENT VIEW
HILLTHORPE DR
HADRIAN CL
SANDAL RISE
Hillthorpe Farm
Pear Tree Farm
Hillthorpe House
Gingerbread Plantation
PEARTREE FIELD LA
DARNING LA
FORUM VIEW
HALL GARTH RD
CHARIOT WAY
OAKFIELD PK
Went Farm
Thorpe Manor
CAUSEWAY GARTH LA
WATCHIT HOLE LA
DONCASTER RD
THORPE LA
Thorpe Audlin
BRIDGE LA
Hepworth Farm
Shooters Hill Farm
THORPE GATE EST
Barr's Drain
COMMON LA
Thorpe Grange Farm
Poultry Farm
COAL PIT LA
Walton Wood House
A639
Walton Wood
Harewood La
Beacon Covert
Sheepwalk La
Tower
Coal Pit Plantation
BEACONFIELD RD
GREEN LA
SHINWELL DR
8
7
17
6
5
16
4
3
15
2
1
14
47
48
49

165

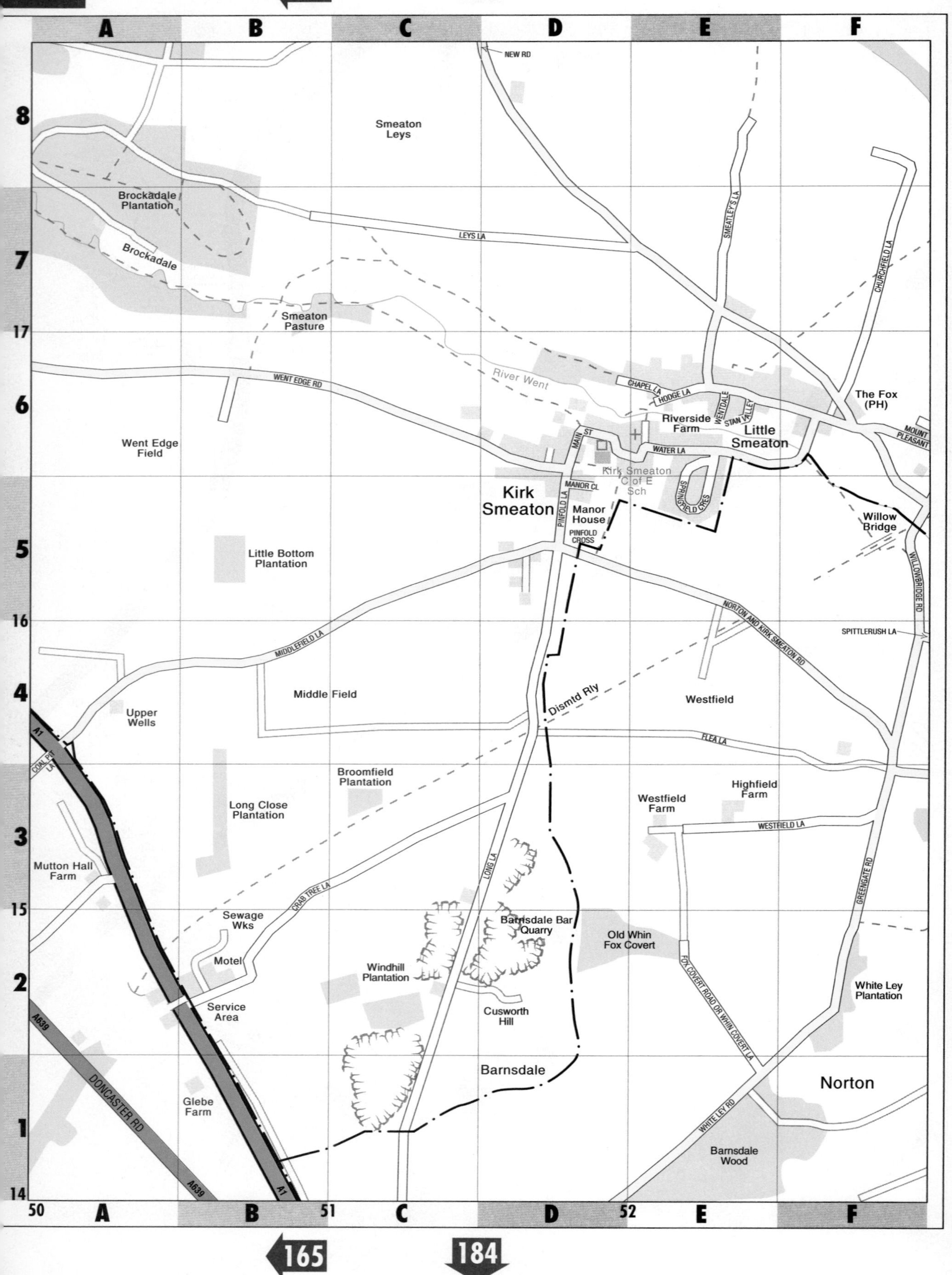

A
B
C
D
E
F
8
7
17
6
5
16
4
3
15
2
1
14
50
51
52
NEW RD
Smeaton
Leys
Brockadale
Plantation
Brockadale
LEYS LA
SMEATLEY'S LA
CHURCHFIELD LA
Smeaton
Pasture
River Went
WENT EDGE RD
CHAPEL LA
HODGE LA
WENTDALE
STAN VALLEY
The Fox
(PH)
Riverside
Farm
Little
Smeaton
MOUNT
PLEASANT
Went Edge
Field
MAIN ST
WATER LA
Kirk Smeaton
C of E
Sch
MANOR CL
SPRINGFIELD CRES
Kirk
Smeaton
PINFOLD LA
Manor
House
PINFOLD
CROSS
Willow
Bridge
Little Bottom
Plantation
WILLOWBRIDGE RD
NORTON AND KIRK SMEATON RD
SPITTLERUSH LA
MIDDLEFIELD LA
Middle Field
Dismtd Rly
Westfield
Upper
Wells
A1
COAL PIT LA
FLEA LA
Broomfield
Plantation
Long Close
Plantation
Westfield
Farm
Highfield
Farm
WESTFIELD LA
Mutton Hall
Farm
CRAB TREE LA
LONG LA
GREENGATE RD
Sewage
Wks
Barnsdale Bar
Quarry
Old Whin
Fox Covert
Motel
Windhill
Plantation
FOX COVERT ROAD OR WHIN COVERT LA
White Ley
Plantation
Service
Area
Cusworth
Hill
A639
DONCASTER RD
Barnsdale
Norton
Glebe
Farm
WHITE LEY RD
Barnsdale
Wood
A639
A1

165
184

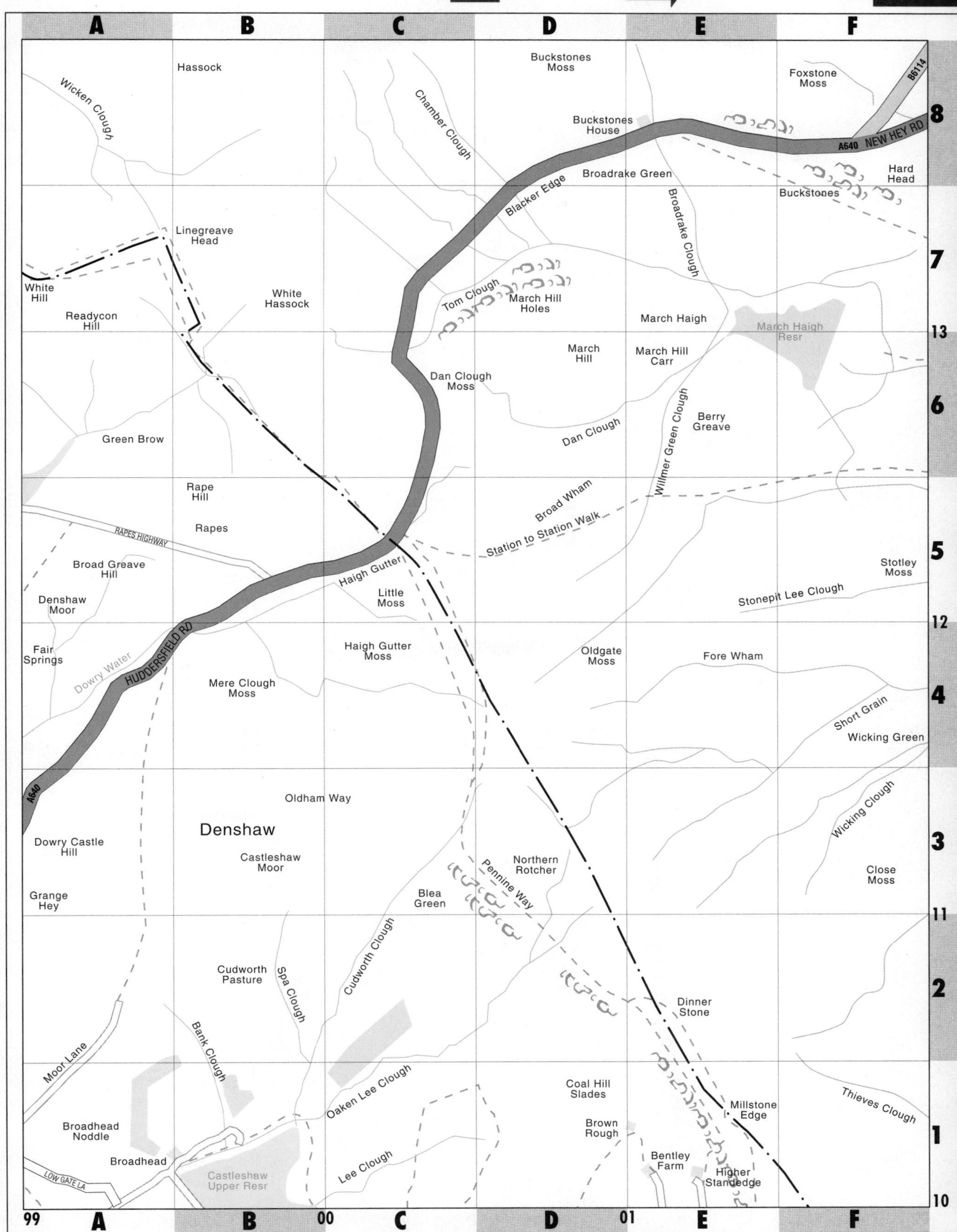
A
B
C
D
E
F
Hassock
Wicken Clough
Chamber Clough
Buckstones Moss
Foxstone Moss
B6114
Buckstones House
A640 NEW HEY RD
Broadrake Green
Blacker Edge
Hard Head
Buckstones
Broadrake Clough
Linegreave Head
White Hill
Readycon Hill
White Hassock
Tom Clough
March Hill Holes
March Haigh
March Haigh Resr
March Hill
March Hill Carr
Dan Clough Moss
Willmer Green Clough
Berry Greave
Dan Clough
Green Brow
Rape Hill
Broad Wham
Rapes
RAPES HIGHWAY
Station to Station Walk
Broad Greave Hill
Haigh Gutter
Stotley Moss
Denshaw Moor
Little Moss
Stonepit Lee Clough
Fair Springs
Haigh Gutter Moss
Oldgate Moss
Fore Wham
Dowry Water
HUDDERSFIELD RD
Mere Clough Moss
Short Grain
Wicking Green
A640
Oldham Way
Wicking Clough
Denshaw
Dowry Castle Hill
Castleshaw Moor
Northern Rotcher
Pennine Way
Close Moss
Grange Hey
Blea Green
Cudworth Clough
Cudworth Pasture
Spa Clough
Dinner Stone
Bank Clough
Moor Lane
Oaken Lee Clough
Coal Hill Slades
Thieves Clough
Millstone Edge
Broadhead Noddle
Brown Rough
Broadhead
Bentley Farm
Lee Clough
Higher Standedge
LOW GATE LA
Castleshaw Upper Resr
8
7
13
6
5
12
4
3
11
2
1
10
99
00
01

167
150

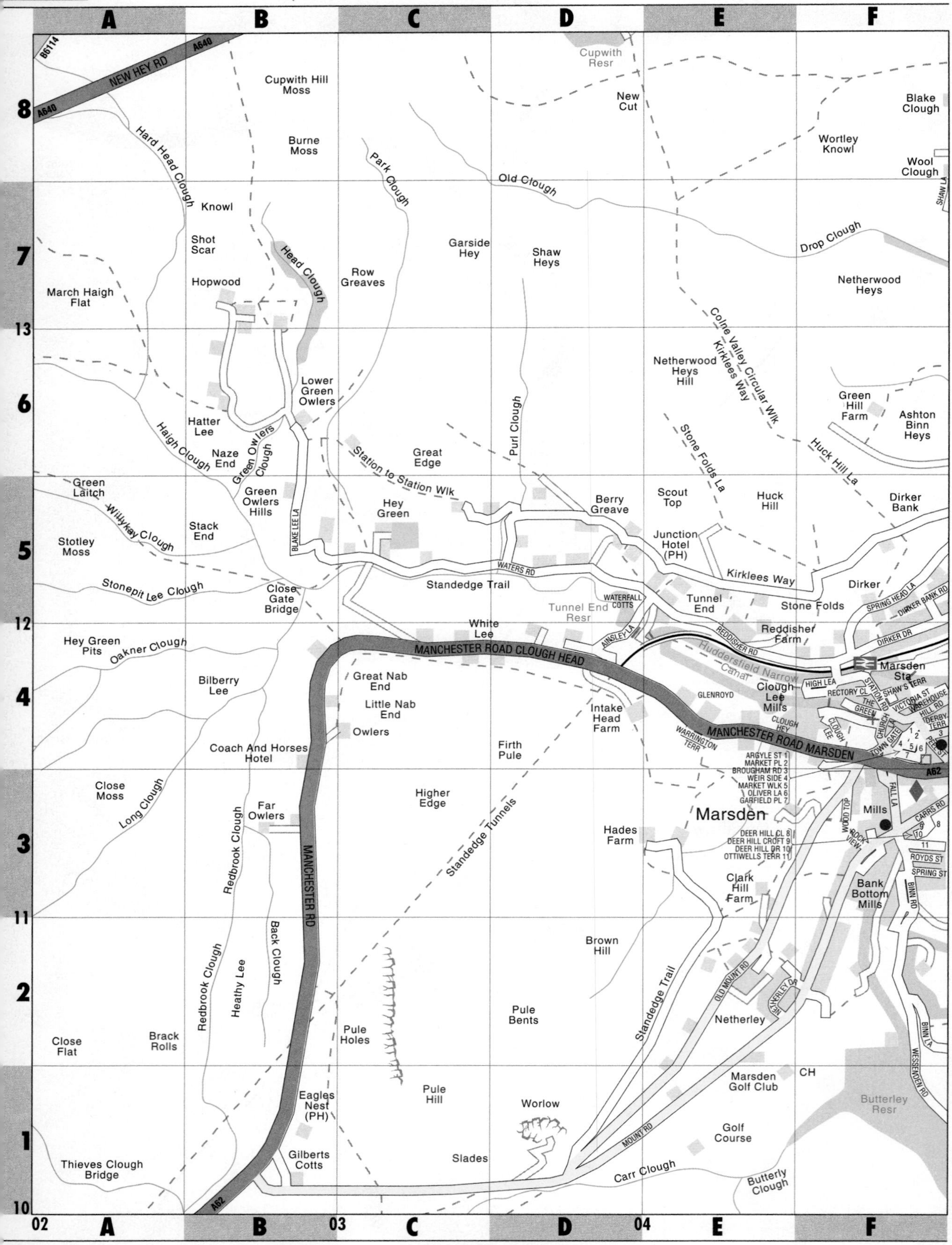

A B C D E F

8

B6114 NEW HEY RD A640

A640

Cupwith Resr

New Cut

Blake Clough

Cupwith Hill Moss

Hard Head Clough

Burne Moss

Park Clough

Old Clough

Wortley Knowl

Wool Clough

SHAW LA

Knowl

7

Shot Scar

Head Clough

Row Greaves

Garside Hey

Shaw Heys

Drop Clough

Netherwood Heys

March Haigh Flat

Hopwood

13

Lower Green Owlers

Netherwood Heys Hill

Colne Valley Circular Wlk

Kirklees Way

Green Hill Farm

Ashton Binn Heys

6

Hatter Lee

Haigh Clough

Green Owlers Clough

Naze End

Station to Station Wlk

Great Edge

Purl Clough

Stone Folds La

Huck Hill La

Green Laitch

Green Owlers Hills

Hey Green

Berry Greave

Scout Top

Huck Hill

Dirker Bank

5

Stotley Moss

Willykay Clough

Stack End

BLAKE LEE LA

WATERS RD

Junction Hotel (PH)

Kirklees Way

Dirker

Stonepit Lee Clough

Close Gate Bridge

Standedge Trail

WATERFALL COTTS

Tunnel End

Stone Folds

SPRING HEAD LA

DIRKER BANK LA

12

Hey Green Pits

Oakner Clough

White Lee

Tunnel End Resr

AINSLEY LA

Reddisher Farm

DIRKER DR

MANCHESTER ROAD CLOUGH HEAD

REDDISHER RD

Marsden Sta

4

Bilberry Lee

Great Nab End

Little Nab End

Intake Head Farm

Huddersfield Narrow Canal

HIGH LEA

Clough Lee Mills

RECTORY CL

SHAW'S TERR

WAREHOUSE HILL RD

VICTORIA ST

Close Moss

Long Clough

REDBROOK CLOUGH

Owlers

GLENROYD

WARRINGTON TERR

MANCHESTER ROAD MARSDEN

CLOUGH HEY

THE GREEN

CHURCH

TOWN GATE

DERBY TERR

A62

Coach And Horses Hotel

Firth Pule

ARGYLE ST 1
MARKET PL 2
BROUGHAM RD 3
WEIR SIDE 4
MARKET WLK 5
OLIVER LA 6
GARFIELD PL 7

Mills

3

Close Flat

Far Owlers

MANCHESTER RD

Higher Edge

Standedge Tunnels

Hades Farm

Marsden

DEER HILL CL 8
DEER HILL CROFT 9
DEER HILL DR 10
OTTIWELLS TERR 11

FALL LA

OLD MOUNT RD

BLOCK VIEW

Bank Bottom Mills

CARRS RD

ROYDS ST

SPRING ST

BINN RD

11

Redbrook Clough

Heathy Lee

Back Clough

Brown Hill

Clark Hill Farm

2

Brack Rolls

Pule Holes

Pule Bents

Standedge Trail

Netherley

ICKERLEY CO

OLD MOUNT RD

Close Flat

1

Thieves Clough Bridge

Eagles Nest (PH)

Pule Hill

Worlow

Slades

Carr Clough

MOUNT RD

Marsden Golf Club

CH

Golf Course

Butterly Clough

Butterley Resr

WESSENDEN RD

Gilberts Cotts

A62

10

02 A B 03 C D 04 E F

167
185

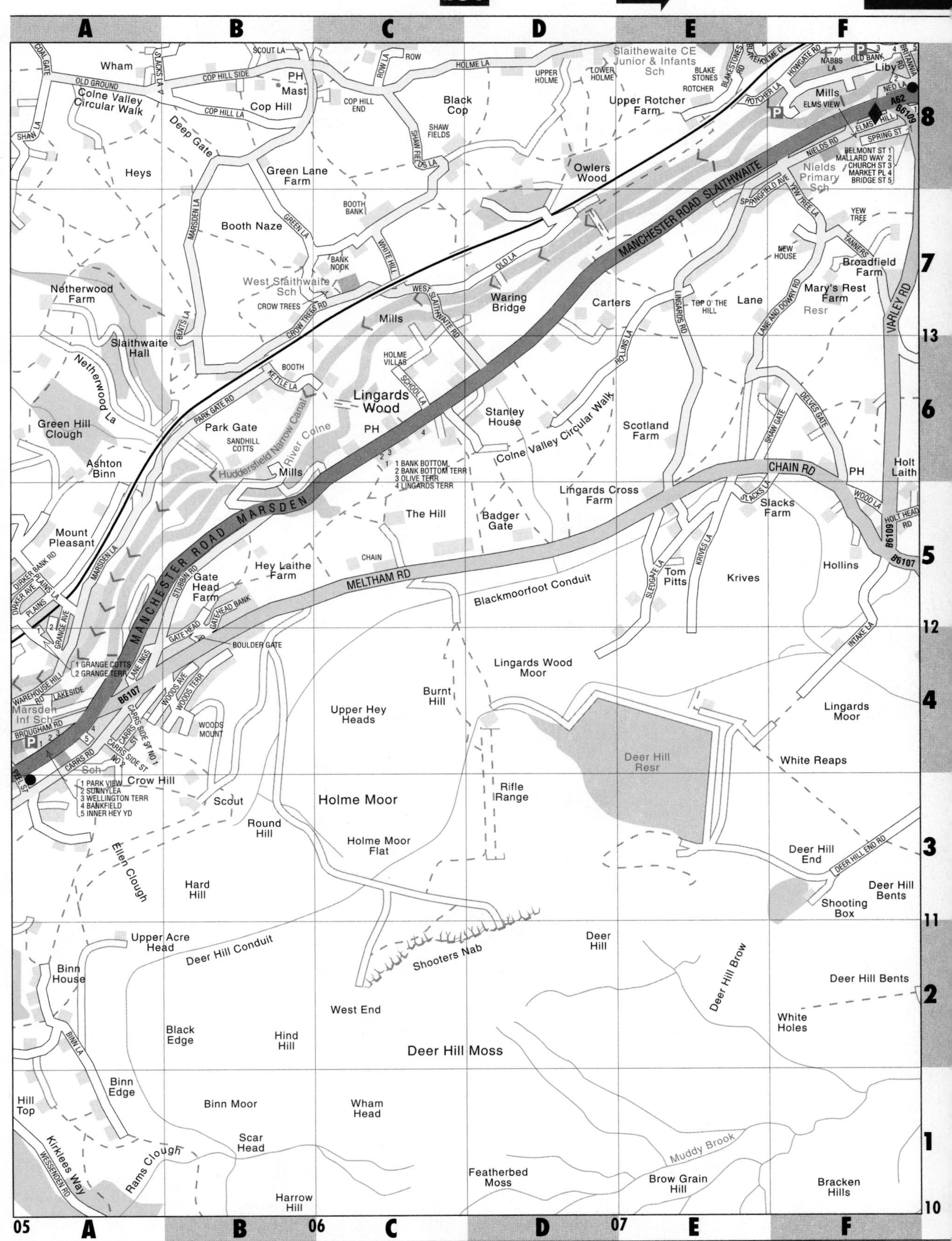
Wham
Colne Valley Circular Walk
Cop Hill
Deep Gate
Heys
Green Lane Farm
Booth Naze
Black Cop
Upper Rotcher Farm
Owlers Wood
Slaithwaite CE Junior & Infants Sch
Netherwood Farm
Slaithwaite Hall
Netherwood La
Green Hill Clough
Ashton Binn
Mount Pleasant
West Slaithwaite Sch
Waring Bridge
Carters
Lane
Broadfield Farm
Mary's Rest Farm
Lingards Wood
Park Gate
Stanley House
Scotland Farm
Huddersfield Narrow Canal
River Colne
MANCHESTER ROAD SLAITHWAITE
MANCHESTER ROAD MARSDEN
Lingards Cross Farm
Slacks Farm
The Hill
Badger Gate
Hey Laithe Farm
Gate Head Farm
MELTHAM RD
CHAIN RD
Blackmoorfoot Conduit
Tom Pitts
Krives
Hollins
Holt Laith
Lingards Wood Moor
Burnt Hill
Upper Hey Heads
Lingards Moor
White Reaps
Deer Hill Resr
Crow Hill
Scout
Holme Moor
Rifle Range
Round Hill
Holme Moor Flat
Deer Hill End
Deer Hill Bents
Shooting Box
Ellen Clough
Hard Hill
Upper Acre Head
Deer Hill Conduit
Shooters Nab
Deer Hill
Deer Hill Brow
Binn House
White Holes
West End
Black Edge
Hind Hill
Deer Hill Moss
Binn Edge
Hill Top
Binn Moor
Wham Head
Scar Head
Rams Clough
Kirklees Way
Muddy Brook
Featherbed Moss
Brow Grain Hill
Bracken Hills
Harrow Hill
Marsden Inf Sch
1 BANK BOTTOM
2 BANK BOTTOM TERR
3 OLIVE TERR
4 LINGARDS TERR
1 PARK VIEW
2 SUNNYLEA
3 WELLINGTON TERR
4 BANKFIELD
5 INNER HEY YD
BELMONT ST 1
MALLARD WAY 2
CHURCH ST 3
MARKET PL 4
BRIDGE ST 5

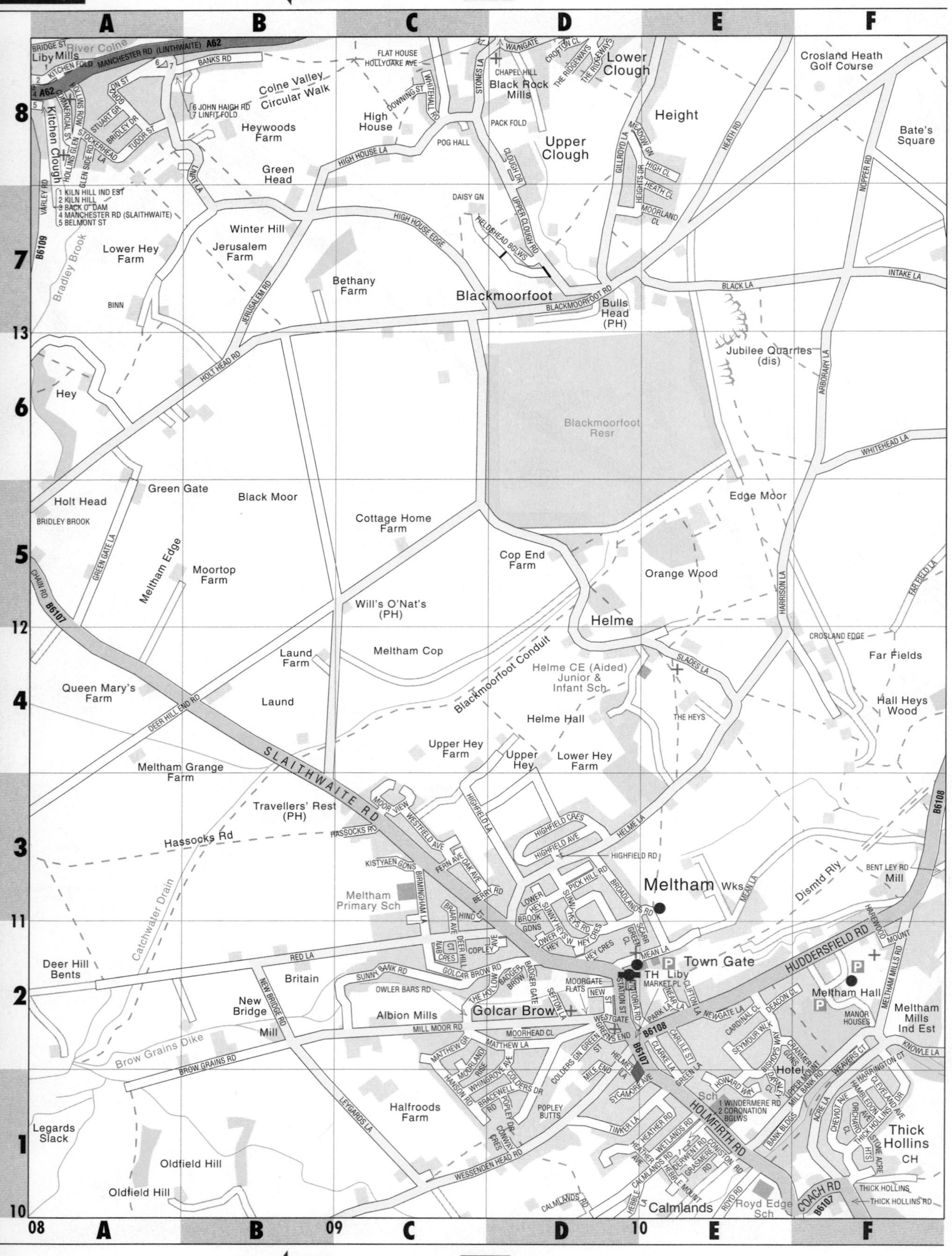
A
B
C
D
E
F
8
7
13
6
5
12
4
3
11
2
1
10
08
09
10
Liby Mills
River Colne
MANCHESTER RD (LINTHWAITE)
A62
BANKS RD
Kitchen Clough
Colne Valley Circular Walk
6 JOHN HAIGH RD
7 LINFIT FOLD
Heywoods Farm
High House
FLAT HOUSE
HOLLYOAKE AVE
WANIGATE
CHAPEL HILL
Black Rock Mills
CROFTON CL
Lower Clough
Crosland Heath Golf Course
PACK FOLD
POG HALL
Upper Clough
Height
Bate's Square
Green Head
HIGH HOUSE LA
1 KILN HILL IND EST
2 KILN HILL
3 BACK O' DAM
4 MANCHESTER RD (SLAITHWAITE)
5 BELMONT ST
DAISY GN
HIGH HOUSE EDGE
FIELDHEAD BGLWS
UPPER CLOUGH RD
HEATH RD
NOPPER RD
Winter Hill
Jerusalem Farm
Lower Hey Farm
Bradley Brook
B6109
Bethany Farm
Blackmoorfoot
BLACKMOORFOOT RD
Bulls Head (PH)
BLACK LA
INTAKE LA
BINN
JERUSALEM RD
HOLT HEAD RD
Jubilee Quarries (dis)
ARBORARY LA
Hey
Blackmoorfoot Resr
WHITEHEAD LA
Holt Head
Green Gate
Black Moor
Cottage Home Farm
Edge Moor
BRIDLEY BROOK
GREEN GATE LA
Meltham Edge
Moortop Farm
Cop End Farm
Orange Wood
HARRISON LA
CHAIN RD
B6107
Will's O'Nat's (PH)
Helme
CROSLAND EDGE
Far Fields
Laund Farm
Meltham Cop
Blackmoorfoot Conduit
Helme CE (Aided) Junior & Infant Sch
SLADES LA
Queen Mary's Farm
DEER HILL END RD
Laund
Helme Hall
THE HEYS
Hall Heys Wood
SLAITHWAITE RD
Upper Hey Farm
Upper Hey
Lower Hey Farm
Meltham Grange Farm
Travellers' Rest (PH)
B6108
HIGHFIELD CRES
HIGHFIELD AVE
HELME LA
HIGHFIELD RD
Hassocks Rd
HASSOCKS RD
Catchwater Drain
KISTYAEN GDNS
Meltham
Wks
Dismtd Rly
BENT LEY RD
Mill
Meltham Primary Sch
BIRMINGHAM LA
BROADLANDS RD
HUDDERSFIELD RD
RED LA
Town Gate
TH
Liby
MARKET PL
Deer Hill Bents
Britain
GOLCAR BROW RD
OWLER BARS RD
MOORGATE FLATS
Meltham Hall
MANOR HOUSES
New Bridge
Albion Mills
Golcar Brow
WESTGATE
Meltham Mills Ind Est
NEW BRIDGE RD
Mill
MILL MOOR RD
MOORHEAD CL
KNOWLE LA
Brow Grains Dike
BROW GRAINS RD
Hotel
Sch
1 WINDERMERE RD
2 CORONATION BGLWS
HOLMFIRTH RD
LEYGARDS LA
Halfroods Farm
POPLEY BUTTS
Legards Slack
Thick Hollins
CH
Oldfield Hill
WESSENDEN HEAD RD
THICK HOLLINS
THICK HOLLINS RD
COACH RD
Calmlands
Royd Edge Sch
CALMLANDS RD

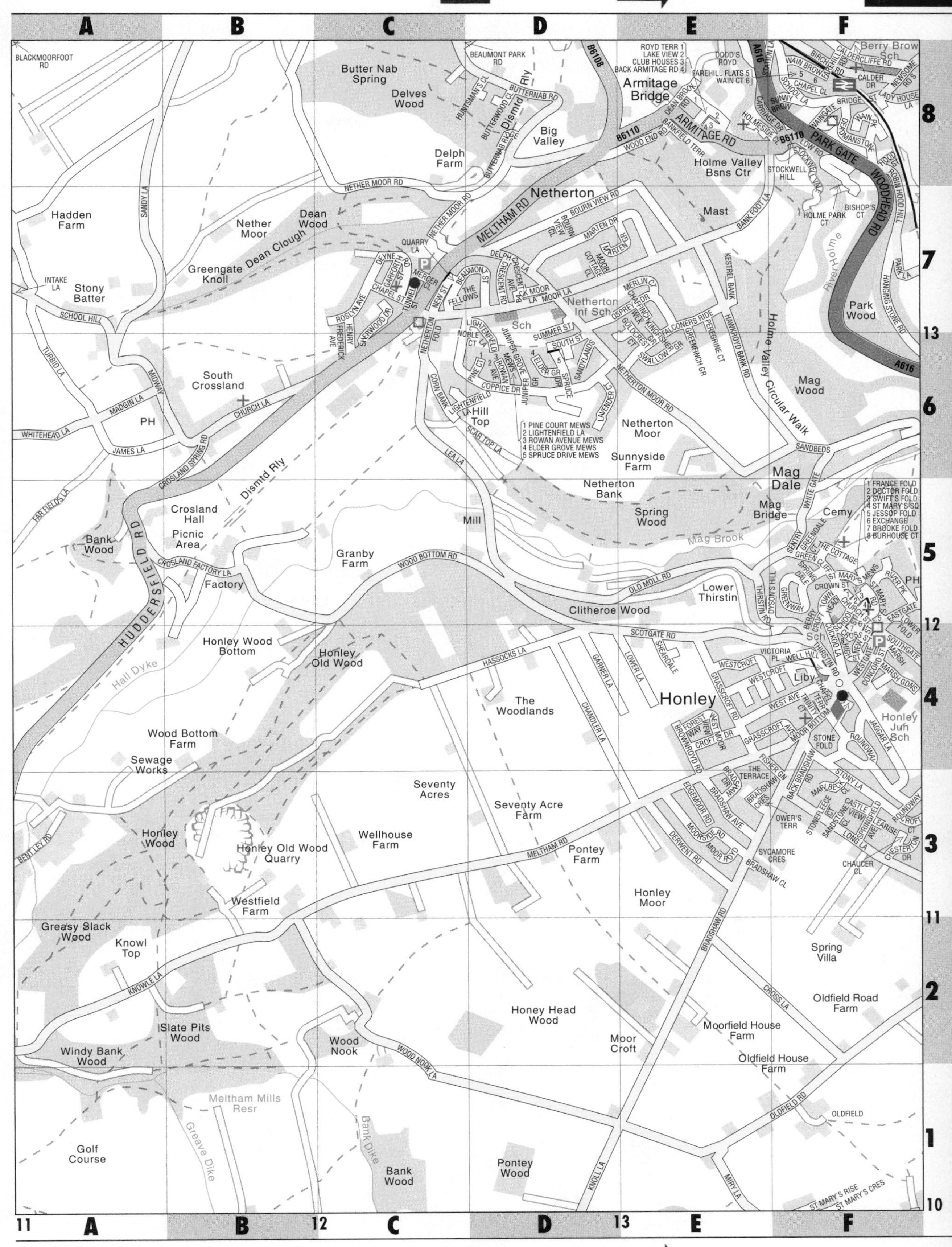
A
B
C
D
E
F
8
7
13
6
5
12
4
3
11
2
1
10
11
12
13
Butter Nab Spring
Delves Wood
Big Valley
Delph Farm
Armitage Bridge
Holme Valley Bsns Ctr
Stockwell Hill
Mast
Netherton
Hadden Farm
Nether Moor
Dean Wood
Dean Clough
Greengate Knoll
Stony Batter
South Crossland
PH
Netherton Inf Sch
Sch
Hill Top
Netherton Moor
Sunnyside Farm
Netherton Bank
Spring Wood
Mag Dale
Mag Bridge
Mag Brook
Mag Wood
Park Wood
Holme Valley Circular Walk
River Holme
Crosland Hall
Picnic Area
Bank Wood
Factory
Granby Farm
Mill
Lower Thirstin
Clitheroe Wood
Cemy
Honley Wood Bottom
Honley Old Wood
Hall Dyke
The Woodlands
Honley
Liby
Honley Jun Sch
Wood Bottom Farm
Sewage Works
Seventy Acres
Seventy Acre Farm
Honley Wood
Honley Old Wood Quarry
Wellhouse Farm
Pontey Farm
Westfield Farm
Honley Moor
Greasy Slack Wood
Knowl Top
Spring Villa
Oldfield Road Farm
Honey Head Wood
Moorfield House Farm
Slate Pits Wood
Wood Nook
Moor Croft
Oldfield House Farm
Windy Bank Wood
Meltham Mills Resr
Greave Dike
Bank Dike
Golf Course
Bank Wood
Pontey Wood
OLDFIELD
Berry Brow Sch
BLACKMOORFOOT RD
BEAUMONT PARK RD
ROYD TERR 1
LAKE VIEW 2
CLUB HOUSES 3
BACK ARMITAGE RD 4
FAREHILL FLATS 5
WAIN CT 6
DODD'S ROYD
ARMITAGE RD
B6108
B6110
A616
PARK GATE
WOODHEAD RD
MELTHAM RD
NETHER MOOR RD
SANDY LA
INTAKE LA
SCHOOL HILL
TURBID LA
MIDWAY
MADGIN LA
CHURCH LA
WHITEHEAD LA
JAMES LA
CROSLAND SPRING RD
FAR FIELDS LA
HUDDERSFIELD RD
CROSLAND FACTORY LA
Dismtd Rly
WOOD BOTTOM RD
OLD MOLL RD
SCOTGATE RD
HASSOCKS LA
GARNER LA
LOWER LA
CHANDLER LA
SANDBEDS
BANK FOOT LA
KESTREL BANK
HAWKROYD BANK RD
BOURN VIEW RD
LEA LA
SCAR TOP LA
1 PINE COURT MEWS
2 LIGHTENFIELD LA
3 ROWAN AVENUE MEWS
4 ELDER GROVE MEWS
5 SPRUCE DRIVE MEWS
1 FRANCE FOLD
2 DOCTOR FOLD
3 SWIFT'S FOLD
4 ST MARY'S SQ
5 JESSOP FOLD
6 EXCHANGE
7 BROOKE FOLD
8 BURHOUSE CT
WESTCROFT
GRASSCROFT RD
WEST AVE
MOOR BOTTOM
BRADSHAW RD
BRADSHAW AVE
BRADSHAW CL
DERWENT RD
EDGEMOOR RD
SYCAMORE CRES
CHAUCER CL
ROUNDWAY
CROSS LA
KNOWLE LA
WOOD NOOK LA
OLDFIELD RD
KNOLL LA
MIRY LA
ST MARY'S RISE
ST MARY'S CRES
BENT LEY RD

171
154

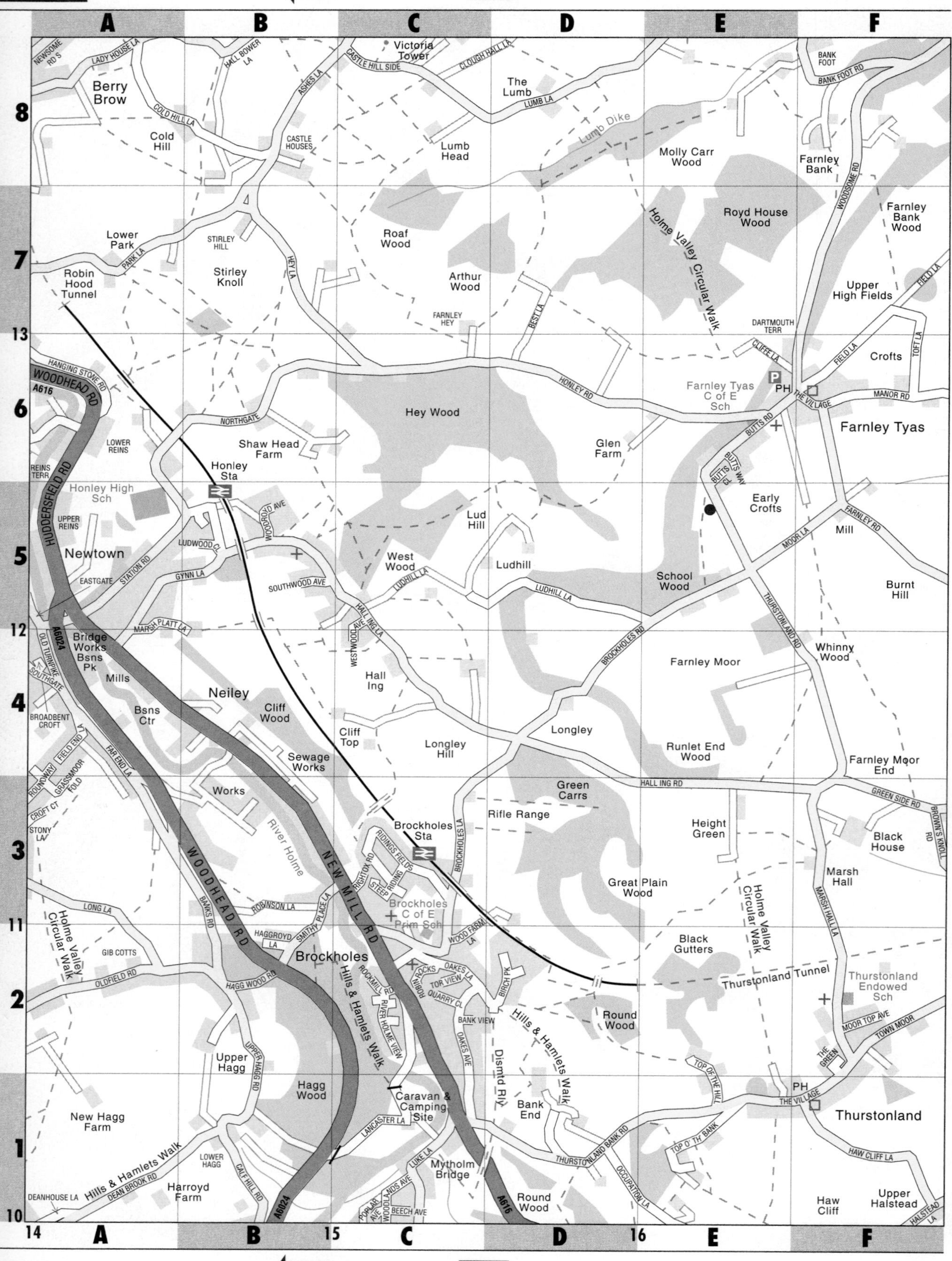
A
B
C
D
E
F
8
7
13
6
5
12
4
3
11
2
1
10
14
15
16
Berry Brow
Cold Hill
Victoria Tower
The Lumb
Lumb Head
Molly Carr Wood
Farnley Bank
Lumb Dike
Royd House Wood
Farnley Bank Wood
Lower Park
Roaf Wood
Arthur Wood
Robin Hood Tunnel
Stirley Knoll
Upper High Fields
Crofts
Holme Valley Circular Walk
Farnley Tyas C of E Sch
Farnley Tyas
Hey Wood
Shaw Head Farm
Glen Farm
Honley Sta
Honley High Sch
Early Crofts
Lud Hill
Mill
Newtown
West Wood
Ludhill
School Wood
Burnt Hill
Bridge Works Bsns Pk
Mills
Hall Ing
Farnley Moor
Whinny Wood
Neiley
Cliff Wood
Bsns Ctr
Cliff Top
Longley Hill
Longley
Runlet End Wood
Sewage Works
Farnley Moor End
Works
Green Carrs
Rifle Range
River Holme
Brockholes Sta
Height Green
Black House
Marsh Hall
Great Plain Wood
Brockholes C of E Prim Sch
Black Gutters
Brockholes
Hills & Hamlets Walk
Thurstonland Tunnel
Thurstonland Endowed Sch
Round Wood
Dismtd Rly
Upper Hagg
Hagg Wood
Caravan & Camping Site
Bank End
PH
Thurstonland
New Hagg Farm
Mytholm Bridge
Harroyd Farm
Haw Cliff
Upper Halstead
WOODHEAD RD
HUDDERSFIELD RD
NEW MILL RD
A616
A6024
HONLEY RD
HALL ING RD
BROCKHOLES RD
MOOR LA
THURSTONLAND RD
LUDHILL LA

171
189

155
174

Lower High Fields
Leigh Fields
Carr Wood
Woodsome Lees
Slate Fields
Range Dike
North Spring Wood
Dean Bottom
Highburton
Highburton C of E (Controlled) First Sch
Kirkburton Middle Sch
Netherton
MANOR RD
The Mansion
Kirkburton
Lincoln House Sch
Kirkburton C of E Sch
Moor Side
Ravensknowle
Riley
Storthes Hall Moor Wood
Storthes Hall
Myers Wood
Storthes Hall Moor
Highfield Farm
Cemy
Saville Wood
Causeway Foot
Blagdens
Boothroyd Wood
Laycock Wood
Joy Wood
Shelley Wood
Wood End
Jenkinson Wood
Smith Wood
Grange
Healey Farm
Healey Greave Wood
Green Side
Clough Wood
Lumb House
Thunder Bridge
Hartley Bank Wood
Hill Top Farm
Brown's Knoll
Brown's Knoll Wood
Birks Wood
Clothiers Arms Inn
Moor Bottom
Stocksmoor
Stocksmoor Sta
Shepley Mill Wood
Round Wood
Wood Lea
Ing Head
Stocks
Lower Stone Wood
Shepley Sta
Lower Halstead Farm
Stone Wood Dike
Stocks Wood
Upper Stone Wood
PENISTONE RD
NORTH RD
GEORGE ST
HUDDERSFIELD RD
Box Ings La
Thunder Bridge Dike
Shepley Dike
BANK HALL GR 1
DYKE BOTTOM 2
FIELD WAY 3

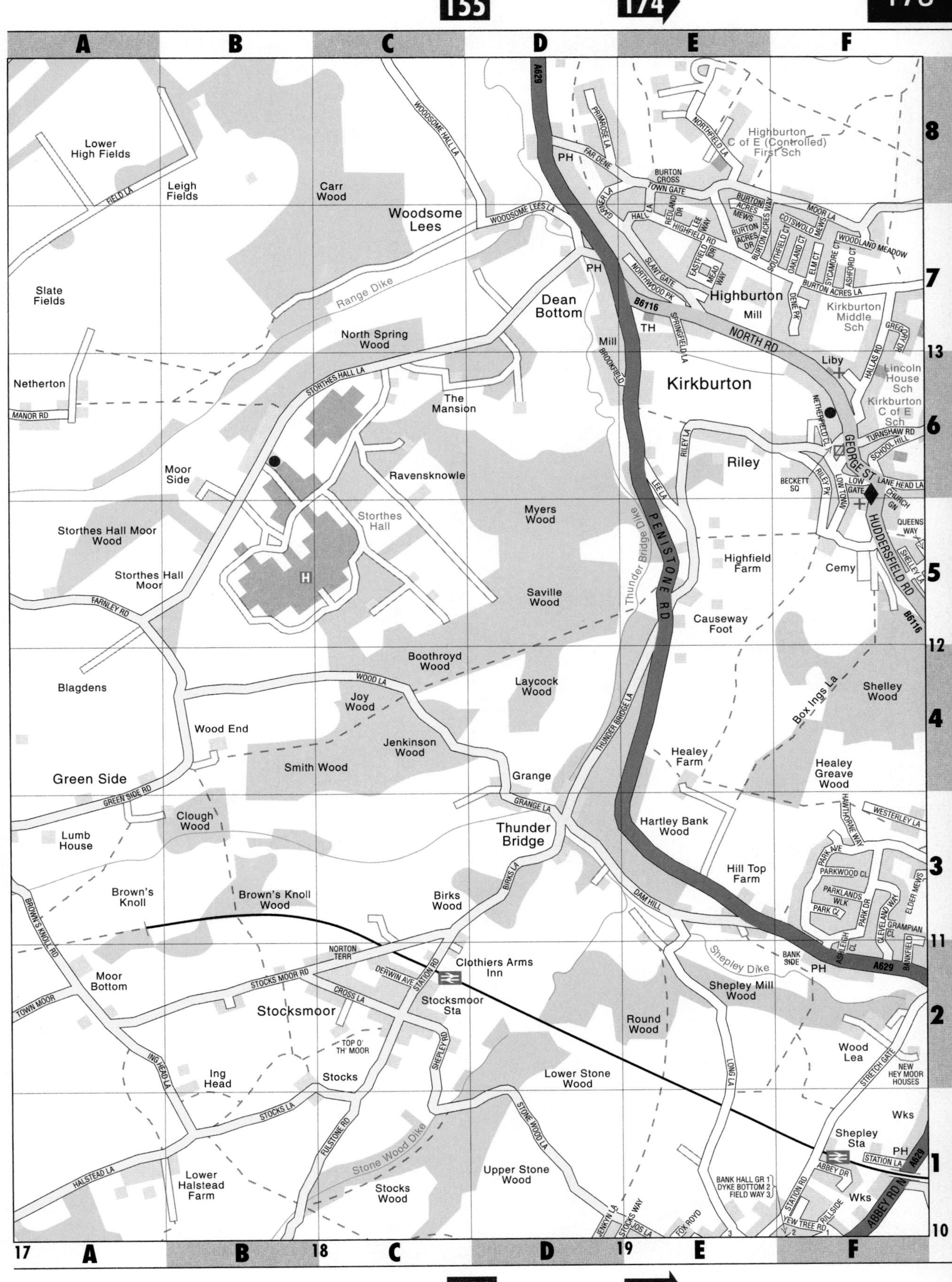

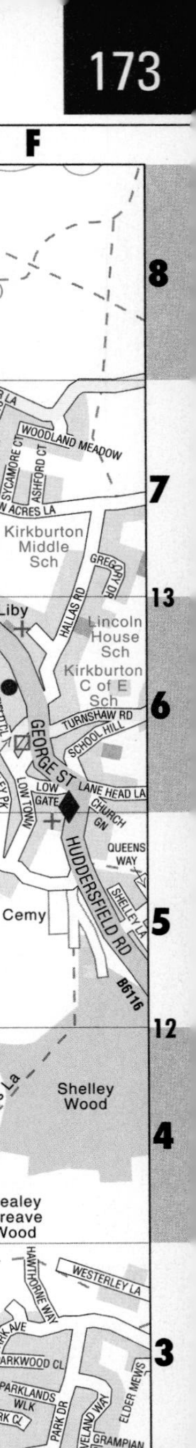

190
174

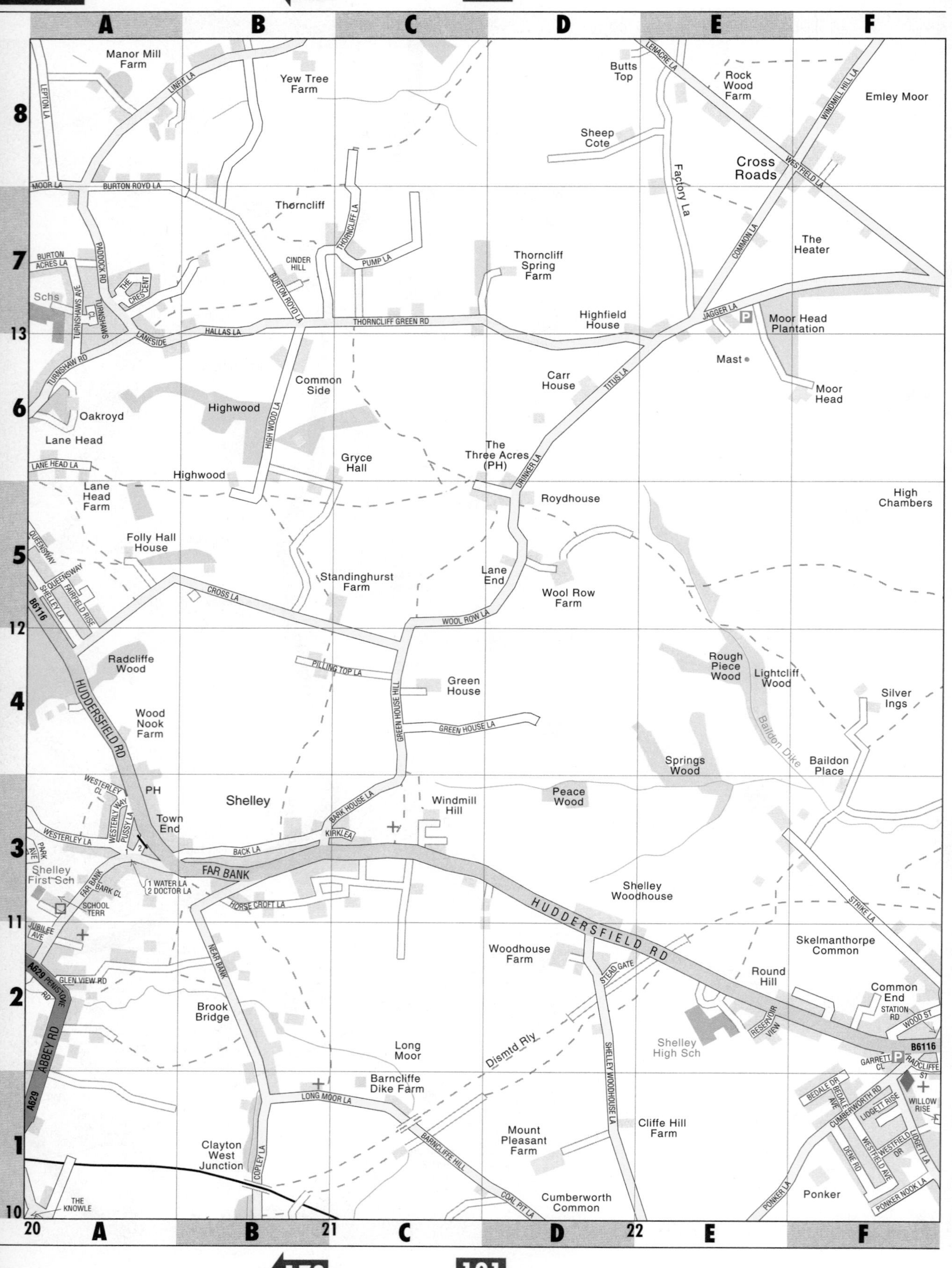
A
B
C
D
E
F
8
7
13
6
5
12
4
3
11
2
1
10
20
21
22
Manor Mill Farm
Yew Tree Farm
Butts Top
Rock Wood Farm
Emley Moor
Sheep Cote
Cross Roads
Thorncliff
Factory La
The Heater
Thorncliff Spring Farm
Highfield House
Moor Head Plantation
Mast
Moor Head
Carr House
Common Side
Highwood
Oakroyd
Lane Head
The Three Acres (PH)
Gryce Hall
Roydhouse
High Chambers
Lane Head Farm
Folly Hall House
Standinghurst Farm
Lane End
Wool Row Farm
Radcliffe Wood
Green House
Rough Piece Wood
Lightcliff Wood
Silver Ings
Wood Nook Farm
Springs Wood
Baildon Dike
Baildon Place
PH
Shelley
Windmill Hill
Peace Wood
Town End
Shelley First Sch
Shelley Woodhouse
Woodhouse Farm
Skelmanthorpe Common
Round Hill
Common End
Brook Bridge
Shelley High Sch
Long Moor
Dismtd Rly
Barncliffe Dike Farm
Mount Pleasant Farm
Cliffe Hill Farm
Clayton West Junction
Cumberworth Common
Ponker
THE KNOWLE
Schs
LEPTON LA
LINFIT LA
MOOR LA
BURTON ROYD LA
BURTON ACRES LA
PADDOCK RD
THE CRESCENT
TURNSHAWS AVE
TURNSHAWS CL
TURNSHAWS
LANESIDE
HALLAS LA
TURNSHAW RD
CINDER HILL
BURTON ROYD LA
THORNCLIFF LA
PUMP LA
THORNCLIFF GREEN RD
LENACRE LA
WINDMILL HILL LA
WESTFIELD LA
COMMON LA
JAGGER LA
TITUS LA
DRINKER LA
HIGH WOOD LA
LANE HEAD LA
QUEENSWAY
SHELLEY LA
FAIRFIELD RISE
B6116
CROSS LA
WOOL ROW LA
PILLING TOP LA
GREEN HOUSE HILL
GREEN HOUSE LA
HUDDERSFIELD RD
WESTERLEY CL
WESTERLY WAY
PUSSY LA
WESTERLEY LA
PARK AVE
BARK HOUSE LA
KIRKLEA
BACK LA
FAR BANK
FAR BANK
BARK CL
1 WATER LA
2 DOCTOR LA
SCHOOL TERR
HORSE CROFT LA
JUBILEE AVE
NEAR BANK
STEAD GATE
STRIKE LA
A629 PENISTONE RD
GLEN VIEW RD
ABBEY RD
A629
RESERVOIR VIEW
STATION RD
WOOD ST
B6116
GARRETT CL
RADCLIFFE ST
SHELLEY WOODHOUSE LA
LONG MOOR LA
BARNCLIFFE HILL
COAL PIT LA
COPLEY LA
BEDALE DR
BEDALE AVE
CUMBERWORTH RD
LIDGETT RISE
WILLOW RISE
WESTFIELD AVE
WESTFIELD DR
LIDGETT LA
DENE RD
PONKER LA
PONKER NOOK LA

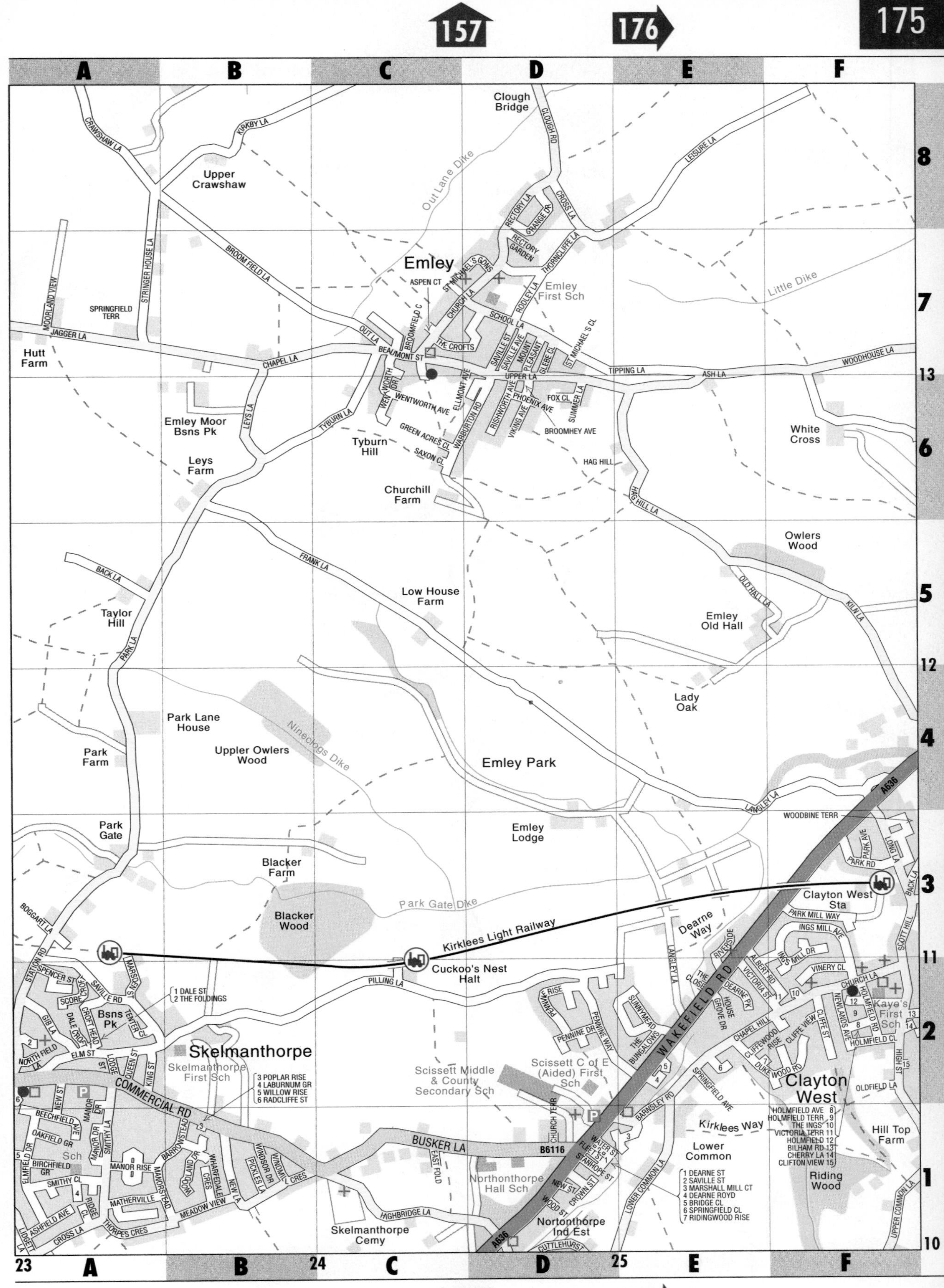
A
B
C
D
E
F
Clough Bridge
CLOUGH RD
CRAWSHAW LA
KIRKBY LA
Upper Crawshaw
Out Lane Dike
LEISURE LA
RECTORY LA
GRANGE DR
CROSS LA
RECTORY GARDEN
THORNCLIFFE LA
STRINGER HOUSE LA
BROOM FIELD LA
Emley
ASPEN CT
ST MICHAEL'S GDNS
Emley First Sch
Little Dike
MOORLAND VIEW
SPRINGFIELD TERR
CHURCH LA
RODLEY LA
SCHOOL LA
ST MICHAEL'S CL
JAGGER LA
Hutt Farm
OUT LA
BROOMFIELD C
THE CROFTS
SAVILLE ST
SAVILLE AVE
MOUNT PLEASANT
GLEBE CL
BEAUMONT ST
CHAPEL LA
TIPPING LA
ASH LA
WOODHOUSE LA
UPPER LA
WENTWORTH DR
ELLMONT AVE
RISHWORTH AVE
PHOENIX AVE
FOX CL
SUMMER LA
WENTWORTH AVE
WARBURTON RD
VIKING AVE
BROOMHEY AVE
Emley Moor Bsns Pk
LEYS LA
TYBURN LA
GREEN ACRES CL
Tyburn Hill
White Cross
SAXON CL
HAG HILL
Leys Farm
Churchill Farm
HAG HILL LA
Owlers Wood
FRANK LA
BACK LA
Low House Farm
OLD HALL LA
KILN LA
Taylor Hill
Emley Old Hall
PARK LA
Lady Oak
Park Lane House
Ninecrogs Dike
Park Farm
Uppler Owlers Wood
Emley Park
LANGLEY LA
A636
WOODBINE TERR
Park Gate
Emley Lodge
PARK AVE
LONG LA
PARK RD
Blacker Farm
BACK LA
Clayton West Sta
Park Gate Dike
BOGGART LA
Blacker Wood
Kirklees Light Railway
Dearne Way
PARK MILL WAY
INGS MILL AVE
INGS MILL DR
SCOTT HILL
STATION RD
SPENCER ST
MARSDEN ST
Cuckoo's Nest Halt
RIVERSIDE
ALBERT RD
VINERY CL
SAVILLE RD
SCORE CROFT
1 DALE ST
2 THE FOLDINGS
PILLING LA
LANGLEY LA
THE CLOSE
VICTORIA ST
CHURCH LA
DALE CROFT
CROFT HEAD
Bsns Pk
TENTER CL
PENNINE RISE
SUNNYMEAD
DEARNE PK
HOUSE GROVE DR
Kaye's First Sch
GIB LA
NEWLANDS AVE
HOLMFIELD RD
PENNINE DR
PENNINE WAY
THE BUNGALOWS
WAKEFIELD RD
CHAPEL HILL
CLIFFEWOOD RISE
CLIFFE VIEW
CLIFFE ST
NORTH FIELD LA
HOLMFIELD CL
ELM ST
LODGE ST
QUEEN ST
KING ST
Skelmanthorpe
Skelmanthorpe First Sch
Scissett Middle & County Secondary Sch
Scissett C of E (Aided) First Sch
HIGH ST
DUKE WOOD RD
Clayton West
OLDFIELD LA
3 POPLAR RISE
4 LABURNUM GR
5 WILLOW RISE
6 RADCLIFFE ST
SPRINGFIELD AVE
NEW ST
COMMERCIAL RD
BARNSLEY RD
HOLMFIELD AVE 8
HOLMFIELD TERR 9
THE INGS 10
VICTORIA TERR 11
HOLMFIELD 12
BILHAM RD 13
CHERRY LA 14
CLIFTON VIEW 15
Hill Top Farm
BEECHFIELD AVE
MANOR DR
Kirklees Way
OAKFIELD GR
SMITHY LA
BARROWSTEAD
BUSKER LA
CHURCH TERR
WATER ST
Lower Common
ELMFIELD DR
BIRCHFIELD GR
MANOR RISE
WOODLAND DR
WHARFEDALE CRES
PICKLES LA
WINDSOR DR
WINDMILL CRES
B6116
EAST FOLD
FLEET ST
STANHOPE ST
SMITHY CL
MANORSTEAD
NEW LA
Northonthorpe Hall Sch
NEW ST
CROWN ST
LOWER COMMON LA
1 DEARNE ST
2 SAVILLE ST
3 MARSHALL MILL CT
4 DEARNE ROYD
5 BRIDGE CL
6 SPRINGFIELD CL
7 RIDINGWOOD RISE
Riding Wood
MATHERVILLE
MEADOW VIEW
ASHFIELD AVE
RIDGE CL
HIGHBRIDGE LA
WOOD ST
Nortonthorpe Ind Est
UPPER COMMON LA
CROSS LA
THORPES CRES
Skelmanthorpe Cemy
LIDGET LA
CUTTLEHURST
8
7
13
6
5
12
4
3
11
2
1
10
23
24
25

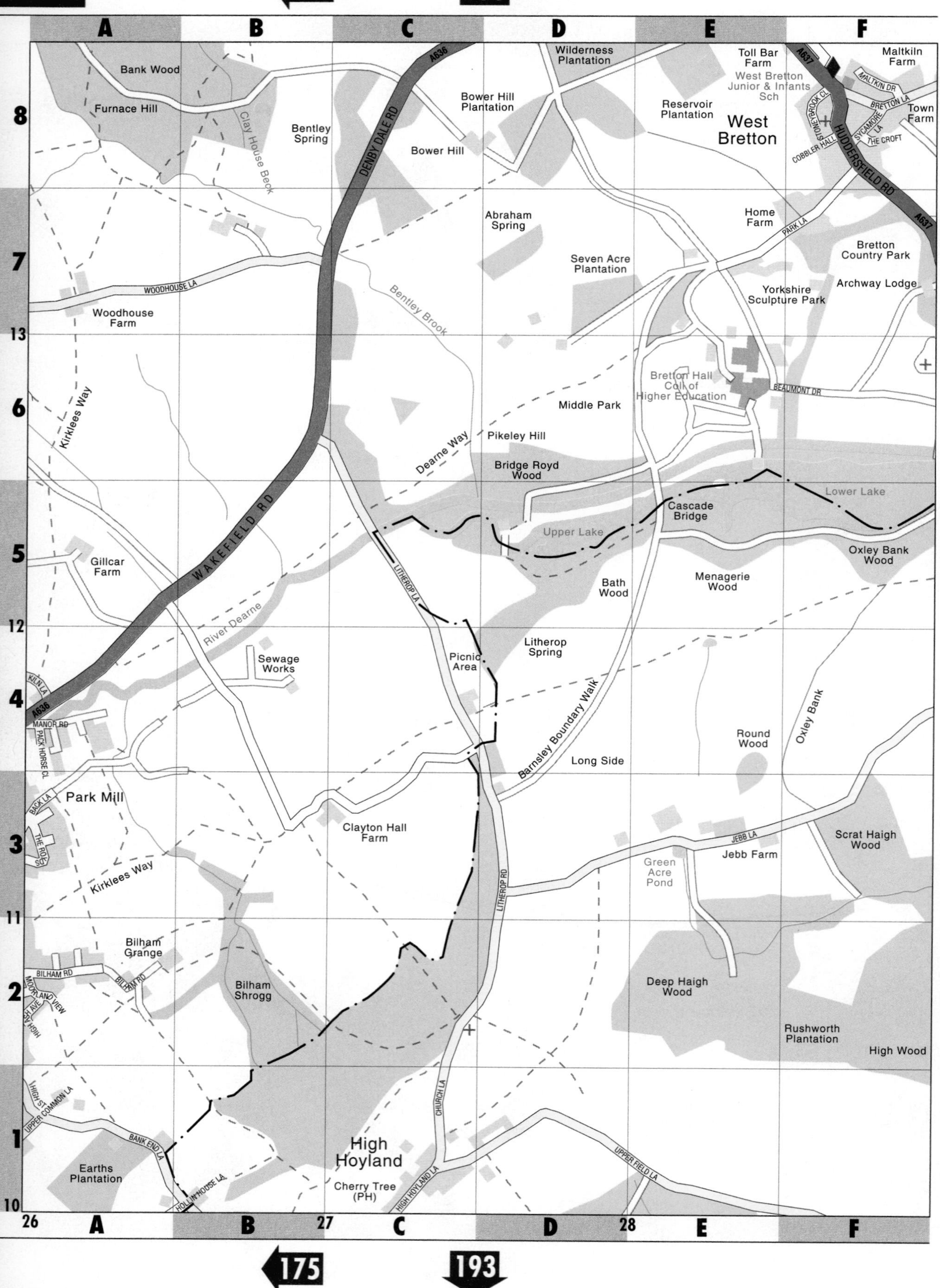
A
B
C
D
E
F
Bank Wood
Furnace Hill
Clay House Beck
Bentley Spring
DENBY DALE RD
A636
Wilderness Plantation
Bower Hill Plantation
Bower Hill
Toll Bar Farm
West Bretton Junior & Infants Sch
Reservoir Plantation
West Bretton
Maltkiln Farm
MALTKIN DR
BRETTON LA
Town Farm
STONEYBROOK CL
COBBLER HALL
SYCAMORE LA
THE CROFT
HUDDERSFIELD RD
A637
Abraham Spring
Home Farm
PARK LA
Bretton Country Park
Seven Acre Plantation
WOODHOUSE LA
Woodhouse Farm
Bentley Brook
Yorkshire Sculpture Park
Archway Lodge
Bretton Hall Coll of Higher Education
BEAUMONT DR
Middle Park
Kirklees Way
Dearne Way
Pikeley Hill
Bridge Royd Wood
Lower Lake
Cascade Bridge
Upper Lake
WAKEFIELD RD
Gillcar Farm
LITHEROP LA
Oxley Bank Wood
Bath Wood
Menagerie Wood
River Dearne
Litherop Spring
Sewage Works
Picnic Area
KILN LA
A636
MANOR RD
PACK HORSE CL
Barnsley Boundary Walk
Round Wood
Oxley Bank
Long Side
BACK LA
Park Mill
THE ROYD
Clayton Hall Farm
JEBB LA
Scrat Haigh Wood
Jebb Farm
Green Acre Pond
Kirklees Way
LITHEROP RD
Bilham Grange
BILHAM RD
BILHAM RD
MOORLAND VIEW
HIGH HALL AVE
Bilham Shrogg
Deep Haigh Wood
Rushworth Plantation
High Wood
HIGH ST
UPPER COMMON LA
CHURCH LA
BANK END LA
High Hoyland
UPPER FIELD LA
Earths Plantation
HOLLIN HOUSE LA
Cherry Tree (PH)
HIGH HOYLAND LA
8
7
13
6
5
12
4
3
11
2
1
10
26
27
28

A B C D E F

8
7
13
6
5
12
4
3
11
2
1
10

Wooley Edge Service Area
Bimshaw Wood
Common La
Water La
Gallows La
Mast
High Moor
Common Doles
Beacon Hill
Picnic Site
Eccle Hill
Ash Farm
Woolley
Backhouse La
Finkle Cl
Wentworth Cl
High St
Sinkle Cl
Savin Royd Wood
Rose Farm
High House Farm
Molly Hurst La
Church St
Church Farm
Back La
Sewage Works
Bretton La
Bramley La
M1
Intake La
Woolley Low Moor La
Common La
Haigh La
Moor House Spring
Middle Field La
Woolley Edge La
Dearne Way & Barnsley Boundary Walk
Bretton Park
Smithy Ridge
Beaumont Dr
Huddersfield Rd
Jobson Wood
Gipsy La
Hartop La
Claphouse Fold
Sewage Works
Haigh Mews
Moorhouse La
Near Moor Farm
Haigh
Jebb La
Haw Top
Haigh Hill
Spoil Heap
Barnsley Boundary Walk
Junction 38
Low Swithen
Windhill La
Windhill Gate
Haigh Hall
Sheep Lane Head
Swithen House
Riverside Farm
River Dearne
Windhill Wood
Woolley First Sch
Husband Wood
Colliery
Top Row
Low Row
Woolley Colliery Rd
Bluebell Rd
Upper Swithen
Fish Pond Halt
Huddersfield Rd
Walk Royd Hill
Park Hill
Swithen Hill
Sewage Works
Spoil Heap
High Wood
Dearne Way
Woolley Colliery Rd
Bloomhouse La
Kingsway
Snapethorpe
Birthwaite Hall
Spring Ram Bsns Pk
Darton Sta
Fountain Sq
Bloomfield Rise
Bloomfield
Bloomhouse
Granborne Dr
Bloomfield
Cowcroft Wood
Brook Hill
Huddersfield Rd
M1
Sike Cl
Falcon Knoll Ing
Allendale Rd
1 Oaks Wood Dr
Howden Cl
Darton Primary Sch
Oaks Farm Cl
Darton Hall Dr
Montrose Ave
Rockwood
Lannvale Fold
Squirrel Hall
Birthwaite Rd
Lambe Flatt
Middle La
Falconer Cl
High Cl
A637
Church St
B6131
Station Rd
Mill La St
School St
Bridge St
Dearne St
Darton Hall Cl
B6131
Church Cl
Kexbrough

29 A 30 B C 30 C D 31 D E F

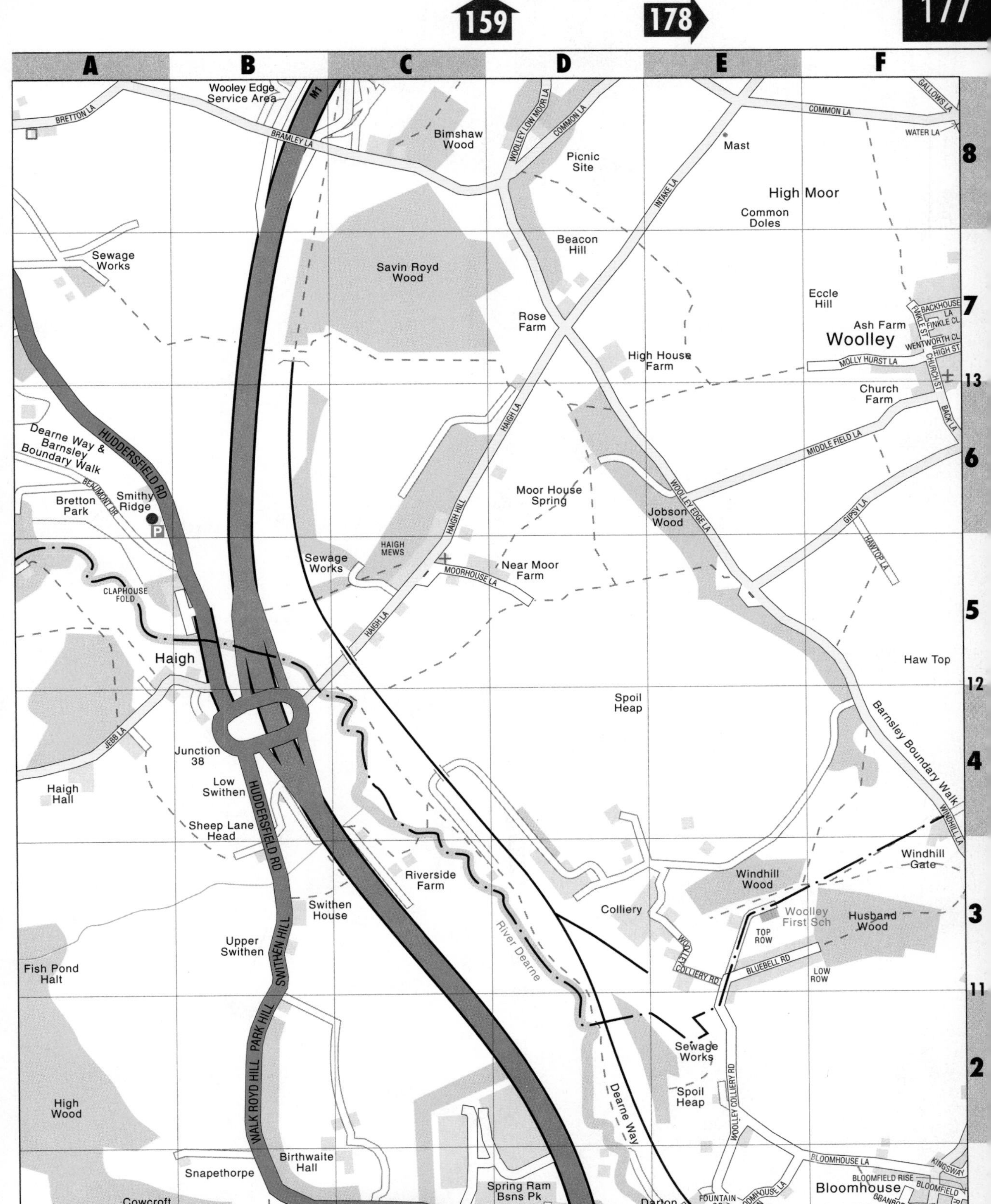

177
160

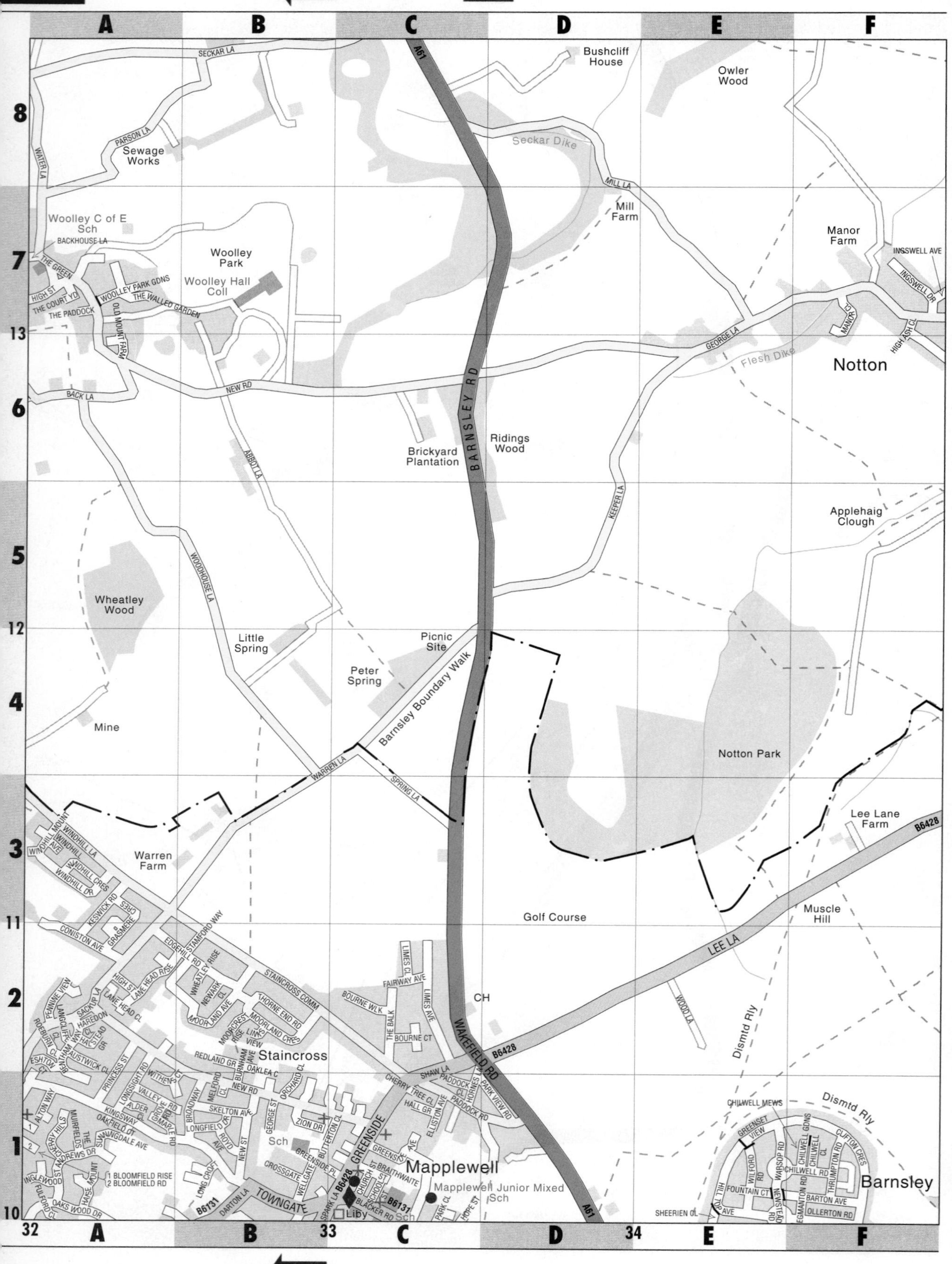
A
B
C
D
E
F
8
7
13
6
5
12
4
3
11
2
1
10
32
33
34
SECKAR LA
A61
Bushcliff House
Owler Wood
Sewage Works
PARSON LA
WATER LA
Seckar Dike
MILL LA
Mill Farm
Woolley C of E Sch
BACKHOUSE LA
Woolley Park
Woolley Hall Coll
Manor Farm
INGSWELL AVE
INGSWELL DR
THE GREEN
HIGH ST
THE COURT YD
THE PADDOCK
WOOLLEY PARK GDNS
THE WALLED GARDEN
OLD MOUNT FARM
GEORGE LA
MANOR CL
HIGH ASH CL
Flesh Dike
Notton
NEW RD
BACK LA
BARNSLEY RD
Ridings Wood
Brickyard Plantation
ABBOT LA
KEEPER LA
Applehaig Clough
WOODHOUSE LA
Wheatley Wood
Little Spring
Picnic Site
Peter Spring
Barnsley Boundary Walk
Mine
Notton Park
WARREN LA
SPRING LA
Lee Lane Farm
B6428
Warren Farm
WINDHILL MOUNT
WINDHILL LA
WINDHILL AVE
WINDHILL CRES
WINDHILL DR
KESWICK RD
GRASMERE CRES
CONISTON AVE
STAMFORD WAY
EDGEHILL RD
Golf Course
Muscle Hill
LEE LA
WHEATLEY RISE
LANE HEAD RISE
HIGH ST
NEWARK CL
STAINCROSS COMM
LIMES CL
FAIRWAY AVE
BOURNE WLK
LIMES AVE
CH
PENNINE VIEW
SACKUP LA
LANE HEAD CL
HAREDON CL
MOORLAND AVE
THORNE END RD
MOORLAND CRES
MOORCREST RISE
LINKS VIEW
LANGCLIFFE
ROEBURN CL
BENTHAM WAY
HALSTEAD GR
AUSTWICK CL
ESHTON CT
REDLAND GR
BURNHAM AVE
Staincross
OAKLEA C
THE BALK
BOURNE CT
WOOD LA
Dismtd Rly
WAKEFIELD RD
B6428
SHAW LA
PADDOCK CL
HORNES LA
PARK VIEW RD
PADDOCK RD
CHERRY TREE CL
HALL GR
ELLISTON AVE
PRINCESS ST
LONGSIGHT RD
WITHENS
VALLEY RD
ALDER GR
OAKFIELD CT
KINGSWAY
SWANGDALE AVE
GROVE RD
MAPLE RD
BROADWAY
MELFORD CL
SKELTON AVE
LONGFIELD DR
ROYD AVE
NEW ST
GEORGE ST
ORCHARD CL
ZION DR
BUTTERTON CL
GREENSIDE
GREENSIDE PL
BRAITHWAITE
CHURCH ST
SCHOOL ST
BLACKER RD
SPARK LA
B6131
Sch
Mapplewell
Mapplewell Junior Mixed Sch
PARK CL
HOPE ST
Liby
ALTON WAY
MUIRFIELDS
CHERRY HILLS
THE ST ANDREWS DR
HAISE MOUNT
1 BLOOMFIELD RISE
2 BLOOMFIELD RD
INGLEWOOD
FULFORD CL
OAKS WOOD DR
LONG CROFT
CROSSGATE
WELLGATE
TOWNGATE
DARTON LA
CHILWELL MEWS
GREENSET VIEW
WILFORD RD
WARSOP RD
CHILWELL GDNS
CHILWELL CL
THRUMPTON RD
CLIFTON CRES
Barnsley
FOUNTAIN CT
NEWSTEAD RD
EGMANTON RD
BARTON AVE
OLLERTON RD
HILL TOP AVE
SHEERIEN CL

177

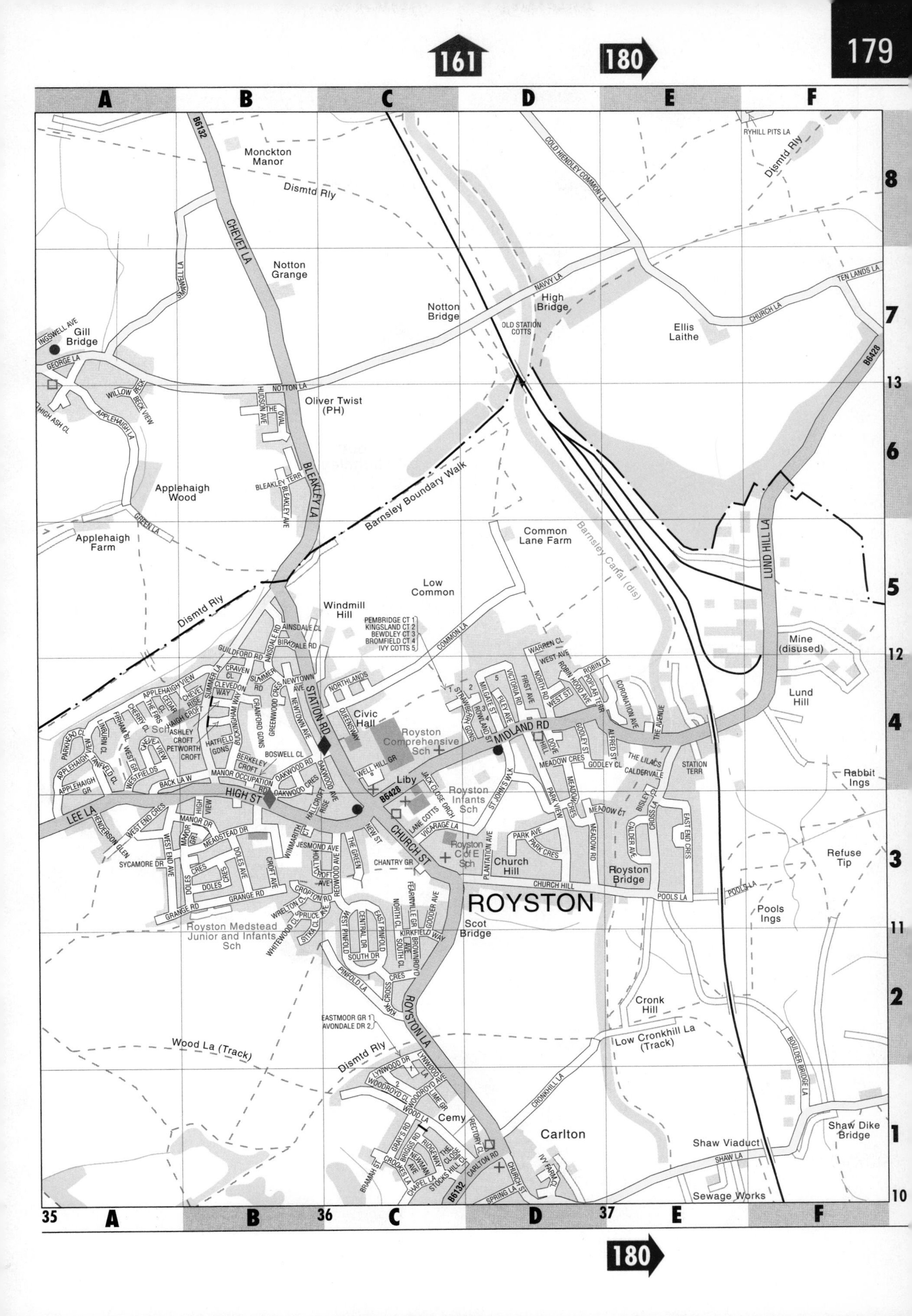
161
180
A
B
C
D
E
F
8
7
13
6
5
12
4
3
11
2
1
10
35
36
37
Monckton Manor
Dismtd Rly
CHEVET LA
Notton Grange
Notton Bridge
NAVVY LA
High Bridge
OLD STATION COTTS
COLD HIENDLEY COMMON LA
RYHILL PITS LA
Ellis Laithe
CHURCH LA
TEN LANDS LA
B6428
Gill Bridge
GEORGE LA
NOTTON LA
Oliver Twist (PH)
WILLOW BECK
BECK VIEW
APPLEHAIGH LA
HIGH ASH CL
Applehaigh Wood
BLEAKLEY LA
BLEAKLEY TERR
BLEAKLEY AVE
Barnsley Boundary Walk
Applehaigh Farm
GREEN LA
Common Lane Farm
Barnsley Canal (dis)
LUND HILL LA
Low Common
Windmill Hill
PEMBRIDGE CT 1
KINGSLAND CT 2
BEWDLEY CT 3
BROMFIELD CT 4
IVY COTTS 5
COMMON LA
Mine (disused)
Lund Hill
STATION RD
Civic Hall
Royston Comprehensive Sch
MIDLAND RD
HIGH ST
LEE LA
Liby
B6428
CHURCH ST
Royston Infants Sch
Royston C of E Sch
Church Hill
CHURCH HILL
ROYSTON
Royston Bridge
POOLS LA
Rabbit Ings
Refuse Tip
Pools Ings
Scot Bridge
Royston Medstead Junior and Infants Sch
ROYSTON LA
Cronk Hill
Low Cronkhill La (Track)
Wood La (Track)
EASTMOOR GR 1
AVONDALE DR 2
CRONKHILL LA
Cemy
Carlton
Shaw Viaduct
SHAW LA
Shaw Dike Bridge
BOULDER BRIDGE LA
Sewage Works
B6132
SPRING LA

180

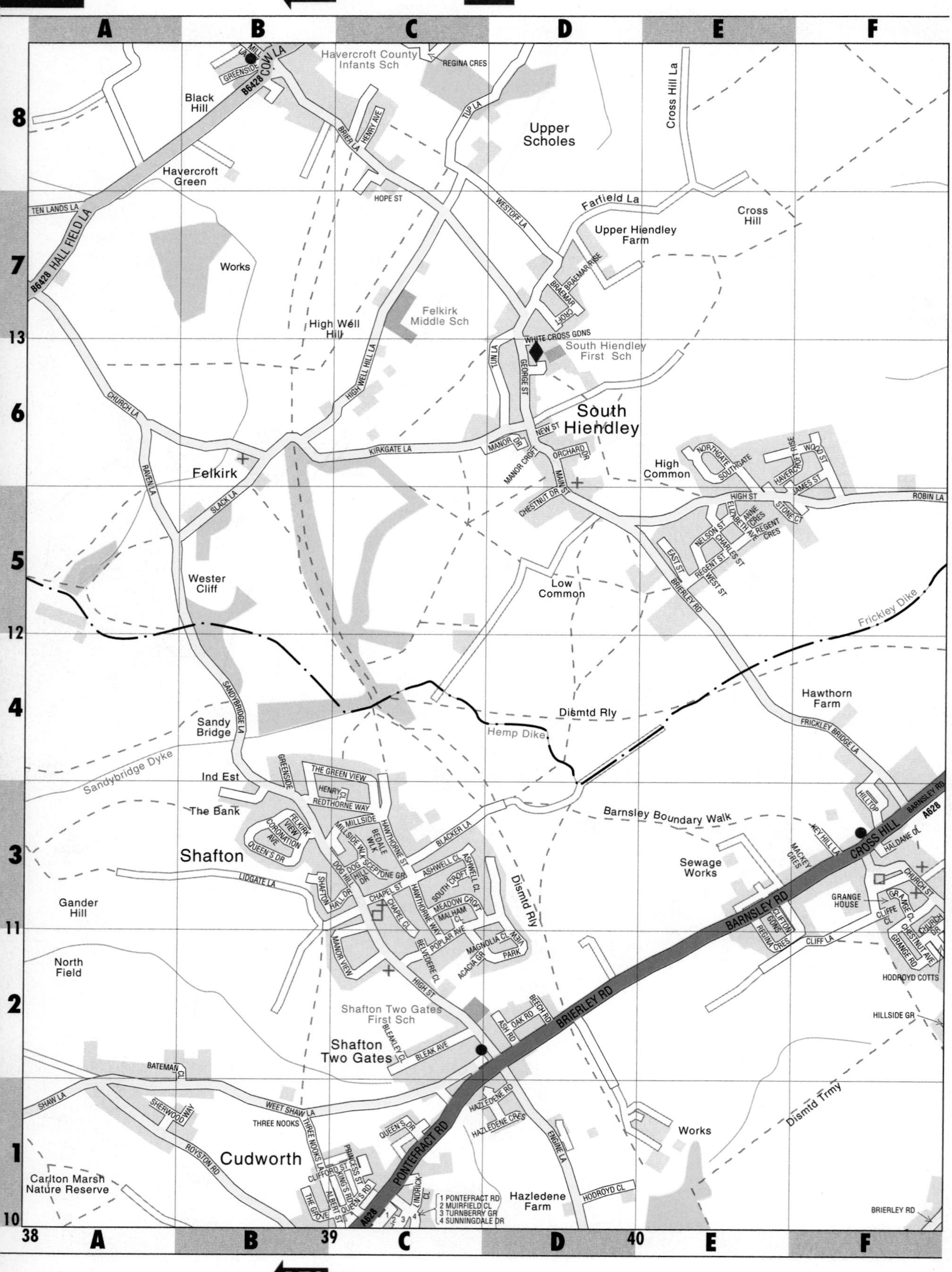
A
B
C
D
E
F
8
7
13
6
5
12
4
3
11
2
1
10
38
39
40
Havercroft County Infants Sch
REGINA CRES
MILL LA
GREENSIDE
COW LA
B6428
Black Hill
Cross Hill La
Upper Scholes
TUP LA
HENRY AVE
BRIER LA
Havercroft Green
HOPE ST
WESTOFF LA
Farfield La
Cross Hill
Upper Hiendley Farm
TEN LANDS LA
HALL FIELD LA
Works
BRAEMAR RISE
BRAEMAR CROFT
High Well Hill
Felkirk Middle Sch
WHITE CROSS GDNS
South Hiendley First Sch
TUN LA
GEORGE ST
HIGH WELL HILL LA
CHURCH LA
South Hiendley
NEW ST
MANOR DR
KIRKGATE LA
ORCHARD DR
MANOR CROFT
High Common
NORTHGATE
SOUTHGATE
HAVERCROFT RISE
WOOD ST
JAMES ST
Felkirk
RAVEN LA
SLACK LA
CHESTNUT DR
MAIN ST
HIGH ST
ELIZABETH AVE
ANNE CRES
REGENT CRES
STONE CT
ROBIN LA
NELSON ST
CHARLES ST
EAST ST
REGENT ST
WEST ST
BRIERLEY RD
Wester Cliff
Low Common
Frickley Dike
SANDYBRIDGE LA
Hawthorn Farm
Sandy Bridge
Dismtd Rly
Hemp Dike
FRICKLEY BRIDGE LA
Sandybridge Dyke
Ind Est
GREENSIDE
THE GREEN VIEW
HENRY CL
REDTHORNE WAY
The Bank
HILLTOP
BARNSLEY RD
A628
Barnsley Boundary Walk
BLACKER LA
MILLSIDE
HAWTHORNE ST
BEDALE WALK
FELKIRK VIEW
CORONATION AVE
QUEEN'S DR
KEY HILL LA
CROSS HILL
HALDANE CL
Shafton
MILLSIDE WALK
DOG HILL DR
SCEPTONE GR
ASHWELL CL
Sewage Works
MACKEY CRES
LIDGATE LA
SHAFTON HALL DR
CHAPEL ST
SOUTH CROFT
Dismtd Rly
CHURCH ST
Gander Hill
CHAPEL CL
HAWTHORNE WAY
MEADOW CROFT
MALHAM CL
GRANGE HOUSE
CLIFFE CL
GRANGE CL
CHESTNUT AVE
CHURCH DR
POPLAR AVE
MAGNOLIA CL
PARK VIEW
CLIFTON GDNS
REGINA CRES
CLIFF LA
GRANGE RD
MANOR VIEW
BELVEDERE CL
ACACIA GR
North Field
HODROYD COTTS
HIGH ST
BIRERLEY RD
BEECH RD
Shafton Two Gates First Sch
OAK RD
ASH RD
HILLSIDE GR
BLEAKLEY CL
Shafton Two Gates
BLEAK AVE
BATEMAN CL
SHAW LA
SHERWOOD WAY
WEET SHAW LA
HAZLEDENE RD
HAZLEDENE CRES
THREE NOOKS
THREE NOOKS LA
QUEEN'S DR
Works
Dismtd Trmy
ROYSTON RD
PONTEFRACT RD
ENGINE LA
Cudworth
PRINCESS ST
Carlton Marsh Nature Reserve
CLIFFORD ST
KING'S RD
QUEEN'S RD
THE GROVE
ALBERT ST
LINDRICK CL
1 PONTEFRACT RD
2 MUIRFIELD CL
3 TURNBERRY GR
4 SUNNINGDALE DR
Hazledene Farm
HODROYD CL
BRIERLEY RD

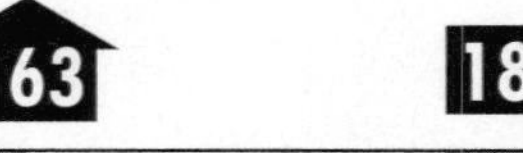

HEMSWORTH

Map column labels (top): A B C D E F

Map row labels (right): 8 7 13 6 12 5 4 3 11 2 1 10

Shaw Hill
Hollins Bank
Marsh Plantation
WAKEFIELD RD
B6273
A628
SPRINGVALE RISE
DORSET CL
SUSSEX CL
WOODLANDS CRES
NORTH WLK
HEREFORD CL
BUTCHER HILL
STATION RD
Church Field Cemy
CEMETERY RD
Hemsworth Archbishop Holgate C of E First Sch
WOOD WEST DALE CL
MARSH LEA GROVE
ST HELEN'S AVE
CENTRE ST
HOLLY ST
LOOSE ST
Hemsworth High Sch
NETTLETON HOUSE
JACKSON HOUSE
COOPER HOUSE
STARLING HOUSE
Wakefield District Coll
LOWFIELD RD
Low Field
Hemsworth West End Middle Sch
SANDYGATE LA
REGENT ST
WEST CROFT RD
MAYFAIR CL
MOUNT AVE
Sch
RECTORY GARTH
CHURCH CL
LOWFIELD CRES
CHEVIOT CL
CHILTERN CT
COTSWOLD CL
MORVERN MEADOWS
TOP ST
WESTFIELD RD
BANK ST
CROSS HILL
EATON PL
LITTLE
LODGE CL
ELM
BREDA
Liby Sch
HIGATE CRES
CLOSE ST
PEARTREE LA
CROSS HILL
Green Hill
MARKET ST
SPRINGSTONE AVE
RIDGESTONE AVE
VALESTONE AVE
GROVE TERR
RINGWOOD WAY
Little Hemsworth
WORTLEY PL
WESTGATE
BRETTEGATE
OLD MILL LA
GRANGEWAY
PLIMSOLL ST
BECK RISE
Cross Hill
PONTEFRACT TERR
Common End
GEORGE ST
LILLEY ST
BANLEE ST
BUSH ST
Vissitt Manor House
EVERDALE MOUNT
BARNSLEY RD
VISSITT CL
LIME TREE LA
OLD MILL VIEW
BEECHWOOD CRES
HAWTHORNE
GRANGE RD
BULLENSHAW RD
Sch
GROVE TERR
BUSH ST
UNION ST
VICTORIA AVE
SPRINGFIELD AVE
OAK TREE GR
ELIZABETH CT
WINDSOR RD
Vissitt Manor Farm
MEADOW
BRONTE DR
CEDAR RD
BEECHWOOD CRES
HIGHFIELD RD
HAMEL RISE
Highfield
Southmoor Highfield Cen
PENLINGTON CL
ST THOMAS ST
KIRKBY RD
HAGUE TERR
TONK ST
OAKWOOD DR
JUBILEE DR
DALE VIEW
CHESTNUT GR
WILLIAM WAY
HOLGATE HOSPITAL
VISSITT LA
MOORSHUTT RD
CLIFTON
MOORFIELD CRES
FERNDALE PL
CRAVEN AVE
RIDDINGS
THORNTON CL
HAGUE CRES
KIRKBYGATE
Dismtd Rly
ROBIN LA
Hemsworth St Helens C of E Middle Sch
CARLTON CL
ASHFIELD RD
MOOR TOP
MEADOW CROFT
Moor Top Farm
HEMSWORTH RD
Hague Hall Cotts
WATER LA
Kennels Farm
WILLOW
GREENFIELD RD
BURNTWOOD BANK
WOOD RD
WHIM LA
B6422
Brierley Tunnel
BARNWELL HILL
Road under construction
Hague Hall Beck
BARNSLEY RD
Brierley
SOUTHMOOR RD
South Moor
Cob Carr Plantation
Ball Park Wood
SAVILE WLK
RINGSTONE GR
SPA WELL GR
PAXTON CL
HOLLY GR
MAGNOLIA DR
BECH CL
RINGSTONE VIEW
Recn Gd
PARK CL
PARK VIEW
PARK AVE
BRIAR RD
ASHLEIGH
Hemsworth Gate
HOLMSLEY LA
WEST ST
SAXON AVE
SAXON MOUNT
ST PAUL'S C of E First Sch
CHURCH DR
CHURCH ST
Pudding Hill
Elms Farm House
COMMON RD
Dunsley
ASHLEY CT
SECOND AVE
CAMP RD
HILLTOP EST
FIRST AVE
BURNS AVE
LEDROYD COTTS
HILLSIDE MOUNT
HILLSIDE GR
Brierley Common
Brierley
HILLSIDE CRES
Barnsley Boundary Walk
COMMON RD
Grimethorpe
Burntwood Sports and Leisure Cen
Brierley Gap
SOUTH KIRKBY COMMON
BRIERLEY RD
Willowgarth High Sch
The Robin Hood (PH)
COMMON RD
BURNT WOOD LA
SANDHILL LA
WINDMILL LANE
Tom Bank Wood
Ringstone Hill
B6273
Windmill Hill

Map column labels (bottom): 41 A B 42 C D 43 E F

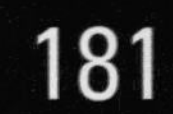

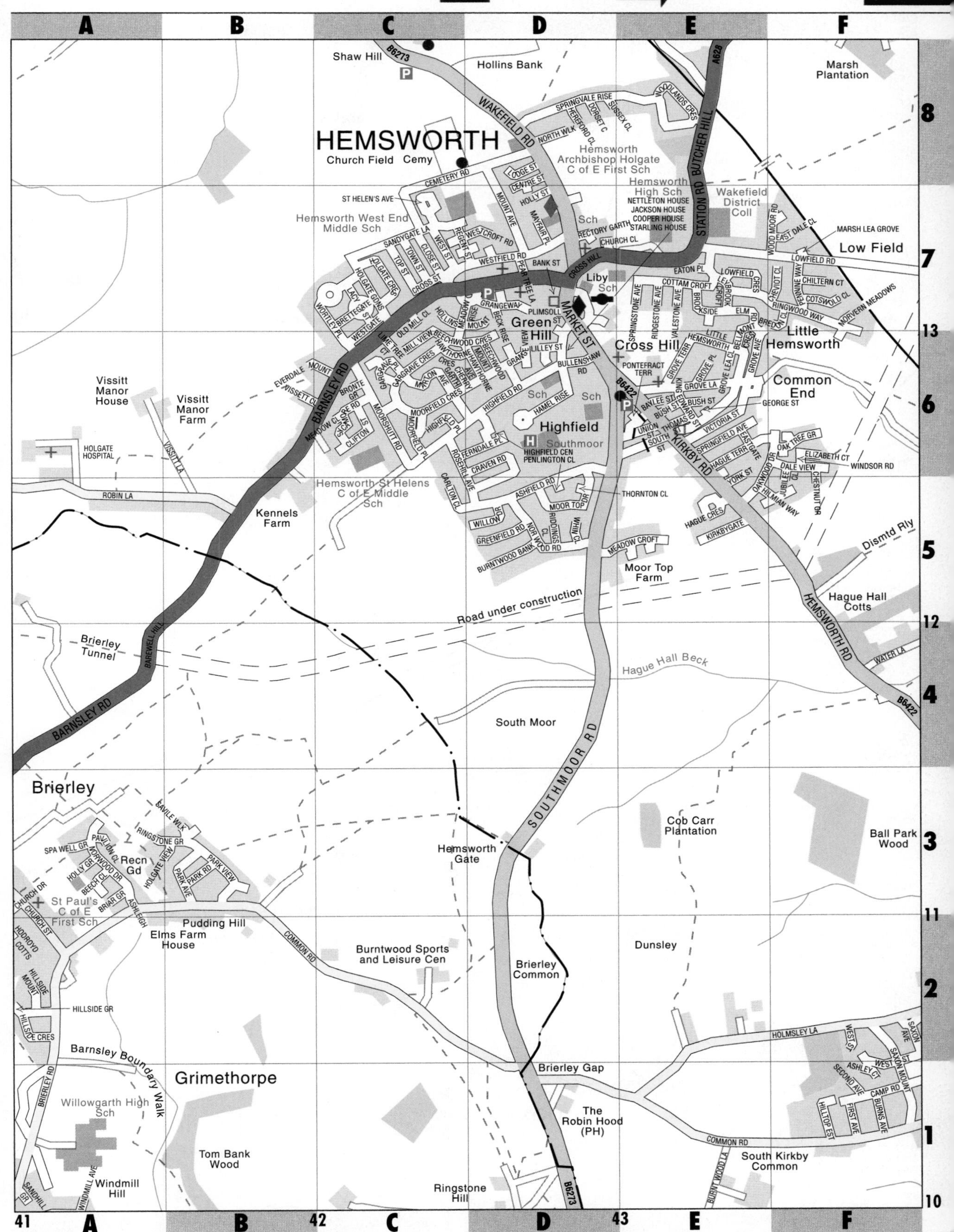

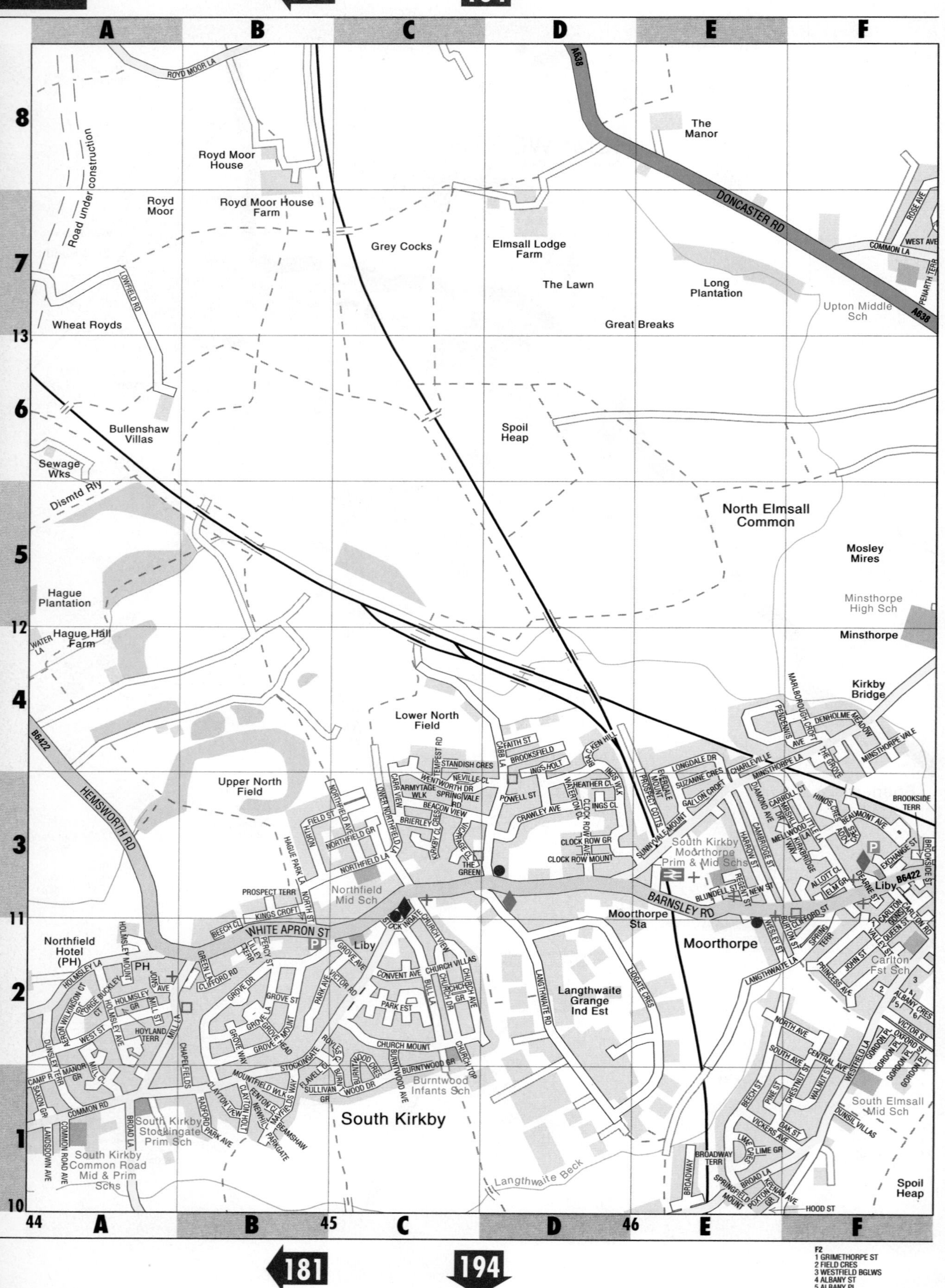

F2
1 GRIMETHORPE ST
2 FIELD CRES
3 WESTFIELD BGLWS
4 ALBANY ST
5 ALBANY PL
6 WOODLEA

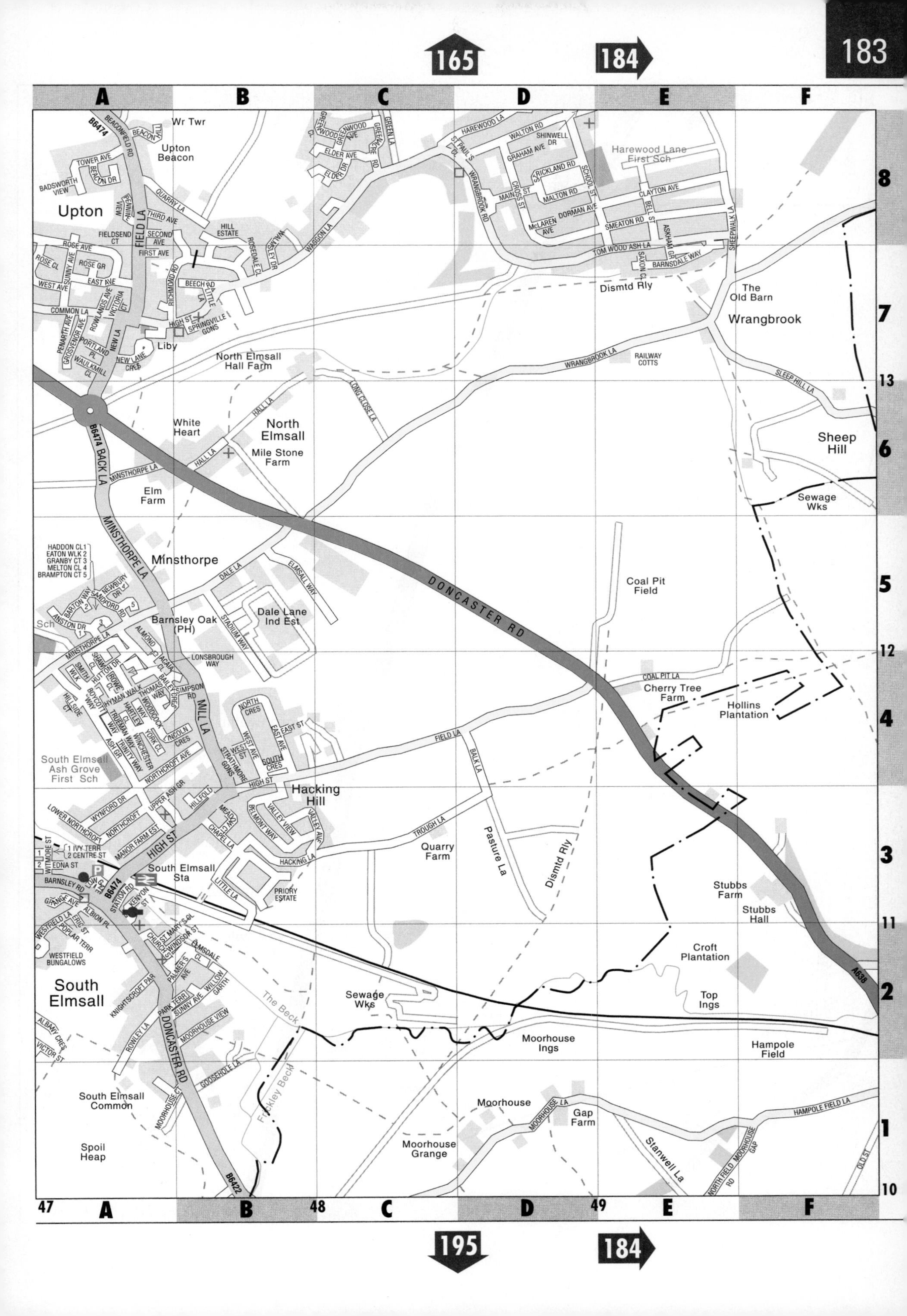
165
184
A B C D E F
8
7
13
6
5
12
4
3
11
2
1
10
47 48 49
Upton
Upton Beacon
Wr Twr
North Elmsall Hall Farm
Liby
White Heart
North Elmsall
Mile Stone Farm
Elm Farm
Minsthorpe
Barnsley Oak (PH)
Dale Lane Ind Est
South Elmsall Ash Grove First Sch
Hacking Hill
South Elmsall Sta
Priory Estate
Quarry Farm
Pasture La
Dismtd Rly
Coal Pit Field
Cherry Tree Farm
Hollins Plantation
Harewood Lane First Sch
The Old Barn
Wrangbrook
Railway Cotts
Sheep Hill
Sewage Wks
Stubbs Farm
Stubbs Hall
Croft Plantation
Top Ings
Hampole Field
Moorhouse Ings
Moorhouse
Gap Farm
Moorhouse Grange
Stanwell La
The Beck
Frickley Beck
South Elmsall
South Elmsall Common
Spoil Heap
Westfield Bungalows
Doncaster Rd
Minsthorpe La
Mill La
High St
Field La
Trough La
Wrangbrook La
Sleep Hill La
Coal Pit La
Hampole Field La
Moorhouse La
Back La
B6474
B6422
A638
195
184

183 166

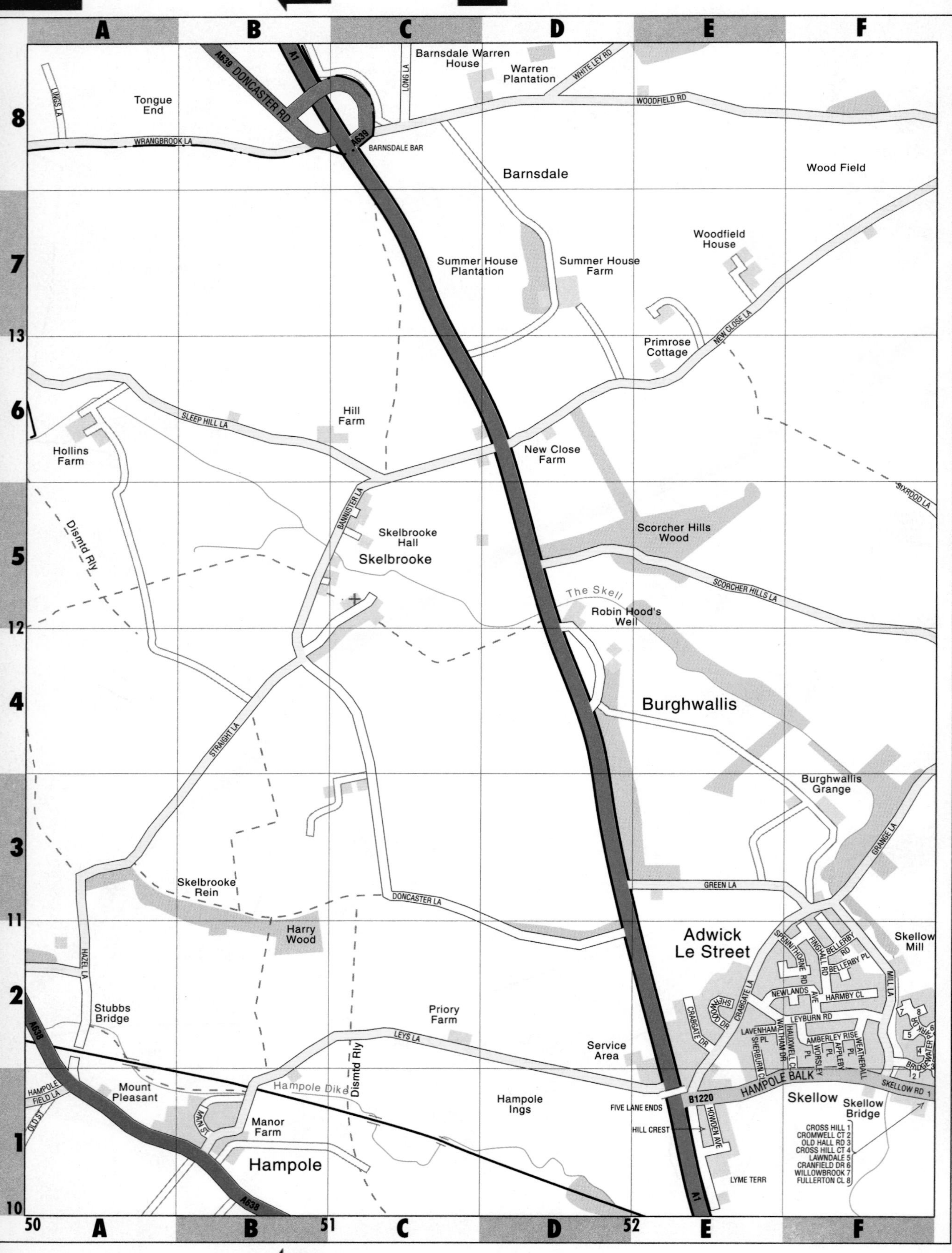
Tongue End
Barnsdale Warren House
Warren Plantation
WHITE LEY RD
WOODFIELD RD
A639 DONCASTER RD
A1
LONG LA
LINGS LA
WRANGBROOK LA
BARNSDALE BAR
Barnsdale
Wood Field
Woodfield House
Summer House Plantation
Summer House Farm
Primrose Cottage
NEW CLOSE LA
SLEEP HILL LA
Hill Farm
Hollins Farm
New Close Farm
SIXROOD LA
BANNISTER LA
Dismtd Rly
Skelbrooke Hall
Skelbrooke
Scorcher Hills Wood
SCORCHER HILLS LA
The Skell
Robin Hood's Well
Burghwallis
STRAIGHT LA
Burghwallis Grange
GRANGE LA
Skelbrooke Rein
DONCASTER LA
GREEN LA
Harry Wood
Adwick Le Street
Skellow Mill
HAZEL LA
Stubbs Bridge
Priory Farm
LEYS LA
Service Area
A638
Mount Pleasant
HAMPOLE FIELD LA
OLD ST
Hampole Dike
MAIN ST
Manor Farm
Hampole
Hampole Ings
FIVE LANE ENDS
HILL CREST
B1220
HAMPOLE BALK
SKELLOW RD
Skellow
Skellow Bridge
HOWDEN AVE
LYME TERR
CRABGATE LA
CRABGATE DR
NEWLANDS AVE
HARMBY CL
LEYBURN RD
LAVENHAM PL
SHERBURN CL
WALTHAM DR
HAUXWELL CL
AMBERLEY RISE
WORSLEY PL
APPLEBY PL
WEATHERALL
BELLERBY RD
BELLERBY PL
FINGHALL RD
SPENNITHORNE RD
MILL LA
CROSS HILL 1
CROMWELL CT 2
OLD HALL RD 3
CROSS HILL CT 4
LAWNDALE 5
CRANFIELD DR 6
WILLOWBROOK 7
FULLERTON CL 8

183

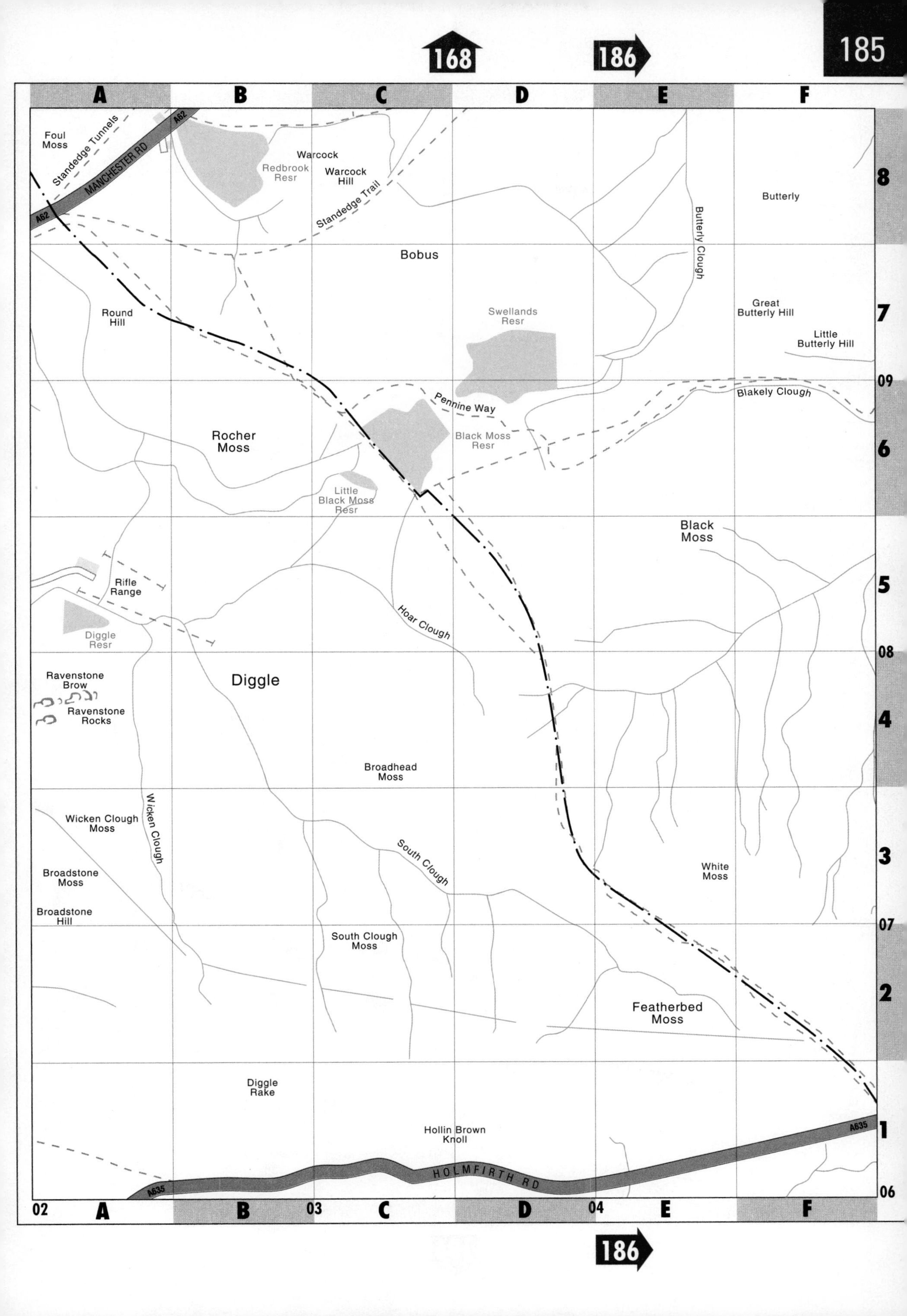
168
186
A
B
C
D
E
F
8
7
09
6
5
08
4
3
07
2
1
06
02
03
04
Foul Moss
Standedge Tunnels
MANCHESTER RD
A62
Redbrook Resr
Warcock
Warcock Hill
Standedge Trail
Butterly
Butterly Clough
Bobus
Round Hill
Swellands Resr
Great Butterly Hill
Little Butterly Hill
Pennine Way
Blakely Clough
Rocher Moss
Black Moss Resr
Little Black Moss Resr
Black Moss
Rifle Range
Diggle Resr
Hoar Clough
Diggle
Ravenstone Brow
Ravenstone Rocks
Broadhead Moss
Wicken Clough Moss
Wicken Clough
South Clough
White Moss
Broadstone Moss
Broadstone Hill
South Clough Moss
Featherbed Moss
Diggle Rake
Hollin Brown Knoll
A635
HOLMFIRTH RD
186

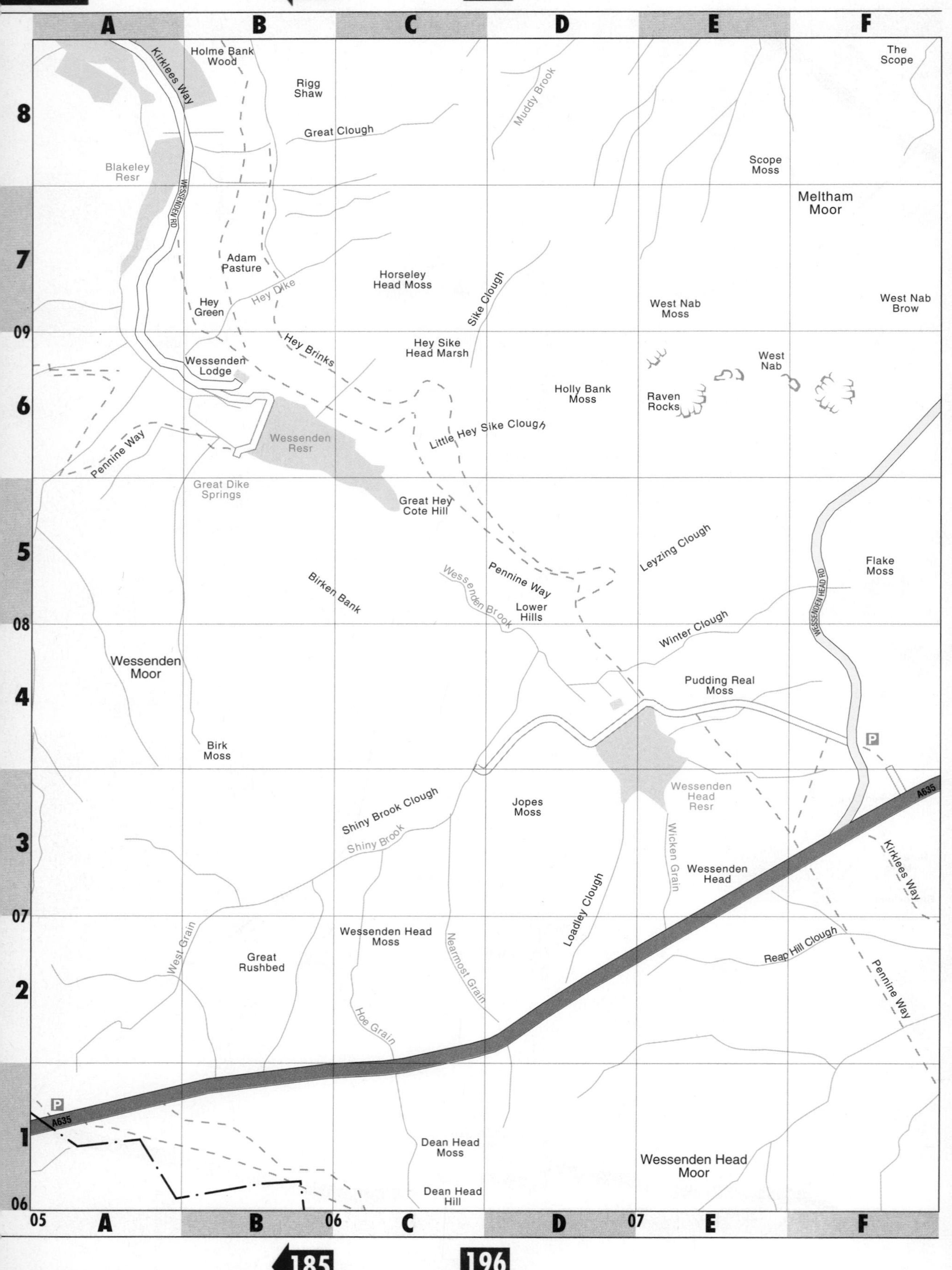

A B C D E F

8

7

09

6

5

08

4

07

3

2

07

1

06

05 A B 06 C D 07 E F

The Scope

Holme Bank Wood

Rigg Shaw

Great Clough

Muddy Brook

Scope Moss

Meltham Moor

Blakeley Resr

Kirklees Way

WESSENDEN RD

Adam Pasture

Hey Dike

Horseley Head Moss

Sike Clough

West Nab Moss

West Nab Brow

Hey Green

Hey Brinks

Hey Sike Head Marsh

Holly Bank Moss

Raven Rocks

West Nab

Wessenden Lodge

Little Hey Sike Clough

Pennine Way

Wessenden Resr

Great Dike Springs

Great Hey Cote Hill

Leyzing Clough

WESSENDEN HEAD RD

Flake Moss

Birken Bank

Wessenden Brook

Pennine Way

Lower Hills

Winter Clough

Wessenden Moor

Pudding Real Moss

Birk Moss

Wessenden Head Resr

Shiny Brook Clough

Shiny Brook

Jopes Moss

Wicken Grain

Wessenden Head

A635

Kirklees Way

West Grain

Great Rushbed

Wessenden Head Moss

Nearmost Grain

Loadley Clough

Reap Hill Clough

Pennine Way

Hoe Grain

A635

Dean Head Moss

Wessenden Head Moor

Dean Head Hill

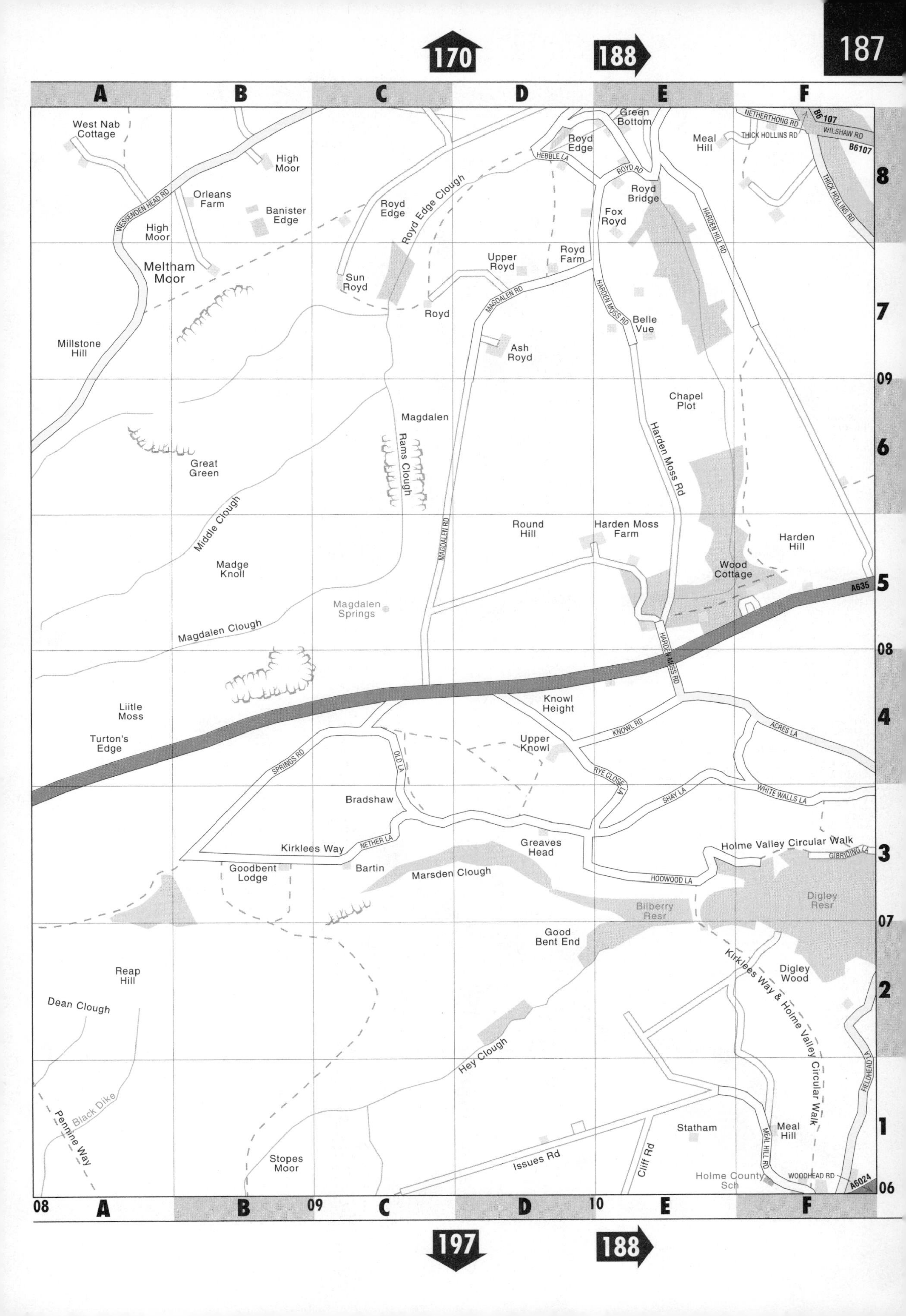

170
188
197
188

West Nab Cottage

High Moor

Orleans Farm

Banister Edge

WESSENDEN HEAD RD

High Moor

High Moor

Meltham Moor

Millstone Hill

Royd Edge

Royd Edge Clough

Sun Royd

Royd

Green Bottom

Royd Edge

HEBBLE LA

ROYD RD

Royd Bridge

Fox Royd

Upper Royd

Royd Farm

Royd

MAGDALEN RD

Ash Royd

Belle Vue

HARDEN HILL RD

NETHERTHONG RD

THICK HOLLINS RD

WILSHAW RD

B6107

B6107

Meal Hill

THICK HOLLINS RD

Chapel Plot

Magdalen

Rams Clough

Great Green

Middle Clough

Madge Knoll

Magdalen Clough

Magdalen Springs

MAGDALEN RD

Round Hill

Harden Moss Farm

Harden Moss Rd

HARDEN MOSS RD

Wood Cottage

Harden Hill

A635

Liitle Moss

Turton's Edge

Knowl Height

Upper Knowl

KNOWL RD

ACRES LA

SHAY LA

WHITE WALLS LA

SPRINGS RD

OLD LA

RYE CLOSE LA

Bradshaw

Kirklees Way

NETHER LA

Goodbent Lodge

Bartin

Marsden Clough

Greaves Head

HOOWOOD LA

Holme Valley Circular Walk

GIBRIDING LA

Bilberry Resr

Digley Resr

Good Bent End

Reap Hill

Dean Clough

Black Dike

Pennine Way

Stopes Moor

Hey Clough

Issues Rd

Kirklees Way & Holme Valley Circular Walk

Digley Wood

Statham

MEAL HILL RD

Meal Hill

FIELDHEAD LA

Cliff Rd

Holme County Sch

WOODHEAD RD

A6024

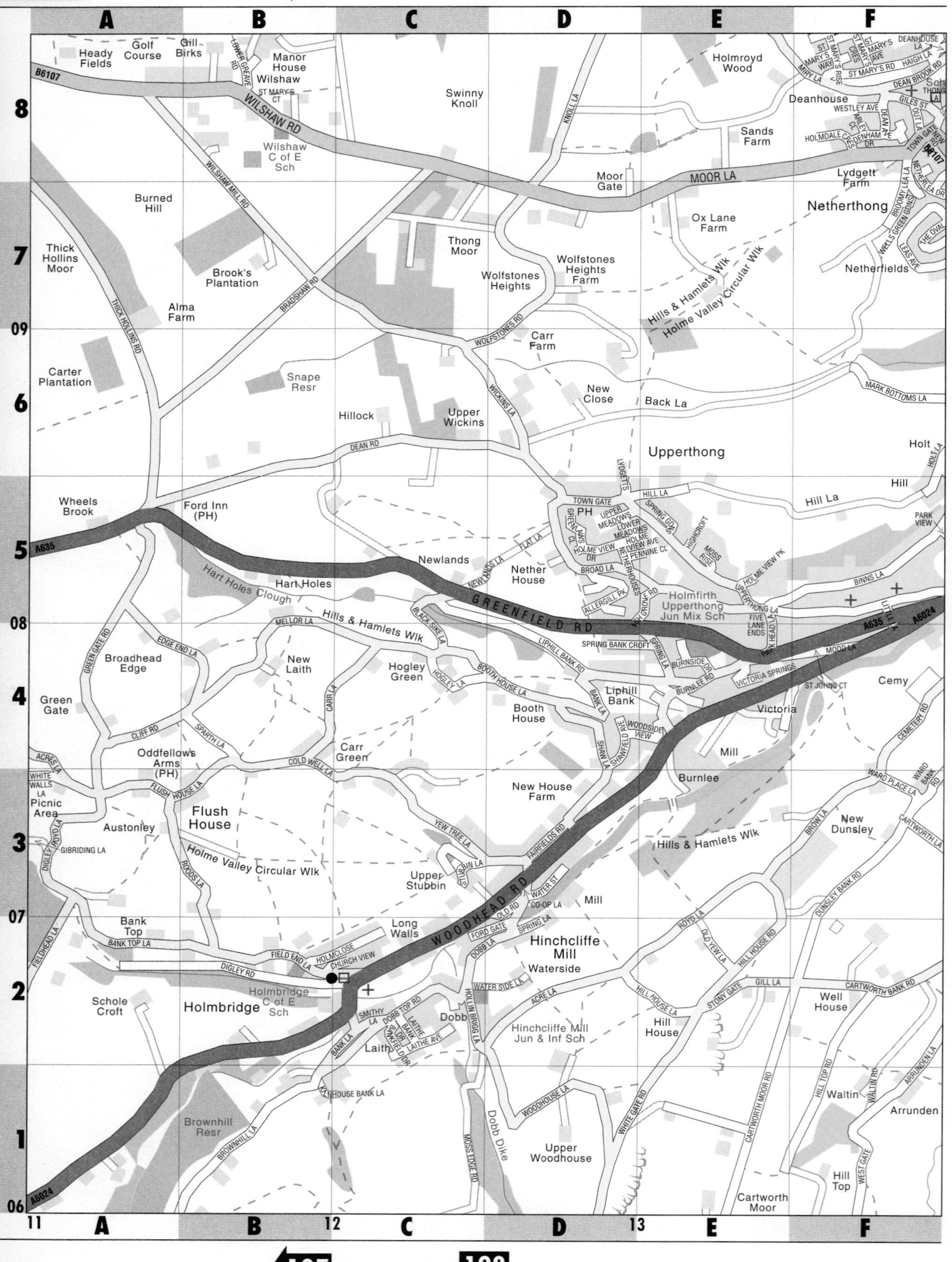
Heady Fields
Golf Course
Gill Birks
Manor House
Wilshaw
Wilshaw C of E Sch
Swinny Knoll
Holmroyd Wood
Deanhouse
Sands Farm
Moor Gate
MOOR LA
Lydgett Farm
Netherthong
Burned Hill
Thick Hollins Moor
Brook's Plantation
Alma Farm
Thong Moor
Wolfstones Heights
Wolfstones Heights Farm
Ox Lane Farm
Netherfields
Hills & Hamlets Wlk
Holme Valley Circular Wlk
Carr Farm
Carter Plantation
Snape Resr
Hillock
Upper Wickins
New Close
Back La
Upperthong
Holt
Hill
Hill La
Wheels Brook
Ford Inn (PH)
Newlands
Nether House
Hart Holes
Hart Holes Clough
GREENFIELD RD
Holmfirth Upperthong Jun Mix Sch
Broadhead Edge
New Laith
Hogley Green
Liphill Bank
Booth House
Green Gate
Oddfellows Arms (PH)
Carr Green
Victoria
Cemy
Mill
Burnlee
Picnic Area
Austonley
Flush House
New House Farm
New Dunsley
Upper Stubbin
Bank Top
Long Walls
WOODHEAD RD
Hinchcliffe Mill
Waterside
Schole Croft
Holmbridge
Holmbridge C of E Sch
Dobb
Laith
Hinchcliffe Mill Jun & Inf Sch
Hill House
Well House
Waltin
Arrunden
Brownhill Resr
Dobb Dike
Upper Woodhouse
Cartworth Moor
Hill Top

172
190

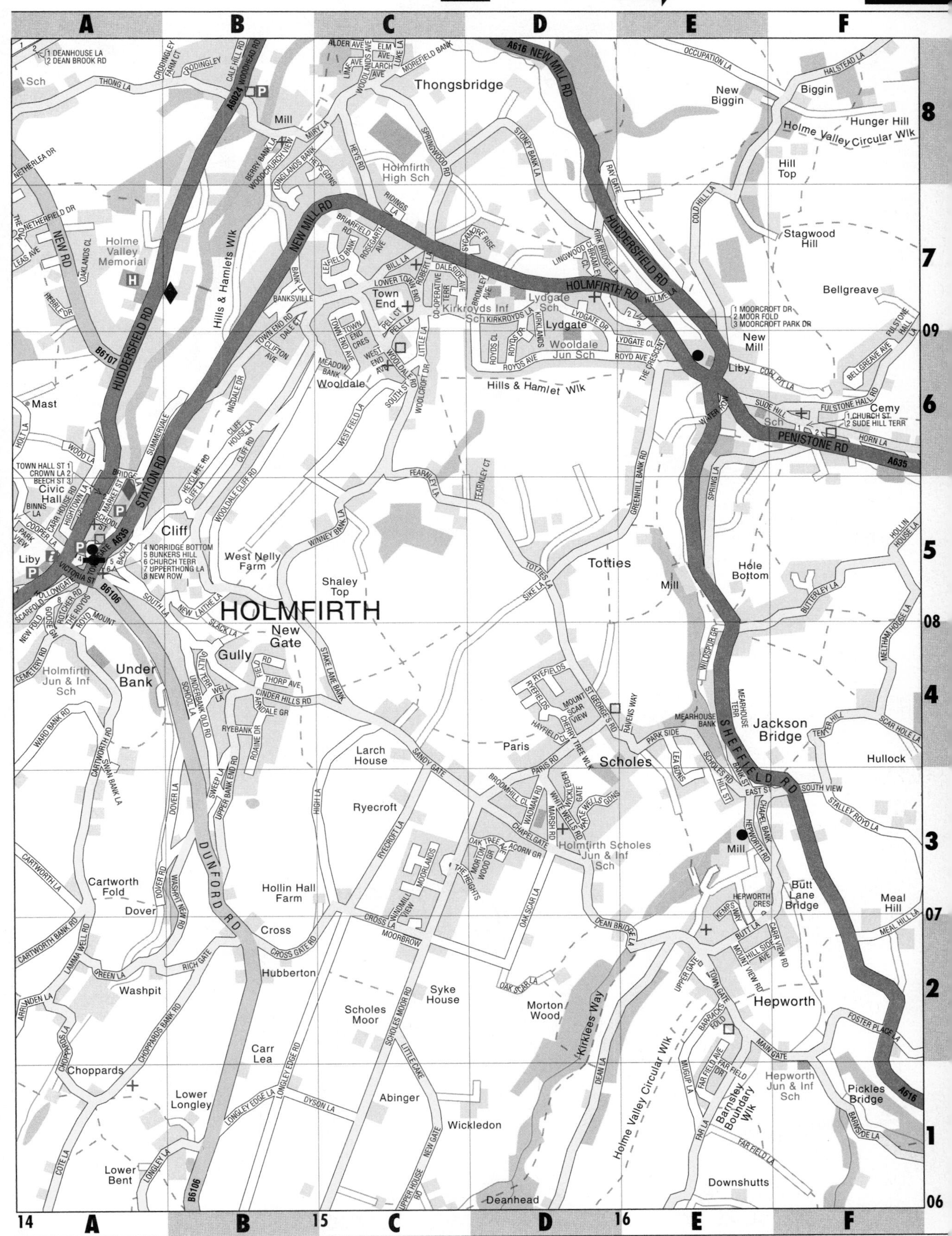
A
B
C
D
E
F
HOLMFIRTH
Thongsbridge
New Biggin
Biggin
Hunger Hill
Holme Valley Circular Wlk
Hill Top
Stagwood Hill
Bellgreave
Holme Valley Memorial
Holmfirth High Sch
Town End
Lydgate
Wooldale
Wooldale Jun Sch
Kirkroyds Inf Sch
New Mill
Liby
Cemy
Hills & Hamlet Wlk
Hills & Hamlets Wlk
Mast
Civic Hall
Cliff
West Nelly Farm
Shaley Top
Totties
Mill
Hole Bottom
New Gate
Gully
Under Bank
Holmfirth Jun & Inf Sch
Paris
Scholes
Jackson Bridge
Hullock
Larch House
Ryecroft
Holmfirth Scholes Jun & Inf Sch
Butt Lane Bridge
Meal Hill
Cartworth Fold
Dover
Hollin Hall Farm
Cross
Hubberton
Washpit
Syke House
Scholes Moor
Morton Wood
Hepworth
Carr Lea
Choppards
Lower Longley
Abinger
Wickledon
Kirklees Way
Hepworth Jun & Inf Sch
Pickles Bridge
Barnsley Boundary Wlk
Lower Bent
Downshutts
Deanhead
A616 NEW MILL RD
HUDDERSFIELD RD
NEW MILL RD
HOLMFIRTH RD
PENISTONE RD
STATION RD
SHEFFIELD RD
DUNFORD RD
NEW RD
1 DEANHOUSE LA
2 DEAN BROOK RD
1 MOORCROFT DR
2 MOOR FOLD
3 MOORCROFT PARK DR
1 CHURCH ST
2 SUDE HILL TERR
TOWN HALL ST 1
CROWN LA 2
BEECH ST 3
4 NORRIDGE BOTTOM
5 BUNKERS HILL
6 CHURCH TERR
7 UPPERTHONG LA
8 NEW ROW
8
7
09
6
5
08
4
3
07
2
1
06
14
15
16

199
190

189
173

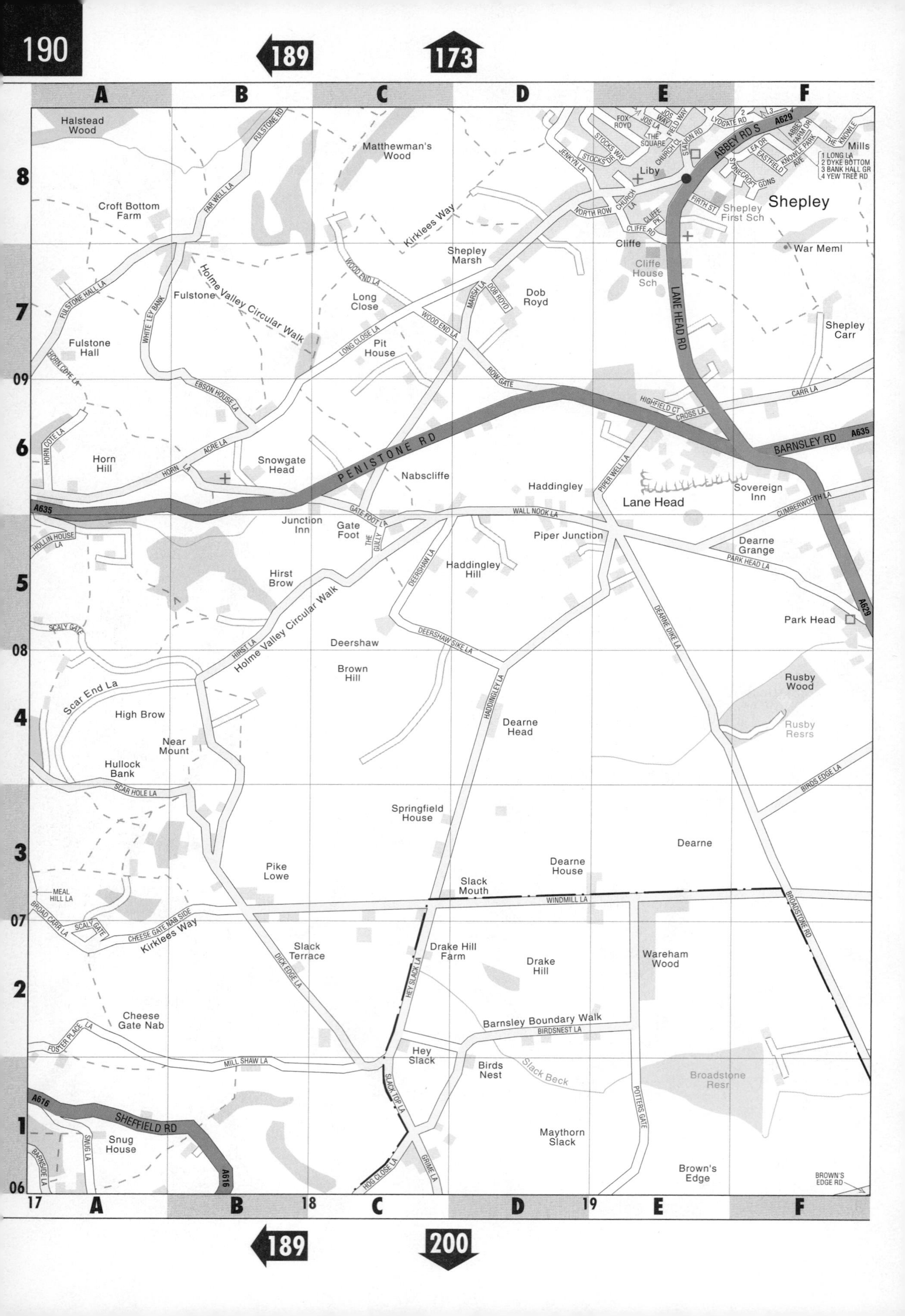
A
B
C
D
E
F
8
7
09
6
5
08
4
3
07
2
1
06
17
18
19
Halstead Wood
Matthewman's Wood
Croft Bottom Farm
Kirklees Way
Shepley Marsh
Fulstone
Holme Valley Circular Walk
Long Close
Dob Royd
Fulstone Hall
Pit House
Horn Hill
Snowgate Head
Nabscliffe
Haddingley
Lane Head
Sovereign Inn
Junction Inn
Gate Foot
Piper Junction
Dearne Grange
Hirst Brow
Haddingley Hill
Park Head
Deershaw
Brown Hill
Rusby Wood
Rusby Resrs
Scar End La
High Brow
Dearne Head
Near Mount
Hullock Bank
Springfield House
Dearne
Pike Lowe
Dearne House
Slack Mouth
Slack Terrace
Drake Hill Farm
Drake Hill
Wareham Wood
Cheese Gate Nab
Barnsley Boundary Walk
Hey Slack
Birds Nest
Slack Beck
Broadstone Resr
Snug House
Maythorn Slack
Brown's Edge
Liby
Shepley
Shepley First Sch
Cliffe
Cliffe House Sch
War Meml
Shepley Carr
Mills
1 LONG LA
2 DYKE BOTTOM
3 BANK HALL GR
4 YEW TREE RD
PENISTONE RD
BARNSLEY RD
A635
A629
A616
SHEFFIELD RD
LANE HEAD RD
ABBEY RD S
FULSTONE RD
FAR WELL LA
FULSTONE HALL LA
WHITE LEY BANK
HORN COTE LA
EBSON HOUSE LA
ACRE LA
HORN LA
WOOD END LA
LONG CLOSE LA
MARSH LA
DOB ROYD
ROW GATE
HIGHFIELD CT
CROSS LA
CARR LA
PIPER WELL LA
WALL NOOK LA
CUMBERWORTH LA
PARK HEAD LA
GATE FOOT LA
THE GULLY
DEERSHAW LA
DEERSHAW SIKE LA
HADDINGLEY LA
DEARNE DIKE LA
HIRST LA
HOLLIN HOUSE LA
SCALY GATE
SCAR HOLE LA
BIRDS EDGE LA
WINDMILL LA
BROADSTONE RD
MEAL HILL LA
BROAD CARR LA
CHEESE GATE NAB SIDE
DICK EDGE LA
HEY SLACK LA
BIRDSNEST LA
FOSTER PLACE LA
MILL SHAW LA
SLACK TOP LA
POTTERS GATE
SNUG LA
BARNSIDE LA
HOG CLOSE LA
GRIME LA
BROWN'S EDGE RD
NORTH ROW
CHURCH LA
CLIFFE PK
CLIFFE RD
FIRTH ST
JENKYN LA
STOCKS DR
STOCKS WAY
FOX ROYD
JOS LA
THE SQUARE
CHURCH CL
STATION RD
FIELD WAY
LYDGATE RD
STONECROFT GDNS
EASTFIELD
LEA DR
KNOWLE PARK AVE
ABBEY FARM DR
THE KNOWLE

189
200

174

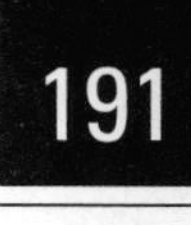

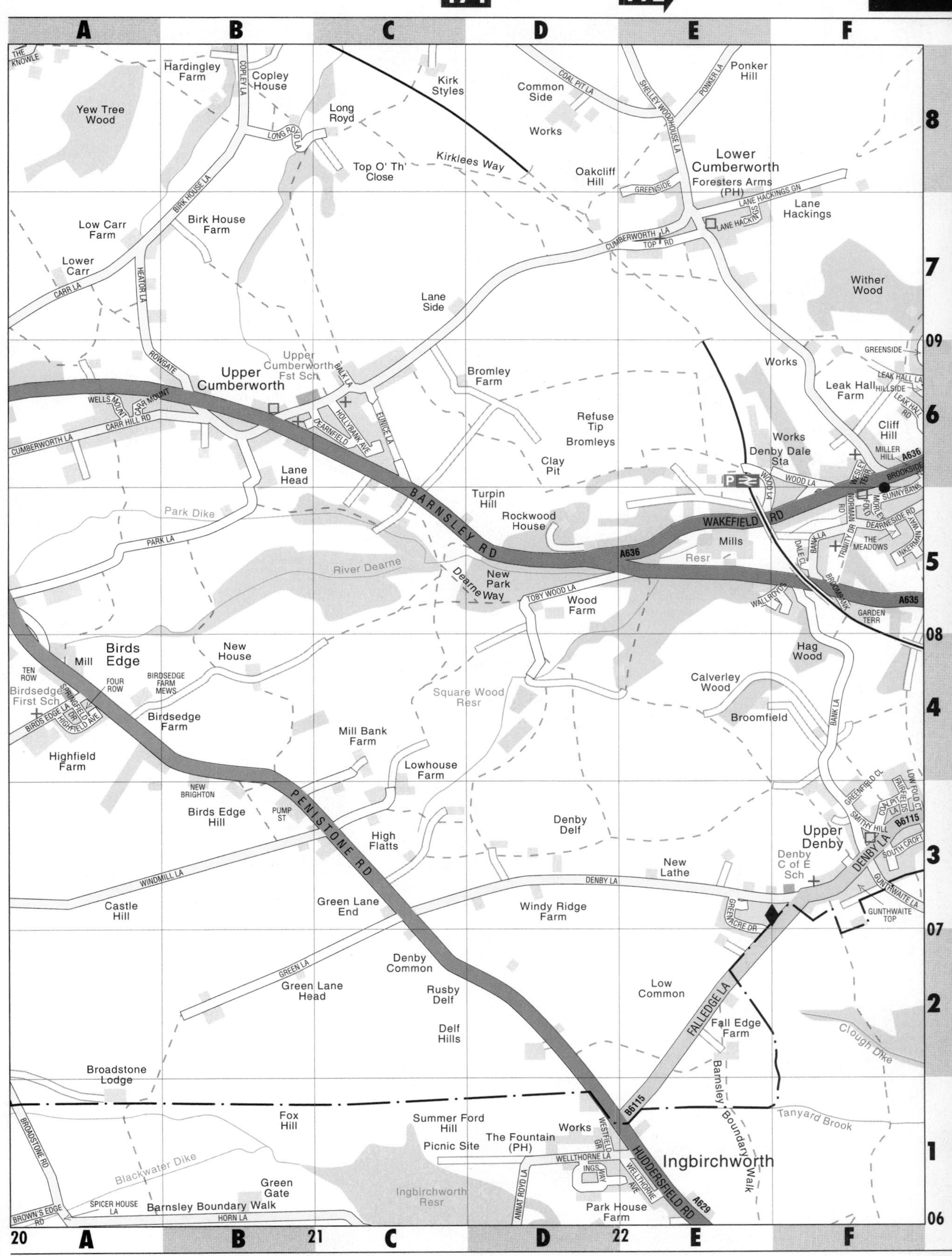

192
A
B
C
D
E
F
8
7
6
5
4
3
2
1
09
08
07
06
20
21
22
Hardingley Farm
Copley House
Yew Tree Wood
Kirk Styles
Common Side
Ponker Hill
Long Royd
Works
Top O' Th' Close
Kirklees Way
Lower Cumberworth
Foresters Arms (PH)
Oakcliff Hill
Lane Hackings
Low Carr Farm
Birk House Farm
Lower Carr
Wither Wood
Lane Side
Upper Cumberworth
Upper Cumberworth Fst Sch
Bromley Farm
Leak Hall Farm
Works
Refuse Tip
Bromleys
Cliff Hill
Denby Dale Sta
Clay Pit
Lane Head
Turpin Hill
Rockwood House
Park Dike
Mills
River Dearne
New Park
Dearne Way
Wood Farm
Resr
Birds Edge
Mill
New House
Hag Wood
Calverley Wood
Birdsedge First Sch
Square Wood Resr
Broomfield
Birdsedge Farm
Mill Bank Farm
Highfield Farm
Lowhouse Farm
Birds Edge Hill
Denby Delf
Upper Denby
High Flatts
Denby C of E Sch
New Lathe
Castle Hill
Green Lane End
Windy Ridge Farm
Denby Common
Green Lane Head
Rusby Delf
Low Common
Delf Hills
Fall Edge Farm
Clough Dike
Broadstone Lodge
Fox Hill
Summer Ford Hill
Works
Tanyard Brook
Picnic Site
The Fountain (PH)
Ingbirchworth
Blackwater Dike
Green Gate
Ingbirchworth Resr
Barnsley Boundary Walk
Park House Farm
BARNSLEY RD
WAKEFIELD RD
PENISTONE RD
HUDDERSFIELD RD
FALLEDGE LA
DENBY LA
WINDMILL LA
GREEN LA
CARR LA
CUMBERWORTH LA
PARK LA
TOBY WOOD LA
A636
A635
A629
B6115
192

191
175

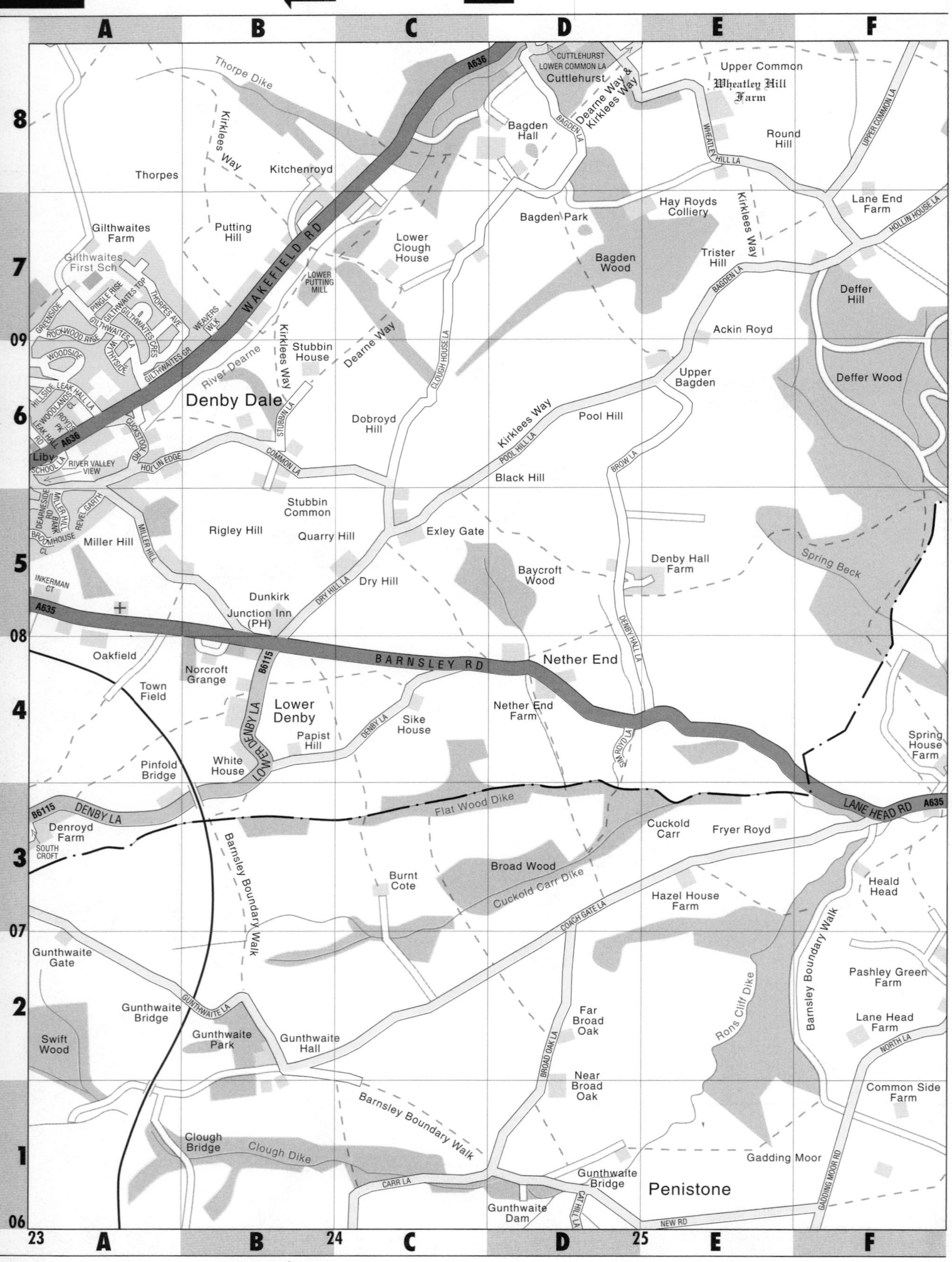
Thorpe Dike
Kirklees Way
Thorpes
Kitchenroyd
A636
Cuttlehurst
Dearne Way & Kirklees Way
Upper Common
Wheatley Hill Farm
Bagden Hall
Round Hill
Putting Hill
Gilthwaites Farm
Gilthwaites First Sch
WAKEFIELD RD
Lower Clough House
Bagden Park
Hay Royds Colliery
Lane End Farm
Bagden Wood
Trister Hill
Deffer Hill
Ackin Royd
Stubbin House
Dearne Way
River Dearne
Denby Dale
Upper Bagden
Deffer Wood
Dobroyd Hill
Kirklees Way
Pool Hill
Black Hill
Liby
Stubbin Common
Rigley Hill
Quarry Hill
Exley Gate
Miller Hill
Denby Hall Farm
Spring Beck
Baycroft Wood
Dry Hill
Dunkirk
Junction Inn (PH)
A635
Oakfield
BARNSLEY RD
Nether End
Norcroft Grange
Town Field
Lower Denby
Nether End Farm
Sike House
Papist Hill
Spring House Farm
Pinfold Bridge
White House
LANE HEAD RD
Flat Wood Dike
DENBY LA
Denroyd Farm
Cuckold Carr
Fryer Royd
Barnsley Boundary Walk
Broad Wood
Burnt Cote
Heald Head
Cuckold Carr Dike
Hazel House Farm
Gunthwaite Gate
Pashley Green Farm
Gunthwaite Bridge
Far Broad Oak
Rons Cliff Dike
Lane Head Farm
Swift Wood
Gunthwaite Park
Gunthwaite Hall
Near Broad Oak
Common Side Farm
Clough Bridge
Clough Dike
Gadding Moor
Gunthwaite Bridge
Penistone
Gunthwaite Dam
A B C D E F
23 24 25
8 7 6 5 4 3 2 1
09 08 07 06

191

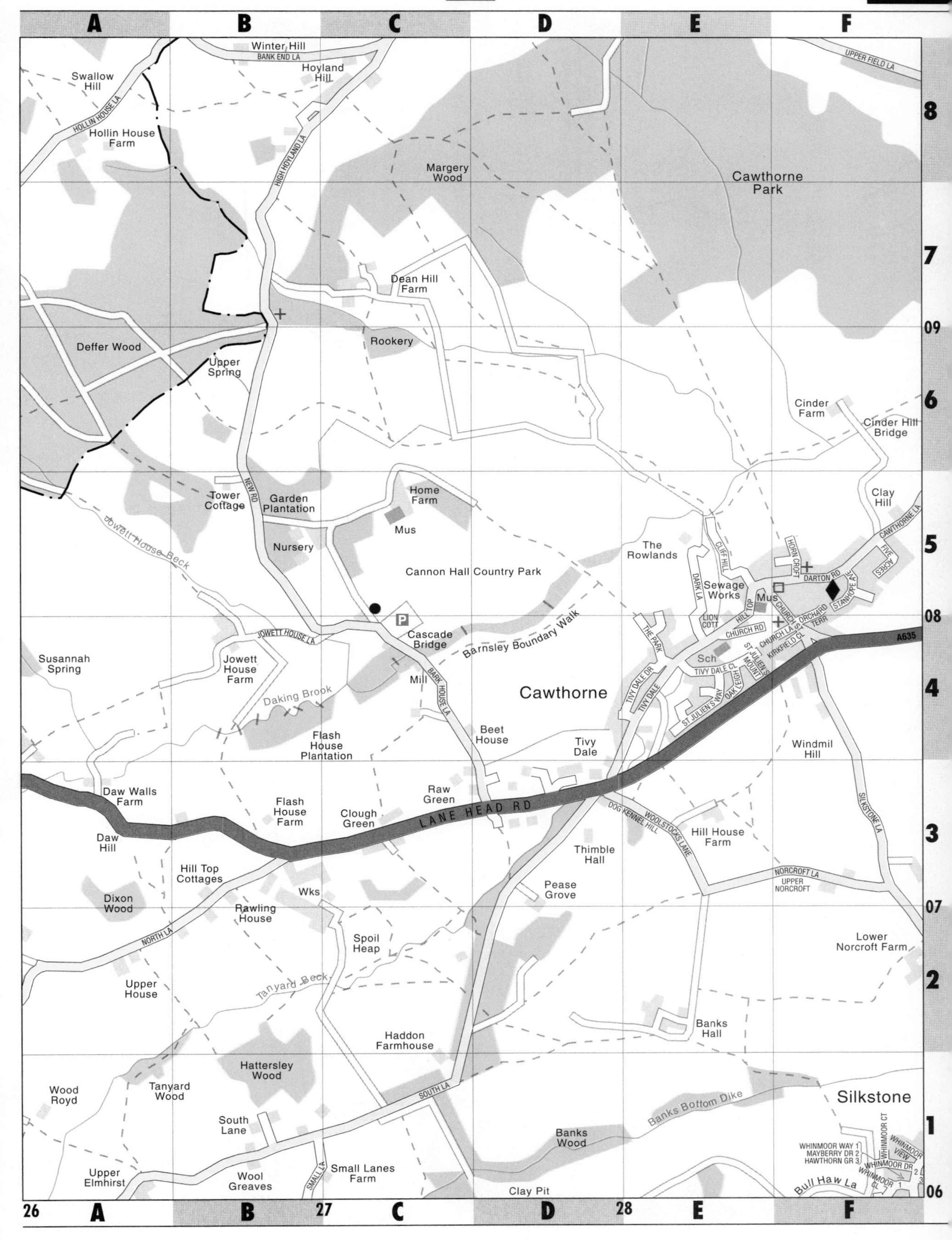

A B C D E F

8
09
7
6
5
08
4
07
3
2
06
1

26 A B 27 C D 28 E F

Winter Hill
BANK END LA
Hoyland Hill
Swallow Hill
Hollin House Farm
HOLLIN HOUSE LA
HIGH HOYLAND LA
Margery Wood
Cawthorne Park
UPPER FIELD LA

Dean Hill Farm
Deffer Wood
Upper Spring
Rookery
Cinder Farm
Cinder Hill Bridge
Clay Hill

Jowett House Beck
NEW RD
Tower Cottage
Garden Plantation
Nursery
Home Farm
Mus
Cannon Hall Country Park
The Rowlands
CLIFF HILL
HORN CROFT
Sewage Works
Mus
DARTON RD
CAWTHORNE LA
FIVE ROW
STANHOPE AV
DARK LA
HILL TOP
LION COTT
CHURCH LA
CHURCH RD
KIRKFIELD CL
ORCHARD TERR

JOWETT HOUSE LA
Susannah Spring
Jowett House Farm
Daking Brook
Cascade Bridge
Mill
BARK HOUSE LA
Barnsley Boundary Walk
Cawthorne
THE PARK
Sch
TIVY DALE DR
TIVY DALE
ST JULIEN'S WAY
ST JULIEN'S MOUNT
OAK RD
A635

Flash House Plantation
Daw Walls Farm
Daw Hill
Flash House Farm
Clough Green
Beet House
Raw Green
Tivy Dale
LANE HEAD RD
DOG KENNEL HILL
WOOLSTOCKS LANE
Hill House Farm
Windmill Hill
SILKSTONE LA

Dixon Wood
Hill Top Cottages
Rawling House
Wks
NORTH LA
Spoil Heap
Thimble Hall
Pease Grove
NORCROFT LA
UPPER NORCROFT
Lower Norcroft Farm

Upper House
Tanyard Beck
Haddon Farmhouse
Banks Hall

Wood Royd
Tanyard Wood
Hattersley Wood
South Lane
SOUTH LA
Banks Wood
Banks Bottom Dike
Silkstone

Upper Elmhirst
Wool Greaves
SMALL LA
Small Lanes Farm
Clay Pit
Bull Haw La
WHINMOOR WAY 1
MAYBERRY DR 2
HAWTHORN GR 3
WHINMOOR VIEW
WHINMOOR CT
WHINMOOR DR

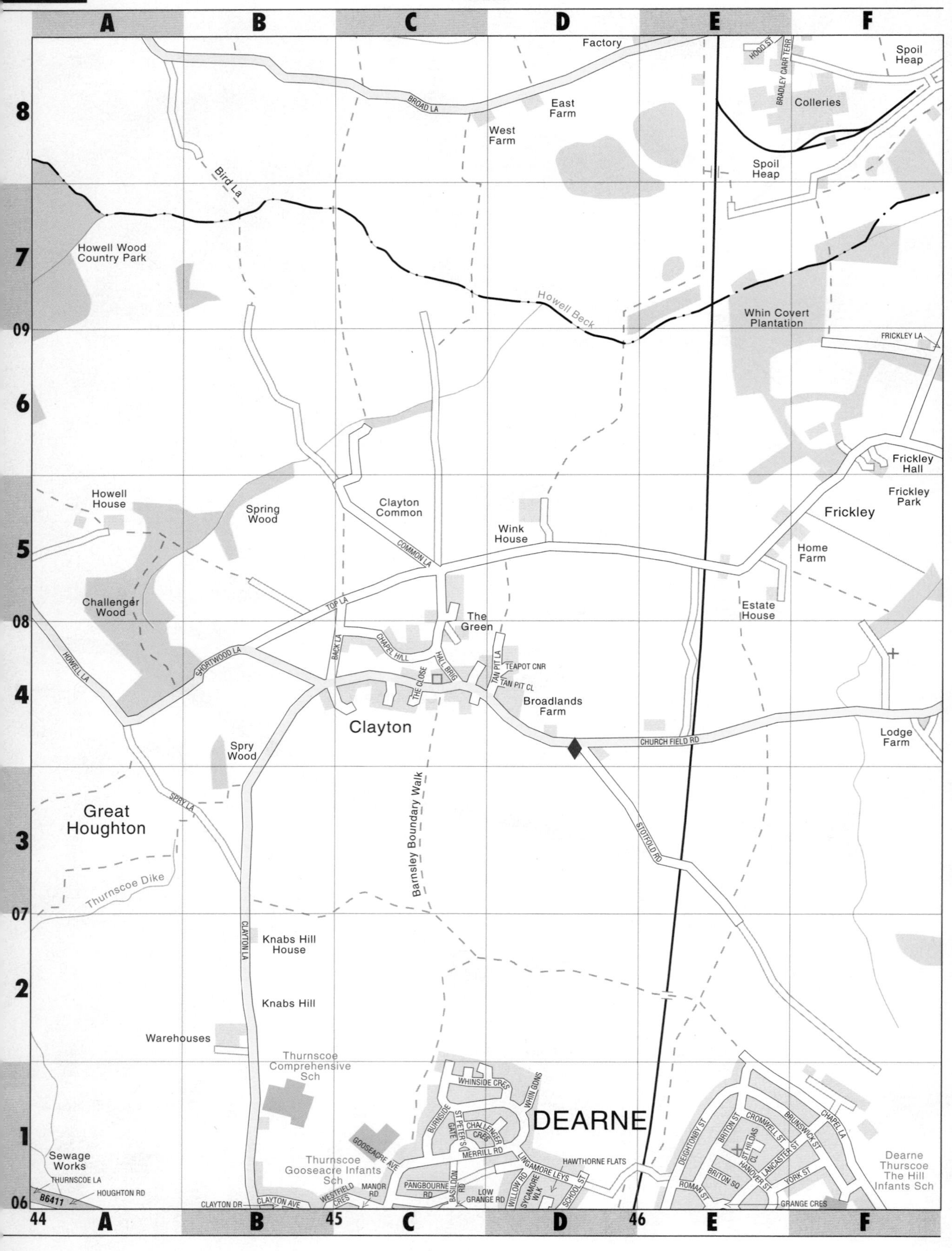

A   B   C   D   E   F

8

Factory

Spoil
Heap

Colleries

BROAD LA

East
Farm

West
Farm

Spoil
Heap

Bird La

7

Howell Wood
Country Park

Howell Beck

Whin Covert
Plantation

FRICKLEY LA

09

6

Frickley
Hall

Frickley
Park

Frickley

Howell
House

Spring
Wood

Clayton
Common

Wink
House

Home
Farm

5

COMMON LA

Challenger
Wood

Estate
House

08

TOP LA

BACK LA

The Green

SHORTWOOD LA

CHAPEL HILL

HALL BRIG

TEAPOT CNR

TAN PIT LA

4

HOWELL LA

THE CLOSE

TAN PIT CL

Clayton

Broadlands
Farm

CHURCH FIELD RD

Lodge
Farm

Spry
Wood

Great
Houghton

SPRY LA

Barnsley Boundary Walk

STOTFOLD RD

3

Thurnscoe Dike

07

CLAYTON LA

Knabs Hill
House

2

Knabs Hill

Warehouses

Thurnscoe
Comprehensive
Sch

WHINSIDE CRES

WHIN GDNS

DEARNE

CROMWELL ST

BRUNSWICK ST

CHAPEL LA

1

BURNSIDE

ST PETER SCT

CHALLENGER
CRES

Hawthorne Flats

DEIGHTON BL ST

BRITON ST

ST HILDAS

CROMWELL ST

LANCASTER ST

YORK ST

Dearne
Thurscoe
The Hill
Infants Sch

Sewage
Works

Thurnscoe
Gooseacre Infants
Sch

GOOSEACRE AVE

GOOSEACRE
GATE

WESTFIELD
CRES

MANOR
RD

PANGBOURNE
RD

BASILDON

MERRILL RD

LOW
GRANGE RD

INGAMORE LEYS

SYCAMORE
WLK

WILLOW RD

SCHOOL ST

ROMAN ST

BRITON SQ

HANOVER ST

GRANGE CRES

THURNSCOE LA

HOUGHTON RD

B6411

CLAYTON DR

CLAYTON AVE

06

44   A   B   45   C   D   46   E   F

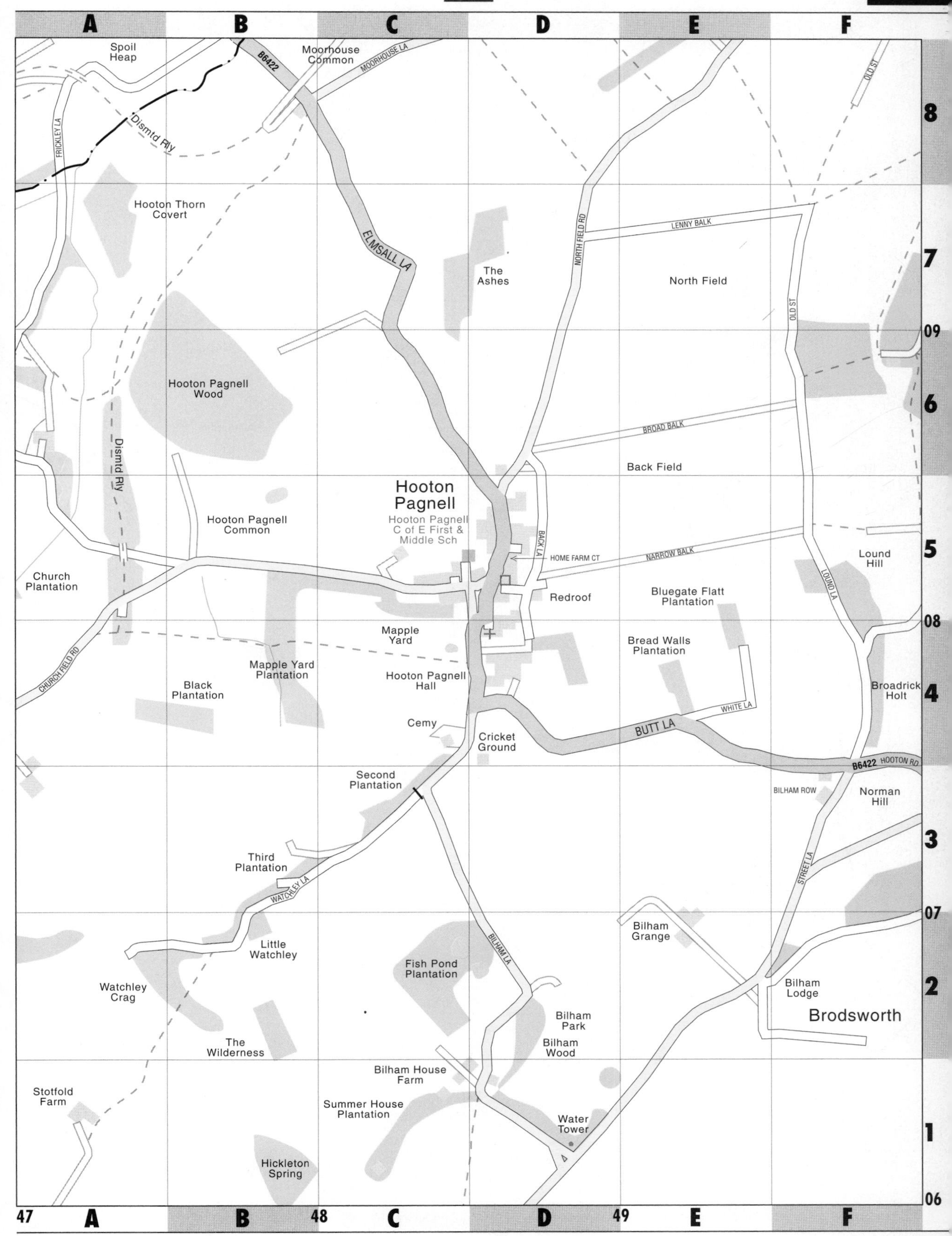

8

7

09

6

5

08

4

3

07

2

1

06

A · B · C · D · E · F

Spoil Heap

Moorhouse Common

B6422

MOORHOUSE LA

FRICKLEY LA

Dismtd Rly

Hooton Thorn Covert

ELMSALL LA

The Ashes

NORTH FIELD RD

LENNY BALK

OLD ST

North Field

Dismtd Rly

Hooton Pagnell Wood

BROAD BALK

Back Field

Hooton Pagnell Common

Hooton Pagnell

Hooton Pagnell C of E First & Middle Sch

BACK LA

HOME FARM CT

NARROW BALK

LOUND LA

Lound Hill

Church Plantation

Redroof

Bluegate Flatt Plantation

CHURCH FIELD RD

Black Plantation

Mapple Yard Plantation

Mapple Yard

Hooton Pagnell Hall

Bread Walls Plantation

08

Broadrick Holt

Cemy

Cricket Ground

BUTT LA

WHITE LA

Second Plantation

B6422 HOOTON RD

BILHAM ROW

Norman Hill

STREET LA

Third Plantation

WATCHLEY LA

07

Little Watchley

Fish Pond Plantation

BILHAM LA

Bilham Grange

Watchley Crag

Bilham Park

Bilham Wood

Bilham Lodge

Brodsworth

The Wilderness

Stotfold Farm

Bilham House Farm

Summer House Plantation

Water Tower

Hickleton Spring

47 · A · B · 48 · C · D · 49 · E · F

186

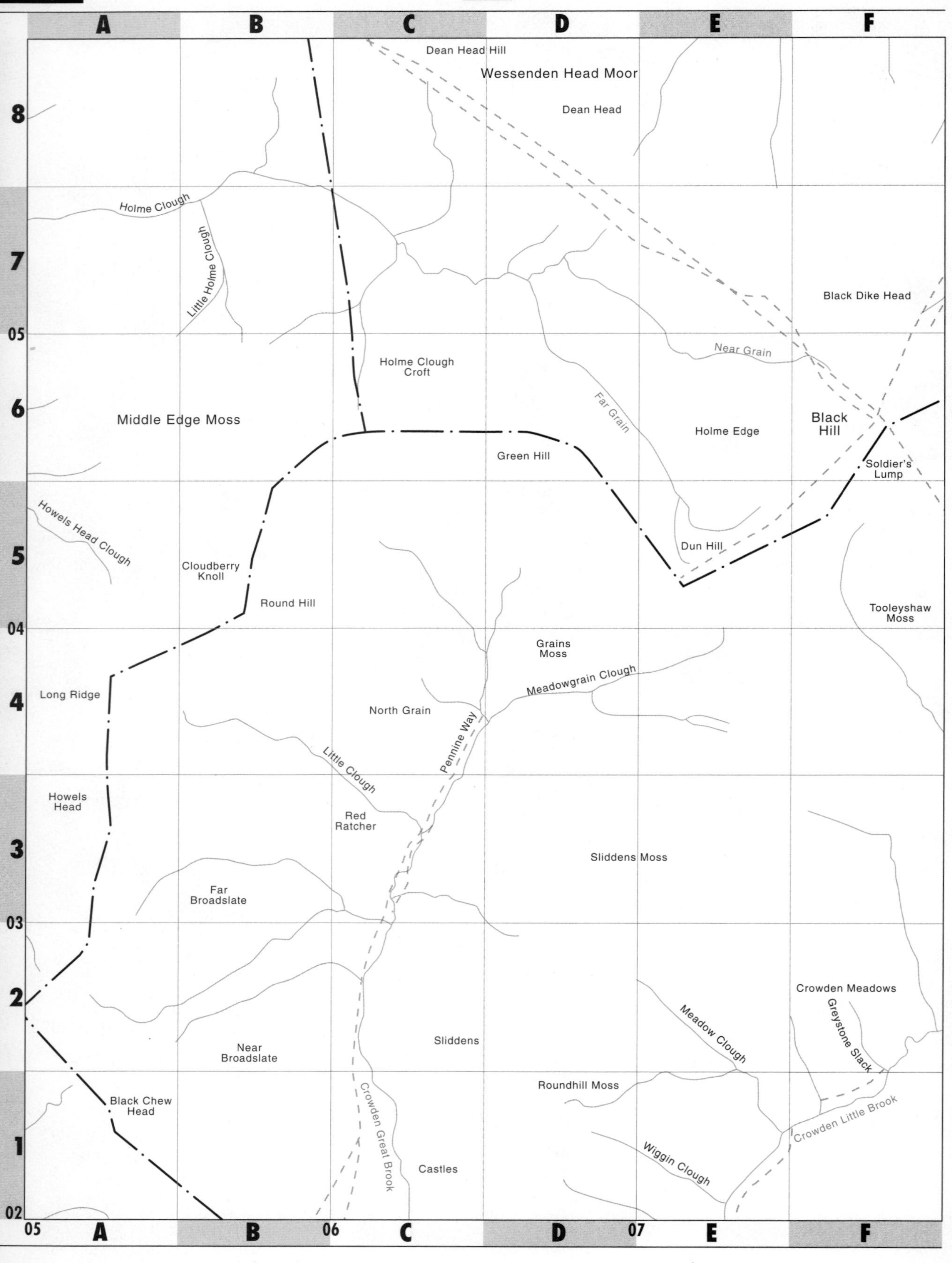

Dean Head Hill

Wessenden Head Moor

Dean Head

Holme Clough

Little Holme Clough

Black Dike Head

Near Grain

Holme Clough
Croft

Middle Edge Moss

Far Grain

Holme Edge

Black
Hill

Green Hill

Soldier's
Lump

Howels Head Clough

Cloudberry
Knoll

Round Hill

Dun Hill

Tooleyshaw
Moss

Grains
Moss

Meadowgrain Clough

Long Ridge

North Grain

Pennine Way

Little Clough

Howels
Head

Red
Ratcher

Sliddens Moss

Far
Broadslate

Crowden Meadows

Meadow Clough

Greystone Slack

Near
Broadslate

Sliddens

Crowden Great Brook

Roundhill Moss

Crowden Little Brook

Black Chew
Head

Wiggin Clough

Castles

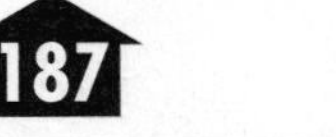

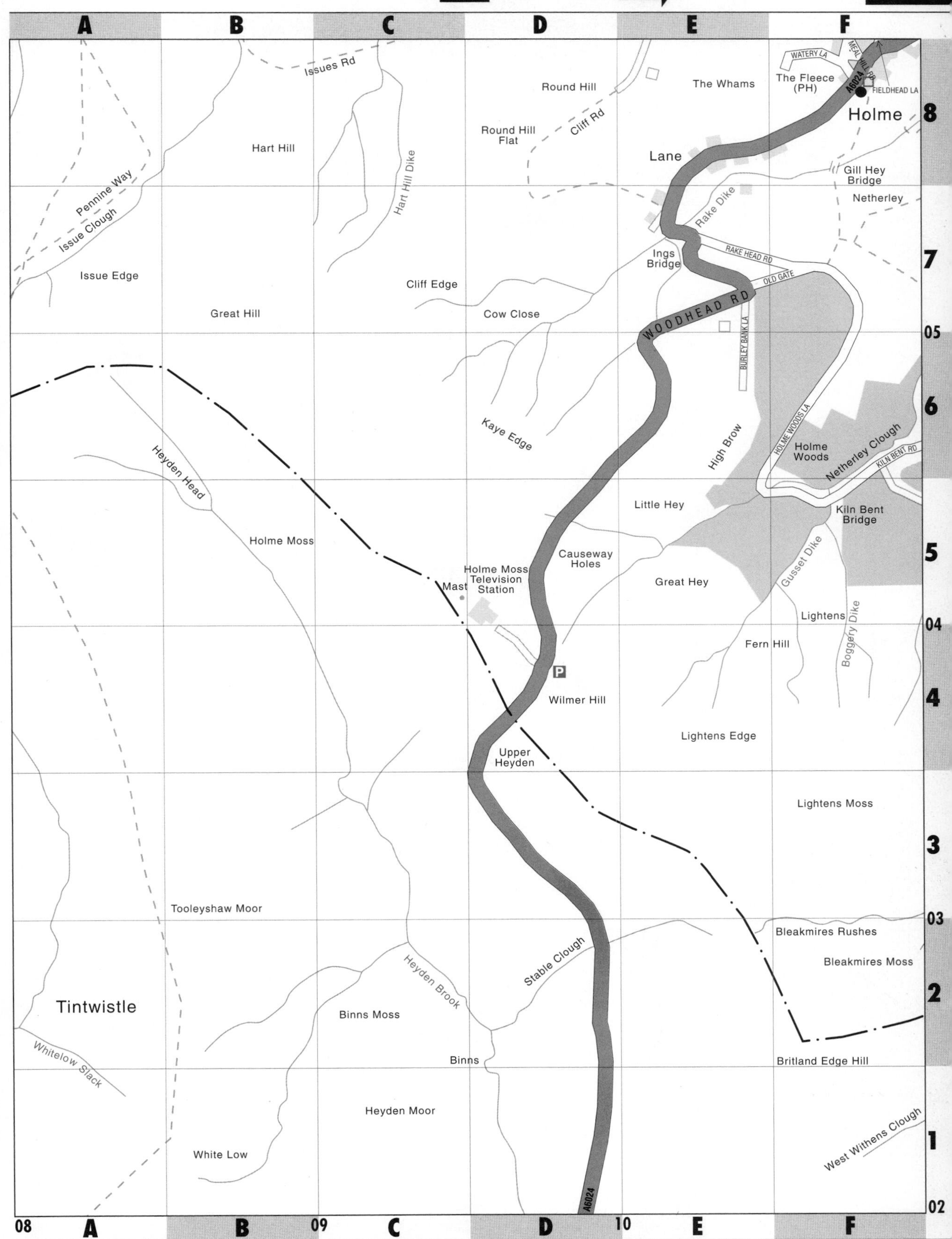

A B C D E F

8
7
05
6
5
04
4
3
03
2
1
02

Issues Rd

Round Hill

The Whams

WATERY LA

The Fleece (PH)

A6024

FIELDHEAD LA

Holme

Hart Hill

Round Hill Flat

Cliff Rd

Lane

Gill Hey Bridge

Netherley

Pennine Way

Issue Clough

Hart Hill Dike

Rake Dike

RAKE HEAD RD

Ings Bridge

OLD GATE

Issue Edge

Cliff Edge

Cow Close

WOODHEAD RD

BURLEY BANK LA

Great Hill

HOLME WOODS LA

Kaye Edge

High Brow

Holme Woods

Netherley Clough

KILN BENT RD

Heyden Head

Little Hey

Kiln Bent Bridge

Holme Moss

Causeway Holes

Great Hey

Gusset Dike

Lightens

Boggery Dike

Holme Moss Television Station

Mast

Fern Hill

04

Lightens Edge

P

Wilmer Hill

Lightens Moss

Upper Heyden

Tooleyshaw Moor

Heyden Brook

Stable Clough

Bleakmires Rushes

Bleakmires Moss

Tintwistle

Binns Moss

Whitelow Slack

Binns

Britland Edge Hill

Heyden Moor

West Withens Clough

White Low

A6024

08 A B 09 C D 10 E F

197
188

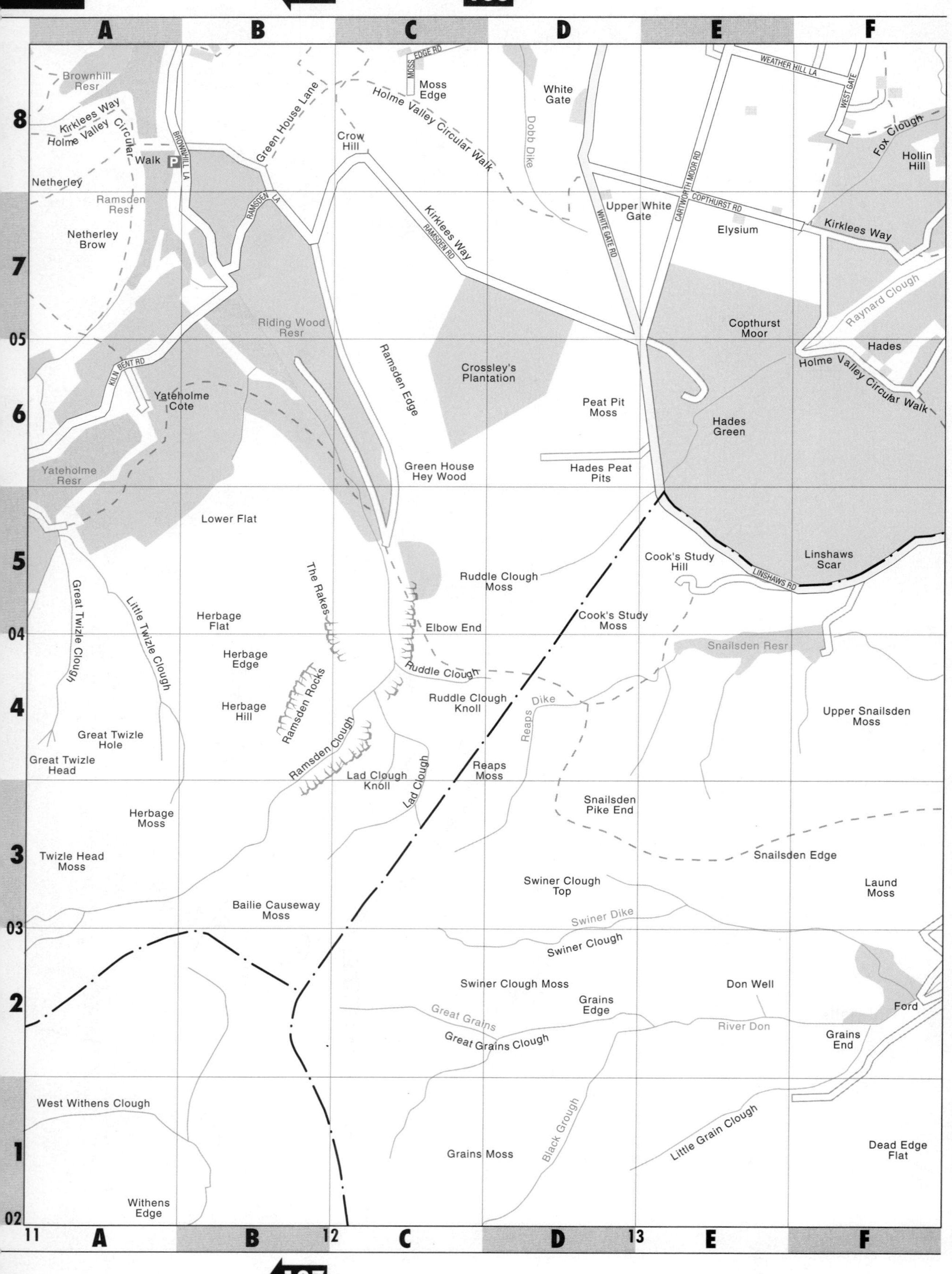
A
B
C
D
E
F
8
7
05
6
5
04
4
3
03
2
1
02
11
12
13
Brownhill Resr
Kirklees Way
Holme Valley Circular Walk
Netherley
Ramsden Resr
Netherley Brow
BROWNHILL LA
Green House Lane
RAMSDEN LA
MOSS EDGE RD
Moss Edge
Crow Hill
Holme Valley Circular Walk
Dobb Dike
White Gate
WEATHER HILL LA
WEST GATE
Fox Clough
Hollin Hill
Kirklees Way
RAMSDEN RD
Upper White Gate
WHITE GATE RD
CARTWORTH MOOR RD
COPTHURST RD
Elysium
Kirklees Way
Raynard Clough
Riding Wood Resr
KILN BENT RD
Yateholme Cote
Ramsden Edge
Crossley's Plantation
Copthurst Moor
Hades
Holme Valley Circular Walk
Peat Pit Moss
Hades Green
Yateholme Resr
Green House Hey Wood
Hades Peat Pits
Lower Flat
Cook's Study Hill
Linshaws Scar
LINSHAWS RD
Ruddle Clough Moss
Great Twizle Clough
Little Twizle Clough
The Rakes
Herbage Flat
Elbow End
Cook's Study Moss
Snailsden Resr
Herbage Edge
Ramsden Rocks
Ruddle Clough
Ruddle Clough Knoll
Reaps Dike
Herbage Hill
Upper Snailsden Moss
Great Twizle Hole
Great Twizle Head
Ramsden Clough
Lad Clough Knoll
Lad Clough
Reaps Moss
Snailsden Pike End
Herbage Moss
Twizle Head Moss
Snailsden Edge
Swiner Clough Top
Laund Moss
Bailie Causeway Moss
Swiner Dike
Swiner Clough
Swiner Clough Moss
Don Well
Grains Edge
Ford
Great Grains
Great Grains Clough
River Don
Grains End
West Withens Clough
Little Grain Clough
Black Grough
Grains Moss
Dead Edge Flat
Withens Edge
Walk

197

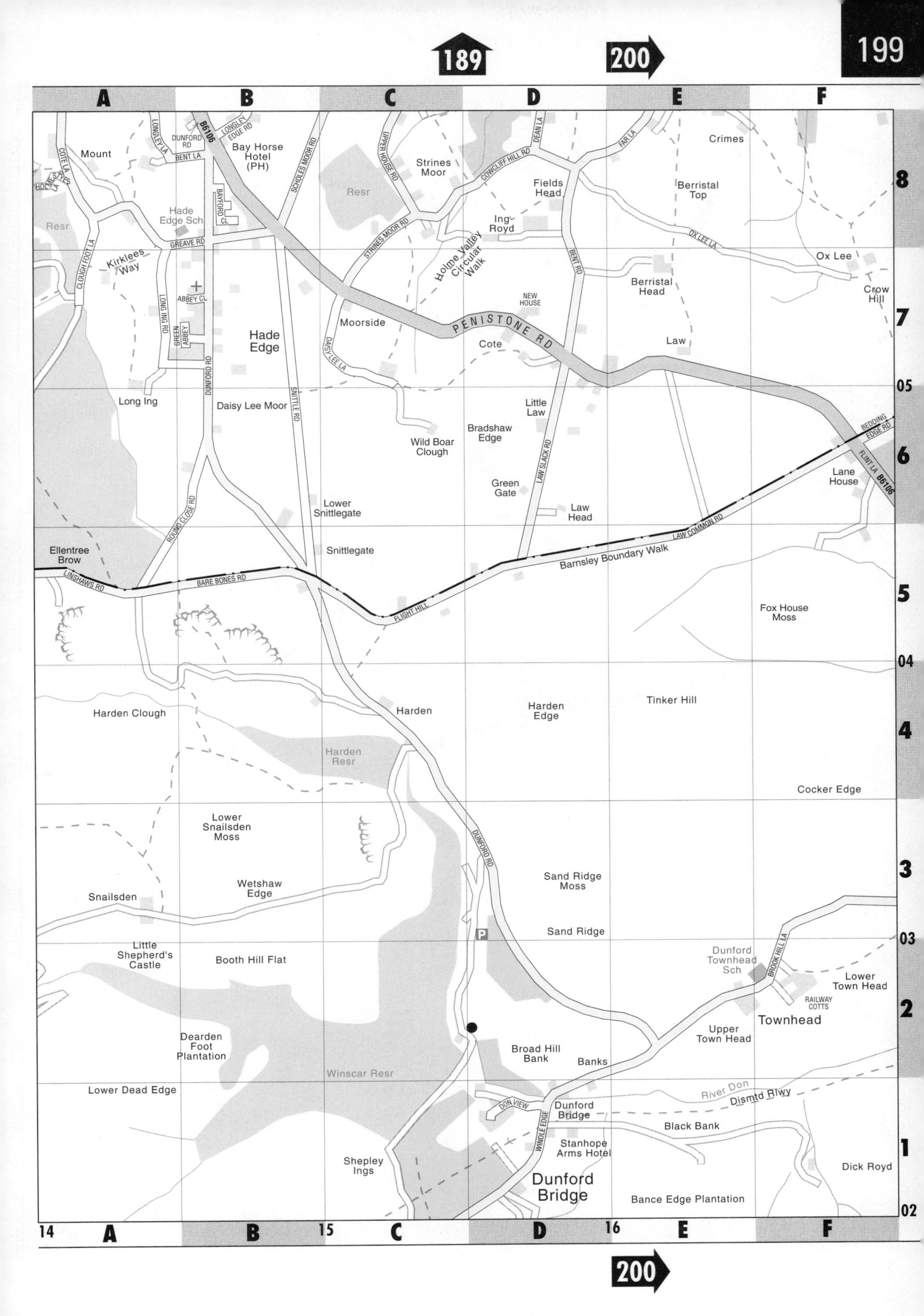
189
200
A
B
C
D
E
F
Mount
Bay Horse Hotel (PH)
Strines Moor
Resr
Fields Head
Crimes
Berristal Top
Hade Edge Sch
Resr
Ing Royd
Kirklees Way
Holme Valley Circular Walk
Ox Lee
Berristal Head
Crow Hill
Moorside
Hade Edge
PENISTONE RD
Cote
Law
Long Ing
Daisy Lee Moor
Little Law
Wild Boar Clough
Bradshaw Edge
Green Gate
Lane House
Law Head
Lower Snittlegate
Snittlegate
Ellentree Brow
Barnsley Boundary Walk
Fox House Moss
Harden Clough
Harden
Harden Edge
Tinker Hill
Harden Resr
Cocker Edge
Lower Snailsden Moss
Sand Ridge Moss
Wetshaw Edge
Snailsden
Sand Ridge
Little Shepherd's Castle
Booth Hill Flat
Dunford Townhead Sch
Lower Town Head
Townhead
Dearden Foot Plantation
Broad Hill Bank
Banks
Upper Town Head
Winscar Resr
Lower Dead Edge
River Don
Dismtd Rlwy
Dunford Bridge
Black Bank
Stanhope Arms Hotel
Shepley Ings
Dick Royd
Dunford Bridge
Bance Edge Plantation
COTE LA
HOLMES RD
LONGLEY LA
DUNFORD RD
BENT LA
B6106
LONGLEY EDGE RD
SCHOLES MOOR RD
UPPER HOUSE RD
DEAN LA
FAR LA
COWCLIFF HILL RD
BAYFORD CL
GREAVE RD
STRINES MOOR RD
CLOUGH FOOT LA
OX LEE LA
BENT RD
LONG ING RD
ABBEY CL
NEW HOUSE
GREEN ABBEY
DAISY LEE LA
DUNFORD RD
SNITTLE RD
LAW SLACK RD
BEDDING EDGE RD
FLINT LA
ROUND CLOSE RD
LAW COMMON RD
LINSHAWS RD
BARE BONES RD
FLIGHT HILL
DUNFORD RD
BROOK HILL LA
RAILWAY COTTS
DON VIEW
WINDLE EDGE
P
8
7
6
5
4
3
2
1
05
04
03
02
14
15
16
200

199
190

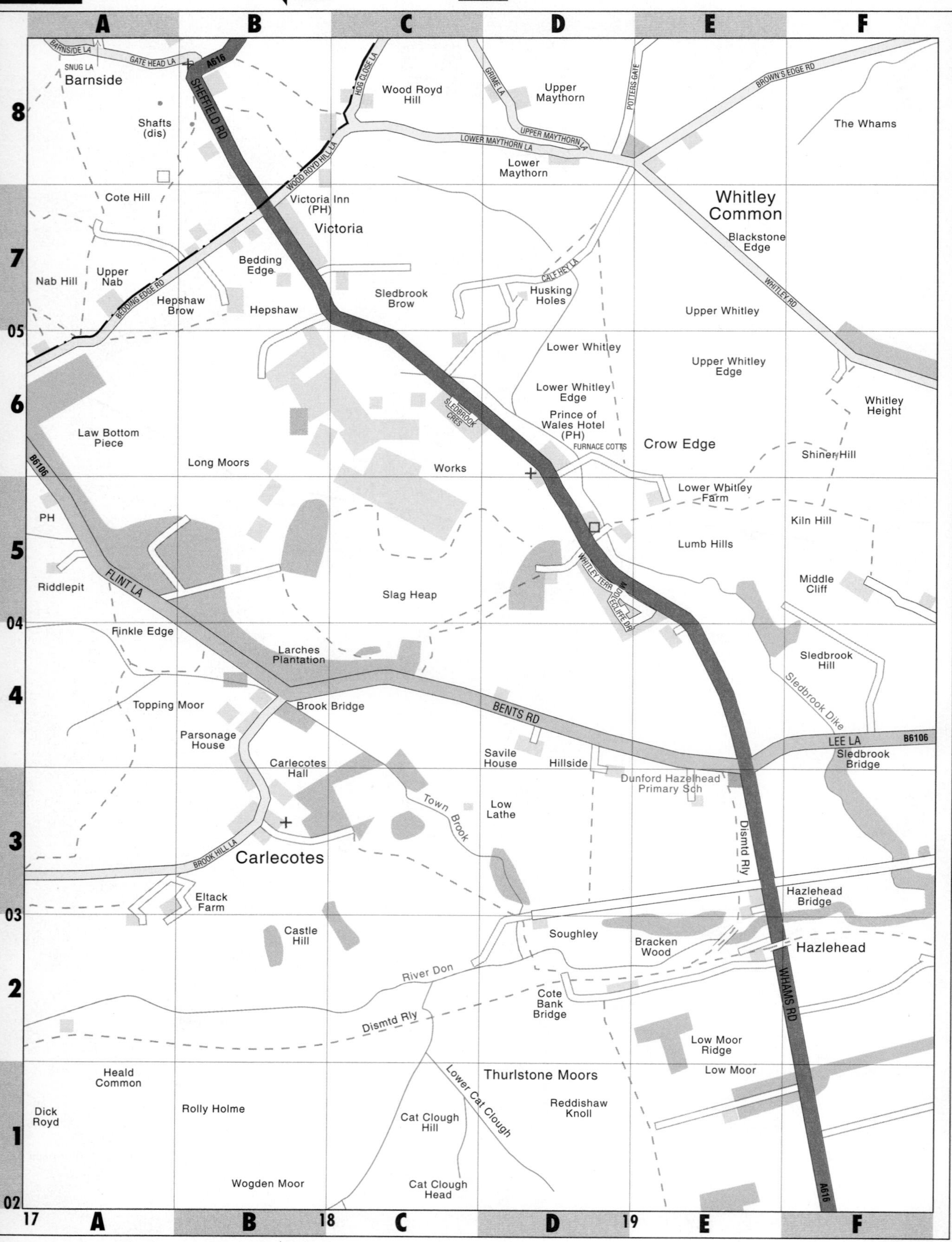

A
B
C
D
E
F
8
7
05
6
5
04
4
3
03
2
1
02
17
18
19
BARNSIDE LA
SNUG LA
Barnside
GATE HEAD LA
A616
SHEFFIELD RD
HOG CLOSE LA
Wood Royd Hill
GRIME LA
Upper Maythorn
POTTERS GATE
BROWN'S EDGE RD
Shafts (dis)
UPPER MAYTHORN LA
LOWER MAYTHORN LA
The Whams
Lower Maythorn
WOOD ROYD HILL LA
Cote Hill
Victoria Inn (PH)
Victoria
Whitley Common
Blackstone Edge
Nab Hill
Upper Nab
Bedding Edge
BEDDING EDGE RD
Hepshaw Brow
Hepshaw
Sledbrook Brow
CALF HEY LA
Husking Holes
WHITLEY RD
Upper Whitley
Lower Whitley
Upper Whitley Edge
Lower Whitley Edge
Whitley Height
SLEDBROOK CRES
Law Bottom Piece
Prince of Wales Hotel (PH)
FURNACE COTTS
Crow Edge
B6106
Long Moors
Works
Shiner Hill
Lower Whitley Farm
PH
Kiln Hill
Lumb Hills
Middle Cliff
Riddlepit
FLINT LA
Slag Heap
WHITLEY TERR
ECLIFFE DR
Finkle Edge
Larches Plantation
Sledbrook Hill
Topping Moor
Brook Bridge
BENTS RD
Sledbrook Dike
LEE LA
B6106
Parsonage House
Savile House
Hillside
Sledbrook Bridge
Carlecotes Hall
Dunford Hazelhead Primary Sch
Town Brook
Low Lathe
Dismtd Rly
BROOK HILL LA
Carlecotes
Hazlehead Bridge
Eltack Farm
Castle Hill
Soughley
Bracken Wood
Hazlehead
River Don
WHAMS RD
Cote Bank Bridge
Dismtd Rly
Low Moor Ridge
Low Moor
Heald Common
Lower Cat Clough
Thurlstone Moors
Dick Royd
Rolly Holme
Cat Clough Hill
Reddishaw Knoll
Wogden Moor
Cat Clough Head
A616

199

A1 Bsns Pk. Knot 126 C3
Aachen Way. Hali HX1 113 A5
Abb Scott La. Brad BD12, BD6 . 94 B6
Abb St. Hud HD1 153 D7
Abbey Ave. Leeds LS5 58 F3
Abbey Cl. Add LS29 7 A8
Abbey Cl. Holmfi HD7 199 B7
Abbey Ct. Hors LS18 58 B6
Abbey Dr. Shep HD8 173 F1
Abbey Farm Dr. Shep HD8 190 F8
Abbey Gorse. Leeds LS5 59 A5
Abbey Grange CE High Sch. Leeds 58 F8
Abbey House Mus. Leeds 58 F5
Abbey La. Hali HX2 111 F7
Abbey Lea. Brad BD15 73 C8
Abbey Mount. Leeds LS5 58 F3 4
Abbey Park Jun & Inf Sch. Hali 91 D6
Abbey Rd. Batley WF17 117 F4
Abbey Rd. Hud HD2 136 B1
Abbey Rd. Leeds LS5 58 E6
Abbey Rd N. Shep HD8 173 F1
Abbey Rd S. Shep HD8 190 F8
Abbey Rd. Shep HD8 174 A2
Abbey St. Leeds LS3 78 F8
Abbey Terr. Leeds LS5 58 F3 3
Abbey View. Leeds LS5 59 A5
Abbey Wlk. Hali HX3 113 C4
Abbey Wlk. Leeds LS5 58 F5
Abbey Wlk S. Hali HX3 113 D4
Abbeydale Garth. Leeds LS5 58 E6
Abbeydale Gdns. Leeds LS5 58 E6
Abbeydale Gr. Leeds LS5 58 E6
Abbeydale Mount. Leeds LS5 58 E6
Abbeydale Oval. Leeds LS5 58 E6
Abbeydale Vale. Leeds LS5 58 E6
Abbeydale Way. Leeds LS5 58 E6
Abbot La. Wool WF4 178 B6
Abbot St. Hud HD1 153 E7
Abbots Pl. Hud HD2 136 F5
Abbots Wood. Brad BD9 55 A3
Abbotside Cl. Brad BD10 56 C6
Abbotsway. Gar LS25 82 D6
Abbott Ct. Leeds LS12 78 D8
Abbott Rd. Leeds LS12 78 D8
Abbott Terr. Wake WF1 142 D3
Abbott View. Leeds LS12 78 D8
Abbott's Ladies Home. Hali HX3 113 C3
Abbotts Cl. Aber LS25 64 E8
Abel St. Brad BD12 94 C4 4
Abelia Mount. Brad BD7 73 F6
Aberdeen Dr. Leeds LS12 78 A8 4
Aberdeen Gr. Leeds LS12 78 A8
Aberdeen Pl. Brad BD7 74 A5
Aberdeen Rd. Leeds LS12 78 A7
Aberdeen Terr. Brad BD14 73 D4
Aberdeen Terr. Brad BD7 74 A6
Aberdeen Wlk. Leeds LS12 78 A7
Aberfield Bank. Midd LS10 99 E6
Aberfield Cl. Midd LS10 99 E7
Aberfield Crest. Midd LS10 99 E6
Aberfield Dr. Crig WF4 159 E4
Aberfield Dr. Midd LS10 99 E6
Aberfield Gate. Midd LS10 99 E7
Aberfield Mount. Midd LS10 99 E6
Aberfield Rd. Midd LS10 99 E7
Aberfield Rise. Midd LS10 99 E7
Aberfield Wlk. Midd LS10 99 E6
Aberford By-Pass. Aber LS25 64 F5
Aberford CE Sch. Aber 64 E7
Aberford Rd. Aber LS25 64 C2
Aberford Rd. B in Elm LS15 63 E7
Aberford Rd. Brad BD8 74 B8
Aberford Rd. Bramham LS23 30 D2
Aberford Rd. Gar LS25 83 A8
Aberford Rd. Loft G WF3 121 F3
Aberford Rd. Roth LS26 101 D6
Aberford Rd. Wake WF1 142 E8
Abingdon St. Brad BD8 55 B1
Abingdon St. Hud HD2 136 A1
Abraham Hill. Roth LS26 100 F5
Abraham Ormerod Day Hospl. Tod 108 B5
Abram St. Brad BD5 74 E4
Acacia Cl. Castle WF10 125 D6
Acacia Dr. Brad BD15 54 A4
Acacia Dr. Brig HX3 115 A7
Acacia Dr. Castle WF10 125 D6
Acacia Gn. Pont WF8 125 F1
Acacia Gr. Heb Br HX7 89 F1
Acacia Gr. Shaf S72 180 C2
Acacia House. Castle WF10 124 E7 8
Acacia Park Cres. Yeadon BD10 39 F2
Acacia Park Dr. Yeadon BD10 . 39 F2
Acacia Park Terr. Yeadon LS19 40 A2
Acacia Wlk. Knot WF11 126 D3
Acaia Cl. S Elm WF9 183 A4
Acaster Dr. Brad BD12 94 C6
Acaster Dr. Gar LS25 83 B5
Accommodation Rd. Leeds LS7 60 A7
Acer Way. Brig BD19 115 F8 8
Ackroyd Ct. Thorn BD13 72 D6
Ackroyd St. Morley LS27 98 B4
Ackroyd St. Tod OL14 86 B1
Ackton Cl. Feath WF7 145 A8
Ackton General Hospl. Feath 124 A1
Ackton Hall Cres. Feath WF7 145 A8
Ackton La. Feath WF7 124 C1
Ackton La. Feath WF7 145 A8
Ackton P'sture La. Castle WF7 124 B4
Ackton Pastures Jun & Inf Sch. Castle 124 A6
Ackworth Ave. Yeadon LS19 40 C6
Ackworth Bell Lane Fst Sch. Ack M T 163 F5
Ackworth Bridle Rd. Ack M T WF8 164 E6
Ackworth Cres. Yeadon LS19 40 C6
Ackworth Dr. Yeadon LS19 40 D6
Ackworth House Cl. Ack M T WF7 164 A8
Ackworth Howards C E Sch. Ack M T 164 B7
Ackworth Mid Sch. Ack M T 163 F4
Ackworth Mill Dam Fst Sch. Ack M T 164 A6
Ackworth Moor Top Sch. Ack M T 163 F4
Ackworth Rd. Feath WF7 145 D3
Ackworth Rd. Pont WF7, WF8 146 C5
Ackworth Sch. Ack M T 164 A7
Ackworth St. Brad BD5 74 E4
Acme Terr. Wake WF1 142 D3
Acorn Dr. Leeds LS14 62 C8
Acorn Gr. Holmfi HD7 189 D3
Acorn Pk. Bail BD17 38 E2
Acorn St. Hali HX1 113 A7
Acorn St. Keigh BD21 35 B5
Acre Ave. Brad BD2 56 B5
Acre Cir. Midd LS10 99 C4
Acre Cl. Brad BD2 56 B5
Acre Cl. Midd LS10 99 B3
Acre Cres. Brad BD2 56 B5
Acre Cres. Midd LS10 99 C4
Acre Dr. Brad BD2 56 B5
Acre Fold. Add LS29 6 E8
Acre Gr. Brad BD2 56 B5
Acre Gr. Midd LS10 99 C4
Acre House Ave. Hud HD3 153 C8
Acre La. Brad BD2 56 B4
Acre La. Brad BD6 74 C1
Acre La. Haw BD22 51 C7
Acre La. Hep HX7 88 C6
Acre La. Holmfi HD7 188 D2
Acre La. Holmfi HD7 190 B6
Acre La. Mel HD7 170 F1
Acre Mount. Midd LS10 99 C4
Acre Pl. Midd LS10 99 C4
Acre Rd. Midd LS10 99 C4
Acre Rise. Bail BD17 38 C4
Acre Sq. Midd LS10 99 C4
Acre St. Hud HD3 153 C8
Acre St. Midd LS10 99 D4
Acre Terr. Midd LS10 99 D4
Acre The. Brad BD12 94 B5
Acre Villas. Heb Br HX7 89 E1 1
Acrehowe Rise. Bail BD17 38 E4
Acres Hall Ave. Pudsey LS28 77 A6
Acres Hall Cres. Pudsey LS28 77 A6
Acres Hall Dr. Pudsey LS28 77 A6
Acres La. Hep HX7 88 F4
Acres La. Holmfi HD7 187 F4
Acres Rd. Loft G WF3 121 C8
Acres St. Keigh BD21 35 B6
Acres The. Add LS29 7 A8
Acres The. Beam LS29 3 A1
Acres The. S in Cra BD20 16 C4
Acton Flat La. Hud HD3 135 A3
Acton St. Brad BD3 75 C7
Acute Terr. Wake WF2 141 E6
Ada St. Bail BD17 38 E2
Ada St. Hali HX3 92 C1 6
Ada St. Keigh BD21 35 A7 11
Ada St. Queen BD13 72 D1 8
Ada St. Ship BD18 54 F8
Ada's Pl. Pudsey LS28 57 E2
Adam Croft. Cull BD13 52 D6
Adam Ct. Hud HD3 135 B1
Adam St. Brad BD6 74 B1 7
Adam St. Tod OL14 108 B6
Adams Gr. Leeds LS15 62 E4
Addi St. Brad BD4 75 C3
Addingford Cl. Hor WF4 159 A8
Addingford Dr. Hor WF4 159 A8
Addingford La. Hor WF4 159 A8
Addingham Fst Sch. Add 2 E1
Addingham Gdns. Leeds LS12 78 A7
Addingham Mid Sch. Add 2 F1
Addison Ave. Brad BD3 56 D1
Addison Ave. Nor WF6 123 C1
Addison Ct. Hor WF4 141 C2
Addison Ct. Leeds LS15 81 D6
Addle Croft La. Lepton HD8 155 F5
Addlethorpe La. Sickl LS22 12 A5
Adey Cres. S Elm WF9 182 F3
Adel CE Sch. Hors 42 D5
Adel Garth. Hors LS16 42 D4
Adel Gn. Hors LS16 42 D4
Adel Grange Cl. Hors LS16 42 C2
Adel Grange Croft. Hors LS16 42 C2
Adel Grange Mews. Hors LS16 42 C2
Adel La. Hors LS16 42 C3
Adel Mead. Hors LS16 42 D4
Adel Mill. Eccup LS16 42 D6
Adel Park Cl. Hors LS16 42 C3
Adel Park Croft. Hors LS16 42 C3
Adel Park Ct. Hors LS16 42 C3
Adel Park Dr. Hors LS16 42 C3
Adel Park Gdns. Hors LS16 42 C3
Adel Pasture. Hors LS16 42 C3
Adel Towers Cl. Hors LS16 42 D3
Adel Towers Ct. Hors LS16 42 D3
Adel Vale. Hors LS16 42 D4
Adel Wood Cl. Hors LS16 42 D3
Adel Wood Dr. Hors LS16 42 D3
Adel Wood Gdns. Hors LS16 42 D3
Adel Wood Gr. Hors LS16 42 D3
Adel Wood Pl. Hors LS16 42 D3
Adel Wood Rd. Hors LS16 42 D3
Adelaide House. Bing BD16 37 B2
Adelaide Rise. Bail BD17 38 C1 1
Adelaide St. Brad BD5 74 E5
Adelaide St. Hali HX1 112 F7 16
Adelaide St. Heb Br HX7 88 F3
Adelaide St. Tod OL14 108 B6 3
Adelaide Terr. Elland HX4 133 F3
Adelphi Rd. Hud HD3 153 C7
Adgil Cres. Hali HX3 114 A4
Administration Rd. Leeds LS9 80 C3
Admiral St. Leeds LS11 79 C4
Adolphus St. Brad BD1 74 F6 4
Adowsley Cl. Ack M T WF7 163 E6
Adwalton Cl. Birk BD11 96 D5
Adwalton Gn. Birk BD11 96 D5
Adwalton Gr. Queen BD13 72 F1
Adwick Gr. Wake WF2 160 B5
Adwick Pl. Leeds LS4 59 C2
Adwick Terr. Pont WF8 125 E2
Aeron Wilkinson Ct. S Kirk WF9 182 A2
Agar St. Brad BD8 73 F8 5
Agar Terr. Brad BD8 73 F8 6
Agbrigg Gr. Wake WF2 142 E2
Agbrigg Rd. Wake WF1, WF2 142 E2
Agincourt Dr. Nor WF6 122 E4
Agnes St. Keigh BD20 18 C1
Agnes Stewart CE High Sch. Leeds 79 E8
Ails La. Hali HX2 90 D1
Aimbry Ct. Hud HD5 154 F2
Ainley Bottom. Elland HX5 135 A5
Ainley Cl. Hud HD3 135 A2
Ainley Pk. Hud HD7 152 E4
Ainley Pl. Mars HD7 151 C2
Ainley Rd. Hud HD3 135 A3
Ainley St. Elland HX5 134 F6 9
Ainleys Ind Est. Elland 135 A5
Ainsbury Ave. Bail BD10 39 B3
Ainsbury Ave. Brad BD10 39 C3
Ainsdale Cl. Roy S71 179 B5
Ainsdale Gr. Cull BD13 52 E6
Ainsdale Rd. Roy S71 179 B5
Ainsley La. Mars HD7 168 D4
Ainsty Cres. Weth LS22 13 E7
Ainsty Dr. Weth LS22 13 E7
Ainsty Garth. Weth LS22 13 E7
Ainsty Rd. Weth LS22 13 D7
Ainsty View. Weth LS22 13 E7
Aintree Cl. Kippax LS25 82 F2
Aintree Ct. Leeds 79 E4
Air St. Leeds LS10 79 E5
Aire and Calder Cotts. Wake WF3 122 B2
Aire Cl. Bail BD17 38 B1
Aire Cres. Glu BD20 16 E6
Aire Ct. Sil BD20 17 E8
Aire Gr. Yeadon LS19 40 C6
Aire Mount. Weth LS22 13 D7
Aire Pl. Leeds LS3 59 E1
Aire Rd. Weth LS22 13 D7
Aire St. Bing BD16 36 E6
Aire St. Brad BD10 39 A1
Aire St. Brig HD6 115 B1
Aire St. Castle WF10 124 D8
Aire St. Dew WF13 138 F5
Aire St. Glu BD20 16 E6
Aire St. Haw BD22 51 D7 3
Aire St. Keigh BD21 35 D8
Aire St. Knot WF11 127 A5
Aire St. Leeds LS1 79 B7
Aire Terr. Castle WF10 103 D1
Aire Valley Cl. L Brad BD20 4 B6
Aire Valley Dr. L Brad BD20 4 B6
Aire View Ave. Ship BD16 54 B8
Aire View Ave. Ship BD18 55 A8
Aire View. Broth WF11 126 C8
Aire View. Con BD20 4 A2
Aire View Dr. Keigh BD20 36 C7
Aire View Inf Sch. Sil 5 E1
Aire View. Keigh BD20 18 F2
Aire View. Knot WF11 126 D5
Aire View. Sil BD20 5 E1
Aire View. Yeadon LS19 40 C6
Aire Way. Bail BD17 38 A1
Airebank. Bing BD16 36 F3
Aireborough L Ctr. Guise 39 E8
Aireburn Ave. Stee BD20 17 D5
Airedale Ave. Ship BD16 54 A7
Airedale Bsns Ctr. L Brad 4 A8
Airedale Cliff. Leeds LS13 58 C5
Airedale College Mount. Brad BD3 56 A1
Airedale College Rd. Brad BD3 56 A1
Airedale College Terr. Brad BD3 56 A1
Airedale Cres. Brad BD3 56 A1
Airedale Croft. Pudsey LS13 57 F5 5
Airedale Ct. Leeds LS14 61 F5
Airedale Dr. Castle WF10 104 C2
Airedale Dr. Gar LS25 83 B6
Airedale Dr. Hors LS18 57 F8
Airedale Dr. Shelf HX3 93 B5
Airedale Fst & Mid Sch. Castle 125 C7
Airedale Gdns. Pudsey LS13 57 F5
Airedale General Hospl. Stee 17 B6
Airedale Gr. Hors LS18 57 F8
Airedale Gr. Roth LS26 101 D6 3
Airedale High Sch. Castle 125 D7
Airedale Hts. Wake WF2 141 C4
Airedale Mews. Sil BD20 5 E1
Airedale Mount. Keigh BD20 36 C8
Airedale Mount. Pudsey LS13 57 E5
Airedale Pl. Bail BD17 38 E2 4
Airedale Quay. Leeds LS13 58 A4
Airedale Rd. Brad BD3 55 F1
Airedale Rd. Castle WF10 125 B7
Airedale Rd. Keigh BD21 35 F8
Airedale Rd. Roth LS26 101 D6
Airedale St. Bing BD16 36 F3
Airedale St. Brad BD2 56 B3
Airedale St. Keigh BD21 35 E8 4
Airedale Terr. Bail BD17 38 D2
Airedale Terr. Morley LS27 98 B4 8
Airedale Terr. Roth LS26 101 D6 2
Airedale Trad Pk. Glu 16 E7
Airedale View. Glu BD20 16 D7
Airedale View. Pudsey LS13 57 F5 4
Airedale View. Roth LS26 101 D6 1
Airedale Wharf. Pudsey LS13 57 F4
Airedale & Wharfdale Coll of F Ed. Hors 57 F7
Airedale & Wharfdale Coll of F Ed. Otley 23 A8
Aireside Ave. Con BD20 4 B2
Aireside. Con BD20 4 B2
Aireside Ctr. Leeds 79 A7
Aireside Terr. Con BD20 4 A3
Airevalley Rd. Keigh BD21 36 B7
Aireview Cres. Bail BD17 38 A1
Aireview Prim Sch. Pudsey 57 F4
Aireview Terr. Keigh BD21 35 E6
Aireville Ave. Ship BD9 55 B5
Aireville Cl. Keigh BD20 18 A2
Aireville Cl. Ship BD18 55 B5
Aireville Cres. Ship BD9 55 B4
Aireville Cres. Sil BD20 5 F1
Aireville Dr. Sil BD20 5 F1
Aireville Grange. Ship BD18 55 B5
Aireville Mount. Keigh BD20 36 C8
Aireville Mouny. Sil BD20 5 F1
Aireville Rd. Ship BD9 55 C5
Aireville Rise. Ship BD9 55 B4
Aireville St. Keigh BD20 18 A2
Aireville Terr. Bur in W LS29 9 E1
Aireworth Cl. Keigh BD21 18 E1
Aireworth Gr. Keigh BD21 35 E8
Aireworth Rd. Keigh BD21 35 E8
Aireworth St. Keigh BD21 35 B6
Airey St. Keigh BD21 35 A7
Airlie Ave. Leeds LS8 60 F4
Airlie Pl. Leeds LS8 60 F4
Airville Dr. Ship BD18 55 B5
Airville Gr. Ship BD18 55 B5
Akam Rd. Brad BD1 74 D7
Aked St. Brad BD1 74 F7 10
Aked's Rd. Hali HX1 113 B6
Aketon Dr. Castle WF10 124 C6
Aketon Rd. Castle WF10 124 C6
Akroyd Ct. Hali HX3 113 C8 3
Akroyd La. Wad M HX7 89 B6
Akroyd Pl. Hali HX1 113 C8 6
Akroyd Terr. Hali HX2 112 F5 23
Alabama St. Hali HX1 112 F7 5
Alan Cres. Leeds LS15 81 A7
Alandale Cres. Gar LS25 82 D6
Alandale Dr. Gar LS25 82 D6
Alandale Gr. Gar LS25 82 D6
Alandale Rd. Gar LS25 82 D6
Alandale Rd. Hud HD2 136 E5
Alaska Pl. Leeds LS7 60 E6
Alban St. Brad BD4 75 B4
Albans Cl. Bard LS17 28 E5
Albany Cres. S Elm WF9 182 F2
Albany Ct. Keigh BD20 35 A8
Albany Ct. Pont WF8 146 D7
Albany Dr. Hud HD5 155 A6
Albany Pl. S Elm WF9 182 F2 5
Albany Rd. Hud HD5 155 A7
Albany Rd. Roth LS26 100 D6
Albany St. Brad BD6 74 C1
Albany St. Brad BD5 74 E4
Albany St. Hali HX3 113 D5
Albany St. Hud HD1 153 F4
Albany St. Leeds LS12 78 A7
Albany St. S Elm WF9 182 F2
Albany Terr. Hali HX3 113 D5
Albany Terr. Leeds LS12 78 A7
Albany Wlk. Ilkley LS29 8 B3
Albert Ave. Brad BD10 56 C8
Albert Ave. Hali HX2 112 E8
Albert Ave. Ship BD18 37 F1
Albert Bldgs. Brad BD10 56 B6
Albert Cl. Batley WF17 118 C2
Albert Cres. Birk BD11 96 B4
Albert Cres. Queen BD13 72 E1
Albert Ct. Hali HX2 112 E8
Albert Dr. Hali HX2 112 E8
Albert Dr. Morley LS27 98 D5
Albert Edward St. Queen BD13 72 E1 4
Albert Gdns. Hali HX2 112 E8
Albert Gr. Leeds LS6 59 D6
Albert La. Tod OL14 108 B6
Albert Pl. Brad BD3 75 E8
Albert Pl. Hors LS18 41 C1
Albert Pl. M'town LS26 102 B3
Albert Prom. Hali HX3 113 A3
Albert Rd. Clay W HD8 175 E2
Albert Rd. Glu BD20 16 D6
Albert Rd. Hali HX6 112 C5
Albert Rd. Hali HX2 112 E8
Albert Rd. Morley LS27 98 C5
Albert Rd. Queen BD13 72 E2
Albert Rd. Roth LS26 101 C6
Albert Rd. Ship BD18 54 F8
Albert Sq. Sil BD20 5 E1
Albert Sq. Yeadon LS19 40 C7
Albert St. Bail BD17 38 C1 2
Albert St. Brad BD10 56 B6
Albert St. Brad BD6 94 B8
Albert St. Brad BD12 94 C2
Albert St. Brig HD6 115 C2
Albert St. Castle WF10 124 D8
Albert St. Clec BD19 116 D8
Albert St. Cud S72 180 C1
Albert St. Elland HX5 134 F6
Albert St. Feath WF7 145 D5
Albert St. Hali HX1 113 B7
Albert St. Haw BD22 51 F8 1
Albert St. Heb Br HX7 89 A3
Albert St. Heb Br HX7 89 E1 7
Albert St. Hud HD1 153 F3
Albert St. Keigh BD21 35 B7
Albert St. Liver WF15 117 C3
Albert St. Nor WF6 123 C3
Albert St. Pudsey LS28 76 D6
Albert St. Queen BD13 72 F1
Albert St. S in Cra BD20 16 E5
Albert St. Thorn BD13 72 D6
Albert St. Tod OL14 108 B6
Albert St. Wils BD15 53 C4
Albert Terr. Brad BD12 94 D2 4
Albert Terr. Brad BD12 94 F5
Albert Terr. Ship BD18 37 F1
Albert Terr. Yeadon LS19 40 C7
Albert View. Hali HX2 112 E8
Albert Way. Birk BD11 96 B4
Albert Wlk. Ship BD18 54 E8 4
Albert Yd. Hud HD1 154 A5
Alberta Ave. Leeds LS7 60 E6
Albion Ave. Leeds LS12 78 D7
Albion Cl. B Spa LS23 30 D5
Albion Croft. Ossett WF5 140 E6
Albion Ct. Batley WF16 117 D4
Albion Ct. Brad BD1 74 E7 11
Albion Ct. Hali HX1 113 C7 3
Albion Ct. Wake WF1 142 C6
Albion Fold. Wils BD15 53 C5
Albion Pk. Leeds 78 E8
Albion Pl. Brig HD6 115 A3 13
Albion Pl. Guise LS20 22 E1
Albion Pl. Leeds LS1 79 C8
Albion Pl. S Elm WF9 183 A3
Albion Pl. Thorn BD13 72 C6
Albion Rd. Brad BD10 56 C8
Albion Rd. Dew WF12 139 E1
Albion Rd. Pudsey LS28 57 E2
Albion Sq. Wake WF2 141 E7
Albion St. B Spa LS23 30 D5
Albion St. Bacup OL13 106 A3
Albion St. Batley WF16 117 D4
Albion St. Batley WF17 118 D4
Albion St. Brad BD1 74 E7
Albion St. Brad BD6 93 F7 3
Albion St. Brig HD6 115 A3
Albion St. Castle WF10 124 C8
Albion St. Clec BD19 116 E7
Albion St. Denh BD13 71 D8
Albion St. Dew WF13 118 C1
Albion St. Dew WF13 138 F5
Albion St. Elland HX5 135 A6
Albion St. Hali HX1 113 C7
Albion St. Haw BD22 51 E8
Albion St. Hem WF9 163 A3
Albion St. Hud HD1 154 A5
Albion St. Leeds LS1, LS2 79 C8
Albion St. Liver WF15 117 B4 1
Albion St. Morley LS27 98 A4
Albion St. Otley LS21 23 B7
Albion St. Pudsey LS28 76 F7 6
Albion St. Queen BD13 72 D1
Albion St. Roth WF3 100 D3
Albion St. Wake WF1 142 C7
Albion Terr. B Spa LS23 30 D5
Albion Terr. Heb Br HX7 88 F3
Albion Yd. Brad BD1 74 E7 12
Alcester Garth. Brad BD3 75 B8
Alcester Pl. Leeds LS8 60 F4 10
Alcester Rd. Leeds LS8 60 F4 8
Alcester St. Leeds LS8 60 F4 7
Alcester Terr. Leeds LS8 60 F4 9
Aldams Rd. Dew WF12 139 C7
Alden Ave. Morley LS27 98 A2
Alden Cl. Morley LS27 98 A2
Alden Cres. Pont WF8 146 B7
Alden Ct. Morley LS27 98 A2 5
Alden Fold. Morley LS27 98 A2 4
Alder Ave. Holmfi HD7 189 C8
Alder Ave. Keigh BD21 35 E5
Alder Ave. Wake WF2 142 A8
Alder Carr. Bail BD17 38 B3
Alder Cl. Mapp S75 178 A1
Alder Dr. Pudsey LS28 76 A8
Alder Garth. Pudsey LS28 76 B8
Alder Gr. Hali HX2 91 E6
Alder Gr. Nor WF6 144 B7
Alder Hill Ave. Leeds LS7 60 A7
Alder Hill Gr. Leeds LS7 60 A7
Alder St. Hud HD1, HD2 136 B1
Aldermanbury. Brad BD1 74 E7
Alderney Rd. Batley WF12 118 F2
Alderscholes Cl. Thorn BD13 72 D6 9
Alderscholes La. Thorn BD13 72 C5
Alderson St. Brad BD6 93 E7 2
Alderstone Rise. Hud HD3 135 A2
Aldersyde. Batley WF17 96 E1
Alderton Bank. Leeds LS17 42 F2
Alderton Cres. Leeds LS17 43 A2
Alderton Hts. Leeds LS17 42 F2
Alderton Mount. Leeds LS17 42 F2
Alderton Pl. Leeds LS17 42 F2
Alderton Rise. Leeds LS17 43 A2
Aldonley. Hud HD5 155 A4
Alegar St. Brig HD6 115 C2
Alexander Ave. Leeds LS15 80 F7
Alexander Cres. Pont WF7 145 E7
Alexander Rd. Feath WF7 145 D6
Alexander Sq. Brad BD14 73 B4 10
Alexander St. Brad BD6 94 B8 5
Alexander St. Leeds LS1 79 B8
Alexander Terr. Hali HX1 112 F7
Alexandra Ave. Batley WF17 96 F1 3
Alexandra Cres. Dew WF13 118 A2
Alexandra Cres. Elland HX5 135 B7
Alexandra Cres. Ilkley LS29 8 A4
Alexandra Dr. Nor WF6 144 B7
Alexandra Gr. Leeds LS6 59 E2 5
Alexandra Gr. Pudsey LS28 76 D6
Alexandra Rd. Batley WF17 118 D4
Alexandra Rd. Brad BD2 56 C5
Alexandra Rd. Heb Br HX7 89 A3 8
Alexandra Rd. Hors LS18 58 C8
Alexandra Rd. Hud HD3 153 C7
Alexandra Rd. Leeds LS6 59 E2
Alexandra Rd. Pudsey LS28 76 C6
Alexandra Rd. Ship BD18 55 A7
Alexandra Rd W. Hud HD3 153 C5
Alexandra Sq. Ship BD18 54 F8 14
Alexandra St. Brad BD7 74 C5
Alexandra St. Hali HX1 113 C7
Alexandra St. Liver WF15 117 A4 4
Alexandra St. Queen BD13 72 E1
Alexandra Terr. Brad BD2 56 C2
Alexandra Terr. Yeadon LS19 40 C7 6
Alford Terr. Brad BD7 74 A7
Alfred E Briggs Almshouses. Brad BD12 94 B6 3
Alfred St. Batley WF16 117 D3 4
Alfred St. Batley WF17 118 B4
Alfred St. Brig HD6 115 B3 5
Alfred St. Dew WF13 118 E1 1
Alfred St E. Hali HX1 113 D7
Alfred St. Elland HX4 134 D7
Alfred St. Hali HX1 112 F7 11
Alfred St. Hud HD1 154 A5 4
Alfred St. Liver WF15 117 B4 3
Alfred St. Morley LS27 98 C8 6
Alfred St. Roy S71 179 E4
Alfreds Way. Batley WF17 118 C5
Alice St. Brad BD8 74 D8
Alice St. Clec BD19 116 D8 2
Alice St. Haw BD22 51 C6 5
Alice St. Keigh BD21 35 C7
Alkincote St. Keigh BD21 35 C6
All Alone. Brad BD10 56 A7
All Alone Rd. Brad BD10 56 A6
All Saint's Circ. Roth LS26 101 D6
All Saint's Dr. Roth LS26 101 C6
All Saint's Rd. Roth LS26 101 D6
All Saint's View. Roth LS26 101 C7
All Saints CE Jun Sch. Otley 23 A8
All Saints CE Prim Sch. Feath 124 D1
All Sts' CE Jun & Inf Sch. Hali 113 C2
All Saints CE Prim Sch. Leeds 79 F8
All Saints Comp Sch. Hud 136 C5
All Saints' Fst Sch. Ilkley 8 B5
All Saints Rd. Brad BD7 74 C5
All Saints' View. Pont WF8 146 E8 2
All Souls' Rd. Hali HX3 92 C1
All Souls' St. Hali HX3 92 C1 3
All Souls' Terr. Hali HX3 92 C1 2
Allan Haigh Cl. Wake WF2 141 D8
Allan St. Brad BD3 75 B6
Allan Terr. Sow Br HX6 112 C3
Allandale Ave. Brad BD6 94 A7
Allandale Rd. Brad BD6 94 A7
Allanfield Terr. Weth LS22 13 E8
Allen Croft. Birk BD11 96 A5
Allenby Cres. Leeds LS11 99 A8
Allenby Dr. Leeds LS11 99 A8
Allenby Gdns. Leeds LS11 99 A8
Allenby Gr. Leeds LS11 99 A8
Allenby Pl. Leeds LS11 99 A8
Allenby Rd. Leeds LS11 99 A8
Allenby View. Leeds LS11 79 B1
Allendale Rd. Kex S75 177 D1
Allerby Gn. Brad BD6 93 F6
Allergill Pk. Holmfi HD7 188 D5
Allerton Ave. Leeds LS17 43 D2
Allerton Bywater Inf Sch. Kippax 103 B4
Allerton Bywater Jun Sch. Kippax 103 B5
Allerton Cl. Brad BD15 54 B1
Allerton Dr. E Kes LS17 28 C6
Allerton Fst & Mid Sch. Brad 54 B1
Allerton Gr. Leeds LS17 43 D2
Allerton Grange Ave. Leeds LS17 43 E1
Allerton Grange Cl. Leeds LS17 60 C8
Allerton Grange Cres. Leeds LS17 60 D8
Allerton Grange Croft. Leeds LS8 60 E8
Allerton Grange Dr. Brad BD15 54 B1
Allerton Grange Dr. Leeds LS17 60 D8
Allerton Grange Gdns. Leeds LS17 60 D8
Allerton Grange High Sch. Leeds 43 E1
Allerton Grange Rise. Leeds LS17 60 D8
Allerton Grange Vale. Leeds LS17 60 D8
Allerton Grange Way. Leeds LS17, LS8 60 D8
Allerton Grnge Wlk. Leeds LS17 60 D8
Allerton High Sch. Leeds 43 B3
Allerton Hill. Leeds LS7 60 C7
Allerton La. Brad BD13, BD15 73 A7
Allerton La. Thorn BD13, BD15 73 A7
Allerton Pk. Leeds LS7 60 E7
Allerton Pl. Hali HX1 113 A7
Allerton Pl. Leeds LS17 43 D2
Allerton Rd. Brad BD15 54 B1
Allerton Rd. Brad BD15, BD8 73 F8
Allerton St. Leeds LS4 59 D2
Allescholes Rd. Tod OL14 129 B7
Alliance St. Leeds LS12 78 A7
Allinson St. Leeds LS12 78 E6 7
Allison Dr. Hud HD2 136 B2
Allison La. Ship BD2 55 D4
Allison St. Feath WF7 145 C5
Allison Terr. Wake WF2 120 B2
Alloe Field View. Hali HX2 91 E6
Allott Cl. S Elm WF9 182 F3
Allums La. Arth LS21 25 F5
Alma Cl. Pudsey LS28 57 C3
Alma Cotts. Leeds LS6 59 D5 12
Alma Dr. Hud HD5 154 D6
Alma Gr. Leeds LS9 60 F2
Alma Gr. Ship BD18 55 D8
Alma La. Batley WF16 117 D6
Alma La. Rip HX6 132 B7
Alma Pl. Keigh BD21 35 C5
Alma Pl. Leeds BD3 60 E2
Alma Rd. Leeds LS6 59 E5
Alma Rd. Tod OL14 108 A1
Alma St. Bacup OL13 106 A2
Alma St. Brad BD4 75 D3
Alma St. Brad BD4 75 D5
Alma St. Elland HX5 135 A6
Alma St. Haw BD22 51 C8
Alma St. Keigh BD21 35 C5
Alma St. Leeds LS9 60 F1
Alma St. Queen BD13 72 D1
Alma St. Roth LS26 101 D7
Alma St. Ship BD18 55 D8
Alma St. Tod OL14 108 A1
Alma St. Yeadon LS19 40 C7
Alma Terr. Keigh BD20 19 E1
Alma Terr. Keigh BD21 35 C5
Alma Terr. Roth LS26 100 D6
Almhouses. Keigh BD21 35 A3
Almond Cl. S Elm WF9 183 A5
Almond St. Brad BD3 75 C6
Almond Way. Batley WF17 96 F1
Almondbury Bank. Hud HD5 154 E5
Almondbury Cl. Hud HD5 155 A3
Almondbury Comm. Hud HD4 154 F1
Almondbury Cty Jun Sch. Hud 155 A4
Almondbury Cty Sec Sch. Hud 154 F4
Almondbury Gram Sch. Hud 155 A2
Almondroyd. Liver WF16 117 C5
Almscliffe Ave. Dew WF12 139 E8
Almshouse Hill. Bramham LS23 30 D2
Almshouse La. Crig WF2 160 B4
Almshouse La. Wake WF1 142 C6
Alpha St. Keigh BD21 35 D6
Alpine Cl. Batley WF17 118 B4
Alpine Rise. Thorn BD13 72 D6
Alpine Terr. Roth LS26 100 D6
Alston Cl. Brad BD9 54 D1
Alston La. Leeds LS14 62 A3
Alston Rd. Keigh BD21 18 D1
Altar Dr. Brad BD9 55 A3
Altar Dr. Keigh BD20 19 A1
Altar La. Harden BD16 36 C4
Altar View. Bing BD16 36 E5
Althorpe Gr. Brad BD10 56 A6
Altinkool St. Wake WF1 142 F2
Altofts Hall Rd. Nor WF6 122 F4
Altofts La. Castle WF10 123 D5
Altofts Lodge Dr. Nor WF6 122 E3
Altofts Mid Sch. Nor 122 F3
Altofts Rd. Nor WF6 123 A2
Alton Ave. Hud HD5 154 F7
Alton Gr. Brad BD9 54 F3
Alton Gr. Ship BD18 55 B5
Alton Way. Mapp S75 178 A1
Alum Ct. Brad BD9 55 A3
Alum Dr. Brad BD9 55 A3
Alvanley Ct. Brad BD8 73 D8
Alverthorpe Rd. Wake WF2 141 F6
Alverthorpe St Paul's CE (A) Fst Sch. Wake 141 E8
Alvo Terr. Ship BD18 55 B6
Alwen Ave. Hud HD2 135 F2
Alwoodley Chase. Leeds LS17 43 E5
Alwoodley Court Gdns. Leeds LS17 43 A6
Alwoodley Ct. Leeds LS17 42 F5
Alwoodley Gdns. Leeds LS17 43 A5
Alwoodley Golf Course. Leeds 43 C6
Alwoodley La. Leeds LS17 43 C6
Alwoodley Prim Sch. Leeds 43 A3
Amber St. Batley WF17 118 A6

Amberley Ct. Brad BD3 ... 75 C6
Amberley Gdns. Leeds LS12 ... 78 C6
Amberley Rd. Leeds LS12 ... 78 C6
Amberley Rise. Ad Le S DN6 .. 184 F2
Amberley St. Brad BD3 ... 75 C7
Amberley St. Leeds LS12 ... 78 D6
Amberton App. Leeds LS8 ... 61 C4
Amberton Cl. Leeds LS8 ... 61 C5
Amberton Cres. Leeds LS8 ... 61 C4
Amberton Garth. Leeds LS8 ... 61 C4
Amberton Gdns. Leeds LS8 ... 61 C4
Amberton Gr. Leeds LS8 ... 61 C4
Amberton La. Leeds LS8 ... 61 C4
Amberton Mount. Leeds LS8 ... 61 C4
Amberton Pl. Leeds LS8 ... 61 B4
Amberton Rd. Leeds LS8, LS9 .. 61 C4
Amberton St. Leeds LS8 ... 61 C4
Amberton Terr. Leeds LS8 ... 61 C5
Amble Tonia. Denh BD13 ... 52 E1
Ambler St. Brad BD8 ... 55 C1
Ambler St. Castle WF10 ... 124 E7
Ambler St. Keigh BD21 ... 35 D7
Ambler Way. Queen BD13 ... 92 C7
Amblers Croft. Brad BD10 ... 39 B2
Amblers Ct. Pudsey LS28 ... 76 E6
Amblers Mews. Bail BD17 ... 38 C4 4
Amblers Mews. Keigh BD20 ... 36 D8
Amblers Terr. Hali HX3 ... 92 C1 10
Ambleside Ave. Brad BD9 ... 54 F8 1
Ambleside Dr. Walton WF2 ... 161 A6
Ambleside Gdns. Pudsey LS28 76 C7
Ambleside Gr. Roth LS26 ... 101 C6
Ambleside Rd. Castle WF10 .. 104 E1
Ambleside Wlk. Weth LS22 ... 13 B6
Ambleton Way. Queen BD13 ... 92 C8
Amelia St. Ship BD18 ... 54 F8 1
America La. Brig HD6 ... 115 C2
America La. S in Cra BD20 ... 16 E1
America Moor La. Morley LS27 98 A2
Amisfield Rd. Brig HX3 ... 114 D8
Amos St. Hali HX1 ... 112 F7
Amport Cl. Brig HD6 ... 115 B1
Amundsen Ave. Brad BD2 ... 56 A5
Amy St. Bing BD16 ... 37 A3 9
Amy St. Hali HX3 ... 92 A2 3
Amyroyce Dr. Ship BD18 ... 55 E7
Anaheim Dr. Loft G WF1 ... 121 D5
Ancaster Cres. Leeds LS16 ... 59 B7
Ancaster Rd. Leeds LS16 ... 59 B7
Ancaster View. Leeds LS16 ... 59 B7
Anchor Pl. Brig HD6 ... 136 D8
Anchor St. Hud HD1 ... 154 B7
Anchor St. Tod OL14 ... 108 C5 4
Anderson Ave. Leeds LS8 ... 60 E2
Anderson House. Bail BD17 ... 38 B1
Anderson Mount. Leeds LS8 ... 60 E2
Anderson St. Brad BD8 ... 55 C1
Anderson St. Pont WF8 ... 125 C1
Anderson St. Wake WF2 ... 142 A6
Anderton St. Glu BD20 ... 16 D7
Anderton St. Wake WF1 ... 142 E3
Andover Gn. Brad BD4 ... 75 E4
Andrew Cl. Hali HX3 ... 114 A4
Andrew Cres. Hud HD4 ... 153 A1
Andrew Cres. Loft G WF1 ... 121 B5
Andrew St. Feath WF7 ... 145 C4
Andrew St. Pudsey LS28 ... 57 D2 10
Andrew St. Pudsey LS28 ... 57 D3 4
Andrew St. Wake WF1 ... 142 B8
Andrews Gr. Ack M T WF7 ... 163 F6
Anerley St. Brad BD4 ... 75 B2
Angel Rd. Hali HX1 ... 113 A8
Angel Row. Roth LS26 ... 100 B5
Angel St. Bail BD17 ... 38 D4
Angel Way. Brad BD7 ... 74 D6
Angerton Way. Brad BD6 ... 94 A6
Anglers Country Park. Ryhill .. 161 F5
Angus Ave. Brad BD12 ... 94 C1
Anlaby St. Brad BD4 ... 75 D5
Ann Pl. Brad BD5 ... 74 E5
Ann St. Denh BD13 ... 52 D1
Ann St. Haw BD22 ... 51 D7
Ann St. Keigh BD21 ... 35 B6
Annat Royd La. Ingb S30 ... 191 D1
Anne Cres. S Hie S72 ... 180 E5
Anne Gate. Brad BD1 ... 74 F7
Anne St. Batley WF17 ... 118 A7
Anne St. Brad BD7 ... 73 F3
Anne's Ct. Hali HX3 ... 114 A4
Annie St. Hali HX6 ... 112 B4 1
Annie St. Haw BD22 ... 51 F8
Annie St. Hem WF9 ... 163 A4
Annie St. Keigh BD21 ... 18 C1
Annie St. Loft G WF1 ... 121 B4
Annie St. Morley LS27 ... 98 B4
Annie St. Ship BD18 ... 55 C6
Annison St. Brad BD3 ... 75 A7
Annotes Croft. Hud HD5 ... 154 F7
Anroyd St. Dew WF13 ... 118 A1
Anson Gr. Brad BD7 ... 73 F2
Anston Dr. S Elm WF9 ... 183 A5
Anthony La. Harden BD16 ... 36 B2
Antony Cl. Hud HD3 ... 134 D1
Anvil Ct. Brad BD8 ... 55 B1
Anvil St. Brad BD8 ... 55 B1
Anvil St. Brig HD6 ... 115 A3
Apex Bsns Ctr. Leeds ... 79 C5
Apex View. Leeds LS11 ... 79 B5
Apex Way. Leeds LS11 ... 79 C5
Apperley Gdns. Brad BD10 ... 56 E8
Apperley La. Yeadon BD10 ... 39 F2
Apperley La. Yeadon LS19 ... 40 A4
Apperley Rd. Brad BD10 ... 56 D8
Apple Cl. Batley WF17 ... 97 A2
Apple House Terr. Hali HX2 ... 90 E1
Apple St. Keigh BD21 ... 35 A3
Apple St. Oxen BD22 ... 51 C2
Apple Tree Cl. E Ard WF3 ... 120 C8
Apple Tree Cl. Pont WF8 ... 146 B6
Apple Tree Ct. E Ard WF3 ... 120 C7
Apple Tree Gdns. Ilkley LS29 ... 7 F4
Apple Tree Rd. Feath WF7 ... 145 E4
Appleby La. Gar LS25 ... 83 B7
Appleby Pl. Ad Le S DN6 ... 184 F2
Appleby Pl. Leeds LS15 ... 80 E8
Appleby Way. Morley LS27 ... 98 B4
Appleby Way. Weth LS22 ... 13 E7
Appleby Wlk. Leeds LS15 ... 80 E8
Applegarth. Roth LS26 ... 101 C7
Applegarth. Wake WF2 ... 160 E7
Applehaigh Gr. Roy S71 ... 179 A4
Applehaigh La. Notton WF4 ... 179 A6
Applehaigh View. Roy S71 ... 179 A4
Appleshaw Cres. Wake WF2 . 120 F3
Appleton Cl. Bing BD16 ... 37 B5
Appleton Cl. Brad BD12 ... 94 F5
Appleton Cl. Leeds LS9 ... 79 F8 5
Appleton Ct. Leeds BD13, LS9 . 79 F8 4
Appleton Gr. Leeds LS9 ... 80 B7
Appleton Sq. Leeds LS9 ... 79 F8 6
Appleton Way. Leeds LS9 ... 79 F8
Appletree Cl. B Spa LS23 ... 30 D7
Appleyard Rd. Heb Br HX7 ... 89 F1
Approach The. B in Elm LS15 ... 62 F7
April Ct. Liver WF15 ... 117 A2
Aprilia Ct. Brad BD14 ... 73 D5
Apsley Cres. Brad BD8 ... 55 C1
Apsley St. Haw BD22 ... 34 D3
Apsley St. Haw BD22 ... 51 D7 7
Apsley St. Keigh BD21 ... 35 B5 8
Apsley Terr. Haw BD22 ... 34 D3
Aquamarine Dr. Hud HD2 ... 136 C2
Aquila Way. Clec WF15 ... 116 D5
Arborary La. Mel HD4 ... 170 F6
Arbour The. Ilkley LS29 ... 8 A6
Arcade The. Dew WF12 ... 139 D8 5
Arcade The. Knot WF11 ... 126 E4
Arcadia St. Keigh BD21 ... 35 B5 12
Archbell Ave. Brig HD6 ... 136 B8
Archbishop Cranmer CE Mid Sch.
Leeds ... 43 B3
Archer Rd. Brig HD6 ... 115 D1
Archer St. Castle WF10 ... 124 C6
Archery Pl. Leeds LS2 ... 60 B2
Archery Rd. Leeds LS2 ... 60 B2
Archery St. Leeds LS2 ... 60 B2
Archery Terr. Leeds LS2 ... 60 B2
Arches St. Hali HX1 ... 113 B6
Arches The. Hali HX3 ... 92 D1
Archibald St. Brad BD7 ... 74 C7
Arctic Par. Brad BD7 ... 74 A4
Arctic St. Haw BD22 ... 51 E8 6
Arctic St. Keigh BD20 ... 18 B1
Arden Ct. Hor WF4 ... 159 A8
Arden Ct. Kirkhe HD5 ... 155 C7
Arden Rd. Brad BD8 ... 73 C7
Arden Rd. Hali HX1 ... 113 B6
Ardennes Cl. Brad BD2 ... 55 F4
Ardsley Cl. Brad BD4 ... 75 F2
Argent Way. Brad BD4 ... 75 F2
Argie Ave. Leeds LS4 ... 59 B3
Argie Gdns. Leeds LS4 ... 59 C2 3
Argie Rd. Leeds LS4 ... 59 C2
Argie Terr. Leeds LS4 ... 59 C2
Argyl Mews. E Kes LS17 ... 28 C5
Argyle Rd. Knot WF11 ... 126 C5
Argyle Rd. Leeds LS9 ... 79 D8
Argyle St. Brad BD4 ... 75 B4
Argyle St. Keigh BD21 ... 35 B7
Argyle St. Mars HD7 ... 168 F4
Argyle St. Ship BD18 ... 55 B6
Argyle St. Wake WF1 ... 142 E4
Argyll Ave. Pont WF8 ... 146 B8 3
Argyll Cl. Bail BD17 ... 38 E2
Argyll Cl. Hors LS18 ... 41 B4
Ark St. Leeds LS9 ... 79 E6
Arkendale Mews. Brad BD7 ... 73 E3 5
Arkenley La. Hud HD4 ... 155 A2
Arkenmore. Hud HD5 ... 154 F7
Arksey Pl. Leeds LS12 ... 78 C8 4
Arksey Terr. Leeds LS12 ... 78 C8 10
Arkwright House. Liver WF15 117 A5 9
Arkwright St. Brad BD14 ... 73 B4
Arkwright St. Brad BD4 ... 75 E6
Arkwright St. Leeds LS12 ... 78 E8
Arlesford Rd. Brad BD4 ... 75 E2
Arley Cl. Holmfi HD7 ... 188 F8
Arley Gr. Leeds LS12 ... 78 C8 1
Arley Pl. Leeds LS12 ... 78 C8
Arley St. Leeds LS12 ... 59 C1 5
Arley Terr. Leeds LS12 ... 78 C8
Arlington Bsns Ctr. Morley ... 98 E8
Arlington Cres. Hali HX2 ... 112 D4
Arlington Gr. Leeds LS8 ... 61 B5
Arlington Rd. Leeds LS8 ... 61 B5
Arlington St. Brad BD3 ... 75 B6
Arlington St. Wake WF1 ... 142 B8
Armadale Ave. Brad BD4 ... 95 B8
Armgill La. Ship BD2 ... 55 D4
Armidale Way. Brad BD2 ... 55 F3
Armitage Ave. Brig HD6 ... 136 B8
Armitage Bldgs. E Ard WF12 . 119 B6
Armitage Rd. Brad BD12 ... 94 F4
Armitage Rd. Hali HX1 ... 112 F5 21
Armitage Rd. Hud HD2 ... 135 F1
Armitage Rd. Hud HD3 ... 153 B5
Armitage Rd. Hud HD4 ... 171 E8
Armitage Rd. Wake WF2 ... 141 D8
Armitage Sq. Pudsey LS28 ... 76 D6 2
Armitage St. Castle WF10 ... 124 C8
Armitage St. Dew WF13 ... 138 D5
Armitage St. Hud HD4 ... 154 A4
Armitage St. Roth LS26 ... 100 E4
Armley Grange Ave. Leeds LS12 78 A8
Armley Grange Cres.
Leeds LS12 ... 58 F1
Armley Grange Dr. Leeds LS12 77 F8
Armley Grange Mount.
Leeds LS12 ... 77 F8
Armley Grange Oval.
Leeds LS12 ... 58 F1
Armley Grange Rise.
Leeds LS12 ... 77 F8
Armley Grange View.
Leeds LS12 ... 78 A8
Armley Grnge Wlk. Leeds LS12 78 A8
Armley Grove Pl. Leeds LS12 ... 78 D7
Armley Lodge Rd. Leeds LS12 . 78 C8 3
Armley Lodge Sch. Leeds ... 78 C8
Armley Mills Ind Mus. Leeds ... 59 D1
Armley Park Rd. Leeds LS12 ... 59 C1
Armley Prim Sch. Leeds ... 78 C8
Armley Rd. Leeds LS12 ... 78 F7
Armley Ridge Cl. Leeds LS12 ... 78 A8
Armley Ridge Rd. Leeds LS12 .. 59 A1
Armley Ridge Rd. Leeds LS12 .. 78 B8
Armoury Ave. Mir WF14 ... 138 A5
Armstrong Cl. Nor WF6 ... 123 A4
Armstrong St. Brad BD4 ... 75 D6
Armstrong St. Pudsey LS28 ... 57 D2 9
Armstrong Terr. Pont WF8 ... 146 B7 2
Armytage Cres. Hud HD1 ... 153 F3
Armytage Rd. Brig HD6 ... 115 D1
Armytage Way. Brig HD6 ... 115 D1
Armytage Wlk. S Kirk WF9 ... 182 C3
Arncliffe Ave. Keigh BD22 ... 35 A5 1
Arncliffe Cres. Brig HD6 ... 135 E8
Arncliffe Cres. Morley LS27 ... 98 C2
Arncliffe Ct. Hud HD1 ... 153 E7
Arncliffe Dr. Knot WF11 ... 126 C4
Arncliffe Garth. Pudsey LS28 ... 57 D2 11
Arncliffe Gdns. Batley WF17 .. 118 B5
Arncliffe Gr. Keigh BD22 ... 35 A6 17
Arncliffe Grange. Leeds LS17 .. 43 D2
Arncliffe Rd. Batley WF17 ... 118 B5
Arncliffe Rd. Keigh BD22 ... 35 A6
Arncliffe Rd. Leeds LS16 ... 59 A8
Arncliffe Rd. Wake WF1 ... 142 F8
Arncliffe St. Pudsey LS28 ... 57 D2
Arncliffe Terr. Brad BD7 ... 74 B6
Arndale Ctr. Leeds LS6 ... 59 D5 5
Arndale Gr. Holmfi HD7 ... 189 B4
Arndale Sh Ctr The. Ship BD18 55 B7
Arnford Cl. Brad BD3 ... 74 F8
Arnold Ave. Hud HD2 ... 135 F1
Arnold Pl. Brad BD8 ... 74 C8
Arnold Royd. Brig HD6 ... 135 E7
Arnold St. Brad BD8 ... 55 C1
Arnold St. Hali HX6 ... 112 B4 4
Arnold St. Hali HX1 ... 113 A7
Arnold St. Hud HD2 ... 135 F1
Arnold St. Liver WF15 ... 117 A4
Arnside Ave. Keigh BD20 ... 18 E1
Arnside Cl. Castle WF10 ... 125 D8
Arnside Cres. Castle WF10 ... 125 D8
Arnside Rd. Brad BD5 ... 74 E2
Arran Cl. Hud HD7 ... 152 D5
Arran Ct. Gar LS25 ... 82 F5
Arran Dr. Gar LS25 ... 82 F5
Arran Dr. Hors LS18 ... 41 B4
Arrunden La. Holmfi HD7 ... 188 F2
Arthington Ave. Leeds LS10 ... 79 D2
Arthington Cl. E Ard WF3 ... 119 D7
Arthington Ct. Leeds LS10 ... 79 D2
Arthington Garth. Arth LS21 ... 24 F6
Arthington Gr. Leeds LS10 ... 79 D2
Arthington La. Arth LS21 ... 25 D6
Arthington La. Pool LS21 ... 24 E6
Arthington Lawns. Pool LS21 ... 24 E6
Arthington Pl. Leeds LS10 ... 79 D2
Arthington Rd. Eccup LS16 ... 25 C2
Arthington Sch. Arth ... 25 B6
Arthington St. Brad BD8 ... 74 C8
Arthington St. Leeds LS10 ... 79 D2
Arthington Terr. Leeds LS10 ... 79 D2
Arthington View. Leeds LS10 ... 79 D2
Arthur Ave. Brad BD8 ... 73 D7
Arthur Gr. Batley WF17 ... 117 F8
Arthur St. Bacup OL13 ... 106 B3
Arthur St. Bing BD16 ... 36 F3
Arthur St. Brad BD10 ... 56 B6
Arthur St. Brig HD6 ... 115 C2
Arthur St. Haw BD22 ... 34 C2
Arthur St. Hud HD7 ... 152 E4
Arthur St. Pudsey LS28 ... 57 D2
Arthur St. Pudsey LS28 ... 57 E2
Arthur St. Wake WF1 ... 142 E3
Arthursdale Cl. B in Elm LS15 .. 62 F7
Arthursdale Dr. B in Elm LS15 . 62 F7
Arthursdale Grange.
B in Elm LS15 ... 62 F7
Artillery St. Batley WF16 ... 117 D3
Artist St. Leeds LS12 ... 78 E7
Arum St. Brad BD5 ... 74 C3
Arundel Cl. Batley WF17 ... 97 B2
Arundel Cl. Wake WF1 ... 142 C7
Arundel St. Gar LS25 ... 83 B8
Arundel St. Hali HX1 ... 112 F7 10
Arundel St. Wake WF1 ... 142 C7
Arundel Wlk. Batley WF17 ... 97 B1
Ascot Ave. Brad BD7 ... 73 E2
Ascot Dr. Brad BD7 ... 73 E2
Ascot Gdns. Brad BD7 ... 73 E2
Ascot Gr. Brig HD6 ... 135 E8
Ascot Par. Brad BD7 ... 73 E2
Ascot Rd. Kippax LS25 ... 82 F2
Ascot Terr. Leeds LS9 ... 79 F7
Asdale Rd. Crig WF2 ... 160 B7
Asdale Rd. Wake WF2 ... 160 B7
Ash Ave. Leeds LS6 ... 59 D5
Ash Brow. Floc WF4 ... 157 C3
Ash Brow Rd. Hud HD2 ... 136 B3
Ash Cl. Brig HX3 ... 114 D8
Ash Cl. Ilkley LS29 ... 7 E4
Ash Cl. Ossett WF5 ... 140 D5
Ash Cres. Leeds LS6 ... 59 D5
Ash Cres. Loft G WF3 ... 121 F5
Ash Croft. Brad BD6 ... 94 A8
Ash Ct. Brig BD19 ... 115 F8
Ash Gdns. Leeds LS6 ... 59 D5
Ash Ghyll Gdns. Bing BD16 ... 36 F4
Ash Gn. Pont WF8 ... 125 F1
Ash Gr. Bing BD16 ... 37 A1
Ash Gr. Birk BD11 ... 96 A6
Ash Gr. Brig HD6 ... 115 C2
Ash Gr. Clec BD19 ... 96 A1
Ash Gr. Clec BD19 ... 116 B6
Ash Gr. Dar WF8 ... 147 C5
Ash Gr. Hors LS18 ... 41 C2
Ash Gr. Ilkley LS29 ... 8 C5
Ash Gr. Keigh BD21 ... 35 B4
Ash Gr. Leeds LS6 ... 59 F3
Ash Gr. Loft G WF3 ... 121 F2
Ash Gr. Otley LS21 ... 22 F7
Ash Gr. Pudsey LS28 ... 76 E6
Ash Gr. S Elm WF9 ... 183 A4
Ash Gr. S in Cra BD20 ... 16 D5
Ash Gr. Stee BD20 ... 17 D5
Ash Grove Rd. Holmfi HD7 ... 188 E5
Ash Grove Terr. Brig HD6 ... 115 A1 6
Ash Hall La. Rip HX6 ... 132 A7
Ash Hill Dr. Thorner LS17 ... 44 F4
Ash Hill Garth. Thorner LS17 ... 44 F4
Ash Hill Gdns. Thorner LS17 ... 44 F4
Ash Hill La. Thorner LS17 ... 44 F4
Ash Hill Wlk. Brad BD4 ... 75 B4
Ash La. Emley HD8 ... 175 E7
Ash La. Gar LS25 ... 83 A8
Ash Lea. Fair WF11 ... 105 B4
Ash Lea. Loft G WF3 ... 121 F3
Ash Meadow Cl. Hud HD2 ... 136 C3
Ash Mount. Brad BD7 ... 74 B5
Ash Mount. Keigh BD21 ... 35 A5
Ash Rd. Leeds LS6 ... 59 C5
Ash Rd. Shaf S72 ... 180 D2
Ash St. Clec BD19 ... 116 C7
Ash St. Crof WF4 ... 162 A7
Ash St. Glu BD20 ... 16 D6
Ash St. Hud HD1 ... 154 A8
Ash St. Ilkley LS29 ... 8 C5
Ash St. Loft G WF3 ... 121 F2
Ash St. Oxen BD22 ... 51 C3
Ash Terr. Bing BD16 ... 36 F2
Ash Terr. Gar LS25 ... 83 A8
Ash Terr. Leeds LS6 ... 59 D5 2
Ash Terr. Rip HX6 ... 132 C3
Ash Tree App. Leeds LS14 ... 62 D4
Ash Tree Ave. Thorn BD13 ... 72 B6
Ash Tree Bank. Leeds LS14 ... 62 D5
Ash Tree Cl. Leeds LS14 ... 62 D5
Ash Tree Ct. Leeds LS14 ... 62 D5 5
Ash Tree Gdns. Hali HX2 ... 91 C5
Ash Tree Gdns. Leeds LS14 ... 62 D5
Ash Tree Gdns. Nor WF6 ... 122 F3
Ash Tree Gr. Leeds LS14 ... 62 D5
Ash Tree Grange. Leeds LS14 . 62 D5 4
Ash Tree Inf Sch. Hali ... 91 C5
Ash Tree Rd. Hali HX2 ... 91 C5
Ash Tree View. Leeds LS14 ... 62 D5 7
Ash Tree Wlk. Bur in W LS29 ... 9 E1
Ash Tree Wlk. Leeds LS14 ... 62 D5 8
Ash View. E Ard WF3 ... 120 C7
Ash View. Leeds LS6 ... 59 D5 3
Ash Wlk. Hud HD7 ... 152 E5
Ashbourne Ave. Brad BD2 ... 55 F3
Ashbourne Ave. Clec BD19 ... 116 D6
Ashbourne Bank. Brad BD2 ... 55 F3
Ashbourne Cl. Brad BD2 ... 55 F4
Ashbourne Cres. Brad BD2 ... 55 F3
Ashbourne Cres. Gar LS25 ... 82 F5
Ashbourne Cres. Queen BD13 . 72 D1
Ashbourne Croft. Clec BD19 .. 116 D6
Ashbourne Dr. Brad BD2 ... 55 F3
Ashbourne Dr. Clec BD19 ... 116 D6
Ashbourne Dr. Pont WF8 ... 146 D5
Ashbourne Garth. Brad BD2 ... 56 A4
Ashbourne Gdns. Brad BD2 ... 55 F3
Ashbourne Gdns. Clec BD19 ... 116 D6
Ashbourne Gr. Brad BD2 ... 55 F3
Ashbourne Gr. Hali HX1 ... 112 F7
Ashbourne Haven. Brad BD2 ... 55 F3
Ashbourne Mount. Brad BD2 ... 55 F3
Ashbourne Oval. Brad BD2 ... 55 F3
Ashbourne Rd. Brad BD2 ... 55 F3
Ashbourne Rd. Keigh BD21 ... 35 A5
Ashbourne Rise. Brad BD2 ... 55 F3
Ashbourne View. Clec BD19 .. 116 D6
Ashbourne Way. Brad BD2 ... 55 F3
Ashbourne Way. Clec BD19 ... 116 D6
Ashbrook Cl. Ossett WF5 ... 140 D7
Ashbrooke Pk. Leeds ... 79 C2
Ashbrow Cty Prim Sch. Hud ... 136 C3
Ashbrow Inf Sch. Hud ... 136 B3
Ashburn Cl. Weth LS22 ... 13 D7
Ashburn Croft. Weth LS22 ... 13 D7
Ashburn Dr. Weth LS22 ... 13 D7
Ashburn Gr. Bail BD17 ... 38 C4
Ashburn Gr. Weth LS22 ... 13 D7
Ashburn Pl. Ilkley LS29 ... 8 A3
Ashburn Way. Weth LS22 ... 13 D7
Ashburnham Gr. Brad BD9 ... 55 B3
Ashbury Chase. Loft G WF1 ... 121 A5
Ashby Ave. Leeds LS13 ... 58 D1
Ashby Cl. Liver WF15 ... 116 F1
Ashby Cres. Leeds LS13 ... 58 D1
Ashby Mount. Leeds LS13 ... 58 D2 4
Ashby Sq. Leeds LS13 ... 58 D2
Ashby St. Brad BD4 ... 75 A4
Ashby Terr. Leeds LS13 ... 58 D2
Ashby View. Leeds LS13 ... 58 D2
Ashcombe Dr. Knot WF11 ... 126 F3
Ashcroft Ave. Feath WF7 ... 145 C4
Ashcroft Rd. Feath WF7 ... 145 C4
Ashdale La. Weth LS22 ... 13 D8
Ashdale. Wake WF2 ... 142 E1
Ashday La. Brig HX3 ... 114 B3
Ashday La. Hali HX3 ... 114 B3
Ashdene App. Crof WF4 ... 143 F1
Ashdene Ave. Crof WF4 ... 143 F1
Ashdene Cl. Pudsey LS28 ... 76 E5
Ashdene Cres. Crof WF4 ... 143 F1
Ashdene Cres. Pudsey LS28 ... 76 E5
Ashdene Ct. Cull BD13 ... 52 D6
Ashdene Dr. Crof WF4 ... 143 F1
Ashdene Garth. Crof WF4 ... 143 F1
Ashdene. Gild LS12 ... 77 D3
Ashdene Gr. Pont WF8 ... 125 F4
Ashdene. Tod OL14 ... 108 B1
Ashdown Cl. Brad BD6 ... 74 B1 9
Ashdown Cl. Hali HX2 ... 112 D6
Ashdown Ct. Ship BD18 ... 55 A7
Ashdown Rd. Wake WF1 ... 142 E3
Ashdown St. Leeds LS13 ... 58 C2 13
Ashenhurst Ave. Hud HD4 ... 154 C3
Ashenhurst Cl. Hud HD4 ... 154 B3
Ashenhurst Cl. Tod OL14 ... 108 A7
Ashenhurst Rd. Hud HD4 ... 154 B3
Ashenhurst Rd. Tod OL14 ... 108 A7
Ashenhurst Rise. Hud HD4 ... 154 B3
Ashes La. Hud HD4 ... 154 C1
Ashes La. Tod OL14 ... 108 D7
Ashfield Ave. Morley LS27 ... 97 F3
Ashfield Ave. Ship BD18 ... 55 B5
Ashfield Ave. Skel HD8 ... 175 A1
Ashfield. Brad BD4 ... 75 D1
Ashfield Cl. Hali HX3 ... 91 F2
Ashfield Cl. Leeds LS15 ... 62 D4
Ashfield Cl. Leeds LS12 ... 77 F4
Ashfield Cres. Bing BD16 ... 37 A2
Ashfield Cres. Pudsey LS28 ... 57 E1
Ashfield Ct. Bing BD16 ... 37 A2 5
Ashfield. Dew WF12 ... 139 D4
Ashfield Dr. Bail BD17 ... 38 D3
Ashfield Dr. Hali HX3 ... 92 A2
Ashfield Dr. Ship BD18, BD9 ... 55 B5
Ashfield Gr. Pudsey LS28 ... 57 E1 6
Ashfield Gr. Ship BD9 ... 55 A4
Ashfield. Leeds LS12 ... 78 A4
Ashfield Pk. Leeds LS6 ... 59 E5 1
Ashfield Pl. Brad BD2 ... 56 D2
Ashfield Rd. Batley WF17 ... 97 A2
Ashfield Rd. Brad BD10 ... 39 C1
Ashfield Rd. Elland HX4 ... 134 B7
Ashfield Rd. Hem WF9 ... 181 D5
Ashfield Rd. Hud HD2 ... 135 E1
Ashfield Rd. Morley LS27 ... 97 F3
Ashfield Rd. Pudsey LS28 ... 57 E1
Ashfield Rd. Ship BD18 ... 54 E7
Ashfield Rd. Thorn BD13 ... 72 D6
Ashfield St. Hud HD2 ... 136 B2
Ashfield St. Keigh BD21 ... 35 B6 9
Ashfield St. Nor WF6 ... 123 C3
Ashfield Terr. Brad BD12 ... 94 D4
Ashfield Terr. Clec BD19 ... 116 E7 10
Ashfield Terr. Elland HX4 ... 134 B8
Ashfield Terr. Haw BD22 ... 51 C6 11
Ashfield Terr. Leeds LS15 ... 62 D4
Ashfield Terr. Midd WF3 ... 99 F2
Ashfield Way. Leeds LS12 ... 77 F4
Ashfield. Weth LS22 ... 13 F6
Ashford Ct. Kirkb HD8 ... 173 F7
Ashford Dr. Pudsey LS28 ... 76 F6
Ashford Gn. Brad BD6 ... 73 F1
Ashford Pk. Hud HD7 ... 152 D5
Ashgap La. Nor WF6 ... 123 B3
Ashgrove Ave. Hali HX3 ... 113 E3 1
Ashgrove. Brad BD2 ... 56 C3
Ashgrove. Brad BD10 ... 56 E7
Ashgrove. Brad BD7 ... 74 D6
Ashgrove Cres. Kippax LS25 ... 83 B3
Ashgrove Croft. Kippax LS25 ... 83 B2
Ashgrove Mews. Pudsey LS13 . 57 F4
Ashgrove Mount. Kippax LS25 . 83 A3
Ashgrove Pl. Hali HX3 ... 113 E3 3
Ashgrove Rd. Hud HD2 ... 136 F2
Ashgrove Rd. Keigh BD20 ... 18 A2
Ashington Cl. Brad BD2 ... 56 D3
Ashlands Fst Sch. Ilkley ... 8 C5
Ashlands Rd. Ilkley LS29 ... 8 C5
Ashlar Gr. Castle WF10 ... 124 F6
Ashlar Gr. Queen BD13 ... 92 D8
Ashlea Ave. Brig HD6 ... 136 B8
Ashlea Cl. Brig HD6 ... 136 B8
Ashlea Cl. Gar LS25 ... 82 F5
Ashlea Ct. Leeds LS13 ... 58 C3
Ashlea Dr. Brig HD6 ... 136 B8
Ashlea Gate. Leeds LS13 ... 58 C3
Ashlea Gn. Leeds LS13 ... 58 C3
Ashleigh Ave. Pont WF8 ... 146 D7
Ashleigh Ave. Wake WF2 ... 141 E5
Ashleigh. Bri S72 ... 181 A3
Ashleigh Cl. Shep HD8 ... 173 F2
Ashleigh Dale. Hud HD2 ... 135 E1
Ashleigh Gdns. Roth LS26 ... 101 C6
Ashleigh Rd. Leeds LS16 ... 59 A8
Ashleigh St. Keigh BD21 ... 35 C8
Ashley Ave. Leeds LS9 ... 61 A2 7
Ashley Cl. Clec BD19 ... 96 A2
Ashley Cl. Wake WF2 ... 120 F2
Ashley Croft. Roy S71 ... 179 B4
Ashley Ct. S Kirk WF9 ... 181 F1
Ashley Gr. Heb Br HX7 ... 89 E1
Ashley Ind Est. Hud ... 137 A4
Ashley Ind Est. Leeds ... 60 C4
Ashley Ind Est. Ossett ... 140 E7
Ashley La. Ship BD17 ... 55 B8
Ashley Rd. Bing BD16 ... 37 A2
Ashley Rd. Brad BD12 ... 94 C2
Ashley Rd. Leeds LS9 ... 61 A2
Ashley Rd. Leeds LS12 ... 78 B6
Ashley St. Hali HX1 ... 112 F7
Ashley St. Ship BD17 ... 55 B8
Ashley Terr. Leeds LS9 ... 61 A2 6
Ashmead. B Spa LS23 ... 30 D5
Ashmead. Batley WF17 ... 118 A3
Ashmere Gr. Hud HD2 ... 136 C2
Ashmews. Brad BD10 ... 56 E7
Ashmore Dr. Ossett WF5 ... 119 C1
Ashmount. Brad BD14 ... 73 D4
Ashroyd. Roth LS26 ... 100 F4
Ashtofts Mount. Guise LS20 ... 22 E1
Ashton Ave. Brad BD7 ... 73 E5
Ashton Ave. Leeds LS8 ... 60 F3
Ashton Clough Rd. Liver WF15 117 A4
Ashton Cres. Roth WF3 ... 100 D3
Ashton Ct. Leeds LS8 ... 61 A3
Ashton Gr. Leeds LS8 ... 60 F2
Ashton Mount. Leeds LS8 ... 61 A2
Ashton Pl. Leeds LS8 ... 60 F2
Ashton Rd. Castle WF10 ... 124 D6
Ashton Rd. Heb Br HX7 ... 89 E1
Ashton Rd. Leeds LS8 ... 61 A3
Ashton Road Ind Est.
Leeds LS8 ... 61 A3
Ashton St. Brad BD1 ... 74 D7
Ashton St. Castle WF10 ... 124 D7
Ashton St. Leeds LS8 ... 60 F3
Ashton Terr. Leeds LS8 ... 60 F2
Ashton View. Leeds LS8 ... 60 F2
Ashtree Gr. Brad BD7 ... 73 F3
Ashtree Gr. Kippax LS25 ... 83 B1
Ashville Ave. Leeds LS6 ... 59 E3
Ashville Croft. Hali HX2 ... 112 D8 4
Ashville Gdns. Hali HX2 ... 112 D8
Ashville Gr. Hali HX2 ... 91 D1
Ashville Gr. Leeds LS6 ... 59 D3
Ashville Rd. Leeds LS4, LS6 ... 59 D3
Ashville St. Hali HX3 ... 92 A1 19
Ashville Terr. Glu BD20 ... 16 D6
Ashville Terr. Haw BD22 ... 34 D3
Ashville Terr. Leeds LS6 ... 59 D3
Ashville Terr. Pudsey LS28 ... 57 D2 14
Ashville View. Leeds LS6 ... 59 E2
Ashwell Cl. Shaf S72 ... 180 C3
Ashwell La. Ship BD9 ... 55 A4
Ashwell Rd. Brad BD8 ... 55 B1
Ashwell Rd. Ship BD9 ... 55 A4
Ashwell St. Brad BD8 ... 55 B1
Ashwood Cl. Hud HD2 ... 136 C3
Ashwood Dr. Gild LS27 ... 97 C7
Ashwood Dr. Keigh BD20 ... 19 A1
Ashwood Gdns. Gild LS27 ... 97 B7
Ashwood Gr. Gild LS27 ... 97 C7
Ashwood Gr. Hor WF4 ... 141 C2
Ashwood. Leeds LS14 ... 45 B1
Ashwood St. Brad BD4 ... 75 D1
Ashwood Terr. Leeds LS6 ... 59 F4
Ashwood Villas. Leeds LS6 ... 59 F4
Ashworth Cl. Dew WF13 ... 139 C8
Ashworth Gdns. Dew WF13 ... 139 C8
Ashworth Gr. Dew WF13 ... 139 C8
Ashworth Pl. Brad BD6 ... 74 D1
Ashworth Rd. Dew WF13 ... 139 C8
Ashworth St. Bacup OL13 ... 106 A3 12
Askam Ave. Pont WF8 ... 125 F4
Asket Ave. Leeds LS14 ... 61 F5
Asket Cl. Leeds LS14 ... 61 E6
Asket Cres. Leeds LS14 ... 61 E5
Asket Dr. Leeds LS14 ... 61 E6
Asket Garth. Leeds LS14 ... 61 E5
Asket Gdns. Leeds LS8 ... 61 D6
Asket Gn. Leeds LS14 ... 61 E6
Asket Hill Cty Prim Sch. Leeds . 61 E6
Asket Hill. Leeds LS8 ... 61 D6
Asket Pl. Leeds LS14 ... 61 E5
Asket Wlk. Leeds LS14 ... 61 E5
Askey Ave. Morley LS27 ... 98 B2
Askey Cres. Morley LS27 ... 98 B2
Askham Gr. Upton WF9 ... 183 E7
Askham Rd. Castle WF10 ... 104 D1
Askrigg Dr. Brad BD2 ... 56 B3
Askwith Cty Prim Sch. Ask ... 9 F5
Askwith La. Ask LS21 ... 10 A6
Aspden St. Tod OL14 ... 108 B6
Aspect Gdns. Pudsey LS28 ... 76 D8
Aspect Terr. Pudsey LS28 ... 76 C8
Aspen Cl. Keigh BD21 ... 35 E5
Aspen Cl. Wake WF2 ... 142 A8
Aspen Ct. Emley HD8 ... 175 C7
Aspen Mount. Hors LS16 ... 41 E2
Aspen Rise. Brad BD15 ... 53 F4
Aspinall St. Hali HX1 ... 112 F6
Aspinall St. Heb Br HX7 ... 89 E1
Aspley Pl. Hud HD1 ... 154 B6
Asquith Ave. Morley LS27 ... 97 F6
Asquith Cl. Morley LS27 ... 97 F5
Asquith Dr. Morley LS27 ... 97 F5
Asquith St. Batley WF17 ... 97 B2
Assembly St. Leeds LS2 ... 79 C7 5
Assembly St. Nor WF6 ... 123 A2
Astley Ave. Swil LS26 ... 82 A1
Astley La. Swil LS26 ... 102 C8
Astley Lane Ind Est. Swil ... 102 B8
Astley Way. Swil LS26 ... 102 B8
Aston Ave. Leeds LS13 ... 58 E2
Aston Cl. Liver WF15 ... 116 F2
Aston Cres. Leeds LS13 ... 58 E2
Aston Ct. Ossett WF5 ... 141 A4
Aston Dr. Leeds LS13 ... 58 E2
Aston Gr. Leeds LS13 ... 58 E2
Aston Mount. Leeds LS13 ... 58 E2
Aston Pl. Leeds LS13 ... 58 E2
Aston Rd. Brad BD5 ... 74 E3
Aston Rd. Leeds LS13 ... 58 D2
Aston St. Leeds LS13 ... 58 D2
Aston Terr. Leeds LS13 ... 58 E2
Aston View. Leeds LS13 ... 58 E2
Astor Gr. Leeds LS13 ... 58 A2
Astor St. Leeds LS13 ... 58 A2
Astral Ave. Brig HX3 ... 114 D8
Astral Cl. Brig HX3 ... 114 D8
Astral View. Brad BD6 ... 74 A2
Atalanta Terr. Hali HX2 ... 112 E4
Atha Cl. Leeds LS11 ... 79 A1
Atha Cres. Leeds LS11 ... 79 A1
Atha St. Leeds LS11 ... 79 A1
Athelstan La. Otley LS21 ... 11 A1
Athene Dr. Hud HD4 ... 154 C3
Atherstone Rd. Brad BD15 ... 73 B7
Atherton La. Brig HD6 ... 136 B8
Athlone Dr. Batley WF12 ... 118 E2
Athlone Gr. Leeds LS12 ... 78 C7
Athlone Rise. Gar LS25 ... 83 B7
Athlone St. Leeds LS12 ... 78 C7
Athlone Terr. Leeds LS12 ... 78 C7
Athol Cl. Hali HX3 ... 92 A3
Athol Cres. Hali HX3 ... 92 A3
Athol Gdns. Hali HX3 ... 92 A3
Athol Gn. Hali HX3 ... 92 A3
Athol Rd. Brad BD9 ... 55 B2
Athol Rd. Hali HX3 ... 92 A3
Athol St. Hali HX3 ... 92 A3
Athol St. Keigh BD21 ... 18 E1
Athold Dr. Ossett WF5 ... 140 F5
Athold St. Ossett WF5 ... 140 F5
Atkinson Ct. Nor WF6 ... 123 A1
Atkinson La. Pont WF8 ... 125 F2
Atkinson St. Leeds LS10 ... 79 E5
Atkinson St. Ship BD18 ... 55 B8
Atlanta St. Leeds LS13 ... 58 A2
Atlas Fst Sch. Brad ... 74 C8
Atlas Mill Rd. Brig HD6 ... 115 A2
Atlas St. Brad BD8 ... 55 B1
Attlee Ave. Ryhill WF4 ... 162 C1
Attlee Cres. Wake WF2 ... 160 E8
Attlee Gr. Loft G WF1 ... 121 C4
Attlee St. Nor WF6 ... 144 B8
Auckland Rd. Brad BD6 ... 74 A1
Audby La. Weth LS22 ... 13 F6
Audrey St. Ossett WF5 ... 140 E4
Audsley's Yd. Hor WF4 ... 140 E1
Augusta Ct. Wake WF2 ... 141 F5
Aurelia House. Brad BD8 ... 55 C2
Austhorpe Ave. Leeds LS15 ... 81 E7
Austhorpe Ct. Leeds LS15 ... 81 E7
Austhorpe Dr. Leeds LS15 ... 81 E7
Austhorpe Gdns. Leeds LS15 ... 81 F8
Austhorpe Gr. Leeds LS15 ... 81 E8
Austhorpe La. Leeds LS15 ... 62 D1
Austhorpe Prim Sch. Leeds ... 81 E8
Austhorpe Rd. Leeds LS15 ... 62 D2
Austhorpe View. Leeds LS15 ... 81 D8
Austin Ave. Brig HD6 ... 114 F4
Austin Rd. Castle WF10 ... 125 D8
Austin St. Keigh BD21 ... 35 D8 11
Austwick Cl. Mapp S75 ... 178 A2
Authorpe Rd. Leeds LS6 ... 59 F6
Autumn Ave. Leeds LS6 ... 59 E2
Autumn Ave. Weth LS22 ... 13 E8
Autumn Cres. Hors LS18 ... 58 D7
Autumn Gr. Leeds LS6 ... 59 E2 14
Autumn Pl. Leeds LS6 ... 59 E2 15
Autumn St. Hali HX1 ... 112 F5 10
Autumn St. Leeds LS6 ... 59 E2
Autumn Terr. Leeds LS6 ... 59 E2
Auty Cres. Loft G WF3 ... 121 F5
Auty Sq. Morley LS27 ... 98 B3 2
Avenel Rd. Brad BD15 ... 73 B8
Avenel Terr. Brad BD15 ... 73 B8
Avenham Way. Brad BD3 ... 75 A8
Avens Cl. Pont WF8 ... 146 D7
Avenue A. Th Arch LS23 ... 15 B3
Avenue B. Th Arch LS23 ... 15 B1
Avenue C E. Th Arch LS23 ... 15 C2
Avenue C W. Th Arch LS23 ... 15 C2
Avenue Cres. Leeds LS8 ... 60 F4
Avenue D. Th Arch LS23 ... 15 B1
Avenue Des Hirondelles.
Pool LS21 ... 24 D6

Avenue E E. Th Arch LS23 15 C1
Avenue E W. Th Arch LS23 31 B8
Avenue F. Th Arch LS23 15 D1
Avenue G. Th Arch LS23 15 D2
Avenue Gdns. Leeds LS17 43 A5
Avenue Hill. Leeds LS8 60 F4
Avenue Lawns. Leeds LS17 42 F5
Avenue No 2. Brig HD6 115 A1
Avenue Rd. Brad BD5 74 F3
Avenue Rd. Wake WF2 142 E1
Avenue St. Brad BD4 75 D1
Avenue Terr. Otley LS21 22 F7
Avenue Terr. Pont WF8 146 A8
Avenue The. B in Elm LS15 62 F8
Avenue The. Batley WF17 96 E1
Avenue The. Batley WF17 117 F3
Avenue The. Batley WF17 118 A7
Avenue The. Brad BD14 73 B4
Avenue The. Brig HX3 114 D8
Avenue The. Coll LS22 13 A1
Avenue The. Crof WF4 143 E1
Avenue The. E Ard WF3 120 A8
Avenue The. Guise BD10 39 E2
Avenue The. Hare LS17 27 A6
Avenue The. Hors LS18 40 F1
Avenue The. Hud HD5 154 D5 4
Avenue The. Leeds LS17 43 A5
Avenue The. Leeds LS8 44 A1
Avenue The. Leeds LS15 62 D3 2
Avenue The. Leeds LS9 79 E7
Avenue The. Leeds LS15 81 E3
Avenue The. Loft G WF1 121 B4
Avenue The. Roy S71 179 E4
Avenue The. Ship BD16 54 B8
Avenue Victoria. Leeds LS8 61 A8
Averingcliffe Rd. Brad BD10 56 D6
Avery Tulip Ct. Brad BD12 94 C6 2
Aviary Gr. Leeds LS12 78 C8
Aviary Mount. Leeds LS12 78 C8
Aviary Pl. Leeds LS12 78 C8 8
Aviary Rd. Leeds LS12 78 C8
Aviary Row. Leeds LS12 78 C8
Aviary St. Leeds LS12 78 C8 7
Aviary Terr. Leeds LS12 78 C8 9
Aviary View. Leeds LS12 78 C8 6
Avison Rd. Hud HD4 153 A3
Avison Yd. Wake WF1 142 D6
Avocet Cl. Brad BD8 73 C7
Avocet Garth. Midd LS10 99 D5 4
Avon Cl. Thorner LS17 44 F4
Avon Ct. Thorner LS17 44 E5
Avon Dr. Gar LS25 82 F6
Avon Wlk. Feath WF7 145 C7
Avondale Cres. Ship BD18 55 A7
Avondale Ct. Leeds LS17 43 D3
Avondale Dr. Loft G WF3 121 E5
Avondale Dr. Roy S71 179 C1
Avondale Gr. Ship BD18 55 A7
Avondale. Keigh BD20 35 A8
Avondale Mount. Ship BD18 55 A7
Avondale Pl. Hali HX3 113 B4 8
Avondale Rd. Ship BD18 54 F7
Avondale St. Leeds LS13 58 C1
Avondale St. Wake WF2 142 C4
Avondale Way. Wake WF2 142 C4
Aydon Way. Shelf HX3 93 E7
Aygill Ave. Brad BD9 54 D3
Aylesbury St. Keigh BD21 35 A4 3
Aylesford Mount. Leeds LS15 62 F3
Aylesham Ind Est. Brad 94 D6
Aynholme Cl. Sil LS29 6 F8
Aynholme Dr. Sil LS29 6 F8
Aynsley Gr. Brad BD15 54 B1
Ayres Dr. Hud HD4 153 A3
Ayresome Ave. Leeds LS8 44 A2
Ayresome Oval. Brad BD15 73 A7
Ayresome Terr. Leeds LS8 43 F2
Ayrton Cres. Bing BD16 37 A3 18
Aysgarth Ave. Brig HX3 115 A6
Aysgarth Cl. Brad BD12 94 C2
Aysgarth Cl. Leeds LS9 79 F7
Aysgarth Cl. Wake WF2 141 D3
Aysgarth Cres. Hali HX2 91 A3
Aysgarth Dr. Leeds LS9 79 F7
Aysgarth Dr. Wake WF2 141 D3
Aysgarth Pl. Leeds LS9 79 F7
Aysgarth Rd. Batley WF17 118 A5
Aysgarth Rd. Hud HD4 154 B2
Aysgarth Wlk. Leeds LS9 79 F7
Ayton Cl. Brad BD3 75 A8
Ayton Rd. Hud HD3 152 E6
Azealea Ct. Brad BD3 75 B8

Baby House Hill La. Wad M HX7 69 A4
Bachelor La. Hors LS18 41 C2
Back Acres St. Keigh BD21 35 B6 8
Back Ada St. Keigh BD21 35 A7 10
Back Aireview Terr. Keigh BD21 35 E6
Back Aireville St. Keigh BD20 18 A2
Back Albert Gr. Leeds LS6 59 D6
Back Albert Terr. Leeds LS6 59 E2
Back Allerton Terr. Leeds LS7 60 D7
Back Alma St. Yeadon LS19 40 C7 5
Back Anderton St. Wake WF1 142 E3
Back Ann St. Denh BD13 52 E1
Back Archery Pl. Leeds LS2 60 B2
Back Archery Rd. Leeds LS2 60 B2
Back Archery St. Leeds LS2 60 B2
Back Archery Terr. Leeds LS2 60 B2
Back Armitage Rd. Hud HD4 171 E8
Back Ash Gr. Leeds LS6 59 F3
Back Ashgrove (W). Brad BD7 74 D6
Back Ashley Ave. Leeds LS9 61 A2 8
Back Ashley St. Leeds LS9 61 A2 9
Back Ashville Ave. Leeds LS6 59 E3
Back Ashville Gr. Leeds LS6 59 E3
Back Ashville Rd. Leeds LS6 59 D3
Back Ashville Terr. Leeds LS6 59 D3
Back Ashwood Terr. Leeds LS6 59 F4
Back Aston Pl. Leeds LS13 58 E2 1
Back Aston Rd. Leeds LS13 58 D2
Back Aston St. Leeds LS13 58 D2
Back Aston Terr. Leeds LS13 58 E2 2
Back Aston View. Leeds LS13 58 E2 3
Back Athlone Ave. Leeds LS12 78 C7 13
Back Athlone Gr. Leeds LS12 78 C7 2
Back Athlone Terr. Leeds LS12 78 C7 3
Back Atlanta St. Leeds LS13 58 A2
Back Austhorpe Rd. Leeds LS15 62 C2
Back Austhorpe Rd. Leeds LS15 62 D2 4
Back Aviary Rd. Leeds LS12 78 C8 11
Back Aylesbury St. Keigh BD21 35 A4 4
Back Baker St. Ship BD18 55 A8
Back Balfour St. Bing BD16 36 F2
Back Balfour St. Keigh BD21 35 B6 5
Back Bank St. Castle WF10 124 D8
Back Bank Terr. Pudsey LS28 57 E2
Back Banstead St. Leeds LS8 60 F3 14
Back Barden Pl. Leeds LS12 78 A7 2
Back Barkly Gr. Leeds LS11 79 A2
Back Barkly Par. Leeds LS11 79 A1 3
Back Barkly Terr. Leeds LS11 79 A2 7
Back Barrowby View. Leeds LS15 81 F7
Back Bath Rd. Leeds LS13 58 C2 15
Back Beacon St. Hud HD2 136 A1
Back Beaumont St. Batley WF17 118 C3
Back Beck La. Sil LS29 6 F8
Back Beech St. Bing BD16 36 F2
Back Beech Terr. Hud HD1 136 B1
Back Beechwood Gr. Leeds LS4 59 D3
Back Beechwood Rd. Leeds LS4 59 D3 9
Back Bellbrooke Gr. Leeds LS9 61 B2 9
Back Bellbrooke Pl. Leeds LS9 61 B2 7
Back Bellbrooke Terr. Leeds LS9 61 B2
Back Belvedere Ave. Leeds LS11 79 B2
Back Belvedere Mount. Leeds LS11 79 B2
Back Bentley Ave. Leeds LS6 59 F6 3
Back Bentley Gr. Leeds LS6 59 F6
Back Berkeley Ave. Leeds LS8 61 A3 12
Back Berkeley Terr. Leeds LS8 61 A3 14
Back Beverley Terr. Leeds LS11 79 B3
Back Blackwood Gr. Hali HX1 112 F8
Back Blenheim Ave. Leeds LS2 60 B2 2
Back Blenheim Mount. Brad BD8 55 C2
Back Blenheim Terr. Leeds LS2 60 B2 12
Back Boundary Terr. Leeds LS3 59 E1
Back Bower Rd. Elland HX5 135 A7
Back Bowling Green Rd. Elland HX4 133 F3
Back Bowman St. Wake WF1 142 F3
Back Bradshaw Rd. Honley HD7 171 F3
Back Branch Pl. Leeds LS12 78 A4 10
Back Breary Ave. Hors LS18 41 D1
Back Breary Terr. Hors LS18 41 D1
Back Briggate. Sil BD20 5 E2
Back Broad La. Leeds LS13 58 D4
Back Broomfield Cres. Leeds LS6 59 D4
Back Broomfield Pl. Leeds LS6 59 D3 4
Back Broomfield Rd. Keigh BD21 35 B7 5
Back Broomfield Rd. Leeds LS4 59 D3
Back Broomfield St. Keigh BD21 35 B7 6
Back Broughton Ave. Leeds LS9 61 A2 21
Back Broughton Terr. Leeds LS9 61 A2 20
Back Brudenell Gr. Leeds LS6 59 F3
Back Brudenell Mount. Leeds LS6 59 E3
Back Brudenell Rd. Leeds LS6 59 E3
Back Brunswick St. Dew WF13 118 A1
Back Brunswick St. Leeds LS2 60 C1
Back Burchett Gr. Leeds LS6 60 A4
Back Burchett Pl. Leeds LS6 60 A4
Back Burley Hill. Leeds LS4 59 D2
Back Burley St. Leeds LS3 79 A8 6
Back Burlington Pl. Leeds LS11 79 B2 22
Back Burlington Rd. Leeds LS11 79 B2
Back Burton Cres. Leeds LS6 59 D6 2
Back Burton Terr. Leeds LS11 79 C3 12
Back Buxton St. Keigh BD21 35 D7 4
Back Byrl St. Keigh BD21 18 C1
Back Byrom St. Tod OL14 108 B6 4
Back Caister St. Keigh BD21 35 B4 4
Back Camberley St. Leeds LS11 79 C3 10
Back Carlinghow La. Bately WF17 117 E7
Back Carter Mount. Leeds LS15 81 C8
Back Cartmel Rd. Keigh BD21 35 A7 12
Back Castle Rd. Keigh BD21 35 B8
Back Cavendish Rd. Brad BD10 56 B7
Back Cavendish St. Keigh BD21 35 C7
Back Cavendish Terr. Hali HX1 113 A7 13
Back Cecil St. Hud HD1 154 A6 8
Back Chapel La. Leeds LS6 59 D4
Back Chapel St. Brad BD1 74 F7 12
Back Charles St. Brig HD6 115 A3 10
Back Chatsworth Rd. Leeds LS8 61 A3 9
Back Chestnut Ave. Leeds LS6 59 F3
Back Chestnut Ave. Leeds LS15 62 D2 2
Back Christ Church View. Leeds LS12 78 B8
Back Church La. Hors LS16 42 D5
Back Church La. Leeds LS5 59 A4
Back Church View. Wake WF1 142 F2
Back Claremont Ave. Leeds LS3 60 A1 8
Back Claremont Gr. Leeds LS3 60 A1 6
Back Claremont St. Roth LS26 101 C6 9
Back Claremont Ter. Leeds LS3 60 A1
Back Clarence Rd. Hors LS18 58 B7 7
Back Clarence St. Hali HX1 113 B7
Back Clarendon Pl. Hali HX1 113 A6
Back Clarkson View. Leeds LS6 60 A4 10
Back Clayton St. Roth LS26 100 F5
Back Cliff Mount. Leeds LS6 60 A4
Back Clifton Rd. Hud HD1 153 E7
Back Clifton Terr. Leeds LS9 61 B2
Back Clipston Ave. Leeds LS6 59 F6
Back Clough. Northo HX3 93 A2
Back Clovelly Pl. Leeds LS11 79 B3 27
Back Coldcotes Ave. Leeds LS9 61 B2
Back Colenso Mount. Leeds LS11 78 F4
Back Colenso Rd. Keigh BD21 18 E1
Back Colenso Rd. Leeds LS11 78 F4
Back Colne Rd. Glu BD20 16 D6
Back Colton Rd. Leeds LS12 78 C7
Back Colwyn Pl. Leeds LS11 79 B2 28
Back Colwyn View. Leeds LS11 79 B2 11
Back Commercial St. Hali HX1 113 C7 14
Back Commercial St. Tod OL14 108 C5 16
Back Compton St. Keigh BD21 35 D8 9
Back Conway St. Leeds LS8 60 F3
Back Cowper Gr. Leeds LS8 61 A3 11
Back Cowper St. Leeds LS7 60 E3
Back Craggwood Rd. Hors LS18 58 C7 6
Back Cranbrook Ave. Leeds LS11 79 A3
Back Cranbrook Terr. Leeds LS11 79 A3
Back Croft House La. Keigh BD20 18 A2
Back Croft. Rip HX6 132 C1
Back Cromer Ave. Keigh BD21 35 B5 16
Back Cromer Gr. Keigh BD21 35 B4 1
Back Cromer Terr. Leeds LS2 60 A2
Back Cromwell Terr. Hali HX1 113 B7 2
Back Cross Flats Row. Leeds LS11 78 F2 3
Back Cross Flatts Ave. Leeds LS11 79 A2
Back Cross Flatts Cres. Leeds LS11 78 F2 4
Back Cross Flatts Gr. Leeds LS11 79 A2 3
Back Cross Flatts Mount. Leeds LS11 79 A2 6
Back Cross Flatts Pl. Leeds LS11 78 F2 6
Back Cross Green Cres. Leeds LS9 79 F6 6
Back Cross Gn La. Leeds LS9 79 F6 8
Back Cross La. Elland HX5 134 E6
Back Crossland Ter. Leeds LS11 79 C3 2
Back Dalton Ave. Leeds LS11 79 A2
Back Dalton Gr. Leeds LS11 79 A2
Back Dalton Rd. Leeds LS11 79 A2
Back Dargai St. Leeds LS7 60 C3
Back Dawlish Ave. Leeds LS9 80 B8 3
Back Dawlish Mount. Leeds LS9 80 B8 2
Back Dawlish Rd. Leeds LS9 80 B8 4
Back De Lacy Mount. Leeds LS5 59 A5
Back Delph Mount. Leeds LS6 60 A4
Back Dent St. Leeds LS9 79 F7
Back Der St. Tod OL14 108 C5 7
Back Devonshire La. Leeds LS8 44 A2
Back Dorset Mount. Leeds LS8 61 A4 9
Back Dorset Rd. Leeds LS8 61 A4 7
Back Dorset Terr. Leeds LS8 61 A3 2
Back Dudley Hill Rd. Brad BD2 56 B2
Back Duke of York St. Wake WF1 142 D7
Back Duke St. Feath WF7 145 C6
Back Dunbar St. Wake WF1 142 F4
Back East Park Rd. Leeds LS9 80 A7 10
Back Eaton St. Keigh BD21 35 A4 2
Back Ecclesburn Gr. Leeds LS9 80 B7 1
Back Ecclesburn St. Leeds LS9 80 A7
Back Edensor Rd. Keigh BD21 35 A7 9
Back Edinburgh Rd. Leeds LS12 78 A8
Back Eldon Rd. Hud HD1 153 D7
Back Elford Pl. Leeds LS8 60 F3
Back Elmfield Terr. Hali HHX1X3 113 B5 3
Back Elsworth St. Leeds LS12 78 D7
Back Emily St. Keigh BD21 35 D8 16
Back Eric St. Keigh BD21 35 C8
Back Eric St. Leeds LS13 58 C5
Back Eshald Pl. Roth LS26 101 D6
Back Esmond Terr. Leeds LS12 78 C7 12
Back Estcourt Ave. Leeds LS6 59 C4
Back Estcourt Terr. Leeds LS6 59 C4
Back Eversley Mt. Hali HX2 112 E6
Back Fairford Pl. Leeds LS11 79 C3
Back Featherbank Terr. Hors LS18 58 B7 2
Back Ferguson St. Hali HX1 113 C6 4
Back Field Ct. Thorn BD13 72 D6
Back Fitzwilliam St. Hud HD1 153 F6
Back Florist St. Keigh BD21 18 E1
Back Fold. Brad BD14 73 B5
Back Foster Rd. Keigh BD21 35 B4 2
Back Garden St. Castle WF10 124 D6
Back Garden St. Wake WF1 142 B6
Back Garton Rd. Leeds LS9 80 A7
Back Garton Terr. Leeds LS9 80 A7
Back Gathorne St. Leeds LS8 60 E3
Back George St. Leeds LS2 79 D8 5
Back Gerrard St. Hali HX1 113 B7
Back Gillett La. Roth LS26 100 F5
Back Girlington Rd. Brad BD8 54 F1
Back Gladstone St. Bing BD16 36 F2
Back Glebe Terr. Leeds LS16 59 D7
Back Glen Terr. Hali HX1 113 B5
Back Glenthorpe Terr. LS9 80 A8 2
Back Glossop St. Leeds LS6 60 B4 3
Back Gn. Morley LS27 98 C7
Back Gooder La. Brig HD6 115 B1 1
Back Gordon St. Wake WF1 142 F2
Back Gordon Terr. Leeds LS6 59 F6
Back Graham Gr. Leeds LS4 59 D3
Back Granby Gr. Leeds LS6 59 D4
Back Grange Ave. Leeds LS7 60 E4
Back Grange Cres. Leeds LS7 60 E4
Back Grange Terr. Leeds LS7 60 D4
Back Grange View. Leeds LS7 60 E4
Back Grant St. Keigh BD21 35 A7
Back Grantley St. Wake WF1 142 D6
Back Graveley St. Leeds LS15 81 A8 6
Back Great Russell St. Brad BD7 74 C7
Back Greaves St. Brad BD5 74 D3
Back Greenhead Rd. Hud HD1 154 A6 2
Back Greenhow Wlk. Leeds LS4 59 D2
Back Greenmount Terr. Leeds LS11 79 B3
Back Greenwood Mount. Leeds LS6 59 E7 4
Back Grosvenor Ter. Hali HX1 113 A7 11
Back Grosvenor Ter. Leeds LS6 59 F4
Back Grouse St. Keigh BD21 35 D8
Back Grove Gdns. Leeds LS6 59 E6
Back Grove Rd. Ilkley LS29 8 B4
Back Grovehall Ave. Leeds LS11 79 A1 5
Back Grovehall Dr. Leeds LS11 79 A1 7
Back Haigh Ave. Roth LS26 100 C7
Back Haigh St. Roth LS26 100 C7
Back Haigh View. Roth LS26 100 C7
Back Halliday Gr. Leeds LS12 78 A8
Back Halliday Pl. Leeds LS12 78 A8 17
Back Hambleton St. Wake WF1 142 C7 5
Back Hamilton Ave. Leeds LS7 60 E4
Back Hamilton View. Leeds LS7 60 E4
Back Harehills Ave. Leeds LS7 60 E4
Back Harehills Park View. Leeds LS9 61 B2 1
Back Hares Mount. Leeds LS8 60 E4
Back Harold Gr. Leeds LS6 59 E2 12
Back Hartley Ave. Leeds LS6 60 B4 1
Back Hartley Gr. Leeds LS6 60 A4 5
Back Hartley St. Morley LS27 98 C3
Back Hatfield St. Wake WF1 142 C7
Back Hawksworth Gr. Leeds LS5 58 D6
Back Headingley Av. Leeds LS6 59 C5
Back Headingley Mount. Leeds LS6 59 C5
Back Heathfield Ter. Leeds LS6 59 D6 5
Back Heddon Pl. Leeds LS6 59 E6
Back Heddon St. Leeds LS6 59 E6
Back Heights Rd. Wils BD13 72 B8
Back Henrietta St. Batley WF17 118 C5 3
Back Hessle Ave. Leeds LS6 59 E3
Back Hessle Mount. Leeds LS6 59 E3
Back Hessle Terr. Leeds LS6 59 E3
Back Hessle View. Leeds LS6 59 E3
Back High St. Thorn BD13 72 D6 12
Back Highbury Terr. Leeds LS6 59 E6
Back Highfield Rd. Leeds LS13 58 E2 4
Back Highthorne View. Leeds LS12 78 B8 1
Back Highth'rne Gr. Leeds LS12 78 A8 12
Back Highth'rne St. Leeds LS12 78 A8 15
Back Hill Top Ave. Leeds LS8 60 F4
Back Hillcrest Ave. Leeds LS7 60 E4
Back Hillcrest View. Leeds LS7 60 E4
Back Hilton Gr. Leeds LS8 60 F4 1
Back Hilton Pl. Leeds LS8 60 F4
Back Hilton Rd. Leeds LS8 60 F4
Back Hird St. Keigh BD21 35 B6 7
Back Hollyshaw Terr. Leeds LS15 81 C8 5
Back Honoria St. Hud HD1 136 A1
Back Hope Hall Terr. Hali HX1 113 C6 14
Back Hovingham Gr. Leeds LS8 61 A4
Back Hovingham Mount. Leeds LS8 61 A4 5
Back Hovingham Terr. Leeds LS8 61 A4 3
Back Hyde Gr. Keigh BD21 35 D8
Back Hyde Terr. Leeds LS2 60 A1
Back Ibbetson Pl. Leeds LS2 60 B1
Back Ingledew Cres. Leeds LS8 44 B2
Back Ivy Ave. Leeds LS9 80 A8 11
Back Ivy Gr. Leeds LS9 80 B7 2
Back Ivy Mount. Leeds LS9 80 A8 9
Back Ivy St. Leeds LS9 80 A8 12
Back John St. Thorn BD13 72 D6
Back Kelso Rd. Leeds LS2 59 F2
Back Kendal La. Leeds LS3 60 A1 1
Back Kennerleigh Wlk. Leeds LS15 62 C1
Back Kensington St. Brad BD8 55 A1
Back Kensington St. Brad BD8 74 A8
Back Kensington Ter. Leeds LS6 59 F3
Back Kirby St. Keigh BD21 35 D8
Back Kirkgate. Ship BD18 55 A7
Back Kitson St. Leeds LS9 79 F7
Back Knowl Rd. Mir WF14 137 F6
Back Knowle Mount. Leeds LS4 59 D3 12
Back La. Bad WF9 164 E2
Back La. Batley WF16 117 D4
Back La. Birk BD11 96 F7
Back La. Brad BD10 56 B8
Back La. Brad BD13, BD14 73 B2
Back La. Bramham LS23 30 D3
Back La. Bur in W LS29 9 F1
Back La. Clay DN5 194 C4
Back La. Clay W HD8 176 A3
Back La. Crof WF4 144 C2
Back La. Dew WF12 138 F2
Back La. Dew WF12 156 F7
Back La. Emley HD8 175 A5
Back La. Floc WF4 156 E5
Back La. Gild LS12 77 C3
Back La. Guise LS20 39 D8
Back La. H Pag DN5 195 D5
Back La. Hali HX2 91 D5
Back La. Haw BD22 50 C6
Back La. Heb Br HX7 88 F1
Back La. Hep HX7 88 F4
Back La. Holmfi HD7 189 A5
Back La. Hors LS18 58 B8
Back La. Keigh BD20 19 D1
Back La. Keigh BD22 34 B7
Back La. Kippax WF10 103 B4
Back La. Leeds LS13 58 D1
Back La. Lepton WF14 156 B7
Back La. Mir WF14 137 E5
Back La. Neth WF4 158 B7
Back La. Ossett WF5 140 D5
Back La. Otley LS29 10 A1
Back La. Pudsey LS28 57 D3
Back La. Rip HX6 132 D4
Back La. Ryhill WF4 162 B4
Back La. S Elm WF9 183 A6
Back La. Shep HD8 174 B3
Back La. Ship BD9 55 A4
Back La. Sickl LS22 12 C5
Back La. Sil BD20 5 E2
Back La. Skip BD23 4 C8
Back La. Thorn BD13 72 E7
Back La W. Roy S71 179 A4
Back La. Wad M HX7 69 A6
Back La. Wake WF1 142 B6
Back La. Wils BD15 53 D3
Back La. Wool WF4 178 A6
Back La. Yeadon LS19 40 A6
Back Laisteridge La. Brad BD7 74 C6
Back Lake St. Leeds LS10 79 D2
Back Landseer Ave. Leeds LS13 58 E3
Back Landseer Gr. Leeds LS13 58 E3
Back Landseer Terr. Leeds LS13 58 E3
Back Langdale Gdns. Leeds LS6 59 C4
Back Langdale Terr. Leeds LS6 59 C4
Back Lascelles Terr. Leeds LS8 60 F3 3
Back Laurel Mount. Leeds LS7 60 D5
Back Leatham St. Dew WF13 118 A1 2
Back Leeming. Oxen BD22 51 D1
Back Lime St. Keigh BD21 35 B3
Back Linden Gr. Leeds LS11 79 C3 3
Back Lindum St. Brad BD8 55 C2
Back Lodge La. Leeds LS11 79 B2 1
Back Lombard St. Yeadon LS19 40 A4
Back Longroyd Terr. Leeds LS11 79 C3
Back Lord St. Hali HX1 113 B7 8
Back Low La. Hors LS18 41 D1
Back Lucas St. Leeds LS6 60 A4 4
Back Lyon St. Queen BD13 72 F1
Back Lytton St. Hali HX3 92 C1 7
Back Mafeking Ave. Leeds LS11 79 A1
Back Mafeking Mount. Leeds LS11 79 A1
Back Malt St. Keigh BD22 35 A4 9
Back Mannville Rd. Keigh BD21 35 A6 10
Back Manor Dr. Leeds LS6 59 E4
Back Manor Gr. Leeds LS7 60 D6
Back Manor St. Brad BD2 56 B3
Back Manor Terr. Leeds LS6 59 E4
Back Market St. Brad BD6 74 C1 3
Back Markham Ave. Leeds LS8 60 F4
Back Marriot St. Dew WF13 118 D1 4
Back Marshall Ave. Leeds LS15 62 D2 3
Back Marshall St. Leeds LS15 62 C2 5
Back Marshall Terr. Leeds LS15 62 C2 6
Back Mary St. E Ard WF3 120 E8
Back Mary St. Glu BD20 16 D8
Back Masham St. Leeds LS12 78 D7
Back Maud Ave. Leeds LS11 79 B2
Back Mayville Ave. Leeds LS6 59 E3
Back Mayville Pl. Leeds LS6 59 E3
Back Mayville St. Leeds LS6 59 E3
Back Mayville Terr. Leeds LS6 59 E3
Back Meadow View. Leeds LS6 59 E3 12
Back Melbourne Gr. Leeds LS13 58 C2 18
Back Methley Dr. Leeds LS7 60 D6
Back Mexborough Ave. Leeds LS7 60 D4
Back Mexb'rough Dr. Leeds LS7 60 D4
Back Mexb'rough Gr. Leeds LS7 60 D4
Back Mexb'rough St. Leeds LS7 60 D4
Back Middle Cross St. Leeds LS12 78 D7 6
Back Middleton Rd. Ilkley LS29 8 A4
Back Middleton View. Leeds LS11 79 A3 1
Back Midland Rd. Leeds LS6 59 F3 7
Back Milan Ave. Leeds LS8 60 F3
Back Milan Rd. Leeds LS8 60 F3
Back Milan St. Leeds LS8 61 A3 3
Back Mitchell Terr. Bing BD16 36 F2
Back Mitford Rd. Leeds LS12 78 D7
Back Model Rd. Leeds LS12 78 D7 10
Back Model Terr. Leeds LS12 78 D7
Back Model View. Leeds LS12 78 D7 3
Back Monk Bridge Dr. Leeds LS6 59 F6 7
Back M'nk Bridge St. Leeds LS6 59 F6
Back Montague St. Wake WF1 142 F3
Back Montpelier Terr. Leeds LS6 60 A4 2
Back Moor La. Hud HD4 171 D7
Back Moorfield St. Hali HX1 113 A5
Back Moorfield Terr. Leeds LS12 78 A8 19
Back Moorland Terr. Leeds LS2 60 A2
Back Morning St. Keigh BD21 35 B4 14
Back Morritt Dr. Leeds LS15 80 F8
Back Mount Ave. Batley WF17 118 D3 2
Back Mount Pleasant. Midd LS10 99 C5
Back Mount Pleasant. Wake WF1 142 D6
Back Mount View. Leeds LS6 59 F4
Back Muff St. Brad BD4 75 B5
Back Myrtle Ave. Bing BD16 36 F2
Back Myrtle Terr. Haw BD22 34 F1
Back Nansen St. Leeds LS13 58 A2
Back Nelson St. Dew WF13 139 C8 14
Back New St. Brig HD6 115 A3 8
Back New York St. Leeds LS2 79 C7 4
Back Newport Gdns. Leeds LS6 59 D3 2
Back Newport Mount. Leeds LS6 59 D3 1
Back Newport Pl. Leeds LS6 59 D3 6
Back Newton Gr. Leeds LS7 60 E4
Back Newton La. Ledsh WF10 104 B5
Back Newton La. Ledst WF10 103 E7
Back Nice View. Leeds LS8 60 F4 17
Back Norman Mt. Leeds LS5 59 A4 1
Back Norman Pl. Leeds LS8 44 A2
Back Norman Terr. Leeds LS8 44 A2
Back North Park Av. Leeds LS8 60 F8
Back North St. Brad BD12 95 A4
Back Northbrook St. Leeds LS7 60 D7
Back Northgate. Pont WF8 125 D1
Back Norwood Gr. Leeds LS6 59 E3
Back Norwood Pl. Leeds LS6 59 E3
Back Norwood Rd. Leeds LS6 59 E3 2
Back Norwood Terr. Leeds LS6 59 E3
Back Nowell Cres. Leeds LS9 61 B1 5
Back Nowell Mount. Leeds LS9 61 B1 4
Back Nowell Pl. Leeds LS9 61 B1
Back Nowell Terr. Leeds LS9 61 B1
Back Nunington St. Leeds LS12 78 D8 2
Back Nunington View. Leeds LS12 59 C1 3
Back Nunroyd Rd. Leeds LS17 43 D1
Back Nursery Mt. Midd LS10 79 E1 2
Back o' Dam. Slai HD7 170 A8
Back o' Th' Height. Rip HX6 131 D1
Back O'Wall. Mars HD7 151 B3
Back Oak Ave. Bing BD16 36 F2
Back Oak Rd. Leeds LS7 60 D5
Back Oakfield Terr. Leeds LS6 59 E6
Back Oakley St. E Ard WF3 99 E1
Back Oakley Terr. Leeds LS11 79 C2
Back Oakwood Ave. Leeds LS8 61 B6
Back Oakwood Dr. Leeds LS8 61 B6
Back of the Mill. Harden BD16 36 A1
Back Osmondthorpe La. Leeds LS9 80 C8
Back Otterburn St. Keigh BD21 35 C8 2
Back Outwood La. Hors LS18 58 C7 5
Back Overdale Ter. Leeds LS15 81 A8 5
Back Oxford Pl. Leeds LS1 79 B8
Back Oxford St. E Ard WF3 120 E8
Back Oxford St. Keigh BD21 35 A6 7
Back Paget St. Keigh BD21 35 A7 8
Back P'rish Ghyll Rd. Ilkley LS29 8 B4
Back Park Cres. Leeds LS8 44 B2
Back Park Terr. Hali HX1 113 A6
Back Park View Ave. Leeds LS4 59 D3
Back Park View. Leeds LS11 79 A3 6
Back Parkfield Pl. Leeds LS11 79 A3 5
Back Parkfield Rd. Leeds LS11 79 A3
Back Parnaby Ave. Midd LS10 79 F1
Back Parnaby St. Midd LS10 79 F1
Back Parnaby Terr. Midd LS10 79 F1
Back Pasture Gr. Leeds LS7 60 D7
Back Pasture Rd. Leeds LS8 60 F4
Back Pawson St. E Ard WF3 120 E8
Back Pleasant St. Hali HX6 112 C4
Back Pollard La. Leeds LS13 58 C5
Back Pollard St. Hud HD2 136 B2
Back Poplar Ave. Leeds LS15 62 D2 1
Back Potternewton La. Leeds LS7 60 C6
Back Potters St. Leeds LS7 60 D6
Back Prospect Pl. Keigh BD21 35 B6
Back Prospect Terr. Leeds LS9 79 F7
Back Providence Ave. Leeds LS6 60 A4 11
Back Providence St. Batley WF17 118 C5 4
Back Purlwell Hall Rd. Batley WF17 118 C3
Back Purwell La. Batley WF17 118 C4
Back Quarry Mount Terr. Leeds LS6 60 A4 9
Back Queen St. Elland HX4 134 D6 2
Back Queen St. Hud HD1 154 B5 2
Back Ravens St. Dew WF13 139 A6
Back Ravenscar Ave. Leeds LS8 61 A6 5
Back Ravenscar Pl. Leeds LS8 61 A6 1
Back Raynville Mount. Leeds LS13 58 E3
Back Rd. Brad BD12 94 C4 19
Back Regent Park Terr. Leeds LS6 59 F4
Back Regent St. Wake WF1 142 E3
Back Regent Terr. Leeds LS6 59 F2
Back Reginald Mount. Leeds LS7 60 D4
Back Reginald Pl. Leeds LS7 60 D4
Back Reginald St. Leeds LS7 60 D4
Back Rhodes St. Hali HX1 113 B7
Back Ribble St. Keigh BD21 35 F8
Back Richardson St. Brad BD12 95 A4
Back Richmond Mount. Leeds LS6 59 E4
Back Ridge Mount Terr. Leeds LS6 60 A4
Back Ridge St. Tod OL14 108 B5
Back Ridge View. Leeds LS7 60 A5
Back Rigging La. Sow Br HX6 111 C3
Back Ripley St. Keigh BD20 18 F1
Back Ripon St. Hali HX1 112 E6
Back Ripon Terr. Hali HX3 92 B1
Back River St. Haw BD22 51 D7 5
Back Roberts St. Roth LS26 101 C6 3
Back Rochester Ter. Leeds LS6 59 D4
Back Rokeby Gdns. Leeds LS6 59 C5 1
Back Roman Gr. Leeds LS8 44 A2
Back Roman Pl. Leeds LS8 44 B2
Back Roman St. Leeds LS8 44 B2
Back Rose Ave. Hors LS18 58 B7
Back Rosebank Cres. Leeds LS3 59 F2
Back Rosemont Wlk. Leeds LS13 58 C2 5
Back Rossall Rd. Leeds LS8 61 A4 1
Back Rossington Rd. Leeds LS8 60 E4
Back Roundhay Ave. Leeds LS8 60 F5
Back Roundhay Cres. Leeds LS8 60 F5
Back Roundhay Gr. Leeds LS8 60 F5
Back Roundhay Pl. Leeds LS8 60 F5
Back Roundhay View. Leeds LS8 60 F5
Back Row. Leeds LS11 79 B6
Back Rowland Terr. Leeds LS11 79 C3 8
Back Rowsley St. Keigh BD21 35 D7 2
Back Rupert St. Keigh BD21 35 C8
Back Russell St. Brad BD5 74 D5
Back Ruthven View. Leeds LS8 61 A3
Back Rydal St. Keigh BD22 35 A6 5
Back Rylstone St. Keigh BD21 35 E8 1
Back Saint Ives Mount. Leeds LS12 78 A8
Back Salisbury Gr. Leeds LS12 78 C8 5
Back Salisbury Terr. Leeds LS12 78 C8
Back Salisbury View. Leeds LS12 78 C8
Back Saltaire Rd N. Ship BD17 55 B8
Back Sandhurst Gr. Leeds LS8 61 A3 8
Back Sandhurst Pl. Leeds LS8 61 A3 7
Back Sandhurst Rd. Leeds LS8 61 A3 6
Back Savile Par. Hali HX1 113 B5 6
Back Savile Pl. Leeds LS7 60 D3
Back Savile Rd. Leeds LS7 60 D3
Back School View. Leeds LS6 59 E3
Back Seaforth Ave. Leeds LS9 61 B2 3
Back Seaforth Pl. Leeds LS9 61 A3 20
Back Seaforth Terr. Leeds LS9 61 A3 22
Back Sefton Ave. Leeds LS11 79 A3
Back Sefton Terr. Leeds LS11 79 A3
Back Shaftesbury Ave. Leeds LS8 44 A2
Back Shaw La. Keigh BD21 35 D3
Back Sholebroke Av. Leeds LS7 60 D5
Back Sholebroke Mount. Leeds LS7 60 D4
Back Sholebroke Pl. Leeds LS7 60 D4
Back Sholebroke Row. Leeds LS7 60 D5
Back Sholebroke Terr. Leeds LS7 60 D5
Back Sholebroke View. Leeds LS7 60 D4
Back Sidlaw Terr. Leeds LS8 60 F4
Back Simpson St. Keigh BD21 35 A7 1
Back Sladen St. Keigh BD21 35 A7 5
Back Slaithwaite Rd. Dew WF12 139 C4
Back Smith Row. Brad BD5 74 C3 6
Back South End Gr. Leeds LS13 58 E1
Back South St. Hud HD1 153 D5
Back Southfield Sq. Brad BD8 55 C1
Back Spring St. Hud HD1 154 A6 4
Back Springfield Mount. Leeds LS12 78 A8 3
Back Springfield Pl. Brad BD8 55 D1
Back Springfield Rd. Elland HX5 135 A7
Back St Alban Cres. Leeds LS9 61 C1
Back St. Bramham LS23 30 C2
Back St Elmo Gr. Leeds LS9 80 A8 5

Back St Luke's Cres. Leeds LS11 .... 79 A4 4
Back St Mary's Rd. Leeds LS7 .. 60 D5
Back St Paul's Rd. Ship BD18 .. 55 A7
Back St. Pont WF8 .... 146 C8
Back Stanley St. Hud HD1 ...... 153 E3
Back Stanley St. Leeds LS9 .. 60 F2 11
Back Stanmore Pl. Leeds LS4 .. 59 C3
Back Stanmore St. Leeds LS4 .. 59 C3
Back Station Rd. Batley WF17 118 D4
Back Station Rd. Glu BD20 ...... 16 D7
Back Station Rd. Mir WF17 ...... 118 D4
Back Stone Hill Rd. Brad BD2 .. 56 B4
Back Storey Pl. Leeds LS14 .... 61 E1
Back Stratford Ave. Leeds LS11 79 A3
Back Stratford St. Leeds LS11 . 79 C3 11
Back Stratford Ter. Leeds LS11 79 B3
Back Strathmore Dr. Leeds LS9 61 A3 16
Back Sunnybank Av. Hors LS18 58 B7 5
Back Sunnydene. Leeds LS14 .. 61 F1
Back Sutton App. Leeds LS14 .. 61 E1
Back Sycamore Ave. Bing BD16 36 F2
Back Tamworth St. Brad BD4 .. 75 E6
Back Tempest Rd. Leeds LS14 .. 61 E1
Back Tempest Rd. Leeds LS11 . 79 A3 2
Back Tempest Rd. Leeds LS11 79 B3 15
Back Temple View. Leeds LS11 79 A3
Back Thornhill Rd. Hud HD3 .. 153 A6
Back Thornhill St. Pudsey LS28 57 B6
Back Tower Gr. Leeds LS12 .... 78 A8 1
Back Trafford Ave. Leeds LS9 . 61 B2 5
Back Trentham Pl. Leeds LS9 .. 79 B2 10
Back Trinity Terr. Brad BD5 .... 74 D5
Back Union St. Hud HD1 .... 154 A6
Back Unity St S. Bing BD16 .... 36 F2
Back Unity St S. Bing BD16 .... 36 F2
Back Unity St S. Bing BD16 .... 37 A2 6
Back Victor Terr. Leeds LS13 .. 113 A8
Back Victoria Ave. Leeds LS9 .. 80 B8 5
Back Victoria Gr. Leeds LS9 .... 80 B8 5
Back Victoria Rd. Hali HX1 .... 113 C7
Back Wakefield Rd. Leeds HX6 . 112 C4
Back Walmsley Rd. Leeds LS6 .. 59 E3
Back Walnut St. Leeds BD21 .... 35 B4 16
Back Webster St. Dew WF13 139 C6 3
Back Welburn Ave. Leeds LS16 59 B7
Back Wellfield Terr. Tod OL14 108 B4
Back Welton Ave. Leeds LS6 .... 59 E3 7
Back Welton Gr. Leeds LS6 ...... 59 E3
Back Welton Mount. Leeds LS6 59 E3 4
Back Welton Pl. Leeds LS6 ...... 59 E3
Back Wentworth St. Hud HD1 153 F7
Back Wesley Rd. Leeds LS12 ... 78 C7
Back Wesley St. Castle WF10 124 D8
Back West St. Sow Br HX6 ...... 112 B3
Back Westbourne Terr.
   Leeds LS2 .... 60 A2
Back Westbury St. Midd LS10 . 79 F1
Back Westfield Rd. Leeds LS3 .. 59 F1
Back Westlock Ave. Leeds LS6 . 61 A1
Back Westmoreland Mount.
   Leeds LS13 .... 58 D4 2
Back Weston Rd. Ilkley LS29 .. 8 B4
Back Westover Rd. Leeds LS13 58 D3
Back Wetherby Gr. Leeds LS4 . 59 C2 4
Back Wetherby Rd. Leeds LS8 . 61 B6
Back Wharf St. Hali HX6 .... 112 C4
Back Wheat St. Keigh BD22 .... 35 A4 7
Back Wickham St. Leeds LS11 . 79 B3
Back William Ave. Leeds LS15 . 80 E8 1
Back Wilton Gr. Leeds LS6 ...... 59 E6 3
Back Winston Gdns. Leeds LS6 59 C5 3
Back Winterburn St. Keigh
   BD21 .... 35 C8
Back Wolsley St. Hali HX1 .... 112 F7 4
Back Wood St. Brad BD8 .... 74 C8 3
Back Wood St. E Ard WF3 .... 120 D8
Back Woodbine Terr. Leeds LS659 E6
Back Woodland Park Rd. Leeds
   LS6 .... 59 E5 3
Back Woodstock St. Leeds LS6 59 E5
Back Wright Ave. Haw BD22 .. 34 D3
Back York Pl. Leeds LS1 .... 79 B7
Back York St. Leeds LS2 .... 79 D7 3
Backhold Ave. Hali HX3 ...... 113 E2
Backhold Dr. Hali HX3 .... 113 E2
Backhold La. Hali HX3 .... 113 D2
Backhold Rd. Hali HX3 .... 113 E2
Backhouse La. Wool WF4 ...... 177 F8
Backstone Gill La. Hare LS17 .. 27 E1
Backstone La. Ilkley LS29 ...... 8 D4
Backstone Way. Ilkley LS29 .... 8 D4
Bacon Ave. Nor WF6 .... 123 C3
Bacon St. Guise LS20 .... 39 F8
Bacup Rd. Tod OL14 .... 107 D4
Baddeley Gdns. Brad BD10 .... 39 A1
Baden Powell Cres. Pont WF8 146 D7
Baden St. Haw BD22 .... 51 C8
Baden Terr. Clec BD19 .... 116 D7 4
Badger Brow. Mel HD7 .... 170 D2
Badger Cl. Crig WF4 .... 159 F7
Badger Gate. Mel HD7 .... 170 D2
Badger Hill. Brig HD6 .... 135 E6
Badger La. B Head HX7 .... 88 B4
Badger La. Brig HX3 .... 114 B7
Badger Wood Glade. Weth
   LS22 .... 13 E7
Badgergate Ave. Wils BD15 ... 53 C4
Badgers Gate. Nes LS29 .... 3 E4
Badgers Mount. Leeds LS15 ... 62 F2
Badgers Way. Brad BD2 .... 55 E4
Badsworth CE (C) Fst Sch. Bad 164 E2
Badsworth Ct. Bad WF9 .... 164 E3
Badsworth Ct. Brad BD14 ...... 73 D5
Badsworth Mews. Bad WF9 .... 164 E2
Badsworth View. Upton WF9 . 183 A8
Bagden Cl. D Dale HD8 .... 192 D8
Bagden La. D Dale HD8 .... 192 E7
Baghill Ct. Pont WF8 .... 146 F8
Baghill Gn. E Ard WF3 .... 119 D6
Baghill La. Pont WF8 .... 146 F8
Baghill Rd. E Ard WF3 .... 119 D6
Baghill Sta. Pont 146 E8
Bagley La. Pudsey LS28 .... 57 E4
Bagnall Terr. Brad BD6 .... 74 B1 2
Bagshaw Mus. Batley 118 A8
Baildon Ave. Kippax LS25 ...... 83 B3
Baildon CE Fst Sch Annexe. Bail 38 D4

Baildon CE Fst Sch. Bail 38 D4
Baildon Chase. Leeds LS14 .... 62 C7
Baildon Cl. Leeds LS14 .... 62 C6
Baildon Dr. Leeds LS14 .... 62 C6
Baildon Gn. Leeds LS14 .... 62 C6
Baildon Golf Course. Bail 38 A6
Baildon Holmes. Bail BD17 .... 38 C1
Baildon Path. Leeds LS14 ...... 62 C6 1
Baildon Pl. Leeds LS14 .... 62 C6
Baildon Rd. Bail BD17 .... 38 D2
Baildon Wlk. Leeds LS14 .... 62 C7
Baildon Wood Ct. Bail BD17 .. 38 C2
Bailey Cres. S Elm WF9 .... 183 A4
Bailey Hall Bank. Hali HX3 .... 113 D7
Bailey Hills Rd. Bing BD16 .... 36 E4
Bailey St. Brad BD4 .... 74 F5
Bailey Towers. Leeds LS14 .... 62 A5 2
Bailey Wells Ave. Brad BD5 ... 74 C3
Bailey's Ct. Leeds LS14 .... 62 A5
Bailey's Hill. Leeds LS14 ...... 62 B5
Bailey's La. Leeds LS14 .... 62 A5
Bailey's Lawn. Leeds LS14 .... 62 A5
Bailiff Bridge Jun & Inf Sch.
   Brig 115 B7
Bainbridge Wharf. Farnh BD20 . 4 C1
Bainbrigge Rd. Leeds LS6 ...... 59 D4
Baines St. Hali HX1 .... 113 A8
Baines St. Roth LS26 .... 100 E5
Baird St. Brad BD5 .... 74 F3
Bairstow La. Hali HX6 .... 112 C6
Bairstow Mount. Hali HX6 .... 112 D5
Bairstow St. Brad BD15 .... 54 A3
Bairstow's Bldgs. Hali HX2 .... 91 F4
Baitings Gate Rd. Rip HX6 .... 131 C2
Baker Cres. Morley LS27 .... 98 A3
Baker Fold. Hali HX1 .... 113 A7
Baker La. Loft G WF3 .... 121 D5
Baker Rd. Morley LS27 .... 98 A3
Baker St. Brad BD2 .... 56 B2
Baker St. Morley LS27 .... 98 A3
Baker St N. Hali HX2 .... 92 A5
Baker St. Ship BD18 .... 55 B7
Baker's St. Heb Br HX7 .... 89 A4 12
Baker's Ter. Brad BD7 .... 74 A4
Balbec Ave. Leeds LS6 .... 59 E5
Balbec St. Leeds LS6 .... 59 E5
Balderstone H'll La. Mir WF14 138 C7
Baldovan Mount. Leeds LS8 ... 60 F4
Baldovan Terr. Leeds LS8 ...... 60 F4 11
Baldwin La. Brad BD13, BD14 . 73 A2
Baldwin La. Queen BD13, BD14 73 A2
Baldwin Terr. Hali HX3 .... 113 D7
Balfour St. Bing BD16 .... 36 F2
Balfour St. Brad BD4 .... 75 A4
Balfour St. Keigh BD21 .... 35 B6 6
Balk Ave. Loft G WF3 .... 122 A2
Balk Cres. Loft G WF3 .... 122 A2
Balk La. Brad BD7 .... 74 B4
Balk La. D Dale HD8 .... 191 C6
Balk La. Kirkhe HD5 .... 155 B7
Balk La. Loft G WF3 .... 122 A2
Balk La. S Elm WF9 .... 183 D4
Balk La. Wake WF2 .... 142 A1
Balk St. Batley WF17 .... 118 B5
Balk. The. Mapp S75 .... 178 C2
Balk. The. Walton WF2 .... 161 B6
Balkcliffe La. Midd LS10 .... 99 A6
Balkram Dr. Hali HX2 .... 91 A5
Balkram Edge. Hali HX2 .... 91 A5
Balkram Rd. Hali HX2 .... 91 B5
Balks. Liver WF15 .... 117 A5
Ball Royd Rd. Hud HD2 .... 136 B2
Ball St. Thorn BD13 .... 72 E6
Ballantyne Rd. Brad BD10 .... 39 A2
Ballater Ave. Hud HD4 .... 153 C2
Ballfield La. Kex S75 .... 177 C1
Ballroyd Clough. Hud HD3 .... 153 A6
Ballroyd Clough. Hud HD3 .... 153 A7
Ballroyd La. Hud HD3 .... 153 A5
Balm Pl. Leeds LS11 .... 79 A5
Balm Rd. Leeds LS10 .... 79 E2
Balm Wlk. Leeds LS11 .... 79 A5
Balme La. Brad BD12 .... 94 D3
Balme Rd. Clec BD19 .... 116 D8
Balme St. Brad BD1 .... 74 F7
Balme St. Brad BD12 .... 94 D3
Balmfield Cres. Liver WF15 ... 117 A1
Balmfield. Liver WF15 .... 117 A1
Balmoral Ave. Hud HD4 .... 153 C2
Balmoral Chase. Leeds LS10 . 79 F3
Balmoral Dr. Knot WF11 ...... 126 C4
Balmoral Pl. Hali HX1 .... 113 C6
Balmoral St. Heb Br HX7 ...... 89 A3 12
Balne Ave. Wake WF2 .... 142 A3
Balne La. Wake WF2 .... 142 A3
Bamborough St. Wake WF1 .. 142 F3
Bamburgh Cl. Leeds LS15 .... 62 E3
Bamburgh Rd. Leeds LS15 .... 62 E3
Bancroft Rd. Hud HD5 .... 154 E5
Bancroft St. Haw BD22 .... 51 F8
Bangor Gr. Leeds LS12 .... 78 A4 12
Bangor Pl. Leeds LS12 .... 78 A4
Bangor St. Leeds LS12 .... 78 A4
Bangor Terr. Leeds LS12 ...... 78 A4 11
Bank Ave. Hors LS18 .... 58 B8
Bank Ave. Morley LS27 .... 98 A5
Bank Bldgs. Heb Br HX7 ...... 89 F2
Bank Bldgs. Mel HD7 .... 170 E1
Bank Bottom. Hali HX3 .... 113 D7
Bank Bottom. Heb Br HX7 .... 90 A2
Bank Bottom. Mars HD7 ...... 169 C6
Bank Bottom Terr. Mars HD7 169 C6
Bank Cl. Brad BD10 .... 56 D6
Bank Cl. Hali HX3 .... 92 A1
Bank Crest Rise. Ship BD18 .. 54 C7
Bank Crest. Bail BD17 .... 38 C3
Bank Edge Gdns. Hali HX2 .... 91 E5
Bank Edge Rd. Hali HX2 ...... 91 E4

Bank End. Elland HX4 .... 133 D7
Bank End La. Clay W HD8 .... 176 A1
Bank End La. H Hoy HD8 ...... 176 A1
Bank End La. Hud HD5 .... 154 E4
Bank End Rd. Slai HD7 .... 152 C3
Bank End. Slai HD7 .... 152 C4
Bank Field Grange. Mark BD4 134 C7
Bank Foot. Kirkb HD4 .... 172 F8
Bank Foot Pl. Batley WF17 .... 118 C5
Bank Foot Rd. Kirkb HD4 ...... 172 F8
Bank Foot St. Batley WF17 .... 118 C5
Bank Gate. Slai HD7 .... 151 F1
Bank Gdns. Hors LS18 .... 58 B8
Bank Gr. Dew WF12 .... 140 A7
Bank Hall Gr. Shep HD8 ...... 190 F8
Bank Hey Bottom La. Rip HX6 132 E3
Bank House Cl. Morley LS27 .. 98 A5
Bank House La. Hali HX2 ...... 90 E4
Bank La. D Dale HD8 .... 191 F4
Bank La. Holmfi HD7 .... 188 C2
Bank La. Holmfi HD7 .... 188 D4
Bank La. Holmfi HD7 .... 189 B7
Bank Nook. Mars HD7 .... 169 C7
Bank Par. Otley LS21 .... 22 F7
Bank Rd. Glu BD20 .... 16 D7
Bank Royd La. Rip HX4 ...... 133 B1
Bank Side. Shep HD8 .... 173 F2
Bank Side St. Leeds LS8 ...... 60 F2
Bank Sq. Morley LS27 .... 98 A5
Bank St. Brad BD1 .... 74 C1
Bank St. Brad BD1 .... 74 E7
Bank St. Castle WF10 .... 124 D8
Bank St. Clec BD19 .... 116 C7
Bank St. Dew WF12 .... 139 D8
Bank St. Hem WF9 .... 181 D7
Bank St. Holmfi HD7 .... 189 E4
Bank St. Hor WF4 .... 141 A1
Bank St. Keigh BD21 .... 35 C7 5
Bank St. Liver WF15 .... 117 B4
Bank St. Mir WF14 .... 138 A4
Bank St. Morley LS27 .... 98 A5
Bank St. Ossett WF5 .... 140 D5
Bank St. Ship BD18 .... 55 B7
Bank St. Tod OL14 .... 108 B4
Bank St. Wake WF1 .... 142 C6
Bank St. Weth LS22 .... 13 E5
Bank Terr. Heb Br HX7 .... 88 E4
Bank Terr. Morley LS27 .... 98 B5
Bank Top. Hali HX3 .... 113 F5
Bank Top. Hali HX3 .... 113 F5
Bank Top. La. Heb Br HX7 .... 109 F5
Bank Top Rd. Holmfi HD7 .... 188 A6
Bank Top Way. Keigh BD21 .. 35 A6
Bank View. Bail BD17 .... 38 B2
Bank View. Dew WF12 .... 140 A8
Bank View. Honley HD7 .... 172 C2
Bank View. Sow Br HX2 ...... 111 D6
Bank View. Sow Br HX6 ...... 112 A5
Bank View Terr. Leeds LS7 .... 60 B7
Bank Wlk. Bail BD17 .... 38 C4
Bank Wood Rd. Dar WF8 .... 147 F4
Banker St. Leeds LS4 .... 59 D2
Bankfield Ave. Kirkhe HD5 .... 155 B8
Bankfield Ave. Ship BD18 .... 54 D7
Bankfield. Bard LS17 .... 28 D4
Bankfield Cl. Ossett WF5 .... 140 F4
Bankfield Ct. Hud HD5 .... 154 D5
Bankfield Dr. Mir WF14 .... 137 F5
Bankfield Gdns. Leeds LS4 .. 59 C2
Bankfield Gdns. Hali HX3 .... 113 E5
Bankfield. Leeds LS4 .... 59 C2 1
Bankfield. Ship BD18 .... 54 D7
Bankfield St. Keigh BD22 .... 34 E8
Bankfield Terr. Bail BD17 .... 38 D2
Bankfield Terr. Hud HD4 ...... 171 E8
Bankfield Terr. Leeds LS4 .... 59 C2
Bankfield View. Hali HX3 .... 92 B1
Bankfield Wlk. Keigh BD22 .. 34 E7
Bankfields Rd. Leeds LS4 .... 59 C2
Bankfoot St. Heb Br HX7 .... 88 F3
Bankholme Ct. Brad BD4 .... 95 F7
Bankhouse La. Hali HX3 ...... 113 D2
Bankhouse La. Pudsey LS28 . 76 D5
Bankhouse. Pudsey LS28 .... 76 D5
Bankhouse Rd. Hud HD3 .... 153 B5
Banklands Ave. Sil BD20 ...... 5 F1
Banklands. Sil BD20 .... 5 F2
Banks App. Hud HD7 .... 152 D5
Banks Ave. Ack M T WF7 .... 163 E5
Banks Ave. Hud HD7 .... 152 D5
Banks Cres. Hud HD7 .... 146 C8
Banks Dr. Hud HD7 .... 152 D5
Banks End Rd. Elland HX5 ... 135 C6
Banks Garth. Knot WF11 .... 126 F4
Banks Gr. Hud HD7 .... 152 D5
Banks La. Knot WF11 .... 126 F4
Banks Mount. Hud HD7 ...... 146 C8 14
Banks Rd. Honley HD7 .... 172 B3
Banks Rd. Hud HD7 .... 152 D5
Banks Side. Hud HD7 .... 170 B8
Banks St. Batley WF17 .... 118 C4
Banksfield Cl. Yeadon LS19 . 40 B8
Banksfield Cres. Yeadon LS19 . 40 B8

Banksfield Gr. Yeadon LS19 .. 40 B8
Banksfield Mount. Yeadon LS19 40 B8
Banksfield Rd. Heb Br HX7 .. 89 E1 8
Banksfield Rise. Yeadon LS19 . 40 B8
Banksfield Terr. Heb Br HX7 . 89 E1
Bankside Terr. Bail BD17 ...... 38 B2
Bankside. Tod OL14 .... 108 A4
Banksville. Holmfi HD7 .... 189 B7
Bankwell Fold. Brad BD6 ...... 74 D1
Bankwell Rd. Hud HD3 .... 153 B4
Bankwood. Batley WF17 ...... 97 B3
Bankwood Way. Batley WF17 . 97 B3
Banner St. Brad BD3 .... 75 A6
Bannerman St. Brad BD12 .... 95 A5
Bannister La. Ham DN6 .... 184 C5
Bannockburn Way. Nor WF6 122 E4
Banstead St E. Leeds LS8 .... 60 F3 9
Banstead St W. Leeds LS8 .... 60 F3 11
Banstead Terr E. Leeds LS8 .. 60 F3 13
Banstead Terr W. Leeds LS8 . 60 F3 13
Bantam Cl. Morley LS27 ...... 98 D4
Bantam Grove La. Morley LS27 98 D4
Bantree Ct. Brad BD10 .... 39 A2
Baptist La. Ossett WF5 .... 141 B4
Baptist Pl. Brad BD1 .... 74 D7
Baptist St. Batley WF17 ...... 118 A3
Bar Croft. Kirkhe HD5 .... 137 B1
Bar House La. Keigh BD20 .... 17 F3
Bar La. Bramham S23 .... 31 A6
Bar La. Gar LS25 .... 83 A7
Bar La. Hors LS18 .... 57 F8
Bar La. Keigh BD20 .... 18 F1
Bar La. Loft G WF1 .... 121 D1
Bar La. Neth WF4 .... 158 B2
Bar La. W Bret WF4 .... 158 B2
Bar Mount. Gar LS25 .... 83 A7
Bar St. Batley WF17 .... 118 D4
Bar St. Tod OL14 .... 108 A4
Barber Row. Slai HD7 .... 152 D1
Barber Sq. Liver WF16 .... 117 C4
Barber Wlk. Dew WF13 .... 139 C8 7
Barberry Ave. Brad BD3 ...... 75 E8
Barclay Cl. Cull BD13 .... 52 E6
Barclay St. Leeds LS7 .... 60 D1
Barcroft Gr. Yeadon LS19 .... 40 A6
Barcroft. Haw BD22 .... 51 F8
Barden Ave. Brad BD6 .... 93 D8
Barden Cl. Batley WF17 ...... 118 B5
Barden Cl. Leeds LS12 .... 78 A7
Barden Dr. Bing BD16 .... 37 C4
Barden Mount. Leeds LS12 .. 78 A7
Barden Pl. Leeds LS12 .... 78 A7
Barden Rd. Brad BD8 .... 55 B1
Barden Terr. Leeds LS12 ...... 78 A7
Bardon Bones Rd. Dun Br HD7 . 199 B5
Bare Head La. Northo HX3 .... 92 D5
Barewell Hill. Bri S72 .... 181 A4
Barfield Ave. Yeadon LS19 .... 40 A6
Barfield Cres. Leeds LS17 .... 43 F5
Barfield Dr. Yeadon LS19 .... 40 A6
Barfield Gr. Leeds LS17 ...... 44 A5
Barfield Mount. Leeds LS17 .. 44 A5
Barfield Rd. Brig HX3 .... 114 C7
Bargate. Slai HD7 .... 152 D1
Barge St. Hud HD1 .... 153 F4
Barge St. Hud HD1 .... 153 F4
Bargrange Ave. Ship BD18 .. 55 B6
Bargreen. Kirkhe HD5 .... 137 B1
Barham Terr. Brad BD10 ...... 56 D4
Baring Ave. Brad BD3 .... 75 D8
Baring Sq. S in Cra BD20 .... 20 A2
Bark Cl. Shep HD8 .... 174 A3
Bark House La. Caw S75 ...... 193 C4
Bark View Terr. Leeds LS7 .... 60 B7
Bark. La. Add LS29 .... 7 A8
Barker Cl. Hali HX3 .... 113 E3
Barker Ct. Hud HD2 .... 135 E1
Barker House. Hali HX3 ...... 113 E3 4
Barker Pl. Leeds LS13 .... 58 D2
Barker St. Liver WF15 .... 117 B4
Barker's Rd. Crig WF4 .... 159 E6
Barkerend Fst Sch. Brad 75 A8
Barkerend Rd. Brad BD1, BD3 . 75 B8
Barkisland Jun & Inf Sch. Rip 133 A5
Barkly Ave. Leeds LS11 .... 79 A1
Barkly Dr. Leeds LS11 .... 79 A1
Barkly Gr. Leeds LS11 .... 79 A2
Barkly Par. Leeds LS11 .... 79 A1 2
Barkly Pl. Leeds LS11 .... 79 A1 1
Barkly Rd. Leeds LS11 .... 79 A1
Barkly St. Leeds LS11 .... 79 A1
Barkly Terr. Leeds LS11 .... 79 A2 8
Barkston Wlk. Brad BD15 .... 73 A7
Barlboro' Pl. Hud HD4 .... 153 A4
Barlby Way. Leeds LS8 .... 61 C6
Barley Cote Ave. Keigh BD20 . 19 A2
Barley Cote Gr. Keigh BD20 .. 19 A2
Barley Cote Rd. Keigh BD20 . 19 A2
Barley Croft. Dew WF13 ...... 138 F8
Barley Field Ct. Leeds LS15 .. 81 A8 3
Barley Mews. Roth WF3 ...... 100 B3
Barley St. Keigh BD22 .... 35 A4
Barleycorn Cl. Wake WF1 .... 121 E1
Barleyfield Cl. Wake WF1 .... 142 E8
Barleyfields Cl. Weth LS22 .. 13 E6
Barleyfields Ct. Weth LS22 .. 13 E6
Barleyfields Rd. Weth LS22 .. 13 E6
Barleyfields Terr. Weth LS22 . 13 E6
Barleyfields Wlk. Weth LS22 . 13 E6
Barlow St. Brad BD3 .... 75 D7

Barmouth Terr. Brad BD3 .... 55 F2
Barn Cl. Men LS29 .... 21 F4
Barn St. Oxen BD22 .... 51 C2
Barnaby Rd. Bing BD16 ...... 37 C4
Barnard Cl. Leeds LS15 ...... 62 E3
Barnard Rd. Brad BD4 .... 75 A5
Barnard Way. Leeds LS15 .... 62 E3
Barnbow La. B in Elm LS15 .. 63 B5
Barnbow La. Leeds LS15 ...... 63 B5
Barnbrough St. Leeds LS4 ... 59 C2
Barnby Royd. Hud HD5 ...... 154 E7
Barncliffe Hill. Shep HD8 .... 174 C1
Barncroft Cl. Leeds LS14 .... 61 F7
Barncroft Ct. Leeds LS14 .... 61 F7
Barncroft Dr. Leeds LS14 .... 61 F7
Barncroft Gdns. Leeds LS14 . 61 E6
Barncroft Grange. Leeds LS14 61 E6
Barncroft Hts. Leeds LS14 .... 61 E7
Barncroft Mount. Leeds LS14 61 E6
Barncroft Rd. Leeds LS14 .... 61 F7
Barncroft Rise. Leeds LS14 .. 61 F7
Barncroft Towers. Leeds LS14 61 E6
Barnes Ave. Wake WF1 ...... 121 A3
Barnes Meadows. Litt OL15 . 129 C1
Barnes Rd. Brad BD8 .... 73 F7
Barnes St. Castle WF10 ...... 124 D6
Barnes St. Tod OL14 .... 108 A1 6
Barnet Gr. Morley LS27 ...... 98 A2 2
Barnet Rd. Leeds LS12 .... 78 D7
Barnsdale Est. Castle WF10 124 D6
Barnsdale Rd. M'town WF10 . 124 C6
Barnside La. Holmfi HD7 ...... 189 F1
Barnside. La. Holmfi HD7 .... 189 F1
Barnsley Beck Gr. Bail BD17 . 38 D3
Barnsley Rd. Ack M T WF7 .. 164 A6
Barnsley Rd. Bri S72 .... 180 E3
Barnsley Rd. Clay W HD8 .... 175 E1
Barnsley Rd.
   Wake WF1, WF2, WF4 ...... 160 C5
Barnsley Rd. Wool WF4 ...... 160 C5
Barnstone Vale. Wake WF1 .. 121 C2
Barnswick Cl. Pont WF8 ...... 146 D6
Barnswick View. Hors LS16 .. 41 E4
Baron Cl. Leeds LS11 .... 79 A4
Baroncourt. Leeds LS15 ...... 81 D8
Baronsmead. Leeds LS15 .... 81 D8
Baronsway. Leeds LS15 ...... 81 C8
Barr St. Hud HD1 .... 154 C8
Barrack St. Leeds LS7 .... 60 D3
Barrack St. Leeds LS7 .... 60 D3
Barracks Fold. Holmfi HD7 .. 189 E2
Barracks St. Liver WF16 ...... 117 A8
Barraclough Bldgs. Brad BD10 56 E7
Barraclough Sq. Brad BD12 .. 94 C4 18
Barraclough St. Brad BD12 .. 94 B6 5
Barran Ct. Leeds LS8 .... 60 F3
Barran St. Bing BD16 .... 37 A3 8
Barras Garth Pl. Leeds LS12 . 78 B6
Barras Garth Rd. Leeds LS12 . 78 B6
Barras Pl. Leeds LS12 .... 78 B6
Barras St. Leeds LS12 .... 78 B6
Barras Terr. Leeds LS12 ...... 78 B6
Barratt's Rd. Wake WF1 ...... 142 C8
Barrett St. Sil BD20 .... 5 D1
Barrington Cl. Hali HX3 ...... 114 A4
Barrington Par. Clec BD19 .. 117 A8
Barrowby Ave. Leeds LS15 .. 81 E7
Barrowby Cr. Men LS29 ...... 22 B4
Barrowby Cres. Leeds LS15 . 81 E8
Barrowby Dr. Leeds LS15 .... 81 F7
Barrowby La. Gar LS25 ...... 82 E8
Barrowby La. Leeds LS15, LS25 . 82 A8
Barrowby La. Swil LS15, LS25 . 82 A8
Barrowby Rd. Leeds LS15 .... 81 E7
Barrowclough La. Hali HX3 . 113 F7
Barrows La. Stee BD20 ...... 17 C4
Barrowstead. Skel HD8 ...... 175 B1
Barry St. Brad BD1 .... 74 F7
Barsey Green La. Rip HX4 .. 133 C6
Barstow Sq. Wake WF1 ...... 142 C6 2
Barthorpe Ave. Leeds LS17 .. 60 B8
Barthorpe Cl. Brad BD4 ...... 75 F2
Barthorpe Cres. Leeds LS17 . 43 B8
Bartle Cl. Brad BD7 .... 73 F3
Bartle Fold. Brad BD7 .... 73 F3
Bartle Gill Dr. Bail BD17 .... 38 E4
Bartle Gill Rise. Bail BD17 .. 38 E4
Bartle Gill View. Bail BD17 .. 38 E4
Bartle Gr. Brad BD7 .... 73 F3
Bartle La. Brad BD7 .... 73 F3
Bartle Pl. Brad BD7 .... 73 F3
Bartle Sq. Brad BD7 .... 74 A4
Barton Ct. Leeds LS15 .... 81 D7
Barton Ct. Leeds LS15 .... 81 D7
Barton Gr. Leeds LS11 .... 79 A4
Barton Hill. Leeds LS11 ...... 79 A4
Barton Manor Cl. Hud HD4 .. 154 A4
Barton Pl. Leeds LS11 .... 79 A4
Barton Rd. Leeds LS11 ...... 79 A4
Barton St. Brad BD5 .... 74 B3
Barton Terr. Leeds LS11 ...... 79 A4
Barton View. Leeds LS11 .... 79 A4
Barton Way. S Elm WF9 .... 183 A5
Barum Top. Hali HX1 .... 113 C7 12
Barwick Gn. Brad BD6 .... 73 E1
Barwick in Elmet CE Jun & Inf Sch.
   B in Elm 63 E7
Barwick Rd. B in Elm LS15, LS25 63 E7
Barwick Rd. Leeds LS15 ...... 62 D4
Barwick Rd. Leeds LS14, LS15 . 62 D4
Basford St. Wake WF2 ...... 142 A5
Basil St. Brad BD5 .... 74 B3
Basil St. Hud HD4 .... 153 D4
Basildon Rd. Dearne S63 .. 194 C1
Baslow Gr. Brad BD9 .... 54 F2
Bassenthwaite Wlk.
   Knot WF11 .... 126 E2

Batcliffe Dr. Leeds LS6 .... 59 C6
Batcliffe Mount. Leeds LS6 .. 59 C6
Bateman Cl. Shaf S72 .... 180 B2
Bateman St. Brad BD8 .... 55 B1
Bates Ave. Sow Br HX6 ...... 111 F3
Bath Cl. Leeds LS13 .... 58 C2
Bath Gr. Leeds LS13 .... 58 C2 14
Bath La. Leeds LS13 .... 58 C2
Bath Pl. Clec BD19 .... 116 D7
Bath Pl. Hali HX3 .... 92 B1
Bath Rd. Clec BD19 .... 116 D7
Bath Rd. Leeds WF16 .... 117 D4
Bath Rd. Hali HX3 .... 113 C4
Bath Rd. Leeds LS13 .... 58 C2
Bath St. Bacup OL13 .... 106 A2 1
Bath St. Batley WF17 .... 118 D5
Bath St. Brad BD3 .... 75 A7
Bath St. Dew WF13 .... 118 C1
Bath St. Elland HX5 .... 134 F6
Bath St. Hali HX1 .... 113 D6 3
Bath St. Hud HD1 .... 153 F3
Bath St. Hud HD1 .... 154 A7
Bath St. Ilkley LS29 .... 8 C5
Bath St. Keigh BD21 .... 35 B7
Bath St. Tod OL14 .... 108 B5 3
Batley Ave. Hud HD1 .... 153 D6
Batley Bsns Ctr. Batley 118 B6
Batley Enterprise Ctr. Batley . 118 B6
Batley Field Hill. Batley WF17 118 C6
Batley Gram Sch. Batley 118 B7
Batley High Sch. Batley 118 B7
Batley Manorfield Inf Sch.
   Batley 118 A4
Batley Parish CE Aided Sch.
   Batley 118 C5
Batley Rd. Batley WF16 ...... 117 F4
Batley Rd. E Ard FW3 .... 119 E5
Batley Rd. Wake WF2 .... 120 B2
Batley St. Hali HX3 .... 92 A1 28
Batley St. Hud HD5 .... 154 D6 7
Batley Sta. Batley 118 C5
Batter La. Yeadon LS19 ...... 40 C4
Battinson Rd. Hali HX1 ...... 112 F8
Battinson St. Hali HX3 ...... 113 E5
Battye Ave. Hud HD4 .... 153 B3
Battye St. Dew WF13 .... 75 D6
Battye Street Inf Sch. Batley . 117 D4
Battyeford CE (C) Jun & Inf Sch.
   Mir 137 E6
Baulk Head La. Tod OL14 .... 108 F6
Bavaria Pl. Brad BD8 .... 55 B1
Bawn App. Leeds LS12 ...... 77 F5
Bawn Ave. Leeds LS12 ...... 77 F6
Bawn Dr. Leeds LS12 .... 77 F6
Bawn Gdns. Leeds LS12 .... 77 F6
Bawn Path. Leeds LS12 ...... 77 F6
Bawn Vale. Leeds LS12 ...... 77 F6
Bawn Wlk. Leeds LS12 ...... 77 F6
Bawson Ct. Clec BD19 ...... 96 A1
Baxandall St. Brad BD5 ...... 74 E3
Baxter La. Northo HX3 ...... 93 A3
Baxter Wood. Glu BD20 ...... 16 C7
Bay Cl. Hud HD3 .... 153 C7
Bay Hall Com'n Rd. Hud HD1 . 154 A8
Bay Horse La. Scar LS14 .... 45 A6
Bay Horse La. Thorner LS17 . 45 A6
Bay of Biscay. Brad BD9 .... 54 B4
Bayford Cl. Holmfi HD7 ...... 199 B8
Bayldons Pl. Batley WF17 .. 118 C5 9
Baylee St. Hem WF9 .... 181 E6
Bayswater Cres. Leeds LS8 .. 60 F3
Bayswater Gr. Brad BD2 .... 56 D2
Bayswater Gr. Leeds LS8 .... 60 F3
Bayswater Mount. Leeds LS8 . 60 F3
Bayswater Pl. Leeds LS8 .... 60 F2
Bayswater Rd. Leeds LS8 .. 60 F3
Bayswater Row. Leeds LS8 .. 60 F3
Bayswater Terr. Hali HX3 .... 113 C3
Bayswater Terr. Leeds LS8 .. 60 F3
Bayton La. Yeadon LS19 .... 40 E5
Beacon Ave. Morley LS27 .. 98 C2
Beacon Brow. Brad BD6 .... 73 D2
Beacon Cl. Bing BD16 ...... 37 B3
Beacon Gr. Brad BD6 .... 73 F1
Beacon Gr. Morley LS27 .... 98 C2
Beacon Hill. Upton WF9 .... 183 A8
Beacon Pl. Brad BD6 .... 73 E1
Beacon Rd. Brad BD6 .... 73 E2
Beacon Rise. Ilkley LS29 .... 7 E4
Beacon St. Add LS29 .... 7 A8
Beacon St. Brad BD7 .... 73 E2 1
Beacon St. Dew WF13 ...... 138 E6
Beacon View. S Kirk WF9 .. 182 C3
Beaconsfield Ct. Gar LS25 .. 82 F8
Beaconsfield Rd. Brad BD14 . 73 D4
Beaconsfield St. Hali HX3 .. 113 E6
Beaconsfield St. Tod OL14 .. 108 B5
Beaden Dr. Lepton HD8 ...... 155 E3
Beadon Ave. Hud HD5 ...... 155 B5
Beagle Ave. Hud HD4 .... 153 C1
Beal La. Beal DN14 .... 127 F2
Beamshaw. S Kirk WF9 .... 182 B1
Beamsley Gr. Bing BD16 .... 37 B3
Beamsley Gr. Leeds LS6 .... 59 E2 3
Beamsley House. Ship BD18 . 55 B5
Beamsley La. Beam BD23 .... 2 F6
Beamsley Mount. Leeds LS6 . 59 E2
Beamsley Pl. Leeds LS6 ...... 59 E2 2
Beamsley Rd. Brad BD9 ...... 55 B2
Beamsley Rd. Ship BD18 .... 55 B5
Beamsley Terr. Leeds LS6 .. 59 E2
Beamsley View. Ilkley LS29 . 7 E4
Beamsley Wlk. Brad BD9 .... 55 A2
Bean St. Elland HX5 .... 135 C6
Beancroft Rd. Castle WF10 . 124 C6
Beancroft St. Castle WF10 . 124 C6
Beanlands Dr. Glu BD20 .... 16 C6
Beanlands Par. Ilkley LS29 .. 8 C5
Beanlands Pl. Glu BD20 .... 16 C6
Bearing Ave. Leeds LS11 .... 79 C2
Beast Fair. Pont WF8 .... 146 C8

Beast Fair Service Rd.
Pont WF8 ... 146 C8 3
Beast Market. Hud HD1 ... 154 B6 4
Beatrice St. Clec BD19 ... 116 D8 1
Beatrice St. Keigh BD20 ... 18 C1
Beatrice St. Oxen BD22 ... 51 C2 5
Beaufort Gr. Brad BD2 ... 56 A3
Beaufort Rd. Bacup OL13 ... 106 A7
Beaumont Ave. Hud HD5 ... 154 D5
Beaumont Ave. Leeds LS8 ... 44 A2
Beaumont Ave. S Elm WF9 ... 182 F3
Beaumont Cl. Loft G WF3 ... 121 F5
Beaumont Dr. W Bret WF4 ... 176 F6
Beaumont Park Rd. Hud HD4 153 D2
Beaumont Pl. Batley WF17 ... 117 F3
Beaumont Rd. Brad BD8 ... 55 B1
Beaumont Sq. Pudsey LS28 ... 76 D6 5
Beaumont St. Batley WF17 ... 118 C3
Beaumont St. Emley HD8 ... 175 C7
Beaumont St. Hud HD3 ... 152 F5
Beaumont St. Hud HD1 ... 154 B7
Beaumont St. Hud HD5 ... 154 D5 14
Beaumont St. Hud HD4 ... 171 D7
Beaumont St. Loft G WF3 ... 121 F5
Beaumont St. Tod OL14 ... 108 A6
Beauvais Dr. Keigh BD20 ... 36 B8
Beaver Dr. Dew WF13 ... 138 F7
Beaver Terr. Bacup OL13 ... 106 A3 10
Becca La. Aber LS25 ... 64 E7
Beck Bottom. Pudsey LS28 ... 56 E6
Beck Bottom. Wake WF2 ... 120 C3
Beck Hill. Brad BD6 ... 93 E7
Beck La. Bing BD16 ... 37 A4
Beck La. Coll LS22 ... 13 B1
Beck La. Liver FW16 ... 117 C3
Beck Meadow. B in Elm LS15 ... 63 E6
Beck Rd. Bing BD16 ... 36 E8
Beck Rd. Hud HD1 ... 154 A8
Beck Rd. Leeds LS8 ... 60 F4
Beck Rise. Hem WF9 ... 181 D7
Beck Side Cl. Con BD20 ... 4 A2
Beck Side. Keigh BD21 ... 35 C6 3
Beck St. Keigh BD21 ... 35 C6
Beck View. Notton WF4 ... 179 A6
Beckbridge Cl. Nor WF6 ... 123 C3
Beckbridge Gn. Nor WF6 ... 123 C3
Beckbridge La. Nor WF6 ... 123 C2
Beckbridge Rd. Nor WF6 ... 123 C3
Beckbridge Way. Nor WF6 ... 123 C2
Beckbury Cl. Pudsey LS28 ... 57 D2 1
Beckbury St. Pudsey LS28 ... 57 D2 2
Beckenham Pl. Hali HX1 ... 112 E8
Beckett Cl. Hor WF4 ... 141 C2
Beckett Cres. Dew WF13 ... 138 F8
Beckett Ct. Leeds LS15 ... 81 D6
Beckett Gr. Dew WF13 ... 138 F7
Beckett La. Dew WF13 ... 138 F7
Beckett Pk Cty Prim Sch. Leeds 59 B5
Beckett Pk. Leeds ... 59 B6
Beckett Rd. Dew WF13 ... 118 B2
Beckett Sq. Kirkb HD8 ... 173 F6
Beckett St. Batley WF17 ... 118 D3
Beckett St. Leeds LS9 ... 60 F1
Beckett Terr. Leeds LS9 ... 60 F1
Beckett Wlk. Dew WF13 ... 138 F7
Beckett's Park Cres. Leeds LS6 59 C5
Beckett's Park Dr. Leeds LS6 .. 59 C6
Beckett's Park Rd. Leeds LS6 .. 59 D5
Becketts Cl. Hep HX7 ... 88 F4
Beckfield Rd. Ship BD16 ... 54 A7
Beckfoot Grammar Sch. Bing .. 37 A1
Beckfoot La. Harden BD16 ... 36 F1
Beckfoot Mill. Harden BD16 ... 36 E1
Beckhill App. Leeds LS7 ... 60 A6
Beckhill Ave. Leeds LS7 ... 60 A6
Beckhill Chase. Leeds LS7 ... 60 A6
Beckhill Cl. Leeds LS7 ... 60 A6
Beckhill Dr. Leeds LS7 ... 60 A7
Beckhill Fold. Leeds LS7 ... 60 A7
Beckhill Garth. Leeds LS7 ... 60 A6
Beckhill Gate. Leeds LS7 ... 60 A6
Beckhill Gdns. Leeds LS7 ... 60 A6
Beckhill Gn. Leeds LS7 ... 60 B6
Beckhill Gr. Leeds LS7 ... 60 A6
Beckhill Lawn. Leeds LS7 ... 60 A6
Beckhill Pl. Leeds LS7 ... 60 A7
Beckhill Row. Leeds LS7 ... 60 A7
Beckhill View. Leeds LS7 ... 60 A6
Beckhill Wlk. Leeds LS7 ... 60 A7
Beckley Rd. Wake WF2 ... 142 A6
Becks Ct. Dew WF12 ... 139 F6
Becks Rd. Keigh BD21 ... 35 A6
Beckside Cl. Bur in W LS29 ... 9 E1
Beckside Cl. Sil LS29 ... 6 F8
Beckside Gdns. Hud HD5 ... 155 C4
Beckside La. Brad BD7 ... 74 A4
Beckside Rd. Brad BD7 ... 74 A5
Beckwith Dr. Brad BD10 ... 56 D5
Bedale Ave. Brig HD6 ... 135 E8
Bedale Ave. Skel HD8 ... 174 F1
Bedale Dr. Brad BD6 ... 73 F1
Bedale Dr. Skel HD8 ... 174 F1
Bedale. E Ard WF3 ... 119 D8
Bedale Wlk. Shaf S72 ... 180 C3
Bedding Edge Rd. Holmfi HD7 200 A7
Bede Ct. Wake WF1 ... 142 C8
Bede House. Wake WF1 ... 142 C8
Bede's Cl. Thorn BD13 ... 72 D6
Bedford Ave. Floc WF4 ... 156 E5
Bedford Cl. Crof WF4 ... 162 A8
Bedford Cl. Feath WF7 ... 145 D4
Bedford Cl. Hors LS16 ... 41 E3
Bedford Cl. Lepton HD8 ... 155 E3
Bedford Ct. Feath WF7 ... 145 D4
Bedford Ct. Leeds LS8 ... 61 C6
Bedford Dr. Hors LS16 ... 41 E3
Bedford Garth. Hors LS16 ... 41 E3
Bedford Gdns. Hors LS16 ... 41 E3
Bedford Gn. Hors LS16 ... 41 E3
Bedford Gr. Hors LS16 ... 41 E2
Bedford Mount. Hors LS16 ... 41 E2
Bedford Row. Leeds LS10 ... 79 D4
Bedford St. Brad BD4 ... 74 F6
Bedford St. Clec BD19 ... 116 C7
Bedford St. Elland HX5 ... 134 F6 7
Bedford St. Hali HX1 ... 113 B7
Bedford St. Keigh BD21 ... 35 B7
Bedford St. Leeds LS1 ... 79 B8
Bedford St N. Hali HX1 ... 113 B7
Bedford View. Hors LS16 ... 41 E3
Bedivere Rd. Brad BD8 ... 73 D7
Bedlam La. Arth LS21 ... 25 F4
Beech Ave. Crof WF4 ... 162 B7
Beech Ave. Denh BD13 ... 52 C3
Beech Ave. Hali HX6 ... 112 B5
Beech Ave. Holmfi HD7 ... 172 C1
Beech Ave. Hors LS18 ... 58 C7
Beech Ave. Hud HD7 ... 152 E5
Beech Ave. Hud HD5 ... 154 F5
Beech Ave. Leeds LS12 ... 78 C8
Beech Ave. Loft G WF3 ... 121 F4
Beech Ave. Tod OL14 ... 108 B6
Beech Ave. Wake WF2 ... 141 F7
Beech Cl. Bacup OL13 ... 106 A3
Beech Cl. Brad BD10 ... 39 B2
Beech Cl. Bri S72 ... 181 A3
Beech Cl. Leeds LS9 ... 61 D3
Beech Cl. Men LS29 ... 22 A6
Beech Cl. S Kirk WF9 ... 182 B2
Beech Cl. Shelf HX3 ... 93 D6
Beech Cres. Bail BD17 ... 37 F1
Beech Cres. Brad BD3 ... 56 B1
Beech Cres. Castle WF10 ... 125 D5
Beech Cres. Dar WF8 ... 147 C5
Beech Cres. Leeds LS9 ... 61 D3
Beech Croft. Walton WF2 ... 161 A7
Beech Ct. Bail BD17 ... 38 B1
Beech Ct. Castle WF10 ... 124 E6
Beech Ct. Ossett WF5 ... 140 C6
Beech Dr. Ack M T WF7 ... 146 A1
Beech Dr. Denh BD13 ... 52 C3
Beech Dr. Leeds LS12 ... 78 C8
Beech Gdns. Castle WF10 ... 125 D6
Beech Gr. B Sal LS25 ... 105 E3
Beech Gr. Bing BD16 ... 37 C5
Beech Gr. Brad BD3 ... 56 B1
Beech Gr. Brad BD14 ... 73 C4 2
Beech Gr. Brig HX3 ... 115 A7
Beech Gr. Clec BD19 ... 96 A1
Beech Gr. Feath WF7 ... 145 E4
Beech Gr. Hem WF9 ... 163 A2
Beech Gr. Liver WF16 ... 117 C5
Beech Gr. Morley LS27 ... 97 F3
Beech Gr. Nor WF6 ... 144 A8
Beech Gr. Roth LS26 ... 100 F6
Beech Gr. Sil BD20 ... 5 D1
Beech Grove Ave. Gar LS25 ... 82 E6
Beech Grove Terr. Gar LS25 ... 82 E6
Beech Grove Terr. Leeds LS2 .. 60 B2
Beech Hill. Otley LS21 ... 23 A8
Beech Hill. Pont WF8 ... 125 E1
Beech Hill Prim Sch. Hali ... 113 B8
Beech Jun & Inf Sch. Hud ... 152 E5
Beech La. Leeds LS9 ... 61 C3
Beech Lees. Pudsey LS28 ... 57 C4
Beech Mount. Leeds LS9 ... 61 D3
Beech Rd. B Spa LS23 ... 30 C8
Beech Rd. Brad BD6 ... 94 C7
Beech Rd. Hali HX6 ... 112 C4
Beech Rd. Shaf S72 ... 180 D2
Beech Rd. Upton WF9 ... 183 B7
Beech Spinney. Weth LS22 ... 13 E8
Beech Sq. Brad BD14 ... 73 C4 3
Beech St. Bacup OL13 ... 106 A3
Beech St. Bing BD16 ... 36 F2
Beech St. E Ard WF3 ... 98 E1
Beech St. Elland HX4 ... 134 A4
Beech St. Elland HX5 ... 134 F6
Beech St. Glu BD20 ... 16 D6
Beech St. Hali HX1 ... 113 B8
Beech St. Holmfi HD7 ... 189 A5
Beech St. Hud HD1 ... 153 D5
Beech St. Keigh BD21 ... 35 E8
Beech St. Mir WF14 ... 138 A5
Beech St. Pont WF8 ... 146 E7
Beech St. S Elm WF9 ... 182 E1
Beech St. Stee BD20 ... 17 C5
Beech Terr. Brad BD3 ... 75 B8
Beech Tree Rd. Feath WF7 ... 145 E4
Beech View. Aber LS25 ... 64 D7
Beech View. Crig WF4 ... 159 F3
Beech View. Hali HX6 ... 112 B5 9
Beech Way. Batley WF17 ... 97 A2
Beech Wlk. Birk BD11 ... 96 B4
Beech Wlk. Dew WF13 ... 139 C8 5
Beech Wlk. Leeds LS9 ... 61 D3
Beechcroft Cl. Morley LS11 ... 78 D1
Beechcroft Mead. Leeds LS17 . 44 A4
Beechcroft. Roth WF3 ... 100 D1
Beechcroft View. Morley LS11 78 D1
Beechdale Ave. Batley WF17 . 118 A7
Beecher St. Hali HX3 ... 92 B2
Beecher St. Keigh BD21 ... 18 E1
Beeches End. B Spa LS23 ... 30 E7
Beeches Rd. Keigh BD21 ... 35 D8
Beeches Rd. Keigh BD21 ... 35 E8
Beeches The. Bail BD17 ... 38 D4
Beeches The. Guise LS20 ... 22 E2
Beeches The. Pudsey LS28 ... 76 B8
Beechfield Ave. Skel HD8 ... 175 A1
Beechfield. Gild LS12 ... 77 D3
Beechfield Rd. Hud HD2 ... 135 E1
Beechfield Terr. Clec BD19 ... 116 E7 13
Beechfield. Wake WF2 ... 160 E8
Beechmount Cl. Bail BD17 ... 38 D4
Beechnut La. Pont WF8 ... 125 C1
Beechroyd. Pudsey LS28 ... 76 E6
Beechroyd Terr. Bing BD16 ... 36 F2
Beechtree Ct. Bail BD17 ... 38 A2
Beechwood Ave. Birk BD11 ... 96 D7
Beechwood Ave. Brad BD6 ... 74 B2
Beechwood Ave. Hali HX2, HX3 92 A5
Beechwood Ave. Keigh BD20 ... 18 F1
Beechwood Ave. Leeds LS4 ... 59 D3
Beechwood Ave. Mir WF14 ... 138 A5
Beechwood Ave. Pont WF8 ... 146 B7
Beechwood Ave. Shelf HX3 ... 93 B5
Beechwood Ave. Ship BD18 ... 54 E7
Beechwood Ave. Sow Br HX6 ... 111 F3
Beechwood Ave. Wake WF2 .. 141 D6
Beechwood Cl. Hali HX2 ... 91 F4
Beechwood Cl. Hors LS18 ... 41 A3
Beechwood Cres. Hem WF9 .. 181 C6
Beechwood Cres. Leeds LS4 ... 59 D3
Beechwood Cres. Pont WF8 .. 146 B7
Beechwood Cres. Sow Br HX6 111 F3
Beechwood Ctr. Roth ... 101 C7
Beechwood Dale.
Ack M T WF7 ... 164 B7
Beechwood Dr. Brad BD6 ... 74 B2
Beechwood Dr. Hali HX2 ... 91 F5
Beechwood Dr. Sow Br HX6 .. 111 F3
Beechwood Gr. Birk BD11 ... 96 D7
Beechwood Gr. Brad BD6 ... 74 B2
Beechwood Gr. Hali HX2 ... 91 F4
Beechwood Gr. Hor WF4 ... 141 C1
Beechwood Gr. Hud HD2 ... 136 A4
Beechwood Gr. Ilkley LS29 ... 7 F4
Beechwood Gr. Leeds LS4 ... 59 D3
Beechwood Gr. Ship BD18 ... 54 E7
Beechwood Mount. Hem WF9 181 D6
Beechwood Mount. Leeds LS4 . 59 D3
Beechwood Pl. Leeds LS4 ... 59 D3
Beechwood. Pont WF8 ... 146 B7 1
Beechwood Prim Sch. Leeds ... 62 A4
Beechwood Rd. Brad BD6 ... 74 A2
Beechwood Rd. Hali HX2 ... 91 F4
Beechwood Rd. Leeds LS4 ... 59 D3 8
Beechwood Rd. Mir WF14 ... 138 A6
Beechwood Rise. Weth LS22 ... 13 E7
Beechwood. Roth LS26 ... 101 D7
Beechwood Row. Leeds LS4 ... 59 D3
Beechwood St. Leeds LS4 ... 59 D3
Beechwood St. Pudsey LS28 ... 57 C1
Beechwood Terr. Leeds LS4 ... 59 D3
Beechwood View. Leeds LS4 ... 59 D3
Beechwood Wlk. Leeds LS4 ... 59 D3
Beecroft Cl. Leeds LS13 ... 58 B3
Beecroft Cres. Leeds LS13 ... 58 B3
Beecroft Gdns. Leeds LS13 ... 58 A3
Beecroft Mount. Leeds LS13 ... 58 B3 3
Beecroft Prim Sch. Leeds ... 59 B3
Beecroft St. Keigh BD21 ... 35 D7
Beecroft St. Leeds LS5 ... 59 A3
Beecroft Wlk. Brad BD15 ... 73 A7 1
Beehive St. Brad BD6 ... 93 F7 6
Beehive Yd. Brad BD6 ... 93 F7 7
Beeston Hill St Luke's CE Sch.
Leeds ... 79 B4
Beeston Pk Croft. Leeds LS11 . 78 E2
Beeston Pk Garth. Leeds LS11 . 78 E2
Beeston Park Gr. Leeds LS11 .. 78 E2
Beeston Park Pl. Leeds LS11 .. 78 E2
Beeston Park Terr. Leeds LS11 78 E2
Beeston Prim Sch. Leeds ... 78 E2
Beeston Rd. Leeds LS11 ... 78 F3
Beeston Rd. Leeds LS11 ... 79 A3
Beestonley. Elland HX4 ... 133 E4
Beestonley La. Elland HX4 ... 133 E4
Bela Ave. Brad BD4 ... 75 C3
Belcross Dr. Hali HX3 ... 113 D8 2
Beldon La. Brad BD7 ... 73 F2
Beldon Park Ave. Brad BD7 ... 73 F1
Beldon Park Cl. Brad BD7 ... 73 F2
Beldon Pl. Brad BD2 ... 56 B2
Beldon Rd. Brad BD7 ... 74 A3
Belfast St. Hali HX1 ... 112 F5
Belford Cl. Brad BD4 ... 75 D3
Belfry Ct. Loft G WF3 ... 121 C5
Belfry The. Yeadon LS19 ... 40 C6
Belgrave Ave. Hali HX3 ... 113 D8
Belgrave Ave. Ossett WF5 ... 140 E4
Belgrave Cl. Hali HX3 ... 113 D8
Belgrave Cres. Hali HX3 ... 113 E8
Belgrave Dr. Hali HX3 ... 113 E8
Belgrave Gdns. Hali HX3 ... 113 D8
Belgrave Gr. Hali HX3 ... 113 D8 4
Belgrave Mews. Yeadon LS19 . 40 A4
Belgrave Mount. Hali HX3 ... 92 D1
Belgrave Mount. Wake WF1 .. 142 D8
Belgrave Pk. Hali HX3 ... 113 D8 3
Belgrave Rd. Bing BD16 ... 37 A3
Belgrave Rd. Keigh BD21 ... 35 B8
Belgrave St. Hali HX6 ... 112 B4 6
Belgrave St. Leeds LS2 ... 79 C8
Belgrave St. Ossett WF5 ... 140 E4
Belgrave Terr. Hud HD1 ... 153 F7
Belgrave Terr. Wake WF1 ... 142 D8
Belgravia Rd. Wake WF1 ... 142 B8
Belinda St. Leeds LS10 ... 79 E3
Bell Bank View. Bing BD16 ... 36 E4
Bell Dean Rd. Brad BD15, BD8 73 B7
Bell Hall Mount. Hali HX1 ... 113 A5 24
Bell Hall Terr. Hali HX1 ... 113 A5
Bell Hall View. Hali HX1 ... 113 B5 1
Bell House Ave. Brad BD4 ... 75 B1
Bell La. Ack M T WF7 ... 163 F5
Bell La. Leeds LS13 ... 58 D3
Bell Rd. Leeds LS13 ... 58 C3
Bell Sq. Sil BD20 ... 5 E2
Bell St. Brad BD12 ... 94 C4 17
Bell St. Dew WF13 ... 138 E5
Bell St. Hali HX3 ... 113 D8
Bell St. Hud HD4 ... 154 B4
Bell St. Leeds LS9 ... 79 D8 1
Bell St. Upton WF9 ... 183 E8
Bell St. Wake WF1 ... 142 B7
Bellbrooke Ave. Leeds LS9 ... 61 B2 11
Bellbrooke Gr. Leeds LS9 ... 61 B2 8
Bellbrooke Pl. Leeds LS9 ... 61 B2 6
Bellbrooke St. Leeds LS9 ... 61 B2
Belle Isle Ave. Wake WF1 ... 142 D4
Belle Isle Cir. Midd LS10 ... 99 E8
Belle Isle Cl. Midd LS10 ... 99 E8
Belle Isle Cres. Wake WF1 ... 142 D4
Belle Isle Dr. Wake WF1 ... 142 D4
Belle Isle Par. Midd LS10 ... 79 E1
Belle Isle Rd. Haw BD22 ... 51 C7
Belle Isle Rd. Midd LS10 ... 99 E7
Belle View Rise. Shelf HX3 ... 93 B5
Belle Vue Ave. B in Elm LS15 ... 62 F6
Belle Vue Ave. Leeds LS8 ... 61 D6
Belle Vue Boys Sch. Brad ... 54 C4
Belle Vue. Brad BD8 ... 55 D1
Belle Vue Cres. Hud HD2 ... 136 C3
Belle Vue Cres. Shelf HX3 ... 93 B5
Belle Vue Dr. Pudsey LS28 ... 57 C3
Belle Vue Est. B in Elm LS15 ... 62 F6
Belle Vue Fst Sch. Brad ... 55 D1
Belle Vue Girls Sch. Ship ... 54 C5
Belle Vue. Ilkley LS29 ... 8 C3
Belle Vue. Queen BD13 ... 92 E7
Belle Vue Rd. B in Elm LS15 ... 62 F6
Belle Vue Rd. Leeds LS3 ... 59 F1
Belle Vue Rd. Shelf HX3 ... 93 B5
Belle Vue Rd. Wake WF1 ... 142 E2
Belle Vue Sch (Art & Drama).
Wake ... 142 F4
Belle Vue St. Batley WF17 ... 117 F5
Belle Vue Terr. Guise LS20 ... 39 E8
Belle Vue Terr. Hali HX3 ... 113 E5
Bellerby Brow. Brad BD6 ... 73 E1
Bellerby Pl. Ad Le S DN6 ... 184 F2
Bellerby Rd. Ad Le S DN6 ... 184 F2
Bellevue Terr. Sow Br HX2 ... 111 C7
Bellgreave Ave. Holmfi HD7 .. 189 F6
Bellhouse Cres. Brad BD4 ... 95 B8
Bellmont Cres. Hem WF9 ... 181 E6
Bellmount Cl. Leeds LS13 ... 58 D3
Bellmount Gdns. Leeds LS13 ... 58 C4
Bellmount Gn. Leeds LS13 ... 58 D4 4
Bellmount Pl. Leeds LS13 ... 58 D4
Bellmount View. Leeds LS13 ... 58 D3
Belloe St. Brad BD5 ... 74 D4
Bellshaw St. Brad BD8 ... 73 E7
Bellstring La. Mir WF14 ... 137 E1
Bellwood Ave. B Spa LS23 ... 30 D6
Belmont Ave. Bail BD17 ... 38 B3
Belmont Ave. Brad BD12 ... 94 E7
Belmont Ave. Otley LS21 ... 10 F1
Belmont. Broth WF11 ... 105 C1
Belmont Cl. Bail BD17 ... 38 B3
Belmont Cl. Hud HD1 ... 154 A7 1
Belmont Cres. Brad BD12 ... 94 E7
Belmont Cres. Ship BD18 ... 55 A8
Belmont Gdns. Brad BD12 ... 94 D7
Belmont Gr. Brad BD6 ... 94 D7
Belmont Gr. Leeds LS2 ... 60 A1
Belmont Gr. Yeadon LS19 ... 40 C5
Belmont Grange. Liver WF15 117 A2
Belmont Mid Sch. Bail ... 38 B3
Belmont Pl. Hali HX1 ... 113 A6
Belmont Rd. Ilkley LS29 ... 8 E4
Belmont Rise. Bail BD17 ... 38 B3
Belmont Rise. Brad BD12 ... 94 E7
Belmont St. Brad BD2 ... 56 C5
Belmont St. Feath WF7 ... 144 C5
Belmont St. Hali HX6 ... 112 C4
Belmont St. Hali HX3 ... 113 E8
Belmont St. Hud HD1 ... 154 A7
Belmont St. Slai HD7 ... 169 F8
Belmont St. Wake WF1 ... 142 B8
Belmont Terr. Hali HX2 ... 111 E5
Belmont Terr. Midd WF3 ... 99 F2
Belmont Terr. Ship BD18 ... 55 A8
Belmont Way. S Elm WF9 ... 183 B3
Belton Cl. Brad BD7 ... 74 A3
Belton Gr. Hud HD3 ... 135 B2
Belton Rd. Sil BD20 ... 17 E8
Belton St. Hud HD5 ... 154 E5
Belvedere Ave. Leeds LS17 ... 43 D4
Belvedere Ave. Leeds LS11 ... 79 B2
Belvedere Cl. Shaf S72 ... 180 C2
Belvedere Ct. Leeds LS17 ... 43 E4
Belvedere Gr. Leeds LS17 ... 43 D4
Belvedere Mount. Leeds LS11 . 79 B2
Belvedere Rd. Batley WF17 ... 118 B4
Belvedere Rd. Leeds LS17 ... 43 D4
Belvedere Terr. Brad BD8 ... 74 B8
Belvedere Terr. Leeds LS11 ... 79 B2
Belvedere View. Leeds LS17 ... 43 E4
Belvoir Dr. Knot WF11 ... 126 E4
Belvoir Gdns. Hali HX3 ... 113 C3
Bembridge Ct. Wake WF2 ... 141 E5
Bempton Ct. Brad BD7 ... 74 B4 5
Bempton Gr. Batley WF17 ... 96 F2
Bempton Pl. Brad BD7 ... 74 B4 4
Ben Booth La. Floc WF4 ... 156 F4
Ben Rhydding Dr. Ilkley LS29 ... 8 F3
Ben Rhydding Rd. Ilkley LS29 ... 8 D3
Ben Rhydding Sta. Ilkley ... 8 E4
Benbow Ave. Brad BD10 ... 56 E5
Bendigo Rd. Dew WF12 ... 118 F1
Benjamin Gott High Sch The.
Leeds ... 59 A2
Benjamin St. Liver WF15 ... 117 B3
Benjamin St. Wake WF2 ... 142 A7
Benn Ave. Brad BD7 ... 73 F4
Benn Cres. Brad BD7 ... 73 F4
Benn La. Hud HD3 ... 152 F6
Bennet Ct. Leeds LS15 ... 81 D8
Bennett Ave. Hor WF4 ... 141 C2
Bennett Ct. Otley LS21 ... 10 F1
Bennett House. Brad BD15 ... 73 B7 8
Bennett La. Batley WF12 ... 118 F2
Bennett Rd. Leeds LS6 ... 59 D5
Bennett St. Hali HX3 ... 113 D6
Bennett St. Liver WF15 ... 117 B4 5
Benns La. Hali HX2 ... 90 F2
Benny La. Slai HD7 ... 152 B3
Benny Parr Cl. Batley WF17 ... 118 E5
Benomley Cres. Hud HD5 ... 154 E4
Benomley Dr. Hud HD5 ... 154 E3
Benomley Rd. Hud HD5 ... 154 E3
Benroyd Terr. Elland HX4 ... 134 C4
Benson Gdns. Leeds LS12 ... 78 B6
Benson Gdns. Nor WF6 ... 123 C3
Benson La. Nor WF6 ... 123 C3
Benson St. Leeds LS7 ... 60 D2
Bent Close La. Heb Br HX7 ... 110 E3
Bent Cotts. S in Cra BD20 ... 16 B5
Bent La. Holmfi HD7 ... 199 B8
Bent La. S in Cra BD20 ... 16 C5
Bent Lea. Hud HD2 ... 136 F6
Bent Ley Rd. Mel HD7 ... 171 A3
Bent Rd. Holmfi HD7 ... 199 D7
Bent St. Hud HD4 ... 154 B4
Bentcliff Wlk. Brad BD15 ... 73 B7 1
Bentcliffe Ave. Leeds LS17 ... 43 E2
Bentcliffe Cl. Leeds LS17 ... 43 E1
Bentcliffe Ct. Leeds LS17 ... 43 E1
Bentcliffe Dr. Leeds LS17 ... 43 E2
Bentcliffe Gdns. Leeds LS17 ... 43 E1
Bentcliffe Gr. Leeds LS17 ... 43 E1
Bentcliffe La. Leeds LS17 ... 43 D2
Bentcliffe Mount. Leeds LS17 .. 43 E1
Bentfield Cotts. Brad BD14 ... 73 C5
Bentham Way. Mapp S75 ... 178 A2
Bentley Ave. Brig HX3 ... 115 A7
Bentley Cl. Bail BD17 ... 38 B4
Bentley Ct. Leeds LS6 ... 59 F6 1
Bentley Gr. Leeds LS6 ... 59 F6
Bentley La. Leeds LS6, LS7 ... 59 F6
Bentley Mount. Hali HX6 ... 112 D5
Bentley Mount. Leeds LS6 ... 59 F6
Bentley Par. Leeds LS6 ... 59 F6
Bentley Prim Sch. Leeds ... 59 F6
Bentley Rd. Wake WF2 ... 141 E4
Bentley Sq. Roth LS26 ... 101 C5 2
Bentley St. Brad BD12 ... 94 D3 4
Bentley St. Hud HD1 ... 153 E3
Benton Cres. Hor WF4 ... 141 C2
Benton Park Ave. Yeadon LS19 40 C5 2
Benton Park Cres. Yeadon LS19 40 C5
Benton Park Dr. Yeadon LS19 . 40 C5
Benton Park Rd. Yeadon LS19 . 40 C5
Benton Park Sch. Yeadon ... 40 B5
Bents La. Mars HD7 ... 169 B6
Bents La. Wils BD15 ... 53 A6
Bents Rd. Carl S30 ... 200 D4
Benyon Park Way. Leeds LS12 78 D4
Beresford Rd. Brad BD6 ... 94 B7
Beresford St. Brad BD12 ... 95 A5
Berkeley Ave. Leeds LS8 ... 61 A3
Berkeley Cres. Leeds LS8 ... 61 A3
Berkeley Croft. Roy S71 ... 179 B4
Berkeley Ct. Leeds LS3 ... 59 F1 2
Berkeley Gr. Leeds LS8 ... 61 A3
Berkeley Mount. Leeds LS8 ... 61 A3 15
Berkeley Rd. Leeds LS8 ... 61 A3
Berkeley St. Leeds LS8 ... 61 A3
Berkeley Terr. Leeds LS8 ... 61 A3 13
Berkeley View. Leeds LS8 ... 61 A3
Berking Ave. Leeds LS9 ... 79 F8
Bermerside Sch. Hali ... 113 B2
Bermondsey St. Otley LS21 ... 23 B8
Bernard St. Hud HD2 ... 136 E3
Bernard St. Leeds LS2 ... 79 C8
Bernard St. Roth LS26 ... 101 D6
Berne Gr. Wake WF1 ... 142 C7
Berners St. Wake WF1 ... 142 D6
Berry Bank La. Holmfi HD7 ... 189 B8
Berry Brow Inf Sch. Hud ... 171 F8
Berry Croft. Honley HD7 ... 171 F5
Berry La. Hali HX3 ... 113 D7
Berry La. Hor WF4 ... 141 B1
Berry La. Keigh BD21 ... 35 B6
Berry La. Swil LS26 ... 102 E8
Berry Moor Rd. Sow Br HX6 .. 112 D2
Berry Rd. Mel HD7 ... 170 C3
Berry St. Keigh BD21 ... 35 D7 6
Berry View. Hud HD4 ... 153 F1
Berry's Bldgs. Hali HX2 ... 91 F4
Berry's Yd. Hor WF4 ... 141 B2
Bertha St. Keigh BD21 ... 35 C7
Bertha St. Pudsey LS28 ... 57 D2
Bertie St. Brad BD4 ... 75 C3
Bertram Dr. Bail BD17 ... 38 B2
Bertram Rd. Brad BD8 ... 55 C2
Bertrand St. Leeds LS11 ... 79 A5 10
Berwick Ave. Batley WF16 ... 117 D6
Berwick St. Hali HX1 ... 113 D7
Bescaby Gr. Bail BD17 ... 38 E3
Besha Ave. Brad BD12 ... 94 D6
Besha Gr. Brad BD12 ... 94 D6
Bessingham Gdns. Brad BD6 .. 93 F8
Best La. Kirkb HD4 ... 172 D7
Best La. Oxen BD22 ... 51 C2
Beswick Cl. Brad BD3 ... 75 D7
Beswick St. Tod OL14 ... 129 A7
Bethal Gn. Litt OL15 ... 129 C1
Bethel Rd. Ship BD18 ... 55 D8
Bethel St. Brig HD6 ... 115 B2
Bethel St. Hali HX3 ... 92 A2 2
Bethel St. Keigh BD20 ... 36 D8
Bethel Terr. Hali HX2 ... 90 D1
Bethel Terr. Sow Br HX6 ... 112 D3
Bethesda Row. Heb Br HX7 ... 89 D1
Betteras Hill Rd. Hillam LS25 105 F7
Betula Way. Lepton HD8 ... 155 E3
Beulah Gr. Leeds LS6 ... 60 B3 3
Beulah Mount. Leeds LS6 ... 60 B3 2
Beulah Pl. Hali HX2 ... 111 E5
Beulah St. Leeds LS6 ... 60 B3
Beulah Terr. Leeds LS6 ... 60 B4 4
Beulah Terr. Leeds LS15 ... 62 C2
Beulah View. Leeds LS6 ... 60 B3 1
Bevan Ave. Nor WF6 ... 144 B8
Bevan Pl. Wake WF2 ... 141 C4
Bevedere Gdns. Leeds LS17 ... 43 E4
Beverley Ave. Brad BD12 ... 94 D2
Beverley Ave. Leeds LS11 ... 79 B3
Beverley Cl. Elland HX5 ... 135 B7
Beverley Ct. Hud HD2 ... 136 B2
Beverley Dr. Brad BD12 ... 94 D2
Beverley Dr. Dew WF12 ... 139 F8
Beverley Garth. Ack M T WF7 164 A5
Beverley Gdns. Batley WF17 ... 97 B2
Beverley Mount. Leeds LS11 .. 79 B3 13
Beverley Pl. Hali HX3 ... 92 B1
Beverley Rise. Ilkley LS29 ... 7 E4
Beverley St. Brad BD4 ... 75 D5
Beverley Terr. Hali HX3 ... 92 B1
Beverley Terr. Leeds LS11 ... 79 B3
Beverley View. Leeds LS11 ... 79 B3
Beverley Wlk. Gar LS25 ... 82 F6
Bevin Cl. Loft G WF1 ... 121 C5
Bevin Cres. Loft G WF1 ... 121 C5
Bevor Cres. Batley WF16 ... 117 D6
Bewdley Ct. Roy S71 ... 179 D4
Bewerley Cres. Brad BD6 ... 94 A6
Bewerley Street Prim Sch.
Leeds ... 79 B4
Bewick Gr. Midd LS10 ... 99 F7
Bexhill Cl. Pont WF8 ... 125 F2
Bexley Ave. Leeds LS8 ... 60 F2
Bexley Gr. Leeds LS8 ... 60 F2
Bexley Mount. Leeds LS8 ... 60 F2 9
Bexley Pl. Leeds LS8 ... 60 F2 8
Bexley Rd. Leeds LS8 ... 60 F3
Bexley Terr. Leeds LS8 ... 60 F2
Bexley View. Leeds LS8 ... 60 F2
Beza Rd. Leeds LS10 ... 79 D3
Beza St. Leeds LS10 ... 79 D3
Bickerdike Pl. Kippax WF10 ... 103 B4
Bickerdike Terr. Kippax LS25 ... 83 A1
Bickerton Way. Otley LS21 ... 10 E1
Biddenden Rd. Leeds LS15 ... 62 F2
Bideford Ave. Leeds LS8 ... 43 F2
Bideford Mount. Brad BD4 ... 75 E3
Bierley CE Fst Sch. Brad ... 75 B1
Bierley Hall Gr. Brad BD4 ... 95 B7
Bierley Hall Hospl. Brad ... 95 B8
Bierley House Ave. Brad BD4 .. 75 C1
Bierley La. Brad BD4 ... 95 B8
Bierley View. Brad BD4 ... 75 C1
Big Meadow Dr. Sil LS29 ... 6 D8
Bilham La. H Pag DN5 ... 195 D2
Bilham Rd. Clay W HD8 ... 176 A2
Bilham Row. H Pag DN5 ... 195 F3
Bill La. Holmfi HD7 ... 189 C7
Billam's Hill. Otley LS21 ... 10 F1
Billey La. Leeds LS12 ... 77 E4
Billing Ct. Yeadon LS19 ... 40 D3
Billing Dr. Yeadon LS19 ... 40 E3
Billing View. Brad BD10 ... 56 C7
Billing View. Yeadon LS19 ... 40 D3
Billingbauk Dr. Leeds LS13 ... 58 D1
Billingham Cl. Wake WF2 ... 141 D8
Billingsley Terr. Brad BD4 ... 75 B4
Billingwood Dr. Yeadon LS19 ... 40 D3
Billy La. Wad M HX7 ... 89 C5
Bilsdale Grange. Brad BD6 ... 93 F8
Bilsdale Way. Bail BD17 ... 38 A2
Bilton Pl. Brad BD8 ... 74 C8
Bingley Bank. Bard LS17 ... 28 C2
Bingley CE Fst Sch. Bing ... 36 F3
Bingley Grammar Sch. Bing ... 36 E4
Bingley Hospl. Bing ... 37 A3
Bingley Rd. Bail BD17 ... 38 B6
Bingley Rd. Brad BD9 ... 54 D4
Bingley Rd. Cull BD13 ... 35 B1
Bingley Rd. Cull BD13 ... 52 E7
Bingley Rd. Guise LS29 ... 21 C2
Bingley Rd. Men LS29 ... 21 F3
Bingley Rd. Ship BD18 ... 54 E8
Bingley St. Brad BD8 ... 74 A7
Bingley (St Ives) Municipal Golf
Course. Harden ... 36 B4
Bingley St. Leeds LS3 ... 78 F8
Bingley Sta. Bing ... 36 F3
Bingley Stoney Lea Mid Sch.
Ship ... 54 B6
Binham Rd. Hud HD2 ... 153 D8
Binks Fold. Brad BD12 ... 94 D2 3
Binks St. Loft G WF1 ... 121 C4
Binn La. Mars HD7 ... 169 A2
Binn Rd. Mars HD7 ... 168 F3
Binn. Slai HD7 ... 170 A7
Binnie St. Brad BD3 ... 75 B7
Binns Hill La. Hali HX2 ... 112 B6
Binns La. Brad BD7 ... 73 F5
Binns La. Glu BD20 ... 16 A6
Binns La. Holmfi HD7 ... 188 F5
Binns St. Bing BD16 ... 37 A3
Binns Top La. Hali HX3 ... 114 B2
Binswell Fold. Bail BD17 ... 38 C4 9
Birch Ave. Brad BD5 ... 74 F2
Birch Ave. Leeds LS15 ... 81 A8
Birch Ave. Lepton HD8 ... 155 E2
Birch Ave. Rip HX6 ... 132 C1
Birch Ave. Tod OL14 ... 108 A7
Birch Cl. Brad BD5 ... 74 F2
Birch Cl. Brig HD6 ... 115 C3
Birch Cliff. Bail BD17 ... 38 B2
Birch Close La. Bail BD16 ... 37 F8
Birch Cres. Leeds LS15 ... 81 A8
Birch Ct. Morley LS27 ... 98 B2
Birch Dr. Kippax LS25 ... 83 A3
Birch Gn. Pont WF8 ... 125 F1
Birch Gr. Batley WF17 ... 118 A8
Birch Gr. Brad BD5 ... 74 E1
Birch Gr. Castle WF10 ... 125 D6
Birch Gr. Hud HD7 ... 152 E5
Birch Gr. Keigh BD21 ... 35 B4
Birch Gr. Kippax LS25 ... 83 A3
Birch Hill Rise. Hors LS18 ... 58 E8 1
Birch House. Castle WF10 ... 124 E7 7
Birch La. Brad BD5 ... 74 E3
Birch La. Brad BD5 ... 74 F2
Birch La. Hali HX2 ... 111 F8
Birch Pk. Honley HD7 ... 172 D2
Birch Rd. Hud HD4 ... 171 F8
Birch Rd. Kippax LS25 ... 83 A3
Birch Rd. Nor WF6 ... 144 B7
Birch St. Brad BD8 ... 74 A8
Birch St. Morley LS27 ... 98 B2
Birch St. Wake WF1 ... 142 F4
Birch Tree Gdns. Keigh BD21 ... 35 E6
Birch Way. Brad BD5 ... 74 F2
Birchcliffe Rd. Heb Br HX7 ... 89 A3
Birchdale. Bing BD16 ... 36 F5
Birchen Ave. Ossett WF5 ... 140 C6
Birchen Hills. Ossett WF5 ... 140 C5
Birchencliffe Hill Rd. Hud HD3 135 B2
Birchenlee Cl. Heb Br HX7 ... 89 F1
Birches The. Bramho LS16 ... 24 F2
Birches The. Guise LS20 ... 22 E2
Birchfield Ave. Gild LS27 ... 97 C6
Birchfield Garth. Leeds LS14 ... 62 C8
Birchfield Gr. Skel HD8 ... 175 A1
Birchfields Ave. Leeds LS14 ... 62 C8
Birchfields Cl. Leeds LS14 ... 62 C7
Birchfields Cres. Leeds LS14 ... 62 C8
Birchfields Ct. Leeds LS14 ... 62 C8 5
Birchfields Rise. Leeds LS14 ... 62 C8
Birchington Ave. Hud HD3 ... 135 B2
Birchington Cl. Hud HD3 ... 135 B2
Birchington Dr. Hud HD3 ... 135 A2
Birchlands Ave. Wils BD15 ... 53 B6
Birchlands Gr. Wils BD15 ... 53 B6
Birchroyd. Roth LS26 ... 100 F4
Birchtree Cl. Wake WF1 ... 142 F8
Birchtree Way. Hors LS16 ... 41 E2
Birchtree Wlk. Knot WF11 ... 126 D3
Birchwood Ave. Batley WF17 .. 96 F2
Birchwood Ave. Keigh BD20 ... 18 B2
Birchwood Ave. Leeds LS17 ... 44 A3
Birchwood Cl. Hud HD2 ... 135 D2
Birchwood Ct. Ilkley LS29 ... 8 A4
Birchwood Ct. Liver WF15 ... 117 B3 2
Birchwood Dr. Keigh BD20 ... 18 B2
Birchwood Hill. Leeds LS17 ... 44 A4
Birchwood Mount. Leeds LS17 44 A4
Birchwood Rd. Keigh BD20 ... 18 A2
Bird La. Rip HX6 ... 132 C3
Birdale Field La. Coll LS22 ... 29 D8
Birdcage Hill. Hali HX3 ... 113 A3
Birdcage La. Hali HX3 ... 113 B3
Birdcage Wlk. Otley LS21 ... 23 A6
Birds Edge La. D Dale HD8 ... 190 F4
Birds Royd La. Brig HD6 ... 115 C1
Birdsedge Farm Mews.
D Dale HD8 ... 191 A4
Birdsedge Fst Sch. D Dale ... 191 A4
Birdsnest La. Wh Com HD7 ... 190 D2
Birdswell Ave. Brig HD6 ... 115 D3
Birfed Cres. Leeds LS4 ... 59 B3
Birk House La. Shep HD8 ... 191 B8
Birk La. Morley LS27 ... 97 E4
Birk Lea St. Brad BD5 ... 74 F4
Birkby Brow Cres. Batley WF17 97 B2
Birkby Hall Rd. Hud HD2 ... 135 E1
Birkby Haven. Brad BD6 ... 93 E8
Birkby Jun Sch. Hud ... 136 A1
Birkby La. Brig HD6 ... 115 D7
Birkby Lodge Rd. Hud HD2 ... 153 F8
Birkby Rd. Hud HD2 ... 135 D1

Birkby St. Brad BD12 ... 94 D4
Birkdale Ave. Hud HD3 ... 153 A8
Birkdale Cl. Cull BD13 ... 52 E6
Birkdale Cl. Leeds LS17 ... 43 B4
Birkdale Dr. Leeds LS17 ... 43 B4
Birkdale Gn. Leeds LS17 ... 43 B4
Birkdale Gr. Dew WF13 ... 118 A1
Birkdale Gr. Hali HX2 ... 91 F7
Birkdale Gr. Leeds LS17 ... 43 A4
Birkdale High Sch. Dew ... 118 A2
Birkdale High Sch. Dew ... 118 B2
Birkdale Mount. Leeds LS17 ... 43 B4
Birkdale Pl. Leeds LS17 ... 43 A4
Birkdale Rd. Dew WF13 ... 118 B1
Birkdale Rd. Roy S71 ... 179 B5
Birkdale Rise. Leeds LS17 ... 43 A4
Birkdale Way. Leeds LS17 ... 43 B4
Birkdale Wlk. Leeds LS17 ... 43 A4
Birkenshaw CE Fst Sch. Birk ... 96 A6
Birkenshaw Cty Fst Sch. Birk ... 96 B6
Birkenshaw La. Birk BD11 ... 96 C4
Birkenshaw Mid Sch. Birk ... 96 B4
Birkett St. Clec BD19 ... 116 D8
Birkhead St. Batley WF16 ... 117 E3
Birkhill. Castle WF10 ... 125 C8
Birkhill Cres. Birk BD11 ... 96 B5
Birkhouse La. Brig HD6 ... 115 D6
Birkhouse La. Hud HD1, HD4 . 153 E5
Birkhouse La. Hud HD5 ... 154 E5
Birkhouse Rd. Brig HD6 ... 115 C6
Birkin La. Birkin WF11 ... 127 D8
Birklands Rd. Hud HD2 ... 135 F2
Birklands Rd. Ship BD18 ... 55 B7
Birklands Terr. Ship BD18 ... 55 B7
Birks Ave. Brad BD7 ... 73 F5
Birks Fold. Brad BD7 ... 73 F6
Birks Hall St. Hali HX1 ... 113 A8
Birks Hall Terr. Hali HX1 ... 113 A8
Birks La. Hud HD4 ... 155 A3
Birks La. Kirkb HD8 ... 173 D3
Birks La. Rip HX6 ... 132 E5
Birks La. Sow Br HX6 ... 132 D8
Birks La. Tod OL14 ... 129 B8
Birks Rd. Hud HD3 ... 153 A5
Birkshall La. Brad BD4, BD3 ... 75 B6
Birkshead. Wils BD15 ... 53 D5
Birksland Ind Est. Brad ... 75 B5
Birksland Moor. Birk BD11 ... 96 B3
Birksland St. Brad BD3 ... 75 B6
Birkwith Cl. Leeds LS14 ... 62 B8
Birkwood Ave. Crof WF4 ... 144 B2
Birkwood Rd. Nor WF6 ... 122 C3
Birmingham La. Mel HD7 ... 170 C3
Birnam Gr. Brad BD4 ... 75 A4
Birr Rd. Brad BD9 ... 55 B3
Birstall Cty J & I Sch. Batley ... 96 F1
Birstall La. Birk BD11 ... 96 E5
Birstall St Peter's CE Prim Sch.
Batley ... 96 E2
Birthwaite Rd. Kex S75 ... 177 B1
Bishop St. Brad BD9 ... 55 B2
Bishop Way. E Ard WF3 ... 119 F8
Bishop's Ct. Hud HD4 ... 171 F7
Bishopdale Dr. Coll LS22 ... 13 A1
Bishopdale Holme. Brad BD6 .. 93 E8
Bishopgate St. Leeds LS1 ... 79 B7
Bishops Way. Mel HD7 ... 170 E2
Bishops Way. Mir WF14 ... 137 D7
Bisley Cl. Roy S71 ... 179 E4
Bismarck Dr. Leeds LS11 ... 79 B4
Bismarck St. Leeds LS11 ... 79 B4
Bittern Rise. Morley LS27 ... 98 C3
Black Abbey La. Glu BD20 ... 16 C6
Black Brook Way. Elland HX4 134 C6
Black Bull St. Leeds LS10 ... 79 D6
Black Dyke La. Wils BD13 ... 53 B1
Black Edge La. Denh BD13 ... 71 D6
Black Gates Ct. E Ard WF3 ... 119 F8
Black Gates Rise. E Ard WF3 . 119 F8
Black Hill La. Eccup LS16 ... 25 D1
Black Hill La. Keigh BD20 ... 17 E1
Black Hill Rd. Arth LS21 ... 25 C5
Black Hill. Wad M HX7 ... 89 B8
Black La. Mel HD7 ... 170 E7
Black Moor Rd. Leeds LS17 ... 43 A2
Black Moor Rd. Oxen BD22 ... 51 E4
Black Rd. Crof WF4 ... 143 B3
Black Sike La. Holmfi HD7 ... 188 C5
Black Wlk. Pont WF8 ... 125 E2
Black Wood Gr. Hors LS16 ... 41 D3
Black Wood Mount. Hors LS16 41 D3
Black Wood Rise. Hors LS16 ... 41 D3
Blackbird Gdns. Brad BD8 ... 73 B7 11
Blackburn Bldgs. Brig HD6 ... 115 C2
Blackburn Cl. Brad BD8 ... 73 D7
Blackburn Cl. Hali HX3 ... 91 F3
Blackburn Ct. Pont WF8 ... 146 C8 13
Blackburn Ct. Roth LS26 ... 100 F5
Blackburn House. Hali HX3 ... 92 A3
Blackburn La. Knot WF11 ... 127 C3
Blackburn Pl. Batley WF17 ... 118 D5
Blackburn Rd. Batley WF17 ... 96 E1
Blackburn Rd. Brig HD6 ... 115 A4
Blacker Cres. Neth WF4 ... 158 E6
Blacker La. Neth WF4 ... 159 B5
Blacker La. Shaf S72 ... 180 C3
Blacker Rd. Hud HD1, HD2 ... 153 F8
Blacker Rd. Mapp S75 ... 178 C1
Blacker Rd N. Hud HD1, HD2 . 153 F8
Blackers Ct. Dew WF12 ... 139 B4
Blackett St. Pudsey LS28 ... 57 B7
Blackgates Cres. E Ard WF3 .. 119 F8
Blackgates Dr. E Ard WF3 ... 119 F8
Blackgates Fold. E Ard WF3 .. 119 F8
Blackgates Inf Sch. E Ard ... 98 E1
Blackgates Jun Sch. E Ard ... 119 F8
Blackhouse Rd. Hud HD2 ... 136 B2
Blackledge. Hali HX1 ... 113 D7
Blackley Rd. Elland HX5 ... 134 E4
Blackman La. Leeds LS2 ... 60 B2
Blackmires. Hali HX2 ... 92 A5
Blackmoor Ct. Leeds LS17 ... 42 F5
Blackmoor La. Bard LS17 ... 28 A1
Blackmoorfoot Rd. Hud HD4 .. 153 E4
Blackmoorfoot Rd. Slai HD7 .. 170 D7
Blackpool Gr. Leeds LS12 ... 78 A4
Blackpool Pl. Leeds LS12 ... 78 A4
Blackpool St. Leeds LS12 ... 78 A4 7
Blackpool Terr. Leeds LS12 ... 78 A4 6
Blackpool View. Leeds LS12 ... 78 A4 8
Blackshaw Beck La. Shelf BD13 93 A8
Blackshaw Clough Rd. Rip HX6 132 A6
Blackshaw Dr. Brad BD6 ... 93 D8
Blackshaw St. Tod OL14 ... 108 D5
Blacksmith Fold. Brad BD7 ... 74 A4
Blacksmith La. Eccup LS16 ... 25 F1
Blacksmiths Fold. Hud HD5 ... 154 F3
Blackstone Ave. Brad BD12 ... 94 C2
Blackstone Edge Rd.
Heb Br HX7 ... 131 B7
Blackstone Edge Rd. Rip HX6 130 F5
Blackthorn Way. Wake WF2 .. 142 A8
Blackthorne Ct. Midd LS10 ... 99 D8 4
Blackwall. Hali HX1 ... 113 C6
Blackwall La. Hali HX6 ... 112 B5
Blackwall Rise. Hali HX6 ... 112 B5
Blackwood Ave. Hors LS16 ... 41 D3
Blackwood Gdns. Hors LS16 ... 41 D3
Blackwood Gr. Hali HX1 ... 112 F8
Blackwood Hall La. Hali HX2 . 111 D7
Blacup Moor View. Clec BD19 116 D7
Blagden La. Hud HD4 ... 153 F1
Blairsville Gdns. Leeds LS13 ... 58 B4
Blairsville Gr. Leeds LS13 ... 58 C4
Blaith Royd La. Heb Br HX7 ... 109 F4
Blaithroyd La. Hali HX3 ... 113 E6
Blake Cres. Guise LS20 ... 39 F8
Blake Gr. Leeds LS7 ... 60 D6
Blake Hall Dr. Mir WF14 ... 138 C4
Blake Hall Rd. Mir WF14 ... 138 C4
Blake Hill End. Northo HX3 ... 92 F5
Blake Hill. Northo HX3 ... 92 E3
Blake Law La. Brig WF15 ... 115 F2
Blake Law La. Liver HD6 ... 116 A2
Blake Lee La. Mars HD7 ... 168 B5
Blake Stones. Slai HD7 ... 169 E8
Blakehill Ave. Brad BD2 ... 56 C2
Blakehill Fst Sch. Brad ... 56 A6
Blakehill Terr. Brad BD2 ... 56 C2
Blakeholme Cl. Slai HD7 ... 169 E8
Blakelaw Dr. Brig HD6 ... 115 D3
Blakeley Gr. Wake WF2 ... 141 F6
Blakeney Gr. Midd LS10 ... 79 D1
Blakeney Rd. Midd LS10 ... 79 D1
Blakeridge La. Batley WF17 .. 118 B5
Blakestones Rd. Slai HD7 ... 169 E8
Blakey Rd. Wake WF2 ... 141 F8
Blamires Pl. Brad BD7 ... 73 F3
Blamires St. Brad BD7 ... 73 F3
Blanche St. Brad BD4 ... 75 D6
Bland St. Hali HX1 ... 113 B7 6
Bland St. Hud HD1 ... 153 F4
Bland's Cl. Castle WF10 ... 124 E7
Blandford Gdns. Leeds LS2 ... 60 B2 9
Blandford Gr. Leeds LS2 ... 60 B2 10
Blands Ave. Kippax WF10 ... 103 A5
Blands Cres. Kippax WF10 ... 103 A5
Blands Gr. Kippax WF10 ... 103 A5
Blands Terr. Kippax WF10 ... 103 A5
Blanket Hall St. Liver WF16 ... 117 D3
Blayd's Mews. Leeds LS1 ... 79 C7 7
Blayd's Yd. Leeds LS1 ... 79 C7 6
Blayds St. Leeds LS9 ... 79 F7
Bleach Mill La. Men LS29 ... 21 E5
Bleak Ave. Shaf S72 ... 180 C2
Bleak St. Clec BD19 ... 117 C8
Bleak St Lower. Clec BD19 ... 117 C8
Bleakley Ave. Notton WF4 ... 179 B6
Bleakley Cl. Shaf S72 ... 180 C2
Bleakley La. Notton WF4 ... 179 B6
Bleakley Terr. Notton WF4 ... 179 B6
Bleasdale Ave. Hud HD2 ... 135 F1
Bleasdale Ave. Knot WF11 ... 126 F4
Blencarn Cl. Leeds LS14 ... 61 F4
Blencarn Garth. Leeds LS14 ... 61 F4
Blencarn Lawn. Leeds LS14 ... 61 F4
Blencarn Path. Leeds LS14 ... 61 F4
Blencarn Rd. Leeds LS14 ... 61 F4
Blencarn View. Leeds LS14 ... 61 F4
Blencarn Wlk. Leeds LS14 ... 61 F4
Blenheim Ave. Leeds LS2 ... 60 B2 1
Blenheim Cl. Knot WF11 ... 126 C4
Blenheim Cres. Leeds LS2 ... 60 B2
Blenheim Ct. Hali HX1 ... 113 B8
Blenheim Ct. Leeds LS2 ... 60 B2 3
Blenheim Dr. Batley WF17 ... 118 C6
Blenheim Dr. Dew WF13 ... 118 A1
Blenheim Gr. Leeds LS2 ... 60 B2
Blenheim Hill. Batley WF17 ... 118 D7
Blenheim Mid Sch. Leeds ... 60 B3
Blenheim Mount. Brad BD8 ... 55 C2
Blenheim Pl. Brad BD10 ... 39 B1
Blenheim Prim Sch. Leeds ... 60 B2
Blenheim Rd. Brad BD8 ... 55 C2
Blenheim Rd. Wake WF1 ... 142 B8
Blenheim Sq. Batley WF17 ... 118 C6
Blenheim Sq. Leeds LS2 ... 60 B2
Blenheim St. Heb Br HX7 ... 89 B3
Blenheim St. Keigh BD21 ... 35 B5 10
Blenheim Terr. Leeds LS2 ... 60 B2
Blenheim View. Leeds LS2 ... 60 B2
Blenheim Wlk. Leeds LS2 ... 60 B2 4
Blenkinsop Ct. Morley LS27 ... 98 B2
Blessed English Martyrs' Inf & Jun
Sch. Wake ... 141 D5
Blind La. Bick LS24 ... 15 F8
Blind La. Birk BD11 ... 96 F8
Blind La. E Ard WF3 ... 120 A5
Blind La. Hali HX2 ... 91 E8
Blind La. Harden BD16 ... 36 D3
Blind La. Heb Br HX2 ... 111 B7
Blind La. Thorner LS17 ... 44 E4
Blind La. Tod OL14 ... 108 B6
Bloomfield Rd. Mapp S75 ... 177 F1
Bloomfield Rise. Mapp S75 ... 177 F1
Bloomhouse La. Mapp S75 ... 177 F1
Blucher St. Brad BD4 ... 75 D6
Blue Ball La. Rip HX6 ... 131 E3
Blue Ball Rd. Rip HX6 ... 131 D3
Blue Bell Hill. Hud HD4 ... 153 F2
Blue Bell La. Tod OL14 ... 86 D2
Blue Butts. Ossett WF5 ... 140 D5
Blue Hill Cres. Leeds LS12 ... 78 A6
Blue Hill. Denh BD13 ... 52 D1
Blue Hill Gr. Leeds LS12 ... 78 A5
Blue Hill Grange. Leeds LS12 .. 78 A5
Blue Hill La. Leeds LS12 ... 78 A6
Bluebell Cl. Pont WF8 ... 146 D7
Bluebell Ct. Batley WF17 ... 96 E2
Bluebell Rd. Wool S75 ... 177 E3
Bluebell Wlk. Hali HX2 ... 111 E8
Blundell St. Leeds LS1 ... 60 B1
Blundell St. S Elm WF9 ... 182 E3
Blythe Ave. Brad BD8 ... 74 A8
Blythe St. Brad BD7 ... 74 D7
Boar La. Leeds LS1 ... 79 C7
Boardman St. Tod OL14 ... 108 B6
Boat La. Kippax WF10 ... 103 B3
Boat La. M'town WF10 ... 103 A3
Boathouse La. Mir WF14 ... 138 C3
Bob La. Hali HX2 ... 112 D7
Bobbin Mill Cl. Stee BD20 ... 17 C5
Bobbin Mill Cl. Tod OL14 ... 86 B1
Bobbin Mill Ct. Stee BD20 ... 17 C5
Bobbin St. Tod OL14 ... 86 C1
Bodiham Hill. Gar LS25 ... 83 B8
Bodington Hall. Hors ... 42 C2
Bodkin La. Oxen BD22 ... 50 E3
Bodley Terr. Leeds LS4 ... 59 D1
Bodmin App. Midd LS10 ... 99 A5
Bodmin Ave. Ship BD18 ... 55 F7
Bodmin Cres. Midd LS10 ... 99 B5
Bodmin Croft. Midd LS10 ... 99 B4
Bodmin Dr. Nor WF6 ... 123 B3
Bodmin Garth. Midd LS10 ... 99 A4
Bodmin Gdns. Midd LS10 ... 99 A4
Bodmin Pl. Midd LS10 ... 99 B4
Bodmin Rd. Midd LS10 ... 99 A5
Bodmin Sq. Midd LS10 ... 99 A4
Bodmin St. Midd LS10 ... 99 A4
Bodmin Terr. Midd LS10 ... 99 A4
Bog Green La. Kirkhe HD5 ... 137 C4
Bog La. B in Elm LS15 ... 63 A5
Boggart Hill Cres. Leeds LS14 . 61 F6
Boggart Hill Dr. Leeds LS14 ... 61 F6
Boggart Hill Gdns. Leeds LS14 61 E6
Boggart Hill. Leeds LS14 ... 61 E6
Boggart Hill Rd. Leeds LS14 ... 61 E6
Boggart La. Skel HD8 ... 175 A3
Boggart La. Sow Br HX6 ... 112 B3
Boland Cres. Haw BD22 ... 34 E3
Boldgrove St. Dew WF12 ... 140 A6
Boldmere Rd. Leeds LS15 ... 80 E7
Boldron Holt. Brad BD6 ... 93 F8
Boldshay St. Brad BD3 ... 75 B8
Bolehill Pk. Brig HD6 ... 114 E6
Bolingbroke St. Brad BD5 ... 74 D2
Bolland St. Brad BD12 ... 94 E5 3
Bolling Hall (Mus). Brad ... 75 A3
Bolling Rd. Brad BD4 ... 74 F5
Bolling Rd Fst Sch. Ilkley ... 8 E4
Bolling Rd. Ilkley LS29 ... 8 D4
Bolsover Cl. Gar LS25 ... 83 B7
Bolstermoor Rd. Slai HD7 ... 152 A4
Boltby La. Brad BD6 ... 93 E8
Bolton Bridge Rd. Ilkley LS29 ... 8 A4
Bolton Brow. Hali HX6 ... 112 D4
Bolton Brow Jun & Inf Sch.
Hali ... 112 D4
Bolton Cres. Brad BD2 ... 56 B4
Bolton Ct. Brad BD2 ... 56 A2
Bolton Dr. Brad BD2 ... 56 B4
Bolton Gdns. Yeadon LS19 ... 40 C6
Bolton Gr. Brad BD2 ... 56 B4
Bolton. Hali HX2 ... 91 E7
Bolton Hall Rd. Brad BD2 ... 55 E5
Bolton Hall Rd. Ship BD2 ... 55 E5
Bolton La. Brad BD2 ... 55 E3
Bolton Lane Fst Sch. Brad ... 55 F3
Bolton Rd. Add LS29 ... 2 F4
Bolton Rd. Brad BD2, BD3 ... 55 F2
Bolton Rd. Draug LS29 ... 2 F4
Bolton Rd. Sil BD20, LS29 ... 5 F4
Bolton Rd. Yeadon LS19 ... 40 C6
Bolton Royd Prim Sch. Pudsey . 76 A8
Bolton St. Brad BD3 ... 75 A7
Bolton St. Brad BD12 ... 94 C6
Bolton Terr. Sil BD20 ... 5 E2
Bolton Way. B Spa LS23 ... 30 C7
Bolton Wife Hill. Crig WF4 ... 159 F1
Bolton Woods Fst Sch. Ship ... 55 D4
Bolus Cl. Loft G WF1 ... 121 C4
Bolus La. Loft G WF1 ... 121 C4
Bonaccord Sq. Batley WF17 .. 118 C4
Bonaccord Terr. Batley WF17 118 C4
Bond Ct. Leeds LS1 ... 79 B8 6
Bond St. Batley WF17 ... 96 E1 6
Bond St. Batley WF17 ... 118 C6
Bond St. Brig HD6 ... 115 A3
Bond St. Dew WF13 ... 139 C8
Bond St. Hali HX1 ... 113 B6
Bond St. Heb Br HX7 ... 89 A3
Bond St. Leeds LS1 ... 79 B8
Bond St. Pont WF8 ... 125 E2
Bond St. Tod OL14 ... 108 B5
Bond St. Wake WF1 ... 142 B7
Bond Street Ctr. Leeds ... 79 C7
Bondgate. Hare LS17 ... 27 A7
Bondgate. Otley LS21 ... 23 A7
Bondgate. Pont WF8 ... 125 F2
Bonegate Ave. Brig HD6 ... 115 B3
Bonegate Rd. Brig HD6 ... 115 B3
Bonn Rd. Brad BD9 ... 55 A2
Bonwick Mall. Brad BD6 ... 93 E7
Boocock St. Pudsey LS28 ... 57 E1 2
Bookers Cl. Clec DB19 ... 117 C7
Bookers Field. Clec BD19 ... 117 C7
Booth Bank. Mars HD7 ... 169 C7
Booth. Hali HX2 ... 90 E3
Booth Hill. Hali HX2 ... 90 E4
Booth House La. Holmfi HD7 . 188 D4
Booth House Rd. Sow Br HX2 111 C7
Booth House Ter. Sow Br HX2 111 C7
Booth. Mars HD7 ... 169 B6
Booth Royd. Brad BD10 ... 39 B1
Booth Royd Dr. Brad BD10 ... 39 B1
Booth Royd La. Brig HD6 ... 135 D8
Booth St. Brad BD10 ... 56 B7
Booth St. Bur in W LS29 ... 9 E2
Booth St. Castle WF10 ... 124 D8
Booth St. Clec BD19 ... 116 D8
Booth St. Queen BD13 ... 72 D1 5
Booth St. Ship BD18 ... 55 D7
Booth's Bldgs. Brig HD6 ... 115 B7
Bootham Pk. Brad BD9 ... 54 D2
Boothman Wlk. Keigh BD21 ... 35 A5 4
Boothroyd Dr. Hud HD4 ... 153 B3
Boothroyd Gn. Dew WF13 ... 139 B8
Boothroyd Jun & Inf Sch. Dew 139 A7
Boothroyd La. Dew WF13 ... 139 A8
Boothroyd Lane Inf Sch. Dew ... 139 B8
Boothroyd Lane Mid Sch. Dew 139 B8
Boothtown Rd. Hali HX3 ... 92 B2
Border Cl. Hud HD3 ... 134 F1
Borough Market. Hali ... 113 C7
Borough Rd. Wake WF1 ... 142 C7
Boroughgate. Otley LS21 ... 23 A8
Borrins Way. Bail BD17 ... 38 D3
Borrough View. Leeds LS8 ... 60 E8
Borrowdale Cres. Leeds LS12 ... 58 F2
Borrowdale Croft. Yeadon LS19 40 B7
Borrowdale Dr. Castle WF10 . 104 D1
Borrowdale Rd. Batley WF12 118 E2
Borrowdale Rd. Wake WF2 ... 141 E7
Borrowdale Terr. Leeds LS14 .. 61 F3
Boston Ave. Leeds LS5 ... 58 F3
Boston Hill. Wad M HX7 ... 89 B6
Boston Mews. B Spa LS23 ... 30 E7
Boston Rd. B Spa LS23 ... 30 D6
Boston Rd. Weth LS22 ... 13 E3
Boston Spa CE Prim Sch. B Spa 30 E7
Boston Spa Comp Sch. B Spa .. 30 B7
Boston Spa Inf Sch. B Spa ... 30 C8
Boston Spa Jun Sch. B Spa ... 30 D7
Boston St. Castle WF10 ... 124 E8
Boston St. Hali HX1 ... 112 F7
Boston St. Sow Br HX6 ... 112 A3
Boston Towers. Leeds LS9 ... 60 E1
Boston Wlk. Brad BD6 ... 93 F8
Boswell Cl. Roy S71 ... 179 B4
Bosworth Ave. Nor WF6 ... 122 E4
Bosworth Cl. Brad BD15 ... 54 B1
Botany Ave. Brad BD2 ... 55 F4
Botany Dr. Keigh BD20 ... 19 E2
Botany La. Lepton HD8 ... 155 F4
Botham Hall Rd. Hud HD3 ... 152 F5
Bottom Boat Rd. Loft G WF3 .. 122 D6
Bottomley La. Rip HX4 ... 133 C2
Bottomley Rd. Tod OL14 ... 129 C6
Bottomley St. Brad BD5 ... 74 D4
Bottomley St. Brad BD6 ... 93 F7
Bottomley St. Brig HD6 ... 115 B4 2
Bottomley's Bldgs. Leeds LS6 .. 60 B3 8
Bottoms. Hali HX3 ... 113 D3
Bottoms La. Birk BD11 ... 96 B4
Boulder Bridge La. Roy S71 ... 179 F1
Boulder Gate. Mars HD7 ... 169 B4
Boulevard The. Brad BD6 ... 93 E8
Boulevard The. Pudsey LS28 ... 57 D2
Boundary Ave. Glu BD20 ... 16 D6
Boundary Cl. Leeds LS15 ... 81 E7
Boundary Farm Rd. Leeds LS17 43 A3
Boundary La. Crof WF6 ... 143 F7
Boundary Pl. Leeds LS7 ... 60 E2
Boundary Rd. Batley WF13 ... 117 F2
Boundary St. Leeds LS7 ... 60 E2
Boundary St. Liver WF16 ... 117 C4
Bourbon Cl. Brad BD6 ... 94 B8
Bourn View Cl. Hud HD4 ... 171 D7
Bourn View Rd. Hud HD4 ... 171 D7
Bourne Ct. Mapp S75 ... 178 C2
Bourne St. Brad BD10 ... 39 B2
Bourne Wlk. Mapp S75 ... 178 C2
Bow La. B Head HX7 ... 88 A4
Bow St. Hud HD1 ... 153 F5
Bow St. Keigh BD21 ... 35 C7
Bow St. Leeds LS9 ... 79 E7
Bowbridge Rd. Brad BD5 ... 74 E4 9
Bowcliffe Rd. Bramham LS23 .. 30 D2
Bower Gn. Brad BD3 ... 75 C7
Bower La. Batley WF13 ... 117 F3
Bower Rd. Leeds LS15 ... 62 E3
Bower Slack Rd. Sow Br HX7 110 F1
Bower St. Brad BD5 ... 74 E6 3
Bower The. Batley WF17 ... 117 F7 1
Bowers La. Rip HX4 ... 133 D6
Bowes Nook. Brad BD6 ... 93 E7
Bowfell Cl. Leeds LS14 ... 62 A4
Bowland Ave. Bail BD17 ... 37 E1
Bowland Cl. Leeds LS15 ... 80 E7
Bowland St. Brad BD1 ... 74 D8
Bowler Cl. Brad BD12 ... 94 C6
Bowling Alley. Brig HD6 ... 136 A8
Bowling Ave. Wake WF2 ... 120 F2
Bowling Back La. Brad BD4 ... 75 B5
Bowling Court Ind Est. Brad ... 75 C5
Bowling Ct. Brig HD6 ... 114 F3
Bowling Dyke. Hali HX1 ... 113 C8 8
Bowling Green Ct. Hud HD3 .. 152 E7
Bowling Green Jun & Inf Sch.
Elland ... 133 F3
Bowling Green Rd. Elland HX4 133 F3
Bowling Green Terr.
Leeds LS11 ... 79 B5
Bowling Hall Rd. Brad BD4 ... 75 A3
Bowling Old La. Brad BD5 ... 74 D2
Bowling Old La. Brad BD5 ... 74 E4
Bowling Park Cl. Brad BD4 ... 74 F4
Bowling Park Dr. Brad BD4 ... 74 F3
Bowling Park Fst Sch. Brad ... 74 F3
Bowling St. Hud HD4 ... 153 A4
Bowman Ave. Brad BD6 ... 94 B7
Bowman Gr. Hali HX1 ... 113 A7
Bowman La. Leeds LS10 ... 79 D7
Bowman Pl. Hali HX1 ... 113 A7 5
Bowman Rd. Brad BD6 ... 94 B7
Bowman St. Hali HX1 ... 113 A7 6
Bowman St. Wake WF1 ... 142 F3
Bowman Terr. Hali HX1 ... 113 A7
Bownas Rd. B Spa LS23 ... 30 C8
Bowness Ave. Brad BD10 ... 56 D4
Bowness Ave. Castle WF10 ... 104 E1
Bowness Dr. Hud HD5 ... 154 D7
Bowood Ave. Leeds LS7 ... 60 A7
Bowood Cres. Leeds LS7 ... 60 A7
Bowood Gr. Leeds LS7 ... 60 A7
Bowood La. Sow Br HX6 ... 111 D1
Bowwood Dr. Keigh BD20 ... 36 C8
Box La. Pont WF8 ... 125 E2
Box Tree Cl. Brad BD8 ... 54 E1
Box Trees La. Hali HX2 ... 91 D3
Boxhill Rd. Elland HX5 ... 134 F7
Boxwood Rd. Elland HX5 ... 134 F5
Boy La. Brad BD4 ... 95 B7
Boy La. Hali HX3 ... 91 D2
Boycott Dr. Ack M T WF7 ... 164 A5
Boycott Way. S Elm WF9 ... 183 A4
Boyd Ave. Brad BD3 ... 56 E1
Boyle & Petyt Sch The. Beam ... 2 F6
Boyle The. B in Elm LS15 ... 63 D8
Boyne Dr. Wake WF2 ... 160 A5
Boyne Hill. Crig WF4 ... 160 A4
Boyne St. Hali HX1 ... 113 B7
Boynton House. Brad BD15 ... 73 B8 9
Boynton St. Brad BD5 ... 74 E3
Boynton Terr. Brad BD5 ... 74 E3
Boys La. Hali HX3 ... 113 D5
Boys Scarr. Hali HX2 ... 111 D6
Bracewell Ave. Brad BD15 ... 73 A8
Bracewell Bank. Hali HX3 ... 92 A2
Bracewell Dr. Hali HX3 ... 91 F2
Bracewell Gr. Hali HX3 ... 92 A1 1
Bracewell Hill. Hali HX3 ... 91 F2
Bracewell Rd. Mel HD7 ... 170 D1
Bracewell St. Keigh BD21 ... 35 F7
Bracken Ave. Brig HD6 ... 115 A5
Bracken Bank Ave. Keigh BD22 34 F3
Bracken Bank Cr. Keigh BD22 . 35 A3
Bracken Bank Gr. Keigh BD22 . 34 F3
Bracken Bank Wy. Keigh BD22 34 F3
Bracken Bank Wlk. Keigh BD22 34 F2
Bracken Cl. Brig HD6 ... 115 A5
Bracken Cl. Mir WF14 ... 137 D7
Bracken Ct. Leeds LS17 ... 43 C1
Bracken Edge. Brad BD10 ... 56 C7
Bracken Edge. Leeds LS8 ... 60 F5
Bracken Edge Prim Sch. Leeds 60 E5
Bracken Ghyll Dr. Sil BD20 ... 5 D2
Bracken Gr. Hud HD2 ... 136 B4
Bracken Gr. Mir WF14 ... 137 D7
Bracken Hall Rd. Hud HD2 ... 136 C3
Bracken Hill. Ack M T WF7 ... 163 D6
Bracken Hill. Leeds LS17 ... 43 C1
Bracken Hill. Mir WF14 ... 137 D7
Bracken Hill. S Kirk WF9 ... 182 D4
Bracken Mount. Sil BD20 ... 5 D2
Bracken Pk. Scar LS14 ... 45 A7
Bracken Rd. Brig HD6 ... 115 A5
Bracken Rd. Keigh BD22 ... 35 A4
Bracken Rd. Stee BD20 ... 17 A5
Bracken Sq. Hud HD2 ... 136 C4
Bracken St. Keigh BD21 ... 35 B4
Brackenbeck Rd. Brad BD7 ... 73 F4
Brackenbed Grange. Hali HX2 . 91 E1
Brackenbed La. Hali HX2 ... 91 F1
Brackendale Ave. Brad BD10 .. 39 A2
Brackendale. Brad BD10 ... 39 A2
Brackendale Dr. Brad BD10 ... 38 F2
Brackendale Gr. Brad BD10 ... 38 F2
Brackendale Par. Brad BD10 ... 38 F2
Brackenhill Fst Sch. Brad ... 73 F3
Brackenholme Royd. Brad BD6 93 E8 10
Brackens La. Shelf HX3 ... 93 B7
Brackenwood Cl. Ilkley LS29 ... 8 E4
Brackenwood Cl. Leeds LS8 ... 60 E7
Brackenwood Ct. Loft G WF1 . 121 D5
Brackenwood Dr. Leeds LS8 ... 60 E8
Brackenwood Gn. Leeds LS8 ... 60 E8
Brackenwood Rd. Loft G WF1 121 D5
Bradbeck Rd. Brad BD7 ... 73 F7
Bradburn Rd. Roth WF3 ... 100 A3
Bradbury St. Dew WF13 ... 138 E5
Bradcroft. Hud HD1 ... 136 B1
Bradd Cl. Liver WF15 ... 117 B5
Bradfield Cl. Hud HD2 ... 136 E5
Bradford and Heckmondwike Rd.
Birk BD4 ... 95 F8
Bradford and Wakefield Rd.
Birk BD4, BD11 ... 96 C7
Bradford Bsns Pk. Brad ... 55 E1
Bradford City Tech Coll. Brad .. 74 D7
Bradford City Tech Coll. Brad .. 74 E4
Bradford Coll. Brad ... 74 D6
Bradford Forster Sq Sta. Brad . 74 E7
Bradford Girls' Grammar Sch.
Brad ... 54 E1
Bradford Golf Course. Guise ... 39 A7
Bradford Grammar Sch. Brad ... 55 C3
Bradford & Ilkley Community Coll.
Ilkley ... 8 A3
Bradford Ind Mus. Brad ... 56 C3
Bradford Int'change Sta. Brad . 74 F6
Bradford Moor Fst Sch. Brad ... 75 C8
Bradford Moor Golf Course.
Brad ... 56 B1
Bradford Old Rd. Hali HX3 ... 92 C2
Bradford Old Rd. Ship BD16 ... 54 B7
Bradford Rd. Batley WF17 ... 118 D5
Bradford Rd. Bing BD16 ... 37 A1
Bradford Rd. Birk BD11 ... 96 A5
Bradford Rd. Birk BD11 ... 96 D7
Bradford Rd. Brad BD10 ... 56 B6
Bradford Rd. Brad BD14 ... 73 D5
Bradford Rd. Brad BD12, BD19 95 B3
Bradford Rd. Brig HD6 ... 115 B2
Bradford Rd. Brig HD6 ... 115 B5
Bradford Rd. Bur in W LS29 ... 21 F8
Bradford Rd. Clec BD19 ... 96 C2
Bradford Rd. Clec BD19 ... 116 E8
Bradford Rd. Dew WF13 ... 118 D1
Bradford Rd. E Ard WF3 ... 120 B8
Bradford Rd. Gild LS27 ... 97 B5
Bradford Rd. Guise LS29 ... 22 B3
Bradford Rd. Hud HD1, HD2 .. 136 B3
Bradford Rd. Keigh BD20, BD21 18 E1
Bradford Rd. Liver WF15 ... 117 B4
Bradford Rd. Loft G WF2 ... 120 E5
Bradford Rd. Men LS29 ... 22 B3
Bradford Rd. Northo HX3 ... 93 A1
Bradford Rd. Northo HX3 ... 93 A3
Bradford Rd. Otley LS21 ... 22 D6
Bradford Rd. Pudsey LS28 ... 57 C1
Bradford Rd. Ship BD18 ... 54 C7
Bradford Rd. Ship BD18 ... 55 B6
Bradford Rd. Wake WF2 ... 120 F3
Bradford Royal Infmy. Brad ... 54 F1
Bradford St. Dew WF13 ... 118 D1
Bradford St. Keigh BD21 ... 35 D8
Bradfords Cl. Bramham LS23 .. 30 C3
Bradlaugh Rd. Brad BD6 ... 74 B1
Bradlaugh Terr. Brad BD6 ... 74 C1 2
Bradley Ave. Castle WF10 ... 124 C8
Bradley Ave. Sil BD20 ... 5 D2
Bradley Bvd. Hud HD2 ... 136 C3
Bradley Carr Terr. S Elm WF9 194 E8
Bradley Dr. Sil BD20 ... 5 D2
Bradley Gr. Sil BD20 ... 5 D2
Bradley Grange Gdns.
Hud HD2 ... 136 F6
Bradley Junction Ind Est. Hud 136 F4
Bradley La. Elland HX4 ... 134 B6
Bradley La. Pudsey LS28 ... 76 B7
Bradley Mills La. Hud HD1 ... 154 C8
Bradley Mills Rd. Hud HD5 ... 154 D8
Bradley Park Golf Course. Hud 136 E6
Bradley Quarry Cl. Hud HD2 .. 137 A6
Bradley Rd. Hud HD2 ... 136 D6
Bradley Rd. Sil BD20 ... 5 D2
Bradley Rise. Sil BD20 ... 5 D2
Bradley St. Bing BD16 ... 36 F3
Bradley St. Castle WF10 ... 124 D8
Bradley St. Hud HD1 ... 154 B6 13
Bradley St. Ship BD9 ... 55 C4
Bradley Terr. Leeds LS17 ... 44 A4
Bradley Voluntary CE Prim Sch.
Hud ... 136 F5
Bradleys Both Cty Prim Sch.
L Brad ... 4 C6
Bradshaw Ave. Honley HD7 ... 171 E3
Bradshaw Cl. Honley HD7 ... 171 E3
Bradshaw Cty Prim Sch. Hali ... 71 F1
Bradshaw Cres. Honley HD7 . 171 E3
Bradshaw Dr. Honley HD7 ... 171 E3
Bradshaw La. Hali HX2 ... 72 A2
Bradshaw La. Mars HD7 ... 151 A1
Bradshaw Rd. Honley HD7 ... 171 E2
Bradshaw Rd. Mel HD7 ... 188 B7
Bradstock Gdns. Morley LS27 . 98 A6
Bradwell La. Ossett WF5 ... 140 E5
Brae Ave. Brad BD2 ... 55 F3
Braemar Croft. S Hie S72 ... 180 D7
Braemar Dr. Gar LS25 ... 83 B8
Braemar Rise. S Hie S72 ... 180 D7
Brafferton Arbor. Brad BD6 ... 93 E8
Braim Wood Mid Sch. Leeds ... 61 D7
Braine Rd. Weth LS22 ... 13 F6
Braithwaite Ave. Keigh BD22 .. 34 F7
Braithwaite Cres. Keigh BD22 . 34 F7
Braithwaite Dr. Keigh BD22 ... 34 F7
Braithwaite Edge Rd.
Keigh BD22 ... 34 D8
Braithwaite Gr. Keigh BD22 ... 34 F7
Braithwaite Rd. Keigh BD22 ... 34 E8
Braithwaite Row. Leeds LS10 .. 79 E2 6
Braithwaite Sch. Keigh ... 34 E8
Braithwaite St. Leeds LS11 ... 78 F6
Braithwaite St. Mapp S75 ... 178 C1
Braithwaite Way. Keigh BD22 . 34 F7
Braithwaite Wlk. Keigh BD22 .. 34 F7
Bramah St. Roy S71 ... 179 C1
Bramble Ave. B Spa LS23 ... 30 B7
Bramble Cl. Brad BD14 ... 73 C3
Bramble Cl. Pont WF8 ... 146 B7
Bramble Wlk. Batley WF17 ... 96 F1
Brambles The. Ilkley LS29 ... 7 F4
Bramham Dr. Bail BD17 ... 38 D4
Bramham La. Bard LS23 ... 29 B3
Bramham Park. Bramham ... 47 A7
Bramham Prim Sch. Bramham 30 D4
Bramham Rd. B Spa LS23 ... 30 D4
Bramham Rd. Bing BD16 ... 37 A4
Bramham Rd. Castle WF10 ... 124 A6
Bramham Rd. Thorner LS14 ... 46 C7
Bramhope Old La. Otley LS21 .. 23 E4
Bramhope Prim & Mid Schs.
Bramho ... 24 E2
Bramhope Rd. Clec BD19 ... 116 C8
Bramleigh Dr. Morley LS27 ... 98 A6
Bramleigh Gr. Morley LS27 ... 98 A6
Bramley Cl. Holmfi HD7 ... 189 D7
Bramley Cres. Loft G WF1 ... 121 B4
Bramley Ctr. Leeds ... 58 D3
Bramley Fold. Brig HX3 ... 114 D8
Bramley Gdns. Leeds LS14 ... 45 C1
Bramley Grange Coll. Leeds ... 45 D1
Bramley Grange. Leeds LS13 .. 58 C1 7
Bramley Hill Prim Sch. Leeds .. 58 B2
Bramley La. Brig HX3 ... 114 D8
Bramley La. W Bret WF4 ... 177 B8
Bramley St. Brad BD5 ... 74 E4
Bramley St. Leeds LS13 ... 58 C1 5
Bramley Sta. Leeds ... 58 B1
Bramley View. Brig HX3 ... 114 E8
Brampton Ct. S Elm WF9 ... 183 A5
Brampton. Heb Br HX2 ... 90 B1
Bramstan Ave. Leeds LS13 ... 58 A3
Bramstan Cl. Leeds LS13 ... 58 A3
Bramstan Gdns. Leeds LS13 ... 58 A3
Bramstan Recn Ctr. Leeds ... 58 A4
Bramston St. Brig HD6 ... 115 A1
Bran St. Keigh BD21 ... 35 B4 8
Brancepeth Pl. Leeds LS12 ... 78 E7
Branch Cl. Leeds LS12 ... 78 A4
Branch End. Gild LS27 ... 97 E7
Branch La. Hud HD2 ... 135 B3
Branch Pl. Leeds LS12 ... 78 A4
Branch Rd. Batley WF17 ... 118 C5
Branch Rd. Brig BD19 ... 94 F1
Branch Rd. Crig WF4 ... 159 C4
Branch Rd. Dew WF13 ... 139 C8
Branch Rd. Elland HX4 ... 133 D5
Branch Rd. Hud HD2 ... 135 B4
Branch Rd. Leeds LS12 ... 78 A4
Branch Rd. Leeds LS12 ... 78 C8
Branch St. Hud HD1 ... 153 D5
Branch St. Leeds LS12 ... 78 A4
Brand Hill App. Crof WF4 ... 143 E1
Brand Hill Dr. Crof WF4 ... 143 E1
Brander App. Leeds LS9 ... 61 D1
Brander Cl. Leeds LS9 ... 61 D1
Brander Dr. Leeds LS9 ... 61 D1
Brander Gr. Leeds LS9 ... 61 C1
Brander House. Brad BD15 ... 73 A7 4
Brander Rd. Leeds LS9 ... 61 D1
Brander St. Leeds LS9 ... 61 D2
Brandfort St. Brad BD7 ... 74 A5
Brandon Cres. Hare LS17 ... 44 F6
Brandon Ct. Leeds LS17 ... 44 C5
Brandon La. Scar LS17 ... 44 F6
Brandon Rd. Leeds LS3 ... 60 A1 5
Brandon St. Leeds LS12 ... 78 F7
Brandon Terr. Leeds LS17 ... 44 C5
Brandon Way. Leeds LS7 ... 60 D5
Brandy Carr Rd. Wake WF2 ... 120 C3
Branksome Cres. Brad BD9 ... 54 F2
Branksome Ct. Brad BD9 ... 54 F2
Branksome Dr. Ship BD18 ... 54 D8
Branksome Gr. Ship BD18 ... 54 C8
Branksome Pl. Leeds LS6 ... 59 E2
Branksome St. Leeds LS6 ... 59 E2 9
Branksome Terr. Leeds LS6 ... 59 E2 8
Bransby Cl. Pudsey LS28 ... 57 E2
Bransby Ct. Pudsey LS28 ... 57 E2 1
Bransby Rise. Pudsey LS28 ... 57 E2
Bransdale Ave. Guise LS20 ... 39 E8
Bransdale Ave. Nor WF6 ... 123 A4
Bransdale Cl. Bail BD17 ... 38 A2
Bransdale Cl. Guise LS20 ... 39 E8

Bransdale Cl. Nor WF6 .... 123 A4
Bransdale Clough. Brad BD6 ... 73 E1
Bransdale Garth. Guise LS20 .. 39 E8
Bransdale Gdns. Guise LS20 ... 39 E8
Bransdale Mews. Nor WF6 .... 123 A4
Bransdale Wlk. Nor WF6 .... 123 A4
Branshaw Dr. Keigh BD22 .... 34 E5
Branshaw Golf Course. Keigh .. 34 D4
Branshaw Gr. Keigh BD22 .... 34 E5
Branshaw Mount. Keigh BD22 . 34 E5
Branshaw Sch. Keigh 35 A6
Branstone Gr. Ossett WF5 ...... 119 D1
Brant Ave. Hali HX2 .... 91 F4
Brant Bank La. Nes LS29 .... 7 D6
Brantcliffe Dr. Bail BD17 .... 38 C4
Brantcliffe Way. Bail BD17 .... 38 C5
Brantdale Cl. Brad BD9 .... 54 C4
Brantdale Rd. Brad BD9 .... 54 C4
Brantford St. Leeds LS7 .... 60 D6
Brantom Farm. Sow Br HX2 .. 111 C5
Brantwood Ave. Brad BD9 .... 54 C4
Brantwood Cl. Brad BD9 .... 54 C4
Brantwood Cres. Brad BD9 .... 54 C4
Brantwood Dr. Brad BD9 .... 54 C4
Brantwood Gr. Brad BD9 .... 54 B4
Brantwood Oval. Brad BD9 .... 54 C4
Brantwood Rd. Brad BD9 .... 54 B4
Brantwood Villas. Brad BD9 ..... 54 C4
Branwell Ave. Batley WF17 .... 96 F3
Branwell Dr. Haw BD22 .... 51 C8
Branxholme Ind Est. Brig 115 B7
Brassey Rd. Brad BD4 .... 75 A4
Brassey St. Hali HX1 .... 113 B6
Brassey Terr. Brad BD4 .... 75 A4
Brathay Gdns. Leeds LS14 .... 62 A3
Bray Cl. Brad BD7 .... 73 D2
Braybrook Ct. Brad BD8 .... 55 C3
Brayshaw Dr. Brad BD7 .... 73 D2
Brayshaw Rd. E Ard WF3 .... 120 C7
Brayside Ave. Hud HD2 .... 135 F2
Brayton App. Leeds LS14 .... 62 C5
Brayton Cl. Leeds LS14 .... 62 C5
Brayton Garth. Leeds LS14 ...... 62 D5 10
Brayton Gn. Leeds LS14 .... 62 D5
Brayton Gr. Leeds LS14 .... 62 C5
Brayton Grange. Leeds LS14 .... 62 D5 12
Brayton Pl. Leeds LS14 .... 62 D5 13
Brayton Sq. Leeds LS14 .... 62 D5 11
Brayton Terr. Leeds LS14 .... 62 C5 1
Brayton Wlk. Leeds LS14 .... 62 C5 2
Brazil St. Castle WF10 .... 124 E8
Bread St. Wake WF1 .... 142 C6 14
Break Neck. Hali HX3 .... 114 A8
Breakmoor Ave. Sil BD20 .... 5 E3
Breaks Rd. Brad BD12 .... 94 E6 4
Brearcliffe Cl. Brad BD6 .... 94 A8 3
Brearcliffe Dr. Brad BD6 .... 94 A8
Brearcliffe Gr. Brad BD6 .... 94 A7
Brearcliffe Rd. Brad BD6 .... 94 B7
Brearcliffe St. Brad BD6 .... 94 A7
Brearley La. Heb Br HX2 .... 111 B8
Brearley St. Batley WF17 .... 118 B4
Brearton St. Brad BD1 .... 74 E8
Breary Ave. Hors LS18 .... 41 D1
Breary Ct. Bramho LS16 .... 24 E3
Breary La. Bramho LS16 .... 24 E3
Breary La E. Bramho LS16 .... 25 A3
Breary Rise. Bramho LS16 .... 24 E3
Breary Terr. Hors LS18 .... 41 D1
Breary Wlk. Hors LS18 .... 41 D1
Breck Lea. Sow Br HX6 .... 112 A3
Breck Willows. Sow Br HX6 ... 111 F2
Brecks Gdns. Kippax LS25 .... 82 F3
Brecks La. Kippax LS25 .... 82 F3
Brecks La. Swil LS26 .... 82 C4
Brecks Rd. Brad BD14 .... 73 D5
Brecon App. Leeds LS9 .... 61 D1
Brecon Ave. Hud HD3 .... 135 A1
Brecon Cl. Brad BD10 .... 56 B7
Brecon Ct. Leeds LS9 .... 61 D1
Brecon Rise. Leeds LS9 .... 61 D1
Bredon Ave. Ship BD18 .... 55 F7
Bredon Cl. Hem WF9 .... 181 F7
Breighton Adown. Brad BD6 ..... 93 D8
Bremner St. Otley LS21 .... 23 B8
Brendan Ct. Brad BD10 .... 56 D6
Brendon Ct. Brad BD4 .... 75 D3
Brendon Ct. Mir WF14 .... 137 F2
Brendon Dr. Hud HD2 .... 135 D1
Brendon Wlk. Brad BD4 .... 75 D2
Brentford Rd. Brad BD12 .... 94 C6
Brentlea Ave. Wake WF2 .... 142 B3
Brentwood Cl. Batley WF17 .... 118 E5
Brentwood Cl. Th Aud WF8 .... 165 A5
Brentwood Gdns. Brad BD6 ...... 94 D8
Brentwood Gr. Leeds LS12 ...... 78 C7 9
Brentwood St. Leeds LS12 .... 78 C7 10
Brentwood Terr. Leeds LS12 .... 78 C7 11
Bretfield Ct. Dew WF12 .... 139 D5
Brett Gdns. Leeds LS11 .... 79 B4
Brettegate. Hem WF9 .... 181 C7
Bretton Country Pk. W Bret 176 F7
Bretton Hall Coll (Annexe).
Castle 124 C7
Bretton Hall Coll of Higher Ed.
W Bret 176 E6
Bretton La. Crig WF4 .... 159 C3
Bretton La. W Bret WF4 .... 159 B2
Bretton St. Dew WF12 .... 139 D5
Brevitt St. Wake WF1 .... 142 E3
Brewerton La. Batley WF13 ..... 117 F2
Brewery Dr. Hud HD4 .... 153 E2
Brewery La. Dew WF12 .... 139 C4
Brewery La. Knot WF11 .... 126 F4
Brewery La. Queen BD13 .... 72 D3
Brewery La. Queen BD13 .... 92 C7
Brewery Rd. Ilkley LS29 .... 8 C4
Brewery Rd. Keigh BD21 .... 35 A3
Brewery St. Batley WF16 .... 117 D3 5
Brewery St. Hali HX3 .... 92 C2 1
Brewery St. Keigh BD21 .... 35 D7
Brewery St. Tod OL14 .... 107 E8
Brewery Wharf Mus. Leeds 79 D7
Brewery Yard. Hud HD5 .... 155 C3
Brexdale Ave. Kippax LS25 .... 82 F3
Brian Ave. Hud HD5 .... 154 E5
Brian Cres. Leeds LS15 .... 62 B3
Brian Pl. Leeds LS15 .... 62 B3
Brian Royd La. Elland HX4 ...... 133 F7
Brian St. Hud HD3 .... 135 B1
Brian View. Leeds LS15 .... 62 C3
Briar Ave. Mel HD7 .... 170 C3
Briar Bank. Hem WF9 .... 163 A2
Briar Cl. Batley WF16 .... 117 D5
Briar Cl. Elland HX5 .... 134 E5
Briar Cl. Pudsey LS28 .... 57 D3
Briar Dr. Batley WF13 .... 117 F2
Briar Gate. Weth LS22 .... 13 E7
Briar Gr. Bri S72 .... 181 A3
Briar Gr. Wake WF1 .... 142 E3
Briar Rhydding. Bail BD17 .... 38 E2
Briar St. Bacup OL13 .... 106 A1 5
Briar Wood. Ship BD18 .... 55 E7
Briardale Rd. Brad BD9 .... 54 B4
Briarfield Ave. Brad BD10 .... 56 A7
Briarfield Cl. Brad BD10 .... 56 A7
Briarfield Cl. Ilkley LS29 .... 8 D3
Briarfield Gdns. Ship BD18 .... 55 C6
Briarfield Gr. Brad BD10 .... 56 A7
Briarfield Rd. Holmfi HD7 .... 189 C7
Briarfield Rd. Ship BD18 .... 55 C5
Briarlea Cl. Yeadon LS19 .... 39 F5
Briarlyn Ave. Hud HD3 .... 135 A2
Briarlyn Rd. Hud HD3 .... 135 B2
Briarmains Rd. Batley WF17 ..... 96 F2
Briarsdale Croft. Leeds LS8 ...... 61 C3
Briarsdale Ct. Leeds LS8 .... 61 C3
Briarsdale Garth. Leeds LS8 ...... 61 B3
Briarsdale Hts. Leeds LS9 .... 61 C3
Briarwood Ave. Brad BD6 .... 74 B1
Briarwood Ave. Keigh BD20 ...... 18 F1
Briarwood Cl. Loft G WF1 .... 121 D5
Briarwood Cres. Brad BD6 .... 74 B1
Briarwood Dr. Brad BD6 .... 74 B1
Briarwood Gr. Brad BD6 .... 74 B2
Brick and Tile Terr. Brig HD6 .. 115 A1
Brick Mill Rd. Pudsey LS28 .... 76 F6
Brick Row. Brad BD12 .... 94 C3
Brick St. Clec BD19 .... 116 C7
Brick St. Leeds LS9 .... 79 D7
Brick St. Wake WF2 .... 141 D7
Brick Terr. Brig HD6 .... 115 B1
Brickbank. Hud HD5 .... 154 F3
Brickfield Gr. Hali HX2 .... 92 A5
Brickfield La. Hali HX2 .... 92 A5
Brickfield Terr. Hali HX2 .... 92 A5
Brickyard. Mir WF14 .... 137 F5 7
Bride St. Tod OL14 .... 108 B6
Bridge Ave. Otley LS21 .... 23 A8
Bridge Cl. B Spa LS23 .... 30 E8
Bridge Cl. Clay W HD8 .... 175 E2
Bridge Cl. Hor WF4 .... 140 E1
Bridge Cotts. Aber LS25 .... 64 E7
Bridge Croft. Hud HD3 .... 153 B4
Bridge Ct. Hem WF9 .... 163 A2
Bridge Ct. Morley LS27 .... 98 B3
Bridge End. Brig HD6 .... 115 A1
Bridge End. Glu BD20 .... 16 B6
Bridge End. Leeds LS1 .... 79 C7
Bridge End St. Tod OL14 .... 86 C1
Bridge Fold. Leeds LS5 .... 59 A4
Bridge Foot. Th Arch LS23 .... 30 E8
Bridge Garth. B Spa LS23 .... 30 D6
Bridge Gate. Heb Br HX7 .... 89 A3
Bridge La. Holmfi HD7 .... 189 A6
Bridge La. Ilkley LS29 .... 8 A4
Bridge La. Knot WF11 .... 126 F5
Bridge La. Shelf HX3 .... 93 B7
Bridge La. Th Aud WF8 .... 165 B4
Bridge Lanes. Heb Br HX7 .... 88 F3
Bridge Paddock. Coll LS22 .... 13 B1
Bridge Rd. B Spa LS23 .... 30 E8
Bridge Rd. Brig HD6 .... 115 A2
Bridge Rd. Hor WF4 .... 140 E1
Bridge Rd. Hud HD2 .... 137 B5
Bridge Rd. Leeds LS5 .... 59 A4
Bridge Rd. Leeds LS11 .... 79 A6
Bridge Rd. Pudsey LS13 .... 57 E5
Bridge Rd. S in Cra BD20 .... 16 D5
Bridge Rd. Sil BD20 .... 5 E2
Bridge St. Batley WF17 .... 117 E8
Bridge St. Batley WF17 .... 118 D5
Bridge St. Brad BD1 .... 74 F6
Bridge St. Castle WF10 .... 124 E8
Bridge St. Haw BD22 .... 34 B2
Bridge St. Hud HD4 .... 153 F3
Bridge St. Hud HD4 .... 171 F8
Bridge St. Keigh BD21 .... 35 B6
Bridge St. Leeds LS2 .... 79 D8 3
Bridge St. Liver WF16 .... 117 C4
Bridge St. Mapp S75 .... 177 E1
Bridge St. Morley LS27 .... 98 B2
Bridge St. Nor WF6 .... 123 C3
Bridge St. Otley LS21 .... 23 A8
Bridge St. Pont WF8 .... 146 D8 7
Bridge St. Sil BD20 .... 5 E2
Bridge St. Slai HD7 .... 152 A1
Bridge St. Sow Br HX6 .... 112 B3
Bridge St. Thorn BD13 .... 72 E6 1
Bridge St. Tod OL14 .... 108 B5
Bridge St. Wake WF1 .... 142 D4
Bridge Terr. Hali HX2 .... 90 E6
Bridge View. Pudsey LS13 .... 57 E6
Bridge Wood Cl. Hors LS18 .... 41 D2
Bridge Works Bsns Pk. Honley 172 A4
Bridgegate Way. Brad BD10 ...... 56 D5
Bridgehouse La. Haw BD22 ...... 51 C6
Bridgewater Ct. Leeds LS6 .... 59 F6
Bridgewater Park Dr.
Ad Le S DN6 .... 184 F2
Bridgewater Rd. Leeds LS9 .... 79 F5
Bridgeway. Brad BD4 .... 75 D3
Bridgland Ave. Men LS29 .... 22 A5
Bridgwater Rd. Brad BD9 .... 55 A2
Bridle Ave. Ossett WF5 .... 140 C8
Bridle Cl. Neth WF4 .... 158 E7
Bridle Dene. Shelf HX3 .... 93 C5
Bridle La. Neth WF4 .... 158 E7
Bridle La. Ossett WF5 .... 140 C8
Bridle Path Rd. Hare LS17 .... 44 E5
Bridle Path Rd. Leeds LS15 ...... 62 A2
Bridle Path Wlk. Leeds LS15 .... 62 A2 3
Bridle Pl. Ossett WF5 .... 140 D8
Bridle St. Batley WF17 .... 118 E5
Bridle Stile La. Queen BD13 ...... 72 E2
Bridle Stile. Shelf HX3 .... 93 C5
Bridley Brook. Slai HD7 .... 170 A5
Bridley Dr. Slai HD7 .... 170 A8
Brier Hey Cl. Heb Br HX7 .... 89 F1
Brier Hey La. Heb Br HX7 .... 89 F1
Brier Hill Cl. Clec BD19 .... 116 A6
Brier Hill View. Hud HD2 .... 136 D5
Brier La. Brig HD6 .... 114 E2
Brier La. Ryhill WF4 .... 180 C8
Brier St. Hali HX3 .... 92 B2
Brier St. Keigh BD21 .... 35 B4
Brierdene. Sil BD20 .... 5 E2
Brierfield Gdns. Gild LS27 .... 97 C6
Brierlands Cl. Gar LS25 .... 83 B8
Brierlands Fold. Gar LS25 .... 83 B8
Brierlands La. Gar LS25 .... 83 B8
Brierley Cl. Ship BD18 .... 55 C6
Brierley Cres. S Kirk WF9 .... 182 C3
Brierley Rd. Grim S72 .... 181 A1
Brierley Rd. S Hie S72 .... 180 E5
Brierley Rd. Shaf S72 .... 180 D2
Briery Cl. Ilkley LS29 .... 7 E4
Briery Field. Ship BD18 .... 55 B5
Briery Gr. Mir WF14 .... 138 A2
Briestfield Rd. Dew WF12 .... 156 E6
Brig Royd. Rip HX6 .... 132 E5
Brigg Gdns. Keigh BD22 .... 34 F7
Brigg's Ave. Castle WF10 .... 124 E6
Briggate. Brig HD6 .... 115 A2
Briggate. Elland HX5 .... 134 F7
Briggate. Hud HD5 .... 155 A7
Briggate. Leeds LS1 .... 79 C7
Briggate. Ship BD17 .... 55 B8
Briggate. Ship BD18 .... 55 C7
Briggate. Sil BD20 .... 5 E2
Briggland Ct. Wils BD15 .... 53 C5
Briggs Ave. Brad BD6 .... 74 A1
Briggs Gr. Brad BD6 .... 74 A1
Briggs Pl. Brad BD6 .... 74 A1
Briggs Rd. Roy S71 .... 179 C1
Briggs Row. Feath WF7 .... 145 D4
Briggs St. Queen BD13 .... 72 E1
Briggs Terr. Hud HD5 .... 154 D6 2
Brighouse and Clifton CE (A) Prim
Sch. Brig 115 E2
Brighouse and Denholme Gate Rd.
Northo HX3 .... 93 B4
Brighouse and Denholme Gate Rd.
Queen HX3 .... 92 F6
Brighouse and Denholme Gate Rd.
Shelf HX3 .... 93 B4
Brighouse and Denholme Rd.
Queen BD13 .... 72 B3
Brighouse Cemy. Brig 115 A5
Brighouse Eastfield Sec Sch.
Brig 114 F7
Brighouse F Ed Ctr. Brig 115 A3
Brighouse High Sch. Brig 114 F5
Brighouse High Sch. Brig 115 A2
Brighouse Liby & Smith Art Gal.
Brig 115 A3
Brighouse Rd. Brad BD12 .... 94 D6
Brighouse Rd. Brig HX3 .... 114 D7
Brighouse Rd. Denh BD13 .... 71 E6
Brighouse Rd. Hud HD3 .... 135 B3
Brighouse Rd. Queen BD13 .... 92 F7
Brighouse Rd. Shelf BD13, HX3 92 F7
Brighouse Wood La. Brig HD6 114 F3
Brighouse Wood Rw. Brig HD6 114 F3
Brighouse Woodhouse Jun & Inf
Sch. Brig 136 B8
Bright St. Brad BD15 .... 54 B1
Bright St. Brad BD14 .... 73 B4
Bright St. Dew WF13 .... 118 C1 3
Bright St. E Ard WF3 .... 120 E8
Bright St. Farnh BD20 .... 4 D1
Bright St. Hali HX6 .... 112 B5
Bright St. Haw BD22 .... 51 D7 8
Bright St. Mir WF14 .... 138 A8
Bright St. Morley LS27 .... 98 A4
Bright St. Pudsey LS28 .... 57 F2
Bright St. Queen BD13 .... 72 F1
Bright St. Tod OL14 .... 108 A3
Brighton Ave. Morley LS27 .... 97 F5
Brighton Cl. Batley WF17 .... 117 E6
Brighton Cliff. Leeds LS13 .... 58 C2
Brighton Gr. Hali HX1 .... 113 A8 5
Brighton Gr. Leeds LS13 .... 58 D1
Brighton Rd. Ilkley LS29 .... 8 E3
Brighton St. Batley WF16 .... 117 D4
Brighton St. Brad BD10 .... 39 A1
Brighton St. Hali HX3 .... 92 A1 21
Brighton St. Ship BD17 .... 55 B8
Brighton St. Tod OL14 .... 86 C1
Brighton St. Wake WF2 .... 142 A5
Brighton Terr. Brig BD19 .... 94 F1
Brignall Croft. Leeds LS9 .... 60 F1
Brignall Garth. Leeds LS9 .... 60 F1
Brignall Way. Leeds LS9 .... 60 F1
Brigshaw Comprehensive Sch.
Kippax 102 F7
Brigshaw Dr. Kippax WF10 ...... 102 F6
Brigshaw La.
Kippax LS25, WF10 .... 103 A8
Brindley Gr. Brad BD8 .... 73 C7
Brindley Rd. Sil BD20 .... 17 F8
Brindley Way. Loft G WF2 .... 120 F4
Brindley Way. Loft G WF2 .... 121 A4
Brisbane Ave. Brad BD2 .... 55 E3
Briscoe La. Elland HX4 .... 134 B7
Bristfield Rd. Dew WF12 .... 157 A8
Bristol Ave. Keigh BD20 .... 36 B8
Bristol St. Hali HX3 .... 113 D3
Bristol St. Leeds LS7 .... 60 D1
Britannia Ave. Bacup OL13 ..... 106 A2
Britannia Bldgs. Morley LS27 .. 97 F2
Britannia Cl. Pudsey LS28 .... 57 F2 8
Britannia Ct. Pudsey LS13 .... 77 A8
Britannia Rd. Hud HD3, HD7 .. 152 F4
Britannia Rd. Morley LS27 .... 98 A2
Britannia Rd. Slai HD7 .... 169 F8
Britannia Sq. Morley LS27 .... 97 F2
Britannia St. Bing BD16 .... 37 A3
Britannia St. Brad BD5 .... 74 F6
Britannia St. Leeds LS1 .... 79 B7
Britannia St. Pudsey LS28 .... 58 A2
Britannia Terr. Clec BD19 .... 116 D8
British Liby Document Supply Ctr
The. Th Arch 15 B3
Briton Sq. Dearne S63 .... 194 E1
Briton St. Dearne S63 .... 194 E1
Britton St. Liver BD19 .... 116 F6
Broad Acres. Crig WF4 .... 160 A7
Broad Balk. H Pag DN5 .... 195 E6
Broad Carr La. Elland HX4 ...... 134 C4
Broad Carr La. Holmfi HD7 ..... 190 A2
Broad Cut Rd. Crig WF4 .... 159 D7
Broad Gate. Tod OL14 .... 108 D6
Broad Gate. Tod OL14 .... 109 A5
Broad Head La. Haw BD20 .... 33 D3
Broad Ings Way. Shelf HX3 .... 93 C5
Broad La. Brad BD4 .... 75 D5
Broad La. Heb Br HX7 .... 88 F1
Broad La. Hep HX7 .... 88 B6
Broad La. Holmfi HD7 .... 188 D5
Broad La. Hud HD5 .... 154 D6
Broad La. Leeds LS5, LS13,
LS28 .... 58 C3
Broad La. Pont WF8 .... 125 D1
Broad La. S Elm WF9 .... 182 E1
Broad La. S Kirk WF9 .... 194 C8
Broad La. Sow Br HX2 .... 111 C5
Broad La. Tod OL14 .... 87 D1
Broad Lane Cl. Leeds LS13 .... 58 E4
Broad Lane Mid Sch. Leeds 58 C3
Broad Oak. Hud HD7 .... 152 E2
Broad Oak La. Brig HX3 .... 114 D6
Broad Oak La. Ingb S30 .... 192 D2
Broad Oak Pl. Brig HX3 .... 114 D6
Broad Oak St. Brig HX3 .... 114 D6
Broad St. Brad BD1 .... 74 E7
Broad St. Dew WF13 .... 139 A6
Broad St. Hali HX1 .... 113 C7
Broad St. Pudsey LS28 .... 57 C3
Broad St. Tod OL14 .... 108 B6
Broad Tree Rd. Hali HX3 .... 92 A2
Broad View. Ossett WF5 .... 140 F5
Broad Way Ct. Dew WF12 .... 139 E1
Broadacre Rd. Ossett WF5 ...... 140 F5
Broadbent Croft. Honley HD7 .. 172 A4
Broadcroft Chase. E Ard WF3 .. 119 E7
Broadcroft Dr. E Ard WF3 .... 119 E8
Broadcroft Gr. E Ard WF3 .... 119 E8
Broadcroft Way. E Ard WF3 .... 119 E8
Broadfield Cl. Brad BD4 .... 75 E1
Broadfield Ind Est. Hud 153 F3
Broadfield Way. Sil LS29 .... 6 D8
Broadfolds. Brad BD14 .... 73 C4
Broadgate Ave. Hors LS18 .... 41 D1
Broadgate Cres. Hors LS18 .... 58 C8
Broadgate Cres. Hud HD5 .... 154 D4
Broadgate Dr. Hors LS18 .... 41 D1
Broadgate. Elland HX4 .... 134 A2
Broadgate. Hud HD5 .... 154 D4
Broadgate Inf Sch. Hors 41 C1
Broadgate Jun Sch. Hors 41 C1
Broadgate La. Hors LS18 .... 41 C1
Broadgate. Ossett WF5 .... 140 E5
Broadgate Rise. Hors LS18 .... 58 D8
Broadgate Wlk. Hors LS18 .... 58 C8
Broadlands. Keigh BD20 .... 35 A8
Broadlands Rd. Mel HD7 .... 170 D3
Broadlands St. Brad BD4 .... 75 D4
Broadlea Ave. Leeds LS13 .... 58 E4
Broadlea Cl. Leeds LS13 .... 58 E4
Broadlea Cres. Brad BD5 .... 74 F3
Broadlea Cres. Leeds LS13 .... 58 E4
Broadlea Gdns. Leeds LS13 ...... 58 E4
Broadlea Gr. Leeds LS13 .... 58 E4
Broadlea Hill. Leeds LS13 .... 58 E4
Broadlea Mount. Leeds LS13 ... 58 F3
Broadlea Oval. Leeds LS13 .... 58 E4
Broadlea Pl. Leeds LS13 .... 58 E3
Broadlea Rd. Leeds LS13 .... 58 E4
Broadlea St. Leeds LS13 .... 58 E4
Broadlea Terr. Leeds LS13 .... 58 F4
Broadlea View. Leeds LS13 ...... 58 D4
Broadley Ave. Hali HX2 .... 91 B2
Broadley Cl. Hali HX2 .... 91 C1
Broadley Cres. Hali HX2 .... 91 C1
Broadley Gr. Hali HX2 .... 91 C1
Broadley Lathe. Hali HX2 .... 91 C2
Broadley Rd. Hali HX2 .... 91 B1
Broadmead. Castle WF10 .... 124 F8
Broadmeadows. Loft G WF1 .. 121 D5
Broadoaks Cl. Dew WF12 .... 140 A7
Broadowler La. Ossett WF5 ..... 140 F5
Broadstone Rd. D Dale HD8 .. 190 F3
Broadstone Rd. Ingb S30 .... 191 A1
Broadstone St. Tod OL14 .... 108 D6
Broadstone Way. Brad BD4 ...... 75 E3
Broadwalk. Otley LS21 .... 10 E1
Broadway Ave. Brad BD5 .... 74 D2
Broadway Ave. Leeds LS6 .... 59 E2
Broadway. Bing BD16 .... 37 A2
Broadway. Brad BD1 .... 74 F7
Broadway Cl. Brad BD5 .... 74 D2
Broadway Ct. Sow Br HX6 .... 111 E3
Broadway Dr. Hors LS18 .... 58 B8 4
Broadway. Guise LS20 .... 39 C8
Broadway. Hali HX3 .... 113 F5
Broadway. Hors LS18 .... 58 C8
Broadway. Hud HD1 .... 154 B7 8
Broadway. Leeds LS5 .... 58 E7
Broadway. Leeds LS15 .... 80 F7
Broadway. Mapp S75 .... 178 B1
Broadway. Pont WF8 .... 146 E7
Broadway. S Elm WF9 .... 182 E1
Broadway. Sow Br HX6 .... 111 E3
Broadway Terr. S Elm WF9 ...... 182 E1
Broadway. Wake WF2 .... 141 D4
Broadwell Rd. Ossett WF5 .... 140 F5
Broadwood Ave. Hali HX2 .... 91 C1
Brock Bank. Hud HD5 .... 154 F7
Brockadale Ave. Pont WF8 ...... 146 D5
Brockholes CE Prim Sch.
Honley 172 C2
Brockholes La. Honley HD7 .... 172 C3
Brockholes Rd. Honley HD4 .... 172 D4
Brockholes Rd. Kirkb HD4 ...... 172 D4
Brockholes Sta. Honley 172 C3
Brocklesby Dr. Brad BD15 .... 73 B8
Brocks. Sow Br HX2 .... 111 C6
Brockstones. Elland HX4 .... 133 F7
Brockswood Ct. Walton WF2 . 161 C5
Brockwell Gdns. Sow Br HX6 . 112 A3
Brockwell La. Sow Br HX6 ..... 111 F2
Brockwell La. Sow Br HX6 ..... 112 A2
Brodetsky Jewish Prim Sch.
Leeds 43 C4
Brodrick Ct. Leeds LS6 .... 59 D5
Broken Cross. Hud HD5 .... 154 E2
Broken Way. Brad BD5 .... 74 D2
Bromet Pl. Brad BD2 .... 56 B4
Bromfield Ct. Roy S71 .... 179 D4
Bromford Rd. Brad BD4 .... 75 B3
Bromley Ave. Holmfi HD7 ...... 189 D7
Bromley Gr. Keigh BD22 .... 34 E5
Bromley Mount. Wake WF1 ... 142 D4
Bromley Rd. Batley WF17 .... 118 E3
Bromley Rd. Bing BD16 .... 36 F4
Bromley Rd. Hud HD2 .... 135 F1
Bromley Rd. Ship BD18 .... 54 E8
Bromley St. Batley WF17 .... 118 D3
Brompton Ave. Brad BD4 .... 75 A4
Brompton Gr. Leeds LS11 .... 79 B2 2
Brompton Mount. Leeds LS11 . 79 B2 5
Brompton Rd. Brad BD4 .... 75 B4
Brompton Row. Leeds LS11 ..... 79 B3 28
Brompton Terr. Leeds LS11 ...... 79 B2 4
Brompton View. Leeds LS11 .... 79 B2 3
Bronshill Gr. Brad BD15 .... 54 C1
Bronte Ave. Knot WF11 .... 126 B4
Bronte Bridge. Haw 50 B4
Bronte Cl. Batley WF13 .... 117 F2
Bronte Cl. Brad BD9 .... 54 E2
Bronte Cl. Clec BD19 .... 96 B1
Bronte Cl. Hud HD4 .... 153 D3
Bronte Dr. Keigh BD22 .... 34 F3
Bronte Gr. Hem WF9 .... 181 C6
Bronte Gr. Mir WF14 .... 138 C4
Bronte House Sch. Yeadon 39 F2
Bronte Mid Sch. Haw 34 E3
Bronte Old Rd. Thorn BD13 ..... 72 E6
Bronte Parsonage Mus. Haw .. 51 B7
Bronte Pl. Thorn BD13 .... 72 E6
Bronte Rd. Batley WF17 .... 96 E1
Bronte St. Haw BD22 .... 51 B7 1
Bronte St. Keigh BD21 .... 35 D8
Bronte Way. Mir WF14 .... 138 C4
Brook Cl. Ossett WF5 .... 140 F3
Brook Cotts. Rip HX6 .... 132 B7
Brook Dr. Elland HX4 .... 134 C4
Brook Field. Mir WF14 .... 137 F2
Brook Gdns. Dew WF13 .... 139 B8 10
Brook Gdns. Mel HD7 .... 170 D3
Brook Grain Hill. Brig HD6 ...... 136 A8
Brook Grains La. Rip HX6 .... 132 D2
Brook Hill. Bail BD17 .... 38 D3
Brook Hill La. Carl S30 .... 200 B3
Brook Hill La. Dun Br S30 .... 199 F2
Brook La. Clec WF15 .... 116 C4
Brook La. Hud HD7 .... 152 D4
Brook Rd. Dew WF12 .... 139 B7 4
Brook Side. Slai HD7 .... 152 A2
Brook St. Brad BD12 .... 95 B5
Brook St. Castle WF10 .... 104 C3
Brook St. Dew WF13 .... 117 F1
Brook St. Elland HX5 .... 135 A6
Brook St. Heb Br HX7 .... 89 A4 3
Brook St. Hud HD1 .... 153 E4
Brook St. Hud HD1 .... 154 A7
Brook St. Hud HD5 .... 154 D6
Brook St. Ilkley LS29 .... 8 B4
Brook St. Keigh BD21 .... 35 B5 11
Brook St. Nor WF6 .... 122 F3
Brook St. Ossett WF5 .... 140 D5
Brook St. Tod OL14 .... 108 B5 10
Brook St. Wake WF1 .... 142 C6
Brook Terr. Hali HX2 .... 90 E2
Brook Terr. Slai HD7 .... 152 A2
Brook The. Litt OL15 .... 129 C1
Brook's Yd. Hud HD1 .... 154 A6 17
Brookdale Ave. Ossett WF5 .... 119 D1
Brookdale. Tod OL14 .... 108 A2
Brooke Ct. Pont WF8 .... 146 D5
Brooke St. Batley WF16 .... 117 D3 8
Brooke St. Brig HD6 .... 115 A1
Brooke St. Clec BD19 .... 116 E7
Brookeville Ave. Brig HX3 .... 114 C7
Brookfield Ave. Castle WF10 . 124 F7
Brookfield Ave. Clec BD19 .... 95 E1
Brookfield Ave. Leeds LS8 .... 60 F4
Brookfield Ave. Pudsey LS13 .... 57 D6
Brookfield Ave. Ship BD18 .... 55 D8
Brookfield Ct. Nor WF6 .... 123 C2
Brookfield Ct. Pudsey LS13 ...... 57 D6
Brookfield Dr. Ack M T WF7 .. 164 C8
Brookfield Fst Sch. Brad 56 E6
Brookfield Gdns. Pudsey LS13 . 57 D6
Brookfield. Kirkb HD8 .... 173 E6
Brookfield Pl. Leeds LS6 .... 59 E6
Brookfield Rd. Brad BD3 .... 75 A8
Brookfield Rd. Leeds LS6 .... 59 E6
Brookfield Rd. Ship BD18 .... 55 D8
Brookfield St. Leeds LS10 .... 79 D5
Brookfield St. Tod OL14 .... 86 C1
Brookfield Terr. Clec BD19 .... 95 E1
Brookfield Terr. Leeds LS10 ..... 79 D5
Brookfield View. Clec BD19 ...... 95 E1
Brookfields Ave. Brig BD12 ...... 94 E1
Brookfields. Neth WF4 .... 158 D5
Brookfields Rd. Brig BD12 .... 94 E1
Brookfoot Ave. Birk BD11 .... 96 A5
Brookfoot La. Brig HD6 .... 114 E3
Brookgreen. Brig HX3 .... 114 C8
Brookhill Ave. Leeds LS17 .... 43 E4
Brookhill Cl. Leeds LS17 .... 43 E4
Brookhill Cres. Leeds LS17 .... 43 E4
Brookhill Dr. Leeds LS17 .... 43 E4
Brookhill Gr. Leeds LS17 .... 43 E4
Brookhouse Gdns. Brad BD10 .. 56 F8
Brookland Towers. Leeds LS14 62 A5 3
Brooklands Ave. Elland HX4 .. 134 B4
Brooklands Ave. Leeds LS14 ..... 62 A4
Brooklands Ave. Walton WF2 161 B7
Brooklands. Brig HX3 .... 114 D7
Brooklands Cl. Elland HX4 ...... 134 B4
Brooklands Cl. Leeds LS14 .... 61 E4
Brooklands Cl. Men LS29 .... 22 B5
Brooklands Cres. Leeds LS14 .. 61 E4
Brooklands Cres. Ryhill WF4 . 162 D1
Brooklands Cres. Yeadon LS19 40 B6
Brooklands Ct. Ossett WF5 ... 141 A4
Brooklands Dr. Leeds LS14 .... 61 E4
Brooklands Dr. Yeadon LS19 ..... 40 B6
Brooklands. E Kes LS17 .... 28 C5
Brooklands Garth. Leeds LS14 61 F4
Brooklands Gr. Men LS29 .... 22 B5
Brooklands. Hud HD2 .... 136 F5
Brooklands La. Leeds LS14 ...... 61 F4
Brooklands La. Men LS29 .... 22 B5
Brooklands Rd. Walton WF2 .. 161 C7
Brooklands View. Leeds LS14 .. 61 F4
Brooklands View. Walton WF2 161 C7
Brooklands Way. Men LS29 ...... 22 A5
Brooklands Wlk. Men LS29 ...... 22 B5
Brookleigh. Pudsey LS28 .... 57 B6
Brooklyn Ave. Hud HD5 .... 155 A6
Brooklyn Ave. Leeds LS12 .... 78 D7
Brooklyn Ct. Clec BD19 .... 116 D8
Brooklyn Dr. Clec BD19 .... 116 D8
Brooklyn Pl. Leeds LS12 .... 78 C7
Brooklyn Rd. Clec BD19 .... 116 D8
Brooklyn St. Keigh BD20 .... 18 A2
Brooklyn St. Leeds LS12 .... 78 C7
Brooklyn Terr. Brig HD6 .... 114 E5
Brooklyn Terr. Leeds LS12 .... 78 C7
Brookroyd Ave. Brig HD6 .... 115 B6
Brookroyd Gdns. Batley WF17 117 F8 3
Brookroyd La. Batley WF17 .... 117 F8
Brooks Terr. Brad BD13 .... 73 B2
Brooks Yd. Dew WF13 .... 139 B7
Brooks Yd. Hud HD1, HD2 ...... 137 A5
Brooksbank Ave. Brad BD7 .... 73 E5
Brooksbank Dr. Leeds LS15 ...... 81 A8
Brooksbank Gdns. Elland HX5 134 F6
Brooksbank Sch The. Elland .. 134 E6
Brooksbank. Wake WF2 .... 142 B6
Brooksfield. S Kirk WF9 .... 182 D4
Brookside. Coll LS22 .... 29 B8
Brookside. D Dale HD8 .... 191 F6
Brookside Fold. Oxen BD22 ...... 51 C2 2
Brookside. Heb Br HX7 .... 88 E4
Brookside. Hem WF9 .... 181 E7
Brookside. Leeds LS17 .... 43 E5
Brookside St. S Elm WF9 .... 182 F3
Brookside Terr. S Elm WF9 ..... 182 F3
Brookway. Feath WF7 .... 145 D5
Broom Cl. Midd LS10 .... 99 F7
Broom Cres. Midd LS10 .... 99 E7
Broom Cross. Midd LS10 .... 99 E7
Broom Field La. Emley HD8 ... 175 B7
Broom Garth. Midd LS10 .... 99 F7
Broom Gdns. Midd LS10 .... 99 E7
Broom Gr. Midd LS10 .... 99 F6
Broom Hall Ave. Wake WF1 .. 121 A2
Broom Hall Cres. Wake WF1 . 121 A2
Broom Hill Rd. Elland HX4 ..... 151 D8
Broom Lawn. Midd LS10 .... 99 E7
Broom Mount. Midd LS10 .... 99 F6
Broom Nook. Midd LS10 .... 99 F7
Broom Pl. Midd LS10 .... 99 F6
Broom Rd. Midd LS10 .... 99 E7
Broom St. Brad BD4 .... 74 F6
Broom St. Clec BD19 .... 116 B6
Broom St. Keigh BD21 .... 35 C6 7
Broom Terr. Midd LS10 .... 99 F7
Broom View. Midd LS10 .... 99 F7
Broom Wlk. Batley WF17 .... 118 E5
Broombank. D Dale HD8 .... 191 F5
Broombank. Hud HD2 .... 135 D2
Broomcroft. Brad BD14 .... 73 B4 11
Broomcroft Ct. Ossett WF5 .... 140 D4
Broome Ave. Brad BD2 .... 55 E3
Broome Cl. Nor WF6 .... 123 A4
Broomer St. Dew WF13 .... 138 E6
Broomfield Ave. Hali HX3 .... 113 B3
Broomfield Cl. Emley HD8 ..... 175 C7
Broomfield Cres. Leeds LS6 ..... 59 D4
Broomfield. Elland HX5 .... 134 D6
Broomfield Gdns. Hud HD2 .... 136 A5
Broomfield. Hors LS16 .... 42 B4
Broomfield Pl. Brad BD14 .... 73 A3
Broomfield Pl. Keigh BD21 .... 35 B7 3
Broomfield Pl. Leeds LS6 .... 59 D3
Broomfield Rd. Hud HD1, HD2 136 A5
Broomfield Rd. Hud HD1, HD2 153 D6
Broomfield Rd. Keigh BD21 ...... 35 B7 4
Broomfield Rd. Leeds LS6 .... 59 D4
Broomfield Sch. Midd 99 F7
Broomfield St. Keigh BD21 .... 35 B7
Broomfield St. Leeds LS6 .... 59 D3 3
Broomfield St. Queen BD13 ...... 72 E1
Broomfield Terr. Clec BD19 .... 116 B7
Broomfield Terr. Hud HD1 ..... 153 D7
Broomfield Terr. Leeds LS6 ...... 59 D3
Broomfield View. Leeds LS6 ..... 59 D3 5
Broomhey Ave. Emley HD8 ..... 175 D6
Broomhill Ave. Keigh BD21 ..... 35 A5
Broomhill Ave. Knot WF11 ...... 127 B3
Broomhill Ave. Leeds LS17 .... 43 D1
Broomhill. Castle WF10 .... 125 A6
Broomhill Cl. Holmfi HD7 .... 189 D3
Broomhill Cl. Knot WF11 .... 127 B3
Broomhill Cres. Knot WF11 .... 127 B3
Broomhill Cres. Leeds LS17 ..... 43 D2
Broomhill Dr. Keigh BD21 .... 35 A5 2
Broomhill Dr. Knot WF11 .... 127 B3
Broomhill Dr. Leeds LS17 .... 43 C1
Broomhill Gr. Keigh BD21 .... 35 A5
Broomhill Gr. Knot WF11 .... 127 B3
Broomhill Mount. Keigh BD21 . 35 A5
Broomhill Pl. Knot WF11 .... 127 B3
Broomhill Sq. Knot WF11 .... 127 B3
Broomhill St. Keigh BD21 .... 35 A5
Broomhill Terr. Batley WF17 . 118 D4
Broomhill Way. Keigh BD21 ..... 35 B5
Broomhill Wlk. Keigh BD21 ...... 35 A5
Broomhill Wlk. Knot WF11 ..... 127 B3
Broomhouse Cl. D Dale HD8 .. 192 A5
Broomroyd. Hud HD3 .... 152 F6
Broomsdale Rd. Batley WF17 .. 118 E5
Broomwood Mid Sch. Brad 75 D1
Broomy Lea La. Holmfi HD7 ... 188 F7
Broster Ave. Keigh BD22 .... 34 F7
Brotherton Ave. Wake WF1 ... 142 E7
Brotherton Prim Sch. Broth 126 C8
Brougham Rd. Hali HX3 .... 92 C1 11
Brougham Rd. Mars HD7 .... 169 A4
Brougham St. Hali HX3 .... 92 C1 12
Brougham Terr. Hali HX3 .... 92 C2 13
Broughton Ave. Brad BD4 .... 75 B1
Broughton Ave. Leeds LS9 .... 61 A2 22
Broughton Rd. Hud HD4 .... 153 B3
Broughton St. Heb Br HX7 .... 89 A4
Broughton Terr. Leeds LS9 .... 61 A2 19
Broughton Terr. Pudsey LS28 .. 76 E8 7
Broughtons Yd. Knot WF11 .... 126 C5
Brow Bottom La. Hali HX2 .... 91 B6
Brow Foot Gate La. Hali HX2 . 112 D6
Brow Grains Rd. Mel HD7 .... 170 B2
Brow La. D Dale HD8 .... 192 D6
Brow La. Hali HX3 .... 92 B6
Brow La. Holmfi HD7 .... 188 F3
Brow La. Northo HX3 .... 92 E4
Brow La. Shelf HX3 .... 93 D6
Brow La. Thorn BD14 .... 72 F3
Brow Quarry Ind Est. Brig 114 D6
Brow Rd. Haw BD22 .... 51 D6
Brow Rd. Hud HD1 .... 153 E5
Brow St. Keigh BD21 .... 35 D6
Brow Top Rd. Haw BD22 .... 51 E7
Brow Wood Cres. Brad BD2 ...... 55 E3

Brow Wood Rd. Shelf HX3 ... 93 D6
Brow Wood Rise. Shelf HX3 ... 93 D6
Browcliff. Sil BD20 ... 5 E2
Browfield Terr. Sil BD20 ... 5 E2
Browfoot Dr. Hali HX2 ... 112 D6
Browfoot. Ship BD18 ... 55 D8
Browgate. Bail BD17 ... 38 C4
Brown Ave. Leeds LS11 ... 78 E4
Brown Bank La. Sil BD20 ... 6 B4
Brown Bank Terr. Glu BD20 ... 16 E7
Brown Birks St. Tod OL14 ... 86 B1 1
Brown Hill Ave. Leeds LS9 ... 61 A2
Brown Hill Cl. Birk BD11 ... 96 A7
Brown Hill Cres. Leeds LS9 ... 61 A2
Brown Hill Dr. Birk BD11 ... 96 A6
Brown Hill La. B Head HX7 ... 87 E5
Brown Hill Terr. Leeds LS9 ... 61 A2
Brown La E. Leeds LS11 ... 78 F5
Brown La W. Leeds LS11, LS12 78 E5
Brown Lee La. Wils BD15 ... 53 A4
Brown Pl. Leeds LS11 ... 78 E4
Brown Rd. Leeds LS11 ... 78 E4
Brown Royd Ave. Hud HD5 ... 154 D8
Brown St. Keigh BD21 ... 35 D8 15
Brown St. Mir WF14 ... 137 F5
Brown's Edge Rd.
Wh Com S30 ... 200 E8
Brown's Knoll Rd. Kirkb HD4 . 173 A3
Brown's Pl. Batley WF17 ... 118 B4
Brown's St. Batley WF17 ... 118 C4
Brown's Terr. Batley WF17 ... 118 B4
Brownberrie Ave. Hors LS18 ... 41 C3
Brownberrie Cres. Hors LS18 .. 41 B3
Brownberrie Dr. Hors LS18 ... 41 C3
Brownberrie Gdns. Hors LS18 . 41 B3
Brownberrie La. Hors LS18 ... 41 B3
Brownberrie Wlk. Hors LS18 ... 41 C3
Brownberry Gr. Shelf HX3 ... 93 D7
Brownhill Cl. Batley WF17 ... 96 F1
Brownhill Cres. Hem WF9 ... 163 A1
Brownhill Garth. Batley WF17 . 96 F1
Brownhill La. Holme HD7 ... 198 B8
Brownhill Prim Sch. Leeds ... 61 A1
Brownhill Rd. Batley WF17 ... 96 F1
Brownhill St Saviour's CE Sch.
Batley ... 97 A1
Browning Ave. Hali HX3 ... 113 D4
Browning Rd. Hud HD2 ... 136 D3
Browning St. Brad BD3 ... 75 B7
Brownings The. Brig HX3 ... 114 C7
Brownlea Cl. Yeadon LS19 ... 39 F5
Brownroyd Ave. Roy S71 ... 179 C2
Brownroyd Hill Rd. Brad BD6 .. 74 B2
Brownroyd Rd. Honley HD7 ... 171 E4
Brownroyd St. Brad BD7 ... 74 B6
Brownroyd St. Brad BD8 ... 74 B7
Brownroyd Wlk. Brad BD6 ... 74 B2
Browsfield Rd. Sil LS29 ... 6 D8
Browsholme St. Keigh BD21 .. 35 C6 2
Browwood Terr. Brad BD6 ... 93 F7
Bruce Gdns. Leeds LS12 ... 78 E7
Bruce Lawn. Leeds LS12 ... 78 E7
Bruce St. Hali HX1 ... 112 F6
Brudenell Ave. Leeds LS6 ... 59 F3
Brudenell Gr. Leeds LS6 ... 59 F3
Brudenell Mount. Leeds LS6 ... 59 F3
Brudenell Prim Sch. Leeds ... 59 E3
Brudenell Rd. Leeds LS6 ... 59 E3
Brudenell St. Leeds LS6 ... 59 F3
Brudenell View. Leeds LS6 ... 59 F3 2
Brunel Cl. Brad BD9 ... 55 A2
Brunel Ct. Hali HX3 ... 92 B2 3
Brunel Gdns. Brad BD5 ... 74 C3 7
Brunel Rd. Loft G WF2 ... 120 F4
Brunswick Arc. Keigh BD21 ... 35 C7 8
Brunswick Ct. Leeds LS2 ... 60 D1
Brunswick Dr. Dew WF13 ... 118 A1
Brunswick Gdns. Gar LS25 ... 82 F7
Brunswick Gdns. Hali HX1 ... 113 B7 5
Brunswick Gr. Wake WF1 ... 142 D6 8
Brunswick House. Bing BD16 .. 37 B2
Brunswick Pl. Brad BD10 ... 56 D7
Brunswick Pl. Morley LS27 ... 98 B4 3
Brunswick Rd. Brad BD10 ... 56 D7
Brunswick Rd. Pudsey LS28 ... 76 E8
Brunswick Row. Leeds LS2 ... 60 D1
Brunswick. Ryhill WF4 ... 162 B2
Brunswick St. Batley WF16 ... 117 D3
Brunswick St. Batley WF17 ... 118 C5 6
Brunswick St. Bing BD16 ... 37 B3
Brunswick St. Cull BD13 ... 52 E6
Brunswick St. Dearne S63 ... 194 F1
Brunswick St. Dew WF13 ... 118 A1
Brunswick St. Heb Br HX7 ... 88 F3
Brunswick St. Hud HD1 ... 154 A6
Brunswick St. Morley LS27 ... 98 A5
Brunswick St. Queen BD13 ... 72 F1 1
Brunswick St. Wake WF1 ... 142 D6
Brunswick Street Bglws.
Wake WF1 ... 142 D6 9
Brunswick Terr. Leeds LS2 ... 60 C1
Brunswick Terr. Morley LS27 .. 98 B4
Bruntcliffe Ave. Morley LS27 ... 97 E5
Bruntcliffe Cl. Morley LS27 ... 97 F4
Bruntcliffe Dr. Morley LS27 ... 97 F4
Bruntcliffe High Sch. Morley ... 97 E4
Bruntcliffe La. Morley LS27 ... 97 E4
Bruntcliffe Rd. Morley LS27 ... 97 E4
Bruntcliffe Way. Morley LS27 .. 97 E4
Brunthwaite Bdge La. Sil BD20 18 A8
Brunthwaite La. Sil BD20 ... 6 B1
Brussels St. Leeds LS9 ... 79 D7
Bryan Cl. Castle WF10 ... 124 A8
Bryan Rd. Elland HX5 ... 134 D6
Bryan Rd. Hud HD2 ... 135 D1
Bryan St. Brig HD6 ... 115 A1 5
Bryan St N. Pudsey LS28 ... 57 D4
Bryan St. Pudsey LS28 ... 57 D3
Bryan Terr. Hud HD7 ... 152 E6
Bryanstone Rd. Brad BD4 ... 75 D5
Bryer St. Dew WF13 ... 139 C8
Bryngate. Roth LS26 ... 101 C6
Bryony Ct. Midd LS10 ... 99 F5
Buck La. Bail BD17 ... 38 F3
Buck Mill La. Brad BD10 ... 39 A2
Buck St. Brad BD3 ... 75 A6
Buck St. Denh BD13 ... 71 E8
Buck Stone Ave. Leeds LS17 ... 42 F4
Buck Stone Cl. Leeds LS17 ... 43 A4
Buck Stone Cres. Leeds LS17 .. 43 A4
Buck Stone Dr. Leeds LS17 ... 42 F4
Buck Stone Gdns. Leeds LS17 . 43 A4
Buck Stone Gn. Leeds LS17 ... 42 F4
Buck Stone Gr. Leeds LS17 ... 42 F4
Buck Stone La. S in Cra BD20 .. 16 A1
Buck Stone Mount. Leeds LS17 42 F4
Buck Stone Oval. Leeds LS17 .. 42 F4
Buck Stone Rd. Leeds LS17 ... 42 F5
Buck Stone Rise. Leeds LS17 .. 42 F4
Buck Stone View. Leeds LS17 .. 42 F4
Buck Stone Way. Leeds LS17 .. 42 F4
Buckden Ct. Sil BD20 ... 5 E2
Buckden Rd. Hud HD3 ... 153 D8
Buckfast Ct. Brad BD10 ... 56 B7
Buckingham Ave. Leeds LS6 ... 59 E4
Buckingham Cres. Brad BD14 . 73 D5
Buckingham Ct. Wake WF1 ... 142 F4
Buckingham Dr. Leeds LS6 ... 59 E4
Buckingham Dr. Wake WF1 ... 142 F3
Buckingham Gr. Leeds LS6 ... 59 E4
Buckingham Mount. Leeds LS6 59 E3
Buckingham Rd. Leeds LS6 ... 59 E4
Buckingham Way.
Byram WF11 ... 126 E7
Buckingham Way. Roy S71 ... 179 B4
Buckland Pl. Hali HX1 ... 112 E6
Buckland Rd. Brad BD8 ... 73 F8 3
Buckle La. Men LS29 ... 22 C4
Buckle La. Nor WF6 ... 123 A2
Buckley Ave. Leeds LS11 ... 79 B3
Buckley La. Hali HX2 ... 91 C2
Buckley View. Tod OL14 ... 108 A6
Buckrose St. Hud HD1 ... 136 A1
Buckstone Dr. Yeadon LS19 ... 40 B3
Buckthorne Cl. E Ard WF3 ... 120 D8
Buckthorne Ct. E Ard WF3 ... 120 D8
Buckthorne Dr. E Ard WF3 ... 120 D8
Buckthorne Fold. E Ard WF3 .. 120 D8
Buckton Cl. Leeds LS11 ... 79 A4
Buckton Mount. Leeds LS11 ... 79 A4
Buckton View. Leeds LS11 ... 79 A4
Bude Rd. Brad BD5 ... 74 F1
Bude Rd. Leeds LS11 ... 79 B3
Bugler Terr. Hor WF4 ... 140 E1
Bula Cl. Kippax LS25 ... 83 B2
Bulay Rd. Hud HD1 ... 153 F4
Bull Close La. Hali HX1 ... 113 C6
Bull Gn. Hali HX1 ... 113 C7
Bull Green Rd. Hud HD3 ... 152 F6
Bull Hill. Oxen BD22 ... 51 C1
Bull La. Crig WF4 ... 159 F5
Bull La. S Kirk WF9 ... 182 C2
Bull Ring. Wake WF1 ... 142 C6
Bull Royd Ave. Brad BD8 ... 73 E8
Bull Royd Cres. Brad BD8 ... 73 E8
Bull Royd Dr. Brad BD8 ... 73 E8
Bull Royd La. Brad BD8 ... 73 E8
Bullace Trees La. Liver WF15 116 E3
Bullenshaw Rd. Hem WF9 ... 181 D6
Buller Cl. Leeds LS9 ... 61 B1
Buller Ct. Leeds LS9 ... 61 C1
Buller Gr. Leeds LS9 ... 61 B1
Buller St. Brad BD4 ... 75 C5
Buller St. Roth LS26 ... 101 C6 6
Bullerthorpe La.
Leeds LS15, LS26 ... 81 E4
Bullfield The. Harden BD16 ... 53 B8
Bullfields Cl. Dew WF12 ... 139 E2
Bullough La. Leeds LS26 ... 81 A1
Bullough La. Roth LS26 ... 100 F8
Bullstyle Rd. Pont WF8 ... 146 C6
Bungalow Rd. Glu BD20 ... 16 C6
Bungalows The. Clay W HD8 . 175 E2
Bungalows The . Hali HX2 ... 91 D1
Bungalows The. Hali HX3 ... 92 A2
Bungalows The. Hali HX3 ... 113 E2
Bungalows The. Leeds LS15 ... 62 D3
Bungalows The. Nor WF6 ... 123 A5
Bungalows The. Ossett WF5 . 140 C6
Bunker's Hill La. Keigh BD22 ... 34 D5
Bunkers Hill. Aber LS25 ... 64 E6
Bunkers Hill. Guise BD17 ... 39 B5
Bunkers Hill. Holmfi HD7 ... 189 A5
Bunkers Hill. Wake WF2 ... 120 F2
Bunkers La. Batley WF17 ... 117 F4
Bunney Gr. Northo HX3 ... 92 F4
Burbeary Rd. Hud HD1 ... 153 E3
Burberry Cl. Brad BD4 ... 95 C8
Burchett Gr. Leeds LS6 ... 60 A4
Burchett Pl. Leeds LS6 ... 60 A4
Burchett Terr. Leeds LS6 ... 60 B4
Burcote Dr. Elland HD3 ... 134 B1
Burdale Pl. Brad BD7 ... 74 B6
Burdett Terr. Leeds LS4 ... 59 C2 5
Burdock Way. Hali HX1 ... 113 B7
Burfitts Rd. Hud HD3 ... 153 B7
Burgh Mill La. Dew WF13 ... 139 A7
Burhouse Ct. Honley HD7 ... 171 F4
Burkill St. Wake WF1 ... 142 D2
Burking Rd. Dew WF13 ... 139 B8
Burlees La. Heb Br HX7 ... 89 C3
Burleigh St. Hali HX1 ... 112 F5 13
Burley Bank La. Holme HD7 ... 197 E6
Burley C E Fst Sch. Bur in W ... 9 E1
Burley Ct. Stee BD20 ... 17 C5
Burley Grange Rd. Leeds LS4 .. 59 C2 2
Burley Hill Cres. Leeds LS4 ... 59 B3
Burley Hill Dr. Leeds LS4 ... 59 C3
Burley La. Hors LS18 ... 58 B7
Burley La. Men LS29 ... 21 F5
Burley Lodge Pl. Leeds LS6 ... 59 E1
Burley Lodge Rd. Leeds LS6 ... 59 E2
Burley Lodge St. Leeds LS6 ... 59 E1
Burley Lodge Terr. Leeds LS6 .. 59 E1
Burley Mews. Stee BD20 ... 17 C5
Burley Mid Sch. Bur in W ... 9 F1
Burley Park Sta. Leeds ... 59 D3
Burley Pl. Leeds LS4 ... 59 E1
Burley Rd. Leeds LS3, LS4 ... 59 D2
Burley Rd. Men LS29 ... 22 A6
Burley St. Elland HX5 ... 134 F6 10
Burley St. Leeds LS3 ... 78 F8
Burley St Matthias' Sch. Leeds 59 D2
Burley St. Ship BD2 ... 55 D4
Burley Wlk. Batley WF17 ... 118 B5
Burley Wood Cres. Leeds LS4 . 59 C2
Burley Wood La. Leeds LS4 ... 59 C3
Burley Wood Mount. Leeds LS4 59 B3
Burley Wood View. Leeds LS4 . 59 C3
Burley & Woodhead CE Sch.
Bur in W ... 21 F8
Burlington Ave. Brad BD3 ... 56 E1
Burlington Pl. Leeds LS11 ... 79 B2 21
Burlington Rd. Leeds LS11 ... 79 B2
Burlington St. Brad BD8 ... 55 D1
Burlington St. Hali HX1 ... 112 F7 2
Burlington Works. Brad ... 56 E1
Burmantofts St. Leeds LS9 ... 79 E8
Burn Rd. Hud HD2, HD3 ... 135 C3
Burned Gr. Shelf HX3 ... 93 C7
Burned Rd. Shelf HX3 ... 93 D7
Burneston Gdns. Brad BD6 ... 93 E8 12
Burnett Ave. Brad BD5 ... 74 D3
Burnett Pl. Brad BD5 ... 74 D3
Burnett Rise. Queen BD13 ... 92 C8
Burnett St. Brad BD1 ... 74 F7
Burnham Ave. Brad BD4 ... 75 C1
Burnham Ave. Mapp S75 ... 178 B1
Burnham Ct. Weth LS22 ... 13 C6
Burnham Rd. Gar LS25 ... 82 F6
Burnhill La. Bad WF9 ... 164 F5
Burniston Cl. Wils BD15 ... 53 C4
Burniston Dr. Hud HD3 ... 153 A8
Burnlee Rd. Holmfi HD7 ... 188 E4
Burnley Hill Terr. Shelf HX3 ... 93 B4
Burnley Rd. Bacup OL13 ... 85 A1
Burnley Rd. H Chap BB10 ... 85 C4
Burnley Rd. Hali HX2 ... 111 D6
Burnley Rd. Hali HX2, HX6 ... 112 C6
Burnley Rd. Tod OL14 ... 85 C4
Burnley Road Jun & Inf Sch.
Heb Br ... 89 E1
Burnleyville. Clec BD19 ... 96 B1
Burnroyd Ave. Glu BD20 ... 16 D6
Burns Ave. S Kirk WF9 ... 181 F1
Burns Ct. Clec WF17 ... 96 D2
Burns Hill. Sil LS29 ... 6 E8
Burns St. Hali HX3 ... 91 F3
Burns Way. B Spa LS23 ... 30 D5
Burnsall Ave. Batley WF17 ... 118 A5
Burnsall Croft. Leeds LS12 ... 78 B7
Burnsall Ct. Leeds LS12 ... 78 B8
Burnsall Gdns. Leeds LS12 ... 78 B8
Burnsall Grange. Leeds LS12 .. 78 C8 17
Burnsall Rd. Batley WF17 ... 118 A5
Burnsall Rd. Brad BD3 ... 75 B7
Burnsall Rd. Brig HD6 ... 135 E8
Burnsall Rd. Liver WF15 ... 116 F4
Burnsdale. Brad BD15 ... 54 A3
Burnside Ave. Shelf HX3 ... 93 C6
Burnside Cl. Batley WF17 ... 97 A1
Burnside. Dearne S63 ... 194 C1
Burnside Dr. Holmfi HD7 ... 188 E4
Burnt Acres La. Heb Br OL14 . 109 B8
Burnt Edge La. B Head HX7 ... 87 D4
Burnt House Cl. Tod OL14 ... 108 C6
Burnt Plats La. Mars HD7 ... 151 B3
Burnt Side Rd. Gild LS12 ... 77 C2
Burnt Wood Cres. S Kirk WF9 182 C2
Burnt Wood La. S Kirk WF9 ... 181 E1
Burntwood Ave. S Kirk WF9 .. 182 C2
Burntwood Bank. Hem WF9 ... 181 D5
Burntwood Dr. S Kirk WF9 ... 182 C1
Burntwood Gr. S Kirk WF9 ... 182 C1
Burntwood Inf Sch. S Kirk ... 182 C2
Burntwood Sports & Leisure Ctr.
Bri ... 181 C2
Burnup Gr. Clec BD19 ... 116 C7
Burnwells Ave. Brad BD10 ... 39 A2
Burnwells. Brad BD10 ... 39 A2
Burr Tree Dr. Leeds LS15 ... 81 D7
Burr Tree Garth. Leeds LS15 ... 81 D7
Burr Tree Vale. Leeds LS15 ... 81 D7
Burrage St. Bing BD16 ... 36 F3
Burras Ave. Otley LS21 ... 22 F7
Burras Dr. Otley LS21 ... 22 F7
Burras La. Otley LS21 ... 22 F7
Burras Rd. Brad BD4 ... 75 B2
Burrel Cl. Weth LS22 ... 14 A5
Burrell St. Wake WF1 ... 142 D6
Burrow St. Brad BD5 ... 74 E6
Burrows The. Batley WF17 ... 117 F7
Burrwood Terr. Elland HX4 ... 134 B5
Burrwood Way. Elland HX4 ... 134 B5
Burton Acres Dr. Kirkb HD8 ... 173 E7
Burton Acres La. Kirkb HD8 ... 173 F7
Burton Acres Mws. Kirkb HD8 173 E7
Burton Acres Way. Kirkb HD8 173 E7
Burton Ave. Leeds LS11 ... 79 C3
Burton Com'n La. B Sal LS25 .. 105 F4
Burton Cres. Leeds LS6 ... 59 D6
Burton Cross. Kirkb HD8 ... 173 E8
Burton Mews. Leeds LS17 ... 43 D5
Burton Rd. Leeds LS11 ... 79 C3
Burton Row. Leeds LS11 ... 79 C4
Burton Royd La. Kirkb HD8 ... 174 A7
Burton Salmon Pr Sch. B Sal . 105 E3
Burton St. Brad BD4 ... 75 A4
Burton St. Hali HX2 ... 92 A5
Burton St. Keigh BD20 ... 18 B2
Burton St. Leeds LS11 ... 79 C4
Burton St. Pudsey LS28 ... 57 D3
Burton St. S Elm WF9 ... 182 F2
Burton St. Wake WF1 ... 142 B7
Burton Terr. Leeds LS11 ... 79 C3 13
Burton Way. Leeds LS9 ... 61 A1
Burwood Rd. Hud HD3 ... 153 C8
Busfield St. Bing BD16 ... 36 F3
Busfield St. Brad BD4 ... 75 B3
Bush St. Hem WF9 ... 181 E6
Bushill Fold. Queen BD13 ... 72 C2
Busker La. Skel HD8 ... 175 C1
Buslingthorpe Gn. Leeds LS7 ... 60 C3
Buslingthorpe La. Leeds LS7 ... 60 C4
Buslingthorpe Vale. Leeds LS7 60 C4
Bussey Ct. Leeds LS6 ... 60 A3
Busy La. Ship BD18 ... 38 E1
Butcher Hill. Hem WF9 ... 181 E8
Butcher Hill. Leeds LS16, LS18 58 F8
Butcher La. Roth LS26 ... 100 E5
Butcher St. Brad BD7 ... 74 D7
Butcher St. Leeds LS11 ... 79 B6
Bute Ave. Brig HD6 ... 115 A5
Bute St. Ship BD2 ... 55 D4
Butler La. Bail BD17 ... 38 D4
Butler St E. Brad BD3 ... 75 A7
Butler St W. Brad BD3 ... 75 A8
Butt Hill. Kippax LS25 ... 83 A1
Butt La. Brad BD10 ... 56 B8
Butt La. H Pag DN5 ... 195 E4
Butt La. Haw BD22 ... 51 C7
Butt La. Holmfi HD7 ... 189 E2
Butt La. Leeds LS12, LS13 ... 77 D6
Butterbowl Dr. Leeds LS12 ... 77 F5
Butterbowl Garth. Leeds LS12 . 77 E5
Butterbowl Gdns. Leeds LS12 . 77 F5
Butterbowl Gr. Leeds LS12 ... 77 E5
Butterbowl Lawn. Leeds LS12 . 77 E5
Butterbowl Mount. Leeds LS12 77 F5
Butterbowl Rd. Leeds LS12 ... 77 F5
Butterfield Homes. Glu BD20 .. 16 C6
Butterfield Homes. Ship BD16 . 54 B6 5
Butterfield Homes. Wils BD15 . 53 B6
Butterfield St. Leeds LS9 ... 79 F7 2
Butterley La. Holmfi HD7 ... 189 F5
Butterley St. Leeds LS10 ... 79 C6
Buttermere Ave. Weth LS22 ... 13 C6
Buttermere Crft. Walton WF2 161 A6
Buttermere Dr. Hud HD5 ... 154 D6
Buttermere Rd. Brad BD2 ... 56 B3
Buttermere Wlk. Knot WF11 . 126 E2
Butternab Rd. Hud HD4 ... 171 D8
Butternab Ridge. Hud HD4 ... 171 D8
Buttershaw Comp Sch. Brad ... 93 F8
Buttershaw Dr. Brad BD6 ... 73 E1
Buttershaw Fst Sch. Brad ... 93 F7
Buttershaw La. Brad BD6 ... 94 B8
Buttershaw La. Clec WF15 ... 116 B5
Buttershaw Mid Sch. Brad ... 93 F7
Butterton Cl. Mapp S75 ... 178 C1
Butterwick Gdns. Weth LS22 ... 13 C5
Butterwood Cl. Hud HD4 ... 171 D8
Butterworth End La.
Sow Br HX6 ... 133 A7
Butterworth Hill. Slai HD3 ... 152 A7
Butterworth La. Sow Br HX6 . 111 E1
Buttholme Gate. Brad BD6 ... 93 F8
Button Hill. Leeds LS7 ... 60 D4
Button Pk. Pont WF8 ... 146 C7
Buttress La. Hali HX2 ... 90 F1
Butts Cl. Kirkb HD4 ... 172 E6
Butts Ct. Leeds LS1 ... 79 C8
Butts Garth. Thorner LS14 ... 45 F5
Butts Garth Vw. Thorner LS14 . 45 F5
Butts Green La. Hali HX2 ... 112 A7
Butts Green Rd. Hali HX2 ... 111 F7
Butts Hill. Clec BD19 ... 117 B8
Butts La. Guise LS20 ... 22 E1
Butts La. M Fry LS25 ... 105 D8
Butts La. Neth WF4 ... 158 B7
Butts La. S Mil LS25 ... 105 D8
Butts La. Tod OL14 ... 108 E8
Butts Mount. Leeds LS12 ... 78 D7
Butts Rd. Kirkb HD4 ... 172 E6
Butts Terr. Guise LS20 ... 22 E1
Butts The. Keigh BD20 ... 36 D8
Butts The. Pont WF8 ... 125 D1
Butts Way. Kirkb HD4 ... 172 E6
Butts Yd. Clec BD19 ... 116 D7 8
Buxton Ave. Ship BD9 ... 55 C4
Buxton La. Ship BD9 ... 55 C4
Buxton Pl. Wake WF1 ... 142 B8
Buxton St. Brad BD9 ... 55 B2
Buxton St. Hali HX3 ... 92 A1 8
Buxton St. Keigh BD21 ... 35 D7 3
Byeway. Guise LS20 ... 22 C1
Byland Cl. B Spa LS23 ... 30 C7
Byland Gr. Brad BD15 ... 53 F1
Byland. Hali HX2 ... 91 E7
Bylands Ave. Keigh BD20 ... 18 E2
Byram Arc. Hud HD1 ... 154 A6 22
Byram Park Ave. Byram WF11 126 E8
Byram Park Rd. Byram WF11 126 E8
Byram St. Hud HD1 ... 154 B6
Byrom St. Tod OL14 ... 108 B6
Byron Ave. Hali HX6 ... 112 B5 6
Byron Ct. Knot WF11 ... 126 B4
Byron Fst Sch. Brad ... 75 B8
Byron Gr. Batley FW13 ... 117 E2
Byron Gr. Loft G WF3 ... 121 E6
Byron St. Brad BD3 ... 75 B8
Byron St. Hali HX6 ... 112 B5 16
Byron St. Hali HX1 ... 112 F7 15
Byron St. Leeds LS2 ... 60 D1
Byways The. Pont WF8 ... 146 D6
Bywell CE (C) Mid Sch. Dew ... 118 F1
Bywell Cl. Dew WF12 ... 140 A8
Bywell Rd. Dew WF12 ... 118 F1

Cabb La. S Kirk WF9 ... 182 D4
Cabbage Hill. Leeds LS12 ... 78 B6
Cabin Rd. Pool LS21 ... 24 B5
Cable St. Hud HD1 ... 154 A4
Cad Beeston Mws. Leeds LS11 79 A3
Cadney Croft. Hali HX1 ... 113 C6 5
Cadogan Ave. Hud HD3 ... 153 B8
Caenarvon Cl. Batley WF17 ... 97 A1
Caernarvon Ave. Gar LS25 ... 83 B7
Cain Cl. Leeds LS9 ... 79 F7 8
Cain La. Hali HX3 ... 114 A4
Cairns Cl. Brad BD2 ... 55 F3
Caister Cl. Batley WF17 ... 97 A2
Caister Gr. Keigh BD21 ... 35 B4 5
Caister St. Keigh BD21 ... 35 B4 3
Caister Way. Keigh BD21 ... 35 B4
Calde Ct. Brad BD12 ... 94 E6
Caldene Ave. Brad BD12 ... 94 E6
Caldene Ave. Heb Br HX7 ... 89 D1
Calder Ave. Hali HX2 ... 112 F5
Calder Ave. Roy S71 ... 179 E3
Calder Bank Rd. Dew WF13 ... 139 B7
Calder Banks. Queen BD13 ... 73 A1
Calder Cl. Castle WF10 ... 125 B8
Calder Cl. Elland HX4 ... 134 D7
Calder Cl. Ossett WF5 ... 140 C5
Calder Cl. Weth LS22 ... 13 D8
Calder Coll of F Ed. Tod ... 108 B5
Calder Dr. Hud HD4 ... 171 F8
Calder Gr. Heb Br HX7 ... 89 E1 3
Calder High Sch. Heb Br ... 89 F1
Calder House. Elland HX5 ... 134 F7 10
Calder House. Mir WF14 ... 138 A4
Calder Mount. Crig WF4 ... 159 E5
Calder Rd. Dew WF13 ... 138 F5
Calder Rd. Mir WF14 ... 138 A3
Calder St. Brig HD6 ... 115 C1
Calder St. Castle WF10 ... 124 C8
Calder St. Elland HX4 ... 134 D7
Calder St. Hali HX4 ... 113 D6
Calder St. Tod OL14 ... 108 B5
Calder St. Wake WF1 ... 142 D4
Calder Terr. Elland HX3 ... 113 A1
Calder Terr. Heb Br HX7 ... 88 F3
Calder Terr. Hor WF4 ... 159 C8
Calder Vale Rd. Wake WF1 ... 142 E5
Calder View. Brig HD6 ... 115 A1
Calder View. Crig WF4 ... 159 E5
Calder View. Ossett WF5 ... 140 B5
Calder Way. Sil BD20 ... 17 E8
Calderbrook Rd. Litt OL15 ... 129 C2
Caldercliffe Rd. Hud HD4 ... 153 F1
Caldercroft. Elland HX5 ... 135 B6
Calderdale Bsns Pk. Hali ... 91 F3
Calderdale Way. Elland HX5 .. 134 F7
Calderdale Way. Elland HX5 .. 135 B6
Calderstone Ave. Brad BD6 ... 93 E8
Caldervale. Roy S71 ... 179 E4
Caldicott Cl. Tod OL14 ... 107 F3
Caledonia Ct. Wake WF2 ... 120 B2
Caledonia Rd. Batley WF17 ... 118 D5
Caledonia Rd. Keigh BD21 ... 35 D8
Caledonia St. Brad BD4, BD5 .. 74 F5
Caledonian Rd. Dew WF12 ... 139 C5
Calf Hey La. Wh Com S30 ... 200 D7
Calf Hey Terr. Tod OL14 ... 108 A1 3
Calf Hill Rd. Holmfi HD7 ... 172 B1
Calgary Cres. E Ard WF3 ... 119 F7
Calgary Pl. Leeds LS7 ... 60 D6
California Dr. Castle WF10 ... 123 D5
California Dr. Hor WF4 ... 141 C1
California Dr. Tod OL14 ... 108 A3
California La. Clec BD19 ... 117 B7
California Mews. Morley LS27 . 98 B6
California St. Morley LS27 ... 98 B4 10
Call La. Leeds LS1 ... 79 C7
Calls The. Leeds LS2 ... 79 D7
Cally Hall Farm Cotts.
B Head HX7 ... 88 A4
Calmlands Rd. Mel HD7 ... 170 D1
Calpin Cl. Brad BD10 ... 56 B8
Calton Gr. Keigh BD21 ... 35 F6
Calton Rd. Keigh BD21 ... 35 F6
Calton St. Hud HD1 ... 154 B8
Calton St. Keigh BD21 ... 35 B6
Calver Ave. Keigh BD21 ... 35 A8
Calver Gr. Keigh BD21 ... 35 A7
Calver Rd. Keigh BD21 ... 35 A7
Calverley Ave. Brad BD3 ... 75 D8
Calverley Ave. Leeds LS13 ... 58 B3
Calverley CE Prim Sch. Pudsey 57 B7
Calverley Ct. Leeds LS13 ... 58 B3
Calverley Ct. Roth LS26 ... 101 B5
Calverley Cutting. Pudsey BD10 56 F8
Calverley Dr. Leeds LS13 ... 58 B3
Calverley Garth. Leeds LS13 ... 58 B3
Calverley Gdns. Leeds LS13 ... 58 A4
Calverley Gr. Leeds LS13 ... 58 B3 1
Calverley Green Rd. Nor WF6 122 F3
Calverley La. Hors LS18 ... 58 A8
Calverley La. Leeds LS13 ... 58 A3
Calverley La. Pudsey LS28 ... 57 C5
Calverley La. Yeadon LS18 ... 57 E7
Calverley Moor Ave.
Pudsey LS28 ... 57 A1
Calverley Parkside Cty Prim Sch.
Pudsey ... 57 B6
Calverley Rd. Roth LS26 ... 101 C5
Calverley St. Leeds LS1 ... 60 B1
Calverley Terr. Leeds LS13 ... 58 B3 2
Calversyke Mid Sch. Keigh ... 34 F7
Calversyke St. Keigh BD21 ... 35 A7
Calvert Cl. Kippax LS25 ... 83 A3
Calverts Wlk. Ossett WF5 ... 140 E4
Cam La. Brig HD6 ... 115 D3
Camargue Fold. Brad BD2 ... 55 F4
Cambell St. Keigh BD21 ... 35 C7
Camberley Mount. Brad BD4 ... 75 E4
Camberley St. Leeds LS11 ... 79 C3 9
Camborne Dr. Hud HD2 ... 135 F3
Camborne Rd. Hud HD2 ... 135 F3
Camborne Way. Keigh BD22 ... 34 E5
Cambrian Bar. Brad BD12 ... 94 B6
Cambrian St. Leeds LS11 ... 79 A4
Cambrian Terr. Leeds LS11 ... 79 A4
Cambridge Cl. Morley LS27 ... 98 B5
Cambridge Cres. Crof WF4 ... 143 C3
Cambridge Ct. Morley LS27 ... 98 B4
Cambridge Dr. Leeds LS13 ... 58 B3
Cambridge Dr. Otley LS21 ... 23 C7
Cambridge Gdns. Leeds LS13 .. 58 B3
Cambridge Gr. Kippax LS25 ... 83 A1
Cambridge Gr. Otley LS21 ... 23 B7
Cambridge Pl. Brad BD3 ... 74 F8
Cambridge Pl. Queen BD13 ... 72 E1
Cambridge Pl. Tod OL14 ... 108 B5 12
Cambridge Rd. Batley WF17 ... 96 D2
Cambridge Rd. Hud HD1 ... 154 A7
Cambridge Rd. Leeds LS7 ... 60 C3
Cambridge St. Batley WF16 ... 117 E4
Cambridge St. Batley WF17 ... 118 C5
Cambridge St. Brad BD14 ... 73 B4
Cambridge St. Brad BD7 ... 74 B4
Cambridge St. Castle WF10 ... 124 D7
Cambridge St. Guise LS20 ... 22 E1
Cambridge St. Heb Br HX7 ... 88 F3
Cambridge St. Nor WF6 ... 123 A1
Cambridge St. Otley LS21 ... 23 A8
Cambridge St. Queen BD13 ... 72 F1 13
Cambridge St. S Elm WF9 ... 182 E3
Cambridge St. Tod OL14 ... 108 C5
Cambridge St. Wake WF2 ... 142 A5
Cambridge Terr. Otley LS21 ... 23 B7
Cambridge Way. Otley LS21 ... 23 B7
Camden Rd. Castle WF10 ... 125 D8
Camden St. Sow Br HX6 ... 112 B3
Camellia Cl. Wake WF2 ... 141 D3
Camellia Mount. Brad BD7 ... 73 E6
Camelot Ct. Pont WF8 ... 146 E8
Cameron Ave. Brad BD12 ... 94 C1
Camerton Gn. Brad BD5 ... 74 F2
Camilla Ct. Dew WF12 ... 139 F7
Camm La. Mir WF14 ... 138 B6
Camm St. Brig HD6 ... 115 B3
Camp Hill. Mars HD3 ... 151 B5
Camp Mount. Pont WF8 ... 146 B8
Camp Rd. Bramho LS16 ... 24 E1
Camp Rd. S Kirk WF9 ... 181 F1
Camp Rise. Pont WF8 ... 146 B8
Camp Sq. Thorner LS14 ... 45 F5
Campbell St. Glu BD20 ... 16 D7
Campbell St. Pudsey LS28 ... 57 E2
Campbell St. Queen BD13 ... 72 F1
Campden Rd. Heb Br HX7 ... 88 E4
Campinot Vale. Slai HD7 ... 151 F1
Campion Cl. Pont WF8 ... 146 D7
Campus Rd. Brad BD7 ... 74 C6
Camroyd St. Dew WF13 ... 118 D1
Canada Cres. Yeadon LS19 ... 40 C4
Canada Dr. Yeadon LS19 ... 40 C5
Canada Rd. Yeadon LS19 ... 40 C5
Canada Terr. Yeadon LS19 ... 40 C4
Canal Ct. Loft G WF3 ... 121 D6
Canal La. Loft G WF3 ... 121 E6
Canal La. Sil BD20 ... 18 A7
Canal Pl. Leeds LS12 ... 78 F7
Canal Rd. Bing BD16 ... 36 F5
Canal Rd. Brad BD1 ... 74 F8
Canal Rd. Hali HX6 ... 112 E4
Canal Rd. Keigh BD20 ... 18 E1
Canal Rd. Leeds LS12 ... 78 D8
Canal Rd. Pudsey LS13 ... 57 E5
Canal Rd. Ship BD1, BD2 ... 55 D3
Canal St. Brig HD6 ... 115 B2
Canal St. Hali HX3 ... 113 D6
Canal St. Hud HD1 ... 154 C8
Canal St. Leeds LS12 ... 78 E7
Canal St. Tod OL14 ... 108 B5
Canal Wharf. Leeds LS11 ... 79 B7
Canal Wlk. Loft G WF3 ... 121 F6
Canary St. Clec BD19 ... 116 D8
Canberra Cl. Haw BD22 ... 51 F8 6
Canberra Dr. Haw BD22 ... 51 F8
Canby Gr. Hud HD5 ... 155 B5
Cancel St. Leeds LS10 ... 79 D5
Canford Dr. Brad BD15 ... 54 C1
Canford Gr. Brad BD15 ... 54 C1
Canford Rd. Brad BD15 ... 54 B1
Canker La. Hali HX3 ... 92 B3
Canker La. Hud HD2 ... 136 D1
Canning Ave. Wake WF2 ... 141 D8
Cannon Gr. Batley WF16 ... 117 E5
Cannon Hall Cl. Brig HD6 ... 115 D2
Cannon Hall Country Pk. Caw 193 D5
Cannon Hall Dr. Brig HD6 ... 115 D2
Cannon Mill La. Brad BD7 ... 74 A4
Cannon St. Bing BD16 ... 37 A2
Cannon St. Castle WF10 ... 124 E5
Cannon St. Hali HX1 ... 112 F5 15
Cannon St. Tod OL14 ... 108 A3
Cannon Way. Dew WF13 ... 139 C7
Canonbury Terr. Leeds LS11 ... 78 E3
Canteen Mill Ind Est. Tod ... 107 E8
Canterbury Ave. Brad BD5 ... 74 C4
Canterbury Cres. Hali HX3 ... 92 B1
Canterbury Dr. Leeds LS6 ... 59 C4
Canterbury Rd. Dew WF12 ... 118 F1
Canterbury Rd. Leeds LS6 ... 59 C4
Capas Heights Way.
Batley WF16 ... 117 E3
Cape Mills Ind Est. Pudsey ... 57 E3
Cape St. Brad BD1 ... 74 E8
Capel St. Brig HD6 ... 115 A1
Capel St. Pudsey LS28 ... 57 B6
Captain St. Bacup OL13 ... 106 A7 7
Captain St. Brad BD1 ... 74 F8
Carberry Pl. Leeds LS6 ... 59 E2
Carberry Rd. Leeds LS6 ... 59 E2
Carberry Terr. Leeds LS6 ... 59 E2 7
Cardan Dr. Ilkley LS29 ... 8 E4
Cardigan Ave. Leeds LS15 ... 80 E8
Carden Rd. Brad BD4 ... 75 E5
Cardigan Ave. Morley LS27 ... 98 A2
Cardigan Cl. Batley WF17 ... 118 E5
Cardigan Ct. Leeds LS6 ... 59 E4
Cardigan La. Leeds LS4, LS6 ... 59 D2
Cardigan La. Leeds LS4, LS6 ... 59 E3
Cardigan La. Ossett WF5 ... 141 A3
Cardigan St. Queen BD13 ... 72 F1
Cardigan Terr. Wake WF1 ... 142 C7
Cardigan Trad Est. Leeds ... 59 D1
Cardinal Ave. Leeds LS11 ... 98 F8
Cardinal Cl. Mel HD7 ... 170 E2
Cardinal Cres. Leeds LS11 ... 98 F8
Cardinal Gdns. Leeds LS11 ... 98 E8
Cardinal Gr. Leeds LS11 ... 98 E8
Cardinal Heenan High Sch.
Leeds ... 43 A1
Cardinal Rd. Leeds LS11 ... 78 F1
Cardinal Sq. Leeds LS11 ... 78 E1
Cardinal Wlk. Leeds LS11 ... 98 F8
Cardwell Terr. Dew WF12 ... 139 C6
Carforth St. Hud HD1 ... 154 C5
Carisbrooke Cres. Brad BD6 ... 94 C8
Carisbrooke La. Gar LS25 ... 83 B8
Cariss St. Leeds LS10 ... 79 D3
Cark Rd. Keigh BD21 ... 35 C8
Carlby Gr. Keigh BD22 ... 35 A6 3
Carlby St. Keigh BD22 ... 35 A6
Carleton Cl. B Spa LS23 ... 30 B8
Carleton Cl. Pont WF8 ... 146 D7
Carleton Crest. Pont WF8 ... 146 E6
Carleton Dr. B Spa LS23 ... 30 B7
Carleton Gate. Pont WF8 ... 146 D6
Carleton Glen. Pont WF8 ... 146 D7
Carleton Green Cl. Pont WF8 146 E5
Carleton High Sch. Pont ... 146 E5
Carleton House. Brad BD6 ... 93 E8 1
Carleton Park Ave. Pont WF8 146 D6
Carleton Park Prim Sch. Pont 146 D6
Carleton Park Rd. Pont WF8 .. 146 D6
Carleton Rd. Pont WF8 ... 146 E6
Carleton St. Keigh BD20 ... 18 C1
Carleton View. Pont WF8 ... 146 D6
Carlile St. Mel HD7 ... 170 E2
Carlinghow Hill. Batley WF17 118 B7
Carlinghow La. Batley WF17 .. 117 F6
Carlinghow Mills. Batley ... 118 B6
Carlinghow Princess Royal Jun &
Inf Sch. Batley ... 118 A7
Carlisle Ave. Yeadon LS19 ... 40 C6
Carlisle Cl. Dew WF13 ... 118 C2
Carlisle Dr. Pudsey LS28 ... 76 E6
Carlisle Gr. Pudsey LS28 ... 76 D6
Carlisle Pl. Brad BD8 ... 55 C1
Carlisle Rd. Brad BD8 ... 55 C1
Carlisle Rd. Leeds LS10 ... 79 D6
Carlisle Rd. Pudsey LS28 ... 76 D6
Carlisle St. Brad BD8 ... 55 C1
Carlisle St. Hali HX2 ... 112 E8 8
Carlisle St. Keigh BD21 ... 35 D7
Carlisle St. Pudsey LS28 ... 57 C1
Carlisle Terr. Brad BD8 ... 55 C1
Carlrayne La. Men LS29 ... 22 A5
Carlton App. Weth LS22 ... 13 C6
Carlton Ave. Batley WF17 ... 118 B3
Carlton Ave. Castle WF10 ... 124 F7
Carlton Ave. Pudsey LS28 ... 76 E7
Carlton Ave. Ship BD18 ... 54 F8
Carlton Carr. Leeds LS7 ... 60 C2

Carlton Cl. Clec BD19 .... 116 D7 1
Carlton Cl. Hem WF9 .... 181 C5
Carlton Cl. Leeds LS7 .... 60 C2
Carlton Cl. Nor WF6 .... 123 B2
Carlton Croft. Leeds LS7 .... 60 C2
Carlton Croft. Wake WF2 .... 160 D6
Carlton Ct. Clec BD19 .... 116 D8
Carlton Ct. Ossett WF5 .... 140 D6
Carlton Dr. Bail BD17 .... 38 C4
Carlton Dr. Gar LS25 .... 82 F5
Carlton Dr. Guise LS20 .... 22 F2
Carlton Dr. Ship BD18 .... 55 A5
Carlton Dr. Ship BD9 .... 55 B4
Carlton Fst Sch. S Elm 182 F2
Carlton Garth. Leeds LS17 .... 44 A5
Carlton Garth. Leeds LS7 .... 60 C2
Carlton Gate. Leeds LS7 .... 60 C2
Carlton Gdns. Leeds LS7 .... 60 C2
Carlton Gdns. S Elm WF9 .... 182 F3
Carlton Gr. Brad BD5 .... 74 D3 2
Carlton Gr. Elland HX5 .... 135 C7
Carlton Gr. Leeds LS7 .... 60 C2
Carlton Gr. Ship BD18 .... 55 B5
Carlton Hill. Leeds LS2, LS7 .... 60 C2
Carlton House Terr. Hali HX1 .... 113 A5
Carlton Jun & Inf Sch. Dew 118 B2
Carlton Jun & Inf Sch. Roth 100 D3
Carlton La. E Carl LS19 .... 23 C3
Carlton La. Guise LS20 .... 23 C3
Carlton La. Roth LS26 .... 100 C1
Carlton La. Roth LS26 .... 100 E4
Carlton Marsh Nature Reserve.
Cud 180 A1
Carlton Moor Mews. Midd LS10 .... 99 F5
Carlton Mount. Yeadon LS19 .... 40 C8
Carlton Pl. Hali HX1 .... 113 C6 1
Carlton Pl. Leeds LS7 .... 60 C2
Carlton Rd. Batley WF16 .... 117 C6
Carlton Rd. Dew WF13 .... 118 C1
Carlton Rd. Liver WF15 .... 117 A3
Carlton Rd. Roy S71 .... 179 D1
Carlton Rd. S Elm WF9 .... 182 F3
Carlton Rd. Ship BD18 .... 54 E8
Carlton Rise. Leeds LS7 .... 60 C2
Carlton Rise. Pudsey LS28 .... 76 E7
Carlton Row. Leeds LS12 .... 78 A7
Carlton St. Bacup OL13 .... 106 A3 2
Carlton St. Brad BD7 .... 74 D6
Carlton St. Castle WF10 .... 124 D8
Carlton St. Feath WF7 .... 145 D7
Carlton St. Hali HX1 .... 113 C6 1
Carlton St. Haw BD22 .... 51 D7 10
Carlton St. Heb Br HX7 .... 89 A3 19
Carlton St. Hor WF4 .... 141 A1
Carlton St. Nor WF6 .... 123 C2
Carlton St. Otley LS21 .... 23 B7
Carlton St. Wake WF2 .... 142 A5
Carlton Terr. Batley WF17 .... 118 A3
Carlton Terr. Dew WF12 .... 139 D6
Carlton Terr. Hali HX1 .... 113 C6 6
Carlton Terr. Pudsey LS28 .... 76 E8 2
Carlton Terr. Yeadon LS19 .... 40 C7
Carlton View. Kippax WF10 .... 102 F6
Carlton View. Leeds LS7 .... 60 C2
Carlton Way. Clec BD19, OL2 .... 116 D7 2
Carlton Wlk. Ship BD18 .... 54 F8
Carlton-Bolling Sch. Brad 56 A1
Carlyle Cres. Castle WF10 .... 125 B7
Carlyle Rd. Castle WF10 .... 125 B7
Carmel Rd. Hali HX3 .... 92 C2
Carmine Cl. Hud HD5 .... 154 E6
Carmona Ave. Ship BD18 .... 55 B5
Carmona Gdns. Ship BD18 .... 55 B5
Carnaby Rd. Brad BD7 .... 73 E2
Carnegie Coll. Leeds 59 B6
Carnegie Dr. Ship BD18 .... 55 C7
Carnlea Gr. Wake WF2 .... 142 C3
Carnoustie Gr. Ship BD16 .... 54 B7
Carolan Ct. Hud HD7 .... 152 D5
Caroline St. Clec BD19 .... 116 D8 10
Caroline St. Ship BD18 .... 54 F8
Carperley Cres. Denh BD13 .... 71 E8
Carr Bank Bottom. Otley LS21 .... 10 F2
Carr Bank. Keigh BD20 .... 19 C1
Carr Bank. Otley LS21 .... 11 A2
Carr Bottom Ave. Brad BD5 .... 74 C2
Carr Bottom Fold. Brad BD5 .... 74 C1
Carr Bottom Gr. Brad BD5 .... 74 B2
Carr Bottom Rd. Brad BD10 .... 56 E7
Carr Bottom Rd. Brad BD5 .... 74 C2
Carr Bridge Ave. Hors LS16 .... 41 D3
Carr Bridge Cl. Hors LS16 .... 41 D3
Carr Bridge Dr. Hors LS16 .... 41 D3
Carr Bridge View. Hors LS16 .... 41 D3
Carr Cl. Yeadon LS19 .... 40 D3
Carr Crofts Dr. Leeds LS12 .... 78 B7
Carr Crofts. Leeds LS12 .... 78 B7
Carr Field Dr. Hali HX2 .... 111 E8
Carr Gate Cres. Loft G WF2 .... 120 D5
Carr Gate Dr. Loft G WF2 .... 120 E5
Carr Gate Mount. Loft G WF2 .... 120 D5
Carr Gr. Keigh BD20 .... 19 A1
Carr Green Ave. Brig HD6 .... 135 F6
Carr Green Cl. Brig HD6 .... 135 F6
Carr Green Dr. Brig HD6 .... 135 F6
Carr Green Jun & Inf Sch. Brig 135 F7
Carr Green La. Brig HD6 .... 135 F7
Carr Green La. Hud HD5 .... 154 D6
Carr Hall La. Elland HX4 .... 134 A4
Carr Hall Rd. Brad BD12 .... 94 C3
Carr Head La. S in Cra BD20 .... 16 A5
Carr Hill Ave. Pudsey LS28 .... 57 A6
Carr Hill Dr. Pudsey LS28 .... 57 A6
Carr Hill Gr. Pudsey LS28 .... 57 A6
Carr Hill Nook. Pudsey LS28 .... 57 A6
Carr Hill Rd. D Dale HD8 .... 191 A6
Carr Hill Rd. Pudsey LS28 .... 57 A6
Carr Hill Rise. Pudsey LS28 .... 57 A6
Carr House Fold. Tod OL14 .... 108 D6 1
Carr House Gate. Brad BD12 .... 94 C4
Carr House Gr. Brad BD12 .... 94 C4
Carr House La. Brad BD12 .... 94 B4
Carr House La. Shelf HX3 .... 93 D7
Carr House La. Tod OL14 .... 108 D6
Carr House Mount. Brad BD12 .... 94 C4
Carr House Rd. Holmfi HD7 .... 189 A5
Carr House Rd. Shelf HX3 .... 93 D7
Carr House. Wake WF1 .... 142 C6 20
Carr Houses. M'town LS26 .... 123 E8
Carr La. Bing BD16 .... 36 E8
Carr La. Brad BD12 .... 94 D5
Carr La. Castle WF10 .... 124 F5
Carr La. Denh BD13 .... 52 E2
Carr La. Dew WF16 .... 117 E1
Carr La. Dew WF12, WF13 .... 157 C8
Carr La. Hem WF4 .... 162 F2
Carr La. Holmfi HD7 .... 188 B4
Carr La. Ingb S30 .... 192 C1
Carr La. Keigh BD20 .... 19 A1
Carr La. Keigh BD20 .... 36 C8
Carr La. Neth WF4 .... 158 B6
Carr La. Roth WF3 .... 100 E3
Carr La. Shep HD8 .... 190 F6
Carr La. Ship BD18 .... 55 D7
Carr La. Slai HD7 .... 152 A1
Carr La. Thorner LS14 .... 45 D5
Carr La. Wake WF2 .... 160 E7
Carr La. Weth LS22 .... 14 A7
Carr La. Yeadon LS19 .... 40 D3
Carr Lane Ave. Castle WF10 .... 124 E5
Carr Manor Ave. Leeds LS17 .... 43 B1
Carr Manor Cty Pr Sch. Leeds 60 B8
Carr Manor Cres. Leeds LS17 .... 60 B8
Carr Manor Croft. Leeds LS17 .... 60 B7
Carr Manor Dr. Leeds LS17 .... 60 B8
Carr Manor Garth. Leeds LS17 .... 43 B1
Carr Manor Gdns. Leeds LS17 .... 60 B8
Carr Manor Gr. Leeds LS17 .... 60 B8
Carr Manor High Sch. Leeds 60 A7
Carr Manor Mount. Leeds LS17 .... 60 B8
Carr Manor Par. Leeds LS17 .... 60 B8
Carr Manor Pl. Leeds LS17 .... 60 B8
Carr Manor Rd. Leeds LS17 .... 60 B8
Carr Manor View. Leeds LS17 .... 60 C8
Carr Manor Wlk. Leeds LS17 .... 60 B7
Carr Moor Side. Leeds LS11 .... 79 C3
Carr Moor St. Leeds LS10 .... 79 D2
Carr Mount. D Dale HD8 .... 191 A6
Carr Mount. Kirkhe HD5 .... 155 E7
Carr Pit Rd. Hud HD5 .... 154 C5
Carr Rd. Brad BD12 .... 94 C3
Carr Rd. Pudsey LS28 .... 57 A7
Carr Rd. Tod OL14 .... 107 A8
Carr Side Cres. Batley WF17 .... 118 C3
Carr St. Batley WF17 .... 96 E1
Carr St. Batley WF16 .... 117 C4 3
Carr St. Batley WF17 .... 118 C2
Carr St. Brad BD5 .... 74 D2
Carr St. Brig HD6 .... 115 A4
Carr St. Clec BD19 .... 116 D7
Carr St. Hud HD3 .... 153 C7
Carr St. Keigh BD21 .... 35 C7
Carr St. Liver WF15 .... 117 A5
Carr Top Cl. Batley WF17 .... 118 B2
Carr Top La. Hud HD7 .... 152 D4
Carr View Rd. Holmfi HD7 .... 189 F2
Carr View. S Kirk WF9 .... 182 C3
Carr Wood Cl. Pudsey LS28 .... 57 A6
Carr Wood Gdns. Pudsey LS28 .... 57 A7
Carr Wood Ind Est. Castle 124 F5
Carr Wood Rd. Castle WF10 .... 124 F5
Carr Wood Way. Pudsey LS28 .... 57 A7
Carr's Cl. Batley WF13 .... 117 F3
Carrfield Dr. B in Elm LS15 .... 63 D7
Carrfield La. B in Elm LS15 .... 63 D7
Carrfield Rd. B in Elm LS15 .... 63 D7
Carrfield Villas. Tod OL14 .... 86 A1
Carrgate. Hem WF9 .... 163 B2
Carrholm Cres. Leeds LS7 .... 60 B7
Carrholm Dr. Leeds LS7 .... 60 B7
Carrholm Gr. Leeds LS7 .... 60 B7
Carrholm Mount. Leeds LS7 .... 60 B7
Carrholm Rd. Leeds LS7 .... 60 B7
Carrholm View. Leeds LS7 .... 60 B7
Carriage Dr. Hali HX1 .... 113 A8
Carriage Dr. Hud HD4 .... 171 F8
Carriage Dr The. Elland HX4 .... 134 A4
Carriage Dr The. Leeds LS8 .... 61 C8
Carriage La. Elland HX4 .... 134 C8
Carricks Cl. Brad BD12 .... 94 E6
Carrier St. Hali HX1 .... 113 C7 17
Carrington St. Brad BD3 .... 75 C7
Carrington Terr. Guise LS20 .... 39 D8
Carroll Ct. S Elm WF9 .... 182 E3
Carroll St. Brad BD3 .... 75 A6
Carrs Rd. Mars HD7 .... 169 A4
Carrs Side St No 1. Mars HD7 .... 169 A4
Carrs Side St No 2. Mars HD7 .... 169 A4
Carrs St. Mars HD7 .... 169 A4
Carter Ave. Leeds LS15 .... 81 C8 2
Carter La. Leeds LS15 .... 81 C8 6
Carter La. Queen BD13 .... 72 D3
Carter Mount. Leeds LS15 .... 81 C8
Carter St. Brad BD4 .... 74 F6
Carter St. Wake WF1 .... 142 B6
Carter Terr. Leeds LS15 .... 62 C1 4
Carter's La. H Hill LS29 .... 8 E7
Cartmel Rd. Keigh BD21 .... 35 A7
Cartmell Dr. Leeds LS15 .... 80 D7
Cartref House. Brad BD15 .... 73 A7 5
Cartworth Bank Rd. Holmfi
HD7 .... 188 F2
Cartworth La. Holmfi HD7 .... 189 A3
Cartworth Moor Rd. Holme
HD7 .... 198 E8
Cartworth Moor Rd. Holmfi
HD7 .... 188 E1
Cartworth Rd. Holmfi HD7 .... 189 A4
Cartwright Gdns. Hud HD4 .... 153 C3
Cartwright House. Liver WF15 .... 117 A5 7
Cartwright Memorial Hall. Brad 55 C3
Cartwright St. Liver WF15 .... 116 F6
Carver St. Clec BD19 .... 116 D8
Caryl Rd. Brad BD4 .... 75 A3
Cashmere St. Keigh BD21 .... 35 A7
Casleford Smawthorne Inf Sch.
Castle 124 D6
Casson Ave. E Ard WF3 .... 99 B1
Casson Dr. E Ard WF3 .... 120 B8
Casson Gr. E Ard WF3 .... 99 B1
Casterton Gdns. Leeds LS14 .... 62 A3
Castle Ave. Brig HD6 .... 135 F8
Castle Ave. Hud HD4 .... 154 A1
Castle Ave. Wake WF2 .... 142 D2
Castle Carr Rd. Hali HX2 .... 90 D6
Castle Carr Rd. Wad M HX7 .... 70 A1
Castle Cl. Bard LS17 .... 28 D3
Castle Cl. Batley WF17 .... 97 A1
Castle Cres. Dew WF12 .... 139 D1
Castle Cres. Wake WF2 .... 160 D8
Castle Croft. Harden BD16 .... 36 A1
Castle Ct. Keigh BD21 .... 35 C8 1
Castle Garth. Pont WF8 .... 125 E1
Castle Gate. Heb Br HX7 .... 110 C4
Castle Gate. Ilkley LS29 .... 8 B4
Castle Gate. Loft G LS26 .... 122 A8
Castle Gate. Weth LS22 .... 13 E5
Castle Gr. Bard LS17 .... 28 D3
Castle Gr. Harden BD16 .... 36 A1
Castle Gr. Hor WF4 .... 159 C8
Castle Grove Ave. Leeds LS6 .... 59 D6
Castle Grove Dr. Leeds LS6 .... 59 D6
Castle Grove Fst Sch. Wake 142 E2
Castle Hall Mid Sch. Mir 138 B5
Castle Head Cl. Roth WF3 .... 100 C1
Castle Head La. Loft G WF3 .... 121 A8
Castle Hill. Brig HD6 .... 135 F8
Castle Hill. Ilkley LS29 .... 8 B4
Castle Hill Jun & Inf Sch. Tod 108 D6
Castle Hill Rd. Liver BD19 .... 117 B6
Castle Hill Side. Hud HD4 .... 172 C8
Castle Hill View. Batley WF16 .... 117 F3
Castle Hill. Wake WF2 .... 141 C4
Castle Houses. Hud HD4 .... 172 B8
Castle Ings Cl. Gild LS12 .... 77 D3
Castle Ings Dr. Gild LS12 .... 77 D3
Castle Ings Gdns. Gild LS12 .... 77 D2
Castle La. Rip HX6 .... 132 C3
Castle La. Slai HD7 .... 151 E2
Castle La. Tod OL14 .... 108 D6
Castle Lane Cl. Tod OL14 .... 108 D6
Castle Mount. Dew WF12 .... 139 D1
Castle Par. Castle WF10 .... 124 F6
Castle Pl. Brig HD6 .... 135 F8
Castle Rd. Ilkley LS29 .... 8 B4
Castle Rd. Keigh BD21 .... 35 B8
Castle Rd. Roth LS26 .... 100 D5
Castle Rd. Ship BD18 .... 55 B7
Castle Rd W. Wake WF2 .... 142 D1
Castle Rd. Wake WF2 .... 142 E1
Castle Sch The. Castle 125 C7
Castle Sch The. Tod 107 F4
Castle St. Brad BD5 .... 74 E5
Castle St. Leeds LS1 .... 79 A8
Castle St. Wake WF2 .... 141 F5
Castle Syke Hill. Ack M T WF8 .... 146 B3
Castle Syke View. Pont WF8 .... 146 C6
Castle Terr. Wake WF2 .... 160 D8
Castle Vale. Pont WF8 .... 125 F2
Castle View. Honley HD7 .... 171 F3
Castle View. Hor WF4 .... 159 C8
Castle View. Leeds LS17 .... 43 B1
Castle View. Mir WF14 .... 138 B5
Castle View. Pont WF8 .... 125 D1
Castle View. Wake WF2 .... 160 D8
Castle Wood Cl. Hare LS17 .... 27 A7
Castle Wood Cl. Hors LS18 .... 58 D8
Castle Yd. Ilkley LS29 .... 8 B4
Castlefield Ct. Castle WF10 .... 124 D8
Castlefields Cres. Brig HD6 .... 135 F8
Castlefields Dr. Brig HD6 .... 135 F8
Castlefields Ind Est. Bing 36 D5
Castlefields Inf Sch. Brig 114 F1
Castlefields La. Bing BD16 .... 36 E5
Castlefields Rd. Bing BD16 .... 36 D6
Castlefields Rd. Brig HD6 .... 135 F8
Castleford Glasshoughton Fst Sch.
Castle 124 F7
Castleford High Sch. Castle 124 F8
Castleford La. Feath WF7 .... 124 B2
Castleford La. Knot WF11 .... 126 B5
Castleford Normanton & District
Hospl (General). Castle 124 B6
Castleford Oyster Park Inf Sch.
Castle 125 D8
Castleford Oyster Park Jun Sch.
Castle 125 D8
Castleford Rd. Nor WF6 .... 123 C3
Castleford Sta. Castle 124 D7
Castleford Three Lane Ends Fst &
Mid Schs. Castle 124 A8
Castleford Whitwood Fst Sch.
Castle 123 F5
Castlegate Dr. Brad BD10 .... 56 C6
Castlegate Dr. Pont WF8 .... 146 C5
Castlegate House. Elland HX5 .... 134 F7 17
Castlegate. Hud HD1 .... 154 A6
Castlegate Loop. Hud HD1 .... 154 A6
Castlegate Slip. Hud HD1 .... 154 A7
Castlemore Rd. Bail BD17 .... 38 D2
Castlerigg Gn. Brad BD6 .... 93 F6
Castleton Cl. Leeds LS12 .... 78 F7
Castleton Prim Sch. Leeds 78 E7
Castleton Rd. Leeds LS12 .... 78 E8
Castletown Dr. Bacup OL13 .... 106 B1
Castley La. Cast LS21 .... 25 B8
Castley La. Leath LS21 .... 24 E8
Cat Hill La. Pen S30 .... 192 D1
Cat La. Elland HX4 .... 133 F7
Cat La. Sow Br HX7 .... 111 B5
Cater St. Brad BD1 .... 74 F7
Cath Ch of St Peter The. Brad 74 F7
Cathcart St. Hali HX3 .... 92 B1 6
Cathcart St. Leeds LS6 .... 60 A3
Cathedral Church of All Saints The.
Wake 142 C6
Cathedral Cl. Brad BD1 .... 74 F7 6
Cathedral Cl. Wake WF1 .... 142 B7
Cathedral Wlk. Wake WF1 .... 142 C6 21
Catherine Cl. Hud HD3 .... 135 A2
Catherine Cres. Elland HX5 .... 134 F6 15
Catherine Gr. Leeds LS11 .... 79 B3 17
Catherine House La.
Wad M HX2 .... 90 A6
Catherine Rd. Hud HD2 .... 136 B4
Catherine Slack. Brig HD6 .... 114 F6
Catherine Slack Fst Sch. Queen 92 C6
Catherine Slack. Queen BD13 .... 92 C6
Catherine St. Brig HD6 .... 115 A3
Catherine St. Elland HX5 .... 134 F6
Catherine St. Hem WF9 .... 163 A4
Catherine St. Keigh BD21 .... 35 B5 5
Catlow St. Castle WF10 .... 124 C7
Cattle La. Aber LS25 .... 64 E7
Cattle Market St. Otley LS21 .... 23 A8
Cattlelaith La. Knot WF11 .... 126 D2
Caudle Hill. Fair WF11 .... 104 F4
Cauldwell Gdns. Brad BD5 .... 74 E4 2
Caulms Wood Rd. Dew WF13 .... 118 D1
Causeway Cres. Slai HD7 .... 152 D1
Causeway Foot. Hali HX2 .... 71 D3
Causeway Garth La.
Th Aud WF8 .... 165 C4
Causeway. Hali HX1 .... 113 D7
Causeway Head La. Rip HX6 .... 132 B5
Causeway. Rip HX6 .... 133 A2
Causeway Side. Slai HD7 .... 152 D1
Causeway. Slai HD7 .... 151 F4
Causeway Wood Rd. Tod OL14 .... 108 E4
Cautley Rd. Leeds LS9 .... 79 F6
Cavalier App. Leeds LS9 .... 79 F6
Cavalier Cl. Leeds LS9 .... 79 F6 5
Cavalier Ct. Leeds LS9 .... 79 F6
Cavalier Dr. Brad BD10 .... 56 E8
Cavalier Gate. Leeds LS9 .... 79 F6
Cavalier Gdns. Leeds LS9 .... 79 F6
Cavalier House. Leeds LS9 .... 79 E7
Cave Cres. Wake WF2 .... 141 E4
Cave Hill. Northo HX3 .... 92 F4
Cave La. E Ard WF3 .... 120 E7
Cavendish Ct. Brad BD10 .... 56 C5
Cavendish Ct. Keigh BD21 .... 35 C7 2
Cavendish Dr. Bing BD16 .... 37 B4
Cavendish Dr. Guise LS20 .... 39 D8
Cavendish Fst Sch. Brad 56 D5
Cavendish Gr. Guise LS20 .... 39 D8
Cavendish Mews. Leeds LS17 .... 43 D4
Cavendish Pl. Pudsey LS28 .... 57 E1
Cavendish Rd. Brad BD10 .... 56 B7
Cavendish Rd. Brad BD2 .... 56 C5
Cavendish Rd. Guise LS20 .... 39 D8
Cavendish Rd. Leeds LS2 .... 60 B2
Cavendish Rise. Pudsey LS28 .... 77 A7
Cavendish Sq. Pudsey LS28 .... 57 E1 3
Cavendish St. Hali HX1 .... 113 A7 15
Cavendish St. Keigh BD21 .... 35 C7
Cavendish St. Leeds LS3 .... 78 F8
Cavendish St. Pudsey LS28 .... 77 A7
Cavendish St. Yeadon LS19 .... 40 C7 3
Cavendish Terr. Hali HX1 .... 113 A7 14
Cavewell Cl. Ossett WF5 .... 140 F3
Cavewell Gdns. Ossett WF5 .... 140 F3
Cawcliffe Dr. Brig HD6 .... 115 A5
Cawcliffe Rd. Brig HD6 .... 115 A4
Cawley Garth. Batley WF16 .... 117 E3
Cawley La. Batley WF16 .... 117 E3
Cawood Haven. Brad BD6 .... 93 E8
Cawthorne Ave. Hud HD2 .... 136 A2
Cawthorne CE Prim Sch. Caw 193 E4
Cawthorne La. Caw S75 .... 193 F5
Cawthorne Rd. Wake WF2 .... 160 B6
Caxton Rd. Otley LS21 .... 22 E7
Caxton St. Weth LS22 .... 13 E5
Caycroft Nook. Hep HX7 .... 88 F5
Caygill Terr. Hali HX1 .... 113 C6
Caythorne Wlk. Brad BD10 .... 56 C5
Caythorpe Rd. Leeds LS16 .... 59 B7
Cecil Ave. Bail BD17 .... 38 C4
Cecil Ave. Brad BD7 .... 74 B4
Cecil Ave. Brig HX3 .... 114 E8
Cecil Gr. Leeds LS12 .... 78 C8 3
Cecil Mount. Leeds LS12 .... 78 C8 2
Cecil Rd. Leeds LS12 .... 78 C8
Cecil St. Haw BD22 .... 51 E8 11
Cecil St. Hud HD1 .... 154 A6 9
Cecil St. Leeds LS12 .... 78 C8 4
Cedar Ave. Hud HD1 .... 153 F7
Cedar Ave. Leeds LS12 .... 78 C7
Cedar Ave. Ossett WF5 .... 140 E4
Cedar Cl. Hud HD7 .... 152 F5
Cedar Cl. Leeds LS12 .... 78 C7
Cedar Cl. Pont WF8 .... 146 C5
Cedar Cl. Roy S71 .... 179 A4
Cedar Covert. Weth LS22 .... 13 E8
Cedar Ct. Castle WF10 .... 124 E7
Cedar Dr. Brad BD12 .... 94 E4
Cedar Dr. Dew WF12 .... 140 B7
Cedar Gr. Elland HX4 .... 134 B7
Cedar Gr. Feath WF7 .... 145 D7
Cedar Gr. S in Cra BD20 .... 16 C5
Cedar Mount. Hud HD1 .... 153 F7
Cedar Mount. Leeds LS12 .... 78 C7
Cedar Pl. Leeds LS12 .... 78 C7
Cedar Rd. Dew WF12 .... 140 A7
Cedar Rd. Leeds LS12 .... 78 C7
Cedar Rd. Nor WF6 .... 144 B7
Cedar St. Bing BD16 .... 36 E5
Cedar St. Hali HX1 .... 112 F6
Cedar St. Hud HD1 .... 153 E7
Cedar St. Keigh BD21 .... 35 B4
Cedar St. Leeds LS12 .... 78 C7
Cedar St. Tod OL14 .... 129 A8
Cedar Terr. Leeds LS12 .... 78 C7
Cedar Way. Clec BD19 .... 117 A8
Cedar Wlk. Feath WF7 .... 145 D6
Cedar Wlk. Knot WF11 .... 126 E2
Cedars The. Bramho LS16 .... 24 F2
Celandine Ave. Hud HD3 .... 152 E8
Celandine Cl. Pont WF8 .... 146 D7
Celandine Dr. Hud HD3 .... 152 E8
Cemetery La. Hali HX6 .... 112 A4
Cemetery La. Keigh BD20 .... 18 B2
Cemetery La. Roth WF3 .... 100 C2
Cemetery Rd. Batley WF16 .... 117 D4
Cemetery Rd. Batley WF17 .... 118 B5
Cemetery Rd. Bing BD16 .... 36 E4
Cemetery Rd. Brad BD7, BD8 .... 73 F6
Cemetery Rd. Brad BD12, BD6 .... 94 B7
Cemetery Rd. Dew WF13 .... 139 B7
Cemetery Rd. Haw BD22 .... 50 F6
Cemetery Rd. Hem WF9 .... 181 C8
Cemetery Rd. Holmfi HD7 .... 188 F4
Cemetery Rd. Hud HD1 .... 153 F7
Cemetery Rd. Leeds LS11 .... 79 A4
Cemetery Rd. Nor WF6 .... 123 C2
Cemetery Rd. Pudsey LS28 .... 76 D8
Cemetery Rd. Ryhill WF4 .... 162 B1
Cemetery Rd. Yeadon LS19 .... 40 C8
Centenary Rd. Bail BD17 .... 38 F4
Centenary Sq. Dew WF12 .... 139 B4
Centenary Way. Batley WF17 .... 118 B6
Central Arc. Clec BD19 .... 116 E7
Central Ave. Bail BD17 .... 38 B2
Central Ave. Brad BD5 .... 74 C4
Central Ave E. Clec WF15 .... 116 B5
Central Ave. Clec WF15 .... 116 B5
Central Ave. Hem WF9 .... 163 A4
Central Ave. Hud HD2 .... 136 B2
Central Ave. Keigh BD22 .... 34 F3
Central Ave. S Elm WF9 .... 183 A3
Central Ave. Ship BD18 .... 55 B7
Central Cl. Hud HD2 .... 136 B3
Central Dr. Castle WF10 .... 124 A7
Central Dr. Hud HD2 .... 136 B3
Central Dr. Keigh BD22 .... 34 F3
Central Dr. Roy S71 .... 179 C3
Central (Kayes) Coll. Hud 153 F7
Central Par. Clec BD19 .... 116 E7 6
Central Par. Leeds LS9 .... 80 C3
Central Pk. Hali HX1 .... 113 B5
Central Pk. Leeds 79 B6
Central Rd. Hud HD2 .... 136 B3
Central Rd. Leeds LS1 .... 79 C7
Central St. Dew WF13 .... 139 C8
Central St. Hali HX1 .... 113 C7 10
Central St. Heb Br HX7 .... 89 A3
Central St. Leeds LS1 .... 79 B8
Central Street Inf Sch. Heb Br 89 A3
Central View. Bacup OL13 .... 106 A2
Centre 27 Bsns Pk. Batley 97 B3
Centre St. Brad BD5 .... 74 C3 4
Centre St. Hem WF9 .... 181 D8
Centre St. Liver WF16 .... 117 C4 1
Centre St. S Elm WF9 .... 183 A3
Centre The. Pont S66 .... 146 E7
Centuria Wlk. Hud HD3 .... 152 E8
Century Pl. Brad BD8 .... 55 C1
Century Rd. Elland HX5 .... 134 F7
Ceres Rd. Weth LS22 .... 14 A5
Chaddlewood Cl. Hors LS18 .... 41 C1
Chadwell Springs. Ship BD16 .... 54 A7
Chadwick La. Mir WF14 .... 137 F3
Chadwick St. Leeds LS10 .... 79 D6
Chaffinch Rd. Brad BD8 .... 73 C7 6
Chaffinch Wlk. Hud HD4 .... 171 E7
Chain. Mars HD7 .... 169 C5
Chain Rd. Mel HD7 .... 170 A5
Chain Rd. Slai HD7 .... 169 F6
Chain St. Brad BD1 .... 74 D7
Chain St. Castle WF10 .... 124 C8
Chalcroft Cl. Batley WF16 .... 117 E5
Chald La. Wake WF2 .... 142 B5
Chalfont Rd. Leeds LS16 .... 59 B8
Chalice Cl. Midd LS10 .... 99 E7
Challenge Way. Batley WF12 .... 119 A3
Challenger Cres. Dearne S63 .... 194 D1
Challis Gr. Brad BD5 .... 74 E3
Chalner Ave. Morley LS27 .... 97 F2
Chalner Cl. Morley LS27 .... 97 F2
Chalwood. Hud HD2 .... 136 E4
Chancellor St. Leeds LS6 .... 60 C3
Chancery Cl. Hud HD1 .... 154 A6 20
Chancery La. Hud HD1 .... 154 A6 19
Chancery La. Ossett WF5 .... 140 C8
Chancery La. Wake WF1 .... 142 C6 4
Chancery Rd. Ossett WF5 .... 140 B8
Chandler Cl. Batley WF17 .... 96 E1
Chandler La. Honley HD7 .... 171 D4
Chandlers Cl. Loft G WF1 .... 121 B5
Chandlers The. Leeds LS2 .... 79 D7
Chandos Ave. Leeds LS8 .... 60 E8
Chandos Fold. Leeds LS8 .... 60 E7
Chandos Garth. Leeds LS8 .... 60 E8
Chandos Gdns. Leeds LS8 .... 60 E8
Chandos Gn. Leeds LS8 .... 60 E8
Chandos Pl. Leeds LS8 .... 60 F8
Chandos St. Brad BD4 .... 74 F6
Chandos St. Keigh BD21 .... 35 B5 4
Chandos Terr. Leeds LS8 .... 60 F8
Chandos Wlk. Leeds LS8 .... 60 E7
Change La. Hali HX3 .... 113 E2
Change View. Bacup OL13 .... 106 B4
Changegate Ct. Haw BD22 .... 51 B7 2
Changegate. Haw BD22 .... 51 B7
Channing Way. Brad BD1 .... 74 E6
Chantrell Ct. Leeds LS2 .... 79 D7 5
Chantry Bridge Ind Est. Wake 142 D5
Chantry Cl. Ilkley LS29 .... 8 B3
Chantry Cl. Pont WF8 .... 146 B7
Chantry Croft. Leeds LS15 .... 81 D7
Chantry Dr. Ilkley LS29 .... 8 B4
Chantry Garth. Leeds LS15 .... 81 D7
Chantry Gr. Roy S71 .... 179 C3
Chantry La. Stut LS24 .... 48 E5
Chantry Rd. Wake WF2 .... 141 E5
Chapel Allerton Hospl. Leeds 60 E6
Chapel Allerton Pr Sch. Leeds 60 D6
Chapel Ave. Batley WF16 .... 117 E5
Chapel Ave. Heb Br HX7 .... 89 B3
Chapel Bank. Holmfi HD7 .... 189 E3
Chapel Cl. Dew WF12 .... 139 D2
Chapel Cl. Elland HX4 .... 134 B4
Chapel Cl. Gar LS25 .... 82 E7
Chapel Cl. Hud HD4 .... 171 F8
Chapel Cl. Shaf S72 .... 180 C3
Chapel Cl. W Har WF4 .... 162 F7
Chapel Cl. W Har WF9 .... 163 A7
Chapel Croft. Brig HD6 .... 135 F7
Chapel Fold. Batley WF17 .... 118 A3
Chapel Fold. Brad BD6 .... 74 B1
Chapel Fold. Brig BD12 .... 115 C8
Chapel Fold. Leeds LS6 .... 59 D3
Chapel Fold. Leeds LS11 .... 78 E2
Chapel Fold. Loft G WF1 .... 121 B3
Chapel Fold. Pudsey LS28 .... 76 E6 3
Chapel Garth. Ack M T WF7 .... 164 A6
Chapel Gn. Pudsey LS28 .... 76 D6 1
Chapel Gr. Bing BD16 .... 36 E5
Chapel Grange Sch. Brad 73 D8
Chapel Hill. Clay DN5 .... 194 C4
Chapel Hill. Clay W HD8 .... 175 E2
Chapel Hill. Hud HD1 .... 154 A5
Chapel Hill La. Mars HD3 .... 151 B5
Chapel Hill. Midd LS10 .... 99 D5 1
Chapel Hill. Mir WF14 .... 137 F2
Chapel Hill. Morley LS27 .... 98 A5
Chapel Hill. Slai HD7 .... 152 D1
Chapel Hill. Yeadon LS19 .... 40 B7 2
Chapel House Rd. Brad BD12 .... 94 D2 4
Chapel La. B in Elm LS15 .... 63 E7
Chapel La. B Spa LS23 .... 30 D5
Chapel La. Bad WF9 .... 164 E2
Chapel La. Batley WF17 .... 96 F1 6
Chapel La. Batley WF16 .... 117 E4
Chapel La. Brad BD13 .... 73 B2
Chapel La. Brad BD13, BD15 .... 73 C8
Chapel La. Dearne S63 .... 194 F1
Chapel La. Dew WF12 .... 139 D2
Chapel La. Emley HD8 .... 175 B7
Chapel La. Gar LS25 .... 82 E7
Chapel La. Guise BD17 .... 39 C5
Chapel La. Hal E BD23 .... 1 E8
Chapel La. Hali HX2 .... 90 B2
Chapel La. Hali HX6 .... 112 D4
Chapel La. Hali HX3 .... 113 D3
Chapel La. Hali HX3 .... 114 B4
Chapel La. Hud HD7 .... 152 D4
Chapel La. Hud HD5 .... 154 D5
Chapel La. Ilkley LS29 .... 8 A4
Chapel La. K Smea WF8 .... 166 E6
Chapel La. Keigh BD22 .... 34 C7
Chapel La. Keigh BD21 .... 35 B7
Chapel La. Kippax LS25 .... 83 B1
Chapel La. Leeds LS6 .... 59 D4
Chapel La. Leeds LS12 .... 77 E5
Chapel La. Leeds LS12 .... 78 C7 7
Chapel La. Queen BD13 .... 72 E1
Chapel La. Roy S71 .... 179 C1
Chapel La. S Elm WF9 .... 183 B3
Chapel La. Yeadon LS19 .... 40 B7
Chapel Pl. Leeds LS6 .... 59 D5 10
Chapel Rd. Bing BD16 .... 36 E5
Chapel Rd. Brad BD12 .... 94 D6
Chapel Rd. Brad BD12 .... 94 E6
Chapel Rd. Leeds LS7 .... 60 D5
Chapel Rd. Stee BD20 .... 17 C5
Chapel Row. Wils BD15 .... 53 C6
Chapel Sq. Leeds LS6 .... 59 D5 1
Chapel St. Bing BD16 .... 36 E5
Chapel St. Brad BD2 .... 56 D4
Chapel St. Brad BD6 .... 74 C1
Chapel St. Brad BD5 .... 74 D4
Chapel St. Brad BD1 .... 74 F7
Chapel St. Brig HD6 .... 114 E5
Chapel St. Clec WF15 .... 116 C5
Chapel St. Clec BD19 .... 116 E8
Chapel St. Denh BD13 .... 71 D8
Chapel St. Dew WF12 .... 139 C6
Chapel St. E Ard WF3 .... 98 F1
Chapel St. E Ard WF3 .... 120 C7
Chapel St. Elland HX4 .... 134 B4
Chapel St. Hali HX2 .... 112 E8 7
Chapel St. Hud HD4 .... 153 E2
Chapel St. Hud HD1 .... 154 A5
Chapel St. Hud HD5 .... 154 D5 7
Chapel St. Hud HD4 .... 171 C7
Chapel St. Knot WF11 .... 127 A5
Chapel St. Leeds LS6 .... 59 D5
Chapel St. Leeds LS15 .... 81 A8
Chapel St. Litt OL15 .... 129 D2
Chapel St. Liver FW15 .... 117 C4
Chapel St. Loft G WF3 .... 121 E5
Chapel St. Mir WF14 .... 138 A5
Chapel St N. Hali HX3 .... 91 F3
Chapel St. Ossett WF5 .... 141 A4
Chapel St. Pudsey LS28 .... 57 B6
Chapel St. Pudsey LS28 .... 57 E1
Chapel St. Pudsey LS13 .... 57 E5
Chapel St. Queen BD13 .... 72 E1
Chapel St. Roth WF3 .... 100 D3
Chapel St. Ryhill WF4 .... 162 B1
Chapel St S. Tod OL14 .... 108 A1 7
Chapel St. Shaf S72 .... 180 C3
Chapel St. Sil BD20 .... 5 E2
Chapel St. Sil LS29 .... 6 F8
Chapel St. Slai HD7 .... 152 B5
Chapel St. Thorn BD13 .... 72 D6
Chapel St. Tod OL14 .... 108 D6 4
Chapel St. Yeadon LS19 .... 40 B4
Chapel Terr. Brad BD15 .... 54 B1
Chapel Terr. Honley HD7 .... 171 F4
Chapel Terr. Hud HD4 .... 153 D4
Chapel Terr. Leeds LS6 .... 59 D5 9
Chapel Terr. Rip HX6 .... 133 C7
Chapel Terr. Sow Br HX6 .... 111 D3
Chapel Terr. Thorn BD13 .... 72 D6
Chapel Wlk. Bing BD16 .... 36 F3
Chapel Wlk. Brad BD2 .... 56 D4
Chapel Yd. Leeds LS15 .... 81 D6
Chapelfields. S Kirk WF9 .... 182 B1
Chapelgate. Holmfi HD7 .... 189 D3
Chapeltown. Hali HX1 .... 113 B7
Chapeltown. Pudsey LS28 .... 76 D6
Chapeltown Rd. Leeds LS7 .... 60 D4
Chapman St. Brad BD4 .... 75 D6
Chapman St. Leeds LS9 .... 60 E1
Chariot Way. Th Aud WF8 .... 165 A4
Charles Ave. Brad BD3 .... 75 D7
Charles Ave. Hali HX3 .... 114 A4
Charles Ave. Hud HD3 .... 153 A8
Charles Ave. Leeds LS9 .... 79 F6
Charles Ave. Loft G WF1 .... 121 B5
Charles Ave. Wake WF1 .... 142 F3
Charles Cotton Cl. Wake WF2 .... 141 D8
Charles Ct. Oxen BD22 .... 51 C2 7
Charles Gdns. Leeds LS11 .... 79 A5
Charles Gr. Roth LS26 .... 101 C6
Charles St. Batley WF17 .... 118 C4
Charles St. Bing BD16 .... 36 F3
Charles St. Brad BD1 .... 74 F7 8
Charles St. Brig HD6 .... 115 A3
Charles St. Castle WF10 .... 124 E7
Charles St. Clec BD19 .... 117 B8
Charles St. Dew WF13 .... 138 E5
Charles St. Dew WF13 .... 138 F8
Charles St. Dew WF12 .... 139 E8
Charles St. Elland HX5 .... 134 F6
Charles St. Hali HX6 .... 112 B5 15
Charles St. Hali HX1 .... 113 D7
Charles St. Hor WF4 .... 159 D7
Charles St. Hors LS18 .... 58 B7
Charles St. Hud HD4 .... 153 D4
Charles St. Morley LS27 .... 98 B4
Charles St. Ossett WF5 .... 140 F3
Charles St. Otley LS21 .... 23 A7
Charles St. Pudsey LS28 .... 57 D3
Charles St. Queen BD13 .... 72 D1
Charles St. Ryhill WF4 .... 162 A1
Charles St. S Hie S72 .... 180 E5
Charles St. Ship BD17 .... 55 B8
Charles St. Wake WF1 .... 142 D5
Charlestown Est. Ack MT WF7 .... 164 A4
Charlestown Rd. Hali HX3 .... 113 D8
Charlesworth Gr. Hali HX2 .... 112 E8
Charlesworth La. Wake WF2 .... 142 B5
Charlesworth Pl. Loft G WF3 .... 122 C6
Charlesworth Sq. Clec BD19 .... 117 A8
Charlesworth St. Dew WF12 .... 139 E8
Charlesworth Terr. Hali HX2 .... 112 E8
Charlesworth's Bldgs.
Hor WF4 .... 141 A1
Charleville. S Elm WF9 .... 182 E4
Charlotte Cl. Batley WF17 .... 96 F3
Charlotte Ct. Haw BD22 .... 51 E8
Charlotte Gr. Leeds LS15 .... 81 B8
Charlotte Gr. Ossett WF5 .... 140 F4
Charlotte St. Wake WF1 .... 142 D5
Charlton Ct. Hali HX2 .... 112 E8
Charlton Gr. Leeds LS9 .... 80 A7

Charlton Gr. Sil BD20 .... 17 F8
Charlton Mount. Leeds LS9 .... 79 F7
Charlton Pl. Leeds LS9 .... 80 A7
Charlton Rd. Leeds LS9 .... 80 A7
Charlton St. Leeds LS9 .... 80 A7
Charnwood Bk. Batley WF16 . 117 E4
Charnwood Cl. Brad BD2 .... 56 C2
Charnwood Gr. Brad BD2 .... 56 C2
Charnwood Rd. Brad BD2 .... 56 C2
Charterhouse Rd. Brad BD10 .. 39 B1
Charteris Rd. Brad BD8 .... 73 C7
Chartists Way. Morley LS27 .... 98 A3
Chartwell Ct. Leeds LS17 .... 44 B5
Charville Gdns. Thorner LS17 .. 44 F3
Chase The. Bur in W LS29 .... 22 A7
Chase The. Gar LS25 .... 83 B7
Chase The. Keigh BD21 .... 34 F8
Chase The. Loft G WF3 .... 122 A6
Chase The. Weth LS22 .... 13 F6
Chase The. Yeadon LS19 .... 40 A4
Chassum Gr. Brad BD9 .... 55 B2
Chaster St. Batley WF17 .... 118 A6
Chat Hill Rd. Thorn BD13 .... 72 F5
Chatham St. Brad BD3 .... 56 A1
Chatham St. Hali HX6 .... 112 B5 8
Chatham St. Hali HX1 .... 113 B7
Chatswood Ave. Leeds LS11 ... 98 F8
Chatswood Cres. Leeds LS11 .. 98 F8
Chatswood Dr. Leeds LS11 ...... 78 F1
Chatsworth Ave. Pudsey LS28 . 76 A8 1
Chatsworth Cl. Hud HD5 .... 154 D4
Chatsworth Cl. Leeds LS8 .... 61 A3
Chatsworth Cres. Pudsey LS28 76 A8
Chatsworth Ct. Dew WF12 ...... 139 F7
Chatsworth Dr. Pudsey LS28 ... 76 A8 2
Chatsworth Dr. Weth LS22 ...... 13 C6
Chatsworth Fall. Pudsey LS28 . 76 A8
Chatsworth Mws. Morley LS27 98 B3 5
Chatsworth Pl. Brad BD8 .... 55 B2
Chatsworth Rd. Leeds LS8 .... 61 A3
Chatsworth Rd. Pudsey LS28 ... 76 A8
Chatsworth Rise. Pudsey LS28 76 A8
Chatsworth St. Keigh BD21 ..... 35 D7
Chatsworth Terr. Dew WF12 . 139 F7
Chatts Wood Fold. Brad BD12 . 95 B5
Chaucer Ave. Loft G WF3 .... 121 E6
Chaucer Ave. Pudsey LS28 ...... 76 F6
Chaucer Cl. Honley HD7 .... 171 F3
Chaucer Gdns. Pudsey LS28 .... 76 F6
Chaucer Gr. Pudsey LS28 .... 76 F6
Chaucer St. Hali HX1 .... 112 F6
Cheapside. Batley WF17 .... 118 D5
Cheapside. Brad BD1 .... 74 E7
Cheapside. Clec BD19 .... 116 E7
Cheapside. Hali HX1 .... 113 C7
Cheapside. Nor WF6 .... 123 B2
Cheapside. Shelf HX3 .... 93 C6
Cheapside. Wake WF1 .... 142 B6
Cheddington Gr. Brad BD15 .... 73 B8
Cheese Gate Nab Side.
Holmfi HD7 .... 190 A2
Cheetham St. Heb Br HX7 .... 89 A3 20
Chelburn View. Litt OL15 .... 129 C1
Chellow Grange Rd. Brad BD9 . 54 C3
Chellow La. Brad BD9 .... 54 D1
Chellow St. Brad BD5 .... 74 D2
Chellow Terr. Brad BD9 .... 54 D1
Chellow Way. Dew WF12 .... 139 C7
Chelmsford Rd. Brad BD3 .... 75 C8
Chelmsford Rd. Brad BD3 .... 75 D7
Chelmsford Terr. Brad BD3 ..... 75 C7
Chelsea Cl. Leeds LS12 .... 78 C6
Chelsea Mansions. Northo HX3 93 A2
Chelsea Rd. Brad BD7 .... 73 F4
Chelsea St. Keigh BD21 .... 35 B6
Chelsfield Ct. Leeds LS15 .... 62 F3
Chelsfield Way. Leeds LS15 .... 62 F3
Cheltenham Ave. Ilkley LS29 ..... 8 F4
Cheltenham Gdns. Hali HX3 .... 113 D4
Cheltenham Pl. Hali HX3 .... 113 D4
Cheltenham Rd. Brad BD2 .... 55 F5
Cheltenham St. Leeds LS12 .... 78 D6
Chelwood Ave. Leeds LS8 .... 43 E3
Chelwood Cres. Leeds LS8 ...... 43 F2
Chelwood Dr. Brad BD15 .... 73 A7
Chelwood Dr. Leeds LS8 .... 43 F2
Chelwood Gr. Leeds LS8 .... 43 F3
Chelwood Mount. Leeds LS8 ... 43 F3
Chelwood Pl. Leeds LS8 .... 43 E3
Chenies Cl. Leeds LS14 .... 61 E1
Chepstow Cl. Gar LS25 .... 83 B7
Chequerfield Ave. Pont WF8 .. 146 F8
Chequerfield Cl. Castle WF10 124 A6
Chequerfield Dr. Pont WF8 .... 146 F7
Chequerfield Inf Sch. Pont 146 F7
Chequerfield La. Pont WF8 .... 146 F8
Chequerfield Mount. Pont
WF8 .... 146 F7
Chequerfield Rd. Pont WF8 .... 146 F7
Chequers Cl. Pont WF8 .... 146 F7
Chequers Ct. Pont WF8 .... 146 F8
Cheriton Dr. Queen BD13 .... 72 F1
Cherry Cl. Roy S71 .... 179 A4
Cherry Ct. Leeds LS9 .... 60 E1
Cherry Fields. Brad BD2 .... 55 E4
Cherry Garth. Hem WF9 .... 181 C6
Cherry Gr. Ilkley LS29 .... 7 F4
Cherry Hills. Mapp S75 .... 178 A1
Cherry La. Clay W HD8 .... 175 F2
Cherry Lea Ct. Yeadon LS19 .... 40 B5
Cherry Nook Rd. Hud HD2 ...... 136 E3
Cherry Pl. Leeds LS9 .... 60 E1
Cherry Rise. Leeds LS14 .... 62 C8
Cherry Row. Leeds LS9 .... 60 E1
Cherry St. Haw BD22 .... 51 E8 2
Cherry St. Keigh BD21 .... 35 E8
Cherry Tree Ave. Brad BD10 ... 56 D7
Cherry Tree Ave. Castle WF10 125 D5
Cherry Tree Cl. Hud HD7 .... 152 F5
Cherry Tree Cl. Mapp S75 ...... 178 C1
Cherry Tree Cres. Pudsey LS28 57 D3
Cherry Tree Cr. Walton WF2 . 161 B7
Cherry Tree Ct. E Ard WF3 .... 120 C7
Cherry Tree Ctr. Hud HD1 ...... 154 A6 15
Cherry Tree Dr. Elland HX4 .... 134 C7
Cherry Tree Dr. Pudsey LS28 .. 57 D3
Cherry Tree Dr. Walton WF2 . 161 B7
Cherry Tree Gdns. Brad BD10 . 38 F1
Cherry Tree Rd. Walton WF2 161 B7
Cherry Tree Rise. Keigh BD21 . 35 E6
Cherry Tree Row. Wils BD16 ... 53 B7
Cherry Tree Wlk. E Ard WF3 . 120 C7
Cherry Tree Wlk. Holmfi HD7 189 D4
Cherrywood Cl. Leeds LS14 .... 45 B1
Cherrywood Gdns. Leeds LS14 45 B1
Cherwell Croft. Gar LS25 .... 83 B5
Chesham St. Brad BD7 .... 74 C6
Chesham St. Keigh BD21 .... 35 D8
Chesil Bank. Hud HD3 .... 153 B6
Chesilton Ave. Hud HD3 .... 153 B7
Chesney Ave. Leeds LS10 .... 79 D4
Chesnut End. B Spa LS23 .... 30 E7
Chessington Dr. Floc WF4 ...... 157 D3
Chester Cl. Hali HX3 .... 92 B1 3
Chester Ct. Hali HX3 .... 92 B1 1
Chester Gr. Hali HX3 .... 92 B1 2
Chester Pl. Hali HX3 .... 92 B1 4
Chester Rd. Hali HX3 .... 92 B1
Chester St. Brad BD5 .... 74 E6
Chester St. Hali HX3 .... 92 B1
Chester St. Hali HX6 .... 112 B4 3
Chester St. Leeds LS12 .... 78 C8
Chester Terr. Hali HX3 .... 92 B1
Chesterton Ct. Hor WF4 .... 141 C2
Chesterton Ct. Leeds LS15 ...... 81 D6
Chesterton Dr. Honley HD7 ..... 171 F3
Chestnut Ave. B Spa LS23 .... 30 C8
Chestnut Ave. Batley WF17 ..... 118 A4
Chestnut Ave. Bri S72 .... 180 F2
Chestnut Ave. Leeds LS6 .... 59 E3
Chestnut Ave. Leeds LS15 .... 62 D2
Chestnut Ave. Tod OL14 .... 108 A7
Chestnut Ave. Walton WF2 ...... 161 A6
Chestnut Ave. Weth LS22 .... 13 D6
Chestnut Cl. Elland HX4 .... 134 B7
Chestnut Cl. Hud HD4 .... 154 A2
Chestnut Cl. Ilkley LS29 .... 8 E3
Chestnut Cl. Keigh BD22 .... 34 F6
Chestnut Cres. Nor WF6 .... 144 A7
Chestnut Ct. Rip HX6 .... 132 D4
Chestnut Ct. Ship BD18 .... 54 F7
Chestnut Dr. S Hie S72 .... 180 D5
Chestnut Garth. Hud HD3 .... 153 B7
Chestnut Gdns. Leeds LS12 ..... 78 B6
Chestnut Gn. Pont WF8 .... 125 F1
Chestnut Gr. B Spa LS23 .... 30 C8
Chestnut Gr. Crof WF4 .... 143 F1
Chestnut Gr. Hem WF9 .... 181 F6
Chestnut Gr. Leeds LS6 .... 59 E3
Chestnut Gr. Pont WF8 .... 146 D6
Chestnut Gr. Pudsey LS28 .... 57 B6
Chestnut Gr. Ship BD2 .... 55 E4
Chestnut Meadows. Mir WF14 137 F8
Chestnut Pl. Leeds LS6 .... 59 E3
Chestnut Rd. Leeds LS6 .... 59 E3 6
Chestnut St. Glu BD20 .... 16 D6
Chestnut St. Hali HX1 .... 112 F6
Chestnut St. Hud HD2 .... 136 D3
Chestnut St. Leeds LS6 .... 59 E3
Chestnut St. S Elm WF9 .... 182 F1
Chestnut Terr. Dew WF12 .... 139 C3
Chestnut Wlk. Knot WF11 .... 126 D3
Chestnut Wlk. Wake WF2 .... 142 A8
Chestnuts The. Rip HX6 .... 132 C3
Chevet Croft. Wake WF2 .... 160 E7
Chevet Gr. Wake WF2 .... 160 E7
Chevet Hill. Walton WF2 .... 160 F3
Chevet La. Notton WF4 .... 179 B8
Chevet La. Wake WF2, WF4 .. 160 F6
Chevet La. Walton WF2, WF4 160 F6
Chevet La. Walton WF2 .... 161 B2
Chevet Level. Walton WF2 ...... 160 F4
Chevet Mount. Brad BD15 .... 73 A8
Chevet Park Ct. Walton WF2 . 160 E3
Chevet Rise. Roy S71 .... 179 B4
Chevet Terr. Crof WF1 .... 143 A1
Chevet View. Roy S71 .... 179 A4
Chevin Ave. Men LS29 .... 22 A5
Chevin Ave. Otley LS21 .... 23 B6
Chevin End Rd. Guise LS20 ..... 22 D3
Chevin Forest Park. Otley 23 D5
Chevin Side. Otley LS21 .... 23 A6
Chevinedge Cres. Hali HX3 ..... 113 D1
Chevington Ct. Yeadon LS19 .... 40 A3
Chevins Cl. Batley WF17 .... 117 F8
Cheviot Ave. Mel HD7 .... 170 F1
Cheviot Cl. Hem WF9 .... 181 F7
Cheviot Ct. Gar LS25 .... 82 F5
Cheviot Gate. Brad BD12 .... 94 B6
Cheviot Pl. Knot WF11 .... 126 F4
Cheviot Way. Mir WF14 .... 137 F2
Cheyne Wlk. Keigh BD22 .... 35 A6 12
Chichester St. Leeds LS12 .... 78 C8
Chickenley Cty Inf Sch. Dew ... 140 A7
Chickenley Cty Jun Sch. Dew .. 140 A8
Chickenley La. Dew WF12 .... 140 B7
Chidswell Gdns. Batley WF12 119 B3
Chidswell La. Batley WF12 ...... 119 A3
Chidswell La. Ossett WF5 .... 119 B2
Child La. Liver WF15 .... 116 F1
Childs La. Ship BD18 .... 55 E6
Childs Rd. Wake WF2 .... 141 D8
Chiltern Ave. Castle WF10 .... 123 F5
Chiltern Ave. Hud HD3 .... 135 A1
Chiltern Ave. Knot WF11 .... 126 E4
Chiltern Cl. Gar LS25 .... 82 F5
Chiltern Ct. Gar LS25 .... 82 F5
Chiltern Ct. Hem WF9 .... 181 F7
Chiltern Dr. Ack M T WF7 .... 163 F5
Chiltern Dr. Mir WF14 .... 137 F2
Chiltern Rd. Dew WF12 .... 118 F1
Chiltern Way. Clec WF15 .... 116 D5
Chilwell Cl. Barn S71 .... 178 F1
Chilwell Gdns. Barn S71 .... 178 F1
Chilwell Mews. Barn S71 .... 178 F1
Chilwell Rd. Barn S71 .... 178 F1
Chimney La. Lepton HD8 .... 155 D4
Chinewood Ave. Batley WF17 . 118 B6
Chippendale Ct. Men LS29 .... 22 B4
Chippendale Rise. Brad BD8 .... 73 D8
Chippendale Rise. Otley LS21 .. 11 A1
Chirton Gr. Leeds LS8 .... 61 A5
Chislehurst Pl. Brad BD5 .... 74 C4
Chiswick St. Leeds LS6 .... 59 E2
Chiswick Terr. Leeds LS6 .... 59 E2
Choppards Bank Rd. Holmfi
HD7 .... 189 A2
Choppards La. Holmfi HD7 ...... 189 A2
Chorley La. Leeds LS2 .... 79 A8 3
Chrisharben Pk. Brad BD14 ..... 73 C4
Christ Church Ave. Leeds LS12 78 B8
Christ Church CE Jun & Inf Sch.
Hali 112 D8
Christ Church CE Jun Sch. Hali 112 C5
Christ Church Mt. Leeds LS12 . 78 B8 11
Christ Church Par. Leeds LS12 78 B8
Christ Church Pl. Leeds LS12 ... 78 B8 12
Christ Church Rd. Leeds LS12 78 B8
Christ Church St. Bacup OL13 106 A3 3
Christ Church Terr. Leeds LS12 78 B8 10
Christ Church Vw. Leeds LS12 . 78 B8
Christ the King RC Prim Sch.
Leeds 58 E1
Christiana Terr. Morley LS27 ... 98 B5
Christopher Rd. Leeds LS6 .... 60 A4
Christopher St. Brad BD5 .... 74 C3 1
Christopher Terr. Brad BD5 ..... 74 C3 2
Church App. Gar LS25 .... 82 F7
Church Ave. Crof WF1 .... 143 D7
Church Ave. Gild LS27 .... 97 C8
Church Ave. Hors LS18 .... 41 B1
Church Ave. Hud HD7 .... 152 E2
Church Ave. Hud HD4 .... 153 E4
Church Ave. Leeds LS6 .... 59 F7
Church Ave. S Kirk WF9 .... 182 C2
Church Ave. Swil LS26 .... 82 A2
Church Bank. Brad BD1 .... 74 F7
Church Bank. Hali HX6 .... 112 C4
Church Bank. Hali HX2 .... 112 D6
Church Bank La. Heb Br HX7 . 110 C3
Church Cl. Crof WF4 .... 144 B2
Church Cl. Hali HX2 .... 91 D5
Church Cl. Hali HX1 .... 113 B7
Church Cl. Hem WF9 .... 181 D7
Church Cl. Leeds LS14 .... 62 B4
Church Cl. M'field LS25 .... 84 A8
Church Cl. Mapp S75 .... 177 E1
Church Cl. Pool LS21 .... 24 C7
Church Cl. Shep HD8 .... 190 E8
Church Cl. Sow Br HX6 .... 111 E3
Church Cl. Swil LS26 .... 82 A2
Church Cres. Hors LS18 .... 41 B1
Church Cres. Leeds LS17 .... 43 C3
Church Cres. Neth WF4 .... 158 E6
Church Cres. Swil LS26 .... 82 B1
Church Cres. Yeadon LS19 .... 40 A6
Church Cswy. Th Arch LS23 ..... 14 F1
Church Ct. Brad BD7 .... 73 F5
Church Ct. Nor WF6 .... 123 A1
Church Ct. Ossett WF5 .... 140 D7
Church Ct. Yeadon LS19 .... 40 B6
Church Dr. Bri S72 .... 180 F3
Church Dr. E Kes LS17 .... 28 B5
Church Dr. S Kirk WF9 .... 182 C2
Church Farm Cl. Nor WF6 .... 122 F4
Church Farm Cl. Roth WF3 ...... 100 C1
Church Farm. Thorner LS14 ..... 45 F6
Church Farm View.
B in Elm LS15 .... 63 E7
Church Field Rd. Clay DN5 ...... 194 E4
Church Fields. Brad BD2 .... 56 D2
Church Garth. Castle WF10 ..... 124 F6
Church Garth. Pool LS21 .... 24 C7
Church Gate. Hors LS18 .... 41 B1
Church Gdns. Gar LS25 .... 82 F6
Church Gdns. Gild LS27 .... 97 C7
Church Gdns. Leeds LS17 .... 43 D3
Church Gn. Hali HX2 .... 91 E1
Church Gn. Kirkb HD8 .... 173 F6
Church Gr. Hors LS18 .... 41 B1
Church Gr. S Kirk WF9 .... 182 C2
Church Grange. Clec BD19 ...... 116 E7 4
Church Hill. Bail BD17 .... 38 D4
Church Hill. Bramham LS23 ..... 30 D2
Church Hill. Bramho LS16 .... 24 D3
Church Hill Gdns. Pudsey LS28 57 F2
Church Hill Gn. Pudsey LS28 ... 57 F2
Church Hill. Hali HX2 .... 90 D1
Church Hill Mt. Pudsey LS28 ... 57 F2
Church Hill. Roy S71 .... 179 D3
Church Hill. Thorner LS14 .... 46 A6
Church House. Elland HX5 ...... 134 F7 13
Church La. Bard LS17 .... 28 C2
Church La. Batley WF16 .... 117 D3
Church La. Brad BD6 .... 94 B8
Church La. Brig HX3 .... 114 C4
Church La. Brig HD6 .... 115 A2 3
Church La. Brig HD6 .... 115 B2
Church La. Brig HD6 .... 135 D7
Church La. Caw S75 .... 193 F4
Church La. Clay W HD8 .... 175 F2
Church La. Clec BD19 .... 117 C8
Church La. Clift LS21 .... 10 B2
Church La. Coll LS22 .... 13 B1
Church La. Crig WF4 .... 160 A4
Church La. Dar WF8 .... 147 D5
Church La. Dew WF13 .... 138 F8
Church La. Dew WF12 .... 139 E2
Church La. E Ard WF3 .... 119 D7
Church La. E Ard WF3 .... 120 C7
Church La. Elland HX4 .... 134 A4
Church La. Emley HD8 .... 175 C7
Church La. Feath WF7 .... 124 C1
Church La. Feath WF7 .... 144 D8
Church La. Gar LS25 .... 82 F7
Church La. Guise BD17 .... 39 C5
Church La. H Hoy S75 .... 176 C1
Church La. Hali HX2 .... 91 E1
Church La. Hare LS17 .... 26 F7
Church La. Heb Br HX7 .... 88 E3
Church La. Hep HX7 .... 88 F5
Church La. Hors LS18 .... 41 B1
Church La. Hors LS16 .... 42 C5
Church La. Hud HD7 .... 152 E1
Church La. Hud HD4 .... 154 A2
Church La. Hud HD5 .... 154 D6
Church La. Hud HD4 .... 171 B6
Church La. Kippax LS25 .... 83 B1
Church La. Kirkhe HD5 .... 155 B7
Church La. Leeds LS6 .... 59 F7
Church La. Leeds LS7 .... 60 D6
Church La. Leeds LS15 .... 62 D3
Church La. Liver WF15 .... 116 B3
Church La. Liver WF15 .... 117 A5
Church La. Loft G WF1 .... 121 B5
Church La. M'Field LS25 .... 83 F7
Church La. M'town LS26 .... 102 C2
Church La. Mars HD3 .... 150 F5
Church La. Mars HD7 .... 168 F4
Church La. Mir WF14 .... 138 C5
Church La. Neth WF4 .... 158 E7
Church La. Nor WF6 .... 123 A1
Church La. Pont WF8 .... 146 D8 2
Church La. Pool LS21 .... 24 C7
Church La. Pudsey LS28 .... 76 E7
Church La. Ryhill S71 .... 179 F7
Church La. Shep HD8 .... 190 E8
Church La. Swil LS26 .... 82 A1
Church Lane Ave. Loft G WF1 121 B5
Church Meadows. Batley WF17 96 D1
Church Meadows.
Bramham LS23 .... 30 D3
Church Mews. B Spa LS23 .... 30 D8
Church Mews. Brad BD6 .... 93 E7 5
Church Mount. Hors LS18 .... 41 B1
Church Mount. S Kirk WF9 ...... 182 C2
Church Pl. Gar LS25 .... 82 F7
Church Pl. Hali HX1 .... 113 B7
Church Rd. Batley WF17 .... 117 F8
Church Rd. Brad BD6 .... 94 B8
Church Rd. Caw S75 .... 193 E4
Church Rd. Hors LS18 .... 41 B1
Church Rd. Leeds LS12 .... 78 C7
Church Rd. Leeds LS9 .... 79 E7
Church Rd. Liver FW15 .... 116 E2
Church Rd. Loft G WF3 .... 121 F5
Church Rd. Nor WF6 .... 122 E4
Church Rd. S in Cra BD20 .... 16 D5
Church Rd. Swil LS26 .... 102 E8
Church Rd. Tod OL14 .... 107 E8
Church Row. Denton LS29 .... 9 A6
Church Sch The. Thorn 72 E6
Church Side. M'town LS26 ...... 102 C2
Church Sq. Gar LS25 .... 82 F7
Church St. Add LS29 .... 7 A8
Church St. B Spa LS23 .... 30 D8
Church St. Batley WF17 .... 96 E1
Church St. Batley WF16 .... 117 D3
Church St. Bing BD16 .... 37 A2
Church St. Brad BD8 .... 55 C1
Church St. Brad BD6 .... 93 E7
Church St. Brig HD6 .... 135 F8
Church St. Broth WF11 .... 126 C8
Church St. Castle WF10 .... 124 D8
Church St. Caw S75 .... 193 F4
Church St. Clec WF15 .... 116 C5
Church St. Clec BD19 .... 116 E7
Church St. Cull BD13 .... 52 D6
Church St. Dew WF13 .... 138 E5
Church St. Dew WF13 .... 139 D8
Church St. Elland HX4 .... 134 D7
Church St. Elland HX5 .... 134 F7
Church St. Gild LS27 .... 97 C7
Church St. Glu BD20 .... 16 D7
Church St. Guise LS20 .... 22 F1
Church St. Hali HX1 .... 113 D6
Church St. Haw BD22 .... 51 B7
Church St. Heb Br HX7 .... 110 E8
Church St. Hep HX7 .... 88 F5
Church St. Holmfi HD7 .... 189 F6
Church St. Honley HD7 .... 171 F5
Church St. Hor WF4 .... 141 B1
Church St. Hud HD7 .... 152 D4
Church St. Hud HD3 .... 153 A6
Church St. Hud HD1 .... 153 D5
Church St. Hud HD4 .... 153 E4
Church St. Hud HD1 .... 154 B6
Church St. Hud HD5 .... 154 D6
Church St. Ilkley LS29 .... 8 B4
Church St. Keigh BD21 .... 35 C6
Church St. Keigh BD21 .... 35 D7
Church St. Leeds LS5 .... 59 A4
Church St. Leeds LS10 .... 79 E3
Church St. Liver WF15 .... 117 A5
Church St. Mapp S75 .... 177 E1
Church St. Mapp S75 .... 178 C1
Church St. Morley LS27 .... 98 A5
Church St. Ossett WF5 .... 140 D7
Church St. Oxen BD22 .... 51 C2
Church St. Roth LS26 .... 100 E5
Church St. Roth LS26 .... 101 C7
Church St. Roy S71 .... 179 C3
Church St. Roy S71 .... 179 D1
Church St. S Elm WF9 .... 183 A2
Church St. Ship BD18 .... 55 D8
Church St. Slai HD7 .... 169 F8
Church St. Tod OL14 .... 107 E8
Church St. Wake WF1 .... 142 C4
Church St. Weth LS22 .... 13 E5
Church St. Wool WF4 .... 177 F7
Church St. Yeadon LS19 .... 40 A6
Church Terr. Clay W HD8 .... 175 D1
Church Terr. Hali HX4 .... 91 D5
Church Terr. Holmfi HD7 .... 189 A5
Church Top. S Kirk WF9 .... 182 C2
Church View Cl. Ryhill WF4 .... 162 C1
Church View. Clec BD19 .... 116 B8
Church View. Crig WF4 .... 159 F5
Church View. Feath WF7 .... 145 C5
Church View. Hali HX6 .... 112 C4
Church View. Holmfi HD7 .... 188 C2
Church View. Kippax LS25 .... 83 D2
Church View Mws. B Spa LS23 30 D5
Church View. S Kirk WF9 .... 182 C2
Church View. Thorner LS14 ...... 45 F6
Church View. Wake WF1 .... 142 E2
Church Villas. S Kirk WF9 .... 182 C2
Church Way. Keigh BD21 .... 35 C6
Church Way. Morley LS27 .... 98 A5 3
Church Wlk. Batley WF17 .... 118 A3
Church Wlk. Dew WF12 .... 139 E2
Church Wlk. Leeds LS2 .... 79 D7
Church Wlk. Northo HX3 .... 93 A2
Church Wlk. Tod OL14 .... 108 B1
Church Wood Ave. Leeds LS16 59 C7
Church Wood Mount.
Leeds LS16 .... 59 C7
Church Wood Rd. Leeds LS16 .. 59 C6
Churchbalk Dr. Pont WF8 .... 146 E6
Churchbalk La. Pont WF8 .... 146 E6
Churchfarm Garth.
Thorner LS17 .... 44 F4
Churchfield Cl. Liver WF15 ..... 117 A4 5
Churchfield Croft. Nor WF6 .... 122 F4
Churchfield Croft. Roth LS26 . 100 F5
Churchfield Gr. Roth LS26 ...... 100 E6
Churchfield La. Castle WF10 .. 124 F7
Churchfield La. K Smea WF8 . 166 F7
Churchfield La. Roth LS26 .... 100 E6
Churchfield Rd. Roth LS26 ...... 100 E6
Churchfield St. Batley WF17 .. 118 C5 1
Churchfield Terr. Liver WF15 117 A4 6
Churchfields. Crof WF4 .... 144 A1
Churchfields. Hud HD2 .... 136 F3
Churchfields Rd. Brig HD6 ...... 115 A3
Churchfields. Ryhill WF4 .... 162 B2
Churchgate. Bramho LS16 .... 24 D3
Churchill Flats. Pool LS21 .... 24 C7
Churchill Gdns. Leeds LS2 .... 60 B2 11
Churchill Gr. Batley WF16 ...... 117 E3
Churchill Gr. Wake WF2 .... 160 E8
Churchill Rd. Thorn BD13 .... 72 F6
Churchill St. Tod OL14 .... 107 E8
Churchill Way. Glu BD20 .... 16 E7
Churchside Villas.
M'town LS26 .... 102 C2
Churchtown Cres. Bacup OL13 106 B1
Churchville Ave. M'Field LS25 . 83 F7
Churchville Dr. M'field LS25 .... 84 A7
Churchville. M'field LS25 .... 84 A8
Churchville Terr. M'field LS25 . 84 A7
Churchway. Crof WF4 .... 144 A1
Churchwood Cl. Slai HD7 .... 151 F1
Churn La. Hali HX2 .... 112 D7
Churn Milk La. Hali HX3 .... 92 A4
Churwell Ave. Batley WF13 .... 117 F3 3
Churwell Cl. Castle WF10 .... 124 D6
Churwell Prim Sch. Morley 98 B7
Cinder Hill. Kirkb HD8 .... 174 B7
Cinder Hill Rd. Tod OL14 .... 108 E6
Cinder Hills Rd. Holmfi HD7 ... 189 B4
Cinder La. B Spa LS23 .... 30 E6
Cinder La. Castle WF10 .... 124 C8
Cinder La. Lindley LS21 .... 11 F5
Cinderhills La. Hali HX3 .... 113 E3
City Hall. Brad 74 E6
City La. Hali HX3 .... 91 E2
City of Leeds Coll of Music.
Leeds 60 B1
City of Leeds Sch. Leeds 60 A4
City of Leeds Sch. Leeds 79 C8
City Park Ind Est. Leeds 78 C3
City Rd. Brad BD8 .... 74 C8
City Sq. Leeds LS1 .... 79 B7
Cityway Ind Est. Brad 75 A5
Clapgate La. Rip HX6 .... 132 E7
Clapgate. Otley LS21 .... 23 A8
Clapgate Prim Sch. Midd 99 F5
Clapham Dene Rd. Leeds LS15 62 B1
Clapham St. Denh BD13 .... 71 E8
Claphouse Fold. W Bret S75 .. 177 A5
Clapton Ave. Hali HX1 .... 113 A6
Clara Dr. Pudsey LS28 .... 57 A8
Clara Rd. Brad BD2 .... 55 F5
Clara St. Brig HD6 .... 115 A1
Clara St. Hud HD4 .... 153 A3
Clara St. Pudsey LS28 .... 57 D2
Clare Cres. Brad BD12 .... 94 C2
Clare Hall La. Hali HX1 .... 113 C6 11
Clare Hill. Hud HD1 .... 154 A7
Clare Rd. Brad BD12 .... 94 C2
Clare Rd. Clec BD19 .... 116 D7
Clare Rd. Hali HX1 .... 113 C6
Clare Rd. Heb Br HX7 .... 89 D1
Clare St. Hali HX1 .... 113 C6
Claremont Ave. Leeds LS3 .... 60 A1 9
Claremont Ave. Ship BD18 ...... 55 E6
Claremont. Batley WF16 .... 117 D4
Claremont. Brad BD7 .... 74 D6
Claremont Cres. Crof WF4 ..... 161 F8
Claremont Cres. Leeds LS6 ..... 59 F5
Claremont Cres. Ship BD18 ..... 55 E6
Claremont Ct. Leeds LS6 .... 59 E6
Claremont Dr. Leeds LS6 .... 59 E6
Claremont Gdns. Bing BD16 .... 37 A4
Claremont Gdns. Pudsey LS28 57 D2
Claremont Gr. Leeds LS3 .... 60 A1 4
Claremont Gr. Pudsey LS28 .... 76 E7
Claremont Gr. Ship BD18 .... 55 F6
Claremont Pl. Leeds LS12 .... 78 A7
Claremont. Pudsey LS28 .... 76 F8
Claremont Rd. Dew WF13 .... 118 B1
Claremont Rd. Leeds LS6 .... 59 E6
Claremont Rd. Ship BD18 .... 55 E6
Claremont St. Clec BD19 .... 116 D8 7
Claremont St. Hali HX6 .... 112 C5
Claremont St. Hud HD1 .... 154 A7
Claremont St. Leeds LS12 .... 78 A7
Claremont St. Roth LS26 .... 101 C6
Claremont St. Wake WF1 .... 142 E4
Claremont Terr. Brad BD5 .... 74 D6
Claremont Terr. Leeds LS12 .... 78 A7 1
Claremont Terr. Tod OL14 .... 129 D5
Claremont Terr. Wake WF2 .... 142 A5
Claremont View. Leeds LS3 ..... 60 A1 3
Claremont View. Roth LS26 ... 101 C6 8
Claremount Rd. Hali HX3 .... 92 C1
Claremount Terr. Hali HX3 ...... 92 C2 3
Clarence Dr. Hors LS18 .... 58 B7
Clarence Dr. Men LS29 .... 21 F6
Clarence Gdns. Hors LS18 .... 58 B7
Clarence Mews. Hors LS18 ...... 58 B7
Clarence Rd. Hors LS18 .... 58 B7
Clarence Rd. Leeds LS10 .... 79 D7
Clarence Rd. Leeds LS10 .... 79 E6
Clarence Rd. Ship BD18 .... 54 F8
Clarence Rd. Wake WF2 .... 142 B3
Clarence St. Batley WF17 .... 118 D5
Clarence St. Clec BD19 .... 116 D7
Clarence St. Hali HX1 .... 113 B7
Clarence St. Leeds LS13 .... 58 C1
Clarence Terr. Dew WF12 .... 139 D6
Clarence Terr. Pudsey LS28 .... 76 E8 1
Clarendon Ct. Wake WF1 .... 142 C7 1
Clarendon Pl. Hali HX1 .... 113 A6
Clarendon Pl. Leeds LS2 .... 60 A2
Clarendon Pl. Queen BD13 ...... 92 C8 3
Clarendon Rd. B Spa LS23 .... 30 C8
Clarendon Rd. Bing BD16 .... 37 B4
Clarendon Rd. Leeds LS2 .... 60 A1
Clarendon St. Haw BD22 .... 51 C6 9
Clarendon St. Keigh BD21 .... 35 B5
Clarendon St. Wake WF1 .... 142 C7 2
Clarendon Terr. Pudsey LS28 .. 76 E6
Clarendon Way. Leeds LS2 ...... 60 A1
Clarges St. Brad BD5 .... 74 D3
Clarion Field. Men LS29 .... 22 D5
Clarion St. Wake WF1 .... 142 E4
Clark Ave. Leeds LS9 .... 79 F7
Clark Cres. Leeds LS9 .... 79 F7
Clark Gr. Leeds LS9 .... 79 F6
Clark La. Leeds LS9 .... 79 F7
Clark Mount. Leeds LS9 .... 79 F7
Clark Rd. Leeds LS9 .... 79 F7
Clark Row. Leeds LS9 .... 79 F6
Clark Spring Cl. Morley LS27 ... 98 A7
Clark Spring Rise. Morley LS27 98 B7
Clark Terr. Leeds LS9 .... 79 F7
Clark View. Leeds LS9 .... 79 F6
Clarke Cres. Nor WF6 .... 144 A7
Clarke Gr. Wake WF1 .... 121 E1
Clarke La. Mel HD7 .... 170 E2
Clarke Rd. E Ard FW3 .... 119 E5
Clarke St. Dew WF13 .... 118 A1
Clarke St. Pudsey LS28 .... 57 B6
Clarkson Ave. Batley WF16 ..... 117 E4
Clarkson Ct. Nor WF6 .... 123 C1
Clarkson St. Dew WF13 .... 138 E6
Clarkson St. Wake WF2 .... 142 A5
Clarkson View. Leeds LS6 .... 60 A4
Clarydon Pl. Batley WF16 .... 117 D4 2
Clattering Stones Rd.
Heb Br HX7 .... 110 E2
Clay Butts. Hud HD2 .... 135 E2
Clay Hill Dr. Brad BD12 .... 94 D4
Clay House La. Elland HX4 ...... 134 D7
Clay La. Slai HD7 .... 152 A1
Clay Pit La. Leeds LS2, LS7 ...... 60 C1
Clay Pits La. Hali HX1 .... 112 F8
Clay Pits La. Rip HX6 .... 132 B7
Clay St. Hali HX6 .... 112 B4
Clay St. Hali HX6 .... 112 C5
Clay St. Hali HX1 .... 112 F7
Clay Well. Hud HD7 .... 152 D4
Clayborn View. Clec BD19 .... 116 E6
Clayfield Bglws. Knot WF11 ..... 126 C4
Clayfield Dr. Brad BD7 .... 74 A2
Claypit La. Ledsh LS25 .... 104 C7
Claypit La. Thorner LS14 .... 45 F5
Clayton Ave. Dearne S63 .... 194 B1
Clayton Ave. Kippax LS25 .... 83 C2
Clayton Ave. Upton WF9 .... 183 E8
Clayton (C E) Fst Sch. Brad 73 B4
Clayton CE Fst Sch. Brad 73 C4
Clayton Cl. Leeds LS10 .... 79 F2
Clayton Cotts. Hor WF4 .... 141 A1 2
Clayton Ct. Feath WF7 .... 145 C5
Clayton Ct. Leeds LS16 .... 58 F8
Clayton Ct. Leeds LS10 .... 79 F2
Clayton Dr. Leeds LS10 .... 79 F2
Clayton Fields. Hud HD2 .... 153 F8
Clayton Gr. Yeadon LS19 .... 40 B7
Clayton Grange. Leeds LS16 .... 58 F8 2
Clayton Holt. S Kirk WF9 .... 182 B1
Clayton Hospl. Wake 142 B7
Clayton La. Brad BD14 .... 73 B4
Clayton La. Brad BD5 .... 74 E4
Clayton La. Dearne S63 .... 194 B2
Clayton Mews. Nor WF6 .... 123 A4
Clayton Mid Sch. Brad 73 C4
Clayton Pl. Nor WF6 .... 123 A4
Clayton Rd. Brad BD7 .... 73 F5
Clayton Rd. Leeds LS10 .... 79 F2
Clayton Rise. Keigh BD20 .... 35 A8
Clayton Rise. Loft G WF1 .... 121 B5
Clayton St. Roth LS26 .... 100 F5
Clayton St. Wake WF2 .... 142 A5
Clayton Terr. Cull BD13 .... 52 D5
Clayton View. S Kirk WF9 .... 182 B1
Clayton Way. Leeds LS10 .... 79 F2
Clayton West Sta. Clay W 175 F3
Clayton Wood Bank. Hors LS16 41 F1
Clayton Wood Cl. Leeds LS16 .. 41 F1
Clayton Wood Ct. Leeds LS16 .. 41 F1
Clayton Wood Rd. Leeds LS16 . 41 F1
Clayton Wood Rise. Leeds LS16 41 F1
Claytons Bldgs. Feath WF7 ..... 145 D8
Cleasby Rd. Men LS29 .... 22 A4
Cleavesty La. E Kes LS17 .... 28 B6
Cleckheaton Golf Course. Brad 95 A2
Cleckheaton Rd. Brad BD12 ..... 94 D6
Cleeve Hill. Yeadon LS19 .... 40 B4
Cleevethorpe Gr. Wake WF2 . 142 E1
Clegg La. Elland HX4 .... 133 F7
Clegg St. Brad BD12 .... 94 C3 10
Clement St. Brad BD8 .... 73 F8 9
Clement St. Hali HX6 .... 112 B4 5
Clement St. Hud HD1, HD4 ..... 153 D4
Clement St. Hud HD1 .... 153 F8
Clement St. Wake WF2 .... 141 F5
Clement Terr. Dew WF12 .... 139 C6
Clement Terr. Roth LS26 .... 100 E4
Cleopatra Pl. Leeds LS13 .... 58 C1 4
Clerk Green St. Batley WF17 . 118 B4
Clervaux Ct. Brad BD14 .... 73 D5
Clevedon Pl. Hali HX3 .... 92 A2 4
Clevedon Way. Roy S71 .... 179 B4
Cleveland Ave. Hali HX3 .... 113 D4
Cleveland Ave. Hor WF2 .... 141 D2
Cleveland Ave. Knot WF11 ...... 126 E4
Cleveland Ave. Mel HD7 .... 170 F1
Cleveland Garth. Hor WF2 ...... 141 D2
Cleveland Gr. Hor WF2 .... 141 D2
Cleveland Pl. Heb Br HX7 .... 89 A3 3
Cleveland Rd. Brad BD9 .... 55 B3
Cleveland Rd. Hud HD1 .... 153 D7
Cleveland St. Tod OL14 .... 86 B1
Cleveland Way. Shep HD8 ...... 173 F3
Cleveley Gdns. Heb Br HX7 .... 110 E8
Cleveleys Ave. Hali HX6 .... 112 B5 14
Cleveleys Ave. Leeds LS11 ...... 78 F4
Cleveleys Ct. Leeds LS11 .... 78 F4 9
Cleveleys Gdns. Hali HX6 .... 112 B5 12
Cleveleys Mount. Leeds LS11 .. 78 F4 8
Cleveleys Rd. Leeds LS11 .... 78 F4
Cleveleys St. Leeds LS11 .... 78 F4 6
Cleveleys Terr. Leeds LS11 ...... 78 F4 7
Cliff Cl. Hud HD3 .... 153 B6
Cliff Cres. Hali HX2 .... 112 E5
Cliff Cres. Kippax LS25 .... 83 C1
Cliff Ct. Leeds LS6 .... 60 A4 1
Cliff Ct. Liver WF15 .... 117 A3
Cliff Dr. Crig WF4 .... 159 D5
Cliff Gdns. Hali HX2 .... 112 E5
Cliff Gr. Crig WF4 .... 159 C4
Cliff Hill. Caw S75 .... 193 E5
Cliff Hill La. Hali HX2 .... 112 B6
Cliff Hollins La. Birk BD12, BD4 95 C6
Cliff House La. Holmfi HD7 ...... 189 B6
Cliff House Sch. Leeds 78 A5
Cliff La. Bri S72 .... 180 F2
Cliff La. Holmfi HD7 .... 189 B5
Cliff La. Leeds LS6 .... 59 F4
Cliff La. Rip HX6 .... 132 D2
Cliff La. Wake WF1 .... 142 B6
Cliff Mount. Leeds LS6 .... 60 A4
Cliff Mount St. Leeds LS6 .... 60 A4
Cliff Mount Terr. Leeds LS6 ..... 60 A4
Cliff Par. Wake WF1 .... 142 B6

Cliff Park Ave. Wake WF1 ...... 142 B7
Cliff Rd. Crig WF4 .... 159 D4
Cliff Rd. Holmfi HD7 .... 188 A4
Cliff Rd. Holmfi HD7 .... 189 B6
Cliff Rd. Leeds LS6 .... 60 A4
Cliff Road Gdns. Leeds LS6 ...... 60 A4
Cliff Side Gdns. Leeds LS6 ...... 60 A4
Cliff St. Haw BD22 .... 51 D7
Cliff St. Pont WF8 .... 146 C8 12
Cliff St. Wake WF2 .... 141 F7
Cliff Terr. Leeds LS6 .... 60 A4
Cliff Terr. M'field LS25 .... 84 B6
Cliff Vale Rd. Ship BD18 .... 55 B5
Cliff Villas. Pont WF8 .... 146 C8 11
Cliff Wood Ave. Ship BD18 ...... 55 B4
Cliffdale Rd. Leeds LS6 .... 60 B4
Cliffdale Road Light Ind Est.
  Leeds 60 B4
Cliffe Ash. Hud HD7 .... 152 D4
Cliffe Ave. Bail BD17 .... 38 C3
Cliffe Ave. Brig HX3 .... 115 A7
Cliffe Ave. Harden BD16 .... 36 A1
Cliffe Castle Mus. Keigh 18 B1
Cliffe Cl. Bri LS27 .... 180 F3
Cliffe Cres. Keigh BD20 .... 36 B8
Cliffe Crest. Hor WF4 .... 141 B2
Cliffe Ct. Keigh BD21 .... 35 B8
Cliffe Ct. Yeadon LS19 .... 40 C7
Cliffe Dr. Yeadon LS19 .... 40 B3
Cliffe End Rd. Hud HD3 .... 153 B6
Cliffe Gdns. Ship BD18 .... 55 B6
Cliffe Hill Jun Mix & Inf Sch.
  Brig 115 A6
Cliffe House Ave. Gar LS25 .... 83 A5
Cliffe House Sch. Shep 190 E7
Cliffe La. Bail BD17 .... 38 C1
Cliffe La. Clec BD19 .... 95 F1
Cliffe La. Kirkb HD4 .... 172 E6
Cliffe La. S. Bail BD17 .... 38 C1
Cliffe La W. Bail BD17 .... 38 C2
Cliffe La. Thorn BD13 .... 72 E7
Cliffe La. Yeadon LS19 .... 40 C3
Cliffe Mill Fold. Keigh BD20 .. 36 E8
Cliffe Mount. Clec BD19 .... 96 A1
Cliffe Park Chase. Leeds LS12 . 78 A6
Cliffe Park Cl. Leeds LS12 .... 78 A6
Cliffe Park Cres. Leeds LS12 .. 78 A6
Cliffe Park Dr. Leeds LS12 .... 78 A6
Cliffe Park Rise. Leeds LS12 .. 78 A6
Cliffe Pk. Shep HD8 .... 190 E8
Cliffe Rd. Brad BD3 .... 55 F1
Cliffe Rd. Brig HD6 .... 115 B2
Cliffe Rd. Shep HD8 .... 190 E8
Cliffe Rd. Batley WF17 .... 117 F4
Cliffe St. Clay W HD8 .... 175 F2
Cliffe St. Dew WF13 .... 118 D1
Cliffe St. Heb Br HX7 .... 89 A3 9
Cliffe St. Keigh BD21 .... 35 B8
Cliffe St. Litt OL15 .... 129 D2
Cliffe St. Thorn BD13 .... 72 D7
Cliffe Terr. Bail BD17 .... 38 C1
Cliffe Terr. Brad BD8 .... 55 D1
Cliffe Terr. Hali HX6 .... 112 A5
Cliffe Terr. Hud HX3 .... 113 C2
Cliffe Terr. Keigh BD21 .... 35 C4
Cliffe Terr. With LS22 .... 13 E5
Cliffe View. Brad BD15 .... 53 F2
Cliffe View. Clay W HD8 .... 175 F2
Cliffe View. Morley LS27 ...... 97 D3
Cliffe Wood Cl. Brad BD9 ...... 54 E3
Cliffestone Dr. Keigh BD20 .... 36 D8
Cliffewood Rise. Clay W HD8 ... 175 E2
Clifford Ave. Ilkley LS29 ..... 8 A5
Clifford Ave. Wake WF2 .... 142 D2
Clifford Cty Prim Sch. B Spa .. 30 E5
Clifford Ct. Ossett WF5 .... 140 C6
Clifford Moor Rd. B Spa LS23 .. 30 C7
Clifford Pl. Morley LS27 ...... 98 B7 3
Clifford Rd. B Spa LS23 .... 30 E7
Clifford Rd. Bail BD17 .... 38 C2
Clifford Rd. Bramham LS23 ..... 30 D3
Clifford Rd. Ilkley LS29 ...... 8 A5
Clifford Rd. S Kirk WF9 .... 182 B2
Clifford St. Brad BD5 .... 74 E5
Clifford St. Cud S72 .... 180 C1
Clifford St. S Elm WF9 .... 182 F2
Clifford St. BD20 .... 5 D2
Clifford View. Wake WF2 .... 142 D2
Clifton Ave. Hali HX1 .... 112 F6
Clifton Ave. Holmfi HD7 .... 189 B6
Clifton Ave. Hor WF4 .... 141 A2
Clifton Ave. Leeds LS9 .... 61 B2
Clifton Ave. Loft G WF1 .... 121 E5
Clifton Ave. Pont WF8 .... 146 B8 6
Clifton Cl. Hor WF4 .... 141 A2
Clifton Comm. Brig HD6 .... 115 C3
Clifton Cres. Barn S71 .... 178 F1
Clifton Cres. Hor WF4 .... 141 A2
Clifton Ct. Pudsey LS28 .... 76 E8 11
Clifton Dr. Hor WF4 .... 141 A2
Clifton Dr. Pudsey LS28 .... 76 E8
Clifton Forge Bsns Pk. Knot ... 126 E4
Clifton Gdns. Leeds LS9 .... 280 E3
Clifton Gr. Leeds LS9 .... 61 B1
Clifton Hill. Pudsey LS28 ..... 76 E8
Clifton Inf Sch. Hor 140 F2
Clifton La. Clift LS21 .... 10 E5
Clifton La. Mel HD7 .... 170 E2
Clifton Mount. Leeds LS9 ...... 61 A2
Clifton Pl. Pudsey LS28 .... 76 F8
Clifton Pl. Ship BD18 .... 55 B6
Clifton Rd. Wake WF1 .... 142 B8
Clifton Rd. Brig HD6 .... 115 B2 3
Clifton Rd. Crof WF4 .... 144 B3
Clifton Rd. Hali HX3 .... 113 C4
Clifton Rd. Hor WF4 .... 141 A2
Clifton Rd. Hud HD1 .... 153 E7
Clifton Rd. Ilkley LS29 .... 8 D3
Clifton Rd. Pudsey LS28 .... 76 E8
Clifton Side. Hud HD2 .... 136 F6
Clifton St. Brad BD8 .... 55 D1
Clifton St. Hali HX3 .... 92 A1 13
Clifton St. Hali HX6 .... 112 C4
Clifton St. Hem WF9 .... 181 C6
Clifton St. Keigh BD22 .... 35 A6
Clifton St. Queen BD13 .... 72 E1 10
Clifton Terr. Batley WF17 ..... 118 D5
Clifton Terr. Leeds LS9 .... 61 A2
Clifton Terr. Ossett WF5 ...... 140 C8
Clifton View. Clay W HD8 ...... 175 F2

Clifton View. Pont WF8 .... 146 B8 5
Clifton Villas. Brad BD8 ...... 55 D1
Clipston Ave. Leeds LS6 .... 59 F6
Clipston Mount. Leeds LS6 ..... 59 F6
Clipston St. Leeds LS6 .... 59 F6
Clipston Terr. Leeds LS6 ...... 59 F6 9
Clitheroe St. Brad BD5 .... 74 E2 2
Clive Pl. Brad BD7 .... 74 B5
Clive St. Brad BD7 .... 74 B5
Cliviger-Holme C E Prim Sch.
  H Chap 85 B6
Cloberry St. Leeds LS2 .... 60 A2
Clock La. Denh BD13 .... 71 D8
Clock Row Ave. S Kirk WF9 ..... 182 D3
Clock Row Gr. S Kirk WF9 ...... 182 D3
Clock Row Mount. S Kirk WF9 ... 182 D3
Clock View St. Keigh BD20 ..... 18 B2
Clog Bridge. Sil BD20 .... 5 E1
Clog Sole Rd. Brig HD6 .... 114 F4
Cloisters The. Hali HX1 .... 113 A5 1
Close Head Dr. Thorn BD13 ..... 72 B6
Close Head La. Thorn BD13 ..... 72 B6
Close Head. Thorn BD13 .... 72 B6
Close Hill La. Hud HD4 .... 153 F2
Close Lea Ave. Brig HD6 .... 114 F1
Close Lea. Brig HD6 .... 115 A1
Close Lea Dr. Brig HD6 .... 114 F1
Close Lea Way. Brig HD6 .... 114 F1
Close Rd. Caste WF10 .... 124 F7
Close St. Hem WF9 .... 181 C7
Close The. B in Elm LS15 ...... 63 D6
Close The. B Spa LS23 .... 30 E8
Close The. Brad BD2 .... 55 F6
Close The. Clay DN5 .... 194 C4
Close The. Clay W HD8 .... 175 E2
Close The. Coll LS22 .... 29 B8
Close The. E Ard WF3 .... 120 D7
Close The. E Kes LS17 .... 28 C5
Close The. Guise LS20 .... 39 C8
Close The. Kippax LS25 .... 83 A1
Close The. Leeds LS17 .... 43 A5
Close The. Leeds LS6 .... 59 E7
Close The. Pont WF8 .... 146 F7
Close The. Roy S71 .... 179 C1
Close The. Thorner LS14 .... 46 A6
Closes Rd. Brig HD6 .... 115 A1 2
Cloth Hall St. Dew WF13 .... 139 D8
Cloth Hall St. Hud HD1 .... 154 A6
Cloth Hall St. Leeds LS2 ...... 79 C7 2
Cloudsdale Ave. Brad BD5 ...... 74 E4
Clough Ave. Stee BD20 .... 17 C6
Clough Bank. Hali HX2 .... 91 B5
Clough Bank La. Keigh BD22 .... 34 B6
Clough Bldgs. Sow Br HX6 ...... 111 D4
Clough Dr. Batley WF17 .... 97 A2
Clough Dr. Lepton HD8 .... 155 D2
Clough Dr. Slai HD7 .... 170 D8
Clough Foot La. Holmfi HD7 .... 199 A7
Clough Gate. Floc WF4 .... 156 D5
Clough Gate. Haw BD22 .... 34 D2
Clough Hall La. Hud HD4 .... 154 D1
Clough Hey. Mars HD7 .... 168 E4
Clough House La. D Dale HD8 ... 192 C6
Clough House La. Rip HX4 ...... 133 B2
Clough House La. Slai HD7 ..... 151 D1
Clough House. Slai HD7 .... 151 D1
Clough Houses. Haw BD22 .... 34 C2
Clough La. Brig HD6 .... 115 D6
Clough La. Brig HD6 .... 135 F6
Clough La. Hali HX2 .... 91 B5
Clough La. Haw BD22 .... 34 A6
Clough La. Hali HX2 .... 135 F6
Clough La. Hud HD1, HD2 .... 153 C5
Clough La. Lepton WF14 .... 156 C7
Clough La. Liver BD19 .... 116 D3
Clough La. Wad M HX7 .... 90 B5
Clough Lee. Mars HD7 .... 168 F4
Clough Pk. Lepton HD8 .... 155 D2
Clough Pl. Hali HX2 .... 91 B5
Clough Rd. Bacup OL13 .... 106 A3
Clough Rd. Emley HD8 .... 157 D1
Clough Rd. Hud HD7 .... 136 A2
Clough Rd. Slai HD7 .... 152 A2
Clough Rd. Slai HD7 .... 152 A4
Clough Rd. Sow Br HX6 .... 112 D1
Clough Rd. Tod OL14 .... 108 A1 4
Clough St. Brad BD5 .... 74 E3
Clough St. Morley LS27 .... 98 C4
Clough The. Lepton HD8 .... 155 D2
Clough The. Mir WF14 .... 137 E6
Clough Way. Lepton HD8 .... 155 D2
Clovelly Ave. Leeds LS11 ...... 79 B3 25
Clovelly Gr. Leeds LS11 .... 79 B3 24
Clovelly Pl. Leeds LS11 .... 79 B3 26
Clovelly Row. Leeds LS11 ...... 79 B3 23
Clovelly Terr. Leeds LS11 ..... 79 B3
Clover Cres. Pudsey LS28 ...... 57 A7
Clover Cres. Pudsey LS28 ...... 57 A7
Clover Hill Cl. Hali HX1 ...... 113 B6
Clover Hill. Clec WF15 .... 116 D5
Clover Hill Rd. Hali HX1 ...... 113 B5
Clover Hill Terr. Hali HX1 .... 113 B5 7
Clover Hill View. Hali HX1 .... 113 B5 7
Clover St. Bacup OL13 .... 106 A3
Clover St. Brad BD5 .... 74 B3
Cloverdale. Shelf HX3 .... 93 D7
Cloverville App. Brad BD6 ..... 94 C7
Club Houses. Hud HD4 .... 91 F3
Club Houses. Hud HD4 .... 171 E8
Club La. Hali HX2 .... 91 F3
Club La. Pudsey LS13 .... 57 E5
Club Row. Leeds LS7 .... 60 D7
Club Row. Wils BD15 .... 53 C5
Club Row. Yeadon LS19 .... 40 C7
Club St. Brad BD7 .... 73 F5
Club St. Tod OL14 .... 86 B1
Club Terr. Hem WF9 .... 163 B3
Clubhouses Croft. Hor WF4 ..... 141 A1 8
Clumber Dr. Clec BD19 .... 117 B7
Cluntergate. Hor WF4 .... 141 B1
Clunters La. Sow Br HX2 .... 111 B6
Clutton St. Batley WF17 .... 118 E5
Clyde App. Leeds LS12 .... 78 E6
Clyde Chase. Leeds LS12 .... 78 E6 5
Clyde Ct. Leeds LS12 .... 78 E6 3
Clyde Gdns. Leeds LS12 .... 78 E6 4
Clyde Grange. Leeds LS12 ...... 78 E6 3
Clyde St. Bing BD16 .... 36 F3
Clyde St. Sow Br HX6 .... 112 C3
Clyde St. Wake WF1 .... 142 E4

Clyde View. Leeds LS12 .... 78 E6
Clyde Wlk. Leeds LS12 .... 78 E6 4
Clydesdale Dr. Brad BD6 .... 93 F7
Co-op Bldgs. Hali HX3 .... 91 F2
Co-op La. Holmfi HD7 .... 188 D3
Co-operation Rd. Bacup OL13 ... 106 A2 2
Co-operation St. Leeds LS12 ... 78 A4 9
Co-operative Bldgs. Brig HD6 .. 115 B7
Co-operative St. Dew WF12 ..... 140 B8
Co-operative St. Hor WF4 ...... 141 A1
Co-operative St. Keigh BD21 ... 35 A3
Co-operative St. Mir WF14 ..... 138 A3
Co-operative St. Morley LS27 .. 98 A5 12
Co-operative St. Roth WF3 ..... 100 C1
Co-operative St. Wake WF2 ..... 142 A5
Co-operative Terr. Elland HX4 . 133 F4
Co-operative Terr. Holmfi HD7 . 189 C7
Co-operative Terr. Hor WF4 .... 141 A1
Coach Fold. Hali HX3 .... 113 C8
Coach Gate La. Ingb S30 .... 192 D3
Coach La. Clec BD19 .... 116 E8 1
Coach La. Lindley LS21 .... 11 F6
Coach La. Thorn BD13 .... 72 F6
Coach Rd. Bail BD17 .... 38 A1
Coach Rd. Brig HD6 .... 114 F4
Coach Rd. Guise LS20 .... 39 D7
Coach Rd. Hud HD2 .... 135 F2
Coach Rd. Loft G WF1 .... 121 C4
Coach Rd. Mel HD7 .... 170 F1
Coach Rd. Rip HX6 .... 132 D4
Coal Clough Rd. Tod OL14 ...... 86 B2
Coal Gate. Mars HD7 .... 151 A1
Coal Gate Rd. Rip HX6 .... 131 F5
Coal Hill Dr. Pudsey LS13 ..... 57 F4
Coal Hill Fold. Pudsey LS13 ... 57 F4
Coal Hill Gate. Pudsey LS13 ... 57 F4
Coal Hill Gdns. Pudsey LS13 ... 57 F4
Coal Hill Gn. Pudsey LS13 ..... 57 F4
Coal Hill La. Pudsey LS28,LS13 . 57 F4
Coal Pit La. Bacup OL15 .... 106 B3
Coal Pit La. Batley WF17 ...... 118 A6
Coal Pit La. Brig HD6 .... 115 E2
Coal Pit La. D Dale HD8, S30 .. 191 D8
Coal Pit La. Holmfi HD7 .... 189 F6
Coal Pit La. Hud HD4 .... 153 F3
Coal Pit La. S Elm WF9 .... 183 E4
Coal Pit La. Upton WF8 .... 165 F3
Coalpit La. D Dale HD8 .... 191 F3
Coalpit La. Hali HX3 .... 113 F4
Coate's La. Sil BD20 .... 4 F4
Coates Cl. Dew WF12 .... 118 F1
Coates Terr. Brad BD5 .... 74 D4
Coates Terr. Brad BD5 .... 74 D4
Cobb Ave. Wake WF2 .... 141 F4
Cobble Hall Golf Course. Leeds . 44 C1
Cobbler Wall. W Bret WF4 ...... 176 F8
Cobblers La. Pont WF8 .... 147 A8
Cobbydale Ct. Sil BD20 .... 5 D1
Cobcroft La. C Stub WF11 ...... 127 F1
Cobcroft Rd. Hud HD1, HD2 ..... 136 A1
Cobden Ave. Leeds LS12 .... 78 A4 3
Cobden Cl. Batley WF17 .... 118 C5 8
Cobden Mews. Leeds LS11 .... 113 B8
Cobden Gr. Leeds LS12 .... 78 A4 4
Cobden Mews. Morley LS27 ...... 98 A5 10
Cobden Pl. Leeds LS12 .... 77 F4
Cobden Rd. Leeds LS12 .... 77 F4
Cobden Rd. Brad BD15 .... 54 B1
Cobden St. Brad BD13 .... 56 B7
Cobden St. Brad BD14 .... 73 B4
Cobden St. Leeds LS12 .... 77 F4
Cobden St. Morley LS27 .... 98 A5 9
Cobden St. Queen BD13 .... 72 F1
Cobden St. Tod OL14 .... 108 B5
Cobden Terr. Elland HX5 .... 134 C8
Cobden Terr. Leeds LS12 .... 77 F4
Cobham Par. Loft G WF1 .... 121 B4
Cobham Wlk. Leeds LS15 .... 62 F2
Cock Hill La. Shelf HX3 .... 93 B6
Cock La. Crof WF4 .... 143 F2
Cock Pit La. Rip HX4 .... 132 A2
Cockburn Way. Leeds LS11 ...... 79 C3 1
Cockcroft La. Rip HX6 .... 132 A1
Cockermouth La. Lepton WF4 .... 156 D2
Cockin La. Thorn BD14 .... 72 E4
Cocking End. Add LS29 .... 7 C5
Cocking La. Sil LS29 .... 6 E6
Cockley La. Kirkhe HD5 .... 155 D8
Cockley Meadows. Kirkhe HD5 ... 137 C1
Cockshott Cl. Leeds LS12 ...... 58 F1 2
Cockshott Dr. Leeds LS12 ...... 58 F1
Cockshott Hill. Pudsey LS28 ... 57 D3
Cockshott La. Brad BD10 .... 56 A8
Cockshott La. Leeds LS12 ...... 58 F1
Cockshott Pl. Sil LS29 .... 6 E8
Coggil St. Leeds LS12 .... 80 A2
Coiners Fold. Heb Br HX7 ...... 110 C8
Colbeck Row. Batley WF17 ...... 96 E1
Colbert St. Leeds LS12 .... 78 C4
Colby Rise. Leeds LS15 .... 80 E7
Cold Edge Rd. Hali HX7 .... 70 D3
Cold Edge Rd. Hali HX2 .... 90 F6
Cold Hiendley Common La.
  Ryhill WF2 .... 161 D1
Cold Hill La. Holmfi HD7 ...... 189 E7
Cold Hill La. Hud HD4 .... 172 A8
Cold Royd La. Hud HD5 .... 155 A8
Cold St. Haw BD22 .... 51 C6
Cold Well La. Holmfi HD7 ...... 188 B4
Cold Well Rd. Leeds LS15 ...... 62 B1
Cold Well Sq. Leeds LS15 ...... 62 B1
Coldbeck Dr. Brad BD6 .... 93 E8
Coldcotes Ave. Leeds LS9 ...... 61 B2
Coldcotes Cir. Leeds LS9 ...... 61 C2
Coldcotes Cres. Leeds LS9 ..... 61 C2
Coldcotes Dr. Leeds LS9 .... 61 C2
Coldcotes Garth. Leeds LS9 .... 61 C2
Coldcotes Gr. Leeds LS9 .... 61 D2
Coldcotes View. Leeds LS9 ..... 61 D2
Coldcotes Wlk. Leeds LS9 ...... 61 D2
Colden Cl. Heb Br HX7 .... 88 F3

Colden Jun & Inf Sch. Hep 88 B6
Colden La. Hep HX7 .... 88 A6
Colden La. Heb Br HX7 .... 88 E4
Colders Dr. Mel HD7 .... 170 D1
Colders Gn. Mel HD7 .... 170 D2
Coldhill La. S in Elm LS25 .... 65 E4
Coldhill La. Saxton LS24 ...... 65 E4
Coldshaw Top. Haw BD22 .... 51 C6
Coldwell St. Slai HD7 .... 152 D1
Coldwells Hill. Elland HX4 .... 133 F3
Coleman St. Brad BD1 .... 55 F1
Coleman St. Leeds LS12 .... 78 F6
Colenso Gdns. Leeds LS11 ...... 78 F4 1
Colenso Gr. Keigh BD21 .... 18 E1
Colenso Gr. Leeds LS11 .... 78 F4
Colenso Mount. Leeds LS11 ..... 78 F4
Colenso Pl. Leeds LS11 .... 78 F4
Colenso Rd. Keigh BD21 .... 18 E1
Colenso Rd. Leeds LS11 .... 78 F4
Colenso Terr. Leeds LS11 ...... 78 F4
Colenso Way. Keigh BD21 .... 18 E1
Coleridge Cl. Roth LS26 .... 101 C3
Coleridge Cres. Wake WF2 ...... 120 F3
Coleridge La. Pudsey LS28 ..... 76 F5
Coleridge St. Hali HX1 .... 113 C6
Coles Way. Keigh BD20 .... 18 D2
Coley La. Brig HX3 .... 93 D2
Coley Hall La. Brig HX3 .... 93 C3
Coley Rd. Northo HX3 .... 93 C3
Coley St. Shelf HX3 .... 93 C3
Coley View. Northo HX3 .... 93 A2
Coll of the Resurrection. Mir . 137 E6
Coll Pl. Brad BD6 .... 94 D8 7
Collbrook Ave. Brad BD6 .... 94 C8
Colleen Rd. Crig WF4 .... 159 E5
College Cl. L Brad BD20 .... 4 C5
College Farm La. Coll LS22 .... 13 B3
College Gr. Castle WF10 .... 124 A6
College Gr. Wake WF1 .... 142 C8
College Grove Cl. Wake WF1 .... 142 C8
College Grove Rd. Wake WF1 .... 142 C8
College La. L Brad BD20 .... 4 D6
College of the Blessed Virgin.
  Leeds 59 E4
College Rd. Bing BD16 .... 37 A6
College Rd. Castle WF10 .... 125 B7
College Rd. Gild LS27 .... 97 D6
College Rd. L Brad BD20 .... 4 D5
College St. Batley WF17 .... 96 E1 1
College St. E. Hud HD4 .... 153 D4
College St. Hud HD4 .... 153 D4
College St. Tod OL14 .... 86 C1
College Terr. Ack M T WF7 ..... 163 E6
College Terr. Hali HX1 .... 112 F5
College View. Ack M T WF7 ..... 163 E6
College Wlk. Leeds LS17 .... 35 C7 6
Collier La. Aber LS25 .... 65 A5
Collier La. Bail BD17 .... 38 C4
Colliers Cl. Ship BD18 .... 54 E7
Colliers La. Thorner LS17 ..... 44 E4
Collin Moor La. Elland HX4 .... 134 C8
Collin Rd. Leeds LS14 .... 61 F1
Collindale Cl. Brad BD10 ...... 56 E6
Collinfield Rise. Brad BD6 .... 93 F6
Collingham Ave. Brad BD6 ...... 93 F8
Collingham Dr. Gar LS25 .... 82 F6
Collingwood Rd. Nor WF6 .... 123 B2
Collins St. Brad BD7 .... 74 A3
Collins St. Brad BD4 .... 75 B4
Collinson St. Clec BD19 .... 116 D8
Collyer View. Ilkley LS29 ..... 8 E3
Colmore Cl. Leeds LS12 .... 78 D6
Colmore Rd. Leeds LS12 .... 78 D5
Colne Hurst. Hud HD2 .... 136 E4
Colne Rd (Chapel La).
  Haw BD22 .... 34 C2
Colne Rd (Church St).
  Haw BD22 .... 34 B2
Colne Rd. Glu BD20 .... 16 B6
Colne Rd (Goodley). Haw BD22 .. 34 C2
Colne Rd. Hud HD1 .... 154 A4
Colne St. Hud HD1 .... 153 E5
Colne St. Hud HD1 .... 154 A4
Colne Vale Rd. Hud HD3 .... 153 A4
Colne Valley Bsns Pk. Slai 152 D1
Colne Valley Marsden Cty Jun Sch.
  Mars 169 A4
Colonel's Wlk. Pont WF8 .... 125 C1
Colston Cl. Brad BD8 .... 54 E1
Colton Croft. Leeds LS15 ...... 81 D7
Colton Garth. Leeds LS15 ...... 81 D7
Colton La. Leeds LS15 .... 81 D7
Colton Pl. Knot WF11 .... 126 E1
Colton Prim Sch. Leeds 81 E6
Colton Rd E. Leeds LS15 .... 81 E6
Colton Rd. Leeds LS12 .... 78 C7
Colton Rd. Leeds LS15 .... 81 D6
Colton Ret Pk. Leeds 81 E7
Colton St. Leeds LS12 .... 78 C7
Coltsfoot Cl. Pont WF8 .... 146 D7
Columbus St. Hali HX3 .... 92 A1 18
Colville Terr. E Ard WF3 ...... 99 E1
Colville Terr. Leeds LS11 ..... 79 B4
Colwyn Ave. Leeds LS11 .... 79 B2 14
Colwyn Mount. Leeds LS11 ...... 79 B2 15
Colwyn Pl. Leeds LS11 .... 79 B2 19
Colwyn Rd. Leeds LS11 .... 79 B2
Colwyn St. Hud HD1 .... 153 D7
Colwyn Terr. Feath WF7 .... 145 D6
Colwyn Terr. Leeds LS11 .... 79 B2 18
Colwyn View. Leeds LS11 .... 79 B2 12
Colyton Mount. Brad BD15 ...... 54 A1
Combs Hill Sch. Dew 139 F3
Combs Rd. Dew WF12 .... 139 E3
Combs The. Dew WF12 .... 139 E3
Comet St. Bacup OL13 .... 106 A3
Commerce St. Brad BD1 .... 74 E7 5
Commercial Bldgs. Brad BD12 ... 95 B4
Commercial Rd. Dew WF13 .... 118 C3
Commercial Rd. Leeds LS5 ...... 59 A3
Commercial Rd. Skel HD8 .... 175 B2
Commercial St. Batley WF17 .... 118 C5
Commercial St. Brig HD6 .... 115 B2
Commercial St. Castle WF10 .... 124 D8 8
Commercial St. Clec BD19 ...... 116 D7
Commercial St. Denh BD13 ...... 71 D8
Commercial St. Dew WF12 .... 139 F7
Commercial St. Hali HX1 .... 113 C7

Commercial St. Haw BD22 .... 34 B2
Commercial St. Heb Br HX7 ..... 89 A3
Commercial St. Hud HD1 .... 154 B5
Commercial St. Leeds LS1 ...... 79 C8
Commercial St. Morley LS27 .... 98 B5
Commercial St. Queen BD13 ..... 72 D1 4
Commercial St. Roth LS26 ...... 100 F5
Commercial St. Ship BD18 ...... 55 B8
Commercial St. Slai HD7 .... 170 A8
Commercial St. Tod OL14 .... 108 C5
Commercial St. Wake LS1 .... 142 D4
Commercial Vill's. Pudsey LS28 . 76 D6
Common End La. Lepton HD8 ..... 155 D2
Common Holme La. Nes LS29 ..... 7 E6
Common Ing La. Ryhill WF4 ..... 162 B2
Common La. Clay DN5 .... 194 C5
Common La. D Dale HD8 .... 192 B3
Common La. E Ard WF3 .... 99 C1
Common La. Emley HD8 .... 174 E7
Common La. Hali HX3 .... 113 C5
Common La. Knot WF11 .... 127 B4
Common La. Knot WF11 .... 127 D3
Common La. Roy S71 .... 179 C5
Common La. Th Aud WF8 .... 165 B3
Common La. Wool WF4 .... 177 D8
Common Rd. Batley WF17 .... 117 F4
Common Rd. Brad BD12 .... 94 C6
Common Rd. Bri S72 .... 181 B2
Common Rd. Elland HX5 .... 135 C6
Common Rd. Hem WF9 .... 163 A4
Common Road Av. S Kirk WF9 .... 182 A1
Common Road Ind Est. Brad 94 D6
Common Side La. Feath WF7 ..... 145 A6
Common Terr. Brig HD6 .... 115 B2
Common The. Dew WF12 .... 139 E3
Commonside. Batley WF17 .... 118 D3
Commonside. Liver FW15 .... 116 D2
Como Ave. Brad BD8 .... 54 F1 3
Como Gdns. Brad BD8 .... 73 F8
Como Gdns. Brad BD8 .... 54 F1 2
Como Gr. Brad BD8 .... 54 F1
Compeigne Ave. Keigh BD21 ..... 18 F1
Compton Ave. Leeds LS9 .... 61 A2 15
Compton Cres. Leeds LS9 .... 61 A2
Compton Gr. Leeds LS9 .... 61 A2 13
Compton La. Bard LS22 .... 29 B6
Compton Mount. Leeds LS9 ...... 61 A2 18
Compton Pl. Leeds LS9 .... 61 A2
Compton Rd. Leeds LS9 .... 61 A2
Compton Row. Leeds LS9 .... 61 A2
Compton St. Keigh BD21 .... 35 D8 10
Compton Terr. Leeds LS9 .... 61 A2 17
Compton View. Leeds LS9 .... 61 A2 16
Comuit St. Brad BD8 .... 55 C1
Cona La. Keigh BD21 .... 35 A8
Concord St. Leeds LS2 .... 79 E5 17
Concord St. Leeds LS2 .... 60 D1
Concordia St. Leeds LS1 .... 79 C7
Concrete St. Hali HX3 .... 92 A1 27
Conduit St. Brad BD8 .... 55 C1
Coney La. Keigh BD21 .... 35 A7
Coney Moor Gr. M'town LS26 .... 102 F3
Coney Warren La. Loft G WF3 ... 121 E8
Coney Wlk. Dew WF13 .... 138 F8
Conference Gr. Leeds LS12 ..... 78 A7
Conference Pl. Leeds LS12 ..... 78 A7
Conference Rd. Leeds LS12 ..... 78 A7
Conference Terr. Leeds LS12 ... 78 A7
Congress Mount. Leeds LS12 .... 78 A7
Congress St. Leeds LS12 .... 78 A7
Congreve App. Bard LS17 .... 28 E6
Congreve Way. Bard LS17 .... 28 E6
Conisborough La. Gar LS25 ..... 83 B7
Coniston Ave. Hud HD5 .... 154 D6
Coniston Ave. Leeds LS6 .... 59 E5 2
Coniston Cl. Elland HX5 .... 135 B7
Coniston Cl. Queen BD13 .... 92 D8 2
Coniston Cl. Loft G WF3 .... 121 B6
Coniston Dr. Castle WF10 ...... 125 E7
Coniston Gdns. Castle WF10 .... 125 E7
Coniston Gr. Bail BD17 .... 37 F1
Coniston Gr. Brad BD9 .... 54 F2
Coniston House. Elland HX5 .... 134 F7 15
Coniston Pl. Knot WF11 .... 126 E1
Coniston Rd. Batley WF12 ...... 118 F2
Coniston Rd. Brad BD7 .... 73 E3 4
Coniston Rd. Mel HD7 .... 170 E1
Coniston Rd. Roth LS26 .... 101 C2
Coniston Way. Roth LS26 .... 101 C6
Coniston Way. Weth LS22 .... 13 B5
Connaught Fold. Hud HD7 .... 136 E5
Connaught Rd. Ilkley LS29 ..... 8 D3
Connolley Cty Prim Sch. Con ... 4 A3
Cononley La. Con BD20 .... 4 B2
Cononley Rd. Glu BD20 .... 16 B8
Consort Ave. Leeds LS3 .... 59 F1
Consort Terr. Leeds LS3 .... 59 F1
Consort View. Leeds LS3 .... 59 F1
Consort Wlk. Leeds LS3 .... 59 F1
Constable Gr. Loft G WF3 ...... 121 E6
Constable Rd. E Ard WF3 .... 119 F8
Constable Rd. Ilkley LS29 ..... 8 E3
Constance St. Ship BD18 .... 54 F8
Constitutional St. Hali HX1 ... 113 A5 2
Convent Ave. S Kirk WF9 .... 182 C2
Conway Ave. Leeds LS8 .... 60 F3
Conway Cres. Batley WF17 ...... 118 C2
Conway Cres. Mel HD7 .... 170 D1
Conway Dr. Leeds LS8 .... 60 F3
Conway House. Brad BD15 .... 73 B7 2
Conway Mount. Leeds LS8 .... 60 F3
Conway Pl. Leeds LS8 .... 61 A3
Conway Rd. Leeds LS8 .... 60 F3
Conway St. Brad BD4 .... 74 F5
Conway St. Hali HX1 .... 113 A6
Conway St. Leeds LS8 .... 60 F3
Conway St. Pudsey LS28 .... 57 D1 5
Conway Terr. Leeds LS8 .... 60 F3
Conway View. Leeds LS8 .... 60 F3
Cook La. Liver WF16 .... 117 C4
Cooke Cres. Clec BD19 .... 117 A8

Cooke La. Keigh BD21 .... 35 C7
Cooke St. Keigh BD21 .... 35 C7 3
Cookridge Ave. Hors LS16 ...... 41 E6
Cookridge Cty Prim Sch. Hors .. 41 E4
Cookridge Dr. Hors LS16 .... 41 E6
Cookridge Gr. Hors LS16 .... 41 E6
Cookridge Hall Golf Course.
  Hors 41 F6
Cookridge Hospl. Hors 41 E2
Cookridge La. Hors LS16 .... 41 E7
Cookridge St. Leeds LS1, LS2 .. 79 B8
Cooksland La. Feath WF7 .... 144 E8
Cookson Cl. Castle WF10 .... 125 D5
Cookson St. Brig HD6 .... 114 F3
Coombe Hill. Brad BD13 .... 73 B2
Coombe Rd. Hud HD3 .... 152 F5
Cooper Bridge Rd. Hud WF14 .... 137 B6
Cooper Cl. Bing BD16 .... 37 A5
Cooper Fields. Hali HX2 .... 111 E6
Cooper Gr. Shelf HX3 .... 93 D7
Cooper Hill. Pudsey LS28 ...... 76 F5
Cooper House. Hem WF9 .... 181 D6
Cooper La. Brad BD6 .... 93 D8
Cooper La. Holmfi HD7 .... 189 A5
Cooper La. Shelf BD6, HX3 ..... 93 D8
Cooper Lane Fst Sch. Brad 73 D1
Cooper St. Weth LS22 .... 13 E5
Cooper St. Tod OL14 .... 108 E6
Cooperative St. Tod OL14 ...... 129 A7
Cop Hill End. Mars HD7 .... 169 C8
Cop Hill La. Mars HD7 .... 169 C8
Cop Hill Side. Mars HD7 .... 169 B8
Copeland St. Brad BD4 .... 75 D5
Copeworth Dr. Crig WF4 .... 159 F3
Copgrove Cl. Brad BD4 .... 75 E3
Copgrove Ct. Brad BD4 .... 75 E3
Copgrove Rd. Brad BD4 .... 75 E3
Copgrove Rd. Leeds LS8 .... 61 B5
Copley Ave. Hali HX2 .... 112 F5
Copley Ave. Mel HD7 .... 170 D2
Copley Bank Rd. Slai HD7 ...... 152 C3
Copley Hall St. Hali HX3 ...... 113 B1
Copley Glen. Hali HX3 .... 113 B2
Copley Gr. Hali HX3 .... 113 B2
Copley Hall St. Hali HX3 ...... 113 B2
Copley Hall Terr. Hali HX3 .... 113 B2
Copley Hill. Batley WF17 ...... 96 F1
Copley Hill. Leeds LS12 .... 78 E6
Copley Hill Trad Est. Leeds ... 78 E6
Copley Jun & Inf Sch. Hali 113 B2
Copley La. Aber LS25 .... 65 D5
Copley La. Hali HX3 .... 113 B2
Copley La. Roth WF3 .... 100 B4
Copley La. Saxton LS25 .... 65 D5
Copley Mill House. Elland HX3 . 114 B1
Copley Mount. Hali HX3 .... 113 B2
Copley St. Batley WF17 .... 118 A7
Copley St. Brad BD5 .... 74 B3
Copley St. Leeds LS12 .... 78 E6
Copley Terr. Hali HX3 .... 113 B2
Copley Yd. Leeds LS12 .... 78 E6
Coplowe La. Wils BD15 .... 53 D6
Copmanroyd. Clift LS21 .... 11 C3
Copper Beech Cl. Pont WF8 ..... 146 E6
Copper Beech Ct. Walton WF2 ... 161 A6
Copperas House Terr.
  Tod OL14 .... 108 A2
Copperas Row. Elland HX4 ...... 133 E7
Copperfield Ave. Leeds LS9 .... 79 F6 20
Copperfield Cres. Leeds LS9 ... 79 F6 19
Copperfield Dr. Leeds LS9 ..... 79 F6
Copperfield Gr. Leeds LS9 ..... 80 A6 4
Copperfield Mount. Leeds LS9 .. 80 A6 3
Copperfield Pl. Leeds LS9 ..... 79 F6 19
Copperfield Row. Leeds LS9 .... 79 F6 19
Copperfield Terr. Leeds LS9 ... 80 A6
Copperfield View. Leeds LS9 ... 79 F6 18
Copperfield Wlk. Leeds LS9 .... 79 F6 23
Coppice Cl. Wake WF1 .... 142 E8
Coppice Dr. Hud HD4 .... 171 D6
Coppice The. B in Elm LS15 .... 63 D6
Coppice The. Glu BD20 .... 16 C6
Coppice The. Hud HD2 .... 136 B4
Coppice The. Ilkley LS29 ...... 8 A8
Coppice The. Mir WF14 .... 138 A8
Coppice The. Yeadon LS19 ...... 39 F5
Coppice View. Brad BD10 .... 56 A8
Coppice Way. Leeds LS8 .... 61 B6
Coppice Wood Ave. Brad BD7 .... 74 A6
Coppice Wood Cl. Guise LS20 ... 23 A1
Coppice Wood Cres.
  Yeadon LS19 .... 23 B1
Coppice Wood Gr. Brad BD7 ..... 74 A6
Coppice Wood Gr. Yeadon LS20 .. 40 A8
Coppice Wood Rise.
  Yeadon LS19 .... 40 B8
Coppies The. Brad BD12 .... 94 B8
Coppin Hall Gr. Mir WF14 ...... 137 D6
Coppin Hall La. Mir WF14 ...... 137 D6
Coppy Cl. Ship BD16 .... 54 A6
Coppy La. Haw BD22 .... 33 C7
Coppy La. Leeds LS13 .... 58 C4
Coppy La. Wad M BD10 .... 72 C3
Coppy Nook La. Heb Br HX7 ..... 110 E3
Coppy Rd. Sil LS29 .... 6 E8
Coppy Rd. Stee BD20 .... 17 B5
Coppy Row. Haw BD22 .... 34 B2
Copse The. Bing BD16 .... 37 C3
Copse The. Brig BD19 .... 115 F7
Copse The. Feath WF7 .... 124 C5
Copt Royd Gr. Yeadon LS19 ..... 40 A7
Copthorne Fst Sch. Brad 74 C4
Copthorne Gdns. Hud HD2 .... 136 F5
Copthurst Rd. Holme HD7 .... 198 E7
Copy Bottom. H Chap BB10 ...... 85 A3
Corban St. Brad BD4 .... 75 C3
Corby St. Hud HD1 .... 136 A1
Corcroft Cl. Brad BD4 .... 75 E1
Cordingley Cl. Brad BD4 .... 75 E1
Cordingley St. Brad BD4 .... 75 E1
Corfe Cl. Batley WF17 .... 97 B3
Corn Bank. Hud HD4 .... 171 C6
Corn Exchange. Leeds LS1 ...... 79 C7
Corn Market. Hali HX1 .... 113 C7 19
Corn Market. Pont WF8 .... 146 C8

212 Cor - Cro

Corn Mill Ct. Leeds LS13 77 D7
Corn Mill La. Otley LS29 10 A1
Corn Mill La. Thorn BD13 72 F5
Corn Mill. Men LS29 22 B4
Corn St. Keigh BD21 35 A4 6
Cornfield Ave. Hud HD3 153 A7
Cornfield St. Tod OL14 108 D6 3
Cornholme Jun & Inf Sch. Tod 86 A1
Cornholme Terr. Tod OL14 86 B1 7
Cornmill Ave. Liver WF15 117 C3
Cornmill Cl. Bard LS17 28 D3
Cornmill Cres. Liver WF15 117 B2
Cornmill Dr. Liver WF15 117 B3
Cornmill La. Bard LS17 28 D3
Cornmill La. Liver WF15 117 B3
Cornrace View. Hud HD4 154 B4
Cornus Gdns. Midd LS10 99 D8 2
Cornwall Ave. Sil BD20 5 C1
Cornwall Cl. Roth LS26 100 D6
Cornwall Cres. Bail BD17 38 B4
Cornwall Cres. Brig HD6 115 B6
Cornwall Cres. Roth LS26 100 D6
Cornwall House. Elland HX5 134 F7 16
Cornwall Pl. Brad BD8 55 D1
Cornwall Rd. Bing BD16 37 B2
Cornwall Rd. Brad BD8 55 D1
Cornwall Rd. Keigh BD21 18 E1
Cornwall Terr. Brad BD8 55 D1
Coronation Ave. Guise BD10 39 D4
Coronation Ave. Kippax LS25 83 C1
Coronation Ave. Nor WF6 122 F3
Coronation Ave. Roy S71 179 E4
Coronation Ave. Shaf S72 180 B3
Coronation Bglws. Kippax LS25 83 C1 3
Coronation Bglws. Knot WF11 126 D4
Coronation Bglws. Mel HD7 170 E1
Coronation Bsns Ctr. Keigh 18 C1
Coronation Hospl. Ilkley 8 C3
Coronation Mount. Keigh BD22 34 F7
Coronation Par. Leeds LS15 80 E7
Coronation Rd. Crof WF4 144 B3
Coronation Rd. Hali HX3 113 D4
Coronation St. Brad BD12 95 A4
Coronation St. Castle WF10 103 F1
Coronation St. Elland HX4 134 C7
Coronation St. Elland HX5 134 F6
Coronation St. Roth WF3 100 D3
Coronation St. Wake WF2 120 F1
Coronation Terr. Batley WF17 96 F1 2
Coronation Terr. Castle WF10 125 A6
Coronation Terr. Rip HX6 132 E6
Coronation Way. Keigh BD22 34 F8
Coronation Wlk. Keigh BD22 34 F8
Corporal La. Shelf HX3 92 F6
Corporation St. Brad BD2 56 C3
Corporation St. Dew WF13 139 D8
Corporation St. Hali HX6 112 B4
Corporation St. Hali HX1 113 C8
Corporation St. Hud HD1 154 A5 2
Corporation St. Morley LS27 98 A4
Corpus Christi High Sch. Leeds 80 E8
Corpus Christi Prim Sch. Leeds 80 D8
Corrance Rd. Brad BD12 94 D1
Corrie St. Thorn BD13 72 E6
Cote Farm Cotts. Brad BD10 38 F1
Cote La. Brad BD15 54 A1
Cote La. Brig HD2 135 E5
Cote La. Holmfi HD7 199 A8
Cote La. Pudsey LS28 57 C2
Cote Rd. Rip HX6 132 B4
Cote The. Pudsey LS28 57 C2
Cote Wall. Mir WF14 138 D3
Cotefields Ave. Pudsey LS28 57 C2
Coteroyd Ave. Morley LS27 98 C8
Coteroyd Dr. Morley LS27 98 C7
Cotewall Rd. Brad BD5 74 D3
Cotswold Ave. Ship BD18 55 E7
Cotswold Cl. Hem WF9 181 F7
Cotswold Dr. Clec WF15 116 D5
Cotswold Dr. Gar LS25 82 F5
Cotswold Dr. Knot WF11 126 E4
Cotswold Dr. Roth LS26 100 D6
Cotswold Mews. Kirkb HD8 173 F7
Cotswold Rd. Roth LS26 100 E6
Cotswold Rd. Wake WF2 141 D5
Cottage Gn. Brad BD8 73 F8 12
Cottage Homes. Hud HD5 155 A6
Cottage Rd. Brad BD10 56 D7
Cottage Rd. Leeds LS6 59 D6
Cottage The. Honley HD7 171 F5
Cottam Ave. Brad BD7 74 B6
Cottam Croft. Hem WF9 181 E7
Cottam Terr. Brad BD7 74 B6
Cotterdale. Brad BD15 54 A3
Cotterdale Holt. Coll LS22 13 A1
Cotterdale View. Leeds LS15 80 E6
Cotterill Rd. Knot WF11 126 D3
Cottingley App. Morley LS11 78 D1
Cottingley Chase. Morley LS11 78 D1
Cottingley Cliffe Rd. Ship BD16 54 C6
Cottingley Cty Prim Sch. Morley 78 C1
Cottingley Cres. Morley LS11 78 D1
Cottingley Dr. Morley LS11 78 C2
Cottingley Dr. Ship BD16 54 A8
Cottingley Fst Sch. Ship 54 B7
Cottingley Fold. Morley LS11 78 C2
Cottingley Gdns. Morley LS11 78 D1
Cottingley Gn. Morley LS11 78 D1
Cottingley Gr. Morley LS11 78 D1 4
Cottingley Hghts. Morley LS11 78 D1 1
Cottingley Manor Sch. Ship 54 B7
Cottingley Moor Rd. Ship BD16 54 A5
Cottingley New Rd. Ship BD16 54 B7
Cottingley Rd. Brad BD15 54 A4
Cottingley Rd. Morley LS11 78 C2
Cottingley Sta. Morley 78 C1
Cottingley Terr. Brad BD8 55 D1
Cottingley Twrs. Morley LS11 78 D1 2
Cottingley Vale. Morley LS11 78 D1
Cotton St. Leeds LS9 79 D7
Cotton St. Wake WF2 142 C4
Couford Gr. Hud HD2 136 F4
Coule Royd. Hud HD5 154 F7
Coultas Cl. Men LS29 22 B4
Cty Arc. Leeds 79 C8
Cty Cl. Batley WF17 118 C6
Cty Ct. Brad 74 E7
Cty Works. Bail 38 C1
Coupe Gr. Nor WF6 122 F5
Coupland Pl. Leeds LS11 79 B4
Coupland Rd. Gar LS25 82 E7
Coupland Rd. Leeds LS11 79 B4
Coupland St. Leeds LS11 79 B3
Coupland St. Tod OL14 108 B5 6
Court Dr. Leeds LS5 58 E6
Court La. Hali HX2 112 D7
Court No 6. Batley WF17 118 C4
Court The. Leeds LS17 42 F5
Court The. Liver WF15 116 E4
Court The. Ship BD18 54 E7
Court Way The. Ack M T WF7 164 B8
Court Yard Mews. Sil BD20 17 F6
Court Yd The. Wool WF4 178 A7
Courtenay Cl. Brad BD3 75 E7
Courthouse St. Otley LS21 23 A8
Courts Leet. Brad BD12 94 C4 1
Courtyard The. Bacup OL13 106 A3 5
Courtyard The. Batley WF17 96 F2
Courtyard The. Hud HD4 153 D4
Cousen Ave. Brad BD7 73 F5
Cousen Rd. Brad BD7 74 B4
Cousin La. Hali HX2 91 E4
Coutances Way. Ilkley LS29 9 B3
Coventry St. Brad BD4 75 B4
Coventry St. Hali HX2 112 E7 3
Cover Dr. Brad BD6 94 A8 2
Coverdale Garth. Coll LS22 29 A8
Coverdale Way. Bail BD17 38 E4
Coverley Garth. Yeadon LS19 39 F7
Coverley Rise. Yeadon LS19 39 F7
Covert The. Batley WF17 117 F7
Covey Clough Ct. Mir WF14 137 F1
Cow and Calf. Ilkley 8 E2
Cow Close Gr. Leeds LS12 78 A4
Cow Close La. Brad BD12 94 E2
Cow Close Rd. Leeds LS12 78 A4
Cow Gate. Hud HD3 152 F6
Cow Gn. Hali HX1 113 C7
Cow Hey La. Wad M BB10 68 D3
Cow Heys. Hud HD5 154 F7
Cow Hill Gate La. Hali HX2 71 E1
Cow La. Brig HX3 114 D4
Cow La. Crof WF4 144 A4
Cow La. Hali HX3 113 C2
Cow La. Knot WF11 127 A4
Cow La. Rip HX6 132 D6
Cow La. Ryhill WF4 162 C1
Cow La. Wad M HX7 88 E8
Cowcliff Hill Rd. Holmfi HD7 199 D8
Cowcliffe Hill Rd. Hud HD2 135 F3
Cowdray Dr. Brig BD19 115 F8 9
Cowdry Cl. Dew WF12 139 E2
Cowfold St. Tod OL14 108 B6 1
Cowgill St. Bacup OL13 106 A3 13
Cowgill St. Brad BD8 55 C1
Cowhurst Ave. Tod OL14 107 F7
Cowhurst Ave. Tod OL14 108 A7
Cowlersley Cty Jun & Inf Sch.
Hud 152 F3
Cowlersley La. Hud HD4 152 F3
Cowley Cres. Brad BD9 54 D4
Cowley Rd. Pudsey LS13 57 F5
Cowpasture Rd. Ilkley LS29 8 C3
Cowper Ave. Leeds LS9 61 A2 1
Cowper Cres. Leeds LS9 61 A2 2
Cowper Gr. Leeds LS8 61 A3 10
Cowper Mount. Leeds LS9 61 A2
Cowper Rd. Leeds LS9 61 A2
Cowper St. Dew WF12 139 C6
Cowper St. Leeds LS7 60 E3
Cowper Terr. Leeds LS9 61 A2
Cowrakes Cl. Hud HD3 135 A1
Cowrakes Rd. Hud HD3 135 A1
Cowroyd Pl. Hali HX3 113 D8
Cowslip St. Hud HD1 153 D5
Cowtoot La. Bacup OL13 106 A4
Coxley Cres. Neth WF4 158 D6
Coxley La. Neth WF4 158 D7
Coxley View. Neth WF4 158 C5
Coxwold Hill. Weth LS22 13 E7
Coxwold View. Weth LS22 13 E6
Coxwold Wlk. Brad BD15 73 A7 3
Crab Hill. Pont WF8 146 C8
Crab La. Crig WF2 160 B4
Crab La. Leeds LS12 78 C8
Crab Tree La. K Smea WF8 166 B3
Crabgate Dr. Ad Le S DN6 184 E2
Crabgate La. Ad Le S DN6 184 E2
Crabtree Ave. Bacup OL13 106 A1
Crabtree Ave. Batley WF16 117 E5
Crabtree Gn. Coll LS22 29 B7
Crabtree Hill. Coll LS22 29 B8
Crabtree La. E Kes LS17 28 C7
Crabtree Pl. Brad BD7 74 A4 5
Crabtree St. Brad BD7 74 A4 6
Crabtree St. Hali HX1 112 F7
Crabtree Way. E Ard WF3 119 F7
Crack La. Wils BD15 53 D5
Crackenedge La. Dew WF13 118 D1
Crackenedge Terr. Dew WF13 118 D1
Cracoe Rd. Brad BD3 75 B6
Crag Cl. Hali HX2 91 D4
Crag Cl. S in Cra BD20 16 C5
Crag Ct. Hali HX2 91 D4
Crag Gdns. Bramham LS23 30 D2
Crag Hill Ave. Hors LS16 41 E6
Crag Hill Rd. Brad BD10 39 A2
Crag Hill View. Hors LS16 41 E6
Crag La. Hali HX2 91 D3
Crag La. L Brad BD20 4 C4
Crag La. Leeds LS17 42 F5
Crag La. S in Cra BD20 16 C4
Crag Mount. Pont WF8 146 C8 16
Crag Pl. Keigh BD21 35 C4
Crag Rd. Ship BD18 55 C7
Crag The. Bramham LS23 30 D2
Crag Top. Fair WF11 105 A4
Crag Vale Terr. Glu BD20 16 B6
Crag View. Brad BD10 56 D6
Crag View. S in Cra BD20 16 C5
Cragg Ave. Hors LS18 58 C8
Cragg Bottom Rd. Haw BD22 49 E8
Cragg Dr. Ilkley LS29 8 F3
Cragg Hill. Hors LS18 58 C8
Cragg La. Brad BD7 74 A3
Cragg La. Denh BD13 71 E6
Cragg La. Heb Br HX7 110 D6
Cragg La. Thorn BD13 72 A5
Cragg Rd. Heb Br HX7 109 F5
Cragg Rd. Heb Br HX7 110 D6
Cragg Rd. Hors LS18 58 C8
Cragg St. Brad BD7 74 A3
Cragg Terr. Brad BD7 74 A3
Cragg Terr. Hors LS18 58 B8
Cragg Terr. Yeadon LS19 40 B2
Cragg Top. Denh BD13 71 E5
Cragg Vale Jun & Inf Sch.
Heb Br 110 C3
Cragg View. Sil BD20 5 E2
Cragg Wood Dr. Yeadon LS19 40 A2
Craggwell Terr. Hors LS18 58 C7 7
Craggwood Cl. Hors LS18 58 C7
Craggwood Rd. Hors LS18 58 C8
Craggwood Terr. Hors LS18 58 C7 8
Cragside. Brad BD10 38 F1
Cragside Cl. Leeds LS5 58 E7
Cragside Cres. Leeds LS5 58 E7
Cragside Gdns. Leeds LS5 58 E7
Cragside Gr. Leeds LS5 58 D6
Cragside Mount. Leeds LS5 58 E7
Cragside Pl. Leeds LS5 58 E6
Cragside Wlk. Leeds LS5 58 E7
Craig Cl. Batley WF17 118 C6
Craig House. Brad BD15 73 B8 6
Craig-y-don. Dew WF12 139 F7
Craiglands. Brig HX3 114 D8
Craiglands Rd. Ilkley LS29 8 C3
Craiglea Dr. Brad BD12 94 D2
Craigmore Ct. Brad BD4 75 F2
Craigmore Dr. Ilkley LS29 8 E4
Cranberry Ave. Tod OL14 129 B7
Cranborne Dr. Mapp S75 177 F1
Cranbourne Rd. Brad BD9 54 D1
Cranbrook Ave. Brad BD6 94 C8
Cranbrook Ave. Leeds LS11 79 A3
Cranbrook Pl. Brad BD5 74 E3 3
Cranbrook St. Brad BD14 73 B4 4
Cranbrook St. Brad BD5 74 E3
Cranbrook View. Pudsey LS28 77 A5
Cranewells Dr. Leeds LS15 81 D6
Cranewells Gn. Leeds LS15 81 C6
Cranewells Rise. Leeds LS15 81 C6
Cranewells Vale. Leeds LS15 81 C6
Cranewells View. Leeds LS15 81 C7
Cranfield Dr. Ad Le S DN6 184 F2
Cranford Gdns. Roy S71 179 B4
Cranford Pl. Wils BD15 53 C5
Cranleigh Mount. Keigh BD21 35 A5
Cranmer Bank. Leeds LS17 43 A3
Cranmer Cl. Leeds LS17 43 A3
Cranmer Gdns. Leeds LS17 43 A3
Cranmer Gdns. Mel HD7 170 F2
Cranmer Rd. Brad BD3 55 F1
Cranmer Rd. Leeds LS17 43 A3
Cranmer Rise. Leeds LS17 43 A3
Cranmore Cres. Midd LS10 99 E5
Cranmore Dr. Midd LS10 99 F6
Cranmore Garth. Midd LS10 99 E5
Cranmore Gdns. Midd LS10 99 E5
Cranmore Gn. Midd LS10 99 E5
Cranmore Gr. Midd LS10 99 E5
Cranmore La. Midd LS10 99 F5
Cranmore Rd. Midd LS10 99 E5
Cranmore Rise. Midd LS10 99 F5
Cranwood Dr. Hud HD5 155 A6
Craven Ave. Sil BD20 5 E1
Craven Ave. Thorn BD13 72 E6
Craven Cl. Clec BD19 117 C8
Craven Cl. Roy S71 179 B4
Craven Cres. Sil LS29 6 E8
Craven Ct. Brad BD8 73 F8 10
Craven Ct. Hali HX1 113 A6 2
Craven Ct. Sil BD20 5 F1
Craven Dr. Clec BD19 117 C8
Craven Dr. Sil BD20 5 E1
Craven Gr. Sil BD20 5 F1
Craven House. Tod OL14 129 A8
Craven La. Clec BD19 117 C8
Craven Pk. Men LS29 21 F5
Craven Rd. Dew WF13 139 A6
Craven Rd. Hem WF9 181 D6
Craven Rd. Keigh BD21 35 E8
Craven Rd. Leeds LS6 60 B3
Craven St. Brad BD3 74 F8 4
Craven St. Dew WF13 138 E6
Craven St. Hud HD4 153 A4
Craven St. Otley LS21 23 B7
Craven St. Wake WF1 142 C7
Craven Terr. Brad BD2 56 C3
Craven Terr. Hali HX1 113 A6
Craven Terr. Otley LS21 23 B7
Cravendale Rd. Dew WF13 138 D6
Crawford Ave. Brad BD6 94 C8
Crawford Dr. Wake WF2 141 F7
Crawford St. Brad BD4 75 A4
Crawford St. Tod OL14 129 B8
Crawley Ave. S Kirk WF9 182 D3
Crawshaw Ave. Pudsey LS28 76 F7
Crawshaw Cl. Pudsey LS28 76 E7 1
Crawshaw Gdns. Pudsey LS28 76 F7
Crawshaw Hill. Pudsey LS28 76 E7 2
Crawshaw La. Emley HD8 175 A8
Crawshaw La. Floc WF4 156 F2
Crawshaw La. Floc WF4 157 A1
Crawshaw Pk. Pudsey LS28 76 E7
Crawshaw Rd. Pudsey LS28 76 E7
Crawshaw Rise. Pudsey LS28 76 E6
Crawshaw St. Dew WF13 138 F6
Crawthorne Cres. Hud HD2 136 E4
Cray La. Elland HX4 133 E2
Crayford Dr. Crof WF4 143 F1
Crediton Ave. Brad BD15 73 B8
Crescent Ave. Dew WF13 138 D5
Crescent Ave. Hud HD4 171 D7
Crescent Ave. Roth LS26 100 F7
Crescent Bglws. Midd WF3 99 D2
Crescent Grange. Leeds LS11 79 C4 1
Crescent Rd. Hud HD2 136 A1
Crescent Rd. Hud HD4 171 D7
Crescent Rd. Ryhill WF4 162 D1
Crescent Royd. Hud HD5 155 A5
Crescent St. Tod OL14 108 B5 1
Crescent Terr. Ilkley LS29 8 B4
Crescent The. Bail BD17 38 C2
Crescent The. Bing BD16 36 E6
Crescent The. Birk BD11 96 A7
Crescent The. Brad BD6 93 E8
Crescent The. Brig HD6 115 B3 3
Crescent The. Bur in W LS29 21 E8
Crescent The. Castle WF10 124 F6
Crescent The. Clec WF15 116 D5
Crescent The. Dew WF13 138 D5
Crescent The. E Ard WF3 120 A8
Crescent The. Elland HX4 134 A4
Crescent The. Elland HX5 134 F5
Crescent The. Feath WF7 144 D5
Crescent The. Gar LS25 83 A7
Crescent The. Guise LS20 39 C8
Crescent The. Hali HX3 113 F6
Crescent The. Holmfi HD7 189 E6
Crescent The. Hors LS16 42 B4
Crescent The. Ilkley LS29 8 E5
Crescent The. Kippax LS25 83 A1
Crescent The. Kirkb HD8 174 A7
Crescent The. Leeds LS17 42 F6
Crescent The. Leeds LS15 81 B8
Crescent The. M'field LS25 84 A6
Crescent The. Men LS29 22 B4
Crescent The. Neth WF4 158 D5
Crescent The. Nor WF6 122 F4
Crescent The. Otley LS21 11 A2
Crescent The. Pudsey LS28 76 F8
Crescent The. Sickl LS22 12 C5
Crescent Towers. Leeds LS11 79 C4 2
Crescent View. Keigh BD22 35 A3
Crescent View. Leeds LS17 42 F6
Crescent Wlk. Brad BD14 73 D5
Crescent Wlk. Dew WF13 138 D5
Cresent The. Brig HX3 114 D8
Creskeld Cres. Bramho LS16 24 F3
Creskeld Dr. Bramho LS16 24 F3
Creskeld Garth. Bramho LS16 24 F3
Creskeld Gdns. Bramho LS16 24 F3
Creskeld La. Arth LS21 25 A5
Creskeld La. Bramho LS16 24 F3
Creskeld Pk. Bramho LS16 24 F3
Creskeld Way. Brad BD15 53 F2
Creskell Rd. Leeds LS11 79 B5
Cressfield Rd. Hud HD3 153 C8
Cresswell La. Batley WF13 117 F3
Cresswell Mount. Brad BD7 73 E2
Cresswell Pl. Brad BD7 73 E2
Cresswell Terr. Brad BD7 73 E2 2
Crest Ave. Brad BD12 94 C1
Crest Ave. Hud HD5 154 E5
Crest Dr. Pont WF8 146 E6
Crest Hill Rd. Hud HD2 136 C3
Crest Mount. Pont WF8 146 E6
Crest Pl. Brig HD6 114 E5
Crest Rd. Hud HD3 135 A3
Crest The. Hud HD2 136 E6
Crest The. Kippax LS25 83 A1
Crest The. Leeds LS14 61 E6
Crest The. Swil LS26 82 A1
Crest View. Brig HD6 114 E5
Crestfield Ave. Elland HX5 134 E6
Crestfield Cres. Elland HX5 134 E5
Crestfield Dr. Elland HX5 134 E5
Crestfield Dr. Hali HX2 112 E5
Crestfield Rd. Elland HX5 134 E5
Crestville Cl. Brad BD14 73 D5
Crestville Rd. Brad BD14 73 C5
Crestville Terr. Brad BD14 73 D5
Crewe Ave. Knot WF11 126 B4
Crewe Rd. Castle WF10 125 D7
Crib La. Hali HX1 113 C8
Cricketers App. Wake WF2 120 E3
Cricketers Cl. Ack M T WF7 164 A5
Cricketers Gn. Yeadon LS19 40 C5
Cricketers Terr. Leeds LS12 78 C7
Cricketers Way. Leeds LS5 59 B4
Cricketers Wlk. Leeds LS15 81 E7
Cricketers Wlk. Stee BD20 17 D5
Cricklegate. Leeds LS15 81 B8
Crigglestone Dane Royd Fst Sch.
Crig 159 F2
Crigglestone Fst Sch. Crig 159 D4
Crigglestone Mid Sch. Crig 159 F3
Crimble Bank. Slai HD7 152 A1
Crimble Cl. Brig HX3 114 E7
Crimble Clough Rd. Slai HD7 152 A3
Crimbles Ct. Pudsey LS28 76 F7
Crimbles Pl. Pudsey LS28 76 F7
Crimbles Rd. Pudsey LS28 76 F7
Crimbles Terr. Pudsey LS28 76 F7
Crimea La. Slai HD7 151 E4
Crimea St. Bacup OL13 106 A2 5
Crimple Gn. Gar LS25 83 B6
Crimshaw La. Ship BD18 55 D5
Crimsworth Dean. Wad M 68 F2
Crimsworth La. Wad M HX7 89 A8
Crinan Ct. Nor WF6 123 A4
Cringles La. Sil BD20 5 F7
Cripplegate. Hali HX1 113 D7
Crodingley Farm Ct.
Holmfi HD7 189 B8
Crodingley. Holmfi HD7 189 B8
Croft Ave. Bing BD16 36 D6
Croft Ave. E Ard WF3 120 D7
Croft Ave. Knot WF11 127 A5
Croft Ave. Nor WF6 122 F3
Croft Ave. Nor WF6 123 C3
Croft Ave. Otley LS21 10 F1
Croft Ave. Pudsey LS28 57 D3
Croft Ave. Roy S71 179 B3
Croft Bridge. Roth LS26 101 C5
Croft Chantry. Hem WF9 163 A2
Croft Cl. Men LS29 21 F4
Croft Cottage La. Hud HD1 154 B8 3
Croft Ct. Honley HD7 171 F3
Croft Ct. Honley HD7 172 A3
Croft Ct. Hors LS18 41 C1
Croft Ct. Men LS29 21 F4
Croft Dr. Bramham LS23 30 D3
Croft Dr. Honley HD7 171 E4
Croft Dr. Men LS29 22 A4
Croft End. Weth LS22 13 C5
Croft Field. Sil BD20 17 E8
Croft Foulds Ct. Gar LS25 82 F7
Croft Gdns. Hud HD2 135 E1
Croft Head. Guise LS20 22 E1
Croft Head La. Crof WF1 143 E6
Croft Head. Skel HD8 175 A2
Croft Head Terr. Glu BD20 16 C6
Croft Hill. S in Cra BD20 16 C5
Croft House Ave. Morley LS27 98 B5
Croft House Cl. Brad BD6 94 B8
Croft House Cl. Morley LS27 98 B5
Croft House Ct. Pudsey LS28 76 E8 6
Croft House Dr. Morley LS27 98 B5
Croft House Dr. Otley LS21 10 F1
Croft House. Elland HX4 134 F7 11
Croft House Fold. Add LS29 7 A8
Croft House Gdns. Morley LS27 98 B5
Croft House Gr. Morley LS27 98 B5
Croft House La. Hud HD1 153 E7
Croft House La. Keigh BD20 18 A2
Croft House La. Morley LS27 98 B5
Croft House Mews.
Morley LS27 98 B5
Croft House Mount. Morley LS27 98 B6
Croft House Rd. Brad BD6 94 B8
Croft House Rd. Morley LS27 98 B5
Croft House Rd. Slai HD3 151 D5
Croft House Rise. Morley LS27 98 B6
Croft House View. Morley LS27 98 B5
Croft House Way. Morley LS27 98 B6
Croft House Wlk. Morley LS27 98 B6
Croft La. Tad LS24 31 E6
Croft La. Th Arch LS23 15 A4
Croft Pk. Men LS29 21 F4
Croft Pl. Brig HD6 115 B4 1
Croft Rd. Bing BD16 36 D6
Croft Rd. Bramham LS23 30 D3
Croft Rd. Keigh BD20 19 D1
Croft Rise. Men LS29 22 A4
Croft Row. Denh BD13 71 E6
Croft St. Birk BD11 96 A5
Croft St. Brad BD10 56 C8
Croft St. Brad BD6 74 C1
Croft St. Brad BD5 74 F6
Croft St. Brig HD6 115 A2 6
Croft St. Dew WF13 139 C8
Croft St. Glu BD20 16 C6
Croft St. Hali HX6 112 C4
Croft St. Haw BD22 51 C7
Croft St. Heb Br HX7 89 A3 22
Croft St. Hud HD1 153 C5
Croft St. Keigh BD21 35 B6
Croft St. Liver WF16 117 D3
Croft St. Otley LS21 23 B7
Croft St. Pudsey LS28 57 D3
Croft St. Ship BD18 55 B8
Croft St. Stee BD20 17 C5
Croft Terr. Gild LS12 77 E3
Croft The. Bad WF9 164 D3
Croft The. Birk BD11 96 E5
Croft The. Castle WF10 124 F6
Croft The. Coll LS22 29 A8
Croft The. Draug BD23 1 D5
Croft The. E Ard FW12 119 D5
Croft The. Knot WF11 127 A5
Croft The. Leeds LS15 62 B1
Croft The. Roth LS26 101 C5
Croft The. Scar LS14 45 D8
Croft The. W Bret WF4 176 F8
Croft Way. Men LS29 22 A4
Croft's Ct. Leeds LS1 79 B8
Croftdale Gr. Leeds LS15 62 D2
Crofters Gn. Brad BD10 56 A8
Croftlands. Batley WF12 118 F2
Croftlands. Brad BD10 56 A8
Croftlands. Hud HD4 154 A2
Croftlands. Knot WF11 127 A5
Crofton Cl. Slai HD7 170 D8
Crofton High Sch. Crof 161 F8
Crofton Inf Sch. Crof 162 A8
Crofton Jun Sch. Crof 162 A8
Crofton Rd. Brad BD9 54 F3
Crofton Rd. Ship BD9 55 A4
Crofton Rise. Thorner LS17 45 A4
Crofton Shay Jun & Inf Sch.
Crof 143 E1
Crofton Terr. Thorner LS17 45 A4
Crofts The. Batley WF17 117 F4
Crofts The. Emley HD8 175 D7
Crofts The. Farnh BD20 4 E1
Crofts The. S in Cra BD20 16 C4
Croftside Cl. Leeds LS14 62 B3
Croftway. B in Elm LS15 63 E7
Croisdale Cl. Liver WF15 116 E4
Cromack View. Pudsey LS28 76 C7
Cromarty Ave. Hud HD4 153 C2
Cromarty Dr. Hud HD4 153 C2
Cromer Ave. Keigh BD21 35 B5 15
Cromer Gr. Keigh BD21 35 B5 17
Cromer Pl. Leeds LS2 60 A2
Cromer Rd. Keigh BD21 35 B5
Cromer Rd. Leeds LS2 60 A2
Cromer St. Hali HX1 112 F5 4
Cromer St. Keigh BD21 35 B5 14
Cromer St. Leeds LS2 60 A2
Cromer Terr. Leeds LS2 60 A2
Cromwell Cl. Byram WF11 126 D8
Cromwell Cl. Hali HX3 114 A4
Cromwell Cres. Pont WF8 146 E8
Cromwell Ct. Ad Le S DN6 184 F1
Cromwell Ct. Birk BD11 96 D5
Cromwell Ct. Ship BD9 54 C5
Cromwell Hts. Leeds LS9 79 E8 2
Cromwell Mount. Leeds LS9 60 E1
Cromwell Pl. Ossett WF5 140 E7
Cromwell Rd. Castle WF10 125 D7
Cromwell Rd. Hali HX3 114 A4
Cromwell Rise. Kippax LS25 103 B8
Cromwell St. Dearne S63 194 E1
Cromwell St. Leeds LS9 60 E1
Cromwell Terr. Hali HX1 113 B7 1
Cromwell View. Hali HX3 114 B4
Cronkhill La. Roy S71 179 D1
Crook Farm Caravan Pk. Bail 37 F3
Crooke La. Wils BD15 53 C4
Crooked La. Brad BD10 39 A1
Crooked La. Hali HX3 92 B6
Crookes La. Roy S71 179 C1
Cropper Gate. Leeds LS1 79 A8
Cropredy Cl. Queen BD13 72 F1
Cropstones. Bramham LS23 30 D2
Cropton Rd. Roy S71 179 B3
Crosby Ave. Leeds LS11 78 F4 2
Crosby Pl. Leeds LS11 79 A5
Crosby Rd. Leeds LS11 79 A4 8
Crosby St. Keigh BD21 35 B8
Crosby St. Leeds LS11 78 F5
Crosby Terr. Leeds LS11 79 A5
Crosby View. Leeds LS11 79 A5 9
Croscombe Wlk. Brad BD5 74 E5
Crosland Ct. Hud HD3 134 F1
Crosland Edge. Mel HD7 170 F4
Crosland Factory La. Mel HD4 171 B5
Crosland Heath Golf Course.
Hud 152 F1
Crosland Hill Rd. Hud HD4 153 B3
Crosland Moor. Hud 153 C3
Crosland Moor Inf Sch. Hud 153 C3
Crosland Rd. Hud HD3 135 A1
Crosland Rd. Hud HD1 153 E4
Crosland Spring Rd. Hud HD4 171 B6
Crosland St. Hud HD4 153 E4
Crosley View. Bing BD16 37 C2
Crosley Wood Rd. Bing BD16 37 B2
Cross Albert Pl. Leeds LS12 78 D6
Cross Alma St. Leeds LS9 60 F1
Cross Aston Gr. Leeds LS13 58 E2
Cross Ave. Roth LS26 100 F7
Cross Bank Rd. Batley WF17 118 B6
Cross Bank St. Mir WF14 138 A2
Cross Banks. Ship BD18 55 B7
Cross Banstead St. Leeds LS8 60 F3 12
Cross Barstow St. Leeds LS11 79 C6
Cross Bath Rd. Leeds LS13 58 C2
Cross Belgrave St. Leeds LS2 79 C8 1
Cross Bell St. Leeds LS9 79 D8 2
Cross Bellbrooke Ave.
Leeds LS9 61 B2 10
Cross Bentley La. Leeds LS6 59 F6
Cross Burley Lodge Rd.
Leeds LS6 59 E2
Cross Cardigan Mount.
Leeds LS4 59 C1
Cross Cardigan Terr. Leeds LS4 59 C1
Cross Catherine St. Leeds LS9 79 E7
Cross Chancellor St. Leeds LS6 60 B3
Cross Chapel St. Leeds LS6 59 D5 4
Cross Chestnut Gr. Leeds LS6 59 E3 5
Cross Church St. Clec BD19 116 E7 8
Cross Church St. Hud HD1 153 D5
Cross Church St. Hud HD1 154 B6 14
Cross Cliff Rd. Leeds LS6 59 F4
Cross Cotts. Hud HD1 153 D7
Cross Cowper St. Leeds LS7 60 E3
Cross Crown St. Clec BD19 116 D7 5
Cross Dawlish Gr. Leeds LS9 80 B8 7
Cross Dikes Rd. Rip HX6 132 A7
Cross Easy Rd. Leeds LS9 79 F6
Cross Elford St. Leeds LS8 60 F3
Cross Emily St. Keigh BD21 35 C8 11
Cross End Fold. Add LS29 7 A8
Cross Ends La. Wad M HX7 69 A4
Cross Eric St. Leeds LS13 58 C5
Cross Evanston Ave. Leeds LS4 59 C2
Cross Farm Ct. Oxen BD22 51 C3
Cross Field. Elland HX4 134 A4
Cross Fields. Hud HD5 154 E7
Cross Firs St. Hud HD3 153 B5
Cross Flats Row. Leeds LS11 78 F2
Cross Flatts Ave. Leeds LS11 79 A2
Cross Flatts Cres. Leeds LS11 78 F2
Cross Flatts Dr. Leeds LS11 78 F2 8
Cross Flatts Gr. Leeds LS11 79 A2
Cross Flatts. Leeds LS11 79 A2
Cross Flatts Mount. Leeds LS11 79 A2
Cross Flatts Par. Leeds LS11 78 F2
Cross Flatts Park Prim Sch.
Leeds 79 B2
Cross Flatts Pl. Leeds LS11 78 F2
Cross Flatts Rd. Leeds LS11 78 F2
Cross Flatts St. Leeds LS11 78 F2
Cross Flatts Terr. Leeds LS11 78 F2
Cross Foundry St. Dew WF13 138 E5
Cross Fountaine St. Leeds LS2 79 B8 4
Cross Francis St. Leeds LS7 60 D3
Cross Gate Rd. Holmfi HD7 189 B2
Cross Gates Ave. Leeds LS15 62 B3
Cross Gates Ctr. Leeds LS15 62 C2
Cross Gates La. Harden BD16 36 C3
Cross Gates La. Leeds LS15 62 B3
Cross Gates Mid Sch. Leeds 62 A2
Cross Gates Prim Sch. Leeds 62 B2
Cross Gates Rd. Leeds LS15 62 B2
Cross Gates Sta. Leeds 62 C1
Cross Glen Rd. Leeds LS16 59 C7
Cross Gn. Brad BD4 75 E4
Cross Gn. Otley LS21 23 B8
Cross Granby Terr. Leeds LS6 59 D5 8
Cross Grange Ave. Leeds LS7 60 E4
Cross Grasmere St. Leeds LS12 78 D7 8
Cross Green App. Leeds LS9 80 A5
Cross Green Ave. Leeds LS9 79 F6 9
Cross Green Cl. Leeds LS9 80 A5
Cross Green Comprehensive Sch.
Leeds 80 A6
Cross Green Cres. Leeds LS9 79 F6 7
Cross Green Ct. Leeds LS9 80 B5
Cross Green Dr. Hud HD5 155 A6
Cross Green Dr. Leeds LS9 80 A5
Cross Green Garth. Leeds LS9 80 A5
Cross Green Gr. Leeds LS9 79 F6
Cross Green La. Leeds LS9 79 F6
Cross Green La. Leeds LS15 81 B8
Cross Green Light Ind Est.
Leeds 80 B5
Cross Green Rd. Hud HD5 155 A6
Cross Green Rd. Leeds LS9 79 F6
Cross Green Rise. Leeds LS9 80 A5
Cross Green Row. Leeds LS6 59 E7
Cross Green Vale. Leeds LS9 80 B5
Cross Green Way. Leeds LS9 80 A5
Cross Greenwood Mount.
Leeds LS6 59 E7 1
Cross Grove St. Hud HD1 154 A5
Cross Hands La. W Har WF9 163 B6
Cross Hartley Ave. Leeds LS6 60 A4
Cross Heath Gr. Leeds LS11 78 E3
Cross Henley Rd. Leeds LS13 58 C2
Cross Hill. Ad Le S DN6 184 F1
Cross Hill. Bri S72 180 F3
Cross Hill Ct. Ad Le S DN6 184 F2
Cross Hill. Elland HX4 134 C7
Cross Hill. Fair WF11 105 A4
Cross Hill. Hali HX1 113 C8
Cross Hill. Hem WF9 181 D7
Cross Hill La. Liver WF15 116 C1
Cross Hills Ct. Kippax LS25 83 A1 3
Cross Hills Dr. Kippax LS25 83 A1
Cross Hills Ent Ctr. Glu 16 E7
Cross Hills Gdns. Kippax LS25 83 A1 2
Cross Hills. Kippax LS25 83 B1
Cross Hilton Gr. Leeds LS8 60 F5
Cross Ingledew Cres.
Leeds LS8 44 B2
Cross Ingram Rd. Leeds LS11 78 F5
Cross Ivy Mount. Leeds LS9 80 A8 7
Cross Kelso Rd. Leeds LS2 59 F1 1
Cross Keys. Wake WF5 141 A7
Cross La. Bing BD16 36 F3
Cross La. Birk BD11 96 B7
Cross La. Brad BD7 74 A4
Cross La. Brig HD6 115 F1

Cross La. Elland HX5 134 E6
Cross La. Emley HD8 175 D8
Cross La. Guise LS20 23 A4
Cross La. Holmfi HD7 189 C2
Cross La. Honley HD7 171 F2
Cross La. Hud HD4 154 A3
Cross La. Kirkb HD4 173 C2
Cross La. Kirkb HD8 174 B5
Cross La. Leeds LS12 77 E5
Cross La. Leeds LS12 78 B7
Cross La. Oxen BD22 51 C3
Cross La. Queen BD13 92 C8
Cross La. Roy S71 179 E3
Cross La. Shelf HX3 93 A6
Cross La. Shelf HX3 93 B4
Cross La. Shep HD8 190 E6
Cross La. Skel HD8 175 A1
Cross La. Tod OL14 108 F4
Cross La. Wake WF2 141 F5
Cross La. Wils BD16 53 D7
Cross Lane Bsns Pk. Liver 117 B4
Cross Lea Farm Rd. Leeds LS5 58 F7
Cross Lee Gate. Tod OL14 107 F7
Cross Lee Rd. Tod OL14 107 F7
Cross Lee. Tod OL14 107 F7
Cross Leeds St. Keigh BD21 35 B7 13
Cross Lidgett Pl. Leeds LS8 60 E4
Cross Linden Terr. Leeds LS11 79 C3 5
Cross Louis St. Leeds LS7 60 D3
Cross Maude St. Leeds LS2 79 D7
Cross Milan Rd. Leeds LS8 61 A3 4
Cross Mill St. Leeds LS9 79 D7
Cross Mitford Rd. Leeds LS12 78 D7 5
Cross Osmondthorpe La. Leeds LS9 80 C8
Cross Park Ave. Castle WF10 124 F7
Cross Park St. Batley WF17 118 D5
Cross Park St. Dew WF12 139 F8
Cross Park St. Hor WF4 141 A1 7
Cross Park St. Leeds LS15 81 A8 7
Cross Peel St. Morley LS27 98 B4 2
Cross Pipes Rd. Wake WF2 141 E8
Cross Platts. Brig HX3 114 C4
Cross Quarry St. Leeds LS6 60 A4 14
Cross Queen St. Nor WF6 123 A2
Cross Rd. Brad BD8 55 B1
Cross Rd. Brad BD10 56 C8
Cross Rd. Brad BD12 94 F4
Cross Rd. Crig WF4 159 F3
Cross Rd. Dew WF12 139 D1
Cross Rd. Hors LS18 58 A8
Cross Rd. Neth WF4 158 B7
Cross Reginald Mt. Leeds LS7 60 D4
Cross Rink St. Batley WF17 118 D3 3
Cross River St. Keigh BD21 18 E1
Cross Roseville Rd. Leeds LS8 60 E3
Cross Rosse St. Ship BD18 55 B8
Cross Roundhay Ave. Leeds LS8 60 F5
Cross Row. Swil LS15 82 A6
Cross Rydal St. Keigh BD22 35 A6 6
Cross Ryecroft St. Ossett WF5 140 C7
Cross Speedwell St. Leeds LS6 60 B3
Cross Spr'gwell St. Leeds LS12 78 F6 1
Cross Sq. Wake WF1 142 C6 15
Cross St. Bacup OL13 106 A3
Cross St. Batley WF17 118 C5
Cross St. Brad BD14 73 C4 5
Cross St. Brad BD6 93 F7 2
Cross St. Brad BD12 95 A4
Cross St. Brig HD6 115 B4
Cross St. Castle WF10 124 B8
Cross St. Castle WF10 124 C8
Cross St. Dew WF12 139 D7
Cross St. Dew WF12 139 E8
Cross St. E Ard WF3 120 E8
Cross St. Elland HX4 134 B4 1
Cross St. Elland HX4 134 D7 7
Cross St. Hali HX1 113 C7
Cross St. Hali HX1 113 D6 1
Cross St. Hem WF9 181 C7
Cross St. Honley HD7 171 F4
Cross St. Hor WF4 141 B1 2
Cross St. Hud HD4 153 E4
Cross St. Leeds LS15 81 A8
Cross St. Liver WF15 117 A2
Cross St Michael's La. Leeds LS6 59 D4
Cross St. Ossett WF5 119 C1
Cross St. Pont WF8 146 D8 3
Cross St. Roth LS26 100 E5
Cross St. Slai HD7 152 A1
Cross St. Upton WF9 183 D8
Cross St W. Hali HX2 112 E8 2
Cross St. Wake WF1 142 C6
Cross St. Weth LS22 13 E5
Cross Stamford St. Leeds LS7 60 D1
Cross Stone Rd. Tod OL14 108 D6
Cross Sun St. Brad BD1 74 F8 6
Cross Terr. Roth LS26 100 E5
Cross The. B in Elm LS15 63 E7
Cross The. Bramho LS16 24 D3
Cross Union St. Leeds LS2 79 D8
Cross Valley Dr. Leeds LS15 62 B1
Cross Wellington St. Brad BD1 74 F7 1
Cross Wells Rd. Rip HX6 132 C5
Cross Westfield Rd. Leeds LS3 59 F1 4
Cross Wingham St. Leeds LS7 60 D2
Cross Woodstock St. Leeds LS2 60 B2 5
Cross Woodv'w St. Leeds LS11 79 B2 17
Cross York St. Leeds LS2 79 D7 2
Crossbeck Cl. Ilkley LS29 8 B3
Crossbeck Rd. Ilkley LS29 8 C3
Crossdale Ave. Brad BD6 93 E8
Crossfield Cl. Oxen BD22 51 B3
Crossfield Ct. Neth WF4 157 F6
Crossfield Rd. Oxen BD22 51 C3
Crossfield St. Leeds LS2 60 A3
Crossfields. Neth WF4 158 A6
Crossflatts Fst Sch. Bing 36 E6
Crossflatts Sta. Bing 36 E5
Crossgate. Mapp S75 178 B1
Crossgate. Otley LS21 23 A7
Crosshills Mount. Elland HX4 134 C7
Crosshills Rd. Con BD20 4 A2
Crossings The. Batley WF17 117 F8
Crossland Rd. Morley LS27 98 B7
Crossland St. Leeds LS11 79 C3
Crossland Terr. Leeds LS11 79 C3
Crosslane Ind Est. Liver 117 A4
Crossley Cl. Hali HX1 113 A7
Crossley Cl. Mir WF14 138 A8
Crossley Gdns. Hali HX1 113 A8
Crossley Gr. Mir WF14 138 A8
Crossley Hall Fst Sch. Brad 73 E8
Crossley Hall St. Brad BD8 73 D7
Crossley Heath Sch. Hali 113 A4
Crossley Hill. Hali HX3 113 D3
Crossley La. Hud HD5 155 A7
Crossley La. Mir WF14 138 B8
Crossley New Rd. Tod OL14 87 F1
Crossley St. Batley WF15 117 C2
Crossley St. Brad BD7 74 B5
Crossley St. Brig HD6 115 B1
Crossley St. Crof WF4 143 F6
Crossley St. Crof WF4 144 A5
Crossley St. Feath WF7 145 D5
Crossley St. Hali HX1 113 C7
Crossley St. Queen BD13 72 F1
Crossley St. Tod OL14 108 B5 15
Crossley St. Weth LS22 13 E5
Crossley Terr. Batley WF17 118 C3
Crossley Terr N. Hali HX3 92 A4
Crossley Terr S. Hali HX3 92 A4
Crossman Dr. Nor WF6 123 C3
Crossmoor Cl. Sil BD20 5 C1
Crossmount St. Batley WF17 118 C3
Crossroads Cotts. Stut LS24 47 E5
Crossway. Ship BD16 53 F7
Crossways The. Otley LS21 11 A2
Crow Hill End Rd. Sow Br HX7 110 F2
Crow Hill Rd. Sow Br HX7 110 F2
Crow La. Hud HD3 153 A5
Crow La. Otley LS21 23 A7
Crow Nest La. Leeds LS11 78 E2
Crow Nest Rd. Heb Br HX7 89 B2
Crow Nest Terr. Dew WF13 139 B7 2
Crow Nest View. Dew WF13 139 A7
Crow Tree Cl. Bail BD17 38 D3
Crow Tree La. Brad BD8 54 E1
Crow Trees. Mars HD7 169 C7
Crow Trees Pk. Yeadon LS19 40 B4
Crow Trees Rd. Mars HD7 169 B7
Crow Wood La. Rip HX4 133 D2
Crow Wood Pk. Hali HX2 112 D5
Crowgill Rd. Ship BD18 55 B8
Crowlees CE Sch. Mir 138 B4
Crowlees Cl. Mir WF14 138 B4
Crowlees Gdns. Mir WF14 138 B5
Crowless Rd. Mir WF14 138 B4
Crown & Anchor Yd. Pont WF8 146 C8 6
Crown Cl. Dew WF12 140 A7
Crown Dr. Brad BD12 94 C4
Crown Flatt Way. Dew WF12 118 E1
Crown La. Holmfi HD7 189 A5
Crown Point Cl. Ossett WF5 140 C6
Crown Point Dr. Ossett WF5 140 C7
Crown Point Rd. Leeds LS10 79 D6
Crown Point Rd. Ossett WF5 140 C6
Crown Point Ret Pk. Leeds 79 C6
Crown Rd. Hali HX3 92 B2
Crown St. Brad BD1 74 C7
Crown St. Brad BD12 94 C4 9
Crown St. Brig HD6 115 A3
Crown St. Bur in W LS29 9 F1
Crown St. Clay W HD8 175 D1
Crown St. Clec BD19 116 D7
Crown St. Elland HX5 134 F7
Crown St. Hali HX1 113 C7
Crown St. Heb Br HX7 89 A3 18
Crown St. Honley HD7 171 F5
Crown St. Leeds LS2 79 C7
Crown St. Liver WF15 117 B4
Crown St. Ossett WF5 140 E3
Crownest La. Bing BD16 37 A3
Crownest Rd. Bing BD16 37 A3
Crownlands La. Ossett WF5 140 D6
Crowther Ave. Pudsey LS28 56 F6
Crowther Cl. Slai HD7 152 A2
Crowther Fold. Harden BD16 36 B1
Crowther Pl. Castle WF10 124 D7
Crowther Pl. Leeds LS6 60 B3
Crowther Rd. Batley WF16 117 E5
Crowther Rd. Mir WF14 138 A5
Crowther St. Batley WF17 117 F5
Crowther St. Brad BD10 56 D7
Crowther St. Brad BD12 94 C4 8
Crowther St. Castle WF10 124 D7
Crowther St. Clec BD19 116 D8 6
Crowther St. Hud HD1 153 F3
Crowther St. Hud HD1 154 B5
Crowtrees Cres. Brig HD6 135 F7
Crowtrees Ct. Yeadon LS19 40 B3
Crowtrees La. Brig HD6 135 F7
Crowtrees Pk. Brig HD6 135 F8
Croxall Dr. Loft G WF3 121 E5
Croydon Rd. Brad BD7 73 F6
Croydon St. Leeds LS11 78 F6
Croydon St. Queen BD13 72 E1 12
Crumack La. Oxen BD22 51 F3
Crummock Pl. Knot WF11 126 E2
Cryer Row. S in Cra BD20 16 D4
Crystal Ct. Hali HX1 113 A7 9
Crystal Pl. Wake WF1 142 D6 7
Crystal Terr. Brad BD4 75 C3
Cubley Ave. Wake WF2 160 B6
Cuckoo La. Honley HD7 171 F4
Cuckoo Nest Ind Est. Brad 74 C7
Cuckoo's Nest Halt. Skel 175 C2
Cuckstool Rd. D Dale HD8 192 A6
Cudbear St. Leeds LS10 79 D6
Cullingworth Fst Sch. Cull 52 D6
Cullingworth Parkside Mid Sch. Cull 52 E6
Cullingworth Rd. Cull BD13 52 E5
Cullingworth St. Batley WF13 118 A3
Culpans Rd. Sow Br HX7 111 A5
Culver St. Hali HX1 113 C7 4
Cumberland Ave. Hud HD2 136 B5
Cumberland Cl. Hali HX2 91 E3
Cumberland Rd. Brad BD7 74 A5
Cumberland Rd. Castle WF10 104 E2
Cumberland Rd. Leeds LS6 59 F4
Cumberworth La. D Dale HD8 190 F6
Cumberworth La. D Dale HD8 191 E7
Cumberworth Rd. Skel HD8 174 F1
Cumbrian Way. Wake WF2 141 E2
Cunliffe La. Guise BD17 39 B5
Cunliffe Rd. Brad BD8 55 D3
Cunliffe Rd. Ilkley LS29 8 A4
Cunliffe Terr. Brad BD8 55 D2
Cunliffe Villas. Brad BD8 55 D3
Cure Hill. Haw BD22 34 B3
Curlew Cl. Castle WF10 124 D6
Curlew Cl. Ilkley LS29 7 E4
Curlew Rise. Morley LS27 98 D3
Curlew St. Brad BD5 74 C3
Curly Hill. Ilkley LS29 8 B6
Currer Ave. Brad BD4 75 B1
Currer La. Nes LS29 3 C4
Currer St. Brad BD1 74 F7
Currer Wlk. Stee BD20 17 B6
Curwen Cres. Batley WF16 117 E6
Curzon Rd. Brad BD3 75 B7
Curzon St. Hud HD2 137 A6
Cut Rd. Broth WF11 105 C1
Cut Rd. Fair WF11 105 A4
Cuthberts Cl. Queen BD13 92 D8
Cutler Heights La. Brad BD4 75 D3
Cutler La. M'town LS26 102 E4
Cutler Pl. Brad BD4 75 D4
Cutsyke Ave. Castle WF10 124 B5
Cutsyke Crest. Castle WF10 124 B5
Cutsyke Hill. Castle WF10 124 B6
Cutsyke Rd. Castle WF7 124 B3
Cutsyke Rd. Feath WF7 124 B3
Cypress Fold. Lepton HD8 155 E3
Cypress House. Castle WF10 124 E7 10
Cypress Rd. Nor WF6 144 C8
Cyprus Ave. Brad BD10 38 F1
Cyprus Ave. Wake WF1 142 A8
Cyprus Cres. Mir WF14 138 D7
Cyprus Dr. Brad BD10 39 A1
Cyprus Gr. Gar LS25 82 E7
Cyprus Gr. Wake WF1 142 A8
Cyprus Mount. Wake WF1 142 A8
Cyprus Rd. Gar LS25 82 E7
Cyprus St. Wake WF1 142 B8
Cyprus Terr. Gar LS25 82 E7
Czar St. Leeds LS11 79 A6
Dacre Ave. Wake WF2 141 C4
Dacre Cl. Liver WF15 116 F5
Daffels Wood Cl. Brad BD4 95 B8
Daffil Ave. Morley LS27 98 B7
Daffil Gr. Morley LS27 98 B8
Daffil Grange Mews. Morley LS27 98 B7 1
Daffil Grange Way. Morley LS27 98 B7
Daffil Rd. Morley LS27 98 B7
Dagenham Rd. Brad BD4 75 C3
Daisy Bank. Hali HX1 113 B5
Daisy Bank St. Tod OL14 86 B1 2
Daisy Cl. Batley WF17 96 E2
Daisy Croft. Sil BD20 5 F1
Daisy Gn. Slai HD7 170 C7
Daisy Hill Ave. Morley LS27 98 C6
Daisy Hill Back La. Brad BD9 54 E2
Daisy Hill. Brad BD12 94 C3 5
Daisy Hill Cl. Morley LS27 98 C6
Daisy Hill. Dew WF13 139 C8
Daisy Hill Gr. Brad BD9 54 E2
Daisy Hill La. Brad BD9 54 E2
Daisy Hill Mid Sch. Brad 54 E2
Daisy Hill. Morley LS27 98 C5
Daisy Hill. Sil BD20 5 F1
Daisy Lea. Elland HD3 152 A8
Daisy Lea La. Hud HD3 135 C1
Daisy Lee La. Holmfi HD7 199 C7
Daisy Mount. Hali HX6 112 A5
Daisy Pl. Ship BD18 54 F8 12
Daisy Rd. Brig HD6 136 B8
Daisy Row. Leeds LS13 58 D1 3
Daisy Royd. Hud HD4 154 A2
Daisy St. Brad BD7 74 A3
Daisy St. Brig HD6 115 A2 5
Daisy St. Hali HX1 113 B6
Daisy St. Haw BD22 51 E8 1
Daisy Vale Terr. E Ard WF3 99 E1
Daisyfield Rd. Leeds LS13 58 D2 2
Dalby Ave. Brad BD3 56 C1
Dalby St. Brad BD3 75 C8
Dalcross Gr. Brad BD5 74 F4
Dalcross St. Brad BD5 74 F4
Dale Ave. Tod OL14 108 D5
Dale Cl. Batley WF17 118 C3
Dale Cl. D Dale HD8 191 F5
Dale Cl. Guise LS20 39 B8
Dale Cl. Ossett WF5 140 E6
Dale Cres. Stee BD20 17 C5
Dale Croft. Gar LS25 82 E8
Dale Croft. Ilkley LS29 7 E4
Dale Croft Rise. Brad BD15 54 A2
Dale Croft. Skel HD8 175 A2
Dale Ct. Holmfi HD7 189 B7
Dale Ct. Pont WF8 146 D5
Dale Garth. Bail BD17 38 B3
Dale Gr. Ship BD10 38 E1
Dale La. Batley WF16 117 E5
Dale La. S Elm WF9 183 B5
Dale Lane Ind Est. S Elm 183 B5
Dale Mews. Pont WF8 146 D5
Dale Park Ave. Hors LS16 41 D4
Dale Park Cl. Hors LS16 41 D4
Dale Park Gdns. Hors LS16 41 D4
Dale Park Rise. Hors LS16 41 D4
Dale Park View. Hors LS16 41 D4
Dale Park Wlk. Hors LS16 41 D4
Dale Rd. Gild BD11 97 A8
Dale St. Brad BD1 74 E7
Dale St. Dew WF12 139 C4
Dale St. Hali HX6 112 B4
Dale St. Hud HD3 153 A5
Dale St. Hud HD1 154 A5
Dale St. Keigh BD21 18 E1
Dale St. Ossett WF5 140 D6
Dale St. Ship BD18 55 B7
Dale St. Skel HD8 175 A2
Dale St. Tod OL14 108 B5
Dale Stone Cl. Broth WF11 105 C1
Dale The. Aber LS25 47 E1
Dale View Cl. Keigh BD21 35 E6
Dale View Gr. Keigh BD21 35 E6
Dale View. Hali HX2 111 D6
Dale View. Hem WF9 181 F6
Dale View. Ilkley LS29 7 E4
Dale View. Pont WF8 146 D5
Dale View Rd. Keigh BD21 35 E6
Dale View. Sil BD20 5 E2
Dale View. Stee BD20 17 C5
Dale Wlk. Feath WF7 145 C4
Dalefield Ave. Nor WF6 123 B1
Dalefield Rd. Nor WF6 144 B8
Dales Dr. Guise LS20 39 B8
Dales Way. Guise LS20 39 B8
Daleside Ave. Holmfi HD7 189 C7
Daleside Ave. Pudsey LS28 76 A8
Daleside Cl. Brad LS28 56 F1
Daleside. Dew WF12 139 C1
Daleside. Elland HX4 134 A7
Daleside Gr. Brad BD12 94 F4
Daleside Gr. Pudsey LS28 76 A7
Daleside Rd. Keigh BD20 19 A1
Daleside Rd. Pudsey LS28 75 F8
Daleside Rd. Ship BD18 55 E8
Daleside Wlk. Brad BD5 74 F2
Daleson Cl. Northo HX3 93 A3
Dalesway. Bing BD16 37 B5
Daleview Ct. Bail BD17 38 A2
Dallam Ave. Ship BD18 54 E8
Dallam Gr. Ship BD18 54 E8 3
Dallam Rd. Ship BD18 54 E8
Dallam Wlk. Ship BD18 54 F8
Dalmeny Ave. Hud HD4 153 C3
Dalmeny Cl. Hud HD4 153 C3
Dalton Ave. Leeds LS11 79 A2
Dalton Bank Rd. Hud HD5 137 A3
Dalton Clowes. Hud HD5 154 E7
Dalton Fold Rd. Hud HD5 154 D7
Dalton Gr. Hud HD5 154 E7
Dalton Gr. Leeds LS11 79 A2
Dalton Green La. Hud HD5 155 A6
Dalton Jun & Inf Sch. Hud 154 F6
Dalton La. Coll LS23 29 E3
Dalton La. Keigh BD21 35 E7
Dalton Rd. Keigh BD21 35 E7
Dalton Rd. Leeds LS11 79 A2
Dalton St. Hali HX6 112 B5 2
Dalton St. Tod OL14 108 B5
Dalton Terr. Brad BD8 74 B8
Dalton Terr. Castle WF10 124 D7
Dalton Terr. Keigh BD21 35 E8
Dalton Works. Hud 136 F1
Dam Head La. Lepton HD8 155 F5
Dam Head Rd. Hali HX6 112 C5
Dam Hill. Shep HD8 173 E3
Dam La. Saxton LS24 65 F6
Dam La. Yeadon LS19 40 C7
Damask St. Hali HX1 113 B8
Damems La. Keigh BD22 35 A2
Damems Rd. Keigh BD21 35 A3
Damon Ave. Brad BD10 56 E4
Dampier St. Tod OL14 108 A1
Damside. Keigh BD21 35 B6
Damside Rd. Hud HD4 154 B4
Dan La. Brad BD13 73 C2
Danby La. Wake WF2 160 C4
Danby Wlk. Leeds LS9 79 F7
Dandy Mill Ave. Pont WF8 125 F2
Dandy Mill Croft. Pont WF8 125 F2
Dane Hill Dr. Brad BD4 75 E3
Danebury Rd. Brig HD6 115 B1
Danecourt Rd. Brad BD4 75 F3
Danefield Terr. Otley LS21 23 B8
Danehurst. Pont WF8 146 E8
Danella Cres. Wake WF2 120 F3
Danella Gr. Wake WF2 120 F2
Danes La. Neth WF4 158 B6
Danesleigh Dr. Neth WF4 158 B6
Daniel Ct. Brad BD4 75 F2
Daniel St. Brad BD3 75 D7
Danny La. Hali HX2 111 D7
Dansk Way. Ilkley LS29 8 D5
Danum Dr. Bail BD17 38 C2
Darbyfields. Hud HD7 152 E6
Darcey Hey La. Hali HX2 112 E5
Darcy Ct. Leeds LS15 81 C8
Darfield Ave. Leeds LS8 61 A3
Darfield Cres. Leeds LS8 61 A2
Darfield Gr. Leeds LS8 60 F3 16
Darfield Pl. Leeds LS8 61 A3
Darfield Rd. Leeds LS8 61 A3
Darfield St. Brad BD1 74 D8
Darfield St. Leeds LS8 61 A3
Dark La. B Head HX7 88 C3
Dark La. B in Elm LS15 63 D8
Dark La. Batley WF17 96 F3
Dark La. Batley WF17 118 B4
Dark La. Caw S75 193 E5
Dark La. Hali HX2 112 B6
Dark La. Haw BD22 33 F1
Dark La. Hud HD4 155 A3
Dark La. Oxen BD22 51 D3
Dark La. Pont WF8 146 C7
Darkfield La. Pont WF8 125 F4
Darkwood Cl. Leeds LS17 44 A4
Darkwood Way. Leeds LS17 44 A4
Darley Ave. Midd LS10 99 D7
Darley Rd. Liver WF15 116 F5
Darley St. Batley WF16 117 D4
Darley St. Brad BD1 74 E7
Darley St. Keigh BD20 18 B1
Darnell Terr. Leeds LS11 79 C6
Darnes Ave. Hali HX2 112 E5
Darning La. Th Aud WF8 165 B5
Darnley Ave. Wake WF2 142 A6
Darnley Cl. Mel HD7 170 E1
Darnley La. Leeds LS15 81 C7
Darnley Rd. Leeds LS16 59 B7
Darren St. Brad BD4 75 E6
Darrington CE Jun & Inf Sch. Dar 147 D5
Darrington La. Dar WF8 146 E2
Darrington Sch. Dar 147 C5
Dartmouth Ave. Hud HD5 155 A3
Dartmouth Ave. Morley LS27 98 A2
Dartmouth Park. Morley 97 E3
Dartmouth Terr. Brad BD8 55 C2
Dartmouth Terr. Kirkb HD4 172 E6
Dartmouth Way. Leeds LS11 79 C2
Darton Hall Cl. Mapp S75 177 F1
Darton Hall Dr. Mapp S75 177 F1
Darton La. Mapp S75 178 B1
Darton Mapplewell Cty Inf Sch. Mapp 178 B1
Darton Prim Sch. Mapp 177 F1
Darton Rd. Caw S75 193 F5
Darton Sta. Mapp 177 E1
Darwin St. Brad BD5 74 C3
Davey La. B Head HX7 87 F3
David La. Dew WF13 118 C2
David St. Castle WF10 124 B7
David St. Leeds LS11 79 B6
David St. Wake WF1 142 E4
Davies Ave. Leeds LS8 61 A8
Davis Ave. Castle WF10 125 D6
Daw Green Ave. Crig WF4 159 E4
Daw La. Crig WF4 159 D4
Daw La. Hor WF4 159 C8
Daw Royds. Hud HD5 155 A4
Dawes Ave. Castle WF10 124 F6
Dawlish Ave. Leeds LS9 80 B8
Dawlish Cres. Leeds LS9 80 B8
Dawlish Gr. Leeds LS9 80 B7
Dawlish Mount. Leeds LS9 80 B8
Dawlish Pl. Leeds LS9 80 B8 1
Dawlish Rd. Leeds LS9 80 B8
Dawlish Row. Leeds LS9 80 B8
Dawlish St. Leeds LS9 80 B8
Dawlish Terr. Leeds LS9 80 B8
Dawnay Rd. Brad BD5 74 C4
Dawson Ave. Brad BD6 94 C8
Dawson Gdns. Dew WF13 139 C8 1
Dawson Hill. Morley LS27 98 A5
Dawson Hill Yd. Hor WF4 141 B1 3
Dawson La. Birk BD4 76 E2
Dawson La. Brad BD4 75 C1
Dawson La. Roth LS26 100 E6
Dawson Mount. Brad BD4 75 C1
Dawson Pl. Brad BD4 75 D1
Dawson Pl. Keigh BD21 35 C5
Dawson Rd. Hud HD4 154 B3
Dawson Rd. Keigh BD21 35 C5
Dawson Rd. Leeds LS11 79 A3
Dawson St. Brad BD10 39 B2
Dawson St. Brad BD4 75 C2
Dawson St. E Ard WF3 98 D1
Dawson St. Pudsey LS28 57 D1 7
Dawson Terr. Brad BD4 75 C1
Dawson Way. Keigh BD21 35 C5
Dawson's Corner. Pudsey LS28 57 C2
Dawsons M'dow. Pudsey LS28 57 C2
Dawtrie Cl. Castle WF10 125 D7
Dawtrie St. Castle WF10 125 D7
Day St. Dew WF13 138 E5
Day St. Hud HD1 154 C5
De Lacey Mews. Brad BD4 75 C2
De Lacy Ave. Brad BD4 95 B8
De Lacy Ave. Feath WF7 124 C1
De Lacy Ave. Hud HD5 154 F4
De Lacy Mount. Leeds LS5 59 A4
De Lacy Terr. Pont WF8 146 E8
De Trafford St. Hud HD4 153 D4
Deacon Cl. Mel HD7 170 E2
Deaconess Ct. Ilkley LS29 8 B3
Deadmanstone. Hud HD4 171 F8
Deal St. Hali HX1 113 D6
Deal St. Keigh BD21 35 E8
Dealburn Rd. Brad BD12 94 E4
Dean Ave. Holmfi HD7 188 F8
Dean Ave. Leeds LS8 61 A6
Dean Beck Ave. Brad BD6 74 E1
Dean Beck Ct. Brad BD6 94 F8
Dean Bridge La. Holmfi HD7 189 E2
Dean Brook Rd. Holmfi HD7 172 A1
Dean Brook Rd. Hud HD4 171 E8
Dean Cl. Brad BD8 54 D1
Dean Cl. Wake WF2 120 F2
Dean Clough. Hali HX1 113 C8
Dean Ct. Elland HX3 113 A2
Dean Ct. Leeds LS8 61 A6
Dean Edge Rd. Haw BD22 50 A8
Dean End. Elland HX4 134 C8
Dean Hall Cl. Morley LS27 97 F4
Dean Head. Hors LS18 41 A8
Dean House La. Hali HX2 90 E2
Dean La. E Carl LS16 24 A1
Dean La. Guise LS20 38 F8
Dean La. Holmfi HD7 189 D1
Dean La. Hors LS18 41 A8
Dean La. Keigh BD22 33 F6
Dean La. Sow Br HX6 111 E2
Dean La. Sow Br HX6 132 E8
Dean La. Wils BD13 53 C1
Dean Park Ave. Birk BD11 96 E7
Dean Park Dr. Birk BD11 96 E6
Dean Rd. Brad BD6 94 D8
Dean Rd. Holmfi HD7 188 C6
Dean St. Elland HX4 134 D7
Dean St. Elland HX5 134 F6 8
Dean St. Haw BD22 51 D7
Dean St. Hud HD3 153 B8
Dean St. Ilkley LS29 8 C5
Dean Villas. Tod OL14 129 B7
Dean Wood View. Hali HX3 113 C2
Deane The. Leeds LS15 80 D7
Deanery Gdns. Brad BD10 56 C5
Deanfield Ave. Morley LS27 97 F6
Deanfield Jun & Inf Sch. Hali 91 E3
Deanhouse La. Holmfi HD7 189 A8
Deanhurst Gdns. Gild LS27 97 D6
Deanhurst Ind Ctr. Gild 97 D6
Deanroyd Rd. Tod OL14 129 B7
Deanstones Cres. Queen BD13 92 E8
Deanstones La. Queen BD13 92 E8
Deansway. Morley LS27 97 F6
Deanswood Cl. Leeds LS17 43 A3
Deanswood Dr. Leeds LS17 42 F3
Deanswood Garth. Leeds LS17 43 A3
Deanswood Gdns. Leeds LS17 42 F3
Deanswood Gn. Leeds LS17 42 F3
Deanswood Hill. Leeds LS17 43 A3
Deanswood Pl. Leeds LS17 43 A3
Deanswood Rise. Leeds LS17 43 A3
Deanswood View. Leeds LS17 43 A3
Deanwood Ave. Brad BD15 54 A3
Deanwood Cres. Brad BD15 54 A2
Deanwood Wlk. Brad BD15 54 A2
Dearden St. Hali HX6 112 B5
Dearden St. Ossett WF5 140 D5
Dearne Croft. Weth LS22 13 E8
Dearne Dike La. D Dale HD8 190 E5
Dearne Fold. Hud HD3 135 B1
Dearne Pk. Clay W HD8 175 E2
Dearne Royd. Clay W HD8 175 E2
Dearne St. Clay W HD8 175 D1
Dearne St. Mapp S75 177 F1
Dearne St. S Elm WF9 182 F3
Dearne Thurscoe The Hill Inf Sch. Dearne 194 F1
Dearneside Rd. D Dale HD8 191 F5
Dearnfield. D Dale HD8 191 C6
Dearnley St. Dew WF13 138 E6
Dee Ct. Haw BD22 34 C2
Deep Dale. B Spa LS23 14 C1
Deep La. Brad BD13 73 C5
Deep La. Brig HD6 115 F2
Deep La. Hali HX2 111 F7
Deep La. Hud HD4 153 B3
Deep La. Sow Br HX6 132 B8
Deep La. Thorn BD13 72 A5
Deepdale Cl. Bail BD17 38 A2
Deepdale La. B Spa LS23 14 C1
Deer Croft Ave. Hud HD3 152 F8
Deer Croft Cres. Hud HD3 152 F8
Deer Croft Dr. Hud HD3 152 F8
Deer Croft Rd. Hud HD3 134 F1 2
Deer Hill Cl. Mars HD7 168 F3
Deer Hill Croft. Mars HD7 168 F3
Deer Hill Ct. Mel HD7 170 C2
Deer Hill Dr. Mars HD7 168 F3
Deer Hill End Rd. Mel HD7 170 A4
Deershaw La. Holmfi HD7 190 C5
Deershaw Sike La. Holmfi HD7 190 C5
Deerstone Ridge. Weth LS22 13 E8
Defarge Ct. Brad BD5 74 E3
Deffer Rd. Wake WF2 160 C6
Deganwy Dr. Kirkhe HD5 137 C2
Deighton Cl. Weth LS22 13 F6
Deighton Cty Jun Sch. Hud 136 D4
Deighton Cty Sec Sch. Hud 136 D4
Deighton Gates Jun & Inf Sch. Weth 13 E8
Deighton La. Batley WF17 118 A4
Deighton Rd. Hud HD2 136 E3
Deighton Rd. Weth LS22 13 E7
Deighton Sta. Hud 136 E3
Deightonby St. Dearne S63 194 E1
Delacy Cres. Castle WF10 104 D1
Delamere St. Brad BD5 74 D2
Delf Hill. Brig HD6 135 E7
Delf Hill Mid Sch. Brad 94 C6
Delf La. Tod OL14 86 D3
Delf La. Wad M HX7 89 C8
Delf Pl. Brig HD6 135 E7
Delfs La. Sow Br HX7 110 F1
Delius Ave. Brad BD10 56 E5
Dell Croft. Sil BD20 5 C2
Dell The. Bard LS17 28 D3
Dell The. Cull BD13 52 D6
Dell The. Cull BD13 52 E6
Dell The. Hud HD2 136 B4
Delmont Cl. Batley WF17 117 E6
Delph Cres. Brad BD14 73 B4
Delph Ct. Leeds LS6 60 A4
Delph Dr. Brad BD14 73 B4
Delph Gr. Brad BD14 73 B4
Delph Hill. Bail BD17 38 C4 10
Delph Hill. Hali HX2 113 A4 5
Delph Hill La. Hali HX2 90 D2
Delph Hill. Pudsey LS28 76 E8
Delph Hill Rd. Hali HX2 112 F4
Delph Hill Terr. Hali HX2 112 F4 3
Delph La. Hud HD4 171 D7
Delph La. Leeds LS6 60 A4
Delph Mount. Leeds LS6 60 A4
Delph St. Hali HX1 113 B6
Delph Terr. Brad BD14 73 B4
Delph The. Feath WF7 145 F5
Delph View. Leeds LS6 60 A4
Delph Wood Cl. Bing BD16 37 C3
Delverne Gr. Brad BD2 56 C3
Delves Gate. Slai HD7 169 F6
Delves Wood Rd. Hud HD4 153 C1
Denard Ind Est. Hud 153 B4
Denbigh App. Leeds LS9 61 D2
Denbigh Croft. Leeds LS9 61 D2
Denbigh Hts. Leeds LS9 61 D2
Denbrook Ave. Brad BD4 75 F1
Denbrook Cl. Brad BD4 75 F1
Denbrook Cres. Brad BD4 95 F8
Denbrook Way. Brad BD4 75 F1
Denbrook Wlk. Brad BD4 75 F1
Denbury Mount. Brad BD4 75 E2
Denby CE Sch. D Dale 191 F3
Denby Cl. Batley WF17 96 D1
Denby Cl. Liver WF15 116 F5
Denby Crest. Dar WF8 147 D5
Denby Ct. Haw BD22 34 B2
Denby Dale Rd. Crig WF4 159 C5
Denby Dale Rd E. Crig WF4 159 F7
Denby Dale Rd. W Bret WF4 158 E2
Denby Dale Rd W. Crig WF4 159 D6
Denby Dale Rd. Wake WF2 142 B3
Denby Dale Sta. D Dale 191 E6
Denby Dr. Bail BD17 38 B1
Denby Grange La. Flock WF4 157 A5
Denby Hall La. D Dale HD8 192 D4
Denby Hill Rd. Haw BD22 34 B2
Denby La. Brad BD15 54 B1
Denby La. D Dale HD8 191 D3
Denby La. D Dale HD8 192 A3
Denby La. D Dale HD8 192 C4
Denby Lane Cres. Floc WF4 156 E5
Denby Mount. Oxen BD22 51 C2
Denby Park Dr. Floc WF4 156 E5
Denby Pl. Hali HX6 112 B5 5
Denby Rd. Dar WF8 147 C5
Denby Rd. Keigh BD21 35 C5
Denby St. Brad BD8 74 C8
Denby View. Dew WF12 139 D1
Dence Gn. Brad BD4 75 E5
Dence Pl. Leeds LS15 80 E8
Dene Cl. Elland HX5 134 E5
Dene Cres. Brad BD7 73 E4
Dene Gr. Sil BD20 5 E2
Dene Hill. Bail BD17 37 F3
Dene Mount. Brad BD15 54 C1
Dene Pk. Kirkb HD8 173 F7
Dene Pl. Hali HX1 113 B8
Dene Rd. Brad BD6 73 D1
Dene Rd. Skel HD8 174 F1
Dene Royd Ct. Elland HX4 133 F3
Dene View. Hali HX2 111 D8
Denehill. Brad BD9 54 D2
Deneside Mount. Brad BD5 74 D2
Deneside. Ossett WF5 140 C7
Deneside Terr. Brad BD5 74 D2
Denesway. Gar LS25 83 A5
Deneway. Pudsey LS28 57 C2
Denfield Ave. Hali HX3 91 F2
Denfield Cres. Hali HX3 91 F2
Denfield Edge. Hali HX3 91 F2
Denfield Gdns. Hali HX3 91 F2
Denfield La. Hali HX3 91 E2
Denfield Sq. Hali HX3 91 F2
Denhale Ave. Wake WF2 141 F6
Denham Ave. Morley LS27 98 A2
Denham Dr. Holmfi HD7 188 F8
Denham St. Batley WF17 118 A7

Denham St. Brig HD6 115 A1 4
Denholme Dr. Ossett WF5 140 D7
Denholme Fst Sch. Denh 52 D1
Denholme Gate Rd. Brig HX3 93 C1
Denholme Gte Rd. Northo HX3 93 C1
Denholme M'dow. S Elm WF9 182 F4
Denholme Rd. Oxen BD22 51 D1
Denison Rd. Leeds LS3 79 A8
Denison St. Batley WF17 118 C4
Denison St. Yeadon LS19 40 B7
Denmark St. Wake WF1 142 E4
Dennil Cres. Leeds LS15 62 D4
Dennil Rd. Leeds LS15 62 D3
Dennington La. Crig WF4 159 C3
Dennis La. Sil BD20 5 A4
Dennison Fold. Brad BD4 75 E5
Dennison Hill. Otley LS21 23 B8
Dennistead Cres. Leeds LS6 59 D5
Denshaw Dr. Morley LS27 98 C4
Denshaw Gr. Morley LS27 98 C4
Denshaw La. Midd WF3 98 F3
Denstone St. Wake WF1 142 D7
Dent Dr. Wake WF1 142 F8
Dent St. Leeds LS9 79 F7
Denton Ave. Leeds LS8 60 F8
Denton Dr. Bing BD16 37 C4
Denton Gdns. Ack M T WF7 164 A5
Denton Gr. Leeds LS8 60 F8
Denton House. Brad BD6 93 E8 9
Denton Rd. Denton LS29 8 F8
Denton Rd. Denton LS29 9 A6
Denton Rd. Ilkley LS29 8 D5
Denton Row. Denh BD13 71 D8
Denton Row. Elland HX4 134 C4
Denton Terr. Castle WF10 124 E8
Denwell Terr. Pont WF8 125 D1
Der St. Tod OL14 108 C5
Derby Pl. Brad BD3 75 D7
Derby Rd. Brad BD3 75 E7
Derby Rd. Yeadon LS19 40 B4
Derby St. Bing BD16 36 F3
Derby St. Brad BD14 73 B4 3
Derby St. Brad BD7 74 B4
Derby St. Hali HX6 112 D4
Derby St. Queen BD13 72 D1
Derby St. Tod OL14 108 D5
Derby Terr. Brad BD10 56 E8
Derby Terr. Mars HD7 168 F4
Derbyshire St. Leeds LS10 79 F3
Derdale St. Tod OL14 108 C5
Derry Hill Gdns. Men LS29 21 F4
Derry Hill. Men LS29 21 F4
Derry La. Men LS29 21 F4
Derwent Ave. Bail BD17 37 E1
Derwent Ave. Gar LS25 82 F6
Derwent Ave. Roth LS26 101 C6
Derwent Ave. Wils BD15 53 C4
Derwent Cl. Heb Br HX7 89 A4
Derwent Ct. Sil BD20 17 E8
Derwent Dr. Castle WF10 104 E1
Derwent Dr. Hors LS16 42 D4
Derwent Dr. Hud HD5 154 D7
Derwent Gr. Wake WF2 141 F6
Derwent Pl. Knot WF11 126 E1
Derwent Pl. Leeds LS11 79 A6
Derwent Rd. Batley WF12 118 F2
Derwent Rd. Brad BD2 56 A3
Derwent Rd. Honley HD7 171 E3
Derwent Rd. Mel HD7 170 E1
Derwent Rd. Wake WF2 141 F6
Derwent Rise. Weth LS22 13 D8
Derwent St. Keigh BD21 35 F8
Derwentwater Gr. Leeds LS6 59 D5
Derwentwater Terr. Leeds LS6 59 D5
Derwin Ave. Kirkb HD4 173 C2
Detroit Ave. Leeds LS15 81 E8
Detroit Dr. Leeds LS15 81 E8
Deveron Gr. Hud HD2 153 E8
Devon Cl. Leeds LS2 60 B2
Devon Gr. Ossett WF5 140 C4
Devon Rd. Leeds LS2 60 B2
Devon St. Hali HX1 112 F6
Devon Way. Brig HD6 115 B6
Devon Wlk. Dew WF13 139 B8 4
Devonshire Ave. Leeds LS8 44 A2
Devonshire Cl. Leeds LS8 44 A2
Devonshire Cres. Leeds LS8 44 A1
Devonshire Ct. Knot WF11 127 A4
Devonshire Gdns. Leeds LS2 60 B3
Devonshire La. Leeds LS8 44 A2
Devonshire Pl. Yeadon LS19 40 B7 3
Devonshire St. Hud HD1 153 E3
Devonshire St. Keigh BD21 35 B7
Devonshire St W. Keigh BD21 35 A7
Devonshire Terr. Brad BD9 55 C2
Dewar Cl. Coll LS22 13 B1
Dewhirst Cl. Bail BD17 38 D2
Dewhirst Pl. Brad BD4 75 D6
Dewhirst Rd. Bail BD17 38 D2
Dewhirst Rd. Brig HD6 115 A4
Dewhirst St. Wils BD15 53 C5
Dewhurst Rd. Hud HD2 136 B2
Dewsbury and Batley Tech & Art Coll. Batley 118 C5
Dewsbury and Batley Tech & Art Coll. Dew 118 C1
Dewsbury District Golf Course. Mir 138 D3
Dewsbury District Hospl. Batley 118 A2
Dewsbury Gate Rd. Batley WF13 117 F3
Dewsbury Mills. Dew WF12 139 C6
Dewsbury Moor Crem. Dew 139 A8
Dewsbury Moor Inf Sch. Batley 117 F2
Dewsbury Mus & Art Gal. Dew 139 A7
Dewsbury Rd. Brig HD6 135 C6
Dewsbury Rd. Clec BD19 96 B2
Dewsbury Rd. Clec BD19 116 E7
Dewsbury Rd. E Ard WF12 119 C7
Dewsbury Rd. Elland HX5 135 C6
Dewsbury Rd. Leeds LS11 79 C2
Dewsbury Rd. Midd LS27 98 F5
Dewsbury Rd. Ossett WF5 140 D7
Dewsbury Rd. Wake WF2 141 D5
Deyne Rd. Hud HD4 171 C7
Diadem Dr. Leeds LS14 61 E1
Dial St. Leeds LS9 79 F6
Diamond Ave. S Elm WF9 182 E3
Diamond St. Batley WF17 118 B6
Diamond St. Brad BD1 74 F6
Diamond St. Hali HX1 113 A8
Diamond St. Hud HD1 154 B8
Diamond St. Hud HD5 154 D5 10
Diamond St. Keigh BD22 35 A4
Diamond Terr. Hali HX1 113 A8
Dib Cl. Leeds LS8 61 D5
Dib La. Leeds LS8 61 D5
Dibb La. Yeadon LS19 39 F7
Dick Dean La. Wad M HX7 69 A5
Dick Edge La. Holmfi HD7 190 B2
Dick La. Brad BD3, BD4 75 E6
Dick's Garth Rd. Men LS29 21 F4
Dicken's St. Hali HX2 112 E7
Dickens St. Brad BD5 74 E3
Dickinson Ct. Wake WF1 142 C8
Dickinson Gdns. Dew WF13 139 B8 11
Dickinson St. Hors LS18 41 C2
Dickinson St. Wake WF1 142 C7
Dickinson Terr. Feath WF7 145 D6
Dickson Fold. Liver WF15 116 F4
Dicky Sykes La. Ack M T WF7 163 D5
Digby Rd. Men LS29 22 A4
Digley Rd. Holmfi HD7 188 B2
Digley Royd La. Holmfi HD7 188 A3
Dimple Gdns. Ossett WF5 140 D4
Dimple Well Inf Sch. Ossett 140 D4
Dimple Wells Cl. Ossett WF5 140 D4
Dimple Wells La. Ossett WF5 140 D4
Dimple Wells Rd. Ossett WF5 140 D4
Dimples La. Haw BD22 51 B6
Dimples La. Keigh BD20 36 D8
Dineley Ave. Tod OL14 108 A7
Dingle Rd. Hud HD1 153 D6
Dingley Rd. Hud HD3 153 C8
Dinsdale's Bldgs. Yeadon LS19 40 A6
Dirker Ave. Mars HD7 169 A5
Dirker Bank Rd. Mars HD7 168 F5
Dirker Dr. Mars HD7 168 F4
Dirkhill Rd. Brad BD7 74 C5
Dirkhill St. Brad BD7 74 B5
Discovery Rd. Hali HX1 113 D6
Dish Hill Fly-over. Broth WF11 126 D8
Disney Cl. Hud HD4 153 D3
Dispensary Wlk. Hali HX1 113 D7
Disraeli Gdns. Leeds LS11 79 B4
Disraeli Terr. Leeds LS11 79 B4
Dixon Ave. Brad BD7 73 F5
Dixon Cl. Elland HX4 134 B8
Dixon Cl. Stee BD20 17 C5
Dixon La. Leeds LS12 78 C5
Dixon Lane Rd. Leeds LS12 78 C5
Dixon St. Feath WF7 145 D7
Dixon St. S in Cra BD20 16 E5
Dixon's Yd. Wake WF1 142 D6
Dob La. Sow Br HX6 111 D3
Dob Park Rd. Clift LS21 10 E8
Dob Royd. Shep HD8 190 D7
Dob The. Sow Br HX6 111 D3
Dobb La. Holmfi HD7 188 C2
Dobb Top Rd. Holmfi HD7 188 C2
Dobroyd Rd. Tod OL14 108 A4
Dobson Ave. Leeds LS11 79 C3
Dobson Gr. Leeds LS11 79 C3
Dobson Pl. Leeds LS11 79 C3
Dobson Terr. Leeds LS11 79 C3
Dobson View. Leeds LS11 79 C3
Dobsons Wharf. Sil BD20 17 E8
Dock La. Ship BD17, BD18 55 C8
Dock St. Leeds LS10 79 C7
Dockery. Hud HD1 153 F3
Dockfield Pl. Ship BD17 55 C8
Dockfield Rd. Ship BD17 55 C8
Dockfield Terr. Ship BD17 55 C8
Dockroyd La. Haw BD22 34 D2
Doctor Fold. Honley HD7 171 F5
Doctor Hill. Brad BD10 56 A6
Doctor Hill. Brad BD10 56 B7
Doctor Hill. Hali HX2 91 E1
Doctor La. Brad BD10 39 B1
Doctor La. Floc WF4 157 B2
Doctor La. Mir WF14 138 A5
Doctor La. Shep HD8 174 A3
Dodd's Royd. Hud HD4 171 E8
Dodge Holme Ct. Hali HX2 91 D4
Dodge Holme Dr. Hali HX2 91 D4
Dodge Holme Gdns. Hali HX2 91 D4
Dodge Holme Rd. Hali HX2 91 D4
Dodgeholme Cl. Hali HX2 91 D4
Dodgson Ave. Leeds LS7 60 E3
Dodgson St. Elland HX5 134 F5
Dodlee La. Hud HD3 152 E7
Dodsworth Cres. Nor WF6 144 B8
Dodworth Dr. Wake WF2 160 B5
Dog Hill Dr. Shaf S72 180 C3
Dog Hill. Shaf S72 180 C3
Dog Kennel Bank. Hud HD5 154 C4
Dog Kennel Hill. Caw S75 193 E3
Dog Kennel La. Hali HX3 113 E5
Dog La. Elland HX4 133 E2
Dog La. Elland HX4 133 E7
Dog Pits La. Bacup OL13 106 A6
Doghouse La. Tod OL14 108 A5
Dogley La. Lepton HD4 155 D1
Dogley Villa Ct. Lepton HD8 155 D1
Doldram La. Sow Br HX6 112 A1
Dole La. Heb Br HX7 89 A1
Dole St. Thorn BD13 72 E6
Doles Ave. Roy S71 179 B3
Doles Cres. Roy S71 179 B3
Dolfin Pl. Hud HD2 136 F5
Doll La. Cull BD13 52 E4
Dolly La. Leeds LS9 60 E2
Dolphin La. Midd WF3 99 F2
Dolphin Rd. Midd LS10 99 E5
Dombey St. Hali HX1 113 A7
Domestic Rd. Leeds LS12 78 F5
Domestic St. Leeds LS11 78 F5
Domestic Street Ind Est. Leeds 78 F6
Dominion Ave. Leeds LS7 60 E7
Dominion Ind Pk. Brig 114 C8
Don Ave. Weth LS22 13 D8
Don Ct. Sil BD20 5 E1
Don Pedro Ave. Nor WF6 123 D2
Don Pedro Cl. Nor WF6 123 D2
Don St. Keigh BD21 35 B8
Don View. Dun Br S30 199 D1
Donald Ave. Brad BD6 94 C8
Donald St. Pudsey LS28 57 D2 5
Doncaster La. Ham DN6 184 C3
Doncaster Rd. Ack M T WF9 163 B6
Doncaster Rd. Crof WF4 143 D2
Doncaster Rd. Dar WF7 164 B3
Doncaster Rd. Ham WF9 183 D5
Doncaster Rd. Knot WF11 126 C4
Doncaster Rd. S Elm WF9 183 D5
Doncaster Rd. Th Aud WF8 165 C4
Doncaster Rd. Upton WF9 166 A1
Doncaster Rd. Upton WF9 182 E7
Doncaster Rd. W Har WF9 163 B6
Doncaster Rd. Wake WF1 142 E4
Doncaster Road Est. Ack M T WF7 164 A5
Doncaster Sq. Knot WF11 126 D5
Doncaster St. Hali HX3 113 D3
Donisthorpe St. Brad BD5 74 E3
Donisthorpe St. Leeds LS10 79 E5
Dorchester Ave. Pont WF8 146 B8
Dorchester Cres. Bail BD17 38 F4
Dorchester Cres. Brad BD4 75 E2
Dorchester Ct. Brad BD4 75 E3
Dorchester Dr. Hali HX2 112 E5
Dorchester Dr. Yeadon LS19 40 D6
Dorchester Rd. Hud HD2 136 B5
Dorian Cl. Brad BD10 56 C6
Dorman Ave. Upton WF9 183 D8
Dorothy St. Keigh BD21 35 A3
Dorset Ave. Leeds LS8 61 A4
Dorset Cl. Brad BD5 74 C3
Dorset Cl. Hem WF9 181 D8
Dorset Gr. Pudsey LS28 76 E8
Dorset Mount. Leeds LS8 61 A3 1
Dorset Rd. Leeds LS8 61 A3
Dorset St. Brad BD5 74 D3
Dorset St. Hud HD1 153 F8
Dorset St. Leeds LS8 61 A4 10
Dorset Terr. Leeds LS8 61 A3
Dorset Wlk. Dew WF13 139 B8 6
Dortmund Sq. Leeds LS2 79 C8 3
Doubting La. Dew WF12 139 D1
Doubting Rd. Dew WF12 139 D1
Douglas Ave. Batley WF17 118 F5
Douglas Ave. Hud HD3 153 B6
Douglas Ave. Hud HD5 154 E5
Douglas Cres. Ship BD18 55 D6
Douglas Dr. Brad BD4 75 C4
Douglas Rd. Bacup OL13 106 A1
Douglas Rd. Brad BD4 75 C4
Douglas St. Dew WF12 139 C4
Douglas St. Hali HX3 92 B2
Douglas St. Haw BD22 51 E8 8
Dove Cl. Weth LS22 13 E8
Dove Dr. Castle WF10 125 B8
Dove St. Haw BD22 51 D7 16
Dove St. Ship BD18 54 F8
Dovecote Cl. Hor WF4 141 B2
Dovecote Dr. Ledst WF10 103 E6
Dovecote La. Hor WF4 141 A2
Dovedale Cl. Crof WF4 144 A1
Dovedale Cl. Shelf HX3 93 B6
Dovedale Garth. Leeds LS15 62 F3
Dovedale Gdns. Leeds LS15 62 F3
Dovelands. S in Cra BD20 16 D4
Dover La. Holmfi HD7 189 B3
Dover Rd. Holmfi HD7 189 A3
Dover St. Brad BD3 56 A1
Dover St. Gar LS25 83 B7
Dover St. Tod OL14 108 D5
Dovesdale Gr. Brad BD5 74 D2
Dovesdale Rd. Brad BD5 74 D2
Dowkell La. Th Arch LS23 14 F1
Dowker St. Hali HX1 112 F5 8
Dowker St. Hud HD3 153 B5
Dowley Gap La. Bing BD16 37 B1
Downham St. Brad BD3 75 A6
Downing Cl. Brad BD3 75 B7
Downing St. Slai HD7 170 C8
Downland Cres. Knot WF11 127 B2
Downside Cres. Brad BD15 54 A1
Dowry La. Rip HX6 132 A3
Dracup Ave. Brad BD7 73 E5
Dracup Rd. Brad BD7 73 F3
Dradishaw Rd. Sil BD20 5 D1
Dragon Cres. Leeds LS12 78 D5
Dragon Dr. Leeds LS12 78 D5
Dragon Rd. Leeds LS12 78 D5
Drake La. Birk BD11 96 E5
Drake Rd. Litt OL15 129 C1
Drake St. Brad BD1 74 F6
Drake St. Keigh BD21 35 C8
Drakes Ind Est. Hali 92 A4
Draper Corner. Hep HX7 88 E6
Draper La. Hep HX7 88 F6
Draughton Gr. Brad BD5 74 D1
Draughton St. Brad BD5 74 D1
Dray View. Batley WF13 117 F2
Draycott Wlk. Brad BD4 75 E3
Drayton Manor Yd. Leeds LS11 79 C4
Drewry Rd. Keigh BD21 35 B7
Drewton Rd. Brad BD1 74 E8
Driftholme Rd. Birk BD11 96 F7
Drighlington Cty Inf Sch. Birk 96 E6
Drighlington Jun Sch. Birk 96 F7
Drill Par. Brad BD8 55 D1
Drill St. Haw BD22 51 C6 10
Drill St. Keigh BD21 35 C7
Drinker La. Kirkb HD8 174 D6
Drive The. Bard LS17 28 D5
Drive The. Batley WF17 118 A6
Drive The. Bing BD16 36 E6
Drive The. Brad BD10 56 D6
Drive The. Brig HX3 114 D8
Drive The. Bur in W LS29 21 E8
Drive The. Heb Br HX7 89 D1
Drive The. Kippax LS25 83 A1
Drive The. Leeds LS17 43 A6
Drive The. Leeds LS8 60 F8
Drive The. Leeds LS15 62 D2
Drive The. Leeds LS9 79 E7
Drive The. Swil LS26 82 A1
Driver Pl. Leeds LS12 78 E6
Driver St. Leeds LS12 78 E6
Driver Terr. Leeds LS12 78 E6
Driver Terr. Sil BD20 5 E2
Drivers Row. Pont WF8 146 B7
Drub La. Clec BD19 95 F2
Druggist La. Sil LS29 6 F8
Druids St. Brad BD14 73 B4
Druids View. Bing BD16 36 D6
Drummer La. Slai HD7 152 B4
Drummond Ave. Leeds LS16 59 C7
Drummond Ct. Leeds LS16 59 C6
Drummond Mid Sch. Brad 55 C1
Drummond Rd. Brad BD8 55 C1
Drummond Rd. Leeds LS16 59 C7
Drummond Trad Est. Brad 74 D8
Drury Ave. Hors LS18 58 B8
Drury Cl. Hors LS18 58 B8
Drury La. Elland HX4 133 F4
Drury La. Hors LS18 58 B8
Drury La. Nor WF6 122 F3
Drury La. Wake WF1 142 B6
Dry Carr La. Hali HX2 90 C4
Dry Hill La. D Dale HD8 192 B5
Dryclough Ave. Hud HD4 153 C2
Dryclough Cl. Hali HX3 113 C3
Dryclough La. Hali HX3 113 C3
Dryclough Rd. Hud HD4 153 C2
Dryden St. Bing BD16 36 F3
Dryden St. Brad BD1 75 A6
Dubb La. Bing BD16 37 A3
Duchy Ave. Brad BD9 54 E3
Duchy Cres. Brad BD9 54 E3
Duchy Dr. Brad BD9 54 E3
Duchy Gr. Brad BD9 54 E3
Duchy Villas. Brad BD9 54 E3
Duchywood. Brad BD9 54 E3
Ducie St. Brad BD10 39 B1
Duck Hill. Wad M HX7 69 A1
Duckett Gr. Pudsey LS28 75 F8
Duckett La. Brad BD1 74 E7
Duckworth Gr. Brad BD9 54 F1
Duckworth La. Brad BD9 54 F1
Duckworth Terr. Brad BD9 54 F1
Dudfleet La. Hor WF4 159 B8
Dudley Ave. Batley WF17 97 A2
Dudley Ave. Hud HD1 153 D6
Dudley Cres. Hali HX2 91 D5
Dudley Gr. Brad BD4 75 E5
Dudley Hill Fst Sch. Brad 75 C3
Dudley Hill Rd. Brad BD2 56 B3
Dudley Rd. Hud HD1 153 D6
Dudley St. Brad BD4 75 B3
Dudley St. Brad BD4 75 E5
Dudwell Ave. Hali HX3 113 C2
Dudwell Gr. Hali HX3 113 C2
Dudwell La. Hali HX3 113 C2
Dufton App. Leeds LS14 62 A3
Duich Rd. Brad BD6 93 E6
Duinen St. Brad BD5 74 F5
Duke of York Ave. Wake WF2 142 D1
Duke of York St. Wake WF2 120 F1
Duke of York St. Wake WF1 142 D7
Duke St. Brad BD1 74 E7 4
Duke St. Castle WF10 124 B8
Duke St. Dew WF13 138 E5
Duke St. Elland HX5 134 F6
Duke St. Hali HX2 90 D1
Duke St. Haw BD22 51 D7 11
Duke St. Hem WF9 163 A3
Duke St. Keigh BD20 18 C1
Duke St. Leeds LS9 79 D7
Duke Wood Rd. Clay W HD8 175 F2
Dulverton Cl. Morley LS11 78 D1
Dulverton Cl. Pont WF8 125 F3
Dulverton Ct. Morley LS11 78 D1 3
Dulverton Garth. Morley LS11 78 C1
Dulverton Gdns. Morley LS11 78 C2
Dulverton Gn. Morley LS11 78 D1
Dulverton Gr. Brad BD4 75 D3
Dulverton Gr. Morley LS11 78 C1
Dulverton Pl. Morley LS11 78 C1
Dulverton Rise. Pont WF8 125 F3
Dulverton Sq. Morley LS11 78 D1
Dulverton Way. Pont WF8 125 F3
Dunbar Cft. Queen BD13 72 F1
Dunbar St. Wake WF1 142 F4
Dunbottle Cl. Mir WF14 138 C5
Dunbottle La. Mir WF14 138 B6
Duncan Ave. Otley LS21 22 D6
Duncan Ave. Wake WF2 142 E2
Duncan St. Brad BD5 74 E5
Duncan St. Leeds LS1 79 C7
Dunce Park Cl. Elland HX5 134 F5
Duncombe Rd. Brad BD8 74 A7
Duncombe St. Brad BD8 74 A7
Duncombe St. Leeds LS1 79 A8
Duncombe Way. Brad BD8 74 A7
Dundas St. Hali HX1 112 F5 18
Dundas St. Hud HD1 154 A6 25
Dundas St. Keigh BD21 35 D6
Dundee Rd. Tod OL14 107 D8
Dunford Hazelhead Prim Sch. Carl 200 E3
Dunford Rd. Dun Br HD7 199 D3
Dunford Rd. Holmfi HD7 189 B3
Dunford Rd. Holmfi HD7 199 B7
Dunford Townh'd Sch. Dun Br 199 F2
Dungeon La. Roth LS26 101 A1
Dunhill Cres. Leeds LS9 80 E8
Dunhill Rise. Leeds LS9 80 E8
Dunkirk Cres. Hali HX1 112 E6
Dunkirk Gdns. Hali HX1 112 E5
Dunkirk La. Hali HX1 112 F6
Dunkirk Rise. Keigh BD20 18 E2
Dunkirk St. Hali HX1 112 E6
Dunkirk Terr. Hali HX1 112 F6
Dunlin Croft. Midd LS10 99 D5 8
Dunlin Ct. Midd LS10 99 D5 6
Dunlin Dr. Midd LS10 99 D5
Dunlin Fold. Midd LS10 99 D5 7
Dunlin Way. Brad BD8 73 C7 3
Dunn Cl. Wake WF2 120 F3
Dunningley La. Midd WF3 98 F2
Dunningley La. Midd WF3 98 F4
Dunnington Wlk. Brad BD6 94 A6
Dunrobin Ave. Gar LS25 83 B8
Dunsford Ave. Brad BD4 95 B8
Dunsil Villas. S Elm WF9 182 F1
Dunsley Bank Rd. Holmfi HD7 188 F3
Dunsley Terr. S Kirk WF9 182 A2
Dunsmore Dr. Hud HD3 152 F8
Dunstan Cl. Ossett WF5 140 E4
Dunstarn Dr. Hors LS16 42 D3
Dunstarn Gdns. Hors LS16 42 E3
Dunstarn La. Hors LS16 42 D2
Durban Ave. Leeds LS11 78 F2
Durban Cres. Leeds LS11 78 F2
Durham Rd. Brad BD8 55 A1
Durham St. Castle WF10 124 E6
Durham St. Hali HX2 112 E7 2
Durham Terr. Brad BD8 55 A1
Durkar Fields. Crig WF4 159 F6
Durkar La. Crig WF4 159 F6
Durkar Low La. Crig WF4 160 A7
Durkar Rise. Crig WF4 159 F6
Durkheim Ct. Brad BD3 75 C7
Durley Ave. Brad BD9 55 A3
Durling Dr. Ship BD18 55 E7
Durlston Gr. Brad BD12 94 D4
Durlston Terr. Brad BD12 94 D4
Durn St. Tod OL14 86 A1
Durrance St. Keigh BD22 34 F6
Durrant Cl. Weth LS22 13 F4
Dutton Gn. Leeds LS14 62 A8
Dutton Way. Leeds LS14 62 A7
Duxbury Rise. Leeds LS7 60 B2
Dyas Bldgs. Feath WF7 144 E5
Dye House La. Sow Br HX6 112 E1
Dye House La. Wils BD15 53 B5
Dyehouse La. Brig HD6 115 B1
Dyehouse La. Pudsey LS28 76 A6
Dyehouse Rd. Brad BD12 95 A5
Dyer La. Hali HX3 91 F2
Dyer St. Leeds LS2 79 D8
Dyers Ct. Leeds LS6 59 F4
Dyke Bottom. Shep HD8 190 F8
Dyke Cl. Mir WF14 138 A8
Dyke End. Slai HD7 152 B3
Dyke La. Heb Br OL14 109 B7
Dymond Gr. Liver WF15 117 A3
Dymond Rd. Liver WF15 117 B3
Dymond View. Liver WF15 117 A3
Dyneley House. Brad BD15 73 B7 10
Dyson La. Holmfi HD7 189 C1
Dyson La. Rip HX6 132 C2
Dyson Pl. Hali HX3 113 E3
Dyson Rd. Hali HX1 112 F8
Dyson St. Brad BD1 74 D7
Dyson St. Brig HD6 115 A3
Dyson St. Hud HD5 154 E6
Dyson St. Ship BD9 55 A4
Dyson's Hill. Honley HD7 171 E5

Eagle Gr. Wake WF2 141 D6
Eagle St. Haw BD22 51 E8
Eagle St. Keigh BD21 35 B7
Eagle St. Tod OL14 108 B6
Eaglesfield Dr. Brad BD6 94 A6
Ealand Ave. Batley WF17 118 A7
Ealand Cres. Batley WF17 118 A7
Ealand Rd. Batley WF17 117 F7
Ealand Rd. Batley WF17 118 A7
Ealing Ct. Batley WF17 118 A6
Earl Cowper Mid Sch. Leeds 60 E4
Earl St. Dew WF12 140 B8
Earl St. Haw BD22 51 C6
Earl St. Hem WF9 163 A3
Earl St. Keigh BD21 35 B8
Earl St. Wake WF1 142 D7
Earl Terr. Hali HX3 92 A2 5
Earle St. Feath WF7 145 C6
Earles Ave. Hud HD5 154 E5
Earls View. S in Cra BD20 16 C4
Earlsheaton High Sch. Dew 139 E8
Earlsheaton Inf Sch. Dew 139 F7
Earlsmere Dr. Morley LS27 97 F5
Earlswood Ave. Leeds LS8 43 F2
Earlswood Chase. Pudsey LS28 76 E6
Earlswood Cres. Kippax LS25 83 A2
Earlswood Mead. Pudsey LS28 76 E6
Easby Ave. Batley WF17 117 F4
Easby Cl. Ilkley LS29 7 F4
Easby Dr. Ilkley LS29 7 F4
Easby Rd. Brad BD7 74 D5
Easdale Cl. Leeds LS14 61 F5
Easdale Cres. Leeds LS14 62 A5
Easdale Rd. Leeds LS14 61 F4
Easingwood Dr. Kirkhe HD5 137 B1
East Acres. Byram WF11 126 E7
East Ardsley Prim Sch. E Ard 120 D8
East Ave. Glu BD20 16 D6
East Ave. Hor WF4 141 C1
East Ave. Hud HD3 135 C1
East Ave. Keigh BD21 35 C8
East Ave. Pont WF8 146 B7
East Ave. S Elm WF9 183 B4
East Ave. Upton WF9 183 A7
East Bath St. Batley WF17 118 D5
East Beck Ct. Ask LS21 9 F5
East Bierley CE Fst Sch. Birk 95 F7
East Bolton. Hali HX2 91 E7
East Busk La. Otley LS21 23 C8
East Byland. Hali HX2 91 E6
East Causeway Cl. Hors LS16 42 D5
East Causeway Cr. Hors LS16 42 D4
East Causeway Vale. Hors LS16 42 E4
East Chevin Rd. Otley LS21 23 C5
East Cl. Hud HD2 136 B2
East Cl. Pont WF8 146 F5
East Cliffe. Hali HX3 113 E6
East Cswy. Hors LS16 42 D5
East Dale Cl. Hem WF9 181 F7
East Dene. Sil BD20 5 E2
East Down. Castle WF10 125 A8
East Dr. Gar LS25 83 B5
East Dr. Pont WF8 146 F7
East End Cres. Roy S71 179 E3
East Field St. Leeds LS9 79 E7
East Fold. Skel HD8 175 C1
East Garforth Jun & Inf Sch. Gar 83 B8
East Garforth Sta. Gar 83 A7
East Gr. Kirkhe HD5 155 C8
East Grange Cl. Midd LS10 79 E1
East Grange Dr. Midd LS10 79 E1
East Grange Garth. Midd LS10 79 E1
East Grange Rd. Midd LS10 79 E1
East Grange Rise. Midd LS10 79 E1
East Grange Sq. Midd LS10 79 E1
East Grange View. Midd LS10 79 E1
East Hardwick Cty Prim Sch. Dar 146 E2
East Keswick CE Jun & Inf Sch. E Kes 28 C5
East La. Leeds LS2 79 D8
East Lee La. Tod OL14 109 A7
East Leeds High Sch. Leeds 61 F4
East Moor Ave. Leeds LS8 43 F1
East Moor Community Home Sch. Hors 42 E4
East Moor Cres. Leeds LS8 43 F2
East Moor Dr. Leeds LS8 44 A1
East Moor Rd. Leeds LS8 43 F2
East Morton Fst Sch. Keigh 36 D8
East Mount. Brig HD6 115 A3 3
East Mount Pl. Brig HD6 115 A3 4
East Par. Bail BD17 38 D4
East Par. Brad BD1 74 F7 4
East Par. Hali HX6 112 D4
East Par. Ilkley LS29 8 C4
East Par. Keigh BD21 35 C7
East Par. Leeds LS1 79 B8
East Par. Men LS29 22 A4
East Par. Stee BD20 17 D5
East Park Dr. Leeds LS9 80 A7
East Park Gr. Leeds LS9 80 A7
East Park Mount. Leeds LS9 80 A7 7
East Park Par. Leeds LS9 80 A7
East Park Pl. Leeds LS9 80 A7
East Park Rd. Hali HX3 92 A1
East Park Rd. Leeds LS9 79 F7
East Park St. Leeds LS9 80 A7
East Park St. Morley LS27 97 F3
East Park Terr. Leeds LS9 80 A7 8
East Park View. Leeds LS9 80 A7
East Pinfold. Roy S71 179 C2
East Rd. Brad BD12 94 E6
East Royd. Haw BD22 34 D2
East Side Ct. Pudsey LS28 77 A5
East Squire La. Brad BD8 55 C1
East St. Batley WF17 118 C5
East St. Brig HD6 115 A1
East St. Brig HX3 115 A7
East St. Holmfi HD7 189 E3
East St. Hud HD3 135 B1
East St. Hud HD7 152 E4
East St. Leeds LS2, LS9 79 E7
East St. Loft G WF1 121 C2
East St. Loft G WF3 122 A2
East St. Ryhill WF4 162 D1
East St. S Elm WF9 183 B4
East St. S Hie S72 180 E5
East St. Sow Br HX6 111 E1
East Terr. Haw BD22 51 E8
East View. Brad BD13 73 C2
East View. Brig HX3 115 A7
East View. Castle WF10 124 A7
East View. Clec BD19 116 A6
East View Cotts. Pudsey LS28 76 F8 5
East View. Gild LS27 97 C5
East View. Glu BD20 16 D7
East View. Kippax LS25 83 B2
East View. Knot WF11 127 A4
East View. Leeds LS15 62 C2
East View. M'field LS25 84 B6
East View. Mir WF14 137 F5 6
East View. Ossett WF5 140 E3
East View. Pudsey LS28 76 E5
East View Rd. Yeadon LS19 40 C6
East View. Roth LS26 101 C5
East View. Sil BD20 5 E2
East View Terr. Brad BD12 94 E4
East View Terr. Otley LS21 23 B7
East View. Yeadon LS19 40 C6
East-Thorpe Pl. Mir WF14 138 B4
Eastborough Cres. Dew WF13 118 D1
Eastborough Jun & Inf Sch. Dew 139 D8
Eastbourne Ave. Feath WF7 145 E6
Eastbourne Cl. Pont WF8 147 A7
Eastbourne Cres. Pont WF8 147 A8
Eastbourne Dr. Pont WF8 147 A8
Eastbourne Rd. Ship BD9 55 B5
Eastbourne Terr. Pont WF8 147 A8
Eastbourne View. Pont WF8 147 A8
Eastbrook La. Brad BD1 74 F6 2
Eastbrook Well. Brad BD1 74 F7
Eastburn Jun & Inf Sch. Stee 16 F6
Eastbury Ave. Brad BD6 73 D1
Eastdean Bank. Leeds LS14 62 A6
Eastdean Dr. Leeds LS14 62 A6
Eastdean Gate. Leeds LS14 62 B5 7
Eastdean Gdns. Leeds LS14 62 B6
Eastdean Gr. Leeds LS14 62 B6
Eastdean Grange. Leeds LS14 62 B5 8
Eastdean Rd. Leeds LS14 62 A6
Eastdean Rise. Leeds LS14 62 B6
Easterly Ave. Leeds LS8 61 B4
Easterly Cl. Leeds LS8 61 B3
Easterly Cres. Leeds LS8 61 A4
Easterly Cross. Leeds LS8 61 B4
Easterly Garth. Leeds LS8 61 B4
Easterly Gr. Leeds LS8 61 A4
Easterly Mount. Leeds LS8 61 B4
Easterly Rd. Leeds LS8 61 C5
Easterly Sq. Leeds LS8 61 B4
Easterly View. Leeds LS8 61 B4
Eastfield Ave. Knot WF11 126 F3
Eastfield Cres. Roth LS26 101 B6
Eastfield Dr. Kirkb HD8 173 E7
Eastfield Dr. Pont WF8 125 F1
Eastfield Dr. Roth LS26 101 B6
Eastfield Gdns. Brad BD4 75 E3
Eastfield Gr. Nor WF6 123 C3
Eastfield La. Castle WF10 124 E8
Eastfield Pl. S in Cra BD20 16 D5
Eastfield Rd. Knot WF11 126 F3
Eastfield Rd. Mir WF14 138 D6
Eastfield. Shep HD8 190 F8
Eastgate. Bramho LS16 24 D3
Eastgate. Elland HX5 134 F7
Eastgate. Hem WF9 181 E6
Eastgate. Honley HD7 171 F5
Eastgate. Leeds LS2 79 D8
Easthorpe Ct. Brad BD2 56 D4
Eastland Wlk. Leeds LS13 58 E1 3
Eastlands. Hud HD5 155 A4
Eastleigh Ct. E Ard WF3 120 A8
Eastleigh Dr. E Ard WF3 120 A8
Eastleigh Gr. Brad BD5 74 C3
Eastmoor Gr. Roy S71 179 C2
Eastmoor Rd. Wake WF1 142 D8
Easton Pl. Hud HD3 153 B7
Eastville Rd. Crof WF4 144 B3
Eastway. Mir WF14 137 F7
Eastway Pk. Mir WF14 138 A7
Eastwood Ave. Hali HX2 91 E7
Eastwood Ave. Sow Br HX6 111 F3
Eastwood Ave. Wake WF2 141 E7
Eastwood Cl. Crig WF4 159 F7
Eastwood Cl. Hali HX2 91 E7
Eastwood Cres. Leeds LS14 62 D4
Eastwood Cres. Ship BD16 54 B8
Eastwood Ct. Hali HX3 113 A4 7
Eastwood Dr. Leeds LS14 62 D5
Eastwood Fst Sch. Keigh 35 D8

Eastwood Garth. Leeds LS14 62 D4
Eastwood Gdns. Leeds LS14 62 C4
Eastwood Gr. Gar LS25 83 A5
Eastwood Gr. Hali HX2 91 E7
Eastwood La. Leeds LS14 62 D4
Eastwood Nook. Leeds LS14 62 D4
Eastwood Rd. Tod OL14 87 D2
Eastwood St. Brad BD4 74 F5
Eastwood St. Brig HD6 115 B3 8
Eastwood St. Hali HX3 92 A2 7
Eastwood St. Hud HD5 154 D5 8
Easy Rd. Leeds LS9 79 F6
Eaton Hill. Hors LS16 41 F3
Eaton Mews. Midd LS10 99 C5
Eaton Pl. Hem WF9 181 E7
Eaton Rd. Ilkley LS29 8 A3
Eaton Sq. Midd LS10 99 C5
Eaton St. Keigh BD21 35 A4 1
Eaton Wlk. S Elm WF9 183 A5
Eaves Ave. Heb Br HX7 88 E4
Eaves Rd. Heb Br HX7 88 E4
Ebberston Gr. Leeds LS6 59 F3
Ebberston Pl. Leeds LS6 59 F3
Ebberston Terr. Leeds LS6 59 F3
Ebenezer Pl. Brad BD7 74 A4
Ebenezer St. Brad BD1 74 F6
Ebenezer St. Leeds LS2 79 C8 7
Ebenezer St. Pudsey LS28 57 D3 6
Ebenezer St. Roth WF3 100 B3
Ebor Gardens Cty Prim Sch. Leeds 79 F8
Ebor Gdns. Mir WF14 137 F5
Ebor La. Haw BD22 51 D8
Ebor Mount. Kippax LS25 83 A2
Ebor Mount. Leeds LS6 59 F2
Ebor Pl. Leeds LS6 59 F2
Ebor St. Leeds LS6 59 F2
Ebor Terr. Leeds LS10 79 E2
Ebridge Ct. Bing BD16 37 A3 17
Ebson House La. Holmfi HD7 190 B6
Ebury Cl. Batley WF17 118 D6
Ebury St. Batley WF17 118 D6
Eccles Ct. Brad BD2 56 B4
Eccles Parlour. Rip HX6 132 A7
Ecclesburn Ave. Leeds LS9 80 A7
Ecclesburn Rd. Leeds LS9 80 A7
Ecclesburn St. Leeds LS9 80 A7
Ecclesburn Terr. Leeds LS9 80 A7 13
Eccleshill North Mid Sch. Brad 56 D6
Eccleshill Sch & F Ed Ctr. Brad 56 E5
Eccup La. Eccup LS16 25 F2
Eccup La. Hare LS16 26 A5
Eccup Moor Rd. Eccup LS16 42 E8
Echo St. Liver WF15 116 F2
Edale Ave. Hud HD4 153 F1
Edale Cl. Kirkhe HD5 137 B1
Edale Gr. Queen BD13 92 C8
Edale Way. Hors LS16 41 F3
Eddercliff Cres. Liver WF15 117 A6
Edderthorpe St. Brad BD3 75 A6
Eddison Cl. Hors LS16 42 D5
Eddison St. Pudsey LS28 57 D2
Eddison Wlk. Hors LS16 42 D5
Eddystone Rise. Knot WF11 126 D3
Edelshain Gr. Wake WF2 160 F8
Eden Ave. Ossett WF5 140 D6
Eden Ave. Wake WF2 141 D5
Eden Cl. Brad BD12 94 D3
Eden Cres. Leeds LS4 59 B4
Eden Dr. Leeds LS4 59 C4
Eden Gdns. Leeds LS4 59 B3
Eden Gr. Leeds LS4 59 B3
Eden Mount. Leeds LS4 59 B3
Eden Rd. Leeds LS4 59 B4
Eden Way. Leeds LS4 59 B3
Eden Wlk. Leeds LS4 59 B3
Edendale. Castle WF10 124 F8
Edensor Rd. Keigh BD21 35 A7
Ederoyd Ave. Pudsey LS28 57 B1
Ederoyd Cres. Pudsey LS28 57 B1
Ederoyd Dr. Pudsey LS28 57 B1
Ederoyd Gr. Pudsey LS28 57 B1
Ederoyd Mount. Pudsey LS28 57 B1
Ederoyd Rise. Pudsey LS28 57 A1
Edgar St. Brad BD14 73 D3
Edgbaston Cl. Leeds LS17 43 A6
Edgbaston Wlk. Leeds LS17 43 A6
Edge Ave. Dew WF12 139 D1
Edge Cl. Dew WF12 139 E1
Edge Cl. Hud HD7 152 E4
Edge End. Denh BD13 52 E1
Edge End Gdns. Brad BD6 93 E7 1
Edge End La. Holmfi HD7 188 A4
Edge End Rd. Brad BD6 93 E7
Edge Hill Cl. Hud HD5 154 D7
Edge Junc. Dew WF12 139 D1
Edge La. Dew WF12 139 E1
Edge La. Hep HX7 87 F7
Edge Rd. Dew WF12 139 F1
Edge Terr. Hud HD3 152 F7
Edge Top Rd. Dew WF12 139 C2
Edge View. Dew WF12 139 E1
Edge View. Hud HD7 152 E4
Edgebank Ave. Brad BD6 93 F6
Edgehey Gn. Hep HX7 88 B6
Edgehill Cl. Queen BD13 72 F1 6
Edgehill Rd. Mapp S75 178 B2
Edgeholme La. Hali HX2 112 B7
Edgemoor Cl. Hali HX3 113 B4
Edgemoor Rd. Crig WF4 159 F2
Edgemoor Rd. Honley HD7 171 E3
Edgerton Gn. Hud HD1 153 E7
Edgerton Grove Rd. Hud HD1 153 E7
Edgerton La. Hud HD1 153 E7
Edgerton Rd. Hud HD1 153 E8
Edgerton Rd. Leeds LS16 59 B8
Edgeware Rd. Hud HD5 155 A6
Edgware Ave. Leeds LS8 60 F2 7
Edgware Gr. Leeds LS8 60 F2 3
Edgware Mount. Leeds LS8 60 F2 1
Edgware Pl. Leeds LS8 60 F2 2
Edgware Row. Leeds LS8 60 F2 6
Edgware St. Leeds LS8 60 E2 6
Edgware Terr. Leeds LS8 60 F2 5
Edgware View. Leeds LS8 60 F2 4
Edinburgh Ave. Leeds LS12 78 A8 7
Edinburgh Gr. Leeds LS12 78 A8
Edinburgh Pl. Gar LS25 83 B7
Edinburgh Pl. Leeds LS12 78 A8 6
Edinburgh Rd. Leeds LS12 78 A8
Edinburgh Terr. Leeds LS12 78 A8 5
Edlington Cl. Brad BD4 75 E3
Edmonton Pl. Leeds LS7 60 D6
Edmund Campion R C Sch. Brad 73 D8
Edmund St. Brad BD5 74 D6
Edmund St. Tod OL14 129 A8
Edna St. S Elm WF9 183 A3
Edrich Cl. Brad BD12 94 E6
Edroyd Pl. Pudsey LS28 57 D3
Edroyd St. Pudsey LS28 57 D3
Education Rd. Leeds LS7 60 C3
Edward Cl. Dew WF12 139 B3
Edward Cl. Hali HX3 114 A4
Edward Dr. Loft G WF1 121 C5
Edward Rd. Mir WF14 137 F5
Edward St. Bacup OL13 106 A3
Edward St. Brad BD4 74 F6
Edward St. Brad BD4 75 E1
Edward St. Brig HD6 115 A3
Edward St. Brig HD6 115 C2
Edward St. Hali HX6 112 B4
Edward St. Heb Br HX7 89 A3
Edward St. Leeds LS2 79 C8
Edward St. Liver WF15 117 A4
Edward St. Liver WF15 117 A5
Edward St. Nor WF6 123 A5
Edward St. Ship BD18 37 F1
Edward St. Wake WF1 142 D7
Edward Turner Cl. Brad BD12 94 C6 1
Edwards Rd. Hali HX2 112 E5
Edwin Rd. Leeds LS6 59 F2
Eel Holme View St. Keigh BD20 18 B2
Eel Mires Garth. Weth LS22 13 F6
Effingham Rd. Harden BD16 36 A1
Egerton Gr. Brad BD15 54 A1
Egerton St. Hali HX6 112 B4 7
Egerton Terr. Yeadon LS19 40 D3
Eggleston Dr. Brad BD4 75 F2
Eggleston St. Pudsey LS13 57 F5
Egglestone Sq. B Spa LS23 30 C7
Egham Gn. Brad BD10 56 B7
Egmanton Rd. Barn S71 178 F1
Egremont Cres. Brad BD6 93 F6
Egremont St. Sow Br HX6 112 A3
Egremont Terr. Sow Br HX6 112 A3
Egypt Rd. Wils BD13 72 C8
Eiffel Bldgs. Heb Br HX7 89 A3
Eiffel St. Heb Br HX7 89 A3
Eighth Ave. Clec WF15 116 B5
Eighth Ave. Leeds LS12 78 E6
Eighth Ave. Roth LS26 101 A7
Eightlands Ave. Leeds LS13 58 D2
Eightlands La. Leeds LS13 58 D2
Eightlands Rd. Dew WF13 139 C8
Elam Wood Rd. Keigh BD20 18 C3
Eland House. Elland HX5 134 F7 8
Elba Terr. Ossett WF4 141 B3
Elbow La. Brad BD2 56 B2
Elbow La. Hali HX2 90 E1
Elder Ave. Upton WF9 183 C8
Elder Ave. Wake WF2 142 A7
Elder Bank. Cull BD13 52 D6
Elder Cl. Batley WF17 96 F2
Elder Croft. Leeds LS13 58 C1
Elder Dr. Dew WF12 139 D3
Elder Dr. Upton WF9 183 C8
Elder Garth. Gar LS25 83 B6
Elder Gn. Wake WF2 142 A7
Elder Gr. Hud HD4 171 D6
Elder Gr. Wake WF2 142 A7
Elder Grove Mews. Hud HD4 171 D6
Elder La. Hud HD2 137 A5
Elder Mount. Leeds LS13 58 C1 1
Elder Pl. Leeds LS13 58 C1 2
Elder Rd. Leeds LS13 58 C1
Elder St. Brad BD10 56 E7
Elder St. Keigh BD20 18 A2
Elder St. Leeds LS13 58 C1 3
Eldon Pl. Brad BD1 74 D8
Eldon Pl. Clec BD19 116 E7
Eldon Rd. Hud HD1 153 D7
Eldon St. Batley WF16 117 D4
Eldon St. Hali HX3 113 C8
Eldon St. Ossett WF5 140 F7
Eldon St. Tod OL14 108 C5
Eldon Terr. Brad BD1 74 D8
Eldroth Mount. Hali HX1 113 A5 20
Eldroth Rd. Hali HX1 113 A5
Eldwick Fst Sch. Bing 37 C5
Eleanor Dr. Pudsey LS28 56 F7
Eleanor St. Brig HD6 115 A1
Eleanor St. Hud HD1 154 A8 2
Eleventh Ave. Clec WF15 116 C5
Elford Gr. Leeds LS8 60 F3
Elford Pl E. Leeds LS8 60 F3
Elford Pl W. Leeds LS8 60 F3
Elford Rd. Leeds LS8 60 F3
Elgar Wlk. Loft G WF3 121 E6
Elgin Cl. Hud HD4 153 C2
Eli St. Brad BD5 74 F3
Elia St. Keigh BD21 35 D8
Elim Wlk. Dew WF13 139 C8 4
Eliot Gr. Guise LS20 39 F8
Elizabeth Ave. Brad BD12 94 D4
Elizabeth Ave. S Hie S72 180 E5
Elizabeth Cl. Brad BD12 94 D4
Elizabeth Cres. Brad BD12 94 D4
Elizabeth Ct. Castle WF10 125 C8
Elizabeth Ct. Coll LS22 29 A8
Elizabeth Ct. Hem WF9 181 F6
Elizabeth Dr. Brad BD12 94 D4
Elizabeth Dr. Castle WF10 125 D8
Elizabeth Dr. Knot WF11 126 C4
Elizabeth Gdns. Wake WF1 142 C8
Elizabeth Gr. Morley LS27 98 C5
Elizabeth House. Hali HX2 91 E3
Elizabeth St. Bing BD16 37 A3 15
Elizabeth St. Brad BD5 74 E5
Elizabeth St. Brad BD12 94 D4
Elizabeth St. Elland HX4 134 D7 1
Elizabeth St. Elland HX5 134 F6
Elizabeth St. Haw BD22 34 D3
Elizabeth St. Hud HD4 154 A3
Elizabeth St. Leeds LS6 59 E3
Elizabeth St. Liver FW15 116 E4
Elizabeth St. Wake WF1 142 E2
Elizabethan Ct. Pont WF8 125 E2
Ella St. Hem WF9 163 A4
Elland Bridge. Elland HX5 134 F7
Elland CE Sch. Elland 134 F7
Elland Golf Course. Elland 134 C5
Elland Independent Hospl. Elland 135 A7
Elland Inf Sch. Elland 134 E5
Elland La. Elland HX5 135 A7
Elland La. Elland HX5 135 B7
Elland Rd. Brig HD6, HX5 114 E2
Elland Rd. Hali HD6, HX5 114 E2
Elland Rd. Leeds LS11 78 E3
Elland Rd. Morley LS11 78 E3
Elland Rd. Morley LS27 98 C8
Elland Rd. Rip HX6 132 E4
Elland Road Ind Est. Leeds 78 D3
Elland Road Stadium. Leeds 78 E3
Elland St. Castle WF10 103 E1
Elland Way. Leeds LS11 78 D3
Elland Wood Bottom. Hali HX3, HX5 113 D1
Elland-Riorges' Link. Elland HX5 135 A7
Ellar Carr Rd. Brad BD10 39 C1
Ellar Carr Rd. Cull BD13 52 C7
Ellen Holme Cotts. Hali HX2 111 D5
Ellen Royd La. Hali HX2 111 C8
Ellen Royd St. Hali HX3 113 C8
Ellen St. Bing BD16 37 A3 13
Ellenthorpe Rd. Bail BD17 37 E2
Ellerby La. Leeds LS9 79 E6
Ellerby Rd. Leeds LS9 79 E7
Ellercroft Ave. Brad BD7 74 A6
Ellercroft Rd. Brad BD7 74 A6
Ellercroft Terr. Brad BD7 74 A6
Ellerker La. Thorner LS14 46 B5
Ellerker Rd. Thorner LS14 46 A6
Ellers Gr. Leeds LS8 60 F4
Ellers Rd. Leeds LS8 60 F4
Ellers Rd. S in Cra BD20 16 D4
Ellerton St. Brad BD3 75 C7
Ellicott Ct. Men LS29 22 A4
Ellin's Terr. Nor WF6 144 A8
Ellinthorpe St. Brad BD4 75 B5
Elliot Ct. Queen BD13 72 D1 11
Elliott St. Ship BD18 55 A8
Elliott St. Sil BD20 5 D1
Ellis Fold. Leeds LS12 78 B7
Ellis La. B in Elm LS25 63 E3
Ellis Pl. Leeds LS11 79 B3 7
Ellis St. Brad BD5 74 D3
Ellison St. Hali HX3 92 A1 7
Ellison St. Hud HD4 153 D4
Elliston Ave. Mapp S75 178 C1
Ellistones Gdns. Elland HX4 134 A7
Ellistones La. Elland HX4 134 A6
Ellistones Pl. Elland HX4 134 A6
Ellmont Ave. Emley HD8 175 D7
Ellton Gr. Brad BD6 74 A1 4
Elm Ave. Hali HX6 112 B5
Elm Ave. Holmfi HD7 189 C8
Elm Ave. Kippax LS25 82 F3
Elm Ave. Loft G WF3 121 F4
Elm Ave. Tod OL14 108 B6
Elm Cl. Dar WF8 147 C5
Elm Cl. Ossett WF5 140 E3
Elm Cres. Keigh BD20 36 D8
Elm Croft. Leeds LS14 62 C8
Elm Ct. Birk BD11 96 B4
Elm Ct. Kirkb HD8 173 F7
Elm Gdns. Castle WF10 125 D5
Elm Gr. Bur in W LS29 21 F8
Elm Gr. Clec BD19 117 A8
Elm Gr. Keigh BD21 35 B4
Elm Gr. Keigh BD20 36 D8
Elm Gr. Liver WF16 117 C5
Elm Gr. S Elm WF9 182 F3
Elm Gr. Shelf HX3 93 D6
Elm Gr. Ship BD18 55 E7
Elm Gr. Sil BD20 5 D1
Elm Pk. Pont WF8 146 C6
Elm Pl. Hali HX6 112 B5 11
Elm Pl. Knot WF11 126 E3
Elm Rd. Dew WF13 138 F8
Elm Rd. Hem WF9 181 E7
Elm Rd. Nor WF6 144 B7
Elm Rd. S in Cra BD20 16 C5
Elm Rd. Ship BD18 55 D7
Elm St. Bacup OL13 106 A3
Elm St. Crof WF4 162 B7
Elm St. Elland HX4 134 A4
Elm St. Hud HD4 154 B4
Elm St. Leeds LS6 60 B4
Elm St. Oxen BD22 51 C3
Elm St. Skel HD8 175 A2
Elm Terr. Brig HD6 115 B5
Elm Terr. Otley LS21 23 C8
Elm Terr. Pont WF8 146 C8 4
Elm Tree Ave. Brad BD6 94 C8
Elm Tree Cl. Batley WF15 117 C2
Elm Tree Cl. Brad BD6 94 D8
Elm Tree Cl. Keigh BD21 35 D6
Elm Tree Gdns. Brad BD6 94 C8
Elm Tree St. Wake WF1 142 F4
Elm View. Hali HX3 113 C4 3
Elm View. Stee BD20 17 B6
Elm Way. Batley WF17 97 A2
Elm Wood St. Brig HD6 115 B4
Elmet Dr. B in Elm LS15 63 E7
Elmet Rd. B in Elm LS15 63 E6
Elmet Towers. Leeds LS14 62 C4
Elmete Ave. B in Elm LS15 62 F6
Elmete Ave. Leeds LS8 61 C7
Elmete Cl. Leeds LS8 61 D6
Elmete Croft. B in Elm LS15 62 F6
Elmete Ct. Leeds LS8 61 C6
Elmete Dr. Leeds LS8 61 D6
Elmete Gr. Leeds LS8 61 C7
Elmete Grange. Men LS29 22 A4
Elmete Hill. Leeds LS8 61 D6
Elmete La. Leeds LS8 44 E2
Elmete Mount. Leeds LS8 61 D6
Elmete Rd. Castle WF10 104 D1
Elmete Way. Leeds LS8 61 D6
Elmete Wlk. Leeds LS8 61 D6
Elmete Wood Sch. Leeds 61 D8
Elmfield Ave. Hud HD3 152 F5
Elmfield. Bail BD17 38 D3
Elmfield Bsns Pk. Gar 83 A8
Elmfield Ct. Morley LS27 98 B3
Elmfield Dr. Brad BD6 94 D8
Elmfield Dr. Skel HD8 175 A1
Elmfield Gr. Leeds LS12 78 D6
Elmfield Pl. Leeds LS12 78 D6
Elmfield Rd. Glu BD20 16 E7
Elmfield Rd. Hud HD2 135 E1
Elmfield Rd. Leeds LS12 78 D6 3
Elmfield Rd. Morley LS27 98 B2
Elmfield Terr. Hali HX1 113 B5
Elmfield Terr. Hud HD5 154 D5 3
Elmfield Way. Leeds LS13 58 D1
Elmhurst Cl. Leeds LS17 44 B4
Elmhurst Gdns. Leeds LS17 44 A4
Elmhurst Gr. Knot WF11 126 F3
Elmore Terr. Glu BD20 16 E7
Elmroyd. Roth LS26 100 F4
Elms Hill. Slai HD7 169 F8
Elms The. Guise LS20 22 E1
Elms View. Slai HD7 169 F8
Elmsall La. H Pag DN6 195 C7
Elmsall St. Brad BD1 74 D8
Elmsall Way. S Elm WF9 183 B5
Elmsdale Cl. S Elm WF9 183 B2
Elmsley St. Stee BD20 17 C5
Elmton Cl. Midd LS10 99 D7
Elmtree La. Leeds LS10 79 D4
Elmwood Ave. B in Elm LS15 63 D7
Elmwood Ave. Hud HD1 154 A7 4
Elmwood Ave. Walton WF2 161 B7
Elmwood Chase. B in Elm LS15 63 D7
Elmwood Cl. Hud HD1 154 A7 5
Elmwood Cl. Mir WF14 137 F1
Elmwood Cl. Walton WF2 161 B7
Elmwood Dr. Brig HD6 114 F3
Elmwood Dr. Keigh BD22 35 A4
Elmwood Dr. Walton WF2 161 B7
Elmwood Garth. Walton WF2 161 B7
Elmwood Gr. Batley WF17 118 D3
Elmwood Gr. Hor WF4 141 C1
Elmwood La. B in Elm LS15 63 D7
Elmwood La. Leeds LS7 60 C1
Elmwood Rd. Keigh BD22 34 F4
Elmwood Rd. Leeds LS2 60 C1
Elmwood St. Hali HX1 113 A5
Elmwood Terr. Dew WF13 118 C1
Elmwood Terr. Keigh BD22 34 F4
Elphaborough Cl. Heb Br HX7 110 E8
Elphin Ct. Heb Br HX7 110 D8
Elsdon Gr. Brad BD5 74 E5
Elsham Terr. Leeds LS4 59 C2
Elsicker La. Crof WF1 143 F6
Elsie St. Keigh BD20 18 B2
Elsinore Ave. Elland HX5 134 F5
Elsinore Ct. Elland HX5 134 E6
Elstone View. Loft G WF1 121 A4
Elswick House. Brad BD15 73 A7 7
Elsworth Ave. Brad BD3 56 D1
Elsworth St. Leeds LS12 78 D7
Elsworth Terr. Leeds LS12 78 D7 4
Eltham Cl. Leeds LS6 60 B3
Eltham Ct. Leeds LS6 60 B3 4
Eltham Dr. Leeds LS6 60 B3
Eltham Gdns. Leeds LS6 60 B3
Eltham Gr. Brad BD6 94 A8
Eltham Rise. Leeds LS6 60 B3
Elvaston Rd. Morley LS27 98 A3
Elvey Cl. Brad BD2 56 D4
Elvey St. Wake WF1 142 C7
Elwell Cl. Shelf HX3 93 D7
Elwell St. E Ard WF3 99 E1
Elwyn Gr. Brad BD5 74 E3
Elwyn Rd. Brad BD5 74 F3
Ely St. Elland HX4 134 D6
Ely St. Leeds LS12 78 C8
Embankment The. Leeds LS1 79 C7
Emblem Terr. Wake WF1 142 D3
Embleton Rd. M'town LS26 123 C8
Embsay Steam Rly. Hal E 1 C7
Emerald St. Batley WF17 118 B6
Emerald St. Hud HD1 154 B8
Emerald St. Keigh BD22 35 A4 11
Emerson Ave. Brad BD9 54 D3
Emily St. Keigh BD21 35 D8
Emley Fst Sch. Emley 175 D7
Emley Moor Bsns Pk. Emley 175 B6
Emm La. Brad BD9 55 B3
Emmanuel Terr. Hud HD4 153 F2
Emmanuel Trad Est. Leeds 78 F6
Emmeline Cl. Brad BD10 56 B8
Emmet Cl. Birk BD11 96 B5
Emmfield Dr. Ship BD9 55 A4
Emmott Dr. Yeadon LS19 40 E3
Emmott Farm Fold. Haw BD22 51 C6 2
Empsall Row. Brig HD6 115 B3 4
Emscote Ave. Hali HX1 113 A5
Emscote Gdns. Hali HX1 113 A5 18
Emscote Gr. Hali HX1 113 A5
Emscote Pl. Hali HX1 113 A5
Emscote St S. Hali HX1 113 A5
Emsley Cl. Brad BD4 95 B8
Emsley Pl. Leeds LS10 79 E5
Emville Ave. Leeds LS17 44 C5
Enderley Rd. Thorn BD13 72 D6 8
Endor Cres. Bur in W LS29 21 F7
Endor Gr. Bur in W LS29 21 F7
Endsleigh Pl. Brad BD14 73 B4 5
Enfield Ave. Leeds LS7 60 E2
Enfield Cl. Batley WF17 117 F6
Enfield Dr. Batley WF17 117 F6
Enfield Dr. Brad BD6 74 A1
Enfield Par. Brad BD6 74 A1
Enfield Rd. Bail BD17 38 C2
Enfield Side Rd. Haw BD22 50 E5
Enfield St. Keigh BD21 35 B7
Enfield St. Leeds LS7 60 D2
Enfield Terr. Leeds LS7 60 E2
Enfield Wlk. Brad BD6 74 A1
Enfield. Yeadon LS19 40 B6
Engine La. Hor WF4 140 F1
Engine La. Shaf S72 180 D1
Engine La. W Har WF4 163 A7
Englefield Cres. Brad BD4 75 E2
Ennerdale Ave. Batley WF12 118 E2
Ennerdale Cl. Weth LS22 13 C6
Ennerdale Cres. Batley WF12 118 E2
Ennerdale Dr. Brad BD2 56 B3
Ennerdale Dr. Knot WF11 126 E2
Ennerdale Rd. Batley WF12 118 E2
Ennerdale Rd. Brad BD2 56 B3
Ennerdale Rd. Gild LS12 77 D2
Ennerdale Rd. Wake WF2 141 F7
Ennerdale Way. Gild LS12 77 D3
Enoch La. Hud HD4 153 F3
Enterprise Park Ind Est. Leeds 78 F1
Enterprise Way. Brad BD10 56 B6
Enterprise Way. Castle WF10 124 C8
Enterprise Way. Midd LS10 79 F1
Envoy St. Leeds LS11 79 C4
Epsom Rd. Kippax LS25 82 F2
Epsom Way. Kirkhe HD5 137 C1
Epworth Pl. Leeds LS10 79 E4
Eric St. Keigh BD21 35 C8
Eric St. Leeds LS13 58 C5
Eric St. S Elm WF9 183 A3
Ernest St. Dew WF13 139 D8 8
Ernest St. Tod OL14 86 C1
Erringden Rd. Heb Br HX7 89 D1
Erringden St. Tod OL14 108 C5 12
Escroft Cl. Brad BD12 94 D1
Eshald La. Roth LS26 101 D6
Eshald Mansions. Roth LS26 101 D6 4
Eshald Pl. Roth LS26 101 D6
Esholt Ave. Guise LS20 39 D7
Esholt La. Bail BD17 38 F4
Esholt La. Guise BD17 39 A4
Eshton Ave. Brad BD12 94 F5
Eshton Ct. Mapp S75 178 A2
Esk Ave. Castle WF10 125 B8
Esk Gdns. Weth LS22 13 E8
Eskdale Ave. Nor WF6 123 A4
Eskdale Ave. Shelf HX3 93 B5
Eskdale Cl. Batley WF12 118 E3
Eskdale Cl. Guise LS20 39 E8
Eskdale Cl. Nor WF6 123 A4
Eskdale Croft. Guise LS20 39 E8
Eskdale Croft. Nor WF6 123 A4
Eskdale Ct. Nor WF6 123 A4
Eskdale Gr. Gar LS25 83 A5
Eskdale Mount. Heb Br HX7 89 A4
Eskdale Mount. Leeds LS14 61 F4
Eskdale Rd. Wake WF2 141 E7
Eskdale Rise. Brad BD15 73 C8
Eskine Par. Brad BD6 93 F6
Esmond St. Brad BD7 73 F3
Esmond St. Leeds LS12 78 C7 14
Esmond Terr. Leeds LS12 78 C7
Essex Park Ind Est. Brad 75 A6
Essex St. Brad BD4 75 A5
Essex St. Hali HX1 112 F6
Essex St. Heb Br HX7 89 A2 1
Estcourt Ave. Leeds LS6 59 C4
Estcourt Dr. Dar WF8 147 D4
Estcourt Gr. Brad BD7 74 A5
Estcourt Rd. Brad BD7 74 A5
Estcourt Rd. Dar WF8 147 C5
Estcourt Terr. Leeds LS6 59 C4
Esther Ave. Wake WF2 141 F4
Esther Gr. Wake WF2 141 F5
Esthwaite Gdns. Leeds LS15 80 E6
Ethel St. Keigh BD20 18 B1
Ethel St. S in Cra BD20 16 D4
Etna St. Brad BD7 73 F3
Eton Ave. Hud HD5 154 F6
Eton St. Hali HX1 112 F7
Eton St. Heb Br HX7 88 F3
Euden Edge Rd. Slai HD7 152 A3
Eunice La. D Dale HD8 191 C6
Euroway Trad Est. Brad 95 A7
Euston Gr. Leeds LS11 78 F4
Euston Mount. Leeds LS11 78 F4
Euston Terr. Leeds LS11 78 F4
Evanston Ave. Leeds LS4 59 C1
Evelyn Ave. Brad BD3 75 E8
Evelyn Pl. Leeds LS12 78 C6
Evens Terr. Brad BD5 74 E2
Everard St. Hud HD4 153 D4
Everdale Mount. Hem WF9 181 C6
Everdale Mount. S Elm WF9 182 E3
Everest Ave. Ship BD18 55 E7
Everleigh St. Leeds LS9 80 A7
Eversley Dr. Brad BD4 75 E4
Eversley Pl. Hali HX2 112 E6
Eversley Rd. Heb Br HX7 89 A4
Every St. Tod OL14 108 C5 9
Evesham Gr. Brad BD10 56 B7
Ewart Pl. Brad BD7 74 A3
Ewart St. Brad BD7 74 A3
Ewart St. Queen BD13 72 E1
Ewood Dr. Heb Br HX7 90 A1
Ewood Hall Ave. Heb Br HX7 89 F1
Ewood La. Tod OL14 107 F6
Exchange Bldgs. Glu BD20 16 D7
Exchange. Honley HD7 171 F5
Exchange St. Clec BD19 95 D1
Exchange St. Elland HX4 134 D6 3
Exchange St. Nor WF6 123 A2
Exchange St. S Elm WF9 182 F3
Exe St. Brad BD5 74 C3
Exeter Dr. Midd LS10 99 E7
Exeter St. Hali HX6 112 C4
Exeter St. Hali HX3 113 D3
Exhibition Rd. Ship BD18 54 F8 7
Exley Ave. Keigh BD21 35 A4
Exley Bank. Hali HX3 113 D2
Exley Bank Top. Hali HX3 113 D1
Exley Cres. Keigh BD21 35 A5
Exley Dr. Keigh BD21 35 A5
Exley Gdns. Hali HX3 113 D2
Exley Gr. Keigh BD21 35 A5
Exley Head View. Keigh BD22 34 E8
Exley La. Elland HX5 134 E8
Exley La. Hali HX5 113 E1
Exley Mount. Brad BD7 73 F6
Exley Mount. Keigh BD21 35 A5
Exley Rd. Keigh BD21 35 A5
Exley Sec Sch. Hali 113 E2
Exley St. Keigh BD22 35 A6 11
Exley Way. Keigh BD21 35 A4
Exmoor St. Hali HX1 112 F6
Exmouth Pl. Brad BD3 55 F1
Express Way. Castle WF10 123 D5
Exton Pl. Leeds LS15 80 E7
Eyre St. Batley WF17 118 D4
Eyre St. Dew WF12 139 B4
Eyres Ave. Leeds LS12 78 C8
Eyres Gr. Leeds LS12 78 C8
Eyres Mill Side. Leeds LS12 78 B8
Eyres St. Leeds LS12 78 C8
Eyres Terr. Leeds LS12 78 C8
Eyrie App. Morley LS27 98 C3

Factory La. Brad BD4 75 B2
Factory La. Hud HD3 153 B4
Factory St. Brad BD4 75 C2
Fagley Cres. Brad BD2 56 C2
Fagley Croft. Brad BD2 56 D2
Fagley Dr. Brad BD2 56 C2
Fagley Fst Sch. Brad 56 D2
Fagley La. Brad BD2 56 D3
Fagley Pl. Brad BD2 56 C1
Fagley Rd. Brad BD2 56 D2
Fagley Terr. Brad BD2 56 C1
Fair Bank. Ship BD18 55 C6
Fair Lea Rd. Hud HD4 153 E1
Fair Mount. Tod OL14 108 A1
Fair Rd. Brad BD6 74 B1
Fair St. Hud HD1 153 F4
Fair View Cres. Bacup OL13 106 B3
Fair View. Liver WF15 116 F5
Fair View. Pont WF8 146 E5
Fair Ways. Mir WF14 137 F2
Fairbank Rd. Brad BD8 55 A1
Fairbank Terr. Brad BD8 55 A1
Fairbourne House. Brad BD6 93 E8 8
Fairbrook Rd. Crig WF2 160 A4
Fairburn Dr. Gar LS25 83 B6
Fairburn Gdns. Brad BD2 56 C4
Fairburn Ings Nature Reserve. Ledsh 104 B4
Fairburn Prim Sch. Fair 105 A4
Fairclough Gr. Hali HX3 91 F3
Fairfax Ave. Birk BD11 97 A5
Fairfax Ave. Brad BD4 75 C1
Fairfax Ave. Feath WF7 124 C1
Fairfax Ave. Knot WF11 126 D3
Fairfax Ave. Men LS29 22 A5
Fairfax Cl. Leeds LS14 62 B3
Fairfax Community Sch. Brad 75 B3
Fairfax Cres. Brad BD4 75 C1
Fairfax Cres. Hali HX3 114 A5
Fairfax Gdns. Men LS29 22 A5
Fairfax Gr. Yeadon LS19 39 F7
Fairfax Rd. Bing BD16 36 F5
Fairfax Rd. Cull BD13 52 E7
Fairfax Rd. Leeds LS11 79 A3
Fairfax Rd. Men LS29 22 A5
Fairfax Rd. Pont WF8 146 E8
Fairfax St. Brad BD4 74 F5
Fairfax St. Haw BD22 51 D7
Fairfax St. Otley LS21 23 B7
Fairfax St. Sil BD20 5 D1
Fairfax View. Hors LS18 41 B4
Fairfield Ave. Batley WF16 117 E5
Fairfield Ave. Dew WF12 139 F8 3
Fairfield Ave. E Ard WF3 119 D7
Fairfield Ave. Leeds LS13 58 A2
Fairfield Ave. Nor WF6 122 E3
Fairfield Ave. Ossett WF5 140 F4
Fairfield Ave. Pont WF8 146 B8
Fairfield Ave. Pudsey LS28 76 F8 7
Fairfield Cl. Castle WF10 104 E1
Fairfield Cl. Leeds LS13 58 B2
Fairfield Cl. Ossett WF5 140 F4
Fairfield Cres. Dew WF13 118 A1 5
Fairfield Cres. Leeds LS13 58 B2
Fairfield Ct. Bail BD17 38 E4
Fairfield Ct. Castle WF10 125 A7
Fairfield Ct. Gar LS25 82 D7
Fairfield Ct. Liver WF15 116 F4
Fairfield. Denh BD13 71 D8
Fairfield Dr. Bail BD17 38 E4
Fairfield Dr. Batley WF16 117 E5
Fairfield Dr. Ossett WF5 140 F4
Fairfield. Fair WF11 105 A5
Fairfield Gdns. Ossett WF5 140 F5
Fairfield Gr. Leeds LS13 58 B2
Fairfield Hill. Leeds LS13 58 B2
Fairfield Mount. Leeds LS13 58 B2
Fairfield Mount. Ossett WF5 140 F4
Fairfield Par. Batley WF16 117 E5
Fairfield Rd. Batley WF16 117 E5
Fairfield Rd. Brad BD8 55 B1
Fairfield Rd. Brad BD12 94 D3
Fairfield Rd. Leeds LS13 58 A2
Fairfield Rd. Ossett WF5 140 F4
Fairfield Rise. Kirkb HD8 174 A5
Fairfield Sch. Batley 117 E5
Fairfield Sq. Leeds LS13 58 B2
Fairfield St. Brad BD4 75 D1
Fairfield St. Leeds LS13 58 B2
Fairfield Terr. Clec BD19 116 E7 9
Fairfield Terr. Dew WF12 139 F8
Fairfield Terr. Leeds LS13 58 B2
Fairfield Terr. Ossett WF5 140 E4
Fairfield Wlk. Ossett WF5 140 F4
Fairfields. Castle WF10 125 E7
Fairfields. D Dale HD8 191 F3
Fairfields Rd. Holmfi HD7 188 D3
Fairford Ave. Leeds LS11 79 C3
Fairford Terr. Leeds LS11 79 C3
Fairhaven Gn. Brad BD10 56 C7
Fairlea Ave. Hud HD4 153 E1
Fairlea Cotts. Hud HD4 153 E1
Fairleigh Cres. E Ard WF3 119 F8
Fairleigh Cres. E Ard WF3 120 A8
Fairleigh Rd. E Ard WF3 120 A8
Fairless Ave. Brig HX3 115 A7
Fairmoor Way. Batley WF16 117 E5
Fairmount. Brad BD9 55 C2
Fairmount Pk. Ship BD18 54 E7
Fairmount Terr. Dew WF12 139 E6
Fairmount Terr. Keigh BD21 35 F6
Fairview Ave. Batley WF17 117 F6
Fairview Cres. Batley WF17 118 A6
Fairview Ct. Bail BD17 38 B1
Fairview Rd. Batley WF17 118 A6
Fairview Terr. Hali HX3 92 B1
Fairway App. Nor WF6 123 C2
Fairway Ave. Brad BD7 73 F2
Fairway Ave. Mapp S75 178 C2
Fairway Ave. Nor WF6 123 C2
Fairway. Brad BD7 73 F1
Fairway Cl. Brad BD7 73 F1
Fairway Cl. Guise LS20 39 C8
Fairway Cl. Nor WF6 123 C1
Fairway Cres. Haw BD22 51 D6
Fairway Dr. Brad BD7 73 F2
Fairway Dr. Nor WF6 123 C1
Fairway Gr. Brad BD7 74 A2
Fairway. Guise LS20 22 C1
Fairway Ind Pk. Batley 96 F2
Fairway. Nor WF6 123 C1
Fairway. Ship BD18 54 F7
Fairway The. Feath WF7 124 D1
Fairway The. Hali HX2 91 F7
Fairway The. Hud HD2 136 A4
Fairway The. Leeds LS17 43 B6
Fairway The. Pudsey LS28 57 B1
Fairway Wlk. Brad BD7 73 F2
Fairway. Yeadon LS19 40 A2
Fairways The. Ship BD9 54 E5

Fairweather Green Mid Sch. Brad ... 73 E7
Fairweather Mews. Brad BD8 . 73 E7
Fairy Dell. Ship BD16 ... 54 B7
Fairy Hill La. Castle WF8 ... 125 D5
Faith St. S Kirk WF9 ... 182 D4
Falcon Cl. Otley LS21 ... 23 A7
Falcon Cliffe. Stee BD20 ... 17 D5
Falcon Dr. Castle WF10 ... 124 C6
Falcon Knowl Ing. Kex S75 ... 177 D1
Falcon Mews. Brad BD8 ... 73 C8
Falcon Mews. Morley LS27 ... 98 C3
Falcon Rd. Bing BD16 ... 36 F5
Falcon Rd. Dew WF12 ... 139 D6
Falcon St. Brad BD7 ... 74 B4
Falcon St. Hali HX3 ... 113 D3
Falcon St. Hud HD4 ... 153 F2
Falconer Cl. Kex S75 ... 177 D1
Falconers Ride. Hud HD4 ... 171 E7
Falhouse La. Dew WF4 ... 156 D7
Falkland Cres. Leeds LS17 ... 43 C1
Falkland Gdns. Leeds LS17 ... 43 D1
Falkland Gr. Leeds LS17 ... 43 C1
Falkland Mount. Leeds LS17 ... 43 C1
Falkland Rd. Brad BD10 ... 56 E4
Falkland Rd. Leeds LS17 ... 43 C1
Falkland Rise. Leeds LS17 ... 43 C1
Falklands Ct. Leeds LS17 ... 43 C1
Fall Ings Rd. Wake WF1 ... 142 E4
Fall La. Dew WF13 ... 139 B6
Fall La. E Ard WF3 ... 120 D8
Fall La. Hali HX6 ... 112 D4
Fall La. Liver WF15 ... 116 D1
Fall La. Mars HD7 ... 168 F3
Fall La. Northo HX3 ... 92 E4
Fall Rd. Mir WF14 ... 137 E8
Fall Spring Gdns. Elland HX4 . 133 F3
Fall Spring Gn. Elland HX4 ... 133 F3
Fall Wood St. Haw BD22 ... 51 D6
Falledge La. D Dale HD8 ... 191 E2
Fallow Croft. Hud HD2 ... 136 F5
Fallow La. Keigh BD22 ... 34 A6
Fallowfield Cl. Brad BD4 ... 95 C8
Fallowfield Dr. Brad BD4 ... 75 C1
Fallowfield Gdns. Brad BD4 ... 75 C1
Fallswood Gr. Leeds LS13 ... 58 D4
Falmouth Ave. Brad BD3 ... 55 F1
Falmouth Ave. Nor WF6 ... 123 B3
Falmouth Cres. Nor WF6 ... 123 B3
Falmouth Rd. Nor WF6 ... 123 B3
Falsgrave Ave. Brad BD2 ... 56 D2
Faltis Sq. Brad BD10 ... 56 C6
Fanny Moor Cres. Hud HD4 ... 154 C2
Fanny Moor La. Hud HD4 ... 154 C2
Fanny St. Keigh BD21 ... 35 B6
Fanny St. Ship BD18 ... 37 F1
Far Bank. Shep HD8 ... 174 B3
Far Common Rd. Mir WF14 ... 137 E8
Far Croft. Lepton HD8 ... 156 A2
Far Croft Terr. Leeds LS12 ... 78 D6 1
Far Dene. Kirkb HD8 ... 173 D8
Far End La. Honley HD7 ... 172 A4
Far Field Ave. Holmfi HD7 ... 189 E1
Far Field Dr. Holmfi HD7 ... 189 E1
Far Field La. Holmfi HD7 ... 189 E1
Far Field La. Mel HD7 ... 170 F5
Far Fields La. Mel HD7 ... 171 A5
Far La. Heb Br HX2 ... 90 A2
Far La. Holmfi HD7 ... 189 E1
Far Moss. Leeds LS17 ... 43 A5
Far Reef Cl. Hors LS18 ... 41 C2
Far Richard Cl. Ossett WF5 ... 140 D7
Far View Bank. Hud HD5 ... 154 E4
Far View Cres. Hud HD5 ... 154 E4
Far View. Hali HX2 ... 91 E6
Far Well Fold. Yeadon LS19 ... 40 D3
Far Well La. Holmfi HD7 ... 190 B8
Far Well Rd. Yeadon LS19 ... 40 D3
Faraday Sq. Hud HD3 ... 153 A4
Farcliffe Pl. Brad BD8 ... 55 B1
Farcliffe Rd. Brad BD8 ... 55 B1
Farcliffe Terr. Brad BD8 ... 55 B1
Fardene St. Sil BD20 ... 5 D2
Fardew Ct. Bing BD16 ... 36 F4
Fardew Golf Course. Keigh ... 36 C8
Farehill Flats. Hud HD4 ... 171 F8
Farehill Rd. Hud HD4 ... 171 F8
Farfield Ave. Batley WF17 ... 117 F6
Farfield Ave. Brad BD6 ... 93 E7
Farfield Ave. Pudsey LS28 ... 57 C3
Farfield Cty Inf Sch. Pudsey ... 57 C3
Farfield Cres. Brad BD6 ... 93 F7
Farfield Ct. Leeds LS17 ... 43 E5
Farfield Dr. Pudsey LS28 ... 57 C2
Farfield Gr. Brad BD6 ... 93 F7
Farfield Gr. Pudsey LS28 ... 57 C3
Farfield Rd. Bail BD17 ... 38 D2
Farfield Rd. Brad BD6 ... 94 A7
Farfield Rd. Hud HD5 ... 154 F3
Farfield Rd. Ship BD18 ... 55 A7
Farfield Rise. Pudsey LS28 ... 57 C3
Farfield St. Brad BD9 ... 55 A2
Farfield St. Clec BD19 ... 95 D1
Farfield Terr. Brad BD9 ... 55 A2
Farlea Dr. Brad BD2 ... 56 C3
Farleton Dr. Brad BD2 ... 56 D3
Farm Croft. Feath WF7 ... 144 E5
Farm Ct. Leeds LS15 ... 62 B2
Farm Gdns. Feath WF7 ... 144 E5
Farm Hill Cres. Leeds LS7 ... 60 A5
Farm Hill Ct. Brad BD10 ... 56 B5
Farm Hill N. Leeds LS7 ... 60 A6
Farm Hill Rd. Brad BD10 ... 56 B6
Farm Hill Rd. Morley LS27 ... 97 F5
Farm Hill Rise. Leeds LS7 ... 60 A5
Farm Hill S. Leeds LS7 ... 60 A5
Farm Hill Way. Leeds LS7 ... 60 A5
Farm La. Hem WF9 ... 163 A3
Farm Mount. Leeds LS15 ... 62 C2
Farm Pond Dr. Brig HD6 ... 114 E5
Farm Rd. Feath WF7 ... 145 D5
Farm Rd. Leeds LS15 ... 62 B2
Farmfield Dr. Hem WF9 ... 163 A3
Farmstead Rd. Brad BD10 ... 56 C6
Farnboro St. Tod OL14 ... 108 A2
Farndale App. Leeds LS14 ... 62 C5
Farndale Cl. Leeds LS14 ... 62 C5
Farndale Cl. Weth LS22 ... 13 B6
Farndale Ct. Gar LS25 ... 82 F5
Farndale Ct. Leeds LS14 ... 62 C5 3
Farndale Garth. Leeds LS14 ... 62 C6
Farndale Gdns. Leeds LS14 ... 62 C6 10
Farndale Pl. Leeds LS14 ... 62 C6
Farndale Rd. Bail BD17 ... 38 A2
Farndale Rd. Wils BD15 ... 53 C4
Farndale Sq. Leeds LS14 ... 62 C5 5
Farndale Terr. Leeds LS14 ... 62 C5 4
Farndale View. Leeds LS14 ... 62 C6 11
Farne Ave. Wake WF2 ... 141 F6
Farnham Cl. Bail BD17 ... 38 D4
Farnham Cl. Leeds LS14 ... 45 B1
Farnham Croft. Leeds LS14 ... 45 B1
Farnham Fst Sch. Brad ... 74 B5
Farnham Rd. Brad BD7 ... 74 B5
Farnham Way. Crof WF4 ... 143 F1
Farnlee. Hud HD3 ... 135 B1
Farnley CE Prim Sch. Farnley ... 11 D5
Farnley Cl. Men LS29 ... 22 B4
Farnley Cres. Haw BD22 ... 34 B3
Farnley Cres. Leeds LS12 ... 77 E6
Farnley Hey. Kirkb HD4 ... 172 C7
Farnley La. Farnley LS21 ... 11 B3
Farnley La. Otley LS21 ... 11 B3
Farnley Park High Sch. Leeds ... 77 E4
Farnley Pk. Farnley LS21 ... 11 E2
Farnley Rd. Kirkb HD4 ... 172 F5
Farnley Rd. Men LS29 ... 22 B4
Farnley Tyas CE Sch. Kirkb ... 172 E6
Farnley View. Birk BD11 ... 97 A6
Farr Royd. Bur in W LS29 ... 9 E2
Farr Royd Terr. Bur in W LS29 ... 9 E2
Farra St. Oxen BD22 ... 51 C2
Farrar Ave. Mir WF14 ... 137 F6
Farrar Cl. Hors LS16 ... 42 A4
Farrar Dr. Mir WF14 ... 137 F6
Farrar Height La. Rip HX6 ... 132 B4
Farrar La. Hors LS16 ... 42 A4
Farrar Mill La. Hali HX3 ... 113 D3
Farrer La. Roth LS26 ... 101 C5
Farriers Croft. Brad BD2 ... 55 F4
Farriers Pl. Castle WF10 ... 125 B6
Farringdon Cl. Brad BD4 ... 75 E4
Farringdon Dr. Brad BD4 ... 75 E4
Farringdon Gr. Brad BD6 ... 94 A7
Farrow Bank. Leeds LS12 ... 77 E7
Farrow Gn. Leeds LS12 ... 77 F7
Farrow Hill. Leeds LS12 ... 77 F7
Farrow Rd. Leeds LS12 ... 77 F7
Farrow Vale. Leeds LS12 ... 77 E7
Farside Gn. Brad BD5 ... 74 C3
Farsley Farfield Jun Sch. Pudsey ... 57 C2
Farsley Springbank Jun Sch. Pudsey ... 57 D3
Fartown Cl. Pudsey LS28 ... 76 E5
Fartown Green Rd. Hud HD2 . 136 B2
Fartown High Sch. Hud ... 136 C2
Fartown. Pudsey LS28 ... 76 E5
Farway. Brad BD4 ... 75 E4
Fascination Pl. Queen BD13 ... 72 C2 1
Faugh La. Hep HX7 ... 88 C6
Favell Ave. Nor WF6 ... 123 B1
Faversham Wlk. Brad BD4 ... 75 E4
Fawcett Ave. Leeds LS12 ... 78 B5
Fawcett Bank. Leeds LS12 ... 78 A5
Fawcett Cl. Leeds LS12 ... 78 A5
Fawcett Dr. Leeds LS12 ... 78 A5 1
Fawcett Gdns. Leeds LS12 ... 78 A5
Fawcett La. Leeds LS12 ... 78 B5
Fawcett Pl. Brad BD4 ... 95 C8
Fawcett Rd. Leeds LS12 ... 78 A5 2
Fawcett St. Wake WF2 ... 142 C4
Fawcett Vale. Leeds LS12 ... 78 A5
Fawcett Way. Leeds LS12 ... 78 A5
Fawkes Dr. Otley LS21 ... 22 D6
Faxfleet St. Brad BD5 ... 74 D2
Faye Gdns. Brad BD4 ... 75 D1
Fearnley Ave. Ossett WF5 ... 140 D7
Fearnley Cl. Leeds LS12 ... 78 D7
Fearnley Ct. Holmfi HD7 ... 189 D5
Fearnley Dr. Ossett WF5 ... 140 C7
Fearnley La. Holmfi HD7 ... 189 C6
Fearnley Pl. Leeds LS12 ... 78 D7
Fearnley St. Dew WF13 ... 139 B7
Fearnley St. Feath WF7 ... 145 C5
Fearnside's Cl. Hor WF4 ... 141 A1 10
Fearnsides St. Brad BD8 ... 74 B8
Fearnsides Terr. Brad BD8 ... 74 B8
Fearnville Ave. Leeds LS8 ... 61 D4
Fearnville Cl. Leeds LS8 ... 61 D5
Fearnville Dr. Brad BD4 ... 75 D5
Fearnville Dr. Leeds LS8 ... 61 D4
Fearnville Gr. Leeds LS8 ... 61 D4
Fearnville Gr. Roy S71 ... 179 C3
Fearnville Mount. Leeds LS8 ... 61 D4
Fearnville Pl. Leeds LS8 ... 61 E4
Fearnville Rd. Leeds LS8 ... 61 D4
Fearnville Sch. Leeds ... 61 D4
Fearnville Terr. Leeds LS8 ... 61 E4
Fearnville View. Leeds LS8 ... 61 D4
Feast Field. Hors LS18 ... 41 B1
Feather Bed La. Elland HX4 ... 134 D6 5
Feather Rd. Brad BD3 ... 75 B7
Feather St. Keigh BD21 ... 35 D6
Featherbank Ave. Hors LS18 ... 58 B7
Featherbank Gr. Hors LS18 ... 58 B8 5
Featherbank La. Hors LS18 ... 58 B7
Featherbank Mount. Hors LS18 58 B8 6
Featherbank Terr. Hors LS18 ... 58 B7 3
Featherbank Wlk. Hors LS18 ... 58 B7 1
Featherbed Cl. Elland HX4 ... 134 D6 4
Featherbed La. Bick LS24 ... 15 E6
Featherbed La. Wig LS24 ... 15 E6
Featherstone High Sch. Feath 145 F4
Featherstone La. Feath WF7 . 145 D7
Featherstone Purston St Thomas CE Mid Sch. Feath ... 145 F5
Featherstone Sta. Feath ... 145 C6
Featherstone Streethouse Fst Sch. Feath ... 144 C5
Federation St. Brad BD5 ... 74 F2
Feetham's Fold. Leeds LS9 ... 79 E7
Felbrigg Ave. Keigh BD22 ... 35 A6
Felcote Ave. Hud HD5 ... 154 E5
Felcourt Dr. Brad BD4 ... 75 E2
Felkirk Mid Sch. S Hie ... 180 C7
Felkirk View. Shaf S72 ... 180 B3
Felks Stile Rd. Hud HD4 ... 153 A1
Fell Cres. Keigh BD22 ... 34 F6
Fell Gr. Hud HD2 ... 136 C4
Fell Gr. Keigh BD22 ... 34 F6
Fell Greave Cres. Hud HD2 ... 136 C4
Fell Greave Rd. Hud HD2 ... 136 C4
Fell La. Keigh BD22 ... 34 F6
Fellows The. Hud HD4 ... 171 C7
Fellowsides La. Ossett WF5 .. 140 E5
Fellside. Tod OL14 ... 109 B5
Fellwood Ave. Haw BD22 ... 51 E8
Fellwood Cl. Haw BD22 ... 51 E8
Felnex Cl. Leeds LS9 ... 80 C6
Felnex Cres. Leeds LS9 ... 80 C6
Felnex Rd. Leeds LS9 ... 80 C5
Felnex Sq. Leeds LS9 ... 80 B5
Felnex Way. Leeds LS9 ... 80 C5
Fenay Bankside. Lepton HD8 . 155 D3
Fenay Bridge Rd. Lepton HD8 155 C4
Fenay Cres. Hud HD5 ... 155 A3
Fenay Dr. Lepton HD8 ... 155 C3
Fenay La. Hud HD5 ... 155 B3
Fenay Lea Dr. Hud HD5 ... 155 C4
Fenby Ave. Brad BD4 ... 75 C3
Fenby Cl. Brad BD4 ... 75 C3
Fenby Gdns. Brad BD4 ... 75 C3
Fenby Gr. Brad BD4 ... 75 C3
Fencote Cres. Brad BD2 ... 56 D3
Fender Rd. Brad BD6 ... 73 F1
Fenny Royd Est. Brig HX3 ... 114 B8
Fenton Cl. S Kirk WF9 ... 182 B1
Fenton Rd. Hali HX1 ... 112 F5
Fenton Rd. Hud HD1 ... 153 F3
Fenton Rd. Loft G WF3 ... 121 F7
Fenton Sq. Hud HD1 ... 153 F5
Fenton St. Bur in W LS29 ... 9 F1
Fenton St. E Ard WF3 ... 98 F1
Fenton St. Leeds LS1 ... 60 B1
Fenton St. Mir WF14 ... 138 A4
Fentonsgate. Roth WF3 ... 100 C1
Fenwick Dr. Brad BD6 ... 94 A6
Ferguson St. Hali HX1 ... 113 C6 2
Fern Ave. Mel HD7 ... 170 C3
Fern Bank. Otley LS21 ... 23 B8
Fern Chase. Scar LS14 ... 45 A7
Fern Cl. Batley WF17 ... 118 F5
Fern Croft. Clec WF15 ... 116 C4
Fern Croft. Scar LS14 ... 45 A7
Fern Ct. Keigh BD20 ... 18 A2
Fern Ct. Wake WF2 ... 120 E3
Fern Gdns. Ilkley LS29 ... 8 A3
Fern Hill Ave. Ship BD18 ... 54 F7
Fern Hill Gr. Ship BD18 ... 54 F7
Fern Hill Mount. Ship BD18 ... 54 F7
Fern Hill Rd. Ship BD18 ... 54 F7
Fern Lea Flats. Hud HD3 ... 135 A1
Fern Lea. Queen BD13 ... 72 F1
Fern Lea Rd. Hud HD3 ... 135 A1
Fern Lea St. Hali HX6 ... 112 B5 4
Fern Lea View. Pudsey LS28 ... 57 E2
Fern St. Brad BD4 ... 75 D3
Fern St E. Hud HD1 ... 154 C6
Fern St. Hali HX3 ... 92 B2
Fern St. Haw BD22 ... 51 C6 8
Fern St. Hud HD1 ... 136 A1
Fern St. Hud HD1 ... 154 A8 4
Fern St. Keigh BD21 ... 35 C8
Fern Terr. Pudsey LS28 ... 57 E2 3
Fern Way. Scar LS14 ... 45 A7
Fernbank Ave. Bing BD16 ... 37 A3 1
Fernbank Ave. Keigh BD22 ... 34 F4
Fernbank Ave. Pudsey LS13 ... 57 F3
Fernbank Cl. Pudsey LS13 ... 57 F3
Fernbank Dr. Bail BD17 ... 38 A1
Fernbank Dr. Bing BD16 ... 37 B3
Fernbank Dr. Pudsey LS13 ... 57 F3
Fernbank Gdns. Pudsey LS13 ... 57 F3
Fernbank Pl. Pudsey LS13 ... 57 F3
Fernbank Rd. Brad BD3 ... 56 B1
Fernbank Rd. Pudsey LS13 ... 57 F3
Fernbank St. Bing BD16 ... 37 A3
Fernbank Terr. Bing BD16 ... 37 A3
Fernbank Wlk. Pudsey LS13 ... 57 F3
Ferncliffe Dr. Bail BD17 ... 38 B3
Ferncliffe Dr. Keigh BD20 ... 18 A2
Ferncliffe Rd. Bing BD16 ... 37 A3
Ferncliffe Rd. Leeds LS13 ... 58 C2
Ferncliffe Rd. Ship BD18 ... 54 F8 15
Ferncliffe Terr. Leeds LS13 ... 58 C2
Ferndale Ave. Brad BD14 ... 73 A3
Ferndale Gr. Ship BD9 ... 55 C4
Ferndale Pl. Hem WF9 ... 181 D6
Ferndene Ave. Batley WF17 ... 96 F3
Ferndene. Bing BD16 ... 37 B2
Ferndown Gn. Brad BD5 ... 74 D3
Ferney Lee Jun & Inf Sch. Tod 108 A6
Ferney Lee Rd. Tod OL14 ... 108 A6
Fernfield Terr. Hali HX3 ... 92 B2 7
Fernhill. Bing BD16 ... 37 A5
Fernhurst Cl. Mir WF14 ... 138 A6
Fernhurst Cres. Mir WF14 ... 138 B6
Fernhurst Lea. Mir WF14 ... 138 B6
Fernhurst Rd. Mir WF14 ... 138 B6
Fernhurst Way. Mir WF14 ... 138 A6
Ferniehurst Fst Sch. Bail ... 38 C2
Fernlea Cl. Batley WF16 ... 117 E3
Fernlea Cl. Crof WF4 ... 162 A8
Fernlea Gr. Hud HD7 ... 152 E3
Fernlea. Roth LS26 ... 100 F6
Fernleigh Ct. Wake WF2 ... 141 F5
Fernley Gdns. Brad BD12 ... 94 C4
Fernley Green Cl. Knot WF11 127 B4
Fernley Green Ind Est. Knot ... 127 B4
Fernley Green Rd. Knot WF11 127 B4
Fernley Hill Dr. Nor WF6 ... 122 F5
Ferns The. Bacup OL13 ... 106 A1 3
Fernside Ave. Hud HD5 ... 154 F4
Fernside Cl. Hud HD5 ... 155 A5
Fernside Cres. Hud HD5 ... 155 A5
Fernside. Crof WF4 ... 144 C3
Fernwood Ct. Leeds LS8 ... 44 A1
Fernwood. Leeds LS8 ... 44 A1
Ferrand Ave. Brad BD4 ... 95 C8
Ferrand La. Bing BD16 ... 36 F3
Ferrand La. Clec BD19 ... 96 A1
Ferrand St. Bing BD16 ... 37 A3
Ferrands Cl. Harden BD16 ... 36 B1
Ferrands Park Way. Harden BD16 ... 36 B1
Ferriby Cl. Brad BD2 ... 56 D3
Ferriby Towers. Leeds LS9 ... 60 E1
Ferry La. Loft G WF3 ... 121 F2
Ferry Top La. Ryhill WF4 ... 162 A3
Ferrybridge By-Pass. Knot WF11 ... 126 C5
Ferrybridge Power Sta. Castle 126 B7
Ferrybridge Rd. Castle WF10 124 F7
Ferrybridge Rd. Knot WF11 ... 126 D4
Ferrybridge Rd. Pont WF8 ... 125 F3
Festival Ave. Ship BD18 ... 55 D5
Feversham Fst Sch. Brad ... 75 A6
Feversham St. Brad BD3 ... 75 A6
Fewston Ave. Leeds LS9 ... 79 F6
Fewston Ave. Wake WF1 ... 142 F8
Fewston Ct. Leeds LS9 ... 79 F6
Fiddle La. Rip HX6 ... 132 F4
Fiddler Hill. Dew WF12 ... 139 B4
Fidler Cl. Gar LS25 ... 82 E7
Fidler La. Gar LS25 ... 82 E7
Field Cl. Batley WF16 ... 117 D6
Field Cres. S Elm WF9 ... 182 F2 2
Field Ct. Thorn BD13 ... 72 E6
Field End Cl. Leeds LS15 ... 81 A7
Field End Cres. Leeds LS15 ... 81 A7
Field End Ct. Leeds LS15 ... 81 A7
Field End Garth. Leeds LS15 ... 81 A7
Field End Gdns. Leeds LS15 ... 81 A7
Field End Gn. Leeds LS15 ... 81 A7
Field End Gr. Leeds LS15 ... 81 B8
Field End La. Holmfi HD7 ... 188 B2
Field End La. Honley HD7 ... 172 A4
Field End. Leeds LS15 ... 81 A7
Field End Mount. Leeds LS15 ... 81 A7
Field End Rd. Leeds LS15 ... 81 A7
Field Head. Hud HD7 ... 152 D5
Field Head La. Batley WF17 ... 96 E3
Field Head La. Hali HX2 ... 91 D7
Field Head La. Heb Br HX7 ... 110 B4
Field Head La. Oxen BD22 ... 51 A5
Field Head Way. Hali HX2 ... 91 D7
Field House. Aber LS25 ... 64 E8
Field House Cl. Weth LS22 ... 13 C5
Field Hurst. Brig BD19 ... 115 F7
Field La. Aber LS25 ... 64 E8
Field La. Batley WF17 ... 118 D4
Field La. Brig HD6 ... 135 F8
Field La. Dew WF13 ... 138 D6
Field La. Kirkb HD4 ... 173 A8
Field La. Ossett WF5 ... 140 D6
Field La. S Elm WF9 ... 183 C4
Field La. Upton WF9 ... 183 A8
Field La. Wake WF2 ... 142 C3
Field Lane Cty Jun & Inf Sch. Batley ... 118 D4
Field Lane Prim Sch. Brig ... 135 E7
Field Pl. Wake WF2 ... 142 A5
Field Rd. Holmfi HD7 ... 189 B4
Field Side. Hali HX1 ... 112 F8
Field St. Brad BD1 ... 74 F7 9
Field St. Dew WF13 ... 138 E6
Field Terr. Leeds LS15 ... 81 A8
Field Top Rd. Brig HD6 ... 114 F1
Field Way. Shep HD8 ... 190 E8
Fieldcroft Ct. Mir WF14 ... 137 F5 3
Fieldedge La. Keigh BD20 ... 19 A2
Fielden Sq. Tod OL14 ... 108 B4
Fielden St. Tod OL14 ... 108 E6
Fieldens Pl. Batley WF17 ... 118 A6
Fieldgate Rd. Brad BD10 ... 56 D7
Fieldhead Cl. Pont WF8 ... 125 F1
Fieldhead Cres. Batley WF17 .. 96 E3
Fieldhead Ct. B Spa LS23 ... 30 C7
Fieldhead Dr. B in Elm LS15 ... 63 F8
Fieldhead Dr. Glu BD20 ... 16 D7
Fieldhead Dr. Guise LS20 ... 39 C8
Fieldhead Gdns. Batley WF12 119 B3
Fieldhead Gr. Guise LS20 ... 39 C8
Fieldhead Hospl. Loft G ... 121 D1
Fieldhead Jun & Inf Sch. Batley 96 F3
Fieldhead La. Holme HD7 ... 187 F1
Fieldhead Paddock. B Spa LS23 30 C8
Fieldhead Rd. Guise LS20 ... 39 D8
Fieldhead St. Brad BD7 ... 74 C7
Fieldhouse Cl. Leeds LS17 ... 43 C2
Fieldhouse Cotts. Hali HX1 ... 113 A5 15
Fieldhouse Dr. Leeds LS17 ... 43 C2
Fieldhouse Dr. Slai HD7 ... 152 A1
Fieldhouse Gr. Pudsey LS28 ... 57 C2
Fieldhouse Lawn. Leeds LS17 .. 43 C2
Fieldhouse Rd. Hud HD1 ... 154 C8 2
Fieldhouse St. Brad BD3 ... 75 D7
Fieldhouse St. Wake WF1 ... 142 F3
Fieldhouse Wlk. Leeds LS17 ... 43 C2
Fieldhurst Ct. Brad BD4 ... 95 C8
Fielding Gate. Leeds LS12 ... 78 D8
Fielding St. Heb Br HX7 ... 89 A3 28
Fields Rd. Brad BD12 ... 94 E5
Fields Rd. Lepton HD8 ... 155 D2
Fields Rise. Kirkhe HD5 ... 137 C1
Fields The. Roth WF3 ... 100 D1
Fields Way. Kirkhe HD5 ... 137 C1
Fieldsend Ct. Upton WF9 ... 183 A7
Fieldshead Bglws. Slai HD7 ... 170 D7
Fieldside Rd. Hem WF9 ... 163 B2
Fieldway Ave. Leeds LS13 ... 58 A4
Fieldway. Brad BD14 ... 73 B5
Fieldway Chase. Roth LS26 ... 101 D5
Fieldway Cl. Leeds LS13 ... 58 A4
Fieldway. Ilkley LS29 ... 8 E4
Fieldway Rise. Leeds LS13 ... 58 A4
Fife St. Haw BD22 ... 51 D7 15
Fifth Ave. Brad BD3 ... 56 C1
Fifth Ave E. Clec WF15 ... 116 B5
Fifth Ave. Roth LS26 ... 101 A7
Fifth Ave W. Clec WF15 ... 116 B5
Fifth St. Brad BD12 ... 94 E6
Fifth St. Crof WF4 ... 162 B7
Filbert St. Hud HD1 ... 136 A1
Filey Ave. Roy S71 ... 179 D4
Filey St. Brad BD1 ... 74 F6 3
Filey St. Brad BD1 ... 75 A6
Filley Royd. Clec BD19 ... 116 E6
Fillingfir Dr. Leeds LS16 ... 58 F8
Fillingfir Rd. Leeds LS16 ... 58 F8
Fillingfir Wlk. Leeds LS16 ... 58 F8
Finch Ave. Wake WF2 ... 160 D5
Finch St. Brad BD5 ... 74 D4
Finching Gr. Mir WF14 ... 138 A8
Finchley St. Brad BD5 ... 74 D3
Finchley Way. Morley LS27 ... 98 A3 4
Findon Terr. Brad BD10 ... 56 E4
Fine Garth Cl. Bramham LS23 . 30 D3
Finghall Rd. Ad Le S DN6 ... 184 F2
Fink Hill. Hors LS18 ... 58 A8
Finkil St. Brig HD6 ... 114 F5
Finkin Ave. Loft G WF3 ... 121 E2
Finkin Croft. Loft G WF3 ... 121 E2
Finkin La. Loft G WF3 ... 121 E2
Finkle Cl. Wool WF4 ... 177 F7
Finkle La. Gild LS27 ... 97 D6
Finkle St. Pont WF8 ... 125 D1
Finkle St. Sow Br HX6 ... 111 D4
Finkle St. Wool WF4 ... 177 F7
Finsbury Dr. Brad BD2 ... 55 F5
Finsbury Rd. Leeds LS1 ... 60 B1
Finthorpe La. Hud HD5 ... 155 A3
Fir Ave. Dew WF13 ... 138 D5
Fir Bank. Dew WF13 ... 118 A1 6
Fir Par. Dew WF13 ... 138 D5
Fir Rd. Hud HD1 ... 153 D6
Fir St. Haw BD22 ... 51 C6
Fir St. Keigh BD21 ... 35 B4 12
Fir St. Tod OL14 ... 129 A8
Fir Tree App. Leeds LS17 ... 43 C3
Fir Tree Cl. Leeds LS17 ... 43 C4
Fir Tree Cty Prim Sch. Leeds ... 43 C3
Fir Tree Gdns. Brad BD10 ... 56 D7
Fir Tree Gdns. Leeds LS17 ... 43 B4
Fir Tree Gn. Leeds LS17 ... 43 C4
Fir Tree Gr. Leeds LS17 ... 43 C4
Fir Tree La. Leeds LS17 ... 43 D3
Fir Tree Rise. Leeds LS17 ... 43 C3
Fir Tree Vale. Leeds LS17 ... 43 C3
Fir Wlk. Dew WF13 ... 138 D5
Firbank Gn. Brad BD2 ... 56 D3
Firbank Gr. Leeds LS15 ... 80 E6
Firbeck. Harden BD16 ... 53 B8
Firbeck Rd. Bramham LS23 ... 30 D3
Firethorn Cl. Brad BD8 ... 74 A8
Firham Cl. Roy S71 ... 179 A4
Firs The. Roy S71 ... 179 A4
Firs The. Scar LS14 ... 45 C7
First Ave. Bard LS17 ... 28 E5
First Ave. Brad BD3 ... 56 C1
First Ave. Clec WF15 ... 116 C5
First Ave. Hali HX3 ... 113 B4
First Ave. Hem WF9 ... 163 A4
First Ave. Hor WF4 ... 140 F1
First Ave. Hud HD7 ... 152 D4
First Ave. Hud HD5 ... 154 F7
First Ave. Keigh BD21 ... 35 B6 3
First Ave. Leeds LS12 ... 78 D7
First Ave. Loft G WF1 ... 121 C2
First Ave. Pudsey LS28 ... 57 E1
First Ave. Roth LS26 ... 100 F7
First Ave. Roy S71 ... 179 D4
First Ave. S Kirk WF9 ... 181 F1
First Ave. Upton WF9 ... 183 A7
First Ave. Weth LS22 ... 13 F5
First Ave. Yeadon LS19 ... 40 C5
First Avenue Ind Est. Pudsey .. 57 E1
First St. Brad BD12 ... 94 E6
First St. Crof WF4 ... 162 B7
Firth Ave. Brig HD6 ... 115 A3 5
Firth Ave. Leeds LS11 ... 79 A2
Firth Cl. Loft G WF3 ... 121 E5
Firth Gr. Leeds LS11 ... 79 A2
Firth House La. Brig HD6 ... 136 C7
Firth House La. Rip HX4 ... 133 C1
Firth House. Wake WF1 ... 142 C6 19
Firth La. Wils BD15 ... 53 C5
Firth Mount. Leeds LS11 ... 79 A2
Firth Rd. Brad BD9 ... 55 A3
Firth Rd. Leeds LS11 ... 79 A2
Firth Row. Brad BD4 ... 95 B8
Firth St. Brig HD6 ... 115 A1
Firth St. Hud HD1 ... 154 B5
Firth St. Leeds LS9 ... 60 E1
Firth St. Shep HD8 ... 190 E8
Firth St . Thorn BD13 ... 72 D6 4
Firth Terr. Leeds LS9 ... 60 E1
Firth View. Leeds LS11 ... 79 A2 5
Firthcliffe Dr. Liver WF15 ... 117 B5
Firthcliffe Gr. Liver WF15 ... 117 C5
Firthcliffe La. Liver WF15 ... 117 B5
Firthcliffe Mount. Liver WF15 117 B5
Firthcliffe Par. Liver WF15 ... 117 B5
Firthcliffe Pl. Liver WF15 ... 117 C5
Firthcliffe Rd. Liver WF15 ... 117 B5
Firthcliffe Terr. Liver WF15 ... 117 B5
Firthcliffe View. Liver WF15 .. 117 B5
Firthcliffe Wlk. Liver WF15 ... 117 B5
Firthfield La. Bad WF9 ... 164 F4
Firthfields. Gar LS25 ... 83 A7
Firtree Ave. Gar LS25 ... 83 B6
Firville Ave. Nor WF6 ... 123 B1
Firville Cres. Nor WF6 ... 144 B8
Firwood Cl. Tod OL14 ... 108 A1
Fish St. Leeds LS1 ... 79 C8
Fishbeck La. Add BD20 ... 6 A4
Fisher Gn. Honley HD7 ... 171 F4
Fisher Gr. Ossett WF5 ... 140 F4
Fisher St. Knot WF11 ... 126 E4
Fishergate. Knot WF11 ... 126 D5
Fishpond La. Crig WF4 ... 159 F4
Fishponds Dr. Crig WF4 ... 159 F5
Fitts La. Hare LS17 ... 27 A8
Fitzgerald St. Brad BD5 ... 74 E5
Fitzroy Dr. Leeds LS8 ... 61 A6
Fitzroy Rd. Brad BD3 ... 75 C7
Fitzwilliam Fst Sch. Hem ... 163 A4
Fitzwilliam St. Brad BD4 ... 74 F5
Fitzwilliam St. Hem WF9 ... 163 B1
Fitzwilliam Sta. Hem ... 163 A3
Five Acres. Caw S75 ... 193 F5
Five Lane Ends. Ad Le S DN6 . 184 E1
Five Lane Ends. Brad BD2 ... 56 A5
Five Lane Ends. Eccup LS16 ... 42 D8
Five Lane Ends. Holmfi HD7 ... 188 E5
Five Oaks. Bail BD17 ... 38 A2
Fixby Ave. Hali HX2 ... 112 E5
Fixby Cty Prim Sch. Hud ... 136 A4
Fixby La. Dew WF13 ... 156 E6
Fixby Park Dr. Hud HD2 ... 135 F2
Fixby Rd. Hud HD2 ... 136 A5
Fixby View Yd. Brig HD6 ... 135 E6
Flanshaw Ave. Wake WF2 ... 141 E6
Flanshaw Cres. Wake WF2 ... 141 E6
Flanshaw Fst Sch. Wake ... 141 F7
Flanshaw Gr. Wake WF2 ... 141 E6
Flanshaw La. Wake WF2 ... 141 D6
Flanshaw Rd. Wake WF2 ... 141 E6
Flanshaw St Michael's C E Sch. Wake ... 141 E5
Flanshaw St. Wake WF2 ... 141 E6
Flanshaw View. Wake WF2 ... 141 E6
Flanshaw Way. Wake WF2 ... 141 D7
Flappit Spring. Cull BD13 ... 52 A6
Flasby St. Keigh BD21 ... 35 C8
Flash La. Mir WF14 ... 138 B6
Flass La. Castle WF10 ... 124 C5
Flat House. Slai HD7 ... 170 C8
Flat La. Holmfi HD7 ... 188 D5
Flat Nook. Bing BD16 ... 37 B3
Flats La. B in Elm LS15 ... 63 D6
Flats The. Hali HX1 ... 113 C6 12
Flavell Cl. S Kirk WF9 ... 182 B1
Flawith Dr. Brad BD2 ... 56 D2
Flax Meadow. Hud HD3 ... 135 A2
Flax Mill Rd. Leeds LS10 ... 79 E3
Flax Pl. Leeds LS9 ... 79 E7
Flaxton Cl. Leeds LS11 ... 79 B3 2
Flaxton Gdns. Leeds LS11 ... 79 B3 1
Flaxton Gn. Brad BD2 ... 56 D2
Flaxton Pl. Brad BD7 ... 74 B6
Flaxton St. Leeds LS11 ... 79 B3
Flaxton View. Leeds LS11 ... 79 B3
Flea La. Norton WF8 ... 166 E4
Fledborough Rd. Weth LS22 ... 13 C5
Fleece St. Brad BD6 ... 93 F7
Fleece St. Keigh BD21 ... 35 C7
Fleet La. M'town LS26 ... 102 A4
Fleet La. Queen BD13 ... 72 D1
Fleet La. Roth LS26 ... 101 E5
Fleet St. Clay W HD8 ... 175 D1
Fleet Thro Rd. Hors LS18 ... 58 B6
Fleming Ct. Hud HD5 ... 155 A5
Fleming House. Brad BD15 ... 73 A7 6
Fleming St. Batley WF17 ... 118 C5
Fleminghouse La. Hud HD5 ... 155 A5
Fletcher Ave. Sil BD20 ... 5 E2
Fletcher Cres. Brig HD6 ... 135 E6
Fletcher Homes. Dew WF13 .. 139 A8
Fletcher La. Ship BD2 ... 55 D4
Fletcher Rd. Brad BD6 ... 74 B1
Fletton Terr. Brad BD2 ... 56 B2
Flexbury Ave. Morley LS27 ... 98 A3
Flight Hill. Dun Br HD7 ... 199 C5
Flight House Rd. Rip HX6 ... 131 F4
Flint La. Carl HD7, S30 ... 200 A5
Flint St. Hud HD1 ... 136 B1
Flintmill La. Th Arch LS23 ... 14 D3
Flinton Gr. Brad BD2 ... 56 D3
Flockton Ave. Brad BD4 ... 75 A4
Flockton (CE) Fst Sch. Floc ... 157 C2
Flockton Cl. Brad BD4 ... 75 A4
Flockton Cres. Brad BD4 ... 75 A4
Flockton Dr. Brad BD4 ... 75 A4
Flockton Gr. Brad BD4 ... 75 A4
Flockton Rd. Brad BD4 ... 75 A4
Floral Ave. Leeds LS7 ... 60 C6
Floreat Cl. Batley WF17 ... 118 A8
Florence Ave. Leeds LS9 ... 61 A2
Florence Ave. Wils BD15 ... 53 B6
Florence Gr. Leeds LS9 ... 61 A2
Florence Mount. Leeds LS9 ... 61 A2 4
Florence Pl. Leeds LS9 ... 61 A2 3
Florence St. Brad BD3 ... 75 C6
Florence St. Castle WF10 ... 124 D8
Florence St. Hali HX1 ... 113 A7
Florence St. Leeds LS9 ... 61 A2
Florence Terr. Morley LS27 ... 98 B4 9
Florida Rd. Brad BD15 ... 54 A4
Florist St. Keigh BD21 ... 18 E1
Flounders Hill. Ack M T WF7 . 163 F6
Flower Acre. Elland HX5 ... 134 F6
Flower Bank. Brad BD2 ... 55 F4
Flower Bank. Sow Br HX6 ... 111 F3
Flower Cl. Yeadon LS19 ... 40 A7
Flower Croft. Keigh BD21 ... 34 F5
Flower Garth. Brad BD10 ... 56 D6
Flower Haven. Brad BD9 ... 54 D4
Flower Hill. Brad BD9 ... 54 F4
Flower Mount. Bail BD17 ... 38 D4
Flower Mount. Yeadon LS19 ... 40 C7 8
Flower Scar Rd. Tod OL14 ... 107 B7
Flowerlands. Brig HX3 ... 114 E8
Floyd St. Brad BD5 ... 74 E3
Flush House La. Holmfi HD7 .. 188 A3
Flush. Liver FW15 ... 117 C4
Fold La. Hep HX7 ... 88 A6
Fold The. Haw BD22 ... 51 B7 4
Fold The. Leeds LS15 ... 62 E4
Foldings Ave. Brig BD19 ... 115 F8
Foldings Cl. Brig BD19 ... 115 E8
Foldings Ct. Brig BD19 ... 115 E8
Foldings Gr. Brig BD19 ... 115 E8
Foldings Par. Brig BD19 ... 115 E8
Foldings Rd. Brig BD19 ... 115 F8
Foldings The. Skel HD8 ... 175 A2
Foljambe St. Wake WF2 ... 142 C4
Folkestone St. Brad BD3 ... 75 C7
Folkton Holme. Brad BD2 ... 56 E2
Follett Ave. Hud HD4 ... 153 C2
Follingworth La. Slai HD7 ... 151 D1
Follingworth Rd. Batley WF17 118 F5
Folly Hall Ave. Brad BD6 ... 94 B8
Folly Hall Cl. Brad BD6 ... 94 B8 2
Folly Hall Gdns The. Brad BD6 . 94 B8
Folly Hall. Hud HD1 ... 154 A4
Folly Hall La. Heb Br HX7 ... 110 E2
Folly Hall Mount. E Ard WF3 .. 119 E8
Folly Hall Rd. Brad BD6 ... 94 B8
Folly Hall Rd. E Ard WF3 ... 119 E8
Folly Hall Wlk. Brad BD6 ... 94 B8
Folly La. Bramham LS23 ... 30 D2
Folly La. Leeds LS11 ... 79 B4
Folly Rd. Hud HD2 ... 136 A3
Folly View. Bramham LS23 ... 30 D2
Folly View Rd. Haw BD22 ... 51 D6
Fontmell Cl. Brad BD4 ... 75 E2
Football. Yeadon LS19 ... 40 C6
Forber Gr. Brad BD4 ... 75 E5
Ford Dr. Mir WF14 ... 137 E6
Ford Gate. Holmfi HD7 ... 188 D3
Ford Hill. Queen BD13 ... 92 D8
Ford House Sch. Leeds ... 59 E4
Ford. Queen BD13 ... 92 C8
Ford St. Hem WF9 ... 163 B1
Ford St. Keigh BD21 ... 18 E1
Fore La. Sow Br HX6 ... 112 A3
Fore Lane Ave. Sow Br HX6 ... 112 A3
Foreside Bottom La. Denh BD13 71 D5
Forest Ave. Hali HX2 ... 91 E4
Forest Bank. Gild LS27 ... 97 C7
Forest Cl. Wake WF1 ... 121 F1
Forest Cres. Hali HX2 ... 91 E4
Forest Gate. Otley LS21 ... 23 A7
Forest Gn. Hali HX2 ... 91 E3
Forest Hill Gdns. Elland HD3 . 152 A8
Forest Hill Rd. Elland HX4 ... 133 E1
Forest Rd. Hud HD5 ... 154 E5

Forest Way. Honley HD7 .... 171 E4
Forge Hill La. Knot WF11 .... 126 E4
Forge La. Batley WF15 .... 117 C2
Forge La. Dew WF12 .... 139 B4
Forge La. Hare LS17 .... 27 D1
Forge La. Hor WF4 .... 159 C8
Forge La. Leeds LS12 .... 78 D8
Forge La. Liver WF15 .... 117 B3
Forge Row. Gild LS12 .... 77 D3
Forge View. Stee BD20 .... 17 C5
Forman's Dr. Roth WF3 .... 100 A3
Formby Ave. Hud HD2 .... 135 F3
Forrest Ave. Hud HD1 .... 153 D7
Forrest Terr. Dew WF12 .... 139 E6
Forrester Cl. Hem WF9 .... 163 A3
Forster Ct. Brad BD1 .... 74 F7
Forster Dr. Batley WF16 .... 117 E3
Forster Pl. Leeds LS12 .... 78 B4
Forster Sq. Brad BD1 .... 74 F7
Forster St. Leeds LS10 .... 79 E5
Forsythia Ave. E Ard WF3 ...... 120 C7
Fort Ann Rd. Batley WF17 ...... 118 F4
Fortis Way. Hud HD3 .... 152 E8
Fortshot La. Hare LS17 .... 27 B1
Forum View. Th Aud WF8 .... 165 A5
Foss Ave. Weth LS22 .... 13 D7
Foss Wlk. Castle WF10 .... 104 B1
Fosse Way. Gar LS25 .... 83 B6
Foster Ave. Hud HD4 .... 153 C2
Foster Ave. Nor WF6 .... 123 A1
Foster Ave. Sil BD20 .... 5 D2
Foster Ave. Thorn BD13 .... 72 F6
Foster Beaver Coll The. Brad .. 54 F1
Foster Cl. Bur in W LS29 .... 9 F1
Foster Cl. Morley LS27 .... 98 A5 8
Foster Cres. Morley LS27 .... 98 A5 7
Foster Gdns. Keigh BD22 .... 34 F7
Foster La. Heb Br HX7 .... 89 A4
Foster Park Gr. Denh BD13 ..... 52 E1
Foster Park Rd. Denh BD13 ..... 52 E1
Foster Park View. Denh BD13 . 52 E1
Foster Pk. Denh BD13 .... 52 E1
Foster Place La. Holmfi HD7 .. 189 F2
Foster Rd. Keigh BD21 .... 35 B4
Foster Sq. Denh BD13 .... 71 D8
Foster St. Morley LS27 .... 98 A5 11
Foster St. Queen BD13 .... 72 E1 1
Foston Cl. Brad BD2 .... 56 E2
Foston La. Brad BD2 .... 56 E2
Fothergill Ave. Ack M T WF7 . 163 E6
Foul Clough Rd. Tod OL14 ...... 128 D8
Foulcauseway La. Otley LS21 .. 23 D7
Foulds' Terr. Bing BD16 .... 37 A4 6
Foundry App. Leeds LS9 .... 61 B3
Foundry Ave. Leeds LS8, LS9 ... 61 B3
Foundry Dr. Leeds LS9 .... 61 B3
Foundry Hill. Bing BD16 .... 36 F3
Foundry La. Brad BD4 .... 75 B5
Foundry La. Knot WF11 .... 127 A4
Foundry La. Leeds LS14, LS9 ... 61 E3
Foundry La. Pudsey LS28 .... 57 E2
Foundry Mill Cres. Leeds LS14 61 F3
Foundry Mill Dr. Leeds LS14 .... 61 E3
Foundry Mill Gdns. Leeds LS14 61 E5
Foundry Mill Mt. Leeds LS14 .... 61 F3
Foundry Mill St. Leeds LS14 .... 61 F3
Foundry Mill Terr. Leeds LS14 . 61 F3
Foundry Mill View. Leeds LS14 61 F3
Foundry Mill Wlk. Leeds LS14 . 61 F3
Foundry Pl. Leeds LS9 .... 61 B3
Foundry St. Brig HD6 .... 115 C1
Foundry St. Clec BD19 .... 116 E8
Foundry St. Dew WF13 .... 138 E5
Foundry St. Dew WF13 .... 139 D8
Foundry St. Hali HX1 .... 113 C8
Foundry St. Leeds LS11 .... 79 B6
Foundry St. Leeds LS9 .... 79 E7
Foundry St N. Hali HX3 .... 91 F3
Foundry St. Sow Br HX6 .... 112 B3
Foundry St. Tod OL14 .... 108 A4
Foundry Terr. Clec BD19 .... 116 E7
Foundry Wlk. Leeds LS8 .... 61 B3
Fountain Cl. Liver WF15 .... 116 F1
Fountain Ct. Mapp S75 .... 177 E1
Fountain Ct. Barn S71 .... 178 E1
Fountain Dr. Liver WF15 .... 116 F1
Fountain Gr. Hud HD4 .... 153 C4
Fountain Sq. Mapp S75 .... 177 E1
Fountain St. Batley WF16 ...... 117 D5
Fountain St. Brad BD1 .... 74 E8
Fountain St. Brad BD12 .... 94 C6
Fountain St. Hali HX1 .... 113 C6
Fountain St. Heb Br HX7 .... 89 A3 29
Fountain St. Leeds LS1 .... 79 A8
Fountain St. Liver WF15 .... 116 F1
Fountain St. Morley LS27 .... 98 C8 3
Fountain St. Queen BD13 .... 72 E1 14
Fountain St. Rip HX6 .... 132 D4
Fountain St. Thorn BD13 .... 72 D6 7
Fountain St. Tod OL14 .... 108 E6
Fountain Terr. Brad BD12 .... 94 D3
Fountain Way. Ship BD18 .... 55 C7
Fountain Wlk. Leeds LS14 .... 62 B5 1
Fountains Ave. B Spa LS23 .... 30 C7
Fountains Ave. Batley WF17 .. 117 F4
Fountains Way. Wake WF1 ..... 121 F1
Four Acres. Mir WF14 .... 138 A3
Four Lane Ends. Castle WF10 124 A6
Four Lane Ends. Dew WF12 ... 139 F2
Four Lane Ends. Guise LS20 .... 39 C7
Four Row. D Dale HD8 .... 191 A4
Fourlands Cres. Brad BD10 ..... 56 C8
Fourlands Ct. Brad BD10 .... 56 C8
Fourlands Dr. Brad BD10 .... 56 C8
Fourlands Gdns. Brad BD10 ..... 56 C8
Fourlands Gr. Brad BD10 .... 56 C8
Fourlands Rd. Brad BD10 .... 56 C8
Fourteenth Ave. Leeds LS12 .... 78 D6
Fourth Ave. Brad BD3 .... 56 C1
Fourth Ave. Clec WF15 .... 116 B5
Fourth Ave. Keigh BD21 .... 35 A6 9
Fourth Ave. Loft G WF1 .... 121 B2
Fourth Ave. Roth LS26 .... 101 A7
Fourth Ave. Weth LS22 .... 13 F5
Fourth Ct. Leeds LS11 .... 79 A6
Fourth St. Brad BD12 .... 94 E6 1
Fourth St. Crof WF4 .... 162 B7
Fowler St. Brad BD4 .... 75 B5
Fowler's Pl. Pudsey LS28 .... 57 E2
Fox Cl. Emley HD8 .... 175 D6
Fox Covert Road or Whin Covert
La. Norton WF8 .... 166 E2
Fox Ct. Crig WF4 .... 159 F7
Fox Ct. Elland HX4 .... 134 D7
Fox Heads La. Spoff LS22 .... 12 A8
Fox Hollies Rd. Hud HD2 .... 136 B4
Fox La. Crig WF4 .... 159 F7
Fox La. Wake WF1 .... 121 A1
Fox Royd Ave. Mir WF14 .... 137 F6
Fox Royd Dr. Mir WF14 .... 137 F6
Fox Royd La. Mir WF14 .... 137 F6 3
Fox Royd. Shep HD8 .... 173 E1
Fox Royd View. Mir WF14 .... 137 F6 4
Fox St. Batley WF17 .... 118 D4
Fox St. Bing BD16 .... 36 F3
Fox St. Brad BD5 .... 74 C3 5
Fox St. Clec BD19 .... 116 B7
Fox St. Dew WF13 .... 138 E5
Fox St. Hud HD1 .... 154 A6
Fox Terr. Pont WF8 .... 125 E1
Fox View. Batley WF13 .... 118 A3
Fox Wood Ave. Leeds LS8 .... 61 E5
Fox Wood Cl. Leeds LS8 .... 61 E5
Fox Wood Gr. Leeds LS8 .... 61 E5
Fox Wood Rise. Leeds LS8 .... 61 E5
Fox Wood Wlk. Leeds LS8 .... 61 E5
Foxbridge Way. Feath WF6 ..... 123 E3
Foxcliff. Broth WF11 .... 105 D1
Foxcroft Cl. Leeds LS6 .... 59 B5
Foxcroft Cl. Queen BD13 .... 92 C7
Foxcroft Dr. Brig HD6 .... 114 F1
Foxcroft Dr. Brig HD6 .... 135 F8
Foxcroft Gn. Leeds LS6 .... 59 B5
Foxcroft Mount. Leeds LS6 .... 59 C5
Foxcroft Rd. Leeds LS6 .... 59 B5
Foxcroft Way. Leeds LS6 .... 59 B5
Foxdale Cl. Bacup OL13 .... 106 A1 1
Foxen La. Rip HX6 .... 132 C6
Foxglove Ave. Leeds LS8 .... 61 C6
Foxglove Rd. Batley WF17 .... 96 E2
Foxglove Rd. Hud HD5 .... 154 E4
Foxhill Ave. Leeds LS16 .... 42 C1
Foxhill Ave. Queen BD13 .... 72 D1
Foxhill. Bail BD17 .... 38 B3
Foxhill Cl. Queen BD13 .... 72 D1
Foxhill Cres. Leeds LS16 .... 42 D1
Foxhill Ct. Leeds LS16 .... 42 C1
Foxhill Dr. Leeds LS16 .... 42 D1
Foxhill Dr. Queen BD13 .... 72 D1
Foxhill Fst Sch. Queen 72 D2
Foxhill Gn. Leeds LS16 .... 42 D1
Foxhill Gr. Leeds LS16 .... 42 D1
Foxhill Gr. Queen BD13 .... 72 D1
Foxhill. Weth LS22 .... 13 E6
Foxhole La. Pudsey LS28 .... 57 B6
Foxholes Cres. Pudsey LS28 ...... 57 B6
Foxholes La. Nor WF6 .... 122 F5
Foxlow Ave. Hud HD5 .... 154 E8
Foxroyd La. Dew WF12 .... 139 B1
Foxstone Rise. Bail BD17 .... 38 E3
Foxstones La. Rip HX6 .... 132 D2
Foxwood Farm Way. Leeds LS8 61 E5
Foxwood Wlk. Weth LS22 .... 13 E7
Frain Cl. Pont WF8 .... 146 E7
France Fold. Honley HD7 .... 171 F5
France St. Batley WF17 .... 118 E4
Frances Ave. Hud HD4 .... 153 C3
Frances Rd. Dew WF12 .... 139 F7
Frances St. Brig HD6 .... 115 A3 9
Frances St. Elland HX5 .... 134 F6 11
Frances St. Keigh BD21 .... 35 A8
Frances St. Pudsey LS28 .... 57 D2
Francis Ave. Hud HD3 .... 153 A4
Francis Catholic Prim Sch.
Morley 97 F4
Francis Cl. Hali HX1 .... 113 A7
Francis Ct. Leeds LS7 .... 60 D3
Francis Gr. Leeds LS11 .... 79 B3 18
Francis House. Brad BD2 .... 56 B2
Francis Rd. Crof WF4 .... 144 B3
Francis St. Ack M T WF7 .... 163 D5
Francis St. Batley WF16 .... 117 E3
Francis St. Brad BD4 .... 75 A5
Francis St. Castle WF10 .... 124 E8
Francis St. Hali HX1 .... 113 A6
Francis St. Hud HD3 .... 153 A4
Francis St. Leeds LS7 .... 60 E3
Francis St. Mir WF14 .... 137 F5
Francis Terr. Ack M T WF7 ...... 163 D5
Francis View. Mir WF14 .... 137 F5
Frank Cl. Dew WF12 .... 139 E2
Frank La. Dew WF12 .... 139 E2
Frank La. Emley HD8 .... 175 C5
Frank La. Heb Br HX2 .... 90 B1
Frank Parkinson Ct. Guise LS20 22 E1
Frank Parkinson Homes.
Guise LS20 .... 22 E1
Frank Peel Cl. Batley WF16 .... 117 D4 4
Frank Pl. Brad BD7 .... 74 B4 3
Frank St. Brad BD7 .... 74 B4
Frank St. Hali HX1 .... 113 A6
Frankland Gr. Leeds LS7 .... 60 E3
Frankland Pl. Leeds LS7 .... 60 E3
Fraser Ave. Hors LS18 .... 58 A8
Fraser House. Brad BD6 .... 93 E8 2
Fraser Rd. Pudsey LS28 .... 56 F6
Fraser St. Brad BD8 .... 74 C8
Fraser St. Leeds LS9 .... 60 F1
Freakfield La. Liver WF15 .... 116 B2
Fred St. Keigh BD21 .... 35 B6
Fred's Pl. Brad BD4 .... 75 C3
Frederick Ave. Leeds LS9 .... 80 A6
Frederick Ave. Wake WF1 .... 142 F3
Frederick Cl. Brad BD10 .... 38 F1
Frederick St. Brad BD1 .... 74 F6
Frederick St. E Ard WF3 .... 120 E8
Frederick St. Hud HD4 .... 153 C4
Frederick St. Keigh BD21 .... 35 D7
Frederick St. Liver WF15 .... 117 B3 5
Frederick St. Pudsey LS28 .... 57 C3
Frederick St. Wake WF1 .... 142 C6
Frederick Walker Gdns. Batley
WF17 .... 118 D4
Free Sch La. Hali HX1& HX3 .. 113 B5
Freely La. Bramham LS23 .... 30 D2
Freeman Rd. Hali HX3 .... 114 A5
Freemans Way. Weth LS22 .... 14 A6
Freemont St. Leeds LS13 .... 58 A2
Freeston Ct. Nor WF6 .... 123 B3
Freeston Dr. Nor WF6 .... 123 B3
Freestone Way. Nor WF6 .... 122 E4
Fremantle Gr. Brad BD4 .... 75 E5
Fremantle Pl. Leeds LS15 .... 80 E7
Frensham Ave. Morley LS27 .... 97 F3
Frensham Dr. Brad BD7 .... 73 D3
Frensham Dr. Castle WF10 ..... 125 D6
Frensham Gr. Brad BD7 .... 73 D3
Frensham Way. Brad BD7 .... 73 D3
Freshfield Gdns. Brad BD15 ..... 54 B1
Freston Ave. Crof WF1 .... 143 D7
Freston Dr. Crof WF1 .... 143 D7
Friar Ct. Brad BD10 .... 56 C6
Friar Pl. Hud HD2 .... 136 F5
Friar's Cl. Feath WF7 .... 145 D4
Friars Ind Est. Brad 56 B7
Friars Nook. Pont WF8 .... 146 E7
Friarwood La. Pont WF8 .... 146 D8
Frickley Bridge La. Bri S72 ..... 180 F4
Frickley La. Clay WF9 .... 195 A8
Frickley La. S Elm WF9 .... 195 A8
Frieldhurst Rd. Tod OL14 .... 86 C1
Friendly Ave. Hali HX6 .... 112 A5
Friendly Fold Rd. Hali HX3 ...... 92 A2
Friendly St. Hali HX3 .... 92 A2 1
Friendly St. Hud HD1 .... 154 B6 3
Friendly St. Thorn BD13 .... 72 D6
Friends Adult Sch. Morley 98 B4
Frimley Dr. Brad BD5 .... 74 C2
Frith House. Brig HD6 .... 136 C7
Frith St. Haw BD22 .... 51 E8 14
Frizinghall Fst Sch. Ship 55 C5
Frizinghall Mid Sch. Ship 55 C5
Frizinghall Rd. Ship BD9 .... 55 C4
Frizinghall Sta. Ship 55 C4
Frizley Gdns. Ship BD9 .... 55 C4
Frober Pl. Leeds LS15 .... 80 E7
Frobisher Gr. Wake WF2 .... 141 E5
Frobisher Rd. Litt OL15 .... 129 C1
Frogmoor Ave. Brad BD12 .... 94 F5
Front Row. Leeds LS11 .... 79 B6
Front St. Bramham LS23 .... 30 C2
Front St. Castle WF10 .... 124 F6
Front St. Leeds LS11 .... 79 B6
Front St. Pont WF8 .... 146 C8
Frost Hill. Liver WF15 .... 117 B4
Fruit St. Keigh BD21 .... 35 E8
Fryergate. Wake WF2 .... 141 F7
Fryston La. Castle WF11 .... 125 F7
Fryston Rd. Castle WF10 .... 125 C7
Fulford Ave. Hud HD2 .... 136 A2
Fulford Cl. Mapp S75 .... 178 A1
Fulford St. Castle WF10 .... 124 C7
Fulford Wlk. Brad BD2 .... 56 D2
Fulham Pl. Leeds LS11 .... 79 B3 3
Fulham Sq. Leeds LS11 .... 79 B3 5
Fulham St. Leeds LS11 .... 79 B3
Fullerton Cl. Ad Le S DN6 .... 184 F2
Fullerton St. Brad BD3 .... 75 A6
Fullwood Dr. Hud HD7 .... 152 D4
Fulmar Ct. Midd LS10 .... 99 D5
Fulmar Mews. Brad BD8 .... 73 C7 8
Fulmar Rd. Castle WF10 .... 124 C6
Fulneck Boys' Sch. Pudsey 76 E4
Fulneck Cl. Hud HD2 .... 135 F3
Fulneck Girls' Sch. Pudsey 76 E5
Fulneck Golf Course. Pudsey 76 D4
Fulneck. Pudsey LS28 .... 76 E5
Fulstone Hall La. Holmfi HD7 . 190 A7
Fulstone Rd. Kirkb HD4 .... 173 C1
Fulton St. Brad BD1 .... 74 E7
Fulwood Gr. Wake WF2 .... 160 B5
Furnace Cotts. Wh Com S30 .. 200 D6
Furnace Gr. Brad BD12 .... 94 F5
Furnace Inn St. Brad BD4 .... 75 D5
Furnace La. Birk BD11 .... 96 A6
Furnace Rd. Brad BD12 .... 94 F5
Furnace Rd. Brad BD12 .... 95 A6
Furnbrook Gdns. Kirkhe HD5 . 155 C8
Furness Ave. Hali HX2 .... 91 E4
Furness Ave. Wake WF2 .... 120 E2
Furness Cres. Hali HX2 .... 91 D5
Furness Dr. Hali HX2 .... 91 D4
Furness Dr. Wake WF2 .... 120 E2
Furness Gdns. Hali HX2 .... 91 E4
Furness Gr. Hali HX2 .... 91 E4
Furness Pl. Hali HX2 .... 91 E3
Fusden La. Clec BD19 .... 96 A1
Futures Way. Brad BD4 .... 74 F5
Fyfe Cres. Bail BD17 .... 38 D2
Fyfe Gr. Bail BD17 .... 38 E2
Fyfe La. Bail BD17 .... 38 E2
Gable End Terr. Pudsey LS28 .. 76 F7
Gables The. Keigh BD21 .... 35 A7 13
Gadding Moor Rd. Caw S30 ... 192 F1
Gagewell Dr. Hor WF4 .... 141 B2
Gagewell La. Hor WF4 .... 141 B2
Gagewell View. Hor WF4 .... 141 B2
Gain La. Brad BD2, BD3 .... 56 E1
Gainest. Hali HX2 .... 112 F5
Gainford Dr. Gar LS25 .... 82 F6
Gainsborough Cl. Brad BD3 ...... 56 A2
Gainsborough Pl. Gild LS12 ...... 77 E3
Gainsborough Way. Loft G
WF3 .... 121 E5
Gainsbro Ave. Hors LS16 .... 42 B5
Gainsbro Dr. Hors LS16 .... 42 B5
Gaisby La. Ship BD18, BD2 .... 55 D5
Gaisby Mount. Ship BD18 .... 55 D5
Gaisby Pl. Ship BD18 .... 55 D6
Gaisby Rise. Ship BD18 .... 55 D5
Gaitskell Ct. Leeds LS11 .... 79 A5 6
Gaitskell Grange. Leeds LS11 .. 79 A5 6
Gaitskell Wlk. Leeds LS11 .... 79 A5
Gale St. Haw BD22 .... 51 F8 5
Gale St. Keigh BD21 .... 35 C8
Galefield Gn. Brad BD6 .... 93 F6
Gall La. Tod OL14 .... 86 C3
Gallon Croft. S Elm WF9 .... 182 E3
Galloway Ct. Pudsey LS28 .... 76 A8 3
Galloway La. Pudsey LS28 .... 57 A1
Galloway Rd. Brad BD10 .... 56 D7
Galloway St. Hud HD1 .... 154 C8 1
Gallows Hill. Castle WF10 ...... 125 D7
Gallows La. Wool WF4 .... 159 F1
Galsworthy Ave. Brad BD9 .... 54 D3
Gamble Hill Chase. Leeds LS13 77 D8
Gamble Hill Cl. Leeds LS13 ...... 77 D8
Gamble Hill Croft. Leeds LS13 . 77 D8
Gamble Hill Cross. Leeds LS13 77 D8
Gamble Hill Dr. Leeds LS13 ...... 77 D8
Gamble Hill Fold. Leeds LS13 .. 77 D8
Gamble Hill Gn. Leeds LS13 ..... 77 D8
Gamble Hill Grange. Leeds LS13 77 D8
Gamble Hill Lawn. Leeds LS13 . 77 D8
Gamble Hill. Leeds LS13 .... 77 D8
Gamble Hill Path. Leeds LS13 .. 77 D8
Gamble Hill Pl. Leeds LS13 ...... 77 D8
Gamble Hill Rise. Leeds LS13 .. 77 D8
Gamble Hill Vale. Leeds LS13 .. 77 D8
Gamble Hill View. Leeds LS13 . 77 D8
Gamble Hill Wlk. Leeds LS13 ... 77 D8
Gamble La. Leeds LS12 .... 77 C6
Gambles Hill. Pudsey LS28 .... 57 D3 8
Game Scar La or Goose Eye
Brow. Keigh BD22 .... 34 B6
Gamel View. Stee BD20 .... 17 B6
Gang The. Leeds LS12 .... 78 C7 1
Ganners Cl. Leeds LS13 .... 58 C4
Ganners Gn. Leeds LS13 .... 58 C4
Ganners Gr. Leeds LS13 .... 58 D4
Ganners Hill. Leeds LS13 .... 58 D4
Ganners La. Leeds LS13 .... 58 C4
Ganners Mount. Leeds LS13 ..... 58 C4
Ganners Rd. Leeds LS13 .... 58 C4
Ganners Rise. Leeds LS13 .... 58 D4
Ganners Way. Leeds LS13 .... 58 C4
Ganners Wlk. Leeds LS13 .... 58 C4
Gannerthorpe Cl. Brad BD12 ... 94 C3 4
Gannet Cl. Castle WF10 .... 124 C6
Ganny Rd. Brig HD6 .... 115 B2
Ganton Cl. Leeds LS6 .... 60 B4
Ganton Way. Hud HD2 .... 135 F3
Gaol La. Hali HX1 .... 113 D7
Garden Ave. Liver WF15 .... 117 A6
Garden Cl. Brad BD12 .... 94 C4
Garden Cl. Glu BD20 .... 16 B6
Garden Cl. Liver WF15 .... 117 A5
Garden Cl. Ossett WF5 .... 140 E3
Garden Cres. Dew WF13 .... 138 E6
Garden Dr. Dew WF13 .... 138 E6
Garden Field. Brad BD12 .... 94 D3
Garden Fold. Brig HX3 .... 114 C8
Garden Ho Cl. M'town LS26 ... 102 D3
Garden House La. E Ard WF3 120 A8
Garden La. Brad BD9 .... 54 F3
Garden La. Knot WF11 .... 127 A5
Garden La. Rip HX6 .... 133 C7
Garden Par. Liver WF15 .... 117 A5 1
Garden Pl. Dew WF13 .... 117 F1
Garden Pl. S in Cra BD20 .... 16 E5
Garden Rd. Brig HD6 .... 115 A4
Garden St. Ack M T WF7 .... 163 D5
Garden St. Batley WF16 .... 117 D3 6
Garden St. Castle WF10 .... 124 D6
Garden St. Castle WF10 .... 125 A6
Garden St. Dew WF13 .... 138 E5
Garden St. Haw BD22 .... 51 F8 11
Garden St. Hud HD1 .... 153 F4
Garden St. Leeds LS9 .... 79 D7
Garden St N. Hali HX3 .... 113 D8
Garden St. Nor WF6 .... 122 E3
Garden St. Nor WF6 .... 123 B2
Garden St. Tod OL14 .... 108 B6
Garden St. Wake WF1 .... 142 B6
Garden Terr. Brad BD9 .... 55 A3
Garden Terr. Crig WF4 .... 159 E4
Garden Terr. D Dale HD8 .... 191 F5
Garden Terr. Dew WF13 .... 138 E6
Garden Terr. Heb Br HX7 .... 89 A3 11
Garden View. Bing BD16 .... 37 C3
Garden View Ct. Leeds LS8 .... 44 B1
Garden View. Liver WF15 .... 117 A6
Garden Village. M'field LS25 .... 84 A6
Garden Wlk. Liver WF15 .... 117 A5 2
Gardener's Sq. Brig HX3 .... 114 C8
Gardeners Ct. Leeds LS10 .... 79 D4
Gardens Rd. Dew WF13 .... 138 F5
Gardens St. Brad BD9 .... 54 F4
Gardens The. Bing BD16 .... 37 D3
Gardens The. Hali HX1 .... 113 C5
Gardens The. Morley LS27 .... 97 F2
Gardens The. Pudsey LS28 .... 57 C3
Gardiner Row. Brad BD4 .... 75 B3
Garfield Ave. Brad BD8 .... 55 B2
Garfield Pl. Mars HD7 .... 168 F4
Garfield St. Brad BD15 .... 54 A1
Garfield St. Hali HX3 .... 92 A1 17
Garfield St. Tod OL14 .... 86 C1
Garforth Ave. Stee BD20 .... 17 C6
Garforth Barleyhill Inf Sch. Gar 82 E7
Garforth Cl. Nor WF6 .... 122 E3
Garforth Comprehensive Sch.
Gar 82 E5
Garforth Dr. Nor WF6 .... 122 E3
Garforth Golf Course. B in Elm 63 E3
Garforth Green Lane Jun & Inf
Sch. Gar 83 B6
Garforth Inf Sch. Gar 82 E7
Garforth Ninelands Jun & Inf
Sch. Gar 83 A6
Garforth Rd. Keigh BD21 .... 35 E8
Garforth St. Brad BD15 .... 54 B1
Garforth St. Hud HD4 .... 171 C7
Garforth Sta. Gar 82 F8
Gargrave App. Leeds LS9 .... 60 F1
Gargrave Cl. Brig HD6 .... 135 D7
Gargrave Cres. Hem WF9 .... 181 C6
Gargrave Ct. Leeds LS9 .... 60 F1
Gargrave Pl. Hem WF9 .... 181 C6
Gargrave Pl. Leeds LS9 .... 60 F1
Gargrave Pl. Wake WF2 .... 141 C5
Garibaldi St. Brad BD3 .... 75 E7
Garland Dr. Leeds LS15 .... 81 D8
Garlick St. Brig HD6 .... 135 E6
Garmil Head La. Hem WF9 ...... 162 F5
Garmil La. W Har WF4 .... 162 F6
Garmont Rd. Leeds LS7 .... 60 D6
Garner La. Honley HD7 .... 171 D4
Garner La. Kirkb HD4 .... 173 D8
Garnet Ave. Leeds LS11 .... 79 C3
Garnet Cres. Leeds LS11 .... 79 C3
Garnet Gr. Leeds LS11 .... 79 C3
Garnet La. Stut LS24 .... 48 F8
Garnet Par. Leeds LS11 .... 79 C3
Garnet Pl. Leeds LS11 .... 79 C3
Garnet Rd. Leeds LS11 .... 79 C2
Garnet Terr. Leeds LS11 .... 79 C3
Garnet View. Leeds LS11 .... 79 C3
Garnett St. Batley WF13 .... 117 F3
Garnett St. Brad BD3 .... 75 A7
Garnett St. Heb Br HX7 .... 89 A3
Garnett St. Otley LS21 .... 23 B8
Garrett Cl. Skel HD8 .... 174 F2
Garsdale Ave. Brad BD10 .... 56 C7
Garsdale Cres. Bail BD17 .... 38 E4
Garsdale Fold. Coll LS22 .... 13 A1
Garsdale Gr. Wake WF1 .... 142 F8
Garsdale Rd. Hud HD4 .... 154 B2
Garsdale Wlk. Knot WF11 .... 126 E2
Garth Ave. Coll LS22 .... 29 B8
Garth Ave. Leeds LS17 .... 43 B1
Garth Ave. Nor WF6 .... 144 A8
Garth Barn Cl. Ship BD9 .... 55 A4
Garth Dr. Leeds LS17 .... 43 B1
Garth End. Coll LS22 .... 29 B8
Garth Gr. Men LS29 .... 22 A4
Garth Land Way. Brad BD4 ...... 75 C3
Garth Rd. Leeds LS17 .... 43 B1
Garth St. Castle WF10 .... 124 C6
Garth St. Keigh BD21 .... 35 A7
Garth The. Coll LS22 .... 29 B8
Garth The. Gar LS25 .... 83 A7
Garth The. Leeds LS9 .... 79 E7
Garth Wlk. Leeds LS17 .... 43 C1
Garthwaite Mount. Brad BD15 54 B2
Garton Ave. Leeds LS9 .... 80 A7
Garton Dr. Brad BD10 .... 56 D5
Garton Gr. Leeds LS9 .... 80 A7
Garton Rd. Leeds LS9 .... 80 A7
Garton Terr. Leeds LS9 .... 80 A7
Garton View. Leeds LS9 .... 80 A7 9
Garvey View. Brad BD5 .... 74 E4
Garwick Terr. Elland HX4 ...... 134 D7 9
Gas St. Haw BD22 .... 51 D7 4
Gas Works La. B Spa LS23 .... 30 F7
Gas Works La. Elland HX5 ...... 134 F7
Gas Works Rd. Hali HX6 .... 112 D4
Gas Works Rd. Keigh BD21 .... 35 F7
Gascoigne Ave. B in Elm LS15 . 63 D6
Gascoigne Ct. B in Elm LS15 .... 63 E6
Gascoigne Rd. B in Elm LS15 .... 63 D6
Gascoigne Rd. E Ard WF3 .... 99 E1
Gascoigne View. B in Elm LS15 63 D6
Gaskell Dr. Hor WF4 .... 141 A2
Gaskell St. Wake WF2 .... 142 A5
Gasson St. Hud HD3 .... 153 A4
Gasworks St. Hud HD1 .... 154 B7
Gasworks St. Liver WF15 .... 117 B4
Gate Foot La. Holmfi HD8 ...... 190 C5
Gate Head. Elland HX4 .... 133 F6
Gate Head La. Elland HX4 ...... 133 F6
Gate Head La. Holmfi HD7 ...... 200 A8
Gate Head. Mars HD7 .... 169 B4
Gate Way Dr. Yeadon LS19 ...... 40 A6
Gatefield Mount. Brad BD6 ...... 94 B6
Gatehead Bank. Mars HD7 ..... 169 B5
Gatehouse Ent'prise Ctr. Hud 153 F3
Gateland Dr. Thorner LS17 ...... 44 E4
Gateland La. Thorner LS17 ...... 44 E4
Gateon House La. Bard LS17 ... 28 B4
Gatesgarth Cres. Hud HD3 ..... 135 A1
Gateside View. Leeds LS15 ...... 80 E6
Gateways Girls' Prep & High Sch.
Hare 27 A6
Gateways. Loft G WF1 .... 121 C5
Gathorne Cl. Leeds LS8 .... 60 F3
Gathorne St. Brad BD7 .... 74 B4
Gathorne St. Brig HD6 .... 115 B3
Gathorne St. Leeds LS8 .... 60 E3
Gathorne Terr. Leeds LS8 .... 60 E3
Gauk St. Broth WF11 .... 126 C8
Gauk St. Fair WF11 .... 105 A4
Gaukroger La. Hali HX3 .... 113 D5
Gauxholme Fold. Tod OL14 ..... 107 F3
Gaw La. Hal E BD23 .... 1 F8
Gawcliffe Rd. Ship BD18 .... 55 C7
Gawthorpe Ave. Bing BD16 ..... 37 A5
Gawthorpe Dr. Bing BD16 ...... 37 A5
Gawthorpe Green La. Lepton
HD8 .... 155 E6
Gawthorpe La. Bing BD16 .... 37 A4
Gawthorpe La. Kirkhe HD8 .... 155 D6
Gawthorpe La. Ossett WF5 .... 119 E2
Gawthorpe La. Wake WF2 ...... 120 A2
Gawthorpe Prim Sch. Ossett . 119 C1
Gay La. Otley LS21 .... 23 A7
Gaynor St. Brad BD8 .... 74 D8
Gaythorn Terr. Brig HX3 .... 93 C1
Gaythorne Rd. Brad BD2 .... 56 C2
Gaythorne Rd. Brad BD5 .... 74 E3
Gaythorne Terr. Brad BD14 ..... 73 C4 6
Geecroft La. Sickl LS22 .... 12 B4
Geelong Cl. Brad BD2 .... 55 F3
Gelder Rd. Leeds LS12 .... 78 C7
Gelder Terr. Hud HD5 .... 154 C5
Gelderd Cl. Leeds LS12 .... 78 D4
Gelderd La. Leeds LS12 .... 78 D4
Gelderd Pl. Leeds LS12 .... 78 E6
Gelderd Rd. Batley WF17 .... 97 C5
Gelderd Rd. Gild LS27 .... 97 C5
Gelderd Rd. Leeds LS12 .... 78 D3
Gelderd Trad Est. Leeds 78 E5
General Hospl The. Dew 118 B1
General Infmy at Leeds The.
Leeds 60 B1
Geneva Gr. Wake WF1 .... 142 D7
Genista Dr. Midd LS10 .... 99 D8
George and Crown Yd. Wake
WF1 .... 142 C6 5
George Ave. Hud HD2 .... 153 E8
George Buckley Ct. S Kirk WF9 182 A2
George La. Notton WF4 .... 178 E6
George La. Rip HX6 .... 132 B2
George Sq. Hali HX1 .... 113 C7 11
George St. Bail BD17 .... 38 C1 6
George St. Batley WF16 .... 117 D4
George St. Batley WF17 .... 118 C4
George St. Brad BD1 .... 74 F6
George St. Brig HX3 .... 114 D7
George St. Brig HD6 .... 115 A1
George St. Brig HD6 .... 115 C2
George St. Clec BD19 .... 116 D8
George St. Denh BD13 .... 52 E1
George St. Dew WF13 .... 138 E5
George St. Dew WF13 .... 138 F8
George St. Dew WF13 .... 139 C8
George St. Elland HX4 .... 134 D7 5
George St. Elland HX5 .... 134 F6
George St. Feath WF7 .... 144 D5
George St. Feath WF7 .... 145 C5
George St. Hali HX1 .... 113 C7
George St. Heb Br HX7 .... 110 E8
George St. Hem WF9 .... 181 E6
George St. Hor WF4 .... 141 B1
George St. Hud HD3 .... 135 B1
George St. Hud HD3 .... 153 B5
George St. Hud HD1 .... 153 E4
George St. Hud HD1 .... 154 A6 12
George St. Kirkb HD8 .... 173 F6
George St. Leeds LS1 .... 79 B8
George St. Liver WF15 .... 117 A4 10
George St. Loft G WF1 .... 121 B5
George St. Mapp S75 .... 178 B1
George St. Nor WF6 .... 122 F3
George St. Ossett WF5 .... 140 D7
George St. Ryhill WF4 .... 162 B2
George St. S Hie S72 .... 180 D6
George St. Ship BD18 .... 54 F8
George St. Sil LS29 .... 6 F8
George St. Sow Br HX6 .... 112 B3
George St. Thorn BD13 .... 72 D6
George St. Tod OL14 .... 108 B5 13
George St. Wake WF1 .... 142 C6
George St. Yeadon LS19 .... 40 B4
George's Sq. Cull BD13 .... 52 D6
George's Sq. Keigh BD21 .... 35 B6
George's St. Hali HX3 .... 91 F3
George-a-green Rd. Wake
WF2 .... 141 E4
Georgia Mews. Ossett WF5 ... 140 F4
Geraldton Ave. Brad BD2 .... 55 E3
Gerard Ave. Morley LS27 .... 97 F4
Gernhill Ave. Brig HD2 .... 135 F5
Gerrard St. Hali HX1 .... 113 B7
Gervase Rd. Hor WF4 .... 141 A2
Ghyll Beck Dr. Otley LS21 .... 22 D6
Ghyll Beck Dr. Yeadon LS19 ..... 40 E3
Ghyll Cl. Stee BD20 .... 17 C5
Ghyll Mews. Ilkley LS29 .... 8 A3
Ghyll Mount. Yeadon LS19 .... 39 F6
Ghyll Rd. Leeds LS6 .... 59 A6
Ghyll Royd. Guise LS20 .... 39 E7
Ghyll Royd Sch. Ilkley 7 F3
Ghyll The. Hud HD2 .... 136 A4
Ghyll The. Ship BD16 .... 54 A8
Ghyll Wood Dr. Ship BD16 .... 54 A8
Ghyll Wood. Ilkley LS29 .... 7 E3
Ghyllbank. Sil BD20 .... 5 E2
Ghyllroyd Ave. Birk BD11 .... 96 B5
Ghyllroyd Dr. Birk BD11 .... 96 B4
Gib Cotts. Honley HD7 .... 172 A2
Gib La. Skel HD8 .... 175 A2
Gibb La. Hali HX2 .... 91 B3
Gibbet St. Hali HX1, HX2 .... 112 E7
Gibraltar Ave. Hali HX1 .... 112 E6
Gibraltar Isl Rd. Leeds LS10 .... 79 F4
Gibraltar Rd. Hali HX1 .... 112 E6
Gibraltar Rd. Pudsey LS28 .... 76 B7
Gibraltar Terr. S in Cra BD20 .. 16 C5
Gibriding La. Holmfi HD7 .... 187 F3
Gibson Ave. Wake WF2 .... 141 F7
Gibson Cl. Wake WF2 .... 142 A7
Gibson Dr. Leeds LS15 .... 81 C7
Gibson La. Kippax LS25 .... 83 C2
Gibson Lane Jun Sch. Kippax ... 83 B1
Gibson Mill. Hep HX7 .... 88 C8
Gibson St. Brad BD3 .... 75 B6
Gibson St. Hud HD3 .... 153 C7
Gibson St. Tod OL14 .... 108 C5 6
Gilbert Chase. Leeds LS5 .... 59 A3
Gilbert Cl. Leeds LS5 .... 59 B3
Gilbert Gr. Hud HD4 .... 153 D3
Gilbert Mount. Leeds LS5 .... 59 B3
Gilbert St. Pudsey LS28 .... 57 D2
Gilcar St. Nor WF6 .... 123 D4
Gildersome Birchfield Cty Prim
Sch. Gild 97 C6
Gildersome Jun Sch. Gild 97 C7
Gildersome La. Gild LS27 .... 77 B1
Gildersome Spur. Gild LS27 ..... 97 D5
Gilead Rd. Hud HD3 .... 152 E7
Giles Hill La. Shelf HX3 .... 93 A7
Giles St. Brad BD6 .... 74 A1
Giles St. Brad BD5 .... 74 D5
Giles St. Holmfi HD7 .... 188 F8
Gill Bank Rd. Ilkley LS29 .... 8 A6
Gill Beck Cl. Bail BD17 .... 38 E4
Gill Cl. Sil LS29 .... 6 D8
Gill La. Guise LS19 .... 39 F4
Gill La. Holmfi HD7 .... 188 E2
Gill La. Keigh BD22 .... 34 A4
Gill La. Nes LS29 .... 7 C7
Gill La. Yeadon LS19 .... 39 F4
Gill La. Yeadon LS19 .... 40 A5
Gill Sike Ave. Wake WF2 .... 141 F4
Gill Sike Bglws. Wake WF2 ..... 141 F4
Gill Sike Gr. Wake WF2 .... 141 F4
Gill Sike House. Wake WF2 ... 141 F4
Gill Sike Rd. Wake WF2 .... 141 E4
Gill St. Wake WF1 .... 142 C6 1
Gill's Bldgs. Wake WF2 .... 142 A5
Gill's Yd. Wake WF1 .... 142 C7
Gillann St. Knot WF11 .... 127 A4
Gillett Dr. Roth LS26 .... 100 F5
Gillett La. Roth LS26 .... 100 F5
Gilling Ave. Gar LS25 .... 83 B8
Gillingham Gn. Brad BD4 .... 75 E3
Gillion Cres. Crig WF4 .... 159 E6
Gillrene Ave. Wils BD15 .... 53 D4
Gillroyd La. Slai HD7 .... 170 D8
Gillroyd Par. Morley LS27 .... 98 B3
Gillroyd Pl. Morley LS27 .... 98 B4 7
Gillroyd Terr. Morley LS27 ...... 98 C4
Gills The. Otley LS21 .... 11 A2
Gillstone Dr. Haw BD22 .... 51 D6
Gillygate. Pont WF8 .... 146 D8
Gilmour St. Hali HX3 .... 92 B1 5
Gilpin Pl. Leeds LS12 .... 78 D6
Gilpin St. Brad BD3 .... 75 B7
Gilpin St. Leeds LS12 .... 78 D6 2
Gilpin Terr. Leeds LS12 .... 78 D6
Gilpin View. Leeds LS12 .... 78 D6
Gilroyd Rise. Brad BD7 .... 74 B7
Gilstead Ct. Bing BD16 .... 37 C3
Gilstead Dr. Bing BD16 .... 37 C3
Gilstead La. Bing BD16 .... 37 C3
Gilstead Mid Sch. Bing 37 C4
Gilstead Way. Ilkley LS29 .... 8 B5
Gilthwaites Cres. D Dale HD8 192 A7
Gilthwaites Fst Sch. D Dale 192 A7
Gilthwaites Gr. D Dale HD8 ... 192 A6
Gilthwaites La. D Dale HD8 .... 192 A7
Gilthwaites Top. D Dale HD8 . 192 A7
Gilynda Cl. Brad BD8 .... 73 E7
Gin La. Crof WF7 .... 144 C4
Ginnel The. Bard LS17 .... 28 C2
Gipsy Hill. Roth LS26 .... 101 B6

Gipsy La. Leeds LS11 99 A7
Gipsy La. Midd LS11 99 A7
Gipsy La. Roth LS26 101 B6
Gipsy La. Wake WF2 160 E7
Gipsy La. Wool WF4 177 F6
Gipsy Mead. Roth LS26 101 B6
Gipsy St. Brad BD3 75 E8
Gipton App. Leeds LS9 61 D1
Gipton Ave. Leeds LS8 60 E3
Gipton Gate E. Leeds LS9 61 C3
Gipton Gate W. Leeds LS9 61 B3
Gipton Sq. Leeds LS9 61 D1
Gipton St. Leeds LS8 60 E3
Gipton Wood Ave. Leeds LS8 61 B5
Gipton Wood Cres. Leeds LS8 61 B5
Gipton Wood Gr. Leeds LS8 61 B5
Gipton Wood Pl. Leeds LS8 61 B5
Gipton Wood Prim Sch. Leeds 61 C3
Gipton Wood Rd. Leeds LS8 61 B5
Girlington Fst Sch. Brad 74 A8
Girlington Rd. Brad BD8 55 A1
Girnhill Inf Sch. Feath 145 C4
Girnhill La. Feath WF7 145 C4
Gisbourne Rd. Hud HD2 136 E5
Gisburn Rd. Wake WF1 142 F8
Gisburn St. Keigh BD21 35 B8
Gissing Rd. Wake WF2 141 D4
Glade The. Pudsey LS28 57 A2
Glade The. Scar LS14 45 B7
Gladstonbury Ave. Wake WF1 121 F1
Gladstone Cres. Bacup OL13 106 A2 3
Gladstone Cres. Yeadon LS19 40 B5
Gladstone Ct. Dew WF13 118 A1 3
Gladstone Rd. Hali HX1 113 A7 16
Gladstone Rd. Yeadon LS19 40 B4
Gladstone St. Bacup OL13 106 A2
Gladstone St. Bing BD16 36 F2
Gladstone St. Brad BD15 54 B1
Gladstone St. Brad BD3 75 C7
Gladstone St. Clec BD19 116 D7 3
Gladstone St. Elland HX4 134 A4 3
Gladstone St. Feath WF7 145 D7
Gladstone St. Keigh BD21 35 B6
Gladstone St. Nor WF6 123 C3
Gladstone St. Pudsey LS28 57 D3 1
Gladstone St. Queen BD13 72 F1
Gladstone St. Tod OL14 86 B1 10
Gladstone Terr. Castle WF10 124 E8
Gladstone Terr. Morley LS27 98 A4
Gladstone Terr. Pudsey LS28 57 F2
Gladstone View. Hali HX3 113 E3
Gladwin St. Batley WF17 118 B4
Glaisdale Cl. Sil BD20 17 E8
Glaisdale Ct. Brad BD15 54 A3
Glaisdale Gr. Brig HX3 114 D7
Glamis Cl. Gar LS25 83 B8
Glanville Terr. Roth LS26 100 E5
Glasshouse St. Leeds LS10 79 D5
Glasshouse View. Midd LS10 99 B4
Glastonbury Dr. Hud HD3 152 F5
Glazier Rd. Queen BD13 72 C2
Gleanings Ave. Hali HX2 112 C7
Gleanings Dr. Hali HX2 112 C7
Glebe Ave. Leeds LS5 59 B4
Glebe Cl. Emley HD8 175 D7
Glebe Field Chase. Weth LS22 13 D6
Glebe Field Cl. Weth LS22 13 D6
Glebe Field Croft. Weth LS22 13 D6
Glebe Field Dr. Weth LS22 13 D6
Glebe Field Garth. Weth LS22 13 D6
Glebe Field Holt. Weth LS22 13 D6
Glebe Gate. Dew WF12 139 F1
Glebe La. Knot WF11 126 F4
Glebe Mount. Pudsey LS28 76 E6
Glebe Pl. Leeds LS5 59 B4
Glebe St. Castle WF10 124 D7
Glebe St. Hud HD1 153 E7
Glebe St. Nor WF6 144 C8
Glebe St. Pudsey LS28 76 E6
Glebe Terr. Leeds LS16 59 D7
Glebelands. Beal WF11 127 E4
Glebelands Cl. Gar LS25 82 F6
Glebelands Dr. Leeds LS6 59 D6
Gledcliffe. Hali HX3 113 D8 5
Gleddings Cl. Hali HX3 113 A3
Gleddings Preparatory Sch The. Hali 113 A3
Gledhill Rd. Brad BD3 75 B6
Gledhill St. Tod OL14 108 B6 2
Gledhill Terr. Dew WF13 138 F8
Gledholt Bank. Hud HD1 153 E5
Gledholt Rd. Hud HD1 153 E6
Gledhow Ave. Leeds LS8 60 F8
Gledhow Ct. Leeds LS7 60 E7
Gledhow Dr. Oxen BD22 51 C4
Gledhow Grange View. Leeds LS8 60 F7
Gledhow Grange Wlk. Leeds LS8 60 F7
Gledhow La. Leeds LS7, LS8 60 E7
Gledhow Mount. Leeds LS8 60 E2
Gledhow Park Ave. Leeds LS7 60 E6
Gledhow Park Cres. Leeds LS7 60 E6
Gledhow Park Dr. Leeds LS7 60 E6
Gledhow Park Gr. Leeds LS7 60 E6
Gledhow Park Rd. Leeds LS7 60 E6
Gledhow Park View. Leeds LS7 60 E6
Gledhow Pl. Leeds LS8 60 E2
Gledhow Prim Sch. Leeds 60 F8
Gledhow Rd. Leeds LS8 60 E2
Gledhow Rise. Leeds LS8 61 B6
Gledhow Terr. Leeds LS8 60 E2 1
Gledhow Towers. Leeds LS8 60 E7
Gledhow Valley Rd. Leeds LS17, LS7, LS8 60 E7
Gledhow Wood Ave. Leeds LS8 60 F7
Gledhow Wood Cl. Leeds LS8 60 F7
Gledhow Wood Ct. Leeds LS8 61 A5
Gledhow Wood Gr. Leeds LS8 60 F7
Gledhow Wood Rd. Leeds LS8 60 F6
Gledmow Lane End. Leeds LS7 60 D7
Glen Ave. Batley WF17 118 C6
Glen Ave. Tod OL14 107 F7
Glen Dale. Ship BD16 53 F7
Glen Dene. Men LS29 22 B4
Glen Dene. Ship BD16 53 F7
Glen Field Ave. Hud HD2 136 F3
Glen Garth. Keigh BD21 35 D5
Glen Gr. Morley LS27 98 B3
Glen Lee La. Keigh BD21 35 D5
Glen Mount Cl. Hali HX3 91 E2
Glen Mount. Men LS29 22 B3
Glen Mount. Morley LS27 98 B3
Glen Mount. Ship BD16 53 F7
Glen Rd. Bail BD17 37 D4
Glen Rd. Leeds LS16 59 C7
Glen Rd. Morley LS27 98 C3
Glen Rise. Bail BD17 38 A2
Glen Rly. Ship 37 F2
Glen Side Rd. Slai HD7 170 A8
Glen Terr. Brig HX3 114 C7
Glen Terr. Hali HX1 113 B5
Glen The. Tod OL14 107 F7
Glen View. Hali HX1 113 B5
Glen View. Harden BD16 36 B1
Glen View Rd. Bing BD16 37 C5
Glen View Rd. Heb Br HX7 88 E4
Glen View Rd. Shep HD8 174 A2
Glen View St. Tod OL14 86 B1
Glen Way. Bing BD16 37 C6
Glenaire Dr. Bail BD17 38 A1
Glenaire Fst Sch. Bail 38 A2
Glenaire. Ship BD18 38 E1
Glenbrook Dr. Brad BD7 73 F7
Glencoe Cl. Kippax LS25 102 F8
Glencoe Croft. Kippax LS25 102 F8
Glencoe Gdns. Kippax LS25 102 F8
Glencoe Terr. Kippax LS25 102 F8
Glencoe Terr. Liver WF15 117 B3
Glencoe View. Leeds LS9 79 F6
Glendale Ave. Gar LS25 82 F6
Glendale Cl. Brad BD6 94 A7
Glendale Dr. Brad BD6 94 A7
Glendale. Hor WF4 140 F1
Glendare Ave. Brad BD7 73 F6
Glendare Rd. Brad BD7 73 F6
Glendare Terr. Brad BD7 73 F6
Glendorne Dr. Kirkhe HD5 137 C1
Glendower Pk. Hors LS16 42 D2
Gleneagles Rd. Feath WF7 124 D1
Gleneagles Rd. Leeds LS17 43 B4
Gleneagles Way. Hud HD2 135 F3
Glenfield Ave. Brad BD6 94 D8
Glenfield Ave. Weth LS22 13 F4
Glenfield Mount. Brad BD6 94 D8 8
Glenfield. Ship BD18 38 E1
Glenfields Cl. Neth WF4 158 D5
Glenfields. Neth WF4 158 D5
Glenholm Rd. Bail BD17 38 C3
Glenholm Rd W. Bail BD17 38 C2
Glenholme Heath. Hali HX1 112 E7
Glenholme Rd. Brad BD8 55 B1
Glenholme Rd. Pudsey LS28 57 C2
Glenholme. Ship BD18 38 E1
Glenholme Terr. Ossett WF5 119 C1
Glenhurst Ave. Keigh BD21 35 C5
Glenhurst. Brad BD4 75 D1
Glenhurst Dr. Keigh BD21 35 D5
Glenhurst Gr. Keigh BD21 35 D5
Glenhurst Rd. Ship BD18 54 E8
Glenlea Cl. Leeds LS28 58 A3
Glenlea Gdns. Leeds LS28 58 A3
Glenlee Rd. Brad BD7 73 F7
Glenlow Rd. Batley WF12 118 F3
Glenlyon Ave. Keigh BD20 18 A1
Glenlyon Dr. Keigh BD20 18 A1
Glenmere Mount. Yeadon LS19 40 D7
Glenmore Cl. Brad BD2 56 C1
Glenmore Ct. Bramho LS16 24 E3
Glenrose Dr. Brad BD7 73 E6
Glenroyd Ave. Brad BD6 94 D7
Glenroyd Cl. Pudsey LS28 76 C7
Glenroyd. Mars HD7 168 E4
Glenroyd. Ship BD18 38 E1
Glensdale Gr. Leeds LS9 79 F7
Glensdale Mount. Leeds LS9 79 F7
Glensdale Rd. Leeds LS9 79 F7
Glensdale St. Leeds LS9 79 F7
Glensdale Terr. Leeds LS9 80 A7
Glenside Ave. Ship BD18 38 E1
Glenside Cl. Hud HD3 153 D8
Glenside Rd. Ship BD18 38 E1
Glenstone Gr. Brad BD7 73 F7
Glenthorpe Ave. Leeds LS9 80 A8
Glenthorpe Cres. Leeds LS9 80 A8
Glenthorpe Terr. Leeds LS9 80 A8
Glenton Sq. Brad BD9 55 A2
Glenview Ave. Brad BD9 54 E3
Glenview Cl. Ship BD18 54 C7
Glenview Dr. Ship BD18 54 C6
Glenview Gr. Ship BD18 54 D7
Glenview Rd. Ship BD18 54 D7
Glenview Terr. Ship BD18 54 F8
Glenwood Ave. Bail BD17 37 E1
Global Ave. Leeds LS11 78 E1
Globe Ct. Liver WF15 117 B4
Globe Fold. Brad BD8 74 C8
Globe Rd. Leeds LS11 79 A6
Glossop Gr. Leeds LS6 60 B4
Glossop Mount. Leeds LS6 60 B4
Glossop St. Leeds LS6 60 B4
Glossop View. Leeds LS6 60 B4 2
Gloucester Ave. Brad BD3 56 D1
Gloucester Ave. Sil BD20 5 C1
Gloucester Ct. Leeds LS12 78 E6
Gloucester Gr. Wake WF2 141 D5
Gloucester Pl. Wake WF2 141 D5
Gloucester Rd. Bing BD16 37 B2
Gloucester Rd. Wake WF2 141 D5
Gloucester Terr. Leeds LS12 78 E7
Glover Ct. Brad BD5 74 E4
Glover Way. Leeds LS11 79 C2
Glovershaw La. Bail BD16 37 E6
Glusburn Cty Prim Sch. Glu 16 C6
Glydegate. Brad BD5 74 E6
Glyndon Ct. Brig HD6 136 B8
Glynn Terr. Brad BD8 74 B8
Godfrey Rd. Hali HX3 113 C3
Godfrey St. Brad BD8 73 D7
Godley Branch Rd. Hali HX3 113 E8
Godley Cl. Roy S71 179 D4
Godley Gdns. Northo HX3 92 F1
Godley La. Hali HX3 113 E8
Godley La. Northo HX3 92 F1
Godley Rd. Hali HX3 113 D8
Godley St. Roy S71 179 D4
Godly Cl. Rip HX6 132 C1
Godwin St. Brad BD1 74 E7
Goff Well La. Keigh BD21 35 C2
Gog Hill. Elland HX5 134 F7
Goit Side. Brad BD1 74 E7 15
Goit Side. Hali HX2 90 E4
Goit Stock La. Harden BD16 53 B8
Goit Stock Terr. Harden BD16 53 B8
Golcar Brow Rd. Mel HD7 170 C2
Golcar Cty J & I Schs. Hud 152 D4
Goldcrest Ave. Brad BD8 73 B7 12
Goldcrest Ct. Hud HD4 171 E6
Golden Acre Cnr. Bramho LS16 25 A1
Golden Acre Pk. Eccup 42 C8
Golden Bank. Hors LS18 41 C1
Golden Butts Rd. Ilkley LS29 8 C4
Golden Sq. Hor WF4 141 B1
Golden Terr. Leeds LS12 78 A4
Golden View Dr. Keigh BD21 35 F6
Goldfields Ave. Elland HX4 134 B8
Goldfields Cl. Elland HX4 134 B8 1
Goldfields View. Elland HX4 134 B8 2
Goldfields Way. Elland HX4 134 B8
Goldington Ave. Hud HD3 153 A8
Goldington Dr. Hud HD3 153 A8
Golf Ave. Hali HX2 112 C7
Golf Cres. Hali HX2 112 C7
Golf La. Batley LS27 118 E8
Gomersal Fst Sch. Clec 96 B1
Gomersal La. Clec BD19 117 A7
Gomersal Mid Sch. Clec 96 B1
Gomersal Rd. Liver WF16 117 C6
Gomersal St Mary's CE Fst Sch. Clec 117 B8
Gondal Ct. Brad BD5 74 C3
Good Hope Cl. Nor WF6 123 D3
Goodcomb Pl. Kippax LS25 83 C3
Gooder Ave. Roy S71 179 C3
Gooder La. Brig HD6 115 B1
Gooder St. Brig HD6 115 A2
Goodman St. Leeds LS10 79 E3
Goodrick La. Eccup LS17 43 B7
Goodwin House. Queen BD13 72 E1 5
Goodwin Pl. Hud HD2 136 F5
Goodwin Rd. Leeds LS12 78 C6
Goodwood Ave. Kippax LS25 83 A2
Goodwood. Ilkley LS29 7 F6
Goody Cross La. Swil LS26 82 C2
Goody Cross. Swil LS26 82 C2
Goose Cote La. Haw BD22 34 E2
Goose Cote La. Keigh BD22 34 E2
Goose Cote Way. Haw BD22 34 E3
Goose Eye. Keigh BD22 34 B6
Goose Gn. Holmfi HD7 189 A5
Goose Hill. Batley WF16 117 D4
Goose La. Guise LS20 21 C1
Goose West La. Sow Br HX6 112 B2
Gooseacre Ave. Dearne S63 194 C1
Goosefield Rise. Gar LS25 82 D6
Goosehill La. Crof WF1 143 E7
Goosehill Rd. Nor WF6 144 A8
Goosehole La. S Elm WF9 183 B1
Gordale Cl. Batley WF17 118 B5
Gordale Cl. Brad BD4 75 F3
Gordon Ave. Ossett WF5 140 D6
Gordon Dr. Leeds LS6 59 F6
Gordon Pl. Leeds LS6 59 F6 5
Gordon Pl. S Elm WF9 182 F2
Gordon St. Brad BD14 73 B4 7
Gordon St. Brad BD5 74 F5
Gordon St. E Ard WF3 120 E8
Gordon St. Elland HX5 134 F6
Gordon St. Feath WF7 145 D7
Gordon St. Hali HX3 92 B2
Gordon St. Haw BD22 51 E8 10
Gordon St. Ilkley LS29 8 C4
Gordon St. Keigh BD21 35 B7
Gordon St. S in Cra BD20 16 D5
Gordon St. Slai HD7 170 A8
Gordon St. Sow Br HX6 112 A3
Gordon St. Tod OL14 108 C5 10
Gordon St. Wake WF1 142 F2
Gordon Terr. Brad BD10 39 B1
Gordon Terr. Knot WF11 127 B3
Gordon Terr. Leeds LS6 59 F6
Gordon Terr. Slai HD7 152 D2
Gordon View. Leeds LS6 59 F6
Gordonsfield. Ack M T WF7 163 F5
Goring Park Ave. Ossett WF5 141 A4
Gorple Rd. Worst BB10 66 A5
Gorse Ave. Bail BD17 37 E2
Gorse Lea. Midd LS10 99 D8 5
Gorse Rd. Hud HD3 153 C6
Gorton St. Hem WF9 163 B1
Gosling La. Rip HX6 132 F2
Gosport Cl. Elland HD3 152 A8
Gosport La. Elland HX4 133 F1
Gosport La. Elland HD3 152 A8
Gothic Mount. Feath WF7 145 A8
Gothic St. Queen BD13 72 E1
Gott St. Haw BD22 51 F8
Gott's Terr. Keigh BD20 18 A2
Gotts Park Ave. Leeds LS12 58 F1
Gotts Park View. Leeds LS12 59 A2
Gotts Pk. Leeds 59 A1
Gotts Rd. Leeds LS12 78 F7
Gough La. Rip HX6 132 B7
Goulbourne St. Keigh BD21 35 B6
Governor's Wlk. Wake WF1 142 D7
Gower St. Brad BD5 74 E4
Gower St. Leeds LS2 79 D8
Grace Leather La. Batley WF17 118 E5
Grace St. Keigh BD21 35 D7
Grace St. Leeds LS1 79 A8
Gracechurch St. Brad BD8 74 D8
Gracey La. Brad BD6 73 F1
Grafton Cl. Bail BD17 38 D4
Grafton Cl. Knot WF11 126 F5
Grafton Pl. Hali HX3 92 A3
Grafton Rd. Keigh BD21 35 A5
Grafton Sch. Leeds 60 B3
Grafton St. Batley WF17 118 D3
Grafton St. Brad BD5 74 E5
Grafton St. Castle WF10 124 E5
Grafton St. Keigh BD21 35 B5
Grafton St. Leeds LS7 60 D1
Grafton Villas. Leeds LS15 62 D4
Graham Ave. Leeds LS4 59 D3 10
Graham Ave. Upton WF9 183 D8
Graham Dr. Castle WF10 125 B7
Graham Gr. Leeds LS4 59 D3
Graham Mount. Leeds LS4 59 D3
Graham St. Brad BD9 55 A2
Graham St. Hud HD1 153 F5
Graham St. Leeds LS4 59 D3
Graham Terr. Leeds LS4 59 D3
Graham View. Leeds LS4 59 D3
Graham Wlk. Gild LS27 97 D7
Grain St. Brad BD5 74 B2
Gramfield Rd. Hud HD4 153 C3
Grammar School St. Brad BD1 74 E8
Grampian Ave. Wake WF2 141 E3
Grampian Cl. Shep HD8 173 F3
Granby Ave. Leeds LS6 59 D5
Granby Cl. Leeds LS6 59 D5
Granby Ct. S Elm WF9 183 A5
Granby Dr. Keigh BD20 18 F1
Granby Gr. Leeds LS6 59 D5
Granby La. Keigh BD20 18 F1
Granby Mount. Leeds LS6 59 D5 7
Granby Pl. Leeds LS6 59 D5
Granby Rd. Leeds LS6 59 D5
Granby St. Brad BD4 74 F6 6
Granby St. Leeds LS6 59 D5
Granby St. Queen BD13 72 E1 2
Granby Terr. Leeds LS6 59 D5
Granby View. Leeds LS6 59 D5
Grand Arc. Leeds LS1 79 C8 2
Grand Cross Rd. Hud HD5 154 E6
Grand Stand Rd. Loft G WF2 120 F5
Grand Stand. Slai HD7 152 B5
Grandage Terr. Brad BD8 74 B8
Grandsmere Pl. Hali HX3 113 B4 5
Grange Ave. Batley WF17 118 B3
Grange Ave. Birk BD4 96 A8
Grange Ave. Brad BD15 73 C8
Grange Ave. Brad BD3 75 F8
Grange Ave. Gar LS25 82 F6
Grange Ave. Hali HX2 91 F5
Grange Ave. Hud HD2 135 F1
Grange Ave. Ilkley LS29 8 D4
Grange Ave. Leeds LS7 60 E4
Grange Ave. Mars HD7 169 A4
Grange Ave. Men LS29 21 F5
Grange Ave. S Elm WF9 183 A3
Grange Ave. Ship BD18 54 E8
Grange Ave. Th Arch LS23 15 A3
Grange Ave. Yeadon LS19 40 C6
Grange Bank Cl. Hud HD5 154 D7
Grange Bank. Shelf HX3 93 C6
Grange Castle. Yeadon LS19 40 D6
Grange Cl. Bad WF9 164 E2
Grange Cl. Bard LS17 28 D4
Grange Cl. Bri S72 180 F3
Grange Cl. Elland HD3 152 A8
Grange Cl. Hors LS18 57 F8
Grange Cl. Ilkley LS29 8 D4
Grange Cl. Knot WF11 126 D4
Grange Cl. Leeds LS10 79 D4
Grange Cotts. Mars HD7 169 A4
Grange Cres. Keigh BD20 18 E1
Grange Cres. Leeds LS7 60 E4
Grange Cres. Yeadon LS19 40 C6
Grange Croft. Leeds LS17 43 C5
Grange Ct. B in Elm LS15 62 F6
Grange Ct. Bad WF9 164 E2
Grange Ct. Hali HX3 114 A4
Grange Ct. Leeds LS17 43 C5
Grange Ct. Leeds LS6 59 F5
Grange Ct. Ship BD16 54 A7 4
Grange Dr. Brad BD15 73 C8
Grange Dr. Emley HD8 175 D8
Grange Dr. Hors LS18 57 F8
Grange Dr. Ossett WF5 140 F3
Grange Est. Ilkley LS29 8 D4
Grange Farm Prim Sch. Leeds 61 F6
Grange Fields Mount. Midd LS10 99 F7 6
Grange Fields Rd. Midd LS10 99 F6
Grange Fields Way. Midd LS10 99 F6
Grange Gr. Brad BD3 75 F8
Grange Gr. Keigh BD20 18 E1
Grange Holt. Leeds LS17 43 C5
Grange House. Bri S72 180 F3
Grange Hts. Hali HX3 114 A4
Grange La. Brig HD6 115 E2
Grange La. Burg DN6 184 F3
Grange La. Floc WF4 157 D4
Grange La. Haw BD22 33 F3
Grange La. Kippax LS25 83 B2
Grange La. Kirkb HD8 173 D3
Grange Mid Sch. Keigh 18 E2
Grange Mount. Yeadon LS19 40 C6
Grange Park Ave. Leeds LS8 61 D5
Grange Park Cl. Kippax WF10 103 A5
Grange Park Cl. Leeds LS8 61 D5
Grange Park Cl. Morley LS27 98 B7 9
Grange Park Cres. Leeds LS8 61 D5
Grange Park Dr. Morley LS27 98 B7
Grange Park Dr. Ship BD16 54 B8
Grange Park Gr. Leeds LS8 61 D5
Grange Park Mews. Leeds LS8 61 D5
Grange Park Mews. Morley LS27 98 B7 10
Grange Park Pl. Leeds LS8 61 E5
Grange Park Rd. Leeds LS8 61 E5
Grange Park Rd. Ship BD16 54 A7
Grange Park Rise. Leeds LS8 61 D5
Grange Park Terr. Leeds LS8 61 E5
Grange Park Way. Morley LS27 98 B7
Grange Park Wlk. Leeds LS8 61 D5
Grange Pk. Bail BD17 38 E3
Grange Pk. Hali HX3 113 B3
Grange Rd. Batley WF17 118 A3
Grange Rd. Batley WF17 118 F4
Grange Rd. Batley WF3 119 F8
Grange Rd. Bing BD16 37 B4
Grange Rd. Brad BD15 73 C8
Grange Rd. Bri S72 180 F2
Grange Rd. Bur in W LS29 9 F1
Grange Rd. Castle WF10 104 E1
Grange Rd. Clec BD19 116 C8
Grange Rd. Farnh BD20 4 D1
Grange Rd Fst Sch. Brad 74 B5
Grange Rd. H Chap BB10 85 A7
Grange Rd. Hud HD7 152 E6
Grange Rd. Keigh BD20 18 E1
Grange Rd. Leeds LS10 79 D4
Grange Rd. Roy S71 179 B3
Grange Rd. Stee BD20 17 A5
Grange Rd The. Hors LS16 42 B1
Grange Rd. Yeadon LS19 40 C6
Grange St. Hali HX3 92 A1
Grange St. Keigh BD21 35 C8
Grange St. Wake WF2 142 A5
Grange Terr. Brad BD15 73 C8
Grange Terr. Leeds LS7 60 D4
Grange Terr. Mars HD7 169 A4
Grange Terr. Morley LS27 98 B7 8
Grange Terr. Pudsey LS28 76 E8
Grange Terr. Ship BD18 55 B6
Grange Terr. Stee BD20 17 A5
Grange The. Gar LS25 83 B7
Grange Upper Sch. Brad 74 B2
Grange View. Brad BD3 75 F8
Grange View. Dew WF12 139 D1
Grange View Gdns. Leeds LS17 44 F1
Grange View. Hem WF9 181 D6
Grange View. Leeds LS7 60 E4
Grange View. Otley LS21 10 F1
Grange View. Pudsey LS28 76 E8
Grange View. Stee BD20 17 A5
Grange View. Weth LS22 13 E4
Grangefield Ave. Batley WF17 118 B3
Grangefield Ave. Bur in W LS29 9 F1
Grangefield Ct. Gar LS25 82 F7
Grangefield Ind Est. Pudsey 57 E1
Grangefield Rd. Pudsey LS28 57 E1
Grangefields. Hud HD2 135 E1
Grangeway. Brad BD15 73 C8
Grangeway. Hem WF9 181 D7
Grangewood Ct. Hors LS16 42 B1
Grangewood Ct. Loft G WF1 121 D5
Grangewood Gdns. Hors LS16 42 B1
Granhamthorpe. Leeds LS13 58 C2
Granny Ave. Morley LS27 98 C8
Granny Hall Gr. Brig HD6 114 F4
Granny Hall La. Brig HD6 114 F4
Granny Hall Pk. Brig HD6 114 F4
Granny La. Leeds LS12 78 A5
Granny La. Mir WF14 138 B3
Grant Ave. Leeds LS7 60 E2
Grant St. Brad BD3 75 A7
Grant St. Keigh BD21 35 A7
Grant St. Oxen BD22 51 C2
Grantham Pl. Brad BD7 74 C5
Grantham Pl. Hali HX3 92 B2
Grantham Rd. Brad BD7 74 C5
Grantham Rd. Hali HX3 92 B2
Grantham Terr. Brad BD7 74 C5
Grantham Towers. Leeds LS9 60 E1
Grantley Pl. Hud HD2 136 D5
Grantley St. Wake WF1 142 D6
Grantley Way. Wake WF1 142 D7
Granton Rd. Leeds LS7 60 D5
Granton St. Brad BD3 75 C7
Granville Ave. Pont WF8 146 C8 10
Granville Mount. Otley LS21 22 F7
Granville Pl. Brad BD15 54 B1
Granville Pl. Otley LS21 22 F7
Granville Rd. Leeds LS9 60 E1
Granville Rd. Ship BD18 55 C5
Granville St. Brad BD14 73 C5
Granville St. Castle WF10 124 C5
Granville St. Dew WF13 139 B8
Granville St. Elland HX5 134 F6 6
Granville St. Feath WF7 145 C4
Granville St. Keigh BD21 35 B7
Granville St. Liver WF15 117 B3
Granville St. Nor WF6 123 B2
Granville St. Pudsey LS28 57 F2 2
Granville St. Pudsey LS28 76 C8
Granville St. Tod OL14 108 A1 2
Granville Terr. Bing BD16 37 A3
Granville Terr. Guise LS20 22 F2
Granville Terr. Hud HD1 153 E5
Granville Terr. Otley LS21 22 F7
Granville Terr. Ship BD18 55 B5
Granville Terr. Yeadon LS19 40 C7 2
Grape St. Brad BD15 54 C1
Grape St. Hali HX1 113 B7
Grape St. Keigh BD21 35 E8 2
Grape St. Leeds LS10 79 D5
Grasleigh Ave. Brad BD15 54 A3
Grasleigh Way. Brad BD15 53 F2
Grasmere Ave. Weth LS22 13 C5
Grasmere Cl. Castle WF10 104 E1
Grasmere Cres. Mapp S75 178 A3
Grasmere Dr. Elland HX5 135 B7
Grasmere Dr. Weth LS22 13 C5
Grasmere Rd. Batley WF12 118 E2
Grasmere Rd. Brad BD2 56 A3
Grasmere Rd. Brig BD12 94 E1
Grasmere Rd. Knot WF11 126 E2
Grasmere Rd. Leeds LS12 78 D6
Grasmere Rd. Mel HD7 170 E1
Grasmere Rd. Wake WF2 141 E7
Grasscroft Ave. Honley HD7 171 F4
Grasscroft. Hud HD5 154 F2
Grasscroft Rd. Honley HD7 171 E4
Grasscroft Rd. Hud HD1 153 E7
Grassmere Rd. Hud HD1 153 E7
Grassmoor Fold. Honley HD7 172 A3
Gratrix La. Hali HX6 112 C5
Grattan Rd. Brad BD1 74 D7 8
Graveleythorpe Rd. Leeds LS15 62 B1
Graveleythorpe Rise. Leeds LS15 62 B1 2
Gray Ave. Ship BD18 55 D5
Gray Ct. Leeds LS15 81 D8
Gray Hall Cl. Elland HX4 133 F3
Gray St. Liver FW15 116 E4
Gray's Rd. Roy S71 179 C1
Grayrigg Cl. Leeds LS15 80 E7
Grayrigg Ct. Leeds LS15 80 D7
Grayshon St. Birk BD11 96 E5
Grayson Crest. Leeds LS4 59 B3
Grayson Hts. Leeds LS4 59 B3
Grayswood Cres. Brad BD4 75 D3
Grayswood Dr. Brad BD4 75 D3
Great Albion St. Hali HX1 113 C7
Great Ben La. Slai HD7 151 E3
Great Cross St. Brad BD1 74 F6 1
Great Edge Rd. Hali HX2 111 F6
Great George St. Leeds LS1 79 A8 4
Great George St. Leeds LS1 LS2 79 B8
Great Horton Mid Sch. Brad 74 A4
Great Horton Rd. Brad BD7 73 E3
Great Horton Rd. Brad BD7 74 B5
Great House La. Rip HX6 132 A3
Great House Rd. Tod OL14 108 E8
Great & Little Preston CE Inf Sch. Swil 102 E7
Great & Little Preston Jun Sch. Swil 102 E7
Great North Rd. M'field LS25 84 A6
Great Northern Rd. Keigh BD21 35 C6
Great Northern St. Hud HD1 154 B7
Great Northern St. Morley LS27 98 A3
Great Pasture. Bur in W LS29 9 F2
Great Pond St. Dew WF13 138 F5
Great Russell Ct. Brad BD7 74 C7
Great Russell St. Brad BD7 74 C7
Great Wilson St. Leeds LS11 79 C6
Great Wood St. Batley WF17 118 C4
Greatfield Cl. Ossett WF5 140 E6
Greatfield Dr. Ossett WF5 140 E5
Greatfield Gdns. Ossett WF5 140 E6
Greatfield Rd. Ossett WF5 140 E5
Greave Cl. Hud HD2 136 B4
Greave Clough Cl. Bacup OL13 106 B3 2
Greave Clough Dr. Bacup OL13 106 B3
Greave House Dr. Hali HX2 111 C7
Greave House Flds. Hali HX2 111 E8
Greave House La. Lepton HD8 155 D3
Greave House Pk. Hali HX2 111 D7
Greave House Terr. Lepton HD8 155 D3
Greave Rd. Bacup OL13 106 B3
Greave Rd. Holmfi HD7 199 A8
Greave Rd. Rip HX6 131 E6
Greave St. Tod OL14 108 D5
Greavefield La. Pont WF8 126 B1
Greaves Ave. Wake WF2 141 C5
Greaves Croft. Lepton HD8 155 D3
Greaves Rd. Dew WF13 118 D1
Greaves St. Brad BD5 74 D3
Greaves St. Castle WF10 124 D8
Greek St. Castle WF10 124 E8
Greek St. Leeds LS1 79 B8
Green Abbey. Holmfi HD7 199 B7
Green Acre Cl. Bail BD17 38 D3
Green Acres Cl. Emley HD8 175 C6
Green Acres. Crig WF4 160 A7
Green Acres. Feath WF7 145 E3
Green Ave. Batley WF16 117 E4
Green Ave. Kippax LS25 82 F3
Green Ave. Sil BD20 5 D2
Green Balk La. Lepton HD8 155 F2
Green Bank Ct. Bail BD17 38 B1
Green Bank. Roth WF3 100 D1
Green Chase. Leeds LS6 59 E7 2
Green Cl. Batley WF17 118 E5
Green Cl. Brad BD8 73 E8
Green Cl. Dew WF13 118 A2
Green Cl. L Brad BD20 4 C6
Green Cl. Leeds LS6 59 F7
Green Cl. Stee BD20 16 F6
Green Cliff. Honley HD7 171 F5
Green Cres. Hud HD7 152 E5
Green Cres. Leeds LS6 59 E7
Green Croft. Hem WF9 163 B2
Green Ct. B in Elm LS15 62 F7
Green Ct. Brad BD7 73 F5
Green Ct. Brig BD19 115 F8
Green Edge. Hud HD7 152 C6
Green End. Brad BD14 73 B4
Green End. Brig HD6 115 A1
Green End Cl. Bacup OL13 106 A3 8
Green End La. Wake WF2 142 C3
Green End Rd. Brad BD6 94 B8
Green End Rd. Keigh BD20 19 E2
Green Gate La. Mel HD7 170 A5
Green Gate Rd. Holmfi HD7 188 A4
Green Gdns. Hud HD7 152 E5
Green Hall Pk. Shelf HX3 93 D5
Green Head Ave. Keigh BD20 18 A2
Green Head Dr. Keigh BD20 18 A2
Green Head La. Keigh BD20 18 A2
Green Head Rd. Keigh BD20 18 B2
Green Hill Chase. Leeds LS12 78 B6
Green Hill Cl. Leeds LS12 58 F1
Green Hill Croft. Leeds LS12 78 B6
Green Hill Dr. Leeds LS13 58 E1
Green Hill Gdns. Leeds LS12 78 B6
Green Hill. Hali HX2 112 B6
Green Hill Holt. Leeds LS12 78 B6
Green Hill La. Leeds LS12 78 B5
Green Hill Mount. Leeds LS13 58 E1
Green Hill Pl. Leeds LS13 58 E1
Green Hill Rd. Bacup OL13 106 A1 8
Green Hill Rd. Leeds LS12, LS13 58 E1
Green Hill Way. Leeds LS13 58 E1
Green House Hill. Kirkb HD8 174 C4
Green House La. Shep HD8 174 C4
Green La. Ack M T WF7 163 D6
Green La. Ad Le S DN6 184 E3
Green La. Add LS29 2 E1
Green La. B Spa LS23 30 F6
Green La. Bail BD17 38 A4
Green La. Bail BD17 38 B1
Green La. Brad BD8 55 C1
Green La. Brad BD10 56 A8
Green La. Brad BD10 56 C8
Green La. Brad BD2 56 D3
Green La. Brad BD7 74 A5
Green La. Brad BD12 94 C2
Green La. Brad BD12 94 F4
Green La. Brig HD6 114 E5
Green La. Brig HD6 115 F2
Green La. Bur in W LS29 9 E3
Green La. Castle WF10 103 F1
Green La. Castle WF10 124 C5
Green La. Clec BD19 95 E2
Green La. Coll LS22 29 A8
Green La. D Dale HD8 191 B2
Green La. Dew WF13 118 A1
Green La. Elland HX4 133 F1
Green La. Elland HX4 134 D6
Green La. Feath WF7 145 D6
Green La. Gar LS25 83 A7
Green La. Glu BD20 16 B7
Green La. Hal E BD23 1 E8
Green La. Hali HX2 90 D1
Green La. Hali HX2 91 E8
Green La. Hali HX2, HX3, HX4 92 E6
Green La. Hali HX2 112 E5
Green La. Hali HX3 113 E6
Green La. Haw BD22 33 F4
Green La. Haw BD22 34 D2
Green La. Hep HX7 88 E5
Green La. Holmfi HD7 189 A2
Green La. Hor WF4 159 C8
Green La. Hors LS16 41 D5
Green La. Hors LS18 58 B7
Green La. Kippax LS25 82 F2
Green La. Kippax LS25 82 F3
Green La. L Brad BD20 5 A6
Green La. Ledst WF10 103 E6
Green La. Leeds LS14 62 A8
Green La. Leeds LS15 62 B1 5

Green La. Leeds LS12 .... 77 C5
Green La. Leeds LS12 .... 78 E6
Green La. Leeds LS11 .... 79 A1
Green La. Liver WF15 .... 116 D3
Green La. M'town LS26 .... 102 F2
Green La. Mars HD7 .... 169 B7
Green La. Mel HD7 .... 170 E1
Green La. Men LS29 .... 21 C5
Green La. Neth WF4 .... 157 F6
Green La. Neth WF4 .... 158 E5
Green La. Neth WF4 .... 158 F5
Green La. Notton WF4 .... 179 A5
Green La. Otley LS21 .... 10 F1
Green La. Pont WF8 .... 146 D7
Green La. Pont WF8 .... 146 E5
Green La. Pudsey LS28 .... 76 D6
Green La. Queen BD13 .... 72 B3
Green La. Rip HX6 .... 132 B4
Green La. Rip HX4 .... 150 F8
Green La. Roth WF3 .... 100 D1
Green La. S Kirk WF9 .... 182 B2
Green La. Shelf HX3 .... 93 E6
Green La. Stee BD20 .... 17 A6
Green La. Thorn BD13 .... 72 E6
Green La. Upton WF9 .... 165 C1
Green La. Wake WF2 .... 141 E7
Green La. Yeadon LS19 .... 40 B5
Green Lane Cl. Neth WF4 .... 158 A6
Green Lane Cty Pr Sch. Pont . 146 B6
Green Lane Fst Sch. Brad 55 C1
Green Lane Terr. Slai HD7 .... 152 C6
Green Lea Cl. B Spa LS23 .... 30 E7
Green Lea Mills (Ind Units).
Hud 155 A6
Green Lea Rd. Hud HD5 .... 154 F6
Green Lea. Roth LS26 .... 101 C6
Green Meadow. Wils BD15 .... 53 D4
Green Meadows Sch. Guise 22 C1
Green Mount. Bail BD17 .... 38 B2
Green Mount. Brad BD4 .... 75 D3
Green Mount. Hud HD5 .... 154 D6
Green Mount Rd. Thorn BD13 . 72 E6
Green Mount Ret Pk. Hali 113 B7
Green Park Ave. Hali HX3 .... 113 C2
Green Park Ave. Hor WF4 .... 140 F2
Green Park Ave. Ossett WF5 . 140 E3
Green Park Dr. Hali HX3 .... 113 C2
Green Park Gate. Hali HX3 .... 113 C2
Green Park Rd. Hali HX3 .... 113 C2
Green Park St. Hali HX3 .... 113 C3
Green Pk. Leeds LS17 .... 43 E2
Green Pk. Wake WF1 .... 142 E6
Green Pl. Brad BD2 .... 56 B2
Green Rd. Bail BD17 .... 38 C2
Green Rd. Leeds LS6 .... 59 E7
Green Rd. Liver WF15 .... 117 A5
Green Row. Brad BD10 .... 56 B6
Green Row. Leeds LS6 .... 59 E7 3
Green Royd. Elland HX4 .... 134 C6
Green Royd. Hali HX2 .... 91 B4
Green Side Rd. Kirkb HD4 .... 173 A3
Green Slacks La. Mars HD3 .... 151 B5
Green St. Brad BD1 .... 74 F7 13
Green St. Brad BD12 .... 95 B5
Green St. Castle WF10 .... 103 D1
Green St. Elland HX4 .... 134 B4 3
Green St. Haw BD22 .... 51 C6
Green St. Hud HD1 .... 154 A7
Green St. Mel HD7 .... 170 D2
Green St. Oxen BD22 .... 51 C2 4
Green Sykes Rd. Keigh BD22 .... 34 A7
Green Terr. Dew WF13 .... 118 A2
Green Terr. Guise LS20 .... 39 E8
Green Terr. Leeds LS11 .... 79 C3
Green Terr. Mir WF14 .... 137 F6
Green Terrace Sq. Hali HX1 .... 113 A5
Green The. Batley WF17 .... 96 F2
Green The. Bing BD16 .... 36 E7
Green The. Bing BD16 .... 37 A6
Green The. Bing BD16 .... 37 D3
Green The. Bing BD16 .... 37 D6
Green The. Birk BD4 .... 95 F7
Green The. Brad BD10 .... 56 B8
Green The. Castle WF10 .... 125 D8
Green The. Crof WF4 .... 144 C2
Green The. Feath WF7 .... 145 E4
Green The. Gar LS25 .... 83 A7
Green The. Guise LS20 .... 39 E8
Green The. Hors LS18 .... 58 B8
Green The. Hud HD2 .... 136 D5
Green The. Kippax LS25 .... 83 A1 1
Green The. Kirkb HD4 .... 172 F2
Green The. Leeds LS17 .... 43 E2
Green The. Leeds LS5 .... 58 E7
Green The. Mars HD7 .... 168 F4
Green The. Mir WF14 .... 137 E6
Green The. Ossett WF5 .... 140 E4
Green The. Otley LS21 .... 10 F1
Green The. Pudsey LS28 .... 57 D4
Green The. Roy S71 .... 179 C3
Green The. S Kirk WF9 .... 182 C3
Green The. Wake WF2 .... 120 E3
Green The. Wool WF4 .... 178 A7
Green Top Gdns. Leeds LS12 .... 78 B5
Green Top. Leeds LS12 .... 78 B5
Green Top St. Brad BD8 .... 73 E7
Green View. Leeds LS6 .... 59 E7
Green View. Scar LS14 .... 45 C8
Green View The. Shaf S72 .... 180 C4
Green Way. Glu BD20 .... 16 C7
Green Way. Hali HX2 .... 91 E8
Green Way. Scar LS14 .... 45 C8
Green Wood Pk. Leeds LS6 .... 59 E7
Green's Sq. Hali HX2 .... 112 E8 3
Green's Sq. Kippax LS25 .... 83 B1
Greenacre Ave. Brad BD12 .... 94 D2
Greenacre Cl. Brad BD12 .... 94 D2 1
Greenacre Dr. Brad BD12 .... 94 D2
Greenacre Dr. D Dale HD8 .... 191 E3
Greenacre Park Ave. Yeadon
LS19 .... 40 B5
Greenacre Park Mews. Yeadon
LS19 .... 40 C5 1
Greenacre Park Rise. Yeadon
LS19 .... 40 C5
Greenacre Pk. Yeadon LS19 .... 40 B5
Greenacre Rd. Upton WF9 .... 183 C8
Greenacre Way. Brad BD12 .... 94 D2
Greenacre Wlk. Ryhill WF4 .... 162 D2
Greenacres Ave. Shelf HX3 .... 93 D6
Greenacres Cl. Ossett WF5 .... 119 D1
Greenacres Dr. Batley WF17 .... 97 A2
Greenacres Dr. Keigh BD20 .... 18 A1
Greenacres Dr. Shelf HX3 .... 93 D6
Greenacres Gr. Shelf HX3 .... 93 D6
Greenacres. Ossett WF5 .... 119 D1
Greenacres. Rip HX6 .... 132 E4
Greenacres. Shelf HX3 .... 93 D6
Greenaire Pl. Brad BD1 .... 74 D7 10
Greenbank Gr. Nor WF6 .... 122 F3
Greenbank Rd. Brad BD15 .... 73 C8
Greenbank Rd. Nor WF6 .... 122 F3
Greenbanks Ave. Hors LS18 .... 41 C2
Greenbanks Cl. Hors LS18 .... 41 C2
Greenbanks Dr. Hors LS18 .... 41 B2
Greencliffe Ave. Bail BD17 .... 38 C3
Greencroft Ave. Northo HX3 .... 93 B3
Greendale Cl. H Chap BB10 .... 85 A7
Greendale Ct. Honley HD7 .... 171 F5
Greendown Cl. Ilkley LS29 .... 8 D4
Greeney Hill. Wils BD15 .... 53 B4
Greenfell Cl. Keigh BD22 .... 34 F6
Greenfield Ave. Brig HX3 .... 115 A7
Greenfield Ave. Gild LS27 .... 97 B7
Greenfield Ave. Guise LS20 .... 39 B7
Greenfield Ave. Hud HD3 .... 153 A7
Greenfield Ave. Kippax LS25 .... 83 A2
Greenfield Ave. Ossett WF5 .... 141 A4
Greenfield Ave. Ship BD18 .... 55 C5
Greenfield Cl. D Dale HD8 .... 191 F3
Greenfield Cl. Elland HX4 .... 133 F2
Greenfield Cl. Kippax LS25 .... 83 A2
Greenfield Cl. Northo HX3 .... 93 A3
Greenfield Cl. Ossett WF5 .... 141 A4
Greenfield Cl. Wake WF2 .... 120 F2
Greenfield Cres. Cull BD13 .... 52 E6
Greenfield Ct. Keigh BD21 .... 35 A7
Greenfield Dr. Brig BD19 .... 115 F8 6
Greenfield Dr. Gild LS27 .... 97 B7
Greenfield Garth. Kippax LS25 .... 83 A2
Greenfield Gdns. Stee BD20 .... 16 F6
Greenfield. Haw BD22 .... 51 C8
Greenfield La. Brad BD10 .... 39 B1
Greenfield La. Brad BD7 .... 73 F3
Greenfield La. Brad BD4 .... 95 B7
Greenfield La. Guise LS20 .... 39 B7
Greenfield Mount. Wake WF2 .... 120 F2
Greenfield Pl. Brad BD8 .... 55 C1
Greenfield Pl. Brig HX3 .... 115 A7
Greenfield Rd. Hem WF9 .... 181 D5
Greenfield Rd. Holmfi HD7 .... 188 D5
Greenfield Rd. Leeds LS9 .... 79 E7
Greenfield Rd. Nor WF6 .... 122 F2
Greenfield Rd. Ossett WF5 .... 141 A4
Greenfield Rise. Kippax LS25 .... 83 A2
Greenfield Sch. Brad 39 B1
Greenfield Terr. Haw BD22 .... 51 C8
Greenfield Terr. M'town LS26 .... 102 E3
Greenfield Terr. Tod OL14 .... 86 A1
Greenfield Vale. Kippax LS25 .... 83 A2
Greenfield View. Kippax LS25 .... 83 A2
Greenfield Way. Wake WF2 .... 120 F2
Greenfields. Batley WF16 .... 117 C5
Greenfields Way. Bur in W LS29 .... 21 F7
Greenfinch Gr. Hud HD4 .... 171 E7
Greenfold La. Weth LS22 .... 13 F5
Greengate Rd. Keigh BD21 .... 35 C6
Greengate Rd. Norton WF8 .... 166 F3
Greengate. Roth LS26 .... 101 C6
Greengate. Sil BD20 .... 5 D2
Greengates Ave. Brad BD12 .... 94 C1 3
Greengates Fst Sch. Brad 56 E7
Greenhead Ave. Hud HD5 .... 154 F5
Greenhead Coll. Hud 153 F6
Greenhead Ct. Hud HD1 .... 153 E7
Greenhead Gram Sch. Keigh 18 B2
Greenhead La. Brig HD6 .... 135 E6
Greenhead La. Hud HD5 .... 154 F5
Greenhead Rd. Hud HD1 .... 153 F6
Greenhead Rd. Leeds LS16 .... 59 B8
Greenhill Ave. Pont WF8 .... 146 E6
Greenhill Bk Rd. Holmfi HD7 .... 189 E5
Greenhill Cty Prim Sch. Leeds . 77 E7
Greenhill Cres. Leeds LS12 .... 78 C6
Greenhill Dr. Bing BD16 .... 36 E7
Greenhill Ind Est. Heb Br 110 F8
Greenhill La. Bing BD16 .... 36 F6
Greenhill La. Brad BD3 .... 75 C7
Greenhill Mid Sch. Leeds 77 D8
Greenhill Mount. Pont WF8 .... 146 E6
Greenhill Rd. Hud HD3 .... 152 E7
Greenhill Rd. Wake WF1 .... 142 D7
Greenhill St. Brad BD3 .... 75 C7
Greenhills. Yeadon LS19 .... 40 C3
Greenholme Ct. Brad BD4 .... 75 F2
Greenholme Tr Est. Bur in W 9 F2
Greenhouse Rd. Hud HD2 .... 136 A1
Greenhow Cl. Leeds LS4 .... 59 D2
Greenhow Gdns. Leeds LS4 .... 59 D2
Greenhow Pk. Bur in W LS29 .... 9 D1
Greenhow Rd. Leeds LS4 .... 59 D2
Greenhow Wlk. Leeds LS4 .... 59 D2
Greenland Ave. Queen BD13 .... 92 E8
Greenland Rd. B Head HX7 .... 87 C6
Greenland Villas. Queen BD13 92 E8
Greenlaws Cl. Holmfi HD7 .... 188 D5
Greenlay Dr. Wake WF2 .... 120 B2
Greenlea Ave. Yeadon LS19 .... 39 F6
Greenlea Cl. Yeadon LS19 .... 39 F5
Greenlea Fold. Yeadon LS19 .... 39 F5
Greenlea Mount. Yeadon LS19 39 F6
Greenlea Rd. Yeadon LS19 .... 39 F5
Greenmoor Ave. Roth WF3 .... 100 C1
Greenmoor Cl. Roth WF3 .... 100 C1
Greenmoor Cres. Roth WF3 .... 100 D1
Greenmount Ct. Leeds LS11 .... 79 B3 4
Greenmount La. Leeds LS11 .... 79 B3
Greenmount Pl. Leeds LS11 .... 79 B3
Greenmount St. Leeds LS11 .... 79 B3
Greenmount Terr. Leeds LS11 .... 79 B3
Greenock Pl. Leeds LS12 .... 78 A8 10
Greenock Rd. Leeds LS12 .... 78 A8
Greenock St. Leeds LS12 .... 78 A8 8
Greenock Terr. Leeds LS12 .... 78 A8 9
Greenroyd Ave. Clec BD19 .... 95 D2
Greenroyd Ave. Hali HX3 .... 113 B3
Greenroyd Croft. Hud HD2 .... 135 E1
Greenroyd Ct. Dar WF8 .... 147 C5
Greenroyd Dr. S in Cra BD20 .... 16 D4
Greenroyd Gr. S in Cra BD20 .... 16 D4
Greenroyd La. Hali HX2 .... 91 E1
Greens End Rd. Mel HD7 .... 170 D2
Greens La. Bacup OL13 .... 106 A3
Greenset View. Barn S71 .... 178 E1
Greenshank Mews. Morley
LS27 .... 98 D3
Greenshaw Terr. Guise LS20 .... 22 D1
Greenside Ave. Hud HD5 .... 155 A5
Greenside Ave. Leeds LS12 .... 78 B5
Greenside Ave. Mapp S75 .... 178 C1
Greenside. Brad BD12 .... 95 A4
Greenside Cl. Leeds LS12 .... 78 C5
Greenside. Clec BD19 .... 116 E7
Greenside Cty Inf Sch. Hud 155 A4
Greenside Cres. Hud HD5 .... 155 A5
Greenside Ct. Gild LS27 .... 97 D7
Greenside. D Dale HD8 .... 192 A7
Greenside Dr. Hud HD5 .... 155 A5
Greenside Dr. Leeds LS12 .... 78 C5
Greenside Est. Mir WF14 .... 138 A7
Greenside. Feath WF7 .... 145 D6
Greenside Gr. Pudsey LS28 .... 76 D6
Greenside La. Brad BD8 .... 73 F7
Greenside La. Cull BD13 .... 52 E6
Greenside. Liver WF16 .... 117 C4 4
Greenside. Mapp S75 .... 178 C1
Greenside Mount. Mir WF14 .... 138 B7
Greenside Pl. Mapp S75 .... 178 C1
Greenside. Pudsey LS28 .... 76 D6 3
Greenside Rd. Leeds LS12 .... 78 C5
Greenside Rd. Mir WF14 .... 138 B7
Greenside. Ryhill S72 .... 180 B8
Greenside. Shaf S72 .... 180 B4
Greenside Terr. Leeds LS12 .... 78 B5
Greenside. Walton WF2 .... 161 A7
Greenside Wlk. Leeds LS12 .... 78 B5
Greensnook La. Bacup OL13 .... 106 A3
Greensnook Terr. Bacup OL13 106 A3 1
Greensway. Gar LS25 .... 82 E7
Greenthorpe Hill. Leeds LS13 .... 77 E8
Greenthorpe Mount. Leeds
LS13 .... 77 E8
Greenthorpe Rd. Leeds LS13 .... 77 E8
Greenthorpe St. Leeds LS13 .... 77 E7
Greenthorpe Wlk. Leeds LS13 . 77 E8
Greenton Ave. Brig BD19 .... 94 E1
Greenton Cres. Queen BD13 .... 92 D8
Greentop. Pudsey LS28 .... 76 D6
Greentrees. Brad BD6 .... 94 B6 1
Greenups Terr. Hali HX6 .... 112 B4
Greenview Cl. Leeds LS9 .... 61 C2
Greenview Mount. Leeds LS9 .. 61 D2
Greenville Ave. Leeds LS12 .... 78 B5
Greenville Dr. Brad BD12 .... 94 E7
Greenville Gdns. Leeds LS12 .... 78 B5
Greenway Cl. Leeds LS15 .... 62 C1
Greenway Dr. Brad BD15 .... 73 B7
Greenway. Guise LS20 .... 39 C7
Greenway. Honley HD7 .... 171 F5
Greenway. Hud HD3 .... 152 F5
Greenway. Leeds LS15 .... 62 C1
Greenway Rd. Brad BD5 .... 74 E2
Greenwell Row. Brad BD14 .... 73 B4 6
Greenwood Ave. Brad BD2 .... 56 A4
Greenwood Ave. Dew WF12 .... 139 F7
Greenwood Ave. Upton WF9 .... 183 C8
Greenwood Bldgs. Kirkhe HD5 155 C8
Greenwood Cl. Nor WF6 .... 144 B7
Greenwood Cl. Upton WF9 .... 183 C8
Greenwood Cres. Roy S71 .... 179 B4
Greenwood Ct. Brad BD1 .... 74 F6
Greenwood Ct. Leeds LS6 .... 59 E7
Greenwood Dr. Brad BD2 .... 56 A4
Greenwood Ho. Wake WF1 .... 142 C6 24
Greenwood Mount. Brad BD2 .. 56 A4
Greenwood Mount. Leeds LS6 . 59 E7
Greenwood Prim Sch. Leeds 79 C4
Greenwood Rd. Bail BD17 .... 38 B1
Greenwood Rd. E Ard WF3 .... 119 F7
Greenwood Rd. Wake WF1 .... 142 E7
Greenwood Row. Pudsey LS28 76 F7
Greenwood St. Dew WF12,
WF13 .... 139 B8
Greenwood St. Dew WF12 .... 139 C6
Greenwood St. Heb Br HX7 .... 89 A3 5
Greenwood St. Hud HD4 .... 154 A4
Greetland Jun & Inf Sch.
Elland 134 B7
Greetland Rd. Rip HX4 .... 133 B6
Gregory Cres. Brad BD7 .... 73 E2
Gregory Ct. Brad BD14 .... 73 C4 1
Gregory Dr. Kirkb HD8 .... 173 F7
Gregory La. Lepton WF14 .... 156 A7
Gregory Rd. Castle WF10 .... 124 E5
Gregory Springs La. Mir WF14 138 B3
Gregory Springs Mount. Mir
WF14 .... 138 B2
Gregory Springs Rd. Mir WF14 138 B3
Gregory St. Batley WF17 .... 118 E5
Grenfell Dr. Brad BD3 .... 75 D8
Grenfell Rd. Brad BD3 .... 75 D8
Grenfell Terr. Brad BD3 .... 75 D8
Grenley St. Knot WF11 .... 127 A4
Grenville Wlk. Crig WF4 .... 159 F3
Gresham Ave. Brad BD2 .... 55 F4
Gresley Rd. Keigh BD21 .... 35 C7
Gresley Road Ind Est. Keigh 35 C7
Grey Cl. Loft G WF1 .... 121 B3
Grey Ct. Loft G WF1 .... 121 B3
Grey Gables. Neth WF4 .... 158 E6
Grey Hall. Elland HX4 .... 133 F3
Grey Scar Cr. Haw BD22 .... 34 B2
Grey Scar Rd. Haw BD22 .... 34 A2
Grey St. Loft G WF1 .... 121 B3
Grey Stone La. Tod OL14 .... 108 F8
Grey Stones La. Wad M HX7 .... 69 B5
Greycourt Cl. Brad BD10 .... 56 A6
Greycourt Cl. Hali HX1 .... 113 A5
Greyfriar Wlk. Brad BD7 .... 73 E3
Greyfriars Ave. Hud HD2 .... 136 E4
Greyshiels Ave. Leeds LS6 .... 59 C4
Greyshiels Cl. Leeds LS6 .... 59 C4
Greyshon Dr. Brad BD6 .... 74 C1
Greystone Ave. Elland HX5 .... 134 E5
Greystone Cl. B Spa LS23 .... 30 E7
Greystone Cres. Brad BD10 .... 56 C6
Greystone Ct. Brig HD6 .... 136 A7
Greystone Mount. Leeds LS15 . 80 E7
Greystone Pk. Aber LS25 .... 47 E1
Greystones Cl. Aber LS25 .... 47 E1
Greystones Dr. Keigh BD22 .... 34 F3
Greystones Dr. Ossett WF5 .... 140 E3
Greystones La. Keigh BD22 .... 33 D7
Greystones Mount. Keigh BD22 34 F2
Greystones Rd. Hali HX2 .... 111 E7
Greystones Rise. Keigh BD22 .. 34 F3
Griff House La. E Ard WF3 .... 120 B8
Griffe Dr. Brad BD12 .... 94 C1
Griffe Gdns. Haw BD22 .... 34 B2
Griffe Head Cres. Brad BD12 .. 94 C2 2
Griffe Head Rd. Brad BD12 .... 94 C2
Griffe Rd. Brad BD12 .... 94 C1
Griffe Rd. Haw BD22 .... 50 D8
Griffe View. Haw BD22 .... 34 B2
Grime La. Crof WF4 .... 144 B2
Grime La. Wh Com HD7 .... 200 D8
Grimes Dyke Prim Sch. Leeds . 62 D6
Grimescar M'dows. Hud HD2 135 D2
Grimescar Rd. Hud HD2 .... 135 D3
Grimethorpe St. S Elm WF9 .... 182 F2 1
Grimscar Ave. Hud HD2 .... 135 F1
Grimthorpe Ave. Leeds LS6 .... 59 C5 4
Grimthorpe Pl. Leeds LS6 .... 59 D5
Grimthorpe St. Leeds LS6 .... 59 C5
Grimthorpe Terr. Leeds LS6 .... 59 D5
Grindlestone Bank. Hali HX2 .. 91 C4
Grisedale Ave. Hud HD2 .... 135 F1
Grizedale Cl. Weth LS22 .... 13 B6
Grosmont Pl. Leeds LS13 .... 58 C3
Grosmont Rd. Leeds LS13 .... 58 C2
Grosmont Terr. Leeds LS13 .... 58 C3
Grosvenor Ave. Lepton HD8 .. 155 E3
Grosvenor Ave. Pont WF8 .... 146 B8
Grosvenor Ave. Ship BD18 .... 54 F8
Grosvenor Ave. Upton WF9 .... 183 A7
Grosvenor Ct. Hors LS16 .... 41 D4
Grosvenor Fst Sch. Brad 55 C1
Grosvenor Hill. Leeds LS7 .... 60 C2
Grosvenor Mews. Yeadon LS19 40 A4
Grosvenor Mount. Leeds LS6 .. 59 F4
Grosvenor Park Gdns. Leeds
LS6 .... 59 F4
Grosvenor Pk. Leeds LS7 .... 60 C7
Grosvenor Rd. Batley WF17 .. 118 D6
Grosvenor Rd. Brad BD8 .... 55 D1
Grosvenor Rd. Hud HD5 .... 154 F6
Grosvenor Rd. Leeds LS6 .... 59 F4
Grosvenor Rd. Ship BD18 .... 54 F7
Grosvenor St. Batley WF16 .. 117 D5 2
Grosvenor St. Brad BD8 .... 55 D1
Grosvenor St. Dew WF12 .... 139 C7
Grosvenor St. Elland HX5 .... 134 F6
Grosvenor St. Wake WF1 .... 142 F3
Grosvenor Terr. Batley WF16 117 D4 1
Grosvenor Terr. Brad BD8 .... 55 D1
Grosvenor Terr. Hali HX1 .... 113 A7 12
Grosvenor Terr. Leeds LS6 .... 59 F4
Grosvenor Terr. Otley LS21 .... 23 B8
Grosvenor Terr. Weth LS22 .... 13 E6
Grosvenor Way. Lepton HD8 . 155 E3
Grouse Moor La. Queen BD13 . 72 C2
Grouse St. Keigh BD21 .... 35 D8 8
Grove Ave. Hali HX3 .... 92 A3
Grove Ave. Hem WF9 .... 181 E6
Grove Ave. Ilkley LS29 .... 7 F3
Grove Ave. Leeds LS6 .... 59 E6
Grove Ave. Pont WF8 .... 146 E8
Grove Ave. Pudsey LS28 .... 76 D7
Grove Ave. S Kirk WF9 .... 182 C2
Grove Ave. Ship BD18 .... 55 B5
Grove Cl. Brad BD2 .... 56 A4
Grove Cl. Clec BD19 .... 96 B1
Grove Convalescent Hospl The.
Ilkley 8 B3
Grove Cotts. Brig HD6 .... 114 E2
Grove Cres. B Spa LS23 .... 30 F7
Grove Cres. Hali HX2 .... 111 E7
Grove Cres S. B Spa LS23 .... 30 F7
Grove Cres. Walton WF2 .... 161 B7
Grove Croft. Hali HX3 .... 91 F2
Grove Ct. Hali HX3 .... 92 A2
Grove Ct. Leeds LS6 .... 59 E6
Grove Ct. Pudsey LS28 .... 76 D7
Grove Dr. Hali HX3 .... 91 F3
Grove Dr. S Kirk WF9 .... 182 B2
Grove Edge. Hali HX3 .... 91 F2
Grove Farm Cl. Hors LS16 .... 41 F4
Grove Farm Cres. Hors LS16 .... 41 E4
Grove Farm Croft. Hors LS16 .. 41 E4
Grove Farm Dr. Hors LS16 .... 41 E4
Grove Gdns. B Spa LS23 .... 30 F7
Grove Gdns. Dew WF12 .... 140 A6
Grove Gdns. Hali HX3 .... 92 A3
Grove Gdns. Leeds LS6 .... 59 E6
Grove Hall Park Homes. Dar
WF8 .... 147 D8
Grove Head. S Kirk WF9 .... 182 B2
Grove House Cres. Brad BD2 .. 56 A4
Grove House Dr. Brad BD2 .... 56 A3
Grove House Fst Sch. Brad 56 A4
Grove House Rd. Brad BD2 .... 56 A3
Grove La. Bad WF9 .... 164 E3
Grove La. Clec BD19 .... 96 B1
Grove La. Hem WF9 .... 181 E6
Grove La. Knot WF11 .... 126 E4
Grove La. Leeds LS6 .... 59 E6
Grove La. S Kirk WF9 .... 182 B2
Grove Lea Cl. Hem WF9 .... 181 E6
Grove Lea Cres. Pont WF8 .... 146 E7
Grove Lea Wlk. Pont WF8 .... 146 E7
Grove Mill La. Hali HX3 .... 92 A2
Grove Mount. Pont WF8 .... 146 E8
Grove Mount. S Kirk WF9 .... 182 B2
Grove Pk. Crig WF4 .... 159 E6
Grove Pk. Hali HX3 .... 92 A3
Grove Pl. B Spa LS23 .... 30 E7
Grove Pl. Hem WF9 .... 181 E6
Grove Rd. B Spa LS23 .... 30 E7
Grove Rd. Batley WF16 .... 117 E3
Grove Rd. Elland HX5 .... 135 B7
Grove Rd. Heb Br HX7 .... 89 A4
Grove Rd. Hor WF4 .... 141 A1
Grove Rd. Hors LS18 .... 58 C8
Grove Rd. Hud HD1 .... 154 B7
Grove Rd. Ilkley LS29 .... 7 F4
Grove Rd. Leeds LS6 .... 59 E5
Grove Rd. Leeds LS10 .... 79 E3
Grove Rd. Leeds LS15 .... 81 A7
Grove Rd. Mapp S75 .... 178 A1
Grove Rd. Men LS29 .... 22 A4
Grove Rd. Pont WF8 .... 146 E8
Grove Rd. Pudsey LS28 .... 76 D7
Grove Rd. Ship BD18 .... 55 B5
Grove Rd. Wake WF1 .... 142 D5
Grove Rise. Leeds LS17 .... 42 F5
Grove Rise. Pont WF8 .... 146 E8
Grove Royd. Hali HX3 .... 92 A2
Grove Sq. Clec BD19 .... 96 B1
Grove Sq. Hali HX3 .... 91 F2
Grove St. Bacup OL13 .... 106 A3
Grove St. Batley WF15 .... 117 C2
Grove St. Batley WF16 .... 117 E4
Grove St. Brig HD6 .... 115 B2
Grove St. Dew WF13 .... 139 C8
Grove St. Hali HX2 .... 91 F3
Grove St. Hali HX6 .... 112 D4
Grove St. Hud HD3 .... 152 F6
Grove St. Leeds LS1 .... 79 A8
Grove St. Mir WF14 .... 138 B6
Grove St. Ossett WF5 .... 140 D4
Grove St. Pudsey LS28 .... 57 E2 4
Grove St S. Hali HX1 .... 112 F7 7
Grove St. S Kirk WF9 .... 182 B2
Grove St. Slai HD7 .... 151 F1
Grove St. Wake WF1 .... 142 D5
Grove Terr. B Spa LS23 .... 30 E7
Grove Terr. Birk BD11 .... 96 A4
Grove Terr. Brad BD7 .... 74 D6
Grove Terr. Brig HD6 .... 114 E2
Grove Terr. Heb Br HX7 .... 110 E8
Grove Terr. Hem WF9 .... 181 E6
Grove Terr. Pudsey LS28 .... 76 D7
Grove The. Bail BD17 .... 38 C4
Grove The. Batley WF16 .... 117 C6
Grove The. Batley WF17 .... 118 A7
Grove The. Bing BD16 .... 36 E6
Grove The. Brad BD10 .... 56 B7
Grove The. Brad BD10 .... 56 D7
Grove The. Brig HX3 .... 114 D8
Grove The. Cud S72 .... 180 B1
Grove The. E Ard WF3 .... 120 B8
Grove The. E Kes LS17 .... 28 B6
Grove The. Hors LS18 .... 41 B1
Grove The. Hud HD2 .... 136 B2
Grove The. Ilkley LS29 .... 8 B4
Grove The. Kippax LS25 .... 83 A1
Grove The. Leeds LS17 .... 42 F5
Grove The. Nor WF6 .... 123 B2
Grove The. Pudsey LS28 .... 76 D7
Grove The. Queen BD13 .... 72 D1 7
Grove The. Ryhill WF4 .... 162 A1
Grove The. S Elm WF9 .... 182 F4
Grove The. Shelf HX3 .... 93 C6
Grove The. Ship BD18 .... 54 E7
Grove The. Swil LS26 .... 82 B2
Grove The. Walton WF2 .... 161 B6
Grove The. Yeadon LS19 .... 40 B6
Grove Way. S Kirk WF9 .... 182 B2
Grove Wilmington. Leeds LS7 .. 60 D2
Grovehall Ave. Leeds LS11 .... 79 A1
Grovehall La. Pont WF8 .... 147 B8
Grovehall Par. Leeds LS11 .... 78 F1
Grovehall Rd. Leeds LS11 .... 78 F1
Grovelands. Brad BD2 .... 56 A4
Groves Hall Rd. Dew WF13 .... 138 F8
Groveville. Brig HX3 .... 93 C1
Groveway. Brad BD2 .... 56 A4
Grunberg Rd. Leeds LS6 .... 59 D5
Grunberg St. Leeds LS6 .... 59 D5 6
Guard House Ave. Keigh BD22 35 A7
Guard House Dr. Keigh BD22 .. 35 A7
Guard House Fst Sch. Keigh 34 F7
Guard House Gr. Keigh BD22 .. 34 F7
Guard House Rd. Keigh BD22 .. 35 A7
Guernsey Rd. Batley WF12 .... 118 F2
Guild Way. Hali HX2 .... 112 B7
Guildford Rd. Roy S71 .... 179 B5
Guildford St. Heb Br HX7 .... 89 A2
Guildford St. Ossett WF5 .... 140 D4
Guillemot App. Morley LS27 .... 98 D3
Guiseley Dr. Guise LS29 .... 22 B2
Guiseley Inf Sch. Guise 22 E1
Guiseley Sch. Guise 39 D8
Guiseley Sta. Guise 22 D1
Guisley Queensway Jun & Inf Sch.
Yeadon 40 A8
Gulley Rd. Leeds LS9 .... 80 D3
Gully Terr. Holmfi HD7 .... 189 B4
Gully The. Holmfi HD7 .... 190 C5
Gunson Cres. Ossett WF5 .... 140 D6
Gunter Rd. Weth LS22 .... 14 A5
Gunthwaite La. Ingb S30 .... 192 B2
Gunthwaite Top. D Dale HD8 . 191 F3
Gurbax Ct. Brad BD3 .... 75 E7
Gurney Cl. Brad BD5 .... 74 D3
Guy St. Brad BD4 .... 74 F6 5
Guycroft. Otley LS21 .... 22 F7
Gwynne Ave. Brad BD3 .... 56 E1
Gynn La. Honley HD7 .... 172 B5
Gypsy Ct. Castle WF10 .... 125 C6
Gypsy La. Castle WF10 .... 125 C5
Gypsy Wood Cl. Leeds LS15 .... 81 D7
Gypsy Wood Crest. Leeds LS15 81 D7

Hacking La. S Elm WF9 .... 183 B3
Hadassah St. Hali HX3 .... 113 D4
Haddingley La. Holmfi HD7 .... 190 D4
Haddon Ave. Hali HX3 .... 113 C3
Haddon Ave. Leeds LS4 .... 59 C2
Haddon Cl. Clec BD19 .... 117 B8
Haddon Cl. S Elm WF9 .... 183 A5
Haddon Pl. Leeds LS4 .... 59 C2
Haddon Rd. Leeds LS4 .... 59 D2
Hade Edge Sch. Holmfi 199 B8
Hadfield House. Brad BD6 .... 93 E8 3
Hadfield Rd. Batley WF16 .... 117 D5
Hadleigh Ct. Leeds LS17 .... 43 D2
Hadleigh Rise. Pont WF8 .... 146 B5
Hadrian Cl. Castle WF10 .... 104 C1
Hadrian Cl. Th Aud WF8 .... 165 A5
Hag Farm Rd. Bur in W LS29 .. 21 E7
Hag Farm Rd. Men LS29 .... 21 E7
Hag Hill. Emley HD8 .... 175 E6
Hag Hill La. Emley HD8 .... 175 E6
Hag La. Hali HX3 .... 92 D3
Hagg La. Mir WF14 .... 138 C2
Hagg Wood Rd. Honley HD7 .. 172 B2
Haggroyd La. Honley HD7 .... 172 B2
Haggs Hill Rd. Ossett WF5 .... 141 A5
Haggs La. Wake WF2 .... 141 C5
Hague Cres. Hem WF9 .... 181 E5
Hague Park La. S Kirk WF9 .... 182 B3
Hague Terr. Hem WF9 .... 181 E6
Haigh Ave. Roth LS26 .... 100 C7
Haigh Beck View. Brad BD10 .. 56 C7
Haigh Cnr. Brad BD10 .... 56 D7
Haigh Croft. Roy S71 .... 179 B4
Haigh Fold. Brad BD2 .... 56 C3
Haigh Gdns. Roth LS26 .... 100 C7
Haigh Hall. Brad BD10 .... 56 D7
Haigh Hall Rd. Brad BD10 .... 56 D7
Haigh Hill. Wool S75, WF4 .... 177 C6
Haigh House Hill. Elland HD3 134 E3
Haigh La. Floc WF4 .... 157 A2
Haigh La. Hali HX3 .... 113 D4
Haigh La. Holmfi HD7 .... 188 F8
Haigh La. Wool S75, WF4 .... 177 C5
Haigh Mews. Wool S75 .... 177 C5
Haigh Moor Ave. E Ard WF3 .. 119 E6
Haigh Moor Cres. E Ard WF3 119 E6
Haigh Moor Rd. E Ard WF3 .. 119 E6
Haigh Moor St. Wake WF1 .... 142 D8
Haigh Moor View. E Ard WF3 119 E6
Haigh Park Rd. Leeds LS10 .... 80 B2
Haigh Rd. Roth LS26 .... 100 F6
Haigh Road Sch. Roth 100 E6
Haigh St. Brad BD4 .... 75 B3
Haigh St. Brig HD6 .... 115 A3 16
Haigh St. Elland HX4 .... 134 B7
Haigh St. Hali HX1 .... 112 F8 5
Haigh St. Hud HD1 .... 153 F3
Haigh Terr. Roth LS26 .... 100 C7
Haigh View. Roth LS26 .... 100 C7
Haigh Wood Cres. Hors LS16 .. 41 D3
Haigh Wood Gn. Hors LS16 .... 41 D2
Haigh Wood Rd. Hors LS16 .... 41 D2
Haigh's Sq. Hud HD5 .... 154 D7
Haighside Cl. Roth LS26 .... 100 D6
Haighside Dr. Roth LS26 .... 100 C6
Haighside. Roth LS26 .... 100 C6
Haighside Way. Roth LS26 .... 100 C6
Hailhead Dr. Pont WF8 .... 125 F1
Haincliffe Pl. Keigh BD21 .... 35 B4 11
Haincliffe Rd. Keigh BD21 .... 35 B4
Haines Pk. Leeds 60 E2
Hainsworth Moor Cres. Queen
BD13 .... 92 D8 5
Hainsworth Moor Dr. Queen
BD13 .... 92 D8 6
Hainsworth Moor Garth. Queen
BD13 .... 92 D8 4
Hainsworth Moor Gr. Queen
BD13 .... 92 D8
Hainsworth Moor Mid Sch.
Queen 92 D8
Hainsworth Moor View. Queen
BD13 .... 92 D8
Hainsworth Rd. Sil BD20 .... 17 F8
Hainsworth Sq. Pudsey LS28 .. 57 D3 7
Hainsworth St. Leeds LS12 .... 78 E6 6
Hainsworth St. Roth BD20 .... 100 E4
Hainworth Crag Rd. Keigh BD21 35 A2
Hainworth La. Keigh BD21 .... 35 B3
Hainworth Rd. Keigh BD21 .... 35 B3
Hainworth Rd. Keigh BD21 .... 35 C4
Hainworth Wood Rd. Keigh
BD21 .... 35 B4
Hainworth Wood Rd N. Keigh
BD21 .... 35 C5
Haise Mount. Mapp S75 .... 178 A1
Halcyon Hill. Leeds LS7 .... 60 C8
Halcyon Way. Brad BD5 .... 74 C3
Haldane Cl. Bri S72 .... 180 F3
Haldane Cres. Wake WF1 .... 142 F8
Hales Rd. Leeds LS12 .... 78 B4
Halesworth Cres. Brad BD4 .... 75 E3
Haley Hill. Hali HX3 .... 113 C8
Haley's Yd. Leeds LS13 .... 58 C3
Half Acre Rd. Denh BD13 .... 72 B7
Half Acres Fst & Mid Schs.
Castle 124 C7
Half House La. Brig HD6 .... 114 D5
Half Mile Cl. Pudsey LS28 .... 57 F2
Half Mile Gdns. Pudsey LS13 .... 57 F2
Half Mile Gn. Pudsey LS28 .... 57 F2
Half Mile La. Pudsey LS13 .... 57 F3
Half Mile. Pudsey LS13 .... 57 F2
Half Moon La. Crof WF1 .... 143 C6
Half Moon St. Hud HD1 .... 154 A6 13
Half St. Keigh BD21 .... 35 B8
Halfpenny La. Pont WF8 .... 146 A8
Halfpenny Lane Jun & Inf Sch.
Pont 146 B8
Halifax Catholic High Sch. Hali 92 A6
Halifax General Hospl. Hali 113 D3
Halifax Golf Course. Hali 71 B1
Halifax High Sch The. Hali 113 C6
Halifax Ind Ctr The . Hali 113 A8
Halifax La. B Head HX7 .... 87 E4
Halifax La. Hali HX2 .... 111 E8
Halifax Rd. Batley WF17 .... 118 B2
Halifax Rd. Brad BD6 .... 94 B7
Halifax Rd. Brig HX3 .... 114 B8
Halifax Rd. Brig HD6 .... 114 E5
Halifax Rd. Brig HD6 .... 115 E7
Halifax Rd. Clec WF15 .... 116 C5
Halifax Rd. Cull BD13 .... 52 A5
Halifax Rd. Cull BD13 .... 52 D6
Halifax Rd. Denh BD13 .... 71 E5
Halifax Rd. Denh BD13 .... 71 E7
Halifax Rd. Dew WF13 .... 118 B2
Halifax Rd. Dew WF13 .... 139 D8
Halifax Rd. Elland HX5 .... 134 E7
Halifax Rd. Hali HX3, HX5 .... 134 E8
Halifax Rd. Heb Br HX7 .... 88 C2
Halifax Rd. Keigh BD21, BD22 . 35 A2
Halifax Rd. Litt HX6 .... 148 A7
Halifax Rd. Northo HX3 .... 93 B4
Halifax Rd. Queen BD13 .... 92 C7
Halifax Rd. Rip HX6 .... 132 E6
Halifax Rd. Shelf HX3 .... 93 B4
Halifax Rd. Slai HD7 .... 152 B5
Halifax Rd. Tod OL14 .... 108 D6
Halifax Sta. Hali 113 D6
Hall Ave. Brad BD2 .... 56 D5
Hall Ave. Hud HD1 .... 153 F5
Hall Ave. S in Cra BD20 .... 16 D4
Hall Bank Dr. Bing BD16 .... 36 F4
Hall Bank La. Heb Br HX7 .... 110 E8
Hall Bower. Hud HD4 .... 154 B1
Hall Bower La. Hud HD4 .... 154 B1
Hall Brig. Clay DN5 .... 194 C4
Hall Cl. B Spa LS23 .... 30 E7
Hall Cl. Bramho LS16 .... 24 E4
Hall Cl. Bur in W LS29 .... 9 D1
Hall Cl. Liver WF15 .... 117 A3
Hall Cl. Ossett WF5 .... 119 B1
Hall Cl. S in Cra BD20 .... 16 D4
Hall Cliffe Cres. Hor WF4 .... 141 A2

Hall Cliffe Ct. Hor WF4 ... 141 A2
Hall Cliffe Gr. Hor WF4 ... 141 A2
Hall Cliffe Rd. Hor WF4 ... 141 A2
Hall Cliffe Rise. Hor WF4 ... 141 B2
Hall Croft. Neth WF4 ... 158 E6
Hall Cross Gr. Hud HD5 ... 154 D3
Hall Cross Rd. Hud HD5 ... 154 D3
Hall Ct. Broth WF11 ... 126 C8
Hall Ct. Leeds LS7 ... 60 D4
Hall Ct. S in Cra BD20 ... 16 D4
Hall Dr. Bramho LS16 ... 24 E4
Hall Dr. Bur in W LS29 ... 9 D1
Hall Dr. Liver WF15 ... 117 B2
Hall Dr. S in Cra BD20 ... 16 D4
Hall Field La. Ryhill S72 ... 180 A7
Hall Garth Rd. Th Aud WF8 ... 165 A4
Hall Gdns. Farnh BD20 ... 4 E1
Hall Gr. Leeds LS6 ... 59 F2
Hall Gr. Mapp S75 ... 178 C1
Hall Green La. Rip HX6 ... 150 D8
Hall Ing La. Honley HD7 ... 172 C5
Hall Ing Rd. Honley HD4 ... 172 E3
Hall Ing Rd. Kirkb HD4 ... 172 E3
Hall Ings. Brad BD1 ... 74 E6
Hall Ings. Hali HX3 ... 114 A3
Hall La. Ask LS21 ... 9 E6
Hall La. Brad BD4 ... 74 F5
Hall La. Dew WF12 ... 139 F2
Hall La. Hors LS18 ... 41 A1
Hall La. Hors LS16 ... 41 F6
Hall La. Kirkb HD8 ... 173 E7
Hall La. Ledst WF10 ... 103 F6
Hall La. Leeds LS7 ... 60 D4
Hall La. Leeds LS12 ... 77 D5
Hall La. Leeds LS12 ... 78 D7
Hall La. Northo HX3 ... 92 F4
Hall La. S Elm WF9 ... 183 B6
Hall La. S in Elm LS25 ... 84 F5
Hall La. Ship BD18 ... 55 D8
Hall La. Slai HD3 ... 152 B6
Hall Mews. B Spa LS23 ... 30 E7
Hall Orchards Ave. Weth LS22 14 A6
Hall Park Ave. Crof WF4 ... 143 F2
Hall Park Ave. Hors LS18 ... 41 A1
Hall Park Ave. Liver WF15 ... 117 A2
Hall Park Cl. Hors LS18 ... 41 A1
Hall Park Croft. Kippax LS25 .. 103 B8
Hall Park Ct. Kippax LS25 ... 83 B1
Hall Park Garth. Hors LS18 ... 41 A1
Hall Park Meadows. Kippax LS25 ... 103 B8
Hall Park Mount. Hors LS18 ... 41 A1
Hall Park Orch. Kippax LS25 ... 83 B1
Hall Park Rd. Th Arch LS23 ... 15 B5
Hall Park Rise. Hors LS18 ... 41 B1
Hall Park Rise. Kippax LS25 ... 83 B1
Hall Pl. Leeds LS9 ... 79 F7
Hall Rd. Brad BD2 ... 56 D5
Hall Rd. Leeds LS12 ... 78 C7
Hall Rd. Swil LS26 ... 82 B1
Hall Rd. Wake WF2 ... 141 D4
Hall Rise. Bramho LS16 ... 24 E3
Hall Rise. Bur in W LS29 ... 9 D1
Hall Rise Cl. Bramho LS16 ... 24 E3
Hall Rise Croft. Bramho LS16 .. 24 E3
Hall Royd. Ship BD18 ... 55 B7
Hall Sq. Pudsey LS28 ... 57 B7
Hall St. Brad BD6 ... 74 C1 6
Hall St. Brig HD6 ... 115 B2 5
Hall St. Feath WF7 ... 145 E4
Hall St. Glu BD20 ... 16 D7
Hall St. Haw BD22 ... 34 D2
Hall St. Haw BD22 ... 51 C6
Hall St. Hud HD3 ... 152 F7
Hall St N. Hali HX3 ... 92 B2
Hall St. Tod OL14 ... 108 B5
Hall Stone Ct. Shelf HX3 ... 93 C5
Hall Way. S in Cra BD20 ... 16 D4
Hallam Field Houses. Guise LS20 ... 39 E8
Hallam La. Ask LS21 ... 10 B5
Hallam St. Guise LS20 ... 39 D8
Hallamshire Mws. Wake WF2 141 C4
Hallas Bridge. Wils BD13 ... 52 F6
Hallas Gr. Hud HD5 ... 154 F5
Hallas Hall Farm Cotts. Cull BD13 ... 52 E6
Hallas La. Cull BD13 ... 52 E5
Hallas La. Kirkb HD8 ... 174 B6
Hallas La. Wils BD13 ... 52 F5
Hallas Rd. Kirkb HD8 ... 173 F6
Hallbank Cl. Brad BD5 ... 74 D1
Hallbank Dr. Brad BD5 ... 74 D1
Hallcliffe. Bail BD17 ... 38 D4
Hallcroft Cl. Hor WF4 ... 141 B1 5
Hallcroft Dr. Add LS29 ... 7 B7
Hallcroft Dr. Hor WF4 ... 141 B1
Hallcroft Rise. Roy S71 ... 179 B3
Halley St. Bacup OL13 ... 106 A7 8
Hallfield Ave. M'Field LS25 ... 83 F7
Hallfield Cres. Weth LS22 ... 13 F5
Hallfield Dr. Bail BD17 ... 38 C3
Hallfield La. Weth LS22 ... 13 F5
Hallfield Pl. Brad BD1 ... 74 E8
Hallfield Rd. Brad BD1 ... 74 D8
Hallfield St. Brad BD1 ... 74 E8
Hallfield Terr. M'Field LS25 ... 83 F7
Hallgate. Brad BD1 ... 74 E8
Halliday Ave. Leeds LS12 ... 78 A8
Halliday Dr. Leeds LS12 ... 78 A8 16
Halliday Gr. Leeds LS12 ... 78 A8
Halliday Mount. Leeds LS12 ... 78 A8
Halliday Pl. Leeds LS12 ... 78 A8
Halliday Rd. Gar LS25 ... 82 E7
Halliday Rd. Leeds LS12 ... 78 A8 18
Halliday St. Pudsey LS28 ... 76 E8
Halliley Gdns. Dew WF13 ... 139 C8 2
Halliley St. Dew WF13 ... 139 B8
Halling Pl. Tod OL14 ... 108 A4
Hallowes Gr. Cull BD13 ... 52 D5
Hallowes Park Rd. Cull BD13 ... 52 D6
Hallows Rd. Keigh BD21 ... 18 E1
Hallows The. Keigh BD20 ... 35 A8
Hallroyd Cres. Tod OL14 ... 108 C5
Hallroyd Pl. Tod OL14 ... 108 C5
Hallroyd Rd. Tod OL14 ... 108 C5
Hallwood Gn. Brad BD10 ... 56 E5
Halstead Dr. Men LS29 ... 22 A5
Halstead Gr. Mapp S75 ... 178 A2
Halstead La. Kirkb HD4 ... 173 A1
Halstead Pl. Brad BD7 ... 74 B3
Halsteads Way. Stee BD20 ... 17 C6
Halton Cl. Hud HD5 ... 154 F4
Halton Dr. Leeds LS15 ... 81 A8
Halton Moor Ave. Leeds LS9 ... 80 D7
Halton Moor Rd. Leeds LS15, LS9 ... 80 D6
Halton Pl. Brad BD5 ... 74 B3
Halton Rd. Wake WF1 ... 142 F8
Halton St. Feath WF7 ... 145 D7
Hambledon Ave. Brad BD4 ... 95 B8
Hambledon Ave. Mel HD7 ... 170 F1
Hambledon Fst Sch. Brad ... 95 B8
Hambleton Bank. Hali HX2 ... 91 B6
Hambleton Cotts. B Abby BD23 . 2 B8
Hambleton Cres. Hali HX2 ... 91 B5
Hambleton Dr. Hali HX2 ... 91 B5
Hambleton St. Wake WF1 ... 142 C7 6
Hame The. Elland HX4 ... 133 F3
Hamel Rise. Hem WF9 ... 181 D6
Hamilton Ave. Leeds LS7 ... 60 E4
Hamilton Ct. Nor WF6 ... 123 B3
Hamilton Gdns. Leeds LS7 ... 60 E3
Hamilton House. Brad BD15 ... 73 B8 5
Hamilton Pl. Leeds LS7 ... 60 E3
Hamilton Prim Sch. Leeds ... 60 E4
Hamilton St. Brad BD1 ... 74 D8
Hamilton Terr. Leeds LS7 ... 60 E4
Hamilton Terr. Otley LS21 ... 23 B8
Hamilton View. Leeds LS7 ... 60 E4
Hamm Strasse. Brad BD1 ... 74 E8
Hammer La. Crof WF4 ... 144 B4
Hammerstone Leach La. Elland HX5 ... 134 D5
Hammerstones Rd. Elland HX5 134 D6
Hammerton Dr. Gar LS25 ... 83 A5
Hammerton Gr. Pudsey LS28 .. 76 F7 4
Hammerton Rd. Hud HD2 ... 136 A2
Hammerton St. Brad BD3 ... 75 A6
Hammerton St. Pudsey LS28 ... 76 E7
Hammerton Terr. Tod OL14 ... 108 B6 5
Hammond Cres. Birk BD11 ... 96 E7
Hammond Pl. Brad BD9 ... 55 A3
Hammond Rd. Knot WF11 ... 126 D3
Hammond Sq. Brad BD9 ... 55 A3
Hammond St. Hali HX1 ... 112 F6
Hammond St. Hud HD2 ... 136 B1
Hammond St. Leeds LS9 ... 79 E6
Hampden Cl. Knot WF11 ... 126 B5
Hampden Pl. Brad BD5 ... 74 D4
Hampden Pl. Hali HX1 ... 113 B7
Hampden St. Brad BD5 ... 74 D4
Hampole Balk. Ad Le S DN6 ... 184 E1
Hampole Field La. Ham DN6 ... 183 F1
Hampshire Cl. Ilkley LS29 ... 8 D4
Hampshire St. Hud HD5 ... 154 D6 3
Hampson St. Batley WF17 ... 118 A7
Hampton Pl. Brad BD10 ... 56 B8
Hampton Pl. Leeds LS9 ... 79 F7
Hampton St. Hali HX1 ... 112 F5 6
Hampton St. Leeds LS9 ... 79 E7
Hampton Terr. Leeds LS9 ... 79 F7 7
Hamworth Dr. Haw BD22 ... 34 D2
Hanby Ave. Nor WF6 ... 122 F3
Hand Bank La. Mir WF14 ... 138 A2
Hand Carr La. Sow Br HX2 ... 111 C7
Handel St. Brad BD7 ... 74 C7
Handel St. Hud HD7 ... 152 D4
Handel Terr. Hud HD5 ... 154 D5 2
Handsworth Rd. Wake WF2 ... 160 A4
Hanging Gate La. Oxen BD22 ... 51 B5
Hanging Heaton CE Sch. Batley 118 F3
Hanging Royd. Slai HD7 ... 152 D3
Hanging Stone Rd. Hud HD4 ... 171 F7
Hanging Stones La. Rip HX6 ... 132 F5
Hangingroyd Cl. Heb Br HX7 ... 89 A3
Hangingroyd La. Heb Br HX7 ... 89 A3 4
Hangingroyd Rd. Heb Br HX7 .. 89 A3 26
Hangingstone Rd. Ilkley LS29 ... 8 E2
Hangram St. Brig HD6 ... 115 B2 2
Hanley Rd. Morley LS27 ... 98 A3
Hannah Ct. Brad BD12 ... 94 C3
Hannah St. Bacup OL13 ... 106 A3 11
Hanover Ave. Leeds LS3 ... 79 A8
Hanover Cl. Brad BD8 ... 55 B1
Hanover Cres. Pont WF8 ... 146 C5
Hanover Ct. Dew WF13 ... 118 A1 4
Hanover Ct. Keigh BD20 ... 18 A2
Hanover Gdns. Bur in W LS29 .. 21 E8
Hanover Gdns. Dew WF13 ... 139 B8
Hanover House. Hali HX2 ... 112 E5
Hanover La. Leeds LS3 ... 79 A8
Hanover Mount. Leeds LS3 ... 60 A1
Hanover Pl. Batley WF17 ... 118 D5
Hanover Pl. Broth WF11 ... 105 C1
Hanover Sq. Brad BD1 ... 74 D8
Hanover Sq. Leeds LS3 ... 79 A8
Hanover St. Batley WF17 ... 118 C5
Hanover St. Dearne S63 ... 194 E1
Hanover St. Dew WF13 ... 139 B8
Hanover St. Farnh BD20 ... 4 D1
Hanover St. Hali HX6 ... 112 D4
Hanover St. Hali HX1 ... 113 B6
Hanover St. Keigh BD21 ... 35 C7
Hanover St. Wake WF2 ... 142 A5
Hanover Way. Bur in W LS29 .. 21 E8
Hanover Way. Leeds LS3 ... 79 A8
Hansby Ave. Leeds LS14 ... 62 B5
Hansby Bank. Leeds LS14 ... 62 B5
Hansby Cl. Leeds LS14 ... 62 B4
Hansby Dr. Leeds LS14 ... 62 B4
Hansby Gate. Leeds LS14 ... 62 B5
Hansby Gdns. Leeds LS14 ... 62 B4
Hansby Grange. Leeds LS14 ... 62 B5 10
Hansby Pl. Leeds LS14 ... 62 B5
Hanson Ave. Nor WF6 ... 123 B1
Hanson Ct. Brad BD12 ... 94 B2
Hanson Fold. Brad BD12 ... 94 C3 8
Hanson La. Hali HX1 ... 113 A7
Hanson La. Hud HD4 ... 153 E2
Hanson Mount. Brad BD12 ... 94 C2
Hanson Pl. Brad BD12 ... 94 C3 7
Hanson Rd. Brig HD6 ... 135 E8
Hanson Rd. Mel HD7 ... 170 C1
Hanson Sch. Brad ... 56 A4
Hanworth Rd. Brad BD12 ... 94 D6
Harbeck Dr. Harden BD16 ... 36 B1
Harbour Cres. Brad BD6 ... 94 A8
Harbour Pk. Brad BD6 ... 93 F8 2
Harbour Rd. Brad BD6 ... 94 A8
Harclo Rd. Keigh BD21 ... 35 E8
Harcourt Ave. Thorn BD13 ... 72 D7
Harcourt Dr. Add LS29 ... 2 F1
Harcourt Pl. Leeds LS1 ... 79 A8
Harcourt St. Brad BD4 ... 75 B3
Harcourt St. Wake WF2 ... 141 F5
Hard Ings Rd. Keigh BD21 ... 18 C1
Hard Nese La. Oxen BD22 ... 50 F1
Hard Nese La. Oxen BD22 ... 51 B2
Hard Platts La. Elland HX4 ... 133 F2
Hardaker La. Bail BD17 ... 38 A2
Hardaker St. Brad BD8 ... 74 D8
Hardaker's La. Ack M T WF7 . 163 E6
Hardakers App. Ack M T WF7 163 F5
Hardcastle Ave. Pont WF8 ... 125 C1
Hardcastle Crags. Wad M ... 68 C1
Hardcastle La. Floc WF4 ... 157 E4
Hardcastle La. Neth WF4 ... 157 E4
Harden Brow La. Harden BD16 36 A1
Harden Fst Sch. Harden ... 36 B1
Harden Gr. Brad BD10 ... 56 E3
Harden Gr. Keigh BD21 ... 35 E5
Harden Hill Rd. Mel HD7 ... 187 E8
Harden La. Harden BD15 ... 53 B7
Harden La. Wils BD15 ... 53 B7
Harden Moss Rd. Holmfi HD7 187 E4
Harden Moss Rd. Mel HD7 ... 187 E7
Harden Rd. Harden BD16 ... 36 D2
Harden Rd. Keigh BD21 ... 35 F5
Hardgate La. Haw BD22 ... 51 F7
Hardie Rd. Ryhill WF4 ... 162 C1
Harding Houses. Glu BD20 ... 16 E7
Hardings La. Glu BD20 ... 16 F7
Hardings La. H Hill LS29 ... 8 A8
Hardings La. Ilkley LS29 ... 8 A7
Hardistry Dr. Pont WF8 ... 146 B8
Hardknot Cl. Brad BD7 ... 73 E3
Hardrow Gn. Leeds LS12 ... 78 D5
Hardrow Gr. Leeds LS12 ... 78 D5
Hardrow Rd. Leeds LS12 ... 78 D5
Hardrow Terr. Leeds LS12 ... 78 D5
Hardwick Cres. Pont WF8 ... 146 D5
Hardwick Croft. Leeds LS7 ... 60 D6
Hardwick Ct. Pont WF8 ... 146 C7
Hardwick La. W Har WF4 ... 145 B1
Hardwick Rd. Dar WF7, WF8 . 146 F3
Hardwick Rd. Feath WF7 ... 145 C4
Hardwick Rd. Pont WF7, WF8 146 D5
Hardwick St. Keigh BD21 ... 35 A6 8
Hardy Ave. Brad BD6 ... 94 C8
Hardy Ave. Morley LS27 ... 98 C8
Hardy Croft. Wake WF1 ... 142 D6 5
Hardy Ct. Morley LS27 ... 98 B4
Hardy Gr. Leeds LS11 ... 79 A3 8
Hardy Pl. Brig HD6 ... 114 E5
Hardy St. Brad BD6 ... 74 C1
Hardy St. Brad BD4 ... 74 F6
Hardy St. Brig HD6 ... 115 B3
Hardy St. Leeds LS11 ... 79 A3
Hardy St. Morley LS27 ... 98 B4
Hardy Terr. Leeds LS11 ... 79 B3 8
Hardy View. Leeds LS11 ... 79 A3 7
Hare Farm Ave. Leeds LS12 ... 77 D7
Hare Farm Cl. Leeds LS12 ... 77 D7
Hare La. Pudsey LS28 ... 76 F4
Hare Park Ave. Clec WF15 ... 116 C4
Hare Park Cl. Clec WF15 ... 116 C4
Hare Park La. Clec WF15 ... 116 C4
Hare Park La. Crof WF4 ... 161 F8
Hare Park Mount. Leeds LS12 . 77 D7
Hare Park View. Crof WF4 ... 161 F8
Hare St. Hali HX1 ... 113 A6 1
Harecroft Rd. Otley LS21 ... 11 A1
Haredon Cl. Mapp S75 ... 178 A2
Harefield Cl. Stee BD20 ... 17 A5
Harefield Dr. Batley WF17 ... 97 A1
Harefield E. Leeds LS15 ... 80 E7
Harefield Rd. Pont WF8 ... 146 F8 2
Harefield W. Leeds LS15 ... 80 E8
Harehill Ave. Tod OL14 ... 108 A6
Harehill Cl. Brad BD10 ... 39 B1
Harehill Rd. Brad BD10 ... 39 B1
Harehill St. Tod OL14 ... 108 A6
Harehills Ave. Leeds LS7, LS8 . 60 F4
Harehills La. Haw BD22 ... 33 D1
Harehills La. Leeds LS7, LS8, LS9 ... 61 B1
Harehills Mid Sch. Leeds ... 60 F3
Harehills Park Ave. Leeds LS9 . 61 B2 1
Harehills Park Rd. Leeds LS9 .. 61 B2 16
Harehills Park Terr. Leeds LS9 61 B2 17
Harehills Park View. Leeds LS9 61 B2 13
Harehills Pl. Leeds LS8 ... 60 F3
Harehills Prim Sch. Leeds ... 61 A3
Harehills Rd. Leeds LS8 ... 60 F3
Harepark Dr. Clec WF15 ... 116 C4
Hares Ave. Leeds LS8 ... 60 F4 6
Hares Mount. Leeds LS8 ... 60 E4
Hares Rd. Leeds LS8 ... 60 F4 4
Hares Terr. Leeds LS8 ... 60 F4
Hares View. Leeds LS8 ... 60 F4 5
Harewood Ave. Batley WF16 . 117 E3
Harewood Ave. Hali HX2 ... 112 D8
Harewood Ave. Hare LS17 ... 27 D7
Harewood Ave. Nor WF6 ... 123 C3
Harewood Ave. Pont WF8 ... 146 E8
Harewood Ave. Stee BD20 ... 17 A5
Harewood CE Prim Sch. Hare .. 27 A7
Harewood Cl. Knot WF11 ... 126 C4
Harewood Cres. Haw BD22 ... 34 E2
Harewood Ct. Leeds LS17 ... 43 D1
Harewood Ct. Leeds LS14 ... 62 A4
Harewood Gate. Hare LS17 ... 27 A7
Harewood Gr. Batley WF16 ... 117 E3
Harewood House. Hare ... 26 E6
Harewood La. Upton WF9 ... 183 D8
Harewood La Fst Sch. Upton . 183 E8
Harewood Mews. Hare LS17 ... 27 A7
Harewood Mount. Mel HD7 ... 170 F2
Harewood Mount. Pont WF8 . 146 E8
Harewood Pl. Hali HX2 ... 112 E6
Harewood Rd. Coll LS17 ... 28 C7
Harewood Rd. E Kes LS17 ... 28 C7
Harewood Rd. Keigh BD22 ... 34 F3
Harewood Rd. Wake WF1 ... 142 F8
Harewood Rise. Keigh BD22 ... 34 F3
Harewood St. Brad BD3 ... 75 B7
Harewood St. Leeds LS2 ... 79 C8
Harewood View. Pont WF8 ... 146 E8
Harewood Way. Pudsey LS13 .. 77 B8
Hargrave Cres. Men LS29 ... 21 F4
Hargreaves Ave. Loft G WF3 . 121 E5
Hargreaves St. Glu BD20 ... 16 E6
Harker Rd. Brad BD12 ... 94 C7
Harker St. Knot WF11 ... 127 B4
Harker St. S in Cra BD20 ... 16 E5
Harker Terr. Pudsey LS28 ... 57 D1 1
Harland Cl. Brad BD2 ... 55 E2
Harland Sq. Leeds LS2 ... 60 A3
Harlech Ave. Leeds LS11 ... 79 B2
Harlech Cres. Leeds LS11 ... 79 B2
Harlech Gr. Leeds LS11 ... 79 B2
Harlech Mount. Leeds LS11 ... 79 B2
Harlech Rd. Leeds LS11 ... 79 B2
Harlech St. Leeds LS11 ... 79 B2
Harlech Terr. Leeds LS11 ... 79 B2
Harlech Way. Gar LS25 ... 83 B7
Harley Cl. Pudsey LS13 ... 77 A8
Harley Ct. Pudsey LS13 ... 77 A8
Harley Dr. Pudsey LS13 ... 77 A8
Harley Gdns. Pudsey LS13 ... 77 A8
Harley Gn. Pudsey LS13 ... 77 A8
Harley Pl. Brig HD6 ... 115 A1
Harley Rd. Pudsey LS13 ... 77 A8
Harley Rise. Pudsey LS13 ... 77 A8
Harley St. Brig HD6 ... 115 A1 7
Harley St. Tod OL14 ... 108 B6
Harley Terr. Pudsey LS13 ... 77 B8
Harley View. Pudsey LS13 ... 77 A8
Harley Wlk. Pudsey LS13 ... 77 A8
Harley Wood. Tod OL14 ... 107 E8
Harlington Ct. Morley LS27 ... 98 A2 3
Harlington Rd. Morley LS27 ... 98 A2
Harlock St. Wake WF1 ... 142 E2
Harlow Ct. Leeds LS8 ... 61 C7
Harlow Rd. Brad BD7 ... 74 A5
Harmby Cl. Ad Le S DN6 ... 184 F2
Harmon Cl. Brad BD4 ... 95 C8
Harold Ave. Leeds LS6 ... 59 E2
Harold Gr. Leeds LS6 ... 59 E2
Harold Mount. Leeds LS6 ... 59 E2
Harold Pl. Leeds LS6 ... 59 E2
Harold Pl. Ship BD18 ... 54 F8 13
Harold Rd. Leeds LS6 ... 59 E2
Harold Sq. Leeds LS6 ... 59 E2
Harold St. Bing BD16 ... 36 E4
Harold St. Leeds LS6 ... 59 E2
Harold Terr. Leeds LS6 ... 59 E2
Harold View. Leeds LS6 ... 59 E2
Harold Wilson House. Nor WF6 ... 123 A1
Harold Wlk. Leeds LS6 ... 59 E2
Harp Rd. Hud HD3 ... 153 B5
Harpe Inge. Hud HD5 ... 154 E7
Harper Ave. Brad BD10 ... 39 B1
Harper Cres. Brad BD10 ... 39 C1
Harper Gr. Brad BD10 ... 39 B1
Harper Gr. S in Cra BD20 ... 16 D4
Harper La. Yeadon LS19 ... 40 B6
Harper Pl. Leeds LS2 ... 79 D8
Harper Rock. Yeadon LS19 ... 40 B6
Harper Royd La. Sow Br HX6 . 112 C2
Harper St. Leeds LS2 ... 79 D7
Harper Terr. Yeadon LS19 ... 40 B6 8
Harpers Sq. S in Cra BD20 ... 16 D4
Harrap St. Wake WF2 ... 141 D7
Harrier Cl. Brad BD8 ... 73 B7
Harrier Way. Morley LS27 ... 98 D4
Harriet St. Brad BD8 ... 74 B8
Harriet St. Brig HD6 ... 115 A4
Harriet St. Leeds LS7 ... 60 D3
Harrington Ct. Mel HD7 ... 170 F1
Harris Ct. Brad BD7 ... 74 A4
Harris St. Bing BD16 ... 37 A2 3
Harris St. Brad BD1 ... 75 A7
Harrison and Potter Trust Homes The. Leeds LS2 ... 60 A3 6
Harrison and Potter Trust Homes The. Leeds LS7 ... 60 C1
Harrison Cres. Leeds LS9 ... 61 D1
Harrison La. Mel HD7 ... 170 E5
Harrison Pl. Glu BD20 ... 16 B6
Harrison Rd. Crof WF4 ... 143 F1
Harrison Rd. Hali HX1 ... 113 C6
Harrison St. Bing BD16 ... 37 A2
Harrison St. Leeds LS1 ... 79 C8
Harrison St. Tod OL14 ... 86 B1
Harrisons Ave. Pudsey LS28 ... 57 F2 5
Harrogate Ave. Brad BD3 ... 56 A2
Harrogate Pl. Brad BD3 ... 56 A2
Harrogate Rd. Brad BD10, BD2 56 D5
Harrogate Rd. E Carl LS16 ... 23 F2
Harrogate Rd. Hare LS17 ... 27 A4
Harrogate Rd. Leeds LS17 ... 43 E5
Harrogate Rd. Spoff LS22 ... 13 B7
Harrogate Rd. Yeadon LS19 ... 40 C5
Harrogate St. Brad BD3 ... 56 A2
Harrogate Terr. Brad BD3 ... 56 A2
Harrogate View. Leeds LS17 ... 44 C5
Harrop Ave. Morley LS27 ... 98 B2
Harrop Gr. Morley LS27 ... 98 B2
Harrop La. Wils BD15 ... 53 B3
Harrop Terr. Morley LS27 ... 98 B2
Harrop Well La. Pont WF8 ... 146 D8 12
Harrow St. Hali HX1 ... 112 F7
Harrow St. S Elm WF9 ... 182 E3
Harrowby Cres. Leeds LS16 ... 59 B7
Harrowby Rd. Leeds LS16 ... 59 B7
Harry La. Brad BD14 ... 73 B4
Harry La. Oxen BD22 ... 51 C3
Harry St. Brad BD4 ... 75 C3
Hart St. Brad BD7 ... 74 B4
Hart St. Hud HD4 ... 154 A2
Hart's Hole. Slai HD7 ... 152 A5
Harthill Ave. Gild LS27 ... 97 D7
Harthill Cl. Gild LS27 ... 97 D7
Harthill. Gild LS27 ... 97 D7
Harthill La. Gild LS27 ... 97 D8
Harthill Par. Gild LS27 ... 97 D7
Harthill Rise. Gild LS27 ... 97 C7
Hartington Mid Sch. Haw ... 51 C7
Hartington St. Batley WF17 ... 118 C3
Hartington St. Keigh BD21 ... 35 C8 9
Hartington Terr. Brad BD7 ... 74 A5
Hartland Rd. Brad BD4 ... 75 E4
Hartley Cl. S Elm WF9 ... 183 A4
Hartley Cres. Leeds LS6 ... 60 B4
Hartley Gdns. Leeds LS6 ... 60 B4
Hartley Gr. Dew WF13 ... 118 C1
Hartley Gr. Leeds LS6 ... 60 A4
Hartley Hill. Leeds LS2 ... 60 C1
Hartley Park Ave. Pont WF8 .. 146 B8
Hartley Park View. Pont WF8 146 B8
Hartley Pl. Morley LS27 ... 98 B3 3
Hartley St. Brad BD4 ... 75 B5
Hartley St. Castle WF10 ... 124 C7
Hartley St. Dew WF13 ... 118 C1
Hartley St. Glu BD20 ... 16 A6
Hartley St. Hali HX1 ... 113 A8
Hartley St. Morley LS27 ... 98 B7
Hartley St. Morley LS27 ... 98 C4
Hartley Terr. Feath WF7 ... 145 C4
Hartley's Bldgs. Morley LS27 .. 98 B3 6
Hartley's Sq. Keigh BD20 ... 19 D1
Hartlington Ct. Bail BD17 ... 38 E3
Hartman Pl. Brad BD9 ... 54 F2
Hartshead H'll La. Liver WF15 116 D1
Hartshead Jun Mix & Inf Sch. Liver ... 116 C2
Hartshead La. Liver WF15 ... 116 C2
Hartshead Moor Sch. Clec ... 116 A6
Hartwell Rd. Leeds LS6 ... 59 E2
Harvelin Pk. Tod OL14 ... 109 A5
Harvest Croft. Bur in W LS29 ... 9 D1
Harvey Royd. Hud HD5 ... 155 A4
Harvey St. Wake WF1 ... 142 E3
Harwill App. Morley LS27 ... 98 C7
Harwill Ave. Morley LS27 ... 98 C7
Harwill Croft. Morley LS27 ... 98 C7
Harwill Gr. Morley LS27 ... 98 C7
Harwill Rd. Morley LS27 ... 98 C7
Harwill Rise. Morley LS27 ... 98 C7
Harwood Cl. Hud HD5 ... 154 F5
Harwood Cl. Wake WF2 ... 142 E1
Haselden Cres. Wake WF2 ... 141 E5
Haselden Rd. Wake WF2 ... 141 E5
Haslam Cl. Brad BD3 ... 75 A8
Haslam Gr. Ship BD18 ... 55 E6
Haslemere Cl. Brad BD4 ... 75 D3
Haslewood Cl. Leeds LS9 ... 79 E8
Haslewood Ct. Leeds LS9 ... 79 F8 1
Haslewood Dene. Leeds LS9 ... 79 F8
Haslewood Dr. Leeds LS9 ... 79 F8 2
Haslewood Gn. Leeds LS9 ... 79 F8
Haslewood Mews. Leeds LS9 ... 79 F8
Haslewood Pl. Leeds LS9 ... 79 F8
Haslewood Sq. Leeds LS9 ... 79 F8
Hasley Rd. Bur in W LS29 ... 21 F8
Haslingden Dr. Brad BD9 ... 54 F2
Hassocks La. Honley HD7 ... 171 D4
Hassocks Rd. Mel HD7 ... 170 C3
Haste St. Castle WF10 ... 124 B8
Hastings Ave. Brad BD5 ... 74 D2
Hastings Ave. Wake WF2 ... 142 D2
Hastings Cres. Castle WF10 ... 125 B7
Hastings Ct. Coll LS22 ... 29 B8
Hastings Ct. Nor WF6 ... 122 E4
Hastings Ct. Thorner LS17 ... 44 E4
Hastings Gr. Wake WF2 ... 142 D2
Hastings Pl. Brad BD5 ... 74 D3
Hastings St. Brad BD5 ... 74 D2
Hastings Terr. Brad BD5 ... 74 D2
Hastings Way. Coll LS22 ... 28 F8
Hastings Wlk. Castle WF10 ... 125 B7
Hatchet La. Brad BD12 ... 95 A4
Hatfield Gdns. Roy S71 ... 179 B4
Hatfield Pl. Ryhill WF4 ... 162 D2
Hatfield Rd. Brad BD2 ... 56 B2
Hatfield St. Wake WF1 ... 142 C7
Hathaway Ave. Brad BD9 ... 54 D3
Hathaway Dr. Leeds LS14 ... 45 B1
Hathaway La. Leeds LS14 ... 62 B8
Hathaway Mews. Leeds LS14 .. 45 B1
Hathaway Wlk. Leeds LS14 ... 62 B8 1
Hathershelf La. Heb Br HX7 .. 111 A7
Hatton Cl. Brad BD6 ... 94 D8
Haugh End La. Sow Br HX6 ... 112 A3
Haugh Rd. Tod OL14 ... 108 E6
Haugh Shaw Croft. Hali HX1 .. 113 A5 16
Haugh Shaw Jun & Inf Sch. Hali ... 113 A5
Haugh Shaw Rd. Hali HX1 ... 113 A5
Haugh Shaw Rd W. Hali HX1 . 112 F5 24
Haugh Shaw Sec Sch. Hali ... 113 A5
Haughs La. Hud HD3 ... 153 A7
Haughs Rd. Hud HD3 ... 153 A7
Hauxley Ct. Ilkley LS29 ... 8 D5
Hauxwell Cl. Ad Le S DN6 ... 184 F2
Hauxwell Dr. Yeadon LS19 ... 40 B6
Havelock Sq. Thorn BD13 ... 72 E6 2
Havelock St. Brad BD7 ... 74 A4
Havelock St. Dew WF13 ... 138 E5
Havelock St. Thorn BD13 ... 72 E6
Haven Chase. Hors LS16 ... 41 E3
Haven Croft. Hors LS16 ... 41 F3
Haven Ct. Hors LS16 ... 41 E3
Haven Ct. Pont WF8 ... 146 B5
Haven Garth. Hors LS16 ... 41 E3
Haven Gdns. Hors LS16 ... 41 E3
Haven Gn. Hors LS16 ... 41 E3
Haven La. Heb Br HX7 ... 110 B8
Haven Mount. Hors LS16 ... 41 E3
Haven Rise. Hors LS16 ... 41 E3
Haven St. Tod OL14 ... 108 C5 15
Haven The. Brad BD10 ... 56 C6
Haven The. Leeds LS15 ... 81 D8
Haven View. Hors LS16 ... 41 E3
Havercroft Cty Inf Sch. Ryhill 180 B8
Havercroft La. Dar WF8 ... 147 E5
Havercroft. Ossett WF5 ... 140 E5
Havercroft Rise. S Hie S72 ... 180 E6
Havercroft Way. Batley WF17 117 D5
Haverdale Rd. Ryhill WF4 ... 162 C1
Haveroid La. Crig WF4 ... 159 F4
Haveroid Way. Crig WF4 ... 159 F5
Haverthwaites Dr. Aber LS25 .. 47 E1
Havertop La. Feath WF6 ... 123 F2
Haw Ave. Yeadon LS19 ... 40 C8
Haw Cliff La. Kirkb HD4 ... 172 F1
Haw Hill View. Nor WF6 ... 123 C3
Haw La. Yeadon LS19 ... 40 B8
Haw Park La. Ryhill WF4 ... 161 F3
Haw Park La. Walton WF2 ... 161 B2
Haw View. Yeadon LS19 ... 40 C8
Hawber Cote Dr. Sil BD20 ... 5 F2
Hawber Cote La. Sil BD20 ... 5 F2
Hawber La. Sil BD20 ... 5 F1
Hawes Ave. Brad BD5 ... 74 C2
Hawes Ave. Hud HD3 ... 153 B6
Hawes Cl. Castle WF10 ... 125 B8
Hawes Cres. Brad BD5 ... 74 C2
Hawes Dr. Brad BD5 ... 74 C2
Hawes Gr. Brad BD5 ... 74 C2
Hawes Mount. Brad BD5 ... 74 C2
Hawes Rd. Brad BD5 ... 74 C2
Hawes Terr. Brad BD5 ... 74 C2
Haweswater Cl. Weth LS22 ... 13 B5
Haweswater Pl. Knot WF11 ... 126 E1
Hawk St. Keigh BD21 ... 35 D8 4
Hawk's Nst Gdns E. Leeds LS17 43 D4
Hawk's Nest Gdns S. Leeds LS17 ... 43 D4
Hawk's Nst Gdn W. Leeds LS17 43 D4
Hawk's Nest Rise. Leeds LS17 43 D4
Hawkcliffe View. Sil BD20 ... 5 C1
Hawke Ave. Batley WF16 ... 117 E4
Hawke Way. Brad BD12 ... 94 E6
Hawkesworth La. Guise LS20 .. 39 B7
Hawkhill Dr. Guise LS20 ... 39 D8
Hawkhill Ave. Leeds LS15 ... 62 B2
Hawkhill Dr. Leeds LS15 ... 62 B2
Hawkhill Gdns. Leeds LS15 ... 62 B2
Hawkhills. Leeds LS7 ... 60 E7
Hawkhurst Rd. Leeds LS12 ... 78 C6
Hawkingcroft Rd. Hor WF4 ... 140 F1
Hawkins Dr. Leeds LS7 ... 60 C2
Hawkins Way. Litt OL15 ... 129 C1
Hawkroyd Bank Rd. Hud HD4 171 E6
Hawksbridge La. Oxen BD22 .. 51 A3
Hawkshead Cl. Brad BD5 ... 74 E5
Hawkshead Cres. Leeds LS14 . 62 A3
Hawkshead Dr. Brad BD5 ... 74 E5
Hawkshead Way. Brad BD5 ... 74 E5 5
Hawkshead Wlk. Brad BD5 ... 74 E5 6
Hawkstone Ave. Guise LS20 ... 39 C7
Hawkstone Dr. Keigh BD20 ... 18 A1
Hawkstone View. Guise LS20 .. 39 D7
Hawkswood Ave. Brad BD9 ... 54 F3
Hawkswood Ave. Leeds LS5 ... 58 E7
Hawkswood Cres. Leeds LS5 ... 58 E7
Hawkswood Gr. Leeds LS5 ... 58 E7
Hawkswood Mount. Leeds LS5 58 E7
Hawkswood Pl. Leeds LS5 ... 58 F6
Hawkswood St. Leeds LS5 ... 58 E6
Hawkswood Terr. Leeds LS5 ... 58 F6
Hawkswood View. Leeds LS5 ... 58 E7
Hawksworth Ave. Guise LS20 .. 39 D8
Hawksworth CE Prim Sch. Guise ... 38 F8
Hawksworth Cl. Men LS29 ... 22 A3
Hawksworth Cty Prim Sch. Leeds ... 58 E7
Hawksworth Dr. Guise LS20 ... 39 D7
Hawksworth Dr. Men LS29 ... 22 A4
Hawksworth Gr. Leeds LS5 ... 58 D6
Hawksworth Hall Sch. Guise ... 38 F8
Hawksworth Mid Sch. Leeds ... 58 E7
Hawksworth Rd. Bail BD17 ... 38 C6
Hawksworth Rd. Hors LS18 ... 58 D7
Hawksworth St. Ilkley LS29 ... 8 B4
Hawley Cl. Morley LS27 ... 97 F2
Hawley Terr. Brad BD10 ... 56 E4
Hawley Way. Morley LS27 ... 97 F2
Haworth Cl. Mir WF14 ... 137 F6
Haworth Fst Sch. Haw ... 51 C7
Haworth Gr. Brad BD9 ... 54 E3
Haworth La. Yeadon LS19 ... 40 B7
Haworth Rd. Batley WF17 ... 96 F2
Haworth Rd. Brad BD9 ... 54 C4
Haworth Rd. Haw BD22 ... 51 E8
Haworth Rd. Wils BD15 ... 53 C4
Haworth Sta. Haw ... 51 C7
Hawthorn Ave. Batley WF17 ... 118 A3
Hawthorn Ave. Brad BD3 ... 75 E8
Hawthorn Ave. Crof WF4 ... 143 E1
Hawthorn Ave. Knot WF11 ... 126 E3
Hawthorn Ave. Yeadon LS19 ... 40 C7
Hawthorn Cl. Brig HD6 ... 115 C3
Hawthorn Cl. Wake WF2 ... 120 B3
Hawthorn Cres. Bail BD17 ... 38 D3
Hawthorn Cres. Leeds LS7 ... 60 D7 4
Hawthorn Cres. Yeadon LS19 .. 40 B7
Hawthorn Ct. Crof S65 ... 143 E1
Hawthorn Dr. Brad BD10 ... 56 C7
Hawthorn Dr. Pudsey LS13 ... 57 D6
Hawthorn Dr. Yeadon LS19 ... 40 C8
Hawthorn Gr. Ack M T WF7 ... 163 F5
Hawthorn Gr. Bur in W LS29 ... 21 F8
Hawthorn Gr. Pudsey LS13 ... 57 D5
Hawthorn Gr. Roth LS26 ... 100 F4
Hawthorn Gr. Silk S75 ... 193 F1
Hawthorn La. Leeds LS7 ... 60 D7 6
Hawthorn Mill. Leeds LS12 ... 78 A4 5
Hawthorn Mount. Leeds LS7 ... 60 D7 3
Hawthorn Pl. Tod OL14 ... 108 B6 9
Hawthorn Rd. Bacup OL13 ... 106 A2
Hawthorn Rd. Leeds LS7 ... 60 D7
Hawthorn Rd. Slai HD7 ... 151 F1
Hawthorn Rd. Yeadon LS19 ... 40 C7
Hawthorn St. Brad BD3 ... 75 E8
Hawthorn St. Brig HX3 ... 114 D8
Hawthorn St. Hali HX1 ... 113 A5 6
Hawthorn Terr. Hali HX1 ... 113 A5 7
Hawthorn Terr. Hud HX1 ... 154 B8
Hawthorn Terr. Ossett WF5 .. 140 E3
Hawthorn Vale. Leeds LS7 ... 60 D7 7
Hawthorn View. Bail BD17 ... 38 E3
Hawthorn View. Leeds LS7 ... 60 D7 5
Hawthorne Ave. Castle WF10 125 B6
Hawthorne Ave. Feath WF7 ... 145 C4
Hawthorne Ave. Hem WF9 ... 181 D6
Hawthorne Ave. Ship BD18 ... 55 D5
Hawthorne Ave. Weth LS22 ... 13 D7
Hawthorne Cl. Floc WF4 ... 157 D3
Hawthorne Cl. Lepton HD8 ... 155 D3
Hawthorne Cres. Hem WF9 ... 181 C6
Hawthorne Flats. Dearne S63 194 D1
Hawthorne Gr. Wake WF2 ... 141 E7
Hawthorne Mount. Nor WF6 . 144 B7
Hawthorne Rise. Leeds LS14 ... 62 C8
Hawthorne St. Shaf S72 ... 180 C3
Hawthorne St. Sil BD20 ... 5 D1
Hawthorne Terr. Hud HD4 ... 153 C4
Hawthorne Terr. Swil LS25 ... 82 C5
Hawthorne Terr. Wake WF2 . 141 E7
Hawthorne Way. Keigh BD20 .. 36 E8
Hawthorne Way. Shaf S72 ... 180 C3
Hawthorne Way. Shep HD8 ... 173 F3
Hawthorns The. Glu BD20 ... 16 C6
Hawthorns The. Loft G WF1 ... 121 D5
Hawthorns The. Ossett WF5 . 140 F4
Hawtop La. Wool WF4 ... 177 F5
Hayburn Gdns. Batley WF17 .. 118 B5
Hayburn Rd. Batley WF17 ... 118 A5
Haycliffe Ave. Brad BD7 ... 74 A2
Haycliffe Dr. Brad BD7 ... 73 F2
Haycliffe Gr. Brad BD7 ... 74 A2
Haycliffe Hill Rd. Brad BD5 ... 74 B3

Haycliffe La. Brad BD5, BD6 .... 74 B2
Haycliffe Rd. Brad BD5 .... 74 B3
Haycliffe Terr. Brad BD5 .... 74 B3
Hayclose Mead. Brad BD6 .... 94 A6
Hayden St. Brad BD3 .... 75 B6
Haydn Ave. Loft G WF3 .... 121 E6
Haydn's Terr. Pudsey LS28 .... 57 E2
Hayfield Ave. B Spa LS23 .... 30 C8
Hayfield Ave. Hud HD3 .... 153 A7
Hayfield Cl. Bail BD17 .... 38 E4
Hayfield Cl. Holmfi HD7 .... 189 D4
Hayfield Terr. Leeds LS12 .... 78 C6
Hayfields The. Haw BD22 .... 51 C8
Haygill Nook. Sil BD23 .... 1 E1
Hayhills La. Sil BD20 .... 5 D4
Hayhills Rd. Sil BD20 .... 5 E2
Hayleigh Ave. Leeds LS13 .... 58 C3 9
Hayleigh Mount. Leeds LS13 .... 58 C3
Hayleigh St. Leeds LS13 .... 58 C3 8
Hayleigh Terr. Leeds LS13 .... 58 C3 7
Hayley Ct. Hali HX3 .... 113 C8 4
Hayne La. Neth WF4 .... 157 E5
Haynes St. Brad BD21 .... 35 D6
Hays La. Hali HX2 .... 91 C7
Hayson Ct. Dew WF12 .... 118 F1
Haythorns Ave. Sil BD23 .... 5 D1
Haythorns Mount. Sil BD20 .... 5 D1
Hayton Dr. Weth LS22 .... 13 F4
Hayton Wood View. Aber LS25 .... 64 E8
Haywain The. Ilkley LS29 .... 8 D3
Haywood Ave. Hud HD3 .... 153 C7
Hazebrouck Dr. Bail BD17 .... 38 B4
Hazel Ave. Dew WF12 .... 140 B7
Hazel Ave. Leeds LS14 .... 62 C8
Hazel Beck. Ship BD16 .... 54 A8
Hazel Cl. Birk BD11 .... 96 A6
Hazel Cl. Dew WF12 .... 140 B7
Hazel Cres. Dew WF12 .... 140 B7
Hazel Croft. Ship BD18 .... 55 D7
Hazel Ct. Roth LS26 .... 100 F4
Hazel Ct. Wake WF2 .... 142 A8
Hazel Dr. Dew WF12 .... 140 B7
Hazel Gdns. Castle WF10 .... 125 D6
Hazel Gr. Bacup OL13 .... 106 B3
Hazel Gr. Batley WF17 .... 118 A4
Hazel Gr. Brig HX3 .... 115 A7
Hazel Gr. Floc WF4 .... 157 D3
Hazel Gr. Hud HD2 .... 136 B5
Hazel Gr. Hud HD7 .... 152 F2
Hazel Gr. S in Cra BD20 .... 16 C5
Hazel Grove Rd. S in Cra BD20 .... 16 C5
Hazel Hurst Gr. Queen BD13 .... 92 D7
Hazel Hurst Rd. Queen BD13 .... 92 D7
Hazel La. Ham DN6 .... 184 A2
Hazel Mount. Ship BD18 .... 55 C7
Hazel Rd. Knot WF11 .... 126 E2
Hazel Rise. M'town LS26 .... 102 C1
Hazel Wlk. Brad BD9 .... 54 D2
Hazelcroft. Brad BD2 .... 56 D4
Hazeldene Cotts. Sickl LS22 .... 12 C5
Hazeldene. Queen BD13 .... 92 D8
Hazelheads. Bail BD17 .... 38 C5
Hazelhurst Ave. Ship BD16 .... 37 A1 1
Hazelhurst Brow. Brad BD9 .... 54 D2
Hazelhurst Ct. Brad BD9 .... 54 D2
Hazelhurst Ct. Pudsey LS28 .... 76 F7
Hazelhurst Rd. Brad BD9 .... 54 D2
Hazelhurst Terr. Brad BD9 .... 54 D2
Hazelmere Ave. Ship BD16 .... 54 A8
Hazelwood Ave. Gar LS25 .... 83 A5
Hazelwood Ave. Keigh BD20 .... 18 E1
Hazelwood Ct. Loft G WF1 .... 121 D5
Hazelwood Rd. Brad BD9 .... 54 C3
Hazelwood Rd. Loft G WF1 .... 121 D5
Hazelwood Rd. Hem WF9 .... 163 B1
Hazelwood St. Tod OL14 .... 108 B5
Hazledene Cres. Shaf S72 .... 180 D1
Hazledene Rd. Shaf S72 .... 180 D1
Headfield CE Mid Schs. Dew 139 C5
Headfield Ave. Dew WF12 .... 139 C5
Headfield Rd. Dew WF12 .... 139 D5
Headfield Rd. Hud HD4 .... 154 A3
Headfield View. Dew WF12 .... 139 D4
Headingley Ave. Leeds LS6 .... 59 C5
Headingley Cres. Leeds LS6 .... 59 D4
Headingley Ct. Leeds LS6 .... 59 F4
Headingley Golf Course. Eccup 42 D6
Headingley Grounds (Cricket & Rugby League). Leeds 59 D4
Headingley La. Leeds LS6 .... 59 E4
Headingley Mount. Leeds LS6 .... 59 D5
Headingley Prim Sch. Leeds 59 D5
Headingley Sta. Leeds 59 B4
Headingley View. Leeds LS6 .... 59 D4
Headland Gr. Brad BD6 .... 73 F1
Headland La. Dew WF12 .... 139 F6
Headlands Ave. Ossett WF5 .... 140 C5
Headlands CE (C) Jun & Inf Sch. Liver 117 A4
Headlands Cl. Liver WF15 .... 117 B3
Headlands Gr. Ossett WF5 .... 140 C5
Headlands La. Knot WF11 .... 126 E4
Headlands La. Pont WF8 .... 125 D1
Headlands Pk. Ossett WF5 .... 140 C5
Headlands Rd. Hud HD1 .... 154 A7
Headlands Rd. Liver WF15 .... 117 A4
Headlands St. Ossett WF5 .... 140 C5
Headlands St. Liver WF15 .... 117 A3
Headlands The. Liver WF15 .... 117 A3
Headlands Wlk. Ossett WF5 .... 140 C5
Headley Cotts. Bramham LS24 .... 48 A8
Headley Golf Course. Thorn 72 D5
Headley La. Bramham LS23 .... 30 E1
Headley La. Thorn BD13 .... 79 C8
Headrow The. Leeds LS1 .... 79 C8
Headwall Gn. Slai HD7 .... 152 B3
Heald La. Bacup OL13 .... 106 A8
Heald St. Castle WF10 .... 124 F8
Heald Terr. Rip HX4 .... 133 A5
Healdfield Rd. Castle WF10 .... 124 F8
Healds Ave. Liver WF15 .... 117 B4
Healds Rd. Dew WF13 .... 118 A2
Healdwood Rd. Castle WF10 .... 125 A8
Healdwood Rd. Castle WF10 .... 125 A8
Healey Ave. Bing BD16 .... 37 A2
Healey Cl. Batley WF17 .... 117 F5
Healey Cres. Ossett WF5 .... 140 D3
Healey Croft La. Ossett WF5 .... 140 D4
Healey Gn La. Leeds WF17 .... 155 F7
Healey Jun Inf Sch. Batley 117 F5

Healey La. Batley WF17 .... 117 F5
Healey La. Batley WF17 .... 118 B5
Healey La. Bing BD16 .... 37 A2 2
Healey La. Dew WF12 .... 157 A7
Healey Rd. Ossett WF5 .... 140 D3
Healey St. Batley WF17 .... 117 F5
Healey Wood Cres. Brig HD6 .... 115 A1
Healey Wood Gdns. Brig HD6 .... 136 B8
Healey Wood Gr. Brig HD6 .... 136 B8
Healey Wood Rd. Brig HD6 .... 115 B1
Heap La. Brad BD3 .... 75 A8
Heap St. Brad BD1 .... 75 A7
Heap St. Hali HX3 .... 92 C2
Heath Ave. Hali HX3 .... 113 B4
Heath Cl. Dew WF12 .... 140 B8
Heath Cl. Slai HD7 .... 170 E7
Heath Cres. L Brad BD20 .... 4 C6
Heath Cres. Leeds LS11 .... 78 E3
Heath Dr. B Spa LS23 .... 30 B7
Heath Dr. L Brad BD20 .... 4 C6
Heath Gdns. Hali HX3 .... 113 B4
Heath Gr. Keigh BD20 .... 36 D8
Heath Gr. Leeds LS11 .... 78 E3
Heath Gr. Pudsey LS28 .... 76 C6
Heath Hall Ave. Brad BD4 .... 75 B1
Heath Hall. Hali HX1 .... 113 C5
Heath House La. Slai HD7 .... 152 B4
Heath La. Hali HX3 .... 113 C4
Heath Lea. Hali HX1 .... 113 C6
Heath Mount. Leeds LS11 .... 78 E3
Heath Mount Rd. Brig HD6 .... 136 A8
Heath Park Ave. Hali HX1 .... 113 C5
Heath Pl. Leeds LS11 .... 78 E3
Heath Rd. Brad BD3 .... 56 B1
Heath Rd. Dew WF12 .... 140 B8
Heath Rd. Hali HX1, HX3 .... 113 C5
Heath Rd. Hud HD7 .... 152 F1
Heath Rd. Leeds LS11 .... 78 E3
Heath Rd. Slai HD7 .... 170 E8
Heath Rise. Leeds LS11 .... 78 E2
Heath Royd. Hali HX3 .... 113 C4
Heath St. Bing BD16 .... 37 A3
Heath St. Brad BD3 .... 75 C7
Heath St. Hali HX3 .... 113 C4
Heath St. Liver WF15 .... 117 B2
Heath Terr. Brad BD3 .... 75 C7
Heath Trng & Dev Ctr (Coll.). Hali 113 C4
Heath View St. Hali HX1 .... 113 D6
Heath Villas. Hali HX3 .... 113 C4
Heath Wlk. Dew WF12 .... 140 B8
Heathcliff. Haw BD22 .... 51 B7
Heathcliffe Cl. Batley WF17 .... 96 F3
Heathcroft Bank. Leeds LS11 .... 78 E2
Heathcroft Cres. Leeds LS11 .... 78 E2
Heathcroft Dr. Leeds LS11 .... 78 E2
Heathcroft Lawn. Leeds LS11 .... 78 E2
Heathcroft Rise. Leeds LS11 .... 78 E2
Heathcroft Vale. Leeds LS11 .... 78 E2
Heathdale Ave. Hud HD2 .... 135 F1
Heather Ave. Mel HD7 .... 170 E1
Heather Bank Cl. Cull BD13 .... 52 D5
Heather Bank. Tod OL14 .... 108 B1
Heather Cl. Loft G WF1 .... 121 D5
Heather Cl. Ossett WF5 .... 140 F3
Heather Cl. S Kirk WF9 .... 182 D3
Heather Cl. Batley WF17 .... 96 E2
Heather Ct. Hud HD3 .... 152 F8
Heather Ct. Loft G WF1 .... 121 E5
Heather Dr. Hali HX2 .... 91 A3
Heather Gdns. Leeds LS13 .... 77 E8
Heather Gdns. Scar LS14 .... 45 C7
Heather Gr. Brad BD9 .... 54 B3
Heather Gr. Keigh BD21 .... 35 A8
Heather Gr. Leeds LS13 .... 77 E8
Heather Rd. Bail BD17 .... 38 D4
Heather Rd. Mel HD7 .... 170 E1
Heather Rise. Bur in W LS29 .... 21 F8
Heather Side. Bail BD17 .... 38 B4
Heather Vale. Scar LS14 .... 45 B7
Heather View. Bing BD16 .... 37 D5
Heather View. Ossett WF5 .... 140 F3
Heatherbank Ave. Keigh BD22 .... 34 F4
Heathercroft. Leeds LS7 .... 60 E6
Heatherdale Ct. E Ard WF3 .... 119 E8
Heatherdale Dr. E Ard WF3 .... 119 E8
Heatherdale Rd. E Ard WF3 .... 119 E8
Heatherfield Cres. Hud HD1 .... 153 D6
Heatherfield Rd. Hud HD1 .... 153 D6
Heathergrove Fold. Hud HD1 .... 153 D7
Heatherlands Ave. Denh BD13 .... 52 D2
Heatherstones. Hali HX3 .... 113 B4 3
Heathfield Cl. Bing BD16 .... 37 A4
Heathfield Cl. E Ard WF3 .... 119 F8
Heathfield Gr. Brad BD7 .... 73 E4
Heathfield Gr. Hali HX3 .... 113 C4 1
Heathfield. Hors LS16 .... 42 B4
Heathfield Mews. Hud HD7 .... 152 E4
Heathfield. Mir WF14 .... 137 F6
Heathfield Pl. Hali HX3 .... 113 C4 2
Heathfield Rd. Hud HD7 .... 152 E4
Heathfield Rd. Ossett WF5 .... 140 C8
Heathfield Rise. Rip HX6 .... 132 C1
Heathfield Sq. Leeds LS6 .... 59 D6 1
Heathfield St. Elland HX5 .... 135 A6
Heathfield Terr. Hali HX3 .... 113 C4
Heathfield Terr. Leeds LS6 .... 59 D6
Heathfield Wlk. Hors LS16 .... 42 A5
Heathmoor Cl. Brad BD10 .... 56 A7
Heathmoor Cl. Hali HX2 .... 91 D6
Heathmoor Mount. Hali HX2 .... 91 D6
Heathmoor Park Rd. Hali HX2 .... 91 D6
Heathmoor Way. Hali HX2 .... 91 D6
Heathness Rd. Add LS29 .... 2 D1
Heathview Inf Sch. Wake 142 D7
Heathwood Dr. Slai HD7 .... 152 C5
Heathy Ave. Hali HX2 .... 92 A5
Heathy La. Hali HX2 .... 92 A5
Heaton Ave. Clec BD19 .... 116 C7
Heaton Ave. Dew WF12 .... 139 E8
Heaton Ave. Keigh BD20 .... 36 C7
Heaton Ave. Kirkhe HD5 .... 137 C1
Heaton Ave. Leeds LS12 .... 78 C5
Heaton Avenue Fst Sch. Clec 116 C7
Heaton Cl. Bail BD17 .... 38 B4

Heaton Cl. Bing BD16 .... 37 B4
Heaton Cres. Bail BD17 .... 38 B5
Heaton Cres. Bing BD16 .... 37 B4
Heaton Dr. Bail BD17 .... 38 B4
Heaton Dr. Bing BD16 .... 37 B4
Heaton Fold La. Hud HD1 .... 153 D6
Heaton Gdns. Hud HD1 .... 153 D6
Heaton Gr. Clec BD19 .... 116 C7
Heaton Gr. Ship BD9 .... 55 B4
Heaton Gr. Ship BD18 .... 55 C7
Heaton Hill. Brad BD6 .... 93 E7
Heaton Moor Rd. Kirkhe HD5 .... 137 C1
Heaton Park Dr. Brad BD9 .... 55 A3
Heaton Park Rd. Brad BD9 .... 54 F3
Heaton Rd. Batley WF17 .... 118 C7
Heaton Rd. Brad BD8, BD9 .... 55 B2
Heaton Rd. Hud HD1 .... 153 D6
Heaton Royds Hospl. Ship 54 D5
Heaton Royds La. Ship BD9 .... 54 F5
Heaton Royds Sch. Ship 55 A5
Heaton St. Ack M T WF7 .... 163 E5
Heaton St. Brad BD4 .... 75 A5
Heaton St. Brig HD6 .... 115 A2 4
Heaton St. Clec BD19 .... 116 D8
Heaton's Ct. Leeds LS1 .... 79 C7
Heatons Yd. Brig HD6 .... 115 B1
Heator La. D Dale HD8 .... 191 A7
Hebb View. Brad BD6 .... 73 E2
Hebble Ct. Hali HX2 .... 91 D4
Hebble Dean. Hali HX2 .... 91 F1
Hebble Dr. Holmfi HD7 .... 189 A7
Hebble End. Heb Br HX7 .... 88 F3
Hebble Gdns. Hali HX2 .... 91 E1
Hebble La. Hali HX3 .... 91 F1
Hebble La. Mel HD7 .... 187 D8
Hebble Mount. Mel HD7 .... 170 E1
Hebble Row. Haw BD22 .... 34 C1
Hebble St. Dew WF13 .... 138 F5
Hebble St. Hud HD1 .... 154 B8 4
Hebble Vale Dr. Hali HX2 .... 91 E1
Hebden App. Leeds LS14 .... 62 B6
Hebden Bridge Sta. Heb Br 89 B2
Hebden Chase. Leeds LS14 .... 62 B6
Hebden Cl. Leeds LS14 .... 62 B6
Hebden Gn. Leeds LS14 .... 62 C6
Hebden Path. Leeds LS14 .... 62 B6
Hebden Pl. Leeds LS14 .... 62 B6
Hebden Rd. Haw BD22 .... 51 D6
Hebden Rd. Wake WF1 .... 142 E8
Hebden Royd CE Jun & Inf Sch. Heb Br 88 E3
Hebden Terr. Wad M HX7 .... 89 B8
Hebden Wlk. Leeds LS14 .... 62 C6 2
Heber Cl. Sil BD20 .... 5 E2
Heber St. Keigh BD21 .... 35 B6
Heber's Ghyll Dr. Ilkley LS29 .... 7 E3
Heber's Gr. Ilkley LS29 .... 7 E4
Heckmondwike Cty Prim Sch. Batley 117 E6
Heckmondwike Cty Sec Sch. Batley 117 E6
Heckmondwike Gram Sch. Batley 117 D4
Heckmondwike Rd. Batley WF13 .... 117 F1
Heckmondwike Rd. Dew WF13 138 F8
Heckmondwike The Royds Inf Sch. Batley 117 D5
Hector Cl. Brad BD6 .... 74 C1 7
Heddon Cl. Brad BD5 .... 74 E5
Heddon Gr. Brad BD5 .... 74 E5
Heddon Pl. Leeds LS6 .... 59 E6
Heddon St. Leeds LS6 .... 59 E6 4
Heddon Wlk. Brad BD5 .... 74 E5
Hedge Cl. Brad BD8 .... 73 E8
Hedge Side. Brad BD8 .... 73 E8
Hedge Top La. Northo HX3 .... 93 B2
Hedge Way. Brad BD8 .... 73 E8
Hedley Chase. Leeds LS12 .... 78 E7
Hedley Cl. Leeds LS12 .... 78 E7
Hedley Gdns. Leeds LS12 .... 78 E7
Heeley Rd. Wake WF2 .... 160 A4
Heidelberg Rd. Brad BD9 .... 55 A2
Height Gn. Hali HX6 .... 112 B4
Height La. Draug BD23 .... 1 D3
Height La. Oxen BD22 .... 51 D2
Height Rd. Heb Br HX7 .... 89 E8
Height Rd. Wad M HX7 .... 90 A2
Heights Bank. Leeds LS12 .... 77 F7
Heights Cl. Leeds LS12 .... 77 F7
Heights Dr. Leeds LS12 .... 77 F7
Heights E The. Leeds LS12 .... 77 F7
Heights Garth. Leeds LS12 .... 77 F7
Heights La. Batley WF16 .... 117 E3
Heights La. Bing BD16 .... 37 B6
Heights La. Brad BD9 .... 54 D3
Heights La. Leeds LS12 .... 77 F7
Heights Par. Leeds LS12 .... 77 F7
Heights The. Holmfi HD7 .... 189 C3
Heights W The. Leeds LS12 .... 77 F7
Heights Wlk. Leeds LS12 .... 77 F7
Helen Rose Ct. Ship BD18 .... 38 E1
Helen St. Hud HD1 .... 153 E3
Helen St. Ship BD18 .... 54 F8
Helen Terr. Brig HD6 .... 114 F3
Helena Pl. Kippax LS25 .... 102 F8
Helena St. Kippax LS25 .... 102 F8
Helena Way. Brad BD4 .... 95 C8
Helene Cl. Hud HD3 .... 152 E8
Hell La. Crof WF4 .... 143 E4
Hellewell St. Brad BD6 .... 93 F7 4
Hellewell's Rd. Nor WF5 .... 140 D1
Hellwood La. Scar LS14 .... 45 D7
Helm La. Mir WF14 .... 137 D5
Helm La. Sow Br HX6 .... 132 C8
Helme (Aided) Jun & Inf Sch. Mel 170 E4
Helme La. Mel HD7 .... 170 D3
Helmet La. Mel HD7 .... 170 D2
Helmsley Dr. Leeds LS16 .... 59 B7
Helmsley Rd. B Spa LS23 .... 30 C7
Helmsley Rd. Leeds LS16 .... 59 B7
Helmsley St. Brad BD4 .... 75 A4
Helmsley St. Wake WF2 .... 142 D1
Helmton Croft. Midd LS10 .... 99 A5
Helston Garth. Midd LS10 .... 99 A5

Helston Cl. Midd LS10 .... 99 A5
Helston Pl. Midd LS10 .... 99 A5
Helston Rd. Midd LS10 .... 99 A6
Helston Rd. Nor WF6 .... 123 B3
Helston St. Midd LS10 .... 98 F6
Helston Way. Midd LS10 .... 99 A6
Helston Wlk. Midd LS10 .... 99 A5
Hemingway Cl. Leeds LS10 .... 79 E3
Hemingway Garth. Leeds LS10 .... 79 E3
Hemingway Gn. Leeds LS10 .... 79 E3
Hemishor Dr. Swil LS26 .... 102 E8
Hemsby Gr. Keigh BD21 .... 35 B4 7
Hemsby Rd. Castle WF10 .... 124 C6
Hemsby St. Keigh BD21 .... 35 B4 6
Hemsworth Archbishop Holgate CE Fst Sch. Hem 181 D7
Hemsworth Grove Lea Fst Sch. Hem 181 E7
Hemsworth High Sch. Hem 181 E7
Hemsworth Hollygarth Sch. Hem 181 D7
Hemsworth Kinsley Fst Sch. Hem 163 B2
Hemsworth Kinsley Mid Sch. Hem 163 B3
Hemsworth La. Hem WF9 .... 163 A5
Hemsworth Rd. S Kirk WF9 .... 181 F4
Hemsworth St Helens CE (Aided) Mid Sch. Hem 181 C6
Hemsworth Water Pk. Hem 163 D1
Hemsworth West End Mid Sch. Hem 181 C7
Hen Holme La. Sil BD20 .... 17 F7
Henacrewood Ct. Queen BD13 .... 92 E7
Henage St. Queen BD13 .... 72 D10
Henbury St. Leeds LS7 .... 60 D1
Henconner Ave. Leeds LS7 .... 60 C6
Henconner Cres. Leeds LS7 .... 60 C6
Henconner Dr. Leeds LS7 .... 60 C6
Henconner Gdns. Leeds LS7 .... 60 C6
Henconner Garth. Leeds LS7 .... 60 C6
Henconner La. Leeds LS7 .... 60 C6
Henconner La. Leeds LS13 .... 77 E8
Henconner Rd. Leeds LS7 .... 60 C6
Hendal La. Wake WF2 .... 160 A5
Henderson Ave. Nor WF6 .... 144 B8
Henderson Glen. Roy S71 .... 179 A3
Henderson Pl. Brad BD6 .... 74 C1 8
Hendford Dr. Brad BD3 .... 75 B8
Henley Ave. Brad BD5 .... 74 E2
Henley Ave. Dew WF12 .... 139 E2
Henley Ave. Yeadon LS19 .... 40 A3
Henley Cl. Yeadon LS19 .... 40 B3
Henley Cres. Leeds LS13 .... 58 C2
Henley Cres. Yeadon LS19 .... 40 A3
Henley Croft. Hud HD5 .... 154 E6
Henley Dr. Yeadon LS19 .... 40 A3
Henley Gr. Brad BD5 .... 74 E2
Henley Gr. Leeds LS13 .... 58 C2 2
Henley Hill. Yeadon LS19 .... 40 A3
Henley Mount. Yeadon LS19 .... 40 A3
Henley Pl. Leeds LS13 .... 58 C2
Henley Rd. Brad BD5 .... 74 F2
Henley Rd. Dew WF12 .... 139 E2
Henley Rd. Leeds LS13 .... 58 C2
Henley St. Leeds LS13 .... 58 C2 3
Henley Terr. Leeds LS13 .... 58 C2
Henley View. Leeds LS13 .... 58 C2
Henrietta St. Batley WF17 .... 118 C5 2
Henry Ave. Leeds LS12 .... 78 C5
Henry Ave. Ryhill WF4 .... 180 C8
Henry Cl. Shaf S72 .... 180 C3
Henry Frederick Av. Hud HD4 .... 171 C6
Henry Moore Ct. Castle WF10 .... 125 B7
Henry Pl. Morley S64 .... 98 A4
Henry Ralph Ave. Hud HD4 .... 153 C1
Henry St. Batley WF17 .... 118 C2
Henry St. Brad BD14 .... 73 C4
Henry St. Brig HD6 .... 115 A4
Henry St. Hali HX1 .... 113 B6
Henry St. Hud HD1 .... 154 A6
Henry St. Keigh BD21 .... 35 C7
Henry St. Thorn BD13 .... 72 D6
Henry St. Wake WF2 .... 142 A6
Henry Terr. Yeadon LS19 .... 39 F7
Henshaw Ave. Yeadon LS19 .... 40 B6
Henshaw Cres. Yeadon LS19 .... 40 B6
Henshaw La. Yeadon LS19 .... 40 B6
Henshaw Oval. Yeadon LS19 .... 40 B6
Henshaw Rd. Tod OL14 .... 108 B1
Henson Gr. Castle WF10 .... 125 B6
Hepton Dr. Hep HX7 .... 88 F4
Heptonstall Jun & Inf Sch. Hep 88 F5
Hepworth Ave. Morley LS27 .... 98 B8
Hepworth Ave. Mir WF14 .... 138 B6
Hepworth Cres. Holmfi HD7 .... 189 E3
Hepworth Cres. Morley LS27 .... 98 B8
Hepworth Dr. Mir WF14 .... 138 C6
Hepworth Jun & Inf Sch. Holmfi 189 F1
Hepworth Rd. Holmfi HD7 .... 138 F1
Hepworth Rd. Holmfi HD7 .... 189 E3
Hepworth St. Castle WF10 .... 103 F1
Hepworths Bldgs. Hud HD2 .... 136 D3
Herbalist St. Leeds LS12 .... 78 E6
Herbert St. Brad BD8 .... 75 E8
Herbert St. Brad BD14 .... 73 C4
Herbert St. Brad BD5 .... 74 D4
Herbert St. Hali HX3 .... 92 A1
Herbert St. Mir WF14 .... 138 A5
Herbert St. Ship BD18 .... 37 F1
Herbert St. Ship BD18 .... 54 B6
Hereford Cl. Hem WF9 .... 181 D8
Hereford Cl. Nor WF6 .... 123 D1
Hereford St. Leeds LS12 .... 78 C8
Heritage Rd. Batley WF17 .... 118 C4
Heritage Way. Haw BD22 .... 34 C2
Hermit St. Keigh BD21 .... 35 A2
Hermitage Pk. Lepton HD8 .... 155 E2
Hermon Ave. Hali HX1 .... 113 A6
Hermon Gr. Hali HX1 .... 113 A6
Hermon Rd. Leeds LS15 .... 62 B1
Heron Cl. Leeds LS17 .... 43 F4
Heron Cl. Morley LS27 .... 98 D4 4
Heron Dr. Wake WF2 .... 160 C5
Heron Gr. Leeds LS17 .... 43 F4

Herschel Rd. Brad BD8 .... 73 D7
Hertford Chase. Leeds LS15 .... 81 D8
Hertford Cl. Leeds LS15 .... 81 D8
Hertford Croft. Leeds LS15 .... 81 D8
Hertford Fold. Leeds LS15 .... 81 D8
Hertford Lawn. Leeds LS15 .... 81 C6
Heseltine Cl. Nor WF6 .... 123 A2
Heseltine La. Heb Br HX7 .... 110 B4
Heshbon St. Brad BD4 .... 75 C3
Hesketh Ave. E Ard WF3 .... 119 D8
Hesketh La. E Ard WF3 .... 119 D8
Hesketh Mount. Leeds LS5 .... 59 A5
Hesketh Pl. Leeds LS5 .... 59 A5
Hesketh Rd. Leeds LS5 .... 59 A5
Hesketh Terr. Leeds LS5 .... 59 A4
Hesley Rd. Wake WF2 .... 160 B5
Hessle Ave. Leeds LS6 .... 59 E3
Hessle Common La. W Har WF7 .... 163 D7
Hessle La. W Har WF7 .... 163 D8
Hessle Mount. Leeds LS6 .... 59 E3
Hessle Pl. Leeds LS6 .... 59 E3 17
Hessle Rd. Leeds LS6 .... 59 E3 10
Hessle Terr. Leeds LS6 .... 59 E3 10
Hessle View. Leeds LS6 .... 59 E3
Hessle Wlk. Leeds LS6 .... 59 E3 9
Hetchell View. Bard LS17 .... 28 D2
Hetton Rd. Leeds LS8 .... 61 B4
Heuthwaite Ave. Weth LS22 .... 13 F4
Hew Clews. Brad BD7 .... 73 E3
Hexham Gn. Hud HD3 .... 152 F5
Hey Beck La. E Ard WF12 .... 119 C5
Hey Cres. Mel HD7 .... 170 D2
Hey Head La. Litt OL14 .... 129 A1
Hey Head La. Tod OL14 .... 108 D7
Hey La. Hud HD5 .... 154 D3
Hey La. Hud HD7 .... 172 B7
Hey La. Kirkb HD7 .... 172 B7
Hey La. Rip HD3 .... 151 D2
Hey Slack La. Wh Com HD7 .... 190 C2
Hey St. Brad BD7 .... 74 D7
Hey St. Brig HD6 .... 115 B4
Hey St. Tod OL14 .... 108 C5 1
Hey's Bldgs. Nor WF6 .... 122 F4
Heybeck Wlk. Brad BD4 .... 75 F2
Heycliffe Rd. Holmfi HD7 .... 189 B5
Heyford Ct. Brad BD2 .... 55 D3
Heygate Cl. Bail BD17 .... 38 D4
Heygate La. Bail BD17 .... 38 D4
Heygate La. Bramham LS23 .... 30 F3
Heygate La. Bramham LS23 .... 31 A5
Heys Ave. Thorn BD13 .... 72 F6
Heys Cres. Thorn BD13 .... 72 F6
Heys Gdns. Holmfi HD7 .... 189 C8
Heys La. Hali HX2 .... 90 B6
Heys La. Rip HX6 .... 132 D1
Heys La. Slai HD7 .... 151 D2
Heys Rd. Holmfi HD7 .... 189 C8
Heys The. Mel HD7 .... 170 E4
Heysham Dr. Brad BD4 .... 75 F3
Heywood Cl. Northo HX3 .... 93 A2
Heywood Pl. Hali HX1 .... 113 B7
Heywood St. Hali HX1 .... 113 A7 17
Hick La. Batley WF17 .... 118 D5
Hick St. Brad BD1 .... 74 F7 11
Hicks La. M'town LS26 .... 102 B3
Higgin Chamber. Sow Br HX2 .... 111 C5
Higgin La. Hali HX3 .... 113 E5
High Ash Ave. Clay W HD8 .... 176 A2
High Ash Ave. Leeds LS17 .... 43 F5
High Ash Cl. Notton WF4 .... 178 F7
High Ash Dr. Leeds LS17 .... 43 E5
High Ash. Leeds LS17 .... 43 F5
High Ash Mount. Leeds LS17 .... 43 F5
High Ash Pk. Brad BD15 .... 53 F1
High Ash. Ship BD18 .... 55 E7
High Bank App. Leeds LS15 .... 81 D7
High Bank Cl. Leeds LS15 .... 81 D8
High Bank Cl. Sil BD20 .... 6 E8
High Bank Gate. Leeds LS15 .... 81 D7
High Bank Gdns. Leeds LS15 .... 81 E7
High Bank La. Brad BD20 .... 4 C6
High Bank Pl. Leeds LS15 .... 81 D7
High Bank Way. Leeds LS15 .... 81 D7
High Banks Cl. Keigh BD20 .... 18 F2
High Binns La. Oxen BD22 .... 51 D3
High Bradley La. L Brad BD20 .... 4 C7
High Brooms. Hud HD7 .... 155 E1
High Bury Cl. Queen BD13 .... 92 C8
High Busy La. Brad BD10 .... 56 A8
High Busy La. Ship BD18 .... 55 F8
High Cl. Guise LS20 .... 39 B8
High Cl. Hud HD5 .... 154 E3
High Cl. Kex S75 .... 177 D1
High Cl. Ossett WF5 .... 119 D1
High Cl. Yeadon LS19 .... 40 B3
High Cliffe Cl. Thorn BD13 .... 72 D6
High Cliffe Terr. Weth LS22 .... 13 D6 11
High Cote. Keigh BD20 .... 18 F2
High Court La. Leeds LS2 .... 79 D7
High Crest. Hud HD7 .... 152 E2
High Croft Cres. Hud HD5 .... 154 F3
High Croft. Queen BD13 .... 72 E1
High Croft Rd. Tod OL14 .... 108 C6
High Cross La. Shelf HX3 .... 93 F7
High Cross Rd. Nor WF6 .... 122 E3
High End. Guise BD17 .... 39 C5
High Fernley Ct. Brad BD12 .... 94 C4 10
High Fernley Fst Sch. Brad 94 B3
High Fernley Rd. Brad BD12 .... 94 B3
High Field La. Haw BD22 .... 34 C3
High Fold La. Keigh BD20 .... 18 A2
High Fold. Bail BD17 .... 38 C4
High Green Dr. Sil BD20 .... 5 D2
High Green Rd. Nor WF6 .... 122 E3
High Grove La. Hali HX3 .... 113 E5
High House Ave. Brad BD2 .... 56 A4
High House Edge. Slai HD7 .... 170 C7
High House La. Hali HX2 .... 90 C4

High House La. Slai HD7 .... 170 C8
High House Mews. Sil LS29 .... 6 F8
High House Rd. Brad BD2 .... 56 A4
High Hoyland La. A Hoy S75 .... 193 B8
High La. Cowl BD22 .... 32 A8
High La. Hali HX2 .... 112 B8
High La. Heb Br HX7 .... 110 D3
High La. Holmfi HD7 .... 189 B3
High La. Hud HD4 .... 154 C1
High Lea. Mars HD7 .... 168 F4
High Lees Rd. Hali HX2 .... 91 B5
High Level Way. Hali HX1 .... 112 F8
High Malsis. S in Cra BD20 .... 16 A5
High Meadow. Keigh BD20 .... 18 A1
High Meadows. Dew WF12 .... 139 C1
High Meadows. Elland HX4 .... 134 C7
High Meadows. Walton WF2 .... 161 B6
High Mill. Add LS29 .... 3 A1
High Mill La. Add LS29 .... 3 A1
High Moor Ave. Leeds LS17 .... 43 E2
High Moor Cl. Leeds LS17 .... 43 E3
High Moor Cres. Leeds LS17 .... 43 E3
High Moor Ct. Leeds LS17 .... 43 E3
High Moor Dr. Leeds LS17 .... 43 E3
High Moor Gr. Leeds LS17 .... 43 E3
High Oxford St. Castle WF10 .... 124 C7
High Park Cres. Brad BD9 .... 54 E3
High Park Dr. Brad BD9 .... 54 E3
High Park Gr. Brad BD9 .... 54 E3
High Poplars. Brad BD2 .... 55 F4
High Rd. Dew WF12 .... 139 E7
High Ridge Ave. Roth LS26 .... 100 E6
High Ridge Ct. Roth LS26 .... 100 E6
High Ridge. Neth WF4 .... 158 E6
High Ridge Pk. Roth LS26 .... 100 E6
High Ridge Way. Bramho LS16 .... 24 F2
High Royds Dr. Guise LS29 .... 22 B3
High Royds Hospl. Guise 22 B2
High Spirit Sch. Batley 117 D4
High Spring Gardens La. Keigh BD20 .... 35 A8
High Spring Rd. Keigh BD21 .... 35 F6
High St. B Spa LS23 .... 30 D8
High St. B Spa LS23 .... 30 E5
High St. Batley WF17 .... 96 E1
High St. Brad BD10 .... 56 B8
High St. Bramham LS23 .... 30 D2
High St. Brig HD6 .... 115 B3
High St. Broth WF11 .... 105 C1
High St. Castle WF10 .... 124 C7
High St. Clay W HD8 .... 175 F2
High St. Clec BD19 .... 116 D8
High St. Crig WF4 .... 159 E5
High St. Crof WF4 .... 144 B5
High St. Crof WF4 .... 161 F8
High St. Dew WF12, WF13 .... 139 B7
High St. Dew WF12 .... 139 C1
High St. Dew WF12 .... 139 F7
High St. Elland HX4 .... 133 F3
High St. Elland HX4 .... 134 D7 8
High St. Hali HX2 .... 90 E1
High St. Hali HX1 .... 113 B6
High St. Honley HD7 .... 171 F4
High St. Hor WF4 .... 141 A1
High St. Hud HD1 .... 153 E5
High St. Hud HD1 .... 154 A6
High St. Keigh BD21 .... 35 B7
High St. Kippax LS25 .... 83 B1
High St. Knot WF11 .... 126 C5
High St. Mapp S75 .... 178 A2
High St. Morley LS27 .... 98 A3
High St. Nor WF6 .... 122 F3
High St. Nor WF6 .... 123 B2
High St. Ossett WF5 .... 119 C1
High St. Pudsey LS28 .... 57 D3
High St. Queen BD13 .... 72 E1
High St. Roy S71 .... 179 B3
High St. S Elm WF9 .... 183 A3
High St. S Hie S72 .... 180 E5
High St. S in Cra BD20 .... 16 D4
High St. Shaf S72 .... 180 C2
High St. Slai HD7 .... 152 B5
High St. Stee Brad BD20 .... 17 C5
High St. Thorn BD13 .... 72 D6
High St. Tod OL14 .... 108 A3
High St. Upton WF9 .... 183 B7
High St. Wool WF4 .... 178 A7
High St. Yeadon LS19 .... 40 C7
High Stones Rd. Heb Br HX7 .... 110 E3
High Street Pl. Brad BD10 .... 56 B8
High Sunderland La. Hali HX3 .... 92 D1
High Top. B Head HX7 .... 88 B4
High Trees La. Elland HX4 .... 133 E6
High Trees St. B Spa 30 E6
High View. Crig WF4 .... 159 E5
High View. Roy S71 .... 179 B3
High Weardley La. Hare LS17 .... 26 A6
High Well Hill La. S Hie S72 .... 180 C7
High Wheatley. Ilkley LS29 .... 8 F3
High Wicken Cl. Thorn BD13 .... 72 D6
High Wood Ct. Leeds LS6 .... 59 E5
High Wood. Ilkley LS29 .... 8 F3
High Wood La. Kirkb HD8 .... 174 A8
High Woodlands. E Ard WF3 .... 120 C7
Higham and Dob La. Sow Br HX6 .... 111 C3
Highbridge La. Skel HD8 .... 175 C1
Highbridge Terr. Brad BD5 .... 74 F1
Highburton CE (C) Fst Sch. Kirkb 173 D6
Highbury Cl. Leeds LS6 .... 59 E6
Highbury La. Leeds LS6 .... 59 E6
Highbury Mount. Leeds LS6 .... 59 E6
Highbury Pl. Leeds LS6 .... 59 E6
Highbury Pl. Pudsey LS13 .... 77 A8
Highbury Rd. Brad BD4 .... 75 C6
Highbury Rd. Leeds LS6 .... 59 E6
Highbury St. Leeds LS6 .... 59 E6
Highbury Terr. Dew WF12 .... 139 D8 9
Highbury Terr. Leeds LS6 .... 59 E6
Highcliffe Ave. Hud HD8 .... 135 F2
Highcliffe Ct. Weth LS22 .... 13 F5
Highcliffe Dr. Hali HX2 .... 112 D7
Highcliffe Ind Est. Morley 97 E5
Highcliffe Rd. Batley WF17 .... 118 C3

Highcliffe Rd. Morley LS27 97 F4
Highcroft. Batley WF17 118 C3
Highcroft Cl. Pudsey LS28 76 C8
Highcroft. Coll LS22 29 A8
Highcroft Gdns. Keigh BD21 35 F6
Highcroft. Holmfi HD7 188 E5
Highdale. Batley WF12 118 E2
Highdale Croft. Brad BD10 56 B8
Higher Ashenhurst. Tod OL14 108 A7
Higher Back La. B Head HX7 87 F4
Higher Brockwell. Sow Br HX6 112 A3
Higher Calderbrook. Litt OL15 129 C1
Higher Calderbrook Rd. Litt
OL15 129 C2
Higher Change Villas. Bacup
OL13 106 B4
Higher Coach Rd. Bail BD17 37 F2
Higher Downs. Brad BD8 73 D8
Higher Grge Rd. Pudsey LS28 76 E8
Higher Hartley St. Glu BD20 16 B6
Higher Intake Rd. Brad BD2 56 C1
Higher Lodge St. Glu BD20 16 B6
Higher Park Royd Dr. Rip HX6 132 E6
Higher Scholes. Haw BD22 33 F1
Higher School St. Ship BD18 54 F8 4
Higherwood Cl. Keigh BD21 35 E6
Highfield Ave. Brad BD10 56 A7
Highfield Ave. Brig HD6 115 B8
Highfield Ave. D Dale HD8 191 A4
Highfield Ave. Elland HX4 134 B7
Highfield Ave. Leeds LS12 78 D5
Highfield Ave. Mel HD7 170 D3
Highfield Ave. Pont WF8 126 A4
Highfield Ave. Pont WF8 146 C7
Highfield Ave. Shelf HX3 93 D7
Highfield. Brad BD4 75 D1
Highfield Cl. Feath WF7 145 D8
Highfield Cl. Gild LS27 97 E7
Highfield Cl. Keigh BD20 19 D1
Highfield Cl. Leeds LS12 78 D5
Highfield Cty Prim Sch. Leeds 43 E4
Highfield Cres. Bail BD17 38 C4
Highfield Cres. Brad BD9 54 E4
Highfield Cres. Heb Br HX7 89 A4 5
Highfield Cres. Kippax LS26 102 F5
Highfield Cres. Leeds LS12 78 D6
Highfield Cres. Mel HD7 170 D3
Highfield Cres. Neth WF4 157 F6
Highfield Cres. Pudsey LS28 76 D8
Highfield Cres. Roth LS26 101 C7
Highfield Ct. Castle WF10 124 D6
Highfield Ct. Haw BD22 34 C2
Highfield Ct. Shep HD8 190 E6
Highfield Ctr. Hem WF9 181 D6
Highfield Dr. Batley WF17 96 E2
Highfield Dr. Brad BD9 54 E4
Highfield Dr. Gar LS25 82 F5
Highfield Dr. Gild LS27 97 D7
Highfield Dr. Hali HX2 111 E8
Highfield Dr. Kippax LS26 102 F5
Highfield Dr. Liver FW15 116 E4
Highfield Dr. Wake WF2 141 E8
Highfield Dr. Yeadon LS19 40 C3
Highfield. E Ard WF3 98 D1
Highfield Garth. Leeds LS12 78 D5
Highfield Gdns. Brad BD9 54 D4
Highfield Gdns. Dew WF12 139 D3
Highfield Gdns. Gild LS27 97 D7
Highfield Gdns. Leeds LS12 78 C5
Highfield Gn. Kippax WF10 102 F6
Highfield Gn. Pudsey LS28 76 D8
Highfield Gr. Brad BD10 56 A6
Highfield Gr. Hali HX5 134 E8
Highfield Gr. Kippax WF10 102 F6
Highfield La. B in Elm LS15 63 E5
Highfield La. Batley WF13 117 F4
Highfield La. Keigh BD21 35 B8
Highfield La. Lepton HD8 155 D5
Highfield La. Mel HD7 170 C3
Highfield La. Roth LS26 101 C7
Highfield La. S in Elm LS25 84 D5
Highfield La. Sil BD20 5 E2
Highfield Mews. Bail BD17 38 C4 1
Highfield Mews. Keigh BD20 19 D1
Highfield Mid Sch. Keigh 35 B7
Highfield Mount. Dew WF12 139 E1
Highfield Mount. Roth LS26 101 C6
Highfield Pl. Brad BD8 55 C1
Highfield Pl. Hali HX1 112 F6
Highfield Pl. Hem WF9 181 C6
Highfield Pl. Kippax WF10 103 A6
Highfield Pl. Morley LS27 98 B3
Highfield Rd. Aber LS25 64 E8
Highfield Rd. Brad BD2, BD10 56 B7
Highfield Rd. Brig HD6 135 E8
Highfield Rd. Clec BD19 116 C7
Highfield Rd. Elland HX5 134 F6
Highfield Rd. Hali HX2 111 E8
Highfield Rd. Hem WF9 181 D6
Highfield Rd. Hor WF4 141 A1
Highfield Rd. Keigh BD21 35 A8
Highfield Rd. Kirkb HD8 173 E7
Highfield Rd. Leeds LS13 58 D2
Highfield Rd. Mel HD7 170 D3
Highfield Rd. Neth WF4 158 D5
Highfield Rd. Pont WF8 146 C6
Highfield Rd. Pudsey LS28 76 C8
Highfield Rd. Ship BD9 55 C5
Highfield Rd. Slai HD7 151 F4
Highfield Rise. Wake WF2 141 E8
Highfield. Shelf HX3 93 C5
Highfield St. Keigh BD21 35 B7
Highfield St. Leeds LS13 58 D2
Highfield St. Pudsey LS28 76 C8
Highfield Terr. Dew WF12 139 D3
Highfield Terr. Pudsey LS28 76 C8
Highfield Terr. Queen BD13 92 D8
Highfield Terr. Rip HX6 132 E6
Highfield Terr. Ship BD18 54 D8
Highfield Terr. Yeadon LS19 40 C3
Highfield View. Gild LS27 97 E7
Highfields. Hud HD1 153 F7
Highfields. Neth WF4 158 D5
Highfields Rd. Hud HD1 153 F7
Highfields. Ryhill WF4 162 D2
Highfields Sch. Hud 153 F7
Highfold. Yeadon LS19 40 A5
Highgate Ave. Lepton HD8 155 F3
Highgate. Brad BD9 54 F4
Highgate Cl. Brad BD13 73 C2
Highgate Cres. Lepton HD8 155 E3
Highgate Dr. Lepton HD8 155 F3
Highgate. Glu BD20 16 C7
Highgate Gr. Brad BD13 73 C2
Highgate La. Kirkhe HD5 137 D1
Highgate La. Lepton HD8 155 E3
Highgate Rd. Brad BD13 73 B2
Highgate Rd. Dew WF12 139 D8
Highgate St. Batley WF12 118 F3
Highgate Terr. Dew WF12 139 D8 10
Highgate Wlk. Lepton HD8 155 F3
Highland Cl. Pont WF8 125 F3
Highland Ville. Brig HX3 114 D8
Highlands Ave. Hud HD5 154 F3
Highlands Cl. Brad BD7 73 E3 1
Highlands Cl. Midd LS10 99 F8
Highlands Dr. Midd LS10 99 F8
Highlands Gr. Brad BD7 73 E3
Highlands Gr. Midd LS10 99 F8
Highlands Grammar Sch. Hali 91 F6
Highlands La. Hali HX2 91 F6
Highlands Pk. Hali HX2 91 F6
Highlands The. Clec WF15 116 D5
Highlands Wlk. Midd LS10 99 F8
Highlea Cl. Yeadon LS19 39 F5
Highlee La. Rip HX6 132 A1
Highley Hall Croft. Brig HD6 115 D3
Highley Pk. Brig HD6 115 E2
Highmoor. Bail BD17 38 A3
Highmoor Cres. Brig HD6 115 D3
Highmoor La. Brig HD6 115 E4
Highmoor La. Brig HD6 115 F5
Highmoor La. Clec HD6 116 A6
Highmoor Wlk. Bail BD17 38 A3
Highroad Well La. Hali HX2 112 C7
Highroyd Cres. Hud HD5 154 D5 1
Highroyd La. Hud HD5 154 D6
Highroyd. Lepton HD8 155 F3
Highthorne Ave. Brad BD3 56 C1
Highthorne Dr. Leeds LS17 43 F4
Highthorne Gr. Leeds LS17 44 A4
Highthorne Gr. Leeds LS12 78 A8 11
Highthorne Mount. Leeds LS17 43 F4
Highthorne St. Leeds LS12 78 A8
Highthorne View. Leeds LS12 78 A8 14
Hightown Fst Sch. Clec 116 C5
Hightown La. Holmfi HD7 189 A5
Hightown Rd. Clec WF15 116 D6
Hightown View. Clec WF15 116 D5
Highway. Guise LS20 22 B1
Highways. Leeds LS14 61 E1
Highwood Ave. Leeds LS17 43 C3
Highwood Cres. Leeds LS17 43 C3
Highwood Gr. Leeds LS17 43 C2
Hilberoyd Rd. Batley WF17 118 D5
Hilda St. Ossett WF5 140 E4
Hilda St. Ship BD9 55 A4
Hill Brow Cl. Brad BD15 54 A1
Hill Cl. Bail BD17 38 B2
Hill Cl. Hud HD3 134 F1
Hill Cl. Pont WF8 146 D7
Hill Clough Gr. Keigh BD22 34 D7
Hill Cres. Batley WF17 97 A1
Hill Cres. Bur in W LS29 21 F7
Hill Cres. Hali HX3 113 F5
Hill Cres. Yeadon LS19 40 C5
Hill Crest. Ad Le S DN6 184 E1
Hill Crest Ave. Denh BD13 52 E1
Hill Crest Ave. Hali HX6 112 B5 3
Hill Crest. Coll LS22 28 E8
Hill Crest Dr. Denh BD13 52 D1
Hill Crest. Hali HX6 112 B5 1
Hill Crest Mount. Denh BD13 52 D1
Hill Crest Rd. Denh BD13 52 D1
Hill Crest Rd. Dew WF12 139 C5
Hill Crest Rd. Thorn BD13 72 D7
Hill Crest. Rip HX6 132 C1
Hill Crest. Ryhill WF4 162 C1
Hill Crest. Swil LS26 82 A1
Hill Crest View. Denh BD13 52 D1
Hill Croft Cl. Dar WF8 147 D5
Hill Croft. Rip HX6 132 C1
Hill Croft. Thorn BD13 72 E7
Hill Dr. Ack M T WF7 164 A8
Hill End Cl. Brig HX3 94 A2
Hill End Cl. Leeds LS12 77 F8
Hill End Cres. Leeds LS12 77 F8
Hill End. Dew WF12 139 E8
Hill End Gr. Brad BD7 73 E3
Hill End La. Cull BD13 52 F8
Hill End La. Harden BD16 36 A1
Hill End La. Queen BD13 92 D8
Hill End Rd. Leeds LS12 77 F8
Hill Estate. Upton WF9 183 B7
Hill Foot. Ship BD18 54 E7
Hill Gr. Hud HD3 134 F1
Hill Gr S. Midd LS10 99 F7
Hill Green Ct. Birk BD4 76 E2
Hill Grove Lea. Hud HD3 134 F1
Hill House Edge La. Oxen HX7 70 B8
Hill House La. Holmfi HD7 188 E2
Hill House La. Oxen BD22 51 C1
Hill House Rd. Holmfi HD7 188 E2
Hill La. Holmfi HD7 188 E5
Hill Lands. Brad BD12 94 C5
Hill Park Ave. Hali HX3 91 F1
Hill Rd. Castle WF10 124 F6
Hill Rd. Wake WF2 160 C4
Hill Rise Ave. Leeds LS13 58 C4
Hill Rise Gr. Leeds LS13 58 C4
Hill Side Ave. Holmfi HD7 189 E2
Hill Side Mount. Pudsey LS28 57 E2
Hill Side Rd. Bing BD16 36 F3
Hill Side Rd. Brad BD3 75 A7
Hill Side Terr. Brad BD3 75 A8
Hill St. Brad BD6 74 A1
Hill St. Brad BD4 75 B5
Hill St. Clec BD19 116 C7
Hill St. Hali HX1 113 B6
Hill St. Haw BD22 51 C6
Hill St. Holmfi HD7 189 E3
Hill St. Leeds LS9 60 E1
Hill St. Leeds LS11 79 B3
Hill Top Ave. Barn S71 178 E1
Hill Top Ave. Hud HD2 135 B4
Hill Top Ave. Leeds LS8 60 F4
Hill Top. Brig HX3 114 E7
Hill Top. Bur in W LS29 9 E1
Hill Top CE Fst Sch. Brad 94 C6
Hill Top. Castle WF10 123 F7
Hill Top. Caw S75 193 E5
Hill Top Cl. E Ard WF3 119 E6
Hill Top Cl. Hem WF9 163 A3
Hill Top Cl. Leeds LS12 77 F8
Hill Top Cotts. Brad BD9 54 E2
Hill Top Cres. Mir WF14 137 F1
Hill Top Ct. E Ard WF3 119 E6
Hill Top Ct. Wake WF2 160 C4
Hill Top Dr. Hud HD3 153 A8
Hill Top Est. Batley WF16 117 E4
Hill Top Fold. Slai HD7 151 F1
Hill Top Gdns. E Ard WF3 119 E6
Hill Top Gn. E Ard WF3 119 D6
Hill Top Gr. Brad BD15 54 A1
Hill Top Gr. E Ard WF3 119 E6
Hill Top. Hali HX2 112 A3
Hill Top. Hem WF9 163 A3
Hill Top. Ilkley LS29 8 A2
Hill Top Inf Sch. E Ard 119 D5
Hill Top. Knot WF11 126 F4
Hill Top La. Bing BD16 36 F8
Hill Top La. Brad BD15 54 A1
Hill Top La. E Ard WF3 119 E6
Hill Top La. Heb Br HX7 110 B4
Hill Top La. W Har WF7 145 C1
Hill Top Mews. Knot WF11 126 F4
Hill Top Mount. Leeds LS8 60 F4
Hill Top Pl. Leeds LS6 59 F2
Hill Top Pl. Leeds LS8 60 F4 15
Hill Top Rd. Floc WF4 157 D3
Hill Top Rd. Haw BD22 34 B2
Hill Top Rd. Holmfi HD7 188 F1
Hill Top Rd. Hud HD3 153 A8
Hill Top Rd. Hud HD1 153 E5
Hill Top Rd. Hud HD5 154 D6
Hill Top Rd. Keigh BD21 35 A2
Hill Top Rd. Leeds LS12 77 F8
Hill Top Rd. Slai HD7 152 A1
Hill Top Rd. Thorn BD13 72 C7
Hill Top Rd. Wake WF2, WF4 160 C4
Hill Top Sch. Castle 125 C7
Hill Top St. Leeds LS6 59 F2 2
Hill Top. Stee BD20 17 C5
Hill Top View. E Ard WF3 119 D6
Hill Top View. Nor WF6 144 A7
Hill Top Way. Keigh BD22 34 F7
Hill Top Wlk. Keigh BD22 34 F7
Hill View Ave. Leeds LS7 60 D7
Hill View. Hali HX2 91 F7
Hill View Mount. Leeds LS7 60 D7
Hill View Pl. Leeds LS7 60 D7 1
Hill View Terr. Leeds LS7 60 D7 2
Hillam La. B Sal LS25 105 E5
Hillam La. Hillam LS25 105 E5
Hillam Rd. Brad BD2 55 D3
Hillam St. Brad BD5 74 B3
Hillary Pl. Leeds LS2 60 B2
Hillary Rd. Ship BD18 55 E7
Hillary St. Batley WF13 117 F3 2
Hillbrook Rise. Ilkley LS29 7 F3
Hillcote Dr. Brad BD5 74 E4
Hillcourt Ave. Leeds LS13 58 C4
Hillcourt Croft. Leeds LS13 58 C4
Hillcourt Dr. Leeds LS13 58 C4
Hillcourt Gr. Leeds LS13 58 C4
Hillcrest Ave. Batley WF17 118 A5
Hillcrest Ave. Castle WF10 125 D6
Hillcrest Ave. Feath WF7 145 B5
Hillcrest Ave. Leeds LS7 60 E4
Hillcrest Ave. Ossett WF5 140 C8
Hillcrest Ave. Queen BD13 92 F8
Hillcrest Ave. Sil BD20 5 E2
Hillcrest Cl. Castle WF10 125 D7
Hillcrest Cl. Swil LS26 81 F1
Hillcrest Dr. Castle WF10 125 E6
Hillcrest Dr. Queen BD13 92 F8
Hillcrest Mount. Brig BD19 115 F7
Hillcrest Mount. Castle WF10 125 E6
Hillcrest Mount. Hors LS16 41 E4
Hillcrest. Nor WF6 122 E4
Hillcrest Pl. Leeds LS7 60 E4
Hillcrest Rd. Castle WF10 125 E7
Hillcrest Rd. Queen BD13 92 F8
Hillcrest Rise. Hors LS16 41 E4
Hillcrest View. Leeds LS7 60 E4
Hillesley Rd. Batley WF12 119 A3
Hillfold. S Elm WF9 183 B3
Hillfoot Ave. Pudsey LS28 76 B8
Hillfoot Cres. Pudsey LS28 76 B8
Hillfoot Dr. Pudsey LS28 76 B8
Hillfoot Rise. Pudsey LS28 76 B8
Hillgarth. Dew WF12 139 D3
Hillgarth. Knot WF11 126 E3
Hillhead Dr. Batley WF17 97 A1
Hillhouse La. Hud HD1 154 B8
Hillidge Rd. Leeds LS10 79 D4
Hillidge Sq. Leeds LS10 79 D4
Hillingdon Way. Leeds LS17 43 B6
Hillings La. Guise LS20, LS29 21 E3
Hillings La. Men LS29 21 E3
Hillside Ave. Guise LS20 22 D3
Hillside Ave. Hali HX2 111 D7
Hillside Ave. Haw BD22 34 B2
Hillside Ave. Hud HD2 136 B2
Hillside Ave. Rip HX6 132 E6
Hillside. Byram WF11 126 D7
Hillside Cl. Sil LS29 6 E8
Hillside Cl. Wake WF2 141 D3
Hillside Cres. Bacup OL13 106 A7 6
Hillside Cres. Bri S72 181 A2
Hillside Cres. Hud HD4 154 B2
Hillside Ct. Men LS29 21 F4
Hillside Ct. S Elm WF9 183 A4
Hillside. D Dale HD8 192 A6
Hillside. Gar LS25 83 B6
Hillside Gr. Bri S72 181 A2
Hillside Gr. Haw BD22 34 B2
Hillside Gr. Pudsey LS28 76 F7 7
Hillside Gr. Pudsey LS28 77 A7
Hillside Mid Sch. Leeds 79 B4
Hillside Mount. Bri S72 181 A2
Hillside Mount. Pont WF8 146 E8
Hillside Mount. Pudsey LS28 77 A7
Hillside Rd. Ack M T WF7 164 A6
Hillside Rd. Leeds LS7 60 D7
Hillside Rd. Pont WF8 146 E8
Hillside Rd. Ship BD18 55 D5
Hillside Rise. Guise LS20 22 D3
Hillside Rise. Liver WF15 117 A3
Hillside Special Sch. Brig 135 E7
Hillside Terr. Bail BD17 38 C3
Hillside View. Hali HX6 112 A4
Hillside View. Pudsey LS28 77 A7
Hillside View. Slai HD7 152 E1
Hillside Works Ind Est. Clec 95 D2
Hillthorpe Dr. Th Aud WF8 165 A5
Hillthorpe Rd. Pudsey LS28 76 E5
Hillthorpe Rise. Pudsey LS28 76 E5
Hillthorpe Sq. Pudsey LS28 76 E5 1
Hillthorpe St. Pudsey LS28 76 E5 2
Hillthorpe Terr. Pudsey LS28 76 E5 3
Hilltop. Bri S72 180 F3
Hilltop Est. S Kirk WF9 181 F1
Hillview Gdns. Northo HX3 93 A1
Hillway. Guise LS20 39 C8
Hilmian Way. Hem WF9 181 F5
Hilton Ave. Ship BD18 55 B5
Hilton Cres. Bail BD17 38 C2
Hilton Dr. Ship BD18 55 B5
Hilton Gr. Brad BD7 74 B6
Hilton Gr. Leeds LS8 60 F5
Hilton Gr. Ship BD18 55 B5
Hilton Grange Sch. Bramho 24 B4
Hilton Pl. Leeds LS8 60 F4
Hilton Rd. Brad BD7 74 A6
Hilton Rd. Leeds LS8 60 F4
Hilton Rd. Ship BD18 55 B5
Hilton St. Heb Br HX7 89 A3 27
Hilton St. Leeds LS8 60 F4 2
Hilton Terr. Leeds LS8 60 F4 3
Hinchcliffe Ave. Ossett WF5 140 F5
Hinchcliffe Mill Jun & Inf Sch.
Holmfi 188 C2
Hinchcliffe St. Brad BD3 75 B8
Hinchliffe Ave. Bail BD17 38 D2
Hind Ct. Mel HD7 170 C3
Hind St. Brad BD8 74 C8 5
Hind St. Brad BD12 94 C2
Hindle Pl. Morley LS27 98 B7 2
Hindley Rd. Liver WF15 117 A3
Hindley Wlk. Brad BD7 73 D2
Hinds Cres. S Elm WF9 182 F3
Hinton La. Castle WF11 126 A6
Hipperholme CE (C) Inf Sch.
Brig 114 C7
Hipperholme Gram Sch. Brig 114 C8
Hipswell St. Brad BD3 75 C8
Hird Ave. Brad BD6 94 C8
Hird Rd. Brad BD12 94 D6
Hird St. Keigh BD21 35 B5
Hird St. Leeds LS11 79 A3
Hird St. Ship BD17 55 B8
Hirst Ave. Batley WF16 117 D6
Hirst Gr. Heb Br HX7 89 B3
Hirst La. Holmfi HD7 190 B5
Hirst La. Ship BD18 54 E8
Hirst Lodge Ct. Brad BD2 55 F5
Hirst Mill Cres. Ship BD18 37 E1
Hirst Rd. Dew WF13 118 C1
Hirst Rd. Wake WF2 141 D5
Hirst St. Kippax WF10 102 F7
Hirst St. Mir WF14 138 A3
Hirst St. Tod OL14 86 B1
Hirst Wood Cres. Ship BD18 54 E8 1
Hirst Wood Rd. Ship BD18 54 E8
Hirstlands Ave. Ossett WF5 140 C7
Hirstlands Dr. Ossett WF5 140 C8
Hive St. Keigh BD22 35 A6
HMS Ceres Communication
Trng Ctr. E Carl 23 E1
Hoads The. Brig HD6 135 F7
Hob La. Haw BD22 50 C7
Hob La. Hud HD4 153 B2
Hob La. Rip HX6 132 C5
Hob La. Sow Br HX6 112 B1
Hobart Bldgs. Heb Br HX7 89 D1
Hobart Rd. Castle WF10 125 D8
Hobart Rd. Dew WF12 118 F1
Hobb Nook La. Ask LS21 10 A7
Hobberley La. Thorner LS17 44 F3
Hobson Fold. Brad BD12 94 D2 4
Hockney Rd. Brad BD8 74 B8
Hodge La. K Smea WF8 166 E6
Hodgewood La. Dar WF8 147 D6
Hodgson Ave. Brad BD3 56 D1
Hodgson Ave. Leeds LS17 44 A3
Hodgson Cres. Leeds LS17 44 A3
Hodgson La. Birk BD11 96 C6
Hodgson Pl. Morley LS27 98 B7 6
Hodgson St. Morley LS27 98 C1
Hodgson St. Wake WF1 142 B7
Hodgson Terr. Dew WF12 139 D6
Hodroyd Cl. Shaf S72 180 D1
Hodroyd Cotts. Bri S72 180 F2
Hoffman St. Hud HD3 153 A4
Hog Close La. Wh Com HD7 200 C8
Hogley La. Holmfi HD7 188 C4
Holays. Hud HD5 154 E7
Holbeck La. Leeds LS11 78 F6
Holbeck Moor Rd. Leeds LS11 79 A5
Holbeck Towers. Leeds LS11 79 A5 5
Holborn App. Leeds LS6 60 A3
Holborn Ct. Brad BD12 94 C6
Holborn Ct. Leeds LS6 60 B3 9
Holborn Gdns. Leeds LS6 60 A3 4
Holborn Gn. Leeds LS6 60 A3
Holborn Gr. Leeds LS6 60 A3
Holborn St. Leeds LS6 60 B3
Holborn Terr. Leeds LS6 60 B3
Holborn Towers. Leeds LS6 60 B3 10
Holborn View. Leeds LS6 60 A3
Holborn Wlk. Leeds LS6 60 A3
Holden Ing Way. Batley WF17 97 A4
Holden La. Bail BD17 38 D4
Holden La. Sil BD20 18 C6
Holden Rd. Brad BD6 74 B1 1
Holden St. Keigh BD22 34 F5
Holderness Rd. Knot WF11 126 E4
Holderness St. Tod OL14 108 C5 14
Holdforth Cl. Leeds LS12 78 E7
Holdforth Gdns. Leeds LS12 78 E7
Holdforth Gn. Leeds LS12 78 E7
Holdforth Pl. Leeds LS12 78 E7
Holdsworth Ave. Batley WF17 117 E7
Holdsworth Ct. Clec BD19 116 D7 6
Holdsworth Rd. Hali HX2, HX3 92 A6
Holdsworth Sq. Brad BD2 56 D4
Holdsworth St. Brad BD1 74 F8
Holdsworth St. Clec BD19 116 D8
Holdsworth St. Ship BD18 55 C6
Holdsworth Terr. Hali HX1 113 D5
Hole Bottom Rd. Tod OL14 108 B7
Hole La. Sil BD20 5 B3
Holes La. Knot WF11 126 E4
Holgate Ave. Hem WF9 163 B3
Holgate Cres. Hem WF9 181 C7
Holgate Gdns. Hem WF9 181 C7
Holgate Hospital. Hem WF9 181 A6
Holgate Rd. Pont WF8 146 C5
Holgate Terr. Hem WF9 163 B3
Holgate View. Bri S72 181 B3
Holgate View. Hem WF9 163 B3
Holker St. Brad BD8 74 B8
Holker St. Keigh BD21 35 C8
Holland Rd. Kippax LS25 83 C2
Holland St. Batley WF17 118 D5
Hollas La. Hali HX3, HX6 112 F3
Hollas La. Sow Br HX6 112 E2
Hollerton La. E Ard WF3 119 F7
Hollin Ave. Hud HD3 153 D7
Hollin Brigg La. Holmfi HD7 188 C2
Hollin Close La. Brad BD2 55 E3
Hollin Cres. Leeds LS16 59 E7
Hollin Dr. Crig WF4 159 E5
Hollin Dr. Leeds LS16 59 E7
Hollin Edge. D Dale HD8 192 A6
Hollin Gate. Otley LS21 10 D2
Hollin Gdns. Leeds LS16 59 C7
Hollin Greaves La. Hali HX3 92 D1
Hollin Hall Dr. Ilkley LS29 7 E3
Hollin Hall. Hud HD7 152 C5
Hollin Hall La. Hud HD7 152 C5
Hollin Hall La. Kirkhe WF14 137 D2
Hollin Head. Bail BD17 38 F4
Hollin Hill Ave. Leeds LS8 61 C5
Hollin Hill Dr. Leeds LS8 61 C5
Hollin House La. Clay W HD8 193 A8
Hollin House La. Holmfi HD7 189 F5
Hollin La. Crig WF4 159 D6
Hollin La. Leeds LS16 59 D7
Hollin La. Rip HX6 132 A3
Hollin La. Ship BD18 55 D6
Hollin La. Sow Br HX6 112 C2
Hollin La. Wad M HX2 90 B5
Hollin Mews. Leeds LS16 59 D7
Hollin Mount. Leeds LS16 59 D7
Hollin Park Ave. Leeds LS8 61 D5
Hollin Park Cres. Leeds LS8 61 D5
Hollin Park Ct. Pudsey LS28 57 A6
Hollin Park Dr. Pudsey LS28 57 A6
Hollin Park Mount. Leeds LS8 61 D5
Hollin Park Par. Leeds LS8 61 C5
Hollin Park Pl. Leeds LS8 61 D5
Hollin Park Rd. Leeds LS8 61 D5
Hollin Park Rd. Pudsey LS28 57 A6
Hollin Park Terr. Leeds LS8 61 D5
Hollin Park View. Leeds LS8 61 C5
Hollin Rd. Leeds LS16 59 D7
Hollin Rd. Ship BD18 55 C6
Hollin Rise. Ship BD18 55 C6
Hollin St. Sow Br HX6 111 E1
Hollin Terr. Hud HD3 153 C7
Hollin Terr. Ship BD18 55 C6
Hollin View. Leeds LS16 59 D7
Hollin Wood Cl. Ship BD18 54 E7
Hollinbank La. Batley WF16 117 E5
Hollingbourne Rd. Leeds LS15 62 F2
Hollings Rd. Brad BD8 74 B8
Hollings Sq. Brad BD8 74 B8
Hollings St. Brad BD8 74 B8
Hollings St. Ship BD16 54 B7
Hollings Terr. Brad BD8 74 B8
Hollings The. M'town LS26 102 B3
Hollingthorpe Ave. Crig WF4 159 F3
Hollingthorpe Ct. Crig WF4 159 F2
Hollingthorpe Gr. Crig WF4 159 E3
Hollingthorpe La. Crig WF4 159 E3
Hollingthorpe Rd. Crig WF4 159 E2
Hollingwood Ave. Brad BD7 73 F4
Hollingwood Ct. Brad BD7 73 E3
Hollingwood Dr. Brad BD7 73 E4
Hollingwood Fst Sch. Brad 73 E3
Hollingwood Gate. Ilkley LS29 7 F3
Hollingwood La. Brad BD7 73 E3
Hollingwood Mount. Brad BD7 73 E4
Hollingwood Rise. Ilkley LS29 7 F3
Hollingworth La. Knot WF11 127 A4
Hollingworth La. Tod OL14 129 B8
Hollinhirst La. Neth WF4 158 F6
Hollinhurst. Kippax WF10 102 F6
Hollinroyd Rd. Dew WF12 139 E8
Hollins Ave. Batley WF13 117 F3
Hollins Bank. Hali HX6 112 B4
Hollins Bank La. Stee BD20 17 E4
Hollins Cl. Keigh BD20 17 F2
Hollins Glen. Slai HD7 170 A8
Hollins Gr. Kippax WF10 102 F6
Hollins Hey Rd. Elland HX4 134 D4
Hollins Hill. Guise BD17, LS20 39 B6
Hollins La. Hali HX2 91 C5
Hollins La. Hali HX6 112 B5
Hollins La. Keigh BD20 17 F2
Hollins La. Slai HD7 169 E6
Hollins La. Sow Br HX6 111 C5
Hollins Meadow. Tod OL14 108 A1
Hollins Mill La. Hali HX6 112 B4
Hollins Mount. Hem WF9 181 C7
Hollins Pk. Kippax LS25 83 A1
Hollins Pl. Heb Br HX7 89 A3
Hollins Pl. Tod OL14 108 A1 13
Hollins Rd. Batley WF13 117 F2 2
Hollins Rd. Tod OL14 108 A1
Hollins Row. Slai HD7 170 A8
Hollins. Sow Br HX6 111 C5
Hollins St. Tod OL14 129 B8
Hollins The. Tod OL14 108 B6
Hollinwood View. Keigh BD16 36 D7
Hollis Pl. Leeds LS3 59 F1
Hollow The. Mel HD7 170 D2
Hollowfield Croft. Brad BD12 95 B5
Hollowgate. Holmfi HD7 189 A5
Holly Ave. Hors LS16 41 D3
Holly Bank. Ack M T WF7 163 E6
Holly Bank Dr. Brig HX3 114 D8
Holly Bank. Gar LS25 83 B6
Holly Bank. Guise LS20 39 D8
Holly Bank Pk. Brig HD6 135 F8
Holly Bank Rd. Brig HD6 135 F8
Holly Bank Rd. Hud HD3 135 C1
Holly Bank. S in Cra BD20 16 C5
Holly Bush Ct. B Spa LS23 30 E7
Holly Cl. Crof WF4 143 E1
Holly Cl. Midd LS10 99 B4
Holly Cres. Crof WF4 143 E1
Holly Cres. Rip HX6 132 C3
Holly Ct. E Ard WF3 119 E6
Holly Ct. Guise LS20 39 E8
Holly Ct. Loft G WF1 121 C5
Holly Dr. Hors LS16 41 D3
Holly Gr. Batley WF17 118 B3
Holly Gr. Bri S72 181 A3
Holly Gr. Hali HX1 113 A6
Holly Gr. Hud HD3 135 C1
Holly Hall La. Brad BD12 94 C4
Holly House. Castle WF10 124 E7 6
Holly Park Dr. Brad BD7 73 E4
Holly Park Gr. Brad BD7 73 E4
Holly Rd. B Spa LS23 30 B8
Holly Rd. Hud HD1 153 E4
Holly St. Brad BD6 73 D2
Holly St. Hem WF9 181 D7
Holly St. Wake WF2 141 F7
Holly Terr. Hud HD1 154 B8
Hollybank Ave. Batley WF17 118 C7
Hollybank Ave. D Dale HD8 191 C6
Hollybank Gdns. Brad BD7 73 F3
Hollybank Gr. Brad BD7 73 E3
Hollybank House. Brig HD6 135 F8
Hollybank Rd. Brad BD7 73 F3
Hollybush Gn. Coll LS22 29 C8
Hollycroft Ave. Roy S71 179 B3
Hollycroft Ct. Hors LS16 42 A3
Hollyfield Ave. Hud HD3 153 A7
Hollyns Terr. Elland HX4 134 C7 6
Hollynsmill. Elland HX4 134 D7
Hollyoake Ave. Slai HD7 170 C8
Hollyshaw Cres. Leeds LS15 81 C8
Hollyshaw Gr. Leeds LS15 81 C8
Hollyshaw La. Leeds LS15 81 C8
Hollyshaw St. Leeds LS15 81 C8
Hollyshaw Terr. Leeds LS15 81 C8 4
Hollyshaw Wlk. Leeds LS15 62 C1 5
Hollywell La. Leeds LS12 78 B8 9
Holman Ave. Gar LS25 82 F5
Holmbridge CE Sch. Holmfi 188 B2
Holmcliffe Ave. Hud HD4 153 F1
Holmclose. Holmfi HD7 188 C2
Holmdale Cres. Holmfi HD7 188 F8
Holmdene Dr. Mir WF14 138 A6
Holme Ave. Hud HD5 154 E5
Holme Cl. Floc WF4 156 E5
Holme Cl. Glu BD20 16 D6
Holme Cty Sch. Holme 187 F1
Holme Croft. Crig WF4 159 F7
Holme Dr. Hali HX2 112 B6
Holme Farm La. Bard LS23 28 F3
Holme Field. Ossett WF5 140 C7
Holme Ghyll. Glu BD20 16 B6
Holme Gr. Bur in W LS29 21 F7
Holme House La. Hali HX2 90 E4
Holme House La. Keigh BD22 34 C5
Holme House Rd. Tod OL14 86 C1
Holme House St. Litt OL15 129 D1
Holme Ings. Nes LS29 7 C7
Holme La. Brad BD4 75 F1
Holme La. Brad BD4 75 F2
Holme La. Glu BD20 16 D6
Holme La. Hal E BD23 1 D8
Holme La. Holmfi HD7 189 E7
Holme La. S in Cra BD20 16 D6
Holme La. Slai HD7 151 E1
Holme La. Wake WF2 142 B3
Holme Leas Dr. Ossett WF5 140 C7
Holme Mid Sch. Brad 75 D3
Holme Mid Sch. Brad 75 D7
Holme Mill La. Keigh BD22 34 F6
Holme Pk. Bur in W LS29 21 F7
Holme Pl. Heb Br HX7 89 A4
Holme Pl. Hud HD1 153 D7
Holme Rd. Hali HX2 112 B6
Holme St. Brad BD5 74 D4
Holme St. Brig HX3 115 A7
Holme St. Heb Br HX7 89 A3
Holme St. Liver WF15 117 B4
Holme St. Oxen BD22 51 C2
Holme St. Tod OL14 107 E7
Holme Styes La. Holme HD7 199 A8
Holme Terr. Litt OL15 129 D1
Holme Top La. Brad BD5 74 D4
Holme Top St. Brad BD5 74 D4
Holme Valley Bsns Ctr. Hud 171 E8
Holme Valley Memorial Hospl.
Holmfi 189 A7
Holme View. Arth LS21 25 C6
Holme View Ave. Holmfi HD7 188 D5
Holme View Dr. Holmfi HD7 188 D5
Holme View Pk. Holmfi HD7 188 E5
Holme Villas. Mars HD7 169 C6
Holme Way. Ossett WF5 140 C7
Holme Well Rd. Midd LS10 99 E5
Holme Wood Rd. Brad BD4 75 D3
Holme Wood Rd. Keigh BD22 34 F6
Holme Woods La. Holme HD7 197 F6
Holme's Terr. Hali HX2 112 E8 9
Holmefield Fst Sch. Brad 75 E4
Holmefield Rd. Hud HD3 152 E6
Holmes Rd. Hali HX6 112 C4
Holmes St. Brad BD1 74 D8
Holmes St. Leeds LS11 79 C6
Holmeside Cl. Hud HD4 171 F8
Holmfield Ave. Clay W HD8 175 F2
Holmfield Ave. Wake WF2 142 B3
Holmfield Chase. Loft G WF3 122 B6
Holmfield Cl. Clay W HD8 175 F2
Holmfield Cl. Pont WF8 125 F4
Holmfield. Clay W HD8 175 F2
Holmfield Cotts. M'town LS26 102 E3
Holmfield Dr. Hud HD7 152 F5
Holmfield Dr. Leeds LS8 44 A1
Holmfield Gdns. Hali HX2 92 A5
Holmfield Gr. Wake WF2 142 B3
Holmfield Ind Est. Hali 92 A7
Holmfield La. Castle WF11,
WF8 125 F5
Holmfield La. Wake WF2 142 B3
Holmfield Rd. Clay W HD8 175 F2
Holmfield Rd. S in Cra BD20 16 D5
Holmfield St. Brad BD1 74 D7
Holmfield Terr. Clay W HD8 175 F2
Holmfirth High Sch. Holmfi 189 C8
Holmfirth Jun & Inf Sch.
Holmfi 189 A4
Holmfirth Rd. Diggle OL3 185 D1
Holmfirth Rd. Holmfi HD7 189 F7
Holmfirth Rd. Mel HD7 170 E1
Holmfirth Scholes Jun & Inf Sch.
Holmfi 189 D3
Holmfirth Upperthong Jun Mix Sch.
Holmfi 188 E4

Holmroyd Ave. Glu BD20 .... 16 D6
Holmsley Ave. S Kirk WF9 ...... 182 A2
Holmsley Crest. Roth LS26 ...... 101 A6
Holmsley Field Ct. Roth LS26 . 101 C6
Holmsley Field La. Roth LS26 101 C6
Holmsley Garth. Roth LS26 ...... 101 B7
Holmsley Gr. S Kirk WF9 .... 182 A2
Holmsley La. Roth LS26 .... 101 B6
Holmsley La. S Kirk WF9 .... 181 F2
Holmsley Mount. S Kirk WF9 . 182 A2
Holmsley Wlk. Roth LS26 .... 101 B6
Holmwood Ave. Leeds LS6 ...... 59 E8
Holmwood Cl. Leeds LS6 .... 59 F8
Holmwood Cres. Leeds LS6 ..... 59 F8
Holmwood Dr. Leeds LS6 .... 59 F8
Holmwood Gr. Leeds LS6 .... 59 F8
Holmwood Mount. Leeds LS6 .. 59 F8
Holmwood View. Leeds LS6 ..... 59 E8
Holroyd Hill. Brad BD6 .... 74 C1
Holroyd Sq. Elland HX4 .... 133 F4
Holroyd St. Leeds LS7 .... 60 D2
Holsworthy Rd. Brad BD4 .... 75 E3
Holt Ave. Hors LS16 .... 42 C5
Holt Ave. Hud HD2 .... 136 C4
Holt Cl. Hors LS16 .... 42 C4
Holt Cres. Hors LS16 .... 41 F5
Holt Dr. Hors LS16 .... 42 A5
Holt Farm Cl. Hors LS16 .... 42 A5
Holt Farm Rise. Hors LS16 .... 41 F5
Holt Garth. Hors LS16 .... 42 A5
Holt Gdns. Brad BD10 .... 55 F8
Holt Gdns. Hors LS16 .... 42 C5
Holt Head Rd. Slai HD7 .... 170 B6
Holt La. Holmfi HD7 .... 188 F6
Holt La. Hors LS16 .... 42 A5
Holt Lane Ct. Hors LS16 .... 42 B4
Holt Park App. Hors LS16 .... 42 A5
Holt Park Ave. Hors LS16 .... 42 A5
Holt Park Cl. Hors LS16 .... 42 A5
Holt Park Dis Ctr. Hors LS16 ... 41 F5
Holt Park Dr. Hors LS16 .... 42 A5
Holt Park Gate. Hors LS16 .... 42 A5
Holt Park Gdns. Hors LS16 .... 42 A5
Holt Park Gn. Hors LS16 .... 42 A5
Holt Park Gr. Hors LS16 .... 41 F5
Holt Park Grange. Hors LS16 .. 42 A5
Holt Park La. Hors LS16 .... 42 A5
Holt Park Mid Sch. Hors 42 A4
Holt Park Rd. Hors LS16 .... 42 A5
Holt Park Rise. Hors LS16 .... 42 A5
Holt Park Vale. Hors LS16 .... 42 A5
Holt Park Way. Hors LS16 .... 42 A5
Holt Rd. Hors LS16 .... 42 A5
Holt Rise. Hors LS16 .... 42 A5
Holt St. Litt OL15 .... 129 D2
Holt The. Ship BD18 .... 55 C8
Holt Vale. Hors LS16 .... 42 A5
Holt View. Hors LS16 .... 41 F5
Holt Way. Hors LS16 .... 42 A5
Holt Wlk. Hors LS16 .... 42 A5
Holtby Gr. Brig HX3 .... 115 A7
Holtdale App. Hors LS16 .... 41 F5
Holtdale Ave. Hors LS16 .... 41 F5
Holtdale Cl. Hors LS16 .... 41 F5
Holtdale Croft. Hors LS16 .... 41 F5
Holtdale Dr. Hors LS16 .... 41 F5
Holtdale Fold. Hors LS16 .... 41 F5
Holtdale Garth. Hors LS16 .... 41 F5
Holtdale Gdns. Hors LS16 .... 41 F5
Holtdale Gn. Hors LS16 .... 41 F5
Holtdale Gr. Hors LS16 .... 41 F5
Holtdale Lawn. Hors LS16 .... 41 F5
Holtdale Pl. Hors LS16 .... 41 F5
Holtdale Rd. Hors LS16 .... 41 F5
Holtdale View. Hors LS16 .... 41 F5
Holtdale Way. Hors LS16 .... 41 F5
Holts La. Brad BD14 .... 73 B4
Holts La. Brad BD14 .... 73 B5
Holts Terr. Hali HX3 .... 113 D4
Holy Family RC Prim Sch. Leeds 78 D7
Holy Family Sch The. Keigh 18 B1
Holy Name Sch. Hors 42 A3
Holy Rood La. Ledsh LS25 .... 104 E8
Holy Trinity CE (Aided) Sch. Hali 92 A6
Holy Trinity CE (Aided) Sch.
Ossett 140 D6
Holy Trinity CE Fst Sch. Bing ... 37 A2
Holy Trinity CE Inf Sch. Hali ... 113 B6
Holy Trinity Jun Sch. Hali 113 B6
Holy Trinity Mid Sch. Hors 41 D5
Holybrook Ave. Brad BD10 .... 56 D6
Holycroft Fst Sch. Keigh 35 B6
Holycroft St. Keigh BD21 .... 35 B6
Holyoake Ave. Batley WF17 ..... 118 A5
Holyoake Ave. Bing BD16 .... 36 F1
Holyoake St. Tod OL14 .... 86 A1
Holyoake Terr. Hor WF4 .... 140 E1
Holyoake Terr. Slai HD7 .... 152 D1
Holyrood Cres. Nor WF6 .... 122 F4
Holywell Ash La. Brad BD8 .... 55 D1
Holywell Dene. Castle WF10 . 125 A6
Holywell Gdns. Castle WF10 . 125 A6
Holywell Gr. Castle WF10 ...... 125 A6
Holywell Green Jun & Inf Schs.
Elland 134 B4
Holywell Halt. Skip 1 B7
Holywell La. Castle WF10 .... 125 B6
Holywell La. Thorner LS17 .... 44 D5
Holywell Mount. Castle WF10 125 B6
Home Farm Ct. H Pag DN5 .... 195 D5
Home Lea Dr. Roth LS26 .... 100 D6
Home Lea. Roth LS26 .... 100 D7
Home View Terr. Brad BD8 .... 55 B1
Homefield Ave. Morley LS27 .... 98 A2
Homepaddock House. Weth
LS22 .... 13 F6
Homestead Dr. Wake WF2 ...... 141 F6
Homestead The. Batley WF16 117 E4
HomesThe. Hud HD2 .... 136 F3
Honey Hole Cl. Tod OL14 .... 108 B4
Honey Hole Rd. Tod OL14 .... 108 B4
Honey Holme La. H Chap BB10 85 A7
Honley CE (C) Inf Sch. Honley 171 F5
Honley CE (C) Jun Sch. Honley 171 F4
Honley High Sch. Honley 172 A5
Honley Rd. Kirkb HD4 .... 172 D6
Honley Sq. Hor WF4 .... 141 A1
Honley Sta. Honley 172 B5
Honoria St. Hud HD1 .... 136 A1
Hood St. Hud HD4 .... 171 F8
Hood St. S Elm WF9 .... 182 E1
Hooton Cres. Ryhill WF4 .... 162 A1
Hooton Pagnell CE Fst & Mid Sch.
H Pag 195 C5
Hooton Rd. Brod DN5 .... 195 F4
Hoowood La. Holme HD7 .... 187 E3
Hopbine Ave. Brad BD5 .... 74 E2
Hopbine Rd. Brad BD5 .... 74 E2
Hope Ave. Brad BD5 .... 74 C2
Hope Ave. Ship BD18 .... 55 D8
Hope Bldgs. Tod OL14 .... 108 C5 11
Hope Hall St. Hali HX1 .... 113 C6
Hope Hall Terr. Hali HX1 .... 113 C6 13
Hope Hill View. Ship BD16 .... 54 A7
Hope La. Bail BD17 .... 38 B3
Hope Pl. Keigh BD21 .... 35 B5
Hope Rd. Leeds LS9 .... 79 D8
Hope St. Castle WF10 .... 104 C2
Hope St. Dew WF13 .... 118 C1
Hope St E. Castle WF10 .... 124 D8 10
Hope St. Hali HX1 .... 113 B7
Hope St. Heb Br HX7 .... 89 A3 21
Hope St. Hud HD3 .... 153 B5
Hope St. Hud HD3 .... 154 A4
Hope St. Mapp S75 .... 178 C1
Hope St. Morley LS27 .... 98 A4
Hope St. Nor WF6 .... 144 A8
Hope St. Ossett WF5 .... 140 F3
Hope St. Ryhill WF4 .... 180 C8
Hope St. Sow Br HX6 .... 112 C3
Hope St W. Castle WF10 .... 124 C7
Hope St. Wake WF1 .... 142 C7
Hope Terr. Slai HD7 .... 152 D3
Hope View. Ship BD18 .... 55 D7
Hopefield Chase. Roth LS26 .. 100 B4
Hopefield Cl. Roth LS26 .... 100 B4
Hopefield Ct E Ard WF3 .... 120 C7
Hopefield Ct. Roth LS26 .... 100 B4
Hopefield Dr. Roth LS26 .... 100 B4
Hopefield Gdns. Roth LS26 ..... 100 B4
Hopefield Gn. Roth LS26 .... 100 B4
Hopefield Gr. Roth LS26 .... 100 B4
Hopefield Mews. Roth LS26 ... 100 B4
Hopefield Way. Roth LS26 .... 100 B4
Hopefield Wlk. Roth LS26 .... 100 B4
Hopes Farm Mount. Midd LS10 99 F7 3
Hopes Farm Rd. Midd LS10 ...... 99 F7
Hopes Farm View. Midd LS10 100 A7
Hopetown Wlk. Nor WF6 .... 123 C3
Hopewell Pl. Leeds LS6 .... 59 E2 11
Hopewell St. Batley WF17 .... 118 B6
Hopewell Terr. Kippax LS25 ..... 83 B1
Hopewell View. Midd LS10 .... 99 D5
Hopewell Way. Crig WF4 .... 159 E5
Hopkin St. Brad BD4 .... 75 E1
Hopkinson Dr. Brad BD4 .... 95 C8
Hopkinson Rd. Hud HD2 .... 136 B4
Hopkinson St. Hali HX3 .... 91 F3
Hopkinsons Bldgs. Hali HX3 .... 91 F3
Hopps's Rd. Glu BD20 .... 16 C7
Hopton Ave. Brad BD4 .... 75 B1
Hopton Ave. Mir WF14 .... 137 E2
Hopton Dr. Mir WF14 .... 137 E2
Hopton Fst Sch. Mir 137 F4
Hopton Hall La. Mir WF14 ...... 137 F1
Hopton La. Mir WF14 .... 137 F2
Hopton New Rd. Mir WF14 ..... 138 A3
Hopwood Bank. Hors LS18 .... 41 C2
Hopwood Cl. Hors LS18 .... 41 C2
Hopwood Gr. Castle WF10 ..... 125 B7
Hopwood La. Hali HX1 .... 113 A6
Hopwood Rd. Hors LS18 .... 41 C2
Horbury Bridge CE Jun & Inf Sch.
Hor 140 E1
Horbury Fst Sch. Hor 141 C1
Horbury Rd. Ossett WF5 .... 140 E3
Horbury Rd. Wake WF2 .... 141 E3
Horbury Sch. Hor 141 C1
Horbury St Peter CE Sch. Hor 141 B1
Horley Green La. Hali HX3 .... 92 E2
Horley Green Rd. Hali HX3 ..... 113 E8
Horn Cote La. Holmfi HD7 ...... 190 A6
Horn Croft. Caw S75 .... 193 F5
Horn La. Holmfi HD7 .... 190 A6
Horn La. Ingb S30 .... 191 B1
Horn La. Sil BD20 .... 5 C4
Hornbeam Ave. Wake WF2 ...... 142 A8
Hornbeam Gn. Pont WF8 .... 125 F1
Hornbeam Way. Leeds LS14 .... 62 C8
Hornby St. Hali HX1 .... 112 F5
Horncastle St. Clec BD19 .... 116 E7 2
Horncastle View. Ryhill WF4 . 162 D2
Horne St. Hali HX1 .... 113 B7
Horne St. Wake WF2 .... 142 C4
Horner Ave. Batley WF17 .... 117 F6
Horner Cres. Batley WF17 .... 117 F6
Hornes La. Mapp S75 .... 178 C1
Hornsea Dr. Wils BD15 .... 53 C4
Horse Croft La. Shep HD8 ...... 174 B3
Horse Fair Flats. Pont WF8 ..... 125 D1
Horse Fair. Pont WF8 .... 125 D1
Horse Pond La. Slai HD3 .... 152 A7
Horsefair. Weth LS22 .... 13 E5
Horsehold La. Heb Br HX7 .... 88 E2
Horsehold Rd. Heb Br HX7 .... 88 E2
Horsfall St. Hali HX1 .... 113 A5
Horsfall St. Morley LS27 .... 97 F6
Horsfall St. Tod OL14 .... 108 E6
Horsforth Featherbank Inf Sch.
Hors 58 B7
Horsforth Golf Course. Yeadon 40 F5
Horsforth Nw Rd. Pudsey LS13 57 E4
Horsforth Sch & F Ed Ctr. Hors 41 B1
Horsforth St Margaret's CE Prim
Sch. Hors 41 B1
Horsforth Sta. Hors 41 C3
Horsham Ct. Keigh BD22 .... 34 E5
Horsham Rd. Brad BD4 .... 75 E2
Horsley St. Brad BD6 .... 74 C1 5
Horsman St. Brad BD4 .... 75 B6
Horton Bank Top Fst Sch. Brad 73 E2
Horton Cl. Pudsey LS13 .... 57 F4
Horton Garth. Pudsey LS13 ...... 57 F4
Horton Grange Rd. Brad BD7 .. 74 B5
Horton Hall Cl. Brad BD5 .... 74 D5
Horton Park Ave. Brad BD5,
BD7 .... 74 C5
Horton Pl. Hali HX2 .... 91 F8
Horton Rise. Pudsey LS13 .... 57 F4
Horton St. Batley WF16 .... 117 D3
Horton St. Hali HX1 .... 113 D6
Horton St. Ossett WF5 .... 140 C6
Hospital La. Hors LS16 .... 41 F3
Hospital Rd. Keigh BD20 .... 19 A1
Hostingley La. Dew WF12 ...... 140 B2
Hothfield St. Sil BD20 .... 5 D1
Hothfield Street Jun Sch. Sil 5 D1
Hough End Ave. Leeds LS13 ..... 58 D1
Hough End Cl. Leeds LS13 .... 58 D1
Hough End Cres. Leeds LS13 .... 58 C1
Hough End Ct. Leeds LS13 .... 58 D1
Hough End Garth. Leeds LS13 . 58 C1
Hough End Gdns. Leeds LS13 .. 58 D1 2
Hough End La. Leeds LS13 .... 58 C1
Hough Gr. Leeds LS13 .... 58 C2 16
Hough La. Leeds LS13 .... 58 C2
Hough. Northo HX3 .... 93 A1
Hough Side Cl. Pudsey LS28 .... 77 B7
Hough Side High Sch. Pudsey .. 77 B8
Hough Side La. Pudsey LS28 .... 77 A7
Hough Side Rd. Pudsey LS28 .... 77 A7
Hough Terr. Leeds LS13 .... 58 C2 17
Hough Top. Pudsey LS13 .... 77 B8
Hough Tree Rd. Pudsey LS13 .. 77 C8
Hough Tree Terr. Pudsey LS13 77 C8
Houghley Ave. Leeds LS12 ...... 58 F2
Houghley Cl. Leeds LS13 .... 58 E2
Houghley Cres. Leeds LS12 ..... 58 F3
Houghley La. Leeds LS12, LS13 58 E1
Houghley Pl. Leeds LS12 .... 58 F2
Houghley Rd. Leeds LS12 .... 58 F2
Houghley Sq. Leeds LS12 .... 58 F2
Houghton Ave. Knot WF11 ..... 126 B5
Houghton Pl. Brad BD1 .... 74 D8
Houghton Rd. Dearne S63 ...... 194 A1
Houghton St. Brig HD6 .... 115 B3
Houghton Twrs. Hali HX6 ...... 112 B4 10
Houghton's Almshouses. Hud
HD5 .... 154 F3 1
Hoults La. Elland HX4 .... 134 C8
Houndhill La. Feath WF7 .... 145 F5
House Grove Dr. Clay W HD8 175 E2
Hovingham Ave. Leeds LS8 ...... 61 A4
Hovingham Gr. Leeds LS8 .... 61 A4
Hovingham Mount. Leeds LS8 . 61 A4 6
Hovingham Prim Sch. Leeds 61 A4
Hovingham Terr. Leeds LS8 ..... 61 A4 4
Howard Ave. Hud HD3 .... 153 C7
Howard Ave. Leeds LS15 .... 80 F7
Howard Cres. Crig WF4 .... 159 E6
Howard Ct. Leeds LS15 .... 80 F7
Howard Pk. Clec BD19 .... 116 E7
Howard Pl. Batley WF17 .... 118 C3
Howard Rd. Hud HD3 .... 153 C7
Howard St. Batley WF17 .... 118 C3
Howard St. Brad BD5 .... 74 D6
Howard St. Hali HX1 .... 113 A8
Howard St. Ossett WF5 .... 140 D7
Howard St. Wake WF1 .... 142 C7
Howard Villas. Clec BD19 .... 116 E7
Howard Way. Litt OL15 .... 129 C1
Howard Way. Mel HD7 .... 170 E1
Howarth Ave. Brad BD2 .... 56 A5
Howarth Cres. Brad BD2 .... 56 A5
Howarth La. Hud HD1 .... 153 E3
Howarth Pl. Leeds LS7 .... 60 C1
Howarth Rd Fst Sch. Brad 54 D3
Howbeck Ave. Keigh BD20 .... 19 A1
Howbeck Dr. Keigh BD20 .... 36 A8
Howcans La. Hali HX3 .... 92 B5
Howden Ave. Ad Le S DN6 ...... 184 E1
Howden Ave. Keigh BD20 .... 18 A2
Howden Cl. Brad BD4 .... 75 F1
Howden Cl. Hud HD4 .... 152 F2
Howden Cl. Mapp S75 .... 177 F1
Howden Clough High Sch.
Batley 97 B1
Howden Clough Ind Est. Batley 97 C3
Howden Clough Rd. Batley LS27 97 D3
Howden Gdns. Leeds LS6 .... 59 E2
Howden Pl. Leeds LS6 .... 59 E2
Howden Rd. Sil BD20 .... 5 F1
Howden Way. Wake WF1 .... 142 E6
Howdenbrook. Shelf HX3 .... 93 E7
Howell La. G Hou DN5 .... 194 A4
Howell Wood Country Pk.
S Kirk 194 A7
Howes La. Northo HX3 .... 92 F2
Howgate. Brad BD10 .... 56 C8
Howgate Rd. Slai HD7 .... 169 F8
Howgill Gn. Brad BD6 .... 94 A6
Howlett Cross. Roth LS26 .... 100 B4
Howley Hall Golf Course.
Batley 118 F8
Howley Mill La. Batley WF17 . 118 D7
Howley Park Cl. Morley LS27 ... 97 F2
Howley Park Rd E. Morley LS27 98 A1
Howley Park Rd. Morley LS27 . 97 F2
Howley Park Trad Est. Morley . 97 F2
Howley St. Batley WF17 .... 118 D6
Howley Wlk. Batley WF17 .... 118 E5
Howley Wlk. Batley WF17 .... 118 E6
Howroyd La. Dew WF12 .... 156 E7
Howroyd La. Rip HX4 .... 133 B4
Howson Cl. Guise LS20 .... 22 F1
Hoxton Mount. Leeds LS11 ...... 78 F3
Hoxton St. Brad BD8 .... 74 A8
Hoylake Ave. Hud HD2 .... 135 F3
Hoyland Rd. Wake WF2 .... 160 B5
Hoyland Terr. S Kirk WF9 .... 182 A2
Hoyle Court Ave. Bail BD17 ...... 38 E3
Hoyle Court Dr. Bail BD17 .... 38 E3
Hoyle Court Fst Sch. Bail 38 E2
Hoyle Court Rd. Bail BD17 .... 38 E3
Hoyle Fold. Keigh BD22 .... 34 F5
Hoyle House Fold. Slai HD7 .... 152 D1
Hoyle Ing Rd. Thorn BD13 .... 72 F6
Hoyle Ing. Slai HD7 .... 152 D1
Hoyle Mill Rd. Hem WF9 .... 163 D2
Hubberton Green Rd. Sow Br
HX6 .... 111 C2
Hubert St. Brad BD3 .... 75 B6
Hubert St. Hali HX2 .... 112 D7
Hubert St. Hud HD3 .... 134 E1
Hud Hill. Shelf HX3 .... 93 B4
Huddersfield Coll of Ed. Hud .. 135 C1
Huddersfield Crem. Hud 136 A6
Huddersfield New Coll. Hud .. 152 F7
Huddersfield Rd. Batley WF17 117 E8
Huddersfield Rd. Brad BD12 .... 94 C4
Huddersfield Rd. Brig HD6 ..... 136 B7
Huddersfield Rd. Densh OL3 .. 167 A4
Huddersfield Rd. Dew WF13 . 138 D4
Huddersfield Rd. Dew WF13 . 139 A7
Huddersfield Rd. Elland HX5 .. 135 A4
Huddersfield Rd. Hali HX3 ..... 113 C4
Huddersfield Rd. Holmfi HD7 . 189 A6
Huddersfield Rd. Holmfi HD7 . 189 E7
Huddersfield Rd. Honley HD7 172 A5
Huddersfield Rd. Hud HD3 ..... 135 A4
Huddersfield Rd. Ingb S30 ...... 191 E1
Huddersfield Rd. Kirkb HD8 .. 174 A4
Huddersfield Rd. Mel HD7 ...... 171 A5
Huddersfield Rd. Shep HD8 .... 174 B4
Huddersfield Rd. Skel HD8 ..... 174 D2
Huddersfield Rd. W Bret WF4 177 A6
Huddersfield Royal Infmy. Hud 153 C8
Huddersfield Sta. Hud 154 A6
Huddersfield Tech Coll. Hud .. 153 F2
Huddersfield Tech Coll. Hud .. 153 F5
Huddersfield Tech Coll. Hud .. 154 A6
Huddersfield Univ. Hud 154 B5
Huddleston Ct. Dew WF12 ..... 139 F8
Hudroyd. Hud HD5 .... 154 F3
Hudson Ave. Brad BD7 .... 74 B3
Hudson Ave. Notton WF4 .... 179 B6
Hudson Cl. Brad BD7 .... 74 B3 1
Hudson Cl. Weth LS22 .... 13 E5
Hudson Cres. Brad BD7 .... 74 B3
Hudson Gdns. Brad BD7 .... 74 B4
Hudson Gr. Leeds LS9 .... 61 A1
Hudson Mews. B Spa LS23 .... 30 E7
Hudson Mill Rd. Hep HX7 .... 88 C5
Hudson Pl. Leeds LS9 .... 61 A1
Hudson Rd. Leeds LS9 .... 61 A1
Hudson St. Brad BD3 .... 75 D7
Hudson St. Leeds LS9 .... 61 A1
Hudson St. Pudsey LS28 .... 57 D1 2
Hudson St. Tod OL14 .... 86 C1
Hudson The. Brad BD12 .... 94 C3
Hudson's Terr. Yeadon LS19 ... 40 C7 4
Hudswell Rd. Leeds LS10 .... 79 D4
Hudswell St. Wake WF1 .... 142 E3
Huggan Row. Pudsey LS28 .... 76 F7 5
Hugh Gaitskell Mid Sch. Leeds 78 F2
Hugh St. Castle WF10 .... 124 D7
Hughenden View. Morley LS27 98 A6
Hughendon Dr. Thorn BD13 ...... 73 A6
Hughendon Wlk. Thorn BD13 .. 73 A6
Hugill St. Thorn BD13 .... 72 D6
Hulbert Croft. Hud HD5 .... 154 F4
Hulbert St. Bing BD16 .... 37 A2
Hull St. Morley LS27 .... 98 B4
Hullen Rd. Elland HX5 .... 134 D6
Hullenedge Gdns. Elland HX5 134 D6
Hullenedge La. Elland HX5 .... 134 D5
Hullenedge Rd. Elland HX5 .... 134 E6
Hullett Cl. Heb Br HX7 .... 89 F1
Hullett Dr. Heb Br HX7 .... 89 F1
Hulme Sq. Castle WF10 .... 104 D1
Hulme St. Sow Br HX6 .... 112 B3
Humber Cl. Castle WF10 .... 125 B8
Humber Cl. Slai HD7 .... 152 D1
Humboldt St. Brad BD1 .... 75 A7
Hume Crest. Batley WF17 ...... 118 C5 7
Humley Rd. Wake WF2 .... 160 B5
Hundhill La. Dar WF8 .... 146 D2
Hungate La. M'town LS26 ...... 122 E8
Hunger Hill. Hali HX1 .... 113 C6
Hunger Hill. Ilkley LS29 .... 8 C7
Hunger Hill. Morley LS27 .... 98 A3
Hunger Hills Ave. Hors LS18 ..... 41 A1
Hunger Hills Dr. Hors LS18 ...... 41 A1
Hungerford Rd. Hud HD3 .... 153 D8
Hunslet Bsns Pk. Leeds 79 E5
Hunslet Carr Prim Sch. Leeds .. 79 E2
Hunslet Green Way. Leeds LS10 79 D4
Hunslet Hall Rd. Leeds LS11 .... 79 B4
Hunslet Hall Sh Ctr. Leeds 79 B4
Hunslet La. Leeds LS10 .... 79 C6
Hunslet Moor Prim Sch. Leeds 79 C3
Hunslet Rd. Leeds LS10 .... 79 C6
Hunslet Rd. Leeds LS10 .... 79 D5
Hunslet St Mary's CE Prim Sch.
Leeds 79 E3
Hunslet Trad Est. Leeds 79 F3
Hunston Ave. Hud HD3 .... 153 B7
Hunsworth La. Birk BD19, BD4 95 E4
Hunsworth La. Clec BD19 .... 95 E4
Hunt Ct. Wake WF2 .... 141 E6
Hunt St. Castle WF10 .... 103 D1
Hunt St. Castle WF10 .... 124 B8
Hunt Yd. Brad BD7 .... 74 A4 3
Hunter Hill Rd. Hali HX2 .... 91 A5
Hunters Ct. Brad BD9 .... 54 C4
Hunters La. Tod OL14 .... 107 F6
Hunters Meadow. Sil BD20 .... 5 E2
Hunters Park Ave. Brad BD14 . 73 E5
Hunters Wlk. Weth LS22 .... 13 E7
Huntingdon Ave. Hud HD2 ..... 136 F4
Huntingdon Rd. Brig HD6 .... 115 C1
Huntock Pl. Brig HD6 .... 114 F5
Huntsman Fold. Wake WF2 .... 141 D6
Huntsman's Cl. Hud HD4 .... 171 D8
Huntsman's Way. Bad WF9 .... 164 E2
Huntsmans Cl. Bing BD16 .... 37 C5
Huntsmans Cl. Keigh BD20 .... 35 A8
Huntwick Ave. Feath WF7 .... 145 C4
Huntwick Cres. Feath WF7 ..... 145 B4
Huntwick Dr. Feath WF7 .... 145 B4
Huntwick La. Feath WF7 .... 145 A5
Huntwick La. W Har WF7 .... 144 F3
Huntwick Rd. Feath WF7 .... 145 C4
Hurst Knowle. Hud HD5 .... 155 A4
Hurst La. Mir WF14 .... 138 B4
Hurst Rd. Heb Br HX7 .... 89 A4
Hurstville Ave. Birk BD4 .... 95 F6
Hurstwood. Hud HD2 .... 136 E4
Husler Gr. Leeds LS7 .... 60 D3
Husler Pl. Leeds LS7 .... 60 D3
Hustings The. Liver WF15 .... 117 A4 3
Hustler St. Brad BD3 .... 56 A1
Hustler's Row. Leeds LS6 .... 59 D8
Hustlergate. Brad BD1 .... 74 E7 7
Hutchinson La. Brig HD6 .... 115 B2 1
Hutchinson's Pl. Leeds LS5 ...... 59 A3
Hutson St. Brad BD5 .... 74 D4
Hutton Dr. Batley WF16 .... 117 E4
Hutton Dr. S Elm WF9 .... 183 A4
Hutton Mid Sch. Brad 56 C5
Hutton Rd. Brad BD5 .... 74 C2
Hutton Terr. Brad BD2 .... 56 D5
Hutton Terr. Pudsey LS28 .... 76 E7
Hydale Ct. Brad BD12 .... 94 C6
Hydale Ct. Keigh BD21 .... 35 E5
Hyde Park Cl. Leeds LS6 .... 59 F2
Hyde Park Cnr. Leeds LS6 .... 59 F3 5
Hyde Park Pl. Leeds LS6 .... 59 F3
Hyde Park Rd. Hali HX1 .... 113 A5
Hyde Park Rd. Leeds LS6 .... 59 F2
Hyde Park St. Hali HX1 .... 113 A5
Hyde Park Terr. Leeds LS6 .... 59 F3
Hyde Pk. Hali HX1 .... 113 A6
Hyde Pk. Wake WF1 .... 142 E6
Hyde Pl. Leeds LS2 .... 60 A1
Hyde St. Brad BD10 .... 39 B1
Hyde St. Leeds LS2 .... 60 A1
Hyde Terr. Leeds LS2 .... 60 A1
Hydro Cl. Ilkley LS29 .... 8 F3
Hyman Wlk. S Elm WF9 .... 183 A4
Hyne Ave. Brad BD4 .... 75 C1
Hyrst Garth. Batley WF17 .... 118 B2
Hyrst Wlk. Batley WF17 .... 118 C3
Hyrstlands Rd. Batley WF17 ... 118 C3
Hyrstmount Jun Sch. Batley .. 118 C3
Ibbetson Cl. Morley LS27 .... 98 A7
Ibbetson Croft. Morley LS27 .... 98 A7
Ibbetson Ct. Morley LS27 .... 98 A7
Ibbetson Dr. Morley LS27 .... 98 A7
Ibbetson Oval. Morley LS27 ..... 98 A7
Ibbetson Rd. Morley LS27 .... 98 A7
Ibbetson Rise. Morley LS27 ...... 98 A7
Ibbotroyd Ave. Tod OL14 .... 108 A7
Ibbotson Flats. Hud HD1 .... 154 B6 6
Ibbottson St. Wake WF1 .... 142 F3
Ida & Robert Arthington Hospl.
Hors 41 F2
Ida St. Brad BD5 .... 74 C3
Ida St. Leeds LS10 .... 80 A2
Iddesleigh St. Brad BD4 .... 75 D6
Ideal L Ctr. Brad 74 D1
Idle CE Fst Sch. Brad 39 B1
Idle Rd. Brad BD2 .... 56 B3
Idlecroft Rd. Brad BD10 .... 56 B8
Idlethorp Way. Brad BD10 .... 56 C7
Ilbert Ave. Brad BD4 .... 75 C1
Ilford St. Morley LS27 .... 98 B4
Ilkley Golf Course. Nes 7 D6
Ilkley Grammar Sch. Ilkley 8 C3
Ilkley Hall Mews. Ilkley LS29 .... 8 B3
Ilkley Hall Pk. Ilkley LS29 .... 8 B3
Ilkley Mid Sch. Ilkley 8 E4
Ilkley Rd. Add LS29 .... 7 B6
Ilkley Rd. Bur in W LS29 .... 9 D3
Ilkley Rd. Keigh BD20 .... 19 C5
Ilkley Rd. Otley LS21 .... 22 F7
Ilkley Sta. Ilkley 8 B4
Illingworth Ave. Hali HX2 .... 91 E7
Illingworth Ave. Nor WF6 ...... 122 E3
Illingworth Cl. Hali HX2 .... 91 E7
Illingworth Cl. Yeadon LS19 ..... 40 C5
Illingworth Cres. Hali HX2 .... 91 E7
Illingworth Dr. Hali HX2 .... 91 E7
Illingworth Gdns. Hali HX2 ...... 91 E7
Illingworth Gr. Hali HX2 .... 91 E7
Illingworth Rd. Brad BD12 .... 94 F4
Illingworth Rd. Hali HX2 .... 91 E7
Illingworth St. Ossett WF5 .... 140 D5
Illingworth Way. Hali HX2 .... 91 E7
Imperial Arc. Hud HD1 .... 154 A6 23
Imperial Ave. Wake WF2 .... 120 F2
Imperial Rd. Hud HD1, HD3 ... 153 D7
Inchfield Rd. Tod OL14 .... 129 A8
Incline The. Hali HX3 .... 113 E8
Independent St. Brad BD5 .... 74 C3
Industrial Ave. Batley WF17 .... 96 D1
Industrial Rd. Hali HX6 .... 112 B4
Industrial St. Bacup OL13 ...... 106 A2
Industrial St. Bing BD16 .... 36 F3
Industrial St. Brig HD6 .... 115 B3
Industrial St. Brig BD19 .... 115 F8 13
Industrial St. Hor WF4 .... 159 C8
Industrial St. Hud HD4 .... 154 A4
Industrial St. Keigh BD22 .... 35 A6
Industrial St. Leeds LS9 .... 60 F1
Industrial St. Liver FW15 ...... 116 E4
Industrial St. Tod OL14 .... 108 C5
Industrial St. Wake WF1 .... 142 C7 4
Industrial Terr. Hali HX1 .... 113 B5 2
Industrial Terr. Hud HD5 .... 155 A5
Industry St. Thorn BD13 .... 72 E6 3
Industry St. Tod OL14 .... 108 A1
Infirmary St. Brad BD1 .... 74 D7
Infirmary St. Leeds LS1 .... 79 B8
Ing Field. Brad BD12 .... 95 A4
Ing Head La. Kirkb HD4 .... 173 A2
Ing Head. Slai HD7 .... 151 E1
Ing Head Terr. Shelf HX3 .... 93 B4
Ing La. Hud HD4 .... 154 A3
Ing St. Brad BD3 .... 75 D7
Ingdale Dr. Holmfi HD7 .... 189 B6
Ingfield Ave. Hud HD5 .... 154 D6
Ingfield Ave. Ossett WF5 .... 140 E6
Ingham Cl. Hali HX2 .... 91 F8
Ingham Cl. Mir WF14 .... 138 C4
Ingham Croft. Mir WF14 .... 138 C4
Ingham Garth. Mir WF14 .... 138 C5
Ingham La. Hali HX2 .... 71 E1
Ingham Rd. Dew WF12 .... 139 D3
Ingham St. Leeds LS10 .... 79 D5
Ingham's Ave. Pudsey LS28 ..... 76 B8
Ingham's View. Pudsey LS28 .. 76 B8
Inghams Ct. Hali HX3 .... 92 A1 23
Inghams Terr. Pudsey LS28 ..... 76 B8
Inghead Gdns. Shelf HX3 .... 93 B4
Ingle Ave. Morley LS27 .... 97 F6
Ingle Cres. Morley LS27 .... 98 A5
Ingle Dean. Heb Br HX7 .... 88 D2
Ingle Gr. Morley LS27 .... 98 A5
Ingle Row. Leeds LS7 .... 60 D6
Ingleborough Dr. Morley LS27 98 C2
Ingleborough Dr. Morley LS27 98 C3
Ingleby Pl. Brad BD7 .... 74 A6
Ingleby Rd. Brad BD7, BD8 ...... 74 A7
Ingleby St. Brad BD7 .... 74 A7
Ingleby Way. Midd LS10 .... 99 E7
Ingledew Cres. Leeds LS8 .... 44 B2
Ingledew Ct. Leeds LS17 .... 43 D4
Ingledew Dr. Leeds LS8 .... 44 B2
Ingleton Cl. Leeds LS11 .... 79 B3 10
Ingleton Dr. Leeds LS15 .... 80 E7
Ingleton Gr. Leeds LS11 .... 79 B3 11
Ingleton Pl. Leeds LS11 .... 79 B3
Ingleton Rd. Hud HD4 .... 154 B2
Ingleton St. Leeds LS11 .... 79 B3 12
Inglewood App. Leeds LS14 ...... 62 B3
Inglewood Ave. Hud HD2 .... 135 C1
Inglewood Dr. Leeds LS14 .... 62 B3
Inglewood Dr. Otley LS21 .... 22 F7
Inglewood. Mapp S75 .... 178 A1
Inglewood Pl. Leeds LS14 .... 62 B3
Ingram Cl. Leeds LS11 .... 78 F5
Ingram Cres. Knot WF11 .... 126 D3
Ingram Cres. Leeds LS11 .... 78 F4
Ingram Ct. Leeds LS11 .... 79 A5 1
Ingram Gdns. Leeds LS11 .... 78 F5
Ingram Par. Roth LS26 .... 100 E5
Ingram Rd. Leeds LS11 .... 78 F5
Ingram Road Prim Sch. Leeds . 78 F5
Ingram Row. Leeds LS11 .... 79 B6
Ingram Sq. Hali HX1 .... 113 A5 22
Ingram St. Hali HX1 .... 113 A5
Ingram St. Keigh BD21 .... 35 B3
Ingram St. Leeds LS11 .... 79 B6
Ingram View. Leeds LS11 .... 78 F5 1
Ingrow Fst Sch. Keigh 35 A4
Ingrow La. Keigh BD21, BD22 . 35 A4
Ingrow West Sta. Keigh 35 B4
Ings Ave. Guise LS20 .... 22 D2
Ings Cl. Ryhill WF4 .... 162 C1
Ings Cl. S Kirk WF9 .... 182 D3
Ings Cres. Dew WF12 .... 139 C2
Ings Cres. Guise LS20 .... 22 C1
Ings Cres. Leeds LS9 .... 80 B7
Ings Cres. Liver WF15 .... 117 B4
Ings Croft. Shelf HX3 .... 93 C6
Ings Ct. Guise LS20 .... 22 C1
Ings Dr. L Brad BD20 .... 4 C5
Ings Dr. M'town LS26 .... 102 E3
Ings Holt. S Kirk WF9 .... 182 D4
Ings La. Castle WF10 .... 103 F2
Ings La. Con BD20 .... 4 A4
Ings La. Dew WF12 .... 139 C2
Ings La. Guise LS20 .... 22 C2
Ings La. L Brad BD20 .... 4 C5
Ings La. Ledst WF10 .... 103 E4
Ings La. Th Arch LS23 .... 31 A8
Ings La. Wig LS24 .... 31 F8
Ings Mere Ct. Fair WF11 .... 105 A4
Ings Mill Ave. Clay W HD8 ...... 175 F3
Ings Mill Dr. Clay W HD8 .... 175 F2
Ings Mill Yd. Batley WF16 ...... 117 D4
Ings Rd. Batley WF16 .... 117 D4
Ings Rd. Batley WF17 .... 118 A6
Ings Rd. Dew WF13 .... 118 E1
Ings Rd. Hem WF9 .... 163 B1
Ings Rd. Hud HD5 .... 155 A4
Ings Rd. Leeds LS9 .... 80 B8
Ings Rd. Liver WF15 .... 117 B5
Ings Rd. Stee BD20 .... 17 B7
Ings Rd. Wake WF1 .... 142 C5
Ings The. Brig HX3 .... 115 A6
Ings The. Clay W HD8 .... 175 F2
Ings View. Castle WF10 .... 125 B8
Ings View. M'town LS26 .... 102 E3
Ings Villa. Batley WF15 .... 117 C2
Ings Way. Brad BD8 .... 73 E8
Ings Way. Ingb BD8, S30 .... 191 D1
Ings Way. Lepton HD8 .... 155 F3
Ings Way. Sil BD20 .... 17 F8
Ings Way W. Lepton HD8 .... 155 E3
Ings Wlk. S Kirk WF9 .... 182 D3
Ingswell Ave. Notton WF4 ...... 179 A7
Ingswell Dr. Notton WF4 .... 178 F7
Ingwell Ct. Wake WF1 .... 142 D6 6
Ingwell St. Wake WF1 .... 142 D6
Ingwell Terr. Clec BD19 .... 116 E7
Inholmes La. Th Arch LS24 ...... 15 C4
Inkerman Ct. D Dale HD8 .... 192 A5
Inkerman St. Bacup OL13 ...... 106 A2 6
Inkerman St. Brad BD2 .... 56 D4
Inkerman St. Brad BD4 .... 75 D4
Inkerman Way. D Dale HD8 .. 191 F5
Inner Hey. Mars HD7 .... 169 A4
Inner Hey Yd. Mars HD7 .... 169 A4
Inner Ring Rd. Leeds LS1, LS2 . 60 C1
Institute Rd. Brad BD2 .... 56 C5
Institute St. Glu BD20 .... 16 C6
Intake Cl. Loft G WF3 .... 121 F5
Intake Gr. Brad BD2 .... 56 C2
Intake High Sch. Leeds 58 A4
Intake. Hud HD7 .... 152 E5
Intake La. Loft G WF3 .... 121 F5
Intake La. Mel HD4 .... 170 F7
Intake La. Midd LS10 .... 99 C3
Intake La. Ossett WF5 .... 140 E5
Intake La. Pudsey LS13 .... 57 F3
Intake La. Slai HD7 .... 169 F4
Intake La. Stee BD20 .... 17 B4
Intake La. Thorner LS14 .... 45 D3
Intake La. Wool WF4 .... 177 E8
Intake La. Yeadon LS19 .... 40 D3
Intake Mount. Midd LS10 .... 99 C4
Intake Rd. Brad BD2 .... 56 C2
Intake Rd. Pudsey LS28 .... 77 A8
Intake Rd. Slai HD7 .... 151 C2
Intake Sq. Midd LS10 .... 99 C3
Intake Terr. Brad BD2 .... 56 C2
Intake The. Kippax LS25 .... 83 B1
Intake View. Midd LS10 .... 99 C3
Intercity Way. Pudsey LS13 ..... 58 A1
Invargarry Cl. Gar LS25 .... 83 B8
Inverness Rd. Gar LS25 .... 83 B7
Invertrees Ave. Yeadon LS19 .. 40 C4
Iona Pl. Hali HX3 .... 92 C2 8
Iona St. Hali HX3 .... 92 C1
Ireland Cres. Hors LS16 .... 41 F3
Ireland St. Harden BD16 .... 36 E3
Ireland Terr. Harden BD16 .... 36 E3
Ireland Wood Cty Prim Sch.
Hors 42 A4
Ireton St. Brad BD7 .... 74 B6
Iron Row. Bur in W LS29 .... 9 F1
Iron St. Clec BD19 .... 116 C7
Ironwood App. Leeds LS14 .... 62 A3
Ironwood Cres. Leeds LS14 ...... 62 A3
Ironwood View. Leeds LS14 ..... 62 A4
Irvin Terr. Castle WF10 .... 124 C7
Irving St. Hali HX1 .... 112 F5 2
Irving Terr. Brad BD14 .... 73 C3
Irwell St. Brad BD4 .... 75 A5
Irwin App. Leeds LS15 .... 80 F7
Irwin Ave. Wake WF1 .... 142 F7
Irwin Cres. Wake WF1 .... 142 E7
Irwin St. Pudsey LS28 .... 57 D2
Isaac St. Brad BD8 .... 74 B8
Island The. Knot WF11 .... 127 A5
Island View. Dew WF12 .... 139 B6

Isles St. Brad BD8 73 F8
Ivanhoe Rd. Brad BD7 74 E5
Ive House La. Hali HX2 111 E8
Ivegate. Brad BD1 74 E7
Ivegate. Yeadon LS19 40 B7
Ives St. Ship BD17 55 B8
Iveson App. Hors LS16 41 F2
Iveson Cl. Hors LS16 41 F2
Iveson Cres. Hors LS16 41 F2
Iveson Dr. Hors LS16 41 F2
Iveson Garth. Hors LS16 42 A2
Iveson Gdns. Hors LS16 41 F2
Iveson Gn. Hors LS16 41 F2
Iveson Gr. Hors LS16 41 F2
Iveson House Cty Prim Annexe. Hors 41 F2
Iveson House Cty Prim Sch. Hors 42 A2
Iveson Lawn. Hors LS16 42 A2
Iveson Rd. Hors LS16 41 F2
Iveson Rise. Hors LS16 42 A2
Ivory St. Leeds LS10 79 C5
Ivy Ave. Leeds LS9 80 B8
Ivy Bank Ct. Bail BD17 38 D2 1
Ivy Bank La. Haw BD22 51 C6
Ivy Chase. Pudsey LS28 77 B7
Ivy Cl. Wake WF1 142 E8
Ivy Cotts. Roy S71 179 D4
Ivy Cres. Brig HX3 114 E7
Ivy Cres. Leeds LS9 80 A7
Ivy Cres. Leeds LS9 80 A8 10
Ivy Ct. Leeds LS7 60 D6
Ivy Farm Cl. Roy S71 179 D1
Ivy Garth. Leeds LS7 60 D6
Ivy Gdns. Castle WF10 125 D5
Ivy Gr. Leeds LS9 80 B8
Ivy Gr. Ship BD18 54 E7
Ivy Gr. Wake WF1 142 E8
Ivy La. B Spa LS23 30 C7
Ivy La. Brad BD15 54 A1
Ivy La. Hali HX2 91 D6
Ivy La. Wake WF1 142 E8
Ivy Mount. Leeds LS9 80 A8
Ivy Mount. Slai HD7 151 F1
Ivy Pl. Glu BD20 16 D7
Ivy Pl. Leeds LS13 58 D4
Ivy Rd. Keigh BD21 35 E6
Ivy Rd. Leeds LS9 80 B8
Ivy Rd. Ship BD18 54 E7
Ivy St. Brig HD6 114 F3
Ivy St. Feath WF7 145 D6
Ivy St. Hali HX1 113 A5
Ivy St. Hud HD4 153 C4
Ivy St. Hud HD4, HD5 154 C5
Ivy St. Keigh BD21 35 B8
Ivy St. Leeds LS9 80 A8
Ivy St S. Hali HX1 113 A5
Ivy St S. Keigh BD21 35 B3
Ivy Terr. Brig HX3 114 E7
Ivy Terr. Brig HD6 114 F3
Ivy Terr. Keigh BD21 35 F6
Ivy Terr. S Elm WF9 183 A3
Ivy View. Leeds LS9 80 A8 8

Jacinth Ct. Hud HD2 136 C2
Jack Bridge. B Head HX7 88 A5
Jack Close Orch. Roy S71 179 C4
Jack Field La. S in Cra BD20 16 A4
Jack Hill. Hud HD2 136 A1
Jack La. Batley WF17 118 D2
Jack La. Leeds LS11 79 B5
Jack La. Leeds LS10, LS11 79 D5
Jack Royd. Hali HX3 91 F2
Jackdaw La. B Spa LS23 30 C8
Jackie Smart Ct. Leeds LS7 60 E3
Jackie Smart Rd. Brad BD5 74 E4 1
Jackman Dr. Hors LS18 58 D7
Jackroyd La. Hud HD4 154 B2
Jackroyd La. Mir WF14 137 E2
Jackson Ave. Leeds LS8 60 F7
Jackson Hill La. Queen BD13 92 F7
Jackson House. Hem WF9 181 D6
Jackson La. Rip HX4 133 A5
Jackson Meadows. Rip HX4 133 A5
Jackson Pl. S in Cra BD20 16 D4
Jackson Rd. Leeds LS7 60 C3
Jackson St. Brad BD3 75 A6
Jackson St. S in Cra BD20 16 D5
Jackson's La. Dar WF8 165 E7
Jackson's La. Dew WF13 139 A1
Jackson's La. L Brad BD20 4 E5
Jacky La. Haw BD22 51 C6
Jacob Kramer Coll (Art). Leeds 60 B1
Jacob Kramer Coll. Leeds 60 B2
Jacob Kramer Coll. Leeds 78 F6
Jacob St. Brad BD5 74 D4
Jacob St. Leeds LS2 60 C1
Jacob's Row. Hud HD4 153 F3
Jacob's Well. Brad BD1 74 E6
Jacob's Well La. Wake WF1 142 D7
Jacques Gr. Sil BD20 5 F1
Jade Pl. Hud HD2 136 C2
Jaggar La. Honley HD7 171 F4
Jagger Green Dean. Elland HX4 134 B3
Jagger Green La. Elland HD3 134 B2
Jagger La. Emley HD8 175 E7
Jagger La. Hud HD5 155 A8
Jail Rd. Batley WF17 117 F5
Jail Yd. Roth LS26 100 F5
Jakeman Cl. E Ard WF3 119 E8
Jakeman Ct. E Ard WF3 119 E8
Jakeman Dr. E Ard WF3 119 E8
James Ave. Leeds LS8 60 F8
James Ave. Stee BD20 17 A5
James Cl. Gar LS25 83 A7
James Duggan Ave. Feath WF7 145 D6
James Gate. Brad BD1 74 E7 18
James Gibbs Cl. Feath WF7 145 D6
James La. Hud HD7 171 A6
James St. Batley WF17 118 B4
James St. Birk BD11 96 A6
James St. Brad BD15 54 C1
James St. Brad BD1 74 E7
James St. Brig HD6 115 A4
James St. Castle WF10 103 D1
James St. Dew WF13 118 B1
James St E. Keigh BD21 35 C6 8
James St. Elland HX4 134 B4
James St. Elland HX5 135 A6
James St. Glu BD20 16 D7
James St. Haw BD22 34 B2
James St. Hud HD7 152 D4
James St. Liver WF15 117 A4 8
James St. Mir WF14 138 A7
James St. S Hie S72 180 F6
James St. Slai HD7 152 A1
James St. Thorn BD13 72 D6
James St. Yeadon LS19 40 B4
Jamie Ct. Brad BD10 56 D6
Jane Hills. Ship BD17 55 A8
Jane St. Denh BD13 52 D1
Jane St. Ship BD18 54 F8
Janesway. Kippax LS25 82 F2
Janet St. Haw BD22 51 E8 5
Jaques Cl. Leeds LS6 59 B4
Jardine Ave. Feath WF7 145 D6
Jardine St. Bing BD16 37 A3 10
Jarratt St. Brad BD8 55 B1
Jarratt St E. Brad BD8 55 B1
Jarrom Cl. Brad BD4 75 D4
Jarvis House. Brad BD6 93 E8 4
Jarvis Sq. Roth WF3 100 A3
Jarvis Wlk. Roth WF3 100 A3
Jasmin Terr. Brad BD8 74 C8
Jason Terr. Batley WF17 97 A2
Jasper St. Brad BD10 56 B8
Jasper St. Hali HX1 112 F7
Javelin Cl. Brad BD10 56 B6
Jay House La. Brig HD6 115 D5
Jay St. Haw BD22 51 D6
JB Priestley Liby. Brad 74 C6
Jean Ave. Leeds LS15 81 A7
Jebb La. Caw S75 176 E3
Jebb La. H Hoy S75 176 F3
Jenkin Dr. Hor WF4 140 F1
Jenkin La. Hor WF4 140 F1
Jenkin Rd. Hor WF4 141 A1
Jenkinson Cl. Leeds LS11 79 A5
Jenkinson Lawn. Leeds LS11 79 A5
Jenkinson St. Batley WF17 118 C2
Jenkyn La. Shep HD8 190 D8
Jennetts Cres. Otley LS21 22 F7
Jennings Cl. Sil BD20 17 F8
Jennings Pl. Brad BD7 74 A4
Jennings St. Brad BD7 74 A4 7
Jenny La. Bail BD17 38 D4
Jenny La. Mir WF14 138 B7
Jensen Ave. Batley WF13 117 F3
Jepson La. Elland HX5 134 E6
Jer Gr. Brad BD7 73 E2
Jer La. Brad BD7 73 E2
Jeremy La. Batley WF16 117 D4
Jermyn St. Brad BD1 74 F7 5
Jerry Clay Dr. Wake WF2 120 E2
Jerry Clay La. Wake WF2 120 D2
Jerry Fields Rd. Sow Br HX2 111 D6
Jerry La. Add BD20 6 F1
Jerry La. Sow Br HX6 112 A3
Jersey Cl. Batley WF12 118 F2
Jerusalem La. Hali HX2 90 D4
Jerusalem Rd. Slai HD7 170 B7
Jerusalem Sq. Hali HX3 114 B4
Jervaulx Cl. B Spa LS23 30 C7
Jervaulx Cres. Brad BD8 74 D8
Jerwood Hill Cl. Hali HX3 92 D1
Jerwood Hill Rd. Hali HX3 92 D1
Jesmond Ave. Roy S71 179 C3
Jesmond Gr. Brad BD9 54 F2
Jesmond Gr. Dew WF13 118 B1
Jessamine Ave. Leeds LS11 78 F2
Jessamine Pl. Glu BD20 16 E6
Jessamine St. Dew WF13 138 D5
Jesse St. Brad BD8 73 D7
Jesse St. Brad BD8 74 B8
Jessop Ave. Hud HD5 155 A3
Jessop Fold. Honley HD7 171 F5
Jessop St. Castle WF10 124 D8
Jessop St. Wake WF2 142 C4
Jester Pl. Queen BD13 92 C8
Jew La. Oxen BD22 51 C1
Jewitt La. Coll LS22 29 C7
JH Whitley Sec Sch. Hali 91 F6
Jill La. Mir WF14 138 D8
Jilley Royd La. Hud HD2 136 A4
Jim Allen La. Hali HX2 90 C1
Jim La. Hud HD1 153 D6
Jin-Whin Hill. Castle WF10 124 A8
Jinny Moor La. Swil LS26 101 E8
Joan Royd. Batley WF16 117 D6
Joffre Ave. Castle WF10 124 E6
John Baker St. Tod OL14 107 E8
John Booth Cl. Liver WF15 116 F2
John Carr Ave. Hor WF4 141 A2
John Escritt Rd. Bing BD16 37 A2
John Haigh Rd. Slai HD7 170 A8
John Jamieson Sch. Leeds 61 C5
John Naylor La. Hali HX2 111 E5
John Nelson Cl. Batley WF17 96 F1 9
John O'Gaunts Wlk. Roth LS26 100 F6
John Ormsby VC Way. Batley WF12 119 A2
John Smeaton Community High Sch. Leeds 62 E3
John Smeaton Mid Sch. Leeds 62 E3
John Smeaton Spts Ctr. Leeds 62 E3
John St. Bail BD17 38 C1
John St. Batley WF17 96 E1 5
John St. Batley WF16 117 D3 9
John St. Brad BD14 73 C4
John St. Brad BD1 74 E7
John St. Brad BD4 75 E1
John St. Brig HD6 115 A3
John St. Castle WF10 124 C6
John St. Cull BD13 52 D6
John St. Denh BD13 52 D1
John St. Dew WF13 118 C2
John St. Dew WF13 118 E1 2
John St. Dew WF13 138 E5
John St. Elland HX4 134 C7
John St. Elland HX5 134 F6
John St. Hali HX1 113 C7 8
John St. Haw BD22 34 D2
John St. Hud HD3 153 B4
John St. Leeds LS6 59 E3
John St. S Elm WF9 182 F2
John St. Ship BD18 55 A8
John St. Thorn BD13 72 D6
John St. Tod OL14 108 B5 4
John St W. Hali HX6 112 B4 2
John St. Wake WF1 142 D6
John St. Yeadon LS19 40 B4
John Street Mkt. Brad 74 E7
John William St. Clec BD19 116 D8 3
John William St. Elland HX5 134 F6 13
John William St. Hud HD1 154 A6
John William St. Liver WF15 117 B3 1
John William St. Liver WF15 117 C4
John's Cres. Wake WF2 120 E2
Johnny La. Otley LS21 23 A6
Johns Ave. Loft G WF3 121 C6
Johns La. Elland HX5 134 F4
Johnson St. Bing BD16 36 F3
Johnson St. Brad BD3 75 D7
Johnson St. Mir WF14 138 A3
Johnson Terr. Morley LS27 98 B4 1
Johnston St. Leeds LS6 60 B4
Johnston St. Wake WF1 142 D6 10
Jonathan Garth. Sil LS29 6 E8
Jons Ave. S Kirk WF9 182 A2
Jos La. Shep HD8 190 E8
Jos Way. Shep HD8 190 E8
Joseph Ave. Northo HX3 93 A2
Joseph Crossley's Almhouses. Hali HX1 113 A6
Joseph Priestley Coll. Roth 101 B7
Joseph Priestly Coll. Gild 97 E7
Joseph Priestly Inst of F Ed. Morley 98 B2
Joseph St. Brad BD3 75 A7
Joseph St. Brad BD4 75 E1
Joseph St. Leeds LS10 79 E4
Joseph Wright Ct. Brad BD10 39 A1
Josephine Rd. Hud HD4 153 A3
Joshua St. Tod OL14 108 B6 7
Jowett House La. Caw S75 193 B4
Jowett Park Cres. Brad BD10 39 A2
Jowett St. Brad BD1 74 C7
Jowett Terr. Morley LS27 98 A2 7
Jowett's La. Sil BD20 5 D8
Jubilee Ave. Loft G WF1 121 C4
Jubilee Ave. Nor WF6 144 A8
Jubilee Ave. Shep HD8 174 A2
Jubilee Bglws. Knot WF11 126 E4
Jubilee Cl. Hem WF9 181 F6
Jubilee Cres. Birk BD11 97 A7
Jubilee Cres. Crof WF4 144 B3
Jubilee Cres. Loft G WF1 121 C4
Jubilee Croft. Birk BD11 96 F7
Jubilee Ct. Hem WF9 163 A4
Jubilee Dr. Keigh BD21 35 A5 3
Jubilee La. Hud HD4 153 A3
Jubilee Mount. Brig HD6 114 F2
Jubilee Pl. Morley LS27 98 B4 5
Jubilee Rd. Crof WF4 144 B3
Jubilee Rd. Hali HX3 113 D3
Jubilee St. Brad BD1 55 D1
Jubilee St. Brad BD4 75 D4
Jubilee St. Crig WF4 159 F3
Jubilee St. Hali HX3 113 D6
Jubilee St. Heb Br HX7 89 E1 9
Jubilee St. Morley LS27 98 B4 6
Jubilee St N. Hali HX3 92 A3
Jubilee Terr. Hali HX3 113 D6 4
Jubilee Terr. Morley LS27 98 B4 4
Jubilee Terr. Rip HX6 132 E6
Jubilee Trees. Men LS29 21 C7
Jubilee Way. Pont WF8 146 C8
Jubilee Way. Ship BD18 55 D8
Judy Haigh La. Dew WF12 157 D8
Judy La. Hud HD2 136 B3
Julian Dr. Brad BD13 73 C2
Julian St. Hud HD5 154 E5
Julie Ave. Crig WF4 159 E5
Jumb Beck Cl. Bur in W LS29 21 F8
Jumble Dyke. Brig HD6 135 F8
Jumble Hole Rd. B Head OL14 88 B1
Jumble Wood. Lepton HD8 155 D3
Jumbles Ct. Roth WF3 100 C1
Jumbles La. Roth WF3 100 C1
Jumples Cl. Hali HX2 91 D4
Jumples Crag. Hali HX2 91 D4
Jumples Ct. Hali HX2 91 D4
Jumples. Hali HX2 91 D4
Jumps La. Heb Br HX7 88 F1
Jumps La. Tod OL14 107 E8
Jumps Rd. Tod OL14 107 E8
Junction Houses. Kippax WF10 103 C1
Junction La. Ossett WF5 141 A4
Junction Rd. Dew WF13 139 B7 3
Junction Rd. Ship BD17 55 C8
Junction Row. Brad BD2 56 B4
Junction St. Leeds LS10 79 C6
Junction Terr. Brad BD2 56 B4
June St. Keigh BD21 35 C8 4
Juniper Cl. Brad BD8 74 B8
Juniper Gr. Hud HD4 171 D6
Juniper Grove Mews. Hud HD4 171 D6
Juniper Pl. Leeds LS9 61 B1
Justin Way. Hud HD4 153 A1

Kaffir Rd. Hud HD2 153 D8
Karnac Rd. Leeds LS8 60 F4
Karon Dr. Hor WF4 141 B1
Kateholm. Bacup OL13 106 A7
Katherine St. Ship BD18 54 F8 10
Katrina Gr. Feath WF7 145 D4
Kay St. Ship BD18 55 C5
Kay St. Wake WF1 142 D6
Kaycell St. Brad BD4 75 B2
Kaye Hill. Cull BD13 52 D6
Kaye La. Hud HD7 152 E3
Kaye La. Hud HD5 154 E2
Kaye St. Batley WF16 117 D3
Kaye St. Dew WF12 139 D6
Kaye's Fst Sch. Clay W 175 F2
Kearsley Terr. Midd LS10 79 E2 13
Keat St. Hud HD4 153 E4
Keats Ave. Tod OL14 108 D6
Keats Dr. Batley WF16 117 E2
Keats Gr. Loft G WF3 121 E6
Kebble Cl. Clec BD19 117 B7
Keble Garth. Kippax LS25 83 C2
Kebroyd Ave. Rip HX6 132 E7
Kebroyd La. Rip HX6 132 E7
Kebroyd Mount. Rip HX6 132 E6
Kebs Rd. Tod OL14 86 E3
Kedleston Rd. Leeds LS8 43 F3
Keeble House. Brad BD2 56 D2
Keel Moorings. Pudsey LS13 57 F5
Keeldar Cl. Brad BD7 74 B3
Keelham Fst Sch. Thorn 71 F5
Keelham La. Keigh BD20 18 A2
Keelham La. Tod OL14 87 D1
Keenan Ave. S Elm WF9 182 E1
Keeper La. Birk BD4 76 E2
Keeper La. Notton WF4 178 D5
Keeton St. Leeds LS9 79 F8
Keighley Cl. Hali HX2 91 E6
Keighley Coll (Annex). Keigh 35 D7
Keighley Dr. Hali HX2 91 E4
Keighley Golf Course. Sil 18 A4
Keighley Ind Pk. Keigh 18 C1
Keighley Pl. Pudsey LS28 57 E2 6
Keighley Prep Sch. Keigh 18 C1
Keighley Rd. Bing BD16 36 E5
Keighley Rd. Brad BD8 55 C3
Keighley Rd. Cull BD13 52 C7
Keighley Rd. Denh BD13 52 D2
Keighley Rd. Glu BD20 16 E6
Keighley Rd. Hali HX2 91 E5
Keighley Rd. Harden BD16 36 A2
Keighley Rd. Haw BD22 34 E3
Keighley Rd. Heb Br HX7 89 A4
Keighley Rd. Ilkley LS29 7 F2
Keighley Rd. L Brad BD20 4 B5
Keighley Rd. Oxen BD22 51 D3
Keighley Rd. Ship BD9 55 C3
Keighley Rd. Sil BD20 17 D8
Keighley Rd. Skip BD23 4 A8
Keighley Rd. Stee BD20 17 E5
Keighley Rd. Wad M HX7 89 B8
Keighley Road (Lidget). Haw BD22 34 D2
Keighley Sta. Keigh 35 D7
Keighley & Worth Valley Rly. Haw 34 E1
Kelburn Gr. Haw BD22 34 B3
Kelcliffe Ave. Guise LS20 22 E1
Kelcliffe Gr. Guise LS20 22 E1
Kelcliffe La. Guise LS20 22 E2
Keldholme Cl. Pudsey LS13 57 F5
Keldholme Rd. Pudsey LS13 57 F5 2
Keldregate. Hud HD2 136 E4
Kell Beck. Otley LS21 10 F2
Kell La. Hali HX2 90 E6
Kell La. Northo HX3 92 F2
Kell St. Bing BD16 37 A3 6
Kellett Ave. Leeds LS12 78 C4
Kellett Cres. Leeds LS12 78 C4
Kellett Dr. Leeds LS12 78 C4
Kellett Gr. Leeds LS12 78 C4
Kellett La. Leeds LS12 78 B5
Kellett Mount. Leeds LS12 78 C4 2
Kellett Pl. Leeds LS12 78 C4 3
Kellett Rd. Leeds LS12 78 B5
Kellett Terr. Leeds LS12 78 C4 1
Kellett Wlk. Leeds LS12 78 C4
Kelloe St. Clec BD19 95 D1
Kelmore Gr. Brad BD6 93 E7
Kelmscott Ave. Leeds LS15 62 D3
Kelmscott Cres. Leeds LS15 62 D3
Kelmscott Garth. Leeds LS15 62 E4
Kelmscott Gdns. Leeds LS15 62 D3
Kelmscott Gn. Leeds LS15 62 D3
Kelmscott Gr. Leeds LS15 62 D3
Kelmscott La. Leeds LS15 62 D3
Kelsall Ave. Leeds LS6 59 E2
Kelsall Gr. Leeds LS6 59 E2 18
Kelsall Pl. Leeds LS6 59 E2 16
Kelsall Rd. Leeds LS6 59 E2 17
Kelsall Terr. Leeds LS6 59 E2
Kelsey St. Hali HX1 112 F8 3
Kelso Gdns. Leeds LS2 59 F1
Kelso Gr. Hud HD5 155 A6
Kelso Pl. Leeds LS2 59 F2 3
Kelso Rd. Leeds LS2 59 F2
Kelso St. Leeds LS2 59 F2
Keltus Ave. Glu BD20 16 D7
Kelvin Ave. Hali HX2 112 D6
Kelvin Ave. Hud HD5 154 E6
Kelvin Cres. Hali HX2 112 D6
Kelvin Rd. Elland HX5 134 E6
Kelvin Way. Brad BD2 56 C2
Kemp's Bridge. Wake WF2 142 A6
Kemps Way. Holmfi HD7 189 E3
Kempton Rd. Kippax LS25 83 A2
Kemsing Wlk. Leeds LS15 62 F2
Ken Churchill Dr. Ossett WF4 141 A3
Kendal Bank. Leeds LS3 59 F1
Kendal Cl. Castle WF10 125 E7
Kendal Cl. Leeds LS3 59 F1
Kendal Croft. Castle WF10 125 E7
Kendal Dr. Castle WF10 125 D8
Kendal Dr. Crof WF4 143 C2
Kendal Dr. Leeds LS15 80 E7
Kendal Garth. Castle WF10 125 E7
Kendal Gdns. Castle WF10 125 E7
Kendal Gr. Leeds LS3 60 A1
Kendal La. Leeds LS3 60 A1
Kendal Rd. Leeds LS3 60 A1 2
Kendal Rise. Crof WF4 143 C2
Kendal Rise. Walton WF2 161 A6
Kendal St. Keigh BD21 35 D6
Kendal Wlk. Leeds LS3 78 F8 5
Kendall Ave. Ship BD18 54 E8
Kendell St. Leeds LS10 79 C7
Kenilworth Ave. Gild LS27 97 D6
Kenilworth Dr. Brig HX3 115 A6
Kenilworth Gdns. Gild LS27 97 D7
Kenilworth House. Brad BD15 73 B8 4
Kenilworth Rd. Leeds LS12 78 C5
Kenilworth St. Brad BD4 75 B4
Kenley Ave. Brad BD6 74 A2
Kenley Mount. Brad BD6 74 A2
Kenley Par. Brad BD6, BD7 73 F2
Kenmore Ave. Clec BD19 116 C8
Kenmore Cl. Clec BD19 116 C8
Kenmore Cres. Brad BD6 74 A2
Kenmore Cres. Clec BD19 116 C8
Kenmore Dr. Brad BD6 74 A2
Kenmore Dr. Clec BD19 116 C8
Kenmore Gr. Brad BD6 74 A2
Kenmore Gr. Clec BD19 116 C8
Kenmore Rd. Brad BD6 74 A2
Kenmore Rd. Clec BD19 116 C8
Kenmore Rd. Loft G WF2 120 F5
Kenmore View. Clec BD19 116 C8
Kenmore Way. Clec BD19 116 C8
Kenmore Wlk. Brad BD6 74 A2
Kennedy Ave. Hud HD2 136 A5
Kennedy Cl. Batley WF12 118 F3
Kennel La. Oxen BD22 50 E2
Kennel La. Sow Br HX6 132 A8
Kennels La. Bard LS14 29 C1
Kennels La. Scar LS14 46 B8
Kennerleigh Ave. Leeds LS15 62 D1
Kennerleigh Cres. Leeds LS15 62 D1
Kennerleigh Dr. Leeds LS15 62 C1
Kennerleigh Garth. Leeds LS15 62 D1
Kennerleigh Glen. Leeds LS15 62 C1 2
Kennerleigh Gr. Leeds LS15 62 D1
Kennerleigh Rise. Leeds LS15 62 C1 3
Kennerleigh Wlk. Leeds LS15 62 C1
Kennet La. Gar LS25 83 A6
Kenneth St. Leeds LS11 78 F5
Kennion St. Brad BD5 74 D5
Kensington Ave. Thorner LS14 46 A6
Kensington Cl. Batley WF17 118 B4
Kensington Cl. Hali HX3 113 A4
Kensington Gdns. Elland HX5 134 E6
Kensington Rd. Hali HX3 113 A3
Kensington Rd. Wake WF1 142 B8
Kensington St. Brad BD8 55 A1
Kensington St. Keigh BD21 35 B6 12
Kensington Terr. Gar LS25 82 E7
Kensington Terr. Leeds LS6 59 F3
Kenstone Cres. Brad BD10 56 A7
Kent Ave. Pudsey LS28 77 A7
Kent Ave. Sil BD20 5 D1
Kent Cl. Pudsey LS28 77 A7
Kent Cres. Pudsey LS28 77 A7
Kent Dr. Pudsey LS28 77 A7
Kent Rd. Bing BD16 37 B2
Kent Rd. Pudsey LS28 76 F6
Kent St. Hali HX1 113 B6
Kent Wlk. Dew WF13 139 B8 3
Kentmere App. Leeds LS14 61 F5
Kentmere Ave. Brig BD12 94 E1
Kentmere Ave. Gar LS25 83 B6
Kentmere Ave. Leeds LS14 61 F7
Kentmere Cl. Leeds LS14 62 A5
Kentmere Cres. Leeds LS14 61 F6
Kentmere Gate. Leeds LS14 61 F7
Kentmere Gdns. Leeds LS14 61 F6
Kentmere Gn. Leeds LS14 61 F6
Kentmere Rise. Leeds LS14 62 A5
Kenton Dr. Crig WF4 160 A8
Kenton Way. Brad BD4 75 D4
Kenworthy Cl. Hors LS16 42 A5
Kenworthy Garth. Hors LS16 42 A5
Kenworthy Gate. Hors LS16 42 A5
Kenworthy Gdns. Hors LS16 42 A5
Kenworthy La. Rip HX6 132 E6
Kenworthy Rise. Hors LS16 42 A5
Kenworthy Vale. Hors LS16 42 A5
Kenya Mount. Keigh BD21 34 F8
Kenyon La. Hali HX2 112 D7
Kenyon St. S Elm WF9 183 A3
Kepler Gr. Leeds LS8 60 E2 2
Kepler Mount. Leeds LS8 60 E2 3
Kepler Terr. Leeds LS8 60 E2 4
Kepstorn Cl. Leeds LS5 59 A5
Kepstorn Rd. Leeds LS16 59 B7
Kepstorn Rise. Leeds LS5 59 A5 1
Keren Gr. Wake WF2 120 E2
Kerr Mackie Prim Sch. Leeds 61 A7
Kerry Garth. Hors LS18 41 B1
Kerry Hill. Hors LS18 41 C1
Kerry Hill. Hors LS18 58 B8
Kerry St. Hors LS18 41 B1
Kershaw Ave. Castle WF10 125 B7
Kershaw Cres. Hali HX2 111 D7
Kershaw Ct. Hali HX2 111 D8
Kershaw Dene Special Sch. Hali 111 E8
Kershaw Dr. Hali HX2 111 D8
Kershaw La. Knot WF11 126 E3
Kershaw Rd. Tod OL14 108 A1
Kershaw St. Brad BD3 75 D7
Kertland St. Dew WF12 139 C7
Kester Rd. Batley WF17 117 F5
Kesteven Cl. Brad BD4 75 F2
Kesteven Ct. Brad BD4 75 F2
Kesteven Rd. Brad BD4 75 F2
Kestrel Bank. Hud HD4 171 E7
Kestrel Cl. Leeds LS17 43 F4
Kestrel Dr. Brad BD2 56 A4
Kestrel Dr. Wake WF2 160 D5
Kestrel Garth. Morley LS27 98 D4 2
Kestrel Gr. Leeds LS17 43 F4
Kestrel Mount. Brad BD2 56 A4
Keswick Cl. Hali HX3 113 E4
Keswick Cl. Tod OL14 107 F7
Keswick Dr. Castle WF10 104 E2
Keswick Dr. Wake WF2 141 E7
Keswick Grange. E Kes LS17 28 C5
Keswick La. Bard LS17 28 C4
Keswick Rd. Mapp S75 178 A3
Keswick St. Brad BD4 75 D5
Keswick View. Bard LS17 28 E5
Kettle La. Mars HD7 169 B6
Kettlethorpe Hall Dr. Wake WF2 160 C6
Kettlethorpe High Sch. Wake 160 C6
Kettlethorpe Rd. Wake WF2 160 C5
Kettlewell Dr. Brad BD5 74 B3
Kew Hill Bottom. Hud HD3 134 F3
Kew Hill. Elland HD3 134 F3
Key Hill La. Bri S72 180 F3
Key Syke La. Tod OL14 108 C5
Kidacre St. Leeds LS10 79 C5
Kiddal La. B in Elm LS15 46 E3
Kidroyd. Hud HD5 154 D4
Kidroyd La. Hud HD5 154 E4
Kilburn Cl. Hud HD5 154 D5
Kilburn La. Dew WF13 118 C1
Kilburn Rd. Leeds LS12 78 C7
Kilby St. Wake WF1 142 B7
Kildare Cres. Brad BD15 54 A1
Kildare Terr. Leeds LS12 78 E6
Kildwick CE Sch. Farnh 16 E8
Killingbeck Bridge. Leeds LS14 61 E1
Killingbeck Dr. Leeds LS14 61 E2
Killingbeck Hospl. Leeds 61 E2
Killingbeck Ret Pk. Leeds LS14 61 E2
Killinghall Ave. Brad BD2 56 B1
Killinghall Dr. Brad BD2 56 B1
Killinghall Gr. Brad BD2 56 B1
Killinghall Rd. Brad BD2, BD3 75 D8
Kiln Bent Rd. Holme HD7 198 A6
Kiln Brow. Hud HD7 152 E4
Kiln Ct. Hud HD3 134 E1
Kiln Fold. Brig HD6 115 D3
Kiln Hill La. Sil BD20 5 B5
Kiln Hill. Slai HD7 170 A8
Kiln La. Emley HD8 175 F5
Kiln La. Wad M BB10 68 D3
Kilncroft. Elland HX4 133 F3
Kilner Bank. Hud HD5 154 C7
Kilner House. Brad BD2 56 D2
Kilner Rd. Brad BD6 74 A1
Kilnhouse Bk La. Holmfi HD7 188 B1
Kilnhurst Ave. Tod OL14 108 C5 13
Kilnhurst La. Tod OL14 108 D4
Kilnhurst Mount. Tod OL14 108 D5
Kilnhurst Rd. Tod OL14 108 C5
Kilnsea Mount. Brad BD4 75 E3
Kilnsey Gr. Wake WF1 142 E8
Kilnsey Hill. Batley WF17 118 D2
Kilnsey Mews. Bail BD17 38 B3
Kilnsey Rd. Brad BD3 75 B6
Kilnsey Rd. Wake WF1 142 E8
Kilnshaw La. Heb Br HX7 109 F7
Kilpin Hill La. Batley WF13 117 F3
Kilroyd Ave. Clec BD19 95 D2
Kilroyd Dr. Clec BD19 95 E2
Kimberley Pl. Hali HX3 92 A4
Kimberley Pl. Leeds LS9 61 B2
Kimberley Rd. Leeds LS9 61 B2
Kimberley St. Brad BD4 75 C6
Kimberley St. Brig HD6 115 B3
Kimberley St. Dew WF12 139 B4
Kimberley St. Feath WF7 145 C6
Kimberley St. Hali HX3 92 A4
Kimberley St. Ilkley LS29 8 C5
Kimberley St. Wake WF1 142 D3
Kimberley View. Leeds LS9 61 B1 1
Kimberly Cl. Th Aud WF8 165 B5
Kinder Ave. Hud HD4 152 F2
Kineholme Dr. Otley LS21 22 D6
Kineton Ave. Tod OL14 108 C6
King Alfred's Dr. Leeds LS6 43 A1
King Alfred's Gn. Leeds LS6 43 A1
King Alfred's Way. Leeds LS6 43 A1
King Alfred's Wlk. Leeds LS6 43 A1
King Cl. Leeds LS17 43 A4
King Cliff Rd. Hud HD1, HD2 136 A1
King Cliffe Flats. Hud HD1 154 A8 3
King Cross Rd. Hali HX1 112 F5
King Cross Rd. Hali HX1 113 A6
King Cross St. Hali HX1 113 B6
King Dr. Leeds LS17 42 F5
King Edward Ave. Hors LS18 41 C1
King Edward Av. Kippax WF10 102 F6
King Edward Cres. Hors LS18 41 C1
King Edward Rd. Thorn BD13 72 D6 2
King Edward St. Dew WF12 139 B3
King Edward St. Hali HX1 113 C7 15
King Edward St. Hem WF9 181 E6
King Edward St. Leeds LS1 79 C8
King Edward St. Nor WF6 123 A2
King Edward St. S in Cra BD20 16 D5
King Edward Terr. Thorn BD13 72 D6 1
King Edwin's Ct. Leeds LS8 61 A5
King George Ave. Hors LS18 41 C1
King George Ave. Leeds LS7 60 D6
King George Ave. Morley LS27 98 B5
King George Croft. Morley LS27 98 B5
King George Gdns. Leeds LS7 60 D7
King George Rd. Hors LS18 41 C1
King George St. Loft G WF1 121 B3
King George V Playing Fields. Keigh 35 F8
King La. Eccup LS17 42 E6
King La. Leeds LS17 43 B3
King Royd La. W Har WF7 163 C6
King St. Batley WF16 117 D4
King St. Birk BD11 96 F6
King St. Brad BD2 56 C5
King St. Brig HD6 115 B2
King St. Castle WF10 124 E5
King St. Clec BD19 116 E8
King St. Elland HX5 135 A6
King St. Hali HX1 113 D7
King St. Heb Br HX7 88 E3
King St. Heb Br HX7 110 E8
King St. Hem WF9 163 B1
King St. Hor WF4 140 E1
King St. Hud HD3 153 C8
King St. Hud HD1 154 B6
King St. Keigh BD21 35 B6
King St. Leeds LS1 79 B7
King St. Mir WF14 138 A4
King St. Morley LS27 98 A3
King St. Nor WF6 122 F4
King St. Nor WF6 123 A1
King St. Ossett WF5 140 E4
King St. Pont WF8 146 C8
King St. Pudsey LS28 57 E1
King St. Sil BD20 5 E1
King St. Skel HD8 175 A2
King St. Sow Br HX6 111 E3
King St. Tod OL14 108 D6
King St. Wake WF1 142 C6
King St. Yeadon LS19 40 A4
King St. Yeadon LS19 40 C7
King's Ave. Leeds LS6 59 E2
King's Bridge Rd. Hud HD4 154 B4
King's Cres. Pont WF8 146 E7
King's Croft Gdns. Leeds LS17 43 D1
King's Ct. Leeds LS17 43 C1
King's Dr. Batley WF17 96 E2
King's Dr. Brad BD2 55 F6
King's Gate. Brad BD1 55 E1
King's Mead. Pont WF8 146 B7
King's Mill La. Hud HD1 154 B5
King's Mount. Knot WF11 126 B5
King's Mount. Leeds LS17 60 C8
King's Pl. Leeds LS6 59 D4
King's Rd. Bing BD16 36 E6
King's Rd. Brad BD2 55 F4
King's Rd. Cud S72 180 C1
King's Rd. Leeds LS6 59 E2
King's Sq. Leeds LS6 59 F6 4
Kingfield. Guise LS20 22 F2
Kingfisher Cl. Crig WF4 159 F7
Kingfisher Ct. Leeds LS17 43 F4
Kingfisher Gr. Brad BD8 73 C7
Kingfisher Gr. Hud HD4 171 E7
Kingfisher Gr. Wake WF2 160 D5
Kingfisher Way. Leeds LS17 43 F4
Kings Ave. Castle WF10 125 A7
Kings Ave. Ilkley LS29 8 A4
Kings Ave. Nor WF6 122 F5
Kings Chase. Roth LS26 100 F6
Kings Cl. Ack M T WF7 163 D5

Kings Cl. Ilkley LS29 7 E4
Kings Cl. Ossett WF5 140 C7
Kings Cl. Otley LS21 23 C7
Kings Cl. Pont WF8 146 C7
Kings Croft. Gar LS25 82 D6
Kings Croft. Ossett WF5 140 C8
Kings Croft. S Kirk WF9 182 B3
Kings Ct. Batley WF17 96 E1
Kings Ct. Hem WF9 163 B1
Kings Ct. S in Cra BD20 16 D4
Kings Dr. Bramho LS16 25 A1
Kings Dr. Nor WF6 122 F5
Kings Gr. Bing BD16 37 A4
Kings Head Dr. Mir WF14 137 F6 2
Kings Head Rd. Mir WF14 137 F6
Kings Lea. Batley WF15 117 C2
Kings Lea. Hali HX3 113 B2
Kings Lea. Ossett WF5 140 C8
Kings Mead. Roth LS26 101 A6
Kings Meadow Cl. Weth LS22 13 D7
Kings Meadow Dr. Weth LS22 13 D7
Kings Meadow Gr. Weth LS22 13 D7
Kings Meadow Mews. Weth LS22 13 D7
Kings Meadow. Ossett WF5 140 C7
Kings Meadow View. Weth LS22 13 D7
Kings Mount. Rip HX6 132 F3
Kings Paddock. Ossett WF5 140 C7
Kings Rd. Bramho LS16 25 B1
Kings Rd. Eccup LS16 25 B1
Kings Rd. Ilkley LS29 7 F4
Kings Rd. Nor WF6 122 E6
Kings View. Hali HX3 114 A4
Kingsbury Pl. Hali HX1 112 F7 13
Kingsdale Ave. Birk BD11 96 E6
Kingsdale Ave. Brad BD2 56 A3
Kingsdale Cres. Brad BD2 56 A3
Kingsdale Ct. Leeds LS14 61 E6
Kingsdale Dr. Brad BD2 56 A3
Kingsdale Gdns. Birk BD11 96 E6
Kingsdale Gr. Brad BD2 55 F3
Kingsland Ct. Roy S71 179 D4
Kingsley Ave. Birk BD11 96 B4
Kingsley Ave. Brad BD2 55 E3
Kingsley Ave. Crof WF4 143 E2
Kingsley Ave. Feath WF7 145 D8
Kingsley Ave. Hors LS16 42 B5
Kingsley Ave. Hud HD1 153 E4
Kingsley Ave. Knot WF11 126 C5
Kingsley Ave. Loft G WF1 121 B5
Kingsley Ave. Sow Br HX6 111 F3
Kingsley Ave. Wake WF2 160 D6
Kingsley Ave. Wake WF2 160 D7
Kingsley Cl. Birk BD11 96 B4
Kingsley Cl. Crof WF4 143 E2
Kingsley Cl. Loft G WF1 121 B5
Kingsley Cl. Wake WF2 160 C6
Kingsley Cres. Bail BD17 38 C2
Kingsley Cres. Birk BD11 96 B4
Kingsley Dr. Birk BD11 96 B4
Kingsley Dr. Hors LS16 42 B5
Kingsley Garth. Loft G WF1 121 B5
Kingsley Pl. Hali HX1 113 A6 4
Kingsley Rd. Hors LS16 42 B5
Kingsmead Dr. Leeds LS14 44 F1
Kingsmead. Leeds LS14 62 A8
Kingsmead. Ossett WF5 140 C8
Kingsmill Cl. Morley LS27 97 F5
Kingston Ave. Hud HD5 154 E6
Kingston Cl. Hali HX1 112 F6
Kingston Cl. Wils BD15 53 C5
Kingston Ct. Hali HX1 112 F6
Kingston Dr. Hali HX1 112 F6
Kingston Gdns. Leeds LS15 62 B2
Kingston Gr. Brad BD10 39 B1
Kingston Rd. Brad BD10 39 B1
Kingston St. Hali HX1 112 F6
Kingston Terr. Leeds LS2 60 B2
Kingsway. Batley WF17 96 E2
Kingsway. Bing BD16 37 A2
Kingsway. Birk BD11 96 F6
Kingsway. Brad BD2 55 F6
Kingsway Cl. Ossett WF5 140 C7
Kingsway Ct. Leeds LS17 43 D1
Kingsway. Dew WF12 139 D8 1
Kingsway Dr. Ilkley LS29 8 A4
Kingsway. Gar LS25 82 D6
Kingsway Garth. Gar LS25 82 D6
Kingsway. Keigh BD20 19 A1
Kingsway. Leeds LS15 81 C8
Kingsway. Loft G WF3 121 F2
Kingsway. Mapp S75 178 A1
Kingsway. Nor WF6 144 A8
Kingsway. Ossett WF5 140 C6
Kingsway. Pont WF8 125 D3
Kingswear Cl. Leeds LS15 62 D1
Kingswear Cres. Leeds LS15 62 D1
Kingswear Garth. Leeds LS15 62 D1
Kingswear Glen. Leeds LS15 62 D1
Kingswear Gr. Leeds LS15 62 D1
Kingswear Par. Leeds LS15 62 D1
Kingswear Rise. Leeds LS15 62 D1 4
Kingswear View. Leeds LS15 62 D1
Kingswell Ave. Loft G WF1 121 C4
Kingswood Ave. Leeds LS8 44 A3
Kingswood Cres. Leeds LS8 43 F3
Kingswood Dr. Leeds LS8 43 F3
Kingswood Gdns. Leeds LS8 43 F3
Kingswood Gn. Northo HX3 92 F1
Kingswood Gr. Leeds LS8 44 A3
Kingswood Pl. Brad BD7 74 A4 8
Kingswood St. Brad BD7 74 A4
Kingswood Terr. Brad BD7 74 A4 9
Kinnaird Cl. Batley WF17 118 F5
Kinnaird Cl. Hali HX5 134 F8
Kinsley House Cres. Hem WF9 163 A2
Kinsley St. Hem WF9 163 B1
Kipling Cl. Hud HD4 153 D3
Kipling Ct. Brad BD10 56 D7
Kipling Gr. Pont WF8 125 D3
Kippax Greenfield Prim Sch. Kippax 83 A2
Kippax Inf Sch. Kippax 83 B1
Kippax Mount. Leeds LS9 79 F7 9
Kippax North Jun & Inf Sch. Kippax 82 F4
Kippax Pl. Leeds LS9 79 F6
Kipping La. Thorn BD13 72 D6
Kipping Pl. Thorn BD13 72 D6 6
Kirby Cote La. Heb Br HX7 110 D3
Kirby Row. Kirkhe HD5 137 C1
Kirby St. Keigh BD21 18 D1
Kirk Beeston Cl. Leeds LS11 78 F2
Kirk Bridge La. Holmfi HD7 189 D7
Kirk Cl. Dew WF12 140 B8
Kirk Cross Cres. Roy S71 179 C2
Kirk Dr. Bail BD17 38 D4
Kirk Hills. Thorner LS14 46 A5
Kirk La. Brig HX3 114 C8
Kirk La Mills. Yeadon 40 A7
Kirk La. Yeadon LS19 40 A7
Kirk Lea Cres. Hud HD3 135 C1
Kirk Smeaton CE (C) Sch. K Smea 166 D6
Kirkbourne Gr. Bail BD17 38 E2
Kirkbridge Way. S Elm WF9 182 F3
Kirkburn Pl. Brad BD7 74 B6
Kirkburton CE Sch. Kirkb 173 F6
Kirkburton Mid Sch. Kirkb 174 A7
Kirkby Ave. Gar LS25 83 A5
Kirkby Cl. S Kirk WF9 182 C3
Kirkby La. Emley HD8, WF4 175 B8
Kirkby La. Sickl LS22 12 A5
Kirkby Leas. Hali HX1 113 C6
Kirkby Rd. Hem WF9 181 E6
Kirkbygate. Hem WF9 181 E5
Kirkdale Ave. Leeds LS12 78 B4
Kirkdale. Castle WF10 125 C8
Kirkdale Cres. Leeds LS12 78 B3
Kirkdale Dr. Crig WF4 159 D6
Kirkdale Dr. Leeds LS12 78 B4
Kirkdale Gdns. Leeds LS12 78 B4
Kirkdale Gr. Leeds LS12 78 A4
Kirkdale Mount. Leeds LS12 78 B4
Kirkdale Terr. Leeds LS12 78 B3
Kirkdale View. Leeds LS12 78 B4
Kirkfield Ave. Thorner LS14 46 A6
Kirkfield Cl. Caw S75 193 F4
Kirkfield Cres. Thorner LS14 46 A6
Kirkfield Dr. Leeds LS15 81 D7
Kirkfield Gdns. Leeds LS15 81 D7
Kirkfield La. Thorner LS14 46 A5
Kirkfield View. Leeds LS15 81 D7
Kirkfield Way. Roy S71 179 C2
Kirkfields. Bail BD17 38 E3
Kirkgate Arc. Otley LS21 23 A7
Kirkgate. Batley WF17 96 D1
Kirkgate. Batley WF12 118 F3
Kirkgate. Brad BD1 74 E7
Kirkgate Bsns Ctr. Wake 142 D5
Kirkgate Ctr. Brad 74 E7
Kirkgate. Farnh BD20 16 E8
Kirkgate. Hud HD1 154 B6
Kirkgate La. S Hie S72 180 C6
Kirkgate. Leeds LS1, LS2 79 C7
Kirkgate Mkt. Leeds 79 C8
Kirkgate. Otley LS21 23 A7
Kirkgate. Ship BD18 55 A8
Kirkgate. Sil BD20 5 E1
Kirkgate Sta. Wake 142 D5
Kirkgate. Wake WF1 142 D6
Kirkham Ave. Wake WF2 120 B3
Kirkham Rd. Brad BD7 74 B5
Kirkham St. Pudsey LS13 57 F5
Kirkhamgate Jun & Inf Sch. Wake 120 B2
Kirkhaw La. Castle WF11 126 B6
Kirkheaton Fst Sch. Kirkhe 137 B1
Kirklands Ave. Bail BD17 38 E3
Kirklands Cl. Bail BD17 38 E2
Kirklands Cl. Men LS29 22 A4
Kirklands Cl. Yeadon LS19 40 A8
Kirklands Ct. Bail BD17 38 E3
Kirklands Gdns. Bail BD17 38 E3
Kirklands. Holmfi HD7 189 D7
Kirklands La. Bail BD17 38 E3
Kirklands. Liver WF15 117 A4
Kirklands Rd. Bail BD17 38 E3
Kirklands. Thorner LS14 45 F5
Kirklea. Shep HD8 174 C3
Kirklees Cl. Pudsey LS28 57 E4
Kirklees Croft. Pudsey LS28 57 D4
Kirklees Dr. Pudsey LS28 57 D4
Kirklees Garth. Pudsey LS28 57 D4
Kirklees Light Rly. Clay W 175 D3
Kirklees Rd. Brad BD15 73 B7
Kirklees Rise. Pudsey LS28 57 D4
Kirkley Ave. Brad BD12 94 C1
Kirkroyds Inf Sch. Holmfi 189 D7
Kirkroyds La. Holmfi HD7 189 D7
Kirkstall Abbey. Leeds 58 F5
Kirkstall Ave. Leeds LS5 58 F3
Kirkstall Ctr The. Leeds 59 D1
Kirkstall Gr. Brad BD8 73 D7
Kirkstall Hill. Leeds LS4, LS5 59 B3
Kirkstall La. Leeds LS5, LS6 59 B4
Kirkstall Mount. Leeds LS5 58 F3
Kirkstall Rd. Leeds LS4 59 C2
Kirkstall St Stephen's CE Prim Sch. Leeds 59 A4
Kirkstall Valley Prim Sch. Leeds 59 C2
Kirkstone Ave. Hud HD5 154 C6
Kirkstone Dr. Clec BD19 117 B8
Kirkstone Dr. Hali HX2 112 C8
Kirkthorpe La. Crof WF1 143 C6
Kirkwall Ave. Leeds LS9 80 B7 3
Kirkwall Dr. Brad BD4 75 E3
Kirkwall House. Brad BD15 73 B8 7
Kirkwood Ave. Hors LS16 41 D4
Kirkwood Cl. Hors LS16 41 D4
Kirkwood Cres. Hors LS16 41 E5
Kirkwood Dr. Hors LS16 41 E5
Kirkwood Dr. Hud HD3 153 B8
Kirkwood Gdns. Hors LS16 41 E5
Kirkwood Gn. Hud HD3 153 B8
Kirkwood Gr. E Ard LS16, WF3 119 F8
Kirkwood Gr. Hors LS16 41 D4
Kirkwood La. Hors LS16 41 D5
Kirkwood Rise. Hors LS16 41 E5
Kirkwood View. Hors LS16 41 E5
Kirkwood Way. Hors LS16 41 E5
Kistyaen Gdns. Mel HD7 170 C3
Kit La. Sil BD20 5 C6
Kit Wood Cl. Brad BD4 75 F2
Kitchen Fold. Slai HD7 170 A8
Kitchener Ave. Leeds LS9 61 B2
Kitchener Gr. Leeds LS9 61 B2
Kitchener Mount. Leeds LS9 61 B1 3
Kitchener St. Brad BD12 95 A5
Kitchener St. Leeds LS9 61 B1
Kitchener St. Roth LS26 101 C6 5
Kitson Cl. Leeds LS12 78 C6
Kitson Coll. Leeds 99 B8
Kitson Gdns. Leeds LS12 78 C6
Kitson Hill Cres. Mir WF14 137 F6
Kitson Hill Rd. Mir WF14 137 F7
Kitson La. Sow Br HX6 112 D1
Kitson Rd. Leeds LS10 79 D5
Kitson St. E Ard WF3 98 D1
Kitson St. Leeds LS9 79 F7
Kitson St. Ship BD18 55 C7
Kitson Wood Rd. Tod OL14 107 E8
Kliffen Pl. Hali HX3 113 D4
Knaresborough Dr. Hud HD2 136 A2
Knight St. Hali HX1 112 F6
Knight St. Hud HD1 154 B7
Knight's Fold. Brad BD7 74 A4
Knights Croft. Weth LS22 13 F7
Knightsclose. Leeds LS15 81 C8
Knightscroft Ave. Roth LS26 100 E6
Knightscroft Dr. Roth LS26 100 E6
Knightscroft Par. S Elm WF9 183 A2
Knightshill. Leeds LS15 81 D8
Knightsway. Gar LS25 82 E6
Knightsway. Leeds LS15 81 C8
Knightsway. Roth WF3 100 B2
Knightsway. Wake WF2 160 C6
Knoll Cl. Ossett WF5 140 E7
Knoll Gdns. Bail BD17 38 B1
Knoll La. Holmfi HD7 188 D8
Knoll Park Dr. Bail BD17 38 B1
Knoll Pk. E Ard WF3 120 D7
Knoll View. Bail BD17 38 B2
Knoll Wood Pk. Hors LS18 58 D8
Knott La. Stee BD20 16 F5
Knott La. Yeadon LS19 40 E1
Knottingley CE (C) Prim Sch. Knot 127 A4
Knottingley Cty Prim Sch. Knot 127 A3
Knottingley Ferrybridge Fst Sch. Knot 126 C5
Knottingley Ferrybridge Roundhill Mid Sch. Knot 126 B5
Knottingley High Sch. Knot 127 A2
Knottingley Rd. Pont WF8 126 B2
Knottingley Sta. Knot 126 E4
Knottingley Vale Jun & Inf Sch. Knot 126 D4
Knotts Rd. Tod OL14 107 D8
Knotty La. Lepton HD8 156 A3
Knowl Gr. Mir WF14 138 A5
Knowl Rd. Holme HD7 187 E4
Knowl Rd. Hud HD7 152 E4
Knowl Rd. Mir WF14 138 A5
Knowl The. Mir WF14 137 F5 9
Knowl Top. Hep HX7 88 C6
Knowle Ave. Hud HD5 154 E5
Knowle Ave. Leeds LS4 59 D3
Knowle Gr. Leeds LS4 59 D3
Knowle La. Brad BD12 94 D2
Knowle La. Mel HD7 171 A2
Knowle Mount. Leeds LS4 59 D3
Knowle Park Ave. Shep HD8 190 F8
Knowle Pl. Leeds LS4 59 D3 11
Knowle Rd. Leeds LS4 59 D3
Knowle Rd. Slai HD7 152 A1
Knowle Sch. Mir 138 A6
Knowle Spring Rd. Keigh BD21 35 B5 1
Knowle Terr. Leeds LS4 59 D3
Knowle The. Shep HD8 190 F8
Knowle Top Dr. Brig HX3 114 E8
Knowle Top Rd. Brig HX3 114 E8
Knowler Cl. Liver WF15 117 A5
Knowler Hill. Liver WF15 117 A5
Knowler Way. Liver WF15 117 A5
Knowles Ave. Brad BD4 75 D2
Knowles Croft. Dew WF13 117 F2 8
Knowles Hill. Dew WF13 117 F2 6
Knowles Hill Rd. Batley WF13 117 F1
Knowles La. Batley WF17 118 B4
Knowles La. Brad BD4 75 D2
Knowles La. Clec BD19 96 B2
Knowles Rd. Batley WF17 118 B4
Knowles Rd. Brig HD6 136 B8
Knowles St. Brad BD4 75 C2
Knowles St. Denh BD13 71 D8
Knowles View. Brad BD4 75 D2
Knowlwood Rd. Tod OL14 108 A3
Knowsley Ave. Tod OL14 108 A1 14
Knowsley St. Brad BD3 75 A6
Knowsthorpe Cres. Leeds LS9 79 F5
Knowsthorpe Gate. Leeds LS9 80 B5
Knowsthorpe La. Leeds LS9 80 B4
Knowsthorpe La. Leeds LS9 80 E2
Knowsthorpe Rd. Leeds LS9 80 C4
Knowsthorpe Way. Leeds LS9 80 B4
Knox St. Pudsey LS13 57 D5
Knutsford Gr. Brad BD4 75 E2
Krives La. Slai HD7 169 E5
Kyffin Ave. Leeds LS15 80 E8
Kyffin Pl. Brad BD4 75 E5

Laburnum Cl. E Ard WF3 120 C7
Laburnum Ct. Castle WF10 124 E6
Laburnum Ct. Hor WF4 140 F1
Laburnum Dr. Bail BD17 38 D4
Laburnum Gr. Brig HX3 115 A6
Laburnum Gr. Clec BD19 96 A1
Laburnum Gr. Haw BD22 51 E8
Laburnum Gr. Hor WF4 140 F1
Laburnum Gr. Hud HD7 152 F5
Laburnum Gr. Skel HD8 175 A1
Laburnum Pl. Brad BD8 55 C1
Laburnum Pl. Brad BD10 56 E8
Laburnum Rd. Batley FW13 117 E2
Laburnum Rd. Ship BD18 55 D5
Laburnum Rd. Wake WF1 142 B7
Laburnum St. Brad BD8 55 C1
Laburnum St. Pudsey LS28 57 D1
Laburnum St. Pudsey LS28 76 C8
Laburnum Terr. Hud HD1 154 B8
Lacey St. Dew WF13 139 B8
Lacey St. Hor WF4 141 C2
Lacy Ave. Tod OL14 108 A1
Lacy Gr. Weth LS22 13 F4
Lacy St. Hem WF9 181 C7
Lacy Way. Hali HX5 135 A8
Ladbroke Gr. Brad BD4 75 E1
Ladderbanks La. Bail BD17 38 D4
Ladderbanks Mid Sch. Bail 38 E4
Ladstone Towers. Hali HX6 112 B4
Lady Ann Rd. Batley WF17 118 E5
Lady Anne Bsns Pk. Batley 118 E6
Lady Balk La. Pont WF8 125 D3
Lady Beck Cl. Leeds LS2 79 D8 4
Lady Cl. Ossett WF5 140 C8
Lady E Hastings Sch. Ledsh 104 D8
Lady Elizabeth Hastings CE Sch. Coll 13 A1
Lady Elizabeth Hastings CE Sch. Th Arch 14 E1
Lady Heton Ave. Mir WF14 137 F6
Lady Heton Dr. Mir WF14 137 E6
Lady Heton Gr. Mir WF14 137 E6
Lady Hetton Cl. Mir WF14 137 E6
Lady House La. Hud HD4 172 A8
Lady La. Bing BD16 37 A5
Lady La. Leeds LS2 79 D8
Lady La. Wake WF2 142 B5
Lady Lane Park Sch. Bing 37 A5
Lady Park Ave. Bing BD16 37 A5
Lady Pit La. Leeds LS11 79 B3
Lady Wood Rd. Leeds LS8 61 B6
Ladybower Ave. Hud HD4 152 F2
Ladyroyd Dr. Birk BD4 95 E6
Ladysmith Rd. Queen BD13 92 C8
Ladywell Cl. Brad BD5 74 E3
Ladywell La. Clec WF15 116 B3
Ladywood Grange. Leeds LS8 61 D6
Ladywood Mead. Leeds LS8 61 D6
Ladywood Terr. Hali HX1 113 A8
Ladywood Way. Dew WF13 138 E4
Lafflands La. Ryhill WF4 162 B1
Lairum Rise. B Spa LS23 30 D5
Laisterdyke. Brad BD4 75 D6
Laisterdyke Mid Sch. Brad 75 D7
Laisteridge La. Brad BD5, BD7 74 C5
Laith Cl. Hors LS16 41 F3
Laith Garth. Hors LS16 41 F3
Laith Gdns. Hors LS16 42 A3
Laith Gn. Hors LS16 41 F3
Laith Rd. Hors LS16 41 F3
Laith Staid La. S in Elm LS25 65 F1
Laithe Ave. Holmfi HD7 188 C2
Laithe Bank Dr. Holmfi HD7 188 C2
Laithe Cl. Sil BD20 5 E2
Laithe Field. Elland HX4 133 D5
Laithe Gr. Brad BD6 74 B1
Laithe Rd. Brad BD6 74 B1
Laithecroft Rd. Batley WF17 118 E5
Laithes Croft. Dew WF12 139 E7
Laithes Dr. Wake WF2 141 D7
Lake Lock Dr. Loft G WF3 122 A6
Lake Lock Gr. Loft G WF3 122 A5
Lake Lock Rd. Loft G WF3 122 A5
Lake Row. Brad BD4 75 B5
Lake St. Brad BD4 75 B5
Lake St. Keigh BD21 18 E1
Lake Terr. Leeds LS10 79 D2
Lake View. Crig WF2 160 C4
Lake View. Hali HX3 113 B8
Lake View. Hud HD4 171 E8
Lake View. Pont WF8 125 C3
Lake Yd. Loft G WF3 122 A5
Lakeland Cres. Leeds LS17 43 A6
Lakeland Ct. Leeds LS15 80 D6
Lakeland Dr. Leeds LS17 43 B6
Lakeland Way. Walton WF2 161 A6
Lakeside Chase. Yeadon LS19 40 C4
Lakeside Cl. Ilkley LS29 8 B5
Lakeside Ct. Hud HD3 153 B8
Lakeside Ct. Leeds LS10 79 D2
Lakeside Est. Ryhill WF4 162 B2
Lakeside Gdns. Yeadon LS19 40 C4
Lakeside Ind Est. Leeds 77 E7
Lakeside. Keigh BD20 19 E2
Lakeside. Mars HD7 169 A4
Lakeside Rd. Leeds LS12 77 E6
Lakeside Terr. Yeadon LS19 40 C4
Lakeside View. Yeadon LS19 40 C4
Lakeside Wlk. Yeadon LS19 40 C4
Lakeview Ct. Leeds LS8 61 C8
Lamb Cote Rd. Hud HD2 136 D6
Lamb Hall Rd. Hud HD3 152 E8
Lamb Inn Rd. Knot WF11 127 A4
Lambert Ave. Leeds LS8 60 F6
Lambert Cl. Elland HX4 134 D7
Lambert Dr. Leeds LS8 60 F6
Lambert Pl. Brad BD2 56 B2
Lambert St. Elland HX4 134 D7 2
Lambert Terr. Hors LS18 41 E1
Lambourne Ave. Brad BD10 56 E5
Lambrigg Cres. Leeds LS14 62 A4
Lambton Gr. Leeds LS8 60 F4 27
Lambton Pl. Leeds LS8 60 F4 25
Lambton St. Leeds LS8 60 F4 23
Lambton Terr. Leeds LS8 60 F4 24
Lambton View. Leeds LS8 60 F4 26
Lamma Well Rd. Holmfi HD7 189 A2
Lampards Cl. Brad BD15 54 A2
Lamplands. Batley WF17 118 D6
Lanark Dr. Hors LS18 41 B4
Lanark Rise. Crof WF4 162 A8
Lancaster Cl. Pont WF8 146 D6
Lancaster Cres. Hud HD5 154 F4
Lancaster Ct. Keigh BD21 35 B5 9
Lancaster La. Holmfi HD7 172 C1
Lancaster St. Castle WF10 104 D1
Lancaster St. Dearne S63 194 E1
Lancastre Ave. Leeds LS5 58 F3
Lancastre Gr. Leeds LS5 58 F3
Land St. Pudsey LS28 57 D3
Land's Bldgs. Ossett WF5 140 D7
Landor St. Keigh BD21 35 D8
Lands Beck Way. Liver WF15 116 F4
Lands Head La. Northo HX3 93 A4
Lands La. Brad BD10 56 C5
Lands La. Guise LS20 22 E1
Lands La. Leeds LS1 79 C8
Landscove Ave. Brad BD4 75 F2
Landsdown Ave. S Kirk WF9 182 A1
Landseer Ave. E Ard WF3 119 E8
Landseer Ave. Leeds LS13 58 E3
Landseer Cl. Leeds LS13 58 D3
Landseer Cres. Leeds LS13 58 E3
Landseer Dr. Leeds LS13 58 E3
Landseer Gdns. Leeds LS13 58 E3
Landseer Gn. Leeds LS13 58 D3
Landseer Gr. Leeds LS13 58 E3
Landseer Mount. Leeds LS13 58 E3
Landseer Rd. Leeds LS13 58 D3
Landseer Rise. Leeds LS13 58 D3
Landseer Terr. Leeds LS13 58 E3
Landseer View. Leeds LS13 58 E3
Landseer Way. Leeds LS13 58 E3
Landseer Wlk. Leeds LS13 58 D3
Landsholme Ct. Brad BD4 75 F2
Landsmoor Gr. Bing BD16 37 C5
Lane and Dowry Rd. Slai HD7 169 F7
Lane Bottom. B Head HX7 87 F4
Lane Cotts. Roy S71 179 C3
Lane Court No 1. Brig HD6 115 B3 6
Lane Court No 2. Brig HD6 115 B3 7
Lane End. Bail BD17 38 C3
Lane End Croft. Leeds LS17 42 F5
Lane End Ct. Leeds LS17 42 F5
Lane End Fold. Pudsey LS28 76 F8
Lane End La. Bacup OL13 106 A1 2
Lane End Mount. Pudsey LS28 76 F8
Lane End Pl. Leeds LS11 79 B5
Lane End. Pudsey LS28 76 F8
Lane End Rd. Bacup OL13 106 A1
Lane End. Thorn BD13 72 D6
Lane Ends Cl. Brad BD8 73 F8
Lane Ends Cl. Hem WF9 163 A4
Lane Ends Gn. Brig HX3 114 C8
Lane Ends. Hali HX2, HX3 91 E3
Lane Ends La. Wad M HX7 89 C4
Lane Ends Terr. Brig HX3 114 C8
Lane Ends View. Loft G WF3 121 E5
Lane Fox Ct. Yeadon LS19 40 B6 7
Lane Hackings. D Dale HD8 191 E7
Lane Hackings Gn. D Dale HD8 191 E7
Lane Head Cl. Mapp S75 178 A2
Lane Head. Hep HX7 88 E5
Lane Head La. Hali HX2 91 D8
Lane Head La. Kirkb HD8 173 F6
Lane Head Rd. Caw S75 193 D3
Lane Head Rd. Rip HX6 132 C5
Lane Head Rd. Shep HD8 190 E7
Lane Head Rise. Mapp S75 178 A2
Lane House Gr. Hali HX2 111 E8
Lane Ings. Mars HD7 169 A4
Lane Side. Bacup OL13 106 A4
Lane Side Cl. Brad BD12 94 C4
Lane Side La. Kirkhe HD5 155 D7
Lane Side. Queen BD13 72 D3
Lane Side. Wils BD15 53 C4
Lane The. Leeds LS17 42 F5
Lane The. Leeds LS9 79 E7
Lane Top. Denh BD13 52 D2
Lane Top. Hud HD7 152 E1
Lanes The. Pudsey LS28 76 F8
Laneside Cl. Morley LS27 98 B7
Laneside. Elland HX4 134 A4
Laneside Fold. Morley LS27 98 B7 11
Laneside Gdns. Morley LS27 98 B8
Laneside. Kirkb HD8 174 A6
Laneside. Morley LS27 98 B7
Laneside St. Tod OL14 108 A4
Lang Kirk Cl. Farnh BD20 4 E1
Lang La. Ship BD2 55 D5
Langbar App. Leeds LS14 62 D6
Langbar Ave. Brad BD9 54 D3
Langbar Cl. Leeds LS14 62 D6
Langbar Garth. Leeds LS14 62 D6
Langbar Gdns. Leeds LS14 62 D5 2
Langbar Gn. Leeds LS14 62 D6
Langbar Gr. Leeds LS14 62 D5
Langbar Grange. Leeds LS14 62 D5 14
Langbar Pl. Leeds LS14 62 D6
Langbar Rd. Ilkley LS29 8 A6
Langbar Rd. Leeds LS14 62 D5
Langbar Sq. Leeds LS14 62 D5 1
Langbar Towers. Leeds LS14 62 D5 3
Langbar View. Leeds LS14 62 D6
Langcliffe Cl. Mapp S75 178 A2
Langdale Ave. Brad BD8 73 E8
Langdale Ave. Brig BD12 94 E1
Langdale Ave. Leeds LS6 59 C4
Langdale Ave. Loft G WF1 121 D5
Langdale Ave. Nor WF6 123 A4
Langdale Cl. Castle WF10 104 E2
Langdale Cl. Weth LS22 13 D6
Langdale Cres. Hali HX2 91 E1
Langdale Ct. Bing BD16 37 A4
Langdale Dr. Ack M T WF7 164 C7
Langdale Dr. Hud HD5 154 D7
Langdale Dr. Nor WF6 123 A4
Langdale Dr. Queen BD13 72 D1 2
Langdale Dr. Wake WF2 141 F6
Langdale Gdns. Leeds LS6 59 C4
Langdale Jun & Inf Sch. Roth 101 B7
Langdale Mews. Nor WF6 123 A4
Langdale Mount. Walton WF2 161 A6
Langdale Rd. Batley WF12 118 F2
Langdale Rd. Brad BD10 56 E4
Langdale Rd. Roth LS26 101 B6
Langdale Sq. Wake WF2 141 F6
Langdale St. Elland HX5 134 F6
Langdale Terr. Leeds LS6 59 C4
Langford Cl. Bur in W LS29 9 E1
Langford Ct. Bur in W LS29 9 E1
Langford La. Bur in W LS29 9 E1
Langford Mews. Bur in W LS29 9 E1
Langford Rd. Bur in W LS29 9 E1
Langford Ride. Bur in W LS29 9 F1
Langlands Rd. Ship BD16 54 A7
Langlea Terr. Brig HX3 114 C8
Langley Ave. Bing BD16 37 A4
Langley Ave. Brad BD4 75 C1
Langley Ave. Leeds LS13 58 A4
Langley Cl. Leeds LS13 58 A4
Langley Cres. Bail BD17 38 E3
Langley Cres. Leeds LS13 58 B4
Langley Garth. Leeds LS13 58 A4
Langley Gr. Bing BD16 37 A4
Langley La. Bail BD17 38 E4
Langley La. Clay W HD8 175 E2
Langley La. Clay W HD8 175 E4
Langley Mount. Leeds LS13 58 B4
Langley Pl. Leeds LS13 58 A4 3
Langley Rd. Bing BD16 37 A4
Langley Rd. Leeds LS13 58 B4
Langley Terr. Hud HD3 153 A8
Langport Cl. Queen BD13 72 F1
Langsett Croft. Hud HD2 136 E5
Langsett Rd. Wake WF2 160 B5
Langthorne Cres. Morley LS27 98 C2
Langthwaite Grange Ind Est. S Kirk 182 D2
Langthwaite La. S Elm WF9 182 E2
Langthwaite Rd. S Kirk WF9 182 D2
Langton Ave. Brad BD4 75 C1
Langton Cl. Clec BD19 96 A2
Langton St. Hali HX6 112 B5
Langwith Ave. Coll LS22 29 A8
Langwith Dr. Coll LS22 28 E8
Langwith Mews. Coll LS22 29 A8
Langwith Valley Rd. Coll LS22 28 E8
Lansdale Ct. Brad BD4 75 F2
Lansdowne Ave. Castle WF10 124 F7
Lansdowne Cl. Bail BD17 38 F3
Lansdowne Cl. Batley WF17 118 C6
Lansdowne Pl. Brad BD5 74 D6
Lansdowne St. Leeds LS12 78 A6
Lanshaw Bank. Beam BD23 3 B6
Lanshaw Cl. Midd LS10 99 E6
Lanshaw Cres. Midd LS10 99 E5
Lanshaw Pl. Midd LS10 99 E6
Lanshaw Rd. Midd LS10 99 E6
Lanshaw Terr. Midd LS10 99 E6
Lanshaw View. Midd LS10 99 E6
Lapage Mid Sch. Brad 75 C8
Lapage St. Brad BD3 75 C7
Lapage Terr. Brad BD3 75 C6
Lapwing Cl. Brad BD8 73 B7
Larch Ave. Holmfi HD7 189 C8
Larch Cl. Batley WF17 97 A2
Larch Cl. Haw BD22 34 D2
Larch Cl. Kirkhe HD5 137 B1
Larch Cl. Liver WF15 117 C3
Larch Cl. Nor WF6 144 B8
Larch Ct. Castle WF10 124 E6
Larch Dale. Hud HD2 136 A4
Larch Dr. Brad BD6 94 D7
Larch Gr. Bing BD16 36 F5
Larch Hill. Brad BD6 94 D7
Larch Hill Cres. Brad BD6 94 D8
Larch La. Gar LS25 83 B6
Larch Rd. Hud HD1 153 D5
Larch St. Keigh BD21 35 B4
Larch Wood. Scar LS14 45 C7
Larchfield Rd. Leeds LS10 79 E5
Larchmont. Brad BD14 73 C4
Larchmont Fst Sch. Brad 73 C4
Lark Hill Ave. Clec BD19 116 B6
Lark Hill. Batley WF17 118 A8
Lark Hill Cl. Clec BD19 116 B6
Lark Hill Dr. Clec BD19 116 B6
Lark St. Bing BD16 36 F3
Lark St. Haw BD22 34 D2
Lark St. Haw BD22 51 D7
Lark St. Keigh BD21 35 B7
Larkfield Ave. Yeadon LS19 40 C4
Larkfield Cres. Yeadon LS19 40 C4
Larkfield Dr. Yeadon LS19 40 C4
Larkfield Mount. Yeadon LS19 40 C4
Larkfield Rd. Pudsey LS28 76 E8
Larkfield Rd. Yeadon LS19 40 C4
Larkfield Terr. Keigh BD21 35 E6
Larkhill Cl. Leeds LS8 60 E8
Larkhill Gn. Leeds LS8 43 E1
Larkhill Rd. Leeds LS8 43 E1
Larkhill View. Leeds LS8 60 E8
Larkhill Way. Leeds LS8 43 E1
Larkhill Wlk. Leeds LS8 43 E1
Larks Hill. Pont WF8 146 B6
Larwood Ave. Brad BD10 56 E4
Lascelles Hall Rd. Kirkhe HD5 155 C6
Lascelles Mount. Leeds LS8 60 F3 7
Lascelles Pl. Leeds LS8 60 F3 5
Lascelles Rd. Batley WF16 117 E3
Lascelles Rd E. Leeds LS8 60 F3 8
Lascelles Rd W. Leeds LS8 60 F3 10
Lascelles St. Leeds LS8 60 F3 4
Lascelles Terr. Leeds LS8 60 F3 2
Lascelles View. Leeds LS8 60 F3 6
Lastingham Gn. Brad BD6 73 E1
Lastingham Rd. Pudsey LS13 57 F5
Latchmere Ave. Leeds LS16 58 F8
Latchmere Cl. Leeds LS16 59 A8
Latchmere Crest. Leeds LS16 58 F8 4
Latchmere Cross. Leeds LS16 58 F8 3
Latchmere Dr. Leeds LS16 58 F8
Latchmere Gdns. Leeds LS16 59 A8
Latchmere Gn. Leeds LS16 58 F8 5
Latchmere Rd. Leeds LS16 58 F8
Latchmere View. Leeds LS16 58 F8
Latchmere Wlk. Leeds LS16 59 A8 4
Latchmore Rd. Leeds LS12 78 E4
Latchmore Road Ind Est. Leeds 78 E4
Latham Ct. Clec BD19 96 B2
Latham La. Clec BD19 96 A2
Latham Lea. Clec BD19 96 A2
Latimer St. Brad BD3 75 D6
Launceston Dr. Brad BD4 75 E2
Laund Rd. Hud HD3 134 E1
Laund Rd. Mars HD7 151 C3
Laund Rd. Slai HD7 151 C3
Launton Way. Brad BD5 74 D4
Laura St. Brig HD6 115 A1 8
Laura St. Hali HX3 92 C1 4
Laura St. Leeds LS12 78 F6
Laurel Bank. Brig BD12 115 C8
Laurel Bank Cl. Hali HX2 92 A6
Laurel Bank Ct. Leeds LS6 59 C4
Laurel Bank. Hali HX1 113 A5 14
Laurel Cl. E Kes LS17 28 C5
Laurel Cl. Elland HX5 134 E6
Laurel Cl. Shelf HX3 93 C6
Laurel Cres. Hali HX2 91 F3
Laurel Cres. Keigh BD21 35 B8
Laurel Ct. Ossett WF5 140 C6
Laurel Dr. Batley WF17 118 A7
Laurel Fold. Leeds LS12 78 C7 8
Laurel Gr. Batley WF17 117 F7
Laurel Gr. Bing BD16 36 E5
Laurel Gr. Keigh BD21 35 B8
Laurel Gr. Leeds LS12 78 C7
Laurel Gr. Sil BD20 5 D1
Laurel Hill Ave. Leeds LS15 81 D7
Laurel Hill Croft. Leeds LS15 81 D7
Laurel Hill Gdns. Leeds LS15 81 D7
Laurel Hill Gr. Leeds LS15 81 D7
Laurel Hill View. Leeds LS15 81 D7
Laurel Hill Way. Leeds LS15 81 D6
Laurel House. Castle WF10 124 E7 4
Laurel Mount. Batley WF16 117 D4
Laurel Mount. Hali HX1 113 A5 17
Laurel Mount. Leeds LS7 60 D5
Laurel Mount. Pudsey LS28 76 E8
Laurel Pk. Wils BD15 53 C4
Laurel Pl. Leeds LS12 78 C7
Laurel St. Brad BD3 75 C6
Laurel St. Hali HX1 113 A5
Laurel St. Leeds LS12 78 C7

Laurel Terr. Elland HX4 133 F4
Laurel Terr. Leeds LS12 78 C7
Laurel Terr. Pudsey LS28 76 E8
Laurels The. Dew WF12 139 F7
Laurels The. Leeds LS8 60 F7
Laurence Ct. Roth LS26 101 D7
Laurieston Sch. Leeds 59 F4
Lavender Croft. Batley WF16 117 E4
Lavender Ct. Hud HD4 171 D6
Lavender Hill. Brad BD10 56 C5
Lavender Wlk. Leeds LS9 79 F7
Lavenham Pl. Ad Le S DN6 184 E2
Laverack Field. Brad BD12 94 C3 6
Laverhills. Clec WF15 116 D5
Laverock Cres. Brig HD6 114 F5
Laverock La. Brig HD6 114 F5
Laverock Pl. Brig HD6 114 F5
Laverton Rd. Brad BD4 75 B4
Lavinia Terr. Brad BD14 73 D4
Law Cl. Weth LS22 13 F6
Law Common Rd. Carl HD7 199 E5
Law Common Rd. Dun Br HD7 199 E5
Law Cts The. Brad 74 F6
Law Hill. Holmfi HD7 199 D6
Law La. Hali HX3 114 A5
Law Slack Rd. Holmfi HD7 199 D6
Law St. Batley WF17 117 F8
Law St. Brad BD4 75 C2
Law St. Clec BD19 116 D8
Law St. Tod OL14 86 B1
Law St. Tod OL14 129 B7
Lawcliffe Cres. Haw BD22 51 D8
Lawefield Ave. Roth LS26 100 C6
Lawefield Gr. Wake WF2 142 A5
Lawefield La. Wake WF2 142 A5
Lawkholme Cres. Keigh BD21 35 C7 4
Lawkholme La. Keigh BD21 35 C8
Lawn Ave. Bur in W LS29 9 F1
Lawn Rd. Bur in W LS29 9 F1
Lawn's La. Leeds LS10 79 E3
Lawndale. Ad Le S DN6 184 F2
Lawndale Fold. Mapp S75 177 F1
Lawns Ave. Gild LS12 77 D3
Lawns Cl. Gild LS12 77 D3
Lawns Cl. Nor WF6 122 E4
Lawns Cres. Gild LS12 77 D3
Lawns Croft. Gild LS12 77 D3
Lawns Dene. Gild LS12 77 D3
Lawns Dr. Gild LS12 77 D3
Lawns Gn. Gild LS12 77 D3
Lawns Hall Cl. Hors LS16 42 B3
Lawns La. Gild LS12 77 D4
Lawns La. Leeds LS12 77 D4
Lawns La. Loft G WF2 120 E6
Lawns Mount. Gild LS12 77 D3
Lawns Park Prim Sch. Leeds 77 E5
Lawns Sq. Gild LS12 77 D3
Lawns Terr. E Ard WF3 120 D7
Lawns Terr. Gild LS12 77 D3
Lawns The. Batley WF16 117 E4
Lawns The. Ilkley LS29 8 A4
Lawns The. Neth WF4 158 A6
Lawns View. Nor WF6 122 E4
Lawnswood Gdns. Hors LS16 42 B2
Lawnswood Rd. Keigh BD21 35 A5
Lawnswood Sch. Leeds 59 B8
Lawrence Ave. Leeds LS8 61 C4
Lawrence Cres. Batley WF16 117 D6
Lawrence Cres. Leeds LS8 61 C5
Lawrence Dr. Brad BD7 73 E2
Lawrence Gdns. Leeds LS8 61 C5
Lawrence Rd. Hali HX3 113 B3
Lawrence Rd. Hud HD1 153 E6
Lawrence Rd. Leeds LS8 61 C4
Lawrence St. Hali HX3 92 A1 14
Lawrence Wlk. Leeds LS8 61 C4
Lawson House. Brad BD6 93 E8 6
Lawson Rd. Brig HD6 115 B2
Lawson St. Brad BD3 74 F8 1
Lawson St. Leeds LS12 78 B7 2
Lawton St. Hud HD4 154 A3
Lay Garth Cl. Roth LS26 100 E5
Lay Garth Gdns. Roth LS26 100 E4
Lay Garth Gn. Roth LS26 100 E4
Lay Garth Mead. Roth LS26 100 E4
Lay Garth Pl. Roth LS26 100 E4
Lay Garth. Roth LS26 100 E5
Lay Garth Sq. Roth LS26 100 E4
Laycock Fst Sch. Keigh 34 C7
Laycock La. Keigh BD22 34 C7
Laycock Pl. Leeds LS7 60 D3
Laygarth Dr. Kirkhe HD5 155 C6
Laythorp Terr. Keigh BD20 19 D1
Laythorpe Ct. Pont WF8 147 A7
Layton Ave. Yeadon LS19 40 E3
Layton Cl. Yeadon LS19 40 E2
Layton Cres. Yeadon LS19 40 D3
Layton Dr. Yeadon LS19 40 E3
Layton La. Yeadon LS19 40 E2
Layton Mount. Yeadon LS19 40 D3
Layton Park Ave. Yeadon LS19 40 E2
Layton Park Cl. Yeadon LS19 40 D3
Layton Park Croft. Yeadon LS19 40 E2
Layton Park Dr. Yeadon LS19 40 E2
Layton Rd. Yeadon LS18, LS19 40 E3
Layton Rise. Yeadon LS18 40 F3
Lazenby Dr. Weth LS22 13 D6
Lazenby Fold. Weth LS22 13 D6
Le Marchant Ave. Hud HD3 153 C8
Lea Ave. Hali HX3 113 C3
Lea Cl. Brig HD6 115 A4
Lea Croft. B Spa LS23 30 D5
Lea Croft. Otley LS21 23 A7
Lea Ct. Brad BD7 73 E2
Lea Dr. Shep HD8 190 F8
Lea Farm Cres. Leeds LS5 58 F6
Lea Farm Dr. Leeds LS5 58 F6
Lea Farm Gr. Leeds LS5 58 F6
Lea Farm Mount. Leeds LS5 58 F7
Lea Farm Pl. Leeds LS5 58 F6
Lea Farm Rd. Leeds LS5 58 F7
Lea Farm Row. Leeds LS5 58 F6
Lea Farm Wlk. Leeds LS5 58 F7
Lea Gdns. Holmfi HD7 189 E4
Lea La. Feath WF7 145 E4
Lea La. Hud HD4 171 C6
Lea Mill Park Cl. Yeadon LS19 40 A7
Lea Mill Park Dr. Yeadon LS19 40 A7
Lea Park Cl. Midd LS10 99 F7
Lea Park Croft. Midd LS10 100 A7
Lea Park Dr. Midd LS10 99 F7
Lea Park Garth. Midd LS10 99 F7 2
Lea Park Gdns. Midd LS10 99 F7 1
Lea Park Gr. Midd LS10 99 F7
Lea Park Vale. Midd LS10 100 A7
Lea Rd. Batley WF17 117 F8
Lea Rise. Honley HD7 171 F3
Lea Side Gdns. Hud HD3 152 E7
Lea St. Hud HD3 135 C1
Lea St. Hud HD1 136 A1
Lea St. Hud HD1 154 A8
Lea The. Gar LS25 82 F5
Lea View. Batley WF17 117 F8
Leabank Ave. Gar LS25 83 A5
Leach Cres. Keigh BD20 18 E2
Leach Rd. Keigh BD20 18 D2
Leach Rise. Keigh BD20 18 E2
Leach Way. Keigh BD20 18 E2
Leadenhall St. Hali HX1 112 F5 17
Leadwell La. Roth LS26 100 C4
Leaf St. Castle WF10 124 C7
Leaf St. Haw BD22 51 E8 4
Leafield Ave. Brad BD2 56 C3
Leafield Ave. Hud HD3 152 E6
Leafield Bank. Hud HD3 152 E6
Leafield Cl. Hud HD2 136 D4
Leafield Cl. Leeds LS17 43 B2
Leafield Cres. Brad BD2 56 B3
Leafield Dr. Brad BD2 56 C4
Leafield Dr. Leeds LS17 43 B2
Leafield Dr. Pudsey LS28 76 F5 2
Leafield Gr. Brad BD2 56 C3
Leafield Grange. Leeds LS17 43 B2
Leafield Pl. Yeadon LS19 39 F7
Leafield Terr. Brad BD2 56 C3
Leafield Way. Brad BD2 56 C3
Leafland St. Hali HX1 113 A7
Leah Pl. Leeds LS12 78 F6
Leak Hall La. D Dale HD8 192 A6
Leak Hall Rd. D Dale HD8 191 F6
Leake St. Castle WF10 124 E7
Leamington Dr. Brad BD10 56 C8
Leamington Rd. Ilkley LS29 8 C5
Leamington St. Brad BD9 55 B2
Leamington Terr. Dew WF12 139 D6
Leamington Terr. Ilkley LS29 8 C5
Learoyd St. Hud HD1 154 B7
Leas Ave. Holmfi HD7 188 F7
Leaside Dr. Thorn BD13 72 D7
Leasowe Ave. Leeds LS10 79 E2
Leasowe Cl. Leeds LS10 79 E2
Leasowe Ct. Leeds LS10 79 E2 9
Leasowe Garth. Leeds LS10 79 E2
Leasowe Gdns. Leeds LS10 79 F2
Leasowe Rd. Leeds LS10 79 E2
Leatham Ave. Feath WF7 145 E4
Leatham Cres. Feath WF7 145 F4
Leatham Dr. Feath WF7 145 F4
Leatham Park Rd. Feath WF7 145 F4
Leather Bank. Bur in W LS29 9 E3
Leathley Ave. Men LS29 22 B4
Leathley Cres. Men LS29 22 B4
Leathley La. Leath LS21 24 B8
Leathley La. Men LS29 22 B4
Leathley Rd. Leeds LS10 79 D5
Leathley Rd. Men LS29 22 B4
Leathley St. Leeds LS10 79 D5
Leavens The. Brad BD10 56 D8
Leaventhorpe Ave. Brad BD8 73 D7
Leaventhorpe Cl. Brad BD8 73 C7
Leaventhorpe Gr. Brad BD13 73 C6
Leaventhorpe La. Brad BD13, BD8 73 C6
Leaventhorpe Mid Sch. Brad 73 B7
Leaventhorpe Way. Brad BD8 73 D7
Leaverholme Cl. H Chap BB10 85 A7
Leavington Cl. Brad BD6 94 B6
Leconfield Ct. Weth LS22 13 C6
Leconfield House. Brad BD10 56 C7
Ledbury Ave. Midd LS10 99 F4
Ledbury Cl. Midd LS10 99 F4 4
Ledbury Croft. Midd LS10 99 F4 3
Ledbury Dr. Midd LS10 99 F4
Ledbury Gn. Midd LS10 99 F4 1
Ledbury Gr. Midd LS10 99 F4 2
Ledgard Bridge Mills Ind Units. Mir 138 A3
Ledgard Dr. Crig WF4 159 F7
Ledgard Way. Leeds LS12 78 C8
Ledgate La. B Sal LS25 105 E4
Ledger La. Loft G WF1 121 B4
Ledger La. Roth WF3 100 C1
Ledger Pl. Loft G WF1 121 B4
Ledston Ave. Gar LS25 83 A5
Ledston Lady Elizabeth Hastings CE Sch. Ledst 103 E6
Ledston Luck Cotts. Ledst LS25 83 E2
Ledston Luck Ent Pk. Ledst 83 D2
Ledston Luck Villas. Ledst LS25 83 D2
Ledston Mill La. Ledst WF10 103 E4
Ledston Mill La. Ledst WF10 103 F7
Lee Bank. Hali HX3 92 B1
Lee Beck Gr. Loft G WF3 121 E8
Lee Bottom Rd. Tod OL14 109 A5
Lee Bridge. Hali HX3 113 B8
Lee Brig. Nor WF6 122 F3
Lee Cl. Wils BD15 53 C6
Lee Clough Dr. Heb Br HX7 89 F1
Lee Ct. Keigh BD21 35 F6
Lee Ct. Liver WF15 117 A5 10
Lee Ct. Ossett WF5 140 F4
Lee Gn. Mir WF14 138 A6
Lee Hall Rd. Hud HD3 135 C1
Lee Head. Hud HD2 153 F8
Lee La. Ack M T WF7 164 B8
Lee La E. Hors LS18 41 B2
Lee La. Hali HX3 92 D3
Lee La. Hors LS18 41 B2
Lee La. Kirkb HD8 173 E6
Lee La. Mapp S71 178 E2
Lee La. Roy S71 178 E2
Lee La. Tod OL14 108 F3
Lee La W. Hors LS18 41 A2
Lee La. Wh Com S30 200 F4
Lee La. Wils BD16 53 E6
Lee Mill Rd. Wad M HX7 89 A5
Lee Mills Ind Est. Hali 113 B8
Lee Moor La. Loft G WF3 121 E8
Lee Moor Rd. Loft G WF3 121 E6
Lee Mount Gdns. Hali HX3 92 A1 5
Lee Mount Inf Sch. Hali 92 A1
Lee Mount Jun & Inf Sch. Hali 92 A1
Lee Mount Rd. Hali HX3 92 A1
Lee Orchards. B Spa LS23 30 E8
Lee Rd. Dew WF13 138 D5
Lee St. Brad BD1 74 E6
Lee St. Brig HD6 115 A4
Lee St. Dew WF13 138 E6
Lee St. Liver WF15 117 A5
Lee St. Queen BD13 92 D8 3
Lee St. Wake WF1 142 C6
Lee Way. Kirkb HD8 173 E7
Lee Wood Rd. Hep HX7 88 F5
Leech La. Harden BD13 53 A8
Leeches Hill. Hud HD3 134 C1
Leeds 27 Ind Est. Morley 97 E5
Leeds and Bradford Rd. Leeds LS13 58 C4
Leeds & Bradford International Airport. Yeadon 40 F7
Leeds Bsns Pk. Morley 97 E4
Leeds Coll of Building. Leeds 60 D1
Leeds Coll of Building. Leeds 61 F4
Leeds Coll of Tech. Leeds 60 B1
Leeds Combined Court Ctr. Leeds 79 B8
Leeds Crem. Hors 42 B3
Leeds Girls' High Sch. Leeds 59 F4
Leeds Golf Ctr. Hare 44 B8
Leeds Grammar Sch (Jun). Leeds 59 F1
Leeds Grammar Sch. Leeds 59 F2
Leeds Jewish Day Sch. Leeds 43 D3
Leeds La. Swil LS26 82 B4
Leeds Metropolitan Univ. Leeds 59 B6
Leeds Metropolitan Univ. Leeds 60 B1
Leeds Old Rd. Batley WF16 117 D6
Leeds Old Rd. Brad BD3 75 E8
Leeds Polytechnic. Leeds 59 C6
Leeds Polytechnic. Leeds 60 C1
Leeds Rd. B in Elm LS15 63 B6
Leeds Rd. Batley WF17 97 B2
Leeds Rd. Brad BD10 39 B2
Leeds Rd. Brad BD2 56 B3
Leeds Rd. Brad BD2 56 C2
Leeds Rd. Brad BD1& BD3 75 C6
Leeds Rd. Bramho LS16 24 D4
Leeds Rd. Brig HX3 114 E8
Leeds Rd. Castle WF10 124 D5
Leeds Rd. Coll LS22 29 A8
Leeds Rd. Dew WF12 118 E1
Leeds Rd. E Ard WF3 119 B5
Leeds Rd. Guise LS20 39 E8
Leeds Rd. Hud HD2 136 F2
Leeds Rd. Ilkley LS29 8 D5
Leeds Rd. Kippax LS25 83 A2
Leeds Rd. Kippax WF10 103 A5
Leeds Rd. Liver WF16 117 C5
Leeds Rd. Loft G WF1 121 C5
Leeds Rd. Loft G WF3 121 C6
Leeds Rd. M'town LS26 102 B3
Leeds Rd. Northo HX3 114 A8
Leeds Rd. Ossett WF5 119 C1
Leeds Rd. Ossett WF5 140 C8
Leeds Rd. Otley LS21 23 D6
Leeds Rd. Pool LS16 24 D4
Leeds Rd. Roth LS26, WF3 100 B2
Leeds Rd. Roth LS26 100 F7
Leeds Rd. Ship BD18 55 D8
Leeds Rd. Wake WF1 142 B8
Leeds Rd. Yeadon LS19 40 D3
Leeds Road Hospl. Brad 75 B7
Leeds St. Keigh BD21 35 B7
Leeds Sta. Leeds 79 B7
Leeds Univ. Leeds 60 A2
Leef St. Hud HD5 154 D6 6
Leefield Rd. Batley WF17 117 E6
Leeke Ave. Hor WF4 141 A2
Leeming St. Brad BD1 74 F8
Lees Ave. Dew WF12 139 C4
Lees Bank Ave. Haw BD22 51 E8
Lees Bank Dr. Haw BD22 51 E8
Lees Bank Hill. Haw BD22 51 E8
Lees Bank Rd. Haw BD22 51 E8
Lees Bldgs. Brig HX3 114 C7
Lees Cl. Cull BD13 52 C6
Lees Cl. Hud HD5 154 F7
Lees Cres. Crig WF4 159 F7
Lees Dr. Dew WF12 139 C4
Lees Fst Sch. Haw 51 E8
Lees Hall Rd. Dew WF12 139 C3
Lees Holm. Dew WF12 139 C4
Lees House Rd. Dew WF12 139 C5
Lees La. Haw BD22 51 D8
Lees La. Pudsey LS28 57 D4
Lees Mill La. Slai HD7 152 B1
Lees Moor Rd. Cull BD13 52 C6
Lees Rd. Heb Br HX7 89 A4 6
Lees The. H Chap BB10 85 A7
Lees Yd. Heb Br HX7 89 A3 15
Leeside Rd. Batley WF16 117 E6
Leesworth Ct. Haw BD22 51 E8 7
Legrams Ave. Brad BD7 73 F5
Legrams La. Brad BD7 74 A6
Legrams Mill La. Brad BD7 74 A6
Legrams St. Brad BD7 74 C7
Legrams Terr. Brad BD7 74 C7
Leicester Cl. Leeds LS7 60 B2
Leicester Gr. Leeds LS7 60 B2
Leicester Pl. Leeds LS2 60 B2
Leicester St. Brad BD4 75 A4
Leicester Terr. Hali HX3 113 B4 9
Leigh Ave. E Ard WF3 120 A8
Leigh Rd. E Ard WF3 120 A8
Leigh St. Ack M T WF7 163 D5
Leigh St. Hali HX6 112 C5
Leigh View. E Ard WF3 120 A8
Leighton La. Leeds LS1 79 A8 5
Leighton Pl. Leeds LS1 79 B8 1
Leighton St. Leeds LS1 79 A8
Leisure La. Emley HD8 175 E8
Leith Ct. Dew WF12 139 E1
Leith St. Keigh BD21 35 B8
Lemans Dr. Batley WF13 117 F3
Lemington Ave. Hali HX1 113 A6
Lemon St. Brad BD5 74 C3
Lemon St. Hali HX1 112 F6
Lemon Tree Cl. Pont WF8 146 B6
Lenacre La. Emley WF4 156 D1
Lenham Cl. Morley LS27 98 A2 1
Lennie St. Keigh BD21 35 B6
Lennon Dr. Brad BD8 74 B8
Lennox Dr. Wake WF2 141 D3
Lennox Rd. Leeds LS4 59 D1
Lennox Rd. Tod OL14 85 F1
Lennox Rd. Tod OL14 86 A1
Lenny Balk. H Pag DN5 195 E7
Lens Dr. Bail BD17 38 C4
Lentilfield St. Hali HX3 92 A2
Lentilfield Terr. Hali HX3 92 A2 6
Lenton Dr. Leeds LS11 79 C2
Lenton Villas. Brad BD10 39 B1
Leodis Ct. Leeds LS11 79 B6
Leonard St. Bing BD16 37 A2
Leonard St. Brad BD12 94 D3
Leonard St. Hud HD2 136 B1
Leonard's Pl. Bing BD16 37 A2 4
Leopold Gdns. Leeds LS7 60 E3
Leopold Gr. Leeds LS7 60 D3
Leopold Prim Sch. Leeds 60 E3
Leopold St. Leeds LS7 60 E3
Leopold St. Ossett WF5 141 A4
Lepton CE Fst Sch. Lepton 156 A3
Lepton Cty Fst Sch. Lepton 155 D3
Lepton La. Kirkb HD8 174 A8
Lepton Mid Sch. Lepton 155 E2
Lepton Pl. Gild LS27 97 D7
Lesley Way. Hud HD4 153 A1
Leslie Ave. Yeadon LS19 40 C8
Leslie St. Hud HD2 136 A1
Leslie Terr. Leeds LS6 60 A3 5
Lesmere Gr. Brad BD7 73 F2
Lessarna Ct. Brad BD4 75 C5
Leven Gdns. Weth LS22 13 D7
Levens Bvd. Leeds LS15 80 E6
Levens Cl. Leeds LS15 80 E6
Levens Gdns. Leeds LS15 80 E6
Levens Pl. Leeds LS15 80 E6
Leventhorpe Cotts. Swil LS26 101 E8
Leventhorpe Ct. Roth LS26 101 C5 1
Leventhorpe Way. Roth LS26 101 C5
Lever St. Brad BD6 74 A1 5
Lever St. Tod OL14 108 B5
Levita Gr. Brad BD4 75 D4
Levita Pl. Brad BD4 75 E5
Levita Pl. Leeds LS15 80 F8 4
Lewin Gr. Castle WF10 125 D8
Lewis St. Hali HX1 113 B8
Lewisham Ct. Morley LS27 98 B4
Lewisham Gr. Morley LS27 98 B4
Lewisham Rd. Slai HD7 152 A1
Lewisham St. Morley LS27 98 B5
Ley Fleaks Rd. Brad BD10 56 B7
Ley La. Leeds LS12 78 D8
Ley Top Fst Sch. Brad 73 B8
Ley Top La. Brad BD15 73 C8
Leybrook Croft. Hem WF9 181 E7
Leyburn Ave. Batley WF16 117 E6
Leyburn Ave. Brig HX3 114 E8
Leyburn Gr. Bing BD16 37 A4 2
Leyburn Gr. Ship BD18 55 A7
Leyburn Rd. Ad Le S DN6 184 F2
Leyburne St. Brad BD8 55 C1
Leyden Rise. Brad BD15 73 B8
Leyfield. Bail BD17 38 B3
Leyfield Bank. Holmfi HD7 189 C7
Leygards La. Mel HD7 170 C1
Leyland Croft. Hud HD2 136 E6
Leyland Rd. Batley WF17 96 E1
Leyland Rd. Castle WF10 125 D8
Leylands Ave. Brad BD9 54 F3
Leylands Gr. Brad BD9 54 F3
Leylands La. Brad BD9 54 F3
Leylands La. Keigh BD21 35 D6
Leylands Rd. Leeds LS2 60 D1
Leylands Terr. Brad BD9 54 F3
Leymoor Rd. Hud HD7 152 E5
Leys La. B Spa LS23 14 C2
Leys La. Emley HD8 175 B6
Leys La. Ham DN6 184 C2
Leys La. K Smea WF8 166 C7
Leys La. Knot WF11 126 F1
Leys Rd. Dar WF8 147 E6
Leysholme Cres. Leeds LS12 78 A6
Leysholme Dr. Leeds LS12 78 B6
Leysholme Terr. Leeds LS12 78 B6
Leysholme View. Leeds LS12 78 B6
Leyside Dr. Brad BD15 54 B1
Leyton Cres. Brad BD10 56 B7
Leyton Dr. Brad BD10 56 B7
Leyton Gr. Brad BD10 56 B7
Leyton Terr. Brad BD10 56 B7
Lichen Cl. Brad BD7 74 A3
Lichfield Mount. Brad BD2 55 F4
Lichfield Rd. Dew WF12 139 F8
Lickless Ave. Hors LS18 41 D1
Lickless Dr. Hors LS18 41 D1
Lickless Gdns. Hors LS18 41 D1
Lickless Terr. Hors LS18 41 D1
Lidgate Cl. Dew WF13 118 C2
Lidgate Cres. S Kirk WF9 182 E2
Lidgate Gdns. Dew WF13 118 C2
Lidgate La. Dew WF13 118 C2
Lidgate La. Shaf S72 180 B3
Lidget Ave. Brad BD7 73 F5
Lidget Green Fst Sch. Brad 73 F6
Lidget Green Mid Sch. Brad 73 F6
Lidget Hill. Pudsey LS28 76 E7
Lidget La. Crof WF4 144 D1
Lidget Pl. Brad BD7 74 A5
Lidget Rd. L Brad BD20 4 C5
Lidget St. Hud HD3 135 B1
Lidget Terr. Brad BD14 73 D4
Lidget Terr. Brad BD7 73 F5
Lidgett Ave. Leeds LS8 60 F7
Lidgett Cres. Leeds LS8 60 F8
Lidgett Ct. Gar LS25 82 E6
Lidgett Ct. Leeds LS8 60 F8
Lidgett Gr. Leeds LS8 60 F7
Lidgett Hill. Leeds LS8 60 F7
Lidgett La. Gar LS25 82 E6
Lidgett La. Leeds LS8 60 F7
Lidgett La. Skel HD8 174 F1
Lidgett Mount. Leeds LS8 43 F1
Lidgett Park Ave. Leeds LS8 44 A1
Lidgett Park Ct. Leeds LS8 43 F1
Lidgett Park Gdns. Leeds LS8 60 F8
Lidgett Park Gr. Leeds LS8 60 F8
Lidgett Park Mews. Leeds LS8 44 A1
Lidgett Park Rd. Leeds LS8 44 A1
Lidgett Park View. Leeds LS8 43 F1
Lidgett Pl. Leeds LS8 60 F8
Lidgett Rise. Skel HD8 174 F1
Lidgett Towers. Leeds LS8 43 E1
Lidgett Wlk. Leeds LS8 60 F7
Lifton Pl. Leeds LS2 60 A2
Light Bank La. Add BD20 6 C3
Light La. Wake WF2 141 E8
Lightcliffe CE Sch. Brig 114 E8
Lightcliffe Golf Course. Brig 114 E8
Lightcliffe Preparatory Sch. Brig 114 D7
Lightcliffe Rd. Brig HD6 115 A4
Lightcliffe Rd. Hud HD4 153 D4
Lightcliffe Royd La. Rip HX4 133 C6
Lightenfield La. Hud HD4 171 D7
Lightfoot Ave. Castle WF10 124 E6
Lightfoot Cl. Castle WF10 124 D6
Lighthazles Chap Rd. Rip HX6 132 A6
Lighthazles Rd. Rip HX6 132 B6
Lighthouse. Litt OL15 129 C1
Lightowler Cl. Hali HX1 113 A7 10
Lightowler Rd. Hali HX1 113 A7
Lightowler St. Brad BD6 74 C1 10
Lightridge Cl. Hud HD2 136 A4
Lightridge Rd. Brig HD2 135 F5
Lilac Ave. Knot WF11 126 E2
Lilac Ave. Wake WF2 142 C3
Lilac Cl. Add LS29 7 A8
Lilac Cl. Brig HD6 115 C3
Lilac Gr. Brad BD4 75 D6
Lilac Gr. Clec BD19 96 A1
Lilac Gr. Ship BD18 55 D5
Lilac St. Hali HX3 92 A1
Lilac Wlk. Hud HD7 152 E5
Lilacs The. Guise LS20 22 E1
Lilacs The. Roy S71 179 E4
Liley La. Kirkhe WF14 155 F8
Liley La. Lepton WF14 156 C6
Lilian St. Brad BD4 75 C3
Lillands Ave. Brig HD6 114 F2
Lillands La. Brig HD6 114 F2
Lillands Terr. Brig HD6 114 F2
Lilley St. Hem WF9 181 D6
Lilley Terr. S Kirk WF9 182 B2
Lilly La. Hali HX3 113 D6
Lilly St. Sow Br HX6 112 B3
Lily Croft. Brad BD8 55 B1
Lily St. Brad BD8 55 B1
Lily St. Tod OL14 107 E8
Lilycroft Fst Sch. Brad 55 B2
Lilycroft Rd. Brad BD9 55 B2
Lilycroft Wlk. Brad BD9 55 A2
Lilythorne Ave. Brad BD10 56 C8
Lime Ave. Heb Br HX7 88 F3
Lime Ave. Holmfi HD7 189 C8
Lime Ave. Tod OL14 108 A6
Lime Cl. Keigh BD20 18 A1
Lime Cres. S Elm WF9 182 E1
Lime Cres. Wake WF2 142 F1
Lime Ct. Bing BD16 36 E6
Lime Gr. Hud HD7 152 E5
Lime Gr. Roy S71 179 C1
Lime Gr. S Elm WF9 182 E1
Lime Gr. Yeadon LS19 40 A4
Lime Pit La. Loft G WF3 121 F4
Lime St. Bing BD16 36 F3
Lime St. Brad BD7 74 B4
Lime St. Clec BD19 116 C7
Lime St. Haw BD22 51 C6
Lime St. Hud HD1 153 E4
Lime St. Keigh BD21 35 B7
Lime St. Ossett WF5 140 E4
Lime St. Tod OL14 108 A6
Lime Tree Ave. B Spa LS23 30 D8
Lime Tree Ave. Batley WF17 118 A4
Lime Tree Ave. Elland HX5 135 A6
Lime Tree Ave. Leeds LS17 43 E2
Lime Tree Ave. Pont WF8 146 B8
Lime Tree Ct. Hem WF9 181 C6
Lime Tree Gdns. B Spa LS23 30 E7
Lime Tree Gr. Birk BD11 96 A7
Lime-Tree Cres. Kippax LS25 83 C1
Limers Gate. Tod OL14 106 E4
Limes Ave. Hali HX3 113 C4
Limes Ave. Mapp S75 178 C2
Limes Cl. Mapp S75 178 C2
Limetrees. Pont WF8 126 A4
Limewood App. Leeds LS14 62 A7
Limewood Rd. Leeds LS14 62 A6
Linburn Cl. Roy S71 179 A4
Lincoln Ave. Batley WF16 117 D5
Lincoln Cl. Brad BD8 55 C1
Lincoln Cres. S Elm WF9 183 A4
Lincoln Dr. Liver WF15 117 A2
Lincoln Gr. Hud HD5 155 A4
Lincoln Gr. Liver WF15 116 F2
Lincoln Green Rd. Leeds LS9 60 E1
Lincoln House Sch. Kirkb 173 F6
Lincoln Rd. Brad BD8 74 C8
Lincoln Rd. Dew WF12 118 F1
Lincoln Rd. Leeds LS9 60 E1
Lincoln St. Brad BD15 73 C8
Lincoln St. Castle WF10 124 E8
Lincoln St. Hud HD1 154 C6
Lincoln St. Tod OL14 86 B1
Lincoln St. Wake WF2 142 A7
Lincoln Towers. Leeds LS9 60 E1
Lincoln Wlk. Kippax LS25 83 C2
Lincombe Bank. Leeds LS8 60 E8
Lincombe Dr. Leeds LS8 60 E8
Lincombe Mount. Leeds LS8 60 E8
Lincombe Rise. Leeds LS8 60 E8
Lincroft Ave. Hud HD5 154 E5
Lincroft Cres. Leeds LS13 58 E3
Lincs Wold. Clec WF15 116 B4
Lindale Ave. Ack M T WF7 164 C7
Lindale Cl. Midd LS10 99 D7
Lindale Garth. Wake WF2 120 C2
Lindale Gr. Wake WF2 120 D1
Lindale La. Wake WF2 120 C2
Lindale Mount. Wake WF2 120 D1
Linden Ave. Brad BD3 75 E8
Linden Ave. Leeds LS11 79 B3
Linden Ave. Tod OL14 108 A6
Linden Cl. Bard LS17 28 D4
Linden Cl. Brig HD6 115 C3
Linden Cl. Castle WF10 125 D6
Linden Cl. Dew WF12 140 B7
Linden Cl. Knot WF11 126 C4
Linden Ct. Leeds LS16 59 D7
Linden Gdns. Leeds LS11 79 C3 6
Linden Gr. Leeds LS11 79 C3
Linden Mount. Leeds LS11 79 B3
Linden Pl. Heb Br HX7 89 A4 11
Linden Pl. Leeds LS11 79 C3 4
Linden Rd. Elland HX5 134 E6
Linden Rd. Hali HX3 113 C4
Linden Rd. Heb Br HX7 89 A4
Linden Rd. Heb Br HX7 89 D1
Linden Rd. Hud HD2 135 F1
Linden Rd. Leeds LS11 79 C3
Linden Rise. Keigh BD21 35 E5
Linden St. Leeds LS11 79 C3
Linden Terr. Ack M T WF7 163 D5
Linden Terr. Leeds LS11 79 C3
Linden Terr. Pont WF8 146 C8
Linden Way. Weth LS22 13 D7
Lindisfarne Rd. Ship BD18 54 F7
Lindley Ave. Hud HD3 135 A2
Lindley Dr. Brad BD7 73 F2
Lindley House Sch. Brad 75 B3
Lindley Lodge. Hud HD3 135 B1
Lindley Moor Rd. Hud HD3 134 E2
Lindley Rd. Brad BD5 74 D3
Lindley Rd. Elland HX5 134 F4
Lindley St. Hud HD3 153 A5
Lindley Vol Sch & Lindley Cty Jun Sch. Hud 135 B1
Lindon St. Haw BD22 51 C6 12
Lindrick Cl. Cud S72 180 C1
Lindrick Gr. Hali HX2 91 F7
Lindrick Way. Hali HX2 91 F7
Lindrick Wlk. Hali HX2 91 F7
Lindsay Acre. E Ard WF3 120 A8
Lindsay Ave. Wake WF2 141 C5
Lindsay Rd. Gar LS25 82 F6
Lindsey Ct. Leeds LS9 60 E1
Lindsey Gdns. Leeds LS9 60 E1
Lindsey Mount. Leeds LS9 60 E1
Lindsey Rd. Leeds LS9 60 E1
Lindwell Ave. Elland HX4 134 C7 5
Lindwell Gr. Elland HX4 134 C7 2
Lindwell Pl. Elland HX4 134 C7 1
Linefield Rd. Batley WF17 118 D5
Lineham Ct. Liver WF15 117 A2
Lineholme Ave. Tod OL14 107 E7
Linfit Fold. Slai HD7 170 A8
Linfit La. Kirkb HD8 174 B8
Linfit La. Lepton HD8 156 C1
Linfit La. Slai HD7 170 B8
Ling Bob Croft. Hali HX2 91 D1
Ling Bob. Hali HX2 112 D8
Ling Bob Jun & Inf Sch. Hali 112 D8
Ling Croft. B Spa LS23 30 B8
Ling La. Scar LS14 45 B7
Ling Park App. Wils BD15 53 C4
Ling Park Ave. Wils BD15 53 C4
Ling Royd Ave. Hali HX2 112 D8
Lingamore Leys. Dearne S63 194 D1
Lingard St. Brad BD1 74 F8 5
Lingards Rd. Slai HD7 169 E7
Lingards Terr. Mars HD7 169 C6
Lingdale Rd. Brad BD6 94 B5
Lingfield App. Leeds LS17 43 B3
Lingfield Bank. Leeds LS17 43 B4
Lingfield Cl. Leeds LS17 43 C3
Lingfield Cres. Brad BD13 73 C2
Lingfield Cres. Leeds LS17 43 B3
Lingfield Dr. Cull BD22 35 A1
Lingfield Dr. Leeds LS17 43 C3
Lingfield Gate. Leeds LS17 43 B3
Lingfield Gdns. Leeds LS17 43 B3
Lingfield Gn. Leeds LS17 43 B3
Lingfield Gr. Leeds LS17 43 C3
Lingfield Gr. Wils BD15 53 D5
Lingfield Hill. Leeds LS17 43 B3
Lingfield Mount. Leeds LS17 43 C3
Lingfield Rd. Leeds LS17 43 C3
Lingfield Rd. Wils BD15 53 C5
Lingfield Terr. Brad BD13 73 C2
Lingfield View. Leeds LS17 43 B3
Lingfield Wlk. Leeds LS17 43 B3
Lings La. Upton DN6 184 A8
Lingwell Ave. Midd LS10 99 C5
Lingwell Chase. Loft G WF3 121 C6
Lingwell Cres. Midd LS10 99 C5
Lingwell Ct. Loft G WF3 121 A5
Lingwell Gate Cres. Loft G WF1 121 B5
Lingwell Gate Dr. Loft G WF1 121 B5
Lingwell Gate La. E Ard WF3 120 F8
Lingwell Gate La. Loft G WF1 121 A6
Lingwell Gate La. Midd WF3 99 F2
Lingwell Gr. Midd LS10 99 C4
Lingwell Nook La. Loft G WF3 121 A8
Lingwell Nook La. Loft G WF3 121 C6
Lingwell Park Ct. Midd LS10 99 C5
Lingwell Rd. Midd LS10 99 C4
Lingwood Ave. Brad BD8 54 F1
Lingwood Cl. Holmfi HD7 189 D7
Lingwood Rd. Brad BD8 73 F8
Lingwood Terr. Brad BD8 73 F8 1
Link Rd. Dew WF12 139 D7
Link Rd. Hud HD1 153 D6
Link Rd. Wake WF1 142 B8
Link The. Pont WF8 146 C6
Link The. Swil LS26 81 F1
Link The. Swil LS26 82 A1
Links Ave. Clec BD19 95 D2
Links The. Feath WF7 124 D1
Links View. Mapp S75 178 B2
Linkway. Ship BD16 54 A7
Linnburn Mews. Ilkley LS29 8 B3
Linnet Cl. Brad BD8 73 C7
Linnet Cl. Mir WF14 138 A8
Linnet Ct. Morley LS27 98 D3
Linnet Gr. Wake WF2 160 D5
Linnet St. Keigh BD21 35 C8
Linnhe Ave. Brad BD6 93 F6
Linshaws Rd. Dun Br HD7 198 E5
Linthwaite Ardron (CE) Sch. Slai 152 E1
Linthwaite Bsns Ctr. Slai 152 D1
Linthwaite Jun & Inf Sch. Slai 152 D1
Linton Ave. Batley WF17 118 A5
Linton Ave. Leeds LS17 43 F4
Linton Ave. Sil BD20 5 E2
Linton Ave. Weth LS22 13 D6
Linton Cl. Leeds LS17 43 E4
Linton Cl. Liver WF15 116 F5
Linton Comm. Coll LS22 13 A1
Linton Cres. Leeds LS17 43 F4
Linton Croft. Leeds LS16 59 A8 3
Linton Dr. Leeds LS17 43 E4
Linton Gr. Batley WF16 117 E3
Linton Gr. Brig HD6 135 E8
Linton Gr. Leeds LS17 43 F4
Linton Hills Rd. Coll LS22 13 C4
Linton La. Coll LS22 13 C4

Linton La. Spoff LS22 13 A7
Linton Meadows. Weth LS22 13 C5
Linton Rd. Coll LS22 13 B1
Linton Rd. Leeds LS17 43 E4
Linton Rd. Wake WF1 142 F6
Linton Rd. Weth LS22 13 D5
Linton Rise. Leeds LS17 43 E4
Linton St. Brad BD4 74 F4
Linton View. Leeds LS17 43 E5
Lion Cott. Caw S75 193 E4
Lion St. Tod OL14 108 A3
Lionel St. Ossett WF5 140 E4
Liphill Bank Rd. Holmfi HD7 188 D4
Lippersley La. Sil LS29 6 B6
Lipscomb St. Hud HD3 153 B5
Lisbon Sq. Leeds LS1 79 A8 10
Lisbon St. Leeds LS1 79 A8
Lisheen Ave. Castle WF10 124 E6
Lishen Gr. Castle WF10 124 E7
Lisker Ave. Otley LS21 23 B7
Lisker Dr. Otley LS21 23 B7
Lismore Rd. Keigh BD20 35 B8
Lister Ave. Brad BD4 75 B3
Lister Cl. Feath WF7 145 C5
Lister Ct. Hali HX1 113 C7 9
Lister Hill. Hors LS18 41 C2
Lister La. Brad BD2 56 A3
Lister La. Hali HX1 113 A7
Lister Lane Sch. Brad 56 A3
Lister Pk. Brad 55 C3
Lister Rd. Feath WF7 145 C5
Lister St. Brad BD4 75 C2
Lister St. Brad BD4 75 E1
Lister St. Brig HD6 115 A3
Lister St. Castle WF10 124 C8
Lister St. Hali HX1 113 C7
Lister St. Hud HD5 154 E5
Lister St. Ilkley LS29 8 A4
Lister St. Keigh BD21 35 B6
Lister View. Brad BD8 55 C1
Lister Ville. Wils BD15 53 C5
Lister's Rd. Hali HX3 113 E8
Lister's Rd. Hud HD2 136 B3
Listerdale. Liver WF15 117 B5
Listerhills Ind Est. Brad 74 C7
Listerhills Rd. Brad BD7 74 C7
Listers Ct. Ilkley LS29 8 A4
Listing Ave. Liver WF15 117 B5
Listing Ct. Liver WF15 117 B5
Listing Dr. Liver WF15 117 B5
Listing La. Liver BD19, WF15 . 117 B6
Litell Royd. Feath WF7 144 D5
Litherop La. Emley HD8 176 C5
Litherop Rd. H Hoy S75 176 D3
Little Baines St. Hali HX1 113 A7
Little Bradley. Elland HX4 134 C6
Little Brunswick St. Hud HD1 154 A7 6
Little Cake. Holmfi HD7 189 C2
Little Church La. M'town LS26 102 C2
Little Cross St. Brad BD5 74 E2 1
Little Fountain St. Morley LS27 98 A3
Little Green La. Batley WF16 117 C5
Little Hemsworth. Hem WF9 181 E6
Little Horton Gn. Brad BD5 74 D5
Little Horton La. Brad BD5 74 D4
Little Horton La. Brad BD5 74 E6 2
Little King St. Leeds LS1 79 B7
Little La. Brad BD9 54 F1
Little La. Feath WF7 145 E4
Little La. Holmfi HD7 188 F5
Little La. Holmfi HD7 189 C6
Little La. Ilkley LS29 8 C4
Little La. Keigh BD20 19 E1
Little La. Morley LS27 98 C8 7
Little La. Roth WF3 100 E3
Little La. S Elm WF9 182 F3
Little La. S Elm WF9 183 B3
Little La. Upton WF9 183 B7
Little La. Wad M HX7 69 B6
Little Lane Ct. Morley LS27 98 C8 8
Little London. Northo HX3 92 F4
Little London Prim Sch. Leeds 60 C2
Little Moor Pl. Leeds LS12 78 B7 6
Little Neville St. Leeds LS1 79 B7
Little Pk. Brad BD10 39 F1
Little Queen St. Leeds LS1 79 A8
Little St. Haw BD22 51 C8
Little Woodhouse. Brig HD6 115 A2
Little Woodhouse St. Leeds LS2 60 A1
Littlebeck Dr. Bing BD16 37 C3
Littlefield Gr. Ossett WF5 140 E6
Littlefield Rd. Ossett WF5 140 E5
Littlefield Wlk. Brad BD6 94 B8
Littleholme St. Tod OL14 108 A3
Littlelands. Ship BD16 54 A7
Littlemoor Cres. Pudsey LS28 76 E5
Littlemoor Cres S. Pudsey LS28 76 E5
Littlemoor Gdns. Hali HX2 91 E6
Littlemoor Gdns. Pudsey LS28 76 E5
Littlemoor Gr. Mir WF14 137 F5
Littlemoor La. Thorner LS14 45 F5
Littlemoor Rd. Hali HX2 91 E6
Littlemoor Rd. Mir WF14 137 F5 2
Littlemoor Rd. Pudsey LS28 76 F6
Littlemoor View. Pudsey LS28 76 F6
Littlethorpe Hill. Liver WF15 116 D1
Littlethorpe Rd. Liver WF15 116 D2
Littletown Prim Sch. Liver 117 A6
Littleway. Leeds LS17 43 C1
Littlewood Cl. Brad BD6 94 C7
Litton Croft. Wake WF1 142 F7
Litton Rd. Keigh BD22 35 A6
Litton Way. Leeds LS14 62 B8
Littondale Cl. Bail BD17 38 E4
Liversedge Hall La. Liver WF15 117 A3
Liversedge Sec Sch. Liver 117 A3
Livingston House. Brad BD10 56 C6
Livingstone Cl. Brad BD2 55 F6
Livingstone Rd. Brad BD2 55 F5
Livingstone Rd. Ship BD2 55 D4
Livingstone St. Hali HX3 92 A1 11
Livingstone St N. Hali HX2 92 A5
Livinia Gr. Leeds LS7 60 C2
Lloyd St. Tod OL14 108 B6
Lloyds Dr. Brad BD12 94 E6
Lobley St. Batley WF16 117 E4
Locarno Ave. Brad BD9 54 E2
Locherbie Gn. Brad BD15 54 B1
Lochy Rd. Brad BD6 93 F6
Lock La. Castle WF10 103 D1
Lock La. Nor WF6 122 F6
Lock St. Dew WF12 139 D4
Lock St. Hali HX3 113 D6
Lock St. Tod OL14 108 A3
Lock View. Bing BD16 36 E4
Lock Way. Dew WF13 138 E4
Locksley Rd. Brig HD6 115 D1
Lockwood Ave. Mir WF14 138 B7
Lockwood Cl. Leeds LS11 79 C1
Lockwood Ct. Leeds LS11 79 C1
Lockwood Pk. Leeds LS11 79 C1
Lockwood Rd. Hud HD1 153 F3
Lockwood Scar. Hud HD4 154 A2
Lockwood St. Brad BD6 74 C1
Lockwood St. Brad BD12 94 E5
Lockwood St. Ship BD18 54 F8 5
Lockwood Sta. Hud 153 E3
Lockwood Way. Leeds LS11 79 C1
Lockwood's Yd. Hud HD1 154 A6 21
Lode Pit La. Bing BD16 37 D4
Lodge Ave. Castle WF10 125 C7
Lodge Ave. Elland HX5 135 C7
Lodge Cl. Hud HD4 153 E1
Lodge Dr. Elland HX5 135 C7
Lodge Dr. Mir WF14 138 C4
Lodge Farm Cl. Dew WF12 139 D4
Lodge Farm Gdns. Nor WF6 122 F3
Lodge Gate Cl. Denh BD13 52 E1
Lodge Gate. Denh BD13 52 E1
Lodge Hill. Bail BD17 37 F3
Lodge Hill Rd. Ossett WF5 140 D8
Lodge La. Crof WF4 143 E2
Lodge La. Leeds LS11 79 B3
Lodge La. Liver WF15 117 C2
Lodge La. Wake WF2 160 E4
Lodge Pl. Elland HX5 135 C7
Lodge Rd. Pudsey LS28 76 D8
Lodge St. Cull BD13 52 D6
Lodge St. Glu BD20 16 B6
Lodge St. Hem WF9 181 D8
Lodge St. Leeds LS2 60 B1
Lodge St. Skel HD8 175 A2
Lodge Terr. Leeds LS11 79 B2 13
Lodge The. Hud HD7 152 E2
Lodges Cl. Ryhill WF4 162 C2
Lodore Ave. Brad BD2 56 B3
Lodore Pl. Brad BD2 56 B3
Lodore Rd. Brad BD2 56 A3
Loft St. Brad BD8 73 F8
Lofthouse Pl. Leeds LS2 60 B2
Lofthouse Terr. Leeds LS2 60 C2
Logwood St. Hud HD1 154 A4
Lombar House. Brad BD15 73 B7 6
Lombard St. Hali HX1 112 F5
Lombard St. Leeds LS15 80 F7
Lombard St. Yeadon LS19 40 A4
Lombardi Ct. Ossett WF5 140 F4
Lombardy Garth. Wake WF2 142 A8
Lomond Ave. Hors LS18 41 B4
Londesboro Gr. Leeds LS9 80 A7
Londesboro Terr. Leeds LS9 80 A7
London La. Yeadon LS19 40 A4
London Rd. Slai HD7 152 A1
London Rd. Sow Br HX6 112 E3
London Rd. Tod OL14 109 C6
London Spring Rd. Rip HX6 132 A4
London St. Yeadon LS19 40 A4
Long Cl. Brad BD12 94 B4
Long Close La. Holmfi HD8 190 C7
Long Close La. Leeds LS9 79 F7
Long Close La. S Elm WF9 183 C6
Long Crest. Pont WF8 146 E6
Long Croft. Mapp S75 178 B1
Long Croft St. Hud HD7 152 E4
Long Cswy. Denh BD13 71 C8
Long Cswy. Dew WF12 139 D3
Long Cswy. Hal E BD23 1 D7
Long Cswy. Hors LS16 42 D3
Long Cswy. Leeds LS9 79 F5
Long Cswy. Loft G WF3 121 F5
Long Cswy. Rip HX6 131 F1
Long Cswy The. B Head HX7 87 E4
Long Cswy The. H Chap BB10 85 D7
Long Cswy The. Heb Br HX7 111 A6
Long Cswy The. Sow Br HX7 111 A6
Long Cswy. Tod OL14 108 F3
Long Cswy. Wake WF1 142 D8
Long Dam La. Ryhill WF4 162 B3
Long Edge Low Rd. Sow Br HX6 111 B2
Long Edge Rd. Sow Br HX7 111 A3
Long Fallas Cres. Brig HD6 136 B8
Long Gate. Haw BD20 33 B8
Long Gate. Rip HX6 150 A8
Long Gate. S in Cra BD20 33 B8
Long Grove Ave. Hud HD5 154 E6
Long Hey La. Tod OL14 108 C3
Long Heys. Elland HX4 134 C6
Long Hill End. Cowl BD22 32 D8
Long Hill Rd. Hud HD2 136 C4
Long House Rd. Hali HX2 91 C6
Long Ing Rd. Holmfi HD7 199 A7
Long La. Ack M T WF7 146 B1
Long La. B in Elm LS15 63 E5
Long La. Brad BD15 53 D1
Long La. Clay W HD8 175 F3
Long La. Dew WF12 139 F6
Long La. Floc WF4 156 E1
Long La. Hali HX2, HX3 91 E2
Long La. Hali HX3 113 F6
Long La. Harden BD16 36 A1
Long La. Heb Br HX7 88 E1
Long La. Heb Br HX7 109 D3
Long La. Hud HD5 154 E7
Long La. K Smea WF8 166 D3
Long La. Pont WF7, WF8 146 F7
Long La. Queen BD13 92 E7
Long La. Shep HD8 173 E2
Long La. Ship BD9 54 E5
Long La. Sow Br HX6 112 A2
Long Lee Fst Sch. Keigh 35 F5
Long Lee La. Keigh BD21 35 E5
Long Lover La. Hali HX1 112 F8
Long Meadow Ct. Gar LS25 83 A5
Long Meadow Gate. Gar LS25 82 F5
Long Meadows. Brad BD2 55 E4
Long Meadows. Bramho LS16 24 E2
Long Meadows. Gar LS25 82 F5
Long Moor La. Shep HD8 174 B1
Long Reach. Hali HX2 91 A3
Long Riddings. Add LS29 2 E1
Long Ridge. Brig HD6 136 A7
Long Row. Brad BD12 94 D5
Long Row. Crof WF4 144 A5
Long Row Ct. Brad BD5 74 E3 2
Long Row. Hors LS18 41 C2
Long Row. Thorn BD13 72 C7
Long Royd Dr. Bail BD17 38 E4
Long Royd La. Shep HD8 191 B8
Long Royd Rd. Sow Br HX6 111 C2
Long Shaw La. Tod OL14 108 F4
Long St. Brad BD4 75 B5
Long Thorpe La. Roth WF3 100 B1
Long Tongue Scrog La. Kirkhe HD5 155 E7
Long Tongue Scrog La. Lepton WF14 155 F6
Long Wall. Elland HX5 134 E6
Longacre. Castle WF10 124 D6
Longbottom Ave. Sil BD20 5 F1
Longbottom Ave. Sow Br HX6 111 E3
Longbottom Terr. Hali HX3 113 D4
Longcauseway. Dew WF12 139 D7
Longclose Ind Est. Leeds 60 E2
Longcroft. Hud HD5 154 F2
Longcroft Jun Sch. Hud 154 F2
Longcroft. Keigh BD21 35 C6
Longcroft Link. Brad BD1 74 D7 3
Longcroft Pl. Brad BD1 74 D7 4
Longcroft Rd. Ilkley LS29 8 E3
Longdale Dr. S Elm WF9 182 E4
Longden Ave. Hud HD4 153 D2
Longdike Ct. Kippax LS25 83 B1 3
Longdike La. Kippax LS25 103 C8
Longdon Ave. Lepton HD8 155 E3
Longdon Wlk. Lepton HD8 155 E3
Longfellow Gr. Loft G WF3 121 E6
Longfield Ave. Hud HD7 152 E5
Longfield Ave. Hud HD5 154 D7
Longfield Ave. Northo HX3 93 A1
Longfield Ave. Pudsey LS28 76 F7 3
Longfield Cl. Hud HD5 154 D7
Longfield Cl. Tod OL14 108 B4
Longfield Dr. Ack M T WF7 164 C7
Longfield Dr. Leeds LS13 81 A8
Longfield Dr. Mapp S75 178 B1
Longfield Dr. Pudsey LS13 57 F5
Longfield. Elland HX4 134 B4
Longfield Garth. Pudsey LS13 57 F5 3
Longfield Gr. Pudsey LS28 76 F7 2
Longfield Gr. Tod OL14 108 B4
Longfield. Hep HX7 88 F4
Longfield La. Tod OL14 108 B3
Longfield Mount. Pudsey LS28 76 F7 1
Longfield Rd. Batley WF16 117 D4
Longfield Rd. Pudsey LS28 76 E7
Longfield Rd. Tod OL14 108 B5
Longfield Terr. Pudsey LS28 76 E7
Longfield Terr. Tod OL14 108 B4
Longfield Terr. Wake WF2 141 F7
Longfield Way. Tod OL14 108 B4
Longford Terr. Brad BD7 73 F5
Longhouse Dr. Denh BD13 71 D8
Longhouse La. Denh BD13 71 D8
Longlands Ave. Denh BD13 52 D1
Longlands Ave. Slai HD7 151 E1
Longlands Bank. Holmfi HD7 189 B8
Longlands Cl. Ossett WF5 140 E6
Longlands Dr. Haw BD22 51 D8
Longlands Dr. Mapp S75 178 B1
Longlands La. Sickl LS22 12 D4
Longlands Rd. Batley WF13 118 A2
Longlands Rd. Ossett WF5 140 E6
Longlands Rd. Slai HD7 151 E1
Longlands St. Brad BD1 74 D7
Longlands Trad Est. Ossett 140 E6
Longley Edge La. Holmfi HD7 189 B1
Longley Edge Rd. Holmfi HD7 189 B1
Longley La. Holmfi HD7 189 A1
Longley La. Hud HD4 154 D2
Longley La. Sow Br HX6 111 F1
Longley Park Golf Course. Hud 154 C4
Longley Rd. Hud HD5 154 D4
Longmeadow. Rip HX4 133 A5
Longroyd Ave. Leeds LS11 79 C3
Longroyd Cres. Leeds LS11 79 C3
Longroyd Cres N. Leeds LS11 79 C3
Longroyd Cres. Slai HD7 151 E1
Longroyd Gr. Leeds LS11 79 C3
Longroyd La. Hud HD1 153 F5
Longroyd Pl. Hud HD1 153 E5
Longroyd Pl. Leeds LS11 79 C3
Longroyd St. Leeds LS11 79 C3
Longroyd St N. Leeds LS11 79 C3
Longroyd Terr. Leeds LS11 79 C3
Longroyd View. Leeds LS11 79 C3
Longroyde Cl. Brig HD6 114 F1
Longroyde Gr. Brig HD6 135 F8
Longroyde Jun & Inf Sch. Brig 114 F1
Longroyde Rd. Brig HD6 115 A1 3
Longside La. Brad BD7 74 C6
Longsight Rd. Mapp S75 178 A1
Longsight Terr. Hem WF9 163 B1
Longwood Ave. Bing BD16 36 E5
Longwood Cl. E Ard WF3 119 D8
Longwood Cl. Leeds LS17 44 B5
Longwood Cres. Leeds LS17 44 B5
Longwood Ct. E Ard WF3 119 E8
Longwood Edge Rd. Hud HD3 152 E7
Longwood Fold. E Ard WF3 119 E8
Longwood Garth. E Ard WF3 119 E8
Longwood Gate. Hud HD3 152 F6
Longwood House Rd. Hud HD2 136 A3
Longwood Rd. E Ard WF3 119 E8
Longwood Rd. Hud HD3 153 C5
Longwood Vale. E Ard WF3 119 E8
Longwood View. Bing BD16 36 E5
Longwood Way. Leeds LS17 44 B5
Longwoods Wlk. Knot WF11 127 A5
Lonsbrough Ave. Batley WF16 117 D5
Lonsbrough Flats. Hud HD1 154 B6 7
Lonsbrough Way. S Elm WF9 183 A4
Lonsdale Ave. Batley WF17 117 F7 3
Lonsdale Meadows. B Spa LS23 30 D7
Lonsdale Rd. Wake WF1 142 B8
Lonsdale Rise. E Ard WF3 119 E8
Lonsdale St. Brad BD3 75 B8
Lord La. Haw BD22 51 B8
Lord St. Batley WF13 117 F4
Lord St. Dew WF12 140 B7
Lord St. Hali HX6 112 C5
Lord St. Hali HX1 113 C7
Lord St. Haw BD22 51 D7 12
Lord St. Hud HD1 154 B6
Lord St. Keigh BD21 35 C7
Lord St. Leeds LS12 78 F6
Lord St. Slai HD7 151 F1
Lord St. Tod OL14 108 A1
Lord St. Wake WF1 142 F3
Lord Terr. Leeds LS12 78 F6 2
Lord's Bldgs. Morley LS27 98 A2 6
Lord's La. Brig HD6 115 B1
Lordsfield Pl. Brad BD4 75 D1
Lorne Fst Sch. Brad 75 B4
Lorne St. Brad BD4 75 B3
Lorne St. Haw BD22 51 F8 2
Lorne St. Keigh BD21 35 E8
Lorry Bank. Leeds LS7 60 C4
Loscoe Cl. Feath WF6 123 E3
Loscoe La. Feath WF6, WF7 124 A1
Loscoe La. Nor WF6 123 E2
Lothersdale Rd. Glu BD20 16 A7
Lotherton Hall. Aber 65 B5
Lotherton La. Aber LS25 65 A6
Lotherton La. Aber LS25 65 B5
Lotherton Way. Gar LS25 83 A8
Loughrigg St. Brad BD5 74 E3
Louis Ave. Brad BD5 74 C4
Louis Ct. Leeds LS7 60 D3
Louis Gr. Leeds LS7 60 E3
Louis Le Prince Ct. Leeds LS8 60 F3
Louis St. Leeds LS7 60 E3
Louisa St. Brad BD10 56 B8
Louisa St. Castle WF10 124 C8
Lound La. H Pag DN5 195 F5
Lovaine Gr. Wake WF2 142 D1
Love La. Castle WF10 124 C6
Love La. Hali HX1 113 B5
Love La. Ossett WF5 140 C6
Love La. Pont WF8 146 B8
Love La. Roth LS26 100 E5
Love La. Wake WF2 142 B6
Love Lane Terr. Pont WF8 146 C8
Lovell House. Brad BD15 73 B7 4
Lovell Park Cl. Leeds LS7 60 D1
Lovell Park Ct. Leeds LS7 60 C1
Lovell Park Gate. Leeds LS7 60 C1
Lovell Park Grange. Leeds LS7 60 D1
Lovell Park Hill. Leeds LS7 60 D1
Lovell Park Hts. Leeds LS7 60 D1
Lovell Park Rd. Leeds LS2, LS7 60 C1
Lovell Park Towers. Leeds LS7 60 C1
Lovell Park View. Leeds LS7 60 D1
Low Ash Ave. Ship BD18 55 D7
Low Ash Cres. Ship BD18 55 D7
Low Ash Dr. Ship BD18 55 D7
Low Ash Fst Sch. Ship 55 D6
Low Ash Gr. Ship BD18 55 D7
Low Ash Rd. Ship BD18 55 E7
Low Bank Dr. Haw BD22 34 B3
Low Bank La. Haw BD22 34 B2
Low Bank St. Pudsey LS28 57 D3
Low Cl. Bing BD16 37 B2
Low Cl. Ilkley LS29 8 B5
Low Cliff Wlk. Batley FW16 117 E2
Low Close St. Leeds LS2 60 A3
Low Cross Ct. Knot WF11 127 A5
Low Farm La. Ack M T WF7 164 A6
Low Farm. Swil LS26 102 E8
Low Fields Ave. Leeds LS11 78 E4
Low Fields Rd. Leeds LS11 78 E4
Low Fields Rd. Leeds LS12 78 E4
Low Fields Way. Leeds LS11 78 E4
Low Fold. Brad BD2 55 F2
Low Fold. Brig BD19 115 F8
Low Fold. Denh BD13 52 D2
Low Fold. Leeds LS9 79 E6
Low Fold. Stee BD20 17 D5
Low Fold. Yeadon LS19 40 B4
Low Gate. Kirkb HD8 173 F6
Low Gate La. Densh OL3 167 A1
Low Gate. S Elm WF9 183 A3
Low Gipton Cres. Leeds LS8 61 D3
Low Gn. Ack M T WF7 164 B7
Low Gn. Knot WF11 127 B4
Low Gn. Yeadon LS19 40 C3
Low Grange Cres. Midd LS10 79 E1
Low Grange Rd. Dearne S63 194 C1
Low Grange View. Midd LS10 99 E8
Low Green. Brad BD7 74 A3 4
Low Green Terr. Brad BD7 74 B3
Low Hall Cl. Men LS29 22 A4
Low Hall Pl. Leeds LS11 79 A6
Low Hall Rd. Men LS29 22 B4
Low Hall Rd. Yeadon LS18 57 E8
Low Hill. Bail BD17 38 C6
Low Hills La. Hud HD3 135 A1
Low House Dr. Sil BD20 17 E8
Low House Fold. Liver WF15 116 F4
Low La. Batley WF17 96 E1
Low La. Brad BD14 73 A5
Low La. Brig HD6 115 C6
Low La. Draug BD23 1 E6
Low La. Embsay BD23 1 B8
Low La. Hal E BD23 1 B8
Low La. Hors LS18 41 D1
Low La. Neth WF4 158 B8
Low La. Queen BD13 72 C3
Low La. Sil BD20 5 C5
Low La. Sil BD20 18 A6
Low La. Thorn BD14 73 A5
Low La. Wad M HX2 90 A7
Low Laithes Golf Course. Wake 141 B7
Low Mill La. Add LS29 7 B8
Low Mill La. Dew WF13 138 E4
Low Mill La. Keigh BD21 35 D7
Low Mill Rd. Ossett WF5 140 C3
Low Mills Rd. Leeds LS12 78 B4
Low Moor Cres. Crig WF4 159 F3
Low Moor Fst Sch. Brad 94 E6
Low Moor La. Crig WF4 159 E1
Low Moor Side. Gild LS12 77 D3
Low Moor Side La. Gild LS12 77 C2
Low Moor St. Brad BD12 94 D6
Low Moor Terr. Hali HX2 112 D7
Low Moorside Cl. Gild LS12 77 E3
Low Moorside Ct. Gild LS12 77 D3
Low Park Rd. Denton LS29 9 B5
Low Platt La. Mars HD3 151 B5
Low Rd. Dew WF13 138 F8
Low Rd. Dew WF12 139 C1
Low Rd. Dew WF12 139 E7
Low Rd. Hud HD4 171 F8
Low Rd. Leeds LS10 79 F3
Low Road Prim Sch. Leeds 79 E3
Low Row. Mapp S75 177 E3
Low Shops La. Roth LS26 100 C6
Low Spring Rd. Keigh BD21 35 F6
Low St. Broth WF11 126 C7
Low St. Dew WF13 118 C1
Low St. E Ard WF3 98 F1
Low St. Keigh BD21 35 C7
Low Town. Kirkb HD8 173 F6
Low Way. B Spa LS23 30 D6
Low Way. Bramham LS23 30 D2
Low Well Rd. Brad BD5 74 D3 4
Low Whitehouse Row. Leeds LS10 79 D5
Low Wood Ct. Keigh BD20 18 B3
Low Wood Rise. Ilkley LS29 8 F3
Low Wood. Wils BD15 53 D4
Lowcroft. Coll LS22 29 A8
Lowdale. Batley WF12 118 E2
Lowell Ave. Brad BD7 73 F5
Lowell Gr. Pudsey LS13 77 A8
Lowell Pl. Pudsey LS13 77 A8
Lower Ashgrove. Brad BD5 74 D6
Lower Back La. B Head HX7 87 F4
Lower Bank House. Elland HX4 133 D4
Lower Bankhouse. Pudsey LS28 76 D4
Lower Basinghall St. Leeds LS1 79 B7
Lower Bentley Royd. Hali HX6 112 A4
Lower Bower La. Batley WF13 117 F2 1
Lower Brockwell La. Sow Br HX6 111 F2
Lower Brunswick St. Leeds LS2 60 D1
Lower Calderbrook. Litt OL15 129 C1
Lower Cambridge St. Castle WF10 124 E8
Lower Clay Pits. Hali HX1 112 F8
Lower Clifton St. Hali HX6 112 C4
Lower Clyde St. Sow Br HX6 112 B3
Lower Common La. Clay W HD8 175 E1
Lower Constable Rd. Ilkley LS29 8 D3
Lower Cross St. Dew WF13 118 C1 1
Lower Cross St. Hali HX1 113 D7
Lower Crow Nest Dr. Brig HX3 115 B7
Lower Denby La. D Dale HD8 192 B4
Lower Edge Rd. Brig HD6 135 D7
Lower Edge Rd. Elland HX5 135 D7
Lower Exley. Hali HX3 113 D1
Lower Fields Mid Sch. Brad 75 C4
Lower Finkil St. Brig HD6 114 F5
Lower Fitzwilliam St. Hud HD1 154 B7 4
Lower Fold. Brig HD6 135 F6
Lower Fold. Hali HX1 113 C7
Lower Fold. Honley HD7 171 F5
Lower Furney Lee. Tod OL14 108 A6
Lower Gate. Hud HD3 153 C5
Lower George St. Brad BD6 74 B1 5
Lower George St. Tod OL14 108 C5 5
Lower Globe St. Brad BD8 74 C8
Lower Grange Cl. Brad BD8 73 C7
Lower Grange. Hud HD2 136 E6
Lower Grattan Rd. Brad BD1 74 D7 9
Lower Greave Rd. Mel HD7 188 B8
Lower Green Ave. Brig BD19 115 F8 11
Lower Green. Bail BD17 38 B2
Lower Hagg. Holmfi HD7 172 B1
Lower Hall Cl. Liver WF15 116 F4
Lower Hall Cres. Kirkhe HD5 155 C6
Lower Hall Dr. Liver WF15 116 F4
Lower Hall La. Liver WF15 116 F4
Lower Hall Mount. Liver WF15 116 F4
Lower Hall Rd. Kirkhe HD5 155 C6
Lower Haughs. Slai HD7 152 B5
Lower Heights Rd. Thorn BD13 72 C8
Lower Hey. Mel HD7 170 D2
Lower Highfield. Hali HX2 91 B3
Lower Holme. Bail BD17 38 C1
Lower Holme. Slai HD7 169 D8
Lower House La. Lepton HD8 156 B2
Lower Kipping La. Thorn BD13 72 D6 10
Lower Kirkgate. Hali HX1 113 D7
Lower La. B Head HX7 87 E3
Lower La. Birk BD4 95 D5
Lower La. Brad BD4 75 C4
Lower La. Clec BD19 117 B7
Lower La. Honley HD7 171 E4
Lower Laith Ave. Tod OL14 108 C5
Lower Langwith. Coll LS22 29 A8
Lower Lark Hill. Clec BD19 116 B7
Lower Maythorn La. Wh Com HD7 200 D8
Lower Meadows. Holmfi HD7 188 D5
Lower Mickletown. M'town LS26 102 F3
Lower Mill Bank Rd. Sow Br HX6 132 D7
Lower Newlands. Brig HD6 115 B1
Lower North St. Batley WF17 118 B4
Lower Northcroft. S Elm WF9 183 A3
Lower Northfield La. S Kirk WF9 182 C3
Lower Oxford St. Castle WF10 124 D7
Lower Park Gn. Sil BD20 5 C1
Lower Park Royd Dr. Rip HX6 132 E6
Lower Peel St. Dew WF13 118 C1
Lower Putt'g Mill. D Dale HD8 192 B7
Lower Quarry Rd. Hud HD2, HD5 137 A6
Lower Range. Hali HX3 92 C1 9
Lower Rd. Mars HD3 150 F5
Lower Reins. Honley HD7 172 A6
Lower Rushton Rd. Brad BD3 75 E7
Lower Sandhills. Thorner LS14 45 E3
Lower Scholes. Haw BD22 50 F8
Lower School St. Brad BD12 94 C6
Lower School St. Ship BD18 54 F8 3
Lower Skircoat Gn. Hali HX3 113 C2
Lower Smithy. B Head HX7 88 A5
Lower Station Rd. Nor WF6 123 A2
Lower Swift Pl. Rip HX6 132 B2
Lower Taythes La. Pont WF8 126 A1
Lower Top of Hill. Mars HD3 150 F6
Lower Town End Rd. Holmfi HD7 189 C7
Lower Town St. Leeds LS13 58 D2
Lower Viaduct St. Hud HD1 154 B7 6
Lower W'rrengate. Wake WF1 142 D6 2
Lower Wellgate. Elland HX4 134 C7 3
Lower Wellhouse Rd. Slai HD7 152 D3
Lower Wellington Rd. Ilkley LS29 8 B4
Lower Westfield Rd. Brad BD9 55 A1
Lower Wheat Royd. Hud HD5 154 F2
Lower Whitegate Rd. Hud HD4 154 B3
Lower Wormald. Rip HX6 131 F1
Lower Wortley Prim Sch. Leeds 78 B4
Lower Wortley Rd. Leeds LS12 78 B5
Lower Wyke Gn. Brig BD12 115 B8
Lower Wyke La. Brig BD12 115 C8
Lower York St. Wake WF1 142 C7
Lowerhouses CE Inf Sch. Hud 154 D3
Lowerhouses. Hud HD7 152 E2
Lowerhouses La. Hud HD5 154 D3
Lowerhouses Rd. Hud HD3 153 B6
Lowertown. Oxen BD22 51 C2
Lowestwood La. Slai HD7 152 D2
Loweswater Ave. Brad BD6 93 F6
Loweswater Rd. Knot WF11 126 E2
Lowfield Cl. Brad BD12 94 E5
Lowfield Cres. Hem WF9 181 E7
Lowfield Cres. Sil BD20 17 F8
Lowfield La. Beam BD23 3 A4
Lowfield Rd. Dew WF13 138 F8
Lowfields Way. Hali HX5 135 A8
Lowlands Rd. Mir WF14 138 B4
Lowood La. Batley WF17 96 F3
Lowry Rd. E Ard WF3 119 E8
Lowry View. Keigh BD21 35 C6 6
Lowther Ave. Gar LS25 82 E6
Lowther Cres. Swil LS26 82 A2
Lowther Dr. Gar LS25 82 E6
Lowther Gr. Gar LS25 82 E6
Lowther Rd. Gar LS25 82 E6
Lowther St. Brad BD2 56 B2
Lowther St. Leeds LS8 60 F4 22
Lowther Terr. Swil LS15 82 A6
Lowtown Jun & Inf Sch. Pudsey 76 F7
Lowtown. Pudsey LS28 76 F8
Loxley Gr. Weth LS22 13 D8
Loxley St. Batley WF17 118 A7
Lucas Ct. Leeds LS6 60 C3
Lucas Pl. Leeds LS6 60 A4
Lucas St. Leeds LS6 60 A4
Luck La. Hud HD1, HD3 153 D6
Lucy Ave. Leeds LS15 80 E8
Lucy Hall Dr. Bail BD17 37 F3
Lucy La. Lepton HD8 155 E5
Lucy St. Hali HX3 113 D8
Luddenden CE Inf Sch. Hali 111 D8
Luddenden La. Hali HX2 111 D7
Luddenden Prim Sch. Hali 111 D8
Luddendenfoot Jun & Inf Sch. Hali 111 E5
Luddendon Pl. Queen BD13 72 C2 3
Luddite House. Liver WF15 117 A5 8
Ludhill La. Honley HD4 172 D5
Ludlam St. Brad BD5 74 E5
Ludlow Ave. Gar LS25 83 B7
Ludolf Dr. Thorner LS17 44 E4
Ludwell Cl. Dew WF12 139 F1
Ludwood Cl. Honley HD7 172 B5
Luke La. Holmfi HD7 172 C1
Luke La. Honley HD7 172 C1
Luke Rd. Brad BD5 74 C4
Lulworth Ave. Leeds LS15 81 D8
Lulworth Cl. Leeds LS15 62 D1 1
Lulworth Cres. Leeds LS15 62 D1
Lulworth Dr. Leeds LS15 81 D8
Lulworth Garth. Leeds LS15 81 D8
Lulworth Gr. Brad BD4 75 D2
Lulworth View. Leeds LS15 81 D8
Lulworth Wlk. Leeds LS15 62 D1
Lumb Bottom. Birk BD11 96 F7
Lumb Foot. Haw BD22 50 E7
Lumb Gill La. Add LS29 7 B6
Lumb La. Brad BD8 74 D8
Lumb La. Hali HX2 90 F6
Lumb La. Hali HX3 92 B2
Lumb La. Hud HD4 172 D8
Lumb La. Liver WF15 116 F2
Lumb La. Sow Br HX6 132 C7
Lumb Rd. Hep HX7 88 D5
Lumb Terr. Hali HX2 90 F6
Lumbfoot Rd. Haw BD22 50 F7
Lumbrook Cl. Northo HX3 93 C3
Lumbrook. Northo HX3 93 C2
Lumbutts La. Tod OL14 108 F4
Lumbutts Rd. Tod OL14 108 C3
Lumby Cl. Pudsey LS28 76 F5
Lumby La. E Kes LS17 28 B6
Lumby La. Pudsey LS28 76 F6
Lumby Leys La. S Mil LS25 105 A8
Lumby St. Brad BD10 56 B8
Lumley Ave. Castle WF10 124 A7
Lumley Ave. Leeds LS4 59 D3
Lumley Gr. Leeds LS4 59 D3
Lumley Hill. Castle WF10 124 A7
Lumley Mount Bglws. Castle WF10 124 A6
Lumley Mount. Castle WF10 124 A6
Lumley Mount. Leeds LS4 59 D3
Lumley Pl. Leeds LS4 59 D3
Lumley Rd. Batley WF12 118 E2
Lumley Rd. Leeds LS4 59 D3
Lumley St. Castle WF10 124 B7
Lumley St. Leeds LS4 59 D3
Lumley Terr. Leeds LS4 59 D3
Lumley View. Leeds LS4 59 D3
Lumley Wlk. Leeds LS4 59 D3
Lunan Pl. Leeds LS8 60 F4 13
Lunan Terr. Leeds LS8 60 F4 14
Lund Dr. Batley WF16 117 E3
Lund Hill La. Roy S71 179 F5
Lund Hill La. Ryhill S71 179 F5
Lund La. Keigh BD22 34 B6
Lund St. Bing BD16 36 F3
Lund St. Brad BD8 73 E7
Lund St. Keigh BD21 35 C8
Lunnfields La. B Sal LS25, WF11 105 C4
Lupset Cres. Wake WF2 141 E3
Lupton Ave. Leeds LS9 61 B1
Lupton St. Brad BD8 55 E1
Lupton St. Leeds LS10 79 E3
Lustre St. Keigh BD21 35 A7
Luther Pl. Hud HD2 153 E8
Luther St. Pudsey LS13 57 E5
Luther Way. Brad BD2 55 F3
Luton St. Hali HX1 112 F7
Luton St. Hud HD4 152 F3
Luton St. Keigh BD21 35 B7
Luttrell Cl. Hors LS16 42 A2
Luttrell Cres. Hors LS16 42 A2

Luttrell Gdns. Hors LS16 .... 42 A2
Luttrell Pl. Hors LS16 .... 42 A2
Luttrell Rd. Hors LS16 .... 42 A2
Luxor Ave. Leeds LS8 .... 60 F4 20
Luxor Rd. Leeds LS8 .... 60 F4 18
Luxor St. Leeds LS8 .... 60 F4 19
Luxor View. Leeds LS8 .... 60 F4 21
Lydbrook Pk. Elland HX3 .... 113 A2
Lyddon Terr. Leeds LS2 .... 60 A2
Lydgate Cl. Holmfi HD7 .... 189 E6
Lydgate Cty Prim Sch. Batley . 118 F5
Lydgate Dr. Holmfi HD7 .... 189 D7
Lydgate Dr. Lepton HD8 .... 156 A3
Lydgate House. Brad BD15 .... 73 B7 5
Lydgate. Leeds LS9 .... 60 F1
Lydgate. Lepton HD8 .... 156 A3
Lydgate. Northo HX3 .... 93 A3
Lydgate Pk. Brig HX3 .... 114 E7
Lydgate Pl. Pudsey LS28 .... 57 A7
Lydgate Rd. Batley WF17 .... 118 F5
Lydgate Rd. Shep HD8 .... 190 F8
Lydgate Sch. Holmfi 189 D7
Lydgate St. Pudsey LS28 .... 57 A7
Lydgetts. Holmfi HD7 .... 188 D5
Lydia St. Leeds LS2 .... 79 D8
Lyme Chase. Leeds LS14 .... 61 F2
Lyme Terr. Ad Le S DN6 .... 184 E1
Lymington Dr. Brad BD4 .... 75 E4
Lyncroft. Brad BD2 .... 55 F4
Lynda Gr. Ossett WF5 .... 141 A4
Lyndale Cres. Batley WF16 ...... 117 E4
Lyndale Dr. Ship BD18 .... 55 F7
Lyndale Dr. Wake WF2 .... 120 E2
Lyndale Gr. Nor WF6 .... 123 C1
Lyndale. Kippax LS25 .... 103 A8
Lyndale Mews. Batley WF13 . 117 F3
Lyndale Rd. Bing BD16 .... 37 C5
Lynden Ave. Ship BD18 .... 55 E8
Lyndhurst Cl. Brad BD6 .... 94 A7
Lyndhurst Ave. Brig HD6 .... 136 A7
Lyndhurst Cl. B in Elm LS15 .... 62 F7
Lyndhurst Cres. B in Elm LS15 . 62 F7
Lyndhurst Gr. Brad BD15 .... 54 C1
Lyndhurst Grove Rd. Brig HD6 136 A7
Lyndhurst Rd. B in Elm LS15 .... 62 F6
Lyndhurst Rd. Brig HD6 .... 136 A8
Lyndhurst Rd. Hud HD3 .... 153 B8
Lyndhurst. S in Cra BD20 .... 16 C5
Lyndhurst View. B in Elm LS15 62 F6
Lyndon Ave. Bramham LS23 .... 30 C3
Lyndon Ave. Gar LS25 .... 82 E7
Lyndon Cl. Bramham LS23 .... 30 C3
Lyndon Cres. Bramham LS23 ... 30 C3
Lyndon Rd. Bramham LS23 ...... 30 C3
Lyndon Sq. Bramham LS23 ...... 30 C3
Lyndon Terr. Bing BD16 .... 37 A3 3
Lyndon Way. Bramham LS23 ... 30 C3
Lyndum Gr. Kippax LS25 .... 83 A2
Lynfield Dr. Brad BD9 .... 54 C3
Lynfield Dr. Clec WF15 .... 116 B5
Lynfield Mount Hospl. Brad 54 D2
Lynfield Mount. Ship BD18 .... 55 E8
Lynndale Ave. Glu BD20 .... 16 D7
Lynndale Ave. Hud HD2 .... 135 F1
Lynnfield Gdns. B in Elm LS15 . 62 F6
Lynnwood Gdns. Pudsey LS28 . 76 C7
Lynsey Gdns. Brad BD4 .... 95 B7
Lynthorne Rd. Ship BD9 .... 55 C4
Lynton Ave. B Spa LS23 .... 30 D8
Lynton Ave. Brad BD9 .... 54 F2
Lynton Ave. Hud HD1 .... 153 F6
Lynton Ave. Midd WF3 .... 99 E2
Lynton Dr. Brad BD9 .... 54 F2
Lynton Dr. Keigh BD20 .... 18 F1
Lynton Dr. Ship BD18 .... 55 A7
Lynton Gr. Brad BD9 .... 54 F2
Lynton Gr. Hali HX2 .... 71 F1
Lynton Terr. Clec BD19 .... 116 D8 5
Lynton Villas. Brad BD9 .... 54 F2
Lynwood Ave. Leeds LS12 .... 78 C5
Lynwood Ave. Roth LS26 .... 101 D6
Lynwood Ave. Ship BD18 .... 55 E8
Lynwood Cl. Birk BD11 .... 96 B4
Lynwood Cl. Feath WF7 .... 144 E4
Lynwood Cl. Knot WF11 .... 127 A5
Lynwood Cres. Hali HX1 .... 112 F5 1
Lynwood Cres. Hem WF9 .... 163 A4
Lynwood Cres. Leeds LS12 .... 78 C5
Lynwood Cres. Pont WF8 .... 146 D6
Lynwood Cres. Roth LS26 .... 101 D6
Lynwood Ct. Brad BD10 .... 56 A7
Lynwood Ct. Keigh BD22 .... 34 E5
Lynwood Dr. Roy S71 .... 179 C2
Lynwood Dr. Wake WF2 .... 160 C6
Lynwood Gr. Leeds LS12 .... 78 C4
Lynwood La. Roy S71 .... 179 C2
Lynwood Mews. Brad BD4 .... 75 F2
Lynwood Mount. Leeds LS12 ..... 78 C5
Lynwood Rise. Leeds LS12 .... 78 C5
Lynwood View. Leeds LS12 .... 78 C5
Lyon Rd. Pont WF8 .... 146 D6
Lyon Rd. Stee BD20 .... 16 F6
Lyon St. Queen BD13 .... 72 F1
Lyon St. Thorn BD13 .... 72 D7
Lytham Dr. Brad BD13 .... 73 B2
Lytham Gr. Leeds LS12 .... 78 A4
Lytham Pl. Leeds LS12 .... 78 A4 13
Lytham St. Hali HX1 .... 112 F7 14
Lytham Way. Hud HD3 .... 153 B8
Lytton Rd. Brad BD8 .... 73 F8
Lytton St. Leeds LS10 .... 79 D3

Mabel Royd. Brad BD7 .... 73 F5
Mabel St. Heb Br HX7 .... 89 E1
Mabgate Gn. Leeds LS9 .... 79 D8
Mabgate. Leeds LS9 .... 79 D8
Macaulay Rd. Hud HD2 .... 135 F1
Macaulay St. Leeds LS9 .... 60 E1
Macham St. Hud HD1 .... 153 F4
Mackey Cres. Bri S72 .... 180 F3
Mackie Hill Cl. Crig WF4 .... 159 D4
Mackingstone Dr. Haw BD22 ... 34 B3
Mackingstone La. Keigh BD22 . 34 B4
Mackinnon Ave. Nor WF6 .... 123 C3
Mackintosh Memorial Homes
The. Hali HX3 .... 113 A4
Macturk Gr. Brad BD8 .... 55 A1
Maddocks St. Ship BD18 .... 55 A8
Madeley Rd. Ryhill WF4 .... 162 C1
Madeley Sq. Castle WF10 .... 104 C1
Madgin La. Hud HD7 .... 171 A6
Madison Ave. Brad BD4 .... 75 E1
Madni Cl. Hali HX1 .... 113 B7
Madri Muslim Girls Sch. Dew .. 139 D6
Mafeking Ave. Leeds LS11 .... 79 A1
Mafeking Gr. Leeds LS11 .... 79 A1
Mafeking Mount. Leeds LS11 ... 79 A1
Magdalen Rd. Mel HD7 .... 187 C6
Magdalene Cl. Hors LS16 .... 42 A3
Magdalene Rd. Wake WF2 .... 141 D5
Magistrates Ct. Brad 74 E6
Magna Gr. Wake WF2 .... 142 E1
Magnolia Cl. Shaf S72 .... 180 D2
Magnolia House. Castle WF10 124 E7 11
Magpie La. Morley LS27 .... 98 C3
Maidstone St. Brad BD3 .... 75 C7
Mail Cl. Leeds LS15 .... 62 E3
Main Ave. Hud HD4 .... 152 F3
Main Gate. Holmfi HD7 .... 189 E2
Main Rd. Denh BD13 .... 71 D8
Main Rd. Farnh BD20 .... 16 E8
Main Rd. Keigh BD20 .... 36 D8
Main Rd. Stee BD20 .... 16 F6
Main St. Aber LS25 .... 64 E7
Main St. Add LS29 .... 7 A8
Main St. B in Elm LS15 .... 62 F6
Main St. B in Elm LS15 .... 63 D7
Main St. B Sal LS25 .... 105 E3
Main St. Bad WF9 .... 164 E2
Main St. Bing BD16 .... 36 F3
Main St. Brad BD12 .... 94 C4 2
Main St. Brad BD12 .... 94 E6
Main St. Bur in W LS29 .... 9 F1
Main St. Coll LS22 .... 13 C2
Main St. Coll LS22 .... 29 B8
Main St. Con BD20 .... 4 A2
Main St. E Ard WF3 .... 120 D7
Main St. E Kes LS17 .... 28 C5
Main St. Farnh BD20 .... 4 D2
Main St. Gar LS25 .... 82 E7
Main St. Guise LS20 .... 38 F8
Main St. Guise BD17 .... 39 C5
Main St. Ham DN6 .... 184 B1
Main St. Haw BD22 .... 50 D7
Main St. Haw BD22 .... 51 C7
Main St. K Smea WF8 .... 166 D6
Main St. Kippax WF10 .... 103 B4
Main St. L Brad BD20 .... 4 C5
Main St. Ledst WF10 .... 103 E6
Main St. M Fry LS25 .... 105 F8
Main St. M'town LS26 .... 102 D3
Main St. Men LS29 .... 22 A4
Main St. Pool LS21 .... 24 C7
Main St. Roth WF3 .... 100 D3
Main St. S Hie S72 .... 180 D6
Main St. S in Cra BD20 .... 16 D5
Main St. Ship BD16 .... 54 B6
Main St. Sickl LS22 .... 12 C5
Main St. Sil LS29 .... 6 E8
Main St. Tad LS24 .... 31 E7
Main St. Th Arch LS23 .... 15 A4
Main St. Thorner LS17 .... 44 E4
Main St. Thorner LS14 .... 45 F5
Main St. Upton WF9 .... 183 D8
Main St. Wils BD15 .... 53 C5
Mainspring Rd. Wils BD15 .... 53 C5
Maitland Cl. Brad BD15 .... 73 B7
Maitland Cl. Tod OL14 .... 129 A8
Maitland Pl. Leeds LS11 .... 79 A4
Maitland St. Tod OL14 .... 129 A8
Maize St. Keigh BD21 .... 35 A4 5
Maizebrook. Dew WF16 .... 117 F1
Major St. Tod OL14 .... 108 C5
Major St. Wake WF2 .... 142 B3
Makin St. Wake WF2 .... 142 A5
Malais La. S in Cra BD20 .... 16 A5
Malham Ave. Brad BD9 .... 54 C3
Malham Ave. Brig HD6 .... 135 E8
Malham Cl. Leeds LS14 .... 62 A4
Malham Cl. Shaf S72 .... 180 C3
Malham Dr. Batley WF17 .... 118 A5
Malham Dr. Liver WF15 .... 116 F1
Malham Rd. Brig HD6 .... 135 E7
Malham Rd. Wake WF1 .... 142 F7
Malham Sq. Wake WF1 .... 142 F7
Malin Rd. Batley WF12 .... 118 F3
Mallard Ave. Wake WF2 .... 160 C5
Mallard Cl. Brad BD10 .... 56 C5
Mallard Cl. Midd LS10 .... 99 F7
Mallard Ct. Brad BD8 .... 73 C7 1
Mallard Rd. Castle WF10 .... 124 C6
Mallard Way. Morley LS27 .... 98 D4 3
Mallard Way. Slai HD7 .... 169 F8
Mallinson St. Dew WF13 .... 118 A1
Mallory Cl. Brad BD7 .... 73 F6
Malmesbury Cl. Brad BD4 .... 75 E1
Malmesbury Cl. Leeds LS12 .... 78 C6 2
Malmesbury Gr. Leeds LS12 .... 78 C6
Malmesbury Pl. Leeds LS12 .... 78 C6
Malmesbury St. Leeds LS12 .... 78 C6
Malmesbury Terr. Leeds LS12 . 78 C6
Malsis Cres. Keigh BD21 .... 35 A6
Malsis Rd. Keigh BD21 .... 35 B5
Malt Kiln Croft. Wake WF2 ...... 142 E1
Malt Kiln La. Kippax LS25 .... 83 B1 2
Malt Kiln La. Thorn BD13 .... 72 C5
Malt St. Keigh BD22 .... 35 A4 8
Maltby Ct. Leeds LS15 .... 81 D7
Malthouse Cl. Scar LS14 .... 45 C8
Malting Cl. Roth WF3 .... 100 B3
Malting Rise. Roth WF3 .... 100 B3
Maltings Ct. Leeds LS11 .... 79 C4 3
Maltings Rd. Hali HX2 .... 91 D2
Maltings Rd. Leeds LS11 .... 79 C3
Maltings The. Clec BD19 .... 116 C8
Maltings The. Leeds LS6 .... 59 E2
Maltings The. Mir WF14 .... 137 F5
Maltings The. Pont WF8 .... 125 D1
Maltings The. Roth WF3 .... 100 B3
Maltkiln La. Castle WF10 .... 124 E8
Maltkin Dr. W Bret WF4 .... 176 F8
Malton Rd. Upton WF9 .... 183 D8
Malton St. Hali HX3 .... 92 C2
Malton St. Hali HX6 .... 112 B5 7
Malvern Brow. Brad BD9 .... 54 D2
Malvern Cl. Castle WF10 .... 123 F5
Malvern Cres. Keigh BD20 .... 18 E3
Malvern Gr. Brad BD9 .... 54 D1
Malvern Gr. Leeds LS11 .... 79 B4
Malvern Rd. Brad BD9 .... 54 D2
Malvern Rd. Dew WF12 .... 118 F1
Malvern Rd. Hud HD4 .... 154 B4
Malvern Rd. Knot WF11 .... 126 E4
Malvern Rd. Leeds LS11 .... 79 A4
Malvern Rise. Hud HD4 .... 154 B3
Malvern Rise. Leeds LS11 .... 79 A4
Malvern St. Brad BD3 .... 75 A7
Malvern St. Leeds LS11 .... 79 A4
Malvern View. Leeds LS11 .... 79 A4 5
Manchester Rd. Brad BD5 .... 74 D3
Manchester Rd. Hud HD4 .... 153 D4
Manchester Rd. Mars HD7 .... 168 B3
Manchester Rd Marsden.
Mars HD7 .... 168 E4
Manchester Rd (Slaithwaite).
Slai HD7 .... 170 A8
Manchester Road Clough Head.
Mars HD7 .... 168 C4
Manchester Road (Linthwaite).
Slai HD7 .... 152 D1
Manchester Sq. Otley LS21 .... 23 A8
Manchester St. Hud HD4 .... 153 C4
Mandale Gr. Brad BD6 .... 93 D8
Mandale Mid Sch. Brad 93 D8
Mandale Rd. Brad BD6 .... 73 D1
Mandarin Way. Midd LS10 .... 99 F7
Mandela Ct. Leeds LS7 .... 60 D5
Mandeville Cres. Brad BD6 .... 93 F8
Mangrill La. B in Elm LS14 .... 46 E6
Manitoba Pl. Leeds LS7 .... 60 D6
Mankinholes Bank. Tod OL14 .... 108 F3
Manley Ct. Gar LS25 .... 82 F5
Manley Dr. Weth LS22 .... 13 C6
Manley Gr. Ilkley LS29 .... 8 D4
Manley Rd. Ilkley LS29 .... 8 E4
Manley Rise. Ilkley LS29 .... 8 D3
Manley St. Brig HD6 .... 115 A3
Mann's Bldgs. Batley WF17 .... 97 B2
Mannheim Rd. Brad BD9 .... 55 A2
Manningham La. Brad BD1 BD8 55 D1
Manningham Mid Sch. Brad 55 D1
Mannville Gr. Keigh BD22 .... 35 A6
Mannville Pl. Keigh BD22 .... 35 A6 16
Mannville Rd. Keigh BD22 .... 35 A6
Mannville St. Keigh BD22 .... 35 A6 13
Mannville Terr. Brad BD7 .... 74 D6
Mannville Way. Keigh BD22 .... 35 A6 14
Mannville Wlk. Keigh BD22 .... 35 A6 15
Manor Ave. Leeds LS6 .... 59 E4
Manor Ave. Ossett WF5 .... 140 F3
Manor Cl. Bad WF9 .... 164 E2
Manor Cl. Brad BD8 .... 73 D8
Manor Cl. Bramho LS16 .... 24 D3
Manor Cl. Hali HX3 .... 113 B4
Manor Cl. K Smea WF8 .... 166 D5
Manor Cl. Notton WF4 .... 178 F7
Manor Cl. Ossett WF5 .... 140 F3
Manor Cl. Roth LS26 .... 100 E6
Manor Cl. Yeadon LS19 .... 40 B7
Manor Cres. Pool LS21 .... 24 C7
Manor Cres. Roth LS26 .... 100 D5
Manor Cres. Wake WF2 .... 141 E4
Manor Cres. Walton WF2 .... 161 A8
Manor Croft. Heb Br HX7 .... 89 B3
Manor Croft. Leeds LS15 .... 81 C7
Manor Croft. S Hie S72 .... 180 D6
Manor Ct. Ossett WF5 .... 140 F3
Manor Ct. Otley LS21 .... 23 A8
Manor Ct. Ship BD16 .... 54 A7 3
Manor Ct. Thorner LS17 .... 44 F4
Manor Dr. Crof WF4 .... 162 A7
Manor Dr. Feath WF7 .... 124 C1
Manor Dr. Floc WF4 .... 157 D3
Manor Dr. Hali HX3 .... 113 B4
Manor Dr. Heb Br HX7 .... 89 B3
Manor Dr. Leeds LS6 .... 59 E4
Manor Dr. Mir WF14 .... 137 D7
Manor Dr. Ossett WF5 .... 140 F3
Manor Dr. Roy S71 .... 179 B3
Manor Dr. S Hie S72 .... 180 D6
Manor Dr. Ship BD16 .... 54 B7
Manor Dr. Skel HD8 .... 175 A1
Manor Farm. Bad WF9 .... 164 E2
Manor Farm Cl. Midd LS10 .... 99 D6
Manor Farm Cl. Ship BD16 .... 54 B6
Manor Farm Cres. Morley LS27 98 C8
Manor Farm Ct. Crig WF4 .... 159 E4
Manor Farm Dr. Batley WF17 118 F5
Manor Farm Dr. Midd LS10 .... 99 D6
Manor Farm Dr. Morley LS27 ... 98 C8
Manor Farm Est. S Elm WF9 .. 183 A3
Manor Farm Gdns. Midd LS10 .. 99 C6
Manor Farm Gn. Midd LS10 ...... 99 C6
Manor Farm Gr. Midd LS10 .... 99 C6
Manor Farm Rd. Crig WF4 .... 159 E4
Manor Farm Rd. Midd LS10 .... 99 D6
Manor Farm Rise. Midd LS10 .... 99 D6
Manor Farm Way. Midd LS10 ... 99 C5
Manor Farm Wlk. Midd LS10 ..... 99 D6
Manor Fold. Ship BD16 .... 54 B6 4
Manor Garth. Ledsh LS25 .... 104 D8
Manor Garth. Leeds LS15 .... 81 C7
Manor Garth Rd. Dew WF12 ... 139 F7
Manor Garth Rd. Kippax LS25 .. 83 B2
Manor Garth. Walton WF2 .... 161 A8
Manor Gdns. Batley WF12 .... 119 A2
Manor Gdns. Cull BD13 .... 52 D5
Manor Gdns. Pool LS21 .... 24 C7
Manor Gdns. Thorner LS14 .... 46 A6
Manor Gr. Castle WF10 .... 124 E5
Manor Gr. Keigh BD20 .... 36 A8
Manor Gr. Leeds LS7 .... 60 D6
Manor Gr. Ossett WF5 .... 140 F3
Manor Gr. Roy S71 .... 179 B3
Manor Gr. S Kirk WF9 .... 182 A1
Manor Haigh Rd. Wake WF2 . 141 E4
Manor Heath Rd. Hali HX3 ...... 113 B4
Manor House Bglws. Knot
WF11 .... 126 F5
Manor House Croft. Hors LS16 42 D3
Manor House La. Hare LS17 ...... 43 F7
Manor House Mus & Art Gal.
Ilkley 8 B4
Manor House Rd. Wils BD15 ...... 53 C6
Manor House St. Pudsey LS28 ... 76 E7 5
Manor House. Wake WF1 .... 142 D6 4
Manor Houses. Mel HD7 .... 170 F2
Manor La. Ossett WF5 .... 140 F3
Manor La. Ship BD18 .... 55 B7
Manor Mill La. Leeds LS11 .... 78 E1
Manor Occupation Rd. Roy S71 179 B4
Manor Park Ave. Kippax WF10 103 B5
Manor Park Ave. Pont WF8 ..... 125 F3
Manor Park Gdns. Birk BD19 ... 96 B3
Manor Park Rise. Dar WF8 ...... 147 D4
Manor Park Way. Lepton HD8 155 D2
Manor Pk. Brad BD8 .... 73 D8
Manor Pk. Dar WF8 .... 147 D5
Manor Pk. Haw BD22 .... 34 C2
Manor Pk. Mir WF14 .... 137 C7
Manor Pk. Scar LS14 .... 45 C7
Manor Pl. Hor WF4 .... 141 A1 1
Manor Rd. Batley WF17 .... 118 F5
Manor Rd. Beal DN14 .... 127 F7
Manor Rd. Clay W HD8 .... 176 A4
Manor Rd. Dearne S63 .... 194 C1
Manor Rd. Dew WF13 .... 139 B7
Manor Rd. Hor WF4 .... 141 A1
Manor Rd. Hors LS18 .... 58 A8
Manor Rd. Hud HD7 .... 152 D4
Manor Rd. Keigh BD20 .... 18 A2
Manor Rd. Kirkb HD4 .... 172 F6
Manor Rd. Leeds LS11 .... 79 B6
Manor Rd. Morley LS27 .... 98 C8
Manor Rd. Ossett WF5 .... 140 F4
Manor Rd. Roth LS26 .... 100 D6
Manor Rd. Ship BD16 .... 54 B7
Manor Rd. Wake WF2 .... 141 F5
Manor Rd. Walton WF2 .... 161 A7
Manor Rise. Hud HD4 .... 154 B4
Manor Rise. Ilkley LS29 .... 8 D4
Manor Rise. Skel HD8 .... 175 A1
Manor Rise. Walton WF2 .... 161 A8
Manor Row. Brad BD1 .... 74 E7
Manor Row. Brad BD12 .... 94 C7
Manor (Spts Ctr) The. Yeadon . 40 B7
Manor Sq. Otley LS21 .... 23 A8
Manor Sq. Yeadon LS19 .... 40 B7 5
Manor St. Brad BD2 .... 56 B3
Manor St. Brig BD19 .... 115 F6
Manor St. Dew WF12 .... 139 D8
Manor St. Hud HD4 .... 154 B4
Manor St Ind Est. Leeds 60 E2
Manor St. Leeds LS7 .... 60 D2
Manor St. Otley LS21 .... 23 A8
Manor Terr. Brad BD2 .... 56 B3
Manor Terr. Kippax LS25 .... 83 B1
Manor Terr. Leeds LS6 .... 59 E4
Manor View. Castle WF10 .... 124 E5
Manor View. Leeds LS6 .... 59 E4
Manor View. Pudsey LS28 .... 76 E7
Manor View. Shaf S72 .... 180 C2
Manor Way. Batley WF17 .... 118 A4
Manor Way. S in Cra BD20 .... 16 C4
Manorcroft. Nor WF6 .... 123 B2
Manorfield Dr. Hor WF4 .... 141 A2
Manorfield. Leeds LS11 .... 78 F3
Manorfields Ave. Crof WF4 ...... 162 A8
Manorfields. Crof WF4 .... 162 A8
Manorley La. Brad BD6 .... 93 E6
Manorstead. Skel HD8 .... 175 A1
Manscombe Rd. Brad BD15 .... 54 C1
Manse Cres. Bur in W LS29 .... 9 E1
Manse Dr. Hud HD4 .... 153 A3
Manse Rd. Bur in W LS29 .... 9 E1
Manse St. Brad BD3 .... 75 C7
Manse Way. Glu BD20 .... 16 D6
Mansel Mews. Brad BD4 .... 75 E2
Mansfield Ave. Bing BD16 .... 37 C5
Mansfield Pl. Leeds LS6 .... 59 D6
Mansfield Rd. Brad BD8 .... 55 C2
Mansfield Rd. Bur in W LS29 .... 9 E1
Mansion Gdns. Hud HD4 .... 153 F1
Mansion La. Leeds LS8 .... 44 B1
Manston App. Leeds LS15 .... 62 C3
Manston Ave. Leeds LS15 .... 62 C3
Manston Cres. Leeds LS15 .... 62 C2
Manston Dr. Leeds LS15 .... 62 C3
Manston Gdns. Leeds LS15 .... 62 D3
Manston Gr. Leeds LS15 .... 62 C3
Manston La. Leeds LS15 .... 62 E2
Manston Prim Sch. Leeds 62 D3
Manston Rise. Leeds LS15 .... 62 C3
Manston Terr. Leeds LS15 .... 62 D3 5
Manston Towers. Leeds LS14 .. 62 D4 3
Manston Way. Leeds LS15 .... 62 D3
Manygates Ave. Wake WF1 .... 142 D3
Manygates Cres. Wake WF1 . 142 D3
Manygates Ct. Wake WF1 .... 142 D3
Manygates La. Wake WF1WF2 142 D2
Manygates Pk. Wake WF1 .... 142 D3
Manywells Brow. Cull BD13 .... 52 C4
Manywells Cres. Cull BD13 .... 52 D5
Manywells La. Cull BD13 .... 52 B5
Maple Ave. Brad BD3 .... 75 E8
Maple Ave. Haw BD22 .... 34 D2
Maple Ave. Hud HD7 .... 152 F5
Maple Ave. Pont WF8 .... 146 C5
Maple Cl. Castle WF10 .... 124 B5
Maple Cl. Kirkhe HD5 .... 137 C1
Maple Croft. Leeds LS17 .... 43 E3
Maple Croft. Leeds LS17 .... 43 E3
Maple Croft. Leeds LS12 .... 77 D5
Maple Ct. Leeds LS11 .... 78 F2 2
Maple Dr. Leeds LS12 .... 77 D5
Maple Dr. Pont WF8 .... 146 D6
Maple Dr. Weth LS22 .... 13 E7
Maple Fold. Leeds LS12 .... 77 D5
Maple Gr. Clec BD19 .... 96 A1
Maple Gr. Hud HD2 .... 136 A5
Maple Gr. Keigh BD20 .... 18 A1
Maple Gr. Nor WF6 .... 144 A7
Maple Gr. Pont WF8 .... 146 C5
Maple Rd. Dew WF12 .... 140 B7
Maple Rd. Mapp S75 .... 178 A1
Maple Rise. Roth LS26 .... 100 F4
Maple St. Hali HX1 .... 112 F5 14
Maple St. Hud HD5 .... 154 C5
Maple St. Tod OL14 .... 129 A7
Maple St. Wake WF2 .... 141 F8
Maple Terr. Yeadon LS19 .... 39 F7
Maple Way. Leeds LS14 .... 62 C8
Maple Wlk. Dew WF12 .... 140 B7
Maple Wlk. Knot WF11 .... 126 E3
Maplin Ave. Hud HD3 .... 134 F1
Maplin Dr. Hud HD3 .... 134 F1 1
Mapplewell Cres. Ossett WF5 140 E5
Mapplewell Dr. Ossett WF5 ..... 140 E5
Mapplewell Inf Sch. Mapp 178 C1
Mapplewell Jun Mix Sch. Mapp178 C1
Marbridge Ct. Brad BD6 .... 74 B2
March Cote La. Ship BD16 .... 54 A6
March St. Nor WF6 .... 123 A1
Marchant St. Castle WF10 .... 124 C8
Marchbank Rd. Brad BD3 .... 75 C8
Marchwood Gr. Brad BD14 .... 73 D5
Marcus Way. Hud HD3 .... 134 D1
Mardale Cres. Leeds LS14 .... 62 A3
Mardale Rd. Batley WF12 .... 118 E2
Margaret Ave. Bard LS17 .... 28 D4
Margaret Cl. Morley LS27 .... 98 C6
Margaret St. Hali HX1 .... 113 B7
Margaret St. Keigh BD21 .... 35 A8
Margaret St. Loft G WF1 .... 121 A4
Margaret St. Wake WF1 .... 142 B7
Margate Rd. Brad BD4 .... 75 A4
Margate. Roth LS26 .... 101 C6 2
Margate St. Sow Br HX6 .... 112 A3
Margerison Cres. Ilkley LS29 ...... 8 E3
Margerison Rd. Ilkley LS29 .... 8 E3
Margetson Rd. Birk BD11 .... 97 A5
Margram Bsns Ctr. Hali 113 B8
Margrove House. Brad BD15 ...... 73 B8 8
Maria St. Bur in W LS29 .... 9 E2
Marian Gr. Leeds LS11 .... 79 B3 16
Marian Rd. Leeds LS6 .... 60 B3
Marian Terr. Leeds LS6 .... 60 B3
Marie Cl. Kirkhe HD5 .... 155 C6
Marina Cres. Morley LS27 .... 97 F3
Marina Terr. Hud HD7 .... 152 E5
Marine Villa Rd. Knot WF11 ...... 126 F4
Marion Ave. Wake WF2 .... 141 D8
Marion Dr. Ship BD18 .... 55 C7
Marion Gr. Wake WF2 .... 141 D8
Marion St. Bing BD16 .... 37 A3
Marion St. Brad BD7 .... 74 C7
Marion St. Brig HD6 .... 115 A3
Maris St. Leeds LS9 .... 79 D7
Marizon Gr. Wake WF1 .... 142 D7
Mark Bottoms La. Holmfi HD7 188 F6
Mark Cl. Brad BD10 .... 56 C8
Mark La. Leeds LS2 .... 79 C8
Mark La. Tod OL14 .... 108 A7
Mark St. Brad BD5 .... 74 E3
Mark St. Hud HD1 .... 153 E5
Mark St. Liver WF15 .... 117 B4
Mark St. Wake WF1 .... 142 C4
Market Ave. Hud HD1 .... 154 B6 9
Market Ct. Thorn BD13 .... 72 E6 5
Market Pl. Clec BD19 .... 116 E7 1
Market Pl. Dew WF13 .... 139 D8
Market Pl. Hud HD1 .... 154 A6
Market Pl. Keigh BD21 .... 35 C7
Market Pl. Mars HD7 .... 168 F4
Market Pl. Mel HD7 .... 170 D2
Market Pl. Nor WF6 .... 123 A2
Market Pl. Otley LS21 .... 23 A8
Market Pl. Pont WF8 .... 146 D8
Market Pl. Pudsey LS28 .... 76 E7
Market Pl. Slai HD7 .... 169 F8
Market Pl. Weth LS22 .... 13 E5
Market Shops. Nor WF6 .... 123 A2
Market Sq. Batley WF17 .... 118 C5 5
Market Sq. Leeds LS14 .... 62 B5 3
Market Sq. Ship BD18 .... 55 B7
Market St. Batley WF17 .... 96 E1
Market St. Batley WF16 .... 117 D3
Market St. Bing BD16 .... 36 F3
Market St. Brad BD6 .... 74 C1 4
Market St. Brad BD1 .... 74 E7
Market St. Brig HD6 .... 115 B2
Market St. Clec BD19 .... 116 E7
Market St. Dew WF13 .... 139 D8 3
Market St. Feath WF7 .... 145 C6
Market St. Hali HX1 .... 113 C7
Market St. Heb Br HX7 .... 89 A3
Market St. Hem WF9 .... 181 D7
Market St. Holmfi HD7 .... 189 A5
Market St. Hud HD3 .... 153 B5
Market St. Hud HD1 .... 153 E5
Market St. Hud HD1 .... 154 A6
Market St. Keigh BD21 .... 35 C7
Market St. Nor WF6 .... 123 A2
Market St. Otley LS21 .... 23 A8
Market St. Ship BD18 .... 55 B7
Market St. Stee BD20 .... 17 D5
Market St. Thorn BD13 .... 72 E6
Market St. Tod OL14 .... 108 A3
Market St. Wake WF1 .... 142 C6
Market Wlk. Mars HD7 .... 168 F4
Markfield Ave. Brad BD12 .... 94 C5
Markfield Cl. Brad BD12 .... 94 C5
Markfield Cres. Brad BD12 .... 94 C5
Markfield Dr. Brad BD12 .... 94 C5
Markham Ave. Leeds LS8 .... 60 F4
Markham Ave. Yeadon LS19 .... 40 C5
Markham Cres. Yeadon LS19 ... 40 C5
Markham Croft. Yeadon LS19 .. 40 C5
Markham St. Batley WF17 .... 118 B4
Markham St. Wake WF2 .... 142 A6
Marl Pit Hill. Pont WF8 .... 146 A6
Marland Rd. Keigh BD21 .... 35 E8
Marlbeck Cl. Honley HD7 .... 171 F3
Marlborough Ave. Byram
WF11 .... 126 D7
Marlborough Ave. Hali HX3 ...... 113 B4 7
Marlborough Croft. S Elm WF9 182 F4
Marlborough Ct. Men LS29 .... 22 B4
Marlborough Gdn. Dew WF13 118 B2
Marlborough Gdns. Leeds LS2 . 60 B2 7
Marlborough Gr. Ilkley LS29 .... 8 D3
Marlborough Gr. Leeds LS2 .... 60 B2 8
Marlborough Gr'ge. Leeds LS1 79 A8 9
Marlborough House. Elland
HX5 .... 134 F7 9
Marlborough Rd. Brad BD8 .... 55 C1
Marlborough Rd. Brad BD10 .... 56 C8
Marlborough Rd. Heb Br HX7 .. 89 A3
Marlborough Rd. Hud HD2 .... 136 B5
Marlborough Rd. Ship BD18 .... 55 A7
Marlborough Sq. Ilkley LS29 .... 8 D3
Marlborough St. Keigh BD21 ...... 35 D8
Marlborough St. Leeds LS1 .... 79 A8
Marlborough St. Ossett WF5 .... 140 C5
Marlborough St. Wake WF2 .... 142 A6
Marlborough Terr. Heb Br HX7 89 A3
Marlborough Towers. Leeds LS179 A8 8
Marlborough Villas. Men LS29 22 B4
Marlbro' Terr. Batley WF13 ... 118 B2 5
Marldon Rd. Northo HX3 .... 93 A1
Marley Cl. Brad BD8 .... 73 E8
Marley Ct. Bing BD16 .... 36 D7
Marley Gr. Leeds LS11 .... 78 F3
Marley La. Queen BD13 .... 72 E3
Marley Pl. Leeds LS11 .... 78 F3
Marley Rd. Keigh BD21 .... 35 F8
Marley St. Brad BD3 .... 75 A7
Marley St. Keigh BD21 .... 35 C6
Marley St. Leeds LS11 .... 78 F3
Marley Terr. Leeds LS11 .... 78 F3 5
Marley View. Bing BD16 .... 36 D7
Marley View. Leeds LS11 .... 78 F3
Marling Rd. Hud HD2 .... 135 B3
Marlo Rd. Batley WF12 .... 119 A2
Marlott Rd. Ship BD18 .... 55 E8
Marlow Cl. Hud HD5 .... 154 F6
Marlow St. Keigh BD21 .... 35 E8
Marlowe Cl. Pudsey LS28 .... 76 F5 3
Marlowe Ct. Gar LS25 .... 82 F7
Marlowe Ct. Guise LS20 .... 22 D1
Marlpit La. Dar WF8 .... 147 B5
Marmion Ave. Brad BD8 .... 73 C7
Marne Ave. Brad BD14 .... 73 C3
Marne Cres. Brad BD10 .... 56 B7
Marriner Rd. Keigh BD21 .... 35 C6
Marriner's Dr. Ship BD9 .... 55 B4
Marriner's Wlk. Keigh BD21 .... 35 C5
Marriot Gr. Wake WF2 .... 142 F1
Marsden Ave. Leeds LS11 .... 79 A2
Marsden Ct. Pudsey LS28 .... 57 D3 3
Marsden Gate. Elland HX4 .... 151 E7
Marsden Golf Club. Mars 168 E1
Marsden Gr. Leeds LS11 .... 79 A2
Marsden Inf Sch. Mars 169 A4
Marsden La. Mars HD7 .... 169 A5
Marsden La. Mars HD7 .... 169 B7
Marsden Mount. Leeds LS11 ... 79 A2
Marsden Pl. Leeds LS11 .... 79 A2
Marsden St. Skel HD8 .... 175 A2
Marsden Sta. Mars 168 F4
Marsden View. Leeds LS11 .... 79 A2
Marsett Way. Leeds LS14 .... 62 B8
Marsh Croft. Broth WF11 .... 126 C7
Marsh Delves. Hali HX3 .... 113 F6
Marsh Delves La. Hali HX3 ...... 113 F6
Marsh End. Knot WF11 .... 127 B5
Marsh Gdns. Honley HD7 .... 171 F4
Marsh Gr. Brad BD5 .... 74 C3
Marsh Grove Rd. Hud HD3 ...... 153 D8
Marsh Hall La. Kirkb HD4 .... 172 F3
Marsh La. B Head HX7 .... 88 B3
Marsh La. Birk BD11 .... 96 A5
Marsh La. Byram WF11 .... 126 F6
Marsh La. Hali HX3 .... 113 F6
Marsh La. Knot WF11 .... 127 B4
Marsh La. Leeds LS9 .... 79 E8
Marsh La. Oxen BD22 .... 51 B4
Marsh La. Shep HD8 .... 190 D7
Marsh Lea Grove. Hem WF9 . 181 F7
Marsh Platt La. Honley HD7 .. 172 A5
Marsh. Pudsey LS28 .... 76 C7
Marsh Rd. Holmfi HD7 .... 189 D3
Marsh St. Brad BD5 .... 74 D3
Marsh St. Clec BD19 .... 116 E6
Marsh St. Honley HD7 .... 171 F4
Marsh St. Leeds LS6 .... 60 A3
Marsh St. Roth LS26 .... 100 F5
Marsh Terr. Pudsey LS28 .... 76 C7
Marsh Vale. Leeds LS6 .... 60 A3 3
Marsh Way. Wake WF1 .... 142 D7
Marshall Ave. Crig WF4 .... 159 F3
Marshall Ave. Leeds LS15 .... 62 D2
Marshall Cres. Morley LS27 .... 98 B2
Marshall Dr. S Elm WF9 .... 182 F3
Marshall Mill Ct. Clay W HD8 175 E1
Marshall St. Keigh BD20 .... 18 B1
Marshall St. Leeds LS15 .... 62 C2
Marshall St. Leeds LS11 .... 79 B6
Marshall St. Loft G WF3 .... 121 F5
Marshall St. Mir WF14 .... 138 A3
Marshall St. Morley LS27 .... 98 B4
Marshall St. Yeadon LS19 .... 40 B7
Marshall Terr. Leeds LS15 .... 62 C2
Marsham Gr. Hud HD3 .... 153 C7
Marshfield Fst Sch. Brad 74 C2
Marshfield Pl. Brad BD5 .... 74 D3
Marshfield St. Brad BD5 .... 74 D3
Marshway. Hali HX1 .... 113 A8
Marsland Ave. Wake WF1 .... 142 D6
Marsland Ct. Clec BD19 .... 95 D2
Marsland Pl. Brad BD3 .... 75 D7
Marsland Pl. Wake WF1 .... 142 D6
Marsland St. Wake WF1 .... 142 D6
Marsland Terr. Wake WF1 .... 142 D6
Marston Ave. Morley LS27 .... 98 A3
Marston Cl. Queen BD13 .... 72 F1
Marston Ct. Castle WF10 .... 124 A6
Marston Mount. Leeds LS9 .... 60 E1
Marston Way. Weth LS22 .... 13 C6
Marston Wlk. Nor WF6 .... 122 E4
Marten Dr. Hud HD4 .... 171 D7
Marten Gr. Hud HD4 .... 171 E7
Marten Rd. Brad BD5 .... 74 C3
Martin Ct. Leeds LS15 .... 81 D8
Martin Frobisher Dr. Nor WF6 122 F3
Martin Gr. Wake WF2 .... 160 E6
Martin Green La. Elland HX4 . 134 A7
Martin St. Batley WF17 .... 96 E1
Martin St. Brig HD6 .... 115 B3
Martin St. Nor WF6 .... 144 A8
Martin Terr. Leeds LS4 .... 59 C2
Martindale Dr. Leeds LS13 .... 58 E1
Martlett Dr. Brad BD5 .... 74 F2
Marton Ave. Hem WF9 .... 181 C6
Marton Heights. Hali HX6 .... 112 A5
Marwood Rd. Leeds LS13 .... 77 E7
Mary Rose Ct. Feath WF7 .... 145 C4
Mary St. Brad BD4 .... 75 C5
Mary St. Brad BD12 .... 94 C4
Mary St. Brig HD6 .... 115 A4
Mary St. Denh BD13 .... 52 E1
Mary St. E Ard WF3 .... 120 E8
Mary St. Oxen BD22 .... 51 C2 6
Mary St. Pudsey LS28 .... 57 E4
Mary St. Ship BD18 .... 54 F8
Mary St. Thorn BD13 .... 72 D6 5
Maryfield Ave. Leeds LS15 .... 62 A2
Maryfield Cl. Leeds LS15 .... 62 A2
Maryfield Cres. Leeds LS15 .... 62 B2
Maryfield Ct. Leeds LS15 .... 62 B2 5
Maryfield Gdns. Leeds LS15 .... 62 A2
Maryfield Gn. Leeds LS15 .... 62 A2
Maryfield Mews. Leeds LS15 ... 62 A2
Maryfield Vale. Leeds LS15 .... 62 A2 1
Marygate. Wake WF1 .... 142 C6 13
Maryville Ave. Brig HD6 .... 114 E5
Masefield Ave. Brad BD9 .... 54 C3
Masefield St. Guise LS20 .... 39 F8
Masham Gr. Leeds LS12 .... 78 D7

Masham Pl. Brad BD9 .... 54 F2
Masham St. Leeds LS12 .... 78 D7
Mason Sq. Hali HX2 .... 91 F3
Mason St. Heb Br HX7 .... 89 A3
Mason's Green. Hali HX2 .... 91 E5
Masonic St. Hali HX1 .... 112 E6
Master La. Hali HX2 .... 112 F4
Matherville. Skel HD8 .... 175 A1
Matlock St. Hali HX3 .... 92 A1 9
Matlock St. Hud HD4 .... 153 C4
Matterdale Cl. Batley WF12 .. 118 E2
Matterdale Rd. Batley WF12 . 118 E2
Matthew Cl. Keigh BD20 .... 18 F1
Matthew Gr. Mel HD7 .... 170 C2
Matthew La. L Brad BD20 .... 4 C5
Matthew La. Mel HD7 .... 170 D2
Matthew La. Tod OL14 .... 108 E7
Matthew Murray High Sch. Leeds 78 F4
Matty Marsden La. Ossett WF4 .... 140 E2
Maud Ave. Leeds LS11 .... 79 B2
Maud Pl. Leeds LS11 .... 79 B3 14
Maud St. Brad BD3 .... 75 B6
Maude Ave. Bail BD17 .... 38 C2
Maude Cres. Sow Br HX6 .... 111 E3
Maude La. Rip HX6 .... 132 D4
Maude St. Elland HX4 .... 134 D7
Maude St. Hali HX3 .... 92 A3
Maude St. Leeds LS2 .... 79 D7
Maudsley St. Brad BD3 .... 75 B7
Maurice Ave. Brig HD6 .... 114 F4
Mavis Ave. Dew WF13 .... 139 A6
Mavis Ave. Hors LS16 .... 41 E6
Mavis Gr. Hors LS16 .... 41 E6
Mavis La. Hors LS16 .... 41 E6
Mavis Rd. Batley WF13 .... 117 F3
Mavis St. Brad BD3 .... 75 B7
Mavis St. Dew WF13 .... 139 A6
Maw St. Brad BD4 .... 74 F5
Mawcroft Cl. Yeadon LS19 .... 40 A5
Mawcroft Grange Dr. Yeadon LS19 .... 40 A5
Mawson Ct. Brad BD1 .... 74 E7 16
Mawson St. Ship BD18 .... 54 F8 6
Maxwell Ave. Batley WF17 .... 118 C2
Maxwell Rd. Brad BD6 .... 93 F8
Maxwell Rd. Ilkley LS29 .... 8 D3
Maxwell St. Feath WF7 .... 145 C5
Maxwell St. Morley LS27 .... 97 F3
May Ave. Thorn BD13 .... 72 E6
May Bush Rd. Wake WF1 .... 142 E3
May St. Clec BD19 .... 95 D1
May St. Haw BD22 .... 51 D6
May St. Hud HD4 .... 153 E4
May St. Keigh BD21 .... 35 C8
May Terr. Leeds LS9 .... 79 F6
May Tree Cl. Brad BD14 .... 73 D5
Mayberry Dr. Silk S75 .... 193 F1
Maybrook Ind Pk. Leeds 78 E8
Maybury Ave. Crig WF4 .... 160 A7
Mayfair Ave. Elland HX4 .... 133 F1
Mayfair. Brad BD5 .... 74 D4
Mayfair Pl. Hem WF9 .... 181 D7
Mayfair Way. Brad BD4 .... 75 D5
Mayfield Ave. Brad BD12 .... 94 D3
Mayfield Ave. Brig HD6 .... 115 B8
Mayfield Ave. Hali HX1 .... 113 A6
Mayfield Ave. Hud HD5 .... 154 F6
Mayfield Ave. Ilkley LS29 .... 8 D4
Mayfield Cl. Glu BD20 .... 16 C6
Mayfield Cl. Ilkley LS29 .... 8 D4
Mayfield Ct. Ossett WF5 .... 140 E3
Mayfield Dr. Hali HX1 .... 113 A6
Mayfield Dr. Keigh BD20 .... 36 C8
Mayfield Gdns. Hali HX6 .... 112 D5
Mayfield Gdns. Hali HX1 .... 113 A6
Mayfield Gdns. Ilkley LS29 .... 8 D5
Mayfield Gr. Bail BD17 .... 38 E3
Mayfield Gr. Brig HD6 .... 115 B8
Mayfield Gr. Hali HX1 .... 113 A6
Mayfield Gr. Hud HD5 .... 154 F6
Mayfield Gr. Wils BD15 .... 53 B6
Mayfield Mount. Hali HX1 .... 113 A6 3
Mayfield Pl. Brad BD12 .... 94 C3
Mayfield Rd. Heb Br HX7 .... 89 A4
Mayfield Rd. Ilkley LS29 .... 8 C4
Mayfield Rd. Keigh BD20 .... 35 B8
Mayfield Rd. Leeds LS15 .... 81 B8
Mayfield Rise. Brad BD12 .... 94 D3
Mayfield Rise. Ryhill WF4 .... 162 A1
Mayfield St. Hali HX1 .... 113 A5 10
Mayfield Terr. Brad BD14 .... 73 C3
Mayfield Terr. Brad BD12 .... 94 D3 1
Mayfield Terr. Clec BD19 .... 116 E7 12
Mayfield Terr S. Hali HX1 .... 113 A5 11
Mayfield View. Brad BD12 .... 94 D3
Mayfields Way. S Kirk WF9 .. 182 B1
Mayflower St. Leeds LS10 .... 80 A2
Maylea Dr. Otley LS21 .... 22 D6
Mayman Cl. Batley WF17 .... 118 C5
Mayman La. Batley WF17 .... 118 B5
Maynes Cl. Dew WF12 .... 139 D2
Mayo Ave. Brad BD5 .... 74 E2
Mayo Cl. Leeds LS8 .... 61 D6
Mayo Cres. Brad BD5 .... 74 E1
Mayo Dr. Brad BD5 .... 74 E1
Mayo Gr. Brad BD5 .... 74 E1
Mayo Rd. Brad BD5 .... 74 E1
Mayor's Walk Ave. Pont WF8 .... 146 D7
Mayor's Wlk. Pont WF8 .... 146 D7
Mayors Wlk. Castle WF10 .... 125 E7
Maypole Mews. B in Elm LS15 . 63 D8
Maypole Rd. Hud HD2 .... 136 C4
Mayster Gr. Brig HD6 .... 135 F8
Mayster Rd. Brig HD6 .... 135 F7
Maythorne Ave. Batley WF17 .... 118 A4
Maythorne Cres. Brad BD14 .... 73 D4
Maythorne Dr. Brad BD14 .... 73 E4
Mayville Ave. Keigh BD20 .... 36 B8
Mayville Ave. Leeds LS6 .... 59 E3
Mayville Pl. Leeds LS6 .... 59 E3
Mayville Rd. Leeds LS6 .... 59 E3
Mayville St. Leeds LS6 .... 59 E3 16
Mayville Terr. Leeds LS6 .... 59 E3
Mazebrook Ave. Clec BD19 .... 95 E2
Mazebrook. Clec BD19 .... 95 E2
Mazebrook Cres. Clec BD19 .... 95 E2
McBride Way. Weth LS22 .... 13 F5
McBurney Cl. Hali HX3 .... 92 B2 2
McLaren Ave. Upton WF9 .... 183 D8
McMahon Dr. Brad BD13 .... 73 C2
McMillan Sch. Brad 39 C1
Mead St. Hud HD1 .... 136 A1
Mead View. Brad BD4 .... 75 E3
Mead Way. Kirkb HD8 .... 173 E7
Meadow Bank. Ack M T WF7 . 146 A1
Meadow Bank Cres. Mir WF14 137 E5
Meadow Bank. Dew WF13 .... 138 F8
Meadow Bank. Holmfi HD7 .... 189 C6
Meadow Bank. Ryhill WF4 .... 162 C1
Meadow Bottom Rd. Tod OL14 108 B6
Meadow Brook Chase. Nor WF6 .... 123 C1
Meadow Brook Cl. Nor WF6 .. 123 C1
Meadow Brook Ct. Nor WF6 .. 144 C8
Meadow Brook Gn. Nor WF6 . 123 C1
Meadow Cl. B Spa LS23 .... 30 C8
Meadow Cl. Bard LS17 .... 28 E6
Meadow Cl. Batley WF17 .... 97 A1
Meadow Cl. Con BD20 .... 4 A3
Meadow Cl. Harden BD16 .... 36 B1
Meadow Cl. Hem WF9 .... 181 C6
Meadow Cl. Liver WF15 .... 116 F1
Meadow Cl. Loft G WF1 .... 121 D5
Meadow Cl. Shelf HX3 .... 93 D6
Meadow Cres. Hali HX3 .... 91 E2
Meadow Cres. Roy S71 .... 179 D3
Meadow Croft Cl. Brad BD10 .... 55 F8
Meadow Croft. E Kes LS17 .... 28 C5
Meadow Croft. Hem WF9 .... 181 E5
Meadow Croft. Hud HD2 .... 136 F5
Meadow Croft. Keigh BD22 .... 34 E6
Meadow Croft. Leeds LS11 .... 79 B5
Meadow Croft. Loft G WF1 .... 121 C5
Meadow Croft. Shaf S72 .... 180 C3
Meadow Ct. Brad BD15 .... 54 A4
Meadow Ct. Brig HD6 .... 115 E2
Meadow Ct. Castle WF10 .... 125 D6
Meadow Ct. Roy S71 .... 179 D3
Meadow Ct. S Elm WF9 .... 183 B3
Meadow Dr. Hali HX3 .... 91 E2
Meadow Dr. Liver WF15 .... 116 F1
Meadow End. Bramho LS16 .... 24 E2
Meadow Garth. Bramho LS16 .. 24 F1
Meadow Garth. Loft G WF1 .... 121 C5
Meadow Gn. Slai HD7 .... 170 D8
Meadow La. Con BD20 .... 4 A2
Meadow La. Dew WF13 .... 118 C1
Meadow La. Hali HX3 .... 91 E2
Meadow La. Leeds LS11 .... 79 C6
Meadow La. Liver WF15 .... 116 F1
Meadow La. Slai HD7 .... 151 F1
Meadow La. Wake WF2 .... 141 F7
Meadow Lea. Glu BD20 .... 16 C6
Meadow Park Cres. Pudsey LS28 .... 57 B2
Meadow Park Dr. Pudsey LS28 57 B2
Meadow Pk. Kirkhe HD5 .... 137 B2
Meadow Rd. Brad BD10 .... 56 E8
Meadow Rd. Castle WF10 .... 124 B5
Meadow Rd. Gar LS25 .... 83 A7
Meadow Rd. Leeds LS11 .... 79 B5
Meadow Rd. Roy S71 .... 179 D3
Meadow Rise. Hem WF9 .... 181 C7
Meadow St. Hud HD1 .... 153 D7
Meadow The. Nor WF6 .... 144 A7
Meadow Vale. Loft G WF1 .... 121 D5
Meadow Vale. Neth WF4 .... 158 D5
Meadow Valley. Leeds LS17 .... 43 B5
Meadow View. B in Elm LS15 .. 63 E8
Meadow View. Brad BD12 .... 94 C1
Meadow View. Haw BD22 .... 34 D2
Meadow View. Leeds LS6 .... 59 E3 13
Meadow View. Ossett WF5 .... 140 C7
Meadow View. Skel HD8 .... 175 B1
Meadow Way. Ack M T WF7 .... 146 A1
Meadow Way. E Ard WF3 .... 119 D7
Meadow Way. Leeds LS17 .... 43 B5
Meadow Wlk. Bad WF9 .... 164 E3
Meadow Wlk. Hali HX3 .... 91 E2
Meadowbank Ave. Brad BD15 . 54 B1
Meadowcroft Cl. Loft G WF1 . 121 D5
Meadowcroft Ct. Loft G WF1 . 121 D5
Meadowcroft. Draug BD23 .... 1 D6
Meadowcroft La. Rip HX6 .... 132 E5
Meadowcroft. Men LS29 .... 22 A4
Meadowcroft Mews. Leeds LS9 79 E7
Meadowcroft Rd. Loft G WF1 121 D5
Meadowcroft Rise. Brad BD4 .. 95 C8
Meadowfield Cl. Hem WF9 .... 163 A3
Meadowfields Cl. Crof WF4 .. 162 A8
Meadowfields Dr. Crof WF4 .. 162 A8
Meadowfields Rd. Crof WF4 .. 162 A8
Meadowgate Croft. Roth WF3 100 B2
Meadowgate Dr. Roth WF3 ...... 100 B1
Meadowgate. Ossett WF5 .... 140 C7
Meadowgate Vale. Roth WF3 100 B1
Meadowhurst Gdns. Pudsey LS28 .... 76 D7
Meadowlands. Brig BD19 .... 94 E1
Meadows The. D Dale HD8 .... 191 F5
Meadows The. Hors LS16 .... 42 C3
Meadowside Rd. Bail BD17 .... 38 E4
Meadstead Dr. Roy S71 .... 179 B3
Meadway. Brad BD6 .... 93 F6
Meadway. Feath WF7 .... 144 C5
Meagill Rise. Otley LS21 .... 10 E2
Meal Hill La. Holmfi HD7 .... 189 F3
Meal Hill La. Slai HD7 .... 151 F2
Meal Hill Rd. Holme HD7 .... 187 F1
Meal Hill. Slai HD7 .... 151 F2
Mean La. Haw BD22 .... 50 D8
Mean La. Mel HD7 .... 170 E2
Meanwood CE Aided Prim Sch. Leeds 59 E7
Meanwood Cl. Leeds LS7 .... 60 B4
Meanwood Gr. Leeds LS6 .... 42 E1
Meanwood Park Hospl. Leeds .. 42 F1
Meanwood Rd. Leeds LS6, LS7 60 B4
Meanwood St. Leeds LS7 .... 60 C2
Meanwood Towers. Leeds LS6 60 A8
Meanwood Vall'y Dr. Leeds LS7 59 F6
Meanwood Vall'y Gn. Leeds LS7 59 F6
Meanwood Vall'y Gr. Leeds LS7 59 F6 2
Meanwood Valley Mount. Leeds LS7 .... 59 F6
Meanwood Valley Rd. Leeds LS7 59 F6
Meanwood Valley Wlk. Leeds LS7 .... 59 F6
Mearclough Rd. Hali HX6 .... 112 D4
Mearhouse Bank. Holmfi HD7 189 E4
Mearhouse Terr. Holmfi HD7 189 E4
Medeway. Pudsey LS28 .... 57 C2
Medhurst Ave. Kippax LS25 .... 83 B2
Medley La. Northo HX3 .... 92 F4
Medley St. Castle WF10 .... 124 E7
Medlock Rd. Hor WF4 .... 141 A1
Medway Ave. Gar LS25 .... 83 A5
Medway. Kirkhe HD5 .... 137 B2
Medway. Queen BD13 .... 92 F8
Meeting House La. Slai HD7 .. 152 A4
Meg La. Hud HD3 .... 153 B5
Meggison Gr. Brad BD5 .... 74 C4
Megnaway. Brad BD5 .... 74 E4 3
Melba Rd. Brad BD5 .... 74 B3
Melbourne Ave. Wake WF2 .... 120 F3
Melbourne Gr. Brad BD3 .... 75 E8
Melbourne Gr. Leeds LS13 .... 58 C2
Melbourne Mews. Wake WF2 120 E4
Melbourne Pl. Brad BD5 .... 74 D5
Melbourne Rd. Tod OL14 .... 108 A1
Melbourne Rd. Wake WF1 .... 142 A8
Melbourne St. Hali HX3 .... 92 A1 22
Melbourne St. Heb Br HX7 .... 89 A3 25
Melbourne St. Leeds LS2 .... 60 D1
Melbourne St. Liver WF15 .... 117 B3 4
Melbourne St. Morley LS27 .... 98 B4
Melbourne St. Pudsey LS28 .... 57 D2 7
Melbourne St. Ship BD18 .... 55 A8
Melbourne Terr. Brad BD5 .... 74 E5 1
Melcombe Wlk. Brad BD4 .... 75 E4
Melford Cl. Mapp S75 .... 178 B1
Melford St. Brad BD4 .... 75 C2
Mellor Brook. Slai HD7 .... 151 F4
Mellor La. Holmfi HD7 .... 188 B5
Mellor Mill La. Elland HX4 .... 134 B4
Mellor St. Brig HD6 .... 115 B2
Mellor St. Hali HX1 .... 113 A5
Mellor St. Tod OL14 .... 107 E8
Mellor Terr. Hali HX1 .... 113 A5
Mellor's Bldgs. Dew WF4 .... 156 D8
Mellwood La. S Elm WF9 .... 182 F3
Melrose Cl. Hud HD5 .... 155 A6
Melrose Ct. Elland HX5 .... 134 E6
Melrose Dr. Bur in W LS29 .... 9 E2
Melrose Gr. Hors LS18 .... 58 E8
Melrose Pl. Hors LS18 .... 58 D8
Melrose Pl. Pudsey LS28 .... 76 D6
Melrose St. Brad BD7 .... 74 A4
Melrose St. Hali HX3 .... 92 A1 26
Melrose Terr. Bacup OL13 .... 106 A7 9
Melrose Terr. Elland HX5 .... 134 F6
Melrose Wlk. Hors LS18 .... 58 E8
Meltham CE (C) Jun & Inf Sch. Mel 170 E1
Meltham House La. Holmfi HD7 .... 189 F4
Meltham Mills Ind Est. Mel HD7 .... 170 F2
Meltham Mills Rd. Mel HD7 .... 170 F2
Meltham Prim Sch. Mel 170 C3
Meltham Rd. Hud HD1, HD4 .. 153 F3
Meltham Rd. Mars HD7 .... 169 C5
Melton Ave. Midd LS10 .... 99 F4
Melton Cl. Midd LS10 .... 99 F4
Melton Cl. S Elm WF9 .... 183 A5
Melton Garth. Midd LS10 .... 99 F4
Melton Rd. Wake WF2 .... 160 A4
Melton St. Batley WF17 .... 118 B6
Melton Terr. Brad BD10 .... 56 E4
Melton Way. Liver WF15 .... 116 F1
Melville Cl. Leeds LS6 .... 60 B3
Melville Gdns. Leeds LS6 .... 60 B4
Melville Gr. Ilkley LS29 .... 8 E4
Melville Pl. Leeds LS6 .... 60 B4
Melville Rd. Leeds LS6 .... 60 B3
Melville St. Brad BD7 .... 74 C7
Memorial Dr. Leeds LS6 .... 59 F7
Mendip Ave. Hud HD3 .... 135 A1
Mendip Cl. Gar LS25 .... 82 F5
Mendip Rd. Dew WF12 .... 118 F1
Mendip Way. Brad BD12 .... 94 B6
Menin Dr. Bail BD17 .... 38 C5
Menston Dr. Guise LS29 .... 22 A3
Menston Inf Sch. Men 21 F4
Menston Jun Sch. Men 22 A4
Menston Old La. Bur in W LS29 21 F7
Menston Old La. Men LS29 .... 21 F7
Menston Sta. Men 22 B5
Menstone St. Brad BD8 .... 74 C8 6
Mercer Cl. Hud HD4 .... 171 C7
Merchants Ct. Brad BD4 .... 75 A5
Mercia Way. Leeds LS15 .... 62 E3
Mercury Row. Otley LS21 .... 23 A7
Merewood Rd. Castle WF10 .. 123 F7
Meriden Ave. Gar LS25 .... 82 F5
Merlin Cl. Morley LS27 .... 98 C3
Merlin Ct. Batley WF17 .... 118 A8
Merlin Ct. Hud HD4 .... 171 E7
Merlin Gr. Brad BD8 .... 73 C7
Merlyn Rees High Sch. Midd 99 E8
Merrill Rd. Dearne S63 .... 194 C1
Merrion Cres. Hali HX3 .... 113 E5
Merrion Ctr. Leeds 60 C1
Merrion Pl. Leeds LS2 .... 79 C8
Merrion St. Hali HX3 .... 113 E5
Merrion St. Leeds LS1, LS2 .... 79 C8
Merrion Way. Leeds LS2 .... 60 C1
Merrivale Rd. Brad BD15 .... 73 A8
Merry Bent La. Rip HX6 .... 132 A5
Merrybents St. Tod OL14 .... 108 D5
Merrydale Rd. Brad BD4 .... 95 A6
Mersey St. Bacup OL13 .... 106 A1 4
Merton Ave. Pudsey LS28 .... 57 D2
Merton Cl. Kippax LS25 .... 83 C2
Merton Dr. Pudsey LS28 .... 57 C2
Merton Fold. Brad BD5 .... 74 E4 6
Merton Gdns. Pudsey LS28 .... 57 C2
Merton Rd. Brad BD7 .... 74 D5
Merton St. Hud HD1 .... 154 A5
Merville Ave. Bail BD17 .... 38 C5
Metcalfe St. Brad BD4 .... 75 B4
Methley Dr. Leeds LS7 .... 60 C7
Methley Gr. Leeds LS7 .... 60 C6
Methley Inf Sch. M'town 102 C2
Methley Jun Sch. M'town 102 D3
Methley La. Leeds LS7 .... 60 D6
Methley La. Roth LS26 .... 101 E4
Methley Mount. Leeds LS7 .... 60 D6
Methley Park Hospl. M'town .. 102 A3
Methley Pl. Leeds LS7 .... 60 C6
Methley Rd. Castle WF10 .... 124 B8
Methley Terr. Leeds LS7 .... 60 D6
Methley View. Leeds LS7 .... 60 D6
Methuen Oval. Brad BD12 .... 94 C1 2
Mettle Cote. Bacup OL13 .... 106 A1
Mews Ct. Feath WF7 .... 145 D5
Mews The. Nor WF6 .... 123 B3
Mexborough Ave. Leeds LS7 .... 60 D4
Mexborough Dr. Leeds LS7 .... 60 D4
Mexborough Gr. Leeds LS7 .... 60 D4
Mexborough House. Elland HX5 .... 134 F7 3
Mexborough Pl. Leeds LS7 .... 60 D4
Mexborough Rd. Leeds LS7 .... 60 D4
Mexborough Rd. Ship BD2 .... 55 D5
Mexborough St. Leeds LS7 .... 60 D4
Meynell App. Leeds LS11 .... 79 A5
Meynell Ave. Roth LS26 .... 100 E5
Meynell Ct. Leeds LS15 .... 81 D7
Meynell Hts. Leeds LS11 .... 79 A5
Meynell Mount. Roth LS26 .... 100 F5
Meynell Rd. Leeds LS15 .... 81 D6
Meynell Sq. Leeds LS11 .... 79 A5 3
Meynell Wlk. Leeds LS11 .... 79 A5
Meyrick Ave. Weth LS22 .... 14 A6
Miall St. Hali HX1 .... 113 A8
Michael Ave. Loft G WF3 .... 121 E5
Mickledore Cl. Brad BD7 .... 73 E3
Mickledore Ridge. Brad BD7 .... 73 E3
Micklefield CE (C) Prim Sch. M'field 84 A7
Micklefield Ct. Yeadon LS19 ...... 40 B4
Micklefield La. Yeadon LS19 ...... 40 B4
Micklefield Rd. Yeadon LS19 ...... 40 B4
Micklegate. Pont WF8 .... 125 D1
Micklegate Sq. Pont WF8 .... 125 D1
Micklemoss Dr. Queen BD13 .... 72 C2
Micklethwaite Dr. Queen BD13 92 E8
Micklethwaite La. Bing BD16 ...... 36 E7
Micklethwaite Rd. Crig WF4 .. 159 F3
Micklethwaite View. Weth LS22 13 E4
Mickletown Rd. M'town LS26 .... 102 C3
Mickley St. Leeds LS12 .... 78 D7
Mid Yorkshire Nuffield Hospl. Hors 58 E8
Middle Cl. Kex S75 .... 177 C1
Middle Cross St. Leeds LS12 ...... 78 D7 9
Middle Dean St. Elland HX4 .... 134 D6 1
Middle Field La. Wool WF4 .... 177 F6
Middle Hall Cl. Liver WF15 .... 116 F4
Middle La. Brad BD14 .... 73 C5
Middle La. Coll LS22 .... 13 C2
Middle La. Crof WF4 .... 162 B7
Middle La. Knot WF11 .... 127 A3
Middle Oxford St. Castle WF10 124 C7
Middle Rd. Dew WF12, WF13 .... 139 B7
Middle Rd. Dew WF12 .... 139 E7
Middle Rd. Leeds LS9 .... 80 D2
Middle St. Brad BD1 .... 74 E7
Middle St. Sow Br HX6 .... 111 E1
Middle Way. Keigh BD21 .... 35 E7
Middlebrook Cl. Brad BD8 .... 73 E7
Middlebrook Cres. Brad BD8 .... 73 D6
Middlebrook Dr. Brad BD8 .... 73 D7
Middlebrook Hill. Brad BD8 .... 73 D7
Middlebrook Rise. Brad BD8 .... 73 D7
Middlebrook View. Brad BD8 .... 73 E7
Middlebrook Way. Brad BD8 .... 73 E7
Middlebrook Wlk. Brad BD8 .... 73 E7
Middlecliffe Dr. Wh Com S30 . 200 D5
Middlecroft Cl. Midd LS10 .... 99 F8
Middlecroft Rd. Midd LS10 .... 99 F8
Middlefield La. K Smea WF8 .. 166 B4
Middlegate. Batley WF17 .... 96 E1
Middlemoor. Leeds LS14 .... 62 B8
Middlethorne Mid Sch. Leeds .. 44 B5
Middleton Ave. Ilkley LS29 .... 8 B5
Middleton Ave. Leeds LS9 .... 60 F1
Middleton Ave. Roth LS26 .... 100 A5
Middleton Cl. Morley LS27 .... 98 C4
Middleton Cres. Leeds LS11 .... 79 B2
Middleton Ct. Liver WF15 .... 116 E4
Middleton District Ctr. Midd 99 D5
Middleton Gr. Leeds LS11 .... 79 B1
Middleton Gr. Morley LS27 .... 98 C4
Middleton La. Midd WF3 .... 99 D3
Middleton La. Roth LS26 .... 100 A5
Middleton Park Ave. Midd LS10 99 B4
Middleton Park Cir. Midd LS10 99 B5
Middleton Park Cr. Midd LS10 .. 99 C5
Middleton Park Ct. Midd LS10 .. 99 B4
Middleton Park Gn. Midd LS10 99 B4
Middleton Park Gr. Midd LS10 99 B4
Middleton Park High Sch. Midd 99 D4
Middleton Park Mount. Midd LS10 .... 99 B4
Middleton Park Pl. Midd LS10 .. 99 C4
Middleton Park Rd. Midd LS10 99 C5
Middleton Park Sq. Midd LS10 . 99 C4
Middleton Pk Sq N. Midd LS10 . 99 C4
Middleton Pk Sq S. Midd LS10 . 99 C4
Middleton Pk Terr. Midd LS10 .. 99 C4
Middleton Prim Sch. Midd 99 C4
Middleton Rd. Ilkley LS29 .... 8 A4
Middleton Rd. Midd LS10 .... 99 F8
Middleton Rd. Morley LS27 .... 98 C4
Middleton Rly. Leeds 79 C1
Middleton Rly. Midd 99 C8
Middleton St. Brad BD8 .... 55 B1
Middleton Terr. Morley LS27 ...... 98 C4
Middleton Way. Knot WF11 .... 126 F4
Middleton Way. Midd LS10 .... 99 F6
Middleway. Sil BD20 .... 5 F1
Midge Hall Cl. Bur in W LS29 ..... 9 E1
Midgeham Gr. Harden BD16 .... 36 A1
Midgehole La. Wad M HX7 .... 89 A6
Midgehole Rd. Wad M HX7 .... 89 A6
Midgeley Rd. Bail BD17 .... 38 A1
Midgley Almsho's. Haw BD22 .. 51 E8 16
Midgley Gdns. Leeds LS6 .... 60 A3
Midgley Jun Mix & Inf Sch. Hali 90 C1
Midgley Pl. Leeds LS6 .... 60 B3
Midgley Rd. Bur in W LS29 .... 9 E1
Midgley Rd. Heb Br HX7 .... 89 F1
Midgley Row. Brad BD4 .... 75 B1
Midgley Terr. Leeds LS6 .... 60 B3
Midland Cl. Leeds LS10 .... 79 F3
Midland Garth. Leeds LS10 .... 79 F3
Midland Hill. Bing BD16 .... 36 F3
Midland Pas. Leeds LS6 .... 59 F3
Midland Pl. Leeds LS11 .... 79 A6
Midland Rd. Bail BD17 .... 38 D2
Midland Rd. Brad BD8 .... 55 D1
Midland Rd. Leeds LS6 .... 59 F3
Midland Rd. Leeds LS10 .... 79 E3
Midland Rd. Pont WF8 .... 125 E1
Midland Rd. Roy S71 .... 179 D4
Midland Rd. Ship BD9 .... 55 C5
Midland St. Hud HD1 .... 154 B8
Midland St. Roth LS26 .... 101 C6
Midland Terr. Brad BD2 .... 55 E3
Midland Terr. Keigh BD21 .... 35 C8
Midland Terr. Ship BD9 .... 55 C5
Midway Ave. Ship BD16 .... 54 A7 1
Midway. Hud HD4 .... 171 A6
Milan Rd. Leeds LS8 .... 60 F3
Milan St. Leeds LS8 .... 61 A3 5
Mildred St. Brad BD3 .... 56 A1
Mildred Sylvester Way. Nor WF6 .... 123 E2
Mile Cross Gdns. Hali HX1 .... 112 E6
Mile Cross Pl. Hali HX1 .... 112 E6
Mile Cross Rd. Hali HX1 .... 112 E6
Mile Cross Terr. Hali HX1 .... 112 E6
Mile End. Mel HD7 .... 170 D2
Mile Thorn St. Hali HX1 .... 112 F7
Miles Garth. Bard LS17 .... 28 F6
Miles Hill Ave. Leeds LS7 .... 60 B6
Miles Hill Cres. Brad BD4 .... 75 C1
Miles Hill Cres. Leeds LS7 .... 60 B6
Miles Hill Dr. Brad BD4 .... 75 C1
Miles Hill Gr. Leeds LS7 .... 60 B6
Miles Hill Mount. Leeds LS7 ...... 60 A7
Miles Hill Pl. Leeds LS7 .... 60 B7
Miles Hill Prim Sch. Leeds 60 A7
Miles Hill Rd. Leeds LS7 .... 60 B6
Miles Hill Sq. Leeds LS7 .... 60 B6
Miles Hill St. Leeds LS7 .... 60 B6
Miles Hill Terr. Leeds LS7 .... 60 B6
Miles Hill View. Leeds LS7 .... 60 B6
Milestone Ct. Pudsey LS28 .... 57 F2
Milford Gr. Birk BD19 .... 96 A3
Milford Pl. Brad BD9 .... 55 A3
Milford Pl. Leeds LS4 .... 59 D1
Milford St. Hud HD1 .... 154 A5
Milgate St. Roy S71 .... 179 D4
Mill Bank Cl. Sow Br HX6 .... 132 C7
Mill Bank Rd. Mel HD7 .... 170 F1
Mill Bank Rd. Sow Br HX6 .... 132 D7
Mill Banks. Sil BD20 .... 5 E1
Mill Carr Hill Rd. Brad BD12, BD4 .... 95 B5
Mill Cl. Ack M T WF7 .... 164 A6
Mill Cl. S Kirk WF9 .... 182 A1
Mill Cotts. Feath WF7 .... 145 B5
Mill Croft. Gild LS27 .... 97 D7
Mill Ct. Oxen BD22 .... 51 C2 3
Mill Dam. B Spa LS23 .... 30 E5
Mill Dam La. Pont WF8 .... 125 E2
Mill Farm Dr. Crig WF2 .... 160 C4
Mill Fold Way. Rip HX6 .... 132 E4
Mill Garth. Gild LS27 .... 97 D7
Mill Gn. Leeds LS12 .... 78 F6
Mill Grath. Pont WF8 .... 146 C7
Mill Green Cl. Leeds LS14 .... 62 C5
Mill Green Garth. Leeds LS14 .. 62 C5 6
Mill Green Gdns. Leeds LS14 .. 62 C5
Mill Green Pl. Leeds LS14 .... 62 C4
Mill Green Rd. Leeds LS14 .... 62 C5
Mill Green View. Leeds LS14 .. 62 B5
Mill Hey. Haw BD22 .... 51 D7
Mill Hill. Ack M T WF7 .... 164 A8
Mill Hill Ave. Pont WF8 .... 146 C6
Mill Hill Cl. Dar WF8 .... 147 D5
Mill Hill Gn. Roth LS26 .... 100 E5
Mill Hill. Haw BD22 .... 51 C7
Mill Hill Hospl. Hud 155 A7
Mill Hill La. Brig HD6 .... 114 F4
Mill Hill La. Liver HD6 .... 115 F1
Mill Hill La. Pont WF8 .... 146 C7
Mill Hill. Leeds LS1 .... 79 C7
Mill Hill. Nor WF6 .... 123 A1
Mill Hill. Pudsey LS28 .... 76 E5
Mill Hill Rd. Pont WF8 .... 146 C7
Mill Hill. Roth LS26 .... 100 E5
Mill Hill Sq. Roth LS26 .... 100 E5
Mill Hill Top. Harden BD16 .... 53 B8
Mill House La. Sow Br HX6 .... 112 A2
Mill La. Ack M T WF7 .... 164 A6
Mill La. Ad Le S DN6 .... 184 F2
Mill La. Bard LS17 .... 28 E4
Mill La. Batley WF17 .... 97 B2
Mill La. Batley WF17 .... 118 E3
Mill La. Birk BD11 .... 77 A2
Mill La. Birk BD11 .... 96 A6
Mill La. Brad BD4, BD5 .... 74 F5
Mill La. Brad BD6 .... 93 E6
Mill La. Brig HD6 .... 115 B2
Mill La. Castle WF10 .... 103 D1
Mill La. Clec BD19 .... 95 D3
Mill La. Dew WF12 .... 140 A7
Mill La. E Ard WF3 .... 120 E8
Mill La. Elland HX4 .... 134 C4
Mill La. Feath WF7 .... 144 D6
Mill La. Floc WF4 .... 157 D2
Mill La. Gild LS27 .... 97 D7
Mill La. Guise LS20 .... 38 D8
Mill La. Hali HX2 .... 91 D7
Mill La. Hali HX3 .... 92 B2
Mill La. Haw BD22 .... 34 C2
Mill La. Hud HD5 .... 137 B5
Mill La. L Brad BD20 .... 4 C6
Mill La. Leeds LS13 .... 58 A3
Mill La. M'town LS26 .... 102 D3
Mill La. Mapp S75 .... 177 E1
Mill La. Nor WF6 .... 123 D4
Mill La. Notton WF4 .... 178 D8
Mill La. Otley LS21 .... 23 A8
Mill La. Oxen BD22 .... 51 C3
Mill La. Pont WF8 .... 125 F3
Mill La. Pool LS21 .... 24 D7
Mill La. Queen BD13 .... 72 C2
Mill La. Ryhill WF4 .... 162 B1
Mill La. S Elm WF9 .... 183 B4
Mill La. S Kirk WF9 .... 182 A2
Mill La. Stee BD20 .... 17 C5
Mill La. Th Arch LS23 .... 30 E8
Mill Lane Cty Prim Sch. Batley 118 D3
Mill Moor Rd. Mel HD7 .... 170 C2
Mill Pit La. Roth LS26 .... 100 D7
Mill Pk. Mir WF14 .... 137 F2
Mill Rd. Dew WF13 .... 118 C2
Mill Row. Stee BD20 .... 16 F6
Mill Royd St. Brig HD6 .... 115 B2
Mill Shaw La. Holmfi HD7 .... 190 B1
Mill St. Batley WF17 .... 117 E8
Mill St. Brad BD6 .... 74 A1
Mill St. Brad BD1 .... 74 F7
Mill St. Castle WF10 .... 124 B7
Mill St. Cull BD13 .... 52 D6
Mill St E. Dew WF12 .... 139 D6
Mill St. Elland HX3 .... 113 A1
Mill St. Glu BD20 .... 16 E6
Mill St. Hud HD4 .... 153 E4
Mill St. Leeds LS9 .... 79 D7
Mill St. Morley LS27 .... 98 A3
Mill St. S in Cra BD20 .... 16 E5
Mill St. S Kirk WF9 .... 182 A2
Mill St W. Dew WF12 .... 139 C7
Mill View. Hem WF9 .... 181 C6
Mill View. Knot WF11 .... 126 B4
Millbank Ct. Pudsey LS28 .... 76 F6
Millbank Fold. Pudsey LS28 .... 76 F6
Millbank. Pudsey LS28 .... 76 F6
Millbank View. Pudsey LS28 .... 76 F6
Millbeck Cl. Brad BD8 .... 73 C6
Millbeck Gn. Coll LS22 .... 29 A8
Millbridge Inf Sch. Liver 117 B4
Millbridge Upper Jun Mix Sch. Liver 117 B4
Millcroft Est. Pool LS21 .... 24 D7
Miller Ave. Wake WF2 .... 142 D2
Miller Ct. Crig WF2 .... 160 B4
Miller Garth. Ack M T WF7 .... 164 A5
Miller Hill Bank. D Dale HD8 .. 192 A5
Miller Hill. D Dale HD8 .... 192 A5
Millergate. Brad BD1 .... 74 E7 14
Millers Ct. Liver WF15 .... 117 B2
Millersdale Cl. Brad BD4 .... 95 A7
Millfield Cl. Hud HD3 .... 153 C7
Millfield Cres. Pont WF8 .... 146 C6
Millfield Rd. Hor WF4 .... 159 C8
Millfields. Ossett WF5 .... 140 C5
Millfields. Sil BD20 .... 5 D1
Millgarth Ct. Coll LS22 .... 29 B8
Millgarth St. Leeds LS2 .... 79 D8 6
Millgate. Ack M T WF7 .... 164 A5
Millgate. Bing BD16 .... 36 F3
Millgate. Elland HX5 .... 134 F7
Millgate. Hud HD1 .... 153 E5
Millgate. Hud HD4 .... 155 B2
Milligan Ave. Brad BD2 .... 56 A5
Millmoor Cl. Brad BD9 .... 54 D2
Millshaw. Leeds LS11 .... 78 E1
Millshaw. Morley LS11 .... 78 D1
Millshaw Mount. Leeds LS11 .... 78 E1
Millshaw Park Av. Morley LS11 98 D8
Millshaw Park Cl. Morley LS11 98 D8
Millshaw Park Dr. Leeds LS11 .. 78 D1 5
Millshaw Park La. Morley LS11 98 D8
Millshaw Park Way. Morley LS11 .... 78 D1
Millshaw Rd. Leeds LS11 .... 98 E7
Millside. Shaf S72 .... 180 C3
Millside Wlk. Shaf S72 .... 180 C3
Millstone Cl. Ack M T WF7 .... 164 A5
Millstone Rise. Liver WF15 .... 117 B2
Millward St. Ryhill WF4 .... 162 A1
Millwood La. Tod OL14 .... 108 D5
Millwright St. Leeds LS2 .... 60 D1
Miln Rd. Hud HD1 .... 154 A8
Milne Ct. Leeds LS15 .... 81 D6
Milne St. Brad BD7 .... 74 C7
Milne's Ave. Wake WF2 .... 141 F3
Milner Bank. Otley LS21 .... 22 D6
Milner Cl. Elland HX4 .... 134 C7
Milner Gdns. Leeds LS9 .... 79 F6
Milner Ing. Brad BD12 .... 94 C5
Milner La. Bard LS14 .... 28 F1
Milner La. Elland HX4 .... 134 C7
Milner La. Roth WF3 .... 100 A2
Milner La. Scar LS14 .... 45 F7
Milner La. Thorner LS14 .... 45 F7
Milner Rd. Bail BD17 .... 38 A1
Milner Royd La. Sow Br HX6 .. 112 E3
Milner St. Hali HX1 .... 113 B7
Milner St. Hud HD1 .... 153 E3
Milner St. Ossett WF5 .... 119 C1
Milner Way. Ossett WF5 .... 140 E6
Milner's La. Dar WF8 .... 147 D4
Milner's Rd. Yeadon LS19 .... 39 F7
Milnes Gr. Castle WF10 .... 125 B7
Milnes St. Leeds LS12 .... 78 E6
Milnsbridge Cty Sec Sch. Hud 153 A5
Milnthorpe Cl. Bramham LS23 . 30 C3
Milnthorpe Cres. Wake WF2 .. 160 D7
Milnthorpe Dr. Wake WF2 ...... 160 D8
Milnthorpe Garth. Bramham LS23 .... 30 C3
Milnthorpe Gdns. Bramham LS23 .... 30 C3
Milnthorpe La. Bramham LS23 30 C3
Milnthorpe La. Wake WF2 .... 142 D2
Milnthorpe Wy. Bramham LS23 30 C3
Milroyd Cres. Batley WF17 .... 97 A2
Milton Ave. Hali HX6 .... 112 B5
Milton Ave. Liver WF15 .... 117 C3
Milton Cl. Crig WF4 .... 159 D6
Milton Cl. Liver WF15 .... 117 C3
Milton Cres. Wake WF2 .... 141 C4
Milton Ct. Loft G WF3 .... 121 F6
Milton Dr. B in Elm LS15 .... 62 F7
Milton Dr. Batley WF15 .... 117 C2
Milton Dr. Hem WF9 .... 163 B2
Milton Gdns. Batley WF15 .... 117 C2
Milton Gr. Batley WF13 .... 118 C2
Milton Pl. Hali HX1 .... 113 B7
Milton Pl. Ossett WF5 .... 140 D7
Milton Rd. Liver WF15 .... 117 C3
Milton Rd. Wake WF2 .... 141 D4
Milton St. Batley WF16 .... 117 D5
Milton St. Brad BD7 .... 74 C7
Milton St. Castle WF10 .... 124 C8
Milton St. Denh BD13 .... 71 E8
Milton St. Hali HX6 .... 112 B5 11
Milton St. Wake WF2 .... 142 A5
Milton Terr. Clec BD19 .... 116 C8
Milton Terr. Hali HX1 .... 113 B7
Milton Terr. Hem WF9 .... 163 A4
Milton Terr. Leeds LS5 .... 59 A4
Milton Terr. Yeadon LS19 .... 39 F7
Milton Wlk. Dew WF13 .... 139 C8
Minden Cl. Pont WF8 .... 146 A7
Minden Way. Pont WF8 .... 146 A8
Minerva St. Hud HD4 .... 152 F3
Mini Market. Hud HD1 .... 154 C8
Minnie St. Haw BD22 .... 51 C6

Minnie St. Keigh BD21 ... 35 B6
Minor Roads. Mars HD7 ... 169 B6
Minorca Mount. Denh BD13 ... 52 D1
Minstead Ave. Brig HD6 ... 135 D7
Minsthorpe High Sch & Community Coll. S Elm ... 183 A5
Minsthorpe La. S Elm WF9 ... 182 E4
Minsthorpe La. S Kirk WF9 ... 182 E4
Minsthorpe Vale. S Elm WF9 . 182 F4
Mint St. Brad BD2 ... 56 B2
Mint St. Hud HD1 ... 153 D7
Miramar. Hud HD2 ... 136 D5
Mirey Butt La. Knot WF11 ... 126 D3
Mirey La. Sow Br HX6 ... 111 C3
Mirfield Ave. Brad BD2 ... 56 A5
Mirfield Free Gram Sch. Mir .. 137 F7
Mirfield Sports Ctr. Mir ... 137 F7
Mirfield Sta. Mir ... 138 A3
Miriam Lord Fst Sch. Brad ... 55 B1
Miry La. B in Elm LS15 ... 46 F1
Miry La. Clec WF15 ... 116 C5
Miry La. Heb Br HX7 ... 110 F6
Miry La. Holmfi HD7 ... 188 F8
Miry La. Holmfi HD7 ... 189 B8
Miry La. Yeadon LS19 ... 40 B7
Mission St. Brig HD6 ... 115 C1
Mistral Cl. Brad BD12 ... 94 C2
Mistral Gr. Clec WF15 ... 116 B5
Mistress La. Leeds LS12 ... 78 C8
Mitcham Dr. Brad BD9 ... 55 A2
Mitchell Ave. Dew WF13 ... 118 B2 3
Mitchell Ave. Hud HD5 ... 155 B5
Mitchell Cl. Brad BD10 ... 39 C1
Mitchell La. Brad BD10 ... 39 C1
Mitchell La. Sil BD20 ... 5 E1
Mitchell Sq. Brad BD5 ... 74 E4 8
Mitchell St. Brig HD6 ... 115 A3
Mitchell St. Hali HX6 ... 112 C4
Mitchell St. Heb Br HX7 ... 89 A2 6
Mitchell St. Keigh BD21 ... 35 D8
Mitchell St. Tod OL14 ... 107 E8
Mitchell Terr. Bing BD16 ... 36 F2
Mitford Pl. Leeds LS12 ... 78 D7 2
Mitford Rd. Leeds LS12 ... 78 D7
Mitford Terr. Leeds LS12 ... 78 D7
Mitford View. Leeds LS12 ... 78 D7 1
Mitre Ct. Brad BD4 ... 75 D3
Mitre St. Dew WF13 ... 139 A8
Mitre St. Hud HD1 ... 153 E7
Mitton St. Brad BD5 ... 74 C3
Mitton St. Ship BD16 ... 54 B6 2
Mixenden Cl. Hali HX2 ... 91 C5
Mixenden Cty Prim Sch. Hali ... 91 B6
Mixenden Ct. Hali HX2 ... 91 D4
Mixenden La. Hali HX2 ... 91 D6
Mixenden Rd. Hali HX2 ... 91 C5
Mixenden Stones. Hali HX2 ... 91 C6
Moat End. Thorner LS14 ... 45 F5
Moat Hill. Batley WF17 ... 97 A2
Moat Hill Fm Dr. Batley WF17 . 97 A2
Modd La. Holmfi HD7 ... 188 F4
Modder Ave. Leeds LS12 ... 78 B7
Modder Pl. Leeds LS12 ... 78 B7
Model Ave. Leeds LS12 ... 78 D7
Model Rd. Leeds LS12 ... 78 D7
Model Terr. Leeds LS12 ... 78 D7
Moderna Bsns Pk. Heb Br ... 110 F8
Moffat Cl. Brad BD6 ... 93 F7
Moffatt Cl. Hali HX3 ... 91 F3
Moldgreen Jun & Inf Sch. Hud 154 D5
Moles Head. Hud HD7 ... 152 C6
Molly Hurst La. Wool WF4 ... 177 F7
Mona St. Slai HD7 ... 151 F1
Mona St. Wake WF2 ... 141 E6
Mona's Terr. Tod OL14 ... 108 A1 1
Monckton Dr. Castle WF10 ... 125 C6
Monckton Rd. Wake WF2 ... 142 B2
Mond Ave. Brad BD3 ... 56 D1
Monk Barn Cl. Bing BD16 ... 37 A4 1
Monk Bridge Ave. Leeds LS6 ... 59 F6 11
Monk Bridge Dr. Leeds LS6 ... 59 F6 6
Monk Bridge Gr. Leeds LS6 ... 59 E6 2
Monk Bridge Mount. Leeds LS6 59 F6 10
Monk Bridge Pl. Leeds LS6 ... 59 E6
Monk Bridge Rd. Leeds LS6 ... 59 E6
Monk Bridge St. Leeds LS6 ... 59 F6
Monk Bridge Terr. Leeds LS6 .. 59 E6
Monk Ings Ave. Clec WF17 ... 96 C2
Monk Ings. Clec WF17 ... 96 D1
Monk St. Brad BD7 ... 74 C7
Monk St. Wake WF1 ... 142 D5
Monkfield. Mir WF14 ... 137 E6
Monkhill Ave. Pont WF8 ... 125 D2
Monkhill Dr. Pont WF8 ... 125 D2
Monkhill La. Pont WF8 ... 125 D3
Monkhill Mount. Pont WF8 ... 125 D2
Monkhill Sta. Pont ... 125 E2
Monkswood Ave. Leeds LS14 .. 61 F8
Monkswood Bank. Leeds LS14 61 F8
Monkswood Cl. Leeds LS14 ... 61 F8
Monkswood Dr. Leeds LS14 ... 61 F8
Monkswood Gate. Leeds LS14 . 62 A8 6
Monkswood Gn. Leeds LS14 ... 61 F8
Monkswood Hill. Leeds LS14 ... 61 F8
Monkswood. Leeds LS5 ... 58 F6
Monkswood Rise. Leeds LS14 . 61 F8
Monkswood Wlk. Leeds LS14 .. 62 A8
Monkwood Rd. Loft G WF1 ... 121 B5
Mons Rd. Tod OL14 ... 107 F7
Monson Ave. Pudsey LS28 ... 57 B6
Mont Gr. Brad BD5 ... 74 D3 1
Montagu Ave. Leeds LS8 ... 61 C5
Montagu Cres. Leeds LS8 ... 61 C5
Montagu Ct. Leeds LS8 ... 61 B6
Montagu Dr. Leeds LS8 ... 61 B6
Montagu Gdns. Leeds LS8 ... 61 B5
Montagu Gr. Leeds LS8 ... 61 C5
Montagu Pl. Leeds LS8 ... 61 B5
Montagu Rd. Weth LS22 ... 14 A6
Montagu Rise. Leeds LS8 ... 61 C4
Montagu View. Leeds LS8 ... 61 B5
Montague Cres. Gar LS25 ... 83 A7
Montague Pl. Gar LS25 ... 83 A7
Montague St. Brad BD5 ... 74 C3
Montague St. Sow Br HX6 ... 112 A3
Montague St. Wake WF1 ... 142 F2
Montcalm Cres. Leeds LS10 ... 79 E2
Montcalm Cres. Loft G WF3 ... 121 F3
Montfort Cl. Hors LS18 ... 41 B3
Montpelier Terr. Leeds LS6 ... 60 A4 3
Montreal Ave. Leeds LS7 ... 60 D6
Montreal St. Tod OL14 ... 108 A1 9
Montreal Terr. Pudsey LS13 ... 77 A8
Montrose Ave. Mapp S75 ... 177 F1
Montrose Pl. Queen BD13 ... 72 C2
Montrose Pl. Queen BD13 ... 72 C2 2
Montrose St. Ship BD2 ... 55 D4
Montserrat Rd. Brad BD4 ... 75 F1
Monument La. Pont WF8 ... 146 E7
Monument Mews. Pont WF8 . 146 E7
Moody St. Brad BD4 ... 74 F5
Moor Allerton Ave. Leeds LS17 43 E2
Moor Allerton Cty Prim Sch. Leeds ... 43 F1
Moor Allerton Cres. Leeds LS17 43 E2
Moor Allerton Ctr. Leeds ... 43 B2
Moor Allerton Dr. Leeds LS17 . 43 E2
Moor Allerton Gdns. Leeds LS17 43 D2
Moor Allerton Way. Leeds LS17 43 E2
Moor Ave. B Spa LS23 ... 30 D6
Moor Ave. Leeds LS15 ... 80 F7
Moor Ave. Loft G WF3 ... 121 E6
Moor Bottom. Honley HD7 ... 171 F4
Moor Bottom La. Bing BD16 ... 37 B3
Moor Bottom La. Elland HX4 .. 134 A8
Moor Bottom La. Keigh BD21 .. 35 B2
Moor Bottom La. Sow Br HX7 111 A5
Moor Bottom Rd. Hali HX2 ... 91 F6
Moor Bottom Rd. Rip HX6 ... 132 F5
Moor Cl. Hud HD4 ... 153 C1
Moor Cl. Leeds LS10 ... 79 D2
Moor Close Ave. Queen BD13 . 92 C8
Moor Close Farm Mews. Queen BD13 ... 92 C8 2
Moor Close La. Queen BD13 ... 92 C8
Moor Close Par. Queen BD13 .. 72 D1
Moor Close Rd. Queen BD13 ... 92 C8
Moor Cottage Cl. Hud HD4 ... 171 D7
Moor Cres. Leeds LS11 ... 79 C4
Moor Crescent Chase. Leeds LS11 ... 79 C4
Moor Crest Rd. Hud HD4 ... 153 C3
Moor Croft. Bing BD16 ... 37 B5
Moor Croft. Hors LS16 ... 42 D4
Moor Dr. Haw BD22 ... 34 C3
Moor Dr. Leeds LS6 ... 59 E6
Moor Dr. Otley LS21 ... 23 D8
Moor Dr. Pudsey LS28 ... 76 F5
Moor Edge High Side. Harden BD16 ... 36 A2
Moor End Ave. Hali HX2 ... 91 C1
Moor End Gdns. Hali HX2 ... 91 D1
Moor End La. Batley WF13 ... 117 F2
Moor End La. Sow Br HX6 ... 112 D2
Moor End Rd. Hali HX2 ... 91 B2
Moor End Rd. Hud HD4 ... 153 E3
Moor End Sec Sch. Hud ... 153 D2
Moor Farm Gdns. Leeds LS7 ... 60 C7
Moor Flatts Ave. Midd LS10 ... 99 C5
Moor Flatts Rd. Midd LS10 ... 99 C5
Moor Fold. Holmfi HD7 ... 189 E7
Moor Gate. Tod OL14 ... 108 C3
Moor Gr. Loft G WF3 ... 121 E6
Moor Gr. Pudsey LS28 ... 76 F5
Moor Gr. Shelf HX3 ... 93 C7
Moor Grange Ct. Leeds LS16 ... 58 F8 8
Moor Grange Dr. Leeds LS16 ... 59 A8
Moor Grange Rise. Leeds LS16 59 A8
Moor Grange View. Leeds LS16 59 A8
Moor Haven Ct. Leeds LS17 ... 43 A3
Moor Hey La. Elland HD3 ... 133 F2
Moor Hey La. Elland HD2, HX4 135 C5
Moor Hill Rd. Hud HD3 ... 134 F1
Moor House Ct. Leeds LS17 ... 44 B4
Moor Knoll Cl. E Ard WF3 ... 120 D8
Moor Knoll Dr. E Ard WF3 ... 120 D8
Moor Knoll La. E Ard WF3 ... 120 D8
Moor La. Add LS29 ... 2 B1
Moor La. Add LS29 ... 2 D1
Moor La. Ask LS21 ... 10 B7
Moor La. Birk BD11 ... 96 C3
Moor La. Bur in W LS29 ... 21 D7
Moor La. Clec BD19 ... 96 B2
Moor La. Clift LS21 ... 10 C4
Moor La. Coll LS22 ... 29 F7
Moor La. Dar WF8 ... 147 A2
Moor La. E Kes LS17 ... 28 A5
Moor La. Guise LS20 ... 22 E2
Moor La. Hali HX2 ... 91 E4
Moor La. Hare LS17 ... 27 F6
Moor La. Holmfi HD7 ... 188 E8
Moor La. Hud HD4 ... 171 E8
Moor La. Kirkb HD4 ... 172 F5
Moor La. Kirkb HD8 ... 173 F7
Moor La. Men LS29 ... 21 E4
Moor La. Pont WF8 ... 146 E4
Moor La. Sil LS29 ... 6 D8
Moor La. Stut LS24 ... 48 F8
Moor La. Th Arch LS23 ... 14 D5
Moor La. Tod OL14 ... 108 B3
Moor Park Ave. Hud HD4 ... 153 C1
Moor Park Ave. Leeds LS6 ... 59 D6
Moor Park Cl. Brad BD3 ... 75 C8
Moor Park Cl. Sil LS29 ... 6 D8
Moor Park Cres. Sil LS29 ... 6 D8
Moor Park Ct. Dew WF12 ... 118 E1 6
Moor Park Dr. Brad BD3 ... 75 D8
Moor Park Dr. Leeds LS6 ... 59 E6
Moor Park Dr. Sil LS29 ... 6 D8
Moor Park Gdns. Dew WF12 . 118 E1
Moor Park Gr. Sil LS29 ... 6 E8
Moor Park Mount. Leeds LS6 .. 59 E6
Moor Park Rd. Brad BD3 ... 75 C8
Moor Park Villas. Leeds LS6 ... 59 E6
Moor Park Way. Sil LS29 ... 6 E8
Moor Rd. Bramho LS16 ... 24 D2
Moor Rd. Feath WF7 ... 145 D5
Moor Rd. Ilkley LS29 ... 21 C7
Moor Rd. Leeds LS6 ... 59 D6
Moor Rd. Leeds LS10 ... 79 C4
Moor Rd. Leeds LS10 ... 79 D2
Moor Rd. Litt OL15 ... 129 C1
Moor Rd. Loft G WF3 ... 121 E6
Moor Rd. Men LS29 ... 21 C7
Moor Royd. Hali HX3 ... 113 A4
Moor Royd. Honley HD7 ... 171 E3
Moor Side. B Spa LS23 ... 30 B7
Moor Side Cotts. Keigh BD20 .. 19 B3
Moor Side La. Slai HD7 ... 151 D3
Moor St. Haw BD22 ... 34 D3
Moor St. Queen BD13 ... 72 E1 9
Moor Stone Pl. Shelf HX3 ... 93 C5
Moor Terr. Brad BD2 ... 56 C1
Moor Top Ave. Ack M T WF7 . 163 E5
Moor Top Ave. Kirkb HD4 ... 172 F2
Moor Top. Birk BD11 ... 96 D6
Moor Top Dr. Hem WF9 ... 181 D5
Moor Top Gdns. Hali HX2 ... 91 E8
Moor Top. Gild LS12 ... 77 C1
Moor Top. Guise LS20 ... 22 E4
Moor Top La. Lepton WF4 ... 156 D1
Moor Top. Mir WF14 ... 137 E6
Moor Top. Otley LS21 ... 22 E4
Moor Top Rd. Brad BD12 ... 94 B6
Moor Top Rd. Hali HX2 ... 112 B8
Moor Top Rd. Kirkhe HD5 ... 137 C2
Moor Valley Pk. Bail LS20 ... 38 C7
Moor View Ave. Ship BD18 ... 55 A8
Moor View. Bacup OL13 ... 106 A4
Moor View. Batley WF16 ... 117 E2
Moor View Cl. Castle WF10 ... 124 F7
Moor View. Crig WF4 ... 159 F5
Moor View Ct. Keigh BD20 ... 36 C7
Moor View. Leeds LS11 ... 79 A5
Moor View. M'town LS26 ... 102 F3
Moor View. Mel HD7 ... 170 C3
Moor View. Mir WF14 ... 117 A1
Moor View Terr. Haw BD22 ... 50 D7
Moor Way. Haw BD22 ... 34 C3
Moorbank Ct. Leeds LS6 ... 59 E5
Moorbottom. Clec BD19 ... 116 B7
Moorbottom Rd. Hud HD1 ... 153 E4
Moorbrow. Holmfi HD7 ... 189 C2
Moorcock Rd. B Head HX7 ... 87 C5
Moorcrest Rise. Mapp S75 ... 178 B2
Moorcroft Ave. Brad BD3 ... 56 D1
Moorcroft Ave. Haw BD22 ... 34 E3
Moorcroft Avenues. Hud HD7 152 D5
Moorcroft. Dew WF13 ... 118 A1
Moorcroft Dr. Brad BD4 ... 75 F1
Moorcroft Dr. Dew WF13 ... 117 F1
Moorcroft Dr. Holmfi HD7 ... 189 D7
Moorcroft Pk Dr. Holmfi HD7 189 E7
Moorcroft Rd. Brad BD4 ... 75 F1
Moorcroft Rd. Dew WF13 ... 117 F1
Moorcroft Terr. Brad BD4 ... 95 F8
Moorcross CE Inf Sch. Hud ... 153 C3
Moore Ave. Brad BD6, BD7 ... 74 A2
Moore St. Keigh BD21 ... 35 C6 5
Moore View. Brad BD7 ... 73 F3
Moorehouse Gr. Leeds LS9 ... 60 E1
Moorend CE Fst Sch. Clec ... 95 C1
Moorfield Ave. Brad BD3 ... 56 D1
Moorfield Ave. Brig BD19 ... 115 E7
Moorfield Ave. Leeds LS12 ... 78 A8
Moorfield Ave. Men LS29 ... 21 F4
Moorfield Cl. Yeadon LS19 ... 40 D6
Moorfield Cres. Hem WF9 ... 181 C6
Moorfield Cres. Leeds LS12 ... 78 A8
Moorfield Cres. Pudsey LS28 .. 76 D6 4
Moorfield Cres. Yeadon LS19 .. 40 D7
Moorfield Croft. Yeadon LS19 .. 40 D6
Moorfield Ct. Yeadon LS19 ... 40 D6
Moorfield Dr. Bail BD17 ... 38 C5
Moorfield Dr. Haw BD22 ... 34 D3
Moorfield Dr. Yeadon LS19 ... 40 D6
Moorfield Fst Sch. Brad ... 75 C7
Moorfield Gdns. Pudsey LS28 .. 76 D6
Moorfield. Gild LS27 ... 97 C7
Moorfield Gr. Leeds LS12 ... 78 A8
Moorfield Gr. Pudsey LS28 ... 76 D6
Moorfield Pl. Brad BD10 ... 56 B8
Moorfield Pl. Hem WF9 ... 181 C6
Moorfield Rd. Hud HD1 ... 136 B1
Moorfield Rd. Ilkley LS29 ... 8 F4
Moorfield Rd. Leeds LS12 ... 78 A8
Moorfield Rd. Ship BD16 ... 54 A7
Moorfield Rd. Yeadon LS19 ... 40 D7
Moorfield Sch. Ilkley ... 8 D3
Moorfield St. Hali HX1 ... 113 A5
Moorfield St. Leeds LS2 ... 60 A3 8
Moorfield St. Leeds LS12 ... 78 A8
Moorfield Terr. Yeadon LS19 .. 40 C7
Moorfield View. Liver WF15 .. 116 F1
Moorfield Way. Brig BD19, LS29 ... 115 E7
Moorfields. Leeds LS13 ... 58 C3
Moorfoot La. Con BD20 ... 4 A3
Moorgarth Ave. Brad BD3 ... 56 D1
Moorgate Ave. Brad BD3 ... 56 D1
Moorgate Ave. Kippax LS25 ... 83 A2
Moorgate. Bail BD17 ... 38 C4
Moorgate Cl. Kippax LS25 ... 83 A2
Moorgate Dr. Kippax LS25 ... 83 B2
Moorgate Flats. Mel HD7 ... 170 D2
Moorgate Rd. Kippax LS25 ... 83 A3
Moorgate Rise. Kippax LS25 ... 83 A2
Moorgate St. Hali HX1 ... 112 F5 16
Moorhead Cl. Mel HD7 ... 170 D2
Moorhead Cres. Ship BD18 ... 54 E7
Moorhead La. Ship BD18 ... 54 E7
Moorhead Terr. Ship BD18 ... 54 E7
Moorhouse Ave. Brad BD2 ... 56 A5
Moorhouse Ave. Leeds LS11 ... 78 F1
Moorhouse Ave. Loft G WF3 ... 122 B6
Moorhouse Ave. Wake WF2 .. 142 A6
Moorhouse Cl. Loft G WF3 ... 122 B7
Moorhouse Cl. Nor WF6 ... 123 C3
Moorhouse Cl. Oxen BD22 ... 51 C3
Moorhouse Cres. Wake WF2 . 142 A6
Moorhouse Ct. Oxen BD22 ... 51 C3
Moorhouse Ct. S Elm WF9 ... 183 A1
Moorhouse Dr. Birk BD11 ... 95 F7
Moorhouse Gap. H Pag DN6 .. 183 F1
Moorhouse Gr. Loft G WF3 ... 122 B7
Moorhouse La. Birk BD11 ... 96 A7
Moorhouse La. H Pag WF9 ... 183 D1
Moorhouse La. Oxen BD22 ... 51 C4
Moorhouse La. Ryhill WF4 ... 162 C4
Moorhouse La. Wool S75 ... 177 C5
Moorhouse Terr. Loft G WF3 . 122 B7
Moorhouse View. Loft G WF3 122 B7
Moorhouse View. S Elm WF9 183 B2
Moorings The. Brad BD10 ... 56 D8
Moorings The. Leeds LS17 ... 43 E5
Moorings The. Leeds LS10 ... 80 B3
Moorland Ave. Bail BD17 ... 38 D5
Moorland Ave. Bing BD16 ... 37 C5
Moorland Ave. Birk BD11 ... 96 A7
Moorland Ave. Gild LS27 ... 97 C8
Moorland Ave. Guise LS20 ... 22 E1
Moorland Ave. Leeds LS6 ... 59 F2
Moorland Ave. Mapp S75 ... 178 B2
Moorland Cl. Gild LS27 ... 97 C8
Moorland Cl. Hali HX2 ... 91 E3
Moorland Cl. Leeds LS17 ... 43 D1
Moorland Cl. Slai HD7 ... 170 E7
Moorland Cotts. Heb Br HX7 . 131 C8
Moorland Cres. Bail BD17 ... 38 D4
Moorland Cres. Gild LS27 ... 97 B8
Moorland Cres. Guise LS20 ... 22 C2
Moorland Cres. Guise LS20 ... 22 E2
Moorland Cres. Leeds LS17 ... 43 C1
Moorland Cres. Mapp S75 ... 178 B2
Moorland Cres. Men LS29 ... 22 A5
Moorland Cres. Pudsey LS28 .. 57 A1
Moorland Dr. Birk BD11 ... 96 B6
Moorland Dr. Crig WF4 ... 159 F2
Moorland Dr. Guise LS20 ... 22 E2
Moorland Dr. Leeds LS17 ... 43 D1
Moorland Dr. Pudsey LS28 ... 57 A1
Moorland Garth. Leeds LS17 ... 43 C1
Moorland Gdns. Leeds LS17 ... 43 D1
Moorland Gr. Leeds LS17 ... 43 C2
Moorland Gr. Pudsey LS28 ... 76 A8
Moorland Ings. Leeds LS17 ... 43 C1
Moorland Leys. Leeds LS17 ... 43 C1
Moorland Mount. Clec BD19 .. 116 B6
Moorland Pl. Brad BD12 ... 94 E5 4
Moorland Pl. Loft G WF3 ... 121 E8
Moorland Rd. Birk BD11 ... 96 E6
Moorland Rd. Bramho LS16 ... 24 C2
Moorland Rd. Leeds LS6 ... 59 F2
Moorland Rd. Pudsey LS28 ... 57 A1
Moorland Rise. Leeds LS17 ... 43 C2
Moorland Rise. Mel HD7 ... 170 C2
Moorland Terr. Gar LS25 ... 82 E6
Moorland Terr. Keigh BD21 ... 35 F6
Moorland View. Brad BD12 ... 94 E5
Moorland View. Clay W HD8 . 176 A2
Moorland View. Emley HD8 ... 175 A7
Moorland View. Leeds LS17 ... 43 C2
Moorland View. Sow Br HX6 . 111 F3
Moorland View. Wils BD15 ... 53 D4
Moorland Wlk. Leeds LS17 ... 43 C2
Moorlands Ave. Brad BD3 ... 56 D1
Moorlands Ave. Dew WF13 ... 118 C1
Moorlands Ave. Hali HX2 ... 91 E3
Moorlands Ave. Keigh BD22 ... 34 F4
Moorlands Ave. Mir WF14 ... 137 F6 1
Moorlands Ave. Ossett WF5 .. 140 C8
Moorlands Ave. Yeadon LS19 .. 40 D6
Moorlands Cl. Batley WF13 ... 117 F3
Moorlands Cres. Hali HX2 ... 91 E3
Moorlands Cres. Hud HD3 ... 134 D1
Moorlands Ct. Elland HX4 ... 134 B8 3
Moorlands Dr. Hali HX3 ... 91 E2
Moorlands Dr. Yeadon LS19 ... 40 D6
Moorlands Hall Hospl. Dew ... 139 B8
Moorlands. Holmfi HD7 ... 189 C3
Moorlands. Ilkley LS29 ... 8 A2
Moorlands Ind Ctr. Clec ... 95 D1
Moorlands Pl. Hali HX1 ... 113 B5
Moorlands Rd. Birk BD11 ... 96 A7
Moorlands Rd. Dew WF13 ... 139 B8
Moorlands Rd. Elland HX4 ... 134 B8
Moorlands Rd. Hud HD3 ... 134 D1
Moorlands Sch. Dew ... 139 B8
Moorlands Sch. Leeds ... 42 D1
Moorlands Terr. Bacup OL13 . 106 A1 6
Moorlands The. B Spa LS23 ... 30 C8
Moorlands The. Bacup OL13 .. 106 A8
Moorlands The. Leeds LS17 ... 43 E4
Moorlands The. Weth LS22 ... 13 F5
Moorlands View. Hali HX1 ... 113 B5
Moorlea Dr. Bail BD17 ... 38 D3
Moorleigh Cl. Kippax LS25 ... 83 B2
Moorleigh Dr. Kippax LS25 ... 83 B2
Moorroyd St. Ossett WF5 ... 140 C8
Moors The. Ilkley LS29 ... 8 B4
Moorshutt Rd. Hem WF9 ... 181 C6
Moorside App. Birk BD11 ... 96 F5
Moorside Ave. Batley WF13 .. 117 F2
Moorside Ave. Birk BD11 ... 96 A7
Moorside Ave. Birk BD11 ... 96 F5
Moorside Ave. Brad BD2 ... 56 D2
Moorside Ave. Hud HD4 ... 153 D4
Moorside Ave. Stee BD20 ... 17 A5
Moorside. Brad BD9 ... 54 E2
Moorside Cl. Birk BD11 ... 96 F5
Moorside Cl. Brad BD2 ... 56 C3
Moorside. Clec BD19 ... 116 A6
Moorside. Clec BD19 ... 116 C7
Moorside Cres. Bacup OL13 .. 106 A4
Moorside Cres. Batley WF13 . 117 F2
Moorside Cres. Birk BD11 ... 96 F5
Moorside Cres. Crig WF4 ... 159 F2
Moorside Croft. Brad BD2 ... 56 C2
Moorside Dr. Birk BD11 ... 96 F5
Moorside Dr. Leeds LS13 ... 58 C4
Moorside End. Batley WF13 .. 117 F2
Moorside Gdns. Birk BD11 ... 96 F5
Moorside Gdns. Brad BD2 ... 56 C4
Moorside Gdns. Hali HX3 ... 91 F4
Moorside Gn. Birk BD11 ... 96 F6
Moorside Jun & Inf Sch. Hali ... 91 F4
Moorside La. Add LS29 ... 6 E4
Moorside La. Ask LS21 ... 10 A7
Moorside La. Brad BD3 ... 75 D7
Moorside La. Oxen BD22 ... 50 F5
Moorside Maltings. Leeds LS11 79 C4
Moorside Mews. Brad BD2 ... 56 D3
Moorside Mount. Birk BD11 ... 96 E5
Moorside Paddock. Clec BD19 116 B6
Moorside Par. Birk BD11 ... 96 E5
Moorside Pl. Batley WF13 ... 117 F2
Moorside Pl. Brad BD3 ... 75 D7
Moorside Rd. Batley WF13 ... 117 F2
Moorside Rd. Birk BD11 ... 96 E5
Moorside Rd. Brad BD2 ... 56 C3
Moorside Rd. Brad BD3 ... 75 D7
Moorside Rd. Honley HD7 ... 171 E3
Moorside Rd. Kirkhe HD5 ... 137 C1
Moorside Rd. Wils BD15 ... 53 C4
Moorside Rise. Clec BD19 ... 116 B7
Moorside St. Brad BD12 ... 94 B6
Moorside St. Leeds LS13 ... 58 C4
Moorside Terr. Birk BD11 ... 96 F5
Moorside Terr. Brad BD2 ... 56 D2
Moorside Terr. Leeds LS13 ... 58 C4
Moorside Vale. Birk BD11 ... 96 F6
Moorside View. Birk BD11 ... 96 F5
Moorside Wlk. Birk BD11 ... 96 F5
Moorthorpe Ave. Brad BD3 ... 56 D1
Moorthorpe Sta. S Elm ... 182 E3
Moortop. Birk BD11 ... 96 E6
Moortown Corner House. Leeds LS17 ... 43 D2
Moortown Cty Prim Sch. Leeds 43 D2
Moortown Golf Course. Leeds . 43 B6
Moorview Cres. Wils BD16 ... 53 E6
Moorview Croft. Men LS29 ... 21 F5
Moorview Ct. Brad BD10 ... 39 A1
Moorview Dr. Ship BD18 ... 55 F7
Moorview Dr. Wils BD16 ... 53 E6
Moorview Gr. Keigh BD21 ... 35 D5
Moorville Ave. Brad BD3 ... 56 D1
Moorville Cl. Leeds LS11 ... 79 B4
Moorville Ct. Leeds LS11 ... 79 B4
Moorville Dr. Birk BD11 ... 96 A7
Moorville Gr. Leeds LS11 ... 79 A4
Moorville Rd. Leeds LS11 ... 79 B4
Moorway. Guise LS20 ... 39 C8
Moorwell Pl. Brad BD2 ... 56 C4
Moravian Pl. Brad BD5 ... 74 D4
Morefield Bank. Holmfi HD7 .. 189 C8
Moresby Rd. Brad BD6 ... 93 F6
Moresdale La. Leeds LS14 ... 61 F3
Moresdale La. Leeds LS14 ... 62 A3
Morley Ave. Brad BD3 ... 56 D1
Morley Ave. Knot WF11 ... 127 A4
Morley Carr Rd. Brad BD12 ... 94 D5
Morley Cross Hall Inf Sch. Morley ... 97 F2
Morley Cross Hall Jun Sch. Morley ... 97 F3
Morley Elmfield Inf Sch. Morley 98 B2
Morley Fold. D Dale HD8 ... 191 F5
Morley Hall La. Sow Br HX2 ... 111 D6
Morley High Sch. Morley ... 97 F3
Morley La. Hud HD3 ... 153 A4
Morley St. Brad BD7 ... 74 E6
Morley Sta. Morley ... 98 C5
Morley Victoria Prim Sch. Morley ... 98 A5
Morley View. Hali HX3 ... 113 E3
Morning St. Keigh BD21 ... 35 B4 13
Morningside. Brad BD8 ... 55 B1
Morningside. Denh BD13 ... 52 E1
Mornington Rd. Bing BD16 ... 37 A3
Mornington Rd. Ilkley LS29 ... 8 C4
Mornington St. Keigh BD21 ... 35 B8
Mornington Villas. Brad BD8 ... 55 D1
Morpeth Pl. Leeds LS9 ... 79 E7
Morpeth St. Brad BD7 ... 74 C7
Morpeth St. Queen BD13 ... 72 E1
Morphet Terr. Leeds LS7 ... 60 C1
Morrell Cres. Wake WF2 ... 120 F3
Morris Ave. Leeds LS5 ... 59 A5
Morris Cl. Hem WF9 ... 163 B2
Morris Gr. Leeds LS5 ... 59 A4
Morris La. Leeds LS5 ... 59 A5
Morris Mount. Leeds LS5 ... 59 A4
Morris Pl. Morley LS27 ... 97 F5
Morris Silman Jewish Mid Sch. Leeds ... 43 C4
Morris View. Leeds LS5 ... 59 A4
Morrison St. Castle WF10 ... 124 E7
Morrit Ave. Leeds LS15 ... 62 B1
Morritt Dr. Leeds LS15 ... 80 F8
Morritt Gr. Leeds LS15 ... 80 F8
Mortimer Ave. Batley WF17 ... 117 F5
Mortimer Ave. Brad BD3 ... 56 D1
Mortimer Cl. Gar LS25 ... 82 E7
Mortimer Cl. Ossett WF5 ... 140 F6
Mortimer Row. Brad BD3 ... 75 D7
Mortimer Row. Hor WF4 ... 140 F1
Mortimer St. Batley WF17 ... 117 F5
Mortimer St. Brad BD8 ... 73 F8
Mortimer St. Clec BD19 ... 116 D7
Mortimer Terr. Batley WF17 . 117 F5
Morton Gn. Hud HD5 ... 155 A3
Morton Gr. Dew WF12 ... 139 B3
Morton Gr. Keigh BD20 ... 36 D8
Morton La. Bing BD16 ... 36 D7
Morton La. Keigh BD16 ... 36 D7
Morton Par. Wake WF2 ... 142 A6
Morton Rd. Brad BD4 ... 75 D5
Morton Terr. Guise LS20 ... 22 D1
Morton Way. Hud HD3 ... 134 E1
Morton Wood Gr. Holmfi HD7 189 D3
Mortons Cl. Hali HX3 ... 113 E3
Morvern Meadows. Hem WF9 181 F7
Morwick Gr. B in Elm LS15 ... 62 F6
Moselden La. Rip HX6 ... 150 D6
Moseley Pl. Leeds LS6 ... 60 B3
Moseley Wood App. Hors LS16 41 D4
Moseley Wood Ave. Hors LS16 41 D6
Moseley Wood Bk. Hors LS16 41 D5
Moseley Wood Cl. Hors LS16 .. 41 D4
Moseley Wood Cres. Hors LS16 41 D5
Moseley Wood Crft. Hors LS16 41 D4
Moseley Wood Dr. Hors LS16 .. 41 D5
Moseley Wood Gdn. Hors LS16 41 D5
Moseley Wood Gn. Hors LS16 . 41 D5
Moseley Wood Gr. Hors LS16 .. 41 D5
Moseley Wood La. Hors LS16 .. 41 E5
Moseley Wood Rise. Hors LS16 41 D5
Moseley Wood Vw. Hors LS16 41 E6
Moseley Wood Way. Hors LS16 41 D6
Moseley Wood Wlk. Hors LS16 41 D5
Moser Ave. Brad BD2 ... 56 A5
Moser Cres. Brad BD2 ... 56 A5
Moss Bridge Rd. Pudsey LS13 . 57 F5
Moss Carr Ave. Keigh BD21 ... 35 F5
Moss Carr Gr. Keigh BD21 ... 35 F5
Moss Carr Rd. Keigh BD21 ... 35 F5
Moss Dr. Hali HX2 ... 91 E6
Moss Edge Rd. Holmfi HD7 ... 188 C1
Moss Gdns. Leeds LS17 ... 43 A5
Moss Hall La. B Head HX7 ... 87 E4
Moss La. Hali HX2 ... 91 E6
Moss La. Heb Br HX7 ... 89 A4
Moss Lea. Morley LS27 ... 98 B7 4
Moss Rise. Holmfi HD7 ... 188 E5
Moss Rise. Leeds LS17 ... 43 A5
Moss Row. Wils BD15 ... 53 C6
Moss Side. Brad BD9 ... 54 E2
Moss St. Castle WF10 ... 124 C8
Moss St. Haw BD22 ... 51 E8
Moss St. Hud HD4 ... 154 B4
Moss St. Thorn BD13 ... 72 C7
Moss Syke. Scar LS14 ... 45 C8
Moss Valley. Leeds LS17 ... 43 A5
Mossdale Ave. Brad BD9 ... 54 C3
Mosstree Cl. Queen BD13 ... 72 C2
Mossy Bank Cl. Queen BD13 ... 72 E2
Mostyn Gr. Brad BD6 ... 94 A8
Mostyn Mount. Hali HX3 ... 92 A3
Mostyn Wlk. Crig WF4 ... 159 F2
Motley La. Guise LS20 ... 22 E2
Moulson Ct. Brad BD5 ... 74 E3 1
Moulson Terr. Denh BD13 ... 71 D8
Mount Ave. Batley WF16 ... 117 E6
Mount Ave. Batley WF17 ... 118 D3 1
Mount Ave. Brad BD2 ... 56 C5
Mount Ave. Hali HX2 ... 112 C7
Mount Ave. Hem WF9 ... 181 D7
Mount Ave. Hud HD3 ... 134 D1
Mount Ave. Wake WF2 ... 120 F3
Mount Cres. Clec BD19 ... 116 D8
Mount Cres. H Chap BB10 ... 85 A8
Mount Cres. Hali HX2 ... 112 C7
Mount Cres. Wake WF2 ... 141 F3
Mount Dr. Leeds LS17 ... 43 B6
Mount Gdns. Clec BD19 ... 116 D8
Mount Gdns. Leeds LS17 ... 43 B6
Mount Gr. Brad BD2 ... 56 B5
Mount La. Brig HD6 ... 135 E6
Mount La. H Chap BB10 ... 85 A8
Mount La. Tod OL14 ... 86 C3
Mount Pellon Rd. Hali HX2 ... 112 E8
Mount Pisgah. Otley LS21 ... 23 A7
Mount Pl. Ship BD18 ... 55 B8
Mount Pleasant. Ack M T WF7 163 F6
Mount Pleasant. Ack M T WF7 164 A6
Mount Pleasant Ave. Hali HX1 113 B8
Mount Pleasant Ave. Leeds LS8 60 F5
Mount Pleasant. Brad BD6 ... 93 F7 1
Mount Pleasant. Brig HD6 ... 135 E6
Mount Pleasant. Castle WF10 124 F6
Mount Pleasant. Denh BD13 ... 71 D8
Mount Pleasant. Dew WF12 .. 139 E7
Mount Pleasant Dr. Heb Br HX7 89 F1
Mount Pleasant. Emley HD8 .. 175 D7
Mount Pl'sant Gdns. Kippax LS25 83 B1 5
Mount Pleasant Gdns. Leeds LS8 ... 60 F5
Mount Pleasant. Glu BD20 ... 16 B6
Mount Pleasant. Guise LS20 ... 22 E2
Mount Pleasant. Hud HD1 ... 153 F3
Mount Pleasant. Ilkley LS29 ... 8 C3
Mount Pleasant Inf Sch. Hud . 153 F3
Mount Pleasant Jun Sch. Hud 153 F3
Mount Pleasant. K Smea WF8 166 F6
Mount Pleasant. Keigh BD20 .. 36 C7
Mount Pleasant. Kippax LS25 .. 83 B1 4
Mount Pleasant La. Lepton HD8 ... 155 C4
Mount Pleasant. Men LS29 ... 21 F4
Mount Pleasant. Midd LS10 ... 99 C5
Mount Pleasant Rd. Pudsey LS28 ... 76 F8
Mount Pleasant. Rip HX6 ... 132 F4
Mount Pleasant. Sil LS29 ... 6 F8
Mount Pleasant Sports Ctr. Hud ... 153 F3
Mount Pl'sant St. Feath WF7 . 145 D6
Mount Pleasant St. Hud HD5 . 154 D6 1
Mount Pleasant St. Pudsey LS28 ... 76 F8 2
Mount Pl'sant St. Queen BD13 . 72 E1
Mount Pleasant St. Tod OL14 .. 86 A1
Mount Pleasant View. Tod OL14 ... 108 B5 7
Mount Preston. Leeds LS2 ... 60 A1
Mount Preston St. Leeds LS2 .. 60 A1
Mount Prim Sch The. Wake ... 141 F3
Mount Rd. Brad BD2 ... 56 B5
Mount Rd. Brad BD6 ... 74 A1
Mount Rd. Hud HD1 ... 153 D7
Mount Rd. Loft G WF3 ... 121 F6
Mount Rd. Mars HD7 ... 168 D1
Mount Rise. Leeds LS17 ... 43 B6
Mount Royd. Brad BD8 ... 55 C2
Mount Scar View. Holmfi HD7 189 D4
Mount St. Batley WF17 ... 118 D3
Mount St. Brad BD2 ... 56 B5
Mount St. Brad BD3, BD4 ... 75 B6
Mount St. Clec BD19 ... 116 D8
Mount St. Hali HX6 ... 112 B4
Mount St. Hali HX1 ... 113 C7
Mount St. Hud HD3 ... 153 A4
Mount St. Hud HD1, HD4 ... 153 F3
Mount St. Keigh BD21 ... 35 A7
Mount St Mary's High Sch. Leeds ... 79 E7
Mount St W. Hali HX2 ... 112 E8 6
Mount Tabor Rd. Hali HX2 ... 91 A4
Mount Tabor St. Pudsey LS28 . 76 C7
Mount Terr. Batley WF17 ... 118 C3
Mount Terr. Brad BD2 ... 56 B5
Mount The. B in Elm LS15 ... 63 D6
Mount The. Batley WF17 ... 96 E2
Mount The. Castle WF10 ... 125 C7
Mount The. Kippax LS25 ... 83 A1
Mount The. Leeds LS17 ... 43 B6
Mount The. Leeds LS15 ... 62 B1
Mount The. Nor WF6 ... 123 B2
Mount The. Pont WF8 ... 146 C8
Mount The. Roth LS26 ... 100 F7
Mount The. Tod OL14 ... 108 C6
Mount The. Wake WF2 ... 120 D1
Mount The. Wake WF2 ... 141 F3
Mount Vernon Rd. Yeadon LS19 ... 40 C4
Mount View. Hali HX2 ... 91 A3
Mount View. Haw BD22 ... 34 B2
Mount View. Queen BD13 ... 72 D1
Mount View Rd. Holmfi HD7 .. 189 E2
Mount Wlk. Castle WF10 ... 124 D5
Mount Zion Rd. Hud HD5 ... 154 C6
Mountain Cres. Dew WF12 ... 139 D2
Mountain Rd. Dew WF12 ... 139 D2
Mountain View. Ship BD18 ... 55 D6
Mountain Way. Kirkhe HD5 ... 155 C7
Mountbatten Ave. Loft G WF1 121 C5
Mountbatten Ave. Wake WF2 160 E8
Mountbatten Cr. Loft G WF1 .. 121 C5
Mountbatten Ct. Brad BD5 ... 74 E2 4
Mountbatten Gdns. Hud HD3 . 153 B7
Mountbatten Gr. Loft G WF1 121 D4
Mountcliffe View. Morley LS27 98 B7
Mountfield Ave. Hud HD5 ... 155 B4
Mountfield Rd. Hud HD5 ... 155 B5
Mountfield Wlk. S Kirk WF9 .. 182 B1
Mountfields. Brig HX3 ... 114 E8
Mountfields. Leeds LS3 ... 59 F1 3
Mountjoy Prep Sch. Hud ... 153 F7

Mountjoy Rd. Hud HD1 .... 153 F7
Mountleigh Cl. Brad BD4 .... 95 A7
Mouse Hole La. Mir WF14 ...... 138 D1
Moverley Flatts. Pont WF8 ...... 146 E7
Mowat Ct. Clec WF15 .... 116 B5
Mowbray Cl. Cull BD13 .... 52 C5
Mowbray Cres. Leeds LS14 ...... 62 A3
Mowbray Ct. Leeds LS14 .... 62 A3
Moxon Cl. Pont WF8 .... 146 D6
Moxon Gr. Loft G WF1 .... 121 B3
Moxon Pl. Wake WF2 .... 141 C5
Moxon Sq. Wake WF1 .... 142 D7
Moxon St. Loft G WF1 .... 121 C4
Moxon Way. Loft G WF1 .... 121 C4
Mozley Dr. Hali HX2 .... 91 F6
Mucky La. Elland HX5 .... 134 D4
Muddy La. Coll LS22 .... 13 B2
Muff St. Brad BD4 .... 75 B5
Muffit La. Batley BD19 .... 117 D8
Mug Mill La. Dew WF12 .... 157 E8
Mugup La. Holmfi HD7 .... 189 E1
Muirfield Ave. Feath WF7 .... 124 D1
Muirfield Cl. Cud S72 .... 180 C1
Muirfields The. Mapp S75 .... 178 A1
Muirhead Dr. Brad BD4 .... 75 E2
Muirlands The. Hud HD2 .... 136 E5
Mulberry Ave. Hors LS16 .... 42 D4
Mulberry Ave. Ryhill WF4 .... 162 B1
Mulberry Garth. Hors LS16 .... 42 E3
Mulberry Garth. Th Arch LS23 . 14 E1
Mulberry House. Castle WF10 124 E7 12
Mulberry Pl. Ryhill WF4 .... 162 B1
Mulberry Rise. Hors LS16 .... 42 D4
Mulberry St. Hud HD5 .... 154 C5
Mulberry St. Keigh BD21 .... 35 D8 13
Mulberry St. Leeds LS10 .... 79 D5
Mulberry St. Pudsey LS28 .... 76 E7
Mulberry Terr. Hud HD1 .... 154 B8
Mulberry View. Hors LS16 .... 42 D3
Mulcture Hall Rd. Hali HX1 .... 113 D7
Mulehouse La. Elland HD3 .... 134 B1
Mulgrave St. Brad BD3 .... 75 B6
Mullberry Gdns. M'town LS26 102 B2
Mullins Ct. Leeds LS9 .... 79 F7
Mumford St. Brad BD5 .... 74 E3
Munby St. Brad BD8 .... 73 E7
Muncaster Rd. Gar LS25 .... 83 B8
Munster St. Brad BD4 .... 75 B3
Murdoch St. Keigh BD21 .... 35 F8
Murdstone Cl. Brad BD5 .... 74 E3 5
Murgatroyd St. Brad BD5 .... 74 E2
Murgatroyd St. Ship BD17 .... 55 B8
Murray Rd. Hud HD2 .... 153 F8
Murray St. Brad BD5 .... 74 C3 3
Murton Cl. Leeds LS14 .... 62 A4
Museum Ct. Brad BD2 .... 56 C2
Museum St. Leeds LS9 .... 60 F1
Musgrave Bank. Leeds LS13 .... 58 E2
Musgrave Bldgs. Pudsey LS28 76 F8 6
Musgrave Ct. Wake WF2 .... 141 D4
Musgrave Dr. Brad BD2 .... 56 C2
Musgrave Gr. Brad BD2 .... 56 C2
Musgrave Mount. Brad BD2 .... 56 C2
Musgrave Mount. Leeds LS13 . 58 E2
Musgrave Rd. Brad BD2 .... 56 C2
Musgrave Rise. Leeds LS13 .... 58 E2
Musgrave St. Batley WF17 .... 96 E1 2
Musgrave View. Leeds LS13 .... 58 E2
Mushroom St. Leeds LS9 .... 60 E1
Musselburgh St. Brad BD7 .... 74 C7
Mutton La. Wils BD15 .... 53 D2
Myers Ave. Brad BD2 .... 56 A4
Myers Croft. Hud HD5 .... 154 F6
Myers Croft. Otley LS21 .... 23 A7
Myers La. Brad BD2 .... 56 A4
Myrtle Ave. Bing BD16 .... 36 F2
Myrtle Ave. Dew WF13 .... 138 E5
Myrtle Ave. Hali HX2 .... 91 E4
Myrtle Ct. Bing BD16 .... 36 F2
Myrtle Dr. Hali HX2 .... 91 E4
Myrtle Dr. Haw BD22 .... 34 F1
Myrtle Gdns. Hali HX2 .... 91 E4
Myrtle Gr. Bing BD16 .... 36 F2
Myrtle Gr. Hali HX2 .... 91 E4
Myrtle Gr. Hud HD3 .... 153 B6
Myrtle Gr. Queen BD13 .... 92 C8 5
Myrtle Park Fst Sch. Bing 36 F2
Myrtle Pl. Bing BD16 .... 36 F3
Myrtle Pl. Hali HX2 .... 91 E4
Myrtle Pl. Ship BD18 .... 54 F8 11
Myrtle Rd. Dew WF13 .... 138 E5
Myrtle Rd. Elland HX5 .... 134 F6
Myrtle Rd. Hud HD7 .... 152 D4
Myrtle St. Bing BD16 .... 37 A3 11
Myrtle St. Brad BD3 .... 75 C6
Myrtle St. Hud HD1 .... 154 B7 1
Myrtle St. Tod OL14 .... 108 B5
Myrtle View. Haw BD22 .... 34 D3
Myrtle View. Haw BD22 .... 51 F8 12
Myrtle Wlk. Bing BD16 .... 36 F3
Myson Ave. Pont WF8 .... 125 F4
Mytholm Cl. Heb Br HX7 .... 88 F3
Mytholm Ct. Heb Br HX7 .... 88 E3
Mytholm. Heb Br HX7 .... 88 E3
Mytholmes. Haw BD22 .... 51 C8
Mytholmes La. Haw BD22 .... 34 D1
Mytholmes La. Haw BD22 .... 51 C8
Mytholmes Terr. Haw BD22 .... 51 C8
Mytholmroyd Sta. Heb Br 110 E8

Nab Cres. Mel HD7 .... 170 C2
Nab End La. Elland HX4 .... 134 D7
Nab La. Batley WF17 .... 97 B2
Nab La. Mir WF14 .... 137 F6
Nab La. Ship BD18 .... 54 D7
Nab The. Mir WF14 .... 137 E6
Nab View. Sil BD20 .... 5 F3
Nab Water La. Oxen HX7 .... 70 C6
Nab Wood Bank. Ship BD18 .... 54 D7
Nab Wood Cl. Ship BD18 .... 54 E7
Nab Wood Cres. Ship BD18 .... 54 D7
Nab Wood Dr. Ship BD18 .... 54 D6
Nab Wood Gdns. Ship BD18 .... 54 E7
Nab Wood Gr. Ship BD18 .... 54 D7
Nab Wood Grammar Sch. Ship 54 C7
Nab Wood Mid Sch. Ship 54 D7
Nab Wood Mount. Ship BD18 .. 54 D7
Nab Wood Pl. Ship BD18 .... 54 D7
Nab Wood Rd. Ship BD18 .... 54 D6
Nab Wood Rise. Ship BD18 .... 54 D7
Nab Wood Terr. Ship BD18 .... 54 D7
Nabbs La. Slai HD7 .... 151 F1
Nabcroft La. Hud HD4 .... 153 D3
Nabcroft Rise. Hud HD4 .... 153 D4
Naburn App. Leeds LS14 .... 62 C8
Naburn Chase. Leeds LS14 .... 62 B7
Naburn Cl. Leeds LS14 .... 62 C7
Naburn Ct. Leeds LS14 .... 62 C8 3
Naburn Dr. Leeds LS14 .... 62 B7
Naburn Fold. Leeds LS14 .... 62 C7
Naburn Gdns. Leeds LS14 .... 62 B7
Naburn Gn. Leeds LS14 .... 62 B7
Naburn Pl. Leeds LS14 .... 62 B8
Naburn Rd. Leeds LS14 .... 62 B7
Naburn View. Leeds LS14 .... 62 C7
Naburn Wlk. Leeds LS14 .... 62 B7
Nairn Cl. Hud HD4 .... 153 C2
Nancroft Cres. Leeds LS12 .... 78 C7
Nancroft Mount. Leeds LS12 .. 78 C7
Nancroft Terr. Leeds LS12 .... 78 C8
Nanny Goat La. B in Elm LS25 .. 82 D8
Nansen Ave. Leeds LS13 .... 58 C2 9
Nansen Gr. Leeds LS13 .... 58 C2 10
Nansen Mount. Leeds LS13 .... 58 C2 11
Nansen Pl. Leeds LS13 .... 58 B2 1
Nansen St. Leeds LS13 .... 58 A2
Nansen Terr. Leeds LS13 .... 58 B2 3
Nansen View. Leeds LS13 .... 58 B2 2
Naomi Rd. Hud HD4 .... 154 A2
Napier House. Tod OL14 .... 129 A8
Napier Rd. Brad BD3 .... 75 D7
Napier Rd. Elland HX5 .... 134 E6
Napier St. Brad BD3 .... 75 D7
Napier St. Keigh BD21 .... 35 D6
Napier St. Queen BD13 .... 72 F1 2
Napier Terr. Brad BD3 .... 75 D7
Naples St. Brad BD8 .... 55 B1
Nares St. Haw BD22 .... 51 E8 9
Nares St. Keigh BD21 .... 35 B7
Nares St Upper. Keigh BD21 .... 35 B7
Narrow Balk. H Pag DN5 .... 195 E5
Narrow La. Harden BD16 .... 36 B1
Narrows The. Harden BD16 .... 36 B1
Naseby Garth. Leeds LS9 .... 60 E1
Naseby Gdns. Leeds LS9 .... 79 E8 5
Naseby Grange. Leeds LS9 .... 79 E8 4
Naseby Pl. Leeds LS9 .... 79 E8 3
Naseby Rise. Queen BD13 .... 72 F1
Naseby Terr. Leeds LS9 .... 79 E8
Naseby View. Leeds LS9 .... 79 E8 6
Naseby Wlk. Leeds LS9 .... 79 E8
Nashville Rd. Keigh BD22 .... 35 A6 4
Nashville St. Keigh BD22 .... 35 A6 2
Nashville Terr. Keigh BD22 .... 35 A6 1
Nassau Pl. Leeds LS7 .... 60 E4
Nat Mus of Photography & TV. Brad 74 E6
Nathan La. Sow Br HX6 .... 132 C7
Nathaniel Waterhouse Homes. Hali HX1 .... 113 C6 8
National Pk. Leeds 79 E4
National Rd. Leeds LS10 .... 79 E4
Natty Fields Cl. Hali HX2 .... 91 E7
Natty La. Hali HX2 .... 91 E7
Navigation Gdns. Dew WF12 . 139 B4
Navigation Rd. Castle WF10 .. 103 D1
Navigation Rd. Dew WF12 .... 139 B4
Navigation Rd. Hali HX3 .... 113 D6
Navigation Wlk. Leeds LS10 .... 79 C7
Navvy La. Ryhill S71 .... 179 D7
Naylor La. Hali HX2 .... 90 C1
Naylor St. Dew WF13 .... 118 B2
Naylor St. Hali HX1 .... 112 F7 9
Naylor St. Ossett WF5 .... 140 C8
Naylor's Bldgs. Brig BD19 .... 115 F8 5
Naze View. Tod OL14 .... 107 F3
Neal Pl. Leeds LS10 .... 79 D6
Neal St. Brad BD5 .... 74 E6
Neale Rd. Hud HD1 .... 153 F3
Neale St. Heb Br HX7 .... 89 A2 5
Near Bank. Shep HD8 .... 174 B2
Near La. Mel HD7 .... 170 E2
Nearcliffe Rd. Brad BD9 .... 55 A2
Neath Gdns. Leeds LS9 .... 61 D3
Necropolis Rd. Brad BD7 .... 73 F5
Ned Hill Rd. Hali HX2 .... 71 F3
Ned La. Brad BD4 .... 75 F4
Ned La. Slai HD7 .... 169 F8
Needles Inn La. Roth LS26 .... 101 C7
Nell Gap Ave. Neth WF4 .... 158 A7
Nell Gap Cres. Neth WF4 .... 158 A6
Nell Gap La. Neth WF4 .... 158 A6
Nell Gap La. Neth WF4 .... 158 A7
Nelson Croft. Gar LS25 .... 82 D5
Nelson Ct. Morley LS27 .... 97 F2
Nelson Pl. Hali HX6 .... 112 D4
Nelson Pl. Morley LS27 .... 98 A5 1
Nelson Pl. Queen BD13 .... 72 E1
Nelson Rd. Ilkley LS29 .... 8 B4
Nelson St. Batley WF17 .... 96 F1
Nelson St. Batley WF17 .... 118 A5
Nelson St. Brad BD15 .... 54 C1
Nelson St. Brad BD5 .... 74 E5
Nelson St. Dew WF13 .... 139 C8
Nelson St. Hali HX6 .... 112 D4
Nelson St. Haw BD22 .... 51 E8
Nelson St. Hud HD1 .... 153 F4
Nelson St. Liver WF15 .... 117 B3
Nelson St. Nor WF6 .... 123 C3
Nelson St. Otley LS21 .... 23 A7
Nelson St. Queen BD13 .... 72 E1 8
Nelson St. S Hie S72 .... 180 E5
Nelson St. Tod OL14 .... 129 A8
Nene St. Brad BD5 .... 74 C4
Nepshaw La. Gild LS27 .... 97 D4
Nepshaw La. Morley LS27 .... 97 E5
Nepshaw La N. Morley LS27 .... 97 E5
Nepshaw La S. Morley LS27 .... 97 E5
Neptune St. Leeds LS9 .... 79 D7
Nesfield Cl. Midd LS10 .... 99 F6
Nesfield Cres. Midd LS10 .... 99 F6
Nesfield Garth. Midd LS10 .... 99 E6
Nesfield Gdns. Midd LS10 .... 99 E6
Nesfield Rd. Ilkley LS29 .... 7 F5
Nesfield Rd. Midd LS10 .... 99 E6
Nesfield St. Brad BD1 .... 74 E8
Nesfield View. Ilkley LS29 .... 7 E4
Nesfield View. Midd LS10 .... 99 F6
Nesfield Wlk. Midd LS10 .... 99 E6
Nessfield Dr. Keigh BD22 .... 34 F5
Nessfield Fst Sch. Keigh 34 F5
Nessfield Gr. Keigh BD22 .... 34 F5
Nessfield Rd. Keigh BD22 .... 34 F5
Nest Est. Heb Br HX7 .... 110 D8
Nest La. Heb Br HX7 .... 110 D8
Nestfield Cl. Pont WF8 .... 125 D3
Neston Way. Ossett WF5 .... 119 D1
Nether Cl. Hud HD5 .... 154 E8
Nether Cres. Hud HD5 .... 154 E8
Nether Hall Ave. Hud HD5 .... 154 E8
Nether La. Holme HD7 .... 187 C3
Nether Moor Rd. Hud HD4 .... 171 C8
Nether Moor View. Bing BD16 . 37 A3 16
Nether St. Pudsey LS28 .... 57 D4
Netherby St. Brad BD3 .... 75 B7
Nethercliffe Cres. Guise LS20 . 22 D2
Nethercliffe Rd. Guise LS20 .... 22 D2
Netherdale Ct. Weth LS22 .... 14 A6
Netherend Rd. Slai HD7 .... 151 F1
Netherfield Ave. Neth WF4 .... 158 D5
Netherfield Cl. Castle WF10 .. 123 F5
Netherfield Cl. Kirkb HD8 .... 173 F6
Netherfield Cl. Yeadon LS19 .... 40 B7
Netherfield Cres. Neth WF4 .. 158 D5
Netherfield Ct. Guise LS20 .... 22 D1
Netherfield Dr. Guise LS20 .... 22 D1
Netherfield Dr. Holmfi HD7 .... 189 A7
Netherfield Ind Pk. Dew 138 E5
Netherfield Pl. Clec BD19 .... 116 E7
Netherfield Pl. Neth WF4 .... 158 D6
Netherfield Rd. Dew WF13 .... 138 E5
Netherfield Rd. Guise LS20 .... 22 D2
Netherfield Rise. Guise LS20 ... 22 D1
Netherhall Rd. Bail BD17 .... 38 D3
Netherhouses. Holmfi HD7 .... 188 D5
Netherlands Ave. Brad BD6 .... 94 C7
Netherlands Avenue Sch. Brad 94 D7
Netherlands Sq. Brad BD12 .... 94 D7
Netherlea Dr. Holmfi HD7 .... 188 F7
Netherleigh Sch The. Brad 54 F2
Netherley Dr. Mars HD7 .... 168 E2
Netherly Brow. Ossett WF5 .... 140 E3
Netheroyd. Feath WF7 .... 144 C5
Netheroyd Hill Rd. Hud HD2 .. 136 A3
Netheroyd Pl. Crof WF4 .... 144 B4
Netherthong Jun & Inf Sch. Holmfi 188 F8
Netherthong Rd. Mel HD7 .... 187 F8
Netherton Fold. Hud HD4 .... 171 C6
Netherton Hall Gdns. Neth WF4 .... 158 E6
Netherton Inf Sch. Hud 171 D7
Netherton La. Neth WF4 .... 158 E7
Netherton Moor Rd. Hud HD4 171 E6
Netherwood Cl. Hud HD2 .... 136 A3
Nettle Gr. Northo HX3 .... 92 F1
Nettleton Ave. Mir WF14 .... 137 F5
Nettleton Chase. Ossett WF5 119 C1
Nettleton Cl. Birk BD4 .... 76 E2
Nettleton Ct. Leeds LS15 .... 81 D8
Nettleton Hill Rd. Slai HD7 .... 152 B6
Nettleton House. Hem WF9 .... 181 D6
Nettleton Rd. Hud HD5 .... 155 A8
Nettleton Rd. Mir WF14 .... 137 F5
Nettleton St. Loft G WF3 .... 122 B6
Nettleton St. Ossett WF5 .... 140 C6
Nettleton Terr. Hud HD5 .... 155 A8
Nettleton's Almshouses. Hud HD5 .... 154 F3 3
Nevill Gr. Brad BD9 .... 54 D3
Neville App. Leeds LS9 .... 80 C6
Neville Ave. Brad BD4 .... 75 B1
Neville Ave. Leeds LS9 .... 80 C6
Neville Cl. Leeds LS9 .... 80 C6
Neville Cl. S Kirk WF9 .... 182 C3
Neville Cres. Leeds LS9 .... 80 D8
Neville Garth. Leeds LS9 .... 80 C6
Neville Gr. Hud HD5 .... 154 F4
Neville Gr. Leeds LS9 .... 80 C6
Neville Gr. Swil LS26 .... 82 A2
Neville Mount. Leeds LS9 .... 80 C6
Neville Par. Leeds LS9 .... 80 C6
Neville Pl. Leeds LS9 .... 80 D7
Neville Rd. Brad BD4 .... 75 B4
Neville Rd. Leeds LS9 .... 80 D8
Neville Rd. Leeds LS15, LS9 .... 80 E7
Neville Rd. Otley LS21 .... 23 B7
Neville Rd. Wake WF2 .... 141 C5
Neville Row. Leeds LS9 .... 80 C6
Neville Sq. Leeds LS9 .... 80 D8
Neville St. Clec BD19 .... 116 E7
Neville St. Keigh BD21 .... 35 D8 12
Neville St. Leeds LS1 .... 79 B7
Neville St. Nor WF6 .... 123 B1
Neville St. Wake WF1 .... 142 F4
Neville Terr. Leeds LS9 .... 80 C6
Neville View. Leeds LS9 .... 80 C6
Neville Wlk. Leeds LS9 .... 80 C7
Nevins Rd. Dew WF13 .... 138 D6
Nevison Ave. Pont WF8 .... 125 E3
New Adel Ave. Hors LS16 .... 42 A3
New Adel Gdns. Hors LS16 .... 42 A3
New Adel La. Hors LS16 .... 42 A3
New Augustus St. Brad BD1 .... 74 F6
New Ave. Kirkhe HD5 .... 137 B1
New Bank. Hali HX3 .... 113 D8
New Bank St. Morley LS27 .... 98 B5
New Bond St. Hali HX1 .... 113 B7
New Bridge Rd. Mel HD7 .... 170 B2
New Briggate. Leeds LS1, LS2 . 79 C8
New Brighton. D Dale HD8 .... 191 B3
New Brighton. Ship BD16 .... 54 C6
New Brook St. Ilkley LS29 .... 8 B4
New Brunswick St. Hali HX1 .. 113 B7
New Brunswick St. Wake WF1 142 C5
New Cl. Hors LS18 .... 58 B8
New Cl. Mars HD7 .... 151 C1
New Cl. Ship BD18 .... 54 D7
New Clayton Terr. Cull BD13 .. 52 D5
New Close Ave. Sil BD20 .... 5 E1
New Close La. Mars HD7 .... 151 C1
New Close La. Norton DN6 .... 184 E7
New Close Rd. Ship BD18 .... 54 C7
New Clough Rd. Sow Br HX6 .. 112 D1
New Craven Gate. Leeds LS11 79 C4
New Cres. Hors LS18 .... 58 B8
New Cross St. Brad BD5 .... 74 F3
New Cross St. Brad BD12 .... 95 B5
New Dales La. L Brad BD20 .... 4 B7
New Delight. Wad M HX7 .... 69 A1
New England Rd. Keigh BD21 .. 35 C5
New Farmers Hill. Roth LS26 .. 101 D7
New Fold. Brad BD6 .... 93 E7
New Fold. Holmfi HD7 .... 189 A5
New Gate. Holmfi HD7 .... 189 C1
New Grove Dr. Hud HD5 .... 154 E7
New Hall App. Neth WF4 .... 157 F4
New Hall Cl. Crig WF4 .... 159 E4
New Hall La. Neth WF4 .... 157 F4
New Hall Way. Neth WF4 .... 157 F3
New Hey Moor Houses. Shep HD8 .... 173 F2
New Hey Rd. Brad BD4 .... 75 A4
New Hey Rd. Brig HD6 .... 135 D5
New Hey Rd. Elland HD3 .... 152 A8
New Hey Rd. Hud HD2, HD3 .. 135 D5
New Hey Rd. Hud HD2, HD3 .. 152 E8
New Hey Rd. Hud HD2, HD3 .. 153 C7
New Hey Rd. Mars HD3 .... 150 D2
New Hey Rd. Slai HD2, HD3, HD6 .... 151 D5
New Holme Rd. Haw BD22 .... 51 D6
New House. Holmfi HD7 .... 199 D7
New House La. Brad BD13 .... 73 B1
New House Rd. Hud HD2 .... 136 D4
New House. Slai HD7 .... 169 F7
New Inn Ct. Otley LS21 .... 23 A7
New Inn St. Leeds LS12 .... 78 A7
New John St. Brad BD1 .... 74 E7
New Kirkgate. Ship BD18 .... 55 B8
New La. B Head HX7 .... 88 D3
New La. B Sal LS25 .... 105 D3
New La. Birk BD4 .... 76 C2
New La. Brad BD3, BD4 .... 75 D6
New La. Castle WF10 .... 123 D5
New La. Clec BD19 .... 116 A6
New La. Crig WF4 .... 159 E7
New La. E Ard WF3 .... 120 C8
New La. Farnh BD20 .... 4 F2
New La. Gild BD11 .... 97 B8
New La. Hali HX3 .... 113 B2
New La. Hali HX3 .... 113 D4
New La. Heb Br HX7 .... 110 D4
New La. Leeds LS11 .... 79 B6
New La. Mars HD3 .... 150 D4
New La. Midd LS10 .... 99 B5
New La. Skel HD8 .... 175 B1
New La. Slai HD7 .... 152 A3
New La. Slai HD7 .... 152 B6
New La. Sow Br HX7 .... 111 B5
New La. Upton WF9 .... 183 A7
New Laithe Cl. Hud HD4 .... 154 C2
New Laithe Hill. Hud HD4 .... 154 C2
New Laithe La. Holmfi HD7 .... 189 B5
New Laithe Rd. Brad BD6 .... 74 A1 3
New Laithe Rd. Haw BD22 .... 49 E8
New Laithe Rd. Hud HD4 .... 154 C2
New Laithes Jun Sch. Hors 58 A6
New Lane Cres. Upton WF9 .... 183 A7
New Leeds. Leeds LS13 .... 58 B5
New Line. Brad BD10 .... 56 E7
New Longley La. Sow Br HX6 112 A1
New Longley. Sow Br HX6 .... 112 A1
New Market. Otley LS21 .... 23 A7
New Market Pl. Brad BD1 .... 74 E7 8
New Market St. Leeds LS1 .... 79 C7
New Mill La. B Spa LS23 .... 30 E5
New Mill Rd. Holmfi HD7 .... 172 C3
New Mill Rd. Holmfi HD7 .... 189 B7
New Mill Rd. Honley HD7 .... 172 C3
New North Par. Hud HD1 .... 154 A6
New North Rd. Hud HD1 .... 153 F7
New North Rd. Liver WF16 .... 117 C5
New North Rd. Slai HD7 .... 152 A2
New Occupation La. Pudsey LS28 .... 76 C6
New Otley Rd. Brad BD3 .... 75 A8
New Park Ave. Pudsey LS28 .... 57 E3
New Park Cl. Pudsey LS28 .... 57 E3
New Park Croft. Pudsey LS28 .. 57 E3
New Park La. Wake WF2 .... 141 B7
New Park Pl. Pudsey LS28 .... 57 E3
New Park Rd. Queen BD13 .... 72 D1
New Park St. Morley LS27 .... 97 F3
New Park Vale. Pudsey LS28 ... 57 E3
New Park View. Pudsey LS28 ... 57 E2
New Park Way. Pudsey LS28 ... 57 E3
New Park Wlk. Pudsey LS28 .... 57 D2 4
New Popplewell La. Brig BD19 115 F8
New Princess St. Leeds LS11 .. 79 B5
New Rd. B Head HX7 .... 87 F6
New Rd. Bad WF9 .... 164 D2
New Rd. Bramham LS23 .... 30 D3
New Rd. Castle WF11 .... 126 A5
New Rd. Caw S75 .... 193 B5
New Rd. Denh BD13 .... 71 D8
New Rd E. Brig BD19 .... 115 F8
New Rd. Elland HX4 .... 134 B7
New Rd. Elland HX4 .... 134 C2
New Rd. Elland HD3 .... 152 A8
New Rd. Feath WF7 .... 144 E7
New Rd. Hali HX1 .... 113 C6
New Rd. Heb Br HX7 .... 88 F2
New Rd. Heb Br HX7 .... 110 D1
New Rd. Heb Br HX7 .... 110 E8
New Rd. Holmfi HD7 .... 189 A7
New Rd. Hor WF4 .... 141 B1
New Rd. K Smea WF8 .... 166 D8
New Rd. Kirkhe HD5 .... 137 B2
New Rd. Ledsh LS25 .... 84 D2
New Rd. Mapp S75 .... 178 B1
New Rd. Neth WF4 .... 158 B7
New Rd. Pen S30 .... 192 E1
New Rd. Roth WF3 .... 100 D3
New Rd. Sil BD20 .... 5 E1
New Rd. Tod OL14 .... 86 C4
New Rd. Tod OL14 .... 108 F8
New Rd. Tod OL14 .... 109 A5
New Rd. W Har WF7 .... 145 C1
New Rd. Wool WF4 .... 178 B6
New Rd. Yeadon LS19 .... 39 F7
New Road Side. Hors LS18 .... 58 B7
New Road Side. Yeadon LS19 .. 40 B4
New Road Sq. Brig HD6 .... 135 E6
New Row. Bad WF9 .... 164 E2
New Row. Brad BD9 .... 54 E2
New Row Cotts. Dar WF8 .... 147 C5
New Row. Elland HX4 .... 134 C4
New Row. Holmfi HD7 .... 189 A5
New Row. Pudsey LS28 .... 57 A3
New Row. Ship BD16 .... 54 B8
New Row. Wake WF2 .... 120 B2
New Scarbro' Rd. Leeds LS13 . 58 D2 1
New St. Ack M T WF7 .... 163 F5
New St. Batley WF17 .... 118 C5
New St. Batley WF17 .... 118 E3
New St. Bing BD16 .... 36 E7
New St. Brad BD10 .... 56 B8
New St. Brad BD12 .... 95 B5
New St. Brad BD4 .... 95 B8
New St. Brig HD6 .... 115 B7
New St. Brig HD6 .... 115 D2
New St. Castle WF10 .... 103 E1
New St. Clay W HD8 .... 175 D1
New St. Denh BD13 .... 71 D8
New St. Dew WF12 .... 139 F7
New St. Elland HX4 .... 133 F3
New St. Hali HX2 .... 112 E8
New St. Hali HX3 .... 114 A4
New St. Haw BD22 .... 34 D2
New St. Haw BD22 .... 51 C6
New St. Hem WF9 .... 163 C1
New St. Honley HD7 .... 171 F4
New St. Hor WF4 .... 141 B1
New St. Hors LS18 .... 58 B8
New St. Hud HD7 .... 152 E4
New St. Hud HD3 .... 153 A4
New St. Hud HD1 .... 153 E5
New St. Hud HD1 .... 154 A5
New St. Hud HD4 .... 171 C7
New St. Kippax LS25 .... 83 B1
New St. Kirkhe HD5 .... 155 C8
New St. Liver BD19 .... 116 F6
New St. Mapp S75 .... 178 B1
New St. Mel HD7 .... 170 D2
New St. Ossett WF5 .... 140 E5
New St. Pudsey LS28 .... 57 D2
New St. Pudsey LS28 .... 76 E6
New St. Roy S71 .... 179 C3
New St. S Elm WF9 .... 182 E3
New St. S Hie S72 .... 180 D6
New St. Skel HD8 .... 175 A2
New St. Slai HD7 .... 152 A1
New Station St. Leeds LS1 .... 79 B7
New Street Cl. Pudsey LS28 .... 76 E6
New Street Gdns. Pudsey LS28 76 E6
New Street Gr. Pudsey LS28 ... 76 E6
New Sturton La. Gar LS25 .... 83 B7
New Tanhouse. Mir WF14 .... 137 F5 6
New Temple Gate. Leeds LS15 81 A7
New Toftshaw. Brad BD4 .... 95 D8
New Town Ct. Keigh BD21 .... 35 A7 15
New Way. Batley WF17 .... 118 C5
New Way. Guise LS20 .... 22 C1
New Wellgate. Castle WF10 .. 124 F6
New Wells. Wake WF1 .... 142 C5
New Windsor Dr. Roth LS26 .. 100 F6
New Wlk. Leeds LS8 .... 44 B1
New Works Rd. Brad BD12 .... 94 D5
New York La. Yeadon LS19 .... 40 D2
New York Rd. Leeds LS2, LS9 .. 79 D8
New York St. Leeds LS2 .... 79 D7 1
Newall Ave. Otley LS21 .... 10 F1
Newall Carr Rd. Clift LS21 .... 10 F6
Newall Carr Rd. Otley LS21 .... 10 F2
Newall Cl. Men LS29 .... 22 B5
Newall Cl. Otley LS21 .... 10 F1
Newall Cl. Otley LS21 .... 22 F8
Newall Cres. Hem WF9 .... 162 F3
Newall Fst Sch. Otley 11 A1
Newall Hall Pk. Otley LS21 .... 11 A1
Newall Mount. Otley LS21 .... 22 F8
Newall St. Brad BD5 .... 74 D4
Newall St. Tod OL14 .... 129 A8
Newark Cl. Mapp S75 .... 178 B2
Newark Rd. Bing BD16 .... 36 E5
Newark St. Brad BD4 .... 75 B5
Newbridge La. Hal E BD23 .... 1 D8
Newburn Rd. Brad BD7 .... 74 B5
Newbury Dr. S Elm WF9 .... 183 A5
Newbury Rd. Brig HD6 .... 135 F7
Newbury Wlk. Kirkhe HD5 .... 137 C1
Newby Fst Sch. Brad 74 D3
Newby Garth. Leeds LS17 .... 44 B5
Newby Rd. Farnh BD20 .... 16 E8
Newby St. Brad BD5 .... 74 E4
Newby St. Glu BD20 .... 16 D7
Newcastle Cl. Birk BD11 .... 96 D5
Newcastle Fm Ct. Fair WF11 . 105 A4
Newcombe St. Elland HX5 .... 135 A6
Newfield Ave. Castle WF10 .... 124 E7
Newfield Ave. Nor WF6 .... 123 C1
Newfield Cl. Nor WF6 .... 123 C1
Newfield Cres. Nor WF6 .... 123 C1
Newfield Ct. Nor WF6 .... 123 C2
Newfield Dr. Gar LS25 .... 83 B4
Newfield Dr. Men LS29 .... 22 A5
Newfield La. Ledsh LS25 .... 104 D8
Newforth Gr. Brad BD5 .... 74 C2
Newgate La. Mel HD7 .... 170 E2
Newgate. Mir WF14 .... 138 A4
Newgate. Pont WF8 .... 146 C8
Newgate St. Batley WF12 .... 118 F3
Newhall Bank. Midd LS10 .... 99 D5
Newhall Chase. Midd LS10 .... 99 D6
Newhall Cl. Midd LS10 .... 99 D6
Newhall Cres. Midd LS10 .... 99 E6
Newhall Croft. Midd LS10 .... 99 D7
Newhall Dr. Brad BD6 .... 94 F8
Newhall Garth. Midd LS10 .... 99 D5
Newhall Gate. Midd LS10 .... 99 E7
Newhall Gdns. Midd LS10 .... 99 D5
Newhall Gn. Midd LS10 .... 99 D6
Newhall La. Mir WF14 .... 138 B2
Newhall Mount. Brad BD6 .... 94 F8
Newhall Mount. Midd LS10 .... 99 D5
Newhall Rd. Brad BD4 .... 75 B1
Newhall Rd. Midd LS10 .... 99 D6
Newhill. S Kirk WF9 .... 182 B1
Newhold. Gar LS25 .... 83 A8
Newhouse Pl. Hud HD1 .... 154 A7 2
Newill Cl. Brad BD5 .... 75 A2
Newlaithes Cres. Nor WF6 .... 123 D2
Newlaithes Garth. Hors LS18 .. 58 A6
Newlaithes Gdns. Hors LS18 .... 58 B7
Newlaithes Rd. Hors LS18 .... 58 B6
Newland Ave. Hud HD2 .... 135 F1
Newland Cres. Crig WF4 .... 159 E7
Newland Ct. Wake WF1 .... 142 E2
Newland La. Nor WF6 .... 122 F1
Newland Rd. Hud HD5 .... 155 B7
Newland St. Knot WF11 .... 126 B5
Newland St. Wake WF1 .... 142 E2
Newland View. Nor WF6 .... 122 F3
Newlands Ave. Ad Le S DN6 .. 184 F2
Newlands Ave. Brad BD3 .... 56 D1
Newlands Ave. Clay W HD8 .... 175 F2
Newlands Ave. Northo HX3 .... 93 A3
Newlands Ave. Sow Br HX6 .... 111 E3
Newlands Ave. Yeadon LS19 .... 40 A7
Newlands Cl. Brig HD6 .... 115 B1
Newlands Cres. Morley LS27 ... 98 E4
Newlands Dr. Bing BD16 .... 36 E6
Newlands Dr. Glu BD20 .... 16 D7
Newlands Dr. Loft G WF3 .... 121 E5
Newlands Dr. Morley LS27 .... 98 D4
Newlands Dr. Northo HX3 .... 93 A3
Newlands Gr. Northo HX3 .... 93 A3
Newlands Jun Sch. Sow Br 111 E3
Newlands La. Holmfi HD7 .... 188 C5
Newlands Pl. Brad BD3 .... 56 B1
Newlands Prim Sch. Morley 98 D5
Newlands. Pudsey LS28 .... 57 D2
Newlands Rd. Hali HX2 .... 112 B7
Newlands Rise. Yeadon LS19 .. 40 A7
Newlands The. Sow Br HX6 .... 111 E2
Newlands Wlk. Loft G WF3 .... 121 E5
Newlay Bridle Path. Hors LS18 58 C7 2
Newlay Cl. Brad BD10 .... 56 E7
Newlay Gr. Hors LS18 .... 58 B6
Newlay La. Hors LS18 .... 58 B7
Newlay La. Leeds LS13 .... 58 C4
Newlay Lane Pl. Leeds LS13 .... 58 C4
Newlay Wood Ave. Hors LS18 . 58 C7
Newlay Wood Cl. Hors LS18 ... 58 C7
Newlay Wood Cres. Hors LS18 58 C7
Newlay Wood Dr. Hors LS18 ... 58 C7
Newlay Wood Fold. Hors LS18 58 C7 9
Newlay Wood Gdns. Hors LS18 58 C7 3
Newlay Wood Rd. Hors LS18 ... 58 B7
Newlay Wood Rise. Hors LS18 58 C7
Newley Ave. Batley WF17 .... 117 F8
Newley Mount. Hors LS18 .... 58 B6
Newlyn Rd. Keigh BD20 .... 19 A1
Newman Ave. Roy S71 .... 179 C1
Newman St. Brad BD4 .... 75 B2
Newmarket App. Leeds LS9 .... 80 B6
Newmarket Gn. Leeds LS9 .... 80 B6
Newmarket La. Leeds LS9 .... 80 B6
Newmarket La. Loft G WF3 .... 122 D8
Newmillerdam Country Park. Notton 160 D2
Newport Ave. Leeds LS13 .... 58 A2
Newport Cres. Leeds LS6 .... 59 D3
Newport Gdns. Leeds LS6 .... 59 D3
Newport Mount. Leeds LS6 .... 59 D3
Newport Pl. Brad BD8 .... 55 C1
Newport Rd. Brad BD8 .... 55 C1
Newport Rd. Leeds LS6 .... 59 D3
Newport St. Pont WF8 .... 125 C1
Newport View. Leeds LS6 .... 59 D3
Newroyd Rd. Brad BD5 .... 74 E2
Newsam Ct. Leeds LS15 .... 81 A7
Newsam Dr. Leeds LS15 .... 80 E6
Newsam Green Rd. Swil LS26 . 81 E1
Newsholme La. Crig WF4 .... 159 F7
Newsholme New Rd. Keigh BD22 .... 34 B4
Newsome Ave. Hud HD4 .... 154 A2
Newsome Jun Sch. Hud 154 A1
Newsome Rd. Hud HD4 .... 154 B3
Newsome Rd S. Hud HD4 .... 154 A1
Newsome Sec Sch. Hud 153 F1
Newsome St. Dew WF13 .... 118 B1
Newsomes Row. Batley WF17 118 B4
Newstead Ave. Hali HX1 .... 112 E7
Newstead Ave. Hem WF9 .... 163 A3
Newstead Ave. Loft G WF1 .... 121 A5
Newstead Cres. Hem WF9 .... 163 A4
Newstead Dr. Hem WF9 .... 163 A3
Newstead Gdns. Hali HX1 .... 112 E7 8
Newstead Gr. Hali HX1 .... 112 E7
Newstead Gr. Hem WF9 .... 163 A3
Newstead Heath. Hali HX1 .... 112 E7 5
Newstead La. Hem WF4, WF9 162 F3
Newstead Mount. Hem WF9 .. 163 A3
Newstead Pl. Hali HX1 .... 112 E7
Newstead Rd. Barn S71 .... 178 E1
Newstead Rd. Otley LS21 .... 23 B7
Newstead Rd. Wake WF1 .... 142 B7
Newstead Terr. Hali HX1 .... 112 E7
Newstead Terr. Hem WF9 .... 163 A3
Newstead View. Hem WF9 .... 163 A3
Newstead Wlk. Brad BD5 .... 74 D4
Newton Ave. Loft G WF1 .... 121 B2
Newton Cl. Loft G WF1 .... 121 B1
Newton Cl. Roth LS26 .... 100 B4
Newton Ct. Leeds LS8 .... 61 C6
Newton Ct. Loft G WF1 .... 121 B4
Newton Ct. Roth LS26 .... 100 B4
Newton Dr. Castle WF10 .... 125 B7
Newton Dr. H Chap BB10 .... 85 A7
Newton Dr. Loft G WF1 .... 121 C3
Newton Garth. Leeds LS7 .... 60 E5
Newton Gn. Loft G WF1 .... 121 B1
Newton Gr. Leeds LS7 .... 60 E4
Newton Hill Rd. Leeds LS7 .... 60 D5
Newton La. Fair WF11 .... 104 C4
Newton La. Ledsh WF10 .... 104 C4
Newton La. Ledst WF10 .... 103 E4
Newton La. Loft G WF1 .... 121 B4
Newton Lodge Cl. Leeds LS7 ... 60 C5
Newton Lodge Dr. Leeds LS7 ... 60 C5
Newton Par. Leeds LS7 .... 60 D5
Newton Park Ct. Leeds LS7 .... 60 E5
Newton Park Dr. Leeds LS7 .... 60 E5
Newton Park View. Leeds LS7 . 60 E4
Newton Pk. Brig HD6 .... 114 F6
Newton Pl. Brad BD5 .... 74 E4
Newton Rd. Leeds LS7 .... 60 E5
Newton Sq. Gild LS12 .... 77 D3
Newton St. Brad BD5 .... 74 E3
Newton St. Hali HX6 .... 112 B4 9
Newton View. Leeds LS7 .... 60 D5
Newton Way. Bail BD17 .... 38 C4
Newton Wlk. Leeds LS7 .... 60 E4
Newtown Ave. Roy S71 .... 179 B4
Nibshaw La. Clec BD19 .... 117 A8
Nibshaw Rd. Clec BD19 .... 117 A8
Nice Ave. Leeds LS8 .... 60 F4 16
Nice St. Leeds LS8 .... 61 A4
Nice View. Leeds LS8 .... 60 F4
Nicholas Cl. Brad BD7 .... 73 F7
Nichols Cl. Weth LS22 .... 13 C5
Nichols Way. Weth LS22 .... 13 C5
Nicholson St. Castle WF10 .... 124 C7
Nickleby Rd. Leeds LS9 .... 80 A8
Nicolsons Pl. Sil BD20 .... 5 E1
Nidd App. Weth LS22 .... 13 D8

Nidd Ct. Sil BD20 5 E1
Nidd Dr. Castle WF10 125 B8
Nidd St. Brad BD3 75 B6
Nidderdale Cl. Gar LS25 83 B5
Nidderdale Wlk. Bail BD17 38 E4
Nields Cty Prim Sch. Slai 169 F8
Nields Rd. Slai HD7 169 F8
Nightingale Crest. Wake WF2 141 C4
Nightingale St. Keigh BD21 35 D8 3
Nile Cres. Keigh BD22 34 F6
Nile Rd. Ilkley LS29 8 B4
Nile St. Haw BD22 51 E8
Nile St. Hud HD1 153 F5
Nile St. Keigh BD22 34 F6
Nile St. Leeds LS2 79 D8
Nina Rd. Brad BD7 73 F3
Ninelands La. Gar LS25 83 A6
Ninelands Spur. Gar LS25 83 A6
Ninevah La. Bad WF9 164 E3
Ninevah La. Kippax WF10 102 F5
Nineveh Gdns. Leeds LS11 79 A5
Nineveh Par. Leeds LS11 79 A5
Nineveh Rd. Leeds LS11 79 A5
Ninth Ave. Clec WF15 116 B5
Nippet La. Leeds LS9 79 E8
Nixon Ave. Leeds LS9 80 B7
Nixon Cl. Dew WF12 139 F1
Noble Ct. Hud HD4 171 D6
Noble St. Brad BD7 74 B5
Nog La. Ship BD9 55 A4
Nook Gdns. B in Elm LS15 62 F8
Nook Gn. Dew WF12 139 D2
Nook La. Sow Br HX6 131 F8
Nook La. Wad M HX7 89 D4
Nook Rd. B in Elm LS15 62 F8
Nook The. Clec BD19 116 E8
Nook The Cull BD13 52 D6
Nook The. E Ard WF3 119 E6
Nook The. Leeds LS17 43 D5
Nook Wlk. Dew WF13 138 F8
Nooking The. Wake WF2 120 B3
Nooks The. Gild LS27 97 D6
Noon Cl. Loft G WF3 121 E5
Nopper Rd. Hud HD4 170 F8
Nopper Rd. Mel HD7 170 F8
Nor Wood Rd. Hem WF9 181 D5
Nora Pl. Leeds LS13 58 A3
Nora Rd. Leeds LS13 58 A3
Nora Terr. Leeds LS13 58 A3
Norbeck Dr. Haw BD22 51 E8
Norbury Rd. Brad BD10 56 E4
Norcliffe La. Brig HX3 114 A7
Norcliffe La. Hali HX3 114 A7
Norcroft Brow. Brad BD7 74 D6
Norcroft Ind Est. Brad 74 C7
Norcroft La. Caw S75 193 F5
Norcroft St. Brad BD1, BD7 74 C7
Norcross Ave. Hud HD3 153 B7
Norfield. Hud HD2 136 A4
Norfolk Ave. Batley WF17 118 B3
Norfolk Cl. Broth WF11 126 C8
Norfolk Cl. Leeds LS7 60 D7
Norfolk Cl. Litt OL15 129 C1
Norfolk Cl. Roth LS26 101 D5
Norfolk Dr. Roth LS26 101 D5
Norfolk Gdns. Brad BD1 74 E6 1
Norfolk Gdns. Leeds LS7 60 D7
Norfolk Gn. Leeds LS7 60 D7
Norfolk House. Wake WF1 142 F3
Norfolk Mount. Leeds LS7 60 D7
Norfolk Pl. Hali HX1 113 A6
Norfolk Pl. Leeds LS7 60 D7
Norfolk St. Batley WF17 118 B4
Norfolk St. Bing BD16 37 A3 4
Norfolk St. Heb Br HX7 89 A2 3
Norfolk Terr. Leeds LS7 60 D7
Norfolk View. Leeds LS7 60 D7
Norfolk Wlk. Dew WF13 139 B8 5
Norfolk Wlk. Leeds LS7 60 D7
Norgarth Cl. Batley WF17 118 F5
Norham Gr. Brad BD12 94 D2
Norland CE (C) Jun & Inf Sch. Sow Br 112 D2
Norland Rd. Sow Br HX6 112 C3
Norland Rd. Sow Br HX6 133 D8
Norland St. Brad BD7 73 F3
Norland Town Rd. Sow Br HX6 112 D2
Norland View. Hali HX6 112 D4
Norland View. Hali HX2 113 A4 6
Norman Ave. Brad BD2 56 B5
Norman Ave. Elland HX5 135 A6
Norman Cres. Brad BD2 56 B5
Norman Dr. Mir WF14 137 F6
Norman Gr. Brad BD2 56 B5
Norman Gr. Elland HX5 135 A6
Norman Gr. Leeds LS5 59 A4
Norman La. Brad BD2 56 B5
Norman Mount. Brad BD2 56 B5
Norman Mount. Leeds LS5 59 A4
Norman Pl. Hor WF4 141 B1 6
Norman Pl. Leeds LS8 44 A2
Norman Rae Playing Fields. Ship 54 F6
Norman Rd. D Dale HD8 191 F5
Norman Rd. Hud HD2 136 A1
Norman Rd. Mir WF14 137 F6
Norman Row. Leeds LS5 59 A4
Norman St. Bing BD16 37 A3
Norman St. Elland HX5 135 A6
Norman St. Hali HX1 112 F5 3
Norman St. Haw BD22 51 D7 14
Norman St. Leeds LS5 59 A4
Norman St. Ship BD18 55 D7
Norman Terr. Brad BD2 56 B5
Norman Terr. Elland HX5 135 A6
Norman Terr. Leeds LS8 44 A2
Norman View. Leeds LS5 59 A4
Normanon Pl. Leeds LS11 79 A4
Normans Way. Wake WF2 142 F1
Normanton C E (Aided) Fst Sch. Nor 123 B2
Normanton Common Fst Sch. Nor 123 D3
Normanton Cross St. Hor WF4 159 C8
Normanton Freeston High Sch. Nor 123 B1
Normanton Gr. Leeds LS11 79 A4
Normanton Grammar Sch. Nor 123 A1
Normanton Ind Est. Nor 123 D3
Normanton Lee Brigg Fst Sch. Nor 122 E3
Normanton Martin Frobisher Fst Sch. Nor 122 F4
Normanton Queen St Fst Sch. Nor 123 A2
Normanton St. Hor WF4 159 C8
Normanton Woodhouse Fst Sch. Nor 123 A1
Normanton Woodlands Mid Sch. Nor 144 A8
Norr Green Terr. Wils BD15 53 D6
Norridge Bottom. Holmfi HD7 189 A5
Norris Cl. Hud HD5 155 A4
Norristhorpe Ave. Liver WF15 117 A2
Norristhorpe La. Liver WF15 117 B2
Norristhorpe Sch. Liver 117 B2
North App. Stut LS24 48 A5
North Ave. Brad BD8 55 D2
North Ave. Castle WF10 123 F7
North Ave. Hor WF4 141 C1
North Ave. Otley LS21 23 A8
North Ave. Pont WF8 146 B7
North Ave. S Elm WF9 182 F2
North Ave. S in Cra BD20 16 D4
North Ave. Wake WF1 142 C8
North Baileygate. Pont WF8 125 E1
North Bank Rd. Batley WF17 118 A6
North Bank Rd. Hud HD2 135 F1
North Bank Rd. Ship BD16 54 B6
North Bolton. Hali HX2 91 E7
North Bridge. Hali HX1 113 C8 7
North Bridge L Ctr. Hali 113 C8
North Bridge St. Hali HX1 113 C8
North Broadgate La. Hors LS18 41 C1
North Brook St. Brad BD1, BD3 74 F8
North Byland. Hali HX2 91 E7
North Carr Croft. Hud HD5 154 E7
North Carr. Hud HD5 154 E7
North Cl. Feath WF7 124 C1
North Cl. Leeds LS8 61 D6
North Cl. Roy S71 179 C3
North Cliffe Ave. Thorn BD13 72 F6
North Cliffe Cl. Thorn BD13 72 E6 7
North Cliffe Dr. Thorn BD13 72 E6
North Cliffe Gr. Thorn BD13 72 E6 8
North Cliffe La. Thorn BD13 72 F6
North Cliffe. Sow Br HX6 112 B3
North Cres. S Elm WF9 183 B4
North Croft Grove Rd. Ilkley LS29 8 A4
North Cross Rd. Hud HD2 135 F2
North Ct. Leeds LS2 79 C8
North Cut. Brig HD6 114 F2
North Dean Ave. Keigh BD22 34 E7
North Dean Rd. Elland HX4 113 A1
North Dean Rd. Keigh BD22 34 F7
North Dene Rd. Sil BD20 5 E2
North Dr. Bramho LS16 24 F2
North Dr. Gar LS25 83 B4
North Dr. Hud HD7 152 E4
North East Wakefield Coll. Pont 125 B1
North Farm Rd. Leeds LS8, LS9 61 C3
North Featherstone Jun & Inf Sch. Pont 145 E7
North Field La. Skel HD8 175 A2
North Field Rd. H Pag DN5 195 D7
North Fold. Brad BD10 56 B8
North Gate. Kirkhe WF14 137 E3
North Grange Mews. Leeds LS6 59 F4
North Grange Mount. Leeds LS6 59 F5
North Grange Rd. Leeds LS6 59 F4
North Grove App. Weth LS22 13 F7
North Grove Ave. Weth LS22 13 F7
North Grove Cl. Leeds LS8 61 D6
North Grove Cres. Weth LS22 13 F7
North Grove Ct. Weth LS22 13 E6
North Grove Dr. Leeds LS8 61 D6
North Grove Dr. Weth LS22 13 E7
North Grove Mount. Weth LS22 13 E6
North Grove Rd. Weth LS22 13 E7
North Grove Rise. Leeds LS8 61 D6
North Grove Way. Weth LS22 13 F6
North Hall Ave. Brad BD10 39 A2
North Hill Cl. Leeds LS8 61 C6
North Hill Ct. Leeds LS6 59 F5
North Hill Dr. Kirkhe HD5 155 C8
North Hill Rd. Leeds LS6 59 F4
North Hill. Scar LS14 28 D1
North Holme St. Brad BD1 74 E8
North Ives. Oxen BD22 51 C4
North John St. Queen BD13 72 E1 3
North King St. Batley WF17 118 D4
North La. Caw S75 193 A2
North La. Leeds LS6 59 D5
North La. Leeds LS8 61 C6
North La. Roth LS26 101 C6
North La. Slai HD7 151 D1
North Lingwell Rd. Midd LS10 99 C5
North Lodge La. Dar WF8 147 F4
North Mead. Bramho LS16 24 F2
North Moor La. Kirkhe HD5 137 C2
North Ossett High Sch. Ossett 119 D1
North Par. Brad BD15 54 A2
North Par. Brad BD1 74 E7
North Par. Bur in W LS29 9 E2
North Par. Hali HX1 113 C7
North Par. Ilkley LS29 8 C4
North Par. Leeds LS16 59 A8
North Par. Otley LS21 23 A8
North Park Ave. Leeds LS8 44 A1
North Park Gr. Leeds LS8 44 A1
North Park Par. Leeds LS8 60 F8
North Park Rd. Brad BD9 55 B3
North Park Rd. Leeds LS8 61 A8
North Park St. Dew WF13 118 A1
North Park Terr. Brad BD9 55 C2
North Parkway. Leeds LS14 62 A6
North Pl. S in Cra BD20 16 C5
North Queen St. Keigh BD21 35 C7 1
North Rd. Brad BD6 74 B1
North Rd. Dew WF13 138 E6
North Rd. Fair WF11 105 A4
North Rd. Hors LS18 41 B3
North Rd. Kirkb HD8 173 E7
North Rd. Leeds LS15 62 C2
North Rd. Leeds LS9 80 D3
North Rd. Roy S71 179 D4
North Rd. S in Cra BD20 16 C5
North Rise. Hud HD2 136 C2
North Road Terr. Wake WF1 142 B7
North Row. S in Cra BD20 16 C5
North Row. Shep HD8 190 D8
North Royd. Rip HX4 133 B5
North Selby. Hali HX2 91 D7
North St. Add LS29 7 A8
North St. Batley WF16 117 D3
North St. Batley WF17 118 B6
North St. Brad BD10 39 B2
North St. Brad BD1 74 F7
North St. Brad BD12 95 A4
North St. Castle WF10 104 C3
North St. Castle WF10 124 C8
North St. Dew WF13 118 C1
North St. Elland HX4 134 B4
North St. Elland HX4 134 D7 4
North St. Glu BD20 16 D7
North St. Haw BD22 51 B7
North St. Hud HD1 153 D5
North St. Hud HD1 153 E3
North St. Keigh BD21 35 C7
North St. Leeds LS2, LS7 60 D1
North St. Mir WF14 137 F4
North St. Nor WF6 144 A8
North St. Otley LS21 23 A8
North St. Pudsey LS28 76 E8 9
North St. S in Cra BD20 16 D5
North St. S Kirk WF9 182 B3
North St. Sil BD20 5 E2
North St. Weth LS22 13 E5
North St. Yeadon LS19 40 B4
North Terr. Batley WF17 96 F1
North Terr. Leeds LS15 62 C2
North Terr. Yeadon LS19 40 B7
North View. Brad BD15 54 A1
North View. Dew WF12 139 D6
North View. Hem WF9 163 A4
North View. Knot WF11 126 E4
North View. Men LS29 22 A3
North View Rd. Birk BD4 96 A7
North View Rd. Brad BD3 55 F2
North View. S in Cra BD20 16 D5
North View St. Keigh BD20 18 C1
North View St. Pudsey LS28 57 E2
North View. Stee BD20 16 F6
North View Terr. Dew WF13 117 F2 7
North View Terr. Dew WF13 118 B2 2
North View Terr. Haw BD22 51 C8
North View Terr. Pudsey LS28 57 E2 5
North View. Wils BD15 53 C5
North Way. Hud HD2 136 E4
North Way. Leeds LS8 61 D6
North West Rd. Leeds LS6 60 B3
North Wing. Brad BD3 74 F8
North Wlk. Harden BD16 36 A1
North Wlk. Hem WF9 181 D8
North's Pl. Mir WF14 138 A7
Northallerton Rd. Brad BD3 55 F1
Northampton St. Brad BD3 55 F1
Northbrook Pl. Leeds LS7 60 D7
Northbrook St. Leeds LS7 60 D7
Northcliffe Golf Course. Ship 54 E6
Northcliffe Rd. Ship BD18 55 B6
Northcote Cres. Leeds LS11 79 B4
Northcote Dr. Leeds LS11 79 B4
Northcote Fold. Coll LS22 13 B2
Northcote Gn. Leeds LS11 79 B4
Northcote. Ossett WF5 119 C1
Northcote Rd. Brad BD2 56 B2
Northcote St. Pudsey LS28 57 D2
Northcote Terr. Brad BD2 56 B1
Northcroft Ave. S Elm WF9 183 A4
Northcroft Rise. Brad BD8 54 E1
Northcroft. S Elm WF9 183 A3
Northdale Ave. Brad BD5 74 C2
Northdale Cres. Brad BD5 74 C2
Northdale Mount. Brad BD5 74 C2
Northdale Rd. Ship BD9 55 B5
Northedge La. Brig HX3 93 D1
Northedge M'dow. Brad BD10 56 B6
Northedge Pk. Brig HX3 93 D1
Northern Cl. Brad BD7 73 F4
Northern St. Leeds LS1 79 A7
Northfield Ave. Hud HD1 153 E4
Northfield Ave. Knot WF11 126 F3
Northfield Ave. Ossett WF5 140 D6
Northfield Ave. Roth LS26 100 C4
Northfield Ave. S Kirk WF9 182 C3
Northfield Ave. Weth LS22 13 E6
Northfield Cl. Elland HX5 134 F6 1
Northfield Cres. Ship BD16 54 A7
Northfield Dr. Pont WF8 125 F1
Northfield Gdns. Brad BD6 74 C1
Northfield Gr. Brad BD6 74 C1
Northfield Gr. Hud HD1 153 F3
Northfield Gr. S Kirk WF9 182 C3
Northfield La. Hor WF4 141 C1
Northfield La. Kirkb HD8 173 E8
Northfield La. S Kirk WF9 182 C3
Northfield Mid Sch. S Kirk 182 C3
Northfield Pl. Brad BD8 55 C1
Northfield Pl. Dew WF13 118 C1
Northfield Pl. Roth LS26 100 B4
Northfield Pl. Weth LS22 13 E6
Northfield Rd. Brad BD6 74 B1
Northfield Rd. Crof WF4 144 B3
Northfield Rd. Dew WF13 118 B1
Northfield Rd. Knot WF11 126 F3
Northfield Rd. Ossett WF5 140 D7
Northfield St. Dew WF13 118 C1
Northfield St. S Kirk WF9 182 B3
Northfield Terr. Queen BD13 73 A1
Northfield Terr. Slai HD7 152 A2
Northfields. Th Arch LS23 15 A3
Northgate. Bail BD17 38 C4
Northgate. Brad BD1 74 E7 1
Northgate Cl. Pont WF8 125 D1
Northgate. Clec BD19 116 D7
Northgate. Dew WF13 139 D8
Northgate. Elland HX5 134 F7
Northgate. Hali HX1 113 C8
Northgate. Hep HX7 88 F5
Northgate. Honley HD7 172 B6
Northgate. Hor WF4 141 A1
Northgate. Hud HD1 154 B7
Northgate. Hud HD1, HD5 154 F3
Northgate La. Coll LS22 13 A3
Northgate. Liver WF16 117 C4
Northgate Lodge. Pont WF8 125 D1
Northgate. Pont WF8 125 D1
Northgate Rise. Coll LS22 13 B2
Northgate. Roth LS26 101 C6 1
Northgate. S Hie S72 180 E6
Northgate. Wake WF1 142 C6 16
Northgate. Wake WF1 142 C7
Northgates. Weth LS22 13 E5
Northlands. Roy S71 179 C4
Northlea Ave. Brad BD10 39 B1
Northolme Ave. Leeds LS16 59 B7
Northolme Cres. Leeds LS16 59 B7
Northonthorpe Hall Sch. Clay W 175 D1
Northorpe La. Mir WF14 138 C7
Northowram Gn. Northo HX3 93 A3
Northowram Jun & Inf Sch. Northo 93 A3
Northrop Cl. Brad BD8 55 A1
Northside Ave. Brad BD7 74 A6
Northside Bsns Pk. Leeds 60 D2
Northside Rd. Brad BD7 74 A6
Northside Terr. Brad BD7 73 F6
Northstead. Dew WF13 138 D7
Northumberland St. Hud HD1 154 B6 1
Northway Cres. Mir WF14 137 F7
Northway Gdns. Mir WF14 137 F7
Northway. Mir WF14 137 F7
Northways Sch. B Spa 30 D5
Northwell Gate. Otley LS21 10 E2
Northwest Bsns Pk. Leeds 60 B3
Northwood Cl. Pudsey LS28 76 F5
Northwood Cl. Roth LS26 101 C7
Northwood Cres. Brad BD10 56 C6
Northwood Falls. Roth LS26 101 C7
Northwood Gdns. Leeds LS15 81 E7
Northwood Mt. Pudsey LS28 76 F5
Northwood Pk. Kirkb HD8 173 E7
Northwood Pk. Roth LS26 101 C7
Northwood View. Pudsey LS28 76 F5
Norton and Kirk Smeaton Rd. Norton WF8 166 E4
Norton Cl. Elland HX5 134 F5
Norton Cl. Hali HX2 112 B7
Norton Dr. Hali HX2 112 B7
Norton Rd. Leeds LS8 44 A3
Norton Rd. Wake WF1 142 D7
Norton St. Elland HX5 134 F6
Norton St. Sil BD20 5 D1
Norton St. Wake WF1 142 E4
Norton Terr. Kirkb HD4 173 C2
Nortonthorpe Ind Est. Clay W 175 D1
Norwich Ave. Leeds LS10 79 D2
Norwood Ave. Birk BD11 96 B4
Norwood Ave. Bur in W LS29 9 F1
Norwood Ave. Ship BD18 55 B6
Norwood Cl. Bur in W LS29 9 F1
Norwood Cres. Birk BD11 96 B4
Norwood Cres. Pudsey LS28 57 F2
Norwood Croft. Pudsey LS28 57 F2
Norwood. Dar WF8 147 A5
Norwood Dr. Batley WF17 117 F8
Norwood Dr. Birk BD11 96 B4
Norwood Dr. Bri S72 181 A3
Norwood Gr. Birk BD11 96 B4
Norwood Gr. Leeds LS6 59 E3
Norwood Green Hill. Brig HX3 93 F2
Norwood Mount. Leeds LS6 59 E3 1
Norwood Pk. Hud HD2 135 D1
Norwood Pl. Leeds LS6 59 E3 3
Norwood Pl. Ship BD18 55 B6
Norwood Rd. Hud HD2 135 E2
Norwood Rd. Leeds LS6 59 E3
Norwood Rd. Ship BD18 55 B6
Norwood St. Brad BD5 74 D2
Norwood St. Nor WF6 123 D4
Norwood St. Ship BD18 55 B6
Norwood Terr. Brig HX3 94 A2
Norwood Terr. Bur in W LS29 9 F1
Norwood Terr. Leeds LS6 59 E3
Norwood Terr. Ship BD18 55 B6
Norwood View. Leeds LS6 59 E3
Nostell Cl. Brad BD8 74 D8
Nostell La. Ryhill WF4 162 B2
Noster Gr. Leeds LS11 78 F3
Noster Hill. Leeds LS11 78 F3
Noster Pl. Leeds LS11 78 F3
Noster Rd. Leeds LS11 78 F3
Noster St. Leeds LS11 78 F3
Noster Terr. Leeds LS11 79 A3
Noster View. Leeds LS11 78 F3
Notre Dame Sixth Form Coll. Leeds 60 B3
Nottingham St. Brad BD3 75 E7
Notton La. Notton WF4 179 B6
Nova La. Batley WF17 96 D2
Nowell App. Leeds LS9 61 B1
Nowell Ave. Leeds LS9 61 B1
Nowell Cl. Leeds LS9 61 B1 6
Nowell Cres. Leeds LS9 61 B1
Nowell End Row. Leeds LS9 61 B1
Nowell Gdns. Leeds LS9 61 B1 8
Nowell Gr. Leeds LS9 61 B1
Nowell La. Leeds LS9 61 B1
Nowell Mount. Leeds LS9 61 B1
Nowell Par. Leeds LS9 61 B1
Nowell Pl. Hud HD5 154 F4
Nowell Pl. Leeds LS9 61 B1
Nowell St. Dew WF13 118 B1
Nowell St. Leeds LS9 61 B1
Nowell Terr. Leeds LS9 61 B1
Nowell View. Leeds LS9 61 B1
Nowell Wlk. Leeds LS9 61 B1
Nowell's Yd. Dew WF13 139 B8
Nuffield Hospl. Hud 135 E1
Nunburnholme Wlk. Brad BD10 56 C6
Nunington Ave. Leeds LS12 78 C8 12
Nunington St. Leeds LS12 78 D8 1
Nunington Terr. Leeds LS12 78 C8 13
Nunington View. Leeds LS12 59 C1 4
Nunlea Royd. Brig HX3 115 A6
Nunn's Cl. Feath WF7 145 D4
Nunn's Croft. Feath WF7 145 D4
Nunn's Gn. Feath WF7 145 D4
Nunn's La. Feath WF7 145 D4
Nunnery La. Brig HD6 135 D7
Nunns Ave. Feath WF7 145 D3
Nunns Ct. Feath WF7 145 C3
Nunns View. Feath WF7 145 C3
Nunroyd Ave. Guise LS20 39 F8
Nunroyd Ave. Leeds LS17 43 D1
Nunroyd. Batley WF16 117 D5
Nunroyd Gr. Leeds LS17 43 D1
Nunroyd Lawn. Leeds LS17 43 E1
Nunroyd Rd. Leeds LS17 43 D1
Nunroyd St. Leeds LS17 43 D1
Nunroyd Terr. Leeds LS17 43 D1
Nunthorpe Rd. Pudsey LS13 57 F5
Nurser La. Brad BD5 74 C4
Nurser Pl. Brad BD5 74 C4
Nursery Ave. Hali HX3 91 F3
Nursery Cl. Bail BD17 37 E2
Nursery Cl. Hali HX3 91 F2
Nursery Cl. Keigh BD20 18 A3
Nursery Cl. Leeds LS17 43 C4
Nursery Garth. Weth LS22 13 F6
Nursery Gr. Hali HX3 91 F3
Nursery Gr. Leeds LS17 43 A4
Nursery La. Hali HX3 91 F3
Nursery La. Leeds LS17 43 C4
Nursery La. Rip HX6 132 B3
Nursery Mount. Midd LS10 79 E1
Nursery Mount Rd. Midd LS10 79 E2 12
Nursery Rd. Brad BD14 73 B4 12
Nursery Rd. Brad BD7 73 F2
Nursery Rd. Guise LS20 22 D3
Nursery St. Dew WF12 139 C4
Nursery St. Hud HD2 136 A1
Nursery Way. B Spa LS23 30 B8
Nursery Way. B Spa LS23 30 D5
Nursery Wood Rd. Batley WF17 118 D3
Nussey Ave. Batley WF17 96 E2
Nutclough Rd. Heb Br HX7 89 B4
Nutfield St. Tod OL14 108 B6 6
Nuttall Rd. Brad BD3 75 A8
Nuttall St. Bacup OL13 106 B3 1
Nutter La. Clec WF17 96 C2
Nutter St. Clec BD19 116 C7
Nutting Grove Ter. Leeds LS12 77 E5

O'Cot La. Mars HD3 151 B4
O'Grady Sq. Leeds LS9 79 F7 10
Oak Ave. Bing BD16 36 F2
Oak Ave. Brad BD8 55 D2
Oak Ave. Bur in W LS29 21 F8
Oak Ave. Gar LS25 82 F7
Oak Ave. Hali HX6 112 B5
Oak Ave. Hud HD7 152 E5
Oak Ave. Hud HD5 154 E5
Oak Ave. Loft G WF3 121 F4
Oak Ave. Mel HD7 170 C3
Oak Ave. Morley LS27 98 B3
Oak Ave. Nor WF6 144 A8
Oak Ave. Tod OL14 108 A7
Oak Bank. Bing BD16 37 A2 7
Oak Bank. Ship BD18 55 D5
Oak Cl. Bur in W LS29 21 F8
Oak Cres. Gar LS25 82 F7
Oak Cres. Leeds LS15 80 F7
Oak Dr. Gar LS25 82 F7
Oak Dr. Slai HD7 152 D3
Oak Gr. Gar LS25 83 A7
Oak Gr. Keigh BD21 35 A4
Oak Gr. Morley LS27 98 C3
Oak Hall Pk. Crig WF4 159 C4
Oak Head Terr. Glu BD20 16 D8
Oak Hill Rd. Brig HD6 115 B3
Oak Hill. Sow Br HX6 132 E8
Oak House. Castle WF10 124 E7 9
Oak La. Brad BD9 55 C2
Oak La. Hali HX1 113 A7 4
Oak La. Sow Br HX6 132 E8
Oak Leigh. Caw S75 193 E4
Oak Mount. Brad BD8 55 D2
Oak Mount. Tod OL14 108 B6
Oak Pl. Bail BD17 38 F4
Oak Pl. Gar LS25 82 E7
Oak Pl. Hali HX6 112 B5 10
Oak Pl. Hali HX1 113 A7
Oak Rd. Gar LS25 82 E7
Oak Rd. Hud HD2 137 A5
Oak Rd. Leeds LS7 60 D5
Oak Rd. Leeds LS12 78 B7
Oak Rd. Leeds LS15 80 F7
Oak Rd. Morley LS27 97 F3
Oak Rd. Shaf S72 180 D2
Oak Ridge. Weth LS22 13 C5
Oak Rise. Clec BD19 95 D2
Oak Royd. Gar LS25 82 F7
Oak Scar La. Holmfi HD7 189 D3
Oak St. Batley WF16 117 D4
Oak St. Brad BD14 73 B4
Oak St. Crof WF4 162 A7
Oak St. Elland HX5 134 F6
Oak St. Hali HX6 112 B5 18
Oak St. Haw BD22 51 D7
Oak St. Heb Br HX7 89 A4 9
Oak St. Loft G WF3 121 C4
Oak St. Morley LS27 98 B7
Oak St. Oxen BD22 51 C3
Oak St. Pudsey LS28 76 C8
Oak St. S Elm WF9 182 F1
Oak St. Tod OL14 108 A4
Oak Terr. Elland HX4 134 A4 2
Oak Terr. Hali HX1 113 A7 2
Oak Terr. Hud HD2 136 B2
Oak Terr. Leeds LS15 62 D3 1
Oak Tree Ave. Holmfi HD7 189 D3
Oak Tree Ave. Lepton HD8 155 D3
Oak Tree Bsns Pk. Leeds 62 A7
Oak Tree Cl. Leeds LS9 61 C3
Oak Tree Cres. Leeds LS9 61 C3
Oak Tree Ct. Leeds LS9 61 C3
Oak Tree Ct. Sil BD20 5 D2
Oak Tree Dr. Leeds LS8 61 C3
Oak Tree Gr. Hem WF9 181 F6
Oak Tree Gr. Leeds LS9 61 C3
Oak Tree Meadow. Walton WF2 161 A6
Oak Tree Mount. Leeds LS9 61 C3
Oak Tree Pl. Leeds LS9 61 C3
Oak Tree Rd. Lepton HD8 155 D3
Oak Tree Terr. Lepton HD8 155 D3
Oak Tree Wlk. Leeds LS9 61 C3
Oak View. Sil BD20 5 E2
Oak View Terr. Batley WF17 117 F8 4
Oak Villas. Brad BD8 55 D2
Oak Wood Rd. Weth LS22 13 D7
Oakbank Ave. Keigh BD22 34 F5
Oakbank Broadway. Keigh BD22 34 F4
Oakbank Cres. Keigh BD22 34 F5
Oakbank Ct. Keigh BD22 34 F4
Oakbank Dr. Keigh BD22 34 F5
Oakbank Gr. Keigh BD22 34 F5
Oakbank La. Keigh BD22 34 F4
Oakbank Mount. Keigh BD22 34 F4
Oakbank Recn Ctr. Keigh 34 F4
Oakbank Sch. Keigh 34 F4
Oakburn Rd. Ilkley LS29 8 A3
Oakdale Ave. Brad BD6 74 B1
Oakdale Ave. Ship BD18 55 D6
Oakdale. Bing BD16 37 A5
Oakdale Cl. Brad BD10 56 E3
Oakdale Cl. Hali HX3 92 A2
Oakdale Cl. Loft G WF3 121 B6
Oakdale Cres. Brad BD6 74 B1
Oakdale Cres. Hud HD3 153 A8
Oakdale Dr. Brad BD10 56 E3
Oakdale Dr. Ship BD18 55 E6
Oakdale Fst Sch. Ship 55 E6
Oakdale Garth. Leeds LS14 45 B1
Oakdale Gr. Ship BD18 55 E6
Oakdale Meadow. Leeds LS14 45 B1
Oakdale Pk. Pool LS21 24 D6
Oakdale Rd. Ship BD18 55 E6
Oakdale Terr. Brad BD6 74 B1
Oakdean. Hud HD2 136 A4
Oakdene Cl. Pudsey LS28 76 F5
Oakdene Ct. Leeds LS17 44 A4
Oakdene Dr. Leeds LS17 44 A4
Oakdene Gdns. Leeds LS17 44 A4
Oakdene Vale. Leeds LS17 44 A4
Oakdene Way. Leeds LS17 44 A4
Oaken Bank Cres. Hud HD5 154 C4
Oaken Cl. Bacup OL13 106 B3
Oakenclough Rd. Bacup OL13 106 B3
Oakenshaw Ct. Brad BD12 94 C2
Oakenshaw La. Brad BD19 95 A3
Oakenshaw La. Crof WF4 143 A2
Oakenshaw La. Walton WF1, WF2 161 A8
Oakenshaw St. Wake WF1 142 F3
Oakes Ave. Honley HD7 172 C2
Oakes Fold. Lepton HD8 156 A3
Oakes La. Honley HD7 172 C2
Oakes Rd. Hud HD3 153 B8
Oakes Rd S. Hud HD3 153 B7
Oakes St. Wake WF2 141 D6
Oakfield Ave. Bing BD16 37 C2
Oakfield Ave. Roth LS26 100 E6
Oakfield Cl. Elland HX5 134 E6
Oakfield Cl. Gar LS25 82 F6
Oakfield Cres. Knot WF11 126 F3
Oakfield Ct. Mapp S75 178 A1
Oakfield Dr. Bail BD17 38 D2
Oakfield Gr. Brad BD9 55 C2
Oakfield Gr. Skel HD8 175 A1
Oakfield. Leeds LS6 59 E4
Oakfield Pk. Th Aud WF8 165 B4
Oakfield Rd. Hud HD2 135 E1
Oakfield Rd. Keigh BD21 35 B4
Oakfield Terr. Hors LS18 58 E8 4
Oakfield Terr. Ship BD18 55 D7
Oakhampton Ct. Leeds LS8 61 C8
Oakhill Rd. Batley WF17 118 A7
Oakhurst Ave. Leeds LS11 79 A1 6
Oakhurst Gr. Leeds LS11 78 F1
Oakhurst Mount. Leeds LS11 78 F1
Oakhurst Rd. Leeds LS11 79 A1
Oakhurst St. Leeds LS11 79 A1
Oakland Ct. Kirkb HD8 173 F7
Oakland Dr. Neth WF4 158 D5
Oakland Rd. Neth WF4 158 D5
Oakland Rd. Wake WF1 142 E3
Oakland St. Sil BD20 5 D1
Oaklands Ave. Northo HX3 93 B3
Oaklands Ave. Pudsey LS13 57 E5
Oaklands. Brad BD10 56 A8
Oaklands. Brig HD6 114 F1
Oaklands Cl. Holmfi HD7 189 A7
Oaklands Croft. Walton WF2 161 B6
Oaklands Dr. Hors LS16 42 D3
Oaklands Dr. Hud HD5 154 F5
Oaklands Gr. Pudsey LS13 57 E5
Oaklands. Ilkley LS29 8 A3
Oaklands Rd. Pudsey LS13 57 E5
Oaklands. Ship BD18 54 D7
Oaklea Cl. Mapp S75 178 B2
Oaklea Gdns. Hors LS16 42 D2
Oaklea Hall Cl. Hors LS16 42 D2
Oaklea Rd. B in Elm LS15 62 F6
Oakleigh Ave. Brad BD14 73 B3
Oakleigh Ave. Hali HX3 113 C3
Oakleigh Ave. Wake WF2 141 E5
Oakleigh Cl. Brad BD14 73 B4
Oakleigh Gdns. Brad BD14 73 B3
Oakleigh Gr. Brad BD14 73 B3
Oakleigh Rd. Brad BD14 73 B4
Oakleigh Terr. Brad BD14 73 B4
Oakleigh Terr. Tod OL14 86 B1 8
Oakleigh View. Bail BD17 38 B3
Oakley Gr. Leeds LS11 79 C2
Oakley St. E Ard WF3 99 E1
Oakley Terr. Leeds LS11 79 C2
Oakley View. Leeds LS11 79 C2
Oakridge Ave. Men LS29 22 B4
Oakridge Ct. Bing BD16 37 A4
Oakroyd Ave. Brad BD6 74 C1
Oakroyd Cl. Birk BD11 96 A5
Oakroyd Cl. Brig HD6 115 B5
Oakroyd Dr. Birk BD11 96 A4
Oakroyd Dr. Brig HD6 115 B5
Oakroyd Mount. Pudsey LS28 76 E8
Oakroyd Rd. Brad BD6 74 B1 10
Oakroyd Rd. Brad BD6 74 C1 12
Oakroyd. Roth LS26 100 F4
Oakroyd Terr. Bail BD17 38 D2 3
Oakroyd Terr. Brad BD8 55 D2
Oakroyd Terr. Morley LS27 98 C8
Oakroyd Terr. Pudsey LS28 76 E8 8
Oakroyd Villas. Brad BD8 55 D2
Oaks Dr. Brad BD15 73 C8
Oaks Farm Cl. Mapp S75 177 F1
Oaks Farm Dr. Mapp S75 177 F1
Oaks Fold. Brad BD5 74 E3
Oaks Green Mount. Brig HD6 135 F7
Oaks La. B Spa LS23 30 D8
Oaks La. Brad BD15, BD8 73 D8
Oaks Rd. Batley WF17 118 E4
Oaks The. Guise LS20 22 E2
Oaks The. Morley LS27 98 B7
Oaks Wood Dr. Mapp S75 178 A1
Oaksfield. M'town LS26 102 D2
Oaktree La. Bad WF7 164 C5
Oakville Rd. B Head HX7 88 D2
Oakway. Birk BD11 96 B4
Oakwell Ave. Batley WF17 117 F6
Oakwell Ave. Leeds LS8 61 A6

Oakwell Ave. Pont WF8 .... 146 C6
Oakwell Cl. Birk BD11 .... 97 A5
Oakwell Cl. Brad BD7 .... 74 B3
Oakwell Cl. Hem WF9 .... 163 A2
Oakwell Cres. Leeds LS8 .... 61 A6
Oakwell Dr. Leeds LS8 .... 61 A6
Oakwell Gdns. Leeds LS8 .... 61 A6
Oakwell Gr. Leeds LS13 .... 58 C3
Oakwell Hall Country Pk. Clec . 96 D3
Oakwell Ind Pk. Batley 97 A4
Oakwell Mount. Leeds LS8 .... 61 A6
Oakwell Oval. Leeds LS8 .... 61 A6
Oakwell Rd. Birk BD11 .... 97 A5
Oakwell Terr. Pudsey LS28 ...... 57 D3 2
Oakwell Way. Batley WF17 ...... 97 A3
Oakwood Ave. Birk BD11 .... 96 A4
Oakwood Ave. Leeds LS8 .... 61 B6
Oakwood Ave. Roy S71 .... 179 C4
Oakwood Ave. Ship BD2 .... 55 D4
Oakwood Ave. Wake WF2 .... 141 D6
Oakwood Boundary Rd. Leeds LS8 .... 61 B6
Oakwood Cl. Nor WF6 .... 122 F4
Oakwood Cres. Roy S71 .... 179 B4
Oakwood Ct. Brad BD8 .... 74 C8
Oakwood Ct. Leeds LS8 .... 61 C6
Oakwood Dr. Bing BD16 .... 37 A5
Oakwood Dr. Hem WF9 .... 181 E6
Oakwood Dr. Leeds LS8 .... 61 B6
Oakwood Dr. Nor WF6 .... 122 F4
Oakwood Dr. Roth LS26 .... 100 D7
Oakwood Garth. Leeds LS8 ...... 61 C6
Oakwood Gdns. Crig WF4 ...... 159 D6
Oakwood Gn. Leeds LS8 .... 61 C6
Oakwood Gr. Brad BD8 .... 55 A1
Oakwood Gr. Hor WF4 .... 141 C2
Oakwood Gr. Leeds LS8 .... 61 B6
Oakwood Grange La. Leeds LS8 61 C6
Oakwood Grange. Leeds LS8 ... 61 C6
Oakwood La. Leeds LS8, LS9 ... 61 C5
Oakwood Mount. Leeds LS8 ..... 61 B6
Oakwood Nook. Leeds LS8 .... 61 B6
Oakwood Pk. Leeds LS8 .... 61 C6
Oakwood Pl. Leeds LS8 .... 61 B6
Oakwood Prim Sch. Leeds 61 C3
Oakwood Rd. Batley WF17 ...... 118 E5
Oakwood Rd. Roy S71 .... 179 B4
Oakwood Rise. Leeds LS8 .... 61 C6
Oakwood Terr. Pudsey LS28 ..... 76 E6
Oakwood View. Leeds LS8 .... 61 C6
Oakwood. Wake WF2 .... 141 D3
Oakwood Wlk. Leeds LS8 .... 61 C6
Oakworth Fst Sch. Haw 34 D2
Oakworth Hall. Haw BD22 .... 34 C2
Oakworth Rd. Keigh BD21, BD22 .... 35 A6
Oakworth Sta. Haw 34 D1
Oakworth Terr. Haw BD22 .... 34 D2
Oasby Croft. Brad BD4 .... 75 E1
Oast House Croft. Roth WF3 . 100 B3
Oastler Ave. Hud HD1 .... 153 F6
Oastler Pl. Brad BD12 .... 94 D6
Oastler Rd. Pudsey LS28 .... 57 B6
Oastler Rd. Ship BD18 .... 54 F8
Oastler St. Dew WF13 .... 139 B8
Oates St. Dew WF13 .... 139 C8
Oatland Cl. Leeds LS7 .... 60 C2
Oatland Ct. Leeds LS7 .... 60 C2
Oatland Dr. Leeds LS7 .... 60 C2
Oatland Gdns. Leeds LS7 .... 60 D2
Oatland Gn. Leeds LS7 .... 60 C2
Oatland La. Leeds LS7 .... 60 C2
Oatland Pl. Leeds LS7 .... 60 C3
Oatland Rd. Leeds LS7 .... 60 C2
Oatlands Dr. Otley LS21 .... 11 A1
Oats St. Keigh BD22 .... 35 A4
Oban Cl. E Ard WF3 .... 98 D1
Oban Pl. Leeds LS12 .... 78 B8 6
Oban St. Leeds LS12 .... 78 B8 8
Oban Terr. Leeds LS12 .... 78 B8 7
Occupation La. Aber LS24 .... 47 F4
Occupation La. Batley WF13 .. 117 F3
Occupation La. Bramho LS16 .... 24 B2
Occupation La. Hali HX2 .... 91 F6
Occupation La. Holmfi HD7 ..... 189 E8
Occupation La. Honley HD7 ... 172 D1
Occupation La. Keigh BD22 ...... 34 E4
Occupation La. Pudsey LS28 .... 76 C7
Occupation Rd. Hud HD2 .... 136 C3
Occupation Rd. Hud HD2, HD3 153 C8
Ochrewell Ave. Hud HD2 .... 136 E3
Octagon Terr. Hali HX2 .... 112 E4
Odda La. Guise LS20 .... 21 E1
Oddfellow St. Morley LS27 ...... 98 A4
Oddfellows Club Houses. Ack M T WF7 .... 163 D5
Oddfellows' Ct. Brad BD1 .... 74 E7
Oddfellows St. Brig HD6 .... 115 B4 3
Oddfellows St. Brig BD19 .... 115 F8
Oddfellows St. Mir WF14 .... 138 A5
Oddy Pl. Brad BD6 .... 74 B1 6
Oddy Pl. Leeds LS6 .... 59 D6 4
Oddy St. Brad BD4 .... 75 E1
Oddy's Fold. Leeds LS6 .... 59 E8
Odsal Pl. Brad BD6 .... 94 D8 9
Odsal Rd. Brad BD6 .... 94 D8
Offley La. W Har WF9 .... 163 B6
Ogden Cres. Denh BD13 .... 52 D2
Ogden La. Brig HD6 .... 135 F8
Ogden La. Denh BD13 .... 52 D2
Ogden La. Hali HX2 .... 71 D2
Ogden View Cl. Hali HX2 .... 91 D7
Old Allen Rd. Wils BD13, BD15 53 B2
Old Arcade The. Hali HX1 ...... 113 C7 20
Old Bank Fst Sch. Mir 138 A7
Old Bank Fold. Hud HD5 .... 154 D5 13
Old Bank. Hali HX3 .... 113 D7
Old Bank Rd. Dew WF12 .... 139 E8
Old Bank Rd. Mir WF14 .... 138 A4
Old Bank. Rip HX6 .... 132 E4
Old Bank. Slai HD7 .... 169 F8
Old Barn Cl. Leeds LS17 .... 43 A5
Old Bell Ct. Hali HX1 .... 113 C6 9
Old Brandon La. Thorner LS17 44 E4
Old Bridge Rise. Ilkley LS29 .... 8 A5
Old Canal Rd. Brad BD1 .... 74 E8
Old Church St. Ossett WF5 ..... 140 D5
Old Cl. Morley LS11 .... 98 D8
Old Cock Yd. Hali HX1 .... 113 C7 18
Old Corn Mill La. Brad BD7 ...... 74 A4
Old Cross Stone Rd. Tod OL14 108 C5 17
Old Crown Rd. Wake WF2 ..... 141 D3
Old Cswy. Hali HX6 .... 112 C4
Old Dalton La. Keigh BD21 .... 35 D7
Old Earth. Elland HX5 .... 135 B7
Old Earth Jun & Inf Sch. Elland 135 C7
Old Farm App. Leeds LS16 .... 58 F8
Old Farm Cl. Leeds LS16 .... 59 A8
Old Farm Cross. Leeds LS16 ..... 59 A8
Old Farm Dr. Leeds LS16 .... 59 A8
Old Farm Garth. Leeds LS16 .... 59 A8 2
Old Farm Par. Leeds LS16 .... 59 A8
Old Farm Wlk. Leeds LS16 .... 58 F8 6
Old Fieldhouse La. Hud HD2 .. 136 D1
Old Fold. Pudsey LS28 .... 57 D3 9
Old Garth Croft. Fair WF11 ..... 105 A4
Old Gate. Heb Br HX7 .... 89 A3 24
Old Gate. Holme HD7 .... 197 F7
Old Godley La. Northo HX3 ...... 92 F1
Old Great North Rd. Broth WF11 .... 126 D8
Old Great North Rd. Knot WF11 .... 126 C5
Old Ground. Mars HD7 .... 169 A8
Old Guy Rd. Queen BD13 .... 72 C1
Old Hall Cl. Glu BD20 .... 16 B6
Old Hall Court Yd. Crof WF1 .. 143 A5
Old Hall. Hali HX3 .... 113 D4
Old Hall La. Emley HD8 .... 175 E5
Old Hall Mews. Batley WF17 . 118 C7
Old Hall Rd. Ad Le S DN6 .... 184 F2
Old Hall Rd. Batley WF17 .... 118 C7
Old Hall Rd. E Ard WF3 .... 119 F8
Old Hall Rd. Glu BD20 .... 16 B6
Old Hall View. Castle WF10 ... 125 D5
Old Hall Way. Glu BD20 .... 16 B6
Old Haworth La. Yeadon LS19 . 40 B7 6
Old Hollings Hill. Guise LS20, BD17 .... 39 C6
Old La. Birk BD11 .... 96 B5
Old La. Bramho LS16 .... 24 B3
Old La. Brig HD6 .... 115 B3
Old La. Cull BD13 .... 52 D6
Old La. Gild BD11 .... 97 A8
Old La. Guise LS20 .... 38 E8
Old La. Hali HX2 .... 90 E1
Old La. Hali HX3 .... 92 B2
Old La. Haw BD22 .... 49 F7
Old La. Holme HD7 .... 187 C4
Old La. Hud HD2 .... 136 D5
Old La. Ilkley LS29 .... 8 D3
Old La. Leeds LS11 .... 78 F1
Old La. Mars HD7 .... 169 D7
Old La. Nes LS29 .... 7 C7
Old La. Pool LS16 .... 23 F4
Old La. Slai HD7 .... 152 C5
Old La. Tod OL14 .... 108 A3
Old La. Wad M HX7 .... 89 B8
Old Laithe La. Wad M HX7 .... 89 C5
Old Lane Ct. Brig HD6 .... 115 B3 2
Old Langley La. Bail BD17 .... 38 E4
Old Lee Bank. Hali HX3 .... 92 B1
Old Leeds Rd. Hud HD1 .... 154 B6
Old Lees Rd. Heb Br HX7 .... 89 A4
Old Lindley Rd. Elland HD3 ..... 134 D2
Old Lodge Hill or Hardings La. Ilkley LS29 .... 7 F6
Old Main St. Bing BD16 .... 36 F3
Old Malt St. Haw BD22 .... 51 C6 1
Old Market. Hali HX1 .... 113 C7
Old Marsh. Pudsey LS28 .... 76 C6
Old Meadows Rd. Bacup OL13 106 A4
Old Mill Bsns Pk. Leeds 79 F4
Old Mill Cl. Hem WF9 .... 181 C7
Old Mill La. Leeds LS10 .... 79 E4
Old Mill Rd. Ship BD17 .... 55 B8
Old Mill The. Weth LS22 .... 13 E5
Old Mill Yd. Ossett WF5 .... 140 C3
Old Moll Rd. Honley HD7 .... 171 E5
Old Mount Farm. Wool WF4 .. 178 A6
Old Mount Rd. Mars HD7 .... 168 E2
Old Oak Cl. Leeds LS16 .... 59 A7
Old Oak Dr. Leeds LS16 .... 59 A7
Old Oak Garth. Leeds LS16 .... 58 F7
Old Orch The. Pool LS21 .... 24 C7
Old Oxenhope La. Oxen BD22 .. 51 B4
Old Park Rd. Brad BD10 .... 56 C7
Old Park Rd. Leeds LS8 .... 61 A8
Old Pool Bank. Bramho LS21 ... 24 B5
Old Pool Bank. Pool LS21 .... 24 B5
Old Popplewell La. Brig BD19 115 E8
Old Power Way. Hali HX5 .... 135 A8
Old Rd. Brad BD7 .... 73 E2
Old Rd. Denh BD13 .... 71 D8
Old Rd. Holmfi HD7 .... 188 D3
Old Rd. Morley LS27 .... 98 C8
Old Rd. Neth WF4 .... 157 F6
Old Rd. Pudsey LS28 .... 57 D2
Old Rd. Thorn BD13 .... 73 A6
Old Rd. Wad M HX7 .... 69 A2
Old Riding La. Hali HX2 .... 90 F3
Old Robin. Clec BD19 .... 116 D7 9
Old Run Rd. Leeds LS10 .... 79 D1
Old Run Rd. Midd LS10 .... 79 D1
Old Sawmills The. Rip HX6 ..... 132 C2
Old School Mews. Morley LS27 98 C8 4
Old Shaw La. B Head HX7 .... 88 A4
Old Souls Way. Bing BD16 .... 36 E6
Old South St. Hud HD1 .... 154 A6
Old St. H Pag DN5 .... 195 F7
Old St. Ham DN6 .... 183 F1
Old Station Cotts. Ryhill S71 .. 179 D7
Old Station Way. Sil LS29 .... 6 F8
Old Town J & I Sch. Wad M 89 B6
Old Town Mill La. Wad M HX7 . 89 B5
Old Turnpike. Honley HD7 ...... 172 A4
Old Wakefield Rd. Hud HD5 ... 154 D5 5
Old Water Mill The. Rip HX6 .. 132 D7
Old Well Head. Hali HX1 .... 113 C6
Old Westgate. Dew WF13 .... 139 C8
Old Whack House La. Yeadon LS19 .... 39 F6
Old Wood La. Guise BD16 .... 21 B2
Old Yew La. Holmfi HD7 .... 188 E2
Oldfield Ave. Leeds LS12 .... 78 C6
Oldfield Fst Sch. Haw 50 C8
Oldfield Gate. Haw BD22 .... 51 A7
Oldfield. Honley HD7 .... 171 F1
Oldfield La. Batley WF16 .... 117 D3
Oldfield La. Clay W HD8 .... 175 F2
Oldfield La. Coll LS22 .... 13 E1
Oldfield La. Haw BD22 .... 50 C8
Oldfield La. Haw BD22 .... 51 A7
Oldfield La. Leeds LS12 .... 78 D6
Oldfield Rd. Honley HD7 .... 171 F1
Oldfield St. Hali HX3 .... 92 A3
Oldfield St. Hud HD4 .... 153 E4
Oldfield St. Leeds LS12 .... 78 C6 1
Oldgate. Hud HD1 .... 154 B6
Oldham Rd. Rip HX6 .... 150 C6
Oldroyd Cres. Leeds LS11 .... 78 E2
Oldroyd Rd. Tod OL14 .... 108 E4
Oldside Ct. Keigh BD20 .... 19 E1
Olicana Pk. Ilkley LS29 .... 8 A5
Olive Gr. Brad BD8 .... 73 E8
Olive St. Hud HD1 .... 136 B1
Olive Terr. Bing BD16 .... 37 A3
Olive Terr. Mars HD7 .... 169 C6
Oliver Gdns. Mir WF14 .... 137 F7
Oliver Hill. Hors LS18 .... 58 C7
Oliver La. Mars HD7 .... 168 F4
Oliver Rd. Batley WF16 .... 117 E5
Oliver St. Brad BD4 .... 75 A5
Olivers Mount. Pont WF8 .... 146 E8
Ollerdale Ave. Brad BD15 .... 54 A3
Ollerdale Cl. Brad BD15 .... 54 A2
Ollerton Rd. Barn S71 .... 178 F1
Olney St. Slai HD7 .... 152 A1
Olrika Ct. Leeds LS7 .... 60 D4
Oltley Rd. Men LS29 .... 22 B5
Olympic Ct. Brad BD12 .... 94 E5 6
Omar St. Liver WF16 .... 117 C4
Onchan Dr. Bacup OL13 .... 106 B1
One St. Brad BD1 .... 74 D7
Onslow Cres. Brad BD4 .... 75 B2
Ontario Pl. Leeds LS7 .... 60 D6
Opal St. Keigh BD22 .... 35 A4 10
Orange St. Brad BD3 .... 75 C6
Orange St. Hali HX1 .... 113 C7
Orange Terr. Hud HD1 .... 154 B8
Orange Tree Gr. E Ard WF3 .... 120 C7
Orchard Ave. Loft G WF3 .... 121 F5
Orchard Cl. E Ard WF3 .... 120 D6
Orchard Cl. Hali HX2 .... 112 D6
Orchard Cl. Hor WF4 .... 141 A2
Orchard Cl. Mapp S75 .... 178 B1
Orchard Cl. Mel HD7 .... 170 F1
Orchard Cl. Wake WF1 .... 120 F3
Orchard Croft. Leeds LS15 .... 62 B2 2
Orchard Croft. Wake WF2 .... 120 E2
Orchard Croft. Walton WF2 ... 161 A7
Orchard Ct. Bramham LS23 ..... 30 D2
Orchard Dr. Ack M T WF7 ...... 164 A5
Orchard Dr. Coll LS22 .... 13 B3
Orchard Dr. Crig WF4 .... 159 F7
Orchard Dr. Fair WF11 .... 105 B5
Orchard Dr. S Hie S72 .... 180 D6
Orchard Gate. Otley LS21 .... 23 A7
Orchard Gdns. Crig WF4 .... 159 F7
Orchard Gr. Brad BD10 .... 56 D6
Orchard Gr. Men LS29 .... 22 B4
Orchard Head Cres. Pont WF8 125 F4
Orchard Head Dr. Pont WF8 .. 125 E4
Orchard Head Jun Mid & Inf Sch. Pont 125 E4
Orchard Head La. Pont WF8 .. 125 E4
Orchard La. Add LS29 .... 7 A8
Orchard La. Guise LS20 .... 22 E1
Orchard Lees. Kirkhe HD5 ...... 155 C8
Orchard Mount. Leeds LS15 ..... 62 C2
Orchard Rd. Kirkhe HD5 .... 155 C8
Orchard Rd. Leeds LS15 .... 62 B2 1
Orchard Rd. Tod OL14 .... 107 F7
Orchard Rd. Wake WF2 .... 142 E1
Orchard Sq. Leeds LS15 .... 62 B2
Orchard St. Dew WF12 .... 139 D6
Orchard St. Hud HD4 .... 154 A4
Orchard St. Otley LS21 .... 23 B7
Orchard St W. Hud HD3 .... 153 A5
Orchard Terr. Caw S75 .... 193 F4
Orchard Terr. Hud HD4 .... 154 B4
Orchard The. B Spa LS23 .... 30 D8
Orchard The. Crof WF4 .... 144 A1
Orchard The. Elland HX4 .... 133 F3
Orchard The. Feath WF7 .... 124 D1
Orchard The. Keigh BD21 .... 35 F7
Orchard The. Mir WF14 .... 138 B7
Orchard The. Nor WF6 .... 123 B2
Orchard The. Ossett WF5 .... 140 D5
Orchard The. Pont WF8 .... 146 F5
Orchard The. Wake WF2 WF4 120 F3
Orchard View. Broth WF11 .... 126 C8
Orchard View. Dar WF8 .... 147 C5
Orchard View. Weth LS22 .... 13 E8
Orchard Way. Brig HD6 .... 115 A4
Orchard Way. Guise LS20 .... 22 E1
Orchard Way. Roth LS26 .... 100 F6
Orchard Wlk. Heb Br HX7 .... 89 F1
Orchards The. Bing BD16 .... 37 A5
Orchards The. Clec BD19 .... 117 C8
Orchards The. Leeds LS15 .... 62 C2
Orchards The. M'town LS26 .. 102 C2
Orchid Ct. Roth WF3 .... 100 B2
Oriental St. Leeds LS12 .... 78 C7 6
Orion Cres. Midd LS10 .... 99 E7
Orion Dr. Midd LS10 .... 99 E7
Orion Gdns. Midd LS10 .... 99 E7
Orion View. Midd LS10 .... 99 F7
Orion Wlk. Midd LS10 .... 99 F8
Orlando Cl. Mir WF14 .... 137 F7
Orleans St. Brad BD6 .... 93 F7
Ormond Rd. Brad BD6 .... 74 B1
Ormond St. Brad BD7 .... 74 A4
Ormonde Dr. Brad BD15 .... 73 A8
Ormonde Pl. Leeds LS7 .... 60 C3
Ormondroyd Ave. Brad BD6 ..... 94 C8
Orville Gdns. Leeds LS6 .... 59 E4
Orwell Cl. Castle WF10 .... 125 C5
Osborne Ave. Hor WF4 .... 141 C2
Osborne Gr. Brig HX3 .... 114 D7
Osborne Pl. Tod OL14 .... 108 C5 3
Osborne St. Brad BD5 .... 74 D5
Osborne St. Hali HX1 .... 112 F8
Osborne St. Heb Br HX7 .... 89 A3 14
Osborne St. Hud HD5 .... 154 D5 15
Osbourne Ct. Leeds LS13 .... 58 D1
Osmondthorpe Fst Sch. Leeds . 80 D8
Osmondthorpe La. Leeds LS9 .. 80 C7
Osmondthorpe Mid Sch. Leeds 80 D8
Osprey Cl. Leeds LS17 .... 43 F4
Osprey Ct. Brad BD8 .... 73 C7
Osprey Dr. Hud HD4 .... 171 E7
Osprey Gr. Leeds LS17 .... 43 F4
Osprey Meadow. Morley LS27 . 98 D4
Ossett Flushdyke Jun & Inf Sch. Ossett 140 F7
Ossett La. Dew WF12 .... 140 A6
Ossett South Parade Inf Sch. Ossett 140 F4
Ossett South Parade Jun Sch. Ossett 140 F4
Ossett Southdale CE (C) Sch. Ossett 140 E4
Ossett Towngate Jun & Inf Sch. Ossett 140 F6
Osterley Gr. Brad BD10 .... 56 E5
Ostler Sch The. Hali 112 F8
Oswald St. Brad BD8 .... 74 A8
Oswald St. Ship BD18 .... 55 D7
Oswaldthorpe Ave. Brad BD3 .. 56 D1
Otley All Saints Fst Sch. Otley .. 23 B7
Otley Ashfield Fst Sch. Otley 10 E1
Otley Golf Course. Otley 22 C6
Otley La. Yeadon LS19 .... 40 B7
Otley Mount. Keigh BD20 .... 19 E1
Otley Old Rd. Bramho LS16 ...... 24 B1
Otley Old Rd. E Carl LS16 .... 23 F3
Otley Old Rd. E Carl LS16 .... 24 B1
Otley Old Rd. Hors LS16 .... 41 F4
Otley Rd. Bail BD17 .... 38 E2
Otley Rd. Bing BD16 .... 20 B1
Otley Rd. Bing BD16 .... 37 D6
Otley Rd. Bur in W LS29 .... 22 B8
Otley Rd. Guise LS20 .... 22 D1
Otley Rd. Hare LS17 .... 26 C7
Otley Rd. Hors LS16 .... 42 C5
Otley Rd. Keigh BD20 .... 19 F1
Otley Rd. Leeds LS6, LS16 .... 59 D6
Otley Rd. Ship BD17, BD18 .... 55 B7
Otley St. Hali HX1 .... 112 F7
Otley St. Keigh BD21 .... 35 B6
Otley Westgate Fst Sch. Otley . 22 F7
Ottawa Pl. Leeds LS7 .... 60 D6
Otterburn Cl. Brad BD5 .... 74 E5 7
Otterburn Gdns. Hors LS16 ...... 42 B3
Otterburn St. Keigh BD21 .... 35 C8
Otters Holt. Crig WF4 .... 159 F7
Otterwood Bank. Weth LS22 .... 13 F7
Ottiwells Terr. Mars HD7 ...... 168 F3
Ouchthorpe Fold. Loft G WF1 121 C4
Ouchthorpe La. Loft G WF1 ... 121 C2
Queen's Ct. Leeds LS17 .... 43 C1
Oulton Dr. Roth LS26 .... 101 C3
Oulton Inf Sch. Roth 101 B6
Oulton Jun Sch. Roth 101 B6
Oulton La. Roth LS26 .... 100 F5
Oulton La. Roth LS26 .... 101 C6
Oulton Terr. Brad BD7 .... 74 C6
Ounsworth St. Brad BD4 .... 75 B4
Our Lady of Good Counsel RC Sch. Leeds 62 A6
Our Lady of Lourdes RC Prim Sch. Hud 136 C4
Our Lady of Victories RC Prim Sch. Keigh 35 A7
Ouse Dr. Weth LS22 .... 13 D8
Ouse St. Haw BD22 .... 51 D7 2
Out Gang. Leeds LS13 .... 58 D3
Out La. Emley HD8 .... 175 C7
Out La. Holmfi HD7 .... 188 F8
Outcote Bank. Hud HD1 .... 154 A5
Outgang La. Leeds LS13 .... 58 E3
Outlane Cty Prim Sch. Hud 134 D1
Outside La. Oxen BD22 .... 50 F2
Outwood Ave. Hors LS18 .... 58 D7
Outwood Grange Sch. Loft G . 121 A4
Outwood La. Hors LS18 .... 58 D7
Outwood Ledger Lane Jun & Inf Sch. Loft G 121 B4
Outwood Park Ct. Loft G WF1 121 B4
Outwood Wlk. Hors LS18 .... 58 C7
Ouzelwell Cres. Dew WF12 .... 139 B3
Ouzelwell La. Dew WF12 .... 139 A3
Ouzelwell Rd. Dew WF12 .... 139 B4
Ouzlewell Gn. Roth WF3 .... 100 D2
Oval The. Bail BD17 .... 38 B2
Oval The. Beal DN14 .... 127 F5
Oval The. Bing BD16 .... 37 B2
Oval The. Brad BD8 .... 73 E8
Oval The. Clec WF15 .... 116 C5
Oval The . Gar LS25 .... 83 A7
Oval The. Guise LS20 .... 39 C8
Oval The. Holmfi HD7 .... 188 F7
Oval The. Leeds LS14 .... 61 F2
Oval The. Leeds LS10 .... 79 E4
Oval The. Notton WF4 .... 179 B6
Oval The. Otley LS21 .... 10 F1
Oval The. Roth LS26 .... 100 F5
Ovenden Ave. Hali HX3 .... 92 A1
Ovenden Cl. Hali HX3 .... 92 A1 15
Ovenden Cres. Hali HX3 .... 92 A2
Ovenden Gn. Hali HX3 .... 92 A2
Ovenden High Sch The. Hali 91 F3
Ovenden Park. Hali 91 F4
Ovenden Rd. Hali HX3 .... 92 A2
Ovenden Road Terr. Hali HX3 .. 92 A2 9
Ovenden Terr. Hali HX3 .... 92 A2
Ovenden Way. Hali HX3 .... 91 F2
Ovenden Wood Rd. Hali HX2 ... 91 D2
Over Hall Cl. Mir WF14 .... 138 B6
Over Hall Pk. Mir WF14 .... 138 B6
Over Hall Rd. Mir WF14 .... 138 B6
Over La. Yeadon LS19 .... 40 C3
Overburn Rd. S in Cra BD20 ..... 16 D4
Overdale Ave. Leeds LS17 .... 44 A5
Overdale Cl. Weth LS22 .... 13 D6
Overdale Dr. Brad BD10, BD18 38 F1
Overdale Mount. Hali HX6 .... 112 C5
Overdale. Rip HX6 .... 132 E7
Overdale Terr. Leeds LS15 .... 81 A8 4
Overend St. Brad BD6 .... 74 A1 6
Overthorpe Ave. Dew WF12 ... 139 D1
Overthorpe Rd. Dew WF12 ..... 139 D3
Overton Dr. Brad BD6 .... 73 D2
Ovington Dr. Brad BD4 .... 75 E2
Ower's Cres. Honley HD7 .... 171 E3
Owl La. Batley WF12 .... 119 A2
Owl La. Batley WF12 .... 119 B2
Owl La. Ossett WF5 .... 119 B1
Owl Mews. Kirkhe HD5 .... 155 C6
Owl Ridge. Morley LS27 .... 98 C3
Owl St. Keigh BD21 .... 35 D8 6
Owlcotes Ctr. Pudsey 57 D1
Owlcotes Dr. Pudsey LS28 .... 76 C8
Owlcotes Garth. Pudsey LS28 . 76 B8
Owlcotes Gdns. Pudsey LS28 .. 76 C8
Owlcotes La. Pudsey LS28 .... 57 C1
Owlcotes La. Pudsey LS28 .... 76 C8
Owlcotes Rd. Pudsey LS28 ...... 76 B8
Owlcotes Terr. Pudsey LS28 .... 76 C8
Owler Bars Rd. Mel HD7 .... 170 C2
Owler Ings Rd. Brig HD6 .... 115 A2
Owler La. Batley WF17 .... 96 F3
Owler Park Rd. Ilkley LS29 .... 7 F6
Owler's La. Bad WF9 .... 164 F4
Owlers Cl. Hud HD2 .... 136 F5
Owlet Grange. Ship BD18 .... 55 C6
Owlet Hurst La. Liver WF15 ... 117 B2
Owlet Rd. Ship BD18 .... 55 C7
Owlett Mead Cl. E Ard WF3 ...... 99 E1
Owlett Mead. E Ard WF3 .... 99 E1
Ox Heys Meadow. Thorn BD13 73 A6
Ox Lee La. Holmfi HD7 .... 199 E8
Oxenhope CE Aided Fst Sch. Oxen 51 C3
Oxenhope Sta. Oxen 51 C3
Oxfield Ct. Hud HD5 .... 155 A7
Oxford Ave. Guise LS20 .... 22 D1
Oxford Cl. Clec BD19 .... 117 B8
Oxford Cl. Queen BD13 .... 92 C8
Oxford Court Gdns. Castle WF10 .... 124 C7
Oxford Cres. Brad BD14 .... 73 B4
Oxford Cres. Hali HX3 .... 113 D4
Oxford Dr. Clec BD19 .... 117 B8
Oxford Dr. Kippax LS25 .... 83 A2
Oxford La. Hali HX3 .... 113 D3
Oxford Pl. Bail BD17 .... 38 E2
Oxford Pl. Brad BD3 .... 74 F8
Oxford Pl. Hud HD1 .... 153 E3
Oxford Pl. Leeds LS1 .... 79 B8
Oxford Pl. Pudsey LS28 .... 57 E1
Oxford Rd. Batley WF17 .... 96 E1
Oxford Rd. Brad BD2 .... 56 B2
Oxford Rd. Clec BD19 .... 96 B2
Oxford Rd. Dew WF13 .... 118 B1
Oxford Rd. Guise LS20 .... 22 E1
Oxford Rd. Hali HX1 .... 113 C6
Oxford Rd. Leeds LS7 .... 60 C3
Oxford Rd. Queen BD13 .... 92 C8 6
Oxford Rd. Wake WF1 .... 142 B8
Oxford Row. Leeds LS1 .... 79 B8
Oxford St. Batley WF16 .... 117 D4
Oxford St. Batley WF17 .... 118 B4
Oxford St. Brad BD14 .... 73 B4
Oxford St. E Ard WF3 .... 120 E8
Oxford St. Feath WF7 .... 145 C5
Oxford St. Guise LS20 .... 22 E1
Oxford St. Hali HX6 .... 112 D4
Oxford St. Heb Br HX7 .... 88 F3
Oxford St. Hud HD1 .... 154 B7
Oxford St. Keigh BD21 .... 35 A6
Oxford St. Morley LS27 .... 97 F2
Oxford St. Nor WF6 .... 123 C3
Oxford St. S Elm WF9 .... 182 F2
Oxford St. Tod OL14 .... 108 B5
Oxford St. Wake WF1 .... 142 E3
Oxford Terr. Bail BD17 .... 38 E2
Oxford Terr. Batley WF17 .... 118 D4
Oxford Wlk. Clec BD19 .... 117 B8
Oxley Gdns. Brad BD12 .... 94 C7
Oxley Hall. Leeds 59 C8
Oxley Rd. Hud HD2 .... 136 C4
Oxley St. Brad BD8 .... 74 C8
Oxley St. Leeds LS9 .... 79 F7
Oxleys Sq. Hud HD3 .... 134 D1
Oxton Cl. Leeds LS9 .... 79 F8
Oxton Gdns. Leeds LS9 .... 79 F8
Oxton Mount. Leeds LS9 .... 79 F8
Oxton Pl. Leeds LS9 .... 79 F8
Oxton Way. Leeds LS9 .... 79 F8
Oyster Cl. Morley LS27 .... 98 C3

Pacaholme Rd. Wake WF2 ..... 141 D8
Pack Fold. Slai HD7 .... 170 C8
Pack Horse Cl. Clay W HD8 .... 176 A4
Pack Horse Ctr. Hud HD1 ...... 154 B6 5
Pad Cote La. Cowl BD22 .... 32 A8
Padan St. Hali HX3 .... 113 D4
Paddock Cl. Birk BD11 .... 96 E5
Paddock Cl. Brad BD12 .... 94 C1
Paddock Cl. Gar LS25 .... 83 A6
Paddock Cl. Mapp S75 .... 178 C1
Paddock Cty Jun Sch. Hud 153 D5
Paddock Dr. Birk BD11 .... 96 E5
Paddock Foot. Hud HD1 .... 153 E5
Paddock Gn. E Kes LS17 .... 28 C5
Paddock House La. Sickl LS22 . 12 B3
Paddock La. Hali HX2 .... 112 C8
Paddock Rd. Kirkb HD8 .... 174 A7
Paddock Rd. Mapp S75 .... 178 C1
Paddock Rd. Northo HD8, S75 . 92 E5
Paddock. Ship BD9 .... 55 B4
Paddock The. B Sal LS25 .... 105 E3
Paddock The. Bail BD17 .... 38 F4
Paddock The. Brig BD19 .... 115 F8 12
Paddock The. Castle WF10 ..... 125 C6
Paddock The. Cull BD13 .... 52 D6
Paddock The. Dew WF12 .... 139 F6
Paddock The. E Kes LS17 .... 28 C5
Paddock The. Kirkhe HD5 .... 155 C7
Paddock The. Knot WF11 .... 126 F3
Paddock The. Leeds LS6 .... 59 F7
Paddock The. Nor WF6 .... 123 B1
Paddock The. Roth LS26 .... 100 E5
Paddock The. Sil BD20 .... 5 E1
Paddock The. Thorner LS14 ...... 45 F5
Paddock The. Wool WF4 .... 178 A7
Paddock View. Castle WF10 ... 125 B6
Paddy Bridge Rd. Heb Br HX7 . 89 D1
Padgum. Bail BD17 .... 38 C4 12
Padma Cl. Brad BD7 .... 74 B7
Padmans La. B Spa LS23 .... 30 D8
Padstow Ave. Midd LS10 .... 99 A5
Padstow Gdns. Midd LS10 .... 99 A5
Padstow Pl. Midd LS10 .... 99 A4
Page Hill. Hali HX2 .... 91 E2
Page St. Hud HD1 .... 154 B5
Paget Cres. Hud HD2 .... 135 D1
Paget St. Keigh BD21 .... 35 A7
Painthorpe House Country Club. Crig 159 E4
Painthorpe La. Crig WF4 .... 159 E4
Painthorpe Terr. Crig WF4 ..... 159 E4
Paisley Gr. Leeds LS12 .... 78 B8
Paisley Pl. Leeds LS12 .... 78 B8 4
Paisley Rd. Leeds LS12 .... 78 A8
Paisley St. Leeds LS12 .... 78 B8 3
Paisley Terr. Leeds LS12 .... 78 B8 5
Paisley View. Leeds LS12 .... 78 A8 13
Pakington St. Brad BD5 .... 74 D4
Palace House Rd. Heb Br HX7 . 89 A2
Paleside La. Ossett WF5 .... 140 D7
Palesides Ave. Ossett WF5 ... 140 D8
Palestine Rd. Heb Br HX7 .... 89 A4 4
Paley Rd. Brad BD4 .... 75 A4
Paley Terr. Brad BD4 .... 75 A4
Palin Ave. Brad BD3 .... 56 D1
Palm St. Hali HX3 .... 92 B2
Palm St. Hud HD4 .... 154 B4
Palma St. Tod OL14 .... 86 B1
Palmer Rd. Brad BD3 .... 75 B8
Palmer's Ave. S Elm WF9 .... 183 B2
Palmerston St. Brad BD2 .... 56 B2
Pangbourne Rd. Dearne S63 . 194 C1
Pannal Ave. Wake WF1 .... 142 E8
Pannal St. Brad BD7 .... 74 A3
Panorama Dr. Ilkley LS29 .... 7 E3
Papyrus Villas. Tad LS24 .... 31 C6
Parade The. Batley WF17 .... 118 A4
Parade The. Brad BD4 .... 75 E3
Parade The. Leeds LS9 .... 79 E7
Parade The. Otley LS21 .... 10 E1
Parade The. Ship BD16 .... 54 A7 2
Parade The. Yeadon LS19 .... 39 F6
Paradise Fields. Pont WF8 ..... 125 D1
Paradise La. Hali HX2 .... 112 B6
Paradise La. Stut LS24 .... 48 B5
Paradise Pl. Hors LS18 .... 58 E8 3
Paradise Rd. Brad BD9 .... 54 F4
Paradise St. Brad BD1 .... 74 D7
Paradise St. Hali HX1 .... 113 B6
Paradise St. Pudsey LS28 .... 57 D3
Paris Rd. Holmfi HD7 .... 189 D4
Parish Ghyll Dr. Ilkley LS29 .... 7 F3
Parish Ghyll La. Ilkley LS29 .... 7 F3
Parish Ghyll Rd. Ilkley LS29 .... 8 A3
Parish Ghyll Wlk. Ilkley LS29 ...... 8 A3
Park Ave. Bing BD16 .... 36 F2
Park Ave. Birk BD11 .... 96 E6
Park Ave. Brad BD10 .... 39 B2
Park Ave. Bri S72 .... 181 B3
Park Ave. Castle WF10 .... 124 F7
Park Ave. Clay W HD8 .... 175 F3
Park Ave. Crof WF1 .... 143 D7
Park Ave. Dar WF8 .... 147 C5
Park Ave. Dew WF13 .... 139 B7
Park Ave. Elland HX5 .... 134 E6
Park Ave. Haw BD22 .... 34 D2
Park Ave. Hud HD1 .... 153 F6
Park Ave. Keigh BD21 .... 35 B6
Park Ave. Kippax LS25 .... 83 C1
Park Ave. Kippax WF10 .... 103 C4
Park Ave. Leeds LS8 .... 61 C7
Park Ave. Leeds LS15 .... 62 D2
Park Ave. Leeds LS12 .... 78 B8
Park Ave. Liver WF15 .... 117 A2
Park Ave. Loft G WF1 .... 121 A4
Park Ave. Loft G WF3 .... 121 C6
Park Ave. Mir WF14 .... 138 B4
Park Ave. Morley LS27 .... 97 F3
Park Ave. Nor WF6 .... 123 B2
Park Ave. Pont WF8 .... 146 B8
Park Ave. Pudsey LS28 .... 76 E7
Park Ave. Roy S71 .... 179 D3
Park Ave. S in Cra BD20 .... 16 D5
Park Ave. S Kirk WF9 .... 182 B2
Park Ave. Shep HD8 .... 173 F3
Park Ave. Ship BD18 .... 55 A8
Park Ave. Swil LS26 .... 82 A1
Park Ave. Wake WF2 .... 142 B4
Park Ave. Yeadon LS19 .... 40 A7
Park Ave. Yeadon LS19 .... 40 C4
Park Cl. Batley WF17 .... 118 B3
Park Cl. Bing BD16 .... 37 A4
Park Cl. Birk BD11 .... 96 E6
Park Cl. Brad BD10 .... 56 C5
Park Cl. Brig HX3 .... 114 E7
Park Cl. Dar WF8 .... 147 C5
Park Cl. Hali HX2 .... 91 B2
Park Cl. Keigh BD21 .... 35 C5
Park Cl. Leeds LS13 .... 58 C3
Park Cl. Nor WF6 .... 123 A1
Park Cl. Queen BD13 .... 72 D1
Park Cl. Shep HD8 .... 173 F3
Park Cliffe Rd. Brad BD2 .... 56 B2
Park Copse. Hors LS18 .... 41 A1
Park Cotts. Leeds LS8 .... 44 B1
Park Cres. Add LS29 .... 7 A8
Park Cres. Brad BD3 .... 56 A2
Park Cres. Castle WF10 .... 125 C7
Park Cres. Gild LS27 .... 97 D6
Park Cres. Guise LS20 .... 39 C7
Park Cres. Hali HX3 .... 92 A1
Park Cres. Leeds LS8 .... 44 B1
Park Cres. Leeds LS12 .... 78 B8 11
Park Cres. Roth LS26 .... 101 A6
Park Cres. Roy S71 .... 179 D3
Park Croft. Batley WF17 .... 118 B4
Park Croft. Dew WF13 .... 139 A8
Park Cross St. Leeds LS1 .... 79 B8
Park Ct. Brad BD9 .... 55 C2
Park Ct. Ossett WF5 .... 140 F4
Park Ct. Pool LS21 .... 24 D6
Park Dale. Castle WF10 .... 104 C1
Park Dale. Men LS29 .... 22 A4
Park Dr. Batley WF17 .... 118 A7
Park Dr. Bing BD16 .... 37 B5
Park Dr. Hors LS18 .... 58 A8
Park Dr. Hud HD1 .... 153 E7
Park Dr. Loft G WF3 .... 121 C7
Park Dr. Mir WF14 .... 138 B5
Park Dr S. Hud HD1 .... 153 F6
Park Dr. S in Cra BD20 .... 16 D5
Park Dr. Shep HD8 .... 173 F3
Park Dr. Ship BD9 .... 55 B4
Park Drive Rd. Keigh BD21 .... 35 C5
Park Edge Cl. Leeds LS8 .... 61 C7
Park Est. S Kirk WF9 .... 182 C2
Park Farm Ind Est. Leeds 99 B8
Park Field. Men LS29 .... 22 A4
Park Fields. Hali HX2 .... 91 B2
Park Gate. Brad BD1 .... 74 F7
Park Gate Cl. Hors LS18 .... 58 B8
Park Gate Cres. Guise LS20 .... 39 D8
Park Gate. Hud HD8 .... 171 F8
Park Gate Rd. Mars HD7 .... 169 B6
Park Gdns. Hali HX2 .... 112 D5
Park Gdns. Ossett WF5 .... 140 F4

Park Gn. Nor WF6 123 A1
Park Gn. Sil BD20 5 C2
Park Gr. Gild LS27 97 D6
Park Gr. Hor WF4 140 F2
Park Gr. Hors LS18 57 F8
Park Gr. Hud HD1 153 F6
Park Gr. Keigh BD21 35 C8
Park Gr. Mir WF14 138 C4
Park Gr. Queen BD13 72 D1 9
Park Gr. Ship BD18 54 F8
Park Gr. Ship BD9 55 C4
Park Gr. Swil LS26 102 B8
Park Gr. Yeadon LS19 40 A7
Park Grove Ct. Ship BD9 55 C4
Park Grove Rd. Wake WF2 142 A5
Park Head La. D Dale HD8 190 F5
Park Head La. Holmfi HD7 188 E4
Park Hill Cl. Brad BD8 54 D1
Park Hill Dr. Brad BD8 54 D1
Park Hill Gr. Wake WF1 142 F6
Park Hill. Hud HD2 136 F6
Park Hill. Kex S75 177 B2
Park Hill La. Wake WF1 142 E6
Park House Cl. Brad BD12 94 E7
Park House Cres. Brad BD12 94 E7
Park House Dr. Dew WF12 139 D4
Park House Gr. Brad BD12 94 E7
Park House Rd. Brad BD12 94 E6
Park House. Stee BD20 17 C6
Park House Wlk. Brad BD12 94 E7
Park La. Bail BD17 38 F4
Park La. Brad BD14 73 B4
Park La. Brad BD5 74 D4
Park La. D Dale HD8 191 B5
Park La. Elland HX4 133 F1
Park La. Emley HD8 175 A5
Park La. Guise LS20 39 C7
Park La. Hali HX3 113 E2
Park La. Heb Br HX7 110 C8
Park La. Hud HD7 152 D4
Park La. Hud HD4, HD7 172 A7
Park La. Keigh BD21 35 C5
Park La. Kippax WF10 103 C5
Park La. Kippax LS25 103 C8
Park La. Ledsh LS25 104 C8
Park La. Leeds LS8 44 B2
Park La. Leeds LS3 79 A8
Park La. M'town LS26 102 A1
Park La. Mel HD7 170 E2
Park La. Pont WF7, WF8 124 E1
Park La. Queen BD13 72 F1
Park La. Roth LS26 101 A6
Park La. S in Cra BD20 16 D5
Park La. Sickl LS22 12 B5
Park La. W Bret WF4 176 F7
Park Lane Coll of F Ed. Leeds 79 A8
Park Lane Mews. Leeds LS17 44 B4
Park Lea. Hud HD2 136 F6
Park Lodge Cres. Wake WF1 142 E6
Park Lodge Gr. Wake WF1 142 D6
Park Lodge La. Wake WF1 142 F6
Park Mead. Brad BD10 39 B2
Park Mews. Pool LS21 24 D6
Park Mid Sch. Castle 124 E7
Park Mill La. Wake WF5 141 B8
Park Mill Way. Clay W HD8 175 F3
Park Mount Ave. Bail BD17 38 E3
Park Mount. Leeds LS5 59 B4
Park Mount. Leeds LS12 78 A8
Park Mount. Pool LS21 24 B5
Park Mount Terr. Leeds LS5 59 A4
Park Nook. Hali HX3 113 F2
Park Par. Dew WF13 139 B7
Park Par. Morley LS27 97 F3
Park Pl. Brad BD10 39 B2
Park Pl E. Brig HX3 114 E7
Park Pl. Hali HX1 113 A6
Park Pl. Leeds LS1 79 B8
Park Pl. Pont WF8 146 B8
Park Pl W. Brig HX3 114 E7
Park Rd. B Spa LS23 30 C8
Park Rd. Batley WF16 117 D4 3
Park Rd. Batley WF17 118 D5
Park Rd. Bing BD16 37 A4
Park Rd. Brad BD10 39 B2
Park Rd. Brad BD10 56 E6
Park Rd. Brad BD5 74 E5
Park Rd. Brad BD6 94 C7
Park Rd. Bri S72 181 B3
Park Rd. Castle WF10 125 A5
Park Rd. Clay W HD8 175 F3
Park Rd. Dew WF13 118 B1
Park Rd. Dew WF13 138 F6
Park Rd. Dew WF12 139 C6
Park Rd. Dew WF12 139 F7
Park Rd. Glu BD20 16 C6
Park Rd. Guise LS20 39 D8
Park Rd. Hali HX6 112 D5
Park Rd. Hali HX1 113 B6
Park Rd. Hud HD4 153 B4
Park Rd. Hud HD4 153 E4
Park Rd. Leeds LS13 58 C3
Park Rd. Leeds LS12 78 A8
Park Rd. Leeds LS15 81 D6
Park Rd. Men LS29 22 A4
Park Rd. Pont WF8 125 B2
Park Rd. Ship BD18 55 C7
Park Rd. Tod OL14 108 B6
Park Rd W. Hud HD4 153 D4
Park Rd. Yeadon LS19 40 A7
Park Rd. Yeadon LS19 40 B4
Park Rise. Castle WF10 124 F7
Park Rise. Leeds LS13 58 C4
Park Road Jun, Mid & Inf Sch. Batley 118 D5
Park Row. Brig HD6 115 B2 6
Park Row. Bur in W LS29 9 F2
Park Row. Leeds LS1 79 B8
Park Row. Otley LS21 23 B8
Park Row. Pudsey LS28 57 E1
Park Row. S in Cra BD20 16 D4
Park Side. Clec BD19 117 A7
Park Side. Floc WF4 157 C3
Park Side. Holmfi HD7 189 E4
Park Side. Hors LS18 58 A8
Park Side. Kirkhe HD5 137 C1
Park Special Sch The. Wake 142 B5
Park Spring Gdns. Pudsey LS13 58 B1
Park Spring Prim Sch. Pudsey 77 B8
Park Spring Rise. Pudsey LS13 58 B1
Park Sq. Brad BD6 94 A8 1
Park Sq E. Leeds LS1 79 B8
Park Sq. Loft G WF3 121 C6
Park Sq N. Leeds LS1 79 B8
Park Sq. Northo HX3 93 A2
Park Sq. Ossett WF5 140 F4
Park Sq. Pool LS21 24 D6
Park Sq S. Leeds LS1 79 B8
Park Sq W. Leeds LS1 79 B8
Park St. Batley WF17 117 D4
Park St. Batley WF17 117 E8
Park St. Brig HD6 115 B2
Park St. Clec BD19 116 B6
Park St. Clec BD19 117 C8
Park St. Dew WF13 118 D1
Park St. Glu BD20 16 D6
Park St. Hali HX6 112 D4
Park St. Haw BD22 51 D7
Park St. Hor WF4 141 A1
Park St. Leeds LS12 78 A8
Park St. Leeds LS1 79 B8
Park St. Leeds LS15 81 B8
Park St. Morley LS27 98 C8
Park St. Ossett WF5 140 F4
Park St. Ship BD18 55 A8
Park St. Slai HD7 152 C6
Park St. Wake WF1 142 D5
Park St. Yeadon LS19 40 A7
Park Stone Rise. Shelf HX3 93 B5
Park Terr. Brig HX3 114 D7
Park Terr. Hali HX1 113 A6
Park Terr. Keigh BD21 35 D7
Park Terr. Keigh BD21 35 F6
Park Terr. Leeds LS6 59 D6
Park Terr. Otley LS21 23 B8
Park Terr. Pool LS21 24 A5
Park Terr. S Elm WF9 183 A2
Park Terr. Ship BD18 55 A8
Park The. Caw S75 193 E4
Park Top Cotts. Bing BD16 37 B5
Park Top. Pudsey LS28 57 E1
Park Top Rd. Haw BD22 51 A5
Park Towngate The. Hali HX3 114 A4
Park View Ave. Haw BD22 51 E8 13
Park View Ave. Leeds LS4 59 D3
Park View Ave. Northo HX3 93 A1
Park View Ave. Yeadon LS19 40 C4
Park View. Bri S72 181 B3
Park View. Castle WF10 125 B6
Park View. Clec BD19 116 C7
Park View Cres. Leeds LS8 44 B2
Park View. Elland HX4 134 A1
Park View Gr. Leeds LS4 59 D3
Park View. Hali HX1 113 A6
Park View. Hem WF9 163 B1
Park View. Holmfi HD7 189 A5
Park View. Kippax LS25 83 B1 6
Park View. Leeds LS13 58 C3
Park View. Leeds LS11 79 A3
Park View. Loft G WF3 121 C6
Park View. Mars HD7 169 A4
Park View. Mir WF14 138 C4
Park View. Pudsey LS28 76 E7
Park View Rd. Brad BD9 55 B3
Park View Rd. Leeds LS4 59 D2
Park View Rd. Mapp S75 178 D1
Park View. Roy S71 179 D3
Park View. Shaf S72 180 D2
Park View. Swil LS26 82 A1
Park View Terr. Brad BD9 55 B3
Park View Terr. Leeds LS15 81 A8 8
Park View Terr. Yeadon LS19 40 B4
Park View. Wake WF2 141 E6
Park View. Yeadon LS19 39 F7
Park Villa Ct. Leeds LS8 44 A1
Park Villas Dr. Pont WF8 125 B1
Park Villas. Leeds LS8 44 A1
Park W. Roth LS26 100 F5
Park Way. Bail BD17 37 F1
Park Way. Men LS29 22 A4
Park Way. Pool LS21 24 D7
Park Wood Ave. Leeds LS11 98 F8
Park Wood Cres. Leeds LS11 98 F7
Park Wood Dr. Leeds LS11 98 F8
Park Wood Rd. Leeds LS11 98 F8
Parkcroft. Pudsey LS28 57 D2
Parkdale Dr. Rip HX6 132 E7
Parker Ave. Nor WF6 122 E4
Parker La. Mir WF14 138 B5
Parker Rd. Dew WF12 139 C4
Parker Rd. Hor WF4 141 C1
Parker St. Batley WF16 117 D4
Parker St. E Ard WF3 120 C7
Parker St. Glu BD20 16 D7
Parker's La. Keigh BD20 18 A3
Parkfield Ave. Elland HX5 134 F6 14
Parkfield Ave. Leeds LS11 79 A3
Parkfield Ave. Mir WF14 138 C4
Parkfield Cl. Kippax LS25 83 B2
Parkfield Cl. Pudsey LS28 76 E7 3
Parkfield Cres. Mir WF14 138 C4
Parkfield Croft. Mir WF14 138 C4
Parkfield Ct. Leeds LS14 61 E3
Parkfield Dr. B Spa LS23 30 C8
Parkfield Dr. Ossett WF5 141 A5
Parkfield Dr. Queen BD13 72 D1 3
Parkfield Dr. Sow Br HX6 112 A2
Parkfield Gr. Leeds LS11 79 A3
Parkfield La. Feath WF7 124 C2
Parkfield La. Sow Br HX6 112 D3
Parkfield Mount. Leeds LS11 79 A3
Parkfield Mount. Pudsey LS28 76 E7
Parkfield Pl. Leeds LS11 79 A3
Parkfield Rd. Brad BD8 55 D2
Parkfield Rd. Leeds LS11 79 A3 4
Parkfield Rd. Ship BD18 54 E8
Parkfield Row. Leeds LS11 79 A3
Parkfield St. Leeds LS11 79 C5
Parkfield Terr. Pudsey LS28 57 E1
Parkfield Terr. Pudsey LS28 76 E7
Parkfield View. Leeds LS11 79 A3
Parkfield View. Ossett WF5 141 A5
Parkfield Way. Leeds LS14 61 E3
Parkfield Way. Mir WF14 138 B4
Parkgate Ave. Wake WF1 142 E6
Parkgate. Kirk S WF9 182 B1
Parkhead Cl. Roy S71 179 A4
Parkhill Cres. Wake WF1 142 F6
Parkin Hall La. Sow Br HX6 111 B1
Parkin La. Brad BD10 56 F8
Parkin La. Tod OL14 107 E5
Parkin Sq. Slai HD7 152 B5
Parkin St. Clec WF15 116 C5
Parkin's Almsho's. Hud HD5 154 F3 2
Parkinson App. Gar LS25 82 F8
Parkinson Cl. Wake WF1 142 E6
Parkinson La. Hali HX1 112 F6
Parkinson Lane Jun & Inf Sch. Hali 113 A6
Parkinson Rd. Denh BD13 71 E8
Parkinson St. Brad BD5 74 D4
Parkland Ave. Morley LS27 97 E3
Parkland Cres. Leeds LS6 43 A1
Parkland Dr. Brad BD10 56 C7
Parkland Dr. Leeds LS6 43 A1
Parkland Gdns. Leeds LS6 60 A8
Parkland Mid & Fst Schs. Brad 56 D7
Parkland Terr. Leeds LS6 60 A8
Parklands. Bing BD16 37 B5
Parklands. Bramho LS16 24 D3
Parklands. Castle WF10 124 E7
Parklands Cty Prim Sch. Leeds 62 A3
Parklands Cres. Bramho LS16 24 E3
Parklands Cres. Hor WF4 140 E1
Parklands Dr. Hor WF4 140 E1
Parklands Dr. Sow Br HX6 111 E1
Parklands Gate. Bramho LS16 24 E3
Parklands High Sch. Leeds 62 B4
Parklands. Ilkley LS29 8 D4
Parklands. Ossett WF5 140 F4
Parklands Wlk. Shep HD8 173 F3
Parkside Ave. Leeds LS6 59 F7
Parkside Ave. Queen BD13 72 D1
Parkside. Bing BD16 37 B4
Parkside Cl. Leeds LS6 59 F8
Parkside Cl. Tod OL14 86 B1
Parkside. Clec BD19 116 E7
Parkside Cres. Leeds LS6 59 F8
Parkside Ct. Haw BD22 51 E8
Parkside Gdns. Leeds LS6 59 F7
Parkside Gn. Leeds LS6 59 F7
Parkside Gr. Brad BD9 55 A3
Parkside Gr. Leeds LS11 79 A1
Parkside. Hali HX3 113 B4 10
Parkside Ind Est. Leeds 79 C2
Parkside La. Leeds LS11 79 C2
Parkside La. Loft G WF3 121 E2
Parkside Lawns. Leeds LS6 59 F7
Parkside Mount. Leeds LS11 79 A1
Parkside Par. Leeds LS11 79 A1
Parkside Pl. Leeds LS6 59 F8
Parkside Rd. Brad BD5 74 E2
Parkside Rd. Leeds LS16, LS6 59 E8
Parkside Rd. Pudsey LS28 57 D2
Parkside Rd. Tod OL14 86 B1
Parkside Terr. Cull BD13 52 E6
Parkside View. Leeds LS6 59 F8
Parkside Wlk. Pudsey LS28 57 E2
Parkstone Ave. Hors LS16 42 A1
Parkstone Dr. Brad BD10 56 C5
Parkstone Gn. Hors LS16 42 A1
Parkstone Gr. Hors LS16 42 A1
Parkstone. Hud HD2 136 F6
Parkstone Mount. Hors LS16 42 A1
Parkstone Pl. Hors LS16 42 A1
Parkview Ct. Leeds LS8 44 B2
Parkview Ct. Ship BD18 55 A7
Parkville Pl. Leeds LS13 58 C3
Parkville Rd. Leeds LS13 58 C3
Parkway. Brad BD5 74 F2
Parkway Cl. Leeds LS14 61 E4
Parkway. Crof WF4 143 F2
Parkway Ct. Leeds LS14 61 E3
Parkway. Gild LS27 97 D6
Parkway Grange. Leeds LS14 61 E3
Parkway. Keigh BD21 35 C5
Parkway Mews. Leeds LS14 62 B5
Parkway. Queen BD13 72 D1
Parkway. Stee BD20 17 B5
Parkway Towers. Leeds LS14 61 E4
Parkway Vale. Leeds LS14 61 F4
Parkway Vale. Leeds LS14 62 A4
Parkways Ave. Roth LS26 101 B5
Parkways Cl. Roth LS26 101 B6
Parkways Ct. Roth LS26 101 B6
Parkways Dr. Roth LS26 101 B6
Parkways Garth. Roth LS26 101 B5
Parkways Gr. Roth LS26 101 B6
Parkways. Roth LS26 101 B6
Parkwood Ave. Leeds LS8 61 A7
Parkwood Cl. Shep HD8 173 F3
Parkwood Fst Sch. Keigh 35 D6
Parkwood Gdns. Pudsey LS28 57 A6
Parkwood Rd. Hud HD3, HD7 152 E6
Parkwood Rd. Pudsey LS28 57 B6
Parkwood Rd. Ship BD18 54 F7
Parkwood Rise. Keigh BD21 35 C6
Parkwood St. Keigh BD21 35 D7
Parkwood Way. Leeds LS8 61 A7
Parliament Pl. Leeds LS12 78 D7
Parliament Rd. Leeds LS12 78 D7
Parliament St. Wake WF2 142 B6
Parlington Ct. B in Elm LS15 63 E7
Parlington Dr. Aber LS25 64 E7
Parlington House. Aber LS25 64 D7
Parlington La. Aber LS25 64 C4
Parlington Meadow. B in Elm LS15 63 E6
Parma St. Brad BD5 74 E4
Parnaby Ave. Midd LS10 79 F1
Parnaby Rd. Midd LS10 79 F1
Parnaby St. Midd LS10 79 F1
Parnaby Terr. Midd LS10 79 F1
Parratt Row. Brad BD3 75 D7
Parrock La. Wad M HX7 89 B6
Parrott St. Brad BD4 75 D1
Parry La. Brad BD4 75 C5
Parson La. Wool WF4 178 A8
Parson St. Keigh BD21 35 D8
Parson's La. Sil LS29 6 C8
Parsonage La. Brig HD6 115 A2
Parsonage Rd. Brad BD5 74 E3
Parsonage Rd. Brad BD4 75 D5
Parsonage Rd. M'town LS26 102 D3
Parsonage St. Hali S6 92 D1
Parsons Gn. Weth LS22 13 F5
Parsons Rd. Ship BD9 55 A4
Partons Pl. Loft G WF3 121 C6
Partridge Cl. Morley LS27 98 D4 5
Partridge Cres. Dew WF12 139 F1
Pasture Ave. Leeds LS7 60 D7
Pasture Cl. Brad BD14 73 E4
Pasture Cres. Leeds LS7 60 D7
Pasture Gr. Leeds LS7 60 D7
Pasture La. Brad BD14, BD7 73 D4
Pasture La. Leeds LS7 60 D7
Pasture Mount. Leeds LS12 78 B8
Pasture Par. Leeds LS7 60 D7
Pasture Pl. Leeds LS7 60 D7
Pasture Rd. Bail BD17 38 D2
Pasture Rd. Leeds LS8 60 F4
Pasture Rise. Brad BD14 73 D4
Pasture Side Ter E. Brad BD14 73 D4
Pasture Side Ter W. Brad BD14 73 C4 4
Pasture St. Leeds LS7 60 D7
Pasture Terr. Leeds LS7 60 D7
Pasture View. Leeds LS12 78 B8
Pasture View Rd. Roth LS26 100 E5
Pasture Wlk. Brad BD14 73 C4
Pastures Way. Hud HD7 152 D5
Pateley Cres. Hud HD2 136 A2
Patent St. Brad BD9 55 B2
Paternoster La. Brad BD7 74 A4 10
Paterson Ave. Wake WF2 142 A6
Patience La. Nor WF6 122 F3
Patterdale App. Weth LS22 13 B5
Patterdale Dr. Hud HD5 154 D6
Patterdale Rd. Batley WF12 118 E2
Patterson Ct. Wake WF2 120 F3
Pattie St. Keigh BD20 18 B1
Paul La. Kirkhe HD5 137 C4
Paul La. Lepton HD8 156 C2
Paul Row. Litt OL15 129 D1
Pauline Terr. Castle WF10 124 C7
Pavement La. Hali HX2 91 E8
Pavilion Cl. Bri S72 181 A3
Paw La. Queen BD13 92 F7
Pawson St. Brad BD4 75 D6
Pawson St. E Ard WF3 120 E8
Pawson St. Morley LS27 97 F3
Pawson St. Roth WF3 100 B2
Peabody St. Hali HX3 92 A1 6
Peace Hall Dr. Lepton HD8 155 C5
Peace St. Brad BD4 75 C5
Peach Tree Cl. Pont WF8 146 B6
Peach Wlk. Brad BD4 75 B4
Peacock Ave. Wake WF2 141 F7
Peacock Cl. Wake WF2 141 F7
Peacock Gn. Morley LS27 98 D3
Peacock Gr. Wake WF2 141 F7
Peak View. Batley WF13 117 F2
Pear Pl. Tod OL14 86 B1 3
Pear St. Hali HX1 112 F6
Pear St. Hud HD4 153 E4
Pear St. Keigh BD21 35 A3
Pear St. Oxen BD22 51 C2
Pear St. Tod OL14 86 B1 4
Pear Tree Acre. Th Arch LS23 14 E1
Pear Tree Cl. Pont WF8 146 B6
Pear Tree La. Hem WF9 181 D7
Pearl St. Batley WF17 118 A6
Pearl St.Keigh BD22 35 A4 12
Pearson Ave. Leeds LS6 59 E3 15
Pearson Fold. Brad BD12 94 F4
Pearson Gr. Leeds LS6 59 E3
Pearson La. Brad BD9 54 D1
Pearson Rd. Brad BD6, DN35 94 D8 11
Pearson Rd W. Brad BD6 94 D8 4
Pearson Row. Brad BD12 94 D3 3
Pearson St. Brad BD3 75 C6
Pearson St. Clec BD19 116 A6
Pearson St. Clec BD19 116 E6
Pearson St. Leeds LS10 79 D5
Pearson St. Nor WF6 123 A5
Pearson St. Pudsey LS28 57 B7
Pearson Terr. Leeds LS6 59 E3 14
Pearson's La. Dew WF12 156 F7
Pearsons Bldgs. Otley LS21 23 B7
Peartree F'ld La. Th Aud WF8 165 D5
Peas Acre. Bing BD16 36 E8
Peasborough View. Bur in W LS29 21 F8
Pease Cl. Pont WF8 146 D6
Peasehill Cl. Yeadon LS19 40 C4
Peasehill Pk. Yeadon LS19 40 C4
Peaseland Ave. Clec BD19 116 C7
Peaseland Cl. Clec BD19 116 D7
Peaseland Rd. Clec BD19 116 D7
Peaselands. Ship BD18 55 A7
Peat Ponds. Hud HD3 134 E1
Peckett Cl. Hud HD3 153 C7
Peckfield Bar. Gar LS25 83 D4
Peckover Dr. Pudsey LS28 76 A8
Peckover St. Brad BD1 74 F7
Peebles Cl. Hud HD3 135 B1
Peel Ave. Batley WF17 118 C5
Peel Cl. Brad BD4 75 E6
Peel Cl. Hor WF4 141 B1
Peel Cottage Rd. Tod OL14 108 A1
Peel Cottage St. Tod OL14 108 A1 5
Peel Ct. Brad BD2 56 A2
Peel Dr. Bacup OL13 106 B1
Peel House. Bing BD16 37 B2
Peel Park Dr. Brad BD2 56 B2
Peel Park Terr. Brad BD2 56 B2
Peel Park View. Brad BD3 56 A1
Peel Pk. Brad 55 F2
Peel Pl. Bur in W LS29 9 E2
Peel Row. Brad BD7 74 A4
Peel St. Bing BD16 37 B3
Peel St. Hali HX6 112 B4 8
Peel St. Hor WF4 141 B1
Peel St. Hud HD1 154 A5 5
Peel St. Liver WF16 117 C4
Peel St. Mars HD7 168 F4
Peel St. Mars HD7 169 A4
Peel St. Morley LS27 98 B4
Peel St. Queen BD13 72 F1
Peel St. Thorn BD13 72 D6
Peel St. Wils BD15 53 C4
Peel Street Prim Sch. Morley 98 B4
Peep Green Rd. Liver WF15 116 C2
Pegholme Dr. Otley LS21 22 D6
Pelham Ct. Brad BD2 56 B3
Pelham Pl. Leeds LS7 60 C7
Pelham Rd. Brad BD2 56 B3
Pell Ct. Holmfi HD7 189 C7
Pell La. Holmfi HD7 189 C7
Pellon La. Hali HX1 113 A8
Pellon New Rd. Hali HX1, HX2 112 F8
Pellon St. Tod OL14 108 A2
Pellon Terr. Brad BD10 39 B1
Pellon Wlk. Brad BD10 39 B1
Pemberton Dr. Brad BD7 74 D6
Pemberton Rd. Castle WF10 125 B8
Pembridge Ct. Roy S71 179 C4
Pembroke Cl. Morley LS27 97 F5
Pembroke Dr. Morley LS27 97 F5
Pembroke Dr. Pudsey LS28 76 E8 5
Pembroke Gdns. Leeds LS9 61 D2
Pembroke Rd. Pudsey LS28 76 E8
Pembroke Rise. Kippax LS25 83 C2
Pembroke St. Brad BD5 74 E4
Pembroke Towers. Leeds LS9 61 D3
Pembury Mount. Leeds LS15 62 F3
Penarth Ave. Upton WF9 183 A7
Penarth Rd. Leeds LS15 62 B2
Penarth Terr. Upton WF9 182 F7
Penda's Dr. Leeds LS15 62 D2
Penda's Gr. Leeds LS15 62 D3
Penda's Way. Leeds LS15 62 E3
Penda's Wlk. Leeds LS15 62 D2
Pendennis Ave. S Elm WF9 182 F4
Pendil Cl. Leeds LS15 81 C8
Pendle Ave. Bacup OL13 106 A3
Pendle Cl. Bacup OL13 106 A2
Pendle Rd. Bing BD16 37 B3
Pendragon. Brad BD2 56 A3
Pendragon La. Brad BD2 56 B3
Pendragon Terr. Guise LS20 39 D8
Penfield Gr. Brad BD14 73 C4
Penfield Rd. Birk BD11 96 F6
Pengarth. Bing BD16 37 C5
Penistone Hill C'try Pk. Oxen 51 A6
Penistone La. Holmfi HD8 190 D6
Penistone Rd. D Dale HD7, HD8 191 C3
Penistone Rd. Holmfi HD7, HD8 190 C6
Penistone Rd. Holmfi HD7 199 D7
Penistone Rd. Hud HD8 155 C3
Penistone Rd. Kirkb HD8 173 E5
Penistone Rd. Lepton HD8 155 C3
Penistone Rd. Shep HD8 173 E5
Penistone Rd. Shep HD7, HD8 190 C6
Penlands Cres. Leeds LS15 81 D7
Penlands Lawn. Leeds LS15 81 D7
Penlands Wlk. Leeds LS15 81 D7
Penlington Cl. Hem WF9 181 D5
Penn Dr. Clec WF15 116 D6
Penn Gr. Clec WF15 116 D6
Penn St. Hali HX1 113 A8
Pennine Cl. Holmfi HD7 188 D5
Pennine Cl. Queen BD13 92 D7
Pennine Cl. Wake WF2 141 E3
Pennine Cres. Hud HD3 152 E8
Pennine Dr. Clay W HD8 175 D2
Pennine Gdns. Slai HD7 152 D1
Pennine Gr. Tod OL14 108 C6
Pennine Rd. Bacup OL13 106 A2
Pennine Rd. Dew WF12 139 E8
Pennine Rise. Clay W HD8 175 D2
Pennine View. B Head HX7 87 F4
Pennine View. Batley WF17 97 A2
Pennine View. Kirkhe HD5 137 C2
Pennine View. Mapp S75 178 A2
Pennine View. Slai HD7 152 D1
Pennine View. Upton WF9 183 A8
Pennine Way. Clay W HD8 175 D2
Pennine Way. Heb Br HX7 88 D1
Pennine Way. Hem WF9 181 F7
Pennine Way. Hep HX7 88 B6
Pennington Gr. Leeds LS6 60 A4 13
Pennington La. Roth LS26 101 B2
Pennington Pl. Leeds LS6 60 A3 1
Pennington St. Leeds LS6 60 A4
Pennington Terr. Brad BD5 74 C4
Pennington Terr. Leeds LS6 60 A4 12
Pennithorne Ave. Bail BD17 38 C4
Pennwell Croft. Leeds LS14 62 D5 6
Pennwell Dean. Leeds LS14 62 D5
Pennwell Fold. Leeds LS14 62 E5
Pennwell Garth. Leeds LS14 62 D5
Pennwell Gn. Leeds LS14 62 D5
Pennwell Lawn. Leeds LS14 62 E5
Penny Hill Ctr. Leeds 79 E4
Penny Hill Dr. Brad BD14 73 D4
Penny Lane Way. Leeds LS10 79 D4
Penny Spring. Hud HD5 154 E3
Pennyfield Sch. Leeds 42 F1
Pennygate. Bail BD16 37 D6
Penraevon Ave. Leeds LS7 60 C3
Penraevon Ind Est. Leeds 60 C3
Penrith Cres. Castle WF10 104 E1
Penrith Gr. Leeds LS12 78 C6
Penrose Beck Dr. Ack M T WF7 163 F5
Penrose Pl. Northo HX3 93 A2
Penryn Ave. Kirkhe HD5 155 C8
Pentland Ave. Brad BD14 73 C4
Pentland Ave. Knot WF11 126 E4
Pentland Cty Inf Sch. Dew 139 D6
Pentland Dr. Gar LS25 82 F5
Pentland Gr. Wake WF2 141 E3
Pentland Rd. Dew WF12 139 D6
Pentland Way. Morley LS27 98 A3 1
Pepper Gdns. Leeds LS13 58 E4
Pepper Hill. Shelf HX3 93 A6
Pepper Hills. Leeds LS17 43 D4
Pepper La. Leeds LS13 58 D4
Pepper La. Leeds LS10 79 F3
Pepper Rd. Leeds LS10 79 F2
Pepper Royd St. Dew WF13 118 D1
Per La. Hali HX2 91 D8
Percival St. Brad BD3 75 A7
Percival St. Hud HD3 152 F6
Percival St. Leeds LS2 60 B1
Percival Whitley Coll. Hali 113 A6
Percival Whitley Coll of F Ed. Brig 136 A8
Percy St. Bing BD16 37 A3
Percy St. Hud HD2 136 A1
Percy St. Keigh BD21 35 C4
Percy St. Leeds LS12 78 D6
Percy St. S Kirk WF9 182 B2
Peregrine Ave. Morley LS27 98 D4
Peregrine Ct. Hud HD4 171 E7
Peridot Fold. Hud HD2 136 C2
Permain Ct. Hud HD4 154 B4
Perry Cl. Keigh BD22 35 A4
Perseverance St. Pudsey LS28 76 C7
Perseverance La. Brad BD7 74 A4 12
Perseverance Rd. Hali HX3 72 A3
Perseverance Rd. Queen BD13 72 A3
Perseverance St. Bail BD17 38 D4
Perseverance St. Brad BD12 94 C4
Perseverance St. Castle WF10 124 D8 4
Perseverance St. Hali HX6 112 B5 13
Perseverance St. Hud HD4 154 A3
Perseverance Tr. Batley WF17 118 C3
Perseverance Terr. Hali HX1 113 A5
Perseverance Terr. Roth LS26 100 E4
Perseverence St. Hud HD4 153 A3
Perth Ave. Brad BD2 55 E3
Perth Dr. E Ard WF3 119 F8
Perth Mount. Hors LS18 41 B4
Peter Hill. Batley WF17 118 D2
Peter La. Hali HX2 112 B7
Peter La. Morley LS27 98 D4
Peterborough Pl. Brad BD2 56 B3
Peterborough Rd. Brad BD2 56 B2
Peterborough Terr. Brad BD2 56 B3
Petergate. Brad BD1 74 F7
Peterhouse Dr. Otley LS21 23 C7
Petersfield Ave. Midd LS10 99 E7
Petersgarth. Ship BD18 54 E8 5
Peterson Rd. Wake WF1 142 D6
Pether Hill. Elland HX4 133 F3
Petrie Cres. Pudsey LS13 57 D5
Petrie Gr. Brad BD3 75 E7
Petrie Rd. Brad BD3 75 E7
Petrie St. Pudsey LS13 57 D5
Petworth Croft. Roy S71 179 B4
Peverell Cl. Brad BD4 75 E3
Peveril Mount. Brad BD2 56 C3
Pexwood Rd. Tod OL14 107 F3
Pheasant Dr. Batley WF17 97 A3
Pheasant St. Keigh BD21 35 D8
Phil May Ct. Leeds LS12 78 E6 1
Philip Garth. Loft G WF1 121 C5
Philip's Gr. Loft G WF3 121 C6
Philip's La. Dar WF8 147 C5
Philippa Way. Leeds LS12 78 C3
Philips Rd. Bacup OL13 106 A7
Phillips St. Castle WF10 124 B8
Phoebe La. Hali HX3 113 D4
Phoebe Lane Ind Est. Hali 113 D4
Phoenix Ave. Emley HD8 175 D6
Phoenix Ct. Tod OL14 108 D6
Phoenix Ct. Wake WF2 142 A6
Phoenix St. Brig HD6 115 B2
Phoenix St. Tod OL14 108 D6
Phoenix Way. Brad BD4 75 E6
Phoenix Works. Brad 56 E1
Piccadilly. Brad BD1 74 E7
Piccadilly. Wake WF2 142 B6
Pick Hill Rd. Mel HD7 170 D3
Pickard Ct. Leeds LS15 81 C8
Pickard La. Sil BD20 5 E2
Picker St. Tod OL14 107 E8
Pickering Ave. Gar LS25 83 B8
Pickering Dr. Ossett WF5 119 C1
Pickering La. Ossett WF5 119 C1
Pickering Mount. Leeds LS12 78 D8
Pickering St. Leeds LS12 78 D8
Pickerings The. Queen BD13 92 E8
Pickersgill St. Ossett WF5 140 C8
Pickford St. Hud HD3 153 A4
Pickle Top. Slai HD7 151 E2
Pickles Ct. Tod OL14 108 B6 13
Pickles Hill. Haw BD22 33 F1
Pickles La. Brad BD7 73 F2
Pickles La. Skel HD8 175 B1
Pickles St. Batley WF17 118 B2
Pickles St. Keigh BD21 35 B5 13
Picklesfield. Batley WF17 118 B2
Pickthall Terr. Tod OL14 108 D5
Pickwood La. Sow Br HX6 112 E2
Picton St. Brad BD8 55 D1
Pictureville. Brad BD1 74 E6
Piece Hall Yd. Brad BD1 74 E7 6
Piece Wood Rd. Hors LS16 41 D3
Pigeon Cote Cl. Leeds LS14 62 A6
Pigeon Cote Rd. Leeds LS14 62 A6
Piggott St. Brig HD6 115 A3
Pighill Top La. Slai HD7 151 F2
Pike End Rd. Rip HX6 150 C7
Pike Law La. Slai HD7 152 B5
Pike Law Rd. Slai HD7 152 B5
Pike Law. Slai HD7 152 B5
Pildacre Brow. Ossett WF5 140 C6
Pildacre Croft. Ossett WF5 140 C6
Pildacre La. Ossett WF5 140 B6
Pilden La. E Ard WF3 120 C7
Pilgrim Ave. Dew WF13 138 F7
Pilgrim Cres. Dew WF13 138 F7
Pilgrim Dr. Dew WF13 138 F7
Pilkington St. Wake WF2 142 C4
Pill White La. Lindley LS21 11 F6
Pilling La. Skel HD8 175 C2
Pilling Top La. Kirkb HD8 174 C4
Pilmer Ct. Wake WF2 141 D4
Pilot St. Leeds LS9 60 E1
Pin Hill La. Hali HX2 90 D1
Pincheon St. Wake WF1 142 D6 11
Pinder Ave. Leeds LS12 77 F4
Pinder Gr. Leeds LS12 77 F4
Pinder St. Leeds LS12 77 F4
Pinder View. Leeds LS12 77 F4
Pinder's Gr. Wake WF1 142 E8
Pinderfields General Hospl. Wake 121 D1
Pinderfields Rd. Wake WF1 142 C7
Pinders Cres. Knot WF11 126 C5
Pinders Garth. Knot WF11 126 D5
Pinders Gn. M'town LS26 123 C8
Pinders Green Ct. M'town LS26 102 C1
Pinders Green Dr. M'town LS26 102 C1
Pinders Green Fold. M'town LS26 102 C1
Pine Cl. Castle WF10 124 E6
Pine Cl. Weth LS22 13 E7
Pine Court Mews. Hud HD4 171 D6
Pine Croft. Keigh BD20 18 A1
Pine Ct. Hud HD4 171 D6
Pine Ct. Leeds LS2 79 D7
Pine Gr. Batley WF17 118 B3
Pine Rd. Tod OL14 107 F7
Pine St. Bacup OL13 106 A1 7
Pine St. Brad BD1 74 F8
Pine St. Hali HX1 113 C6 10
Pine St. Haw BD22 51 C6
Pine St. Hud HD1 154 B7
Pine St. S Elm WF9 182 E1
Pine Tree Ave. B Spa LS23 30 E8
Pine Tree Ave. Pont WF8 146 B6

Pineapple Cotts. Crof WF1 .... 143 E6
Pinedale. Bing BD16 ... 36 F5
Pinehurst Ct. Hud HD3 ... 135 B1
Pines Gdns. Ilkley LS29 ... 7 F3
Pinewood Ave. Wake WF2 ... 141 D6
Pinewood Cl. Ilkley LS29 ... 8 A3
Pinewood Gdns. Elland HX4 .. 134 B4
Pinewood Pl. Knot WF11 ... 126 E3
Pinfold Cl. Dew WF12 ... 139 E2
Pinfold Cl. Floc WF4 ... 157 C2
Pinfold Cl. Knot WF11 ... 126 C5
Pinfold Cl. Mir WF14 ... 138 B5
Pinfold Cl. Rip HX4 ... 133 A5
Pinfold Cross. K Smea WF8 ... 166 D5
Pinfold Ct. Leeds LS15 ... 81 B8
Pinfold Dr. Crof WF4 ... 144 A1
Pinfold Gr. Leeds LS15 ... 81 A8
Pinfold Gr. Wake WF2 ... 142 E1
Pinfold Hill. Dew WF13 ... 139 B7
Pinfold Hill. Leeds LS15 ... 81 B8
Pinfold La. Brig HD6 ... 135 D5
Pinfold La. Floc WF4 ... 157 C2
Pinfold La. Gar LS25 ... 82 F7
Pinfold La. Hors LS16 ... 41 F7
Pinfold La. K Smea WF8 ... 166 D5
Pinfold La. Leeds LS12 ... 78 B7
Pinfold La. Leeds LS15 ... 81 A8
Pinfold La. Lepton HD8 ... 156 A3
Pinfold La. M'town LS26 ... 102 E2
Pinfold La. Mars HD3 ... 151 C5
Pinfold La. Mir WF14 ... 138 C5
Pinfold La. Roy S71 ... 179 C2
Pinfold La. Slai HD7 ... 152 A4
Pinfold La. Sow Br HX6 ... 111 E4
Pinfold La. Wake WF2 ... 142 E1
Pinfold Mount. Leeds LS15 ... 81 B7
Pinfold Rd. Leeds LS15 ... 81 B7
Pinfold Rise. Aber LS25 ... 64 E8
Pinfold Sq. Leeds LS15 ... 81 A8
Pingle Rise. D Dale HD8 ... 192 A7
Pink St. Haw BD22 ... 51 C6
Pinnacle La. Heb Br HX7 ... 109 E8
Pinnar Croft. Hali HX3 ... 114 A4
Pinnar La. Hali HX3 ... 113 F5
Pioneer St. Dew WF12 ... 139 C4
Pioneer St. Tod OL14 ... 129 A7
Pipe and Nook La. Leeds LS12 . 77 F7
Piper Hill. Fair WF11 ... 105 A4
Piper La. Otley LS21 ... 22 F7
Piper Well La. Shep HD8 ... 190 E6
Pippins Green Av. Wake WF2 120 F4
Pirie Cl. Brad BD2 ... 55 F3
Pit Field Rd. Roth WF3 ... 100 D2
Pit La. Batley WF13 ... 117 F2
Pit La. Clec BD19 ... 96 B2
Pit La. Denh BD13 ... 52 C1
Pit La. M'Field LS25 ... 83 F5
Pit La. M'town LS26 ... 102 D4
Pit La. Queen BD13 ... 72 C4
Pit La. Thorn BD13 ... 72 C4
Pitcliffe Way. Brad BD5 ... 74 F4
Pitfall St. Leeds LS1 ... 79 C7
Pits La. Brig BD19 ... 115 F6
Pitt Hill La. Rip HX4 ... 133 D2
Pitt Row. Leeds LS1 ... 79 C7
Pitt St. Keigh BD21 ... 35 D7
Pitt St. Liver WF15 ... 117 B2
Pitt St. Tod OL14 ... 108 D5
Pitts St. Brad BD4 ... 75 D4
Place's Rd. Leeds LS9 ... 79 E7
Plaid Row. Leeds LS9 ... 79 E8
Plain La. Sow Br HX6 ... 111 C2
Plains La. Hali HX5 ... 134 F8
Plains La. Mars HD7 ... 169 A5
Plains. Mars HD7 ... 169 A5
Plane Gr. Pont WF8 ... 125 F1
Plane St. Hud HD4 ... 154 B3
Plane St. Tod OL14 ... 107 E7
Plane Tree Ave. Castle WF10 125 D5
Plane Tree Ave. Leeds LS17 ... 43 F4
Plane Tree Cl. Leeds LS17 ... 43 F4
Plane Tree Croft. Leeds LS17 .. 43 F4
Plane Tree Gdns. Leeds LS17 .. 43 F4
Plane Tree Gr. Yeadon LS19 ... 40 D6
Plane Tree Nest. Hali HX2 ... 112 E6
Plane Tree Nest La. Hali HX2 112 E5
Plane Tree Rd. Hali HX6 ... 112 B5
Plane Tree Rise. Leeds LS17 ... 43 F4
Plane Tree View. Leeds LS17 .. 43 F4
Plane Trees Cl. Clec BD19 ... 95 D3
Planetrees Rd. Brad BD4 ... 75 C6
Planetrees St. Brad BD15 ... 54 A1
Plantation Ave. Leeds LS17 ... 44 A5
Plantation Ave. Leeds LS15 ... 81 A7
Plantation Ave. Roy S71 ... 179 D3
Plantation Dr. Hud HD4 ... 154 A1
Plantation Gdns. Leeds LS17 ... 44 B5
Plantation Pl. Brad BD4 ... 75 C4
Plantation Way. Bail BD17 ... 38 D3
Platt La. Slai HD7 ... 152 A1
Platt Sq. Clec BD19 ... 116 D7 7
Playfair Rd. Leeds LS10 ... 79 D2
Playground. Gild LS12 ... 77 D3
Pleasance The. Swil LS26 ... 82 A1
Pleasant Ct. Leeds LS6 ... 60 A3 2
Pleasant Mount. Leeds LS11 ... 79 A5
Pleasant Pl. Leeds LS11 ... 79 A5
Pleasant St. Brad BD7 ... 74 A4
Pleasant St. Hali HX6 ... 112 C4
Pleasant St. Leeds LS11 ... 79 A5
Pleasant Terr. Leeds LS11 ... 79 A5
Pleasant View. Loft G WF2 ... 120 F7
Pledwick Cres. Wake WF2 ... 160 D6
Pledwick Dr. Wake WF2 ... 160 D5
Pledwick Gr. Wake WF2 ... 160 C5
Pledwick La. Wake WF2 ... 160 D5
Pledwick Rise. Wake WF2 ... 160 D5
Plevna St. Leeds LS10 ... 80 A2
Plevna Terr. Bing BD16 ... 36 F4
Plimsoll St. Brad BD4 ... 75 A4
Plimsoll St. Hem WF9 ... 181 D7
Ploughcroft La. Hali HX3 ... 92 C3
Ploughmans Croft. Brad BD2 ... 55 E4
Plover Dr. Batley WF17 ... 117 F5
Plover Rd. Hud HD3 ... 153 B8
Plover St. Brad BD5 ... 74 C3
Plover St. Keigh BD21 ... 35 C8
Plover Way. Morley LS27 ... 98 D3
Plum St. Hali HX1 ... 112 F6
Plum St. Keigh BD21 ... 35 A3
Plum Tree Cl. Pont WF8 ... 146 B6
Plumpton Ave. Brad BD2 ... 55 F6
Plumpton Cl. Brad BD2 ... 56 A5
Plumpton Dr. Brad BD2 ... 55 F6
Plumpton End. Brad BD2 ... 56 A6
Plumpton Gdns. Brad BD2 ... 55 F6
Plumpton Lea. Brad BD2 ... 55 F6
Plumpton Mead. Brad BD2 ... 55 F6
Plumpton Pl. Wake WF2 ... 142 A6
Plumpton Rd. Wake WF2 ... 142 A6
Plumpton St. Brad BD8 ... 74 A8
Plumpton St. Wake WF2 ... 142 A6
Plumpton Terr. Wake WF2 ... 142 A5
Plumpton Wlk. Brad BD2 ... 55 F6
Plymouth Gr. Hali HX1 ... 113 A8 3
Poet's Pl. Hors LS18 ... 41 C2
Pog Hall. Slai HD7 ... 170 C8
Pohlman St. Hali HX1 ... 112 F5 11
Pole Gate Branch. Slai HD7 ... 151 D4
Pole Gate. Slai HD7 ... 151 D4
Pole Rd. Keigh BD22 ... 33 F8
Pollard Ave. Bing BD16 ... 37 B5
Pollard Ave. Clec BD19 ... 96 B1
Pollard Cl. Clec BD19 ... 96 B1
Pollard La. Brad BD2 ... 56 B1
Pollard La. Leeds LS13 ... 58 C5
Pollard La. Pudsey LS13 ... 58 C5
Pollard Park Mid Sch. Brad ... 75 B8
Pollard St. Brad BD4 ... 74 F5
Pollard St. Hud HD2 ... 136 B2
Pollard St. Loft G WF3 ... 121 C6
Pollard St N. Hali HX3 ... 113 D8
Pollard St S. Hud HD3 ... 153 B4
Pollard St. Ship BD16 ... 54 B6 1
Pollard St. Tod OL14 ... 107 E8
Pollard Way. Clec BD19 ... 96 B1
Pollard's Fields. Knot WF11 ... 126 B5
Pollit Ave. Sow Br HX6 ... 111 F3
Pollums La. Fair WF11 ... 105 B6
Polperro Cl. Nor WF6 ... 123 B3
Pomfret Ct. Pont WF8 ... 147 A8
Pomfret Pl. Gar LS25 ... 83 B8
Pond Cl. Hud HD4 ... 153 F2
Pond La. Lepton HD8 ... 156 A2
Pond St. Keigh BD21 ... 35 C8
Ponden La. Haw BD22 ... 50 A7
Pondfields Cl. Kippax LS25 ... 83 B2
Pondfields Crest. Kippax LS25 . 83 B2
Pondfields Dr. Kippax LS25 ... 83 B2
Pondfields Rise. Kippax LS25 .. 83 B2
Ponker La. Skel HD8 ... 174 E1
Ponker Nook La. Skel HD8 ... 174 F1
Pontefract Ave. Leeds LS9 ... 79 F7 11
Pontefract Carleton Jun & Inf Sch.
Pont ... 146 E6
Pontefract Castle. Pont ... 125 E1
Pontefract Cobbler's Lane Inf Sch.
Pont ... 126 A1
Pontefract Cobbler's Lane Jun Sch.
Pont ... 147 A8
Pontefract Gen Infmy. Pont ... 146 D8
Pontefract H Fam & St Michaels
Prim Sch. Pont ... 126 A1
Pontefract Jun & Inf Sch. Pont 125 D1
Pontefract Kings High Sch.
Pont ... 146 C7
Pontefract La. Leeds LS15, LS9 80 C5
Pontefract Lane Cl. Leeds LS9 . 79 F7
Pontefract Pk. Pont ... 125 A1
Pontefract Rd. Ack M T WF7 . 146 A1
Pontefract Rd. Ack M T WF7 . 164 A8
Pontefract Rd. Castle WF10 .. 124 E7
Pontefract Rd. Crof WF4 ... 144 A2
Pontefract Rd. Cud S72 ... 180 C1
Pontefract Rd. Feath WF7 ... 145 E5
Pontefract Rd. Hem WF9 ... 163 F2
Pontefract Rd. Knot WF11 ... 126 B4
Pontefract Rd. Knot WF11 ... 126 D4
Pontefract Rd. Leeds LS10 LS26 80 B2
Pontefract Rd. Nor WF6 ... 123 D3
Pontefract St Giles CE Inf Sch.
Pont ... 125 D1
Pontefract St. Leeds LS9 ... 79 F7
Pontefract Terr. Hem WF9 ... 181 E6
Pontefract Willow Park Jun Sch.
Pont ... 146 F8
Pontey Dr. Hud HD5 ... 155 B5
Pontey Mount. Hud HD5 ... 155 B5
Pool Bank Cl. Pool LS21 ... 24 D7
Pool Bank Ct. Pool LS21 ... 24 D6
Pool Bank New Rd. Bramho
LS21 ... 24 D5
Pool Bank New Rd. Leath LS21 24 C5
Pool CE Prim Sch. Pool ... 24 C7
Pool Ct. Brad BD3 ... 75 A7
Pool Hill La. D Dale HD8 ... 192 D6
Pool in Wharfedale CE Prim Sch.
Pool ... 24 D7
Pool Rd. Leath LS21 ... 24 B7
Pool Rd. Otley LS21 ... 23 C8
Pool St. Keigh BD21 ... 18 E1
Poole Cres. Leeds LS15 ... 62 B1
Poole Mount. Leeds LS15 ... 62 B1
Poole Rd. Leeds LS15 ... 62 B1
Poole Row. B Sal LS25 ... 105 E3
Poole Sq. Leeds LS15 ... 62 B1
Pools La. Roy S71 ... 179 E3
Pope St. Keigh BD21 ... 35 D8
Pope St. Nor WF6 ... 123 C5
Popeley Rd. Batley WF16 ... 117 C6
Poplar Ave. Brad BD7 ... 73 F2
Poplar Ave. Castle WF10 ... 125 C7
Poplar Ave. Gar LS25 ... 82 E6
Poplar Ave. Hali HX6 ... 112 C5
Poplar Ave. Holmfi HD7 ... 172 C1
Poplar Ave. Leeds LS15 ... 62 D2
Poplar Ave. Shaf S72 ... 180 C2
Poplar Ave. Ship BD18 ... 55 C5
Poplar Ave. Tod OL14 ... 108 A7
Poplar Ave. Wake WF2 ... 141 E5
Poplar Ave. Weth LS22 ... 13 E7
Poplar Cl. Bur in W LS29 ... 21 F8
Poplar Court. Leeds LS13 ... 77 E8
Poplar Cres. Hali HX2 ... 91 F7
Poplar Cres. Morley LS27 ... 98 C1
Poplar Cres. Ship BD18 ... 55 C5
Poplar Croft. Leeds LS13 ... 77 E8
Poplar Dr. Hors LS18 ... 57 F8
Poplar Dr. Keigh BD20 ... 36 C7
Poplar Dr. Nor WF6 ... 123 A5
Poplar Dr. Ship BD18 ... 55 C5
Poplar Garth. Leeds LS13 ... 77 E8
Poplar Gdns. Leeds LS13 ... 77 E8
Poplar Gn. Leeds LS13 ... 77 E8
Poplar Gn. Pont WF8 ... 125 F1
Poplar Gr. Brad BD7 ... 73 F2
Poplar Gr. Clec BD19 ... 116 C6
Poplar Gr. Harden BD16 ... 36 A1
Poplar Gr. Knot WF11 ... 126 E2
Poplar Gr. Pont WF8 ... 146 B8
Poplar Gr. Ship BD18 ... 55 C5
Poplar House. Castle WF10 ... 124 E7 3
Poplar Mount. Leeds LS13 ... 77 E8
Poplar Rd. Brad BD7 ... 74 A2
Poplar Rd. Ship BD18 ... 55 C6
Poplar Rise. Leeds LS13 ... 58 E1
Poplar Rise. Skel HD8 ... 175 B1
Poplar Sq. Pudsey LS28 ... 57 D2 13
Poplar St. Hali HX3 ... 113 C8
Poplar St. Hud HD2 ... 136 A1
Poplar St. Hud HD5 ... 154 D5 11
Poplar St. Loft G WF3 ... 121 C6
Poplar Terr. Hud HD5 ... 154 D5 17
Poplar Terr. Keigh BD21 ... 35 A7 14
Poplar Terr. Keigh BD20 ... 36 D7
Poplar Terr. Roy S71 ... 179 D4
Poplar Terr. S Elm WF9 ... 183 A2
Poplar View. Brad BD7 ... 73 E2
Poplar View. Brig HX3 ... 115 B6
Poplar View. Leeds LS13 ... 77 E8
Poplar Way. Leeds LS13 ... 77 E8
Poplars Farm Fst Sch. Brad ... 55 E4
Poplars Park Rd. Brad BD2 ... 55 E4
Poplars The. Bramho LS16 ... 24 F2
Poplars The. Guise LS20 ... 22 E2
Poplars The. Knot WF11 ... 127 B2
Poplars The. Leeds LS6 ... 59 E4
Poplars The. Loft G WF3 ... 121 C8
Poplars The. S in Cra BD20 ... 16 C4
Popley Butts. Mel HD7 ... 170 C1
Popley Dr. Mel HD7 ... 170 D1
Popple Wells La. Hali HX2 ... 112 A7
Popples Dr. Hali HX2 ... 91 F7
Popples. Hali HX2 ... 91 F7
Popples Side. Hep HX7 ... 88 D6
Poppleton Ct. E Ard WF3 ... 98 E1 1
Poppleton Dr. E Ard WF3 ... 98 E1
Poppleton Rd. E Ard WF3 ... 98 E1
Poppleton Rise. E Ard WF3 ... 119 E8
Poppleton Way. E Ard WF3 ... 119 E8
Porchester House. Hud HD5 . 154 D6 4
Porritt St. Clec BD19 ... 95 D1
Portage Ave. Leeds LS15 ... 80 F7
Portage Cres. Leeds LS15 ... 80 F7
Portal Cres. Mir WF14 ... 138 A8
Portal Dr. Mir WF14 ... 138 A8
Portland Ave. Pont WF8 ... 125 B1
Portland Cl. Hud HD3 ... 153 C7
Portland Cres. Leeds LS1 ... 60 B1
Portland Ct. Keigh BD21 ... 35 B6
Portland Gate. Leeds LS1 ... 60 B1
Portland House. Elland HX5 .. 134 F7 14
Portland Pl. Bing BD16 ... 37 A2
Portland Pl. Hali HX1 ... 113 C6
Portland Pl. Upton WF9 ... 183 A7
Portland Rd. Hali HX3 ... 113 D8
Portland Rd. Leeds LS12 ... 78 C6
Portland St. Brad BD5 ... 74 E6
Portland St. Hali HX1 ... 113 C7 5
Portland St. Haw BD22 ... 51 D7
Portland St. Hud HD1 ... 153 F6
Portland St. Leeds LS1 ... 79 B8
Portland St. Pudsey LS28 ... 77 A7
Portland St. Wake WF1 ... 142 F3
Portland Way. Leeds LS1 ... 60 B1
Portman St. Pudsey LS28 ... 57 B6
Portobello Gr. Wake WF2 ... 142 D3
Portobello Rd. Wake WF1,
WF2 ... 142 D3
Portree House. Brad BD6 ... 93 E8 7
Portsmouth Ave. Brad BD3 ... 55 F1
Portwood St. Brad BD9 ... 54 D2
Post Hill Ct. Leeds LS12 ... 77 D7
Post Office Rd. Brad BD2 ... 56 C5
Post Office Rd. Feath WF7 ... 145 D5
Post Office St. Liver BD19 ... 116 F6
Pot La. Stee BD20 ... 17 C6
Pothouse Rd. Brad BD6 ... 94 B8
Potovens Ct. Loft G WF3 ... 121 C6
Potovens La. Loft G WF1 ... 121 B5
Potovens La. Wake WF2 ... 120 F4
Potter Ave. Wake WF2 ... 141 E4
Potter Brow Rd. Bail BD17 ... 38 C7
Potternewton Ave. Leeds LS7 .. 60 B6
Potternewton Cres. Leeds LS7 60 B5
Potternewton Ct. Leeds LS7 ... 60 C6
Potternewton Gdns. Leeds LS7 60 B6
Potternewton Gr. Leeds LS7 ... 60 B6
Potternewton Hghts. Leeds LS7 60 C6
Potternewton La. Leeds LS7 ... 60 B6
Potternewton Lane Prim Sch.
Leeds ... 60 B5
Potternewton Mansion Coll of F Ed.
Leeds ... 60 E5
Potternewton Mt. Leeds LS7 ... 60 B6
Potternewton View. Leeds LS7 60 B6
Potters Croft. Loft G WF3 ... 121 C6
Potters Gate. Wh Com HD8 ... 190 E1
Potters Wlk. Hud HD7 ... 152 E4
Potterton Cl. B in Elm LS15 ... 63 E8
Potterton Ct. B in Elm LS15 ... 63 E8
Potterton La. B in Elm LS15 ... 46 E2
Pottery La. Knot WF11 ... 126 D5
Pottery La. Roth LS26 ... 101 D7
Pottery Rd. Leeds LS10 ... 79 D4
Pottery St. Castle WF10 ... 124 B8
Pottery St. Hud HD3 ... 152 E8
Potts' Terr. Nor WF6 ... 144 B8
Poulton Pl. Leeds LS11 ... 79 C3
Poverty La. Sow Br HX7 ... 111 A1
Powell Ave. Brad BD5 ... 74 C4
Powell Rd. Bing BD16 ... 37 B2
Powell Rd. Ship BD18 ... 55 D5
Powell St. Batley WF16 ... 117 E3
Powell St. Castle WF10 ... 124 D8
Powell St. Hali HX1 ... 113 C6 13
Powell St. S Kirk WF9 ... 182 D3
Poxton Gr. S Elm WF9 ... 182 E1
Prail Cl. Pont WF8 ... 125 F1
Pratt La. Mir WF14 ... 138 A6
Pratt La. Ship BD18 ... 55 C6
Precinct The. Feath WF7 ... 145 C5
Premiere Pk. Ilkley LS29 ... 7 E3
Prescott St. Hali HX1 ... 113 C6
Prescott Terr. Brad BD15 ... 54 B1
Preston La. Hali HX2 ... 91 D2
Preston La. Swil LS26 ... 102 E7
Preston Par. Leeds LS11 ... 79 A2
Preston Pl. Hali HX1 ... 113 A7
Preston St. Batley WF17 ... 118 C4
Preston St. Brad BD7 ... 74 C7
Preston St. Dew WF12 ... 139 E6
Preston Terr. Bing BD16 ... 36 E5
Preston View. Swil LS26 ... 82 B1
Prestwich Dr. Hud HD2 ... 135 F3
Prestwick Cl. Otley LS21 ... 22 D6
Pretoria St. Castle WF10 ... 124 E7
Pretoria St. Feath WF7 ... 145 C6
Pretoria St. Slai HD7 ... 151 F1
Pretoria St. Wake WF1 ... 142 D3
Priest Bank Rd. Farnh BD20 ... 16 E8
Priest Hill Gdns. Weth LS22 ... 13 D8
Priest La. Rip HX6 ... 132 E4
Priesthorpe Ave. Pudsey LS28 57 B2
Priesthorpe Ct. Pudsey LS28 ... 57 D4
Priesthorpe High Sch. Pudsey . 57 B2
Priesthorpe La. Pudsey LS28 ... 57 B3
Priesthorpe Rd. Pudsey LS28 .. 57 B4
Priestley Ave. Batley WF16 ... 117 D6
Priestley Ave. Brad BD6 ... 94 C8
Priestley Cl. Pudsey LS28 ... 76 F8
Priestley Dr. Pudsey LS28 ... 76 F8
Priestley Gdns. Pudsey LS28 ... 76 F8
Priestley Gn. Brig HX3 ... 93 E1
Priestley Gr. Hud HD4 ... 153 F1
Priestley Hill. Queen BD13 ... 92 C6
Priestley Pl. Sow Br HX6 ... 112 A3
Priestley Sq. Batley WF17 ... 96 E2
Priestley St. Brad BD1 ... 74 F8 7
Priestley St. Thorn BD13 ... 72 D6
Priestley Terr. Brad BD6 ... 74 C1 1
Priestley View. Pudsey LS28 ... 76 F8
Priestley Wlk. Pudsey LS28 ... 76 F8
Priestman Cl. Brad BD8 ... 55 C1
Priestman Mid Sch. Brad ... 74 C2
Priestman St. Brad BD8 ... 55 C1
Priestthorpe Cl. Bing BD16 ... 37 A4
Priestthorpe Fst Sch. Bing ... 37 A3
Priestthorpe La. Bing BD16 ... 37 A4
Priestthorpe Rd. Bing BD16 ... 37 A4
Priestwell St. Tod OL14 ... 108 C6
Primitive St. Hud HD1 ... 154 B6 8
Primitive St. Roth WF3 ... 100 D3
Primley Gdns. Leeds LS17 ... 43 C4
Primley Park Ave. Leeds LS17 . 43 D4
Primley Park Cl. Leeds LS17 ... 43 D4
Primley Park Cres. Leeds LS17 43 D4
Primley Park Ct. Leeds LS17 ... 43 C5
Primley Park Dr. Leeds LS17 ... 43 D5
Primley Park Garth. Leeds LS17 43 D5
Primley Park Gn. Leeds LS17 ... 43 D5
Primley Park Gr. Leeds LS17 ... 43 C4
Primley Park La. Leeds LS17 ... 43 D4
Primley Park Mount. Leeds
LS17 ... 43 D4
Primley Park Rd. Leeds LS17 ... 43 C4
Primley Park Rise. Leeds LS17 43 D4
Primley Park View. Leeds LS17 43 D5
Primley Park Way. Leeds LS17 43 C5
Primley Park Wlk. Leeds LS17 . 43 D5
Primose Hill. Batley WF17 ... 118 D5
Primrose Ave. Leeds LS15 ... 81 A8 2
Primrose Ave. Swil LS26 ... 82 B1
Primrose Bank. Bing BD16 ... 37 B2
Primrose Cl. Leeds LS15 ... 81 A8
Primrose Cl. Pont WF8 ... 146 D7
Primrose Cres. Leeds LS15 ... 62 A1
Primrose Dene. Byram WF11 126 D7
Primrose Dr. Bing BD16 ... 37 C2
Primrose Dr. Castle WF10 ... 125 B6
Primrose Dr. Leeds LS15 ... 81 A8
Primrose Garth. Leeds LS15 ... 80 F8
Primrose Gdns. Leeds LS15 ... 62 A1
Primrose Gr. Hud HD4 ... 154 A3
Primrose Gr. Keigh BD21 ... 35 E7
Primrose Gr. Leeds LS15 ... 62 A1
Primrose Hill Cl. Swil LS26 ... 82 B1
Primrose Hill Dr. Swil LS26 ... 102 B8
Primrose Hill Garth. Swil LS26 102 B8
Primrose Hill Gdns. Swil LS26 . 82 B1
Primrose Hill Gn. Swil LS26 ... 102 B8
Primrose Hill Gr. Swil LS26 ... 82 B1
Primrose Hill High Sch (Annexe).
Leeds ... 60 E2
Primrose Hill High Sch. Leeds . 60 E1
Primrose Hill. Knot WF11 ... 127 A5
Primrose Hill. Pudsey LS28 ... 57 E1 5
Primrose Hill Rd. Hud HD4 ... 154 A4
Primrose House. Wake WF1 . 142 D5
Primrose La. B Spa LS23 ... 30 C7
Primrose La. Bing BD16 ... 37 C2
Primrose La. Crig WF4 ... 159 D6
Primrose La. Kirkb HD8 ... 173 D8
Primrose La. Leeds LS11 ... 79 C3
Primrose La. Leeds LS15 ... 81 A8
Primrose La. Liver WF15 ... 116 F5
Primrose La. Mir WF14 ... 138 C7
Primrose La. Ship BD2 ... 55 D4
Primrose Rd. Leeds LS15 ... 81 A8
Primrose Row. Bail BD17 ... 38 F4
Primrose St. Brad BD8 ... 74 C8 2
Primrose St. Hud HD4 ... 154 A4
Primrose St. Keigh BD21 ... 35 E7
Primrose Vale. Knot WF11 ... 127 A4
Primrose Way. Shelf HX3 ... 93 D7
Primrose Wlk. Morley LS27 ... 98 C8
Prince Edward Gr. Leeds LS12 78 A4
Prince Edward Rd. Leeds LS12 78 A4
Prince Henry Rd. Otley LS21 ... 11 A1
Prince Henry's Gram Sch. Otley 11 A1
Prince St. Batley WF17 ... 118 C6
Prince St. Brad BD4 ... 75 C2
Prince St. Dew WF13 ... 139 D8 2
Prince St. Haw BD22 ... 51 D7
Prince St. Hud HD4 ... 154 B4
Prince St. Kippax WF10 ... 102 F7
Prince St. Sil BD20 ... 5 D1
Prince William Ct. Feath WF7 145 C4
Prince Wood La. Hud HD2 ... 135 C2
Prince's Ave. Leeds LS8 ... 61 B7
Prince's Cres. Brad BD2 ... 55 E3
Prince's Ct. Leeds LS17 ... 43 C1
Prince's Gate. Hali HX3 ... 113 B4
Prince's St. Brad BD6 ... 93 E7 4
Prince's St. Brad BD6 ... 94 B8
Prince's Way. Brad BD1 ... 74 E6
Princeroyd Way. Brad BD7 ... 74 A7
Princes St. Batley WF16 ... 117 E4
Princess Alexandra Wlk. Hud
HD1 ... 154 B6 10
Princess Ave. Dew WF12 ... 140 A8
Princess Ave. S Elm WF9 ... 182 F2
Princess Cl. Dew WF12 ... 140 A8
Princess Cres. Dew WF12 ... 140 A7
Princess Ct. Leeds LS17 ... 43 D3
Princess Gdns. Dew WF13 ... 139 B8 9
Princess La. Dew WF12 ... 140 A8
Princess of Wales Prec The.
Dew WF13 ... 139 D8 4
Princess Rd. Dew WF12 ... 140 A7
Princess Rd. Ilkley LS29 ... 8 A3
Princess St. Batley WF17 ... 118 C6
Princess St. Brig HD6 ... 115 B2
Princess St. Castle WF10 ... 103 F1
Princess St. Cud S72 ... 180 C1
Princess St. Dew WF12 ... 140 B8
Princess St. Elland HX4 ... 134 D7 3
Princess St. Hali HX6 ... 112 C4
Princess St. Hali HX1 ... 113 C7
Princess St. Hud HD1 ... 154 A5 3
Princess St. Loft G WF1 ... 121 B4
Princess St. Mapp S75 ... 178 A1
Princess St. Mir WF14 ... 138 A4
Princess St. Nor WF6 ... 123 B2
Princess St. Wake WF1 ... 142 E2
Princess St. Yeadon LS19 ... 40 A4
Princeville Fst Sch. Brad ... 74 B6
Princeville Rd. Brad BD7 ... 74 B7
Princeville St. Brad BD7 ... 74 B6
Prior St. Keigh BD21 ... 35 D8
Prior's La. Hal E BD23 ... 1 E7
Priordale Rd. Feath WF7 ... 145 B4
Priory Cl. Bing BD16 ... 37 A4 7
Priory Cl. Mir WF14 ... 137 E6
Priory Cl. Nor WF6 ... 122 F4
Priory Cl. Ossett WF5 ... 140 D4
Priory Cl. Weth LS22 ... 13 F6
Priory Croft. Ossett WF5 ... 140 D5
Priory Ct. Brad BD8 ... 74 D8
Priory Estate. S Elm WF9 ... 183 B3
Priory Gr. Bing BD16 ... 37 A4
Priory Grange. Pont WF8 ... 125 E2
Priory Mews. Loft G WF3 ... 121 F6
Priory Pl. Hud HD2 ... 136 F5
Priory Rd. Brig HD6 ... 115 C2
Priory Rd. Feath WF7 ... 145 C4
Priory Rd. Ossett WF5 ... 140 D5
Priory Sq. Walton WF2 ... 161 A7
Priory Way. Mir WF14 ... 137 E6
Priory Wlk. Mir WF14 ... 137 E6
Privilege St. Leeds LS12 ... 78 B7
Proctor St. Brad BD4 ... 75 D2
Prod La. Bail BD17 ... 37 E2
Progress Ave. Harden BD16 ... 36 A1
Prospect Ave. Hali HX2 ... 112 E4
Prospect Ave. Leeds LS13 ... 58 C3
Prospect Ave. Nor WF6 ... 123 B3
Prospect Ave. Pudsey LS28 ... 76 D8
Prospect Ave. Ship BD18 ... 55 C7
Prospect Bank. Bramham LS23 30 D3
Prospect Cl. Hali HX2 ... 112 E4
Prospect Cl. Ship BD18 ... 55 C7
Prospect Cotts. S Elm WF9 ... 182 E3
Prospect Cres. Keigh BD22 ... 34 E5
Prospect Cres. Leeds LS10 ... 79 D3
Prospect Ct. Hali HX2 ... 112 B8
Prospect Dr. Keigh BD22 ... 34 E5
Prospect Gdns. Leeds LS15 ... 81 B8 4
Prospect Gr. Pudsey LS28 ... 76 D8
Prospect Gr. Ship BD18 ... 55 C7
Prospect La. Birk BD11 ... 96 B5
Prospect Mount. Keigh BD22 ... 34 E5
Prospect Mount. Ship BD18 ... 55 C7
Prospect Pl. Brad BD9 ... 54 F1
Prospect Pl. Brad BD2 ... 56 C2
Prospect Pl. Brig HX3 ... 94 A2
Prospect Pl. Brig HD6 ... 115 A2
Prospect Pl. Elland HD3 ... 151 F8
Prospect Pl. Hali HX2 ... 91 F3
Prospect Pl. Hors LS18 ... 58 B8
Prospect Pl. Leeds LS13 ... 58 C3
Prospect Pl. Queen BD13 ... 72 E1 18
Prospect Pl. Roth WF3 ... 100 B2
Prospect Pl. Roth LS26 ... 100 F4
Prospect Rd. Batley WF16 ... 117 C6
Prospect Rd. Bing BD16 ... 37 C5
Prospect Rd. Brad BD3 ... 55 F1
Prospect Rd. Bur in W LS29 ... 21 F8
Prospect Rd. Clec BD19 ... 116 D7
Prospect Rd. Hud HD3 ... 152 F6
Prospect Rd. Liver WF15 ... 116 D2
Prospect Rd. Ossett WF5 ... 140 D5
Prospect Row. Hali HX2 ... 91 F3
Prospect Row. Men LS29 ... 21 C6
Prospect Sq. Pudsey LS28 ... 57 D2 12
Prospect St. Batley WF17 ... 118 C6
Prospect St. Brad BD10 ... 56 C5
Prospect St. Brad BD4 ... 75 A5
Prospect St. Brad BD6 ... 93 F7
Prospect St. Clec BD19 ... 116 D8 11
Prospect St. Glu BD20 ... 16 D7
Prospect St. Hali HX3 ... 113 D8
Prospect St. Haw BD22 ... 51 C6 7
Prospect St. Hor WF4 ... 159 C8
Prospect St. Hud HD1 ... 154 A5
Prospect St. Keigh BD22 ... 34 F6
Prospect St. Pudsey LS28 ... 57 D3
Prospect St. Pudsey LS28 ... 76 C8
Prospect St. Ship BD18 ... 55 C7
Prospect St. Thorn BD13 ... 72 E6
Prospect St. Yeadon LS19 ... 40 C3
Prospect Terr. Batley WF13 .. 117 F2 3
Prospect Terr. Brad BD15 ... 54 C1
Prospect Terr. Clec BD19 ... 116 D8
Prospect Terr. L Brad BD20 ... 4 C6
Prospect Terr. Leeds LS13 ... 58 C3
Prospect Terr. Liver WF15 ... 117 A4
Prospect Terr. M'field LS25 ... 84 A6
Prospect Terr. Pudsey LS28 ... 57 D2 3
Prospect Terr. Pudsey LS13 ... 57 E5
Prospect Terr. Roth LS26 ... 100 F4
Prospect Terr. S Kirk WF9 ... 182 B2
Prospect View. Leeds LS13 ... 58 D3
Prospect View. Liver WF15 ... 116 E2
Prospect Villas. Weth LS22 ... 13 E6
Prospect Wlk. Ship BD18 ... 55 C7
Prosper St. Leeds LS10 ... 79 E4
Providence Ave. Bail BD17 ... 38 C4
Providence Ave. Leeds LS6 ... 60 A4
Providence Bldgs. Hali HX3 ... 114 A4
Providence Cres. Haw BD22 ... 34 C2
Providence Ct. Haw BD22 ... 34 C2
Providence Ct. Morley LS27 ... 98 A5 5
Providence La. Haw BD22 ... 34 C1
Providence Pl. Brad BD12 ... 94 C4 5
Providence Pl. Brig HD6 ... 115 C1
Providence Pl. Gar LS25 ... 82 E7
Providence Pl. Kippax WF10 .. 103 B3
Providence Pl. Leeds LS2 ... 60 C1
Providence Pl. Pudsey LS28 ... 57 E1 4
Providence Pl. Swil LS15 ... 82 A6
Providence Rd. Leeds LS6 ... 60 A4
Providence Row. Bail BD17 ... 38 C4
Providence Row. Hali HX2 ... 91 F3
Providence Row. Keigh BD20 .. 19 E2
Providence St. Batley WF17 .. 118 C5
Providence St. Brad BD1 ... 74 D7 5
Providence St. Brig BD12 ... 94 E1
Providence St. Clec BD19 ... 116 E8 2
Providence St. Dew WF12 ... 139 F7
Providence St. Elland HX5 ... 134 F7 18
Providence St. Leeds LS9 ... 79 E7
Providence St. Pudsey LS28 ... 57 D2 6
Providence St. Tod OL14 ... 129 A7
Providence St. Wake WF1 ... 142 C7
Providence Terr. Leeds LS2 ... 60 A3
Providence Terr. Thorn BD13 .. 72 D6
Prune Park La. Brad BD15 ... 53 F2
Pudding La. Tod OL14 ... 86 C2
Pudsey Bsns Ctr. Pudsey ... 76 F7
Pudsey Crawshaw Sch. Pudsey 76 F7
Pudsey Grangefield Sch. Pudsey 76 E8
Pudsey Greenside Prim Sch.
Pudsey ... 76 D6
Pudsey Primrose Hill Prim Sch.
Pudsey ... 57 D1
Pudsey Rd. Leeds LS12, LS13 .. 77 D8
Pudsey Rd. Pudsey LS12, LS13 77 B7
Pudsey Rd. Tod OL14 ... 86 B2
Pudsey Tyersal Prim Sch.
Pudsey ... 75 F6
Pudsey Waterloo Inf Sch.
Pudsey ... 76 C7
Pugneys Country Park. Crig ... 160 B8
Pugneys Rd. Wake WF2 ... 142 C2
Pule Green La. Hali HX3 ... 92 C3
Pullan Ave. Brad BD2 ... 56 C4
Pullan Dr. Brad BD2 ... 56 C4
Pullan Gr. Brad BD2 ... 56 C4
Pullan La. Guise BD17 ... 39 C5
Pullan St. Brad BD5 ... 74 D5
Pulmans Pl. Hali HX3 ... 113 C2
Pump La. Dew WF13 ... 138 F8
Pump La. E Ard WF13 ... 119 E5
Pump La. Kirkb HD8 ... 174 C7
Pump La. W Har WF4 ... 163 A8
Pump St. D Dale HD8 ... 191 B3
Pumphouse La. Mir WF14 ... 138 B6
Punch Bowl Yd. Broth WF11 .. 126 C8
Punch Bowl Yd. Clec BD19 ... 116 C7
Pundles. Hali HX2 ... 91 E8
Purbeck Gr. Gar LS25 ... 82 F6
Purcell Dr. Sil BD20 ... 5 D2
Purley Wlk. Brad BD6 ... 94 B8
Purlwell Ave. Batley WF17 ... 118 B3
Purlwell Cres. Batley WF17 ... 118 B3
Purlwell Hall Rd. Batley WF17 118 C4
Purlwell La. Batley WF17 ... 118 C4
Purprise La. Wad M HX7 ... 69 A1
Purston Inf Sch. Feath ... 145 D4
Purston La. Ack M T WF7 ... 145 F1
Purston Park Ct. Feath WF7 .. 145 D4
Purwell Inf Sch. Batley ... 118 B3
Pye Nest Ave. Hali HX2 ... 112 E5
Pye Nest Dr. Hali HX2 ... 112 E4
Pye Nest Gdns. Hali HX2 ... 112 E5
Pye Nest Gr. Hali HX2 ... 112 E5
Pye Nest Rd. Hali HX2 ... 112 E4
Pye Nest Rise. Hali HX2 ... 112 E4
Pyenot Ave. Clec BD19 ... 116 E6
Pyenot Dr. Clec BD19 ... 116 E6
Pyenot Gdns. Clec BD19 ... 116 E6
Pyenot Hall La. Clec BD19 ... 116 E6
Pym St. Leeds LS10 ... 79 D5
Pymont Ct. Roth WF3 ... 100 C1
Pymroyd La. Hud HD4 ... 153 B3
Pynate Rd. Batley WF17 ... 118 A6
Pyrah Fold. Brad BD12 ... 94 C4 6
Pyrah Rd. Brad BD12 ... 94 D7
Pyrah St. Brad BD12 ... 94 D4
Pyrah St. Dew WF13 ... 118 C1

Quail St. Keigh BD21 ... 35 D8
Quaker House. Leeds LS2 ... 60 A3 9
Quaker La. Brad BD5 ... 74 B3
Quaker La. Clec BD19 ... 116 D6
Quaker La. Hud HD1 ... 153 E5
Quakers La. Rip HX6 ... 132 D3
Quakers La. Yeadon LS19 ... 40 B5
Quarmby Croft. Hud HD3 ... 153 A7
Quarmby Fold. Hud HD3 ... 153 A7
Quarmby Rd. Hud HD3 ... 153 B6
Quarrie Dene Ct. Leeds LS7 ... 60 C6
Quarry Ave. Knot WF11 ... 127 A3
Quarry Bank Ct. Leeds LS5 ... 58 F6
Quarry Cl. Honley HD7 ... 172 C2
Quarry Cotts. Stee BD20 ... 17 D5
Quarry Ct. Hud HD3 ... 152 F7
Quarry Dene Pk. Leeds LS16 ... 59 C8
Quarry Dr. Kirkhe HD5 ... 155 C5
Quarry Farm Rd. Pool LS21 ... 24 B5
Quarry Gdns. Leeds LS17 ... 43 A6
Quarry Hill. Hor WF4 ... 140 F1
Quarry Hill. Hud HD5 ... 155 B4
Quarry Hill Ind Est. Hor ... 140 F1
Quarry Hill La. Weth LS22 ... 13 E6
Quarry Hill. Roth LS26 ... 101 C6
Quarry Hill. Sow Br HX6 ... 112 B3
Quarry La. Batley WF17 ... 96 F1 10
Quarry La. E Ard LS27 ... 119 A6
Quarry La. Hud HD4 ... 171 C7
Quarry La. Kirkhe HD5 ... 155 C5
Quarry La. Morley LS27 ... 98 B2
Quarry La. Upton WF9 ... 183 A8
Quarry Mount Pl. Leeds LS6 ... 60 A4 7
Quarry Mount Prim Sch. Leeds 60 A4
Quarry Mount. Ryhill WF4 ... 162 B1
Quarry Mount St. Leeds LS6 ... 60 A4 6
Quarry Mount Terr. Leeds LS6 60 A4 8

Quarry Mount. Yeadon LS19 .... 40 C7 7
Quarry Pl. Brad BD2 .... 56 B2
Quarry Pl. Leeds LS6 .... 60 A3
Quarry Rd. Clec BD19 .... 116 D7
Quarry Rd. Clec BD19 .... 117 B7
Quarry Rd. Dew WF13 .... 139 B7
Quarry Rd. Hali HX3 .... 91 E2
Quarry Rd. Hud HD4 .... 153 B3
Quarry Rd. Hud HD1 .... 153 E6
Quarry Rd. Liver WF15 .... 117 A4
Quarry Rd. Pool LS21 .... 24 B5
Quarry Rd. Roth LS26 .... 101 D6
Quarry St. Ack M T WF7 .... 163 F5
Quarry St. Keigh BD21 .... 35 D7
Quarry St. Leeds LS6 .... 60 A4
Quarry St. Ship BD9 .... 55 A4
Quarry The. Leeds LS17 .... 43 A6
Quarry View. Ack M T WF7 .... 163 E5
Quarry View. Dew WF13 .... 117 F1
Quarrydene Dr. Castle WF10 125 B6
Quarryfield Terr. E Ard WF3 .. 120 D7
Quarryfields. Mir WF14 .... 138 B8
Quarryside Rd. Mir WF14 .... 137 F5
Quay St. Hud HD1 .... 154 B6
Quebec St. Brad BD1 .... 74 E6
Quebec St. Elland HX5 .... 135 A7
Quebec St. Keigh BD21 .... 35 B6
Quebec St. Leeds LS1 .... 79 B7
Quebec St. Tod OL14 .... 108 A1 8
Quebec St. Wake WF2 .... 142 B6
Queen Elizabeth Dr. Nor WF6 144 B8
Queen Elizabeth Gdns. Hud HD1 .... 153 F6
Queen Elizabeth Gr. Wake WF1 .... 142 E7
Queen Elizabeth Grammar Sch. Wake 142 C7
Queen Elizabeth Rd. Wake WF1 .... 142 E7
Queen Eliz'beth St. Loft G WF1 121 B4
Queen Margaret's Dr. Byram WF11 .... 126 D8
Queen Margarets Ave. Byram WF11 .... 126 D8
Queen Margarets Cl. Byram WF11 .... 126 D8
Queen Sq. Leeds LS2 .... 60 C1
Queen St. Bail BD17 .... 38 C1 5
Queen St. Bing BD16 .... 36 F3
Queen St. Brad BD10 .... 56 D7
Queen St. Brad BD6 .... 93 E7 3
Queen St. Castle WF10 .... 124 E8
Queen St. Clec BD19 .... 96 B2
Queen St. Clec BD19 .... 116 E7
Queen St. Dew WF13 .... 138 E6
Queen St. Dew WF12 .... 140 B7
Queen St. E Ard WF3 .... 120 D8
Queen St. Elland HX4 .... 134 C6
Queen St. Haw BD22 .... 51 C6 6
Queen St. Heb Br HX7 .... 110 E8
Queen St. Hor WF4 .... 141 A1
Queen St. Hud HD1 .... 154 B6 15
Queen St. Leeds LS1 .... 79 A8
Queen St. Leeds LS10 .... 80 A2
Queen St. Liver FW16 .... 117 C3
Queen St. Loft G WF1 .... 121 B4
Queen St. Mir WF14 .... 138 A4
Queen St. Morley LS27 .... 98 A5
Queen St. Nor WF6 .... 123 A2
Queen St. Ossett WF5 .... 140 D5
Queen St. Pont WF8 .... 146 C8
Queen St. Roth WF3 .... 100 D3
Queen St. S Elm WF9 .... 182 F2
Queen St S. Hud HD1 .... 154 B5
Queen St. Sil BD20 .... 5 E1
Queen St. Skel HD8 .... 175 A2
Queen St. Sow Br HX6 .... 111 E3
Queen St. Stee BD20 .... 17 C5
Queen St. Swil LS26 .... 102 E6
Queen St. Tod OL14 .... 108 B5
Queen St. Wake WF1 .... 142 C6
Queen St. Wils BD15 .... 53 C4
Queen St. Yeadon LS19 .... 40 A4
Queen Tap Yd. Hud HD1 .... 154 A6 24
Queen Terr. Pont WF8 .... 146 B8 4
Queen Victoria Cres. Northo HX3 .... 93 B3
Queen Victoria St. Leeds LS1 .. 79 C8 6
Queen's Arc. Leeds 79 C8 5
Queen's Ave. Brad BD2 .... 55 F3
Queen's Ave. Pont WF8 .... 146 A7
Queen's Cres. Crof WF4 .... 144 C4
Queen's Cres. Ossett WF5 .... 140 D5
Queen's Dr. Cud S72 .... 180 C1
Queen's Dr. Ilkley LS29 .... 7 F3
Queen's Dr. Ossett WF5 .... 141 A5
Queen's Dr. Shaf S72 .... 180 B3
Queen's Drive La. Ilkley LS29 .... 7 F3
Queen's Gate. Hali HX3 .... 113 B4
Queen's Gdns. Ilkley LS29 .... 8 A3
Queen's Gdns. Ossett WF5 .... 140 D5
Queen's Gr. Morley LS27 .... 97 F3
Queen's Park Dr. Castle WF10 125 B8
Queen's Pl. Morley LS27 .... 98 B4
Queen's Prom. Morley LS27 .... 98 A5
Queen's Rd. B Spa LS23 .... 30 C8
Queen's Rd. Bing BD16 .... 36 E6
Queen's Rd. Brad BD1, BD2, BD8 .... 55 E2
Queen's Rd. Brig HX3 .... 93 F2
Queen's Rd. Cud S72 .... 180 C1
Queen's Rd. Hali HX1 .... 112 F7
Queen's Rd. Hud HD2 .... 153 E8
Queen's Rd. Ilkley LS29 .... 8 A3
Queen's Rd. Keigh BD21 .... 35 B5
Queen's Rd. Leeds LS6 .... 59 E2
Queen's Rd. Morley LS27 .... 97 F3
Queen's Rd. Pont WF8 .... 146 A7
Queen's Rise. Brad BD2 .... 55 F3
Queen's Road Cty Prim Sch (Annexe). Leeds 59 E3
Queen's Road Prim Sch. Hali .. 112 F7
Queen's Sq. Pont WF8 .... 146 A7
Queen's Wlk. Leeds LS6 .... 59 B6
Queen's Wlk. Ossett WF5 .... 140 F5
Queens Cl. Bing BD16 .... 37 B2
Queens Cl. Leeds LS7 .... 60 C8
Queens Ct. Clec BD19 .... 96 B2
Queens Ct. Leeds LS14 .... 62 B5 4
Queens Dr Cl. Ossett WF5 .... 140 F5
Queens Dr. Hali HX3 .... 114 A4
Queens Dr. Roth WF3 .... 100 D3
Queens Dr. Wake WF2 .... 120 E1
Queens Gr. Keigh BD21 .... 35 B5
Queens Mill. Dew WF13 .... 138 E6
Queens Mill Ind Est. Hud 154 A4
Queens Mill Rd. Hud HD1 HD4 154 A4
Queens Par. Leeds LS14 .... 62 B5 2
Queens Park Cl. Castle WF10 125 B8
Queens Pl. Otley LS21 .... 23 A7
Queens Pl. Ship BD18 .... 54 F8
Queens Rd. Castle WF10 .... 125 B7
Queens Rd. Ship BD18 .... 54 F8
Queens Rd W. Hud HD4 .... 153 B4
Queens Sq. Hud HD2 .... 136 D1
Queens Terr. Heb Br HX7 .... 88 F3
Queens Terr. Otley LS21 .... 23 B7
Queens's Ct. Leeds LS1 .... 79 C7
Queensbury Ave. Loft G WF1 . 121 C5
Queensbury Golf C'se. Queen .. 93 A8
Queensbury Rd. Hali HX3 .... 92 B5
Queensbury Sch. Queen 92 E8
Queensbury Sq. Queen BD13 .. 72 E1 6
Queensgate. Brad BD1 .... 74 E7 10
Queensgate. Hud HD1 .... 154 B5
Queenshill App. Leeds LS17 .... 43 C2
Queenshill Ave. Leeds LS17 .... 43 C3
Queenshill Cl. Leeds LS17 .... 43 C2
Queenshill Cres. Leeds LS17 .... 43 C3
Queenshill Ct. Leeds LS17 .... 43 C2
Queenshill Dr. Leeds LS17 .... 43 C2
Queenshill Garth. Leeds LS17 . 43 C2
Queenshill Gdns. Leeds LS17 .. 43 B2
Queenshill Rd. Leeds LS17 .... 43 C2
Queenshill View. Leeds LS17 .... 43 C2
Queenshill Way. Leeds LS17 .... 43 C2
Queenshill Wlk. Leeds LS17 .... 43 C2
Queensthorpe Ave. Leeds LS13 77 E8
Queensthorpe Cl. Leeds LS13 .. 77 E8
Queensthorpe Rise. Leeds LS13 77 D8
Queensway. Bing BD16 .... 37 B2
Queensway. Gar LS25 .... 82 D7
Queensway. Guise LS20 .... 40 A8
Queensway. Hali HX1 .... 112 F8
Queensway. Keigh BD21 .... 35 C7 7
Queensway. Kirkb HD8 .... 174 A5
Queensway. Leeds LS15 .... 81 C8
Queensway. Morley LS27 .... 98 A4
Queensway. Nor WF6 .... 144 A7
Queensway. Pont WF8 .... 125 F3
Queensway. Roth LS26 .... 100 E6
Queensway. Roy S71 .... 179 C4
Queensway. Yeadon LS19 .... 40 A8
Queenswood Cl. Leeds LS6 .... 59 A6
Queenswood Ct. Leeds LS6 .... 59 B4
Queenswood Dr. Leeds LS6 .... 59 A5
Queenswood Gdns. Leeds LS6 59 C4
Queenswood Gn. Leeds LS6 .... 59 A7
Queenswood Hts. Leeds LS6 .. 59 C5
Queenswood Mount. Leeds LS6 59 B5
Queenswood Rd. Leeds LS6 .... 59 B5
Queenswood Rise. Leeds LS6 .. 59 B4
Quincy Cl. Brad BD2 .... 56 C4

Raby Ave. Leeds LS7 .... 60 D3
Raby Pk. Weth LS22 .... 13 D6
Raby St. Leeds LS7 .... 60 D3
Raby Terr. Leeds LS7 .... 60 D3
Racca Ave. Knot WF11 .... 127 B4
Racca Gn. Knot WF11 .... 127 A4
Race Moor La. Haw BD22 .... 34 C3
Rachael St. Hor WF4 .... 140 F1
Racton St. Slai HD7 .... 151 F1
Radcliffe Ave. Brad BD2 .... 56 A5
Radcliffe Gdns. Pudsey LS28 .. 76 E6
Radcliffe Gr. Pudsey LS28 .... 76 E6 2
Radcliffe La. Hali HX2 .... 90 C2
Radcliffe La. Pudsey LS28 .... 76 E7
Radcliffe Pl. Wake WF1 .... 142 C6 7
Radcliffe Rd. Hud HD3 .... 153 B4
Radcliffe Rd. Slai HD7 .... 152 B2
Radcliffe Rd. Wake WF2 .... 141 E4
Radcliffe St. Skel HD8 .... 174 F2
Radcliffe Terr. Pudsey LS28 .. 76 E6 1
Radfield Rd. Brad BD6 .... 74 E1
Radford Park Ave. S Kirk WF9 182 B1
Radnor St. Brad BD3 .... 75 D7
Radnor St. Leeds LS12 .... 78 E6
Radwell Dr. Brad BD5 .... 74 E5
Rae Ct. Loft G WF3 .... 121 E5
Raeburn Dr. Brad BD6 .... 94 A7
Rafborn Ave. Hud HD3 .... 134 E1
Rafborn Gr. Hud HD3 .... 134 E1
Raglan Ave. Keigh BD22 .... 34 F6
Raglan Cl. Castle WF10 .... 124 A8
Raglan Ct. Hali HX1 .... 113 A7 8
Raglan Dr. Brad BD3 .... 75 D7
Raglan Rd. Leeds LS2, LS6 .... 60 A3
Raglan St. Brad BD3 .... 75 D7
Raglan St. Hali HX1 .... 113 A7
Raglan St. Keigh BD22 .... 34 F6
Raglan St. Queen BD13 .... 72 F1
Raglan St. Tod OL14 .... 108 B5 2
Raglan Terr. Brad BD3 .... 75 E7
Raikes La. Batley WF17 .... 96 F2
Raikes La. Birk BD4 .... 76 B2
Raikes La. Birk BD4 .... 95 E7
Raikes La. Brad BD4 .... 76 B2
Raikes Lane CE Inf Sch. Batley 96 E2
Raikes Wood Dr. Birk BD4 .... 95 E7
Railes Cl. Hali HX2 .... 90 D1
Railgate. Whit OL13 .... 106 C1
Railsfield Mount. Leeds LS13 ... 58 C2
Railsfield Rise. Leeds LS13 .... 58 C2
Railsfield Way. Leeds LS13 .... 58 C2
Railway Ave. Pont WF8 .... 125 C1
Railway Cotts. S Elm WF9 .... 183 E7
Railway Cotts. B Abby BD23 .... 2 C7
Railway Cotts. B Sal LS25 .... 105 D4
Railway Cotts. Dun Br S30 .... 199 F2
Railway Cotts. M'field LS25 .... 84 A6
Railway Rd. Brad BD10 .... 56 B8
Railway Rd. Ilkley LS29 .... 8 B4
Railway Rd. Leeds LS15 .... 62 D2
Railway St. Brad BD4 .... 75 C2
Railway St. Brig HD6 .... 115 B1 2
Railway St. Clec BD19 .... 116 D7
Railway St. Dew WF13 .... 139 A6
Railway St. Dew WF12 .... 139 D7
Railway St. Hud HD1 .... 154 A6
Railway St. Keigh BD20 .... 18 C1
Railway St. Leeds LS9 .... 79 E7
Railway St. Liver WF16 .... 117 D3
Railway St. Tod OL14 .... 108 B6
Railway Terr. Brad BD12 .... 94 E5 1
Railway Terr. E Ard WF3 .... 99 C1
Railway Terr. Elland HX3 .... 113 A2
Railway Terr. Feath WF7 .... 145 D5
Railway Terr. Hem WF9 .... 163 A3
Railway Terr. Loft G WF1 .... 121 A5
Railway Terr. Nor WF6 .... 123 A2
Railway View. Castle WF10 .... 124 B7
Railway View. Loft G WF1 .... 121 F6
Raincliffe Gr. Leeds LS9 .... 80 A8
Raincliffe Mount. Leeds LS9 .... 80 A7 11
Raincliffe Rd. Leeds LS9 .... 80 A7
Raincliffe St. Leeds LS9 .... 80 A8 13
Raincliffe Terr. Leeds LS9 .... 80 A7 12
Raines Dr. L Brad BD20 .... 4 C5
Rainsborough Ave. Knot WF11 126 C3
Raistrick Way. Ship BD18 .... 55 D8
Rake Bank. Hali HX2 .... 91 D3
Rake Head Barn La. Tod OL14 129 A8
Rake Head Rd. Holme HD7 .... 197 E7
Rake. Heb Br HX7 .... 109 F8
Rakehill Rd. B in Elm LS15 .... 63 B7
Raleigh Gdns. Litt OL15 .... 129 C1
Raleigh St. Hali HX1 .... 112 F5 12
Ralph Thoresby High Sch. Hors 41 F4
Rampart Rd. Leeds LS6 .... 60 A3
Ramsden Ave. Brad BD7 .... 73 E5
Ramsden Cl. Broth WF11 .... 126 C8
Ramsden Ct. Brad BD7 .... 74 A4
Ramsden La. Holme HD7 .... 198 B7
Ramsden La. Tod OL14 .... 128 F7
Ramsden Mill La. Hud HD7 .... 152 E3
Ramsden Pl. Brad BD14 .... 73 B5
Ramsden Rd. Holme HD7 .... 198 C7
Ramsden Rd. Litt OL12 .... 128 C1
Ramsden St. Castle WF10 .... 124 C5
Ramsden St. Hali HX3 .... 91 F2
Ramsden St. Hud HD7 .... 152 E4
Ramsden St. Hud HD1 .... 154 A5
Ramsden St. Kippax LS25 .... 102 F8
Ramsden St. Tod OL14 .... 129 A7
Ramsden Wood Rd. Tod OL14 129 A7
Ramsey Ave. Bacup OL13 .... 106 A1
Ramsey Cres. Neth WF4 .... 158 B7
Ramsey Rd. Neth WF4 .... 158 A7
Ramsey St. Brad BD5 .... 74 D3
Ramsey View. Neth WF4 .... 158 A7
Ramsgate Cres. Roth WF3 .... 100 B1
Ramsgate. Roth WF3 .... 100 B1
Ramsgate St. Hali HX1 .... 112 F7
Ramshead App. Leeds LS14 .... 62 A6
Ramshead Cl. Leeds LS14 .... 62 A7
Ramshead Cres. Leeds LS14 .... 61 F7
Ramshead Dr. Leeds LS14 .... 62 A6
Ramshead Gdns. Leeds LS14 .. 61 F7
Ramshead Gr. Leeds LS14 .... 62 A6
Ramshead Heights. Leeds LS14 62 A5 1
Ramshead Hill. Leeds LS14 .... 62 A6
Ramshead Pl. Leeds LS14 .... 62 A6
Ramshead View. Leeds LS14 .... 62 A6
Rand Pl. Brad BD7 .... 74 C5
Rand St. Brad BD7 .... 74 C5
Randall Pl. Brad BD9 .... 55 A3
Randall Well St. Brad BD7 .... 74 D6
Randolph St. Brad BD3 .... 75 E8
Randolph St. Hali HX3 .... 113 C8 1
Randolph St. Leeds LS13 .... 58 A2
Random Cl. Keigh BD22 .... 34 F5
Ranelagh Ave. Brad BD10 .... 56 E5
Range Bank. Hali HX3 .... 92 C1
Range Ct. Hali HX3 .... 113 C8 2
Range Gdns. Hali HX3 .... 92 C1
Range La. Hali HX3 .... 92 C1
Range St. Hali HX3 .... 92 C1
Ransdale Dr. Brad BD5 .... 74 D3
Ransdale Gr. Brad BD5 .... 74 D3
Ransdale Rd. Brad BD5 .... 74 D3
Ranter's Fold. Hor WF4 .... 141 A1
Raper View. Aber LS25 .... 64 E8
Rapes Highway. Densh OL3 .... 167 A5
Rashcliffe Hill Rd. Hud HD1 .... 153 F4
Raspberry Pl. S in Cra BD20 .... 16 D4
Rastrick Comm. Brig HD6 .... 136 A8
Rastrick High Sch. Brig 114 F1
Rathlin Rd. Batley WF12 .... 118 F3
Rathmell Rd. Leeds LS15 .... 80 E7
Rathmell St. Brad BD5 .... 74 D1
Ratten Row Rd. Sow Br HX6 .. 111 C1
Raven La. Ryhill S72 .... 180 A6
Raven Rd. Leeds LS6 .... 59 E4
Raven St. Bing BD16 .... 36 F3
Raven St. Hali HX1 .... 112 F7
Raven St. Hud HD1 .... 153 D5
Raven St. Keigh BD21 .... 35 B7
Raven Terr. Brad BD8 .... 73 C7
Ravens Ave. Dew WF13 .... 139 A6
Ravens Ave. Hud HD5 .... 154 E5
Ravens Cres. Dew WF13 .... 139 A6
Ravens Croft. Dew WF13 .... 139 A6
Ravens Gr. Dew WF13 .... 139 A6
Ravens Lodge Ter. Dew WF13 139 A6
Ravens Mount. Pudsey LS28 .... 76 F7
Ravens St. Dew WF13 .... 138 F6
Ravens Way. Holmfi HD7 .... 189 E4
Ravens Wlk. Dew WF13 .... 139 A6
Ravenscar Ave. Leeds LS8 .... 61 A6 6
Ravenscar Mount. Leeds LS8 .. 61 A6 3
Ravenscar Pl. Leeds LS8 .... 61 A6 2
Ravenscar Terr. Leeds LS8 .... 61 A6 4
Ravenscar View. Leeds LS8 .... 61 A6
Ravenscar Wlk. Leeds LS8 .... 61 A6
Ravenscliffe Ave. Brad BD10 .... 56 E4
Ravenscliffe Fst Sch. Brad 56 E4
Ravenscliffe Rd. Pudsey LS28 .. 56 F6
Ravenscourt. Hud HD1 .... 153 D5
Ravensdeane. Hud HD3 .... 153 D8
Ravensfield Rd. Dew WF13 .... 139 A6
Ravenshall Sch. Dew 139 A4
Ravenshouse Rd. Dew WF13 .... 138 F7
Ravensknowle Rd. Hud HD5 .. 154 E5
Ravensmead. Feath WF7 .... 145 F5
Ravensthorpe CE J Sch. Dew 138 E5
Ravensthorpe Inf Sch. Dew 138 E6
Ravensthorpe Soc Ed Ctr & Spec Care Unit. Dew 138 E5
Ravensthorpe Sta. Dew 138 F4
Ravenstone Dr. Elland HX4 .... 134 C6
Ravenstone Gdns. S in Cra BD20 16 E5
Ravensville. Glu BD20 .... 16 E6
Ravenswharf Rd. Dew WF13 . 139 A6
Ravensworth Cl. Leeds LS15 . 62 F3
Ravensworth Way. Leeds LS15 62 F3
Raw End Rd. Hali HX2 .... 112 A8
Raw Hill. Brig HD6 .... 135 F8
Raw La. Hali HX2 .... 91 D5
Raw La. Heb Br HX7 .... 89 D3
Raw Nook Rd. Hud HD3 .... 152 E8
Rawden Hill. Arth LS21 .... 25 F6
Rawdon CE Prim Sch. Yeadon .. 40 D3
Rawdon Dr. Yeadon LS19 .... 40 B3
Rawdon Golf Course. Yeadon .. 40 B3
Rawdon Hall Dr. Yeadon LS19 .. 40 B3
Rawdon Littlemoor Jun & Inf Sch. Yeadon 40 C4
Rawdon Rd. Haw BD22 .... 51 C7
Rawdon Rd. Hors LS18 .... 57 F8
Rawdon St. Keigh BD22 .... 35 A6
Rawfield La. Fair WF11 .... 105 C6
Rawfield La. M Fry LS25 .... 105 C6
Rawfolds Ave. Batley WF17 .... 96 F2
Rawfolds Way. Liver BD19 .... 116 F6
Rawgate Ave. Castle WF10 .... 124 A7
Rawling St. Keigh BD21 .... 35 B5
Rawroyds. Elland HX4 .... 134 C5
Rawson Ave. Brad BD3 .... 75 D8
Rawson Ave. Hali HX3 .... 113 B3
Rawson Jun & Inf Sch. Hali 92 B2
Rawson Mkt. Brad 74 E7
Rawson Pl. Brad BD1 .... 74 E7
Rawson Pl. Sow Br HX6 .... 112 A3
Rawson Rd. Brad BD1 .... 74 E7
Rawson Sq. Brad BD10 .... 39 B1
Rawson Sq. Brad BD1 .... 74 E7 3
Rawson St. Brad BD12 .... 94 D4
Rawson St. Hali HX1 .... 113 C7
Rawson St N. Hali HX3 .... 92 B1
Rawson Terr. Leeds LS11 .... 79 C3
Rawson Wood. Sow Br HX6 .... 111 E2
Rawthorpe CE Inf Sch. Hud 154 E8
Rawthorpe Cres. Hud HD5 .... 154 E8
Rawthorpe Jun Sch. Hud 154 D7
Rawthorpe La. Hud HD5 .... 154 E7
Rawthorpe Sec Sch. Hud 154 E8
Rawthorpe Terr. Hud HD5 .... 154 E8
Rawtonstall Bank. B Head HX7 88 E4
Ray Gate. Holmfi HD7 .... 189 D8
Ray Gate. Hud HD3 .... 152 D8
Ray Gate. Wad M HX7 .... 89 F8
Ray St. Hud HD1 .... 154 B7
Ray Winfield Ind Est. Ack M T 163 E5
Raygill Cl. Leeds LS17 .... 44 B5
Raylands Cl. Midd LS10 .... 99 F6
Raylands Ct. Midd LS10 .... 99 F6
Raylands Fold. Midd LS10 .... 99 F6
Raylands Garth. Midd LS10 .... 99 F6
Raylands La. Midd LS10 .... 99 F6
Raylands Pl. Midd LS10 .... 99 F6
Raylands Rd. Midd LS10 .... 99 F6
Raylands Way. Midd LS10 .... 99 F6
Rayleigh St. Brad BD4 .... 75 A4
Raymond Dr. Brad BD5 .... 74 E2
Raymond St. Brad BD5 .... 74 E2
Raynbron Cres. Brad BD5 .... 74 E3
Raynel App. Hors LS16 .... 42 A3
Raynel Cl. Hors LS16 .... 42 A4
Raynel Dr. Hors LS16 .... 42 A4
Raynel Garth. Hors LS16 .... 42 A3
Raynel Gdns. Hors LS16 .... 42 A4
Raynel Gn. Hors LS16 .... 42 A3
Raynel Mount. Hors LS16 .... 42 A4
Raynel Way. Hors LS16 .... 41 F4
Rayner Ave. Batley WF16 .... 117 D6
Rayner Ave. Brad BD8 .... 54 F1
Rayner Dr. Brig HD6 .... 115 A4
Rayner Mount. Brad BD15 .... 73 A8
Rayner Rd. Brig HD6 .... 115 A4
Rayner St. Hor WF4 .... 141 A1
Rayner Terr. Pudsey LS28 .... 76 F8
Rayners Ave. Clec WF15 .... 116 C4
Raynham Cres. Keigh BD21 .... 34 F8
Raynor Cl. Hud HD3 .... 153 C7
Raynville App. Leeds LS13 .... 58 E3 1
Raynville Ave. Leeds LS13 .... 58 E3
Raynville Cl. Leeds LS13 .... 58 E3
Raynville Cres. Leeds LS12 .... 58 E3
Raynville Ct. Leeds LS13 .... 58 E3 2
Raynville Dene. Leeds LS12 .... 58 F3
Raynville Dr. Leeds LS13 .... 58 E3
Raynville Gn. Leeds LS13 .... 58 E2
Raynville Gr. Leeds LS13 .... 58 E3
Raynville Grange. Leeds LS13 . 58 E3 3
Raynville Mount. Leeds LS13 ... 58 E3
Raynville Pl. Leeds LS13 .... 58 E3 4
Raynville Prim Sch. Leeds 58 E2
Raynville Rd. Leeds LS12, LS13 58 E3
Raynville Rise. Leeds LS13 .... 58 E2
Raynville St. Leeds LS13 .... 58 E3
Raynville Terr. Leeds LS13 .... 58 E3
Raynville Wlk. Leeds LS13 .... 58 E2
Raywood Cl. Yeadon LS19 .... 40 A8
Reap Hirst Rd. Hud HD2 .... 135 D2
Rebecca St. Brad BD1 .... 74 D7
Recreation Ave. Leeds LS11 .... 79 A4 3
Recreation Cres. Leeds LS11 ... 78 F4
Recreation Gr. Leeds LS11 .... 79 A4
Recreation La. Elland HX5 .... 134 E6
Recreation Mount. Leeds LS11 79 A4
Recreation Pl. Leeds LS11 .... 79 A4
Recreation Rd. Hali HX6 .... 112 C4
Recreation Rd. Leeds LS11 .... 78 F2
Recreation Row. Leeds LS11 .... 78 F4
Recreation St. Leeds LS11 .... 79 A4
Recreation Terr. Leeds LS11 .... 79 A4
Recreation View. Leeds LS11 .. 79 A4
Rectory Ave. Castle WF10 .... 124 D8 2
Rectory Cl. Gar LS25 .... 82 F7
Rectory Cl. Mars HD7 .... 168 F4
Rectory Cl. Roy S71 .... 179 D1
Rectory Dr. Batley WF17 .... 97 A1
Rectory Dr. Hud HD5 .... 155 B7
Rectory Garden. Emley HD8 .. 175 D7
Rectory Garth. Hem WF9 .... 181 D7
Rectory La. Emley HD8 .... 175 D8
Rectory Row. Keigh BD21 .... 35 B7 12
Rectory St. Castle WF10 .... 124 D8 3
Rectory St. Leeds LS9 .... 60 E1
Rectory View. Dew WF12 .... 139 E3
Red Beck Rd. Northo HX3 .... 92 F1
Red Beck Vale. Ship BD18 .... 55 A5
Red Brink La. Sow Br HX6 .... 111 B2
Red Deer Park La. Floc WF4 .. 156 E5
Red Doles Ind Est. Hud 136 C1
Red Doles La. Hud HD2 .... 136 C1
Red Doles Rd. Hud HD1, HD2 136 C2
Red Hall App. Leeds LS14 .... 45 A1
Red Hall Ave. Leeds LS17 .... 44 F1
Red Hall Chase. Leeds LS14 .... 45 A1
Red Hall Croft. Leeds LS14 .... 62 A8
Red Hall Ct. Leeds LS14 .... 45 A1
Red Hall Dr. Leeds LS14 .... 45 A1
Red Hall Garth. Leeds LS14 .... 45 A1
Red Hall Gdns. Leeds LS17 .... 44 F1
Red Hall Gn. Leeds LS14 .... 45 A1
Red Hall La. Leeds LS14, LS17 . 45 A1
Red Hall La. Wake WF1 .... 121 A1
Red Hall View. Leeds LS14 .... 45 A1
Red Hall Way. Leeds LS14 .... 45 A1
Red Hall Wlk. Leeds LS14 .... 45 A1
Red House Mus. Clec 96 B1
Red La. Crof WF4 .... 143 E5
Red La. Feath WF7 .... 144 E5
Red La. Mel HD7 .... 170 B2
Red La. Pudsey LS28 .... 57 C3
Red Laithes Ct. Dew WF13 .... 138 E6
Red Laithes La. Dew WF13 .... 138 E6
Red Lees Rd. H Chap BB10 .... 85 A8
Red Lodge Cl. Leeds LS8 .... 61 D4
Redbeck Cotts. Yeadon LS19 .... 57 E8
Redburn Ave. Ship BD18 .... 55 A5
Redburn Dr. Ship BD18 .... 55 A5
Redburn Rd. Ship BD18 .... 55 B5
Redcar La. Stee BD20 .... 17 C2
Redcar Rd. Brad BD10 .... 56 E6
Redcar St. Hali HX1 .... 112 F7
Redcliffe Ave. Keigh BD21 .... 35 A7
Redcliffe Gr. Keigh BD21 .... 35 A7
Redcliffe St. Keigh BD21 .... 35 A7
Redcote La. Leeds LS12 .... 59 B1
Redcote La. Leeds LS4 .... 59 C2
Reddisher Rd. Mars HD7 .... 168 E4
Reddyshore Scout Gate. Tod OL14 .... 129 C5
Redesdale Gdns. Hors LS16 .... 42 B3
Redfearn Ave. Batley WF16 .... 117 D5
Redhall Cl. Leeds LS11 .... 78 E1
Redhall Cres. Leeds LS11 .... 78 E1
Redhall Gate. Leeds LS11 .... 78 E1
Redhill Ave. Castle WF10 .... 125 A6
Redhill Ave. E Ard WF3 .... 119 E5
Redhill Cl. E Ard WF3 .... 119 E5
Redhill Cres. E Ard WF3 .... 119 E5
Redhill Dr. Castle WF10 .... 125 B7
Redhill Dr. E Ard WF3 .... 119 E5
Redhill Fst Sch. Castle 125 C8
Redhill Gdns. Castle WF10 .... 125 A7
Redhill Mid Sch. Castle 125 C8
Redhill Mount. Castle WF10 .. 125 A7
Redhill Rd. Castle WF10 .... 125 A7
Redhill View. Castle WF10 .... 125 A6
Redland Cres. Hem WF9 .... 163 B2
Redland Dr. Kirkb HD8 .... 173 E7
Redland Gr. Mapp S75 .... 178 B2
Redlands Cl. Mir WF14 .... 138 A7
Redmayne Gr. Knot WF11 .... 126 D3
Redmire Ct. Leeds LS14 .... 62 B4
Redmire Dr. Leeds LS14 .... 62 A4
Redmire St. Brad BD3 .... 75 E7
Redmire View. Leeds LS14 .... 62 A4
Redruth Dr. Nor WF6 .... 123 B3
Redshaw Rd. Leeds LS12 .... 78 D6
Redthorne Way. Shaf S72 .... 180 C3
Redvers Cl. Hors LS16 .... 42 A1
Redwood Ave. E Ard WF3 .... 120 A8
Redwood Ave. Roy S71 .... 179 C3
Redwood Cl. Keigh BD21 .... 35 E5
Redwood Cl. Yeadon LS19 .... 39 F7
Redwood Dr. Hud HD2 .... 136 E5
Redwood Gr. Hud HD5 .... 154 D6 5
Redwood Gr. Yeadon LS19 .... 39 F7
Redwood Way. Yeadon LS19 .... 39 F7
Reed Rd. Leeds LS12 .... 78 C6
Reed St. Bacup OL13 .... 106 A3
Reed St. Hud HD3 .... 153 D7
Reedling Dr. Morley LS27 .... 98 C3
Reedsdale Ave. Gild LS27 .... 97 C7
Reedsdale Dr. Gild LS27 .... 97 C7
Reedsdale Gdns. Gild LS27 .... 97 C7
Rees Way. Brad BD3 .... 74 F8
Reeth Rd. Brig HD6 .... 135 E8
Reevy Ave. Brad BD6 .... 93 F8
Reevy Cres. Brad BD6 .... 93 F8
Reevy Dr. Brad BD6 .... 94 A8
Reevy Hill Fst Sch. Brad 73 F1
Reevy Rd. Brad BD6 .... 94 B8
Reevy Rd W. Brad BD6 .... 93 E8
Reevy St. Brad BD6 .... 74 A1
Reevylands Dr. Brad BD6 .... 94 A8
Reform St. Clec BD19 .... 96 B1
Regal Cl. Rip HX6 .... 132 C1
Regal Dr. Rip HX6 .... 132 C1
Regency Ct. Brad BD8 .... 74 B8
Regency Ct. Leeds LS6 .... 59 E4
Regency Gdns. E Ard WF3 .... 120 A8
Regency Park Gr. Pudsey LS28 76 E5 4
Regency Park Rd. Pudsey LS28 76 E5
Regency Rd. Mir WF14 .... 138 A4
Regency View. Brad BD3 .... 56 A2
Regent Ave. Hors LS18 .... 58 C7
Regent Cl. Brig HD6 .... 135 E6
Regent Cl. Hors LS18 .... 58 C7
Regent Cres. Hors LS18 .... 58 C7
Regent Cres. S Hie S72 .... 180 E5
Regent Ct. Hors LS18 .... 58 C7 10
Regent Ct. Leeds LS1 .... 79 C7 1
Regent House. Elland HX5 .... 134 F7 6
Regent Park Ave. Leeds LS6 .... 59 F4
Regent Park Cross Ave. Leeds LS6 .... 59 F4
Regent Park Terr. Leeds LS6 .... 59 F4
Regent Pl. Brad BD10 .... 39 A1
Regent Pl. Hali HX6 .... 112 B5 17
Regent Pl. Heb Br HX7 .... 89 A4 8
Regent Rd. Hors LS18 .... 58 B7
Regent Rd. Hud HD1 .... 153 E7
Regent Rd. Ilkley LS29 .... 8 A4
Regent Rd. Kirkhe HD5 .... 137 C2
Regent St. Bacup OL13 .... 106 A2 4
Regent St. Brad BD10 .... 39 A1
Regent St. Brad BD10 .... 56 D7
Regent St. Castle WF10 .... 124 C7
Regent St. Feath WF7 .... 145 C5
Regent St. Hali HX1 .... 113 B6
Regent St. Haw BD22 .... 51 D7 13
Regent St. Heb Br HX7 .... 89 A3
Regent St. Hem WF9 .... 181 C7
Regent St. Hor WF4 .... 140 F2
Regent St. Leeds LS2, LS7 .... 60 D1
Regent St. Leeds LS7 .... 60 D7
Regent St. Liver FW16 .... 117 C3
Regent St. Mir WF14 .... 138 A3
Regent St. Nor WF6 .... 123 C4
Regent St. Queen BD13 .... 72 F1
Regent St. S Elm WF9 .... 182 E3
Regent St. S Hie S72 .... 180 E5
Regent St. Tod OL14 .... 108 A1
Regent St. Wake WF1 .... 142 E3
Regent Street Fst Sch. Feath . 145 D5
Regent Terr. Leeds LS6 .... 59 F2
Regent Terr. Leeds LS7 .... 60 D7
Regents Pk. Wake WF1 .... 142 E6
Regina Cres. Bri S72 .... 180 E2
Regina Cres. Ryhill WF4 .... 162 C1
Regina Dr. Leeds LS7 .... 60 D6
Regina House. Leeds LS13 .... 77 D8
Reginald Mount. Leeds LS7 .... 60 D4
Reginald Pl. Leeds LS7 .... 60 D4
Reginald Row. Leeds LS7 .... 60 D4
Reginald St. Brad BD5 .... 74 D3
Reginald St. Leeds LS7 .... 60 D4
Reginald Terr. Leeds LS7 .... 60 D4
Reginald View. Leeds LS7 .... 60 D4
Reid Park Ave. Hor WF4 .... 140 E1
Reighton Croft. Brad BD10 .... 56 E6
Rein Ct. Aber LS25 .... 64 E8
Rein Gdns. E Ard WF3 .... 119 C8
Rein Mews. E Ard WF3 .... 119 C8
Rein Rd. Hors LS18 .... 58 C6
Rein Rd. Morley LS27 .... 98 C1
Rein St. Morley LS27 .... 98 C1
Rein The. Leeds LS14 .... 61 F6
Reins Ave. Bail BD17 .... 38 B1
Reins Rd. Brig HD6 .... 135 E8
Reins Terr. Honley HD7 .... 172 A5
Reinwood Ave. Hud HD3 .... 153 B7
Reinwood Ave. Leeds LS8 .... 61 E5
Reinwood Cty Prim Sch. Hud . 153 B7
Reinwood Rd. Hud HD3 .... 153 B6
Rembrandt Ave. E Ard WF3 .... 119 F8
Renee Cl. Brad BD4 .... 95 C8
Renfield Gr. Nor WF6 .... 123 D3
Renshaw St. Brad BD10 .... 39 B1
Renton Ave. Guise LS20 .... 22 D1
Renton Dr. Guise LS20 .... 39 D8
Renton Lea. Guise LS20 .... 39 D8
Reservoir Pl. Dew WF13 .... 118 A1
Reservoir Pl. Queen BD13 .... 72 C2 4
Reservoir Rd. Batley WF17 .... 117 F4
Reservoir Rd. Hali HX2 .... 112 E8
Reservoir Rd. Haw BD22 .... 50 F6
Reservoir St. Dew WF13 .... 118 A1
Reservoir View. Skel HD8 .... 174 E2
Reservoir View. Thorn BD13 .... 72 D7
Restmore Ave. Guise LS20 .... 22 D2
Retford Pl. Brad BD7 .... 74 C5
Reuben St. Liver WF15 .... 117 A5
Reva Cl. Bing BD16 .... 37 B4
Reva Syke Rd. Brad BD14 .... 73 B4
Revel Garth. D Dale HD8 .... 192 A5
Revie Rd. Leeds LS11 .... 78 F3
Reydon Wlk. Brad BD6 .... 73 F1
Reyhill Gr. Brad BD5 .... 74 E5
Reyner House Mews. Brad BD5 74 E5
Reynolds Ave. Brad BD7 .... 73 E5
Rhine St. Brad BD4 .... 75 A5
Rhode's Hill La. Bramham LS23 30 F3
Rhodes Ave. Batley WF16 .... 117 D6
Rhodes Cres. Pont WF8 .... 146 D6
Rhodes Gdns. Loft G WF3 .... 121 C6
Rhodes La. B Spa LS23 .... 30 C6
Rhodes Pl. Ship BD17 .... 55 B8
Rhodes St. Castle WF10 .... 124 B7
Rhodes St. Castle WF10 .... 124 C8
Rhodes St. Hali HX1 .... 113 B7
Rhodes St. Liver FW15 .... 117 C4
Rhodes St. Ship BD18 .... 55 A8
Rhodes Terr. Brad BD2 .... 56 B4
Rhodes Terr. Leeds LS12 .... 78 E6
Rhodesia Ave. Brad BD15 .... 73 C8
Rhodesia Ave. Hali HX3 .... 113 C3
Rhodesia St. Glu BD20 .... 16 D6
Rhodesway. Brad BD8 .... 73 D8
Rhodesway Sch. Brad 73 C8
Rhondda Pl. Hali HX1 .... 112 E6
Rhum Cl. Brad BD6 .... 93 F6
Rhyddings Ave. Ack M T WF7 .... 163 F5
Rhyddings Dr. Ack M T WF7 .. 163 F5
Rhyddings Gdns. Ilkley LS29 .... 8 D4
Rhyl St. Feath WF7 .... 145 D6
Rhylstone Mount. Brad BD7 .... 73 F6
Ribble St. Keigh BD21 .... 35 E8
Ribblesdale Ave. Gar LS25 .... 83 B6
Ribbleton Gr. Brad BD3 .... 75 A8
Ribstone St. Heb Br HX7 .... 89 E1
Riccall Nook. Brad BD10 .... 56 D6
Rice St. Hud HD1 .... 154 B5 1
Rich Gate. Holmfi HD7 .... 189 B2
Richard Dunn Sports Ctr The. Brad 74 D1
Richard Oastler Sch. Leeds 59 D2
Richard Pl. Brig HD6 .... 115 A4 4
Richard St. Bacup OL13 .... 106 A7 3
Richard St. Brad BD3 .... 75 A7
Richard St. Brig HD6 .... 115 A4
Richard St. Wake WF1 .... 142 C7 3
Richard Thorpe Av. Mir WF14 138 B5
Richardshaw Dr. Pudsey LS28 . 57 E1
Richardshaw La. Pudsey LS28 . 76 E8
Richardshaw Rd. Pudsey LS28 57 F1
Richardson Ave. Brad BD6 .... 94 C8
Richardson Cres. Leeds LS9 .... 80 C7
Richardson Rd. Leeds LS9 .... 80 C7
Richardson Sq. Hud HD1 .... 154 A6 5
Richardson St. Brad BD12 .... 95 A4
Richmond Ave. Hud HD2 .... 136 A2
Richmond Ave. Knot WF11 .... 126 B5
Richmond Ave. Leeds LS6 .... 59 E4
Richmond Ave. Sow Br HX6 .... 111 F3
Richmond Cl. Hali HX1 .... 113 C8
Richmond Cl. Leeds LS13 .... 58 A2
Richmond Cl. Morley LS27 .... 98 A3 3
Richmond Cl. Roth LS26 .... 100 F6
Richmond Ct. Crof WF4 .... 162 A8
Richmond Ct. Hud HD4 .... 152 F3
Richmond Ct. Leeds LS9 .... 79 F7 1
Richmond Ct. Pont WF8 .... 125 D1

Richmond Ct. Roth LS26 ... 100 F6
Richmond Flats. Hud HD1 ... 154 B7 7
Richmond Garth. Ossett WF5 140 F4
Richmond Gdns. Pudsey LS28 . 77 A7
Richmond Gdns. Sow Br HX6 . 111 F3
Richmond Green St. Leeds LS9 79 E7
Richmond Hill App. Leeds LS9 . 79 E7
Richmond Hill Cl. Leeds LS9 ... 79 E7
Richmond Hill Prim Sch. Leeds 79 F6
Richmond House Sch. Leeds ... 59 C7
Richmond Lea. Mir WF14 ... 138 A6
Richmond Mews. Ship BD18 ... 54 F8
Richmond Mount. Leeds LS6 ... 59 E4
Richmond Pl. Ilkley LS29 ... 8 C3
Richmond Pl. Ship BD18 ... 54 F8 16
Richmond Rd. Batley WF16 ... 117 E6
Richmond Rd. Batley WF17 ... 118 D2
Richmond Rd. Brad BD7 ... 74 D6
Richmond Rd. Hali HX1 ... 113 B8
Richmond Rd. Leeds LS6 ... 59 E4
Richmond Rd. Pudsey LS28 ... 57 C2
Richmond Rd. Ship BD18 ... 54 F8 17
Richmond Rd. Upton WF9 ... 183 A7
Richmond Rd. Wake WF1 ... 142 B8
Richmond St. Castle WF10 ... 124 D7
Richmond St. Clec BD19 ... 116 D7
Richmond St. Hali HX1 ... 113 B8
Richmond St. Keigh BD21 ... 35 B8
Richmond St. Leeds LS9 ... 79 E7
Richmond St. Tod OL14 ... 108 C5 8
Richmond Terr. Otley LS21 ... 22 F7
Richmond Terr. Pudsey LS28 ... 77 A7
Richmond Way. Gar LS25 ... 82 F5
Richmondfield Ave.
B in Elm LS15 ... 63 E6
Richmondfield Cl. B in Elm LS15 63 E6
Richmondfield Cres.
B in Elm LS15 ... 63 E6
Richmondfield Cross.
B in Elm LS15 ... 63 E6
Richmondfield Dr. B in Elm LS1563 E6
Richmondfield Garth.
B in Elm LS15 ... 63 E7
Richmondfield Gr. B in Elm LS1563 E6
Richmondfield La. B in Elm LS1563 E6
Richmondfield Mount.
B in Elm LS15 ... 63 E6
Richmondfield Way.
B in Elm LS15 ... 63 E6
Rickard St. Leeds LS12 ... 78 F6
Ridding Gate. Otley LS21 ... 10 E1
Riddings Cl. Hem WF9 ... 181 D5
Riddings Cl. Hud HD2 ... 136 D3
Riddings Rd. Hud HD2 ... 136 D3
Riddings Rd. Ilkley LS29 ... 8 B4
Riddings Rise. Hud HD2 ... 136 E3
Riddlesden CE Fst Sch. Keigh .. 18 F2
Riddlesden Golf Course. Sil ... 18 C4
Riddlesden St. Keigh BD20 ... 18 F1
Rider Rd. Leeds LS6 ... 60 B4
Rider St. Leeds LS9 ... 79 E8
Ridge Ave. Neth WF4 ... 158 A7
Ridge Bank. Tod OL14 ... 108 B5
Ridge Cl. Guise LS20 ... 39 C8
Ridge Cl. Hud HD4 ... 154 A3
Ridge Cl. Skel HD8 ... 175 A1
Ridge Cres. Neth WF4 ... 158 A6
Ridge Gr. Leeds LS7 ... 60 A5
Ridge Hill. Brig HD6 ... 114 E1
Ridge La. Sil BD20 ... 5 C7
Ridge Lea. Brig HD6 ... 114 F1
Ridge Mount. Leeds LS6 ... 60 A4
Ridge Rd. Kippax LS25 ... 83 D2
Ridge Rd. Leeds LS7 ... 60 B4
Ridge Rd. Neth WF4 ... 158 A6
Ridge Rd. Tod OL14 ... 108 B5
Ridge St. Hud HD4 ... 154 A3
Ridge Terr. Leeds LS6 ... 59 E5
Ridge The. Coll LS22 ... 13 C3
Ridge View. Elland HX5 ... 135 C6
Ridge View Gdns. Brad BD10 .. 56 C7
Ridge View. Pudsey LS13 ... 77 C8
Ridge View Rd. Brig HD6 ... 115 A1
Ridge Way. Leeds LS8 ... 60 F6
Ridgedale Mount. Pont WF8 .. 125 D4
Ridgefield St. Castle WF10 ... 124 D7
Ridgemount Rd. Keigh BD20 ... 18 E2
Ridgestone Ave. Hem WF9 ... 181 E7
Ridgeway Cl. Hud HD5 ... 154 E7
Ridgeway Cl. Leeds LS8 ... 60 F6
Ridgeway Cres. Roy S71 ... 179 C1
Ridgeway Dr. Batley WF17 ... 97 A1
Ridgeway Gdns. Brig HD6 ... 114 E5
Ridgeway. Guise LS20 ... 39 B8
Ridgeway. Hud HD5 ... 154 E7
Ridgeway Mount. Keigh BD22 . 34 F5
Ridgeway. Queen BD13 ... 92 F8
Ridgeway. Ship BD18 ... 55 E6
Ridgeway Sq. Knot WF11 ... 126 F3
Ridgeway The. Knot WF11 ... 126 F3
Ridgeways The. Slai HD7 ... 170 D8
Ridgewood Cl. Bail BD17 ... 38 E3
Ridgley View. Castle WF10 ... 125 D5
Riding Head La. Hali HX2 ... 90 E1
Riding Hill. Shelf HX3 ... 93 E6
Riding La. Hali HX2 ... 91 D3
Riding St. Batley WF17 ... 117 E6
Ridings Cl. Loft G WF3 ... 121 B6
Ridings Ct. Loft G WF3 ... 121 B6
Ridings Fields. Honley HD7 ... 172 C3
Ridings Gdns. Loft G WF3 ... 121 B6
Ridings La. Holmfi HD7 ... 189 C7
Ridings La. Hud HD7 ... 152 C4
Ridings La. Loft G WF3 ... 121 B6
Ridings Mews. Loft G WF3 ... 121 B6
Ridings Rd. Dew WF13 ... 139 D8
Ridings Sh Ctr. Wake ... 142 C6
Ridings Way. Loft G WF3 ... 121 B6
Ridingwood Rise. Clay W HD8 175 E2
Ridleys Fold. Sil LS29 ... 6 F8
Rievaulx Ave. Brad BD8 ... 74 C8
Rievaulx Cl. B Spa LS23 ... 30 C7
Rifle Fields. Hud HD1 ... 153 F6
Rifle St. Hud HD1 ... 154 B5
Rigg La. Ack M T WF7, WF8 .. 164 E7
Rightox Rd. Honley HD7 ... 172 C3
Rigton App. Leeds LS9 ... 79 E8
Rigton Bank. Bard LS17 ... 28 D4
Rigton Cl. Leeds LS9 ... 79 F8
Rigton Dr. Leeds LS9 ... 79 E8
Rigton Gn. Bard LS17 ... 28 E4
Rigton Gn. Leeds LS9 ... 79 E8
Rigton Lawn. Leeds LS9 ... 79 E8
Rigton Mews. Leeds LS9 ... 79 E8
Rigton St. Brad BD5 ... 74 D3
Riley La. Hali HX2 ... 91 F8
Riley La. Kirkb HD8 ... 173 E6
Riley Pk. Kirkb HD8 ... 173 E6
Riley St. Hud HD4 ... 154 B4
Rillbank La. Leeds LS3 ... 59 F1
Rillbank St. Leeds LS3 ... 59 F2
Rillington Mead. Brad BD10 ... 56 D6
Rills Mead. Otley LS21 ... 23 A7
Rillside. Shep HD8 ... 173 F1
Rilston St. Brad BD7 ... 74 B6
Rimswell Holt. Brad BD10 ... 56 E6
Ring O'Bells Yd. Hor WF4 ... 141 A1 9
Ring Rd Adel. Hors LS16 ... 42 D2
Ring Rd Beeston. Leeds LS12 .. 78 C3
Ring Rd Be'ston Pk. Leeds LS11 98 F7
Ring Rd Beeston Pk. Midd LS10 99 A6
Ring Rd Cross Gates. Leeds
LS15 ... 62 C3
Ring Rd Farsley. Pudsey LS28 . 57 C4
Ring Rd Halton. Leeds LS15 ... 62 C1
Ring Rd (Horsforth). Hors LS18 58 E8
Ring Rd Low Wortley.
Leeds LS12 ... 78 B4
Ring Rd Meanw'd. Leeds LS17 . 42 F2
Ring Rd Middleton. Midd LS10 . 99 F6
Ring Rd Moortown. Leeds LS17 43 D3
Ring Rd Seacroft. Leeds LS14 .. 62 B6
Ring Rd Shadwell. Leeds LS17 . 44 D2
Ring Rd Weetwood. Leeds LS16 42 C1
Ring Rd West Pk. Leeds LS16 .. 42 A1
Ring Road Bramley.
Pudsey LS13 ... 77 C8
Ring Road Farnley. Leeds LS12 77 E7
Ringby La. Hali HX3 ... 92 B4
Ringstone Gr. Bri S72 ... 181 B3
Ringway. Gar LS25 ... 82 D6
Ringwood Ave. Leeds LS14 ... 62 A8
Ringwood Cres. Leeds LS14 ... 62 A8
Ringwood Ct. Loft G WF1 ... 121 D5
Ringwood Dr. Leeds LS14 ... 62 A8
Ringwood Edge. Elland HX5 ... 134 D6
Ringwood Gdns. Leeds LS14 ... 62 A8
Ringwood Mount. Leeds LS14 . 62 A8 1
Ringwood Rd. Brad BD5 ... 74 C3
Ringwood Way. Hem WF9 ... 181 F7
Rink Par. Batley WF17 ... 118 D3 5
Rink St. Batley WF17 ... 118 D3
Rink Terr. Batley WF17 ... 118 D3 4
Ripley Cl. Nor WF6 ... 123 D2
Ripley Ct. Nor WF6 ... 144 B8
Ripley Dr. Nor WF6 ... 123 D3
Ripley La. Guise LS20 ... 22 E2
Ripley Rd. Brad BD4 ... 74 F4
Ripley Rd. Liver WF15 ... 116 F4
Ripley St. Brad BD15 ... 54 A2
Ripley St. Brad BD5 ... 74 F4
Ripley St. Brig HX3 ... 115 A7
Ripley St. Keigh BD20 ... 18 F1
Ripley Terr. Hali HX2 ... 111 D7
Ripon Ave. Hud HD2 ... 136 B2
Ripon House. Elland HX5 ... 134 F7 5
Ripon Rd. Dew WF12 ... 118 F1
Ripon St. Hali HX1 ... 112 E6
Ripon Terr. Hali HX3 ... 92 B1
Rippenden Stones Cty Jun Mix & Inf
Sch. Rip ... 132 C2
Ripponden Jun & Inf School.
Rip ... 132 E5
Ripponden New Bank. Rip HX6 132 E4
Ripponden Old Bank. Rip HX6 132 E4
Ripponden Old La. Rip HX6 ... 132 B3
Rise La. Tod OL14 ... 108 A5
Rise The. Broth WF11 ... 126 C8
Rise The. Kippax LS25 ... 83 A1
Rise The. Leeds LS5 ... 59 A5
Rise The. Northo HX3 ... 93 A2
Rise The. Pont WF8 ... 146 E7
Risedale Ave. Batley WF17 ... 97 B2
Risedale Cl. Batley WF17 ... 97 B2
Rishworth Ave. Emley HD8 ... 175 D6
Rishworth Hall Cl. Rip HX6 ... 132 B1
Rishworth Mill La. Rip HX6 ... 150 D8
Rishworth New Rd. Rip HX6 .. 132 B1
Rishworth Rd. Dew WF12 ... 139 D8
Rishworth Rd. Rip HX4 ... 133 A4
Rishworth Sch. Rip ... 132 C2
Rishworth St. Dew WF13 ... 139 D8
Rishworth St. Keigh BD22 ... 34 F6
Rishworth St. Wake WF1 ... 142 C7
Rishworthian Ct. Elland HX3 .. 113 A1
Ristone Fold. Leeds LS12 ... 78 C5
Rivadale View. Ilkley LS29 ... 8 B5
Rivelin Rd. Castle WF10 ... 124 C6
River Holme Vw. Honley HD7 172 C2
River Pk. Honley HD7 ... 171 F5
River St. Brig HD6 ... 115 C1
River St. Haw BD22 ... 51 D7 6
River St. Keigh BD21 ... 18 E1
River St. Tod OL14 ... 108 C5
River Valley View. D Dale HD8 192 A6
River View. B Spa LS23 ... 30 F7
River View. Castle WF10 ... 124 B8
River View. Ilkley LS29 ... 8 E5
River Wlk. Bing BD16 ... 36 F3
Riverdale Ave. Loft G WF3 ... 121 F2
Riverdale Cl. Loft G WF3 ... 121 F2
Riverdale Cres. Loft G WF3 ... 121 F2
Riverdale Dr. Loft G WF3 ... 121 F2
Riverdale Gdns. B Spa LS23 ... 30 F7
Riverdale Rd. Loft G WF3 ... 121 F2
Riverdale Rd. Otley LS21 ... 23 A8
Riverdale. Weth LS22 ... 13 F4
Rivermead. Wake WF2 ... 142 D3
Riverside Ave. Otley LS21 ... 11 B2
Riverside Cl. Otley LS21 ... 11 B1
Riverside. Clay W HD8 ... 175 E3
Riverside Cotts. Sil BD20 ... 17 D8
Riverside Cres. Otley LS21 ... 11 B1
Riverside Ct. Leeds LS1 ... 79 C7
Riverside Dr. Otley LS21 ... 11 B2
Riverside Est. Ship BD17 ... 55 B8
Riverside Ind Est. Dew ... 139 C7
Riverside Jun Sch. Heb Br ... 89 A3
Riverside. Keigh BD21 ... 35 E7
Riverside Pk. Otley LS21 ... 11 B1
Riverside Villas. Wake WF2 .. 142 D2
Riverside Way. Dew WF13 ... 138 E4
Riverside Wlk. Ilkley LS29 ... 7 F5
Riverwood Dr. Hali HX3 ... 113 B2
Riviera Gdns. Leeds LS7 ... 60 C6
Rivock Ave. Keigh BD20 ... 17 F3
Rivock Ave. Stee BD20 ... 17 D6
Rivock Gr. Keigh BD20 ... 17 F3
RM Grylls Mid Sch. Clec ... 116 B4
Roach Grange Av. Kippax LS25 83 A3
Road End. Elland HX4 ... 134 C7 4
Road Sides. Pont WF8 ... 146 D6
Roaine Dr. Holmfi HD7 ... 189 B4
Roans Brae. Brad BD10 ... 56 E6
Robb Ave. Leeds LS11 ... 79 A1
Robb St. Leeds LS11 ... 79 A1
Robbins Terr. Feath WF7 ... 145 D6
Roberson Terr. Clec BD19 ... 117 A8
Robert Ct. Liver WF15 ... 116 F3
Robert La. Holmfi HD7 ... 189 C7
Robert St. Brad BD3 ... 75 A6
Robert St. Hali HX3 ... 92 A2
Robert St. Haw BD22 ... 51 F8
Robert St N. Hali HX3 ... 92 C2 2
Robert's St. Clec BD19 ... 116 C7
Roberts Ave. Leeds LS9 ... 61 B2
Roberts Ct. Leeds LS9 ... 61 B2
Roberts Pl. Brad BD1 ... 74 D7
Roberts Pl. Leeds LS9 ... 61 C1
Roberts St. Keigh BD22 ... 34 C6
Roberts St. Pudsey LS28 ... 57 E1
Roberts St. Roth LS26 ... 101 C6 4
Roberts Way. Wake WF2 ... 142 F1
Robertsgate. Roth WF3 ... 100 B1
Robertshaw Rd. Heb Br HX7 ... 88 F3
Robertson Ave. Brig HD6 ... 136 A8
Roberttown CE (C) Jun Mix Sch.
Liver ... 116 E2
Roberttown La. Liver WF15 ... 116 F2
Robin Chase. Pudsey LS28 ... 76 F7
Robin Cl. Brad BD2 ... 56 C4
Robin Cl. Pont WF8 ... 125 D3
Robin Dr. Brad BD2 ... 56 C4
Robin Hill. Batley WF17 ... 118 A8
Robin Hood Ave. Roy S71 ... 179 D4
Robin Hood Cres. Wake WF2 141 E4
Robin Hood Gr. Hud HD2 ... 136 C4
Robin Hood Hill. Hud HD4 ... 171 F7
Robin Hood Jun & Inf Sch.
Roth ... 100 B2
Robin Hood Rd. Hud HD2 ... 136 C4
Robin Hood St. Castle WF10 .. 124 E7 1
Robin Hood Way. Brig HD6 ... 115 E2
Robin La. Batley WF13 ... 117 F3
Robin La. Batley WF13 ... 118 B2
Robin La. Hem WF9 ... 181 A5
Robin La. Pudsey LS28 ... 76 E7
Robin La. Roy S71 ... 179 D4
Robin Rocks. Honley HD7 ... 172 C2
Robin Royd Ave. Mir WF14 ... 138 A8
Robin Royd Croft. Mir WF14 .. 138 A8
Robin Royd Dr. Mir WF14 ... 138 A8
Robin Royd Garth. Mir WF14 . 138 A8
Robin Royd Gr. Mir WF14 ... 138 A8
Robin Royd La. Mir WF14 ... 138 A8
Robin St. Brad BD5 ... 74 C4
Robin St. Hud HD1 ... 153 D5
Robin Wlk. Ship BD18 ... 55 D6
Robin's Gr. Roth LS26 ... 100 F5
Robinia Wlk. Wake WF2 ... 142 A8
Robins The. Bur in W LS29 ... 21 E8
Robinson Ct. Brad BD7 ... 73 F6
Robinson La. Honley HD7 ... 172 B3
Robinson La. Kippax LS25 ... 83 B1
Robinson St. Hud HD1 ... 154 C5
Robinson St. Kippax WF10 ... 103 B4
Robinson St. Pont WF8 ... 125 D1
Robinwood Ct. Leeds LS8 ... 44 A1
Robinwood Jun & Inf Sch. Tod 107 E8
Robson Cl. Pont WF8 ... 146 D6
Robson's Rd. Wake WF1 ... 142 B6
Rochdale Rd. Bacup OL13 ... 106 A1
Rochdale Rd. Elland HX4 ... 134 B7
Rochdale Rd. Hali HX2, HX6 .. 112 D5
Rochdale Rd. Rip HX6 ... 131 C2
Rochdale Rd. Slai HD7 ... 151 F4
Rochdale Rd. Sow Br HX6 ... 111 F1
Rochdale Rd. Tod OL14 ... 108 A3
Rochdale Rd. Tod OL14 ... 129 B6
Rocheford Cl. Leeds LS10 ... 79 F3
Rocheford Ct. Leeds LS10 ... 79 F3
Rocheford Gdns. Leeds LS10 ... 79 F3
Rocheford Gr. Leeds LS10 ... 79 F3
Rocheford Wlk. Leeds LS10 ... 79 F3
Rochester Cl. Bacup OL13 ... 106 A7 2
Rochester Ct. Hor WF4 ... 141 C2
Rochester Dr. Hor WF4 ... 141 C2
Rochester Gdns. Pudsey LS13 . 57 F4
Rochester House. Brad BD15 .. 54 B1
Rochester Pl. Elland HX5 ... 134 F6 5
Rochester Rd. Batley WF17 ... 96 F3
Rochester St. Brad BD3 ... 75 C7
Rochester St. Ship BD18 ... 55 C6
Rochester Terr. Leeds LS6 ... 59 D4
Rochester Wynd. Leeds LS17 .. 44 A4
Rock Cliffe Mount. Hali HX2 ... 111 D7
Rock Edge. Liver WF15 ... 117 A5
Rock Fold. Hud HD7 ... 152 D4
Rock Hill. Castle WF10 ... 125 A6
Rock House Dr. Dew WF13 ... 118 C2
Rock La. Leeds LS13 ... 58 B4
Rock La. Slai HD7 ... 152 A3
Rock La. Wils BD13 ... 72 C8
Rock Lea. Queen BD13 ... 72 F1 5
Rock Nook. Litt OL15 ... 129 D1
Rock Rd. Hud HD3 ... 135 B2
Rock St. Brig HD6 ... 115 A3 15
Rock St. Hud HD3 ... 152 E7
Rock Terr. Castle WF10 ... 125 A6
Rock Terr. Hud HD3 ... 135 B1
Rock Terr. Leeds LS15 ... 80 F8 2
Rock Terr. Morley LS27 ... 98 B5
Rock Terr. Thorn BD13 ... 72 D6
Rock Terr. Tod OL14 ... 108 A2
Rock The. Hud HD7 ... 152 E1
Rock View. Elland HX4 ... 134 C4
Rock View. Mars HD7 ... 168 F3
Rockcliffe Ave. Bail BD17 ... 38 C1
Rockery Croft. Hors LS18 ... 41 C2
Rockery Rd. Hors LS18 ... 41 C2
Rockfield Terr. Yeadon LS19 ... 40 C7
Rockhill Cl. Batley WF17 ... 96 F1
Rockhill La. Brad BD4 ... 95 A7
Rockingham Cl. Leeds LS15 ... 62 F3
Rockingham La. Bad WF9 ... 164 E4
Rockingham Rd. Leeds LS15 ... 62 F3
Rockingham St. Hem WF9 ... 163 B3
Rockingham Way. Leeds LS15 . 62 F3
Rockland Cres. Brad BD7 ... 73 E5
Rocklands Ave. Bail BD17 ... 38 C4 2
Rocklands Pl. Bail BD17 ... 38 C4 3
Rockley Cl. Hud HD5 ... 154 E4
Rockley Dr. Wake WF2 ... 160 B6
Rockley Grange Gdn. Gar LS25 82 D5
Rockley St. Dew WF13 ... 139 D8
Rockliffe La. Bacup OL13 ... 106 A1
Rockliffe Rd. Bacup OL13 ... 106 A1
Rockmill Rd. Honley HD7 ... 172 C2
Rocks La. Hali HX2 ... 71 D1
Rocks Rd. Hali HX3 ... 113 A4
Rocks View. Hali HX2 ... 113 A4 3
Rockville Terr. Hali HX1 ... 113 A5 19
Rockville Terr. Yeadon LS19 ... 40 C6
Rockwell La. Brad BD10 ... 56 C6
Rockwood Cl. Hud HD2 ... 136 E6
Rockwood Cl. Mapp S75 ... 177 F1
Rockwood Cres. Crig WF4 ... 159 D6
Rockwood Cres. Pudsey LS28 . 57 A3
Rockwood Gr. Pudsey LS28 ... 57 B3
Rockwood Rd. Pudsey LS28 ... 57 A2
Rockwood Rise. D Dale HD8 .. 192 A7
Roderick St. Leeds LS12 ... 78 B7
Rodger La. Wake WF2 ... 120 F2
Rodillian Sch. Roth ... 100 B1
Rodin Ave. Brad BD8 ... 73 D7
Rodley La. Emley HD8 ... 175 D7
Rodley La. Leeds LS13 ... 58 A4
Rodley La. Pudsey LS28, LS13 . 57 D6
Rodley Prim Sch. Pudsey ... 57 F5
Rodney Yd. Wake WF1 ... 142 C6
Rods Mills La. Morley LS27 ... 98 B3
Rods View. Morley LS27 ... 98 B3 4
Roe House. Bail BD17 ... 38 B1
Roebuck La. Clift LS21 ... 10 F4
Roebuck Memorial Homes.
Hud HD5 ... 154 F6
Roebuck St. Batley WF17 ... 96 F1
Roebuck Terr. Clift LS21 ... 10 F4
Roeburn Cl. Mapp S75 ... 178 A2
Roger Ct. Brad BD2 ... 56 B2
Roger Dr. Wake WF2 ... 142 D1
Roger Fold. Kippax LS25 ... 83 B1 1
Roger Gate. Heb Br HX7 ... 89 C1
Roger La. Hud HD4 ... 154 C3
Rogers Ct. Loft G WF3 ... 121 F6
Rogers Pl. Pudsey LS28 ... 76 F8
Rogerson Sq. Brig HD6 ... 115 A3
Roils Head Rd. Hali HX2 ... 112 C7
Rokeby Gdns. Brad BD10 ... 56 E6
Rokeby Gdns. Leeds LS6 ... 59 C5
Roker La. Pudsey LS28 ... 77 A5
Roman Ave. Hud HD3 ... 134 D1
Roman Ave. Leeds LS8 ... 44 A3
Roman Cl. Hud HD3 ... 134 D1
Roman Cres. Leeds LS8 ... 44 B2
Roman Dr. Hud HD3 ... 134 D1
Roman Dr. Leeds LS8 ... 44 B2
Roman Gdns. Leeds LS8 ... 44 A2
Roman Gr. Leeds LS8 ... 44 B2
Roman Mount. Leeds LS8 ... 44 B2
Roman Pl. Leeds LS8 ... 44 B2
Roman Rd. Batley WF17 ... 117 F8 5
Roman Rise. Pont WF8 ... 146 C5
Roman St. Dearne S63 ... 194 E1
Roman Terr. Leeds LS8 ... 44 A2
Roman View. Leeds LS8 ... 44 B2
Romanby Shaw. Brad BD10 ... 56 D6
Rombald's View. Ilkley LS29 ... 8 D5
Rombalds Ave. Leeds LS12 ... 78 C8
Rombalds Cres. Leeds LS12 ... 59 C1
Rombalds Ct. Men LS29 ... 21 F4
Rombalds Dr. Bing BD16 ... 37 B3
Rombalds Gr. Leeds LS12 ... 78 C8
Rombalds La. Ilkley LS29 ... 8 E3
Rombalds Pl. Leeds LS12 ... 59 C1 1
Rombalds St. Leeds LS12 ... 59 C1
Rombalds Terr. Leeds LS12 ... 78 C8
Rombalds View. Leeds LS12 ... 59 C1
Rombalds View. Otley LS21 ... 10 D2
Romford Ave. Morley LS27 ... 98 A3
Romford Ct. Brad BD6 ... 93 F6
Romney Mount. Pudsey LS28 .. 77 A5
Romsey Cl. Hud HD3 ... 134 F1
Romsey Gdns. Brad BD4 ... 75 E3
Romsey Mews. Brad BD4 ... 75 D3
Ronald Dr. Brad BD7 ... 74 A7
Ronaldsway Cl. Bacup OL13 ... 106 B1
Roods La. Holmfi HD7 ... 188 B3
Rook La. Brad BD4 ... 75 C2
Rook St. Bing BD16 ... 36 F3
Rook St. Hud HD1 ... 154 A7
Rook's Nest Jun & Inf Sch.
Loft G ... 121 C4
Rook's Nest Rd. Loft G WF1 .. 121 D4
Rookery La. Hali HX3 ... 113 D3
Rookery The. Sil LS29 ... 6 F8
Rookes Ave. Brad BD6 ... 94 C8
Rookes La. Brig HX3 ... 94 A1
Rookhill Dr. Pont WF8 ... 146 E7
Rookhill Mount. Pont WF8 ... 146 F7
Rookhill Rd. Pont WF8 ... 146 F7
Rooks Ave. Clec BD19 ... 116 C8
Rooks Cl. Brig BD12 ... 94 D1
Rookwith Par. Brad BD10 ... 56 E6
Rookwood Ave. Kippax LS25 .. 103 A8
Rookwood Ave. Leeds LS9 ... 80 D8
Rookwood Cres. Leeds LS9 ... 80 C8
Rookwood Gdns. Leeds LS9 ... 80 C8
Rookwood Gr. Leeds LS9 ... 80 C8
Rookwood Hill. Leeds LS9 ... 80 C8
Rookwood Mount. Leeds LS9 ... 80 C8
Rookwood Par. Leeds LS9 ... 80 C8
Rookwood Pl. Leeds LS9 ... 80 C8
Rookwood Rd. Leeds LS9 ... 80 C8
Rookwood Sq. Leeds LS9 ... 80 D8
Rookwood St. Leeds LS9 ... 80 C7
Rookwood Terr. Leeds LS9 ... 80 C8
Rookwood Vale. Leeds LS9 ... 80 C7
Rookwood View. Leeds LS9 ... 80 C8
Rookwood Wlk. Leeds LS9 ... 80 C8
Rooley Ave. Brad BD6 ... 74 E1
Rooley Banks. Sow Br HX6 ... 111 E3
Rooley Cl. Brad BD5 ... 74 E1
Rooley Cres. Brad BD6 ... 94 E8
Rooley Ct. Sow Br HX6 ... 111 D3
Rooley Hts. Sow Br HX6 ... 111 D3
Rooley La. Brad BD4, BD5 ... 75 B1
Rooley La. Sow Br HX6 ... 111 D3
Roomfield Ct. Tod OL14 ... 108 B5 11
Roomfield St. Tod OL14 ... 108 B5
Rooms Fold. Morley LS27 ... 98 A6
Rooms La. Gild LS27 ... 98 A8
Rooms La. Morley LS27 ... 98 A6
Rope Wlk. Hali HX2 ... 90 F7
Rope Wlk. Knot WF11 ... 127 A4
Roper Ave. Leeds LS8 ... 60 F8
Roper Gdns. Hali HX2 ... 91 D4
Roper Gn. Hali HX2 ... 91 D4
Roper Gr. Leeds LS8 ... 60 F8
Roper La. Hali HX2 ... 91 F8
Roper La. Queen BD13 ... 72 B2
Roper St. Keigh BD21 ... 35 B7 11
Ropergate End. Pont WF8 ... 146 C8 8
Ropergate. Pont WF8 ... 146 C8
Ropergate Service Rd. Pont
WF8 ... 146 C8 7
Rosary RC Prim Sch. Leeds ... 60 C2
Roscoe St. Leeds LS7 ... 60 D2
Rose Ave. Hors LS18 ... 58 B7
Rose Ave. Hud HD4 ... 152 F3
Rose Ave. Hud HD3 ... 153 C6
Rose Ave. Upton WF9 ... 183 A7
Rose Bank. Bur in W LS29 ... 21 E8
Rose Bank Pl. Brad BD8 ... 73 E7
Rose Bank Rd. Tod OL14 ... 108 A5
Rose Cl. Upton WF9 ... 183 A7
Rose Ct. Gar LS25 ... 83 A7
Rose Croft. E Kes LS17 ... 28 C6
Rose Farm App. Nor WF6 ... 122 F4
Rose Farm Cl. Nor WF6 ... 122 F5
Rose Farm Fold. Nor WF6 ... 122 F5
Rose Farm Rise. Nor WF6 ... 122 F5
Rose Garth. Crof WF4 ... 143 F1
Rose Garth. Men LS29 ... 21 C7
Rose Gr. Heb Br HX7 ... 89 A4 7
Rose Gr. Heb Br HX7 ... 110 E8
Rose Gr. Roth LS26 ... 100 D6
Rose Gr. Upton WF9 ... 183 A7
Rose Grove La. Hali HX2 ... 112 A5
Rose Heath. Hali HX2 ... 91 D7
Rose Hill Dr. Hud HD2 ... 135 E1
Rose La. Hem WF7 ... 163 D4
Rose Meadows. Keigh BD22 ... 34 E5
Rose Mount. Brad BD2 ... 56 A3
Rose Mount. Hud HD2 ... 135 D1
Rose Mount Pl. Leeds LS12 ... 78 D6
Rose Pl. Hali HX2 ... 111 E5
Rose St. Brad BD8 ... 55 B1
Rose St. Hali HX1 ... 112 F6
Rose St. Haw BD22 ... 51 C6
Rose St. Hors LS18 ... 58 B8
Rose St. Keigh BD21 ... 35 F7
Rose St. Tod OL14 ... 108 B5
Rose Terr. Add LS29 ... 6 F8
Rose Terr. Hali HX2 ... 113 A4 2
Rose Terr. Hali HX1 ... 113 A7 3
Rose Terr. Hors LS18 ... 58 A7
Rose Terr. Hud HD1 ... 154 B8
Rose Terr. L Brad BD20 ... 4 C5
Rosebank Cres. Leeds LS3 ... 59 F2
Rosebank Gdns. Leeds LS3 ... 59 F1
Rosebank Rd. Leeds LS3 ... 59 F1
Rosebank Row. Leeds LS3 ... 59 F1
Rosebank St. Batley WF17 ... 118 B6
Roseberry St. Haw BD22 ... 34 D2
Roseberry St. Tod OL14 ... 86 C1
Rosebery Ave. Hali HX3 ... 113 D4
Rosebery Ave. Ship BD18 ... 55 C7
Rosebery Mount. Ship BD18 ... 55 D7
Rosebery Rd. Brad BD8 ... 55 C2
Rosebery St. Elland HX5 ... 134 F6
Rosebery St. Hud HD2 ... 135 C1
Rosebery St. Pudsey LS28 ... 76 C8
Rosebery Terr. Hali HX1 ... 113 A8
Rosebery Terr. Pudsey LS28 ... 57 F2 3
Rosebud Wlk. Leeds LS8 ... 60 E2
Rosecliffe Mount. Leeds LS13 . 58 C2
Rosecliffe Terr. Leeds LS13 ... 58 C2
Rosedale Ave. Brad BD15 ... 53 F4
Rosedale Ave. Hud HD5 ... 154 D5 16
Rosedale Ave. Liver WF15 ... 116 D2
Rosedale Ave. Wake WF2 ... 160 E8
Rosedale Bank. Midd LS10 ... 79 D1
Rosedale Cl. Bail BD17 ... 38 A2
Rosedale Cl. Upton WF9 ... 183 B7
Rosedale Gdns. Midd LS10 ... 79 D1
Rosedale Gn. Midd LS10 ... 79 D1
Rosedale Rise. B Spa LS23 ... 30 C7
Rosedale. Roth LS26 ... 100 F6
Rosedale Wlk. Midd LS10 ... 79 D1
Rosegarth Ave. Holmfi HD7 ... 189 C7
Rosehill Ave. Hem WF9 ... 181 C6
Rosehill Cres. Brad BD12 ... 94 C4
Roselee Cl. Hali HX3 ... 113 E3
Rosemary Cl. Brig HD6 ... 115 A1
Rosemary La. Brig HD6 ... 115 A1
Rosemary La. Hali HX3 ... 113 E1
Rosemont Ave. Leeds LS13 ... 58 C2 7
Rosemont Ave. Pudsey LS28 ... 76 F8 3
Rosemont. Bramho LS16 ... 24 E3
Rosemont Dr. Pudsey LS28 ... 76 F8
Rosemont Gr. Leeds LS13 ... 58 C2 8
Rosemont La. Bail BD17 ... 38 D2 2
Rosemont Pl. Leeds LS13 ... 58 C2
Rosemont Rd. Leeds LS13 ... 58 C2
Rosemont St. Leeds LS13 ... 58 C2
Rosemont St. Pudsey LS28 ... 76 F8 4
Rosemont Terr. Leeds LS13 ... 58 C2
Rosemont Terr. Pudsey LS28 .. 76 F8
Rosemont View. Leeds LS13 ... 58 C2
Rosemont Wlk. Leeds LS13 ... 58 C2 6
Rosemount Ave. Elland HX5 ... 135 A6
Rosemount. Bacup OL13 ... 106 A4
Rosemount Cl. Keigh BD21 ... 35 B7 2
Rosemount Terr. Elland HX5 . 135 A6
Rosemount Wks. Elland ... 135 A5
Rosemount Wlk. Keigh BD21 ... 35 B7 1
Rosendale Cl. Bacup OL13 ... 106 B3 3
Rosendale Cres. Bacup OL13 106 B3
Roseneath Pl. Leeds LS12 ... 78 D6
Roseneath St. Leeds LS12 ... 78 D6
Roseneath Terr. Leeds LS12 ... 78 D6
Rosetta Dr. Brad BD8 ... 73 F8
Roseville Rd. Leeds LS8 ... 60 E2
Roseville St. Leeds LS8 ... 60 E2
Roseville Terr. Dew WF12 ... 139 F8
Roseville Terr. Leeds LS15 ... 62 D3 4
Roseville Way. Leeds LS8 ... 60 E2
Rosewood Ave. Keigh BD20 ... 18 F1
Rosewood Ave. Kippax LS25 ... 82 F3
Rosewood Ct. Roth LS26 ... 100 F7
Rosewood Gr. Brad BD4 ... 75 D5
Rosewood Sq. S in Cra BD20 ... 16 D4
Rosgill Dr. Leeds LS14 ... 62 A5
Rosgill Wlk. Leeds LS14 ... 61 F5
Rosley Mount. Brad BD6 ... 93 F6
Roslyn Ave. Hud HD4 ... 171 C7
Roslyn Pl. Brad BD7 ... 74 B6
Ross Gr. Leeds LS13 ... 58 B4
Ross Terr. Leeds LS13 ... 58 A4
Rossall Gr. Leeds LS8 ... 60 F4
Rossall Rd. Leeds LS8 ... 60 F4
Rosse St. Brad BD8 ... 74 A8
Rosse St. Ship BD18 ... 55 B8
Rossefield App. Leeds LS13 ... 58 D2
Rossefield Ave. Hud HD2 ... 135 E1
Rossefield Ave. Leeds LS13 ... 58 D2
Rossefield Chase. Leeds LS13 . 58 D2
Rossefield Cl. Leeds LS13 ... 58 D2 3
Rossefield Dr. Leeds LS13 ... 58 D2
Rossefield Gn. Leeds LS13 ... 58 D2
Rossefield Gr. Leeds LS13 ... 58 D2
Rossefield Lawn. Leeds LS13 .. 58 D2
Rossefield Par. Leeds LS13 ... 58 D2
Rossefield Pk. Ship BD9 ... 55 B4
Rossefield Pl. Leeds LS13 ... 58 D2
Rossefield Rd. Ship BD9 ... 55 A4
Rossefield Sch. Ship ... 55 A4
Rossefield Terr. Leeds LS13 ... 58 D2
Rossefield View. Leeds LS13 ... 58 D2
Rossefield Way. Leeds LS13 ... 58 C2
Rossefield Wlk. Leeds LS13 ... 58 D2 5
Rossendale Pl. Ship BD18 ... 55 A7
Rossington Gr. Leeds LS8 ... 60 E4 2
Rossington Pl. Leeds LS8 ... 60 E4 3
Rossington Rd. Leeds LS8 ... 61 A5
Rossington St. Leeds LS2 ... 79 B8
Rossiter Dr. Knot WF11 ... 126 D3
Rosslyn Ave. Ack M T WF7 ... 163 F5
Rosslyn Cl. Ack M T WF7 ... 163 F5
Rosslyn Ct. Ack M T WF7 ... 163 F5
Rosslyn Ct. Dew WF12 ... 139 F7
Rosslyn Gr. Ack M T WF7 ... 163 F5
Rosslyn Gr. Haw BD22 ... 51 C6
Rossmore Dr. Brad BD15 ... 54 C1
Rotcher La. Slai HD7 ... 169 E8
Rotcher Rd. Holmfi HD7 ... 189 A5
Rotcher. Slai HD7 ... 169 E8
Rothbury Gdns. Hors LS16 ... 42 B3
Rothesay Terr. Brad BD7 ... 74 C6
Rothwell CE Sch. Roth ... 100 E6
Rothwell Dr. Hali HX1 ... 113 B5
Rothwell Inf Sch. Roth ... 100 E4
Rothwell La. Roth LS26 ... 101 B5
Rothwell Mount. Hali HX1 ... 113 B5
Rothwell Rd. Hali HX1 ... 113 B5
Rothwell Sports Ctr. Roth ... 101 C4
Rothwell St. Hud HD5 ... 154 E6
Rothwell West Prim Sch. Roth 100 E4
Rough Hall La. Hali HX2 ... 90 F5
Rough Side La. Tod OL14 ... 108 C3
Round Close Rd. Holme HD7 . 199 B6
Round Hill Cl. Brad BD14 ... 73 B2
Round Hill Cl. Hali HX2 ... 91 F6
Round Hill. Hali HX2 ... 91 F6
Round Hill La. Kirkhe HD5 ... 137 B3
Round Ings Rd. Slai HD3 ... 152 A6
Round St. Brad BD5 ... 74 E3
Round St. Wake WF1 ... 142 E4
Round Thorn Pl. Brad BD8 ... 74 A8
Round Wood Ave. Hud HD5 ... 155 A6
Roundell Ave. Brad BD4 ... 95 B8
Roundhay Ave. Leeds LS8 ... 60 F5
Roundhay CE Prim Sch. Leeds . 61 D7
Roundhay Cres. Leeds LS8 ... 60 F5
Roundhay Gdns. Leeds LS8 ... 60 F5
Roundhay Gr. Leeds LS8 ... 60 F5
Roundhay Hall Hospl. Leeds ... 61 A7
Roundhay High Sch. Leeds ... 61 A7
Roundhay Mount. Leeds LS8 ... 60 F5
Roundhay Park La. Leeds LS17 44 B4
Roundhay Park. Leeds ... 61 B8
Roundhay Pl. Leeds LS8 ... 60 F5
Roundhay Rd. Leeds LS7, LS8 .. 60 F3
Roundhay Sch. Leeds ... 61 A7
Roundhay St John's CE Prim Sch.
Leeds ... 61 C6
Roundhay View. Leeds LS8 ... 60 F5
Roundhead Fold. Brad BD10 ... 56 E8
Roundhill Ave. Ship BD16 ... 54 B7
Roundhill Mount. Ship BD16 ... 54 B7
Roundhill Pl. Brad BD1 ... 74 D7 6
Roundhill Rd. Castle WF10 ... 124 D7
Roundhill St. Brad BD5 ... 74 D4
Roundthorn Sch. Brad ... 74 E3
Roundway. Honley HD7 ... 171 F4
Roundway. Honley HD7 ... 172 A3
Roundway The. Morley LS27 ... 97 F4
Roundwell Rd. Clec WF15 ... 116 C5
Roundwood Ave. Bail BD17 ... 38 F3
Roundwood Ave. Brad BD10 ... 56 E4
Roundwood Cres. Wake WF2 141 C5
Roundwood Glen. Brad BD10 .. 56 E6
Roundwood Hill Sch. Wake ... 141 D3
Roundwood Ind Est. Wake ... 141 B5
Roundwood Rd. Bail BD17 ... 38 E4
Roundwood Rd. Ossett WF5 .. 141 A4
Roundwood Rise. Wake WF2 141 D4
Roundwood. Ship BD18 ... 54 F7
Roundwood View. Brad BD10 .. 56 E6
Rouse Fold. Brad BD4 ... 74 F5
Rouse Mill La. Batley WF17 ... 118 D4
Rouse St. Liver WF15 ... 117 A4 7
Row Gate. Shep HD8 ... 190 D6
Row La. Mars HD7 ... 169 C8
Row La. Sow Br HX6 ... 111 D3
Row. Mars HD7 ... 169 C8
Row St. Hud HD4 ... 153 E4
Rowan Ave. Brad BD3 ... 75 E7
Rowan Ave. Hud HD4 ... 171 D6
Rowan Ave. Nor WF6 ... 144 A7
Rowan Avenue Mews. Hud
HD4 ... 171 D6
Rowan Cl. Batley WF17 ... 97 A2
Rowan Cl. Knot WF11 ... 126 E2
Rowan Ct. Brad BD2 ... 56 C1
Rowan Ct. Wake WF2 ... 141 F8
Rowan Ct. Yeadon LS19 ... 40 B5
Rowan Dr. Brig HD6 ... 115 C3

Rowan Garth. Glu BD20 .... 16 D6
Rowan Gn. Pont WF8 .... 125 F1
Rowan Pl. Gar LS25 .... 83 B6
Rowan St. Keigh BD20 .... 18 A2
Rowanberry Cl. Brad BD2 .... 56 B4
Rowans The. Bail BD17 .... 37 F3
Rowans The. Bramho LS16 .... 24 F2
Rowans The. Pudsey LS13 .... 57 F3
Rowans The. Weth LS22 .... 14 A6
Rowantree Ave. Bail BD17 .... 38 B4
Rowantree Dr. Brad BD10 .... 56 C6
Rowe Cl. S Elm WF9 .... 183 A4
Rowgate. D Dale HD8 .... 191 B6
Rowland La. Wad M HX7 .... 89 C4
Rowland Pl. Leeds LS11 .... 79 B3
Rowland Rd. Leeds LS11 .... 79 B3
Rowland St. Roy S71 .... 179 D4
Rowland Terr. Leeds LS11 .... 79 C3 7
Rowlands Ave. Hud HD5 .... 154 F6
Rowlands Ave. Upton WF9 ..... 183 A7
Rowlestone Rise. Brad BD10 .... 56 E6
Rowley Dr. Ilkley LS29 .... 8 F3
Rowley Dr. Lepton HD8 .... 155 D3
Rowley La. Lepton HD8 .... 155 E2
Rowley La. S Elm WF9 .... 183 A2
Rowley Lea. Brad BD10 .... 56 E5
Rowsley St. Keigh BD21 .... 35 D7 1
Rowton Thorpe. Brad BD10 ...... 56 E6
Roxburgh Gr. Brad BD15 .... 73 B8
Roxby Cl. Leeds LS9 .... 60 E1
Roxby St. Brad BD5 .... 74 D3
Roxholme Ave. Leeds LS7 .... 60 E5
Roxholme Gr. Leeds LS7 .... 60 E5
Roxholme Pl. Leeds LS7 .... 60 E5
Roxholme Rd. Leeds LS7 .... 60 E5
Roxholme Terr. Leeds LS7 .... 60 E5
Roy Rd. Brad BD6 .... 73 D1
Roy St. Tod OL14 .... 86 A1
Royal Armouries Mus The.
Leeds 79 D6
Royal Cl. Leeds LS10 .... 79 D2
Royal Ct. Leeds LS10 .... 79 D2
Royal Ct. Pont WF8 .... 146 B5
Royal Dr. Leeds LS10 .... 79 D2
Royal Gdns. Leeds LS10 .... 79 D2
Royal Gr. Leeds LS10 .... 79 D2
Royal Halifax Infmy. Hali 113 B5
Royal Park Ave. Leeds LS6 .... 59 F3
Royal Park Gr. Leeds LS6 .... 59 F3
Royal Park Mount. Leeds LS6 .. 59 F3
Royal Park Prim Sch. Leeds 59 E2
Royal Park Rd. Leeds LS6 .... 59 F2
Royal Park Terr. Leeds LS6 .... 59 F3
Royal Park View. Leeds LS6 ...... 59 F3
Royal Pl. Leeds LS10 .... 79 D2
Royal Terr. B Spa LS23 .... 30 E8
Royal Terr. Hud HD3 .... 153 A5
Royd Ave. Batley WF16 .... 117 D6
Royd Ave. Bing BD16 .... 37 C3
Royd Ave. Holmfi HD7 .... 189 E6
Royd Ave. Hud HD3 .... 135 A3
Royd Ave. Hud HD3 .... 153 A5
Royd Ave. Mapp S75 .... 178 B1
Royd Cl. Glu BD20 .... 16 D6
Royd Cres. Hali HX1 .... 112 F8 2
Royd Cres. Heb Br HX7 .... 89 F1
Royd Croft. Hud HD3 .... 153 B6
Royd Edge Sch. Mel 170 E1
Royd Head Farm. Ossett WF5 140 C5
Royd House Gr. Keigh BD21 ..... 35 E5
Royd House La. Slai HD7 .... 152 D1
Royd House Rd. Keigh BD21 ..... 35 E5
Royd House Way. Keigh BD21 .. 35 E5
Royd House Wlk. Keigh BD21 .. 35 E5
Royd Ings Ave. Keigh BD21 ...... 18 D1
Royd La. Hali HX3 .... 92 A3
Royd La. Holmfi HD7 .... 188 E2
Royd La. Keigh BD20 .... 18 B1
Royd La. Rip HX6 .... 132 D4
Royd La. Tod OL14 .... 108 B6
Royd Mill Bsns Pk. Brig 115 C2
Royd Moor La. Bad WF9 .... 164 C1
Royd Mount. Hali HX3 .... 92 C2 4
Royd Mount. Holmfi HD7 .... 189 A5
Royd Mount Mid Sch. Thorn 72 C6
Royd Pl. Hali HX3 .... 92 C2
Royd Rd. Mel HD7 .... 187 E8
Royd Rd. Tod OL14 .... 108 B7
Royd Sq. Heb Br HX7 .... 89 A3 2
Royd St. Brad BD12 .... 94 C4 3
Royd St. Hud HD3 .... 153 A5
Royd St. Keigh BD20 .... 18 B2
Royd St. Slai HD7 .... 151 F1
Royd St. Thorn BD13 .... 72 C6
Royd St. Tod OL14 .... 108 A6
Royd St. Wils BD15 .... 53 C5
Royd Terr. Heb Br HX7 .... 89 A3
Royd Terr. Hud HD4 .... 171 E8
Royd View. Heb Br HX7 .... 89 E1
Royd Way. Keigh BD21 .... 18 C1
Royd Wood. Clec BD19 .... 116 D6
Royd Wood. Oxen BD22 .... 51 D4
Roydfield St. Hud HD2 .... 136 B2
Roydlands St. Brig HX3 .... 114 D7
Roydon Gr. Brad BD9 .... 55 A2
Royds Ave. Birk BD11 .... 96 B5
Royds Ave. Brig HD6 .... 115 B8
Royds Ave. Castle WF10 .... 125 C8
Royds Ave. Holmfi HD7 .... 189 D6
Royds Ave. Hud HD3 .... 153 C5
Royds Ave. Ossett WF5 .... 140 C8
Royds Ave. Slai HD7 .... 152 D2
Royds Cl. Holmfi HD7 .... 189 D6
Royds Cl. Leeds LS12 .... 78 C4
Royds Cres. Brig HD6 .... 115 B7
Royds Dr. Holmfi HD7 .... 189 D6
Royds Farm Rd. Leeds LS12 ...... 78 C3
Royds Gr. Loft G WF1 .... 121 C5
Royds Hall Ave. Brad BD6 .... 94 C8
Royds Hall La. Brad BD6 .... 94 A7
Royds Hall La. Brad BD12, BD6 94 B5
Royds Hall Rd. Leeds LS12 .... 78 C4
Royds Hall Sch. Hud 153 C6
Royds La. Leeds LS12 .... 78 C3
Royds La. Leeds LS12 .... 78 C4
Royds La. Roth LS26 .... 101 A3
Royds Park Cres. Brad BD12 ..... 94 D4
Royds Pk. D Dale HD8 .... 192 A6
Royds Sch. Roth 101 B2
Royds St. Mars HD7 .... 168 F3
Royds The. Clay W HD8 .... 176 A3
Royds The. Holmfi HD7 .... 189 A5
Royds View. Slai HD7 .... 152 D1
Roydscliffe Dr. Brad BD9 .... 54 F4
Roydscliffe Rd. Brad BD9 .... 54 F4
Roydsdale Way. Brad BD4 .... 95 A6
Roydstone Rd. Brad BD3 .... 75 D8
Roydstone Terr. Brad BD3 .... 75 D8
Roydwood Terr (Back).
Cull BD13 .... 52 D6
Roydwood Terr. Cull BD13 .... 52 D6
Royle Fold. Batley WF16 .... 117 D4
Royles Cl. S Kirk WF9 .... 182 C2
Royles Head La. Hud HD3 .... 152 E6
Royston CE Sch. Roy 179 C3
Royston Cl. E Ard WF3 .... 120 D6
Royston Comprehensive Sch.
Roy 179 C4
Royston Hill. E Ard WF3 .... 120 D6
Royston Inf Sch. Roy 179 C3
Royston La. Roy S71 .... 179 C2
Royston Medstead Jun & Inf Sch.
Roy 179 B3
Royston Rd. Cud S72 .... 180 B1
Royston Summer Fields Jun & Inf
Sch. Roy 179 A4
Ruby St. Batley WF17 .... 118 A7
Ruby St. Keigh BD22 .... 35 A4 13
Ruby St. Leeds LS9 .... 60 E1
Rud La. Heb Br HX7 .... 110 A3
Rudby Haven. Brad BD10 .... 56 E5
Rudd St. Brad BD7 .... 74 A4 11
Rudding Ave. Brad BD15 .... 54 A1
Rudding Cres. Brad BD15 .... 54 A1
Rudding Dr. Batley WF17 .... 117 F6
Rudding St. Hud HD4 .... 153 D4
Rudgate HM Prison. Th Arch 15 A2
Rudgate Pk. Th Arch LS23 .... 15 A3
Rudgate. Tad LS24 .... 31 D4
Rudgate. Th Arch LS23, LS24 ... 15 D5
Ruffield Side. Brad BD12 .... 94 C5
Rufford Ave. Yeadon LS19 .... 40 C6
Rufford Bank. Yeadon LS19 .... 40 C6
Rufford Cl. Yeadon LS19 .... 40 C6
Rufford Cres. Yeadon LS19 .... 40 C6
Rufford Dr. Yeadon LS19 .... 40 C6
Rufford Pl. Hali HX3 .... 113 B4 2
Rufford Rd. Elland HX5 .... 134 F6
Rufford Rd. Hali HX3 .... 113 B4
Rufford Rd. Hud HD3 .... 152 F5
Rufford Ridge. Yeadon LS19 ..... 40 C6
Rufford Rise. Yeadon LS19 .... 40 B6
Rufford St. Brad BD3 .... 75 C7
Rufford St. Wake WF2 .... 141 F6
Rufford Villas. Hali HX3 .... 113 B4 4
Rufus St. Brad BD5 .... 74 B3
Rufus St. Keigh BD21 .... 35 C8 6
Rugby Ave. Hali HX3 .... 91 F3
Rugby Dr. Hali HX3 .... 91 F3
Rugby Gdns. Hali HX3 .... 91 F3
Rugby Mount. Hali HX3 .... 91 F3
Rugby Pl. Brad BD7 .... 74 B6
Rugby Terr. Hali HX3 .... 91 F3
Rumble Rd. Dew WF12 .... 118 F1
Rumbold Rd. Hud HD3 .... 153 D7
Rumple Croft. Otley LS21 .... 10 E2
Runnymeade Ct. Brad BD10 ...... 56 B7
Runswick Ave. Leeds LS11 .... 78 F5 3
Runswick Gr. Brad BD5 .... 74 D1
Runswick Pl. Leeds LS11 .... 79 A5
Runswick St. Brad BD5 .... 74 D1
Runswick St. Leeds LS11 .... 79 A5
Runswick Terr. Brad BD5 .... 74 D1
Runswick Terr. Leeds LS11 .... 79 A5
Runtlings La. Ossett WF5 .... 140 C4
Runtlings. Ossett WF5 .... 140 C5
Runtlings The. Ossett WF5 ...... 140 B5
Rupert Rd. Ilkley LS29 .... 8 A5
Rupert St. Haw BD22 .... 51 F8
Rupert St. Keigh BD21 .... 35 C8 5
Ruschcroft Terr. Bail BD17 .... 38 C3
Rushdene Ct. Brad BD12 .... 94 C1
Rushfield Vale. Lepton HD8 ..... 155 C4
Rushmoor Rd. Brad BD4 .... 75 D2
Rushmore Dr. Pudsey LS28 .... 57 C3
Rushton Ave. Brad BD3 .... 75 E8
Rushton Hill Cl. Hali HX2 .... 91 C1
Rushton Rd. Brad BD3 .... 75 E8
Rushton St. Hali HX1 .... 112 F8 6
Rushton St. Pudsey LS28 .... 57 B6
Rushton Terr. Brad BD3 .... 75 E7
Rushworth St. Hali HX3 .... 92 A1 16
Ruskin Ave. Brad BD9 .... 54 D3
Ruskin Ave. Wake WF1 .... 121 A3
Ruskin Cl. Castle WF10 .... 125 B8
Ruskin Cres. Guise LS20 .... 39 F8
Ruskin Ct. Wake WF2 .... 120 F2
Ruskin Dr. Castle WF10 .... 125 B8
Ruskin Gr. Hud HD2 .... 136 D3
Ruskin Pl. Castle WF10 .... 125 B8
Ruskin St. Pudsey LS28 .... 57 C1
Ruskin Terr. Hali HX3 .... 92 A1 24
Russel Ct. Bard LS17 .... 28 D3
Russell Ave. Crig WF4 .... 159 F3
Russell Ave. Queen BD13 .... 92 E8
Russell Cl. Batley WF16 .... 117 E3
Russell Cl. Batley WF17 .... 118 C5
Russell Gr. Birk BD11 .... 96 B5
Russell Hall Fst Sch. Queen 72 E1
Russell Hall La. Queen BD13 ..... 72 E1 15
Russell Rd. Queen BD13 .... 92 D8
Russell St. Brad BD5 .... 74 D5
Russell St. Dew WF13 .... 118 A1
Russell St. Hali HX1 .... 113 C7 21
Russell St. Keigh BD21 .... 35 B7
Russell St. Leeds LS1 .... 79 B8
Russell St. Queen BD13 .... 72 E1
Russell St. Ship BD18 .... 55 C5
Russell St. Tod OL14 .... 108 C5
Russell St. Wake WF1 .... 142 C4
Russets The. Wake WF2 .... 160 E6
Russett Gr. Hud HD4 .... 154 C3
Rustic Ave. Hali HX3 .... 114 A4
Ruswarp Cres. Brad BD10 .... 56 D6
Ruth St. Haw BD22 .... 51 E8 15
Ruth St. Hud HD4 .... 154 A2
Ruthven View. Leeds LS8 .... 61 A3
Rutland Ave. Pont WF8 .... 146 D5
Rutland Ave. Wake WF2 .... 142 C2
Rutland Cl. Kippax LS25 .... 83 B2
Rutland Cl. Roth LS26 .... 101 D6 5
Rutland Ct. Pudsey LS28 .... 76 E8 3
Rutland Dr. Crof WF4 .... 143 C2
Rutland Dr. Kippax LS25 .... 83 B2
Rutland House. Bing BD16 .... 37 A3 5
Rutland Ind Est. Wake 142 D4
Rutland Mount. Leeds LS3 .... 78 F8 2
Rutland Rd. Batley WF17 .... 118 D6
Rutland Rd. Floc WF4 .... 157 C3
Rutland Rd. Hud HD3 .... 153 A5
Rutland St. Brad BD4 .... 75 A5
Rutland St. Keigh BD21 .... 35 B5 7
Rutland St. Leeds LS3 .... 79 A8
Rutland Terr. Leeds S18 .... 78 F8
Rutland Wlk. Dew WF13 .... 139 B8 7
Ryan Gr. Keigh BD22 .... 34 D8
Ryan Mid Sch. Brad 74 F3
Ryan St. Brad BD5 .... 74 D3
Ryburn Golf Course. Sow Br .. 112 C2
Ryburn La. Rip HX6 .... 132 E5
Ryburn Pl. Wake WF2 .... 142 B5
Ryburn Rd. Hud HD3 .... 153 B7
Ryburn St. Sow Br HX6 .... 112 B3
Ryburn Terr. Hali HX1 .... 112 F7 1
Ryburn Terr. Rip HX6 .... 132 C1
Ryburn Valley High Sch.
Sow Br 111 E3
Ryburn View. Rip HX6 .... 132 C3
Rycroft Ave. Pudsey LS13 .... 58 B1
Rycroft Ave. Ship BD16 .... 54 A6
Rycroft Cl. Pudsey LS13 .... 58 B1
Rycroft Ct. Pudsey LS13 .... 58 B1 2
Rycroft Dr. Pudsey LS13 .... 58 B1
Rycroft Gn. Pudsey LS13 .... 58 B1 1
Rycroft Pl. Pudsey LS13 .... 58 B1 3
Rycroft Sq. Pudsey LS13 .... 58 B1
Rycroft St. Ship BD18 .... 55 D5
Rycroft Towers. Pudsey LS13 .. 58 A1
Rydal Ave. Bail BD17 .... 37 E1
Rydal Ave. Gar LS25 .... 82 F6
Rydal Ave. Ship BD9 .... 55 C4
Rydal Cres. Morley LS27 .... 98 D5
Rydal Cres. Wake WF2 .... 141 E7
Rydal Dr. Hud HD5 .... 154 D6
Rydal Dr. Morley LS27 .... 98 D5
Rydal Dr. Wake WF2 .... 141 E7
Rydal Gr. Liver WF15 .... 117 A1
Rydal St. Castle WF10 .... 125 D8
Rydal St. Keigh BD21 .... 35 A6
Rydale Ct. Ossett WF5 .... 140 D4
Rydall Pl. Leeds LS11 .... 78 F5
Rydall St. Leeds LS11 .... 78 F5
Rydall Terr. Leeds LS11 .... 78 F5
Ryder Cl. Pont WF8 .... 146 B8
Ryder Gdns. Leeds LS8 .... 61 A7
Rydings Ave. Brig HD6 .... 115 A3
Rydings Cl. Brig HD6 .... 115 A3 11
Rydings Dr. Brig HD6 .... 114 F3
Rydings Wlk. Brig HD6 .... 114 F3
Rye Close La. Holme HD7 .... 187 E4
Rye Croft. Hali HX2 .... 91 F6
Rye Field La. Mars HD3 .... 150 F6
Rye Field La W. Mars HD3 .... 150 F6
Rye Garth. Weth LS22 .... 13 D8
Rye La. Hali HX2 .... 91 C1
Rye Pl. Leeds LS14 .... 61 F1
Rye St. Keigh BD21 .... 35 B4 9
Rye Way. Castle WF10 .... 125 B8
Ryebank. Holmfi HD7 .... 189 B4
Ryebread. Castle WF10 .... 103 E1
Ryecroft Ave. Ryhill WF4 .... 162 C2
Ryecroft Cl. Loft G WF1 .... 121 C5
Ryecroft Cres. Hali HX2 .... 91 D1
Ryecroft Dr. Hud HD3 .... 135 B1
Ryecroft Fst Sch. Brad 75 F2
Ryecroft. Harden BD21 .... 35 F1
Ryecroft La. Brig HD6 .... 136 C8
Ryecroft La. Hali HX2 .... 91 D1
Ryecroft La. Holmfi HD7 .... 189 C3
Ryecroft Mid Sch. Leeds 77 E6
Ryecroft Rd. Cull BD21 .... 35 E1
Ryecroft Rd. Glu BD20 .... 16 B7
Ryecroft Rd. Harden BD16 .... 36 A1
Ryecroft St. Ossett WF5 .... 140 C7
Ryecroft Terr. Hali HX2 .... 91 D1
Ryecroft Way. Glu BD20 .... 16 C6
Ryedale Ave. Knot WF11 .... 126 E2
Ryedale Ave. Leeds LS12 .... 78 B4
Ryedale Cl. Nor WF6 .... 123 A5
Ryedale Ct. Leeds LS14 .... 61 F5
Ryedale Holt. Leeds LS12 .... 78 C5
Ryedale. Kirkhe HD5 .... 137 B2
Ryedale Pk. Ilkley LS29 .... 8 D3
Ryedale Pl. Nor WF6 .... 123 A5
Ryedale Way. Brad BD15 .... 54 A2
Ryedale Way. E Ard WF3 .... 119 E7
Ryefield Ave. Brad BD14 .... 73 B5
Ryefields Ave. Hud HD3 .... 153 A7
Ryefields. Holmfi HD7 .... 189 D4
Ryefields Rd. Hud HD7 .... 152 E4
Ryeland St. Glu BD20 .... 16 D7
Ryelands Gr. Brad BD9 .... 54 D4
Ryhill Fst Sch. Ryhill 162 B1
Ryhill Ind Est. Ryhill WF4 .... 162 B1
Ryhill Pits La. Ryhill WF4 .... 161 E1
Rylands Ave. Bing BD16 .... 37 B3
Rylstone Gdns. Brad BD3 .... 56 A1
Rylstone Gr. Wake WF1 .... 142 F8
Rylstone Rd. Bail BD17 .... 37 F2
Rylstone St. Keigh BD21 .... 35 D8
Ryndleside. Hud HD3 .... 134 F1 4
Ryshworth Ave. Bing BD16 .... 36 D6
Ryshworth Bridge. Bing BD16 .. 36 D6
Ryshworth Mid Sch. Bing 36 E7
Ryton Dale. Brad BD10 .... 56 E6
Sable Crest. Brad BD2 .... 55 F4
Sackup La. Mapp S75 .... 177 F1
Sackup La. Mapp S75 .... 178 A2
Sackville App. Leeds LS7 .... 60 C3
Sackville Rd. Sil BD20 .... 5 E2
Sackville St. Brad BD1 .... 74 E7 17
Sackville St. Dew WF13 .... 138 E6
Sackville St. Heb Br HX7 .... 89 A4 10
Sackville St. Leeds LS7 .... 60 C3
Sackville St. Tod OL14 .... 108 C5
Sacred Heart RC Pr Sch. Ilkley .. 8 D4
Sacred Heart RC Prim Sch.
Leeds 59 B3
Sacred Heart RC Prim Sch.
Sow Br 112 A3
Saddler St. Brad BD12 .... 94 C4 7
Saddler's La. Broth WF11 .... 105 C1
Saddlers Croft. Castle WF10 .. 125 B6
Saddleworth Rd. Elland HX4 .. 134 C7
Saddleworth Rd. Mars HX4,
HX5 .... 150 E5
Saddleworth Rd. Rip HX4, HX5 133 C5
Sadler Cl. Hors LS16 .... 42 C4
Sadler Copse. Hors LS16 .... 42 C4
Sadler Way. Hors LS16 .... 42 C4
Sadlers Wlk. Weth LS22 .... 13 F6
Saffron Dr. Brad BD15 .... 73 B8
Sagar La. Tod OL14 .... 86 D3
Sagar Pl. Leeds LS6 .... 59 D4
Sagar St. Castle WF10 .... 124 D8
Sage St. Brad BD5 .... 74 C4
Saint St. Brad BD7 .... 74 A4 1
St Abbs Cl. Brad BD6 .... 94 C7
St Abbs Dr. Brad BD6 .... 94 C7
St Abbs Fold. Brad BD6 .... 94 C7
St Abbs Gate. Brad BD6 .... 94 C7
St Abbs Way. Brad BD6 .... 94 C7
St Abbs Wlk. Brad BD6 .... 94 C7
St Agnes Preparatory Sch.
Leeds 59 D6
St Aidan's Rd. Bail BD17 .... 38 D2
St Aidan's Sq. Bing BD16 .... 36 E6
St Aidans Rd. Swil LS26 .... 102 E8
St Aiden's Wlk. Ossett WF5 ..... 141 A4
St Alban App. Leeds LS9 .... 61 C1
St Alban Cl. Leeds LS9 .... 61 C1
St Alban Cres. Leeds LS9 .... 61 C1
St Alban Gr. Leeds LS9 .... 61 C1
St Alban Mount. Leeds LS9 .... 61 C1
St Alban Rd. Leeds LS9 .... 61 C1
St Alban View. Leeds LS9 .... 61 C1
St Alban's Ave. Hali HX3 .... 113 C3
St Alban's Ave. Hud HD3 .... 135 A3
St Alban's Pl. Leeds LS2 .... 60 C1
St Alban's Rd. Hali HX3 .... 113 C3
St Albans Croft. Hali HX3 .... 113 D4
St Aldon's CE (Aided) Fst Sch.
Skel 175 A1
St Andrew's Ave. Morley LS27 97 F3
St Andrew's CE Fst Sch. Keigh 35 A7
St Andrew's CE Inf Sch. Brig .. 115 A4
St Andrew's Cath Sch. Leeds ... 43 D1
St Andrew's CE Jun & Inf Sch.
Brad 95 B4
St Andrew's Cl. Morley LS27 ... 97 E3
St Andrew's Cl. Pudsey LS13 ... 57 E5
St Andrew's Cres. Brad BD12 .. 95 A4
St Andrew's Dr. Brig HD6 .... 115 A4
St Andrew's Gr. Morley LS27 .. 97 F3
St Andrew's Pl. Brad BD7 .... 74 C6
St Andrew's Pl. Leeds LS3 .... 78 F8 6
St Andrew's Rd.
Castle HD1, S11, S74 .... 104 D1
St Andrew's Rd. Hud HD1 .... 154 C7
St Andrew's St. Leeds LS3 .... 78 F8 1
St Andrew's Terr. Glu BD20 ...... 16 D7
St Andrew's Villas. Brad BD7 .... 74 C7
St Andrews CE Jun Sch. Brig .. 115 A4
St Andrews Cl. Hali HX2 .... 92 A5
St Andrews Cl. Yeadon LS19 ..... 40 C7 1
St Andrews Croft. Leeds LS17 .. 43 B4
St Andrews Dr. Feath WF7 ...... 124 D1
St Andrews Dr. Kirkhe HD5 ..... 155 C8
St Andrews Dr. Knot WF11 ...... 126 C5
St Andrews Dr. Leeds LS17 .... 43 C4
St Andrews Dr. Mapp S75 .... 178 A1
St Andrews Rd. Yeadon LS19 ..... 40 C8
St Andrews Wlk. Leeds LS17 .... 43 C4
St Ann St. Leeds LS2 .... 79 B8
St Ann's Ave. Leeds LS4 .... 59 D2
St Ann's Cl. Leeds LS4 .... 59 C4
St Ann's Gdns. Leeds LS4 .... 59 C3
St Ann's La. Leeds LS4 .... 59 C3
St Ann's Mount. Leeds LS4 .... 59 D3
St Ann's Rise. Leeds LS4 .... 59 C3
St Ann's Sq. Leeds LS4 .... 59 C3
St Ann's Sq. Leeds LS9 .... 79 E8
St Ann's Way. Leeds LS4 .... 59 C3
St Anne's Ave. Hud HD3 .... 135 A3
St Anne's Cl. Dew WF12 .... 139 D4
St Anne's Dr. Leeds LS4 .... 59 C4
St Anne's Gn. Leeds LS4 .... 59 C4
St Anne's Pl. Elland HX4 .... 133 E4
St Anne's RC Cath. Leeds 79 B8
St Anne's RC Sch. Keigh 35 B8
St Anne's Rd. Hali HX3 .... 113 C2
St Anne's Rd. Leeds LS6 .... 59 C5
St Anne's St. Ryhill WF4 .... 162 B1
St Annes Villas. Pont WF8 .... 125 E2
St Anns Sq. Hali HX6 .... 112 C4
St Anthony's Dr. Leeds LS11 .... 78 F2
St Anthony's R C Fst Sch. Brad 73 D5
St Anthony's RC Jun Sch. Ship . 55 F8
St Anthony's RC Prim Sch.
Leeds 78 F2
St Anthony's Rd. Leeds LS11 .... 78 F2
St Augustine's CE Fst Sch. Brad 56 A1
St Augustine's Jun & Inf Sch.
Hali 113 A8
St Augustine's Terr. Brad BD3 .. 56 A1
St Augustine's Terr. Hali HX1 113 A8 6
St Augustines R C Prim Sch.
Leeds 61 B3
St Austin's Catholic Inf Sch.
Wake 142 D7
St Austin's Catholic Jun Sch.
Wake 142 D7
St Barnabas Rd. Clec WF15 ...... 116 C5
St Barnabas Rd. Leeds LS11 ...... 79 B6
St Barnabas Sch. Ship 55 A4
St Bartholomew's CE Prim Sch.
Leeds 78 C7
St Bartholomew's Cl.
Leeds LS12 .... 78 C7
St Bartholomews Ct.
Wake WF2 .... 141 C4
St Bede's Grammar Sch. Brad .. 55 A3
St Benedict's Sch. Gar 82 F7
St Benedicts RC Sec Sch. Leeds 58 E5
St Bernard's Ave. Pont WF8 .. 146 B8
St Bevan's Rd. Hali HX3 .... 113 C3
St Blaise Ct. Brad BD5 .... 74 E5
St Blaise RC Sec Sch. Brad 75 B1
St Boltophs Cl. Knot WF11 ...... 127 A4
St Brendan's RC Sch. Brad 56 D6
St Catherine's Cr. Leeds LS13 .. 58 D4
St Catherine's Dr. Leeds LS13 .. 58 D4
St Catherine's Gn. Leeds LS13 58 D4
St Catherine's Hill. Leeds LS13 58 D4
St Catherine's St. Wake WF1 142 F3
St Catherine's Villas. Wake
WF1 .... 142 F3
St Catherine's Wlk. Leeds LS8 . 61 A6
St Chad's Ave. Brig HD6 .... 114 E5
St Chad's Ave. Leeds LS6 .... 59 D6
St Chad's CE Prim Sch. Leeds .. 59 B7
St Chad's CE (Aided) Jun & Inf Sch.
Brig 114 E5
St Chad's Dr. Leeds LS6 .... 59 C6
St Chad's Gr. Leeds LS6 .... 59 C6
St Chad's Rd. Brad BD8 .... 55 B1
St Chad's Rd. Leeds LS16 .... 59 D6
St Chad's Rise. Leeds LS6 .... 59 C6
St Chad's View. Leeds LS6 .... 59 C6
St Christopher's Ave. Roth
LS26 .... 100 F5
St Christophers Dr. Sil LS29 .... 6 F8
St Clair Rd. Otley LS21 .... 23 B7
St Clair St. Otley LS21 .... 23 B8
St Clair St. Wake WF1 .... 142 D6
St Clairs Terr. Otley LS21 .... 23 B8
St Clare's Ave. Brad BD2 .... 56 D2
St Clare's RC Fst Sch. Brad 56 D2
St Clements Ave. Roth LS26 ... 100 E5
St Clements Ct. Roth LS26 ..... 100 D4
St Clements Rise. Roth LS26 .. 100 D5
St Columba's RC Fst Sch. Brad 75 D2
St Cuthbert & the Fst Martyrs RC
Sch Brad 55 A2
St Cuthbert's Ct. Ack M T WF7 146 A1
St Cuthbert's Ct. Ack M T WF7 164 A8
St Cuthbert's RC Inf Sch. Brad 55 B3
St Cyprians Gdns. Leeds LS9 ... 61 B2 12
St Davids Rd. Otley LS21 .... 10 E2
St Davids Sch. Hud 153 C6
St Dominic's RC Mid Sch. Leeds 60 D3
St Edmund's Hall Prep Sch.
Leeds 44 A1
St Edmunds Cl. Castle WF10 . 125 C8
St Edward's RC Pr Sch. B Spa .. 30 D7
St Edward's Terr. B Spa LS23 ... 30 D5
St Edwards Cl. Byram WF11 .. 126 E7
St Elmo Gr. Leeds LS9 .... 80 A8 6
St Eloi Ave. Bail BD17 .... 38 C4
St Enoch's Rd. Brad BD6 .... 74 B2
St Francis Pl. Leeds LS11 .... 79 B6
St Francis Prim Sch. Leeds 79 B3
St Francis' RC Fst Sch. Brad 56 A4
St George RC Sch. Brad 55 F1
St George's Ave. Hud HD3 .... 135 A3
St George's Ave. Roth LS26 ..... 100 C7
St George's Cres. Roth LS26 . 100 C7
St George's Pl. Brad BD5 .... 74 E5 2
St George's Pl. Brad BD5 .... 75 B4
St George's Rd. Hali HX3 .... 92 A1
St George's Rd. Holmfi HD7 .. 189 D4
St George's Rd. Leeds LS1 .... 60 B1
St George's Rd. Wake WF2 ..... 141 D3
St George's Sq. Elland HD3 ..... 152 B8
St George's Sq. Heb Br HX7 ..... 89 A3 17
St George's Sq. Hud HD1 .... 154 A6 18
St George's St. Heb Br HX7 ...... 89 A3 16
St George's St. Hud HD1 .... 154 A6
St Georges Ct. Ryhill WF4 ...... 162 D2
St Georges Wlk. Wake WF2 .. 160 C6
St Giles Ave. Pont WF8 .... 146 B8
St Giles CE Jun Mix Sch. Pont . 125 D1
St Giles Cl. Brig HD6 .... 114 E5
St Giles Garth. Bramho LS16 .... 24 E3
St Giles Rd. Brig HX3 .... 114 E7
St Giles' View. Pont WF8 .... 146 D7
St Gregory's RC Pr Sch. Leeds .. 62 D5
St Helen's Ave. Hem WF9 .... 181 C7
St Helen's Dr. M'Field LS25 ...... 83 F8
St Helen's Gate. Hud HD4 .... 155 A2
St Helen's Gr. Wake WF2 .... 142 F1
St Helen's La. Hors LS16 .... 42 C3
St Helen's Pl. Castle WF10 ..... 124 E7 2
St Helen's Way. Ilkley LS29 .... 8 D4
St Helena Rd. Brad BD6 .... 74 B1
St Helens Ave. Hors LS16 .... 42 D3
St Helens Cl. Hors LS16 .... 42 C3
St Helens Croft. Hors LS16 .... 42 C3
St Helens Gdns. Hors LS16 .... 42 C3
St Helens Gr. Hors LS16 .... 42 C3
St Helens St. Leeds LS10 .... 79 D5
St Helens Way. Hors LS16 .... 42 D3
St Helier Gr. Bail BD17 .... 38 D4
St Hilda's Ave. Leeds LS9 .... 79 F6 14
St Hilda's Cres. Leeds LS9 .... 79 F6 16
St Hilda's Gr. Leeds LS9 .... 79 F6 15
St Hilda's Mount. Leeds LS9 ..... 79 F6 13
St Hilda's Pl. Leeds LS9 .... 79 F6 12
St Hilda's Rd. Leeds LS9 .... 79 F6 11
St Hilda's Sch. Hor 141 A2
St Hilda's Terr. Brad BD3 .... 75 E8
St Hildas Cl. Dearne S63 .... 194 E1
St Ians Croft. Sil LS29 .... 6 F7
St Ignatius Jun & Inf Sch.
Ossett 140 E3
St Ive's Gdns. Hali HX3 .... 113 C3
St Ive's Rd. Hali HX3 .... 113 C3
St Ives Cl. Pont WF8 .... 125 D3
St Ives Gr. Harden BD16 .... 36 C2
St Ives Gr. Leeds LS12 .... 78 A8 20
St Ives Mount. Leeds LS12 .... 78 A8
St Ives Pl. Harden BD16 .... 36 C2
St Ives Rd. Harden BD16 .... 36 C2
St James App. Leeds LS14 .... 62 B4
St James Ave. Hors LS18 .... 41 D1
St James Bsns Pk. Brad 74 F6
St James CE (C) Fst Sch. Crig .. 159 F6
St James CE Sch. Weth 13 F6
St James Cres. Pudsey LS28 ...... 76 B7
St James Ct. Brig HD6 .... 115 B3
St James Ct. Hali HX1 .... 113 C7 2
St James Ct. Ryhill WF4 .... 162 C1
St James Dr. Hors LS18 .... 41 D1
St James Manston CE Mid Sch.
Leeds 62 D3
St James Pk. Wake WF2 .... 141 C4
St James Pl. Bail BD17 .... 38 F4
St James Rd. Bail BD17 .... 38 F4
St James Rd. Hali HX1 .... 113 C7
St James' Rd. Ilkley LS29 .... 8 A4
St James Sq. Northo HX3 .... 93 A3
St James St. Batley WF16 .... 117 D3
St James St. Batley WF17 .... 118 C5
St James St. Hali HX1 .... 113 C7 1
St James Terr. Hors LS18 .... 41 D1
St James Way. Crig WF4 .... 159 F6
St James Wlk. Hors LS18 .... 41 D1
St James's Ct. Leeds LS8 .... 60 E2 5
St James's Mkt. Brad 75 A6
St James's Pk. Wake WF1 .... 142 E6
St James's Rd. Hud HD1 .... 153 D7
St James's Sq. Brad BD5 .... 74 E5
St James's St. Weth LS22 .... 13 E5
St James's Univ Hospl. Leeds . 60 F2
St John Fisher RC High Sch.
Dew 118 B1
St John Par. Dew WF13 .... 139 B7
St John St. Brig HD6 .... 115 A1
St John St. Dew WF13 .... 139 B8
St John the Evangelist Inf & Jun
Sch. Brad 73 E1
St John Wlk. Dew WF13 .... 139 B8
St John's Ave. Batley WF17 ... 118 A6
St John's Ave. Hud HD4 .... 154 A2
St John's Ave. Kirkhe HD5 ...... 137 C1
St John's Ave. Leeds LS6 .... 59 F2
St John's Ave. Ossett WF5 ...... 141 A5
St John's Ave. Pudsey LS28 .... 57 D3 10
St John's Ave. Thorner LS14 .... 45 F5
St John's Ave. Wake WF1 .... 142 B8
St John's CE Fst Sch. Brad 75 D1
St John's CE Inf Sch. Dew 139 A8
St John's Chase. Wake WF1 .... 142 B7
St John's Cl. Aber LS25 .... 47 E1
St John's Cl. Heb Br HX7 .... 89 A3 7
St John's Cl. Leeds LS6 .... 59 F2
St John's Cl. Ossett WF5 .... 141 A5
St John's Cl. Rip HX6 .... 132 C1
St John's Cres. Brad BD8 .... 73 E8
St John's Cres. Hud HD1 .... 154 A8
St John's Cres. Nor WF6 .... 144 A7
St John's Cres. Ossett WF5 .... 141 A5
St John's Croft. Wake WF1 ..... 142 B8
St John's Cross. Hali HX2 .... 91 F8
St John's Ct. Bail BD17 .... 38 E2
St John's Ct. Keigh BD20 .... 18 A2
St John's Ct. Leeds LS7 .... 60 D4
St John's Ct. Lepton HD8 .... 155 F3
St John's Ct. Thorner LS14 .... 45 F5
St John's Ct. Wake WF1 .... 142 B7
St John's Ct. Yeadon LS19 .... 40 A6
St John's Dr. Hud HD1 .... 154 A8
St John's Dr. Yeadon LS19 .... 40 A6
St John's Garth. Aber LS25 .... 64 E8
St John's Gr. Leeds LS6 .... 59 F2
St John's Gr. Wake WF1 .... 142 C8
St John's Hospital (Almshouses).
Ledsh LS25 .... 104 D8
St John's Jun & Inf Sch. Rip .. 132 C1
St John's Jun & Inf Sch. Wake 142 B8
St John's La. Hali HX1 .... 113 C6
St John's Mount. Wake WF1 . 142 B8
St John's N. Wake WF1 .... 142 B7
St John's Pk. Men LS29 .... 21 F5
St John's Pl. Birk BD11 .... 96 A6
St John's Pl. Clec BD19 .... 116 E7 7
St John's Pl. Hali HX1 .... 113 C6
St John's RC Sch. Nor 123 C2
St John's Rd. B Spa LS23 .... 30 D7
St John's Rd. Hud HD1 .... 154 A8
St John's Rd. Ilkley LS29 .... 8 E4
St John's Rd. Keigh BD20 .... 18 A2
St John's Rd. Kirkhe HD5 .... 137 C1
St John's Rd. Leeds LS3 .... 59 F1
St John's Rd. Yeadon LS19 .... 40 A6
St John's Residential Sch for the
Deaf. B Spa 30 D7
St John's Sq. Wake WF1 .... 142 B7
St John's St. Con BD20 .... 4 A2
St John's St. Hor WF4 .... 140 E1
St John's St. Roth LS26 .... 101 C5
St John's St. Sil BD20 .... 5 E1
St John's View. B Spa LS23 ...... 30 C7
St John's View. Batley WF17 . 118 A6
St John's Way. Yeadon LS19 .... 40 A6
St John's Wlk. Roy S71 .... 179 D4
St Johns Ave. Sil LS29 .... 6 F8
St Johns Church Sch. Hud 152 D5
St Johns Cl. Clec BD19 .... 116 E7
St Johns Cl. Dew WF13 .... 139 B8
St Johns Ct. Holmfi HD7 .... 188 F4
St Johns Ctr. Leeds 79 C8
St Johns Mews. Wake WF1 ..... 142 B8
St Johns Way. Keigh BD22 .... 34 F6
St Joseph's Catholic Prim Sch.
Weth 13 E6
St Joseph's Coll. Brad 55 C3
St Joseph's Mount. Pont WF8 146 B7
St Joseph's Prim Sch. Batley . 118 A2
St Joseph's Prim Sch. Tod 108 B6
St Joseph's RC Fst Sch. Bing 37 A3
St Joseph's RC Inf Sch. Brad 74 D4
St Joseph's RC Jun & Inf Sch.
Pont 146 C8
St Joseph's RC Jun Sch. Brad .. 74 D4
St Joseph's RC Prim Sch. Brig 114 F5
St Joseph's RC Prim Sch. Hali 113 D8
St Joseph's RC Prim Sch. Hud 154 F6
St Joseph's RC Prim Sch. Keigh 35 B5
St Joseph's RC Prim Sch. Leeds 79 E4
St Joseph's RC Prim Sch.
Pudsey 76 F8
St Josephs RC Jun Sch. Otley .. 23 A8
St Jude's Pl. Brad BD1 .... 74 D8
St Jude's St. Brad BD8 .... 74 D8
St Jude's St. Hali HX1 .... 113 B5 4
St Julien's Mount. Caw S75 ... 193 E4
St Julien's Way. Caw S75 .... 193 E4
St Laurence's Cl. Ship BD2 .... 55 E5
St Lawrence Cl. Pudsey LS28 ... 76 D7
St Lawrence St. Leeds LS7 .... 60 D6
St Lawrence Terr. Pudsey LS28 76 E6
St Leonard's Ct. Brad BD8 .... 54 F1 4
St Leonard's Gr. Brad BD8 .... 54 F1
St Leonard's Rd. Brad BD8 .... 54 F1
St Leonards Cl. Sil LS29 .... 6 F7
St Luke's Cl. B Spa LS23 .... 30 D5
St Luke's Cl. Clec BD19 .... 116 B7
St Luke's Cres. Leeds LS11 .... 79 A4
St Luke's Gn. Leeds LS11 .... 79 A4
St Luke's Hospl. Brad 74 D4
St Luke's Hospl. Hud 153 C3
St Luke's Rd. Leeds LS11 .... 79 A4
St Luke's St. Leeds LS11 .... 79 A4
St Luke's Terr. Clec BD19 .... 116 B7
St Luke's Terr. Keigh BD20 .... 36 D8
St Luke's View. Leeds LS11 ...... 79 A4 6
St Lukes CE Fst Sch. Brad 56 D4

St Lukes Cl. Batley WF17 .... 118 E4
St Malachy's RC Sch. Hali 91 E3
St Margaret's Ave. Brad BD4 .. 75 D2
St Margaret's Ave. Hors LS18 . 41 B2
St Margaret's Ave. Leeds LS8 . 61 A6
St Margaret's Ave. M'town LS26 .... 102 D3
St Margaret's Cl. Hors LS18 ... 41 B2
St Margaret's Dr. Hors LS18 ... 41 B2
St Margaret's Dr. Leeds LS8 ... 61 A6
St Margaret's Gr. Leeds LS8 ... 61 A6
St Margaret's Home. Leeds 59 D6
St Margaret's Hospl. Leeds 59 D6
St Margaret's Pl. Brad BD7 ...... 74 B5
St Margaret's Rd. Brad BD7 .... 74 B6
St Margaret's Rd. Hors LS18 ... 41 B2
St Margaret's Rd.M'town LS26 102 D3
St Margaret's Terr. Brad BD7 . 74 B5
St Margaret's Terr. Ilkley LS29 . 8 B3
St Margaret's View. Leeds LS8 61 A6
St Mark's Ave. Leeds LS2 .... 60 A2
St Mark's Flats. Leeds LS2 ...... 60 A3 7
St Mark's Rd. Hud HD3 .... 153 A6
St Mark's Rd. Leeds LS6 .... 60 B3
St Mark's St. Leeds LS2 .... 60 A3
St Mark's St. Wake WF1 .... 142 D8
St Mark's Terr. Brad LS22 .... 94 C5
St Marks View. Hud HD3 .... 153 A6
St Martin's Ave. Leeds LS7 ...... 60 D5
St Martin's Cres. Leeds LS7 .... 60 D5
St Martin's Dr. Leeds LS7 .... 60 C6
St Martin's Gdns. Leeds LS7 .... 60 D5
St Martin's Gr. Castle WF10 .. 124 B6
St Martin's Gr. Leeds LS7 .... 60 D5
St Martin's Rd. Leeds LS7 .... 60 D5
St Martin's View. Brig HD6 ..... 115 A3 7
St Martin's View. Leeds LS7 .... 60 D5
St Martins Ave. Brad BD7 .... 74 C7
St Martins Ave. Otley LS21 .... 10 F2
St Martins Cl. Feath WF7 .... 145 C4
St Mary St. Hali HX1 .... 113 B6
St Mary's Ave. Batley WF17 ... 118 B3
St Mary's Ave. Brad BD12 .... 94 C2
St Mary's Ave. Holmfi HD7 ...... 188 F8
St Mary's Ave. Mir WF14 .... 138 C6
St Mary's Ave. Swil LS26 .... 82 A1
St Mary's CE Fst Sch. Wake ... 142 D6
St Mary's CE Jun & Inf Sch. Sow Br 132 C7
St Mary's Cl. Brad BD12 .... 94 B2
St Mary's Cl. E Ard WF3 .... 119 D7
St Mary's Cl. Gar LS25 .... 82 F6
St Mary's Cl. Ilkley LS29 .... 8 C4
St Mary's Cl. Leeds LS7 .... 60 D5
St Mary's Cl. Leeds LS12 .... 78 D6
St Mary's Cl. S Elm WF9 .... 183 A2
St Mary's Comp Sch. Guise 22 C3
St Mary's Cres. Brad BD12 .... 94 B2
St Mary's Cres. Holmfi HD7 ..... 188 F8
St Mary's Ct. Kippax WF10 ..... 103 B4
St Mary's Ct. Leeds LS7 .... 60 D5
St Mary's Ct. Mel HD7 .... 188 B8
St Mary's Dr. Brad BD12 .... 94 C2
St Mary's Fold. Brad BD4 .... 75 D5
St Mary's Garth. E Kes LS17 .... 28 B5
St Mary's Gdns. Brad BD12 ...... 94 C2 1
St Mary's Heights. Hali HX2 ..... 91 D5
St Mary's Hospl. Leeds 77 F8
St Mary's La. Kirkhe HD5 .... 155 C7
St Mary's La. Leeds LS9 .... 79 E8
St Mary's Mews. Honley HD7 ... 171 F5
St Mary's Mount. Brad BD12 ..... 94 B2
St Mary's Pl. Castle WF10 ...... 124 D8 1
St Mary's Pl. Dew WF12 .... 139 D6
St Mary's RC Fst Sch. Brad 74 F7
St Mary's RC Inf Sch. Batley .. 118 B6
St Mary's RC Jun Mix & Inf Sch. Roth 100 F4
St Mary's RC Jun Sch. Batley .. 118 B6
St Mary's RC Prim Sch. Bacup . 106 B2
St Mary's RC Prim Sch. Hali 113 B6
St Mary's RC Sch. Hors 41 C1
St Mary's Rd. Brad BD8, BD9 .. 55 C2
St Mary's Rd. Brad BD4 .... 75 D5
St Mary's Rd. Holmfi HD7 .... 188 F8
St Mary's Rd. Honley HD7 .... 171 F5
St Mary's Rd. Keigh BD20 .... 18 F2
St Mary's Rd. Leeds LS7 .... 60 D5
St Mary's Rd. Nor WF6 .... 122 F3
St Mary's Rise. Holmfi HD7 ..... 188 F8
St Mary's Sq. Brad BD12 .... 94 C2
St Mary's Sq. Honley HD7 .... 171 F5
St Mary's Sq. Morley LS27 .... 98 A4
St Mary's St. B Spa LS23 .... 30 D8
St Mary's St. Leeds LS9 .... 79 D8
St Mary's Way. Holmfi HD7 ...... 188 F8
St Mary's Wlk. M'Field LS25 .... 83 F7
St Mary's Wlk. M'field LS25 ..... 84 A7
St Mary's Wlk. Mir WF14 .... 138 C6
St Marys Ave. Nor WF6 .... 122 F4
St Marys Gate. Elland HX5 ...... 134 F7 12
St Marys Park App. Leeds LS12 77 F8
St Marys RC Prim Sch. Leeds .. 80 A8
St Matthew Rd. Dew WF13 ..... 139 B8
St Matthew's CE Mid Sch.Leeds 60 C7
St Matthew's CE Fst Sch. Brad 74 E1
St Matthew's Dr. Northo HX3 .. 93 A3
St Matthew's R C Sch. Brad 73 B8
St Matthew's Rd. Brad BD5 ...... 74 D1
St Matthew's St. Leeds LS11 ... 79 A5 4
St Matthew's Wlk. Leeds LS7 .. 60 C8
St Matthews Cl. Wils BD15 ...... 53 D4
St Matthews Gr. Wils BD15 ...... 53 C4
St Matthias' Ct. Leeds LS4 .... 59 D2
St Matthias' Gr. Leeds LS4 .... 59 D2
St Matthias' St. Leeds LS4 .... 59 D2
St Matthias' Terr. Leeds LS4 .... 59 D2
St Michael Ct. Leeds LS13 .... 58 D3
St Michael's C E Jun & Inf Sch. Shelf 93 D6
St Michael's CE Sch. Leeds 59 E5
St Michael's Cl. Castle WF10 . 124 D7
St Michael's Cl. Dew WF12 .... 139 E1
St Michael's Cl. Emley HD8 ..... 175 D7
St Michael's Cl. Ship BD16 .... 54 B6 6
St Michael's Cl. Wake WF2 ..... 142 A5
St Michael's Coll. Leeds 59 F1
St Michael's Cres. Leeds LS6 .. 59 D4
St Michael's Fst Sch. Brad 74 B4
St Michael's Gdns. Emley HD8 175 D7
St Michael's Gr. Leeds LS6 ...... 59 D4
St Michael's Ho. Wake WF2 ... 142 A5
St Michael's La. Leeds LS6 .... 59 D4
St Michael's Mount. Dew WF12 .... 139 E1
St Michael's Rd. Brad BD8 .... 74 C8
St Michael's Rd. Leeds LS6 ...... 59 D4
St Michael's Terr. Leeds LS6 ... 59 D5
St Michael's Way. Bur in W LS29 .... 21 F8
St Michaels Ave. Pont WF8 ..... 146 B8 1
St Michaels Way. Sil LS29 .... 6 F7
St Nicholas Catholic Prim Sch. Leeds 61 D3
St Nicholas Rd. Ilkley LS29 .... 8 A5
St Nicholas St. Castle WF10 .. 124 D7
St Oswald Ave. Pont WF8 .... 146 B8
St Oswald Rd. Wake WF2 .... 141 D5
St Oswald St. Castle WF10 ..... 124 D8 6
St Oswald's CE Fst Sch. Brad .. 74 C3
St Oswalds CE Jun Sch. Guise . 39 E8
St Oswalds Garth. Guise LS20 .. 22 F1
St Oswalds Pl. Ossett WF5 ..... 140 E7
St Oswalds Terr. Guise LS20 ... 22 E1
St Patrick's Fst Sch. Brad 74 C8
St Patrick's Prim Sch. Batley ... 96 D2
St Patrick's RC(A) Jun & Inf Sch. Elland 134 D6
St Patrick's RC Prim Sch. Hud 153 E8
St Patricks RC Prim Sch. Leeds 80 A8
St Paul's Ave. Birk BD11 .... 96 B5
St Paul's Ave. Brad BD6 .... 94 B8
St Paul's CE Fst Sch. Bri 181 A3
St Paul's CE Fst Sch. Brad 94 B8
St Paul's Cl. Upton WF9 .... 183 D8
St Paul's Dr. Wake WF2 .... 141 D8
St Paul's Fst Sch. Brad 55 C1
St Paul's Gr. Brad LS29 .... 94 B8
St Paul's Gr. Ilkley LS29 .... 8 D4
St Paul's Pl. Leeds LS1 .... 79 B8
St Paul's RC Prim Sch. Leeds ... 43 A4
St Paul's Rd. Birk BD11 .... 96 B5
St Paul's Rd. Brad BD8 .... 55 C2
St Paul's Rd. Brad BD6 .... 94 B8
St Paul's Rd. Hali HX1 .... 112 F5 20
St Paul's Rd. Keigh BD21 .... 35 D6
St Paul's Rd. Mir WF14 .... 138 A4
St Paul's Rd. Ship BD18 .... 55 A7
St Paul's St. Hud HD1 .... 154 B5 3
St Paul's St. Leeds LS1 .... 79 B8
St Paul's St. Morley LS27 .... 98 B3 1
St Paul's Terr. Mir WF14 .... 138 A4
St Paul's Wlk. Wake WF2 .... 141 D8
St Paulinus Cl. Dew WF13 ...... 139 B8
St Paulinus' RC Jun & Inf Sch. Dew 139 A7
St Pauls Rd. Kirkhe HD5 .... 155 B8
St Pauls Rise. Sil LS29 .... 6 F8
St Peg Cl. Clec BD19 .... 116 E7
St Peg La. Clec BD19 .... 116 E7
St Peter Claver's Coll. Mir 137 E8
St Peter & Paul RC Mid Sch. Midd 99 E5
St Peter & St Pauls RC Prim Sch. Yeadon 39 F6
St Peter's Ave. Roth LS26 ...... 100 F5
St Peter's Ave. Sow Br HX6 .... 111 F3
St Peter's CE Inf Sch. Morley .. 98 B6
St Peter's CE Mid Sch. Leeds ... 79 E8
St Peter's CE Prim Sch. Leeds .. 79 E8
St Peter's Cl. Batley WF17 .... 96 D1
St Peter's Cl. Mir WF14 .... 137 F5 8
St Peter's Cres. Loft G WF3 ... 122 B6
St Peter's Cres. Morley LS27 ... 98 A6
St Peter's Ct. Leeds LS13 .... 58 D3
St Peter's Garth. Thorner LS14 46 A6
St Peter's Gate. Dearne S63 . 194 C1
St Peter's Gate. Tod OL14 ...... 129 B8
St Peter's Gdns. Dew WF12 .... 139 F7
St Peter's Gdns. Leeds LS13 .... 58 C3
St Peter's Gr. Hor WF4 .... 141 B1
St Peter's Inf Sch. Sow Br 111 E3
St Peter's Mount. Leeds LS13 . 58 D2
St Peter's Par. Dew WF12 ...... 139 F7
St Peter's Pl. Leeds LS9 .... 79 D8
St Peter's RC Fst Sch. Brad 75 B6
St Peter's Sq. Leeds LS9 .... 79 D8
St Peter's Sq. Sow Br HX6 .... 111 E3
St Peter's St. Hud HD1 .... 154 B6 2
St Peter's St. Leeds LS2 .... 79 D8
St Peter's Way. Men LS29 .... 21 F4
St Peters Cres. Kirkhe HD5 ..... 155 B8
St Peters Ct. Leeds LS11 .... 79 C4
St Peters Ct. Sil LS29 .... 6 F7
St Peters Gate. Ossett WF5 .... 140 D7
St Philip's Ave. Midd LS10 .... 99 B5
St Philip's CE Fst Sch. Brad 55 A1
St Philip's Cl. Bur in W LS29 .... 9 F1
St Philip's Cl. Dew WF13 .... 118 D1
St Philip's Dr. Bur in W LS29 .... 21 F8
St Philip's Sch. Midd 99 B5
St Philip's Way. Bur in W LS29 21 F8
St Philips Ct. Hud HD3 .... 135 B2
St Richards Rd. Otley LS21 .... 10 F2
St Stephen's CE Fst Sch. Brad . 74 E3
St Stephen's Ct. Leeds LS9 .... 79 F8
St Stephen's Ct. Stee BD20 ...... 17 C6
St Stephen's Rd. Brad BD5 .... 74 E3
St Stephen's Rd. Hud HD1 ...... 153 F4
St Stephen's Rd. Leeds LS9 ...... 79 F8
St Stephen's Rd. Pudsey LS28 . 57 A7
St Stephen's Rd. Stee BD20 ...... 17 C5
St Stephen's St. Elland HX3 .... 113 A2
St Stephen's Terr. Brad BD5 .... 74 D3
St Stephens Ct. Elland HX3 .... 113 A2
St Swithins Dr. Loft G WF3 ..... 121 F2
St Swithins Gr. Loft G WF3 ..... 121 F2
St Theresa's RC Prim Sch. Leeds 62 C4
St Thomas a Beckett Cath Comp Sch. Wake 142 E1
St Thomas CE Jun Sch. Feath . 145 C5
St Thomas Rd. Feath WF7 ...... 145 D5
St Thomas' Rd. Hud HD1 .... 153 F5
St Thomas Row. Leeds LS2 ...... 60 D1
St Thomas's Rd. Brad BD1 .... 74 D7 2
St Thomas's Terr. Pont WF8 ... 125 F3
St Urban's RC Prim Sch. Leeds . 59 C8
St Vincent Rd. Pudsey LS28 ..... 76 F6
St Vincent's Sch. B Spa 30 D7
St Walburga's RC Fst Sch. Ship 54 F7
St Walburga's RC Prim Sch.Ship55 A7
St Wilfrid's St. Pudsey LS28 ..... 57 B7
St Wilfrid's Ave. Leeds LS8 ...... 61 B4
St Wilfrid's Catholic High Sch. Feath 124 C1
St Wilfrid's Cir. Leeds LS8 .... 61 B3
St Wilfrid's Cl. Brad BD7 .... 73 F5
St Wilfrid's Cres. Brad BD7 ...... 73 F5
St Wilfrid's Cres. Leeds LS8 ..... 61 B4
St Wilfrid's Dr. Leeds LS8 .... 61 A4
St Wilfrid's Garth. Leeds LS8 .. 61 B3
St Wilfrid's Gr. Leeds LS8 .... 61 B4
St Wilfrid's Rd. Brad BD7 .... 73 F5
St William's RC Fst Sch. Brad ... 74 B8
St Winefride's RC Sch. Brad 94 B8
St Winifred's Cl. Hali HX2 .... 91 D5
Sal Nook Cl. Brad BD12 .... 94 E7
Sal Royd Rd. Brad BD12 .... 94 E6
Salcombe Pl. Brad BD4 .... 75 E2
Salem Pl. Gar LS25 .... 82 E7
Salem Pl. Leeds LS10 .... 79 C6
Salem St. Brad BD1 .... 74 E8
Salem St. Heb Br HX7 .... 88 F3
Salem St. Queen BD13 .... 92 C8
Salendine Nook High Sch. Hud 152 F7
Salford. Tod OL14 .... 108 B4
Salford Way. Tod OL14 .... 108 A4
Salisbury Ave. Bail BD17 .... 38 C3
Salisbury Ave. Leeds LS12 .... 78 C8
Salisbury Cl. Dew WF12 .... 139 F8
Salisbury Cl. Nor WF6 .... 123 B3
Salisbury Ct. Hors LS18 .... 41 D1
Salisbury Gr. Leeds LS12 .... 78 C8
Salisbury Mews. Hors LS18 ...... 41 D1
Salisbury Pl. Hali HX3 .... 92 B1
Salisbury Pl. Pudsey LS28 .... 57 A7
Salisbury Rd. Brad BD12 .... 94 C6 3
Salisbury Rd. Brig BD19 .... 115 F8
Salisbury Rd. Keigh BD22 .... 35 A6
Salisbury Rd. Leeds LS12 .... 78 C8
Salisbury Rd. Ship BD9 .... 55 C5
Salisbury St. Pudsey LS28 .... 57 A6
Salisbury St. Sow Br HX6 .... 112 A3
Salisbury St. Yeadon LS19 .... 40 B4
Salisbury Terr. Leeds LS12 .... 78 C8
Salisbury View. Hors LS18 .... 41 D1
Salisbury View. Leeds LS12 ...... 78 C8
Salley St. Litt OL15 .... 129 C2
Salmon Cres. Hors LS18 .... 41 C1
Salt Drake. Sow Br HX6 .... 132 B8
Salt Gram Sch. Ship 37 F2
Salt Horn Cl. Brad BD12 .... 94 F5
Salt Pie Alley. Wake WF2 .... 142 B6
Salt St. Brad BD8 .... 55 C1
Salt St. Hali HX1 .... 113 A8
Saltaire Fst Sch. Ship 54 F8
Saltaire. Haw BD22 .... 51 F8 4
Saltaire Rd. Bing BD16 .... 37 D5
Saltaire Rd. Ship BD18 .... 55 A8
Saltaire Sta. Ship 37 F1
Saltburn Pl. Brad BD9 .... 54 F2
Saltburn St. Hali HX1 .... 112 F7 8
Salter Rake Gate. Tod OL14 ... 129 B8
Salter Row. Pont WF8 .... 146 D8 1
Salter St. Batley WF17 .... 118 B2
Salterhebble Hill. Hali HX3 ..... 113 D3
Salterhebble Jun & Inf Sch. Hali 113 D3
Saltersgate Ave. Knot WF11 ... 126 E4
Saltonstall La. Hali HX2 .... 90 D5
Sampson St. Liver WF15 .... 117 B4
Samuel Dr. Loft G WF3 .... 121 E5
Samuel St. Keigh BD21 .... 35 C7
Sand Beds. Queen BD13 .... 72 F1
Sand Hill La. Leeds LS17 .... 43 D3
Sand Hill Lawns. Leeds LS17 .... 43 D3
Sand Moor Golf Course. Leeds .. 43 C6
Sand St. Haw BD22 .... 51 C6
Sand St. Hud HD1 .... 154 B5
Sand St. Keigh BD21 .... 35 C8
Sandal & Agbrigg Sta. Wake . 142 E2
Sandal Ave. Wake WF2 .... 142 E1
Sandal Cliff. Wake WF2 .... 142 E1
Sandal Fst Sch. Bail 38 C3
Sandal Hall Cl. Wake WF2 ...... 142 F1
Sandal Hall Mews. Wake WF2 142 E1
Sandal Magna Endowed CE Mid Sch. Wake 160 E8
Sandal Magna Fst Sch. Wake . 142 E2
Sandal Rise. Th Aud WF8 .... 165 A5
Sandal Way. Batley WF17 .... 96 F1
Sandale Wlk. Brad BD6 .... 93 F7 5
Sandall Cl. Kippax LS25 .... 83 B2
Sandall Magna. Shelf HX3 .... 93 E7
Sandals Rd. Bail BD17 .... 38 C3
Sandbeck Ind Est. Weth 13 F7
Sandbeck La. Weth LS22 .... 14 B8
Sandbeck Way. Weth LS22 .... 13 F7
Sandbed Ct. Leeds LS15 .... 62 D3
Sandbed La. Leeds LS15 .... 62 D3
Sandbed Lawns. Leeds LS15 .... 62 D3 3
Sandbeds Cres. Hali HX2 .... 91 E1
Sandbeds. Honley HD7 .... 171 F6
Sandbeds Rd. Hali HX2 .... 91 E1
Sandbeds Terr. Hali HX2 .... 91 E1
Sandbeds Trad Est. Ossett 140 E7
Sandene Ave. Hud HD4 .... 153 C2
Sandene Dr. Hud HD4 .... 153 C2
Sanderling Ct. Brad BD8 .... 73 C7 7
Sanderling Garth. Midd LS10 ... 99 D5 5
Sanderling Way. Midd LS10 ...... 99 D5
Sanderson Ave. Brad BD6 .... 74 C1
Sanderson Ave. Nor WF6 .... 123 A1
Sanderson La. Loft G LS26 ...... 122 B8
Sanderson La. Roth LS26 .... 101 B1
Sanderson St. Wake WF1 .... 142 D6
Sandfield Ave. Leeds LS6 .... 59 E6
Sandfield Garth. Leeds LS6 ...... 59 E6
Sandfield Rd. Bacup OL13 .... 106 A1
Sandfield Rd. Brad BD10 .... 56 B6
Sandford Mid Sch. Leeds 58 E3
Sandford Pl. Leeds LS5 .... 59 A4
Sandford Rd. Brad BD3 .... 75 C7
Sandford Rd. Leeds LS5 .... 59 B3
Sandford Rd. S Elm WF9 .... 183 A5
Sandforth Ave. Hali HX3 .... 92 C2
Sandgate Dr. Kippax LS25 .... 83 C2
Sandgate La. Kippax LS25 .... 83 C1
Sandgate La. Kippax LS25 .... 83 D3
Sandgate Rise. Kippax LS25 ...... 83 C2
Sandgate Terr. Kippax LS25 ...... 83 C1
Sandhall Ave. Hali HX2 .... 112 D8
Sandhall Cres. Hali HX2 .... 112 D8 5
Sandhall Dr. Hali HX2 .... 112 D7
Sandhall Gn. Hali HX2 .... 112 D7
Sandhall La. Hali HX2 .... 112 D7
Sandhill Cl. Pont WF8 .... 125 D4
Sandhill Cres. Leeds LS17 .... 43 E4
Sandhill Ct. Leeds LS17 .... 43 D3
Sandhill Dr. Leeds LS17 .... 43 E4
Sandhill Gr. Grim S72 .... 181 A1
Sandhill Gr. Leeds LS17 .... 43 E5
Sandhill Lawn. Pont WF8 .... 146 C7
Sandhill Mount. Brad BD10 .... 56 C6
Sandhill Mount. Leeds LS17 ...... 43 E5
Sandhill Oval. Leeds LS17 .... 43 E5
Sandhill Rise. Pont WF8 .... 125 D3
Sandholme Cres. Brig HX3 ...... 114 D7
Sandholme Dr. Brad BD10 .... 56 C6
Sandholme Dr. Bur in W LS29 . 21 F8
Sandholme Dr. Ossett WF5 ..... 140 D5
Sandholme Fold. Brig HX3 ...... 114 D7
Sandhurst Ave. Leeds LS8 .... 61 A3
Sandhurst Gr. Leeds LS8 .... 61 A3
Sandhurst Mount. Leeds LS8 .... 61 A4
Sandhurst Pl. Leeds LS8 .... 61 A3
Sandhurst Rd. Leeds LS8 .... 61 A3
Sandhurst St. Pudsey LS28 .... 57 A7
Sandhurst Terr. Leeds LS8 .... 61 A3
Sandiford Cl. Leeds LS15 .... 62 D3
Sandiford Terr. Leeds LS15 .... 62 D3
Sandiway Bank. Dew WF12 ..... 139 D3
Sandleas Way. Leeds LS15 .... 62 F2
Sandlewood Cl. Leeds LS11 .... 79 A5
Sandlewood Gn. Leeds LS11 .... 79 B5
Sandmead Cl. Brad BD4 .... 75 E3
Sandmead Cl. Morley LS27 .... 98 A6
Sandmead Croft. Morley LS27 . 98 A6
Sandmoor Ave. Leeds LS17 .... 43 D6
Sandmoor Chase. Leeds LS17 ... 43 D5
Sandmoor Cl. Leeds LS17 .... 43 D5
Sandmoor Cl. Thorn BD13 .... 72 E6 6
Sandmoor Ct. Leeds LS17 .... 43 D5
Sandmoor Dr. Leeds LS17 .... 43 D5
Sandmoor Garth. Brad BD10 ..... 39 B1
Sandmoor Gdns. Shelf HX3 .... 93 B5
Sandmoor Gdns. Leeds LS17 ..... 43 C6
Sandmoor La. Leeds LS17 .... 43 D5
Sandmoor Mews. Leeds LS17 .. 43 D5
Sandon Gr. Leeds LS10 .... 79 E2 10
Sandon Mount. Leeds LS10 .... 79 E2
Sandon Pl. Leeds LS10 .... 79 E2
Sandown Ave. Crof WF4 .... 143 F1
Sandown Ave. Hali HX2 .... 91 E4
Sandown Rd. Hali HX2 .... 91 E4
Sandpiper Mews. Brad BD8 ...... 73 C7 5
Sandringham App. Leeds LS17 . 43 E3
Sandringham Ave. Knot WF11 126 C4
Sandringham Ave. Pudsey LS28 76 E6 4
Sandringham Cl. Brad BD14 ...... 73 D5
Sandringham Cl. Pont WF8 ..... 146 C5
Sandringham Cres. Leeds LS17 43 E3
Sandringham Ct. Brad BD14 ..... 73 D5
Sandringham Ct. Hud HD2 ...... 136 E5
Sandringham Dr. Leeds LS17 .... 43 D3
Sandringham Gdns. Leeds LS17 43 D3
Sandringham Gn. Leeds LS17 .. 43 E4
Sandringham Mount. Leeds LS17 .... 43 E3
Sandringham Rd. Brad BD14 .... 73 D5
Sandringham Rd.Byram WF11 126 D7
Sandringham Rd. Weth LS22 .... 13 E6
Sandringham Way. Leeds LS17 43 D3
Sandrock Rd. Pont WF8 .... 125 E2
Sands House La. Hud HD4 ...... 153 B1
Sands La. Dew WF12 .... 139 E7
Sands La. Lepton WF14 .... 155 F6
Sands La. Mir WF14 .... 138 D3
Sands Rd. Dew WF12 .... 139 E6
Sandsend Cl. Brad BD9 .... 54 D3
Sandside Cl. Brad BD5 .... 74 E8
Sandstone Cl. Honley HD7 ...... 171 F3
Sandway Gdns. Leeds LS15 ...... 62 B2
Sandway Gr. Leeds LS15 .... 62 B2
Sandway. Leeds LS15 .... 62 B2
Sandwell St. Slai HD7 .... 151 F1
Sandwich Cres. Hud HD2 .... 135 F3
Sandy Bank Ave. Roth LS26 .... 100 F6
Sandy Banks. Harden BD16 ...... 53 B8
Sandy Beck. Brad BD15 .... 54 A3
Sandy Dyke La. Sow Br HX6 .. 132 E8
Sandy Gate. Hare LS17 .... 26 E7
Sandy Gate. Heb Br HX7 .... 89 B4
Sandy Gate. Holmfi HD7 .... 189 C4
Sandy Gate. Keigh BD20 .... 35 A8
Sandy Gate La. Ack M T WF7 . 146 C3
Sandy Gate La. Wad M HX7 .... 89 C4
Sandy Gr. Roth LS26 .... 100 F6
Sandy La. Hud HD4 .... 171 A7
Sandy La. Neth WF4 .... 158 C7
Sandy Lane Fst Sch. Brad 54 A4
Sandy Lobby. Pool LS21 .... 24 C6
Sandy Way. Yeadon LS19 .... 40 B7 1
Sandy Wlk. Bramho LS16 .... 24 F2
Sandy Wlk. Wake WF1 .... 142 B7
Sandyacres Cres. Roth LS26 .. 100 F6
Sandyacres Dr. Roth LS26 .... 100 F6
Sandyacres. Roth LS26 .... 100 F6
Sandybridge La. Shaf S72 .... 180 B4
Sandyfield Terr. Batley WF17 .. 118 B6
Sandyfoot. Rip HX4 .... 133 B4
Sandygate La. Hem WF9 .... 181 C7
Sandygate Terr. Brad BD4 .... 75 D5
Sandylands. Glu BD20 .... 16 D7
Sandylands. Hud HD4 .... 171 D6
Sandymoor. Brad BD15 .... 54 A4
Sandywood Ct. Hors LS18 .... 58 C7
Sandywood St. Keigh BD21 .... 35 C8
Sangster Way. Brad BD5 .... 75 A1
Sanquah Terr. Nor WF6 .... 123 C3
Santa Monica Cres. Brad BD10 . 56 A7
Santa Monica Gr. Brad BD10 ... 56 A7
Santa Monica Rd. Brad BD10 ... 56 A7
Santingley La. Ryhill WF4 .... 162 A6
Sanworth St. Tod OL14 .... 108 C5 2
Sapgate La. Thorn BD13 .... 72 E6
Saplin St. Brad BD8 .... 55 B1
Sapphire Ct. Batley WF17 .... 118 A6
Sarah St. E Ard WF3 .... 120 D8
Sardinia St. Leeds LS10 .... 79 D5
Saunders Cl. Hud HD3 .... 153 C7
Saunters Way. Nor WF6 .... 123 A4
Savile Ave. Brad BD10 .... 56 C6
Savile Ave. Leeds LS7 .... 60 D4
Savile Bsns Ctr. Dew 139 D7
Savile Cl. Brig HD6 .... 115 D3
Savile Cres. Hali HX1 .... 113 B6
Savile Ct. Mir WF14 .... 138 A6
Savile Dr. Hali HX1 .... 113 B6
Savile Dr. Hor WF4 .... 141 A2
Savile Dr. Leeds LS7 .... 60 D3
Savile Glen. Hali HX1 .... 113 B6
Savile Gn. Hali HX1 .... 113 C6
Savile Gr. Dew WF12 .... 139 C7
Savile House. Elland HX5 .... 134 F7 7
Savile La. Brig HD6 .... 115 D3
Savile Lea. Hali HX1 .... 113 B6
Savile Mews. Dew WF12 .... 139 C5
Savile Mount. Leeds LS7 .... 60 D3
Savile Par. Hali HX1 .... 113 B5 5
Savile Park Gdns. Hali HX1 ..... 113 B5
Savile Park Rd. Clec BD19 .... 95 D3
Savile Park Rd. Hali HX1 .... 113 B5
Savile Park St. Hali HX1 .... 113 A5
Savile Park Terr. Hali HX1 .... 113 A5 21
Savile Pit La. Dew WF12 .... 140 A8
Savile Pk. Hali HX1 .... 113 A5
Savile Pk. Hali HX3 .... 113 B1
Savile Pl. Leeds LS7 .... 60 D3
Savile Pl. Mir WF14 .... 138 A7
Savile Prec. Castle WF10 .... 124 C8
Savile Rd. Castle WF10 .... 124 C8
Savile Rd. Dew WF12 .... 139 C6
Savile Rd. Elland HX5 .... 134 F6
Savile Rd. Hali HX1 .... 113 B6
Savile Rd. Heb Br HX7 .... 88 E3
Savile Rd. Hud HD3 .... 153 C8
Savile Rd. Leeds LS7 .... 60 D3
Savile Rd. M'town LS26 .... 102 D3
Savile Royd. Hali HX1 .... 113 B5
Savile Sq. Mir WF14 .... 138 A5
Savile St. Batley WF17 .... 118 D2
Savile St. Clec BD19 .... 95 D1
Savile St. Hud HD3 .... 153 A5
Savile Town CE Sch. Dew 139 D6
Savile Way. Hali HX5 .... 135 A8
Savile Wlk. Bri S72 .... 181 B3
Savile Wlk. Dew WF13 .... 139 C8 6
Saville Ave. Emley HD8 .... 175 D7
Saville Cl. Roth WF3 .... 100 C1
Saville Ct. Otley LS21 .... 22 F7
Saville Gn. Leeds LS9 .... 79 F8 3
Saville Rd. Skel HD8 .... 175 A2
Saville St. Clay W HD8 .... 175 D1
Saville St. Emley HD8 .... 175 D7
Saville St. Ossett WF5 .... 140 F4
Saville St. Wake WF1 .... 142 C7
Saw Mill. Sow Br HX6 .... 132 E8
Saw Mill St. Leeds LS11 .... 79 B6
Saw Yd. Wake WF1 .... 142 C6 17
Sawley Cl. Wake WF1 .... 142 E8
Sawley St. Keigh BD21 .... 35 B6
Sawood La. Oxen HX7 .... 70 F8
Sawrey Pl. Brad BD5 .... 74 D6
Sawyers Garth. Add LS29 .... 7 A8
Saxon Ave. S Kirk WF9 .... 181 F2
Saxon Cl. Emley HD8 .... 175 C6
Saxon Cl. Upton WF9 .... 183 E7
Saxon Ct. Leeds LS17 .... 43 B3
Saxon Gate. Leeds LS17 .... 43 B2
Saxon Gn. Leeds LS17 .... 43 A2
Saxon Gr. Leeds LS17 .... 43 A2
Saxon Gr. S Kirk WF9 .... 182 A1
Saxon Mount. Leeds LS17 .... 43 B3
Saxon Mount. S Kirk WF9 .... 181 F1
Saxon Rd. Leeds LS17 .... 43 A2
Saxon St. Brad BD8 .... 74 C8
Saxon St. Hali HX1 .... 112 F8
Saxon St. Tod OL14 .... 108 A1 10
Saxon Way. Castle WF10 .... 125 A8
Saxton Ave. Brad BD6 .... 73 F1
Saxton House. Yeadon LS19 ...... 40 B6
Saxton La. Leeds LS9 .... 79 E7
Saxton Pl. Hud HD5 .... 155 A4
Saxton St. Liver WF15 .... 117 C5
Sayers Cl. Leeds LS5 .... 59 B4
Sayle Ave. Brad BD4 .... 75 B1
Sayner La. Leeds LS10 .... 79 E5
Sayner Rd. Leeds LS10 .... 79 D6
Scaitcliffe View. Tod OL14 .... 107 F5
Scale Hill. Hud HD2 .... 136 A2
Scalebor Park Hospl. Bur in W . 21 D8
Scaley St. Brad BD3 .... 75 D7
Scaly Gate. Holmfi HD7 .... 190 A2
Scaly Gate. Holmfi HD7 .... 190 A5
Scammonden Rd. Rip HX4 .... 133 B3
Scape View. Hud HD7 .... 152 E4
Scapegoat Hill Jun & Inf Sch. Slai 152 B6
Scar Bottom La. Elland HX4 ..... 133 F7
Scar Gr. Hud HD4 .... 153 F2
Scar Head Rd. Sow Br HX6 ...... 112 B3
Scar Hill Cotts. Elland HX4 ...... 133 E4
Scar Hole La. Holmfi HD7 .... 190 A3
Scar La. Hud HD3, HD7 .... 152 F4
Scar Top Cotts. Haw BD22 .... 50 B7
Scar Top. Hud HD7 .... 152 E4
Scar Top La. Hud HD4 .... 171 D6
Scar Top Rd. Haw BD22 .... 50 A7
Scarborough Gr. Ship BD18 .... 55 A7
Scarborough Rd. Otley LS21 ...... 22 F7
Scarborough Rd. Ship BD18 ...... 55 A7
Scarborough St. Dew WF12 ..... 139 D6
Scarborough St. E Ard WF3 .... 119 D8
Scarborough Terr. Dew WF12 139 D6
Scarbro' Junc. Leeds LS13 .... 58 D1
Scarbro Terr. Elland HX5 .... 134 F6
Scarcroft Ct. Scar LS14 .... 45 D8
Scarfold. Holmfi HD7 .... 189 A5
Scargill Cl. Leeds LS9 .... 60 F1
Scargill Grange. Leeds LS9 .... 79 F8
Scarhouse La. Hud HD7 .... 152 E4
Scarlet Hts. Queen BD13 .... 72 F1
Scarr Bottom. Hali HX2 .... 112 F4
Scarr End La. Batley WF13 .... 117 F2
Scarr End La. Dew WF12 .... 139 F5
Scarr End View. Batley WF13 .. 117 F2
Scarr Green Cl. Mel HD7 .... 170 E2
Scarsdale La. Bard LS17 .... 28 E6
Scarsdale Ridge. Bard LS17 .... 28 E6
Scarth Ave. Leeds LS9 .... 61 A2 5
Scarth Terr. Loft G WF3 .... 122 B6
Scarwood Cl. Bing BD16 .... 37 A4 8
Scatcherd Gr. Morley LS27 .... 97 F4
Scatcherd La. Morley LS27 .... 97 F4
Scatcherd Park Ave. Morley LS27 .... 98 A5
Scawthorpe Cl. Pont WF8 .... 125 F1
Sceptone Gr. Shaf S72 .... 180 C3
Schofield La. Hud HD5 .... 154 D6
Schofield St. Litt OL15 .... 129 D2
Schofields Ctr. Leeds 79 C8
Scholebrook La. Pudsey BD4 ... 76 C4
Scholemoor Ave. Brad BD7 .... 73 E5
Scholemoor La. Brad BD7 .... 73 E5
Scholemoor Rd. Brad BD7 .... 73 F5
Scholes (Elmete) Jun & Inf Sch. B in Elm 62 F6
Scholes Fst Sch. Brig 115 E8
Scholes La. B in Elm LS15 .... 62 E8
Scholes La. Brig BD19 .... 115 F7
Scholes La. Elland HX4 .... 113 A1
Scholes La. Haw BD22 .... 33 F1
Scholes Moor Rd. Holmfi HD7 189 C2
Scholes Rd. Castle WF10 .... 104 D1
Scholes Rd. Holmfi HD7 .... 189 E3
Scholes Rd. Hud HD2 .... 136 A2
Scholes St. Brad BD5 .... 74 D2
Scholey Ave. Brig HD6 .... 136 A8
Scholey Head La. H Chap BB10 85 A8
Scholey Rd. Brig HD6 .... 136 A8
Scholfield St. Tod OL14 .... 108 B6 11
School Ave. Dew WF13 .... 117 F1
School Cl. Crof WF4 .... 144 B4
School Cl. Gild LS12 .... 77 D3
School Cl. Hali HX2 .... 91 F7
School Cl. Rip HX6 .... 132 E4
School Cote Brow. Hali HX3 ...... 92 B6
School Cote Terr. Hali HX3 .... 92 B6
School Cres. Dew WF13 .... 117 F1
School Cres. Hali HX2 .... 91 F7
School Cres. Wake WF2 .... 141 D4
School Croft. Broth WF11 .... 126 C8
School Croft. Roth LS26 .... 100 E6
School Dr. Knot WF11 .... 126 C5
School Fold. Brad BD12 .... 94 B6
School Gn. Bramho LS16 .... 24 E2
School Gn. Thorn BD13 .... 73 A6
School Gr. Dew WF13 .... 117 F1
School Green Ave. Thorn BD13 72 F6
School Hill. Crig WF2 .... 160 B4
School Hill. Hud HD4 .... 171 A7
School Hill. Kirkb HD8 .... 173 F6
School La. Aber LS25 .... 64 E7
School La. Brad BD6 .... 74 B1 8
School La. Castle WF10 .... 124 F6
School La. Coll LS22 .... 29 B8
School La. D Dale HD8 .... 192 A6
School La. Dew WF13 .... 117 F1
School La. E Kes LS17 .... 28 C5
School La. Emley HD8 .... 175 D7
School La. Hali HX2 .... 91 F7
School La. Hali HX3 .... 114 A3
School La. Hare LS17 .... 44 C8
School La. Holmfi HD7 .... 189 B4
School La. Hor WF4 .... 141 A1
School La. Hud HD1 .... 153 E5
School La. Hud HD5 .... 155 B7
School La. Hud HD4 .... 171 F8
School La. Leeds LS6 .... 59 E6
School La. Leeds LS7 .... 60 C6
School La. Leeds LS15 .... 81 A8
School La. Leeds LS15 .... 81 E7
School La. Liver WF15 .... 116 D2
School La. Mars HD7 .... 169 C6
School La. Ryhill WF4 .... 162 B1
School La. Slai HD7 .... 152 B6
School La. Th Arch LS23 .... 14 F4
School La. Tod OL14 .... 108 B5 9
School La. Wake WF2 .... 120 E2
School La. Walton WF2 .... 161 A7
School Land La. Hep HX7 .... 87 F6
School Pl. Brad16 BD12 .... 94 C4
School Rd. Keigh BD22 .... 34 F7
School Rd. Pont WF8 .... 146 F7
School Rd. Slai HD7 .... 152 B6
School Rd. Wake WF2 .... 141 D4
School Rd. Weth LS22 .... 13 F6
School St. Batley WF17 .... 96 F1 7
School St. Brad BD14 .... 73 B4
School St. Brad BD1 .... 74 E8
School St. Brad BD4 .... 75 C3
School St. Brad BD12 .... 94 C6
School St. Brad BD12 .... 95 A4
School St. Brad BD4 .... 95 B8
School St. Castle WF10 .... 103 E1
School St. Castle WF10 .... 124 C8
School St. Clec BD19 .... 116 B7
School St. Cull BD13 .... 52 D6
School St. Dearne S63 .... 194 D1
School St. Denh BD13 .... 52 E1
School St. Denh BD13 .... 71 E8
School St. Dew WF13 .... 138 E5
School St. Dew WF12, WF13 . 139 D8
School St. Dew WF12 .... 140 B8
School St. E Ard FW12 .... 119 D5
School St. Elland HX4 .... 134 B7
School St. Hali HX1 .... 113 D6
School St. Heb Br HX7 .... 89 A3 13
School St. Holmfi HD7 .... 189 A5
School St. Honley HD7 .... 171 F5
School St. Hud HD5 .... 154 D5
School St. Keigh BD20 .... 18 A2
School St. Liver WF15 .... 116 F2
School St. Liver WF15 .... 117 B2
School St. Mapp S75 .... 177 E1
School St. Mapp S75 .... 178 C1
School St. Morley LS27 .... 98 B4
School St. Morley LS27 .... 98 C8
School St. Ossett WF5 .... 119 C1
School St. Pudsey LS28 .... 57 D3
School St. Pudsey LS28 .... 76 D6
School St. Ship BD16 .... 54 B7
School St. Stee BD20 .... 17 C5
School St. Upton WF9 .... 183 D8
School St W. Hud HD3 .... 153 B8
School St. Wils BD15 .... 53 C5
School Terr. Fair WF11 .... 105 A4
School Terr. Shep HD8 .... 174 A3
School View. Leeds LS6 .... 59 E3
School Wlk. Keigh BD22 .... 34 F7
Schreiber Bsns Pk. Wake 142 D4
Scissett CE (Aided) Fst Sch. Clay W 175 D2
Scissett Mid & Cty Sec Sch. Clay W 175 D2
Sconce La. Bail BD16 .... 38 B7
Scopsley Gn. Dew WF12 .... 156 E8

Scopsley La. Dew WF12 ... 156 E8
Scorcher Hills La. Burg DN6 ... 184 E5
Score Croft. Skel HD8 ... 175 A2
Score Hill. Northo HX3 ... 93 A4
Score Hill. Shelf HX3 ... 93 A4
Scoresby St. Brad BD1 ... 74 F7
Scotch Park Trad Est. Leeds ... 78 D8
Scotchman Cl. Morley LS27 ... 97 F2
Scotchman La. Batley LS27 ... 97 E1
Scotchman Mid Sch. Brad ... 55 A2
Scotchman Rd. Brad BD9 ... 55 A2
Scotgate Rd. Honley HD7 ... 171 E4
Scotland Cl. Hors LS18 ... 41 B4
Scotland La. Hors LS18 ... 41 B5
Scotland Mill La. Leeds LS16 ... 42 F1
Scotland St. Clec WF17 ... 96 C2
Scotland Way. Hors LS18 ... 41 B4
Scotland Wood Rd. Leeds LS17 42 F2
Scott Ave. Batley WF16 ... 117 D6
Scott Cl. S in Cra BD20 ... 16 D5
Scott Cl. Swil LS26 ... 82 A1
Scott Gn. Gild LS27 ... 97 B8
Scott Green Cres. Gild LS27 ... 97 C8
Scott Green Dr. Gild LS27 ... 97 C8
Scott Green Gr. Gild LS27 ... 97 C8
Scott Green Mount. Gild LS27 . 97 B8
Scott Green View. Gild LS27 ... 97 C8
Scott Hall Ave. Leeds LS7 ... 60 C4
Scott Hall Cty Mid Sch. Leeds ... 60 C6
Scott Hall Cres. Leeds LS7 ... 60 B6
Scott Hall Dr. Leeds LS7 ... 60 C4
Scott Hall Gn. Leeds LS7 ... 60 C5
Scott Hall Gr. Leeds LS7 ... 60 C5
Scott Hall Pl. Leeds LS7 ... 60 C5
Scott Hall Rd. Leeds LS6, LS7 ... 60 B6
Scott Hall Row. Leeds LS7 ... 60 D4
Scott Hall Sports Ctr. Leeds ... 60 B6
Scott Hall Sq. Leeds LS7 ... 60 C5
Scott Hall St. Leeds LS7 ... 60 C4
Scott Hall Terr. Leeds LS7 ... 60 C5
Scott Hall Way. Leeds LS7 ... 60 C6
Scott Hall Wlk. Leeds LS7 ... 60 C4
Scott Hill. Clay W HD8 ... 175 F3
Scott House. Tod OL14 ... 129 A8
Scott La. Clec BD19 ... 96 B1
Scott La. Clec BD19 ... 116 E8
Scott La. Keigh BD20 ... 18 E2
Scott La. Morley LS27 ... 97 E3
Scott La W. Keigh BD20 ... 18 E2
Scott La. Weth LS22 ... 13 E5
Scott Mews. Weth LS22 ... 13 E5
Scott St. Brad BD6 ... 94 D8 3
Scott St. Keigh BD21 ... 35 C7
Scott St. Pudsey LS28 ... 76 F6
Scott St. Tod OL14 ... 129 A8
Scott Vale. Hud HD2 ... 136 D3
Scott Wood La. Leeds LS7 ... 60 C4
Scotts Hill Cl. Thorner LS14 ... 45 F5
Scotty Bank. Brig HD6 ... 115 A2 7
Scotty Croft La. Brig HD6 ... 115 A1
Scout Bottom La. Heb Br HX7 110 F8
Scout Cl. Heb Br HX7 ... 110 F8
Scout Hill Rd. Dew WF13 ... 139 A6
Scout Hill Terr. Dew WF13 ... 139 A6 2
Scout Hill View. Dew WF13 ... 139 A6 1
Scout La. Mars HD7 ... 151 B1
Scout Rd. Heb Br HX7 ... 110 F8
Scout Road Jun, Mid & Inf Sch. Heb Br ... 110 F8
Scrapers La. Tod OL14 ... 108 B8
Sculptor Pl. Brig HD6 ... 115 A3 14
Seacroft Arc. Leeds LS14 ... 62 B5 5
Seacroft Ave. Leeds LS14 ... 62 B5
Seacroft Chase. Leeds LS14 ... 62 B5 6
Seacroft Cl. Leeds LS14 ... 62 B5
Seacroft Cres. Leeds LS14 ... 62 B5
Seacroft Gate. Leeds LS14 ... 62 B5 9
Seacroft Grange Cty Prim Sch. Leeds ... 61 F3
Seacroft Hospl. Leeds ... 62 A3
Seacroft Ind Est. Leeds ... 62 B7
Seacroft Park Mid Sch. Leeds ... 62 B3
Seaforth Ave. Leeds LS9 ... 61 A3
Seaforth Gr. Leeds LS9 ... 61 A3 17
Seaforth Mount. Leeds LS9 ... 61 A3 18
Seaforth Pl. Leeds LS9 ... 61 A3 19
Seaforth Rd. Leeds LS9 ... 61 B3
Seaforth Terr. Leeds LS9 ... 61 A3 21
Seagrave Rd. Hud HD4 ... 153 C3
Seaton St. Brad BD3 ... 75 B7
Seckar La. Wool WF4 ... 178 B8
Secker St. Wake WF2 ... 142 B3
Second Ave. Bard LS17 ... 28 E5
Second Ave. Brad BD3 ... 56 C1
Second Ave. Clec WF15 ... 116 B4
Second Ave. Hali HX3 ... 113 B4 6
Second Ave. Hem WF9 ... 163 A4
Second Ave. Hor WF4 ... 140 F1
Second Ave. Hud HD7 ... 152 D4
Second Ave. Hud HD5 ... 154 F7
Second Ave. Keigh BD21 ... 35 B6 2
Second Ave. Kirkhe HD5 ... 137 C1
Second Ave. Leeds LS12 ... 78 E7
Second Ave. Loft G WF1 ... 121 B2
Second Ave. Roth LS26 ... 100 F7
Second Ave. S Kirk WF9 ... 181 F1
Second Ave. Upton WF9 ... 183 A8
Second Ave. Weth LS22 ... 13 F5
Second Ave. Yeadon LS19 ... 40 C5
Second St. Brad BD12 ... 94 E6
Second St. Crof WF4 ... 162 B7
Sedan St. Hali HX1 ... 113 C6 1
Sedbergh Cl. Leeds LS15 ... 80 D7
Sedbergh Dr. Ilkley LS29 ... 8 C3
Sedbergh Pk. Ilkley LS29 ... 8 B3
Sedburgh Rd. Hali HX3 ... 113 D5
Sedge Gr. Haw BD22 ... 51 C8
Sedgewick St. Batley WF17 ... 96 E1 3
Sedgfield Terr. Brad BD1 ... 74 D7 1
Sedgwick Cl. Brad BD8 ... 74 D8
Seed Hill Terr. Hali HX2 ... 91 C6
Seed Hill Terr. Stee BD20 ... 17 C5
Seed Row. Brad BD4 ... 95 B8
Seed St. Brad BD12 ... 94 D6
Sefton Ave. Brig HD6 ... 114 F5
Sefton Ave. Leeds LS11 ... 79 A3
Sefton Cres. Brig HD6 ... 114 F5
Sefton Dr. Brig HD6 ... 114 F5
Sefton Dr. Ilkley LS29 ... 8 B3
Sefton Gr. Brad BD2 ... 56 B3
Sefton La. Mel HD7 ... 170 D2
Sefton Pl. Keigh BD21 ... 35 C8
Sefton Rise. Dew WF12 ... 139 D4
Sefton St. Hali HX1 ... 113 A8
Sefton St. Keigh BD21 ... 35 C8
Sefton St. Leeds LS11 ... 79 B3
Sefton Terr. Hali HX1 ... 113 A8
Sefton Terr. Leeds LS11 ... 79 A3
Selborne Gr. Brad BD9 ... 55 B2
Selborne Gr. Keigh BD21 ... 35 B5
Selborne Mount. Brad BD9 ... 55 C2
Selborne Terr. Brad BD9 ... 55 B2
Selborne Terr. Ship BD18 ... 55 B6
Selborne Villas. Brad BD9 ... 55 B3
Selbourne Ave. Dew WF12 ... 139 C5
Selbourne Dr. Dew WF12 ... 139 C5
Selbourne Rd. Dew WF12 ... 139 C5
Selbourne Villas. Brad BD14 ... 73 C3
Selby Ave. Leeds LS9 ... 80 E8
Selby. Hali HX2 ... 91 D6
Selby Rd. Gar LS25 ... 83 C4
Selby Rd. Ledsh LS25 ... 84 B4
Selby Rd. Ledst LS25 ... 83 C4
Selby Rd. Leeds LS15 LS25 LS9 81 C8
Selby Rd. S Mil LS25 ... 84 B4
Selby Rd. Swil LS15, LS25 ... 82 B6
Selby St. Wake WF1 ... 142 D7
Seldon St. Brad BD5 ... 74 B3
Selene Cl. Clec BD19 ... 96 C2
Sellars Fold. Brad BD7 ... 74 A4 4
Sellerdale Ave. Brad BD12 ... 94 D1
Sellerdale Dr. Brad BD12 ... 94 D2
Sellerdale Rise. Brad BD12 ... 94 D1
Sellerdale Way. Brad BD12 ... 94 D1
Selso Rd. Dew WF12 ... 118 F1
Seminary St. Leeds LS2 ... 60 A1
Semon Ave. Brad BD2 ... 55 F5
Senior St. Dew WF13 ... 139 B7
Senior St. Hud HD5 ... 154 E5
Senior Way. Brad BD5 ... 74 E6
Sentry. Honley HD7 ... 171 F5
Sergeantson St. Hud HD1 ... 154 A6 14
Serpentine Rd. Clec BD19 ... 116 D7
Servia Dr. Leeds LS7 ... 60 C3
Servia Gdns. Leeds LS7 ... 60 C3
Servia Hill. Leeds LS6, LS7 ... 60 B3
Servia Rd. Leeds LS7 ... 60 B3
Service Rd. Leeds LS9 ... 80 D3
Sessions House Yd. Pont WF8 125 C1
Seven Hills Prim Sch. Morley ... 98 B4
Sevenoaks Mead. Brad BD15 ... 54 B1
Seventh Ave. Clec WF15 ... 116 B5
Seventh Ave. Roth LS26 ... 101 A7
Seventh St. Crof WF4 ... 162 B7
Severn Dr. Gar LS25 ... 83 B6
Severn Rd. Brad BD2 ... 56 A3
Severn Rd. Leeds LS10 ... 79 F3
Severn Way. Leeds LS10 ... 79 F3
Sewage Works Rd. Leeds LS9 . 80 C3
Sewell Rd. Brad BD3 ... 75 B6
Sewerbridge La. Feath WF7 ... 145 A8
Seymour St. Brad BD3 ... 75 A6
Seymour St. Wake WF2 ... 142 C4
Seymour Wlk. Mel HD7 ... 170 E2
Shackleton St. Tod OL14 ... 86 C1
Shackleton Terr. Harden BD16 36 A1
Shade Jun & Inf Sch. Tod ... 108 A3
Shade St. Tod OL14 ... 108 A3
Shadwell La. Leeds LS17 ... 43 D2
Shadwell La. Thorner LS17 ... 44 B5
Shadwell Park Ave. Leeds LS17 44 C5
Shadwell Park Cl. Leeds LS17 ... 44 C5
Shadwell Park Ct. Leeds LS17 . 44 C4
Shadwell Park Dr. Leeds LS17 . 44 C4
Shadwell Pk Gdns. Leeds LS17 44 C5
Shadwell Park Gr. Leeds LS17 . 44 C4
Shadwell Prim Sch. Thorner ... 44 F4
Shadwell Sch. Leeds ... 43 F4
Shadwell Wlk. Leeds LS17 ... 43 E3
Shady La. Con BD20 ... 4 A3
Shaftesbury Ave. Beal DN14 ... 127 F5
Shaftesbury Ave. Brad BD9 ... 54 D1
Shaftesbury Ave. Brig HD6 ... 136 B7
Shaftesbury Ave. Leeds LS8 ... 44 A2
Shaftesbury Ave. Ship BD18 ... 55 C7
Shaftesbury Ct. Brad BD9 ... 54 D1
Shaftesbury Rd. Leeds LS8 ... 44 A2
Shafton Hall Dr. Shaf S72 ... 180 B3
Shafton La. Leeds LS11 ... 78 F5
Shafton Pl. Leeds LS11 ... 78 F5 2
Shafton St. Leeds LS11 ... 79 A5
Shafton Two Gates Fst Sch. Shaf ... 180 C2
Shafton View. Leeds LS11 ... 78 F5
Shakespeare App. Leeds LS9 ... 60 F1
Shakespeare Ave. Leeds LS9 ... 60 F1
Shakespeare Ave. Nor WF6 ... 144 A7
Shakespeare Ave. Tod OL14 ... 108 D6
Shakespeare Bldgs. Hud HD1 153 D6
Shakespeare Cl. Guise LS20 ... 39 F8
Shakespeare Cl. Leeds LS9 ... 60 F1
Shakespeare Cl. Litt OL15 ... 129 C1
Shakespeare Ct. Leeds LS9 ... 60 F1
Shakespeare Gdns. Leeds LS9 60 F1
Shakespeare Grange.Leeds LS9 60 F1
Shakespeare Lawn. Leeds LS9 60 F1
Shakespeare Prim Sch. Leeds ... 60 F1
Shakespeare Rd. Guise LS20 ... 39 F8
Shakespeare St. Hali HX1 ... 113 C7
Shakespeare St. Leeds LS9 ... 60 F2
Shakespeare Towers. Leeds LS9 60 F1
Shalimar St. Hali HX1 ... 112 F7
Shambles The. Hud HD1 ... 154 B6 11
Shambles The. Weth LS22 ... 13 E5
Shann Ave. Keigh BD21 ... 34 F8
Shann Cres. Keigh BD21 ... 34 F8
Shann La. Keigh BD20 ... 17 F1
Shann St. Ship BD2 ... 55 D4
Shannon Cl. Brig HD6 ... 135 E7
Shannon Cl. Ilkley LS29 ... 7 F3
Shannon Dr. Hud HD3 ... 134 D1
Shannon Rd. Brig HD6 ... 135 E7
Shannon Rd. Leeds LS9 ... 79 E8
Shannon St. Leeds LS9 ... 79 E8
Share Hill. Slai HD7 ... 152 C3
Sharehill. Slai HD7 ... 152 C4
Sharleston Jun & Inf Sch. Crof 144 B4
Sharnaley Ct. Pont WF8 ... 147 A8
Sharneyford Cty Prim Sch. Bacup ... 106 C5
Sharon Cotts. Ossett WF5 ... 140 D7
Sharp Ave. Brad BD6 ... 94 C8
Sharp House Rd. Midd LS10 ... 99 F4
Sharp La. Hud HD4, HD5 ... 154 F2
Sharp La. Midd LS10, WF3 ... 99 F4
Sharp Royd. Hud HD5 ... 155 A4
Sharp St. Brad BD6 ... 74 C1 11
Sharp St. Dew WF13 ... 118 D1
Sharp's Row. Pudsey LS28 ... 76 E6
Sharpe St. Batley WF16 ... 117 D3
Sharpe St. Brad BD5 ... 74 E6
Shaw Ave. Nor WF6 ... 123 C2
Shaw Barn Croft. Weth LS22 ... 13 C5
Shaw Barn La. Weth LS22 ... 13 C5
Shaw Booth La. Hali HX2 ... 90 F4
Shaw Cl. Elland HX4 ... 134 C4
Shaw Cl. Guise LS20 ... 39 F8
Shaw Cl. Nor WF6 ... 123 C2
Shaw Cl. S Elm WF9 ... 183 A4
Shaw Fields La. Mars HD7 ... 169 C8
Shaw Fields. Mars HD7 ... 169 C8
Shaw Fold. Wake WF2 ... 142 E1
Shaw Gate. Slai HD7 ... 169 F6
Shaw Hill. Hali HX1 ... 113 C5
Shaw Hill La. Hali HX3 ... 113 D5
Shaw La. Cud S71 ... 179 E1
Shaw La. Elland HX4 ... 134 B4
Shaw La. Elland HX5 ... 135 C8
Shaw La. Guise LS20 ... 22 F1
Shaw La. Hali HX4 ... 113 D5
Shaw La. Holmfi HD7 ... 188 D4
Shaw La. Hud HD7 ... 153 B4
Shaw La. Keigh BD21 ... 35 D3
Shaw La. Leeds LS6 ... 59 D6
Shaw La. Mapp S75 ... 178 C2
Shaw La. Mars HD7 ... 169 A8
Shaw La. Oxen BD22 ... 51 B2
Shaw La. Rip HX6 ... 132 C2
Shaw La. Roy S71 ... 179 E1
Shaw La. Shelf HX3 ... 92 F6
Shaw La. Slai HD7 ... 152 C8
Shaw La. Sow Br HX6 ... 112 C1
Shaw La. Tod OL14 ... 86 C3
Shaw Lane Gdns. Guise LS20 ... 22 F1
Shaw Leys. Yeadon LS19 ... 40 A8
Shaw Lodge. Hali HX3 ... 113 D5
Shaw Rise. Nor WF6 ... 123 C2
Shaw Royd. Yeadon LS19 ... 40 A8
Shaw St. Brad BD12 ... 94 B6 4
Shaw St. Clec BD19 ... 116 B7
Shaw St. Elland HX4 ... 134 C4
Shaw St. Mir WF14 ... 138 A5
Shaw Wood Ave. Tod OL14 ... 109 A6
Shaw's Terr. Mars HD7 ... 168 F4
Shawcross Inf Sch. Batley ... 119 A3
Shawfield Ave. Holmfi HD7 ... 188 D4
Shawmount. Hali HX2 ... 111 E8
Shaws La. B in Elm LS15 ... 63 C6
Shaws La. Sow Br HX7 ... 111 A2
Shay Cl. Brad BD9 ... 54 F4
Shay Cres. Brad BD9 ... 54 E4
Shay Ct. Brad BD9 ... 54 E4
Shay Ct. Crof WF4 ... 143 E1
Shay Dr. Brad BD9 ... 54 E4
Shay Fold. Brad BD9 ... 54 E4
Shay Gap Rd. Keigh BD22 ... 34 C7
Shay Gate. Wils BD15 ... 53 E4
Shay Gr. Brad BD9 ... 54 F4
Shay La. Brad BD9 ... 54 F4
Shay La. Crof WF4 ... 143 E1
Shay La. Hali HX2, HX3 ... 92 A4
Shay La. Holme HD7 ... 187 E3
Shay La. Walton WF2 ... 161 C7
Shay La. Wils BD15 ... 53 D4
Shay St. Leeds LS6 ... 60 B3
Shay Syke. Hali HX1 ... 113 D5
Shayfield La. Roth WF3 ... 100 D3
Sheaf St. Leeds LS10 ... 79 D6
Shearbridge Pl. Brad BD7 ... 74 C6
Shearbridge Rd. Brad BD7 ... 74 C6
Shearbridge Terr. Brad BD7 ... 74 C6
Sheardale. Honley HD7 ... 171 E4
Shearing Cross Gdns. Hud HD1 ... 154 B8 1
Shed St. Keigh BD21 ... 35 C7
Sheep Hill La. Brad BD13 ... 73 B2
Sheepridge Gr. Hud HD2 ... 136 C3
Sheepridge Rd. Hud HD2 ... 136 C3
Sheepscar Gr. Leeds LS7 ... 60 D1
Sheepscar Row. Leeds LS7 ... 60 E2
Sheepscar St N. Leeds LS7 ... 60 D3
Sheepscar St S. Leeds LS7 ... 60 D1
Sheepscar Way. Leeds LS7 ... 60 D3
Sheepwalk La. Castle WF10 ... 125 D6
Sheepwalk La. Upton WF9 ... 183 E8
Sheerien Cl. Barn S71 ... 178 E1
Sheffield Rd. Holmfi HD7 ... 189 E3
Sheila Terr. Liver WF16 ... 117 C3
Sheldrake Ave. Brad BD8 ... 73 C7
Sheldrake Rd. Castle WF10 ... 124 D6
Shelf Hall La. Shelf HX3 ... 93 C5
Shelf Jun & Inf Sch. Shelf ... 93 B5
Shelf Moor Rd. Shelf HX3 ... 93 C6
Shelf Moor. Shelf HX3 ... 93 C7
Shell Rd. Heb Br HX7 ... 88 F3
Shell La. Pudsey LS28 ... 57 B5
Shelldrake Dr. Midd LS10 ... 99 D5
Shelley Ave. Batley WF16 ... 117 E2
Shelley Cres. Roth LS26 ... 101 C3
Shelley Dr. Knot WF11 ... 126 B4
Shelley Fst Sch. Shep ... 174 A3
Shelley Gr. Brad BD8 ... 73 E8
Shelley High Sch. Shep ... 174 E2
Shelley La. Kirkb HD8 ... 174 A5
Shelley Wlk. Loft G WF3 ... 121 E6
Shelley Woodhouse La. Shep HD8 ... 174 D1
Shelley Woodhouse La. Skel HD8 ... 174 D1
Shelwith Wlk. Leeds LS14 ... 62 A2
Shepcote Cl. Hors LS16 ... 41 F3
Shepcote Cres. Hors LS16 ... 41 F3
Shepherd St. Brad BD7 ... 74 B4 1
Shepherd's Gr. Leeds LS7 ... 60 E4
Shepherd's La. Leeds LS7, LS8 60 F4
Shepherd's Pl. Leeds LS8 ... 60 F4
Shepherds Gr. Hud HD2 ... 136 E3
Shepherds Thorn La. Hud HD2 136 C6
Shepley Fst Sch. Shep ... 190 E8
Shepley Mount. Mir WF14 ... 138 B7
Shepley Rd. Kirkb HD4 ... 173 C2
Shepley St. Wake WF1 ... 142 E7
Shepley Sta. Shep ... 173 F1
Shepstye Rd. Hor WF4 ... 141 A1
Sherborne Dr. Keigh BD22 ... 34 E5
Sherborne Rd. Brad BD10 ... 39 B1
Sherborne Rd. Brad BD7 ... 74 D6
Sherbrooke Ave. Leeds LS15 ... 80 F7
Sherburn App. Leeds LS14 ... 62 C6
Sherburn Cl. Ad Le S DN6 ... 184 E2
Sherburn Cl. Birk BD11 ... 96 B6
Sherburn Cl. Leeds LS14 ... 62 C6 6
Sherburn Ct. Leeds LS14 ... 62 C6 3
Sherburn Gr. Birk BD11 ... 96 B6
Sherburn Pl. Leeds LS14 ... 62 C6
Sherburn Rd. Brig HD6 ... 135 E8
Sherburn Rd. Leeds LS14 ... 62 C6
Sherburn Rd N. Leeds LS14 ... 62 B7
Sherburn Row. Leeds LS14 ... 62 C6 4
Sherburn Sq. Leeds LS14 ... 62 C6 7
Sherburn Wlk. Leeds LS14 ... 62 C6 5
Sheridan Cl. Pudsey LS28 ... 76 F6
Sheridan Ct. Pudsey LS28 ... 76 F6
Sheridan St. Brad BD4 ... 75 B4
Sheridan St. Loft G WF1 ... 121 C5
Sheridan Way. Pudsey LS28 ... 76 F6
Sheriff La. Bing BD16 ... 37 D4
Sherwell Gr. Brad BD15 ... 54 C1
Sherwell Rise. Brad BD15 ... 54 C1
Sherwood Ave. Clec BD19 ... 117 B8
Sherwood Ave. Hud HD2 ... 136 F5
Sherwood Cl. Batley WF13 ... 117 F3
Sherwood Cl. Bing BD16 ... 37 C5
Sherwood Cl. Clec BD19 ... 117 B8
Sherwood Dr. Ad Le S DN6 ... 184 E2
Sherwood Dr. Hud HD4 ... 171 C7
Sherwood Gn. Roth WF3 ... 100 A3
Sherwood Gr. Ship BD18 ... 54 E8
Sherwood Gr. Wake WF2 ... 141 E4
Sherwood Ind Est. Roth ... 100 B3
Sherwood Pl. Brad BD2 ... 56 B2
Sherwood Rd. Brig HD6 ... 115 C2
Sherwood Way. Cud S72 ... 180 A1
Shetcliffe La. Brad BD4 ... 95 C8
Shetcliffe Rd. Brad BD4 ... 95 B8
Shetland Cl. Brad BD2 ... 55 F4
Shibden Dr. Batley WF17 ... 117 F6
Shibden Garth. Hali HX3 ... 114 A8
Shibden Grange Dr.Northo HX3 92 F1
Shibden Hall Croft. Hali HX3 ... 114 A8
Shibden Hall Rd. Brig HX3 ... 114 A8
Shibden Hall Rd. Hali HX3 ... 113 F8
Shibden Head Fst Sch. Queen . 92 C7
Shibden Head La. Queen BD13 92 D7
Shibden View. Queen BD13 ... 92 D7
Shield Cl. Leeds LS15 ... 62 E3
Shield Hall La. Sow Br HX6 ... 111 C4
Shill Bank Ave. Mir WF14 ... 138 D6
Shill Bank La. Mir WF14 ... 138 C6
Shillbank View. Mir WF14 ... 138 C6
Shilling St. Wake WF1 ... 142 D8
Shillinghill La. Pont WF8 ... 126 B1
Shinwell Dr. Upton WF9 ... 183 D8
Ship St. Brig HD6 ... 115 B2
Ship Yd. Wake WF1 ... 142 D5
Shipley CE Fst Sch. Ship ... 55 B6
Shipley Coll of F Ed. Ship ... 55 A8
Shipley College Mill Annexe. Ship ... 37 F1
Shipley Fields Rd. Ship BD18 ... 55 C5
Shipley Golf Course. Harden ... 36 E1
Shipley Sta. Ship ... 55 C8
Shipley Wycliffe CE Mid Sch. Ship ... 55 A8
Shipton Mews. Morley LS27 ... 98 B3
Shire Cl. Brad BD6 ... 93 F7
Shire Oak Rd. Leeds LS6 ... 59 E5
Shire Oak St. Leeds LS6 ... 59 D5
Shire Oak St. Leeds LS6 ... 59 E5
Shires Gr. Loft G WF3 ... 121 F5
Shires Hill. Hud HD1 ... 153 E5
Shirley Ave. Batley WF17 ... 96 E2
Shirley Ave. Brad BD12 ... 94 C1
Shirley Ave. Clec BD19 ... 117 B8
Shirley Cl. Otley LS21 ... 23 B7
Shirley Cres. Brad BD12 ... 94 C1
Shirley Dr. Leeds LS13 ... 58 C4
Shirley Gr. Brig HX3 ... 115 A7
Shirley Gr. Clec BD19 ... 117 B8
Shirley Manor Prim Sch. Brad . 94 C1
Shirley Mount. Clec BD19 ... 117 B8
Shirley Par. Clec BD19 ... 117 A8
Shirley Pl. Brad BD12 ... 94 C1
Shirley Pl. Clec BD19 ... 117 B8
Shirley Rd. Brad BD7 ... 74 B6
Shirley Rd. Brad BD4 ... 75 D1
Shirley Rd. Clec BD19 ... 117 B8
Shirley Sq. Clec BD19 ... 117 B8
Shirley St. Denh BD13 ... 52 E1
Shirley St. Haw BD22 ... 51 B7 3
Shirley St. Ship BD18 ... 54 F8
Shirley Terr. Clec BD19 ... 117 B8
Shirley Wlk. Clec BD19 ... 117 B8
Shoe Market. Pont WF8 ... 146 D8 4
Shoebridge Ave. Stee BD20 ... 16 F6
Shoebroad La. Tod OL14 ... 108 B4
Sholebroke Ave. Leeds LS7 ... 60 D4
Sholebroke Mount. Leeds LS7 . 60 C4
Sholebroke Pl. Leeds LS7 ... 60 D4
Sholebroke St. Leeds LS7 ... 60 D4
Sholebroke Terr. Leeds LS7 ... 60 D5
Sholebroke View. Leeds LS7 ... 60 D4
Shoolaboards La. Pont WF8 ... 146 F8 3
Shop La. Kirkhe HD5 ... 137 C1
Shop La. Kirkhe HD5 ... 155 C8
Shop La. Loft G WF3 ... 121 B8
Shore End La. Wad M HX2 ... 90 A7
Shore Gn. Tod OL14 ... 86 C2
Shore New Rd. Tod OL14 ... 86 B1
Shoreham Rd. Leeds LS12 ... 78 C6 3
Short Cl. Brad BD12 ... 94 B5
Short La. Leeds LS7 ... 60 C7
Short St. Dew WF12 ... 140 A7
Short St. Feath WF7 ... 145 C5
Short St. Tod OL14 ... 108 B5 5
Shortway. Pudsey LS28 ... 57 A1
Shortway. Thorn BD13 ... 73 A6
Shortwood La. Clay DN5 ... 194 B4
Shroggs Rd. Hali HX3 ... 113 A8
Shroggs St. Hali HX1 ... 113 A8
Shroggs Vue Terr. Hali HX1 ... 113 A8
Shutt The. Hor WF4 ... 159 B8
Shuttleworth La. Brad BD8 ... 73 E8
Shuttocks Cl. Kippax LS25 ... 83 A3
Shuttocks Fold. Kippax LS25 ... 83 B3
Shutts La. Brig HX3 ... 93 E2
Sickle St. Clec BD19 ... 116 E8
Sickleholme Ct. Hud HD2 ... 136 E5
Sicklinghall Cty Prim Sch. Sickl 12 B5
Sicklinghall Rd. Coll LS22 ... 13 B5
Siddal Gr. Hali HX3 ... 113 D4
Siddal Inf Sch. Hali ... 113 E3
Siddal Jun Sch. Hali ... 113 E3
Siddal La. Hali HX3 ... 113 E3
Siddal New Rd. Hali HX3 ... 113 D5
Siddal St. Hali HX3 ... 113 E3
Siddal Top La. Hali HX3 ... 113 E3
Siddall St. Leeds LS11 ... 79 B6
Siddel View. Hali HX3 ... 113 E4
Siddon Dr. Hud HD5 ... 155 A3
Side Copse. Otley LS21 ... 23 B8
Side La. Hud HD3 ... 152 F6
Sidings The. Guise LS20 ... 22 D1
Sidings The. Ship BD18 ... 55 C8
Sidney St. Leeds LS2 ... 79 C8
Siegen Cl. Morley LS27 ... 98 A4
Sigget La. Tod OL14 ... 107 F6
Sigott St. Hud HD3 ... 152 F6
Sike Cl. Kex S75 ... 177 D1
Sike La. Holmfi HD7 ... 189 D5
Sike La. Walton WF2 ... 161 B5
Sikes Cl. Hud HD5 ... 154 F4
Silcoates Ave. Wake WF2 ... 120 E1
Silcoates Dr. Wake WF2 ... 120 E1
Silcoates La. Wake WF2 ... 120 E1
Silcoates Sch. Wake ... 120 E1
Silcoates St. Wake WF2 ... 142 A7
Silk Mill App. Hors LS16 ... 41 E2
Silk Mill Ave. Hors LS16 ... 41 E3
Silk Mill Bank. Hors LS16 ... 41 D2
Silk Mill Cl. Hors LS16 ... 41 D3
Silk Mill Dr. Hors LS16 ... 41 E2
Silk Mill Dr. Keigh BD20 ... 19 E1
Silk Mill Gdns. Hors LS16 ... 41 D2
Silk Mill Gn. Hors LS16 ... 41 E2
Silk Mill Rd. Hors LS16 ... 41 D2
Silk Mill Way. Hors LS16 ... 41 E2
Silk St. Brad BD9 ... 55 A2
Silkstone Cres. Nor WF6 ... 122 F4
Silkstone Cres. Wake WF2 ... 160 C6
Silkstone Ct. Leeds LS15 ... 62 C1 6
Silkstone La. Caw S75 ... 193 F3
Silkstone Rd. Brad BD3 ... 75 B8
Silkstone Way. Leeds LS15 ... 62 C1
Silsbridge St. Brad BD1 ... 74 D7 7
Silsden Golf Course. Sil ... 18 A8
Silsden Rd. Add LS29 ... 6 C7
Silsden Rd. Keigh BD20 ... 18 E4
Silsden Rd. L Brad BD20 ... 4 D5
Silson La. Bail BD17 ... 38 E4
Silver Birch Ave. Brad BD12 ... 94 D2
Silver Birch Cl. Brad BD12 ... 94 D2
Silver Birch Dr. Brad BD12 ... 94 D2
Silver Birch Gr. Brad BD12 ... 94 D2
Silver Court Ind Est. Hud ... 154 C5
Silver Ct. Pudsey LS28 ... 57 F1
Silver La. Yeadon LS19 ... 40 B7
Silver Mill Hill. Otley LS21 ... 23 B6
Silver Royd Ave. Leeds LS12 ... 77 F6
Silver Royd Cl. Leeds LS12 ... 77 F6
Silver Royd Dr. Leeds LS12 ... 77 F6
Silver Royd Garth. Leeds LS12 77 F6
Silver Royd Gr. Leeds LS12 ... 77 F6
Silver Royd High Sch. Leeds ... 78 A6
Silver Royd Hill. Leeds LS12 ... 77 F6
Silver Royd Pl. Leeds LS12 ... 77 F6
Silver Royd Rd. Leeds LS12 ... 77 F6
Silver Royd St. Leeds LS12 ... 77 F6
Silver Royd Terr. Leeds LS12 ... 77 F6
Silver St. Brad BD8 ... 55 B1
Silver St E. Hud HD5 ... 154 C5
Silver St. Fair WF11 ... 105 A4
Silver St. Hali HX1 ... 113 C7
Silver St. Hud HD5 ... 154 C6
Silver St. Leeds LS11 ... 79 A6
Silver St. Loft G WF1 ... 121 B3
Silver St. Tod OL14 ... 129 A7
Silver St W. Hud HD5 ... 154 C5
Silver St. Wake WF1 ... 142 C6 6
Silverdale Ave. Guise LS20 ... 39 E8
Silverdale Ave. Keigh BD20 ... 18 E1
Silverdale Ave. Leeds LS17 ... 44 B5
Silverdale Cl. Guise LS20 ... 39 E7
Silverdale Cres. Guise LS20 ... 39 E8
Silverdale Dr. Guise LS20 ... 39 E7
Silverdale Gr. Guise LS20 ... 39 D8
Silverdale Grange. Guise LS20 39 E7
Silverdale Mount. Guise LS20 ... 39 E7
Silverdale Rd. Brad BD5 ... 74 E2
Silverdale Rd. Guise LS20 ... 39 D8
Silverdale Terr. Elland HX4 ... 134 A6
Silverhill Ave. Brad BD3 ... 56 D1
Silverhill Dr. Brad BD3 ... 56 D1
Silverhill Rd. Brad BD3 ... 56 C1
Silverwood Ave. Hali HX2 ... 91 C1
Silverwood Wlk. Hali HX2 ... 91 C1
Silwood Dr. Brad BD2 ... 56 C3
Sim Royd La. D Dale HD8 ... 192 D4
Simeon St. Tod OL14 ... 129 A8
Simes St. Brad BD1 ... 74 D7
Simm Carr La. Northo HX3 ... 92 D4
Simmonds La. Hali HX3 ... 113 D5
Simms Dene. Brad BD15 ... 54 A4
Simon Cl. Brad BD4 ... 75 F2
Simon Green Rd. Slai HD7 ... 152 B3
Simpson Gr. Brad BD10 ... 39 C1
Simpson Gr. Leeds LS12 ... 78 D7
Simpson Rd. Heb Br HX7 ... 110 D8
Simpson Rd. S Elm WF9 ... 183 B4
Simpson St. E Ard WF3 ... 120 E8
Simpson St. Hali HX3 ... 92 B2 5
Simpson St. Keigh BD21 ... 35 A7
Simpson's Lane Jun & Inf Sch. Knot ... 126 D3
Simpsons La. Knot WF11 ... 126 D3
Sinclair Garth. Wake WF2 ... 160 E8
Sinclair Rd. Brad BD2 ... 55 F5
Sinden Mews. Brad BD10 ... 39 B2
Singleton St. Brad BD1 ... 55 E1
Sion Hill. Hali HX3 ... 113 E3
Sir George Martin Dr. Hors LS16 ... 42 D4
Sir Isaac Holden Pl. Brad BD7 . 74 C7
Sir Karl Cohen Sq. Leeds LS12 78 B7 4
Sir Wilfred Pl. Brad BD10 ... 56 B8
Sisley La. Tod OL14 ... 109 A4
Sissons Ave. Midd LS10 ... 99 B4
Sissons Cres. Midd LS10 ... 99 B3
Sissons Dr. Midd LS10 ... 99 B4
Sissons Gn. Midd LS10 ... 99 B4
Sissons Gr. Midd LS10 ... 99 B4
Sissons La. Midd LS10 ... 99 B4
Sissons Mount. Midd LS10 ... 99 A3
Sissons Pl. Midd LS10 ... 99 B4
Sissons Rd. Midd LS10 ... 99 A3
Sissons Row. Midd LS10 ... 99 B4
Sissons St. Midd LS10 ... 99 B4
Sissons Terr. Midd LS10 ... 99 B3
Sissons View. Midd LS10 ... 99 B3
Sitka Cl. Roy S71 ... 179 B2
Sitlington Middlestown Jun & Inf Sch. Neth ... 158 B7
Sitlington Netherton Jun & Inf Sch. Neth ... 158 E6
Siward St. Hem WF9 ... 163 A4
Six Heights. Rip HX6 ... 132 E3
Sixrood La. Burg DN6 ... 184 F5
Sixth Ave. Brad BD3 ... 56 C1
Sixth Ave. Clec WF15 ... 116 B5
Sixth Ave. Roth LS26 ... 101 A6
Sixth St. Crof WF4 ... 162 B7
Sizers Ct. Yeadon LS19 ... 40 A5
Skelbrooke Dr. Pont WF8 ... 146 D5
Skelda Rise. Ilkley LS29 ... 8 B3
Skellow Rd. Ad Le S DN6 ... 184 F1
Skelmansthorpe Bsns Pk. Skel 175 A2
Skelmanthorpe Fst Sch. Skel . 175 B2
Skelton Ave. Leeds LS9 ... 80 B8
Skelton Ave. Mapp S75 ... 178 B1
Skelton Cres. Hud HD4 ... 153 B3
Skelton Cres. Leeds LS9 ... 80 B8
Skelton Grange Rd. Leeds LS10 80 B2
Skelton Mount. Leeds LS9 ... 80 B8
Skelton Pl. Leeds LS9 ... 80 B8
Skelton Rd. Leeds LS9 ... 80 B8
Skelton St. Leeds LS9 ... 80 B8
Skelton Terr. Leeds LS9 ... 80 B8
Skelton Wlk. Brad BD10 ... 56 D7
Skeltons La. Leeds LS14 ... 45 C1
Skelwith App. Leeds LS14 ... 62 A2
Skinner La. Brad BD8 ... 55 C2
Skinner La. Leeds LS7 ... 60 D1
Skinner La. Pont WF8 ... 125 D2
Skinner St. Leeds LS1 ... 79 A8 11
Skippon Terr. Thorner LS14 ... 45 F6
Skipton Ave. Hud HD2 ... 136 B2
Skipton Rd. Add LS29 ... 2 D1
Skipton Rd. Farnh BD20 ... 4 C1
Skipton Rd. Glu BD20 ... 16 E6
Skipton Rd. Ilkley LS29 ... 7 E4
Skipton Rd. Keigh BD20 ... 18 B2
Skipton Rd. L Brad BD20 ... 4 B6
Skipton Rd. Sil BD20 ... 5 C2
Skipton Rd. Stee BD20 ... 17 B5
Skipton Rise. Gar LS25 ... 83 B7
Skipton St. Batley WF17 ... 118 C2
Skircoat Gn. Hali HX3 ... 113 C2
Skircoat Green Rd. Hali HX3 ... 113 C3
Skircoat Moor Cl. Hali HX3 ... 113 A4
Skircoat Moor Rd. Hali HX3 ... 113 A4
Skircoat Rd. Hali HX1 ... 113 C5
Skirrow St. Ship BD16 ... 54 B6
Skye Rd. Brad BD9 ... 55 A3
Slack Bottom. Hep HX7 ... 88 E6
Slack Bottom Rd. Brad BD6 ... 94 A8
Slack House La. Wad M HX7 ... 89 B7
Slack La. Crof WF4 ... 144 A1
Slack La. Elland HD3 ... 152 A8
Slack La. Hali HX2 ... 90 B4
Slack La. Haw BD22 ... 34 B3
Slack La. Holmfi HD7 ... 189 B4
Slack La. Rip HX6 ... 131 F5
Slack La. Rip HX6 ... 133 A3
Slack La. S Hie S72 ... 180 B5
Slack La. Wake WF2, WF4 ... 160 C5
Slack. Slai HD3 ... 152 A7
Slack Top. Hep HX7 ... 88 D6
Slack Top La. Wh Com HD7 ... 190 C1
Slacks La. Mars HD7 ... 169 A8
Slacks La. Slai HD7 ... 169 E5
Sladdin Row. Queen BD13 ... 92 C8
Slade Cl. B Spa LS23 ... 30 D7
Slade House. Brad BD2 ... 56 D2
Slade La. Brig HD6 ... 135 F6
Slade La. Keigh BD20 ... 18 E2
Slade Wlk. Batley WF17 ... 96 F1
Sladen Bridge. Haw BD22 ... 50 F7
Sladen St. Keigh BD21 ... 35 A7 6
Slades La. Mel HD7 ... 170 E4
Slades Rd. Slai HD7 ... 152 B4
Slaid Hill Ct. Leeds LS17 ... 44 B5
Slaithewaite CE (C) Jun & Inf Sch. Slai ... 169 E8
Slaithwaite Ave. Dew WF12 ... 139 C4
Slaithwaite CE Sch. Slai ... 151 F1
Slaithwaite Cl. Dew WF12 ... 139 C4
Slaithwaite Gate. Slai HD7 ... 152 A5
Slaithwaite Rd. Dew WF12 ... 139 D4
Slaithwaite Rd. Mel HD7 ... 170 B3
Slaithwaite Sta. Slai ... 151 F1
Slant Gate. Hud HD7 ... 152 E2
Slant Gate. Kirkb HD8 ... 173 E7
Slant La. Tod OL14 ... 108 D6
Slater Ave. Heb Br HX7 ... 89 A4
Slater Ing La. Hep HX7 ... 88 C5
Slaters Rd. Pudsey LS28 ... 57 E1
Slates La. Ilkley LS29 ... 8 B7
Slaymaker La. Haw BD22 ... 34 C3
Slead Ave. Brig HD6 ... 114 F4
Slead Cres. Brig HD6 ... 114 F4
Slead Gr. Brig HD6 ... 114 F4
Slead Royd. Brig HD6 ... 114 F4
Slead View. Brig HD6 ... 114 F4
Sledbrook Cres. Wh Com S30 200 C6
Sledgate La. Slai HD7 ... 169 E5
Sledge Gate. Mars HD3 ... 151 A4
Sledmere Croft. Leeds LS14 ... 62 C6
Sledmere Garth. Leeds LS14 ... 62 C6
Sledmere Gn. Leeds LS14 ... 62 C6 9
Sledmere La. Leeds LS14 ... 62 C6
Sledmere Pl. Leeds LS14 ... 62 C6
Sledmere Sq. Leeds LS14 ... 62 C6 8
Sleep Hill La. Ham DN6 ... 184 B6
Sleep Hill La. S Elm DN6 ... 183 F7
Sleights La. Hare LS17 ... 27 B6
Sleningford Gr. Ship BD18 ... 54 E8
Sleningford Rd. Bing BD16 ... 36 E5
Sleningford Rd. Ship BD18 ... 54 E8
Sleningford Rise. Bing BD16 ... 36 F5

Sleningford Terr. Bing BD16 .... 36 E5
Slicer's Yd. Bing BD16 .... 36 F3
Slipper La. Mir WF14 .... 137 E7
Slippery Ford La. Haw BD22 ..... 33 C6
Slippy La. Hali HX2 .... 91 C5
Sloan Sq. Brad BD8 .... 74 B8
Slutwell La. Pont WF8 .... 146 D8
Smalewell Cl. Pudsey LS28 ...... 76 D6
Smalewell Dr. Pudsey LS28 ...... 76 C6
Smalewell Gdns. Pudsey LS28 . 76 C6
Smalewell Gn. Pudsey LS28 ..... 76 D6
Smalewell Rd. Pudsey LS28 ..... 76 C6
Small La. Caw S75 .... 193 B1
Small La. Hud HD7 .... 152 D4
Small Lees Rd. Rip HX6 .... 132 D3
Small Page Fold. Queen BD13 . 72 E1 7
Small Shaw La. Wad M HX7 ..... 69 A1
Smallpage Yd. Wake WF1 ...... 142 C6 9
Smallwood Gdns.Batley WF12 119 A3
Smallwood Rd. Batley WF12 .. 119 A2
Smallwood Rd. Batley WF12 .. 119 A3
Smawell La. Notton WF4 .... 179 B7
Smawthorne Av. Castle WF10 124 D7
Smawthorne Gr. Castle WF10 124 D7
Smawthorne La. Castle WF10 124 D7
Smeatley's La. K Smea WF8 .. 166 E7
Smeaton App. Leeds LS15 .... 62 E3
Smeaton Gr. Swil LS26 .... 82 A2
Smeaton Rd. Upton WF9 .... 183 E8
Smiddles La. Brad BD5 .... 74 D2
Smiddy Hill. Th Arch LS23 .... 15 A4
Smirthwaite St. Wake WF1 .... 142 C8
Smirthwaite View. Nor WF6 .. 123 A1
Smith Ave. Brad BD6 .... 94 C8
Smith Cres. Brig HD6 .... 135 E8
Smith House Ave. Brig HD6 ... 115 A6
Smith House Cres. Brig HD6 . 115 A5
Smith House Gr. Brig HD6 ..... 115 A5
Smith House La. Brig HX3 ..... 115 A6
Smith La. Brad BD9 .... 54 F2
Smith Rd. Brad BD7 .... 74 B3
Smith Rd. Dew WF13 .... 117 F1
Smith St. Brad BD7 .... 74 D7
Smith St. Brad BD4 .... 95 B8
Smith St. Castle WF10 .... 103 F1
Smith St. Castle WF10 .... 104 C2
Smith St. Keigh BD21 .... 35 A8
Smith St. Liver WF15 .... 117 B3
Smith St. Ship BD16 .... 54 B6
Smith Wlk. S Elm WF9 .... 183 A4
Smith's Terr. Hali HX3 .... 92 A3
Smitherd's St. Keigh BD21 ...... 35 C6
Smithfield Ave. Brig HX3 .... 114 C8
Smithies La. Batley WF17 .... 96 E1
Smithies La. Liver FW16 .... 117 D2
Smithies M'r Cl. Batley WF17 117 F7
Smithies Moor Cres. Batley
WF17 .... 117 F8
Smithies M'r La. Batley WF17 117 E7
Smithies Moor Rise. Batley
WF17 .... 117 F8
Smiths Ave. Hud HD3 .... 153 D7
Smithson Ave. Castle WF10 ... 125 C6
Smithson St. Roth LS26 .... 100 F4
Smithville. Keigh BD21 .... 18 F1
Smithwell La. Hep HX7 .... 88 E5
Smithy Carr La. Brig HD6 ..... 115 A4
Smithy Cl. Crof WF4 .... 161 F8
Smithy Cl. Skel HD8 .... 175 A1
Smithy Clough La. Rip HX6 ... 132 B3
Smithy Greaves. Nes LS29 .... 7 C7
Smithy Hill. Brad BD6 .... 74 C1
Smithy Hill. D Dale HD8 .... 191 F3
Smithy Hill. Denh BD13 .... 71 E6
Smithy La. Bard LS17 .... 28 C2
Smithy La. Bur in W LS29 .... 21 E8
Smithy La. Denton LS29 .... 9 B7
Smithy La. E Ard WF3 .... 119 F8
Smithy La. Hep HX7 .... 88 A6
Smithy La. Holmfi HD7 .... 188 C2
Smithy La. Hors LS16 .... 41 E6
Smithy La. Hud HD5 .... 154 C5
Smithy La. Neth WF4 .... 157 F6
Smithy La. Rip HX6 .... 150 D7
Smithy La. Skel HD8 .... 175 A1
Smithy La. Wils BD15 .... 53 C6
Smithy Mills La. Hors LS16 ...... 42 D2
Smithy Mills La. Leeds LS16 .... 42 D1
Smithy Nook. Litt OL15 .... 129 C1
Smithy Par. Dew WF12 .... 139 F1
Smithy Place La. Honley HD7 172 B2
Smithy St. Hali HX1 .... 113 D7
Smithy Wlk. Dew WF12 .... 139 F1
Smyth St. Wake WF1 .... 142 B6
Snail La. Heb Br HX7 .... 110 B8
Snape Dr. Brad BD7 .... 73 D2
Snape St. Keigh BD21 .... 35 C4
Snapethorpe Cres. Wake WF2 141 D3
Snapethorpe Gate. Wake WF2 141 C4
Snapethorpe Mid Sch. Wake . 141 D4
Snapethorpe Rd. Wake WF2 . 141 D4
Snaygill Ind Est. Skip 4 A8
Snelsins La. Clec BD19 .... 95 C1
Snelsins Rd. Clec BD19 .... 95 C1
Snittle Rd. Holmfi HD7 .... 199 B6
Snow Hill Cl. Wake WF1 .... 121 A1
Snow Hill Rise. Wake WF1 ..... 121 A1
Snow Hill View. Wake WF1 ... 142 B8
Snowden App. Leeds LS13 .... 58 E3
Snowden Cl. Leeds LS13 .... 58 D2
Snowden Cres. Leeds LS13 ...... 58 D2
Snowden Fold. Leeds LS13 .... 58 D2
Snowden Gn. Leeds LS13 .... 58 D2
Snowden Gr. Leeds LS13 .... 58 D2
Snowden Lawn. Leeds LS13 ..... 58 D2
Snowden Rd. Ship BD18 .... 55 D7
Snowden Royd. Leeds LS13 ..... 58 D2
Snowden St. Brad BD1 .... 74 E8
Snowden Vale. Leeds LS13 .... 58 D2
Snowden Way. Leeds LS13 .... 58 D3
Snowdens Wlk. Brad BD14 ...... 73 D4
Snowdon Ave. Knot WF11 ..... 126 C4
Snowdon St. Batley WF17 ..... 118 B4
Snug La. Holmfi HD7 .... 190 A1
Snydale Ave. Nor WF6 .... 123 C1
Snydale Cl. Nor WF6 .... 123 C1
Snydale Ct. Nor WF6 .... 123 C1
Snydale Gr. Nor WF6 .... 123 C1
Snydale Rd. Nor WF6 .... 123 C1
Soaper House La. Brig HX3 ..... 93 D1
Soaper La. Brad BD6 .... 93 D8
Soaper La. Shelf HX3 .... 93 D8
Sod House Gn. Hali HX3 .... 92 A3
Soho Gr. Wake WF2 .... 142 A6
Soho St. Brad BD1 .... 74 D7
Soho St. Hali HX1 .... 112 F7
Solid. Hud HD4 .... 153 F2
Solomon Hill. Hali HX2 .... 90 D1
Solway Rd. Batley WF17 .... 118 F5
Somerdale Cl. Leeds LS13 .... 58 D1
Somerdale Gdns. Leeds LS13 .. 58 D1
Somerdale Gr. Leeds LS13 .... 58 D1
Somerdale Wlk. Leeds LS13 ..... 58 D1
Somers Pl. Leeds LS1 .... 79 B8 5
Somers St. Leeds LS1 .... 79 A8
Somerset Ave. Bail BD17 .... 38 B4
Somerset Ave. Brig HD6 .... 136 B7
Somerset Ct. Knot WF11 .... 126 F4
Somerset Rd. Hud HD5 .... 154 D4
Somerset Rd. Pudsey LS28 ...... 76 E8
Somerton Dr. Brad BD4 .... 75 E2
Somerville Ave. Brad BD6 .... 94 B7
Somerville Ave. Leeds LS14 ..... 61 F2
Somerville Dr. Leeds LS14 .... 61 F3
Somerville Gn. Leeds LS14 ...... 61 F2
Somerville Gr. Leeds LS14 .... 61 F3
Somerville Mount. Leeds LS14 62 A2 2
Somerville Pk. Brad BD6 .... 94 B7
Somerville Terr. Otley LS21 ..... 23 C8
Somerville View. Leeds LS14 ... 61 F2
Sonning Rd. Brad BD15 .... 73 B8
Soothill La. Batley WF17 .... 118 E5
Soothill La. E Ard WF17 .... 119 A5
Sorbus Way. Lepton HD8 .... 155 E3
Sorrel Cl. Pont WF8 .... 146 D7
Sorrin Cl. Brad BD10 .... 56 A7
Sotheron Croft. Dar WF8 ...... 147 C5
Soureby Cross Way. Birk BD4 . 95 F7
Sourhall Cotts. Tod OL14 ...... 107 D6
Sourhall Rd. Tod OL14 .... 107 C5
South Accommodation Rd. Leeds
LS10, LS9 .... 79 E5
South App. Bramham LS14 ..... 46 F8
South App. Bramham LS14 ..... 47 C6
South App. Stut LS25 .... 48 A3
South Ave. Castle WF10 .... 123 F7
South Ave. Hor WF4 .... 141 C1
South Ave. Hud HD2 .... 136 B2
South Ave. Hud HD4 .... 152 F3
South Ave. Pont WF8 .... 146 B7
South Ave. S Elm WF9 .... 182 F2
South Baileygate. Pont WF8 .. 125 E1
South Bank. E Kes LS17 .... 28 C6
South Bank. Queen BD13 .... 72 F1 3
South Bank Rd. Batley WF17 . 118 A6
South Bolton. Hali HX2 .... 91 E7
South Bradford Golf Course.
Brad 94 F7
South Brook Terr. Brad BD7 .... 74 D6
South Cl. Guise LS20 .... 39 B8
South Cl. Roy S71 .... 179 C2
South Cliffe. Thorn BD13 .... 72 E6
South Clough Head. Hali HX2 112 A8
South Craven Sch. Glu 16 D6
South Cres. S Elm WF9 .... 183 B4
South Croft Ave. Birk BD11 ..... 96 A6
South Croft. D Dale HD8 .... 191 F3
South Croft Dr. Birk BD11 ...... 96 A7
South Croft Gate. Birk BD11 ... 96 A6
South Croft. Shaf S72 .... 180 C3
South Cross Rd. Hud HD2 ...... 135 F2
South Crossland CE Jun Sch.
Hud 171 D7
South Dr. Guise LS20 .... 39 B8
South Dr. Pudsey LS28 .... 57 D2
South Dr. Roy S71 .... 179 C2
South Dr. Wake WF2 .... 142 E1
South Edge. Keigh BD20 .... 35 A8
South Edge. Ship BD18 .... 54 F7
South Elmsall Ash Grove Fst Sch.
S Elm 183 A4
South Elmsall Mid Sch. S Elm 182 F1
South Elmsall Sta. S Elm 183 A3
South End Ave. Leeds LS13 ...... 58 E1
South End Gr. Leeds LS13 .... 58 E1
South End Mount. Leeds LS13 . 58 E1 2
South End Terr. Leeds LS13 ..... 58 E1
South Farm Cres. Leeds LS9 ... 61 C2
South Farm Rd. Leeds LS9 ...... 61 D2
South Gr. Brig HD6 .... 114 E5
South Gr. Ship BD18 .... 54 D7
South Hawksw'th St. Ilkley LS29 8 B4
South Hiendley Fst Sch. S Hie 180 D6
South Hill Cl. Midd LS10 .... 99 F7
South Hill Croft. Midd LS10 ..... 99 F7
South Hill Dr. Bing BD16 .... 37 C2
South Hill Gdns. Midd LS10 ..... 99 F7
South Hill Rise. Midd LS10 .... 99 F7
South Hill Way. Midd LS10 .... 99 F7
South Holme. Liver WF15 ...... 117 B4
South Kirkby Common Road
Prim & Mid Schs. S Kirk 182 A1
South Kirkby Moorthorpe
Prim & Mid Schs. S Elm 182 E3
South Kirkby Stockingate Prim
Sch. S Kirk 182 A1
South La. Caw S75 .... 193 C1
South La. Elland HX5 .... 134 F4
South La. Elland HX5 .... 134 F5
South La. Holmfi HD7 .... 189 A5
South La. Neth WF4 .... 158 D4
South La. Shelf HX3 .... 93 C7
South Lane Gdns. Elland HX5 134 F5
South Lee. Hors LS18 .... 41 B1
South Leeds Bsns Pk. Leeds 79 D4
South Leeds L Ctr. Leeds 79 B5
South Mead. Bramho LS16 ...... 24 F2
South Mount. E Kes LS17 .... 28 B6
South Nelson St. Morley LS27 .. 98 A5
South Ossett Inf Sch. Ossett . 140 E4
South Par. Brad BD8 .... 55 D1
South Par. Clec BD19 .... 116 C7
South Par. Elland HX4 .... 133 F3
South Par. Elland HX5 .... 134 F5
South Par. Hali HX1 .... 113 D6
South Par. Ilkley LS29 .... 8 A4
South Par. Leeds LS6 .... 59 D5
South Par. Leeds LS1 .... 79 B8
South Par. Morley LS27 .... 98 B4
South Par. Ossett WF5 .... 141 A4
South Par. Otley LS21 .... 23 B7
South Par. Pudsey LS28 .... 76 E6
South Par. Wake WF1 .... 142 C6
South Parade Cl. Pudsey LS28 76 D6
South Park Terr. Birk LS28 ...... 76 F4
South Park Way. Wake WF2 . 120 F4
South Parkway Ap. Leeds LS14 61 E3
South Parkway. Leeds LS14 .... 61 F4
South Parkway. Leeds LS14 .... 62 A4
South Queen St. Morley LS27 .. 98 B3
South Rd. Cull BD13 .... 52 D5
South Rd. Leeds LS9 .... 80 C3
South Rd. Ship BD9 .... 55 C4
South Ridge. Kippax LS25 .... 83 A1
South Royd Ave. Hali HX3 ..... 113 C4
South Selby. Hali HX2 .... 91 D6
South Sq. Thorn BD13 .... 72 D6
South St. Bacup OL13 .... 106 A3
South St. Brad BD5 .... 74 C3
South St. Brad BD12 .... 95 A4
South St. Brig HD6 .... 115 A3
South St. Denh BD13 .... 71 D8
South St. Dew WF13 .... 139 C8
South St. Dew WF12 .... 139 D6
South St. Elland HX4 .... 134 B4
South St. Hali HX1 .... 113 B6
South St. Hem WF9 .... 181 E6
South St. Holmfi HD7 .... 189 C6
South St. Hud HD1 .... 153 D5
South St. Hud HD4 .... 171 D6
South St. Keigh BD21 .... 35 B5
South St. Keigh BD20 .... 36 D8
South St. Liver WF15 .... 117 B4 6
South St. Mir WF14 .... 138 A4
South St. Morley LS27 .... 98 B4
South St. Nor WF6 .... 144 A7
South St. Ossett WF5 .... 140 D4
South St. Ryhill WF4 .... 162 D1
South St. Thorn BD13 .... 72 D7
South St. Wake WF1 .... 142 D5
South St. Yeadon LS19 .... 40 B4
South Terr. Dew WF12 .... 139 E6
South Terr. Ossett WF5 .... 140 E3
South View. Batley WF17 .... 96 F1 1
South View. Brad BD10 .... 56 D7
South View. Castle WF10 ...... 104 C2
South View. Castle WF10 ...... 124 E5
South View Cl. Birk BD4 .... 95 E7
South View Cl. Yeadon LS19 ... 39 F7
South View. Coll LS22 .... 28 F8
South View Cres. Yeadon LS19 39 F7
South View. Crig WF4 .... 159 D4
South View. Dew WF12 .... 139 D6
South View Dr. Birk BD4 .... 95 F7
South View. E Ard WF3 .... 119 D5
South View. Farnh BD20 .... 4 D1
South View. Feath WF7 .... 145 D6
South View Gdns. Pont WF8 .. 147 A8
South View. Glu BD20 .... 16 D6
South View Gr. Clec BD19 ..... 117 B7
South View. Guise LS20 .... 22 E1
South View. Hali HX2 .... 111 F5
South View. Hali HX3 .... 113 E4
South View. Hali HX3 .... 114 A4
South View. Haw BD22 .... 51 C7
South View. Holmfi HD7 .... 189 F3
South View. Hors LS18 .... 58 C7
South View. Hud HD1 .... 153 D5
South View Inf Sch. Yeadon 40 B6
South View. Keigh BD20 .... 19 C1
South View. Keigh BD22 .... 34 E8
South View. Leeds LS15 .... 62 C2 4
South View. Men LS29 .... 22 A3
South View. Pudsey LS28 .... 57 C1
South View. Pudsey LS28 .... 76 F8
South View Rd. Birk BD4 .... 95 F7
South View Rd. Midd LS10 .... 79 E1
South View Rd. Yeadon LS19 ... 40 B7 9
South View. Roth LS26 .... 100 D6
South View. Ship BD9 .... 55 C4
South View St. Sil BD20 .... 5 D1
South View St. Tod OL14 .... 86 C1
South View Terr. Bail BD17 ..... 38 C4 6
South View Terr. Dew WF13 .. 118 B2
South View Terr. Dew WF13 .. 138 E6
South View Terr. Floc WF4 .... 156 E4
South View Terr. Otley LS21 .... 23 B7
South View Terr. Yeadon LS19 40 C6
South View. Weth LS22 .... 13 E8
South View. Yeadon LS19 .... 39 F7
South Way. Birk BD4 .... 95 E7
South Way. Ship BD18 .... 54 D7
South Wlk. Harden BD16 .... 36 A1
Southampton St. Brad BD3 .... 55 F1
Southcliffe Dr. Bail BD17 .... 38 C1
Southcliffe Way. Bail BD17 ...... 38 C1
Southcote Pl. Brad BD10 .... 56 B8
Southdale Gdns. Ossett WF5 . 140 E5
Southdale Rd. Ossett WF5 ..... 140 E5
Southdown Cl. Brad BD9 .... 54 E2
Southdown Rd. Bail BD17 .... 38 B1
Southedge Cl. Brig HX3 .... 114 C7
Southedge Terr. Brig HX3 ...... 114 C7
Southern Rd. Hud HD4 .... 153 A3
Southfield Ave. Brad BD6 .... 94 C8
Southfield Ave. Feath WF7 .... 145 B4
Southfield Ave. Keigh BD20 ..... 19 A2
Southfield Ave. Leeds LS17 ...... 43 E2
Southfield Cl. Hor WF4 .... 141 B1
Southfield Cl. Wake WF2 .... 120 E1
Southfield Ct. Kirkb HD8 .... 173 F7
Southfield Dr. Keigh BD20 .... 19 A2
Southfield Dr. Leeds LS17 .... 43 E2
Southfield Fold. Hor WF4 ...... 159 B8
Southfield. Hep HX7 .... 88 F4
Southfield House. Add LS29 .... 6 F8
Southfield La. Brad BD5, BD7 .. 74 B3
Southfield La. Hor WF4 .... 159 B8
Southfield La. Sil LS29 .... 6 E8
Southfield Mount. Keigh BD20 . 18 F2
Southfield Mount. Leeds LS12 . 78 C7
Southfield Rd. Bing BD16 .... 37 A1
Southfield Rd. Brad BD5 .... 74 C2
Southfield Rd. Bur in W LS29 ..... 9 E1
Southfield Rd. Crof WF4 .... 144 B3
Southfield Rd. Hud HD5 .... 155 A4
Southfield Rd. Knot WF11 ..... 126 F3
Southfield Rd. Sil LS29 .... 6 F8
Southfield Sq. Brad BD8 .... 55 C1
Southfield St. Leeds LS12 .... 78 C7
Southfield Terr. Birk BD11 .... 96 A6
Southfield Terr. Brig HX3 .... 93 C1
Southfield Terr. Sil LS29 .... 6 F8
Southfield Way. Keigh BD20 .... 19 A2
Southfields. Bramho LS16 .... 24 F2
Southfields. Hud HD5 .... 154 E5
Southfields View. Neth WF4 .. 158 D5
Southgate. Brad BD1 .... 74 E7
Southgate. Elland HX5 .... 134 F6
Southgate. Guise LS20 .... 39 B7
Southgate. Hali HX1 .... 113 C7 16
Southgate. Honley HD7 .... 171 F4
Southgate. Hud HD1 .... 154 B6
Southgate. Pont WF8 .... 146 D8
Southgate. Roth LS26 .... 101 C6
Southgate. S Hie S72 .... 180 E6
Southgate. Wake WF1 .... 142 C6
Southlands Ave. Bing BD16 ...... 37 A1
Southlands Ave. Brad BD13 ...... 73 C6
Southlands Ave. Keigh BD20 .... 19 A1
Southlands Ave. Leeds LS17 .... 60 C8
Southlands Ave. Yeadon LS19 .. 40 E2
Southlands. Bail BD17 .... 38 B1
Southlands Cl. Bad WF9 .... 164 E2
Southlands Cl. Leeds LS17 .... 43 C1
Southlands Cres. Leeds LS17 .. 60 C8
Southlands Dr. Hud HD2 .... 136 A3
Southlands Dr. Keigh BD20 ...... 19 A1
Southlands Dr. Leeds LS17 .... 60 C8
Southlands Gr. Bing BD16 .... 37 A1
Southlands Gr. Brad BD13 .... 73 B6
Southlands Gr. Keigh BD20 ...... 19 A1
Southlands Gr W. Keigh BD20 . 19 A2
Southlands. Hali HX2 .... 71 F1
Southlands. Kirkhe HD5 .... 137 B1
Southlands Mount. Keigh BD20 19 A1
Southlands Rd. Keigh BD20 ...... 19 A1
Southlea Ave. Haw BD22 .... 34 E2
Southlea Cl. Brad BD12 .... 95 A5
Southleigh Ave. Leeds LS11 ..... 99 A8
Southleigh Cres. Leeds LS11 ... 99 A8
Southleigh Croft. Leeds LS11 ... 99 B8
Southleigh Dr. Leeds LS11 .... 99 A8
Southleigh Garth. Leeds LS11 . 99 B8
Southleigh Gdns. Leeds LS11 .. 99 A8
Southleigh Gr. Leeds LS11 .... 99 A8
Southleigh Grange. Leeds LS11 99 B8
Southleigh Rd. Leeds LS11 .... 99 A8
Southleigh View. Leeds LS11 ... 99 A8
Southmere Ave. Brad BD7 .... 74 A3
Southmere Cres. Brad BD7 .... 74 A3
Southmere Dr. Brad BD7 .... 73 F3
Southmere Fst Sch. Brad 74 A3
Southmere Gr. Brad BD7 .... 74 A3 3
Southmere Oval. Brad BD7 .... 73 F3
Southmere Rd. Brad BD7 .... 74 A3
Southmere Terr. Brad BD7 .... 74 A3
Southmoor Hospl. Hem 181 D6
Southmoor La. Knot WF11 ..... 127 D3
Southmoor Rd. Hem WF9 ...... 181 D3
Southolme Cl. Leeds LS5 .... 59 A6
Southowram Bank. Hali HX3 . 113 E6
Southowram Jun & Inf Sch.
Hali 114 A4
Southroyd Pk. Pudsey LS28 ..... 76 E5
Southroyd Prim Sch. Pudsey 76 E6
Southroyd Rise. Pudsey LS28 .. 76 E5
Southwaite Cl. Leeds LS14 .... 61 F4
Southwaite Garth. Leeds LS14 61 F4
Southwaite La. Leeds LS14 ...... 61 F4
Southwaite Lawn. Leeds LS14 . 61 F4
Southwaite Pl. Leeds LS14 .... 61 F4
Southway. Bing BD16 .... 37 C5
Southway. Bur in W LS29 .... 9 C3
Southway. Guise LS20 .... 39 B8
Southway. Hors LS18 .... 41 A3
Southway. Hud HD3 .... 135 C1
Southway. Ilkley LS29 .... 8 D3
Southway. Mir WF14 .... 137 F7
Southwell Ave. Hud HD3 .... 153 B7
Southwood Ave. Honley HD7 . 172 B5
Southwood Cl. Leeds LS14 ...... 62 C4
Southwood Cres. Leeds LS14 .. 62 C4
Southwood Gate. Leeds LS14 .. 62 C4
Sovereign Cl. Batley WF17 .... 96 F1
Sovereign Gdns. Nor WF6 ..... 123 A2
Sovereign St. Hali HX1 .... 113 B7 9
Sovereign St. Leeds LS1 .... 79 C7
Sovereign's Way. Dew WF12 139 B3
Sowden Bldgs. Brad BD2 .... 56 B2
Sowden La. Brig HX3 .... 93 F3
Sowden Rd. Brad BD9 .... 54 D3
Sowden St. Brad BD7 .... 74 B3
Sowden's Yd. Bramho LS16 ..... 24 D3 3
Sowerby Bridge High Sch. Hali 112 C5
Sowerby Bridge Sta. Sow Br . 112 C3
Sowerby Croft La. Sow Br HX6 112 C2
Sowerby La. Heb Br HX2 .... 111 C6
Sowerby La. Sow Br HX2 .... 111 C6
Sowerby New Rd. Sow Br HX6 111 F3
Sowerby St. Sow Br HX6 .... 112 B3
Sowgate La. Knot WF11 .... 126 B3
Sowgate La. Pont WF11 .... 126 A3
Sowood Ave. Ossett WF5 .... 140 E3
Sowood Gdns. Ossett WF5 ..... 140 F3
Sowood La. Floc WF12 .... 157 B6
Sowood La. Ossett WF5 .... 140 F3
Sowood St. Leeds LS4 .... 59 C2
Sowood View. Ossett WF5 ..... 140 F3
Soyland Town Rd. Rip HX6 .... 132 D6
Spa Bottom. Lepton HD8 .... 155 C5
Spa Croft Rd. Ossett WF5 ...... 141 A4
Spa Fields Ind Est. Slai 152 B1
Spa Fields. Slai HD7 .... 152 B1
Spa Fold. Loft G WF3 .... 121 F4
Spa Gr. Wake WF2 .... 141 E3
Spa Hill. Batley WF17 .... 118 D5
Spa La. B Spa LS23 .... 30 E7
Spa La. Bing BD16 .... 37 A5
Spa La. Ossett WF5 .... 141 A4
Spa La. Slai HD7 .... 152 B1
Spa St. Batley WF17 .... 118 D5
Spa St. Ossett WF5 .... 141 B4
Spa Well Gr. Bri S72 .... 181 A3
Spaines Rd. Hud HD2 .... 136 A1
Spalding Towers. Leeds LS9 .... 60 E1
Sparable La. Wake WF1 .... 142 E3
Spark House La. Sow Br HX6 112 C3
Spark La. Mapp S75 .... 178 B1
Spark St. Hud HD3 .... 152 F7
Sparks Rd. Hud HD3 .... 153 B7
Spartal La. Ledst LS25 .... 103 E8
Spartan Rd. Brad BD12 .... 94 D5
Sparth La. Holmfi HD7 .... 188 B4
Spawd Bone La. Knot WF11 .. 126 E3
Speak Cl. Wake WF1 .... 142 F8
Spear Fir. Bard LS17 .... 28 A2
Spearhead Way. Keigh BD21 ... 35 C8
Speedwell Mount. Leeds LS6 ... 60 B3 6
Speedwell Rd. Castle WF10 ... 123 E5
Speedwell St. Hud HD1 .... 153 D5
Speedwell St. Leeds LS6 .... 60 B3 7
Speeton Ave. Brad BD7 .... 73 E2
Speeton Gr. Brad BD7 .... 73 D2
Spen App. Leeds LS16 .... 58 F7
Spen Bank. Clec BD19 .... 116 F7
Spen Bank. Leeds LS16 .... 59 A7
Spen Cl. Brad BD4 .... 95 B7
Spen Common La. Bramham
LS24 .... 47 F6
Spen Cres. Leeds LS16 .... 58 F7
Spen Dr. Leeds LS16 .... 59 A8
Spen Gdns. Leeds LS16 .... 59 B8
Spen Gn. Leeds LS16 .... 58 F7
Spen La. Clec BD19 .... 117 A8
Spen La. Leeds LS16 .... 42 A1
Spen La. Leeds LS16, LS5, LS6 59 A7
Spen Lawn. Leeds LS16 .... 58 F7
Spen Mews. Leeds LS16 .... 59 A7
Spen Rd. Leeds LS16 .... 59 B8
Spen Vale St. Liver WF16 ...... 117 D2
Spen Valley Ind Est. Clec 116 F6
Spen Valley Rd. Dew WF13 .... 138 F6
Spen View. Dew WF16 .... 117 F1
Spen View La. Brad BD4 .... 95 B7
Spen Wlk. Leeds LS16 .... 58 F7
Spence La. Leeds LS12 .... 78 F6
Spenceley St. Leeds LS2 .... 60 A2
Spenceley St. Leeds LS2 .... 60 A3
Spencer Ave. Brad BD7 .... 74 A5
Spencer Ave. Morley LS27 .... 98 A2
Spencer Ave. Sil BD20 .... 5 E2
Spencer Cl. Glu BD20 .... 16 E7
Spencer La. Heb Br HX7 .... 89 A1
Spencer Mount. Leeds LS8 ...... 60 E3
Spencer Pl. Leeds LS7 .... 60 E3
Spencer Rd. Brad BD7 .... 74 A5
Spencer St. Keigh BD21 .... 35 B7 7
Spencer St. Mir WF14 .... 138 A3
Spencer St. S in Cra BD20 .... 16 D5
Spencer St. Skel HD8 .... 175 A2
Spencer Terr. Hud HD2 .... 136 D3
Spenfield Ct. Liver WF15 .... 117 A2
Spennithorne Ave. Hors LS16 .. 42 A2
Spennithorne Dr. Hors LS16 .... 42 B1
Spennithorne Rd. Ad Le S DN6 184 F2
Spenser Rd. Guise LS20 .... 39 F8
Spenser Rise. Guise LS20 .... 39 F8
Spenslea Gr. Morley LS27 .... 98 A2
Spibey Cres. Roth LS26 .... 100 D7
Spibey La. Roth LS26 .... 100 D7
Spicer House La. Ingb S30 ..... 191 A1
Spicer St. Brad BD5 .... 74 C3
Spindle St. Hali HX2 .... 92 A5
Spindles The. Midd LS10 .... 99 D8 3
Spink La. Pont WF8 .... 125 D1
Spink Pl. Brad BD8 .... 74 D8
Spink St. Brad BD8 .... 74 D8
Spink Well La. E Ard WF3 .... 98 F1
Spinkfield Rd. Hud HD2 .... 153 F8
Spinks Gdns. Leeds LS14 .... 62 B4
Spinkwell Rd. Dew WF13 ...... 118 C1 4
Spinners Chase. Pudsey LS28 . 76 E7
Spinners The. Haw BD22 .... 51 C6
Spinney The. Brig HD6 .... 115 A5
Spinney The. Draug BD23 .... 1 D5
Spinney The. Keigh BD20 .... 36 D7
Spinney The. Leeds LS17 .... 43 E2
Spinney The. Leeds LS9 .... 79 E7
Spinney The. Wake WF2 .... 160 E7
Spinney The. Weth LS22 .... 13 D6
Spinney The. Yeadon LS19 .... 40 A2
Spinneyfield Ct. Leeds LS9 .... 79 E7
Spinneyfield. Hud HD2 .... 136 A3
Spion Kop. Thorner LS14 .... 45 F5
Spire Ct. Hud HD1 .... 153 F7
Spitalgap La. Dar WF8 .... 147 C6
Spittal Hardwick La. Castle
WF10 .... 125 C5
Spittlerush La. Norton WF8 ... 166 F4
Spofforth Hill. Weth LS22 .... 13 D6
Spofforth Wlk. Gar LS25 .... 83 B7
Spout Fold. Wake WF2 .... 141 D6
Spout Hill. Brig HD6 .... 135 E6
Spout House La. Brig HD6 ..... 114 E6
Spring Ave. Gild LS27 .... 97 C8
Spring Ave. Keigh BD21 .... 35 E6
Spring Bank Cres. Leeds LS6 ... 59 E4
Spring Bank Croft. Holmfi HD7 188 D4
Spring Bank. Cull BD13 .... 52 D5
Spring Bank Dr. Liver WF15 .. 117 B2
Spring Bank. Leeds LS5 .... 59 A4 5
Spring Bank Pl. Brad BD8 .... 55 D2
Spring Bank. Pont WF8 .... 146 D7
Spring Bank Prim Sch. Leeds ... 59 E4
Spring Bank Rise. Keigh BD21 . 35 C4
Spring Bank Terr. Guise LS20 .. 22 E1
Spring Bottom. Tod OL14 .... 128 F7
Spring Cl. Bing BD16 .... 37 B2
Spring Cl. Gar LS25 .... 83 A8
Spring Cl. Gar LS25 .... 83 B6
Spring Cl. Keigh BD21 .... 35 E6
Spring Cl. Morley LS27 .... 98 A7
Spring Close Ave. Leeds LS9 .... 79 F6
Spring Close Gdns. Leeds LS9 .. 79 F6
Spring Close St. Leeds LS9 ...... 79 E6
Spring Close Wlk. Leeds LS9 ... 79 F6
Spring Ct. Brad BD15 .... 54 A3
Spring Dale. Honley HD7 .... 171 F5
Spring Dr. Keigh BD21 .... 35 E6
Spring Edge. Hali HX1 .... 113 A4
Spring Edge N. Hali HX1 .... 113 A5
Spring Edge S. Hali HX1 .... 113 A5
Spring Edge W. Hali HX1 .... 112 F5
Spring End Rd. Ossett WF4 ... 141 B3
Spring Farm La. Harden BD16 . 36 A1
Spring Farm Mews. Wils BD15 53 C5
Spring Garden St. Queen BD13 72 E1
Spring Gardens La. Brad BD9 .. 55 A3
Spring Gardens La. Keigh BD20 18 A1
Spring Gardens Mount. Keigh
BD20 .... 18 B1
Spring Gdns. Bacup OL13 ...... 106 A3 7
Spring Gdns. Batley WF17 ...... 118 B5
Spring Gdns. Birk BD11 .... 96 F6
Spring Gdns. Brad BD1 .... 74 E8
Spring Gdns. Bur in W LS29 .... 9 F1
Spring Gdns. Hare LS17 .... 27 A7
Spring Gdns. Holmfi HD7 .... 188 E5
Spring Gr. Hali HX1 .... 112 E7 4
Spring Gr. Heb Br HX7 .... 89 A4
Spring Grove Cty Prim Sch.
Hud 153 F5
Spring Grove St. Hud HD1 ..... 154 A5
Spring Grove Terr. Leeds LS6 .. 59 E2
Spring Grove View. Leeds LS6 . 59 E2 6
Spring Hall Cl. Shelf HX3 .... 93 B5
Spring Hall Ct. Hali HX1 .... 112 E8 11
Spring Hall Dr. Hali HX2 .... 112 E7
Spring Hall Gdns. Hali HX2 .... 112 E7
Spring Hall Gr. Hali HX2 .... 112 E7 4
Spring Hall La. Hali HX1 .... 112 F7
Spring Hall La. Hali HX3 .... 113 D4
Spring Hall Pl. Hali HX1 .... 112 E7 7
Spring Head. Hali HX2 .... 91 E1
Spring Head La. Mars HD7 ..... 168 F5
Spring Head Rd. Haw BD22 ...... 51 C8
Spring Head Rd. Thorn BD13 ... 72 F6
Spring Head. Shelf HX3 .... 93 C5
Spring Hill. Bail BD17 .... 37 F3
Spring Hill. Hors LS16 .... 42 E4
Spring Hill. Leeds LS7 .... 60 C4
Spring Hill. Ship BD18 .... 55 F7
Spring Holes La. Thorn BD13 ... 72 D7
Spring La. Bail BD17 .... 37 D6
Spring La. Batley WF17 .... 118 B7
Spring La. Crof WF4 .... 162 B7
Spring La. Elland HX4 .... 134 A7
Spring La. Holmfi HD7 .... 188 D2
Spring La. Holmfi HD7 .... 188 E4
Spring La. Holmfi HD7 .... 189 E5
Spring La. Mapp S75 .... 178 C3
Spring La. Roy S71 .... 179 D1
Spring La. Weth LS22 .... 14 C5
Spring Mill Fold. Hali HX2 .... 90 F8
Spring Mill La. Ossett WF5 .... 140 F6
Spring Mill St. Brad BD5 .... 74 E4
Spring Mount. Keigh BD21 .... 35 E5
Spring Park Rd. Wils BD15 .... 53 C6
Spring Pl. Brad BD7 .... 74 C5
Spring Pl. Keigh BD21 .... 35 E5
Spring Ram Bsns Pk. Kex 177 D1
Spring Rd. Leeds LS6 .... 59 E4
Spring Rise. Draug BD23 .... 1 D5
Spring Rise. Keigh BD21 .... 35 E6
Spring Row. Harden BD16 .... 36 B1
Spring Row. Keigh BD21 .... 35 B6
Spring Row. Oxen BD22 .... 51 E1
Spring Row. Queen BD13 .... 72 E1 17
Spring Side Rise. Hud HD7 ..... 152 D5
Spring St. Brad BD10 .... 56 B6
Spring St. Brig HD6 .... 115 A2
Spring St. Dew WF13 .... 118 C1
Spring St. Haw BD22 .... 51 F8 3
Spring St. Hud HD1 .... 154 A6 7
Spring St. Keigh BD21 .... 35 C8
Spring St. Liver WF15 .... 117 B4
Spring St. Mars HD7 .... 168 F3
Spring St. Rip HX6 .... 132 D4
Spring St. Slai HD7 .... 169 F8
Spring St. Tod OL14 .... 86 C1
Spring Terr. Hali HX3 .... 113 D8
Spring Terr. Keigh BD21 .... 35 E6
Spring Terr. S Elm WF9 .... 182 F2
Spring Vale Rd. S Kirk WF9 ... 182 C3
Spring Valley Ave. Leeds LS13 . 58 C1
Spring Valley Cl. Leeds LS13 ... 58 C1
Spring Valley Cl. Liver WF15 . 117 A5
Spring Valley Cres. Leeds LS13 58 C1
Spring Valley Croft. Leeds LS13 58 C1
Spring Valley Ct. Leeds LS13 ... 58 C1
Spring Valley Dr. Leeds LS13 ... 58 C1
Spring Valley. Pudsey LS28 ...... 57 E1
Spring Valley Sq. Liver WF15 . 117 A5
Spring Valley St. Liver WF15 . 117 A5
Spring Valley View. Leeds LS13 58 C1
Spring Valley Wlk. Leeds LS13 . 58 C1
Spring View. Gild LS27 .... 97 C8
Spring View. H Chap BB10 .... 85 A8
Spring View. Ossett WF5 .... 140 F6
Spring View. Sow Br HX2 .... 111 D6
Spring Villas. Tod OL14 .... 86 B1
Spring Way. Keigh BD21 .... 35 E6
Spring Wood Ave. Hali HX3 ... 113 B2
Spring Wood Dr. Hali HX3 ..... 113 B2
Spring Wood Gdns. Brad BD5 . 74 F2
Springbank Ave. Gild LS27 .... 97 C7
Springbank Ave. Pudsey LS28 . 57 E3
Springbank Cl. Pudsey LS28 .... 57 E3
Springbank Cres. Gar LS25 ...... 82 C6
Springbank Cres. Gild LS27 ...... 97 C8
Springbank Cres. Hud HD2 ..... 136 D1
Springbank Dr. Pudsey LS28 .... 57 E4
Springbank. Gar LS25 .... 82 C6
Springbank Gr. Pudsey LS28 ... 57 E3
Springbank Rd. Gild LS27 .... 97 C8
Springbank Rd. Hud HD2 .... 136 D1
Springbank Rd. Pudsey LS28 ... 57 E3
Springbank Rise. Pudsey LS28 57 E3
Springcliffe. Brad BD8 .... 55 B1
Springcliffe St. Brad BD8 .... 55 B1
Springdale Ave. Hud HD1 ...... 153 F4
Springdale Cres. Brad BD10 .... 56 C7
Springdale St. Hud HD1 .... 153 F4
Springfield Ave. Bacup OL13 . 106 A3
Springfield Ave. Batley WF17 118 B5
Springfield Ave. Brad BD7 .... 73 F5
Springfield Ave. Clay W HD8 . 175 E2
Springfield Ave. Hem WF9 ..... 181 E6
Springfield Ave. Honley HD7 .. 171 F3
Springfield Ave. Ilkley LS29 ...... 8 C4
Springfield Ave. Morley LS27 ... 98 A6
Springfield Ave. Pont WF8 ..... 125 F1
Springfield Ave. Slai HD7 .... 169 E7
Springfield. B Spa LS23 .... 30 D5
Springfield. B Spa LS23 .... 30 D8
Springfield Cl. Clay W HD8 ... 175 E2
Springfield Cl. Hors LS18 .... 41 E1
Springfield Cl. Leeds LS10 .... 80 A2
Springfield Cres. Morley LS27 .. 98 A6
Springfield Cres. Norton WF8 166 E5
Springfield Ct. Keigh BD20 ...... 35 A8
Springfield Ct. Yeadon LS19 .... 40 B8
Springfield Dr. Clec WF15 ..... 116 C5
Springfield Dr. D Dale HD8 ... 191 A4
Springfield. Elland HD3 .... 152 B8
Springfield Farm (Riding Sch).
Cull 52 A7
Springfield Gdns. Hors LS18 .... 41 D1

Springfield Gdns. Keigh BD20 ... 35 A8
Springfield Gdns. Pudsey LS28 ... 76 F6
Springfield Gn. Leeds LS10 ... 79 E2
Springfield Gr. Bing BD16 ... 36 F3
Springfield Gr. Brig HD6 ... 115 A5
Springfield Gr'ge. Wake WF2 ... 141 D6
Springfield House. Clec BD19 ... 116 E7 3
Springfield La. Birk BD4 ... 76 F2
Springfield La. Clec FW15 ... 116 E5
Springfield La. Kirkb HD8 ... 173 E7
Springfield La. Morley LS27 ... 98 A6
Springfield Mount. Add LS29 ... 2 F1
Springfield Mount. Hors LS18 ... 41 D1
Springfield Mount. Leeds LS2 ... 60 A1
Springfield Mount. Leeds LS12 ... 78 A8 2
Springfield Mount. S Elm WF9 ... 182 E1
Springfield Pk. Mir WF14 ... 138 B5
Springfield Pl. Brad BD10 ... 56 B6
Springfield Pl. Brad BD1 ... 74 D8
Springfield Pl. Guise LS20 ... 22 E1
Springfield Pl. Leeds LS10 ... 79 E2
Springfield Pl. Otley LS21 ... 22 F7
Springfield. Queen BD13 ... 72 D1
Springfield Rd. Bail BD17 ... 38 B4
Springfield Rd. Elland HX4 ... 135 B7
Springfield Rd. Guise LS20 ... 22 E1
Springfield Rd. Keigh BD20 ... 35 A8
Springfield Rd. Morley LS27 ... 98 A6
Springfield Rise. Hors LS18 ... 41 D1
Springfield Rise. Roth LS26 ... 100 F4
Springfield Sch. Yeadon ... 41 A8
Springfield. Sow Br HX6 ... 112 A3
Springfield St. Brad BD8 ... 74 C8
Springfield St. Roth LS26 ... 100 F4
Springfield St. Thorn BD13 ... 72 E6
Springfield Terr. Brad BD8 ... 74 C8
Springfield Terr. Brig BD19 ... 94 F1
Springfield Terr. Brig HX3 ... 114 C8
Springfield Terr. Cull BD13 ... 52 E5
Springfield Terr. Dew WF13 ... 118 C1
Springfield Terr. Elland HD3 ... 134 B1
Springfield Terr. Emley HD8 ... 175 A7
Springfield Terr. Guise LS20 ... 39 E8
Springfield Terr. Hali HX2 ... 90 C1
Springfield Terr. Pudsey LS28 ... 57 D1 4
Springfield View. Feath WF7 ... 145 A8
Springfield Wlk. Hors LS18 ... 41 D1
Springfields Ave. Knot WF11 ... 127 B4
Springfields. Knot WF11 ... 127 B3
Springhead. Haw BD22 ... 51 C8
Springhead Park Sch. Roth ... 101 A6
Springhead Rd. Roth LS26 ... 101 A6
Springhill Ave. Crof WF4 ... 162 A8
Springhill Dr. Crof WF4 ... 144 A1
Springhill Gr. Crof WF4 ... 144 A1
Springhill Mount. Crof WF4 ... 162 A8
Springhurst Rd. Ship BD18 ... 55 A7
Springlodge Pl. Brad BD8 ... 55 D1
Springmead Dr. Gar LS25 ... 82 F6
Springroyd Terr. Brad BD8 ... 73 F8
Springs La. Bick LS23 ... 14 F6
Springs La. Ilkley LS29 ... 8 C4
Springs La. Th Arch LS23 ... 14 F6
Springs Rd. Guise LS19 ... 39 E6
Springs Rd. Holme HD7 ... 187 B4
Springs The. Wake WF1 ... 142 C6 12
Springstone Ave. Hem WF9 ... 181 E7
Springstone Ave. Ossett WF5 ... 140 D7
Springswood Ave. Ship BD18 ... 55 A7
Springswood Pl. Ship BD18 ... 55 A7
Springswood Rd. Ship BD18 ... 55 A7
Springvale Rise. Hem WF9 ... 181 D8
Springville Gdns. Upton WF9 ... 183 B7
Springville Terr. Brad BD10 ... 56 B7
Springwell Ave. Swil LS26 ... 82 A1
Springwell Cl. Yeadon LS19 ... 40 C6 1
Springwell Ct. Leeds LS12 ... 78 F6 4
Springwell Dr. Brad BD5 ... 74 E4
Springwell Rd. Leeds LS11 ... 79 A6
Springwell Rd. Ossett WF5 ... 140 E5
Springwell Rd. Swil LS26 ... 82 A1
Springwell St. Leeds LS12 ... 78 F6
Springwell Terr. Yeadon LS19 ... 40 C6 2
Springwell View. Batley WF17 ... 96 F1 4
Springwell View. Leeds LS11 ... 79 A6
Springwood Ave. Brad BD5 ... 74 F3
Springwood Ave. Hud HD1 ... 153 F5
Springwood Gdns. Hali HX3 ... 113 B2
Springwood Gr. Leeds LS8 ... 61 C6
Springwood Hall Cl. Hud HD1 ... 153 E6
Springwood Hall Gdns. Hud HD1 ... 153 F6
Springwood Rd. Holmfi HD7 ... 189 C8
Springwood Rd. Leeds LS8 ... 61 C6
Springwood Rd. Yeadon LS19 ... 40 A3
Springwood Sq. Hud HD1 ... 154 A6 6
Springwood St. Hud HD1 ... 154 A6 10
Springwood Terr. Brad BD2 ... 55 E2
Sprinkwell Cl. Brad BD3 ... 55 F1
Spruce Ave. Roy S71 ... 179 B3
Spruce Dr. Hud HD4 ... 171 D6
Spruce Drive Mews. Hud HD4 ... 171 D6
Spruce St. Keigh BD21 ... 35 D8 14
Spruce Wlk. Tod OL14 ... 129 A8
Sprutts La. Wad M HX7 ... 89 B8
Spry La. Dearne S63 ... 194 B3
Spur Dr. Leeds LS15 ... 62 E3
Spur St. Batley WF17 ... 118 D4
Spurr Gr. Walton WF2 ... 161 B6
Spurrier's Ave. Knot WF11 ... 126 C3
Square Rd. Hali HX1 ... 113 D7
Square Rd. Tod OL14 ... 129 A8
Square St. Brad BD4 ... 75 A5
Square The. B Spa LS23 ... 30 E7
Square The. Batley WF17 ... 117 F6
Square The. Brad BD8 ... 73 C7 2
Square The. Castle WF10 ... 125 C7
Square The. Farnley LS21 ... 11 D4
Square The. Hare LS17 ... 27 A7
Square The. Keigh BD20 ... 19 D1
Square The. Kippax LS25 ... 83 A1
Square The. Knot WF11 ... 126 C5
Square The. Shep HD8 ... 190 E8
Square View. Tod OL14 ... 129 B8
Squire Gn. Brad BD8 ... 54 F1
Squire La. Brad BD8, BD9 ... 54 F1
Squirrel Cl. Batley WF13 ... 118 A3
Squirrel Ditch. Hud HD4 ... 154 C3
Squirrel End. Batley WF13 ... 118 A2
Squirrel Hall Dr. Batley WF13 ... 117 F3
Squirrel La. Thorn BD13 ... 72 B5
Squirrel Wlk. Batley WF13 ... 118 A3
Squirrels Drey. Crig WF4 ... 159 F7
Stable Fold. Brad BD12 ... 94 D2
Stable La. Hali HX3 ... 92 B1
Stablers Wlk. Nor WF6 ... 123 A4
Stables La. B Spa LS23 ... 30 E7
Stackgarth. Brig HD6 ... 136 A8
Stackhills Rd. Tod OL14 ... 108 C5
Stacks La. Heb Br HX7 ... 110 F5
Stadium Rd. Brad BD6 ... 94 D8
zStadium Way. Hud HD1 ... 154 C7
Stadium Way. Leeds LS11 ... 78 E3
Stadium Way. S Elm WF9 ... 183 B5
Stafford Ave. Hali HX3 ... 113 C4
Stafford Hill La. Kirkhe HD5 ... 155 C8
Stafford Par. Hali HX3 ... 113 C3
Stafford Pl. Hali HX3 ... 113 C4
Stafford Rd. Hali HX3 ... 113 C3
Stafford Sq. Hali HX3 ... 113 D3
Stafford St. Brad BD4 ... 75 B4
Stafford St. Castle WF10 ... 124 C8
Stafford St. Leeds LS10 ... 79 E4
Stafford St. Morley LS27 ... 97 F2
Stafford Terr. Wake WF2 ... 141 F6
Stainbeck Ave. Leeds LS7 ... 59 F6
Stainbeck Gdns. Brad BD6 ... 93 D8
Stainbeck Gdns. Leeds LS7 ... 60 B7
Stainbeck High Sch. Leeds ... 60 B8
Stainbeck La. Leeds LS7 ... 60 B7
Stainbeck Preparatory Sch. Leeds ... 60 B7
Stainbeck Rd. Leeds LS7 ... 60 A7
Stainbeck Rd. Leeds LS7 ... 60 C8
Stainbeck Wlk. Leeds LS7 ... 60 B7
Stainburn Ave. Castle WF10 ... 125 A5
Stainburn Ave. Leeds LS17 ... 43 E1
Stainburn Cres. Leeds LS17 ... 43 E1
Stainburn Dr. Leeds LS17 ... 43 D1
Stainburn Gdns. Leeds LS17 ... 43 E1
Stainburn Mount. Leeds LS17 ... 60 E8
Stainburn Rd. Leeds LS17 ... 60 D8
Stainburn Terr. Leeds LS17 ... 60 D8
Stainburn View. Leeds LS17 ... 43 E1
Staincliffe CE Jun Mix Sch. Batley ... 118 A3
Staincliffe Cres. Batley WF13 ... 117 F2 4
Staincliffe Ct. Sil BD20 ... 5 D1
Staincliffe Hall Rd. Batley WF17 ... 118 A4
Staincliffe House. Brad BD15 ... 73 B7 9
Staincliffe Rd. Dew WF13 ... 118 A1
Staincross Comm. Mapp S75 ... 178 B2
Stainecross Ave. Hud HD4 ... 153 C2
Staines Croft. Hud HD5 ... 154 E6
Stainland Dean. Elland HX4 ... 133 D2
Stainland Rd. Elland HX4 ... 134 C6
Stainland Rd. Hali HX4 ... 113 D1
Stainland Rd. Rip HX4 ... 133 B4
Stainmore Cl. Leeds LS14 ... 62 A3
Stainmore Pl. Leeds LS14 ... 62 A3
Stainton Cl. Brad BD6 ... 93 E8
Stainton La. Roth WF3 ... 100 D3
Stair Foot La. Leeds LS16 ... 42 E5
Staircase La. Bramho LS16, LS21 ... 24 D5
Stairfoot Cl. Hors LS16 ... 42 D5
Stairfoot View. Hors LS16 ... 42 D5
Stairfoot Wlk. Hors LS16 ... 42 D5
Staithe Ave. Midd LS10 ... 99 D5
Staithe Cl. Midd LS10 ... 99 D5
Staithe Gdns. Midd LS10 ... 99 D5 2
Staithgate La. Brad BD6 ... 94 D7
Stake La. Heb Br HX7 ... 110 F7
Stake Lane Bank. Holmfi HD7 ... 189 C4
Stakes Fold. Batley WF16 ... 117 E4
Stallabrass St. Brad BD8 ... 74 C8 4
Stalley Royd La. Holmfi HD7 ... 189 F3
Stamford Ave. Castle WF10 ... 124 A6
Stamford St. Brad BD4 ... 75 B5
Stamford Way. Mapp S75 ... 178 B2
Stammergate La. Coll LS22 ... 13 C2
Stamp Hill Cl. Sil LS29 ... 6 D8
Stan Valley. K Smea WF8 ... 166 E6
Stanacre Pl. Brad BD3 ... 74 F8 3
Stanage La. Shelf HX3 ... 93 C7
Stanally St. Tod OL14 ... 107 E8
Stanbury Fst Sch. Haw ... 50 D6
Stancliffe Way. Kirkhe HD5 ... 137 B1
Stand Bridge Garth. Crig WF4 ... 159 F5
Standale Ave. Pudsey LS28 ... 76 D8
Standale Cres. Pudsey LS28 ... 76 D8
Standale Rise. Pudsey LS28 ... 76 D8
Standard Dr. Hud HD4 ... 153 B2
Standard Ind Est. Brad ... 56 C3
Standbridge Cl. Wake WF2 ... 160 A5
Standbridge Fst Sch. Wake ... 160 A5
Standbridge La. Wake WF2, WF4 ... 160 B6
Standbridge La. Wake WF2 ... 160 C7
Standiforth La. Hud HD5 ... 154 F6
Standiforth Pl. Hud HD5 ... 154 F6
Standiforth Rd. Hud HD5 ... 154 D6
Standish Cres. S Kirk WF9 ... 182 C4
Stanhall Ave. Pudsey LS28 ... 57 D1 3
Stanhope Ave. Caw S75 ... 193 F5
Stanhope Ave. Hors LS18 ... 41 C2
Stanhope Cl. Hors LS18 ... 41 C1
Stanhope Dr. Hors LS18 ... 58 C8
Stanhope Gdns. E Ard WF3 ... 99 E1
Stanhope Gr. E Ard WF3 ... 99 E1
Stanhope Rd. E Ard WF3 ... 99 E1
Stanhope St. Clay W HD8 ... 175 D1
Stanks App. Leeds LS14 ... 62 D4 1
Stanks Ave. Leeds LS14 ... 62 D4
Stanks Cl. Leeds LS14 ... 62 E4
Stanks Cross. Leeds LS14 ... 62 E4
Stanks Dr. Leeds LS14 ... 62 D5
Stanks Garth. Leeds LS14 ... 62 E4
Stanks Gdns. Leeds LS14 ... 62 D5
Stanks Gn. Leeds LS14 ... 62 E4
Stanks Gr. Leeds LS14 ... 62 D4
Stanks La N. Leeds LS14 ... 62 C5
Stanks La S. Leeds LS14 ... 62 D4
Stanks Par. Leeds LS14 ... 62 D4
Stanks Rd. Leeds LS14 ... 62 D4
Stanks Rise. Leeds LS14 ... 62 E5
Stanks Way. Leeds LS14 ... 62 D4
Stanley Ave. Leeds LS9 ... 60 F2 10
Stanley Cotts. Nor WF6 ... 123 A2
Stanley Ct. Hali HX1 ... 112 F7 6
Stanley Dr. Leeds LS8 ... 44 B2
Stanley Gr. Guise LS20 ... 39 E8
Stanley Grove Jun & Inf Sch. Loft G ... 121 F3
Stanley La. Elland HX4 ... 134 A3
Stanley La. Liver WF15 ... 117 A5
Stanley La. Loft G WF1 ... 121 D4
Stanley Lofthouse Gate Jun & Inf Sch. Loft G ... 121 D6
Stanley Newton Hill Cty Prim Sch. Loft G ... 121 C2
Stanley Pl. Batley WF17 ... 118 D5
Stanley Pl. Hud HD7 ... 152 D4
Stanley Pl. Leeds LS9 ... 61 A2 11
Stanley Rd. Brad BD2 ... 55 D4
Stanley Rd. Hali HX1 ... 112 F5
Stanley Rd. Hud HD3 ... 135 A3
Stanley Rd. Hud HD3 ... 135 C1
Stanley Rd. Keigh BD22 ... 35 A4
Stanley Rd. Leeds LS7 ... 60 D3
Stanley Rd. Leeds LS9 ... 61 A2
Stanley Rd. Liver WF15 ... 117 A2
Stanley Rd. Ship BD2 ... 55 D4
Stanley Rd. Wake WF1 ... 142 D7
Stanley Royd Hospl. Wake ... 142 D8
Stanley St. Bing BD16 ... 37 A3
Stanley St. Brad BD10 ... 56 B8
Stanley St. Brad BD10 ... 56 D7
Stanley St. Brig HD6 ... 115 B3
Stanley St. Castle WF10 ... 124 E8
Stanley St. Clec BD19 ... 116 D8
Stanley St. Feath WF7 ... 145 D7
Stanley St. Hali HX6 ... 112 C4
Stanley St. Haw BD22 ... 51 E8
Stanley St. Hud HD1 ... 153 E3
Stanley St. Keigh BD21 ... 35 B8
Stanley St N. Hali HX2 ... 92 A5
Stanley St Peter's CE (C) Sch. Loft G ... 121 F5
Stanley St. Ship BD18 ... 55 C5
Stanley St. Wake WF1 ... 142 D6
Stanley Terr. Leeds LS9 ... 61 A2 10
Stanley Terr. Leeds LS12 ... 78 C7
Stanley View. Leeds LS12 ... 78 C7
Stanley Wrenthorpe Inf Sch. Wake ... 120 F2
Stanley Wrenthorpe Jun Sch. Wake ... 120 F2
Stanmoor Dr. Loft G WF3 ... 121 E6
Stanmore Ave. Leeds LS4 ... 59 C3
Stanmore Cres. Leeds LS4 ... 59 C3
Stanmore Gr. Leeds LS4 ... 59 C3
Stanmore Hill. Leeds LS4 ... 59 D3
Stanmore Mount. Leeds LS4 ... 59 C3
Stanmore Pl. Brad BD7 ... 74 A5
Stanmore Pl. Leeds LS4 ... 59 C3
Stanmore Rd. Leeds LS4 ... 59 C3
Stanmore St. Leeds LS4 ... 59 C3
Stanmore Terr. Leeds LS4 ... 59 C3
Stanmore View. Leeds LS4 ... 59 C3
Stannard Well Dr. Hor WF4 ... 141 B2
Stannard Well La. Hor WF4 ... 141 C2
Stannary Pl. Hali HX1 ... 113 B8
Stannery End La. Heb Br HX7 ... 110 F7
Stanningley Ave. Hali HX2 ... 91 C5
Stanningley By-Pass. Leeds LS13 ... 58 D1
Stanningley By-Pass. Pudsey LS13 ... 58 B1
Stanningley Ct. Pudsey LS28 ... 57 F2 4
Stanningley Dr. Hali HX2 ... 91 C5
Stanningley Field Cl. Leeds LS13 ... 58 A1
Stanningley Gr. Batley WF16 ... 117 D3 7
Stanningley Gn Jun Sch. Hali ... 91 B5
Stanningley Prim Sch. Pudsey ... 57 F2
Stanningley Rd. Hali HX2 ... 91 C5
Stanningley Rd. Leeds LS12, LS13 ... 58 D1
Stanningley Rd. Pudsey LS28 ... 57 F2
Stanningley Sch. Pudsey ... 57 F2
Stansfield Cl. Castle WF10 ... 125 B8
Stansfield Cl. Hali HX1 ... 113 A7
Stansfield Ct. Sow Br HX6 ... 112 B3
Stansfield Dr. Castle WF10 ... 125 C8
Stansfield Gr'ge. Sow Br HX6 ... 111 E1
Stansfield Hall. Litt OL15 ... 129 C1
Stansfield Hall Rd. Tod OL14 ... 108 C6
Stansfield Mill La. Sow Br HX6 ... 111 F1
Stansfield Pl. Brad BD10 ... 39 B1
Stansfield Rd. Castle WF10 ... 125 B8
Stansfield Rd. Tod OL14 ... 108 B5
Stansfield St. Tod OL14 ... 108 B6 8
Stansfield Terr. Tod OL14 ... 86 B1 6
Stanwell Ave. Hud HD2 ... 135 D1
Stanwick House. Ship BD2 ... 55 D4
Stapleton House. Ship BD2 ... 55 D4
Stapper Gn. Wils BD15 ... 53 B6
Star St. Brad BD5 ... 74 C3
Starbeck Rd. Wake WF1 ... 142 E8
Starkey La. Farnh BD20 ... 4 E1
Starkie St. Keigh BD21 ... 35 B6
Starling House. Hem WF9 ... 181 D6
Starting Post. Brad BD10 ... 55 F7
Starwort Cl. Pont WF8 ... 146 D7
Station App. Bur in W LS29 ... 21 E8
Station App. Tod OL14 ... 108 B5
Station Ave. Leeds LS13 ... 58 C2
Station Cl. Gar LS25 ... 82 F7
Station Cotts. Tad LS24 ... 31 C6
Station Cres. Leeds LS12 ... 78 B7
Station Ct. Gar LS25 ... 82 F8
Station Fields. Gar LS25 ... 82 F7
Station Gdns. Weth LS22 ... 13 D5
Station Gr. Glu BD20 ... 16 D7
Station Gr. Leeds LS13 ... 58 C2 12
Station Ind Est. Hali ... 111 D7
Station La. Birk BD11 ... 96 B6
Station La. Coll LS22 ... 29 B8
Station La. E Ard WF3 ... 98 E1
Station La. E Ard WF3 ... 99 D1
Station La. Feath WF7 ... 145 C5
Station La. Hud HD7 ... 152 D3
Station La. Hud HD4 ... 171 F8
Station La. Liver WF16 ... 117 D3
Station La. Pont WF8 ... 146 E8
Station La. Roth LS26 ... 101 D7
Station La. Shep HD8 ... 173 F1
Station La. Thorner LS14 ... 45 F6
Station Mount. Leeds LS13 ... 58 C2
Station Par. Leeds LS5 ... 59 B4
Station Par. Tod OL14 ... 85 F1
Station Pl. Leeds LS13 ... 58 C2
Station Plaza. Ilkley LS29 ... 8 B4
Station Rd. Ack M T WF7 ... 164 C7
Station Rd. Arth LS21 ... 24 F6
Station Rd. B in Elm LS15 ... 62 F6
Station Rd. Bail BD17 ... 38 D3
Station Rd. Batley WF17 ... 118 D4
Station Rd. Birk BD11 ... 96 E6
Station Rd. Brad BD1 ... 55 E2
Station Rd. Brad BD14 ... 73 C4
Station Rd. Brad BD12 ... 94 B2
Station Rd. Brad BD12 ... 94 E5 5
Station Rd. Brig BD12 ... 94 B2
Station Rd. Brig HX3 ... 114 C7
Station Rd. Brig HD6 ... 115 C2
Station Rd. Bur in W LS29 ... 9 E1
Station Rd. Castle WF10 ... 124 D8
Station Rd. Cull BD13 ... 52 D6
Station Rd. Denh BD13 ... 71 E8
Station Rd. Dew WF12 ... 139 C5
Station Rd. Dew WF12 ... 139 F6
Station Rd. Dew WF12 ... 140 A6
Station Rd. Elland HX4 ... 134 C4
Station Rd. Gar LS25 ... 82 F8
Station Rd. Glu BD20 ... 16 D7
Station Rd. Guise LS20 ... 22 D1
Station Rd. Guise BD17 ... 39 C6
Station Rd. Hali HX3 ... 92 A5
Station Rd. Hali HX2 ... 111 D7
Station Rd. Haw BD22 ... 34 D1
Station Rd. Haw BD22 ... 51 D7
Station Rd. Heb Br HX7 ... 89 B2
Station Rd. Hem WF9 ... 181 E7
Station Rd. Holmfi HD7 ... 189 A5
Station Rd. Honley HD7 ... 172 A5
Station Rd. Hors LS18 ... 41 C3
Station Rd. Hud HD2 ... 137 A5
Station Rd. Hud HD7 ... 152 D4
Station Rd. Ilkley LS29 ... 8 B4
Station Rd. Kippax WF10 ... 103 C4
Station Rd. Kirkb HD4 ... 173 C2
Station Rd. Knot WF11 ... 126 C5
Station Rd. Leeds LS15 ... 62 C1
Station Rd. Leeds LS12 ... 78 B7
Station Rd. Lepton HD8 ... 155 D3
Station Rd. Liver WF16 ... 117 D3
Station Rd. M'town LS26 ... 102 C3
Station Rd. Mapp S75 ... 177 E1
Station Rd. Mars HD7 ... 168 F4
Station Rd. Men LS29 ... 22 B4
Station Rd. Mir WF14 ... 138 A4
Station Rd. Morley LS27 ... 98 B5
Station Rd. Nor WF6 ... 122 F3
Station Rd. Ossett WF5 ... 140 E4
Station Rd. Otley LS21 ... 23 A7
Station Rd. Oxen BD22 ... 51 C2
Station Rd. Queen BD13 ... 72 F2
Station Rd. Roy S71 ... 179 B4
Station Rd. Ryhill WF4 ... 162 A1
Station Rd. S Elm WF9 ... 183 A3
Station Rd. Ship BD18 ... 55 B7
Station Rd. Skel HD8 ... 175 A2
Station Rd. Slai HD7 ... 152 A1
Station Rd. Sow Br HX6 ... 112 C3
Station Rd. Stee BD20 ... 17 D6
Station Rd. Tod OL14 ... 86 C1
Station Rd. Wils BD13 ... 53 A4
Station St. Hud HD1 ... 154 A6
Station St. Mel HD7 ... 170 D2
Station St. Pudsey LS28 ... 76 D6
Station St. Wake WF1 ... 142 E2
Station Terr. Kippax WF10 ... 103 C4
Station Terr. Leeds LS13 ... 58 C2
Station Terr. Roy S71 ... 179 E4
Station View. Leeds LS15 ... 62 C1
Station View. Oxen BD22 ... 51 C3
Station View. Stee BD20 ... 17 D5
Station Way. Leeds LS12 ... 78 B7
Station Works Ind Pk. Keigh ... 35 E7
Staups La. B Head OL14 ... 88 A2
Staups La. Northo HX3 ... 92 F1
Staveley Ct. Bing BD16 ... 36 F4
Staveley Dr. Ship BD18 ... 54 D7
Staveley Gr. Keigh BD22 ... 35 A3
Staveley Rd. Bing BD16 ... 37 A4
Staveley Rd. Brad BD7 ... 74 B6
Staveley Rd. Keigh BD22 ... 35 A4
Staveley Rd. Ship BD18 ... 54 D8
Staveley Way. Keigh BD22 ... 35 A4
Stavely Mews. Bing BD16 ... 37 A4 5
Staverton St. Hali HX2 ... 112 E7 1
Staybrite Ave. Ship BD16 ... 54 A7
Staygate Gn. Brad BD6 ... 74 E1
Staynton Cres. Hud HD2 ... 136 F5
Stead Gate. Shep HD8 ... 174 D2
Stead La. Kirkhe HD5 ... 155 B8
Stead La. Rip HX6 ... 132 C2
Stead La. Thorner LS14 ... 45 F5
Stead Rd. Brad BD4 ... 95 E8
Stead St. Hali HX1 ... 113 B7
Stead St. Ship BD17 ... 55 B8
Stead's Yd. Hors LS18 ... 41 C2
Steadman St. Brad BD3 ... 75 B6
Steadman Terr. Brad BD3 ... 75 B6
Steanard La. Mir WF14 ... 138 C3
Steander La. Leeds LS9 ... 79 D7
Steander. Leeds LS9 ... 79 D7
Steele La. Rip HX4 ... 133 C1
Steep La. Sow Br HX6 ... 111 B4
Steep Riding. Honley HD7 ... 172 C3
Steeplands. Hud HD2 ... 136 F6
Steeple Ave. Floc WF4 ... 156 E4
Steeton Gr. Stee BD20 ... 17 C6
Steeton Hall Gdns. Stee BD20 ... 17 D6
Steeton Jun & Inf Sch. Stee ... 17 D5
Steeton & Silsden Sta. Stee ... 17 D6
Stell Hill. Keigh BD22 ... 34 D5
Stella Gdns. Pont WF8 ... 125 F2
Stephen Cl. Northo HX3 ... 93 A1
Stephen Cres. Brad BD2 ... 55 E3
Stephen Rd. Brad BD6 ... 73 F2
Stephen Row. Northo HX3 ... 93 A2
Stephen St. Heb B HX7 ... 89 A3 10
Stephenson Rd. Wils BD15 ... 53 D2
Stephenson St. Brad BD7 ... 74 B3 2
Stephenson Way. Gild LS12 ... 77 D3
Stephensons Way. Ilkley LS29 ... 8 B4
Steps La. Hali HX6 ... 112 C5
Sterling Ind Pk. Castle ... 124 F5
Sterne Hill. Hali HX2 ... 112 F4
Stevenson Ave. Castle WF10 ... 125 C5
Stewart Cl. Brad BD2 ... 56 C5
Stewart Pl. Leeds LS11 ... 79 B3 6
Stewart St. Haw BD22 ... 51 E8
Sticker La. Brad BD4 ... 75 C4
Stile Common Inf Sch. Hud ... 154 A3
Stile Common Jun Sch. Hud ... 154 A3
Stile Common Rd. Hud HD4 ... 154 B3
Stile Hill Way. Leeds LS15 ... 81 E6
Stile Rd. Tod OL14 ... 108 A7
Stilemoor Rise. Tod OL14 ... 108 A7
Stillington House. Ship BD2 ... 55 D4
Stillwell Dr. Wake WF2 ... 160 E8
Stillwell Garth. Wake WF2 ... 160 E8
Stillwell Gr. Wake WF2 ... 160 E8
Stirley Hill. Hud HD4 ... 172 B7
Stirling Cres. Brad BD4 ... 75 E3
Stirling Cres. Hors LS18 ... 41 B4
Stirling Rd. Bur in W LS29 ... 9 D1
Stirling St. Hali HX1 ... 113 B6
Stirling St. Sil BD20 ... 5 E2
Stirling Way. Gar LS25 ... 83 B7
Stirrup Gr. Brad BD2 ... 55 F4
Stirton St. Brad BD5 ... 74 D3 3
Stithy St. Ossett WF5 ... 140 C8
Stock Hey La. Tod OL14 ... 109 C6
Stock La. Hali HX2 ... 112 C7
Stockeld La. Sickl LS22 ... 12 D6
Stockeld Rd. Ilkley LS29 ... 8 A4
Stockeld Way. Ilkley LS29 ... 8 A5
Stockerhead La. Slai HD7 ... 170 A8
Stockheld La. B in Elm LS15 ... 45 F1
Stockheld La. B in Elm LS15 ... 62 F8
Stockhill Fold. Brad BD10 ... 56 D7
Stockhill Rd. Brad BD10 ... 56 D7
Stockhill St. Dew WF13 ... 139 A8
Stocking La. Aber LS25 ... 65 A7
Stocking La. Knot WF11 ... 127 C4
Stockingate. S Kirk WF9 ... 182 B2
Stockinger La. Sil LS29 ... 6 F8
Stocks App. Leeds LS14 ... 62 B4
Stocks Ave. Heb Br HX7 ... 110 D8
Stocks Bank Rd. Mir WF14 ... 137 E6
Stocks Cres. Heb Br HX7 ... 110 D8
Stocks Dr. Shep HD8 ... 190 E8
Stocks Gdns. Heb Br HX7 ... 110 D8
Stocks Hill Cl. Keigh BD20 ... 19 D1
Stocks Hill Cl. Roy S71 ... 179 C1
Stocks Hill. Leeds LS13 ... 58 D3
Stocks Hill. Leeds LS12 ... 78 C8
Stocks Hill. Leeds LS11 ... 79 A5
Stocks Hill. Men LS29 ... 21 F4
Stocks La. Batley WF17 ... 118 C5
Stocks La. Brad BD13 ... 73 B1
Stocks La. Hali HX2 ... 90 E2
Stocks La. Heb Br HX7 ... 110 D8
Stocks La. Kirkb HD4 ... 173 B1
Stocks La. Sow Br HX6 ... 111 E3
Stocks Lane Fst Sch. Brad ... 73 B1
Stocks Moor Rd. Kirkb HD4 ... 173 B2
Stocks Rd. Leeds LS14 ... 62 C4
Stocks Rise. Leeds LS14 ... 62 B4
Stocks St. Leeds LS7 ... 60 C3
Stocks Way. Shep HD8 ... 190 D8
Stocks Wlk. Hud HD5 ... 154 F3
Stocksbank Dr. Mir WF14 ... 137 D6
Stocksmoor Rd. Neth WF4 ... 158 C2
Stocksmoor Sta. Kirkb ... 173 C2
Stockwell Dr. Batley WF17 ... 118 D6
Stockwell Hill. Hud HD4 ... 171 F8
Stockwell Vale. Hud HD4 ... 171 F8
Stod Fold. Hali HX2 ... 91 C8
Stogoen Hill. Brad BD13 ... 73 B1
Stone Acre Ct. Brad BD5 ... 74 E2 3
Stone Acre Hts. Mel HD7 ... 170 F1
Stone Brig Gn. Roth LS26 ... 100 D4
Stone Brig La. Roth LS26 ... 100 D4
Stone Cliffe. Hali HX3 ... 113 A4 1
Stone Ct. Keigh BD20 ... 36 D8
Stone Ct. S Hie S72 ... 180 E5
Stone Dene. Bing BD16 ... 37 A6
Stone Fold. Honley HD7 ... 171 F4
Stone Gr. Stee BD20 ... 17 C6
Stone Hall Rd. Brad BD2 ... 56 B4
Stone Hill. Bing BD16 ... 37 B5
Stone La. Oxen BD22 ... 51 B2
Stone Pits La. Gild LS27 ... 97 D5
Stone St. Bail BD17 ... 38 E2
Stone St. Brad BD15 ... 54 A3
Stone St. Brad BD1 ... 74 E7
Stone St. Clec BD19 ... 116 C7
Stone St. Haw BD22 ... 51 C6 3
Stone Wood La. Shep HD4, HD8 ... 173 D1
Stonebridge App. Leeds LS12 ... 77 E6
Stonebridge Ave. Leeds LS12 ... 77 F6
Stonebridge. Brad BD10 ... 56 B8
Stonebridge Gr. Leeds LS12 ... 77 E6
Stonebridge La. Leeds LS12 ... 77 E6
Stonebridge La. Leeds LS12 ... 77 F6
Stonecliffe Bank. Leeds LS12 ... 77 E6
Stonecliffe Cl. Leeds LS12 ... 77 E6
Stonecliffe Cres. Leeds LS12 ... 77 E6
Stonecliffe Dr. Leeds LS12 ... 77 E6
Stonecliffe Dr. Neth WF4 ... 158 E7
Stonecliffe Garth. Leeds LS12 ... 77 E6
Stonecliffe Gdns. Leeds LS12 ... 77 E6
Stonecliffe Gn. Leeds LS12 ... 77 E6
Stonecliffe Gr. Leeds LS12 ... 77 E6
Stonecliffe Lawn. Leeds LS12 ... 77 E6
Stonecliffe Mount. Leeds LS12 ... 77 E6
Stonecliffe Pl. Leeds LS12 ... 77 E6
Stonecliffe Terr. Leeds LS12 ... 77 E6
Stonecliffe View. Leeds LS12 ... 77 E6
Stonecliffe Way. Leeds LS12 ... 77 E5
Stonecliffe Wlk. Leeds LS12 ... 77 E5
Stonecroft. Brad BD2 ... 56 C4
Stonecroft Gdns. Shep HD8 ... 190 F8
Stonecroft. Loft G WF3 ... 121 E5
Stonedale Cl. Pool LS21 ... 24 E6
Stonefield Ave. Hud HD4 ... 153 B3
Stonefield Cl. Brad BD2 ... 56 B5
Stonefield Pl. Batley WF17 ... 96 F1
Stonefield Rd. Hud HD4 ... 153 B3
Stonefield. Scar LS14 ... 45 B8
Stonefield St. Clec BD19 ... 116 A6
Stonefield St. Dew WF13 ... 118 C1
Stonefield Terr. Morley LS27 ... 98 C8
Stonegate App. Leeds LS7 ... 59 F6
Stonegate. Bing BD16 ... 37 A5
Stonegate Chase. Leeds LS7 ... 59 F7
Stonegate Cl. Leeds LS17 ... 43 D3
Stonegate Cres. Leeds LS7 ... 60 A7
Stonegate Dr. Leeds LS7 ... 60 A7
Stonegate Dr. Pont WF8 ... 146 C6
Stonegate Edge. Leeds LS7 ... 60 A7
Stonegate Farm Cl. Leeds LS7 ... 59 F7
Stonegate Gdns. Leeds LS7 ... 59 F7
Stonegate Gn. Leeds LS7 ... 59 F6
Stonegate Gr. Leeds LS7 ... 60 A7
Stonegate La. Ack M T WF7 ... 163 E5
Stonegate La. Leeds LS7 ... 59 F7
Stonegate. Leeds LS7 ... 60 C3
Stonegate Mews. Leeds LS7 ... 59 F6
Stonegate. Ossett WF5 ... 140 F3
Stonegate Pl. Leeds LS7 ... 59 F6
Stonegate Rd. Brad BD10 ... 56 C6
Stonegate Rd. Leeds LS17 ... 43 C2
Stonegate Sch. Leeds ... 60 A8
Stonegate View. Leeds LS7 ... 59 F7
Stonegate Wlk. Leeds LS7 ... 59 F7
Stonegate Wlk. Leeds LS7 ... 60 A6
Stonehaven Ct. Keigh BD21 ... 35 E5
Stonehurst. Leeds LS14 ... 62 D4
Stonehurst Rd. Mir WF14 ... 138 A6
Stonehyrst Ave. Dew WF13 ... 118 D1
Stonelea Ct. Leeds LS6 ... 59 D5
Stoneleigh Gr. Ossett WF5 ... 140 D5
Stoneleigh. Queen BD13 ... 72 F1 4
Stonely Dr. Tod OL14 ... 129 A7
Stones Bank. Rip HX6 ... 132 C2
Stones Dr. Rip HX6 ... 132 B2
Stones La. Hud HD7 ... 152 D3
Stones La. Slai HD7 ... 170 C8
Stones La. Tod OL14 ... 107 E4
Stones Rd. Tod OL14 ... 107 F4
Stones Terr. Tod OL14 ... 108 A2
Stoney Back La. Hud HD4 ... 153 E2
Stoney Bank La. Holmfi HD7 ... 189 D8
Stoney Bank St. Dew WF13 ... 139 A6
Stoney Battery. Hali HD1 ... 113 C8 5
Stoney Battery Rd. Hud HD1 ... 153 D4
Stoney Butts La. Rip HX4 ... 133 B5
Stoney Croft. Clec BD19 ... 117 B7
Stoney Cross St. Hud HD4 ... 153 F2
Stoney Ford La. Kirkhe HD5 ... 137 B1
Stoney Garth. Crig WF4 ... 159 F3
Stoney Hill. Brig HD6 ... 115 A2
Stoney La. Batley WF17 ... 118 D6
Stoney La. Brig HX3 ... 115 A6
Stoney La. Crig WF4 ... 159 F2
Stoney La. Hali HX3 ... 92 A3
Stoney La. Hors LS18 ... 58 B8
Stoney La. Hud HD3 ... 152 F6
Stoney La. Hud HD4 ... 153 F2
Stoney La. Loft G WF2 ... 120 D5
Stoney La. Men LS29 ... 21 D6
Stoney La. Thorner LS14 ... 45 B5
Stoney Ridge Ave. Brad BD9 ... 54 B4
Stoney Ridge Hospl. Ship ... 54 C5
Stoney Ridge Rd. Ship BD16 ... 54 C5
Stoney Rise. Hors LS18 ... 58 B8
Stoney Rock Ct. Leeds LS9 ... 60 F1
Stoney Rock Gr. Leeds LS9 ... 60 F1
Stoney Rock La. Leeds LS9 ... 60 F1
Stoney Royd La. Tod OL14 ... 107 F7
Stoney Royd Terr. Hali HX3 ... 113 D4
Stoney St. Keigh BD20 ... 18 B2
Stoneybrook Cl. W Bret WF4 ... 176 F8
Stoneycroft. Hors LS18 ... 58 B8 3
Stoneycroft La. Keigh BD20 ... 18 B2
Stoneyhurst Sq. Brad BD4 ... 75 E3
Stoneys Fold. Wils BD15 ... 53 B6
Stoneythorpe. Hors LS18 ... 58 B8 2
Stonlea Dr. Brig HD6 ... 135 F7
Stony Croft La. Rip HX4 ... 133 B5
Stony Gate. Holmfi HD7 ... 188 E2
Stony La. B Head HX7 ... 88 D2
Stony La. Brad BD15 ... 53 F2
Stony La. Brad BD2 ... 56 C5
Stony La. Brig HX3 ... 114 C4
Stony La. Elland HX4 ... 134 A8
Stony La. Honley BD2 ... 171 F3
Stony La. Rip HX6 ... 132 D5
Stony La. Tod OL14 ... 86 E2
Stony Royd La. Heb Br HX7 ... 110 A4
Stony Royd. Pudsey LS28 ... 57 C3
Stoodley Cl. Tod OL14 ... 109 A5
Stoodley Glen. Tod OL14 ... 109 A7
Stoodley Grange. Tod OL14 ... 109 B5
Stoodley La. Heb Br OL14 ... 109 B7
Stoodley Terr. Hali HX2 ... 112 E5
Stopford Ave. Wake WF2 ... 160 E8
Stopford Garth. Wake WF2 ... 160 E8
Storey Pl. Leeds LS14 ... 61 E1
Storie Cres. Wake WF2 ... 141 E4
Storiths Ct. Add LS29 ... 6 F7
Storiths La. Hazl BD23 ... 3 B8
Stormer Hill La. Sow Br HX6 ... 112 D1
Storr Hill. Brad BD12 ... 94 D4
Storrs Hill Rd. Ossett WF5 ... 140 E2
Storth Ave. Hud HD4 ... 152 F3
Storth Pl. Hud HD2 ... 135 F1
Storthes Hall Hospl. Kirkb ... 173 B5
Storthes Hall La. Kirkb HD8 ... 173 C6
Storths Rd. Hud HD2 ... 135 F1
Stotfold Rd. Clay DN5 ... 194 E3
Stott Hill. Brad BD1 ... 74 F7
Stott Rd. Leeds LS6 ... 59 E3
Stott St. Leeds LS12 ... 78 D7
Stott Terr. Brad BD2 ... 56 D4
Stourton Rd. Ilkley LS29 ... 7 F5
Stowe Gr. Leeds LS9 ... 80 C8
Stowell Mill St. Brad BD5 ... 74 D4
Stradmore Rd. Denh BD13 ... 71 E8
Straight La. Add LS29 ... 6 D5
Straight La. Hali HX2 ... 91 D5
Straight La. Ham DN6 ... 184 B4
Straightacres La. Brad BD10 ... 56 D5
Straits. Bail BD17 ... 38 C4 7
Stralau St. Batley WF17 ... 118 C6
Strands Ct. Neth WF4 ... 158 E6
Stranglands La. Castle WF11 ... 126 B5
Stratford Ave. Leeds LS11 ... 79 A3
Stratford Cl. Hud HD7 ... 152 E5
Stratford House. Brad BD15 ... 73 B7 3
Stratford Rd. Brad BD7 ... 74 B5
Stratford St. Leeds LS11 ... 79 B3
Stratford Terr. Leeds LS11 ... 79 B3
Strathallan Dr. Bail BD17 ... 38 D3
Stratheden Rd. Wake WF2 ... 142 A7
Strathmore Ave. Leeds LS9 ... 61 A3
Strathmore Cl. Brad BD2 ... 56 B3
Strathmore Dr. Bail BD17 ... 38 B4
Strathmore Dr. Leeds LS9 ... 61 A3
Strathmore Gdns. S Elm WF9 ... 183 B4
Strathmore Rd. Ilkley LS29 ... 8 E4

Strathmore St. Leeds LS9 61 B2 1
Strathmore Terr. Leeds LS9 61 A3
Strathmore View. Leeds LS9 61 A2
Stratton Rd. Brig HD6 115 C1
Stratton View. Brad BD4 75 E4
Stratton Wlk. Brad BD15 73 A8
Strawberry Ave. Gar LS25 82 E6
Strawberry Ave. Liver WF15 117 A3
Strawberry Bank. Liver WF15 117 A4
Strawberry Fields. Keigh BD21 35 C8 8
Strawberry Gdns. Roy S71 179 D4
Strawberry La. Leeds LS12 78 C7
Strawberry Rd. Leeds LS12 78 C7
Strawberry Sq. Batley WF16 117 D3 2
Strawberry St. Keigh BD21 35 C8
Strawberry St. Sil BD20 5 D1
Stray The. Brad BD10 56 A6
Stream Head Rd. Wils BD13 53 B2
Streamside Cl. Heb Br HX7 110 E8
Streamside. Leeds LS6 59 E6
Street 1. Th Arch LS23 31 A8
Street 2. Th Arch LS23 31 B8
Street 3. Th Arch LS23 15 B1
Street 5. Th Arch LS23 15 B2
Street 6. Th Arch LS23 15 B3
Street 7. Th Arch LS23 15 C2
Street 8. Th Arch LS23 15 D2
Street Furlong La. Pont WF8 147 B7
Street Head La. Haw BD22 50 E8
Street La. Gild LS27 97 C6
Street La. H Pag DN5 195 F3
Street La. Keigh BD20 19 C2
Street La. Leeds LS17 43 E2
Street The. Sil LS29 6 D8
Streethouse Sta. Feath 144 D5
Strensall Gn. Brad BD6 93 E8 11
Stretch Gate. Shep HD8 173 F2
Stretchgate La. Hali HX2 112 E8
Strickland Ave. Thorner LS17 45 A4
Strickland Cl. Thorner LS17 44 F4
Strickland Cres. Thorner LS17 44 F4
Strickland Rd. Upton WF9 183 D8
Strike La. Shep HD8 174 F3
Strikes La. S in Cra BD20 16 E3
Strines Moor Rd. Holmfi HD7 199 C8
Strines St. Tod OL14 129 A7
Stringer House La. Emley HD8 175 A7
Stringer La. Hor WF4 141 B1 4
Strong Close Gr. Keigh BD21 35 E7
Strong Close Rd. Keigh BD21 35 E7
Strong Close Way. Keigh BD21 35 E7
Stuart Gr. Nor WF6 123 A4
Stuart Gr. Slai HD7 170 A8
Stuart Pl. Hud HD2 136 F5
Stuart Rd. Pont WF8 125 C1
Stuart St. Castle WF10 124 E8
Stuart St. Pont WF8 125 C1
Stubbin La. D Dale HD8 192 B6
Stubbin La. Holmfi HD7 188 C3
Stubbin Rd. Mars HD7 169 B5
Stubbing Brink. Heb Br HX7 88 E3
Stubbing Dr. Heb Br HX7 88 E3
Stubbing Holme Rd.Heb Br HX7 88 E3
Stubbing La. Elland HX4 133 E5
Stubbing La. Sow Br HX6 132 E8
Stubbing Way. Ship BD18 55 C6
Stubbings Cl. Heb Br HX7 110 E8
Stubbings Inf Sch. Heb Br 89 A3
Stubbings Rd. Bail BD17 37 F2
Stubbings St. Heb Br HX7 110 E8
Stubbins. Sow Br HX6 132 E8
Stubbs La. E Ard WF3 120 E7
Stubham Rise. Ilkley LS29 8 A5
Stubley Farm Rd. Batley WF16 117 D6
Stubley Holme. Tod OL14 86 A1
Stubley La. Tod OL14 86 B1
Stubley Rd. Batley WF16 117 C6
Stubley St. Wake WF1 142 B6
Studfold View. Leeds LS14 62 A2
Studio Rd. Leeds LS3 59 E1
Studleigh Terr. Brig HD6 114 E5
Studley Ave. Brad BD6 94 B7
Studley Cl. Keigh BD20 19 D1
Studley Cres. Bing BD16 37 B3
Studley Rd. Brad BD3 55 F2
Stumpcross Cl. Pont WF8 125 F3
Stumpcross Ct. Pont WF8 125 F3
Stumpcross La. Pont WF8 125 F3
Stumpcross Way. Pont WF8 125 F3
Stunsteds Rd. Clec BD19 116 D8
Sturges Gr. Brad BD2 56 B1
Sturton Ave. Gar LS25 83 A7
Sturton Gr. Hali HX2 91 E6
Sturton Grange La. Gar LS25 83 C7
Sturton La. Gar LS25 83 A8
Sturton La. Hali HX2 91 E7
Stutely Gr. Hud HD2 136 E5
Sty La. Bing BD16 36 F6
Styebank La. Roth LS26 100 F6
Styes La. Sow Br HX6 111 D4
Styveton Way. Stee BD20 17 B6
Sude Hill. Holmfi HD7 189 F6
Sude Hill Terr. Holmfi HD7 189 F6
Sudforth La. Beal DN14 127 F5
Suffolk Ave. Batley WF17 118 B3
Suffolk Cl. Ossett WF5 140 C4
Suffolk Ct. Yeadon LS19 40 B7
Suffolk House. Wake WF1 142 F3
Suffolk Pl. Brad BD2 55 F4
Suffolk St. Batley WF17 118 B4
Sufton St. Hud HD2 135 F1
Sugar Hill Cl. Roth LS26 101 C3
Sugar Hill. Sil LS29 6 F8
Sugar La. Dew WF12 139 E8
Sugar La. Wake WF1 142 E3
Sugar Well App. Leeds LS7 60 A5
Sugar Well Mount. Leeds LS7 60 A5
Sugar Well Rd. Leeds LS7 60 A5
Sugarwell Ct. Leeds LS7 60 B4
Sugden St. Brad BD1 74 C7
Sugden St. Brad BD12 94 F4
Sugden's Almshouses. Haw BD22 34 E3
Sulby Gr. Brad BD10 56 E7
Sullivan Cl. Hud HD4 153 D3
Sullivan Gr. S Kirk WF9 182 B1
Summer Hall Ing. Brad BD12 94 C4
Summer Hill Rd. M'town LS26 102 D2
Summer Hill St. Brad BD7 74 A5
Summer La. Emley HD8 175 D6
Summer La. Roy S71 179 B4
Summer Meadow. Pont WF8 146 C7
Summer Rd. Roy S71 179 B4
Summer St. Hali HX1 112 F5 25
Summer St. Hud HD1, HD4 153 F4
Summer St. Hud HD4 171 D7
Summerbridge Cl. Batley WF17 118 A6
Summerbridge Cr. Brad BD10 56 D5
Summerbridge Cres. Clec BD19 96 C2
Summerbridge Dr. Brad BD10 56 D5
Summerdale. Clec BD19 96 B2
Summerfield Ave. Brig HD6 115 B6
Summerfield Ave. Leeds LS13 58 A3
Summerfield Cl. Bail BD17 38 B3
Summerfield Cl. Byram WF11 126 E8
Summerfield Dr. Bail BD17 38 B3
Summerfield Dr. Byram WF11 126 E8
Summerfield Dr. Leeds LS13 58 A3
Summerfield Gdns. Leeds LS13 58 A3
Summerfield Gn. Bail BD17 38 B3
Summerfield Gn. Leeds LS13 58 A3
Summerfield Gr. Bail BD17 38 B3
Summerfield Gr. Lepton HD8 155 D2
Summerfield Pk. Bail BD17 38 B3
Summerfield Pl. Leeds LS13 58 A3
Summerfield Prim Sch. Pudsey 57 F3
Summerfield Rd. Brad BD10 56 C6
Summerfield Rd. Leeds LS13 58 A3
Summerfield Rd. Tod OL14 108 D5
Summerfield Rd W. Tod OL14 108 C5
Summergate Pl. Hali HX1 112 F6
Summergate St. Hali HX1 112 F6
Summerhill Ave. Stee BD20 17 D6
Summerhill Dr. Stee BD20 17 D6
Summerhill Gdns. Leeds LS8 44 B2
Summerhill Gr. Gar LS25 82 D6
Summerhill La. Stee BD20 17 D6
Summerhill Pl. Leeds LS8 44 B3
Summerhill Rd. Gar LS25 82 D6
Summerlands Gr. Brad BD5 75 A2
Summerscale St. Hali HX1 113 A8 4
Summerseat Pl. Brad BD7 74 C5
Summervale. Holmfi HD7 189 A6
Summerville Rd. Brad BD7 74 C6
Summerville Rd. Pudsey LS28 57 C2
Summit St. Keigh BD21 35 B8
Sun Ct. Feath WF7 145 C8
Sun Field. Pudsey LS28 57 D1
Sun Fold. Hali HX1 113 D6
Sun Hill Dr. Bail BD17 37 E3
Sun La. Bur in W LS29 9 E2
Sun La. Haw BD22 50 E7
Sun La. Wake WF1 142 D6
Sun St. Brad BD1 74 F8
Sun St. Haw BD22 51 C6
Sun St. Keigh BD20 19 E1
Sun St. Keigh BD21 35 C6
Sun St. Pudsey LS28 57 E1
Sun St. Stee BD20 17 A5
Sun St. Yeadon LS19 40 C7
Sun Terr. Tod OL14 86 B1
Sun Vale Ave. Tod OL14 129 B7
Sun Way. Hali HX3 113 F5
Sun Wood Ave. Shelf HX3 93 B4
Sunbeam Ave. Leeds LS11 79 B3
Sunbeam Gr. Leeds LS11 79 B3 9
Sunbeam Pl. Leeds LS11 79 B3
Sunbeam Terr. Leeds LS11 79 B3
Sunbridge Rd. Brad BD1 74 D7
Sunbury Gr. Hud HD5 154 E6
Sunderland Ct. Brig HD6 115 A3 6
Sunderland Rd. Brad BD9 55 C2
Sunderland Rd. L Brad BD20 4 D5
Sunderland St. Hali HX1 113 B7 7
Sunderland St. Haw BD22 51 F8
Sunderland St. Keigh BD21 35 B6
Sundown Ave. Brad BD7 73 E4
Sunfield Cl. Pudsey LS28 57 D2
Sunfield Dr. Pudsey LS28 57 D2
Sunfield Gdns. Pudsey LS28 57 D2
Sunfield Pl. Pudsey LS28 57 D2
Sunfield Terr. Clec BD19 116 E7 11
Sunhurst Cl. Haw BD22 34 C2
Sunhurst Dr. Haw BD22 34 C2
Sunningdale Ave. Leeds LS17 43 A4
Sunningdale Ave. Mapp S75 178 A1
Sunningdale. Brad BD8 73 D8
Sunningdale Cl. Leeds LS17 43 A4
Sunningdale Cres. Cull BD13 52 E5
Sunningdale Ct. Hud HD2 135 F3
Sunningdale Dr. Cud S72 180 C1
Sunningdale Dr. Leeds LS17 43 A4
Sunningdale Gn. Leeds LS17 43 A4
Sunningdale. M'Field LS25 83 F8
Sunningdale Rd. Hud HD4 153 D3
Sunningdale Way. Leeds LS17 43 A4
Sunningdale Wlk. Leeds LS17 43 A4
Sunny Ave. S Elm WF9 183 B2
Sunny Ave. Upton WF9 183 A7
Sunny Bank Ave. Brad BD5 74 D1
Sunny Bank Ave. Mir WF14 138 A8
Sunny Bank. Brad BD9 54 D2
Sunny Bank Dr. Hali HX6 112 C4
Sunny Bank Dr. Mir WF14 137 F8
Sunny Bank Gr. Leeds LS8 60 F5
Sunny Bank Gr. Mir WF14 138 A7
Sunny Bank. Heb Br HX7 89 F1
Sunny Bank. Hem WF9 163 A3
Sunny Bank. Knot WF11 127 A4
Sunny Bank La. Batley WF17 118 D7
Sunny Bank La. Brig HX3 114 B6
Sunny Bank La. Heb Br HX7 110 D8
Sunny Bank. Leeds LS8 60 F5
Sunny Bank. Nor WF6 144 B7
Sunny Bank Par. Mir WF14 137 F8
Sunny Bank Rd. Batley WF17 118 D6
Sunny Bank Rd. Brad BD5 74 D1
Sunny Bank Rd. Brig HD6 115 A2
Sunny Bank Rd. Glu BD20 16 C6
Sunny Bank Rd. Hali HX2 91 C5
Sunny Bank Rd. Mel HD7 170 C2
Sunny Bank Rd. Mir WF14 138 A8
Sunny Bank Rd. Slai HD7 152 B3
Sunny Bank Rd. Wad M HX7 69 A3
Sunny Bank. Ryhill WF4 162 A1
Sunny Bank. Ship BD18 55 B7
Sunny Bank St. Hali HX6 112 C4
Sunny Bank Terr. Hali HX3 92 C1 4
Sunny Bank Terr. Tod OL14 86 B1 9
Sunny Bank View. Leeds LS8 60 F5
Sunny Bank Wlk. Mir WF14 138 A7
Sunny Brow. Hud HD4 171 F8
Sunny Brow La. Brad BD9 54 D2
Sunny Dale. Denh BD13 52 D2
Sunny Gr. Morley LS27 98 C8 5
Sunny Heys Rd. Mel HD7 170 D3
Sunny Heys W. Mel HD7 170 D2
Sunny Hill Ave. Keigh BD21 34 F5
Sunny Hill Gr. Keigh BD21 34 F5
Sunny Hill. Wake WF2 120 E1
Sunny Mead. Hud HD5 155 A6
Sunny Mount. Brig HX3 114 C7
Sunny Mount. Harden BD16 36 B1
Sunny Mount. Keigh BD22 34 E8
Sunny Mount. Keigh BD21 35 B8
Sunny Mount. Keigh BD20 36 C7
Sunny Side St. Hali HX3 92 C1 1
Sunny Vale Country Club. Brig 114 C6
Sunny View Cres. Hud HD2 136 D3
Sunny View Terr. Queen BD13 92 C8 4
Sunnybank Ave. Brad BD3 56 F1
Sunnybank Ave. Hors LS18 58 B7 4
Sunnybank Cl. Brig BD19 115 F7
Sunnybank Cres. Elland HX4 134 B7
Sunnybank Cres. Yeadon LS19 40 D7
Sunnybank Ct. Yeadon LS19 40 D7
Sunnybank. D Dale HD8 191 F5
Sunnybank Dr. Elland HX4 134 B7
Sunnybank Gr. Brad BD3 56 F1
Sunnybank Grange. Brig HD6 115 A2 1
Sunnybank La. Brad BD3 56 F1
Sunnybank La. Elland HX4 134 B7
Sunnybank. M'field LS25 84 B6
Sunnybank Rd. Elland HX4 134 B7
Sunnybank Rd. Hors LS18 58 B7 6
Sunnybank Rd. Hud HD3 153 D8
Sunnybank St. Ossett WF5 140 D5
Sunnybank Terr. Brig HD6 115 A3
Sunnybrae Cres. Bing BD16 37 B2
Sunnycliffe. Keigh BD20 36 D8
Sunnydale Ave. Brig HD6 136 A8
Sunnydale Cres. Otley LS21 22 D6
Sunnydale Croft. Ossett WF5 140 E4
Sunnydale Gr. Keigh BD21 35 F6
Sunnydale Pk. Keigh BD20 19 E2
Sunnydale Pk. Ossett WF5 140 E5
Sunnydale Rd. Ossett WF5 140 F5
Sunnydale Ridge. Otley LS21 22 D6
Sunnydale Terr. Ossett WF5 140 E5
Sunnydene. Leeds LS14 61 F1
Sunnyfield Ave. H Chap BB10 85 A8
Sunnyfield Dr. Hem WF9 163 A3
Sunnyfield. E Ard WF3 120 C7
Sunnyhill Cres. Wake WF2 120 D1
Sunnyhill Croft. Wake WF2 120 E2
Sunnylea. Mars HD7 169 A4
Sunnymead. Clay W HD8 175 E2
Sunnymount Terr. Batley WF17 96 F1 5
Sunnyridge Ave. Pudsey LS28 76 B8
Sunnyside Ave. E Ard WF3 119 D8
Sunnyside Ave. Liver WF15 116 F2
Sunnyside. Batley WF16 117 D3
Sunnyside. Brig HD6 136 D8
Sunnyside. Elland HX4 134 A1
Sunnyside. Hud HD2 153 E8
Sunnyside La. Brad BD3 55 F1
Sunnyside Rd. Leeds LS13 58 B1
Sunnyside. Tod OL14 108 A5
Sunnyvale Mount. S Elm WF9 182 E3
Sunnyview Ave. Leeds LS11 78 F3
Sunnyview. E Ard WF3 120 C6
Sunnyview Gdns. Leeds LS11 78 F3
Sunnyview Terr. Leeds LS11 78 F3
Sunroyd Ave. Hor WF4 141 B2
Sunroyd Hill. Hor WF4 141 B2
Sunset Ave. Leeds LS6 59 E8
Sunset Dr. Ilkley LS29 8 D5
Sunset Dr. Leeds LS6 59 E7 6
Sunset Hilltop. Leeds LS6 59 E8
Sunset Mount. Leeds LS6 59 E7 5
Sunset Rd. Leeds LS6 59 E7
Sunset Rise. Leeds LS6 59 E8
Sunset Terr. Ilkley LS29 8 E5
Sunset View. Leeds LS6 59 E8
Surat Rd. Slai HD7 151 F3
Suresnes Rd. Keigh BD21 35 B7
Surgery St. Haw BD22 51 D6
Surrey Gr. Brad BD5 74 E4
Surrey Gr. Pudsey LS28 76 E8
Surrey Rd. Pudsey LS28 76 E8 4
Surrey St. Batley WF17 118 D5
Surrey St. Hali HX1 112 F6
Surrey St. Keigh BD21 35 E8
Surrey St. Tod OL14 108 B6
Sussex App. Leeds LS10 79 F3
Sussex Ave. Hors LS18 41 C3
Sussex Ave. Leeds LS10 79 F3
Sussex Cl. Hem WF9 181 D8
Sussex Cres. Castle WF10 125 E8
Sussex Gdns. Leeds LS10 79 F3
Sussex Gn. Leeds LS10 79 F3
Sussex Pl. Leeds LS10 79 F3
Sussex St. Batley WF17 118 D5
Sussex St. Keigh BD21 35 E8
Sussex St. Leeds LS9 79 F7
Sussex Wlk. Dew WF13 139 B8 2
Sutcliffe Pl. Brad BD6 94 D8 6
Sutcliffe St. Hali HX2 112 E8
Sutcliffe Wood La. Brig HX3 114 C6
Sutherland Ave. Leeds LS8 44 A2
Sutherland Cres. Leeds LS8 44 A2
Sutherland Dr. Hud HD4 153 C2
Sutherland Mount. Leeds LS9 61 A2
Sutherland Rd. Brig HX3 114 E8
Sutherland Rd. Leeds LS9 61 A2
Sutherland St. Leeds LS12 78 E6
Sutherland Terr. Leeds LS9 61 A2
Sutton App. Leeds LS14 61 E1
Sutton Ave. Brad BD2 56 A4
Sutton Ave. Hud HD5 155 A7
Sutton Cres. Brad BD4 75 E5
Sutton Cres. Leeds LS14 61 E1
Sutton Dr. Cull BD13 52 D5
Sutton Dr. Hud HD5 155 A8
Sutton Fields. Glu BD20 16 C6
Sutton Gr. Brad BD4 75 E5
Sutton Gr. Morley LS27 98 A3 2
Sutton La. Byram WF11 126 E7
Sutton La. S in Cra BD20 16 E5
Sutton Rd. Brad BD4 75 E5
Sutton St. Leeds LS12 78 F6
Sutton-in-Craven CE Prim Sch. S in Cra 16 D5
Sutton-in-Craven Cty Prim Sch. S in Cra 16 D5
Suzanne Cres. S Elm WF9 182 E3
Swain House Cres. Brad BD2 56 A5
Swain House Fst & Mid Schs. Brad 56 A5
Swain House Rd. Brad BD2 56 A5
Swain Mount. Brad BD2 56 A5
Swaine Hill Cres. Yeadon LS19 40 A7
Swaine Hill St. Yeadon LS19 40 A7
Swaine Hill Terr. Yeadon LS19 40 A7
Swale Cres. Gar LS25 83 B6
Swale Ct. Sil BD20 17 E8
Swale Dr. Castle WF10 125 B8
Swale Rise. Weth LS22 13 D8
Swales Moor Rd. Hali HX3 92 C4
Swales' Yd. Pont WF8 146 C8 5
Swallow Ave. Leeds LS12 78 A6
Swallow Cl. Leeds LS17 43 F4
Swallow Cl. Pool LS21 24 D6
Swallow Cres. Leeds LS12 78 A6
Swallow Dr. Leeds LS17 44 A4
Swallow Dr. Morley LS27 98 D4
Swallow Dr. Pool LS21 24 D6
Swallow Fold. Brad BD8 73 C7
Swallow Garth. Wake WF2 160 D5
Swallow Gr. Hud HD4 171 E6
Swallow Hill. Batley WF17 118 A8
Swallow La. Hud HD7 152 C5
Swallow La. Slai HD7 152 C5
Swallow Mount. Leeds LS12 78 A6
Swallow St. Hud HD1 154 A5 1
Swallow St. Keigh BD21 35 D8 5
Swallow St. Liver WF16 117 D3
Swan Bank La. Hali HX3 113 D5
Swan Bank La. Holmfi HD7 189 A4
Swan La. Elland HD3 134 B1
Swan La. Hud HD1 153 E3
Swan St. Brad BD5 74 E6
Swan St. Leeds LS1 79 C8
Swanhill La. Pont WF8 146 D7
Swarcliffe App. Leeds LS14 62 C4
Swarcliffe Ave. Leeds LS14 62 D5
Swarcliffe Bank. Leeds LS14 62 C4
Swarcliffe Dr. Leeds LS14 62 C4
Swarcliffe Drive E. Leeds LS14 62 D4 2
Swarcliffe Gn. Leeds LS14 62 C4
Swarcliffe Mid Sch. Leeds 62 C5
Swarcliffe Par. Leeds LS14 62 C4
Swarcliffe Rd. Leeds LS14 62 C5
Swarcliffe Towers. Leeds LS14 62 D5 9
Swardale Gn. Leeds LS14 62 C4
Swardale Rd. Leeds LS14 62 C4
Swarland Gr. Brad BD5 74 E5
Swartha La. Add BD20 6 A2
Sweep La. Holmfi HD7 189 B3
Sweet St. Leeds LS11 79 B6
Sweet St W. Leeds LS11 79 A6
Swift Pl. Rip HX6 132 B2
Swift Way. Wake WF2 160 D5
Swift's Fold. Honley HD7 171 F5
Swillington La. Swil LS26 82 A4
Swillington Prim Sch. Swil 82 A2
Swincar Ave. Yeadon LS19 40 B7
Swincliffe Cl. Birk BD19 96 A4
Swincliffe Cres. Birk BD19 96 B3
Swincroft. Ossett WF5 140 E5
Swindon Rd. Dew WF13 139 C8
Swine La. Keigh BD20 36 B8
Swine La. W Har WF4 162 D5
Swine Market La. Heb Br HX7 110 A3
Swinegate. Leeds LS1 79 C7
Swineshead La. Tod OL14 108 B3
Swineshead Rd. Tod OL14 108 A3
Swinnow Ave. Pudsey LS13 58 A1
Swinnow Cl. Pudsey LS13 58 A1
Swinnow Cres. Pudsey LS28 58 A2
Swinnow Dr. Pudsey LS13 58 A1
Swinnow Garth. Pudsey LS13 58 A1
Swinnow Gdns. Pudsey LS13 58 A1
Swinnow Gn. Pudsey LS28 77 A8
Swinnow Gr. Pudsey LS13 58 A1
Swinnow La. Leeds LS13 58 A1
Swinnow La. Pudsey LS13 LS28 77 B8
Swinnow Mid Sch. Pudsey 77 A8
Swinnow Pl. Pudsey LS13 58 A2
Swinnow Rd. Pudsey LS13 58 B1
Swinnow View. Leeds LS13 58 A1
Swinnow Wlk. Pudsey LS13 58 A1
Swinton Pl. Brad BD7 74 B5
Swinton Terr. Hali HX1 112 F5
Swire Smith Mid Sch. Keigh 35 E6
Swires Rd. Brad BD2 56 C1
Swires Rd. Hali HX1 113 B6
Swires Terr. Hali HX1 113 B6
Swiss St. Castle WF10 103 E1
Swithen Hill. Kex S75 177 B3
Swithen's La. Roth LS26 100 F4
Swithen's St. Roth LS26 100 F4
Swithenbank Ave. Ossett WF5 140 D8
Swithenbank St. Ossett WF5 119 C1
Swithens Ct. Roth LS26 100 F4
Swithens Dr. Roth LS26 100 F4
Swithens Gr. Roth LS26 100 E4
Sycamore Ave. Bing BD16 36 F2
Sycamore Ave. Brad BD7 73 F6
Sycamore Ave. Hud HD3, HD7 152 F5
Sycamore Ave. Kippax LS25 82 F2
Sycamore Ave. Knot WF11 126 D3
Sycamore Ave. Leeds LS8 60 F5
Sycamore Ave. Leeds LS15 81 A8
Sycamore Ave. Mel HD7 170 D1
Sycamore Ave. Tod OL14 108 A7
Sycamore Ave. Wake WF2 120 F3
Sycamore Ave. Wake WF2 141 F7
Sycamore Chase. Pudsey LS28 76 F7
Sycamore Cl. Brad BD3 75 A8
Sycamore Cl. Bramho LS16 24 F1
Sycamore Cl. Knot WF11 126 D2
Sycamore Cl. Leeds LS6 60 A4
Sycamore Cl. Lepton HD8 155 F3
Sycamore Copse. Wake WF2 141 F5
Sycamore Croft. Leeds LS11 79 B3
Sycamore Ct. Brad BD3 75 A8
Sycamore Ct. Hud HD8 152 F5
Sycamore Ct. Ilkley LS29 8 A5
Sycamore Ct. Kirkb HD8 173 F7
Sycamore Dr. Add LS29 7 A8
Sycamore Dr. Brig HX3 115 A6
Sycamore Dr. Clec BD19 116 B7
Sycamore Dr. Elland HX5 134 E6
Sycamore Dr. Roy S71 179 A3
Sycamore Fold. Leeds LS11 79 B3
Sycamore Gn. Pont WF8 125 F1
Sycamore Gr. Nor WF6 144 A8
Sycamore Gr. Stee BD20 16 F5
Sycamore Gr. Wake WF2 141 F7
Sycamore Ho. Castle WF10 124 E7 5
Sycamore Ind Est. Batley 117 D2
Sycamore La. W Bret WF4 176 F8
Sycamore Rd. Hem WF9 181 C6
Sycamore Rise. Holmfi HD7 189 D7
Sycamore Row. Leeds LS13 58 A4
Sycamore St. Wake WF1 142 E4
Sycamore Terr. Honley HD7 171 E3
Sycamore Terr. Hor WF4 159 C8
Sycamore View. Keigh BD22 34 F6
Sycamore Way. Batley WF17 96 F1
Sycamore Way. Feath WF7 145 D6
Sycamore Wlk. Dearne S63 194 D1
Sycamore Wlk. Pudsey LS28 57 D2
Sycamores The. Bramho LS16 24 F1
Sycamores The. Dew WF13 118 B2
Sycamores The. Guise LS20 22 E2
Sycamores The. Hor WF4 141 C1
Sydenham Pl. Brad BD3 56 A2
Sydenham Rd. Leeds LS11 78 F6 3
Sydenham St. Leeds LS11 78 F6
Sydney Gdns. Litt OL15 129 C1
Sydney St. Bing BD16 37 A3 12
Sydney St. Liver WF15 117 B3
Sydney St. Pudsey LS28 57 D2
Sydney St. Roth LS26 101 D6
Syke Ave. Dew WF12 139 F8
Syke Ave. E Ard WF3 119 D7
Syke Cl. E Ard WF3 119 C7
Syke Gdns. E Ard WF3 119 D7
Syke Gn. Scar LS14 45 C8
Syke Gr. Dew WF12 139 F8
Syke House La. Elland HX4 133 F7
Syke Ing Cl. Dew WF12 140 A7
Syke Ing Terr. Dew WF12 140 A7
Syke La. Brig HX3 93 E1
Syke La. Dew WF12 139 F7
Syke La. Hali HX2 71 E2
Syke La. Queen BD13 92 F7
Syke La. Scar LS14 45 B8
Syke La. Sow Br HX6 112 B3
Syke Rd. Dew WF12 139 F8
Syke Rd. E Ard WF3 119 D7
Syke Rd. Weth LS22 14 A5
Syke Side. Keigh BD20 18 B2
Syke St. Dew WF12 139 F7
Syke Terr. E Ard WF3 119 C7
Syke View. Dew WF12 139 F8
Sykes Ave. Batley WF16 117 E5
Sykes Ave. Mir WF14 138 C6
Sykes Cl. Ack M T WF7 163 D5
Sykes Cl. Batley WF17 118 E6
Sykes Fold. Oxen BD22 51 E1
Sykes Gate. Heb Br HX7 131 C7
Sykes La. Batley WF12 119 A4
Sykes La. Brad BD12 95 A4
Sykes La. Haw BD22 34 D2
Sykes Rd. Batley WF17 118 E6
Sykes St. Castle WF10 124 D8 9
Sykes St. Clec BD19 116 D7
Sylhet Cl. Brad BD1 74 D8
Sylvan Ave. Queen BD13 92 D8
Sylvester Ave. Nor WF6 144 A7
Symons St. Wake WF2 142 B5
Syringa Ave. Brad BD15 54 A4
Syringa St. Hud HD1 153 D7

Tabbs Ct. Brig BD19 94 F1
Tabbs La. Brig BD19 94 F1
Tadcaster Grammar Sch. Tad 31 D2
Tadman St. Wake WF1 142 C4
Talbot and Falcon Yd. Wake WF1 142 C6 8
Talbot Ave. Hud HD3 135 C1
Talbot Ave. Leeds LS17, LS8 43 F2
Talbot Ave. Leeds LS4 59 C3
Talbot Cty Prim Sch. Leeds 43 F2
Talbot Cres. Leeds LS8 43 F2
Talbot Gdns. Leeds LS8 43 F2
Talbot Gr. Leeds LS8 43 F2
Talbot House. Elland HX5 134 F6 2
Talbot Mount. Leeds LS4 59 C3
Talbot Rd. Leeds LS8 43 F1
Talbot Rise. Leeds LS17 43 F2
Talbot Row. Batley WF17 118 D5
Talbot St. Batley WF17 118 C4
Talbot St. Brad BD7 74 C7
Talbot St. Keigh BD21 35 A7 4
Talbot St. Nor WF6 123 A2
Talbot Terr. Leeds LS4 59 C3
Talbot Terr. Roth LS26 100 E4
Talbot View. Leeds LS4 59 C3
Talbot View. Mir WF14 138 A6
Tall Trees Dr. Feath WF7 145 D8
Tamar St. Brad BD5 74 C4
Tammy Hall St. Wake WF1 142 C6 3
Tamworth St. Brad BD4 75 E6
Tan House Ct. Brad BD4 95 B7
Tan House La. Ack M T WF7 164 B7
Tan House La. Shelf HX3 93 A5
Tan House La. Wils BD15 53 B6
Tan La. Brad BD4 95 B6
Tan Pit Cl. Clay DN5 194 D4
Tan Pit La. Clay DN5 194 D4
Tandem Ind Est. Kirkhe 155 B6
Tandem Way. Kirkhe HD5 155 B6
Tandy Trad Est The. Leeds 59 D1
Tanfield Cl. Roy S71 179 A4
Tanfield Rd. Hud HD1 153 F8
Tanglewood Ct. Brad BD6 74 A1 2
Tanhouse Hill. Brig HX3 114 C7
Tanhouse Hill. Hors LS18 58 E8 2
Tanhouse La. Lepton WF14 156 B7
Tanhouse Pk. Brig HX3 114 C7
Tanhouse St. Dew WF13 138 F6
Tanner Hill Rd. Brad BD7 73 E3
Tanner St. Clec WF15 116 B5
Tannerbrook Cl. Brad BD14 73 D4
Tanners. Slai HD7 169 F7
Tannett Gn. Brad BD5 74 F2
Tanpits. Heb Br HX7 89 A3 23
Tanshelf Dr. Pont WF8 146 C8
Tanshelf Ind Est. Pont 125 C1
Tanshelf Sta. Pont 125 C1
Tansy End. Oxen BD22 51 E2
Tanton Cres. Brad BD14 73 D4
Tanton Wlk. Brad BD14 73 D4
Tanyard Ave. Hud HD3 153 A7
Tanyard Fold. Crig WF4 160 A3
Tanyard Rd. Hud HD3 153 A7
Tanyard Rd. Hud HD3 153 B4
Tarn Cl. Castle WF10 104 E1
Tarn Ct. Keigh BD20 34 F8
Tarn Ct. Loft G WF1 121 B3
Tarn La. Bard LS17 44 E7
Tarn La. Hare LS17 44 E7
Tarn La. Keigh BD22 34 B8
Tarn Rd. Feath WF7 145 E4
Tarn View Rd. Yeadon LS19 40 D7
Tarnhill Mews. Brad BD5 74 E4
Tarnside Dr. Leeds LS14 62 A3
Tate Naylor St. Dew WF13 118 B2
Tatefield Gr. Kippax LS25 83 A1
Tatefield Pl. Kippax LS25 83 A1
Tateley La. Ossett WF5 119 C1
Tatham Way. Leeds LS8 61 C6
Tatton St. Wake WF1 142 F3
Taunton St. Ship BD18 55 A8
Tavern St. Wake WF1 142 D6
Taverngate. Guise LS20 38 E8
Tavora St. Wake WF1 142 C7
Tawny Cl. Morley LS27 98 D4 1
Tay Ct. Brad BD2 56 D5
Taylor Ave. Sil BD20 5 D1
Taylor Cl. Ossett WF5 140 F4
Taylor Cres. Ossett WF5 140 F4
Taylor Dr. Ossett WF5 140 F4
Taylor Gr. M'town LS26 102 E3
Taylor Hall La. Mir WF14 116 E1
Taylor Hall La. Mir WF14 137 F8
Taylor Hill Rd. Hud HD4 153 E1
Taylor La. B in Elm LS15 63 B5
Taylor La. Hali BD13 72 A3
Taylor La. Slai HD7 152 B5
Taylor Rd. Brad BD6 94 D8 10
Taylor St. Batley WF17 118 C4
Taylor St. Clec BD19 116 C7
Taylor St. Hud HD7 152 E4
Taylor Wood Cotts. W Har WF4 163 B6
Taylor's Bldgs. Hud HD4 154 A2
Taylors Cl. Leeds LS14 62 B4
Teal Cl. Castle WF10 124 D6
Teal Dr. Morley LS27 98 D4
Teal Mews. Midd LS10 99 D5
Tealbeck App. Otley LS21 23 B7
Tealbeck House. Otley LS21 23 B7
Tealby Cl. Hors LS16 41 E2
Teall Ct. Ossett WF5 141 A5
Teall St. Ossett WF5 141 A5
Teall St. Wake WF1 142 C6 11
Teapot Cnr. Clay DN5 194 D4
Teasdale St. Brad BD4 75 B3
Teasel Cl. Brad BD12 95 A4
Technology Dr. Batley WF17 118 E4
Teddington Ave. Hud HD5 154 F6
Tees Cl. Castle WF10 125 B8
Tees St. Brad BD5 74 C3
Teesdale Pl. Knot WF11 126 E2
Telephone Pl. Leeds LS9 60 D1
Telford Cl. Castle WF10 124 B7
Telford Cl. Leeds LS10 79 E2
Telford Cl. Sil BD20 17 F8
Telford Ct. Brad BD7 74 B6
Telford Gdns. Leeds LS10 79 E2
Telford Pl. Leeds LS10 79 E2
Telford St. Leeds LS10 79 E2
Telford Terr. Leeds LS10 79 E2
Telford Way. Loft G WF2 120 F5
Telford Wlk. Leeds LS10 79 E2
Telscombe Dr. Brad BD4 75 D2
Temperance Field. Brad BD12 94 D3
Temperance Fields. Brig BD19 115 F8
Temperance St. Pudsey LS28 57 E1
Tempest Pl. Leeds LS11 79 A3
Tempest Rd. Leeds LS11 79 B2
Tempest Rd. S Kirk WF9 182 C4
Templar Dr. Hud HD5 154 D5
Templar Gdns. Weth LS22 13 F7
Templar La. Leeds LS15 62 D4
Templar La. Leeds LS2 79 D8
Templar Pl. Leeds LS2 79 D8
Templar St. Leeds LS2 79 D8
Templar St. Wake WF1 142 F3
Templar's Way. Brad BD8 73 E8
Templars Cl. Elland HX4 134 A7
Templars Way. Gar LS25 82 F6
Temple Ave. Leeds LS15 81 A6
Temple Ave. Roth LS26 100 F7
Temple Bank Sch. Brad 54 E2
Temple Cl. Hud HD1 154 A6
Temple Cl. Leeds LS15 81 A6
Temple Cres. Leeds LS11 79 A3
Temple Ct. Leeds LS15 80 F7
Temple Ct. Roth LS26 100 F7
Temple Gate Dr. Leeds LS15 81 A7
Temple Gate. Leeds LS15 81 B7
Temple Gdns. Nor WF6 122 F4
Temple Gn. Roth LS26 101 A7
Temple Gr. Leeds LS15 81 A7
Temple La. Leeds LS15 81 B7
Temple La. Litt OL15 129 D1
Temple Lawn. Roth LS26 101 A7
Temple Lea. Leeds LS15 81 B7
Temple Moor High Sch. Leeds 81 B8
Temple Newsam Park Golf Course. Leeds 80 F5
Temple Newsam Pk. Leeds 81 A5
Temple Park Cl. Leeds LS15 81 A7
Temple Park Gdns. Leeds LS15 81 A7
Temple Park Gn. Leeds LS15 81 A7
Temple Rd. Dew WF13 139 A7
Temple Rhydding Dr. Bail BD17 38 C2
Temple Rise. Leeds LS15 81 A6
Temple Row Cl. Leeds LS15 81 E6
Temple Row. Keigh BD21 35 B7
Temple Row. Leeds LS15 81 E6
Temple St. Brad BD9 55 B2
Temple St. Castle WF10 124 C7
Temple St. Hud HD3 135 B1
Temple St. Keigh BD21 35 B7
Temple View Gr. Leeds LS9 80 A7
Temple View Pl. Leeds LS9 79 F7
Temple View Rd. Leeds LS9 79 F7
Temple View. Roth WF3 100 C1
Temple View Terr. Leeds LS9 79 F7
Temple Wlk. Leeds LS15 81 B8
Templegate Ave. Leeds LS15 81 B6

Templegate Cl. Leeds LS15 ... 81 C7
Templegate Cres. Leeds LS15 . 81 B6
Templegate Gn. Leeds LS15 ... 81 B7
Templegate Rd. Leeds LS15 ... 81 B6
Templegate Rise. Leeds LS15 .. 81 A6
Templegate View. Leeds LS15 . 81 B6
Templegate Way. Leeds LS15 . 81 B6
Templegate Wlk. Leeds LS15 .. 81 B7
Templenewsam Halton Prim Sch. Leeds ... 81 A8
Templenewsam Rd. Leeds LS15 81 A5
Templenewsam View. Leeds LS15 ... 80 F6
Templestowe Cres. Leeds LS15 62 C1
Templestowe Dr. Leeds LS15 .. 81 C8 3
Templestowe Gdns.Leeds LS15 81 B8 5
Templestowe Hill. Leeds LS15 . 62 B1 1
Ten Lands La. Ryhill S71 ... 180 A7
Ten Row. D Dale HD8 ... 191 A4
Ten Yards La. Denh BD13 ... 72 A8
Tenbury Fold. Brad BD4 ... 75 E3
Tennis Ave. Brad BD4 ... 75 E1
Tennis Way. Bail BD17 ... 38 A1
Tennyson Ave. Loft G WF3 ... 121 E6
Tennyson Ave. Sow Br HX6 ... 111 F3
Tennyson Ave. Tod OL14 ... 108 D6
Tennyson Cl. Knot WF11 ... 126 B4
Tennyson Cl. Pudsey LS28 ... 76 F6
Tennyson Pl. Brad BD3 ... 75 B8
Tennyson Pl. Brig HX3 ... 114 C8
Tennyson Pl. Clec BD19 ... 116 D8 4
Tennyson Rd. Brad BD6 ... 94 B8
Tennyson St. Guise LS20 ... 39 F8
Tennyson St. Hali HX3 ... 92 A1 12
Tennyson St. Keigh BD21 ... 35 B5 6
Tennyson St. Morley LS27 ... 98 B4
Tennyson St. Pudsey LS28 ... 57 D2 8
Tennyson St. Pudsey LS28 ... 76 F6
Tennyson Terr. Morley LS27 ... 98 B4
Tennyson Way. Pont WF8 ... 125 D2
Tenter Cl. Skel HD8 ... 175 A2
Tenter Croft. Batley WF17 ... 38 C4 5
Tenter Hill. Brad BD14 ... 73 B4
Tenter Hill. Bramham LS23 ... 30 C2
Tenter Hill. Holmfi HD7 ... 189 F4
Tenter Hill La. Hud HD2 ... 136 D4
Tenter La. Leeds LS1 ... 79 C7
Tenterden Way. Leeds LS15 ... 62 F2
Tenterfield Rd. Ossett WF5 ... 140 E5
Tenterfield Rise. Northo HX3 .. 93 A1
Tenterfield Terr. Tod OL14 ... 108 E6
Tenterfields. Brad BD10 ... 56 E8
Tenterfields Bsns Ctr. Hali ... 111 E5
Tenterfields. Hali HX2 ... 111 E5
Tenters Cl. Knot WF11 ... 126 D5
Tenters Gr. Hud HD2 ... 136 C3
Tenth Ave. Clec WF15 ... 116 C5
Tern St. Brad BD5 ... 74 C3
Ternhill Gr. Brad BD5 ... 74 E5
Terrace Gdns. Hali HX3 ... 92 B1
Terrace The. B Spa LS23 ... 30 E7
Terrace The. Honley HD7 ... 171 E3
Terrace The. Pudsey LS28 ... 76 E4
Terrington Crest. Brad BD14 ... 73 D4
Terry Rd. Brad BD12 ... 94 E5 2
Tetley Dr. Birk BD11 ... 96 B4
Tetley La. Northo HX3 ... 93 A2
Tetley Pl. Brad BD2 ... 55 F3
Tetley St. Brad BD1 ... 74 D7
Tew St. Wake WF2 ... 142 C4
Tewit Cl. Hali HX2 ... 91 F7
Tewit Gdns. Hali HX2 ... 91 F7
Tewit Gn. Hali HX2 ... 91 F7
Tewit Hall Gdns. Hali HX2 ... 91 F6
Tewit Hall Rd. Brad BD3 ... 75 C8
Tewit La. Hali HX2 ... 91 F7
Tewitt Cl. Stee BD20 ... 17 B6
Tewitt La. Bing BD16 ... 37 B6
Tewitt La. Wils BD13 ... 53 A2
Texas St. Morley LS27 ... 98 B2
Thacker Gate Rd. Sow Br HX7 111 B4
Thackeray Gr. Hud HD4 ... 153 D3
Thackeray Rd. Brad BD10 ... 56 D4
Thackeray Wlk. Knot WF11 ... 126 B4
Thackley Ave. Brad BD10 ... 39 A2
Thackley Ct. Ship BD18 ... 55 C8
Thackley Fst Sch. Brad ... 39 B1
Thackley Old Rd. Ship BD18 ... 55 D8
Thackley Rd. Brad BD10 ... 39 A2
Thackley View. Brad BD10 ... 39 A2
Thackray Ave. Batley WF16 ... 117 E5
Thackray La. Pont WF8 ... 125 E1
Thackray St. Hali HX2 ... 112 D7
Thackray St. Morley LS27 ... 98 A3
Thames Dr. Gar LS25 ... 83 B6
Thane Way. Leeds LS15 ... 62 E3
Thanes Cl. Hud HD2 ... 135 E1
Thanet Garth. Sil BD20 ... 17 E8
Thatchers Way. Clec BD19 ... 96 B1
Theaker La. Leeds LS12 ... 78 B8
Theakston Mead. Brad BD14 ... 73 C4
Thealby Cl. Leeds LS9 ... 79 E8
Thealby Lawn. Leeds LS9 ... 60 E1
Thealby Pl. Leeds LS9 ... 79 E8 1
Thearne Gn. Brad BD14 ... 73 D4
Theodore St. Leeds LS11 ... 79 A2
Thewlis La. Hud HD4 ... 153 B1
Thick Hollins Dr. Mel HD7 ... 170 F1
Thick Hollins. Mel HD7 ... 170 F1
Thick Hollins Rd. Holmfi HD7 . 188 A7
Thick Hollins Rd. Mel HD7 ... 187 F8
Third Ave. Brad BD3 ... 56 C1
Third Ave. Clec WF15 ... 116 B5
Third Ave. Hali HX3 ... 113 B4
Third Ave. Hud HD7 ... 152 D4
Third Ave. Keigh BD21 ... 35 B6 1
Third Ave. Kirkhe HD5 ... 137 C1
Third Ave. Leeds LS12 ... 78 D6
Third Ave. Loft G WF1 ... 121 C2
Third Ave. Roth LS26 ... 101 A7
Third Ave. Upton WF9 ... 183 A8
Third Ave. Weth LS22 ... 13 F5
Third St. Brad BD12 ... 94 E6 2
Third St. Crof WF4 ... 162 B7
Thirkhill Ct. Brad BD5 ... 74 E4 4
Thirkleby Royd. Brad BD14 ... 73 C4
Thirlmere Ave. Brig BD12 ... 94 E1
Thirlmere Ave. Elland HX5 ... 135 B7
Thirlmere Cl. Leeds LS11 ... 98 E8
Thirlmere Dr. Castle WF10 ... 125 D7
Thirlmere Dr. E Ard WF3 ... 120 A8
Thirlmere Dr. Weth LS22 ... 13 B6
Thirlmere Gdns. Brad BD2 ... 56 B2
Thirlmere Gdns. Leeds LS11 ... 98 E8
Thirlmere Gr. Bail BD17 ... 37 E1
Thirlmere Pl. Knot WF11 ... 126 E2
Thirlmere Rd. Batley WF12 ... 118 F2
Thirlmere Rd. Wake WF2 ... 141 E6
Thirsk Cl. Hud HD2 ... 136 B2
Thirsk Dr. Kippax LS25 ... 83 A2
Thirsk Grange. Brad BD14 ... 73 D4
Thirsk Row. Leeds LS1 ... 79 B7
Thirstin Rd. Honley HD7 ... 171 F5
Thirteenth Ave. Clec WF15 ... 116 B5
Thistle Cl. Hud HD2 ... 135 E2
Thistle Hill Ave. Kirkhe HD5 ... 155 C5
Thistle St. Hud HD1 ... 154 B8
Thistle Way. Gild LS27 ... 97 D5
Thistlewood Rd. Loft G WF1 .. 121 E5
Thomas Ct. Brad BD6 ... 74 C1
Thomas Danby Coll. Leeds ... 60 D2
Thomas Danby Coll. Leeds ... 79 A5
Thomas St. Batley WF16 ... 117 D3
Thomas St. Batley WF17 ... 118 B6
Thomas St. Brig HD6 ... 115 A1
Thomas St. Castle WF10 ... 103 E1
Thomas St. Elland HX4 ... 134 B4
Thomas St. Elland HX5 ... 135 A6
Thomas St. Glu BD20 ... 16 D7
Thomas St. Hali HX1 ... 113 C7
Thomas St. Haw BD22 ... 51 D6
Thomas St. Hem WF9 ... 181 E6
Thomas St. Hud HD3 ... 135 B1
Thomas St. Hud HD1 ... 153 E4
Thomas St. Leeds LS6 ... 60 A3
Thomas St. Liver WF15 ... 117 A4 9
Thomas St S. Hali HX1 ... 113 A6
Thomas St. Tod OL14 ... 86 C1
Thomas St W. Hali HX1 ... 113 A5
Thomas Way. S Elm WF9 ... 183 A4
Thompson Ave. Brad BD2 ... 55 F5
Thompson Ave. Castle WF10 . 125 E6
Thompson Dr. Wake WF2 ... 120 F3
Thompson Gn. Bail BD17 ... 38 A2
Thompson La. Bail BD17 ... 38 A1
Thompson St. Hali HX1 ... 113 B7
Thompson St. Nor WF6 ... 123 A2
Thompson St. Ship BD18 ... 55 A8
Thompson's Yd. Wake WF1 ... 142 B6
Thong La. Holmfi HD7 ... 189 A8
Thoresby Dr. Clec BD19 ... 117 B8
Thoresby Gr. Brad BD7 ... 73 E3
Thoresby Pl. Leeds LS2 ... 60 B1
Thorn Ave. Brad BD9 ... 54 D4
Thorn Ave. Dew WF12 ... 139 C2
Thorn Bank. Bacup OL13 ... 106 A2
Thorn Cl. Bacup OL13 ... 106 A2 8
Thorn Cl. Leeds LS8 ... 61 B3
Thorn Cl. Ship BD18 ... 55 E6
Thorn Cres. Bacup OL13 ... 106 A2 7
Thorn Cres. Leeds LS8 ... 61 B3
Thorn Cross. Leeds LS8 ... 61 C4
Thorn Dr. Bacup OL13 ... 106 A2
Thorn Dr. Brad BD9 ... 54 D4
Thorn Dr. Leeds LS8 ... 61 B3
Thorn Dr. Queen BD13 ... 92 C7
Thorn Garth. Clec BD19 ... 116 C6
Thorn Garth. Keigh BD20 ... 18 A1
Thorn Garth Sch. Brad ... 39 C1
Thorn Gdns. Bacup OL13 ... 106 A2
Thorn Gr. Brad BD9 ... 54 D4
Thorn Gr. Leeds LS8 ... 61 B3
Thorn Hill. Elland HX4 ... 133 F2
Thorn La. Brad BD9 ... 54 D4
Thorn La. Leeds LS8 ... 60 F6
Thorn Mount. Leeds LS8 ... 61 C4
Thorn Park Sch for the Deaf. Brad ... 54 D4
Thorn Rd. Dew WF12 ... 139 C1
Thorn Royd Dr. Brad BD4 ... 75 F2
Thorn St. Bacup OL13 ... 106 A2
Thorn St. Batley WF17 ... 96 E1
Thorn St. Brad BD8 ... 55 A1
Thorn St. Haw BD22 ... 51 E8 3
Thorn Terr. Leeds LS8 ... 61 C4
Thorn Tree St. Hali HX1 ... 112 F5
Thorn View. Elland HX5 ... 135 A6
Thorn View. Hali HX3 ... 92 C2 5
Thorn View. Heb Br HX7 ... 110 E8
Thorn View. Leeds LS8 ... 61 B3
Thorn Wlk. Leeds LS8 ... 61 C3
Thornaby Dr. Brad BD14 ... 73 C4
Thornacre Cres. Ship BD18 ... 55 E7
Thornacre Rd. Ship BD18 ... 55 E7
Thornberry Dr. Clec WF15 ... 116 B5
Thornbridge Mews. Brad BD2 . 56 B4
Thornbury Ave. Brad BD3 ... 75 D8
Thornbury Cres. Brad BD3 ... 75 D8
Thornbury Dr. Brad BD3 ... 75 D8
Thornbury Fst Sch. Brad ... 75 E8
Thornbury Gr. Brad BD3 ... 75 D8
Thornbury Mid Sch. Brad ... 75 E8
Thornbury Pk. Wake WF2 ... 141 F4
Thornbury Rd. Brad BD3 ... 75 D7
Thornbury Rd. Wake WF2 ... 141 F4
Thornbury St. Brad BD3 ... 75 D7
Thorncliff Green Rd. Kirkb HD8 174 C7
Thorncliff La. Kirkb HD8 ... 174 C7
Thorncliffe Est. Batley WF17 .. 118 A3
Thorncliffe La. Emley HD8 ... 175 D7
Thorncliffe Rd. Batley WF17 .. 118 B3
Thorncliffe Rd. Brad BD8 ... 55 D1
Thorncliffe Rd. Keigh BD22 ... 34 F6
Thorncliffe St. Hud HD3 ... 135 B1
Thorncroft Rd. Brad BD6 ... 74 A1
Thorndale Rise. Brad BD2 ... 55 F4
Thorndene Way. Birk BD4 ... 96 A7
Thorne Cl. Nor WF6 ... 123 C1
Thorne Cl. Pudsey LS28 ... 76 B8
Thorne End Rd. Mapp S75 ... 178 B2
Thorne Gr. Roth LS26 ... 101 A6
Thorne Rd. Hud HD1 ... 153 E4
Thorne St. Elland HX4 ... 134 A4 1
Thorner CE Jun & Inf Sch. Thorner ... 46 A6
Thorner Gr. Sil BD20 ... 5 E2
Thorner La. B in Elm LS14 ... 45 E1
Thorner La. Bard LS14, LS23 ... 29 D2
Thorner La. Scar LS14 ... 45 E8
Thorner Rd. B in Elm LS14 ... 46 D8
Thorner Rd. Bard LS14, LS23 ... 29 E1
Thorner Rd. Bramham LS23 ... 30 B2
Thornes House Sch. Wake ... 142 A4
Thornes Ind Est. Wake ... 142 C4
Thornes La. Wake WF1, WF2 142 C4
Thornes Lane Wharf. Wake WF1 ... 142 D4
Thornes Moor Ave. Wake WF2 142 A3
Thornes Moor Cl. Wake WF2 142 A3
Thornes Moor Dr. Wake WF2 142 A3
Thornes Moor Rd. Wake WF2 142 A3
Thornes Office Pk. Wake ... 142 B3
Thornes Pk. Brig HD6 ... 115 A1
Thornes Pk. Ship BD18 ... 55 D5
Thornes Rd. Wake WF2 ... 142 A3
Thorney La. Hali HX2 ... 90 D2
Thornfield Ave. Brad BD6 ... 94 D8
Thornfield Ave. Hud HD4 ... 153 E3
Thornfield Ave. Pudsey LS28 ... 57 C3
Thornfield. Bing BD16 ... 36 E4
Thornfield Ct. Leeds LS15 ... 62 B2 4
Thornfield. Dew WF12 ... 139 D6
Thornfield Dr. Leeds LS15 ... 62 B2 3
Thornfield Hall. Thorn BD13 ... 72 E6 4
Thornfield. Haw BD22 ... 51 D7 9
Thornfield Mews. Bing BD16 ... 36 E7
Thornfield Mews. Leeds LS15 .. 62 B2 2
Thornfield Mount. Batley WF17 97 A1
Thornfield Pl. Brad BD2 ... 56 C3
Thornfield Rd. Hud HD4 ... 153 E3
Thornfield Rd. Leeds LS16 ... 59 B8
Thornfield Rise. Elland HX4 ... 134 B7 2
Thornfield St. Elland HX4 ... 134 B7 1
Thornfield Terr. Wils BD15 ... 53 B4
Thornfield Way. Leeds LS15 ... 62 B2
Thornhill Ave. Haw BD22 ... 34 E3
Thornhill Ave. Hud HD3 ... 153 C7
Thornhill Ave. Ship BD18 ... 55 D5
Thornhill Bridge La. Brig HD6 115 A3
Thornhill CE Prim Sch. Dew ... 139 C2
Thornhill Cl. Neth WF4 ... 158 B7
Thornhill Cl. Pudsey LS28 ... 57 B7
Thornhill Cl. Walton WF2 ... 161 A6
Thornhill Croft. Leeds LS12 ... 78 B6
Thornhill Croft. Walton WF2 .. 161 A7
Thornhill Dr. Pudsey LS28 ... 57 B8
Thornhill Dr. Ship BD18 ... 55 D5
Thornhill Dr. Walton WF2 ... 161 A7
Thornhill Fst & Mid Sch. Dew 139 E1
Thornhill Gr. Pudsey LS28 ... 57 B7
Thornhill Gr. Ship BD18 ... 55 D5
Thornhill Gr. Stee BD20 ... 17 B6
Thornhill Hey. Elland HX4 ... 133 F2
Thornhill High Sch. Dew ... 139 E1
Thornhill Lees CE Inf Sch. Dew 139 C4
Thornhill Mid Sch. Leeds ... 78 C6
Thornhill Park Av. Dew WF12 139 D4
Thornhill Pl. Brad BD3 ... 75 E8
Thornhill Pl. Brig HD6 ... 115 A1 1
Thornhill Pl. Leeds LS12 ... 78 B6
Thornhill Rd. Brig HD6 ... 115 A1
Thornhill Rd. Castle WF10 ... 124 E6
Thornhill Rd.Dew WF12 WF13 139 B7
Thornhill Rd. Dew WF12 ... 139 C5
Thornhill Rd. Hud HD3 ... 153 A6
Thornhill Rd. Hud HD3 ... 153 D8
Thornhill Rd. Leeds LS12 ... 78 C6
Thornhill Rd. Neth WF4 ... 158 A8
Thornhill Rd. Stee BD20 ... 17 B6
Thornhill St. Dew WF12 ... 139 D6
Thornhill St. Leeds LS12 ... 78 B7 3
Thornhill St. Pudsey LS28 ... 57 B6
Thornhill St. Wake WF1 ... 142 C5
Thornhill Street Bglws. Wake WF1 ... 142 C5
Thornhill Terr. Brad BD3 ... 75 D8
Thornhills Beck La. Brig HD6 . 115 B4
Thornhills La. Brig HD6 ... 115 C4
Thornie View. Dew WF12 ... 139 C4
Thornlea Cl. Yeadon LS19 ... 39 F5
Thornleigh Ave. Wake WF2 ... 142 C3
Thornleigh Cres. Wake WF2 .. 142 C3
Thornleigh Croft. Wake WF2 . 142 C4
Thornleigh. Dew WF12 ... 139 D6
Thornleigh Dr. Wake WF2 ... 142 C4
Thornleigh Garth. Wake WF2 142 C3
Thornleigh Gdns. Leeds LS9 ... 79 F6
Thornleigh Gr. Leeds LS9 ... 79 F6 1
Thornleigh Gr. Wake WF2 ... 142 C3
Thornleigh Mount. Leeds LS9 .. 79 F6 3
Thornleigh Rd. Hud HD4 ... 153 C3
Thornleigh Rd. Wake WF2 ... 142 C4
Thornleigh St. Leeds LS9 ... 79 F6 4
Thornleigh View. Leeds LS9 ... 79 F6 2
Thornmead Rd. Bail BD17 ... 38 D2
Thornsgill Ave. Brad BD4 ... 75 C3
Thornton Ave. Leeds LS12 ... 78 A7 3
Thornton Cl. Batley WF17 ... 96 F3
Thornton Cl. Hem WF9 ... 181 D5
Thornton Ct. Brad BD8 ... 73 F8 11
Thornton Fst Sch. Thorn ... 72 D6
Thornton Gdns. Leeds LS12 ... 78 A7
Thornton Gr. Leeds LS12 ... 78 A7
Thornton La. Brad BD5 ... 74 C3
Thornton Lodge Hall. Hud HD1 153 E4
Thornton Lodge Rd. Hud HD1 153 F4
Thornton Moor Rd. Denh BD13 71 B7
Thornton Moor Rd. Oxen BD13 71 B7
Thornton Old Rd. Brad BD8 ... 73 E7
Thornton Rd. Brad BD1, BD13, BD8 ... 73 C7
Thornton Rd. Brig HD6 ... 135 E8
Thornton Rd. Denh BD13 ... 71 F5
Thornton Rd. Dew WF12 ... 139 C4
Thornton Rd. Thorn BD13 ... 72 C6
Thornton Sch. Brad ... 73 B6
Thornton St. Brad BD1 ... 74 C7
Thornton St. Bur in W LS29 ... 9 E2
Thornton St. Clec BD19 ... 116 A6
Thornton St. Clec BD19 ... 116 B6
Thornton St. Dew WF13 ... 139 B8
Thornton St. Hali HX1 ... 112 F5 7
Thornton Terr. Hali HX1 ... 112 F5
Thornton View Rd. Brad BD14 . 73 C3
Thornton's Arc. Leeds ... 79 C8 4
Thorntonville. Clec BD19 ... 116 E8
Thorntree Ave. Crof WF4 ... 143 E1
Thorntree Cl. Dar WF8 ... 147 D4
Thorntree Ct. Crof WF4 ... 143 E1
Thornville Ave. Leeds LS6 ... 59 E2
Thornville Cres. Leeds LS6 ... 59 E3 11
Thornville Ct. Brad BD8 ... 55 D2
Thornville Gr. Leeds LS6 ... 59 E2 4
Thornville. Morley LS27 ... 98 B7 5
Thornville Mount. Dew WF13 139 A6 3
Thornville Mount. Leeds LS6 ... 59 E2 3
Thornville Pl. Dew WF13 ... 139 A6
Thornville Pl. Leeds LS6 ... 59 E2
Thornville Rd. Leeds LS6 ... 59 E2
Thornville Row. Leeds LS6 ... 59 E2 13
Thornville St. Dew WF13 ... 139 A6
Thornville St. Leeds LS6 ... 59 E2
Thornville Terr. Dew WF13 ... 139 B6
Thornville Terr. Leeds LS6 ... 59 E2
Thornville View. Leeds LS6 ... 59 E2 10
Thornville Wlk. Dew WF13 ... 139 A6
Thorp Arch HM Prison. Th Arch 15 A2
Thorp Arch Trad Est. Th Arch .. 15 B2
Thorp Ave. Holmfi HD7 ... 189 B4
Thorp Garth. Brad BD10 ... 56 B8
Thorp Pyn Croft. Hud HD5 ... 154 E7
Thorparch Grange Sch. Th Arch 14 F3
Thorpe Ave. Thorn BD13 ... 73 A6
Thorpe Cl. Guise LS20 ... 39 B8
Thorpe Cres. Midd LS10 ... 99 C3
Thorpe Ct. Midd LS10 ... 99 C3
Thorpe Dr. Guise LS20 ... 22 C1
Thorpe Garth. Midd LS10 ... 99 B3
Thorpe Gate Est. Th Aud WF9 165 A4
Thorpe Gdns. Midd LS10 ... 99 C3
Thorpe Gr. Midd LS10 ... 99 C4
Thorpe Gr. Thorn BD13 ... 73 A6
Thorpe Green Dr. Hud HD7 ... 152 E6
Thorpe Jun & Inf Sch. Midd ... 99 E2
Thorpe La. E Ard WF3 ... 98 F1
Thorpe La. Guise LS20 ... 22 B1
Thorpe La. Hud HD5 ... 155 A4
Thorpe La. Midd WF3 ... 99 A2
Thorpe La. Th Aud WF8 ... 165 A4
Thorpe Lower La. Midd WF3 ... 99 F2
Thorpe Lower La. Roth WF3 .. 100 A3
Thorpe Mid Sch. Brad ... 56 B8
Thorpe Mount. Midd LS10 ... 99 B3
Thorpe Pl. Midd LS10 ... 99 C4
Thorpe Pl. Sow Br HX6 ... 111 C2
Thorpe Rd. E Ard WF3 ... 120 C7
Thorpe Rd. Midd LS10 ... 99 C4
Thorpe Rd. Pudsey LS28 ... 76 E8
Thorpe Rd. Thorn BD13 ... 73 A6
Thorpe Sq. Midd LS10 ... 99 D4
Thorpe St. Hali HX3 ... 92 B2
Thorpe St. Keigh BD21 ... 35 C8
Thorpe St. Leeds LS15 ... 81 A8
Thorpe St. Midd LS10 ... 99 C3
Thorpe Terr. Midd LS10 ... 99 C4
Thorpe View. Midd LS10 ... 99 C3
Thorpe View. Ossett WF5 ... 140 D8
Thorpe View. Wake WF2 ... 141 F6
Thorpes Ave. D Dale HD8 ... 192 A7
Thorpes Cres. Skel HD8 ... 175 A1
Thorverton Dr. Brad BD4 ... 95 E8
Thorverton Gr. Brad BD4 ... 95 E8
Threadneedle St. Hud HD1 ... 154 A6
Threap Croft. Hali HX2 ... 91 F6
Three La Ends. Castle WF10 .. 124 A8
Three Nooks. Cud S72 ... 180 B1
Three Nooks La. Cud S72 ... 180 B1
Three Sisters Sq. Hud HD1 ... 154 A8 1
Threshfield. Bail BD17 ... 38 C3
Threshfield Cres. Birk BD11 ... 96 A6
Thrift Way. Bing BD16 ... 36 F2
Throstle Ave. Midd LS10 ... 99 B3
Throstle Crest. Feath WF7 ... 145 A8
Throstle Dr. Midd LS10 ... 99 A3
Throstle Farm Fst Sch. Knot .. 126 E2
Throstle Farm Mid Sch. Knot . 126 F2
Throstle Hill. Midd LS10 ... 99 B3
Throstle La. Midd LS10 ... 99 C3
Throstle Mount. Hali HX2 ... 111 F5
Throstle Mount. Midd LS10 ... 99 B3
Throstle Nest. Batley WF17 ... 118 A4
Throstle Nest Cl. Clift LS21 ... 10 D2
Throstle Nest Rd. Sil BD20 ... 5 D2
Throstle Nest View. Hors LS18 58 C7 4
Throstle Par. Midd LS10 ... 99 B3
Throstle Pl. Midd LS10 ... 99 B3
Throstle Rd. Midd LS10 ... 99 C3
Throstle Rd. Midd LS10 ... 99 E5
Throstle Row. Midd LS10 ... 99 B3
Throstle Sq. Midd LS10 ... 99 D3
Throstle St. Midd LS10 ... 99 B3
Throstle St. Tod OL14 ... 129 B6
Throstle Terr. Midd LS10 ... 99 C3
Throstle View. Midd LS10 ... 99 D3
Throstle Way. Knot WF11 ... 126 E2
Throstle Wlk. Midd LS10 ... 99 B3
Throxenby Way. Brad BD14 ... 73 C4
Thrum Hall Cl. Hali HX1 ... 112 F7
Thrum Hall Dr. Hali HX1 ... 112 F7
Thrum Hall La. Hali HX1 ... 112 F7
Thrumpton Rd. Barn S71 ... 178 F1
Thrush Hill Rd. Heb Br HX7 ... 89 E1 4
Thrush St. Keigh BD21 ... 35 D8
Thryberg St. Brad BD3 ... 75 A7
Thunder Bridge La. Kirkb HD8 173 D4
Thunderton La. Sow Br HX6 .. 111 C2
Thurgory Gate. Lepton HD8 ... 155 E3
Thurgory La. Lepton HD8 ... 155 E4
Thurley Dr. Brad BD4 ... 75 B2
Thurley Rd. Brad BD4 ... 75 B2
Thurnscoe Comp Sch. Dearne 194 B1
Thurnscoe Gooseacre Inf Sch. Dearne ... 194 C1
Thurnscoe La. G Hou S72 ... 194 A1
Thurnscoe Rd. Brad BD1 ... 74 D8
Thurrish La. Wad M HX7 ... 69 B6
Thursby St. Brad BD3 ... 75 B7
Thurstonland Bank Rd. Honley HD7 ... 172 D1
Thurstonland Endowed Sch. Kirkb ... 172 F2
Thurstonland Rd. Kirkb HD4 .. 172 E5
Thwaite Gate. Leeds LS10 ... 79 F3
Thwaite La. Leeds LS10 ... 80 A3
Thwaites Ave. Ilkley LS29 ... 8 C5
Thwaites Bridge. Keigh BD21 .. 35 F7
Thwaites Brow Rd. Keigh BD21 35 F6
Thwaites La. Keigh BD21 ... 35 E7
Tichborne Rd. Brad BD5 ... 74 E3 4
Tichborne Rd W. Brad BD5 ... 74 E3
Tichborne St. Liver FW15 ... 116 E4
Tichbourne St. Batley WF17 .. 117 F4
Tickhill St. Brad BD3 ... 75 B6
Tiding Field La. Slai HD7 ... 151 D2
Tidswell St. Batley WF16 ... 117 E4
Tilbury Ave. Leeds LS11 ... 78 F4 10
Tilbury Gr. Leeds LS11 ... 78 F4 12
Tilbury Mount. Leeds LS11 ... 78 F4 15
Tilbury Par. Leeds LS11 ... 78 F4 11
Tilbury Rd. Leeds LS11 ... 78 F4
Tilbury Row. Leeds LS11 ... 78 F4
Tilbury Terr. Leeds LS11 ... 78 F4 14
Tilbury View. Leeds LS11 ... 78 F4 13
Tile La. Hors LS16 ... 42 D3
Tile St. Brad BD8 ... 55 B1
Tile Terr. Brig HD6 ... 115 A1
Tiley Sq. Brad BD5 ... 74 E4 5
Till Carr La. Brig HX3 ... 115 A8
Tillotson Ave. Sow Br HX6 ... 112 A3
Tillotson St. Sil BD20 ... 5 D2
Tim La. Haw BD22 ... 34 B1
Timber Pl. Leeds LS9 ... 79 E6
Timber St. Elland HX5 ... 134 F6 3
Timber St. Keigh BD21 ... 35 E8 3
Timbercliffe. Litt OL15 ... 129 D1
Timble Dr. Bing BD16 ... 37 B4
Timmey La. Hali HX2 ... 112 A5
Timothy La. Batley WF17 ... 118 D7
Tinderley Gr. Hud HD5 ... 154 F4
Tingley Ave. E Ard WF3 ... 98 E1
Tingley Comm. E Ard LS27 ... 98 C1
Tingley Comm. Morley LS27 ... 98 C1
Tingley Cres. Morley WF3 ... 98 C1
Tinker La. Lepton HD8 ... 156 B2
Tinker La. Mel HD7 ... 170 D1
Tinkingfield La. Bick LS24 ... 15 C8
Tinsel Rd. Dew WF12 ... 118 F1
Tinshill Ave. Hors LS16 ... 41 E3
Tinshill Cl. Hors LS16 ... 41 E3
Tinshill Cres. Hors LS16 ... 41 E4
Tinshill Dr. Hors LS16 ... 41 E5
Tinshill Garth. Hors LS16 ... 41 E4
Tinshill Gr. Hors LS16 ... 41 F4
Tinshill La. Hors LS16 ... 41 E3
Tinshill Mid Sch. Hors ... 41 E3
Tinshill Mount. Hors LS16 ... 41 E4
Tinshill Rd. Hors LS16 ... 41 D4
Tinshill View. Hors LS16 ... 41 E4
Tinshill Wlk. Hors LS16 ... 41 E5
Tinsworth Rd. Wake WF2 ... 160 A4
Tintagel Ct. Nor WF6 ... 123 B3
Tintern Ave. Brad BD8 ... 73 D7
Tintern Ave. Hud HD3 ... 152 F5
Tippaty La. Byram WF11 ... 127 A7
Tipping La. Emley HD8 ... 175 E7
Tisma Dr. Brad BD4 ... 95 C8
Titan District Ctr. Brad ... 94 C2
Tithe Barn Fold. B in Elm LS15 63 D7
Tithe Barn La. Bard LS17 ... 28 C2
Tithe Barn Rd. Knot WF11 ... 127 A4
Tithe Barn St. Dew WF13 ... 139 D8
Tithe Barn St. Hor WF4 ... 141 A1
Tithe House Way. Hud HD2 ... 136 E6
Titus La. Emley HD8 ... 174 D6
Titus St. Ship BD18 ... 54 F8
Tiverton Wlk. Brad BD4 ... 75 E2
Tivoli Pl. Brad BD5 ... 74 C4
Tivoli Pl. Ilkley LS29 ... 8 C3
Tivy Dale. Caw S75 ... 193 E4
Tivy Dale Cl. Caw S75 ... 193 E4
Tivy Dale Dr. Caw S75 ... 193 E4
Toby La. Brad BD7 ... 74 A5
Toby Wood La. D Dale HD8 ... 191 D5
Todd Terr. Brad BD7 ... 74 B4 2
Todley Hall Rd. Keigh BD22 ... 34 A6
Todmorden High Sch. Tod ... 107 F6
Todmorden Old Rd. Bacup OL13 ... 106 B5
Todmorden Rd. Bacup OL13 ... 106 B4
Todmorden Rd. Litt OL15 ... 129 D2
Todwell La. Brad BD5 ... 74 C3
Toft La. Kirkb HD4 ... 172 F6
Toft St. Leeds LS12 ... 78 D6
Tofts Ave. Brad BD12 ... 94 C2
Tofts Gr. Brig HD6 ... 135 F7
Tofts Grove Gdns. Brig HD6 ... 135 F7
Tofts House Cl. Pudsey LS28 ... 76 E7
Tofts Rd. Clec BD19 ... 116 D7
Tofts Rd. Pudsey LS28 ... 76 D7
Tofts Rd. Pudsey LS28 ... 76 E7
Toftshaw Fold. Brad BD4 ... 95 D8
Toftshaw La. Brad BD4 ... 95 E8
Toftshaw New Rd. Brad BD4 ... 95 D8
Toll Bar La. Wake WF2 ... 120 D1
Toll Bar Rd. Castle WF10 ... 123 F7
Toller Dr. Brad BD9 ... 54 E3
Toller Gr. Brad BD9 ... 54 F3
Toller La. Brad BD8, BD9 ... 55 A1
Toller Pk. Brad BD9 ... 54 F3
Tolson Cres. Hud HD5 ... 154 F7
Tolson Grange. Hud HD5 ... 154 F5
Tolson Memorial Mus. Hud ... 154 E6
Tolson St. Dew WF13 ... 118 C1
Tolson St. Ossett WF5 ... 140 B8
Tolson's Yd. Hud HD5 ... 154 D5 12
Tolworth Fold. Brad BD15 ... 73 B8 1
Tom Dando Cl. Nor WF6 ... 123 E2
Tom La. Hud HD4 ... 153 B3
Tom Wood Ash La. Upton WF9 183 E7
Tombridge Cres. Hem WF9 ... 163 B1
Tomling Cote La. Sil BD20 ... 18 B8
Tommy La. Slai HD7 ... 152 E1
Tonbridge Cl. Brad BD6 ... 93 F8
Tonbridge St. Leeds LS1 ... 60 A1
Tong App. Leeds LS12 ... 77 D6
Tong Dr. Leeds LS12 ... 77 D7
Tong Gate. Leeds LS12 ... 77 D7
Tong Gn. Leeds LS12 ... 77 D6
Tong Hall Bsns Ctr. Birk ... 76 D2
Tong La. Bacup OL13 ... 106 B2
Tong La. Birk BD4 ... 76 E2
Tong Park Fst Sch. Bail ... 38 F4
Tong Rd. Leeds LS12 ... 77 C6
Tong Recn Ctr. Birk ... 96 A8
Tong Sch. Birk ... 96 A8
Tong St. Birk BD4 ... 95 F8
Tong St. Brad BD4 ... 75 D1
Tong Way. Leeds LS12 ... 77 D7
Tong Wlk. Leeds LS12 ... 77 D7
Tongue La. Leeds LS6 ... 42 F1
Toot Hill La. Sow Br HX6 ... 111 B2
Tootal St. Wake WF1 ... 142 D5
Toothill Ave. Brig HD6 ... 136 A7
Toothill Bank. Brig HD6 ... 136 A7
Toothill La. Brig HD6 ... 136 A7
Toothill La S. Brig HD6 ... 135 F6
Top Fold. Fair WF11 ... 105 A4
Top Headlands. Ossett WF5 .. 140 C5
Top House Farm Mews. Fair WF11 ... 105 A4
Top La. Clay DN5 ... 194 C5
Top La. W Bret WF4 ... 158 D1
Top Meadow. Mir WF14 ... 137 F2
Top Moor Side. Leeds LS11 ... 79 A5
Top o' Th' Bank. Honley HD7 . 172 E1
Top o' Th' Close Rd. Tod OL14 129 C6
Top o' Th' Hill Rd. Tod OL14 .. 108 A1
Top o' th' Moor. Kirkb HD4 ... 173 C2
Top o' The Hill. Slai HD7 ... 169 E7
Top of Carr. Batley WF17 ... 118 B2 1
Top of the Hill. Honley HD7 ... 172 E1
Top Orch. Ryhill WF4 ... 162 B1
Top Rd. D Dale HD8 ... 191 E7
Top Row. Mapp S75 ... 177 E3
Top St. Hem WF9 ... 181 C7
Top St. Tod OL14 ... 128 F7
Top Stone Cl. B Sal LS25 ... 105 E3
Topaz Cl. Hud HD2 ... 136 C2
Topcliffe Ave. Morley LS27 ... 98 D4
Topcliffe Ct. Morley LS27 ... 98 D4 8
Topcliffe Fold. Morley LS27 ... 98 C2
Topcliffe Gn. Morley LS27 ... 98 D4 7
Topcliffe Gr. Morley LS27 ... 98 C2
Topcliffe La. Morley LS27 ... 98 C2
Topcliffe La. Morley LS27 ... 98 D2
Topcliffe Mead. Morley LS27 ... 98 D4 6
Topcliffe Mews. Morley LS27 .. 98 D4 9
Tor Ave. Brad BD12 ... 94 C1
Tor View. Honley HD7 ... 172 C2
Torcote Cres. Hud HD2 ... 136 C5
Tordoff Ave. Brad BD7 ... 73 E5
Tordoff Gn. Brad BD6 ... 94 B8 4
Tordoff Pl. Leeds LS5 ... 59 A4
Tordoff Rd. Brad BD12 ... 94 E6 5
Tordoff Terr. Leeds LS5 ... 59 A4
Toronto Pl. Leeds LS7 ... 60 D6
Torre Cl. Leeds LS9 ... 80 A8
Torre Cres. Brad BD6 ... 73 D1
Torre Dr. Leeds LS9 ... 61 A1
Torre Gdns. Leeds LS9 ... 79 F8
Torre Gn. Leeds LS9 ... 79 F8
Torre Gr. Brad BD6 ... 73 D1
Torre Gr. Leeds LS9 ... 61 A1
Torre Hill. Leeds LS9 ... 61 B1
Torre La. Leeds LS9 ... 80 B8
Torre Mount. Leeds LS9 ... 61 A1
Torre Pl. Leeds LS9 ... 80 A8
Torre Rd. Brad BD6 ... 73 D1
Torre Rd. Leeds LS9 ... 80 A8
Torre Sq. Leeds LS9 ... 61 B1 7
Torre View. Leeds LS9 ... 61 B1
Torre Wlk. Leeds LS9 ... 61 B1
Torridon Cres. Brad BD6 ... 93 E6
Torridon Rd. Batley WF12 ... 118 E2
Totties La. Holmfi HD7 ... 189 D5
Toulston La. Bramham LS23 ... 30 F2
Tower Ave. Upton WF9 ... 183 A8
Tower Bldgs. Batley WF16 ... 117 D3 1
Tower Cswy. Tod OL14 ... 107 B7
Tower Dr The. Pool LS21 ... 24 E6
Tower Gdns. Hali HX2 ... 112 F4 2
Tower Gr. Leeds LS12 ... 78 A8
Tower Hill. Hali HX6 ... 112 B4
Tower House St. Leeds LS2 ... 60 C1
Tower La. Leeds LS12 ... 77 F8
Tower La. Leeds LS12 ... 78 A8
Tower Pl. Leeds LS12 ... 77 F8
Tower Rd. Leeds LS9 ... 80 D4
Tower Rd. Ship BD18 ... 54 E8
Tower St. Brad BD2 ... 56 B2
Tower St. Tod OL14 ... 86 A1
Towers Cl. Crof WF4 ... 162 A8
Towers La. Crof WF4 ... 144 B1
Towers Sq. Leeds LS6 ... 60 A8
Towers Way. Leeds LS6 ... 60 A8
Towlerton La. Wake WF2 ... 120 E2
Town Ave. Hud HD1 ... 154 C8
Town Cl. Hors LS18 ... 41 B1
Town Cres. Hud HD1 ... 154 C8
Town End Ave. Ack M T WF7 . 164 C7
Town End Ave. Holmfi HD7 ... 189 C6
Town End. Brad BD7 ... 74 A4
Town End Cl. Glu BD20 ... 16 D6
Town End Cl. Leeds LS13 ... 58 E1
Town End Cres. Holmfi HD7 .. 189 C7
Town End. Gar LS25 ... 82 E8
Town End. Gild LS27 ... 97 D7
Town End. Hud HD7 ... 152 D4
Town End. Hud HD5 ... 154 F4
Town End La. Lepton HD8 ... 156 A3
Town End. Ossett WF5 ... 140 D5
Town End Rd. Brad BD14 ... 73 B5
Town End Rd. Holmfi HD7 ... 189 B7
Town Fields Rd. Elland HX5 .. 134 E6
Town Gate. Brad BD10 ... 56 B8
Town Gate. Brad BD12 ... 94 C3
Town Gate. Brig BD19 ... 115 F8
Town Gate. Guise LS20 ... 22 E1
Town Gate. Heb Br HX2 ... 90 B1
Town Gate. Hep HX7 ... 88 F5
Town Gate. Holmfi HD7 ... 188 D5
Town Gate. Holmfi HD7 ... 188 F8
Town Gate. Holmfi HD7 ... 189 A5
Town Gate. Holmfi HD7 ... 189 E2
Town Gate. Kirkb HD8 ... 173 E8
Town Gate. Lepton HD8 ... 156 A4
Town Gate. Mars HD7 ... 168 F4
Town Gate. Northo HX3 ... 93 A2
Town Gate. Pudsey LS28 ... 57 B6
Town Gate. Sow Br HX6 ... 111 E3
Town Gn. Dew WF12 ... 139 E7
Town Hall Bldgs. Elland HX5 . 135 A6
Town Hall Sq. Yeadon LS19 ... 40 B7 4
Town Hall St E. Hali HX1 ... 113 C7 6
Town Hall St. Elland HX5 ... 134 F6 4
Town Hall St. Hali HX6 ... 112 B4
Town Hall St. Holmfi HD7 ... 189 A5
Town Hall St. Keigh BD21 ... 35 C7
Town Hall St. Mir WF14 ... 138 A4
Town Hall Way. Dew WF12 ... 139 D8
Town Head. Honley HD7 ... 171 F5
Town Hill. Bramham LS23 ... 30 D2
Town Hill St. Ship BD16 ... 54 B6
Town La. Brad BD10 ... 39 B1
Town Moor. Kirkb HD4 ... 172 F2
Town Pl. Hud HD1 ... 154 C8
Town Rd. Kirkhe HD5 ... 137 C1
Town St. Batley WF17 ... 118 C2

Town St. Birk BD11 ... 96 A6
Town St. Dew WF12 ... 139 F7
Town St. Gild LS27 ... 97 D7
Town St. Guise LS20 ... 22 E1
Town St. Hem WF9 ... 181 C7
Town St. Hors LS18 ... 41 B1
Town St. Leeds LS7 ... 60 D7
Town St. Leeds LS12 ... 78 B7
Town St. Leeds LS11 ... 78 E2
Town St. Midd LS10 ... 99 C5
Town St. Pudsey LS28 ... 57 D3
Town St. Pudsey LS28 ... 57 E2
Town St. Pudsey LS13 ... 57 F5
Town St. Roth WF3 ... 100 D2
Town St. Yeadon LS19 ... 40 B7
Town St. Yeadon LS19 ... 40 D3
Town Street Mews. Leeds LS7 60 D7
Town Street Wlk. Leeds LS7 ... 60 D7 8
Town Terr. Hud HD1 ... 154 C8
Town The. Dew WF12 ... 139 D2
Town Top. Kirkhe HD5 ... 137 C1
Town Wells Dr. Pudsey LS28 ... 57 B6
Townend Pl. Glu BD20 ... 16 C6
Townend Pl. Pudsey LS28 ... 76 F8 8
Townend Rd. Leeds LS12 ... 78 B5
Townfield La. Hep HX7 ... 88 F5
Townfield. Wils BD15 ... 53 C5
Townfold. Ossett WF5 ... 140 E6
Towngate Ave. Brig HD6 ... 115 D3
Towngate. Bail BD17 ... 38 C4 8
Towngate. Brig HX3 ... 114 C8
Towngate. Brig HD6 ... 115 E2
Towngate Gr. Mir WF14 ... 138 B5
Towngate. Hali HX3 ... 114 A4
Towngate House. Elland HX5 134 F7 1
Towngate. Hud HD4 ... 154 A2
Towngate. Keigh BD21 ... 35 C7
Towngate. Mapp S75 ... 178 B1
Towngate. Mir WF14 ... 138 B6
Towngate. Ossett WF5 ... 140 F6
Towngate Rd. Batley WF17 ... 118 A5
Towngate. Ship BD18 ... 55 D7
Townhead Fold. Sil LS29 ... 6 E8
Townley Ave. Hali HX3 ... 114 A4
Townley Rd. Wake WF2 ... 141 D4
Townville Dr. Castle WF10 ... 125 D5
Townville Fst Sch. Castle ... 125 C7
Towton Dr. Castle WF10 ... 124 A6
Track Mount. Batley WF17 ... 118 B2
Track Rd. Batley WF17 ... 118 B3
Trafalgar Rd. Dew WF13 ... 118 B1
Trafalgar Rd. Ilkley LS29 ... 8 B4
Trafalgar Sq. Hali HX1 ... 113 A5 4
Trafalgar St. Batley WF17 ... 118 A4
Trafalgar St. Brad BD1 ... 74 E8
Trafalgar St. Hali HX1 ... 113 A5 5
Trafalgar St. Leeds LS2 ... 79 D8
Trafford Ave. Leeds LS9 ... 61 B2 4
Trafford Gr. Leeds LS9 ... 61 B3
Trafford Terr. Leeds LS9 ... 61 B2 2
Tranbeck Rd. Guise LS20 ... 22 B1
Tranfield Ave. Guise LS20 ... 22 C1
Tranfield Cl. Guise LS20 ... 22 C1
Tranfield Ct. Guise LS20 ... 22 C1
Tranfield Gdns. Guise LS20 ... 22 C1
Tranmere Dr. Guise LS20 ... 22 C1
Tranmere Park Jun & Inf Sch. Guise ... 39 C8
Tranquility Ave. Leeds LS15 ... 62 C2
Tranquility Ct. Leeds LS15 ... 62 C2 2
Tranquility. Leeds LS15 ... 62 C2
Tranquility Wlk. Leeds LS15 ... 62 C2 1
Transvaal Terr. Batley WF17 . 118 B7
Tranter Gr. Brad BD4 ... 75 E5
Tranter Pl. Leeds LS15 ... 80 E8
Travis House. Tod OL14 ... 129 A7
Travis Lacey Terr. Dew WF13 139 B8 8
Tredgold Ave. Bramho LS16 ... 24 F2
Tredgold Cl. Bramho LS16 ... 24 E2
Tredgold Cres. Bramho LS16 ... 24 E2
Tredgold Garth. Bramho LS16 . 24 E3
Tree La. Hali HX2 ... 90 F5
Tree Top View. Queen BD13 ... 72 C2
Treefield Ind Est. Gild ... 97 D6
Trees St. Brad BD8 ... 55 C1
Trelawn Ave. Leeds LS6 ... 59 D5
Trelawn Cres. Leeds LS6 ... 59 D5 11
Trelawn Pl. Leeds LS6 ... 59 D5
Trelawn St. Leeds LS6 ... 59 D5
Trelawn Terr. Leeds LS6 ... 59 D5
Tremont Gdns. Leeds LS10 ... 79 E2
Trenam Park Dr. Brad BD10 ... 39 A2
Trenance Dr. Ship BD18 ... 54 F7
Trenance Gdns. Elland HX4 ... 134 A7
Trenholme Ave. Brad BD6 ... 94 B6
Trenic Cres. Leeds LS6 ... 59 D3 7
Trenic Dr. Leeds LS6 ... 59 D3 13
Trent Ave. Gar LS25 ... 83 B6
Trent Ave. Nor WF6 ... 123 A4
Trent Rd. Leeds LS9 ... 61 A1
Trent St. Leeds LS11 ... 79 B5
Trentham Ave. Leeds LS11 ... 79 B2 8
Trentham Gr. Leeds LS11 ... 79 B2 7
Trentham Pl. Leeds LS11 ... 79 B2 9
Trentham Row. Leeds LS11 ... 79 B2 6
Trentham St. Leeds LS11 ... 79 B2
Trentham Terr. Leeds LS11 ... 79 B3 29
Trenton Dr. Brad BD8 ... 55 C1
Trenton Rd. Batley WF12 ... 118 F3
Trescoe Ave. Leeds LS13 ... 58 E1
Tresham Ct. Batley WF12 ... 118 F2
Trevelyan Sq. Leeds LS1 ... 79 C7
Trevelyan St. Brig HD6 ... 115 A5
Trevelyan St. Hud HD5 ... 154 D5 9
Trevor Terr. Loft G WF2 ... 120 E6
Triangle Bsns Pk. Batley ... 97 A3
Triangle CE Inf & Jun Sch. Sow Br ... 111 E1
Triangle The. Hud HD1 ... 153 E5
Triath Ct. Batley WF17 ... 117 E6
Trilby St. Wake WF1 ... 142 D7
Trimmingham La. Hali HX2 ... 112 E6
Trimmingham Rd. Hali HX2 ... 112 E6
Trinity & All Saints' Coll. Hors . 41 A3
Trinity Bsns Ctr. Wake ... 142 D5
Trinity Church Gate. Wake WF1 ... 142 D6
Trinity Ct. Honley HD7 ... 171 F4
Trinity Dr. D Dale HD8 ... 191 F5
Trinity Gr. Brig HD6 ... 115 A4 2
Trinity House. Wake WF1 ... 142 D6 3
Trinity Pl. Bing BD16 ... 37 A2
Trinity Pl. Hali HX1 ... 113 C6
Trinity Rd. Brad BD5 ... 74 D5
Trinity Rd. Hali HX1 ... 113 C6
Trinity Rise. Otley LS21 ... 23 B7
Trinity St. Batley WF17 ... 118 C2
Trinity St. Hali HX1 ... 113 C6
Trinity St. Heb Br HX7 ... 88 F3
Trinity St. Hud HD1 ... 153 F7
Trinity St. Keigh BD21 ... 35 C8
Trinity St. Mir WF14 ... 138 A4
Trinity St. Pont WF8 ... 125 D1
Trinity St. Wake WF1 ... 142 F3
Trinity Street Arc. Leeds ... 79 C7
Trinity View. Brad BD12 ... 94 E7
Trinity View. Hali HX3 ... 113 D6
Trinity View. Ossett WF5 ... 140 D7
Trinity Way. S Elm WF9 ... 183 A4
Trinity Wlk. Brad BD12 ... 94 E7
Trip Garth. Coll LS22 ... 13 B2
Trip La. Coll LS22 ... 13 A2
Tristram Ave. Brad BD5 ... 75 A2
Troon Dr. Hud HD2 ... 135 F3
Trooper La. Hali HX3 ... 113 E5
Trooper Terr. Hali HX3 ... 113 D6
Trough La. Cull BD13 ... 52 A3
Trough La. Denh BD13 ... 52 A3
Trough La. S Elm WF9 ... 183 C3
Trough Well La. Wake WF2 ... 120 E3
Troughton Pl. Pudsey LS28 ... 76 F5
Troughton St. Pudsey LS28 ... 76 F5
Troutbeck Ave. Bail BD17 ... 37 E1
Troy Hill. Morley LS27 ... 98 A5
Troy Rd. Hors LS18 ... 41 C2
Troy Rd. Morley LS27 ... 98 A5
Troy Rise. Morley LS27 ... 98 B5
Troydale Gdns. Pudsey LS28 ... 77 B5
Troydale Gr. Pudsey LS28 ... 77 B5
Troydale La. Pudsey LS28 ... 77 B5
Trueman Ave. Batley WF16 ... 117 E5
Trueman Ct. Brad BD12 ... 94 E6
Trueman Way. S Elm WF9 ... 183 A4
Truncliffe. Brad BD5 ... 74 D1
Trundles La. Knot WF11 ... 127 B4
Truro Dr. Nor WF6 ... 123 B3
Truro St. Leeds LS12 ... 78 C8
Truro Wlk. Nor WF6 ... 123 B3
Tubby La. Hud HD2 ... 136 B1
Tudor Cl. Pont WF8 ... 146 C5
Tudor Croft. Hud HD2 ... 136 F5
Tudor Ct. Pudsey LS28 ... 57 C2
Tudor Gdns. Leeds LS11 ... 78 E2
Tudor House. Wake WF1 ... 142 C6 23
Tudor Lawns. Leeds LS8 ... 61 C7
Tudor Lawns. Loft G WF1 ... 120 E5
Tudor St. Brad BD5 ... 74 D4
Tudor St. Slai HD7 ... 170 A8
Tudor Way. Castle WF10 ... 125 B8
Tudor Way. Dew WF12 ... 139 B3
Tuel La. Hali HX6 ... 112 B4
Tuel Lane Inf Sch. Hali ... 112 B4
Tufton St. Sil BD20 ... 5 E1
Tulip St. Haw BD22 ... 51 C5
Tulip St. Leeds LS10 ... 79 D3
Tumbling Cl. Ossett WF5 ... 140 E6
Tumbling Hill. Dar WF8 ... 147 A5
Tumbling Hill St. Brad BD7 ... 74 D6
Tun La. S Hie S72 ... 180 D7
Tunnacliffe Rd. Hud HD4 ... 154 B3
Tunnel St. Denh BD13 ... 71 D8
Tunnel St. Hud HD4 ... 171 C7
Tunnicliffe Pl. Sil BD20 ... 5 D1
Tunstall Gn. Brad BD4 ... 75 E3
Tunstall Rd. Leeds LS11 ... 79 C3
Tunwell La. Brad BD2 ... 56 C4
Tunwell St. Brad BD2 ... 56 C4
Tup La. Ryhill WF4 ... 180 C8
Turbary Ave. Pudsey LS28 ... 57 E2 2
Turbid La. Hud HD4 ... 171 A6
Turbury La. Elland HX4 ... 133 E8
Turbury La. Sow Br HX4 ... 133 E8
Turf Ct. Cull BD13 ... 52 C5
Turf La. Cull BD13 ... 52 C5
Turgate La. Sow Br HX7 ... 111 A1
Turkey Hill. Pudsey LS28 ... 76 F6
Turley Cote La. Elland HX4 ... 134 C2
Turn o The Nook. Ossett WF5 140 C6
Turnberry Ave. Leeds LS17 ... 43 B4
Turnberry Cl. Leeds LS17 ... 43 B4
Turnberry Dr. Leeds LS17 ... 43 B4
Turnberry Gr. Cud S72 ... 180 C1
Turnberry Gr. Leeds LS17 ... 43 B4
Turnberry Pl. Leeds LS17 ... 43 B4
Turnberry Rise. Leeds LS17 ... 43 B4
Turnberry View. Leeds LS17 ... 43 B4
Turnbridge Rd. Hud HD1 ... 154 C6
Turnbull Ct. Leeds LS8 ... 61 D5
Turner Ave. Batley WF17 ... 118 C5
Turner Ave. Brad BD7 ... 73 F5
Turner Ave N. Hali HX2 ... 91 D5
Turner Ave S. Hali HX2 ... 91 E4
Turner Cl. E Ard WF3 ... 119 E8
Turner Cres. Otley LS21 ... 11 B1
Turner Dr. E Ard WF3 ... 119 E8
Turner La. Hali HX3 ... 92 D1
Turner La. Sil LS29 ... 6 C6
Turner La. Sil LS29 ... 6 D8
Turner Pl. Brad BD7 ... 74 B5
Turner Pl. Hali HX2 ... 91 E5
Turner St. Pudsey LS28 ... 57 D3 5
Turner's Ct. Hali HX3 ... 92 B2 1
Turners Yd. Pudsey LS28 ... 57 D3
Turney St. Hali HX3 ... 92 A2
Turnip La. Dew WF12 ... 139 D2
Turnkey Park. Leeds ... 78 C4
Turnpike St. Elland HX5 ... 135 A7
Turnshaw Rd. Haw BD22 ... 33 F2
Turnshaw Rd. Kirkb HD8 ... 174 A6
Turnshaws Ave. Kirkb HD8 ... 174 A7
Turnshaws Cl. Kirkb HD8 ... 174 A7
Turnshaws Special Sch. Kirkb 174 A7
Turnsteads Ave. Clec BD19 ... 116 B8
Turnsteads Cl. Clec BD19 ... 116 C8
Turnsteads Cres. Clec BD19 ... 116 C8
Turnsteads Dr. Clec BD19 ... 116 C8
Turnsteads Mount. Clec BD19 116 C8
Turnstone Ct. Midd LS10 ... 99 D5 3
Turnways The. Leeds LS6 ... 59 C4
Turret Hall Rd. B Head HX7 ... 88 C2
Turret Royd Rd. B Head HX7 ... 88 D2
Turton Gn. Gild LS27 ... 97 D7
Turton St. Wake WF1 ... 142 D6
Turton Vale. Gild LS27 ... 97 D6
Turver's La. Beal WF11 ... 127 F3
Turvin Rd. Litt HX6 ... 130 D2
Turvin Rd. Rip HX6 ... 130 D2
Twain Cres. Castle WF10 ... 125 C6
Tweed Cl. Batley WF17 ... 97 A1
Tweedale Gdns. Dew WF13 ... 139 B8
Tweedale St. Dew WF13 ... 139 B8 2
Tweedy St. Wils BD15 ... 53 C5
Twelfth Ave. Clec WF15 ... 116 B5
Twickenham Ct. Brad BD8 ... 55 D2
Twitch Hill. Hor WF4 ... 141 B1
Twivey St. Castle WF10 ... 124 C7
Two Dales Sch. Guise ... 39 C8
Two Gates. Slai HD7 ... 151 E1
Two Laws Rd. Haw BD22 ... 49 D8
Tyas Gr. Leeds LS9 ... 80 B7
Tyas La. Mars HD7 ... 151 B2
Tyburn La. Emley HD8 ... 175 C6
Tyersal Ave. Pudsey BD4 ... 75 F6
Tyersal Cl. Pudsey BD4 ... 75 F6
Tyersal Cres. Pudsey BD4 ... 75 F6
Tyersal Ct. Pudsey BD4 ... 75 F6
Tyersal Dr. Pudsey BD4 ... 75 F6
Tyersal Fst Sch. Brad ... 75 D5
Tyersal Garth. Pudsey BD4 ... 75 F6
Tyersal Gn. Pudsey BD4 ... 75 F6
Tyersal Gr. Pudsey BD4 ... 75 F6
Tyersal La. Brad BD4 ... 75 F4
Tyersal La. Pudsey BD4, LS28 . 76 A5
Tyersal Pk. Pudsey BD4 ... 75 F6
Tyersal Rd. Pudsey BD4 ... 75 F6
Tyersal Terr. Pudsey BD4 ... 75 F6
Tyersal View. Pudsey BD4 ... 75 E6
Tyersal Wlk. Pudsey BD4 ... 75 F6
Tyler Cl. Nor WF6 ... 123 E2
Tyndale Ave. Hor WF4 ... 141 C2
Tyndale Wlk. Batley WF16 ... 117 E5
Tyne St. Brad BD3 ... 74 F8
Tyne St. Haw BD22 ... 51 D7 1
Tyne St. Keigh BD21 ... 35 D7
Tynedale Ct. Leeds LS7 ... 60 A6
Tynwald Cl. Leeds LS17 ... 43 A2
Tynwald Dr. Leeds LS17 ... 43 A2
Tynwald Gdns. Leeds LS17 ... 43 A2
Tynwald Gn. Leeds LS17 ... 43 A3
Tynwald Hill. Leeds LS17 ... 43 A2
Tynwald Mount. Leeds LS17 ... 43 A2
Tynwald Rd. Leeds LS17 ... 43 A2
Tynwald Wlk. Leeds LS17 ... 43 A3
Tyrrel St. Brad BD1 ... 74 E7 9
Tyrrell Ct. Wake WF2 ... 141 D7
Tyson St. Brad BD1 ... 74 D8
Tyson St. Hali HX1 ... 112 E6

Ullswater Ave. Batley WF12 ... 118 E3
Ullswater Cl. Batley WF12 ... 118 E2
Ullswater Cl. Knot WF11 ... 126 E1
Ullswater Cres. Leeds LS15 ... 80 E7
Ullswater Cres. Roth LS26 ... 101 C6
Ullswater Dr. Brad BD6 ... 93 F6
Ullswater Dr. Weth LS22 ... 13 C6
Ullswater Rd. Batley WF12 ... 118 E3
Ullswater Rise. Weth LS22 ... 13 C5
Una Pl. Hud HD2 ... 153 E8
Underbank Ave. B Head HX7 ... 88 C1
Underbank Old Rd. Holmfi HD7 189 B4
Undercliffe Fst Sch. Brad ... 56 B1
Undercliffe La. Brad BD3 ... 56 A1
Undercliffe Mid Sch. Brad ... 56 B1
Undercliffe Old Rd. Brad BD2 .. 56 B1
Undercliffe Pl. Brig HX3 ... 114 B7
Undercliffe Rd. Brad BD2 ... 56 B3
Undercliffe Rise. Ilkley LS29 ... 8 E2
Undercliffe St. Brad BD3 ... 56 B1
Undercliffe Terr. Hali HX2 ... 112 F4 1
Underwood Dr. Yeadon LS19 ... 40 C1
Union Cross Yd. Hali HX1 ... 113 C7
Union Gr. Liver WF15 ... 117 B3
Union House La. Brad BD13 ... 73 C2
Union La. Hali HX2 ... 71 D1
Union Pl. Leeds LS11 ... 79 B6
Union Rd. Brad BD7 ... 74 B5
Union Rd. Brad BD12 ... 94 C7
Union Rd. Liver WF15 ... 117 B3
Union Sq. Wake WF1 ... 142 D6
Union St. Bail BD17 ... 38 E2
Union St. Batley WF17 ... 96 F1 8
Union St. Bing BD16 ... 36 E7
Union St. Castle WF10 ... 124 B7
Union St. Dew WF13 ... 139 D8
Union St. Elland HX4 ... 134 D7 6
Union St. Hali HX6 ... 112 C4
Union St. Hali HX1 ... 113 C6
Union St. Hem WF9 ... 181 E6
Union St. Hud HD3 ... 153 B8
Union St. Hud HD1 ... 154 B7 6
Union St. Leeds LS2 ... 79 D8
Union St. Liver WF16 ... 117 C3
Union St. Morley LS27 ... 98 C8 1
Union St. Ossett WF5 ... 140 D6
Union St. Otley LS21 ... 22 F7
Union St. Queen BD13 ... 72 E1 11
Union St S. Tod OL14 ... 108 B5
Union St. Slai HD7 ... 151 F1
Union St. Sow Br HX6 ... 111 E1
Union St. Wake WF1 ... 142 C7
Union Terr. Leeds LS7 ... 60 C6
Union Yd. Brad BD10 ... 56 B8
Unity Cl. Leeds LS6 ... 60 B4
Unity St. Heb Br HX7 ... 89 A4
Unity St. Keigh BD20 ... 18 F2
Unity St N. Bing BD16 ... 36 F2
Unity St. Roth WF3 ... 100 D3
Unity St S. Bing BD16 ... 36 F2
Unity St. Tod OL14 ... 129 A8
Unity Terr. Hali HX1 ... 112 E6
Univ of Bradford. Brad ... 74 D6
Univ of Bradford Management Ctr. Ship ... 55 B4
University Rd. Leeds LS2 ... 60 A2
University St. Castle WF10 ... 124 D7
Unna Way. Hud HD1 ... 154 A7
Unwin Pl. Brad BD9 ... 54 E2
Upland Cres. Leeds LS8 ... 61 A5
Upland Gr. Leeds LS8 ... 61 A5
Upland Rd. Leeds LS8 ... 61 A4
Uplands Ave. Brad BD13 ... 73 B2
Uplands Cl. Brad BD13 ... 73 B2
Uplands Cres. Brad BD13 ... 73 B2
Uplands Dr. Mir WF14 ... 138 A6
Uplands Gr. Brad BD13 ... 73 B2
Uplands. Keigh BD20 ... 18 A1
Uplands The. Pont WF8 ... 146 C7
Upper Accommodation Rd. Leeds LS9 ... 79 E7
Upper Ada St. Ship BD18 ... 54 F8 8
Upper Addison St. Brad BD4 ... 74 F5
Upper Allerton La. Brad BD13 . 72 E8
Upper Armley CE Sch. Leeds ... 78 B8
Upper Ash Gr. S Elm WF9 ... 183 B3
Upper Ashley La. Ship BD17 ... 55 B8
Upper Bank End Rd. Holmfi HD7 ... 189 B3
Upper Bank Hey Bottom. Rip HX6 ... 132 E3
Upper Barker St. Liver WF15 ... 117 A4
Upper Basinghall St. Leeds LS1 79 B8
Upper Batley La. Batley WF17 118 B8
Upper Batley Low La. Batley WF17 ... 118 C8
Upper Battye St. Batley WF16 117 D4
Upper Bell Croft. Hali HX3 ... 114 A4
Upper Bell Hall. Hali HX1 ... 113 A5
Upper Bolton Brow. Hali HX6 112 D4
Upper Bonegate. Brig HD6 ... 115 B3
Upper Brig Royd. Rip HX6 ... 132 E4
Upper Brockholes. Hali HX2 ... 91 D8
Upper Brow Rd. Hud HD1 ... 153 D5
Upper Butts. Clec BD19 ... 116 D7
Upper Calton St. Keigh BD21 ... 35 B5
Upper Camroyd St. Dew WF13 118 D1
Upper Carr La. Pudsey LS28 ... 57 A6
Upper Carr St. Liver WF15 ... 117 A5
Upper Castle St. Brad BD5 ... 74 F4
Upper Chelsea St. Keigh BD21 35 B5
Upper Clough Rd. Slai HD7 ... 170 D7
Upper Commercial St. Batley WF17 ... 118 C5
Upper Common La. Clay W HD8 ... 192 F8
Upper Croft Rd. Batley WF17 118 B4
Upper Cross St. Dew WF13 ... 118 C1 2
Upper Cumberworth CE Aided Fst Sch. D Dale ... 191 B6
Upper Ellistones La. Elland HX4 ... 134 A7
Upper Exley. Hali HX3 ... 113 E1
Upper Ferndown Gn.Brad BD15 54 A1
Upper Field House La. Sow Br HX6 ... 111 D2
Upper Field La. H Hoy S75 ... 176 E1
Upper Field La. Kex S75 ... 176 E1
Upper Fountain St. Hali HX6 .. 112 B4
Upper Fountaine St. Leeds LS2 79 C8
Upper Gate. Holmfi HD7 ... 189 E2
Upper George St.Batley WF16 117 D4
Upper George St. Brad BD6 ... 74 B1 4
Upper George St. Hud HD1 ... 154 A6 3
Upper Grange Ave. Brad BD15 73 B8 3
Upper Green Ave. Brig BD19 . 115 F8 10
Upper Green Ave. E Ard WF3 119 D7
Upper Green. Bail BD17 ... 38 B2
Upper Green. Brad BD7 ... 74 A3 1
Upper Green La. Brig HD6 ... 114 E5
Upper Green Way. E Ard WF3 119 D7
Upper Hagg Rd. Holmfi HD7 ... 172 B2
Upper Hagg Rd. Honley HD7 . 172 B2
Upper Hatfield Pl. Ryhill WF4 162 D2
Upper Haugh Shaw. Hali HX1 113 A5 13
Upper Heaton La. Kirkhe HD5 137 B2
Upper Heights Rd. Thorn BD13 72 C8
Upper Hird St. Keigh BD21 ... 35 A5
Upper Hirst. Hud HD3 ... 152 D8
Upper Holme. Slai HD7 ... 169 D8
Upper Hopton CE (C) 5-9 Sch. Mir ... 137 F1
Upper House La. Clec WF15 .. 116 C4
Upper House Rd. Holmfi HD7 199 C8
Upper House St. Brad BD4 ... 75 B5
Upper Kirkgate. Hali HX1 ... 113 D7
Upper La. Clec BD19 ... 117 B7
Upper La. Emley HD8 ... 175 D6
Upper La. Neth WF4 ... 158 D4
Upper La. Northo HX3 ... 92 F3
Upper La. Tod OL14 ... 87 D1
Upper Langwith. Coll LS22 ... 28 E8
Upper Lombard St.Yeadon LS19 40 A4
Upper Lumb La. Heb Br HX7 .. 110 C4
Upper Marsh. Hali HX3 ... 113 F5
Upper Marsh La. Oxen BD22 ... 51 A5
Upper Martin Gn. Elland HX4 134 A7
Upper Mary St. Ship BD18 ... 54 F8 9
Upper Maythorn La. Wh Com HD7 ... 200 D8
Upper Meadows. Holmfi HD7 188 D5
Upper Meadows. Queen BD13 92 E8
Upper Mill Row. Keigh BD20 ... 19 E2
Upper Millergate. Brad BD1 ... 74 E7 13
Upper Mosscar St. Brad BD3 ... 75 A7
Upper Mount. Mel HD7 ... 170 F1
Upper Mount St. Batley WF17 118 C3
Upper Mount St. Hud HD1 ... 153 F4
Upper Nidd St. Brad BD3 ... 75 B6
Upper Norcroft. Caw S75 ... 193 F3
Upper North St. Batley WF17 118 B4
Upper North St. Leeds LS2 ... 60 B1
Upper Prish Ghyll La.Ilkley LS29 7 F3
Upper Park Gate. Brad BD1 ... 74 F7
Upper Peel St. Dew WF13 ... 118 D1 1
Upper Piccadilly. Brad BD1 ... 74 E7 2
Upper Quarry Rd. Hud HD2 ... 137 A6
Upper Raglan St. Tod OL14 ... 108 B6
Upper Rd. Batley WF17 ... 118 B2
Upper Reins. Honley HD7 ... 172 A5
Upper Rushton Rd. Brad BD3 .. 56 D1
Upper Seymour St. Brad BD3 .. 75 B7
Upper South St. Dew WF13 ... 118 C1
Upper Station Rd. Batley WF17 ... 118 D4
Upper Sutherland Rd.Brig HX3 114 E8
Upper Swain Royd Mews. Brad BD15 ... 53 E4
Upper Town. Oxen BD22 ... 51 C2
Upper Town St. Leeds LS13 ... 58 C3
Upper Warrengate.Wake WF1 142 D6 12
Upper Washer La. Hali HX2 ... 112 F5
Upper Wellhouse Rd. Slai HD7 152 C3
Upper West St. Batley WF17 . 118 E5
Upper Westlock Ave. Leeds LS9 61 A1
Upper Whitley Fst Sch. Floc ... 156 E5
Upper Willow Hall. Hali HX2 .. 112 D6
Upper Woodlands Rd.Brad BD8 55 A1
Upper Woodview Pl.Leeds LS11 79 B2 16
Upper Wortley Dr. Leeds LS12 78 B7 1
Upper Wortley Prim Sch. Leeds 78 B6
Upper Wortley Rd. Leeds LS12 78 B7
Upper Wortley Recn Ctr. Leeds 77 F7
Upper York St. Wake WF1 ... 142 C7
Upperfield Dr. Hud HD7 ... 152 C4
Upperhead Row. Hud HD1 ... 154 A6 11
Uppermoor Cl. Pudsey LS28 ... 76 D6
Uppermoor. Pudsey LS28 ... 76 D7
Upperthong La. Holmfi HD7 ... 189 E5
Upton Mid Sch. Upton ... 182 F7
Upton St. Batley WF17 ... 118 B6
Upwood La. Keigh BD20 ... 19 D2
Upwood Pk. Oxen BD22 ... 51 E3
Urban Terr. Floc WF4 ... 156 E5
Ure Cres. Brad BD8 ... 74 D8
Ure Gr. Weth LS22 ... 13 D8
Usher St. Brad BD4 ... 75 A5
Usher Street Fst Sch. Brad ... 75 A5
Utley Fst Sch. Keigh ... 18 A2
Uttley St. Hali HX3 ... 92 B2 4

Vale Ave. Knot WF11 ... 126 D4
Vale Ave. Leeds LS8 ... 44 A3
Vale Cl. Hud HD5 ... 154 F3
Vale Cres. Knot WF11 ... 126 D4
Vale Crest. Knot WF11 ... 126 D4
Vale Gr. Queen BD13 ... 72 F1
Vale Gr. Sil BD20 ... 5 D1
Vale Head Gr. Knot WF11 ... 126 D4
Vale Head Mount. Knot WF11 126 D4
Vale Mill La. Haw BD22 ... 34 D1
Vale Rd. Hem WF9 ... 163 B1
Vale St. Bacup OL13 ... 106 A3
Vale St. Brig HD6 ... 115 A3
Vale St. Keigh BD21 ... 18 E1
Vale St. Tod OL14 ... 108 B5
Vale Terr. Knot WF11 ... 126 D5
Vale The. Coll LS22 ... 29 A8
Vale The. Leeds LS6 ... 59 F5
Vale View. Ack M T WF7 ... 164 B7
Valentine Ct. Thorn BD13 ... 72 E7
Valestone Ave. Hem WF9 ... 181 E7
Valley Ave. Brig HX3 ... 115 A8
Valley Ave. S Elm WF9 ... 183 B3
Valley Cl. Leeds LS17 ... 43 A5
Valley Cres. Wake WF2 ... 120 F2
Valley Ct. Brad BD1 ... 55 E1
Valley Ct. Liver WF15 ... 117 B5
Valley Dr. Dew WF12 ... 139 E1
Valley Dr. Ilkley LS29 ... 8 E4
Valley Dr. Leeds LS15 ... 62 B1
Valley Dr. Swil LS26 ... 102 E8
Valley Dr. Wake WF2 ... 120 F2
Valley Farm Rd. Midd LS10 ... 79 F1
Valley Farm Rd. Roth LS10 ... 80 A1
Valley Farm Way. Roth LS10 ... 80 A1
Valley Fold. Queen BD13 ... 92 E8
Valley Gdns. Leeds LS7 ... 60 C8
Valley Gn. Pudsey LS28 ... 76 F6
Valley Gr. Hali HX2 ... 91 F7
Valley Gr. Pudsey LS28 ... 76 F6
Valley Head. Hud HD2 ... 135 C2
Valley Hts. Hud HD2 ... 135 C2
Valley Mills Ind Est. Brad ... 56 E8
Valley Mount. Kippax LS25 ... 83 A2
Valley Mount. Pudsey LS13 ... 77 A8
Valley Par. Brad BD8 ... 55 D1
Valley Parade F'tball Gd. Brad . 55 D1
Valley Pl. Brad BD1 ... 55 E1
Valley Rd. Brad BD1 ... 74 E8
Valley Rd. Clec BD19 ... 116 E8
Valley Rd. Dar WF8 ... 147 E4
Valley Rd. Dew WF12 ... 139 F1
Valley Rd. Heb Br HX7 ... 89 A3 6
Valley Rd. Ilkley LS29 ... 8 D5
Valley Rd. Keigh BD21 ... 35 F7
Valley Rd. Kippax LS25 ... 83 A2
Valley Rd. Leeds LS13 ... 58 C5
Valley Rd. Liver WF15 ... 117 B4
Valley Rd. Mapp S75 ... 178 A1
Valley Rd. Morley LS27 ... 98 C5
Valley Rd. Ossett WF5 ... 140 D4
Valley Rd. Pont WF8 ... 146 D8 5
Valley Rd. Pudsey LS28 ... 76 F6
Valley Rd. Ship BD18 ... 55 C6
Valley Ridge. Kippax LS25 ... 82 F2
Valley Ridge. Kippax LS25 ... 82 F3
Valley Rise. Leeds LS13 ... 58 C5
Valley Sq. Pudsey LS28 ... 76 F6
Valley St. S Elm WF9 ... 182 F2
Valley Terr. Leeds LS17 ... 43 F3
Valley The. Leeds LS17 ... 43 A5
Valley View. Bail BD17 ... 38 B1
Valley View Cl. Keigh BD22 ... 34 E3
Valley View Gdns. Haw BD22 .. 51 E8 12
Valley View. Glu BD20 ... 16 C7
Valley View Gr. Brad BD2 ... 56 A2
Valley View. Hali HX2 ... 91 F7
Valley View. Hali HX5 ... 134 F8
Valley View. Harden BD16 ... 36 A1
Valley View Rd. Hep HX7 ... 88 F4
Valley View Rd. Ossett WF5 .. 140 D4
Valley View. S Elm WF9 ... 183 B3
Valley Way. Hali HX2 ... 91 F7
Vancouver Pl. Leeds LS7 ... 60 E6
Varley Rd. Slai HD7 ... 169 F7
Varley St. Pudsey LS28 ... 57 D1
Vaughan St. Brad BD1 ... 74 D7
Vaughan St. Hali HX1 ... 112 F5 5
Vegal Cres. Hali HX3 ... 91 F2
Venn St. Hud HD1 ... 154 B6
Ventnor Cl. Ossett WF5 ... 140 D5
Ventnor Dr. Ossett WF5 ... 140 D5
Ventnor St. Brad BD3 ... 75 A7
Ventnor Terr. Hali HX3 ... 113 B4
Ventnor Way. Ossett WF5 ... 140 D5
Vento Cl. Brad BD6 ... 94 B8
Venture St. Bacup OL13 ... 106 A3
Verdun Rd. Brad BD6 ... 94 A8
Vere Sq. Brad BD5 ... 74 E4 7
Verity Spur. Leeds LS9 ... 80 E8
Verity St. Birk BD4 ... 95 F7
Verity View. Leeds LS9 ... 61 E1
Vermont St. Leeds LS13 ... 58 A2
Verner St. Feath WF7 ... 145 C4
Vernon Ave. Hud HD1 ... 153 F7
Vernon Cl. Hud HD1 ... 153 F7
Vernon Ct. Keigh BD20 ... 35 B8
Vernon House. Brad BD15 ... 73 B7 7
Vernon Pl. Brad BD2 ... 56 B2
Vernon Pl. Pudsey LS28 ... 57 E1
Vernon Pl. Queen BD13 ... 92 C7
Vernon Pl. Wake WF2 ... 142 B3
Vernon Rd. Leeds LS1 ... 60 B1
Vernon Rd. Liver FW15 ... 117 C4
Vernon St. Haw BD22 ... 51 F8
Vernon St. Leeds LS2 ... 60 B1
Vernon St. Tod OL14 ... 108 A3
Vesper Cl. Leeds LS5 ... 58 F6
Vesper Ct. Leeds LS5 ... 58 E6
Vesper Gate Cres. Leeds LS5 .. 58 F6
Vesper Gate Dr. Leeds LS5 ... 58 E5
Vesper Gate Mount. Leeds LS5 58 F6
Vesper Gdns. Leeds LS5 ... 58 F5
Vesper Gr. Leeds LS5 ... 59 A4 2
Vesper House. Brad BD15 ... 73 A7 8
Vesper La. Leeds LS5 ... 58 F5
Vesper Mount. Leeds LS5 ... 59 A4
Vesper Pl. Leeds LS5 ... 59 A4 4
Vesper Rd. Leeds LS5 ... 58 E6
Vesper Rise. Leeds LS5 ... 58 E6
Vesper Terr. Leeds LS5 ... 59 A4 3
Vesper Way. Leeds LS5 ... 58 E6
Vesper Wlk. Leeds LS5 ... 58 E6
Vestry St. Brad BD4 ... 75 B3
Viaduct Rd. Leeds LS4 ... 59 D1
Viaduct St. Hud HD1 ... 154 A7
Viaduct St. Pudsey LS28 ... 57 D1
Viaduct St. Slai HD7 ... 152 A1
Vicar La. Brad BD1 ... 74 F6
Vicar La. Leeds LS1, LS2 ... 79 C8
Vicar La. Ossett WF5 ... 140 E3
Vicar Park Dr. Hali HX2 ... 112 B8
Vicar Park Rd. Hali HX2 ... 112 B8
Vicar St. Liver WF15 ... 117 A5 11
Vicarage Ave. Gild LS27 ... 97 C6
Vicarage Ave. Leeds LS5 ... 59 B4
Vicarage Cl. Brad BD12 ... 94 C2
Vicarage Cl. Loft G WF1 ... 121 C5
Vicarage Cl. S Kirk WF9 ... 182 C3
Vicarage Dr. Pudsey LS28 ... 76 D7
Vicarage Gdns. Birk BD11 ... 96 A5
Vicarage Gdns. Brig HD6 ... 135 F8
Vicarage Gdns. Feath WF7 ... 145 D8
Vicarage La. Bramham LS23 ... 30 D3
Vicarage La. Feath WF7 ... 145 D5
Vicarage La. Roy S71 ... 179 C3
Vicarage Meadows. Mir WF14 138 C5
Vicarage Pl. Leeds LS5 ... 59 B4
Vicarage Rd. Dew WF12 ... 139 C5
Vicarage Rd. Dew WF12 ... 139 D8
Vicarage Rd. Hud HD3 ... 153 B6
Vicarage Rd. Leeds LS6 ... 59 F2 1
Vicarage Rd. Ship BD18 ... 55 E8
Vicarage St. Leeds LS5 ... 59 B4
Vicarage St N. Wake WF1 ... 142 D7
Vicarage St S. Wake WF1 ... 142 D6 1
Vicarage Terr. Batley WF17 ... 118 A7
Vicarage Terr. Leeds LS5 ... 59 B4
Vicarage View. Leeds LS5 ... 59 B4
Vicars Rd. Leeds LS8 ... 60 F4
Vicars Terr. Kippax WF10 ... 103 B4
Vicars Terr. Leeds LS8 ... 60 F4
Vickerman Cres. Hud HD4 ... 153 F1
Vickerman St. Hali HX1 ... 112 F6
Vickers Ave. Leeds LS5 ... 58 F3
Vickers Ave. S Elm WF9 ... 182 E1
Vickers St. Castle WF10 ... 124 D7
Vickers St. Morley LS27 ... 97 F2
Vickers St. Morley LS27 ... 97 F3
Vickersdale. Pudsey LS28 ... 57 E2
Victor Dr. Guise LS20 ... 39 E8
Victor Rd. Brad BD9 ... 55 B2
Victor Rd. S Kirk WF9 ... 182 C2
Victor St. Batley WF17 ... 118 D5
Victor St. Brad BD9 ... 55 B2
Victor St. Brad BD3 ... 75 E7
Victor St. Castle WF10 ... 124 C5
Victor St. S Elm WF9 ... 182 F2
Victor Terr. Brad BD9 ... 55 B2
Victor Terr. Hali HX1 ... 113 A8
Victoria App. Loft G WF1 ... 121 B3
Victoria Ave. Batley WF17 ... 118 C4
Victoria Ave. Brad BD2 ... 56 D4
Victoria Ave. Brig HD6 ... 115 C3
Victoria Ave. Clec BD19 ... 116 D7
Victoria Ave. Elland HX5 ... 134 E6
Victoria Ave. Hali HX6 ... 112 C5
Victoria Ave. Hali HX1 ... 112 F6
Victoria Ave. Haw BD22 ... 51 C8
Victoria Ave. Hors LS18 ... 58 A7
Victoria Ave. Ilkley LS29 ... 7 F4
Victoria Ave. Keigh BD21 ... 35 C8 7
Victoria Ave. Leeds LS9 ... 80 B7
Victoria Ave. Men LS29 ... 22 A5
Victoria Ave. Morley LS27 ... 98 A5
Victoria Ave. Roth LS26 ... 100 E4
Victoria Ave. Ship BD18 ... 54 F8
Victoria Ave. Wake WF2 ... 142 A6
Victoria Ave. Yeadon LS19 ... 40 D8
Victoria Bldgs. Dew WF12 ... 118 E1 5
Victoria Bldgs. Heb Br HX7 ... 110 C2
Victoria Cl. Hors LS18 ... 58 A7
Victoria Cl. Ilkley LS29 ... 8 A4
Victoria Cl. Kippax WF10 ... 103 B4
Victoria Cl. Yeadon LS19 ... 40 D7
Victoria Cotts. B Sal LS25 ... 105 D4
Victoria Cty Prim Sch. Leeds ... 80 B8
Victoria Cres. Dew WF13 ... 118 A2
Victoria Cres. Elland HX5 ... 134 F6
Victoria Cres. Hors LS18 ... 58 A7
Victoria Cres. Pudsey LS28 ... 76 C7
Victoria Ct. Batley WF17 ... 96 F1
Victoria Ct. Castle WF10 ... 124 D6
Victoria Ct. Keigh BD21 ... 35 B8
Victoria Ct. Ship BD18 ... 54 F8 18
Victoria Ct. Upton WF9 ... 183 A7
Victoria Dr. Brad BD2 ... 56 D4
Victoria Dr. Dew WF12 ... 139 C4
Victoria Dr. Hors LS18 ... 58 A7
Victoria Dr. Ilkley LS29 ... 7 F4
Victoria Dr. Morley LS27 ... 98 B6
Victoria Dr. Northo HX3 ... 93 B3
Victoria Gdns. Hors LS18 ... 58 B7
Victoria Gdns. Ilkley LS29 ... 7 F4
Victoria Gdns. Pudsey LS28 ... 76 C7
Victoria Gr. Hors LS18 ... 58 A6
Victoria Gr. Ilkley LS29 ... 7 F4
Victoria Gr. Leeds LS9 ... 80 B8
Victoria Gr. Pudsey LS28 ... 76 C7
Victoria Gr. Wake WF2 ... 141 D3

Victoria Grange Dr. Morley LS27 ... 98 A5
Victoria Grange Way. Morley LS27 ... 98 A5 4
Victoria House. Leeds LS5 ... 59 A4
Victoria Ind Est. Brad ... 56 C4
Victoria La. Hud HD7 ... 152 C4
Victoria La. Hud HD1 ... 154 B6
Victoria Mews. Hors LS18 ... 58 A7
Victoria Mews. Keigh BD21 ... 35 B7
Victoria Mews. Morley LS27 ... 98 A5 6
Victoria Mills. Batley ... 118 B6
Victoria Mount. Hors LS18 ... 58 A7
Victoria Park Ave. Leeds LS13, LS5 ... 58 F3
Victoria Park Gr. Leeds LS13, LS5 ... 58 E3
Victoria Park Sch. Leeds ... 58 E3
Victoria Park St. Keigh BD21 ... 35 D8 7
Victoria Park View. Keigh BD21 35 D8
Victoria Pk. Ship BD18 ... 54 F7
Victoria Pl. B Spa LS23 ... 30 D4
Victoria Pl. Brig HD6 ... 115 B1
Victoria Pl. Castle WF10 ... 124 E8
Victoria Pl. Honley HD7 ... 171 F4
Victoria Pl. Hud HD4 ... 153 A1
Victoria Pl. Hud HD5 ... 154 D5 6
Victoria Pl. Mir WF14 ... 137 F5 5
Victoria Pl. Yeadon LS19 ... 40 A7
Victoria Prim Sch. Roth ... 100 D6
Victoria Rd. Brad BD2 ... 56 C4
Victoria Rd. Brad BD6 ... 94 A8
Victoria Rd. Brig HX3 ... 114 D7
Victoria Rd. Brig HD6 ... 115 B7
Victoria Rd. Bur in W LS29 ... 9 E2
Victoria Rd. Clec BD19 ... 117 C8
Victoria Rd. Dew WF13 ... 118 C1
Victoria Rd. Dew WF12 ... 139 C4
Victoria Rd. Elland HX5 ... 134 E6
Victoria Rd. Glu BD20 ... 16 D6
Victoria Rd. Guise LS20 ... 39 D8
Victoria Rd. Hali HX1 ... 113 A7
Victoria Rd. Haw BD22 ... 34 D2
Victoria Rd. Haw BD22 ... 51 D7
Victoria Rd. Heb Br HX7 ... 89 A4
Victoria Rd. Hud HD1 ... 153 F4
Victoria Rd. Ilkley LS29 ... 7 F4
Victoria Rd. Keigh BD21 ... 35 B5
Victoria Rd. Leeds LS5 ... 59 A4
Victoria Rd. Leeds LS6 ... 59 E3
Victoria Rd. Leeds LS11 ... 79 B6
Victoria Rd. Liver WF15 ... 117 A3
Victoria Rd. Mel HD7 ... 170 D2
Victoria Rd. Morley LS27 ... 98 A6
Victoria Rd. Pudsey LS28 ... 57 D2
Victoria Rd. Pudsey LS28 ... 76 C7
Victoria Rd. Roth LS26 ... 100 D6
Victoria Rd. Roy S71 ... 179 D4
Victoria Rd. Ship BD18 ... 54 F8
Victoria Rd. Sow Br HX6 ... 112 B3
Victoria Rd. Tod OL14 ... 108 B6 10
Victoria Rise. Pudsey LS28 ... 76 C7
Victoria Sh Ctr. Brad ... 74 D8
Victoria Springs. Holmfi HD7 . 188 E4
Victoria Sq. Holmfi HD7 ... 189 A5
Victoria Sq. Leeds LS1 ... 79 B8 3
Victoria St. Ack M T WF7 ... 163 D5
Victoria St. Bail BD17 ... 38 C1 3
Victoria St. Batley WF17 ... 96 F1
Victoria St. Batley WF16 ... 117 D4
Victoria St. Batley WF17 ... 118 B6
Victoria St. Bing BD16 ... 36 E7
Victoria St. Brad BD10 ... 39 B2
Victoria St. Brad BD15 ... 54 A3
Victoria St. Brad BD2 ... 56 D2
Victoria St. Brad BD14 ... 73 B4 9
Victoria St. Brad BD1 ... 74 D8
Victoria St. Brig HD6 ... 115 B1
Victoria St. Brig HD6 ... 115 C2
Victoria St. Castle WF10 ... 124 B8
Victoria St. Clay W HD8 ... 175 E2
Victoria St. Clec BD19 ... 116 D8
Victoria St. Cull BD13 ... 52 E6
Victoria St. Dew WF13 ... 138 E6
Victoria St. Elland HX4 ... 134 D7
Victoria St. Feath WF7 ... 145 D5
Victoria St. Hali HX1 ... 113 C7
Victoria St. Haw BD22 ... 34 D2
Victoria St. Hem WF9 ... 181 E6
Victoria St. Holmfi HD7 ... 189 A5
Victoria St. Hor WF4 ... 140 F1
Victoria St. Hud HD2 ... 136 E3
Victoria St. Hud HD3 ... 153 C8
Victoria St. Hud HD1 ... 154 A4
Victoria St. Hud HD5 ... 154 D5
Victoria St. Kippax WF10 ... 103 B4
Victoria St. Leeds LS2 ... 59 F1
Victoria St. Leeds LS7 ... 60 D7
Victoria St. Leeds LS10 ... 79 D6
Victoria St. Loft G WF1 ... 121 B4
Victoria St. Mars HD7 ... 168 F4
Victoria St. Morley LS27 ... 97 F5
Victoria St. Morley LS27 ... 98 C7
Victoria St. Pont WF8 ... 125 D3
Victoria St. Pudsey LS28 ... 57 B6
Victoria St. Queen BD13 ... 72 F1
Victoria St. S in Cra BD20 ... 16 D5
Victoria St. Ship BD17 ... 55 B8
Victoria St. Sow Br HX6 ... 112 B3
Victoria St. Tod OL14 ... 86 C1
Victoria St. Wake WF2 ... 142 A7
Victoria St. Weth LS22 ... 13 F5
Victoria St. Wils BD15 ... 53 C4
Victoria Street Cty Prim Inf Sch. Batley ... 117 D4
Victoria Terr. Add LS29 ... 6 F8
Victoria Terr. Brig HX3 ... 114 D7
Victoria Terr. Clay W HD8 ... 175 F2
Victoria Terr. Guise LS20 ... 22 E1
Victoria Terr. Hali HX2 ... 111 E5
Victoria Terr. Hali HX2 ... 113 A4 4
Victoria Terr. Hali HX1 ... 113 A6
Victoria Terr. Keigh BD21 ... 35 D7 5
Victoria Terr. L Brad BD20 ... 4 C5
Victoria Terr. Leeds LS3 ... 59 F1
Victoria Terr. Pudsey LS28 ... 57 F2 1
Victoria Terr. Tod OL14 ... 109 A7
Victoria Terr. Yeadon LS19 ... 40 D7
Victoria Way. Loft G WF1 ... 121 B3
Victoria Wlk. Hors LS18 ... 58 A7
Victory Ave. Hud HD3 ... 153 C5
Victory La. Loft G WF3 ... 122 A2
Victory Rd. Ilkley LS29 ... 8 B4
View Croft Rd. Ship BD17 ... 55 C8
View Rd. Keigh BD20 ... 35 A8
View St. Hud HD5 ... 154 D5
View The. Leeds LS17 ... 43 A6
View The. Leeds LS8 ... 61 A8
Viewlands Cres. Men LS29 ... 22 D5
Viewlands. Hud HD2 ... 136 B4
Viewlands Mount. Men LS29 ... 22 D5
Viewlands Rise. Men LS29 ... 22 D5
Vignola Terr. Brad BD14 ... 73 C5
Viking Ave. Emley HD8 ... 175 D6
Viking Rd. Pont WF8 ... 146 E8
Villa Cl. Ack M T WF7 ... 164 B8
Villa Gr. Bing BD16 ... 37 A4
Villa Mount. Brad BD12 ... 94 C1
Villa Rd. Bing BD16 ... 37 A4
Villa St. Hali HX6 ... 112 C4
Village Ave. Leeds LS4 ... 59 D3
Village Gdns. Leeds LS15 ... 81 D6
Village Pl. Leeds LS4 ... 59 D2
Village Rd. Eccup LS16 ... 25 F1
Village St. Brig HX3 ... 94 A2
Village St The. Leeds LS4 ... 59 D2
Village Terr. Leeds LS4 ... 59 D3
Village The. Kirkb HD4 ... 172 F1
Village The. Kirkb HD4 ... 172 F6
Village The. Th Arch LS23 ... 14 E1
Vincent Ave. Stee BD20 ... 17 A5
Vincent St. Brad BD1 ... 74 D7
Vincent St. Hali HX1 ... 112 F6
Vine Ave. Clec BD19 ... 116 C8
Vine Cl. Brig HD6 ... 115 D2
Vine Cres. Clec BD19 ... 116 D8
Vine Cres. Brig HD6 ... 115 D2
Vine Ct. Guise LS20 ... 39 E8
Vine Garth. Brig HD6 ... 115 D3
Vine Gr. Brig HD6 ... 115 D2
Vine St. Brad BD7 ... 74 B4
Vine St. Clec BD19 ... 116 D8
Vine St. Hud HD1 ... 154 C8
Vine Terr E. Brad BD8 ... 73 E8
Vine Terr. Hali HX1 ... 113 B6
Vine Terr. Thorn BD13 ... 72 D6 3
Vine Terr W. Brad BD8 ... 73 E7
Vinery Ave. Leeds LS9 ... 80 A8
Vinery Cl. Clay W HD8 ... 175 F2
Vinery Gr. Leeds LS9 ... 80 A8 3
Vinery Mount. Leeds LS9 ... 80 A7
Vinery Pl. Leeds LS9 ... 80 A7
Vinery Rd. Leeds LS4 ... 59 D2
Vinery St. Leeds LS9 ... 80 A7
Vinery St. Leeds LS9 ... 80 A8 4
Vinery Terr. Leeds LS9 ... 80 A7
Vinery View. Leeds LS9 ... 80 A7
Vineyard. Hud HD7 ... 152 D5
Violet St. Hali HX1 ... 113 A7
Violet St. Haw BD22 ... 51 C6
Violet St N. Hali HX1 ... 113 A8
Virginia Cl. Loft G WF2 ... 121 A6
Virginia Ct. Loft G WF2 ... 121 A6
Virginia Dr. Loft G WF2 ... 121 A6
Virginia Gdns. Loft G WF2 ... 121 A6
Virginia Rd. Hud HD3 ... 153 C7
Virginia St. Brad BD14 ... 73 C3
Virginia Terr. Thorner LS14 ... 45 F5
Vissett Cl. Hem WF9 ... 181 B6
Vissett La. Hem WF9 ... 181 B6
Vivian Pl. Brad BD7 ... 74 A3
Vivien Rd. Brad BD8 ... 73 C8
Vulcan Cl. Dew WF13 ... 139 C8
Vulcan Gdns. Dew WF13 ... 139 C8
Vulcan Rd. Dew WF13 ... 139 C8
Vulcan St. Brad BD4 ... 75 D1
Vulcan St. Brig HD6 ... 115 C1
Vulcan St. Tod OL14 ... 108 A1 11

Waddilove's Hospl. Brad ... 55 D2
Waddington St. Keigh BD21 ... 35 C6 1
Wade House Ave. Shelf HX3 ... 93 C6
Wade House Rd. Shelf HX3 ... 93 C6
Wade St. Brad BD1 ... 74 E6
Wade St. Hali HX1 ... 113 D7
Wade St. Pudsey LS28 ... 57 D3
Wadhouse La. Crig WF4 ... 160 A8
Wadlands Cl. Pudsey LS28 ... 57 D4
Wadlands Dr. Pudsey LS28 ... 57 C4
Wadlands Gr. Pudsey LS28 ... 57 C4
Wadlands Rise. Pudsey LS28 .. 57 C3
Wadman Rd. Holmfi HD7 ... 189 D3
Wadsworth Ave. Tod OL14 ... 108 A4
Wadsworth Ct. Hali HX1 ... 113 A8 2
Wadsworth La. Heb Br HX7 ... 89 C3
Wadsworth St. Hali HX1 ... 112 F8 4
Waggon La. Upton WF9 ... 183 C8
Wagon La. Bing BD16 ... 37 A1
Wain Brow. Hud HD4 ... 171 F8
Wain Ct. Hud HD4 ... 171 F8
Wain Pk. Hud HD4 ... 171 F8
Waincliffe Cres. Leeds LS11 ... 78 F1
Waincliffe Dr. Leeds LS11 ... 98 F8
Waincliffe Garth. Leeds LS11 .. 78 F1
Waincliffe Mount. Leeds LS11 . 98 F8
Waincliffe Pl. Leeds LS11 ... 78 F1
Waincliffe Sq. Leeds LS11 ... 78 F1
Waincliffe Terr. Leeds LS11 ... 98 F8
Waindale Cl. Hali HX2 ... 91 A3
Waindale Cres. Hali HX2 ... 91 A3
Waindike Cl. Nor WF6 ... 123 C3
Waindyke Way. Nor WF6 ... 123 D2
Waingate. Hud HD4 ... 171 F8
Waingate Pk. Slai HD7 ... 152 D1
Wainhouse Rd. Hali HX1 ... 112 F5
Wainhouse Terr. Hali HX2 ... 112 F5 22
Wainman Sq. Brad BD12 ... 94 C3 2
Wainman St. Bail BD17 ... 38 D4
Wainman St. Brad BD12 ... 94 C3 1
Wainman St. Hali HX1 ... 112 F7 17
Wainman St. Ship BD17 ... 55 B8
Wainscott Cl. Wad M HX7 ... 89 B6
Wainsgate La. Wad M HX7 ... 89 B6
Wainsgate. Wad M HX7 ... 89 B6
Wainstalls Cty Prim Sch. Hali .. 90 F5
Wainstalls. Hali HX2 ... 90 F5
Wainstalls La. Hali HX2 ... 90 F5
Wainstalls Lodge La. Hali HX2 90 E5
Wainstalls Rd. Hali HX2 ... 90 F5
Waite St. Wake WF2 ... 141 E6
Waites Croft. Wake WF2 ... 120 B2
Waites Terr. Otley LS21 ... 23 B7
Wakefield 41 Ind Pk. Loft G ... 120 F5
Wakefield Ave. Leeds LS14 ... 61 F1
Wakefield Cathedral CE Sch. Wake ... 142 A3
Wakefield City High Sch.Wake 142 F7
Wakefield Cres. Dew WF12 ... 139 F8
Wakefield District Coll. Hem . 181 E7
Wakefield District Coll. Wake 142 A5
Wakefield District Coll. Wake 142 B7
Wakefield Eastmoor Fst Sch. Wake ... 142 D7
Wakefield Gate. Hali HX3 ... 112 F4
Wakefield Girls High Sch. Wake ... 142 B7
Wakefield Greenhill Fst Sch. Wake ... 142 D7
Wakefield Heath View Mid Sch. Wake ... 142 E7
Wakefield Independent Jun Sch. W Har ... 162 F6
Wakefield Kettlethorpe Fst Sch. Wake ... 160 B5
Wakefield Lawefield Fst Sch. Wake ... 142 A5
Wakefield Lawefield Mid Sch. Wake ... 142 A5
Wakefield (Lupset) Municipal Golf Course. Wake ... 141 E2
Wakefield Manygates Mid Sch. Wake ... 142 D2
Wakefield Meth (C) Fst Sch. Wake ... 142 C3
Wakefield Old Rd. Dew WF12 139 D8 6
Wakefield Rd. Ack M T WF7 .. 163 E5
Wakefield Rd. Birk BD11 ... 97 A5
Wakefield Rd. Brad BD4 ... 75 B4
Wakefield Rd. Brig HD6, HX3 114 E7
Wakefield Rd. Brig HD6 ... 115 B2 4
Wakefield Rd. Brig HD6 ... 115 C1
Wakefield Rd. Clay W HD8 ... 175 E2
Wakefield Rd. D Dale HD8 ... 192 B7
Wakefield Rd. Dew WF12 ... 139 E8
Wakefield Rd. Feath WF7 ... 145 B5
Wakefield Rd. Floc WF4 ... 157 C4
Wakefield Rd. Gar LS25 ... 82 C4
Wakefield Rd. Gild LS27 ... 97 D5
Wakefield Rd. Hali HX3 ... 113 B2
Wakefield Rd. Hem WF9 ... 163 B2
Wakefield Rd. Hor WF4 ... 141 C2
Wakefield Rd. Hud HD1, HD5 154 D5
Wakefield Rd. Leeds LS10 ... 79 F2
Wakefield Rd. Lepton HD8 ... 155 D3
Wakefield Rd. Liver WF15 ... 117 B4
Wakefield Rd. Liver HD6 ... 116 B7
Wakefield Rd. Mapp S75 ... 178 C2
Wakefield Rd. Ossett WF5 ... 140 F7
Wakefield Rd. Pont WF8 ... 146 B7
Wakefield Rd. Roth LS26 ... 100 B6
Wakefield Rd. Roth LS26 ... 101 C2
Wakefield Rd. Swil LS26 ... 82 C4
Wakefield Rd. Wake WF5, WF2 ... 141 B6
Walden Dr. Brad BD9 ... 54 C3
Walden Howe Cl. Feath WF7 . 145 C8
Walden St. Castle WF10 ... 124 D7
Waldorf Way. Wake WF2 ... 142 C5
Walesby Ct. Hors LS16 ... 41 E2
Walford Ave. Leeds LS9 ... 80 A8
Walford Gr. Leeds LS9 ... 80 A8
Walford Mount. Leeds LS9 ... 80 A8
Walford Rd. Leeds LS9 ... 80 A8
Walford Terr. Leeds LS9 ... 80 A8
Walk Royd Hill. Kex S75 ... 177 B2
Walk The. Keigh BD21 ... 35 C6
Walk The. Pudsey LS28 ... 57 C2
Walker Ave. Brad BD7 ... 73 E5
Walker Ave. Wake WF2 ... 141 F7
Walker Cl. Glu BD20 ... 16 B6
Walker Dr. Brad BD8 ... 74 B8
Walker Gn. Dew WF12 ... 139 E2
Walker La. Hali HX6 ... 112 D4
Walker La. Hor WF4 ... 141 B1
Walker La. Wad M HX7 ... 89 C5
Walker Pl. Morley LS27 ... 98 B7 7
Walker Pl. Ship BD18 ... 55 D8
Walker Rd. Brad BD12 ... 94 F4
Walker Rd. Hors LS18 ... 41 B1
Walker Rd. Men LS29 ... 21 F4
Walker St. Brad BD4 ... 95 B8
Walker St. Brig BD19 ... 115 F8 3
Walker St. Clec BD19 ... 116 D8
Walker St. Dew WF13 ... 138 D4
Walker St. Dew WF12 ... 139 D3
Walker St. Dew WF12 ... 139 F6
Walker Terr. Brad BD4 ... 75 B4
Walker Terr. Cull BD13 ... 52 D5
Walker Wood. Bail BD17 ... 37 F2
Walker's La. Leeds LS12 ... 78 C4
Walker's La. Sil BD20 ... 5 D1
Walker's Pl. Sil BD20 ... 17 E8
Walker's Rd. Leeds LS6 ... 59 F5
Walker's Terr. Wake WF1 ... 142 B6
Walkergate. Otley LS21 ... 23 A8
Walkergate. Pont WF8 ... 125 E1
Walkers Gn. Leeds LS12 ... 78 C4
Walkers Mount. Batley WF17 118 C3
Walkers Row. Yeadon LS19 ... 40 A7
Walkley Ave. Batley WF16 ... 117 D3
Walkley Gr. Batley WF16 ... 117 D3 10
Walkley La. Batley WF16 ... 117 D2
Walkley Terr. Batley WF16 ... 117 E2
Walkley Villas. Batley WF16 .. 117 E2
Wall Nook La. Holmfi HD8 ... 190 D6
Wall St. Keigh BD22 ... 34 F6
Wallace Gdns. Loft G WF3 ... 121 B6
Wallace St. Hali HX1 ... 112 F6
Wallbank Dr. Ship BD18 ... 55 C6
Walled Garden The. Wool WF4178 A7
Waller Clough Rd. Slai HD7 ... 151 F4
Wallingford Mount. Brad BD15 73 B7
Wallis St. Brad BD8 ... 73 F7
Wallis St. Brad BD8 ... 74 A7
Wallis St. Hali HX6 ... 112 B4
Wallroyds. D Dale HD8 ... 191 F5
Walmer Gr. Pudsey LS28 ... 76 F5
Walmer Gr. Pudsey LS28 ... 77 A5
Walmer Villas. Brad BD8 ... 55 D1
Walmsley Dr. Upton WF9 ... 183 B7
Walmsley Rd. Leeds LS6 ... 59 E3
Walnut Ave. Dew WF12 ... 140 B7
Walnut Ave. Wake WF2 ... 141 F7
Walnut Cl. Dew WF12 ... 140 A6
Walnut Cl. Leeds LS14 ... 62 C8
Walnut Cres. Dew WF12 ... 140 A6
Walnut Cres. Wake WF2 ... 141 F7
Walnut Dr. Dew WF12 ... 140 B7
Walnut Dr. Nor WF6 ... 144 A7
Walnut Dr. Pont WF8 ... 146 C6
Walnut Gr. Dew WF12 ... 140 B7
Walnut La. Dew WF12 ... 140 A7
Walnut Pl. Dew WF12 ... 140 A7
Walnut Rd. Dew WF12 ... 140 B7
Walnut St. Brad BD3 ... 75 C6
Walnut St. Hali HX1 ... 113 A7
Walnut St. Keigh BD21 ... 35 B4 15
Walnut St. S Elm WF9 ... 182 F1
Walpole Rd. Hud HD4 ... 153 D3
Walsden Est. Tod ... 129 B7
Walsden Est. Tod OL14 ... 129 B7
Walsden Jun Sch. Tod ... 108 A1
Walsh La. Bing BD16 ... 37 A7
Walsh La. Gild LS12 ... 77 D2
Walsh La. Hali HX3 ... 92 B1
Walsh St. Hali HX1 ... 112 F7 12
Walsh's Sq. Hali HX1 ... 113 A5 23
Walsham Dr. Hud HD3 ... 134 F1
Walshaw La. Wad M BB10 ... 68 C3
Walshaw St. Brad BD7 ... 74 A4 2
Walter Clough La. Brig HX3 .. 114 C5
Walter Cres. Leeds LS9 ... 79 F7
Walter St. Brad BD10 ... 56 B8
Walter St. Leeds LS4 ... 59 D1
Walter St. Ship BD2 ... 55 D4
Waltham Dr. Ad Le S DN6 ... 184 E2
Waltin Rd. Holmfi HD7 ... 188 F1
Walton Cl. Bacup OL13 ... 106 A1
Walton Croft. Hud HD5 ... 154 E6
Walton Dr. Birk BD11 ... 96 F5
Walton Fold. Tod OL14 ... 108 D6 2
Walton Garth. Birk BD11 ... 96 F5
Walton Grove Inf Sch. Walton 161 B6
Walton Jun Sch. Walton ... 161 A7
Walton La. Brig BD19 ... 115 F6
Walton La. Wake WF2 ... 160 F8
Walton Rd. Th Arch LS23 ... 14 C4
Walton Rd. Upton WF9 ... 183 D8
Walton Rd. Weth LS22, LS23 ... 14 C4
Walton St. Brad BD4 ... 74 F5
Walton St. Hali HX6 ... 112 B4
Walton St. Leeds LS11 ... 79 B6
Walton St. Leeds LS10 ... 79 D7
Walton Station La. Wake WF2 160 F7
Walton View. Crof WF4 ... 161 F8
Waltroyd Rd. Clec BD19 ... 116 C7
Wansford Cl. Brad BD4 ... 75 E2
Wanstead Cres. Brad BD15 ... 73 B8
Wapping Fst Sch. Brad ... 74 F8
Wapping Nick La. Elland HX4 134 E3
Wapping Rd. Brad BD3 ... 74 F8
Warburton Pl. Brad BD6 ... 74 C1 9
Warburton Rd. Emley HD8 ... 175 D6
Warcock La. Bacup OL13 ... 106 B3
Ward Bank Rd. Holmfi HD7 ... 189 A4
Ward Ct. Brig HD6 ... 135 F7
Ward La. Loft G WF3 ... 122 A2
Ward Place La. Holmfi HD7 ... 188 F3
Ward Sq. Hud HD1 ... 154 A6 26
Ward St. Brad BD7 ... 74 A3
Ward St. Dew WF13 ... 118 D1
Ward St. Keigh BD21 ... 35 B6 4
Ward St. Leeds LS10 ... 79 D5
Ward's End. Hali HX1 ... 113 C6
Wardman St. Keigh BD21 ... 18 E1
Wards Hill. Batley WF17 ... 118 C5
Wards Hill Ct. Batley WF17 ... 118 C5 10
Wareham Cnr. Brad BD4 ... 75 E1
Warehouse Hill Rd. Mars HD7 169 A4
Warehouse St. Batley WF17 . 118 D4
Waring Way. Dew WF12 ... 118 E1
Warlands End Gate. Litt OL14 129 D5
Warlbeck. Ilkley LS29 ... 7 F4
Warley Ave. Brad BD3 ... 75 D8
Warley Dene. Hali HX2 ... 112 B6
Warley Dr. Brad BD3 ... 75 D8
Warley Edge La. Hali HX2 ... 112 C7
Warley Gr. Brad BD3 ... 75 D8
Warley Gr. Hali HX2 ... 112 D7
Warley Rd. Hali HX1, HX2 ... 112 E6
Warley Road Jun & Inf Sch. Hali ... 112 E6
Warley St. Hali HX1 ... 113 A6
Warley Town Cty Prim Sch. Hali ... 112 B6
Warley Town La. Hali HX2 ... 112 A6
Warley View. Hali HX2 ... 112 D7
Warley Wood Ave. Hali HX2 .. 111 F5
Warley Wood La. Hali HX2 ... 111 F5
Warm La. Yeadon LS19 ... 40 A5
Warmfield Heath Parochial Sch. Crof ... 143 B4
Warmfield La. Crof WF1 ... 143 E7
Warmfield View. Wake WF1 . 142 F7
Warmliegh Pk. Queen BD13 ... 72 B1
Warneford Ave. Ossett WF5 . 140 D7
Warneford Rd. Hud HD4 ... 153 A3
Warneford Rise. Hud HD4 ... 153 A3
Warnford Gr. Brad BD4 ... 75 D3
Warrel's Ave. Leeds LS13 ... 58 C3 4
Warrel's Ct. Leeds LS13 ... 58 C2
Warrel's Gr. Leeds LS13 ... 58 C2
Warrel's Mount. Leeds LS13 ... 58 C2
Warrel's Pl. Leeds LS13 ... 58 C3
Warrel's Rd. Leeds LS13 ... 58 C3
Warrel's Row. Leeds LS13 ... 58 C2 4
Warrel's St. Leeds LS13 ... 58 C2
Warrel's Terr. Leeds LS13 ... 58 C2 19
Warren Ave. Bing BD16 ... 37 B5
Warren Ave. Knot WF11 ... 126 D3
Warren Ave. Wake WF2 ... 142 D2
Warren Cl. Liver WF15 ... 117 B2
Warren Cl. Roy S71 ... 179 D5
Warren Ct. Wake WF1 ... 142 D6
Warren Dr. Bing BD16 ... 37 B4
Warren Dr. Feath WF7 ... 145 A8
Warren House La. E Carl LS19 23 D1
Warren House La. Hud HD3 .. 135 A3
Warren House. Wake WF1 ... 142 C6 22
Warren La. Arth LS21 ... 25 A7
Warren La. Bing BD16 ... 37 B4
Warren La. Bramham LS24 ... 31 B1
Warren La. Mapp S75 ... 178 C4
Warren La. Wool S75 ... 178 C4
Warren Park Cl. Brig HD6 ... 114 E5
Warren Pk. Brig HD6 ... 114 E6
Warren St. Dew WF12 ... 139 D6
Warrens La. Birk WF17 ... 96 D5
Warrens La. Clec WF17 ... 96 D3
Warrenside. Hud HD2 ... 136 E4
Warrenton Pl. Brad BD7 ... 74 A5
Warrington Terr. Mars HD7 .. 168 E4
Warsop Rd. Barn S71 ... 178 E1
Warton Ave. Brad BD4 ... 75 B1
Warwick Ave. Hud HD7 ... 152 E5
Warwick Cl. Brad BD4 ... 75 B4
Warwick Cl. Hali HX3 ... 113 B4 1
Warwick Ct. Hors LS18 ... 58 C7 1
Warwick Dr. Brad BD4 ... 75 B4
Warwick Rd. Batley WF17 ... 118 D3
Warwick Rd. Brad BD4 ... 75 B4
Warwick Road Jun & Inf Sch. Batley ... 118 C3
Warwick St. Wake WF1 ... 142 F3
Wasdale Cres. Wake WF2 ... 141 E7
Wasdale Rd. Wake WF2 ... 141 E7
Washburn Ct. Sil BD20 ... 5 E1
Washburn Ct. Weth LS22 ... 13 D8
Washburn Dr. Glu BD20 ... 16 C7
Washer La. Hali HX2 ... 112 F4
Washer Lane Ind Est. Hali ... 112 F4
Washfold Rd. Heb Br HX7 ... 131 B7
Washington Pl. Pudsey LS13 ... 77 A8
Washington St. Brad BD8 ... 54 F1
Washington St. Hali HX3 ... 92 A1 20
Washington St. Leeds LS12 ... 78 E8
Washington St. Pudsey LS13 ... 77 A8
Washington Terr. Pudsey LS13 77 A8
Washpit New Rd. Holmfi HD7 189 B3
Wasp Nest Rd. Hud HD1 ... 136 A1
Waste La. Hud HD5 ... 154 E4
Waste La. Mir WF14 ... 137 F3
Waste La. Mir WF14 ... 138 A3
Waste La. Wad M HX7 ... 69 A5
Waste The. Mir WF14 ... 137 F3
Wastwater Dr. Brad BD6 ... 93 F6
Watchit Hole La. Th Aud WF8 165 C4
Watchley La. H Pag DN5 ... 195 B3
Water Gn. Rip HX6 ... 132 A6
Water Green La. Rip HX6 ... 132 A6
Water Hill La. Hali HX2 ... 112 A5
Water La. Brad BD1 ... 74 D7
Water La. Dar WF8 ... 146 D2
Water La. Dew WF12 ... 139 B6
Water La. Dew WF12 ... 140 A7
Water La. Hali HX3 ... 113 D6
Water La. K Smea WF8 ... 166 E6
Water La. Keigh BD21 ... 35 B6
Water La. Leeds LS12 ... 77 D7
Water La. Leeds LS11 ... 79 A6
Water La. Leeds LS11 ... 79 C7
Water La. Loft G WF3 ... 121 F4
Water La. Neth WF4 ... 158 D8
Water La. Pont WF8 ... 125 F3
Water La. Pudsey LS28 ... 57 D3
Water La. S Kirk WF9 ... 181 F4
Water La. Shep HD8 ... 174 A3
Water La. Wool WF4 ... 178 A8
Water La. Yeadon LS18 ... 40 F1
Water Lane Cl. Neth WF4 ... 158 D8
Water Row. Holmfi HD7 ... 189 E6
Water Royd Ave. Mir WF14 ... 138 A6
Water Royd Cres. Mir WF14 . 138 A6
Water Royd Dr. Mir WF14 ... 138 A6
Water Royd La. Mir WF14 ... 138 A6
Water Side La. Holmfi HD7 ... 188 D2
Water St. Brig HD6 ... 115 B3
Water St. Clay W HD8 ... 175 D1
Water St. Holmfi HD7 ... 188 D3
Water St. Hud HD1, HD4 ... 153 F3
Water St. Hud HD1 ... 153 F5
Water St. Sow Br HX6 ... 112 B3
Water St. Tod OL14 ... 108 B5
Water Stalls Rd. Heb Br HX7 . 110 F2
Watercock St. Brad BD4 ... 75 A5
Watercroft. Hud HD5 ... 154 F3
Waterfall Cotts. Mars HD7 ... 168 D5
Watergate. Brig HX3 ... 114 C7
Watergate. Hud HD1 ... 154 B6
Watergate. M'town LS26 ... 102 B1
Watergate. Pont WF8 ... 125 C1
Watergate Rd. Dew WF12 ... 139 B7
Waterhouse Ct. Hors LS18 ... 58 B7 8
Waterhouse Dr. E Ard WF3 ... 120 B7
Waterhouse Gr. Wake WF2 ... 142 A6
Waterhouse St. Hali HX1 ... 113 C7
Waterhouse St. Keigh BD21 ... 35 B7 8
Waterloo Cl. Castle WF10 ... 123 F5
Waterloo Cres. Brad BD10 ... 56 F8
Waterloo Cres. Leeds LS13 ... 58 D4
Waterloo Fold. Brad BD12 ... 94 D2 2
Waterloo Gr. Pudsey LS28 ... 76 B7
Waterloo Jun Sch. Pudsey ... 76 C7
Waterloo La. Leeds LS13 ... 58 D3
Waterloo Mount. Pudsey LS28 76 B8
Waterloo Rd. Bing BD16 ... 36 F3
Waterloo Rd. Brig HD6 ... 115 A3
Waterloo Rd. Hud HD5 ... 155 B6
Waterloo Rd. Pudsey LS28 ... 76 B7
Waterloo Rise. Hud HD5 ... 155 A5
Waterloo St. Leeds LS10 ... 79 C7
Waterloo St. Wake WF1 ... 142 D4
Waterloo Terr. Hali HX6 ... 112 C6
Waterloo Way. Leeds LS13 ... 58 D3
Waters Rd. Mars HD7 ... 168 D5
Waterside. Bing BD16 ... 36 D5
Waterside Fold. Heb Br HX7 ... 89 A4
Waterside. Hali HX3 ... 113 D6
Waterside. Hud HD4 ... 153 F2
Waterside. Hud HD1 ... 153 F5
Waterside Ind Pk. Leeds ... 80 B2
Waterside Mill. Oxen BD22 ... 51 E1
Waterside. Oxen BD22 ... 51 C2
Waterside Rd. Brad BD8 ... 74 A8
Waterside Rd. Leeds LS10 ... 80 B3
Waterside. Sil BD20 ... 17 F8
Waterside Wlk. Kirkhe WF14 137 D5
Watersole La. Weth LS23 ... 14 B4
Waterton Cl. S Kirk WF9 ... 182 D3
Waterton Cl. Walton WF2 ... 161 A6
Waterton Gr. Wake WF2 ... 141 F5
Waterton Prim Sch. Wake ... 141 D4
Waterton Rd. Wake WF2 ... 141 E4
Waterton St. Castle WF10 ... 124 B7
Waterwood Cl. E Ard WF3 ... 119 F7
Waterworks Rd. Batley WF17 117 F4
Watery La. Holme HD7 ... 197 F8
Watford Ave. Brig HX3 ... 93 F3
Watkin Ave. Thorn BD13 ... 72 F6
Watkinson Ave. Hali HX2 ... 91 F4
Watkinson Bglws. Hali HX2 ... 91 E3
Watkinson Dr. Hali HX2 ... 91 F4
Watkinson Rd. Hali HX2 ... 91 F4
Watling Rd. Castle WF10 ... 104 E1
Watmough St. Brad BD7 ... 74 A3 2
Watroyd La. Slai HD7 ... 152 B2
Watson Ave. Dew WF12 ... 140 B8
Watson Cl. Oxen BD22 ... 51 C2
Watson Cres. Wake WF1 ... 142 E7
Watson Mill La. Sow Br HX6 .. 112 B2
Watson Rd. Leeds LS14 ... 61 F1
Watson St. Morley LS27 ... 97 F3
Watson St. Nor WF6 ... 123 A2
Watson's La. Tad LS24 ... 31 D5
Watt St. Brad BD4 ... 75 D6
Wattlesyke. Coll LS22 ... 29 E8
Watts St. Brad BD14 ... 73 B4
Watty Hall Ave. Brad BD6 ... 74 A2
Watty Hall La. Brad BD6 ... 74 B2
Watty Hall Rd. Brad BD6 ... 74 A2
Watty La. Tod OL14 ... 107 F3
Watty Terr. Tod OL14 ... 107 F3
Wauchope St. Wake WF2 ... 142 B5
Wauds Gates. Bail BD17 ... 38 C1
Waulkmill Cl. Upton WF9 ... 183 A7
Wavell Garth. Wake WF2 ... 160 F7
Wavell Gr. Wake WF2 ... 160 F7
Waveney Rd. Leeds LS12 ... 78 C5
Waverley Ave. Brad BD7 ... 74 B5
Waverley Ave. Keigh BD20 ... 36 B8
Waverley Cres. Brig HX3 ... 114 C7
Waverley Garth. Leeds LS11 .. 79 B4
Waverley Mid Sch. Brad ... 74 B5
Waverley Pl. Brad BD7 ... 74 B5
Waverley Rd. Brad BD7 ... 74 B5
Waverley Rd. Elland HX5 ... 134 F5
Waverley Rd. Hud HD1 ... 153 F7
Waverley Sch. Hud ... 153 E8
Waverley St. Dew WF12 ... 139 C7
Waverley St. Slai HD7 ... 151 F1
Waverley Terr. Brad BD7 ... 74 B5
Waverley Terr. Brig HX3 ... 114 C7
Waverley Terr. Hud HD1 ... 153 D7
Waverton Gn. Brad BD6 ... 93 F7
Wavertree Park Gdns. Brad BD12 ... 94 C4 12
Wayland App. Hors LS16 ... 42 D4
Wayland Croft. Hors LS16 ... 42 D4
Wayland Ct. Hors LS16 ... 42 D4
Wayland Dr. Hors LS16 ... 42 D4
Wayne Cl. Batley WF17 ... 118 C6
Wayside Ave. Bard LS14 ... 28 D1
Wayside Cres. Bard LS14 ... 28 D1
Wayside Cres. Brad BD2 ... 56 B5
Wayside Mount. Bard LS14 ... 28 D1
Weardale Cl. Brad BD4 ... 75 C1
Weardley La. Hare LS17 ... 26 B6
Weather Hill La. Heb Br HX7 . 110 E4
Weather Hill La. Holme HD7 . 198 E8
Weather Hill Rd. Hud HD3 ... 135 A2
Weatherall Pl. Ad Le S DN6 ... 184 F2
Weatherhead Pl. Sil BD20 ... 5 F1
Weatherhill Cres. Hud HD3 ... 135 A2
Weatherhouse Terr. Hali HX2 . 91 D1
Weaver Ct. Brad BD10 ... 56 B8
Weaver Gdns. Morley LS27 ... 98 D3
Weaver St. Leeds LS4 ... 59 D1
Weavers Cotts. Oxen BD22 ... 51 C2 1
Weavers Croft. Brad BD10 ... 39 B2
Weavers Croft. Pudsey LS28 ... 76 F6
Weavers Ct. Leeds LS12 ... 78 B7 5
Weavers Ct. Mel HD7 ... 170 F2
Weavers Ct. Pudsey LS28 ... 76 F5 1
Weavers Hill. Haw BD22 ... 51 C6
Weavers Rd. Pont WF8 ... 125 E1
Weavers Wlk. D Dale HD8 ... 192 B7
Weaverthorpe Rd. Brad BD4 ... 75 E1
Webb Dr. Brad BD2 ... 56 A2
Webb's Terr. Hali HX3 ... 113 D8
Weber Ct. Brad BD3 ... 75 C7
Webster Hill. Dew WF13 ... 139 C8
Webster Pl. Brad BD3 ... 75 B7
Webster Pl. Nor WF6 ... 123 A2
Webster Row. Leeds LS12 ... 78 B6
Webster St. Brad BD3 ... 75 B7
Webster St. Dew WF13 ... 139 C8
Wedgemoor Cl. Brad BD12 ... 94 C4 14
Wedgewood Ct. Leeds LS8 ... 44 A1
Wedgewood Dr. Leeds LS8 ... 44 A1
Wedgewood Gr. Leeds LS8 ... 44 A1
Wedgewood Sch. Brad ... 75 F2
Weeland Ave. Crof WF4 ... 144 B3
Weeland Cres. Crof WF4 ... 144 C4
Weeland Dr. Crof WF4 ... 144 C3
Weeland Rd. Beal DN14 ... 127 D4
Weeland Rd. Crof WF4 ... 144 C3
Weeland Rd. Knot WF11 ... 127 D4
Weet Shaw La. Cud S72 ... 180 B1
Weetlands Cl. Kippax LS25 ... 83 B2
Weetwood Ave. Leeds LS16 ... 59 D7
Weetwood Cty Prim Sch. Leeds 59 D7
Weetwood Cres. Leeds LS16 ... 59 D8
Weetwood Ct. Leeds LS16 ... 59 C8
Weetwood Grange Gr. Leeds LS16 ... 59 B8
Weetwood House Ct. Leeds LS16 ... 59 B8
Weetwood La. Leeds LS16 ... 59 D7
Weetwood Mill La. Leeds LS16 59 D8
Weetwood Park Dr. Leeds LS16 59 B8
Weetwood Rd. Brad BD8 ... 74 A8
Weetwood Rd. Leeds LS16 ... 59 B8
Weetwood Wlk. Leeds LS16 ... 59 C8
Weetworth Ave. Castle WF10 124 F6
Weetworth Pk. Castle WF10 . 124 E6
Weir La. Bacup OL13 ... 106 A7
Weir Side. Mars HD7 ... 168 F4
Weir St. Tod OL14 ... 108 A3
Welbeck Dr. Brad BD7 ... 73 E4
Welbeck La. Wake WF1 ... 143 B8
Welbeck Rd. Batley WF17 ... 96 F2
Welbeck Rd. Leeds LS9 ... 80 A7
Welbeck Rise. Brad BD7 ... 73 E4
Welbeck St. Castle WF10 ... 124 D8
Welbeck St. Wake WF1 ... 142 D3
Welburn Ave. Brig HX3 ... 114 D7
Welburn Ave. Leeds LS16 ... 59 B7
Welburn Cl. Wake WF2 ... 142 F1
Welburn Dr. Leeds LS16 ... 59 B7
Welburn Gr. Leeds LS16 ... 59 B7

Welburn Mount. Brad BD6 93 E8
Welbury Dr. Brad BD8 55 C2
Weldon Dr. Elland HD3 152 A8
Welfare Ave. B in Elm LS15 63 E7
Welham Wlk. Brad BD3 56 A1
Well Cl. Swil LS26 102 E8
Well Cl. Yeadon LS19 40 C3
Well Close Rise. Leeds LS7 60 C2
Well Close St. Brig HD6 115 B3
Well Croft. Ship BD18 55 B7
Well Garth Bank. Leeds LS13 58 B4
Well Garth. Leeds LS15 62 C2
Well Garth Mount. Leeds LS15 62 C2
Well Garth View. Leeds LS13 58 C4
Well Gr. Hud HD2 136 C3
Well Green La. Brig HD6 114 F5
Well Head Dr. Hali HX1 113 C6
Well Head La. Hali HX1 113 C6
Well Head La. Sow Br HX6 111 C3
Well Heads. Denh BD13 72 A6
Well Hill Gr. Roy S71 179 C4
Well Hill. Honley HD7 171 F4
Well Hill. Otley LS21 22 F7
Well Hill. Yeadon LS19 40 B7
Well Holme Mead. Gild LS12 77 E3
Well House Ave. Leeds LS8 61 A5
Well House Cres. Leeds LS8 61 A5
Well House Dr. Leeds LS8 61 A5
Well House Gdns. Leeds LS8 61 A5
Well House Rd. Leeds LS8 61 A5
Well La. Batley WF17 118 D5
Well La. Brig HD6 115 E2
Well La. Dew WF13 138 F8
Well La. Guise LS20 22 E1
Well La. Hali HX1 113 D7
Well La. Holmfi HD7 189 B4
Well La. Kippax LS25 83 A1
Well La. Leeds LS7 60 D7
Well La. Tod OL14 108 B5
Well La. Yeadon LS19 40 B7
Well La. Yeadon LS19 40 C3
Well Royd Ave. Hali HX2 112 C7
Well Royd Cl. Hali HX2 112 D7
Well St. Brad BD1 74 F7
Well St. Denh BD13 71 D8
Well St. Dew WF12 118 E1 3
Well St. Elland HX4 134 B4 2
Well St. Guise LS20 22 E1
Well St. Hud HD1 153 F5
Well St. Keigh BD21 35 B7
Well St. Liver WF15 117 A5
Well St. Pudsey LS28 57 D3
Well St. S in Cra BD20 16 E5
Well St. Tod OL14 108 B4
Well St. Wils BD15 53 C5
Well Terr. Guise LS20 22 E1
Well View. Guise LS20 22 E1
Welland Dr. Gar LS25 83 B6
Wellands Gn. Clec BD19 116 B7
Wellands La. Clec BD19 116 A7
Wellands Terr. Brad BD3 75 C7
Wellcroft Gr. E Ard WF3 119 F7
Wellcroft. Otley LS21 23 B7
Wellesley Gn. Wake WF2 141 E7
Wellesley St. Brad BD1 74 F7 3
Wellfield Ave. Floc WF4 156 E5
Wellfield Cl. Floc WF4 156 E5
Wellfield Cl. Hud HD7 152 E2
Wellfield Rd. Hud HD3 153 C7
Wellfield Terr. Tod OL14 108 B4
Wellgarth. Hali HX1 113 B5
Wellgarth Rd. Feath WF7 145 E4
Wellgate. Castle WF10 124 F6
Wellgate. Elland HX4 134 C8
Wellgate. Mapp S75 178 B1
Wellgate. Slai HD7 152 B3
Wellhead Cl. Bramho LS16 24 E4
Wellhead Mews. Crig WF4 159 F4
Wellholme. Brig HD6 115 B3
Wellhouse Ave. Mir WF14 138 B7
Wellhouse Cl. Mir WF14 138 A7
Wellhouse Fst Sch. Mir 138 B7
Wellhouse La. Hud HD5 137 A1
Wellhouse La. Mir WF14 138 B7
Wellhouse Mid Sch. Mir 138 B7
Wellhouse. Mir WF14 138 B7
Wellington Arc. Brig 115 B2 7
Wellington Bridge St. Leeds LS12 78 F8
Wellington Bridge St. Leeds LS12 79 A7
Wellington Bsns Ctr. Elland 135 A7
Wellington Cres. Ship BD18 55 A7
Wellington Ct. Birk BD11 96 A6
Wellington Ct. Hali HX2 112 E8 4
Wellington Fst Sch. Brad 56 B3
Wellington Garth. Leeds LS13 58 D4 3
Wellington Gdns. Leeds LS13 58 D4
Wellington Gr. Brad BD2 56 B2
Wellington Gr. Leeds LS13 58 D4
Wellington Gr. Pudsey LS28 76 C7
Wellington Hill. Thorner LS14 45 A3
Wellington Mid Sch. Brad 56 B3
Wellington Mount. Leeds LS13 58 D4
Wellington Pl. Hali HX1 113 D6 2
Wellington Pl. Knot WF11 126 D4
Wellington Rd. Brad BD2 56 B3
Wellington Rd. Dew WF13 139 C8
Wellington Rd E. Dew WF13 139 C8 10
Wellington Rd. Ilkley LS29 8 B4
Wellington Rd. Keigh BD21 35 C7
Wellington Rd. Leeds LS12, LS3 78 E6
Wellington Rd. Leeds LS12, LS3 78 F7
Wellington Rd. Tod OL14 108 B6
Wellington Rd. Wils BD15 53 C4
Wellington Sq. Keigh BD21 35 C6 4
Wellington St. Batley WF17 118 C4
Wellington St. Bing BD16 36 F3
Wellington St. Brad BD15 54 C1
Wellington St. Brad BD2 56 B3
Wellington St. Brad BD10 56 B7
Wellington St. Brad BD1 74 F7 2
Wellington St. Brad BD4 75 D6
Wellington St. Castle WF10 124 B8
Wellington St. Dew WF13 139 C8 11
Wellington St. Hud HD3 153 B8
Wellington St. Leeds LS1 79 A7
Wellington St. Liver WF15 117 B3 3
Wellington St. Morley LS27 98 A4
Wellington St. Queen BD13 72 F1
Wellington St S. Hali HX1 113 D6
Wellington St W. Hali HX1 113 B6
Wellington St. Wake WF2 141 E7
Wellington St. Wils BD15 53 C4
Wellington Terr. Leeds LS13 58 D4
Wellington Terr. Mars HD7 169 A4
Wellington Wlk. Dew WF13 139 C8 8
Wells Croft. Leeds LS6 59 E7
Wells Ct. Hali HX3 92 B1
Wells Ct. Ossett WF5 140 C5
Wells Gr. Guise LS20 22 E1
Wells Gn Gdns. Holmfi HD7 188 F7
Wells Mount. D Dale HD8 191 A6
Wells Mount. Guise LS20 22 E1
Wells Prom. Ilkley LS29 8 B3
Wells Rd. Dew WF12 139 E2
Wells Rd. Guise LS20 22 E1
Wells Rd. Ilkley LS29 8 B3
Wells Terr. Brig HX3 94 A2
Wells The. Hali HX2 112 D7
Wells Wlk. Ilkley LS29 8 B3
Wellstone Ave. Pudsey LS13 77 B8
Wellstone Ave. Pudsey LS13 77 C8
Wellstone Dr. Pudsey LS13 58 B1
Wellstone Garth. Pudsey LS13 77 C8
Wellstone Gdns. Pudsey LS13 77 B8
Wellstone Gn. Pudsey LS13 58 B1
Wellstone Rd. Pudsey LS13 77 B8
Wellstone Rise. Pudsey LS13 77 B8
Wellstone Way. Pudsey LS13 77 B8
Wellthorne Ave. Ingb S30 191 E1
Wellthorne La. Ingb S30 191 D1
Welton Gr. Leeds LS6 59 E3
Welton Mount. Leeds LS6 59 E3
Welton Pl. Leeds LS6 59 E3
Welton Rd. Leeds LS6 59 E3
Welwyn Ave. Batley WF17 117 F6
Welwyn Ave. Ship BD18 55 F7
Welwyn Dr. Bail BD17 38 C2
Welwyn Dr. Ship BD18 55 F7
Welwyn Rd. Batley WF12 118 F3
Wembly Ave. Thorn BD13 72 F6
Wenborough La. Brad BD4 75 F3
Wendel Ave. B in Elm LS15 63 D7
Wendron Cl. Liver WF15 116 F1
Wendron Way. Brad BD10 56 B7
Wenlock St. Brad BD3 75 A6
Wenning St. Keigh BD21 35 E8
Wensley Ave. Leeds LS7 60 C7
Wensley Ave. Ship BD18 55 A7
Wensley Bank Ter. Thorn BD13 72 C6
Wensley Bank. Thorn BD13 72 C6
Wensley Bank W. Thorn BD13 72 C6
Wensley Cres. Leeds LS7 60 C7
Wensley Dr. Leeds LS7 60 C7
Wensley Dr. Pont WF8 146 E6
Wensley Gdns. Leeds LS7 60 B8
Wensley Gn. Leeds LS7 60 B7
Wensley Gr. Brig HD6 135 E8
Wensley Gr. Leeds LS7 60 C7
Wensley Rd. Leeds LS7 60 B8
Wensley St E. Hor WF4 141 A1 6
Wensley St. Hor WF4 141 A1 5
Wensley View. Leeds LS7 60 C7
Wensleydale Ave. Leeds LS12 58 F2
Wensleydale Cl. Leeds LS12 58 F2 2
Wensleydale Cres. Leeds LS12 58 F2
Wensleydale Ct. Leeds LS7 60 C7
Wensleydale Dr. Leeds LS12 58 F2
Wensleydale Mws. Leeds LS12 58 F2 1
Wensleydale Par.Batley WF17 117 F8 2
Wensleydale Rd. Brad BD3 75 E7
Wensleydale Rise. Bail BD17 38 E4
Wensleydale Rise. Leeds LS12 58 F2 3
Went Ave. Feath WF7 145 C3
Went Croft. Pont WF8 146 D5
Went Edge Rd. K Smea WF8 165 F6
Went Edge Rd. Th Aud WF8 165 F6
Went Fold. Pont WF8 146 D5
Went Garth. Pont WF8 146 D5
Went Gr. Feath WF7 145 C3
Went Hill Cl. Ack M T WF7 164 A8
Went La. Feath WF4 145 D2
Went La. W Har WF4 163 C3
Went Vale (Special Sch). Pont 146 E5
Went View. Th Aud WF8 165 A5
Went-Dale Rd. Pont WF8 146 D5
Wentbridge La. Th Aud WF8 165 C6
Wentbridge Rd. Feath WF7 145 E4
Wentcliffe Rd. Knot WF11 126 B4
Wentdale. K Smea WF8 166 E6
Wentwell Rd. Feath WF7 144 D5
Wentworth Ave. Emley HD8 175 C6
Wentworth Ave. Leeds LS17 43 C4
Wentworth Cl. Men LS29 22 A4
Wentworth Cl. Wool WF4 177 F7
Wentworth Cres. Leeds LS17 43 C4
Wentworth Ct. Brig HD6 135 F7
Wentworth Dr. Crof WF4 162 A8
Wentworth Dr. Emley HD8 175 C6
Wentworth Dr. Hali HX2 91 F7
Wentworth Dr. S Kirk WF9 182 C3
Wentworth Gate. Weth LS22 13 B6
Wentworth Gr. Hali HX2 91 F7
Wentworth Pk Rise. Dar WF8 147 D5
Wentworth Rd. Feath WF7 145 B4
Wentworth St. Hud HD1 153 F7
Wentworth St. Wake WF1 142 B7
Wentworth Terr. Hem WF9 163 B3
Wentworth Terr. Wake WF1 142 B7
Wentworth Terr. Yeadon LS19 40 D3
Wentworth Way. Leeds LS17 43 C4
Wentworth Way. Wake WF2 142 E1
Wepener Mount. Leeds LS9 61 B1
Wepener Pl. Leeds LS9 61 B1
Wesley App. Leeds LS11 78 F2
Wesley Ave. Brad BD12 94 E7
Wesley Ave. Leeds LS12 78 C7 4
Wesley Ave S. Brad BD12 94 E6 3
Wesley Cl. Batley WF17 96 E1
Wesley Cl. Leeds LS11 78 F3
Wesley Croft. Leeds LS11 78 F3
Wesley Ct. Hali HX1 113 C7 7
Wesley Ct. Leeds LS6 60 A3
Wesley Ct. Leeds LS11 78 F2
Wesley Ct. Ossett WF5 140 C6
Wesley Ct. Yeadon LS19 39 F7
Wesley Dr. Brad BD12 94 E7
Wesley Garth. Leeds LS11 78 F3
Wesley Gn. Leeds LS11 78 F2
Wesley Gr. Brad BD10 39 C1
Wesley Hall Ct. Loft G WF3 121 F2
Wesley House. Leeds LS11 78 F2 1
Wesley Pl. Dew WF13 139 C8
Wesley Pl. Feath WF7 145 D4
Wesley Pl. Keigh BD21 35 B3
Wesley Pl. Leeds LS12 78 C7 5
Wesley Pl. Leeds LS9 79 E7
Wesley Pl. Sil BD20 5 E1
Wesley Rd. Leeds LS12 78 C7
Wesley Rd. Pudsey LS28 57 C2
Wesley Row. Pudsey LS28 76 E8 10
Wesley Sq. Pudsey LS28 76 E7 6
Wesley St. Castle WF10 124 C5
Wesley St. Castle WF10 124 D8 7
Wesley St. Clec BD19 116 D8
Wesley St. Dew WF13 139 C8
Wesley St. Leeds LS11 78 F3
Wesley St. Morley LS27 98 A4
Wesley St. Ossett WF5 140 D6
Wesley St. Otley LS21 23 A8
Wesley St. Pudsey LS28 57 D1
Wesley St. Pudsey LS28 57 D3
Wesley St. Pudsey LS13 57 F5
Wesley St. S Elm WF9 182 E2
Wesley St. Wake WF1 142 E3
Wesley Terr. Bacup OL13 106 A7 1
Wesley Terr. D Dale HD8 191 F6
Wesley Terr. Leeds LS13 58 D3
Wesley Terr. Pudsey LS13 57 F5
Wesley Terr. Pudsey LS28 76 E8
Wesley View. Pudsey LS13 57 F5 1
Wesley View. Pudsey LS28 76 E7
Wesleyan Terr. Brad BD4 75 C3
Wessenden Hd Rd. Mel HD7 170 D1
Wessenden Rd. Mars HD7 169 A1
West Acres. Byram WF11 126 D7
West Ave. B Spa LS23 14 C1
West Ave. Bail BD17 38 C3
West Ave. Brad BD15 53 F3
West Ave. Brig HX3 115 A7
West Ave. Hali HX3 113 B4
West Ave. Honley HD7 171 F4
West Ave. Hor WF4 141 C1
West Ave. Hud HD3 135 C1
West Ave. Leeds LS8 61 C8
West Ave. Pont WF8 146 A8
West Ave. Roy S71 179 D4
West Ave. S Elm WF9 183 B4
West Bank. Brad BD9 54 F4
West Bank Cl. Keigh BD22 34 F8
West Bank Gr. Keigh BD20 18 E2
West Bank. Hali HX2 91 D4
West Bank. Keigh BD22 34 F8
West Bank Rd. Keigh BD20 18 D2
West Bank Rise. Keigh BD22 34 F8
West Bolton. Hali HX2 91 D7
West Bowling Golf Course. Brad 75 A1
West Bradford Golf Course. Brad 54 C2
West Bretton Jun & Inf Sch. W Bret 176 F8
West Busk La. Otley LS21 22 D6
West Byland. Hali HX2 91 D7
West Carr La. Mars HD3 150 E2
West Chevin Rd. Men LS29 22 E5
West Chevin Rd. Otley LS21 22 E5
West Cl. Hud HD2 136 B2
West Cl. Nor WF6 123 A3
West Cl. Pont WF8 146 E5
West Cliffe. Hali HX3 113 E6
West Croft. Brad BD12 94 C2
West Croft. S in Cra BD20 16 D4
West Ct. Leeds LS13 58 C1 6
West Ct. Leeds LS8 61 C8
West Dale. B Spa LS23 14 C1
West Dene. Leeds LS17 43 F6
West Dene. Sil BD20 5 E2
West Dr. Oxen BD22 51 C3
West Dr. Pont WF8 146 E7
West End App. Morley LS27 97 E3
West End Ave. Feath WF7 145 A8
West End Ave. Holmfi HD7 189 C6
West End Ave. Roy S71 179 A3
West End. B Spa LS23 14 C1
West End Cl. Hors LS18 40 F1
West End Cres. Roy S71 179 A3
West End Dr. Clec BD19 116 C6
West End Dr. Hors LS18 41 A1
West End. Gild LS12 77 D3
West End. Gild LS27 97 C7
West End Golf Course. Hali 112 C8
West End Gr. Hors LS18 40 F1
West End. Heb Br HX7 89 A3
West End Jun & Inf Sch. Hors 40 F1
West End La. Hors LS18 40 F2
West End Mid Sch. Clec 116 C7
West End. Queen BD13 92 D8
West End Rd. Hali HX1 112 E6
West End Rd. Hud HD7 152 C4
West End Rd. Pudsey LS28 57 B6
West End Rise. Hors LS18 40 F1
West End Terr. Brad BD2 56 B5
West End Terr. Guise LS20 22 C1
West End Terr. Heb Br HX7 89 E1 5
West End Terr. Ship BD18 55 A8
West Farm Ave. Midd LS10 99 B5
West Field La. Holmfi HD7 189 C6
West Field. Thorner LS14 45 E4
West Garforth Jun Sch. Gar 82 E6
West Gate. Holme HD7 198 F8
West Gate. Holmfi HD7 188 F1
West Gate. Weth LS22 13 E5
West Gr. Bail BD17 38 C4 11
West Gr. Roy S71 179 A4
West Grange Cl. Midd LS10 79 D1
West Grange Dr. Midd LS10 79 D1
West Grange Fold. Midd LS10 79 D1
West Grange Garth. Midd LS10 79 D1
West Grange Gdns. Midd LS10 79 D1
West Grange Gn. Midd LS10 79 D1
West Grange Rd. Midd LS10 79 D1
West Grange Wlk. Midd LS10 79 D1
West Grove Ave. Hud HD5 154 D6
West Grove St. Pudsey LS28 57 D1 10
West Grove Terr. Hali HX1 113 B7 4
West Hall La. Add LS29 3 A1
West Hall Sch. Loft G 122 B6
West Hill Ave. Leeds LS7 60 C7
West Hill St. Hali HX1 113 B7
West House. Elland HX5 134 F7 2
West Ings Cl. Knot WF11 127 B5
West Ings Ct. Knot WF11 127 B5
West Ings La. Knot WF11 127 B5
West La. Ask LS21 9 E5
West La. B Spa LS23 14 C1
West La. Bail BD17 38 A2
West La. Bail BD17 38 B3
West La. Clec BD19 96 B1
West La. Crof WF4 144 B2
West La. Hali HX3 113 F3
West La. Haw BD22 51 B7
West La. Keigh BD21, BD22 35 A7
West La. L Brad BD20 4 C5
West La. S in Cra BD20 16 C4
West La. Thorn BD13 72 D6
West Lea Cl. Leeds LS17 43 B1
West Lea Cres. E Ard WF3 119 D7
West Lea Cres. Yeadon LS19 39 F6
West Lea Dr. E Ard WF3 119 D6
West Lea Dr. Leeds LS17 43 B1
West Lea Garth. Leeds LS17 43 B1
West Lea Gdns. Leeds LS17 43 B1
West Lea Gr. Yeadon LS19 39 F6
West Leeds Boys High Sch. Leeds 78 A7
West Leeds Girls High Sch. Leeds 78 A7
West Leeds St. Keigh BD21 35 A7
West Lodge Cres. Hud HD2 135 B4
West Lodge Gdns. Leeds LS7 60 C6
West Mead. Castle WF10 125 A7
West Moor Rd. Hem WF9 163 A2
West Moor View. Honley HD7 171 E4
West Moorlands Ave. Dew WF13 118 B1
West Mount Pl. Hali HX1 113 A8 7
West Mount St. Leeds LS11 79 A3
West Oaks Special Sch. B Spa 30 D7
West Par. Guise LS20 22 E1
West Par. Hali HX6 112 D4
West Par. Hali HX1 113 B6
West Par. Ilkley LS29 8 C4
West Par. Leeds LS16 59 A8
West Par. Roth LS26 100 F5
West Par. Wake WF1 142 C6
West Parade Ct. Wake WF1 142 C5
West Parade Flats. Hali HX1 113 B6
West Parade St. Wake WF1 142 C5
West Park Ave. Leeds LS8 44 B3
West Park Chase. Leeds LS8 44 A3
West Park Cl. Leeds LS8 44 A3
West Park Cres. Leeds LS8 44 B2
West Park Dr. Dar WF8 147 D2
West Park Dr E. Leeds LS8 44 B3
West Park Dr. Leeds LS16 59 A8
West Park Dr (W). Leeds LS8 43 F3
West Park Gdns. Leeds LS8 44 B2
West Park Gr. Batley WF17 118 A5
West Park Gr. Leeds LS8 44 B2
West Park Pl. Leeds LS8 44 B2
West Park Rd. Batley WF17 117 F4
West Park Rd. Brad BD8 73 F8
West Park Rd. Leeds LS8 44 B2
West Park Sch. Leeds 59 A7
West Park St. Brig HD6 115 B2 8
West Park St. Dew WF13 118 B1
West Park Terr. Batley WF17 118 A5
West Park Terr. Brad BD8 73 F8 8
West Parks. Pudsey LS28 76 D7
West Pasture Cl. Hors LS18 40 F1
West Pinfold. Roy S71 179 C2
West Pk. Guise LS20 22 C2
West Pl. Hud HD5 154 D6
West Primley Park Dr. Leeds LS17 43 D5
West Rd. Leeds LS9 80 C3
West Road (North). Leeds LS9 80 D3
West Royd Ave. Brad BD2 56 B4
West Royd Ave. Hali HX1 113 A6
West Royd Ave. Mir WF14 138 A6
West Royd Ave. Ship BD18 55 E8
West Royd Cl. Hali HX1 113 A5
West Royd Cl. Ship BD18 55 D8
West Royd Cres. Ship BD18 55 E8
West Royd Dr. Mir WF14 138 A6
West Royd Dr. Ship BD18 55 E8
West Royd Gr. Mir WF14 138 A6
West Royd Gr. Ship BD18 55 E8
West Royd Mount. Ship BD18 55 E8
West Royd Pk. Mir WF14 138 A6
West Royd Rd. Ship BD18 55 E8
West Royd Terr. Ship BD18 55 E8
West Royd Villas. Hali HX1 113 A5 3
West Royd. Wils BD15 53 C4
West Royd Wlk. Ship BD18 55 E8
West Scausby Pk. Hali HX2 91 E7
West Shaw La. Oxen BD22 51 A3
West Side Ret Pk. Yeadon 39 F7
West Slaithwaite Rd. Mars HD7 169 C7
West Slaithwaite Sch. Mars 169 C7
West St. Bail BD17 38 C4
West St. Batley WF16 117 C4 2
West St. Batley WF17 118 D5
West St. Batley WF17 118 E5
West St. Birk BD11 96 E5
West St. Brad BD2 56 B3
West St. Brad BD1 74 F6
West St. Brig HD6 115 A3 2
West St. Brig HD6 115 B7
West St. Castle WF10 124 C8
West St. Clec BD19 96 B1
West St. Clec BD19 116 D7
West St. Dew WF12 139 C7
West St. Elland HX4 134 B4
West St. Hali HX1 113 A7
West St. Hud HD3 135 B1
West St. Ilkley LS29 8 B4
West St. Leeds LS3 78 F8
West St. Loft G WF3 121 F2
West St. Morley LS27 98 B3
West St. Nor WF6 123 A2
West St. Pudsey LS28 76 E8
West St. Roy S71 179 D4
West St. Ryhill WF4 162 C1
West St. S Elm WF9 183 B4
West St. S Hie S72 180 E5
West St. S Kirk WF9 182 A2
West St. Shelf HX3 93 B4
West St. Sow Br HX6 112 B3
West St. Tod OL14 108 A6
West St. Wake WF2 141 F5
West Terrace St. Pudsey LS28 57 D1 9
West Vale. Dew WF12 139 B6
West Vale Jun & Inf Sch. Elland 134 D7
West Vale. Leeds LS12 78 E5
West View. Ack M T WF7 163 D5
West View. Arth LS21 24 F6
West View Ave. Bur in W LS29 9 E1
West View Ave. Castle WF10 125 A7
West View Ave. Hali HX2 112 E7
West View Ave. Ship BD18 55 E7
West View. Batley WF17 118 B2
West View. Brad BD4 75 A4
West View. Brig BD19 94 F1
West View Cl. Ship BD18 55 E7
West View Cres. Hali HX2 112 E7
West View. Crig WF4 159 E4
West View Ct. Yeadon LS19 39 F7
West View Dr. Hali HX2 112 E7
West View. Elland HX4 134 A4
West View. H Chap BB10 85 A8
West View. Hali HX3 92 B2
West View. Hali HX1 112 F6
West View. Hud HD1 153 D5
West View. Ilkley LS29 8 B3
West View. Kippax LS25 83 B2
West View. Leeds LS11 79 A4
West View. M'field LS25 84 B6
West View. Otley LS21 23 B8
West View. Pudsey LS28 57 D2 15
West View Rd. Bur in W LS29 9 E1
West View Rd. Hali HX3 92 B2
West View Rise. Hud HD1 153 D5
West View. Roth LS26 101 C5
West View. Sil BD20 5 E2
West View St. Haw BD22 51 F8 8
West View Terr. Hali HX2 112 E8
West View. Wake WF2 120 B2
West View. Yeadon LS19 39 F7
West Villa Rd. Guise LS20 22 E1
West Way. Ship BD18 54 D7
West Wells Cres. Ossett WF5 140 C5
West Wells Rd. Ossett WF5 140 D5
West Wood Ct. Midd LS10 99 A5
West Wood Rd. Midd LS10 98 F4
West Yorks Transport Mus. Brad 74 E5
West Yorkshire Ind Est. Brad 95 E8
Westacres. Brig HD6 136 B8
Westborough Dr. Hali HX2 112 D7
Westborough High Sch. Dew 139 A8
Westbourne Ave. Gar LS25 82 D6
Westbourne Ave. Leeds LS11 79 B3 20
Westbourne Ave. Pont WF8 146 C7 1
Westbourne Cl. Otley LS21 22 E7
Westbourne Cl. Wake WF2 160 C6
Westbourne Cres. Gar LS25 82 D6
Westbourne Cres. Hali HX3 113 D3
Westbourne Cres. Pont WF8 146 B7
Westbourne Dr. Gar LS25 82 D6
Westbourne Dr. Guise LS20 22 C1
Westbourne Dr. Men LS29 22 A5
Westbourne Fst Sch. Brad 55 B2
Westbourne Gdns. Gar LS25 82 D6
Westbourne Gr. Gar LS25 82 D6
Westbourne Gr. Hali HX3 113 D3
Westbourne Gr. Otley LS21 22 E7
Westbourne Mt. Leeds LS11 79 B3 22
Westbourne Mt. Pont WF8 146 C7 2
Westbourne Pl. Leeds LS11 79 B3 21
Westbourne Pl. Pudsey LS28 57 D1
Westbourne Rd. Brad BD8 55 B2
Westbourne Rd. Hud HD1 153 D7
Westbourne Rd. Pont WF8 146 C7
Westbourne St. Leeds LS11 79 B3 19
Westbourne Terr. Gar LS25 82 D6
Westbourne Terr. Hali HX3 113 D3
Westbrook Cl. Hors LS18 41 B2
Westbrook Ct. Hali HX3 113 B8
Westbrook Dr. Hud HD5 155 B6
Westbrook La. Hors LS18 41 B2
Westbrook Lane Jun & Inf Sch. Hors 41 B3
Westbrook St. Brad BD7 74 D6
Westbrook Terr. Batley WF17 118 B6
Westburn Ave. Keigh BD22 34 F5
Westburn Cres. Keigh BD22 34 F5
Westburn Gr. Keigh BD22 34 F5
Westburn Way. Keigh BD22 34 F5
Westbury Cl. Brad BD4 75 D5
Westbury Gr. Leeds LS10 79 F2
Westbury Mount. Midd LS10 79 F1
Westbury Pl. Hali HX1 112 E6
Westbury Pl N. Leeds LS10 79 F2
Westbury Pl S. Midd LS10 79 F1
Westbury Rd. Brad BD6 73 D1
Westbury St. Brad BD4 75 D5
Westbury St. Elland HX5 135 A7
Westbury St. Midd LS10 79 F1
Westbury Terr. Hali HX1 112 E6
Westbury Terr. Midd LS10 79 F1
Westcliffe Ave. Bail BD17 38 B3
Westcliffe Dr. Hali HX2 112 D7
Westcliffe Rd. Clec BD19 116 C7
Westcliffe Rd. Ship BD18 55 B7
Westcliffe Rise. Clec BD19 116 C7
Westcombe Ave. Leeds LS8 44 A2
Westcombe Ct. Brad BD12 94 C4 13
Westcroft Ave. Shelf HX3 93 B4
Westcroft Dr. Ossett WF5 119 C1
Westcroft. Honley HD7 171 E4
Westcroft Rd. Brad BD7 74 A4
Westcroft Rd. Hem WF9 181 D7
Westdale Dr. Pudsey LS28 76 D8
Westdale Gdns. Pudsey LS28 76 D8
Westdale Gr. Pudsey LS28 76 D8
Westdale Rd. Pudsey LS28 76 D8
Westdale Rise. Pudsey LS28 76 D8
Westend St. Brad BD1 74 D7
Westercroft La. Northo HX3 93 B3
Westercroft View. Northo HX3 93 B3
Westerley Cl. Shep HD8 174 A3
Westerley Cres. Sil BD20 5 C1
Westerley La. Shep HD8 174 A3
Westerly Croft. Leeds LS12 78 C8
Westerly Rise. Leeds LS12 78 C8
Westerly Way. Shep HD8 174 A3
Westerman St. Wake WF1 142 E3
Western Ave. Batley WF17 97 A1
Western Ave. Keigh BD20 18 D3
Western Ave. Pont WF8 125 F1
Western Ct. Pont WF8 125 F1
Western Gr. Leeds LS12 78 B5
Western Mount. Leeds LS12 78 B5
Western Pl. Brad BD13 73 B1
Western Rd. Hud HD4 153 A4
Western Rd. Leeds LS12 78 B5
Western St. Leeds LS12 78 B5
Western Way. Brad BD6 94 A7
Westerton Cl. E Ard WF3 120 B8
Westerton Rd. E Ard WF3 119 E7
Westerton Sch. E Ard 119 D7
Westerton Wlk. E Ard WF3 120 B8
Westfell Cl. Keigh BD22 34 F6
Westfell Rd. Keigh BD22 34 F6
Westfell Way. Keigh BD22 34 F6
Westfield Ave. Brig HX3 114 D7
Westfield Ave. Castle WF10 124 C5
Westfield Ave. Dew WF12 140 A8
Westfield Ave. Hud HD3 153 B7
Westfield Ave. Kippax LS25 83 A1
Westfield Ave. Kippax WF10 103 A5
Westfield Ave. Knot WF11 126 F3
Westfield Ave. Leeds LS12 77 F8
Westfield Ave. Mel HD7 170 C3
Westfield Ave. Pont WF8 146 C6
Westfield Ave. Skel HD8 174 F1
Westfield Ave. Yeadon LS19 39 F6
Westfield. Brig HX3 114 D7
Westfield Bungalows. S Elm WF9 183 A2
Westfield Cl. Batley WF16 117 C5
Westfield Cl. Roth LS26 100 C4
Westfield Cl. Yeadon LS19 39 F6
Westfield Cotts. Pont WF8 146 C5
Westfield Cres. Brad BD2 56 B1
Westfield Cres. Dearne S63 194 C1
Westfield Cres. Keigh BD20 18 F2
Westfield Cres. Leeds LS3 59 F1
Westfield Cres. Ossett WF5 140 C5
Westfield Cres. Ryhill WF4 162 A1
Westfield Cres. Ship BD18 55 E6
Westfield Cres. Wake WF2 120 B2
Westfield Ct. Hor WF4 140 F2
Westfield Ct. Mir WF14 138 A5
Westfield Ct. Roth LS26 100 C4
Westfield Dr. Brig HX3 114 D7
Westfield Dr. Keigh BD20 18 F1
Westfield Dr. Ossett WF5 140 C5
Westfield Dr. Skel HD8 174 F1
Westfield Dr. Yeadon LS19 39 F6
Westfield Farm. Ossett WF5 140 C6
Westfield Gdns. Brig HX3 114 D7
Westfield Gdns. Kippax LS25 82 F2
Westfield Gn. Brad BD4 75 E4
Westfield Gr. Ack M T WF7 164 C8
Westfield Gr. Brad BD10 56 A8
Westfield Gr. Castle WF10 124 C5
Westfield Gr. Dew WF13 138 F8
Westfield Gr. Ingb S30 191 D1
Westfield Gr. Kippax WF10 103 A5
Westfield Gr. Ship BD18 55 E6
Westfield Gr. Wake WF1 142 C8
Westfield Gr. Yeadon LS19 39 F6
Westfield Ind Est. Yeadon 40 A7
Westfield La. Brad BD10 56 A8
Westfield La. Brig BD12, BD19 94 D1
Westfield La. Dar WF8 147 C3
Westfield La. Emley HD8 174 F8
Westfield La. Kippax LS25 83 A1
Westfield La. Norton WF8 166 F3
Westfield La. S Elm WF9 182 F2
Westfield La. S Mil LS25 84 F2
Westfield La. Ship BD18 55 F7
Westfield La. Thorner LS14 45 E4
Westfield Mount. Yeadon LS19 39 F6
Westfield Oval. Yeadon LS19 39 E6
Westfield Pk. Wake WF1 142 C8
Westfield Pl. Brig BD19 94 E1
Westfield Pl. Hali HX1 113 A6
Westfield Pl. Wake WF2 120 B2
Westfield Prim Sch. Leeds 59 F1
Westfield. Pudsey LS28 57 D1
Westfield Rd. Batley WF16 117 D5
Westfield Rd. Brad BD9 55 A2
Westfield Rd. Brad BD14 73 B4
Westfield Rd. Hem WF9 181 D7
Westfield Rd. Hor WF4 140 F2
Westfield Rd. Keigh BD20 18 F1
Westfield Rd. Knot WF11 126 F3
Westfield Rd. Leeds LS3 59 F1
Westfield Rd. Morley LS27 98 A4
Westfield Rd. Roth LS26 100 C3
Westfield Rd. Wake WF1 142 C8
Westfield St. Batley WF16 117 C5
Westfield St. Hali HX1 113 B6
Westfield St. Ossett WF5 140 C5
Westfield Terr. Bail BD17 38 C4
Westfield Terr. Brad BD2 56 B1
Westfield Terr. Brad BD14 73 B4 2
Westfield Terr. Hali HX1 113 A8
Westfield Terr. Heb Br HX7 89 E1 2
Westfield Terr. Hor WF4 141 A1
Westfield Terr. Kippax WF10 103 A5
Westfield Terr. Leeds LS3 59 F1
Westfield Terr. Leeds LS7 60 C7
Westfield Terr. Wake WF1 142 C8
Westfield. Thorn BD13 73 A6
Westfield View. Wake WF1 142 C8
Westfield Villas. Hor WF4 140 F1
Westfields Ave. Mir WF14 138 B5
Westfields. Castle WF10 124 C5
Westfields Rd. Mir WF14 138 A5
Westfields. Roy S71 179 A4
Westgarth. Coll LS22 13 B3
Westgate. Bail BD17 38 C4
Westgate. Brad BD2 56 C4
Westgate. Brad BD1 74 D7
Westgate. Brig HD6 115 E2
Westgate Cl. Loft G WF3 121 C8
Westgate. Clec BD19 116 D7
Westgate Ct. Roth WF3 121 C8
Westgate. Dew WF13 139 D8
Westgate. Elland HX5 134 F7
Westgate End. Wake WF2 142 A5
Westgate Gr. Loft G WF3 121 C8
Westgate. Guise LS20 39 B8
Westgate. Hali HX1 113 C7
Westgate. Hem WF9 181 C6
Westgate Hill Fst Sch. Birk 96 A8
Westgate Hill St. Birk BD4 96 B8
Westgate. Honley HD7 171 F4
Westgate. Hud HD1 154 A6
Westgate. Hud HD5 154 F2
Westgate La. Loft G WF3 121 C8

Westgate. Leeds LS1 79 A8
Westgate. Liver WF16 117 C4
Westgate Market. Hali 113 C7
Westgate. Mel HD7 170 D2
Westgate. Otley LS21 22 F7
Westgate. Ship BD18 55 B8
Westgate Sta. Wake 142 B6
Westgate Terr. Birk BD4 96 A8
Westgate Terr. Dew WF13 139 C8 13
Westgate. Wake WF1, WF2 142 C6
Westgrove Ct. Clec BD19 116 C8
Westhill Ave. Cull BD13 52 E5
Westholme Rd. Hali HX1 112 F6
Westholme St. Brad BD1 74 D6
Westland Ct. Leeds LS11 99 B8
Westland Rd. Leeds LS11 79 B1
Westland Sq. Leeds LS11 99 B8
Westlands Dr. Brad BD15 54 C1
Westlands Gr. Brad BD15 54 C1
Westlea Ave. Keigh BD20 18 F1
Westleigh. Bing BD16 37 A4 3
Westleigh Cl. Bail BD17 38 A2
Westleigh Dr. Bail BD17 38 A2
Westleigh Rd. Bail BD17 38 A2
Westleigh Way. Bail BD17 38 A2
Westley Ave. Holmfi HD7 188 F8
Westlock Ave. Leeds LS9 61 A1
Westmead. Pudsey LS28 57 A1
Westminster Ave. Brad BD14 73 A4
Westminster Cl. Pudsey LS13 57 F4
Westminster Cres. Brad BD14 73 A4
Westminster Cres. Leeds LS15 80 E7
Westminster Crft.Pudsey LS13 57 F4
Westminster Dr. Brad BD14 73 A4
Westminster Dr. Pudsey LS13 57 F4
Westminster Gdns. Brad BD14 73 A4
Westminster Pl. Brad BD3 55 F1
Westminster Rd. Brad BD3 55 F1
Westminster Terr. Brad BD3 55 F1
Westmoor Ave. Bail BD17 38 B4
Westmoor Cl. Bail BD17 38 B4
Westmoor Cty Sch. Dew 117 F1
Westmoor Pl. Leeds LS13 58 B3
Westmoor Rd. Leeds LS13 58 B3
Westmoor Rise. Leeds LS13 58 B3
Westmoor St. Leeds LS13 58 B3
Westmoreland Mount. Leeds LS13 58 D4 1
Westmorland House. Wake WF1 142 C6 10
Westmorland St. Wake WF1 142 C6
Westmount St. Pont WF8 146 C8 15
Westoff La. S Hie S72 180 D7
Weston Ave. Queen BD13 92 D8
Weston Cres. Otley LS21 10 F1
Weston Dr. Otley LS21 10 E1
Weston La. Otley LS21 10 E1
Weston Lane Mid Sch. Otley 10 F2
Weston Moor Rd. Clift LS21 10 D8
Weston Park View. Otley LS21 10 D1
Weston Rd. Ilkley LS29 8 B4
Weston Ridge. Otley LS21 10 E1
Weston St. Keigh BD22 34 F5
Weston Vale Rd. Queen BD13 92 D8
Westover Ave. Leeds LS13 58 C3 6
Westover Gdns. Pudsey LS28 76 C7
Westover Gn. Leeds LS13 58 C3
Westover Gr. Leeds LS13 58 C3 3
Westover Mount. Leeds LS13 58 C3 10
Westover Rd. Leeds LS13 58 C3
Westover St. Leeds LS13 58 C3 2
Westover Terr. Leeds LS13 58 C3 1
Westover View. Leeds LS13 58 C3 5
Westridge Dr. Hud HD4 153 C1
Westroyd Ave. Clec BD19 95 D2
Westroyd Ave. Pudsey LS28 76 C6
Westroyd. Clift LS21 11 A3
Westroyd Cres. Pudsey LS28 76 C6
Westroyd Gdns. Pudsey LS28 76 C6
Westroyd Inf Sch. Pudsey 57 D2
Westroyd. Pudsey LS28 76 C6
Westvale Mews. Leeds LS13 58 E1
Westview Ave. Keigh BD20 35 B8
Westview Cl. L Brad BD20 4 C5
Westview Ct. Keigh BD20 35 A8
Westview Gr. Keigh BD20 35 A8
Westview Way. Keigh BD20 35 B8
Westville Ave. Ilkley LS29 8 A4
Westville Cl. Ilkley LS29 8 A4
Westville Rd. Ilkley LS29 8 A4
Westville Way. Thorn BD13 72 D6
Westward Croft. Hud HD3 135 C2
Westward Ho. Hali HX3 92 A4
Westward Ho. Queen BD13 72 E1 16
Westway. Batley WF12 118 F3
Westway. Bing BD16 37 B5
Westway. Brad BD9 54 C2
Westway. Gar LS25 82 D6
Westway. Guise LS20 39 B8
Westway. Keigh BD20 17 F1
Westway. Mir WF14 137 F7
Westway. Pudsey LS28 57 C3
Westways Cl. Wake WF2 120 F2
Westways Dr. Leeds LS8 61 C7
Westways Rise. Wake WF2 120 F2
Westways. Wake WF2 120 F2
Westwinn Garth. Leeds LS14 45 C1
Westwinn View. Leeds LS14 45 C1
Westwood Ave. Brad BD2 56 B5
Westwood Ave. Honley HD7 172 C5
Westwood Cl. Feath WF7 145 D7
Westwood Cl. Morley LS27 98 A6
Westwood Cty Prim Sch. Midd 99 A4
Westwood Cres. Ship BD16 54 A8
Westwood Dr. Ilkley LS29 7 F2
Westwood Edge Rd. Slai HD7 152 A3
Westwood Fold. Slai HD7 152 B2
Westwood Gr. Brad BD2 56 B5
Westwood Hospl. Brad 73 C1
Westwood Rd. Castle WF10 124 B5
Westwood Rd. Ossett WF5 140 F5
Westwood Rise. Morley LS27 98 B6
Westwood Side. Morley LS27 98 B7
Westwood St. Hud HD5 137 A6
Westwood Way. B Spa LS23 30 D8
Wetherby Bsns Pk. Weth 13 F6
Wetherby Cty Prim Sch. Weth 13 F5
Wetherby Gr. Leeds LS4 59 C2 8
Wetherby High Sch. Weth 13 F5
Wetherby Pl. Leeds LS4 59 D2
Wetherby Race Course. Weth 14 B6
Wetherby Rd. Bard LS17 28 E4
Wetherby Rd. Bramham LS23 30 C3
Wetherby Rd. Coll LS22 13 D3
Wetherby Rd. K Deigh LS22 13 E8
Wetherby Rd. Leeds LS8 61 D7
Wetherby Rd. Scar LS14 45 C6
Wetherby Rd. Sickl LS22 12 D5
Wetherby Rd. Th Arch LS23 14 F4
Wetherby Rd. Thorner LS14 45 C6
Wetherby Rd. Weth LS22 13 D3
Wetherby Terr. Leeds LS4 59 C2 6
Wetherhill St. Batley WF17 118 B5
Wetherill Terr. Batley WF13 117 F3 4
Wetlands Rd. Mel HD7 170 E1
Weydale Ave. Hud HD3 153 A8
Weyhill Dr. Brad BD15 73 B8
Weymouth Ave. Brad BD15 73 A8
Weymouth Ave. Hud HD3 153 B7
Whack House Cl. Yeadon LS19 40 A6
Whack House La. Yeadon LS19 40 A7
Whalley La. Denh BD13 52 E2
Whams Rd. Carl S30 200 F2
Wharf St. Brad BD3 74 F8
Wharf St. Brig HD6 115 B2
Wharf St. Dew WF12 139 D7
Wharf St. Hali HX6 112 C4
Wharf St. Leeds LS2 79 D7 4
Wharf St. Ship BD17 55 B8
Wharf St. Tod OL14 108 A1 12
Wharfdale View. Men LS29 22 A4
Wharfe Bank. Coll LS22 28 E8
Wharfe Cl. Hors LS16 42 D4
Wharfe Cres. Pool LS21 24 D7
Wharfe Gr. Weth LS22 13 D5
Wharfe Grange Hospl. Weth 13 D5
Wharfe Mews. Men LS29 22 B4
Wharfe Pk. Add LS29 7 A8
Wharfe Rein. Coll LS22 28 E8
Wharfe St. Otley LS21 23 B8
Wharfe View. Pool LS21 24 C7
Wharfe View Rd. Ilkley LS29 8 B4
Wharfe View. Weth LS22 13 D5
Wharfe Way. Castle WF10 125 B8
Wharfedale Ave. Leeds LS7 60 B4
Wharfedale Cres. Gar LS25 82 F6
Wharfedale Cres. Skel HD8 175 B1
Wharfedale Ct. Leeds LS14 61 F5
Wharfedale Ct. Otley LS21 23 A8
Wharfedale Dr. Ilkley LS29 8 C4
Wharfedale Dr. Nor WF6 123 A4
Wharfedale Gdns. Bail BD17 38 E4
Wharfedale General Hospl. Otley 10 F2
Wharfedale Gr. Leeds LS7 60 B4
Wharfedale Mews. Otley LS21 23 A8
Wharfedale Mount. Leeds LS7 60 B4
Wharfedale Mount. Shelf HX3 93 B5
Wharfedale Pl. Leeds LS7 60 B4
Wharfedale Rd. Brad BD4 95 A7
Wharfedale Rise. Brad BD9 54 C2
Wharfedale Rise. E Ard WF3 119 D7
Wharfedale St. Leeds LS7 60 B4
Wharfedale View. Add LS29 6 E8
Wharfedale View. Leeds LS7 60 B4
Wharfeside La. Ilkley LS29 8 C5
Wharncliffe Cres. Brad BD2 56 D4
Wharncliffe Dr. Brad BD2 56 D4
Wharncliffe Gr. Brad BD2 56 D4
Wharncliffe Gr. Ship BD18 55 B6
Wharncliffe Rd. Ship BD18 55 B6
Wharncliffe Rd. Wake WF2 160 A4
Wharton St. Liver WF15 117 B4 4
Wharton Terr. Batley WF16 117 D3 3
Whartons Mid Sch The. Otley 11 A2
Whartons The. Otley LS21 11 A2
Wheat Cl. Dew WF13 138 F8
Wheat Field Ave. Hud HD3 153 A8
Wheat Head Cres. Keigh BD22 34 E5
Wheat Head Dr. Keigh BD22 34 F5
Wheat Head La. Keigh BD22 34 E5
Wheat St. Keigh BD22 35 A4
Wheatcroft Ave. Batley WF17 118 C4
Wheatcroft. Castle WF10 125 B7
Wheater House. Wake WF1 142 C6 18
Wheater Rd. Brad BD7 74 A5
Wheatfield Ct. Pudsey LS28 76 D6
Wheathouse Rd. Hud HD2 135 F1
Wheathouse Terr. Hud HD2 135 F1
Wheatings The. Ossett WF5 140 F5
Wheatlands Ave. Brad BD9 54 E2
Wheatlands Ave. Glu BD20 16 C7
Wheatlands Cres. Brad BD9 54 E2
Wheatlands Dr. Brad BD9 54 E2
Wheatlands Dr. Liver WF15 116 F2
Wheatlands Gr. Brad BD9 54 E2
Wheatlands. Ilkley LS29 8 C4
Wheatlands La. Glu BD20 16 C7
Wheatlands. Pudsey LS28 57 C2
Wheatlands Sq. Brad BD9 54 E2
Wheatley Ave. Ilkley LS29 8 E4
Wheatley Ave. Nor WF6 123 B1
Wheatley Cl. Hali HX3 92 A1 3
Wheatley Ct. Hali HX2 91 D4
Wheatley Dr. Mir WF14 138 A3
Wheatley Gdns. Ilkley LS29 8 F3
Wheatley Gr. Ilkley LS29 8 F3
Wheatley Hill La. Clay W HD8 192 E8
Wheatley La. Ilkley LS29 8 F4
Wheatley Lane Ends. Hali HX3 91 E2
Wheatley Rd. Hali HX3 91 F2
Wheatley Rd. Ilkley LS29 8 C3
Wheatley Rise. Ilkley LS29 8 E3
Wheatley Rise. Mapp S75 178 B2
Wheaton Ave. Leeds LS15 81 B8
Wheaton Ct. Leeds LS15 81 A8 9
Wheatroyd Cres. Ossett WF5 140 D3
Wheatroyd La. Hud HD5 154 E2
Wheelright Coll. Dew 139 B7
Wheelwright Ave. Leeds LS12 78 A5
Wheelwright Cl. Leeds LS12 78 A5
Wheelwright Dr. Dew WF13 118 B2
Wheelwright St. Dew WF13 139 C8 12
Wheldale La. Castle WF10 104 E2
Wheldon Rd. Castle WF10 104 B2
Whernside Mount. Brad BD7 73 E2
Whernside Way. Hali HX2 91 A3
Wherwell Rd. Brig HD6 136 C8
Whetley Cl. Brad BD8 74 C8
Whetley Fst Sch. Brad 74 A8
Whetley Gr. Brad BD8 55 A1
Whetley Hill. Brad BD8 74 C8
Whetley La. Brad BD8 74 A8
Whetley Mid Sch. Brad 74 A8
Whetley Terr. Brad BD8 74 C8 1
Whewell St. Batley WF17 96 E1 4
Whimbrel Cl. Brad BD8 73 C7 4
Whin Cl. Hem WF9 181 D5
Whin Gdns. Dearne S63 194 D1
Whin Knoll Ave. Keigh BD21 35 A7
Whin Mount. Nor WF6 144 C8
Whin St. Keigh BD21 35 A7
Whin View Ct. Ryhill WF4 162 C1
Whinberry Pl. Batley WF17 96 F3
Whinbrook Cres. Leeds LS17 43 C1
Whinbrook Ct. Leeds LS17 43 C1
Whinbrook Gdns. Leeds LS17 43 C1
Whinbrook Gr. Leeds LS17 43 C1
Whinburn Sch. Keigh 17 F2
Whincop Ave. Castle WF10 124 A7
Whincover Cl. Leeds LS12 77 F5
Whincover Cross. Leeds LS12 77 F5
Whincover Dr. Leeds LS12 77 E5
Whincover Gdns. Leeds LS12 77 F5
Whincover Gr. Leeds LS12 77 F5
Whincover Grange. Leeds LS12 77 F5
Whincover Hill. Leeds LS12 77 E5
Whincover Mount. Leeds LS12 77 F5
Whincover Rd. Leeds LS12 77 F5
Whincover View. Leeds LS12 77 F5
Whincup Gdns. Leeds LS10 79 E2 3
Whinfield Ave. Keigh BD22 34 E7
Whinfield Cl. Keigh BD22 34 F8
Whinfield Dr. Keigh BD22 34 E8
Whinfield. Hors LS16 42 B4
Whinfield Pl. Ossett WF5 141 B4
Whingate Ave. Leeds LS12 78 A7
Whingate Cl. Leeds LS12 78 A7
Whingate Gn. Leeds LS12 78 A7
Whingate Gr. Leeds LS12 78 A7
Whingate. Leeds LS12 78 A7
Whingate Prim Sch. Leeds 78 A7
Whingate Rd. Leeds LS12 78 A7
Whingrove Ave. Mel HD7 170 D1
Whinmoor Cl. Silk S75 193 F1
Whinmoor Cres. Leeds LS14 45 A1
Whinmoor Ct. Leeds LS14 45 A1
Whinmoor Ct. Silk S75 193 F1
Whinmoor Dr. Silk S75 193 F1
Whinmoor Gdns. Leeds LS14 45 A1
Whinmoor La. Thorner LS17 44 B4
Whinmoor Mid Sch. Leeds 45 B1
Whinmoor View. Silk S75 193 F1
Whinmoor Way. Leeds LS14 62 D5
Whinmoor Way. Silk S75 193 F1
Whinmore Gdns. Clec BD19 117 C7
Whinney Cl. Feath WF7 144 D5
Whinney Field. Hali HX3 113 C4
Whinney Hill Pk. Brig HD6 115 B5
Whinney Moor Av. Wake WF2 141 E4
Whinny Royd La. Shelf HX3 93 A5
Whinny La. Feath WF7 144 D5
Whins La. Spoff HG3 12 C8
Whins La. Th Arch LS23 14 F1
Whins The. Keigh BD21 35 A2
Whinside Cres. Dearne S63 194 C1
Whirlaw Ave. Tod OL14 108 A7
Whirlaw La. Tod OL14 108 B8
Whiskers La. Northo HX3 92 E4
Whisperwood Cl. Loft G WF1 121 D5
Whisperwood Rd. Loft G WF1 121 D5
Whitacre Cl. Hud HD2 136 E3
Whitacre St. Hud HD2 136 E3
Whitaker Ave. Brad BD2 56 C3
Whitaker Cl. Brad BD2 56 C3
Whitaker St. Batley WF17 118 D4
Whitaker St. Pudsey LS28 57 D2
Whitby Ave. Hud HD2 136 B2
Whitby Cres. Dew WF12 139 F8
Whitby Rd. Brad BD8 55 A1
Whitby Terr. Brad BD8 55 A1
Whitcliffe Mount Sch. Clec 116 B8
Whitcliffe Rd. Clec BD19 116 D8
Whitcliffe Road Fst Sch. Clec 116 D8
Whitcliffe Sq. Clec BD19 116 D8
White Abbey Rd. Brad BD8 74 C8
White Apron St. S Kirk WF9 182 B2
White Birch Terr. Hali HX3 91 F2
White Castle Ct. Queen BD13 72 B2
White Cross Gdns. S Hie S72 180 D6
White Cross. Hud HD2 136 E5
White Cross Rd. Batley WF12 118 E2
White Field La. Heb Br HX7 110 C8
White Gate. Hali HX2 91 D7
White Gate. Honley HD7 171 F5
White Gate Rd. Holme HD7 198 D7
White Gate Rd. Holmfi HD7 188 D1
White Gr. Leeds LS8 61 A8
White Hart Dr. Hud HD4 154 A2
White Hart Fold. Tod OL14 108 B5 8
White Hill. Mars HD7 169 C7
White Horse Cl. Batley WF17 97 B2
White Horse Yd. Wake WF1 142 C6
White House Bglws. Wake WF2 142 B3
White La. Brad BD6 74 D1
White La. H Pag DN5 195 E4
White La. Haw BD22 33 F3
White Laith Ave. Leeds LS14 62 B8
White Laith Prim Sch. Leeds 62 C7
White Laithe App. Leeds LS14 62 B8 2
White Laithe Cl. Leeds LS14 62 B8
White Laithe Croft. Leeds LS14 62 B8
White Laithe Gdns. Leeds LS14 62 B8
White Laithe Gn. Leeds LS14 62 C8
White Laithe Gr. Leeds LS14 62 C8
White Laithe Rd. Leeds LS14 62 B8
White Laithe Wlk. Leeds LS14 62 C8 4
White Lands. Yeadon LS19 40 A4
White Lane Top. Brad BD6 94 D8 1
White Lee Cl. Batley WF16 117 E6
White Lee Gdns. Heb Br HX7 89 F1
White Lee Rd. Batley WF16 117 E6
White Lee Side. Batley WF16 117 E6
White Ley Bank. Holmfi HD7 190 A7
White Ley Rd. Norton WF8 166 E1
White Rose Ave. Gar LS25 83 A8
White Rose Ave. Hud HD5 154 F6
White Rose Way. Gar LS25 83 A7
White Slack Gate. Tod OL14 129 A6
White St. Roth LS26 101 C6 7
White Walls La. Holmfi HD7 187 F3
White Wells Gdns.Holmfi HD7 189 D3
White Wells. Ilkley 8 B2
White Wells Rd. Holmfi HD7 189 D3
White's Cl. Brad BD9 54 D3
White's Rd. Wake WF1 142 D6
White's Terr. Brad BD8 55 B1
White's View. Brad BD8 74 B8
Whiteacre St. Hud HD2 136 F3
Whitebeam Gn. Pont WF8 125 F1
Whitebeam La. Midd LS10 99 D8 6
Whitebeam Wlk. Brad BD2 56 B5
Whitebridge Ave. Leeds LS9 80 E8
Whitebridge Prim Sch. Leeds 80 E7
Whitebridge Spur. Leeds LS9 61 E1
Whitebridge View. Leeds LS9 61 E1
Whitechapel Cl. Leeds LS8 61 C6
Whitechapel Gr. Brig BD19 95 A1
Whitechapel Mid Sch. Clec 116 C8
Whitechapel Rd. Brig BD19 116 A8
Whitechapel Rd. Clec BD19 116 C8
Whitechapel Way. Leeds LS8 61 B6
Whitecliffe Cres. Swil LS26 82 A2
Whitecliffe Dr. Swil LS26 82 A2
Whitecliffe Rise. Swil LS26 82 A2
Whitecoat Prim Sch. Leeds 58 D4
Whitecote Gdns. Leeds LS13 58 B4
Whitecote Hill. Leeds LS13 58 B4
Whitecote La. Leeds LS13 58 B4
Whitecote La. S Mil LS25 84 F4
Whitecote Rise. Leeds LS13 58 B4
Whitefield Pl. Brad BD8 74 A8
Whitegate Dr. Hali HX3 113 D4
Whitegate. E Kes LS17 28 C6
Whitegate. Hali HX3 113 D4
Whitegate Hill. Dar WF8 164 E8
Whitegate La. Ack M T WF8 164 E8
Whitegate Rd. Hali HX3 113 D4
Whitegate Rd. Hud HD4 154 B4
Whitegate Terr. Hali HX3 113 D4
Whitegate Top. Hali HX3 113 E5
Whitegates Cl. Wake WF1 121 A1
Whitegates Gr. Lepton HD8 155 D2
Whitehall Ave. Brad BD12 94 C1
Whitehall Ave. Mir WF14 138 A7
Whitehall Ave. Wake WF1 121 A1
Whitehall Cres. Wake WF1 121 A1
Whitehall Croft. Roth LS26 100 F5
Whitehall Ct. Hor WF4 141 B1 1
Whitehall Gr. Birk BD11 96 B5
Whitehall Gr. Birk BD11 96 D6
Whitehall Rd. Birk BD11 96 E6
Whitehall Rd. Brad BD12 94 C1
Whitehall Rd. Brig BD12 94 C1
Whitehall Rd . Clec BD19 95 D2
Whitehall Rd E. Birk BD11 96 B5
Whitehall Rd. Gild LS12 77 D2
Whitehall Rd. Leeds LS12 78 A4
Whitehall Rd. Leeds LS12 78 E6
Whitehall Rd. Leeds LS1, LS12 79 A7
Whitehall Rd. Slai HD7 170 C8
Whitehall Rd W. Birk BD11 96 A4
Whitehall Rd W. Clec BD19 95 E3
Whitehall Rise. Wake WF1 142 A8
Whitehall St. Brig HX3 114 D8
Whitehall St. Wake WF2 141 F5
Whitehall Trad Est. Leeds 77 F4
Whitehall Way. Dew WF13 139 D8
Whitehaven Cl. Brad BD6 93 F7
Whitehead Gr. Brad BD2 56 C1
Whitehead La. Hud HD4 154 A3
Whitehead La. Mel HD4 170 F6
Whitehead Pl. Brad BD2 56 C1
Whitehead St. Brad BD3 75 B6
Whitehead's Terr. Hali HX1 112 F7 3
Whitehill Cty Jun & Inf Schs. Hali 91 E6
Whitehill Cres. Hali HX2 91 E6
Whitehill Dr. Hali HX2 91 E6
Whitehill Gn. Hali HX2 91 F6
Whitehill Rd. Hali HX2 91 E6
Whitehill Rd. Haw BD22 33 D5
Whitehouse Ave. Swil LS26 102 D8
Whitehouse Cres. Swil LS26 102 E8
Whitehouse Dr. Swil LS26 102 D8
Whitehouse La. Swil LS26 82 C2
Whitehouse La. Yeadon LS19 40 F8
Whitehouse St. Leeds LS10 79 D5
Whitelands Cres. Bail BD17 38 D3
Whitelands. Pudsey LS28 76 F8 1
Whitelands Rd. Bail BD17 38 D3
Whiteley Ave. Sow Br HX6 111 F3
Whiteley Croft Cl. Otley LS21 23 A7
Whiteley Crft Garth. Otley LS21 22 F7
Whiteley Croft. Otley LS21 23 A7
Whiteley Croft Rd. Otley LS21 22 F7
Whiteley Croft Rd. Otley LS21 23 A7
Whiteley Croft Rise. Otley LS21 23 A7
Whiteley St. Feath WF7 145 C5
Whiteley St. Hud HD3 153 B4
Whiteley Terr. Rip HX6 132 C2
Whitelock St. Leeds LS7 60 D1
Whiteplatts St. Tod OL14 108 B6 12
Whiterose Mead. Gar LS25 83 A7
Whitestone Cres. Yeadon LS19 40 B7
Whitestone La. Hud HD1 154 B8 2
Whiteways. Brad BD2 55 E3
Whitewood Cl. Roy S71 179 B3
Whitfield Ave. Leeds LS10 79 E4
Whitfield Gdns. Leeds LS10 79 E4
Whitfield Pl. Leeds LS10 79 E4
Whitfield Sq. Leeds LS10 79 E4
Whitfield St. Clec BD19 116 D8 9
Whitfield St. Leeds LS8 60 F3
Whitfield Way. Leeds LS10 79 E4
Whitford Freight Ctr. Nor 123 D4
Whitham Cl. B Spa LS23 30 D8
Whitkirk Cl. Leeds LS15 81 E8
Whitkirk La. Leeds LS15 81 D8
Whitkirk Prim Sch. Leeds 81 C7
Whitlam St. Ship BD18 54 F8
Whitley Gdns. Leeds LS8 60 E3
Whitley Grange Hospl. Dew 138 F1
Whitley La. Hali HX3 114 A5
Whitley Lower CE Sch. Dew 156 E8
Whitley Pl. Kippax WF10 103 B4
Whitley Rd. Dew WF12 139 B1
Whitley Rd. Keigh BD21 35 A5
Whitley Rd. Wh Com S30 200 E7
Whitley Spring Cres. Ossett WF5 140 F6
Whitley Spring Rd.Ossett WF5 140 F6
Whitley St. Bing BD16 36 F3
Whitley St. Brad BD3 75 A7
Whitley St. Hali HX1 113 B6
Whitley Terr. Wh Com S30 200 D5
Whitley Way. Floc WF4 156 E5
Whitteron Cl. Hud HD3 135 B1
Whittle Cres. Brad BD14 73 B5
Whitton Croft Rd. Ilkley LS29 8 B4
Whitty La. Hali HX2 112 B6
Whitwell Ave. Elland HX5 135 B7
Whitwell Dr. Elland HX5 135 B7
Whitwell Gr. Elland HX5 135 B7
Whitwell Gn La. Elland HX5 135 B6
Whitwell St. Brad BD4 75 A5
Whitwood Common La. Castle WF10 123 E5
Whitwood Enterprise Pk. Nor 123 B3
Whitwood La. Brig HD6 115 D7
Whitwood La. Castle WF10 123 E6
Whitwood Mining & Tech Coll (Annexe). Castle 124 B8
Whitwood Mining & Tech Coll. Castle 124 A6
Whitwood Terr. Castle WF10 123 E5
Whitworth Rd. Dew WF13 139 B7 1
Wholestone Gate. Slai HD7 152 B5
Whytecote End. Brad BD12 94 C4
Wibsey Fst Sch. Brad 74 B1
Wibsey Mid Sch. Brad 74 B1
Wibsey Park Ave. Brad BD6 94 A8
Wicken La. Thorn BD13 72 B7
Wicket. Pudsey LS28 57 B7
Wickets Cl. Brad BD6 94 D8
Wickets The. Leeds LS6 59 F7
Wickets The. Leeds LS15 81 E7
Wickham Ave. B Spa LS23 30 C8
Wickham Ave. Brad BD6 94 C8
Wickham Cl. B Spa LS23 30 C8
Wickham St. Brig BD19 94 F1
Wickham St. Leeds LS11 79 A3
Wicking La. Rip HX6 132 A8
Wickins La. Holmfi HD7 188 D6
Wickleden Gate. Holmfi HD7 189 D3
Widdop Rd. Hep HX7 88 D6
Wide La. Haw BD22 34 B3
Wide La. Morley LS27 98 C3
Wide La. Morley LS27 98 D4
Wigan St. Brad BD1 74 D7
Wiggan La. Hud HD2 136 D4
Wiggin Cross. Slai HD7 152 E1
Wighill La. Th Arch LS23 15 C2
Wighill La. Wig LS24 15 C2
Wighill St. S in Cra BD20 16 D5
Wightman St. Brad BD3 56 A1
Wignall St. Keigh BD20 18 B2
Wigton Chase. Leeds LS17 44 A5
Wigton Gate. Leeds LS17 43 E6
Wigton Gn. Leeds LS17 43 F6
Wigton Gr. Leeds LS17 43 E6
Wigton Moor Prim Sch. Leeds 43 F5
Wigton Park Cl. Leeds LS17 43 F6
Wike La. Bard LS17 28 B3
Wike Ridge Ave. Leeds LS17 44 B5
Wike Ridge Gr. Leeds LS17 44 B5
Wike Ridge La. Hare LS17 44 C7
Wike Ridge La. Leeds LS17 44 C7
Wike Ridge Mount. Leeds LS17 44 B5
Wilberlee Cty Prim Sch. Slai 151 D2
Wilby St. Clec BD19 116 D7
Wilcock La. L Brad BD20 4 F5
Wild Gr. Pudsey LS28 76 A7
Wild's Yd. Wake WF1 142 D5
Wilday Cl. Bing BD16 36 E6
Wildspur Gr. Holmfi HD7 189 E4
Wilford Rd. Barn S71 178 E1
Wilfred Ave. Leeds LS15 81 B8
Wilfred St. Brad BD14 73 D4
Wilfred St. Leeds LS15 81 B8 2
Wilfrid Terr. Leeds LS12 78 A4
Wilkin St. Keigh BD21 35 B7
Wilkinson Fold. Brad BD12 94 C3 9
Wilkinson Terr. Brad BD7 73 F6
Wilkinson Way. Otley LS21 10 E1
Willan's Rd. Dew WF13 118 C1
Willans Ave. Roth LS26 100 E7
Willerton Cl. Batley WF12 119 B3
Willgutter La. Haw BD22 33 F1
William Ave. Leeds LS15 80 E8 2
William Henry Smith Sch The. Brig 135 E8
William Henry St. Brig HD6 115 A3 1
William Henry St. Ship BD18 54 F8 2
William Hey Ct. Leeds LS9 61 B2
William Horsfall St. Hud HD4 153 C3
William Prince Gr. Wake WF1 142 E4
William Rise. Leeds LS15 80 E8
William St. Batley WF13 117 F3
William St. Brad BD5 74 E6
William St. Brad BD4 75 D1
William St. Brad BD4 75 D5
William St. Brad BD6 93 F7
William St. Brig HD6 115 A1 10
William St. Castle WF10 103 D1
William St. Castle WF10 104 C2
William St. Denh BD13 52 D1
William St. Dew WF13 138 E5
William St. Dew WF12 139 E8
William St. Elland HX4 134 D6
William St. Hud HD4 153 C4
William St. Hud HD1 154 B7 3
William St. Leeds LS6 59 E3
William St. Liver WF15 117 B4 2
William St. Morley LS27 98 C8
William St. Pudsey LS28 57 D1 8
William St. Pudsey LS28 57 F2
William View. Leeds LS15 80 E8
Williams Dr. Stee BD20 17 B5
Williams Rd. Stee BD20 17 B5
Williamson St. Hali HX1 113 A8
Willis St. Leeds LS9 79 E7
Willoughby Terr. Leeds LS11 78 F5
Willow App. Leeds LS4 59 E1
Willow Ave. B Spa LS23 30 D6
Willow Ave. Brad BD2 56 A6
Willow Ave. Leeds LS4 59 E1
Willow Bank. Hali HX1 113 A5
Willow Bank. Tod OL14 108 B6
Willow Beck. Notton WF4 179 A6
Willow Cl. Brad BD6 94 C7
Willow Cl. Bur in W LS29 9 E1
Willow Cl. Clec BD19 117 B7
Willow Cl. Guise LS20 22 E1
Willow Cl. Hali HX2 112 D6
Willow Cl. Leeds LS4 59 E1
Willow Clough. Rip HX6 132 D2
Willow Cres. B Spa LS23 30 D6
Willow Cres. Brad BD2 56 A6
Willow Cres. Hali HX6 112 C5
Willow Cres. Leeds LS15 80 F7
Willow Cres. Nor WF6 144 A8
Willow Croft. Clec BD19 116 C7
Willow Croft. Men LS29 22 A4
Willow Ct. Castle WF10 124 E6
Willow Ct. Feath WF7 124 C1
Willow Ct. Pool LS21 24 D6
Willow Ct. Wake WF2 141 D7
Willow Dene Ave. Hali HX2 112 D5
Willow Dr. Brad BD6 94 C7
Willow Dr. Hali HX2 112 D6
Willow Dr. Hem WF9 181 D5
Willow Dr. Wake WF1 142 E3
Willow Garth Ave. Glu BD20 16 D7
Willow Garth Ave. Leeds LS14 62 B8
Willow Garth Cl. Leeds LS14 62 B8
Willow Garth. Crig WF4 159 F6
Willow Garth. Feath WF7 124 C1
Willow Garth. Leeds LS4 59 E1
Willow Garth. S Elm WF9 183 B2
Willow Gdns. Brad BD2 56 A6
Willow Gdns. Castle WF10 125 D5
Willow Gdns. Guise LS20 22 E1
Willow Gdns. Wake WF2 141 D7
Willow Glade. B Spa LS23 30 D5
Willow Gn. Loft G WF1 121 B3
Willow Gr. B Spa LS23 30 D6
Willow Gr. Brad BD2 56 A6
Willow Gr. Hud HD7 152 E5
Willow Gr. Keigh BD21 35 A3
Willow Gr. Kippax LS25 82 F3
Willow Gr. Ossett WF5 140 E3
Willow Gr. Wake WF1 142 E3
Willow Hall Dr. Hali HX6 112 D5
Willow Hall La. Hali HX6 112 D5
Willow La. B Spa LS23 30 D5
Willow La. Crof WF1 143 D7
Willow La E. Feath WF7 124 C1
Willow La E. Hud HD1 154 B8
Willow La. Feath WF7 124 C1
Willow La. Hud HD1 154 A8
Willow La. Wake WF2 141 D7
Willow Park Dr. Shelf HX3 93 D6
Willow Pk. Loft G WF1 121 B2
Willow Pk. Pont WF8 146 F8
Willow Rd. Batley WF17 118 E4
Willow Rd. Castle WF10 124 D6
Willow Rd. Dearne S63 194 D1
Willow Rd. Knot WF11 127 A5
Willow Rd. Leeds LS4 59 E1
Willow Rd. Pudsey LS28 57 D2
Willow Rd. Wake WF2 141 D7
Willow Rise. Hali HX2 112 D6
Willow Rise. Skel HD8 175 A1
Willow Sq. Roth LS26 101 C5 3
Willow St. Brad BD8 74 A8
Willow St. Clec BD19 95 D1
Willow St. Hali HX6 112 D4
Willow St. Hali HX1 113 A6
Willow Terr. Batley WF17 118 E4
Willow Terr. Hali HX6 112 C5
Willow Terrace Rd. Leeds LS1 60 B1
Willow Tree Cl. Keigh BD21 35 D5
Willow Tree Gdns. Bing BD16 37 C5
Willow Vale. Weth LS22 13 E7
Willow View. Hali HX6 112 C5
Willow Villas. Brad BD2 56 A6
Willow Way. S in Cra BD20 16 C4
Willow Well Rd. Leeds LS15 80 F8
Willow Wlk. Liver WF15 117 A3
Willowbridge La. Castle WF10 124 A6
Willowbridge Rd. Norton WF8 166 F5
Willowbrook. Ad Le S DN6 184 F2
Willowdene La. Pont WF8 125 D3
Willowfield Ave. Hali HX2 112 D5
Willowfield Cl. Hali HX2 112 D6
Willowfield Cres. Brad BD2 56 A6
Willowfield Cres. Hali HX2 112 D6
Willowfield Dr. Hali HX2 112 D5
Willowfield Fst Sch. Brad 74 B6
Willowfield Rd. Hali HX2 112 D6
Willowfield St. Brad BD7 74 B6
Willowfield Terr. Hali HX2 112 E5
Willowfield View. Hali HX2 112 D6
Willowgarth High Sch. Grim 181 A1
Willows The. Hali HX2 91 E7
Willows The. Harden BD16 36 B1
Willows The. Leeds LS17 43 C2
Wills Gill. Guise LS20 22 F1
Willwood Ave. Hud HD3 153 B7
Wilman Dr. Ossett WF5 140 C6
Wilman Hill. Brad BD6 74 B1 3
Wilman Post. Ossett WF5 140 C6
Wilmar Dr. Hud HD3 134 E1
Wilmer Dr. Ship BD9 55 A4
Wilmer Dr. Ship BD18 55 A5
Wilmer Rd. Brad BD9 55 A3
Wilmington Gr. Leeds LS7 60 C2
Wilmington St. Leeds LS7 60 D2
Wilmington Terr. Leeds LS7 60 C2
Wilmot Rd. Ilkley LS29 8 C4
Wilmur Mount. Hali HX2 111 D6
Wilsden Fst Sch. Wils 53 C5
Wilsden Hill Rd. Wils BD15 53 B5
Wilsden Old Rd. Harden BD16 36 B1
Wilsden Rd. Brad BD15 53 F3
Wilsden Rd. Harden BD16 36 B1
Wilshaw CE Sch. Mel 188 B8
Wilshaw Mill Rd. Mel HD7 188 B7
Wilshaw Rd. Mel HD7 188 B8
Wilson Ave. Mir WF14 137 F5
Wilson Ave. Ossett WF5 141 A4
Wilson Ave. Stee BD20 17 B6
Wilson Ct. Loft G WF1 121 C4
Wilson Dr. Loft G WF1 121 B4
Wilson Rd. Bing BD16 36 F4
Wilson Rd. Brad BD12 94 E4
Wilson Rd. Hali HX1 112 F5 19
Wilson Rd. Mir WF14 137 F5
Wilson St. Brad BD8 55 C1
Wilson St. Castle WF10 124 C8
Wilson St. Feath WF7 145 C5
Wilson St. Glu BD20 16 D7
Wilson St. Pont WF8 125 D1
Wilson St. S in Cra BD20 16 E5
Wilson Terr. Mir WF14 137 F5
Wilson Wood St. Batley WF17 118 C2
Wilson's Row. M'town LS26 102 F3

Wilsons Yd. Pudsey LS28 .... 57 D1 6
Wilton Ave. Hud HD2 .... 136 E5
Wilton Gr. Leeds LS6 .... 59 E6
Wilton Rd. Ilkley LS29 .... 8 A3
Wilton St. Brad BD5 .... 74 E6
Wilton St. Brig HD6 .... 114 F3
Wilton St. Dew WF12 .... 139 D7
Wilton Terr. Clec BD19 .... 116 D7
Wimborne Dr. Brad BD15 .... 54 C1
Wimborne Dr. Keigh BD21 .... 34 F8
Winbrooke Terr. Brad BD6 .... 74 A1
Winburg Rd. Brad BD7 .... 74 A5
Winchester St. Leeds LS12 .... 78 D7
Winchester Way. S Elm WF9 . 183 A4
Winden Cl. Crig WF4 .... 159 D6
Winden Cl. Loft G WF3 .... 121 C5
Winden Gr. Loft G WF3 .... 121 B5
Windermere Ave. Men LS29 .... 22 A6
Windermere Dr. Gar LS25 .... 82 F6
Windermere Dr. Knot WF11 .. 126 E1
Windermere Dr. Leeds LS17 ... 42 F6
Windermere Rd. Bacup OL13 106 A4
Windermere Rd. Bail BD17 .... 37 F1
Windermere Rd. Batley WF12 118 E2
Windermere Rd. Brad BD7 .... 73 E3
Windermere Rd. Castle WF10 125 D7
Windermere Rd. Mel HD7 .... 170 E1
Windermere Rd. Wake WF2 .. 141 F7
Windermere Terr. Brad BD7 ... 73 E3 3
Windgate. Sil BD20 .... 17 F8
Windhill Ave. Mapp S75 .... 178 A3
Windhill CE Fst Sch. Ship 55 E8
Windhill Cres. Mapp S75 .... 178 A3
Windhill Cres. Wake WF1 .... 142 E8
Windhill Ct. Wake WF1 .... 142 F8
Windhill Dr. Mapp S75 .... 178 A3
Windhill La. Mapp S75 .... 178 A3
Windhill Mount. Mapp S75 .... 178 A3
Windhill Old Rd. Brad BD10,
BD18 .... 38 F1
Windhill Rd. Wake WF1 .... 142 F8
Winding Rd. Hali HX1 .... 113 C7
Winding Way. Leeds LS17 .... 43 B5
Windle Edge. Dun Br S30 .... 199 D1
Windle La. Con BD20 .... 4 A2
Windle Royd La. Hali HX2 .... 112 C7
Windmill App. Midd LS10 .... 99 E8
Windmill Ave. Grim S72 .... 181 A1
Windmill Chase. Roth LS26 .... 100 E4
Windmill Cl. Midd LS10 .... 99 E7
Windmill Cres. Northo HX3 .... 93 A2
Windmill Cres. Skel HD8 .... 175 B1
Windmill Ct. Leeds LS14 .... 62 B6
Windmill Dr. Northo HX3 .... 93 A2
Windmill Field Rd. Roth LS26 . 100 E4
Windmill Gn. Roth LS26 .... 100 E4
Windmill Gr. Liver BD19 .... 117 B6
Windmill Hill. Brad BD6 .... 74 A1
Windmill Hill La. Emley HD8 .. 174 F8
Windmill Hill La. Floc WF4 .... 156 F1
Windmill Hill. Pudsey LS28 .... 76 C6
Windmill La. Batley WF17 .... 97 A1
Windmill La. Brad BD6 .... 74 C1
Windmill La. Guise LS20 .... 22 D4
Windmill La. Roth LS26 .... 100 E4
Windmill La. Wh Com HD7 .... 190 D3
Windmill La. Yeadon LS19 .... 40 C6
Windmill Prim Sch. Midd 99 E8
Windmill Rd. Bramham LS23 ... 30 E4
Windmill Rd. Midd LS10 .... 99 E8
Windmill Rise. Aber LS25 .... 64 E6
Windmill View. Holmfi HD7 .... 189 C2
Windmill View. Wake WF1 .... 142 D8
Windrose Cl. Nor WF6 .... 123 A4
Windsor Ave. Ack M T WF7 .... 164 C7
Windsor Ave. Leeds LS15 .... 81 B8
Windsor Ave. Sil BD20 .... 5 D1
Windsor Cl. Batley WF12 .... 119 B2
Windsor Cl. Kippax LS25 .... 83 A2
Windsor Cres. Hali HX2 .... 91 E1
Windsor Cres. Haw BD22 .... 34 B2
Windsor Cres. Roth LS26 .... 100 E6
Windsor Cres. Wake WF1 .... 121 A1
Windsor Ct. Leeds LS17 .... 43 E2
Windsor Ct. Morley LS27 .... 98 A4
Windsor Dr. Hud HD5 .... 155 A6
Windsor Dr. Knot WF11 .... 126 B5
Windsor Dr. Liver WF15 .... 117 B2
Windsor Dr. Skel HD8 .... 175 B1
Windsor Gdns. Batley WF12 .. 119 B2
Windsor Gn. Gar LS25 .... 83 B7
Windsor Gr. Haw BD22 .... 34 B2
Windsor Gr. Thorn BD13 .... 72 D6
Windsor Mount. Leeds LS15 .... 81 B8
Windsor Pl. Hud HD2 .... 136 E5
Windsor Rd. Batley WF17 .... 97 B2
Windsor Rd. Batley WF17 .... 119 B2
Windsor Rd. Haw BD22 .... 34 B2
Windsor Rd. Heb Br HX7 .... 89 A4
Windsor Rd. Hem WF9 .... 181 F6
Windsor Rd. Hud HD4 .... 152 F3
Windsor Rd. Ship BD18 .... 55 B7
Windsor Rd. Tod OL14 .... 108 A6
Windsor Rd. Wake WF2 .... 120 F1
Windsor Rise. Pont WF8 .... 146 B5
Windsor St. Brad BD4 .... 75 A5
Windsor St. Hali HX1 .... 113 C6
Windsor St. S Elm WF9 .... 183 A2
Windsor View. Batley WF12 .. 119 B2
Windsor View. Heb Br HX7 .... 89 A4 1
Windsor Wlk. Batley WF17 .... 97 B2
Windsor Wlk. Brig HX3 .... 115 A6
Windy Bank La. Clec WF15 .... 116 B4
Windy Bank La. Liver WF15 .. 116 B4
Windy Bank La. Queen BD13 ... 92 B6
Windy Gr. Wils BD15 .... 53 D4
Windy Harbour La. Tod OL14 .. 87 B1
Windy Ridge. Thorn BD13 .... 72 C7
Windyridge St. Hor WF4 .... 140 F2
Wine St. Leeds LS1 .... 79 B8
Wine Tavern La. Sow Br HX6 111 B3
Wine Tavern Rd. Sow Br HX6 111 B3
Winfield Dr. Hud HD3 .... 152 F8
Winfield Gr. Leeds LS2 .... 60 B2
Winfield Pl. Leeds LS2 .... 60 B2
Winfield Rd. Birk BD4 .... 95 E6
Winfield Terr. Leeds LS2 .... 60 B2
Wingate Ave. Keigh BD22 .... 34 F6
Wingate Croft. Wake WF2 .... 160 F8
Wingate Gr. Wake WF2 .... 160 F8
Wingate Way. Keigh BD22 .... 34 F6
Winget Ave. Hud HD4 .... 152 F3
Wingfield Ct. Bing BD16 .... 37 A4
Wingfield Mount. Brad BD3 .... 75 B8
Wingfield St. Brad BD3 .... 75 B8
Winmarith Ct. Roy S71 .... 179 B3
Winney Bank La. Holmfi HD7 . 189 C5
Winnipeg Pl. Leeds LS7 .... 60 D6
Winnow La. B Spa LS23 .... 30 B7
Winrose App. Midd LS10 .... 99 E7
Winrose Ave. Midd LS10 .... 79 D1
Winrose Cl. Brad BD12 .... 94 C4
Winrose Cres. Midd LS10 .... 99 E8
Winrose Dr. Midd LS10 .... 99 D8
Winrose Garth. Midd LS10 .... 99 E8
Winrose Gr. Midd LS10 .... 99 E8
Winrose Hill. Midd LS10 .... 79 E1
Winsford Dr. Hud HD5 .... 155 B7
Winslow Rd. Brad BD10 .... 56 E4
Winston Ave. Glu BD20 .... 16 E7
Winston Gdns. Leeds LS6 .... 59 C5 2
Winston Mount. Leeds LS6 .... 59 C5
Winston Terr. Brad BD7 .... 74 A5
Winter Ct. Brad BD15 .... 54 A3
Winter Hill. Elland HD3 .... 152 A7
Winter Hill. Hali HX3 .... 114 A3
Winter St. Hali HX1 .... 112 F5 26
Winter's Cotts. B Head HX7 .... 88 C2
Winter's La. B Head HX7 .... 88 C2
Winterbourne Av. Morley LS27 98 B6
Winterburn La. Hali HX2 .... 112 A6
Winterburn St. Keigh BD21 .... 35 C8 3
Winterbutlee Gr. Tod OL14 .... 108 A1 16
Winterbutlee Rd. Tod OL14 .... 108 A1
Winterneb. Hali HX2 .... 111 E5
Wintersett La. Ryhill WF4 .... 162 A5
Winterton Dr. Brad BD12 .... 94 C5
Winthorpe Ave. Midd WF3 .... 99 D2
Winthorpe Cres. Midd WF3 .... 99 D2
Winthorpe St. Leeds LS6 .... 59 F6
Winthorpe View. Midd WF3 .... 99 E2
Winton Gn. Brad BD6 .... 94 B6 2
Winton St. Hud HD1 .... 153 E3
Wintoun St. Leeds LS7 .... 60 D1
Wisbey Bank. Brad BD6 .... 74 D1
Wistons La. Elland HX5 .... 135 A7
Witchfield Hill. Shelf HX3 .... 93 D6
Witham Rd. Ship BD18 .... 54 E8
Witham Way. Gar LS25 .... 83 B6
Withens Ct. Mapp S75 .... 178 A1
Withens End La. Rip HX4 .... 150 E7
Withens Hill Croft. Hali HX2 .... 91 D7
Withens La. Heb Br HX7 .... 109 F3
Withens La. Rip HX4 .... 150 F8
Withens New Rd. Hali HX2 .... 71 B2
Withens New Rd. Heb Br HX7 109 E3
Withens Rd. Batley WF17 .... 96 E2
Withens Rd. Hali HX2 .... 91 A7
Within Fields. Hali HX3 .... 114 A4
Withins Cl. Brad BD5 .... 74 B3
Withyside. D Dale HD8 .... 192 A6
Witmore St. S Elm WF9 .... 183 A3
Witton St. Wake WF1 .... 142 D7
Woburn Dr. Hud HD5 .... 155 B6
Woburn Terr. Brad BD14 .... 73 B4 1
Wold Cl. Thorn BD13 .... 72 D6
Wolfstones Rd. Holmfi HD7 .... 188 D6
Wolley Ave. Gild LS12 .... 77 D3
Wolley Ct. Gild LS12 .... 77 D3
Wolley Dr. Gild LS12 .... 77 D3
Wolley Gdns. Gild LS12 .... 77 D3
Wolseley Rd. Leeds LS4 .... 59 D2
Wolseley St. Brad BD14 .... 73 C5
Wolsey Ave. Pont WF8 .... 146 B8 2
Wolsey Terr. Hali HX1 .... 113 A7 1
Wolston Cl. Brad BD4 .... 75 E2
Womersley Pl. Pudsey LS28 .... 76 D6 4
Womersley Rd. Knot WF11 .... 127 B2
Womersley St. Hali HX1 .... 112 F7 18
Wonder St. Wake WF1 .... 142 D5
Wood Ave. Batley WF16 .... 117 D5
Wood Bottom La. Brig HD6 .... 114 E4
Wood Bottom Rd. Honley HD4 171 C5
Wood Cl. Bail BD17 .... 38 B2
Wood Cl. Hem WF9 .... 163 A2
Wood Cl. L Brad BD20 .... 4 C5
Wood Cl. Leeds LS7 .... 60 C7
Wood Cl. Nor WF6 .... 122 E3
Wood Cl. Roth LS26 .... 100 D6
Wood Cres. Roth LS26 .... 100 D6
Wood Croft. Brig HD6 .... 114 F1
Wood Croft. Sow Br HX6 .... 111 E3
Wood Dr. Roth LS26 .... 100 C6
Wood End Cotts. Mir WF14 .... 137 F3
Wood End Cres. Ship BD18 .... 55 D8
Wood End. Hud HD4 .... 153 F3
Wood End La. Rip HX4 .... 133 D6
Wood End La. Shep HD8 .... 190 C7
Wood End Rd. Hud HD4 .... 171 E8
Wood Farm La. Honley HD7 .. 172 C2
Wood Gn. Castle WF10 .... 123 F5
Wood Gr. Leeds LS12 .... 77 D7
Wood Gr. Ossett WF5 .... 140 D8
Wood Hey La. Heb Br HX7 .... 89 B1
Wood Hill Cres. Hors LS16 .... 41 C3
Wood Hill Ct. Hors LS16 .... 41 D4
Wood Hill Garth. Hors LS16 .... 41 D4
Wood Hill Gdns. Hors LS16 .... 41 D4
Wood Hill Gr. Hors LS16 .... 41 D3
Wood Hill Rd. Hors LS16 .... 41 D4
Wood Hill Rise. Hors LS16 .... 41 D4
Wood Hill. Roth LS26 .... 100 D6
Wood La. B in Elm LS15 .... 62 E6
Wood La. Bard LS17 .... 28 E3
Wood La. Batley WF17 .... 118 D3
Wood La. Brad BD2 .... 55 F5
Wood La. Brig HX3 .... 114 B8
Wood La. Brig HX3 .... 114 D2
Wood La. Castle WF10 .... 123 F5
Wood La. Crig WF4 .... 160 B3
Wood La. D Dale HD8 .... 191 E6
Wood La. Dew WF13 .... 118 D1
Wood La. Gild LS12 .... 77 E2
Wood La. Hali HX2, HX3 .... 91 E2
Wood La. Holmfi HD7 .... 189 A6
Wood La. Hors LS18 .... 58 C8
Wood La. Hud HD4 .... 154 C3
Wood La. Kirkb HD8 .... 173 C4
Wood La. Kirkhe WF14 .... 137 E4
Wood La. Leeds LS13 .... 58 C4
Wood La. Leeds LS6 .... 59 E5
Wood La. Leeds LS7 .... 60 C7
Wood La. Leeds LS12 .... 77 D7
Wood La. Leeds LS12 .... 78 A3
Wood La. Mapp S71 .... 178 E2
Wood La. Neth WF4 .... 157 E7
Wood La. Northo HX3 .... 93 B1
Wood La. Pudsey LS28 .... 57 B7
Wood La. Roth LS26 .... 100 D6
Wood La. Roy S71 .... 179 C1
Wood La. Slai HD7 .... 169 F5
Wood La. Sow Br HX6 .... 111 E4
Wood La. Swil LS26 .... 102 E7
Wood La. Th Arch LS23 .... 14 E3
Wood La. Wad M HX2 .... 90 B5
Wood Land Ct. Leeds LS6 .... 59 E5
Wood Lea. Byram WF11 .... 126 D8
Wood Lea. Tod OL14 .... 107 E8
Wood Moor Rd. Hem WF9 .... 181 F7
Wood Mount. Neth WF4 .... 157 F6
Wood Mount. Roth LS26 .... 100 C6
Wood Nook La. Hali HX6 .... 112 C5
Wood Nook La. Honley HD4 .. 171 C2
Wood Nook Terr. Pudsey LS28 57 C1
Wood Pl. Brad BD8 .... 74 C8
Wood Pl. Leeds LS11 .... 79 A3 3
Wood Rd. Brad BD5 .... 74 E4
Wood Rd. Ship BD9 .... 55 C4
Wood Row. M'town LS26 .... 102 B3
Wood Royd Hill La.Holmfi HD7 200 B8
Wood Sq. Hali HX3 .... 92 B2
Wood St. Bail BD17 .... 38 C1 4
Wood St. Batley WF17 .... 118 C5
Wood St. Bing BD16 .... 36 E6
Wood St. Brad BD15 .... 54 C1
Wood St. Brad BD8 .... 74 C8
Wood St. Brig HD6 .... 115 B2
Wood St. Castle WF10 .... 124 C8
Wood St. Clay W HD8 .... 175 D1
Wood St. Clec BD19 .... 116 C7
Wood St. Crof WF4 .... 144 B3
Wood St. Dew WF13 .... 118 D1
Wood St. E Ard WF3 .... 120 D8
Wood St. Elland HX5 .... 135 A6
Wood St. Haw BD22 .... 51 C6 4
Wood St. Hors LS18 .... 41 C2
Wood St. Hud HD3 .... 153 A5
Wood St. Hud HD1 .... 154 A6
Wood St. Hud HD5 .... 154 D6
Wood St. Keigh BD21 .... 35 C6
Wood St. Morley LS27 .... 97 F5
Wood St N. Hali HX3 .... 92 B2
Wood St. Ossett WF5 .... 140 D8
Wood St. S Hie S72 .... 180 F6
Wood St. Skel HD8 .... 174 F2
Wood St. Slai HD7 .... 151 F1
Wood St. Stee BD20 .... 17 C5
Wood St. Tod OL14 .... 108 B6
Wood St. Wake WF1 .... 142 C6
Wood Terr. Hud HD4 .... 154 A3
Wood Top. Brig HD6 .... 114 E5
Wood Top. Mars HD7 .... 168 F3
Wood Top Rd. Heb Br HX7 .... 89 B2
Wood View Ave. Castle WF10 124 A7
Wood View. Bail BD17 .... 38 A2
Wood View Bglws. Castle
WF10 .... 124 A7
Wood View Cl. Castle WF10 .. 124 A7
Wood View Cres. Castle WF10 124 A7
Wood View. Denh BD13 .... 52 C3
Wood View Dr. Brad BD2 .... 56 D2
Wood View Gr. Brig HD6 .... 114 F4
Wood View. Hud HD2 .... 135 D1
Wood View. Morley LS27 .... 98 C8
Wood Villas. Heb Br HX7 .... 88 C1
Wood Vine Rd. Pudsey LS28 .... 57 C1
Wood Yard Cotts.Walton WF2 161 B8
Wood's Row. Pudsey LS28 .... 57 E1
Woodacre Cres. Bard LS17 .... 28 C3
Woodacre Gn. Bard LS17 .... 28 C4
Woodacre La. Bard LS17 .... 28 C4
Woodale Ave. Brad BD9 .... 54 D3
Woodbine Ave. Pont WF8 .... 146 C8 9
Woodbine Gr. Brad BD10 .... 56 B7
Woodbine Rd. Hud HD1 .... 136 B1
Woodbine St. Brad BD1 .... 75 A7
Woodbine St. Hali HX1 .... 113 A5 8
Woodbine St. Ossett WF5 .... 140 D7
Woodbine Terr. Brad BD10 .... 56 B7
Woodbine Terr. Clay W HD8 . 175 F3
Woodbine Terr. Hali HX1 .... 113 A5 9
Woodbine Terr. Hors LS18 .... 58 C7 9
Woodbine Terr. Leeds LS13 .... 58 C3
Woodbine Terr. Leeds LS6 .... 59 E6
Woodbine Terr. Tod OL14 .... 86 B1
Woodbourne Ave. Leeds LS17 . 43 C1
Woodbourne. Leeds LS8 .... 61 C7
Woodbridge Cl. Leeds LS6 .... 59 B5
Woodbridge Cl. Wake WF1 .... 142 E6
Woodbridge Cres. Leeds LS6 .. 59 A6
Woodbridge Fold. Leeds LS6 .. 59 A5 2
Woodbridge Garth. Leeds LS6 . 59 B5
Woodbridge Gdns. Leeds LS6 .. 59 A5
Woodbridge Gn. Leeds LS6 .... 59 B5
Woodbridge Lawn. Leeds LS6 . 59 A5
Woodbridge Pl. Leeds LS6 .... 59 A5
Woodbridge Rd. Leeds LS6 .... 59 A5
Woodbrook Ave. Hali HX2 .... 91 C5
Woodbrook Cl. Hali HX2 .... 91 C5
Woodbrook Pl. Hali HX2 .... 91 C5
Woodbrook Rd. Hali HX2 .... 91 C5
Woodburn Ave. Dew WF12 .... 139 F6
Woodbury Rd. Brad BD8 .... 55 B2
Woodchurch Vw. Holmfi HD7 189 B8
Woodcliffe Ct. Leeds LS7 .... 60 C7
Woodcock St. Wake WF1 .... 142 D3
Woodcock Way. S Elm WF9 .. 183 A4
Woodcot Ave. Bail BD17 .... 38 D2
Woodcroft. Wake WF2 .... 142 E1
Woodcross End. Morley LS27 .. 98 A7
Woodcross Fold. Morley LS27 . 98 A7
Woodcross Garth. Morley LS27 98 A7
Woodcross Gdns. Morley LS27 98 A6
Woodcross. Morley LS27 .... 98 A6
Woodedge Ave. Hud HD5 .... 155 A6
Woodend Cres. Kippax WF10 102 F5
Woodend Ct. Brad BD5 .... 74 F2
Woodend. Kippax WF10 .... 102 F6
Woodend Mid Sch. Ship 55 D8
Woodend Rd. Mir WF14 .... 137 F4
Woodfield Ave. Batley WF17 . 118 A4
Woodfield Ave. Elland HX4 .... 134 B7
Woodfield Ct. Hud HD2 .... 153 F8
Woodfield Dr. Elland HX4 .... 134 C6
Woodfield Dr. L Brad BD20 .... 4 C5
Woodfield Pk. Walton WF2 .... 161 A6
Woodfield Rd. Cull BD13 .... 52 E7
Woodfield Rd. Norton DN6 .... 184 E8
Woodfield Terr. Pudsey LS28 .. 76 F6
Woodford Ave. Hali HX3 .... 113 D4
Woodford Cl. Brad BD15 .... 73 A8
Woodford Dr. Hud HD5 .... 155 B7
Woodhall Ave. Brad BD3 .... 56 E1
Woodhall Ave. Leeds LS5 .... 58 E6
Woodhall Cl. Crig WF4 .... 159 F6
Woodhall Cl. Neth WF4 .... 158 A6
Woodhall Cl. Pudsey LS28 .... 57 A2
Woodhall Cres. Hali HX3 .... 113 A3
Woodhall Croft. Pudsey LS28 .. 57 A2
Woodhall Ct. Leeds LS15 .... 81 D6
Woodhall Ct. Pudsey LS28 .... 57 A5
Woodhall Dr. Ack M T WF7 .... 163 F6
Woodhall Dr. Batley WF17 .... 118 A4
Woodhall Dr. Leeds LS5 .... 58 E6
Woodhall Gr. M'town LS26 .... 102 D3
Woodhall La. Pudsey LS28 .... 57 A2
Woodhall Park Ave. Pudsey
LS28 .... 57 B2
Woodhall Park Cres E. Pudsey
LS28 .... 57 B1
Woodhall Park Cres W. Pudsey
LS28 .... 57 A1
Woodhall Park Croft. Pudsey
LS28 .... 57 B1
Woodhall Park Dr. Pudsey LS28 57 B1
Woodhall Park Gr. Pudsey LS28 57 A2
Woodhall Park Mount. Pudsey
LS28 .... 57 A2
Woodhall Pl. Brad BD3 .... 56 E1
Woodhall Rd. Brad BD3 .... 56 E2
Woodhall Rd. Pudsey LS28 .... 56 E2
Woodhall Rd. Pudsey LS28 .... 57 A5
Woodhall Terr. Brad BD3 .... 56 E1
Woodhall View. Brad BD3 .... 56 F1
Woodhead Cl. Hud HD2 .... 136 C3
Woodhead La. Brig HD6 .... 115 E2
Woodhead La. Gild LS27 .... 97 C7
Woodhead Rd. Batley WF17 .... 97 B4
Woodhead Rd. Brad BD7 .... 74 B6
Woodhead Rd. Holmfi HD7 .... 172 B3
Woodhead Rd. Holmfi HD7 .... 188 D3
Woodhead Rd. Honley HD7 .... 172 B3
Woodhead Rd. Hud HD4 .... 153 C2
Woodhead St. Clec BD19 .... 116 E7 14
Woodhead St. Hali HX2 .... 112 E8 5
Woodhill Rise. Brad BD10 .... 56 E8
Woodhill View. Weth LS22 .... 13 E6
Woodhouse Ave. Hud HD2 .... 136 C2
Woodhouse Ave. Keigh BD21 .. 35 C5
Woodhouse CE(A) Inf Sch. Hud136 C3
Woodhouse Cl. E Ard WF3 .... 120 B6
Woodhouse Cl. Keigh BD21 .... 35 C5
Woodhouse Cliff. Leeds LS6 .... 60 A4
Woodhouse Cotts. Slai HD3 ... 151 D5
Woodhouse Cres. Nor WF6 .... 144 B8
Woodhouse Dr. Keigh BD21 .... 35 C5
Woodhouse Fst Sch. Nor 144 A8
Woodhouse Gr. Hud HD2 .... 136 C2
Woodhouse Gr. Keigh BD21 .... 35 C5
Woodhouse Gr. Tod OL14 .... 108 D5
Woodhouse Grove Sch. Pudsey 39 F1
Woodhouse Hall Rd. Hud HD2 136 C2
Woodhouse Hill Ave. Leeds
LS10 .... 79 E2
Woodhouse Hill Gr. Leeds LS10 79 E2 8
Woodhouse Hill. Hud HD2 .... 136 C2
Woodhouse Hill Pl. Leeds LS10 79 E2 7
Woodhouse Hill Rd. Leeds LS10 79 E2
Woodhouse Hill Terr. Leeds
LS10 .... 79 E2 5
Woodhouse La. Brig HD6 .... 136 B8
Woodhouse La. E Ard WF3 .... 120 B5
Woodhouse La. Emley HD8 .... 176 A7
Woodhouse La. Hali HX3 .... 113 A3
Woodhouse La. Holmfi HD7 .... 188 D1
Woodhouse La. Leeds LS2 .... 60 A2
Woodhouse La. Wool WF4,
S75 .... 178 B5
Woodhouse Mount. Nor WF6 144 A8
Woodhouse Rd. Keigh BD21 .... 35 C4
Woodhouse Rd. Tod OL14 .... 108 E6
Woodhouse Rd. Wake WF1 .... 142 E7
Woodhouse Sq. Leeds LS3 .... 60 A1 7
Woodhouse St. Leeds LS6 .... 60 A3
Woodhouse Terr. Brad BD6 .... 94 D8 12
Woodhouse Way. Keigh BD21 . 35 C5
Woodhouse Wlk. Keigh BD21 .. 35 C5
Woodkirk Ave. E Ard WF3 .... 119 D8
Woodkirk Gdns. E Ard WF12 . 119 B6
Woodkirk Gr. Brad BD12 .... 94 C1
Woodkirk Gr. E Ard WF3 .... 119 D8
Woodkirk High Sch. E Ard 119 C8
Woodland Ave. Crof WF4 .... 143 C7
Woodland Ave. Swil LS26 .... 82 A1
Woodland Cl. Brad BD9 .... 54 C4
Woodland Cl. Crig WF4 .... 159 F2
Woodland Cl. Leeds LS15 .... 81 C8
Woodland Cres. Roth LS26 .... 100 D6
Woodland Cres. Ship BD9 .... 54 C4
Woodland Cres. Swil LS26 .... 82 A1
Woodland Croft. Hors LS18 .... 41 C2
Woodland Ct. Bing BD16 .... 36 E5
Woodland Dr. Hali HX2 .... 112 D5
Woodland Dr. Leeds LS7 .... 60 D7
Woodland Dr. Skel HD8 .... 175 B1
Woodland Dr. Swil LS26 .... 81 F1
Woodland Dr. Wake WF2 .... 160 D6
Woodland Gr. Ack M T WF7 .... 146 A1
Woodland Gr. Dew WF13 .... 138 F8
Woodland Gr. Leeds LS7 .... 60 E4
Woodland Gr. Ship BD9 .... 54 C5
Woodland Gr. Swil LS26 .... 82 A1
Woodland Hall. B Head HX7 .... 88 A4
Woodland Hill. Leeds LS15 .... 81 B8
Woodland La. Leeds LS7 .... 60 D7
Woodland Meadow.Kirkb HD8 173 F7
Woodland Mount. Leeds LS7 ... 60 E4 1
Woodland Park Rd. Leeds LS6 . 59 F5
Woodland Pk. Roth LS26 .... 101 C5
Woodland Rd. Hud HD2 .... 136 F2
Woodland Rd. Leeds LS15 .... 81 B8
Woodland Rd. Wake WF2 .... 141 D5
Woodland Rise. Leeds LS15 .... 81 C8
Woodland Rise. Wake WF2 .... 141 D6
Woodland Sq. Brig HD6 .... 115 C1
Woodland Terr. Leeds LS7 .... 60 A7
Woodland View. B Head HX7 .. 88 C2
Woodland View. Leeds LS7 .... 60 D7
Woodland View. Pont WF8 .... 146 E6
Woodland View. Pudsey LS28 . 57 A7
Woodlands Ave. Castle WF10 125 C6
Woodlands Ave. Clec BD19 .... 96 A1
Woodlands Ave. Hali HX3 .... 92 C1
Woodlands Ave. Holmfi HD7 . 189 C8
Woodlands Ave. Lepton HD8 . 155 E3
Woodlands Ave. Pudsey LS28 . 57 C1
Woodlands Ave. Tod OL14 .... 108 B6
Woodlands Cl. D Dale HD8 .... 192 A6
Woodlands Cl. E Ard WF3 .... 120 C7
Woodlands Cl. Hud HD2 .... 137 A6
Woodlands Cl. Ilkley LS29 .... 7 E4
Woodlands Cl. Pudsey BD10 ... 39 F1
Woodlands Cl. Scar LS14 .... 45 C8
Woodlands Cres. Clec BD19 .... 96 A1
Woodlands Cres. Hem WF9 .... 181 E8
Woodlands. Crof WF4 .... 143 F1
Woodlands Croft. Kippax LS25 103 B8
Woodlands Ct. Hors LS16 .... 42 B1
Woodlands Dr. Clec BD19 .... 96 A1
Woodlands Dr. E Ard WF3 .... 120 C7
Woodlands Dr. Gar LS25 .... 83 B6
Woodlands Dr. Lepton HD8 .... 155 E2
Woodlands Dr. Morley LS27 .... 97 F6
Woodlands Dr. Pudsey BD10 ... 39 F1
Woodlands Dr. Yeadon LS19 ... 40 C2
Woodlands. E Ard WF3 .... 120 C7
Woodlands End. Lepton HD8 . 155 E3
Woodlands Fold. Birk BD11 .... 96 B5
Woodlands Gr. Bail BD17 .... 37 F2
Woodlands Gr. Brad BD13 .... 73 B1
Woodlands Gr. Hali HX3 .... 92 C1
Woodlands Gr. Ilkley LS29 .... 7 E4
Woodlands Gr. Kippax LS25 ... 103 C8
Woodlands Gr. Pudsey LS28 ... 57 C1
Woodlands Gr. Ship BD16 .... 54 B7
Woodlands. Hor WF4 .... 141 C2
Woodlands. Ilkley LS29 .... 8 D4
Woodlands La. Dew WF13 .... 138 F8
Woodlands. Leeds LS17 .... 43 E2
Woodlands Mount. Hali HX3 ... 92 C2
Woodlands Orthopaedic Hospl.
Yeadon 40 C1
Woodlands. Ossett WF5 .... 140 D7
Woodlands Park Gr. Pudsey
LS28 .... 76 D5
Woodlands Park Rd. Pudsey
LS28 .... 76 D5
Woodlands Rd. Batley WF17 . 118 A8
Woodlands Rd. Bing BD16 .... 37 C4
Woodlands Rd. Brad BD8 .... 55 A1
Woodlands Rd. Brad BD13 .... 73 A1
Woodlands Rd. Clec BD19 .... 96 A1
Woodlands Rd E. Lepton HD8 155 D3
Woodlands Rd. Hali HX3 .... 92 C1
Woodlands Rd. Hali HX5 .... 134 F8
Woodlands Rd. Lepton HD8 ... 155 E3
Woodlands Rise. Haw BD22 .... 51 C6
Woodlands Rise. Ilkley LS29 .... 7 E4
Woodlands. Sow Br HX6 .... 111 F2
Woodlands St. Brad BD8 .... 74 C8
Woodlands Terr. Brad BD8 .... 55 A1
Woodlands Terr. Brad BD12 .... 95 B5
Woodlands Terr. Pudsey LS28 57 C1
Woodlands The. Heb Br HX7 ... 89 A2
Woodlands The. Pont WF8 .... 146 E6
Woodlands View. Hali HX3 .... 92 C1 8
Woodlands Way. Kippax LS25 103 C8
Woodlands Way. Lepton HD8 155 E2
Woodlea App. Yeadon LS19 .... 39 F6
Woodlea. B Spa LS23 .... 30 D8
Woodlea Cl. Yeadon LS19 .... 39 F5
Woodlea Ct. Leeds LS17 .... 44 B4
Woodlea Dr. Yeadon LS19 .... 39 F5
Woodlea Gr. Leeds LS11 .... 78 F3
Woodlea Gr. Yeadon LS19 .... 39 F6
Woodlea Mount. Leeds LS11 ... 79 A3
Woodlea Mount. Yeadon LS19 . 39 F6
Woodlea Pl. Leeds LS11 .... 79 A3
Woodlea Rd. Yeadon LS19 .... 39 F5
Woodlea. S Elm WF9 .... 182 F2 6
Woodlea St. Leeds LS11 .... 78 F3
Woodlea View. Yeadon LS19 ... 39 F5
Woodleigh Ave. Brad BD5 .... 74 E1
Woodleigh Ave. Gar LS25 .... 82 E7
Woodleigh Cres. Ack M T WF7 163 F6
Woodlesford Cres. Hali HX2 ... 91 B2
Woodlesford Jun & Inf Sch.
Roth 101 C7
Woodlesford Sta. Roth 101 D7
Woodliegh Gr. Hud HD4 .... 153 C1
Woodliffe Cres. Leeds LS7 .... 60 C7
Woodliffe Dr. Leeds LS7 .... 60 C7
Woodman Ave. Elland HX5 .... 134 F5
Woodman Ave. Hud HD2 .... 137 A5
Woodman St. Leeds LS15 .... 81 A8
Woodmoor Cl. Crig WF4 .... 159 E4
Woodmoor Dr. Crig WF4 .... 159 E4
Woodmoor Rd. Wake WF2 .... 160 B5
Woodmoor Rise. Crig WF4 .... 159 E5
Woodnook Cl. Hors LS16 .... 41 D2
Woodnook Dr. Hors LS16 .... 41 D3
Woodnook Garth. Hors LS16 ... 41 D3
Woodnook Rd. Hors LS16 .... 41 D3
Woodrow Cres. M'town LS26 ... 102 A3
Woodrow Dr. Brad BD12 .... 94 E6
Woodroyd Ave. Brad BD5 .... 74 F2
Woodroyd Ave. Honley HD7 . 172 B5
Woodroyd Ave. Roy S71 .... 179 C1
Woodroyd Cl. Roy S71 .... 179 C1
Woodroyd Dr. Hali HX3 .... 91 F2
Woodroyd Gdns. Hali HX2 .... 111 F5
Woodroyd Gdns. Ilkley LS29 .... 8 F3
Woodroyd. Hud HD7 .... 152 C5
Woodroyd Mid Sch. Brad 74 E2
Woodroyd Rd. Brad BD5 .... 74 E2
Woodroyd Rd. Brad BD5 .... 74 E3
Woodroyd Terr. Brad BD5 .... 74 F2
Woods Ave. Mars HD7 .... 169 B4
Woods Mount. Mars HD7 .... 169 B4
Woods Terr. Mars HD7 .... 169 B4
Woodside Ave. Crof WF4 .... 144 C3
Woodside Ave. Leeds LS4 .... 59 C2
Woodside Ave. Ship BD16 .... 53 F7
Woodside Ave. Ship BD18 .... 54 E8 2
Woodside Ave. Wake WF2 .... 120 E2
Woodside. Castle WF10 .... 125 C8
Woodside CE Inf Sch. Hors 41 D1
Woodside Cl. Morley LS27 .... 98 A6
Woodside Cres. Batley WF17 118 A4
Woodside Cres. Crof WF4 .... 144 C4
Woodside Cres. Hali HX3 .... 92 B1
Woodside Cres. Ship BD16 .... 53 F7
Woodside Ct. Cull BD13 .... 52 D6
Woodside Ct. Hors LS18 .... 58 E8
Woodside. D Dale HD8 .... 192 A6
Woodside Dr. Morley LS27 .... 98 A7
Woodside Dr. Ship BD16 .... 53 F7
Woodside Dr. Wake WF2 .... 120 E2
Woodside Gdns. Morley LS27 .. 98 A7
Woodside Gr. Elland HX4 .... 134 D6
Woodside Gr. Hali HX3 .... 92 C1
Woodside Gr. Kippax WF10 .... 102 F6
Woodside Hill Cl. Hors LS18 ... 58 E8
Woodside. Keigh BD20 .... 18 A1
Woodside La. Hud HD2 .... 136 B4
Woodside La. Morley LS27 .... 98 A7
Woodside Mid & Fst Schs. Brad 94 A6
Woodside Mount. Hali HX3 .... 113 B8
Woodside Park Ave. Hors LS18 58 D8
Woodside Park Dr. Hors LS18 . 58 D8
Woodside Pl. Hali HX3 .... 92 B1
Woodside Pl. Leeds LS4 .... 59 C2
Woodside Rd. B Spa LS23 .... 30 B7
Woodside Rd. Brad BD12 .... 94 C4
Woodside Rd. Hali HX3 .... 113 B8
Woodside Rd. Hud HD4 .... 153 D2
Woodside Rd. Sil BD20 .... 5 C1
Woodside. Ship BD18 .... 55 D8
Woodside St. Kippax WF10 .... 102 F6
Woodside Terr. Elland HX4 .... 134 D6 6
Woodside Terr. Hali HX3 .... 92 C1
Woodside Terr. Leeds LS4 .... 59 C2 7
Woodside Veiw. Hud HD4 .... 152 F3
Woodside View. Elland HX4 .. 134 D6
Woodside View. Hali HX3 .... 92 B1
Woodside View. Holmfi HD7 . 188 E4
Woodside View. Leeds LS4 .... 59 C2
Woodside View. Ship BD16 .... 54 A7
Woodside. Wake WF2 .... 120 E2
Woodsley Gn. Leeds LS6 .... 59 F2
Woodsley Rd. Brad BD10 .... 56 A6
Woodsley Rd. Leeds LS2, LS3,
LS6 .... 59 F2
Woodsome Ave. Mir WF14 .... 137 E6
Woodsome Dr. Lepton HD8 ... 155 D2
Woodsome Dr. Mir WF14 .... 137 F6
Woodsome Est. Batley WF17 .... 118 B4
Woodsome Rd. Kirkb 155 B1
Woodsome Hall La. Kirkb HD8 173 C8
Woodsome Lees La.Kirkb HD8 173 D7
Woodsome Pk. Lepton HD8 ... 155 D2
Woodsome Rd. Hud HD4 .... 155 B2
Woodstock Cl. Hors LS16 .... 42 D3
Woodstock Cres. Hud HD3 .... 153 B8
Woodstock Wlk. Brad BD5 .... 74 E5 3
Woodthorne Croft. Leeds LS17 44 A4
Woodthorpe Cl. Wake WF2 ... 160 E7
Woodthorpe Dr. Wake WF2 .. 160 E7
Woodthorpe Glades. Wake
WF2 .... 160 E7
Woodthorpe La. Wake WF2 .. 160 E6
Woodthorpe Park Dr. Wake
WF2 .... 160 E7
Woodthorpe Terr. Hud HD1 .... 153 F5
Woodvale Cl. Brad BD4 .... 75 E5
Woodvale Cres. Bing BD16 .... 37 A5
Woodvale Gr. Brad BD7 .... 73 E5
Woodvale Rd. Brig HD6 .... 115 B3
Woodvale Way. Brad BD7 .... 73 E5
Woodview Ave. Bail BD17 .... 38 F4
Woodview. Birk BD11 .... 96 D7
Woodview. Brad BD8 .... 55 D3
Woodview Cl. Hors LS18 .... 41 C2
Woodview Gr. Leeds LS11 .... 79 B2
Woodview Mount. Leeds LS11 79 B2
Woodview Pl. Leeds LS11 .... 79 B2
Woodview Rd. Keigh BD22 .... 34 F4
Woodview Rd. Leeds LS11 .... 79 B2
Woodview St. Leeds LS11 .... 79 B2
Woodview Terr. Brad BD8 .... 55 D3
Woodview Terr. Keigh BD21 ... 35 B4 10
Woodview Terr. Leeds LS11 .... 79 B2
Woodville Ave. Hors LS18 .... 58 D8 2
Woodville Ave. Hud HD7 .... 152 E4
Woodville Cres. Hors LS18 .... 58 D8 4
Woodville Ct. Leeds LS8 .... 44 B1
Woodville Ct. Wake WF2 .... 142 C2
Woodville Gr. Haw BD22 .... 51 F8 9
Woodville Gr. Hors LS18 .... 58 D8 1
Woodville Gr. Midd LS10 .... 79 E1 1
Woodville Pl. Brad BD9 .... 54 F4
Woodville Pl. Hors LS18 .... 58 E8 6
Woodville Pl. Hud HD2 .... 136 E6
Woodville Rd. Dew WF12 .... 139 D8
Woodville Rd. Keigh BD20 .... 35 B8
Woodville Sq. Midd LS10 .... 79 E1
Woodville St. Hali HX3 .... 92 A1 25
Woodville St. Hors LS18 .... 58 E8 5
Woodville St. Ship BD18 .... 55 D8
Woodville Terr. Brad BD5 .... 74 D5
Woodville Terr. Haw BD22 .... 51 F8 10
Woodville Terr. Hors LS18 .... 58 D8 3
Woodward Ct. Mir WF14 .... 138 B7
Woodway Dr. Hors LS18 .... 58 C7
Woodway. Hors LS18 .... 58 C7
Woodway. Ship BD16 .... 53 F7
Woodworth Gr. Keigh BD21 .... 35 B3
Wool Row La. Kirkb HD8 .... 174 C5
Wool St. Liver WF16 .... 117 D3
Woolcroft Dr. Holmfi HD7 .... 189 C6
Wooldale Jun Sch. Holmfi 189 D6
Wooldale Rd. Holmfi HD7 .... 189 C6
Wooler Ave. Leeds LS11 .... 79 A2
Wooler Dr. Leeds LS11 .... 79 A2
Wooler Gr. Leeds LS11 .... 79 A2
Wooler Pl. Leeds LS11 .... 78 F2
Wooler Rd. Leeds LS11 .... 78 F2
Wooler St. Leeds LS11 .... 78 F2
Woolford Way. Loft G WF3 .... 121 D6
Woolgreaves Ave. Wake WF2 160 D6
Woolgreaves Cl. Wake WF2 .. 160 D6
Woolgreaves Croft.Wake WF2 160 D6
Woolgreaves Dr. Wake WF2 . 160 D7
Woolgreaves G'th.Wake WF2 160 D6
Wooller Rd. Brad BD12 .... 94 D5
Woolley CE Sch. Wool 178 A7
Woolley Colliery Rd.Mapp S75 177 E2
Woolley Edge La. Wool WF4 . 177 E6
Woolley Fst Sch. Mapp 177 E3

Woolley Hall Coll. Wool 178 B7
Woolley Low Moor La. Crig
WF4 .... 159 D2
Woolley Park Gdns. Wool WF4 178 A7
Woolley View. Crig WF4 ...... 159 F2
Woollin Ave. E Ard WF3 .... 119 E6
Woollin Cres. E Ard WF3 ...... 119 E6
Woolman St. Leeds LS9 .... 79 D7
Woolmarket. Pont WF8 .... 146 D8 6
Woolpack's Yd. Wake WF1 .... 142 B6
Woolrow La. Brig HD6 .... 115 C6
Woolshops Sq. Hali HX1 .... 113 C7 22
Woolstocks La. Caw S75 ...... 193 E3
Wootton St. Brad BD5 .... 74 E4
Worcester Ave. Midd LS10 ..... 99 F4
Worcester Dr. Midd LS10 .... 99 F4
Worcester Gr. Hud HD4 .... 154 B3
Worcester Pl. Brad BD4 .... 75 A4
Worden Gr. Brad BD7 .... 73 E4
Wordsworth Ct. Roth LS26 .... 101 C3
Wordsworth Dr. Knot WF11 ... 126 B4
Wordsworth Gr. Loft G WF3 .. 121 F5
Wordsworth Way. Bing BD16 .. 37 A5
Workhouse La. Elland HX4 .... 134 D6
Workhouse La. Hali HX2 .... 112 A7
Wormald Row. Leeds LS2 .... 79 C8
Wormald St. Dew WF13 .... 139 C8
Wormald St. Hud HD5 .... 154 F3
Wormald St. Liver WF15 .... 117 C3
Worrall Rd. Wake WF2 .... 160 A4
Worrall St. Morley LS27 .... 97 F3
Worsley Pl. Ad Le S DN6 .... 184 F2
Worsnop Bldgs. Brad BD12 .... 94 C4 15
Worsnop St. Brad BD12 .... 94 D6
Worstead Rd. Haw BD22 .... 51 F8
Worth Ave. Keigh BD21 .... 18 E1
Worth Bridge Rd. Keigh BD21 . 35 E8
Worth Valley Mid Sch. Keigh ... 35 A3
Worth Way. Keigh BD21 .... 35 C6
Worthing Head Cl. Brad BD12 . 94 D3 2
Worthing Head Rd. Brad BD12 94 D3
Worthing St. Brad BD12 .... 94 D3
Worthinghead Fst Sch. Brad ... 94 D3
Worthington St. Brad BD8 ...... 74 C8
Worthville Cl. Keigh BD21 ...... 35 C5
Wortley Heights. Leeds LS12 .. 78 D6
Wortley La. Leeds LS12 .... 78 F6
Wortley Moor La. Leeds LS12 .. 78 B6

Wortley Moor Rd. Leeds LS12 . 78 A7
Wortley Pk. Leeds LS12 .... 78 E6
Wortley Pl. Hem WF9 .... 181 C7
Wortley Rd. Leeds LS12 .... 78 B7
Wortley St. Bing BD16 .... 37 B3
Wortley Twrs. Leeds LS12 ...... 78 E6 8
Worts Hill La. Mars HD3 .... 151 B4
Worts Hill Side. Mars HD7 .... 151 C4
Wrangbrook La. Ham WF9 .... 183 D7
Wrangbrook Rd. Upton WF9 .. 183 D8
Wrangthorn Ave. Leeds LS6 ... 59 F3 1
Wrangthorn Pl. Leeds LS6 ...... 59 F3
Wrangthorn Terr. Leeds LS6 ... 59 F3 3
Wray's Bldgs. Hor WF4 .... 141 A1
Wrelton Cl. Roy S71 .... 179 B3
Wren Ave. Brad BD7 .... 73 E5
Wren Croft. Pont WF8 .... 125 D3
Wren Dr. Morley LS27 .... 98 D3
Wren Garth. Wake WF2 .... 160 D5
Wren Hill. Batley WF17 .... 118 A8
Wren Nest Rd. Rip HX6 .... 132 A4
Wren St. Haw BD22 .... 51 D7 17
Wren St. Hud HD1 .... 153 D5
Wren St. Keigh BD21 .... 35 C8
Wrenbeck Ave. Otley LS21 ..... 11 B2
Wrenbeck Cl. Otley LS21 .... 11 B2
Wrenbeck Dr. Otley LS21 .... 11 B2
Wrenbury Ave. Hors LS16 ...... 41 D5
Wrenbury Cres. Hors LS16 ..... 41 E5
Wrenbury Gr. Hors LS16 .... 41 E5
Wrenthorpe Jerry Clay La Jun &
Inf Sch. Wake 120 E2
Wrenthorpe La. Wake WF2 ... 120 D1
Wrenthorpe La. Wake WF2 ... 120 E1
Wrenthorpe Rd. Wake WF2 .. 120 E2
Wrexhall Rd. Batley WF12 .... 118 E2
Wrexham Rd. Bur in W LS29 ..... 9 D2
Wright Ave. Haw BD22 .... 34 D3
Wright St. Bacup OL13 .... 106 A7 5
Wright St. Haw BD22 .... 34 D2
Wright St. S in Cra BD20 .... 16 D5
Wrigley Ave. Brad BD4 .... 75 B1
Wrigley Hill. Hali HX2 .... 91 E5
Wroe Cres. Brad BD12 .... 94 C3
Wroe Pl. Brad BD12 .... 94 C3
Wroe St. Dew WF13 .... 117 F1
Wroe Terr. Brad BD12 .... 94 C3
Wrose Ave. Brad BD2 .... 56 A5
Wrose Ave. Ship BD18 .... 55 D6
Wrose Brow Rd. Ship BD18 .... 55 D8
Wrose Dr. Ship BD18 .... 55 D6

Wrose Gr. Ship BD18 .... 55 D6
Wrose Hill Pl. Ship BD2 .... 55 D5
Wrose Mount. Ship BD18 .... 55 E6
Wrose Rd. Brad BD2 .... 56 A6
Wrose Rd. Ship BD18 .... 55 E6
Wrose View. Bail BD17 .... 38 C3
Wrose View. Ship BD18 .... 55 D6
Wrosecliffe Gr. Ship BD10 ...... 55 F8
Wycliffe Cl. Pudsey LS13 .... 57 D5
Wycliffe Dr. Leeds LS17 .... 43 D2
Wycliffe Gdns. Ship BD18 ...... 55 A8
Wycliffe Rd. Pudsey LS13 .... 57 D5
Wycliffe Rd. Ship BD18 .... 55 A8
Wycliffe St. Ossett WF5 .... 140 D7
Wycoller Rd. Brad BD12 .... 94 C4
Wycombe Gn. Brad BD4 .... 75 E3
Wyebeck Ave. Leeds LS9 .... 80 D7
Wyke Cres. Brad BD12 .... 94 D2
Wyke La. Brad BD12 .... 94 E3
Wyke Manor Upper Sch. Brad . 94 D3
Wyke Mid Sch. Brad 94 C3
Wyke Old La. Brig HD6 .... 115 B7
Wykebeck Ave. Leeds LS9 ...... 80 D8
Wykebeck Cres. Leeds LS9 ...... 80 D8
Wykebeck Gdns. Leeds LS9 .... 80 D8
Wykebeck Gr. Leeds LS9 .... 80 D8
Wykebeck Mount. Leeds LS9 .. 80 D8
Wykebeck Pl. Leeds LS9 .... 80 E8
Wykebeck Prim Sch. Leeds 61 D2
Wykebeck Rd. Leeds LS9 .... 80 D8
Wykebeck Sq. Leeds LS9 .... 80 D8
Wykebeck St. Leeds LS9 .... 80 D8
Wykebeck Terr. Leeds LS9 ...... 80 D8
Wykebeck Valley Rd. Leeds LS9 61 D2
Wykebeck View. Leeds LS9 ..... 80 D8
Wykelea Cl. Brad BD12 .... 94 D3
Wyncliffe Gdns. Leeds LS17 .... 43 D2
Wyncroft Rise. Ship BD18 ...... 55 D5
Wyndham Ave. Brad BD2 .... 55 F3
Wynford Ave. Hors LS16 .... 42 B1
Wynford Dr. S Elm WF9 .... 183 A3
Wynford Gr. Hors LS16 .... 42 B1
Wynford Mount. Hors LS16 .... 42 A1
Wynford Rise. Hors LS16 .... 42 B1
Wynford Terr. Hors LS16 .... 42 A1
Wynford Way. Brad BD12 .... 94 E7
Wynmore Ave. Bramho LS16 .. 24 F2
Wynmore Cres. Bramho LS16 .. 24 F2
Wynmore Dr. Bramho LS16 .... 24 F2
Wynmore Dr. Hud HD3 .... 134 F1

Wynne St. Brad BD1 .... 74 D8
Wynthorpe Rd. Hor WF4 ...... 141 B1
Wynthorpe Rd. Hor WF4 ...... 159 B8
Wynyard Dr. Morley LS27 ...... 97 F4
Wyther Ave. Leeds LS5 .... 58 F3 2
Wyther Dr. Leeds LS5 .... 59 A3
Wyther Gn. Leeds LS5 .... 59 A3
Wyther La. Leeds LS5 .... 58 F3
Wyther Lane Ind Est. Leeds 58 F3
Wyther Park Ave. Leeds LS12 . 58 F1
Wyther Park Cl. Leeds LS12 ... 58 F1 1
Wyther Park Cty Prim Sch.
Leeds 58 F3
Wyther Park Cres. Leeds LS12 58 F2
Wyther Park Gr. Leeds LS12 .. 58 F2
Wyther Park Hill. Leeds LS12 .. 58 F2
Wyther Park Mt. Leeds LS12 .. 58 F1
Wyther Park Pl. Leeds LS12 ... 58 F2
Wyther Park Rd. Leeds LS12 .. 58 F1
Wyther Park Sq. Leeds LS12 .. 58 E1
Wyther Park St. Leeds LS12 ... 58 F1
Wyther Park Terr. Leeds LS12 . 58 F1
Wyther Park View. Leeds LS12 58 F2
Wyvern Ave. Hud HD3 .... 153 C6
Wyvern Cl. Batley WF17 .... 118 C6
Wyvern Cl. Brad BD7 .... 73 F5
Wyvern Pl. Hali HX2 .... 112 E8
Wyvern Terr. Hali HX2 .... 112 E8 12
Wyverne Rd. Hud HD7 .... 152 E4
Wyvil Cres. Ilkley LS29 .... 8 E5
Wyvil Rd. Ilkley LS29 .... 8 E5

Yarborough Croft. Northo HX3 93 A4
Yard No 1. Batley WF17 .... 118 A3
Yard No 2. Batley WF17 .... 118 A3
Yard No 4. Batley WF17 .... 117 F8 1
Yardley Way. Brad BD12 .... 94 E6
Yarn St. Leeds LS10 .... 79 E4
Yarwood Gr. Brad BD7 .... 73 E3 2
Yate La. Oxen BD22 .... 51 C3
Yates Flat. Ship BD18 .... 55 D6
Yates La. Hud HD3 .... 153 B4
Ye Farre Cl. Brig HD6 .... 115 A4 3
Yeadon Dr. Hali HX1 .... 114 A4
Yeadon House. S in Cra BD20 . 16 C5
Yeadon Moor Rd. Yeadon LS19 40 E6
Yeadon Moor Rd. Yeadon LS18 41 A8
Yeadon Westfield Inf Sch.
Yeadon 39 F6
Yeadon Westfield Jun Sch.
Yeadon 39 F6

Yew Gr. Hud HD4 .... 152 F3
Yew Green Ave. Hud HD4 ...... 153 E3
Yew Green Rd. Hud HD4 .... 153 E3
Yew Pk. Brig HD6 .... 114 E5
Yew St. Hud HD2 .... 136 A1
Yew Tree Ave. Brad BD8 .... 54 D1
Yew Tree Cres. Brad BD8 .... 54 E1
Yew Tree Cl. L Brad BD20 .... 4 C6
Yew Tree Ct. Liver WF15 ...... 117 A5 6
Yew Tree Ct. Tod OL14 .... 129 A8
Yew Tree Gr. Brad BD8 .... 54 E1
Yew Tree La. Brad BD13 .... 72 E8
Yew Tree La. Holmfi HD7 ...... 188 C3
Yew Tree La. Hud HD4, HD7 .. 152 F3
Yew Tree La. Slai HD7 .... 169 F7
Yew Tree Rd. Hud HD2, HD3 . 135 B3
Yew Tree Rd. Shep HD8 .... 173 F1
Yew Tree Slai HD7 .... 169 F7
Yew Tree St. Wake WF1 .... 142 E4
Yew Tree Wlk. Knot WF11 .... 126 E2
Yew Trees Ave. Northo HX3 .... 93 A3
Yew Trees Croft. Hali HX2 ...... 90 C1
Yewbank Cl. Ilkley LS29 .... 8 A4
Yewbank Terr. Ilkley LS29 .... 8 A4
Yewdall Way. Brad BD10 .... 56 C6
Yewdall Rd. Pudsey LS13 .... 57 E5
Yews Hill Rd. Hud HD1, HD4 .. 153 E4
Yews Mount. Hud HD1 .... 153 F4
York Cl. S Elm WF9 .... 183 A4
York Cres. Bing BD16 .... 37 A2 1
York Dr. Batley WF16 .... 117 D6
York Dr. Batley WF17 .... 118 D6
York Gate. Otley LS20 .... 22 F5
York Gate. Otley LS20 .... 23 C4
York Gr. Batley WF17 .... 118 D6
York Gr. Mir WF14 .... 137 F5 4
York House. Brad BD10 .... 56 C7
York House. Elland HX5 .... 134 F7 4
York Pl. Ack M T WF7 .... 164 B7
York Pl. Clec BD19 .... 116 D8 8
York Pl. Leeds LS1 .... 79 B8
York Pl. Tod OL14 .... 108 B5 14
York Pl. Weth LS22 .... 13 F6
York Rd. Batley WF17 .... 118 C6
York Rd. Bick LS22 .... 14 D7
York Rd. Leeds LS14, LS15, LS9 61 E1
York Rd. Leeds LS14, LS15 ..... 62 C6

York Rd. Mir WF14 .... 137 F5
York Rd. Weth LS22 .... 14 D7
York Road Ind Est. Weth 13 F6
York St. Bing BD16 .... 37 A2
York St. Brad BD8 .... 73 E7
York St. Brig HD6 .... 115 A1
York St. Castle WF10 .... 124 E8
York St. Dearne S63 .... 194 F1
York St. Glu BD20 .... 16 D7
York St. Hali HX1 .... 113 B6
York St. Heb Br HX7 .... 89 A2 2
York St. Hem WF9 .... 181 E5
York St. Leeds LS9 .... 79 D7
York St. Nor WF6 .... 122 F3
York St. Queen BD13 .... 72 E1
York St. Tod OL14 .... 108 B6
York Terr. Hali HX3 .... 92 B1
York Villas. Nor WF6 .... 123 B2
Yorkshire Martyrs Collegiate Sch.
Birk 96 A8
Yorkshire Sculpture Pk.W Bret 176 E7
Yorkshire TV Studios. Leeds ... 59 E1
Yorkshire Way. Brad BD7 .... 74 B3
Young St. Brad BD8 .... 73 F8
Young's Ct. Aber LS25 .... 64 E6

Zakira Muslim Girls High Sch.
Batley 118 D4
Zealand St. Brad BD4 .... 75 D4
Zermatt Gr. Leeds LS7 .... 60 C6
Zermatt Mount. Leeds LS7 ..... 60 C6
Zermatt St. Leeds LS7 .... 60 D6
Zermatt Terr. Leeds LS7 .... 60 D6
Zetland Pl. Leeds LS8 .... 60 F3 1
Zetland St. Hud HD1 .... 154 B6 12
Zetland St. Wake WF1 .... 142 C6
Zion Cl. Hud HD3 .... 135 B1
Zion Dr. Mapp S75 .... 178 B1
Zion St. Bacup OL13 .... 106 A3
Zion St. Heb Br HX7 .... 89 E1
Zion St. Leeds LS9 .... 79 E6
Zion St. Ossett WF5 .... 119 C1
Zoar St. Morley LS27 .... 98 A4